D1233928

Third Edition

dictionary of education

Prepared under the Auspices of Phi Delta Kappa

Carter V. Good, Editor

Dean and Professor of Education, Emeritus
University of Cincinnati

Winifred R. Merkel, Assistant Editor

McGraw-Hill Book Company

New York   St. Louis   San Francisco   Düsseldorf   Johannesburg
Kuala Lumpur   London   Mexico   Montreal   New Delhi
Panama   Rio de Janeiro   Singapore   Sydney   Toronto

34567890   KPKP   7987654

This book was set in Times Roman by Rocappi, Inc.
The editors were Robert C. Morgan and Helen Greenberg;
the designer was Nicholas Krenitsky;
and the production supervisor was Thomas J. Lo Pinto.
The printer and binder was Kingsport Press, Inc.

Library of Congress Catologing in Publication Data

Good, Carter Victor, 1897-   ed.
    Dictionary of education.

    1.   Education—Dictionaries.   I.   Phil Delta
Kappa.   II.   Title.
LB15.G6   1973   370'.3   73-4784
ISBN 0-07-023720-4

contents

coordinators, associates and reviewers

Adult and Extension Education (and Correspondence Study)
COORDINATORS: David S. Coleman, Rollins College
Wilson B. Thiede, University of Wisconsin
ASSOCIATES: George F. Aker, Florida State University
H. Mason Atwood, Indiana University
Roger DeCrow, Syracuse University
Glenn Jensen, University of Wyoming
Ann Litchfield, University of Chicago
George D. Russell, North Carolina State University
Coolie Verner, University of British Columbia

Aerospace Education
COORDINATOR: John A. Whitesel, Miami University
ASSOCIATES: James V. Bernardo, National Aeronautics and Space Administration
John E. Cocanougher, Miami University
Wesley Crum, Central Washington State College
John Gordon, Miami University
William L. Hanks, Miami University
Wesley R. Kimball, Wright-Patterson Air Force Base
Margaret Marshall, Indianapolis Public Schools
Robert O'Neil, Federal Aviation Agency
John V. Sorensen, Maxwell Air Force Base
Mervin K. Strickler, Office of General Aviation Affairs
Charles W. Webb, Maxwell Air Force Base
Walter Zaharevitz, National Aerospace Education Council

Agricultural Education (and Agricultural Extension)
COORDINATOR: Lloyd J. Phipps, University of Illinois

Art Education
COORDINATOR: H. James Marshall, University of Illinois
ASSOCIATE: Beverly Jean Davis, National Art Education Association
REVIEWERS: Harlan Hoffa, Pennsylvania State University
Edward L. Mattil, North Texas State University

Audiovisual Education and Instructional Media (Radio, TV, Programmed Instruction, and Teaching Machines)
COORDINATOR: Sidney C. Eboch, Ohio State University
ASSOCIATES: Edwin G. Novak, Ohio State University
Robert W. Wagner, Ohio State University
REVIEWER: Merlyn P. McClure, University of Cincinnati

Business Education (and Consumer and Distributive Education)
COORDINATOR: Mearl R. Guthrie, Bowling Green State University
ASSOCIATES: James D. Bowling, Muskingum Area Technical Institute
M. Lee Goddard, Bowling Green State University
Chester O. Mills, Bowling Green State University

Curriculum and Cocurriculum (and Textbooks in Relation to the Curriculum)
COORDINATOR: Phil C. Lange, Columbia University
ASSOCIATES: Gordon N. Mackenzie, Columbia University
Alice Miel, Columbia University

Developmental and Remedial Instruction (and Remedial Reading)
COORDINATOR: Donald L. Cleland, University of Pittsburgh
ASSOCIATES: Sister Mary Paul Hickey, Carlow College
Richard Kemper, University of South Carolina
Lorraine Morgan, Chatham College

Educational Psychology and Human Development (and Child and Adolescent Development)
COORDINATOR: R. Stewart Jones, University of Illinois

Educational Sociology
COORDINATOR: L. Glenn Smith, Iowa State University

Education in Canada
COORDINATOR: E. Brock Rideout, Ontario Institute for Studies in Education
ASSOCIATES: G. W. Battershill, Department of Education, Manitoba
L. H. Bergstrom, Department of Education, Saskatchewan
C. W. Dickson, Department of Education, Quebec
Fred Kirby, Department of Education, Newfoundland
F. P. Levirs, Department of Education, British Columbia
J. R. McCarthy, Department of Education, Ontario
Earle G. McDonald, Department of Education, Alberta
Lorne R. Moase, Department of Education, Prince Edward Island
R. A. Simpson, Department of Education, Nova Scotia

Education in England and Wales
COORDINATOR: R. E. Bell, The Open University, Bletchley, England

Elementary Education and Early Childhood Education (Preschool, Kindergarten, Primary, and Intermediate)
COORDINATOR: Agnes A. Manney, University of Cincinnati
ASSOCIATE: Patricia O'Reilly, University of Cincinnati

Evaluation and Measurement (Intelligence, Achievement, Aptitude, Personality, and Attitude)
COORDINATOR: Richard C. Pugh, Indiana University
ASSOCIATES: Sabir A. Alvi, Ontario Institute for Studies in Education
H. Glenn Ludlow, Indiana University
James M. Morgan, Indiana University

Foreign Language Instruction
COORDINATOR: Gottfried F. Merkel, University of Cincinnati
ASSOCIATES: Karl W. Obrath, University of Cincinnati
Joseph L. Scott, Pennsylvania State University

Guidance, Counseling, Student Personnel Services and Procedures, and Child Accounting
COORDINATOR: Worth R. Jones, University of Cincinnati
ASSOCIATES: Jack E. Corle, Ohio Northern University
Hope Daugherty, U.S. Department of Agriculture
Forrest E. Orebaugh, Cincinnati Public Schools

Higher Education (Undergraduate and Graduate, Junior and Community Colleges, Professional Education Other than Teacher Education, and Accrediting)
COORDINATOR: August W. Eberle, Indiana University

History of Education, Comparative Education, and International and Intercultural Education
COORDINATOR: L. Glenn Smith, Iowa State University
ASSOCIATES: George A. Kizer, Iowa State University
Franklin Parker, West Virginia University

Home Economics Education
COORDINATOR: Vivian Roberts, Ohio University
ASSOCIATES: Allyne Bane, Ohio University
Wade Bash, School Food Service, State of Ohio
Julia Nehls, Ohio University
Olive Parrish, Ohio State University
Barbara Reed, State Department of Education, Ohio
Dorothy Scott, Ohio State University
Shirley Slater, Ohio University

Industrial Arts Education
COORDINATORS: William F. Tierney, University of Maryland
John A. Whitesel, Miami University
ASSOCIATES: Herbert A. Anderson, Stout State University
Gardner T. Boyd, Kansas City, Missouri, Public Schools
Kenneth W. Brown, State University of New York at Buffalo
Charles A. Bunten, Miami University
Robert E. Buxten, State University of New York at Buffalo
Howard S. Decker, American Industrial Arts Association
Carlton Gerbracht, State University of New York at Oswego
Harold G. Gilbert, Northern Illinois University
Robert C. Hutchcroft, University of Michigan
D. L. Jelden, Colorado State College
Henry A. Loats, Ball State University
Delmar Olson, North Carolina State University
Bernard S. Proctor, Cheyney State College
E. Robert Rudiger, Stout State University
Marshall Schmitt, United States Office of Education
Leslie E. Stephenson, San Jose State College
Robert S. Swanson, Stout State University
Earl M. Weber, Millersville State College

Jewish Education
COORDINATOR: Zalmen Slesinger, American Association for Jewish Education
ASSOCIATES: Hyman Chanover, American Association for Jewish Education
Samuel H. Dinsky, American Association for Jewish Education
Isidor Margolis, American Association for Jewish Education

Language Arts (Reading, Literature, English, Speech, Linguistics, Composition, Journalism, and Handwriting)
COORDINATOR: Helen J. Caskey, University of Cincinnati
ASSOCIATES: Mary E. Coleman, University of Pennsylvania
James Danbury, University of Cincinnati
Helen Tangeman, Cincinnati Public Schools

Libraries and Library Education
COORDINATOR: Maurice F. Tauber, Columbia University
ASSOCIATE: Hilda Feinberg, Research Library, Revlon Research Center, New York

Mathematics Education (and Arithmetic)
COORDINATOR: Edith Robinson, University of Georgia
ASSOCIATES: Joseph R. Hooten, Jr., University of Georgia
Michael L. Mahaffey, University of Georgia
William D. McKillip, University of Georgia
Len Pikaart, University of Georgia
Leslie P. Steffe, University of Georgia
Robert E. Wilcutt, Boston University

Military Education
COORDINATOR: James C. Shelburne, Headquarters, Air University
ASSOCIATES: Oliver T. Albertini, Department of Defense
Rolfe L. Allen, Department of the Army

W. E. Allen, Department of the Navy
V. J. Anania, Department of the Navy
R. K. Biel, United States Marine Corps
C. L. Bueker, United States Air Force
George Fagan, United States Air Force Academy
Woodford Agee Heflin, Air University
R. J. Marcott, United States Coast Guard
Richard W. Moss, Department of Defense

Music Education
COORDINATOR: Simon V. Anderson, University of Cincinnati

Philosophy of Education
COORDINATOR: George A. Kizer, Iowa State University
ASSOCIATES: L. Glenn Smith, Iowa State University
Lloyd P. Williams, University of Oklahoma

Physical and Health Education (Recreation, Outdoor Education, Safety Education, Driver Training, and Modern Dance)
COORDINATOR: William J. Schnitzer, University of Cincinnati
ASSOCIATES: Louis E. Alley, State University of Iowa
Peter J. Cardullias, University of Cincinnati
Robert Korsgaard, Ball State University
Mary E. Wolverton, University of Cincinnati

Religious Education and Character Education
COORDINATOR: Joe D. Mills, Winthrop College

Roman Catholic Education
COORDINATOR: Roland J. Goddu, New England Center for Continuing Education, Durham, N.H.
ASSOCIATE: Sister Mary Sarah Fasenmyer, Catholic University of America

School Administration (Federal, State, Rural; Finance; Law; Plant; Transportation; and Public and Community Relations) and Supervision and Improvement of Instruction
COORDINATOR: Robert D. Price, University of Cincinnati
ASSOCIATES: Glen G. Eye, University of Wisconsin
Willard Fox, Bowling Green State University
Ben M. Harris, University of Texas
William H. Roe, University of Connecticut
Stephen Romine, University of Colorado
Roger M. Shaw, Kent State University
Robert J. Simpson, Miami University
Mike J. Stolee, University of Miami
Dewey H. Stollar, University of Tennessee
Byron A. Zude, University of Cincinnati
Fredrick C. Zumsteg, Indian Hill Schools, Ohio

Science Education
COORDINATOR: Donald D. Christian, Waynesburg College
ASSOCIATES: Lloyd M. Bennett, Texas Women's University
Gene W. Moser, University of Pittsburgh

Secondary Education
COORDINATOR: Robert G. Portune, University of Cincinnati
ASSOCIATES: Subhashani Mohan
Dean Moore

Special Education
COORDINATOR: Godfrey D. Stevens, University of Pittsburgh
ASSOCIATES: Ray H. Barsch, Southern Connecticut State University
Jack W. Birch, University of Pittsburgh
Joseph L. French, Pennsylvania State University
William E. Garove, University of Pittsburgh
I. Ignacy Goldberg, Columbia University
Marjorie S. Greeley, San Francisco State College
Frieda K. Hammermeister, University of Pittsburgh
John L. Johnson, Syracuse University
Melton C. Martinson, University of Kentucky
Jack Matthews, University of Pittsburgh
Joseph Newman, University of Pittsburgh
Ralph L. Peabody, University of Pittsburgh
Jerome H. Rothstein, San Francisco State College
Daniel D. Sage, Syracuse University
George H. Shames, University of Pittsburgh
James M. Wolf, Canal Zone Government, Canal Zone
Naomi Zigmond, University of Pittsburgh

Statistics (and Experimental Design) and Data Processing
COORDINATOR: Howard B. Lyman, University of Cincinnati
ASSOCIATES: Donald A. Schumsky, University of Cincinnati
R. J. Senter, University of Cincinnati

Teacher Education (Program, Staff, Professional Organizations and Ethics, Recruitment, Certification, and Employment)
COORDINATOR: Charles R. Weilbaker, University of Cincinnati

Vocational Trade and Industrial Education, and Technical Institute Education
COORDINATOR: Dennis H. Price, University of Cincinnati

Assistance Not Otherwise Acknowledged
Vincent Cyphers, Colorado State College
Lawrence V. Jordan, New York City Board of Education
Harold R. Rice, University of Cincinnati

preface

First edition—origin of the dictionary project: Phi Delta Kappa voted at the Cincinnati meeting of its National Council (December, 1937) to sponsor preparation of a comprehensive educational dictionary and two years later at the Chicago meeting of the National Council made substantial plans for support of the project. This action had been preceded by a period of preliminary work to which a number of persons and organizations contributed. A committee under the chairmanship of President D. A. Robertson of Goucher College, with the support and sponsorship of the American Council on Education, acting jointly with a committee of the American Educational Research Association (of which the editor was chairman), had contributed generously to the formulation of an initial working plan. The original suggestion that committees of the American Council on Education and of the American Educational Research Association study the problem of educational terminology came from George F. Zook early in 1934, when he was United States Commissioner of Education, and his interest in the project continued after he became president of the American Council on Education.

Purpose and scope: The primary purpose of this volume is to make available a comprehensive dictionary of professional terms in education that will do for educational workers and teachers what already has been accomplished by technical dictionaries for practitioners in such special fields as medicine, law, engineering, and psychology. In clarification of the concepts and terminology employed in educational writing, speaking, and teaching, it is important to remember the statement attributed to Mark Twain: "The difference between the right word and almost the right word is the difference between lightning and lightning bug."

The *Dictionary* is concerned with technical and professional terms and concepts in the entire area of education. As a general policy, it has excluded names of persons, institutions, school systems, organizations, places, and titles of publications and journals, except where a movement, method, or plan is represented.

Only those foreign educational terms most frequently employed in the study of comparative education (particularly the schools of Canada, England, France, Germany, and Italy) are defined (in the first and second editions). An attempt has been made to select from such related fields as psychology, sociology, and philosophy those terms with significant educational connotations.

Another problem of delimitation has been encountered in choosing technical terms for definition, especially in school-subject fields, so as to include only words with definite educational, professional connotations. Obviously, such purely content or subject-matter terms as *test tube* in science, *triangle* in mathematics, and *voting* in civics are not included. *Carpetbagger* has meaning in history but no special professional significance for the field of education; on the other hand, *counterchronological order* has a place in the educational vocabulary of the social-studies field. *Holstein* is an important term in agriculture or animal husbandry, but has no place in a dictionary of education, while *agricultural extension* does have special professional significance in the field of education.

The master list of terms: The first step in compiling the first edition was the preparation of a master list of some 19,000 terms, based largely on examination of the indexes of a wide range of books in education. The major part of this work of compilation was done at Wayne State University under the direction of W. Ray Smittle. This word list was placed in the hands of the various specialists responsible for formulating definitions. The master list was intended only as a starting point in the selection of terms for definition and was suggestive rather than definitive.

The coordinators: After compiling the word list for the first edition, the next step was the selection of more than one hundred specialists to serve as coordinators. Recognized experts in the various areas of education were invited to assume responsibility for selecting terms and formulating definitions in their respective fields of specialization. The fields and authors represented in the

Encyclopedia of Educational Research (Macmillan, 1941) proved very helpful in this phase of the project.

In most instances, the coordinators chose to enlist the assistance of a number of their associates and of their graduate students. This procedure resulted in the cooperation of several thousand persons. Some coordinators formed committees numbering only a few collaborators, while other specialists cooperated with as many as forty or fifty persons.

Preparation and refinement of specialized word lists: Through use of the master list for the first edition and by examining indexes of selected textbooks, articles in professional journals, glossaries, and special dictionaries, each coordinator compiled a list of terms limited as closely as possible to his immediate field of specialization. Copies of these word lists, when forwarded to the Cincinnati editorial office, were examined with a view to discovering and eliminating unnecessary duplications, deleting nonprofessional terms, and adding appropriate words.

In refining the word list for a particular subdivision of education, the editorial office, the coordinator, and his associates employed the following criteria:

1. Is the term a professional one, applicable to the field of education, or a strictly subject-matter term, such as *triangle* or *circle* in mathematics?

2. Is the term given a special meaning or shade of meaning in education?

3. Has the term a direct application to the area in question?

4. Is the term more frequently used in the particular area than in other fields of education?

5. If the term is used in related fields, is it given a special meaning or shade of meaning in the area in question?

6. Can the term be treated adequately in a fifty-word definition? Space limitations and the function of a dictionary required that encyclopedic terms or phrases be omitted; for example, *conflicting psychologies of learning* or the *relation between high school marks and performance in college.* Other items of an encyclopedic nature that were omitted included persons, institutions, school systems, places, educational organizations, fraternities, foundations, national committees, publications, journals, and standard tests. Such terms were defined only where an educational movement, method, or plan was represented; for example, the *Morrison unit organization, Montessori method, Gary plan,*

and *Winnetka plan.* Space limitations made it necessary to dispense with quotations that might otherwise have presented in context the particular term defined.

As another step in identification of the professional vocabulary of the various areas in education, for use in the first edition, the content of the *Encyclopedia of Educational Research* was analyzed. In alternate columns of the *Encyclopedia* the professional terms were underlined preliminary to compilation into an alphabetical check list, for comparison with the definitions already in the files. Some 2,000 new words for definition resulted from this comparison. A less extensive word analysis, based on the topical headings of the *Encyclopedia of Modern Education* (Philosophical Library, 1943), resulted in a relatively small number of additional terms for definition.

Review and collation: Approximately 20,000 definitions were written for the first edition by more than a hundred coordinators or specialists and their numerous assistants, and edited by the staff of the *Dictionary* office. In turn, some one hundred reviewing committees, for the most-part representing national professional organizations, evaluated the definitions in particular areas. Finally the editorial office sought to collate all criticisms received for a particular definition, referring the final version to the original author for approval. In many instances, several definitions for a particular term were listed seriatim to represent special usage in different subdivisions of education, which reduced the total number of terms in the alphabetical listing to approximately 16,000 in the first edition. In these several stages of refinement, several thousand workers gave assistance.

Spelling and pronunciation: In matters of spelling, Webster's *New International Dictionary* has been followed.

Pronunciation is given for common terms in education frequently mispronounced, for certain words derived from Latin or Greek roots, for foreign language terms, and for many medical and psychological expressions related to education.

Order of listing terms: With the exception of educational terms employed in foreign countries, which are grouped by country at the end of the volume, the definitions are arranged alphabetically. As a rule, the compound terms are listed in inverse order, to stress the key word or noun form; for example, *superintendent, school* or *high school, vocational.* For these compound terms a full system of cross reference has been provided.

For the first edition Roland A. Browne and Emily C. Browne served as editorial assistants, and the Advisory Committee included Carter Alexander, W. W. Charters, Henry D. Rinsland, W. Ray Smittle, and Paul M. Cook, with the editor serving as chairman.

The second edition: After 1945, new terms came into general use in many areas of education and in related disciplines; for example, client-centered counseling, nondirective therapy, group dynamics, small-group study, participant observer, and action research.

A tentative master list of new terms was prepared for consideration in revising the *Dictionary of Education*, based on an analysis of the index of the 1950 revised edition of the *Encyclopedia of Educational Research*, the index of the *Review of Educational Research* for a period of years after 1945, and the alphabetical list of topical headings in the *Education Index*, 1950–1953.

One hundred or more specialists or coordinators, with the help of their associates, were asked to analyze the indexes of recent books, journals, and other major bodies of literature in their particular areas of responsibility, for comparison with the definitions in the first edition of the *Dictionary of Education* and for use in identifying new terms. If the one hundred or more coordinators used the assistance of their associates and advanced students as freely as did their predecessors in preparing the 1945 edition, probably 2,000 or more educational workers participated in the preparation of the revised edition.

Somewhat unexpectedly, the preparation of the 1959 edition proved as large a task as that of the first edition. There were many new terms and definitions to be added, some terms to be deleted, new meanings for old terms, and the exacting work of collating the materials prepared for the first and second editions. The terms defined and cross-references total approximately 25,000, but the individual definitions are fewer by several thousand in the second edition.

The third edition: Since 1959, terminology in education and related areas has continued to increase rapidly, as revealed through word analysis of the indexes of the 1960s from the following sources (a survey for which Neville L. Robertson was responsible):

Education Index
Review of Educational Research

Encyclopedia of Educational Research, Third Edition, 1960
Handbook of Research on Teaching
Outstanding Education Books of the Year, as listed annually in the *NEA Journal*
ERIC Thesaurus and Supplement
Standard Terminology for Curriculum and Instruction in State and Local School Systems

Specialized dictionaries and many other sources in the literature have been useful in selecting terms and in preparing definitions.

The problem of dealing with educational terminology in the various foreign languages has become so large that only terms in the English language are included in the third edition, with separate sections for Canada and for England and Wales. It is hoped that some other organization with sufficient resources, such as UNESCO, may be able to provide an educational dictionary of foreign language terms relating to the schools and programs of the countries represented. Information concerning education in foreign countries is found in the ten-volume *Encyclopedia of Education* (Macmillan, 1971). This Encyclopedia and the *Encyclopedia of Educational Research* (Macmillan, 1969) present information on more than a thousand encyclopedic topics.

The word analyses of the literature were made available to the coordinators for the third edition of the *Dictionary,* who were asked to supplement the more general survey of indexes by examining books and periodicals in their own special fields of responsibility. By consolidation and unification of appropriate areas, the number of fields and coordinators is smaller than for the first and second editions. Entries (and cross-references) have increased to 33,000.

Grateful acknowledgment is made to Phi Delta Kappa, which has contributed the financial support for the project during the preparation of the three editions. The University of Cincinnati has been helpful and generous in providing facilities and space for the editorial office throughout the preparation of the three editions.

The valuable contributions of the coordinators and their associates, as in the first and second editions, have made a new edition possible, although the editor is responsible for the final form of the content. A list of the contributors to the third edition appears above. Some of these specialists also contributed to the earlier editions.

Carter V. Good

introduction*

With the publication of the *Dictionary of Education* the science of education [has come] of age. While the art of education is of very ancient lineage, the science of education came into being with the birth of the twentieth century. During the years that have intervened between that date and this [1945], thousands of pioneers have freely coined expressions and given strange new meanings to old words without regard to accepted usage.

It was in the order of natural events that confusion should follow in the train of uncontrolled invention. Words came to have whatever meaning a person wished to give them, and only unusually careful writers defined their terms. This adolescent freedom of play with meanings, while an exhilarating experience, has hindered communication. Conflicts and arguments have been provoked between men who use the same words, but with different meanings. In fact, the lack of clear definition of concepts has led to usages so loose that with too great frequency many writers have not been consistent in their own use of their own terms.

It was to be expected that scholarly thinkers should be concerned with this lack of accuracy. When the science of education was only twenty years old, articles began to appear in the literature to call attention to the confusion. And as normally happens, certain persons made constructive moves to rectify the condition.

The editor of the *Dictionary of Education* was the leader who crystallized feeling into action. Nearly twenty years ago he made his first analyses of usage and wrote his first reports [during the second half of the 1920s]. Ten years ago [1934-1935] he helped enlist the alert sympathy of the then United States Commissioner of Education, George F. Zook, who aided in the appointment of a joint committee of the American Educa-tional Research Association and of the American Council on Education, which worked with meager funds. Thereafter, with the persistence of the pioneer, the editor led the movement to secure the support of the educational fraternity for men, Phi Delta Kappa, which in turn provided sponsorship for the *Dictionary* and the modest funds that have been needed to complete the project. Just as the . . . *Encyclopedia of Educational Research* is the monument of Walter S. Monroe, so the *Dictionary of Education* is the substantial contribution of Carter V. Good.

The *Dictionary of Education* will serve two historical purposes. On the one hand, it is the first instrument of the profession as a whole which is dedicated to exactness of words and the artistry of precision. For the young scholar who is building his vocabulary the definitions of authorities will provide a solid base. In the *Dictionary* he has a source to consult which will acquaint him with commonly accepted meanings. For the mature scholar also the definitions will be useful as he sets his own meanings against the background of meanings of others which have been assembled in terse and convenient form.

On the other hand, this first edition provides a solid base on which to build a more perfect instrument. Those who have closely followed the task of assembling the vocabulary and of securing the cooperation of scholars to define the terms realize the enormous amount of detailed work that has been devoted to the project for the last decade [1935-1945]. Such observers are less concerned about the criticisms of users that must inevitably appear. They see rather that only by the publication of this first substantial solution to the problem of definition can better dictionaries be made by later lexicographers.

W. W. Charters

---

* The late Dr. Charters originally prepared this introduction for the first edition of the *Dictionary of Education*, 1945, but what he says is pertinent today.

key to pronunciation

The following simplified system of indicating pronunciation has been adopted. Pronunciation is not indicated for all terms but is restricted largely to foreign terms and to the more difficult scientific terms.

a	mat	j	joy	u	mug
ā	fate			ū	muse
ã	share	o	hop		
ä	father	ō	rope	y	yes
â	law	ŏ	forward	z	zebra
		ōō	pull, foot	zh	pleasure
ch	choose	ōō	pool, rule		
		oi	toil	ə	represents:
e	let	ou	mouse		
ē	evil			a	in alike
ê	fern	s	set	e	in later
		sh	fish	i	in pencil
g	get			o	in abandon
		th	thick	u	in circus
i	trim	th	there		
ī	fight				

Foreign Sounds:

KH   sounded like *ch* in Scottish *loch* or in German *Bach.*
N   not pronounced, but used to indicate that the vowel preceding it is nasal. There are four nasal sounds in French, represented in the *Dictionary* by the following symbols:
   äN   *a* in *father,* nasalized
   aN   *a* in *mat,* nasalized
   ōN   *o* in *forward,* nasalized
   uN   *u* in *mug,* nasalized
ø   approximately the sound of *u* in *fur.*
r   generally rolled in French, Italian, and German.
Y   (the French sound of u, or the German sound of ü) pronounced like the English *ē* in *evil,* with lips rounded as for *ōō* in *pōōl.*

abbreviations of terms appearing within definitions*

abbr.	abbreviation	lit.	literally
adj.	adjective	masc.	masculine
admin.	administration	math.	mathematics
agric.	agricultural	meas.	measurement
alt.	alternate	mil.	military
anal.	analysis	mus.	music
ant.	antonym	n.	noun
arith.	arithmetic	neurol.	neurology
audiovis.	audiovisual	neut.	neuter
biol.	biology	obs.	obsolete
behav.	behaviorism -istic	obsoles.	obsolescent
bus.	business	pathol.	pathology
cap.	capitalized	philos.	philosophy
comp. w.	compare with	photog.	photography
contr. w.	contrast with	phys.	physical
couns.	counseling	pl.	plural
curric.	curriculum	pol.	political
dev.	development	prim.	primary
dist. f.	distinguish from	psych.	psychology
distrib.	distributive	psychoan.	psychoanalysis
ec.	economics	pup.	pupil
ed.	education	R.C.	Roman Catholic
elem.	elementary	read.	reading
exper.	experimentation	relig.	religious
fact.	factor	res.	research
fem.	feminine	sci.	science
for.	foreign	sec.	secondary
Fr.	French	sing.	singular
genet.	genetics	sociol.	sociology
Ger.	German	sp.	spelling
Gr.	Greek	Span.	Spanish
Heb.	Hebrew	spec.	special
hist.	history	stat.	statistics
ind.	industrial	syn.	synonym
instr.	instruction	theol.	theology
It.	Italian	trans.	transportation
journ.	journalism	U.S.	United States
jun. coll.	junior college	v.	verb
kind.-prim.	kindergarten-primary	var.	variant
lang.	language	vis.	visual
Lat.	Latin	voc.	vocational
libr.	library		

*Italics and boldface type are used primarily to indicate terms defined in the *Dictionary* and for cross-references.

abbreviations and symbols for terms defined

A: arithmetic average.

AA: accomplishment age; achievement age; attainment age.

AD: average deviation.

AM: (1) amplitude modulation; (2) arithmetic mean.

AQ: accomplishment quotient; achievement quotient; attainment quotient.

AR: accomplishment ratio; achievement ratio; attainment ratio.

Aver.: arithmetic average.

β: the Greek lower-case *beta* used as a symbol for the standard regression coefficient and for measures of kurtosis and skewness.

$b_{01 \cdot 23} \ldots n$: symbol for coefficient of partial regression when the variables are expressed in gross scores or in terms of deviations from any origin (usually their respective means), but not in standard scores.

$\beta_{01 \cdot 23} \ldots n$: standard or beta regression coefficient.

bis. η: biserial eta.

CA: chronological age.

CAVD: an abbreviation used to designate the I.E.R. intelligence scale, which consists of a battery of four tests, involving completion, arithmetic, vocabulary, and direction following.

CB: coefficient of brightness.

CC: coefficient of contingency.

$\check{C}$ or CC: cum correction.

χ^2: (kī′ skwãr); chi square, or square contingency.

CI: coefficient of intelligence.

CR: critical ratio.

D: (1) a commonly used abbreviation for difference; sometimes refers to the difference between the ranks of a case on two different variables; (2) the symbol designating the 10 to 90 percentile range; (3) sometimes used as an abbreviation for *decile* (*Dec.* is preferred as less ambiguous).

db: decibel.

Dec.: decile.

d.v.: double vibration.

EA: educational age.

EQ: educational quotient.

ER: education ratio.

η the Greek letter *eta*, symbol for correlation ratio.

f.: (1) (stat.) frequency; (2) (photog.) the symbol used in the f system of designating lens speed; in the United States, represents the reciprocal of the ratio of the maximum aperture of the lens to its focal length; in Europe, represents the ratio itself; *see* f. number; f. system; lens speed.

F_1: (genet.) the first filial generation; the first offspring of the P_1 generation. *See* F_2; P_1.

F_2: (genet.) the offspring of the F_1 generation, produced by mating (either random or selective) within the F_1 generation. *See* F_1; P_1.

FM: frequency modulation.

g: gain (in connection with one method of computing rank correlation).

G: (rare) geometric mean.

GA: guessed average.

GM: geometric mean; also sometimes, guessed mean.

h: index of precision.

i: (1) class interval; (2) as a subscript, it identifies any one observation of the class denoted by the letter to which it is so affixed.

IB: index of brightness.

IQ: intelligence quotient.

k: coefficient of alienation.

ku.: kurtosis.

M: mean or arithmetic mean.

M': arbitrary origin.

MA: mental age.

Md: median.

MD: mean deviation.

Md D: median deviation.

Mdn: median.

Med.: (rare) median. *See* Md.: Mdn.

Mg: (rare) geometric mean.

M_G: geometric mean.

M_H: harmonic mean.

MI: mental index.

Mo: mode.

n: *see* N.

N: a symbol for the total number of cases in a frequency table. (In cases in which a whole group and a subgroup are dealt with, N is commonly used for the entire group and n for the subgroup.)

P: percentile.

P_1: a given parental generation from which are traced succeeding generations; the parents of the F_1 and the grandparents of the F_2 generation. *See* F_1; F_2.

P.A.: public-address system.

Pc. Ave.: percent of average development.

PE: probable error.

Per.: percentile.

Q: quartile deviation; semiinterquartile range.

Q_1: first, or lower, quartile; 25th percentile.

Q_2: second quartile; 50th percentile. (Rarely used, as Q_2 coincides with the median.)

Q_3: third, or upper, quartile; 75th percentile.

r: the lower-case r, used as the general symbol for the coefficient of correlation in a sample. *Contr. w.* ρ.

R: the coefficient of correlation obtained by Spearman's foot-rule method of gains.

$r_{0 \cdot 123} \ldots n$: the symbol sometimes used for coefficient of multiple correlation.

$r_{12 \cdot 34} \ldots n$: coefficient of partial correlation.

$R_{0 \cdot 123} \ldots n$: coefficient of multiple correlation.

r_{bis}: biserial coefficient of correlation.

ρ: the Greek lower-case *rho*, used as the symbol for the rank difference correlation coefficient and also for the correlation in a population. *Contr. w. r.*

r_t: tetrachoric correlation coefficient.

s: standard deviation in a sample. *Contr. w.* σ.

s^2: (s squared) variance in a sample. *Contr. w.* σ^2.

SA: subject age.

SD: standard deviation; sometimes used in place of the symbol σ or s.

σ: the Greek lower-case *sigma*, used as the symbol for standard deviation; often used to denote standard deviation of the population, when it is to be contrasted with s.

σ^2: (sigma squared) variance; *see* V; often used to denote variance of the population, when it is to be contrasted with s^2.

Σ: the Greek capital *sigma*, used as a symbol for summation. *See* σ.

Sk: skewness.

S or *SC:* sine correction.

SQ: subject quotient.

SR: subject ratio.

s.u.: sensation unit. *See* decibel.

V: variance. *See* σ^2 and s^2.

z: mode.

prefixes and suffixes

a-: (Gr.) lacking, without, as in atypical, anesthesia, achromatic; assumes the form *an-* before a vowel or *h;* equivalent to Latin *non-*.

a-: (Lat.) (1) alternative form for **ab-**, as in aversion; (2) alternative form for **ad-**, as in ascend.

ab-: (Lat.) away from, as in abient, aberration, abstract; assumes the form *abs-* before *c, q,* and *t.*

ad-: (Lat.) toward, as in adient; assumes the forms *ac-, af-, ag-, al-, ap-,* and *as-* before *c, f, g, l, p,* and *s,* respectively.

ambi-: (Lat.) both, either, as in ambidextrous, ambilateral.

ana-: (Gr.) up, forward, anew, as in anabolism. *Contr. w.* **cata-**.

auto-: (Gr.) self, as in autogenous, autohypnosis.

bi-: (Lat.) two, double, as in bimanual, bilateral; assumes the form *bin-* before vowels, as in binocular. *Contr. w.* **multi-; uni-**.

cata-: (Gr.) down, destructive, as in catabolism. *Contr. w.* **ana-**.

dys-: *see* **mal-**.

eu-: (Gr.) good, pleasant, as in euthanasia, euphony.

extra-: (Lat.) outside, outward, as in extracurricular, extrasensory. *Contr. w.* **intro-**.

extro-: *var.* **extra-**.

-graphy: (Gr.) writing, delineation, as in photography, geography, historiography.

hemi-: (Gr.) half, as in hemisphere; equivalent to Latin **semi-**.

hetero-: (Gr.) unlike, various, as in heterogeneous. *Contr. w.* **homo-; ortho-**.

histo-: (Gr.) tissue, as in histology.

homo-: (Gr.) like, similar, as in homosexual, homogeneous. *Contr. w.* **hetero-**.

hyper-: (Gr.) to a high degree, excessive, or superior, as in hypertrophy, hypersensitivity. *Contr. w.* **hypo-**.

hypo-: (Gr.) to a low degree, inferior, as in hypochondria. *Contr. w.* **hyper-**.

ideo-: (Gr.) idea, thought, as in ideomotor. *Dist. f.* **idio-**.

idio-: (Gr.) private, personal, as in idiosyncrasy. *Dist. f.* **ideo-**.

intro-: (Lat.) within, inward, as in introspection. *Contr. w.* **extra-**.

-lalia: (Gr.) speech process, as in echolalia.

lalio-, lalo-: (Gr.) speech, as in lalorrhea, laliophobia.

logo-: (Gr.) reasoning, words, as in logorrhea.

-logy: (Gr.) knowledge, science, as in geology, psychology.

macro-: (Gr.) large, as in macrocephaly, macrophotography. *Contr. w.* **micro-**.

mal-: (Lat.) faulty, imperfect, as in malformation, maladjustment; equivalent to Greek **dys-**.

micro-: (Gr.) small, as in microscope, microorganism. *Contr. w.* **macro-**.

mono-: (Gr.) single, as in monosyllabic; equivalent to Latin **uni-**. *Contr. w.* **bi-; multi-; poly-**.

multi-: (Lat.) many, various, as in multilateral; equivalent to Greek **poly-**. *Contr. w.* **bi-; uni-**.

neo-: (Gr.) new, as in Neoplatonism.

ortho-: (Gr.) straight, correct, correction of, as in orthography, orthopedics.

pan-: (Gr.) all, universal, as in panphobia, pantheism.

para-: (Gr.) distorted, perverted, as in paralexia.

-phobia: (Gr.) excessive or pathological fear, as in pyrophobia.

poly-: (Gr.) many, excessive, as in polyglot, polyuria; equivalent to Latin **multi-**.

psycho-: (also *psych-*) (Gr.) mind, mental, as in psychology, psychiatry.

retro-: (Lat.) backward, behind, as in retrospect, retrograde.

scoto-: (Gr.) darkness, as in scotomization, scotophobia.

semi-: (Lat.) half, partly, as in semiconscious; equivalent to Greek **hemi-**.

stereo-: (Gr.) solid, as in stereoscope.

syn-: (Gr.) together, accompanying, as in synthesis, syncretic.

uni-: (Lat.) one, single, as in unimanual, unilateral. *Contr. w.* **bi-; multi-; poly-**.

a cappella (ä kap·pel′lə): *alt. sp.* **a capella**; (It., lit., "from the chapel") a term descriptive of choral music when it is unaccompanied by instruments.

a posteriori: relating to reasoning based upon sense experience or knowledge derived from such reasoning. *Contr. w.* **a priori.**

a posteriori probability: *see* **probability, a posteriori.**

a priori: pertaining to knowledge the validity of which is claimed to be independent of or apart from sense experience. *Contr. w.* **a posteriori.**

a priori existence probability: *see* **probability, a priori existence.**

a priori probability: *see* **probability, a priori.**

A-S-T program: *see* **assign-study-recite formula.**

abac: an arithmetic graph used in computation with solutions indicated by the intersection of lines corresponding to the values of the variables involved. *Syn.* **net table.**

abacist: one who uses an *abacus* for calculating purposes.

abacounter: *see* **abacus.**

abacus (ab′ə·kəs): (1) (math.) a calculating device used in ancient and medieval Europe (and today in some Oriental countries); originally it was a table or board covered with fine dust, but many forms have been developed that use sliding counters on rods or in grooves; (2) (arith.) a calculating device usually composed of beads on a framework of parallel wires which can be used to teach understanding of place value and its relationship with the four fundamental processes in arithmetic; sometimes adapted for use to develop number readiness and number concepts with blind children; *See* **soroban; suan pan.**

abandonment of property: leaving or giving up the use of a school building or other property.

abandonment of teacher's contract: failure by either the teacher or the hiring authority to observe further the terms of a teacher's contract; constitutes a breach of contract if unexcused, for example, if it does not follow a breach by one party that warrants abandonment by the other. *See* **contract, breach of.**

abasia (ə·bā′zhi·ə; -zi·ə): inability to walk due to motor incoordination (often resulting from psychogenic disturbances) or to paralysis.

abasia, atactic: incoordination in walking resulting from *ataxia;* also called *ataxic abasia.*

abatable nuisance: *see* **nuisance, abatable.**

abatement: (school admin.) the reduction of a previously recorded expenditure or receipt item by such things as refunds, rebates, and collections for loss or damage to school property.

abbey school: *syn.* **monastic school.**

ABC method: a method of teaching reading by acquainting the learner first with letters, then with combinations, such as *ab, ac, ad,* and finally with words. *Syn.* **alphabet method;** *contr. w.* **word method.**

abduction: the outward movement of a limb away from the axis of the body. *Contr. w.* **adduction.**

abductive thinking: *see* **thinking, abductive.**

abductor: a muscle that abducts.

abécédaire (a′bā′sā′dār′): (Fr.) (1) *syn.* **abecedarian;** (2) *syn.* **abecedarium.**

abecedarian (ā′bē·sē·dār′i·ən): *n.* (1) a beginning pupil, especially one who is learning to read; (2) a teacher of primary reading and other rudimentary subjects.

abecedarian: *adj.* (1) arranged in alphabetical order; (2) rudimentary or primary.

abecedarium (ā′bē·sē·dār′i·əm): a primer, especially an ABC book. *Syn.* **abécédaire; abecedary.**

abecedary (ā′bē·sē′də·ri): (1) *syn.* **abecedarian;** (2) *syn.* **abecedarium.**

Abelian group: *see* **group, Abelian.**

aberration: any deviation from the usual course.

abient: a term used by Holt to describe a reaction in which the organism displays a continued or persistent orientation away from a stimulus—one in which the organism avoids the stimulus or its repetition or prolongation. *Contr. w.* **adient.**

abilities, primary mental: (1) fundamental elements of intelligence; multiple-factor analyses studies completed by L. L. Thurstone suggest six predominant factors, memory, reasoning, verbal, number, spatial, and word fluency; (2) the least number of independent mental abilities that need be postulated to account for a matrix of correlations.

ability: (1) the actual power present in an organism to carry to completion any given act or to make adjustments successfully, the response being subject to voluntary control and dependent on the motivation of the subject to do his best performance; (2) (gestalt) not a scientific term, but used as a synonym for *skill. Dist. f.* **capacity.**

ability, acquired: what the client can do at the moment in a given field of activity.

ability, adult: differential of learning and performance capacity of adults with respect to younger persons and to general maturity.

ability, artistic: (1) a combination of traits relating to the capacity for aesthetic judgments of expressive form, often indicated by special aptitude or acquired skill in the creative arts, such as drawing, painting, design, and modeling; (2) one's capacity to respond imaginatively to qualities and immediate characteristics of art works.

ability, athletic: motor skills and abilities involved in the performance of athletic sports, measured in terms of achievement.

ability, average: (1) typical ability of all persons in the population, based largely upon subjective opinion; (2) the mean or median ability of all persons in any grade, class, or other group.

ability, basic: (spec. ed.) by the handicapped, demonstrated understanding of terms and tactile discrimination.

ability, cognitive: *see* **intelligence, cognitive.**

ability, crystallized: those cognitive performances in which skilled judgment habits have become crystallized as the result of earlier learning application of some prior, more fundamental, general ability to these fields.

ability, dimension of: ability as measured by a particular aspect of performance, such as speed, range, or power.

ability distribution: *see* **distribution, ability.**

ability, distribution of: *see* **distribution of ability.**

ability, economic: *syn.* **ability, financial.**

ability, educative: the capacity to utilize and to profit from one's intellectual endowment in responding to school demands for mastery of academic subjects.

ability, eductive: the inherent or developed capacity to translate sense impressions into simple concepts or to elicit various types of action responses; ability to develop new relations on the basis of perceived relationships.

ability expectancy: the level of development which a given individual might be expected to reach on the basis of his physical, mental, and emotional attributes, assuming that environmental factors remain generally constant.

ability, extrinsic: an aspect of test performance which is irrelevant to the decision being made; illustrated by the success of coaching in preparing for tests.

ability, final: *see* **final status.**

ability, financial: (1) the extent to which any fund-raising unit, such as a state or school district, has financial resources which might be available for the maintenance of a program; (2) the quality of being able financially to maintain an educational program.

ability, fluid: ability to perform tasks requiring adaptation to new situations. *Dist. f.* **ability, crystallized.**

ability, general: (1) the composite of a number of measured abilities; (2) as used by Spearman in his two-factor theory of intelligence; *syn.* **g-factor;** (3) rough *syn.* **intelligence, general.**

ability grouping: *see* **grouping, ability.**

ability index: *see* **index, ability.**

ability, initial: *see* **initial status.**

ability, intellectual: power to perform a mental act.

ability, intrinsic: an aspect of test performance which is relevant to the decision being made; aids performance on a test and response to later instruction.

ability, language: capability in the command of language or in the acquisition of additional languages.

ability, learning: the inherent or developed capacity to acquire behavioral patterns, attitudes, and methods of responding to stimuli through exercise of the mental and physical processes (memory, reasoning, neuromuscular activity, etc.) which are relevant to stimulation of new responses; the ability to profit through previous experience.

ability, mechanical: (1) intelligent application of the necessary principles of mechanics and facility in the use of tools and the operation of machinery; (2) the individual's ability to deal with mechanisms and mechanical problems (as contrasted with ability to deal with abstract or social problems); frequently found in combination with various types of abstract intelligence. *Syn.* **intelligence, concrete; intelligence, mechanical;** *dist. f.* **intelligence, abstract; intelligence, social.**

ability, mental: (1) a measure of the total activity of a man or animal in responding to internal or external stimulation in relation to experience in the past and expectancy of the future; (2) as commonly used in measurement and testing, a degree of ability represented by performance on a group of tests selected because they have proved their practical value in the prediction of success in academic work and in some vocations.

ability, motor: an individual's efficiency in executing motor skills, that is, the present level of performance in such activities as walking, speaking, writing, and manipulating instruments.

ability, musical: an inherited capacity for musical achievement; sometimes implies development of such an inherited gift. *See* **aptitude, music; musicality.**

ability, olfactory: the ability to distinguish odors and associate smells with known objects.

ability, primary: any one of the seven relatively independent factors of which Thurstone found general intelligence to be composed, including number facility, word fluency, visualizing ability, memory, perceptual speed, induction, and verbal reasoning.

ability, problem-solving: (math.) (1) the degree of capability necessary to find the correct solution to problem situations; (2) an estimate of such ability derived by administering standardized tests.

ability, reading: (1) skill in recognizing directly and interpreting accurately printed or written units of language with eye movements normally characterized by long sweeps that do not overreach their span of recognition; (2) tendency to read carefully, reasoning inductively; measured by rate of reading and by verbal ability and vocabulary (including rate for disconnected facts and chart reading).

ability, receptive language: *see* **decoding, visual.**

ability, scholarship: the ability to do school work or to learn from academically oriented textbooks.

ability, sequencing: the ability to follow one thing after another.

ability, silent-reading: relative efficiency in reading without audible pronunciation; regarded generally as a com-

plex skill made up of subordinate skills, all of which function in an integrated manner to produce efficient reading.

ability, social: (1) competency in getting along with other persons; (2) competency in participating in social interaction and in attaining status in the group; (3) effectiveness in leading or influencing companions and in adjusting oneself to them without strain or conflict.

ability, special: (1) an ability limited to certain types of performance, as distinguished from *general ability,* which is conceived as a factor operating, in varying degrees, in all or most types of performance; (2) an ability that overlaps other abilities only slightly or not at all and is largely independent of general ability and the individual's general level of performance; (3) an ability that is not consistent with other abilities of the individual, deviating markedly from the general level of his other performances.

ability, superior mental: *see* **intelligence.**

ability, synthesizing: the power to put together parts or elements to form a whole; proficiency in combining ideas to form a complex concept.

ability test: *see* **test, ability.**

ability-to-pay tax theory: *see* **tax theory, ability-to-pay.**

Abitur (ä·bi·tōor'): (Lat., lit., "one goes away") in German-speaking countries, a state examination given at the end of 6, 7, or 9 years to students who have completed their course at a secondary school at the Gymnasium level; required for admission to a university or other university-level institution; can be taken without attending a regular secondary school after private tutoring or after special courses for exceptionally gifted students. *See* **Gymnasium.**

abjection: depression of spirits; a downcast state of mind.

abjudicate: (law) to give away or transfer by judgment.

abjure: to take an oath declaring a renunciation.

ablactation: the process of weaning a child or young animal.

able student: *see* **student, able.**

abnormal: either statistically or qualitatively different from the mean (the usual).

abnormal child: *syn.* **child, exceptional.**

abnormal mental process: *see* **mental process, abnormal.**

abnormal psychology: *see* **psychology, abnormal.**

abnormality, breathing: any unusual pattern or form of inspiration and expiration; inefficient utilization of respiration in speaking, the more relevant abnormalities being shallow breathing, holding of the breath, and unusually rapid, slow, or irregular inhaling and exhaling.

abnormality, congenital: any microscopic or macroscopic structural abnormality attributable to faulty development and present at birth.

abortive guidance: *see* **guidance, abortive.**

abortive trial: *see* **trial, abortive.**

aboulia (ə·bōō'li·ə): *alt. sp.* **abulia;** loss of ability to reach a decision or to perform an act; a mental state characterized by hesitation and conflict.

abreaction: reliving an emotional experience so as to decrease its present effect upon the individual; a psychotherapeutic technique. *See* **catharsis.**

abrogation: an annulment or repeal of a legal instrument.

abscissa: the first number of the pair of numbers assigned a point in the plane when Cartesian coordinates are used. *See* **coordinates, Cartesian.**

absence: the failure of a pupil to be present at school; generally understood as failure to be present at more than half the session. (The interpretation of what constitutes absence varies, however, according to different rules, some demanding total absence and some only a moment's absence.) *See* **attendance, a day's.**

absence, aggregate days: the sum of the days of absence of all pupils when school is in session during a given reporting period. *See* **session, days in.**

absence and tardiness report, teacher's daily: *see* **report, teacher's daily absence and tardiness.**

absence, average daily: the aggregate days absence of a given school during a given reporting period divided by the number of days school is in session during this period; for groups of schools having varying lengths of terms, the sum of the average daily absences obtained for the individual schools. *See* **absence, aggregate days; absence, day of; session, days in.**

absence, day of: a day when school is in session during which a pupil is in membership but not in attendance. *See* **absence.**

absence, excused: absence from school for any reason recognized as legitimate by the school, for example, attendance at religious ceremonies, illness of the pupil or of a member of the pupil's family, or death in the home.

absence, legal: absence from school for reasons in accordance with regulations established by law. (Illness is commonly recognized by law as a legitimate reason for absenting oneself from school; holidays and religious ceremonies are occasions for legal absence.)

absence, percentage of: *see* **percentage of absence.**

absence record: *see* **record, absence.**

absence, teacher: failure on the part of a teacher to be present for school duties; may be excused, as for illness, or unexcused.

absence, unexcused: absence from school for reasons that are not recognized by the school as legitimate, for example, absence because of play, truancy, illegal work, etc.

absolute: (philos.) unlimited, unconditional, underived, not relative; perfect or whole; descriptive of any standard not instituted or modified by the consequences of its operational application, but a standard by virtue of its own inherent constitution and properties which are perfect and complete.

absolute accuracy: *see* **accuracy, absolute.**

absolute blindness: *see* **blindness, total.**

absolute brilliance limen: *syn.* **absolute brilliance threshold.**

absolute brilliance threshold: a measure of the lowest intensity of light that an individual can distinguish from complete darkness after the eyes have become accommodated to darkness. *Syn.* **absolute brilliance limen.**

absolute deviation: *see* **deviation, absolute.**

absolute error: *see* **error, absolute.**

absolute humidity: *see* **humidity, absolute.**

absolute mind: *see* **mind, absolute.**

absolute music: *see* **music, absolute.**

absolute perceptual span: *see* **perceptual span, absolute.**

absolute pitch: *see* **pitch, absolute.**

absolute programming: *see* **programming, absolute.**

absolute, the: (philos.) the self-contained; that which is unrelated to anything beyond itself; the point of ultimate reference; that which is universally valid; independent, ultimate ground of all being; opposite of mere appearance, as *being* is to *becoming* or *the infinite* to *the finite*; God, universal spirit (Hegel), the unknowable, *noumenon* (Kant).

absolute threshold of audibility: *see* **threshold of audibility.**

absolute value: *see* **value, absolute.**

absolute-variability: *see* **variability, absolute.**

absolutism: (1) (philos.) the doctrine that holds to the existence of the absolute or to the absolute character of certain abstractions, as absolute values, truths, etc.; *see* **absolute; absolute, the**; (2) (pol. sci.) the doctrine of unconditioned power exercised by rulers bound neither by the laws of nature nor by any kind of moral or legal limitations; (3) in social theory particularly, the doctrine that social laws, normative and regulative, exist at all periods and under all circumstances of proper social life with finality and everlastingness.

absorbent mind: *see* **Montessori method.**

absorption unit: *see* **unit, absorption.**

abstract: *n.* a descriptive or informative summary or abridgment of a statement, speech, or document.

abstract: *v.* to summarize; to proceed to broader and broader generalizations by a process of leaving out and relating details.

abstract: *adj.* (philos.) (1) considered apart from any particular or concrete object; expressing a quality as independent of any particularly qualified object; thus, honesty is the abstract expression for honest behavior; (2) (Hegelian usage) pertaining to any part of any whole; pertaining to one aspect separated from a totality; thus, the leaf of a tree is regarded as abstract.

abstract algebra: *see* **algebra, abstract.**

abstract average: *see* **average, abstract.**

abstract concept: *see* **concept, abstract.**

abstract expressionism: *see* **action painting.**

abstract intelligence: *see* **intelligence, abstract.**

abstract learning: *see* **learning, abstract.**

abstract number: *see* **number, abstract.**

abstract problem: *see* **problem, abstract.**

abstract reasoning: *see* **reasoning, abstract.**

abstract-reasoning test: *see* **test, abstract-reasoning.**

abstract relationships, transfer of: *see* **transfer of abstract relationships.**

abstraction: (1) the process of recognizing the common characteristics which relate specific objects or situations and identifying these characteristics; (2) the mental process in which one neglects or cuts off certain impressions in the interest of emphasis upon a single line of thought; (3) in animal experimentation, the ability of an animal to respond to the common element in a number of different stimuli, as to the concept of triangularity; (4) sometimes, transfer of training which has been effected by generalization of common experiences; *see* **generalization, response; generalization, stimulus**; (5) loosely, intense absorption with extraneous incidents or marked inattention to present situations; (6) in programmed instruction, a response which the student makes to a single property of a complex stimulus, such as "pachyderm" in response to a picture of an elephant.

abstraction, levels of: steps or levels involved in the process of developing successively broader generalizations (abstracting proceeds from more detailed or specific levels to less specific or detailed levels by a process of omitting particular characteristics); a basic notion in the field of general semantics, the tendency to confuse different levels of abstraction being regarded by general semanticists as indicative of inadequate language behavior. *See* **allness; extensionalization; therapy, general semantic.**

abstractor: one who extracts for an information storage and retrieval system a brief summary of the essentials of a published piece of research, including research material published in foreign languages.

absurdities test: *see* **test, absurdities.**

abulia (ə·bū′li·ə): *alt. sp.* **aboulia.**

abused child: *syn.* **child, battered.**

-ac: a suffix meaning automatic computer, as in the acronyms ENIAC, SWAC, UNIVAC, etc., coined as trade names.

academe (a·kə·dēm′): a poetic term for the academic milieu, derived from Plato's Academy and the Roman poet Horace's subsequent use of the name in the line "and seek for truth in the groves of Academe."

academia (a·kə·dēm′yə): (New Lat., lit., "university") a generic term referring to the system or total aspect or atmosphere of higher education; generally used in flowery, oratorical, or humorous speech. *See* **academe.**

academic: (1) (sec. ed.) pertaining to the fields of English, foreign languages, history, economics, mathematics, and science; (2) (higher ed.) traditionally pertaining to the liberal arts fields but more recently used to relate to all instructional activities as distinguished from noninstructional activities; (3) pertaining to the realm of ideas or abstractions. *See* **nonacademic.**

academic acceleration: *see* **acceleration, academic.**

academic achievement: *see* **achievement, academic.**

academic administration: *see* **administration, academic.**

academic aptitude: *see* **aptitude, academic.**

academic-aptitude test: *see* **test, academic-aptitude.**

academic building: *see* **building, academic.**

academic costume: outer garments, consisting of special caps, gowns, and hoods of various forms, worn on special academic occasions by students, graduates, faculties, and officials in colleges, universities, and other institutions of learning.

academic course: see course, academic.

academic dean: see dean, academic.

academic degree: see degree, academic.

academic department: see department, academic.

academic disability: see disability, academic.

academic dissertation: syn. dissertation.

academic enrichment: see enrichment, curriculum.

academic freedom: see freedom, academic.

academic game: syn. game, simulation.

academic goal: see goal, academic.

academic high school: see high school, academic.

academic inventory: see inventory, academic.

academic marketplace: a term used by some specialists in educational sociology to describe universities in terms of a marketplace where academic skills and the people who possess them are bought, sold, and bartered.

academic method: (art ed.) a method of art teaching in which the main interest is in the product, with stress on authoritarianism, imitation, naturalism, and technical proficiency; may apply to modern as well as to traditional approaches.

academic persistence: see persistence, academic.

academic probation: syn. probation, scholastic (2).

academic progress: see progress, academic.

academic promotion: see promotion, academic.

academic record: see record, academic.

academic retardation: syn. progress, slow.

academic standard: see standard, academic.

academic tenure: see tenure, academic.

academic training: see training, academic.

academic travel abroad: see travel abroad, academic.

academic year: the period covering the annual session (excluding the summer session) of an educational institution of university level, usually divided into two semesters or three quarters or, in some colleges, into two trimesters of about 15 weeks each, usually coordinated with a summer trimester; the total period is usually about 9 months. Also called *school year.*

academical plan: (1) a plan of teacher education under which state funds were granted to academies for the establishment of a separate department offering a course preparing students to teach in elementary schools; first established by New York in 1834; (2) the general practice of offering courses for the training of teachers by academies, whether publicly or privately supported; fairly common during the middle period of the nineteenth century.

academically handicapped: see handicapped, academically.

academically talented child: see child, academically talented.

Academician: (1) the title of the first important educational journal in the United States, beginning publication in 1818; (2) (not cap.) one distinguished for scholarship or bookish learning.

academy: (1) (cap.) the gymnasium on the northwest side of Athens where Plato taught; (2) (cap.) the intellectual tradition initiated by Plato, called the Old Academy to the early fourth century B.C., thereafter the New Academy until the formal closing of the Academy along with all the other pagan Greek schools by the Emperor Justinian in 529 A.D.; (3) the privately supported secondary schools, prominent in the United States from about 1750 to 1875, which superseded the Latin grammar schools and were replaced by the high schools; (4) sometimes used to designate institutions of higher education, as United States Military Academy; (5) sometimes used to designate a body of scholars, as American Academy of Fine Arts and Sciences.

academy, free: In New York State, the designation of certain educational institutions which were once private academies but which are now operated under public auspices. Syn. **high school.**

Academy leader: see leader, Academy.

academy, military: a school for boys and young men, organized and equipped somewhat on the pattern of a military post and in which military training and military science form an essential part of the curriculum.

academy of fine arts: a school or institute of learning where courses of instruction are given in drawing, painting, sculpture, design, architecture, and other fine arts.

academy, service: any of several institutions of higher education maintained by the Federal government to prepare students for a professional career as officers in one of the armed services.

academy, tuition: an independent secondary school supported largely or entirely through tuition fees; usually designates a school maintained for the profit of an owner or stockholders.

acalculia: inability to carry out mathematical calculations in the absence of mental deficit; usually associated with aphasia as a result of an extensive lesion involving the temporal, parietal, and occipital lobes in the dominant hemisphere of the brain. Syn. **dyscalculia.**

acatalepsia (ə·kat'ə·lep'si·ə): inability to understand commands or instructions, whether delivered by language, signs, gestures, or symbols.

accelerated child: see child, accelerated.

accelerated college entrance: see college entrance, accelerated.

accelerated course: see course, accelerated.

accelerated program: see program, accelerated.

accelerated progress: syn. acceleration.

accelerated promotion: see promotion, accelerated.

accelerated pupil: syn. child, accelerated (1).

acceleration: (1) the process of progressing through the school grades at a rate faster than that of the average child, either by skipping grades or by rapidly mastering the work of one grade and moving on to the next higher grade; (2) advancement in mental growth or achievement beyond the average for the individual's chronological age; (3) a general term including all administrative practices which result in completing a school program in less than the usual time allotted.

acceleration, academic: any process whereby a pupil makes educational progress faster than is usual, whether measured by advancement in school grade (American) or standard (British), or by actual educational advancement; the means to such faster progress are many and should not be restricted to faster progress by grade skipping. Also called *educational acceleration* or *scholastic acceleration.*

acceleration, negative: (stat.) the curve that results when each successive change is smaller than the preceding one.

acceleration, positive: (stat.) the curve that results when each successive change is greater than the preceding one.

acceleration time: see start time.

accelerator, reading: see reading accelerator.

accent: (1) (read.) the stress laid by the voice on a syllable of a word to make it more prominent than the other syllables; (2) a fallacy of ambiguity in which unclear or distorted meaning results from undue emphasis upon any part of a statement at the expense of its whole or intended meaning; for example, " 'Love thy neighbor as thyself' means that I need not love you, for you are not my neighbor"; see **ambiguity, fallacy of.**

acceptability, social: degree to which a child is accepted or rejected as indicated by his associates' response to him.

acceptable transcript: syn. transcript, mailable.

acceptance: in counseling, the therapist's positive, uncensuring attitude toward the client, implying understanding of the counselee's feelings and behavior and recognition of his worth as an individual, without condoning antisocial behavior.

acceptance of false hypothesis: syn. error, beta.

acceptance, peer: liking by one's own age group and inclusion in its activities, evidenced by the fact that the group praises one's accomplishments and listens to one's ideas.

acceptance region: *see* **region, acceptance.**

acceptance sampling: *see* **sampling, acceptance.**

acceptee, administrative: a registrant who has been accepted for military service following an administrative determination that he possesses the required capacity to achieve the minimum score on the prescribed mental test, notwithstanding his failure to achieve such score.

access, immediate: the ability to obtain data from or place data in a storage device, usually in a short period of time.

access, parallel: (data processing) the process of obtaining information from or placing information into storage where access time is dependent on the simultaneous transfer of all elements of a word from a given storage location.

access, random: (1) the function of a computer, slide projector, or tape playback unit that enables one to go to any storage location at any time and with equal facility and get a piece of information or place it in storage at that location; the time required for such access is independent of the location of the information just previously obtained or placed in storage; (2) in automatic data processing, access in a storage device under conditions such that the next address from which information is to be obtained is chosen at random.

access, serial: the process of obtaining information from or placing information into storage where access is dependent on waiting while nondesired locations are processed.

access time: (data processing) the interval between the point of time at which the arithmetic unit calls for information from the storage unit and the moment at which the information is completely available; or the interval between the point of time at which the arithmetic unit is ready to send information to the storage unit and the moment at which the storage of the information in the memory unit is complete.

accessibility: the quality of being easy to approach or reach. (A school is accessible if there are good highways or railroads, buses, or other means of transportation by which it can be reached; a room is accessible if it opens to a communicating corridor.)

accession: a library term describing all the administrative work necessary to receive, inspect, catalog, mark and identify, and place material in storage for distribution.

accession, teacher: the addition of an instructor to the teaching staff of a school system, because of a vacancy or the creation of a new position.

accessory, bus: *see* **bus accessory.**

accessory material: workbooks, charts, cards, and other devices that are used to supplement the basic textbook in reading.

accessory room: a separate *science room* planned and equipped for such essential and desirable uses as reading, preparation, project work, photography, storage, and construction.

accessory space: parts of a building or room used for activities supplementary to teaching (storage space, darkroom, etc.).

accidence: that branch of linguistic study which deals with the changes of form employed to denote the different numbers, cases, tenses, moods, etc.

accident drill: a practiced plan for rapidly discharging pupils from a school bus.

accident insurance: *see* **insurance, accident.**

accident, lost-time: an unexpected event resulting in injury to a person to the extent that he is unable to perform his duties during a period extending beyond the remainder of the day or shift.

accident prevention training: *see* **training, accident prevention.**

accident-prone: having a tendency to many accidents or near accidents.

accident report: *see* **report, accident.**

accident, school: an injury or mishap occurring to an individual while he is in school.

accident, school-bus: (1) an accident involving a school bus, which results in property damage or personal injury, as when a child is injured by the bus, by a vehicle near the bus, or while on the bus; (2) an accident involving a child immediately before boarding or after leaving the bus if it is at the scene of the accident.

accident, school-bus, associated-type: an accident in which a school child or children are injured before boarding or after alighting from the school bus, but which does not involve the school bus itself.

accident spot map: a map upon which accident locations, drivers' and pedestrians' residences, and other significant facts concerning accidents are shown by means of pins or other markers, size and shape of pins or marks indicating the various types of accidents.

accidental: (1) happening without having been foreseen; descriptive especially of an event which is or seems to be unpremeditated; (2) incidental or circumstantial to the essential nature of a thing; for example, all education involves both a teacher and a pupil, but the ages of teacher and pupil are accidental.

accidental error: *see* **error, accidental.**

accidental sample: *syn.* **sample, incidental.**

accidentals: *syn.* **chromatics.**

accommodation: (1) (psych.) the act of changing one's behavior consciously or unconsciously so as to make better adjustment to demands of the environment; as used by Piaget, changes made by the child in his schemata in adaptation to changing stimulus situations; (2) (soc.) as a condition, a state of equilibrium between individuals or groups in which certain working arrangements have been accepted; as a process, the social adjustment between individuals or groups, aimed at temporarily suspending conflict, common forms of accommodation being conciliation, arbitration, compromise, and tolerant participation; also called *antagonistic accommodation;* (3) the act of making adjustive muscular movements that prepare the sense organs to receive distinct impressions from stimuli, for example, the adjustments made in the shape of the lens and the size of the pupil of the eye for seeing objects at different distances and under different conditions of light.

accommodation, antagonistic: *see* **accommodation** (2).

accommodation, binocular: (1) the act of adjusting the two eyes on a central point in such a manner as to produce a clear image; (2) the posturing of the focusing mechanism of both eyes for maximum interpretation. *Syn.* **binocular focusing.**

accommodation, near point of: *see* **near point of accommodation.**

accommodation strategy: (1) (spec. ed.) the particular procedure used by a teacher or therapist to facilitate the accommodation of a learner to his disability or environment; (2) a procedure adopted by middle-class Negroes for achievement of aspirations by adaptation to white middle-class mores.

accomplishment: *syn.* **achievement.**

accomplishment age: rare *syn.* **age, achievement.**

accomplishment quotient (AQ): *syn.* **quotient, achievement.**

accomplishment ratio: rare *syn.* **quotient, achievement.**

accomplishment test: *syn.* **test, achievement.**

account approach: a method of teaching the principles of bookkeeping and accounting by starting with consideration of the ledger account, on the assumption that the student may see the source of the transactions and the classification of those items for use in the balance sheet, and in the profit and loss statement. *Syn.* **ledger approach.**

account, charge: *see* **charge account.**

account, subsidiary: (school finance) an account which contains detailed information in support of control accounts in the same ledger or in a general ledger. *See* **accounts, inventory controlling.**

accountability: (admin.) liability for results which have been obtained through the responsible exercise of delegated authority.

accountability, educational: the theory that teachers and school systems may be held responsible for actual improvement in pupil achievement and that such improvement is measurable through tests of teacher effectiveness constructed by outside agencies. *See* **testing, accountability.**

accountability, pupil: the responsibility for carrying out an obligation or trust to each pupil appropriately assigned to a specific school or a school district. *See* **attendance data.**

accountability testing: *see* **testing, accountability.**

accountant: one who is qualified through training and experience to plan and direct the keeping of financial records and to summarize, analyze, and interpret the results.

accounting: (1) the art of recording, classifying, and summarizing, in a significant manner and in terms of money, transactions and events that are, in part at least, of a financial character and interpreting the results thereof; (2) a recognized area of instruction in schools and colleges, leading to facility in performing the functions listed in (1).

accounting and computing operations training: *see* **training, accounting and computing operations.**

accounting, child: *syn.* **accounting, pupil.**

accounting classification: the grouping of expenditures and revenues according to purpose or source. *See* **character classification.**

accounting, cost: a method of accounting that provides for the assembling and recording of all the elements of cost incurred to accomplish a purpose, to carry on an activity or operation, or to complete a unit of work or a specific job.

accounting department: *see* **department, accounting.**

accounting equation: *syn.* **bookkeeping equation.**

accounting, financial: the classification and summarization of financial records for the purpose of conducting, controlling, and interpreting the financial and business transactions of a school.

accounting, internal: the recording of financial transactions in such a form as to supply information needed for management purposes. *See* **accounting.**

accounting period: a period of time for which records are maintained and at the end of which financial statements are prepared. *See* **fiscal period; fiscal year.**

accounting, property: the accounts and related records required for fixed assets.

accounting, pupil: a system for collecting, computing, and reporting information about pupils needed for the maintenance of essential records of the individual child during his school life. Also called *child accounting.*

accounting, secretarial: an area of study infrequently offered on both college and high-school levels that deals with the bookkeeping and accounting phases of secretarial work; includes simple statement analysis, personal records for executives, banking operations, simple bookkeeping systems, etc.

accounting, student: the recording of information relating to students, including such items as records of previous achievement, grades and credits earned, and honors and awards received.

accounting system: (1) a method and procedure for recording transactions and preparing financial statements; (2) a set of records and a plan of procedure for bookkeeping and accounting adapted to a particular situation.

accounting system, uniform school: a system of accounting involving pupil accounting and financial accounting, so organized that each form used within the system dovetails with each of the other forms of the system.

accounting, teacher: the recording of information relating to individual teachers, including the recording of time for payroll purposes and numerical data or statements concerning such facts as education, experience, personality, conduct, efficiency, and achievement.

accounting, uniform: any system of accounting in which items are defined identically and are recorded in similar places on similar forms.

accounting, uniform paper: a system of child accounting based on a common system of record, report, and administrative forms.

accounts, budgetary: accounts necessary to reflect budget operations as distinguished from those which represent actual assets and liabilities and income and expense items.

accounts, inventory controlling: (school admin.) summary accounts in the organization's general ledger that are set up by the accounting department for the items or accounts in a given classification of materials; the individual store's ledger accounts are closed into the controlling account for the particular classification.

accounts receivable: amounts owing on open account from private persons, firms, or corporations or from governmental units (but not including amounts due from other funds).

accredit: to designate an educational institution as meeting required standards or accepted criteria of quality established by a competent agency. (Use of the word is frequently accompanied by an indication of the agency that does the accrediting.)

accreditation: the recognition accorded to an educational institution in the United States through inclusion on a list of accredited or approved institutions issued by some agency or organization (professional, regional, or state), which sets up standards or requirements that must be complied with in order to secure approval; membership is voluntary and extralegal.

accredited elementary school: *see* **elementary school, accredited.**

accredited high school: *see* **high school, accredited.**

accredited school: a school that has met accepted standards applied to it by a competent agency or an official accrediting agency or association.

accrediting agency: an organization that sets up criteria for judging the quality of educational institutions and programs, determines the extent to which institutions and programs meet these criteria, and issues some sort of public announcement concerning the institutions and programs found to be of acceptable quality; may be either a governmental bureau, such as a state department of education, or a voluntary organization, such as a regional association of colleges and secondary schools.

accrediting agent: *syn.* **accrediting agency.**

accrediting association: a nongovernmental or voluntary accrediting agency; may be one of several types: (*a*) a regional association of colleges and secondary schools; (*b*) an association composed of practitioners in a given profession, such as the American Medical Association or the American Bar Association, which sets up agencies or committees for the accrediting of professional schools; (*c*) an association of specialized professional schools or colleges, such as the National Association of Schools of Music; (*d*) a council representing several interested groups or associations, such as the professional schools, the practitioners, and the state licensing or certificating agencies, such as the Council on Dental Education.

accrediting association, regional: an organization set up to administer an accrediting procedure in a territory covering several states but not the entire nation.

accrediting procedure: the process by which an accrediting agency determines whether an educational institution or a program is to be accredited.

accreditment: *syn.* **accreditation.**

accretionary growth: *see* **growth, accretionary.**

accrual: in accounting, sums of money that have accrued.

accrual basis: the basis of a system of accounting in which revenues are accounted for when earned or due, even though not collected, and expenditures are accounted for as soon as liabilities are incurred, whether paid or not.

acculturation: (1) the absorption by any group of certain features of the culture of another group, as a result of contact or interaction between the two; (2) the merging of two or more cultures, ranging from accommodative arrangements to full assimilation or synthesis of cultures; (3) the entire sequence of processes involved in a contact and subsequent intermixture of the traits and patterns of two or more cultures. *See* **socialization.**

accumulative average: *syn.* **average, grade point.**

accumulative error: *syn.* **error, constant.**

accumulator: (data processing) a register in the arithmetic unit where the results of arithmetic or logic operations are stored temporarily.

accuracy: (1) correspondence of statement with fact or reality; exactness within the limits of completeness demanded by the purpose of the investigator or observer; (2) the ratio of the number of test items correctly done to the number attempted; (3) freedom from both variable and constant errors, as on the part of a set of test scores; to be distinguished from *reliability*, which is affected directly by variable errors only; (4) agreement between the result of a calculation or measurement and the accepted value for that calculation or measurement; evaluated in terms of the relative error made, the smaller the relative error, the greater the accuracy; (5) (read.) exactness or precision in the pronunciation of a word; exactness of comprehension in reading.

accuracy, absolute: complete agreement between the true or accepted value and an observed or a computed value; unattainable in psychological measurement.

accuracy, degree of: *see* **error, relative.**

accuracy, false: the seemingly exact but actually inaccurate result obtained by the application of correct calculation techniques to inaccurate raw data.

accuracy in computation: the degree of agreement between the result of a calculation or measurement and the accepted value for that calculation or measurement; evaluated in terms of the relative error made.

accuracy in measurement: *see* **measurement, accuracy in.**

accuracy in reasoning: reasoning which involves not only valid logical principles but also the selection of appropriate assumptions at the outset.

accuracy, relative: *see* **error, relative.**

accuracy score: *see* **score, accuracy.**

accuracy test: *see* **test, accuracy.**

accusation: (school law) a legal charge, implicating one or many, of guilt of a punishable offense.

accused: *n.* the defendant or defendants charged with commission of a punishable offense.

ace: (phys. ed.) a point, in a game such as handball or tennis, scored by a shot that the opponent is unable to touch.

acetate: a plastic sheet which may be (*a*) clear, permitting a high degree of light transmission, resulting in a transparent appearance, (*b*) treated with a special coating on either side so that, though appearing clear, it will accept ordinary drawing inks, or (*c*) matte or frosted, with one side etched or roughed so as to take regular inks and colored pencil markings easily.

acetate-base film: *see* **film, acetate-base.**

acetylcholine: chemical substance which apparently functions within the neuromuscular system to produce responses.

achievement: (1) accomplishment or proficiency of performance in a given skill or body of knowledge; (2) progress in school; theoretically different from intelligence but overlaps with it to a great degree.

achievement, academic: knowledge attained or skills developed in the school subjects, usually designated by test scores or by marks assigned by teachers, or by both.

achievement age: *see* **age, achievement.**

achievement battery: *see* **battery, achievement.**

achievement gap: the difference in academic success between culturally disadvantaged and middle-class children caused by the formers' learning style, which is slow, physical, nonverbal, problem-centered, and concrete-oriented.

achievement mark: *see* **mark, achievement.**

achievement motivation: *see* **motivation, achievement.**

achievement need: *see* **motivation, achievement.**

achievement, objective: commonly, a measure of the student's ability in terms of standardized test results.

achievement, pupil: the status of a pupil with respect to attained skills or knowledge as compared with other pupils or with the school's adopted standards.

achievement quotient (AQ): *see* **quotient, achievement.**

achievement ratio: *syn.* **quotient, achievement.**

achievement, reading: attainment in any of a number of reading skills, habits, and attitudes; usually estimated by performance on some criterion measure such as formal or informal reading tests, or by reading grade levels.

achievement scale: *syn.* **test, achievement.**

achievement score: *see* **score, achievement.**

achievement standards: *see* **standards, achievement.**

achievement test: *see* **test, achievement.**

achievement test, general: *see* **battery, achievement; measurement, multiple.**

achiever, high general: a child who achieves high scores on arithmetic, reading, and spelling tests.

achiever, latent: a person who possesses hidden ability to succeed in specified areas but who has not yet reached the culmination stage of this process, possibly because of developmental or motivational factors. *See* **underachievement.**

achromatic vision: *see* **color blindness.**

acouasm (ə·kōō′az′m): false perception of indefinite sounds, as hissing, ringing, whistling.

acoumeter (ə·kōō′mə·tər; -mē′tər): an instrument used for testing the hearing, for example, the Politzer acoumeter, which produces a fixed clicking tone and which normally can be heard at distances up to about 45 feet.

acoustic: pertaining to sounds, with particular reference to their perception as against their production.

acoustic basis: the phonetic foundation of a language used in determining the significance of variations in pronunciation.

acoustic class: *see* **class, acoustic.**

acoustic feedback: *see* **feedback, acoustic.**

acoustic image: a mental picture of sound, pitch, and rhythm sequences.

acoustic method: a method of teaching the deaf to understand speech and to speak through training of the auditory and tactile sense organs by sound vibrations produced by the voice or sonorous instruments; devised by Dr. Max A. Goldstein.

acoustic training: *syn.* **training, auditory;** *see* **acoustic method.**

acoustic trauma: *see* **trauma, acoustic.**

acoustical sound trap: *see* **sound trap, acoustical.**

acoustically handicapped: *syn.* **handicapped, hearing.**

acousticist: a linguist who believes that the origin of language is to be looked for in the imitation of sounds rather than in spontaneous articulation.

acoustics: (1) the science of sound; an area of study concerned with the cause, nature, and phenomena of vibrations that affect the organs of hearing; (2) loosely, the sound characteristics of an enclosure, such as a room, an open-air theater, etc.

acquiescent learning: *see* **learning, acquiescent.**

acquired: not ascribable to hereditary causes.

acquired ability: *see* **ability, acquired.**

acquired aphasia: *see* **aphasia, acquired.**

acquired character: *see* **character, acquired.**

acquired characteristic: *syn.* **character, acquired.**

acquired deafness: *syn.* **deafness, adventitious.**

acquired disability: *see* **disability, acquired.**

acquired hearing impairment: *see* **hearing impairment, acquired.**

acquired reaction: *syn.* **response, acquired.**

acquired reflex: *syn.* **reflex, conditioned.**

acquired response: *see* **response, acquired.**

acquired virtues: *see* **virtues, acquired.**

acquisition, library: the branch of library service concerned with acquiring books, periodicals, and other library materials by purchase, exchange, gift, or deposit, together with the development and maintenance of essential records of these accessions.

acquisition program, Library of Congress foreign: *see* **program, Library of Congress foreign acquisition.**

acquisitiveness: (1) the tendency to emphasize individual ownership, or a desire to collect; sometimes extended to include an excessive desire to acquire friends, facts, fads, etc.; (2) the gathering or collecting instinct in insects and animals.

acquittal: a court release, generally a verdict, absolving one of a legal *accusation.*

acreation: activities that are not recreational but are engaged in during leisure time. *See* **leisure; recreation.**

acronym: an expression formed from the initial letters or group of letters of words in a set phrase.

acrylics: (art) a painting medium in which color pigments are suspended in a polymerized acrylic acid (or derivatives or other similar acids); they have plastic qualities similar to oil pigments, produce both transparent and opaque colors, are water soluble, and dry hard more quickly than oils yet possess greater permanency.

act, creative social: *see* **social act, creative.**

act of creation, conscious: *see* **creation, conscious act of.**

act of skill: any muscular coordination or mental process that has been brought to a high level of proficiency through practice.

Act of Supremacy: an act by Parliament in 1534 breaking England's ties with the Roman Catholic Church; in 1559 a second Act of Supremacy required the clergy, all judges, and royal officials to take an oath accepting the supremacy of the crown in all church matters; its chief educational significance lies in the fact that charity was called upon to fill the vacuum left when the Roman Catholic Church was forced to abandon its efforts in the education of poor children.

act of thought: a complete act of thought involves (*a*) a felt difficulty; (*b*) definition and location of the difficulty; (*c*) emergence of a tentative solution; (*d*) mental elaboration of the solution; (*e*) experimental verification or testing of the proposed solution; in Dewey, defined as "active, persistent, and careful consideration of any belief or supposed form of knowledge in the light of the grounds that support it and the further consequences to which it tends."

Act of Toleration: the act by the English Parliament in 1689 granting rights to dissenters from the Anglican faith; recognized the existence of *dissenting schools* and authorized their incorporation.

Act of Uniformity: one of a series of acts by the English Parliament, passed between 1549 and 1662, which marked the foundation of the English church of protestantism; the act of 1662 aimed at the expulsion of all those clergymen from their benefices and all those teachers from their schools who refused to conform to the established church; legal suits, however, later permitted dissenters to teach in private schools. *See* **Act of Supremacy; Act of Toleration.**

act, tortious: an act that results in the commission of a *tort.*

action: (legal) (1) a court proceeding for the redress of a wrong, the protection of a right, or the punishment of an offense; (2) a lawsuit.

action at law: court action in a law case, as distinguished from *equity.*

action, bodily: *see* **bodily action.**

action, civil: a law suit brought to recover some civil right or to obtain redress for some wrong.

action, contract: (legal) an action brought to enforce rights under a contract.

action, criminal: proceedings by which a party charged with a crime is brought to trial.

action exercise: *see* **exercise, action.**

action, group: discussion or work that produces results not likely to have been achieved by the same people acting separately; commonly used in problem solution as well as in construction, dramatization, art, etc. *Syn.* **group activity.**

action, impulsive: behavior that occurs without deliberation or delay although not at the reflex level; it may be engaged in regardless of the consequences. *Contr. w.* **action, reflective.**

action, integrative: *see* **integrative action.**

action, internalized: in the theory of Piaget, mental manipulation, or operation, as the central component in the structure of knowledge.

action painting: a mid-twentieth-century movement in painting which is characterized by spontaneity and unpremeditated response to the emerging image which prior painting action has produced; many such paintings are large scale and may involve forms which were created by pouring, splattering, vigorous brush strokes, etc.; formerly called *abstract expressionism;* (such artists as Jackson Pollack, Franz Kline, Willem De Kooning, and others are identified with this movement).

action pattern: (1) the formula for the logical procession from an assumption to a procedure designed to accomplish an objective based upon that assumption; (2) the successive derivation of an assumption, a principle, an objective, a criterion, and a procedure; (3) *see* **supervision, pattern of.**

action-pattern program: *see* **program, action-pattern.**

action play: a poem or verse accompanied by bodily movements, the purpose being to develop in a child a sense of rhythm and to bring large muscles into use through purposeful activity, thus releasing the child from tensions.

action-potential technique: a technique for measuring the presence of muscular activity of the speech organs in silent reading by the use of a galvanometer.

action-potential waves: *see* **waves, action-potential.**

action project: an instructional project originating in the school but in which there is a definite planned carry-over into the out-of-school life of the pupil.

action, purposive: *see* **purposive action.**

action, reflective: behavior that occurs after a conscious selection of the response believed to be most appropriate. *Contr. w.* **action, impulsive.**

action research: *see* **research, action.**

action series: in foreign language instruction, a type of learning method in which children in groups or as individuals perform a series of sequential actions and say what they are doing as they perform each action; also called the Gouin Series.

action song: *see* **song, action.**

action, tort: a legal action, generally for damages, based upon the commission of a tort. *See* **tort.**

action word: *see* **word, action.**

actionable negligence: *see* **negligence, actionable.**

activation of passive image: *see* **image, activation of passive.**

active census file: *see* **census file, active.**

active duty for training: *see* **training, active duty for.**

active image: *see* **image, active.**

Active National Guard: *see* **National Guard, Active.**

active negativism: *see* **negativism (1).**

active vocabulary: *see* **vocabulary, active.**

activism: (1) (philos.) any theory or tendency that emphasizes activity; in metaphysics, the theory that reality or some aspect of it must be essentially active in nature; in social philosophy, a designation for the characteristic of any person or group of being continually busy to no significant end; *ant.* **intellectualism;** (2) the doctrine of aims that holds that creative activity is itself the objective of education, as opposed to the view that the ideal is a perfect or final state or condition; (3) in practice, emphasis on an activity curriculum and pupil activity; (4) the designation of the philosophy of Rudolf Christoph Eucken. *See* **pedagogy of action.**

activism, student: the student movements and procedures on college campuses in the 1960s designed to force changes in rules and practices, to increase opportunity for students to participate significantly in institutional government, and generally to hasten social change. *See* **power, student.**

activist: one who adheres to the belief that meaning arises out of the active experience of the individual and that experience is a continuous stream of minute, complicated, integrated responses.

activist, student: a leader in campus activism. *See* **activism, student.**

activities, adult-interest: those adult-sponsored activities brought into the school which are apart from regular school activities but in which pupil participation is requested.

activities alcove: an alcove at one end of a regular classroom containing equipment and space necessary to allow pupils to indulge in activities involving manual work, construction, modeling, etc.

activities, campus: college extraclass activities. *See* **activities, extraclass.**

activities, cocurricular: those school-sponsored child activities which require administrative provision and organizational involvements somewhat different from the more typical classroom instruction.

activities, coordinate: those activities of the school which are closely related to instruction but not a part of it, such as medical and dental inspection, nurse service, and enforcement of compulsory-attendance laws.

activities curriculum, classroom: *see* **curriculum, classroom activities.**

activities, daily living: (spec. ed.) the normal day-to-day routines and other activities for which social and personal management skills are required of the individual. *See* **Montessori method.**

activities, developmental: the sequentially organized activities in study and learning which focus upon the attainment of the objectives of a particular unit or lesson.

activities, extraclass: that area of the total curriculum which includes experiences not usually provided in typical classes, such as work experiences, out-of-school experiences, camp experiences, clubs, assembly programs, interscholastic and intramural athletics, student participation in government, and other activities under the guidance of the school. (The present trend is toward use of this term instead of *extracurricular activities* which is misleading in the light of the new definitions of the *curriculum.*)

activities, extracurricular: *syn.* **activities, extraclass.**

activities, follow-up: (read.) workbook or other exercises which follow a reading lesson, the purpose of which is to give practice to some reading skill and to strengthen it; seatwork activities following a reading lesson.

activities, functional: (1) useful, practical pursuits which relate directly to everyday living and contribute to the development of an individual; (2) (spec. ed.) activities which assist in the restoration of articular and muscular function, improve the general physical condition, and build physical endurance.

activities, initiatory: those activities provided at the beginning of a new instructional unit or lesson which are designed to acquaint pupils with objectives, materials, and learning experiences and to motivate them in study.

activities, instruction-related: activities intended to influence directly the quality of instruction offered to students, including lecturing, lesson planning, analyzing teacher behavior, preparing materials, etc.

activities, intermission: those activities which occur during the time not scheduled for regular classwork or recitations; more specifically, those activities which occur during the usual school recess period, during the noon hour, or during short vacation periods.

activities, language: activities in which speaking or writing plays the major role, such as conversing, letter writing, making reports, and storytelling.

activities, mimetic: (elem. ed.) dramatic gestures which help interpret a story, song, etc.; provide an outlet for the need of primary children for physical activity and gratify their desire to imitate and impersonate; primary teachers emphasize those large motor responses such as throwing, running, jumping, galloping, bending, twisting, turning, etc.

activities, music: those guitar clubs, barbershop quartets, dance bands, madrigal groups, etc. which lie outside the normal musical endeavors of the public school curriculum. *See* **club, music.**

activities, noncourse: any school activities which exist to aid students in understanding the variety, depth, and breadth of personal experiences, the opportunities available, and the choices and alternatives open to them by helping them recognize, interpret, and act upon their personal strengths and resources; takes place apart from work in connection with a student's regular subjects.

activities, nonschool: any undertakings of an organization composed chiefly of pupils that are carried on under auspices other than those of the school but which through study and analysis of each individual attempt to provide formal and informal experiences to encourage growth toward the individual's highest potential developmental level. *Syn.* **out-of-school activities.**

activities, ontogenetic (on'tō·jə·net'ik): a term employed by M. McGraw to designate learned responses (especially learned motor responses involving large-muscle activity) as distinguished from phylogenetic activities. *Contr. w.* **activities, phylogenetic.**

activities, out-of-school: *see* **activities, nonschool.**

activities, phylogenetic (f ī'lō·jə·net'ik): a term used by M. McGraw to denote activities which are identical with or correspond closely to those of the phyletic forebears of the species and which are determined primarily by hereditary factors common within the species. *Contr. w.* **activities, ontogenetic.**

activities, prevocational: (spec. ed.) the first phase of a work-study program for the mentally retarded which involves course work and activities related to the world of work.

activities, reading-readiness: activities which prepare a child to learn to read, such as storytelling, speech development, and vocabulary development.

activities, routine: (elem. ed.) activities engaged in by teacher and children which are necessary for efficient classroom management, so conducted as to provide a classroom conducive to group learning and wholesome personality development, for example, health inspection, collection of lunch money, recording of attendance, etc.

activities, school-life: a term used to designate extraclass activities conducted in the elementary school.

activities, self-defense: a general term applied to boxing, wrestling, hand-to-hand contests, jujitsu, and other bodily contact activities.

activities, self-testing: a term applied to such physical-education activities as "stunts," in which the individual competes against his previous record.

activities, social service: (1) work carried on by civic, religious, welfare, and health organizations for the purpose of helping disadvantaged individuals and families improve their living conditions and opportunities; often classified into four large groups—family welfare, child welfare, public health, and neighborhood work; (2) a major area of study in social work.

activities, student: *see* **activities, extraclass.**

activities, student body: nonclassroom experiences in which all persons enrolled for study at an educational institution may participate and which are designed to assist students in understanding themselves and their world.

activities supervisor: *see* **supervisor, activities.**

activity: any large learning situation in which children willingly engage, because to do so is satisfying and serves as a means of reaching a worthwhile goal desirable to the children; usually involves investigation, experience, and study in several related areas of knowledge cogent to the problem at hand, without, however, recourse to formal or traditional classroom procedures. *See* **unit, activity.**

activity, after school: the nonacademic portion of the regular school program that is conducted at the close of the school day. *See* **activities, extraclass; activity, out-of-class.**

activity analysis: *see* **analysis, activity.**

activity, art: (1) productive or appreciative participation in an experience of aesthetic nature by an individual or group; includes activities in all the fine arts and the arts of literature, drama, music, and the dance; (2) an activity of the school curriculum employing art experience.

activity, athletic: the trend in physical education away from calisthenics and formalized drill towards games and free play, offering students greater opportunities to participate in those sports and games which they enjoy most.

activity book: *see* **book, activity.**

activity center: *syn.* **work center.**

activity checklist: *see* **checklist, activity.**

activity coefficient: *see* **coefficient, activity.**

activity, community: any group activity undertaken by a person or persons in the community and carried out under the direction of those authorized to act for some official or voluntary agency of the community.

activity concept: the generalization that activities, whether physical or intellectual, are necessary if learning is to occur.

activity, cooperative: group experience, physical, intellectual, or emotional, designed to achieve a common purpose.

activity, corecreational: a recreational activity participated in by both sexes together.

activity, creative: (1) activity that initiates new interests or facilitates the seeing of new relationships in thinking and learning; (2) play or work activity that originates in a person's own ideas, thoughts, and feelings and results in expressive form; (3) free and spontaneous self-expression resulting in painting, drawing, or another form of expressional art, provision for which is made in the organization of a unit of teaching.

activity, culminating: (1) the high point of achievement, performance, or development toward which an individual or group directs its learnings, such as a play production for a theater group, a research report by an individual or a committee; (2) the instructional plan for the concluding procedures in a major class project or teaching unit, such as summary accounts or exhibits to conclude a series of related field trips and study assignments; (3) an exhibit, demonstration, or program by which a project or unit of work is brought to a significant conclusion.

activity, curricular: (1) any student or teacher activity suggested in the courses of study or provided for in the curriculum; (2) any revision, modification, adaptation, or development of teaching materials or courses of study.

activity curriculum: *syn.* **curriculum, classroom activities.**

activity, directed: (art. ed.) experience with the information and materials of art that is guided or controlled by the teacher.

activity, directed reading: a reading activity carried on under the guidance of the teacher, including the reading of specific references, the solving of problems, and the answering of questions.

activity, discovery: activity that confronts the learner with a problem situation that creates bafflement and starts the process of inquiry; also, activity that results from withholding from him certain kinds of information and certain kinds of generalizations to challenge the search behavior and to preserve the opportunity for autonomous exploration and experimentation. *See* **learning, discovery.**

activity, discussion: that phase of classroom teaching in which there is a free exchange of questions and opinions on mutually agreeable topics between teachers and students.

activity, expressive: (1) the making or doing of something as a means of learning or of confirming knowledge; (2) the use of language (possibly of other mediums of communication) in an endeavor to express concepts or feelings.

activity fee: *syn.* **tax, blanket.**

activity, fine motor: any physical activity which requires highly developed small muscle coordination.

activity, free-creative: (art) free and spontaneous self-expression, resulting in art form. *See* **art, creative.**

activity, goal-directed: a planned, purposeful approach to learning where the goal is recognized by the learner and

the culminating action is within the possible achievement of the learner.

activity, gross motor: activity involving muscles that are not capable of a great degree of precision, as determined by the ratio of motor neurons to muscle fibers in each motor unit. *See* **movement, fundamental;** *contr. w.* **activity, fine motor.**

activity, group: *syn.* **action, group.**

activity-group therapy: *see* **therapy, activity-group.**

activity, idiographic: the personal dimension of activity in a social system, comprising three major elements, the individual, personality, and need disposition. *See* **data, idiographic.**

activity, locomotor: those movements of the child or other living organism which serve to transport it from place to place; specifically, creeping and walking; in a wider sense, stepping movements, rolling, hitching, etc.

activity, manual: movement or motion of the hands and fingers; differs from *manipulation* in that manual activity does not necessarily involve the use of an external object.

activity, marginal: (1) a semiconscious or unconscious response to stimuli barely perceived by the organism, for example, shifting the weight from one foot to the other while engaged in an absorbing conversation; (2) activity taking place on the fringe of consciousness as opposed to that taking place at the focus of consciousness.

activity, mass: (1) the intensive involvement of the organism in a reaction, characteristic of the behavior of young infants; opposed to *specific activity*, which is more localized; (2) the actions and reactions of a large group, such as a mob, a crowd, an audience, or a public.

activity, mental: (1) classically, the activity of the mind as distinguished from that of the body; (2) according to the functional view of mind, the integrated response of the organism to stimuli, with emphasis on such active processes as attention and interpretation as against the passivity of sensation and the automatism of reflex and habit; may or may not be accompanied by overt motor action.

activity method: a method of instruction that stresses the participation of pupils in meaningful learning activities through activity units. *See* **project method.**

activity, motor: a mode of action involving physical and muscular coordination.

activity movement: a trend in education representing a reaction against undue verbalistic learning and excessive use of books as the primary source of curriculum materials; emphasizes the value of overt mental activity, such as making things, going on excursions, and playing games; advocates respecting the interests and needs of the child and recommends education through pupil enterprises that reproduce or approximate life situations.

activity, neuromuscular: a vigorous or energetic action which relates to or stimulates the nerves and muscles or nerve and muscle tissue.

activity, oral-language: (1) a game, program, or other device for bringing speech into play for training purposes; (2) the employment of the techniques suited to effective oral expression; (3) a speaking activity such as taking part in conversation, using the telephone, or giving a talk.

activity, out-of-class: any school-connected activity, participated in by students or teachers, apart from work in regularly scheduled classes, as, for example, participation in athletics, clubs, forensics, and activities connected with home room, music, publications, student councils, etc.

activity, out-of-school: (1) any undertaking of an organization chiefly of pupils that is carried on under auspices other than those of the school, for example, a Sunday-school class, a Boy Scout troop, or a 4-H club; (2) any undertaking with which pupils commonly concern themselves when not in school, such as selling papers, taking music lessons, or watching television.

activity period: *see* **period, activity.**

activity, physical: a vigorous or energetic action performed by the body.

activity plan: (1) an administrative device providing for specialized instruction in such activity fields as music, art, and physical education; (2) *syn.* **activity method.**

activity, playground: a vigorous or energetic action, usually organized or supervised, which occurs on a piece of ground ordinarily having facilities for recreation.

activity program: *syn.* **classroom activities; curriculum.**

activity, pupil: activity in which the pupil engages freely with a maximum of self-direction and self-motivation and a minimum of teacher direction and external motivation. *Syn.* **pupil self-activity.**

activity, purposeful: (1) action motivated and directed by reference to an anticipated result and involving (*a*) the projection of a desired goal, (*b*) the construction of a plan of action toward its attainment, and (*c*) persistence and reflective action in carrying out the plan; (2) any persistent goal-oriented behavior whether or not there is awareness of the goal. *Syn.* **purposive activity.**

activity, purposive: *syn.* **activity, purposeful.**

activity, random: (1) the activity of newborn infants that, to some observers, appears to be chaotic or unorganized; (2) movement or motion that is not directed toward the achievement of a goal; restless or aimless movement of any member of the body or of the body as a whole.

activity record: *see* **record, activity.**

activity, recreational: an active or passive pursuit voluntarily engaged in during leisure and primarily motivated by the satisfaction or pleasure derived from it.

activity school: a school in which the principal instructional procedure is that of free pupil participation in meaningful activities having educative value.

activity, segmental: movement of a single member of the body. *Contr. w.* **activity, mass.**

activity, social: (1) normative function of human beings in association with one another; may involve mutual cooperation and effort, as in an occupation or recreation; (2) a way of approaching the problem of curriculum building through the technique of analyzing the activities of the group.

activity, specific: *ant.* **activity, mass** (1).

activity, spontaneous: (1) external movement that arises from internal stimulation; movement for which an observer cannot discern an external stimulus; (2) self-initiated activity, as contrasted with activity initiated at the suggestion or demand of another person.

activity, supervised club: an undertaking of any organization of the club type that is carried on with the approval of the school authorities and under the supervision of a member of the faculty.

activity ticket: *see* **ticket, activity.**

activity unit: *see* **unit, activity.**

actor-judger: (philos.) one who deliberates upon a situation and seeks to determine and verify the grounds of his action, thus reconstructing his own character in accordance with the requirements of the situation as judged.

actual class limit: *syn.* **class limit, real.**

actuality: in the philosophy of Aristotle (1) the mode of being of whatever is completely real; (2) the realization of some potentiality, either in a form that supervenes to perfect its appropriate matter or in a movement of some faculty into operation and use. *See* **entelechy; form; potentiality.**

actuality broadcast: *see* **broadcast, actuality.**

actualizing tendency: the inherent tendency of the organism to develop all its capacities in ways which serve to maintain or enhance the organism.

actuarial prediction: *syn.* **prediction, statistical.**

actuarially sound retirement program: *see* **retirement program, actuarially sound.**

acuity: clarity of discrimination; perception of minute differences in sensory stimuli. *See* **acuity, auditory; visual acuity.**

acuity, auditory: ability of an individual to discriminate between two auditory stimuli in terms of intensity, pitch, timbre, or duration. *Syn.* **aural acuity.**

acuity, sensory: the power of perceiving stimuli of low intensity or brief duration, or of distinguishing among them, as measured by the stimulus threshold or the differential threshold.

acuity, visual: *see* **visual acuity.**

acute hallucinosis: *see* **hallucinosis, acute.**

ad hoc (ad hăc): (Lat., lit., "for this [purpose]") established for a particular purpose without reference to wider applications, as ad hoc committee, ad hoc policy, etc.

ad lib program: *see* **program, ad lib.**

ad valorem (ad və·lō′rəm): (school finance) a tax referring to a tax rate levied according to value on all taxable property.

ADA: *see* **attendance, average daily.**

adaptability: the power to adjust oneself to the environment or to the changes in the environment. *See* **adjustment.**

adaptation: *syn.* **behavior, adaptive.**

adaptation, biological: the process of biological change occurring in species of plants or animals by means of which the organism is better fitted to cope with its environment.

adaptation board: a board with openings in which the individual inserts pegs to make a pattern like one seen, but facing in a different direction.

adaptation, dark: accommodation of retina and iris for varying intensities of light from brightness to darkness.

adaptation, form: the utilization of perceptions of shape, dimension, and depth in making a selective response.

adaptation, individual: (1) the process whereby a person, consonant with his needs and capacities, meets the demands of his environment physiologically, psychologically or socially; (2) *see* **adaptation of schools to individual differences; adjustment to individual differences.**

adaptation, light: power of the eye to adjust itself to variations in the amount of light; accommodation of the retina and iris for varying intensities of light from darkness to brightness. *See* **adaptation, dark.**

adaptation, negative: the phenomenon in which the threshold of response to a stimulus becomes increasingly high upon continued reapplication of the stimulus, so that increasingly weak responses are elicited by the original stimulus or increasingly strong stimuli are necessary to elicit a response of equal strength. *Contr. w.* **adaptation, positive.**

adaptation of instruction: adjustment of teaching to the individual abilities, needs, and interests of the members of the class.

adaptation of schools to individual differences: the provision of curriculums, courses of study, methods, materials, and differentiated rates of progress to meet individual differences in abilities, interests, purposes, and needs. *See* **Cambridge plan; curriculum, enriched; differentiation of content; grouping, ability.**

adaptation, positive: (1) adjustment to the environment; (2) the phenomenon in which the threshold of response to a stimulus becomes increasingly low upon continued reapplication of the stimulus, so that increasingly strong responses are elicited by the original stimulus or increasingly weak stimuli elicit a response of equal strength. *Contr. w.* **adaptation, negative.**

adaptation, social: the process by which individuals and groups gradually and with varying degrees of awareness modify their behavior to fit the social environment.

adapted physical education: *see* **physical education, adapted.**

adaptive behavior: *see* **behavior, adaptive.**

adaptive-behavior norm: *see* **norm, adaptive-behavior.**

adaptive conditioning: *see* **conditioning, adaptive.**

adaptive procedure: any procedure intended to meet an educational situation with respect to individual differences in ability or purpose or with respect to the purposes of the educational program itself.

adaptive teaching machine: *see* **teaching machine, adaptive.**

addend code: *syn.* **code, geometric.**

addiction, drug: *see* **drug addiction.**

adding by endings: *see* **addition, higher-decade.**

addition: (1) (lang.) adding an unnecessary sound or letter to a word, as in the pronunciation akrost for across or the spelling librarry for library; (2) a reading error that consists in supplying a letter, word, or syllable not present in the context; (3) a part of a building constructed after completion of the original structure.

addition, decade: *syn.* **addition, higher-decade.**

addition facts: the list of statements which specify the sums when adding two of the whole numbers from 0 through 9; in earlier literature this list was considered to contain 100 such statements; currently the list is more likely to be thought of as containing 45 statements by considering combinations involving 0 separately and by making use of the commutative law. *See* **law, commutative.**

addition, higher-decade: addition in which the sum of a one-digit and a two-digit numeral is computed mentally, such as $27 + 5$ or $49 + 2$.

addition method: *see* **subtraction, methods of.**

additional aid: *see* **aid, additional.**

additional aid district: *see* **district, additional aid.**

additive cancellation: *see* **law, cancellation.**

additive constant: *see* **constant, additive.**

additive numeration system: *see* **numeration system.**

additivity: in a rows-by-columns experimental design, the tendency for treatments to induce uniform or constant changes from row to row or column to column (the concept may be expanded to more complex designs); absence of a real or intrinsic reaction implies additivity if any treatment effects exist; may be a function of the measuring scale.

address: (1) an identification (label, name, number, etc.) that designates a device, register, or location within an electronic computer where information is stored; (2) the part of an instruction for the computer that specifies the location of an operand for the instructions. *See* **operand.**

address, direct: (data processing) an address which indicates where the referenced operand is to be found, with no reference to an index register. *See* **address, level of; B-register; operand.**

address, indexed: an address which is to be modified or has been modified by an index register. *See* **B-register.**

address, indirect: an address in a computer instruction which indicates where the address of the referenced operand is to be found. *See* **address, level of; operand.**

address, level of: in automatic data processing, any of three main ways for specifying operands in an instruction, as follows: zero level, in which the operand specification symbols appearing in the instruction are the operand itself ("literal" addressing); first level, in which the operand specification symbols appearing in the instruction are the address of the operand ("direct" addressing); second level, in which the operand specification symbols appearing in the instruction are the address of the address of the operand ("indirect" addressing).

address, literal: in automatic data processing, an operand; a zero-level address. *See* **address, level of.**

address, machine: (data processing) an absolute, direct, unindexed address.

address modification: *see* **instruction modification.**

address, relative: in automatic data processing, a symbolic address that includes specific indication of the number of absolute addresses by which it is separated from some origin.

adduction: the inward movement of a limb toward the axis of the body. *Contr. w.* **abduction.**

adductor: a muscle that adducts.

adenoids: lymphoid tissue normally located in the mucous membrane of the vault, the posterior wall of the nasopharynx, or around the Eustachian tubes. [The term is often used loosely to mean *hypertrophied* (enlarged) *adenoids.*]

adequacy: (1) feeling of ability to cope with one's problems; (2) (meas.) characteristic of a good examination, evidenced by its sufficient length to sample widely the behavior it is designed to measure.

adequacy, emotional: the condition in which a person has an appropriate kind and degree of emotional response to environmental stimuli.

adequacy, numerical: (admin.) a condition in which there is a sufficient number of people in an organization to accomplish its goals in a satisfactory manner.

adequate response: *see* **response, adequate.**

adequate sample: *see* **sample, adequate.**

adequate stimulus: *see* **stimulus, adequate.**

adiadochokinesis (-ki·nē′sis): inability to make coordinated successive movements, such as arm or finger movements; this occurs in persons with cerebellar lesions. *See* **diadochokinesia.**

adient: (1) a term used by Holt to describe the behavior of an organism that tends toward additional contact with the stimulus; (2) characterized by approach responses in contrast to avoidance reactions, for example, descriptive of behavior associated with curiosity, imitation, and aggressiveness. *Contr. w.* **abient.**

adjourn: in law, the postponement of a court session or legal body for a specified purpose and/or time.

adjourned meeting: (school admin.) a continuation of a meeting that was adjourned at some former time; the same rules apply to the adjourned meeting as applied to the original meeting which was adjourned.

adjudication: a given legal conclusion or judgment.

adjunct professor: *see* **professor, adjunct.**

adjusted birth rate: *see* **birth rate, corrected.**

adjusted compensation: (1) remuneration that has been increased or decreased for some reason; (2) remuneration in the form of a pension; (3) a form of pension annuity, or other contract, conditioned in the manner of life insurance, drawing interest, but not available until certain conditions are met.

adjusted death rate: *see* **death rate, corrected.**

adjusted individual: one who has established wholesome relationships with his physical and social environment, with the result that he is emotionally stable.

adjustive behavior: *see* **behavior, adjustive.**

adjustive phase of guidance: *see* **guidance, adjustive phase of.**

adjustment: (1) (psych.) the process of finding and adopting modes of behavior suitable to the environment or to changes in the environment; (2) (psych.) the favorable, neutral, or unfavorable adaptation of an organism to external and internal stimulation; (3) (biol.) a change or acquired characteristic in an organism that enables it to meet the requirements of its environment; (4) (sociol.) the process by which individuals or groups accept, compromise with, or acquiesce with social forces or one another; (5) (stat.) *syn.* **smoothing;** (6) (stat.) any change made in a statistical value in order to correct for the effect of a measured constant error; (7) (pupil trans.) a minor change made in a mechanism to improve its operation, for example, resetting the ignition points or changing the carburetor mixture in a gasoline engine; to be distinguished from a repair.

adjustment, administrative: a shift in current administrative practice to facilitate pupil adjustment, for example, double promotions.

adjustment, binocular: (1) the act of directing the two eyes so that they work harmoniously in producing clear images upon the retinas which are interpreted as a single clear, sharp image; (2) the state in which the two eyes work together to produce clear, sharp vision.

adjustment case: (1) a pupil whose behavior pattern and problems seem to school officials to require analysis and treatment of home, school, and community factors; (2) a problem or set of difficulties presented by such a pupil.

adjustment, child: a dynamic condition in which the child's behavior fulfills his emotional needs and also is consistent with the demands of his cultural milieu; the child manifests adjustment when he is happy and free from extreme moodiness (depression to elation), when he can and does meet internal and external stimuli with appropriate and consistent behavior, and when he is able to obtain satisfactions through the effective use of his abilities; an integrating process within the child which is a basal factor in his personality development.

adjustment class: *see* **class, adjustment.**

adjustment, cost-of-living: a salary adjustment made to keep salaries in a constant relationship to the cost of living as measured by the *cost-of-living index;* these adjustments may or may not be automatic.

adjustment counselor: *see* **counselor, adjustment.**

adjustment, education as: *see* **education as adjustment.**

adjustment, emotional: the process by which one becomes able to cope with emotions in relation to one's psychological and mental makeup.

adjustment, instructional: a shift in current instructional practice to facilitate pupil adjustment.

adjustment, interpersonal: *syn.* **adjustment, social.**

adjustment inventory: *see* **inventory, adjustment.**

adjustment mechanism: a group of related actions utilized by the individual in his adaptation to his environment, such as projection or aggression, and believed to have anxiety-reducing properties.

adjustment, moral: the balance that an individual obtains when the demands of self and the customs of society must be reconciled with the imperatives of higher principle, these being viewed as either self-determined or imposed by an outside authority.

adjustment, occupational: response of a person to stimuli furnished by a job and its circumstances correlated with personal values, abilities, and interests.

adjustment of aspiration: the degree to which the individual sets his goals realistically in relation to his physical and mental attributes and in accordance with his environment.

adjustment, personality: the process of bringing one's personality into closer harmony with the demands of one's environment or reference group.

adjustment problem: a circumstance of a situation which disrupts or interferes with the normal process of psychological development.

adjustment, psychosocial: psychological development of the child from the point of view which stresses social interaction.

adjustment, pupil: (1) the correction of a maladjustment of a given pupil, involving the discovery and removal of the cause or causes of the maladjustment; frequently necessitates changes in habits and the sublimation of desires, through repeated interviews; (2) the act or process of harmonizing the pupil's needs with his educational environment.

adjustment, school: the process of fitting the school environment to the needs of the pupils.

adjustment, social: (1) the process whereby the individual attempts to maintain or further his security, comfort, status, or creative inclinations in the face of the ever-changing conditions and pressures of his social environment, or the state or condition attained through such efforts; (2) a harmonious relationship between one's self and other people; requires understanding of one's self, suitable relationships with parents and siblings, desirable relationships in neighborhood and community, and eventually, established long-term congenial relationships with contemporaries; involves a continuous modification of personality; *syn.* **interpersonal adjustment;** *see* **accommodation, social;** *contr. w.* **maladjustment, social.**

adjustment, substitute: an acceptable mode of behavior used to replace a "usual" mode of behavior.

adjustment teacher: (spec. ed.) a teacher whose major function is to instruct certain pupils having special social-emotional adjustment problems; aids them to meet their desires and to adapt them to the demands of society. *Syn.* **therapeutic teacher.**

adjustment to blindness: the process of adapting modes of behavior to lack of sight.

adjustment to community: the fitting of the individual into the life, mores, and activities of a local area or unit of population.

adjustment to individual differences: the provision, not only of adapted materials and methods, but also of personal attention necessary for the individual's wholesome development as an integrated personality; implies and includes adaptation of schools to individual differences.

adjustment, vocational: (1) the degree to which a person is suited by personality, interests, and training to his occupation; (2) (couns.) the establishment of a satisfactory, harmonious, or otherwise proper relationship to one's employment, occupation, or profession; an aspect of personal development.

Adlerian psychology: *see* **psychology, Adlerian.**

ADM: *see* **membership, average daily.**

administrability: a characteristic of a measuring instrument involving the ease with which an examiner may understand and present the instructions for the test, the availability of alternate forms, the ease with which the individuals tested comprehend how they are to proceed, and the efficiency with which the test may be scored.

administration: all those techniques and procedures employed in operating the educational organization in accordance with established policies.

administration, academic: supervision, organization, and operation of instructional activities and personnel in higher education, usually headed by a chief academic administrator, such as a dean of instruction, dean of faculties, or vice-president for instruction (or education) who is directly responsible to the president. *See* **academic; administration, educational.**

administration, building: the management or supervision of the operation, maintenance, and general use of university, college, or school buildings. *See* **administration, physical plant.**

administration, bureaucratic: (1) strictly, the management and control of a school system through the agency of one or more bureaus or offices, variously charged with duties and powers relative to the schools, for example, the administrative system used in France; (2) loosely (and often derogatorily), any type of control, direction, and management that is characterized by inflexibility and uniform and mechanical standardization; (3) the exercise of control through officials remote from those who are immediately responsible for rendering school services. *See* **ombudsman.**

administration, business: (1) those aspects of school administration which are not directly related to classroom instruction but are primarily concerned with the provision of proper working facilities in terms of the materials and equipment required for instruction; distinguishable but not properly separable from *educational administration;* (2) the designation of a subject offered in college and (occasionally) in secondary school, dealing with the organization and management of business enterprises; (3) the designation of a college curriculum designed to prepare students for positions of responsibility in business.

administration, central: (1) the principal educational authority having jurisdiction over a school system or major division thereof; may apply to a city, county, state, national, or other school system, depending on the governmental level of the unit being considered; (2) the act or process of exercising control over educational matters on the part of an authority as above defined; (3) a plan or type of organization by which the authority and responsibility for operating the school system of an educational unit are concentrated in a single policy-forming and jurisdictional body or bureau, for example, the system used in Ontario or France; usually aims at and results in relatively uniform educational practices in the unit so administered; (4) (higher ed.) the offices and acts of the chief administrative officer, usually the president, and those directly responsible to him in a college or university, which may be a single institution with one or more campuses or a multi-institutional organization.

administration, centralized: (1) an administrative system in which authority for direction, control, and management is located at one point; (2) that system of administering education in which the major responsibility for direction, control, and management is exercised by the state or national government, as has been the case in France; (3)

a system which may provide opportunity for delegating responsibility to subordinate agencies; (4) *syn.* **administrative organization, unit type of.**

administration, city-school: (1) the direction, control, and management of schools in an incorporated municipality; (2) the direction, control, and management of education by a body representing the municipality as the local unit for school administration, education being legally a state function.

administration, classroom: the management of all business affairs connected with the work of a teacher and all duties connected with the material things about the classroom.

administration, decentralized: (1) any plan for the operation of schools according to which scope is provided for local initiative in adapting programs to local educational needs; in a state, for example, this might imply initiative on the part of city or district school systems, in a city, initiative on the part of persons, groups, or individual schools; (2) any plan for operation of higher education institutions according to which provision is made for initiative, decision making, and control at lower administrative levels such as academic departments.

administration, division of: a major unit in an educational institution or organization, charged with responsibility for the management, direction, and maintenance of educational enterprises or the general supervision of other units that perform these functions.

administration, dual type of: that system of local school, college, and university administration in which executive activity and responsibility are divided between two executive officers, generally of equal rank, who are independent of each other and are responsible directly to the same board, the division generally being between educational and business functions. *Syn.* **double-headed plan of administrative organization.**

administration, educational: (1) the direction, control, and management of all matters pertaining to school affairs, including business administration, since all aspects of school affairs may be considered as carried on for educational ends; *syn.* **general administration;** (2) the direction, control, and management of those aspects of school administration most directly related to the instructional process, but not related to the business aspects of administration, such as teacher and pupil personnel, program of studies, program of activities, curricula, methods, instructional aids, and guidance; *see* **administration, academic.**

administration, financial: (1) the managing or conduct of an office or group of functions pertaining to fiscal affairs; (2) the performance of those executive duties of an institution, business, or governmental body which involve monetary affairs; (3) the management of the funds belonging to an enterprise, especially the permanent funds (to be distinguished from *business administration,* which relates to the management of matters concerning current income and expenditures of the enterprise).

administration, general: *syn.* **administration, educational** (1).

administration, institutional: (spec. ed.) the leadership and coordinative staff of a specialized, usually residential, treatment center.

administration, line: the control, direction, and management of an enterprise, particularly a school or school system, through the issuance of executive directives, each officer in the line receiving directives from an officer above and passing them on to one below; includes the delegating of responsibility and authority along this line. *See* **supervision, line-and-staff organization of.**

administration, line-and-staff: *see* **organization, line-and-staff.**

administration, local school: the control, direction, and management of schools by an agency representing a limited local area such as the city, county, borough, town, township, or other unit designated by law, which exercises powers delegated to it by the state.

administration of buildings, grounds, and equipment: *see* **administration, building; administration, physical plant.**

administration of supplies: the general supervision of materials necessary for the operation of schools and for instruction, involving the ascertaining of needs, purchasing, distribution, and use.

administration of teaching: the application of procedures and principles to the use of school facilities and the scheduling of teacher-pupil enterprises so that the desired teaching acts and learning experiences may take place under the best conditions.

administration, office: the conduct of the work in a school or school system that pertains to the office of the administrative head and to the business affairs of the school directed from that office.

administration office: an office for the use of an administrator or manager in his official capacity or for the use of his staff, for example, superintendent's office, business office, registrar's office, president's office, and dean's office.

administration, personnel: (1) the task of handling the problems arising from the varied relationships of the school staff, such as the appointing, supervising, and dismissing of teachers, principals, and other employees of a school system; (2) the administering of those agencies dealing with pupil-personnel activities; (3) (higher ed.) management of the groups of persons involved in the activities of an institution of higher education, including academic staff, nonacademic personnel, and students.

administration, physical plant: the management or supervision of the operation, maintenance, and general use of college and university campuses, including buildings, grounds, equipment, security, and services such as power, water, disposal of waste, etc.

administration room: a room in a school building in which attention is given to the business affairs of the school.

administration, school: *see* **administration, educational** (1).

administration, state school: (1) the activities of the executive, judicial, and legislative branches of the state government in the educational affairs of the state; (2) the direction or control of the school system of a state by the elected or appointed state school officers, whether or not such direction or control is highly centralized.

administration, township school: the control, direction, and management of schools in the township or other similar local government unit used for school purposes.

administration, tridimensional concept of educational: a taxonomical approach that poses an analytical model involving the human, technical, and conceptual dimensions of educational administration.

administrational: pertaining to the functions of direction, control, and management of schools.

administrative acceptee: *see* **acceptee, administrative.**

administrative adjustment: *see* **adjustment, administrative.**

administrative bulletin: *see* **bulletin, administrative.**

administrative certificate: *see* **certificate, administrative.**

administrative code: that body of rules and regulations enacted by a state board of education or the chief executive of a state system (superintendent of public instruction, commissioner of education) under statutory authority, to govern the operation of schools.

administrative committee: (1) a committee dealing with general administrative policies, usually consisting of the principal administrative officers of an agency or institution; (2) a committee to which executive rather than policy-making functions are assigned.

administrative control: (1) the exercise of authority in managing, directing, and administering the affairs of an educational institution or system; (2) a regulation, curb, rule, or check exercised by the executive officer in pursuance of action authorized by a legislative body such as the state legislature or the local or state board of education; (3) the cumulative decisions and actions of a governing body of a school or school system. *See* **control, decentralized; control, operative.**

administrative control, centralization of: the process of consolidating administrative authority into fewer divisions and of reducing the number of autonomous divisions.

administrative council: a group or council of top administrators of a higher education institution who meet regularly to assist the chief administrative officer, such as the president, in making decisions on significant issues, problems, or procedures; typically not made up of faculty members.

administrative credentials: *syn.* **certificate, administrative.**

administrative effectiveness: the extent to which satisfactory results have been produced through the control, direction, and management exercised by the executive authority; satisfactory results shall be judged in terms of the objectives of the activity.

administrative form: a form used to convey information from one school official to another or from a school official to a pupil or to a person outside the school; usually of temporary importance and not kept permanently.

administrative internship: *see* **internship, administrative.**

administrative machinery: (1) the organization or means through which the educational service is carried on and the desired results are obtained; not to be considered as necessarily leading to standardization or uniformity; (2) inflexible and frequently mechanical rules and practices in the control, direction, and management of an educational institution or system.

administrative officer: (1) a member of an educational staff with responsibilities in the direction, control, or management of a school or schools in an educational system; (2) (higher ed.) the college or university official who has the primary duty of carrying out the administrative rulings and policies of the governing body of the institution; usually consulted in the formulation of such policies.

administrative organization: (1) the scheme or plan used in the assignment of duties and responsibilities and the determination of staff relationships so that all phases of operating a school system may be efficiently managed, produce maximum results in meeting educational objectives, and result in optimum personnel relationships; (2) the personnel responsible for the management and direction of the affairs of a school or school system, regarded collectively.

administrative organization, double-headed plan of: *syn.* **administration, dual type of.**

administrative organization, dual type of: *syn.* **administration, dual type of.**

administrative organization, line type of: *syn.* **administration, line.**

administrative organization, multiple type of: that plan or system for control, direction, and management in which there are two or more principal executive officers, coordinate in rank, independent of each other, and responsible directly to the board of education or to its committees. (The dual type of administrative organization has been the most common multiple organization found, although some cities have had as many as eight coordinate principal executives, each responsible to the board of education or to its committees.)

administrative organization, unit type of: the type of system or plan for administration that has one chief executive officer, generally the superintendent of schools, responsible to the board of education for the administration of all aspects of the system, the business manager and all other employees of the school system being subordinate to the chief executive. *Syn.* **centralized administration; unitary administrative system.**

administrative policy: (1) a statement adopted by a board of education or an administrative agency outlining principles to be followed with respect to specific matters; usually requires rules or regulations to be adopted for its implementation and is broad enough to provide for administrative decision regarding the manner in which it shall be implemented although its implementation in some manner is mandatory; (2) a fixed procedure or practice of administration, which is carried out over an indefinite period without specific authorization and from which departures are made only by specific authorization.

administrative position: a position involving performance of major duties in organizing, managing, or supervising duties of other employees and calling for the carrying of certain responsibilities in the direction, control, or management of an educational or other institution.

administrative rule: a directive for implementing policy.

administrative system, unitary: *syn.* **administrative organization, unit type of.**

administrative technique: a method or device employed by an administrative officer in the direction and management of schools.

administrative theory: the schematic organization of principles, derived from contemplation and analysis of facts, assumptions, experiences, observations, records, and purposes, which may be applied to explain conditions or occurrences and to give plausible direction to administrative procedures.

administrative unit: that geographic unit comprising all the area under a single system of school administration; generally constitutes a local taxing or fiscal unit for school purposes; usually controlled by a board of education of which the superintendent of schools is the executive officer. *Dist. f.* **attendance area; attendance unit.**

administrative unit, basic: fundamentally, an administrative unit which may often exercise complete administrative functions, except those reserved by the state, or which, in other instances, may be dependent on an intermediate unit for the performance of certain administrative functions.

administrative unit, intermediate: a unit smaller than the state which exists primarily to provide consultative, advisory, or statistical services to local basic administrative units or to exercise certain regulatory and inspectoral functions over local basic administrative units; an intermediate unit may operate schools and contract for school services, but it does not exist primarily to render such services; it may or may not have taxing and bonding authority.

administrative unit, local school: the geographical area whose public school facilities are part of a common system, the whole being controlled by a single board of education. (This has slight variations, as in Illinois and California, where separate boards of education govern elementary and secondary education within the same geographical areas.)

administrative unit, minimum: generally thought of as a unit having 2,000 pupils in grades 1 to 12; recommended from the standpoint of administrative economy in maintaining a school program of desirable quality.

administrator, chief: a generic term referring to the person responsible for the total administration of an educational system, institution, or division of either; may refer to state superintendents or commissioners, city, county, or district superintendents, principals, deans, chancellors, and presidents.

administrator, educational: *syn.* **administrator, chief.**

administrator, participative: an educational official who joins the group under his direction in creating a climate in which he has no need to impose controls since they emerge from group processes as the need is perceived and then are mediated by group or organization objectives and by such relevant data as deadlines and target dates.

admissible evidence: *see* **evidence, admissible.**

admissible mark: any one of the elementary units or basic symbols in a symbol system, such as the letters of the English alphabet or the digits 0, 1, 2, 3, 4, 5, 6, 7, 8, 9 in the decimal number system.

admission: acceptance of an applicant for enrollment in a school or other educational institution.

admission age: *see* **age, admission.**

admission, early: (1) the practice of acceleration by enrolling mentally advanced children when they are below the minimum legally permitted school age; an administrative practice usually dependent upon the recommendation of a school psychologist; (2) school enrollment of a handicapped child at a preschool age level; (3) *syn.* **college entrance, accelerated.**

admission, elastic: an arrangement by which a child may be admitted to school at the particular time during the year when he reaches the minimum age as set by the board of education, regardless of his classmates' progress.

admission examination: *see* **examination, admission.**

admission form: *syn.* **application blank for admission.**

admission, mandatory: the ruling, as laid down by statute in some states, which provides that admission to the state colleges and universities shall not be denied if the applicant holds a diploma from an accredited high school.

admission office: *see* **director of admission.**

admission, open: a policy of some colleges and universities of accepting any candidate who presents a high school diploma or high school equivalency certificate; nonselective admission, instituted in some cases to make higher education more accessible to minority group students; occasionally referred to as *open-door admission. Contr. w.* **admission, selective.**

admission, open-door: *see* **admission, open.**

admission policy: the school policy that controls the standards for admission into school, such as admission age, second-grade admission age, etc.

admission, postponement of: *see* **postponement of admission.**

admission requirements: specifications of the educational and other experiences required of new students for admission to a college; usually stated in terms of pattern and amount of credits, scores on standardized psychological and achievement examinations, age, and sometimes length of residence in a state or city. *See* **examinations, college entrance.**

admission, selective: admission of applicants to an educational institution by selection on the basis of legal residence or of predictive measures or other criteria of scholastic aptitude, personal fitness, and probable future success. *Contr. w.* **admission, open.**

admissions counselor: *syn.* **admissions officer.**

admissions, director of: *syn.* **admissions officer.**

admissions officer: one of the administrative persons of a higher education institution who inform prospective students about the offerings and advantages of the college or institution and who handle, process, and screen their applications for entrance; in private colleges they have considerable powers of selection and the opportunity to make effective use of clinical data in arriving at a decision regarding the admission of students. *Syn.* **admissions counselor; director of admissions.**

adolescence: a period in human development occurring between puberty and maturity and extending roughly from 13 or 14 years of age into the early 20's; initiated by a short period of puberty, it continues for many years after the advent of sexual maturity; in highly industrialized societies, adolescence is a long twilight zone in which society does not accord the adolescent full adult responsibility.

adolescent behavior: *see* **behavior, adolescent.**

adolescent delinquency: *see* **adolescence; delinquency, juvenile.**

adolescent education: education that begins at the onset of adolescence and continues until adulthood, that is, until the individual actually assumes the role of an adult in such matters as social and economic independence and the ability to have and maintain a family; does not terminate at any given age, grade, or accumulation of credit. *Contr. w.* **adult education; childhood education.**

adolescent music: *see* **music, adolescent.**

adolescent-needs approach: a method of attack on the problem of selecting materials for the core curriculum in secondary education, based on consideration of the educational, social, emotional, and physical needs of adolescents.

adolescent psychology: *see* **psychology, adolescent.**

adolescent spurt: a positively accelerated increase in growth, especially in height, usually occurring shortly before or during the early years of pubescence. (It does not appear in all individuals, and the increase in such aspects as height is neither relatively nor absolutely as great as during the first year or two of life.)

adoption: the act of voluntarily accepting a child of other parents for one's own.

adoption home: an institution designed to care for a child during the interim from his separation from his natural parents until his adoption.

adoption of practices: the process by which an idea gets from its source or origin to its place of ultimate use;

usually thought of as consisting of five stages, namely awareness, interest, evaluation, trial, adoption; sometimes called the *diffusion process.*

ADP: *see* **data processing, automated.**

adrenal cortex: the outermost layer of the adrenal glands, cells of which secrete cortin, a substance that plays a part in development of sex cells and in body growth.

adult: a person who has come into that stage of life in which he has assumed responsibility for himself and usually for others and who has concomitantly accepted a functionally productive role in his community.

adult ability: *see* **ability, adult.**

adult agricultural class: *see* **class, adult agricultural.**

adult basic education: an instructional program for the undereducated adult planned around those basic and specific skills most needed to help him function more adequately as a member of society. *See* **fundamental education** (2); **teaching, remedial.**

adult business and office education supervisor: *see* **supervisor, adult distributive education.**

adult center: *see* **center, adult education; evening school** (2).

adult center, residential: *see* **center, residential.**

adult counseling: *see* **counseling, adult.**

adult development program: *see* **program, adult development.**

adult distributive education certificate: *see* **certificate, adult distributive education.**

adult distributive education supervisor: *see* **supervisor, adult distributive education.**

adult education: any process by which men and women, either alone or in groups, try to improve themselves by increasing their knowledge, skills, or attitudes, or the process by which individuals or agencies try to improve men and women in these ways. *See* **continuing education.**

adult education broadcasting: *see* **broadcasting, adult education.**

adult education by public library: informally, the basic function of bringing together books and people, long carried on by the public library; in recent years, formal programs, that is, discussion groups, planned reading courses, book reviews, films, concerts, classes, etc., using the considerable library resources available. (More and more such activities are being centered in public libraries.)

adult education center: *see* **center, adult education.**

adult education council: a voluntary association of agency and individual representatives of the community engaged in developing and implementing various types of adult educational activities in a community, state, or region, furthering exchange of information, developing cooperation and coordination of effort by its constituent agencies, and furnishing information to the public on available educational opportunities for adults.

adult education department: *see* **department, adult education.**

adult education, liberal: any learning experience aimed at helping adults become better and more complete human beings; held to be worthwhile on its own account and not designed primarily to further any additional end.

adult education, library: educational activities sponsored by libraries, usually public, for the benefit and enlightenment of adult users.

adult education, public school: educational activities of a wide variety offered by public schools for adults, usually at night. *See* **evening school.**

adult education, religious: an educational program dealing with religious matters and conducted by a religious institution for adults.

adult education, rural: the developing and cultivating of the various physical, intellectual, aesthetic, and moral faculties and the economic welfare of adults living in rural communities, through such agencies as the agricultural extension service, evening classes by agricultural occupations instructors, university and college extension courses, rural organizations, the rural press, the church, libraries, community clubs, child-welfare institutions, parent-teacher associations, Chautauquas, rural pageants, the drama, music, radio, television, and parental education conferences.

adult educator: a person with specialized training, education, and/or significant professional experience in the field of adult education, involved in the planning and directing of educational activities for adults. *See* **change agent.**

adult evening distributive education class: *see* **class, adult evening distributive education.**

adult extension program, distributive education: *see* **program, distributive education adult extension.**

adult-farmer class: *see* **class, adult-farmer.**

adult guidance: *see* **guidance, adult.**

adult homemaking education: *see* **homemaking education, adult.**

adult institute: *syn.* **institute** (2).

adult instructor, distributive education: *see* **instructor, distributive education adult.**

adult intelligence: *see* **intelligence, adult.**

adult interest activities: *see* **activities, adult interest.**

adult leader: *see* **leader, adult.**

adult library service: *see* **library service, adult.**

adult population: *see* **population, adult.**

adult reading: *see* **reading, adult.**

adult reading program: *see* **program, adult reading.**

adult reading vocabulary: *see* **vocabulary, adult reading.**

adult school: a separate institution or a department within a university, college, public school, or corporation; established for the instruction of adults with programs and courses which may but do not usually carry academic credit. *See* **center, extension; college, evening.**

adult school, residential: *see* **center, residential.**

adult spelling list: *see* **spelling list, adult.**

adult spelling need: *see* **spelling need, adult.**

adult vocational education: *see* **vocational education, adult.**

adult writing vocabulary: *see* **vocabulary, adult writing.**

adulthood: a period in human development between adolescence and old age; extends roughly from 21 to about 65 years of age, the latter figure being extremely variable, depending on factors of physical and mental health, nature of occupation, and social status; the period of adulthood is the longest of the various groupings; associated with adulthood are maturity, independence, occupational attainments, marriage, etc., but only a portion of individuals in this age group attain all the developmental tasks associated with being an adult. *See* **task, developmental.**

advance organizer: (ed. psych.) an overview of new material presented in advance so as to counteract the effects of *proactive inhibition;* the term grows out of Ausubel's theory of meaningful verbal learning. *See* **subsumption, obliterative.**

advanced algebra: *see* **algebra, advanced.**

advanced arithmetic: *see* **arithmetic, advanced.**

advanced course: *see* **course, advanced.**

advanced flying training: *see* **training, advanced flying.**

advanced grade: *see* **grade, advanced.**

advanced individual training: *see* **training, advanced individual.**

advanced, mentally: *see* **mentally advanced.**

advanced military course: *see* **military course, advanced.**

advanced pilot training: *see* **training, advanced pilot.**

advanced placement: *see* **placement, advanced.**

advanced placement program: *see* **program, advanced placement.**

advanced reconditioning training: *see* **training, advanced reconditioning.**

advanced standing: *syn.* **placement, advanced.**

advanced student: *see* **student, advanced.**

advanced trainer: *see* **trainer, advanced.** .

advanced training, ROTC: *see* **training, ROTC advanced.**

advanced unit training: *see* **training, advanced unit.**

advancement, horizontal: the advancement of a teacher or other educational worker within a given branch of the educational service. *Dist. f.* **advancement, vertical.**

advancement in rating: *see* **rating, advancement in.**

advancement, vertical: advancement of a teacher or other educational worker from a lower to a higher branch of the educational service, usually involving increased responsibilities and higher remuneration. *Dist. f.* **advancement, horizontal.**

advancements: accounts that involve the advancement of money for books, supplies, etc., that are later rented or resold to pupils or others at cost or at a slight profit. (Such accounts are not regular disbursements, and their gross amounts should not figure in the statement of total expenditures.) Sometimes called *revolving fund receipts.*

advantageous seat: *syn.* **favorable seat.**

adventitious: acquired, not inherited.

adventitious blindness: *see* **blindness, adventitious.**

adventitious deafness: *see* **deafness, adventitious.**

adventitious hearing impairment: *syn.* **hearing impairment, acquired.**

adventure school: *syn.* **hedge school.**

adversary: a term applied to the opponents in litigation.

advertising: (bus. ed.) the study of the use of persuasion to present and promote identifiable ideas, goods, and services by means of mass communication; recent areas of development in the study of advertising are motivational research, creation of markets through mass advertising, truth in advertising, improved mechanical production for newspaper, magazine, radio, and television media, and advertising campaigns.

advertising art: *see* **art, advertising.**

advertising, consumer: any paid effort to stimulate demand for consumer goods and services and to influence consumers in their choice making.

advertising, school: (1) paid notices placed in newspapers or periodicals for the purpose of bringing public attention to a school; (2) publicity concerning an educational institution.

advice: (couns.) careful and considered recommendations as to a proposed course of conduct.

advisee: a student who is assigned to or voluntarily seeks the help of an adviser for purposes of consulting, gaining information, and receiving suggestions and direction concerning his problems, usually of a personal, scholastic, or vocational nature.

advisement: thoughtful consideration of a problem, prior to making a decision or offering counsel.

adviser: *alt. sp.* **advisor;** an informed person in a given area who provides specific information for another individual or individuals; in education, an adviser may provide information about such things as course selection or future education plans.

adviser, class: a member of the faculty assigned to guide students in the organization and activities of a given class.

adviser, educational: *see* **advisor, educational.**

adviser, faculty: a faculty member of an institution functioning chiefly in the area of academic counseling, as by examination and approval of the student's registration in courses of study, with performance in personal-social counseling and vocational counseling taking a minor place or being referred to other professionals; occasionally called *faculty counselor.*

adviser, foreign-student: one who assists foreign students in college or university in making an academic, personal-social, and environmental adjustment to campus and community life.

adviser, foundation: a person, agency, or association acting in an advisory capacity to the staff of a philanthropic foundation concerning the merits of applications for financial assistance in various areas of specialization or concerning its investments.

adviser, homeroom: *syn.* **homeroom teacher.**

adviser, major: a college or university faculty member in the student's area of scholastic concentration who is responsible for advising him in the choice of subjects and registration for courses therein.

adviser, minor: a college or university faculty member assigned to advise a student about his field of minor concentration as distinguished from his field of major concentration.

adviser of publications: a member of a college or high school faculty assigned to guide students in the publication of school newspapers, magazines, handbooks, or yearbooks. *Syn.* **publication adviser; publication sponsor; publication supervisor; supervisor of publications.**

adviser, personal: *syn.* **counselor, personal.**

adviser, publication: *syn.* **adviser of publications.**

adviser, reader's: a library staff member responsible for assisting patrons in the selection of reading material bearing on their special interests and for promoting individual and group adult education activities.

adviser, remedial: *syn.* **counselor, personal.**

adviser, social: *syn.* **counselor.**

adviser, student: an upperclassman among college students, appointed to assist freshmen with scholastic and social adjustment problems.

adviser, student activity: a faculty member or student personnel administrator or staff member assigned to assist and guide a student group or organization in the conduct of its program of activities.

adviser, teacher: an instructor who serves as an adviser for students.

adviser, vocational: a qualified person who assists individuals in choosing an occupation, preparing for it, entering it, and progressing in it; also aids in helping an individual to make satisfactory adjustment to his environment in all of its aspects. *See* **counselor, vocational.**

advisership, homeroom: guidance of pupils by the teacher of the homeroom; may include such phases as guidance in schedule planning, course planning, extraclass activities, vocations, health, leisure-time activities, and social behavior.

advisor, educational: (mil. ed.) a person professionally qualified who advises a commandant on matters pertaining to educational methods and techniques; the spelling "advisor" is current usage throughout the Air Force.

advisory committee: a group of persons usually outside the educational profession chosen to advise regarding an educational program; does not have final decision-making powers; offers advice to legally constituted administrative officials; used extensively in the cooperative extension service and in vocational education in agriculture. *Syn.* **citizens' advisory committee; citizens' commission; lay advisory committee.**

advisory committee, agricultural: *see* **committee, agricultural citizens'.**

advisory committee, business and office education: *see* **committee, business and office education advisory.**

advisory-committee certificate: *see* **certificate, advisory-committee.**

advisory committee, citizens': *syn.* **advisory committee.**

advisory committee, craft: a group of local craftsmen selected from a specific trade or occupation, appointed to advise the school on matters pertaining to teaching the particular occupation.

advisory committee, distributive education: *see* **committee, distributive education advisory.**

advisory committee, lay: *syn.* **advisory committee.**

advisory committee, merchants': *syn.* **committee, distributive education advisory.**

advisory council: *see* **advisory committee.**

advisory program: *see* **program, advisory.**

advocacy: support of a cause by argument; especially, that prerogative of freedom which gives anyone the right (privilege) not only to object to the beliefs of the majority but to urge their abandonment or alteration.

aeolian harp: *see* **harp, aeolian.**

aerial field trip: *see* **field trip, aerial.**

aerial perspective: *see* **perspective, aerial.**

aero club: *see* **club, aero.**

aerodynamics: the science that treats of the motion of air and other gaseous fluids and of the forces acting on bodies when the bodies move through such fluids; usually a prime course in an aeronautics program.

aerology: that branch of meteorology which treats of the free atmosphere, that is, the atmosphere unaffected by surface effects, usually on the basis of direct observations. *See* **meteorology.**

aeromedical: (1) of or pertaining to aviation medicine, as in aeromedical center, aeromedical knowledge, aeromedical therapy, etc. or, in a restricted sense, of or pertaining to aviation medicine as applied to diseases incident to flight in the atmosphere as distinguished from flight in space; (2) of or pertaining to the use of aircraft in the practice of medicine.

aeronautical engineering: *see* **engineering, aeronautical.**

aeronautical rating: *see* **rating, aeronautical.**

aeronautical technology: (1) that phase of technology dealing with aeronautics; (2) a curriculum usually in the form of a four-year undergraduate university program preparing students in the technological aspects of aeronautics.

aeronautics: an area of study dealing with the design, production, and flight of aircraft through the atmosphere.

aeronautics, preflight: in the Air Force, that branch of aeronautics pursued by a student previous to studies involving actual flight.

aeronomy: a study concerned with the physical and chemical properties of the upper atmosphere and with the processes occurring with it; usually taught as a graduate course in aerospace engineering programs.

aerospace: of or pertaining to the earth's envelope of atmosphere and the space above it; two separate entities considered as a single realm for activity in launching, guidance, and control of vehicles which will travel in both entities.

aerospace biology: *see* **biology, aerospace.**

aerospace curriculum: *see* **curriculum, aerospace.**

aerospace education: (1) an educational program, subject, or curriculum encompassing a study of the various aspects of both aviation and space science, exploration, and travel and their significance in present-day life; (2) that branch of general education concerned with communicating knowledge, skills, and attitudes about aerospace science and activities and their total impact on society today; includes both aviation education and space education; (3) (mil. ed.) acquisition of knowledge and understanding of the nature of aerospace power and of the physical and psychological environments in which it evolves, especially such power as affects complex relationships in political, diplomatic, military, cultural, and economic affairs.

aerospace education instructor: *see* **instructor, aerospace education.**

aerospace education workshop: *see* **workshop, aerospace education.**

aerospace industry: *see* **industry, aerospace.**

aerospace medical training: *see* **training, aerospace medical.**

aerospace navigation: *see* **navigation, aerospace.**

aerospace science: *see* **science, aerospace.**

aerospace studies program: *see* **program, aerospace studies.**

aerospace training: *see* **training, aerospace.**

aesthete: one sensitive to or highly appreciative of the beautiful; a person of artistic taste.

aesthetic: *n.* variant of aesthetics, used especially to designate Kant's theories on space and time. *See* **aesthetics.**

aesthetic: *adj.* (1) pertaining to aesthetics or to the beautiful as the quality either of an object or of an experience; (2) pertaining to whatever is immediately experienced or felt, as distinguished from what is arrived at by mediate inference or reasoning. (Thus Kant, regarding space and time as a priori forms of intuition, calls them aesthetic elements of experience.)

aesthetic appreciation: *see* **appreciation, aesthetic.**

aesthetic education: education pertaining to the theories of beauty, its essential character, and methods of recognizing, analyzing, and evaluating beauty; in the public schools, aesthetic education is generally developed in connection with or as a by-product of the program of art appreciation. *See* **aesthetics; appreciation, art.**

aesthetic experience: *see* **experience, aesthetic.**

aesthetic expression: *see* **expression, aesthetic.**

aesthetic growth: *see* **growth, aesthetic.**

aesthetic judgment: discriminatory judgment in matters of artistic values based, either consciously or unconsciously, on the laws and principles of aesthetics. *See* **aesthetic education; aesthetics.**

aesthetic organization: *see* **aesthetics; design.**

aesthetic perception, types of: a term that refers to special types of perception which seem to depend on general physical constitution and to be the expression of an individual's personality; such types are sometimes divided into objective, physiological, associative, and character types and bear relationship to the thinking, sensation, feeling, and intuitive types of Jung and to the modern artistic styles of realism, expressionism, surrealism, and constructivism.

aesthetic response: *see* **response, aesthetic.**

aesthetics: (1) the systematic study of beauty, especially as manifested in the fine arts; *see* **arts, fine;** (2) the branch of inquiry that deals with the nature of beauty and the principles governing its production and evaluation; (3) the study of one's responses to artistic and immediately sensuous phenomena. *See* **aesthetic education.**

aesthetics of movement: *see* **eurythmics.**

aesthetics of music: a discipline in which it is attempted to define the nature of the musical experience, that is, the experience in either producing or appreciating music, and to formulate principles which govern the production of this experience and which determine its ultimate meaning in the psychic life of the race. *See* **musicology, historical.**

affect (a'fekt): *n.* the feeling component of mental life as contrasted with the cognitive, or thinking, elements of mental activity.

affect development: (1) the progressive growth of feelings and emotions; (2) the formulation of conscious, subjective aspects of emotions considered apart from bodily changes.

affect, lack of: absence or weakness of emotional response to interpersonal or intrapersonal problems.

affection: (1) the feeling function or functions, as distinguished from the knowing and willing functions known, respectively, as *cognition* and *volition;* (2) fondness (distinguished from passion in degree of intensity and by absence of any necessary sexual connotation); (3) according to structural psychology, a simple feeling, viewed by some as an attribute of sensation, by others as a mental element on the bipolar continuum of pleasantness-unpleasantness, and by still others as a mental element characterized by subjectivity but not necessarily hedonic.

affective domain: *see* **domain, affective.**

affective psychosis: *see* **psychosis, affective.**

affective response: *see* **response, affective.**

affective score: *see* **score, affective.**

affective space: *see* **space, affective.**

affective tone: (1) pleasantness or unpleasantness accompanying perception; (2) the subjective aspects of acceptance-rejection responses; (3) an elemental feeling adjustment; to be contrasted with *emotion,* which is a more complex adjustment. *Syn.* **feeling tone.**

afferent nerves: those nerves which carry impulses from the sensory endings to the central nervous system.

affiant (ə·fī'ənt): a person making an *affidavit.*

affidavit: a statement or declaration reduced to writing and sworn to or affirmed before some officer who has authority to administer an oath or affirmation. *See* **affirmation.**

affiliated school: (1) an off-campus school whose facilities are used for student teaching in the program of teacher education; not an integral part of the teacher-education institution itself, but by agreement provides opportunities for student teaching or research; *syn.* **cooperating school;** (2) a school closely associated with another, usually larger, school but separately operated.

affine geometry: *see* **geometry, affine.**

affirmation: a solemn statement made as a substitute for a sworn statement by a person whose conscience will not permit him to swear.

affix: a term used to designate either a prefix or a suffix; anything that is added to a root word to modify its meaning.

AFROTC: Air Force ROTC. *See* **Reserve Officers' Training Corps.**

after-effect masking: *syn.* **fatigue, auditory.**

after school activity: *see* **activity, after school.**

aftercare movement: program of assistance for mental patients following their release from the hospital.

afterimage, negative: the prolongation or renewal of a visual image, but in colors complementary to those of the original image, after the cessation of the visual stimulation.

afterimage, positive: the prolongation or renewal of a visual image in its original colors after the cessation of visual stimulation.

afterimage, visual: the continuation of a visual sensation after the stimulus is removed, as commonly experienced upon closing the eyes after staring at a bright light. *See* **afterimage, positive; persistence of vision.**

afternoon Hebrew school: *see* **Hebrew school.**

afterquestion: a question introduced at the end of an illustration, example, or unit of work to test comprehension or guide review of the material.

age, accomplishment (AA): rare *syn.* **age, achievement.**

age, achievement (AA): the age equivalent of an individual's achievement in all subjects or in specified subjects as shown on a standardized achievement test. *Syn.* **accomplishment age.**

age, admission: (1) the age at which pupils are admitted to a given grade or division of the school system; (2) the minimum age for admission to the public school as established by ruling of the board of education; *syn.* **age, entrance** (1); **age, school.**

age, anatomical: the expression of the anatomical development of an individual in terms of the median chronological age of typical individuals having the same degree of anatomical development. (Similar to *physiological age,* except that anatomical development usually is determined by x-rays of the bones, frequently of the wrist bones.)

age-and-schooling certificate: an authorization granted by school authorities which shows that a child has met the age, schooling, and other requirements necessary in order to work. *Syn.* **work certificate.**

age-and-schooling certificate, limited: an age-and-schooling certificate that permits a youth to be employed in a limited number of types of work, the work permitted being dependent on his physical condition.

age-and-schooling certificate, nonstandard: an age-and-schooling certificate granted to youths who have not completed a prescribed grade but who are unable to profit from further schooling or who could profit by it but are exempt from it for other reasons.

age-and-schooling certificate, part-time: an age-and-schooling certificate granted to youths permitting them to engage in work not forbidden by law, either on alternate days, weeks, or months as a portion of a part-time schooling program, or during those hours in which school is not in session.

age, arithmetic: an expression of the relative arithmetic achievement of a pupil, found by comparing his score on an arithmetic achievement test with standardized age norms for that test.

age as of September 1: (pupil accounting) age at last birthday on or prior to September 1; may be recorded and reported by years; for example, an official school age reported as 8 years means that the child has reached his eighth birthday on or prior to September 1, but has not reached his ninth birthday; also may be recorded and reported by years and months, as of September 1. *See* **age, proof of.**

age-at-grade norm: *see* **norm, age-at-grade.**

age-at-grade score: *see* **score, age-at-grade.**

age, attainment (AA): rare *syn.* **age, achievement.**

age, basal: a term used with the Stanford-Binet intelligence test, representing the age level assigned to the most advanced section of the test for which the subject answers all items correctly; used together with the additional months of credit earned at higher age levels to estimate the *mental age* of the child.

age-behavior norm: *see* **norm, age-behavior.**

age calibration: the act or process of standardizing a test in terms of age levels, generally on the basis of chronological age.

age, carpal: the degree of development of the bones of the wrist as compared with normal development at a particular chronological age.

age, census: *see* **age, school census.**

age certificate: *see* **certificate, age.**

age, child-bearing: variously specified as ages 14 to 44, 15 to 44, 20 to 44.

age, chronological (CA): the amount of time that has elapsed since an individual's birth. *Syn.* **life age;** *see* **age, corrected chronological;** *dist. f.* **age, lunar;** *contr. w.* **age, anatomical; age, mental; age, physiological.**

age, compulsory school: *see* **age limit, compulsory-attendance.**

age, corrected chronological: the postnatal chronological age of a prematurely born child, less the amount of time by which the child's gestation period is estimated to differ from normal or full term. (The modal period for "normal" or "full term" is 280 days following the first day of the last menstrual period.)

age, dental: a measure of an individual's maturity stated in years and months which is obtained by recording tooth eruption and subsequent dental development as related to the average boy or girl.

age differences: *see* **differences, age.**

age distribution chart: *see* **chart, age distribution.**

age, educational (EA): a measure similar to the achievement age, but differing in that it is ordinarily applied only to a pupil's average standing in a number of school subjects expressed in terms of an age score, whereas achievement age may refer to a single subject or to the average of several. *See* **age, achievement; age, subject.**

age, entrance: (1) the age at which children are permitted to enroll in school, quite generally fixed by the various states at 6 years; *syn.* **age, admission** (2); (2) the age at which a given child first enrolls in school; (3) sometimes used to designate the age at which pupils are compelled to enter school.

age equivalent: the corresponding age score for a raw score on a test, established by determining the average score made by pupils of the same age; an age norm. *See* **norm, age.**

age-grade distribution: *see* **distribution, age-grade.**

age-grade group, modal: *see* **group, modal age-grade.**

age-grade index: *see* **index, age-grade.**

age-grade norm, modal: *syn.* **norm, age-at-grade.**

age-grade progress: *see* **progress, age-grade.**

age-grade-progress report: *see* **report, age-grade-progress.**

age-grade-progress survey: *see* **survey, age-grade-progress.**

age-grade report: *see* **report, age-grade.**

age-grade status: *see* **status, age-grade.**

age-grade survey: *see* **survey, age-grade.**

age-grade table: *see* **table, age-grade.**

age, grip: a measure of an individual's maturity in strength of grip, commonly obtained by the use of the hand dynamometer; stated in terms of age in years and months; thus, a boy whose right-hand dynamometer grip is 19 kg may be said to have a grip age of about 11 years, that is, to have the hand-grip strength of the typical boy of 11 years of age chronologically.

age group, modal: *syn.* **group, modal age-grade.**

age, height: a measure of one aspect of an individual's physical maturity; stated in terms of age in years and months, and derived by use of an age-height table; thus, a boy who is 60 inches tall may be said to have a height age of about 14 years and 9 months, that is, to be as tall as the typical boy 14 years and 9 months of age chronologically.

age, life: *syn.* **age, chronological.**

age limit, compulsory-attendance: that age below which or that age above which a child or youth is not required by the attendance law to be in school.

age, lunar: chronological age expressed in terms of lunar months (taken uniformly as 28 days each); of value in exact research for expressing the age of an infant; sometimes also used to express estimated age of a fetus.

age-mates: individuals of approximately the same age as the child under consideration.

age, median: in pupil accounting, the age for a given group of pupils that evenly divides the distribution of pupils when classified by age, that is, the age so selected that 50 percent of the total number of pupils is older and 50 percent is younger.

age, menarchial: the time or age at which menstruation begins.

age, mental (MA): the level of intellectual development expressed as equivalent to the chronological age at which the average child attains that level; the term should be interpreted in terms of a specified mental test and is not appropriate for use with adults.

age, mental-maturity: *syn.* **age, mental.**

age, modal: that age or range which is most typical or characteristic of pupils of specified grade placement.

age, moral: an expression of an individual's ethical and spiritual maturity; it is believed that the normal individual reaches an age of competency or discretion in the course of growth at which point he can make moral judgments with a full view to consequences. *See* **development, moral.**

age, motor-ability: a score for the degree of muscle control of a child expressed in terms of years or months and derived from his performance in a series of tests standardized by age levels.

age norm: *see* **norm, age.**

age norm, modal: *syn.* **norm, age-at-grade** (1).

age, normal: the typical chronological age for average pupils for entering a given school grade, usually age 6 for grade 1, 7 for grade 2, etc. (In schools in which pupils normally advance at the rate of one school grade per year, the normal age for entering a given grade may be calculated by adding the grade number to the legal school-entrance age and subtracting 1.)

age of arrest: the age at which some type of normal development ceases, resulting in a holding to the habits and attitudes of this earlier period; maintenance of a specific stage of development.

age of compulsory school attendance: that period of a pupil's life during which the pupil must be enrolled and remain in an instructional program approved by a state department of education.

age of pupils, average: the total of the ages (expressed in years and months) of the pupils of a given group divided by the number of pupils in the group.

age, optimum: that point in, or segment of, an individual's life span which is most advantageous or suitable for a specific performance or activity; in education, the normative and desirable chronological age at which a particular activity or instruction in a particular subject of study should begin and can be effectively undertaken; this indicates somewhat greater maturity than the initial *readiness* stage.

age, organismic: an individual's average of several "growth ages" at a selected chronological age point; for example, the average of the following ages taken at a given chronological age: reading age, weight age, mental age, anatomical age, height age, dental age; used as an indication of the level of general development.

age, personality: relative personality development expressed in terms of the age for which the degree of development is typical; thus, a child whose personality age is 7 years has attained a level of personality development typical of children whose chronological age is 7 years.

age, physiological: an expression of a person's level of maturity of physiological function, especially sexual maturity, in terms of years and months; based on the typical age at which persons usually achieve an equivalent degree of physiological maturity; thus, a boy of 13 having a physiological age of 15 years would be as physiologically and sexually mature as the average boy having a chronological age of 15 years.

age, proof of: any authentic evidence of the date of birth, often required before a child is admitted to the first grade, and usually required in a school census; evidences commonly accepted are birth certificates, Bible records, baptismal certificates, passports, life-insurance policies, etc.

age, pupil: *see* **age, chronological**.

age range of class: the span of ages of members of a class, from youngest to oldest, usually expressed as a maximum allowable in groups of children having special instructional needs for which class grouping has been employed.

age, reading: an expression of reading ability in terms of age, based on preestablished norms; thus, if a child reads as well as the typical 12-year-old, his reading age is 12 years, regardless of his actual chronological age.

age record, permanent: *see* **record, permanent age**.

age scale: *see* **scale, age**.

age, school: (1) any age within the period, as designated by law, during which all children physically or mentally capable of doing so are required to attend school, generally extending from the age of 7 to 16 years but with some variation from state to state; (2) any age within the period during which children are legally permitted to attend the public schools (usually from 6 to 21 years); (3) *syn.* **age, admission** (2); **age, school admission**.

age, school admission: the minimum age for admission to the public school as established by ruling of the board of education or by state law.

age, school census: the age span of children and youth included in the school census. *See* **census, school**.

age, school entrance: *syn.* **age, school admission**.

age, school-leaving: the earliest age, varying from state to state, at which pupils are no longer required by law to attend school.

age score: *see* **score, age**.

age, skeletal: a measure of the extent to which ossification of the bones of the body has progressed from that typical for the infant to that typical for the adult.

age, social: relative social development expressed in terms of the age for which the degree of development is typical; thus, a person with a social age of 9 years has reached a stage of social competence equal to that of the typical child of 9 chronological years.

age, sociological: *syn.* **age, social**.

age-specific birth rate: *see* **birth rate, age-specific**.

age-specific mortality rate: *see* **mortality rate, age-specific**.

age standard per grade: the age range accepted as normal for a given school grade.

age structure: the number of individuals falling into age groups, given by most census publications both in absolute numbers and in percentages.

age, subject (SA): a pupil's achievement in a given school subject, expressed in terms of age; a subject age of 8 in arithmetic indicates achievement in arithmetic typical for 8-year-old pupils.

age, test: loosely and ambiguously used as a synonym for *mental age*; strictly, an age used to describe performance on any test whatever.

age, weight: a measure of one aspect of an individual's maturity; stated in terms of age in years and months and derived by use of an age-weight table.

agency, accrediting: *see* **accrediting agency**.

agency, community: any of the service agencies in the community, including health clinics, psychological and psychiatric services, social service agencies, family and children's agencies, civic and professional clubs, placement agencies, churches, and other similar groups.

agency contacts: interviews with the personnel of social agencies by school personnel workers.

agency, cultural: *see* **cultural agency**.

agency, Federal rehabilitation: *see* **Federal rehabilitation agency**.

Agency for International Development program: *see* **program, Agency for International Development**.

agency funds: *see* **funds, agency**.

agency, group work: (1) a community agency which cooperates with a teacher education institution in providing group work experiences for prospective teachers in training; (2) (guidance) an organization which meets the needs of boys and girls, especially adolescents, which cannot be met through traditional agencies or community foster care resources.

agency referral: an administrative form used to refer indigent children to the public-welfare or other agency, or the act itself of referring such children to an agency. (The form lists the names of the children and of their parents and the articles or services needed.)

agency, social: one of the nonprofit, voluntary, or tax-supported agencies or organizations which offer health and welfare services.

agency, state: *see* **state agency**.

agency, talent: *see* **talent agency**.

agency, training: *see* **training agency**.

agency, training support: *see* **training support agency**.

agent: one who undertakes to transact some business or to manage some affair for another, by the authority and on account of the latter, and to render an account of it.

agent, agricultural: *see* **extension worker, county**.

agent, change: *see* **change agent**.

agent, county: *syn.* **extension agent**; *see* **extension worker, county**.

agent, curriculum-change: *see* **curriculum-change agent**.

agent, extension: *see* **extension agent**.

agent, Four-H Club: *see* **extension worker, county**.

agent, home: *see* **extension worker, county**.

agent, home demonstration: *see* **extension worker, county**.

aggregate: *n.* a number of persons who are classified together because they share some characteristic but who do not necessarily interact with one another.

aggregate attendance: *see* **attendance, aggregate**.

aggregate days absence: *see* **absence, aggregate days**.

aggregate days attended: the sum of the number of days attended by all pupils enrolled. *Syn.* **attendance, aggregate**.

aggregate days enrolled: the sum of the number of days of enrollment for all pupils. (After being once enrolled, a pupil remains on the roll until he has been legally withdrawn by the superintendent's office for such reasons as (*a*) death, (*b*) removal from the district, (*c*) grant of a permit to work, or (*d*) passing the compulsory-attendance age and leaving school.)

aggregate days membership: *see* **membership, aggregate days**.

aggregate load: *see* **load, aggregate**.

aggregate pupil miles: *see* **miles, aggregate pupil**.

aggression: *syn.* **aggressiveness** (1).

aggression, displaced: the turning of hostile and aggressive impulses, thoughts, or overt behaviors toward a new (perhaps completely innocent) target, such as kicking a dog when the aggression was actually produced by a traffic ticket.

aggressive behavior: *see* **behavior, aggressive.**

aggressive disorder: *see* **disorder, classroom.**

aggressiveness: (1) a tendency toward forceful, outgoing action, characterized by taking the initiative, making vigorous defense, and losing few opportunities to exhibit the self or that with which the self is identified; the opposite of the tendency to avoid danger or conflict by withdrawal; (2) hostile behavior directed toward hurting another individual; (3) (psychoan.) a behavior trait thought to result from the operation of the death instinct. *Contr. w.* **submissiveness.**

aggressor forces: forces engaged in aggressive military action; in the context of training exercises, the "enemy" is created to add realism in training maneuvers and exercises; this method replaces the less realistic system of fictional red and blue armies.

agility: (phys. ed.) the ability to change direction swiftly, easily, and under control.

agitation: exaggerated motor restlessness motivated by fear or apprehension.

agitophasia: *see* **cluttering.**

agnosia: a condition of losing the ability to recognize the character of objects through the senses of touch, taste, sight, or hearing.

agnosia, auditory music: inability to recognize music, although it can be heard, or to connect any meaning with it.

agnosia, color: an inability to name and sort colors. *Dist. f.* **color blindness.**

agnosia, tactile: *syn.* **astereognosis.**

agnosticism: in theology, the theory that it is impossible for man to have knowledge of God; in philosophy generally, any theory that affirms an intrinsically unknowable phenomenon.

agorophobia (ag'ə·rə·fō'bi·ə): a morbid fear of open spaces, such as streets, parks, or fields.

agrammatism: (1) failure to utter words in their grammatically correct order; (2) a symptom in motor (expressive) aphasia characterized by omission of connectives and related words, resulting in telegraphic sentences.

agraphia: an inability to express thoughts in writing due to a lesion of the central nervous system; often associated with the *aphasias. Comp. w.* **dysgraphia.**

agreement and difference, method of: *see* **method of agreement and difference.**

agreement, coefficient of: *see* **coefficient of agreement.**

agreement, cooperative training: *syn.* **contract, cooperative student.**

agreement, method of: *see* **method of agreement.**

agreement, project: *see* **project agreement.**

agreement, training: *syn.* **contract, cooperative student.**

agribusiness education: *see* **agricultural mechanics education; agricultural products education; agricultural supplies education.**

agricultural activities, supervised: *see* **program, supervised agricultural experience.**

agricultural advisory committee: *see* **committee, agricultural citizens'.**

agricultural agent: *see* **extension worker, county.**

agricultural business education: *syn.* **agribusiness education;** *see* **agricultural mechanics education; agricultural products education; agricultural supplies education.**

agricultural citizens' committee: *see* **committee, agricultural citizens'.**

agricultural class, adult: *see* **class, adult agricultural.**

agricultural college: *see* **college, agricultural.**

agricultural coordinator: *see* **coordinator, agricultural.**

agricultural counseling: *see* **counseling, agricultural.**

agricultural counselor: *see* **counselor, agricultural.**

agricultural course: *see* **course, agricultural.**

agricultural curriculum: *see* **curriculum, agricultural.**

agricultural demonstration plot: *see* **demonstration plot, agricultural.**

Agricultural Development Service, International (IADS): an agency in the U.S. Department of Agriculture, established in 1963 to administer and coordinate the department's participation in foreign technical assistance and training; provides an effective way to utilize the resources, capabilities, and experiences of the department in planning and executing foreign programs in agriculture and home economics. *See* **agricultural education, international.**

agricultural education: (1) education for duties and responsibilities related in some way to agriculture; provided for persons engaged in or expecting to engage in production agriculture or in nonfarm agricultural occupations and for persons who are not and who do not expect to be engaged in agricultural occupations; included in the programs of elementary schools, secondary schools, and colleges; *see* **agriculture, nonvocational; agriculture, vocational;** (2) education for students preparing to become teachers of vocational education in agriculture.

agricultural education, international: a curriculum to prepare Americans and nationals of countries other than the United States to provide agricultural education in the countries of these nationals.

agricultural education, secondary: agricultural education in high schools or in other schools offering agricultural studies below the college level and above the elementary.

agricultural evening class: *see* **class, adult agricultural.**

agricultural evening school: *see* **class, adult agricultural.**

agricultural experiment station: *see* **experiment station, agricultural.**

agricultural extension: *see* **extension, agricultural.**

agricultural extension agent: *see* **extension worker, county.**

agricultural extension, director of: *see* **director of agricultural extension.**

agricultural extension division: *see* **extension division, agricultural.**

agricultural extension work, cooperative: *see* **extension service in agriculture and home economics, cooperative.**

agricultural guidance: *see* **guidance, agricultural.**

agricultural high school: *see* **high school, agricultural.**

agricultural mathematics: *see* **mathematics, agricultural.**

agricultural mechanics education: (1) a program of instruction and on-job experiences offered as a part of vocational education in agriculture at the high school and postsecondary school levels and designed to prepare or upgrade students for employment in nonfarm agricultural machinery and equipment businesses that supply and service the mechanical and equipment needs of production agriculture; (2) the instruction of a mechanical nature offered in any vocational education in an agriculture course, for example, agricultural machinery, agricultural buildings, soil and water conservation, rural electrification, and agricultural processing machinery.

agricultural mechanics shop: *syn.* **shop, agricultural.**

agricultural occupation experience program: *see* **program, supervised agricultural experience.**

agricultural occupation, nonfarm: an occupation in which a worker needs knowledge and skill in agricultural subjects. *Syn.* **off-farm agricultural occupation.**

agricultural occupation, off-farm: *syn.* **agricultural occupation, nonfarm.**

agricultural occupations teacher: a teacher of vocational education courses designed to prepare or upgrade students for employment in occupations, both nonfarm and farm, requiring knowledge and skill in agricultural subjects. Also called *agricultural teacher.*

agricultural on-job training: *see* **training, agricultural on-job.**

agricultural part-time class: *syn.* **class, young farmer** (1).

agricultural placement for experience: *see* **on-job training, agricultural.**

agricultural postsecondary education: *see* **postsecondary education, agricultural.**

agricultural preparatory program: *see* **program, agricultural preparatory.**

agricultural production education: a program of instruction and on-job experiences offered as a part of vocational education in agriculture at the high school and postsecondary school levels and designed to prepare or upgrade students for employment in occupations involving the production of plants and animals.

agricultural products education: a program of instruction and on-job experiences offered as a part of vocational education in agriculture at the high school and postsecondary school levels and designed to prepare and upgrade students for employment in nonfarm agricultural firms that process, handle, transport, inspect, control quality of, store, or market the products of production agriculture.

agricultural project: *see* **project, agricultural.**

agricultural resources education: a program of instruction and on-job experiences offered as a part of vocational education in agriculture at the high school and postsecondary school levels and designed to prepare and upgrade students for employment in nonfarm occupations such as soil and water conservation, game management, and rural recreation.

agricultural school: a school of lower than college grade or one that emphasizes the teaching of agriculture though it offers other subjects also.

agricultural school laboratory experience program: *see* **program, agricultural school laboratory experience.**

agricultural shop: *see* **shop, agricultural.**

agricultural supervised occupational experience program: *see* **program, supervised agricultural experience.**

agricultural supplemental program: *see* **program, agricultural supplemental.**

agricultural supplies education: a program of instruction and on-job experiences offered as a part of vocational education in agriculture at the high school and postsecondary school levels and designed to prepare or upgrade students for employment in agricultural businesses that supply and service production agriculture.

agricultural teacher: *see* **agricultural occupations teacher.**

agricultural technical education: *see* **technical education, agricultural.**

agricultural technician: *see* **technical education, agricultural.**

agricultural work experience: *see* **training, agricultural on-job.**

agriculture: all the processes and services, both nonfarm and farm, involved in producing plants and animals and their products and in getting them to the consumer.

agriculture laboratory: *see* **laboratory, land.**

agriculture, nonvocational: one of the practical arts taught usually in the lower grades of the high school to provide appropriate education in agriculture for persons who are not and who do not expect to be engaged in an agricultural occupation, either nonfarm or farm.

agriculture, prevocational: instruction in agriculture previous to vocational instruction to prepare for an agricultural occupation, either nonfarm or farm. *Contr. w.* **agriculture, nonvocational; agriculture, vocational.**

agriculture, technical: agricultural subjects, as distinguished from nonagricultural subjects, taught at the postsecondary level in an area vocational school, junior college, or in an agricultural college or division of a university. *See* **technical education, agricultural.**

agriculture, vocational: education in agriculture for persons engaged in or expecting to engage in an agricultural occupation, either nonfarm or farm. *See* **establishment in agriculture;** *contr. w.* **agriculture, nonvocational; agriculture, prevocational.**

aid, additional: a term sometimes applied to the money distributed to financially weak school districts under a state program of support to enable these districts to finance a minimum required program of education. *See* **equalization aid.**

aid, audio: any device by means of which the learning process may be encouraged or carried on through the sense of hearing, for example, tape and disc recordings, public address systems, and radio programs. *Dist. f.* **aid, audiovisual.**

aid, audiovisual: any device by means of which the learning process may be encouraged or carried on through the senses of hearing and/or sight. *Syn.* **audiovisual material.**

aid, auditory: *syn.* **aid, audio.**

aid, automated: (mil. ed.) any aid employed in an automatic system for scheduling flight simulator missions and evaluating results so as (*a*) to predict probable transfer of training to real-world tasks, (*b*) to help the instructor determine areas of strength or weakness, rate of learning, and when trainee should be advanced to next more difficult level of training, and (*c*) to measure efficiency of various teaching techniques and help to refine performance criteria.

aid, categorical: aid funded by the Federal government and restricted to the conduct of research operating within Federally cited categories or peripheries. *Contr. w.* **general aid.**

aid, conditioned: (1) in general, assistance given provided that certain requirements are met; (2) more specifically, financial assistance given by a larger unit to a smaller one if certain requirements, usually stipulated in the law, are met.

aid, educational: financial assistance through grants of money for educational purposes.

aid, emergency: financial assistance granted to meet unforeseen educational situations that call for immediate action.

aid, engineering: one who assists an engineer or scientist; usually has some post-high-school technical education.

aid, equalization: in school finance, the principle whereby State and/or Federal monies are given in inverse proportion to a school district's local resources. *See* **aid, additional.**

aid, ergogenic: (phys. ed.) a special foodstuff, drug, or other aid which may or may not improve skill performance or hasten recovery.

aid, Federal: *syn.* **aid for education, national.**

aid, financial: (1) the expenditure of public or Federal funds for the conservation of both natural and human resources; these funds are made available to deserving individuals or projects when for certain reasons the expenses of education or training or of conservation cannot otherwise be met; (2) a program of assistance by both private and public educational institutions designed to aid students in paying educational expenses; this assistance is usually granted on the basis of academic promise, personal integrity, and need and may be in the form of fellowships, scholarships, grants-in-aid, loans, student employment or cooperative housing, or teaching, research, or counseling assistantships.

aid for education, national: support given by the Federal government to school systems and educational institutions through grants, appropriations, and allotments to further the carrying out of educational programs. *Syn.* **Federal aid.**

aid for pupil transportation, state: aid granted by a state, amounting to all or a portion of the cost, to school districts for the purpose of pupil transportation. *See* **transportation, pupil.**

aid, general: *see* **aid, categorical.**

aid, hearing: *see* **hearing aid.**

aid, instructional: *see* **instructional aid.**

aid, low-vision: one of the optical devices of various types useful to persons with vision impairment.

AID program: *see* **program, Agency for International Development.**

aid, scholarship: *see* **scholarship (2).**

aid, school: financial help, support, or relief extended by a board of education to a child of compulsory school age to enable him to attend school.

aid, sensory: an object or device used in teaching to stimulate interest, extend perception, and facilitate learning.

aid, special education: any material or device provided to facilitate learning by pupils having special disabilities, for example, special equipment in partially sighted classes and in classes for the hard of hearing and for the mentally retarded.

aid, speech training: *see* **speech training aid.**

aid, state: grants by the state to local or intermediate school administrative units for the support of an educational program.

aid, student: financial assistance to students in the form of loans, scholarships, fellowships, and work that enables them to earn a part or all of their expenses while attending school.

aid, study: (1) help given to a student in his studies; (2) a device that aids one who studies, such as a study guide or outline.

aid, teaching: an auxiliary instructional device, such as a chart, drawing, picture, film, mock-up, or working model, intended to facilitate learning.

aid, three-dimensional: a model used to demonstrate height, width, and depth to the blind.

aid to education, Federal: *syn.* **aid for education, national.**

aid, visual: any device by means of which the learning process may be encouraged or carried on through the sense of sight, for example, motion pictures, photographs, graphics, etc. *Dist. f.* **aid, audio; aid, audiovisual.**

aid, voice training: *see* **speech training aid.**

aide: a person who helps the teacher in the nursery school classroom as needed with such things as setting up activities, making transitions, and assisting individual children; suggested training includes brief orientation in human development, social relations, and the school's goals and procedures, as well as some basic skill training; may be called *teacher technician*. *See* **head teacher** (2).

aide, management: *see* **management aide.**

aide, special-education: *see* **teacher aide.**

aide, teacher: a *paraprofessional* addition to the school staff, sometimes paid, sometimes unpaid, performing a variety of noninstructional duties and sometimes even tutoring small groups or individuals; also used frequently in school programs for handicapped children. *See* **personnel, auxiliary.**

aikido: a unique method of unaggressive self-defense and physical culture training; no dangerous holds or blows are used and no attacking techniques are included; the mental training involved is based on principles of Zen Buddhism. *See* **judo; jujitsu.**

aim: a foreseen end that gives direction to an activity and motivates behavior. *Syn.* **end-in-view; goal.**

aim, deferred: an objective whose attainment is not expected until after one or more intermediate goals or objectives have been reached.

aim, immediate: in education, a particular concrete task to be accomplished, such as the learning of arithmetical processes; may or may not be a necessary means to the ultimate aims of education.

aim, proximate: a necessary means to the ultimate aims of education. *See* **aim, ultimate.**

aim, specific: an objective that has been reduced to such definite character and restricted range that it can be used as a practical guide for immediate steps in action.

aim, ultimate: the final end(s) for which education exists, for example, growth, self-realization, knowledge of and service to God, or perfection of the intelligence.

aiming error: *see* **error, aiming.**

aims, cultural: objectives of education or of social policy in terms of the personal enrichment traditionally called "culture." (Use of the term should be made with the understanding that in sociology the term *culture* is used to mean the total social heritage of any group of people.)

aims, reading: (1) purposes or objectives that stimulate the reader to engage in reading and that guide his activity; (2) authoritatively stated objectives or purposes of the reading program in schools.

air conditioning: the process of air treatment designed to control its temperature, humidity, circulation, and purity.

air conduction: *see* **conduction, air.**

air duct: (1) a pipe or tube for conveying air to or from various rooms of a building for purposes of ventilation; (2) a heat conductor in certain types of heating systems.

air explorer: a member of the Boy Scouts of America participating in nonmilitary aviation studies and receiving Air Force advice and assistance.

air filter: a screen, spray of water, or other device through which air is drawn for the purpose of removing impurities and sometimes of adding moisture content.

Air Force cadet, distinguished: *see* **cadet, distinguished Air Force.**

Air Force Junior ROTC mission: the AFJROTC mission is to acquaint secondary school students with the aerospace age, to develop informed citizens, strengthen character, promote an understanding of the role of the citizen soldier in a democratic society, and motivate students for careers in the U.S. Air Force.

Air Force Reserve Officer Training Corps objectives: AFROTC objectives are to (*a*) identify, motivate, and select qualified students to complete the AFROTC program, (*b*) provide college-level education that will qualify cadets for commissioning in the U.S. Air Force, (*c*) heighten each cadet's appreciation of and dedication to American principles, give him an understanding of how the U.S. Air Force serves the national interest, and develop his potential as a leader and manager and his understanding of officer professionalism in the U.S. Air Force, and (*d*) commission in the U.S. Air Force second lieutenants who are dedicated to their assignment, accept responsibility willingly, think creatively, and speak and write effectively.

Air Force Reserve Officers' Training Corps detachment: an Air Force organization manned by active duty Air Force personnel assigned to AFROTC, with duty station at a civilian educational institution; with concurrence of the institution, the AFROTC detachment has the academic title *Department of Aerospace Studies*, and as such is an integral academic subdivision of the educational institution; it includes all AFROTC activities conducted at the institution as stipulated in the contract with the Air Force.

Air Force Reserve Officers' Training Corps mission: the AFROTC mission is to commission, through a college campus program, career-oriented second lieutenants in response to Air Force requirements.

Air Force specialty: a grouping of duties and tasks related in skill, knowledge, difficulty, operational sequence, or the like, and making up a job or specialty. *See* **code, Air Force specialty; utilization field.**

Air Force specialty code: *see* **code, Air Force specialty.**

air maneuver: *see* **maneuver, air.**

air navigation: *see* **navigation, air.**

air-raid drill: *see* **drill, air-raid.**

air-raid shelters: *see* **shelters, air-raid.**

air science and tactics: the Air Force counterpart of the Army's *military science and tactics*. *See* **military science.**

air training command: a major air command with headquarters at Randolph Air Force Base, Texas, having the mission of providing pilot, navigation, and technical training for Air Force officers and airmen.

airborne training, joint: *see* **training, joint airborne.**

aircraft simulator: *see* **simulator, aircraft.**

airman, basic: (1) a person holding the lowest rank in the Air Force, normally one unskilled in an Air Force specialty or yet unassigned for on-the-job training; (2) the rank of such a person; (3) an airman undergoing basic military training.

airman career program: *see* **program, airman career.**

airman education and commissioning program: *see* **program, airman education and commissioning.**

airplane pilot: (voc. ed.) a licensed individual who is trained in the field of air transportation and capable of flying aircraft. *See* **pilot, instructor.**

akinesia: (a·ki·nē′zhi·ə): loss of movement for any reason.

alalia: (1) delayed development of speech in childhood; (2) absence of speech due to psychogenic causes. *Comp. w.* **aphasia; aphemia; aphonia.**

alarm reaction: *syn.* **reaction, emergency.**

alarm system: an electrically operated gong or siren or a series of them located on various floors of a building, the purpose of which is to sound the alarm for immediate evacuation of the building in case of fire or other danger; also used for practice in orderly and systematic evacuation of the building during fire drills.

alchemist: in the Middle Ages one who studied or practiced *alchemy*, or primitive chemistry.

alchemy: the practice of chemistry in the Middle Ages, often associated with magic, concerned with transmutation of base metals into gold, or devoted to a search for the elixir of life.

alcohol education: instruction in the facts and principles of the use of fermented and distilled liquors and in the effects of their use.

aleatory music: *see* **music, aleatory.**

alert signal: (safety ed.) part of a signal system, employed as a means of providing a person or persons with the ability to detect and recognize emergencies and take proper steps for protection, such as a civil defense alert signal. *See* **civil defense; warning signal system.**

alertness test: *see* **test, alertness.**

alexia: a type of aphasia resulting from lesions in any one of a variety of locations from the occipital to the frontal lobe of the brain, causing a loss of motor patterns which interferes with the patient's ability to organize abstract visual symbols of written language into meaningful terms, resulting in inability to read; sometimes called *word blindness.*

algebra: (1) the branch of mathematics that uses symbolic representation to study the relationships between the numbers of a given number field and the results of operations on these numbers in accordance with accepted postulates; (2) a generalization of arithmetic.

algebra, abstract: algebra in which the characteristic structure of groups, rings, etc., is studied formally and in detail.

algebra, advanced: (1) a term sometimes used to designate a second course in high school algebra; in accelerated programs, may include many topics usually taught in college algebra; *see* **algebra, intermediate;** (2) any algebra course which is not introductory in nature.

algebra, Boolean: a mathematical system having, in addition to other properties, union and intersection as its binary operations; examples of Boolean algebra can be found in logic, sets, and computer components.

algebra, commercial: *see* **mathematics, business.**

algebra, elementary: (1) a term used to refer to the first formal course in algebra in junior or senior high school; (2) any algebra studied prior to *abstract algebra;* (3) any introductory algebra course, such as elementary *matrix algebra.*

algebra experience materials: a set of physical materials consisting of blocks of various sizes and shapes and a beam balance with weights; a set of instruction cards directs the student in activities which lead to the development of algebraic and arithmetic concepts.

algebra, fundamental laws of: an expression usually referring to the principles taught in elementary high school algebra, such as the field properties of real numbers, laws of exponents, and computation with polynomials.

algebra, intermediate: in accelerated high school programs this term is sometimes used to denote a second course in algebra, reserving the term *advanced algebra* for a course including topics from college algebra.

algebra, linear: algebra in which the theory of vector spaces, matrices, and transformations of certain types is studied. *See* **matrix.**

algebra, matrix: algebra in which the properties of matrices are studied within the framework of a mathematical system. *See* **mathematical system; matrix.**

algebraic formula: *see* **formula, algebraic.**

algebraic language, international: *see* **language, international algebraic.**

algebraic methods: (1) procedures which employ algebraic computation such as factoring polynomials, solving equations etc.; (2) in some contexts, procedures which do not require the calculus.

algebraic process: *see* **algebraic methods.**

algebraic structure: classification of mathematical systems according to their characteristic properties, such as group structure, field structure, etc.; in elementary mathematics emphasis on structure means learning to recognize patterns such as the *commutative* and *distributive laws* and on determining which properties hold in specific examples of mathematical systems. *See* **mathematical system.**

algebraic system: *see* **mathematical system** (1).

algebraic value: *see* **value, algebraic.**

algedonic (al'jə·don'ik): dealing with or relating to the pain-pleasure feeling tone.

algedonic ethics: *syn.* **ethics, pleasure-pain.**

algedonics (al'jə·don'iks): a term coined by H. R. Marshall to designate the science of pain and pleasure, without regard to their philosophical or ethical implications or to their influence as goals of human conduct.

algesia (al·jē'si·ə): capacity to experience pain. *Ant.* **analgesia.**

ALGOL: an automatic coding language used internationally in programming computational applications for the computer; an acronym formed from ALGOrithmic Language, or ALGebraic Oriented Language. *See* **algorithm** (2).

algophobia: morbid fear of bodily pain.

algorism: *alt. sp.* **algorithm.**

algorithm: (1) in elementary mathematics, a specific, often standard, procedure for carrying out a particular computation such as the long division process or the procedure for extracting square root; *syn.* **algorism;** (2) for the computer, a sequence of well-defined steps leading to the solution of a problem; *comp. w.* **heuristic;** (3) in general, a particular procedure specifying a sequence of operations for solving a problem of a given type.

algorithm, spelling: *see* **spelling algorithm.**

algorithm translation: *see* **translation, algorithm.**

alien: (1) a person belonging or owing allegiance to another family, race, or nation; (2) a foreign-born resident of a country in which he does not possess citizenship privileges.

alien education: adult education programs in the United States designed to eliminate illiteracy among foreign-born persons resident in the United States and to educate immigrant groups in American history, the English language, and the principles of citizenship. *See* **Americanization; class, Americanization.**

alien learner: *see* **student, foreign.**

alienation: (1) (sociol.) a feeling of being removed from or out of sympathy with the prevalent goals, trends, or mores of society or of one's cultural group; characteristic responses include withdrawal, rebellion, and *anomie;* (2) (stat.) the extent to which there is absence of relationship between two variables; the extent of departure from perfect correlation between two variables; *see* **coefficient of alienation.**

alienation coefficient: *syn.* **coefficient of alienation.**

alienation, coefficient of: *see* **coefficient of alienation.**

alignment: (1) arrangement in a line; for example, numbers are aligned when they are so arranged that their decimal points, if any, will fall along a straight vertical line; (2) (hand-writing) that characteristic of writing in which successive upper- and lower-case letters are based on a straight line and extend a uniform distance above and below this line, as normally specified for these letters.

alignment chart: *see* **chart, alignment.**

alignment, head: adjustment of the record-playback head so that the angle of its gap is exactly perpendicular to the tape as it moves past.

alimentary canal: the system of organs in the body dealing with food; includes mouth, pharynx, esophagus, stomach, and small and large intestines.

alimentation: the general process of nourishing the body; includes mastication, swallowing, digestion, absorption, and assimilation.

alimentation of state funds: (1) the act or process of "feeding" the state treasury; (2) the provision of funds to the state treasury to be allocated for educational purposes.

alinement: *var.* **alignment.**

all-call switch: *see* **switch, all-call.**

all-day class: *see* **class, all-day.**

all-day school: a school attended by pupils throughout most of the day between breakfast and dinner or supper, usually a "country day," nonpublic school.

all-day school, Jewish: *see* **day school, Jewish.**

all-day session: *see* **session, all-day.**

all-day student teaching: *see* **student teaching, all-day.**

all-day trade classes: *see* **classes, all-day trade.**

all-metal: a type of bus-body construction in which no wood is used; also called *all-steel.*

all-or-none law: *see* **law, all-or-none.**

all-or-none learning: *see* **learning, all-or-none.**

all-purpose classroom: *see* **classroom, all-purpose.**

all-round mechanic: *see* **mechanic, all-round.**

all-school scheduling: *see* **scheduling, all-school.**

all-school style sheet: *see* **style sheet, all-school.**

all-steel: *see* **all-metal.**

all-year school: a school that operates a complete program or curriculum throughout the calendar year.

allegation: in law, a statement in the pleadings of what it is expected will be proved.

allege: to make an allegation.

allegiance, oath of: *see* **oath of allegiance.**

allergen: a substance that produces symptoms of allergy; allergens include various foods, feathers, dust, pollens, etc.

allergic child: *see* **child, allergic.**

allergy: a condition in which the body reacts defensively to a substance, usually some foreign protein contained in food, pollen, dust, etc.; the reaction may be similar to what happens in any inflammation with a concentration of white blood cells and fluids causing swelling, itching, etc.

alley maze: a confusing set of walled runways having turns and blind paths, including a pathway that leads to a reward, usually food; much used in learning experiments with small animals.

allied trades: closely related trades having many common factors of knowledge and skill.

allness: behavior characterized by the tendency to assume that what one knows is all that can be known; drawing final conclusions from insufficient data; reacting to a higher level of abstraction as if it were identical with a lower one; regarded by general semanticists as a basic symptom of inadequate language behavior. *See* **abstraction, levels of.**

allocate: in computer programming, to assign absolute addresses to parts of a program, especially one written with symbolic addresses (thereby, in effect, assigning absolute addresses to most of the other symbolic addresses), or to assign groups of addresses for particular functions, as for storing input data, etc. *See* **segment.**

allocation of book funds: *see* **book funds, allocation of.**

allocation of places: the practice of setting quotas at various levels of schooling and of selecting only enough students to fill the quota for any given level; usually refers to secondary or university levels.

allocation of supervision: *see* **supervision, allocation of.**

allocation of supervisory talent: *see* **supervisory talent, allocation of.**

allocation, talent: *see* **talent allocation.**

alloeroticism (al′ō·ə·rot′i·siz′m): (psychoan.) a tendency to love others. *Dist. f.* **autoeroticism; narcissism.**

allokurtic: having skewness (said of an array of a double-entry table). *Dist. f.* **isokurtic.**

allopsychic: having a predominant interest in the outer world rather than in one's inner life.

allotment: (1) the portion of Federal vocational-education funds to which each state is entitled for each type of vocational education program carried on in the state; based on various state-national population ratios as determined by the most recent United States census; (2) Federal funds for various kinds of war-production training distributed on the basis of types of population; (3) Federal funds allotted to the state by the Federal government for use in purchasing equipment for vocational education programs; (4) state funds distributed to local communities for vocational education programs.

almonry school (al′mən·ri): a type of charity-school practice, somewhat common in England beginning in the fourteenth century, by which boys could attend an existing monastic, abbey, or charity school as charity students, being supported by almonry, which usually was in the form of money or food.

alogia (ə·lō′ji·ə): absence of speech in association with severe mental retardation (idiots, imbeciles).

alpha error: *see* **error, alpha.**

alpha hypothesis: *see* **hypothesis, alpha.**

alpha risk: *see* **risk, alpha.**

alphabet: a set of letters or other graphic symbols, arranged in some customary fixed order, each letter or symbol representing a sound or combination of sounds of the language.

alphabet, augmented Roman: *see* **alphabet, initial teaching.**

alphabet, finger: an alphabet in which letters are indicated by various positions of the fingers; used by the deaf for purposes of communication; two types exist, differentiated according to whether one hand or two hands are used to form the characters, namely, the *one-hand alphabet* and the *two-hand alphabet. See* **dactylology.**

alphabet, initial teaching (i.t.a./ITA): an augmented alphabet of 44 characters, each symbol representing one speech sound; designed by Sir James Pitman and used largely in the early stages of reading instruction; also called *augmented Roman alphabet. See* **orthography, traditional; Unifon.**

alphabet, international phonetic: an alphabetically arranged set of special symbols and letters used for the exact written rendition of sounds in nearly any language; widely used in the study of foreign languages and phonetics, and adopted by scholars on an international basis.

alphabet, manual: *syn.* **alphabet, finger.**

alphabet method: *syn.* **ABC method.**

alphabet, one-hand: *see* **alphabet, finger.**

alphabet, phonemic: an alphabet in which each basic sound in a language is represented by only one symbol. *See* **Unifon.**

alphabet, phonetic: (1) a system of representing speech in which each character always refers to the same speech sound and each sound is represented by a single character; (2) (mil. ed.) a list of standard words used (in training as well as in operations) to identify letters in a message transmitted by radio or telephone; the following phonetic alphabet is authorized for use in the military services of the United States when pronouncing isolated letters and spelling out words normally difficult to understand over voice communications:

A	Alpha	N	November
B	Bravo	O	Oscar
C	Charlie	P	Papa
D	Delta	Q	Quebec
E	Echo	R	Romeo
F	Foxtrot	S	Sierra
G	Golf	T	Tango
H	Hotel	U	Uniform
I	India	V	Victor
J	Juliett	W	Whiskey
K	Kilo	X	X-Ray
L	Lima	Y	Yankee
M	Mike	Z	Zulu

alphabet spelling: *see* **spelling, alphabet.**

alphabet, two-hand: *see* **alphabet, finger.**

alphabet wheel: a wheellike device used for teaching letters and letter combinations, so constructed that when it is revolved various letter combinations are produced.

alphabetic filing: *see* **filing plan.**

alphabetic punch-card machine: *see* **punch-card machine, alphabetic.**

alphabetic spelling: *see* **spelling, alphabetic.**

alphabetico-classed catalog: *syn.* **catalog, alphabetico-classified.**

alphabetico-classified catalog: *see* **catalog, alphabetico-classified.**

alphameric: *syn.* **alphanumeric.**

alphameric punch-card machine: *syn.* **punch-card machine, alphabetic.**

alphanumeric: pertaining to alphabetic characters, numerals, and other symbols such as punctuation or mathematical signs; for example, an alphanumeric machine is one which can process both numeric and alphabetic data. *Syn.* **alphameric.**

alter ego (al'tər ē'gō): (Lat., lit., "other I," "other self") a friend who has one's interests so thoroughly at heart and with whom so much experience is shared that he mirrors the self or is a sort of second self.

alterations, bus: any changes made in the construction or appearance of the bus.

alteregoism (al'tər·ē'gō·iz'm): a tendency to have sympathy only with those individuals who resemble the self in some way.

alternate cooperative plan: *see* **cooperative plan, alternate.**

alternate driver: *see* **driver, alternate.**

alternate-form reliability: *see* **reliability, alternate-form.**

alternate forms: *syn.* **equivalent forms.**

alternate-response item: *see* **item, alternate-response.**

alternate-response test: *see* **test, alternate-response.**

alternate school: a type of platoon organization within which the school day is divided into quarters and the pupils alternately go to home rooms and special rooms, spending two quarters in each. *Syn.* **duplicate school; programmed school.**

alternating squint: *see* **squint, alternating.**

alternating suppression: *see* **suppression, alternating.**

alternating vision: *see* **vision, alternating.**

alternation of grades: the combining of the pupils of two grades into a single class, the entire class doing the work of one of the grades one year and the work of the other grade the next year.

alternation of studies: a plan or technique of rotating or alternating at regular intervals the subjects studied or activities engaged in, in order to avoid excessive fatigue or loss of interest; thus, a difficult subject may be followed by physical activity.

alternation of subjects: a scheduling plan by which two or more subjects are offered singly in rotation on successive days or in successive years or semesters.

alternation, plan of: *syn.* **alternation of grades.**

alternative, plausible: *syn.* **distracter.**

alternatives: (philos.) competing courses of action or beliefs between which a choice is involved; a "forked-road" situation in which one must decide which of various ways to go.

alternatives, cultural: (1) various possibilities of action with reference to the same object, situation, or problem, all of which are approved by the society in question; that is, the individual has a choice among a number of permitted courses of action; (2) any of the possible directions or goals toward which a given social order may move.

altitude, social: *see* **social altitude.**

alto: *syn.* **contralto.**

alto-tenor: an adolescent male voice in the process of changing; has an approximate range from the F below middle C to the C above middle C. *Syn.* **cambiata.**

altruism: (1) a system of ethics, after Comte and Spencer, based on the notion of the ultimate obligation of each man to achieve a selfless devotion to others; opposed both to the ethical doctrine of egoism and to the theological doctrines of the individual pursuit of charity and beatitude; (2) more generally, the pursuit of the good of others as an obligation, however motivated, whether by self-interest, by selfless devotion to society, or by disinterested duty. *See* **egoism; ethics; hedonism.**

altruism, social: regard for and devotion to the best interests of the group rather than of the individual.

aluminum screen: *see* **screen, aluminum.**

alumna (ə·lum'nə): *pl.* **alumnae** (-nē); a female graduate.

alumni college: *see* **college, alumni.**

alumni education (ə·lum'nī): educational activities carried on by a college or university for the benefit of its graduates and former students, including postcollegiate professional instruction and the opportunity to hear analyses of problems and to participate in discussions sponsored by the institution.

alumni fund: *see* **fund, alumni.**

alumni placement bureau: *see* **placement bureau, alumni.**

alumnus (ə·lum'nəs): *pl.* **alumni** (-nī); a male graduate.

alveolar (al·vē'ə·lər, al'vē·ō-): (1) referring to the ridgelike formations on the hard palate immediately behind and above the teeth of the upper jaw; (2) a consonant sound in the production of which movement or placement of the tongue in relation to this ridge plays an important part; *t, d, n, l, r, s, z,* and *sh* are alveolar consonants.

am ha-aratzut (äm·hä·ə·rä·tsōōt'): *n. fem.* (Heb.) a term used to signify ignorance of Jewish law, literature, history, etc. *See* **am ha-aretz.**

am ha-aretz (äm·hä·ä'rets): *n. masc.; pl.* **ammei ha-aretz** (ä'mä. . .); (Heb., lit., "people of the land") a term of opprobrium applied to an individual Jew who is ignorant of Torah; originally referred to the peasant class (usually less learned than the urban population) without any derogatory implication; later, however, under the influence of the Pharisees and their successors, as great emphasis was placed on learning, the phrase began to connote ignorance of the Torah and became a term of reproach.

AM radio: *see* **modulation, amplitude.**

amalgamation: (sociol.) the biological union of previously distinct racial or subracial groups.

amateur art: *see* **art, amateur.**

amateur musician: *see* **musician, amateur.**

amaurosis (am'ô·rō'sis): (1) blindness resulting from a defect of the optic nerve; (2) absolute blindness, from whatever cause.

ambidexterity: the ability to use both hands with equal skill and ease. *Syn.* **ambidextrality.**

ambidextrality: *syn.* **ambidexterity.**

ambieyedness: a condition characterized by a lack of dominance of either eye. (Applied to eyedness as *ambidexterity* is used with respect to handedness.)

ambiguity: (1) in general, the quality of being subject to variable interpretations or of being easily influenced by subjective factors; (2) in language, varying meanings expressed by a word, depending upon both its historical development and the context of the sentence in which it appears; (3) (meas.) the quality of a test item that makes possible more than one logical interpretation of its intent or meaning.

ambiguity, fallacy of: *see* **fallacy of ambiguity.**

ambiguity in counseling: *see* **counseling, ambiguity in.**

ambiguity, space: (art) the representation of uncertain and shifting space as is found in *cubism* and other twentieth-century styles.

ambiguity, tolerance for: the ability of the individual to withstand the frustration generated by stimuli which are equivocal or unstructured.

ambiguity value: *see* **value, ambiguity.**

ambiguous figures: *see* **figures, ambiguous.**

ambilateral: pertaining to or affecting both sides of the body.

ambivalence: (1) a state characterized by the simultaneous existence of contradictory feelings such as love and hate, or contradictory relations such as attack and withdrawal with respect to the same object; (2) a state of indecision arising from the inability to give preference to either one of two conflicting feelings or opinions. *See* **conflict, approach-avoidance.**

ambiversion: (1) a quality of the personality representing a condition somewhere between the extremes of *extroversion* and *introversion*; (2) a trait complex including some characteristics of behavior and attitude classified as extroverted as well as some classified as introverted.

ambivert: one whose interests are equally divided between personal and environmental factors.

amblyopia (am'bli·ō'pi·ə): (1) weakness of vision, without any apparent change in the structure of the eye itself; (2) weakness or loss of vision in which no pathological condition can be discerned in the eye. (Often qualified as congenital amblyopia, hysterical amblyopia, or tonic amblyopia.)

amblyopia ex anopsia (an·op'si·ə): (1) weakness of vision resulting from functional disuse of the eyes; (2) partial loss of vision due to a positive act of inhibition or suppression, a defense mechanism that operates to prevent diplopia, as in squint. *See* **diplopia.**

amblyopia, hysterical: weakness of vision caused by a psychological mechanism.

amblystoma (am·blis'tō·mə): a group or class of salamander frequently used in developmental research, especially that concerned with the prenatal period.

ambulate: (spec. ed.) to walk; usually refers to walking with braces or crutches.

ambulatory: descriptive of a person, usually one who is disabled but who possesses the ability to walk or move about with or without prosthetic appliances or other aids.

ament: one lacking in intelligence; a mentally retarded person. *See* **amentia.**

amentia: lack of intelligence. *See* **retardation, mental;** *contr. w.* **dementia.**

amentia, nevoid: *alt. sp.* **naevoid;** a rare condition characterized by extensive blood-vessel tumors, convulsions, hemiplegia, and severe mental deficiency which usually results in early death.

amentia, phenylpyruvic: *syn.* **phenylketonuria.**

amentia, primary: imperfect mental development due to prenatal factors of unknown etiology.

amentia, secondary: imperfect mental development resulting from adverse environmental influences, whether operating before or after birth.

American English language: *see* **language, American English.**

Americana: books and other printed materials, manuscripts, or artifacts having some connection with American history and culture; in the bibliographic sense, limited to printed materials and manuscripts published in or about America or by American authors.

Americanization: a movement with roots in the nineteenth century which came to prominence in the United States just prior to World War I; as conducted in its earlier phases by several government bureaus, including the U.S. Office of Education, consisted primarily of adult education classes designed to bring non-English-speaking immigrants closer to United States cultural norms; during the conservative reaction of the 1920s, the movement took on xenophobic overtones and with the severely restrictive immigration quotas inaugurated in 1924 gradually ceased to be prominent. *See* **alien education; class, Americanization.**

Americanization class: *see* **class, Americanization.**

Americanization theory: the doctrine that proposes that newcomers from foreign lands should rid themselves as quickly as possible of their old characteristics and obliterate all ethnic and cultural distinctions by taking over completely the language, customs, hopes, and aspirations of the dominant American type; one of the methods suggested for the ethnic adjustment of immigrants to American culture. *See* **community theory.**

ametropia (am'ə·trō'pi·ə): (1) a refractive error in which the eye when in a state of rest does not focus the image of an object upon the retina; includes *hyperopia, myopia,* and *astigmatism;* (2) a general term indicating a condition of *astigmatism, hyperopia,* or *myopia.*

amicus curiae (ə·mē'kəs kū'rē·ī): *pl.* **amici** (ə·mē'kē) (Lat., lit., "friend of the court") bystander or third party in litigation who gives information or expert testimony to aid deliberations; may be permitted to testify to protect his interests and, when a judge is doubtful or mistaken in a matter of law, may inform the court.

amimia (ə·mim'i·ə): loss of ability to comprehend gestures or to express ideas by gestures or mimicry; when motor, a form of *apraxia;* when sensory, an *agnosia;* when sign language is impaired, a form of sensory *aphasia.*

Amish school: one of the schools maintained by a small sect of Mennonites (most of whom reside in Pennsylvania); often thought to fall short of or to be in conflict with the principles of universal education as promulgated and practiced in the United States.

ammoniator: a device for adding ammonia to swimming-pool water as it passes through a filtration system, for purposes of sanitation.

amnesia (am·nē'zhi·ə; -zi·ə): a disorder usually due to fatigue, shock, fever, injury to the brain, or extreme repression and characterized by partial or complete inability to remember or identify past experiences; may be organic or functional.

amnesia, anterograde: loss of recent memory for a period following a shock or trauma of some kind.

amnesia, functional: amnesia occurring without head injury or other ascertainable organic pathological condition. *See* **amnesia.**

amnesia, infantile: the normal and characteristic absence of memory for the period of infancy and early years.

amnesia, retroactive: *syn.* **amnesia, retrograde.**

amnesia, retrograde: loss of memory for a limited or circumscribed period preceding some sort of trauma. *Syn.* **retroactive amnesia.**

amoral: a term designating characters, acts, attitudes, or discriminatory judgments to which moral terms such as right, wrong, good, or bad cannot appropriately be applied; morally or ethically indifferent or neutral. *See* **moral.**

amortization: the gradual redemption, liquidation, or extinction of a liability, asset, profit, or loss over a given period of time through regular, periodic payments.

amortization, bond: *see* **bond retirement.**

amphibology: a fallacy of ambiguity due to the way in which words are combined in a sentence, as in the question, "How much is twice six and four?", which may mean either "How much is $(2 \times 6) + 4$?" or "How much is $2 \times (6 + 4)$?" *Syn.* **amphiboly;** *see* **ambiguity, fallacy of.**

amphiboly: *see* **amphibology.**

amplification, broad-band: amplification across the audio band (20–20,000 cycles per second); the typical modern acoustic devices are not broad-band; rather they suppress selectively the amplification outside the normal speech sound range (250–5,000 cycles per second) or according to prescription.

amplifier: an electrical unit for increasing the amplitude of electrical impulses of sound.

amplifier, power: an amplifier designed to boost signal energy sufficiently to operate a loudspeaker. *See* **preamplifier.**

amplitude modulation: *see* **modulation, amplitude.**

amplitude of response: *see* **response, amplitude of.**

amputation, congenital: a condition in which a child is born with one or both lower or upper extremities missing in whole or in part.

amputee: a person crippled through amputation. *See* **amputation.**

amusia (ə·mū'zi·ə): a mental disorder characterized by loss or absence of the ability to recognize or to reproduce musical sounds.

anabolism: a synthetic or constructive process by which nutritive matter is converted by living cells into more complex compounds; the regenerative aspects of *metabolism*. *See* **metabolism**; *contr. w.* **catabolism**.

anaclisis (ə·nak′lə·sis): (psychoan.) a condition of dependence upon another for care and support; usually viewed, when it occurs in an older person, as a fixation at the developmental level at which a necessary relation of dependence obtains between the infant and its mother or nurse.

anaclitic depression: *see* **depression, anaclitic**.

anaclitic object choice (an′ə·klit′ik): the choice by an individual of a love object similar in its characteristics to those persons—usually mother or nurse—on whom the individual in infancy was dependent for his comfort.

anacusis (an′ə·kū′sis): a disorder of hearing caused by loss of the peripheral organ of hearing, of the auditory nerve, or of its immediate nervous connections in the brain; either a profound threshold shift downward or an otoneural dysfunction which cannot be corrected by medical or prosthetic techniques to a practical hearing level. *See* **audiometric threshold**.

anaerobic reaction: *see* **reaction, anaerobic**.

anaglyph: a specially prepared picture (either still or motion) which when viewed with special glasses produces the effect of third dimension. *Dist. f.* **stereograph**.

anagrams: a reading game consisting in making a word or phrase by transposing the letters of another word or phrase.

anal character: *see* **character, anal**.

anal eroticism: *see* **eroticism, anal**.

anal erotism: *syn.* **eroticism, anal**.

anal personality: *syn.* **character, anal**.

anal stage of development: *see* **stage of development, anal**.

analog: the representation of numeric quantities by means of electrical or other physical variables, rather than by digital representation.

analog computer: *see* **computer, analog**.

analog model: *see* **model, analog**.

analogical thinking: *see* **thinking, analogical**.

analogies test: *see* **test, analogies**.

analogous reasoning: *see* **reasoning, analogous**.

analogy: a resemblance of principle between objects, situations, or ideas superficially unlike; should similarity be extensive, reasoning from analogy may be helpful; if resemblance is merely partial or superficial, masking significant differences, reasoning from analogy may be misleading; to treat electronic devices as "brains" with "memories," that is, as analogous to the human brain and memory, may be misleading in overlooking purposiveness in man and lack of purposiveness in a machine.

analogy drill: *see* **drill, analogy**.

analogy item: *see* **item, analogy**.

analogy, logic of: *see* **logic of analogy**.

analysand: a person undergoing psychoanalysis.

analysis: (1) the process of resolving any problem or situation into its component elements; (2) the process that starts with an assumption of the truth of that which is sought and then passes through a chain of sufficient conditions to the given data or to something accepted as true; (3) (math.) currently, the term frequently refers to the basic principles of the calculus; (4) in some contexts, it is used in the classic sense in contrast to synthesis; thus in the *analysis of a proof* one begins with what is to be proved and analyzes the steps needed immediately, then those which must immediately precede them, etc., ending with the given statements; these steps are then synthesized into the final written proof; (5) (psych.) a process that consists in distinguishing the elements or factors that go to make up a complex state of mind; (6) *syn.* **psychoanalysis**; (7) the breakdown of a communication into its constituent elements or parts such that the relative hierarchy of ideas is made clear and/or the relations between the ideas expressed are made explicit; includes analysis of elements, relationships, and organizational principles; *contr. w.* **synthesis**; (8) (couns.) the process of

critically evaluating personnel information about students as a necessary step for the remediation or treatment phase of counseling; (9) the study of musical form and harmonic structure; *see* **form** (5).

analysis, activity: the breaking down of large-scope behavior into specifics; used in curriculum planning, objectives of education being isolated by resolving life activities into their constituent elements.

analysis, auditory: the act or process of breaking down words or word parts into their fundamental sound elements.

analysis, behavior: (curric.) an approach to curriculum development that initially renders educational aims into descriptions of terminal behaviors and then describes the sequence of behaviors and enabling tasks that students must be capable of performing en route to the desired curricular outcome.

analysis, billet: critical examination and interpretation of tasks, functions and responsibilities of a military billet to determine its staffing and performance requirements. *See* **billet** (2).

analysis, biochemical: the chemical analysis of or determination of chemical elements and compounds in biological materials, for example, the chemical analysis of protoplasm.

analysis, bulletin: (teacher ed.) a research technique involving the collection and examination of institutional publications that contain information on various aspects of teacher education, such as courses, curricula, and admission requirements. *Syn.* **catalog analysis**.

analysis, catalog: *syn.* **analysis, bulletin**.

analysis, causal: (philos. of ed.) that branch of analysis concerned with the dynamic aspects of a situation that promote change or activity.

analysis chart: *see* **chart, analysis**.

analysis, child: treatment of a child according to psychoanalytic principles, but utilizing play diagnosis and less formal techniques than the usual analysis.

analysis, classroom interaction: a systematic pattern for analyzing and studying the observable or recordable behaviors of teachers and pupils and factoring out the ways that these behaviors are interrelated.

analysis, cluster: a simple form of correlational analysis in which clusters are formed of those variables (in a *matrix*) which have high intercorrelations with each other and relatively low correlations with the remaining variables in the matrix.

analysis, cohort: *syn.* **cohort-survival technique**.

analysis, comparative linguistic: the analysis of the relationships between languages.

analysis, content: a detailed evaluation and appraisal of the manifest and latent content of various types of communication; used in curriculum research.

analysis, cost: the systematic analysis of items and patterns of expenditure. *See* **accounting, cost**.

analysis, critical: *see* **thinking, critical**.

analysis, dimensional: a separation of anything into its component parts under conditions necessary and sufficient for the complete characterization of its elements.

analysis, dispersion: *syn.* **analysis, scatter**.

analysis, educational systems: *see* **systems analysis, educational**.

analysis, empirical: a method of studying the nature of anything by the division of the contents into component parts or factors, the division being guided only by the practical experience of the person making the analysis. *Contr. w.* **analysis, technical**.

analysis, empiriological: analysis of individual things and events at the level of experience and nature. *Dist. f.* **analysis, ontological**.

analysis, factor: *see* **factor analysis**.

analysis, field unit: a system involving on-the-spot coding and the scoring and statistical analysis of successive behavior units and selected variables of behavior and situations. *See* **observation, approaches to**.

analysis, financial: (school admin.) the function of evaluating financial data for the purpose of assisting management in planning, organizing, and controlling the activities of a business; a staff function that is usually performed at the level of general administrative management. *See* **functions, staff.**

analysis, functional: (1) breaking items to be taught into specifics in terms of relative use; (2) the act of varying the conditions under which a phenomenon takes place to ascertain the conditions necessary for its existence; (3) the inductive method as interpreted in gestalt theory.

analysis, graphical: the use of the graph as an aid in the discovery of relationships.

analysis, individual: (1) a description of the ways in which men are alike (what is consistent in human nature) and the ways in which men differ (how each individual is unique); (2) in attempting solution of personal problems, individual interviews with a counselor trained in counseling techniques; *see* **counseling, individual.**

analysis, interaction: in group dynamics, the study of all the reactions of each person to every other within the group; systematic records are made and interactions are placed into some scheme of categories.

analysis, item: (1) any one of several methods used in test validation or improvement to determine how well a given question or item discriminates among individuals of different degrees of ability or among individuals differing in some other characteristic; (2) the act or process of determining any systematic information, such as discrimination, difficulty, etc., about a test item.

analysis, job: (1) the basic method used to obtain salient facts about a job, involving observation of workers and conversations with those who know the job, in order to describe in detail the work involved, the conditions for performance, and the qualifications necessary for the worker who must perform it; (2) (voc. ed.) a detailed listing of duties, operations, and skills necessary to perform a clearly defined, specific job, organized into a logical sequence which may be used for teaching, employment, or classification purposes; *see* **study, motion and time.**

analysis, kinesiologic: (1) an analysis of motor skills broken down into basic skills; (2) the identification, anatomically and mechanically, of the factors which contribute to or detract from skillful performance.

analysis, language: a movement in the United States and Great Britain, generally traced to the work of Ludwig Wittgenstein, in which the principal interest is the resolution of philosophical problems arising from the misuse of language.

analysis, linguistic: the identification and classification of the structural properties (semantic, phonetic, analogic) of a verbal or orthographic message.

analysis, literary: detailed study of a literary work, intended to show the characteristics of its composition, style, and ideas and its aesthetic, moral, or philosophical values.

analysis, mathematical: (1) any investigation of data or phenomena through the techniques of mathematics; (2) the process of discovering the relations existing among variables and of determining the laws governing these relations; (3) the process of mathematical proof by which the result is assumed to be true and the reasoning is carried back logically, through a chain of sufficient conditions, to the existing data or to established principles.

analysis, mental health: *see* **inventory, adjustment.**

analysis, morphological: (group dynamics) a method of group problem solving which involves the combining of major attributes of variables into a pattern so that all possible combinations of solutions can be considered.

analysis, multiple-choice item: a technique for determining the number of students who select a given response on multiple-choice tests and for discovering why students select incorrect responses; thus, a critical analysis of test effectiveness.

analysis, multiple scalogram (MSA): selection of an item from a set to be analyzed, location of that item among the remaining items which is most like it and having the fewest errors, determination of the number of errors between the candidate item and all of its predecessors, and finally, application of a statistical test of significance to adjacent item pairs. *See* **analysis, scalogram.**

analysis, multivariate: any statistical procedure that is designed to describe, interpret, and predict the behavior of two or more variables that change or interact simultaneously.

analysis, musical: the intellectual examination of the printed score of a musical composition to determine the character of its melodic, harmonic, rhythmic, and organizational means; several rather fully codified systems exist for musical analysis.

analysis, numerical: a branch of mathematics which deals with methods of obtaining approximate numerical answers to problems, determining the accuracy of approximations, and determining the time required to get an answer.

analysis, occupational: *syn.* **analysis, job.**

analysis of a proof: *see* **analysis** (4).

analysis of covariance: *see* **covariance, analysis of.**

analysis of variance: *see* **variance, analysis of.**

analysis, ontological: the process of trying to reach knowledge of ultimate reality by analyzing the concept of "being" (or "reality") into its component parts or attributes and determining the interrelation of these parts within the whole. *Dist. f.* **analysis, empiriological.**

analysis, operations: (school admin.) application of scientific method to study of complex operations; a sophisticated approach to problem solving utilizing mathematics research and educational and computer technology. *See* **analysis, systems.**

analysis, pattern: any process of combining several responses or scores of individuals into clusters or syndromes, in order to discover whether such patterns differentiate individuals or groups.

analysis, philosophical: a term used to designate a number of techniques for the treatment of erroneous and misused concepts, for the clarification of their logical operations, and for the reinterpretation of their role in education.

analysis, phonetic: (1) analysis of speech sounds; (2) analysis of words into the elements that correspond to speech sounds, for example, breaking up the word spend into the initial consonant blend sp and the final phonogram end.

analysis, planning-program-budgeting: (school finance) the development of program structures representing output-oriented classifications of government expenditures. *See* **program structure.**

analysis, position: *see* **analysis, job.**

analysis, problem: consideration of various aspects of or approaches to a problem in order to solve it.

analysis, profile: (1) a method for appraising individual uniqueness and trait organization, consisting in a search for characteristic patterns in the trait profiles of an individual; (2) any of several methods for studying similarity between sets of scores, whether for the purpose of (a) identifying "types" of people, (b) studying self-consistency over a period of time, (c) differentiating groups, or (d) other type of study; may be based upon Q-technique factor analysis, an index of pattern similarity, or a measure of distance. *See* **analysis, scatter; profile.**

analysis, propaganda: an attempt to recognize and appraise propaganda by a scrutiny of its purposes, agencies, techniques, devices, and truth content.

analysis, reading: examination of the reading behavior of an individual to determine the strength and weakness of his reading. *See* **diagnosis, reading.**

analysis, referential: a method of word study in which each word is divested of its emotional associations, in order to determine its basic meaning.

analysis, scale: *syn.* **analysis, scalogram.**

analysis, scalogram: Guttman's technique of attitude scaling which purports to measure unidimensionality and intensity of attitude. *Syn.* **scale analysis;** *see* **analysis, multiple scalogram; reproducibility.**

analysis, scatter: (1) analysis of a subject's performance on subtests and specific items of a scale; especially, analysis of the range and nature of the items passed and failed on the Stanford-Binet or other test, with special reference to (a) the scale distance between the basal age and the highest age level at which any test item is passed or (b) the different types of tasks passed by adults thought to be mentally deteriorated; (2) study of the difference between successes of a selected examinee and successes of his peers on certain test items or tests; (3) the attempt to find significant relationships or patterns among various subtest scores; may deal either with amount or qualitative pattern of scatter. *Syn.* **dispersion analysis;** *dist. f.* **analysis, pattern.**

analysis, semantic: (1) a process in the study of the relations of signs to that to which they are applicable; (2) the logical analysis of language.

analysis, sequential: a statistical procedure that leads to an inference of predetermined precision based on the fewest possible successive cases or items, when these items are taken one at a time; that is, the procedure indicates when sufficient cases have been acquired to accept or reject a null hypothesis within the predetermined risks of error; enables the investigator to save time and effort by testing for significance as he samples and, if needed, adding observations in the same manner until there is sufficient evidence for accepting or rejecting a null hypothesis. *See* **hypothesis, null.**

analysis, situational: a method of approaching personal and social problems in terms of the total setting rather than single causes or individual traits; in such analysis, cultural or environmental factors which give rise to deviate behavior are seen as more significant than the individual deviate.

analysis, statistical: the application of statistical processes and theory to the compilation, presentation, discussion, and interpretation of numerical data.

analysis, structural: (read.) analysis of a word to identify its root, prefix, and/or suffix, or the syllables which compose it; the purpose is to identify pronunciation units which may be blended to produce the sound of the word.

analysis, substrata-factor: an extension by Holmes (1948) of the Wherry-Doolittle multiple correlation test selection method making it applicable to the analysis of successive sublevels of abilities which are organized by an individual in the solution of a criterion problem.

analysis, systems: the examination of an enterprise, institution, or occupation through resolving into elements or constituent parts its objectives, responsibilities, requirements, and outputs in order to determine what must be accomplished and how it may be accomplished best; a study approach which yields the best results among various objectives and criteria by comparing the risks, effectiveness, and cost of the alternatives; designed to help a decision maker to identify the preferred choice among the possible alternatives.

analysis, systems and procedures: (school admin.) the extensive study of administrative and data processing systems and procedures, from their beginning to their logical conclusion, for simplification and improvement.

analysis, task: reduction of the components of a task to its basic behavioral elements, usually for purposes of determining the best methods of training to perform it, but also to understand better the learning process.

analysis, technical: the division of any educational process into its component parts, or factors, the process of division being accomplished through the application of the results of controlled experimentation and of other techniques of scientific research. *Contr. w.* **analysis, empirical.**

analysis, techniques of: ways of using analytical tools such as tests, case histories, etc., to derive an understanding of students' aptitudes, interests, motives, adjustment problems, and other characteristics; employment of these techniques precedes the personal-interview or treatment phase of counseling.

analysis, trade: the procedure of breaking down a trade or occupation to determine the teachable content in terms of operations, tools, processes, and technical information to be organized into a course of study and arranged according to a sequence of difficulty.

analysis, trend: a technique for analyzing treatment effects when the treatments represent varying degrees of the same variable and can, therefore, be ordered.

analysis, visual: the process of breaking up a word into familiar parts that are known by sight and blending these parts into whole words, for example, recognizing the simple verb form go and the suffix ing in the word going and recombining these parts into the whole word.

analysis, word: (1) the act or process of breaking up words into visual or phonetic elements for the purpose of blending these into word wholes; (2) the act or process of analyzing the likenesses and differences among words, as to both form and meaning.

analyst: (data processing) a person skilled in the definition of a problem and the development of techniques for its solution, especially those techniques for solutions on a computer.

analytic approach to phonics: *see* **phonics, analytic approach to.**

analytic geometry: *see* **geometry, analytic.**

analytic interview: *see* **interview, analytic.**

analytic method: (1) *see* **analysis;** (2) (art ed.) in a creative activity such as modeling from clay, the analytic method consists in pulling out the single details from the whole; akin to observing as a way of thinking and therefore characteristic of the visually minded; *ant.* **synthetic method** (5).

analytic proof: *see* **proof, analytic.**

analytic psychology: *see* **psychology, analytic.**

analytic-synthetic method: the combined method of teaching reading in which each word is first broken up into familiar parts, which are then fused into a whole.

analytical approach: (1) the method of diagnosing reading difficulties that seeks to identify the specific elements in reading ability that are weak and need remedial training; (2) the theoretical assumption that reading ability is made up of specific skills that can be identified.

analytical method: (1) a method of teaching reading in which the whole is first presented and then is broken down into its smaller elements; (2) in the teaching of phonics, the analysis of a word for pronunciation purposes; (3) the close textual study of a literary selection, with attention to the exact meanings and implications of words and allusions and to the techniques of structure and style by which the writer achieves his effects; (4) a method of teaching shorthand devised by Frick, the aim of which is to teach word writing through the use of transfer elements called *sound patterns.*

analytical philosophy: *see* **philosophy, analytical.**

analytical reading test: *see* **test, analytical reading.**

analytical reasoning: *see* **analysis, mathematical.**

analytical research: *see* **research, analytical.**

analytical scale: *syn.* **test, diagnostic.**

analytical study: *see* **study, analytical.**

analytical test: *see* **test, analytical.**

analytical tools: tests, case histories, cumulative records, interviews, and reports used in arriving at an understanding of the characteristics and adjustment problems of a student preceding the counseling interview.

analytically oriented counseling: *see* **counseling, analytically oriented.**

analyzing: (1) (couns.) collecting personal information about students by means of analytical techniques preceding counseling; *see* **analysis, techniques of;** (2) (admin.) identifying the significant parts of the teaching-learning operation.

anamnesis (an'əm·nē'sis): the family and personal history of a patient or client and an account of the circumstances leading to the present illness or investigation. *Contr. w.* **catamnesis.**

anamorphic lens: *see* **lens, anamorphic.**

anarthria (an·är'thri·ə): inability to articulate speech sounds due to a lesion of the central nervous system.

anatomical age: *see* **age, anatomical.**

anatomical development: *see* **development, anatomical.**

anatomical growth: *see* **growth, anatomical.**

anatomy: the branch of biology that relates to the structure of a living organism or any of its parts.

anatomy, applied: knowledge of anatomy as applied to diagnosis and treatment.

anchor test: *see* **test, anchor.**

ancient history: *see* **history, ancient.**

ancillary services: (spec. ed.) specialized services which support educational programs and practices, such as counseling, social work, psychological services, and rehabilitation.

ancillary services and activities, distributive education: *see* **services and activities, distributive education ancillary.**

ancillary statistic: *see* **statistic, ancillary.**

androgen: a hormone secreted by the adrenal cortex and gonads in both males and females but in greater quantities by males; influences the development of secondary sex characteristics and body structure.

anecdotal behavior journal: *see* **journal, anecdotal behavior.**

anecdotal method: (1) a method of analyzing child behavior, chiefly characterized by reliance on records made of isolated occurrences; *dist. f.* **observational method;** (2) a technique by means of which a student's behavior and responses are recorded, as they occur, by the teachers observing them, for use by the counselor in studying and analyzing the student's problems; *see* **event-sampling.**

anecdotal record: *see* **record, anecdotal.**

anecdote: (couns.) a "word snapshot" of an isolated incident of behavior which suggests some special significance.

anethopath: a person with a pathological lack of development in the moral-ethical aspects of personality. *See* **psychopath.**

angelology: the study of spiritual beings, commonly called angels (from the Greek word for "messengers"), who are deemed to be creatures with intelligence but of pure spirit and therefore noncorporeal. *See* **anthropology** (2); *comp. w.* **demonology.**

anger: (1) (child dev.) a pattern of behavior elicited by restraint or thwarting and consisting of a strong unpleasant emotional factor (affect) and defensive or offensive movements (termed *rage* in Watson's hypothesis of three primary emotions); (2) a feeling of displeasure and antagonism so strong and specifically directed against the cause of injury, insult, or pain, real or imaginary, as to be classified as an emotion or passion.

angular transformation: *see* **transformation, angular.**

anhedonia (an′he·dō′ni·ə): a state of apathy characterized by loss of pleasure in the normally pleasurable functions of life.

anima (an′im·ə): (Lat., lit., "spirit") a term used by Jung to signify *personality.*

animal experimentation: *see* **experimentation, animal.**

animal intelligence: *see* **intelligence, animal.**

animalistic nature of man: *see* **nature of man, animalistic.**

animation: a motion-picture technique that gives an illusion of motion to drawings, models, lines, arrows, etc., through the projection of a sequence of frames on which successive positions of the objects, drawings, etc., have been photographed.

animatism (an′i·mə·tiz′m): a form of animism common to primitive peoples and characterized by the belief that all things are alive and that plants and the less complex animals possess the psychological traits of human beings without possessing souls. *See* **animism.**

animism: (1) the theory that the world of nature is inhabited by spirits, some good and some bad; *see* **animatism;** (2) as used by Piaget, a logic of young children that attributes lifelike qualities to inanimate objects such as the sails of a ship.

annexation: legal absorption of one entity into another, for example, a school district. *See* **consolidation** (2); **reorganization, school** (2).

annotated bibliography: *see* **bibliography, annotated.**

annoyers and satisfiers: rewards and punishments, failures and successes, pleasantness and unpleasantness, satisfactions and dissatisfactions to the learner. (The terms are used by Thorndike to clarify his *law of effect* in learning.)

annual: an illustrated record of the school year, usually in book form, written, edited, and published by a class or group of students in a university, college, or high school. *Syn.* **yearbook.**

annual contract: *see* **contract, annual.**

annual current expenditures per pupil in ADA: *see* **expenditures per pupil in ADA, annual current.**

annual current expenditures per pupil in ADM: *see* **expenditures per pupil in ADM, annual current.**

annual dropout rate: *see* **dropout rate, annual.**

annual holding power: *see* **holding power, annual.**

annual, offset: an illustrated college or high school annual printed from pasted-up photoengraved pages, rather than with letterpress and separate engravings of individual pictures. *Syn.* **offset yearbook.**

annual promotion: *see* **promotion, annual.**

annual report: *see* **report, annual.**

annual tabulation report: *see* **report, annual tabulation.**

annual transfer rate: *see* **transfer rate, annual.**

annual transportation report: *see* **report, annual transportation.**

annual withdrawal rate: *see* **withdrawal rate, annual.**

annuitant: the person on whose life an annuity payable under an annuity agreement is based and at whose death the payment of the annuity ceases. (The annuitant usually is the payee also, although this is not always the case.)

annuity: an annual or regular payment made on the basis of an annuity agreement or under a bequest; sometimes designates payments of the nature of pensions to retired members of an institutional staff; an annual allowance or income.

annuity agreement: an agreement by which money or other property is made available to an institution on the condition that the institution binds itself to hold and administer the property and to pay periodically to the donor or other designated individual a stipulated amount, this payment to cease at the time of the annuitant's death; sometimes called *annuity bond.*

annuity bond: *syn.* **annuity agreement,** the latter term being preferred.

annuity funds: *see* **funds, annuity.**

annuity plan of bond payments: a bond issue that provides for annual payments on the principal.

annunciator: a system built into the circuitry of the language laboratory so that a student may press a button in his booth to attract the teacher's or monitor's attention.

anoetic (an′ō·et′ik): pertaining to the fringe of consciousness; hazy.

anomaly (ə·nom′ə·lē): (1) deviation from rule, form, or type; (2) irregularity in development.

anomaly, congenital: a defect of structure or form present at birth.

anomia (ə·nō′mi·ə): (1) a term used by Benjamin Rush to indicate absence of moral sense; (2) a variety of amnesic aphasia characterized by inability to name objects although they are immediately recognized.

anomic: (1) a heteroclitic system of arrays (differing in skewness) in which the skewness of the arrays changes irregularly with the position of the array; *contr. w.* **nomic** (1); (2) a heteroscedastic system of arrays (differing in variability) in which the standard deviation of the arrays changes irregularly with the position of the array; *contr. w.* **nomic** (2).

anomie: (1) a condition of society marked by failure to evolve norms or by lack of values and goals; (2) the cleavage among groups resulting from basic disagreements over values, goals, and norms, sometimes leading to social disintegration; (3) often a characteristic of those individuals in a mass society who suffer from cultural alienation; *see* **alienation.**

answer categories, precoded: *see* **precoded answer categories.**

answer, compound: (1) an answer involving several parts not necessarily related to one another; (2) an answer to a multiple-choice question in which several correct alternatives may be included, all of which must be indicated if the examinee is to receive full credit.

answer, directed: in foreign language teaching, an oral drill in which the student is given a statement plus a cue word which he must use properly in his response. *Syn.* **directed response;** *see* **passage, directed.**

answer grid: an objective test answer sheet with the correct answers for each item punched out; when it is placed atop a student's answer sheet, all student pencil marks indicating correctly answered questions show through the holes.

answer key: *see* **key, answer.**

answer pattern: the pattern of an examinee's responses to either (*a*) several questions where at least one answer is required to each or (*b*) one question where more than one category of elected answers is allowable and acceptable. (Thus, if in answer to the questions "What is your sex?" "What is your race?" a questionnaire respondent replies, respectively, "Male" and "White," then Male-White is the answer pattern of that respondent.)

answer, plausible wrong: *syn.* **distractor.**

answer print: *see* **print, answer.**

answer sheet: the separate sheet on which the examinee may record his responses for a test.

antagonistic accommodation: *see* **accommodation** (2).

antagonistic cooperation: *syn.* **accommodation** (2).

antecedent events: (couns.) those prior experiences or happenings which relate to subsequent behavior; in the behavior-theoretical approach to counseling, to the extent to which these antecedents can be manipulated and controlled, human behavior is potentially controllable.

antedating response: *see* **response, antedating.**

anterograde amnesia: *see* **amnesia, anterograde.**

anthropocentric philosophy: *see* **philosophy, anthropocentric.**

anthropogeography: the science which deals with the adaptation of human groups to natural environment. *Comp. w.* **anthroposociology.**

anthropography: the branch of anthropology which studies the geographical distribution of races and cultures.

anthropoid: resembling man, as the primates, such as chimpanzees and gorillas.

anthropokinetics: the study of the total human being in action, with integrated applications from the special fields of the biological and physical sciences, psychology, and sociology. *Syn.* **biokinetics;** *see* **kinesiology; kinetics.**

anthropological approach: the principle of organization for the study of the interrelation between man, his environment, race, language, and culture, and the sources of the differentiated forms of social life.

anthropology: (1) the science concerned with man, both normatively and historically, dealing with his physical characteristics, his racial, geographical, and historical distribution, classification, and relationships, and his cultural, environmental, and social development and relationships; embraces *anthropography, anthropometry, anthropogeography, ethnology, anthroponomy, demography, sociology, human paleontology, archaeology, folklore,* and *comparative religion;* (2) (relig. ed.) as used by theologians, the study of man as contrasted with *theology,* the study of God, or with *angelology* or *demonology,* the study of spiritual beings.

anthropology, cultural: a subdivision of anthropology used to distinguish the study of human, social, and cultural behavior from physical anthropology; usually includes archaeology, ethnology, social anthropology, comparative religion, and folklore.

anthropology, physical: a subdivision of anthropology concerned with the biological evolution of man and the classification of living races.

anthropology, social: a subdivision of anthropology concerned with developing and testing generalizations about human social and cultural behavior; based on information derived from a comparative study of different societies and cultures throughout the world.

anthropometric index: *see* **index, anthropometric.**

anthropometric measurement: *see* **measurement, anthropometric.**

anthropometry: a branch of physical anthropology concerned with human anatomical measurements; used to gather data for studies of race, growth, physical constitution, evolution, etc.

anthropomorphism: the theory that attributes human characteristics to anything nonhuman, including transcendent or religious beings, especially God. *See* **theriomorphism.**

anthroponomy (an'thrō·pon'ə·mē): a branch of anthropology dealing with the study of human behavior; related to social psychology.

anthroposociology: the study of the reciprocal action of race and environment. *Comp. w.* **anthropogeography.**

anthroposophy: an applied spiritual science founded by Rudolph Steiner, having historical affinities with *theosophy,* with a highly developed philosophy of education carried out in several private schools both in the United States and in Europe.

anti-intellectualism: (1) those tendencies, especially active in modern times, which restrict the process of open inquiry, the freedom of the mind to inquire into all its problems, and the freedom to teach accordingly; (2) the tendency to emphasize emotion or feeling at the expense of thought and reflection; disrespect for or active hostility toward the life of the mind; (3) a term used in criticism of modern education, particularly higher and secondary education, to the effect that the intellectual content of the scholarly disciplines and the pursuit of truth for its own sake have been largely replaced by trivia, practical procedures, and isolated snatches of information.

anticipated-achievement grade-placement score: *see* **score, anticipated-achievement grade-placement.**

anticipated response: *see* **response, anticipated.**

anticipation warrant: a warrant or check for the payment of debt, issued by a governmental agency before money for its redemption is available or due; frequently, under specified conditions, such warrants bear interest.

anticipatory goal response, fractional: *see* **response, fractional anticipatory goal.**

anticipatory response: *syn.* **response, antedating.**

anticlericalism: a political movement of the eighteenth, nineteenth, and twentieth centuries in countries hostile to the excessive power of the church; its aims were to establish the supremacy of the state over all religious faiths and to eliminate or reduce church influences in government and politics.

anticonvulsant: descriptive of an agent relieving or preventing convulsions.

antideterminism: a counseling philosophy which emphasizes that the counselor should help the counselee to defeat those predictions which might be derived from background information in order to free him for making his choices and decisions with a greater degree of freedom than he had before coming into counseling.

antidiscrimination: the policy of refusing to use or permit the use of nonrelevant factors, such as race, creed, color, or ethnic origin, in the employment of faculty and other staff members or in the admission of students to an educational institution or to any of its activities, services, or facilities.

antifeminism: a movement opposing economic, social, and political equality of the sexes.

antinomy (an·tin'ə·mē): mutually contradictory principles or conclusions, each of which may be established by reason, but which cannot both be true; Kant cites as such contradiction the conception of the world as both finite and infinite.

Antioch plan: a plan of cooperative education, as developed at Antioch College. *See* **cooperative education.**

antisocial: pertaining to conduct that is in conflict with or disregards existing social institutions and social norms;

descriptive of the tendency to disrupt approved social relationships. *Dist. f.* **asocial; unsocial.**

antithesis: a proposition opposed to a given *thesis* which expresses a fact or affirmation; (Hegel) the second phase of a dialectical process (either logical or existential), denying or rejecting the first concept or condition and contributing to the emergence of a *synthesis* which both blends and transcends the partial truths of the *thesis* and the *antithesis.*

antonym: a word opposite in meaning to another word; for example, hot is the antonym of cold.

antonym test: *see* **test, antonym.**

anxiety: apprehension, tension, or uneasiness characterized by fear, dread, or uncertainty, the source of which is largely unknown or unrecognized by the individual; may consist in persistent apprehensions of future events as well as in generalized emotional reactions to any choice point or decision.

anxiety, free-floating: a state in which the person has developed general anxiety reactions to almost any problem or decision which he faces so that anxiety has become a part of his personality and occurs without any objective justification for it.

anxiety hysteria: *see* **hysteria, anxiety.**

anxiety neurosis: *see* **neurosis, anxiety.**

anxiety, neurotic: anxiety without or disproportionate to its rational justification, as contrasted with fear of real danger.

anxiety, social: *see* **social anxiety.**

anxiety, test: *see* **test anxiety.**

apathy: (1) in general, lack of feeling; (2) a pathological mental condition characterized by extreme or exaggerated indifference.

aperiodic review: *see* **review, aperiodic.**

aperture: (1) in still cameras, motion-picture cameras, and enlargers, the opening (usually variable in size) provided for the passage of light through the lens; (2) in projectors, the opening between the light source and focusing lens which defines the area of the transparency that will be projected.

aperture card: *see* **card, aperture.**

aperture gate: *see* **gate, aperture.**

aphasia (ə·fā′zhi·ə; -zhə): a disorder consisting essentially in an inability to produce or to comprehend language; may involve both spoken and written language; more specifically, loss of the significance of the symbol; the main types are nominal, syntactical, verbal, and semantic, according to Head, or expressive, receptive, and expressive-receptive, according to Weisenburg and McBride; believed to be caused by various lesions (traumatic, vascular, inflammatory, etc.) of the brain, particularly in the region of the inferior frontal gyrus (Broca's area) and in association areas of the dominant hemisphere.

aphasia, acquired: the loss of ability to comprehend, manipulate, or express words in speech, writing, or signs; acquired after birth due to some injury or disease in the brain centers controlling such processes.

aphasia, auditory: defect, loss, or nondevelopment of the ability to comprehend spoken words, due to disease, injury, or maldevelopment of the hearing centers of the brain; also called *word deafness.*

aphasia, expressive: *see* **aphasia, motor-expressive.**

aphasia, motor-expressive: loss of ability of expression, although the words may be recognized if seen in print; commonly associated with a lesion of the inferior frontal gyrus (Broca's area) of the dominant hemisphere; also called *expressive aphasia. See* **aphasia.**

aphasia, receptive: *syn.* **aphasia, sensory-receptive.**

aphasia, sensory-receptive: interference with adequate comprehension of spoken or written words, often as a result of a lesion of the temporal lobe in the dominant hemisphere; also called *receptive aphasia. See* **aphasia.**

aphemia (ə·fē′mi·ə): a speech disorder without apparent organic cause in which the person afflicted knows what he wishes to say but cannot produce the words; a form of *dysphemia.*

aphonia (a·fō′ni·ə): loss of voice due to a peripheral lesion, which may be structural (trauma, tumor), neurological (recurrent laryngeal nerve), or psychogenic.

aphoristic: *syn.* **axiomatic.**

Apollonian art: *see* **art, Apollonian.**

apologetics: a theological science that seeks to offer from history, science, and/or systematic explanation a defense of the reasonableness of Christianity; also called *fundamental theology,* as a study preparatory to dogmatic theology.

apologist: (1) one who publicly writes or speaks in defense of any cause, policy, or institution; (2) one who defends Christian beliefs and practices, especially any of the early Christian writers, such as Justin Martyr and Clement of Alexandria, who defended Christian doctrine against pagan attack.

apopathetic behavior: *see* **behavior, apopathetic.**

apotheosis (ə·poth′ē·ō′sis): *syn.* **deification.**

apparatus, gymnastic: horses, bucks, mats, parallel bars, ropes, booms, and other devices used as objects on which to perform controlled movements in a gymnasium.

apparatus, tangible: *see* **tangible apparatus.**

apparent class limit: *see* **class limit, apparent.**

apparent error: *syn.* **error, maximum.**

apparent mode: *syn.* **mode, crude.**

apparent quotient method: a method of estimating a partial quotient in a long division problem when the divisor has two digits; the scheme is to use the number in the ten's place as a trial divisor.

apparent weight: *see* **weight, apparent.**

appeal authorities: law courts or educational officers or bodies before which legal appeals may be brought for judgment.

appeal to custom: the invocation of long-established usages and tradition as a method of arriving at a judgment or a decision, contrasted with the appeal to reason and to rigorous scientific evidence.

appearance: (philos.) that which comes to an observer through common sense and sensory impressions; that which an object or event is observed to be, as opposed to that which it really is.

appellant (ə·pel′ənt): the party who appeals the decision of a lower court to a higher court or who takes an appeal from one judicial or administrative body to another, for example, a teacher who appeals dismissal by a local school authority to a higher authority. *Contr. w.* **appellee.**

appellate body: a tribunal or individual having review powers of the judicial actions of lower (inferior) courts or quasi-judicial agencies.

appellee (ap′ə·lē′): one against whom an appeal is taken; the respondent. *Contr. w.* **appellant.**

appendix: matter supplementing the text of a book or dissertation but not essential to its completeness, as a bibliography, statistical tables, and explanatory material.

apperception: the process of relating new material to one's background of experience and of evaluating it in the light of the experience.

apperceptive mass: one's total knowledge or experience in relation to new facts or situations; suggestive of some of the principles proposed by modern gestalt psychology, as, for example, *regulation* (the dominance of wholes over parts).

appetite: a specific desire for food, water, air, sexual activity, rest, sleep, exercise, and the like, that is based upon organic processes and acquired or modified through experience. *Contr. w.* **aversion.**

appetitive powers: (1) in Plato's "Republic" the appetitive powers are specifically hunger, thirst, sex, or generically (on the ground that the satisfaction of such appetites tended to be expensive) the money-loving appetite; (2) in the philosophy of St. Thomas, those powers of the human being which strive for the possession of objects apprehended as good or for avoidance of objects apprehended as evil.

application: (1) the use in particular and concrete situations of abstractions in the form of general ideas, rules of procedure, or generalized method, or of technical principles, ideas, and theories which must be remembered and applied; (2) outcomes of learning and instruction involving the use of skills, knowledges, concepts, and understandings in practical situations; (3) the act of concentrating the attention on the material at hand when called upon to master printed or written matter.

application blank for admission: a record form for collecting educational and other personnel data on students seeking to be admitted to college from high school or to be transferred from one college or university to another.

application level: (read.) a term used by Gray to designate each of the stages in the application of word-analysis techniques to the identification and recognition of new and strange words; he identifies five application levels of increasing complexity and difficulty.

applications, technological: *see* **technological applications.**

applied anatomy: *see* **anatomy, applied.**

applied art: *see* **art, applied.**

applied arts: *see* **arts, applied.**

applied biological science: *see* **science, applied biological.**

applied decoration: *see* **decoration, applied.**

applied design: *see* **design, applied.**

applied mathematics: *see* **mathematics, applied.**

applied music: *see* **music, applied.**

applied philosophy: *see* **philosophy, applied.**

applied reading: *see* **reading, applied.**

applied research: *see* **research, applied.**

applied science: *see* **science, applied.**

appointive board: a board of education or a similar body whose members are appointed by an official or group with properly constituted authority; sometimes appointment may be approved or rejected by qualified electors at a school election.

appointive member: a member of a board of education or a similar body appointed by an official or board.

appointive office: a position in a school system filled by appointment by a regularly constituted board or official, usually for a stipulated period of time. *Dist. f.* **elective office.**

appointment, basis of: the principle or principles by which funds, materials, or services are allocated to operating units from a central source.

appointment of state board: the act of designating members of a state board by a governmental official or body without participation of the electorate.

appointments bureau: *syn.* **placement bureau.**

apportionment, basis of: the system or plan by which funds, materials, or services are distributed to operating units from a central source.

apportionment of equalizing funds: the act of dividing and distributing equalizing funds. *See* **fund, equalization.**

apportionment of school funds: the act of dividing and distributing money for school purposes by a central agency, such as a state, to its subordinate units according to an established basis.

appraisal: (1) formal and accurate valuation of property usually made by persons familiar with such values; generally used to determine the amount of insurance to be carried; (2) (couns.) the process of synthesizing and interpreting data concerning a pupil or student; (3) *see* **evaluation** (3).

appraisal, health: (phys. ed.) the evaluation of the health status of the individual through the utilization of varied organized and systematic procedures such as medical and dental examinations, laboratory tests, health history, teacher observation, etc.

appraisal of buildings: determination of the value of buildings of a university, college, or school on an approved basis, usually replacement value or original value less depreciation; may be made on the basis of market or salable value, but this basis is seldom used in the case of university and college buildings.

appraisal, personal: assessment by means of a personality test and/or interview.

appraisal, task: *see* **task appraisal.**

appreciation: (1) an emotionally tinged awareness of the worth, value, or significance of anything; (2) (art ed.) identification with the artist, especially as concerns his subject matter and his means of expression; the total response of the individual to the modes of expression of others; an integrated response to works of art in which the whole being is involved.

appreciation, aesthetic: an intellectual and emotional awareness of or sensitivity to the aesthetic phenomena, often concerned with critical evaluation and understanding of aesthetic principles, as applied to the visual arts, literature, music, drama, natural beauty, etc. *See* **aesthetic education; aesthetic judgment; aesthetics; appreciation, art.**

appreciation, art: the act of evaluating, understanding, and experiencing any expression of art through sensitive awareness of intrinsic worth or value; generally considered as having two distinguishable but inseparable components, emotional appreciation, based on the pleasure and satisfaction derived from beauty of the object, design, color, tone, etc., and intellectual appreciation, resulting from the understanding of aesthetic principles and artistic techniques; applied to the visual arts, literature, and music.

appreciation course: *see* **course, appreciation.**

appreciation, literature: ability to comprehend, interpret, and value with discrimination the literature read.

appreciation, mathematical: aesthetic value judgment of the beauty of mathematics, particularly with reference to the elegance of a proof.

appreciation, music: (1) intelligent enjoyment of music; (2) the response of a hearer to music, whether emotional or intellectual.

appreciation project: *see* **project, appreciation.**

appreciation unit: *see* **unit, appreciation.**

appreciational experience: *see* **experience, appreciational.**

apprehension: (1) the direct grasp or understanding of the meaning-content of an object or of an act and its object; according to some views, this understanding is of warranted knowledge immediately grasped prior to and independent of inquiry; according to other views, this direct grasp is of meaning-content, mediated by retention and habit, of products of prior experiences and mediated conclusions drawn from them; (2) dread, anticipation of evil or danger, as in "nervous apprehension."

apprehension-span test: *see* **test, apprehension-span.**

apprehension, visual: perception in reading.

apprentice: a young person who, with his parent or guardian, has entered into an agreement with an employer under which the employer is to provide an opportunity for the apprentice to learn a skilled trade or occupation. (Written agreements are specified under Federal apprenticeship standards.)

apprentice class: *see* **class, apprentice.**

apprentice coordinator: *see* **coordinator, apprentice.**

apprentice indenture: a written contract or agreement among parent or guardian, apprentice, and employer concerning the terms of employment and training experiences of the apprentice during his learning period.

apprentice method: a plan of instruction whereby an inexperienced performer or worker is matched with one or more experienced, well-qualified workers for learning skills and competencies in a vocation or profession. *See* **apprenticeship.**

apprentice, paying: an apprentice who pays part or all of the cost of his training through the value of his work.

apprentice school: a formalized training plan for developing apprentices to become journeymen in skilled trades. (The term is not in common use.)

apprentice teacher: (1) in colonial America, a young man apprenticed or indentured to a schoolmaster to learn the trade of schoolteacher (a relatively infrequent practice); (2) in contemporary usage, a term sometimes used to indicate either a recent graduate of or an advanced student in a teacher-training institution who, as a part of his training, works in an elementary or secondary school for a period of 6 weeks to 1 year, performing many of the duties of a regular teacher under the general guidance of the principal and supervisors; he usually receives a small salary for his services; *see* **internship plan**; *contr. w.* **student teacher**; (3) a certified teacher who is employed by a school system, especially in a large city, and is serving a probationary period before being regularly appointed.

apprentice teaching: *syn.* **internship plan.**

apprentice training: *see* **training, apprentice.**

apprenticeship: a practice in which a person, under written agreement, learns a skilled or semiskilled industrial occupation requiring two or more years of supervised work experience on the job supplemented by related classroom instruction.

apprenticeship council, joint: a group of representatives of employers and labor, organized to cooperate with vocational schools in setting up, conducting, and maintaining standards for apprenticeship programs.

apprenticeship education: a type of training commonly provided youth preparing for a trade before the advent of the factory system; usually possessed three distinguishing characteristics: (*a*) the binding of the apprentice to a master for a term of years, often 7; (*b*) the contracting of the master to train and initiate the apprentice in a trade; and (*c*) the custom of lodging the apprentice in the house of the master. (The apprenticeship system was common both in Europe and in America. In some American colonies the master was also required to teach the apprentice reading, writing, and the principles of religion.)

approach: (1) (read.) a method of teaching a child to read based upon some theory of how reading should be learned, such as the experience approach, the alphabetical approach, etc.; (2) (phys. ed.) that part of an exercise on gymnastic apparatus in which the performer comes up to the piece.

approach, analytical: *see* **analytical approach.**

approach, anthropological: *see* **anthropological approach.**

approach-approach conflict: *see* **conflict, approach-approach.**

approach-avoidance conflict: *see* **conflict, approach-avoidance.**

approach, balance sheet: *see* **balance sheet approach.**

approach, basal-reader: the approach to teaching the child to read which uses preprimers, charts, cards, and other materials that are prepared in advance by authors and publishers to be used as tools by the teacher in teaching children to read.

approach, child-development: (read.) an approach to the teaching of reading in which it is recognized that learning to read is a growth process and that reading instruction must be adjusted to the developing abilities of the child.

approach, child-experience: *see* **child-experience approach.**

approach, contemporary problems: *see* **contemporary problems approach.**

approach, creative-values: *see* **creative-values approach.**

approach, cross-media: *see* **cross-media approach.**

approach, cycle: *see* **cycle approach.**

approach, direct: a counseling approach with emphasis on actual overt responses and the direct control of behavior.

approach, documentary: *see* **documentary approach.**

approach, drill: *see* **drill approach.**

approach, equation: *see* **equation approach.**

approach, experience: (read.) a method of teaching beginning reading in which the material to be read is based upon some activity of a group of children which is developed and written or printed by the teacher on the blackboard or on a chart. *See* **approach, basal-reader.**

approach, Fernald-Keller: (read.) a method of teaching children to read involving a kinesthetic procedure: employs tracing and sounding as sensory aids to the visual and speech-motor methods commonly used; used especially with nonreaders.

approach, functional: *see* **functional approach.**

approach, incidental: *see* **incidental approach.**

approach, indirect: a counseling approach with emphasis on verbal reports of behavior and changing mediating responses.

approach, inquiry: *see* **inquiry approach.**

approach, institutional: primary direction of attention to particular institutions, such as schools, hospitals, libraries, and adult associations, by community services in adult education and university extension, whereby leadership training is intensified and broadened.

approach, integrated experience: *see* **integrated experience approach.**

approach, interdisciplinary: *see* **interdisciplinary approach.**

approach, laboratory: *see* **laboratory approach.**

approach, language experience: *see* **language experience approach.**

approach, linguistic: *see* **linguistic approach.**

approach, manipulative: *see* **manipulative approach.**

approach, meaningful: *see* **meaningful approach.**

approach, microeconomic: *see* **microeconomic approach.**

approach, multimedia: *see* **multimedia approach.**

approach, occupational: *see* **occupational approach.**

approach, pressure cooker: *see* **pressure cooker approach.**

approach, process: *see* **process approach.**

approach, psychological: *see* **psychological approach.**

approach reaction: *see* **reaction, approach.**

approach, sequential: *see* **sequential approach.**

approach, social: *see* **social approach.**

approach, social processes: *see* **social processes approach.**

approach, social-values: *see* **social-values approach.**

approach, socioeconomic: *see* **socioeconomic approach.**

approach, sociohistorical: *see* **sociohistorical approach.**

approach, sociological: *see* **sociological approach.**

approach, subject-matter: *see* **subject-matter approach.**

approach, systems: *see* **systems approach.**

approach to a subject, logical: *see* **logical approach to a subject.**

approach, unified-studies: *see* **unified-studies approach.**

approach, word-picture: the use of pictures in identifying words in reading, particularly at first-grade level. *See* **clue, picture.**

approach, writing: *see* **writing approach.**

approaches to observation: *see* **observation, approaches to.**

appropriation: (1) an authorization granted by the legislative body to make expenditures and to incur obligations for specific purposes; usually limited in amount and as to time when it may be expended; *contr. w.* **appropriation, indeterminate**; (2) as the title of a ledger account, designates an account set up for budgetary control to which is credited the amount authorized to meet expenditures and to which are charged encumbrances and expenditures.

appropriation account: (1) a financial record of the amounts of money that have been provided for particular purposes; (2) a particular financial record that lists the appropriations set aside for specific purposes; (3) an account set up to record an appropriation that may include the encumbrances and expenditures chargeable to it.

appropriation, contingency: an appropriation to provide for unforeseeable expenditures.

appropriation, indeterminate: an appropriation that is not limited to any definite period of time but is in effect until the purpose for which it is made is accomplished.

appropriation, line-item: an appropriation whereby a definite amount of money is provided for a specific purpose. *Contr. w.* **appropriation, lump-sum.**

appropriation, lump-sum: an appropriation made for a stated purpose or for a named department, without further specifying the amounts that may be spent for specific activities or for particular objects of expenditure.

appropriation, public school: public moneys set apart by formal action for financing public schools; generally designates moneys voted for schools by the state legislature, town meeting, or local board of education or, in cities with fiscally dependent boards of education, by the city council or board of finance.

appropriational budget: *see* **budget, appropriational.**

approval, social: acceptance by peers and others of the behavior that characterizes an individual.

approved training, certificate of: *see* **certificate of approved training.**

approximate computation: *see* **computation, approximate.**

approximate data: *see* **data, approximate.**

approximate measure: *see* **measure, approximate.**

approximate number: *see* **number, approximate.**

approximate result: (1) a value, accepted in place of the true value, which is obtained by appropriate means of calculation or investigation with approximate numbers or by the application of methods of approximation to exact numbers; (2) *syn.* **round number.**

approximate value: *see* **value, approximate.**

approximation: (1) a value that differs from a correct value by an amount which can be neglected for certain specific purposes; (2) a method, nonexact, for arriving at such a value, for example, a short-cut method.

apraxia: loss of ability to perform voluntarily various purposive movements in the absence of paralysis, ataxia, or disturbances in sensation; there are several types—motor, ideomotor, ideational, etc., examples of which are loss of manipulative patterns, such as inability to relate the word symbol to the motor symbol for writing and disabilities in use of organs of articulation for speech.

apraxia, verbal: the inability to produce words vocally in a patterned, sequential, meaningful manner.

aprosexia (ap'rō-sek'si-ə): a condition characterized by difficulty in fixing the attention.

apsychical (ap·sī'ki·kəl; ā·sī'ki·kəl): not mental.

aptitude: (1) a group of characteristics deemed to be symptomatic of an individual's ability to acquire proficiency in a given area; examples might be a particular art, school subject, or vocational area; (2) ability measured by the amount of time required by the learner to acquire mastery of a task; thus, given enough time, all students can conceivably attain such mastery.

aptitude, academic: the ability of a person to deal in abstractions and to engage successfully in activities that involve literary or classical learning experiences.

aptitude, artistic: an inherent tendency to adapt oneself effectively to artistic expression, such as drawing, painting, designing, modeling, and handcraft. (Both technical skill and creativeness are factors of *aptitude*, but creativeness or inventive ability is generally considered to be the basic index of success in the arts.) *See* **ability, artistic; skill, art.**

aptitude, college: (couns.) indicated capacities for succeeding in college.

aptitude, educational: a combination of characteristics and abilities which, considered together, can be used as a basis for prediction of a certain level of achievement that can be attained through further development.

aptitude index: *see* **index, aptitude.**

aptitude, language: the natural aptness or bent for the learning of a foreign language, often determined by prognosis tests.

aptitude, learning: potential ability to acquire knowledge or skill.

aptitude, mechanical: potential ability to use and understand machines or mechanical processes.

aptitude, music: physical and mental capacities fundamental to success in music; these capacities include a sense of pitch, a sense of rhythm, a sense of time, a strong tonal memory, and other attributes. *See* **musicality.**

aptitude, phonetic: (1) ability to recognize blends or combinations of sounds in various words; (2) ability to identify and remember component sounds and to recall words containing such sounds.

aptitude, reading: innate capacity for reading; believed to be related to intelligence as measured by verbal intelligence tests; also determined by a test specially devised for the purpose, such as the Durrell-Sullivan reading-capacity test.

aptitude, social: (1) a readiness for participating in approved ways in group life; (2) the degree of ability for satisfactory performance in social situations.

aptitude, special: (1) ability, talent, or potential capacity for learning a certain mental or physical operation; (2) mental capacity that indicates the probability of success in a particular line of endeavor.

aptitude test: *see* **test, aptitude.**

aptitude test, modern language: *see* **test, modern language aptitude.**

aptitude, vocational: innate or acquired capacity for a vocation or occupation, indicated by the ability to develop specific skills and to acquire knowledge and information which enable the learner to prepare for or to be more proficient in his chosen trade, occupation, or profession.

AQ: *see* **quotient, accomplishment.**

aquarium: (elem. ed.) a glass enclosure for goldfish and other water life; an integral part of the science program at the primary level.

aquatics: water activities of all kinds; includes swimming, diving, skiing, skin and scuba diving, synchronized water games, boating, and sailing.

Arabic numerals: *see* **numerals, Hindu-Arabic.**

Arbeiter Ring Shule (är'bī·tər ring shoo'lə): *n. fem.; pl. . . .* **Shulen:** (Yiddish, lit., "Workmen's Circle School") a school maintained by the Jewish workers' fraternal order called "The Workmen's Circle"; a supplementary school in which the language of instruction is Yiddish. *See* **Peretz Shule.**

arbitrary: despotic; absolute; fixed or arrived at through whim or caprice; in law, without fair, solid, and substantial cause or without cause based upon law. (Courts will review a determination by a board of education when it appears that it was made in willful disregard of the rights of a party concerned or in disregard of pertinent evidence, that is, arbitrarily.)

arbitrary association: *see* **association, arbitrary.**

arbitrary charges: unsupported accusations against a school employee that constitute the basis for disciplinary action. *See* **dismissal charges.**

arbitrary origin: *see* **origin, arbitrary.**

arbitrary weight: *see* **weight, arbitrary.**

arbitration: in collective negotiations, as between teachers and school administration, a process whereby if both parties fail to reach agreement they may submit their dispute to an impartial individual or panel which recommends a course of action which is often a compromise; also called *mediation,* but often the mediator's findings are advisory rather than requiring compliance; if the parties are required to accept the decision, the process is called *binding arbitration.*

arbitration, binding: *see* **arbitration.**

arbitrator: a private, extraordinary judge, to whose decision matters in controversy are referred by consent of the parties.

archaeology: the study of antiquities, particularly the material remains of ancient peoples such as monuments of art and architecture, pottery and other implements of daily life, inscriptions, etc.

archaeology, biblical: the study of the way of life of peoples described in the Bible; based upon the discovery of the material artifacts and written records of these extinct communities or past epochs.

archery: the art and practice of shooting with the bow and arrow.

archery golf: a game resembling golf, but played by shooting an arrow rather than by hitting a ball. *Syn.* **bonarro.**

architect, school: an architect who specializes in the design and construction of school buildings, not only from the standpoint of architecture in the strict sense, but also from the standpoint of school serviceability and use for instruction and auxiliary purposes.

architect, supervising: an architect employed to check the materials and workmanship of a building in process of construction with the plans and specifications and to see that the provisions of the contract are fulfilled.

architectural drafting: *see* **drafting, architectural.**

architectural drawing: *see* **drawing, architectural.**

architecture: the art and science of designing and constructing buildings, based on aesthetic and scientific knowledge and skill.

architecture, interior: *syn.* **interior design.**

archives: (1) a repository for public records or documents of historic importance; (2) documents or records concerning the activities, rights, claims, treaties, and constitutions of a nation, community, corporation, family, or historical figure; (3) any detailed record or body of data.

arcsin transformation: *syn.* **transformation, angular.**

area: (1) (ind. arts) a section of a shop or laboratory set aside for a particular kind of work; (2) a group of activities, a section of a curriculum, or a part of a program, for example, applied electricity, child development, housing, or radio theory and practice; (3) (stat.) the plane surface covered by a graph, especially that enclosed by a frequency polygon; (4) (stat.) the two-dimensional space under a frequency curve, proportional to the number of observations or cases involved; in the unit normal curve and in curves of sampling distributions, the area under the curve between any two values of the variables is equal to the probability that a given observation will have a value in that interval.

area, assembly: (ind. arts) a space within the laboratory large enough for all, even in the largest class, to assemble as a group for purposes such as discussion, planning, and testing.

area, attendance: *see* **attendance unit** (1).

area, core: *see* **core area.**

area diagram: *syn.* **graph, area.**

area graph: *see* **graph, area.**

area, impacted: *see* **impacted area.**

area of exceptionality: *see* **exceptionality, area of.**

area of living: a group of related life activities.

area of study concept, distributive education: a provision for flexibility in curriculum organization that makes the depth of instruction depend on occupational objectives and competencies needed by individual students and on their abilities.

area sampling: *see* **sampling, area.**

area, speech: *see* **speech area.**

area, standard metropolitan statistical: *see* **metropolitan statistical area, standard.**

area, state economic: *see* **economic area, state.**

area studies: (1) scholarly investigations, monographs, articles, or books dealing with recognized geographical areas, such as Latin America, East Asia, or Africa; (2) the practice followed by some American universities of offering academic majors built around selected geographic areas; *see* **major, broad-fields.**

area, study: a space set aside in a school or library where study activities may be carried on without interference or interruption.

area supervisor, business and office education: *see* **supervisor, business and office education assistant state.**

area supervisor, distributive education: *see* **supervisor, distributive education assistant state.**

area training: *see* **training, area.**

area vocational school: *see* **vocational school, area.**

areas-of-living curriculum: *see* **curriculum, areas-of-living.**

argument: an attempt to establish belief through a course of reasoning.

argument, cosmological: the argument that since the universe exists God must exist, for whatever exists has a cause.

argument, eternal-truths: the belief that there are fundamental realities which are absolute, lasting, unchanging, and knowable and that these "universals" can be expressed in propositions which are existential.

argument, first-cause: the logical development of the premise that the proof of the existence of God can be traced to causality; through the process of reasoning it can be shown that all subordinate causes have had a beginning and that these series must have been caused by a Being who is Himself uncaused.

argument, heuristic: an argument, nonrigorous in the mathematical sense, which convinces.

argument, ontological: the argument based upon the idea that God, being perfect, must necessarily exist, for perfection implies existence; St. Anselm, who provided the classic formulation of this argument, defined God as "a being than which nothing greater can be conceived." (The proper interpretation of Anselm, and hence the proper way to formulate this argument, is a subject of dispute among scholars.)

argument, physicotheological: a process of reasoning which utilizes natural phenomena and relations to illustrate supernatural purposes, designs, and propositions.

argument, teleological: the argument that since the universe exhibits purpose there must be an all-encompassing intelligence (God) responsible for that purpose; William Paley provided a classic exposition of this position.

argumentum ad hominem: (Lat., lit., "argument to the man") an argument, generally held to be fallacious, that is directed to the character of a man rather than to the merits of his argument.

argumentum ad misericordiam: (Lat., lit., "argument to compassion") an argument, generally held to be fallacious, that makes an appeal to the emotions, especially pity, rather than to the merits of the argument.

argumentum ad populum: (Lat., lit., "argument to the populace") an argument, generally held to be fallacious, that makes an appeal to the prejudices of the people rather than to the merits of the argument.

aristocracy: (1) a form of government in which power is held by a minority, theoretically those best qualified to rule; (2) a social class distinguished by wealth or hereditary privilege; (3) a privileged class distinguished by any mark of superiority.

aristocracy, natural: an expression sometimes used to mean an aristocracy based on biologically inherited distinctions.

aristocratic view of education: the view that the opportunities of education should belong to the privileged rather than to the rank and file of common people.

Aristotelian method: (1) strictly, the method of revealing relations between the particular and the general, both in nature and in thought, by means of (*a*) investigation of the general through induction, perception, memory, experience, etc., and (*b*) determination of the particular from the general (or of the less general from the more general) through deduction, proof, and explanation; (2) popularly, the method of explaining particular facts, phenomena, etc., by means of already accepted principles, laws, etc.

Aristotelian realism: *see* **realism** (1).

Aristotelianism: (1) the system of thought which follows the principles and teachings of Aristotle; (2) a moderate *realism* in contrast to *nominalism* which holds that universal ideas have no real existence in things, and in contrast to *Platonism* which holds that such ideas exist or subsist independently of the mind; specifically, Aristotelianism holds that the object of the universal idea is real in nature because it represents the reality of each individual essence, but the universality of the universal idea is mental because the individual essence is itself not universal in nature. *See* **nominalism; Platonism; realism.**

arithmetic: (1) that group of elementary rules and principles giving the existing relations among and methods of computing with numbers; (2) as a school subject, those number experiences centered in a specific class period or systematically related to other subjects and designed to develop the skills and habits associated with understanding of the number processes.

arithmetic, advanced: arithmetical topics or applications given in addition to or going beyond that subject matter of arithmetic generally accepted as belonging to the curriculum of the elementary school.

arithmetic age: *see* **age, arithmetic.**

arithmetic average: *syn.* **mean, arithmetic.**

arithmetic blocks, multibase: *see* **blocks, multibase arithmetic.**

arithmetic, business: *see* **mathematics, applied.**

arithmetic chart: *see* **chart, arithmetic.**

arithmetic, clock: *see* **arithmetic, modular.**

arithmetic, corrective: arithmetic designed to discover and correct mistakes made by pupils in arithmetic. Rough *syn.* **remedial arithmetic.**

arithmetic, fixed point: a method of calculation in which operations take place in an invariant manner, and in which the computer does not consider the location of the radix point.

arithmetic, floating point: a method of calculation by computer which automatically accounts for the location of the radix point.

arithmetic, formal: arithmetic in which all major objectives, methods, and curricula are determined by the inherent nature of the number system and which reflects little of the culture in which it is taught, as contrasted with informal or incidental work in arithmetic done in conjunction with other curricular areas.

arithmetic, functional: (1) arithmetic in which content and method derive from personal and social experiences such as making purchases in a classroom store, playing games, and planning the family budget; (2) arithmetic so taught that it can be used in vocational and social situations.

arithmetic, fundamental theorem of: a theorem whose precise statement differs according to the number system in question; a common form states that every natural number greater than 1 can be written as a product of primes in one and only one way except for order; for example, $12 = 2 \times 2 \times 3$.

arithmetic, fundamentals of: *see* **mathematics, fundamentals of.**

arithmetic graph: *syn.* **chart, arithmetic.**

arithmetic-logic device: the mechanism within a computer that performs calculating operations.

arithmetic mean: *see* **mean, arithmetic.**

arithmetic, mechanical: arithmetic taught and studied by repetition, drill, and rules, with little or no understanding.

arithmetic, modular: a kind of arithmetic involving finite sets of numbers; a typical system uses only the 12 numbers appearing on an ordinary clockface, sums and products being determined by reference to the clock, so that $10 + 4 = 2$ and $5 \times 3 = 3$; technically the arithmetic is one of classes of integers, the classes being determined by remainder on division by some fixed positive integer called the *modulus* (12 for the ordinary clock). *Syn.* **clock arithmetic.**

arithmetic, primary: the examination of the numbers 0,1,-2,3, . . . under the operations of addition, subtraction, multiplication, and division; normally associated with arithmetic in grades 1, 2, and 3.

arithmetic progression: *see* **progression, arithmetic.**

arithmetic quotient: *see* **quotient, subject.**

arithmetic reasoning: *see* **reasoning, arithmetic.**

arithmetic, remedial: any form of teaching and study effort designed to correct faults in performance in any phase of arithmetic.

arithmetic scale: *see* **scale, arithmetic.**

arithmetic, social: topics in arithmetic included for reasons of social utility rather than or in addition to their mathematical importance.

arithmetic, structural: a method of teaching arithmetic, introduced by Catherine Stern, in which the structure of mathematics is learned through the use of concrete material consisting in a set of wooden blocks, called *Stern blocks*, which fit into slots in wooden boards and are accompanied by printed materials which picture the blocks.

arithmetic, traditional: (1) a designation applied to those parts of the arithmetic curriculum which have come down from the past, including some now largely discarded, for example, *true discount*, which is a purely theoretical subject having no functional use; some refer only to the discarded parts as traditional arithmetic; (2) a designation applied to those arithmetic programs which are characterized by methods, objectives, curricula, and materials considered to be outmoded.

arithmetic unit: that part of the hardware of an automatic computer in which arithmetic and logic operations are performed on symbols representing information.

arithmetic value: *syn.* **value, absolute.**

arithmetic, vocational: arithmetic taught and studied from the standpoint of its application to a specific vocation, with emphasis on the techniques and processes most useful for that vocation.

arithmomania (ə·rith′mō·mā′ni·ə): an obsessive compulsion to count objects.

arm-hand control: the ability to control and coordinate the parts and muscles of the arm and hand in performing motor activities involving these members. (In infants, arm-hand control develops in the following temporal sequence: the whole arm, the elbow, the fingers, and the wrist.)

arm-hand posture: the position and relation of the arm and hand in performing a motor act; a term used in descriptions of normative behavior.

arm-movement method: a procedure in teaching handwriting that stresses the movement of the arm in writing and tends to reduce or eliminate the movements of the fingers and hand.

armchair philosophy: *see* **philosophy, armchair.**

Armed Forces education program: *see* **program, Armed Forces education.**

Armed Forces training program: *see* **program, Armed Forces training.**

armory: a building or part thereof used by units of the Army, such as the ROTC; usually contains officers' quarters, storage space for weapons and ammunition, and room for practice drills.

armory training: *see* **training, armory.**

Army Alpha test: *see* **test, Army Alpha.**

Army Beta test: *see* **test, Army Beta.**

Army college: *see* **college, Army.**

Army extension course program: *see* **program, Army extension course.**

Army method teaching: *see* **Army Specialized Training Program.**

Army program of general educational development: that part of Army training which provides all military personnel on active duty with nonmilitary academic and vocational education, with the objective of increasing the efficiency of the Army by raising the educational level of its personnel.

Army school: an educational institution authorized by Headquarters, Department of the Army; with the exception of the U.S. Military Academy, Army schools are classified as Army colleges, branch schools, or specialist schools. *See* **branch school; college, Army; specialist school.**

Army school training: *see* **training, Army school.**

Army Specialized Training Program (ASTP): a method used in World War II by the U.S. Army to prepare personnel for a 9-month period to go to occupied or conquered areas, to take over the military government of those areas, and to be able to talk to the foreign man in the street; specifically, teaching a foreign language by constant and intensive work, oral use, writing, and reading in it day by day, with primary emphasis upon speaking and being understood in the language.

Army standard score: *see* **score, Army standard.**

Army training center training: *see* **training, Army training center.**

Army training program: *see* **program, Army training.**

Army training structure: the total environment in which a soldier develops the knowledge and skills required to accomplish his assigned duties.

Army training test: *see* **test, Army training.**

arousal: the degree to which the cortex is ready to respond; similar to the concept of *threshold* but at a central level; level of arousal is controlled by the arousal area of the midbrain.

arousal response: *see* **response, arousal.**

arrange: to adapt a musical composition to the demands of performance in a medium other than that for which it was composed, for example, to transcribe an orchestral composition for piano.

array: (1) all the measures in a double-entry table that fall within any single given class interval of either of the two variables concerned; (2) any row or column in a double-entry table; (3) any display of objects forming a recognizable pattern, such as triangular array, circular array, etc.; (4) (math.) a display of members of a set arranged in rows and columns, for example, the members of the Cartesian set A × B where A = (a,b,c) and B = (1,2) written

(a,1)   (b,1)   (c,1)
(a,2)   (b,2)   (c,2).

arrest, age of: *see* age of arrest.

arrested development: *see* development, arrested.

arrhythmia: *see* arrythmia.

arrythmia: *alt. sp.* **arrhythmia;** the condition in which no flow of action is manifest and no pattern of regularity can be observed. *Dist. f.* **dysrhythmia;** *contr. w.* **rhythmic action.**

art: human activities aimed at the accomplishment of or participation in aesthetic experience; in common usage activities that involve creative ability, ingenuity, judgment, and skill, resulting in an object or artifact.

art activity: *see* activity, art.

art, advertising: art forms relating to commercial communication and similar activities; includes art forms used by business to increase sales or to popularize ideas such as posters, letterheads, newspaper and magazine advertising, and other types of advertising display. Rough *syn.* **art, commercial.**

art, amateur: the art work of (*a*) one who engages in producing visual art objects, writing, drama, or dance as a pastime or for pleasure rather than as a professional artist, or (*b*) one who lacks experience or formal preparation in a particular art.

art, Apollonian: according to Nietzsche, art pertaining to lyrical qualities.

art, applied: an area of study dealing with the principles of art as related to the design, manufacture, or arrangement of such commodities as food, clothing, shelter, and household furniture and equipment. *Syn.* **related art.**

art appreciation: *see* appreciation, art.

art-appreciation test: *see* test, art-appreciation.

art-aptitude test: *see* test, art-aptitude.

art, baroque: a seventeenth-century art style characterized by emotional intensity, by dramatic effects of color, light and dark, movement, and gesture, and by structural tensions; El Greco, Rembrandt, Correggio, Rubens, and Bernini are representative of the baroque style.

art, Byzantine: the highly decorative, transcendent religious expression which reached its peak in the fifth and sixth centuries A.D.; typified by abstraction, rich ornamentation, and mystical symbolism; the style was centered in the city of Byzantium (Constantinople).

art, Carolingian: a Western European cultural movement during the dynasties of the Frankish kings, circa 613-987 A.D.; reaching a peak in the reign of Charlemagne, it is characterized by a renaissance of Roman classical influences.

art, civic: a broad field of art that has as its object the improvement of conditions in a community, including architecture and the relationship of parks, boulevards, buildings, monuments, bridges, etc., to civic plans and civic beauty in general; art in relation to standards of living in a community.

art club: *see* club, art.

art, commercial: (1) the use of art in the realm of consumer economics for the purpose of product or service presentation; (2) a curriculum of art subjects providing training in art applied to commercial purposes such as advertising.

art concept: a principle or a proposition pertaining to any phase of art; for example, the normal human body is considered to be eight heads in height for purposes of graphic representation; orange and blue are regarded as complementary colors; fitness for function is an essential attribute of design.

art coordinator: *syn.* director, art.

art, costume: art in relation to dress and to the accessories of dress; as presented in schools, a study of personality types, harmony of line, mass, and color, and appropriateness of the costume ensemble for an individual, as well as the evolution of costume from the historical standpoint, and the study of costume for special purposes such as the theater.

art, creative: art based on creative effort rather than reproductive skill and involving original thought, imagination, structural organization, and personal expression or interpretation.

art criticism: *see* criticism, art.

art curriculum: *see* curriculum, art.

art, decorative: all phases of art utilized as a means of ornamentation, enrichment, or decoration rather than as a structural necessity. See **decoration, applied; design, applied.**

art department: *see* department, art.

art, developmental stages in child: such theories as were formulated by Lowenfeld and others during the years 1900-1955. *Syn.* **representational stages in child art;** *see* **developmental stage, dawning realism; developmental stage, period of decision; developmental stage, preschematic; developmental stage, pseudorealistic; developmental stage, schematic; developmental stage, scribbling.**

art, Dionysian: according to Nietzsche, art which expresses temperament and passion.

art director: *see* director, art.

art, domestic: an obsolete term formerly used to denote a phase of home economics relating chiefly to the selection and making of clothing. See **home economics; instruction, clothing.**

art education: instruction and practice in the visual and spatial arts, as carried on in the schools; frequently recognized major areas are fine, industrial, graphic, advertising or commercial, domestic or household, civic, and theater arts; specific visual arts include drawing, design, color, construction, history of art, and art appreciation. See **curriculum, art.**

art elements: the basic structural factors in the visual and spatial arts, namely, *line, mass, tone* (light and dark), *color,* and *texture.* See **art structure.**

art, environmental: *syn.* happening.

art experience: *see* experience, art.

art expression: *see* expression, art.

art, extracurricular: art activities participated in with no consideration of class organization or credit and carried on outside the regular class schedule.

art, figurative: visual art in which some representation of objects is involved.

art, fine: the conscious use of creative imagination in the production of objects or expressive forms and intended for one's aesthetic experience. *Contr. w.* **art, applied.**

art, fine and industrial: the designation of an organization of art in public elementary and secondary schools, according to which all arts are studied; may include the study of painting, sculpture, architecture, commercial art, handcraft, industrial design, and other phases.

art form: (1) an expression of art, such as a picture, statue, poem, or play; (2) a technique of art expression, for example, *etching* or *blank verse;* (3) the entire formation of a work of art, including design, medium, and construction. See **form.**

art, functional: art in which both material and aesthetic needs are met efficiently and directly through the use of art media, such as functional architecture; art in which the function or use of the end-product determines its design.

art, glyphic (glif'ik): the branch of art concerned principally with modeling plastic material and with carving. *Syn.* **modeling; sculpture.**

art, Gothic: a western European style in art of the twelfth to the fourteenth centuries A.D. which was characterized by ornateness, emotional power, and the refinement of earlier medieval forms into a more graceful and natural expression.

art, graphic: (1) (newer usage) those expressions of art produced by printing from various kinds of blocks, plates, or type, such as etching, drypoint, lithography, wood and linoleum block printing, serigraph, rotogravure, offset, letterpress, and all other forms of printing (usually book art is considered a part of graphic art, though sometimes included under commercial art); (2) (older usage) all forms of representation by means of lines, strokes, drawings, and paintings.

art, Greek: art of ancient Greek culture, which extended from the geometric period of the seventh century B.C. through the classical era of the fifth to the more realistic orientation of the Hellenistic style of the second century B.C.

art guidance: *see* **guidance, art.**

art, Hellenistic: the art of ancient Greece in the third and second centuries B.C.; a style characterized by genre subjects, naturalism, and general humanization of earlier religious themes.

art, history of: *see* **history of art.**

art, home: *see* **art, household; interior decoration.**

art, household: a phase of art concerned with the selection, arrangement, furnishing, care, and maintenance of the home and of its immediate surroundings, often including a study of exterior and interior architecture, landscape design, and period styles of furniture and furnishings. (This phase of the art curriculum overlaps the work of the household arts and home economics departments as generally organized.) *See* **interior design.**

art, ideoplastic: art that expresses concepts and ideas.

art, industrial: (1) the art of the machine in which manufacture and, usually, production in quantity are sought; (2) art as made use of in industry. *Dist. f.* **industrial arts.**

art institute: *see* **institute, art.**

art interpretation: (1) a specialized study of art objects with a view to developing habits of critical judgment; (2) the meaning, implications, or expression one derives from his responses to an art form; does not imply the first definition.

art, kinetic: twentieth-century sculpture which is designed to permit parts of the form to move (similar in principle to a *mobile*); movement may be created by air current, electricity, solar energy, and other means.

art material: that which the artist reshapes, organizes, builds with, and imposes his ideas upon, for example, clay, marble, paint, canvas, etc. *See* **art medium.**

art medium: (1) the instrumentality or material means employed by the individual or group in order to achieve a finished art product, including tools or machines, materials, processes, and techniques; *see* **art material;** (2) the particular mode or way of presenting expressive qualities such as are presented in visual arts, drama, dance, literature, and music; (3) term referring to qualities of sound, tone, color, etc.; (4) a visual technique such as television, film, slides, etc.

art metals: the study of metals which are used in the manufacture or fabrication of ornamental products; learning experiences generally include experimenting and designing, constructing, and evaluating art metal products.

art metalwork: *syn.* **metalcraft.**

art, methods of teaching: procedures employed by teachers for guiding the various art experiences of pupils.

art, minimal: an artistic approach, particularly in painting and sculpture, in which the artist severely limits and simplifies the composition, color, form, and other characteristics of his work; in the mid-twentieth century most generally identified with the artist Ad Reinhardt.

art music: *see* **music, art.**

art of the blind: the art peculiar to those who are sightless and depend upon sensory receptors other than sight; signified by an autonomous sense for space determined by touch, sound, and kinesthesia and the emotional value of both to the creator.

art, op: a mid-twentieth-century style, nonobjective in approach, which is based upon optical illusions, specifically the creation of vibrations, apparent movement, and ambiguities through minute tensions between lines, shapes, and colors.

art, physioplastic: art expression derived from direct observation of, or physical contact with, nature.

art, plastic: (1) changing malleable materials into art products through modeling or molding; generally used in connection with modeling in clay, but in recent years includes working with modern synthetic "plastics"; (2) the use of any medium which is formable, reshaped, extended, or combined with other materials.

art, pop: a movement of the 1960s emerging as a reaction against traditional and established art trends; themes are drawn from the commonplace, the trivial, and from commercial imagery and objects; purports to be a social commentary exposing the values of vulgarity, conventionality, and the mass media of the current time.

art, prehistoric: art existing in times prior to written history, including the cave paintings of Lascaux, France, and Altamira, Spain; applies to the work created prior to 3000 B.C., approximately.

art, primitive: (1) a type of art referring to cultures or societies passing through the Neolithic Revolution but showing no signs of evolving in the direction of the historic civilizations; essentially rural and self-sufficient, isolated and static societies, they perpetuate themselves by custom and tradition; (2) activity of an artist of an early period of a culture or artistic movement; (3) product of an artist whose work is marked by directness and naïveté.

art principles: *see* **design principles.**

art product: the culmination of the creative process, the concrete embodiment of ideas and feelings in material form or expression resulting from experience and involving the use of an art medium or performance. *See* **forming products.**

art product, final: the object resulting from creative activity, generally subordinated in importance to the working process with younger children but becoming more and more important with increasing age and with the concern for critical and intellectual awareness. *See* **awareness, critical.**

art rating scale: *see* **rating scale, art.**

art, related: *syn.* **art, applied.**

art, religious: (1) the work of artists who are committed to religious sects or are members devoted to the divine or that which is held to be of ultimate importance; (2) works of art based on ritual or religious themes.

art, representational stages in child: *syn.* **art, developmental stages in child.**

art, rococo: art in the courtly style of the eighteenth century, a refinement of the *baroque,* characterized by elegance, grace, and mannerism; painters of this style were Fragonard, Watteau, Boucher, and Lancret.

art, Roman: art produced during the time of the ancient Roman Republic and Empire (200 B.C.-400 A.D. approximately), particularly applied to the characteristics of classical forms in sculpture, painting, and architecture.

art, Romanesque: a transitional period between the late Byzantine (Carolingian in the West) and the Gothic periods (950-1150 A.D. approximately), in architecture reflecting influences of the classical Roman era and in sculpture indicating a transition from the static to dynamic human and ornamental forms.

art school: an institution for the teaching of art. *See* **academy of fine arts; institute, art.**

art skill: *see* **skill, art.**

art song: *see* **song, art.**

art structure: the design, composition, or pattern of a work of art; the arrangement of basic elements according to principles of artistic judgment and functional integrity.

art, styles of: refers to philosophical and psychological theories concerning types of creative activity; usually describes a manner of expression characteristic of an individual artist, group, or period.

art supervisor: *syn.* **director, art.**

art supplies: *see* **supplies, art.**

art teacher: *see* **teacher.**

art technique: the specific way in which an artist manipulates a medium and executes or renders his work of art.

art, theater: art involved in theater or dramatic activities, as setting the stage, providing lighting, designing and making costumes, properties, and scenery. *See* **design, stage.**

art therapy: *see* **therapy, art.**

art topic: *see* **unit, art.**

art typing: the utilization of various typewriter characters arranged and typed in an artistic or decorative border design, illustration, or picture.

art unit: *see* **unit, art.**

art values: (1) consideration of an art product relating to material, form, and decoration, suitability of form with regard to function (in articles of use), significance of expression, and aesthetic quality; (2) the concepts or assumptions one believes or applies when responding to or estimating the worth of an artistic experience.

art, visual: art the products of which can be seen or comprehended through the eye, such as paintings, sculpture, or architecture; may include the performing arts such as theater and dance. *See* **arts, spatial; arts, visual and spatial.**

art, vocational: any art serving as an occupation or means of livelihood.

art workshop: *see* **workshop, art.**

articulated curriculum: *see* **curriculum, articulated.**

articulated tests: *see* **tests, articulated.**

articulation: (1) (curric.) the organization of classroom instruction, cocurricular activities, and other interdependent and interrelated services of the school system so as to facilitate the continuous and efficient educational progress of students from grade to grade and from school to school; also, the interrelation of the school's instructional program with the educational programs of other available institutions or with work opportunities; (2) (couns.) communication and cooperation between two or more groups in developing their guidance programs so that quick and easy orientation of individuals shifting from one program to another is facilitated; (3) (meas.) the act or process of developing different editions, forms, and especially levels of the same test to yield results that are comparable; (4) (speech) the production of the sounds of speech by a modification of the stream of voiced or unvoiced breath, principally through movements of the jaws, lips, tongue, and soft palate.

articulation, basis of: the neutral position of the various parts of the speech organ characteristic of a group speaking a certain language or dialect.

articulation disorder: *see* **disorder, articulation.**

articulation, horizontal: relationship of continuity existing among the various parts of a curriculum at a given level with respect to successive age and grade levels of instruction, such that, taken together, the parts have some degree of unity and coherence.

articulation of plane and solid geometry: *see* **geometry, articulation of plane and solid.**

articulation, program: (1) the process of so arranging the instructional programs of the successive grades and divisions of the school system that a closely interlocking, continuous, and consistent educational environment is provided for pupils as they progress through the system; (2) the degree of continuity, consistency, and interdependence in the offerings of the successive grades and divisions of the school system.

articulation, random: the utterance of syllabic sounds at random, frequently with much repetition; a common activity of infants during the early period of learning to talk, and believed to be fundamental to the development of the speech function.

articulation, sluggish: abnormally slow or inadequate movements of the tongue, lips, jaw, or velum, resulting in defective speech.

articulation, subject: systematic interrelationship between two or more subjects of study; usually applied to the relationship between the consecutive segments of the same subject, as between English I and English II.

articulation test: *see* **test, articulation.**

articulation, vertical: the degree to which the interlocking and interrelation of the successive levels of the educational system facilitate the continuous, economical, and efficient educational progress of pupils.

articulatory defect: any defective manner of utterance of speech sounds, either separately or in connected speech; usually a relatively constant condition, the most frequently found such defects being sound substitutions, sound distortions, sound omissions, foreign dialect, oral inaccuracy, and lisping; not to be confused with mispronunciation or voice defect. *Dist. f.* **stuttering.**

articulatory signal practice: a technique used in teaching a person to employ a newly learned speech sound. (The student prolongs or repeats the new sound and, at a given signal, instantly says the sounds that follow to make a word, as *s . . . alt,* or *s-s-s-salt.*)

artifact: (1) an object produced by human skill; often used in archaeology with reference to primitive art objects; (2) an extraneous error, trick of the setup, conscious or unconscious result of human activity, for example, wires crossed in an IBM programming board.

artificial ear: *see* **ear, artificial.**

artificial intelligence: *see* **intelligence, artificial.**

artificial language: *see* **language, artificial.**

artificial lighting: *see* **lighting, artificial.**

artificial limb: a device used to replace an arm or leg lost by injury or disease. *See* **prosthesis.**

artificial respiration: *see* **respiration, artificial.**

artificial selection: *see* **selection, artificial.**

artificial sign: *see* **sign, artificial.**

artisan: a person skilled in the techniques of an art or a craft whose work does not necessarily require creation, invention, or originality. *Dist. f.* **artist.**

artist: a person skilled in the practice of an art in which creative activity is dependent on aesthetic judgment, imagination, and originality.

artistic ability: *see* **ability, artistic.**

artistic aptitude: *see* **aptitude, artistic.**

artistic categories: *see* **categories, artistic.**

artistic taste: *see* **taste, artistic.**

arts and crafts: (1) originally, the designation of a movement initiated in England by Ruskin, Morris, and others to make art serve the needs of the people; (2) an area of activity in which the principles of design are made use of in craftwork, including metalwork, leatherwork, ceramics, wood carving, plastics, textiles, and woodworking.

arts and humanities: (1) a broadly used term usually designating courses of study or curricular programs in which appreciation and knowledge of the arts are combined with and/or related to other subject areas; (2) a combination of terms which indicates an attempt to provide understanding of the arts, such as music, drama, literature, and visual arts in relationship to one another, for the purpose of enriching and developing the cultural awareness in a society.

arts, applied: the principles underlying the fine arts as applied to utilitarian things, for example, the principles of color composition and design as applied to machine-woven fabrics; the decorative arts.

arts college: *syn.* **college, liberal arts.**

arts, elementary industrial: *see* **industrial arts, elementary.**

arts, elementary school industrial: *see* **consultant, elementary school industrial arts; industrial arts, elementary.**

arts, fine: (1) the common generic term for painting, sculpture, and architecture; (2) in a broader sense, painting, sculpture, architecture, literature, music, drama, and the dance.

arts for exceptional children, industrial: *see* **industrial arts for exceptional children.**

arts, general industrial: *see* **industrial arts, general.**

arts, graphic: (ind. ed.) the study of the various graphic reproduction and binding methods used in the printing, publishing, and allied industries; learning activities include a variety of forms of relief, intaglio, and stencil methods of printing such as block printing, letterpress printing, rubber stamp construction, lithography, drypoint engraving, photography, thermography, type composition, silk screen printing, and various methods of binding; subject matter and learning experiences are organized under various descriptive titles such as *graphic arts, photography, photolithography (photo-offset-lithography, or offset).*

arts, industrial: *see* **industrial arts.**

arts, liberal: *see* **liberal arts.**

arts, manual: a former school subject which replaced *manual training* and which emphasized the artistic aspect in the design and construction of projects; it in turn was replaced by *industrial arts* in which the emphasis is on the study and interpretation of industry. *See* **industrial arts; training, manual.**

arts, mechanic: a type of school shopwork predominant during the latter part of the nineteenth century designed to teach the trades and related science.

arts, nautical: principles, knowledge, and skills concerned with ships, boats, and water transportation; frequently taught on the industrial arts levels through the building of small boats or models.

arts, practical: a term sometimes used to denote a type of functional education of a manipulative nature on a nonvocational basis; usually includes agriculture, business education, home economics, and industrial arts.

arts, spatial: those arts such as painting, sculpture, and architecture which are particularly concerned with space, light, and color, that is, either those which deal with the representation of forms in space (as painting or drawing) or those of which the products are constructed in space (as sculpture and architecture); term generally implies enclosed, defined, or modulated space as a central concern. *See* **arts, visual and spatial.**

arts, visual and spatial: a term used by artists, authors, and art educators to embrace the entire field of art variously designated as visual arts, spatial arts, or fine, industrial, and related arts; introduced into the nomenclature of art education in an attempt to coin a term that would avoid the distinction implied between fine and not fine, practical and impractical, or useful and nonuseful concepts of art; includes the following areas of study: art appreciation, architecture, sculpture, painting, industrial art, graphic art, advertising art, domestic or household art, civic art, theater art, and history of art. *See* **art, fine and industrial.**

ascendance: (1) the tendency to assume a dominant role in face-to-face relationships; (2) the quality of being able to command, control, or influence others. *Syn.* **dominance;** *contr. w.* **submissiveness.**

ascendance score: *see* **score, ascendance.**

ascendant behavior: *see* **behavior, ascendant.**

ascending: (math.) passing through a range of values from lower to higher values.

ascending letter: *see* **letter, ascending.**

ascetic theology: *see* **theology, ascetic.**

asceticism: self-denial of bodily desires; usually practiced for religious reasons but also used by some as a means toward the end of leading a calm life.

asemia (ə·sē′mi·ə): loss of ability to understand or communicate by signs and gestures. *Syn.* **asymbolia.**

Ashkenazit (äsh·kə·nä′zit): (from Heb. *Ashkenaz*, "Germany," lit., "German pronunciation") the way of pronouncing Hebrew characteristic of the Jews of Germany, Eastern Europe, and other countries where Jews from these areas have settled; this form of pronunciation is the one most frequently used in religious services in the United States and other countries where the dominant element of the Jewish population is of Central and East European origin.

asocial: (1) indifferent to existing social customs or usual social relationships; (2) devoid of social values or meanings. *Dist. f.* **antisocial; unsocial.**

asocial child: *see* **child, asocial.**

asonia (ə·sō′ni·ə): *syn.* **deafness, tone** (1).

aspirate: a speech sound characterized by passage of the breath through a relatively open channel, as in the sound *h.*

aspiration, adjustment of: *see* **adjustment of aspiration.**

aspiration level: the goal or quality of performance desired by an individual (or group) in a specified activity.

assault: (law) an attempt to beat another without touching him. *See* **battery.**

assault course: area of ground used for training soldiers in attacking an enemy in close combat.

assemble: (1) to combine routines to form a program; (2) to translate a source program into a machine language, usually producing one machine language instruction for each source language instruction.

assembler: (data processing) a computer program which operates on symbolic input data to produce from such data machine instructions by carrying out such functions as translation of symbolic operation codes into computer operating instructions, assignment of locations in storage for successive instructions, or computation of absolute addresses from symbolic addresses; generally translates input symbolic codes into machine instructions item for item and produces as output the same number of instructions or constants which were defined in the input symbolic codes. *See* **compiler.**

assembly area: *see* **area, assembly.**

assembly consultation: *syn.* **interview, group.**

assembly program: *see* **program, assembly.**

assembly room: an auditorium or other special room where students gather for announcements, addresses, entertainments, instruction, and other large-group activities.

assertibility, warranted: (Dewey) the purpose of the enterprise of inquiry, a phrasing that refers to knowledge or belief which testing reveals to be acceptable as of the time of testing; emphasis upon inquiry as a process of securing conclusions that are warrantably assertible.

assessed valuation: *syn.* **value, assessment.**

assessment: (1) the process of making the official valuation of property for the purpose of taxation; (2) the valuation placed upon property during this process. (NOTE: Assessment is sometimes used to denote the amount of the tax levied, but such usage is not recommended since it fails to distinguish between the valuation and tax-levy processes.)

assessment, eyesight: a general test of the visual functions of the eye, which may include tests for color blindness, peripheral vision, binocular vision, and central visual acuity. *Syn.* **eyesight test.**

assessment, individual: (couns.) the process by which as many data as possible are gathered and used to evaluate a person more accurately. *See* **analysis, individual.**

assessment rate: the ratio applied to the assessed valuation of property for purposes of determining the amount of tax to be levied. *Syn.* **assessment ratio.**

assessment ratio: *syn.* **assessment rate.**

assessment, special: a compulsory levy made by a local government against certain properties to defray part or all of the cost of a specific improvement or service that is presumed to be of general benefit to the public and of special benefit to the owners of such properties. (NOTE: The term should not be used without a modifier, for example, "special assessments for improvements," unless the intention is to have it cover both improvements and services or unless the particular use is apparent from the context.)

assessment value: *see* **value, assessment.**

assets: (1) property owned; (2) (school accounting) a term used to include cash, accounts receivable, supplies on hand, deferred charges, land, buildings, equipment, and taxes or appropriations accrued, due, and uncollected.

assets, basic: positive qualities of an individual, utilized in guidance and counseling.

assets, capital: *syn.* **assets, fixed.**

assets, fixed: assets of a permanent character having continuing value, such as land, buildings, machinery, furniture, and other equipment. (NOTE: The term denotes probability or intent to continue use or possession; it does not indicate the immobility of an asset.) *Syn.* **capital assets.**

assign-study-recite formula: a teaching formula identified with subject-centered teaching and traditional subject curricula; emphasizes assimilation of knowledge by students and the method of explanation by the teacher; includes (a) explanation and assignment, (b) study through readings, exercises, or research, and (c) application in recitations or tests (with possible provision for remedial instruction); other variations of this formula are assign-study-test-reteach, assign-study-test, and prepare-present-follow-up. *See* **Herbartian method; Morrison plan.**

assigned listening: *see* **listening, assigned.**

assigned value: *see* **value, assigned.**

assignment: (1) the act of allotting to classes or individuals specific mental or physical tasks; (2) the work that has been allotted to the pupil or class.

assignment booklet: a small book in which are written by or for pupils certain lessons, exercises, or other tasks they are to do during work or study periods or before the next regular class period.

assignment cards: (1) cards used in some schools to indicate a piece of reading or other work to be done, generally arranged so that children can use them individually; (2) cards on which are recorded reading tasks for the guidance of individual pupils.

assignment, cooperative: an assignment that is developed through the joint efforts of the teacher and pupils and related to their needs and interests.

assignment, full-time equivalency of: the amount of employed time normally required of a staff member to perform a less than full-time assignment divided by the amount of time normally required in performing a corresponding full-time assignment; usually expressed as a decimal fraction to the nearest 10th.

assignment, indeterminate: an assignment organized around a subject, topic, unit, or principle in which there are no formal minimum or maximum requirements, each pupil merely being required to work to the best of his ability.

assignment, lesson: (1) the act of dividing the assignment of work into definite units known as lessons, equivalent in ordinary practice to a day's work; (2) the work assigned to be prepared as a single lesson.

assignment notification blank: a printed or mimeographed slip to be filled out with the date, subject, and teacher's name, as an advance notice to a school librarian of detailed assignments requiring use of library material.

assignment, oral: a spoken announcement of a piece of work to be done by a pupil or group.

assignment, professional educational: an assignment to a staff member to perform activities designated as professional in the field of education by the laws and regulations governing certification in the state or by other professional educational requirements.

assignment, school direction and management: an assignment to a staff member to perform the professional activities of heading a school.

assignment, school librarian: an assignment to a staff member to perform professional school library service activities such as ordering, cataloging, processing, and circulating books and other materials, planning the use of the library by teachers, pupils, and others, selecting books and materials, participating in faculty planning for the use of books and materials, and guiding teachers, pupils, and others in the use of the library in school programs.

assignment sheet: (1) a sheet containing a statement of the job or project to be undertaken, problems to be solved, instructions or other information to be read and studied, and materials to be used; (2) an advance schedule of tasks for members of a publication staff or journalism class.

assignment, teacher: (1) the appointment of an instructor to a certain position or to certain duties in a school system; (2) the position and duties to which an instructor is appointed.

assignment, teaching: *syn.* **assignment, teacher;** *dist. f.* **assignment, lesson.**

assignment to school, notice of: an administrative form used (a) to inform a child and his parents of the school he

is to attend or (b) to inform the pupil of his daily period assignments during a given term.

assignment, unit: (1) a piece of work of an integrated character assigned to the pupil or student; (2) an assigned problem, project, or job having a central idea or theme and usually extending over a relatively long period of time.

assignment, written: (1) directions for study given to pupils in writing; usually typewritten and duplicated in some way; (2) a piece of work to be done in writing by a pupil or class.

assignments, differentiated: tasks of various degrees of complexity and difficulty or differing in subject matter, assigned to the various members of a class according to their individual abilities, needs, and interests.

assimilation: (1) the act of incorporating material to be learned into one's thought pattern; (2) one of the steps in the *Morrison plan* of directing learning; (3) the act or process of fully comprehending language to the point of using it freely and fully for purposes of reading or expression; (4) (sociol.) the fusion of divergent habits, attitudes, and ideas of two or more groups or societies into a common set of habits, attitudes, and ideas.

assimilation, law of: *syn.* **generalization, stimulus.**

assimilative reading: *see* **reading, assimilative.**

assistant: (higher ed.) a person below the rank of instructor who assists a regular faculty member in the conduct of instruction by performing such duties as grading themes and examination papers, keeping records, and preparing and arranging laboratory materials. (An assistant rarely has complete responsibility for the instruction of a class.) *Syn.* **graduate assistant.**

assistant, graduate: *syn.* **assistant.**

assistant, nursery school: a staff member who has an involvement with the instructional process; often has responsibility for part of the group; assists *head teacher* by sharing duties; suggested training includes high school diploma or equivalent and either one year of in-service training or one year in college with practicum; can be on a work-study basis while working as an *aide,* in preparation for the position of assistant. *See* **head teacher** (2).

assistant principal: *see* **principal, assistant.**

assistant professor: *see* **professor.**

assistant, residence: a student member of the residence hall advisory staff who is responsible for maintaining an interpersonal relationship with the residents of the hall to encourage and enhance educational, personal, and social development.

assistant state supervisor, business and office education: *see* **supervisor, business and office education assistant state.**

assistant state supervisor, distributive education: *see* **supervisor, distributive education assistant state.**

assistant superintendent: *see* **superintendent, assistant.**

assistant teacher: a teacher who is an aide to one or more regularly employed teachers, engaged especially when large classes are necessary because of overcrowding.

assistant, teaching: (1) *syn.* **assistant teacher;** (2) (higher ed.) *see* **assistant.**

assistantship: a work scholarship for college students, usually at the graduate level, carrying a stipend and, frequently, exemption from fees.

associate: a staff member in a nursery school who has more responsibility with less supervision by the professional teacher than an aide or an assistant; suggested training: A.A. degree from 2-year college or 2-year special program in a 4-year college; can be on work-study basis while working as an assistant. *See* **aide; assistant, nursery school; head teacher** (2); **teacher-intern.**

associate degree: *see* **degree, associate.**

associate in arts: the title or degree conferred by some colleges for the completion of 2 years of college work in arts and sciences beyond high school or for the completion of the curriculum of a junior college.

associate in science: the title or degree conferred by some colleges for the completion of 2 years of college work beyond the high school, emphasizing science, or for the completion of a science curriculum in a junior college.

associate learning: *see* **learning, associate.**

associate professor: *see* **professor.**

associate superintendent: *see* **superintendent, associate.**

associate superintendent of public instruction: an official appointed by the state superintendent of public instruction or by the state board of education to serve as a deputy to the superintendent; usually performs a particular function such as the supervision of secondary education.

associate title: synonymous with *associate degree,* but used in many junior colleges because of the traditional connection of *degree* with 4-year colleges and universities. (First proposed in the United States by President William Rainey Harper and conferred by him in 1900 on graduates of the junior colleges of the University of Chicago.)

association: (1) the process of establishing functional relations among psychological activities and states in the course of individual experience; (2) the functional relations established among psychological activities and states; (3) loosely, a statistical term for *correlation;* (4) (sociol.) a group of interacting persons; sometimes used to mean a consciously formed group, usually of a secondary sort; (5) a special-interest group, for example, a trade association or a *teachers' association.*

association, accrediting: *see* **accrediting association.**

association, arbitrary: associative learnings where the linkages are arbitrarily determined, as in the names of objects or symbols.

association area: the area of the central nervous system in which experiences are related. (In reading, this area is supposed to furnish the physical means of connecting word symbols and meanings.)

association, auditory-vocal: the ability to derive relationships from what is heard and express them vocally.

association by contiguity: a state of functional relationship between two or more stimuli, situations, ideas, or concepts as a result of their having been experienced in temporal or spatial proximity (or both), so that the one will evoke the other; for example, each letter of the alphabet seems to suggest or evoke the succeeding letter, since they were learned in that order. (Cause-and-effect concepts appear to result from a constant temporal contiguity in experience; conditioning also is regarded by many as being an example of association by contiguity.) *See* **contiguity.**

association, controlled: (1) a technique whereby the subject is instructed to make specific kinds of responses to a series of stimulus words, for example, to respond by synonyms, opposites, etc.; *see* **association, free;** (2) (sociol.) functional relations regulated by some outside force.

association, corner test of: *see* **test of association, corner.**

association, direct: a mental mechanism by which a student is immediately reminded of a word for an object upon seeing that object.

association, free: a technique used to probe unconscious but learned connections. *See* **test, free-association.**

association, library: a group of librarians organized on a local, district, state, national, or international basis for consideration of and action on professional matters.

association, local teachers': *see* **teachers' association, local.**

association, negative: a tendency for the presence of one trait to be associated with the absence of another, there being fewer observed instances of the presence of both traits and of the absence of both traits than would be the case if the two were mathematically independent. *Contr. w.* **association, positive.**

association of teachers, county: *see* **association, local teachers'.**

association, parent-teacher: *see* **parent-teacher association.**

association, positive: a tendency for the presence or absence of one trait to be associated with the presence or absence, respectively, of another trait, there being more observed instances of the presence of both traits and of the absence of both traits than would be the case if the traits were mathematically independent. *Contr. w.* **association, negative.**

association psychology: *see* **psychology, association.**

association reflex: *see* **reflex, association.**

association-sensory ratio: *see* **ratio, association-sensory.**

association, teachers': *see* **teachers' association.**

association test: *see* **test, association.**

association theory of learning: *see* **psychology, association.**

associational fluency: *see* **fluency, associational.**

associational learning: *see* **learning, associational.**

associational living: *see* **living, associational.**

associational reading: *see* **reading, associational.**

associationism: *syn.* **psychology, association.**

associations, kinesthetic-auditory: (read.) those connections an individual makes when tracing with a finger and sounding a word at the same time. *See* **kinesthetic method** (1).

associations, meaning: the meanings suggested to the reader by the rapid visual impressions of words in reading.

associations, visual-kinesthetic: (read.) those connections an individual makes when tracing and observing a word at the same time.

associative generalization: *syn.* **generalization, stimulus.**

associative inhibition, Muller-Schumann paradigm of: the view that when an association has been formed between any two items it is more difficult to form any association between either of the two and a third item.

associative law: *see* **law, associative.**

associative-learning test: *see* **test, associative-learning.**

associative mode: *see* **mode, associative.**

associative play: *see* **play, associative.**

associative shifting: Thorndike's principle that when two stimuli occur together, one originally eliciting a response, the other may come to substitute for the original in producing a response; Thorndike thought conditioning a special case of this general principle. *See* **conditioning** (1).

associative spread: *syn.* **generalization, stimulus.**

associative transfer: *see* **transfer, associative.**

assumed mean: *syn.* **average, guessed.**

assumption: (1) a broad term to cover any one of the propositions from which a train of reasoning starts or which is necessary to the solution of a problem; ordinarily taken as self-evident but may be true only hypothetically; sometimes not stated but left implicit; not to be confused with the hypothesis, which should be limited in use to the forecast solution of the problem; *see* **hypothesis; postulate; premise; presupposition;** (2) (math.) in a theorem, problem, etc., a given statement; in a deductive system, one of the axioms (postulates) and definitions.

assumption, fundamental: scarcely different from premise; a proposition that is accepted as true because it appears to the investigator to be reasonable in the light of available evidence and because it forms the basis for the train of proof which leads to desired conclusions; an assumption necessary to a theory. *See* **assumption; postulate; premise; presupposition.**

astasia: motor incoordination with inability to stand erect.

astasia-abasia (ə·stā′zhi·ə-ə·bā′zhi·ə): a hysterical condition resulting from mental conflict and manifested by inability to walk or to stand erect.

astereognosis: inability to recognize articles by touch. *Syn.* **tactile agnosia.**

asthenia (as·thē′ni·ə): loss of strength; general debility.

asthenic feelings: feelings such as grief or despondency in which physical activity is inhibited.

asthenic type: a type of body build described by Kretschmer as slender, flat in front, and having a long chest and poor muscular development. *See* **body builds, classification of.**

asthenopia (as′thə·nō′pi·ə): (1) a condition characterized by weakness and rapid fatigue of the eyes; (2) a broad term used to designate discomfort or a group of symptoms resulting from the performance of a visual task.

asthmatic child: *see* **child, asthmatic.**

astigmatism: a refractive error in which light rays are not brought to a single focus because of a difference in the degree of refraction in the different meridians of the eye; results from irregular curvature of cornea or lens.

ASTP: *see* **Army Specialized Training Program.**

astraphobia (as'trə·fō'bi·ə): anxiety amounting to panic during thunderstorms. *Dist. f.* **astrophobia.**

astridecile: an interval, measured in centile units, that exactly straddles the several deciles and throws the two extremes of ability into greater relief by including only 5, instead of 10, centile units in the two extreme intervals; thus, astridecile 0 = 1-5 centiles; astridecile 5 = 45-55; astridecile 9 = 85-95; astridecile 10 = 96-100, etc.; rarely used.

astrionics: a study of electronics as applied to astronautics. *See* **avionics.**

astrobiology: a branch of biology concerned with the study of life on other planets. *See* **ecology.**

astrogation: *see* **astronavigation.**

astrology: the practice of predicting the course of human affairs from the position and movements of heavenly bodies.

astronaut: (1) a person who rides in, or is selected and trained to ride in, a space vehicle; also used as a title, as in "Astronaut Shepard"; (2) in the pre-sputnik era (*a*) an animal sent into space as a means of testing equipment and obtaining data, and (*b*) a person engaged in developing equipment and techniques for space flight and space exploration.

astronaut training: *see* **training, astronaut.**

astronautic centrifuge: *see* **centrifuge, astronautic.**

astronautics: the art, skill, or activity of operating space vehicles; in a broader sense, the art or science of designing, building, and operating space vehicles, manned or unmanned.

astronavigation: the plotting and directing of the movement of a spacecraft from within the craft by means of observations on celestial bodies; sometimes contracted to *astrogation* or called *celestial navigation.*

astronomy: a study of the science which treats of the celestial bodies, their compositions, distances, motions, and the laws which control them.

astronomy, radar: the study of celestial bodies within the solar system by means of radiation originating on earth but reflected from the body under observation.

astrophobia: morbid fear of the sky and celestial space. *Dist. f.* **astraphobia.**

astrophysics: the branch of astronomy that deals with the physical characteristics of heavenly bodies.

asylum: an obsolescent term designating an institution for mental defectives or deranged persons. (Sanitarium and hospital are more modern terms.)

asymbolia (as'im·bō'li·ə): (1) *syn.* **asemia;** (2) *syn.* **aphasia, sensory-receptive;** (3) obs. *syn.* **agnosia.**

asymmetry: (1) lack of similarity between the opposite sides of the body, whether in terms of structure or of function; (2) (stat.) *syn.* **skew;** *ant.* **symmetry;** (3) lack of similarity in opposite ends of a frequency curve.

asymmetry, principle of functional: the emergence of laterality of behavior as a necessary prerequisite for effective attentional adjustment in a bilaterally symmetrical organism; examples are *eyedness, handedness, tonic neck reflex,* etc.

asymptote: a line which a curve approaches as a limit, when the curve is indefinitely extended; for example, the *x* axis is the asymptote of the normal probability curve.

asymptotic: approaching some definite straight line as a limit; for example, the retention curve is asymptotic. *See* **curve, retention.**

asynchronous computer: *see* **computer, asynchronous.**

asynchrony: (1) in programmed instruction, presentation of such items as offer changing stimuli but require the same response or of such items as offer a fixed stimulus but require changing responses; examples of the former items are 5 + 1 = 6, 4 + 2 = 6, 3 + 3 = 6, of the latter, 6 = 4 + 2, 6 = 3 + 3, 6 = 5 + 1; (2) in development,

the differential growth rate of various systems which leads to some unevenness, for example, in early adolescence more rapid growth of the forehead and nose than of the jaw.

atactic abasia: *see* **abasia, atactic.**

atavism: (1) the reappearance of a characteristic present in a remote ancestor which has not been in evidence for many generations; (2) reversion to the primitive.

ataxia: (1) motor incoordination manifest during purposive movement by irregularity and lack of precision; (2) a type of muscular incoordination characterized by lack of balance and/or directional control; one of the types of cerebral palsy; *see* **athetosis; cerebral palsy; rigidity; spasticity; tremor.**

ataxia, static: (1) loss of deep sensibility causing inability to preserve equilibrium in standing; (2) a form of ataxia in which an individual tries to maintain a fixed position or posture.

ataxiagraph: an apparatus giving a graphic record of the degree and nature of muscular coordination in ataxic conditions.

ataxiameter (ə·tak'si·am'ə·tər): an apparatus that gives the total amount of sway at the head, laterally and from front to back, of an individual who is trying to maintain an erect posture.

ataxic abasia: *see* **abasia, atactic.**

ataxic gait: *see* **gait, ataxic.**

ataxic writing: *see* **writing, ataxic.**

atheism: (1) denial of the existence of a God or Supreme Being; (2) denial of a personal God; *ant.* **theism.**

athetoid: descriptive of a patient afflicted with a disorder characterized by slow, squirming, twisting, purposeless movements. *See* **athetosis.**

athetoid, tension: one afflicted with *athetosis* who voluntarily tenses his muscles in an endeavor to stop the involuntary movements.

athetosis: a neuromuscular disability found in the cerebral palsied; characterized by uncontrolled movements; caused by injury to the basal ganglia of the midbrain, which accounts for about 40 percent of all cerebral palsies. *See* **athetoid.**

athlete: one trained to compete in contests of physical ability, stamina, or strength; a trained competitor in a sport, exercise, or game requiring physical skill.

athlete's foot: an infection of the feet caused by the ringworm fungus *(Tinea trichophyton),* most commonly found between the toes, and characterized by inflammation, itching, and pain; aggravated by failure to wash and dry properly between the toes.

athletic ability: *see* **ability, athletic.**

athletic activity: *see* **activity, athletic.**

athletic association: an organization of individuals within a school, community, or other area for support and promotion of athletic contests.

athletic association, state: a voluntary association limited to residents of the state, the purpose of which is to determine policies in the regulation of athletic contests between member schools.

athletic club: *see* **club, athletic.**

athletic coach: *see* **coach, athletic.**

athletic committee, faculty: a committee of the faculty that supervises the athletic-competition activities of a school.

athletic conference: *see* **conference, athletic.**

athletic council: a committee of students and teachers in a school or college, organized as a policy-forming body to guide and regulate interschool competitive athletics.

athletic field: *syn.* **playfield.**

athletic grant-in-aid: *syn.* **scholarship, athletic.**

athletic index: *see* **index, athletic.**

athletic intelligence: *see* **intelligence, athletic.**

athletic official: arbitrator of fair play; the prime justification of an athletic official is to keep the game going within the rules with as little interference as possible, and to make the game more enjoyable for the players; titles are *umpire* and *referee.*

athletic program: *see* **program, athletic.**

athletic quotient: *see* **quotient, athletic.**

athletic scholarship: *see* **scholarship, athletic.**

athletic-strength index: *see* **index, athletic-strength.**

athletic training: *see* **training, athletic.**

athletic-trip card: a form recording the fact that the parent or guardian of an athlete consents to the latter making a trip.

athletic type: a type of body build described by Kretschmer as having broad shoulders, a well-developed chest, thick neck, flat abdomen, and large muscles. *See* **body builds, classification of.**

athleticism: a term used to characterize the low status of physical education in Greece during the Roman Era, when the old ideals of health, military fitness, sportsmanship, and virtue were abandoned for physical professionalism and men would train highly in one particular physical skill or feat and then perform only for pay.

athletics: games and physical contests engaged in on a competitive basis between teams or individuals representing organizations or groups, most commonly schools and colleges.

athletics, director of: *see* **director of athletics.**

athletics, extramural: athletic contests and sports involving individual players and teams representing two or more educational institutions at any level of education. *Contr. w.* **athletics, intramural.**

athletics, intercollegiate: athletic contests and sports involving individual players or teams representing two or more different institutions of higher learning. *See* **athletics, extramural;** *contr. w.* **athletics, intramural.**

athletics, interscholastic: team or individual contests in games or sports, the players representing elementary or secondary schools (particularly the latter), and recognized and managed by school authorities.

athletics, intramural: athletic contests and sports involving only students of the same institution. *Contr. w.* **athletics, extramural; athletics, intercollegiate.**

athletics, mass: a type of competition in games and sports in which the total achievement of a team or group is used in determining the winner.

athletics, track: contests in running, jumping, vaulting, and throwing, especially the running events. *See* **track and field.**

atlas: (1) a bound collection of maps; (2) a bound collection of charts, tables, or plates illustrating any particular subject.

atmosphere, autocratic group: a group situation in which the leader determines all policies; atmosphere tends to be hostile; productiveness, solidarity, and identification with group goals are low.

atmosphere, democratic group: a group situation in which all policies are a matter of group discussion and decision; atmosphere is friendly; productiveness, solidarity, and identification with group goals are high.

atmosphere, group: (1) the summation of forces, including intellectual expectancies and emotional feelings, determining desirable or acceptable behavior in a group; (2) the ethos or emotional climate of a group; *syn.* **group climate.**

atmosphere, permissive: the feeling existing among individuals or groups which encourages differences of opinion and free discussion.

atmosphere, psychological: the total effect that an environment or situation has on an individual's feelings about himself, others, and the world in general; also called *psychological climate.*

atomic-age education: (1) in a broad sense, educational content and instructional emphasis that are up to date and appropriate to a modern culture which is harnessing atomic energy; (2) in a narrower sense, instruction dealing with the various facets of atomic energy, especially its socioeconomic implications, both nationally and internationally; later than air-age education and prophetic of outer-space-age education.

atomism (at'əm·iz'm): (1) narrowly, the philosophical theory that reality consists solely of minute, indivisible,

and discrete particles in space; (2) broadly, any position in politics, psychology, etc., that assumes the priority, independence, and plurality of the units constituting any whole.

atomism, logical: the view that the world (or experience) may be analyzed into ultimate units which are not physical but logical, that is, which are conceptual in content as well as in form; sometimes applied to the philosophy of Leibnitz, whose ultimate units, or *monads,* are spiritual, and to the philosophy of Hume, whose ultimate units, "conjoined but not connected," are impressions; more properly applied to present-day theories, such as those associated with the name of E. B. Holt.

atomism, psychological: (1) narrowly, the theory that all mental states are discrete entities or responses to such entities, for example, materialistic hedonism, the theory that measurable units of pleasure and pain are the sole determinants of psychological experience; (2) broadly, any position that assumes the priority, independence, and plurality of the units producing behavior.

atomistic theory: a psychological theory according to which conduct is traceable to a single isolated cause. *Contr. w.* **field theory.**

atonality: absence of a tonal center; a characteristic of much music of the twentieth century having as its chief harmonic and melodic dogma the deliberate absence of a tonal center.

atonement: (psych.) self-penalty to make up for a feeling of guilt; thought by some mental hygienists to be one of the common defense mechanisms.

atonicity: reduction of the contraction of muscles; flaccidity of posture.

atony (at'ə·ni): lack of muscular tone.

atopognosia: a form of agnosia characterized by a loss of the body schema, for example, right hand–left hand disorientation, failure to locate a pinprick on the skin, etc.

atrophy: a wasting away or diminution in size of a cell, organ, or part.

attachment: taking into custody of the law the person or property of one already before the court, or of one whom it is sought to bring before it; also, a writ for the accomplishment of this purpose.

attack: (1) a sudden manifestation of some physical or mental disorder such as epilepsy; *syn.* **seizure;** (2) an acute spell of sickness.

attack, meaning: *see* **meaning attack.**

attainment age: rare *syn.* **age, achievement.**

attainment, levels of: (read.) the stages of achievement reached by children in reading, generally expressed in terms of grade levels, such as fifth-grade level, first-grade level, etc.

attainment quotient (AQ): rare *syn.* **quotient, achievement.**

attainment ratio (AR): rare *syn.* **quotient, achievement.**

attendance: the act of being present, particularly at school. (Certain court decisions have defined attendance at school as not merely being bodily presence but including actual participation in the work and activities of the school.)

attendance, a day's: variously defined by different regulations, the two extremes being the mere appearance of the pupil at school and the pupil's presence during the whole day.

attendance, age of compulsory school: *see* **age of compulsory school attendance.**

attendance, aggregate: the sum of all the days attended by all the pupils in a school system or any subdivision during the entire school year or any part of it, not counting days on which the schools are closed for any reason whatever. (In schools having two sessions a day, if the attendance of pupils is limited to half-day sessions because of congestion or other reasons, each pupil present is counted as being present for a full day.)

attendance area: *see* **attendance unit** (1).

attendance area, school: *see* **attendance unit** (2).

attendance, average annual percent of: the average attendance for the entire year, divided by the average membership for the same time period.

attendance, average daily: a statistic computed by the formula: the sum of the days attended by each student enrolled divided by the number of days school is in session; this statistic is usually figured for the period of one school year. *See* **session, days in.**

attendance case: (1) a pupil, referred to the attendance department, who is so frequently absent from school that the help of the department is needed in improving his attendance; (2) any pupil referred to the attendance department for adjustment purposes.

attendance center: (1) an office that houses attendance officers and their clerks and records; specifically, the office of the attendance supervisor and of the attendance officers with whom he works; (2) sometimes used synonymously with *bureau of attendance* or *attendance department;* (3) the headquarters within an attendance area for administering attendance-department services; the office to which attendance officers report.

attendance, certificate of: *see* **certificate of attendance.**

attendance clerk: (1) a member of the clerical staff of the schools who works in the attendance department; (2) a member of the clerical staff, serving a school principal, who keeps the attendance records of the school.

attendance, compulsory: *see* **compulsory education.**

attendance, compulsory school: the requirement established by the state legislature that all children, with certain specified exceptions, must attend school; the lower age limits vary from 6 to 8 years, the upper age limits from 16 to 18 years in the various states.

attendance data: information which is used in calculating *pupil accountability.*

attendance department: *see* **department, attendance.**

attendance district: *see* **district, attendance.**

attendance enforcement: the ensuring of regular attendance at school by young people of school age; methods of securing such enforcement vary from old-fashioned procedures based on legal force to more modern measures based on study of causes of nonattendance and their removal.

attendance, full day of: (pupil accounting) a school day during which a pupil is present for an entire school session under the guidance and direction of teachers; when he is present for only part of the session, his attendance is counted according to the nearest half day of attendance; if a school holds two separate sessions per day, a pupil attending for all of either session is considered as having completed a full day of attendance; attendance at a state-approved half-day session for kindergarten or nursery school is also counted as a full day of attendance; an excused absence during examination periods or because of sickness or for any other reason is not counted as a day of attendance. *Syn.* **day of attendance;** *see* **attendance, half day of; session, day in.**

attendance, half day of: attendance for approximately half of a full-day school session or an approved curtailed session; for example, a pupil who is present a major part of either the morning or afternoon portion of a school session usually is counted as being in attendance for that half session; this is the smallest unit of time recorded for attendance purposes during the regular school term of elementary and secondary schools. *See* **attendance, full day of.**

attendance law: the law of a state that specifies those conditions under which the youths of that state must attend school; varies greatly with respect to the ages of youths who are required to attend, length of school year, etc. *Syn.* **compulsory school-attendance legislation.**

attendance laws, compulsory state: *see* **compulsory education.**

attendance, monthly percent of: the average attendance for a single month, divided by the average membership for the same month.

attendance officer: a school officer charged with the duty of studying cases of nonattendance, determining reasons for nonattendance, and getting pupils back in school.

attendance officer's report to bureau: *see* **report to bureau, attendance officer's.**

attendance officer's report to principal: *see* **report to principal, attendance officer's.**

attendance, percentage of: *see* **percentage of attendance.**

attendance record: *see* **record, attendance.**

attendance record card: *see* **record card, attendance.**

attendance record system: *see* **record system, attendance.**

attendance register: a record containing (*a*) the names of pupils who have entered, or are expected to enter, a class or a school, (*b*) identification information about each pupil such as sex, date of birth, and address, and (*c*) information concerning his entry or reentry, membership, attendance, absence, tardiness, and withdrawal. *Syn.* **register.**

attendance report: *see* **report, attendance.**

attendance service: the activity carried on·by the attendance worker or by any school agency to ensure prompt and regular attendance at school. (In some school districts, this service may be confined to law enforcement in its most restricted meaning; in other districts, it has developed into a well-rounded type of social service.)

attendance services: activities such as prompt identification of patterns of nonattendance, promotion of positive pupil and parental attitudes toward attendance, analysis of causes of nonattendance, early action on problems of nonattendance, and enforcement of compulsory attendance laws.

attendance supervision: *see* **supervision, attendance.**

attendance supervisor: *see* **supervisor, attendance.**

attendance teacher: (1) the teacher who is responsible for keeping a record of or reporting on the attendance of a given child; (2) the teacher responsible for improving the attendance of the pupils of the entire school.

attendance unit: (1) (pupil accounting) a school, a school district, or a defined part of a school district for which *pupil accountability* is determined; (2) an administrative unit or subdivision of it consisting of the territory from which children legally may attend a given school building or school center.

attendance unit, minimum elementary school: the minimum number of pupils recommended‚from the standpoint of administrative economy in maintaining a school program of desirable quality: approximately 240 pupils in grades 1 to 6.

attendance worker: the person in charge of pupil attendance at school or any individual on the school staff who is responsible for the understanding and enforcement of the attendance law; duties could also include child accounting, admission and registration of pupils, the school census, work permits, truancy, and discipline.

attention: (1) (structural psych.) the attributive state of sensory clearness; (2) the active selection and emphasis of one component of a complex experience; (3) a sensory adjustment providing for optimal stimulation of a sense modality; (4) (behav. psych.) adjustment of the sense organs to facilitate response to a particular stimulus or situation and to inhibit response to extraneous stimuli or situations by using a perceptual set for one object or class of objects and excluding objects of other classes.

attention chart: *see* **chart, attention.**

attention, fluctuation of: *see* **fluctuation of attention.**

attention, measurement of: metric methods of considering attention have included (*a*) determiners, for example, the ordinal arrangement of the "attention-catching-and-holding power" of advertisements; (*b*) fluctuations of attention, that is, changes in strength, duration, or shifts to other parts of the stimulus field; (*c*) immediate verbal report, wherein the observer reports, for example, road signs seen while driving along an unfamiliar road; (*d*) recall, such as tests of number and accuracy of advertisements as remembered from a magazine; (*e*) recognition or identification of things seen mixed with similar items not seen; (*f*) eye-movement photography; (*g*) resistance to distraction; (*h*) span of attention, or the determination of the number of words, digits, consonants, or geometric forms which can be perceived in a single tachistoscopic exposure. (Classification of metric methods is frequently challenged because of lack of satisfactorily rigorous definition of the category *attention.*)

attention seeking: annoying behavior which is evidenced by the child who constantly wants to be "in the center of the stage" in the classroom, evidencing his desire by such activities as repeated attempts to make others laugh, to pick fights, etc.

attention span: the period of time in which a student can concentrate on a specific learning task.

attention-span test: *syn.* **test, apprehension-span.**

attention, test for: *see* **test for attention.**

attenuation: (1) a weakening or reduction of energy, usually by the dissipation of energy; (2) (meas.) the reduction of a coefficient of correlation from its theoretical value due to errors of measurement in the variance being correlated.

attenuation, correction for: *see* **correction for attenuation.**

attenuator: in electrical circuits, a resistance device that is designed to control the ratio of output to input voltages in steps of a decibel or multiples thereof.

attitude: the predisposition or tendency to react specifically towards an object, situation, or value; usually accompanied by feelings and emotions; some writers differentiate a *verbal attitude* (what the reacting person says) from a *behavioral attitude* (what he actually does when confronted with the affect-producing stimuli); attitudes cannot be directly observed but must be inferred from overt behavior, both verbal and nonverbal.

attitude, behavioral: *see* **attitude.**

attitude cluster: (meas.) a group of related attitudes which tend in any population to be covariant, that is, scores on one attitude tend to be accompanied by corresponding scores on the other attitudes.

attitude, complex: an attitude having two or more components. *Syn.* **multidimensional attitude;** *contr. w.* **attitude, unidimensional.**

attitude, emotionalized: an attitude based primarily on an emotional reaction rather than on critical thought, that is, an effectively loaded attitude.

attitude, general: an attitude toward an attitude object at a higher level of abstraction than a *specific attitude,* for example, attitude toward foreigners instead of attitude toward the Chinese.

attitude master scale: *see* **scale, attitude master.**

attitude, moralistic: *see* **moralistic attitude.**

attitude, multidimensional: *syn.* **attitude, complex.**

attitude object: the stimulus that evokes affective tone.

attitude, professional: a state of mental and emotional readiness on the part of professionals to react to any educationally significant situation in a manner that gives first place to the interests of society and the profession, that demonstrates appreciation of the situation's educational implications, and that indicates ability and desire to cooperate with others toward the solution of the problems involved.

attitude questionnaire: *see* **questionnaire, attitude.**

attitude scale: *see* **scale, attitude.**

attitude, scientific: a set of emotionally toned ideas about science and scientific method and related directly or indirectly to a course of action; in the literature of science education the term implies such qualities of mind as intellectual curiosity, passion for truth, respect for evidence, and an appreciation of the necessity for free communication in science.

attitude score: *see* **score, attitude.**

attitude, social: (1) the attitude of a person or group with respect to a social object or phenomenon such as a person, race, institution, or trait; (2) readiness to respond in a certain way (such as impartially, aggressively, positively, or negatively) to a given social phenomenon; (3) sociability.

attitude, specific: an attitude toward a narrowly defined, relatively concrete attitude object, such as labor unions, the school, or a teacher. *Contr. w.* **attitude, general.**

attitude survey: *see* **survey, attitude.**

attitude test: *see* **test, attitude.**

attitude therapy: *see* **therapy, attitude.**

attitude, unidimensional: an attitude which, when measured, represents one and only one factor. *Contr. w.* **attitude, complex; attitude, multidimensional.**

attitude, verbal: *see* **attitude.**

attitudes, employee: *see* **employee attitudes.**

attitudinal cluster: (sociol.) the related specific or unidimensional attitudes that comprise the total attitude toward an abstract concept such as internationalism, freedom, or justice. *See* **attitude, specific.**

attitudinal orientation: *see* **orientation, attitudinal.**

attitudinizing: the act of assuming an attitude or posture and, often, of maintaining it for long periods; frequently seen in *catatonia* and *hysteria.*

attorney, board: legal counsel for a board of education; may be a paid employee of the board or a local government official with such duties included in his office. *Syn.* **school attorney.**

attorney, school: *syn.* **attorney, board.**

attractive nuisance: *see* **nuisance, attractive.**

attribute: (1) a trait, quality, or characteristic that is regarded as either present or absent in the person or thing being measured; (2) a qualitative trait whose distribution consists of two or more discrete classes; sometimes used in contradistinction to *variable; syn.* **characteristic;** (3) any of the several possible classes of a qualitative variable, for example, eye color.

attribute blocks: *see* **blocks, attribute.**

attribute listing: a method of group problem solving which involves looking at all facets of a problem and alternative methods of solving it until a solution is reached. *See* **dynamics, group; problem solving, cooperative.**

attribute, nonvariable: *syn.* **category.**

atypical: differing to a marked degree in one or more characteristics from others of a given class or category. (The term is relative. Thus, among children in general the blind child is atypical, while among blind children the anophthalmic child, born without eyes, is atypical. Moreover, a reaction, like *echolalia,* may be typical in early childhood, but its persistence atypical.) *See* **exceptional.**

atypical behavior: *see* **behavior, atypical.**

atypical characteristic: *see* **characteristic, atypical.**

atypical child: *see* **child, exceptional.**

atypical condition: *see* **condition, atypical.**

atypical growth: *see* **growth, atypical.**

atypical pupil: *see* **pupil, atypical.**

audibility range: *syn.* **range, audio-frequency.**

audibility threshold: *see* **threshold, audibility.**

audible frequency range: *see* **range, audible frequency.**

audience: a physically contiguous group whose members are subject to the same stimuli. *See* **crowd.**

audience-participation program: *see* **program, audience-participation.**

audience reading: *see* **reading, audience.**

audience situation: a situation in which the pupils of a class serve as an audience while a member of the group reads aloud, speaks, or acts.

auding: (lang. arts) listening to spoken symbols in order to recognize and interpret them.

audio: of or pertaining to sound; when used as a noun, specifically, a sound recording; loosely, any part or all of the complex of sound equipment, facilities, and personnel.

audio-active-compare method: a language-laboratory mode in which the student hears the master, responds with an utterance, records his response, then replays the recording of his own response and master track for self-evaluation.

audio aid: *see* **aid, audio.**

audio channel, movie sound: one of several electrical circuits available in a language laboratory for broadcasting programs that include sound tracks from movies.

audio-frequency range: *syn.* **range, audible frequency.**

audio-oral: *syn.* **audiolingual.**

audio privacy: isolation provided by the closed booth and the electronic circuit in a language laboratory, thus permitting the student to be free from embarrassment and inhibitions while engaged in oral practice.

audio-video mixer: a device that combines the video signal from a TV camera and the audio signal from a microphone or similar source and impresses them on a carrier signal for transmission on a closed-circuit system.

audioactive laboratory: *see* **laboratory, audioactive.**

audiogram: a graphic recording of *audiometric test* results; shows any hearing loss in decibels for pure tones as a function of frequency.

audiogram, threshold: a graph that shows hearing level as a function of frequency.

audiolingual: *adj.* a new term replacing aural-oral, distinguishing that element of language (sound) which is spoken in everyday conversational interchange as differentiated from language as gesture or as writing.

audiolingual drill: *see* **drill, audiolingual.**

audiolingual method: an approach to foreign language teaching that considers languages a set of habits that are mastered by repetition drills and overlearning; listening and speaking are considered the central skills that are followed by reading and writing.

audiology: that interdisciplinary professional area encompassing, among others, the fields of biology, education, medicine, speech, psychology, and physics, that has to do with the measurement and treatment of impaired hearing.

audiometer: an instrument for measuring and testing auditory acuity; measurements may be made with tone or speech signals.

audiometer, delayed feedback: a diagnostic device used in the measurement of hearing that allows for the recording of sounds (usually speech) which can be played back shortly after recording.

audiometer, group: *syn.* **audiometer, phono.**

audiometer, phono: an instrument consisting of an electric phonograph on which are played special disk-type recordings of a voice repeating two- or three-digit numbers in diminishing volume; used to test relatively large groups (up to about 40 persons) for the purpose of discovering those whose hearing is defective. *Syn.* **group audiometer; phonograph audiometer;** *dist. f.* **audiometer, pure-tone.**

audiometer, phonograph: *syn.* **audiometer, phono.**

audiometer, pitch-range: *syn.* **audiometer, pure-tone.**

audiometer, pitch-tone: *syn.* **audiometer, pure-tone.**

audiometer, pure-tone: an instrument consisting of (*a*) an electronic oscillator regulated to produce a series of fixed-tone frequencies (100 to 11,000 cycles per second) with calibrated intensities, standardized in relation to the acuity of the so-called "normal ear," (*b*) an *amplifier* to boost sound energy to suitable levels, (*c*) an attenuator to control the final voltages on the decibel scale, and (*d*) an earphone to transmit the sounds to the ear.

audiometer, speech: an instrument used to measure speech intelligibility; the input may be fed either from a microphone or from the pickup of a phonograph, and the output either to an earphone or to a loud-speaker.

audiometric test: *see* **test, audiometric.**

audiometric threshold: the upper and lower limits of hearing as determined by the use of an audiometer.

audiometrist: a person trained to administer audiometric tests.

audiometry, free-field: an audiometric testing procedure in which the tones are introduced to the subject by a loudspeaker rather than by earphones; an especially useful method of measuring hearing in cases of severe conductive loss combined with good bone conduction. *See* **testing, free-field hearing.**

audiometry, monitoring: a relatively quick method of testing hearing that has developed in connection with conservation of hearing programs in industry; two objectives are to establish the state of hearing in a relatively large number of individuals and to provide reference *audiograms* from which subsequent changes in their hearing are measured.

audiometry, psychogalvanic skin response: a method of testing hearing by Pavlovian conditioning of the psychogalvanic skin response; the subject is conditioned to expect an electric shock after hearing each test tone, and his ability to hear the tones is established by observation of the skin response to that expectation.

audiometry, screening: a part of preventive medicine with particular orientation to the conservation of hearing in school children; the objective is to identify rapidly those children who require closer examination and perhaps medical treatment. *See* **test, screen.**

audiometry, speech: use of a hearing test to measure the threshold for speech directly; the test material is speech—words or sentences may emanate from a microphone or a record with the listener determining when he can identify the words.

audiometry, threshold: the level at which the human ear first becomes sensitive to sound at different frequencies.

audiopassive: *adj.* pertaining to listening practice in which no oral response is expected; also may describe facilities in which students are equipped with headphones only.

audiopassive laboratory: *see* **laboratory, audiopassive.**

audiotutorial method: a self-pacing multimedia system of instruction that features tape recorded lessons with kits of learning materials and instruction sheets for individual learning in study carrels.

audiovisual aid: *see* **aid, audiovisual.**

audiovisual communications: *see* **communications, audiovisual.**

audiovisual director: *see* **director, audiovisual.**

audiovisual education: a broad term to describe all education based on the use of materials (other than books) that appeal directly to the senses of hearing and sight, such as charts, models, still, motion, and sound pictures, phono and tape recordings, etc. *See* **instruction, audiovisual.**

audiovisual instruction: *see* **instruction, audiovisual.**

audiovisual instruction, supervisor of: *syn.* **director, audiovisual.**

audiovisual-kinesthetic method: a method of teaching lipreading, in which motion pictures serve as the basis of instruction. *See* **visual-hearing method.**

audiovisual library: *see* **library, audiovisual.**

audiovisual material: *syn.* **aid, audiovisual.**

audiovisual room: an instructional space designed or provided with special built-in equipment for audiovisual material storage, screening, and listening; it is separate from the school library and does not serve as an adjunct to another room or area.

audiovisual services: *see* **services, audiovisual.**

audit, centralized: the school audit function when assumed by a centralized school agency such as the state department of education or county office of education.

audit, external: an audit performed by persons not on the staff of the organization whose accounts are being audited.

audit, internal: an audit made by persons on the staff of the organization whose accounts are being audited. (An internal audit is usually a continuous audit.)

audit, performance: in the supervision of instruction, a methodical examination and review of a teacher's performance in the classroom; includes all aspects of the teaching-learning situation and environment.

audit, personal: (couns.) a checking of one's weaknesses and strengths and the viewing of them in relation to goals set for oneself.

audit, school: an official examination and verification of school accounts and records.

auditing: the act or procedure of checking the sources of information and the accuracy of a set of bookkeeping records; the verification of accounting statements.

audition: (1) critical listening to a person's voice and other dramatic talent as displayed by a *tryout;* (2) a musical performance intended to reveal competence either to receive training or to engage in a musical activity; (3) the process of advance listening to specific audio material or an oral performance in order to appraise its instructional value and quality; (4) hearing of a musical composition or performance; (5) the sense of hearing or the ability to hear.

auditor: (1) one who attends a course as a listener only and does not receive college credit for the course; (2) (school admin.) a public officer who verifies and examines accounts and the accuracy of the statements contained therein.

auditorily handicapped: *syn.* **handicapped, hearing.**

auditorium: a building or a room in a school building, usually equipped with a stage and arranged much like a theater, used for school assemblies and other meetings, as well as for the presentation of plays, motion pictures, and other programs.

auditorium-gymnasium: *see* **gymnasium-auditorium.**

auditory acuity: *see* **acuity, auditory.**

auditory aid: *syn.* **aid, audio.**

auditory analysis: *see* **analysis, auditory.**

auditory aphasia: *see* **aphasia, auditory.**

auditory awareness: *see* **awareness, auditory.**

auditory comprehension: *see* **comprehension, auditory.**

auditory curve: *see* **curve, auditory.**

auditory decoding: *see* **decoding, auditory.**

auditory decoding test: *see* **test, auditory decoding.**

auditory defect: *see* **defect, auditory.**

auditory discrimination: *see* **discrimination, auditory.**

auditory education: preparing the hearing-impaired individual for the acoustical situations in real life by offering natural situations of perception under normal conditions.

auditory efficiency: (1) the degree to which the organs of hearing function effectively; (2) keenness of hearing.

auditory fatigue: *see* **fatigue, auditory.**

auditory feedback: *see* **feedback, auditory.**

auditory fusion: *see* **fusion, auditory.**

auditory gain: the amount of amplification provided by a hearing aid.

auditory handicap: *see* **handicapped, hearing.**

auditory image: *see* **image, auditory.**

auditory imagery: *see* **imagery, auditory.**

auditory localization: *see* **localization, auditory.**

auditory masking: *see* **masking, auditory.**

auditory memory: *see* **memory, auditory.**

auditory memory span: *see* **memory span, auditory.**

auditory music agnosia: *see* **agnosia, auditory music.**

auditory perception: *see* **perception, auditory.**

auditory presentation: (1) presentation by appeal to the sense of hearing, for example, the introduction of spelling words by pronouncing them for the class; (2) teaching primarily by means of audio aids, such as recordings and the radio.

auditory readiness: *see* **readiness, auditory.**

auditory recruitment: *see* **recruitment, auditory.**

auditory reeducation: *see* **reeducation, auditory.**

auditory sensation area: the sound intensities included between the threshold sound intensities, between the threshold of audibility and the threshold of feeling.

auditory span: the number of letters, words, or numbers that can be repeated immediately after one hearing. *See* **memory span; memory span, auditory.**

auditory teaching aid: *syn.* **aid, audio.**

auditory test: *see* **test, auditory.**

auditory tone limits: the range of tones from lowest to highest that can be heard by the human ear; normally, from about 20 to 20,000 cycles per second.

auditory training: *see* **training, auditory.**

auditory training equipment, group: an amplifying device that permits sound transmission to several persons simultaneously usually through individual "headset" speakers.

auditory-vocal association: *see* **association, auditory-vocal.**

Aufgabe (ouf'gä·bə): (Ger., lit., "lesson assignment") (psych.) in an experiment, the task assigned to the subject.

Aufstehen pattern, (ouf'shtä·ən): (Ger., lit., "standing-up" pattern) the typical way in which a young child gets to his feet from a position flat on the back; three patterns are recognized: (*a*) the child (14 months) rolls over to stomach, then gets to his feet; (*b*) the child (22½ months) rolls over on side, then gets to his feet; (*c*) the child (33 months) sits up, then gets to his feet.

augmented Roman alphabet: *see* **alphabet, initial teaching.**

augmenting item: *see* **item, augmenting.**

Augustinianism: the philosophy of St. Augustine, Bishop of Hippo (345-430 A.D.) (not to be confused with the missionary to the British Isles); emphasizes, among other things, (*a*) the synthesis of Platonic and Christian thought, (*b*) the saving power of God's grace, (*c*) the sinfulness of man, (*d*) divine predestination, and (*e*) reconciliation of grace, the Fall, and free will; an imaginative position overshadowed in the history of Catholicism by the intellectualism of St. Thomas; also called Augustinism.

aura: a distinctive, subjective experience occurring in persons with epilepsy shortly before the advent of an epileptic seizure.

aural acuity: *syn.* **acuity, auditory.**

aural defect: *see* **defect, auditory.**

aural harmonic: *see* **harmonic, aural.**

aural-oral method: *see* **oral-aural.**

aural rehabilitation: *see* **reeducation, auditory.**

aural theory: the study of music theory by ear.

aural training: *see* **training, auditory.**

auricular training: *see* **training, auditory.**

Aussage test: *see* **test, Aussage.**

Austrian method: *syn.* **addition method;** *see* **subtraction, methods of.**

author index: *see* **index, author.**

author notation: *see* **book number.**

author number: *see* **book number.**

authoritarian control: *see* **control, authoritarian.**

authoritarian discipline: *see* **discipline, authoritarian.**

authoritarian personality: *see* **personality, authoritarian.**

authoritarianism: (1) the method of controlling others in which one person sets the tasks, prescribes procedures, and judges results without permitting others to share in the decision process; (2) belief in the principle of authority in social relations; (3) belief in authority as a source of truth; (4) a personal tendency to crave or demand obedience and subordination, or the complex of traits said to be associated with that tendency. *See* **discipline, authoritarian.**

authoritative relationship: the basic relationship existing between a school official, such as a superintendent, and a second school employee in a subordinate position, such as a teacher, over whom the first has direct line authority.

authority: (1) in general, an accepted source of information, direction, or guidance; (2) more precisely, a function of concrete human situations in which a person requires guidance from a source outside himself and grants obedience to that source as a condition of the assistance given; (3) the power to make decisions which guide the actions of another.

authority-centered supervision: *see* **supervision, authority-centered.**

authority, delegated: the right or power to act transferred by a legislative body or responsible officer to a person, institution, or corporate body.

authority, implied: authority not specifically granted but which may be exercised if conditions warrant.

authority library: *see* **library, authority.**

authority, managerial: (school admin.) the right to plan, organize, and control the activities of the organization for which the executive is responsible; consists principally of the rights of decision and command for this purpose; authority, both managerial and operative, is a derivative of *responsibility. See* **authority, operative.**

authority, moral: (1) the source of guidance in ethical conduct; (2) in Freudian theory, the superego; internal control developed by the ego; inhibitions of ego strivings to permit gradual adaptation to reality.

authority, operative: (school admin.) the right of the operative employee to make operative decisions concerning the performance of a specific work assignment, within whatever limits are established by his superior. *See* **authority, managerial.**

authority, parental: according to the teaching of the Roman Catholic Church, the God-given rights of parents to care for and instruct their children; this authority includes privileges and obligations.

authority, school building: a type of public corporation authorized by law to construct school buildings, to rent them to a board of education under a lease rental agreement by which the board eventually obtains ownership, and to issue and sell securities and pledge for the payment thereof the rentals received from the board.

authority, sources of legitimate: (school admin.) a generally accepted basis for the exercise of authority, such as the traditional established belief in the sanctity of the traditions under which the one in authority exercises his power; the charismatic devotion to the exemplary character or general wisdom of an individual which arouses personal trust in him and the normative patterns ordained by him; the rational, superior knowledge and technical competence of the administrator for allocating and integrating roles and facilities required for attaining the institutional goals.

authority, staff: (school admin.) certain rights of decision concerning the staff services rendered to the line or other staff organizations, but without rights of command; the staff executive has rights both of decision and of command within his own staff organization, however. *See* **organization, line-and-staff.**

autism (â′tiz′m): (1) a mental condition marked by a disposition to turn away from reality, to dwell upon imaginary scenes and events, and to gain satisfaction from wishful thinking; (2) a type of thinking dominated by the thinker's personal desires and relatively unchecked by any need to make it conform with reality.

autistic child: *see* **child, autistic.**

autistic personality: *see* **personality, autistic.**

autistic thinking: *see* **thinking, autistic.**

auto body repairman: (voc. ed.) a person who restores damaged bodies and/or body parts of automotive vehicles.

auto parts man: (voc. ed.) the occupation of a person who purchases, stores, and issues parts for automotive and industrial equipment.

autobiography: (couns.) the individual's report of his life or one or more segments of his life; a pupil-centered instrument which can provide insight into the life of the individual; one of the more common documents which can be employed in appraising an individual's interpretation of himself.

autobiography, family: (couns.) a structured or unstructured device for securing an inventory of a family's interests and activities; consists of records of the lives of the members of a family as set down by themselves, which the couselor analyzes to seek to understand behaviors of the members individually and in interaction with one another for the purpose of gaining insight into the characteristics which underlie achievement or underachievement; when the record is set down by others the term *family biography* is used.

autocinesis: *alt. sp.* **autokinesis.**

autocompetition: competition with oneself: the attempt to better one's previous performance. *Syn.* **autorivalry.**

autocratic group atmosphere: *see* **atmosphere, autocratic group.**

autocratic supervision: *see* **supervision, autocratic.**

autoeroticism: a state or condition characterized by the derivation of erotic gratification from body manipulations and body processes that are independent of any direct stimulus proceeding from another person. *Syn.* **autoerotism;** *dist. f.* **narcissism;** *contr. w.* **alloeroticism.**

autoerotism (â′tō·er′ə·tiz′m): *syn.* **autoeroticism.**

autogenous development: *see* **development, autogenous.**

autogenous reinforcement: *see* **reinforcement, autogenous.**

autoharp: a zither-type stringed instrument on which primary chords can be played merely by depressing specific buttons and by strumming; often used in public school music for simple folk-song accompaniments.

autoinstruction: *syn.* **instruction, programmed.**

autoinstructional device: (1) any of various machines and technological systems devoted to mass instruction, including various applications of television and the massed film systems, such as EBF's physics and chemistry series; (2) systems and machines for individual instruction including individual reading pacers, individual viewing and listening equipment, language laboratories, programmed printed materials, and the true teaching machine of the Skinner or Pressey type which presents verbal and pictorial programs in various ways (electronic and mechanical) so that the individual responds and is informed of errors and progress without the aid of a live teacher.

autoinstructional methods: programmed instruction, programmed learning, automated teaching, use of self-instructional materials, etc. *See* **autoinstructional device.**

autoinstructional reading method: *see* **reading method, autoinstructional.**

autokinesis (â·tō·ki·nē′sis): the power of voluntary movement.

autokinetic effect: the phenomenon occurring when a fixed dot of light, projected against a screen or wall in darkness, appears to move in a slow drifting fashion; has been used by social psychologists who tell subjects which way the light will drift in order to attempt to measure *suggestibility.* *Syn.* **autokinetic streaming.**

autokinetic streaming: *syn.* **autokinetic effect.**

automated aid: *see* **aid, automated.**

automated data processing: *see* **data processing, automated.**

automated teaching: *syn.* **instruction, programmed.**

automatic action: any purposeful movement, such as writing, carried on without apparent attention or volition.

automatic annual increment: *see* **increment, automatic annual.**

automatic bladder: *see* **bladder, automatic.**

automatic coding: *see* **coding, automatic.**

automatic computer: *see* **computer, automatic.**

automatic data processing: *see* **data processing, automatic.**

automatic data processing system: *see* **data processing system, automatic.**

automatic light control: *see* **light control, automatic.**

automatic promotion: *syn.* **promotion, continuous.**

automatic test pacing: *see* **pacing, automatic test.**

automatic typewriter: *see* **typewriter, automatic.**

automatic writing: *see* **writing, automatic.**

automaticity: a state of apparent automatic behavior; frequently observed in convulsive disorders (epileptic equivalent states or psychomotor spells) due to damage of the temporal lobe.

automation: the process of getting work performed without any human effort except that of instructing one or more machines what to do and when to do it.

automation, library: application of computers and other electronic and related processing equipment to information storage and retrieval problems of libraries and information centers.

automatism (â·tom′ə·tiz′m): automatic performance of the various acts involved in the use of language, such as understanding a foreign language without a thought of translation, or automatic recall of appropriate terms in speaking or writing.

automatization: the process by which an act becomes so habitual and routine that it is performed without any conscious thought or mental effort.

automonitor: (1) *v.* to make an automatic computer control its own data-processing operation; (2) *n.* a program or routine for this purpose, such as a *trace routine* or an *executive routine.*

automotives: the study of the operating principles, design, construction, maintenance, and repair of automobiles and other internal combustion engines, including the development of understandings of the applied physical and chemical principles.

autonomic nervous sytem: *see* **nervous system, autonomic.**

autonomy: (1) in general, self-regulation; more narrowly, self-regulation of that part of a larger whole which has some relatively independent functions; (2) freedom to act without external control, for example, local control in education as opposed to Federal control; commonly employed in opposition to *heteronomy,* subjection to external authority; *syn.* **local control.**

autonomy of school district: (1) the area of control granted to a school district or its officials through either expressed or implied authority of the state; (2) the power of the authorities of a school district to make decisions concerning those educational matters not governed by the constitutional, legislative, executive, or judicial provisions of the state. *Syn.* **local control.**

autoplastic experience of form: *see* **experience of form, autoplastic.**

autopsyche (â'tō·sī'kē): one's own mind or "inner self."

autorivalry: *syn.* **autocompetition.**

autotelic trait: *see* **trait, autotelic.**

autotutor: a self-scoring device developed by Pressey; a face plate containing holes through which students punch answer sheets; the term *punchboard* is sometimes used to describe this device.

auxiliary agencies: (1) a financial-accounting classification that includes those activities carried on by the school which, while sometimes similar to actual instruction, are distinctly social in nature and are not classified as instructional or coordinate activities; usually includes all costs of public libraries paid by the school, transportation of children, free lunches for children, community activities, school gardens, playgrounds, and costs of school banks; (2) (higher ed.) *syn.* **auxiliary enterprises and activities.**

auxiliary class: *see* **class, auxiliary.**

auxiliary enterprises and activities: enterprises and activities of a business character, operated for the service of students and faculty members, that are not directly related to the educational functions of an institution, for example, residence halls, dining halls, student hospitals, student unions, and bookstores.

auxiliary personnel: *see* **personnel, auxiliary.**

auxiliary services: a financial-accounting classification used by some schools to include both *auxiliary agencies* and *coordinate activities.*

auxiliary services counseling: *see* **counseling, auxiliary services.**

auxiliary storage: *see* **storage, auxiliary.**

auxiliary teacher: *see* **teacher aide.**

available time: *see* **up time.**

avant-gardism (a·vänt·gar'diz·m): a term used to designate the emergence and development of new, often bold, controversial theories, ideas, institutions, etc.

avant-gardists (a·vänt·gärd'ɔsts): (1) those especially in the arts who create, produce, or apply new, original, or experimental ideas and techniques; a group that seems extremist, or bizarre, by traditional or commonly accepted standards; (2) in mid-twentieth century, the "in" group artists enjoying popularity in the current art business world.

average: (1) a generic term variously used to designate such measures of central tendency as the arithmetic mean, median, and mode; (2) loosely, the arithmetic mean; (3) of behavior, typical or ordinary.

average ability: *see* **ability, average.**

average-ability group: *see* **group, average-ability.**

average, abstract: an average that may be used as a substitute for each of the individual values in a series of distributions for purposes of future computations; an average that, when substituted for the individual values, will give the same result in a computation. *Syn.* **substitutional average;** *dist. f.* **average, typical.**

average, accumulative: *syn.* **average, grade point.**

average age of pupils: *see* **age of pupils, average.**

average annual percent of attendance: *see* **attendance, average annual per cent of.**

average, arithmetic: *syn.* **mean, arithmetic.**

average, calculated: an average mathematically determined and dependent on the magnitude of all observations in the series; any measure of central tendency except a position average. *Contr. w.* **average, position.**

average, class: a measure of central tendency, usually the mean, for a class of pupils on some test or measure; commonly used in determining the direction and degree of individual pupil deviation from the group mean for assigning marks or for other purposes. *See* **average, grade.**

average, concrete: *syn.* **average, typical.**

average, cumulative: *syn.* **average, grade point.**

average daily absence: *see* **absence, average daily.**

average daily attendance: *see* **attendance, average daily.**

average daily enrollment: *syn.* **membership, average daily.**

average daily membership: *syn.* **membership, average daily.**

average daily register: *see* **register, average daily.**

average departure: *syn.* **deviation, average.**

average deviation: *see* **deviation, average.**

average enrollment: *see* **enrollment, average.**

average error: *syn.* **deviation, average.**

average, geometric: *syn.* **mean, geometric.**

average, grade: a measure of central tendency, usually the mean, for a grade group of pupils on some test or measure; commonly used in determining the direction and degree of individual pupil deviation from the grade mean for assigning marks or for other purposes. *See* **average, class.**

average, grade point: a measure of average scholastic success in all school subjects taken by a student during a certain term or semester, or accumulated for several terms or semesters; obtained by dividing grade points by hours of course work taken, when course marks are weighted by some such system as the following to obtain grade points: A-40, B-30, C-20, D-10, F-0; most commonly used at the college level. *Syn.* **accumulative average; cumulative average; grade-point ratio; quality point average.**

average, guessed (GA): an arbitrary origin taken at some point in a frequency distribution (usually, but not necessarily, near the middle) in order to facilitate the computation of the arithmetic mean or other statistics. *Syn.* **assumed mean; guessed mean; working mean;** *see* **origin, arbitrary.**

average, harmonic: *syn.* **mean, harmonic.**

average intelligence: *see* **intelligence, average.**

average, logarithmic: *syn.* **mean, geometric.**

average mark: *see* **mark, average.**

average membership: *see* **membership, average daily.**

average, modal: *syn.* **mode (4).**

average number belonging: *syn.* **membership, average daily.**

average number of children per attendance area: the total number of children of school age in an administrative unit divided by the number of attendance areas within the administrative unit. *See* **attendance unit** (1).

average number of children per local basic administrative unit: the total number of children of school age in a given state (or intermediate unit) divided by the number of local basic administrative units within the state (or intermediate unit).

average number of pupils served lunch per day: the total number of pupils served lunch during a given reporting period divided by the number of days during which lunch was served.

average operation time: *see* **operation time, average.**

average, position: any measure of central tendency that is determined by its location at a certain position in a definite arrangement or array of the observations, for example, the median and mode. *Contr. w.* **average, calculated.**

average, quality point: *syn.* **average, grade point.**

average range: *see* **range, average.**

average rank: *see* **rank, average.**

average sample number (ASN): a term used in sequential analysis to describe the mean number of observations that must be made before making a decision to accept or reject a hypothesis with prestated risks of alpha and beta error.

average score: *see* **score, average.**

average, substitutional: *syn.* **average, abstract.**

average transportation cost per pupil transported: *see* **transportation cost per pupil transported, average.**

average, typical: an average that characterizes or typifies the variable. *Syn.* **concrete average;** *dist. f.* **average, abstract.**

average, unweighted arithmetic: *syn.* **mean, unweighted arithmetic.**

average use of classrooms: (1) the ratio of the number of classrooms used to the total number of classrooms available for all periods of a day or week; (2) the ratio of hours of use of classroom stations (seats) to total classroom station-hours available; usually expressed in terms of percent of use. *See* **capacity; utilization, percent of; utilization of classrooms.**

average use of laboratories: (1) the ratio of the number of laboratories used to the total number of laboratories available for use for all periods of a day or week; (2) the ratio of hours of use of laboratory stations (tables or desks) to total laboratory station-hours available; usually expressed in terms of percent of use.

average variation: *syn.* **deviation, average.**

average, weighted arithmetic: *syn.* **mean, weighted arithmetic (1).**

averages, law of: *see* **law of averages.**

averment: (law) a positive statement of facts, as opposed to an argumentative or inferential one.

aversion: (1) a negative attitude; (2) a turning away from some person, situation, or thing, typically with dislike or unpleasant feeling. *Contr. w.* **appetite; interest.**

aversion therapy: *see* **therapy, aversion.**

aversive stimulus: *see* **stimulus, aversive.**

aviation: the art of operating heavier-than-air aircraft.

aviation cadet: *see* **cadet, aviation.**

aviation education: (1) a curriculum, educational program, or subject encompassing a study of the various aspects of aeronautical science and air travel and their significance to modern everyday life; (2) that branch of general education concerned with communicating knowledge, skills, and attitudes about aviation and its impact upon society.

aviation training: *see* **air training command; naval aviation school.**

avionics: a field of applied research in which electronic devices are adapted to use in aeronautics and astronautics. *See* **astrionics.**

avocation: a leisure-time activity, pursued consistently for recreation in the areas of crafts, sports, music, etc.; contributes to personal enrichment and may also be used for therapy values; considered increasingly important as social progress tends to give workers more leisure time. *Syn.* **hobby.**

avocational interests: *see* **interests, avocational.**

avoidance–avoidance conflict: *see* **conflict, avoidance–avoidance.**

avoidance conditioning: *see* **conditioning, avoidance.**

avoidance reaction: *see* **reaction, avoidance.**

award: a device used to stimulate, reinforce, or reward initiative; may be verbal or material.

award: (phys. ed.) a prize, usually a sweater, letter, or medal, given a school athlete in recognition of team membership.

award, student: the award to a student of a medal, letter, ribbon, certificate, pin, or public recognition as acknowledgment of achievement or demonstrated qualities of character.

awards, Caldecott: awards offered yearly to the illustrators of children's books for excellence.

awards, Newbery medal: awards offered annually to the authors of children's books for excellence in plot, style, and content.

awareness: the act of having or showing realization, perception, or knowledge. *See* **consciousness.**

awareness, auditory: the capacity of the organism to process information on both a receiving and a sending basis from the world of sound and to attach appropriate labels and attribute appropriate relationships to the world of sound.

awareness, body: the capacity of the organism to achieve a conscious appreciation of the relationship of all body segments to movement, and the ability to label body parts and to appreciate the functional properties of various body parts.

awareness, critical: in creative activity, controlled imaginative activity, such as is typical for adults; more detailed and more determined interpretation of the self or strongly visual observation on the conscious level.

awareness, kinesthetic: cognizance of the sense by which muscular motion, position, or weight are perceived. *See* **kinesthesia; perception, kinesthetic.**

awareness, nonverbal: with reference to discovery learning, the ability of the learner to apply a principle or generalization correctly without necessarily being able to state that generalization.

awareness, olfactory: identification of the existence of distinct odors.

awareness, spatial: a movigenic term which indicates the capacity of the organism to identify his own position in space relative to his surroundings with constant orientation to surface, elevation, periphery, back, and front.

awareness, tactile: *see* **perception, tactile.**

axes, orthogonal: two or more axes passing through the same point and so related that each axis is perpendicular to all the remaining axes.

axiology: the study of the nature and standard(s) of value and evaluation; one of the six major branches of philosophy.

axiom: (1) a generally accepted principle or rule used as a basis for reasoning; *syn.* **assumption;** (2) (math.) *syn.* **postulate.**

axiomatic: pertaining to propositions possessing the nature of an axiom; referring to that which is self-evident or a universally accepted truth taken for granted as the basis for reasoning. *Syn.* **aphoristic.**

axiomatic thinking: *see* **reasoning, axiomatic.**

axis: *syn.* **axis, coordinate.**

axis, coordinate: *see* **coordinate system.**

axon: the nerve-cell process or long slender extension which transmits impulses from the cell body toward the next nerve cell.

axonometric chart: *see* **chart, axonometric.**

B-box: *see* **B-register.**

B coefficient: the coefficient of belonging; the ratio of the average intercorrelations of the variables in a cluster to their average correlation with variables not in the cluster; thus, a B coefficient of 1.00 indicates that the variables in the cluster correlate no more highly among themselves than they do with the variables outside the cluster. *See* **coefficient, beta regression.**

B-line: *see* **B-register.**

B-register: in data processing by automatic computer, a control-unit counter that facilitates instruction modification; also known as *index register, B-box, B-line, base register.*

B-score: a type of grade score named in tribute to Binet and Buckingham. *See* **score, grade.**

babble-luck theory: a theory of original language development which postulates that primitive babbling accidentally produced sounds that could be repeated by another and hence led to first communication.

babble stage: a stage in language development in infants characterized by the repetition of monosyllabic sounds; the circular-reflex stage of repetition.

babbling: (1) the language activity characteristic of the *babble stage;* (2) a type of speech therapy in which the patient is encouraged to produce meaningless sounds until he produces correctly a certain sound previously produced incorrectly, this new sound then being used as the basis for further corrective instruction.

Babinski reflex: *see* **reflex, Babinski.**

Babinski sign: *syn.* **reflex, Babinski.**

baby biography: *see* **biography, baby.**

baby talk: defective speech characterized by incorrect sound production imitating or carried over from infant speech, taking the form principally of substitutions of one sound for another, as in *pway* for *play* or *witta* for *little;* may also involve sound omissions and distortions and infantile inflectional patterns.

baccalaureate degree: *syn.* **degree, bachelor's.**

baccalaureate sermon: a sermon preached for a graduating class as a part of commencement activities; used properly only in connection with the graduation exercises of institutions of higher education, but popularly used also in reference to the graduation ceremonies of secondary schools.

bachelor of arts: the degree conferred by institutions of higher education for the completion of a 4-year curriculum in liberal arts, originally with emphasis on the humanities but more recently without regard to the special field of emphasis.

bachelor of arts in education (B.A. in Ed.): a degree approximately equivalent to *bachelor of science in education,* usually conferred upon graduates of teacher-education curricula.

bachelor of divinity: *see* **degree, bachelor's (2).**

bachelor of education (Ed. B.): a degree conferred at the completion of a 4-year program of studies in a teacher-training institution. *See* **bachelor of science in education.**

bachelor of laws (LL.B.): *see* **degree, bachelor's (2).**

bachelor of music: a degree conferred by institutions of higher education for the completion of a 4-year curriculum with emphasis on the composition or performance of music.

bachelor of nursing (B.N.): *see* **nursing school.**

bachelor of science: the degree conferred by institutions of higher education for the completion of a 4-year curriculum with emphasis on science or for the completion of a 4-year curriculum in certain technical or professional fields.

bachelor of science in education (B.S. in Ed.): the degree conferred at the completion of a 4-year program of studies in a teacher-training institution; has tended to come into prominence because of widespread adoption, since 1900, as the baccalaureate degree by normal schools as they developed into teachers' colleges; also frequently used by universities to distinguish the baccalaureate degree awarded students in the university college of education from baccalaureate degrees awarded students in other colleges and schools in the university.

bachelor of science in nursing (B.S.N.): *see* **nursing school.**

bachelor's degree: *see* **degree, bachelor's.**

back-and-leg dynamometer: *see* **dynamometer, back-and-leg.**

backboard: the wood or glass surface, 4 by 6 feet in size, on which a basketball goal is fastened.

background, cultural: *see* **cultural background.**

background, experiential: *see* **experiential background.**

background, meaning: *see* **meaning background.**

background music: *see* **music, background.**

background, socioeconomic: *see* **socioeconomic background.**

backhand writing: *see* **writing, backhand.**

backward branching: *see* **branching, backward.**

backward buildup: (for. lang. teaching) a technique for teaching utterance of more than six or seven segments; breaking them from the end into small, logical segments helps teachers and children maintain the appropriate intonation; each segment is modeled by the teacher and repeated by the students; after the individual segments are learned, the entire utterance is repeated.

backward child: *see* **child, backward.**

backward pupil: *see* **pupil, backward.**

Baconian method: a method of research based on the work of Sir Francis Bacon (1561-1626), which emphasizes objective study and proceeds from observation and classification of particular and individual cases to the formulation of general conclusions; omits any function of *hypothesis* as a guide for the selection of particulars to be observed.

badminton: a game played by two to four players on a court 20 by 44 feet, in which a bird or shuttlecock is batted with rackets back and forth between players over a net.

balance: (1) stability or equilibrium maintained through proper distribution of elements; may be physical, as in balancing the human body, emotional, as contributing to poise, aesthetic, consisting in a pleasing integration of the elements of a work of art, etc.; (2) the difference between the two sides of an account; sometimes used on the balance sheet to refer to the credit balance of such funds as restricted current funds, unexpended plant funds, and agency funds; (3) (audiovis. ed.) the proper relationship between high and low frequency levels of an audio signal.

balance board: a device consisting of a narrow, slightly elevated, horizontal rail (about 2½ inches wide, 6 inches high, and 9 feet long) used for testing and training young children in maintaining equilibrium.

balance, dynamic: the capacity of the organism to activate antigravity muscles in proper relationship to one another against the force of gravitational pull to maintain alignment, sustain a transport pattern, and aid in recovery.

balance, eye-muscle: *see* **eye-muscle balance.**

balance-of-stores record: *see* **record, balance-of-stores.**

balance, operational: in supervision of instruction, balance in the utilization of a variety of behaviors and techniques so as to provide the kind of stimulation and direction of others through which the purposes of the instructional program can be achieved.

balance, racial: *see* **racial balance.**

balance, Rorschach experience: Rorschach's "Erlebnistypus"; in the Rorschach test, the ratio of the number of human movement responses to the sum of weighted numbers of three classes of color responses; hypothesized to reflect the individual's predominant mode of balancing his responding to his own inner promptings in contrast with outer stimulation.

balance sheet: a statement, ordinarily prepared from books kept by double entry, showing assets and other resources, liabilities and other obligations (debits), and surplus (credits) of a fund or governmental unit at a specified date after an actual or constructive closing of books.

balance sheet approach: a method of teaching the principles of bookkeeping and accounting by starting with consideration of the balance sheet, analyzing effects of various business transactions on it, and relating other steps in the bookkeeping cycle to it.

balance, static: the ability to maintain one's balance under unfavorable circumstances. *See* **equilibrium.**

balance, test of: *see* **test of balance.**

balanced grouping: *see* **grouping, balanced.**

balanced program: *see* **program, balanced.**

balanced reading program: *see* **program, balanced reading.**

balancing: (phys. ed.) the coordinated ability to maintain body position within a base of support.

balancing reaction: *see* **reaction, balancing.**

ball-and-chicken test: *see* **test, ball-and-chicken.**

ball-and-field test: *see* **test, ball-and-field.**

ballad: (1) simple narrative told in simple verse; (2) in music, an uncomplicated, lyric melody and a relatively straightforward harmonic setting.

ballet: an art form using dancing in which conventional poses and steps are combined with light, flowing figures and movements to convey a story, theme, or atmosphere.

ballet, water: *see* **swimming, synchronized.**

ballistic movement: *see* **movement, ballistic.**

ballot: (1) a piece of paper or other object used in voting; (2) the total number of votes cast; (3) method of voting by paper slips or other objects or by voting machines; (4) to vote or decide by using ballots.

band: (1) an instrumental ensemble performing chiefly or entirely on wind and percussion instruments; (2) in computers, a group of tracks, usually on a drum, used to store characters in serial fashion; the bits constituting one character are stored in parallel, one track for each bit; *see* **bit.**

band chart: *see* **chart, band.**

band, confidence: *see* **region, acceptance.**

band, percentile: *see* **percentile band.**

band, rhythm: *see* **rhythm band.**

band, school: an ensemble of wind and percussion instruments organized in educational institutions for (*a*) the training of young musicians and (*b*) for the social, recreational, and utilitarian needs of the institution.

bandstration: the scoring of a musical composition for performance by a wind band; a term, not yet widely accepted, coined on the analogy of *orchestration.*

bandwidth: in testing, the amount or complexity of information one tries to obtain in a given space or time; the classical psychometric ideal is the instrument with high fidelity and low bandwidth; for example, a college aptitude test tries to bring the answer to just one question with great accuracy.

bank, data: *see* **data bank.**

banking: an area of study of college grade that deals with the principles governing the management of public and private banks; frequently combined with the study of money in a subject called *money and banking.*

baptismal certificate: *see* **certificate, baptismal.**

baptismal record: *see* **record, baptismal.**

bar chart: *syn.* **graph, bar.**

bar diagram: *syn.* **graph, bar.**

bar diagram, hundred percent: *see* **diagram, hundred percent bar.**

bar graph: *see* **graph, bar.**

bar graph, pictorial: *see* **graph, pictorial bar.**

bar mitzvah (bär mits′va): *n. masc.* (Aramaic-Heb., lit., "a son of commandment") (1) a boy who has reached his thirteenth birthday when, in accordance with Jewish tradition, he becomes responsible for the observance of the precepts of Judaism; (2) the religious ceremony for boys who have attained the age of 13.

bar mitzvah requirements: educational requirements set up by Jewish schools, synagogues, and/or communities, to be met by boys before attaining the age of 13 in order to qualify for the *bar mitzvah* ceremony to be performed in the synagogue at a public service. *See* **bar mitzvah.**

barber school: an institution for the training of individuals for the vocation of cutting and dressing hair, shaving and trimming beards, and performing related services.

baritone: a male voice intermediate in range and quality between bass and tenor, usually from A flat, a tenth below middle C, to the G immediately above middle C.

baroque art: *see* **art, baroque.**

barring of teacher: the act of preventing a teacher's participation in educational activities (*a*) by enforcing certification standards for teaching or (*b*) by revoking a certificate for legal cause.

Bartlett test: *see* **test, Bartlett.**

barylalia (bar·i·lā′li·ə): thickness of speech.

bas-relief (bä′rə·lēf′): low relief; a kind of sculpture in which forms are only slightly raised from the flat background.

basal age: *see* **age, basal.**

basal metabolic rate (BMR): *see* **metabolism, basal.**

basal metabolism: *see* **metabolism, basal.**

basal reader: *see* **reader, basal.**

basal-reader approach: *see* **approach, basal-reader.**

basal-reader materials: textbooks, charts, cards, workbooks, manuals, seatwork materials, and tests used in teaching the basal reading skills to children.

basal reading: *see* **reading, basal.**

basal reading level: *see* **reading level, basal.**

basal reading program: *see* **program, basal reading.**

basal reading series: *see* **reading series, basal.**

basal study skills: *see* **study skills, basal.**

basal techniques: techniques that are fundamental in reading, such as word-recognition techniques, comprehension techniques, etc.

base: (stat.) an origin of reference value entering into ratio comparisons; (*a*) in percent, the base is the value that would be assigned 100 percent and is therefore the denominator of the ratio (note that this usage is different from that of interest problems); (*b*) in index numbers, the base is a value (statistic) calculated for a defined group of cases, usually representing a period of time (as one or several years) or a selected geographical area (such as a state, county, or city), and such a value is used as the principal reference point, normally having an index value of 100. (Loosely, the time period or area specified is itself spoken of as the base.)

base line: (art ed.) space symbol appearing in children's drawings around the ages of 7 to 9 years, having its origin in the kinesthetic experience of moving along a line; an indication of the child's conscious relation with his environment, since he relates all things standing on the ground to this symbol.

base, numeration: in a numeration system having place value, the number of units which are grouped together to form the next place; for example, in the conventional decimal system of numeration, 10 is the base, since the grouping is always by 10s. *Syn.* **radix;** *see* **binary system.**

base rate: (meas.) (1) the proportion of persons who succeed prior to the use of a test; represents the proportion of correct decisions which are made when selecting individuals, without the use of the particular test under evaluation; (2) diagnostic and prognostic statements made with a high degree of accuracy purely on the basis of actuarial and/or experience tables; a psychometric device, to be efficient, must make possible a greater number of correct decisions than could be made in terms of the base rates alone. *See* **sign, psychometric; validity, incremental.**

base rate of pay: *see* **pay, base rate of.**

base register: *see* **B-register.**

base, retirement: *see* **retirement base.**

base, training: *see* **training base.**

base year: *see* **age, basal.**

baseball: a game played with a wooden bat and a hard ball by two teams, properly of nine players each, one team being at bat and the other in the field, alternately, for a minimum of nine innings; the game is played on a field having four bases marking the course each player must take in scoring a run.

baseball, little league: a commercially sponsored, out-of-school sport program in which interleague competitive baseball games are organized for teams of boys 9 through 12 years of age; also occasionally called *knothole league baseball.*

basement: the story of a building below the first or main story; usually partly below the ground surface.

bashfulness: an attitude or mental set characterized by the partial or complete inhibition of social responses, especially in the presence of strangers; frequently accompanied by blushing, uncoordinated movements of the body, stammering, etc.; not necessarily a manifestation of emotional disturbance.

basic ability: *see* **ability, basic.**

basic administrative unit: *see* **administrative unit, basic.**

basic airman: *see* **airman, basic.**

basic assets: *see* **assets, basic.**

basic blend vocabulary: *see* **vocabulary, basic blend.**

basic business course: *see* **business education, basic.**

basic business education: *see* **business education, basic.**

basic cadet: *see* **cadet, basic.**

basic combat training: *see* **training, basic combat.**

basic course: *see* **course, basic.**

basic education: (1) (adult ed.) *see* **adult basic education;** (2) *see* **program, common-learnings** (2).

basic education, adult: *see* **adult basic education.**

Basic English: *see* **word list, basic.**

basic flying training: *see* **training, basic flying.**

basic intelligence: *see* **intelligence, basic.**

basic language: *see* **language, basic.**

basic mathematics: *syn.* **mathematics, general.**

basic military course: *see* **military course, basic.**

basic military training: *see* **training, basic military.**

basic motive: *see* **motive, basic.**

basic motor skills: *syn.* **movement, fundamental.**

basic movement: *syn.* **movement, fundamental.**

basic needs: *see* **needs, basic.**

basic occupational outline: a list of topics that must be covered in order to give a satisfactory description of an occupation.

basic personality structure: *see* **structure, basic personality.**

basic pilot training: *see* **training, basic pilot.**

basic program: (school finance) the cost of education of resident pupils in grades preprimary through 12 in average daily membership for the reference year as determined by the mandated program level.

basic reader: *see* **reader, basal.**

basic reading: *see* **reading, basic.**

basic reading vocabulary: *see* **vocabulary, basic reading.**

basic research: *see* **research, basic.**

basic science: *see* **science, basic.**

basic sight vocabulary: *see* **vocabulary, basic sight.**

basic skill: *syn.* **skill, fundamental.**

basic-skills test: *see* **test, basic-skills.**

basic socialization course: *see* **program, common-learnings** (2).

basic spelling list: *see* **spelling list, basic.**

basic subject: *see* **subject, basic.**

basic subtraction facts: *see* **subtraction facts.**

basic test battery: *see* **battery, basic test.**

basic trainee: *see* **trainee, basic.**

basic training: *see* **training, basic.**

basic training school: (mil. ed.) a school that gives basic military training or basic training in any specialty.

basic vocabulary: *see* **vocabulary, basic.**

basic word list: *see* **word list, basic.**

basis, meal: *see* **meal basis.**

basis of apportionment: *see* **apportionment, basis of.**

basis of articulation: *see* **articulation, basis of.**

basis of matching: *see* **matching, basis of.**

basis of public education, moral: *see* **moral basis of public education.**

basis, yield: (school admin.) the price stated as a percentage of yield to be obtained if a bond is held to maturity.

basket system: a method of locker-room arrangement in which small baskets are used for the storage of individual gymnasium uniforms, while large lockers are provided to hold street clothes.

basket system, La Porte: a self-service system of storing gymnasium costumes so devised that attendants can pass behind the tiers of baskets and remove clothes for laundering.

basket-type locker: *see* **locker, basket-type.**

basketball: a game played by two teams, five or six players on each team, on a rectangular court having a raised basket or a goal at each end, points being scored by tossing the ball through the opponent's basket.

bass: the lowest male voice, having a range usually from about E, one octave and a sixth below middle C, to the E or F immediately above middle C.

bass-baritone: a male voice with the range of the baritone, but with a decidedly deeper and more powerful quality of tone, especially in the lower notes.

bat mitzvah (bät mits'vä): *n. fem.* (Heb., lit., "a daughter of commandment") (1) a girl who has reached her twelfth or thirteenth birthday; (2) the religious ceremony for girls who have reached their twelfth or thirteenth birthday— a recent innovation in line with the *bar mitzvah* ceremony for boys which is based on established Jewish religious tradition.

batch data processing: *see* **data processing, batch.**

batch job: *see* **job, batch.**

batch mode computing: *see* **computing, batch mode.**

batch mode computing, remote: *see* **computing, remote batch mode.**

bathophobia (bath'ō·fō'bi·ə): a condition characterized by morbid anxiety pertaining to depths or by a morbid fear of falling from an elevated position.

battered child: *see* **child, battered.**

battery: (law) an unlawful beating or other wrongful physical violence inflicted on another without his consent; the offer or attempt to commit a battery is always an *assault;* there can be an assault without a battery, but battery always includes assault; the two terms are usually used together.

battery, achievement: a group of achievement tests standardized on the same population and thus yielding comparable scores; frequently the tests are designed for measuring outcomes in most of the major instructional areas of specified grade levels; sometimes loosely applied to any group of tests administered to a given set of individuals, even though the tests were not standardized on the same population. *See* **measurement, multiple.**

battery, basic test: (mil. ed.) a series of tests given to all recruits to measure their intelligence, aptitudes, and potential skills.

battery, differential aptitude: a group of tests designed with the intention of showing an individual's relative chances of success in each of a variety of different activities; such batteries are usually developed with the assistance of *factor analysis.*

battery of tests: (1) a group of several tests intended to be administered in succession to the same subject or group of subjects; usually the tests are designed to accomplish a closely related set of measurement objectives; (2) a number of specially selected tests employed together to predict a single criterion. *See* **battery, achievement; measurement, multiple.**

battery plan: a teaching situation in a business machines course whereby a group of identical or very similar business machines are located in one classroom, thus allowing the instructor more time to teach the procedures and techniques.

batting cage: (1) a movable screen placed behind home plate to stop baseballs during batting practice; (2) a net or cage surrounding the batter so that though he may bat the ball hard, it is contained within a small area (usually indoors).

battledore: (lang. arts) a small folded cardboard with alphabets, reading lessons, and woodcut illustrations, used by children about 1750.

BCD code: *see* **code, binary coded decimal.**

Beacon reading method: *see* **reading method, Beacon.**

beaded screen: *see* **screen, beaded.**

bearer bond: *see* **bond, bearer.**

becoming: (1) a metaphysical term referring to any transition from potentiality to actuality, even if it is from nonexistence to existence; *change* is a mode of becoming, the transition from one positive state of being to another positive state; *contr. w.* **being;** (2) for Hegel, becoming is the third member of a triadic relation between *being* and *not-being* and expresses the truth of each as it enters a higher synthesis; *see* **dialectic, Hegelian;** (3) an existential concept in which self-actualization is viewed as a continuous, never-ending process which can be understood only by observing what a person is moving toward.

bed-wetting: *See* **enuresis.**

begging the question, fallacy of: *see* **fallacy of begging the question.**

beginning reader: *see* **reader, beginning.**

beginning reading: *see* **reading, beginning.**

beginning teacher: (1) any person in his first teaching position; (2) more specifically, a person who has completed a regular course, including practice teaching, in a teacher-training institution and is legally certified to teach, and who is just entering upon the work of his first teaching position.

behavior: the action or activities of an organism, that is, anything that an organism does, including overt, physical action, internal physiological and emotional processes, and implicit mental activity.

behavior, adaptive: originally, change in structure or behavior that has survival value; now, more generally, any beneficial changes to meet environmental demand; settling down to the conditions for work or learning, with the elimination of unnecessary preparatory behavior. *Syn.* **adaptation.**

behavior, adjustive: behavior achieved when in the satisfaction of his various needs a person's overt behavior results in the minimum of internal friction or feelings of guilt; the long-term view may also be contemplated.

behavior, adolescent: the characteristic types of behavior displayed by youth of ages from approximately 12 to 18 as regards play, dress, reading, sex relationships, intellectual interests, and the like.

behavior, aggressive: behavior characterized by vigorous efforts toward self-assertion over others, self-preservation against others, or self-advancement over others.

behavior analysis: *see* **analysis, behavior.**

behavior analysis, comparative: study of the various forms of behavior of different organisms in an effort to find parallelisms of sequence, form, or origin.

behavior, antisocial: *see* **antisocial.**

behavior, apopathetic: behavior that is not overtly directed toward others but is influenced or modified by their presence, for example, the behavior of a person "showing off" before others.

behavior, ascendant: a type of aggressive behavior, characterized by the desire to dominate a social situation.

behavior, atypical: behavior differing from that considered normal for or characteristic of a given group or class.

behavior, bell: a technique used in the observation of child behavior, according to which a bell is held near each ear of the child but out of his line of vision; one of the bells has no clapper, but both bells are moved or agitated simultaneously, the response being credited when the subject immediately turns toward the intact bell.

behavior center: an obsolete term for a school or organization of classes for socially or emotionally disturbed pupils.

behavior change: any observable alteration in physical activity which can be measured against a prior criterion of activity. *Comp. w.* **behavior modification.**

behavior, child: a term referring to the actions of the developing individual generally between 2 and 12 years of age.

behavior, civic: an individual or group act designed to perpetuate or advance community, state, or national affairs.

behavior, clay: the designation of an experimental technique used by Gesell, according to which the child is given clay to play with, his reactions and constructions providing a means of studying aesthetic behavior.

behavior clinic: *see* **clinic, behavior.**

behavior, collective: (1) cooperative behavior on the part of the members of a group as a result of such controls as a common danger, common attitudes, common purposes, or a common mood; (2) *syn* **group behavior.**

behavior, combining: behavior involved in bringing together or placing in functional contact such objects as cubes, pellets, and bottles or a cup and spoon; observed in the study of normative behavior of infants.

behavior, compulsory: pupil activities carried out because of pressure from teacher or other school or legal authorities and in accordance with the official rulings or policies of the school.

behavior contract: *see* **contract, behavior.**

behavior, criterion: a combination of responses and performances of individuals or groups designated as a standard against which other responses of individuals or groups are appraised or evaluated; often used in validating tests, inventories, and personnel procedures.

behavior, cup-and-cube: the designation of a technique used in determining the stage or degree of development in children of 1 to 3 years, according to which the child's proficiency in and method of extracting a wooden cube from a cup are observed and compared with age norms for that activity.

behavior, cup-and-spoon: the designation of a technique used in determining the stage or degree of development of very young children, according to which the child's proficiency in and method of eating with a spoon from a cup are observed and compared with age norms for that activity.

behavior-description record: *see* **record, behavior.**

behavior, disintegrative: actions that appear to be maladaptive, disorganized, and out of sequence and character for an individual, probably a consequence of strong disintegrative emotions such as intense fear or anger.

behavior disorder: *see* **disorder, behavior.**

behavior disorder, experimental: *syn.* **neurosis, experimental.**

behavior, dominance: behavior that operates to put the individual in the position of directing others or bending others to his will.

behavior, dominative: a way of responding to others that is characterized by absence of compromise, disregard for the desires of others, and a tendency to use force or threats to attain one's objectives.

behavior, draw-a-man: the designation of a technique used in measuring the stage of development (especially mental development) in young children, according to which the child is instructed to draw a picture of a man, the resulting drawing being then subjected to analysis for accuracy and detail in comparison with developmental norms.

behavior, emotional: that part of total behavior involving or caused by the individual's feelings; the nonvolitional, affective area of total behavior, which is determined principally by the functioning of the glands, the smooth muscles, and the autonomic nervous system and which powerfully influences the individual's overt behavior and mental processes.

behavior, enabling: the prerequisite skills and abilities needed to make the response on a test; these enable a pupil to make a response but are not meant to be critical factors in the measurement; for example, the most important enabling behavior in objective testing is reading skill.

behavior, entry: in programmed learning, the level of knowledge and experience that the learner brings to the task. *Syn.* **readiness.**

behavior, group: (1) conduct or reactions of an aggregate; (2) the activity of a number of individuals reacting together; (3) the behavior of a person as affected by a number of individuals acting as a whole.

behavior, human: manifest action in terms of muscular movements and glandular secretions or in terms of detectable chemical, electrical, and physical change within the organism.

behavior, implicit: the internal responses of an organism, including not only the secretions of glands, circulatory and respiratory changes, peristaltic movements, etc., but also such categories as language habits, imagery, and thinking.

behavior, individual choice: (couns.) action initiated by an individual following a study of alternatives.

behavior, infant: actions of babies between 2 weeks and 2 years of age.

behavior, infantile: (1) in general, behavior similar to that of an infant, regardless of the age of the person so acting; (2) (psychoan.) a regression to modes of behavior characteristic of the young child, or the fixation and retention by the subject of modes of behavior characteristic of the young child.

behavior, integrative: a type of behavior in which the individual's various conscious purposes are harmoniously working together.

behavior journal: *see* **journal, behavior.**

behavior journal, anecdotal: *see* **journal, anecdotal behavior.**

behavior, learned: activity that results largely from training. *See* **conditioning; habit; learning.**

behavior, maladaptive: a pattern of behavior which does not lead to the satisfactions one desires.

behavior management: *see* **behavior modification.**

behavior, matched-dependent: similar predicted performances or achievements frequently used in study designs where equivalent results are often traced to different predictive factors.

behavior, maternal: those responses involved in caring for the young such as nursing, protecting, and training.

behavior model: *see* **model, behavior.**

behavior modification: techniques for dealing with maladaptive behavior either through *classical conditioning* (for example, avoiding anxiety in a specified situation by conditioning a response incompatible with anxiety) or through *operant conditioning* (as by arranging and managing reinforcement contingencies so that desired behaviors are increased in frequency and maintained and undesired

behaviors are decreased in frequency and/or removed) when used with the nonfunctioning or disruptive school child, behavior changes are measurable by continuous assessment and graphic means; *behavior management,* though using many of the same techniques, is a less precise method.

behavior, molar: the approach to behavior study which is concerned with the individual as a whole. *See* **behaviorism, molar;** *contr. w.* **behavior, molecular.**

behavior, molecular: the study of behavior whereby single acts, traits, or events are studied. *See* **behaviorism, molecular;** *contr. w.* **behavior, molar.**

behavior, moral: (1) behavior to which the terms right, wrong, good, or bad can be legitimately applied; opposed to amoral behavior; (2) behavior to which only positive moral terms, right or good, can be legitimately applied; opposed to *immoral* behavior. *See* **amoral; moral.**

behavior, negative: the activity of rejecting, disapproving, or avoiding some person, situation, or thing. *See* **abient;** *contr. w.* **behavior, positive.**

behavior norm: *see* **norm, behavior.**

behavior, normal: the way in which an organism acts, thinks, or feels which is consistent with a norm or standard set to promote the society in which he lives.

behavior, obsessional: conduct resulting from an idea that persists in consciousness in spite of efforts to banish it.

behavior, operant: behavior for which the specific eliciting stimulus is not determined, for which there is no observed antecedent, or which cannot be described adequately in terms of the simple stimulus-response formula. *Contr. w.* **behavior, respondent.**

behavior, overt: a general term for the observable, external responses of an organism.

behavior, paper-and-crayon: the designation of a technique used in determining the stage or degree of development in infants and young children, according to which the child's proficiency in and method of handling paper and crayon are observed and compared with age norms for that activity.

behavior, paper-folding: the designation of a technique for measuring the intelligence of young children, according to which the child's proficiency in folding a piece of paper in a stipulated way is observed and compared with developmental norms; used as a test item in some tests of intelligence, such as the Kuhlmann-Binet and the Ontario.

behavior, parental: maternal and paternal behavior concerned with the rearing, care, and protection of the young.

behavior pattern: a constellation of responses that possess intrinsic unity; since these responses are largely automatic and result from deep psychological needs, the individual has little conscious control over them.

behavior pattern, integration of: *see* **integration of behavior pattern.**

behavior, patterning of: exercises and guided bodily movements such as crawling and alternate flexion of leg and arm used as a general remedial activity for children with developmental or learning disabilities on the assumption that such children somehow missed various motor learnings in infancy.

behavior, pellet-and-bottle: the designation of a technique used in determining the stage or degree of development in infants, according to which the child's proficiency in and method of dropping a pellet into a bottle are observed and compared with age norms for that activity.

behavior, perceptual-motor: the total activity of the child in which input (sensory or perceptual) is directly related to output (motor or muscular control); also called perceptual-movement behavior.

behavior, positive: the activity of accepting, approving, or moving toward some person, situation, or thing. *See* **adient;** *contr. w.* **behavior, negative.**

behavior, prehensory: the flexion of palm and fingers or the flexion and opposition of thumb and fingers upon contact with objects. *See* **prehension; prehension, pellet; prehension, pincer.**

behavior, prenatal: the reactions and movements of the fetus within the uterus.

behavior, problem: (1) behavior that is disapproved of by dominant social groups; (2) behavior that is perceived as being actually or potentially damaging to the individual or group, whether physically, mentally, or socially; (3) antisocial behavior which does not yield to outside pressure or change to acceptable behavior.

behavior problem: *see* problem, behavior.

behavior, problem-solving: the process of selecting from a number of alternatives those that lead to a desired goal.

behavior, prone: postural and locomotor sequences in the behavior of the young infant when placed in the face-downward position.

behavior rating: *see* rating, behavior.

behavior, reading: anything that the organism does when engaged in the act of reading; may be physical, mental, or emotional; believed to be very complex, since reading is a complex rather than a simple process.

behavior record: *see* record, behavior.

behavior, resistant: (1) behavior in an opposite direction from that of an applied force; may be physical or mental; (2) (psychoan.) behavior revealing opposition in bringing material from the unconscious into the conscious.

behavior, respondent: behavior elicited by a known external unconditioned stimulus over which the organism has little or no control, as contrasted with *operant behavior*, which is emitted. *See* conditioning, operant.

behavior science: *see* science, behavioral.

behavior segment: the smallest unit convenient or appropriate for characterizing or describing the reaction of an individual to a stimulus or a pattern of stimuli.

behavior sequence: *see* sequence, behavior.

behavior, sex: acts of an individual or group in relation to sexual matters.

behavior, shaping: the process by which a target response or series of responses is developed through the use of strategically placed reinforcers; a term used primarily by those who identify themselves with B. F. Skinner's *operant conditioning.*

behavior, social: (1) the actions of the individual as a member of society; (2) group action; (3) behavior approved by culturally dominant groups of society.

behavior, spontaneous: action that comes about without any known or observable external stimuli.

behavior, stereotypic: *see* blindism.

behavior, substitute: reaction patterns that result in satisfaction in the place of thwarted or inhibited reactions; compensatory acts.

behavior, supervisory: *see* supervisory behavior.

behavior, supine: developmental sequences in the postural and manipulative responses of the young infant when placed on its back.

behavior survey: *see* survey, behavior.

behavior, terminal: (1) in programmed instruction, the behavior the student is expected to have acquired at the end of a program or programmed sequence; evidence that such behavior has indeed been acquired is provided by successful responses to *terminal items* and/or by performance on a *criterion test;* (2) in general, the behavior desired of a student when he completes a course of instruction or a major segment thereof; a special concern of any instructional system.

behavior-theoretical counseling: *see* counseling, behavior-theoretical.

behavior theory: a view which regards human behavior as primarily rooted in the experiential history of the organism, as having been learned, and as susceptible to modification by psychological means; emphasis is on the nature of the learning processes that underlie behavioral change, and these processes are regarded as essentially identical to those involved in any other kind of complex human learning.

behavior therapy: *see* therapy, behavior.

behavior trait: *see* trait, behavior.

behavior unit: an integrated response of an organism as a whole to a complex stimulus pattern or to one detail of the pattern in relation to other details.

behavior, unlearned: any behavior form that accrues as a result of the development, differentiation, and redifferentiation of body structure independently of any learning or training.

behavior, withdrawn: (1) behavior that operates to separate the individual from contact with others; (2) behavior that operates to separate the individual, mentally at least, from the realities of the world. *See* autism.

behavioral attitude: *see* attitude.

behavioral counseling: *see* counseling, behavioral.

behavioral objectives: *see* objectives, behavioral.

behavioral processes of structure: *see* structure, behavioral processes of.

behavioral theory in counseling: a counseling approach emphasizing the fact that most human behavior is learned and consequently is modifiable by manipulation and creation of learning conditions; the counseling process becomes the judicious and expert arrangement of learning or relearning experiences. *See* behavior theory.

behaviorism: a systematic approach to, or school of psychology, which regards objective, observable manifestations such as motor and glandular responses as the key to an understanding of human behavior; consciousness, feeling, and other subjective phenomena are rejected as unnecessary; places much reliance on the study of behavior of animals under controlled conditions; originated with the work of M. F. Meyer, A. P. Weiss, and J. B. Watson during the first two decades of the present century; the most widely known contemporary exponent is B. F. Skinner.

behaviorism, molar: the variety of behaviorism that holds that behavior is emergent and cannot be deduced from muscle twitches and glandular secretions. *Contr. w.* behaviorism, molecular.

behaviorism, molecular: the variety of behaviorism that holds that behavior is completely described in terms of muscle twitches, glandular secretions, and the stimuli that bring them about. *Contr. w.* behaviorism, molar.

Behrens-Fisher test: *see* test, Behrens-Fisher.

being: (1) that which exists or can exist in any way whatsoever; at one extreme (negatively), being is whatever is not nothing; at the other extreme (positively), being is existence in its most complete and perfect form, the *ens realissimum* or absolute; in *realism*, being is an analogous, not a univocal, concept; hence, it is not an ultimate genus and cannot be defined in the ordinary manner; (2) for Hegel, being is a genus so empty as to be almost equivalent to nothing. *See* becoming.

bel: a unit for expressing the ratio of two values of power, the number of bels being the logarithm to the base 10 of the power ratio.

belief: (1) the acceptance of a proposition as true or of a situation or object as actually existent; (2) (relig.) a proposition which is accepted as true but which, even though not contradictory to reason, cannot be substantiated by reason; (3) the object of belief, or the thing believed in; (4) escape from doubt to the settlement of opinion, not an individual matter only but one that occurs in a community.

belief, reconstruction of: *see* reconstruction of belief.

bell behavior: *see* behavior, bell.

bell-shaped curve: *see* curve, bell-shaped.

belles-lettres (bel'le'trə): (Fr., lit., "beautiful letters") a term used to designate the more artistic, classical, and imaginative forms of literature.

belonging: *syn.* belongingness.

belonging, law of: *see* law of belonging.

belongingness: (1) a sense of security an individual has as a result of being a member of a chosen peer group; *syn.* belonging; (2) (Thorndike) a law of connectionism probably deriving from principles of associative shifting to the effect that we associate many items simply because they occur together, hence come to belong together, as, for example, Abraham Lincoln and Gettysburg; *see* associative shifting; connectionism.

below average child: *see* **pupil, slow.**

below par: below the normal level of health.

belt, confidence: *syn.* **region, acceptance.**

belt graph: *syn.* **chart, band.**

bench trainer: *see* **trainer, bench.**

benchwork: (ind. arts) various types of handwork operations such as filing, assembling, and adjusting, usually performed at a worktable or bench.

beneficiary: a recipient of benefits, such as those received under retirement programs, wills, and trusts, consistent with statutes.

beneficiary student: *see* **student, beneficiary.**

benefit, fringe: any value that the employee receives in addition to direct compensation for services rendered, such as retirement benefits, paid vacations, etc.

benefit, spillover: any benefit which is a result of education and which accrues to people other than those who are being educated.

benefit theory, child: *see* **child benefit theory.**

benefit theory of taxation: a doctrine maintaining that the tax burden imposed on each taxpayer should be determined by the direct benefits which he receives from government. *Comp. w.* **tax theory, ability to pay.**

Bennett filing plan: *see* **filing plan, Bennett.**

Bernoulli's distribution: *see* **distribution, Poisson sampling.**

Bernoulli's law: *syn.* **Bernoulli's theorem.**

Bernoulli's theorem: the view that the ratio of successes to trials of a given event may be made to differ less than any preassigned amount from the true probability of the occurrence of that event by increasing the number sufficiently; a currently accepted explanation of probability. *Syn.* **Bernoulli's law.**

best-answer item: *see* **item, best-answer.**

best-answer test: *see* **test, best-answer.**

best fit: *see* **fit, best.**

best-reason test: *see* **test, best-reason.**

bet ha-yeled (bet hä·yel′ed): *n. masc.* (Heb., lit., "the child's house") a school starting with nursery education and continuing through the second or third grade of the elementary school in which Jewish religious education is integrated with general education, with emphasis on bicultural experience and development of personality. *See* **foundation school, Jewish.**

bet midrash (bet mid·räsh′): *n. masc.; pl.* **batai** . . . (bä·tä′); (Heb., lit., "house of study") (1) a school for higher learning; (2) a part of a synagogue used for study and prayer.

bet midrash le-morim (bet mid·räsh′ lə·mō·rim′): *n. masc.; pl.* **batai** . . . (bä·tä′); (Heb., lit., "a house of study for teachers") a college or institute for the education of teachers.

bet midrash le-rabbanim (bet mid·räsh′ lə·räb·bä·nim′): *n. masc.; pl.* **batai** . . . (bä·tä′); (Heb., lit., "house of study for rabbis") a school for the training of rabbis; a theological seminary.

beta coefficient: *syn.* **coefficient, beta regression.**

beta error: *see* **error, beta.**

beta hypothesis: *see* **hypothesis, beta.**

beta regression coefficient: *see* **coefficient, beta regression.**

beta regression weight: *syn.* **coefficient, beta regression.**

beta risk: *see* **risk, beta.**

beta weight: *syn.* **coefficient, beta regression.**

between-group variance: *see* **variance, between-group.**

bias: (1) (philos.) tendency to weight a situation in favor of some interests or values at the expense of others; providing selection and interpretation rather than being equally open to all possibilities; not to be eliminated but made less arbitrary, more significant, through criticism; (2) prejudice; the intention to influence or alter conditions in an investigation so as to affect the result in a desired way; (3) any irrelevant characteristic of the experimental design or procedure, other than those deliberate variations in the experimental variable, that will systematically affect the differences (in the criterion measure) between treatments.

bias, cultural: (1) the tendency to distort perceptually or cognitively in favor of one's own cultural or ethnic group and contrarily to distort in a reverse direction for other cultural or ethnic groups or individuals; (2) (meas.) bias in test items or test content for or against various cultural groups.

bias in teaching, middle-class: instruction emphasizing the value systems accepted by people belonging to the middle socioeconomic group; historically, a common characteristic of American public education; a frequent contemporary source of difficulty in schools whose populations are drawn partly or wholly from lower socioeconomic levels.

bias, response: *see* **response bias.**

biased sample: *see* **sample, biased.**

Bible: the sacred book of Christians, containing two collections of writings, commonly called the Old and New Testaments, the former being also accepted as the sacred scriptures of Judaism.

Bible class: *see* **class, Bible.**

Bible course: *see* **course, Bible.**

Bible reading: the reading aloud of selected portions of the Bible at a stated time (often early morning) during the school day; a widespread practice in nineteenth- and twentieth-century American public education; declared illegal in 1963 by the U.S. Supreme Court, but some local school districts retain the practice. *See* **prayer decisions.**

Bible school: a school under church auspices where the Bible is studied under the supervision of a teacher, as in Sunday school and similar organizations.

Bible school, vacation: *syn.* **vacation church school.**

Bible teacher: a teacher of the Bible, either in a Sunday school program or in secular and church-related schools where courses in the Bible are offered.

biblical archaeology: *see* **archaeology, biblical.**

biblical research: *see* **research, biblical.**

bibliographic coupling: separation of a body of literature into small related groups through correlation of similar sets of references or bibliographies cited, based upon the hypothesis that if two papers have similar bibliographies there is a relationship between the subjects of the papers.

bibliographical center: *see* **center, bibliographical.**

bibliographical techniques: those processes or skills by the use of which information existing in printed form may be located and utilized; involve an understanding of library practices, an acquaintance with bibliographical aids, and a knowledge of bibliographical form or style; include some understanding of principles of note taking.

bibliography: (1) the study of the material form of books, with comparison of variations in issues and copies, as a means of determining the history and transmission of texts; (2) the process of describing books correctly with respect to authorship, editions, physical form, etc.; (3) the preparation of lists of books, maps, etc.; (4) a list of books, maps, etc., for example, a list of works relating to a particular subject or person or a list of the works of a particular writer.

bibliography, annotated: a list of references accompanied by notes that may indicate the subject, content, method, findings, etc., or may give evaluations, of each publication listed.

bibliology: the science of books, embracing knowledge of the physical book in all its aspects, as printing, bookbinding, bookselling, libraries, and library science.

bibliotherapy: (1) (couns.) assignment of books to be read on various subjects to help a child or a parent understand a problem or to help him see the problem in a different way; (2) the use of reading as a therapeutic aid for ill patients.

biconditional sentence: *see* **sentence, biconditional.**

bicycle safety training: *see* **training, bicycle safety.**

bid: an offer, usually written, to furnish materials or services for a specified sum of money. (Public school boards are generally required by law to secure competitive bids before awarding contracts.)

bid, split-rate: a bid for the purchase of bonds in which interest rates are differentiated according to the length of maturity of the bonds in a particular issue.

bid, straight: a bid for the purchase of bonds in which the interest rate is the same on all bonds of the particular issue.

bidding, competitive: a system of tendering offers whereby the prospective purchaser (for example, a board of education) invites bids or estimates from a number of contractors, dealers, wholesalers, etc., for specified services or merchandise, such bids being made separately, in writing, with the understanding that the lowest bid may be accepted or all bids rejected.

BIE day: (business-industry-education day) a day of visits by teachers to local business and industrial establishments for the purpose of broadening the teachers' understanding of the local community and thereby fostering business-industry-education cooperation; planned usually by a committee of local industry and teaching staff. See **EIB day.**

bifactor method: a method of factoring a matrix that assumes a general factor plus a number of uncorrelated group factors. See **centroid method; tetrad difference.**

bifactor test: see **test, bifactor.**

Big Brother: (1) a term, borrowed from George Orwell's novel *1984*, often used pejoratively in reference to detailed surveillance of individual actions, opinions, and attitudes carried on by bureaucratic governing agencies, especially when these depend on such surveillance for their existence and maintenance of excessively concentrated power and authority; (2) an older male person, either a member of the faculty or an upperclassman whose responsibility it is to assist a younger student on an informal and friendly basis; *syn.* **student sponsor.**

Big Sister: an older female person, either a member of the faculty or an upperclassman, whose responsibility it is to assist a younger student on an informal and friendly basis. *Syn.* **student sponsor.**

big ten: a designation for the Western Conference athletics league, which is made up of 10 universities.

big three: a term that traditionally refers to Harvard, Princeton, and Yale universities in connection with athletic activities.

bilateral: having to do with or affecting both sides.

bilateral lighting: see **lighting, bilateral.**

bilateral transfer: see **transfer, bilateral.**

bilaterality: the capacity of the organism to interweave reciprocal action of the two sides of the body as they perform a task in a balanced relationship of thrusting and counterthrusting patterns around the three coordinates of the vertical, the horizontal, and depth in proper alignment from initiation to completion of the task.

bilingual: having equal facility in the use of two languages. See **multilingual; trilingual;** *contr. w.* **monolingual.**

bill: (1) (law) a written complaint setting forth certain particulars; (2) (mil. ed.) an assignment, with names, for training, administrative, or emergency activities, for example, "fire and rescue bill"; confined to Navy usage.

bill, class: (law) a case in which one or more in a numerous class, having a common interest in the issue, sue in behalf of themselves and all others of the class; also called *class suit.*

bill of particulars: (law) a detailed, informal statement of a plaintiff's cause of actions or of the defendant's setoff; it is an account of the items of the claim and shows the manner in which they arose.

Bill of Rights, GI: see **GI Bill of Rights.**

bill, training: see **training bill.**

billet: (1) a shelter for troops, or, as a verb, to quarter troops; (2) a personnel position or assignment which may be filled by one person.

billet analysis: see **analysis, billet.**

billet evaluation: see **evaluation, billet.**

billfold certificate: see **certificate, billfold.**

bimanual: (1) two-handed; (2) requiring the use of both hands.

bimodal: (said of a frequency distribution or of a frequency curve) having two modes; having a distinct tendency toward concentration of observations or scores

at two different points or regions; having two peaks. *Dist. f.* **multimodel;** *contr. w.* **unimodal.**

bimodalism: *syn.* **bimodality.**

bimodality: the property of having two modes; often occurs if a sample is drawn from two distinct populations. *Syn.* **bimodalism.**

binary code: see **code, binary.**

binary coded decimal code: see **code, binary coded decimal.**

binary digit: (1) a character used to represent one of the two digits, 0 and 1, used in a binary number system; *see* **bit;** (2) in information theory, a measure of information expressed as logarithmic units to the base 2.

binary number: see **number system, binary.**

binary number system: see **number system, binary.**

binary numeral: see **number system, binary.**

binary operation: see **operation, mathematical.**

binary search: in automatic data processing, a technique for finding a particular item in an ordered set of items by repeatedly dividing in half the portion of the ordered set containing the sought-for item until only the sought-for item remains.

binary system: see **number system, binary.**

binaural fusion: see **fusion, binaural.**

binaural hearing: see **hearing, binaural.**

binaural recording: see **recording, binaural.**

binding arbitration: see **arbitration.**

binding, edition: a decorative binding for books, frequently made of leather or simulated leather.

binding, library: a strong, durable cloth binding for books.

Binet class: see **class, Binet.**

Binet scale: see **scale, Binet-Simon.**

Binet school (bē′nā′): (obs.) a term used to name public schools for the mentally retarded in the eastern United States up to World War II.

Binet-Simon scale: see **scale, Binet-Simon.**

Binet test: see **test, Binet.**

binocular: two-eyed.

binocular accommodation: see **accommodation, binocular.**

binocular adjustment: see **adjustment, binocular.**

binocular field of vision: see **field of vision, binocular.**

binocular fixation: see **fixation, binocular.**

binocular flicker: the flickering sensation caused by presenting stimuli to the left and right eyes alternately and with great rapidity.

binocular focusing: *syn.* **accommodation, binocular.**

binocular fusion: *syn.* **fusion, visual.**

binocular incoordination: see **incoordination, binocular.**

binocular parallax: the apparent change in the position of an object when viewed first with one eye and then with the other, the head having remained stationary.

binocular reading test: see **test, binocular reading.**

binocular regression: *syn.* **regression** (3) and (4).

binocular rivalry: failure to achieve binocular fusion, with a consequent alternation of the images seen by the two eyes when different stimuli (such as two different colors or objects) are simultaneously presented to the two eyes. See **fusion** (3).

binocular vision: see **vision, binocular.**

binomial curve: (1) a curve drawn to represent the successive terms of the expansion $(p + q)^n$, where $p + q = 1$ and n may be any positive integral number; (2) *syn.* **curve, normal probability.**

binomial distribution: *syn.* **distribution, binomial sampling.**

binomial sampling distribution: see **distribution, binomial sampling.**

bioastronautics: astronautics considered for its effects upon animal or plant life.

biobibliography: (1) a bibliography concerned with the biographical history of the authors involved; (2) a biography, ordinarily brief, with emphasis on a complete bibliography of the writings of the subject of the biography.

biocenology: the division of biology which considers the factors binding populations of animals together as units in relation to environmental conditions; a subdivision of ecology. *See* **ecology; ecology, human.**

biochemical analysis: *see* **analysis, biochemical.**

biochemistry: the branch of science dealing with the chemical reactions occurring in living organisms.

biogenetic study: *see* **study, biogenetic.**

biogenic: arising within and on the basis of the physical structure of the organism, as, for example, biogenic needs, which are those arising from deficits within various tissue systems of the body.

biographical data: data concerning an individual's past experiences, characteristics, and environmental background. *Comp. w.* **autobiography.**

biographical method: (1) a method of studying the development of the child, according to which behavior is systematically recorded as it occurs; (2) a method of organizing historical materials for teaching purposes, using for centers of interest persons of significant historical importance.

biographical study: *see* **study, biographical.**

biography: a narrative which seeks to record the actions and recreate the personality of an individual.

biography, baby: diary-type recording of an infant's behavioral development; observation largely uncontrolled and anecdotal. *See* **biographical method.**

biography, family: *see* **autobiography, family.**

biography, fictionalized: (lang. arts) a biography which utilizes material based on careful research but which is presented in episodes as the author presumed they may have occurred.

biography, occupational: (couns.) a book written about the career of a famous or ordinary person, real or fictitious, with a view to explaining in detail a particular occupation.

biokinetics: the scientific study of the movement of living organisms. *Syn.* **biomechanics;** *see* **anthropokinetics.**

biologic rhythm: the rhythmic system of an organism, consisting of a built-in regularity of respiration, heartbeat, pulse rate, brain waves, digestive actions, etc.

biological adaptation: *see* **adaptation, biological.**

biological differentiation: *see* **differentiation, biological.**

biological intelligence: *see* **intelligence, biological.**

biological science: *see* **science, biological.**

biological science, applied: *see* **science, applied biological.**

biologically mentally retarded: *see* **mentally retarded, biologically.**

biology, aerospace: the science of human and animal responses to flight conditions in both aviation and space flight.

biology, civic: a study of living organisms, stressing life problems having to do with community relations.

biology, developmental: those processes and events in development which relate to or induce growth, cellular differentiation, and *morphogenesis.*

biology, economic: the part of the study of living organisms that deals with the relation of such organisms to the making or saving of wealth.

biology, molecular: the area of biology which considers the living organism at the molecular level and gives consideration to such topics as molecular structure and process, metabolic energy, respiration, and photosynthesis.

biology, social: (1) the study of the conditioning effects of the human organism, especially its hereditary aspects, on the functioning of the group and society in general; (2) a study of the biological aspects of human groups (race, age, sex, etc.) and of biosocial behavior (birth, death, reproduction, etc.).

biology, space: a branch of biology concerned with life as it may exist in space. *See* **planetology.**

biomechanics: *syn.* **biokinetics.**

biometrics: the science of measurement and statistics as used in connection with plants and animals.

bionics: the application of knowledge gained from the analysis of living systems to the creation of hardware that will perform functions in a manner analogous to the more sophisticated functions of the living system, thus adapting biological phenomena to man's technological uses.

biosocial: possessed of characteristics that stem both from biological and from social forces or processes.

biotechnology: technology concerned with the adaptation of technological theory and practice to the improvement of human life or to the mutual adjustment of man and machine.

bipolar factor: *see* **factor, bipolar.**

bipolarity: (1) the condition of having two projecting fibers in a neuron, one of which conducts toward and the other away from the nerve cell; (2) the existence of different electric properties at two poles.

bipolarity, principle of: asserts that entities, ideas, processes, and realities are best understood in terms of their reciprocal relationships between two coexistent and reciprocal poles; and that a reality or process is constituted by diverse forces in a unified relation, such as structure-function, theory-practice, external-internal, logical-psychological.

biracial committee: any committee deliberately composed of an approximately equal number of black and white community influentials; such committees were appointed in many areas in the 1960s in an effort to reduce racial tensions and seek solutions to community problems arising from racial segregation and discrimination.

birth certificate: *see* **certificate, birth.**

birth certificate, hospital: *see* **certificate, hospital birth.**

birth control: (1) the purposeful control of human procreation; (2) purposeful avoidance of conception; usually implies the avoidance of pregnancy at undesired times by natural or artificial contraceptive measures, including continence. *See* **family planning.**

birth date: the day, month, and year of a person's birth.

birth injury: any injury suffered by a child during parturition, such as a fracture of a bone, subluxation of a joint, injury to peripheral nerves, or intracranial hemorrhage.

birth record: *syn.* **record, permanent age.**

birth trauma: (1) a physical injury to the child during the birth process; (2) (psychoan.) according to Rank, the supposed psychological shock to the child resulting from the process of being born, which, it is alleged, may in later life be manifested in neurotic anxiety or fear.

birth-trauma theory: *see* **birth trauma** (2).

birthrate: an expression of the number of children born during a given period of time per hundred or thousand of the population of a given territory or group.

birthrate, adjusted: *syn.* **birthrate, corrected.**

birthrate, age-specific: the annual number of births per thousand women in each 5- or 10-year age group within the child-bearing ages; age-specific birthrates are now widely used in making projections for areas in which natural increase or decrease (the excess or deficiency of births compared to deaths) is expected to be the predominant source of population change.

birthrate, corrected: the number of live births in a given area in a certain group of the population divided by the total living population of that group, usually expressed in number per thousand of population; groups may be determined on the basis of sex, age, race, etc.; when used by the Bureau of Vital Statistics, the term connotes the correction to show all births rather than only those officially recorded. *Syn.* **adjusted birthrate;** *contr. w.* **birthrate, crude.**

birthrate, crude: the number of live births per thousand of the population in a given area during a year; determined by the proportion of married women of childbearing age in the population and the propensity of these women to have children; this propensity is commonly measured by the fertility rate. *See* **ratio, fertility;** *contr. w.* **birthrate, corrected.**

bisect: to partition into two parts having the same measure.

biserial coefficient of correlation: *syn.* **correlation, biserial.**

biserial eta: (bis η) a number between 0 and 1 indicating the degree of relationship between one variable expressed in alternative categories and another expressed in multiple categories that are not ordinarily expressible in numbers, where it is assumed that the dichotomized variable is in reality continuously measurable and normally distributed even though expressed dichotomously. *See* **correlation, biserial.**

biserial r: *syn.* **correlation, biserial.**

bisexuality: having secondary sex characteristics of both sexes.

Bishop method of clothing construction: *see* **clothing construction, Bishop method of.**

bit: in automatic data processing, an admissible mark in the *binary number system,* as the symbol 1 or the symbol 0; a unit quantity of information, the smallest part of an array of coded characters which can be interpreted. *See* **band (2); binary digit.**

bivariate correlation: *syn.* **correlation, simple.**

black line print: *see* **print.**

blackboard: *see* **chalkboard.**

blackboard by wire: for long-distance lectures transmitted during delivery over telephone wire to another location, the simultaneously transmitted display on a TV monitor of illustrative material, diagrams, etc., as they are drawn by the lecturer with an electronic pen. *See* **telelecture.**

bladder, automatic: a bladder trained to empty itself at regular intervals.

bladder control: voluntary retention of the urine; control of the urge to urinate except under socially suitable circumstances.

bladder reflex: *see* **reflex, bladder.**

Blakeman's criterion: *syn.* **test, Blakeman's.**

Blakeman's test: *see* **test, Blakeman's.**

blank, psychosomatic-experience: *see* **psychosomatic-experience blank.**

blanket tax: *see* **tax, blanket.**

blanket teaching certificate: *see* **certificate, blanket teaching.**

bleeding: (photog., etc.) the elimination of white margins in printing or mounting pictures.

blend: (1) a combination of two or more shorthand characters designed to merge when written together; (2) the fusion of two or more sounds without the identity of either sound being lost, for example, the blend of *b* and *l* in *black.*

blend, consonant: a combination of consonants that must be fused in pronunciation, such as *ch* or *br.*

blend, final: a combination of letters occurring at the end of a word that, when fused in pronunciation, represents a fundamental sound, such as *and* in *hand* or *all* in *wall.*

blend, initial: the combination of one or more consonants with a vowel at the beginning of a word or syllable, such as *ca* in *catch* or *thi* in *thick,* that, when pronounced together and added to the remaining letters of the word or syllable, enables the pupil to determine the pronunciation. *Contr. w.* **blend, final.**

blending inheritance: *see* **inheritance, blending.**

blimp: a soundproofing device that fits over the camera to prevent camera noise from reaching the microphone; though some blimps are integral with the camera, others are containers capable of housing more than one type of camera.

blind: *see* **blindness.**

blind-alley vocation: *see* **vocation, blind-alley.**

blind approach training: *see* **training, blind approach.**

blind, art of the: *see* **art of the blind.**

blind, central registry for the: *see* **registry for the blind, central.**

blind deaf: (1) descriptive of an individual who has auditory and visual handicaps which together cause such severe communication and other developmental and educational problems that he cannot properly be accommodated in special educational programs either for the hearing handicapped or for the visually handicapped; (2)

having both hearing and vision so defective as to be nonfunctional for the ordinary purposes of life.

blind, educationally: lacking sufficient vision to benefit from instruction by ordinary visual methods. (The border line is commonly regarded as 20/200 Snellen measurement.)

blind, home teaching of the: *see* **home teaching of the blind.**

blind, library for the: *see* **library for the blind.**

blind mannerism: *see* **blindism.**

blind, mobility of the: *see* **mobility.**

blind, partially: *see* **partially seeing.**

blind residential school: *see* **residential school for the blind.**

blind, residential school for the: *see* **residential school for the blind.**

blind sixth sense: the idea that a loss of vision is compensated by increased acuity of other sensations. (The weight of experimental findings is at present against this hypothesis.)

blind writing: *see* **writing, blind.**

blind-writing system: one of the organized methods of teaching the blind to write regular script or to print script forms.

blindism: a behavior pattern of the blind, frequently developed during childhood, such as shaking the head rapidly or swaying the body back and forth; interpreted as an act of self-stimulation. *See* **mannerism, blind; stereotypy.**

blindness: a condition of severe visual impairment; such loss of sight as to result in no measurable vision or vision which is so limited as to be of little if any practical use as a channel of learning.

blindness, absolute: *see* **blindness, total.**

blindness, adjustment to: *see* **adjustment to blindness.**

blindness, adventitious: a condition of serious visual impairment occurring after birth as a result of trauma from accident or illness.

blindness, color: lack of perception of one or more colors but rarely of all.

blindness, congenital: a general term for blindness acquired at or before birth. *Dist. f.* **blindness, adventitious.**

blindness, day· a condition in which a person sees better in dim light.

blindness, economic: the inability to do any kind of work for which sight is essential.

blindness, educational: *see* **blindness.**

blindness, functional: *syn.* **blindness, psychic.**

blindness, hysterical: *syn.* **blindness, psychic.**

blindness, legal: as defined by the Social Security Act of 1935, central visual acuity of 20/200 or less in the better eye with correcting glasses or central visual acuity of more than 20/200 if there is a field defect in which peripheral field has contracted to such an angle that the widest diameter of visual field subtends an angle no greater than 20 degrees; the definition varies among the states.

blindness, night: an imperfection of vision, congenital or acquired, in which the sight is deficient at night or under poor illumination; may indicate the presence of serious ocular disease, especially retinitis pigmentosa, or of diminished ocular nutrition, due chiefly to vitamin A deficiency.

blindness, psychic: loss of conscious visual sensation owing to the influence of some psychological mechanism such as hysteria rather than as the result of any known physical cause. *Syn.* **functional blindness; hysterical blindness; psychical blindness.**

blindness, total: the inability to perceive light.

blindness, vocational: impairment of vision to such a degree as to make it impossible for a person to do work at which he had previously earned a living.

blindness, word: *syn.* **alexia.**

block: (1) (voc. ed.) a group of jobs that contain similar elements causing learning difficulties; (2) a large unit or division of instruction; (3) (data processing) a group of characters, words, or fields of data handled as a unit.

block and gap course: *see* **course, block and gap.**

block base: (voc. ed.) a source of learning difficulty (such as a machine, material, operation, or type of construction) that is common to certain jobs in a trade and that forms a basis for considering such jobs as a natural group.

block building: an activity in which children learn to manipulate blocks of various types, sizes, and shapes in the construction of child-sized structures that express their ideas and experiences.

block, counting: *see* **counting block.**

block-design test: *see* **test, block-design.**

block diagram: (1) a graph, describing a computer system, which shows the sequential operations by which data are to be processed; (2) *syn.* **histogram.**

block, independent: a division of a trade or other occupation, as determined by analysis, that can be taught as a unit by itself; a term derived from the Allen block method of course analysis.

block, laboratory: *see* **laboratory block.**

block method of class scheduling: *syn.* **scheduling, group method of class.**

block of instruction: (mil. ed.) a group of related units of instruction covering a major subject area, shown on course chart and plan of instruction for Air Force technical training and as subjects or phases in a flying training syllabus.

block of time: an approach to business and office education that provides a teacher with two or more successive periods for depth instruction and integration of skills and related areas necessary to prepare a student for an office career. *See* **business and office education, intensive; instruction, business and office education related.**

block plan of student teaching: *see* **student teaching, block plan of.**

block play: *see* **play, block.**

block play accessories: complementary toys or equipment used in block building which add to the effectiveness of the building, such as small cars, airplanes, people, animals, boards, spools, cones, etc.

block progression method: (voc. ed.) a learning order in which the learner masters the jobs in one block before starting those in another. *See* **block** (1).

block, psychological: an emotional experience that adversely affects a person's attitude toward learning.

block sort: *see* **sort, block.**

block, time: a long period of time (often 60 to 90 minutes) in a school day which is usually allocated to the pursuit of activity work and integration of basic learnings in experience units.

block transfer: *see* **transfer, block.**

blocked time: (1) procedure used in some high schools in which two or more successive periods within the school day are combined to provide more effective integration; (2) division of time within the college term which permits student teachers to alternate full-time teaching in off-campus centers with double time devoted to courses for which they are enrolled on the campus.

blockflöte (blok'flə̇tə): *syn.* **recorder** (2).

blocking: the prevention or inhibition of the final or consummatory response that would remove a persistent stimulus. *See* **blocking, emotional.**

blocking, emotional: (1) stoppage of a neural or muscular impulse or the break in a train of thought or association because of mental conflict; (2) (psychoan.) the inability to recall a repressed idea.

blocking, mental: the inability or hesitancy to recall appropriate responses at a specific time.

blocks, attribute: (1) in general, plastic or wooden blocks so designed with respect to such attributes as shape, color, thickness, and size as to permit grouping them according to one or more attributes, for example, the set of all those blocks that are red and square; (2) a particular set of blocks developed by Zoltan B. Dienes, usually referred to as *logic blocks.*

blocks, hollow building: hollow wood boxes in three graduated sizes; light in weight, flexible, easily stored; used for construction activities in dramatic play; usually found in kindergartens.

blocks, multibase arithmetic: manipulative materials used to teach the meaning of base and place in the conventional numeration system; by manipulating the blocks, which are made to represent different bases, the child learns to generalize the "rate of exchange" concept inherent in a *place value numeration system. See* **base, numeration; value, place.**

blocks, Patty Hill: (elem. ed.) trade name for a set of heavy wood blocks and posts, in various sizes, held together with removable iron rods; frequently used for large construction activities usually associated with social studies units; in declining use because of relative inflexibility.

blocks, Stern: *see* **arithmetic, structural.**

blocks, unit: blocks made of solid hardwood, in multiple shapes and sizes, having a basic unit of measure.

blue-backed speller: a famous combination speller and reader published by Noah Webster in 1783, which later appeared in many editions, eventually appearing purely as a speller.

blue book: (higher ed.) a blue paper-backed notebook 7 by $8\frac{1}{2}$ inches in size with varying numbers of sheets (4, 8, or 16) ruled on both sides and bound in booklet form, widely used for essay examinations; occasionally other colors are used for the cover.

blue laws, teacher: restrictions on personal freedom and action that are imposed on teachers by some employing authorities, usually written into the contracts signed by the teachers or stated in the rules and regulations of the school boards.

blueprint: (1) the reproduction of a drawing on a chemically treated paper giving a white line on a blue background; (2) (ed.) a detailed specification of the traits desired in persons or in societies, with the intention that the attainment of these traits be made the objective of education.

BMR: basal metabolic rate. *See* **metabolism, basal.**

board attorney: *see* **attorney, board.**

board, bristol: *see* **bristol board.**

board, bulletin: *see* **bulletin board.**

board, buzz: *see* **board, electric.**

board committee report: *see* **report, board committee.**

board, control: *see* **plugboard.**

board, coordinating: *see* **coordinating board.**

board, counting: *see* **abacus.**

board, district school: *see* **district school.**

board election, nonpartisan: *see* **election, nonpartisan board.**

board, electric: a generic term for numerous devices created to test, drill, or demonstrate; the device usually features an electrical circuit which activates a buzzer, bell, or light when appropriate contacts or switches are manipulated in response to questions or pictorial materials displayed on the board; also called a *buzz board.*

board, elementary school: a school board charged with the responsibility for an elementary school district. *See* **school board.**

board examinations: *see* **examinations, board.**

board, flying evaluation: *see* **evaluation board, flying.**

board for vocational education, state: *see* **state board for vocational education.**

board, form: *see* **form board.**

board functions, discretionary: powers and duties of a board of education which are not strictly prescribed by law and which a board may exercise or fail to exercise by its own choice made in terms of the board's concepts and desires and its interpretation of the desires of the community it serves. *Dist. f.* **board functions, mandatory.**

board functions, mandatory: powers and duties of a board of education which are strictly prescribed by law and which a board must exercise. *Dist. f.* **board functions, discretionary.**

board functions, ministerial: powers and duties of a board of education which are administrative in nature as opposed to legislative; present theory of the functions of a board of education allows few strictly ministerial functions to a board of education.

board, governing: *see* **governing board.**

board, hook-and-loop: a presentation board consisting of a cloth surface containing countless nylon loops on which display materials backed with strips of tape having numerous nylon hooks will intermesh and hold firmly.

board immunity: legal exemption of a board of education from liability for suit arising from circumstances as prescribed by law or court rulings; varies considerably from state to state in the United States.

board, intramural: *see* **intramural board.**

board liability: *see* **liability, board.**

board liner: a mechanical device holding pieces of chalk at specified distances from one another so that a number of parallel horizontal lines may be drawn on the blackboard in one operation; used especially in music instruction for drawing staffs and in handwriting instruction to indicate the spaces bounding letters of various heights. *Syn.* **staff liner.**

board, magnetic: a sheet of metal to which objects may be attached by means of magnets; this same surface may be coated with paint or enamel and used also as a *chalkboard.*

board meeting: a gathering of members of a board of education, in accordance with legal requirements, to conduct official school business. *See* **meeting, special.**

board meeting notice: *see* **notice, board meeting.**

board member: *syn.* **school-board member.**

board, murder: *see* **murder board.**

board of control: a governing body having jurisdiction over a particular organization, institution, or governmental unit or division. *Syn.* **board of regents; policy board;** *see* **board of trustees; governing board.**

board of control, central: the board within a governmental unit that has the supervision of or responsibility for certain educational institutions within that unit.

board of control, state: a board charged with the supervision of expenditures in a state.

board of directors: *syn.* **school board.**

board of education: *syn.* **school board.**

board of education, church: a body of officers whose duty it is to give general oversight and direction to the educational activities of a church.

board of education, county: a corporate body provided by statute to supervise the program of education within specified territorial limits of counties, parts of counties, or groups of counties; in some states is responsible for all local administrative functions, in others has specified functions only.

board of education, dependent: a board of education that has its budget or determination of the amount of tax to be levied for educational purposes subject to revision or veto by another government authority such as the city council, mayor, budget director, board of finance, or county board of review.

board of education, district: a corporate body legally constituted and authorized, usually chosen by popular election from the district at large, to direct the program of education within the specified territorial limits of the *school district. See* **school board.**

board of education, independent: a board of education that has the power to decide on budget items or the amount of money to be raised for educational purposes, its decision not being subject to veto or modification by a governmental official or reviewing body but usually subject to a hearing before the citizens of the school district governed by the board.

board of education, state: a group of persons appointed or elected as officials to sit in council to perform certain functions in connection with the management or direction of public education in a state.

board of educational examiners, state: *see* **board of examination, state.**

board of examination, state: a board, frequently under the authority of the chief state school officer or the state board of education, having one or more of the following functions: the general determination of policies, objectives, and methods of administering testing programs within the schools of the state; the examination of pupils wishing to enter high school; the examination of students wishing to enter college; the examination of persons applying for state certificates to teach or to practice a trade, etc.; or the examination of any person for the purpose of determining whether he should be sent to the penitentiary, to a mental hospital, to a home for the aged, etc. *See* **board of examiners, state.**

board of examiners, state: a board, authorized and appointed by a governmental official or body of the state, charged with the responsibility of conducting state examinations. *See* **board of examination, state.**

Board of License: a board composed of representatives of Jewish teacher-training institutions, teachers' and principals' organizations, rabbinic organizations, and the Jewish public that examines and licenses men and women to teach in the weekday Hebrew schools of New York City and certain other cities in accordance with a schedule of requirements that it has elaborated for its own guidance.

board of regents: *syn.* **board of control.**

board of trustees: (1) a group of persons responsible for the direction of the educational affairs of an administrative unit or of an educational institution; usually composed of laymen who select or approve the selection of the professional staff, pass on policies, and take the ultimate responsibility for financing the work of the institution; (2) the titular holders of property for an institution; (3) *syn.* **board of education, district.**

board of visitors: a group of people, usually interested laymen, charged with the responsibility of visiting, investigating, and reporting on the operation of a higher education institution to the board of trustees; relatively rare, often primarily honorary, very rarely synonymous with *board of control, board of trustees, governing board,* etc.

board-owned: a term used to designate equipment or property that a board of education has acquired through purchase, bequest, or donation. *Syn.* **county-owned; district-owned**

board, paper-form: *see* **paper-form board.**

board, peg: a device of pegs fitted in a board; used in a test of manual dexterity.

board, policy: *syn.* **board of control.**

board, proprietary function of: the concept of the local school board as the proprietor of the local school property as the representative of the citizens of the school district or of the state, who are the legal owners.

board, regional education: *syn.* **conference, regional education.**

board, rocking: *see* **rocking board.**

board, scalogram: *see* **scalogram board.**

board, school: *see* **school board.**

board school: a type of nondenominational elementary school established in England in 1870 which was built and supported largely by funds raised by local taxation and controlled by a local school board. (These schools were the "public" schools of England, in the American meaning of the term.)

board selection, ward method of: a method of electing or appointing members to a board of education in which each board member must reside in a given ward of a city and is the representative of that ward on the board.

board, terminal: *syn.* **plugboard.**

boarding around: an arrangement under which the teacher lives for one to several weeks of each school term with each family that has children in school.

boarding child: *see* **child, boarding.**

boarding club, teacher: *see* **club, teacher boarding.**

boarding home: a private home where students reside while attending special day schools; usually requires approval of social welfare personnel.

boarding mother: the woman in charge of a boarding home.

boarding pupil: *see* **pupil, boarding.**

boarding school: an educational institution at the primary or secondary level in which pupils are in residence while enrolled in an instructional program, as opposed to a school to which pupils commute from their homes; includes schools which offer regular and/or special education curricula. *See* **residential school.**

boarding school, nonreservation: a boarding school for Indians that is not located on an Indian reservation and that in most cases is operated by the Federal government.

boarding school, reservation: a school on an Indian reservation operated by the Federal government and providing boarding facilities for the students.

boccie (bo'chē): *alt. sp.* **bocci, boccia;** (Ital. bocce, lit., "balls") Italian lawn bowling played in a long narrow court.

bodily action: (lang. arts) the movement of the body to express feeling and ideas in order to augment communication through speech.

bodily feelings: *see* **experience of form, autoplastic.**

body: (stat.) (1) the main part of a frequency curve or frequency distribution; *contr. w.* **tail;** (2) the main portion of a table, that is, the tabled entries.

body awareness: *see* **awareness, body.**

body build theory: a theory that correlates personality traits with body form; best known are the theories formulated by Kretschmer and by Sheldon.

body builds, classification of: as classified by Kretschmer, three basic physical types are recognized, namely: (*a*) the *athletic type* (broad shoulders, well-developed chest, thick neck, flat abdomen, large muscles), (*b*) the *asthenic type* (slender body, long legs and arms, thin neck, long flat chest, poor muscular development), and (*c*) the *pyknic type* (broad head, short neck, thick shoulders, deep chest, rounded body, short, sturdy arms and legs); intermediate types are recognized, designed by such compounds as asthenic-athletic.

body, bus: *see* **bus body.**

body corporate: a formal, legal synonym for corporate body.

body image: *see* **image, body.**

body mechanics: the application of *kinesiology* to the use of the body in daily life activities and to the prevention and correction of problems related to posture. *Syn.* **anthropomechanics.**

body schema: *syn.* **image, body.**

body size: (typography) the size of a type measured from the top to the bottom of a letter.

body type: *see* **type, body.**

boiler inspection: checking of the condition and order of safety devices, cleanliness, and general condition of steam or hot-water boilers for approval or condemnation.

boiler operation: the work connected with the firing, care, regulation, and cleaning of boilers and accessory equipment.

boiler pressure: the number of pounds of steam carried by a boiler when operating normally.

boiler room: the room that contains the heating plant, consisting of furnaces, boilers, stokers, pumps, ash-handling équipment, etc. *Syn.* **furnace room.**

bonarro: *syn.* **archery golf.**

bond: a written promise, generally under seal, to pay a specified sum of money (called the face value), at a fixed time in the future (called the date of maturity), and carrying interest at a fixed rate, usually payable periodically. (The difference between a note and a bond is that the latter runs for a longer period and requires greater legal formality.)

bond amortization: *see* **bond retirement.**

bond anticipation note: *see* **note, bond anticipation.**

bond, bearer: a bond, negotiable by delivery, with detachable coupons which are presented through proper channels for payment by paying agent.

bond, callable: a bond containing a "callable clause" in which the issuing party reserves the right to call the bond for payment prior to its date of maturity.

bond, contractor's: surety given that contracted work will be performed, usually in the form of a written legal document received from a contractor.

bond, coupon: a bond on which interest is payable to bearer upon presentation of current coupons to paying agent.

bond default: neglect or omission to fulfill a debt obligation covered by a bond.

bond, fidelity: a bond which guarantees the school district against losses resulting from the actions of the employees of the school district.

bond, funding: a bond issued when current obligations are in excess of current revenue.

bond, general obligation: a bond secured by issuer's pledge of its full resources, taxing power, and credit for payment of bond.

bond issue: any given number of bonds, issued by one obligor, that may be of one or several denominations, that are all of like tenor, and that, if secured, are all and equally secured under one mortgage.

bond, limited tax: a *general obligation bond* limited to a specified maximum tax rate.

bond, municipal: a bond issued by a state, territory, or possession of the United States or by any municipality, political subdivision, or public agency or instrumentality to construct, repair, or improve public facilities.

bond, noncallable: a bond that cannot be recalled by the issuer prior to maturity.

bond premium: an amount of money that is to be deducted by the issuing agency from the principal to be paid in the retirement of a bond issue. (In bidding for bonds, investors frequently name a premium as well as a rate of interest.)

bond, public: evidence of debt incurred by a governmental subdivision for which the issuer has pledged all or part of its current and future resources for payment of interest and principal.

bond, refunding: a new bond issued to take the place of one falling due; deferment of debt payments is thus accomplished.

bond, registered: a bond registered for principal or interest or both; if fully registered, coupons are detached and interest and principal are sent directly to owner as they come due.

bond resolution: an enactment by the appropriate body of government for the purpose of authorizing a bond issue.

bond retirement: the act of paying off and withdrawing from circulation bonds that have been outstanding.

bond, revenue: a bond the retirement of which is dependent upon receipts from the facility for the construction of which the bond was issued, for example, a residence hall.

bond, self-liquidating: a *revenue bond* backed by sufficient earnings to meet interest and principal obligations; commonly used by municipalities to finance such projects as city utilities.

bond, serial: a bond that is one of a total issue that is retired by payments made at regular intervals, interest being paid annually, semiannually, or quarterly. *Contr. w.* **bond, straight.**

bond, short-term: one of those securities having less than 5 years to run to maturity.

bond, sinking fund: a bond the payment of which is provided for by means of a sinking fund. *See* **fund, sinking.**

bond, special assessment: a bond payable from a levy assessed against property that presumably benefits by the improvement.

bond, special tax: a bond payable only from special taxes, such as gasoline tax for highways.

bond, straight: a bond issue all of which matures at the same time; less frequently used in school finance than the *serial bond.*

bond, surety: a written promise by an insurer (the surety) to reimburse the party named in the bond (the insured) against the failure of performance of obligations or duties undertaken by another party (the principal) for the benefit of the insured.

bond, term: a bond paid at end of bonding period with only interest paid during intervening period.

bond yield: the net income received from a bond if held to maturity.

bonded debt: *see* debt, bonded.

bonded indebtedness: *syn.* debt, bonded.

bonding, chemical: *see* chemical bonding.

bonding limits: a limitation, specified by state law, upon the indebtedness which a school district may incur and amortize through the issuance of bonds.

bonds, depository: bonds furnished by school depositories as security for the protection of the school's deposits.

bone conduction: *see* conduction, bone.

bone-conduction test: *see* test, bone-conduction.

bone-conduction vibrator: a device on an *audiometer* that delivers vibrations to the mastoid process of the temporal bone instead of generating sound waves in an earphone.

bone cyst: a slow growing, bone-destructive lesion near one end of the shaft of a long bone.

bonus, teachers': payment made to instructors above the contractual salary, usually a payment of a certain percentage of the regular salary that is uniform throughout the school system or unit in which it is made. (Sometimes payment is for summer school attendance, extension-course work, or travel.)

book, activity: a book of coupons, issued to or purchased by college or high school students, entitling the holder to certain privileges such as passes to athletic events and plays and giving him the right to receive issues of the school newspaper, magazine, and yearbook.

book-and-tape correlation: *see* correlation, book-and-tape.

book automobile: *syn.* bookmobile.

book, blue: *see* blue book.

book, braille: a book embossed or printed in braille.

book car: *syn.* bookmobile.

book, career: *see* career book.

book catalog: *see* catalog, book.

book, children's: any book that has a vocabulary and thought content suitable for children.

book, children's trade: in instruction in children's literature, any book other than a textbook written expressly for children.

book classic, children's: *see* classic, children's book.

book classification: *see* classification, book.

book, clip: *see* clip book.

book club, children's: *see* club, children's book.

book, coloring: a children's workbook with figures to be colored with crayons, pencils, or watercolors.

book, comic: *see* comic book.

book, factual: in school libraries, an informational book interesting enough to be used for recreational reading, for example, a book on science or a biography.

book fair: generally a school-community project in which books recommended for young people are displayed for sale.

book funds, allocation of: a division of a portion of the library book budget among the various departments of a college or university; usually a division by rule of thumb but sometimes accomplished by the use of a formula including factors such as the number of students in the department, number of faculty members, number of undergraduate and graduate courses offered, nature of the courses offered, and relative costs of materials.

book jacket: a detachable paper cover, often illustrated, used to protect a book.

book, juvenile: a book containing materials based on the abilities, interests, and tastes of the immature or undeveloped.

book, large-type: a book printed on off-white or cream-colored paper in 18- or 24-point type. *See* reading materials, large-type.

book learning: *see* learning, book.

book lending: *syn.* circulation, library.

book list: (1) a list of books to be used for a given purpose; (2) a list of books read or to be read, compiled by a pupil or class; (3) a list of books believed, as a result of research, to be suitable for children of a given age or grade level, for example, the Winnetka Graded Book List.

book list, graded: *syn.* book list (3).

book number: a symbol, usually consisting of a combination of letters and figures, which serves (*a*) to identify a given book among others having the same class number and (*b*) to place books bearing the same class number in the desired order on the shelf; when used to arrange books alphabetically by author it is called *author number* or *author notation*. *See* classification, book.

book, picture: a book for children, with very little or no text, which relies on pictures to tell the story.

book, picture story: a book for young children in which the pictures are closely related to the text and contribute largely to the presentation of the total content.

book, reference: a book that is used for the purpose of obtaining information, as contrasted with a book that is read chiefly for relaxation or for fun; examples are the dictionary, the encyclopedia, etc.

book, rental: a borrowed book for which a fee is paid; a book obtained from a rental library as contrasted with a free book obtained from a public or other free library.

book report: *see* report, book.

book review: *see* review, book.

book, scrambled: in programmed instruction, a book which presents an intrinsic program; the pages are not read consecutively; following the information presentation a multiple-choice question is given; the answer the student selects refers him to a particular page for confirmation or correction; he may be sent either forward or backward in the text, the numbering of the pages in either direction being randomized so that no clue as to which alternative is correct can be found in the page reference accompanying each alternative; thus each student follows a different path through the book in accordance with his own responses. *See* programming, intrinsic.

book selection: (1) the process of choosing books for library collections; (2) a library-school course on the principles underlying the choice of material for various kinds of libraries and types of readers.

book, talking: a phonograph record or tape recording of readings from a book or other literary matter for use by the blind.

book, the: (obs.) the designation of the school register during the early period of American public education.

book, trade: a book published for the purpose of giving the reader pleasure and of feeding his interest in reading for pleasure. *Contr. w.* book, reference; textbook.

book wagon: *syn.* bookmobile.

bookbinding: the art or process of applying covers to books.

bookkeeping: the act or process of keeping a systematic record of business transactions and preparing financial statements.

bookkeeping cycle: the steps that are fundamental to all bookkeeping systems, from the financial transactions through the journal and ledger to the financial statements.

bookkeeping equation: the relationship between accounts and their ownership, used as the basis of balancing accounts in bookkeeping and accounting; expressed as "assets equal liabilities plus proprietorship" or "assets minus liabilities equal proprietorship," *Syn.* accounting equation.

bookkeeping narrative: *syn.* narrative of transactions.

bookkeeping, personal-use: principles of bookkeeping taught from the standpoint of usefulness to the individual as a means of keeping his personal financial accounts, without regard to vocational usefulness; often less technical in treatment than vocational bookkeeping.

bookkeeping practice set: a valuable teaching tool used as an integrating activity in the teaching of bookkeeping; consists of a set of materials for each student for which he is responsible and which includes journals, ledgers, ruled forms for the preparation of financial statements, and a narrative of transactions (or business papers) of a hypothetical business organization for one or more fiscal periods.

bookkeeping, socialized: the procedures and theories of bookkeeping taught from the standpoint of their usefulness to the individual, in keeping records not only of personal and family financial matters but also of church, club, and social affairs, with no emphasis on the vocational possibilities of bookkeeping. *See* **bookkeeping, personal-use.**

bookkeeping, vocational: the principles and methods of recording financial business transactions, taught with a view to preparing students to become professional bookkeepers or to perform clerical recording functions in business.

booklet, cutback-page: a booklet with each page narrower on the unbound edge than the preceding one turned and with an answer sheet placed under the narrowest page so that its right edge extends beyond the rest of the text far enough to provide answer blanks for the frames in the text; the correct answers are in such position on the answer sheet that those that match the frames on any given page are exposed only upon turning that page.

bookmobile: an automobile truck specially equipped to carry books and serve as a traveling branch library. *Syn.* **book automobile; book car; book wagon.**

bookplate: a label bearing an owner's or donor's name, often bearing also a distinctive design, to be affixed to the inside of the front cover of a book; sometimes called *ex libris* (eks lib'rēs) (Lat., lit., "from the books [of]"), words which often appear on the bookplate.

Boolean algebra: *see* **algebra, Boolean.**

booster club: *see* **club, booster.**

boot: slang for a recruit (a newly enlisted Marine or sailor).

boot camp: slang for a recruit training center.

booth: a sound-treated cubicle for a student as a station in an electronic learning laboratory; the acoustical partitions are usually on three sides; the front partition may be a collapsible, sliding, or folding panel, or it may be made of transparent materials such as plexiglass; the booth is furnished with sound reproducing and/or recording equipment when used for individualized language study or with special electronic apparatus for individual use in other fields of study; also called *study carrel.*

bootstrap: in automatic data processing, the instructions at the beginning of a program together with a few instructions entered from the control console used to load a program into automatic computer storage.

bootstrap commissioning program: *see* **program, bootstrap commissioning.**

bootstrap, operation: an Air Force program that (*a*) provides opportunities (through tuition assistance grants) for officers and airmen during off-duty time to pursue educational programs of personal development or to meet Air Force requirements and (*b*) includes programs through which participants may be released from normal duty for resident study, up to one year, in a college or university to complete degree requirements. *See* **program, bootstrap commissioning.**

border line: a theoretical region presumed to exist between mental or physical health and disease or between normality and abnormality and having some of the characteristics of each.

borderline case: any instance where there is doubt regarding the appropriateness of placement in one or another of two contiguous diagnostic or administrative categories.

borderline child: *see* **child, backward; child, slow-learning.**

borderline defective: *see* **defective, borderline.**

borderline intelligence: *see* **intelligence, borderline.**

borderline mental deficiency: *see* **defective, borderline.**

borderline mentally retarded: *see* **mentally retarded, borderline.**

borderline normal: *see* **normal, borderline.**

borderline vision: *see* **vision, borderline.**

borrow-and-repay method: *syn.* **equal-additions method;** *see* **subtraction, methods of.**

borrow method: *see* **subtraction, methods of.**

borrower's card: *see* **card, library.**

borrowing capacity: *syn.* **debt capacity.**

borrowing power, margin of: difference between legal debt limitation of a governmental unit and present outstanding debt.

Borstal system: *see* **Borstal institution** (Education in England and Wales).

botany, economic: the part of the study of plant life that deals with the relation of plants to wealth and with the structure and development of commercially important plants.

bounce: a repetitive speech pattern employed by some speech correctionists in treating stuttering; the stutterer is instructed to adopt as a consistent stuttering pattern the bounce, as in *b-b-b-boy,* on the assumption that this practice will serve to reduce tension and anxiety associated with attempts to speak.

boundary line: the streets, alleys, or other markings that divide one school district from another; any geographical limits of areas designated as school districts or subschool districts.

bourgeoisie: a term used to designate the class in which ownership of the modes of production and distribution is vested in capitalistic society; historically, the term refers to the postmedieval urban commercial and manufacturing class that successfully challenged the power of the rural nobility and aristocracy.

bowel control: voluntary retention of the feces; control of the urge to evacuate the bowels except under socially suitable circumstances; this control, established in child training, actually means the learning of the internal cues which serve to anticipate the event.

bowling: a game in which a ball is rolled down a wooden alley to knock down ten triangularly set pins at the end of the alley.

box: (1) a piece of gymnasium apparatus having a flat top about 12 inches wide and 5 feet long, padded and leather-covered, and sloping down to a wider base, the height being adjustable by removing sections; (2) (stat.) that part of a table which includes the captions and brace headings.

box heading: (1) *syn.* **brace heading;** (2) *syn.* **caption** (1); *dist. f.* **stub heading.**

box locker: *see* **locker, box.**

boycott, school: *see* **school boycott.**

Boys' and Girls' County Government: a program of county government education, sponsored in some states by the American Legion and the Legion Auxilliary, in which local schools send boys and girls, elected to the several county offices, to the county seat for a day in order to participate in and learn from close observation the duties of the various county officials.

Boys' Club of America, Inc.: the national organization of Boys Clubs in the United States. (In 1971 it had member organizations in 524 cities in 49 states, and operating 1,000 Boys Clubs and serving a million boys in 1972.)

boys' counselor: *see* **dean of boys.**

boys' home economics: *see* **home economics, boys'.**

Boys' State: a program of education in state government, sponsored by the American Legion, in which local groups send boys as representatives to the state capital for approximately one week so that they may have first-hand experiences in a mock state government. (The boys are usually divided into two political parties; elections are held; appointive offices are filled; the government is organized; and attention is given to pertinent problems actually confronting the state.)

brace: an appliance for support of a body part to relieve weakness or to maintain alignment.

brace heading: a heading designation appearing above two or more columns in a table. *Syn.* **box heading.**

bracero program: *see* **program, bracero.**

braces: mechanical devices that are sometimes used after surgery to reinforce or stabilize certain muscles while others are being trained.

brachycephalic (brak·i·sə·fal′ik): characterizing a human with a skull which is relatively short from front to back, that is, in the sagittal direction. *Contr. w.* **dolichocephalic.**

bradykinetic (brad′i·ki·net′ik): pertaining to extremely slow motion, for example, bradykinetic analysis of a physical action by means of motion pictures.

bradylalia (brad·i·lā′li·ə): abnormally slow utterance.

Brahman: the highest major caste of Hindus in India; members of this caste, along with *Kshatriyas* and *Vaisyas*, are supposed to be pure-blooded Aryans and are called twice-born; they alone may wear the sacred thread and enjoy the privilege of formal cultural education; the Brahmans represented the priesthood and the teachers in ancient India.

braille: a touch system of reading and writing for the blind, adapted from the older system of Barbier by Louis Braille (1809-1852), in which the letters of the alphabet are represented by various combinations of raised dots in a cell two dots wide by three dots high; may be written by hand with a stylus and slate or on a mechanical braille writer, or may be printed from metal plates.

braille book: *see* **book, braille.**

braille cell: six raised dots arranged in a group two dots wide and three dots high, all the possible combinations of which constitute the 63 signs used in the braille system. *See* **braille.**

braille class: *see* **class, braille.**

braille contraction: a symbol in the punctographic code read and written by the blind which conserves space by standing, by definition, for a larger group of letters or a word.

braille grade one: an uncontracted system of braille. *See* **braille grade two, standard English.**

braille grade two, standard English: a contracted system of braille including the alphabet, punctuation marks, and 185 contractions, adopted in 1932 for the English-speaking world by duly authorized representatives of the United States and the British Empire. (An uncontracted and a less highly contracted system are known, respectively, as braille grade 1 and braille grade 1½; a more highly contracted system is known as braille grade 3.)

braille, interpoint: a method of printing braille on both sides of the page so that the embossed dots on the two sides do not coincide.

braille slate: a device which acts as a guide for the blind in writing braille; a braille stylus is used to punch dots downward, which necessitates writing from right to left and turning the paper over to read the braille dots.

braille stylus: an awl-like punch for making braille dots by hand on a braille slate.

braille typewriter: *see* **brailler.**

brailler: a portable machine used to produce braille; also called *braille typewriter* or *braillewriter.*

braillewriter: *see* **brailler.**

braillist: one who writes the punctographic system called braille or transcribes print materials into braille for visually handicapped readers.

brain: that portion of the central nervous system enclosed within the skull; an organ important for consciousness, ideation, and voluntary muscular control, receiving impressions from the organs of special sense and regulating functions necessary to life, such as respiration, circulation, and continuing adjustments.

brain-injured child: *see* **child, brain-injured.**

brain injury: any damage to or destruction of the tissues of the brain; any damage leading to impairment of the function of the brain.

brain lesion: a localized macroscopic damage to the brain; destruction of brain tissue.

brain potentials: measurable oscillating electrical impulses of low voltage originating in the cerebral cortex.

brain syndrome, chronic: brain damage from various causes, including psychosis and head injury, and resulting in a behavior pattern characterized by confusion, forgetfulness, poor judgment, and other features similar to those of senility. *See* **syndrome.**

brain-wave intelligence testing: *see* **testing, brain-wave intelligence.**

brain waves: *see* **waves, brain.**

brainstorming: a popular nontechnical term for certain techniques for the stimulation of creative thinking in the development of new ideas; consists of individual or, more generally, small-group activity in which a deliberate attempt is made to think uncritically but creatively about all possible approaches and solutions to a given problem, the group participating in spontaneous and unrestrained discussion which usually involves evaluative feedback.

brainwashing: a metaphorical term for the process of inducing a person to depart radically from his former behavior patterns and standards and to adopt those imposed on him by his captors.

branch: in programmed instruction, a point of choice at which students are sent to alternative items depending on their responses to the particular item; may consist of a single item explaining why a particular answer is incorrect and returning the student to the original item for another try; may also refer to the point at which a criterion item is inserted in a linear program; by successful response to this item the student is sent forward several items, otherwise he takes an intervening sequence of review or remedial items or may be sent backward in the program to repeat inadequately mastered items; branching is based more often on multiple-choice responses than on constructed responses. *See* **branching, backward; branching, forward; item, multiple-choice; programming, intrinsic; programming, linear; response, constructed.**

branch junior college: *see* **junior college, branch.**

branch library: *see* **library, branch.**

branch material curriculum: *see* **curriculum, branch material.**

branch school: an army school which conducts an officer basic and/or advanced course; such schools, under the supervision of the U.S. Continental Army Command, are the Adjutant General School, Air Defense School, Armor School, Artillery and Missile School, Chaplain School, Chemical School, Engineer School, Finance School, Infantry School, Intelligence School, Medical Service Veterinary School, Military Police School, Ordnance School, Quartermaster School, Signal School, Southeastern Signal School, Transportation School, and Women's Army Corps School.

branch, university: *see* **university branch.**

branching: a technique of intrinsic programming developed by Dr. Norman Crowder whereby the student may be routed through one or more remedial sequences of frames if he misses a question or skipped ahead if he evidences mastery of content in a sequence; may also provide optional enrichment of a subject; in either case, student eventually is returned to the main line. *Contr. w.* **programming, linear.**

branching, backward: in programmed instruction, sending the student backward in the program to repeat items he has already seen but inadequately mastered. *Syn.* **washback.**

branching, forward: in linear programming of instruction, sending the student forward several items if he passes successfully a criterion item of the program or sending him to an intervening review or a remedial sequence if he does not pass.

brass instruments: *see* **instruments, brass.**

breach of contract: *see* **contract, breach of.**

break: the point of change from one register to another in voice or instrument.

breakdown, job: *see* **job breakdown.**

breakfast program: *see* **program, breakfast.**

breaking of contract: *syn.* **contract, breach of.**

breaking point, tape: the degree of tension required to break audiotape; acetate tape, when pulled hard from the ends, breaks off cleanly and may be spliced back together; polyester tape stretches before it breaks, thus distorting any sound already on it.

breakpoint: a point in a program at which an automatic computer may be made to stop automatically for a check on the progress of the data handling.

breakthrough: a sudden advance in science or technology that opens the way to a new and greater capability, as in "the breakthrough of Einstein in his $E = mc^2$."

breath control: the efficient use of the breath in playing an instrument or in singing. *See* **breathing, diaphragmatic.**

breath group: a sense-making group of words in a reading drill which should be read by the eye as a unit, just as they would be spoken in a single breath.

breathing abnormality: *see* **abnormality, breathing.**

breathing, diaphragmatic: the direct and conscious use of the diaphragm in the storage, control, and release of the airstream in singing and in playing wind instruments. *See* **breath control.**

Brethren of the Common Life: an association formed in Holland in the late fourteenth century for the purpose of educating boys in the simple Christian virtues, piety, and a little Latin; the movement spread through the Low Countries and northern France and Germany.

breve (brēv): a short half circle placed over a vowel to indicate the short sound.

bricklayer: (voc. ed.) a person who lays building materials such as bricks, concrete or cinder blocks, or glass bricks by spreading mortar and applying courses of the building material.

brief: *n.* (1) (legal) an abbreviated and generally written viewpoint in a case at law; (2) (mil. ed.) an oral presentation dealing with a military subject given by a military person to another military person, usually upon specific request of the latter.

brief: *v.* to give a person or group of persons such as an air crew specific advance instructions or information.

brief form: (shorthand) an abbreviated outline for the word or words that occur most often in our spoken or written language; to be memorized in order to facilitate automatization and thus help the student gain more speed in writing shorthand.

brief, occupational: *see* **occupational brief.**

bright: well above the norm in mental capacity and academic achievement.

bright child: *see* **child, bright.**

brightness: the degree of general intellectual ability, usually assumed to be due largely to the person's nature or constitution. *See* **index of brightness.**

brightness, coefficient of: *see* **coefficient of brightness.**

brightness, index of: *see* **index of brightness.**

brightness ratio: the ratio of the brightest to the darkest part of a central visual area.

bristol board: a fine quality cardboard sometimes used for making charts and posters; lighter than *oak tag*; it lends itself especially to working in black or colored inks. *See* **manila tagboard.**

British and Foreign School Society: a nondenominational organization founded in England in 1814 for the education of the poor, largely owing to the influence of Joseph Lancaster.

British thermal unit (Btu): the quantity of heat required to raise the temperature of one pound of water one degree Fahrenheit at or near its point of maximum density; used as a unit in calculations and specifications for the purchase of fuel.

broad-band amplification: *see* **amplification, broad-band.**

broad-field course: *see* **course, broad-field.**

broad-field organization: organization of the curriculum on the basis of fewer, more inclusive subject fields (such as language arts, mathematics, social studies, sciences) as distinguished from organization on the basis of separated subjects (such as reading, writing, spelling, literature, composition, arithmetic, algebra). *See* **course, broad-field.**

broad-field specialization: *see* **field of concentration, major.**

broad-fields curriculum: *see* **curriculum, broad-fields.**

broad-fields major: *see* **major, broad-fields.**

broad subject field: *see* **subject field.**

broad unit: *see* **unit, activity.**

broadcast: *n.* any transmitted radio or television program, announcement, or signal.

broadcast: *v.* to transmit any radio or televison program, announcement, or signal.

broadcast, actuality: a program based on facts or existing conditions rather than on imaginative creation. Archaic *syn.* **documentary broadcast.**

broadcast, classroom: (1) a broadcast program listened to during school hours as part of the instructional process; (2) a specially prepared broadcast lesson intended to supplement or replace teacher and/or textbook presentation of subject matter.

broadcast course: *see* **college of the air.**

broadcast, delayed: the presentation at a time later than the original production of a broadcast recorded for such subsequent use.

broadcast demonstration lesson: *see* **lesson, broadcast demonstration.**

broadcast, documentary: *syn.* **broadcast, actuality.**

broadcast, educational: (1) a broadcast intended for classroom use; (2) in a broader sense, any program intended primarily to present an educational message; may be a sustaining program or a commercial offering that has educational and/or cultural appeal.

broadcast, foreign: a radio program presented in a foreign language; an instructional device being used increasingly in the United States, especially on the Atlantic Coast, as an aid in the direct-method plan of foreign language instruction.

broadcast, international: a broadcast originating in or beamed to another country.

broadcast lesson: *see* **lesson, broadcast.**

broadcast-lesson guide: material prepared in advance of broadcast for the purpose of aiding preparation, listening, and follow-up of the broadcast; frequently includes a bibliography and questions.

broadcast, on-the-spot: a broadcast originating from the scene of an event, as distinguished from a broadcast originating in the studio. *Syn.* **remote broadcast.**

broadcast, remote: *syn.* **broadcast, on-the-spot.**

broadcast, remote-control: any broadcast originating outside the regular studios. *Syn.* **on-the-spot broadcast.**

broadcast, school: a broadcast program presented by students and/or faculty members of a school. (Such a program may or may not be intended for classroom use.) *Dist. f.* **lesson, broadcast.**

broadcast, studio: broadcast originating from a studio. *Dist. f.* **broadcast, on-the-spot.**

broadcast, talk: a radio program that consists entirely or almost entirely of the spoken word.

broadcaster, educational: (1) one who broadcasts educational or instructional programs; (2) all personnel, including owner, engaged in educational broadcasting.

broadcasting, adult education: the production of broadcasts for the purpose of giving the public definite information about a subject, project, etc.; used extensively by institutions of higher education and public school systems, stressing especially historical relationships and motives as these lend themselves to dramatization.

broadcasting, documentary: the production of radio programs based on historical, factual data.

broadcasting, public relations: the presentation of broadcasts for the purpose of drawing favorable attention to educational activities and ideals.

broadcasting, remote: *see* **broadcast, on-the-spot.**

broadcasting, remote-control: the production of a broadcast program at some distance from the main station, for example, interviewing people on the street or producing a program in a factory; necessitates the use of portable or at least movable transmitters or the use of telephone lines connected with the main station.

broadcasting, shortwave: the transmission of radio programs by means of electric waves of 60 meters or less; enables messages to be sent over greater distances than is possible with high-frequency broadcasting and accordingly has been used for the international dissemination of information and propaganda. (Some school systems, such as those of Cleveland and New York City, disseminate radio lessons by *shortwave broadcasting.*) *Contr. w.* **broadcasting, ultrahigh-frequency.**

broadcasting, ultrahigh-frequency: *see* **frequency, ultrahigh.**

Broca's area: a term applied to the inferior frontal gyrus of the dominant cerebral hemisphere; a lesion of this area is often associated with motor aphasia. *See* **aphasia, motor.**

broken home: any home where one or both parents are dead or where the parents are divorced or separated.

broken-line graph: *see* **graph, line.**

broken series: *syn.* **series, discrete.**

Bronxville goal card: *see* **goal card, Bronxville.**

brother: (R.C. ed.) in religious community life, one voluntarily bound by vows of poverty, chastity, and obedience; a teaching brother devotes his time to instruction; a lay brother devotes his time to manual labor and other secular activity; brothers do not receive Holy Orders.

brotherhood of man: the doctrine that men are brothers because they are created by God, their common Father; the belief and practice of equality deriving from this doctrine.

brotherhood, religious: a religious community, usually organized along monastic lines, consisting of men (clergy and/or laity) dedicated to education or to some religious or charitable activity.

brotherhood week: an annual program observed in many communities to promote good will among various racial and religious groups, usually emphasizing their similarities and pursuit of common social goals.

Brothers of the Christian Schools, Institute of: a Roman Catholic organization founded by St. Jean Baptiste de la Salle in 1684 to provide gratuitous elementary instruction for poor children. (The first school was in Reims, and others were soon opened elsewhere in France and in Italy.)

Brothers of the Common Life: a nonmonastic religious order or brotherhood that, during the period from the fourteenth to the sixteenth century, organized secondary civic and ecclesiastical schools in Western Europe, especially in the Netherlands.

Brown-Spearman formula: *syn.* **Spearman-Brown prophecy formula.**

Brown-Spearman prophecy formula: *syn.* **Spearman-Brown prophecy formula.**

Brown's formula: *syn.* **Spearman-Brown prophecy formula.**

browsing period: *see* **period, free-reading.**

browsing room: a special room (or corner of a larger reading room) housing books and periodicals for recreational reading, usually equipped with comfortable furniture, thus providing generally an atmosphere conducive to reading for pleasure; books are easily accessible to the reader so that he may examine and read them without formally withdrawing them.

Bruhn method (brōōn): an adaptation of the Müller-Walle method of teaching lipreading, stressing speech movements and utilizing syllable drill to build sentences. *See* **Müller-Walle method.**

buccal cavity: the inside of the mouth, that is, the cavity formed by the cheeks, palate, and other interior surfaces of the mouth.

buccal whisper: *see* **whisper, buccal.**

buck: a half-length gymnastic horse without pommels.

Buddhism: the religion, dating from the sixth century B.C., originating in the teaching of the Hindu seer, Gautama Siddhartha, known as the *Buddha,* "the enlightened one"; regards conscious existence as essentially evil and seeks escape from it to nirvana, a state of individual extinction, by means of emancipation from all desire, until which time the soul is condemned to successive reincarnations; holds the view that there is no god, but that each individual may become a Buddha.

buddy system: (safety ed.) a plan of pairing all bathers in groups according to their respective abilities and making each member of the pair responsible for knowing the other's whereabouts during swimming; also used to denote similar pairing in camps, the military, and other youth groups; outside of bathers there can be more than two buddies in a group.

budget: (1) an estimate of proposed expenditures for a given period or purpose and the proposed means of financing them; (2) a forecast of the content of one issue of a student publication; (3) (typewriting) a number of typewriting exercises, usually pertaining to one type of problem, included in an extensive assignment to be completed within a week or longer period of time.

budget, appropriational: a budget, characterized by the designation of sums available for specific items of expenditure, the adoption of which automatically authorizes the expenditure listed.

budget calendar: a statement or register in table form listing the days, weeks, and months of the year together with an indication of the time when particular portions of the budget should be made, by whom they should be made, and other similar data.

budget, capital outlay: (school finance) proposed program for construction, additions to facilities, or other permanent improvements; usually contains priorities and timetable for completion. *See* **capital outlay.**

budget, consumer: (1) systematic plan designed by an individual or family to obtain maximum utility from the available money; (2) a published model designed to assist consumers in planning their expenditures.

budget estimate: an estimate of the expenditures necessary to provide for the program of the school over a designated period of time.

budget, family: *see* **budget, household.**

budget form: (1) the order and arrangement of the contents of the budget; (2) a particular blank or blanks on which the official budget estimates are to be entered according to prescribed order and arrangement of items.

budget, household: a plan for weekly or monthly expenditures needed for the operation of the household, incuding housing, food, and clothing for the family; may include the yearly distribution of the total family income and establish a pattern for its use, in this case including financial plans for education, recreation, health, savings, etc.

budget, performance: a budget set up on the expenditure side in terms of amounts to be used for each element or project in the total program; contrasts with a budget set up in terms of amounts for various objects, such as salaries, wages, supplies, and equipment.

budget period: (school admin.) the period of time, usually a year, for which future income and expenditures are estimated.

budget, preliminary: the tentative, temporary, or prefatory budget; the budget that is temporarily used or followed until the final actual budget is available. *See* **budget.**

budgetary accounts: *see* **accounts, budgetary.**

budgetary control: the limitation of the amount and type of school expenditures according to the sums for such expenditures provided in the budget. (Budget appropriations are usually entered on the accounting ledgers in red and serve as a constant control to prevent expenditures in any account from exceeding the amount allocated in the budget for that account.)

budgetary procedure: (1) the established or approved practice or method of action followed in establishing or administering a budget; (2) the use of an adopted budget in keeping expenditures within the limitations of appropriation (the latter use is better expressed by the term *budgetary control*).

budgeting, time: planning efficient use of time whether on an hourly, daily, weekly, or extended basis; allows time for school activities, study, recreation, personal responsibilities, and rest; in the classroom or laboratory, time schedules must be set up (by the teacher or student) to assure the completion of the project or experiment by the end of the period.

budgets, state approval of: an administrative procedure, which may be required by state law, whereby the chief state school officer or state board of education reviews and approves the budget of a school district.

buffer: in automatic computers, an isolating circuit used to avoid any reaction of a driven circuit upon the corresponding driving circuit.

buffer storage: *see* **storage, buffer.**

bug: (1) an error in a computer program; (2) a malfunction in a computing machine.

building: an edifice or structure having outside walls and a roof enclosing space for use, but not a structure on wheels or one designed to float on water; presumed to be permanently attached to the ground and considered as belonging to the real estate.

building, academic: a building of a university, college, or school district devoted to classroom instruction.

building administration: *see* **administration, building.**

building authority, school: *see* **authority, school building.**

building blocks, hollow: *see* **blocks, hollow building.**

building, club: a building used for lounging and recreation purposes; may have provision for the serving of food and soft drinks and for sleeping quarters for guests of the university, college, or school; a faculty club building or a student club building; a union building.

building code: the requirements in the form of laws, ordinances, and regulations relating to the construction of buildings.

building construction: *see* **construction, building.**

building construction, types of: five types of school and college buildings, defined as follows: type *A*, constructed of fire-resistive materials in gross structure and interior; types *B*, *C*, and *D*, progressively less fire-resistive; type *E*, constructed chiefly of wood.

building contract: *see* **contract, building.**

building costs: *see* **costs, building.**

building debt: *see* **debt, building.**

building depreciation: *see* **depreciation, building.**

building equipment: *see* **equipment, building.**

building estimate: calculation of the probable cost of a building or buildings in accordance with plans and specifications for construction.

building evaluation: the determination of the merits or usefulness of a building.

building, fire-resistive: a building having little flammable material in its construction. *See* **building, fireproof-structure; building construction, types of; construction, fireproof; construction, fire-resistive.**

building, fireproof-structure: a building having no flammable material in its construction. *See* **construction, fireproof.**

building, frame: a building in which the main structural material is wood.

building illumination: *see* **illumination, building.**

building inspection: *see* **inspection, building.**

building insurance: *see* **insurance, building.**

building, library: a building in which books are housed in classified order and which provides reading rooms for students.

building material: the substances used in the construction of buildings, for example, brick, wood, stucco, steel, concrete, and various metals.

building of background: *see* **preparation** (2).

building orientation: *see* **orientation, building.**

building pass: a properly authorized form showing that the student holder is entitled to go to a room or part of a building in which he is not ordinarily expected to be at the time; it usually designates his name, the time, and the place to which he is authorized to go.

building, per pupil cost of a: *see* **cost of a building, per pupil.**

building, placement of: *see* **placement of building.**

building, portable: a building designed and constructed so that after temporary use in some location it can be transported elsewhere, either as a whole or disassembled. *Comp. w.* **classroom, mobile.**

building principal: *see* **principal, building.**

building program: *see* **program, building.**

building sanitation: *see* **sanitation, building.**

building scale: *see* **scale, building.**

building, science: a building containing laboratories equipped with science apparatus, devoted entirely or largely to instruction or research in science, and with other rooms for lectures, storage, and the like.

building score: *see* **score, building.**

building score card: *see* **score card, building.**

building service facilities, school: the school building provisions for hot and cold water, electric light and power, telephone service, fire alarms, clock-and-bell system, public-address system, etc.

building site: *see* **site, building.**

building specifications: the itemized requirements to be furnished or produced, as for a building, grounds, or equipment; a written or printed description of work to be done, the manner in which the work is to be executed, type and quality of material to be furnished, and the dimensions of the structure or other unit, all of which are a corporate part of the contract.

building standards: *see* **standards, building.**

building, student-union: a special building in which are housed the facilities for and organizations concerned with student recreational, social, and governmental activities; usually equipped and maintained by a special fee paid by all students and governed by a board composed of elected students and appointed faculty members. *See* **student union.**

building superintendent: *see* **superintendent, building.**

building survey: *see* **survey, building.**

building-up process: *see* **synthetic method** (5).

building, useful life of school: the number of years it is estimated a school building can be used for public school purposes before becoming unfit for use because of deterioration or obsolescence.

building, utility: a building containing electric generators and other mechanical equipment to produce and/or regulate the power, light, and other utilities for an educational or other institution.

building valuation: *see* **valuation, building.**

building work schedule: *see* **schedule, building work.**

buildings and grounds, department of: *see* **department of buildings and grounds.**

buildings, appraisal of: *see* **appraisal of buildings.**

buildings, flexibility of: *see* **flexibility of buildings.**

buildings, grounds, and equipment, administration of: *see* **administration, building; administration, physical plant.**

buildings, maintenance of: *see* **maintenance of buildings.**

buildings, operation of: *see* **operation of buildings.**

buildings, orientation of: *see* **orientation, school.**

buildings, planning of: *see* **planning of buildings.**

buildings, remodeling of: *see* **remodeling of buildings.**

built-in check: *see* **check, built-in.**

built-in features: stationary cupboards, closets, cases, seats, wall benches, tables, and the like built into a school building.

bulbar poliomyelitis: *see* **poliomyelitis, bulbar.**

bulk eraser: *see* **erase** (1).

bulkhead delusions: *see* **compartmentalization.**

bulletin, administrative: a publication that originates from the administrative offices of a school or school system and that contains information pertaining to the direction, control, and/or management of the schools; may be intended for administrative officers, other members of the school staff, parents, or the general citizenry of the school district.

bulletin analysis: *see* **analysis, bulletin.**

bulletin board: a board to which can be fastened pictures or other materials that are intended for display. *Syn.* **tackboard** (1).

bulletin, curriculum: *see* **curriculum bulletin.**

bulletin, office: statement of news, information, or policies issued by an administrative officer; a means of conveying information to the staff.

bullying: a type of aggressive behavior, found mostly in boys, that obtains for the person a status position of leadership; such behavior is considered to be an over-compensation for failure or threatened behavior.

bureau, appointments: *syn.* **placement bureau.**

bureau, juvenile aid: *see* **juvenile aid bureau.**

bureau, materials: *see* **materials bureau.**

bureau of attendance: *syn.* **department, attendance.**

bureau of child accounting: (1) the local office of the school system that is responsible for planning, coordinating, and supervising the system's child-accounting activities, including attendance service; (2) *syn.* **department, attendance.**

bureau of compulsory education: *syn.* **department, attendance.**

bureau of institutional research: *syn.* **bureau of research.**

bureau of Jewish education: a term applied to a central community agency which services Jewish educational institutions and plans overall programs of Jewish education in the community; also designated as board, council, or committee on Jewish education.

Bureau of Naval Personnel (BuPers): a board generally concerned with the procurement, training, promotion, assignment, and discipline of officer and enlisted personnel of the Navy.

bureau of pupil personnel: the local division of the public school system that is responsible for planning, coordinating, and supervising all pupil-personnel activities. (The title is recent; now in the process of being adopted by a number of cities; in cities using the title, attempts are being made to bring all pupil-personnel agencies under a single administrative control.) *See* **personnel, pupil.**

bureau of recommendations director: *syn.* **director of placement.**

bureau of research: a part of an association or an agency organized usually within a university or a state or city school system for the purpose of carrying on research functions; often called *bureau of institutional research* or bureau of institutional research and planning. *See* **research, institutional.**

bureau of teacher recommendations: *syn.* **placement bureau, teacher.**

bureau, placement: *see* **placement bureau.**

bureau, speakers: *see* **speakers bureau.**

bureau, university extension: *see* **extension bureau, university.**

bureaucracy: (1) an organization for administering a formal structure characterized by rules, a hierarchy of offices, and centralized authority; (2) sometimes used pejoratively to imply cumbersomeness resulting from excessive complexity of organization. *See* **ombudsman.**

bureaucratic administration: *see* **adminstration, bureaucratic.**

burgher school: a type of school, developed during the later Middle Ages in most of the Hanseatic towns, that was established and controlled by the municipal authorities although tuition usually was charged. (Such schools were very common in the Netherlands.)

Burpee: *syn.* **squat-thrust.**

bursar: the treasurer of an educational institution such as a college; commonly used in England and Canada but less frequently in the United States.

bursary: (1) the treasury of a public institution or a religious order; (2) a grant or foundation for maintenance of beneficiary students.

bus: in an automatic computer, a pathway (such as an electrically protected cable) for the transmission of data, usually in the form of electrical pulses.

bus accessory: equipment that is not essential to the mechanical operation of a school bus but which adds to the convenience or safety of its passengers. *Dist. f.* **bus equipment.**

bus alterations: *see* **alterations, bus.**

bus body: that portion of the vehicle mounted on the bus chassis and in which the passengers are carried.

bus capacity: *see* **capacity, bus.**

bus capacity utilization: *see* **capacity utilization, bus.**

bus chassis: the under part of a bus, consisting of wheels, motor, mechanical parts, controls, and frame on which the bus body is mounted.

bus, church: a bus used by a religious organization to transport individuals for the purpose of worship, study, recreation, etc.

bus construction: (1) the material used and the process of manufacturing or assembling the bus; (2) the nature of the vehicle's component parts and their assemblage.

bus, contract: a school bus owned by an individual, partnership, or corporation which is provided, operated, and maintained in accordance with a stipulated agreement with school authorities.

bus contract: *see* **contract, bus.**

bus, conventional type: a bus having its engine encased in a hood located forward and outside the body.

bus depreciation: *see* **depreciation, bus.**

bus driver: a person assigned to drive and to be responsible for the operation of the school bus.

bus-driver certificate: *see* **certificate, bus-driver.**

bus equipment: those items generally considered essential to the safe and comfortable operation of the school bus but which are not a part of the original construction, such as heaters, fire extinguishers, and first-aid kits. *Dist. f.* **bus accessory.**

bus, extended use of: *syn.* **vehicle, nonroutine use of.**

bus fleet: several buses owned or controlled by one operating unit, individual, organization, or school district.

bus garage: (1) a building or addition used for the purpose of storing school buses; (2) a building used for the repair of school buses.

bus lease: a written agreement that arranges for the provision of a school bus without supplies, maintenance, or the services of a driver.

bus, leased: a bus owned by an individual or organization but leased and operated by a governmental unit such as a state, county, town, or school district.

bus load: a term that refers to the passengers in a school bus.

bus maintenance: (1) those services which keep a bus in safe and efficient operating condition; (2) services designed to retard depreciation.

bus mile: *see* **mile, bus.**

bus, privately owned: (1) a bus owned by an individual, partnership, or corporation as distinguished from a vehicle owned by the public school district; (2) a car owned by a parent or neighbor who is paid from public funds to transport his own and sometimes other children to school.

bus, publicly owned: a vehicle owned by a school district, municipality, or other unit of governmental organization and used for the transportation of pupils.

bus, relief: (1) a bus for temporary use while the regular bus is out of service; (2) a motor bus for temporary use in addition to the buses in the regular fleet.

bus route: the entire way traveled by a bus in transporting children to and from school, not including the distance from the bus garage to the starting point; it may be composed of one or more trips. *See* **bus trip.**

bus, school: a motor coach approved by a controlling board for transportation of pupils.

bus, spare: *syn.* **bus, relief.**

bus trip: the travel of a bus from the point of departure to the first place where the bus is completely unloaded.

buses, routing of: *see* **routing of buses.**

buses, state provision for purchase of: state legislation permitting or requiring school districts to purchase, operate, and maintain buses for the transportation of school children.

business administration: *see* **administration, business.**

business agent: a member of the faculty of an educational institution who acts as the agent of the president in administering its business, assisting the president in preparing the budget and controlling its operation.

business and office education advisory committee: *see* **committee, business and office education advisory.**

business and office education area supervisor: *see* **supervisor, business and office education assistant state.**

business and office education assistant state supervisor: *see* **supervisor, business and office education assistant state.**

business and office education certification: *see* **certification, business and office education.**

business and office education, core intensive: a combination of intensive business and office education and cooperative office education designed for students who, entering their senior year of high school, decide that they are interested in but unprepared for an office occupation; they receive intensive instruction in the first semester and cooperative instruction and actual work experience in the second semester. *See* **business and office education, intensive; office education, cooperative.**

business and office education, intensive: a combination or sequence of subjects, locally determined and state approved, developed for students who need depth training in skills and related areas of vocational business and office education. *See* **block of time; instruction, business and office education related.**

business and office education preemployment instruction: *see* **instruction, business and office education preparatory.**

business and office education preparatory instruction: *see* **instruction, business and office education preparatory.**

business and office education related instruction: *see* **instruction, business and office education related.**

business and office education taxonomy: *see* **taxonomy, business and office education.**

business and office education teacher educator: *see* **educator, business and office education teacher.**

business and office education training plan: *see* **training plan, business and office education.**

business and office education training sponsor: *see* **training sponsor, business and office education.**

business and office occupational group: *see* **group, business and office occupational.**

business arithmetic: *see* **mathematics, applied.**

business club: *see* **club, business.**

business college: *see* **college, business.**

business, college of: a school or college of a university providing study at the undergraduate and/or graduate level in business, commerce, and related areas; degrees awarded are typically bachelor of business administration (B.B.A.), master of business administration (M.B.A.), and doctor of business administration (D.B.A.); also called *school of business. Contr. w.* **college, business.**

business communications: *see* **communications, business.**

business correspondence: (1) intercourse by letter between business individuals or business firms; the written communications themselves; (2) the designation of a subject, taught in secondary school or college, dealing with the principles underlying the writing of business letters and other written business communications; (3) the designation of an abridged course in business English.

business course, basic: *see* **business education, basic.**

business data processing systems occupations training: *see* **training, business data processing systems occupations.**

business economics: *see* **economics, business.**

business education: (1) that area of education which develops skills, attitudes, and understandings essential for the successful direction of business relationships; (2) an area of study dealing with the principles and practices of teaching business subjects. *Syn.* **commercial education.**

business education, agricultural: *syn.* **agribusiness education;** *see* **agricultural mechanics education; agricultural products education; agricultural supplies education.**

business education, basic: a study of business functions for everyday living which are common to all people; designed to help the student understand the role of business in our democratic society, to develop an understanding of the interrelationship of business and the community, to help the student attain competency in economic planning, financing, and consuming, and to develop the necessary solutions for dealing with business problems in a changing social and economic environment; the most usual basic business subjects are (*a*) a ninth-grade course variously titled *elementary business training, general business, general business science, business* I, etc., (*b*) *economic geography,* (*c*) *marketing,* (*d*) *business law,* (*e*) *personal record keeping,* (*f*) *consumer education* (when offered by the business education department), and (*g*) an eleventh- or twelfth-grade course variously titled *business economics, consumer economics, economics, business* II, *business* IV, etc. *Syn.* **general business education; social business education; socioeconomic education.**

business education, consumer: the elements of economics, finance, and business relationships as they affect the individual as a consumer; the basic elements of business education taught from the consumer viewpoint.

business education, general: *syn.* **business education, basic.**

business education, social: *syn.* **business education, basic.**

business, elementary: *syn.* **training, junior business.**

business English: an area of study dealing with the principles of English, both written and oral, that are applicable to business; may include the principles governing business-letter writing as well as advertisement writing, business reports, sales talks, the preparation of telegrams, and the writing of minutes.

business ethics: *see* **ethics, business.**

business executive, coordinate: a school business officer responsible to the board of education and coordinate with the superintendent of schools. (An organization having officers of this kind is termed the *multiple type* of organization, as contrasted with the *unit type,* in which the chief business officer is subordinate to the superintendent of schools.)

business experience in distribution: *see* **experience in distribution, business.**

business, general: *syn.* **training, junior business.**

business geography: *syn.* **geography, commercial.**

business high school: *see* **high school, business.**

business, industry, education day (BIE day): a type of in-service training for teachers and guidance counselors; schools are closed and the teachers have the opportunity to visit local businesses and industries; in addition to a tour they receive information about employment procedures, employee-employer problems, manufacturing problems, finance, etc.; results of the experience include better community cooperation and better informed counselors. *See* **education, industry, business day.**

business-labor relations: *see* **relations, business-labor.**

business law: *see* **law, business.**

business management: *see* **administration, business.**

business manager: the officer of the school directly responsible for its business affairs. (Frequently in public schools the business manager is designated as assistant superintendent in charge of business affairs and as such is subordinate to the superintendent of schools; in some school systems, however, he is coordinate with the superintendent of schools and directly responsible to the school board.)

business mathematics: *see* **mathematics, applied.**

business organization course: *see* **course, business organization.**

business report: *see* **report, business.**

business school: *syn.* **college, business.**

business school, private: *syn.* **college, business.**

business staff: (journ.) the members of the staff of a student publication who are concerned with advertising, circulation, promotion, accounting, and finances.

business subject, technical: a specialized business subject (such as typewriting) usually integrating the development of a motor skill with other abilities.

business teacher: an accredited teacher of the business subjects, such as shorthand, typewriting, office machines, bookkeeping, basic business, and other business courses.

business training: *syn.* **training, junior business.**

business writing: *see* **writing, business.**

bust: (mil. slang) (1) to reduce in military rate; (2) to fail or make a mistake.

busy-work: an outmoded term formerly used by primary teachers to designate time-filling assignments given to one group of young children during the period when the teacher was engaged in teaching another group.

buying, impulsive: *see* **impulsive buying.**

buying, installment: *see* **credit, installment.**

buymanship: skill in using money, time, and energy in order to yield the greatest total satisfaction of consumer wants.

buzz board: *see* **board, electric.**

buzz group: *see* **group, buzz.**

buzz session: informal discussion of a specific topic or question for a relatively brief period by small groups within a class or other large group to discuss and pool ideas of all individuals and to report their thinking verbally or in writing to the larger group for consideration.

bylaws: the code or collection of rules adopted by a board or other similar continuing association for the regulation of its own organization and proceedings; must not conflict with the statute or charter by which the board is created but may go further into detail in order to effectuate the intent of the statute or charter.

bypass looping: in programmed instruction, the employment of subgroups, (*1a, 1b, 1c; 2a, 2b, 2c;* etc.); if a student answers *a* correctly, he goes on, skipping *b* and *c* items, thus yielding a fast program; but a slow program is also provided, for if a student misses *a*, he goes on to *b*, and so on; bypassing allows a bright student to work through faster than a less bright student while preserving essentially the same linear sequence for all; this can be done for constructed responses or multiple-choice items or something in between.

bypassing: a programmed instructional technique which allows the learner to skip certain portions of the materials because of prior knowledge or greater learning ability. *See* **programming, intrinsic; programming, linear.**

byte: a term used in computer machine language for a collection of eight *binary digits. See* **bit.**

Byzantine art: *see* **art, Byzantine.**

C scale: a scale of derived scores having a mean of 5 and a standard deviation of 2; a variant of this is the *stanine scale* with a slightly lower standard deviation due to the fact that the two tail categories at either end of the distribution are combined to make 9 steps rather than 11.

C score: a normalized standard score of 11 units with a mean of 5 and a standard deviation of 3; a derived score expressed in terms of a *C scale.*

cab-over-engine: the designation of a type of school bus or other motor vehicle having the driver's cab located immediately above the engine.

cabinet, isolation: *see* **isolation cabinet.**

cabinet plan of supervision: *see* **supervision, cabinet plan of.**

cable tensiometer: *see* **tensiometer, cable.**

CAD properties: (math.) commutative, associative, and distributive properties. *See* **law, associative; law, commutative; law, distributive.**

cadence: (1) the modulation of the voice to form the rhythmic rise and fall of speech; *see* **pitch;** (2) the fall of the voice at the end of a sentence.

cadet: in a general sense, a student in a military school; specifically, within the Department of Defense, students in the United States Air Force Academy, Military Academy, and Air Force or Army ROTC. *See* **candidate, officer; midshipman; trainee, officer.**

cadet, aviation: (1) a person in training to become a commissioned Air Force or naval officer with an aeronautical rating; (2) the grade or status of such a person.

cadet, basic: a cadet in his first eight weeks at the Air Academy being prepared to enter the Cadet Wing fully qualified in basic military skills, physically fit for athletic participation, and mentally conditioned with a sense of honor and duty toward his academic studies.

cadet, distinguished Air Force: a student enrolled in an AFROTC unit who is judged to possess the qualities and attributes of a regular Air Force officer. *See* **graduate, distinguished.**

cadet officer: a cadet (either in an ROTC or in a military or an essentially military school) chosen to serve as an officer over his fellow students in the corps of cadets. (In the typical college or university the jurisdiction of the cadet officer is limited to military training class or drill periods; in a military or essentially military school the jurisdiction is somewhat extended.)

cadet program, Civil Air Patrol: *see* **program, Civil Air Patrol cadet.**

cadet, ROTC: a student enrolled in the senior ROTC of the Army, Navy, or Air Force. *See* **ROTC, senior.**

cadet teacher: *syn.* **apprentice teacher.**

cadet teaching: *see* **internship plan.**

cadet training: *see* **training, cadet.**

cafeteria feeding: *see* **feeding, cafeteria.**

cafeteria report: *see* **report, cafeteria.**

cafeteria, school: a room or building in which public school pupils or college students select prepared foods and serve themselves or are served plate lunches.

cafetorium: a multiple-purpose room used as a cafeteria and also as an auditorium.

cage, batting: *see* **batting cage.**

calculated average: *see* **average, calculated.**

calculating machine: *see* **machine, calculating.**

calculating operation: *see* **operation, calculating.**

calculation: *see* **computation.**

calculation, mechanical: *see* **computation, mechanical.**

calculator: (1) a keyboard-operated machine used to perform arithmetic computations; (2) a punched-card machine that reads data punched on cards, performs calculations, and punches the results of the calculation into cards.

calculator, printing: a simple keyboard calculator in which the calculations are recorded on a roll of paper.

calculus (kal'kū·ləs): (1) the branch of mathematics that deals with infinitesimal changes among related quantities or with those relationships among quantities implied by interdependent infinitesimal changes in the quantities; (2) any method of reasoning or computation that utilizes symbols.

Caldecott awards: *see* **awards, Caldecott.**

calendar, school: *see* **school calendar.**

calisthenics (kal'is·then'iks): formalized arm, leg, and trunk exercises done without apparatus.

calisthenics, continuous: calisthenic exercises in which one exercise follows another without interruption, instructions for the next exercise being given while one exercise is under way.

call: *v.* in automatic data processing, to place the necessary initial values of variables in the required addresses and then to transfer control to a *subroutine*.

call-in service: a telephone "listening" system, often manned 24 hours a day, which persons in need of help may call; usually not a counseling service per se but rather a liaison to appropriate helping organizations.

call instructor: *see* **instructor, call.**

call number: a symbol comprising the *class number* and the *book number*, by which the location of a book on the library shelf is indicated. *See* **classification, book.**

callable bond: *see* **bond, callable.**

callback: *syn.* **verification of census information.**

calligraphy (ka·li'grə·fi): (1) the art of lettering and/or handwriting as in medieval, Oriental, or other manuscript art forms; (2) an elaborate, flowing line in drawing and painting which resembles the continuous rhythms of an elegant handwriting.

calling-the-throw drill: *see* **drill, calling-the-throw.**

Calvert method: a system of reading instruction developed by Hillyer at Calvert School in Baltimore, Maryland; used in distant regions by parents, such as missionaries, to teach their children to read.

Calvinism: the body of Christian theological doctrine originating in the teachings of John Calvin (1509–1564); formally stated in the Five Points of Calvinism: predestination, limited atonement, total depravity, irresistibility of grace, and the perseverance of the saints; teaches that most are damned, some are saved.

cambiata (käm·byä'tə): (It., lit., "changed") (1) *syn.* **alto-tenor;** (2) (mus.) a nonharmonic note of a melody reached by a skip of a third and resolved by a step.

Cambridge plan: a type of elementary school organization devised in Cambridge, Massachusetts, intended to accelerate the progress of bright pupils under a graded system consisting of two parallel courses. *See* **parallel curriculum plan.**

camera angle, objective: (photog. and TV) spatial relationship between subject and camera which results in scenes as they would be viewed by a third person rather than as viewed by the protagonist. *Ant.* **camera angle, subjective.**

camera angle, subjective: (photog. and TV) spatial relationship between subject and camera which results in views or scenes giving the impression of being perceived through the eyes of the protagonist. *Ant.* **camera angle, objective.**

camera chain: a television camera connected to a control unit and viewing monitor. *See* **monitor, viewing.**

camera club: *see* **club, camera.**

camera gate: *see* **gate, camera.**

camera lens: *see* **lens, camera.**

camera, ophthalmograph: *syn.* **oculophotometer.**

camera, stereo: a camera with two lenses which takes two pictures simultaneously; when the finished pictures are properly mounted, the viewer gets a three-dimensional image.

camera switcher: *see* **switcher, camera.**

camera viewfinder: *see* **viewfinder, camera.**

camp counseling: *see* **counseling, camp.**

camp counselor: *see* **counselor, camp.**

camp director: *see* **director, camp.**

camp, institutional: (1) a camp generally operated by some character-building organization such as Boy Scouts, Girl

Scouts, or YMCA; (2) a camp operated by a charitable organization for the benefit of underprivileged children; the fee is sharply reduced or no fee at all is charged.

camp, leadership: a camp in which a major objective is training for social leadership.

camp, municipal: a camp owned and operated by a town or city as a part of its recreation program.

camp, music: a summer program of lessons and rehearsals for public school musicians; frequently located in a rustic environment, with appropriate recreational facilities and activities scheduled for all enrollees.

camp, private: a summer camp owned and operated primarily as a business venture.

camp, school: a camp, operated as a part of the educational function of a school, intended to place certain educative experiences in their natural environment; also may continue remedial treatments for crippled children during the summer months.

camp, summer: an established community where individuals live for a specified length of time participating in an organized camping program. *See* **camping.**

camp, summer church: a period (usually a week during the summer) of organized outdoor camping activity for young people and adults, sponsored by one or more church denominations and designed to contribute to the individual's social and religious welfare through the use of study courses, discussion groups, recreation, campfire programs, and outdoor worship.

campcraft: the building and use of equipment and devices for camping and/or instruction in camping techniques.

camping: simple living out of doors; usually implies that the individual assumes some responsibility for his own food and shelter and engages in activities related to his surroundings.

campus: the grounds of a university or college on which the buildings of the institution are situated; includes the grounds around the buildings but not those belonging to the institution at a distance from the buildings; often limited to the part of the grounds that is improved by landscaping. *See* **grounds** (1).

campus activities: *see* **activities, campus.**

campus care: the work connected with keeping a campus in an orderly, beautiful, and clean condition; includes care of trees, shrubs, grass, and flowers, removal of paper and rubbish, and work on walks and drives.

campus development: the gradual improvement of a campus through planting and caring for trees, shrubs, flowers, and grass.

campus recreation: *see* **recreation, campus.**

campus school: *syn.* **university school.**

canalization: the acquired specificity for a preferred outlet of expression, or fulfillment of a need, which facilitates the discharge of an emotion.

cancellation, additive: *see* **law, cancellation.**

cancellation law: *see* **law, cancellation.**

cancellation test: *see* **test, cancellation.**

candid camera: any camera having lens and shutter equipment suitable for work in poor light conditions and which can be used unobtrusively for taking unposed photographs without the knowledge of the subject.

candidacy: *see* **matriculation.**

candidate: (1) a person under favorable consideration by an employer for a position; (2) (mil. ed.) any individual under consideration for military status or for a military service program whether voluntary (appointment, enlistment, ROTC, etc.) or involuntary (induction).

candidate, naval aviation officer: a student attending the naval aviation officer candidate school. *See* **cadet; candidate, officer; Mister; naval aviation school.**

candidate, officer: a person undergoing training, especially rigorous, short-term training, to qualify for an officer's commission; more specifically, designates a student in the Army, Navy, or Marine officer candidate schools. *See* **cadet; trainee, officer.**

candidate, warrant officer: an enlisted man in the United States Army who is undergoing initial entry pilot training; upon successful completion of this training, the individual will be qualified as an Army aviator in either fixed-wing or rotary-wing aircraft; he will also be commissioned a warrant officer in the United States Army.

cane technique: a technique to aid the blind person in orienting himself and in walking alone; consists of the rhythmic movement of the cane he holds, from a focal point in front of the body, one full step in advance of him as he walks; he then steps into an arc of scanned area, this known area (scanned in advance by his long cane) changing every time he takes a step; known also as the *Hoover* or *touch technique.*

cannery, school: *see* **school cannery.**

canon: (1) any absolute standard or rule; (2) a rule or principle of logic accepted as true and axiomatic and used in the development of logical conclusions; (3) a form of music in which each part in turn takes up the melody, one a few beats behind the other, in strict imitation; (4) an ecclesiastical decree, as the canons of the Council of Trent.

canon law: the body of ecclesiastical rules or laws established by authority and used as a guide in church organization and administration in matters of faith, morals, and discipline; with the fragmentation of the Western Church at the Reformation, the separated communions developed distinct legal systems showing varying degrees of continuity with the past corpus of ecclesiastical law.

cantata (kän·tä′tə): an extended choral form of the baroque period based on a continuous narrative, often religious, and consisting of choruses, solos, duets, etc., without stage setting, costumes, or dramatization; an enlarged form of the very same description is known as an *oratorio.*

CAP: *see* **Program, Community Action.**

cap and gown: *see* **academic costume.**

capability: the ultimate limit of an individual's possible development as determined at a given time, assuming optimum environment and training from that time onward.

capacities: in guidance, measurement of abilities indicating the degree to which individuals accept self-potentiality; this is a process and is the continuation and culmination of all other behavioral dynamics.

capacity: (1) the ultimate limit to which an individual could develop any function, given optimum training and environment; (2) the extent of room or space; (3) the number of students that can be accommodated by a university, college, or school plant, by a building, or by a room; (4) the number of seats or laboratory stations in a building or room; *see* **capacity use.**

capacity, bus: the number of pupils a school bus is designed to carry, usually determined by allowing 13 inches of linear seating space per pupil. *See* **capacity utilization, bus.**

capacity, intellectual: *see* **capacity, mental.**

capacity, learning: the power of receiving and retaining concepts, data, and skills; the comprehensiveness or receptiveness of the mind; more generally, the potential, determined by heredity and environment, for latent change in or actual overt modification of the behavior of an organism.

capacity level, probable: (read.) the highest probable level of reading capacity, supposed to be indicated by the hearing comprehension level, as in the Durrell-Sullivan reading capacity test.

capacity, memory: *see* **memory capacity.**

capacity, mental: a generally determined maximum level of potential performance of the mind, as contrasted with ability, which describes the current level of mental achievement.

capacity, motor: (1) the maximum amount of muscular movement of which one is capable; (2) an individual's innate potentiality for all motor skill performance; (3) (pup. trans.) the ultimate limit of ability in motor performance of a vehicle, usually stated in terms of its weight per certified unit of horsepower.

capacity of chassis: the certified weight that the running gear of a motor vehicle will safely support.

capacity of classroom (or school laboratory): (1) the number of seats (student stations) that can be placed in a classroom, due allowance being made for aisles, instructors' desks and other furniture, and open space; (2) the number of students that can be accommodated in a classroom; sometimes computed on the basis of an allowance of a certain number of square feet of floor area per student or a certain number of cubic feet of space per student.

capacity of laboratory: (1) the number of student stations or places at tables or desks in a laboratory; (2) the number of students that can be accommodated in a laboratory at one time; sometimes computed as an allowance of a certain number of square feet of floor area or a certain number of cubic feet of space per student. *See* **station, work.**

capacity of laboratory, maximum: the largest number of students that can be accommodated in a laboratory at one time; determined either by computing the number of square feet per student and comparing the result with an accepted standard or by the number of student stations in the laboratory.

capacity of school plant, pupil: the membership that can be accommodated in the classrooms and other instruction areas of a given school plant for the school day according to existing state-approved standards, exclusive of multiple sessions; also called *normal capacity of school plant.*

capacity of vehicle: (1) *syn.* **capacity, motor** (3); (2) *syn.* **capacity, bus.**

capacity, physical: the limit of ability in motor activities.

capacity, physical working: the maximum level of metabolism (work) of which an individual is capable.

capacity, reading: (1) the ability to learn to receive ideas from the printed or written word and to make the necessary physical and mental adaptations required in the act of reading; (2) aptitude for reading as distinguished from acquired ability due to experience and training; (3) undeveloped capability for reading.

capacity reading level: *see* **reading level, capacity.**

capacity, sensory: the degree of stimulation or the range of stimuli to which a given receptor will respond; for example, the eye has capacity to respond to radiant energy vibrations between approximately 400 and 760 millimicrons.

capacity, social: the extent of one's ability to adjust to his cultural environment, to achieve and to maintain satisfactory relationships with other individuals and with groups, and to effect such relationships among others.

capacity, supervisory: *see* **supervisory capacity.**

capacity test: *syn.* **test, aptitude.**

capacity, usable: the proportion of the space, particularly floor area, of a building that can be used for instruction purposes, such as classrooms, laboratories, and gymnasiums, but exclusive of corridors, rotundas, storage rooms, or rooms not equipped with instruction furniture.

capacity use: the greatest amount of use that can be secured from a classroom, laboratory, building, or other unit, based on the standard schedule of hours the building is in use.

capacity utilization, bus: an expression in percent indicating the ratio between the number of pupils actually on the bus and the maximum rated capacity, obtained by dividing the former by the latter. *See* **capacity, bus.**

capacity, vital: the volume of air that can be forcefully expelled from the lungs as measured by a spirometer.

capacity, weight: the certified weight that a vehicle can safely transport.

capital assets: *syn.* **assets, fixed.**

capital cost: *see* **cost, capital.**

capital expenditure: *see* **expenditure, capital.**

capital fund: *see* **fund, capital.**

capital goods: *see* **goods, capital.**

capital improvement: *see* **improvement, capital.**

capital investment: funds invested in capital or fixed assets such as land, as contrasted with investments in liquid or short-term assets.

capital outlay: an expenditure that results in the acquisition of fixed assets or additions to fixed assets; it is an expenditure for land or existing buildings, improvement of grounds, construction of buildings, additions to buildings, remodeling of buildings, or initial or additional equipment; includes installment or lease payments on property which have a terminal date and result in the acquisition of the property.

capital outlay budget: *see* **budget, capital outlay.**

capitalism: a theory and system of economic organization based upon the following principles: (*a*) the right of private ownership in land, goods, and instruments of production; (*b*) the right of purchase and sale at the discretion of the individual; (*c*) the right to make a profit; (*d*) the inviolability of legal contracts; (*e*) the efficacy of competition; (*f*) the necessity of a market free of government controls; (*g*) the role of government restricted to the maintenance of order and the enforcement of contracts; and (*h*) a freely contracting, mobile labor force.

capitalist class: (commonly) those people who live from the income of stocks, bonds, or various forms of wealth and occupy the higher positions devoted to direction and control of capital and of the labor of others; one of the most powerful groups in a modern Western economic order; based on acquisition, in contrast with *caste.*

capitalist school: a school of economic thought that would place strict limitations on governmental activity in economic affairs and leave the economic development of the nation largely to private enterprise. *See* **laissez faire;** *contr. w.* **socialist school.**

capitation tax: *see* **tax, capitation.**

caption: (1) the heading or title for a column of entries in a table, placed at the top of the column it describes; *syn.* **box heading; column heading;** (2) the row across the top of a table containing the titles of the several columns of the table; (3) a printed explanation to accompany any of the visuals of audiovisual material.

captioned films for deaf: *see* **films for deaf, captioned.**

capture of data: *see* **data, capture of.**

carbon arc projector: *see* **projector, carbon arc.**

carbon pack: a preassembled pack of carbons and paper for typing multiple copies in one typing operation; also called carbon set.

card, aperture: a punch card, usually tab card size, in which a rectangular hole is die cut to accommodate mounting a frame of microfilm; may include bibliographic and descriptive information concerning the item involved.

card, borrower's: *see* **card, library.**

card catalog: an indexed list of books, periodicals, etc., printed or written on cards and arranged alphabetically.

card, check-out: *syn.* **guidance dismissal blank.**

card, control: in automatic data processing, a card which contains input data for application of a general routine.

card, cumulative record: *see* **cumulative record card.**

card, edge-notched: a card having a coding area around its perimeter into which coded data are entered by notching or punching holes in the perimeter.

card field: *see* **field, card.**

card, introduction: a small card issued by business and office education and distributive education coordinators to introduce prospective part-time cooperative students to employers.

card, item: one of the individual cards, maintained in an *item file,* on which questions or other items for tests are typed for easy reference and efficient construction of tests of foreign language proficiency.

card, job-opportunity: a record used in the distributive education program to list positions that are available to cooperative part-time students.

card, library: a card issued by a circulating library entitling individuals to borrow books.

card, load: a punched card with machine language instructions which are executed immediately by the automatic computer; often serves as a bootstrap.

card, master: a punched card storage means for common data that has frequent use (IBM).

card, officer's data: a card maintained in the Bureau of Naval Personnel containing data needed for assignment to duty and career planning.

card, punch: a heavy, stiff paper of constant size and shape, suitable for punching in a pattern that has meaning and for being handled mechanically; the punched holes are sensed electrically by wire brushes, mechanically by metal fingers, or photoelectrically by photocells.

card punching: the act or process of recording data by punching holes into cards by means of a mechanical punch called a *key punch;* a machine somewhat similar to a typewriter. See **card, punch.**

card punching unit: in automatic data processing, a machine that takes and converts data into coded holes in standard cards.

card reading unit: in an automatic computer, a unit which reads the holes punched in standard cards.

card reproducer: a device that reproduces a punch card by punching another similar card.

card, school-leaving: *syn.* **guidance dismissal blank.**

card, soldier's qualification: (mil. ed.) basic classification record of every enlisted man; contains a summary of his personal history, schooling, occupational and military experience, test scores, and other information.

card sorter: a machine for sorting punch cards electrically or mechanically, for example, an *IBM sorter.*

card-sorting test: *see* **test, card-sorting.**

card-to-tape converter: *see* **converter, card-to-tape.**

card, unit: (libr. sci.) a basic main entry catalog card which, when duplicated, may be utilized in the card catalog as a unit for all other catalog entries for a particular work by adding the appropriate heading.

cardiac case: any person suffering from either a congenital or an acquired form of heart disease.

cardiac class: *see* **class, cardiac.**

cardinal number: *see* **number, cardinal.**

cardinal principles: *see* **seven cardinal objectives or principles.**

cardinal virtues: *see* **virtues, cardinal.**

cardiogram: a tracing produced by means of the cardiograph.

cardiograph: an instrument used to indicate the force and form of the heart's movements.

cardiotachometer: an instrument that makes a continuous record of the heart rate.

cardiovascular endurance: *see* **endurance, cardiovascular.**

cardiovascular test: *see* **test, cardiovascular.**

care and guidance of children: an area of study in home economics in secondary schools, vocational schools, and technical institutes which prepares for employment in a variety of situations as assistants in day-care centers, nursery schools, and recreation centers. *See* **guidance, child; guidance, nursery.**

care, custodial: *see* **custodial care.**

care, institutional: specialized services provided for the education and training of individuals requiring intensive and extensive support; usually on a residential basis.

care, purchase of: *see* **purchase of care.**

career: the progress or general course of action of a person through some phase of life, as in some profession or undertaking; the occupation or profession, especially one requiring special training, followed as one's lifework.

career area: (mil. ed.) a grouping of utilization fields broadly related on the basis of required skills and knowledge.

career areas, related: (mil. ed.) a group of career areas broadly related on the basis of similarity of skills and knowledge.

career book: (couns.) a type of scrapbook collected and organized by the student; concerned with the type of career or vocation which he plans to enter; causes him to investigate the field more thoroughly on his own.

career chart: *see* **chart, career.**

career club: *see* **club, career.**

career conference: *see* **conference, career.**

career counseling: *see* **counseling, career.**

career course: *see* **course, career.**

career day: an arranged informational program involving a meeting or a series of meetings on a single day in order that occupational, educational, and social information may be presented directly to the student by adults in the community. *See* **conference, career; workshop, career.**

career development: (mil. ed.) the process of assignment, reassignment, and training of an Air Force military person within a given career field to acquaint him with the occupations within that field and establish a groundwork for his advancement.

career development course: *see* **course, career development.**

career exploration: investigative activities or inquiries undertaken inside and outside the classroom to search out the necessary information about a future occupational or professional interest or goal.

career fiction: (couns.) an account of an occupation, portrayed through the experiences of one or more fictional characters, which may encompass qualifications, preparation, conditions, duties, nature of work, and possibilities of advancement.

career field: (mil. ed.) one of the fields offered Air Force military persons, consisting of occupations grouped on a functional basis, each requiring similar basic skills and knowledge.

career film: *see* **film, career.**

career guidance: *see* **guidance, career.**

career management: (mil. ed.) the employment of personnel in such a way as to afford an adequate measure of manpower for each function and at the same time to provide for individual differences in ability and temperament in the assignment of tasks or responsibilities.

career notebook: a book in which organized notes are kept concerning a way of living, an occupation, or a profession.

career objective: *see* **occupational objective.**

career objective, tentative: *see* **objective, tentative career.**

career pattern: a number of career and life goals, alternate goals, and ways of attaining such goals.

career planning: the development by the student, with the assistance of counselors and teachers, of well considered steps in his progression toward entry into a specific job or profession; a process which unfolds at varying rates for different individuals.

career program, airman: *see* **program, airman career.**

career workshop: *see* **workshop, career.**

caries (kā′ri-ēz): (Lat., lit., "rottenness") a localized molecular death or disintegration of bone or teeth.

Carnegie library: *see* **library, Carnegie.**

Carnegie unit: *see* **unit, Carnegie.**

carol: a song of devotion or praise, usually celebrating a religious festival.

Carolingian art: *see* **art, Carolingian.**

Carolingian Revival: a movement in the Frankish Empire of the eighth and ninth centuries, initiated primarily by Charlemagne and guided by Alcuin, which promoted an improved educational program for clergy and nobles, the restoration of classical culture, the founding of libraries, and the correction and copying of texts.

carpal age: *see* **age, carpal.**

carpentry laboratory: *see* **laboratory, carpentry.**

carrel: (1) a small cubicle or study desk set aside, usually in the library stacks, for the use of faculty members and students for individual study; (2) a student study station with unitized desk, table, or booth designed to facilitate effective study by the student; described as *wet* when it includes electronic devices and as *dry* when it lacks such devices; usually established in connection with a system that makes available packaged sets or kits of learning materials for self-managed instruction; a separately identified location, although generally considered part of the room into which it opens and which it serves, for example, a study hall, regular classroom, or laboratory.

carry method: *syn.* **equal-additions method.**

carry-over effect: *syn.* **practice effect.**

carry-over sports: *see* **sports, carry-over.**

Cartesian coordinates: *see* **coordinates, Cartesian.**

Cartesian geometry: *see* **geometry, coordinate.**

Cartesian product: *syn.* **set, Cartesian.**

Cartesian set: *see* **set, Cartesian.**

Cartesianism: the philosophy of René Descartes (1596–1650) and his followers; based on application of the logic of mathematics to questions about what is true and what is real; a dualistic philosophy, emphasizing the distinction between thought and extension, that is, between mind and matter.

cartogram: a map on which is shown the distribution of a given variable according to geographical location, usually by means of various shades of color or crosshatching or by dots, for example, a map showing population density. *Syn.* **graded map; statistical map.**

cartography: the group of activities involved in making charts and maps.

cartoon: (1) an interpretive picture, usually a drawing, intended to convey a message or point of view about things, events, or situations; may make free use of exaggeration and symbolism; (2) the original full-scale drawing for a mural.

cartoon graph: *syn.* **graph, pictorial.**

cartridge, tape: *see* **tape cartridge.**

case: (1) an individual, family, or situation being investigated or examined and/or under treatment for the purpose of achieving more adequate physical, mental, or social adjustment; a recipient of assistance from a social agency, worker, or institution; (2) the problem represented by such an individual, family, or situation; (3) an analysis and write-up of the data collected in a case history, including an analysis of the interrelationships in the data; (4) (mil. ed.) a written narrative which presents a realistic and challenging problem; may be a fictionalized statement of an actual military problem which may or may not have been solved, intended to be the focal point of discussion so that students may discover probable truths for future use; (5) a cause, suit, or action at law.

case, adjustment: *see* **adjustment case.**

case, attendance: *see* **attendance case.**

case, borderline: *see* **borderline case.**

case conference: *see* **conference, case.**

case, court: *see* **court case.**

case history: factual material gathered and organized by a teacher or guidance specialist about an individual pupil's behavior and development; this should not be confused with *case study*, which is the analysis and interpretation of this material; a *developmental case history* involves a continuous and systematic gathering of data by trained personnel, such as the guidance counselor.

case-history course: *see* **course, case-history.**

case history, developmental: *see* **case history.**

case-history method: *syn.* **case method.**

case-history records, verification of: *see* **verification of case-history records.**

case history, social: *see* **history, social** (1).

case load: the number of individuals or families with whom a social worker, school counselor, or other official or agency is working at a given moment or during a stated period of time.

case material: a collection of available evidence—social, psychological, physiological, biographical, environmental, vocational—that promises to help explain a single individual or a single social unit such as a family; forms the basis of a *case history.*

case method: (1) in research, the use of detailed studies of single individuals as a basis for induction of principles; (2) a diagnostic and remedial procedure based on thorough investigation of a person in order to shed light upon and to acquire knowledge of his history, his home conditions, and all other influences that may cause his maladjustment or behavior difficulties; *see* **case history**; (3)

(mil. ed.) a method which requires student to participate actively in problem situations, hypothetical or real; he receives a *case*, a report containing pertinent data; he then analyzes data, evaluates the nature of the problem, decides upon applicable principles, and finally recommends a solution or course of action.

case notes: the counselor's, investigator's, or social worker's record of personal interviews with an individual or family and of treatment and progress toward adjustment.

case problem: *see* **problem, case.**

case record: *see* **record, case.**

case reopened: a family or individual whose problem has previously been considered, treated, and solved and who now comes up for reconsideration owing to an unsatisfactory adjustment of the old problem or the development of a new problem.

case report: *see* **report, case.**

case study: an analysis of the origin of individual and family problems and of the methods used in counseling; generic term for individualized counseling methods which utilize cumulative records or other collection of all available evidence—social, psychological, physiological, biographical, environmental, vocational—that promises to help explain a single individual or a single social unit such as a family. *See* **case history; case method.**

case-study method: *syn.* **case method.**

case-study technique: *syn.* **case method.**

case summary: assembled, interpreted data that briefly present a clear analysis of an individual's or family's situation and the result of remedial measures.

case system: the practice of using actual experiences as laboratory material in such subjects as journalism, civics, and debating, approaching as nearly as possible the case system used in schools of law.

casework: (1) the professional application of the *case method;* (2) specifically, the use of thorough studies of individual cases by social workers in their professional practice of planning for and assisting individuals or families in making better personal, social, economic, or other adjustments; (3) in behavior clinics, usually designates the preliminary fact gathering and subsequent carrying out of recommendations and follow-up by the social worker.

casework council, central: a group of persons, representing various social agencies, before which the agencies may bring cases for consideration, discussion, and recommendation and discuss the policies and responsibilities of the agencies represented.

casework method: specific activities directed toward a treatment whose goal is to help people cope with certain psychosocial and cultural-economic problems.

casework, social: *syn.* **casework** (2).

caseworker: (1) a person responsible for obtaining knowledge about the client, his family, and his relationship with the community; (2) a school social worker or visiting teacher whose major function involves the utilization of casework procedures. *See* **casework.**

caseworker, client: a caseworker whose primary concern is the adjustment of the individual client rather than the adjustment of the family of which the client is a member.

caseworker, social: a professional worker functioning in the traditional model of individual support services, usually psychosocial in orientation.

cash disbursements: *see* **disbursements, cash.**

cash receipts: *see* **receipts.**

cassette: a magnetic tape recording medium which houses the tape in a compact sealed plastic case, facilitating both use and protection of the material recorded.

cassette recorder: *see* **recorder, cassette.**

caste system: a closed, endogamous social organization resulting from stratification in which status in a hierarchy of power relations is defined and permanently fixed by ancestry.

casting: the art of throwing, hurling, or flinging an artificial or natural lure attached to a line connected to a reel; a skill in fishing taught as part of an outdoor education program.

casting out nines: a method of checking arithmetical calculations based on the principle that the excess of nines in a given number equals the excess of nines in the sum of its digits; generally used with multiplication and division but applicable also to addition and subtraction; for example, to check the calculation

$$\begin{array}{r} 196 \\ 76 \\ \hline 1176 \\ 1372 \\ \hline 14896 \end{array}$$

the following procedure would be used: (a) add each digit in the multiplicand and subtract as many nines as possible $(1 + 9 + 6 = 16; 16 - 9 = 7)$; (b) do the same for the multiplier $(7 + 6 = 13; 13 - 9 = 4)$; (c) multiply the remainders found in steps (a) and (b) and cast out the nines $(7 \times 4 = 28; 2 + 8 = 10; 10 - 9 = 1)$; (d) repeat the procedure of steps (a) and (b) with the product $(1 + 4 + 8 + 9 + 6 = 28; 2 + 8 = 10; 10 - 9 = 1)$; since the same remainder is obtained in steps (c) and (d), the original calculation $196 \times 76 = 14,896$ is correct unless one of the following errors has been made: transposition of any numbers in the product, any error in the product that is a multiple of nine, a mistake involving zeros or the placement of the decimal point; the method is similar for checking examples in division, as well as in addition and subtraction.

castration complex: *see* **complex, castration.**

catabolism (kə·tab'ə·liz'm): the breaking down of complex bodies of living matter into waste products; the destructive or retrograde aspects of metabolism. *See* **metabolism;** *contr. w.* **anabolism.**

catalog: (1) any pamphlet or book that describes an institution; (2) an exposition of the objectives, viewpoint, curricula, tuition, calendar, and other data concerning an institution, usually issued annually; may be limited to a single school or college of an institution.

catalog, alphabetico-classified: a catalog with entries under broad subject categories alphabetically arranged and subdivided by topics in alphabetical order. *Syn.* **alphabetico-classed catalog.**

catalog analysis: *syn.* **analysis, bulletin.**

catalog, book: library catalog entries printed page-by-page and bound together in book form into one volume or set of volumes.

catalog, card: *see* **card catalog.**

catalog, children's: a catalog of children's books published by the H.W. Wilson Company for the information of teachers and the staffs of children's departments in libraries.

catalog, class: *syn.* **catalog, classified.**

catalog, classed: *syn.* **catalog, classified.**

catalog, classified: a catalog arranged by subject according to the systematic scheme of classification used by a particular library. *Syn.* **class catalog; classed catalog; classified subject catalog;** *see* **classification, book.**

catalog, classified subject: *syn.* **catalog, classified.**

catalog, dictionary: a library catalog in which all entries—including authors, titles, subjects, and other added entries—are interfiled to form a single alphabetical list.

catalog, divided: a library catalog in which the different varieties of entry are filed in separate alphabets by (a) separating all subject entries from other entries, (b) separating all names into a single catalog regardless of whether they are authors or subjects, or (c) dividing entries into separate catalogs of authors, titles, and subjects. *Syn.* **split catalog.**

catalog, library: a listing of all the books or other materials in a library with bibliographic data for each work included; may be arranged by author, title, or subject; most common in American libraries is dictionary arrangement with author, title, and subject entries in one alphabet; most American library catalogs are on cards, the printed catalog in book form being largely outdated.

catalog, split: *syn.* **catalog, divided.**

catalog, subject: a library catalog consisting of listings under subject headings only.

catalog, union: a listing in one arrangement of the resources of two or more libraries.

catalogia (kat·ə·lō′ji·ə): frequent repetition of words and phrases in which there is no coherence of thought; usually confined to cases of mental retardation.

cataloging, machine-readable (MARC): a project under the direction of the Information Systems Office of the Library of Congress to develop techniques for converting catalog card data into machine-readable form for processing by computers so that libraries can prepare catalog cards for their particular needs.

catamnesis (kat′əm·nē′sis): the family and personal history of a patient or client after coming under the care of a physician or agency, including the subsequent notes and records. *Contr. w.* **anamnesis.**

cataphasia (kat′ə·fā′zhi·ə): inappropriate repetition of words, phrases, and sentences which may have been initially used in correct form; it has been observed in organic (syntactical aphasia) and functional (fatigue) problems.

catarrhal deafness: *see* **deafness, catarrhal.**

catastrophic reaction: *see* **reaction, catastrophic.**

catatonia (kat′ə·tō′ni·ə): a mental disorder characterized by purposeless excitement and restless activity, alternating with trancelike stupor sometimes accompanied by rigidity of the muscles.

catechetical method (kat′ə·ket′i·kəl): an ancient method of teaching based on having pupils learn by rote set answers to set questions and recite the answers orally in response to the questions.

catechetical school: a type of early Christian school in which advanced instruction in the Christian faith and general culture, especially philosophy and theology, was given; also served in some cases as a seminary for the training of the clergy. *Dist. f.* **catechumenal school.**

catechism: a compendium of religious doctrine arranged in the form of questions and answers.

catechism class: *see* **class, catechism.**

catechist: a teacher who gave religious instruction in catechumenal schools to pagans preparatory to Christian baptism and church membership.

catechumen: (1) a person who is under instruction and probation preparatory to admission to membership in a sect of the Christian church; (2) more generally, a person being tutored in any set of fundamental principles.

catechumenal instruction: *see* **instruction, catechumenal.**

catechumenal school: a type of early Christian school in which elementary instruction in Christian doctrine was given in preparation for the sacrament of baptism. *Dist. f.* **catechetical school.**

categorical: admitting of no exceptions; unconditional; especially applied to propositions (statements) that assert unconditionally.

categorical aid: *see* **aid, categorical.**

categorical imperative: *see* **imperative, categorical.**

categorical proposition: *see* **proposition, categorical.**

categorical series: *see* **series, categorical.**

categories, artistic: the a priori categories of matter, form, and content, which every work of art must possess; specifically, (*a*) the sensuous beauty of material, (*b*) the formal beauty of design, and (*c*) the expressive beauty of meaning; corresponding to the manipulative, form-experimental, and early expressive stages of creative development of the young child.

categories of children's drawing: *see* **drawing, types of children's.**

categories of pure reason: the organization by Immanuel Kant (1724–1804) of all concepts or ultimate forms of thought into the four categories of (*a*) quantity (unity, plurality, totality), (*b*) quality (reality, negation, limitation), (*c*) relation (substance-and-accident, cause-and-effect, reciprocity), and (*d*) modality (possibility, existence, and necessity).

category: (stat.) (1) a concept embracing observations or cases that are similar; usually one of several conceptual divisions of a larger class; specifically, any one of the divisions into which a qualitative or quantitative variable has been subdivided; *see* **class** (7*b*); (2) a unit of homogeneous cases with respect to some given purpose.

category, compound: (res.) a category that represents a unique combination of single classes from each of two or more variables; it therefore satisfies the conditions of two or more classes simultaneously (for example, French boy, eighth-grade American-born girl, etc.); each cell in a double-entry table represents a compound category.

category, diagnostic: *see* **diagnostic category.**

category, discrete: a classification or subdivision of a discrete, that is, discontinuous, variable. *See* **variable, discrete.**

catharsis: (Gk., lit., "cleansing") the release of tension or anxiety by reliving, through speech or emotional reaction, those incidents or events in the past which contribute to the present difficulty.

catharsis, theory of: (1) the theory of the psychotherapeutic value of uninhibited, expressive behavior; frequently accompanied by the assumption or theory that expression through such behavior in a given situation may reduce or eliminate the need for expression in another; *see* **catharsis**; (2) a traditional folk theory picturing childhood or adolescence as the period for working off the "baser instincts" (for example, "sowing wild oats"), such behavior supposedly serving to immunize the individual in part against later wrongdoing.

cathartic method: *see* **catharsis.**

cathartic projective method: *see* **projective method, cathartic.**

cathedral school: an institution under the management of a head schoolmaster and open to pupils being prepared for life in the world as well as to those destined for the church; developed in the eighth century from the episcopal schools founded originally by bishops, who conducted them chiefly for clerics and were themselves the teachers.

cathexis: (psychoan.) a concentration of psychic energy.

cathode ray tube: *see* **tube, cathode ray.**

Catholepistemiad: the title of the first University of Michigan, founded in 1817 (when half the population was French), which embodied the idea of the University of France; it was not a teaching institution but the department of education providing for the organization of education from the elementary school to the university for the territory of Michigan.

Catholic Action: a term used in the Roman Catholic Church for the cooperative effort of laymen in the pursuit of personal Christian perfection and the participation in social activity aided and sustained by the authority of the bishops.

Catholic education: the comprehensive school system established by the Roman Catholic Church in America is broadly termed Catholic education; the program includes the establishment and maintenance of schools and other educational agencies to provide religious information in accord with the Christian ideal and to maintain a complete educational service in accord with the goals of American society; schools are maintained from the pre-kindergarten level to the final degree at the graduate level; in large measure these schools are supported by the Catholic Church as well as by tuitions and other offerings supplied by the patrons of the schools.

Catholic education, philosophy of: *see* **philosophy of Catholic education.**

catholicism: (1) the faith of the ancient, undivided Christian church, or a church or churches claiming historical continuity from it; (2) the faith of that body of Christians, or that church, of which the Pope, the bishop of Rome, is the spiritual head; (3) the faith of a body of Christians belonging to any of various churches which claim apostolic succession in their historic episcopate; (4) the faith of the entire body of Christian believers or that part of it which accepts the Apostles' Creed.

caucus: as used in collective negotiations between teachers and school administration, the technique of one or both parties withdrawing from the bargaining table for the purpose of conferring in private.

causal analysis: *see* **analysis, causal.**

causal-comparative method: a research method (sometimes referred to as the *inferred causal method*) that seeks to ascertain causation through noting the conditions that are usually or invariably present when certain results are observed and comparing (contrasting) them with conditions that are not found to produce these results. (The method does not go so far as to study mechanisms of causation and does not typically quantify conditions and results, as correlation does, but attempts simply to ascertain what factors seem to be necessary and sufficient for, or at least conducive to, the occurrence of the observed effects; does not involve manipulating the conditions; hence is not notably analytical, explanatory, quantitative, or experimental. Ecology, in certain of its aspects, is an illustration. It is likely to represent the cruder stages of knowledge about causation, presumably to be followed by more refined methods.)

causal method: the patterns of research represented by studies that seek to ascertain the causes of observed phenomena or the results of specified causes, partly through the process of ruling out as many alternative possibilities as is feasible; often (though not necessarily) the causes and results can be reproduced at will and both be expressed in quantitative terms; includes experimental studies, most laboratory studies, and certain types of statistical analysis. *See* **causal-comparative method.**

causal variable: *see* **variable, causal.**

causality: the relation between a cause and its effect or between regularly correlated events or phenomena. *See* **determinism.**

cause-and-effect test: *see* **test, cause-and-effect.**

cause-effect relationship: the situation in which a result is traceable to that which may be marked off specifically as a factor that produced or determined it; the relating of a specific cause to a given effect. *See* **cause, efficient; cause, final; cause, first; cause, formal; cause, material.**

cause, efficient: in the philosophy of Aristotle, the immediate or proximate source of change or of rest from change; for example, if a man is making a statue, the efficient cause is the contact of the chisel with the marble; in modern terminology, the unmodified word cause would be confined in sense to efficient cause. *See* **causes, four.**

cause, final: in the philosophy of Aristotle, the end or good for the sake of which a thing comes to be and is; for example, if a man is making a statue, the final cause is the end the sculptor has in mind. *See* **causes, four.**

cause, first: in the philosophy of Aristotle, the prime mover or God, which originally started the movement of all moving things in heaven and nature; the entire chain of *efficient causes,* not by itself being moved but by being the primary object of thought, love, and desire.

cause, formal: in the philosophy of Aristotle, the form, pattern, or archetype of something, which is stated in the definition of its essence; for example, if a man is making a statue, the formal cause is the essence of the statue to be produced. *See* **causes, four; form.**

cause, material: in the philosophy of Aristotle, that out of which a thing comes to be and which persists in it as an immanent substratum; for example, marble may be the material cause of a statue. *See* **causes, four; matter (2).**

cause, proximate: (1) the agent that directly produces the effect without having the natural sequence disturbed by an intervening independent agent; (2) (legal) the reason, under the law, for the injury.

cause, ultimate: the final or primary agent in a sequence of logical events which lead up to an effect; the Supreme Creator or First Originator; that last cause which is incapable of further analysis.

causes, four: in the philosophy of Aristotle, the necessary conditions for the existence or occurrence of any natural or artificial object or process and the appropriate objects of all scientific inquiry. *See* **cause, efficient; cause, final; cause, formal; cause, material.**

CAVD test: *see* **test, CAVD.**

caveat emptor (kā'vē·at em(p)'tər): (Lat., lit., "let the buyer beware") a rule for governing relations between the seller and the buyer of goods and services.

caveat venditor (kā'vē·at ven'də·tər): (Lat., lit., "let the seller beware") a basic rule governing relations between sellers and buyers of goods and services.

CCTV: *see* **television, closed-circuit.**

cecutient: an individual who is visually handicapped.

ceiling, debt: *see* **debt ceiling.**

ceiling, test: *see* **test ceiling.**

celestial navigation: *see* **astronavigation.**

cell: (1) in automatic data processing, the physical location on or in a storage device that is identified by an address; *see* **address;** (2) (stat.) a compartment of a double-entry table, formed by the intersection of a column and a row; *syn.* **compartment;** (3) a transparency made of acetate for use in projectors; usually 3 × 5 inch, but may be 2 × 2 inch, 6 × 8 inch, etc.

cell assembly: (psych.) a group of neurons functionally linked together into a circuit by previous stimulation of them all together as a consequence of such basic perceptual acts as viewing a triangle or other such object.

cell, braille: *see* **braille cell.**

cell, data: *see* **data cell.**

cell frequency: *see* **frequency, cell.**

cement industry: *see* **industry, cement.**

censor: (psychoan.) to Freudians, the superego (conscience), which operates somewhat as a censor by keeping below the conscious level thoughts and impulses that would threaten the ego.

censorship: the act of examining printed matter, motion pictures, etc., for the purpose of eliminating objectionable content; by its practitioners considered necessary to protect youth, preserve public order and morality, or aid national security; by its opponents held, as usually applied, to have narrowed truth to the limits of some partisan doctrine and inhibited the growth of free thought and open inquiry.

censorship, literary: the scrutiny of literature with the intention of suppressing content deemed to be detrimental to public morals.

census: an enumeration of the population, usually conducted by agents of the government or other authorities, for the purpose of determining the number of people living in the country or area under investigation as well as certain facts relative to the population, such as assessed value of real estate, number, age, and value of motorcars, age of population, number of people married and single, and size of families.

census age: *see* **age, school census.**

census card: a card on which census data regarding a student are recorded.

census card, permanent school: a card for recording permanent cumulative census data about each child in the community.

census, church: (1) an enumeration of the population of a given area in accordance with church membership or preference; (2) an enumeration of a given denomination's membership in regard to certain basic types of information, such as number of baptisms, number of church schools, etc.

census class: *see* **class, census.**

census class projection: *see* **projection, census class.**

census, continuing school: *syn.* **census, continuous school.**

census, continuous school: (pupil accounting) an individual record of every resident child from birth to 21 years of age (or to some other age limit) which is checked regularly with all sources of information available to the school so as to provide an accurate current list of all children residing in a given administrative unit. *Syn.* **continuing school census.**

census department: *see* **department, census.**

census enumerator: a person responsible for making a house-to-house visitation for the purpose of locating all young people of school-census age and collecting needed information about them.

census, family: (1) collection of data relative to all members of a family and comprising a record of the members as a group, as distinguished from a data sheet on a separate individual; (2) a tabulation of data, in a given geographic or political area, concerning the families of that area.

census file: an orderly collection of all census cards, sheets, or folders filed alphabetically or by streets.

census file, active: (1) *syn.* **census file, live;** (2) sometimes includes *live census file, exemption census file, postschool census file,* and *preschool census file.*

census file, dead: the file containing data about children who have died, moved out of the school district, left school, or passed the school-census age.

census file, exemption: a file containing the cards of those children of school age who, for whatever reason, have been exempted from attendance at school in the given school district. *See* **exemption.**

census file, family: (1) a file that contains a card for every family in a given area, arranged alphabetically by street names and numerically by numbers on streets; (2) a file that contains a card for every family in a given area, arranged alphabetically by family name.

census file, inactive: the file that contains the cards of those children of census age who are unaccounted for. (As soon as they are discovered, they are discharged to the proper census file—*active, preschool,* etc.)

census file, live: the file that contains the census cards of all children of compulsory school age, minus the exemptions, plus the cards of those children who enter school before the compulsory period and of those who remain in school until after the compulsory period. *Syn.* **active census file.**

census file, permanent: *syn.* **census file, dead.**

census file, postschool: the file that contains cards of all children past school age who have left school but are still within the census-age limits.

census file, preschool: (1) the file that contains the cards of all children in the district from birth to school age, less those who have entered school (if census ages do not begin at birth, this file will have cards of those children between the lower census-age limit and the lower compulsory-attendance age limit who are not enrolled in school); (2) the file that contains cards for children from birth to census age.

census forms: those cards or sheets needed in taking and maintaining a census.

census record, continuous school: a permanent school census record that is constantly brought up to date. *Dist. f.* **census file, dead.**

census record, family: a record kept by schools or social service agencies containing data about children as parts of their families, each card of which is filed by the name of the head of the household. *Dist. f.* **census file, dead.**

census record, permanent school: a collection of a wide range of pertinent data concerning children of a school district who are of prescribed ages (known as *census ages*), systematically and continuously compiled and kept indefinitely either in the office of the school superintendent or in the census bureau. (Theoretically, among other information, it should contain the name and present address of every child of census age living in the school district.)

census, school: an enumeration and collection of data to determine the number of children of certain ages resident in a given district and to secure information such as date of birth, names of parents, and occupation of parents. *Syn.* **school enumeration.**

census supervisor: *see* **supervisor, census.**

census tract: (1) one of the small areas, with about 4,000 population, into which large cities and adjacent areas are divided for the purpose of providing comparable small-area population; for the United States Census of 1970, all standard metropolitan statistical areas plus other areas were tracted; (2) in many cities, a subdivision of the school district, consisting of a group of enumeration districts or zones, used in the administration of the school census; these subdivisions may conform to city wards or elementary school districts or may be determined on some other basis.

census zone: a geographical area of variable size assigned to a census enumerator; the standard unit for the taking of the school census.

center: (1) (home ec.) space and equipment within the home economics department where a certain activity is carried on; (2) *syn.* **center, student-teaching.**

center, adult: *see* **center, adult education; evening school** (2).

center, adult education: a physical facility designed or adapted expressly for the educational use of adults, sponsored by schools, colleges, universities, communities, organizations, industries, etc.; within some of them are included residential quarters for the participants. *Syn.* **adult center; center for continuation study; center for continuing education;** *see* **center, extension; center, residential.**

center, bibliographical: a collection of bibliographical materials, including a union catalog, provided by the cooperative effort of a number of libraries in an area in order to coordinate their resources and to aid research; may have a book collection either owned by the center or drawn from resources of member libraries or both.

center, child care: *see* **center, day care.**

center, child development: an organized facility for preschool children, with classrooms and outdoor play space; also supplies space for health services, parent interviews, counseling, feeding of the children, and community meetings; originally used in connection with Head Start programs for a center in which a cooperative relationship of family, community, and professional staff assistance contributes to the total development of the child. *See* **Project Head Start.**

Center, Civilian Conservation: one type of Job Corps center; located primarily in rural areas which provide, in addition to other training and assistance, programs or work experience focused upon activities to conserve, develop, or manage public natural resources or public recreational areas or to assist in developing community projects in the public interest. *See* **program, Job Corps.**

center, college clearing: *see* **clearinghouse, college.**

center, community: *see* **community center.**

center, community guidance: *see* **guidance center, community.**

center, counseling: *syn.* **center, guidance.**

center, curriculum materials: *syn.* **laboratory, curriculum materials.**

center, data processing: a computer installation providing data processing service for others, sometimes called customers, on a reimbursable or nonreimbursable basis.

center, day care: (1) an educational or custodial facility where children may be enrolled on a half-day or full-day basis, returning to their own homes each night; the main function of such a center is to supplement parental care for children of working parents or of those who, for other reasons, cannot provide adequate parental supervision; (2) a public or private facility for the training and education of the handicapped in the community; usually for the mentally retarded; stresses personal and social development. *Syn.* **child care center; day care service;** *see* **day nursery.**

center, demonstration: a classroom or group of classrooms set up within a school to serve as a means for attempting the solution of certain educational problems through practice and experimentation and for conducting research.

center, ecumenical: *see* **ecumenical center.**

center, education information: a small local or large-scale multiple-school data collection center; usually associated with data processing and conceptual innovations for storing and retrieval of various forms of educational information.

center, educational materials: *see* **center, instructional materials.**

center, educational service: a unique educational organization designed for service to schools without being a part of the administrative structure of the schools served; offers an array of services to school districts within a geographically defined area or region including research, curriculum development, instructional materials, purchasing, and psychological services among others. *Syn.* **intermediate service unit.**

center, equipment: an area which houses and distributes instructional equipment; provides adequate facilities and staff to coordinate selection and evaluation of instructional equipment and to organize, distribute, and maintain instructional equipment.

center, extension: a physical facility, on or off a college or university campus, for use by adults who come for educational purposes; found particularly among the land-grant colleges and universities.

center for continuation study: *see* **center, adult education.**

center for continuing education: *see* **center, adult education.**

center for the deaf, special: *see* **deaf, special center for the.**

center, guidance: a professionally staffed agency in a school or community setting which is designed to provide guidance services to students who are referred to it or who are seeking help on their own. *Syn.* **counseling center.**

center, health: *syn.* **clinic, health.**

center, homemaking: a facility equipped to teach the various aspects of the homemaking program; usually includes a living area as well as laboratory space; may be a cottage, an apartment, or a special room allocated for the program.

center, independent study: *see* **center, study.**

center, information analysis: *see* **information analysis center.**

center, instructional materials: (1) a well-planned center set up by a school system, situated conveniently within the service area of the system and consisting of at least a library and an audiovisual center which contain a variety of instructional material and equipment and provide for constant evaluation of these media; *syn.* **educational materials center; multimedia center; supplementary resource center;** (2) an area set aside within a single school in which the multimedia approach is utilized for individual and group discovery and for experiences providing enrichment learning.

center, interlibrary: a center collecting and housing seldom-used research materials for a large geographical area; operated cooperatively by a group of libraries.

center, Job Corps: one of the centers, residential or nonresidential, designed and operated to provide Job Corps enrollees, in a well-supervised setting, with education, vocational training, work experience, counseling, and other services to meet their needs; three types of centers are available—conservation centers and men's and women's training centers; the latter two are located in either urban or rural areas where services and facilities allow for successful training for specific types of skilled and semiskilled employment. *See* **Center, Civilian Conservation; program, Job Corps.**

center, juvenile diagnostic: an agency that serves a diagnostic function with problem children.

center, language and area: a college or department, often in a university setting, which specializes in the study of a specific language and civilization, especially one which is non-Western.

center, learning: a loose term for an area in the classroom or some designated area in the school where there is a wide assortment of resources for learning and where the emphasis is upon making observable gains in learning and improving the pupil's self-management of that learning.

center, learning resources: a specially designed space containing a wide range of supplies and equipment for the use of individual pupils and/or small groups pursuing independent study; frequently provided are an open-stock library (including books and programmed materials), a variety of audiovisual equipment and supplies (including projectors and films, tape recorders and tapes, maps, globes, and models), and spaces for individual and small groups to study, preview films, and hold meetings. *See* **center, study.**

center, living: an area in a home economics department which is equipped with furnishings suited to informal group living.

center, local production: an area with adequate facilities and staff to design and produce—with teachers, psychologists, and content specialists—materials to supplement those commercially available or to design and implement instructional systems with administrators, curriculum specialists, supervisors, and teachers; also called *materials preparation center.*

center, materials: *syn.* **materials bureau.**

center, materials preparation: *see* **center, local production.**

center, migrant child: a school and child care center for children of migrant workers; operates for the duration of the harvest season, coinciding with work hours, and focuses on special learning, health, and social problems of migrant children.

center, mobile counseling: *see* **counseling center, mobile.**

center, multimedia: *syn.* **center, instructional materials.**

center, nature: an outdoor area, either run by the school on the school grounds or by an interested group at a location away from the area's schools, with the purpose of providing experiences with nature for the students. *Syn.* **nature conservation center; outdoor learning center; outdoor science laboratory.**

center, nature conservation: *syn.* **center, nature.**

center-of-gravity method: *syn.* **centroid method.**

center of interest: (1) a phase of the group culture around which activities evolving from a variety of related interests tend to group themselves or within which a variety of activities or objects of interest may be classified; (2) a source of environmental or imaginative experiences to which learners are attracted and which the school may utilize in its educational program; (3) (kind.-prim. ed.) a harmonious grouping of materials and equipment so arranged as to emphasize some particular idea, principle, or theme growing out of children's various learning activities; (4) a topic, subject, or unit of reading matter that holds the interest of the pupil.

center of population: (stat.) a point that represents an average for a population distributed over an area; may be applied to any set of observations distributed over a plane. *See* **geographical center; mean center of population; median center of population.**

center, outdoor learning: *syn.* **center, nature.**

center, planning: (1) space equipped with a desk, files, and storage for books and magazines and other materials used by teacher and students; (2) (ind. arts) a central area within the industrial arts laboratory reserved for use in the planning and research required or desired in relation to the learning activities; equipped with planning and reference facilities such as drafting tables, drafting instruments, reference library, opaque slide and overhead projectors, and individual study carrels.

center, reading: (1) a room or part of a room set aside for reading instruction and/or pleasure reading; (2) a service center provided by a school, furnished with equipment to help people who are experiencing difficulty in learning to read; sometimes includes diagnostic, developmental, and remedial services for all age levels; *syn.* **reading clinic.**

center, rehabilitation: a specialized facility for personal, social, and vocational development; usually at least partially supported by public funds; stresses psychological and social aspects of rehabilitation.

center, residence: an extension center that is officially designated as a place where students may have their credits accepted as residence credit.

center, residential: a facility specifically designed or adapted for use by adults for the purpose of learning for short periods, during which time the adults eat, sleep, and carry on their learning activities on the premises. *Syn.* **residential adult center; residential adult school;** *see* **center, adult education; center, extension.**

center, residential adult: *see* **center, residential.**

center, science service: *syn.* **center, science teaching.**

center, science teaching: a cooperative formed by large numbers of school systems with the prime purpose of providing up-to-date services and programs for both teachers and pupils in science education. *Syn.* **school cooperative service organization; science service center.**

center, self-instructional: an area of the *instructional materials center* where a library of programmed and other self-instructional (or autoinstructional) materials and equipment is maintained for students and teachers.

center, student resource: *see* **center, study.**

center, student-teaching: the local school and community in which prospective teachers spend a period of time under the guidance of a supervising teacher in cooperation with a teacher-training institution.

center, study: a place within a school building, outfitted with equipment and materials, where students can study independently using materials other than library books. *Syn.* independent study center; learning resources center; student resource center; *see* nongraded school.

center, supplementary education: a place for school children to visit which has materials and displays to provide supplementary education programs not available in the regular classroom.

center, supplementary resource: *syn.* center, instructional materials.

center-to-center contact: *see* contact, center-to-center.

center, training: *see* training center.

center, university extension: *syn.* center, extension.

centesimal grade: *see* grade, centesimal.

centile: *syn.* percentile.

centile interval: *see* interval, centile.

centile range: *syn.* interval, centile.

centile rank: *syn.* rank, percentile.

central administration: *see* administration, central.

central board of control: *see* board of control, central.

central casework council: *see* casework council, central.

central city: (United States Census of 1970) the largest city in a standard metropolitan statistical area (SMSA) is always called a central city and must have at least 50,000 inhabitants; one or two more cities in the SMSA may be central cities if they have at least 250,000 inhabitants or if they have a population of $\frac{1}{3}$ or more of the largest city and a minimum population of 25,000 (15,000 if contiguous to another city, with a combined population of 50,000). *See* metropolitan statistical area, standard.

central city school: *see* inner city school.

central council: a schoolwide organization made up of representatives of all home rooms or student clubs in the school, serving as a clearing house for these groups and as a unifying force in the school.

central deafness: *see* deafness, central.

central dominance: *see* dominance, central.

central education agency: a central office of the Federal government or of a state or local school system that exercises certain controls over and provides services to subordinate school units.

central fan ventilation: *see* ventilation, central fan.

central hearing impairment: *see* hearing impairment, central.

central heating plant: *see* heating plant, central.

central high school: *syn.* high school, union.

central library: *see* library, central.

central nervous system: *see* nervous system, central.

central oligophasia: *see* oligophasia, central.

central process: an organizing action of the central nervous system and more especially the higher brain centers, as contrasted with activity of either (*a*) the *peripheral* (sensory or motor) nerves or (*b*) the *autonomic* nervous system governing the vegetative life processes.

central processing unit: *see* unit, central processing.

central registry for the blind: *see* registry for the blind, central.

central school: *syn.* consolidated school.

central sound system: an intercommunication system which permits messages, music, and programs to be transmitted to rooms throughout a building or group of buildings; provides communication for administrative or instructional purposes.

central tendency: the tendency of the observations or cases in a distribution to cluster about a point with respect either to absolute value or to frequency of occurrence; usually, but not necessarily, about midway between the extreme high and extreme low values in the distribution. *See* measure of central tendency.

central tendency, error of: *see* error of central tendency.

central thought: *syn.* whole meaning.

central-thought test: *see* test, central-thought.

central vision: *see* vision, central.

centralization: the practice of unifying administration and supervision under fewer organizations, particularly as applied to educational units.

centralization, functional: (school admin.) control over activities, personnel, and materials vested in one person.

centralization of administrative control: *see* administrative control, centralization of.

centralization of certification authority: *see* certification authority, centralization of.

centralization of schools: *syn.* consolidation of schools.

centralized administration: *see* administration, centralized.

centralized audit: *see* audit, centralized.

centralized guidance: *see* guidance, centralized.

centralized library: *see* library, centralized.

centralized purchasing: *see* purchasing, centralized.

centralized school: *syn.* consolidated school.

centrifuge: a machine with a long arm which, when rotated at different speeds, may be used to simulate the accelerations encountered by a human or animal in high-performance aircraft or rocket vehicles.

centrifuge, astronautic: a laboratory facility for achieving centrifugal acceleration so as to test the ability of animals or men to withstand stresses of space flight.

centroid: (fact. anal.) a center of gravity; an average point or position from which the sum of distances (with signs) of all observed points or positions is zero.

centroid method: a method of factoring a matrix in which the first factor is placed so as to pass through the centroid of the test vector termini and each succeeding factor is located orthogonally to the previously extracted factors. *See* bifactor method; factorization, group method of; tetrad difference.

cephalic index: *see* index, cephalic.

cephalization: a functional or organic gradient in which domination and localization of control tend toward the cephalic region, or head.

ceramic industries: *see* industries, ceramic.

ceramics: (1) the art and technology concerned with the manufacture from inorganic, nonmetallic substances of products that are subjected to a high temperature (usually above barely visible red heat, about 540° C or 1000° F) during manufacture or use; (2) activities involving work with clay, glazes, cement, enamels, glass, and similar materials treated by fire; (3) articles made of ceramic materials.

cerebellum: a part of the brain behind and below the cerebrum and occupying the back part of the skull; concerned with the coordination of movements.

cerebral: pertaining to the brain.

cerebral cortex: *see* cortex (2).

cerebral dominance: the normal condition in which one hemisphere of the brain dominates or leads the other in initiating or controlling bodily movements, this dominance normally residing in the left hemisphere in right-handed persons and in the right hemisphere in left-handed persons.

cerebral dominance, mixed: a theoretical condition of alternating or confused dominance of the cerebral hemispheres in regard to a language function, supposedly the cause of certain reading and language disabilities.

cerebral dominance test: *see* test, Wada sodium amytal.

cerebral-dominance theory: the theory that the hemisphere of the brain that controls the most used hand (the left hemisphere in right-handed persons) also normally controls and initiates higher mental functions, speech, abstraction, etc., and that when this dominance is lacking, various incoordinations ensue that are manifested in nervous disorders, speech defects, personality disorders, etc.

cerebral dysfunction: *see* dysfunction, cerebral.

cerebral palsied child: *see* child, cerebral palsied.

cerebral palsy: a neurological condition caused by a defect, lesion, or maldevelopment of the central nervous system which may be congenital or acquired; incoordination, paralysis, weakness, and/or tremor ensue due to a pathological condition in the motor control centers of the brain; sensory, mental, and emotional disorders, singly or in combination, may accompany the motor dysfunction; the major diagnostic classifications are spasticity, athetosis, rigidity, tremor, ataxia, and mixed types. *See* **ataxia; athetosis; rigidity; spasticity; tremor.**

cerebral spastic paralysis: a type of *cerebral palsy* by which the affected person's muscles contract involuntarily and to such an extent that orthopedic deformities may result. *See* **spasticity.**

cerebral type: a type of habitus characterized by a large head, small limbs, and a poorly developed muscular system. *See* **habitus.**

cerebrospinal nervous system: *see* **nervous system, cerebrospinal.**

cerebrum: the main portion of the brain occupying the upper part of the cranium; consists of two equal portions, called hemispheres, which are united at the bottom by a mass of white matter called the corpus callosum.

certainty: (1) assurance or conviction regarding any matter of belief or knowledge; the opposite of doubt; commonly identified with world views in which reality is in some sense changeless; a psychological factor, at least, in the belief that all things change; (2) (stat.) probability approaching 1.0.

certifiable mental defective: *see* **mental defective, certifiable.**

certificate, administrative: a certificate permitting a person who has met certain requirements to hold specified administrative positions in the schools. *Syn.* **administrative credentials.**

certificate, adult distributive education: a certificate awarded to those who satisfactorily complete an extension course in distributive education.

certificate, advisory-committee: a certificate that is given to members of an advisory committee for distributive education in recognition of their cooperation with education.

certificate, age: (1) a statement from the state or local bureau of vital statistics certifying the age of a person; (2) an administrative form used by a school system to certify the age of a pupil.

certificate, age-and-schooling: *see* **age-and-schooling certificate.**

certificate, baptismal: a form issued by a church certifying the baptism of a child; records his date of birth and is therefore used by the school as an authentic record of that date.

certificate, billfold: a small certificate in card form awarded to those who satisfactorily complete an extension course in distributive education or some other area of vocational education.

certificate, birth: (1) a statement in written form issued by the attending physician at the birth of a child, verifying its name and date of birth; (2) a statement written by the Bureau of Vital Statistics and reported by the attending physician at the birth of the child, verifying its name and date of birth.

certificate, blanket teaching: a license to teach all subjects at a specified level, as that of the elementary or the secondary school, rather than a permit to teach a specific school subject.

certificate, bus-driver: a written statement, signed by one or more persons having authority, indicating that the holder is qualified or has met established requirements to operate a school bus.

certificate, compulsory health: *see* **health certificate, compulsory.**

certificate, conditional life: a teaching certificate, valid as long as the teacher remains in active service upon condition that the teacher fulfill a further requirement in continued in-service training.

certificate, counselor: a license to function as a public school counselor, granted by the appropriate certification authority.

certificate, elementary: a license certifying that the holder is qualified to teach in the elementary grades in schools supported by public funds.

certificate, emergency: a certificate, valid for only a limited period of time, which indicates that the holder has not fulfilled the minimum requirements prescribed for a *standard certificate* but is considered competent to fill a teaching position for which a teacher holding a standard certificate is not available; sometimes erroneously called a *temporary certificate. See* **certificate, special** (3).

certificate, employment: a certificate which must be obtained by persons to show that they are of legal age for the work they will do and also to show status, qualifications, and privileges.

certificate, equivalency: *see* **certificate, high school equivalency.**

certificate, first-aid: a card issued by the American Red Cross or other authorized agency indicating that the person named has completed a course of study on emergency treatment of the ill or injured.

certificate, grade of: refers to the period of time for which the certificate is valid; for example, *temporary certificate, life certificate,* etc.; sometimes referred to as class of certificate.

certificate, Hebrew teacher's: an official recognition of the right of the holder to teach in a Jewish weekday school; issued by a board of license of a particular city, or by the National Board of License and a national licensing agency.

certificate, high school equivalency: a formal document issued by a state department of education or other authorized agency certifying that an individual has met the state requirements for high school graduation equivalency either by attaining satisfactory scores on an approved examination or by earning the required number of credits in an organized program of approved instruction; sometimes shortened to *equivalency certificate;* the usual examination is the nationally available *G.E.D. test,* consisting of a battery of five tests in which the minimum passing score is a standard score of 40 in each test and the overall average passing score 48. *See* **test, general educational development.**

certificate, hospital birth: a certificate issued by a hospital verifying the name and date of birth of a child; includes names of parents and is usually signed by both attending physician and hospital administrator.

certificate, initial: a license to teach which certifies that the holder has satisfied the minimum requirements prescribed by the state in an approved teacher-training institution; after a specified period of active teaching, the holder becomes eligible for a higher-grade certificate which certifies his status as an experienced teacher.

certificate, junior college: a license issued in a few states which certifies the holder as being qualified to teach at the junior college level.

certificate, kindergarten extension: a certificate extending kindergarten teaching credentials to permit the holder to teach in the first grade.

certificate, librarian's: a license issued by constituted authority stating that the holder is qualified to hold a library position of a specified kind or level; may be a *teacher's certificate* or *license for school librarians.*

certificate, life state: a written authorization that permits the holder to teach for life within the state in which the certificate is issued; in some states it must be kept in force by active teaching, no additional training usually being required.

certificate, life teaching: *see* **certificate, life state.**

certificate, limited: *syn.* **certificate, provisional.**

certificate, limited age-and-schooling: *see* **age-and-schooling certificate, limited.**

certificate, nonstandard age-and-schooling: *see* **age-and-schooling certificate, nonstandard.**

certificate of approved training: a statement by a teacher-training institution to the effect that the holder has satisfactorily fulfilled the training requirements as established by the school which is approved by the state as a teacher-training institution.

certificate of attendance: an administrative form used either to certify to perfect attendance on the part of a pupil, usually for a month, a semester, or a year, or to certify to some agency, such as the court, the presence of the pupil at school on a given day or days.

certificate of completion: written recognition granted to members of vocational classes when they have satisfactorily completed the requirements of a course of instruction; such certificates are presented when courses are not taken for credit toward graduation; also called certificate of training.

certificate of proficiency: (mil. ed.) written testimonial denoting completion of a prescribed course of instruction.

certificate, overage: a certificate issued by the attendance department or the office of the superintendent of schools certifying that the holder is above compulsory school age.

certificate, part-time age-and-schooling: see age-and-schooling certificate, part-time.

certificate, performer's: a certificate indicating that the holder has completed a special course of study of the standard literature in voice or on a musical instrument and has achieved a high degree of proficiency therein; may be in the form of a *performer's diploma.*

certificate, permanent: usually the highest grade of teaching certificate, valid for the entire professional life of the holder as long as he remains in good standing professionally. *Syn.* **permanent license.**

certificate, physician's: (1) the statement of a physician regarding the health of a youth; a prerequisite to the granting of an *age-and-schooling certificate;* (2) the statement of a physician testifying to the illness of a child, used as a legal excuse for absence from school.

certificate, professional: usually an advanced grade of certificate identifying the holder as an experienced teacher who has completed professional training beyond that required for the *initial certificate.*

certificate, provisional: usually the lowest grade of *standard certificate;* it indicates that the holder has satisfied the minimum requirements prescribed by the certificating authority in an approved teacher-education institution. *Syn.* **provisional license.**

certificate, reading: a written or printed statement given to a child as a reward for having read a certain number of books.

certificate, regular or nonemergency: *syn.* **certificate, standard.**

certificate revocation: the official retraction of a teaching license for violation of law or established regulations of the issuing body.

certificate, special: (1) a certificate, issued by a state, county, or township or by an accrediting agency, permitting a person who has met certain requirements to teach certain subjects on certain levels or to hold certain administrative or supervisory positions within the precincts of the agent; (2) a certificate entitling a qualified person to teach a special subject, that is, a so-called "nonacademic" subject such as agriculture, art, commerce, business, home economics, music, and industrial arts; (3) in time of emergency, a special certificate or permit issued to certain persons of less than standard preparation or qualifications, entitling them to hold educational positions for a limited time.

certificate, standard: a certificate indicating that the holder has fulfilled the minimum teaching requirements as prescribed by the authority issuing the certificate; includes all grades of certificates except the *emergency certificate.*

certificate, substandard: a license to teach, issued on a temporary basis, indicating that the bearer has not fulfilled all the minimum standard requirements for certification.

certificate, supervisory: a license issued by the appropriate authority stating that a teacher is qualified to oversee the instruction given in specified grades, subjects, or school units.

certificate, teacher's: a license stating that a teacher is qualified to instruct in specified grades, subjects, or school units. *Syn.* **teacher's credential.**

certificate, teacher's health: see health certificate, teacher's.

certificate, teaching: *syn.* **certificate, teacher's.**

certificate, temporary: a state or local teaching license, issued to a teacher who meets all minimum standards,

that will be made permanent when certain additional requirements are met, such as graduate work or teaching experience; in some areas all certificates are temporary.

certificate, type of: the field of service for which a certificate is valid, for example, elementary certificate, administrative certificate, etc.

certificate, work: *syn.* **age-and-schooling certificate.**

certificated personnel: *see* **personnel, certificated.**

certificated teacher: a teacher who has been licensed to teach by the agency legally authorized by the state to grant such license.

certificating office: the school office that issues *age-and-schooling certificates.*

certification: *syn.* **certification, teacher.**

certification, administrative provision for teacher: administrative authority given by the state legislature to the state department of education or some representative unit thereof for the purpose of issuing, renewing, and revoking teachers' certificates.

certification authority, centralization of: the movement of the authority to issue teaching certificates from numerous town or township officials to county superintendents until it is now largely concentrated in the state departments of education.

certification, business and office education: minimum state qualifications for certification to teach in the business and office education field.

certification by professional organizations: the certifying by a nonacademic authority that the members of a certain profession are competent to perform their professional functions, for example, *counselor certification* by the American Psychological Association or the National Vocational Guidance Association.

certification by subject: the issuing of a license or certificate to teach one or more specified school subjects.

certification, distributive education: state minimum qualifications for certification or licensing to teach in the distributive education field.

certification, examination for: a test, oral and/or written, given to a candidate for a teaching position to determine his knowledge of academic subject matter or principles of teaching or both; the usual method of determining teaching fitness during the colonial period and the first half of the nineteenth century, when there were few teacher-preparing institutions. (At first, such tests were administered only by local district boards, but later many states adopted plans of county or state examinations. In recent years, the practice of basing certification upon examinations has tended to disappear as the practice of securing certificates by submission of credits earned in a teacher education institution has become common.)

certification law: a statute providing for the licensing of teachers, administrators, supervisors, and other professional employees in a public school system. See **certification, state.**

certification, librarian: the action taken by a legally authorized state body on the professional or technical qualifications of librarians and library workers in publicly supported libraries, based on standards adopted by the body; or similar action on a voluntary basis by a professional group such as a state library association.

certification, school counselor: in guidance, authorization that an individual has received, after having met specific requirements, enabling him to become a practicing school counselor.

certification, state: the act, on the part of a state department of education, of granting official authorization to a person to accept employment in keeping with the provisions of a certificate; applies chiefly to professional services such as teaching, supervision, and administration of education below college level.

certification, state teacher: see **teacher certification, state.**

certification system, semistate: a system whereby the power to issue teaching certificates is shared by the state with other authorities such as cities or, in some cases, individual schools.

certification system, state-county: a system whereby the authority to issue teaching certificates is shared by the counties and the state department of education.

certification, teacher: the act of designating persons whom public boards of education may legally employ as teachers in public schools and of issuing teaching certificates to these qualified persons.

certified mental defective: *syn.* **mental defective, certifiable.**

certiorari (sẽr'shi·ō·rãr'ī): (from the Latin phrase *certiorari volumus,* literally, "we wish to be certified," used in the Latin form of the writ) a writ by which a superior appellate court is asked to review a case decided in a lower court on questions of law.

certitude: that state of mind which gives a firm assent to a judgment without fear of error; incompatible in its extreme forms with the tentative spirit of modern science.

cessatio: a means of redressing grievances against either town or church authority sometimes exercised by the faculty and students of medieval universities, by going on strike or changing the location of the university; for example, the Oxford Cessatio of 1209 led to the founding of Cambridge University.

chain drill: *see* **drill, chain.**

chain feeding: *see* **feeding, chain.**

chain reflex: *see* **reflex, chain.**

chain transformation: *see* **transformation, chain.**

chaining: in programmed instruction, the linking together of a series of discriminable responses in a particular order; the completion of the first response provides the stimulus for the second response; in typical laboratory examples, *reinforcement* is given at the end of the chain of responses; a classroom parallel can be seen in the solution of a long-division problem; each step in the procedure could be separately taught, even in a random order, but the final performance requires a prescribed order to achieve the solution; to provide a student *knowledge of results* at the end of the solution sequence parallels the provision of reinforcement following the final response in a chain. *See* **reinforcer, conditioned; stimulus, discriminative.**

chair: (ed.) a teaching position in an institution of higher education, the incumbent of which is considered eminent in the field represented; often used for professorships having a special endowment for their support.

chair-desk: a form of seating for pupils consisting of a four-legged chair with an attached desk fastened to one side of the chair and extending in front of the seated pupil, usually with a compartment underneath the seat for the storage of books and school supplies.

chairman, department: *see* **department chairman.**

chalk, fluorescent: chalk that becomes luminescent in a darkened room under special ultraviolet lighting.

chalk talk: a visual presentation, drawn or written on a *chalkboard,* accompanied by narration and frequently used to supplement a lecture or discussion; drawings are usually essential to the chalk talk.

chalkboard: a smooth surface of slate, glass, or other material used for group presentation by writing or drawing with chalk, crayon, or other easily erased material. *Syn.* **blackboard.**

chalkboard, magnetic: a presentation board consisting of a metal sheet, covered with chalkboard paint, to which magnetic-backed objects will adhere and on which chalk marks may be made.

challenge tournament: a series of contests in which players may challenge others ranked above them and change their ranking if they win. *Syn.* **perpetual tournament ladder.**

chamber concert: *see* **concert.**

chamber music: *see* **music, chamber.**

chamber opera: *see* **opera, chamber.**

chamber orchestra: *see* **orchestra, chamber.**

chamber recital: *see* **concert.**

champion: one who has defeated all opponents in competition, thus holding first place.

chance: (1) an event resulting solely from random error or subject to no systematic influence; *see* **error, random;** (2) an outcome resulting from unmeasured or unmeasurable factors whose detailed operations are not understood.

chance difference: *see* **difference, chance.**

chance error: (1) *syn.* **error, random** (1); (2) *syn.* **difference, chance.**

chance factor: *syn.* **error, random** (1).

chance-halves correlation coefficient: *see* **split-halves method.**

chance, improvement over: *see* **index of forecasting efficiency.**

chance music: *syn.* **music, aleatory.**

chancellor: (1) the chief administrative officer of a university (a usage confined to a small number of universities); (2) the chief executive officer for a group of institutions of higher education; (3) a title primarily honorary in nature recently given with increasing frequency to a president of a higher education institution who has retired from the presidency; may involve some duties; (4) a title increasingly being used to denote the chief administrative officer of each campus of a multicampus institution the chief central administrator of which is called *president.*

change: the complete or partial alteration of an item in form, quality, or relationship; philosophically, a basic principle of existence in contrast to permanence or changelessness; a principle of education based on the recognition of creativeness including the genuinely novel and not the mere discovery of the preexistent, universal, and invariant; on the whole, change characterizes education that is dynamic rather than static.

change agent: a person, group, agency, or other medium that attempts to alter, change, or restructure concepts, conditions, or processes; for example, a change agent in the curriculum area seeks to make different the learning opportunities provided at a given time and place.

change, behavior: *see* **behavior change.**

change, coercive: alteration of procedures, techniques, or goals as the result of the real or imaginary threat of retaliation by superordinates. *See* **superordinate relationship.**

change, culture: *see* **culture change.**

change, cumulative: (admin.) alterations increasing in size or strength by successive additions in the change process.

change, curriculum: *see* **curriculum change.**

change, educational: *see* **educational change.**

change, emulative: (admin.) alteration brought about by a form of identification, possibly unconscious, of subordinates with the "power figures."

change, indoctrination: (admin.) alterations occurring deliberately as a result of mutual goal setting by both parties concerned but involving an imbalanced power ratio.

change, interactional: (admin.) alterations occurring on both sides of a relationship through mutual goal setting and a fairly equal power distribution and without deliberateness.

change, management of : (admin.) planned direction of the evolutionary aspects of education and control of the educational processes.

change, methodology of: a systematic arrangement of the processes of school administration resulting in a formulated procedure to bring about change.

change, natural: (admin.) change which comes about with no apparent deliberateness and no goal setting on the part of those involved in it.

change of symbol: *see* **symbol, change of.**

change, planned: (admin.) designed change, which comes about as a result of some scheme or system of action.

change score: *see* **score, change.**

change-sensitive test: *see* **test, change-sensitive.**

change, social: *see* **social change.**

change, socialization: change which has a direct kinship with the interactional hierarchial control, parent-child relationships serving as the most obvious example.

change tape: *see* **tape, change.**

change, technocratic: (admin.) planned change to be effected solely through reliance upon collecting and interpreting data.

change, theory of cultural: *see* **cultural change, theory of.**

change, vehicle of: any organizational attack on the instructional program, for example, the Montessori plan, on methods of instruction, such as the core curriculum or on materials used, the purpose being to bring about change or enhance its possibility.

changes of drive accompanying maturity: see **drive, changes of, accompanying maturity.**

changing voice: modification of voice range and quality at adolescence.

channel: (1) in automatic data processing, a shielded line over which pulses travel from one unit to another within the calculator; also, a path parallel to the edge of a memory device along which information may be stored by means of the presence or absence of changes in state, as by spots or holes; see **bus**; (2) (radio/television) a specific band of frequencies assigned to each radio or television station; (3) in an electronic learning laboratory, the conduit for a *dual tape recording* of program signal and student signal or for a *multitape recording* for simultaneous transmission of recorded messages from several program sources to selected student positions.

channel of distribution: the path taken by a product from the producer to the ultimate consumer.

channel selector: a multiposition switch for selecting signals on a tape recording.

channel system: (information theory) a complete system for transmitting a signal from an input location to an output location; the channel includes the properties not only of the apparatus or equipment in the system but of the code of language used; the channel may be an organism, in which case the sense organ is the input location and the motor mechanism is the output location, but it may also be purely mechanical, as is telephony, or it may be an institution such as a newspaper or news service, or any combination of physical, organic, and social transmitting media.

channel-transportation test: see **test, channel-transportation.**

channeling: syn. **canalization.**

chantry school: during the later medieval period, usually an elementary school, staffed by priests, who were supported by endowments to instruct poor boys and to say masses for the repose of the souls of the donors.

chapbook: a kind of crudely prepared and inexpensive small book sold by itinerant peddlers (chapmen) in the seventeenth and eighteenth centuries; some contained stories that appealed to children.

chapel exercises: a gathering of the student body of a secondary school, college, or university in a chapel for religious purposes; formerly, especially in church-related schools, held frequently and at regular intervals with attendance required; in more recent years held less frequently, attendance being usually voluntary and the purposes not necessarily religious; popularly called most often simply "chapel."

chaperon: an adult present at an organized social party for purposes of general supervision of the conduct of students.

character: (1) structural or enduring elements or characteristics which give continuity to personality over time; (2) personality viewed in relation to some system of morality or criterion of value; see **morality; value;** (3) the personality or some part of personality seen as the determinant of moral judgment; see **moral judgment;** (4) (genet.) a distinctive feature or sum of features of an organism (in Mendelian terms, a character is the end product of a line of development that has been controlled by a definite gene); syn. **characteristic; trait** (5); (5) one symbol of a set of elementary symbols such as those corresponding to the keys on a typewriter, including the digits 0 through 9, the letters A through Z, punctuation marks, and operation symbols, also any other single symbols which a computer can read, store, or write; (6) the electrical, magnetic, or mechanical profile used to represent a character in a computer and its various storage and peripheral devices.

character, acquired: (genet.) a noninheritable structural or functional modification of the organism, the result of special environmental forces or of special activities of the organism itself, for example, an act of skill, such as

playing the violin, or a physical mutilation, such as circumcision. See **phenotype.**

character, anal: (psychoan.) a type of character or personality pattern that in its major aspects allegedly can be traced back to the habits, attitudes, feelings, and values stimulated and crystallized during the early years of development when training in the control of defecation and urination was in progress; traits alleged to be characteristic of persons fixated at the anal expulsive stage are conceit, suspiciousness, ambition, interest in money, and a tendency to give gifts instead of love, whereas persons fixated at the anal retentive stage are said to be characterized by such traits as overmeticulousness, petulance, parsimoniousness, pedantry, obstinacy, constipation, and interest in collecting; the ascendance in the personality of the trait complexes mentioned is alleged to be a reflection of an inability in the individual, persisting from the time when he was being trained in bowel and bladder control, to resolve successfully the conflicts arising between his own primitive drives and his desire for social approval. *Contr. w.* **character, genital; character, oral.**

character classification: a financial-accounting classification of expenditures according to their character; in public school financial accounting, this generally includes the following divisions: general control, instruction, auxiliary agencies, coordinate activities, operation of plant, fixed charges, maintenance of plant, debt service, and capital outlay, all but the last two being grouped under *current expenditures.* (Note: Frequently the classifications *auxiliary agencies* and *coordinate activities* are subsumed under the heading *auxiliary services,* especially in some public school systems.)

character education: (1) education designed to develop characters that conform to some system of morality; sometimes viewed as setting an aim for and defining a criterion relevant to all instruction and school experience and sometimes as a separable part of the school program in which direct instruction in some moral code is given; sometimes confused with indoctrination for life in an institution which is seen as imposing major sanctions upon moral behavior, for example, with religious instruction, where the church is seen as the source of sanctions, or with civic education, when civil society or the state is seen in the major sanctioning role; (2) education based on the belief that control of behavior must come from within the individual; emotional and social outcomes of education are stressed as much as intellectual factors. See **character; character, moral; morality; civic.**

character, ethical: an individual's personality traits and behavior evaluated in terms of some set of ethical principles; usually connotes positive factors; listed in 1918 as one of the seven cardinal principles of education. See **character, moral; seven cardinal objectives or principles.**

character, genital: (psychoan.) a type of personality or character pattern alleged to emerge normally when the genitals become the focal erotogenic zones and which, with varying emphases from the preschool to adult years, is characterized by homosexual or heterosexual interests, by some degree of sublimation of aggression, and by striving on the part of the ego toward a socially approved ideal.

character-impersonation sale: a form of demonstration or mock sale used in salesmanship and distributive education classes in which participants assume the mannerisms, speech, and reactions of specific types of persons. See **role-playing.**

character, judgmental: see **judgmental character.**

character measurement, inferential method of: see **measurement, inferential method of character.**

character, moral: a person's system of habits, ideals, attitudes, and beliefs as seen in relation to group-accepted norms and/or to an ideal system of moral standards; commonly used synonymously with *ethical* character. See **character, ethical.**

character, native: syn. **trait, native.**

character, neurotic: see **neurotic character.**

character, objectification of: see **objectification of character.**

character of man as rational being: see **rational being, character of man as.**

character, oral: (psychoan.) a type of character or personality pattern that in its major aspects, it is alleged, can be traced back to the habits, attitudes, values, and feelings stimulated and crystallized during the suckling period; traits alleged to be characteristic or diagnostic of *oral character* associated with a particularly gratifying suckling period are optimism, carefree indifference, and generosity, whereas failure to receive adequate oral gratification is alleged to be associated with pessimism, apprehensiveness, and demandingness. *Contr. w.* **character, anal; character, genital.**

character pattern: a set of action, thought, and feeling tendencies of an individual, group, or culture which provides a basis for prediction of conduct.

character, pregenital: (psychoan.) a type of character or personality pattern alleged to be typical of or to represent a fixation at the *oral* or *anal* periods. *See* **character, anal; character, oral.**

character reader: *see* **reader, character.**

character, secondary sex: a physical characteristic dependent for its development on the hormones of the male or female gonads but not necessary to the reproductive function, for example, male facial hair, female fat distribution, etc.

character, sex-linked: a trait the hereditary transmission of which depends on genes believed to be located in the sex chromosomes and which, accordingly, is associated with a particular sex; a trait of which the presence or absence in the individual is biologically determined by the sex of the individual; thus, under certain controlled conditions, it may be possible to predict the eye color of offspring according to whether they are male or female.

character sketches: brief, paragraph-length characterizations of hypothetical or real personalities; used, among other ways, in a form of reputation test in which the subjects are asked to designate the person or persons in a specified group whom they believe to be well characterized by each sketch. *See* **pupil portraits; test, reputation.**

character test: *see* **test, character.**

character trait: one of an indefinite number of specific characteristics of which the total constitutes the *moral character* of an individual.

character trait, negative: a character trait that correlates negatively with desirable traits, for example, dishonesty.

character trait, positive: a term denoting any type of reaction that may be considered as either of social value or as evidence of an ego that exercises constructive control over the psyche.

character, unit: a hereditary trait or feature that is transmitted directly and is independent of the transmission of other unit characters, being determined only by a single gene or its allelomorphs. *See* **allelomorph; character; gene; genes, complementary; inheritance, blending; inheritance, two-factor.**

characteristic: (1) *syn.* **attribute** (2); (2) *syn.* **statistic** (1); (3) *syn.* **character** (4).

characteristic, atypical: a characteristic of an individual in a given chronological age group which is markedly different from that of the mean. *See* **child, exceptional; condition, atypical; exceptionality, area of.**

characteristic curve, item: *see* **curve, item characteristic.**

characterization: (art ed.) the child's depiction in his drawings of what he regards as most characteristic of an object, action, etc.; simple characterization, such as pants on a figure to indicate a boy, is merely for recognition and does not relate to visual observation, which begins where mere characterization ends; meaningful objects may be given special characteristics.

characterologist: (1) a pseudoscientific advocate of systems by which attempts are made to estimate, in a rapid way, the character, temperament, physical stamina, and mental abilities of the individual; (2) a research or clinical worker in the field of character and personality tests (coming into use in this sense among some authorities).

charge account: an arrangement between a buyer and a seller which permits the buyer to receive goods or services without making full payment; payment is made at a later date.

charitable trust: *see* **trust, charitable.**

charity advertising: advertisements in publications of schools, colleges, or other nonprofit organizations which are solicited not on the basis of business return to the advertiser but as an obligation to the school.

charity education: (1) in religious schools of Reform Jews, where the concept of charity is taught as evolving from the Hebrew word for *justice* (*ts'duh-kuh*), a program that concerns itself with ethical conduct toward others less fortunate and gives practice in making decisions in regard to allocation of funds for charitable purposes; (2) philanthropic education found in early times in Virginia and the Carolinas in institutions often called *old-field schools;* a step in the development of schools in America; fostered by the church and the English government, with some payment made by upper- and middle-class society.

charity school: a type of free or nearly free school provided by gifts or public tax for children of the poor; the term was common in Europe and in the United States until the middle of the nineteenth century but is now obsolete. *Syn.* **pauper school.**

chart: (1) a systematic arrangement of facts in graphic or pictorial form presenting for convenient reference comparisons of quantity, distributions, trends, summaries, etc.; (2) *syn.* **diagram, scatter;** (3) (math.) *see* **graph.**

chart, age distribution: a sheet having various ages listed in one column and the number of pupils of these given ages shown in a second parallel column.

chart, alignment: a chart in which three variables are plotted on straight lines in such a way that, if any two are known, the third can be determined with the use of the straightedge.

chart, analysis: (testing) a chart, usually prepared in connection with a battery of achievement tests, that shows the relative performance of members of a class on the several parts of the battery.

chart, arithmetic: (1) any chart constructed to a uniform scale such that equal divisions on the chart represent equal quantities; *syn.* **arithmetic graph;** *contr. w.* **chart, logarithmic;** (2) any chart used as an aid in the teaching of arithmetic.

chart, attention: an instrument designed for the purpose of denoting the extent of pupil attention at designated intervals of the class period, for example, the *Morrison attention chart.*

chart, axonometric: a chart, showing three dimensions in two-dimensional space, in which the three dimensions are measured along three axes in the two-dimensional space. *Dist. f.* **orthographic chart.**

chart, band: a chart or graph composed of a number of irregular belts or bands, each usually differently shaded or colored, the widths of which are proportional to the magnitudes of the various classes.

chart, bar: *syn.* **graph, bar.**

chart board: (mil. ed.) a small portable board upon which charts and other data pertaining to a flight or mission are mounted and used for instructional purposes.

chart book: a series of reading charts bound into the form of a large book by the use of rings or other devices; frequently used in primer classes.

chart, career: (1) a graphic presentation of some phase of occupational information, generally showing successive stages of progress from one job to another; (2) a chart showing each school subject or type of training as the center of several life careers to which that subject or type of training makes some very definite contribution.

chart, class analysis: a chart used to indicate the relative performance of students on various types of measurements, including sections of a test battery, ability and achievement tests, or other measures of performance.

chart, classification: a chart showing detailed pupil measurements and records for the purpose of classification.

chart, computing: *syn.* **diagram, computing.**

chart, control: a graph drawn to show the limits of variability that will be tolerated; determined empirically for each operation, the limits are based on sampling distributions and provide a basis for *quality control;*

operations are said to be in *statistical control* when sampled items fall within the *tolerance limits* of the control chart.

chart, correlation: (1) *syn.* **table, double-entry;** (2) *syn.* **diagram, scatter;** (3) any of several specially designed forms for computing correlation coefficients.

chart, creative writing: a group composition dictated by pupils and written in chart form by the teacher; the composition is generally based on a common experience of interest to the group.

chart, cumulative: a graph showing any cumulative data as, for example, the total up to each plotted date or the cumulative frequency up to each given point. *See* **ogive.**

chart, curriculum: a chart that shows the sequence of learning tasks or allocation of topics according to grade levels, as shown in a correlation chart, for subject-matter placement of topics in an elementary school textbook series. *See* **map, curriculum.**

chart, diagnostic: a device used for analyzing test results; typically arranged to identify persons in the group tested and to record the nature of each person's response for each skill tested.

chart, dot: (1) *syn.* **map, dot;** (2) *syn.* **diagram, scatter.**

chart, double logarithmic: *syn.* **graph, double logarithmic.**

chart, E: a chart for testing vision made up of lines of symbols similar to the letter E, drawn in various sizes according to the Snellen scale. *Syn.* **symbol-E chart;** *see* **chart, Snellen.**

chart, experience: (read.) a printed or handwritten chart prepared by the teacher and based upon some experience in which the children participate.

chart, fingering: a diagram indicating the application of the fingers to the keys, strings, valves, or holes of a musical instrument. (In class piano instruction, pupils may be required to practice by moving their fingers on full-scale fingering charts made to imitate the keyboard.)

chart, flannel: *see* **feltboard.**

chart, flip: an integrated, graphic easel presentation consisting of separate sheets hinged together so that they may be flipped over the top of the unit into or out of view with progress in the presentation; most useful for tabletop presentation to small rather than large audiences.

chart, flow: (1) a systematic arrangement of data in graphic form symbolically depicting trends, movement, comparisons of quantity or quality, or organization of factors being considered, such as the substrata factors that underlie reading ability; may portray, for example, the flow of administrative responsibility, sequence of steps in a job, number of persons selected or eliminated from a group at successive stages in a research project, etc.; also, a systems analysis technique; not to be confused with a *flow diagram;* (2) (math.) a diagrammatic representation of a sequence of operations required to carry out some procedure; steps in the procedure are usually in rectangles, circles, etc., with arrows leading from one figure to the next; of particular importance in making a flow chart is the insertion of instructions for making decisions and for repeating part of the procedure; *syn.* **logical diagram.**

chart, form distribution: a graphic presentation of the flow of copies of a multicopy form.

chart, form procedure: graphic presentation of the use to which copies of a multicopy form are put.

chart, frequency: *syn.* **graph, frequency.**

chart, grade-distribution: a sheet having the various grades listed in one column and the number of pupils enrolled in each of these grades listed in a second parallel column.

chart, historical: *syn.* **historigram.**

chart, isometric: an axonometric chart in which the three axes are equally foreshortened to show three dimensions in two-dimensional space; in an isometric cube, three faces are visible and all nine of the visible edges are drawn equal in length.

chart, logarithmic: *syn.* **graph, logarithmic.**

chart, machine process: a graphic description of individual machine operations by sequence and movement.

chart, man process: a graphic presentation of both sequence and movement of the successive activities of an individual.

chart, multiple bar: a bar graph in which two or more categories are represented (*a*) by as many bars distinguished by color or crosshatching or (*b*) by separate bands on each of several bars in the graph.

chart, Northampton: one of the charts, with their secondary spellings, which represent the letters and combination of letters used most frequently in the English language and are intended to show how to pronounce the written word.

chart, operation: one complete cycle or the details of one activity represented by a single symbol on a flow process chart. *See* **chart, flow.**

chart, operation flow: a graphic representation of a sequence of operations, usually including time and distances.

chart, operation process: a graphic presentation showing operations and inspections.

chart, organization: a graphic or semigraphic presentation of certain information concerning functions, functional groupings, and lines of responsibility, authority, and accountability in the organization.

chart, orthographic: a chart on which the projecting lines are at right angles to the plane of projection. *Dist. f.* **axonometric chart.**

chart, participation: a device for recording the frequency and sometimes the general character of a pupil's participation in classroom activities; a predetermined code is used to designate various types of responses.

chart, phonovisual: a chart giving either consonants or vowel sounds with pictures to illustrate the sounds; for example, the letter *d* accompanied by the picture of a duck to illustrate the consonant in the initial position.

chart, place value: a chart with columns headed by consecutive powers of the base, used as an aid in the teaching of computation. *See* **value, place.**

chart, procedural flow: (school admin.) a device for summarizing in graphic form the principal facts and functional relationships in a procedure; also called a *routine chart* or *systems chart.*

chart, process: a graphic presentation of the successive steps in an operation or procedure.

chart, profile: (1) a graph used to indicate the relative position of one person or group on each of a battery of tests; (2) a form on which a profile may be charted. *Syn.* **profile; profile graph; psychograph.**

chart, progress: (1) a graphic representation of achievement in schoolwork, usually consisting of a series of test scores or other marks taken from time to time and plotted in graphic form; (2) (typewriting) a chronological record of the individual student's error and speed scores (often kept in graph form) which shows at a glance the student's progress in typewriting skills; (3) a listing of the names of a student group, with provisions for recording observations and evaluation of achievement in schoolwork.

chart, progress distribution: a sheet listing in one column the years spent in school by half years from 9 to 20 years or more and showing in a parallel column the number of pupils who have spent these various periods in school.

chart, rating: *syn.* **rating scale.**

chart, ratio: a chart that shows the rate of change rather than the amount of change; usually drawn as a *logarithmic graph.* *See* **graph, logarithmic.**

chart, reading: *see* **reading chart.**

chart, relative bar: *syn.* **graph, bar.**

chart, routine: *syn.* **chart, procedural flow.**

chart, self-corrective handwriting: a device for individualizing instruction that provides guidance in detecting and overcoming handwriting faults; specific exercises are provided to overcome each type of defect; for example, when the movement is restrained, free-running ovals may be used to loosen the movement; such elements as slant, spacing alignment, unit stroke, letter formation, and speed may be singled out for attention and practice.

chart, semilogarithmic: *syn.* **graph, semilogarithmic.**

chart, Snellen: a white chart with black letters or other symbols of graded sizes, used to measure visual acuity. *See* **scale, Snellen; Snellen notation.**

chart, symbol-E: *syn.* **chart, E.**

chart, systems: *syn.* **chart, procedural flow.**

chart, thinking: a chart analyzing the principal phases of a problem, used to help a conference group think through the problem.

chart, trend: a graphic representation of data (generally by a line graph) used to show changes in frequencies, percentages, or proportions over a period of time, for example, curves of learning.

chart, vertical bar: a graph in which each class is represented by a vertical bar of equal width but with length corresponding to its frequency or value.

chart, vision test: a chart made up of a series of letters or symbols of various sizes, used for testing central visual acuity, for example, the *Snellen chart* or the *E chart.*

charter: a written instrument, granting certain powers and specifying duties, responsibilities, and liabilities, given to an individual or a group of incorporators by the sovereign authority of a nation, political subdivision, or specially empowered official thereof; usually granted in the United States by officials acting under laws of general authorization or through special enactment of the Federal Congress or state legislatures. (A privately controlled school usually has a charter granted by authority of the state legislature.)

charter, philanthropic: a charitable or eleemosynary charter issued under the same authorization as a charter for a private profit corporation but differing from the latter in purpose and in having a longer life, greater freedom of action, and exemption from taxation.

charting: the act or process of summarizing and/or analyzing data by means of charts or graphs.

chartometer: an instrument used for determining the length of a curved or irregular line; usually consists of a disk that is rolled along the line and a series of gears connected to dials from which the distance traversed by the disk may be read.

chassis, bus: *see* **bus chassis.**

chassis capacity: *see* **capacity of chassis.**

chautauqua (shə·tâ′kwə): (1) an adult education institution centered at Chautauqua, New York, utilizing summer assemblies and systematic, extended courses of home reading and correspondence study; (2) a short session of popular entertainment, concerts, educational lectures, etc., produced by an itinerant chautauqua staff or troupe and held in a community, often annually, for several days or weeks. (Traveling chautauquas ceased operation in the early 1930s.)

check, built-in: in automatic computers, any verification operation directly and automatically provided by the hardware.

check, code: *see* **code check.**

check digit: (data processing) a digit used for checking the transcription of numbers.

check flight: *see* **flight, check.**

check, good-faith: (school admin.) a check for a sum of money included with bond bid to guarantee performance of functions by successful bidder.

check-out card: *syn.* **guidance dismissal blank.**

check pilot: the pilot who checks another pilot on a check flight.

check, redundant: in computer operation, a check which uses extra *bits* or characters in a word, but not complete duplication, to help detect errors.

check ride: *syn.* **flight, check.**

check, rough: (math.) a process of estimating the correctness of an operation or series of measures without minute attention to details.

check, sight: *v.* to verify visually the sorting or punching of punched cards by examining the patterns of punched holes.

check, spot: the act or process of reviewing or testing (usually not thoroughly) some of the items, objects, or

cases in a sample, the selection being made either randomly or in some predetermined manner; used primarily in industry.

checking: (1) the practice of reworking a problem using the same or a different pattern of operations in order to make sure that the work is correct; (2) the use of some device or technique, such as casting out nines, to determine whether the answer to an example is correct; *see* **casting out nines.**

checking level: (voc. ed.) (1) a designated point or stage in a course of study at which the instructor may measure the learners' achievement, to ensure adequate testing without the necessity of testing achievement upon the completion of each small unit of work; (2) a certain point or stage of a long or involved job at which a check is made for errors, the purpose being to have the student note and correct errors during the progress of the job.

checklist: a prepared list of items that may relate to a person, procedure, institution, building, etc., used for purposes of observation and/or evaluation, and on which one may show by check marks the presence, absence, or frequency of occurrence of each item on the list.

checklist, activity: a survey of a student's activities to assess pupil readiness for new learning experiences and for general curriculum planning.

checklist, diagnostic: a device used in the classroom, laboratory, or clinic to aid in determining the deficiencies of a pupil or student in reading, language, or other fundamental skills.

checklist, evaluative: *syn.* **checklist, teacher-evaluation.**

checklist, tasks: (admin.) a list of selected, specific tasks used as a resource in implementing a program.

checklist, teacher-evaluation: a checklist of teacher qualities, teaching activities or techniques, or conditions to be observed in a teaching situation; used by an observer for recording or appraisal or by the teacher for purposes of self-improvement.

checkup: an examination performed on people or things as to health, fitness, condition, readiness, etc.

cheerleader: a high school or college student, usually elected by the student body, sometimes appointed, who assumes the responsibility of directing and leading the cheering at athletic events.

cheerleaders' club: *see* **club, cheerleaders'.**

chemical bonding: a branch of chemistry concerned with the study of bonding among atoms in ions and molecules—types, lengths, and strengths of bonds, geometry of molecules, relationships of bonds to physical and chemical properties of substances, and energy considerations.

chemistry: the study of the composition, structure, and properties of matter and of changes in matter, including the accompanying energy phenomena.

chemistry, inorganic: the study of the chemistry of noncarbon compounds.

chemistry, organic: the study of the chemistry of carbon compounds—their properties, chemical behavior, preparation, and uses.

chemistry, physical: the study of the application of physical principles to chemical systems, namely, gas laws, thermodynamics, kinetics, solubility phenomena, and equilibrium.

chemistry, radiation: the branch of chemistry that is concerned with the chemical effects, including decomposition, of energetic radiation or particles on matter. *See* **radiochemistry.**

chemotherapy: use of chemicals—such as tranquilizers, energizers, convulsive agents, in short, chemicals of any sort—to produce alterations of behavior, emotionality, personality, or learning ability.

chest, community: *syn.* **fund, community.**

chest tone: *see* **tone, chest.**

chest voice: *see* **voice, chest.**

chi square (kī): (χ^2) a statistic used to test the agreement of obtained and theoretical distribution; mathematically equal to the sum of the quotients obtained by dividing the square of each difference between the actual and the theoretical frequency (for each category) by the theoretical frequency for that category. *Syn.* **square contingency;** *see* **chi square test of goodness of fit.**

chi square test of goodness of fit: a statistical procedure by means of which the probability can be estimated that a given set of data or one showing a greater discrepancy might arise if a certain law or cause were in operation;

based on the formula $\chi^2 = \sum \left[\dfrac{(f_o - f_t)^2}{f_t} \right]$ where f_o is

each observed frequency and f_t is each theoretical frequency; determined by calculating χ^2 and then finding the probability that a chi square of that or greater magnitude might occur by chance alone by reference to a table of the sampling distribution of χ^2.

Chicago plan: the former arrangement at the University of Chicago by which the freshman and sophomore years were administered as a separate unit with a single curriculum for all entering students, the usual work in arts and sciences was administered through four divisions, and the granting of degrees and certificates was based on comprehensive examinations administered by a semi-independent agency within the university.

chief academic officer: *see* **dean, academic.**

chief administrator: *see* **administrator, chief.**

chief state-school officer: *see* **superintendent of public instruction.**

child: (1) in the broadest sense, a boy or girl at any age before maturity; (2) strictly, a person between infancy and adolescence (puberty). (Sometimes arbitrarily used to designate a person of any age from birth to 12 years.)

child abuse: *see* **child, battered.**

child, abused: *syn.* **child, battered.**

child, academically talented: a child who can be expected to attend college and benefit from enriched experiences in high school as well as college; a term used first by the Conference on the Academically Talented.

child, accelerated: (1) a child who has negotiated the school grades more rapidly than one grade per year; *syn.* **accelerated pupil;** (2) a child whose achievement or mental growth is beyond that of the average child of the same chronological age.

child accounting: *syn.* **accounting, pupil.**

child accounting, director of: *see* **director of child accounting.**

child-accounting records: *see* **records, child-accounting.**

child adjustment: *see* **adjustment, child.**

child, allergic: a child who is susceptible to allergy; may need special education as in a class for the emotionally disturbed or those with low vitality or health problems.

child analysis: *see* **analysis, child.**

child art, representational stages in: *syn.* **art, developmental stages in child.**

child, asocial: a child whose behavior demonstrates that he or she is lacking in understanding or appreciation of existing social customs, social relationships, or moral codes.

child, asthmatic: a child susceptible to or suffering from asthma; may need special education as in a class for emotionally disturbed children or for those with low vitality or health problems.

child, atypical: *syn.* **child, exceptional.**

child, autistic: a child who withdraws and responds only to a narrow class of objects; in severe cases such children may make no normal social responses to parents or other children. *See* **thinking, autistic.**

child, backward: a child who is 1 to 2 years retarded in academic grade placement. *See* **child, slow-learning.**

child, battered: an infant or child on whom severe injury has been inflicted by a parent or other adult; usually caused by exhaustion, frustration, and pressures afflicting the adult, who releases his or her pent-up tensions by beating the child. *Syn.* **child, abused.**

child behavior: *see* **behavior, child.**

child, below average: *see* **pupil, slow.**

child benefit theory: the theory growing out of the *Cochran v. Louisiana State Board of Education* case (281 U.S. 370,

1930) that certain types of expenditure of public funds for students in private or parochial schools are regarded as aids to the child rather than to the institution; textbook and transportation expenditures are examples.

child, boarding: (1) a child not living with his own parents; (2) a child living in a home other than his own and for whose maintenance payment is made.

child, borderline: *see* **child, backward; child, slow-learning.**

child, brain-injured: a child who before, during, or after birth has received an injury to or suffered an infection of the brain; as a result of such organic impairment, defects of the neuromotor system may show disturbances in perception, thinking, and emotional behavior, either separately or in combination, which can be demonstrated by specific tests and which prevent or impede a normal learning process. *Syn.* **neurophrenic child.**

child, bright: (1) a child who is above the average in intellectual ability; (2) a child who learns relatively easily.

child care center: *see* **center, day care.**

child-centered curriculum: *syn.* **curriculum, activity.**

child-centered education: an educational approach in which the child's own interests, rather than external authority exclusively, play a significant role in determining curriculum and procedures; the child is engaged in reconstructing his own real and concrete experience rather than in learning exclusively from books and subject fields; the approach enjoyed less popular and critical acclaim in the 1950s and 1960s than in the 1920s and 1930s.

child-centered school: a school that is organized around the needs, purposes, and interests of the children.

child, cerebral palsied: a child afflicted with cerebral palsy. See **cerebral palsy.**

child, crippled: a child who has an orthopedic impairment interfering with the normal functions of the bones, joints, or muscles to such an extent that special arrangements for the child's transportation and activities must be made by the school.

child, culturally deprived: a child from a social environment which tends to be identifiably inferior to that of the rest of the community, using middle-class standards as reference.

child, culturally different: a child with a cultural background different from that of the white middle-class American which is frequently considered standard by teachers.

child, culturally disadvantaged: a term used to identify lower-class children, particularly of Afro-American heritage; such children are also described as educationally disadvantaged and economically deprived.

child, deaf: a child who from infancy or early childhood has sustained a sufficiently severe impairment of hearing (in the better ear, roughly more than 75 decibels in frequencies in the speech range) so that his language and speech do not develop normally; he must be taught a means of communication by use of special educational techniques. *Dist. f.* **child, deafened; child, educationally deaf; child, hard-of-hearing.**

child, deafened: a child whose language patterns were well established by the time he sustained a severe enough hearing loss through accident or illness to wipe out almost all his usable hearing.

child, defective: (1) as commonly used, a child who is mentally retarded; *see* **retardation, mental;** (2) also frequently used to refer to a child who is retarded educationally, socially, emotionally, or physically.

child, delicate: *syn.* **child, physically below par;** *see* **lowered-vitality case.**

child, delinquent: a youthful offender against the standards of society; (judicial) a child or youth who is apprehended in violating the law; (general) a child or youth who disregards discipline or regulations of the school or other institution. (Upper age differentiation between delinquent and adult offender varies by states.)

child, dependent: (1) in a broad sense, any child whose parents do not care for him properly, and who, therefore, must look to society for support; legally, a distinction usually is made between the dependent child, whose parents cannot provide for him, and the *neglected child*, whose parents will not do so; (2) a child who is not self-supporting and who requires financial or other assistance from his parents or from society.

child development: *see* **development, child.**

child-development approach: *see* **approach, child-development.**

child development center: *see* **center, child development.**

child development laboratory: *see* **laboratory, child development.**

child development specialist: *see* **specialist, child development.**

child, disadvantaged: a child who has an impoverished range of experience and whose physical needs are usually met at a mere subsistence level.

child, disturbed: a child who, because of organic and/or environmental influences, chronically displays (*a*) inability to learn at a rate commensurate with his intellectual, sensory-motor, and physical development, (*b*) inability to establish and maintain adequate social relationships, (*c*) inability to respond appropriately in day-to-day life situations, and (*d*) a variety of behavior ranging from hyperactive, impulsive responses to depression and withdrawal. *See* **child, emotionally disturbed.**

child, dull: *see* **child, backward; child, slow-learning.**

child, educable mentally retarded: a child who because of slow mental development is unable to profit to any great extent from the programs of the regular schools but who has potentialities for development, that is, minimum educability in reading, writing, spelling, arithmetic, etc.; capacity for social adjustment to a point where he can get along independently in the community; and minimum occupational adequacy such that he can later support himself partially or totally at a marginal level.

child, educationally deaf: a child whose impairment of hearing from birth or early childhood has been severe enough (in the better ear, roughly between 60 and 75 decibels in the frequencies in the speech range) to interfere with the natural development of language and speech but whose trainable residual hearing allows for rather rapid growth in speech and language when proper techniques are employed.

child, educationally handicapped: a child whose learning problems are associated with a behavioral disorder or a neurological handicap or a combination thereof and who exhibits a significant discrepancy between ability and achievement.

child, elementary school age: a child served by the elementary school; in a six-grade elementary school, normally any child from age 6 to 12.

child, emancipation of: *see* **emancipation of child.**

child, emotionally disturbed: a child with a deep-rooted problem who habitually expresses his feelings in a manner to hurt himself or others; if, in his attempts to adjust, he hurts others or their property, he may also be considered socially maladjusted; these children may develop the tendency to withdraw within themselves and express excessive fears and frustrations; such difficulties may eventuate in social maladjustment.

child, exceptional: a child who deviates intellectually, physically, socially, or emotionally in his growth and development so markedly from what is considered to be normal that he cannot receive maximum benefit from a regular school program and requires a special class or supplementary instruction and services. *Syn.* **atypical child.**

child-experience approach: (1) a method of teaching new subject matter or ideas by utilizing the previous experiences of the children who are being taught, both as a means of introducing the new subject matter and in order to show applications once the subject matter is learned; (2) a technique of individual counseling in which the experiences of the child are used to show the value of advice given; *see* **psychological approach;** (3) a method of attack upon the problem of curriculum revision, especially in the lower grades, in which an attempt is made to select materials and methods of instruction in such a way

as to harmonize not only with the present interest and ability levels of the children but also with their eventual adult educational needs.

child, feral: a child reportedly living in association with wild animals and whose behavioral peculiarities, such as going about on all fours, are ascribed to this association, for example, *wolf-child.*

child, foster: (1) an adopted child; (2) a child not the biological offspring of the adult person or persons rearing it.

child, gifted: (1) a child whose mental age is considerably higher than his actual age compared with children in the general population; (2) a child who is far more educable than the generality of children; (3) a child whose performance is consistently remarkable in a worthwhile type of human endeavor.

child guidance: *see* **guidance, child.**

child guidance clinic: *see* **clinic, child guidance.**

child, handicapped: a mentally retarded, hard of hearing, deaf, speech-impaired, visually handicapped, seriously emotionally disturbed, crippled, or other health-impaired child who by reason thereof requires special education and related services.

child, hard of hearing: a child in whom the sense of hearing, although defective, is functional with or without a hearing aid.

child, homebound: *see* **pupil, homebound.**

child, hyperactive: the child who seems to be always in motion and whose motion is always in double time.

child, hyperkinetic: a child who is unable to control his body movement; muscular movement is abnormally increased and usually purposeless.

child, incorrigible: a term commonly used to describe a child who cannot be controlled by parents; rapidly falling into disuse.

child, indigent: a child of an indigent family.

child labor: the gainful employment of children outside their home or family; the age at which children may be gainfully employed without violating child-labor laws varies with the states (also defined by Federal statutes).

child, latchkey: a metaphorical term used, especially during World War II, to describe children who were given the door keys of their homes and who fended for themselves while the parents worked.

child, low-vision: a child who, because of visual disabilities, cannot handle easily and at the same rate the same educational materials and tasks that normally sighted children manage with facility; often included in the larger traditional group of *partially seeing* who function with a severe visual disability, but also frequently found within the group described as legally blind. *See* **blindness, legal.**

child, maladjusted: (1) a child whose behavior is so different that he cannot participate in normal activities with other children; (2) a child who cannot benefit from the school situation because of deep psychological problems that bring about deviant behavior and resistance to learning, development, and growth.

child, malnourished: (spec. ed.) a child who is thought to possess specific learning disabilities as a result of nutritional deficits.

child, mentally gifted: *see* **child, gifted.**

child, mentally retarded: a child who is characterized by a condition of arrested or incomplete development or who manifests this condition to the degree that special educational services should be provided. *See* **retardation, mental.**

child, migrant: (1) a child whose parents move from one country to another with the intention of establishing a permanent residence; (2) a child whose parents move from one portion of a country to another with the intention of establishing a permanent home (the term is ordinarily used in this sense only when groups of families make such a change of location); (3) a child whose parents are migrant workers moving periodically for seasonal employment and who is within the age limits for which the local school district provides free public education. *See* **child, transient.**

child, minority group: a child whose parents are classified according to race, religion, or nationality as belonging to groups whose membership is less than 50 percent of a given population.

child, morning-glory: a poetic reference to a child who, slow to mature and for years behind his classmates, does well at a later period in his education; sometimes referred to as a *late bloomer.*

child, needs of: *see* **needs of child.**

child, neglected: a child with regard to whom its parents or society fail in fulfilling their normal responsibilities for support, guidance, or discipline.

child, nervous: a child who for some reason, whether physical or mental, is high-strung and easily excited.

child, neurophrenic: *syn.* **child, brain-injured.**

child, neurotic: strictly, a child who is suffering from a neurosis or pattern of neuroses; loosely used to designate an overimaginative or high-strung child.

child, normal: a child whose age-grade and age-progress status or physical, mental, social, and moral development is average or typical for his age group.

child, normalized: in Montessori terminology, a child who loves to work and who loves the order that work involves.

child, overgrown: a child who is physically developed beyond the norm for his age and sex.

child-parent fixation: *see* **fixation, child-parent.**

child, perceptually disabled: a child who has experienced a disturbance of some sort in normal cephalocaudal neural maturation, prenatally, perinatally, or postnatally, which results in an inability to progress normally in learning situations related to the various sensory modalities.

child, perceptually handicapped: *syn.* **child, brain injured.**

child, perceptually impaired: *syn.* **child, brain-injured.**

child, physically below-par: a child who shows such symptoms as lassitude, early fatigue, lack of stamina, frequent illness, failure to gain weight over a period of several months, or behavior that suggests need for medical advice.

child placement: *see* **placement, child.**

child, precocious: a child who is exceptionally advanced beyond the norm mentally or physically.

child, preschool: the child up to 5 years of age.

child, problem: a child with social, emotional, or educational problems that seriously interfere with school life and with personal life; this child finds it hard to study, can't get along with teachers or classmates, and is constantly "out of sorts" with his family.

child, pseudogifted: a child who, having displayed certain gifts at an early age, has been coached and pushed beyond his mental ability with resulting emotional strain and inability to maintain early levels of achievement.

child psychology: *see* **psychology, child.**

child, psychoneurotic: a child with a morbid mental condition due to psychic causes or whose mind is influenced by a depressive physical condition.

child, refugee: a child who has been displaced from his native country or area of residence.

child, resident: a child who lives within a given school administrative unit.

child, retarded: a child who fails to develop at the rate of the average child because of intellectual, social, emotional, educational, or physical factors, singly or in combination.

child, rural: according to United States census criteria, a child living outside incorporated cities or villages of 2,500 inhabitants or more; less specifically, a child living in the open country.

child, school: (1) a child who is of school age; (2) a child actually enrolled in school.

child, slow-learning: a child who, though capable of achieving a moderate degree of academic success, will do so at a slower rate and with less than average efficiency; can usually be adequately cared for in the regular classroom if limitations are recognized and accepted; may be more competent than average in other than academic subjects.

child socialization: (1) the process by which the child accomplishes his personal adjustment to himself and the peer group; (2) the process and activities whereby children interact in the development of social communication and social groupings; (3) the process of presenting alternative channels of behavior to the young person, some to be positively rewarded and others to be negatively sanctioned. *See* **acculturation; socialization.**

child, socially disadvantaged: a child whose social class background has provided skills, values, outlooks, and behavior patterns significantly different from those reflected by the major institutions of society; such a child is usually from lower-working-class (called by some sociologists lower-lower-class) background and is at a disadvantage in competitive social and educational situations where the experience of lower-middle-class or upper-middle-class children constitutes the norm. *See* **deprivation, environmental.**

child, socially maladjusted: a child who, in trying to solve his problems, comes into conflict with the value system held by dominant society; for example, truancy, used as a temporary solution to a school problem, brings the child into conflict with local school attendance laws; similarly, his behavior in school often becomes so aggressive that he cannot be tolerated because of the harm done to others in the class; he often exhibits serious emotional disturbance. *See* **child, emotionally disturbed.**

child society: an expression which implies recognition that there exists in its own right a child society with its own customs, fads, values, games, and even to some extent its own esoteric forms of communication.

child study: services designed for social, educational, intellectual, and emotional appraisal of children; usually multidisciplinary in composition, generally found in the public schools.

child-study clinic: *syn.* **laboratory, child-study.**

child-study department: *see* **department, child-study.**

child-study group: *see* **group, child-study.**

child-study laboratory: *see* **laboratory, child-study.**

child-study movement: the investigation of the growth and development of children as directed by the belief that the curriculum and instructional procedures should be the result of an intimate understanding of the nature, needs, and interests of children.

child, subnormal: a child with less than normal intelligence; sometimes designated *mentally deficient* when one of the neuropathological group and *mentally retarded* when the subnormality is associated with environmental causes.

child, superior: a child who is considerably above the norm in regard to a number of traits and abilities; usually applied to those children who have outstanding intellectual ability; frequently also implies better than usual social and physical development; a broader term than *gifted child.*

child, trainable mentally retarded: a child incapable of achieving any significant proficiency in academic skills but who is capable of profiting from programs of training in self-care and in social and simple job or vocational skills.

child, transient: a child whose parents change residence frequently. *See* **child, migrant.**

child, typical: a child whose ability, achievement, appearance, attitude, or other characteristics are equivalent to the average—variously defined in terms of the median, mean, mode, or "normality"—of a designated group.

child, underprivileged: *see* **child, culturally deprived.**

child, unstable: a child characterized by emotional instability.

child voice: *see* **voice, child.**

child, vulnerable: (1) an individual between infancy and the age of maturity who is susceptible to harmful or negative influences; (2) a child of average or better intelligence who is not achieving up to his full academic potential because of any one of a number of dysfunctions; *see* **underachiever.**

child welfare: specific and general services to promote and maintain child protection and support; usually of socio-economic and legal nature.

child, whole: the physical, emotional, mental, and social characteristics of the child which comprise the totality of his being.

child, withdrawn: (1) a child who seeks to avoid social contacts and receives relatively few of his gratifications from activities involving other people; (2) a child who gives little overt expression to his thoughts, finding more satisfaction in fantasy and contemplation. *See* **introversion.**

childbearing age: *see* **age, childbearing.**

childhood education: education that begins at infancy and continues until the onset of adolescence; does not end at any given age, grade, or accumulation of credits. *Contr. w.* **adolescent education; adult education.**

children, care and guidance of: *see* **care and guidance of children.**

children's book: *see* **book, children's.**

children's book classic: *see* **classic, children's book.**

children's book club: *see* **club, children's book.**

children's bureau: an agency or office that gives particular attention to studying, helping, and protecting children.

children's catalog: *see* **catalog, children's.**

children's classic: a selection for reading by children written by an author of repute and possessing true literary merit, for example, *Little Women, Robinson Crusoe,* or *Huckleberry Finn.*

children's court: *syn.* **court, juvenile.**

children's drawing, categories of: *see* **drawing, types of children's.**

children's drawing, types of: *see* **drawing, types of children's.**

children's library: *see* **library, children's.**

children's literature: *see* **literature, children's.**

children's newspaper: *see* **newspaper, children's.**

children's play: *see* **play, children's.**

children's present spelling need: *syn.* **spelling need, children's.**

children's spelling need: *see* **spelling need, children's.**

children's trade book: *see* **book, children's trade.**

children's writing vocabulary: *see* **vocabulary, children's writing.**

child's vocabulary: *see* **vocabulary, child's.**

chinning: the act of hanging from a bar, flexing the arms, raising the body so as to bring the chin above the bar, lowering the body, and repeating; an exercise or test of strength.

chirography (kī·rog'rə·fi): (largely obs.) the art of writing or engraving by hand.

chivalric education: a type of training provided the sons of nobles during the period of feudalism, involving the three stages of page, squire, and knight, and concerned largely with physical exercises, social graces, religious obligations, and sometimes academic attainments.

chlorinator: a device for adding chlorine to swimming-pool water as a part of a recirculating filtering system.

choice: (1) making a free decision as to action among possible alternatives; (2) the existence of freedom in making decisions and acting upon them.

choice behavior, individual: *see* **behavior, individual choice.**

choice, consumer: the selection by the consumer of the goods and services he wishes to purchase with his money income or with consumer credit.

choice, freedom of: *see* **free will, doctrine of.**

choice, inappropriate vocational: *see* **vocational choice, inappropriate.**

choice making: an area of consumer education aimed at the development of a sound sense of what is most worth the expenditure of income, time, and energy and what is least worth such expenditure, all in terms of needs, wants, and satisfactions; education toward discrimination in regard to the general classes of goods and services that are worth buying, as distinguished from the more specific skills of actually buying them. *Dist. f.* **buymanship.**

choice-making process: the steps in learning to make choices, which include considering consequences, acting upon the choices made, and evaluating the results.

choice, occupational: (couns.) a decision-making process, usually extending over several years, in which the individual decides upon a specific job or occupation on the basis of his needs, interests, or abilities.

choice, realistic: any choice, made in terms of values and desires and based on knowledge, feeling, and environmental pressures.

choice, vocational: a decision-making process in which an individual chooses a skill or a trade to be pursued as a career; the end result of vocational planning.

choices, mutual: (sociometry) individuals indicating a mutual preference for each other in a friendship, work-companion, or similar test used in sociometry as the basis for constructing a *sociogram.*

choir: (1) a vocal ensemble; *see* **chorus** (1); (2) an ensemble of like instruments, for example, voices, strings, wood-winds, brasses, or percussion.

choir, a cappella: a choral group singing without accompaniment. *See* **a cappella.**

choir, verse: a group of children or young people who speak poetry or other literature together with special attention to meaning and tonal quality.

cholinesterase: an enzyme which plays an important part in transmission of nerve impulses.

choral music: *see* **music, choral.**

choral reading: *see* **choral speaking.**

choral recitation: *see* **recitation, choral.**

choral response: unison oral repetition, by a group learning a foreign language, of a word, phrase, or sentence.

choral speaking: the balanced, blended recitation or reading of poetry, rhythmic prose, or dramatic passages by a chorus in unison, antiphonally, or in orchestral arrangement.

chorale: a religious choral number of the German Protestant church analogous to the hymns of the English and American Protestant churches.

chorditis nodosa: a diseased condition of the vocal folds (cords) involving callouslike growths or thickenings (singer's nodes) that affect the quality of the voice; usually the result of voice strain. *See* **singer's nodule.**

chorea (kō·rē'ə): a nervous disorder of the motor control centers, usually occurring in youth, which is characterized by irregular, jerky, and spasmodic involuntary movements of the face and extremities.

choreography: (1) the art of composing ballet and other dances; planning and arranging the movements, steps, and patterns of the dancers; (2) technique of representing the various movements in dancing through a system of notation.

choreology: in systematic study of the dance, the science of creating rhythmic patterns.

chorus: (1) a large vocal ensemble; the distinction between a chorus and a *choir* is rather arbitrary; the term choir suggests a somewhat more select and sophisticated approach to the art of ensemble singing, but in actual practice no such distinction obtains; (2) a composition for singers; (3) a recurrent portion of a song; a refrain.

chorus, mixed: a chorus of male and female voices, usually consisting of sopranos, altos, tenors, and basses. *Syn.* **choir** (1).

Christian education: that form of religious education which is specifically Christian in content. *See* **religious education.**

Christian education, director of: *see* **director, religious education.**

Christian morals: *see* **morals, Christian.**

chromatic pitch pipe: *see* **pitch pipe, chromatic.**

chromatics: in music, the appearance of sharps, flats, and natural signs which do not derive from the given key signature of the composition. *Syn.* **accidentals;** *see* **composition, musical.**

chrome, national school-bus: *see* **school-bus chrome.**

chromosome: (biol.) one of a number (definite in a given species) of microscopic bodies which can be demonstrated in the nucleus of a cell during the process of mitosis by staining with certain dyes (hence the form chromo-), and which are thought to carry the genes. [The chromosomes can be paired in respect to shape, size, and other characteristics (homologous pairs), and the two phases of a given gene (dominant and recessive, the allelomorphs) are thought to occupy corresponding positions on the members of the chromosome pair.] *See* **allelomorph; dominant; gene; maturation division; mitosis.**

chromosome map: *see* **map, chromosome.**

chronic: pertaining to disorders that persist over a long period.

chronic brain syndrome: *see* **brain syndrome, chronic.**

chronic health problem: *see* **health problem, chronic.**

chronicle filing plan: *see* **filing plan, chronicle.**

chronological age: *see* **age, chronological.**

chronological age, corrected: *see* **age, corrected chronological.**

chronological order: arrangement according to time, from first to last, or from the oldest or most remote to the most recent.

chronology: (1) the science dealing with the measurement of time and with its division into units, such as the year, month, week, day, hour, minute, and second; (2) a list or table or written account of events or things arranged according to their order of occurrence, usually from first to last or from most remote to most recent; (3) the designation of the earliest type of written history, consisting merely of a running narrative of events set down in the order of their occurrence, for example, the *Anglo-Saxon Chronicle.*

chronoscope (kron'ə·skōp): a device for the precise measurement of time intervals; distinguished from ordinary clocks, watches, and stop watches in that it is more accurate, makes use of different mechanical or electric devices, and is adapted for the measurement of time intervals in units as small as a thousandth of a second.

church and state, separation of: *see* **separation of church and state.**

church board of education: *see* **board of education, church.**

church bus: *see* **bus, church.**

church census: *see* **census, church.**

church conference: *see* **conference, church.**

church council: *see* **council, church.**

church education: education provided or supported by the church.

church history: *see* **history, church.**

church-related college: *see* **college, church-related.**

church-related junior college: *syn.* **junior college, denominational.**

church school: (1) an educational program operated by a local church; (2) a school connected with a religious denomination, the degree of connection ranging from present and complete control to historical association.

church school curriculum: *see* **curriculum, church school.**

church school department: *see* **department, church school.**

church school, Sunday: the program of classes designed for Christian education and held on the first day of the week, usually in conjunction with a church's worship service; typical of contemporary Protestant churches.

church school, vacation: *see* **vacation church school.**

church school, weekday: an organization of classes dealing chiefly with moral and religious training conducted on days other than Sunday by teachers appointed by the churches in a community; teachers may be sent to the public-school building, or classes may be provided in church or other buildings.

church-sponsored nursery school: *see* **nursery school, church-sponsored.**

Ciceronianism: a type of humanism developed after the Renaissance characterized by servile imitation of the literary style of Cicero; stressed form rather than thought.

cinema: (1) motion pictures (in collective sense); (2) a motion-picture theater.

cinemanalysis: the examination and study of behavior based on cinematographic records.

cinemascope: an optical system for distorting by means of an anamorphic lens a wide-angle view onto a standard motion-picture frame; in projection the image is again distorted by an anamorphic projection lens to create an image with a coefficient of 2.55.

cinematographer: a motion-picture director of photography, cameraman, or assistant cameraman.

cinematography: (1) motion-picture photography; the creation of the illusion of motion through motion-picture techniques; loosely, the entire complex of activities involved in the staging, direction, photography, editing, and presentation of motion pictures; (2) (phys. ed.) the definition of a specific skill or group of skills through the use of recorded motion.

cinemicrography: the science or technique of taking motion pictures through a microscope in which the subjects appear on the screen enlarged in size to a greater extent than they would if ordinary photographic techniques were used, for example, motion pictures of one-celled animals such as amoebae or paramecia.

cinemicrophotography: the science or technique of making motion pictures in which the subjects appear on the screen reduced in size. *Syn.* **microcinematography.**

Cinerama: a trade name for a motion-picture process of simultaneous triple camera and projector operation; in projection a curved screen partly encircling the audience is used which, together with stereophonic sound, attains to a marked degree the illusion of depth and realism.

cinesitherapy: the use of active and passive movements for therapeutic purposes; the first part of the term is derived from the Greek *kinesis*, "motion."

circle game: a game in which the players stand in a circle or form a ring; formerly recommended for use in classes of small children because of the simplicity of the formation.

circle graph: *see* **graph, circle.**

circle map: *syn.* **map, single-dot.**

circle, reading: *see* **reading circle.**

circuit route: *see* **route, circuit.**

circuit teacher: (1) a teacher employed by two or more schools to divide his time between the schools; usually a teacher in a special area (music, art, etc.); (2) an instructor or specialist employed by the state to travel from school to school or from home to home to bring material help to certain types of handicapped children, homebound children, and others. *Syn.* **itinerant teacher.**

circuit training: *see* **training, circuit.**

circular definition: *see* **definition, circular.**

circular interaction: *see* **interaction, circular.**

circular reaction: *see* **reaction, circular.**

circular reasoning: *see* **reasoning, circular.**

circular scribbling: *see* **scribbling, circular.**

circularity: an argumentative fallacy arising when the sequential elements are tautological; the logic of the premise is inherent in the conclusion rather than standing as a self-evident statement.

circulating library: *see* **library, circulating.**

circulation, library: the lending of books and library materials to library users. *Syn.* **book lending.**

circumpuberal period: *see* **period, circumpuberal.**

citation: (1) an official notice to a child, his parents, or both to appear either before a representative of the attendance department or before the children's, or juvenile, court; (2) a formal statement of commendation, often printed, for example, a citing or enumerating of achievements of a candidate for an honorary degree; (3) (libr. sci.) a reference to and description of a prior document which relates to the document being written.

citation index: *see* **index, citation.**

citation, judicial: a reference to a court decision. (In law, a uniform system of abbreviating citations is used.)

citation, statutory: a reference to a particular statute or law.

citizen: a native-born inhabitant of a country or a foreign-born inhabitant who has become naturalized.

citizens' advisory committee: *syn.* **advisory committee.**

citizens' commission: *syn.* **advisory committee.**

citizens' committee, agricultural: *see* **committee, agricultural citizens'.**

citizenship: (1) membership in some form of governmental organization, with consequent rights and responsibilities; (2) *syn.* **behavior, social.**

citizenship, consumer: the obligation and privilege of every consumer to cooperate with others to improve the standard of living and to increase the satisfaction each consumer gets from his personal resources (time, energy, money).

citizenship education: emphasis in the curriculum and methods aimed at promoting approved social behavior, that is, at making good citizens.

Citizenship Education Project: a project of Teachers College, Columbia University, conceived by Dwight D. Eisenhower when president of the university and by William F. Russell, former president of Teachers College, and financed by the Carnegie Corporation; designed to help ·schools teach more effectively the premises of American liberty by putting good citizenship to work in actual laboratory practices carried out in the communities served by the schools.

citizenship, good: *see* **good citizenship.**

citizenship training: *see* **training, citizenship.**

citizenship, training for: *see* **training, citizenship.**

city, central: *see* **central city.**

city college: rare *syn.* **college, municipal.**

city net enrollment: *see* **enrollment, city net.**

city school: (1) a type of school (elementary, secondary, vocational, evening) or junior college that is directly administered by the authorities of a city school district; (2) a school, public or private, located approximately within a geographical area commonly known as a city.

city school administration: *see* **administration, city school.**

city school district: *see* **district, city school.**

city school society: a type of organization formed in certain American cities where no free public schools existed for the purpose of establishing free schools for poor children not already provided for by a religious society. (One of the earliest was formed in Baltimore in 1799 and another in New York City in 1805.)

city school system: *see* **school system, city.**

city superintendent of schools: *see* **superintendent of schools, city.**

civic art: *see* **art, civic.**

civic behavior: *see* **behavior, civic.**

civic biology: *see* **biology, civic.**

civic cohesion: *see* **cohesion, civic.**

civic education: (1) education that seeks to develop in youth a sincere and conscientious acceptance of the responsibilities of citizenship; (2) a kind of adult education dealing with public affairs and contemporary problems and designed to fortify public opinion with social informátion essential to enlightenment. *See* **public affairs education.**

Civic Education Project: a project in civic education carried on under the sponsorship of the Civic Education Foundation of Cambridge, Massachusetts. The project has developed a number of pamphlet materials which constitute *The Living Democracy Series,* centering about individual and group problems in democratic living.

civic health: *see* **health, civic.**

civic ideals: standards of conduct in relation to matters of good citizenship.

civic indoctrination: *see* **indoctrination, civic.**

civic institution: *see* **institution, social.**

civic morality: *see* **morality, civic.**

civic objectives: *see* **objectives, civic.**

civic orchestra: *see* **orchestra, civic.**

civic organization: broadly, an organized group of members of a community having as its common purpose the promoting or furthering of a public cause or enterprise.

civic organization, junior: an organization of young people frequently imitating or paralleling adult organizations for the control or improvement of governmental affairs.

civic pride: a feeling of esteem and responsibility for the physical and social environment of the community.

civic responsibility: a sense of being responsible to society as a whole rather than to the political manifestations of society as revealed in any single institution; placing social values above private and personal vested interests; includes social understanding, critical judgment, tolerance, a concern for social justice, and participation in social activities.

civics: (1) the elements of political science or that branch of political science dealing with the rights and duties of citizens; (2) since about 1915, the accepted title for studies in government, used especially in secondary schools, replacing the former designation civil government but with a current tendency for the content to be included in courses with changed titles such as *Problems in Democracy;* (3) a course of study, usually in the junior high school, fusing political, social, and economic phases of group life.

civics, community: a branch of the study of civics that emphasizes the individual's relation to his social environment, which is conceived as a series of successively enlarged communities, local, state, and national.

civics, economic: a subject of study, commonly offered in junior high schools, especially in the ninth grade, that deals particularly with economic principles in government and private business, including information about money, banks, business methods, etc., in addition to other topics more frequently included in courses in civics.

civics, vocational: (1) the study of occupational problems in relation to community welfare; (2) study of civics based on the consideration and selection of the pupil's lifework.

civil action: *see* **action, civil.**

Civil Air Patrol Cadet program: *see* **program, Civil Air Patrol Cadet.**

Civil Air Patrol (CAP): a volunteer, semimilitary civilian auxiliary air organization supervised and administered by the Air Force and trained and equipped to assist in national and local emergencies.

civil defense: (1) the provision of adequate defense by the citizens against anything that may endanger lives or cause the loss of life or property, whether the source of such danger is war or natural causes; (2) more specifically, a civil program of the government providing for the safety of citizens on the home front in the event of enemy attack. *See* **alert signal.**

civil liberty: exemption from arbitrary governmental interference with person, property, or opinion; *pl.* specific exemptions named and guaranteed in a document like the *Bill of Rights* or, commonly, secured through tradition and moral principles.

civil service examination: *see* **examination, civil service.**

Civilian Conservation Center: *see* **Center, Civilian Conservation.**

Civilian Conservation Corps (CCC): a project of the Federal government, established in 1933 and abandoned in 1942 which had as its purposes the provision of work relief, the conservation and development of natural resources, and the provision of vocational training activities for young men.

civilian contract school: (mil. ed.) any of several civilian schools having a contract with the Air Force to offer instruction to certain Air Force personnel.

civilian institutions program: *see* **program, civilian institutions.**

civilian rehabilitation: *see* **rehabilitation, civilian.**

civilization: (1) a state of the culture of the social group (such as a tribe, state, or nation) characterized by some degree of artistic, industrial, scientific, governmental, moral, and intellectual achievement; (2) especially, in distinction from barbarism, a state of such culture characterized by a high degree of such achievement; likely to be interpreted, from the standpoint of our own civilization, as involving a high degree of urbanization, industrialization, mechanization, and complexity of social organization; (3) the process of gradually developing such achievement in a group or individual.

clang association clue: *see* **clue, clang association.**

clarette: *see* **recorder** (2).

clarolet: *see* **recorder** (2).

clasping reflex: *syn.* **reflex, Moro.**

class: (1) a group all members of which possess at least one common characteristic; (2) a group of pupils or students scheduled to report regularly at a particular time to a particular teacher; (3) in nondepartmental elementary schools, a group of pupils enrolled with a particular teacher; (4) the total of all pupils or students pursuing a particular subject, frequently at different levels, within a school, for example, the class in French in a high school; (5) (sec. and higher ed.) all pupils or students in an educational institution who entered at the same time and who may graduate, or who graduated, together, for example, the junior class or the class of 1958; (6) (sociol.) a division of the population based on differences in rank; usually thought of as arranged in a hierarchy from lower to higher; according to Marx, any group of persons having, in respect to the means of production, such a common economic relationship as to be brought thereby into conflict with other groups having a different economic relationship to these means; (7) (stat.) (*a*) a group of phenomena or observations that are similar in some respect; hence, cases that exhibit characteristics that fall within defined limits, such as within a *category,* or *class interval,* of a distribution; (*b*) the characteristics (qualitative or quantitative) that define and distinguish one group of phenomena from another; hence, a *category;* specifically, in the case of a quantitative distribution, a *class interval* having given limits.

class, acoustic: (spec. ed.) one of the classes operated for the purpose of providing for instructional needs of children handicapped by impaired hearing.

class, adjustment: a special class providing remedial teaching for pupils who are handicapped in their school progress by specific disabilities, as in reading or arithmetic. *Syn.* **coaching class; restoration class;** *see* **class, auxiliary; class, individual; ungraded room.**

class, adult agricultural: a class or course offered for the adults in a community who are engaged in agricultural occupations, both nonfarm and farm, and for adults who have an economic or a vocational interest in agriculture. *Syn.* **agricultural evening school.**

class, adult evening distributive education: a class for employed retail, wholesale, or service employees or prospective distributive personnel offered as a part of the evening educational program.

class, adult-farmer: commonly a class in agriculture or other farm-related subject which an evening school offers for adults established in farming, usually those over 25 years of age; occasionally one of a group of classes in an evening school.

class adviser: *see* **adviser, class.**

class, age range of: *see* **age range of class.**

class, agricultural evening: *see* **class, adult agricultural.**

class, agricultural part-time: *syn.* **class, young-farmer.**

class, all-day: a group of students regularly enrolled in school for full time; used particularly to describe certain types of classes in vocational education; in agricultural education, a class for high school students in vocational agriculture.

class, Americanization: an organized group of persons, usually immigrants preparing for naturalization, studying the English language and United States history, institutions, and culture. *See* **alien education; Americanization.**

class analysis chart: *see* **chart, class analysis.**

class, apprentice: a group receiving brief, systematic training in a library for the lower grades of library work through directed practice and instruction by members of the staff.

class, auxiliary: a special class for certain pupils providing instruction supplementing the work of the regular curriculum. *See* **class, adjustment.**

class average: *see* **average, class.**

class, Bible: any group of persons meeting together, either formally or informally, to study the Judeo-Christian scriptures, most often under the direction of a clergyman or layman with a special knowledge of the Bible.

class bill: *see* **bill, class.**

class, Binet (bē'nā'; Fr. bē'ne'): a term sometimes used to designate a *special class* for backward and mentally deficient pupils.

class book: (1) a record book used by secondary school and college teachers and serving for these teachers a purpose similar to that of the school register or daily register for elementary teachers; usually gives less attention to attendance data and more attention to data on scholarship; (2) historically, a term used as the partial title of many old American school textbooks, for example, William Sullivan's *The Political Class Book,* published in 1830, as a textbook in civil government.

class boundary, integral: *syn.* **class limit, apparent.**

class boundary, real: *syn.* **class limit, real.**

class, braille: a special class in which blind children receive all their education.

class, cardiac: a special class for pupils with organic heart disease or others who, because of recent or active infection, as in rheumatic fever, may develop such a condition.

class catalog: *syn.* **catalog, classified.**

class, catechism: (1) (R.C. ed.) a class, organized in connection with a parish church, in which Roman Catholic children (usually those attending public schools) and sometimes adults are given instruction in the doctrines and beliefs of the Roman Catholic Church; (2) in certain Protestant churches, a class in which children and sometimes adults of the congregation are given instruction based on Martin Luther's catechism.

class, census: any age group in a given year.

class, coaching: *syn.* **class, adjustment.**

class, competitive: a classified civil service post requiring an examination as a prerequisite to employment eligibility. *See* **classified.**

class, compound: (1) *syn.* **category, compound;** (2) loosely, the objects belonging in such a class or category.

class, convalescent home: a class which provides for the education of children in one of the convalescent homes which perform an intermediate service between care for the chronically or acutely ill in hospitals and the return of the patient to his or her home.

class, cooperative: a plan in which the blind child is enrolled with a teacher of blind children in a special room from which he goes to the regular classrooms for a portion of his school day; the special room becomes his homeroom from which, in cooperation with the regular classroom teachers, his program planning stems.

class, corrective: *syn.* **class, remedial** (2).

class, correspondence: a group of students enrolled in a correspondence, or home-study, course (instruction being given by mail) but doing some of the work as a group under the direction of a leader or supervisor.

class counselor: *see* **counselor, class.**

class, day: a public or private school class where children are enrolled on a day basis; children enrolled in such classes return either to their own homes or to a boarding home each night; such a class may be held at any time of day or evening.

class, day-unit: a high school class in vocational agriculture taught by a teacher who serves several communities, devoting only certain days of each week to any one community.

class, demonstration: (teacher ed.) a class that is used to illustrate to an observing group of prospective or experienced teachers materials, procedures, or techniques used in schoolwork. *See* **teaching, demonstration;** *dist. f.* **class, observation.**

class-descriptive method: in programmed instruction, presentation to the learner of material in frames displaying simultaneously sets of objects with common and significant characteristics, such as a set of different coins displayed heads up. *Contr. w.* **object-descriptive method.**

class, development: a special class for retarded and subnormal pupils.

class diary: a record or written account of various individual or group activities and accomplishments of the members of a class at school.

class, emergency: a type of adult education class organized by the FERA and WPA education divisions primarily for the purpose of providing work relief for unemployed teachers and other white-collar workers during the depression and postdepression years.

class, evening: (1) a high school class in any subject area offered to others than regularly enrolled high school pupils either for attainment of a high school diploma or for acquisition of specific knowledge or skills; (2) (voc. ed.) a class which is supplemental to the daily employment of business or industrial employees, organized by public schools and given outside the working hours of the students; does not necessarily indicate the time of day during which the class is in session; (3) a class usually organized by a higher education institution in a separate division which offers courses in any subject area for both matriculated and nonmatriculated students; does not necessarily indicate time of day class is held; *see* **class, extension.**

class, evening industrial: a class maintained under the provisions of the Smith-Hughes and George-Barden laws, operated in a public school and offering instruction of less than college grade relating to a particular trade or industrial pursuit; held outside the hours of the regular working day, and admitting learners over 16 years of age who are already engaged in the particular trade or industrial pursuit taught. (Evening industrial classes need not be limited to those operating under the Smith-Hughes and George-Barden acts. However, the term usually refers to such classes.)

class, extension: (1) a group of part-time students meeting in regularly spaced sessions and pursuing a course under the auspices of a college, university, or other adult education agency; (2) a part-time day or evening class offered to adults for the purpose of extending the resources of the sponsoring institution; usually held off the main campus when offered by a higher education institution. *See* **class, extramural.**

class, extramural: a class conducted for part-time adult students under the auspices of a college or university and taught on or off the campus; especially a British usage. *See* **class, extension.**

class formation: the organization or arrangement of the members of a class for purposes of instruction.

class, fractional special: an administrative arrangement whereby more than one local school district may share the costs and benefits of a special class; frequently this arrangement is extended to include staff support services such as guidance, counseling, and psychological services.

class frequency: *syn.* **class size** (2).

class, general industrial: a class operated under the Smith-Hughes law (in some states), maintained in a public school in a city of less than 25,000 population, offering instruction of less than college grade in several closely related trades (such as plumbing, steam fitting, and sheet-metal work), and admitting students over the age of 14 years who are not employed and who wish to prepare themselves for entrance into a trade or industrial pursuit.

class group: *see* **group, class.**

class grouping: *see* **grouping, class.**

class, health-improvement: a class for children with low vitality; sometimes referred to as *fresh-air class.*

class, homogeneous special: a class organized with the intent of containing a group of children possessing maximum similarity on one particular dimension or attribute in order to provide appropriate instruction focused on that attribute; in practice usually recognized as falling short of the intent.

class, honors: a group selected for advanced instruction because of demonstrated high achievement; usually applied in secondary schools or colleges.

class, hospital: teaching of hospitalized children in hospital classes, including both group and individual bedside instruction.

class, in-and-outer: a type of short vocational educational class organized to train individuals for employment in a new field or to upgrade them in their present occupation. *See* **upgrading.**

class index: *syn.* **mark, class.**

class, individual: one of a number of kinds of special class for atypical pupils; most frequently a class for backward or mentally deficient pupils or for pupils transferred temporarily to this class for individual instruction. *See* **class, adjustment; class, special.**

class, individual gymnastic: *syn.* **class, remedial** (2).

class instruction: *see* **instruction, class.**

class, instrumental: a class designed for group instruction in playing musical instruments, relatively small in numbers, and best confined to players on identical or closely related instruments, a violin class, for example.

class, intermediate: in an ungraded type of instructional organization, a class composed of pupils between the ages of 9 and 12 years.

class interval: *see* **interval, class.**

class, kindergarten extension: a first grade class taught by a kindergarten teacher who has continued with children promoted from kindergarten; sometimes termed *prefirst, preprimary,* or *transition class.*

class, latent: a hypothetical subgroup of persons into which a population may be divided with respect to the property being measured; each member of the subgroup is assumed to be at the same point or level on a latent continuum. *See* **continuum, latent.**

class librarian: *syn.* **librarian, classroom.**

class, library training: a program of systematic training for library service that emphasizes practical work and is conducted by a library primarily for members of its own staff; distinguished from *apprentice class* by its more formal and extensive instruction.

class limit, actual: *syn.* **class limit, real.**

class limit, apparent: the upper or lower limiting score value of any class interval; thus, if the intervals 1 to 4, 5 to 8, etc., are used, the values 1 and 4 represent the apparent class limits of the lowest class and the values 5 and 8 represent the apparent class limits of the second class, etc. *Syn.* **integral class boundary; integral class limit;** *see* **class** (7); *dist. f.* **class limit, real; interval, class.**

class limit, expressed: *syn.* **class limit, apparent.**

class limit, integral: *syn.* **class limit, apparent.**

class limit, real: the point of division between two successive classes; thus, if the intervals 1 to 4, 5 to 8, etc., are used, the value 4.5 represents the upper real class limit of the first class and the lower real class limit of the second class; all scores between 0.5 and 4.5 would be tabulated in the first class, and all scores between 4.5 and 8.5 in the second class; used in preference to apparent class limits in tabulating data, particularly when the data are continuous. *Syn.* **actual class limit; real class boundary;** *see* **class** (7); *dist. f.* **class limit, apparent; interval, class.**

class limits: the upper and lower limits of a given class interval; the highest and lowest values that can be included in the class interval; frequently used synonymously with apparent class limits, but may also be used in the sense of real class limits. *See* **class limit, apparent; class limit, real; class range; interval, class.**

class load: *see* **load, class.**

class log: a type of class diary that contains entries of the day-by-day activities of a group of children at school.

class, major work: a special class for pupils of superior intelligence providing an enriched curriculum without acceleration in grade progress.

class, makeup: a class organized for pupils who are behind in certain phases of their grade or course work and who wish to overcome their deficiencies.

class management: the administration or direction of class activities with special reference to such problems as discipline, democratic techniques, use and care of supplies and reference materials, the physical features of the classroom, general housekeeping, and the social relationships of pupils. *See* **school management.**

class mark: *see* **mark, class.**

class, master: a group of advanced students instructed simultaneously in some particular musical instrument or, in the case of chamber music, in the instruments used in chamber performance, the instructor being a master artist who usually has one member or chamber group from the class perform under the critical direction of the instructor while the rest of the class observes.

class method: (mus. ed.) procedures designed for use in teaching applied music, vocal or instrumental, to more than one person at a time. *See* **ensemble method;** *contr. w.* **private method.**

class, music methods: a class designed to train music teachers in the general and specific techniques and materials of public group instruction.

class, myope (mī'ōp): a type of special class organized in England in 1908 for the education of children suffering from severe or progressive myopia.

class, noncredit: any class sponsored by a college, university, or other adult education agency for which the work may not be counted toward a degree or diploma; frequently composed of part-time adult students but usually more extended in scope than a lecture series, institute, or conference.

class, nongraded: *see* **class, ungraded.**

class, normal training: during the latter part of the nineteenth century, the name for a special high school class for training elementary school teachers; its work included either only a special course or two during the senior year or requirements covering an entire postgraduate year.

class number: a symbol assigned to a book indicating the class to which it belongs in the classification scheme used by the library. *See* **classification, book.**

class, nutrition: a class organized to present information regarding adequate diet, assimilation of foods, and desirable food habits; may be formed (*a*) for the purpose of instructing individuals how to prevent malnutrition or (*b*) for the purpose of providing both instruction and hygienic measures for the benefit of malnourished pupils.

class, observation: a class in a teacher-preparing institution that studies educational problems through observation of school activities. *Dist. f.* **class, demonstration.**

class, occupations: a class designed to increase the student's occupational information. *See* **occupational information.**

class, open-air: (1) a classroom, used by some public school systems, utilizing a maximum amount of fresh air and sunshine, designed to benefit children who are undernourished, anemic, subject to respiratory infections, or otherwise below par physically; (2) a special class for malnourished, tuberculous (but not actively tubercular), or other pupils with special health problems providing a sheltered unenclosed space for play or rest periods, midday lunch, and other hygienic conditions favorable to the amelioration of their physical condition; *syn.* **open-air school.**

class, open-window: *syn.* **class, open-air.**

class, opportunity: (1) a euphemistic term for a class organized for the special and individual instruction of pupils who have fallen seriously behind in the work of their grades for reasons other than lack of mental ability and who may expect to rejoin their regular classes when their deficiencies are made up; in actual practice, it is found not infrequently that these classes contain pupils like the above and, in addition, children who are mentally retarded or who are handicapped by sensory or other defects to which the ordinary class is not adjustable; (2) sometimes, a class for adolescents for vocational or prevocational training; (3) less frequently, a class for gifted pupils. *See* **opportunity school.**

class, orthogenic: a special class for mentally handicapped or maladjusted pupils, providing corrective or remedial procedures.

class, orthopedic: a special class for crippled children, usually in a room equipped with adjustable school furniture and with provision for physiotherapy, corrective exercises, and occupational therapy.

class, overage: a special class composed of pupils who are above the age that is normal for the grade level of the work being done.

class, part-time: *see* **part-time class.**

class, partially seeing: a special class in which partially seeing children receive all their education. *See* **class, sight-conservation; class, sight-saving; partially seeing.**

class period: *see* **period, class.**

class, practice: (1) a course or classwork in a teacher-preparing institution that requires students to participate directly in the type of activities under consideration or study; (2) a class or group of pupils in a laboratory school used for practice teaching by student teachers.

class, prefirst: *see* **class, kindergarten extension.**

class, preinstrument: a class devoted to the study of and performance on simple instruments such as recorder, tonette, rhythm band instruments, etc., in preparation for later study on a full-fledged musical instrument. *See* **instrument, preorchestral.**

class preparation: *see* **preparation, class.**

class, preprimary: *syn.* **extension, kindergarten** (1).

class, preprimer: *syn.* **extension, kindergarten** (1).

class, prereading: (1) a class operated for the purpose of preparing children for learning to read; (2) (spec. ed.) a class conducted in accordance with a group instructional plan for retarded children who do not read; instruction is aimed at getting the children prepared for learning to read.

class, preschool: a class operated for the purpose of providing early training to enhance the readiness of children for regular school instruction; usually focusing on ages 3 to 4.

class project: *see* **project, class.**

class, radio: a group assembled for the purpose of receiving instruction by radio.

class, radio-production: an instructional unit, usually at the high school or college level, in which techniques of radio production and programming are studied and put into practice.

class range: the width of a class interval, that is, the interval between lower and upper limits of a class interval; especially the interval between *real class limits.*

class register: *syn.* **record book, teacher's class.**

class, regular: the general type of class in which most pupils receive instruction, including most classes other than those composed of exceptional pupils. *Comp. w.* **class, special.**

class, reimbursable: in vocational education, a class organized by a local school system and conducted according to the regulations of the Federal and state laws and policies in order to fulfill their purposes so that a portion of its costs may be refunded.

class, remedial: (1) a specially selected group of pupils in need of more intensive instruction in some area of education than is possible in the regular classroom; (2) a physical education class for students who need special corrective exercises; *syn.* **corrective class; individual gymnastics class; remedial gymnastics.**

class, remedial reading: a group of children specially organized for corrective instruction in reading; generally a smaller group than a regular class group.

class report: *see* **report, class.**

class, restoration: *syn.* **class, adjustment.**

class, sanatorium: a class held in the institution to provide education for children who are resident patients, usually long-time, with such diseases as bone and joint tuberculosis. *See* **class, hospital.**

class schedule: *syn.* **schedule, room.**

class scheduling, block method of: *syn.* **scheduling, group method of class.**

class scheduling, group method of: *see* **scheduling, group method of class.**

class scheduling, mosaic method of: *see* **scheduling, mosaic method of class.**

class sectioning: *see* **sectioning, class.**

class, self-contained: *see* **classroom, self-contained.**

class, sight-conservation: an obsolescing term for *partially seeing class.*

class, sight-saving: an obsolescing term for *partially seeing class.*

class, sight-singing: a class devoted to training music students to read and sing, at first sight, musical examples of increasing complexity.

class size: (1) the number of children enrolled in a class; (2) (stat.) the number of observations or measures falling within any one of the class intervals of a frequency distribution; *syn.* **class frequency; variable frequency;** (3) (stat.) the size of the class interval; *syn.* **class range.**

class, slow reading: an instructional group composed of children who are slow to learn reading or who are otherwise retarded.

class, social: *see* **social class.**

class sociogram: *see* **sociogram, class.**

class, special: (1) a class organized to provide a curriculum differing from the standard school curriculum in content, method of instruction, and rate of progress for any one of various groups of exceptional pupils; (2) a broad term designating a day or evening class for adults and out-of-school youth, often organized on a part-time basis.

class, special-education: a class composed of pupils segregated because of similar physical, mental, or social abnormalities.

class, special help: a class, meeting outside regular school hours, for the purpose of giving special help to pupils having difficulty in certain areas; generally associated with the platoon type of curriculum design.

class, speech-correction: a group of children having some deficiency or difficulty in speech who are segregated for special treatment under teachers especially qualified to deal with them.

class, speech-improvement: a class in which speech improvement is carried on by or with the cooperation of a speech-correction teacher.

class, speech therapy: a small group of speech-defective pupils or a speech-defective pupil segregated for special instruction under a qualified speech therapist.

class sponsor: one who advises and supervises the activities of a group of pupils (such as the sophomore class) who expect to be graduated in the same year.

class struggle: according to Marx (1818–1883), the theory that social classes are in competition, in open or in disguised and subtle form, to possess and control the means of economic production; new means of production or new uses of them are championed by classes that stand to gain by the change; the class struggle is a basic dynamic of history.

class suit: *see* **bill, class.**

class, summer makeup: a class meeting during the summer vacation for the purpose of giving pupils help in areas in which they are having difficulty.

class, television: a class assembled for the purpose of receiving instruction by television.

class, textile: (1) a class organized for the purpose of preparing individuals for profitable employment and advancement in the clothing and allied trades; (2) a class organized to secure consumer information or nonvocational education dealing with textile materials.

class, trade extension: *see* **part-time trade extension class.**

class, transition: (read.) a class of children between kindergarten and first-grade level who are not yet developed sufficiently to make it advisable to teach them to read; the term was first used in this sense in San Fernando Valley, California.

class, tutorial: a type of extension education developed by English universities, for individual adults not in residence but pledged to a continuous course of study under college instructors. *See* **tutorial; university, open** (Ed. in England and Wales).

class, ultimate: any one of the smallest classifications into which the data of an investigation may be subdivided, all other larger classes being obtained by combination of the ultimate classes.

class, ungraded: a class to which children are assigned according to achievement rather than according to age or standard grade classification. *Syn.* **nongraded class; ungraded room;** *see* **special instruction room** (1).

class, ungraded primary: a class having a flexible system of grouping in which children in the primary grades are grouped together regardless of age and in which extensive effort is made to adapt instruction to individual differences.

class, ungraded special: a special class in which all mentally handicapped children from 6 to 16 years of age are enrolled; although not the ideal type of organization, the only practical solution for a small school system which has within the school only 12 to 18 children who require assignment to a special class.

class, vestibule: *syn.* **extension, kindergarten** (1).

class visitation: *see* **visitation, class.**

class, voice: a class designed for group instruction in the techniques of resonant tone development, projection, enunciation, and related principles of good singing.

class, welfare: a term used in Los Angeles to designate special classes for boys or girls who are socially maladjusted. *See* **welfare school.**

class, young-farmer: (1) commonly a class for young men, usually not more than 25 years of age, who have not yet become established in an agricultural occupation, either nonfarm or farm; *syn.* **agricultural part-time class;** (2) occasionally one of a group of classes in an agricultural school.

classed catalog: *syn.* **catalog, classified.**

classes, all-day trade: courses conducted for persons regularly enrolled in a full-time school who have selected a trade or industrial pursuit and who wish to prepare for useful employment in that occupation; training is comprehensive and includes instruction in manipulative processes and also in those technical and other related subjects which are needed by the skilled and competent worker.

classes, duplicate: sections or groups of students receiving instruction in the same subject, at the same level, and doing approximately the same work.

classes, exchange: the designation of a plan by which two or more teachers exchange class groups in order that pupils or students may obtain training in a wider range of problems than is possible under one teacher; most commonly practiced by teachers of home economics, agriculture, and industrial arts.

classes, integrative: a plan in which the blind child is enrolled in the regular classroom; available to him and to his regular teachers is a full-time qualified teacher of blind children and also a resource room; the regular teachers turn to the teacher of blind children for assistance in planning the child's program, for guidance in adapting the classroom procedures, and for providing, as necessary, specialized instruction appropriate to the blind child's needs.

classes, preparatory: *see* **instruction, distributive education preparatory.**

classic, children's book: a book for children that has lasting merit and has had sustained appeal; has often influenced later writing for children.

classical conditioning: *see* **conditioning, classical.**

classical curriculum: *see* **curriculum, classical.**

classical education: a Renaissance secondary-school training of the middle and higher classes of society; flourished from 1450 to 1850; a humanistic education, based on the great intellectual inheritance just recovered from the ancient world and emphasizing the ideal of a cultured gentleman, "fit for the demands of citizenship, the new world of commerce, the affairs at court, diplomatic and otherwise—." *See* **humanism; humanism, classical.**

classical humanism: *see* **humanism, classical.**

classical languages: *see* **languages, classical.**

classical literature: *see* literature, classical.

classical music: *see* music, classical.

classical realism: *see* realism, classical.

classical school: a secondary school emphasizing the study of Latin or Latin and Greek and other traditional subject matter.

classicism: (1) the principles of style embodied in the literature, art, or architecture of ancient Greece and Rome; (2) a style of literature, architecture, music, and other arts in the European tradition, distinguished by authoritative excellence and its relationship to the style of the literature and art of classical antiquity; (3) adherence to traditional standards such as simplicity, restraint, proportion, etc., in any activity.

classics: works or writings that are outstanding artistically, especially, though not only, those of noted Greek and Roman authors.

classification: (1) the act of grouping pupils for purposes of instruction, commonly thought of as ability grouping within given grade groups where the most able of a given grade are grouped for instructional purposes and where the average and the least able form other groups; (2) placement of a pupil in his proper grade on the basis of test results and other data that seem to indicate he is ready to do the work of that grade; (3) (phys. ed.) the grouping of pupils into comparable and somewhat homogeneous groups on the basis of age, weight, strength, skill, interest, other factors, or a combination of such factors; (4) the process of grouping statistical data into mutually exclusive categories or classes on the basis of attributes or magnitudes; requires multiple predictors whose validity is individually determined by each criterion; a classification battery requires a different regression equation for each criterion; (5) in vocational decision making, assignment of each person to the position he can fill best, subject to limitations imposed by the number of vacancies available; the decision maker is concerned about the subsequent performance of everyone, not just those assigned to one category.

classification and selection, personnel: a system whereby individuals are evaluated, categorized, and appointed to appropriate positions of responsibility.

classification, book: a systematic grouping of books according to predetermined categories or characteristics. (Most modern classification systems applicable to books, such as the Dewey decimal system and the Library of Congress system, group books according to subject content. A scheme for symbolic notation usually accompanies a classification schedule and ensures ease in locating specific items.) *See* book number; call number.

classification chart: *see* chart, classification.

classification, decimal: a schematic system usually applied to the organization of book collections according to subject content; the classification of knowledge proceeds from the general to the specific by a division of all knowledge into 10 main categories and subdividing decimally; the system is represented graphically by a symbolic notation in Arabic numerals; devised by Melvil Dewey, it is more widely used in the United States than any other classification system for books. *See* classification, universal decimal (Brussels).

classification, Dewey decimal: *syn.* classification, decimal.

classification exercise: *see* exercise, classification.

classification, flexible: a plan of assigning pupils to classes or grades that permits of modification to suit individual cases, especially facilitating transfer from one class to another at any time during the school year.

classification, functional: grouping or arranging in terms of the action performed as opposed to classification in terms of physical structure or appearance.

classification index: *see* index, classification.

classification, item: in foreign language instruction, filing of each item to be tested, usually by (*a*) chapter or unit of the textbook, (*b*) knowledge or skill tested, and (*c*) type of item.

classification, job: *see* job classification.

classification, Library of Congress: a system of classification particularly applicable to books, developed by the staff of

the Library of Congress; classes of knowledge are represented by a mixed notation of letters and numbers, which permits almost unlimited flexibility and expansion as new subjects are added; used chiefly by large university and research libraries.

classification, object: the act of ordering phenomena into groups, families, or systems on the basis of designated characteristics.

classification of body builds: *see* body builds, classification of.

classification, organizational: the act of ordering related phenomena into categories according to specific purposes or to render the greatest number of general propositions regarding the objects; dividing into classes in order to facilitate a systematic survey.

classification, personnel: (mil. ed.) collection of information regarding education, abilities, pre-Navy training, performance, and experience of men and officers.

classification, pupil: (1) the process of placing pupils in categories according to characteristics or attributes such as age, subject achievement, aptitude, or combinations of these; (2) the act or procedure of organizing children into grades, classes, or groups for instruction and work in various school subjects and activities; (3) the category or group in which the pupil has been placed.

classification scheme: a systematic or orderly arrangement of the elements of a body of knowledge.

Classification, Standard Industrial: *see* Standard Industrial Classification.

classification table: *see* table, classification.

classification, teacher: (1) a systematic arrangement of teachers in groups on the basis of one or more factors, such as type of certificate and salary rank; (2) the place that a teacher holds in a systematic scheme of grouping, such as one based on the kind, amount, and quality of academic and professional preparation or on the duties performed.

classification test: *see* test, classification.

classification, universal decimal (Brussels): a development of the *Dewey decimal classification* distinguished from Dewey largely by extensive expansions and by the use of various symbols in addition to Arabic numerals.

classification, vertical pupil: the placement of grouping of pupils in the successive levels of the educational system.

classified: (1) descriptive of information which is confidential; (2) (school admin.) pertaining to personnel who may be employed but are not certificated; *see* certificated teacher; (3) in civil service, relating to skilled workers.

classified catalog: *see* catalog, classified.

classified content: (voc. ed.) the part of teaching materials that can be grouped under specific headings.

classified filing: *see* filing plan.

classified subject catalog: *syn.* catalog, classified.

classifier: *syn.* table, classification.

classless society: *see* society, classless.

classroom: a room for recitations, teaching, etc., of a class in a school or college. *See* class (2) and (3).

classroom activities curriculum: *see* curriculum, classroom activities.

classroom administration: *see* administration, classroom.

classroom, all-purpose: (home ec.) a room that offers a flexibility of space and a variety of equipment which make it possible to offer instruction in the different areas of home economics.

classroom broadcast: *see* broadcast, classroom.

classroom climate: *see* climate, classroom.

classroom collection: *syn.* library, classroom (1).

classroom committee system: the organization of a classroom into committees to take charge of and regulate matters of thrift, health, etc.

classroom control: *see* discipline (3).

classroom deposit: *syn.* library, classroom (1).

classroom disorder: *see* disorder, classroom.

classroom, electronic: a type of language laboratory which is quickly and easily convertible to a normal classroom by means of drawers, collapsible panels, etc., used to store or conceal electronic apparatus.

classroom environment: *see* **environment, classroom.**

classroom experiment: *see* **experiment, classroom.**

classroom film: *see* **film, classroom.**

classroom, flying: a popular name for the Air Force plane used for teaching navigation.

classroom guidance: *see* **guidance, classroom.**

classroom, ideal climate of: *see* **climate of classroom, ideal.**

classroom instruction: *see* **instruction, classroom.**

classroom instruments: *see* **instruments, classroom.**

classroom interaction analysis: *see* **analysis, classroom interaction.**

classroom inventory: *see* **inventory, classroom.**

classroom-laboratory: a unified room in which the major portion of instruction in a given course in science takes place, including laboratory as well as class activities.

classroom librarian: *see* **librarian, classroom.**

classroom library: *see* **library, classroom.**

classroom loan: *see* **loan, classroom.**

classroom management: *syn.* **class management.**

classroom, mobile: a vehicle, trailer, or other attachment to a vehicle which is used as a classroom and which may easily be moved from place to place at any time.

classroom observational schedule: *see* **schedule, classroom observational.**

classroom, open: a relatively large instructional area or multiple-classroom space not separated by walls, as is the case in the traditional classroom, in which a variety of groups or classes may be working at the same time; for example, in high school, English at several grade levels, and in the elementary school, several grade levels or a variety of groups at the same grade level.

classroom organization: a plan or procedure for bringing the various activities in the classroom into harmonious and effective working relationship.

classroom, parabolic: a classroom so designed as to feature a parabola-shaped wall on the windowed side for the purpose of greater natural illumination.

classroom program: *see* **program, classroom.**

classroom, regular: (1) a term sometimes used to indicate a classroom of one of the more common sizes, such as 24 by 30 feet or 24 by 32 feet (with wide variations in sizes of rooms in modern school buildings, it is becoming improper to use the term in this sense); (2) a classroom designated for "regular," or academic, work as opposed to classrooms for "special" work such as music, industrial arts, or homemaking.

classroom routine: the aggregate of the routine duties carried on in a classroom by teacher and pupils. *See* **activities, routine.**

classroom schedule: *syn.* **schedule, room.**

classroom, self-contained: a classroom in the form of school organization in which classes are composed of groups of children which remain in one location, with one teacher (or team of teachers), for all or nearly all instructional work; to be distinguished from a departmentalized classroom.

classroom size: the dimensions of length and width of a classroom. *See* **floor area, classroom.**

classroom, special: (1) a room used for classes in the special subjects, such as music, homemaking, or physical education; *contr. w.* **classroom, regular** (2); (2) (spec. ed.) a specialized classroom environment providing individualized learning opportunity; grouping is usually done by handicapping characteristics; students may attend on a full- or part-time basis.

classroom, special-education: a room used to instruct groups of children with abnormal physical, mental, or social characteristics.

classroom teacher: one who plans and guides the development of the learning experiences of pupils in classroom situations and is responsible for the activities and conduct of pupils in class situations.

classroom technique: the particular method of execution chosen by the teacher to transmit to students in the classroom the knowledge of some skill, theory, or idea.

classroom test: *see* **test, classroom.**

classroom unit: (1) a measure of need for school support used in connection with state-aid plans; (2) an index of need, representing a number of pupils in average daily attendance or average daily membership, that reflects the cost of maintaining a typical teacher and a typical class of pupils in school; (3) a certain fixed amount of money representing the cost of maintaining one classroom for a given period of time; (4) an expression of the relationship between the need for school services and the varying size of classes and types of schools. (Usually a classroom unit, in larger schools, represents about 29 elementary pupils or about 21 secondary pupils, the exact number varying with the size of the school.)

classroom unit, weighted: a classroom unit that has been adjusted or modified to correct for some specific purpose. *See* **classroom unit.**

classwork, organized: planned activities for a class group for orderly, methodical procedure in learning in both class and study periods.

clause, dehydrated: uninflected words which the student of a foreign language is to use in their appropriate inflected form to complete a given partial sentence.

clause, grandfather: *see* **grandfather clause.**

claustrophobia (klôs′trə·fō′bi·ə): a morbid fear or anxiety concerning closed spaces such as elevators, closets, or small rooms.

clay: pliable earthy substance, potter's clay, used in creative activities or as an emotional outlet through pounding, squeezing, or cutting it. *See* **behavior, clay.**

clay behavior: *see* **behavior, clay.**

clay modeling: the forming of objects in clay. *See* **modeling; sculpture.**

clean: the term descriptive of audio material that is undistorted and noise-free.

clear type: a trade name given to the 24-point type in which textbooks and other educational materials are printed for the use of pupils in sight-saving classes.

clear-type book: *syn.* **book, large-type.**

clearance form: *syn.* **release form.**

clearinghouse, college: a center which obtains the records and credentials of selected students who are seeking college admission and makes the information available to admission officers of accredited institutions; also called *college clearing center.*

clearinghouse, information: (couns.) a center through which one may receive, verify, or provide information from a number of sources for a given individual.

clergy: the ordained ministry of the church, as distinct from the laity, the nonordained people of God; such a dichotomy is not precisely correct according to biblical exegesis.

cleric: a member of the clergy; in the Roman Catholic Church, regular clerics are members of religious orders who live according to a Rule (Regula); secular clerics are not members of a religious order but are under the jurisdiction of a bishop.

clerical practice: (1) a business subject offered in secondary schools dealing with the various duties of clerical workers in offices, such as filing and the operation of duplicators, comptometers, billing machines, etc.; (2) a course intended to prepare less capable business students to perform simple clerical tasks.

clerical subjects: *see* **subjects, clerical.**

clerical test: *see* **test, clerical.**

clerical test, general: *see* **test, general clerical.**

clerical work: (1) office work performed by a clerk, especially that pertaining to written records, including the filling out of office forms, the keeping of accounts, the compilation of statistics, and correspondence; *syn.* **office work;** (2) (classroom admin.) activities of a routine, mechanical nature such as checking attendance and keeping records in order.

clericalism: an excessively professional outlook of the clergy and their undue influence in the life of the church or of society.

clerk, general: as used in business education, the designation of one of a large group of office workers who are not employed in the more clearly defined occupations, such as stenography, bookkeeping, or accounting, but who do a variety of office tasks including the preparation of office forms and statistics and the operation of various office appliances.

clerk, school: (1) an employee of a school who does routine and mechanical clerical work in the school office; (2) an officer of the school district who is responsible for keeping minutes and sometimes financial records also and who may conduct the board's business routine; sometimes synonymous with *secretary of board of education.*

client: the person in the counseling interview who has a concern toward which both the counselor's and his own attention are turned in an attempt to find possible solutions for a dilemma or resolution for future action; school counselors tend to use for their client the term *counselee.*

client caseworker: *see* **caseworker, client.**

client-centered: pertaining to the activity of a school or welfare agency where the emphasis is shifted from what the agency considers best for the client to the attempt to help the client draw on his own resources for the solution of his problem.

client-centered counseling: *see* **counseling, client-centered.**

client-centered psychotherapy: *see* **counseling, client-centered.**

client-centered therapy: *see* **therapy, client-centered.**

client-counselor relationship: *syn.* **counseling relationship.**

client, involuntary: a counselee who does not come to a counselor of his own free will.

client readiness: *see* **readiness, client.**

climate, classroom: the learning environment in a classroom; includes not only physical environment but also emotional tone.

climate, emotional: (1) all environmental conditions or qualities that tend to produce a given type of feeling or emotional response, especially the teacher-pupil and pupil-pupil relationships as environmental influences during the teaching-learning process; (2) the feeling tone present in any human relationship or social situation.

climate, group: *syn.* **atmosphere, group.**

climate of classroom, ideal: in the United States, a democratic atmosphere in the classroom in which the child is encouraged to learn to respect the rights of others, to accept responsibility, to do his share of the work, and to act unselfishly and cooperatively as a member of a social group.

climate of ideas: (1) *syn.* **climate of opinion;** (2) in any culture, the concepts which are so universally used that people ordinarily reach for them as the proper tools to think with without even considering possible alternative sets of notions, thereby not so much predetermining what particular answers they will accept for important questions as unconsciously limiting what questions they will set themselves and what entire range of possibilities they will even consider as answers.

climate of opinion: in any culture, the beliefs which are so nearly universally held that they tend to be almost unconsciously adopted by the young and accepted by the mature as proper answers to important questions and therefore to determine the mode of social life in important ways; sometimes interpreted as a part of the spirit of the times which influences individual and group decisions.

climate, organizational: the pattern of social interaction that characterizes an organization.

climate, psychological: *syn.* **atmosphere, psychological.**

climate setting process: (couns.) permissive action by which one person allows others present in a group or in a one-to-one relationship to express their feelings, whether positive or negative.

climate, social: *see* **social climate.**

climate, supervisory: *see* **supervisory climate.**

climatology: the study of the types, causes, and manifestations of climate.

climatology, military: the science and study of climates employed specifically to serve military ends.

clinic: an organization of trained workers qualified to consider the cases of individuals or families in need of assistance, whether medical, psychological, or philanthropic, and qualified to give such assistance; usually connected with an institution, court, or social settlement.

clinic, behavior: an agency for the study and treatment of persons exhibiting problem behavior; used as a generic term including or synonymous with *psychiatric clinic, psychoeducational clinic,* and *psychological clinic.*

clinic, child guidance: a specialized support facility for direct service to children with adjustive or emotional problems; may work with school personnel and families; core staff generally includes a psychiatrist, a psychologist, and a psychiatric social worker; children may spend the school day in the clinic program, returning home at night.

clinic, child study: *syn.* **laboratory, child study.**

clinic, counselors': a workshop or seminar arrangement wherein guidance workers seek or discover any questions or answers pertaining to the guidance techniques or functions while discussing, sharing, and solving their problems.

clinic, demonstration: a device for showing accepted guidance procedures to those less expert in the field or for demonstrating a new technique before it becomes accepted as a common practice.

clinic, dental: among school health services, an institution for diagnosis and/or treatment of dental problems; may be set up in school buildings where this is a community center agreed upon by all local groups as the best site for this service.

clinic, driver: a work conference for the instruction and improvement of driving skills through discussion, demonstration, and practice.

clinic, educational guidance: a place to which persons come for specialized, individual help involving diagnosis and counseling relating to adjustment to school, special learning problems, behavior problems, and vocational adjustment; such a clinic, functioning under private auspices, is designed to supplement the work of the school with students presenting especially difficult problems.

clinic, extension: *syn.* **clinic, mobile.**

clinic, guidance: a centralized agency, either a part of a public school system or under state or private sponsorship, staffed by a group of specialists, such as psychiatrists, psychologists, social workers, and counselors, devoted to the problems of guidance and providing technical diagnosis and sometimes treatment in especially difficult case problems beyond the ability of teachers and advisers to handle.

clinic, health: an institution associated with a hospital, medical school, or health department for treatment of outpatients.

clinic, hearing: an agency providing services in the evaluation of hearing, in hearing-aid selection, and in rehabilitation for persons with impaired hearing; generally operated in conjunction with schools, colleges, universities, or hospitals, though there are some private clinics.

clinic, homemaking-problems: a nonclass technique used to help individuals identify specific problems and discover possible solutions.

clinic, mobile: a clinic unit that travels from place to place serving clients in each area for a short time, usually for 2 or 3 days each month; in the field of counseling, a mental health clinic which, moving to the client, provides services to many school districts. *Syn.* **extension clinic; traveling clinic.**

clinic, music: a workshop designed to cover certain facets of music teaching and performance; such topics as rehearsal techniques, tone production, articulation, and literature for orchestra, band, or chorus may be covered.

clinic, pediatric speech: a specialized facility for speech and language problems in children; usually associated with a hospital or medical clinic and sometimes providing specialized services for cleft palate conditions.

clinic, prenatal: a community program usually organized by health or welfare agencies to promote good health practices during the period preceding birth; this service aims to familiarize prospective parents with the requirements for proper fetal development and maintenance of health for both mother and baby. *See* **preparental education.**

clinic, preschool: (1) a clinic devoted to the investigation and study of children who are under school age; (2) a clinic composed of local doctors and nurses in which physical examinations are made of children about to enroll in school for the first time.

clinic, psychiatric: a type of behavior clinic concerned with diagnosis and treatment of mental or personality disorders with emphasis on psychiatric methods and usually directed by a psychiatrist; may or may not employ the services of other professional groups.

clinic, psychoeducational: a type of behavior clinic, operated under educational auspices, that is concerned primarily with behavior problems of schoolchildren, especially as these are related to their general adjustment to the school environment, including academic, personal, and social adjustments, with special emphasis on adjustment of school tasks to individual abilities and needs.

clinic, psychological: an organization of psychologists engaging in diagnosis and treatment of personality, behavior, or learning disorders; may use a variety of diagnostic procedures and treatment strategies.

clinic, reading: *syn.* **center, reading.**

clinic, referral: *see* **clinic; fixed point of referral.**

clinic, school: any clinic supported by the school or by the local educational authorities and conducted on school property for the benefit of pupils or students.

clinic, speech: an agency providing examination, diagnosis, and treatment for speech defectives; frequently includes audiometric evaluations; generally operated in conjunction with schools, colleges or universities, and hospitals.

clinic, sport: short-term courses for instruction in the skills required for participating in or officiating at a specific sport; involves laboratory and classroom experiences.

clinic, traveling: *syn.* **clinic, mobile.**

clinic, vocational: a conference of a counselor and other specialists (such as psychologists) to consider the case data and problems of a person relating to the selection of an occupation and adjustment to it.

clinic, well-baby: an adult education program usually organized by health agencies, nursing associations, or nutritionists to instruct young mothers in the development and care of the baby, feeding practices, and common disorders or diseases and their prevention; in some cases medication may be provided.

clinic, well-child: a program similar to the *well-baby clinic* but related primarily to the preschool child; in addition to health and feeding practices for good physical development, mental and social factors are also considered; medication may or may not be provided.

clinical approach: the method of analyzing reading difficulties that makes use of technical aids and studies each case individually in an attempt to detect specific needs.

clinical counseling: *see* **counseling, clinical.**

clinical crib: a crib specially constructed for use in giving developmental tests to babies. *Syn.* **normative crib.**

clinical experience: firsthand participation in patient and patient-related services occurring as a part of an educational program.

clinical method: (1) (couns.) an approach to guidance counseling which stresses the use of psychological tests, clinical tests, and analytical diagnostic studies so that the clinician can understand his client better and arrive at the client's problems more promptly; (2) (medical ed.) instruction for medical students given at the patient's bedside or in the clinical setting where actual symptoms

are studied and treatment given; (3) (teacher ed.) instruction which incorporates the treatment of actual educational problems or problem students.

clinical prediction: *see* **prediction, clinical.**

clinical professor: *see* **professor, clinical.**

clinical prognosis: *see* **prediction, clinical.**

clinical psychologist: *see* **psychologist, clinical.**

clinical psychology: *see* **psychology, clinical.**

clinical report: *see* **report, clinical.**

clinical services: (couns.) services characterized by the cooperation of a number of specialists involved in remedial functions such as the alleviation of personal conflicts which obscure or distort the self-concept. *See* **counseling, auxiliary services.**

clinical teacher: (spec. ed.) a teacher whose major function is to instruct pupils in an individual or small-group setting rather than in a regular-sized classroom, focusing instruction on specifically diagnosed learning needs of the pupils.

clinical type: any one of a number of types of feebleminded individuals, readily recognizable as such by reason of typical physical traits. *Syn.* **pathological type;** *contr. w.* **subcultural type.**

clinical vision test: *syn.* **test, vision.**

clip book: a printed booklet containing a variety of commercially prepared black-and-white line drawings on various subjects.

clique: (sociometry) a narrow circle of persons associated by common interests.

clock-and-bell system: an electrically operated master clock that shows the time on dials installed in the various rooms of a building and regulates the ringing of electric bells at desired times or set intervals.

clock arithmetic: *see* **arithmetic, modular.**

clock golf: a game, derived from golf, involving putting to a central hole from points in a surrounding circle corresponding to the numbers on the dial of a clock.

clock-hour: a total of 60 minutes of actual classwork or instruction.

cloistral school: a school, set up in various Western European countries during the Middle Ages, semimonastic in nature, for the purpose of training students to become priests or teachers. (In Germany the cloistral school later had the function of preparing students who expected to enter a university.)

clonic spasm: *see* **spasm.**

clonic stuttering: *see* **stuttering, clonic.**

close-order drill: *see* **drill, close-order.**

close work: work such as reading, sewing, or drawing normally done at a short distance from the eyes and hence requiring an effort of accommodation.

closed case: (1) a situation involving an individual or a group with a problem which has been either solved or officially abandoned; (2) a pupil whose problem has been solved or who has been transferred to another agency, lost track of, or given up as hopeless.

closed-circuit television: *see* **television, closed-circuit.**

closed curve: *see* **curve, closed.**

closed loop instruction: *see* **instruction, closed loop.**

closed sentence: *see* **sentence, closed.**

closed set: *see* **set, closed.**

closed shop: *see* **shop, closed.**

closed stacks: *see* **stacks, library.**

closed syllable: *see* **syllable, closed.**

closely graded curriculum: *see* **curriculum, closely graded.**

closest fit: *syn.* **fit, best.**

closet: a small room, within or leading from a classroom or laboratory, designed for the purpose of storing clothing, apparatus, or materials temporarily so that they can be easily and frequently removed for use.

closing day: the last attendance day of the school term or year when schoolwork for this period comes to an end; may be marked by special day exercises.

closing entries: *see* **entries, closing.**

closure: (1) a term used in the gestalt description of behavior that signifies pattern completion, goal realization, the resolution of tension, or the process of effecting a balance; (2) (math.) relative to some binary operation, a set has the closure property if each pair of elements is associated with some member of that same set; for example, the *natural numbers* have the closure property relative to addition but not to subtraction (3 + 5 is associated with the natural number 8 while 3 − 5 is not associated with any natural number).

clothing construction, Bishop method of: a method devised by Mrs. Edna Bryte Bishop to expedite and simplify the construction of clothing in the classroom and the home; shortcuts and speed are achieved by combining many manufacturing methods with home practices.

clothing instruction: *see* **instruction, clothing.**

clothing laboratory: *see* **laboratory, clothing.**

clothing management, production, and services: a technological course of study in home economics which trains people for positions in clothing and textiles; areas would include fitting and altering ready-made garments, dressmaking, and assisting in laundry and dry-cleaning work.

clothing requisition: (1) an administrative form used in requesting clothing for children of indigent parents; (2) the process or act of requesting clothing for children of indigent parents.

cloze procedure: a procedure used to estimate readability of printed material and to evaluate and improve reading comprehension; based on the gestalt concept of closure and involving a cloze test composed of reading selections from which words have been deleted; completion of the test requires that the testee fill the blanks left by the deletion. *See* **closure** (1).

cloze test: *see* **test, cloze.**

club: a formally organized, congenial group.

club, aero: a club organized often in connection with flight instruction to encourage increased flying practice and time.

club, art: an extracurricular organization or society composed of pupils whose common interests are in art.

club, athletic: an organization devoted to one or more games or sports and appealing to persons who have a deep interest in these activities and whose desires for participation are not fully satisfied by existing public facilities.

club, booster: a group of people organized for the purpose of supporting school activities, particularly athletic contests; membership is usually made up of parents and other people not in the student body or on the faculty of the school.

club building: *see* **building, club.**

club, business: an organized group of high school or college-level students who have a primary interest in business education.

club, camera: a group of students whose common interest is photography.

club, career: a group of students within a school who have a common vocational interest; they meet regularly to hear speakers, see films or other material, take field trips, and discuss opportunities available in a particular vocation; an adult adviser usually takes part in the club activities.

club, cheerleaders': a high school or college organization comprising students responsible for leading the student body in cheering at athletic events.

club, children's book: an arrangement by which books for reading supplementary to school readers are purchased from commercial suppliers by parents for their children on a regular subscription basis at a reduction in price.

club, commercial: (obs.) *syn.* **club, business.**

club, distributive education: a local organization of students enrolled in distributive education courses in secondary schools and colleges.

club, extension homemaker: any local adult group organized primarily for participation in the extension home

economics program; formerly called *home demonstration club. See* **program, home economics extension.**

club, forensic: an organization of high school or college students whose common interest is public speaking such as debating, panels, and forums.

club, home demonstration: *see* **club, extension homemaker.**

club, industrial arts: (1) a hobby or recreational organization of students or adults who are interested in one or more types of industrial arts activities; (2) a club for high school and college students interested in becoming industrial arts teachers, sponsored at the college level by The American Industrial Arts Association.

club, library: (1) in a school library, a club that assists in the work of the library and may or may not follow a reading program; (2) in a library school or college, a group studying for librarianship or interested in library work.

club, mathematics: an organized group of individuals, having a somewhat homogeneous level of interest and ability in mathematics who meet periodically to discuss mathematical topics.

club movement: a movement toward organizing physical education classes or intramural athletic activities in the form of clubs.

club, music: (1) an organization of patrons and music teachers who promote and sponsor contests and festivals for aspiring young musicians; (2) (mus. ed.) the organization of after-school groups to take group lessons on guitars, accordions, organs, and other instruments not included in the traditional public school music curriculum. *See* **activities, music.**

club, photography: an organized group of students whose common interest is photography.

club, press: an extracurricular group of students interested in journalistic publications, sometimes the center of student publication activities in a high school or college.

club, projectionist: a voluntary organization for providing projection services, usually in a school or church.

club, reading: (1) a group, with or without formal organization, that meets at specified times under the supervision of a librarian to discuss and review books; (2) a class or group of children formed into a club for the purpose of reading together and discussing what they have read; (3) *syn.* **reading circle.**

club, school-affiliated: an organized group of children in the community connected by sponsorship or otherwise with the school; for example, a Boy Scout troop may be sponsored by a school and therefore affiliated with it.

club, service: a student organization formed to promote and support community welfare projects.

club, special-interest: a group of pupils at various grade levels organized for the purpose of pursuing some activity in which all members of the group are interested.

club, study: a group of students organized for the study of a particular problem or topic.

club study course: *see* **course, club study.**

club, teacher boarding: a group of teachers within a community who have associated themselves in an informal organization for the purpose of eating their meals together.

club, teachers': an organization of teachers for the purpose of providing living quarters and developing recreational and cultural interests.

club, trade and industrial education: an organization composed of students in vocational industrial education whose objectives are to develop leadership qualities as they perfect their shop skills and knowledges; also called *vocational-industrial club.*

clubhouse: *see* **building, club.**

clue: (1) (spec. ed.) in education of the visually handicapped, any sound, odor, temperature, or tactile stimulus affecting the senses which can be readily converted in determining one's position or a line of direction; (2) (testing) a word or phrase that gives unintended assistance to the examinee, in answering objective-type test items; *syn.* **cue;** *see* **clue, clang association; clue, grammatical; clue, length cue; clue, specific determiner; prompt.**

clue, clang association: in testing, words or phrases in the stem and keyed answer which sound alike or have similar meanings such that the student can select the correct response on this basis. *See* **stem** (3).

clue, configuration: (1) a hint as to the identity of a word that is gained from an examination of its general outline, or configuration, as distinct from an examination of its detailed parts; (2) a clue as to meaning gained from the pattern of the ideas found in the context rather than from careful consideration of the specific words making up the context.

clue, context: suggestions as to the meaning of a word gained from the words immediately adjacent in a phrase, clause, or other context or found in the same general setting, such as a sentence or paragraph.

clue, grammatical: a fault in the form of a test item enabling an examinee to infer the right answer through knowledge of language usage.

clue, language-rhythm: a clue to the recognition of a word derived from the rhythm of language; useful especially in poetry, where one word at the end of one line suggests a rhyming word at the end of the next, but helpful also in reading prose.

clue, length cue: a clue in a test resulting from a general tendency for true statements to be longer than false ones because of the necessity of including qualifications and limitations to make the statement true.

clue, meaning: a suggestion as to the meaning of a word or sentence in reading matter gained from pictures and context.

clue, picture: (read.) (1) an element in a picture that gives meaning to a part of the context; (2) an illustration that suggests the general theme or significance of a unit of reading material.

clue, rhythm: (1) *syn.* **clue, language rhythm;** (2) a guide to the rhythm to be followed in oral reading of poetry gained from a preliminary examination of the meter, which indicates the stress to be placed on the words and phrases.

clue, secondary: (read.) a hint as to the form of a word derived from touch or sound as contrasted with that derived from sight.

clue, specific determiner: some characteristic in the statement of a true-false test item which supplies an unintended clue to the correct answer.

clue, verbal context: *syn.* **clue, context.**

clue, visual: a peculiarity in the form of a word which gives the reader a clue to its identity.

clue, word-form: a clue to the recognition of words derived from their general shape, configuration, and structure.

cluster: a group of variables, usually fewer than the original, representing tests or reflections of tests whose intercorrelations are high and positive.

cluster analysis: *see* **analysis, cluster.**

cluster, attitude: *see* **attitude cluster.**

cluster, attitudinal: *see* **attitudinal cluster.**

cluster college: *see* **college, cluster.**

cluster sample: *see* **sample, cluster.**

cluster score: *see* **score, cluster.**

cluster, trait: *see* **trait cluster.**

clutch: the device on a motion-picture projector by which the film can be stopped to allow a single frame to be projected as a still picture.

cluttering: excessive rapidity of speech with poor pronunciation, usually on a psychogenic basis. *Syn.* **spluttering.**

co-ed recreation: *see* **recreation, co-ed.**

co-twin control, method of: a design for experiments utilizing identical twins in which one of the twins is kept under one set of environmental conditions while the other is subjected to another set, on the assumption that the factor of inheritance of the twins is identical and that, under similar environmental conditions, their development would be alike; hence any differences that appear in the experiment will be due to environmental factors.

coach and pupil method: (mil. ed.) method of training in which pairs of students take turns teaching each other a procedure previously explained by the instructor.

coach, athletic: an instructor in one or more sports, such as football or golf.

coach, study: (1) a person responsible for instructing and aiding pupils in the techniques of studying; (2) especially, one who tutors a pupil or pupils in a specific area of study in preparation for an examination or in mastering a certain body of knowledge.

coaching: (1) the act of tutoring a student or group of students, such as failing students or those preparing for special assignments or examinations; (2) in-service training of teachers through close supervision of teaching procedures.

coaching class: *syn.* **class, adjustment.**

coacting group: *syn.* **group, secondary.**

coathletics: athletic activities engaged in by both sexes together.

COBOL: an acronym for *Common Business Oriented Language. See* **FORTRAN; language, common business oriented.**

cochlear-palpebral reflex: *see* **reflex, cochlear-palpebral.**

Cochran-Cox test: *see* **test, Cochran-Cox.**

cocurricular activities: *see* **activities, cocurricular.**

code: *n.* (1) a systematic compilation of laws; (2) the whole body of statutes in force in a state (sometimes those parts of the statutes applicable to public schools are juxtaposed to form a *school code*); (3) a systematic statement of principles of conduct, such as a *code of ethics;* (4) (stat.) a set of symbols, usually numbers, employed to convert a given set of numerical, verbal, or categorical data into a series of values having certain desired properties or a transformation scheme by means of which such data are so converted; *see* **code, geometric; decoding; precoding;** (5) a list, table, chart, figure, or some combination of these giving one set of symbols to be substituted for another; used in some psychological and vocational tests and probably derived from the cryptic codes used in military communications; (6) (data processing) an agreed transformation or set of unambiguous rules whereby messages are converted from one representation to another. *See* **coding.**

code: *v.* (1) (stat.) to substitute systematically a set of symbols (usually numbers) for some other set of numerical, verbal, or categorical data; commonly applied in preparing data for treatment by tabulating equipment, such as by assigning a numerical value to each of the responses on a questionnaire, substituting an identification number for a name, grouping values into class intervals, changing the origin and/or scale units of a series of values, or employing a more elaborate *code,* such as a *geometric code,* in order to conserve space on punch cards or tabulation sheets; (2) sometimes applied to the conversion of raw scores into derived scores, such as standard scores; (3) in programmed instruction, to write the instructions constituting a program. *See* **code, geometric; decoding; precoding.**

code, addend: *syn.* **code, geometric.**

code, administrative: *see* **administrative code.**

code, Air Force specialty (AFSC): a numerical code of five digits indicating the career field, particular job, and skill level of an airman; thus in the AFSC 43150 (helicopter mechanic), the first two digits represent the aircraft maintenance career field, the third digit combined with the first two identifies the career field subdivision, the fourth digit shows the skill level (3, 5, 7, or 9, as case may be), and the fifth digit further delimits the specialty; letter prefixes or suffixes may be added to AFSCs, such as 43151A (aircraft mechanic, reciprocal engine) and 43151C (jet aircraft mechanic, two engines). *See* **code, military occupational specialty; code, Navy enlisted classification.**

code, binary: a coding system in which the encoding of data is done through the use of bits. *See* **band** (2); **bit.**

code, binary coded decimal (BCD code): a code in which individual decimal digits are represented by a group of binary digits, as in the 8-4-2-1 binary-coded-decimal notations.

code, building: *see* **building code.**

code check: a testing for the presence of forbidden or illegal codes.

code, coding: a code arranged according to some characteristic of the data to be coded so as to facilitate coding, for example, alphabetical arrangement of states, with the corresponding code numbers. *Contr. w.* **code, decoding.**

code, compound: a code by means of which each possible combination of the values or categories of two or more variables can be identified, for example, a code designed to identify such combinations as Ohio male wage earners or New York female nonwage earners. *Contr. w.* **code, simple.**

code, computer: *syn.* **language, machine.**

code, decoding: a code arranged in the order of magnitude of the code numbers so as to facilitate the determination of the proper meaning to attach to any given code value. *Contr. w.* **code, coding.**

code designation: a number or other symbol assigned to a specific item or category of information for identification purposes.

code, DOT: a code system based on the Dictionary of Occupational Titles compiled by the U.S. Department of Labor which gives number codes for all occupations; volume I defines occupations and titles; volume II classifies jobs according to job descriptions. *See* **occupations, related; training occupational.**

code, forbidden: in automatic data processing, an out-of-code representation, for example, 1111 in the binary coded decimal system.

code, geometric: a form of addend code in which the code numbers assigned to the successive categories of a variable represent a geometric series, as 1, 2, 4, 8, etc., and the code for any given combination of categories is obtained by adding the code numbers for the categories concerned. *Syn.* **addend code; geometric addend code.**

code, geometric addend: *syn.* **code, geometric.**

code, geometrical: *see* **code, geometric.**

code, honor: "We will not lie, steal, or cheat, nor tolerate among us anyone who does." is the code established by cadets in service academies to provide the basis for a personal code of ethics.

code, meaningful: a code made up of meaningful code numbers. *See* **code number, meaningful.**

code, military occupational specialty (MOSC): the Army or Marine Corps job code consisting of a fixed number which indicates a given military occupational specialty; the Coast Guard does not use numbers but rather job titles. *See* **code, Air Force specialty; code, Navy enlisted classification.**

code, minimal addend: a code, found from addends, that in addition to fulfilling the first of the criteria of a unique code number also has addends of the smallest possible practicable size. *See* **code number, unique.**

code, moral: a more or less systematized set of moral laws or maxims of conduct. *See* **moral law.**

code, Navy enlisted classification (NEC): a 4-digit skill identifier assigned to some enlisted billets and personnel; when assigned to a billet, it identifies specific skills required to operate and maintain the growing inventory of complex weapon systems and other equipments, which are not specifically identified by ratings alone, as well as identifying many special skills on training not specifically associated with any rating; when assigned to personnel, it identifies those who have received training or performed duties resulting in effective skills more clearly defined by the NEC than by their individual rating.

code number: a number assigned, either arbitrarily or meaningfully to an individual, case, or observation in order to retain identity for eventual future use. *See* **code number, meaningful.**

code number, meaningful: a code number that serves to distinguish each individual from every other individual in a particular population and also conveys certain information about the individual; for example, the separate code numbers for the month, day, and year of birth may be combined with the code numbers for the individual's sex and score on an intelligence test; written

together, these might form a meaningful code number which would be used as the individual's serial number and from which could be deduced information as to his age, sex, and test score.

code number, officers' qualifications: a four-digit number which marks a Naval officer as having certain basic qualifications for duty.

code number, unique: a code number compiled from addends and fulfilling both the following criteria: (*a*) every answer pattern has a code number; (*b*) every code number within the range of allotted code numbers has a corresponding pattern.

code of ethics: a set of moral standards and principles to guide conduct, formulated by an individual for himself or by a group (such as a society or a profession) for the guidance of its membership.

code of ethics, professional: (1) those ideals, principles, and standards of individual conduct as related to professional duties and responsibilities; (2) a specific set of standards of professional conduct approved by and enforced by the membership of a professional group or association.

code of ethics, teachers': *see* **code of ethics, professional.**

code, operation: in automatic data processing, an instruction, in the form of a coded group of characters, which tells the computer what is to be done. *See* **address; command.**

code, primary Air Force specialty (AFSC): code in which an airman is most highly qualified; he may possess other AFSCs from time to time to meet Air Force training and manpower requirements.

code, prime number: a code number the factors of which are prime numbers.

code, school: *see* **code** *n.* (2).

code, simple: a code by means of which each value or category of a single variable can be identified. *Contr. w.* **code, compound.**

code, standard: a carefully compiled coding list that, because of its general utility and the care used in its compilation, is recognized and widely used as a standard for the coding of the variable or variables in question, for example, the *Standard List of the Causes of Death* compiled by the U.S. Census Bureau.

code, state school: *see* **code** (2).

code test: *see* **test, code.**

code, uniform vehicle: *see* **vehicle code, uniform.**

code, unique addend: a code, formed from addends, that fulfills both the criteria of unique code numbers. *See* **code number, unique.**

coded filing: *see* **filing plan.**

coded values: numerical values derived from observed numerical or categorical data by any form of systematic transformation; applied usually to data that have been adapted for treatment by tabulating equipment through the application of a numerical code; applied frequently to derived scores formed by subtracting and/or dividing original values by a constant, in order to facilitate computation of statistics. *See* **code.**

codification: the process of collecting and arranging the laws, or certain types of laws, of a particular state into a code, such as the bringing together of the school laws of a particular state into a **school code.** *See* **code** (1) and (2).

coding: the act or process of using a code to substitute systematically one set of symbols for another.

coding, automatic: a method of making the computer do part of its own programming and coding through the use of macrocodes, subroutines, compiling routines, etc.

coding code: *see* **code, coding.**

coding, color: the assignment of various colors to instructional materials to indicate level of difficulty, area or level of interest, etc.

coding, compound: *see* **code, compound.**

coding key: *see* **key, coding.**

coding manual: *see* **manual, coding.**

coding, symbolic: coding for machines in which symbolic notation for operators, operands, and locations are used instead of machine instruction codes and addresses, for example, the symbol "L" for load instead of the code "07."

coding table: *see* **table, coding.**

coding tree: a branching device for quickly finding the coded value appropriate to a compounded classification such as sex, race, and marital status; for example, the two classes male and female may be indicated as each broken down into three classes, white, Negro, and others, and each of the six classes so produced then may be broken down according to marital status.

coeducation: an educational practice according to which both boys and girls attend the same school; was begun at the elementary level in the Protestant countries during the Reformation but did not reach the secondary and higher levels until begun in the United States in the early part of the nineteenth century.

coefficient: (1) (stat.) a statistical constant that is independent of the unit of measurement; a statistic that is pure number; *syn.* **statistical coefficient;** (2) a value expressing the degree to which some characteristic or relation is to be found in specified instances; (3) (math.) any factor which is expressly indicated in the representation of a product; for example, in the expression "6*bxy*," 6*y* may be considered the coefficient of *bx;* in practice, the term is frequently used to mean numerical coefficient (the numeral 6 in the example cited) or a parameter; *see* **parameter (3).**

coefficient, activity: a numerical coefficient (employed by Harl Douglass) that takes into account the number of hours or class periods devoted to the supervision of extracurricular activities in relation to the total responsibilities of the job.

coefficient, alpha: (α) the mean of all split-half coefficients from different splittings of a test; an estimate of the correlation between two random samples of items from a universe of items like those in the test. *See* **coefficient of split-half.**

coefficient, beta: *syn.* **coefficient, beta regression.**

coefficient, beta regression: ($\beta_{01 \cdot 23 \ldots n}$) the weight assigned to or the coefficient of one of the independent variables in a partial regression equation, when the variables are expressed in terms of standard scores, indicating the net contribution of that variable to the dependent variable. *Syn.* **beta coefficient; beta regression weight; beta weight; standard regression coefficient.**

coefficient, chance-halves correlation: *see* **split-halves method.**

coefficient, confidence: a statement of the confidence with which a statistically based statement may be made, equal to 1.00 minus the confidence level; thus, if the probability that a parameter is beyond certain limits (confidence limits) is .05 (confidence level), the confidence coefficient that the parameter is within the limits is 1.00—.05, or .95. *See* **confidence level; confidence limits; region, acceptance.**

coefficient, correlation: a pure number, varying usually from +1 through 0 to −1, that denotes the degree of relationship existing between two (or more) series of observations. *See* **correlation.**

coefficient, entire correlation: *syn.* **coefficient, total correlation.**

coefficient, experimental: (1) the difference between two means divided by 2.78 times the standard error of that difference; the standard difference divided by 2.78; (2) *syn.* **ratio, critical.**

coefficient, first-order correlation: any correlation coefficient based on the relationship of three variables; this may be either a partial or a multiple correlation coefficient in which only three variables are involved.

coefficient, frequency: *syn.* **frequency, relative.**

coefficient, gross correlation: *syn.* **coefficient, total correlation.**

coefficient, intercorrelation: any of the $n (n − 1) / 2$ coefficients of correlation that may be computed among n variables.

coefficient, lambda: a ratio expressing the correlation between a subject's responses and those of the members

of a defined group; a simple function of the proportion sums; the upper limit is 1.00 for all groups regardless of the degree of *homogeneity.*

coefficient, mean square contingency: *syn.* **coefficient of contingency.**

coefficient, multiple: *syn.* **coefficient of multiple correlation.**

coefficient, objectivity: the correlation coefficient between two independent ratings or scorings of the same set of products by the same judge. *Syn.* **inter-rater reliability.**

coefficient of agreement: a correlation technique developed by Kendall to measure the agreement among m observers, each making the $n/2$ paired-comparison ratings of n items through use of the formula

$$u = \frac{2\Sigma j}{(m/2)\,(n/2)} - 1,$$ where Σj is the total agreements among judges. *See* **coefficient of concordance; coefficient of consistence in paired comparisons.**

coefficent of alienation: *(k)* a measure of departure from perfect correlation, expressed by the formula $k = \sqrt{1 - r^2}$; the ratio of the standard error of estimate to the standard deviation of the dependent variable. *Syn.* **alienation coefficient.**

coefficient of brightness (CB): a rarely used measure of mental ability, obtained by dividing a pupil's score on a given mental test by the score that is normal for pupils of his age; thus, a CB of 1.00 would indicate average brightness, corresponding to an intelligence quotient (IQ) of 100; however, while a CB of more than 1.00 indicates superior intelligence and a CB of less than 1.00 indicates inferior intelligence, these measures are not comparable with IQ's. *See* **index of brightness.**

coefficient of colligation: a crude measure of relationship between two dichotomous qualitative variables, the measure being a function of the square roots of the products of frequencies in opposite cells of the fourfold table.

coefficient of concordance: a correlation technique developed by Kendall to measure the extent of agreement among the ranking of n items by m raters through use of the formula $W = \dfrac{12\,S}{m^2(n^3 - n)}$, where S is the sum of squares of deviation from the mean, $m (n + 1) / 2$. *See* **coefficient of agreement.**

coefficient of concurrent deviations: a statistic devised to indicate the extent to which a change in one quantity is accompanied by a change in another quantity, either in the same or in the opposite direction, the function not being dependent on the size but only on the direction of the changes.

coefficient of consistence in paired comparisons: a correlation technique developed by Kendall to measure the consistency of an observer in making the $n(n − 1)/2$ paired-comparison ratings of n items. *See* **coefficient of agreement.**

coefficient of contingency (CC): a measure of the degree of association between two variables when each is expressed in several categories (which are usually qualitative, such as hair color or grade placement). (The coefficient of contingency is a function of the *square contingency* and becomes identical with the *Pearson product moment coefficient of correlation* if the categories are successive values of a quantitative variable, the number of categories is sufficiently large to eliminate grouping error, the sample is large, and the correlation surface is normal.) *Syn.* **contingency coefficient; mean square contingency coefficient.**

coefficient of correlation: *syn.* **coefficient, correlation.**

coefficient of correlation, biserial: *syn.* **correlation, biserial.**

coefficient of correlation, Pearson product moment (r): a pure number, limited by the values +1.00 and −1.00, that expresses the degree of relationship between two continuous variables when the arrays of each are homoscedastic; may be calculated from various formulas; for example, $r_{xy} = \dfrac{\Sigma_{xy}}{N\sigma_x\,\sigma_y}$ where Σ_{xy} is the sum of products of the paired values of x and y (expressed as deviations from their respective means), σ_x and σ_y are the standard deviations of the two distributions, and N is the number of paired observations.

coefficient of correlation, product moment: *syn.* **coefficient of correlation, Pearson product moment.**

coefficient of correspondence: *syn.* **index of forecasting efficiency.**

coefficient of determination (d): the square of any coefficient of correlation, *r;* the proportion of the variance of one variable which is accounted for by its correlation with a second variable; thus, these relationships prevail: $d = r^2$; $d = 1 - k^2$, where k = coefficient of alienation. See **coefficient of alienation; coefficient of nondetermination.** *Dist. f.* **index of determination.**

coefficient of dispersion: any one of several measures of relative variability used in an attempt to make due allowance for unequal means; consists of 100 times any measure of variability divided by a measure of central tendency, for example, the *coefficient of variation. Dist. f.* **measure of dispersion.**

coefficient of equivalence: a coefficient of reliability of the type based on a correlation between scores from two forms of the same test or evaluation instrument given at essentially the same time. See **coefficient of reliability; reliability.**

coefficient of intelligence (CI): *syn.* **coefficient of brightness.**

coefficient of internal consistency: a coefficient of reliability of the type based on internal analysis of data obtained on a single trial of a test or other evaluation instrument, for example, by the *analysis of variance method* or the *split-halves method.* See **coefficient of reliability; reliability.**

coefficient of mean square contingency: *syn.* **coefficient of contingency.**

coefficient of multiple correlation: ($R_{y123 \ldots k}$) a pure number lying between the limits of 0.00 and 1.00, indicating the degree of relationship between a criterion or dependent variable and the optimally weighted sum of a number of independent variables, the independent variables being so weighted as to make the multiple correlation coefficient a maximum. *Syn.* **multiple correlation; multiple correlation coefficient.**

coefficient of net correlation: *syn.* **coefficient of partial correlation.**

coefficient of nondetermination: (k^2) the proportion of the variance of one variable which is not accounted for by a second variable with which it is correlated to some degree; the square of the coefficient of alienation, $\sqrt{1 - r^2}$. See **coefficient of alienation; coefficient of determination.**

coefficient of part correlation: the linear correlation between an independent variable and a dependent variable from which the net variations associated with other variables have been removed. *Syn.* **part correlation coefficient;** *dist. f.* **coefficient of partial correlation.**

coefficient of partial correlation: a measure of the net degree of relationship existing between two variables when the common influence of one or more other variables has been removed by holding the latter constant. *Syn.* **coefficient of net correlation; partial correlation coefficient;** *dist. f.* **coefficient of part correlation.**

coefficient of partial regression: ($b_{01\cdot23\ldots n}$ or $\beta_{01\cdot23\ldots n}$) the weight assigned to any one of the independent variables in a partial regression equation; represented by the symbol $b_{01\cdot23\ldots n}$ when each variable is expressed in gross scores or in terms of raw-score deviations from any origin, but not in standard scores; represented by the symbol $\beta_{01\cdot23\ldots n}$ when the variables are expressed in standard scores. See **coefficient, beta regression.**

coefficient of pattern similarity: (1) any statistic used for describing the degree of similarity between two sets of scores; examples are *tau, D, r_p,* etc.; (2) (fact. anal.) a statistic used in matching two factor-loading patterns.

coefficient of regression: (1) (with two variables) an expression of the slope of the regression line; the average number of units of change (increase or decrease) in the dependent variable occurring with a unit change in the independent variable; *syn.* **regression coefficient; regression weight;** (2) (with three or more variables) *syn.* **coefficient of partial regression.**

coefficient of relative variation, Pearson: a statistic used in comparing the relative variability of two or more variables when the means of these variables are not similar; computed from the formula $V = \dfrac{100\sigma}{M}$, where σ is the standard deviation of the distribution and M is the arithmetic mean of the distribution.

coefficient of reliability: (r_{1I}, r_{2II}, etc.) indicates the degree of consistency with which a test or other instrument measures: (a) the coefficient of correlation between a series of observations or scores and an equivalent but independent series of observations or scores of the same type on the same individuals, for example, the coefficient of correlation between the scores obtained by the same group on two forms of the same test; (b) an estimate of consistency derived from item-test data obtained from a single administration, as the Kuder-Richardson formulas. *Syn.* **index of consistency; reliability coefficient;** *see* **Kuder-Richardson formulas;** *dist. f.* **index of reliability.**

coefficient of reproducibility: an indication of the extent to which a person's response pattern to a set of items in an attitude scale can be reproduced from a knowledge of his rank score on the scale. See **reproducibility.**

coefficient of skewness: any one of several measures used to express the degree of skewness or asymmetry of a frequency distribution, for example, the ratio of the cube root of the third moment about the mean to the standard deviation, or the mean minus the mode, divided by the standard deviation. *Syn.* **measure of skewness.**

coefficient of stability: a coefficient of reliability of the type based on correlation between test and retest, with an intervening period of time. See **coefficient of reliability; reliability (2); reliability, stability.**

coefficient of validity: (1) the coefficient of correlation between a criterion variable and one or more independent variables that purport to measure or are used to predict the criterion; (2) the coefficient of correlation found to exist between the results secured from the measuring device being evaluated and those secured through the use of a criterion measure. *Syn.* **validity coefficient.**

coefficient of variability: *syn.* **coefficient of variation.**

coefficient of variation: a measure of dispersion or relative variability equal to 100 times the standard deviation divided by the arithmetic mean; the standard deviation expressed as a percentage of the mean. *Syn.* **coefficient of variability;** *see* **coefficient of dispersion.**

coefficient, phi (ϕ): an index of correlation between two dichotomous variables; based on the ratio of frequencies or proportions in the cells of a fourfold table; a statistic, closely related to chi square, for estimating the correlation between two truly dichotomous variables (or, with modifications, between one true dichotomy and one arbitrarily dichotomized variable or between two artificially dichotomized variables).

coefficient, rank correlation: a somewhat loose term, generally used to mean the *rank difference correlation coefficient* but sometimes designating the coefficient obtained through the *Spearman foot-rule method of gains.*

coefficient, rank difference correlation: (1) (ρ; rho) a measure of the relationship existing between the rank orders of the observations of two variables, as, for example, the rank order of the pupils of a class in each of two examinations; secured by application of the formula $\rho = 1 - \dfrac{6\Sigma D^2}{N(N^2 - 1)}$, in which ΣD^2 equals the sum of the squared differences in rank for each pair of scores and N equals the number of pairs; *syn.* **rho coefficient;** *dist. f.* **Spearman's foot-rule method of gains;** (2) (τ; tau) less commonly, a similar statistic developed by Kendall; *see* **coefficient, tau.**

coefficient, reflection: a factor expressing the relationship between the amount of light reflected and that absorbed by a given surface; used especially to express the reflection value of colors and shades of paints and various ceiling and wall surfaces.

coefficient, reliability: *see* **coefficient of reliability.**

coefficient, rho: *syn.* **coefficient, rank-difference correlation (1).**

coefficient, standard regression: *syn.* **coefficient, beta regression.**

coefficient, statistical: *syn.* **coefficient.**

coefficient, subject: a numerical coefficient used in the formula derived by Harl Douglass and employed in determining a teaching load to allow for differences in the work involved in teaching different subjects.

coefficient, tau: a method proposed by Kendall for measuring the relationship between rank orders, especially when N is larger than 10 but too small for the normal approximation.

coefficient, tetrachoric correlation: (r_{tet}) a coefficient of correlation computed from a fourfold table on the assumption that each of the dichotomous variables is in reality continuous and normally distributed. *See* **correlation, tetrachoric.**

coefficient, total correlation: the coefficient of correlation between two variables in their original form (not residuals). *Syn.* **entire correlation coefficient; gross correlation coefficient; zero-order correlation coefficient;** *contr. w.* **coefficient of partial correlation.**

coefficient, transformed correlation: *syn.* **Fisher's z.**

coefficient, validity: *syn.* **coefficient of validity.**

coefficient, zero-order correlation: *syn.* **coefficient, total correlation.**

coenotrope (sē′nə·trōp; sen′ə-): (behav. psych.) learned behavior common to the race or species because of common experience.

coercion: (couns.) the use of extreme authority when requiring or ordering that a counselee behave in a specific fashion.

coercive change: *see* **change, coercive.**

Coghillian sequence: (1) in general, development of a finer, more differentiated pattern of behavior from an initially more diffuse, gross, crude, undifferentiated response; (2) more particularly, the differentiation of local motor-reflex responses to tactile stimulation in the fetus or very young infant from a more diffuse "total pattern" or mass reaction. *See* **individuation.**

cogito ergo sum (kō′gi·tō er′gō sōōm): (Lat., lit., "I think, therefore I am") the basis of Descartes' attempt firmly to establish himself and, thereby, a foundation for knowledge.

cognate: (1) a speech sound formed in the same way as another sound but differing in the presence or absence of voice; for example, k is the cognate of g, and d is the cognate of t; (2) in two or more languages which have a common origin in an earlier language, one of those words in the languages which may be grouped on the basis of common origin in the earlier language; for example, *madre* (It.) and *mere* (Fr.), cognates meaning "mother."

cognition: in general, the process of knowing; in particular, the process of knowing based upon perception, introspection, or memory.

cognitive ability: *see* **intelligence, cognitive.**

cognitive deficit: a condition characterized by the inability to solve problems and other cognitive tasks.

cognitive development: *see* **development, cognitive.**

cognitive dissonance: *see* **dissonance, cognitive.**

cognitive experience: *see* **experience, cognitive.**

cognitive growth: *see* **growth, cognitive.**

cognitive identity: *see* **law of identity.**

cognitive intelligence: *see* **intelligence, cognitive.**

cognitive map: *see* **map, cognitive.**

cognitive process: *see* **process, cognitive.**

cognitive structure: the organized mass of previously acquired knowledge which serves as a guide for the comprehension and assimilation of new ideas and concepts.

cognitive time: the amount of time it takes for the individual to convert energy forms into useful information through processing which covers the span from receipt of stimulation to the terminal conversion into meaning.

cognitive trait: *see* **trait, cognitive.**

cognitive working system: a hypothetical construct describing or referring to a dynamic set of subabilities mobilized for the purpose of solving a particular problem. *See* **reading, dynamic substrata-factor theory of.**

coherence: (1) (logic) such a relation between the parts of a discourse or chain of reasoning that each supports and at no point contradicts the others; (2) (philos.) a term used to designate the theory that the criterion of truth is coherence, or harmony, among all experiences relating to the object or situation in question; defined by Royce in terms of harmony with thought of the *absolute.*

coherence theory of knowledge: *see* **knowledge, coherence theory of.**

coherence theory of truth: *see* **truth, coherence theory of.**

cohesion: (1) the tendency of successive or simultaneous acts to become connected with learning; (2) (gestalt) the condition of being held together in a psychological field through closure; an implied field force.

cohesion, civic: (1) the state of clinging together; solidarity of members in any political group due to common ideals of citizenship and civil affairs; (2) adherence to and cooperation with the civic unit.

cohesion, group: (1) the act or state of cohering or cleaving together; usually applied to a group of persons strongly associated by common interests or by a feeling of rapport which unites the group to the point where it will present a common front if challenged; (2) the surplus of psychological forces holding members within the group over those forces which encourage a withdrawal from the group; also called *cohesiveness.*

cohesion, social: *see* **cohesion, group.**

cohesiveness: *see* **cohesion, group.**

cohort analysis: *syn.* **cohort-survival technique.**

cohort-survival technique: the most precise of the techniques used for the projection of natural increase in population; the *cohort-survival* procedure does not directly measure natural increase itself; the population projection is obtained by adding the survivors of the resident population, the expected net migration, and the survivors of the babies born to former residents and to newcomers during the period; this procedure shows not only the size of the projected population but also its expected sex and age distribution.

coincidental markers, method of: a method of matching factors in two or more separate researches.

coinsurance: a form of insurance policy in which the insured agrees to carry insurance equal to a specified percentage of the value of the property insured (usually 80 percent) and receives a reduction in rate on the understanding that, if he should fail to maintain the stipulated amount of insurance, he will be unable to collect the full amount of his claim in the event of a partial loss, since he becomes a coinsurer and is responsible for his proportion of the loss.

cold stuttering: *see* **stuttering, pseudo.**

collage (ko·läzh′): (from Fr. *coller,* "to glue") a composition or picture made up of actual materials, such as wood, cloth, metal, etc., cut out and glued to a base material such as paper or mounting board; used for posters, placards, etc., and sometimes reproduced for use as illustrations.

collate: (data processing) to merge two or more ordered sets of data in order to produce one or more ordered sets which still reflect the original ordering relations; the collation process is the merging of two sequences of cards, each ordered on some mutual key, into a single sequence ordered on the mutual key.

collateral attack: (law) an attempt to destroy the effect of a judgment by reopening the merits of a case or by showing reasons why the judgment should not have been given in an action other than that in which the judgment was given, that is, not in an appeal.

collateral inheritance: *see* **inheritance, collateral.**

collateral learning: *syn.* **learning, concomitant.**

collateral objectives: *see* **objectives, collateral.**

collateral reading: *see* **reading, collateral.**

collateral training: *see* **training, collateral.**

collator: (1) (data processing) a device used to *collate* or merge sets or decks of cards or other units into a sequence; a typical example of a card collator has two *input* feeds, so that two ordered sets may enter into the process, and four *output* stackers, so that four ordered sets can be generated by the process; three comparison stations are used to route the cards to one stacker or the other on the basis of comparison of criteria as specified by plugboard wiring; *see* **input; output;** (2) a component of a teaching machine which measures and records the learning process by collecting and recording data such as number of errors, type of error, time intervals required for response, etc., each item being brought together with that part of the program to which it pertains.

collator-recorder: that component of a teaching machine which records by frame number the number of errors, type of error, response latency, etc.

collection, laboratory: (1) a small group of books belonging to a college or university library but kept in a laboratory, a professor's office, or a department office as a direct help in teaching certain subjects; (2) a group of books in a teacher-education institution, a library school, or other similar institution organized for purposes of demonstration, practice, and project work.

collective bargaining: attempt of employee-employer representatives to reach an agreement on wages and working conditions; presence of a union is often implied; to be contrasted with *professional negotiations,* a method which assumes the employing board's legal right to adopt the final policy concerning wages and conditions governing contractual employment; the distinction has, however, faded over the years. *See* **good faith.**

collective behavior: *see* **behavior, collective.**

collective mind: *see* **mind, collective.**

collective monologue: *see* **monologue, collective.**

collective negotiations: *see* **negotiations, collective.**

college: (1) an institution of higher education usually offering only a curriculum in the liberal arts and sciences and empowered to confer degrees or, in junior colleges, associate titles; (2) a major division of a university (usually the division of arts and sciences), especially one that requires for admission no study beyond the completion of secondary education; *see* **school** (3) and (4); (3) an institution of higher education, such as the French "college"; *see* **lycée;** not a frequent usage in the United States; (4) the building or buildings housing a college; (5) sometimes used in a general sense in referring to an institution of higher education, as when one "goes to college," obtains a "college education," or receives a "college degree," even though in fact one may be attending a university; (6) occasionally still used in its original sense, to designate an association or group, such as the electoral college, the College of Cardinals, or the College of Surgeons.

college, 4-year: (1) a college offering a 4-year curriculum above the high-school level; (2) occasionally, a 4-year junior college beginning with the junior year of high school.

college, agricultural: a college devoted to instruction and research in agriculture and associated subjects; may be an independent college or a part of a university; sometimes used incorrectly to designate a *college of agriculture and mechanic arts* or a *land-grant college.* (In a few instances independent agricultural colleges offer instruction in engineering, home economics, and other fields.)

college, alumni: a program developed as formal and informal extension of instruction for graduates and others who have left college, including single lectures or courses during the academic year and short conferences, courses, and study programs on the campus at commencement time for visiting alumni. *See* **alumni education.**

college aptitude: *see* **aptitude, college.**

college, army: either of the two army schools which present the two highest levels of career courses, the U.S. Army War College and the U.S. Army Command and General Staff College.

college, arts: *syn.* **college, liberal arts.**

college boards: a series of tests offered by a private testing organization to help determine one's ability to do college work; consists of a general test and a series of optional achievement tests; often a requirement for candidates for

admission to a higher education institution. *See* **College Entrance Examination Board; examinations, prematriculation.**

college-bound student: *see* **student, college-bound.**

college, business: a privately operated educational institution offering courses (varying in length from a few months to 4 years) in preparation for technical business occupations such as stenography and bookkeeping; rarely empowered to grant degrees. *Syn.* **business school; private business school.**

college, church-related: a college related to a religious denomination or sect through such means as charter requirement, selection of board members or other officers, financial contributions, and theological or religious belief.

college clearing center: *see* **clearinghouse, college.**

college clearinghouse: *see* **clearinghouse, college.**

college, cluster: one of a group of colleges, typically sharing a common site or at least physically located in close proximity to one another, which make their individual offerings available to one another's students and share facilities and services such as auditorium, library, business administration, graduate school, etc., in the interest of avoiding duplication, reducing costs, and strengthening programs; involves deeper coordination and much closer ties than a consortium. *See* **consortium;** *comp. w.* **college, satellite.**

college, community: a college typically set up to meet the educational needs of a particular community and offering 2-year training, either terminal or preparatory, in prepro-fessional and liberal arts fields; most community colleges are publicly controlled and are coeducational.

college, commuter: a higher education institution serving primarily commuter students. *Ant.* **college, residential.**

college counselor: *see* **counselor, college.**

college credit: *see* **credit, college.**

college day: (couns.) a planned program in which arrangements are made for the meeting of high school seniors (or juniors and seniors) and their parents with representatives of various colleges and universities for the purpose of discussing matters pertaining to possible enrollment in the institutions concerned; an evening program is called a *college night.*

college, denominational: a college having an organic connection with a religious denomination or sect.

college, dental: a school or college of dentistry, usually a professional school of a university, which prepares students who have already completed baccalaureate programs to be dentists; awards degree of *doctor of dental science* (D.D.S.).

college, endowed: a college holding endowment funds or participating in income from productive funds held in trust for the college.

college entrance, accelerated: the admission of able students before they have completed high school; these programs are highly individual with colleges, but some have enrolled freshmen after only three of the usual four years of secondary school training. *Syn.* **early admission.**

College Entrance Examination Board: a board with offices in Princeton, New Jersey, and Los Angeles, California, organized in 1900 by a group of colleges and universities to consider problems involved in the preparation and administration of college entrance examinations and to conduct such examinations.

college entrance examinations: *see* **examinations, college entrance.**

college, essentially military: a classification employed by the military services of the United States to designate those degree-granting institutions having the characteristics of an *essentially military school* and in which the military training is supervised and directed by detailed army officers.

college, evening: (1) an independent institution or a separate administrative unit of a college, junior college, or university the function of which is to organize and administer classes to be held in the late afternoon and evening; primarily intended to accommodate part-time or irregular students, but usually having full academic parity with the parent institution; (2) a center of instruction for both credit and noncredit students, full-time and part-time, maintained by a college or university to extend the program beyond the traditional pattern to a wider clientele. (Evening colleges are in most respects similar to university colleges and extension centers.) *See* **center, extension; college, university.**

college fraternity: *see* **fraternity, college.**

college, general: a name used in some universities for the separately organized freshman and sophomore years, organized either as a distinct unit for a special group of freshmen and sophomores, or as a distinct unit for all freshmen and sophomores.

college housing loans: *see* **housing loans, college.**

college, incorporated: a college established as a corporate body under the laws of a state or of the United States.

college, Jesuit: a school of higher learning administered by the Society of Jesus; such institutions in the United States and elsewhere today commonly meet all the standards of contemporary higher education in addition to providing instruction in the traditional philosophical and theological disciplines. *See* **Jesuit Society.**

college, junior: *see* **junior college.**

college, labor: (1) a center for instruction, study, and propaganda, organized for union members by a trade or industrial union or by a group of union leaders, with a curriculum stressing economics, sociology, history, labor leadership, and problems of unionism; (2) a similar center not restricted to union members, but admitting all workers or those interested in the welfare of workers.

college, land-grant: a college maintained to carry out the purposes of the first Morrill Act (1862) and supplementary legislation, so called because that act granted public lands to the states for the establishment of colleges that would "promote the liberal and practical education of the industrial classes in the several pursuits and professions in life"; the institutions are known collectively as *colleges of agriculture and mechanic arts* or as *land-grant colleges and universities.*

college, liberal arts: (1) an institution of higher education that maintains a 4-year curriculum leading to the bachelor's degree, with a central program of liberal arts and in many cases with one or two closely associated professional schools such as a school of music or fine arts; (2) one of the major divisions of a university, comprising the various departments offering the liberal arts or nonprofessional subjects; referred to by various local names such as *arts college, college of arts and sciences,* or *college of science, literature, and arts.*

college library: *see* **library, college.**

college loan fund: *see* **loan fund, college.**

college, medical: a school or college of medicine, usually a professional school of a university, which prepares students who have already completed baccalaureate programs to be physicians; awards degree of *doctor of medicine* (M.D.).

college, municipal: a college maintained by a municipality.

college night: *see* **college day.**

college, nondenominational: a college having no organic connection with a religious denomination or sect.

college, nonsectarian: a privately controlled college that does not indoctrinate its students in the creed of a particular denomination or sect; sometimes used as a synonym for *nondenominational college.*

college, normal: (obs.) *see* **normal school.**

college of agriculture: a division of a university concerned with teaching and research in agriculture.

college of agriculture and mechanic arts: a college (a separate institution or a part of a state university) whose principal function is offering courses and doing research in agriculture and engineering. *See* **college, land-grant; Morrill Act.**

college of arts and sciences: *syn.* **college, liberal arts.**

college of business: *see* **business, college of.**

college of education: an institution offering at least one program of studies of at least 4 years' duration for the preparation of teachers and other workers in education fields; may be an independent institution or one of the colleges or schools of a university; in many instances has evolved from a former *normal school* or an education department of a university; has had greatest period of development since about 1915. *See* **teachers college.**

college of engineering: a school or college of a university providing study at the undergraduate and/or graduate level in engineering; degrees awarded are typically *bachelor of science in engineering* (B.S.E.) and *master of science in engineering* (M.S.E.); sometimes referred to as *school of engineering.*

college of home economics: an administrative division of a university which deals with teaching and research in the various areas of home economics; sometimes called college of family living.

college of Jewish studies: an institution for Jewish adult study on an academic level which may also carry on a program for the education of teachers and group workers.

college of liberal arts: *syn.* **college, liberal arts.**

college of science, literature, and arts: *syn.* **college, liberal arts.**

college of the air: a series of college courses broadcast as lessons on a regular schedule with provision for directed study and supplementary course outlines and materials.

college-operated station: *see* **station, college-operated.**

college philanthropy: *see* **philanthropy, college.**

college placement: *see* **placement, college.**

college-preparatory curriculum: *see* **curriculum, college-preparatory.**

college prerequisites: *see* **prerequisites, college.**

college, private: a college under control of a governing board independent of public governmental agencies except for charter and statutory limitations; more properly designated as *privately controlled college.*

college residence, head of: *see* **director of dormitory.**

college, resident: a college or university in which the majority of students reside in facilities provided by the institution or are in off-campus facilities nearby which are not the family homes of the students. *Syn.* **residential college;** *see* **college within a college;** *ant.* **college, commuter.**

college, residential: *syn.* **college, resident.**

college, satellite: a unit college, to some degree autonomous, of a larger college or university with which it shares some facilities; may be a spin-off from an established institution with its own complex of buildings, including class and seminar rooms, reference library, residence and dining halls, and social and recreational facilities and with its own staff and specialized program; sometimes the term is applied to one of a group of cluster colleges which together make up the full university. *See* **college, cluster.**

college scholarship service: *see* **scholarship service, college.**

college, sectarian: a college controlled by a board of trustees or other body selected from or representing a religious denomination or sect.

college, senior: a division of a 4-year college consisting of the last 2 (junior and senior) years.

college, state: a college maintained by a state; often used within a state to designate the land-grant college offering technical curricula in agriculture, home economics, and engineering, as distinguished from the state university.

college student: *see* **student, college.**

college supervisor: *see* **supervisor, college.**

college, teachers: *see* **teachers college.**

college, training: *syn.* **training school** (1).

college, university: a name given occasionally to a form of combined day and evening school or extension center conducted by a university and sometimes stressing academic courses leading to degrees; a phase of university extension especially for part-time adult students.

college within a college: an undergraduate instructional unit concerned primarily with general education or the liberal arts in which students and faculty live and study in the same area; recently tried in some places as a means of overcoming problems attributed to large enrollments and depersonalization; sometimes called *residential college.* *See* house plan.

college work study program: *see* **program, college work study.**

collegiate church: a church of the later Middle Ages in Europe having a considerable staff and which, when provided with a fund or foundation for the education of poor scholars, was also considered a school. (Winchester and Eton in England began as collegiate churches.)

collegiate church school: a term used to refer to the teaching of youth, usually free, at collegiate churches during the later Middle Ages in Europe. *See* **collegiate church.**

collegiate journalism: *see* **journalism, collegiate.**

collegium musicum (kə·lē′ji·əm mu′si·kəm): an organization of players of music emphasizing the study and performance of music written from the late Middle Ages through the baroque period; the music is performed either on extant instruments from these earlier periods or on authentic replicas.

collinearity: the characteristic of lying on or belonging to the same straight line.

colloquial pronunciation: *see* **pronunciation, colloquial.**

colloquialism: a word, phrase, or pronunciation used ordinarily in conversation and accepted in informal speech and writing but not used or accepted in formal speech and writing.

colloquium: a class organization, usually at the graduate level, in which a conference related to advanced research projects constitutes the essential part of the class activity and serves as a means for planning, executing, and evaluating progress on research projects. *See* **seminar.**

colloquy: a method of collective inquiry characterized by the presentation of testimony by a group of experts and questions, answers, and discussion by both the experts and the audience on the matter under consideration.

colophon: (Gk., lit., "summit," "finishing touch") (1) an inscription included at the end of a book giving such data as names of designer, illustrator, and printer and type faces and paper used; (2) an emblem on the cover, title page, or elsewhere on a book serving as the publisher's identification mark.

color agnosia: *see* **agnosia, color.**

color and object relationships: *see* **color, objective stage of.**

color blindness: *see* **blindness, color.**

color circle: *syn.* **color wheel.**

color coding: *see* **coding, color.**

color, decorative stage of: (art ed.) in children's paintings, the stage of color in which the child merely enjoys the use of color without referring it to meaning or object.

color discrimination: *see* **discrimination, color.**

color dynamics: *see* **dynamics, color.**

color, emotional characteristics of: (1) attributes arising from color used as an extension and reflection of one's emotions; (2) emotional qualities attributed to color which are largely determined associatively through the effect of past experiences and which are of a highly individualized nature; for example, horror might be red to one person, possibly associated with blood, whereas to another it might be green.

color film: *see* **film, color.**

color, haptic: color use or description that is the outcome of emotional or body reactions; in the most general and bold sense, the repetition of one and the same color for the same emotional experience; in the individual and sensitive meaning, color relationships that are determined by the emotional effects color has on us.

color harmony: agreement, conformity, and unity of effect achieved in accordance with aesthetic principles through the existence of color relationship among the components of a design, composition, or other art form.

color, objective stage of: (art ed.) the schematic stage of children's creative growth, when the child discovers that there is a relationship between color and object and

through repetition and the feeling of self-assurance achieved thereby develops a color schema, such as brown for the ground. *See* **developmental stage, schematic; schema, color.**

color, personification of: seeing and dealing with color as if it were a living being, introducing it as a living symbol; for example, two friends, close and harmonious in their relationship, represented by colors close in value and intensity, harmonious in hue.

color plates, Ishihari: *see* **Ishihari color plates.**

color, realistic: color use or description done according to our visual percept; in the most general and bold sense, the assignment of one local color always to the same object; in the individual and more sensitive meaning, concern with the changing effects of colors, as with distance, light and shadow, or with the optically perceivable influences of one color on another.

color schema: *see* **schema, color.**

color sensation: the perception in terms of color of stimuli received by the optic nerve and transmitted to the brain, consisting of differing wavelengths of light broken into the spectral hues, such as red, orange, yellow, green, blue, and violet. [Properties of color sensation generally considered in teaching the subject are modifications of *hue* (red, orange, yellow, etc.), value (tints and shades), and intensity (grayness or vividness of a hue or its modifications toward gray).] *See* **teaching, color.**

color sense: an innate feeling for color that implies the ability to recognize, match, select, or harmonize colors without conscious recourse to thought or reason.

color, subjective stage of: (art ed.) the stage of dawning realism in children's creative growth, from 9 to 11 years of age, when their color relationships are related to their emotional reactions and are highly subjective. *See* **developmental stage, dawning-realism.**

color teaching: *see* **teaching, color.**

color theory: one of a number of bodies of systematized knowledge dealing with the phenomena of color perception, variously based on specific observation of color phenomena from the chemical, physical, or psychological points of view or on individual systems of organizing this knowledge; generally designated by the point of view represented (the pigmental, spectrum, or optical theories of color) or by the theorist's name, Munsell, Ostwald, Brewster, etc. *See* **color harmony; color sensation; teaching, color.**

color, tone: *see* **tone color.**

color vision: *see* **vision, color.**

color-vision test, illuminant-stable: *see* **test, illuminant-stable color-vision.**

color, visual: *syn.* **color, realistic.**

color wheel: a device used in teaching color theory, consisting of a circle divided into a number of segments corresponding to some system of color organization, and by means of which the following typical color groups may be shown: analogous colors, complements, split complements, and triads. *Syn.* **color circle.**

color, words in: *see* **words in color.**

coloring book: *see* **book, coloring.**

Columbian primer: *see* **primer, Columbian.**

column diagram: *see* **diagram, column.**

column form: the vertical, single arrangement in which spelling words are presented, in isolation from related words that make up connected discourse, for purposes of study or testing. *Contr. w.* **context form.**

column graph: *syn.* **diagram, column.**

column heading: *syn.* **caption** (1).

combat drill: *see* **drill, combat.**

combat readiness training: *see* **training, combat readiness.**

combative exercises: activities involving hand-to-hand or bodily contact, such as hand wrestling, boxing, and wrestling, used for developing an aggressive spirit and self-defense skills.

combative measures training: *see* **training, combative measures.**

combination: (stat.) one of the different sets into which a number of objects may be grouped, the arrangement of the objects within the group not being considered. *Dist. f.* **permutation.**

combination laboratory: *see* **laboratory, combination.**

combination, number: *see* **number combination.**

combination of classes: putting children registered for two or more distinct subjects into a single class to be taught by a single teacher.

combination of grades: grouping pupils of two or more grades into a single class for the purpose of carrying on classroom activities and keeping the class size at a desirable level.

combination of measures: (stat.) (1) the forming of a *composite;* (2) a *composite* itself.

combination plan: the procedure whereby conferences in foreman training for employed workers are carried on partly in company time and partly in the workers' time.

combination room: *syn.* **multipurpose room.**

combinational effect: association or insightful response through meaning or discovery of relationships; integration.

combined dimensions: a term used to designate two or more related measures of pupil performance expressed in a single score; thus, if the number of exercises done correctly in a uniform test is taken as the test score, this single score represents the combined dimensions of rate and accuracy.

combined method: (1) in communication with the deaf, the simultaneous use of speech, speech reading, finger spelling, and hearing aids by the speaker and the observer; *syn.* **Rochester method;** (2) a method of teaching reading that combines elements from several methods such as the ABC method, phrase method, and sight method.

combined operation: *see* **operation, combined.**

combined school: a school composed of two or more horizontal units of grade-level groups, such as a combined elementary and junior high school.

combined system in the education of the deaf: an educational system operating with both oral and nonoral classes in the same school.

combined training: *see* **training, combined.**

combined variation: *see* **variation, combined.**

combining behavior: *see* **behavior, combining.**

combo: a term used in popular music and in jazz to designate a small group ("combination") of musicians who perform as a consistently unified organization.

combustible construction: *see* **construction, combustible.**

comedy, musical: *see* **musical comedy.**

comic book: a cheap magazine entirely devoted to comic strips.

comic opera: *see* **opera, comic.**

comic strip: one of a series of cartoon drawings, usually four-panel, printed daily for entertainment in newspapers; originally humorous in content and primarily for children, they have become in many cases serious, often tragic, daily series of adventure or detective stories for adults; such series are printed in color in special Sunday supplements.

comics: certain cheap pamphlets using the comic-strip technique to present stories and other matter mainly for children; sometimes represent pictorially stories which are taken from children's literature; not necessarily funny; commonly sold on the book stands in stations, drugstores, etc.

comma blunder: *syn.* **comma splice.**

comma splice: the use of the comma instead of a full stop (period, question mark, etc.) or a semicolon between sentences or independent clauses, for example, "This is an amusing book, I enjoyed reading it." *Syn.* **comma blunder.**

command: in automatic data processing, a set of signals initiating specific action in an automatic computer; one part of an *instruction.*

command and staff exercise: *see* **exercise, command and staff.**

command post exercise: *see* **exercise, command post.**

command, transfer: in automatic data processing, a signal which conditionally or unconditionally specifies the location of the next instruction and directs the automatic computer to that instruction. *See* **transfer, conditional; transfer, unconditional.**

commandant: any officer commanding an Army or Air Force school.

commandant of cadets: (mil. ed.) an officer who executes the leadership and military program in a service academy and in ROTC detachments. *See* **superintendent.**

commando exercises: training and conditioning exercises resembling movements and activities engaged in by commando or guerrilla troops.

commencement: *syn.* **graduation·(2).**

commensurable: characteristic of two or more measurable quantities if the same unit of measure can be applied to each an integral number of times; for example, a distance of 3 inches is commensurable with a distance of $2\frac{3}{4}$ inches since each is an integral multiple of $\frac{1}{4}$ inch. *Contr. w.* **incommensurable.**

commentary: the verbal sound accompaniment to a motion picture, filmstrip, or other visual material; spoken by a commentator. *Syn.* **narration.**

commentator: a person who gives a commentary for radio, television, sound film, or sound filmstrip. *Syn.* **narrator.**

commercial algebra: *see* **mathematics, business.**

commercial art: *see* **art, commercial.**

commercial club: (obsoles.) *syn.* **club, business.**

commercial education: (obsoles.) *syn.* **business education.**

commercial geography: *see* **geography, commercial.**

commercial high school: *syn.* **high school, business.**

commercial history: *see* **history, commercial.**

commercial law: (obsoles.) *syn.* **law, business.**

commercial museum: *see* **museum, commercial.**

commercial music: *see* **music, commercial.**

commercial school: *syn.* **college, business.**

commercial studies: (obs.) *syn.* **business education, basic; business subject, technical.**

commercialized recreation: *see* **recreation commercialized.**

commission: (mil. ed.) (1) *v.* to make ready for or put in service or use, as, to commission an aircraft or a ship; (2) *n.* a written order giving a person rank and authority as an officer in the armed forces; also, rank and authority given by such an order.

commission, citizens': *syn.* **advisory committee.**

commission of inquiry, Mosely: a British group, led by Alfred Mosely, which visited representative American schools in 1903 to check "their bearing upon national commerce and industry"; an early example of *comparative education* in practice.

commissioner, county: *see* **superintendent, county.**

commissioner of education: (1) the designation sometimes used for the chief school official and executive head of the state public school authority; *see* **director of education; superintendent of public instruction;** (2) the designation used for the chief executive officer of the United States Office of Education of the Department of Health, Education, and Welfare.

commissioning program, bootstrap: *see* **program, bootstrap commissioning.**

commissions: payments, usually on a percentage basis, made to solicitors of advertising and subscriptions for student publications.

commitment: (1) a personal or group engagement to support and follow a line of action, an orientation, a point of view, or a choice; usually involves some public declaration of the engagement; used especially in the vocabularies of writers on religion, existentialism, and group dynamics; (2) the legal act of assigning a person to an institution, including but not limited to a school located in a correctional institution or detention home.

committed truant: *see* **truant, committed.**

committee, ad hoc: *see* **ad hoc.**

committee, advisory: *see* **advisory committee.**

committee, agricultural advisory: *see* **committee, agricultural citizens'.**

committee, agricultural citizens': a term used extensively in agricultural education in referring to *advisory committees* composed of lay citizens.

committee, biracial: *see* **biracial committee.**

committee, business and office education advisory: a group of local business representatives selected by the school administration and the business and office education teachers to advise the school in regard to new developments and needs of businesses in the community.

committee, citizens' advisory: *syn.* **advisory committee.**

committee, distributive education advisory: a group of persons representative of both the school and the business community which gives advice that may be used for the development and improvement of the distributive education program.

committee, guidance: a group consisting primarily of teachers, counselors, and the principal of a particular school elected or appointed to study the existing guidance program of the school and to offer advice regarding its functions, activities, and proposed plans; where appropriate this committee should be involved in planning student assemblies and staff and PTA programs which are designed to support the school's guidance program; students are often included as members.

committee, lay advisory: *syn.* **advisory committee.**

committee, library: *see* **library committee.**

committee, merchants' advisory: *syn.* **committee, distributive education advisory.**

committee, production: a committee charged with the responsibility of making available to staff members copies of newly developed courses of study, units, outlines, and other curriculum materials.

committee, school: *see* **school committee.**

committee, social service: *see* **social service committee.**

committee, steering: a committee generally representative of the various interests involved and responsible for the overall determination and sometimes implementation of policies in regard to a project or activity that is to be undertaken; may function on national, state, or local level, for example, a *curriculum steering committee* within a particular school.

committee system: (1) (elem. ed.) a plan by which a number of classroom committees are organized for appropriate pupil participation in various activities of the school; (2) a method of determining policies or procedures through committee action.

committee, town school: *see* **town system.**

commodity economics: *see* **economics, commodity.**

commodity taxes: *see* **taxes, commodity.**

common activities of living: the common living and social functions such as production, distribution, consumption, conservation, and communication as incorporated and integrated into the curriculum and handled in such a way as to assist children with their developmental tasks and persistent life situations.

common branches: (obs.) the elementary-school subject-matter curriculum.

common business-oriented language: *see* **language, common business-oriented.**

common elements: *syn.* **identical elements.**

common factor: *see* **factor, common.**

common-factor space: *see* **space, common-factor.**

common-factor variance: *syn.* **communality.**

common labor: work for which little or no training is required.

common-language media: magnetic or punched tape or cards that may be used in various kinds of equipment to print or compute administrative business records automatically.

common law: *see* **law, common.**

common learnings: the knowledges, abilities, skills, attitudes, and appreciations that a school regards as essential for all children and youth.

common-learnings program: *see* **program, common-learnings.**

common machine language: *see* **language, common machine.**

common school: (obsoles.) designation for the traditional 8-year public elementary school providing a foundation program of education.

Common School Revival: a term sometimes used to designate the complex of educational movements in the first half of the nineteenth century which resulted in the establishment of free public schools; the improvement of curriculum, teaching methods, and schoolhouses; and the establishment of teacher-training institutions; sometimes restricted to the designation of steps taken after 1830 to improve administrative control, to provide more liberal financial support for educational institutions at all levels, and to secure legislative establishment of state systems of education. (In recent years, historians of education have avoided use of the term because it is too restricted to include the many educational movements of the period and because the period was not one of "revival" but of pioneering educational progress.)

common-school subjects: *see* **subject, common-school.**

common sense: (1) in Aristotelian psychology, a faculty by which particular sensibles are brought together and common sensibles perceived; (2) a faculty of mind, thought (by themselves) to be possessed by some school administrators and other practical men, which sets limits to processes of philosophic or scientific criticism and analysis and which locates and characterizes *reality* despite these processes; used as an antidote for the skepticism and subjectivism thought to be engendered by too much philosophizing; (3) the more or less consistent social beliefs held by men in a culture group; such beliefs operate as important determinants of choice and action and are held subconsciously by most men moved by them; (4) preanalytic comprehension or judgment of a situation or object (usually untrained if not untrainable).

common-sense realism: *see* **realism, common-sense.**

common specialist training: *see* **training, common specialist.**

common trait: *see* **trait, common.**

commons: a dining hall of a university or college where meals are eaten in common, with no distinction for rank.

Commonwealth List of Teacher Traits: a list of the 25 qualities desirable for the classroom teacher developed by W. W. Charters and Douglas Waples and which includes adaptability, attractiveness, breadth of interest, carefulness, consideration, cooperation, dependability, enthusiasm, fluency, forcefulness, good judgment, health, honesty, industry, leadership, magnetism, neatness, open-mindedness, originality, progressiveness, promptness, refinement, scholarship, self-control, and thrift.

communal function: *see* **function, communal.**

communal Sunday school, Jewish: *see* **Sunday school, Jewish communal.**

communal weekday school, Jewish: *see* **weekday school, Jewish communal.**

communality: that part of the variance which a test shares with other tests in the same battery; the sum of the squares of the orthogonal factor loadings on a test.

communicable disease: *see* **disease, communicable.**

communication: (1) the arousal of common meanings, with their resulting reactions, between communicator and interpreter through the use of language or other signs and symbols; a social act involving two or more persons in a field situation; face-to-face the roles of the communicator and interpreter are constantly shifting; in other situations there is less possibility for this interaction; (2) the establishment of a social unit among human beings by the use of language signs and by the sharing of common sets of rules for various goal-seeking activities; (3) (philos.) the process whereby a human society continues to exist by transmitting its values, concepts, attitudes, habits, and skills (nonmaterial cultural components) so that the young may participate in the common life.

communication, confidential: (couns.) secret information revealed in a private counseling setting where a spirit of trust and confidence prevails.

communication disability: *see* **disability, communication.**

communication, human: (1) as used in communications theory, the subscience that investigates the relations between persons who select messages (sources) and persons (destinations) who interpret and are affected by them; (2) the study of mass media of communication and their effects on mass audiences, other cultures, etc.; this usage somewhat arbitrarily restricts the meaning of the term.

communication in counseling: the process of interchanging ideas and information in a counseling setting through such means as words, nonverbal cues, symbolizations, nuances of tone, bodily gestures, and silence. See communication (1).

communication model: a display of the steps in a communication.

communication net: a pattern, usually formally organized, through which communication takes place. See communication (1).

communication, nonverbal: the meaningful transfer of thought or emotion through means other than words or speaking; based on an internal process leading to subverbal insight. See communication in counseling.

communication, privileged: communication between persons which neither can be legally required to reveal; generally reserved to the communication between doctor and patient, lawyer and client, and clergyman and confessant; in most instances school counselors do not have privileged communication.

communication, satellite: the use of one or a series of orbiting man-made satellites which are equipped to receive, amplify, and retransmit (or merely reflect from its surface) microwave signals from and to specially adapted transmitters and receivers several hundred or thousand miles apart. (The first experimental application for transmission of radio, television, and telephone signals between Europe and the United States was made by Telstar satellite in July 1962.)

communication theory: see information theory.

communication unit: (lang. arts) a group of words which cannot be further divided without the loss of their essential meaning as a group; grammatically, an independent clause with any of its modifiers.

communications: (ind. arts) study of and experiences with the mechanical devices and methods used in the transmission, reception, and recording of verbal and graphic messages.

communications, audiovisual: that branch of educational theory and practice concerned primarily with the design, use, and evaluation of messages which control the learning process both as components and as entire instructional systems; emphasis is on instruction and learning procedures employing nonprinted materials including motion pictures, television, sound and silent filmstrips, slide sets, recordings, transparencies, projected opaque pictures, and a variety of graphic arts.

communications, business: an area of study dealing with the transmission of ideas; business letters, oral and written reports, charts, graphs, and interviews are common forms of business communication.

communications specialist: a person having broad knowledge of audiovisual media and capable of organizing the content of audiovisual materials to be produced so that the stated purposes will best be served.

communications theory: a technology (not a theory) that deals with communication in all its aspects—physical, psychological, sociological. (The parallels between processes of communication in machines, organisms, and institutions are described, and common terms for parallel processes are invented or adapted from old ones.) See information theory.

communicative skill: see skill, communicative.

community: (1) any group of people, not necessarily in spatial proximity, who share basic interests, for example, the community of scientists; (2) a group or company of people living fairly close together in a more or less compact, contiguous territory, who are coming to act together in the chief concerns of life; see neighborhood; (3) (R.C. ed.) a group of men or of women who bind themselves by vow to live a celibate common life and who dedicate their lives to the service of Christ and his church; see order, religious.

Community Action Program: see Program, Community Action.

community activity: see activity, community.

community, adjustment to: see adjustment to community.

community agency: see agency, community.

community center: a meeting place in a city or rural community where people living nearby come together to participate in social, recreational, cultural, and philanthropic activities and to build up a democratic organization that will minister to the needs of the community.

community-center school: a school attempting to serve not only persons of school age but all ages and groups of a community, in the evening as well as during the day; its workshop, library, swimming pool, gymnasium, assembly hall, and other rooms are open for use by the people of the community; sometimes used synonymously with community school.

community center school, Jewish: a communal school located in a Jewish community center.

community center, university: a cooperative project carried on by a university and a community to promote the public welfare by making the community a center of educational and welfare enterprises.

community-centered curriculum: see curriculum, community-centered.

community-centered problem: see problem, community-centered.

community chest: syn. fund, community.

community civics: see civics, community.

community college: see college, community.

community control: see control, community.

community coordinating council: a council of civic, social, educational, service, and other agencies and organizations that correlates the interests and services of those agencies and combines their efforts for the elimination of overlapping of effort and for a better understanding and solution of local problems; school and youth programs are included in these activities.

community council: syn. community coordinating council.

community council of social agencies: syn. community coordinating council.

community day school: a school for day pupils and adults developed by the Federal government to meet the educational and social needs of Indian communities.

community development: (1) the efforts of a community to identify its problems and to attempt to establish and reach its goals primarily through the application of the educational process; (2) the induction and educational management of that kind of interaction between the community and its people which leads to the improvement of both; (3) local, state, or Federal projects to improve the economic and/or social standards of an area by development of industry and improved housing, transportation, and educational, recreational, and health facilities; (4) special activities or projects undertaken in developing countries for the general improvement of living conditions in a village or area; may include but not be limited to such activities as sanitation, erecting community buildings, developing industries, or providing recreational facilities.

community educational survey: see survey, community educational.

community fund: see fund, community.

community game: any game that may be participated in by both children and adults.

community guidance center: see guidance center, community.

community health: see health, community.

community high school: see high school, community.

community hygiene: see hygiene, community.

community influential: one of the relatively small number of people in any community whose social and/or economic power or standing is greater than most and whose opinions and preferences carry more than ordinary weight; most people occupying positions of community leadership are community influentials, but not all community influentials occupy formal positions as civic leaders or even appear overtly active in civic affairs. *Contr. w.* **community leader.**

community institution: a local social institution, such as a church or school, serving chiefly the people of a small area and supported by the local group.

community interest: (1) the common concerns shared, directly or vicariously, by community members; (2) the index of communality, of identification of members with an assumed public good.

community journalism: *see* **journalism, community.**

community, lagging: a community that is backward in respect to providing effective economic, social, and aesthetic opportunities for its members and is generally in arrears in its facilities for public school education.

community leader: any of those people in any community who take responsibility for seeing that policy is executed and that jobs or programs bearing on the welfare of the community or subgroups of the community are carried out. *Contr. w.* **community influential.**

community music: *see* **music, community.**

community nursery school: *see* **nursery school, community.**

community occupational survey: *see* **survey, community occupational.**

community of persuasion: *see* **persuasion, community of.**

community organization: (1) broadly, any organized group of the community, particularly an educational, recreational, religious, political, or welfare agency; (2) specifically, the movement toward integration and condensation of the work of these agencies, as, for example, in the case of an adult education council.

community program: *see* **program, community.**

community recreation: *see* **recreation, community.**

community resources: *see* **resources, community.**

community room: a room in a school building, usually equipped with a stage or platform, designed for meetings of community groups.

community, rural: *see* **rural community.**

community school: (1) a school that is intimately connected with the life of the community and that tries to provide for the educational needs of all in the community; sometimes serves as a center for many community activities and utilizes community resources in improving the educational program; (2) a somewhat ambiguous synonym for consolidated school; *see* **consolidated school;** (3) sometimes used as a synonym for evening school; *see* **evening school;** *contr. w.* **neighborhood school.**

community service: activities and enterprises conducted by persons, institutions, and the community as a whole for the maintenance and improvement of desirable social conditions in a locality.

community services, structured: coordination services available on a multiagency basis, developed and maintained by a central information processing agency.

community singing: *see* **singing, community.**

community study: *see* **study, community.**

community supervisor: *see* **supervisor, community.**

community survey: *see* **survey, community.**

community theory: the doctrine proposing that immigrants should foster, in addition to the major American civilization, the cultural, historic, and religious inheritance of their respective minority groups. *See* **Americanization theory.**

community trust: a type of philanthropic foundation that holds the gifts and bequests of many donors and administers them according to a trust agreement.

community-unit school: a school in which a community, as defined by some geographical and sociological boundaries, becomes the attendance area served by the school; the school may represent an administrative unit or may be part of a larger administrative unit.

commutative group: *see* **group (4).**

commutative law: *see* **law, commutative.**

commuter: (higher ed.) a student who travels daily between his home and the institution he attends for classes, study, and other activities. *Ant.* **student, resident** (2).

commuter college: *see* **college, commuter.**

commuting student: *see* **student, commuting.**

companion: (voc. ed.) a person who cares for the elderly or for convalescent people, acting as an aide or friend and attending to the employer's personal needs.

company school: *syn.* **corporation school.**

comparability: the condition existing when scores on two or more different tests or subscales of the same test have been converted to standard scores with the same mean and standard deviation so that they may be compared; that is, conversion to standard scores makes scores on the different tests comparable.

comparable forms: *syn.* **equivalent forms.**

comparable groups: *see* **groups, comparable.**

comparable information: *see* **information, comparable.**

comparable measures: *see* **measures, comparable.**

comparable scores: *see* **scores, comparable.**

comparable test: *see* **test, comparable.**

comparative behavior analysis: *see* **behavior analysis, comparative.**

comparative education: a field of study dealing with the comparison of educational theory and practice in different countries for the purpose of broadening and deepening understanding of educational problems beyond the boundaries of one's own country and sometimes also helping to solve problems in one country by looking at the ways they have been solved in other settings.

comparative-education society: an organization of university professors, administrators, and governmental and other workers in the fields of comparative and international education, such as the Comparative and International Education Society, founded in 1956, to promote the study of comparative and international education in universities, to conduct field trips to foreign school systems, to encourage research projects, and to cooperate with international educational agencies.

comparative journalism: *see* **journalism, comparative.**

comparative jurisprudence: *see* **jurisprudence, comparative.**

comparative linguistic analysis: *see* **analysis, comparative linguistic.**

comparative literature: *see* **literature, comparative.**

comparative method: (pol. sci.) (1) a system of study which aims, through the examination of existing polities or those which have existed in the past, to assemble a definite body of material from which the investigator, by selection, comparison, and elimination, may discover the ideal types and progressive forces of political history; (2) a system of study which involves the collection, classification, analysis, and description of governmental theory and practice in more than one governmental unit so as to ascertain similarities and differences.

comparative musicology: *see* **ethnomusicology.**

comparative negligence: *see* **negligence, comparative.**

comparative prediction: *see* **prediction, comparative.**

comparative psychology: *see* **psychology, comparative.**

comparative religion: *see* **religion, comparative.**

comparative study: *see* **study, comparative.**

comparative subtraction: *see* **subtraction, comparative.**

comparator: (1) that component of a teaching machine which, after the pupil's response, makes an evaluation of it; transmission follows to the pupil, the reinforcement dispenser, the collator, and/or the sequence control unit depending on the mode of operation of the machine; *see* **selector unit;** (2) in automatic computers, a circuit which compares two signals and supplies an indication of their agreement or disagreement; also called *comparer.*

comparer: *see* **comparator** (2).

comparison drill: *see* **drill, comparison.**

comparison, graphical: *see* **graphical comparison.**

comparison, orthogonal: (stat.) a method by which a subdivision of a sum of scores is further divided into components so that each has one degree of freedom; used in analysis of variance.

comparison, paired: *see* **paired comparison.**

compartment: (stat.) *syn.* **cell.**

compartmentalization: a kind of thinking that isolates from each other facts and principles that ought logically to be related; believed to be an unconscious defensive measure to prevent contradictions; in older psychology the extreme case of compartmentalization was termed *bulkhead delusions.*

compatibility, equipment: (data processing) the characteristics of computers by which one computer may accept and process data prepared by another computer without conversion or code modification.

compatible: capable of existing together in harmony; without conflict of interest in law, as would be the two positions of one person who is both teacher and board member in the same district. *See* **incompatible offices.**

compensating error: *see* **error, compensating.**

compensation: (1) a psychological mechanism by which the individual overcomes conscious or unconscious feelings of incompetence, inferiority, or inadequacy by excelling in a particular line of endeavor or by adopting a particular type of behavior or attitude; (2) the total paid to or for a faculty member, usually including primarily salary, payments into retirement funds, and insurance premiums; (3) indemnification, payment of damages, making amends by giving an equivalent or substitute of equal value.

compensation neurosis: *syn.* **neurosis, traumatic.**

compensation, sensory: the counterbalancing of any defect in the sensory system by increased functioning of another sense organ or unimpaired parts of the defective organ.

compensatory education: an education program that seeks to compensate for environmental and experiential deficits in relation to such areas as schooling, housing, employment, poverty, civil rights, and the cultural patterns and life-styles of minority groups; attempts to discover and develop the latent potential of the learner, with emphasis on experiences, activities, and materials specifically designed for cognitive and motivational growth.

compensatory language experience: *see* **language experience, compensatory.**

compensatory movement: any movement of the body or one of its members resulting in the restoration of equilibrium when the body or one of its members has been off balance.

compensatory reflex: *see* **reflex, compensatory.**

competence, functional: ability to apply to practical situations the essential principles and techniques of a particular subject-matter field.

competence, socioindustrial: *see* **socioindustrial competence.**

competencies, general occupational: those skills, concepts, and attitudes needed by all workers regardless of their occupations or specific jobs. *Syn.* **general related learnings; occupational relations learnings.**

competencies, occupational: *see* **competencies, general occupational; competencies, specific job; competencies, specific occupational.**

competencies, specific job: those concepts, skills, and attitudes which are highly specialized and relate directly to (*a*) the single job classification in which the student-learner is interested and (*b*) the specific requirements of the student-learner's training station position.

competencies, specific occupational: those concepts, skills, and attitudes essential to a broad occupational grouping, those with common usefulness to a family of occupations.

competency, economic: the ability of an individual to practice effectively the business activities of everyday living, for example, using credit wisely, making proper use of various bank services, investing money, buying insurance, and other similar activities; sometimes referred to as *economic literacy.*

competition: (1) in its pure form, the struggle between individuals or groups which is unconscious, unrecognized, and impersonal; (2) conscious struggle or rivalry in which one person or group seeks the same object that is sought for by others at the same time; a contention of two or more persons or groups, short of open conflict, for the same object or goal; (3) sometimes rivalry with the previous record of the individual or group; *contr. w.* **cooperation;** (4) (consumer ed.) a condition in which many buyers and many sellers are competing so that no one of them can control supply, demand, or price.

competition festival: a concert or series of concerts in which a number of individuals or musical organizations compete before judges not for awards but for ratings of merit; performers may also receive from the judges criticism and advice. *See* **music contest.**

competition, forced: (art ed.) in creative activity, that which does not grow from a natural situation but which is introduced through standards and prizes, thus fixing attention on extrinsic motivations.

competition, intercollegiate: interschool participation of colleges and universities in athletic competition in such sports as soccer, lacrosse, basketball, water polo, etc.

competition, interscholastic: scheduled competition between elementary or secondary schools, usually in athletics but also in such activities as speech, dramatics, and music.

competition, mental: a source of mental inhibition consisting of conflict between disconnected processes, with consequent direction of attention into divergent channels.

competition, natural: (art ed.) in creative activity, the innate desire to improve one's own standards and achievements; competition with oneself to do better than one has done; intrinsic motivation.

competition, unit of: *see* **unit of competition.**

competitive bidding: *see* **bidding, competitive.**

competitive class: *see* **class, competitive.**

competitive consumption: *see* **comsumption, competitive.**

competitive sport: *see* **sport, competitive.**

competitive unit: *see* **unit, competitive.**

compile: in automatic data processing, to produce a machine language routine from a routine written in source language by selecting appropriate subroutines.

compiler: (data processing) a computer program more powerful than an assembler; in addition to its translating function, which is generally the same process as that used in an assembler, it is able to replace certain items of input with series of instructions, usually called *subroutines;* thus, where an assembler translates item for item and produces as output the same number of instructions or constants which were put into it, the machine-language program which results from compiling is a translated and expanded version of the original. *Syn.* **compiling routine;** *see* **assembler.**

compiler language: *see* **language, compiler.**

compiling routine: *see* **routine, compiling.**

complacency: the state in which an organism is in a satisfactory working relationship with its surroundings.

complaint, presenting: (couns.) the stated problem of the counselee, as distinguished from the real problem, which may differ in fact or affect.

complementary course: *see* **course, complementary.**

complementary genes: *see* **genes, complementary.**

complementary method: a method of performing subtraction when a minuend figure is smaller than the corresponding subtrahend figure, according to which one finds the complement (with respect to 10) of the subtrahend figure and adds this complement to the minuend figure; thus, in the example $74 - 25$, the student thinks, "5 from 10 is 5, 5 plus 4 is 9; put down the 9"; 2 is then subtracted from 6, either by the *addition,* or *Austrian, method* or by the *take-away method. See* **subtraction, methods of.**

complementary principles: principles that are correlative or reciprocal in that they complete or reinforce one another; principles analogous in their relationships to the organs of the body or to the relationships of complementary colors in art; to be distinguished from bipolarity, which asserts two-poled interdependence, while complementary principles may be many, that is, twofold or manifold relations. *See* **bipolarity, principle of.**

complementary sets: *see* **sets, complementary.**

complete factorial design: *see* **design, complete factorial.**

completion: (correspondence study) the finishing of objectives or lessons and examinations required in a course.

completion education: *syn.* **terminal education.**

completion item: *see* **item, completion.**

completion question: *syn.* **item, completion.**

completion rate: (correspondence study) ratio of the completions to the enrollments minus the cancellations.

completion test: *see* **test, completion.**

complex: (psychoan.) a group of related ideas united by a strong emotional bond that has undergone repression, thus becoming unconscious. *Contr. w.* **constellation.**

complex attitude: *see* **attitude, complex.**

complex, castration: (psychoan.) a fear of loss of genitals, alleged to be a universal experience. (Psychoanalytic theory maintains that a male child, when he first realizes that not all human beings possess a penis, interprets its absence in some as a loss, a belief which prompts a fear of the loss of his own genitals as a punishment, especially for sex offenses and for his incestuous desires in relation to his mother; in the case of the female child, the failure to possess a penis, it is claimed, is interpreted at first as a defect for which the mother is responsible; resentment of the mother is alleged to be harbored by the female child because of this belief.)

complex, culture: *see* **culture complex.**

complex, Electra: (1) the fixation of the daughter's affection upon the father; (2) (psychoan.) the alleged desire, whether conscious or unconscious, on the part of the daughter for sexual relations with the father, with a resultant hostility to the mother rival as well as feelings of guilt about both relations; alleged to be a universal experience of girls during the later preschool period; analogous to the *Oedipus complex* in boys.

complex, father: (1) *syn.* **complex, Electra;** (2) loosely, excessive devotion of a child, whether male or female, to the father. *Contr. w.* **complex, mother; complex, Oedipus.**

complex, guilt: an emotional state of variable intensity in which the individual is dominated by a sense of wrongdoing produced by the belief or knowledge that he has contravened some social custom, ethical principle, or legal regulation.

complex, infantile: (psychoan.) a pathological emotional condition in adult life, resulting from a fixation at a pregenital level, in which the subject's feelings and reactions resemble those of an infant.

complex, inferiority: as used in Adlerian psychoanalytic theory, a repressed complex of feelings and emotions, stemming usually from experienced organ inferiority; also attributed to thwarting of self-love during infancy; sometimes, but ambiguously, used as a synonym for *castration complex. Dist. f.* **inferiority feeling.**

complex, mother: (1) *syn.* **complex, Oedipus;** (2) loosely, excessive devotion of a child, whether male or female, to the mother. *Contr. w.* **complex, Electra; complex, father.**

complex number: *see* **number complex.**

complex, Oedipus (ed′i·pəs; ē′di-): (1) sexual interest of an offspring in a parent of the opposite sex; (2) sexual interest of the son in the mother; *contr. w.* **complex, Electra;** (3) (psychoan.) the constellation of conflicting, emotionally toned thoughts and feelings, partly conscious and partly unconscious, arising in all children as a result of identification with the parent of the same sex and affection for and sexual interest in the parent of the opposite sex, together with a resultant jealousy of the parent of the same sex.

complex transfer: *see* **transfer, complex.**

complex variable: *see* **variable, complex.**

compliance: the act or trait of submitting to the wishes, requests, or dictates of another person or of a group. *Contr. w.* **negativism.**

component, ectomorphic: one of the three chief components of physique named by Sheldon and indicating a fragile, delicate, and linear body structure.

components, intelligence: *see* **intelligence components.**

composite: (1) (stat.) a variable consisting of a mathematical function (usually a weighted sum) of two or more variables, often used to index a more general or complex trait, the constituent variables being thought of as parts of the general trait or at least as saturated with different portions of it, so that when taken together they represent the general trait more faithfully than they would singly; the values of the several variables for each case are merged and lose their identity in a total value for that case, in contradistinction to what occurs when data are intermingled to form a *compound;* test scores may be thought of as composites; (2) (pup. trans.) the designation of a type of bus body construction in which both metal and wood are used.

composite industrial arts laboratory: *see* **laboratory, composite industrial arts.**

composite norm: *see* **norm, composite.**

composite number: *see* **number, composite.**

composite print: *see* **print, composite.**

composite rank: *see* **rank, composite.**

composite rating of teaching: *see* **rating of teaching, composite.**

composite score: *see* **score, composite.**

composite shop: *see* **laboratory, composite industrial arts.**

composition: (1) the act or art of combining a number of parts or elements to make a single entity, the resulting ensemble having some underlying and recognizable unity, as visual structure (line, mass, shape, color, tone), sense, sound, or purpose; applies to all the arts, visual, musical, choreographic, dramatic, and literary; (2) the basic design or underlying structure of any artistic expression, as of a painting, poem, sculpture, or piece of music; *syn.* **design** (4); (3) the tangible result of the act of composing, as the resulting piece of music, painting, or literature; (4) in photography, planned arrangement of items or objects which make up the picture; (5) (lang.) the selection, arrangement, and development of ideas and their expression in appropriate written or spoken form; (6) a fallacy of ambiguity in which one argues from the distributive to the collective use of a word; that is, one presupposes that what is true of a part is also true of the whole, as, "Each of these musicians is outstanding. Therefore, an orchestra made up of them would be equally outstanding"; *see* **division** (5); **fallacy of ambiguity.**

composition, free: a nondirected oral composition spoken by the foreign-language student.

composition, group: composition done jointly by a class or other instructional group, often orally; for example, the writing of a ballad by a class through contributions of the entire class group.

composition, imitative: (for. lang.) composition based on the use of studied material and involving the comprehension and application of selected expressions and constructions.

composition, musical: (1) the act of creating and ordering all the manifold tonal resources of music into a coherent whole; (2) the completed product which results from such an act.

composition, oral: a drill technique to develop active speaking ability in a foreign language wherein a student is asked to describe a single drawing or a series of drawings in a variety of ways.

composition scale: *see* **scale, composition.**

composition, semicontrolled: in foreign language instruction, a technique to develop active speaking and writing skills by requiring the student to describe aspects of a photograph or drawing in a predetermined way.

compound: (stat.) a combination of data resulting from the intermingling of two or more sets of cases (as when two or more correlation tables are combined), each case retaining its own identity, and individual values not being added to or combined with other values; a compound has a population equal to the sum of the populations of the constituent groups, in contradistinction to a composite, which has the population of any one of the component series of observations. *Dist. f. composite.*

compound answer: *see* **answer, compound.**

compound category: *see* **category, compound.**

compound class : *see* **class, compound.**

compound code: *see* **code, compound.**

compound coding: *see* **code, compound.**

compound curve: *syn.* **compound stroke.**

compound number: *see* **number, compound.**

compound phonogram: *see* **phonogram, compound.**

compound probability: *see* **probability, compound.**

compound reflex: *see* **reflex, compound.**

compound sentence: *see* **sentence, compound.**

compound stimulus: *see* **stimulus, compound.**

compound stroke: a unified stroke or writing movement within which there is a reversal of arcs, a convex curve being followed by a concave curve (or the reverse), as in the letter s.

comprehension: the act of understanding the meaning of printed or spoken language as contrasted with the ability to perceive and pronounce words without reference to their meaning.

comprehension, auditory: the ability to understand spoken language.

comprehension level, hearing: the highest level at which an individual can comprehend spoken language; usually the hearing comprehension level is somewhat lower than the reading comprehension level.

comprehension, listening: the understanding of material heard, with respect to the listener's grasp of the meaning of words and phrases, of main ideas, and of supporting or illustrating details.

comprehension, literal: (read.) the understanding of the primary or literal meaning of a word, phrase, or sentence.

comprehension, mechanical: a combination of understanding of spatial relations and mechanical information.

comprehension, paragraph: the ability to read entire paragraphs with full and exact understanding.

comprehension, phrase: the ability to grasp the meaning of word groups or phrases.

comprehension score: *see* **score, comprehension.**

comprehension, sentence: the ability to grasp the meaning of a sentence.

comprehension skills: *see* **skills, comprehension.**

comprehension test: *see* **test, comprehension.**

comprehension, visual: the ability to see and understand written language, pictures, or graphic representations.

comprehension vocabulary: *see* **vocabulary, comprehension.**

comprehension, word: the ability to grasp the meaning or meanings of words.

comprehensive achievement test: *see* **test, comprehensive achievement.**

comprehensive examination: *see* **test, comprehensive achievement.**

comprehensive general industrial arts: *see* **industrial arts, comprehensive general.**

comprehensive general industrial arts laboratory: *see* **laboratory, comprehensive general industrial arts.**

comprehensive high school: *see* **high school, comprehensive.**

comprehensive home economics instruction: *see* **instruction, comprehensive home economics.**

comprehensive shop: *see* **laboratory, comprehensive general industrial arts.**

comprehensive student report: *see* **report, comprehensive student.**

comprehensiveness: that characteristic of a point of view or *Weltanschauung* or philosophical mind which strives for a maximum of inclusiveness so that the whole picture rather than scattered or isolated segments is in view; arises from an intellectual dissatisfaction unless all relevant considerations have been explored.

compressed speech: *see* **speech, compressed.**

compression of information: any means employed, such as taking pauses out of speech or removing nonessential elements in written communication, so as to present more information in a given time span.

comptroller: an officer who examines and certifies accounts according to correctness and legality and limits expenditures to budgetary restrictions.

compulsion neurosis: *see* **neurosis, compulsion.**

compulsive idea: *see* **idea, compulsive.**

compulsive personality: *see* **personality, compulsive.**

compulsory age span: *see* **compulsory school age span.**

compulsory attendance: *see* **compulsory education.**

compulsory-attendance age limit: *see* **age limit, compulsory-attendance.**

compulsory-attendance laws, state: *see* **compulsory education.**

compulsory behavior: *see* **behavior, compulsory.**

compulsory education: (1) the practice, now common to all states, territories, and possessions of the United States, of requiring school attendance by law; responsibility is placed on the parents in some states; (2) historically, the requirement that every child should be able to read and write by a certain age, commonly 12 years, school attendance not being mandatory; (3) the requirement that a political subdivision provide education for the school-age population.

compulsory health certificate: *see* **health certificate, compulsory.**

compulsory-maintenance attitude: a term used to characterize the attitude and practice of colonial New England in regard to education; in Massachusetts the law of 1642 made it compulsory to learn to read and write, and the law of 1647 required the appointment of teachers in towns having over 50 families; later all colonies of New England except Rhode Island enacted similar laws.

compulsory military training: *see* **military training, compulsory.**

compulsory retirement: *see* **retirement, compulsory.**

compulsory school age: *see* **age limit, compulsory-attendance.**

compulsory school age limits: *see* **age limit, compulsory-attendance.**

compulsory school age, maximum: the age, varying from state to state, at which children cease to be required to attend school.

compulsory school age, minimum: the age, varying from state to state, at which children are first required to enter school.

compulsory school age span: the number of years during which children are required to attend school.

compulsory school attendance: *syn.* **compulsory education** (1).

compulsory school attendance, age of: *see* **age of compulsory school attendance.**

compulsory school-attendance legislation: *syn.* **attendance law.**

compulsory school year: *see* **school year, compulsory.**

computation: a term applied to a large number of activities of varying complexity whose common characteristic is the manipulation of symbols, for example, computing sums and products of natural numbers, integers, or polynomials, or computing a logarithm; may or may not be accompanied by reflective thinking. *Syn.* **calculation.**

computation, approximate: (1) computation that involves the use of approximate numbers; (2) the application of methods of approximation in computation with either approximate or exact numbers.

computation, mechanical: (1) computation done by machine; (2) computation done without understanding or as a habitual skill.

computational mathematics: *see* **mathematics, computational.**

computed mode: *syn.* **mode, refined.**

computer: (1) a machine, now usually electric or electronic, for the rapid solution of simple or complex calculations; (2) somewhat imprecisely, a data processing machine that compares and analyzes but does not necessarily calculate; supplies output information which is derived from the accepted input information.

computer, analog: a computer system or machine the input and output of which are basically continuous variables—usually measurements, length, depth, temperature, etc.; there is no point at which absolute values are considered available as absolute; in contrast to a *digital computer,* which counts, the analog computer measures.

computer assisted individually paced instruction: *see* **instruction, computer assisted individually paced.**

computer assisted instruction: *see* **instruction, computer assisted.**

computer, asynchronous: an automatic computer in which the performance of the next command starts as a result of a signal that the preceding command has been completed.

computer, automatic: a machine that manipulates symbols according to given rules in a predetermined and self-directed manner; more specifically, a high-speed automatic electronic digital data-handling machine.

computer-based teaching machine: *see* **machine, computer-based teaching.**

computer code: *syn.* **language, machine.**

computer, digital: a computer which operates with clearly defined or discrete numbers, as opposed to physical quantities of variables. *Comp. w.* **computer, analog.**

computer, electronic digital: a high-speed electronic device for performing arithmetic operations in accordance with a program specified by the user; modern computers accept the program of instructions as coded numbers, operate upon numbers stored in an internal "memory," and can select from alternative routines in accordance with the magnitude or algebraic sign of computed intermediate results; instructions covering all possible contingencies must be written in advance, but complex problems may be handled easily at speeds up to thousands of operations per second. *See* **analog.**

computer, fixed program: a computer in which the sequence of instructions is permanently stored and which performs automatically.

computer graphics: a technique which allows the computer operator to manipulate, modify, repeat, and expand or contract displayed images; dynamic displays of three-dimensional objects can be produced and then translated, rotated, and scaled continuously by applying a light pen, hand-held, which must be pointed at the tube; useful for the study of learning and perception.

computer kit: a do-it-yourself kit for building a computer, marketed under such trademarks as Brainiac, Minivac, etc.; may be relatively sophisticated, containing switches, wires, sockets, etc., or, in simpler format, may have only plans which are cut out and assembled with pins and glue.

computer language: *syn.* **language, machine.**

computer mathematics: *see* **mathematics, computer.**

computer, multiaddress: an automatic computer that has a built-in ability to use more than one address in the address part of each instruction; in some computers, one of the additional addresses may take over the function of the *control counter.*

computer music: *see* **music, computer.**

computer, one-address: an automatic computer whose capacity is restricted to instructions having one command and only one address. *See* **computer, multiaddress.**

computer programming: *see* **programming, computer.**

computer scheduling: *see* **scheduling by computer.**

computer storage device: a device into which data can be inserted, in which they can be retained, and from which they can be retrieved.

computer, time-shared: a computer that performs for a large number of users.

computerize: to put in a form which may be utilized on or fed into a computer or calculator; to program information for a punched card, punched tape, or magnetic tape.

computing, batch mode: use of a computer on a process or task prepared and presented in its entirety in the form of decks of punched cards which are read into the computer in groups. *Contr. w.* **computing, conversational.**

computing chart: *syn.* **diagram, computing.**

computing, conversational: employment of teletype or typewriter by the computer user to input his messages via telephone to his program; messages, preferably limited to two or three lines of type, will be responded to within from 1 to 15 seconds; all messages between the user and the computer can be recorded inside the computing system for later analysis; this method of computing permits successive messages to the computer to be contingent on the previous response, so that the method is useful in computer-assisted instruction and in the conduct of experiments. *See* **interaction, conversational.**

computing diagram: *see* **diagram, computing.**

computing, remote batch mode: batch mode computing in which the information in the user's source deck of punched cards (batch) is transmitted over a telephone line to the computer and the output is then returned by telephone line for printout at the remote location for the user. *Contr. w.* **computing, conversational.**

conation: that aspect of man's psychic life having to do with striving and will; traditionally distinguished from *cognition* and *affection;* in the light of modern organismic psychology, these distinctions are probably artificial.

conative: striving or having the power to strive or struggle toward a goal which may be conscious or unconscious; descriptive of one of the three great divisions of the mind or soul (historically), namely, the will as contrasted with terms descriptive of the feelings (*affective*) or the power of knowing (*cognitive*).

conative intelligence: *see* **intelligence, conative.**

concatenated reflexes: *see* **reflex, chain.**

concatenated theory: a theory of which the component laws enter into a network of relations so as to constitute an identifiable configuration or pattern; most typically, they converge on some central point, each specifying one of the factors which plays a part in the phenomenon which the theory explains; a theory of the factor type.

concatenation: any connected series or chain, as of events, phenomena, circumstances, thoughts, emotions, or reflexes.

concentration: (1) the state or act characterized by the centering or focusing of attention upon a task or problem or upon certain elements of an experience; the conscious and intense application of mental or physical forces, or both, in an effort to perform a task or activity or to solve a problem; (2) the centering of a college student's program of study in one department or field of learning in which he does work of advanced grade; (3) a plan of curriculum organization in which one subject, such as history, becomes the center and other subjects are integrated with it.

concentration, major field of: *see* **field of concentration, major.**

concentration plan: *see* **concentration** (3).

concentration requirement: the minimum amount of college or university work required of a student in the scope or sequence of his primary field of specialization. *See* **field of concentration.**

concentric-circles plan: *syn.* **organization by cycles.**

concept: (1) an idea or representation of the common element or attribute by which groups or classes may be distinguished; (2) any general or abstract intellectual representation of a situation, state of affairs, or object; (3) a thought, an opinion, an idea, or a mental image.

concept, abstract: an idea or aggregation of ideas that has been acquired as a symbol or generalization for an intangible, for example, the concept of square, circle, soft, ten, fast, long, over, etc.

concept, art: *see* **art concept.**

concept, concrete: an idea or image of an object that can be perceived by the senses, for example, the concept of a block, ball, fur, money, etc.

concept, darkness: the erroneous idea that blindness imposes a black void or complete darkness.

concept, distributive education area of study: *see* **area of study concept, distributive education.**

concept, empty-organism: a term used by some psychologists and educators to describe the outmoded view that learning is a process of "pouring" knowledge into a passive organism.

concept extension: use of a concept for a wider set of data than that for which it was introduced.

concept, form: *see* **schema.**

concept formation: the development, through abstraction, of a mental process which refers to more than one object or experience or to one object in relation to others. *See* **abstraction** (1).

concept, function: *see* **function concept.**

concept, mathematical: (1) in reference to form, an idea or set of ideas used to classify a set of understandings and almost always specified by a word, phrase, or symbol which names the concept; the cognitive process by which this word is associated with the set is called *learning the concept;* (2) in reference to content, a term used by different writers to mean anything in or related to mathematics which is not considered a skill; *see* **skill, mathematical.**

concept, multiple-causation: (read.) the idea that most reading disabilities are the result of a variety of causes rather than of a single cause.

concept, number: terms commonly referred to as number concepts are cardinal number, ordinal number, one-to-one correspondence, and order ("greater than," "less than"). *See* **concept, mathematical.**

concept, Piagetian: one of the mathematical concepts related to the psychological theory of Jean Piaget. *See* **conservation.**

concept, place: place sense; the ability to locate or identify one place with or in reference to another place or places.

concept teaching: *see* **teaching, concept.**

conception: (1) (psych.) the formulation of a general idea representing the common element or attribute of a group or class; (2) (biol.) the fertilization of an ovum.

concepts of supervision: *see* **supervision, concepts of.**

conceptual framework: the main ideas arranged as to sequence and scope for teaching a *unit* or area of study.

conceptual intelligibility: *syn.* **intelligibility, structural.**

conceptual model: *see* **model, conceptual.**

conceptual thinking: *see* **thinking, conceptual.**

conceptualism: a philosophy or theory, expounded by Abélard during the twelfth century, according to which universals are existent but are not independent of the phenomenal objective form in which they exist (except as conceptions in the Divine Mind before creation).

concert: a prepared performance by an organized group of musicians for an audience which has assembled, ordinarily for the express purpose of attending; performances by soloists are commonly called *recitals,* those by small groups *chamber recitals* or *chamber concerts.*

concert, chamber: *see* **concert.**

concert, neighborhood: a concert given in the inner city or in a suburban or rural area by a large professional group or part of the group for the purpose of bringing live performers and live audiences into greater and more rewarding intimacy outside of the concert hall; may be held in a school or other auditorium or outdoors.

concert reading: *see* **reading, concert.**

concert recitation: *syn.* **recitation, choral.**

concerted reading: *see* **choral speaking.**

concerts, exchange: concerts resulting from a performance agreement between two organizations in which one group host-sponsors a concert for another group in return for the same host-sponsorship, later, by the second group.

conclusion: (1) (logic) the end product of some reasoning process; (2) (math.) the sentence q in a statement of the form "If p, then q"; for example, the expression or sentence $a^2 \geq 0$ is the conclusion of the sentence "If a is a real number, then $a^2 \geq 0$"; *contr. w.* **hypothesis** (2).

concomitant deviation: *syn.* **deviation, concurrent.**

concomitant learning: *see* **learning, concomitant.**

concomitant variable: *see* **variable, concomitant.**

concomitant variation: *syn.* **correlation** (1).

concomitant variations, method of: *see* **method of concomitant variations.**

concordance: an alphabetic list of words and phrases appearing in the body of a work; it cites the locations in the document where the particular words are used and may also exhibit a small amount of text material preceding and following the particular word or phrase at each location.

concordance, coefficient of: *see* **coefficient of concordance.**

concrete: *n.* theory in the abstract proposes generalizations and principles that guide theory in the concrete which, in turn, is related to the daily tasks of experience. *Contr. w.* **abstract.**

concrete: *adj.* referring to an object or idea familiar to the individual through experience.

concrete average: *syn.* **average, typical.**

concrete concept: *see* **concept, concrete.**

concrete intelligence: *see* **intelligence, concrete.**

concrete materials: *see* **materials, concrete.**

concrete mathematics: *see* **mathematics, concrete.**

concrete music: *see* **music, concrete.**

concrete number: *see* **number, concrete.**

concrete operations stage of development: *see* **stage of development, concrete operations.**

concrete problem: *see* **problem, concrete.**

concreteness: inability or loss of ability to think in abstract terms, even when increased effort is put forth; ability to do better spontaneously than when consciously trying.

concurrency: (mil. ed.) the meeting together at one time of several different scientific, technological, training, and other developments so as to reduce the amount of lead time in achieving a given capability.

concurrent deviation: *see* **deviation, concurrent.**

concurrent deviations, coefficient of: *see* **coefficient of concurrent deviations.**

concurrent validity: *see* **validity, concurrent.**

condemnation: the proceeding whereby private property is taken for public use, including the ascertainment of the compensation to be paid.

condition, atypical: a condition of an individual in a given chronological age group which is markedly different from that of the mean; an individual having an atypical condition may reveal one or more atypical characteristics which enable an identification of the condition.

condition, initial: (math.) any one of the conditions, stated or implied in a problem, upon which all further action, discussion, and computation are based.

conditional fee: *see* **fee, conditional.**

conditional grant: *see* **grant, conditional.**

conditional life certificate: *see* **certificate, conditional life.**

conditional promotion: *syn.* **promotion, probationary.**

conditional transfer: *see* **transfer, conditional.**

conditioned aid: *see* **aid, conditioned.**

conditioned emotion: *see* **emotion, conditioned.**

conditioned emotional reaction: *see* **reaction, conditioned emotional.**

conditioned inhibition: *syn.* **inhibition, differential.**

conditioned reflex: *see* **reflex, conditioned.**

conditioned reflex, trace: a type of conditioned reflex in which there is a definite lapse of time between the termination of the stimulus and the beginning of the response, as though the organism reacted to the *trace* of the original stimulus in the central nervous system. (For example, a dog is given tactile stimulation on the left shoulder for 30 seconds, and then, after an interval of 2 minutes, food is administered, with consequent salivation; if this is repeated often enough, the dog will salivate 2 minutes after being given tactile stimulation on the shoulder, even though no food is given.)

conditioned reinforcer: *see* **reinforcer, conditioned.**

conditioned response: *see* **response, conditioned.**

conditioned stimulus: *see* **stimulus, conditioned.**

conditioned student: *see* **student, conditioned.**

conditioning: (1) the process by which an originally inadequate stimulus is substituted for an originally adequate stimulus in calling forth a certain response, through presentation of both stimuli in temporal or spatial contiguity; the building up of responsiveness to a specific stimulus by association; frequently used experimentally for the purpose of controlling reactions or for providing controls for experimentation; *see* **associative shifting;** (2) (gestalt) the emergence or individuation of a particular response from a previous response less differentiated in character; the emergence induced by the repetition of certain details of a stimulus pattern; (3) (phys. ed.) the process of gradually preparing the body for strenuous physical activity.

conditioning, adaptive: the formation of conditioned responses which have value in the adjustment of the individual.

conditioning, avoidance: a form of conditioning in which the organism tries to bypass, escape from, or avoid an aversive stimulus by responding to some cue that the unpleasant stimulus is about to occur; similar to *instrumental conditioning.*

conditioning, classical: Pavlovian conditioning in which conditioned and unconditioned stimuli are invariably paired until the conditioned reflex has been established; usually involves responses controlled by the autonomic nervous system. *Syn.* **respondent conditioning;** *see* **behavior, respondent.**

conditioning, delayed: a type of conditioning in which the conditioned response follows the unconditioned response at an interval proportional to that at which the conditioning stimulus has in practice followed the unconditioned stimulus.

conditioning exercise: *see* **exercise, conditioning.**

conditioning, inhibitory: conditioning that results in the restraint of a particular response to a stimulus and the substitution of a different response. *Syn.* **negative conditioning;** *dist. f.* **extinction.**

conditioning, instrumental: a type of conditioning in which the organism's own response (for example, withdrawal) is instrumental in determining whether or not it receives the unconditioned stimulus.

conditioning, negative: *syn.* **conditioning, inhibitory.**

conditioning, operant: (1) (Skinner) a type of conditioning in which the emitted rather than the elicited behavior of the organism is manipulated; contrasted to *classical conditioning* or *respondent conditioning,* which are used to describe association in elicited behavior; *see* **behavior, operant; behavior, respondent;** (2) in guidance, a procedure which involves the *direct reinforcement* or reward of those emergent behaviors which the therapist regards as appropriate, with little concern about anxiety extinction; *see* **reinforcement.**

conditioning, respondent: *see* **conditioning, classical.**

conditioning, semantic: use of words as conditioned stimuli; useful as a means of investigating semantic generalization; for example, where "red" is the conditioned stimulus paired with an electric shock, what will the reaction be to the words "orange," "bed," "vermilion," and "dead"?

conditioning, stimulus: *syn.* **generalization, stimulus.**

conditions of a problem: the requirements that must be met (*a*) by any hypothesis proposed as a guide to the solution of a problem and (*b*) by the plans of testing the hypothesis as the solution is sought.

conditions, standard: requirement that the circumstances in which a test is taken be identical for all students taking it; one of the checks on reliability of the test.

conduct: *n.* (1) the behavior of persons, usually when viewed ethically; (2) a single act of an individual in one situation; (3) the characteristic quality of action of an individual which familiarity leads his associates to expect of him; the same for groups or classes, for example, gangs, mobs, adolescents, nationality groups, or man (generically).

conduct: (mus.) *v.* to lead an ensemble in the performance of a musical composition, chiefly by movements of the hands and arms intended to indicate the interpretation desired from the performers. (Manual movements are frequently supplemented by those of a light stick, the baton, held in one hand.)

conduct, controls of: *see* **controls of conduct.**

conduct curriculum: *see* **curriculum, conduct.**

conduct disorder: *see* **disorder, conduct.**

conduct, improper: (school law) such conduct as a person of ordinary and reasonable care and prudence would not have been guilty of under the same circumstances.

conducted study: *see* **study, conducted.**

conducting: (1) the art of directing a musical ensemble; (2) the field of study of which this art is the subject.

conduction, air: the process by which sound is conducted to the inner ear through the air in the outer ear canal.

conduction, bone: transmission of sound waves to the hearing mechanism through the bones of the skull, bypassing the middle ear.

conduction deafness: *see* **deafness, conduction.**

conductive hearing impairment: *see* **deafness, conduction.**

conductive hearing loss: *see* **hearing loss, conductive.**

conductivity: a term borrowed from electricity to describe the property of tissues, especially nerve tissues, of transmitting neural impulses. *Contr. w.* **resistance** (1).

conductor, music: a person who leads a musical ensemble; usually shortened to "conductor"; may be the *music director* of the group. *See* **conduct** *v.;* **director, music.**

confabulation: a symptom of certain forms of psychosis consisting in making ready answers and reciting experiences without regard to truth. *Syn.* **fabrication.**

confact: a term used by Symonds to describe transfer because of partial identity, that is, due to the detection of minute perceptual identities. *See* **identity, partial.**

conference: a meeting of two or more persons of common interest who come together primarily for consultation, discussion, and interchange of opinions and ideas.

conference, athletic: an association of schools or colleges formed to provide guidance for and control of competition in athletic sports among member schools, in accordance with rules and regulations agreed upon.

conference book: (supervised study) a book in which the teacher records the results of conferences with pupils concerning individual study problems.

conference, career: in guidance, a group meeting held by the school with the participation of representatives of occupations from the community or neighboring geographical areas. *See* **career day.**

conference, case: the cooperative effort of the school staff in a meeting under the leadership of a guidance specialist to contribute, analyze, and interpret data about an individual pupil so that efforts may be undertaken to assist the student in realizing his full potentiality; case conferences can also be used for in-service training of teachers and counselors, for securing faculty support of a guidance program, and for stimulating teachers to learn more about their students and themselves.

conference, church: (1) a formal meeting of Christians for the purposes of fellowship, study, and spiritual growth; normally an integral part of the church's religious education program; frequently held in denominationally controlled centers designed for conferences; (2) the governing body of certain Protestant denominations, for example, the Methodist church.

conference, departmental: a meeting of all teachers of a given subject or group of subjects within a school or school system, usually for the discussion of curriculum problems, evaluation of pupil accomplishment, or the use of certain teaching methods; may also be used in promoting desired uniformity in the department and in enlarging the services of the department.

conference, free: a conference in which procedures and sometimes the selection of the problems are left to members of the group.

conference group: (1) a meeting of a supervisor or supervisors with a group of teachers or teachers and administrators to discuss problems common to the group; includes general faculty meetings, departmental conferences, meetings of department heads, study groups, committee meetings, and grade conferences; (2) (teacher ed.) a consultation involving a discussion of educational problems; (3) (teacher ed.) a planned or scheduled meeting between an instructor and a group of students for the discussion of a problem previously assigned; (4) (couns.) an aggregate of people in face-to-face communication with one another, having a degree of interaction among themselves and the counselor, with the primary aim of establishing a growth goal.

conference group, master: an organization of individuals in industry that sets the pattern for all subordinate conference groups by meeting regularly and serving as the guiding force for the entire conference program.

conference, guided: (1) a service for assisting members of a conferring group in resolving their problems; may include one or a number of functions and may be available for individuals or groups of varying age levels; (2) (couns.) organized group services to help pupils acquire needed experiences for intelligent personal planning; *see* **guidance, group.**

conference, individual: (1) a meeting of a supervisor and a teacher for the discussion of instructional policies or other problems; may be initiated either by the supervisor or by the teacher; (2) a consultation between a student teacher and the supervising or critic teacher or between a student teacher and a supervisor for a discussion of problems encountered during student teaching.

conference-leadership course: *see* **course, conference-leadership.**

conference leading: *see* **conference procedure.**

conference method: teaching method which employs directed discussion of a topic rather than a lecture by the instructor.

conference, parent-student-counselor: a face-to-face counseling interview involving a counselor, a student, and one or both parents of the student, wherein the counselor attempts to aid the participants in an exploration of mutually pertinent issues and concerns in an effort to reach an agreement on a course of action.

conference, parent-teacher: *syn.* **conference, teacher-parent.**

conference, parent-teacher-student: a discussion carried on by a parent, a teacher, and a student in which there is an attempt at individual assistance or instruction.

conference period: *see* **period, conference.**

conference, postvisitation: a discussion between a supervisor and a teacher subsequent to a classroom visit by the supervisor.

conference, presession: a planning conference participated in by teachers and administrators preceding the opening of the school session.

conference, press: in school journalism, a convention—national, regional, state, district, or local—of representatives of collegiate or scholastic publications.

conference, preteaching: a meeting of a supervisor and a teacher prior to a visit by the supervisor for the purpose of planning and discussing the lesson that is to be observed.

conference procedure: a type of class procedure in which discussion by class members predominates; originally used only when members of the class possessed all or nearly all the information required for dealing with the subject of the conference; more recently applied to any kind of class discussion.

conference, regional: (voc. ed.) a meeting, usually annual, called by the U.S. Office of Education in one of the four officially established regions of the nation for the purpose of dealing with problems of common interest to the states represented; may be confined to a single phase of vocational education or may include all phases.

conference, regional education: a consortium including a number of states, such as the Southern Regional Education Board, New England Board of Higher Education, or Western Interstate Conference of Higher Education. *Syn.* **regional education board;** *see* **consortium.**

conference, residential: a meeting of persons to discuss and exchange ideas and opinions usually for a brief but intensive period, during which time the participants normally eat, sleep, and carry on their learning experiences in a common setting.

conference room: (1) a room (usually in a school or college library) set aside for the use of small groups when work with library materials is necessary to the development of an assignment or project; (2) any room set aside for use by small discussion groups.

conference, supervisory: a conference among school workers to secure improvements in methods of teaching and in the devices and materials used, for example, a conference between a subject supervisor and a teacher or between a principal and a teacher.

conference, teacher-parent: the face-to-face communication between a child's teacher and his parent for the purpose of exchanging information and suggestions to facilitate the child's development. *Syn.* **parent-teacher conference.**

conference, teacher-pupil: the face-to-face communication of the teacher with the individual pupil or with a small group of pupils, designed to help direct learning efforts through conference activities in such fields as planning, evaluation, expectations, responsibilities, behavior, cultivation of new interests, goal-setting, and discussion of pertinent material in the pupil's personal record folder.

conference techniques: *see* **techniques, conference.**

confidence band: *syn.* **region, acceptance.**

confidence belt: *syn.* **region, acceptance.**

confidence coefficient: *see* **coefficient, confidence.**

confidence interval: *syn.* **region, acceptance.**

confidence level: the probability of obtaining a value more extreme than that obtained solely on the basis of sampling error; determines the confidence limits, the confidence interval or acceptance region, and the confidence coefficient; sometimes confused with the confidence coefficient. *Syn.* **fiducial level; level of confidence; level of probability;** *see* **coefficient, confidence; confidence limits; region, acceptance; significance level.**

confidence, level of: *syn.* **confidence level.**

confidence limits: (stat.) those limits, determined by the confidence level selected, which set off the extreme values of the confidence interval, within which an obtained value provides a basis for accepting a null hypothesis, and beyond which an obtained value provides a basis for rejection of the null hypothesis; the points that divide a sampling curve into acceptance and rejection regions. *Syn.* **fiducial limits; probability limits; significance limits;** *see* **coefficient, confidence; confidence level; region, rejection.**

confidence weighting: *see* **weighting, confidence.**

confidential: (1) entrusted with the confidence of another or with his secret affairs or purposes; (2) intended to be held in confidence or kept secret.

confidential communication: *see* **communication, confidential.**

confidential information: *see* **communication, confidential; communication, privileged.**

confidential records: *see* **records, confidential.**

Confidential Statement, Parents': *see* **Parents' Confidential Statement.**

confidentiality: (couns.) a state of trust or intimacy of thought between parties in which communicated information is rendered unknowable to anyone other than the parties. *See* **communication, confidential; communication, privileged.**

configuration: (1) any experience or example of behavior when considered as a whole; (2) (psych.) the unified background or total perceptual pattern into which an afferent impulse is fused or integrated with loss of its identity, thus resulting in a unitary experience (the nearest equivalent to the German term *Gestalt*); (3) (read.) the general outline or pattern of a word; (4) (math.) a general term for any combination of geometrical elements, such as points, lines, and surfaces; (5) (data processing) a group of machines which are interconnected and programmed to operate as a system.

configuration clue: *see* **clue, configuration.**

configuration of points: an arrangement representing relative positions of test vectors in space as determined by their intercorrelations and without regard to any specific reference frame.

confirmation: (1) one of the seven sacraments accepted by the churches of the Catholic tradition and administered variously by chrism or imposition of hands (by bishops) in the Anglican, Orthodox, and Roman Catholic communions; (2) in Lutheran and some other Protestant communions, confirmation is practiced as a solemn rite in which a person renews the promises made on his behalf by sponsors in baptism; confirmation normally presupposes an extended period of preparation (including formal instruction) and admits the person to full membership into the church; (3) a group ceremony of induction into Jewish religious responsibilities upon completion of a course of studies in the Jewish religious school varying in length from 8 to 10 years, depending upon whether the age requirement is set at 14, 15, or 16 years; first introduced in America by rabbis of Reform congregations; now also in vogue in Conservative and some Orthodox congregations; (4) information given the student concerning the correctness or incorrectness of the responses he makes to programmed instructional materials; *see* **knowledge of results.**

conflict: (1) (psych.) a painful or unhappy state of consciousness resulting from a clash or contest of incompatible desires, aims, drives, etc.; (2) (sociol.) direct and open antagonistic struggle of persons or groups for the same object or end; the aim of the conflict is the annihilation, defeat, or subjection of the other person or group as a way of obtaining the goal; *contr. w.* **competition;** (3) (social) *see* **class** (6); **class struggle; communism; conflicts, culture.**

conflict, approach-approach: a type of psychological conflict in which the individual is attracted toward two mutually exclusive goals. *See* **conflict.**

conflict, approach-avoidance: a type of psychological conflict which may arise in an individual who entertains bipolar feelings toward the same person, object, or situation. *See* **ambivalence.**

conflict, avoidance-avoidance: a type of psychological conflict arising when two unpleasant consequences face an individual in which retreat from one moves him toward the other.

conflict, cultural: *see* **conflicts, culture.**

conflict, religious: *see* **religious conflict.**

conflict theory: a psychological theory which states that many normal and most abnormal manifestations of personality are the result of mental conflicts.

conflicts, culture: (1) within a culture, expressions of the fears and irritations resulting from the real or imagined threat to one group of people and its values by another group, the means of aggression and resistance being any social device, economic, political, military, aesthetic, religious, psychological, etc.; (2) conflicts arising from different values held in different cultures.

conflicts, inner: conflicts resulting from suppression into the subconscious of emotion-provoking ideas (generally taboo) which may sometimes find outlet in disguised forms of socially unacceptable behavior.

conformity: the essential adjustment to a social environment over which one has no control; can also be considered to be submission to explicit or implicit coercion or the acceptance, ordinarily without awareness, of prevailing customs and usages.

confounding: (design) a condition arising in incomplete factorial designs in which, for the sake of reducing the number of experimental groups, the effect of one factor or of one of the interactions is mixed with error in such a way that its effect cannot be isolated; loosely used to refer to the mixing of the effect of the experimental variable and some extraneous variable or variables; for example, in a methods experiment in which each treatment is carried out in a different classroom under a different

teacher, the effects of classroom and teacher differences would be confounded with methods.

confusion, directional: *see* **directional confusion.**

confusion, symbolic: a term used to describe a pattern of difficulties in reading which includes confusion in right-left discrimination, lack of right-left dominance, awkwardness, and difficulties in writing and spelling.

congeniality group: *see* **group, congeniality.**

congenital: actually or potentially present in the individual at birth, because of heredity or intrauterine accidents or environmental factors. *Syn.* **connate;** *dist. f.* **innate.**

congenital abnormality: *see* **abnormality, congenital.**

congenital amputation: *see* **amputation, congenital.**

congenital anomaly: *see* **anomaly, congenital.**

congenital blindness: *see* **blindness, congenital.**

congenital cretinism: *see* **cretinism, congenital.**

congenital deafness: *see* **deafness, congenital.**

congenital hearing impairment: *see* **hearing impairment, congenital.**

congregation: in the Roman Catholic Church, (*a*) a group of bishops or cardinals engaged in executive work relating to the government of the Church; (*b*) a religious community whose superior is responsible only to the Pope; (*c*) a parish.

congregation, Jewish junior: a children's congregation conducting daily, Sabbath, and festival services for the pupils of a Jewish school.

congregational Sunday school, Jewish: *see* **Sunday school, Jewish congregational.**

congregational weekday school, Jewish: *see* **weekday school, Jewish congregational.**

Congressional township grants for education: a system of Federal land-grant aid to education, beginning with the admission of Ohio, by which the sixteenth section (1 square mile) of each congressional township was given for schools. (After 1850 two and after 1896 four sections were granted.)

congruency, image: *see* **image congruency.**

congruent: (1) in geometry, a term descriptive of a relation between pairs of point sets, meaning that one point set is an exact replica of the other, as, for example, congruent line segments or congruent triangles; (2) in number theory, a term characterizing a relation between pairs of integers when they have the same remainder on division by a third integer; 7 and 10, for example, have the same remainder on division by 3 and are said to be congruent modulo 3; *see* **arithmetic, modular.**

conjugal family: *see* **family, conjugal.**

connate: *syn.* **congenital.**

connection: a reaction pattern aroused because of the connection or juxtaposition of one stimulus with another; similar to the conditioned reflex but applied to more complex situations. *See* **reflex, conditioned.**

connectionism: (Thorndike) the theory of psychology that is the parent of most prominent learning theories today; essentially a stimulus response or association theory postulating the formation of neural bonds through strengthening of associations by various laws of association, particularly the *law of effect. See* **psychology, association.**

connotation: the sum of the qualities implied by a term or essential to the thing named; stipulates the meaning of a term by describing the characteristics common to the individual members of a class, as the connotation of cow is four-leggedness, domestication, bovine, milkgiving, etc.; the intensive as distinguished from the extensive or denotative meaning of a term. *See* **denotation.**

consanguine family: *see* **family, extended.**

conscience: (1) the process by which a person is made aware of an inner imperative or admonition as to what he ought or ought not to intend, feel, or do in a given situation; (2) the complex of moral urges, concepts, judgments, and beliefs which is believed to be the source of moral imperatives; (3) in psychoanalysis, conscience is analogous to the *superego* (Freud).

conscience, social: (1) a sense of what is right or wrong in terms of the good of the total group (society); (2) the conscience of a group based on the beliefs, ideals, and mores of that group.

conscience, spelling: *see* **spelling conscience.**

conscious act of creation: *see* **creation, conscious act of.**

consciousness: (1) the sum of all experiences that are known to a person at a given time; (2) (gestalt) total awareness at any given time defined as an oversummative field property of a total behavior pattern, paralleling the condition of being alive. *See* **awareness.**

consciousness, group: *see* **group consciousness.**

consciousness, self-: *see* **self-consciousness.**

consensus: (1) general accord or agreement in matters of opinion, belief, value, and attitude; (2) (group dynamics) individual involvement in the group decision-making process to give a "we-feeling."

consensus, social: *see* **social consensus.**

consent form, cooperative office education parental: a form that is signed by parents giving permission for their child to be enrolled in a cooperative office education program.

consent form, distributive education parental: a form that is signed by parents giving permission for their child to be enrolled in the distributive education program.

consent, parental: permission, usually in writing, by a parent or guardian, allowing the child to participate in some extra or special school activity, such as a field trip, varsity athletics, etc.

consequences: (1) the outcomes of an activity; the natural or necessary results, as contrasted with mere sequences; John Dewey maintained that the intelligent anticipation of consequences is a vital goal of education and a necessary underpinning for democratic living; (2) in logic, refers to inferences; *see* **inference.**

conservation: (math.) invariance of a property under some transformation, as, for example, invariance of the cardinal number of a set under rearrangement of the elements (conservation of numerousness); a concept related to the psychological theory of Jean Piaget. (The term is sometimes used to denote the recognition of invariance on the part of the learner.)

conservation, consumer: the preservation, protection, and intelligent use of natural resources for the continued satisfaction of consumer wants.

conservation of hearing: (1) measures taken to preserve and utilize the residual hearing possessed by a person with impaired hearing; (2) measures taken to prevent deafness through the detection and correction of hearing deficiencies.

conservation of human resources: (1) creating, maintaining, or improving the conditions necessary for human growth, development, and efficient social activity; (2) establishing or preserving the physical, intellectual, and economic security of the members of a social group.

conservation of natural resources: (1) the use of natural resources (such as forests, lands, minerals, and waters) without waste, and the development of these resources to their fullest permanent usefulness; (2) a movement first clearly started in the United States in 1908, sponsored by President Theodore Roosevelt, to protect the public lands, forests, etc., under the control of the government.

conservation of vision: *syn.* **sight conservation.**

conservation principle: (Piaget) the principle that mass, number, etc., retain their properties when spatial and form changes are made; that is, a pint is a pint whether in a gallon jug or in a soup bowl; children before age 6 or 7 have not yet acquired this principle, and according to some investigators they do not really incorporate the principle even when it is taught to them.

conservation, sight: *see* **sight conservation.**

conservatism: (1) a point of view or, more exactly, a mood, which favors a minimum of change and stresses the importance of preserving values already achieved, as opposed to liberalism and reactionism; *see* **liberalism; radicalism; reaction;** (2) popularly used to designate the tendency to avoid extremes.

conservative religious school, Jewish: *see* **religious school, Jewish conservative.**

conservatory: (1) an institution for the teaching of music; generally subsidized by the state in Continental Europe and privately owned in Great Britain and America; (2) a name given, occasionally, to the school or college of music in a university complex; provides instruction in nearly all areas of musical discipline.

consistence in paired comparisons, coefficient of: *see* **coefficient of consistence in paired comparisons.**

consistency: (philos.) (1) agreement or harmony of parts in a structural philosophical point of view, particularly between recommended actions and philosophical assumptions; (2) a theory of knowledge that uses as a test for the truth of a given proposition its logical coherence with other relevant judgments assumed to be true.

consistency, index of: *syn.* **coefficient of reliability.**

consistency, internal: the quality in a test of having items which all measure the same thing, which are highly intercorrelated, and which, therefore, correlate highly with the total test score. *See* **coefficient of internal consistency.**

consistent differences, small: *see* **differences, small consistent.**

consistent statistic: *syn.* **statistic, efficient.**

consolation tournament: a series of contests between losers in an eliminating tournament to decide third place.

console: (1) in a language laboratory, a cabinet desk or counter containing control panels, program sources, etc., from which the electronic system is controlled; (2) (data processing) a computer mechanism that shows a machine operator what the computer is doing and the results of its operations; *syn.* **display panel; display unit.**

console, control: a piece of equipment that incorporates monitors for viewing separate images picked up by various TV cameras in a system, in addition to the switching and other control devices required; when remote-controlled cameras are used, special iris, lens focus, and pan-tilt circuits are included.

console, teacher's: instructor's control center in an electronic laboratory where a distribution panel controls the transmission of program signals and may include facilities for two-way communication with individual students or an entire group.

consolidated report: *see* **report, consolidated.**

consolidated school: an enlarged school formed by uniting smaller schools, for the purpose of providing better school facilities and increased educational opportunities. *Syn.* **centralized school.**

consolidated school district: *see* **district, consolidated school.**

consolidation: (1) (behav. psych.) a term used by Watson to describe the tendency of separate parts of an act or movement to become unified into a single act or movement; (2) the act of forming a consolidated school or school district; *see* **consolidated school; district, consolidated school.**

consolidation, county-unit: a merger of all the school districts within a county so that the boundaries of the consolidated district coincide with those of the county. (Cities lying within a county unit are usually organized as independent school districts.)

consolidation of schools: (1) usually defined as the abandonment of one or more attendance units and the bringing of their pupils together into a larger attendance unit; a single attendance unit is the chief characteristic of a consolidated school, when this definition is used, the resulting school being termed either *consolidated* or *centralized school;* (2) the term is often used to denote the merger of school districts for administrative purposes. (Some states permit the abandonment of attendance units and the education of their pupils on a tuition basis, without a change in district organization. Such situations have many of the earmarks of consolidated schools but are not referred to as such.) *Syn.* **centralization of schools.**

consolidation, township-unit: a merger of school districts so that the boundaries of the resulting district coincide with those of a political township.

consonance: a highly controversial relative term used to describe the effect produced by certain musical intervals on the listener, consonant intervals being agreeable, dissonant intervals, disagreeable; controversial because based on subjective judgments, which may change because of reason or habit; what is consonant in one era may be dissonant in another.

consonance, sense of: judgment of the smoothness, purity, blending, and fusion of two or more tones; measured by one of the parts of the Seashore Measures of Musical Talent (original version). *See* **harmonic sensitivity.**

consonant: a class of speech sounds produced by the obstruction or blocking of the free passage of air in the oral cavity. *Contr. w.* **vowel.**

consonant blend: *see* **blend, consonant.**

consonant digraph: *see* **digraph.**

consonant substitution: *see* **substitution, consonant.**

consonant trigraph: a combination of three consonants, for example, *str, tch.*

consortium (kən·sôr′sh(ē)əm); *n. pl.* consortia (kən·sôr′sh(ē)ə); (1) a combination or organization of higher education institutions to share offerings or other educational resources, conduct research and experiments, and/or develop new programs primarily for the purposes of enriching without duplication the opportunities offered by all and of reducing costs; *see* **college, cluster;** (2) (teacher ed.) a group of specialists from different universities who are knowledgeable in certain fields and constitute a steering committee on a research project by means of which they arrive at a new set of programs or innovations applicable to education.

conspicuous consumption: *see* **consumption, conspicuous.**

constancy: (1) the relative stability of the appearance of objects or situations, despite differences in the condition of the organism perceiving them or in the local stimulating conditions; thus, a chair is perceived as a chair, despite normal variations in the external or the internal environment of the organism perceiving it; (2) a tendency to steadiness in purpose or direction of activity; (3) the tendency for members of a group to retain within fairly close limits similar relative positions over a period of time in regard to one or more characteristics, such as intelligence, dominance, popularity, etc. (note that constancy in respect to living organisms is relative and does not imply fixity); (4) relative freedom from errors of measurement, resulting in an approximately stable score or measure for an individual.

constancy hypothesis: (1) the theory that a positive correlation exists between stimulation and sensation; that is, if a given stimulus is observed to call forth a particular sensation on one occasion, the same stimulus will bring about the same response upon another occasion, provided that the condition of the organism remains unchanged; (2) the hypothesis of constancy of relative position (such as in a percentile rank or standard score) for an individual upon remeasurement at different ages or periods; *see* **constancy** (3).

constancy of intelligence: *see* **intelligence, constancy of.**

constant: *adj.* unvarying; retaining the same value throughout the process of a discussion or computation. *Contr. w.* **variable** *adj.*

constant: *n.* (math.) (1) a number that retains the same value through a series of calculations; *contr. w.* **variable** *n.;* (2) *syn.* **parameter;** (3) *syn.* **statistic;** (4) (curric.) any course or subject of study required of all students enrolled in a particular curriculum; *syn.* **required course; required subject;** *contr. w.* **elective.**

constant, additive: a constant term (whether positive or negative) which is added in an equation; for example, in the formula $y = ax + b$, b is an additive constant, a is a multiplying constant, and x and y are variables.

constant, curriculum: any course required of all or nearly all pupils, regardless of the curriculum being pursued.

constant error: *see* **error, constant.**

constant fundamentals, philosophy of: *syn.* **essentialism.**

constant, multiplying: a constant by which values of a variable are to be multiplied; for example, in the formula $y = ax + b$, a is a multiplying constant, b is an additive constant, and x and y are variables.

constant, statistical: *syn.* **statistic** (1).

constants-with-variables curriculum: *see* **curriculum, constants-with-variables.**

constellation: (1) a group of related ideas invested with emotion that has not been repressed and hence is accessible to consciousness; *contr. w.* **complex;** (2) (fact. anal.) (*a*) a grouping of trait vectors within the trait configuration; similar to a cluster in *cluster analysis;* (*b*) the general arrangement of loadings among factors.

constellation, emotional: a group of related ideas invested with emotion that is accessible to consciousness and influences the personality.

constellation, family: the pattern of the family described in terms of the age, sex, personal qualities, and personal relationships of its members.

constitution: (1) the body of fundamental laws or principles formulated by the sovereign people it governs, instituting the form of their government, securing their rights, and defining their duties; ordinarily embodied in written documents but sometimes implied in customs and usages; (2) the physical makeup of an organism, considered as the aggregate of its physical and vital powers; (3) the mental, intellectual, or psychological makeup of an organism, considered as the aggregate of its intellectual powers, character traits, etc.; (4) the totality of the physical and psychological attributes of an organism, with emphasis on inherited characters (the concept includes such features as structure, size and form, metabolism, rate and condition of growth, nutritional status, and resistance to disease); *see* **genotype; heredity; phenotype;** *dist. f.* **habitus; personality; temperament;** (5) the aggregate of interrelated factors, parts, and elements that characteristically compose a given thing, concept, or datum of any sort.

constitution, rigid: a constitution, such as that of the United States, that cannot be modified in its express terms except through such processes as the constitution itself ordains.

constitutional: consistent with the constitution; authorized by the constitution; not conflicting with any provision of the constitution or fundamental law of the state.

constitutional disorder: any disorder to which a person is especially prone by reason of his particular mental and physical makeup; may be inherited or deeply ingrained and of long standing; does not include disorders adventitiously or situationally acquired.

constitutional government: *see* **government, constitutional.**

constitutional habitus: *see* **habitus.**

constitutional history: *see* **history, constitutional.**

constitutional inferiority: mental defectiveness or susceptibility to disease because of an inherent weakness.

constitutive projective method: *see* **projective method, constitutive.**

constriction: (psych.) restriction of attention to a rather narrow range of environmental stimuli.

construct: (1) a property ascribed to two or more objects as a result of scientific observation; generally, a model designed with an awareness of the relationship which exists between data and the model; (2) (testing) some postulated attribute of people, assumed to be reflected in test performance; in test validation, an attribute, such as intelligence, verbal fluency, or anxiety, about which we make statements in interpreting a test.

construct, diagnostic: *syn.* **diagnostic category.**

construct, hypothetical: a "best guess," a scientifically unsupportable explanation or model used in order to allow the imagination of the scientist to go beyond present knowledge and currently orthodox but inadequate theories; an explanation of causal relationships considered to be a temporary expedient because it is based upon conceptualizations which, though operationally inadequate, still contain some empirical support and also an element of testability; nonoperational inadmissible hypothetical constructs may acquire through experimentation supportive evidence which may transform them into the more admissible (operationally valid) intervening variables, the only kinds of constructs upon which sound scientific theory is based. *See* **validity, operational; variable, intervening.**

construct validity: *see* **validity, construct.**

constructed matter: spoken or written language composed unit by unit from the stock of linguistic matter (words, phrases, principles of grammar and composition, etc.) at one's command.

constructed response: *see* **response, constructed.**

construction: (1) (art ed.) the translation of an idea into art form through building with materials such as wood, stone, metal, or clay; used in connection with project work of various kinds such as paper construction, sand tables, and model villages; *see* **experience, motor-constructive;** (2) (ind. arts) the study of the technology, socioeconomic contributions, and architectural problems of industries concerned with residential and commercial structures; learning activities, which are usually centered on scaled structures, involve research, design, engineering, masonry, carpentry, electricity, and plumbing.

construction, building: (1) all the activities or processes involved in the erection of buildings; (2) the program for buildings recently built and in process of being built; (3) the material of which a building is constructed, such as wood, steel, masonry, or brick.

construction, bus: *see* **bus construction.**

construction, combustible: a type of building construction consisting in considerable part of combustible materials.

construction contract: *syn.* **contract, building.**

construction, fire-resistive: the manner of building largely with incombustible materials, such as brick, stone, tile, concrete, and steel; to be *fire-resistant,* a building must have relatively little combustible material even in the interior construction. *See* **building, fire-resistive.**

construction, fireproof: (1) a type of construction designed to withstand a complete burnout of the contents for which the building was intended without impairment of structural integrity; use of incombustible materials and certain fire-resistance requirements for structural members, including exterior walls, are customarily stated in codes; (2) occasionally loosely used as a synonym for *fire-resistive construction.*

construction industry: *see* **industry, construction.**

construction occupations: *see* **occupations, construction.**

construction paper: heavy-bodied paper, rectangular in shape, available in varied colors for use in drawing, cutting, pasting, and other creative activities.

construction service: specialized and professional service, as that of contractors and supervising architects, rendered to university, college, or school authorities to ensure the construction of a building or buildings in accordance with plans and specifications. *See* **architect, supervising.**

construction, type A: a school building constructed of fire-resistive materials, including its walls, windows, doors, floors, and finish.

construction, type B: a building of fire-resistive construction in its walls, floors, stairways, and ceilings, but with wood or composition floor surfaces and wood roof construction over fire-resistive ceilings.

construction, type C: a building with masonry walls and fire-resistive corridors and stairways, but with ordinary construction otherwise, namely, combustible floors, partitions, rooms, and finish.

construction, type D: a building with masonry walls, but otherwise having ordinary or joist construction and wood finish.

construction, type E: a building constructed with wood above the foundations, with or without slate or other semi-fireproof material on the roof.

construction, unit: a type of schoolhouse design according to which a unit of measurement—usually 10 or 15 feet—is taken as a constant and the entire building is planned in terms of this unit or of its multiples, to ensure convenient readjustment of room sizes in the event of later alterations.

construction work: (1) any type of schoolwork that uses construction as a valuable part of the learning process, as is common in art or industrial arts work; (2) constructive or manipulative activity indirectly associated with academic learning.

constructive credit: *see* **credit, constructive.**

constructive discipline: *see* **discipline, constructive.**

constructive experience: *see* **experience, constructive.**

constructive method: (res.) a cumulative, culminating process in which the findings of descriptive, causal, and evaluative or other types of investigations are integrated to arrive at a recommended program of action or other large conclusion; the general nature, purpose, and setting of the product to be constructed are determined, and suggestions are widely sought, evaluated, and synthesized; it is more elaborate, painstaking, and systematic than simple productive effort, such as writing a text, or than simple descriptive methods, such as frequency counts. *See* **integrative method; philosophical method; research, deliberative.**

constructive projective method: *see* **projective method, constructive.**

constructive proof: *see* **proof, constructive.**

constructive seeing: *see* **seeing, constructive.**

constructive thinking: *syn.* **thinking, creative.**

constructivism: an early twentieth century movement originating in sculpture; nonfigurative art concerned with formal organization of planes and expression of volume in three-dimensional form, the fourth dimension being implied through the use of motion and time concepts; refers to the work of artists such as Antoine Pevsner and Naum Gabo.

consultancy services, distributive education: *see* **services, distributive education consultancy.**

consultant: (1) an expert in a specialized field, without administrative authority, whose advice is sought in improving an educational program, the facilities offered, or methods of cooperation; (2) a professionally trained person on call to offer guidance and help in promoting and improving the educational program; *see* **supervisor.**

consultant, curriculum: *syn.* **curriculum specialist.**

consultant, educational: a specialist in any area of educational work who is invited by a school official or a professional or lay group to serve as an adviser in the determination and implementation of school policies.

consultant, elementary school industrial arts: a person engaged to work with elementary classroom teachers to assist with construction activities, develop instructional and resource materials, and provide leadership in the study of industry and industrial technology.

consultant, guidance: a staff member who is responsible for providing assistance to other school staff members, to parents, and to pupils in connection with the solution of individual adjustment problems.

consultant, instructional: a specialist in a particular area and level of schoolwork who is invited to serve as an adviser in reference to problems pertaining to curriculum and teaching; generally refers to a specialist from outside the local school system.

consultant, international: a specialist in any field invited by a ministry, a school administrator, or an international agency to serve as an adviser in the development of educational, agricultural, or technical programs in other countries.

consultant, library: one who gives professional, expert advice to librarians, institutions, organizations, or governmental bodies, or to lay groups interested in the stimulation, administration, or development of improved library services, library buildings, and library equipment.

consultant, music: an expert in music or in music teaching who is engaged to clarify and correct problems confronting administrators and music teachers in their professional work.

consultant, reading: a person who has as his major responsibility the improvement of classroom instruction in reading.

consultant, school plant: a specialist consulted by boards of education, architects, or others for the purpose of getting assistance in the planning of school buildings and equipment; may be an employee of a state department of education, a university, or a private firm or individual.

consultant, speech-hearing: a teacher trained in speech correction and services for the hard of hearing; works with children presenting speech and hearing problems and also is available for consultation with classroom teachers, parents, physicians, or anyone responsible for the welfare of such children.

consultant, technical: a person with specialized knowledge in practical, industrial, or mechanical arts or in applied sciences who has contracted to give his advice in his designated field of specialization.

consultation, assembly: *syn.* **interview, group.**

consultative services: *see* **services, consultative.**

consulting psychologist: *see* **psychologist, consulting.**

consumer: (1) (consumer ed.) the ultimate user of economic goods and services as opposed to the producer of them; for example, everyone is a consumer of food, while the farmer is a producer as well as a consumer of food; (2) the ultimate user of any goods, services, products, etc.; for example, the listener at a concert is a consumer of music, while the concert artist is a producer of music.

consumer-acceptance panel: *see* **panel, consumer-acceptance.**

consumer advertising: *see* **advertising, consumer.**

consumer and homemaking education: a term which is replacing "vocational home economics," since the Federal Vocational Education Amendments of 1968 provide for a broader program in home economics; greater consideration is given to (a) meeting social and cultural conditions and needs, especially in economically depressed areas, (b) preparing youths and adults for the dual role of homemakers and wage earners, and (c) providing consumer education programs. *See* **program, reimbursed consumer and homemaking education; programs in vocational home economics, occupational.**

consumer budget: *see* **budget, consumer.**

consumer business education: *see* **business education, consumer.**

consumer choice: *see* **choice, consumer.**

consumer citizenship: *see* **citizenship, consumer.**

consumer conservation: *see* **conservation, consumer.**

consumer credit: *see* **credit, consumer.**

consumer debt: *see* **credit, consumer.**

consumer democracy: *see* **democracy, consumer.**

consumer-directed economy: *syn.* **democracy, consumer.**

consumer economics: *see* **economics, consumer.**

consumer education: education designed to (a) aid the consumer in using his income wisely, (b) develop responsible consumers in an effort to establish a *consumer democracy,* and (c) analyze the role of government in the area of consumption.

consumer goods: *see* **goods, consumer.**

consumer goods, durable: *see* **goods, durable consumer.**

consumer goods, nondurable: *see* **goods, nondurable consumer.**

consumer information: *see* **information, consumer.**

consumer laws: *see* **laws, consumer.**

consumer learnings: *see* **learning, consumer.**

consumer loyalty: *see* **loyalty, consumer.**

consumer mathematics: *see* **mathematics, consumer.**

consumer maturity: *see* **maturity, consumer.**

consumer movement: *see* **movement, consumer.**

consumer needs.: *see* **needs, consumer.**

consumer price index: *see* **index, consumer price.**

consumer problems: *see* **problems, consumer.**

consumer protection: *see* **protection, consumer.**

consumer research: *see* **research, consumer.**

consumer science: *see* **science, consumer.**

consumer welfare: *see* **welfare, consumer.**

consumers' councils: *see* **councils, consumers'.**

consummatory experience: *see* **experience, consummatory.**

consummatory response: *see* **response, consummatory.**

consummatory value: *see* **value, consummatory.**

consumption, competitive: the purchase of goods and services in an effort to equal or excel consumption by others; often called "keeping up with the Joneses." *Syn.* **emulation.**

consumption, conspicuous: the purchase and use of goods and services to impress others with one's buying power.

consumption-directed economy: *see* **economy, consumption-directed.**

consumption tax: *see* **tax, consumption.**

contact case: a person who is known to have been near enough to another person suffering from a communicable disease to contract and/or transmit the disease.

contact, center-to-center: (couns.) contact on the part of the counselor with the center area of the field of experiences of his client, as opposed to contact with the client's defensive fringe area; forms the essential part of therapy that includes the counselor's obligation to understand his own feelings throughout the therapeutic process as well as the feelings of his client.

contact, eye: *see* **eye contact.**

contact, home-school: *see* **home-school contact.**

contagious disease: *see* **disease, contagious.**

contamination, criterion: *see* **criterion contamination.**

contemplation: (1) the focusing of attention and dwelling upon an experience or idea; (2) mere awareness, divorced from practical action, as in (a) idle reverie or (b) mystical contemplation, where the world of objects and the contemplator's own self lose their distinguishing outlines and fuse in a feeling of unity with God, the Absolute, Ultimate Reality, the One, etc.

contemporary: (1) pertaining to two or more art objects which are produced during the same period of time; (2) descriptive of an art object marked by the characteristics of the current period.

contemporary affairs examination: *see* **examination, contemporary affairs.**

contemporary history: *see* **history, contemporary.**

contemporary-problems approach: a method of attack on the problem of curriculum reorganization in which the principal criterion for selecting material to be studied in the school is whether it contributes to an understanding and appreciation of important current issues.

contemporary society: *see* **society, contemporary.**

contempt of court: any act which is calculated to embarrass, hinder, or obstruct court in the administration of justice, or which is calculated to lessen its authority or its dignity.

content: (lang.) the ideas or meanings presented, or to be presented, in speech or writing.

content analysis: *see* **analysis, content.**

content course: *see* **course, content.**

content, differentiation of: *see* **differentiation of content.**

content examination: *see* **examination, content.**

content reading: *see* **reading, content.**

content reliability: *see* **reliability, content.**

content standard test score: *see* **score, content standard test.**

content subject: *see* **subject, content.**

content theory: a theory of language teaching advocating the utmost possible use of materials and activities of social and cultural significance.

content validity: *see* **validity, content.**

content word: *see* **word, content.**

contest, intergroup: (elem. ed.) any form of organized competitive activity carried on among different school groups, as distinguished from competition among members of a single group.

contest, interschool: *syn.* **competition, interscholastic.**

contest, music: *see* **music contest.**

contest, school: one of numerous types of organized competition in academic subjects, athletics, and other activities connected with the school curriculum or program, often sponsored or promoted by state and national agencies and institutions, including university extension.

contest, speech: *see* **speech contest.**

contest, spelling: *syn.* **spelling match.**

context: (1) the textual material in which a particular word, phrase, or statement is found; may apply to written or spoken material; (2) by extension of meaning, the environment or particular circumstances in which anything occurs or is found.

context clue: *see* **clue, context.**

context clue, verbal: *syn.* **clue, context.**

context evaluation: *see* **evaluation, context.**

context exercises: *see* **exercises, context.**

context form: the presentation of words for spelling drill in the form of phrases, sentences, or paragraphs, rather than individually or in columns. *Contr. w.* **column form.**

context, law of: *see* **law of context.**

context method of lipreading: *see* **lipreading, context method of.**

context reader: *see* **reader, context.**

contextual method: a method of teaching word recognition that depends largely on guessing the word or meaning from its use in a word group or large unit.

contextual theory of knowledge: *see* **knowledge, contextual theory of.**

contextual theory of meaning: *see* **meaning, contextual theory of.**

contiguity: the state of being close together, whether in temporal or spatial relationships, or both. *See* **association by contiguity.**

contiguity, association by: *see* **association by contiguity.**

contiguity, law of: *see* **law of contiguity.**

contingencies of reinforcement: *see* **reinforcement, contingencies of.**

contingency: chance, irregularity, indeterminateness; according to John Dewey, a characteristic of nature (reality), which he calls a mixture of completeness, order, recurring events making possible prediction and control, and of singular cases, uncertain possibilities and processes going toward consequences not yet determinate.

contingency appropriation: *see* **appropriation, contingency.**

contingency coefficient: *syn.* **coefficient of contingency.**

contingency, coefficient of: *see* **coefficient of contingency.**

contingency management: a type of contract planning with students; determines reasonable rewards that the students prize and then establishes the schedule of increments of learning by which the students can earn the rewards. *See* **contract plan.**

contingency method: a method of measuring the degree of association between two variables by employing a formula involving the differences between the actual frequencies in the cells of a two-way (or contingency) table and the frequencies that would be expected if the two variables were independent. *See* **chi square.**

contingency table: *see* **table, contingency.**

contingent fund: *see* **fund, contingent.**

contingent liability: *see* **liability, contingent.**

continuant: a consonant sound that is prolonged in vocal expression such as *f, v,* or *s.*

continuation class, part-time general: a class conducted in a public school on a part-time basis for employed youths over 14 years of age, as a means of increasing their civic or vocational competence and to help them bridge the gap between their withdrawal from full-time schooling and their permanent occupational establishment.

continuation education: the term applied in some countries, especially British Commonwealth nations, to a form of postsecondary schooling, usually part-time, taken by employed people who wish additional formal study but who for some reason cannot attend a university.

continuation school: (voc. ed.) a public part-time school in which young workers may continue their education even though they are employed. (To meet state and Federal standards, classes must meet a minimum of 144 hours per year, and learners must be 14 to 18 years of age. This term was in common use during the period 1910-1930 but has gradually fallen into disuse.)

continuation study, center for: *see* **center, adult education.**

continuation training: *see* **training, continuation.**

continued sum: *syn.* **cumulative total.**

continuing contract: *syn.* **contract, continuous.**

continuing education: (1) any extension of opportunities for reading, study, and training to young persons and adults following their completion of or withdrawal from full-time school and college programs; (2) education for adults provided by special schools, centers, colleges, or institutes that emphasizes flexible rather than traditional or academic programs. *See* **adult education.**

continuing education, center for: *see* **center, adult education.**

continuing education, distributive education: a program in distribution at the postsecondary and/or adult level which meets the continuing vocational interests and needs of individuals so that they may upgrade themselves, retrain themselves, and/or learn new knowledges in distributive occupations.

continuing guidance: *see* **guidance, continuing.**

continuing legal education: *see* **continuing professional education.**

continuing medical education: *see* **continuing professional education.**

continuing professional education: the continuing education of adults for occupational updating and improvement conducted by a wide variety of institutions, organizations, and businesses; usually consists of short-term, intensive, specialized learning experiences often categorized by general field of specialization, such as *continuing medical education* or *continuing legal education.*

continuing school census: *syn.* **census, continuous school.**

continuity: (1) the logical relationship of one scene leading to the next one and the smooth flow of action and narration within the total audiovisual material; (2) a script for radio, television, or film production that specifically outlines the sequence of events to be presented; (3) loosely, spoken interpolated remarks, such as those of an announcer or master of ceremonies, that serve to give sequence to a program.

continuity, correction for: *see* **correction for continuity.**

continuity hypothesis: *see* **hypothesis, continuity.**

continuity of experience: flow of experience from one, earlier, stage to another, later, stage; experience free of dead endings or blocks that remove potential of later enriching experience; educationally, it is a teacher's responsibility to judge among experiences, selecting those which promise continuity of experience in growth in general, in contrast to specialized growth that narrows and delimits future experience.

continuity, social: uninterrupted connection, continuation, or succession, due to social processes, especially communication among individuals; in contrast with biological continuity.

continuity theory: a theory developed by Froebel during the early nineteenth century in which he said that education was but a phase of the general process of evolution, a development by which the individual comes into realization of the life of the all-encompassing unity of which he is but a small unit.

continuity, Yates correction for: *see* **correction for continuity.**

continuous: (stat.) capable of changing by infinitesimal increments; being subdivided infinitely without break or irregularity. *Syn.* **graduated;** *ant.* **discontinuous; discrete.**

continuous calisthenics: *see* **calisthenics, continuous.**

continuous contract: *see* **contract, continuous.**

continuous data: *see* **data, continuous.**

continuous distribution: *see* **distribution, continuous.**

continuous guidance: *see* **guidance, continuous.**

continuous loop: *see* **loop, continuous.**

continuous measure: *see* **measure, continuous.**

continuous progress: *see* **progress, continuous.**

continuous progress promotion: *see* **promotion, continuous progress.**

continuous projection: *see* **reel, continuous projection.**

continuous projection reel: *see* **reel, continuous projection.**

continuous promotion: *see* **promotion, continuous.**

continuous reconstruction of experience, education as the: *see* **education as the continuous reconstruction of experience.**

continuous registration: *see* **registration, continuous.**

continuous reinforcement: *see* **reinforcement.**

continuous scale: *see* **scale, continuous.**

continuous school census: *see* **census, continuous school.**

continuous school census record: *see* **census record, continuous school.**

continuous series: *see* **series, continuous.**

continuous-tone subject: (audiovis. ed.) an illustration consisting of shades of gray, varying from black to white.

continuous variability: *see* **variability, continuous.**

continuous variable: *see* **variable, continuous.**

continuous variates: *see* **variates, continuous.**

continuous variation: *see* **variation, continuous.**

continuum, experiential: *see* **experiential continuum.**

continuum, latent: the continuum or scale for the underlying characteristic or property which a test is devised to measure.

contour map: *see* **map, contour.**

contract: (1) an agreement between two or more persons or corporations to do or forbear something, made under such conditions that it will be appropriately enforced by courts of law or equity (school authorities make contracts for the erection of buildings, for the purchase of land, equipment, and supplies, and for the employment of teachers and other employees); (2) in the Dalton plan, an organized unit of work that can be pursued at the student's own rate and usually completed within 20 school days; the printed or duplicated outline of such a unit of work.

contract action: *see* **action, contract.**

contract, annual: (1) a teacher's contract the terms of which are binding for only one school term or year; (2) any contract continuing for the period of 1 year. *See* **contract, teacher's; contract, term.**

contract, behavior: a technique described by Keirsey and used in the case of aggressive, destructive, or disruptive acts by children in school; a contract is prepared and signed by each party who agrees to play a certain role for a certain period of time; the child agrees that any disruptive act on his part will immediately result in his being asked to leave school; the teacher agrees to signal the child to leave the classroom whenever the child makes a disruptive act; the principal agrees to enforce the agreement; the parent agrees to avoid conversation with the child about school and to avoid punishing or scolding the child for being sent home; and the psychologist negotiates the contract and agrees to be available for counsel.

contract, breach of: failure to fulfill the terms of a written or oral agreement between two parties guaranteeing the performance of a specified service; ordinarily implies the termination of the contract by one party without the consent of the other.

contract, building: a legal agreement for the construction or alteration of a building according to accepted plans and specifications and at specified cost.

contract bus: *see* **bus, contract.**

contract, bus: a type of transportation contract. *See* **contract, transportation.**

contract, construction: *syn.* **contract, building.**

contract, continuing: *syn.* **contract, continuous.**

contract, continuous: a contract that remains in effect for the following year or any predetermined period of employment, on the same terms, unless the teacher is specifically notified by a given date of the termination of his employment; also called *continuing contract. Contr. w.* **contract, annual; contract, term.**

contract, cooperative student: a written agreement sometimes made between a vocational cooperative class and business, professional, or industrial employers, providing

for the employment of certain cooperative students according to the provisions of the Federal vocational acts.

contract, executed: a completed contract as opposed to one which is executory. *See* **contract, executory.**

contract, executory: (school admin.) an incompletely performed contract; something yet to be done in the future.

contract, freedom of: *see* **freedom of contract.**

contract, game: an agreement relative to division of receipts and expenses entered into by two competing teams.

contract, implied: a contractual agreement inferred solely from the acts or conduct of the parties involved, no explicit contractual statement having been made, either orally or in writing. *Contr. w.* **contract, unauthorized.**

contract, initial: the first legal agreement entered into, for example, by a teacher and a school board.

contract, joint: (pup. trans.) a written agreement involving two or more districts or schools, arranging for the common use of one or more buses in transporting children to and from the several schools represented.

contract operation: (1) the plan of supplying pupil transportation service in buses owned by individuals or corporations rather than by school districts or other governmental units; (2) the provision of pupil transportation in accordance with a written agreement.

contract plan: (1) a plan of instruction, adaptable to individual differences, in which the course content is divided into a number of long-term assignments (usually one assignment per month), prepared in printed or duplicated form, each pupil receiving a contract and being allowed to proceed to the next contract when he has completed the previous one; usually provides not only for self-instruction but also for drill, activities, and appraisal of progress; the basis of the *Dalton plan; see* **contingency management;** (2) a method of remedial speech instruction that consists in a series of prescribed, or "contracted," tasks or skills to be mastered by the student; depends on dividing a complicated procedure into short units, on motivation supplied by the student's understanding of the problem, and on the student's assuming the responsibility for correction of the defect.

contract, plant employees': an agreement as to the terms of service and remuneration of employees who operate and maintain a physical plant.

contract, purchase: a legal statement of the obligations created by agreement between vendor and vendee for the exchange of certain values and the conditions governing the discharge of these obligations.

contract, quasi: a contract not based upon agreement of the parties but implied from some relation between them or from a voluntary act of one of them.

contract service: pupil transportation provided by an individual or corporation in accordance with a written agreement. *Syn.* **contract operation** (2).

contract, social: *see* **social contract.**

contract, teacher's: a formal agreement, usually in writing, entered into by a teacher and the employing authority, stating the salary to be paid and the length of the term of the contract, and setting forth the general duties to be performed by the teacher. *See* **contract, annual; contract, continuing; contract, term.**

contract, term: a contractual agreement limited to a definite time, such as 1, 2, or 3 school years. *See* **contract, annual.**

contract, transportation: a written agreement between school authorities and an individual, partnership, or corporation, stipulating the compensation and the amount of service to be rendered for a specified period in transporting pupils to and from school, usually over a specified route.

contract, unauthorized: a purported contractual agreement entered into without regard for legal requirements. *Contr. w.* **contract, implied.**

contract, verbal: (school admin.) a contract expressed in words, not written.

contracted services: *see* **services, contracted.**

contracting family: *see* **family, contracting.**

contracting, performance: a procedure whereby a board of education engages a private firm to conduct a program of educational improvement guaranteed by the firm to achieve satisfactorily predetermined objectives, called *performance criteria,* with compensation paid by the board on a scale related to performance.

contraction, braille: *see* **braille contraction.**

contraction, dynamic: *see* **contraction, phasic** (1).

contraction, isometric: a contraction in which a muscle is unable to shorten, the total tension developed eventually being dissipated as heat. *Syn.* **static contraction.**

contraction, isotonic: *syn.* **contraction, phasic** (1).

contraction, phasic: (1) in general, a term used for muscle shortening during contraction, while the load remains the same; *syn.* **dynamic contraction; isotonic contraction;** (2) occasionally used to mean any change in length, either shortening or lengthening.

contraction, static: *syn.* **contraction, isometric.**

contractor ownership: the designation of a plan of supplying pupil transportation in buses owned by individuals or corporations rather than by the school authorities.

contractor's bond: *see* **bond, contractor's.**

contractual capacity: as applied to the public schools, the authority granted public school officials to enter into legal agreements involving the schools.

contracture, flexion: *see* **flexion contracture.**

contradiction, principle of: the assertion that a proposition cannot be both true and false at the same time and place and under the same conditions; two propositions are said to be related as contradictories when not both can be true but either the one or the other is true; thus, if "All intelligence tests are valid" is true, then "Some intelligence tests are not valid" is false, and vice versa.

contradictory propositions: *see* **propositions, contradictory.**

contraharmonic mean: *see* **mean, contraharmonic.**

contralto: the lowest female voice or a boy's voice of corresponding range, usually from A below middle C to F an eleventh higher. *Syn.* **alto.** (Some musicians use the term contralto to refer to a voice lower in range and deeper in quality than the alto.)

contraposition, rule of: *see* **inference, rules of.**

contrapositive: the contrapositive form of the sentence "*p* implies *q*" is the sentence "not-*q* implies not-*p*"; for example, the contrapositive of the sentence "If a figure is a rectangle, then it is a parallelogram" is "If a figure is not a parallelogram, then it is not a rectangle." *See* **converse.**

contrapposto: (art) the representation of the human body in standing position; the balanced nonsymmetrical position of the body in a relaxed and eased stance.

contrariety: (1) a tendency to behave in a fashion contrary to the wishes, desires, or dictates of others; *syn.* **negativism** (1); (2) inconsistency.

contrariety, principle of: two propositions are said to be related as contraries when not both can be true although both can be false; thus, if "All scientists are objective" is true, then "No scientists are objective" is false; but if "No scientists are objective" is false, then "All scientists are objective" may be either true or false.

contrary classes: (stat.) two classes such that every attribute in the symbol for one is the contrary or negative of the corresponding attribute in the symbol for the other; for example, native-born male and foreign-born female are contrary classes.

contrary propositions: *see* **propositions, contradictory.**

contrast, phonemic: *see* **phonemic contrast.**

contrast, phonetic: *see* **phonetic contrast.**

contrast, subject: (photog.) the scale of tonal values exhibited by a subject; if the scale is short, with little range of tone, it is called flat, whether generally dark or generally light; if it is reasonably long, with good gradation from black to white, it is regarded as normal; when the subject tonal range is great and intermediate tones are relatively lacking, the subject is termed contrasty.

contrasting pairs method: (for. lang. instr.) a method of teaching or testing phonemic discrimination through the use of pairs of words that differ in only one phoneme. *See* **minimal pairs; phonemic contrast.**

contrasuggestibility: a condition in which there is a marked tendency for the individual to act in a manner contrary to that suggested. *Syn.* **negative suggestibility.**

contributed services: a term used to represent the estimated monetary value of the services rendered without remuneration by members of religious organizations in institutions conducted by religious orders, societies, or similar groups, as, for example, various orders of the Roman Catholic Church.

contribution to delinquency: *see* **delinquency, contribution to.**

contributory function of supervision: *see* **supervision, contributory function of.**

contributory negligence: *see* **negligence, contributory.**

contributory retirement system: *see* **retirement system, contributory.**

contrived experiences: *see* **experiences, contrived.**

contrived material: (for. lang. instr.) reading material prepared by individuals or committees in which unfamiliar language items are interspersed among known words so that children are helped to guess at the meaning of the new words from the surrounding familiar words; should be used as a third step in the development of reading skills; the first step being reading of basic utterances, sentences, dialogues, songs, etc., which duplicate material that has been learned thoroughly audiolingually, and the second step consisting of recombined utterances or sentences.

control, administrative: *see* **administrative control.**

control, arm-hand: *see* **arm-hand control.**

control, authoritarian: in education, a type of relationship between teacher and pupils, or between administrator and teaching staff, in which policy and practice tend to be determined primarily and sometimes entirely by those of higher rank; sometimes used to emphasize a domineering relationship in contrast to democratic or cooperative or sympathetic attitude toward co-workers or pupils.

control board: *see* **plugboard.**

control, bowel: *see* **bowel control.**

control card: *see* **card, control.**

control chart: *see* **chart, control.**

control, classroom: *see* **discipline** (3).

control, community: an experimental approach to decentralization of control of inner-city schools as a means of giving ghetto communities equal access to the process of making decisions vitally affecting the education of their children through delegation by the central board of education of specific areas of authority to a governing board of the local school, made up of elected community members and responsible directly to the superintendent of schools of the city and to the state commissioner of education; it is expected that increased parental and community involvement will have an important effect on the achievement of the children in school and result in a teaching staff and program better adapted to their needs. *Syn.* **school decentralization;** *see* **administration, decentralized.**

control console: *see* **console, control.**

control counter: *see* **counter, control.**

control, decentralized: the assignment by the responsible person of some or all of the work of controlling a particular action to a subordinate executive who is closer to the point of performance; increasing decentralization of control results in an increasing separation of administrative control from operative control. *See* **administrative control; control, operative.**

control, delegated: duties or responsibilities in a certain activity that have been transferred by the one actually responsible for such duties or responsibilities to another person; the person receiving such delegated control becomes responsible to the one delegating it for the successful carrying out of the duties or responsibilities, but the one delegating such control cannot delegate the ultimate responsibility which always rests with him.

control, democratic: (1) a system of group organization and action in which there is a high degree of (*a*) sharing in determination of policy, (*b*) respect for minority views, (*c*) common consent, and (*d*) joint responsibility for results; (2) a contrasting term to authoritarian, dictatorial, or totalitarian relations or imposed regulations; (3) the principle of utilizing intelligence wherever it may occur in directing individual or group action; (4) respect for those of lesser rank or position. (The principle of democratic control may apply to a whole school system, to a particular school, or to a single classroom.)

control, emotional: *see* **emotional control.**

control, experimental: the attempt to equalize, by direct methods, the effects of one or more extraneous factors on the criterion measures in an experiment; for example, in an experimental comparison of two methods of instruction, an effort may be made to control the pupil variable (that is, to equalize the initial ability of the experimental groups to profit by these methods of instruction) by deliberately selecting two groups of pupils with identical distributions of scores on a general intelligence test, or an effort may be made to control the teacher variable by having the same teacher for both groups.

control group: *see* **group, control.**

control, hierarchy of: *see* **hierarchy of control.**

control, indirect: a process of directing individual or group action and thought through artful or subtle means which may be unrecognized or willingly tolerated by those who are governed; it minimizes emphasis upon superior-inferior relationships and specific rules.

control, institutional: the control of athletics or other activities by the governing body of a school or college.

control, inventory: (school admin.) the staff function of controlling, coordinating, and regulating the work of procuring and disbursing materials in accordance with inventory and manufacturing plans. *See* **functions, staff.**

control, invisible: limitation in the quality of the results of the teaching-learning process arising from inadequacies present in the instructional or supervisory personnel.

control, local: *syn.* **autonomy (3); autonomy of school district.**

control, locomotor: ability to perform those physical skills which allow a person to move from one place to another effectively.

control, manipulatory: ability to use and to control the movements of the upper limbs.

control, numerical: the study of industrial automation in which specific commands to perform desired machine-tool operations are supplied to the machine-control mechanisms by means of information previously programmed by punched card, punched tape, or magnetic tape; symbolized as N/C.

control, operative: project control, that is, the control of action by individuals and groups who are performing the steps or operations that have been prescribed for the execution of a specific project or undertaking. *See* **administrative control; control, decentralized.**

control panel: (1) a device to tell one or more data-processing machines what columns to read and what operations to perform; *syn.* **plugboard;** (2) that part of a computer *console* which contains manual controls to enable an operator to control the computer; (3) the nerve system of an accounting machine, consisting of a panel plugged with wires that relay data from the cards to the various machine functions to render desired results.

control, popular: the assignment of the control of an activity to the people who are served by the activity; such control may be exercised through meetings and elections or may be delegated to a person or persons selected by the people.

control, preliminary: (school admin.) those functions that seek to establish control of an action before that action commences; includes routine planning, scheduling, preparation, and dispatching.

control, psychological: (1) the control and direction of an individual or group through understanding and applying established principles of human behavior; artfulness in restraining, guiding, or motivating an individual or group through a superior insight into needs, resources, etc.; the

application of a system of indirect pressures to gain a desired pattern of action on the part of others; (2) the indoctrination of a particular system of values in which ideals are construed as fixed rules of conduct; in a bad sense, the art of taking advantage of the comparative ignorance or inexperience of the young, the uninformed, or the weak, without arousing opposition or resentment.

control, quality: (stat.) a set of statistical methods, generally based on sequential analysis, for ensuring the uniformity of a product. *See* **chart, control.**

control register: *see* **instruction register.**

control, remote: *see* **remote control.**

control room: a room usually located adjacent to, or as part of, a television, radio, or electronic learning laboratory or studio, with glass panels installed to permit visual contact between the two areas; contains control console, audio equipment, and other accessories employed by the director, teacher, and/or staff.

control, self-: *see* **self-control.**

control sequence: in data processing, the order in which instructions are executed.

control, social: (1) either the means or the result of applying pressures in order to exercise influence on an individual in the direction of securing conformity to generally accepted ways of action and thought; (2) the efforts of an organized pressure group to gain or exercise power over its own members or over nonmembers; (3) the resultant of several forces or groups working in various degrees of collaboration or opposition, and collectively instrumental in ensuring certain preferred changes or in maintaining certain relationships or behavior patterns.

control, span of: the extent to which a person in an administrative hierarchy exercises effective authority over persons at a lower level in the hierarchy; the maximum number of persons reporting directly to a recognized higher-level position in an administrative organization. *Syn.* **span of supervision; units of supervision.**

control, state: *see* **state control.**

control, statistical: (1) the maintenance of satisfactory uniformity by successive sampling of items to ensure that they all fall within predetermined limits of quality; *see* **chart, control; control, quality;** (2) the act or process of adjusting or correcting results of an experiment so as to make allowance for or to eliminate the effects of one or more extraneous factors that can be measured but that cannot reasonably be directly (that is, experimentally) controlled.

control, superinstitutional: any kind of control over an educational institution or school system that is lodged in an agency outside the institution or system itself, such as the central government, a church, or an accrediting association.

control, tension: *see* **tension control.**

control, thought: any effort to get persons or groups to adopt particular points of view with respect to politics, economics, religion, social values, education, etc., with little or no tolerance of alternate points of view; it stems from (*a*) the greatly increased facilities in means of mass communication such as radio, travel, television, etc., and (*b*) the concept that education is or should be primarily a process of indoctrination in contrast to enlightenment.

control tower operator training program: *see* **program, control tower operator training.**

control unit: the part of the hardware of an automatic computer that directs the sequence of operations, interprets the instructions, initiates action, and directs the circuits that execute the commands.

control, visible: (admin.) clearly understood controls over behavior, readily identified by source. *Contr. w.* **control, invisible.**

controlled association: *see* **association, controlled.**

controlled-association test: *see* **test, controlled-association.**

controlled experimental method: *syn* **experimental method.**

controlled reader: *see* **reader, controlled.**

controlled reading: *see* **reading, controlled.**

controlled responding: *see* **responding, controlled.**

controlled variable: *see* **variable, controlled.**

controlled vocabulary: *see* **vocabulary, controlled.**

controlling accounts, inventory: *see* **accounts, inventory controlling.**

controls, electronic: *see* **electronic controls.**

controls, external: the regulations, restraints, or pressures placed upon an individual by others; a contrasting term to the *internal controls,* feelings, or pressures which an individual may impose upon himself; sometimes indicates or suggests a lack of basic purpose, or the absence of self-discipline, on the part of an individual with an expressed or implied need for direction by others. *Contr. w.* **controls, internal.**

controls, internal: the restraints or regulations of behavior which an individual may place upon his own actions because of conscience, or through feelings of propriety or justice; in contrast to imposed or *external controls* or pressures exerted upon the individual by others; may reflect a childish or adolescent idealism, or a mature, self-disciplined, and responsible adult. *Contr. w.* **controls, external.**

controls of conduct: those rules, accepted practices, social codes, authorities, or influences which act as restraints upon and provide direction for the activities of individuals or groups.

convalescent home class: *see* **class, convalescent home.**

convent: a building or house occupied by a community of nuns; popularly but incorrectly used as a synonym for *convent school.*

convent school: a school operated in connection with a convent, with the sisters as teachers; may be at any level from the kindergarten through college; usually limited to girls, except in the lower grades, where boys may be admitted, according to local custom; popularly but incorrectly called *convent.*

convention: (1) a meeting or assembly; (2) an agreement between parties; (3) a general agreement on which is based a custom, institution, rule of behavior, or matter of taste; hence, by extension, the abuse of such an agreement, whereby the rules based upon it become "conventional," that is, lifeless and artificial.

convention, laws of: *see* **laws of convention.**

convention, teachers': a scheduled gathering of teachers from a single geographical area.

conventional laboratory: *see* **laboratory, conventional.**

conventional morality: *see* **morality, conventional.**

conventional school: a school that is the outgrowth of custom or common practice.

conventional-type bus: *see* **bus, conventional-type.**

convergence: the act of turning the eyes inward to obtain binocular fixation for objects less than 20 feet from the eyes.

convergence, near point of: *see* **near point of convergence.**

convergent squint: *see* **squint, convergent.**

convergent strabismus: *syn.* **esophoria.**

convergent thinking: *see* **thinking, convergent.**

convergent validity: *see* **validity, convergent.**

conversation: a language activity characterized by informality, by the absence of a deliberately assigned question or problem to be discussed, by absence of the need of reaching a decision, and by frequent change of topic. *Dist. f.* **discussion.**

conversation, directed: a technique of controlled oral drill in foreign language teaching wherein utterances are suggested to each student in a conversation to move those conversing smoothly through a planned sequence of familiar utterances.

conversation period: *see* **period, conversation.**

conversational computing: *see* **computing, conversational.**

conversational count: a rhythmic or semirhythmic count used chiefly in handwriting, characterized by running informal oral directions, the count being secured by directed emphasis on certain syllables so as to indicate appropriate upstrokes or other cues in the writing.

conversational interaction: *see* **interaction, conversational.**

conversational method: (1) a method of teaching in which children are given abundant opportunity to share orally their experiences, interests, and activities; represents a reaction against the method of conducting class exercises by means of formal questions and answers; (2) (for. lang. instr.) oral class practice in the form of conversation between students or between students and instructor on subjects chosen with a view toward mastery of the vocabulary and colloquial idiom of the language.

converse: (logic) the converse of the sentence "*p* implies *q*" is the sentence "*q* implies *p*"; for example, the converse of "If two sides of a triangle are equal, the angles opposite those sides are equal" would be "If two angles of a triangle are equal, the sides opposite these angles are equal." *Comp. w.* **contrapositive.**

conversion: (1) wrongful appropriation to one's own use of the goods of another; (2) an adjustment in the burden of interest on debt by some process of substitution; (3) a legal business transaction that decreases the burden of interest rate on a debt or obligation; (4) any mental mechanism in which the accompanying emotional dissociation becomes converted into a physical expression; for example, sensory or motor disturbances may occur as a conversion from anxiety.

conversion base: the skill, experience, and knowledge in one trade that may be of value as a foundation in another trade.

conversion hysteria: *see* **hysteria, conversion.**

conversion of scores: the process or act of changing a series of test scores from one unit of measurement to another; for example, the changing of raw scores to derived scores; a process that usually makes possible direct comparison of an individual's results on more than one test or with other individuals.

converter: (1) in data processing, a machine that changes information in one kind of machine language or code into another kind of machine language or code; (2) an electronic device capable of changing radio and television signals from one class of frequencies to another; attached to a TV receiver, allows a VHF set to tune in UHF channels; similarly installed at the antenna site it can perform the same function to permit distribution of the modified signals to many television receivers not ordinarily equipped to receive such signals.

converter, card-to-tape: a device that converts information directly from punched cards to punched or magnetic tape.

converter, tape-to-card: a device that converts information directly from punched or magnetic tape to cards.

conveyance: any vehicle or equipment in which pupils are transported to and from school, such as train, streetcar, bus, automobile, wagon, or sled.

cooling system: (1) mechanical means of lowering the temperature in a building, usually accompanied by a means for humidity control; *see* **air conditioning;** (2) means of dissipating heat in projection and broadcasting equipment.

cooperating employer: a company or person employing a student-learner who is enrolled in a recognized cooperative program under the regulations of technical and vocational programs.

cooperating merchant: *see* **merchant, cooperating.**

cooperating school: *syn.* **affiliated school** (1).

cooperating school district: *see* **district, cooperating school.**

cooperating teacher: *syn.* **supervising teacher.**

cooperation: action on the part of individuals or groups integrated toward a single effect or toward the achievement of a common purpose. *Contr. w.* **competition.**

cooperation, antagonistic: *syn.* **accommodation** (2).

cooperation, horizontal: agreeable, helpful relations beyond those actually required among persons of equal rank in a department or industry.

cooperation, interinstitutional: an arrangement whereby two or more educational institutions share in the provision and use of certain facilities or services, or take common action for solution of educational problems or for accomplishment of some other common purpose.

cooperation, library: the association of two or more libraries in such efforts as limitation in their collection policies, development of services in particular fields, contribution of cards to union catalogs or lists, or provision of other services to clientele from various areas without regard to political boundaries.

cooperation, vertical: agreeable, helpful relationships beyond those actually required by the tasks at hand among persons of different ranks in industry or in any hierarchical organization.

cooperative: an enterprise in which a number of persons having common interests combine to produce, purchase, or distribute goods jointly so as to eliminate the profits of middlemen. (Most cooperatives in the United States are for purchase and distribution rather than production.)

cooperative activity: *see* **activity, cooperative.**

cooperative assignment: *see* **assignment, cooperative.**

cooperative buying: *syn.* **cooperative purchasing.**

cooperative class: *see* **class, cooperative.**

cooperative course: *see* **course, cooperative.**

cooperative diversified education: a secondary school cooperative work-experience program in which students are given vocational instruction in (*a*) any one of a variety of business or trade and industrial occupations, (*b*) trade and industrial occupations only, or (*c*) business occupations only, such as retailing, office work, business management, etc. *See* **cooperative education.**

cooperative education: a program for persons enrolled in a school that provides for alternating study in school with a job in industry or business, the two experiences being so planned and supervised cooperatively by the school and the employer that each contributes definitely to the student's development in his chosen occupation; work periods and school attendance may be on alternate half-days, weeks, or other periods of time. *Syn.* **cooperative work experience program;** *see* **program, cooperative.**

cooperative employment: *see* **cooperative education.**

cooperative evaluation: *syn.* **grading, cooperative.**

cooperative extension: *see* **extension, cooperative.**

cooperative extension service: *see* **extension service, cooperative.**

cooperative extension service in agriculture and home economics: *see* **extension service in agriculture and home economics, cooperative.**

cooperative extension work: *see* **extension service in agriculture and home economics, cooperative.**

cooperative factors: *see* **factors, cooperative.**

cooperative grading: *see* **grading, cooperative.**

cooperative group plan: (1) a plan of organization in which the teacher directs the experiences of the pupils by dividing them into small groups, each with a chairman; (2) a plan, proposed by J. F. Hosic, for the internal organization of an elementary school; provides for a small group of teachers who work together with the same group of children, the purpose being to achieve more effective coordination of teacher efforts, each teacher offering one phase of the curriculum, but all working toward common aims.

cooperative housing: *see* **housing, cooperative.**

cooperative housing and dining plan: an association of college students to provide for themselves housing and eating facilities in which each member is assigned, usually in rotation or other varying order, duties in the preparation and serving of meals and other housekeeping functions as partial payment of expenses.

cooperative learning: *see* **learning, cooperative.**

cooperative method, distributive education: a means by which an organized sequence of on-the-job learning experiences to develop competencies related to each student's distributive occupational interest is correlated with classroom instruction.

cooperative movement: (1) an organized effort to secure the establishment of the cooperative system as a social institution; *see* **cooperative;** (2) the continued practice of setting up cooperatives.

cooperative nursery school: *see* **nursery school, cooperative.**

cooperative occupational training: *see* **training, cooperative occupational.**

cooperative office education: *see* **office education, cooperative.**

cooperative office education parental consent form: *see* **consent form, cooperative office education parental.**

cooperative part-time class: *see* **part-time class, cooperative.**

cooperative plan: (1) a kind of educational organization where a pupil who is being prepared for employment may spend part of his time in school and part of his time in actual employment in the community; a teacher-coordinator employed by the school usually coordinates the in-school and out-of-school learning experiences; (2) (spec. ed.) a plan whereby the partially-seeing child is usually enrolled in the special classroom for his close eye work and the blind child for reading and writing in braille, where they may receive the help of the special teacher in a special classroom setting.

cooperative plan, alternate: a plan for the budgeting of time in cooperative classes in which each student is paired with another on the same job, one student working full time for a specified number of days or weeks and then returning to school, while his alternate takes his place for the same length of time.

cooperative plan, distributive education: an organizational pattern of instruction which involves regularly scheduled part-time employment and which gives students an opportunity to apply classroom learning in practice; it enables them to develop occupational competencies through training on jobs related to their distributive educational interests.

cooperative plan, nonalternate: a plan for the part-time work of cooperative pupils that assigns only one pupil to each job and allows him to work on a regular schedule of hours for the whole period of the cooperative course.

cooperative planning: *see* **planning, cooperative.**

cooperative problem solving: *see* **problem solving, cooperative.**

cooperative program: *see* **program, cooperative.**

cooperative project: *see* **project, cooperative.**

cooperative pupil control: control of or restraint upon the free exercise of pupil activity, secured through the united efforts of teachers, parents, and other interested parties.

cooperative purchasing: a method by which two or more school districts or a school district and other governmental units or municipalities combine their purchases and thereby frequently secure lower prices.

cooperative purchasing of insurance: a plan by which universities and colleges pool their insurance needs for the purpose of securing lower insurance rates through elimination of brokerage costs, adjustment of rates, and other economies.

cooperative, school: a pupil-planned activity involving the purchase (or manufacture) and sale of school knick-knacks and supplies at or near cost, with some form of profit-sharing plan. (In some schools, especially in isolated areas in the South, the cooperative may be organized on the Rochdale principle, whereby all profits are distributed among customers in ratio to their patronage, and may involve the sale of basic staple goods to the adult community.)

cooperative school: *syn.* **part-time school** (1).

cooperative society: *syn.* **cooperative.**

cooperative student: *see* **student, cooperative.**

cooperative student contract: *see* **contract, cooperative student.**

cooperative supervision: *see* **supervision, cooperative.**

cooperative test: *see* **test, cooperative.**

cooperative testing: *see* **testing, cooperative.**

cooperative training: *see* **cooperative plan, distributive education.**

cooperative training agreement: *syn.* **contract, cooperative student.**

cooperative training plan: *syn.* **contract, cooperative student.**

cooperative work experience program: *syn.* **cooperative education.**

cooperativeness: the willingness of two or more persons to work together to achieve a common end or purpose.

cooperativeness, test of: *syn.* **test, cooperative.**

coordinate: (math.) the number, or one of the ordered set of numbers, assigned a point in space under some coordinate system. *See* **coordinate system; ordinate.**

coordinate activities: *see* **activities, coordinate.**

coordinate axis: *see* **coordinate system.**

coordinate business executive: *see* **business executive, coordinate.**

coordinate geometry: *syn.* **geometry, analytic.**

coordinate hyperplane: *see* **hyperplane, coordinate.**

coordinate organization of supervision: *see* **supervision, coordinate organization of.**

coordinate paper: paper printed with reference lines to show a coordinate system for the plane; commonly called *graph paper;* according to the coordinate system used there is rectangular coordinate paper, polar coordinate paper, double logarithmic coordinate paper, etc. *See* **coordinate system; cross-section paper.**

coordinate relationship: the relationship existing among teachers and other workers in somewhat similar school positions.

coordinate system: (math.) a scheme, when given a space (set of points), for assigning a number or ordered collection of numbers to each point in such a way that each point is assigned a different number or ordered collection of numbers and the different numbers (ordered collections) designate different points; a common scheme is to select a collection of lines, called coordinate axes, through a single point called the origin, with no three of the lines in the same plane; each axis becomes a number line with the origin assigned as 0; if there is more than one axis, an order is assigned to each as first, second, etc.

coordinated eye movements: *see* **eye movements, coordinated.**

coordinated writing: *see* **writing, coordinated.**

coordinates, cartesian: coordinates derived from a coordinate system in which the axes are mutually perpendicular and in which each point on each axis is associated with a real number, the scale being uniform on each axis. *See* **coordinate; coordinate system.**

coordinating: (admin.) the process of unifying the contributions of people, materials, and other resources toward the achievement of a recognized purpose.

coordinating board: a board established at the state level to coordinate the activities and development of colleges and universities in the state, especially public institutions; usually made up of some members of individual institution boards plus some state official or officials and some lay members.

coordinating council: (1) *syn.* **community coordinating council;** (2) a group of reasonably representative community leaders and professional workers who study and plan ways of dealing with community problems, such as juvenile delinquency, through policy formulation and integrating the efforts of a number of agencies.

coordinating council, community: *see* **community coordinating council.**

coordination: in cooperative office education those functions of a teacher-coordinator necessary to the operation of the program, for example, selection of training stations, advisory committee, and students, promotion of the program, related in-class instruction, placement, follow-up, etc. *See* **committee, business and office education advisory; job rotation; office education, cooperative; station; training; teacher-coordinator.**

coordination, distributive education: the process of organizing, developing, and maintaining effective relationships among all groups involved in the distributive education program to the end that the student may receive the best possible preparation for a career in distribution.

coordination, eye: *see* **eye coordination.**

coordination, eye-hand: *see* **eye-hand coordination.**

coordination, eye-muscle: *see* **eye-muscle coordination.**

coordination, locomotor: the ability to maintain balance and smooth movement while moving from one place to another through the use of physical skills.

coordination, motor: synchronization of neuromuscular systems.

coordination, muscular: (1) the combination of the movements of muscles in a suitable relation to give harmonious results; (2) functioning of muscles in cooperation and normal sequence in performing a physical task.

coordination, neuromuscular: in general, the acting together in a smooth, harmonious, concerted way of the muscles and nerves; in a specific instance, the nervous control of muscle contractions in the performance of a motor act.

coordination, perceptual-motor: smooth and efficient functioning of sensory and motor nerves and the connections between them, resulting in rapid reaction to stimuli with a minimum of effort.

coordination, visual and motor: (art ed.) in drawing, the psychological factor of motor control, involving the ability to relate motor activity to visual experience, for example, the motions of the arm in drawing related to seeing the lines so produced.

coordinator: (1) a person responsible for coordinating classroom work with the work of industry, commerce, and home; (2) a person employed in connection with vocational courses to adjust the work of the school to the needs of business and industry; may also supervise pupils; (3) a term used in recent years as an alternative designation of the newer type of well-trained attendance worker; (4) a person responsible for integrating an instructional program in which several persons participate, as in offering a course or group of courses on preparation for marriage; (5) a person responsible for the coordination of various curricular offerings either within a single school or between schools in a school district, county school office, or state department of education; comparable to a supervisor but with emphasis on voluntary cooperation and mutual sharing of ideas and plans; *see* **supervisor;** (6) a title or designation used for a variety of school district central office positions carrying largely staff rather than line responsibility but involving supervisory and/or administrative functions, usually encompassing more than one specific area of activity.

coordinator, agricultural: a member of a school's staff of teachers of agriculture responsible for integrating the classroom instruction and the on-the-job activities of the students employed in agricultural firms; acts as liaison between the school and employers in agricultural firms in programs of cooperative education or other part-time job training.

coordinator, apprentice: a person, usually a vocational school employee, who is charged with maintaining close contact with industry and the work of employed apprentices for the purposes of securing proper apprentice placement and training arrangements and tying together the work of the school and the activities of the apprentices.

coordinator, art: *syn.* **director, art.**

coordinator, cooperative education: a member of the school staff responsible for administering the school program and resolving all problems that arise between the school regulations and the on-the-job activities of the employed student.

coordinator core counselor: *see* **counselor, coordinator core.**

coordinator counselor: *see* **counselor, coordinator.**

coordinator, health: a health educator who relates school health efforts to those of the home and community.

coordinator of guidance: a person who is assigned the responsibility for coordinating the guidance program of a school, a school district, or a county school office.

coordinator of guidance and testing: *syn.* **director of guidance.**

coordinator of placement: an administrative officer at the college level who supervises and coordinates activities of placement officers in job-placement service for students and graduates; develops placement-office procedures, establishes workloads, assigns tasks, and reviews results;

conducts in-service programs for placement personnel; interviews applicants to determine their qualifications and eligibility for employment and assists individuals to develop employment plans based on their aptitudes, interests, and personality characteristics and to plan curricula accordingly; contacts prospective employers to determine their needs and to explain placement service and arranges on-campus interviews between employers and graduating students to facilitate placement of graduates; collects, organizes, and analyzes occupational, educational, and economic information for use in job-placement activities, directs maintenance of occupational library, assists in conducting community surveys to gather labor market information, such as prevailing wages, hours training, and employment possibilities, and coordinates job analysis program of university jobs. *Syn.* **director of placement.**

coordinator, parent-volunteer: a salaried individual who serves as liaison and coordinator between the school and the parent-volunteers and/or parents' groups and enlists parent aid in school and school-community projects.

coordinator, reading: a supervising teacher, or supervisor, appointed to coordinate the reading instruction of a group of teachers, direct activities, and help the teachers with their problems.

coordinator, student-personnel: (1) a person responsible for the integration of all personnel agencies on the campus and for the initiation of new functions; (2) a college officer responsible for developing and fostering cooperation among personnel officers and for integration of personnel programs.

coordinator-teacher: *see* **teacher-coordinator.**

coordinator, training: a representative of the training department of an industry or other business establishment who is responsible for harmonizing the work of the training department with the work of the other departments.

coordinator, vocational: a member of the school staff responsible for integrating the classroom instruction and the on-the-job activities of the employed student; acts as liaison between the school and employers in programs of cooperative education or other part-time job training.

coordinator, vocational adjustment: a certified teacher of retarded children employed by the cooperating school district and assigned to work full time; his duties in addition to the special education responsibility include functioning as a teacher-coordinator in the local *work-study program.*

coprolalia (kop'rə·lā'li·ə): uncontrollable utterance of obscene words or phrases; a symptom of certain psychoses and obsessional neuroses.

coprophobia (kop'rə·fō'bi·ə): a morbid or abnormal repugnance to filth, as repugnance to the act of defecation.

copy, hard: *see* **hard copy.**

copy reading: (1) the act of revising a manuscript for the printer, usually involving editing, headline writing, and marking instructions to the printer; (2) the designation of an advanced journalism course involving practice in preparing newspaper and periodical manuscripts for the printer.

copy setting: the practice on the part of a handwriting instructor of writing model exercises for the pupils to imitate, these being placed on the blackboard for all the class or on sheets before each pupil for individual guidance.

copy theory of knowledge: *see* **knowledge, copy theory of.**

copybook: a book or manual in which writing exercises are printed or inscribed and which is placed before the student of handwriting as a guide to his own practice.

copyholder: a device for holding the copy to be typed; usually placed to the right of the typewriter in alignment with the carriage and at the correct slant and distance from the typist.

copying form: a technique for testing intelligence in young children in which the subject is required to copy a geometrical figure such as a circle, square, diamond, triangle, or cross; used in certain individual intelligence tests.

copyist: a term usually applied to a monk who devoted his time to copying manuscripts and books before the invention of the printing press.

copyright: the exclusive privilege of publishing and selling a work, granted by a government to an author, composer, artist, etc.

core area: the subject or subjects used to form the central core of the core curriculum.

core course: *see* **course, core.**

core curriculum: *see* **curriculum, core.**

core curriculum, social-functions: *see* **curriculum, social-functions core.**

core curriculum, social-problems: *see* **curriculum, social-problems core.**

core dump: *see* **storage dump.**

core, home-economics: *see* **home-economics core.**

core intensive business and office education: *see* **business and office education, core intensive.**

core, magnetic: *see* **magnetic core.**

core program: *see* **program, core.**

core subject: *see* **subject, core.**

core subject matter: *see* **subject matter, core.**

core supervision: *see* **supervision, core.**

core teacher: a teacher who is assigned to teach a class for a *core-curriculum* type of instructional program.

corecreational activity: *see* **activity, corecreational.**

corneal-reflection method: a technique employed in the study of eye movements in reading, in which light is shone into the subject's eyes while he is reading, the light being reflected back from the cornea of each eye and registered by means of an optical apparatus upon light-sensitive material; the basic principle employed in the ophthalmograph.

corneal reflex: *see* **reflex, corneal.**

Cornelian corner: a movement in child development, named after the Roman Cornelia, famed mother of the Gracchi whom she called her jewels; founded in 1942 by a group of psychoanalytically oriented specialists who were working toward adoption of much greater leniency in infant care in such matters as feeding schedule, toilet training, and weaning; adherents of this group hold that psychological mothering, such as allowing the newborn to be in bed with the mother instead of in a hospital nursery, is a very important ingredient in proper psychological development of the child.

Cornell index: *see* **index, Cornell.**

Cornell technique: a technique developed by L. Guttman to test unidimensionality of attitude. *See* **scalogram board.**

corner, number: *see* **number corner.**

corner, science: *see* **science corner.**

corner test of association: *see* **test of association, corner.**

corollary: a theorem that is an immediate consequence of a more general theorem.

corporal punishment: *see* **punishment, corporal.**

corporal-punishment report: *see* **report, corporal-punishment.**

corporate body: a group of individuals who compose the membership of a corporation; also called *body corporate.* *See* **legal person.**

corporate life: a stipulated period for which a franchise or charter is granted by the sovereign authority. (The corporate life usually is without stipulated limit in the case of philanthropic and charitable corporations, the charters being granted in perpetuity.)

corporate trustee: *see* **trustee, corporate.**

corporation: a body of associated persons created by law, with the capacity of perpetual succession and of acting, within its charter, as an individual.

corporation, educational: an incorporated enterprise engaged in education, such as a private school, college, or university, or a philanthropic foundation dedicated to an educational purpose.

corporation, municipal: a body politic created by law as the result of the incorporation of the inhabitants; an agency of the state in the administration and regulation of the affairs thereof; a voluntary corporation.

corporation organization tax: *see* **tax, corporation organization.**

corporation, public: a corporation, created for public purposes only and connected with the administration of the government; the whole interests and franchises of such a corporation are the exclusive property and domain of the government itself, for example, an incorporated school district or city.

corporation, quasi: a public corporation, such as a school district, created by the state for governmental purposes, which, while having many of the characteristics of municipal corporations, is not vested with the general powers of a municipal corporation; it is an involuntary corporation, one not created at its own request.

corporation, quasi municipal: *see* **corporation, quasi.**

corporation school: (1) a program of formal intramural training in a large business or industrial organization, such as a bank, department store, factory, public utility, or other company, for its executives, club members, production and sales staff, foremen, and other employees; (2) a series of lectures or classes (sometimes propagandistic in nature) provided by an industry or business organization to inform its customers on matters concerning foods, clothing, interior decoration, health, etc., or plant or company policies and operations.

corporation tax: *see* **tax, corporation.**

correct-principle score: *see* **score, correct-principle.**

correct pronunciation: *see* **pronunciation, correct.**

correct usage: (1) the use of words according to currently accepted standards of correctness; (2) use of words, punctuation marks, capital letters, and other mechanics of language according to currently accepted standards of correctness.

correct words: (typewriting) actual number of correct words typed, negating any word in which an error is made, thus providing a one-word penalty for each error; in development drills five strokes (characters or spaces) equal one word.

correctable error: *see* **error, correctable.**

correctable letter: a typewritten letter containing one or more errors that may be corrected sufficiently well to make the letter fit to send out. *Dist. f.* **mailable letter.**

corrected birth rate: *see* **birth rate, corrected.**

corrected chronological age: *see* **age, corrected chronological.**

corrected death rate: *see* **death rate, corrected.**

corrected raw score: *see* **score, corrected raw.**

correction: *syn.* **error, absolute** (3).

correction for attenuation: (1) a correction applied to a coefficient of correlation as a means of estimating the magnitude of the correlation that would exist between the two variables if neither contained chance errors; (2) occasionally, a correction applied to a coefficient of correlation to estimate the correlation that would exist if the criterion variable, but not the independent variable, were error-free.

correction-for-chance formula: any of several formulas used in computing the score on alternate-response and multiple-choice tests in order to compensate for the fact that items may have been answered correctly by chance; one common formula is $R - W / (N - 1)$, where R = number of right answers, W = number of wrong answers, and N = number of alternatives in each item.

correction for coarse grouping: *syn.* **correction, Sheppard's.**

correction for continuity: an allowance for the discontinuous nature of data, made in contingency tables having only one degree of freedom and involving small numbers in the cells; each difference is reduced by 0.5 before squaring in the computation of chi square. (Although it is not used, "correction for discontinuity" would be more descriptive.) *Syn.* **Yates correction.**

correction for continuity, Yates: *see* **correction for continuity.**

correction for guessing: *see* **scoring formula.**

correction procedure: *syn.* **practice mode.**

correction, Sheppard's: a correction subtracted from the variance (σ^2) to correct for the use of coarse (that is,

broad) class intervals; mathematically equal to $i^2/_{12}$, where i is the width of the class interval. *Syn.* **correction for coarse grouping.**

correction, sparsity: in analyses of the cost and quality of educational programs, a correction applied to take into account the additional cost of operation of schools in sparsely populated areas. *See* **study, cost-quality.**

correction, speech: *see* **speech correction.**

correction, Yates: *syn.* **correction for continuity.**

correctional education: vocational, cultural, and recreational activities carried on in correctional institutions for the purpose of effecting the social and economic rehabilitation of the inmates.

corrective arithmetic: *see* **arithmetic, corrective.**

corrective class: *syn.* **class, remedial.**

corrective discipline: *see* **discipline, corrective.**

corrective drill: *see* **drill, corrective.**

corrective gymnastics: *see* **gymnastics, corrective.**

corrective institution: *see* **institution, corrective.**

corrective physical education: *see* **physical education, corrective.**

corrective program: *see* **program, corrective.**

corrective reading: *see* **reading, corrective.**

corrective training: *see* **gymnastics, corrective; physical education, corrective.**

correlated: (1) related in such a way that the distribution of one variable depends on another, thus having a coefficient of correlation different from zero; so related that the direction and magnitude of the fluctuations in one variable are directly or inversely associated with the fluctuations in the other; (2) having had the coefficient of correlation computed between two or more variables. *See* **correlation** (1); **correlation, primary; correlation, secondary.**

correlated course of study: *see* **course of study, correlated.**

correlated curriculum: *see* **curriculum, correlated.**

correlated instruction, distributive education: *see* **instruction, distributive education correlated.**

correlated sample: *see* **sample, matched; sample, paired.**

correlation: (1) (stat.) the tendency for corresponding observations in two or more series to vary together from the averages of their respective series, that is, to have similar relative position; if corresponding observations (for example, the scores made by each pupil on two tests) tend to have similar relative positions in their respective series, the correlation is *positive;* if the corresponding values tend to be divergent in position in their respective series, the correlation is *negative;* absence of any systematic tendency for the corresponding observations to be either similar or dissimilar in their relative positions indicates *zero correlation; syn.* **covariation;** *see* **regression;** (2) (stat.) a shortened form commonly used for *correlation coefficient;* (3) (stat.) the act or process of ascertaining the degree of relationship between two or more variables; (4) (curric.) bringing together the elements of two or more different subject-matter fields that bear on the same large problem or area of human experience in such a way that each element is reinforced, broadened, and made richer through its association with the elements from the other subject fields.

correlation, biserial: (r bis) a coefficient of correlation between a two-categoried variable and a continuous variable, assuming that the dichotomized variable is in reality continuously and normally distributed, although expressed in only two degrees. *Syn.* **biserial coefficient of correlation; biserial r;** *dist. f.* **correlation, point biserial.**

correlation, bivariate: *syn.* **correlation, simple.**

correlation, book-and-tape: the degree to which taped material corresponds in content and coverage with the book used as a text in a course.

correlation chart: *see* **chart, correlation.**

correlation coefficient: *see* **coefficient, correlation.**

correlation, coefficient of: *see* **coefficient, correlation.**

correlation coefficient, transformed: *syn.* **Fisher's z.**

correlation curve: *see* **curve, correlation.**

correlation, curvilinear: a correlation in which the relationship between two variables can be expressed only by a curved line. *Syn.* **correlation ratio;** *contr. w.* **correlation, rectilinear.**

correlation, direct: *syn.* **positive correlation;** *see* **correlation** (1).

correlation, distributive education: instruction both in the school and on the job, organized and planned around the activities associated with both the student's individual job and his career objective.

correlation, entire: *syn.* **correlation, total.**

correlation, foot-rule: *syn.* **Spearman's foot-rule method of gains.**

correlation, grade variate: a rank difference correlation corrected on the assumption that both variables are normally distributed.

correlation graph: *syn.* **diagram, scatter.**

correlation, gross: *syn.* **correlation, total.**

correlation index: *syn.* **index of correlation.**

correlation, index of: *see* **index of correlation.**

correlation, indirect: *syn.* **negative correlation;** *see* **correlation** (1).

correlation, interclass: correlation between two separate classes of measurements, such as the correlation between test score and school progress. *Contr. w.* **correlation, intraclass.**

correlation, intraclass: a correlation in which the variables are interchangeable and thus have a common mean and a common standard deviation, for example, the correlation between the stature of brothers, where each pair of brothers is, in effect, plotted twice—once as (X_1, X_2) and once as (X_2, X_1). *Contr. w.* **correlation, interclass.**

correlation, inverse: *syn.* **negative correlation;** *see* **correlation** (1).

correlation, item: the correlation between performance on a single item or question on the test and performance on the total test; this statistic (actually a *point biserial correlation*) shows that those who answered the item correctly also received higher scores on the total test than those who answered the item incorrectly when the statistic is high positive and vice versa when high negative.

correlation line: *syn.* **regression line.**

correlation, linear: *syn.* **correlation, rectilinear.**

correlation machine: a machine for computing simultaneously the several moments necessary to a solution of a particular correlation coefficient, usually the *Pearson product-moment coefficient of correlation.*

correlation matrix: *see* **matrix, correlation.**

correlation matrix, reduced: *see* **matrix, reduced correlation.**

correlation, multiple: *syn.* **coefficient of multiple correlation.**

correlation, negative: *syn.* **indirect correlation; inverse correlation;** *see* **correlation** (1).

correlation, net: *syn.* **correlation, partial.**

correlation, nonlinear: *syn.* **correlation, curvilinear.**

correlation, part: the correlation between a dependent variable and a given independent variable after the additional influences of other independent variables have been removed from the dependent variable.

correlation, part-whole: the correlation between a part measurement and the whole of which it is a part.

correlation, partial: a measure of the degree of relationship existing between two variables after the linear influence of one or more other variables has been removed. *Syn.* **net correlation.**

correlation, perfect: a degree of relationship between two variables (indicated by a coefficient of correlation of $+1.00$ or -1.00), such that the value of either variable may be determined exactly from the value of the other.

correlation plan: *see* **course of study, correlated.**

correlation, point biserial: the correlation between a two-categoried, or dichotomous, variable and an *n*-categoried variable when the variate values of the two categories of the dichotomous variable are assumed to be separate points and not divisions of a continuous variate as in a biserial correlation. *Dist. f.* **correlation, biserial.**

correlation, polychoric (pol'i·kō'rik): the correlation between two variables that are plotted in a table containing more than four cells, when it is assumed that both variables, though expressed qualitatively, are really continuous and normally distributed. *Contr. w.* **correlation, tetrachoric.**

correlation, positive: *see* **correlation** (1).

correlation, primary: a relationship between two variables that apparently cannot be ascribed to the influence of a third variable; a casual relationship. *See* **correlated;** *contr. w.* **correlation, secondary.**

correlation, rank: a method of computing the degree of relationship between two variables by the use of a function of the rank order of the magnitudes of the observations rather than the magnitudes themselves, for example, the *rank difference correlation coefficient* and *Spearman's foot-rule method of gains.*

correlation ratio: (η) the ratio of the standard deviation of the weighted means of the arrays of a variable to the standard deviation of the individual measures of that variable; has an absolute value equal to or greater than the coefficient of correlation; often called *eta,* from the symbol η used to represent it; used in determining the relationship between two variables which are not linearly related. *Syn.* **ratio of correlation;** *dist. f.* **correlation ratio, linear.**

correlation ratio, linear: an estimate of the product-moment coefficient of correlation between two variables, one expressed quantitatively and the other qualitatively. *Dist. f.* **correlation ratio.**

correlation, rectilinear: a correlation in which the relationship between two variables can be expressed graphically by a straight line. *Syn.* **linear correlation;** *contr. w.* **correlation, curvilinear.**

correlation, secondary: a relationship between two variables that is due to the operation of a third variable contributing to the variability of both the first two variables. *See* **correlated;** *contr. w.* **correlation, primary.**

correlation, simple: correlation between two variables, these being correlated on the basis of magnitude. *Syn.* **bivariate correlation;** *see* **correlation** (1).

correlation, skew: *syn.* **correlation, curvilinear.**

correlation, spatial: (art ed.) the mutual relation represented between two things or bodies existing in children's drawings, indicating that they relate themselves meaningfully to their environment and suggesting that they are ready for cooperation.

correlation, spurious: a correlation between two variables which is due, at least in part, to factors other than those which determine values of the two variables.

correlation study: *see* **study, correlation.**

correlation surface: *syn.* **frequency surface** (1).

correlation table: (1) *syn.* **correlation chart; table, double-entry;** (2) *syn.* **diagram, scatter.**

correlation, tetrachoric (tet'rə·kō'rik): (t) the correlation between two variables, both assumed to be continuous and normally distributed, but each expressed in terms of two classes only. *Contr. w.* **correlation, polychoric.**

correlation, total: the correlation between two variables in their original form (not residuals). *Syn.* **entire correlation; gross correlation; zero-order correlation;** *see* **correlation** (1); *contr. w.* **correlation, partial.**

correlation, true: the value of a correlation coefficient existing in the universe, or population, as contrasted with the value appearing in a sample; seldom known in any practical situation.

correlation, zero: *see* **correlation** (1).

correlation, zero-order: any correlation coefficient involving the relationship between two, and only two, variables.

correspondence class: *see* **class, correspondence.**

correspondence, coefficient of: *syn.* **index of forecasting efficiency.**

correspondence course: (1) a method of providing for the systematic exchange between student and instructor of materials sent by mail for the purpose of instruction in units of subject matter; (2) a set of printed lessons or assignments based on textual materials and/or other instructional media with directions for study, exercises, tests, etc., to be used as primary or supplemental aids to learning outside a regular classroom environment. *See* **instruction, correspondence; study, independent.**

correspondence instruction: *see* **instruction, correspondence.**

correspondence instruction, supervised: *see* **correspondence study, supervised.**

correspondence, one-to-one: (math.) a matching of the members of one set, *A*, to the members of another, *B*, in such a way that each member of *A* is associated with exactly one member of *B* and each member of *B* is associated with exactly one member of *A*; sets which can be placed in one-to-one correspondence are equivalent, that is, have the same number of members.

correspondence outline: *see* **correspondence study guide.**

correspondence school: a school giving instruction by mail or by mail and radio or television.

correspondence study: formal study and instruction conducted by mail, using texts, course outlines, and other materials, with lesson reports, corrections, and examinations.

correspondence study guide: a set of instructions, textual materials, and assignments which guide a student through a course.

correspondence study, supervised: a system by which material for study and instruction by mail and other media (such as those issued by the extension division of a university) are obtained by a school (often a high school), that provides regular periods in the school day or in the evening (as in an adult evening school) to guide the work of the students that is to be returned in the form of written responses to the correspondence center for correction and evaluation.

correspondence syllabus: *see* **correspondence study guide.**

correspondence theory of truth: *see* **truth, correspondence theory of.**

corresponding values: *see* **values, corresponding.**

cortex: (1) the bark of a tree or root; (2) the outer layer of an organ as separated from its inner substance, for example, adrenal cortex, the cortical portion of the adrenal gland, or cerebral cortex, the cortex of the brain, consisting mainly of gray matter.

cortex, cerebral: *see* **cortex** (2).

Corti, organ of: *see* **organ of Corti.**

cortical analyzer: a term used by Pavlov to designate a hypothetical analyzing mechanism, apparently a part of the nervous system and particularly of the cerebral hemispheres, by means of which the organism is able to differentiate among the stimuli received by its sense organs, distinguishing those which are biologically favorable from those which are dangerous or destructive.

cortical deafness: *see* **deafness, cortical.**

cosmogony: that branch of metaphysics concerned with the origin of the universe; necessarily speculative and hence frequently mystical or imaginary. *See* **metaphysics.**

cosmological argument: *see* **argument, cosmological.**

cosmology: (1) the branch of philosophy that studies the origin and development of the universe, its order, and its basic constituents; sometimes referred to also as the philosophy of nature; (2) as a unit in a course in astronomy, the science or theory of the universe as a whole, its parts, and its laws; the study of the general nature of the universe in space and time—what it was in the past, what it is now, and what it is likely to be in the future.

cosmos: the universe conceived as a harmonious system; the term excludes chaos as a fundamental characteristic of the complex cosmic system.

cost accounting: *see* **accounting, cost.**

cost analysis: *see* **analysis, cost.**

cost, capital: (pup. trans.) expenditure for permanent transportation facilities such as school buses, garages, and garage equipment. *Syn.* **expenditure, capital;** *dist. f.* **cost, operating.**

cost control records: (pup. trans.) a system of recorded data that identifies the costs of specific expenditures for a fleet of buses, including amounts expended for gasoline, oil, tires, driver's salary, repairs, and servicing.

cost, differential: method of equalizing local district costs for special education wherein state funds are given to local districts in amounts equal to the difference in per-pupil instructional cost between special and regular education. *See* **cost, excess.**

cost, direct operating: (pup. trans.) any expenditure that may be directly charged to the operation of individual vehicles, such as fuel, oil, tires, parts, or driver's salary.

cost, educational: the amount of money or money's worth paid or charged for a particular educational service.

cost, excess: the difference between per-pupil current operative expenditures for students receiving special education services and such expenditures for those receiving only the normal instructional services.

cost, indirect operating: (pup. trans.) items such as "overhead" that cannot be charged directly to any particular vechile but that must be charged to all vehicles operated, such as administration, supervision, and garage expense.

cost of a building, per-pupil: the cost of a building divided by the pupil capacity of the building.

cost of living: the amount of money one must have to buy all the commodities and services that he needs in order to maintain a certain scale of living.

cost-of-living adjustment: *see* **adjustment, cost-of-living.**

cost-of-living index: *see* **index, cost-of-living.**

cost of maintenance: the amount of money expended to keep furniture and equipment in repair.

cost of operation: expenditures (other than those for repairs) made for the purpose of keeping a building in condition for use, for example, expenditures for the employment of janitors, engineers, groundmen, supervisors of these employees, and other employees to care for buildings and grounds; expenditures made for the supplies and materials to be consumed in use by these employees; expenditures for heat, light, water, and power, etc.

cost of transportation: *syn.* **cost, total.**

cost, operating: (pup. trans.) obligations incurred and money expended during a given period for the maintenance and operation of a bus or fleet of buses; does not include capital outlay or debt service.

cost per bus per mile: (pup. trans.) an expression in dollars and cents, determined by dividing either the operating cost or the total cost of one bus during a given period by the total number of miles driven during that period. *See* **cost, operating; cost, total.**

cost per classroom unit: the cost involved in conducting one class for a stipulated period, usually one school year.

cost per cubic foot: a method of expressing the cost of construction per cubic foot of building space, frequently used for purposes of comparison.

cost, per-pupil: (pup. accounting) (1) annual current expenditures per pupil in average daily attendance, annual current expenditures per pupil in average daily membership, current expenditures per pupil, current expenditures per pupil per day (average daily attendance), and current expenditures per pupil per day (average daily membership); (2) the average cost of transporting one pupil, figured variously per day, month, year, mile, per day per bus mile, etc.

cost per pupil per day: (pup. trans.) an expression in dollars and cents derived by dividing either the operating cost or the total cost of transportation over a given period by the number of days in that period and dividing the resulting quotient by the average daily number of pupils transported during that period. *See* **cost, operating; cost, total.**

cost per pupil per mile: (pup. trans.) an expression in dollars and cents derived by dividing either the operating cost or the total cost of transportation for a given period by the aggregate pupil miles. *See* **cost, operating; cost, total; mile, pupil; miles, aggregate pupil.**

cost per pupil per year: (pup. trans.) an expression in dollars and cents derived by dividing either the operating cost or the total cost of transportation during 1 year by the average daily number of pupils transported. *See* **cost, operating; cost, total.**

cost per seat mile: (pup. trans.) an expression in dollars and cents obtained, for a single bus, by dividing either the operating cost or the total cost per bus mile by the seating capacity of the bus; or, for two or more buses, by dividing either the operating cost or the total cost per bus mile for all buses by the aggregate seating capacity of the buses. *See* **cost, operating; cost, total; mile, seat.**

cost-quality study: *see* **study, cost-quality.**

cost, recommended: a reasonable amount to pay for a certain material or service, as established by an authority.

cost, standard credit: a unit of measurement in school finance that expresses in dollars the expense of providing one student with one unit of academic credit (usually a so-called *"Carnegie unit"*).

cost, student: the average amount of money expended per student for a designated service for a given period of time.

cost, student-clock-hour: the average amount of money expended per student per clock-hour instruction for a specified service. (In the case of elementary education, the use of *student* instead of *pupil* is not strictly correct but is an accepted usage.) *See* **clock-hour.**

cost, student-credit-hour: the quotient obtained by dividing the total number of student-credit-hours produced into the total expenditure occasioned in producing them. *See* **student-credit-hour.**

cost, terminal: (1) the final, or end, cost of an undertaking, enterprise, or process; (2) the total outlay for a school building financed by bonds, the terminal cost being the total payments of principal and interest, plus or minus an adjustment if the bonds were sold at a discount or premium.

cost, total: (pup. trans.) all money expended and obligations incurred for transportation during a given period; includes capital outlay, fixed charges, and all operating and administrative costs.

cost, unit: *see* **unit cost.**

cost, unit of: (pup. trans.) any one of several bases on which the cost of transportation is computed, for example, per pupil per year, per pupil per mile, per bus per year, etc.; may be based either on operating cost or on total cost. *See* **cost, operating; cost, total.**

cost value: *see* **value, cost.**

costs, building: the amount of money that must be paid for buildings and plant equipment at particular times, based on costs of materials and labor; usually estimated as price per cubic foot, square foot, or classroom.

costs, instructional: a financial accounting classification that includes all items of expense directly concerned with teaching, for example, teachers' salaries, supervisors' salaries, and instructional supplies.

costs, plant: the amount of money that has been expended on land, buildings, equipment, and improvements other than buildings, exclusive of those items which have been charged to current expense.

costs, school: the amount of money or money's worth paid or charged for educational service in a particular school.

costume art: *see* **art, costume.**

costume design: *see* **art, costume.**

coterminous debt: *see* **debt, coterminous.**

council, administrative: *see* **administrative council.**

council, adult education: *see* **adult education council.**

council, central casework: *see* **casework council, central.**

council, church: (1) a representative body from a local parish or congregation that functions in an advisory or governing capacity; (2) an interdenominational agency designed to coordinate the interests and activities of the participating churches at the local, state, national, or international level; (3) a convention or meeting of church leaders on a universal basis as, for example, the ecumenical council of the early church.

council, community coordinating: *see* **community coordinating council.**

council, coordinating: *see* **coordinating council.**

council, faculty: *see* **faculty council.**

council, guidance: *see* **guidance council.**

council, health: *see* **health council.**

council, joint apprenticeship: *see* **apprenticeship council, joint.**

Council of Carthage: a council of the Roman Catholic Church in 401 A.D., the educational significance of which lies in the act of officially banning the Greek classics and works of the other pagan authors from the literature available to the Catholic faithful; sometimes referred to as the beginning of the "Dark Ages," when Greek and Roman learning passed into an eclipse.

Council of Trent: a council summoned by Pope Paul III in 1545 in response to the challenges of the Protestant Reformation; the effects of the Council, sometimes referred to as the Catholic Counter Reformation, included the placing of renewed emphasis on education, particularly with regard to the Society of Jesus (the Jesuit Order).

Council, Pan-Hellenic: *see* **Pan-Hellenic Council.**

council, pupil-personnel: *syn.* **guidance council.**

council, school-development: (1) a lay group, somewhat similar to an *advisory committee,* but usually concerned with less specific problems and devoting study to the broad problems of the growth or change in function or organization of a school or school system; usually more care is taken for a council of this nature to ensure complete representation of every interest group in a community; *syn.* **school-study council;** (2) a group composed of educators, or of lay citizens and educators, representing a number of school systems, which plans, assists in carrying through, and reviews various studies and research efforts which are carried forward in the cooperating school systems.

council, school-study: *syn.* **council, school-development.**

council, student: *see* **student council.**

council, student guidance: *see* **guidance council, student.**

council, supervision: an advisory group composed of persons chiefly responsible for studying and maintaining supervisory functions within an organization.

councils, consumers': organizations formed to promote consumers' interests and to provide protection, information, and services to the consumer.

counselee: a student being assisted by means of counseling.

counseling: (1) a relationship in which one or more persons with a problem or concern desire to discuss and work toward solving it with another person or persons attempting to help them reach their goals; (2) individualized assistance through (*a*) personal interviews in which the student is aided in the making of his own decisions and choices, such as the vocation he will follow, and (*b*) referral to personnel specialists for professional and personal assistance with problems and adjustments; (3) the personal-treatment phase of assistance, with or without diagnosis of causes of the student's problems; one of the basic services in the body of services constituting *guidance.*

counseling, adult: a counseling process emphasizing the continued personal growth and development of adults and their achievement of harmony with themselves and their individual environments.

counseling, agricultural: conferring with a person for the purpose of assisting him in problems connected with his choice of an agricultural occupation, either nonfarm or farm, training for that occupation, and obtaining employment. *See* **guidance, agricultural.**

counseling, ambiguity in: a characteristic of a therapeutic relationship between a counselor and a client providing for a free associative process in which there is less certainty and less control of the client's reaction.

counseling, analytically oriented: counseling in which the therapist assumes the existence of unconscious mental processes, such as urges, wishes, and fears, of which the client is unaware and for which the primary process places continuous demands on the ego to find outlets for gratification.

counseling, auxiliary services: services that supplement and augment those provided by counselors and other guidance workers, such as special placement services, health and medical services, clinical services, and welfare services. *Syn.* **referral services;** *see* **clinical services.**

counseling, behavior-theoretical: the application of behavior-theoretical conceptualizations to counseling, in which the emphasis is almost always on the effects of prior experiences or happenings on the event under scrutiny; it is taken for granted that these antecedent events are identifiable by some observational procedures and that the relation between antecedents and behavior is regarded as investigable by the procedures and methods of the other natural sciences. *See* **behaviorism.**

counseling, behavioral: the process of effecting change in client behavior by lifting repressions, reducing anxiety, and encouraging new responses through operant conditioning, verbal labeling, discrimination, and generalization. *See* **conditioning, operant** (2).

counseling, behavioral theory in: *see* **behavioral theory in counseling.**

counseling bureau director, student: *see* **director, student counseling bureau.**

counseling, camp: the carrying out of a broad and varied program of camping. *See* **counselor, camp.**

counseling, career: (mil. ed.) the act of orienting an Air Force military person with regard to the Air Force career program and of advising him in the choice of a career field in accordance with his interest and aptitude.

counseling center: *syn.* **center, guidance.**

counseling center, mobile: a vehicle designed to function as a counseling center which moves from one school to another serving as a model to stimulate the development of exemplary and innovative guidance services in regular school programs.

counseling, client-centered: counseling based on the belief that the client can solve his own problems if given assistance in utilizing his personal resources; some of the main principles accepted by a client-centered counselor are that (a) the client can be responsible for himself, (b) the counselor creates a psychological atmosphere which is warm and accepting, and (c) within the individual is a life force which will be positive if the tensions and anxieties in the person's life are released. *Syn.* **nondirective counseling;** *see* **therapy, client-centered.**

counseling, clinical: the method of counseling that emphasizes the counselor's role in gathering and analyzing data, diagnosing the difficulty, and then projecting possible solutions for treating the client; any decision about action is made by the counselee. *See* **counseling, directive.**

counseling, communication in: *see* **communication in counseling.**

counseling, counselor-centered: *syn.* **counseling, directive.**

counseling, crisis: emotional aid on the spot in those adjustment demands of daily life a client cannot well manage on his own, for example, drain-off of frustration, support for the management of panic fury with guilt, communication maintenance in moments of relationship decay, regulation of behavioral and social interaction, and umpire services in decision crises.

counseling, decentralization of: the delegation of counseling responsibility to specifically designated members of the faculty, as opposed to the centering of direct counseling responsibility in the office of one professional counselor.

counseling, differential factors in elementary school: all the forces impinging on the individual that dictate techniques best utilized for assisting the child in developing a harmonious and integrated personality core through carefully planned school experiences.

counseling, directive: counseling in which the counselor takes direct part in the solution of his client's problem by suggesting alternative decisions and plans of action and by offering possible interpretations of the client's aptitudes, interests, and personality as indicated by tests and historical data. *Syn.* **counselor-centered counseling;** *see* **counseling, clinical; counseling, trait and factor theory of.**

counseling, disciplinary: a term that relates to the role of a counselor in discipline cases in which the school administrator may ask for a report on all available nonconfidential information about the individual to provide the basis for making a fair judgment for a course of action; the counselor attempts to help the student achieve greater self-understanding, to accept the consequences of his behavior, and to profit from experience.

counseling, eclectic: counseling in which various techniques are selected and used because of relevancy and applicability to the problems of the individual counselee, as opposed to techniques based on a unitary theory of counseling.

counseling, educational: that phase of the counseling program that is concerned strictly with the student's success and well-being in his educational career and is designed to aid him through the counseling relationship to select the best program of studies in the light of his capacities, interests, plans, and general circumstances. *See* **guidance, educational.**

counseling effectiveness: the extent to which the process of counseling aids or facilitates a client in obtaining some degree of control over his subsequent development in respect to his decision-making processes, overt behavior, interpersonal relationships, self-understanding, and self-acceptance.

counseling, elementary school: *see* **guidance, elementary school.**

counseling, empirical-inductive: a counseling approach to problems in which the counselor focuses attention on the goals and behaviors of each client and sets as his task the planning of an experience that can yield satisfaction to the client and at the same time move him in the direction of the goal he has set.

counseling ethics: *see* **ethics, counseling.**

counseling, existentialism in: *see* **existentialism in counseling.**

counseling, family: the promotion of social interaction by facilitating communication within the family, usually involving the following: (a) an orientation phase, (b) a child-centered phase, (c) a parent-child interaction, (d) a father-mother interaction, (e) a sibling interaction, and (f) a terminal phase.

counseling, goals of: objectives of counseling whereby the counselee is stimulated (a) to evaluate himself and his opportunities, (b) to choose a feasible course of action, (c) to accept responsibility for his choice, and (d) to initiate a course of action in line with his choice.

counseling, group: *syn.* **counseling, multiple.**

counseling, guidance: *syn.* **counseling.**

counseling, individual: direct, personal help given to the individual in solving a problem by gathering all the facts together and focusing all the individual's experiences on the problem.

counseling instructional program: *see* **program, counseling instructional.**

counseling internship: *see* **internship, counseling.**

counseling interview: *see* **interview, counseling.**

counseling, job: assisting the individual to take the next step toward further education for an occupation or helping the student to obtain full-time or part-time employment. *See* **counseling, vocational; guidance, occupational; placement service.**

counseling, marriage: a field of family counseling concerned with problems of marital adjustment, choosing a mate, preparing for marriage, and resolving personal difficulties involving family relationship.

counseling, multiple: a term that refers to the act of counseling with a small group of individuals identified as having one or more common problems; some authorities question this concept, maintaining that true counseling must be on a one-to-one basis.

counseling, nondirective: *syn.* **counseling, client-centered.**

counseling, occupational: *syn.* **counseling, vocational.**

counseling, parent: a counseling process in which parents are helped to understand themselves, to understand their children, and to assist and plan with their children's teachers more effectively.

counseling, pastoral: a therapy consistent with the insights of contemporary dynamic psychology yet rooted firmly in Christian tradition, through which the counselor helps the counselee to cope with personal or religious problems. *Syn.* **religious counseling.**

counseling, permissive: counseling wherein the counselor exhibits an attitude which encourages the free, unlimited expression of feelings on the part of the counselee, and maintains complete acceptance of whatever is expressed.

counseling, personality: counseling, the objective of which is an integration of the patterns of behavior, goals, and environment of the student; performed by teachers and counselors trained in psychology as distinguished from psychiatrists.

counseling practicum: a series of supervised laboratory or field experiences involving counselors-in-training that provide opportunities for them to synthesize the more or less fragmented phases of their previous academic work and to bring these learnings to a focus upon the actual problems of individual students. *See* **practicum.**

counseling, precollege: counseling that aids a student enrolling in college to make social, vocational, and educational decisions, such as the choice of a professional program and specific courses.

counseling, preemployment: the assistance given to students by a counselor, involving information about occupations and occupational fields, specific methods of finding the type of work desired, and occupational ethics.

counseling program: *see* **program, counseling.**

counseling program, evening: *see* **program, evening counseling.**

counseling, protocols for: general policies and principles that, when followed, should permit a school counselor to satisfy the employing school's requirements while simultaneously meeting the counselor's responsibility to himself, the profession, the persons he serves, and the public.

counseling, psychoanalytic theory in: *see* **psychoanalytic theory in counseling.**

counseling psychologist: *see* **psychologist, counseling.**

counseling psychology: *see* **psychology, counseling.**

counseling, rehabilitation: a relationship in which a professionally trained individual attempts to help mentally, emotionally, and physically handicapped persons appraise their strengths and weaknesses in relation to their own particular needs so that they may function occupationally, socially, and personally in a more adequate manner.

counseling, reinforcement theory in: a principle, basic to *behavioral counseling,* which relates to the creation of desirable consequences that will strengthen or facilitate certain behavior. *See* **reinforcement.**

counseling relationship: the mutual and purposeful rapport existing between a counselor and a counselee characterized in the main by warmth and acceptance with a stress upon understanding the counselee's needs and feelings. *Syn.* **client-counselor relationship.**

counseling, religious: *syn.* **counseling, pastoral.**

counseling room: *see* **guidance room.**

counseling, self theory in: *see* **self theory in counseling.**

counseling, semantic: counseling based on the assumption that the counselee is prevented from forming a true picture of reality by the emotional connotations and tensions associated with word meanings.

counseling service: one of the basic services in an organized guidance program involving a person-to-person relationship and providing the individual student with the best opportunity for self-study, decision-making planning, and the resolution of personal problems.

counseling, social: personal or group assistance primarily concerned with aiding persons to form or develop social skills that will enable them to derive satisfactions from social experiences and to make useful contributions to society as social beings.

counseling system: organization of the functions of the counselor or counselors into a unified plan to provide counseling services.

counseling techniques: methods, procedures, and approaches used by counselors in working with counselees.

counseling theory: any of a collection of assumptions, interpretations, and hypotheses about human behavior that help to explain what is happening in counseling and that give an observer (counselor) a framework in which to make his future observations, evaluations, and predictions about client behavior.

counseling, therapeutic: the alleviation of behavior difficulties by counseling; denotes activities that are in no sense medical and designed to remedy conditions that are not directly medical.

counseling, trait and factor theory of: a counseling approach, when less formally applied called *directive* or *counselor-centered,* which stresses diagnosis as a fundamental counselor function; the counselor is responsible for deciding what data are needed, collecting them, and presenting them to the counselee; he also presents his points of view with definiteness and enlightens the counselee through expository statements. *See* **counseling, directive.**

counseling treatment: any interviewing procedure that is designed by a counselor for aiding the student to solve his personal problems; also, procedures used by the counselor in enlisting the cooperation of specialized personnel departments such as a counseling bureau and health service.

counseling, vocational: (1) the continuous process of helping an individual through interpersonal relationships and a reliable fund of information to understand himself and his possible role in the world or work, to test this concept of himself against reality, and to change it into reality with satisfaction to himself and benefit to society; (2) conferring with a person for the purpose of assisting him in problems connected with his choice of occupation, training for that occupation, obtaining employment, etc. *See* **guidance, vocational.**

counselor: (1) one who assists individual students to make adjustments and choices especially in regard to vocational, educational, and personal matters; *syn.* **guidance counselor;** (2) an adviser or personnel specialist.

counselor, adjustment: a general term used to describe a person, in the role of counselor, who seeks to assist a counselee in bringing about a condition of harmonious relation to the environment wherein the counselee is able to obtain satisfaction for most of his needs and to meet fairly well the demands, both physical and social, put upon him.

counselor, admissions: *syn.* **admissions officer.**

counselor, agricultural: one who helps students solve their problems relating to occupational choice in agriculture, training, placement, and adjustment on the job.

counselor boys': *syn.* **dean of boys.**

counselor, camp: a person who functions as a personal adviser to children in typical summer camps or in specialized camps; training, skills, and duties of such workers vary considerably.

counselor-centered counseling: *syn.* **counseling, directive.**

counselor certificate: *see* **certificate, counselor.**

counselor certification, school: *see* **certification, school counselor.**

counselor, class: one who is assigned to counsel pupils enrolled in a particular school class, such as the freshman class.

counselor, college: (1) one who functions as a counselor in a college or university, primarily for students in higher education; (2) a secondary school counselor who may be assigned the task of helping and advising students who expect to continue their formal education beyond high school.

counselor, coordinator: a person who has the responsibility of bringing about a harmonious adjustment of the activities of the various counselors of a given system.

counselor, coordinator core: the person within a school organization who has the responsibility of maintaining a proper balance between subject-matter requirements and administrative practices, giving special emphasis to guidance involving such core subjects as English and mathematics.

counselor, dormitory: *syn.* **counselor, residence.**

counselor education: the program of graduate studies designed to prepare enrollees for guidance positions such as school counselor and director of guidance or for careers as counselor educators and guidance supervisors.

counselor educator: a staff member who teaches or assists in a program of graduate studies designed to prepare enrollees for guidance positions.

counselor, elementary school: a counselor working as a member of the professional staff of an elementary school, with the responsibility for working with pupils, teachers, and parents and having as his major concern the developmental needs of all pupils.

counselor, employment: an employee of a personnel department who interviews and advises persons applying for work or who acts as a consultant to persons employed in the plant or corporation.

counselor evaluation: *see* **evaluation, counselor.**

counselor, faculty: *see* **adviser, faculty.**

counselor for boys: *syn.* **dean of boys.**

counselor for girls: *syn.* **dean of girls.**

counselor function: *see* **function, counselor.**

counselor functions, taxonomy of: *see* **taxonomy of counselor functions.**

counselor, girls': *see* **dean of girls.**

counselor, guidance: *syn.* **counselor.**

counselor, head: *syn.* **director of guidance.**

counselor, health: one whose duties involve guidance in health matters.

counselor, home-visitor: one who visits the homes of pupils or students for the purpose of facilitating adjustment or guidance by gathering information about the pupils, establishing better understanding between the home and the school, and gaining family cooperation in a plan of treatment.

counselor institute: *see* **institute (2).**

counselor, junior high school: a person who functions as a school counselor for students usually enrolled in grades 7, 8, or 9.

counselor, men's: *syn.* **dean of men.**

counselor of men: *syn.* **dean of men.**

counselor of women: *syn.* **dean of women.**

counselor performance: the mode of operation by which a counselor proceeds toward stated or defined aims and objectives.

counselor, personal: a staff member who counsels students who manifest problems of a personal and social nature, uses the results of psychological tests, and performs therapy within limits of interview technique.

counselor, personal-adjustment: *syn.* **counselor, personal.**

counselor, placement: a member of a counseling staff who is assigned special responsibilities for assisting students to find jobs.

counselor, psychological: *syn.* **counselor, personal.**

counselor-pupil ratio: one full-time counselor to a given number of counselees. (The assignment of counselees to counselor is conditioned by many factors such as counseling time, number of counselors available, supplemental duties of the counselor, and many more.)

counselor, reading: a person who helps others with their reading problems, aids them in securing reading materials, and helps them plan their reading activities. *See* **adviser, readers'.**

counselor, rehabilitation: a person who functions in a private or public rehabilitation setting guiding disabled persons through the growing complexities and the many technical and social considerations that are involved in the rehabilitation process and balancing its operations with the personal problems of the disabled and, in many cases, of their families. *See* **rehabilitation.**

counselor, religious: one who assists individuals with problems that are primarily of a religious or spiritual nature.

counselor, remedial: *syn.* **counselor, personal.**

counselor, residence: one who renders individual counseling and group-guidance services to students in a dormitory relative to problems of a scholastic, educational, vocational, and personal-social nature; coordinates and directs work of student counselors in dormitories; the work is on the college or university level. *Syn.* **dormitory counselor.**

counselor, school: a person who is trained to assist individual students in making adjustments and choices especially with regard to vocational, educational, and personal matters and who is assigned the responsibility of providing counseling services to students.

counselor, secondary school: a counselor working in a secondary school setting concerned with and accepting a responsibility for assisting all pupils and having as his major concern the developmental needs and problems of youth. *See* **counselor, junior high school; counselor, senior high school.**

counselor, senior high school: a person who functions as a school counselor for high school students, usually those enrolled in grades 10, 11, or 12.

counselor, student: a student, generally a senior, who assists in the counseling program of an educational institution, not only by guiding younger students, but also by aiding older students to attain insight into their problems and helping them to gain social and educational experience.

counselor, teacher: a member of the faculty whose daily assignment consists of one or more periods of counseling and at least one period of classroom teaching.

counselor training, in-service: *see* **training, in-service counselor.**

counselor, visiting-student: *syn.* **adviser, foreign-student.**

counselor, vocational: one who helps students solve their problems relating to occupational choice, training, placement (in summer, part-time, and full-time employment), and adjustment on the job. *See* **adviser, vocational.**

counselor, women's: *syn.* **dean of women.**

counselors' clinic: *see* **clinic, counselors'.**

counselors, specialization of: the utilization of individual counselors within a school to perform specific duties in providing guidance services; for example, one counselor may be identified as the *college counselor* while another may be referred to as the *placement counselor.*

count, fog: (mil. ed.) a count made of the words in a given piece of writing to measure the degree of difficulty in understanding the piece.

count, item: *syn.* **response count.**

count, response: *see* **response count.**

countable set: *see* **set, countable.**

counter: (1) in automatic computers, a *register* that has an ability (limited) to add or substract because of an associated special adder; used to accumulate or hold data, such as the number of cards running through a machine; (2) (math.) one of the small objects used by primary pupils to match one-to-one so as to learn about cardinal number; (3) (math.) a mechanical device which will, when a button or lever is depressed, display in order the numerals for the counting numbers in some additive place value system of numeration, the binary counter being an example; *see* **numeration system.**

counter, control: a register that contains the address of the next instruction to be executed (not always present in multiaddress computers).

counter, digital: *syn.* **counter, index.**

counter, graphic item: a device that may be attached to the IBM test-scoring machine to count the number of times any response to a multiple-choice test item is marked in a particular set of test papers.

counter, index: a device on tape recorders that counts the revolutions of the feed reel as a rough guide to the position of recorded material on magnetic tape. *Syn.* **digital counter.**

Counter Reformation: *see* **Council of Trent.**

counterbalanced design: *see* **design, counterbalanced.**

counterconditioning: *syn.* **therapy, aversion.**

counterexample: (math.) given a sentence that makes an assertion about all members of a set or all situations of a particular type, a single example that shows the assertion is not always true is called a counterexample to that assertion; for example, 2 would be a counterexample to the assertion "All prime numbers are odd."

counterinsurgency training: *see* training, counterinsurgency.

counterpoint: (1) a form of musical composition characterized by the simultaneous employment of two or more melodies; (2) this form of composition as a field of study.

countersuggestion: (psych.) a suggestion tending to inhibit or reverse the effect of a previous suggestion.

countertransference: (couns.) the development of certain emotional attitudes toward the counselee by the counselor, as contrasted with transference, that describes the counselee's emotional reactions directed toward the counselor. *See* transference.

counting: a method by which a handwriting instructor or learner indicates each successive letter, stroke, or upstroke by speaking a number; in writing the letter n, for example, the count might be "1-2-3-4-5" or "1-2-3."

counting block: (1) a rectangular piece of wood about 1½ inches thick, 10 inches long, and 3 inches wide, containing a single row of 10 holes and two parallel rows of 10 holes each; placement of wooden pegs in designated holes can then be used to show the meaning of any one- or two-place number; (2) a cube, usually of wood or plastic contruction, with numbered, lettered, and figured sides; large enough to be grasped by a young child and used as a child's toy in block building as well as for object identification and simple counting.

counting board: *see* abacus.

counting number: *see* number, counting.

counting, rational: counting by 1s, 2s, 3s, 5s, etc., either forward or backward; sometimes restricted to instances in which the numbers of a specific set are being counted.

counting, rote: reciting the names of the numbers 1, 2, 3, . . . in the correct order with or without understanding their meaning.

country day school: a school, usually private, with sufficient campus and facilities to provide a long school day with a maximum of outdoor recreational activities.

country, developing: a term used to designate any countries that are in a relatively low state of industrial development but presumably wish to become more industrialized; though it is an inexact term, many people prefer it to the term *undeveloped countries*, since all countries are developed to some degree, and to *underdeveloped* countries, since the latter term is judgmental and sometimes insulting. *See* country, third-world.

country, third-world: a term used to designate any countries not considered allies (or satellites) either of the North American-Western European-Australian-New Zealand group or of the communist bloc countries; most third-world countries are developing countries, but the terms are not strictly synonymous. *See* country, developing.

county agent: *syn.* extension agent; *see* extension worker, county.

county association of teachers: *see* association, local teachers'.

county board of education: *see* board of education, county.

county commissioner: *see* superintendent, county.

county extension worker: *see* extension worker, county.

county high school: *see* high school, county.

county institute: *see* institute, county.

county junior college: *see* junior college, county.

county library: *see* library, county.

county-owned: *syn.* board-owned.

county school: a school administered by a board of education that functions on a county-wide basis; may or may not enroll pupils from the whole county, as in the case of a county high school, or may serve an attendance district smaller than a county.

county school association: a society or group of people, organized for the promotion of an educational object, that draws its membership from the county as a whole.

(For educational purposes, the society might draw membership from one or more of the following groups: classroom teachers, administrators, supervisors, school-board members, and patrons.)

county school district: *see* district, county school.

county school system: *see* school system, county.

county superintendent: *see* superintendent, county.

county system, intermediate: a type of school organization in which the county is an intermediate unit set up between local units (district, town, or township) and the state; various methods of administration are employed, but generally there is a county superintendent and sometimes a county board of education. (The intermediate county system differs from the *county unit plan*, in which the administration of the schools of the county is under one board of education and one administrator.)

county unit: a school administrative unit whose boundaries are coterminous with the boundaries of the civil county, except that certain territory (usually cities or villages) within the county may be excluded as independent districts. *See* administrative unit.

county-unit consolidation: *see* consolidation, county-unit.

coupling, bibliographic: *see* bibliographic coupling.

coupon bond: *see* bond, coupon.

courage: an attitude or mode of response, characterized by comparatively calm, intentionally directed, usually aggressive behavior in a situation that the individual knows is likely to result in danger, pain, or other unpleasant experience.

course: organized subject matter in which instruction is offered within a given period of time, and for which credit toward graduation or certification is usually given.

course, academic: (1) in general, a course of study dealing with "cultural" or "pure" subject matter, as opposed to one dealing with "practical" or "applied" subject matter; regarded as necessary for general cultural reasons or as a means of acquiring knowledge in one's field of specialization; (2) (teacher ed.) a course on the college level other than a professional course, particularly a course in one's field of specialization, for example, a course in French for a prospective language teacher or one in biochemistry for a prospective science teacher (in this sense, a professional course may also be an academic course; thus, to a prospective professor of educational psychology, a course in educational psychology would be both a professional and an academic course).

course, accelerated: a course that can be completed in less than the normal amount of time, for example, a six-week course that can be completed in two or three weeks.

course, advanced: (1) a course that presents material and concepts beyond the introductory or the elementary; (2) a course that carries on from an introductory or elementary course given in the same school.

course, advanced military: *see* military course, advanced.

course, agricultural: a course consisting of practical work and instruction in some technical agricultural subject, preparing the student for competent service in an agricultural occupation, either farm or nonfarm.

course, appreciation: a course in which emphasis is placed on enjoyment, aesthetic values, and broadening of interest, rather than on the historical or material values of the subject being studied.

course, basic: (1) a course that presents only the fundamental or essential subject matter in a subject field; (2) a general introductory course that gives the student the necessary general foundation in an area and that is followed by advanced courses in the same general area (thus, trigonometry is a basic course for engineering, anatomy for medicine, etc.).

course, basic business: *see* business education, basic.

course, basic military: *see* military course, basic.

course, basic socialization: *see* program, common-learnings (2).

course, Bible: a course in Biblical literature or literatures with little or much doctrinal interpretation, depending on the school. (In nonsectarian schools and colleges the course ordinarily involves little or no doctrinal interpretation and is usually an elective subject. In parochial or church schools it involves much doctrinal interpretation.)

course, block-and-gap: (sci. ed.) a course designed to investigate fully a few concepts while others are purposely omitted; often cuts across traditional discipline lines, drawing from several academic areas and integrating basic ideas and knowledge; usually problems are selected which do not cover an extensive array of facts from all scientific fields or all details of a single field but rather stress unity among the sciences and relationships between the sciences and other academic studies.

course, broad-field: a course in which traditionally separate subjects (such as geography, history, civics, and social problems) have been fused into a general course, such as a social-science course, stress being placed on the interrelationships of the subjects so combined.

course, business organization: a body of knowledge designed primarily to acquaint the high school or college student with the characteristics, organization, and operations of a business entity; topics such as business organization, finance, personnel, purchasing operations, marketing operations, traffic management, and production are usually included.

course, career: (mil. ed.) one of four sequential courses that prepare an army officer for the general demands of progressive career phases, namely, officer basic course, officer advanced course, command and general staff officer course, and the Army War College resident course.

course, career development: in the Extension Courses Institute of Air University, one of the courses that provides the knowledge phase of the USAF dual channel on-the-job training program; mandatory for airmen in the official up-grade training.

course, case-history: (sci. ed.) instruction organized around illustrative case histories of scientific discoveries, enlightenment, or controversy; it employs original writings and accounts of research by eminent scientists, often edited for reading by students and accompanied by notes and readings from standard textbooks.

course, club study: an extension course, usually outlined by a subject-matter expert for study by the members of a club and supplemented by textbook, library, and syllabus aids; often provided by various national organizations.

course, complementary: a course offering subsidiary material, for example, civilization or background material in connection with the teaching of a foreign language.

course, conference-leadership: a course or series of meetings intended to develop the ability to lead conferences.

course, content: a course in which formal or conventional facts are less emphasized than natural facts. *See* **subject, content.**

course, cooperative: (voc. ed.) a course of study designed to form a basis of related technical knowledge or shop techniques to supplement the work experiences of students working on a part-time basis. *See* **cooperative education; student, cooperative.**

course, core: (1) that part of the school curriculum in which an endeavor is made to assist all pupils in meeting needs believed most common to them and to society without regard to subject-matter classification; (2) a course required of all students, giving instruction in minimum and basic essentials of living.

course, correspondence: *see* **correspondence course.**

course, credit: a course that carries academic credit.

course, defense: *see* **defense school.**

course, demonstration: a course offered by a teacher education institution to show prospective teachers or others the practical application of educational theory in actual school situations. *See* **class, demonstration.**

course, disciplinary: a school subject or other course of study that is valued because of its presumed effect in disciplining the mind or some mental function; a term somewhat related to *faculty psychology* and *formal discipline.*

course, discontinued: (mil. ed.) a course that is permanently discontinued; resources for conducting the course are not retained but are channeled to other uses; however, a file copy of training material is maintained.

course, education: (teacher ed.) a course of study in a university or liberal arts college that is designed to give preparation in one or more phases of such professional content as the understanding of the pupil's growth and development; the psychology of learning; the history and status of educational institutions; teaching, supervision, or administration of schools; the objectives, content, methods, and outcomes of instruction; guidance; the methods and conclusions of educational research; educational philosophy; or the professional and welfare problems of the teacher; may be a course in student or practice teaching.

course, educational orientation: a measured unit of instruction wherein a new group of individuals becomes better acquainted with an established group's traditions, purposes, rules, regulations, policies, facilities, and special services. *See* **course, orientation.**

course, elective: *see* **elective.**

course, elementary: a program of instruction in some elementary school subject or area of experience requiring a school term or year for its completion, for example, a sixth-year course in arithmetic.

course, evening: a series of spaced learning experiences presented in evening class sessions by a school, college, university, or other agency.

course, exploratory: (1) a course intended to acquaint the school officials with the characteristics of those about to enter the school or a new field of study and to help the prospective entrants evaluate the opportunities of the school or an unfamiliar field of study; may be a tryout course, a general course, or a combination of both; *see* **course, general; course, tryout;** (2) a course affording students firsthand contacts and experiences in a variety of subject fields or occupational situations; designed to open up new vistas and stimulate new activities in order to discover and develop the interests and capacities of students and to contribute to their guidance in occupational selection or plans for further education.

course, extension: a series of spaced learning experiences presented by correspondence or on- or off-campus class instruction and offered by a university extension division or other adult education agency. *See* **class, extension.**

course, formal: a course in a formal subject, for example, spelling, arithmetic, formal grammar. *See* **subject, formal.**

course, fusion: a course in which various subjects of one or more fields are grouped and merged into larger wholes.

course, general: a type of exploratory course in which the material studied consists primarily of descriptive and informative material about the field of study rather than samples in the field; thus, a general course in foreign languages may deal with language as a social institution, the origin and development of language, the nature of language as a tool, etc. *See* **course, exploratory;** *contr. w.* **course, tryout.**

course, general methods: *see* **course, methods.**

course, "great issues": a term used to designate a course or courses centering around the major issues of Western culture or around some other significant aspects of living.

course, group-guidance: (couns.) a course planned especially for the consideration of problems peculiar to a whole group.

course, guidance: a course for those pursuing professional training in the guidance field, including academic subject areas and practical field experience related to personnel services.

course, home reading: an annotated list of books with instructions as to how to pursue consecutive reading in a definite subject area, usually provided as an extension service by universities and public libraries.

course, home study: *see* **correspondence course.**

course, honors: a course, at high school or college level, that limits enrollment to exceptionally capable students; provides for independent or tutorial work, places the responsibility for student progress more on the student than on the teacher, emphasizes reading and self-instruction, and usually frees the student from regular classroom attendance and regular course requirements.

course, how-to-study: a course designed to teach students the specific educational skills (such as note taking, use of reference books, etc.) required for successful scholastic work.

course, informal: *see* **course, noncredit.**

course instructions: an outline intended for the guidance of the teacher and listing the work that is to be covered in teaching all or part of a course.

course, instructor-foreman: a conference course for foremen designed to improve their instructional abilities.

course, integrating: *see* **program, common-learnings** (2).

course, integration: (teacher ed.) (1) a course included in a teacher education program that is conducted so as to provide preservice or inservice teachers with concrete assistance in applying educational theory and academic preparation to specific types of classroom problems; (2) a course that brings together for intercorrelation the outcomes derived from a variety of departments, courses, or divisions, whether academic or professional.

course, intensive: (lang.) several hours each day devoted to lectures, study, and directed oral practice to ensure rapid mastery of a foreign language.

course, interdisciplinary: a course, usually experimental, that attempts to utilize the findings and principles of more than one academic discipline, usually topic-centered, focusing on some new area of concern for analysis regardless of how it fits the traditional points of view of established disciplines; instituted in both universities and high schools for the solution of problems involving subject matter from various fields.

course, interservice: *see* **interservice school.**

course, introductory: a preliminary course that leads to or is to be followed by an advanced course or courses in the same subject or area. *Dist. f.* **course, exploratory; course, orientation; course, survey.**

course, janitors' training: a program of instruction designed for the improvement of the work of school janitors and engineers; several plans are in use, the most common being the intensive summer course of lectures, conferences, demonstration, and practice held for 1 or 2 weeks.

course, joint: *see* **joint school.**

course, junior-executive training: any of the courses in a program of study designed for junior executives, buyers, and department heads in retail stores or other distributive organizations; offered in extension classes under the distributive-education program.

course, laboratory: (1) a course in which units of instruction consist of laboratory experiments usually conducted in laboratory buildings or rooms set apart for practical investigation in any of the sciences, as in physics or chemistry; (2) a course in which the laboratory techniques of problem solving through individual and group research and experimentation are applied to specific problems in a field (as in a social science laboratory, a writing laboratory, or a laboratory course in the teaching of English).

course, lecture: a course conducted by the lecture method. *See* **lecture method.**

course, management training: a course designed for owners, managers, and executives in retail stores or other distributive organizations; offered in extension classes under the distributive-education program.

course, methods: (1) a course in how to teach a particular subject; sometimes called a *special methods course;* (2) a course in general classroom procedures that may be used in teaching any subject; sometimes called a *general methods course.*

course, mobilization: (mil. ed.) a course which contains the minimum fundamental instruction required to ensure the student's effective performance in wartime in a particular skill, specialty, or area of professional responsibility.

course, noncredit: a course that does not carry academic credit.

course, nonlaboratory: a course in which laboratory experiments or laboratory techniques are not introduced.

course, normal: (1) historically, a curriculum offered by a university for the specific purpose of training elementary school teachers (the university normal course began to disappear during the last quarter of the nineteenth century, when universities established departments of education for the purpose of preparing both elementary and high school teachers); (2) a teacher-preparing curriculum in a high school or academy.

course, observation: *see* **class, observation.**

course of instruction: a general plan of instruction prepared by the teacher for his own use with a particular group of pupils for a specific period of time.

course of study: (1) strictly, an official guide prepared for use by administrators, supervisors, and teachers of a particular school or school system as an aid to teaching in a given subject or area of study for a given grade, combination of grades, or other designated class or instruction group; may include the aims of the course, the expected outcomes, and the scope and nature of the materials to be studied, with suggestions as to suitable instructional aids, textbooks, supplementary reading, activities, suggested learning experiences, teaching methods, and measurement of achievement; (2) sometimes loosely and incorrectly used as a synonym for *curriculum. Dist. f.* **program, school; program of studies.**

course of study, correlated: (1) a course of study in which textual references are made for relating materials in one subject field with pertinent materials in other subject fields; (2) a course of study that outlines a program to interrelate the instruction of two or more subject areas relative to specific topics and that lists under the respective subject-area headings the activities, knowledges, skills, or appreciation that each subject area can or should contribute to the understanding of the topic in question.

course of study, fused: *syn.* **course of study, integrated.**

course of study, integrated: a course of study in which pupil activity is centered in themes or areas of living and which draws on the content of the various school subjects as mutually associated in some genuine life relation. *Syn.* **fused course of study;** *see* **curriculum, fused.**

course, office-machines: a course of study in which instruction is given in the operation of machines commonly found in the business office; some of these machines are the full-keyboard adding-listing machines, the ten-key adding machines, rotary calculators, and electronic calculators.

course, orientation: (1) a course the aim of which is to introduce the student to some phase of life or education or help him adjust to it; (2) especially, a college course the aim of which is to help the student adjust to college life and which treats of study habits, library methods, utilization of college facilities, social practices, etc.; (3) a course of study, generalized in nature, used to guide pupils and students in the selection of further courses of study.

course, preview: *syn.* **course, survey.**

course, prevocational: (1) (obsoles.) an exploratory industrial arts course preceding general industrial arts education; (2) subject matter related to the world of work usually taught in the beginning phase of a work-study program for the mentally retarded.

course, professional: a course or sequence of courses intended to prepare a person for the practice of a profession and dealing with some phase or aspect of practice.

course, radio-appreciation: a course of study in some high schools, introduced about 1938, to encourage in pupils the habit of listening to better radio programs in the hope that this might continue into adulthood.

course, radio extension: a course of instruction broadcast by an institution of higher education, fees being collected (as for traditional campus or correspondence courses) and academic credit being granted when requirements are successfully met; has been tried experimentally by a number of institutions.

course, reading: a list of books selected for an individual or a group as a guide to systematic, consecutive reading on a definite subject.

course, refresher: (1) a course designed to retrain in subject areas previously covered by the individual or group; intended to update; (2) (voc. ed.) a classroom or correspondence course for persons already engaged in a particular occupation (or who were formerly so engaged) for the purpose of reviewing basic studies or mastering new material applicable to their work.

course, reimbursed: a course in a vocational curriculum meeting state and Federal standards and receiving reimbursement under the Smith-Hughes or George-Barden act or under a state act.

course, reporting: the standard elementary course in news reporting that is the usual introduction to a curriculum in professional journalism.

course, required: *syn.* **constant** *n.* (4).

course, science survey: a scheme of organization used in some college science courses in which an attempt is made to cover the entire scope or an important branch of natural science in a semester or in a year; the intent is to enable students to discover relationships that extend across usual subject-matter boundaries.

course, secretarial-practice: a terminal course designed to simulate actual office settings and help the student master the many secretarial duties performed in the total office environment; this course focuses upon such areas as the further development of office-style dictation and transcription, competency in dealing with people over the telephone or at the reception desk, and competency and skill in operating office equipment.

course, service: (1) any one of several required college courses in physical education; (2) (mil. ed.) a course which presents a curriculum developed and approved by a service to meet a military education and training requirement of that service.

course, short: a form of class or correspondence course for adults, less extended and formalized than regular courses offered by colleges or universities.

course, short-unit: a course of study of relatively short duration organized for the purpose of achieving certain somewhat limited objectives, such as giving instruction in the operation of a particular machine.

course, slack-season: a course, usually in agriculture and related subjects, offered at a time of year when the farming activities of the students require little of their time.

course, special-interest: a course intended to meet the special needs, interests, and abilities of particular pupils.

course, special methods: a type of course in education emphasizing methods or techniques of instruction as well as the content and related problems for one of the various teaching fields, for example, methods of teaching English, as distinguished from a *general methods course,* which has general affiliation with all teaching fields. *See* **course, methods.**

course, specialist: in Army usage, a course given for the purpose of preparing the student for immediate utilization of a particular skill or specialty.

course, stem: *see* **program, common-learnings** (2).

course, subfreshman: any beginners' course in college below the college level, usually carrying no academic credit, that is provided and frequently made obligatory for those freshmen entering college with faulty or insufficient preparation in certain fields of study.

course, subject: a course in which instruction emphasizes knowledge and understandings rather than skills, for example, history.

course, survey: (1) a course designed to give a general view of an area of study, often as a means of introducing an unfamiliar field to pupils or students before undertaking specialized work or of providing them with broad general concepts about an area in which they may or may not plan to specialize; (2) a brief introduction to the structure and forms of a foreign language to serve advanced students as a basis for private study; (3) a series of lectures with extensive literary and cultural readings in a foreign language for students with a reading knowledge of that language or similar lectures and readings in English for orientation of students not familiar with the foreign language in question.

course, teacher-training: *syn.* **course, professional.**

course, terminal: (1) any course in a subject-matter sequence designed for students who do not intend to have further formal instruction in this subject field; (2) a course consisting of practical work and instruction in technical subjects and social studies, the purpose of which is to make the individual more efficient socially, more intelligent as a citizen, and more competent in a nonprofessional or semiprofessional occupation (especially in commercial, engineering, agricultural, secretarial, and health fields); best suited to the needs of high school seniors and junior college students.

course, theory: one of a variety of courses dealing with different aspects of education and enlarging the understanding of students of education, for example, introduction to, history of, and philosophy of education, also educational psychology and sociology; to be distinguished from operational courses such as practice teaching and also from subject-matter area courses.

course training standard: *see* **training standard, course.**

course, tryout: a course in which the pupil is given opportunity to try his ability to succeed in a given field of study or work before attempting more advanced or complex activities; thus a course in first year Latin might be a *tryout* for second year Latin, or a course in occupations might offer *tryouts* for several different types of work. *See* **course, exploratory;** *contr. w.* **course, general.**

course, unit trade: instruction organized for persons attending full-time school and preparing for advantageous entrance into a specific trade or industrial pursuit. *See* **unit trade school or class.**

course, United States Air Force extension: a correspondence course for students enrolled in the Extension Course Institute of Air University.

course, vestibule: an introductory course whose chief aim is to reveal the nature, scope, and occupational possibilities of industrial activities available for later study and participation.

course, vocational: a course consisting of practical work and instruction in some technical subject, preparing the student for competent service in a nonprofessional or semiprofessional occupation (for example, courses in welding, carpentry, etc.); the term is ordinarily used to distinguish such a course from cultural courses (such as English literature and music appreciation) and professional courses (such as medicine, teaching, engineering, etc.).

courses of study, state: suggested courses of study for the various subjects taught in the public elementary and secondary schools of the state, prepared and distributed by authority of the state department of education.

court case: (1) a child or other person who has been officially brought before the court for trial; (2) the legal problem that has been officially presented to the court for decision.

court, children's: *syn.* **court, juvenile.**

court commitment: *see* **commitment** (2).

court hearing: the process of getting statements from those persons involved in a court case, together with testimony from others called as witnesses.

court, juvenile: a court dealing with youthful offenders or juvenile dependents and with adults who contribute to the delinquency of children. (Courts of this type first operated in the United States at about the beginning of the twentieth century.) *Syn.* **children's court.**

court notice: the statement from the court notifying the principals and witnesses in a court case to be present at the hearing.

court of domestic relations: a court having jurisdiction over cases involving the settlement of family difficulties such as desertion and neglect.

court of record: a court whose judgments may be revised by writs of error and whose proceedings and judgments import absolute verity and, until reversed, protect all who obey them.

court officer: an employee of a pupil-personnel department assigned to represent the board of education in matters pertaining to pupil-personnel work in various courts, particularly the juvenile court and courts of record.

court order: a judgment or conclusion of a court on any motion or proceeding by which affirmation relief is granted or relief is denied.

court school: a type of secondary school developed during the Renaissance in connection with the courts of the city-states of Italy, sponsored by the rulers of these cities chiefly to provide a courtly education for the sons of the nobility.

courtesy: an acceptable mode of behavior based on consideration for the feelings of others.

covariance: the arithmetic mean of the products of the paired deviations of two variables, measured from their respective means.

covariance, analysis of: an extension of the methods of analysis of variance in which adjustments are made in the data for the criterion variable on the basis of data collected on one or more other variables which vary concomitantly with the criterion variable.

covariance matrix: *see* **matrix, covariance.**

covariance, unit: the scaling of covariance from its observed value to 1.00.

covariation: *syn.* **correlation** (1).

covariation, measure of: *syn.* **measure of relationship.**

covert response: *see* **response, covert.**

CPS (certified professional secretary): the holder of a certificate issued by the National Secretaries Association to those who pass a 12-hour examination administered by the Institute for Certifying Secretaries; the applicant must meet certain age, experience, and education requirements before he or she is permitted to take the examination, which covers the areas of personal adjustment and human relations, business law, business administration, secretarial accounting, secretarial skills, and secretarial procedures.

cradle school: *syn.* **crèche.**

craft: *syn.* **handcraft; handicraft (obs.).**

craft advisory committee: *see* **advisory committee, craft.**

crafts: *see* **arts and crafts.**

crafts laboratory: *see* **laboratory, crafts.**

craftsman: (1) a skilled worker who works with established crafts, for example, baker, boilermaker, carpenter, electrician, locomotive engineer, machinist, plasterer, upholsterer, industrial foreman, and all types of repairmen and mechanics; (2) (art) one who is skilled in the technical processes and use of media in producing objects of art; generally used for the worker in ceramics, metalwork, jewelry, and weaving but can include the painter and other artists.

craftwork: (1) participation in one of the crafts; (2) objects produced by hand or machine with emphasis on creative design.

Craig method: a method of teaching children to read, consisting of a modified kinesthetic approach employing script letters and word forms covered with carborundum powder; used with normal children of 3 to 5 years of age. *See* **kinesthetic method** (1).

crawl: (1) a long sheet of paper installed on rollers and containing a series of titles or credits relating to a television program; when placed in an opaque projector connected to a film chain, each line appears in sequence as the roller is turned; (2) (phys. ed.) a descriptive name for a swimming technique.

crawl rack: a wide shelf above head height used for training military personnel in clambering up onto an overhead support.

crawling: locomotor movement of the child in which the abdomen is in contact with the surface; occurs between the fourth and ninth months. *Contr. w.* **creeping.**

creamery: a building of an agricultural college used for the manufacture of butter, cheese, and other dairy products.

creation, conscious act of: (art ed.) an instance of the child's creative activity at the time in his creative growth when

he becomes aware of the significance of techniques and the resulting final product; usually found when the child approaches puberty.

creation, unaware: the unconscious imaginative activity of children, which is uninhibited and intuitive and moves directly from subjective experiences into creation.

creationism: (1) philosophically, the theory that the universe and its processes are the result of God's will or of a Creative Force; *contr. w.* **evolutionism;** (2) according to F. S. Breed, the fallacy of subjectivism in the philosophy of John Dewey, whose position is said to be that the process of knowing something constitutes or creates, rather than discovers, the object known; (3) theologically, indicates that for every individual human born there is created a separate soul; (4) biologically, the theory that each species of life was separately created and will reproduce itself without mutations that could be the basis for newly evolved species.

creative activity: *see* **activity, creative.**

creative-activity individualization: *see* **instruction, individualized.**

creative art: *see* **art, creative.**

creative development: *see* **development, creative.**

creative dramatics: *see* **dramatics, creative.**

creative education: education intended to promote and encourage learning and development through original or self-expressive activity on the part of those being taught.

creative experience: *see* **experience, creative.**

creative expression: any free expression of the child through such mediums as language, visual art, music, or rhythms spontaneously evoked by the child's own feelings and experiences and furthered by any means that promote adequacy and clarity of perception and deepen the emotional drive prompting expression.

creative growth: *see* **growth, creative.**

creative music: *see* **music, creative.**

creative playwriting: *see* **playwriting, creative.**

creative reading: *see* **reading, creative.**

creative rhythm: the bodily rhythmical expression of an idea inspired by personal contact or experience; the idea expressed in rhythmical movement is usually some simple thought such as that of ducks swimming in a pond or the wind blowing through the trees, the children, with the guidance of their leader, inventing and executing the movements believed to express the idea and its mood.

creative social act: *see* **social act, creative.**

creative story: a child's story made up from his experiences or imagination and told spontaneously.

creative supervision: *see* **supervision, creative.**

creative therapy: *see* **therapy, creative.**

creative thinking: *see* **thinking, creative.**

creative types: *see* **haptic type; visual type.**

creative-values approach: a method of working with the problem of curriculum revision in which the principal criterion for the selection of materials and methods of instruction is the extent of their contribution to the general goal of encouraging and developing thinking and self-expression on the part of pupils.

creative writing: *see* **writing, creative.**

creative writing chart: *see* **chart, creative writing.**

creativity: the human attribute of constructive originality; may include such factors as associative and ideational fluency, adaptive and spontaneous flexibility, and ability to elaborate in detail; may be fostered or inhibited by teaching procedures; operationally defined by specific productions such as inventions, paintings, discovery of principles, etc., or by standardized tests; beyond a fairly low minimum level does not appear to correlate either positively or negatively with *intelligence. Contr. w.* **conformity.**

creator as spectator: *see* **visual type.**

crèche (kresh): (Fr., lit., "cradle") a day nursery for children 1 to 3 years of age; frequently offers group or class instruction in child care for the mothers and medical attention for the children; first started in France in 1884. *Syn.* **cradle school.**

credential, teacher's: *syn.* **certificate, teacher's.**

credentials: (1) a certificate stating that the student has graduated from a certain curriculum or has passed certain subjects with indicated marks; (2) a signed statement that a student is entitled to represent the school in certain specified capacities; (3) the record of an applicant for a teaching position, including transcripts of college work completed and testimonials relative to previous experience and character.

credentials, administrative: *syn.* **certificate, administrative.**

credit: (1) acknowledgment of the reduction of a debt; (2) trust given or received; (3) official certification of the completion of a course of study; (4) a unit for expressing quantitatively the amount of content of a course of instruction, especially with reference to the value of the course in relation to the total requirements for a degree or certificate. *See* **credit hour, semester.**

credit by examination: academic credit the granting of which involves the use of approved examinations; may be used to shorten the time required for a capable student to earn an academic degree.

credit, college: a unit used in measuring and recording the work completed by an undergraduate student in an institution of higher education. *See* **credit** (4); **credit hour, quarter; credit hour, semester.**

credit, constructive: (mil. ed.) credit granted as the equivalent of completion of all or parts of school courses to certain military personnel who are qualified through length of service, field experience, and demonstrated ability.

credit, consumer: debt incurred by the consumer for the purchase of goods and services. *See* **charge account; credit, installment; credit, open-account.**

credit course: *see* **course, credit.**

credit, extension: credit earned by students in extension classes and correspondence study, of which arbitrary amounts are accepted to meet degree requirements.

credit-for-quality plan: *see* **honor points.**

credit hour: a unit used in measuring and recording the work completed by a student in an institution of higher education. (Usually 1 credit hour represents 1 hour's instruction per week in a given subject for a designated number of weeks in the term. There are two main kinds: *quarter credit hours* and *semester credit hours,* representing approximately 12 and 18 weeks of instruction, respectively, frequently referred to simply as *semester hours* or *quarter hours;* the latter are converted into the former by multiplying them by ⅔.

credit hour, quarter: a unit for expressing quantitatively the content of a course at the level of higher education; a student making normal progress will complete 45 to 48 quarter credit hours of course work in an academic year of 9 months or 3 quarters.

credit hour, semester: (1) a unit for expressing quantitatively the content of a course at the level of higher education (a student making normal progress will complete 30 to 32 semester credit hours of course work in an academic year of 9 months); (2) a specified fraction (usually $\frac{1}{120}$ to $\frac{1}{128}$) of the total content of a 4-year program leading to the bachelor's degree.

credit, installment: a plan of paying for acquired goods or services whereby the customer remits a portion of the account at regular intervals over a period of time. *Syn.* installment buying; *see* **credit, consumer.**

credit, open-account: the oldest and most convenient form of credit which grants the buyer a week to a month in which to pay his account without paying a service charge.

credit, public: confidence or trust in the probity of the whole people and their financial ability to repay debts incurred by or for them.

credit, residence: (1) allocated time units a student must meet by study at the seat (campus) of a school, college, or university to fulfill the requirements for a diploma or degree; (2) allocated time units granted for extension courses (off-campus study credits) completed at specified places which are officially designated as *residence centers.*

credit, secured: credit granted after collateral has been presented as insurance against failure to pay.

credit title: a listing of those who participated in or cooperated with the audiovisual project.

credit union: a cooperative association formed for the purpose of saving money and making small loans at low interest rates to members.

credit union, teachers': an organization or association formed, owned, and controlled by teachers, the purpose of which is to accept funds from teachers for savings accounts and to make loans to teachers from these.

credit, unit of: *syn.* **unit** (3).

credit, weighted: credit that is increased or decreased usually by reason of quality of work done; for example, 1.2 times normal credit may be given for work of A grade.

credits, school: a means of designating the amount of schoolwork a pupil has completed. (In the secondary school, these credits are commonly expressed in units, a unit generally being defined as one subject taken for 1 year, the class meeting 1 hour daily 5 days each week.)

creed: (1) the general belief system of a given individual or religious community; (2) the formal authoritative statement of belief of a church, such as the traditional Christian formularies, the Apostles' Creed and the Nicene Creed.

creeping: locomotor movement of a child, starting from about the ninth month; movement is on the hands and knees with the trunk elevated and parallel to the floor. *Contr. w.* **crawling.**

cretinism, congenital: a condition resulting from severe thyroid deficiency, which reduces the body metabolism to such a degree that there are dwarfism and severe mental retardation. *See* **hypothyroidism; retardation, mental.**

crew training: *see* **training, operational readiness.**

crib: a literal, line-by-line translation of a foreign text, often interlineated with the original; inadequate for proper understanding of literary works since no attempt is made to reflect qualities of style; misused by some students in preparing or reciting a foreign language assignment to simulate a fluency they lack. *See* **pony; trot.**

criminal action: *see* **action, criminal.**

criminology: the science or study of crime as a social problem and the investigation of the causes, detection, and prevention of crime and the treatment of criminals.

crippled child: *see* **child, crippled.**

crippled child services: *see* **services, crippled child.**

crippled children, school for: *see* **school for crippled children.**

crisis counseling: *see* **counseling, crisis.**

crisis, culture: *see* **culture crisis.**

crisis teacher: a teacher within the regular school program who provides emotional support to children with behavior problems through individual or small-group tutoring.

criteria, evaluation: *see* **evaluation criteria.**

criteria, lesson observation: a set of variables which can be rated according to a scale by an observer for the purpose of evaluating a teacher and the teacher's lesson.

criteria, objective: (art ed.) evaluation of the final product as the tangible, objective proof of a creative development, focusing attention on (*a*) the stage of development, (*b*) technique and skill, and (*c*) the organization of the work; considered as supplementing but not replacing *subjective criteria.*

criteria of institutional quality: *see* **institutional quality, criteria of.**

criteria, performance: *see* **contracting, performance.**

criteria, subjective: (art ed.) those criteria in children's drawings which are indicative of certain aspects of personality characteristics, as opposed to criteria which refer to the quality of the aesthetic product. *See* **criteria, objective.**

criterion: *pl.* **criteria;** (1) a standard, norm, or judgment selected as a basis for quantitative and qualitative comparison; (2) the dependent variable in a study; (3) that which one is trying to predict. *See* **measure, criterion; test, criterion.**

criterion behavior: *see* **behavior, criterion.**

criterion contamination: a possible source of error in test validation in which the criterion ratings are affected or "contaminated" by the rater's knowledge of the test scores; since the rater may give higher ratings to those with higher scores, this tends to produce a spuriously high correlation.

criterion frame: *syn.* **frame, terminal.**

criterion group: *see* **group, criterion.**

criterion keying: the act or process of developing a test's scoring key empirically, through noting characteristic differences in answers made by different groups of individuals; the Strong Vocational Interest Blank is a good example of the application of this process.

criterion measure: *see* **measure, criterion.**

criterion measurement: *see* **measurement, criterion.**

criterion programming: *see* **programming, criterion.**

criterion-related validity: *see* **validity, criterion-related.**

criterion score: *syn.* **measure, criterion.**

criterion step: *syn.* **frame, terminal.**

criterion test: *see* **test, criterion.**

criterion variable: *see* **variable, criterion.**

critic teacher: a teacher who is a member of the staff of a laboratory school or affiliated school in a teacher education institution and who has as one of his major responsibilities the supervision of student teaching done in his classroom. (The term is gradually being replaced by other designations, especially *supervising teacher.*)

critical analysis: *see* **thinking, critical.**

critical awareness: *see* **awareness, critical.**

critical incident: some occurrence involving a person which is taken to indicate unusual competence or lack of competence on his part; has been used as a basis for defining job requirements and for developing proficiency tests.

critical-incidents method: a method for determining what abilities are needed to do a particular job in order to establish standards of success through actual incidents occurring on the job; used by Flanagan to develop charts of the personal and social development of elementary school children; critical-incident films or tapes are sometimes used in teaching to study the causes and possible solutions of problems encountered in achieving success in the activity illustrated by such an incident.

critical listening: *see* **listening, critical.**

critical morality: *see* **morality, reflective.**

critical ratio: *see* **ratio, critical.**

critical reading: *see* **reading, critical.**

critical realism: *see* **realism, critical.**

critical region: *syn.* **region, rejection.**

critical score: *syn.* **score, cutting.**

critical thinking: *see* **thinking, critical.**

critical writing: (1) the written evaluation of books, plays, art, musical events, motion pictures, records, and radio and television programs; (2) the designation of a journalism course offering training in such writing.

criticism: the art of evaluating or analyzing with knowledge and propriety; when the analysis results in an unfavorable evaluation, criticism is *negative;* a sympathetic evaluation is called *positive criticism.*

criticism, art: (1) evaluating and/or analyzing with knowledge and rational criteria works of art, literature, drama, etc.; (2) an attempt to explain or give reasons for one's response to, liking for, or evaluation of an art work.

criticism, external: the science of determining the authenticity of historical materials.

criticism, historical: (1) the determination of the relative value and proper utilization of historical records through the combined use of the techniques of external criticism and internal criticism; (2) the science of evaluating a work of history in terms of accepted rules of historical method. *See* **criticism, external; criticism, internal; historical method.**

criticism, internal: the act of determining the meaning and trustworthiness of statements or other evidence found in historical materials, such as documents and remains, and of evaluating such statements and evidence; internal criticism is preceded by *external criticism.*

criticism, negative: *see* **criticism.**

criticism, positive: *see* **criticism.**

critique: (1) criticism or critical examination; (2) (literature) scholarly analysis of an essay, article, or other literary work; (3) (philos.) careful and thorough investigation into the grounds of the claims of a belief or position, as opposed to dogmatic assertion or settlement of a claim (Kant); (4) a critical estimate of an activity designed primarily for the purpose of improving one's future performance therein; (5) review of work with a student teacher to point out his strong and weak points in practice teaching and offer suggestions for improvement.

cross-check question: a question included in a questionnaire to ensure the accuracy of the information given in response to a previous question; thus, birth date may serve as a check on age, separate questions being asked on each.

cross-classification table: *syn.* **table, contingency.**

cross country: a competitive or leisure time sport involving individuals running a course across various terrains.

cross-cultural educational studies: *see* **educational studies, cross-cultural.**

cross education: (1) specifically, the transfer of skill training from one part of the body to another, for example, from the right hand to the left; (2) in a broader sense, synonymous with *transfer of training.*

cross-eye: *syn.* **esotropia.**

cross hearing: *see* **hearing, cross.**

cross-media approach: methodology based on the principle that a variety of audiovisual media and experiences correlated with other instructional materials overlap and reinforce the value of each other; some materials may be used to motivate interest; others, to communicate basic facts; still others, to clear up misconceptions and deepen understanding. *See* **multimedia approach.**

cross-national educational studies: *see* **educational studies, cross-national.**

cross-out test: *syn.* **test, cancellation.**

cross reference: a reference directing attention from one part of a book, index, or other publication to another related word or item in another part of the work.

cross-section paper: paper that is divided into small sections by means of two sets of parallel lines, usually intersecting at right angles to each other. *Syn.* **graph paper;** *see* **coordinate paper; squared paper.**

cross-section study: *see* **study, cross-section.**

cross-sectional genetic method: *see* **genetic method, cross-sectional.**

cross-sectioning: a type of course organization in agriculture that cuts across such fields as animal husbandry, agronomy, agricultural engineering, and agricultural economics, combining materials from each field in each year of a 3- or 4-year sequence. (Sometimes known as a *horizontal* as distinguished from a *vertical* organization of subject matter.)

cross-service training: *see* **training, cross-service.**

cross talk: (audiovis. ed.) (1) interference of one channel with another; (2) leakage of sound in a system causing one student to hear an additional program signal or another student through his headphones; (3) the inadvertent mixing of electronic signals by induction or direct contact during the use of recordings.

cross training: (1) (phys. ed.) training in the contraction of a muscle which may cause the appearance of the action potentials in the identical muscles of the other side of the body; (2) (mil. ed.) training in two or more specialties within a career field.

cross validation: (1) empirical validation of a test or other measuring device by the administration of the unmodified test to a group other than the one(s) on which the test was standardized or from which the scoring key was derived; the process of seeing whether a decision derived from data obtained in the original validation experiment on one sample of persons is actually effective when the decision is applied to another independent sample of persons from the same population; (2) a method or process of validation or item analysis which involves the determination of the probability of occurrence of similar results in both of two samples.

crossed dominance: *see* **dominance, eye-hand.**

crosshatch map: *see* **map, crosshatch.**

crossover design: *see* **design, crossover.**

crosswalk: (1) that portion of a roadway ordinarily included within the prolongation or connection of the lateral lines of sidewalks at intersections; (2) any portion of a roadway distinctly indicated for pedestrian crossing by lines or other markings on the surface.

crowd: a large assembly of persons, relatively unorganized, who are all attending and responding in a similar manner to some object of common attraction; a crowd characterized by strong emotion and excitement is called a *mob.*

crowd mind: the relatively unified thought and volition of a crowd uncritically designated as a mental characteristic of the aggregate without reference to the individuals who compose the aggregate.

crowd psychology: *see* **psychology, crowd.**

crucial result: a result or finding that is of central importance in the testing of a hypothesis or in the practical implications of an experiment.

crucial test: *see* **test, crucial.**

crude birth rate: *see* **birth rate, crude.**

crude data: *see* **data, crude.**

crude death rate: *see* **death rate, crude.**

crude median: *syn.* **median, rough.**

crude mode: *see* **mode, crude.**

crude score: *see* **score, crude.**

crush: a term used to describe an intense, usually short-lived interest on the part of a child or adolescent in an older, glamorous, or better established person of the same or opposite sex.

cryptology: (mil. ed.) that branch of knowledge which treats of hidden, disguised, or encrypted communications.

cryptosystem: the associated items of cryptomaterial which are used as a unit and which provide a single means of encrypting and decrypting.

crystallized ability: *see* **ability, crystallized.**

cubage: the actual cubic space enclosed within the outer surfaces of the outside of enclosing walls and contained between the outer surface of the roof and 6 inches below the finished surfaces of the lowest floors. (The cubic space of dormers, penthouses, vaults, pits, enclosed porches, and other enclosed appendages is included as a part of the cubage. The cubic space of courts or light shafts, open at the top, or of outside steps, cornices, parapets, or open porches or loggias is not included.)

cubarithme slate: a frame, used in arithmetic by the blind, containing rows of square cells in which are placed cubes having on their faces braille letters to represent the digits; since each braille letter can be placed in different positions, only five letters are needed to represent all the digits. *Dist. f.* **Taylor slate.**

cubby: a child's private cubicle for his coat and/or boots; may have a drawer or shelf for personal belongings.

cubic contents: the cubic feet of space in a room or building. *See* **cubage.**

cubism: (art) the interpretation of objects and forms in geometric shapes and planes, organizing them in multiple views of the same object; a movement following the post-impressionists, most generally attributed to Pablo Picasso and Georges Braque.

cue: (1) a reaction to a stimulus which is not of itself strong enough to act as a drive; however, when such a cue is associated with situations in which responses are rewarded, the connections between the cues and the reinforced responses are strengthened and cues can impel responses; *see* **prompt** *n.;* (2) *syn.* **clue.**

cue drill: *see* **drill, cue.**

cue, perceptual: an index or sign, a guide to the visual organization of impressions of the environment.

cue reduction: (read.) the gradual reduction in the number of cues which a reader uses in the identification and recognition of words; believed to be one indication of maturation in reading skill; in a general sense, the perceptual ability to respond to a whole on the basis of only a portion of the total perceptual object or situation.

cuing: eliciting a response to programmed materials by such means as capitalizing, underscoring, italicizing, or other means.

Cuisenaire-Gattegno rods: a set of colored wooden blocks developed by George Cuisenaire and introduced into the United States by Caleb Gattegno; the rods are so designed that the smallest, a 1-centimeter cube, can represent 1; each of the others is a centimeter square in cross section and, in length, a varying multiple of 1 centimeter, each length being of a different color; very useful, in the hands of skilled teachers, in teaching many mathematical concepts to young children.

culminal education: *syn.* **terminal education.**

culminating activity: *see* **activity, culminating.**

cultural agency: (1) a person or organization effective in influencing the behavior and learning of a child or adolescent; for example, parents, teachers, policemen, movie stars, etc.; (2) a person or organization assisting the acculturation process by providing knowledge and training appropriate to the society or by aiding in the transmission of the knowledge, skills, and attitudes of one generation to the next.

cultural aims: *see* **aims, cultural.**

cultural alternatives: *see* **alternatives, cultural.**

cultural anthropology: *see* **anthropology, cultural.**

cultural approach: (psych.) the point of view holding that behavior stems rather from the social than from the biological heritage of the individual or group. *See* **culture; heritage.**

cultural background: the collection of mores, folkways, and institutions that constitutes the social heritage of an individual or group. *See* **culture; heritage.**

cultural bias: *see* **bias, cultural.**

cultural change, theory of: any theory isolating the dynamic factor or factors accounting for changes in cultural modes; may be monistic, claiming there is one universally present basic factor, such as change in means of production (Marx), or pluralistic, maintaining that empirical research shows various causes in various combinations (Dewey); the theories differ on the role of education and of human thought and planning.

cultural conflict: *see* **conflicts, culture.**

cultural deprivation: *see* **deprivation, cultural.**

cultural determinism: *see* **determinism, cultural.**

cultural dynamics: *see* **dynamics, cultural.**

cultural education: (1) all education insofar as it serves as a process of transmitting the folkways and mores of a people or nation; (2) education that is not strictly practical or vocational but that emphasizes the classical and human values of history, science, literature, and art; (3) progressive enlightenment and refinement by enriched experience and understanding.

cultural evolution: *see* **evolution, cultural.**

cultural exchange: *see* **exchange, cultural.**

cultural-familial mentally retarded: *see* **mentally retarded, cultural-familial.**

cultural gap: the differences existing between one culture and another or the differences within a culture resulting from *culture lag.*

cultural geography: *see* **anthropogeography.**

cultural guidance: *see* **guidance, cultural.**

cultural idealization: *see* **idealization, cultural.**

cultural island: the total immersion of the foreign language class into the foreign culture through the continuous, uninterrupted use of the language of that culture, the display of its authentic materials, the listening to its speakers, its music, its drama, and any other activity that duplicates an activity in the foreign land.

cultural lag: *see* **culture lag.**

cultural mathematics: *see* **mathematics, cultural.**

cultural model: (couns.) a behavior model stressing that behavior should be judged in relation to the cultural setting within which it occurs, since what is appropriate for one setting may be entirely inappropriate for another.

cultural myth: *see* **myth, cultural.**

cultural pluralism: *see* **pluralism, cultural.**

cultural process: the mechanism by which the folkways, mores, institutions, and ideals of a society are devised, modified, and passed on from one generation to the next. *See* **culture.**

cultural reading: *see* **reading, cultural.**

cultural recapitulation theory: *syn.* **culture-epochs theory.**

cultural revolution: *see* **revolution, cultural.**

cultural shift: a change in some direction of some of the points of view, institutions, techniques, or other elements in the culture of a given society.

cultural transmission: the passing on, from older members of a group to its younger members, of the most important and distinguishing *culture patterns* of the group.

cultural value: *see* **value, cultural.**

culturally deprived child: *see* **child, culturally deprived.**

culturally different child: *see* **child, culturally different.**

culturally disadvantaged child: *see* **child, culturally disadvantaged.**

culturally disadvantaged pupil: *see* **pupil, culturally disadvantaged.**

culture: (1) the aggregate of the social, ethical, intellectual, artistic, governmental, and industrial attainments characteristic of a group, state, or nation and by which it can be distinguished from or compared with other groups, states, or nations; includes ideas, concepts, usages, institutions, associations, and material objects; (2) (psych.) the level attained by the individual or social group in the accumulation of knowledge and the integration of social behavior patterns; (3) good taste in personal conduct; knowledge of the intellectual heritage of the race; appreciation of art and letters and of beauty in nature, and a reasonably consistent personal philosophy of life. *See* **cultural background; determinism, cultural;** *contr. w.* **philistinism.**

culture accumulation: the process by which beliefs, usages, associational forms, arts, and skills come to be deposited by various peoples, times, and regions on the previously established base, becoming, in varying degrees, the common heritage of mankind.

culture change: the modification of the form of culture traits in the course of time.

culture complex: a constellation of social characteristics, having structured and functional relations, clustered about a central trait; together these form a recognizable social pattern such as the rice complex of oriental civilizations.

culture conflicts: *see* **conflicts, culture.**

culture crisis: the state of confusion which characterizes any cultural entity when its members find its institutions, habits, symbols, beliefs, and faiths infected by chronic instability and uncertainty; often induced by an inability to cope with culture lag. *See* **culture lag.**

culture epoch: a stage in the growth of culture in the history of a given group.

culture-epoch curriculum: *see* **curriculum, culture-epoch.**

culture-epochs theory: (1) the hypothesis that there is a typical evolution in human culture which all societies tend to follow: from hunting to pastoral to agriculture, etc.; (2) belief that the individual child tends in his mental development to pass through the cultural stages or levels typical of the race and that education should be so timed

as to take account of these phases; ontogeny recapitulates phylogeny (G. Stanley Hall); *see* **recapitulation theory.**

culture-fair item: *see* **item, culture-fair.**

culture-fair test: *see* **test, culture-fair.**

culture-free test: *see* **test, culture-fair.**

culture group: *see* **group, culture.**

culture, ideational: *see* **culture, sensate.**

culture lag: (1) the delay occurring between change in one part of culture and change in another dependent part of culture; (2) failure of social institutions to keep pace with the more rapid advances of science; (3) the tendency of social customs to be retarded in relation to the most advanced social theories; (4) the amount or degree of such social retardation.

culture, medieval: the state of civilization, arts, and sciences in the Middle Ages.

culture pattern: an interrelated, interwoven, and virtually inseparable group or cluster of culture traits that, taken together, produce an established and typical result, such as a way of thinking, living, or acting, or a particular and distinctive collection of material objects, for example, the culture pattern of American public education, which represents a cluster of such culture traits as occupational specialization, general literacy, and universal suffrage.

culture, personal: a term proposed to replace the word *culture* in the sense of personal enlightenment and refinement.

culture, sensate: a civilization characterized by the conception that the true reality and value are sensory; a materialistic, empirical, and utilitarian society in which men seek sensuous enjoyment primarily, in contrast with the *ideational culture* which stresses the religious and the ascetic.

culture, target: the culture of the language being learned or taught.

culture trait: *see* **trait, culture.**

culture values: the fundamental standards of any culture group used for the determination and direction of desirable and worthy thought or action, whether of the individual or of the entire group, and on the basis of which punishments and rewards are evaluated.

culture, youth: *see* **subculture.**

cum correction (kum; kŏŏm): (C̄ or CC); with correction; said of vision with glasses prescribed. *Contr. w.* **sine correction.**

cumulated points rating scale: *see* **rating scale, cumulated points.**

cumulating error: *syn.* **error, constant.**

cumulation: a summation in which the sum of the successive quantities of the series is obtained and recorded for each successive item or class of the series.

cumulative: formed by successive additions.

cumulative average: *syn.* **average, grade point.**

cumulative change: *see* **change, cumulative.**

cumulative chart: *see* **chart, cumulative.**

cumulative error: *syn.* **error, constant.**

cumulative frequency: *see* **frequency, cumulative.**

cumulative frequency curve: *syn.* **ogive.**

cumulative frequency distribution: *see* **distribution, cumulative frequency.**

cumulative frequency graph: *syn.* **ogive.**

cumulative frequency table: *see* **table, cumulative frequency.**

cumulative holding power: *see* **holding power, cumulative.**

cumulative-leave plan: a plan whereby the unused days allowed for sick leave with pay are allowed to accumulate, sometimes for as long as 10 years and for as many as 100 days; these accumulated days may be used by the teacher in the case of an extended illness or for a leave, with pay, for professional improvement.

cumulative method: a technique of instruction in foreign languages that at the outset introduces in graded reading material the simpler forms in various grammatical fields and carries them on concurrently, adding new matter in each field from time to time instead of presenting the grammatical material as a series of isolated topics.

cumulative percentage: *see* **percentage, cumulative.**

cumulative percentage curve: *syn.* **ogive.**

cumulative personnel record: *see* **personnel record, cumulative.**

cumulative record: an instrument used to collect and make available a variety of information about each pupil which will enable the school staff to plan an optimum educational program for him; information is collected through pupil observation, interview, testing, sociometric analysis, and other techniques; information recorded will typically include school marks achieved throughout the school experience, comments concerning general factors of adjustment, facts describing curricular and extracurricular activities, medical history, and social adjustment data.

cumulative record card: any pupil record card that is maintained permanently and has data added to it constantly so that all the information is corrected as of any date; in a more restricted meaning, in the newer sense, it is a record card that follows the student not only from school to school but from teacher to teacher within the school.

cumulative record folder: (1) a folded receptacle used as a convenient filing device for accumulating data over a period of time; (2) a folded form on which is recorded in orderly fashion a succession of pertinent data accumulating over a period of time.

cumulative record form: a developmental record containing such information as standardized test results, report card information, pertinent remarks from parent-teacher conferences, information of a confidential nature, and other important information concerning the student.

cumulative record, permanent: *see* **cumulative record.**

cumulative sampling: *see* **analysis, sequential.**

cumulative scale: *see* **scale, cumulative.**

cumulative sum: *syn.* **cumulative total.**

cumulative tale: a simple story with much repetition of the main theme and the addition of characters or incidents as the tale proceeds, for example, "The Gingerbread Boy" or "The House That Jack Built."

cumulative total: the sum of those figures in a series which precede any given point. *Syn.* **continued sum; cumulative sum.**

cup-and-cube behavior: *see* **behavior, cup-and-cube.**

cup-and-spoon behavior: *see* **behavior, cup-and-spoon.**

curative workshop: *see* **workshop, curative.**

curiosity: a tendency to wonder, to inquire, or to investigate, frequently expressed in exploratory or manipulative activities; hence the term *curiosity drive,* believed by some to be as basic as the hunger drive or the sex drive.

curling: a game played by four persons in which heavy stones are made to slide over smooth ice toward a target at the end of the rink.

current: (finance) (1) pertaining to operating funds as distinct from permanent funds; *see* **capital outlay; funds, current;** (2) pertaining to the present fiscal period as contrasted with past or future periods.

current events: present happenings and developments in all fields of human interest and activity.

current expenditure: *see* **expenditure, current.**

current expense: *see* **expense, current.**

current funds: *see* **funds, current.**

current income: *see* **income, current.**

curricula, differentiated: (1) varied selections and sequences of subjects for pupils having different abilities, interests, needs, and purposes and therefore being differently educated, for example (at the secondary school level), the college-preparatory curriculum, the industrial-education curriculum, the commercial curriculum; (2) varied selections and sequences of professional courses available at a teacher-education institution for the purpose of educating for specific positions (such as kindergarten-primary teacher, or rural teacher) or to make provision for adjustments to individual needs, interests, and capacities.

curricular activity: *see* **activity, curricular.**

curricular board: a committee appointed to unify, edit, and distribute the curriculum materials collected or developed by a large number of teachers and to revise, reorganize, and prepare courses of study. *Syn.* **curriculum board.**

curricular content: any subject matter, instructional materials, situations, or experiences that may help to develop understandings, skills, appreciations, and attitudes.

curricular event, instructional: those acts of the teacher and learner with potential in a specific curricular situation for influencing the reconstruction and reorganization of the learner's experiences.

curricular program: *syn.* **curriculum program.**

curricular reading: *see* **reading, curricular.**

curricular reading program: *see* **program, curricular reading.**

curricular validity: *see* **validity, curricular.**

curriculum: *pl.* **curricula;** (1) a systematic group of courses or sequences of subjects required for graduation or certification in a major field of study, for example, social studies curriculum, physical education curriculum; (2) a general overall plan of the content or specific materials of instruction that the school should offer the student by way of qualifying him for graduation or certification or for entrance into a professional or a vocational field; (3) a group of courses and planned experiences which a student has under the guidance of the school or college; may refer to what is intended, as planned courses and other activities or intended opportunities or experiences, or to what was actualized for the learner, as in actual educational treatment or all experiences of the learner under the direction of the school. *See* **learning opportunities;** *dist. f.* **course of study; program, school.**

curriculum, activity: *syn.* **curriculum, classroom activities.**

curriculum, aerospace: a curriculum especially designed to encompass the knowledge and exploration of the science and cultural significance of aviation and space.

curriculum, agricultural: the courses, both agricultural and other, in a program designed to prepare or upgrade students for an agricultural occupation; each cluster of agricultural occupations is served by a different agricultural curriculum.

curriculum, areas-of-living: a curriculum organized around classifications of life activities or areas of living, as, for example, protecting life and health, living in and improving the home, getting a living, securing an education, etc.; in general, it is determined by broad categories of social activity without reference to individual needs or to subject boundaries. *See* **curriculum, personal-problems-of-living; curriculum, social-functions core; curriculum, social-problems core; curriculum, sociological determination of.**

curriculum, art: the total program of pupil activity in the arts, particularly the actual work going on in the classroom as distinguished from a course of study, which merely outlines the work for the teacher at a particular grade or school level. *See* **art education; course of study; experience, art; unit, art.**

curriculum, articulated: a continuous curriculum in which there is a close relationship between elementary school, high school, and college curricula in order to prevent needless repetition and bring about coordination.

curriculum board: *syn.* **curricular board.**

curriculum, branch material: programs of instruction conducted in service schools and in Reserve Officers' Training Corps programs in colleges and universities which prepare students for duties in certain branches of the Army.

curriculum, broad-fields: a curriculum design in which an intensive effort at integration is made in closely related fields; several related subjects are combined into a broad subject area; for example, reading, spelling, writing, and other language activities become a single broad subject area, *language arts;* assumes that life's problems cut across subject-matter lines and that subject matter should serve problems and be mustered around important problems of living.

curriculum building: the systematic procedure of developing a suitable curriculum for a particular school or school system, involving the organization of working committees under expert direction, the choice of general and specific aims of instruction, the selection of appropriate curricular materials, methods of instruction, and means of evaluation, the preparation of official courses of study, the trial and adoption of such courses of study, and the provision for continuous, methodical study, evaluation, and improvement of the existing educational program. *Syn.* **curriculum construction;** *see* **curriculum development.**

curriculum building, socioeconomic approach to: *see* **socioeconomic approach.**

curriculum bulletin: (1) a regular progress report of any curriculum program; (2) a report of the proceedings of committees of the curriculum program; (3) any publication, usually a periodical, that may report curricular activities or present or contain courses of study, teaching aids, suggestions, or materials to help teachers in curriculum planning and teaching.

curriculum change: an alteration of the curriculum consisting in making different or restructuring the learning opportunities provided pupils at a given time and place; may include a basic change in the design of the learning opportunities.

curriculum-change agent: a person, agency, or group, acting directly or through media, that attempts to and may succeed in altering or restructuring the learning opportunities provided at a given time and place.

curriculum chart: *see* **chart, curriculum.**

curriculum, child-centered: *syn.* **curriculum, activity.**

curriculum, church school: the educational program of the church, usually planned for and carried out by specific agencies of the congregation, such as the *Sunday church school, vacation church school,* or *youth fellowship.*

curriculum, classical: (1) a systematic group or sequence of so-called "traditional" courses or subjects required for graduation that includes studies in Latin or Greek or both; (2) (hist. of ed.) the offerings of schools giving instruction in Latin or Greek or both; (3) sometimes designates the seven liberal arts of the medieval schools and the preliminary instruction in Latin and Greek, especially as organized in the *Gymnasium.*

curriculum, classroom activities: a pattern of instruction which seeks to promote learning through cooperative group activities; concerned with the development through group interaction of effective habits and skills of cooperative planning, fact-finding, and evaluation and with development of socially effective citizens; includes teacher participation with pupils in planning and executing learning activities while establishing and practicing basic principles of democratic living.

curriculum, closely graded: a Christian education program which contains separate lessons for each age level corresponding to the needs and capacities of each group. *See* **curriculum, church school; curriculum, cycle graded.**

curriculum, college-preparatory: (1) a sequence of subjects or group of courses prerequisite for college enrollment; (2) a body of educative activities and experiences (in secondary education) prescribed for pupils who wish to enroll at institutions of higher learning.

curriculum, community-centered: an educational program based on and adjusted to the life, culture, resources, needs, activities, and interests of the community in which it is offered.

curriculum compatibility: degree to which courses or programs of various school districts or states are similar; estimated in recent years on the basis of the communication of data on school programs through the use of coding and computers.

curriculum, conduct: (elem. ed.) a socialized curriculum intended to develop in the pupils those attitudes and knowledges deemed necessary for good citizenship through active pupil participation in democratic activities and situations, particularly those connected with the planning and execution of the classwork and the management of the classroom; may be divided into three progressive stages, from the first stage in which the teacher maintains almost complete control to the third stage in which the children devise their own rules, recognize and discuss problems, and offer solutions to difficulties.

curriculum constant: *see* **constant, curriculum.**

curriculum, constants-with-variables: a curriculum pattern consisting of (*a*) subjects required of all students, (*b*) subjects required within specialized curricula, and (*c*) elective subjects.

curriculum construction: *syn.* **curriculum building.**

curriculum consultant: *syn.* **curriculum specialist.**

curriculum, core: a plan intended to develop unified studies based upon the common needs of the learners and organized without restriction by subject matter; in the secondary school the core comprises that part of the school day devoted to general education (common learnings and the common activities program); the remainder of the day is available for the exploration and development of special-interest education (specialized knowledge). *See* **program, core.**

curriculum, correlated: a subject curriculum in which two or more subjects are articulated in such a manner that the relationships of the subject fields are made a part of the instruction without destroying the boundaries of the respective subject fields. *See* **curriculum, fused; curriculum, subject; unified studies approach.**

curriculum, culture-epoch: a plan of organizing the curriculum into a series of epochs such as "the colonial period," "the westward movement," and "the industrial revolution"; applied most frequently in the social studies and literature, often combining the two, thus facilitating study of the economic, social, political, and cultural aspects of the epoch.

curriculum, cycle graded: a Christian education program which contains materials suited for an entire church school department, such as primary or junior, and which is repeated in 2- or 3-year cycles in order to reduce repetition possibility for the individual student. *See* **curriculum, closely graded; department, church school.**

curriculum department: *see* **department, curriculum.**

curriculum design: (1) the way in which the component parts of the curriculum have been arranged in order to facilitate learning and teaching and to enable schools to formulate feasible daily and weekly schedules; (2) a process of conceptualizing a set of systematic relationships between pupils, teacher behavior, materials, content, time, and instructional outcomes; a guide for instruction describing a specific arrangement of all factors relating to instructional practice toward specific outcomes. *Comp. w.* **curriculum building.**

curriculum development: a task of supervision directed toward designing or redesigning the guidelines for instruction; includes development of specifications indicating what is to be taught, by whom, when, where, and in what sequence or pattern.

curriculum, didactic: a plan of instruction that emphasizes precept, principle, doctrine, or rule.

curriculum, differentiated: *see* **curricula, differentiated.**

curriculum director: *syn.* **director of curriculum.**

curriculum, director of: *see* **director of curriculum.**

curriculum, elementary school: the sum total of educative activities in which pupils engage under the auspices of the elementary school.

curriculum-embedded test: *see* **test, curriculum-embedded.**

curriculum, emerging: (1) a curriculum that uses teacher-pupil planning in the process of reconstruction to meet more effectively the needs and interests of children and youth as presently perceived and as anticipated for the future; (2) in early childhood education, a curriculum which develops from a child's questions and spontaneous interests as opposed to a teacher's presentation of material; both may be combined to strengthen the curriculum.

curriculum, enriched: *see* **enrichment, curriculum.**

curriculum enrichment: *see* **enrichment, curriculum.**

curriculum evaluation: *see* **evaluation, curriculum.**

curriculum expansion: (admin.) the increase in the number of organized educative experiences which are under the direction and control of the school.

curriculum, experience: a curriculum in which the content, activities, and structures of instruction are designed to provide a series of purposeful experiences growing out of the interests, purposes, and needs of the learners; characterized by exploration, critical inquiry, replanning in terms of new data and understandings, teacher-pupil planning, and cooperative problem-solving approaches; common learnings are expected results when the curriculum has been properly built on common interests and needs; meanwhile special interests may be developed in projects, individualized activities, or for groups in special subject courses. *See* **curriculum, classroom activities; teaching, pupil-centric;** *contr. w.* **curriculum, subject.**

curriculum for social intelligence: a junior college curriculum designed primarily to train for social citizenship in American civilization through courses that are broadly organized along comprehensive rather than intensive lines and are intended to promote effective social behavior.

curriculum, functional: (1) a curriculum aimed at usefulness in meeting life-adjustment problems; (2) a curriculum that is perceived by the students as being relevant and operational in meeting their existing recognized needs. *See* **functional approach.**

curriculum, fused: a combination of courses into broad areas, drawing for content on all the narrower subjects.

curriculum, general military science: a Reserve Officers' Training Corps program of instruction conducted in colleges and universities which prepares the student for appointment in most branches of the Army.

curriculum, graduate: a course of study leading to a degree beyond the bachelor's or first professional degree.

curriculum guidance: *see* **guidance, curriculum.**

curriculum guidance, vocational: *see* **guidance, vocational curriculum.**

curriculum guide: a substitute for a formal course of study in which desirable content is suggested rather than prescribed; includes important goals and a variety of learning experiences, teaching aids, and evaluation techniques from which those considered best suited to a particular situation may be selected.

curriculum, individual: (1) an organization of subjects, subject matter, and activities designed for a particular individual; (2) an organization of subjects and suggested activities designed to achieve a particular purpose or objective.

curriculum, integrated: a curriculum organization which cuts across subject-matter lines to focus upon comprehensive life problems or broad areas of study that bring together the various segments of the curriculum into meaningful association.

curriculum, intensive: the curriculum of daily Jewish religious schools, whether the afternoon school, or *Talmud Torah,* or the all-day school, or *Yeshivah;* usually extends over a period of 6 years or more with at least 7 hours of instruction per week, the core subjects of instruction being the Bible in the original Hebrew, religious beliefs and practice, modern Hebrew language and literature, Jewish history, and current Jewish events. *See* **Talmud Torah; Yeshivah.**

curriculum, kindergarten: a program of social experiences embodying social studies, language arts, natural science, creative arts, and physical activities through which children, as they learn to work and play together happily and constructively, gain an understanding of the world about them.

curriculum laboratory: *see* **laboratory, curriculum.**

curriculum, legislative control of: *see* **legislative control of curriculum.**

curriculum library: *syn.* **laboratory, curriculum materials.**

curriculum, life: (1) the totality of out-of-school and in-school learning experiences of the individual student; (2) the developmental combination of human needs, social opportunities, and individual learning that the student perceives as personally relevant in giving direction to his individual educational development; to be distinguished from the curriculum of the school. *See* **curriculum.**

curriculum map: *see* **map, curriculum.**

curriculum materials center: *syn.* **laboratory, curriculum materials.**

curriculum materials laboratory: *see* **laboratory, curriculum materials.**

curriculum, multiple-track: a school curriculum which provides two or more different ways of progressing through the levels or grades, the usual provision being a combination of automatic promotion in all tracks and differences in difficulty and in degrees of enrichment among the tracks.

curriculum, occupational: *syn.* **curriculum, vocational.**

curriculum organization: *syn.* **curriculum design.**

curriculum organization, multiple: the plan of providing more than one combination of required and elective subjects for students to follow toward graduation.

curriculum organization, stem-elective: *see* **stem (4).**

curriculum, personal-problems-of-living: an individual-centered approach to curriculum development with a particular group of learners, usually in a core curriculum or general education course, in which the personalized approach to universal social functions is expected to help students gain a deeper understanding of their social and self roles in the social circumstances in which they find themselves; typical units of work might be establishing personal relationships, establishing independence, finding yourself in the group, etc. *See* **curriculum, areas-of-living; curriculum, social-functions core; curriculum, social-problems core.**

curriculum, personalizing of the: the process of making intelligible to the pupil experiences that have been selected as universals, specialties, and alternatives of the culture for the student.

curriculum, preeducation: the program of courses or the sequence of activities, usually during the first and second undergraduate years of work in a teacher education institution, designed to serve as a background of cultural and academic preparation before the technical work of professional education is undertaken. *Syn.* **preeducation sequence;** *dist. f.* **preservice education.**

curriculum, preschool: the program in a school for preschool children, based on the stage of development of the individual children and the specific needs of the group; geared to promote maximum intellectual, social, physical, and emotional development. *See* **child, preschool; nursery school.**

curriculum prescription: (1) a learning unit or specific task defined for and assigned to a student based upon a diagnosis of his capability and need; *see* **instruction, individually prescribed;** (2) a course or sequence of courses required of students who will be graduated from a particular curriculum; *contr. w.* **elective; elective, free; option.**

curriculum, problem-centered: a program of instruction in which learning is stimulated by presenting challenging situations that demand solution.

curriculum, professional: (1) a program or sequence of courses designed to prepare for the practice of a profession; (2) (teacher ed.) a program or sequence of courses, sometimes extending over 4 or 5 years but often including only 1 or 2, designed to prepare specifically for the responsibilities of particular types of teaching positions as well as to fulfill appropriate certification requirements for teaching. (This term is broader than *professional course* and applies to the entire pattern of general academic preparation, specialization for teaching fields, and professional courses in education.) *Syn.* **teachers' curriculum;** *see* **course, professional.**

curriculum program: (1) a program, preferably involving the entire school personnel, designed to improve the experiences of the pupils by modifying or improving any aspect of the school; (2) in general, a concrete presentation of educational aims and points of view and scope and sequence of content as incorporated in courses of study and other curriculum bulletins.

curriculum program, state: (1) a program of curriculum revision of statewide significance, the purpose of which is to bring about teacher growth by means of regional and local curriculum programs, curriculum bulletins, and state courses of study; usually sponsored by the state department of education, a statewide organization of teachers, or state supervisors, and often utilizing the thought of representative educators and laymen; (2) the pattern of courses outlined by a state board of education or state superintendent of public instruction, in courses of study based on statutory school studies and state-adopted texts, specifying the minimum amount of work in each subject each school year.

curriculum, project: *syn.* **curriculum, classroom activities.**

curriculum proposal: (admin.) the stated presentation, for administrative consideration, of a plan for educative experiences under the direction and control of the school.

curriculum, pupil-teacher planned: a curriculum organized by a group of teachers on the basis of consultation with the pupils to be taught, for the purpose of suiting the offerings of the school to the background, experience, present interests, and immediate and future needs of the pupils.

curriculum, readiness: a program planned to meet the developmental needs of children through broadened experiences, with the introduction of academic skills at the most teachable time.

curriculum research: *see* **research, curriculum.**

curriculum revision: *see* **curriculum building.**

curriculum, social: a curriculum based on the study of social conditions, forces, conflicts, and trends, their interrelations, and the possibility of social improvement.

curriculum, social-functions core: a core curriculum in which the scope is defined in terms of social-function categories, these being social activities believed to be universal, such as living in the home, citizenship, leisure, etc. *See* **curriculum, areas-of-living; curriculum, social-problems core; curriculum, sociological determination of.**

curriculum, social-problems core: a core curriculum in which the scope is defined in terms of social-problem categories as evidenced in classifications of crucial social problems and believed to be of real significance in the choices and lives of people; illustrative units are school government, universal military training, crime, marriage, world government; differs from social-functions core curriculum by reason of more problem-solving structuring and from personal-problems-of-living curriculum by its society-centered emphasis. *See* **curriculum, areas-of-living; curriculum, personal-problems-of-living; curriculum, social-functions core; curriculum, sociological determination of.**

curriculum, society-centered: a curriculum design pointing toward discipline and curriculum mastery based almost exclusively on social objectives, striving to mold the child into the kind of person desired by society.

curriculum, sociological determination of: society-centered approaches to curriculum development based upon social reality, as contrasted with subject-matter-centered approaches; thus curriculum content, activities, or experiences may be guided by (*a*) analysis of current social practices, job analysis, etc., (*b*) study of universal and fundamental social institutions, (*c*) study of current social trends, or (*d*) analysis of persisting social problems of the society in which the school or program is located. *See* **curriculum, areas-of-living; curriculum, social-functions core; curriculum, social-problems core;** *contr. w.* **curriculum, subject.**

curriculum specialist: (1) a member of the supervisory staff of a school district or other educational organization specializing in curriculum development and the implementation of curricular designs; (2) a specialist in some specific content field of the school curriculum who works in a supervisory capacity with teachers; (3) a scholar associated with a college or university who does research, fieldwork, and writing in one or more areas of the school curricula. *Syn.* **curriculum consultant; curriculum worker; curriculum supervisor.**

curriculum, spiral: a school curriculum developed around a hierarchy of concepts through the inclusion of the same subjects or topics at various grade levels and at correspondingly varying levels of depth, abstraction, and sophistication. *See* **organization by cycles; spiral approach; spiral progression.**

curriculum, state: (1) a general plan or guide for public school instruction in a particular state at stipulated levels, recommended or enforced by the educational authorities of the state; usually outlines objectives, sequences of experiences, suggested materials for study,

and alternative instructional procedures; (2) the courses or subjects prescribed by law for study in the schools of a particular state.

curriculum, subject: a curriculum in which the learning activities and content are planned within organized fields of knowledge or subjects, such as history, science, mathematics, reading; characterized by emphasis on assimilation of subject content; explanation is the basic teaching method, with assign-study-recite a common procedure; subjects may be extremely compartmentalized into separate courses or related by correlation; required courses (constants) constitute general education offerings, while elective courses (variables) serve special interests. *Contr. w.* **curriculum, classroom activities; curriculum, experience; curriculum, project.**

curriculum supervision: *see* **supervision, curriculum.**

curriculum supervisor: *syn.* **curriculum specialist.**

curriculum, teacher education: the total experiences provided for the college student studying to be a teacher for the purpose of training him to meet the needs of the classroom.

curriculum, teachers': *syn.* **curriculum, professional.**

curriculum, traditional: a vague term frequently applied to the academic, cultural type of curriculum.

curriculum, unified: an educational program in which all parts are systematically selected and arranged on the basis of their contribution to the aim of providing a well-balanced education.

curriculum, vocational: a carefully selected group of courses or a sequence of subjects the content of which will provide the necessary skill and knowledge for success in a specific occupation.

curriculum, watered-down: the practice of telescoping the content and simplifying the curriculum to meet the learning ability rather than merely the basic needs of retarded children.

curriculum worker: *syn.* **curriculum specialist.**

cursive writing: *see* **writing, cursive.**

curtailed: (said of a frequency distribution) broken off at either end, so that the frequencies at that end are markedly lower than would be so except for special influences.

curtailed session: *see* **session, curtailed.**

curtailment: (of a frequency distribution) the quality of being curtailed. *See* **curtailed.**

curve, auditory: a graphical representation of the acuity or the intensity of hearing at different sound frequencies as developed by means of an audiometer test and expressed as a curved or irregular line.

curve, bell-shaped: a curve having the characteristic form of the normal probability curve, that is, one that is symmetrical, unimodal, and shaped somewhat like a bell; often loosely used as a synonym for *normal probability curve.*

curve, closed: intuitively, a path in the plane or in three-dimensional space which can be thought of as going from one point to another and returning or as a path from a point to itself, for example, a figure eight, a circle, a triangle, etc.

curve, correlation: any curve drawn to show graphically the relationship existing between two variables. *Syn.* **curve of relation; line of relation;** *contr. w.* **curve, regression; regression line.**

curve, cumulative frequency: *syn.* **ogive.**

curve, cumulative percentage: *syn.* **ogive.**

curve, distribution: *syn.* **curve, frequency** (1).

curve fitting: (1) the process of finding the constants for the equation of a specified type of curve in such a manner that the curve may agree as closely as possible with the data when graphed; (2) the process of finding those parameters for a curve that can be represented by a mathematical equation in such a manner that some function of the errors is minimized.

curve, frequency: (1) any curve or broken line that represents a frequency distribution; the graph corresponding to a frequency table; *syn.* **distribution curve; frequency**

polygon; (2) an estimate of the limit that probably would be approached by a frequency polygon or histogram if the number of observations were indefinitely increased and the widths of class intervals were indefinitely decreased while the total area under the curve remained constant.

curve, Gauss': *syn.* **curve, normal probability.**

curve, Gauss-Laplace: *syn.* **curve, normal probability.**

curve, Gaussian: *syn.* **curve, normal probability.**

curve, generalized growth: (1) the composite of curves of growth of various body dimensions and structures by which the growth of a person as a whole may be described; (2) a curve depicting the general characteristics of growth of the members of a particular group—boys, girls, American whites, etc.

curve, graduated: *syn.* **curve, smoothed.**

curve, growth: a graphic representation of the changes that occur in a trait or function as a result of maturation; may apply to either physical or mental growth.

curve, item characteristic: (1) the curve representing the proportion of individuals at each level of the ability being measured who answer a test item correctly; (2) a plot of the proportion of correct answers given to an item by persons at each score level against that level which portrays both the item difficulty and the item discrimination.

curve, J: the curve produced by measuring conformity reactions in an area in which conformity to a standard is enforced, such as stopping an automobile at a red light.

curve, J-shaped: a frequency curve, shaped somewhat like a J, in which the frequency density declines rapidly at first and then more slowly from the greatest frequency, which is at one end or the other of the distribution. *Contr. w.* **curve, U-shaped.**

curve, Laplace-Gaussian: *syn.* **curve, normal probability.**

curve, Laplacian: *syn.* **curve, normal probability.**

curve, learning: a graphic representation of certain aspects of progress in learning during successive periods of practice, usually having practice periods plotted on one axis and time required or achievement units plotted on the other; used in some types of instruction to enable pupils to keep a graphic record of progress; widely used in research.

curve, normal: *syn.* **curve, normal probability.**

curve, normal frequency: *syn.* **curve, normal probability.**

curve, normal probability: the graphical representation of the theoretical distribution of an infinitely large number of observations of a continuous variable varying purely by chance, resulting in a perfectly smooth, symmetrical, bell-shaped curve, having the mean, median, and mode coinciding, and which is expressed in mathematical terms as a curve whose height taken at any point on the horizontal axis is in inverse proportion to the antilogarithm of half the squared sigma distance of that point from the mean; the normal probability curve and the normal distribution are purely theoretical mathematical concepts which may be approached in practice but never actually attained. *Syn.* **Gauss' curve; Gaussian curve; Gauss-Laplace curve; Laplace-Gaussian curve; Laplacian curve; normal curve; normal curve of error; normal frequency curve.**

curve of distribution: *syn.* **curve, frequency.**

curve of error, normal: *syn.* **curve, normal probability.**

curve of forgetting: traditionally plotted in terms of quantitative units, the curve of forgetting expresses the amount of measured relative retention of learned material after various units of time have elapsed; the early work of Ebbinghaus on nonsense syllables indicated an initially rapid loss followed by an asymptotic curve where the rate of forgetting continually decreases.

curve of relation: *syn.* **curve, correlation.**

curve, percentile: a cumulative frequency curve in which the cumulative frequency at each class, plotted as the abscissa, is stated as a percentage of the total number of observations. *Syn.* **percentile graph.**

curve, polynomial: a curve drawn to represent an equation consisting of the sum of integral powers of a variable.

curve, positively accelerated: a line graph in which a series of measures increases in value at a more rapid rate for each successive point that is plotted; thus, the curve is less steep at the beginning than at other points along the abscissa variable.

curve, probability: in general, any curve showing the expected distribution of a given kind of event, measure, etc.; often used as a synonym for *normal probability curve.*

curve, regression: *syn.* **curve, correlation.**

curve, retention: a curve which depicts the amount retained after learning. *See* **asymptotic;** *ant.* **curve of forgetting.**

curve, smooth: a curve, such as a frequency curve, that does not change its direction in a sudden or erratic manner. *Dist. f.* **curve, smoothed.**

curve, smoothed: (1) any curve that has had the sudden and erratic changes in its direction removed by some method such as the use of a moving average or freehand smoothing; *syn.* **graduated curve;** *dist. f.* **curve, smooth;** (2) sometimes loosely used to designate a curved line drawn so as to pass through all the points of a graphically represented distribution but somewhat rounded off so as to eliminate angles (not good usage).

curve, standard normal: *syn.* **curve, unit normal.**

curve, true regression: the regression curve that would be obtained if there were an infinite number of observations and the class intervals of both variables were made infinitely small.

curve, U-shaped: a frequency curve or line graph in which the ordinates decrease to a minimum and then increase so that the curve has the general shape of a U; rarely obtained. *Contr. w.* **curve, J-shaped.**

curve, unit normal: a normal probability curve in which the area and the standard deviation are both set equal to unity. *Syn.* **standard normal curve.**

curvilinear: not capable of being represented (statistically or graphically) by a straight line. *Syn.* **nonlinear;** *contr. w.* **rectilinear.**

curvilinear correlation: *see* **correlation, curvilinear.**

curvilinear movement: *see* **movement, curvilinear.**

curvilinear regression: *syn.* **regression, nonlinear.**

curvilinear relation: *syn.* **correlation, curvilinear.**

curvilinear relationship: *syn.* **correlation, curvilinear.**

curvilinearity: the state or condition of being representable by a curve rather than by a straight line. *Syn.* **nonlinearity;** *contr. w.* **linearity; rectilinearity.**

custodial care: care given a person who, in the interests of society, should be kept in an institution for the care of delinquents or incompetents.

custodial mentally retarded: *see* **mentally retarded, custodial.**

custodial service: *syn.* **janitorial service.**

custodian: the caretaker of a school building or the person in charge of all school housekeeping duties. *Syn.* **janitor.**

custodian's handbook: *syn.* **handbook, janitor's.**

custodian's report: *see* **report, custodian's.**

custom: a complex mode of socially established behavior not due to biological inheritance which is enforced by social disapproval of its violation.

custom, appeal to: *see* **appeal to custom.**

customs and ceremonies (Jewish): the patterns and observances of Jewish religious life; a basic course of study in the program of instruction of the Jewish religious school.

cut: *n.* (1) (motion pictures) the instantaneous change from one scene to another; successive frames contain the last frame of one scene and the first frame of the following scene; (2) unexcused absence of a student from class.

cut: *v.* (1) (audiovis.) to sever or splice film in the editing process; (2) to stop operation of camera, action, and/or sound recording equipment; (3) to absent oneself from class.

cutaway: (1) (motion pictures) a scene photographed at the site of principal action, interrupting the flow of action but containing only a part of the view visible in other scenes; used to bridge two scenes that do not move smoothly from one to the other; (2) a real object or a model, made to scale or magnified, in which the outer covering or a portion has been wholly or partially removed so as to reveal the inner structure or framework or working parts.

cutback-page booklet: *see* **booklet, cutback-page.**

cutout: a part of a picture cut out of its surroundings and, frequently, mounted on cardboard or plywood of the same size and shape.

cutting: (motion pictures) *syn.* **editing.**

cutting score: *see* **score, cutting.**

CWPM (correct words per minute): the typewriting rate per minute when a one-word penalty for each error is charged. *Dist. f.* **NWPM.**

cy pres, doctrine of (sē-prā): (Norman Fr., lit., "as nearly as possible") a legal doctrine by which a court may interpret the terms of a bequest so that the trustees may follow the spirit rather than the letter of the stipulations of the bequest; for example, an endowment left for the care of aged sailors on square-rigged ships might be applied to the care of aged sailors on steamships through application by a court of the doctrine of cy pres.

cybernetics (sī·bĕr·net′iks): the comparative study of the control and internal communications systems of information-handling machines and the central nervous systems of animals and men in order to understand better the functioning of information transfer and processing in such systems. *See* **automation; servomechanism.**

cycle approach: (bus. ed.) a method of teaching bookkeeping in which the steps of the bookkeeping cycle (journal entries, adjustments, and financial reports for one fiscal period) are first presented in an elementary manner and then enlarged upon as new materials are introduced.

cycle, evaluation: *see* **evaluation cycle.**

cycle, family: *see* **family cycle.**

cycle graded curriculum: *see* **curriculum, cycle graded.**

cycle plan: (1) (voc. ed.) a plan of organizing the curricular offerings of a general continuation school by which the curriculum is divided into a number of units of vocational work, each relating to a specific trade and having a definite time allotment; each unit is correlated closely with the work done in related subjects and the students progress from one unit to another; for example, while the student is studying a unit on plumbing, all his work in related subjects is based on their application to the plumbing trade, with a complete shift in the emphasis in related subjects when he enters the next unit of work; (2) a plan by which a number of independent lessons are presented in rotation, thus enabling the student to enter the class at any time, start at the point of the cycle at which the class happens to be, and proceed to take each lesson in the cycle as it is presented; (3) (math.) the plan followed in presenting certain mathematical topics whereby more advanced concepts concerning each topic

are introduced as the mathematical maturity of the individual increases.

cycle test: *see* **test, cycle.**

cycle time: the time required to restore data read from a storage device having a destructive read-out.

cyclic: (psych.) occurring in alternating moods, as of excitement and depression.

cyclical motor learning: *see* **learning, cyclical motor.**

cyclical unemployment: *see* **unemployment, cyclical.**

cycling: a competitive or leisure-time activity in which individuals ride a two-wheeled vehicle.

cyclograph: a method of investigating the path of motions, such as change of direction of a worker's hands or a moving part, by attaching lights to the hands and photographing the movements with a time exposure.

cycloid: characteristic of a person who shows relatively marked but normal swings of mood.

cycloplegic (sī′klə·plē′jik): a drug that temporarily puts the ciliary muscles at rest and dilates the pupil; used to obtain the total error of refraction.

cyclorama: an extended scene, or panorama, painted and constructed on a semicircular background where the viewer stands in the center facing the scene; often used as the backdrop for a dramatic production.

cyclothyme (sī′klə·thīm): a personality type distinguishable by alternation of elated and depressed moods; supposedly, one predisposed toward manic-depressive psychosis.

cyclothymic temperament (sī′klə·thī′mik): a temperament characterized by fluctuations in mood within normal limits; similar in nature but not in degree to the mood swings seen in manic-depressive psychosis.

cynic: in modern usage, one who doubts the reality of human goodness or progress and who sneers at man's efforts to improve his condition; he is frequently bitter and sarcastic; in the classical formulation, the school of the Cynics taught that self-control in the face of external circumstances was the highest form of virtue; Diogenes was the most eminent member of this sect. *See* **cynicism.**

cynicism: (1) the philosophy of the Greek school of thought founded by Antisthenes (about 444 B.C.), which exalted the attitude of independence, or even contempt, toward the material goods of the world, pleasure, and the conventions of society, with a consequent tendency toward asceticism and the rejection of family ties; (2) in general usage, an attitude characterized by general skepticism and biting criticism of human motives. *See* **cynic.**

cytology: the area of biology which considers the cell as a unit of organization in plants and animals and gives consideration to the structure, function, pathology, and life history of cells, that is, all cellular phenomena.

D-statistic: the square root of the sum of the squared differences between a student's interest or ability scores and the mean scores for each of the relevant occupational profiles; inferior to the multiple regression equation in predicting success from ability test scores but possibly potentially superior for factors that fail to show a linear relationship to success, such as interests or personality characteristics. *See* **index of dissimilarity; regression equation, partial.**

dactylology: the art of visual language communication in which the fingers form the various letters of the alphabet to construct words. *See* **alphabet, finger.**

dadaism: (art) a post-World War II artistic movement

based on deliberate irrationality and negation of the laws of beauty and organization; a nihilistic declaration toward established (and meaningless) moral and aesthetic values.

daily attendance, average: *see* **attendance, average daily.**

daily health inspection: *see* **health inspection.**

daily-lesson-plan book: a handbook intended for the use of the teacher and containing a tentative plan of the activities of the class each day, noting the opportunities for developing the pupils' intellects and personalities.

daily living activities: *see* **activities, daily living.**

daily load: *see* **load, daily.**

daily log: *see* **log, daily.**

daily mileage: *see* **mileage, daily.**

daily plan: a schedule or timetable indicating the sequences of educational activities for a particular school day.

daily program: *see* **program, daily.**

daily record: *see* **record, daily.**

daily register: *syn.* **record book, teacher's class.**

daily schedule: *see* **schedule, daily.**

daily vacation church school: short-term summer classes for children of the community and neighborhood, offering religious education, hobby interests, and recreation appropriate for various age groupings.

Dalcroze Eurythmics: *see* **eurythmics.**

Dale-Chall readability formula: *see* **readability formula, Dale-Chall.**

Dalton plan: a plan of organizing the curriculum, program of studies, and learning activities adopted in Dalton, Massachusetts, in 1920 and organized as follows: each pupil was given monthly assignments, known as jobs, in each school subject, each job being divided into about 20 units; workbooks and instruction sheets enabled the pupil to work individually at his jobs, while a job card enabled him to record his progress; pupil-teacher conferences were held whenever necessary to take the place of recitations; classrooms were known as laboratories; pupils were free to plan their own work schedules but were obliged to finish each monthly job before proceeding to the job for the succeeding month; cooperation and group work were encouraged.

damages for dismissal: pecuniary compensation or indemnity recoverable in the courts by a person who has suffered loss, detriment, or injury as a result of wrongful discharge.

dame school: a type of private primary school (recognized and frequently subsidized by the community) that existed during the early period of American history and served the purpose of teaching children to read and spell in order that they might qualify for admission to the regular schools; based on the English dame school, which existed long before the institution was taken up in the colonies; operated and taught by women, usually in their own homes (hence the name).

dance: a form of rhythmic motor activity employed by mankind for its recreational, social, and expressive values; as movement enjoyed for its own sake, it becomes a recreational activity; as dance that is performed for its social values, it is often social and recreational; as an expressive medium, dance becomes art.

dance, ethnic: a dance performed by a people in the original place in living form, at the present time or in the past; it is transferred to a new place without any change and performed as it was originally; the music is played without adaptation so that through the rhythm, melodies, and words of the songs one becomes a cocreator of the feeling of another people.

dance, folk: a traditional dance of a people within a specific culture, evolved by them and embodying a characteristic national or regional flavor; for example, the American square dance is a folk dance unique to the United States.

dance job: *see* **job, dance.**

dance, modern: a creative art which expresses and communicates ideas and controlled emotions through the medium of body movement; a living, growing, changing art of personalized dance differing from *ballet* and *folk dance*, which are based on traditional forms.

dance notation: *see* **notation, dance.**

dance, social: dance designed to bring people together for group participation and enjoyment; in the twentieth century refers specifically to ballroom dancing.

dance therapy: *see* **therapy, dance.**

dancing-master education: a term applied to the aristocratic education of children of the nobility of France in connection with the drawing-room life of the court of Louis XIV and his successors. (Rousseau condemned it as making miniature adults of young children and denying them the privilege of developing naturally.)

dark adaptation: *see* **adaptation, dark.**

darkness concept: *see* **concept, darkness.**

Dartmouth College case: a decision by the Supreme Court of the United States in 1819, overruling an act of the legislature of the state of New Hampshire that attempted to alter the charter of the college, "that a corporation is established for purposes of general charity, or for education generally, does not per se make it a public corporation, liable to the control of the legislature"; generally regarded as protecting privately maintained colleges against state control.

Darwinian reflex: *see* **reflex, Darwinian.**

Darwinism, social: *see* **social Darwinism.**

data: *n. pl.; sing.* **datum;** (Lat., lit., "things given") facts in isolation, before exploration of their bearing on the subject inducing their choice.

data, approximate: (1) a set of quantitative values obtained from measurements or from estimations; (2) numerical data not known to be exact.

data, attendance: *see* **attendance data.**

data bank: a total file of stored integrated information from which data can be secured.

data, biographical: *see* **biographical data.**

data blank, pupil: an answer blank which is designed to gain information about the pupil; generally provides cross-sectional information. *Syn.* **pupil information blank; pupil inventory blank;** *see* **evaluation, guidance program.**

data, capture of: recording of information, when it is first received into some organization, on tape or punched cards, so that it can be processed from that point with a minimum of human intervention, with subsequent machines reading the information from the common-language media.

data card, officer's: *see* **card, officer's data.**

data cell: in computer operation, a secondary storage device employing thin magnetic strips of tape; the data cell retrieves and positions the appropriate strips for reading information from it or writing information on it. *See* **file, disk; file, line.**

data, continuous: observed values of a continuous variable that may take any values between the lower and the upper limits of the variable. *Syn.* **graduated data;** *contr. w.* **data, discrete.**

data, crude: (1) most frequently, *syn.* **data, raw;** (2) occasionally used to designate data that are inexact, approximate, or otherwise relatively unrefined.

data, discontinuous: *syn.* **data, discrete.**

data, discrete: observed values of a discrete variable; observations of a variable that may take only certain variate values and no intermediate values. *Contr. w.* **data, continuous.**

data, engineered time: *see* **time data, engineered.**

data, experimental: data obtained by observation of events when certain conditions have been carefully prearranged, controlled, and/or varied by the observer, that is, data obtained by conducting an experiment. *Dist. f.* **data, observational.**

data field: (data processing) (1) one or more (usually adjacent) card columns in a punched card; each data field must be used only for designated information within a given study; (2) sometimes used to indicate a storage location within the computer memory for a given set of data.

data-gathering schedule: *see* **schedule, data-gathering.**

data, graduated: *syn.* **data, continuous.**

data-handling system: an automatically operated or integrated routine used to process data; can be composed of several different combinations of its parts to provide for the processing of normal, rush, or exceptional situations.

data, historical: data that may be represented by a time series.

data, idiographic: (couns.) information about an individual which derives its meaning from the life pattern or a group of traits found in that individual, in contrast with *normative data*, that is, information which derives its meaning from a comparison of the individual with others.

data, input: (data processing) data which are entered into a computer. *Contr. w.* **data, output.**

data, multiple-categoried: data expressed in terms of several classes or categories.

data, normative: *see* **data, idiographic.**

data, observational: (1) data obtained by an examination of the behavioral events of individuals or groups; conditions under which the data are obtained may be structured or unstructured, depending upon the purposes of the observer; *dist. f.* **data, experimental;** (2) data collected in any investigation or sampling study.

data, output: information transferred from the internal storage of a computer to output devices or external storage.

Data-Phone: (1) a device developed for and used by American Telephone & Telegraph Co. and the Bell System in the transmission of data over telephone wires; (2) the system using this device; (3) commonly but loosely, any device (and its related system) for the transmission of data over telephone or telegraph wires.

data processing: (1) the preparation of source media which contain data or basic elements of information and the handling of such data according to precise rules of procedure to accomplish such operations as classifying, sorting, calculating, summarizing, and recording; (2) the production of records and reports; (3) more narrowly, the systematic handling of information by machines.

data processing, automated (ADP): a system for processing data which has been converted to automation; sometimes used loosely for computer data processing.

data processing, automatic: obtaining input information in machine language as close to the point of origin as economically possible, processing the information by automatic computer and by other machines without human intervention as far as economically justified, and having the output information produced in accordance with the needs of management and the more advanced techniques of data processing.

data processing, batch: a technique by which items to be processed in a data processing machine are collected into groups prior to their processing.

data processing center: *see* **center, data processing.**

data processing, delayed-time: automatic data processing that operates with historical information, that is, information after it can no longer affect its source, such as information about the amount of goods shipped after the shipment has been made. *Comp. w.* **data processing, real-time.**

data processing, electronic (EDP): handling of recorded information by means of a machine using electronic circuitry at electronic speed, as opposed to electromechanical equipment.

data processing, in-line: the processing of data without sorting or any prior treatment other than storage. *See* **data processing, on-line.**

data processing, integrated (IDP): specifically, the use of paper-tape-producing equipment and paper-tape-actuated equipment for data handling; more generally, an approach to automatic data processing involving ideally only one manual transcription of input data into machine language.

data processing occupations: *see* **occupations, data processing.**

data processing, off-line: a system in which the operation of peripheral equipment is not under the control of the central processing unit.

data processing, on-line: a system in which the operation of the peripheral equipment or devices is under control of the central processing unit and in which information reflecting current activity is introduced into the data processing system as soon as it occurs; thus it is directly in line with the main flow of transaction processing, as, for example, in processing airline ticket reservations, items for inventory control, etc.

data processing, real-time: the processing of data in a rapid manner so that the results of the processing are available in time to influence the process being monitored, such as the movements of a freight train. *Comp. w.* **data processing, delayed-time.**

data processing system, automatic: a term descriptive of an interacting assembly of procedures, processes, methods, personnel, and automatic equipment to perform a series of data processing operations.

data, raw: data that have not been subjected to statistical or logical analysis; for example, the data contained in a set of test papers before they are scored, in a set of raw scores, or in a distribution of values that have not yet been summarized (statistically), transformed, or evaluated in any manner. *Syn.* **crude data.**

data reduction: the application of arithmetical, mathematical, or statistical techniques to obtain or extract only the needed information from a larger amount of related information, as in the preparation of computer input.

data remoting: the storage and handling of data through mechanical-electronic systems which permit electronic distribution of recorded images without removing the original material from the depository.

data, representative: data that are typical of or that represent fairly a given universe or class of phenomena. *Syn.* **typical data.**

data sheet: a paper form upon which pertinent data about a case or, usually, many cases can be tabulated or assembled; thus, a device for recording in usable form the *raw data* obtained from a study.

data sheet, personal: a pupil data questionnaire giving the school staff personal information that enables them to see the student as he is now and provides extensive data dealing with the present life situation of the student. *See* **data blank, pupil.**

data-storage tube: a modified TV kinescope or picture tube equipped to retain selected images for as long as desired.

data, subjective: ratings or reports that are substantially dependent on the personal judgment of the rater, reporter, or observer.

data, typical: *syn.* **data, representative.**

date book: *syn.* **future book.**

DAVY: *see* **program, disadvantaged youth.**

dawning-realism developmental stage: *see* **developmental stage, dawning-realism.**

day, BIE: *see* **BIE day.**

day blindness: *see* **blindness, day.**

day, business, industry, education: *see* **business, industry, education day.**

day camp: a place in the country with shelter provided, operated usually during the summer months for the benefit of physically below-par persons, especially children, with stress upon rest, feeding, and outdoor activity, usually under medical supervision.

day camping: a program for children in which camping activities are carried out, except that the children return home each night to sleep.

day care center: *see* **center, day care.**

day care program: *see* **program, day care.**

day care service: a facility which provides care for preschool children who come from broken homes or homes where both parents must work. *Syn.* **child care service.**

day, career: *see* **career day.**

day class: *see* **class, day.**

day, college: *see* **college day.**

day, education, industry, business: *see* **education, industry, business day.**

day, EIB: *see* **EIB day.**

day, extended school: *see* **school day, extended.**

day nursery: an institution for the organized care of young children outside their homes; differentiated from the *nursery school* in that it cares for children of a greater age range, tends to have a longer day, and places more emphasis on custodial care than on the promotion of the physical, motor, emotional, intellectual, aesthetic, and social development of the preschool child; in some areas called *child care center, day care center,* or *day nursery school.*

day nursery school: *see* **nursery school, day.**

day of absence: *see* **absence, day of.**

day of attendance: *see* **attendance, full day of.**

day of membership: *see* **membership, day of.**

day of recollection: *syn.* **retreat.**

day, orientation: *see* **orientation day.**

day school: a school attended by pupils during a part of the day, as distinguished from a *residential school* where pupils are boarded and lodged as well as taught.

day school, Jewish: a school, also called Yeshivah, that provides both religious and secular education; usually designated as *day school* or *all-day school* to differentiate it from other Jewish schools that are supplementary schools where the education provided is confined to Jewish education and is regarded as supplementary to that of the public school; there are several types of *day schools,* the two dominant ones being (a) those where Jewish instruction is confined to a given portion of the school day separate from that of the general instruction and (b) those where an attempt is made to integrate the Jewish and the general elements in the curriculum. *See* **Lubavitcher school; supplementary education, Jewish; Yeshivah** (2).

day school program: *see* **program, day school.**

day school, special: a day school operated for the purpose of providing for special instructional needs of certain pupils such as the handicapped or otherwise exceptional.

day student: *see* **student, day.**

day, study: *see* **study day.**

day trade school: a public school offering trade instruction in the daytime to prepare youths or adults for definite trades or occupations. *See* **unit trade school or class.**

day-unit class: *see* **class, day-unit.**

day-unit teacher: a teacher to whom has been assigned the responsibility of completing a teaching unit of work in the daytime; may be a full-time teacher.

daydream: a series of imagined pictures and events in an imaginary environment, constituting an escape from reality.

daylight screen: *see* **screen, daylight.**

daymare: an attack of anxiety and fear occurring during waking hours, brought on by indulgence in daydreaming.

days belonging: *syn.* **aggregate days enrolled.**

days in session: *see* **session, days in.**

days, professional: *see* **professional days.**

de facto (dē fak'tō): (Lat., lit., "from the fact") actually; in reality; an adjectival phrase used to denote a situation derived from fact as distinguished from one derived from law; specifically used of an officer, board, or corporation actually exercising powers as such, though the legal right to do so may be technically questionable or defective because of expiration of term, contest of election, invalid charter, or similar reasons.

de facto officer: *see* **officer, de facto.**

de facto segregation: *see* **segregation, de facto.**

de jure (dē jōō're): (Lat., lit., "from the law") derived from law; used of an officer, board, or corporation having full legal right to exercise powers as such, especially in contradistinction to a *de facto* officer, board, or corporation that may be usurping the same powers under color of authority.

de jure officer: *see* **officer, de jure.**

de jure segregation: *see* **segregation, de jure.**

dead census file: *see* **census file, dead.**

dead-hand control: *syn.* **mortmain control.**

dead time: *see* **time, dead.**

deadhead mileage: *see* **mileage, deadhead.**

deaf: descriptive of a general group of persons in whom the sense of hearing is nonfunctional for the ordinary purposes of life; made up of two distinct classes based

entirely on the time of loss of hearing: (a) those whose hearing losses range from 70 to 75 decibels in the speech range to inability to distinguish more than one or two frequencies at the highest measurable level of intensity in the better ear, so that they are not able to understand and acquire speech and language through the sense of hearing even when sound amplification is provided, and (b) those whose hearing losses average 50 or more decibels in the speech range in the better ear and who, having had a sustained loss from very early childhood or babyhood, do not learn language and speech through the unaided ear.

deaf blind: *see* **blind deaf.**

deaf, captioned films for: *see* **films for deaf, captioned.**

deaf child: *see* **child, deaf.**

deaf-multiply handicapped: descriptive of the deaf whose hearing impairment is combined with other physical or neurological deficiencies.

deaf mute: lacking the sense of hearing and the ability to speak.

deaf, preschool training for the: *see* **training for the deaf, preschool.**

deaf, residential school for the: *see* **residential school for the deaf.**

deaf, special center for the: a system in which deaf children are enrolled in their own school districts, the special teacher being at a given central school; at stated intervals the hard-of-hearing come from other schools for training in speech reading.

deafened: descriptive of a person having profound sensory-neural deafness occurring subsequent to the age at which the use of language is retained, that is, after 5 years of age.

deafened child: *see* **child, deafened.**

deafism: one of certain types of errors which occur in the written language of deaf children.

deafness: a condition in which hearing is either totally absent or so defective as to be nonfunctional for the ordinary purposes of life. *See* **deafness, adventitious; deafness, congenital.**

deafness, acquired: *syn.* **deafness, adventitious.**

deafness, adventitious: a condition occurring after birth (in a person born with normal hearing) as a result of accident or disease and varying in degree from mild impairment to total loss of hearing or hearing so defective as to be nonfunctional for the ordinary purposes of life; may be classified according to the nature of the disorder, as *conduction deafness, hysterical deafness, perception deafness,* and *toxic deafness.*

deafness, catarrhal: hearing loss caused by inflammation of the mucous membrane of the air passages in the head and throat with blockage of the Eustachian tube.

deafness, central: the type of hearing impairment located in the central nervous system.

deafness, conduction: an impairment of hearing due to damage or obstruction of the ear canal, drum membrane, or the ossicular chain in the middle ear; a failure of air vibrations to be adequately conducted to the cochlea. *Syn.* **obstruction deafness;** *see* **otosclerosis.**

deafness, congenital: a general term for deafness dating from birth or earlier. *See* **deafness, true congenital.**

deafness, cortical: hearing impairment that is not a loss of sensitivity but a loss of understanding; involves a difficulty in discrimination but appears more clearly in an articulation test than in a test for the difference limen of pitch or of loudness, since it cannot be explained by abnormality of the auditory organ or the acoustic nerve.

deafness, experimental: an experiment in which hearing people temporarily plug their ears in order to understand the problems of the deaf.

deafness, functional: *syn.* **deafness, psychic** (1).

deafness, hysterical: *syn.* **deafness, psychic** (1).

deafness, mental: *syn.* **deafness, cortical.**

deafness, mixed: the type of hearing impairment which is the combination of perceptive and conductive hearing loss. *See* **deafness, conduction; deafness, perception.**

deafness, nerve: deafness due to defect or disease of the neural apparatus in the inner ear and of the acoustic nerve; often indicated by deficient bone conduction.

deafness, obstruction: *syn.* **deafness, conduction.**

deafness, perception: deafness due to diminished or completely lost functioning of the sound-perceiving apparatus, usually indicated by partial or complete loss of bone conduction.

deafness, peripheral: any hearing impairment that is caused by an abnormality in either the sense organ or the auditory nerve. *Comp. w.* **deafness, central.**

deafness, postlingual: deafness that occurs after language has developed, usually after the age of 3 years.

deafness, potential: threatened loss of hearing, usually indicated by a slight, nonhandicapping impairment that, if not treated, may become progressively worse.

deafness, prelingual: deafness that occurs before language has developed, usually before the age of 3 years.

deafness, progressive: hearing impairment that becomes slowly or rapidly worse, even under expert treatment.

deafness, psychic: (1) strictly, inability to hear owing to the influence of some psychological mechanism such as hysteria, rather than as the result of any known physical cause; *syn.* **functional deafness; hysterical deafness; psychical deafness; psychogenic deafness;** (2) sometimes used as a synonym for *cortical deafness,* that is, deafness caused by defect or impairment of the cerebral cortex, rather than of the ear.

deafness, psychogenic: *see* **deafness, psychic.**

deafness, sensory-neural: any hearing loss which derives from trauma, maldevelopment, or disease affecting the normal function of the inner ear.

deafness, tone: (1) a condition characterized by one or more gaps in the auditory range, the subject being unable to hear certain tones; *syn.* **asonia;** (2) a condition characterized by relative insensitivity to differences between musical tones, sometimes manifested by inability to distinguish one tune from another.

deafness, toxic: deafness resulting from poisons taken into or generated in the system.

deafness, true congenital: deafness present at birth and clearly traceable to hereditary causes. *See* **deafness, congenital.**

deafness, word: the inability to perceive as words the sounds which are heard; inability to associate spoken sounds with their appropriate referents; not due to damage to the mechanism within the ear or other auditory impairment.

dean: a major officer of an independent college or of a division, college, or school of a university, who is responsible, under the president or someone responsible to the president, for the administration and supervision of instructional activities or of student relations.

dean, academic: the officer directly in charge of the instructional program in a school or college and usually responsible immediately to the president for (*a*) the direction of the faculty, (*b*) nominating to the president new members of the faculty on the recommendation of department heads, and (*c*) the appraisal of the services of the faculty members. *Syn.* **chief academic officer; dean of faculties; dean of instruction.**

dean of boys: the administrative person in the school who is assigned the responsibility of coordinating and administering class scheduling and extracurricular activities of the male students in the school.

dean of faculties: *syn.* **dean, academic.**

dean of girls: the administrative person in the school who is assigned the responsibility of coordinating and administering class scheduling and extracurricular activities of the female students in the school.

dean of instruction: *syn.* **dean, academic.**

dean of men: an official in a college or university having charge of student personnel services (such as counseling or discipline) which pertain to men students.

dean of students: a person in a higher education institution concerned with all phases of student life, who, in addition to the administration of student personnel services, also facilitates student growth and development through individual counseling on personal, social, and academic problems and through group contacts and official information and assistance regarding part-time employment, placement, veterans' affairs, housing, student activities, and the social calendar; sometimes called dean of student affairs, director of student affairs, vice-president for student personnel programs, etc.; often supervises work of a *dean of men* and a *dean of women,* although recently these latter titles are often changed to assistant or associate dean of students.

dean of women: an official in a college or university having charge of student personnel services (such as counseling or discipline) which pertain to women students.

dean's list: *syn.* **honor roll.**

death rate, adjusted: *syn.* **death rate, corrected.**

death rate, corrected: the death rate obtained by multiplying the specific death rates found for each age, race, and sex combination in a given population by the number of such persons in a standard population, adding, and dividing by the total number of persons in the standard population. (The standard population may be further specified as to distribution by occupation, nationality, religion, etc.) *Syn.* **adjusted death rate; refined death rate; standardized death rate;** *contr. w.* **death rate, crude.**

death rate, crude: the number of deaths per thousand population in an area during a year.

death rate, refined: *syn.* **death rate, corrected.**

death rate, standardized: *syn.* **death rate, corrected.**

death tax: *see* **tax, death.**

debate: a formal presentation of arguments on both sides of a question before an audience in accordance with standardized procedure; used as a form of training in public speaking and as a competitive intramural or interschool student activity.

debate, problem-solving: a combination of discussion and debate in which the proposition is stated as a problem; the intent is to arrive at a useful solution to the problem through cooperative effort.

debit: in accounting, a notation of the acquisition of debt.

debt: the amount of money, goods, or services owed by one person or corporation to another.

debt, bonded: that portion of indebtedness represented by outstanding bonds.

debt, building: the amount of money borrowed or remaining to be paid for the cost of a building or buildings that constitute all or part of a university, college, or school plant.

debt capacity: the difference between the net outstanding debt of a school district and the maximum debt permitted by law.

debt ceiling: maximum amount of debt to which an issuer may commit itself legally; usually stated as a percentage of assessed valuation of property for tax purposes.

debt, consumer: *see* **credit, consumer.**

debt control: an activity by a group of people or a legislature to restrict the volume of debt or the purposes for which debt may be incurred.

debt, coterminous: debt of governmental units with coterminous boundaries which also have power to levy taxes on the same real and personal property.

debt, floating: obligations other than bonds payable on demand or at an early date; in school finance, usually includes items such as short-term loans, bills payable, and warrants.

debt, funding: debt which usually indicates overspending by local government.

debt limit, school-district: the maximum debt, set by the constitution, statute, or authorized administrative officer, that the local school district may incur; generally expressed as a percentage of the assessed valuation of taxable property in the district.

debt limitation: a legal restriction on the power of a corporation, government, or other agency to incur debt.

debt-maturity schedule: a schedule showing the dates of maturation of serial bonds in a particular bond issue.

debt, net bonded: a misused term that may mean gross debt minus certain debt; the excluded debt varies from region to region.

debt, overlapping: (school admin.) total debt of two or more governmental units that have common authority to tax property located in their jurisdictions.

debt, oxygen: *see* **oxygen debt.**

debt, perpetual: a type of governmental obligation incurred with no definite date of maturity, which can be retired at the pleasure of the government, on which only the interest payments are due, on whose principal the government is never in default, and which the government can redeem or convert into a new obligation at will, for example, the English consols or the French rentes.

debt redemption: the act of returning a commodity, usually money, to the lender in payment of a debt when the debt is due, as agreed upon in the contract or as specified by law.

debt reorganization: a revision of the agreements that were made when the debt was incurred in order to make possible a fulfillment of obligation or to give an extension of time.

debt restriction: a limitation on the incurring of debts, usually a statement of purposes for which debts may be incurred. *See* **debt limitation.**

debt service: the payment of interest and amortization charges of a debt.

debug: *v.* to locate and correct any errors in a computer program, to detect and correct malfunctions in the computer itself, or to test-run and check out a program of machine instructions for a digital computer for the purpose of eliminating mistakes.

decade addition: *syn.* **addition, higher-decade.**

Decalogue: the Ten Commandments, claimed to have been given to Moses by God on Mount Sinai and recorded in the Bible.

decathlon (de·kath'lon): a series of 10 athletic events in which scores are converted into points in accordance with prepared tables or scales.

deceleration time: *see* **stop time.**

decentralization: (school admin.) a process whereby some higher central source of responsibility and authority assigns certain functions and duties to subordinate positions; accomplished through delegation.

decentralization of counseling: *see* **counseling, decentralization of.**

decentralization, school: *see* **control, community.**

decentralized administration: *see* **administration, decentralized.**

decentralized control: *see* **control, decentralized.**

decentralized guidance: *see* **guidance, decentralized.**

decentralized library: *see* **library, decentralized.**

decibel (db): a unit used to measure the relative loudness of sounds; one decibel is considered to be the faintest sound that can be heard by a normally hearing person; each decibel thereafter approximates the smallest perceptible difference in loudness of sounds; 140 decibels, a pressure 10 million times as great as one decibel, is considered to be the pain level in the normal ear; sometimes inaccurately called a *sensation unit.*

decile: $(D_1, D_2, \ldots, D_9)$ one of the nine points, measured along the scale of a variable, that divide the frequency distribution into 10 groups of equal frequency; thus, each tenth percentile (for example, D_1 is the 10th percentile, D_4 is the 40th percentile). *Dist. f.* **interval, decile.**

decile interval: *see* **interval, decile.**

decile range: *syn.* **interval, decile.**

decile rank: *see* **rank, decile.**

decimal classification: *see* **classification, decimal.**

decimal classification, Dewey: *syn.* **classification, decimal.**

decimal classification, universal (Brussels): *see* **classification, universal decimal (Brussels).**

decimal code, binary-coded: *see* **code, binary-coded-decimal.**

decimal system: the conventional system of numeration which is additive, has place value, and in which the grouping is done by tens. *Comp. w.* **binary system; duodecimal system.**

decision: (1) a practical judgment with respect to what is to be done in a particular situation as distinguished from determination of policy which is a judgment regarding a class of situations; (2) in computer operation, the processes of detecting the existence of specified patterns of relationships in the data being handled and of taking alternative courses of action based upon the differences detected.

decision, individual: a choice which must be made in some situation by the individual (or, sometimes, on his behalf) rather than by an institution; for example, the choice of a career.

decision, institutional: (meas.) a choice which must be made in some situation by the testing agency on behalf of an institution (a school or company) rather than by the individuals tested, for example, which applicants to select and which to reject; tests are demonstrably of greater value in such situations than in situations demanding *individual decision.*

decision language: *see* **language, decision.**

decision making: as a scientific process, a method whereby a situation is studied and evaluated, the problems are identified, and alternative solutions to the problems are considered before a course of action with intent to execute it is formulated. *See* **decision.**

decision, period of: *see* **developmental stage, period-of-decision.**

decision, placement: (meas.) assignment of persons to different levels of treatment rather than to quite different types of treatment, so as to maximize the effectiveness of "outcomes."

decision, quality: *see* **quality decision.**

decision, statistical: a practical inference drawn from research of a statistical nature.

decision table: *see* **table, decision.**

decision theory: (1) an attempt to put the decision-making process into mathematical form so that available information may be used to reach the most effective decisions under specified circumstances; (2) in counseling, a concept related to *information theory* in that a decision must be made as to whether the client should leave counseling with a fixed plan of procedure or should go forth prepared to adapt it; in daily life, the concept that a person has the choice of modifying his responses with each change of condition or of modifying them only when unmistakable evidence points to the necessity of change.

deck, source: *see* **program, source.**

deck, tape: *syn.* **tape transport.**

declaratory judgment: *see* **judgment, declaratory.**

decoding: (1) (stat.) the act or process of converting code symbols to the original values or information for which the code symbols stand; sometimes done by application of a mathematical formula and sometimes (especially in the case of geometric codes) through the use of tabulating and sorting machines; (2) (read.) the process of translating printed or written symbols into the spoken word.

decoding, auditory: the ability to understand what is heard.

decoding code: *see* **code, decoding.**

decoding key: *syn.* **code, decoding.**

decoding test, auditory: *see* **test, auditory decoding.**

decoding, visual: the process of obtaining meaning from visual stimuli; indicative of receptive language ability.

decompensation: ego or personality disorganization under excessive stress.

decomposition method: *see* **subtraction, methods of.**

decoration, applied: the application of decorative ornament to any object, as applying carving to a piece of furniture or decalcomania designs to a household article. *See* **art, decorative; design, applied.**

decoration, interior: *see* **interior decoration.**

decoration, interior building: (1) the surface finish (painting, varnishing, etc.) of the interior of buildings; (2) the appearance of walls, ceilings, and trim with respect to paint, varnish, etc.

decorative art: *see* **art, decorative.**

decorative stage of color: *see* **color, decorative stage of.**

decoy: as used in testing, synonymous with *distractor.*

decree: an order of a court of equity concerning the legality of the facts found to exist.

decremental reinforcement: *see* **reinforcement, decremental.**

dedicated tax: *see* **tax, earmarked.**

deduction: that process of logical thought moving from general principles to particular cases; *see* **deductive method;** *contr. w.* **induction;** (2) as a product, a deductive proof; *see* **proof, deductive.**

deduction test: *see* **test, deduction.**

deductive approach: *syn.* **deductive method.**

deductive attack: *syn.* **deductive method.**

deductive lesson: *see* **lesson, deductive.**

deductive method: method of teaching, study, or argument which proceeds from general or universally applicable principles to particular applications of these principles and shows the validity of the conclusions. *See* **RULEG;** *comp. w.* **inductive method** (1) and (2).

deductive proof: *see* **proof, deductive.**

deductive reasoning: *see* **reasoning, deductive.**

deductive study: *see* **study, deductive.**

deductive syllogism: *syn.* **syllogism.**

deductive system: (math.) a system in which the undefined terms are specified and the definitions and axioms explicitly set forth and in which theorems are derived from the axioms and definitions by acceptable methods of proof.

defamation: (law) communication, without lawful right, which injures the reputation of another. *See* **communication, privileged; libel; slander.**

default: failure to do what is required by duty or law.

default, bond: *see* **bond default.**

default, judgment by: *see* **judgment by default.**

defect, articulatory: *see* **articulatory defect.**

defect, auditory: inability to recognize sounds and/or to place sounds in the correct temporal sequence, thus creating confusion not only in the recognition of words but also in their emission; sound reversals may be understood as a confusion in spatial and temporal orientation.

defect, eye: *see* **eye defect.**

defect, mental: a physical or constitutional defect from birth or early age, being the result either of incomplete or arrested growth of certain brain cells or of deficient somatic organization. *See* **retardation, mental.**

defect, ocular: *syn.* **eye defect.**

defect of rhythm: an abnormality in the rhythm or fluency of speech, especially *stuttering* or *cluttering.*

defect, optical: *see* **optical defect.**

defect, physical: *see* **physical defect.**

defect, speech: *see* **speech defect.**

defect, visual: *see* **visual defect.**

defective, borderline: the designation of a person who is just above the level of the highest type of mental deficiency.

defective, certifiable mental: *see* **mental defective, certifiable.**

defective child: *see* **child, defective.**

defective delinquent: *see* **delinquent, defective.**

defective hearing: *see* **hearing loss.**

defective, mental: a term used to describe a child who has organic deficits which permanently reduce the capacity for intellectual functioning.

defective phonation: *see* **disorder, voice.**

defective, physically: descriptive of an individual who has an imperfect or subnormal development of some part of his body.

defective, scholastic: a person having any permanent or temporary mental, emotional, physical, and/or social hindrance to the attainment of individual potentialities to the normal level of expectancy.

defective speech: *see* **speech, defective.**

defective vision: *see* **vision, defective.**

defects, hearing: *see* **hearing loss.**

defendant: the party against whom an action is brought in a court of law.

defense, civil: *see* **civil defense.**

defense course: *see* **defense school.**

defense mechanism: (1) a device (idea, attitude, act) adopted by an organism to protect its physical safety, mental and physical comfort, and personal status or to further its inclinations if these are threatened with thwarting, for example, deception, withdrawal, attack, rationalization, etc.; (2) a form of behavior pointed toward protecting the individual by deceiving others and, on occasion, even the self. *See* **dynamism;** *dist. f.* **reflex, defense.**

defense reaction: *syn.* **defense mechanism.**

defense reflex: *see* **reflex, defense.**

defense school: a school, utilized by two or more military services, which is administered by a coordinating agency of the services and which presents a curriculum developed under the policy guidance and approval authority of an agency element of the Secretary of Defense; a *defense course* is similar in all respects.

defensible minimum program: *see* **program, defensible minimum.**

deferred aim: *see* **aim, deferred.**

deferred charges: prepaid insurance and such other prepayments for anticipated services, or benefits that are to be received over a period of years and that have been paid for in advance; interest due on bank balances, accrued but not payable, may be included.

deferred income credits: payments made to an institution for services to be rendered during a subsequent period, for example, *tuition* or room rentals.

deferred tuition payment plan: *see* **tuition payment plan, deferred.**

deficiency bill: any statute or law authorizing supplementary appropriations to meet increases in current needs that were not expected and included in the original appropriation.

deficiency, familial mental: a condition of mental retardation of hereditary or social-cultural etiology.

deficiency, mental: *see* **retardation, mental.**

deficiency, mild: level two on the adaptive behavior classification system, with an IQ range of 55 to 69. *See* **mentally retarded, educable.**

deficiency, nutritional: *see* **undernourishment.**

deficient, mentally: *see* **mentally deficient.**

deficit: (1) an excess of expenditures over income; (2) the excess of the liabilities and liability reserves of a fund over its assets; where a fund has also other resources and obligations, the excess of its obligations over its resources.

deficit, cognitive: *see* **cognitive deficit.**

deficit spending: in government, expenditures which make borrowing necessary because more money is being spent than is being taken in from taxes and other sources.

definition: (1) the process of determining the meaning or signification of a word, idea, or proposition in general and within a given context; (2) the statement by which the meaning or signification of words, ideas, or propositions is determined; (3) (math.) a statement which sets forth the meaning to be assigned to a word, phrase, symbol, or operation and specifies all conditions, and only those, under which they can be substituted for something else; *see* **term, undefined;** (4) appearance of sharpness or of being in focus of an image such as a photograph, of an object viewed through the microscope, etc.

definition, circular: a defining statement employing words that are themselves defined by the use of the term under definition, for example, "Thinking is the activity of the mind. The mind is that which thinks."

definition, operational: a definition by means of description of observed properties or behaviors; also, a definition by means of outlining the procedure for reproducing the object or phenomenon being described.

deflector, window: a glass or board panel to be set at an angle in front of a partially open window for the purpose of deflecting incoming air toward the ceiling in window ventilation.

deformation, orthopedic: a condition in which muscular movement is so far restricted by accident or disease as to affect a person's capacity for self-support.

deformity: a deviation in body structure; may result from the unopposed action of the sound muscle against a paralyzed muscle.

degaussing: demagnetizing recording and playback heads.

degeneracy, social: a term not widely used by sociologists because of its value implications; however it has legitimate uses when defined as (*a*) a condition of society characterized by the breaking down of ethical, economic, or intellectual standards without the substitution of equivalent standards having equal social desirability or worth; often accompanied by the failure of members of the group to cooperate and by a regression to a more primitive state; (*b*) the condition of a group having an abnormal proportion of individual degeneration; (*c*) the condition of a group whose typical members would seem degenerate from the standpoint of an outside observer.

degree: a title bestowed by a college or university as official recognition for the completion of a course of study or for a certain attainment.

degree, academic: (1) a degree conferred for attainment in liberal education; (2) more broadly, a degree conferred by an institution of higher education, regardless of the field of study.

degree, associate: a degree commonly conferred at the end of a 2-year junior college or technical institute course of study; examples are associate in arts (A.A.), associate in science (A.S.), associate in education (A.Ed.), associate in fine arts (A.F.A.), associate in music (A.M.), associate in commerce (A.C.), associate in engineering (A.Eng.), etc. (The associate title, or degree, is now used in most junior colleges and in many technical institutes in the United States; first authorized by the University of Durham, England, in 1865.)

degree, baccalaureate: *syn.* **degree, bachelor's.**

degree, bachelor's: (1) the first degree in arts and sciences or in certain professional and technical fields, the requirements usually including 4 years of work of college grade; *syn.* **baccalaureate degree;** (2) also used in *bachelor of laws* (LL.B.) and *bachelor of divinity* (B.D.), typically for 2 or 3 years of study beyond the first 4-year degree, although recently there is a trend to replace the LL.B. degree with that of *doctor of jurisprudence* (J.D.).

degree, doctor of education (Ed.D.): the highest professional degree in education awarded by colleges or universities for the advanced study of education, usually granted at the completion of the equivalent of a minimum of 2 to 3 years of graduate work in a teacher education school, college, or university and the writing, defense, and subsequent acceptance of a doctor's dissertation on a project of individual research dealing with some problem having either practical or theoretical application to education. (Depending on the institution granting it, the doctor of education degree may be parallel and equivalent in requirements to the *doctor of philosophy degree* or may be characterized by a shorter period of study and greater emphasis on practical rather than theoretical research. In some institutions the language and dissertation requirements of the Ph.D. degree are modified.) *Dist. f.* **doctor of philosophy in education.**

degree, doctor of medicine: *see* **degree, doctor's** (2).

degree, doctor of music education (Mus.Ed.D.): a doctor's degree conferred for mastery within the field of music education, attested by a dissertation demonstrating rigorous research into an area of public music instruction.

degree, doctor of music (Mus.D.): an honorary doctor's degree conferred for outstanding contribution to the field of music at large.

degree, doctor of musical arts (D.M.A.): (1) a doctor's degree conferred for mastery in the field of musical composition, attested by a final musical composition of symphonic proportions; (2) a doctor's degree conferred for mastery in the field of musical performance, attested by several final recitals of virtuoso professional quality.

degree, doctor of pedagogy: a rarely used title for a degree formerly equivalent to the *doctor of education degree.*

degree, doctor of philosophy (Ph.D.): a doctor's degree conferred for mastery within a field of knowledge and for proved ability in research attested by a dissertation; usually involves a program of approximately 3 years of study and research beyond the *bachelor's degree.*

degree, doctor's: (1) the highest academic degree for attainment in graduate study, as *doctor of philosophy;* (2) the first degree awarded for completion of a curriculum in certain fields of professional education, as *doctor of medicine.*

degree, Future Homemaker's: one of the awards for individual achievement in the Future Homemakers of America organization, based upon achievements in the home, the chapter, the school, and the community; three awards may be earned, the Junior award, the Chapter award, and the State award designated as the Future Homemaker's degree.

degree, graduate: a degree granted for completion of a course of study by one who has previously received a bachelor's or first professional degree in the same field of study.

degree-granting institution, Federal: *see* **institution, Federal degree-granting.**

degree, honorary: a degree bestowed as recognition of outstanding achievement or merit, without reference to the fulfillment of academic requirements for degrees in course.

degree in course: a degree bestowed in recognition of the fulfillment of certain academic requirements.

degree in cursu, master: a degree awarded after successful completion of a 3-year course of study in liberal arts beyond the baccalaureate degree; conferred on thousands of graduates before 1870.

degree, master of education (M.Ed. or Ed.M.): a degree representing an advanced stage of professional educational preparation, usually granted at the completion of either a 5-year curriculum in a special field or a year of graduate work beyond the baccalaureate degree in a teacher education institution, with major specialization either in education or in a teaching field; frequently characterized by a modification of the language and thesis requirements. *See* **master of arts degree in education; master of science degree in education.**

degree, master of music (M.Mus.): a degree representing an advanced stage of achievement in any of several categories within the musical discipline, such as performance, composition, music education, historical musicology, etc.

degree, master's: in the United States, an academic degree of advanced character, usually a second degree, ranking above the bachelor's degree and below the Ph.D., Ed.D., or other equivalent doctor's degrees.

degree of accuracy: *see* **error, relative.**

degree of disability: *see* **disability, degree of.**

degree of freedom: any way an element (such as body, point, or statistic) may move or change; in general, any system will have as many degrees of freedom as it contains independent variables.

degree of mental retardation: *see* **mental retardation, degree of.**

degree, specialist in education: a bachelor's or master's degree, offered at some colleges, which involves teacher preparation in a specialized area in education rather than in general preparation.

degressive taxation: *see* **taxation, degressive.**

dehydrated clause: *see* **clause, dehydrated.**

dehydrated sentence: *see* **sentence, dehydrated.**

deification: the act of revering as a god or the state of being exalted to divine honors. *Syn.* **apotheosis.**

deism: the theory that God created the universe but has no intimate relation with it; affirms a transcendent God rather than an immanent one; implies a denial of revelation; sometimes identified as the "watchmaker theory of the universe."

dejection: a mood of sadness, melancholy, or despondency.

delay study, ratio: *see* **study, ratio delay.**

delayed broadcast: *see* **broadcast, delayed.**

delayed conditioning: *see* **conditioning, delayed.**

delayed feedback audiometer: *see* **audiometer, delayed feedback.**

delayed reaction: *see* **reaction, delayed.**

delayed recall: *see* **recall, delayed.**

delayed reflex: *see* **reflex, delayed.**

delayed-response technique: method of measurement of the duration of retention in an animal or young infant following one presentation of the stimulus situation or object. *See* **test, ball-and-chicken.**

delayed review item: *see* **item, delayed review.**

delayed speech: *see* **speech, delayed.**

delayed-time data processing: *see* **data processing, delayed-time.**

delegated authority: *see* **authority, delegated.**

delegated control: *see* **control, delegated.**

delegated powers: *see* **powers, delegated.**

delegation, executive: a process whereby certain of the executive's functions, responsibilities, and authorities are released and committed to designated subordinate positions; the direction of delegation is always downward in business organizations. *See* **decentralization.**

delegation of legislative power: violation of the constitutional principle that the lawmaking power vested in Federal, state, and local legislative bodies must be exercised by them directly, and not entrusted to other officers or bodies. (In state government, the line between the true legislative power, which must be exercised only by the state legislature, and the quasi-legislative and general administrative powers, which may properly be delegated to state and local boards of education, is very difficult to trace, but the tendency is for the scope of the delegable quasi-legislative power to increase.)

deliberate generalization: *see* **generalization, deliberate.**

deliberative research: *see* **research, deliberative.**

delicate child: *syn.* **child, physically below par;** *see* **lowered-vitality case.**

delinquency: behavior that is in violation of the conduct norms of a society; the definition of the violation may be based on legal or extra-legal norms; social scientists, while accepting the legal definition, prefer to emphasize the extralegal; delinquency is a product of the individual's behavior and experience and to that individual is a way of reacting to frustrations and deprivations; the term is used in juvenile court law to define juvenile offenses which come under the jurisdiction of the court; it is important to distinguish between the criminal act and the delinquent act because of the theory that juveniles are not motivated by the same considerations as are adults.

delinquency, adolescent: *see* **adolescence; delinquency, juvenile.**

delinquency, contribution to: a legal category defined as the act of encouraging or leading a youth to become a delinquent.

delinquency, juvenile: the antisocial acts of young persons who are under age; the age limits are defined variously by the state codes, but most set the upper limit at 16 to 18 years of age, with the lower limit usually at the discretion of the judge; legally the definition of juvenile delinquency refers to behavior in violation of (*a*) statutes designed particularly for juveniles and (*b*) the regular criminal legal code; criminologists and social scientists generally do not limit the definition to strictly legal deviation but include a wide range of antisocial conduct.

delinquency, tax: *see* **tax delinquency.**

delinquent: an offender against the laws of society whose misdeeds are not sufficiently serious to brand him a criminal; usually applied to youthful offenders over whose offenses the juvenile court has jurisdiction; in addition to the legal definition, the term delinquent is being broadened to include all antisocial deviants whether or not they are brought to the attention of the court.

delinquent child: *see* **child, delinquent.**

delinquent, defective: a person whose delinquency is attributable to or associated with mental or other types of deficiency.

delinquent, juvenile: any child whose conduct deviates sufficiently from normal social usage that it may be labeled antisocial; while state legal codes vary considerably, the following common denominators may be noted in regard to the legal definition of the term; (*a*) the individual is under the ages of 16 to 18; (*b*) he has violated any law of the state that if committed by a person above this age group would be an offense punishable other than by death or life imprisonment; (*c*) he has violated laws particularly designed for juveniles, such as those dealing with truancy, incorrigibility, ungovernability, and habitual disobedience; the various state laws have an average of eight or nine such items in addition to the violation of already enacted laws; in addition to the legal definitions, the term juvenile delinquent includes detected antisocial deviants brought to the attention of social agencies.

delinquent, school: *see* **truant.**

Deluder Act: the Law of 1647 enacted by the General Court of Massachusetts requiring towns of 50 families or more to employ a teacher of reading and writing and towns of 100 families to establish and maintain a (Latin) grammar school; called the Deluder Act because of the mention in the preamble of "that old deluder, Satan."

delusion: a false belief that cannot be corrected by logical evidence. *Dist. f.* **hallucination; illusion.**

delusions, bulkhead: *see* **compartmentalization.**

delusions of grandeur: a generally exaggerated misconception of one's origin, position, wealth, ability, or accomplishments, common to certain types of mental disorder.

delusions of reference: the delusional belief that ordinary acts or occurrences have special or hidden meanings and that they refer to the individual with intent to insult or annoy him.

demand: (consumer ed.) the quantity of any goods that consumers are willing to buy at various prices. *See* **supply.**

demand elasticity: (1) in general, the extent to which there is variability or difference in the demand for goods or services; (2) in a market, the degree to which the amount demanded is affected by unit changes in price.

dementia: loss of mental powers. *Contr. w.* **amentia.**

dementia praecox (prē′koks): (Lat., lit., "precocious dementia") a group of deteriorating mental disorders occurring mainly in persons still young; includes *hebephrenia, paranoia,* and *catatonia. See* **schizophrenia.**

dementia, traumatic: dementia sometimes following severe head injuries.

democracy, consumer: an economy in which consumers participate continuously in deciding what goods and services will be produced. *Syn.* **consumer-directed economy;** *ant.* **economy, consumption-directed.**

democratic control: *see* **control, democratic.**

democratic discipline: *see* **discipline, democratic.**

democratic group atmosphere: *see* **atmosphere, democratic group.**

democratic methodology: *see* **methodology, democratic.**

democratic morality: *see* **moral basis of public education.**

democratic supervision: *syn.* **supervision, cooperative.**

democratization of education: the extension of educational opportunity to all persons irrespective of class status or ethnic and racial identification; this would include broadening the scope of the curriculum and school program so that the needs of people of all types and ages would be met, including equality of educational opportunity regardless of variable regional financial ability.

demography: the science or study of the vital statistics of populations, concerned particularly with the rate of population change and the causes of such change; involves a study of moral, intellectual, physical, physiological, and economic factors affecting births, marriages, and mortality.

demonology: (1) the study of supernatural beings known as demons (from the Greek "daimones") who are thought in the Christian tradition to be less than divine and either good or bad, though usually bad; (2) the study of belief in such beings. *See* **anthropology** (2); *comp. w.* **angelology**.

demonstration: (1) the method or process of presenting or establishing facts; (2) the procedure of doing something in the presence of others either as a means of showing them how to do it themselves or in order to illustrate a principle, for example, showing a group of students how to set the tilting table on a circular saw, how to prepare a certain food product, or performing an experiment in front of a class to show the expansion of metals under heat; *see* **demonstration, laboratory;** (3) a term loosely applied to any planned or semi-planned assemblage of people, the primary purpose of which is to call attention to the groups' support for or disapproval of an idea, position, policy, program, law, institution, etc.; demonstrations, which may take many forms ranging from marching to lying down or from singing to silent vigil, have most recently been associated with student or minority groups pressing for social, political, or economic change; demonstrations are differentiated from riots and other forms of mob action such as looting and lynching by being less violent, less random, more consciously directed, and more socially constructive in intent; *see* **activism, student.**

demonstration center: *see* **center, demonstration.**

demonstration class: *see* **class, demonstration.**

demonstration clinic: *see* **clinic, demonstration.**

demonstration course: *see* **course, demonstration.**

demonstration, discovery: a method of science teaching designed to pose problem situations to which answers are not immediately apparent; an inquiry activity, the purpose of the demonstration being to have students discover the principles or concepts involved.

demonstration guidance project: *see* **project, demonstration guidance.**

demonstration, laboratory: (home ec.) a learning experience in which a manipulative process is demonstrated. *See* **demonstration** (2).

demonstration-lecture method: a method of teaching in which the instructor gives an oral presentation of subject matter while showing objects, actions, and occurrences to which the subject matter refers; for example, a physics instructor may illustrate a lecture on expansion by showing how heat expands an object.

demonstration lesson: *see* **lesson, demonstration.**

demonstration lesson, broadcast: *see* **lesson, broadcast demonstration.**

demonstration, logical: a term used in philosophy of education to emphasize a reasoned *demonstration*, as opposed to experimental or empirical proof or verification; refers more specifically to the logical proof of a proposition deductively; more technically, it means a direct, or positive, *demonstration*, in which the conclusion is the immediate sequence of reasoning from axiomatic or established premises.

demonstration method: a method of teaching that relies heavily upon showing the learner a model performance that he should match or surpass; the demonstration may be live, filmed, or electronically presented; provides for practice with real equipment or simulators and evaluates student performance in comparison with the demonstrated standard.

demonstration-performance method: a method of teaching a mental or physical skill in which the student learns by listening, observing, and practicing under supervision the skill as demonstrated by the instructor.

demonstration plot, agricultural: a plot of land controlled by the school which is used to demonstrate approved practices in producing and handling plants and animals; often used in the instructional program in vocational education in agriculture. *See* **laboratory, land.**

demonstration, result: (home ec.) a project carried on for a substantial period of time under the supervision of a professional worker to show the value of a recommended practice, during which time records are kept and comparisons made.

demonstration sale: an illustrative sale before a group of students in which the person acting the part of a salesperson attempts to illustrate the principles of salesmanship as applied to various typical selling situations.

demonstration school: (1) any school with the special purpose of being a model in exemplifying school practices for wider dissemination; (2) (teacher ed.) a campus or off-campus school that presents activities of learning, instruction, etc., planned for the purpose of illustrating methods, techniques, or experiments in school work, featuring such demonstrations rather than practice teaching; *see* **model school.**

demonstration stand: *see* **stand, demonstration.**

demonstration teaching: *see* **teaching, demonstration.**

demonstrative geometry: *see* **geometry, demonstrative.**

demotic writing: *see* **writing, demotic.**

demotion: a reduction in rank or salary or both, which results in a lowering of professional prestige.

demurrer: a plea or allegation by one of the parties to a court action, which, while it has the effect of admitting all the material facts properly pleaded by the opposing party, alleges or contends that the existence of the facts does not constitute grounds for action.

denasality: reduced nasal resonance in speech, especially in sounding consonants m and n and ng.

denominate number: *see* **number, denominate.**

denominate number fact: *see* **number fact, denominate.**

denominational college: *see* **college, denominational.**

denominational junior college: *see* **junior college, denominational.**

denominational school: *see* **church school.**

denominator, lowest common: the smallest number divisible without remainder by each of two or more denominators; in this example $\frac{5}{6} - \frac{3}{4}$, 12 would be the lowest common denominator; in another example $\frac{1}{2} + \frac{3}{8} + \frac{3}{4}$, 8 would be the lowest common denominator.

denotation: the aggregate or class of individuals or instances falling under a conception or named by a term; terms may be used to denote or symbolically point out any member or members of a class of entities which come under the term; thus, the denotation of "man" might be Shakespeare, Beethoven, or simply "that man," and using the term so to designate any member or members of the class Homo sapiens would be a denotative use of the term. *See* **connotation.**

density: (1) (population) the number of persons per square mile; (2) (photog.) the ability of photographic film to transmit light; (3) technically, the logarithm of the opacity, in general terms, the relative darkness of an image area.

density, fact: *see* **fact density.**

density formula: (1) a plan for allocating transportation funds to local school districts on the basis of the number of transported pupils per square mile or per mile of public road; (2) a procedure for calculating the number of individuals per unit for transported pupils. *See* **density of transported pupils.**

density of transported pupils: the number of transported pupils per square mile.

density, variable: a concept governing sampling of variables from a conceived total population of variables, such as the "personality sphere."

density, vocabulary: *see* **vocabulary density.**

dental age: *see* **age, dental.**

dental clinic: *see* **clinic, dental.**

dental college: *see* **college, dental.**

dental examination: *see* **examination, dental.**

dental hygienist: a dental worker who inspects and cleans teeth but does not treat or repair them.

dental report: *see* **report, dental.**

dental sound: a speech sound in the production of which air is expelled between the tongue tip and the upper teeth, as th in think or that.

dentiphone: a hearing aid based on bone conduction and designed to collect sound waves and convey them to the ear through the teeth.

denumerable set: *syn.* **set, countable.**

department: (1) an administrative subdivision of a school or college giving instruction in a branch of study, as the department of English or the department of surgery; (2) a noninstructional unit of a school or college, as the *department of buildings and grounds;* (3) sometimes loosely used to designate a major subdivision of a college or university, as the department of arts and sciences or the medical department.

department, academic: a division of an institution of higher education which is responsible for instruction in the theory and special knowledge of such subjects as literature, languages, science, English, and mathematics and in which emphasis is on "pure" knowledge as distinguished from technical and vocational courses or applied knowledge.

department, accounting: (1) the division of the school administration that is responsible for administering the accounts and other financial records; (2) the department of a college or secondary school that teaches courses in accounting and related subjects.

department, adult education: (1) an administrative unit in a school, university, college, or voluntary association having a program of educational services for adults; (2) an academic unit within a university, usually at the graduate level, organized to provide professional training for adult educators and to conduct research in adult education.

department, art: the part of a school organization that is responsible for the carrying on of art education.

department, attendance: the division of the public schools that is responsible for all activities involved in enforcing the state's compulsory school attendance law. (The term is displacing the term *bureau of compulsory education;* this represents an attempt to break with the tradition of "compelling" children to attend school.)

department, census: the division of the public school system that is responsible for making the school enumeration and maintaining the school census.

department chairman: a faculty member who, in addition to performing the usual duties of teaching in a department, has been designated to preside over staff meetings and to carry on certain administrative duties involved in managing the affairs of the department. (Often it is synonymous with *department head,* but the latter usually implies more authority over the determination of policy. In some institutions the department chairman is elected by the members of the department.)

department, child-study: an agency established in a school system for the purpose of collecting and interpreting data concerning individual pupils; the personnel of the agency consists of such specialists as psychologists, guidance experts, physicians, and nurses; usually found only in the larger school systems and in teacher-education institutions.

department, church school: one of the age-grade divisions of a religious education curriculum, namely, primary, junior, junior high, and senior high.

department, curriculum: that portion of the school system or personnel responsible for directing the development or improvement of the curriculum and the coordination of the curricular offerings within a school system.

department, education: an academic organization, usually found in liberal arts colleges but also in teachers colleges and universities, coordinate with departments of academic subjects and offering professional courses related to teaching, supervision, or administration. (Not to be confused with a *college of education* or a *school of education,* which are complete collegiate organizations controlling all or most of the phases of the curricula used to prepare teachers.)

department, extension: (1) an administrative unit of a school, college, or university in charge of extending the resources of the institution to adults; (2) a subordinate unit of an extension division.

department head: a faculty member who, in addition to doing some teaching in a department, has some responsibility for administering the affairs of the department such as recommending the new staff members, preparing the departmental portion of the daily schedule, assigning duties to the members of the department, preparing the department budget, and requisitioning supplies; in some schools also responsible for some supervision and for dealing with disciplinary cases; usually selected by the principal, the dean, or other officer acting as head of the institution, or appointed by the board of education, especially in large cities.

department, kindergarten-primary: (1) the division of an elementary school composed of the kindergarten and first three grades; (2) a division of an educational institution concerned with the preparation of teachers for kindergarten and the first three grades.

department, maintenance: a division of the school organization responsible for keeping the school property in repair. *See* **maintenance of the school plant.**

department meeting: a meeting of the teachers in a subject-matter field where the work is organized by departments, such as the department of English in a large high school or the department of art in a school system.

department, multiple-room: the homemaking department housed in two or more rooms, in each of which instruction is offered in one area of homemaking.

department, normal: (1) in the nineteenth century, the department or division of an academy or high school offering a program of studies for the preparation of teachers; (2) in the late nineteenth and twentieth centuries, the department of a *teacher education institution* offering courses in methods and principles of teaching, as distinguished from the academic departments; now infrequently used.

department of buildings and grounds: the organization of all employees whose duty it is to care for the physical plant of a school, college, or university; includes a superintendent or director, engineers, firemen, janitors, matrons, various kinds of tradesmen, watchmen, groundmen, other employees, and the supervisors of these groups of employees. (The larger organizations also provide architects and professional engineers.)

department of education, state: a collective term for the chief state school officer and his staff; sometimes includes one state board of education.

department, personnel: (1) a grouping of offices and agencies within an institution that deal with the advising and counseling of students, particularly with respect to personal and academic matters, and with a wide variety of other services that may include almost all services to students except actual classroom instruction; (2) the division of the school administration that is responsible for gathering, compiling, and maintaining records concerning the teaching and nonteaching personnel of a school system and for developing solutions to personnel problems; usually found only in very large school districts.

department, purchasing: the division of a school organization that has the responsibility of buying all needed materials.

department, recreation: a division of some unit of government, such as a city, county, or state, having responsibility for the promotion and control of public recreation.

department, reference: (1) the part of a library in which its reference books are kept for consultation; (2) the administrative unit in charge of the reference work of a library; *see* **reference work.**

department, school: *syn.* **department, school-libraries.**

department, school-libraries: (1) the administrative unit of a public library that supervises libraries in schools and/or has charge of the distribution of books or other reading matter to schools; *syn.* **school (or schools) department;** (2) the section of a board of education responsible for the activities of school libraries in a school system.

department, service: a department set up for the purpose of performing services to education or operating departments, for example, a printing plant, laundry, repair shop, etc.

department, subject-matter: *syn.* **department, academic.**

departmental conference: *see* **conference, departmental.**

departmental library: *see* **library, departmental.**

departmental major: *see* **major, departmental.**

departmental organization: *see* **organization, departmental.**

departmental plan: a plan of teaching under which each teacher teaches one subject or one group of closely related subjects.

departmental school: (1) a school in which the curricular offerings are divided into subject fields and each teacher is made responsible for giving instruction in a particular subject or combination of subjects, the pupils of each grade being taught by several teachers instead of by a single teacher; (2) a type of school organization once prominent in the New England states in which a vertical division was made, separating the school into a reading school and a writing school; pupils attended each department alternately, changing from one school to the other at the end of a half-day or day's session.

departmental study hall: *see* **study hall, departmental.**

departmental supervision: *see* **supervision, departmental.**

departmental supervisor: *see* **supervisor, departmental.**

departmentalization: an arrangement whereby each instructor teaches only one or two subjects in which he is a specialist; either the teacher moves from room to room to teach the various classes or the pupils shift from room to room during the successive periods of the school day.

dependence: (1) a state of leaning or reliance upon; (2) inability to care for one's own needs; (3) contingency; a state of being causally related to something else; (4) (arith.) the state or quality of being so related that what affects one affects all others; for example, a state of dependence exists between the numerator and denominator of a fraction with constant value, since a change in either necessitates a compensatory change in the other.

dependence, functional: (math.) a term used to emphasize the relationship of the dependent to the independent variable in a function. See **function** (3); **variable; variable, dependent.**

dependency case: a problem involving children who are not self-supporting.

dependent board of education: *see* **board of education, dependent.**

dependent child: *see* **child, dependent.**

dependent mentally retarded: *see* **mentally retarded, custodial.**

dependent variable: *see* **variable, dependent.**

dependents' school: a school located on or near a military base, consisting of grades 1-12 and run by the U.S. Department of Defense for the children of American military personnel stationed outside the United States; teachers are civilians recruited from schools within the United States; curricula, activities, and procedures are similar to those in American public schools.

depersonalization: loss of the feeling of unity of the personality.

deposit: (1) money placed with a banking or other institution or with a person, either as a general deposit subject to check or as a special deposit made for some specified purpose; (2) securities lodged with a banking or other institution or with a person for some particular purpose; (3) a sum deposited by contractors and others to accompany and guarantee their bids.

deposition: an affidavit; an oath; the written testimony of a witness given in the course of a judicial proceeding, in law or in equity, in response to interrogatories either oral or written, and where an opportunity is given for cross-examination.

depository bonds: *see* **bonds, depository.**

depository, film: *see* **film depository.**

depository library: *see* **library, depository.**

depository, school: a bank in which school funds are placed.

depot: a designated school bus stop for receiving or discharging pupils.

depraved, human nature as: the doctrine of some Protestant reformers that through original sin human nature was totally vitiated and hence, whatever proceeds from it is accounted sinful.

depreciation: loss in service life of fixed assets, attributable to wear and tear through use and lapse of time, obsolescence, inadequacy, or other physical or functional cause.

depreciation, building: the reduction of the value of a building due to wear and tear and obsolescence and for which provision must be made in the account of profit and loss before the actual present value can be determined. (Depreciation seldom enters into the accounting for public buildings; rather, they are carried at cost until abandoned.)

depreciation, bus: (1) the decrease in value of a bus as a result of age, miles of operation, or other factors; (2) a planned devaluation of the bus so that the investment in the vehicle will reach a zero value at approximately the time the bus has no further value or usefulness.

depreciation reserve: *see* **reserve, depreciation.**

depression: an emotional state characterized by dejection, unpleasant ruminations, or foreboding.

depression, anaclitic: type of depression found in infants separated from their mothers; in severe cases may produce marasmus and death. *See* **anaclisis.**

depression, reactive: a reaction to events (such as death) which would normally arouse profound depression with marked depression and retardation of mental and physical responses.

deprivation, cultural: lack of opportunity to partake of the experiences provided in the homes, schools, and communities of the modal culture; the term is now falling into disuse since it is considered to be inaccurate in view of the fact that all people have a culture. *See* **child, socially disadvantaged; deprivation, environmental.**

deprivation, environmental: inadequate development related to negative circumstances in the child's milieu; reflected in poor school adjustment.

deprivation, maternal: taking away or failing to provide the infant with the psychological mothering believed by some to be an essential prerequisite to normal development.

deprivation, sensory: (1) the reduction of input stimulation of a sense organ to an absolute minimum; (2) lack of stimulation and development of the various sensory modes, arising from a want of experience in *associative transfer* with the senses.

deprivation, stimulus: a loss of something that stirs one to action or effort.

deprived child, culturally: *see* **child, culturally deprived.**

deprived, human nature as: the Roman Catholic doctrine that through original sin the human intellect was darkened and the human will weakened.

depth discrimination: *see* **discrimination, depth.**

depth-essay questionnaire: *see* **questionnaire, depth-essay.**

depth interview: *see* **interview, depth.**

depth of field: the latitude or range within which a lens will keep an object in sharp focus at a given setting. *Syn.* **depth of focus.**

depth of focus: *syn.* **depth of field.**

depth perception: *see* **perception, depth.**

depth psychology: *see* **psychology, depth.**

deputy commissioner of education: an appointive official who carries the responsibilities of the commissioner of education during his absence and who otherwise serves as an assistant to the commissioner performing certain designated functions.

deputy superintendent: *see* **superintendent, deputy.**

derivation of a formula: a process of determining a symbolic representation of some rule or generalization.

derivative form: a word derived from a base or root word by the addition of a prefix, suffix, or both, such as *undemonstrative* from *demonstrate*.

derivative group: *syn.* **group, secondary.**

derived lesson: *see* **lesson, derived.**

derived measure: *see* **measure, derived.**

derived properties, doctrine of: the theory that the various phases or parts of an experience derive their properties or meanings from the total situation in which they emerge; a substitute for the concept of innate qualities or inherent characteristics.

derived score: *see* **score, derived.**

desatellization: in theory of personality development, the process by which the child who originally was a satellite (satellized) with his parents turns instead toward his peer group for identification, values, etc.

descending: (math.) passing through a range of values from higher to lower value.

descending letter: *see* **letter, descending.**

description, diary: *see* **diary description.**

description, job: *see* **job description.**

description, occupational: *see* **occupational description.**

description, specimen: *see* **specimen description.**

descriptive: referring to what is, to matters of fact, as distinct from *normative*, which has reference to ideals, standards, canons, norms, or necessary conditions to be met; a descriptive statement is in the indicative mood, a normative statement is in the optative or imperative mood.

descriptive count: a form of count used in handwriting instruction that is designed to make practice more interesting and that consists for the most part of oral descriptions of the movements or combinations of movements to be used in executing the forms, for example, *up, over, down, around, swing, stop, swing, over,* etc.

descriptive generalization: *see* **generalization, descriptive.**

descriptive geometry: *see* **geometry, descriptive.**

descriptive grammar: *see* **grammer, descriptive.**

descriptive hypothesis: *see* **hypothesis, descriptive.**

descriptive linguistics: *see* **linguistics, descriptive.**

descriptive method: (1) (res.) the general procedures employed in studies that have for their chief purpose the description of phenomena, in contrast to ascertaining what caused them or what their value and significance are (according to some, the term should be restricted to status studies, including simple surveys; according to others, the term is extended to include descriptions of change, as historical studies or growth studies); (2) an approach to the study of political science based on objective, factual, unbiased descriptions of governmental forms, functions, and processes; (3) (philos.) that aspect of inquiry directed toward noting the characteristics or facts in a situation without regard to their meaning, value, or use.

descriptive rating scale: *see* **rating scale, descriptive.**

descriptive record: *syn.* **record, anecdotal.**

descriptive report: *see* **report, descriptive.**

descriptive statistics: *see* **statistics, descriptive.**

descriptor: (libr. sci.) one of a limited set of subject terms (up to several hundred) used to characterize the documents in a particular kind of collection. *See* **uniterm; word, key.**

desegregation: any process of bringing nonwhite and white children into the same schools; involves biracial or multiracial classes and, in some cases, biracial or multiracial faculties and administration. *See* **integration, racial.**

desensitization: (1) therapeutic process by which traumatic experiences are reduced in intensity by repeated exposures of the individual to them either in reality or in fantasy; (2) (couns.) the lessening, by various methods and procedures, of sensitivity with respect to some personal defect, some social inferiority, etc.; (3) (spec. ed.) a type of adaptation-to-stress therapy used, for example, for beginning stutterers.

design: (1) *syn.* **design, experimental;** (2) a plan or layout—including decoration, if any—of the structural form of a work of art in whatever medium of expression, visual, musical, or literary; (3) a decorative pattern of lines, forms, colors, tones, and textures, with attention to proportion, harmony of parts, unity, and structure; (4) the structural form of a piece of art expression, regardless of the medium employed; *syn.* **composition** (2); (5) a visualized rendering of a concept in the graphic or glyphic arts; *see* **art elements; art structure; composition; design principles.**

design, applied: a pattern used to decorate an object, as differentiated from the structural planning of the object itself. (For example, a piece of pottery may be embellished by the application of ornament through painting, incising, or modeling.) *See* **art, decorative; decoration, applied.**

design, complete factorial: a factorial design in which each treatment is studied in all possible combinations with the other treatments; hence a design which is completely counterbalanced with reference to treatment effects.

design, costume: *see* **art, costume.**

design, counterbalanced: an experimental scheme involving a rotation of treatments; often used to neutralize the effect of sequence or order of presentation in situations in which the same group is subjected to more than one treatment, or to neutralize the effect of using different forms of the same test. *Syn.* **rotation technique;** *see* **design, factorial.**

design, cross-over: a modification of a Latin square research design in which each condition appears an equal number of times in each order of presentation, but in which the conditions of the experiment are otherwise assigned in a random manner. *See* **square, Latin.**

design, curriculum: *see* **curriculum design.**

design, dress: designing of garments; a course in home economics so designated may include, in addition to *sketching,* one or more of the following design methods: *flat-pattern design, draping,* and/or *drafting. See* **art, costume.**

design, emotional: (art ed.) design that is stimulated through the inclusion of strong experiences of the self; also, more or less abstract designs in materials inviting free use of forms, where the individual is not restricted to rigid patterns and where a connection is easily established between kinesthetic experiences (arm movements used in producing shapes) and other body sensations.

design experience: *see* **experience, design.**

design, experimental: the plan according to which experimental groups are selected and experimental treatments are administered and their effect is measured, the adequacy of the design depending, in general, on the extent to which it provides for (*a*) control (experimental and/or statistical) of important extraneous factors, the means of control being such that due allowance may be made for their effect in estimating the experimental error; (*b*) randomization (with reference to the experimental treatments) of the effects of uncontrolled factors, such that an error estimate may be secured in which due allowance is made for these randomized factors; and (*c*) computation of an unbiased estimate of experimental error and/or the application of a valid test of the statistical significance of the findings.

design, factorial: (1) the plan of the experiment that permits the simultaneous evaluation of more than one experimental factor, as contrasted with the single variable design, for example, a design that will permit the experimenter to study in the same experiment the effects of both size and style of type on reading rate; (2) the plan for a factor analytic study.

design, flat-pattern: (home ed.) a method of design by which a basic pattern for a garment is cut, slashed, and altered to make a new design.

design, functional: design in which primary consideration is given the use to which an article will be put.

design, incomplete block: a research design in which not all possible treatments or conditions are included within each replication; may be employed in certain situations where an overall general effect is to be measured, rather than the individual effect of each of the possible treatments or conditions.

design, incomplete factorial: a factorial design that omits some of the possible treatment combinations.

design, industrial: the study of industrial products with special consideration being given to (*a*) the aesthetic and appropriate use of industrial materials and processes, and (*b*) their value to society; learning activities involve the development of skills and creative abilities in the use of media for conveying ideas graphically.

design, interior: *see* **interior design.**

design principles: a number of laws, more or less universally observed and utilized, whether consciously or unconsciously, as compositional factors of expression in all the arts, for example, the principles of repetition, rhythm, balance, proportion, emphasis, etc.

design, random replication: an experimental design involving a repetition of the same basic experiment with independent random samples of subjects.

design, randomized block: a research design in which there are two or more replications, with each replication containing a complete set of all treatments or conditions under study, the treatments or conditions usually being systematically arranged within each replication.

design, randomized groups: a plan for an experiment in which the subjects are classified with reference to a control variable into a number of relatively homogeneous groups, each of which is further divided into proportional subgroups, randomly assigned, one to each of the experimental treatments; thus, the entire experiment consists of a number of similar experiments, each of which is performed with a group more homogeneous than the whole.

design, simple randomized: an experimental design in which the subjects or basic sampling units comprising each treatment group are selected at random from the same parent population and the treatments are assigned at random to the treatment group.

design, split-plot: a type of incomplete-block research design. *See* **design, incomplete block.**

design, stage: a phase of theater art pertaining to the designing of curtains, scenery, properties, costumes, lighting effects, and stage sets in general. *See* **art, theater.**

design, systems: *see* **systems design.**

design, ungrouped randomized: a research design in which individuals for two or more groups are selected randomly from the same population and each case or item is subjected individually to one of the treatments or conditions under study.

designer, systems: *see* **systems designer.**

designs, systematic: experimental designs in which observations are taken according to some fixed pattern other than a randomized pattern, for example, a Latin or Graeco-Latin square organization.

desirability, social: *see* **social desirability.**

desirable education and training pattern: *see* **education and training pattern, desirable.**

desire: a conscious wish to achieve some goal whether by approach or by avoidance. *See* **appetite; aversion.**

desired learning outcome: *see* **outcome, desired learning.**

desk: a piece of classroom furniture, on legs or a pedestal, having a flat or sloping surface on which books are placed for reading or on which writing, construction, and other activities are performed.

despondency: an emotional state of sadness and discouragement.

detached study: *see* **study, detached.**

detachment, Air Force Reserve Officers' Training Corps: *see* **Air Force Reserve Officers' Training Corps detachment.**

detachment, rule of: *see* **inference, rules of.**

detention: (1) the act of confining or detaining a pupil after school in the detention hall or room for a limited period of time daily and for a specified number of days; (2) the action of a juvenile court in keeping a child in a detention home, pending court action, on a 24-hour-a-day basis.

detention hall: (1) *syn.* **detention home;** (2) a classroom in which pupils are detained for limited periods of time after school.

detention home: a building, made as homelike as possible, that houses children who are waiting for a hearing before the juvenile court; a practice in juvenile court procedures that avoids the necessity of placing children in city or county prisons.

detention period: *see* **period, detention.**

deterioration index: *see* **index, deterioration.**

deterioration test: *see* **test, deterioration.**

determinable fee: *syn.* **fee, qualified.**

determinant: (Δ) a polynomial function that is composed of the sum of certain types of products of specific quantities and that may be represented symbolically by a square array of these quantities; this square array is frequently referred to as the determinant as well as the polynomial function; thus,

$$\begin{vmatrix} a_1b_1c_1 \\ a_2b_2c_2 \\ a_3b_3c_3 \end{vmatrix} \text{ is the square array}$$

which represents the polynomial function $a_1b_2c_3 + a_2b_3c_1 + a_3b_1c_2 - a_3b_2c_1 - a_1b_3c_2 - a_2b_1c_3$; either may be called the determinant of the nine quantities given. *See* **matrix.**

determinate: (1) having well-defined limits; (2) having values that can be found through appropriate calculations.

determinate evolution: *see* **evolution, determinate.**

determinateness: the state of being fixed through the operation of some constant cause or causes.

determination, coefficient of: *see* **coefficient of determination.**

determination, index of: *see* **index of determination.**

determination of curriculum, sociological: *see* **curriculum, sociological determination of.**

determined action, doctrine of: (gestalt) the view that the part of any integrated experience, behavior pattern, or phenomenon is conditioned or regulated by the experience or phenomenon as a whole.

determining set: a mental set involving conscious or implied goals.

determinism: the doctrine that an event is completely explicable in terms of its antecedents; applied to human actions it holds that, given complete knowledge of conditions, one would also have complete knowledge of precisely how a person will, and indeed must, act. *See* **causality; cause-effect relationship.**

determinism, cultural: (1) the theory that "culture comes from culture"; viewing culture as a closed system, it excludes purely biological, physiological, and psychological factors as causes of human behavior; (2) the process by which cultural environment fixes, limits, or shapes individual potentiality.

determinism, environmental: a theory or working principle that human behavior is determined almost exclusively by factors of the physical and social environment; it would relegate to extremely minimal importance such influences as hereditary factors, geographic influences, or individual motivations.

determinism, psychic: the psychoanalytic theory that acts are motivated by the unconscious.

determinism, psychological: the theory that mental abilities are completely innate and not affected by environmental influences.

detour problem: *see* **problem, detour.**

Detroit plan: a plan of grouping in which pupils are placed in one of three groups on the basis of intelligence test results. *See* **grouping, tripartite.**

deus ex machina (dā'ōōs eks mä'ki·nə): (Lat., lit., "a god from a machine") in literary analysis, any person or thing artificially introduced, especially into fiction, to solve a plot or difficulty; such intervention is frequently supernatural, as in ancient Greek drama, where, in the Greek language, the phrase originated.

deuterolearning: *syn.* **learning to learn.**

developing country: *see* **country, developing.**

development: (1) growth or change in structure, function, or organization, constituting an advance in size, differentiation, complexity, integration, capacity, efficiency, or degree of maturity; a broad term inclusive of but not synonymous with *maturation;* may include lasting changes due to lengthy or extended learning, whether deliberate or incidental; loosely used as synonymous with *growth,* but more often and correctly restricted to sequences involving qualitative changes or changes in quantitative relations among constituent elements or factors, whether with or without merely incremental growth; to be distinguished from most types of *learning* by the comparative durability or permanence of the developmental outcome and by the *gradualism* in genesis of the factors basic to it; (2) (photog.) the process by which the invisible latent image on a sensitized surface formed by the action of light is transformed into a visible image; (3) (scientific method) an extension of basic or applied research through which laboratory findings are reduced to practice; *see* **research and development;** (4) (higher ed.) the title given an office, an officer, and the activity of an officer of a higher education institution who is concerned with the raising of funds and the institutional planning and public relations activities related to the description of needs for funds to potential donors; in some respects a euphemism for fund raising.

development, affect: *see* **affect development.**

development, anal stage of: *see* **stage of development, anal.**

development, anatomical: normal change in structure of the developing human organism; promotes the growth process.

development, arrested: incomplete growth resulting from a check or complete stop at some point in the course of the development of an individual during his life cycle, due to either intrinsic or extrinsic factors.

development, autogenous (â·toj′ə·nəs): development determined primarily by native (maturational) factors but assisted to some extent by self-initiated practice. *See* **maturation.**

development center: a school in which promising ideas or procedures are tested before they are recommended for general use. (The term is used principally in agricultural education.)

development, child: interdisciplinary approach to the study of children, drawing upon such sciences as biology, physiology, embryology, pediatrics, sociology, psychiatry, anthropology, and psychology; emphasis is placed on the importance of understanding children through study of their mental, emotional, social, and physical growth; particular emphasis is laid on the appraisal of the impacts on the growing personality of home, school, and community.

development class: *see* **class, development.**

development, cognitive: according to Piaget, development in the child's thought process through his adaptation to the environment and assimilation of information.

development, community: *see* **community development.**

development, concrete operations stage of: *see* **stage of development, concrete operations.**

development, creative: the ontological process of a person's capacity to act, invent, or produce expressive forms; growth of capacity to engage in imaginative thought.

development, desatellization stage of: *see* **desatellization.**

development, differentiation in: *see* **differentiation in development.**

development, dysplastic (dis·plas′tik): *see* **dysplasia.**

development, educational: changes in the ability to deal adequately with situations as a result of self-direction or direction by others.

development, emotional: the process of psychic evolution that in the mature individual has progressed from infantile dependence to the capacity for assuming adult responsibility and forming adult love relationships.

development, formal operations stage of: *see* **stage of development, formal operations.**

development, group: *see* **group development.**

development, harmonious: the concept of a balanced way of life, such as the "fine proportionativeness" found in the writings of the ancients; the theory that this should be the aim of the educated man is sometimes expressed as "nothing too much" (Delphic oracle), the "golden mean" (Aristotle, Horace), or as "a sense of order and decorum and measure in words and deeds" (Cicero); the concept is found also in Matthew Arnold and Irving Babbitt. *See* **humanism, literary.**

development, hierarchy of: *see* **hierarchy of development.**

development, integration of: *see* **integration of development.**

development, language: the evolution, whether in the race or in the individual, of communication by means of vocal or written symbols.

development, level of: (1) strictly, a stage, region, or point in a developmental sequence or hierarchy of development; sometimes more loosely or broadly used, as in reference to the level of development reached by a child's emotional responses, which are not generally considered to follow any closely fixed developmental sequence; (2) the phylogenetic stage to which a given stage, region, or point of development most closely corresponds.

development, mental: (1) the progressive growth and organization of the mental functions and psychological behavior of the individual, from the prenatal stage to maturity; (2) the stage reached in the process at the moment under consideration. *Dist. f.* **evolution, mental;** *contr. w.* **mental decay.**

development method: *syn.* **problem method** (1).

development, moral: the process of individual experience and growth by which the capacity to distinguish between standards of right and wrong is gradually achieved and becomes progressively influential in the individual's social behavior.

development, motor: the sequences of maturation in postural, locomotor, and manipulative responses; used during the first two years of life as one of the bases of intelligence rating.

development, multidimensional: complex growth or development, in which changes take place in more than one respect or direction, at more than a single rate, etc.

development norm: *see* **norm, development.**

development of perception: *see* **perception, development of.**

development, omnipotence stage of: *see* **stage of development, omnipotence.**

development, oral stage of: *see* **stage of development, oral.**

development, organismic concept of: *see* **organismic concept of development.**

development, percent of average: a device sometimes used for expressing level of mental development in relation to chronological age; secured by dividing the mental age stated in mental growth units by the chronological age stated in similar units and multiplying by 100; assumed to compensate for progressive reduction in amount of mental growth per year or other time unit as the individual develops from birth to maturity and to furnish a quotient result similar to, but more reliable than, the intelligence quotient. *See* **quotient, intelligence; unit, mental growth.**

development, perceptual: the continuing organizing process which is an intermediate stage between sensation and response.

development, personality: the changes in structure and form of the personality that occur as an individual makes the transition from birth to maturity; these personality changes develop as the individual adjusts to inner demands and social impacts.

development, physical: the change in size, shape, function, etc., of structures of the body, for example, the progressive calcification of the bones, changes in size of face, shape of chest, etc., or more efficient functioning due to physical training.

development, plasticity of: *see* **plasticity of development.**

development, preoperational stage of: *see* **preoperational period.**

development, program: *see* **program planning.**

development program, adult: *see* **program, adult development.**

development program, educational: *see* **program, educational development.**

development program, resource: *see* **program, resource development.**

development program, staff: *see* **program, staff development.**

development, psychology of: *see* **psychology of development.**

development, rate of: (audiovis. ed.) speed or tempo with which a given amount of factual information is presented.

development, resatellization stage of: *see* **resatellization.**

development, satellization stage of: *see* **satellization.**

development, social: (1) the pattern of change through the years exhibited by the individual as a result of his interaction with such forces as people, social institutions, social customs, and social organizations; (2) the entire series of progressive changes from birth to death in social behavior, feelings, attitudes, values, etc., that are normal for the individuals of a species; (3) the state at any moment of an individual's social or socially significant reactions, evaluated in accordance with what is regarded as normal for an individual of that age in that culture; (4) the growth of the culture of the group in the direction of the more complete satisfaction of the needs of its members.

development, somatic: growth of body substance as distinguished from growth of mind.

development, specificity of: *see* **specificity of development.**

development, symbolic: as used in early childhood education, cognitive growth in concept formation, verbal language, and visual language (reading).

development, vocabulary: the extension of word meanings.

development, vocational: (1) the individual process of proceeding along a continuum from earliest vocational fantasies toward a final *vocational choice;* (2) a general term pertaining to the overall objective of a work-study program for the mentally retarded.

developmental: pertaining to, or characteristic of, the process of development; a general term applied to many types of age, growth, or maturation, such as mental, anatomical, physiological, educational, or social.

developmental activities: *see* **activities, developmental.**

developmental approach: a method of teaching in which the learner is led to the proper conclusion by means of a step-by-step thinking process.

developmental biology: *see* **biology, developmental.**

developmental case history: *see* **case history.**

developmental direction, law of: the doctrine that growth of the body proceeds in the cephalocaudal direction (from the head downward) and proximodistally (from the mid-line outward) in the extremities. (This law also applies to the assumption of postural and motor control.)

developmental exercise: *see* **exercise, developmental.**

developmental factors in learning: *see* **learning, developmental factors in.**

developmental growth: *see* **growth, developmental.**

developmental guidance: *see* **guidance, developmental.**

developmental lesson: *see* **lesson, developmental.**

developmental model: *see* **model, developmental.**

developmental pattern: *see* **pattern, developmental.**

developmental period: *see* **period, developmental.**

developmental physical education: *see* **physical education, developmental.**

developmental psycholinguistics: *see* **psycholinguistics, developmental.**

developmental psychology: *see* **psychology, developmental.**

developmental quotient: *see* **quotient, developmental.**

developmental reading: *see* **reading, developmental.**

developmental reading disability: *see* **reading disability, developmental.**

developmental reading period: *see* **period, developmental reading.**

developmental scale: *see* **scale, developmental.**

developmental sequence: (1) the more or less regular order of change characterizing the development of a given structure, function, capacity, or skill; (2) the anatomical, physiological, and psychological steps or stages included within a developmental process; roughly synonymous with *genetic sequence;* (3) the organization of activities and materials of instruction in relation to the learners' perceptual backgrounds.

developmental stage, dawning-realism: (art ed.) (1) the period in the child's creative development characterized by his discovery of the meaning of social independence (from adults), that he is more powerful in the group than alone, usually between 9 and 11 years of age; (2) the period when the child becomes aware of differences between boys and girls and as a result characterizes his figures in his drawings as girls and boys, thus giving them an apparent realistic character indicative of a "dawning realism" in his development. *See* **color, subjective stage of.**

developmental stage, gang-age: *see* **developmental stage, dawning-realism** (1).

developmental stage, period-of-decision: (art ed.) the period of creative development in general referred to as *adolescence,* in which the individual loses confidence in his unconscious, childish creative approaches; usually characterized by an increased critical awareness toward the final product.

developmental stage, preschematic: (art ed.) the stage in the creative development of the child in which he searches for a relationship between his representation and the thing represented, usually between 4 and 7 years of age; the kind of relationship is highly individualized and depends on the active knowledge which the child has of things and his emotional relationship to them; for example, "My father has a head and two big legs; my drawing has a head and two big legs"; therefore, "My drawing is Daddy."

developmental stage, pseudorealistic: (art ed.) the period in the creative development of children of about 11 to 13 years in which they become increasingly aware of their final products, yet in their reactions are still childish, that is, uncritical; usually characterized by an increased ability to reason.

developmental stage, schematic: (art ed.) the period in which a child arrives at definite concepts of man and his environment, generally occurring between 7 and 9 years of age; these concepts, or *schemas,* obtain general validity through repetition; the child wants to assure himself of his concepts and therefore repeats them unless significant experiences incite changes or deviations. *See* **color, objective stage of; schema** (2).

developmental stage, scribbling: (art ed.) the period in the child's creative development in which he documents his desire for motor activity by different kinds of linear motions on the paper, usually between 2 and 4 years of age. *See* **scribbling, circular; scribbling, longitudinal; scribbling, naming of; scribbling, uncontrolled.**

developmental stages in child art: *see* **art, developmental stages in child.**

developmental status: *see* **status, developmental.**

developmental task: *see* **task, developmental.**

developmental theory, family: *see* **family developmental theory.**

Devereaux readability formula: *see* **readability formula, Devereaux.**

deviancy: (1) the state of being deviate; *see* **deviate** (1); (2) behavior or physical appearance which differs to a degree from what is generally considered normal; restricted to an undesirable trait or constellation of traits.

deviate: (1) a person who varies markedly from the norm, whether physically, mentally, socially, or emotionally; (2) that which differs from some reference point, usually the mean, of a series; (3) the amount by which a value differs from some reference point, usually the mean, of a series; *syn.* **deviate score; deviation** (2).

deviate education: instruction provided to meet the needs of individuals who vary markedly from the norm in respect to mental abilities, physical condition, or emotional status.

deviate score: *syn.* **deviate** (3).

deviation: (1) the spread or *variability* of the measures of a distribution with reference to a measure of central tendency such as the mean or median; usually expressed by such a measure of *variability* as the quartile deviation or standard deviation; (2) as applied to a single measure, the distance of the score from a selected reference point on the scale; roughly synonymous with *variability*.

deviation about the median, root-mean square: the square root of the arithmetic mean of the squares of the deviations of values from their median; sometimes incorrectly called *standard deviation about the median*.

deviation, absolute: the absolute value of the difference between an observation or score and any measure, such as the arithmetic mean, used as a point of origin or reference. *Syn.* **numerical deviation;** *see* **value, absolute.**

deviation, average (AD): a measure expressing the average amount by which the individual items in a distribution deviate from a measure of central tendency, such as the mean or median; obtained by adding the absolute deviations of items from a measure of central tendency and dividing the sum by the number of items; equals 0.7979σ in a normal distribution. *Syn.* **average departure; average variation; mean absolute error; mean deviation; mean error; mean variation.**

deviation, concomitant: *syn.* **deviation, concurrent.**

deviation, concurrent: a deviation in the same direction as the corresponding deviation for the same individual in the other variable. *Syn.* **concomitant deviation.**

deviation, error: *syn.* **error, absolute** (2).

deviation from schema: *see* **schema, deviation from.**

deviation intelligence quotient: *see* **quotient, deviation intelligence.**

deviation, mean (MD): *syn.* **deviation, average.**

deviation, mean square: *see* **variance.**

deviation, median (MdD): the median of the absolute values of the deviations about some measure of central tendency; sometimes confused with probable error; in a normal distribution, the median deviation is equal to 0.6745σ, to the probable error, and to the quartile deviation. *Syn.* **median error;** *dist. f.* **deviation, average.**

deviation, numerical: *syn.* **deviation, absolute.**

deviation, probable: *syn.* **error, probable.**

deviation, product: a term used in the calculation of the product-moment correlation coefficient, referring to the product of the deviations of each pair of measures from their respective means. *See* **coefficient of correlation, Pearson product moment.**

deviation, quartile (Q): half the interquartile range, that is, half the distance from the third quartile (75th percentile) to the first quartile (25th percentile); equal to the probable error in a normal distribution. *Syn.* **quartile measure of dispersion; semi-interquartile range.**

deviation, root-mean-square: the square root of the arithmetic mean of the squares of the deviations about any origin; may be expressed by the formula $\sqrt{\Sigma d^2/N}$, where d is the deviation of each measure from the origin selected; this value is a minimum when taken about the mean (in which case it is the standard deviation). *Syn.* **root-mean-square error.**

deviation score: *see* **score, deviation.**

deviation, standard (σ, s, or SD): a widely used measure of variability, consisting of the square root of the mean of the squared deviations of scores from the mean of the distribution; may be expressed by the formula $\sigma = \sqrt{\Sigma x^2/N}$, where Σx^2 is the sum of the squared deviations of each score from the mean and N is the number of scores; in a normal distribution, if a distance equal to the standard deviation is laid off on each side of the mean, 68.26 percent of the observations will be included. *Syn.* **index of variability; mean discrepancy.**

deviation, step: the deviation of the observations in a series from an arbitrary origin measured in terms of the class interval used; thus a value in the second class interval above the arbitrary origin would have a step deviation of $+2$; one falling in the ninth class interval below the arbitrary origin would have a step deviation of -9, etc.

device, arithmetic-logic: *see* **arithmetic-logic device.**

device, autoinstructional: *see* **autoinstructional device.**

device, flash: *see* **flash device.**

device, input: *see* **input device.**

device, magnetic-tape input output: *see* **input output device, magnetic-tape.**

device, master: *see* **master device.**

device, mnemonic: *see* **mnemonic device.**

device, motivating: *see* **motivating device.**

device, Pressey: *see* **Pressey device.**

device, response: *see* **response device.**

device, stimulus: *see* **stimulus device.**

device, stimulus-response: *see* **stimulus-response device.**

device, storage: *see* **storage device.**

device, teaching: *see* **teaching device.**

devotional reading: *see* **reading, devotional.**

Dewey decimal classification: *syn.* **classification, decimal.**

dexterities, manual: capacities of muscular coordination.

dexterity test: *see* **test, dexterity.**

dextral: pertaining to the right side of the body.

dextral writing: *see* **writing, dextral.**

dextrality: (1) specifically, a preference for the right hand or side in the performance of a motor act; (2) loosely, a generic term for *handedness.*

dextrosinistral: left-handed by natural preference, but having the right hand trained for skilled operations such as writing.

diachronic linguistics: *see* **linguistics, diachronic.**

diacritical mark: a special symbol, usually placed above a letter to indicate the pronunciation, for example, ¨, ˜, ^, ˌ, ˎ, etc.

diadochokinesia (dī·ad·ə·kō·ki·nē′si·ə): the normal ability to perform rapid alternating movements such as pronation and supination of the hand. *See* **adiadochokinesis.**

diagnosis: (1) the procedure by which the nature of a disorder, whether physical, mental, or social, is determined by discriminating study of the history of the disorder and of the symptoms present; (2) in guidance, the analyzing of performance of clients and the development of tests which elicit maximum information, also, the results obtained by these activities; (3) (curric.) the process of determining the existing capabilities of a student by analyzing his performance of a hierarchy of essential tasks in a specific subject, such as mathematics or music, with the intent of facilitating his learning by assigning appropriate remedial or advanced learning tasks.

diagnosis, differential: (1) search for the areas of a person's relative strengths and/or weaknesses in ability, personality, and achievement through the use of tests and other means of obtaining information about an individual; (2) the delineation of particular dynamic patterns showing how one child differs from another; (3) in medical practice, the process of determining a significant factor which is found in only one of two or more seemingly similar conditions, thus distinguishing between them; extended by analogy from its medical use to other fields such as guidance.

diagnosis, educational: determination of the nature of learning difficulties and deficiencies.

diagnosis, instruments of: (couns.) standardized procedures for the measurement of abilities, achievements, interests, and personality traits. *See* **analytical tools.**

diagnosis, play: (phys. ed.) the result of analyzing learning difficulties and therefore giving clear, explicit directions to the student to be followed on his own, enabling him to acquire a new pattern of movement.

diagnosis, psychological: a diagnostic procedure for determining the patient's intellectual capacity, motivations, conflicts, ego defenses, environmental and self-evaluations, interests and aptitudes, and general personality organization. *See* **diagnosis, differential.**

diagnosis, reading: the analysis of reading behavior for the purpose of identifying the causes of reading retardation or disability. *See* **analysis, reading.**

diagnosis, techniques of: methods of interpreting data provided by diagnostic instruments and interviews to arrive at diagnostic and prognostic conclusions about a student being counseled.

diagnosogenic: having an origin in diagnosis; of or pertaining to symptoms or behavior characteristics that constitute a person's reactions to the experience of being diagnosed; for example, stuttering is sometimes regarded as diagnosogenic in the sense that certain stuttering symptoms may constitute the person's reactions of anxiety and tension to the experience of being labeled a stutterer.

diagnostic category: (couns.) one of various categories or groupings of symptoms that are believed to be useful as a general framework for examining the problems of students, so that specific therapies may be applied; also called *diagnostic constructs.*

diagnostic center, juvenile: *see* **center, juvenile diagnostic.**

diagnostic chart: *see* **chart, diagnostic.**

diagnostic checklist: *see* **checklist, diagnostic.**

diagnostic construct: *syn.* **diagnostic category.**

diagnostic guidance technique: the use of diagnostic tests and of analysis of cumulative and biographical records in discovering special abilities, difficulties, interests, and problems, thereby gaining the benefits of individual appraisal through interviewing before attempting to guide the individual.

diagnostic profile: *see* **profile, diagnostic.**

diagnostic reading test: *see* **test, diagnostic reading.**

diagnostic routine: *see* **routine, diagnostic.**

diagnostic scale: *see* **scale, diagnostic.**

diagnostic sensitivity: *see* **sensitivity, diagnostic.**

diagnostic study: *see* **study, diagnostic.**

diagnostic teaching: *see* **teaching, diagnostic.**

diagnostic test: *see* **test, diagnostic.**

diagonal, major: (1) the diagonal (of a table of intercorrelation coefficients) about which the doubly recorded coefficients are symmetrical; diagonal cells may contain 1.00's, reliability coefficients, communalities, other values, or blanks; *syn.* **diagonal, principal;** (2) the diagonal running from the upper left corner to the lower right corner of a determinant; *syn.* **diagonal, principal;** (3) the diagonal of a scatter diagram running from the corner containing low values of both variables to the corner containing high values in both variables.

diagonal matrix: *see* **matrix, diagonal.**

diagonal method of factorization: *see* **factorization, diagonal method of.**

diagonal, principal: (of a matrix) the diagonal line of entries from upper left to lower right; in a correlation matrix, these entries would correspond to self-correlations (for example, r_{ii}, r_{jj}, r_{kk}) and other entries would be symmetric about the principal diagonal since $r_{jk} = r_{kj}$, etc. *Syn.* **diagonal, major** (1) and (2).

diagonal row frequency: *see* **frequency, diagonal row.**

diagonal seating plan: *see* **seating plan, diagonal.**

diagonal square: *see* **square, diagonal.**

diagram: a graphic device for illustrating a statement and/or for elaborating upon a demonstration.

diagram, area: *syn.* **graph, area.**

diagram, bar: *syn.* **graph, bar.**

diagram, block: *see* **block diagram.**

diagram, circle: *syn.* **graph, circle.**

diagram, column: any representation or comparison of statistical data by means of a series of bars or rectangles, for example, a histogram or bar graph. *Syn.* **column graph.**

diagram, computing: any graphic device for facilitating numerical computations; for example, an abac or a nomograph. *Syn.* **computing chart.**

diagram, dot: (1) *syn.* **map, dot;** (2) *syn.* **diagram, scatter.**

diagram, flow: in programming, a chart setting forth the particular sequence of operations to be done in a computer to handle a particular application. *Comp. w.* **chart, flow.**

diagram, form flow: a graphic summary of the movements of each copy of a form from its origin to its final disposition.

diagram, frequency: *syn.* **graph, frequency.**

diagram, hundred percent bar: *see* **graph, hundred percent bar.**

diagram, logical: *syn.* **chart, flow.**

diagram, map: *syn.* **graph, map.**

diagram, percentage pie: *syn.* **graph, circle.**

diagram, PERT: *see* **program evaluation and review technique.**

diagram, scatter: a double-entry table in which a tally mark, dot, or other symbol is centered for each observation at the intersection of the column and row corresponding to the X and Y scores of that observation; frequently used for determining the coefficient of correlation between two variables, as well as for inspection of data, curve fitting, etc. (sometimes applied to a correlation table after the entries have been tallied). *Syn.* **correlation chart; correlation graph; correlation table; dot diagram; scattergram; scatterplot; scatterpoint.**

diagram, three-dimensional: a representation of positional or operational relationships in which parts and/or objects are represented by conventionalized symbols depicting height, width, and depth.

diagram, vector: a diagram involving directed line segments such as those representing forces or velocities.

diagram, Venn: (math.) a diagram used to represent subset relations, with a rectangular region representing the *universal set* and including circular regions in the interior representing subsets of the universal set; to show two disjoint subsets, for example, the circles could be made nonoverlapping; useful in solving problems relating to sets.

diagramming: (lang.) showing the structure of sentences by means of a visually presented diagram.

dial-a-tape system: an arrangement whereby special telephone numbers may be dialed for tape-recorded information by students who have forgotten the homework assignment or have difficulty preparing it and by parents interested in hearing school news.

dial-access information retrieval system: *see* **information retrieval system, dial-access.**

dial access laboratory: *see* **laboratory, dial access.**

dialect: a form of a language, differing from the most generally accepted form in peculiarities of inflection, vocabulary, pronunciation, vowel quality, idiom, etc., and characteristic of a definite locality, social class, nationality, extraction, etc.

dialect, foreign: stress, intonation, phrasing, rhythm, and sound production characteristic of some language foreign to the one being spoken, as in the use of the distinctive phonetic and inflectional characteristics of German in the speaking of English.

dialect, nonstandard: a dialect which differs from the language customarily used by educated speakers in positions of leadership in a given speech area. *See* **English, standard.**

dialect, regional: speech characteristic of a given limited geographical area and differing from the standard or more general form in matters of pronunciation, intonation, idiom, etc. *See* **dialect.**

dialectic: (1) in general, the logic of argument, such as the method of question and answer of Socrates; (2) more technically, discourse in which the mutually exclusive ideas contained in opposed concepts are resolved in a higher conceptual synthesis; for example, the process of development said to be characteristic of the universal spirit (Hegel), of the history of societies (Marx), of the dialectics of nature (Engels), and of the science of first principles (Plato); *see* **dialectic, Hegelian; materialism, dialectical.**

dialectic, Hegelian: the ontological and cosmological theory of G. W. F. Hegel (1770-1831) that reality universally exhibits a structure of fact, possibility, and value in a harmonious system in which movement takes place through the emergence of a condition (antithesis) contrary in part to its source (thesis), to be replaced in turn by a condition (synthesis) which both blends and transcends the preceding two and is in turn replaced by a new antithesis; also, the method of logical analysis that resolves differences by finding the higher category that blends and transcends the two less inclusive, conflicting categories.

dialectic method: (1) a method of learning or teaching in which the dynamic interaction of the participants in discussion leads to a clarification of ambiguities and misunderstandings arising from a subject matter or experience; (2) a method of philosophizing or thinking in which the mutually exclusive ideas contained in opposed concepts are resolved in a higher conceptual synthesis.

dialectical materialism: *see* **materialism, dialectical.**

dialectical process: a dialogue between two persons; as applied to counseling, a procedure in which the counselor participates to the same degree as the counselee.

dialectical psychology: *syn.* **psychology, Marxian.**

dialectology: the study of speech peculiar to certain localities.

dialogue: (1) (for. lang. instr.) an artificially constructed model conversation employing and presenting familiar or new linguistic structures and vocabulary; (2) (audiolingual instr.) the fundamental pedagogic element in each unit, which the student is required to memorize to the point of total recall; (3) (relig. ed.) a conversation between individuals or groups of different religious persuasions, carried on especially for the purpose of mutual instruction and understanding.

dialogues, living room: a semiofficial program for small group discussion within the intimate setting of each other's homes among Catholics, Protestants, Anglicans, and Orthodox to explore the implications of their respective faiths in the cause of Christian understanding and unity.

dianoetic: a relationship in knowing in which the human mind is thought of as penetrating to and participating in the essence of the thing known.

diaphragm: (1) the partition of muscle and membrane that separates the chest cavity from that of the abdomen, the action of which is involved in breathing; (2) a dividing or covering membrane or thin partition in pneumographic or air-pressure recording instruments.

diaphragm, iris: (photog.) mechanism of overlapping metal leaves by means of which the effective aperture or light opening of the lens can be varied.

diaphragmatic breathing: *see* **breathing, diaphragmatic.**

diapositive: a positive photographic image, made on transparent or translucent material and having a degree of density and contrast suitable for projection or for viewing by transmitted light.

diapositive film: *syn.* **film, positive** (2).

diary description: day-to-day recordings by a student detailing his selection of activities and his relationship with peers and adults; such accounts usually revolve around (*a*) the nature of the activity, (*b*) the purpose of the activity, (*c*) the outcome of the activity, and (*d*) the student's feelings and attitudes about the activity. *See* **observation, approaches to.**

diary method: (1) a supervisory technique in which teachers are expected to keep a record of methods and procedures of teaching and of problems encountered in teaching, such records serving as a basis for conferences between teacher and supervisor; (2) sometimes designates a supervisory method involving the recording by a supervisor of suggestions for improvement of teaching.

diary record: *syn.* **record, anecdotal.**

diascope: a device for projecting transparencies by transmitted light.

diathesis (dĭ·ath′ə·sĭs): an inherited or acquired constitutional predisposition to a particular disease or disorder, whether mental or physical.

dichotomize: to divide a distribution or variable into two nonoverlapping categories or classes.

dichotomous classification (dĭ·kot′ə·məs): *see* **dichotomy.**

dichotomy (dĭ·kot′ə·mi): (1) (logic) the exhaustive division of a genus into two mutually exclusive classes; (2) (stat.) the division of a population or sample into two exclusive classes, for example, male and female; (3) in general, any sharp division into two opposed alternatives.

dicta: *sing.* **dictum;** in law, opinions by a judge on a matter not essential to the decision of the question before him; gratuitous pronouncements of an authoritative nature.

dictation: (1) (shorthand) words and thoughts uttered by one person and written in shorthand by another, to be transcribed into letters, articles, memos, manuscripts, books, and other kinds of typed copy; (2) (mus. ed.) an important facet of the ear training of musicians, usually conducted by playing melodies, rhythms, chords, or various combinations of all three, which the student is to recognize and translate into musical symbols; (3) (for. lang.) a teaching or testing technique in which the instructor reads to students a selection to be copied verbatim, the purpose being to develop the student's ability to distinguish between individual sounds, words, and phrases.

dictation exercise: *see* **exercise, dictation.**

dictation, harmonic: (mus. ed.) dictation dealing solely with the recognition and recording of harmonic patterns. *See* **dictation** (2).

dictation, individualized: (shorthand) speed of dictation which is geared to the proficiency of the individual taking the dictation and not to the class as a whole.

dictation, melodic: dictation dealing solely with the recognition and recording of melodic patterns. *See* **dictation** (2).

dictation, office-style: (shorthand) untimed and irregular dictation patterned after the usual thinking and expressions needed by a dictator in an office to compose a letter; marked by spurts, pauses, and alterations, as opposed to reading dictation from a book without interruptions, changes, or repetitions.

dictation record: *see* **record, dictation.**

dictation, rhythmic: dictation dealing with the recognition and recording of rhythmic patterns. *See* **dictation** (2).

dictation test of writing: *see* **test of writing, dictation.**

dictation, tonal: the performance of music for the purpose of training students to reproduce the appropriate musical symbols. *See* **dictation** (2).

dictatorial planning: organizing a social system by autocratic methods; opposed to cooperative and democratic planning.

diction: the choice of words in speech; good when appropriate for the occasion and the ideas expressed.

dictionary catalog: *see* **catalog, dictionary.**

dictionary, picture: a dictionary for small children consisting of pictures and words arranged in alphabetical order; used for teaching the dictionary idea to young children and helping them to identify strange words.

dictionary, polyglot: a dictionary composed of correlative text in various languages.

dictionary readiness: *see* **readiness, dictionary.**

dictionary skills: *see* **skills, dictionary.**

dictum: *pl.* **dicta;** opinion of a judge that is advisory on a legal point during proceedings in a case at law rather than pertinent to the decision; also known as "obiter dictum."

didache (dĭ·da·khē′): (Gr., lit., "teaching") the teaching of the church in regard to the ethical principles and obligations of the Christian life; teaching as contrasted with preaching. *See* **kerygma.**

didactic curriculum: *see* **curriculum, didactic.**

didactic materials: *see* **Montessori method.**

didactic method: (1) (obs.) any method of teaching or instruction; (2) a method of instruction that emphasizes rules, principles, standards of conduct, and authoritative guidelines; *see* **curriculum, didactic.**

didactics: (obs.) the art of teaching.

didascaleum (dĭ·das′kə·lē′əm): a place of instruction or music school in ancient Athens where "music" was studied for the culture of the soul, the term being interpreted to include all that came under the patronage of the nine muses—literary subjects, reading, writing, etc.; the studies constituted intellectual and ethical, as well as aesthetic, training.

dietitian: a person professionally trained in nutrition and food service management, with related science courses; training is usually followed by a year's internship in a hospital or other institution approved by the American Dietetic Association.

difference, chance: (1) the difference in value between corresponding statistics based on random samples from the same population; (2) the difference in value between a statistic based on a random sample and the corresponding population parameter; (3) any difference between statistic and parameter or hypothesized value of parameter which is no larger than could reasonably be attributed to the effect of random sampling fluctuations.

difference formula: *see* **formula, difference.**

difference, group: a difference in the central tendency, variability, or other feature of a given characteristic in different groups. *Contr. w.* **differences, individual.**

difference, just noticeable: (meas.) a very small difference between two stimuli, one which under the experimental conditions is barely above the *threshold.*

difference, method of: *see* **method of difference.**

difference norms: *see* **norms, difference.**

difference, parameter: (1) a difference between the same summary measures obtained from two or more populations; (2) a theoretically true difference in summary measures in contrast to a difference between statistics.

difference, rank: *see* **rank difference.**

difference score: *syn.* **score, change.**

difference, sex: any significant difference in mental, physical, social, or emotional traits that depends only on the sex of the individual. *See* **difference, group; differences, age.**

difference, significant: (1) a difference which is so great that it may not be reasonably attributed to chance factors (that is, sampling errors or errors of random sampling); usually determined on the basis of a statistical test such as t, F, or x^2; (2) a difference whose probability of occurrence through chance alone is less than the selected significance level (that is, confidence level, fiducial probability, etc.), thus permitting the rejection of a null hypothesis; (3) (poor usage) rarely, a difference that appears to be significant practically, even though the difference has not been demonstrated to be significant statistically, as in (1) and (2) above.

difference, standard: the difference between two means or other statistics divided by the standard error of that difference. *Syn.* **standard ratio;** *see* **ratio, critical.**

difference, statistically significant: (1) a difference between two comparable statistics, computed from separate samples, that is of such magnitude that the probability that the difference may be imputed to chance is less than some defined limit; (2) often arbitrarily defined as a difference that exceeds two or three times the standard error of difference, or that would arise by chance 1 time in 20 or 1 time in 100, the constant employed depending on the concept of "significance" as well as on the size of the sample and the nature of the data; a statistically significant difference does not necessarily imply practical importance.

difference, true: (1) the mean of an infinite number of measures of the difference between paired values; (2) the difference between the true measures of variables or statistics; a hypothetical concept, since true measurements are never attainable.

differences, age: (1) variations, as a result of age, among members of a group; (2) variations within the same individual at different times, due to the length of time lived.

differences, individual: (couns.) variations in characteristics that bring about the uniqueness of the individual child as he impresses himself upon the school and upon educators and lay public as evidencing the need for special attention. *Contr. w.* **difference, group.**

differences, interfamily environmental: *see* **environmental differences, interfamily.**

differences, intrafamily environmental: *see* **environmental differences, intrafamily.**

differences, mental: variations among individuals with respect to those capacities, abilities, and behaviors designated by the terms intelligence, aptitudes, emotions, skills, interests, and attitudes; also, variations in respect to other observable responses that represent sensory functions, memory, attention, etc. (The term mental is used and interpreted with various shades of meaning by different writers. Educationally, the term mental differences commonly refers to variations in learning ability and their related factors such as interest, purpose, need, and emotion.)

differences, race: variations among individuals supposedly due to membership in a group having a more or less common ancestry, this group being loosely designated as a *race;* studied as a branch of *differential psychology.* (Alleged race differences are often cited to support *race prejudice.*)

differences, small consistent: differences between two or more samples which are in the same direction on several variables or on several replications, but which are individually too small to be regarded as statistically significant at any reasonable confidence level; such differences are likely to be the result of using an inefficient research design or excessively small samples. *Contr. w.* **difference, significant.**

differential-aptitude battery: *see* **battery, differential-aptitude.**

differential-aptitude test: *see* **test, differential-aptitude.**

differential cost: *see* **cost, differential.**

differential diagnosis: *see* **diagnosis, differential.**

differential effect: (1) the presence of variations in the effectiveness of an experimental factor from one level to another of some other experimental factor; (2) in analysis of variance procedures, the effect that is measured by interaction.

differential factors in elementary school counseling: *see* **counseling, differential factors in elementary school.**

differential fertility: *see* **fertility, differential.**

differential growth: *see* **growth, differential.**

differential inhibition: *see* **inhibition, differential.**

differential instruction: *see* **instruction, individualized.**

differential prediction: *see* **prediction, differential.**

differential prognosis: *syn.* **prediction, differential.**

differential psychology: *see* **psychology, differential.**

differential, response: *see* **response differential.**

differential response: *see* **response, differential.**

differential, salary: a difference in salary, usually among classes of employees, based upon specified criteria; normally, salary schedules for teachers are differentiated according to the number of years of college preparation or degrees earned; salary differentials for principals are frequently based on size of school.

differential scoring: *see* **scoring, differential.**

differential, semantic: *see* **semantic differential.**

differential validity: *see* **validity, differential.**

differentiated assignments: *see* **assignments, differentiated.**

differentiated-course plan: a promotion plan based on varying the promotion standards according to the ability of each child.

differentiated curricula: *see* **curricula, differentiated.**

differentiated high school diploma: *see* **diploma, differentiated high school.**

differentiated instruction: *see* **instruction, differentiated.**

differentiated mimetic reaction: *see* **reaction, differentiated mimetic.**

differentiation, biological: the development of a difference, or differences, among individuals, groups, or races, through the operation principally of biological factors; contrasted with differentiation having its basis in historical development, geography, climate, culture, individual experience, etc.

differentiation, functional: (school admin.) the process of separating functions for the purpose of regrouping them in assignable work units, either general or specific; tends to take place concurrently with an increase in the volume of business that an organization must handle.

differentiation in development: (1) (anatomy) the process by which special parts and organs are built up through progressive cell division and regional modification; (2) (behavior) the progressive series of changes by which specific adaptive movements of local parts, usually involving more participation of the small-muscle groups, gradually become separated from the nonadaptive generalized movements that characterize the behavior of the fetus and the young infant, thus leading to greater independence in the movement of local parts and increasing adaptiveness to specific stimuli.

differentiation index: *see* **index, differentiation.**

differentiation of content: a plan for meeting individual differences whereby all pupils progress through the grades at the same rate but the content of instruction may differ in a variety of ways, such as degree of difficulty, areas of student interest, quantity of content, or context (field trips, work experience, etc.).

difficulty, level of: an approximation made in order to fit the content of reading materials to the reading ability of the child by different testing procedures.

difficulty scale: *see* **scale, difficulty.**

difficulty score: *see* **score, difficulty.**

difficulty, spelling: *see* **spelling difficulty.**

diffused response: *see* **response, diffused.**

diffusion process: *see* **adoption of practices.**

digest: a brief condensation of a written work, not necessarily in the words of the original.

digestive type: a type of habitus characterized by a large lower jaw, strong masticatory muscles, and a voluminous abdomen; similar to the *pyknic type. See* **habitus; macrosplanchnic.**

digit: (math.) any one of the ten symbols 0, 1, 2, 3, 4, 5, 6, 7, 8, 9 used to write numerals in the Hindu-Arabic system.

digit, binary: *see* **binary digit.**

digit, check: *see* **check digit.**

digit repetition: a technique for testing intelligence in which the subject is required to repeat series of digits either forward or backward after a single presentation, which may be visual or auditory; included in some individual intelligence tests.

digit-span test: *see* **test, digit-span.**

digit-symbol test: *see* **test, digit-symbol.**

digital computer: *see* **computer, digital.**

digital computer, electronic: *see* **computer, electronic digital.**

digital counter: *syn.* **counter, index.**

digital sort: *see* **sort.**

digiting: (stat.) the act or process of reducing operations with multiple-digit numbers to operations involving only the separate digits of these numbers; used especially in connection with calculations to be performed on tabulating machines. *Syn.* **progressive digiting.**

digiting, progressive: *syn.* **digiting.**

dignity, human: *see* **human dignity.**

digraph: a single speech sound represented by letters for two consonants (or two vowels), as th or ou in thought.

dilemma: (1) strictly, a form of syllogism combining hypothetical and disjunctive premises which, on the assumption that the disjunctions are exhaustive, leads to a conclusion that forces choice between two alternatives, usually though not necessarily undesirable; (2) more generally, any argument that forces a choice among a limited number of (usually two) undesirable alternatives; (3) also a situation involving a limited number of (usually two) unpalatable alternatives among which a choice must be made.

diligence: the expending of persistent painstaking effort to accomplish what is undertaken.

dimension: (1) a term used to denote a geometric magnitude measured in a specified direction, such as length, width, or height; (2) a degree of freedom, or independent condition, in the control of the action of an element; for example, time is a very important dimension in the study of the motion of an airplane.

dimension of ability: *see* **ability, dimension of.**

dimension of personality: the aspect of personality that can be measured or that is hypothesized to vary quantitatively along a continuum, for example, extroversion-introversion.

dimensional analysis: *see* **analysis, dimensional.**

dimensionality: (math.) the number of independent conditions that are both necessary and sufficient for the complete characterization of component elements; a line or curve is one-dimensional since points are identified by one independent condition; a plane or surface is two-dimensional since points are fixed by two independent conditions; space is three-dimensional since points are fixed by three independent conditions.

dimensions of mental growth: the view, prevalent among contemporary psychologists, that cognitive functions grow both in breadth (horizontally) and in altitude (vertically), thus laying the foundation for considering transfer of training in either dimension; the view does not rule out the possibility of the existence of other dimensions.

dimensions of observation: *see* **observation, dimensions of.**

dimensions of pupil performance: the distinguishing characteristics of pupil performance, namely, (*a*) the amount or rate of work, (*b*) the quality or accuracy of the performance, and (*c*) the character, often expressed as the level of difficulty, of the work done.

Ding an sich, das (dos ding′ on sikh′): (Ger., lit., "the thing in itself") a term used by Kant to refer to that entity lying beyond sense experience.

dingdong theory: a theory of the origin of language, according to which given environmental objects or situations are supposed to have forcibly called forth certain unlearned gestures or vocalizations, which then came to represent them.

diocesan high school: *see* **high school, diocesan.**

diocesan school: a church-related school under the auspices of a diocese, with episcopal sanction and, normally, control. *Comp. w.* **parochial school.**

diocesan superintendent of schools: *see* **superintendent of schools, diocesan.**

diocesan supervisor: *see* **supervisor, diocesan.**

diocese: in ecclesiastical use, an administrative area of church jurisdiction under the care of a bishop, divided into *parishes;* all territorial areas wherein the Roman Catholic, Anglican, Eastern Orthodox, and Oriental Churches are located are so subdivided for purposes of church government.

Dionysian art: *see* **art, Dionysian.**

diorama (dī′ō-rä′mə; -ram′ə): a three-dimensional representation composed of various symbolic and real materials such as pictures and specimens, frequently utilizing both transmitted and reflected light to produce a natural scenic effect.

dip: an arm-support exercise, done from a prone position on the floor or from a cross rest on parallel bars, in which the body is lowered and raised by bending and straightening the elbows. *Syn.* **push-up.**

diphthong: a sound produced by joining two vowels into a single syllable that carries a single *stress;* this is done through a smooth and continuous glide from the articulation of the first vowel into that of the second, as ĕ into ī in the word "vein."

diplegia (dī-plē′ji·ə): a form of paralysis in which both hemispheres of the brain are involved; paralysis affecting like parts on both sides of the body; bilateral paralysis.

diploma: a formal documentary credential given by an educational institution certifying the completion of a curriculum.

diploma, differentiated high school: a diploma certifying completion of a curriculum consisting of varied selections and sequences of subjects for pupils having different abilities, interests, needs, and purposes, therefore being differently educated; for example, at the secondary school level, a college preparatory curriculum, an industrial-education curriculum, or a commercial curriculum.

diploma, high school equivalency: *syn.* **certificate, high school equivalency.**

diploma mill: an institution that confers educational degrees fraudulently, primarily for profit, without demanding the usual academic achievement from the student.

diploma, performer's: *see* **certificate, performer's.**

diploma, uniform high school: a formal document certifying the completion of the prescribed work of a secondary school, without differentiation according to type of program.

diplopia (di·plō′pi·ə): a defect of vision, as in *cross-eyedness* or *squint,* characterized by seeing single objects as two. *Syn.* **double vision.**

DIQ: *see* **quotient, deviation intelligence.**

direct address: *see* **address, direct.**

direct approach: *see* **approach, direct.**

direct association: *see* **association, direct.**

direct correlation: *see* **correlation** (1).

direct curve: *syn.* **overcurve.**

direct experience: *see* **experience, direct.**

direct heating: *see* **heating, direct.**

direct lighting: *see* **lighting, direct.**

direct measurement: *see* **measurement, direct.**

direct method: (1) a method of teaching foreign languages which stresses complete or nearly complete reliance on the use of the foreign tongue rather than the vernacular for purposes of instruction and in which every effort is made to approximate the ideal of having the students think entirely in the foreign language from the beginning of the course; usually involves much practice in understanding the spoken word and in speaking, reading, and writing the foreign language; (2) a method of teaching shorthand devised by Ann Brewington, based on the recognition of shorthand symbols and their use to record meaning without recourse to phonetic analysis or ordinary English written symbols; (3) (math.) the use of argumentation in an attempt to prove a statement as given, rather than refuting related but mutually exclusive statements; *see* **indirect method; proof, deductive** (1); (4) a method of character education in which attempts are made to teach ethical and moral principles and practice by a direct verbal approach, involving admonition, codes, mottoes, "memory gems," etc.

direct movement: any handwriting movement involving the making of a curve in a clockwise direction; for example, the making of an arch from left to right.

direct operating cost: *see* **cost, direct operating.**

direct oral method: a procedure in language teaching that stresses the use of the spoken language prior to work in reading or writing, without reference to the student's native tongue if the language is foreign.

direct oval: handwriting drill that consists in constructing either retraced or running ovals in a clockwise movement. *Contr. w.* **indirect oval.**

direct-process duplicator: *see* **duplicator, direct-process.**

direct proof: *see* **proof, deductive** (1).

direct reading technique: a procedure in foreign-language teaching stressing reading as a means of language learning from the start, with reference to grammar and syntax only as the need arises.

direct reasoning: *see* **direct method** (3).

direct reinforcement: *see* **conditioning, operant.**

direct relationship: *syn.* **positive correlation;** *see* **correlation** (1).

direct tax: *see* **tax, direct.**

direct teaching: *see* **teaching, direct.**

direct-view receiver: *see* **receiver, direct-view.**

directed activity: *see* **activity, directed.**

directed answer: *see* **answer, directed.**

directed conversation: *see* **conversation, directed.**

directed discussion: *see* **discussion, directed.**

directed learning: *see* **learning, directed.**

directed number: *see* **number, directed.**

directed observation: *see* **observation, directed.**

directed passage: *see* **passage, directed.**

directed play: *see* **play, directed.**

directed practice: *see* **practice, directed.**

directed reading activity: *see* **activity, directed reading.**

directed response: *syn.* **answer, directed.**

directed sentence: *see* **sentence, directed.**

directed speaking test: *see* **test, directed speaking.**

directed study: *see* **study, directed.**

directed-study period: *see* **period, directed-study.**

directed teaching: *see* **teaching, directed.**

directed thinking: *see* **thinking, directed.**

directing method: (art ed.) a practice that requires the child to follow certain prescribed rules and directions; the product is of prime importance, and its nature is predetermined by the teacher. *See* **eclectic method;** *contr. w.* **free-expression method.**

direction signals: *syn.* **turn signals.**

direction taker: (spec. ed.) any straight-lined object whose surface lines when projected into space will give a course or line of travel in a given direction or to an objective.

direction taking: the act of getting a line or course from an object or sound to facilitate traveling in a straight line toward an objective.

directional confusion: (1) uncertainty on the part of the reader of the direction to pursue in reading; (2) the tendency in reading to attack a word first from the right and then the left, which often leads to *reversals* and *substitutions. See* **orientation, directional.**

directional orientation: *see* **orientation, directional.**

directional-process goal: *see* **goal, directional-process.**

directions test: *see* **test, directions.**

directive counseling: *see* **counseling, directive.**

directive method: (couns.) the use of such procedures as advice, suggestion, reassurance, and coercion, and similar active and direct techniques.

directive therapy: *see* **therapy, directive.**

director, art: one who administers the art education program in a school or school system; may also refer to a director of art activities in an advertising agency or other commercial firm; also called **art supervisor, art coordinator,** etc.

director, audiovisual: the person who supervises and/or administers an audiovisual program. *Syn.* **instructional-materials director; supervisor of audiovisual instruction.**

director, bureau of recommendations: *syn.* **director of placement.**

director, camp: the person responsible for the administration and leadership of a camp program.

director, curriculum: *syn.* **director of curriculum.**

director, educational broadcast: a person who has the responsibility of producing and/or presenting broadcasts possessing definite educational values; may be a staff member of a broadcasting station assigned specific educational duties or a staff member in an educational institution with the responsibility of developing broadcasts of an educational nature.

director, instructional-materials: *syn.* **director, audiovisual.**

director, motion-picture: the person controlling action and dialogue in front of the camera, as well as the angle of the camera itself; the person who realizes or puts on film the ideas inherent in the shooting script.

director, music: a person, either the chief conductor of a musical ensemble or someone other than the conductor, who chooses the music to be performed, schedules the performances, and arranges all details related to the actual conducting functions. *See* **conductor, music.**

director, nursery school: a staff member responsible for interviewing, enrolling, and carrying through administrative duties of the program; in a large school, a director may not teach; in a small setting, he or she may also be *head teacher. See* **aide; assistant, nursery school; associate; head teacher** (2); **teacher-intern.**

director of activities: a teacher or administrative official who directs and manages, under the authority of the principal, the nonclass activities of a school, such as athletics, clubs, and group events, and also supervises the work of supervisors of such activities.

director of admissions: *syn.* **admissions officer.**

director of agricultural extension: the title most frequently used for the administrative head of the major unit of a college or university dealing with extramural or extension services in agriculture in land-grant colleges.

director of athletics: the person designated as administrative head in charge of a program of athletics.

director of child accounting: the school official who is the directing head of the bureau or division of child accounting. *See* **bureau of child accounting.**

director of Christian education: *see* **director, religious education.**

director of curriculum: usually a staff officer who works with administrative officials in the planning and development of the educational program of the school and directs the activities of supervisors or coordinators of instructors, teachers, and lay citizens in planning a curriculum and then carrying such plans into effect in the schools.

director of demonstration school: *see* **director of student teaching.**

director of dormitory: an administrative officer responsible for budgetary and recreational functions in student dormitories. *Syn.* **director of residence.**

director of driver training: the person designated as chiefly responsible for the organization, management, and supervision of a program designed to give instruction in driving cars, trucks, and buses.

director of education: formerly the designation of the chief state school officer and executive head of the central educational authority of the state of Rhode Island.

director of employment: a member of the faculty of an educational institution whose responsibility it is to gather information pertaining to the students or alumni of a school, in order to present their qualifications to prospective employers, to guide students in making applications, and to bring employers and prospective employees together for interviews; often conducts conferences and guides students to prepare themselves to meet the demands of the respective occupations or professions. *See* **director of placement.**

director of extension: a title frequently used for the administrative head of the major unit of a college or university dealing with extramural or extension services, especially in land-grant colleges. *See* **extension, university.**

director of guidance: the school staff member who exercises leadership and assists in policy information for the guidance services and carries out such other functions as supervising counselors, communicating with administrative officers of the school, maintaining financial accounts, and controlling provision of physical facilities; has also responsibility for general guidance program development and management; also called *director of guidance services, coordinator of guidance and testing,* or *head counselor.*

director of guidance and special services: a counselor who is qualified to accept delegated leadership and administrative responsibilities both for development and integration of the guidance services and for special programs of education for children in a school or group of schools who are mentally accelerated (gifted) and for those who are mentally retarded or physically handicapped (hard of hearing, impaired in vision, etc.).

director of guidance services: *see* **director of guidance.**

director of health service: the administrative official in charge of the program for protection of health in an organization such as a college.

director of instruction: a member of the faculty of an educational institution who is directly responsible for the program of courses and curricula of the institution; may determine faculty loads, make schedules and see that they are carried out, or supervise instruction; often serves as chairman of the curriculum committee, and may be responsible for directing the research of the institution.

director of personnel: (1) the administrative official in charge of personnel selection, transfer, and dismissal, the maintenance of records concerning teachers and, in some instances, other personnel, the conduct of studies, and the development of the personnel program; usually found only in large school systems; recommends action to the superintendent rather than directly to the school board; (2) a college administrator responsible for supervising the student personnel program; (3) frequently used as the title of the head counselor.

director of personnel and placement bureau: *syn.* **director of guidance.**

director of physical education: the administrative head of physical education, especially required in teacher preparation programs, in a school or college.

director of placement: *syn.* **coordinator of placement.**

director of practice teaching: *see* **director of student teaching.**

director of pupil-personnel services: an administrator responsible for the coordination and planning for a whole school system of guidance services, psychological services, pupil accounting services, school social work or visiting teacher services, and school health services. *Syn.* **director, student-personnel services; director of student affairs** (1).

director of research: a member of the staff of an educational institution or agency whose duties consist of one or more of the following functions: conducting research projects, formulating policies concerning research, approving research policies, deciding what use is to be made of research findings.

director of residence: *syn.* **director of dormitory.**

director of schools: the designation of the chief school officer of Guam.

director of special education: the position in an educational administrative unit (state, county, intermediate, local), existing for the purpose of providing administrative leadership for all existing programs of instruction and services for exceptional children.

director of special services: in early childhood education, an individual, preferably with a degree in nursing, who plans, coordinates, and directs the services of the medical, dental, psychological, speech therapy, and nutrition staffs for *child development centers;* usually found also in Head Start centers.

director of student affairs: (1) *syn.* **director of pupil-personnel services;** (2) *syn.* **director of student personnel.**

director of student personnel: an administrator in a college or university who directs and coordinates the student personnel program; is responsible for the following functions: establishing objectives based upon continuous research, providing for policy determination by instructional and personnel staff and students, coordinating decentralized personnel services and integrating them with the instructional and business phases of the college, selecting, instructing, assigning and supervising student personnel staff, developing a high quality of interpersonal relationship and cooperation, financing and providing for continuing-in-service training and professional development of staff, establishing record keeping and reporting procedures essential for personnel program development and coordination and for research and evaluation, initiating critical self-study of processes, tools, and techniques of the student-personnel program, and evaluating the extent to which objectives of the program are being attained. *See* **dean of men; dean of students; dean of women.**

director of student teaching: the supervisory or administrative head of teacher-education work done in campus demonstration or laboratory schools or in off-campus affiliated schools; other titles often used synonymously, or with slight modifications of implied duties, are *director of demonstration school, director of practice teaching, director of training, supervisor of practice teaching,* and *supervisor of student teaching. Dist. f.* **director of teacher education.**

director of teacher education: the supervisory or administrative head of the department or college responsible for the complete program relating to the professional education of teachers; sometimes referred to as the *dean* or *chairman* of the department. *Dist. f.* **director of student teaching.**

director of training: *see* **director of student teaching.**

director of transportation: a person responsible for the selection of drivers, routing of buses, organization, supervision, and administration of the pupil transportation system.

director of vocational education, local: the school administrator appointed to supervise the total vocational education program in a school district.

director of vocational education, state: the state official directly in charge of the state program of vocational education, especially in connection with the program subsidized by Federal funds.

director of vocational guidance and placement: the college or university administrator who heads and coordinates the program that assists the student in choosing, preparing for, entering upon, and progressing in an occupation.

director, playground: one who is responsible for the organization and supervision of the activities of children in a place for outdoor play. *Dist. f.* **supervisor, playground.**

director, public relations: a staff member charged with responsibility for public relations activities of a school or higher education institution—that is, with public information, news, and interpretation of programs and activities; also called public information officer, university relations officer, or development officer. *See* **development (4).**

director, religious education: a professionally trained person in the fields both of education and of religion (or in some combination of the two) who functions as a supervisor of the religious education program of a local church or a denomination; in Christian denominations sometimes called *director of Christian education.*

director, spiritual: an individual, ordinarily a clergyman, who assumes the responsibility for the guidance of another individual in the pursuit of personal holiness.

director, student counseling bureau: the person with the authority to promote and coordinate the services of an office or department at the posthigh school level that provides counseling services for students.

director, student-personnel services: *syn.* **director of pupil-personnel services.**

director, vocational: the administrative head of a program of vocational education; presumably has technical training in the field and supervises other personnel teaching and administering vocational education classes and programs.

directors, board of: *syn.* **school board.**

directory: (law) an advisory opinion where compliance is not required.

directory, educational: a listing of the numerous professional organizations for teachers, published by the U.S. Office of Education; includes state, regional, and departmental subdivisions of the National Education Association and many unaffiliated organizations.

directory law: *see* **law, directory.**

directress: a trained adult woman in a Montessori classroom who acts as preparer of the environment and guide, protector, and examplar to the children.

disability: *syn.* **handicap.**

disability, academic: a condition rendering an individual incapable of profiting from usual schooling or standard curricula.

disability, acquired: a loss of body organ function, which develops after birth.

disability, communication: an inability to communicate through either one sensory mode or a number of sensory modes; the child might be able to communicate with sign language, for example, but not with his voice or in writing.

disability, degree of: a particular level or relative condition of a physical or mental impairment, illness, or injury;

may be categorized clinically as mild, moderate, or severe.

disability, developmental reading: *see* **reading disability, developmental.**

disability, invisible: any loss of a body organ function that cannot be readily recognized except by some type of diagnostic testing; for example, in contrast to disability of a cerebral palsied child, which can be seen, a disability in form perception cannot be visibly recognized and can only be determined through some type of diagnostic testing or an activity designed to indicate lack of form perception.

disability, learning: an educationally significant discrepancy between a child's apparent capacity for language behavior and his actual level of language functioning; may be either a retardation, a disorder, or a delayed development in one or more of the processes of speech, language, reading, spelling, writing, or arithmetic, resulting from a possible cerebral dysfunction and/or emotional behavioral disturbance and not from mental retardation, sensory deprivation, or cultural or instructional factors.

disability, legal: *see* **legal disability.**

disability, multiple: dysfunction or general loss of two or more body organ functions.

disability, neurological: loss of function as a result of disease or damage or improper structure of the central nervous system.

disability, neuromuscular: low coordination resulting in inability to perform test of balance or to stand unaided.

disability, organic reading: *see* **reading disability, organic.**

disability, permanent: a loss of body organ functions that is persistent for all time without change and renders the individual wholly unable to work.

disability, reading: *see* **reading disability.**

disability, specific reading: *see* **reading disability, specific.**

disabled child, perceptually: *see* **child, perceptually disabled.**

disabled, industrially: (1) not capable of working in industry because of a mental or motor disability; (2) disabled by accidents related to one's work.

disadvantaged child: *see* **child, disadvantaged.**

disadvantaged child, socially: *see* **child, socially disadvantaged.**

disadvantaged pupil, culturally: *see* **pupil, culturally disadvantaged.**

disadvantaged youth: *see* **child, disadvantaged.**

disadvantaged youth program: *see* **program, disadvantaged youth.**

disapproval, group: *see* **group disapproval.**

disarranged-sentence test: *see* **test, disarranged-sentence.**

disbursements, cash: money paid out in cash or by voucher checks that have been signed by the bookkeeper and approved and countersigned by the principal. (Entries noting the amounts of disbursement are usually made in the cashbook.)

disc recording: *see* **disk recording.**

disciple: a follower; one who voluntarily follows the leadership or adheres to the teaching of another; one who has adopted a particular philosophy or set of values originally ascribed to another.

disciplinarian: one who administers discipline or enforces order, who demands and secures a high degree of conformity to rules or regulations or of submission to authority; usually implies a rigorous and direct control over others.

disciplinary counseling: *see* **counseling, disciplinary.**

disciplinary course: *see* **course, disciplinary.**

disciplinary lesson: *see* **lesson, disciplinary.**

disciplinary officer: a person appointed to enforce the rules established by the faculty or administration of an educational institution.

disciplinary subject: *syn.* **course, disciplinary.**

discipline: (1) the process or result of directing or subordinating immediate wishes, impulses, desires, or interests for the sake of an ideal or for the purpose of gaining more effective, dependable action; (2) persistent, active, and self-directed pursuit of some considered course of action in the face of distraction, confusion, and difficulty; (3) direct authoritative control of pupil behavior through punishments and/or rewards; (4) negatively, any restraint of impulses, frequently through distasteful or painful means; (5) a branch of knowledge; (6) a course of training designed to develop a mental or physical ability or an attitude.

discipline, authoritarian: a rigid conception of discipline as a preventive force, used as a means of correcting the faults in the individual's personality. *See* **authoritarianism.**

discipline, constructive: a program (usually in higher education) aimed at preventing misconduct or at providing reeducation or therapy for persons with tendencies toward delinquency.

discipline, corrective: disciplinary principles and practices deliberately selected and applied as teaching devices or methods, usually with an attitude of helpfulness, and usually based on comprehensive insight into normal human frailties and causes of misbehavior.

discipline, democratic: the procedure by which members in a group take responsibility for their behavior by sharing in the determination of the controls which must apply within the group.

discipline, formal: *syn.* **discipline, mental.**

discipline, mental: the theory that the mind has a number of distinct and general powers and faculties, such as memory and will power, which can be strengthened by appropriate exercise; optimum *mental development* is thought to accrue from the study of appropriate subject matter (Latin and mathematics have been historic favorites); a person trained by this method is thought to be able thereafter to deal with other quite unrelated situations and subject matter; involves, thus, the automatic *transfer of training* through the proper exercise of general powers; William Torrey Harris (1835–1909) was the most influential exponent of this position in American educational history. *Syn.* **formal discipline.**

discipline, military: (1) a comprehensive system of ideals, loyalties, and conduct based on law and custom, to which every member of the military service is required to subject himself and of which the basic features are identification of the individual with the group and unswerving obedience to authority; (2) obedience to and exercise of all military loyalties, orders, and regulations; (3) training afforded by military education, particularly as it pertains to conduct and relationships with superiors and fellow students; (4) punishment by military authorities for infractions of military laws and regulations or civil law; (5) occasionally used to designate school discipline that is severe, rigid, and authoritative.

discipline, preventive: negatively, a term applied to efforts to discourage disorder or misbehavior before it actually occurs; it may express itself in providing busy work, inflicting exemplary punishments, individualizing assignments, encouraging pupil cooperation with the teacher, or in any of numerous other devices depending on the insights and abilities of the individual teacher; on the positive side, it involves persistent and planned efforts on the part of the teacher to change fragmentary and whimsical interests of the child or class into better integrated and far-reaching purposes, more consistent with the teacher's purposes.

discipline, punitive: (1) the act of exercising control through punishment, inflicting pain, or imposing penalties for misbehavior; (2) the rigorous or severe treatment of individuals either to be a lesson to others or to create fear as a deterrent to subsequent misbehavior; it may apply not only in the classroom and the home but also in military, political, or prison organizations, and even in religion through fear of hell, excommunication, and the like.

discipline record: *see* **record, discipline.**

discipline, scholastic: formal discipline, especially as applied to the classroom. *See* **discipline, mental.**

discipline, school: the characteristic degree and kind of orderliness in a given school or the means by which that order is obtained; the maintenance of conditions conducive to the efficient achievement of the school's functions.

discipline, self-: *see* **self-discipline.**

discipline, student: participation by students in both the making and the enforcing of regulations governing students' activities, need for and enforcement of rules being recognized.

discipline, therapeutic: a corrective type of disciplinary procedure and practice based upon rather complete and diagnostic analysis of the specific case and more or less prescribed treatment relating thereto; it implies a scientific viewpoint on the part of a specially trained person or specialist in human behavior.

disclaimer: as commonly used in school law, an affidavit denying any present or past affiliation with a group or belief, allegedly subversive in nature, as specified in the affidavit; loyalty oaths often include the disclaimer features and promise or imply that no such affiliation will be made in the future.

disclosure model: *syn.* **model, analog.**

discontinued course: *see* **course, discontinued.**

discontinuous: *syn.* **discrete.**

discontinuous data: *syn.* **data, discrete.**

discontinuous part-time class: *see* **part-time class, discontinuous.**

discontinuous variability: *see* **variability, discontinuous.**

discontinuous variable: *syn.* **variable, discrete.**

discontinuous variation: *syn.* **variation, discrete.**

discoverance: the psychoanalytic therapeutic concept of development of insight as applied by L. L. Tyler to the teaching-learning process; for example, clarification by students of their own ideas by seeking references on a topic, asking questions, indicating insight into their own understanding or behavior, etc.

discovery activity: *see* **activity, discovery.**

discovery demonstration: *see* **demonstration, discovery.**

discovery learning: *see* **learning, discovery.**

discovery method: a procedure in teaching which emphasizes individual study, manipulation of objects, and other experimentation by the student before generalization; requires delay in verbalization of important discoveries until the student is aware of a concept. *See* **inductive method; laboratory method; learning, heuristic; problem method** (1).

discovery teaching: *see* **teaching, discovery.**

discrepancy, expectation: *see* **expectation discrepancy.**

discrepancy, mean: *syn.* **deviation, standard.**

discrepancy score: *see* **score, discrepancy.**

discrete: permitting of no graduation or gradual transition from one value to another; capable of change only by definite amounts (usually successive integral numbers). *Syn.* **discontinuous;** *ant.* **continuous.**

discrete category: *see* **category, discrete.**

discrete data: *see* **data, discrete.**

discrete measure: *see* **measure, discrete.**

discrete scale: *see* **scale, discrete.**

discrete series: *see* **series, discrete.**

discrete variability: *syn.* **variability, discontinuous** (1).

discrete variable: *see* **variable, discrete.**

discrete variates: *see* **variates, discrete.**

discrete variation: *see* **variation, discrete.**

discretionary board functions: *see* **board functions, discretionary.**

discretionary duty: *see* **duty, ministerial.**

discretionary power: *see* **power, discretionary.**

discriminant function: *see* **function, discriminant.**

discriminant function, method of: a statistical technique for prediction of a variable dichotomy through the use of an empirically derived equation which weights optimally each of several variables; the act or process of deriving such a formula; its application is similar to the use of a multiple-regression equation in predicting a numerical criterion.

discriminant validation: *see* **validation, discriminant.**

discriminating power: *syn.* **discrimination** (2).

discrimination: (1) a response, either overt or implicit, that varies according to the nature (that is, type, intensity, etc.) of the stimulus (discriminative responses may be inborn or learned, adaptive or nonadaptive; in the child after language develops, discrimination may apply to judgments concerning values, for example, right vs. wrong, beautiful vs. ugly, etc.); (2) the power of a test or test item to distinguish between good, average, and poor individuals in achievement, aptitude, interest, or some other characteristic; thus, a test is said to discriminate well if the best students score highest, average students earn scores near the mean, and the least able students score lowest; positive discrimination is implied unless negative or zero is definitely stated; *syn.* **positive discrimination;** *contr. w.* **discrimination, negative; discrimination, zero;** (3) the policy of using nonrelevant factors, such as race, creed, color, or ethnic origin, in the employment of faculty or other staff members, or in the admission of students to an educational institution or to any of its activities, services, or facilities.

discrimination, auditory: ability to discriminate between sounds of different frequency, intensity, and pressure-pattern components; ability to distinguish one speech sound from another.

discrimination, color: the act of distinguishing colors.

discrimination, depth: apprehension of the distance of an object from the observer, of the relation between given objects and the observer, or of the spatial relation from front to back of a single solid object.

discrimination, figure-ground: (1) (auditory) the phenomenon evidenced as the auditor perceives and identifies phonemes and sequences of phonemes against the total auditory field; (2) the phenomenon evidenced as the observer recognizes the separate parts of a configuration and mentally organizes them into a meaningful whole so that they stand as figures against the remaining part of the perceptual field.

discrimination, form: the act of distinguishing among geometrical forms, such as squares or triangles, or the ability to do so; used to test the formation of concepts.

discrimination, frequency: the auditory ability to discriminate between different tone frequencies as opposed to the mere detection of sound.

discrimination, hearing: *see* **hearing discrimination.**

discrimination index: *see* **index, differentiation.**

discrimination, index of: *see* **index of discrimination.**

discrimination, intensity: the ability to detect variations in loudness of sounds; measured in various music tests.

discrimination learning: *see* **learning, discrimination.**

discrimination, loudness: *see* **discrimination, intensity.**

discrimination, negative: erroneous indication of good and poor ability or some other characteristic; typical of a test item that is answered correctly more often by the poorest students than by the best students; usually caused by faulty construction of test items. *See* **discrimination** (2); *contr. w.* **discrimination, zero.**

discrimination, olfactory: variation in response according to the type, intensity, or other characteristics of the chemical substance constituting the olfactory stimulus. *See* **discrimination** (1); **response, differential.**

discrimination, pattern: perceiving the whole and the interrelationship of parts; for example, reacting to a person we recognize not on the basis of separate elements but as a *gestalt.*

discrimination, perceptual: (1) the act of discerning the differences among objects or symbols and of distinguishing one from another; in reading, the seeing of differences; (2) the power of identifying differences.

discrimination, pitch: the ability to distinguish between tones of differing frequencies of vibrations; measured in various music tests. *Syn.* **sense of pitch.**

discrimination, positive: *see* **discrimination** (2).

discrimination, quality: *syn.* **discrimination, timbre;** *see* **tone color.**

discrimination, racial: the denial of certain rights or privileges to some individuals on the basis of race or color. *See* **discrimination** (3); **racism.**

discrimination, religious: unjust or unequal treatment accorded individuals or groups on the basis of their religious beliefs or practices.

discrimination, rhythm: the ability to recall and distinguish between rhythmic patterns in which there are time or intensity variations; measured in various music tests. *Syn.* **sense of rhythm.**

discrimination, shape: ability to discriminate between shapes, for example, between a triangle and a square.

discrimination, size: ability to discriminate between various sizes; for example, the ability to tell the difference between a large square and a small square.

discrimination, sound: (1) the act of perceiving two phonetic units or speech sounds as different; *see* **test, sound-discrimination;** (2) (mus.) *see* **discrimination, timbre.**

discrimination, taste: a response that varies according to the type, intensity, or other characteristics of the chemical substance constituting the taste stimulus. *See* **discrimination** (1); **response, differential.**

discrimination, timbre: the ability to distinguish between tones differing in overtones or quality, such as the tones produced by different musical instruments; measured in various music tests. *Syn.* **discrimination, quality;** *see* **tone color.**

discrimination, time: the ability to judge the relative duration of intervals of time or of sounds; measured in various music tests. *Syn.* **sense of time.**

discrimination, tone: the ability to distinguish between tones from baseline frequencies of 200, 250, 1000 h; for example, between

	250	250	250	250	250
and	200	210	220	230	240.

discrimination, visual: the process of distinguishing one object from another visually.

discrimination, word: the act of differentiating one word from another as well as recognizing words, associating meanings with them, and pronouncing them correctly.

discrimination, zero: inability of a test or test item to distinguish among examinees on the desired basis. *See* **discrimination** (2); *contr. w.* **discrimination, negative.**

discriminative stimulus: *see* **stimulus, discriminative.**

discursive reasoning: *see* **reasoning, discursive.**

discussion: an activity in which people talk together in order to share information about a topic or problem or to seek answers to a problem based on all possible available evidence; frequently used as a learning procedure. *Dist. f.* **debate.**

discussion activity: *see* **activity, discussion.**

discussion, directed: (1) group discussion that is controlled by its leadership, fixed agenda, or some other group structures, to move through its stated agenda; (2) a group situation where the structuring and announced expectations call for an orderly discussion of stated agenda; (3) the term is sometimes applied to discussions excessively forced in the direction of the leader's purpose, in contrast to *permissive discussion.*

discussion examination: *syn.* **examination, essay.**

discussion, group: (1) a method of involvement in group work by talking over pertinent problems either to increase the degree of participation on the part of the students or to bring about decision making; (2) (adult ed.) a purposeful, cooperative exploration of a topic of mutual interest to a group of adults, carried on under the guidance of a leader. *See* **discussion.**

discussion group: *see* **group, discussion.**

discussion, guided: (1) a method of teaching by which students develop an understanding of the subject through discussion of pertinent points related to that subject; their discussion is generated and guided by the instructor who uses various types of questions to do this; (2) a method of instruction which seeks to achieve planned learning through the interchange of ideas and experiences in group discussion.

discussion, leaderless group: group interaction in which a leader who is essentially passive is used mainly as a source for information.

discussion period: *see* **period, discussion.**

discussion, permissive: (1) group discussion that moves freely and adjusts to the expressed interests and participation of the members; (2) a group situation where the structuring or expectation does not call for any specific discussion procedure or any fixed outcome of agreements, as contrasted with a group situation that is structured with a stated discussion schedule and expected outcomes. *See* **permissive;** *contr. w.* **discussion, directed.**

disease, communicable: a disease that may be transferred from one person to another without actual contact. *See* **disease, contagious.**

disease, contagious: a disease that may be transferred from person to person by contact. *See* **disease, communicable.**

disease entity: a specific entity which is the sum total of the numerous expressions of one or more pathological processes; the cause of a disease entity is represented by the cause of the basic pathological process in combination with important secondary causative factors.

disease, marginal: any departure from, failure in, or perversion of normal physiological action in the material constitution or functional integrity of the living organism which is of borderline or uncertain classification.

disengagement, psychological: the state of being in conflict or imbalance in a given environment or situation.

disenrollment: (correspondence study) the termination of a student's enrollment in a course prior to its completion; there are the following subdivisions: (*a*) cancellation, no lesson submitted; (*b*) dropped, one or more lessons submitted; (*c*) transfer, change from one course to another.

disinhibition: the temporary removal of an inhibiting response through action of an excitatory stimulus. (For example, a person in a formal social situation where laughter would be a breach of good manners may be inhibiting laughter; under such circumstances, nearly any sudden stimulus such as the dropping of a book may suffice to make the person laugh.)

disintegrative behavior: *see* **behavior, disintegrative.**

disjoined prefix: *see* **prefix, disjoined.**

disjoined suffix: *see* **suffix, disjoined.**

disjoint sets: *see* **sets, disjoint.**

disjunctive proposition: *see* **proposition, disjunctive.**

disk file: *see* **file, disk.**

disk, magnetic: in automatic data processing, a storage device on which information is recorded.

disk recorder: *see* **recorder, disk.**

disk recording: *see* **recording, disk.**

disk storage: *see* **storage, magnetic disk.**

dislocated hip: a displacement of the head of the femur, which does not lie entirely within the shallow acetabulum; congenital dislocations of the hip are believed to be due to lack of embryonic development of the joint.

dismissal: *syn.* **disqualification.**

dismissal blank, guidance: *see* **guidance dismissal blank.**

dismissal charges: accusations that specify the reasons for dismissal of an employee.

dismissal, damages for: *see* **damages for dismissal.**

dismissal from school: *see* **dismissal of pupil; exclusion; exclusion, temporary.**

dismissal hearing: a proceeding in which the plaintiff and the defendant may present evidence before a board or committee relative to the proposed dismissal of a school employee; ordinarily provided for by indefinite-tenure laws. *See* **tenure, indefinite.**

dismissal of pupil: the act of dropping a pupil's name from the roll, whether at the demand of the school authorities or as the result of the pupil's voluntary and legal withdrawal. *See* **dismissal of teacher.**

dismissal of teacher: the separation of an instructor from a school system by requesting his resignation or by a discharge effected by proper authority before the termination of the contract.

dismissal record: *see* **record, dismissal.**

dismissal report: *syn.* **record, dismissal** (1).

dismissed time: official dismissal of students for a part or the whole of a school day, usually at the elementary or secondary school level, so as to facilitate staff meetings, special events, etc. *Dist. f.* **released time.**

disorder, aggressive: *see* **disorder, classroom.**

disorder, articulation: a speech condition in which the speaker omits or distorts sounds or substitutes one sound for another.

disorder, behavior: a conduct problem as contrasted with a personality problem; generally functional rather than organic in origin; in these disorders a child may appear to be "acting out" his emotional difficulties aggressively; the term is nearly synonymous with *conduct disorder* but is more inclusive of all forms of overt behavior that are socially unacceptable.

disorder, classroom: (1) pupil or class actions that are characterized by absence of significant motive on the part of the pupil or by the presence of conditions that interfere with learning or achievement of other educational objectives; in a superficial sense, it sometimes refers to any whispering or movement about the room on the part of the pupils while school is in session, but this is not its chief characteristic, since conversation, activity, and associating of pupils may represent valuable group experience; different kinds of disorder may be recognized: incipient disorder designates a tense or poorly controlled situation in which disorder is likely to rise at any moment; incidental disorder is that which just happens; habitual disorder may apply to the individual pupil because he is experiencing some personal or emotional problem, or it may apply to a particular segment of a class or to the majority of the class; in the last case the primary cause may lie in poor teaching or poor administration, although it may also result from factors over which teacher or administrator has little control; the terms aggressive disorder and pernicious disorder cover actions definitely intended to interrupt or interfere with usual schoolwork, to challenge the status or influence of the teacher, to gain personal attention, etc.; (2) may refer to disarranged furniture and lack of system in handling supplies and equipment, but it should be recognized that an unusual arrangement may be deliberately planned.

disorder, conduct: behavior that is socially disturbing or antisocial in nature.

disorder, functional: *see* **functional disorder.**

disorder, functional speech: *see* **speech disorder, functional.**

disorder, habitual: *see* **disorder, classroom.**

disorder, incidental: *see* **disorder, classroom.**

disorder, incipient: *see* **disorder, classroom.**

disorder, learning: deficient ability in learning school subjects, particularly the *three R's.*

disorder, pernicious: *see* **disorder, classroom.**

disorder, voice: a nontechnical term applied to any irregularity in the vocal production of speech; also called *defective phonation.*

disorganization: state of being in which the organic, regular, or systematic order of items is disarranged or destroyed.

disorganization, social: *see* **social disorganization.**

disorientation: a condition characterized by loss of ability to comprehend oneself in one's environment with reference to location, the approximate time, and persons who should be recognized.

dispatching: (school admin.) a function of control that assures proper time coordination by means of a controlled release of authority to act.

dispersion: the scatter or variability of the observations of a distribution about some measure of central tendency, for example, the standard deviation, variance, quartile deviation, etc. *Syn.* **scatter; spread; variability; variation** (1).

dispersion analysis: *syn.* **analysis, scatter.**

dispersion, coefficient of: *see* **coefficient of dispersion.**

dispersion, relative: *syn.* **variability, relative.**

displaced aggression: *see* **aggression, displaced.**

displacement: a hypothetical mechanism (used in dream fantasy interpretations) which designates how an unconscious emotional impulse is shifted from an important object to an unimportant one at the conscious level; (2) *syn.* **aggression, displaced.**

displacement table: *see* **table, displacement.**

display: *n.* (1) an area of study in the distributive education curriculum concerned with the principles of merchandise arrangement within the store and in store windows; (2) an exhibit or showing of articles, merchandise, products, or school materials.

display: *v.* in programmed instruction, to present an organized pattern of sensory data to a learner. *See* **readout.**

display equipment: *see* **equipment, display.**

display panel: *syn.* **console.**

display room: a room fitted and used for the purpose of displaying the products of a school, university, or college, or of some department of such an institution, for example, a department of art or agriculture.

display unit: *syn.* **console.**

display window: a replica of a store window used for teaching the principles of merchandise display in the classroom; usually a part of the equipment in the distributive education laboratory.

disposable income: *see* **income, disposable.**

disposition: the complex of general traits, attitudes, or temperamental qualities that make a person likely to respond in a certain way, for example, "Her disposition is to punish the children first and then find out why they did what they did."

dispositions, need: *see* **need dispositions.**

disputation: a method of verbal combat indulged in by many philosophers of ancient Athens, particularly the later philosophers known as *Sophists,* and revived in the later medieval universities, particularly by the *Scholastics;* it was sometimes carried out by a single reasoner, who alternately presented both sides of an argument, but usually by two or more disputants defending different points of view.

disqualification: (higher ed.) official action of refusing to allow a student to continue in the institution unless he is formally readmitted; usually results from failure to fulfill terms of academic probation. *Syn.* **dismissal;** *comp. w.* **suspension.**

dissected relief map: *see* **map, dissected relief.**

dissemination, information: *see* **information dissemination.**

dissemination of information, selective: an arrangement designed to keep the various members of an organization fully informed in their areas of interest by screening all incoming documents and automatically sending to each of the members notice of all material relating to his field.

dissent: reasoned disagreement; disagreement between persons on an issue, with full understanding of each other's view and of the reasons for the disagreement.

dissenter school: a term used in the history of education in England for schools operated by religious groups dissenting from the official Anglican faith. *See* **Act of Toleration.**

dissertation: a formal treatise based on original investigation or research in partial fulfillment of the requirements for a doctor's degree; sometimes used interchangeably with *thesis.*

dissertation, academic: *syn.* **dissertation.**

dissimilarity, index of: *see* **index of dissimilarity.**

dissociation: a mental disorder in which one or several groups of ideas become separated by the process of repression from the main body of the personality and so are not accessible to memory or consciousness. *See* **personality, dual.**

dissolution of district: the breaking up of a consolidation through legal process, with a return of each district that formed the original consolidation to the independent status that existed before the consolidation took place; also, the reversion of a school district to unorganized territory (as, for example, in Maine and Wisconsin).

dissolve: an optical effect in motion pictures involving two superimposed scenes in which the second one gradually appears as the first one gradually disappears.

dissonance: *see* **consonance.**

dissonance, cognitive: (1) presence within the cognitive structure of two elements (facts, ideas, principles, etc.) that are discordant, as, for example, when a person who believes his ethnic group superior reads of a Nobel Prize winner who belongs to another race, the existing belief and the new fact are in dissonance; (2) (couns.) the situation existing when there is a break in the continuity of youth's relationships with peers and with adults and when there may be a discrepancy between anticipated events and those already actually experienced, as, for example, in the youth's anticipated move from the junior high school to the senior high school.

dissonance theory: *see* **dissonance, cognitive.**

distance clause: an exception in compulsory attendance laws with provides for children upon whom school attendance would be an undue hardship because of their extreme distance from any school.

distance from school: (pup. trans.) the distance in miles (to the nearest tenth) from the point in the public highway directly opposite the home of the child to the door of the school, measured along public roads and over school property. (In some states it may include the distance from the yard gate of the child's home, or from the entrance of the home, to the public highway.)

distance, social: *see* **social distance.**

distance vision: *see* **vision, distance.**

distance, walking: the distance a pupil is required to walk to school or to a point where he is picked up by a school bus.

distinction: a difference based on the concept that a thing is what it is and not some other thing; a specification of the elements of a thing which identifies it as what it is, and relieves it of elements which confuse it with other things.

distinguished Air Force cadet: *see* **cadet, distinguished Air Force.**

distinguished military graduate: *see* **graduate, distinguished military.**

distinguished military student: *see* **student, distinguished military.**

distinguished professor: *see* **professor, distinguished.**

distortion: (1) a change in original sound attributable to the recording or reproducing mechanism; (2) a technique often used in drawing and painting in which figures or objects are presented in unusual or unfamiliar proportions; the relation of one part to another or to the whole may be unbalanced or asymmetrical; a quality may be exaggerated to emphasize a form or express a feeling.

distractibility: (1) variation in the ability of a person to refrain from reaction to external or internal stimuli which are extraneous to a mental task in hand, resulting in a poorer performance in terms of error or speech; (2) (spec. ed.) inability to fix attention on any subject; a symptom of the mental functioning of persons with brain injuries, whose attention is attracted by every stray stimulus coming into their sensory field.

distraction: a state in which the attention is diverted from the main portion of an experience or is divided among the various portions of it.

distractor: *alt. sp.* **distracter;** any incorrect alternative in a test item providing two or more alternatives from which the examinee must select the correct response; designed to be attractive to (hence, to distract) the respondent who does not know the correct answer. *Syn.* **decoy; foil; plausible wrong answer.**

distributed learning: *see* **learning, distributed.**

distributed practice: *see* **practice, distributed.**

distributed repetition: a laboratory or teaching procedure utilizing practice periods repeated at intervals.

distribution: (1) a tabulation showing the frequencies or percentages of the values of a variable arranged in a sequence as to time, magnitude, etc.; *see* **distribution,**

frequency; distribution, historical; distribution, quantity; (2) the act of moving finished goods to the ultimate consumer.

distribution, ability: a frequency tabulation composed of scores representative of some ability.

distribution, age-grade: the number or percentage of pupils of each age in each grade, and vice versa, usually shown by an age-grade distribution table.

distribution, Bernoulli's: see distribution, Poisson sampling.

distribution, binomial: syn. distribution, binomial sampling.

distribution, binomial sampling: the sampling distribution of the expected proportions for random samples out of a two-class population, the terms of the distributions giving the probability of each possible value that p may take in a random sample of n items; the binomial sampling distribution is given by the successive terms of the expansion of $(p + q)^n$.

distribution, business experience in: see experience in distribution, business.

distribution, continuous: the frequency distribution of a continuous variable.

distribution, cumulative frequency: a tabulation of the frequencies of a series of observations such that each entry gives the sum of all frequencies up to the upper limit of the corresponding class interval or, less frequently, the sum of all frequencies through any other series of points (for example, interval midpoints).

distribution curve: syn. curve, frequency (1).

distribution, F: the sampling distribution of the ratio of the larger to the smaller of two independent estimates of variance arising from the same population variance; the significance level of an F ratio depending upon its magnitude and upon the number of degrees of freedom in both estimates of variance. See variance, analysis of.

distribution, fan-shaped: a bivariate distribution in which there is closer agreement of scores at lower (or higher) levels; for such a distribution, a single correlation coefficient may be misleading.

distribution, field: in data processing, the spreading of data from one field to several for printing, punching, or accumulating in accordance with signals from the cards.

distribution, flat: in the distribution of state moneys to local school districts, that money which is distributed on the same basis (for example, a specified amount per pupil or per classroom unit) to all school districts of the state; normally a feature of state foundation programs having as a second major factor the distribution of *additional aid* to financially weak districts.

distribution-free statistics: syn. statistics, nonparametric.

distribution-free test: syn. test, nonparametric.

distribution, frequency: (1) a tabulation showing the frequencies of the values of a variable when these values are arranged in order of magnitude; often shortened to *distribution; contr. w.* distribution, historical; distribution, quantity; (2) a tabulation of scores from high to low or low to high showing the number of persons who obtain each score or group of scores.

distribution, historical: a tabulation showing the frequencies of any variable in successive intervals of time; a distribution in which time is the basis of classification. *Syn.* temporal distribution; time distribution; *contr. w.* distribution, frequency; distribution, quantity.

distribution, intelligence: the range of variation in mental ability within a group of individuals and the frequency with which cases occur at each of the levels within the total range; usually represented by means of a *frequency table* and a graph representing the number and percentage of cases at each level or interval.

distribution, Lexian: syn. distribution, Lexis.

distribution, Lexis: the frequency distribution obtained when the probability of occurrence of an event is constant from trial to trial within a set but varies from set to set; a frequency distribution with a Lexis ratio greater than 1.00; a frequency distribution having hypernormal dispersion; a series of frequencies whose standard deviation is greater than $\sqrt{Npq}$. *Syn.* Lexian distribution.

distribution, noncentral t: the distribution of t when the mean of t is not equal to zero; used in testing the significance of a point biserial correlation coefficient.

distribution, normal: (1) a frequency distribution in which the quantities are so distributed that a normal probability curve is the best-fitting curve; *syn.* normal frequency distribution; *see* curve, normal probability; (2) a distribution of scores or measures that in graphic form has a distinctive bell-shaped appearance; scores or measures are distributed symmetrically about the mean, with as many cases at various distances above the mean as at equal distances below it and with cases concentrated near the average and decreasing in frequency the further one departs from the average, according to a precise mathematical equation.

distribution, normal frequency: syn. distribution, normal.

distribution of ability: (1) the variation in ability (whether general ability or a specific ability) present in any group of individuals under consideration; (2) the frequency of occurrence of ability at each of successive levels; usually shown by means of a table or a graph, or both, representing the number and percentage of cases in each level or division, from high to low or from low to high.

distribution of marks: (1) the act or procedure of assigning school marks according to a predetermined plan to all pupils completing certain work at school; (2) a tabulation of the frequency of occurrence of each score, mark, or grade earned by the various members of a group whose work has been evaluated by a test or other means.

distribution of scores: a tabulation or enumeration of the frequency of occurrence of each score in a given set of scores.

distribution of workers: distribution of the labor force in terms of geographical location, sex, race, age, education, and income.

distribution panel: see panel, distribution.

distribution, phonetic: the sum of phonetic contexts in which a particular phone may appear in a given language. See phone.

distribution, Poisson: syn. distribution, Poisson sampling.

distribution, Poisson sampling: a theoretical distribution with many practical uses (primarily industrial) in situations where these three conditions prevail: (a) the probability of occurrence is very small, (b) the obtained probability is based on many observations, and (c) the probability of nonoccurrence is indeterminate (it is impossible, for example, to determine the probability of lightning *not* striking, of mistakes *not* being made, or of touchdowns in football *not* occurring); successive terms may be expressed mathematically as $e^{-m}(1, m, m^2/2!, \ldots, m^r/r!, \ldots)$, where e = 2.7183, the base of natural logarithms, and where m = the mean number of occurrences per sample; the distribution is completely specified by the mean, for the mean always equals the variance. *Syn.* Poisson distribution.

distribution, probability: a relative frequency distribution, showing the probability of occurrence of observations of the various possible magnitudes; a frequency distribution each ordinate of which is proportional to the probability of occurrence of an observation with the corresponding abscissa value.

distribution, quantity: a distribution showing the aggregate amount for each class, rather than the class frequency, for example, a table showing the total income received by the people at each of several income levels. *Contr. w.* distribution, frequency; distribution, historical.

distribution, rectangular: a frequency distribution in which successive equal intervals along the score scale include the same frequency or number of scores.

distribution, sampling: the relative frequency distribution of an infinity of determinations of the value of a statistic, each determination being based on a separate sample of the same size and selected independently but by the same prescribed procedure from the same population.

distribution, skewed: an asymmetrical distribution in which most of the scores are closer to one end of the distribution than they are to the other. See skewness, negative; skewness, positive.

distribution, surplus property: *see* **surplus property distribution.**

distribution switch: a switch in the control panel in a language laboratory which determines what program course a student will receive in his booth.

distribution, *t*: the sampling distribution of the ratio of a difference to its standard error; the significance level of *t* is a function of both its magnitude and the number of degrees of freedom. *Syn.* ***t* function.**

distribution, temporal: *syn.* **distribution, historical.**

distribution, time: *syn.* **distribution, historical.**

distribution, truncated: (1) a frequency distribution that is cut off by the removal of (or failure to obtain) certain classes of observations that would all fall at one extreme; (2) term used to describe a distribution of scores that is cut off artificially or arbitrarily at some point, whatever the reason; for example, a distribution of test scores in which many examinees receive the maximum possible score, thereby not enabling these examinees to score as high as they could have if the test had a suitable ceiling.

distribution, U-shaped: a distribution in which frequencies are greatest at the two extremes; thus, when shown graphically, the distribution resembles the letter U.

distributive education: a public vocational instructional program designed to meet the needs of persons over 14 years of age who have entered or are preparing to enter a distributive occupation; a program of instruction in marketing, merchandising, and management.

distributive education adult extension program: *see* **program, distributive education adult extension.**

distributive education adult instructor: *see* **instructor, distributive education, adult.**

distributive education advisory committee: *see* **committee, distributive education advisory.**

distributive education ancillary services and activities: *see* **services and activities, distributive education ancillary.**

distributive education area of study concept: *see* **area of study concept, distributive education.**

distributive education area supervisor: *see* **supervisor, distributive education assistant state.**

distributive education assistant state supervisor: *see* **supervisor, distributive education assistant state.**

distributive education certification: *see* **certification, distributive education.**

distributive education class, adult evening: *see* **class, adult evening distributive education.**

distributive education club: *see* **club, distributive education.**

Distributive Education Clubs of America: a national youth organization providing a program of activities which complements and enriches distributive curricula.

distributive education consultancy services: *see* **services, distributive education consultancy.**

distributive education continuing education: *see* **continuing education, distributive education.**

distributive education cooperative method: *see* **cooperative method, distributive education.**

distributive education cooperative plan: *see* **cooperative plan, distributive education.**

distributive education coordination: *see* **coordination, distributive education.**

distributive education correlated instruction: *see* **instruction, distributive education correlated.**

distributive education correlation: *see* **correlation, distributive education.**

distributive education entry occupation: *see* **occupation, distributive education entry.**

distributive education laboratory: *see* **laboratory, distributive education.**

distributive education parental consent form: *see* **consent form, distributive education parental.**

distributive education participating experiences: *see* **experiences, distributive education participating.**

distributive education pilot program: *see* **program, distributive education pilot.**

distributive education post-high school instruction: *see* **distributive education, postsecondary.**

distributive education, postsecondary: continuing education in marketing and distribution beyond the high school; may be thought of as the thirteenth and fourteenth years of school, but may be offered at a technical school or a community or junior college.

distributive education preemployment instruction: *see* **instruction, distributive education preparatory.**

distributive education preemployment training: *see* **instruction, distributive education preparatory.**

distributive education preparatory instruction: *see* **instruction, distributive education preparatory.**

distributive education programmed instruction: *see* **instruction, distributive education programmed.**

distributive education project: *see* **project, distributive education.**

distributive education project method: *see* **project method, distributive education.**

distributive education project plan: *see* **project plan, distributive education.**

distributive education related instruction: *see* **instruction, distributive education preparatory.**

distributive education, state supervisor of: *see* **supervisor of distributive education, state.**

distributive education store unit: *see* **store unit, distributive education.**

distributive education student recruitment: *see* **recruitment, student.**

distributive education supervised occupational experience: *see* **experience, distributive education supervised occupational.**

distributive education supervisor, adult: *see* **supervisor, adult distributive education.**

distributive education taxonomy: *see* **taxonomy, distributive education.**

distributive education teacher educator: *see* **educator, distributive education teacher.**

distributive education training sponsor: *see* **training sponsor, distributive education.**

distributive education work record: *see* **work record, distributive education.**

distributive law: *see* **law, distributive.**

distributive occupations: those occupations followed by proprietors, managers, or employees engaged primarily in the distribution and merchandising of goods and services; may be found in retailing, wholesaling, and service establishments and in production industries where the marketing function appears.

distributive occupations program: *see* **program, distributive occupations.**

distributive phase of guidance: a function of guidance which involves discovering individual student needs and making these needs known to the student himself and to the teachers who plan the school program.

distributive subjects: *see* **subjects, distributive.**

distributive variable: *see* **variable, distributive.**

distributive worker: *see* **worker, distributive.**

district, additional aid: a district which, by reason of financial inadequacy, qualifies to receive an amount of money from the state which, together with certain other revenues, will provide that district a minimum level of support for its educational program.

district, attendance: (1) *syn.* **attendance area** (1); (2) that section or part of a school district served by one attendance supervisor and his corps of fieldworkers.

district board of education: *see* **board of education, district.**

district, city school: a geographical area, generally coterminous with a legally established municipality, of which the population may be relatively high in number and density and which has been designated as a local school unit, often by state authority, to be governed by a local school board in terms of powers and duties delegated by the state.

district, consolidated school: a term limited in some states to districts, usually rural, maintaining a single attendance unit, while in other states it applies to any school district serving territory once served by two or more districts.

district, cooperating school: a member of a group of legally constituted school districts cooperatively providing a service or program of instruction that could not feasibly be offered in each district separately; commonly used for services for exceptional children.

district, county school: a unit of school administration in which school affairs of the county as a whole (sometimes with specified exceptions) are controlled by a county board of education.

district, dissolution of: *see* **dissolution of district.**

district, elementary: a school district in which no provision is made for public school work beyond the elementary grades.

district, enumeration: (1) any area in which a count of population is made; (2) (United States census) the smallest area for which the U.S. Census Bureau supplies tabulations of the population as to sex, color, nativity, age distribution, and size of family; each political unit, whether incorporated place, township, or election district, consists of one or more enumeration districts, each organized to contain 1,500 to 2,000 people. *Dist. f.* **census tract.**

district, exempted village: (1) a school district or village that has autonomy or freedom from county control and supervision in matters pertaining to the schools; (2) a village school district that is exempt from taxes imposed for special purposes such as maintaining a county high school. (Almost any type of school district may be exempted from certain legal provisions applying to the nonexempted districts.)

district, high school: *see* **high school district.**

district, independent school: any of the over 21,000 independent local school districts in the United States tabulated in the U.S. census of 1970.

district, inspection: the specific geographical area for which a school inspector is responsible.

district institute: *see* **institute, district.**

district, intermediate: an administrative unit, generally following county boundaries, to facilitate state-local school cooperation.

district, joint school: (1) a school district that includes within its boundaries territory in two or more counties; (2) *syn.* **district, consolidated school; district, union school.**

district junior college: *see* **junior college, district.**

district library: *syn.* **library, regional** (1).

district, local school: a generic term applied to the smallest unit within any type of legal hierarchical structure for school organization.

district meeting: an assembly of the resident legal voters of the school district, called to elect officers and to transact business or to decide educational matters of local importance.

district, metro: a reorganization proposal for large cities in which school district lines would be drawn in a general way from the center of the inner city outward, in pie fashion, including the suburbs; one of the major purposes of such a plan would be achievement of a representative cross section of all the city's divergent elements brought into each school district, thus breaking down the financial and legal devices which work to perpetuate *de facto segregation* and socioeconomic fragmentation in big city education; many advocates of metro districts believe that educational parks should serve these expanded school districts; like educational parks, metro districts were confined largely to the suggestion and planning stages in the mid-1960s. *See* **educational park.**

district-owned: *syn.* **board-owned.**

district playground: *see* **playground, district.**

district principal: *see* **principal, district.**

district reorganization, school: *see* **school district reorganization.**

district, rural school: (1) a rural area designated according to state law as a local school administrative unit; (2) a body corporate and politic in an open-country area that, with such help as it may receive from the state or county, provides and maintains its own school or schools under the immediate control of its own board of trustees or directors, generally three in number. (Sometimes erroneously applied only to open-country schools.)

district, school: (1) the area that is under the supervision of a given school board; (2) that territory within which children may attend a given school building or center.

district school: (1) historically, a school in a district that is small enough to enable children to walk to school; (2) an elementary one- or two-teacher school maintained by the rural school district and usually cared for by a locally elected representative body, generally three in number and known as the district school trustees or district school board; more generally spoken of as a *rural school.*

district school association: an organization of persons connected with or interested in schools, formed within the territorial limits of the district for the promotion of some object or purpose relating to education.

district, special school: (1) an agency of the state, usually organized under legislative authority, charged with particular and limited educational duties authorized by law; (2) a school district incorporated by a special act of legislature.

district, submarginal: a school district whose financial resources are inadequate to support a satisfactory educational program.

district superintendent: *syn.* **principal, district.**

district supervisor: *see* **supervisor, district.**

district system: a form of educational organization in which the school district is the local unit of administration, largely independent except for supervision by county and state boards of education.

district tax rate: *see* **tax rate, district.**

district, unified: a school district providing a public school program from kindergarten or grade 1 to grade 12.

district, union high school: *see* **high school district, union.**

district, union school: a type of local school unit formed by the uniting of two or more contiguous school districts for the purpose of providing elementary or secondary education, or both.

district unit: *syn.* **district, rural school** (1).

districts, joint vocational school: *see* **vocational school, area.**

disturbance, emotional: a deep-rooted problem involving the control and expression of feelings.

disturbance, figure-background: inability to discriminate figure from background.

disturbance, perceptual: a condition in which an individual makes different responses from the normal to stimuli, such responses being judged as inferior.

disturbed child: *see* **child, disturbed.**

disturbed child, emotionally: *see* **child, emotionally disturbed.**

disuse, law of: *see* **law of disuse.**

divergent squint: *see* **squint, divergent.**

divergent strabismus: *syn.* **exophoria.**

divergent strategy: *see* **strategy, divergent.**

divergent thinking: *see* **thinking, divergent.**

diversified-activity individualization: *see* **instruction, individualized.**

diversified-activity industrial arts laboratory: *syn.* **laboratory, composite industrial arts.**

diversified-activity shop: *see* **laboratory, composite industrial arts.**

diversified education, cooperative: *see* **cooperative diversified education.**

diversified occupations program: *see* **program, diversified occupations.**

diversified program: *see* **program, diversified.**

diversion: (finance) (1) the act of diverting funds from one account to another; (2) a reassignment or reallotment of funds from one planned category of expenditure to another category of expenditure.

diversional therapy: *see* **therapy, diversional.**

diversity in taxation: (1) variety in sources of tax receipts; (2) a plan or system by which the proper coordination of several taxes to form a unified tax system ensures a uniform amount of income and prevents concentration on a few forms of taxation.

diversity, vocabulary: *see* **vocabulary diversity.**

divided catalog: *see* **catalog, divided.**

divided organization: *syn.* **administration, dual type of.**

divided period plan: a plan of supervised study in which the recitation period is divided into two parts, one for teaching and recitation and the other for supervised study.

divided school: in early New England district school systems, a school in which a town supported and paid several teachers, one of whom spent all his time in one district.

dividing net: a type of net made of rope and used as a partition to divide a gymnasium into two or more floor areas.

diving: a highly specialized aquatic sport that utilizes principles of physics and body mechanics in patterns of body flight above and into water.

diving, scuba: underwater diving in which a swimmer wears swim fins and a face mask and carries strapped to his back an aqualung, an open-circuit device which enables the user to breathe compressed air from the tank and exhale the expired air into the water; *scuba* is an acronym formed from the words self-contained underwater breathing apparatus.

diving, skin: underwater diving in which a swimmer is equipped with swim fins on the feet, a face mask, a snorkel, and other optional equipment the swimmer may elect to carry such as a camera, spear, gun, knife, or compass. *See* **diving, scuba.**

divinity school: *syn.* **theological school.**

division: (1) an administrative unit of a college or school usually consisting of more than one department, as the division of the humanities; (2) a unit of a college or university consisting of a combination of years, as the junior division, comprising the first 2 years; (3) a branch of the college or university, either instructional or noninstructional, that is separate from the program of resident instruction, as the *extension division;* (4) occasionally, any of the principal administrative units of a college or university, as the division of arts and sciences; (5) a fallacy of ambiguity in which one argues from the collective to the distributive use of a word, that is, one presupposes that what is true of the whole is also true of its parts, as "This is an outstanding team. Therefore, each member of the team is an outstanding athlete"; *see* **composition** (6); **fallacy of ambiguity.**

division, extension: *see* **extension division.**

division facts: the set of statements about quotients which derive from the *multiplication facts* and the properties of 1, for example, $54 \div 9 = 6$ and $56 \div 7 = 8$; the number of facts to be learned depends upon the way in which the multiplication facts are handled; in no case will this number exceed 90.

division, junior: *see* **division** (2).

division, long: the form of division that requires the written notation of multiplications, partial dividends, and subtractions; for example,

$$
\begin{array}{r}
32r6 \\
15\overline{)486} \\
45 \\
\hline
36 \\
30 \\
\hline
6
\end{array}
$$

division of administration: *see* **administration, division of.**

division, short: a form of division that requires the person who uses it to carry in his mind the required multiplications, subtractions, and partial dividends; for example,

$$
\begin{array}{r}
2.54r2 \\
3\overline{)764}
\end{array}
$$

division superintendent: *see* **superintendent, county.**

divisional library: *see* **library, divisional.**

divisional organization: *see* **organization, divisional.**

dizygotic twins: *see* **twins, dizygotic.**

docent (dō′sənt): (1) one who explains exhibits in a museum; (2) a member of a teaching staff below professional rank in a college or university.

doctor of dental science (D.D.S.): *see* **college, dental.**

doctor of education degree: *see* **degree, doctor of education.**

doctor of jurisprudence (J.D.): *see* **degree, bachelor's** (2).

doctor of laws (LL.D.): a high degree granted by an American college or university, usually honorary and given to a person who has achieved distinction in a professional field or in public service.

doctor of medicine degree: *see* **degree, doctor's** (2).

doctor of medicine (M.D.): *see* **college, medical.**

doctor of music degree: *see* **degree, doctor of music.**

doctor of music education degree: *see* **degree, doctor of music education.**

doctor of musical arts degree: *see* **degree, doctor of musical arts.**

doctor of pedagogy degree: *see* **degree, doctor of pedagogy.**

doctor of philosophy degree: *see* **degree, doctor of philosophy.**

doctor of philosophy in education (Ph.D.): the highest earned degree awarded by universities for the advanced study of education, usually granted at the completion of the equivalent of a minimum of 3 years of graduate work; similar to the Ph.D. or Ed.D. degree except that the major field of specialization is recognized in the title itself. *Dist. f.* **degree, doctor of education.**

doctor, public school: a physician employed by the board of education for health supervision and health services to children in a public school system.

doctor's degree: *see* **degree, doctor's.**

doctrine: (1) a rule, proposition, or teaching that has such official sanction or authority as to be used to guide and direct those who are bound by such sanction or authority; collectively, a body of such rules or teachings; may be a teaching on the nature of a thing and on what can be done with it or a teaching on how to do something, or on what to do in a given situation, cast in the form of a practical rule, command, or exhortation; (2) (mil. ed.) fundamental principles by which the military forces or elements thereof guide their actions in support of national objectives; authoritative, but requiring judgment in application.

doctrine of determined action: *see* **determined action, doctrine of.**

doctrine of equality: *see* **equality, doctrine of.**

doctrine of free will: *see* **free will, doctrine of.**

doctrine of interest: *see* **interest, doctrine of.**

doctrine of maternal impressions: *see* **maternal impressions, doctrine of.**

doctrine of mental states: *see* **mind, mental states doctrine of.**

doctrine of mind, mental states: *see* **mind, mental states doctrine of.**

doctrine of native goodness: *see* **native goodness, doctrine of.**

doctrine of ratification: *see* **ratification, doctrine of.**

doctrine of respondeat superior: *see* **respondeat superior, doctrine of.**

doctrine of specificity of traits: *see* **specificity of traits, doctrine of.**

doctrine of the mean: *see* **mean, doctrine of the.**

doctrine, racial: *see* **racism.**

document: (1) in a general sense, any publication; (2) more narrowly, a publication by some branch of the government; (3) in historical research, one of the several types of original sources containing a written record that represents a writer's report on a condition or activity with which he had firsthand contact.

documentary: a motion-picture or television program that purports to show reality and in which techniques are generally secondary to the theme; a realistic filmic presentation with the impact of drama.

documentary approach: a method of taking pictures, often without preplanning or detailed script preparation, in which realism of content is emphasized.

documentary broadcast: archaic *syn.* **broadcast, actuality.**

documentary broadcasting: *see* **broadcasting, documentary.**

documentary evidence: the facts, including their evaluation and interpretation, that may be obtained from documents.

documentary film: *see* **documentary.**

documentary frequency study: *see* **study, documentary frequency.**

documentary source: *see* **document** (3).

documentation: (1) the process (or result) of citing illustrative or supporting references for statements made, usually through the use of footnotes; (2) in library science, (*a*) collecting, storing, and organizing recorded informational materials for optimum access and (*b*) collection and conservation, classification and selection, and dissemination and utilization of all information; (3) the group of techniques necessary for the orderly presentation, organization, and communication of recorded knowledge.

dodecaphonic music: *see* **music, dodecaphonic.**

dogma: (1) doctrines based upon authority and closed to criticism; (2) a body of doctrines authoritatively proclaimed by a church or sect for belief by its adherents.

dogmatic: (1) (of persons) given to highly authoritative pronouncements; (2) (of statements) without critical scrutiny and challenge as to grounds and evidence; (3) (of systems) based on assumptions that cannot be scrutinized; (4) (of teaching) characterized by authoritative statements on the part of the teacher intended for acceptance by the pupils without question; to be contrasted with teaching that guides pupils in thinking their own way through problems.

dogmatism: (1) positiveness in asserting an opinion, tenet, or belief as though it were established beyond question; (2) a philosophy or system of beliefs that assumes its fundamental postulates uncritically.

doing method: a method of teaching that provides for the active physical involvement of the pupil, as contrasted with the lecture, demonstration, discussion, and study methods. *Comp. w.* **telling method.**

dolichocephalic: characterizing a human with a skull that has a relatively long anterior-posterior cephalic diameter. *Contr. w.* **brachycephalic.**

domain: (math.) (1) the set on which a function or relation is defined; *see* **function**; (2) the set from which replacements for a variable in an *open sentence* are to be chosen; sometimes called the *universe* for the variable; (3) an integral domain; *see* **mathematical system.**

domain, affective: the area pertaining to the feelings or emotions.

domestic art: *see* **art, domestic.**

domestic economy: *see* **economy, domestic.**

domestic science: *see* **science, household.**

domicile: a place where a person lives, his home; in strict legal sense, the place where he has his true, fixed, permanent home and principal establishment and to which place he has, whenever he is absent, the intention of returning.

dominance: *syn.* **ascendance.**

dominance behavior: *see* **behavior, dominance.**

dominance, central: (1) dominance in language and reading of neither the right nor the left hemisphere of the brain, as opposed to the theory of lateral dominance held by Orton and others; (2) balance between the two hemispheres of the brain in controlling voluntary action.

dominance, cerebral: *see* **cerebral dominance.**

dominance, crossed: *see* **dominance, eye-hand.**

dominance, eye: *syn.* **eye preference.**

dominance, eye-hand: the superior development of or preference for use of the left or the right hand and the corresponding eye in reading, writing, and the perfor-

mance of certain motor tasks; *crossed dominance* is said to be present when the dominant eye and the dominant hand are on opposite sides of the body.

dominance feeling: self-esteem coupled with confidence in one's ability to get his own way in social relationships.

dominance, hand: *see* **handedness.**

dominance, lateral: the consistent preference for use of the muscles on one side of the body. *See* **cerebral dominance.**

dominance, mixed cerebral: *see* **cerebral dominance, mixed.**

dominance, ocular: *syn.* **eye preference.**

dominance, social: ascendance in social relationships; a social position of relative superiority; in the general pattern of accommodation, a positioning of ascendance or of inferiority emerges; it is the former to which we refer as social dominance.

dominant: a character present in one parent that appears in all the hybrid offspring, to the exclusion of a contrasting character present in the other parent. [Strictly speaking, the gene for such a character is the dominant entity and, whenever present in an individual, is able to overcome (dominate) the influence of its recessive *allelomorph* (that is, the gene for the contrasting character).] *See* **Mendel's law.**

dominant eye: *see* **eye, dominant.**

dominant-letter theory: (read.) a theory, not held by all experts, that words are recognized more in terms of their dominant letters than in terms of their general shape, pattern, or configuration.

dominant letters: *see* **letters, dominant.**

dominative behavior: *see* **behavior, dominative.**

Dominican education: a type of teaching developed in the thirteenth century by the Dominicans, or Black Friars, who strongly established themselves in connection with many universities and sought to control higher education and to defend Roman Catholic orthodoxy.

door, emergency: a door located at or near the rear of the bus to be used for evacuation of passengers when exit by the service door is impossible or unsafe.

door, service: a power-operated or manually operated door located on the right side of the bus and normally used for loading and discharging pupils.

dormitory: a building, as at a college, containing a number of private or semiprivate rooms for residents, usually along with common bathroom facilities and recreation areas. *Syn.* **residence hall;** *contr. w.* **dormitory** (Education in England and Wales).

dormitory counselor: *syn.* **counselor, residence.**

dormitory, director of: *see* **director of dormitory.**

dormitory library: *see* **library, dormitory.**

dot chart: (1) *syn.* **map, dot;** (2) *syn.* **diagram, scatter.**

DOT code: *see* **code, DOT.**

dot diagram: (1) *syn.* **map, dot;** (2) **diagram, scatter.**

dot map: *see* **map, dot.**

dotting test: *see* **test, dotting.**

double-alternation problem: *see* **problem, double-alternation.**

double-aspect theory: the view that both mind and matter are aspects of a more fundamental, unknown reality, which is *mind* when experienced subjectively, *matter* when viewed objectively.

double-entry table: *see* **table, double-entry.**

double-frame filmstrip: *see* **filmstrip, double-frame.**

double-frequency table: *syn.* **table, double-entry.**

double gymnasium: *see* **gymnasium, double.**

double-headed plan of administrative organization: *syn.* **administration, dual type of.**

double implication: *see* **sentence, biconditional.**

double logarithmic chart: *syn.* **graph, double logarithmic.**

double logarithmic graph: *see* **graph, double logarithmic.**

double period: *see* **period, double.**

double promotion: *see* **promotion, double.**

double-rating table: *syn.* **table, double-entry.**

double-session day: a school day divided into two parts, usually one before noon and one after noon.

double sessions: *see* **sessions, double.**

double-tailed test: *syn.* **test, two-tailed.**

double taxation: *see* **taxation, double.**

double-testing testing technique: *see* **testing technique, double-testing.**

double-track plan: a promotional plan of school organization providing courses of study on the two-track principle and a number of points for transfer from either track to the other to permit of different rates of progress at various times during a pupil's school career.

double trip: *see* **trip, double.**

double vibration (d.v.): one complete oscillatory cycle of a sound wave; used as a measure of pitch.

double vision: *syn.* **diplopia.**

double wing: an offensive formation in football in which both halfbacks line up behind or outside the ends.

doubling: the immediate repetition of a letter in a word, whether incorrectly, as in *raate* for *rate*, or correctly, as in *bitten*; a common source of error in spelling.

doubt: a state of uncertainty, hesitancy, or suspended judgment in coming to a conclusion or belief; an irritating condition brought on by an indeterminate situation in which action and belief are in question; the opening phase of inquiry in which one feels that a situation needs attention.

doubt, reasonable: (legal) doubt arising from candid consideration of the evidence; actual and substantial, not merely possible or capricious.

dough: *see* **equipment, early childhood education.**

Douglass formula for teaching load: an equation devised by Harl R. Douglass for measuring the load of the high school teacher, which considers such factors as the complexity of the subjects taught, the number of class periods taught per week, the number of pupils in each class, the length of the class period, the time spent in preparation for classes, and the amount of time spent on supervising extracurricular activities, in guidance, and on other duties.

dovetailing item: *see* **item, dovetailing.**

down time: time when an automatic computer is not operating correctly or is not in a condition to operate correctly owing to component failures; *contr. w.* **up time;** (2) (school admin.) inactivity of a machine or department during normal operating hours.

Down's syndrome: *see* **mongolism.**

downstroke: a movement of the writing instrument toward the line of writing from above or away from the line of writing below the line.

DQ: *see* **quotient, developmental.**

draft, final: in composition instruction, the pupils' revised written work which is carefully proofread before submission as a finished product.

draft, first: in composition instruction, the first writing done, generally rapidly, with attention to punctuation, spelling, and grammatical correctness left to later revisions.

drafting: (1) the study of the communication of ideas through drawings, sketches, charts, graphs, and maps; learning experiences include the development of knowledge and skills through the use of instruments involved in lettering, sketching, and various forms of instrumental drawings; (2) (home ec.) a method of design by which specified body measurements are used to create individual garment patterns or design; *comp. w.* **draping.**

drafting, architectural: the study of the means of communicating, through the use of lines and symbols, information about buildings; learning activities include the development of preliminary sketches, plans, elevations, sections, and detail drawings and the study of architectural design, the history of structures, building ordinances, and building materials.

drafting technology: the study of graphic representation with special emphasis on technical requirements, specifications, and standards.

drafting, trade: drafting related to a particular trade, for example, machine drafting.

draftsman: (voc. ed.) a person who prepares plans and detail drawings from sketches or notes to specified dimensions.

drainage: (1) provision for the removal of water from a campus or school grounds by means of pipes or ditches; (2) the running off of water due to the contour of the campus or school grounds.

drama, music: a term used, generally, to denote the operatic works of Richard Wagner (1813-1883); Wagner's texts, music, dramatic substance, and overall aesthetic intent are much more closely interwoven into a unified whole than are these same components in traditional *opera*.

drama, open-end: a procedure used in the testing of attitudes, particularly with respect to the determination of attitudes and beliefs; makes use of a dramatic situation in which the student or students supply their own ending or solution.

drama, school: (1) a play presented by pupils as a definite part of their school activity, either before audiences of their fellow pupils or more rarely before general audiences; (2) the systematic organization of dramatic presentations as a recognized part of school procedure.

drama, social: *see* **sociodrama.**

drama, student: a play produced by students with a minimum of teacher aid or participation.

drama, university: a dramatic performance before a student or general audience as a recognized part of the curriculum of the university; frequently used as a part of training in dramatics, playwriting, etc.

dramatic methods: *see* **methods, dramatic.**

dramatic play: *see* **play, dramatic.**

dramatic representation: *see* **representation, dramatic.**

dramatic rhythm: an activity involving the interpretation and acting out of an idea or story rhythmically, with or without musical accompaniment.

dramatics: (1) the activities of any organization devoted primarily to the creation, preparation, and production of plays; (2) activities in the creation, preparation, and production of plays as a part of classroom work.

dramatics, creative: a dramatic presentation, usually based upon a familiar story, cooperatively planned by children, with spontaneous dialogue rather than written lines memorized by the actors.

dramatics, formal: presentation of plays in the classroom or on a stage through the use of a prepared script.

dramatics, informal: a situation in which pupils, in the course of speech instruction, dramatize a story as they remember it but without the planning intended by the author of a selection.

dramatization: (1) the recasting into the form of a play or drama of a story or other material not already in dramatic form; (2) a form of psychotherapy in which the patient acts out life situations related to his difficulties; a technique to help the individual disclose indirectly feelings and attitudes he may not be able to express directly and to help group members to express, practice, and facilitate interpersonal skills; also, a therapeutic device for releasing feelings; *see* **play, dramatic; psychodrama; role playing; sociodrama.**

draping: (home ec.) a method of clothing design by which fabric is draped on a model or dress form into the lines desired for each particular garment. *Comp. w.* **drafting** (2).

draw-a-man behavior: *see* **behavior, draw-a-man.**

draw-a-man test: *see* **test, draw-a-man.**

drawing: depicting on a surface, such as paper, with pencil, crayon, pen, brush, or other graphic means; may be freehand or instrumental, representational or purely informational, or diagrammatic.

drawing, architectural: a construction drawing used by architects and engineers in the planning and erection of buildings; includes freehand and instrumental representation in plan, elevation, and perspective, involving isometric and orthographic projection, and rendered in pencil, pen and ink, and other mediums. *See* **drawing; drawing, instrumental.**

drawing board: a large board of any convenient size used by a draftsman to hold the sheet of paper on which he is drawing.

drawing, categories of children's: *syn.* **drawing, types of children's.**

drawing, engineering: a study of the communication of ideas through lines, symbols, and drawings depicting the mechanical details associated with machine parts, including machine design; learning activities involve the use of technical drawing instruments and technical methods.

drawing, figure: drawing involving the human form.

drawing, freehand: drawing done by hand without the aid of mechanical instruments such as rulers, triangles, and compasses. (Types of freehand drawing frequently mentioned in art curricula are pictorial, object, figure, animal, illustrative, and contour drawing.)

drawing, instrumental: drawing done with the aid of instruments, for example, mechanical, geometric, and architectural drawing done with the help of such instruments as ruler, triangle, compass, French curve, T square, parallel rule, or drafting machine. *See* **drawing.**

drawing instruments: (ind. arts) a set of different-sized compasses, dividers, and ruling pens used by draftsmen.

drawing, mechanical: a study of the communication of ideas through lines, symbols, and drawings; learning activities involve the use of technical drawing instruments to convey ideas graphically through, for example, orthographic projection, pictorial views, and assembly drawings. *See* **drawing, instrumental.**

drawing, memory: representing an image on a surface through recall, from memory. *See* **drawing.**

drawing, mirror: copying or tracing a drawing perceived in a mirror while the subject's drawing hand and the pencil and paper are concealed.

drawing, perspective: representation on a two-dimensional surface of three-dimensional objects surrounded by space so that they appear in the picture as they do to the eye; may be divided into linear and aerial types, each based on special principles of representation; linear representation may be divided into parallel, or one-point; angular, or two-point; and oblique, or three-point perspective; the terms *curvilinear* and *rectilinear* are also applied to perspective drawing.

drawing, pictorial: various forms of representation on a two-dimensional surface of objects surrounded by space so that they appear in the picture very nearly as they do to the eye; pictorial drawing includes *perspective* and a number of other methods.

drawing, prerepresentative: spontaneous symbolic drawing done by children before feeling a desire or need to represent objects and things realistically according to adult standards.

drawing, raised line: tactile adaptation of drawings in which lines can be explored by the visually handicapped.

drawing, representative: *see* **representation.**

drawing scale: *see* **scale, drawing.**

drawing, scaled: a picture or diagram made according to regularly graded proportions, for example, a drawing made to the scale of 1 inch = 1 foot.

drawing, schematic: (1) a preliminary plan or diagram; (2) an imaginative or symbolic type of expression practiced by kindergarten and primary grade children before reaching the stage of realism. *See* **drawing, prerepresentative; schema.**

drawing, scribble: *see* **scribbling, circular; scribbling, longitudinal; scribbling, naming of; scribbling, uncontrolled.**

drawing, technical: a broad term applied to any drawing used to express technical ideas; suggests the scope of the graphic language.

drawing, trade: *syn.* **drafting, trade.**

drawing, types of children's: stylistic and psychological classifications of children's drawing empirically derived and defined; the best-known systems are Lowenfeld's (visual and haptic) and Herbert Read's (enumerative, organic, empathetic, expressionist, decorative, imaginative, rhythmical pattern, and structural form). *Syn.* **categories of children's drawing.**

dress design: *see* **design, dress.**

dressage (dres'əj; Fr., dres·azh'): (Fr., lit., "training") (behav. psych.) a term used by Bechterev to designate the process of training an animal for experimental purposes by conditioning.

dressing frame: *see* **equipment, early childhood education.**

dressing room: a room used for the purpose of changing apparel; usually connected with a gymnasium or auditorium. *See* **locker room.**

drill: (1) a teaching technique intended to bring about automatic accuracy and speed of performance in any subject; (2) repetitive practice of fundamental skills for purposes of instruction in physical education activities; (3) (mil. ed.) a training exercise in which actual operation is simulated, such as a general quarters drill; may be short form for *close-order drill.*

drill, air-raid: practice in the systematic, safe exodus of children and teachers to a predetermined shelter area prescribed by Civilian Defense.

drill, analogy: in foreign language instruction, an exercise which uses a statement plus a tag question to form the stimulus for responses analogous to the original statement.

drill approach: a method of teaching arithmetic which is based on the idea that through systematic practice on number facts and processes presented authoritatively, with few applications, a pupil will be able to develop skill and power in arithmetic.

drill, audiolingual: oral exercises employed in foreign language teaching to give intensive practice in the application of structural and phonetic principles.

drill, calling-the-throw: (typewriting) a form of drill, used to increase speed and control in typewriting and transcription, in which typists are given a certain number of seconds to complete a designated number of words; at the end of each period of time the teacher calls the "guide" or "throw" and students return their carriages and start retyping the copy immediately.

drill, chain: a type of pupil activity in the language classroom; after the teacher models a statement, one student repeats it, then the student seated next to him repeats it, then the student seated next to the second student repeats it, etc., until about eight children have participated; can also be used effectively in question and response drills, in substitution exercises, in adding to previous sentences, and in many other practice activities.

drill, close-order: (mil. ed.) a marching drill performed at normal or close interval; may be executed in marching, parades, and reviews or in exercises involving the manual of arms, that is, drill in handling a rifle.

drill, combat: (mil. ed.) drill conducted for the purpose of giving training in formations and movements designed for a small unit's use in battle; usually conducted at extended intervals and distances.

drill, comparison: a type of oral drill which requires the student to supply the comparative form of the adjective or adverb.

drill, corrective: (1) repetitive practice for the purpose of eliminating errors; (2) (business ed.) practice material and procedures used to help eliminate the most frequent errors of typewriting students, as previously determined by an analysis of student errors. *Syn.* **remedial practice; skill-improvement practice.**

drill, cue: a type of language drill in which a stimulus utterance by the instructor cues a student response in accordance with a previously established pattern. *See* **drill, tape.**

drill, emergency: instruction and practice in the proper procedures for leaving a school bus in case of emergency.

drill, equivalence: a type of oral drill requiring the student of a foreign language to give the *target language* equivalent of an utterance in the source language.

drill field: a level plot of ground used by students for military drill.

drill, fire: *see* **fire drill.**

drill, fixation: (typewriting) repetitive practice of various letters, words, or manipulative controls; used to overcome uncertainty and hesitancy in making reach strokes to various keys of the typewriter.

drill, fixed increment: a type of oral drill requiring the student to use a standard phrase in each response to a succession of different cue sentences, accommodating each cue sentence to the fixed increment.

drill, flash-card: word recognition drill in which cards with words printed or written on them are exposed to children quickly to be recognized and pronounced at sight; used to perfect rapid sight recognition of words; thought by some experts to widen the span of recognition.

drill, formal: any type of drill or repetitive activity in which the form of the activity is stressed and the goal is an automatic response to a stimulus.

drill, formal handwriting: practice by learners during handwriting instruction that involves copying and recopying set exercises, especially such materials as running ovals and push-and-pull exercises.

drill, four-phase: an oral drill format consisting of (*a*) stimulus, (*b*) student response, (*c*) correct response, and (*d*) student repetition.

drill, free-response: *syn.* **drill, rejoinder.**

drill, general quarters: on a naval vessel, a training exercise designed to simulate a condition of readiness when action against an enemy is imminent and where all battle stations are fully manned and alert, ammunition is ready for instant loading, and guns and guided missile launchers may be loaded.

drill, military: a pattern of, practice in, or the execution of military exercises, formations, and evolutions in both close and extended order.

drill, narration: a linguistic exercise requiring a student to make a statement based on previously cued circumstances; another form of this drill requires a student to narrate a sequence of events based on a number of cues.

drill, negation: in foreign language instruction, a type of pattern drill which requires the student to negate all sentences according to a model.

drill, paired sentence: a type of linguistic exercise in which a student combines two sentences in a predetermined manner, using relative pronouns, conjunctions, or other connectives.

drill, pattern: in language instruction, an oral exercise using basic or model utterances in which several small and consistent changes in sound, form, order, and vocabulary are made repeatedly to promote the student's control over the specific grammatical (or other) structure involved and to make that control habitual through frequent repetition and minimal variation of the linguistic patterns.

drill, phonemic discrimination: in foreign language instruction, a drill in which the student is asked to distinguish between minimal pairs until he is assured he hears different phonemes.

drill, rejoinder: an oral exercise used in foreign language instruction in which the teacher gives the student a cue in the form of a statement or question to which he may freely respond as long as his answer or statement logically advances the conversation; also called *free-response drill.*

drill, replacement: a type of drill which requires the student to substitute one word or group of words for another in an utterance and to restate the new utterance.

drill, rhythmic: exercise in the performance of various rhythmic patterns of music notation.

drill, rhythmical: a handwriting exercise consisting of successive strokes or stroke combinations of about the same length, to be inscribed while following a set rhythm.

drill, speed: (1) repetitive practice aimed at increasing speed of performance; (2) (read.) an exercise for increasing reading speed by having the subject read under time control or by having him read words and phrases exposed in quick succession.

drill subject: *see* **subject, drill.**

drill, tape: an audiolingual language laboratory cue drill in which the cues are prerecorded on magnetic tape. *See* **drill, cue.**

drill, transformation: a linguistic exercise in which a student is required to transform part of an utterance according to a preassigned grammatical criterion and to restate the utterance, including all correct consequences of that transformation. *Comp. w.* **transformation, chain.**

drinking fountain: a fixture in or out of a building from which a jet of water may be released for drinking.

drive: (1) a physiological tension that induces activity that will relieve the tension, for example, hunger, thirst, sex desire, etc.; *syn.* **physiological drive;** (2) loosely, any motive or determinant of behavior, such as a persistent wish.

drive, changes of, accompanying maturity: the gradual shift in the direction of the release of primary energy which is related to and attendant upon maturational phenomena; while primary drives change as the organism matures biologically, secondary drives change only as the individual learns, as he matures.

drive, curiosity: *see* **curiosity.**

drive, nature of: a drive provides impetus for the organism to continue to act until a relatively definite goal is reached and the need which created that drive is satisfied; the strength of the drive depends both upon the strength of the need and the distance to the goal which is perceived as satisfying that need.

drive, physiological: *syn.* **drive** (1).

drive, primary: (1) the tendency for an organism to respond directly to its environment without the intervention of experience; (2) internal biological stimuli which are homostatic in origin; (3) the motivation arising from a fundamental, elemental need.

drive reduction theory: a belief or hypothesis that all behavior has a tension reducing function, the tensions deriving from unsatisfied drives, the behavior being acquired and strengthened when it satisfies the drives by reducing them; similar to Freud's pleasure principle and consistent with Cannon's concept of *homeostasis.*

drive, second-order: (1) a hypothetical construct postulated to explain how primary biological drives become associated with specific and culturally oriented patterns of stimuli as representing to the organism significant goal objects or likely patterns of behavior; (2) a symbolic expression indicating the probable relationships between primary and secondary drives.

drive, secondary: an urge or motivation that has been acquired through experience and education, in distinction to a primary drive, which arises out of the direct needs of the organism.

drive, tape: *syn.* **tape transport.**

driver, alternate: a bus operator available when needed to operate a bus but not regularly assigned to a bus or route. *Syn.* **substitute driver.**

driver clinic: *see* **clinic, driver.**

driver education: *see* **driver safety education.**

driver-mechanic: a school-bus operator who also works part time as a mechanic; usually drives a bus and keeps one or more buses in repair.

driver, pupil: a pupil who attends school and who operates a school bus. *Syn.* **student driver** (2).

driver safety education: learning experiences, including behind-the-wheel driver training, provided by the school for the purpose of helping students to become good traffic citizens and to use motor vehicles safely and efficiently. *Dist. f.* **training, driver;** *syn.* **driver education.**

driver, student: (1) a student in *driver education* receiving road instruction behind the wheel of a motor vehicle, usually preceded by or carried on simultaneously with classroom instruction; (2) a high school or college student who operates a school bus; *syn.* **pupil driver.**

driver, substitute: *syn.* **driver, alternate.**

driver training: *see* **driver, student.**

driver training, director of: *see* **director of driver training.**

driver's assistant: a person responsible to the driver of the bus who watches the pupils, helps them on and off the school bus, flags the bus across railroad tracks, and otherwise helps to provide safe pupil transportation.

driver's daily report: *see* **report, driver's daily.**

drives, socialization of: a means of providing direction and acceptable outlets for drives; the individual learns acceptable techniques for need satisfaction.

driving range, multiple-car: an off-street area on which a number of cars are used simultaneously to provide laboratory instruction under the supervision of one or more teachers.

driving simulation: a teaching method, employing both films and electromechanical devices designed to represent the driver's compartment of the automobile, through which students develop proper judgment and behavior responses as well as manipulation skills.

drivometer: (1) a device attached to an automobile to measure and sometimes record a driver's manipulation of controls in response to highway and traffic situations; (2) a device simulating the controls of an automobile, used to measure and sometimes record a driver's reactions to simulated highway and traffic situations.

drivometer test: *see* **test, drivometer.**

dromedary gait: *see* **gait, dromedary.**

dromomania: a strong impulsion toward running away from home.

drop temporarily: *see* **dropping of pupils** (1).

dropout: (1) most often designates an elementary or secondary school pupil who has been in membership during the regular school term and who withdraws or is dropped from membership for any reason except death or transfer to another school before graduating from secondary school (grade 12) or before completing an equivalent program of studies; such an individual is considered a dropout whether his dropping out occurs during or between regular school terms, whether it occurs before or after he has passed the compulsory school attendance age, and, where applicable, whether or not he has completed a minimum required amount of school work; *see* **mortality, educational;** (2) in programmed instruction, a frame which, when appropriately responded to by the student, is eliminated by the teaching machine from his subsequent repetitions of the program; a dropout device may also be incorporated into the machine for frames answered erroneously, so that the errors may be reviewed at the end of the set sequence.

dropout, potential: a student identified as one who may leave an educational program prior to graduation.

dropout prevention: the forestalling of a pupil's leaving school before graduation.

dropout problem: the educational and social consequences which result when pupils become school dropouts.

dropout program: *see* **program, dropout.**

dropout rate: an expression of the comparison between the number of people who enter schooling at one level and the number who successfully complete a later level, for example, the number of people who enter first grade as compared with the number twelve years later who graduate from high school.

dropout rate, annual: (pupil accounting) the percentage of pupils for whom the school was arithmetically accountable on June 30 who dropped out between July 1 of the preceding year and June 30 of the current year.

dropout rehabilitation: *see* **rehabilitation, dropout.**

dropout returnee: a dropout who returns to the same school during the same academic year or the succeeding academic year.

dropout, rural: a student who resides in an unincorporated area and who leaves school before graduating.

dropout, urban: (pupil accounting) a youth who resides in a population center of 50,000 or more and who leaves school before graduation.

dropping, decimal: *see* **decimal dropping.**

dropping of pupils: (1) the act of removing pupils from the rolls of a school because of absences of 3, 5, 10, or more

days (this practice was so common as to be almost universal in the United States during the latter part of the nineteenth and the early part of the twentieth centuries; it exists today but has been rapidly dying out); (2) the practice of obliging a probation pupil to withdraw from a particular school or course because of consistent failure or inability to do the work of the school or course.

dropping out: leaving a school as a dropout. *See* **dropout.**

drug abuse education: the approach used to discredit the misbeliefs and misconceptions which hamper public understanding of the facts about drug abuse; calls for a broad program of public and professional education aided by the resources of the Federal government.

drug addiction: craving for and actual reliance upon any narcotic drug to the point that relatively normal physiological and psychological functioning depends upon gradually increasing dosages and cannot take place in the absence of the drug.

drum corps: an ensemble of drums, used independently, in company with fifes, or as part of a band; employed chiefly to accompany marching groups.

drum dump: *see* **storage dump.**

drum, magnetic: a rotating cylinder, the surface of which is coated with a magnetic material on which information may be stored as small polarized spots.

dry carrel: *see* **carrel.**

dry mount: *see* **mount, dry.**

dry run: practice or rehearsal of a speech or lesson alone, with or without a tape recorder, or before one or more persons who are present to make suggestions for improvement; this may be recorded on videotape for self-review and critique.

drying rack: *see* **equipment, early childhood education.**

dual channel: a tape recording on which two signals are recorded and retrievable, alternately or simultaneously, by a channel selector.

dual-channel concept of on-the-job training: *see* **training, dual-channel concept of on-the-job.**

dual-channel recording: *see* **recording, dual-channel.**

dual control: (driver ed.) the duplication of the controls of an automobile, so that either of two persons in the driving compartment may control the vehicle; commonly used in driver-training classes.

dual-control system: the system by which vocational education is administered separately from general education; may involve the establishment of separate school boards for vocational education, with their own staffs of professional workers, as in the system followed in Wisconsin; uncommon in the United States. *Contr. w.* **unit-control system** (2).

dual enrollment: *see* **enrollment, dual.**

dual instruction: *see* **instruction, dual.**

dual marking: *see* **marking, dual.**

dual organization: *syn.* **administration, dual type of.**

dual personality: *see* **personality, dual.**

dual routing: (1) *syn.* **route, multiple;** (2) the operation of two or more buses over the same route.

dual sport: *see* **sport, dual.**

dual system of operation: *see* **operation, dual system of.**

dual tape recording: *see* **recording, dual tape.**

dual-track head: *see* **head, dual-track.**

dual-track recorder: *see* **recorder, dual-track.**

dual-track system: *see* **curriculum, multiple-track.**

dual type of administration: *see* **administration, dual type of.**

dualism: in general, the theory that is applied to anything held to be composed of two distinct parts, such as the theory that man is both mind and body; in metaphysics, the theory that the universe is reducible to two kinds of reality, the natural and the supernatural; in epistemology, the theory that the object of knowledge is not identical with the object known.

dualism, psychophysical: the doctrine that mental and physical activity are dissimilar but harmonious; first stated by Leibnitz (1695) and taken over by Titchener (1896). *Syn.* **psychophysical parallelism.**

dualistic ethics: *see* **ethics, dualistic.**

dualistic metaphysics: *see* **metaphysics, dualistic.**

dub: *v.* (audiovis. instr.) (1) to duplicate a tape recording; (2) to record two signals on the same tape.

dubbing: the transfer of recorded sound from one unit to another; commonly record-to-tape, tape-to-tape, tape-to-film; sometimes called a duplicate or a *dup*.

due process: the exercise of the powers of government in such a way as to protect individual rights.

dull child: *see* **child, backward; child, slow-learning.**

dull normal: the designation of children or adults who are just below the average in general intelligence.

dullard: a child who is unable to keep up with his grade in school because of a moderately subnormal intelligence.

dummy: in automatic data processing, a substitute used to fulfill formal specifications that is replaced by the required thing or data when needed; for example, a dummy address, such as 00000, is often used in writing programs when the required address will be provided by address modification.

dummy carton: an empty merchandise container used in the distributive education laboratory for practice work in display.

dump, core: *see* **storage dump.**

dump, drum: *see* **storage dump.**

dump, memory: *see* **storage dump.**

dump, storage: *see* **storage dump.**

duodecimal system: an additive system of numeration having place value and with 12 as its base; thus 12 different symbols are used in writing duodecimal numerals. *See* **decimal system.**

dup: *see* **dubbing.**

duplicate classes: *see* **classes, duplicate.**

duplicate forms: *syn.* **equivalent forms.**

duplicate master: a first-generation copy of a master tape, for daily use in the language laboratory.

duplicate school: *syn.* **alternate school.**

duplicate section: *see* **section, duplicate.**

duplicated newspaper: *see* **newspaper, duplicated.**

duplication, photographic: processes used to make copies of documents by employing techniques similar to those of photography (using light, sensitized paper, etc.).

duplicator, direct-process: a duplicating machine employing a master copy made by placing a sheet of direct-process carbon paper behind the master and tracing, writing, typing, etc., on the face of the master; the carbon (or dye) remains on the back of the master at the point of imprint from the pressure applied by pen or typewriter; the carbon-typed side of the master clamped to the cylinder of the duplicator then comes in contact with blank sheets of paper moistened by a minute amount of alcoholic fluid dispensed on the sheets as they pass through the machine under pressure; the fluid, dissolving the carbon (or dye), transfers the impressions from master to copies which dry instantly; a rapid, economical, and widely used copying process for small jobs. *Syn.* **fluid duplicator; spirit duplicator.**

duplicator, fluid: *syn.* **duplicator, direct-process.**

duplicator, spirit: *syn.* **duplicator, direct-process.**

duplicator, stencil: (mimeograph) stencil duplicators are of two major types: (*a*) the hollow single-drum machine, with which the stencil is clamped over the ink pad on the hollow revolving drum filled with ink, which then seeps through small perforations in the drum to the ink pad and the openings or markings on the stencil, ink from which is deposited on paper fed into the machine under pressure, and (*b*) the twin-cylinder duplicator, with which a silk screen acts as an ink pad covering two closed cylinders between which paste ink is forced through the screen and the stencil clamped over it; as blank paper is fed into the machine, the ink coming through the markings on the stencil prints the copy.

durable consumer goods: *see* **goods, durable consumer.**

duties, housekeeping: *see* **housekeeping duties.**

duty: (1) what one is under obligation to do, such obligation being usually moral but sometimes legal or contractual; (2) the claim of more remote or more significant interests or considerations as opposed to the claim of those which are more immediate or less significant.

duty, discretionary: *see* **duty, ministerial.**

duty, ministerial: (legal) duty not involving the use of discretion, imposed upon a person or body.

dwarf: a person of abnormally small size for his age (under 4 feet tall at maturity). (Dwarfs may be classified, broadly, as well-proportioned, disproportioned, and malformed. In the disproportioned dwarf, the head is comparatively large and the limbs are extremely short. Dwarfs having malformations, always the result of disease, may exhibit a curved spine, bent bones in the limbs, and a deformed pelvis.) ●

dynamic: (1) motivating behavior through the release of energy; for example, a physiological drive is a dynamic process; (2) energetic, stimulating, actively and forcefully influential; (3) a term used to designate a type of psychology that developed largely from psychoanalysis and that is concerned with human motivation; *see* **psychodynamics; psychology, dynamic.**

dynamic air war game: *see* **war game, dynamic air.**

dynamic balance: *see* **balance, dynamic.**

dynamic contraction: *see* **contraction, phasic** (1).

dynamic lattice: *see* **lattice, dynamic.**

dynamic morality: *see* **morality, dynamic.**

dynamic psychology: *see* **psychology, dynamic.**

dynamic range: *see* **range, dynamic.**

dynamic splint: *see* **splint, dynamic.**

dynamic substrata-factor theory of reading: *see* **reading, dynamic substrata-factor theory of.**

dynamic supervision: *see* **supervision, dynamic.**

dynamics: (1) active, functional relationships of importance in the causation of the phenomenon in question; the term often has the connotation of energetic interaction and shifting equilibriums; frequently used in connection with emotional factors underlying behavior; to be contrasted with pure (static) description or normative data and distinguished from the Freudian concept of *dynamism;* (2) in music, variations in volume of sound, indicated by words, symbols, or abbreviations, for example, *pp* (pianissimo) = very soft, *f* (forte) = loud.

dynamics, color: science of the impact of color upon human beings.

dynamics, cultural: (1) the study of the modifications produced in a culture by the invention or borrowing of new traits or the disappearance of old traits; (2) the modifications themselves viewed as a dynamic process.

dynamics, group: an interactive psychological relationship in which members of a group develop a common perception based on shared feelings and emotions; this common perception is affected by the norms of the culture, but the immediate action of the group is based on the spontaneous mood of the immediate collection of individuals; the behaving group provides an outlet for the shared feelings and emotions which in each member separately had no adequate expression; these interstimulative relationships may be described by the term group dynamics, the study of which under the late Kurt Lewin has become a branch of social psychology. *See* **analysis, interaction; discussion, group; research, small-group; T-group.**

dynamics, social: the branch of social inquiry dealing with the laws, forces, and social phenomena of change in society.

dynamism: (1) a defense mechanism; (2) in general, any mechanism; (3) (psychoan.) a device by which the ego placates the id or subdues its demands.

dynamogenesis: (1) hypermental and hypermotor activity resulting from increased stimulation of a sensory organ; (2) the principle that changes in sensory activity invariably result in increased motor activity (Brown-Sequard, 1860); (3) (phys. ed.) the development of muscular power through a physiological process whereby exhausted muscle groups are revived as other muscle groups are brought into action; also called *dynamogenics.*

dynamogenics: *see* **dynamogenesis** (3).

dynamometer (dī'nə·mom'ə·tər): any one of a number of instruments used to measure the strength of muscular exertion, for example, one used to measure the strength of grip.

dynamometer, back-and-leg: a device consisting of a handle attached to a strong spring connected with a dial and pointer and fastened to a small wooden platform; used for measuring lifting strength.

dynamometer, hand: an instrument, used to measure strength of handgrip, in which resistance is usually provided by powerful springs that must be compressed, the number of pounds of pressure exerted being registered on a dial.

dysarthria (dis·är'thri·ə): faulty articulation of speech sounds due to lesions or defects in the central nervous system. *Dist. f.* **anarthria; dyslalia.**

dyscalculia: *syn.* **acalculia.**

dyschronometria: a defect in the sense of time, a learning disorder of the central nervous system affecting all aspects of the time concept, so that a child who is dyschronometric cannot normally learn to tell time from the clock, learn the days of the week, months of the year, or the meaning of before, after, until, in a minute, next week, or tomorrow; the condition, commonly associated with *dyslexia,* can occur in children who are normal intellectually.

dysdiadochokinesia: derangement of the function of diadochokinesia. *See* **diadochokinesia.**

dysfunction: partial disturbance, impairment, or abnormality of the functioning of an organ.

dysfunction, cerebral: absence of completely normal function of the cerebrum, manifested by impairment in intellectual, motor, behavioral, or sense functioning and resulting in hyperactive behavior, emotional instability, perceptual difficulties, transient or persistent motor awkwardness, and various educational difficulties.

dysfunctionality: (school admin.) the persistence of parts or operations that are no longer functional.

dysgenic (dis·jen'ik): referring to anything that tends to impair the qualities of future generations. *Ant.* **eugenic.**

dysgraphia: a disability characterized by any of various degrees of difficulty in writing: *Comp. w.* **agraphia.**

dyskinesia: impairment of the power of voluntary movement, resulting in fragmentary or incomplete movements.

dyslalia (dis·lā'li·ə): faulty articulation of speech sounds due to causes other than lesions or defects in the central nervous system. *Dist. f.* **dysarthria.**

dyslexia: (1) *syn.* **reading disability;** (2) a type of visual aphasia with the associative learning difficulty; (3) a mild form of *alexia.*

dyslogia (dis·lō'ji·ə): a pathological condition that causes impairment of the power of reasoning so that ideas cannot be expressed in speech except with great difficulty; the condition is often present in certain types of feeble-mindedness, in certain psychoses, or as the result of brain damage.

dysphasia (dis·fā'zhi·ə): any impairment of language functioning due to brain damage; generally synonymous with *aphasia,* although the latter term usually refers to a more profound or severe condition of linguistic disorder.

dysphemia: (1) any disorder of speech due to a psychoneurotic condition and having no known organic basis; includes aphemia, paraphemia, spasmophemia, and tachyphemia; (2) sometimes used to designate a condition or predisposition assumed to underlie stuttering or a poorly timed control mechanism for coordinating sequential utterance.

dysphonia (dis·fō'ni·ə): any disturbance of vocalization or phonation, differing from *aphonia* in degree of severity. *See* **aphonia.**

dysphoria: a feeling of anxiety, restlessness, and depression of spirits. *Ant.* **euphoria.**

dysplasia: abnormality of development.

dysplastic development: *see* **dysplasia.**

dyspraxia: the inability to plan a motor act ideationally.

dysrhythmia: any disturbance to the flow of a motor act, speech pattern, thought flow, or language expression which serves to interrupt or interfere with regularity. *Comp. w.* **rhythmic action; arrythmia.**

dysteleology (dis'tel·ē·ol'ə·ji; dis'tē·lē-): the doctrine of purposelessness, particularly the theory that nature operates without purpose or ends. *Ant.* **teleology.**

dystonia: disordered tonicity of any tissues.

dystonia musculorum deformans: a disorder characterized by muscular contractions which produce distortion of the spine and hips; the muscles are hypotonic when at rest and hypertonic when in action; the condition occurs chiefly in children.

dystrophy (dis'trə·fi): imperfect or faulty nutrition or development.

dystrophy, muscular: a group of diseases involving the progressive weakening and wasting of the skeletal muscles; not contagious and appears to have a hereditary basis, but the exact cause is unknown; classified according to appearance of the muscles, the group of muscles primarily involved, the age of onset, and the changes in the muscle tone and reactivity.

e: a mathematical constant, 2.7183, which is the base for natural or Napierian logarithms and is useful in describing the sampling distributions of certain statistics.

E chart: *see* **chart, E.**

ear, artificial: a device for the measurement of earphones which presents an acoustic impedance to the earphone equivalent to the impedance presented by the average human ear and which is equipped with a microphone for measurement of the sound pressures developed by the earphone.

ear examination: *see* **examination, ear.**

ear training: *see* **training, ear.**

early admission: *see* **admission, early.**

early childhood education: usually refers to the program and curriculum for children in nursery school, kindergarten, and/or the primary grades 1 through 3. *See* **kindergarten; preschool education; primary education.**

early childhood education equipment: *see* **equipment, early childhood education.**

early departure: approved leaving of school on a regular schedule before the official close of the school session.

early entrance: *see* **admission, early.**

early expressive stage: (art ed.) the third stage in the young child's creative development, following the *manipulative stage* and the *form-experimental stage;* naming of objects in his painting now occurs, indicating that content or meaning is now important. *See* **form-experimental stage; manipulative stage** (2).

early reading: *see* **reading, early.**

early room: a schoolroom provided for supervised play activities before school begins in the morning.

early school leaver: *syn.* **dropout.**

earmarked tax: *see* **tax, earmarked.**

earmarked tax sources: *see* **tax sources, earmarked.**

earmarking: the allocating of money to a specified purpose.

earth and space science: *see* **science, earth and space.**

earth science: *see* **science, earth.**

easel: an upright frame on which paper may be tacked for young children's exploratory experiences with art mediums.

easy book: a book for young children, such as a picture book or reader.

ecclesiastical foundation: *see* **foundation, ecclesiastical.**

ecclesiastical year: *see* **year, ecclesiastical.**

echelon (esh'ə·län): (Fr., lit., "rung of a ladder") a level of service within an organization.

echo speech technique: (spec. ed.) a technique in which the subject is trained to repeat instantly what he is hearing, following almost simultaneously the utterance of another person; also called **shadowing.**

echolalia (ek'ō·lā'li·ə): (1) a disorder characterized by involuntary repetition of words heard spoken by others; sometimes a symptom of dementia praecox; (2) more commonly, a stage in the development of the child's speech in which he repeats, or echoes with relatively low degree of awareness of meaning, the speech of others in his environment.

echopraxia (ek'ō·prak'si·ə): a condition characterized by the meaningless imitation of motions and gestures made by others; met with in dementia praecox.

eclectic: (1) selected from a group of items or from various sources; (2) descriptive of the practice of drawing doctrines from different schools of thought with or without regard to their coherence or contradiction.

eclectic counseling: *see* **counseling, eclectic.**

eclectic method: (1) (art ed.) an attempt to compromise between directing and free-expression methods by allowing some freedom along with definite directions in the hope of developing skills and techniques along with expression; a logical integration of directing and free-expression methods is thought by many to be impossible; *see* **directing method; free-expression method;** (2) a method of teaching foreign languages combining features of various methods as need arises.

eclectic programming: *see* **programming, eclectic.**

eclectic reasoning: *see* **reasoning, eclectic.**

eclecticism: (1) a school of philosophy that endeavors to construct a coherent and harmonious system of thought or belief by adopting selected beliefs from various rival schools or systems; (2) the practice, commonly attractive to beginning students of philosophy of education, of building an organized philosophy for oneself by collecting a composite body of thought made up of views chosen from various philosophical positions or systems; contains the danger of developing a whimsical picking and choosing rather than a coherent and critically integrated philosophical position; (3) (couns.) the selection of features from a number of theories and the organization of these features into a comprehensive system within the counseling process.

ecology: the field of biology which deals with the mutual relations between organisms and their environment.

ecology, human: that branch of science which deals with the reciprocal relations between man and his environment and the distribution of human beings in relation to social-cultural phenomena and the processes involved in that distribution; includes the study of spatial-areal patterns that rise and change by virtue of the distributive processes.

economic approach: the consideration of an issue from the standpoint of its relation to economic factors, namely, the creating and using of wealth.

economic area, state: an area defined by the Bureau of the Census for the 1950 census report, comprising one or more adjacent counties (or parishes) "with relatively homogeneous agricultural, industrial, social, and demographic characteristics."

economic biology: *see* **biology, economic.**

economic blindness: *see* **blindness, economic.**

economic botany: *see* **botany, economic.**

economic civics: *see* **civics, economic.**

economic competency: *see* **competency, economic.**

economic conditions: (1) situations composed of all factors associated with the production, distribution, and consumption of goods and services; (2) conditions relating to making a living in a community that affect materially the growth and development of the individual and the group.

economic education: a broad term for all education that is aimed at increasing the individual's understanding, knowledge, and appreciation of the economic structure of modern life; includes business, consumer, and distributive education as well as the study of such areas as economics, economic geography, banking, finance, and foreign trade.

economic-factor method: *syn.* **multiple-factor method.**

economic geography: *see* **geography, economic.**

economic history: *see* **history, economic.**

economic literacy: *syn.* **competency, economic.**

economic motive: a drive that is based on considerations of wealth-getting or wealth-using as a means of achieving status or survival.

economic science: *see* **science, economic.**

economic surplus: (1) monetary return in excess of normal, expected profits; (2) monetary return in excess of the minimum yield necessary for the continuance of enterprise.

economic welfare: (1) the standard of living of a group; (2) the goal of a desirable standard of living for the whole group; (3) the establishment of a reasonable standard of living for the whole people.

economics: the branch of social study that deals with the production, distribution, and consumption of commodities having exchange value and with the social phenomena arising from such activities.

economics, business: a study concerned principally with such business operations as financing and funding commercial enterprises, accounting, methods and practices of buying and selling, and personnel and public relations.

economics, commodity: a major branch of economics primarily concerned with the production, distribution, and consumption of material commodities.

economics, consumer: (1) the science that deals with the use of resources to satisfy the needs and wants of consumers as individuals and as a group; (2) the study of economic principles and forces and the interpretation of economic theories in terms of consumer interest as distinguished from producer interest.

economics, historical school of: a school of thought in economics principally concerned with the historical study of economic systems and theories, without any attempt to evaluate them in terms of desirability. *See* **institutionalism.**

economics, labor: a field of study primarily concerned with labor problems, including the welfare of laborers (accidents, old age, pensions, etc.), labor unions, and job security.

economics, land: a major branch of economics primarily concerned with the production, distribution, and consumption of agricultural products and other products taken from the earth, such as minerals, petroleum, and timber.

economics of consumption: *syn.* **economics, consumer.**

economics, personal: *syn.* **economics, consumer.**

economy: in testing, that characteristic of a good examination evidenced by a no greater than reasonable outlay of school personnel time and of money; expressed by the efficiency index divided by the cost per minute of testing time.

economy, consumer-directed: *syn.* **democracy, consumer.**

economy, consumption-directed: an economy in which the consumer has little voice in determining what is to be produced; the producers make available what they would like to sell. *See* **democracy, consumer.**

economy, domestic: orderly arrangement and management of the affairs of a community, estate, or establishment directly concerned with its maintenance or productiveness; regulation with respect to production and consumption; to be contrasted with international or world economy.

economy, law of: *syn.* **law of parsimony.**

economy of abundance: a way of economic life based on the ideal of producing and distributing sufficient goods, foodstuffs, and services so that everyone may have all the necessities and some of the comforts of life.

economy of potential plenty: roughly synonymous with economy of abundance, but with the implication that through defective distribution not all needy persons are supplied with sufficient quantities of the necessities and comforts of life. *See* **economy of abundance.**

economy of scarcity: an organization of economic life in which output is restricted in order to regulate prices. *Contr. w.* **economy of abundance.**

economy, planned: an economic system purposefully organized by the mind of man; opposed to what are considered by the planners to be weaknesses in the competitive system, such as wasteful duplication of effort, inequitable distribution of goods and services, and wastes caused by conflict between capital and labor. *See* **social order, telic.**

economy, political: (1) an old name for the science now usually called *economics;* (2) the economic activities and relations of the state, such as taxation, expenditure of state money, and control of state over business.

economy, principle of: *syn.* **law of parsimony.**

economy, test: a criterion used in conjunction with the time necessary for the examinee to take a test; this term is also used in connection with the financial outlay for test materials.

ecstasy: a trancelike state, sometimes seen in hysteria and catatonia, resembling a powerful emotion of happiness.

ectomorph: an individual of an extremely thin, wiry, and active type.

ectomorphic component: *see* **component, ectomorphic.**

ecumenical center: a center concerned specifically with church reunion and normally sponsored by two or more churches (denominations) devoted to the cause of restoring Christian unity.

ecumenical movement: *see* **ecumenism.**

ecumenism: (from the Gr. oikoumene, lit., "the whole inhabited world") the movement toward the restoration of unity among the various branches of the Christian church—Catholic, Orthodox, Protestant, and Anglican. *Syn.* **ecumenical movement.**

edge-notched card: *see* **card, edge-notched.**

editing: (1) in preparation of films, both picture and sound, the process of cutting and putting together scenes to produce the desired complete film; *syn.* **cutting;** (2) splicing together certain sections of a tape recording or sections from different tape recordings in a desired sequence.

editing, music: the act of providing marks of expression, speed, and style for a composer's work or, in the absence of clearly defined intent, the act of suggesting appropriate possibilities for expression, speed, and style.

edition binding: *see* **binding, edition.**

edition, educational: *syn.* **edition, school.**

edition, reinforced: *syn.* **edition, school.**

edition, school: an edition of a trade book printed on strong paper, with the same illustrations as appear in the trade edition but with specially reinforced binding and usually selling at a lower price than the trade edition. *Syn.* **educational edition; reinforced edition.**

EDP: *see* **data processing, electronic.**

educability: (1) the capacity of an organism to profit from experience and to adjust to conditions that recur; (2) the capacity to master academic skills.

educability, motor: the ability of an individual to learn new motor skills.

educable: capable of learning to a degree that exceeds mere repetition.

educable mentally handicapped: *syn.* **mentally retarded, educable.**

educable mentally retarded: *see* **mentally retarded, educable.**

educable mentally retarded child: *see* **child, educable mentally retarded.**

educand: a general term for a pupil or student; anyone undergoing the process of education.

education: (1) the aggregate of all the processes by means of which a person develops abilities, attitudes, and other forms of behavior of positive value in the society in which he lives; (2) the social process by which people are subjected to the influence of a selected and controlled environment (especially that of the school) so that they may attain social competence and optimum individual development; (3) ordinarily, a general term for the so-called "technical" or more specifically classified professional courses offered in higher institutions for the preparation of teachers and relating directly to educational psychology, philosophy and history of education, curriculum, special and general methods, instruction, administration, supervision, etc.; broadly, the total pattern of preparation, formal and informal, that results in the professional growth of teachers; *see* **teacher education;** (4) the art of making available to each generation the organized knowledge of the past.

education, adapted physical: *see* **physical education, adapted.**

education, adolescent: *see* **adolescent education.**

education, adult: *see* **adult education.**

education, adult basic: *see* **adult basic education.**

education, adult homemaking: *see* **homemaking education, adult.**

education, adult vocational: *see* **vocational education, adult.**

education, aerospace: *see* **aerospace education.**

education, aesthetic: *see* **aesthetic education.**

education, agribusiness: *syn.* **agricultural business education;** *see* **agricultural mechanics education; agricultural products education; agricultural supplies education.**

education, agricultural: *see* **agricultural education.**

education, agricultural business: *syn.* **agribusiness education;** *see* **agricultural mechanics education.**

education, agricultural mechanics: *see* **agricultural mechanics education.**

education, agricultural postsecondary: *see* **postsecondary education, agricultural.**

education, agricultural production: *see* **agricultural production education.**

education, agricultural products: *see* **agricultural products education.**

education, agricultural resources: *see* **agricultural resources education.**

education, agricultural supplies: *see* **agricultural supplies education.**

education, agricultural technical: *see* **technical education, agricultural.**

education, alcohol: *see* **alcohol education.**

education, alien: *see* **alien education.**

education, alumni: *see* **alumni education.**

education and commissioning program, airman: *see* **program, airman education and commissioning.**

education and training of mentally retarded: *see* **mentally retarded, education and training of.**

education and training pattern, desirable: (mil. ed.) an education and training pattern that relates education and training to the development of professionally competent officers.

education, apprenticeship: *see* **apprenticeship education.**

education, aristocratic view of: *see* **aristocratic view of education.**

education, art: *see* **art education.**

education as adjustment: the conception of education as growth and change in the individual, enabling him the better to meet and deal with the varied aspects of the environment affecting his development and activities; generally associated with the progressive movement in education in America; the philosophy of the Commission on Life Adjustment Education for Youth sponsored by the U.S. Office of Education from 1945 to 1954.

education as growth: the view of education as process, holding further growing to be the sole directing end; present growth evaluated in terms of its release of potential for further growing; growing considered as the active pursuit of ends which also serve as instruments to release further growing (Dewey).

education as the continuous reconstruction of experience: (John Dewey) the conception that education is to provide for growth or the continuous enlargement and enrichment of human experience, as opposed to conceptions that identify a terminal or fulfilled end of the educative process.

education, atomic-age: *see* **atomic-age education.**

education, audiovisual: *see* **audiovisual education.**

education, auditory: *see* **auditory education.**

education, aviation: *see* **aviation education.**

education, basic: (1) (adult ed.) *see* **adult basic education;** (2) *see* **program, common-learnings** (2).

education, basic business: *see* **business education, basic.**

education, business: *see* **business education.**

education, camping: one of the educative functions of many schools recognizing the educative value of camping; a form of experience education in which certain learnings are placed in their natural environments.

education, Catholic: *see* **Catholic education.**

education center, adult: *see* **center, adult education.**

education, character: *see* **character education.**

education, charity: *see* **charity education.**

education, child-centered: *see* **child-centered education.**

education, childhood : *see* **childhood education.**

education, Christian: *see* **Christian education.**

education, church: *see* **church education.**

education, citizenship: *see* **citizenship education.**

education, civic: *see* **civic education.**

education, classical: *see* **classical education.**

education, college of: *see* **college of education.**

education, commercial: *syn.* **business education.**

education committee: in connection with boards of education employing the committee system, a committee charged with the examination and direction of matters pertaining directly to instruction.

education, comparative: *see* **comparative education.**

education, compensatory: *see* **compensatory education.**

education, completion: *syn.* **terminal education.**

education, compulsory: *see* **compulsory education.**

education, consumer: *see* **consumer education.**

education, consumer and homemaking: *see* **consumer and homemaking education.**

education, consumer business: *see* **business education, consumer.**

education, continuation: *see* **continuation education.**

education, continuing: *see* **continuing education.**

education, continuing legal: *see* **continuing professional education.**

education, continuing medical: *see* **continuing professional education.**

education, continuing professional: *see* **continuing professional education.**

education, cooperative: *see* **cooperative education.**

education, cooperative office: *see* **office education, cooperative.**

education, core intensive business and office: *see* **business and office education, core intensive.**

education, correctional: *see* **correctional education.**

education council, adult: *see* **adult education council.**

education, counselor: *see* **counselor education.**

education course: *see* **course, education.**

education, creative: *see* **creative education.**

education, culminal: *syn.* **terminal education.**

education, cultural: *see* **cultural education.**

education, democratization of: *see* **democratization of education.**

education department: *see* **department, education.**

education, deviate: *see* **deviate education.**

education, director of: *see* **director of education.**

education, distributive: *see* **distributive education.**

education, distributive education continuing: *see* **continuing education, distributive education.**

education, driver: *see* **driver safety education.**

education, driver safety: *see* **driver safety education.**

education, drug abuse: *see* **drug abuse education.**

education, early childhood: *see* **early childhood education.**

education, economic: *see* **economic education.**

education, elementary: *see* **elementary education.**

education, environmental: *see* **environmental education.**

education, ethical: *see* **moral education.**

education, experimental: *see* **experimental education.**

education, extension: *see* **extension education.**

education, family: *see* **family education.**

education, family-life: *see* **family-life education.**

education, farm mechanics: *see* **agricultural mechanics education.**

education, fire prevention: *see* **fire prevention education.**

education, floriculture: *see* **floriculture education.**

education, folk: *see* **folk education.**

education for an elite: the view, more compatible with an oligarchical form of government than a democracy, that a select few should receive an education for leadership suited to the natural distinctions among men; an education founded on the responsibility of those qualified to deal with problems of social policy while a different kind of education is provided for the masses. *See* **elite, theory of; equalitarianism.**

education for democracy: that type of education in which the relation of the individual to democratic society is stressed. (There are two rather distinct poles of thought among philosophers of education as to procedure in education for democracy. One stresses the content and goals of democracy as the crucial area of treatment by the schools, and the other would stress the methods and ways of thinking as to how democratic goals can most effectively be realized.)

education, forestry: *see* **forestry education.**

education, formal: *see* **formal education.**

education, Franciscan: *see* **Franciscan education.**

education, free: *see* **free education.**

education, freedmen: *see* **freedmen education.**

education, functional: *see* **functional education.**

education, fundamental: *see* **fundamental education.**

education, general: *see* **general education.**

education, general business: *see* **business education, basic.**

education, general science: *see* **general science education.**

education, gentlemanly: *see* **gentlemanly education.**

education, graduate: *syn.* **study, graduate.**

education, health: *see* **health education.**

education, higher: *see* **higher education.**

education, history of: *see* **history of education.**

education, home: *see* **home education.**

education, home-and-family-life: *see* family-life education.

education, home economics: *see* home economics education.

education, homemaking: *see* homemaking education.

education, human-relations: *see* human-relations education.

education in agriculture, vocational: *see* agriculture, vocational.

education in cooperating schools, intergroup: *see* intergroup education in cooperating schools.

education in human sexuality: *see* sex education.

education, in-service: *see* in-service education.

education, in-service teacher: *see* in-service education.

education, industrial: *see* industrial education.

education, industrial arts: *see* industrial arts education.

education, industrial arts teacher: *see* teacher education, industrial arts.

education, industry, business day (EIB day): a day on which representatives of local business and industry make systematically planned, not incidental, visits to schools. *See* business, industry, education day.

education information center: *see* center, education information.

education, intensive business and office: *see* business and office education, intensive.

education, intercultural: *see* intercultural education.

education, intergroup: *see* intergroup education.

education, international: *see* international education.

education, international agricultural: *see* agricultural education, international.

education, interservice: *see* interservice education.

education, Jewish: *see* Jewish education.

education, Jewish extension: *see* extension education, Jewish.

education, Jewish informal: *see* informal education, Jewish.

education, Jewish supplementary: *see* supplementary education, Jewish.

education, labor: *see* labor education.

education, language arts: *see* language arts education.

education, liberal: *see* liberal education.

education, liberal adult: *see* adult education, liberal.

education, library: *see* library education.

education, library adult: *see* adult education, library.

education, life-adjustment: *see* life-adjustment education.

education, mass: *see* mass education.

education, mathematical: *see* mathematics education.

education, mathematics: *see* mathematics education.

education, military: *see* military education.

education, moral: *see* moral education.

education, moral basis of public: *see* moral basis of public education.

education, movement: *see* movement education.

education, museum: *see* museum education.

education, music: *see* music education.

education, narcotics: *see* narcotics education.

education, nursery: *see* nursery education.

education, nutrition: *see* nutrition education.

education, occupational: *see* occupational education.

education, occupational experience: *see* work experience education.

education of mentally deficient: educational and training services for the mentally deficient provided through day or residential classes.

education of the deaf, combined system in the: *see* combined system in the education of the deaf.

education of the mentally superior: *see* mentally superior, education of the.

education, organic philosophy of: *see* organic philosophy of education.

education, ornamental horticulture: *see* ornamental horticulture education.

education, outdoor: *see* outdoor education.

education, parent: *see* parent education.

education, pauper: *see* pauper education.

education personnel: *see* personnel, education.

education, philanthropic: *see* philanthropic education.

education, philosophy of: *see* philosophy of education.

education, philosophy of Catholic: *see* philosophy of Catholic education.

education, physical: *see* physical education.

education, physical and health: *see* physical and health education.

education, police: *see* police education.

education, political: *see* political education.

education, postdoctoral: *see* postdoctoral education.

education, postentry: *see* postentry education.

education, postgraduate: *see* postgraduate education.

education, postsecondary distributive: *see* distributive education, postsecondary.

education, posture: *see* posture education.

education, practical arts: *see* practical arts education.

education, practical nurse: *see* practical nurse education.

education, preentry: *see* preentry education.

education, preparental: *see* preparental education.

education, preprimary: *see* preprimary education.

education, preschool: *see* preschool education.

education, preservice: *see* preservice education.

education, prevocational: *see* prevocational education.

education, primary: *see* primary education.

education, primitive: *see* primitive education.

education, prison: *see* prison education.

education, private: *see* private education.

education, private denominational: *see* church school.

education, professional: *see* course, professional; curriculum, professional; preparation, professional; teacher education.

education, professional military: *see* military education, professional.

education profile: *see* profile, education.

education program: *see* program, education.

education program, Armed Forces: *see* program, Armed Forces education.

education, progressive: *see* progressive education.

education, public: *see* public education.

education, public affairs: *see* public affairs education.

education, public health: *see* public health education.

education, public school adult: *see* public school adult education.

education, radio: *see* radio and television education.

education, radio and television: *see* radio and television education.

education, reformatory: *see* reformatory education.

education, religious: *see* religious education.

education, religious adult: *see* religious adult education.

education, remedial: *see* (1) adult basic education; (2) teaching, remedial.

education, resource-use: *see* resource-use education.

education, rural: *see* rural education.

education, rural adult: *see* adult education, rural.

education, safety: *see* safety education.

education, science: *see* science education.

education, science of: *see* science of education.

education, secondary: *see* secondary education.

education, secondary agricultural: *see* agricultural education, secondary.

education, sensory: *see* sensory education.

education services program: *see* program, education services.

education, sex: *see* sex education.

education, social: *see* social education.

education, social aspects of: *see* social aspects of education.

education, social business: *see* business education, basic.

education, social foundations of: *see* social foundations of education.

education, social interpretation of: *see* social interpretation of education.

education, socialization of: *see* socialization of education.

education, socioeconomic: *see* business education, basic.

education, space: *see* space education.

education, special: *see* special education.

education, specialized: *see* specialized education.

education, speech: *see* speech education.

education, teacher: *see* teacher education.

education, technical: *see* technical education.

education, technical professional: *see* technical education.

education, technological: *see* technological education.

education, telic function of: *see* telic function of education.

education, terminal: *see* terminal education.

education, theological: *see* theological education.

education, tobacco use: *see* tobacco use education.

education, trade: *see* trade and industrial education.

education, trade and industrial: *see* trade and industrial education.

education, universal: *see* universal education.

education, veterans': *see* veterans' education.

education, visual: *see* visual education.

education, vocational: *see* vocational education.

education, vocational agriculture: *see* agriculture, vocational.

education, vocational and technical: *see* vocational and technical education.

education, vocational trade and industrial: *see* vocational trade and industrial education.

education, work experience: *see* work experience education.

education, workers': *see* workers' education.

education, world affairs: *see* world affairs education.

educational accountability: *see* accountability, educational.

educational administration: *see* administration, educational.

educational administration, tridimensional concept of: *see* administration, tridimensional concept of educational.

educational administrator: *syn.* administrator, chief.

educational adviser: *see* adviser, educational.

educational age: *see* age, educational.

educational aid: *see* aid, educational.

educational and occupational planning service: *see* planning service, educational and occupational.

educational aptitude: *see* aptitude, educational.

educational assignment, professional: *see* assignment, professional educational.

educational background: the pupil's past educational experience as shown by his school record and school history.

educational blindness: *see* blindness.

educational broadcast: *see* broadcast, educational.

educational broadcast director: *see* director, educational broadcast.

educational broadcaster: *see* broadcaster, educational.

educational change: current alterations in education in regard to size and scope of the total educational endeavor, including curriculum, teaching methods, and social climate among students in educational institutions.

educational consultant: *see* consultant, educational.

educational corporation: *see* corporation, educational.

educational cost: *see* cost, educational.

educational counseling: *see* counseling, educational.

educational development: *see* development, educational.

educational development program: *see* program, educational development.

educational development test, general: *see* test, general educational development.

educational diagnosis: *see* diagnosis, educational.

educational directory: *see* directory, educational.

educational edition: *syn.* edition, school.

educational effort: *see* effort, educational.

educational endowment: *see* endowment, educational.

educational environment: *see* environment, educational.

educational equalization: *see* equalization, educational.

educational ethics: *see* ethics, educational.

educational examiners, state board of: *see* board of examination, state.

educational exchange grants: *see* exchange grants, educational.

educational exchange, international: *see* exchange, international educational.

educational extension: *see* extension, educational.

educational film: *syn.* film, classroom.

educational finance: *see* finance, educational.

educational foundation: *see* foundation, educational.

educational fraternity: *see* fraternity, educational.

educational frontier: the partly explored or experimental region where new educational developments are taking place.

educational growth: *see* growth, educational.

educational guidance: *see* guidance, educational.

educational guidance clinic: *see* clinic, educational guidance.

educational hierarchy: *see* hierarchy, educational.

educational information: *see* information, educational.

educational interpretation: *syn.* interpretation (2).

educational laboratory, regional: *see* laboratory, regional educational.

educational ladder: a form of educational system in which each level is succeeded by a higher level of public education; in the American educational system, this succession is in the following order: kindergarten, elementary school, junior high school, senior high school, junior college, and state university. See **ladder system.**

educational loading: *see* loading, educational.

educational maladjustment: *see* maladjustment, educational.

educational materials center: *see* center, educational materials.

educational measurement: *see* measurement, educational.

educational media: (pl.) the means of communication that are available for educational purposes; do not usually include the live teacher, the student's peers, or other human resources, although the classroom teacher is the primary medium of instruction in most schools. *See* **medium of instruction.**

educational media, new: term used in various titles of the National Defense Education Act of 1958 to describe pertinent materials and technological devices such as TV, teaching machines, programmed learning material, electronic learning laboratories; also includes many well-established audiovisual media such as motion pictures, filmstrips, slides, and recorders; the term has not been widely accepted.

educational mortality: *see* mortality, educational.

educational motion picture: *syn.* film, classroom.

educational need: *see* need, educational.

educational objective: *see* objective *n.*

educational office employee: *see* employee, educational office.

educational orientation course: *see* course, educational orientation.

educational park: a schooling arrangement proposed in the 1960s by some theorists as a replacement for *neighborhood schools;* a few examples have been started; each park, consisting of a complex of schools ranging from kindergarten through high school or junior college, draws students from all over a *metro district* and is intended to minimize de facto segregation and equalize educational opportunity. *See* **metro district; segregation, de facto.**

educational personnel: *see* personnel, educational.

educational philanthropy: *see* philanthropy, educational.

educational philosophy: *see* philosophy of education.

educational placement: *see* placement, educational.

educational policy: a judgment, derived from some system of values and some assessment of situational factors, operating within institutionalized education as a general plan for guiding decisions regarding means of attaining educational objectives.

educational prediction: *see* prediction, educational.

educational prognosis: *see* prognosis, educational.

educational program: *syn.* program, school (1).

educational propaganda society: an organization (common near the middle of the past century) whose purpose usually was to promote the establishment or improvement of public schools; one of the earliest was the Pennsylvania Society for the Promotion of Public Schools, organized in 1828.

educational psychology: *see* psychology, educational.

educational publicity: *see* publicity, educational.

educational quotient: *see* quotient, educational.

educational radio program: *see* broadcast, educational.

educational radio station: *see* radio station, educational.

educational ratio (ER): *syn.* quotient, achievement.

educational research: *see* research, educational.

educational retardation: *see* retardation, educational.

educational service center: *see* center, educational service.

educational shortages approach: a method of attack on the problem of curriculum revision in which analysis is made of the shortcomings of the existing educational system and material for study selected with a view to correcting these shortcomings; a supplementary method useful in determining the amount of emphasis that should be placed on the various aspects of the curriculum rather than a fundamental method of deciding on the scope, direction, and philosophy of the curriculum.

educational society: an organization whose purpose is to concern itself with ideas and problems of education. (An outstanding example is the National Herbart Society formed in 1895, which still functions actively as the National Society for the Study of Education.)

educational sociology: *see* sociology, educational.

educational specifications: *see* specifications, educational.

educational station: *see* station, educational.

educational studies, cross-cultural: investigations of schools and other related educational institutions, either within the same country or in different countries, across two or more cultural groups, for example, Mexican-American, Japanese-American, Indian-American, Maori-New Zealander. *Contr. w.* educational studies, cross-national.

educational studies, cross-national: investigations of schools and other related educational institutions in two or more countries. *Contr. w.* educational studies, cross-cultural.

educational supplies: *see* supplies, educational.

educational survey: *see* survey, community educational.

educational survey, community: *see* survey, community educational.

educational systems analysis: *see* systems analysis, educational.

educational technology: *see* technology, educational.

educational television: *see* television, educational.

educational test: *see* test, educational.

educational therapy: *see* therapy, educational.

educational toy: *see* toy, educational.

educational voucher: *see* voucher plan.

educationally blind: *see* blind, educationally.

educationally deaf child: *see* child, educationally deaf.

educationally handicapped child: *see* child, educationally handicapped.

educationally operated station: *see* station, educationally operated.

educationally paralyzed: a term descriptive of a learner with a condition that incapacitates him from profitable utilization of his intelligence. *See* autism.

educationally retarded: *see* handicapped, academically.

educationally subnormal: (British) *syn.* mentally retarded, educable; *see* subnormal, mentally.

educationist: (1) one who has achieved competence through specialization in the field of educational theory and practice; often used specifically to refer to instructors or professors in professional departments of education as distinguished from other educators; (2) a specialist in pedagogy; sometimes used pejoratively to indicate a pedantic specialist in education. *Dist. f.* educator.

educative ability: *see* ability, educative.

educative experience: *see* experience, educative.

educator: one who teaches, instructs, or otherwise contributes to the educational development of others; as often used, it implies a quality of achievement or performance higher than usual. *See* education; *dist. f.* educationist.

educator, adult: *see* adult educator.

educator, business and office education teacher: that person at the university or state department of education level charged with the activities needed for preparing teachers or prospective teachers in the professional knowledges, skills, understandings, and appreciations that will enable them to qualify for certification as teachers in vocational business and office education programs.

educator, counselor: *see* counselor educator.

educator, distributive education teacher: that person at the university, college, or state department of education level charged with the activities needed for preparing teachers or prospective teachers in the professional knowledges, skills, understandings, and appreciations that will enable them to qualify for certification as teachers in vocational distributive education.

educator, radio: a person who is primarily interested in developing the instructional and educational possibilities of radio broadcasting; may be connected with an educational institution or with a broadcasting company.

educator, teacher: a qualified professional person responsible for the preparation and in-service training of teachers; also called *teacher trainer*.

eduction: the process of deriving a generalization, concept, theory, etc., as a result of observation and reflection.

eductive ability: *see* ability, eductive.

effect, autokinetic: *see* autokinetic effect.

effect, halo: *see* halo effect.

effect, Hawthorne: *see* Hawthorne effect.

effect, law of: *see* law of effect.

effect, main: (stat.) the weighted average of the simple effects over all levels or values of the control variable.

effect, order: the effect upon treatments of the rank order in which they are administered in an experiment in which all treatments are administered to the same subject or group of subjects. *See* effect, sequence.

effect, practice: (1) a change that follows practice in taking a test; usually an increase in the score of an individual when he takes the same test, or essentially the same test, more than once; such increase may invalidate subsequent use of the test; (2) the difference in accomplishment that is due to repetition of the skill during the interval between two tests; (3) the apparent gain in accomplishment (often only a portion of the entire gain) resulting from using the same test on two or more occasions.

effect, Pygmalion: *see* Pygmalion effect.

effect, regression: *see* regression effect.

effect, sequence: (res. design) the effect upon treatments of the sequence in which they are administered in an experiment in which all treatments are administered to the same subject or group of subjects; to be distinguished from *order effect* in which treatment *A* is third in either presentation *BCA* or *CBA*, though in these presentations the sequence differs.

effect, simple: the treatment effect or the effect of an experimental factor for a given level or value of a control variable; the effect of an experimental factor under controlled conditions, that is, with other factors held constant.

effect, Zeigarnik: observation that memory for incomplete tasks is greater than for completed ones; believed to be related to *gestalt* principle of closure. *See* **closure.**

effective intelligence: *see* **intelligence, effective.**

effective order: the order presenting the ideas and activities involved in a teaching unit that most facilitates the regular and systematic development of the learner.

effective purchasing power: *syn.* **income, real.**

effective range: *see* **range, effective.**

effective teaching: *see* **teaching, effective.**

effective weight: *see* **weight, effective.**

effectiveness, teacher: *see* **teacher effectiveness.**

effector: a nerve end organ that serves to distribute impulses that activate muscle contraction and gland secretion; may be (*a*) a somatic effector, one of the nerve end organs in the striated skeletal muscles, or (*b*) a visceral effector, one of the end organs in involuntary muscles.

efficiency: the ability to achieve desired results with economy of time and effort in relation to the amount of work accomplished.

efficiency of plant: (1) the effectiveness with which a plant lends itself to use; (2) the degree of absence of waste space in a plant.

efficiency of prediction: *see* **index of forecasting efficiency.**

efficiency orientation: *see* **orientation, efficiency.**

efficiency, predictive: *see* **predictive efficiency.**

efficiency principle: a term used by Paul Mort and others to designate the concept that the state should make adequate provisions for local initiative within the minimum program of education as defined by the state; also implies the idea that local school districts should have tax leeway over and above the minimum program.

efficiency, psychovisual: *see* **psychovisual efficiency.**

efficiency rating: *syn.* **rating, merit.**

efficiency records: *see* **records, efficiency.**

efficiency, social: *see* **social efficiency.**

efficiency, test: *see* **test efficiency.**

efficient cause: *see* **cause, efficient.**

efficient statistic: *see* **statistic, efficient.**

effort: the mental or physical energy exerted to achieve an end or to overcome any kind of obstacle. (The question of whether effort results or should result from utilizing or stimulating the learner's interest, or whether effort is or should be primarily an act of will, resulting from and contributing to strength of character, is an important educational issue.) *See* **interest, doctrine of.**

effort, educational: (1) the relative degree of power or economic backing with which a governmental unit supports a given or proposed educational program; (2) a variable factor in the evaluation of educational programs designed to express the extent to which a school administrative unit tries to support public schools; (3) the relation between the available resources of a school administrative unit and the amount of money actually devoted to educational purposes.

effort, financial: (school admin.) the fiscal support which a state or locality gives its school system; there are several possible measures of effort; for example, local effort may be measured by dividing the local tax revenue of a school district by its equalized assessed valuation.

egalitarianism: *syn.* **equalitarianism.**

ego: (1) (metaphysics) that in the person which knows and hence is not itself directly known but rather inferred; (2) (metaphysics) that which is experienced as the subject of the individual's experiences and which provides awareness of personal identity; (3) primitive selfishness; (4) that in the individual which demands realization of its ends and controls perception, thought, feeling, and behavior; (5) (gestalt) a central subsystem within the life space of the individual that is activated when the individual enters into novel or dangerous relations with his environment; (6) (psychoan.) that part of the psyche, involving both conscious and unconscious processes, which has as its chief function perceiving reality and mediating between the primitive drives of the individual (namely, the *id*) and the physical and social pressures of his environment; (7) the self; (8) that part of the self which is distinguished from other selves and the physical world.

ego alien: excluded by the ego. *See* **ego dystonic.**

ego dystonic (dis·ton′ik): unacceptable to the ego. *Ant.* **ego syntonic.**

ego, empirical: the central core of personality made evident in experience by what it does (seeking ends, controlling perception, thought, feeling, and behavior); held by some to be no more than its actions and experiences; in terms of field psychology, a central subsystem within the life space of the individual; in terms of psychoanalysis, that part of the psyche which perceives reality and mediates between one's primitive drives and the environment.

ego ideal: a standard of personal perfection envisioned through self-identification with a personality conceived as ideal—a personality that may never be equaled but may be constantly approached. *See* **self-ideal.**

ego instinct: (psychoan.) any nonsexual instinct.

ego involvement: (1) a process by which an individual becomes identified with external events, ideas, or objects; (2) a mechanism by which events, ideas, or objects are able to serve an individual's ego needs.

ego libido (li·bī′dō): (psychoan.) (1) inversion of sexual impulses; expression of sexual impulse through attachment to the self; (2) failure in normal extension of sexual impulses to involve others. *See* **narcissism.**

ego needs: *see* **needs, ego.**

ego psychology: *see* **psychology, ego.**

ego, pure: the living subject from which the actions and responses of a person emanate and which is more than these; that in a person which is the knower and therefore is not known directly except by the most fleeting and reflexive observation, direct objects of self-knowledge being acts in which the ego has engaged; that in a person which is distinct from other persons and the world; the self, the soul.

ego relevance: the quality in which the relationship under consideration is established as pertinent to the ego, that is, to the self-conscious phase of personality.

ego strength: ability of the ego to withstand stress without personality disorganization.

ego syntonic (sin·ton′ik): acceptable to the ego. *Ant.* **ego dystonic.**

egocentric: (1) selfish, or unheeding of the interests of others; (2) self-centered; (3) of or pertaining to a state alleged to obtain in the early development of children and characterized by a partial or total lack of discrimination between the self and that which is not the self.

egocentric predicament: a term first defined and used by R. B. Perry to designate the difficulty of achieving objectivity in truth seeking and in recognizing the realities of a world external to one's own mental processes, since each person perceives the external world through the medium of his own senses and gives his perceptions an exclusively personal interpretation.

egocentric response: *see* **response, egocentric.**

egocentric speech: *see* **speech, egocentric.**

egocentricity: *syn.* **egocentrism.**

egocentrism: (1) selfishness; (2) self-centeredness; (3) a stage in mental development characterized by lack of discrimination between the self and the rest of the world; (4) a state of limited awareness of the social aspects and implications of one's reactions.

egoism: (1) the ethical theory that one's own welfare should take precedence over that of others; (2) a theory of motivation positing that each individual as a matter of fact does ultimately seek only his own welfare. *See* **altruism; ethics; hedonism.**

egomania: extreme self-esteem or self-interest.

EGRUL: in programmed instruction, an inductive approach that leads the student through a series of examples (EGs) before having him formulate the rule (RUL) himself. *See* **inductive method;** *contr. w.* **RULEG.**

EIA standards: *see* **standards, EIA.**

EIB day: (education-business-industry day) a day on which representatives of local business and industry make systematically planned, not incidental, visits to schools. *See* **BIE day.**

eidetic image: *see* **image, eidetic.**

eight-four plan: the administrative organization of the educational program of a school system into an elementary school of 8 years exclusive of kindergarten (grades 1 to 8) and a secondary school of 4 years (grades 9 to 12).

eight-grade elementary school: *syn.* **elementary school, eight-year.**

eight-year elementary school: *see* **elementary school, eight-year.**

Eight Year Study: the Eight Year Experimental Study of Secondary Education (1933–1941) of the Progressive Education Association, carried out by its Commission on the Relation of School and College; a plan for experimentation, in terms of new understanding of learning and youth needs, by which 30 secondary schools throughout the nation were permitted by representative colleges to experiment with school content and instruction, while the graduates of these schools for a 5-year period beginning in 1936 were to be admitted to college without regard to the traditional course and unit requirements or entrance examinations generally required of all students.

eiren (ī'rēn): a term applied to the Spartan youth when he reached the age of 20 and his training became practically that of real military life; he then took the oath of loyalty to Sparta and entered the army.

ejection: a special case of *projection* in which the child infers that other persons and things have inner experiences similar to his own in given situations.

ejusdem generis, rule of (e·jus'dəm jen'ə·ris): (Lat., lit., "of the same class") in law, a rule of construction which holds that, where general words follow a specific enumeration, such general words are not to be construed in their broadest sense, but are to be held as applying only to those persons or things of the same general class as those specifically enumerated.

élan vital (ā·län' vē·tal'): a term used by Henri Bergson (1859-1941) indicating a life force that is self-causative and explains the ongoing process of life in many directions and with increasing complexity from species to species and from generation to generation of a given species.

elastic admission: *see* **admission, elastic.**

elasticity: (finance) that quality of a tax system manifested by prompt and reliable responses in the tax yield to changes in the tax rate.

election, nonpartisan board: an election in which candidates for office as members of a board of education neither campaign as nor are identified on the ballot as members of a political party and in which contributions of any kind from a political party are neither solicited nor accepted by a candidate.

election notice: *see* **notice, election.**

election, popular: the choice of a person or persons for office of any kind by the voting of a body of qualified or authorized electors (the people); the common method of electing members of local boards of education.

election, representation: a vote conducted by appropriate agencies to determine whether a majority of the teaching staff in a school system desire to be represented by a given union or other organization.

elective: any of a number of studies from which the student is allowed to select. *Syn.* **option** (2); **variable;** *contr. w.* **constant; course, required; subject, required.**

elective, free: any subject or course that is not required in the curriculum being pursued. *Contr. w.* **elective, group.**

elective, group: one of a number of courses that a pupil or student may select from an area in which he is required

to do a certain amount of work; for example, a high school pupil may be required to take 2 years of one modern foreign language from an offering of French, German, and Spanish and may elect to take Spanish I and II. (NOTE: certain areas may be compulsory for all pupils or students or only for those following a certain curriculum.) *Contr. w.* **elective, free.**

elective music: *see* **music, elective.**

elective office: a position in a school system filled by public election, usually for a stipulated period of time. *Dist. f.* **appointive office.**

elective program: *see* **program, elective.**

elective, restricted: a subject that a student may choose from among a limited number of specific courses.

elective system: (1) the practice of permitting a student to make certain choices in planning his school program; (2) formerly, the practice of permitting each student to determine his own program. (In a few schools, graduation was based merely on the number of courses taken; in other schools, election of courses was permitted only among alternative courses in the same general field, such as foreign languages.)

Electra complex: *see* **complex, Electra.**

electric board: *see* **board, electric.**

electric system: the electric facilities of a school building, consisting of light and power facilities, switchboard, clock-and-bell system, telephones, etc.

electrical appliance serviceman: (voc. ed.) a person who installs, services, and repairs stoves, refrigerators, dishwashing machines, and other electrical household appliances, using hand tools and test meters and following wiring diagrams and manufacturer's specifications.

electrical occupations: *see* **occupations, electrical.**

electrician: (voc. ed.) a person who plans layout and installs and repairs wiring, electrical fixtures, apparatus, and control equipment.

electricity/electronics: (ind. arts) the study of the theory, sources, applications, measurement, and control of electrically powered equipment used in heating, air conditioning, refrigeration, and illumination as well as that used in communications, such as the telephone, telegraph, radio, television, radar, and computers; learning activities include demonstration of electrical devices, experimenting with them, their design, construction, and testing; subject matter and learning experiences are organized under various descriptive titles such as *electricity,* electricity/electronics, and *electronics.*

electrocardiogram (EK; EKG): a graphic tracing of the electric current produced by the contraction of the heart muscle.

electrocardiograph: the instrument used in making an electrocardiogram.

electroconvulsive shock therapy: *see* **therapy, electroconvulsive shock.**

electrodermal response (E.D.R.): *syn.* **response, galvanic skin.**

electroencephalograph: an instrument for recording minute electrical oscillations of the cerebral cortex, which are known as brain waves.

electromechanical technician: *see* **technician, electromechanical.**

electromyogram: a tracing that records the electric response in a contracting muscle.

electromyograph: *see* **myograph.**

electronic classroom: *see* **classroom, electronic.**

electronic controls: (voc. ed.) controls that direct and keep quantity within certain limits through the use of electrical and electronic devices such as pushbuttons, limit switches, sensing devices, and other pilot devices to furnish the information that is used to establish the requirements to be controlled, relays and static switching devices as the logic elements that make decisions based on the information, and contactors and power-activated switches that perform the action called for by the decision-making elements.

electronic data processing: *see* **data processing, electronic.**

electronic digital computer: *see* **computer, electronic digital.**

electronic finger reading: *see* **reading, electronic finger.**

electronic learning laboratory: *see* **laboratory, electronic learning.**

electronic machine: *see* **machine, electronic.**

electronic mixer: *see* **mixer, electronic.**

electronic music: *see* **music, electronic.**

electronics industry: *see* **industry, electronics.**

electropiano system: a group of pianos, usually miniature pianos with 66 keys, that feed their amplified sounds into earphone outlets for the performers and into a line going to the teacher who sits at a master console control board built around his miniature piano, at which he monitors and corrects the students, demonstrates correct techniques, etc., either providing individual instruction via the headsets without disturbing other students or directing ensemble playing; each piano is equipped with a tape deck for playback to the student as a means of self-criticism, while the earphone hookup enables students and instructor to converse when the proper switches are flipped. *See* **laboratory, piano class.**

electrotherapy: the use of repeated, brief, nonconvulsive electric shock as part of the treatment for mental or bodily ills. *See* **therapy, electroconvulsive shock.**

element of a matrix: *see* **matrix, element of a.**

element, undefined: *see* **term, undefined.**

elementary algebra: *see* **algebra, elementary.**

elementary business: *syn.* **training, junior business.**

elementary certificate: *see* **certificate, elementary.**

elementary course: *see* **course, elementary.**

elementary curriculum: *see* **curriculum, elementary school.**

elementary district: *see* **district, elementary.**

elementary education: (1) the period of formal education beginning in childhood, usually at the age of 5 to 7 years, and ending approximately with adolescence; defined as including grades 1 to 8 and sometimes nursery school and kindergarten, or as ending with grade 6, as in places in which the six-six and six-three-three plans are in common use; (2) the division of any educational program that is concerned primarily with general education, including those skills, facts, and attitudes which are required by society of all its members; opposed to secondary and higher education as being less specialized in content and less selective as to pupils or students.

elementary family: *see* **family, elementary.**

elementary grade: *see* **grade, elementary.**

elementary grade, intermediate: one of those elementary grades between the primary level and the junior high school level; grade 4, 5, or 6.

elementary grade, upper: one of the elementary grades above the intermediate level; grade 7 or 8.

elementary industrial arts: *see* **industrial arts, elementary.**

elementary instruction: *see* **instruction, elementary.**

elementary pupil: *see* **pupil, elementary school.**

elementary pupil, unclassified: *see* **pupil, unclassified elementary.**

elementary school: a school having a curriculum offering work in any combination of grades 1 to 8 or from the preprimary grades to grade 8. *Syn.* **grade school.**

elementary school, accredited: an elementary school that has met the criteria set up by its accrediting agency.

elementary school age child: *see* **child, elementary school age.**

elementary school attendance unit, minimum: *see* **attendance unit, minimum elementary school.**

elementary school board: *see* **board, elementary school.**

elementary school counseling: *see* **guidance, elementary school.**

elementary school counseling, differential factors in: *see* **counseling, differential factors in elementary school.**

elementary school counselor: *see* **counselor, elementary school.**

elementary school curriculum: *see* **curriculum, elementary school.**

elementary school, eight-grade: *syn.* **elementary school, eight-year.**

elementary school, eight-year: a school of eight grades for children of elementary school age that normally requires 8 years to complete the work provided. *Syn.* **eight-grade elementary school.**

elementary school guidance: *see* **guidance, elementary school.**

elementary school industrial arts: *see* **industrial arts, elementary; consultant, elementary school industrial arts.**

elementary school principal: *see* **principal, elementary school.**

elementary school pupil: *see* **pupil, elementary school.**

elementary school, reorganized: an elementary school from which one or two of the upper grades have been subtracted, the latter having been incorporated into the program of secondary education.

elementary school, six-grade: *syn.* **elementary school, six-year.**

elementary school, six-year: a school for children of elementary school age that normally requires 6 years to complete the work provided. *Syn.* **six-grade elementary school.**

elementary school, summer: a school offering instruction for children of elementary school age during the summer months when the regular school is not in session.

elementary school supervisor: *see* **supervisor, elementary school.**

elementary school unit, minimum attendance: *see* **attendance unit, minimum elementary school.**

elementary school, university: an elementary school, usually on a university campus, used by the university for experimental, participation, demonstration, or practice teaching purposes in the preparation of elementary teachers, supervisors, and principals. *See* **laboratory school.**

elementary science: *see* **science, elementary.**

elements, art: *see* **art elements.**

elements, common: *syn.* **identical elements.**

elements, identical: *see* **identical elements.**

elements in transfer, specific: *syn.* **identical elements;** *dist. f.* **transfer, nonspecific.**

elevation: (meas.) the mean of all scores for a given person from a single instrument or battery.

elevation, mixture of plan and: *see* **plan and elevation, mixture of.**

eleven-year school: a school for children of elementary and high school age that normally requires 11 years to complete the work provided.

eligible for transportation: *see* **transportation, eligible for.**

elimination: (1) the act or process of dropping a pupil or student from membership in a class or school, usually by reason of failure or expulsion; (2) the evolutionary disappearance of structures or characteristics unfavorable to environmental adaptation; (3) the act or process of removing a quantity, symbol, or object from the domain of a discussion; for example, in the equation $b(cd) = b(ef)$, b (b not equal to 0) can be eliminated by dividing both sides of the equation by b, the result being the equation $cd = ef$; (4) (math.) a process of solving a system of simultaneous equations by reducing the number of variables in some of the equations, at the same time maintaining a system equivalent to the original.

elimination tournament: *see* **tournament, elimination.**

elite (ā·lēt′): (1) a select subgroup which is considered to be superior in one or more ways to the large general group of which it is a part; (2) a term used for small typewriter type in which there are 12 spaces to a horizontal inch.

elite, education for an: *see* **education for an elite.**

elite, technical: those members of a social order whose power derives primarily from possession of the highly specialized knowledge necessary for the maintenance of technologically sophisticated economic/industrial systems; found in highly industrialized societies.

elite, theory of: in social and political philosophy, the view that some kind of oligarchy should prevail or that a group made up of a few should hold the ultimate power of determination over the will of the many; thus, in Pareto, and more recently in such varied authors as Lawrence Dennis, James Burnham, and George Santayana, an aristocracy of powerful men, of managers, or of natural leaders will supply order and direction in economic and social affairs.

elocution: a term for training in speech techniques, especially public speaking and recitations, that is no longer in common use because of its emphasis on artificial gestures and tones.

em: a unit of measure in typography; the square of a type body; a unit of length equal to the height of a capital letter of a designated font; a 12-point *em* is one *pica*; it is called either the *em* or the *pica em.*

emancipation of child: surrender of the right to care for, the custody of, and the earnings of a child by its parents, who at the same time renounce parental duties.

embeddedness: (arith.) a condition occurring in a learning situation in which a child's personal association with or interest in materials as such interferes with his use of the materials as a means of developing number ideas.

embossed type: any raised-line or raised-dot type for finger or touch reading, for example, *braille type* or *Moon type.*

embroidery: the art of making raised and ornamental designs on cloth or other fabrics; this skill is used as a creative hobby, as a home industry for the purpose of increasing the family income, or as therapy for retarded or handicapped individuals.

embryology: the study of the development of animals, especially the formation and development of the embryo.

emergency aid: *see* aid, emergency.

emergency certificate: *see* certificate, emergency.

emergency class: *see* class, emergency.

emergency door: *see* door, emergency.

emergency drill: *see* drill, emergency.

emergency program, state education agencies': those programs, other than the operation of schools, which are established to cope with conditions of pressing necessity and are not considered a permanent part of the activities of a state education agency, for example, the state administration of the Veterans Program, Surplus Property, etc.

emergency reaction: *see* reaction, emergency.

emergency, road: any instance of bus failure or other circumstance during the time a school bus is en route and has pupil passengers aboard which prevents the bus from completing its route.

emergency room: a room of the health suite equipped for first aid in case of serious illness or accident.

emergency transportation: *see* transportation, emergency.

emergent evolution: *see* evolution, emergent.

emergent theory of mind: *see* mind, emergent theory of.

emerging curriculum: *see* curriculum, emerging.

emerging expectations: *see* expectations, emerging.

emerging self: *see* self, emerging.

eminent domain: (1) the power to take private property for public use, whether exercised by the sovereign directly or by one to whom sovereign power has been delegated for quasi-public purposes; (2) the superior right of property subsisting in a sovereignty by which private property may in certain cases be taken or its use controlled for the public benefit, without regard to the wishes of the owner.

Emmert's law: *see* law, Emmert's.

emmetropia (em′ə·trō′pi·ə): the condition of the normal eye which, without effort of accommodation, focuses the image exactly upon the retina; the condition in which there is no manifest ametropia (hyperopia, myopia, or astigmatism).

emotion: general descriptive term applied to observed behavior, physiological changes, and subjective feelings, all of which are associated with a state of high *arousal.*

emotion, conditioned: an emotional response that has become elicitable by originally inadequate stimuli.

emotional adequacy: *see* adequacy, emotional.

emotional adjustment: *see* adjustment, emotional.

emotional behavior: *see* behavior, emotional.

emotional blocking: *see* blocking, emotional.

emotional characteristics of color: *see* color, emotional characteristics of.

emotional climate: *see* climate, emotional.

emotional constellation: *see* constellation, emotional.

emotional control: the degree to which one is able to direct or inhibit overt emotional response to his environment.

emotional design: *see* design, emotional.

emotional development: *see* development, emotional.

emotional disturbance: *see* disturbance, emotional.

emotional growth: *see* growth, emotional.

emotional instability: *see* instability, emotional.

emotional maladjustment: *see* maladjustment, emotional.

emotional maturity: *see* maturity, emotional.

emotional-maturity scale: *see* scale, emotional-maturity.

emotional pattern: the grouping or organization of overt responses which characterizes a particular emotional state and by which it can be distinguished from other emotional states. (Some parts of the overt response are under voluntary control; others are not.) *See* anger.

emotional rapport: *see* rapport, emotional.

emotional reaction, conditioned: *see* reaction, conditioned emotional.

emotional reinforcement: *see* reinforcement, emotional.

emotional stability: *see* stability, emotional.

emotional stereotype: *see* stereotype, emotional.

emotional stereotypy: *syn.* stereotype, emotional.

emotional suppression: *see* suppression, emotional.

emotional tension: *see* tension.

emotionalized attitude: *see* attitude, emotionalized.

emotionally disturbed child: *see* child, emotionally disturbed.

emotionally loaded expressions: *see* expressions, emotionally loaded.

emotions, primary: the complex innate patterns of behavior aroused by certain stimulus situations; Watson held that there were three of these emotions in newborn infants: fear, rage, and love.

empathy: the comprehension of the feelings of others without actually having these feelings; empathic understanding is characterized by intellectual knowledge of another person's concerns rather than an emotional response to those concerns.

emphasis prompt: *see* prompt, emphasis.

empire building: in school administration and supervision of instruction, the process of gaining prestige or power by increasing the numbers of people and functions within a specific area of responsibility.

empirical: (1) in general, derived from or based on experience or observation; (2) in a derogatory use, sometimes opposed to scientific, in the sense that one does something because it works without being able to explain why it works.

empirical analysis: *see* analysis, empirical.

empirical ego: *see* ego, empirical.

empirical formula: *see* formula, empirical.

empirical-inductive counseling: *see* counseling, empirical-inductive.

empirical key: *see* key, empirical.

empirical naturalism: *see* experimentalism; humanism, scientific; instrumentalism; pragmatism.

empirical probablility: *syn.* probability, a posteriori.

empirical regression line: *syn.* line of means.

empirical test: *see* test, empirical.

empirical validation: *syn.* validation, external.

empirical validity: *see* validity, empirical.

empiricism: (1) traditionally, the doctrine that stresses the importance of observation, experience, or the senses in obtaining knowledge, as opposed to rationalism, which stresses reason or thought in obtaining knowledge; *see* **rationalism;** (2) in older forms of empiricism, as in the philosophy of John Locke (1632-1704), the mind is a tabula rasa that receives simple ideas through the senses; closely associated with nominalism; *see* **nominalism; sensationalism; tabula rasa;** (3) modern empiricism, as in Dewey, stresses experience as the interaction between organism and field, and knowledge as controlled and reorganized experience, communicated through symbols, and public in character.

empiricism, logical: a doctrine that employs the methodology of science, verification or confirmation of factual knowledge in experience; rejects metaphysical speculation and stresses scientific attitude, symbolic logic, and language analysis; the latter distinguishes it from older empiricism and positivism. *Syn.* **scientific empiricism.**

empiricism, radical: the theory or conception that all ideas are derived from sensations and experience which are therefore the criteria of reality.

empiricism, scientific: *syn.* **empiricism, logical.**

empiriological analysis: *see* **analysis, empiriological.**

employability standard: a criterion by which achievement is measured in the vocational areas of business education; an individual has met the standard of employability when he has attained the minimum achievement in a business occupational skill equivalent to the degree of proficiency required for initial employment.

employee attitudes: the conceptual predispositions of persons employed by others in positions below the executive level.

employee, educational office: one who holds any of the office positions such as file clerk, stenographer, or secretary in a school or school system; duties vary from routine operations to responsibilities involving personnel management and other similar duties.

employee, financial office: one who holds any of a number of positions in a school business office; may include payroll clerk, business machine operator, file clerk, or secretary to business officials.

employee personnel: *see* **personnel, employee.**

employer, cooperating: *see* **cooperating employer.**

employer's report to attendance officer: *see* **report to attendance officer, employer's.**

employment bureau: *syn.* **placement bureau.**

employment certificate: *see* **certificate, employment.**

employment counselor: *see* **counselor, employment.**

employment, director of: *see* **director of employment.**

employment experiences in agriculture: an integral part of the vocational education in an agriculture program; students are placed for supervised on-job experiences in either nonfarm agricultural businesses or production agriculture.

employment, extended: *see* **extended employment.**

employment interview: *see* **interview, employment.**

employment of minors: the act of hiring children or youths to work full time for pay.

employment, part-time: employment engaged in by holders of a *part-time age-and-schooling certificate.* (Employment may be on alternate weeks or months or for a similar period, or it may be outside of regular school hours.)

employment permit: an authorization granted by school authorities which shows that a child has met the age, schooling, and other requirements necessary in order to work. *See* **certificate, employment.**

employment projection: a forecast of employment based on past and current records of employment.

employment services: *see* **services, employment.**

employment services, state: *see* **services, state employment.**

employment survey: *see* **survey, employment.**

employment, teacher: the state of being employed in the instructional services of the field of education, usually under the terms of a written, oral, or implied contract.

employment test: *see* **test, employment.**

employment tests: (mil. ed.) *see* **tests, employment.**

empty mileage: *syn.* **mileage, deadhead.**

empty-organism concept: *see* **concept, empty-organism.**

empty set: *see* **set.**

emulation: (consumer ed.) *syn.* **consumption, competitive.**

emulative change: *see* **change, emulative.**

en: half of an em. *See* **em.**

enabling behavior: *see* **behavior, enabling.**

encipher: (mil. ed.) to convert a plain-text message into unintelligible language by means of a cipher system. *See* **cryptosystem.**

encode: to convert a plain-text message into unintelligible language by means of a code book.

encoding: (1) process whereby a message is transformed into signals that can be carried by a communication channel; (2) process whereby a person transforms his intention into behavior that will serve as a signal in a communication system—usually oral or graphic language, but gestures, signs, etc., may also serve; may involve several steps; for example, a person writes a telegram (first encoding) which is in turn transformed by another into electric signals (second encoding).

encopresis: fecal incontinence, after the second year of life, which is not due to disease or organic conditions.

encounter group: *see* **group, encounter.**

encrypt: (mil. ed.) to convert a plain-text message into unintelligible form (a cryptogram) by means of a cryptosystem. *See* **cryptosystem.**

encumbrances: obligations, in the form of purchase orders or contracts as yet unpaid, which are to be met from an appropriation and for which a part of the appropriation is reserved. (They cease to be encumbrances when paid or approved for payment.)

encyclical, papal: a letter dealing with matters concerning the Roman Catholic Church written by the Pope and addressed to all Ordinaries of the Church and the faithful.

encyclopedia: (1) one or more volumes including information on subjects in all branches of knowledge; articles are usually in alphabetic order; (2) (lit., "circle of studies") the secondary curriculum of the Greek schools following the Age of Pericles (fifth century B.C.); training embraced grammar, literature, music, drawing, geography, geometry, arithmetic, theories of the nature philosophers, and gymnastics.

Encyclopedists: the eighteenth-century writers of the great French Encyclopedia; the work embodied the thought of the Enlightenment period; contributors included Voltaire, Rousseau, Turgot, Duclos, and Jaucourt; editors were Diderot and d'Alembert.

end: a limit, conclusion, purpose; in the philosophy of Aristotle, the final cause of something; whatever stage in natural growth is last, most complete, or best; whatever a voluntary agent wills to accomplish, or whatever product an artist intends to create. *See* **cause, final.**

end-in-view: *syn.* **aim; goal.**

end of data: an expression used as a signal identifying the termination of some quantity of data, as at the end of a reel of magnetic tape.

end of file: an expression used to signal the end of data for a file.

end test: *see* **test, end.**

end title: *see* **title, end.**

endex: a teaching machine technique used for automated testing and immediate scoring by means of audio tape and screen projections.

endings, adding by: *see* **addition, higher-decade.**

endocrine gland: any one of several ductless glands of internal secretion (such as the thyroid) producing chemical substances (hormones) that are passed directly or indirectly into the body fluids and that frequently have a regulatory effect on the body.

endocrinology (en′dō·krī·nol′ə·ji): the study of the endocrine glands and their secretions.

endogamy: the custom of marrying only within the tribal unit, community, political group, or caste.

endogenous: due to causes within the developing organism itself; when applied to mental deficiency, familial.

endogenous feeblemindedness: *see* **feeblemindedness, endogenous.**

endogenous mental retardation: *see* **mental retardation, endogenous.**

endomorph: an individual of the extremely ponderous, soft-fleshed type.

endophasia (en'dō·fā′zhi·ə): the silent, implicit reproduction of a word or sentence without motion of the vocal organs.

endowed college: *see* **college, endowed.**

endowed institution: *see* **institution, endowed.**

endowed public school: *see* **public school, endowed.**

endowed school: any school receiving a considerable portion of its operating budget from invested funds that must be held in perpetuity. *See* **free school.**

endowed university: *see* **university, endowed.**

endowment: (1) a permanent financial provision for any purpose or object (such as funds provided for the use of a school, church, or research agency), the principal of which must be kept intact and prudently invested, while the income may be expended for the purpose for which the provision was made; may be general, as for all the purposes of a college, or special, as for the support of a chair in American history; (2) natural capacity for physical or mental development as determined by the heredity of the individual.

endowment, educational: an endowment provided for some purpose deemed by law to be educational. (There is no legal distinction between educational endowments and other charitable or eleemosynary endowments; they differ only in the purposes to which they are devoted.) *See* **endowment.**

endowment fund: *see* **fund, endowment.**

endowment, hypothecation of: *see* **hypothecation of endowment.**

endowment income: *see* **income, endowment.**

endowment, native: the total inherited capacity of the individual for mental and physical function, as contrasted with any capacity resulting from experience. *See* **trait, native.**

endowment of research: the provision of a principal fund to be held in perpetuity and prudently invested, the income from which is to be used to advance the boundaries of knowledge by means of research.

endowment, plant: money set aside, the earnings of which are restricted to expenditures for land, buildings, or equipment.

endurance: (phys. ed.) the ability of the body to withstand the stresses set up by prolonged activity.

endurance, cardiovascular: the ability of the heart and blood vessels to withstand stress produced by prolonged activity.

endurance, muscular: the ability of a muscle to work against a moderate resistance for long periods of time.

energies, hormic: *see* **hormic energies.**

engineer, school: a man employed to operate mechanical equipment connected with heating and air conditioning a school building.

engineer, systems: *see* **systems engineer.**

engineered time data: *see* **time data, engineered.**

engineering, aeronautical: a university engineering program at both the undergraduate and graduate levels dealing with the science of the design and construction of aircraft.

engineering aid: *see* **aid, engineering.**

engineering, college of: *see* **college of engineering.**

engineering drawing: *see* **drawing, engineering.**

engineering, human: interdisciplinary science wherein engineers and psychologists study the design of equipment to increase man–machine interaction for maximum efficiency, comfort, and safety.

engineering, instructional systems: the process of applying science and technology to the study and planning of an overall instructional system, whereby the relationships of various parts of the system and the utilization of various subsystems are fully planned and validated prior to system implementation; sometimes referred to as the *systems approach.*

engineering, social: the application of scientific principles to the analysis of social processes and the designing of methods of control of the component elements in social interaction with the aim of effecting optimum functioning of the social structure.

engineering, systems: (mil. ed.) the process of applying science and technology to the study and planning of an overall missile or space system, whereby the relationships of the various parts of the system and the utilization of various subsystems are fully planned and comprehended prior to the time that hardware designs are committed.

engineering technician: *see* **technician, engineering.**

English, basic: *see* **word list, basic.**

English laboratory: *see* **laboratory, English.**

English language, American: *see* **language, American English.**

English, oral: a school subject dealing with oral communication in English; intended to improve both extemporaneous speech and oral delivery of literary material; includes practice in attentive listening.

English, standard: the written and spoken English used by educated persons. *See* **dialect, nonstandard.**

engram (en′gram): a term originated by R. Semon to designate a memory trace or pattern assumed to be left in the cells of the brain following a mental stimulus. *Syn.* **neurogram.**

engraving: one of the intaglio printing methods in graphic arts from a plate on which the design has been incised by the engraving tool.

enjoin: to prohibit by official order or decree.

enlisted personnel schools file: *see* **file, enlisted personnel schools.**

enriched curriculum: *see* **enrichment, curriculum.**

enriched program: *see* **program, enriched.**

enrichment, academic: *see* **enrichment, curriculum.**

enrichment, art: (1) the cultural values derived from art; (2) the contribution made by art to the total school curriculum. *See* **enrichment, subject.**

enrichment, curriculum: (1) the process of selectively modifying a curriculum by adding educational content to that which already exists; intended to supply the means to meet the individual educational needs and interests of learners enrolled in a class; curriculum enrichment may be either *horizontal* or *vertical;* (2) a program for the gifted within the framework of the regular classes; consists of deliberate differentiation of curriculum content and activities for the superior pupils in a heterogeneous class.

enrichment, extensive: provision of a great deal of additional educational content to an existing course of study, thus allowing maximum flexibility in accommodating the individual differences of learners within a class.

enrichment, horizontal: (1) curricular provisions for the addition of new learning opportunities on the learner's present achievement level; (2) a program to provide opportunities for gifted pupils to broaden their experience by working in areas not ordinarily explored by the average child, who lacks time or inclination to do so.

enrichment, intensive: provision of curriculum content that permits the pupil to penetrate more deeply into any given area than does the average child; accomplished by providing opportunities for specialization in the given area of activity or working at a more mature level; particularly applicable to skills such as reading, arithmetic, and some areas of science; allows for the inclination of many gifted children to pursue an activity or develop a skill until they become proficient in it or reach a saturation point, so that they satisfy their curiosity and reach a sense of "closure," a feeling of completion; may fluctuate in intensity through the various grade levels.

enrichment, lateral: *syn.* **enrichment, horizontal.**

enrichment, mathematical: that part of the mathematical learning experience of a student or group of students which is considered an extension of the standard curriculum; often dichotomized as *vertical enrichment*, or acceleration (the act of teaching more advanced mathematics at an earlier date than is standard) and *horizontal enrichment* (the study of topics that are very seldom found in a standard curriculum).

enrichment of experience: development of or provision for ascertaining wider and deeper meanings about a given topic or area already partly familiar.

enrichment plan of promotion: *see* **differentiated-course plan; multiple-course plan.**

enrichment, program: greater concentration of services, instructional materials, and supplies for children in depressed areas.

enrichment program: *see* **program, enrichment.**

enrichment, subject: the act or process of increasing the quality or quantity of the offering in a unit of instruction by the inclusion of pertinent illustrative and related material with the basic subject matter or lesson to be taught.

enrichment, vertical: the curricular provision for advanced work or further specialization in the same area of learning.

enrolled pupils: *syn.* **enrollment** (2).

enrollment: (1) the process of entrance into a school, college, university, or course that eventuates in the act of writing the student's name on the roll, register, or files of the institution; (2) (in schools under the college or university level) the total of all the different pupils who are registered in a state, city, school district, school, or classroom during any given period of time such as a school year, semester, term, or month, each name being counted only once (to avoid duplication, students who move or transfer from one school to another during the school year are counted as being enrolled only by the first school attended during that school year); *syn.* **enrolled pupils;** (3) the number of pupils on the roll of a given school at any given date; (4) (in colleges and universities) the total number of different students registered during a given quarter or semester, as of a given date, minus withdrawals previous to that date; for two or more quarters or semesters, it is the sum of the enrollments for those quarters or semesters minus all duplications. *Syn.* **registration.**

enrollment, average: an average of the total number of children enrolled during a given month or year.

enrollment, average daily: *syn.* **membership, average daily.**

enrollment, city net: the sum of the net enrollments of all schools within the city.

enrollment, dual: an arrangement for the regular attendance of a pupil at two schools concurrently, with both schools sharing the direction and control of his studies; for example, he may take some of his courses at a public school and others at a nonpublic school, or he may attend a public secondary school part time and an area vocational school part time. *Syn.* **shared time.**

enrollment, net: the number of pupils on the school roll as of a given date, consisting of the original enrollment plus all later enrollees and minus all withdrawals.

enrollment, open: a policy in some school systems of permitting parents or guardians of school-age children to send them to the school of their choice within the system; that is, the children are not required to attend their neighborhood school.

enrollment, original: (1) *syn.* **enrollment** (2); (2) pupil's act of enrolling in school for the first time during a given school year; (3) a pupil whose first enrollment in a given school year was within the school in question, for example, "John was an original enrollment in school *A.*"

enrollment, projected school: school enrollment, either by grade or by total enrollment, forecast by means of several scientifically developed methods: graphical or mathematical projection of the curve of past population growth; projections based on relationships of population growth in one area to growth in other areas; projections of net migration and of natural increase; and forecasts derived directly from specific estimates of future employment. *See* **cohort-survival technique; grade-retention-rate method; projection, census class; projection, housing; projection, population trend; projection, retention ratio.**

enrollment rate: the ratio of school enrollment to school age population.

enrollment rate, single-year-of-age-grade specific: the proportion or percentage of the population at a given age that is enrolled in a specific grade at any time in a given period; for example, based on the 1950 census, for the United States as a whole, 35 percent of the children 10 years of age were enrolled in grade 4, and about 42 percent were enrolled in grade 5; each of these represents an age-grade specific enrollment rate.

enrollment, state net: the sum of the net enrollments of all the separate, individual school districts within the state.

enrollment status: for the United States Census of 1970, school enrollment ascertained for persons 3 years and older who are classified as enrolled in a school if they attended regular school or college at any time since Feb. 1, 1970; regular schooling includes nursery school, kindergarten, and schooling leading to an elementary school certificate, a high school diploma, or a college degree.

enrollment, total: the entire number of pupils who have been on the roll at any time during the period for which total enrollment is being reported. (Total enrollment is never a decreasing figure; it either remains constant, as when no new pupils enroll after the first day, or is an increasing figure.)

ensemble (än·säm'bəl): (1) a group of performers rather than a soloist; (2) the degree of cooperation, of unity, and of balance attained among a group of performers, designated as "bad ensemble," "good ensemble."

ensemble method: the method of group instruction in the technique of instrumental musical performance; all the instruments of the band or orchestra are taught simultaneously. *See* **class method;** *contr. w.* **private method.**

entelechy (en·tel'e·ki): in the philosophy of Aristotle, (1) the form or essence of something; (2) the mode of being of a thing whose essence is completely realized; the actualization or perfection of the form in a thing, in virtue of which that thing attains its fullest realization of function; for example, the soul is the entelechy of the body. *See* **actuality; essence; form.**

entire correlation: *syn.* **correlation, total.**

entire correlation coefficient: *syn.* **coefficient, total correlation.**

entrance: (1) a passage through a doorway to a school building or through a gateway to school grounds; (2) in programmed instruction, a means of beginning iterative action; the place in the routine that serves as the beginning point.

entrance age: *see* **age, entrance.**

entrance credit: *see* **admission requirements.**

entrance, early: *see* **admission, early.**

entrance examination: *see* **examination, entrance.**

entrance examinations, college: *see* **examinations, college entrance.**

entrance requirements: *syn.* **admission requirements.**

entrance training: *see* **training, entrance.**

entries, closing: (school accounting) entries that are made at the end of the accounting period to transfer balances in general ledger receipt, expenditure, appropriation, and estimated revenue accounts to the fund balance account.

entropy: the measure of unavailable energy in a thermodynamic system; by analogy, in communication theory, a measure of the efficiency of a system such as a language or code in transmitting information; indicates the degree of initial uncertainty that can be resolved by any one message; the clearer the message, the more efficient the system, so that the measure resembles negative entropy.

entry: (1) a child who has just placed his name on the school register or roll; (2) a vestibule.

entry behavior: *see* **behavior, entry.**

entry notice: an administrative form used by the school teacher or principal to inform the central office (county or city) of the enrollment of a pupil.

entry occupation, distributive education: *see* **occupation, distributive education** entry.

entry, original: a term used in pupil accounting designating a pupil entering elementary or secondary school for the first time during a given regular school term in a given state; there are two types of original entries, of which the first, designated by the symbol E1, includes pupils who enter, for the first time during a given regular school term, either a public or nonpublic school in the United States or its outlying areas; the second type, designated by the symbol E2, includes pupils who previously entered a public or nonpublic school in another state during the same regular school term but who have not previously entered a school in the given state; the total number of original entries in a state is the sum of the original entries in public and nonpublic schools, including laboratory, model, and practice schools, and is a cumulative total which increases during the term and never decreases.

entry, vocabulary: *syn.* **word**, entry.

entry word: *see* **word**, entry.

entry worker: *see* **worker**, entry.

enucleation, eye: *see* **eye** enucleation.

enumeration: (1) (arith.) the act of determining the number of objects in a set by counting; (2) (admin.) the counting of all young people of the school district who are of school age.

enumeration district: *see* **district**, enumeration.

enumeration item: *see* **item**, enumeration.

enumeration, school: *see* **census**, school.

enumeration sheet: a type of form used in taking a school census for the purpose of recording essential, pertinent data concerning each child from birth to the age of 18.

enumeration statistics: *see* **statistics**, enumeration.

enunciation: (1) vocal production of articulated sounds; (2) careful pronunciation of the parts of words so as to make them clearly audible to the listener; (3) correct use of lips, teeth, and tongue in clearly sounding words so that they can readily be distinguished.

enuresis (en'ū·rē'sis): involuntary discharge of the urine; may be diurnal, occurring during the day, or nocturnal, occurring during the night.

environment: a general term designating all the objects, forces, and conditions that affect the individual through such stimuli as he is able to receive. *See* **environment, external; environment, internal.**

environment, classroom: *see* **environment**, educational.

environment, educational: the emotional, physical, and intellectual climate that is set up by the teacher and students to contribute to a wholesome learning situation.

environment, external: everything outside the organism which stimulates and to which the organism responds consciously or unconsciously. *Contr. w.* **environment, internal.**

environment, internal: all physical conditions and processes, emotions, and mental processes that influence the organism and modify response to external stimuli. *Dist. f.* **milieu, social;** *contr. w.* **environment, internal.**

environment, learning: the setting and conditions that create an atmosphere for learning. *See* **climate, classroom; environment, educational.**

environment, prepared: a triad consisting of the children, their teachers, and their physical surroundings in which a child is motivated, stimulated, and encouraged to choose his own work and execute it to his own satisfaction.

environment, qualitative: that element in the total environment which is nonmaterial; also, that characteristic in material environment which is effective because of values held concerning the material, for example, beliefs, taboos, connotations.

environment, responsive: an environment that provides a rich supply of feedback to the learner.

environment, simulated: a learning situation in which the learners are faced with simulated or gamelike reproductions of reality and asked to respond.

environment study: (1) the examination and analysis of that which surrounds the individual or group being considered; (2) ecological investigations; (3) that area in the modern curriculum designed to demonstrate the significance of the physical and social environment.

environmental art: *syn.* **happening.**

environmental deprivation: *see* **deprivation, environmental.**

environmental determinism: *see* **determinism, environmental.**

environmental differences, interfamily: the ways in which one home environment is unlike another in such features as family income, social status, and educational level of parents. *Dist. f.* **environmental differences, intrafamily.**

environmental differences, intrafamily: those factors present in a home which cause some difference in the influences affecting each member of that home; factors which account for the fact that no two people live in the same family environment or total situation. *Dist. f.* **environmental differences, interfamily.**

environmental education: recognition and clarification of the values, attitudes, and concepts concerned with man's relationships to his culture and biophysical environment.

environmental technology: *see* **technology, environmental.**

environmentalism: that viewpoint or school of thought which emphasizes the influences of the aggregate of things, conditions, and pressures which surround the organism (particularly man) and minimizes heredity as a causal factor.

eonism (ē'on·iz'm): a perversion, named after the Chevalier d'Eon, a French diplomat who posed as a woman, characterized by the subject's assumption of the clothing, appearance, and attitudes of the opposite sex. *Syn.* **transvestitism.**

ephebi (e·fē'bī): a name given in ancient Athens to a class of young men from 18 to 20 years of age who formed a sort of college under state control; the training was primarily military and gymnastic in nature and was designed only for the future leaders of Athens; in a later Greek period and in Roman times literary studies were included.

ephebic oath: a sworn statement of devotion to the city or state in which a college is located, taken by students upon their graduation from the institution; patterned after an oath of allegiance to Athens required in Greece in ancient times of all youth in the city; once a part of the graduation exercises at some colleges, as Brooklyn College, New York. *See* **ephebi.**

ephebic training: *see* **training, ephebic.**

epicritic sensibility: *see* **sensibility, epicritic.**

Epicureanism: the ethical theory developed by Epicurus (about 342-270 B.C.) affirming pleasure to be the highest goal of life, particularly pleasure that is certain and lasting, of which the most distinguishing feature is the absence of pain; corrupted in the modern period to mean immediate physical pleasure. *See* **hedonism.**

epidemic: a term descriptive of the spread of a disease to many persons in the same area at the same time; through exposure in the classroom many childhood infectious diseases may become epidemic; the term is applied also to the rapid spreading of ideas and fads in fashion, behavior, etc.

epidiascope: a device that combines episcopic and diascopic projection. *See* **diascope; projector, opaque.**

epigenetic: referring to those views which trace the origin of and change in behavior patterns of organisms to the operation of environmental factors; these may be extraorganismic, extratissual, or extracellular.

epigraphy: the systematic study of style and content of inscriptions on stone, metal, pottery, etc., which are often important primary source materials for the historian. *See* **paleography.**

epilepsy: any of a variety of disorders marked by disturbed electrical rhythms of the central nervous system and typically manifested by convulsive attacks, usually with clouding of consciousness. *See* **grand mal; petit mal.**

epilepsy, focal: *see* **epilepsy, Jacksonian.**

epilepsy, Jacksonian: a type of epilepsy in which there is a progression of clonic movements from one part of the body to another in orderly fashion; clonic or tonic movements or paresthesias may be limited to one part of the body while consciousness is retained, or movements may become generalized; consciousness is then lost.

epilepsy, psychomotor: a psychic equivalent of epilepsy; period of amnesia during which certain stereotyped actions and, at times, apparently purposeful behavior are carried out.

epiphenomenalism (ep'i·fə·nom'ə·nəl·iz'm): a theory according to which mind is only a secondary phenomenon accompanying a bodily process, consciousness but an incidental result of the organization and action of the nervous system, and matter primary and real.

epiphenomenon (ep'i·fə·nom'ə·non): a secondary manifestation or occurrence that accompanies a primary process and that is merely incidental, having no effect on the furtherance of the process, as the squeak on the wheel.

episcopal school: see **cathedral school.**

episcope: syn. **projector, opaque.**

epistemological idealism: see **idealism, epistemological.**

epistemology: the study of the origin, nature, and limitations of knowledge; one of the six major branches of philosophy.

epistemology, materialistic: the branch of epistemology that finds the nature, grounds, limits, and criteria of knowledge in *materialism.*

epochal psychosis: see **psychosis, epochal.**

epsilon (ε): the term given to a correlation ratio that has been corrected for the bias introduced by the size of sample and the number of class intervals. See **correlation ratio.**

epsilon square (ε²): a statistic used in testing the significance of *epsilon,* a correlation ratio corrected for bias of the size of sample and the number of class intervals.

EQ: see **quotient, educational.**

equal: (math.) identical; in contemporary literature the statement $x = y$ means that x and y are two names for the same object; thus, $\underline{/ABC} = \underline{/DEF}$ means that $\underline{/ABC}$ and $\underline{/DEF}$ are two names for the same angle.

equal-additions method: see **subtraction, methods of.**

equal-intervals scale: see **scale, equal-intervals.**

equal opportunities: the absence of racial, ethnic, and/or religious barriers to educational, economic, or social advancement.

equal weight: see **weight, equal.**

equalitarianism: the view that men are essentially or naturally or by right equal, especially politically or socially; when associated with revolutionary movements the term takes on a doctrinaire quality. Syn. **egalitarianism;** see **equality, doctrine of.**

equality, doctrine of: a basic concept of democracy; originally, the doctrine that all men are created equal; in modern usage, the belief that all persons are equally entitled to opportunities for optimum development; the doctrine does not mean that all men are equal in actual capacity or endowment, but rather implies that men have equal rights as members of genus Homo sapiens. See **equalitarianism.**

equalization aid: see **aid, equalization.**

equalization, educational: (1) an even or equal distribution of the burden or cost of supporting public education among the subordinate units within a central governmental unit, in terms of the principles of taxpaying ability; (2) the act of equalizing or state of being more nearly equal with respect to the support of education.

equalization fund: see **fund, equalization.**

equalization grant: see **aid, equalization; fund, equalization; grant.**

equalization of teaching load: a redistribution of load so as to reduce the variation in load among teachers, usually accomplished with the help of the Douglass formula.

equalization program, state: a plan, endorsed and supported by the state government, for equalizing or distributing more equitably the costs of a basic educational program required in all school administrative units in the state.

equalized valuation, state: see **valuation, state equalized.**

equate: (1) to match individuals or groups in terms of one or more factors; for example, groups may be equated on the basis of age, sex, mental ability, past achievement, etc.; (2) (math.) to put in the form of an equation.

equated scores: see **scores, equated.**

equating test: syn. **test, matching** (2).

equation: a statement that two expressions or two quantities are equal; the term is commonly used for conditional equations in algebra. See **equal.**

equation approach: (bus. ed.) an approach to the teaching of bookkeeping in which an understanding of the fundamental equation (assets equal liabilities plus proprietorship) is developed through the use of a series of transactions each of which is analyzed as to its effect on the fundamental bookkeeping equation. See **bookkeeping equation;** dist. f. **balance sheet approach.**

equation of teacher service: the act of establishing a reasonable average teaching load for teachers in a given school or school system, taking into consideration (a) current practices in similar schools of the locality or state and (b) what is considered to be a reasonable per pupil cost for instruction.

equation, personal: syn. **error, subjective.**

equation, regression: see **regression equation.**

equation, specification: an equation that indicates an individual's performance on a test in terms of loadings and factor endowments.

equilibrium: the ability of a person to keep his center of gravity over his base of support so that he can remain balanced.

equipment: articles such as furniture, machinery, and books that are used without being consumed; to be distinguished from *supplies.* See **supplies, educational.**

equipment, building: the equipment that is a part of or goes with a building to make it usable, such as desks, seats, tables, etc. Dist. f. **supplies, educational.**

equipment, bus: see **bus equipment.**

equipment center: see **center, equipment.**

equipment compatibility: see **compatibility, equipment.**

equipment, display: T stands, mannequins, hat forms, coat forms, and other equipment used to display merchandise in a distributive education laboratory.

equipment, early childhood education: items such as *dough,* a combination of flour, salt, and water (alum and oil optional), mixed to a consistency that can be molded, formed, and worked with the hands; *dressing frames,* fabric with various kinds of openings, such as zippers, buttons, snaps, laces, etc., enclosed in wooden frames, for children to practice dressing skills; *drying racks,* collapsible structures connected by various-sized rods spaced several feet apart, used for hanging wet papers, towels, or anything needing space to dry; *easels,* child-size painting surfaces, usually two sided, large enough to hold paper that is 18 × 24 inches in size; *powdered tempera,* a dry powder paint soluble in water; *finger paint,* a thick paint, the consistency of library paste, which may be applied to wet glazed paper or any smooth surface; *flannel boards,* flat surfaces covered with flannel or felt, used to display items which will cling, and any materials without intrinsic value which children may use creatively.

equipment, group auditory training: see **auditory training equipment, group.**

equipment, instructional: the furnishings, accessories, or other manufactured appurtenances which are used in the activity of teaching; to be distinguished from *instructional facilities* such as buildings and grounds.

equipment inventory: see **inventory, equipment.**

equipment, janitors': see **janitors' equipment.**

equipment, large muscle: play equipment which includes several varieties of structures essential to preschool programs for development of large muscle coordination;

examples are boxes, large, wooden, rectangular or square structures, usually with at least one side open for climbing, hiding, etc. (a standard size is 5 × 5 feet, walls 2½ inches thick); barrels, hollow cylinders used for climbing, hiding, rolling, or as connecting pieces for walking boards; climber (jungle gym), a group of connected bars forming a maze, on which a number of children can climb at the same time; a nesting bridge or a triangular climber, easily stacked for storage, and flexible for location, which can be used with ladders for versatility in play (standard sizes are 36 and 60 inches).

equipment, library: the furniture and fittings of a library building, such as stacks, books, tables, or lamps.

equipment, manipulative: (1) (kind.-prim.) items that encourage development of small muscles and eye-hand coordination, for example, scissors, beads, puzzles, newsprint (unprinted newspaper), open-ended hollow blocks, pegs and pegboards; (2) (audiovis. ed.) three-dimensional equipment and supplies by means of which learning is enhanced through the sense of touch, for example, objects, models, and specimens, including raised relief maps and manipulative aids for primary pupils retarded in arithmetic.

equipment, mark-sensing: any equipment of an electronic construction that operates on the basis of impulses received from small graphite pencil marks; the information coded by graphite pencil marks on a card or sheet of paper controls various types of electronic control and sorting equipment; the popular machine scoring of tests provides an excellent example of the mark-sensing principle.

equipment, mathematical: materials used in the teaching or learning of mathematics, such as calculators, geometric models, slide rules, etc.

equipment, off-line: (data processing) the peripheral equipment or devices not in direct communication with the central processing unit of a computer.

equipment, on-line: (data processing) peripheral equipment or devices in a system in which the operation of such equipment is under control of the central processing unit and in which information reflecting current activity is introduced into the data-processing system as soon as it occurs; thus, it is directly in line with the main flow of transaction processing.

equipment, output: the equipment used for transferring information from a computer.

equipment, partially sighted: *see* **equipment, sight-saving.**

equipment, perceptual: items which stimulate any or all of the senses of perception, such as puzzles, matching games, blocks of various sizes, sound cylinders, rhythm instruments, etc.

equipment, playback: *see* **playback equipment.**

equipment, punch-card: *see* **punch-card equipment.**

equipment, service: machinery, tools, and other articles used for building service, such as floor machines, brushes, or coal conveyors.

equipment, sight-saving: an older term used to describe equipment such as books printed in large type, large-size maps, large-type typewriters, etc., employed in the education of partially seeing children.

equipment, value of: *see* **value of equipment.**

equipollent sets: *syn.* **sets, equivalent.**

equipotentiality: a term used to designate the capacity of an uninjured part of the brain to take over and perform functions lost by destruction of other areas in the cortex (Lashley); equipotentiality is subject to the *law of mass action* and seems to hold not only in cortical destruction but in subcortical destruction as well.

equipotentiality, functional: a hypothetical construct describing or referring to the idea that (*a*) an individual may solve the same problem or perform the same task at different times by drawing upon a different cognitive working system and (*b*) different individuals may solve the same problem or perform the same task to the same degree of performance by drawing upon different cognitive working systems. *See* **cognitive working system.**

equiprobable events: outcomes which have equal likelihood of occurring; for example, in one toss of a fair coin "heads" and "tails" are considered equally likely outcomes.

equity: a system of law that affords a remedy when there is no complete or adequate remedy at law.

equity in taxation: (1) fairness, justice, or equality with respect to the impact of taxation; (2) one of the so-called "requisites of sound taxation" that relates to the fairness or justice of the tax or tax system.

equivalence class set: *see* **set, equivalence class.**

equivalence, coefficient of: *see* **coefficient of equivalence.**

equivalence drill: *see* **drill, equivalence.**

equivalence of groups: the condition or characteristic of the groups under consideration of having similar distributions on one or more variables; usually ascribed to groups so selected that corresponding measures of central tendency and variability differ by amounts small enough to be accounted for, with a high probability, by chance errors in random sampling from a single population; the equivalence of groups is not necessarily general, but only in regard to one or more specific variables.

equivalence of studies: the principle that stresses the equal value of any studies, whether literary or practical, when they have been pursued for equal lengths of time. (This concept has bestowed dignity upon vocational training equal to the honor accorded academic training.)

equivalency certificate: *see* **certificate, high school equivalency.**

equivalency certificate, high school: *see* **certificate, high school equivalency.**

equivalency, full-time: *see* **full-time equivalency.**

equivalent, age: *see* **age equivalent.**

equivalent forms: two forms of a test which are so similar that they can be used interchangeably and yet are not identical; two test forms that yield about the same mean and variability of scores, and whose items are similar with respect to type, difficulty, distribution of item-test correlations, and representative coverage of content. *Syn.* **alternate forms; comparable forms; duplicate forms; parallel forms; similar forms.**

equivalent, grade: *see* **grade equivalent.**

equivalent groups: *see* **groups, equivalent.**

equivalent methods in transfer: a view emphasizing the idea that methods of learning may differ but still achieve functionally the same end or goal.

equivalent sets: *see* **sets, equivalent.**

equivalents: words or expressions in one language that convey the same meaning as those in another language although they are not word-by-word translations of each other; for example, French *Il y a une heure que je parle* (lit. "there is one hour that I speak") is the equivalent of English "I have been speaking for an hour."

equivocation: a fallacy of ambiguity in which some part of a sentence or proposition is unclear because the meaning of the words used shifts without one's being aware and in control of the movement, as "All criminal action is punishable by law. Prosecution for theft is a criminal action. Therefore, prosecution for theft is punishable by law." *See* **fallacy of ambiguity.**

erase: (1) in tape recording, to remove the magnetic pattern on a tape by placing the tape in the strong magnetic field of an *erase head* or *bulk eraser;* (2) in data processing, to destroy the information stored on the surface of a magnetic tape, magnetic drum, or cathode ray tube in order to make this storage space available for new information; also, to blank out or replace with zeros whatever symbols may have been in an address, register, or storage medium.

erase head: *see* **head, erase.**

eraser, bulk: *see* **erase** (1).

ergasiomania (ĕr·gā′zhi·ō·mā′ni·ə): a condition characterized by morbid activity in work projects (which are often left uncompleted); characteristic of overactive phases of manic excitement.

ergogenic aid: *see* **aid, ergogenic.**

ergometer: a mechanical apparatus used to measure the amount of work done by a muscle.

ergonomics: laws of work or theories of energy expenditure.

erogenous zone: an area of the body surface such as the lips and genitals sensitive to tactual stimulation and releasing sexual feelings and reactions.

eros (ē'rəs): (Gr., lit., "sexual love") the life instinct. *Contr. w.* **thanatos.**

eroticism: (1) (psychoan.) a broad term for sexual arousal or desire; may be associated with the urethral or anal tract or the mouth, skin, or muscles, as well as with the genitals; (2) (pathol.) an overdevelopment of sex reactions.

eroticism, anal: (psychoan.) a state in which value is attached to and satisfaction derived in large measure from the objects, habits, attitudes, and feelings associated with the functions of defecation and urination and with the experiences that accompanied the training for the control of these functions. *Contr. w.* **eroticism, genital; eroticism, oral.**

eroticism, genital: (1) a condition in which pleasure is derived from the stimulation of the genitals; (2) a condition in which sexual excitement is aroused by the stimulation of the genitals; (3) (psychoan.) a stage in libidinal development in which the genitals are the focal erotogenic zone.

eroticism, oral: (psychoan.) a condition in which the chief source of the individual's erotic gratification is in such oral activities as sucking.

erotism, anal: *syn.* **eroticism, anal.**

erotism, genital: *syn.* **eroticism, genital.**

erotism, oral: *syn.* **eroticism, oral.**

error: (1) *syn.* **error, absolute;** (2) in programmed instruction, a response not acceptable to the programmer though it may be valuable for training purposes; *intrinsic programs* handle errors by *branching* students to simpler presentations (type 2) or to remedial sequences (type 3); *linear programs* are revised to prevent such errors.

error, absolute: (1) a generic term for those elements in a test and testing situation that operate to keep it from giving perfectly valid results; (2) the observed or obtained value of a measurement of a quantity minus the true value or mean value; *syn.* **error; deviation, error;** *contr. w.* **error, relative;** (3) the true value or mean value minus the observed or obtained value of a measurement of a quantity; *syn.* **correction;** *contr. w.* **error, relative;** (4) (math.) *syn.* **error, maximum.**

error, accidental: (1) (stat.) *syn.* **error, variable;** (2) (arith.) a mistake in computation ascribable to carelessness rather than to faulty understanding.

error, accumulative: *syn.* **error, constant.**

error, aiming: (mil. ed.) in missilery, an error that results from a miscalculation in such matters as longitude, distance, speed, reentry deflection, or the like.

error, alpha: the rejection of a null or other hypothesis when it is really true; the likelihood of occurrence is equal to the level of significance or confidence. *Syn.* **error of the first kind;** *ant.* **error, beta.**

error, apparent: *syn.* **error, maximum.**

error, average: *syn.* **deviation, average.**

error, beta: the acceptance of a null or other hypothesis when it is really false. *Syn.* **error of the second kind;** *ant.* **error, alpha.**

error, chance: *syn.* **error, random** (1).

error-choice technique: a technique to determine the subject's tendency to guess in a direction determined by the subject's attitude; the respondent is forced to choose between two equally incorrect alternatives reflecting opposed biases.

error, compensating: (1) *syn.* **error, random** (1); (2) an error, regardless of source, that is in a direction opposite from that of some other error which it may therefore be said to counteract.

error, constant: (1) an error that consistently affects all observations or measurements by an equal amount in the same direction and that, accordingly, introduces a systematic bias into the observations or measurements; (2) a factor influencing a set of measurements or observations in the same direction, but not necessarily by equal amounts. *Syn.* **accumulative error; cumulating error; cumulative error; persistent error; systematic error.**

error, correctable: (typewriting) an error that can be corrected in such a way as to make the typewritten material (letter, thesis, manuscript, etc.) usable and acceptable in appearance.

error count: the frequency of specific errors by categories, such as errors in spelling in children's compositions, errors in computation in arithmetic, or errors in punctuation.

error, cumulating: *syn.* **error, constant.**

error, cumulative: *syn.* **error, constant.**

error deviation: *syn.* **error absolute** (2).

error, estimate of: an objective estimate of the magnitude of the experimental error; commonly consists of the standard error or error variance; may be errors of measurement, errors of estimate, or sampling errors.

error, experimental: the error in the result of an experiment that may be due to any combination of such factors as the indirect character of measurement, the lack of precise definitions of the quality or characteristic to be measured, sampling, the influence of irrelevant factors, the inadequacies of testing instruments, the fluctuating character of the individuals involved in the experiment, etc.

error, fortuitous: *syn.* **error, random** (1).

error, grammatical: (1) any mistake made in choosing the conventionally accepted forms of words, such as using *seen* when *saw* is needed; (2) any mistake made in the arrangement of words within one of the conventionally accepted sentence structures.

error, greatest possible: *syn.* **error, maximum.**

error, grouping: (1) the error introduced by the assumption that all cases in a given interval are concentrated at the midpoint of that class interval when a continuous series of observations is divided into class intervals; (2) the error introduced by any stated assumption as to the manner of distribution of data within a class interval when the data have been grouped into class intervals, thereby losing the separate identity of the separate values which collectively constitute a class interval. *Syn.* **error of grouping.**

error in estimation: *syn.* **error of estimate.**

error, law of: any mathematical formula that will give approximately the probability of an error of a given magnitude.

error, logical: (personality measurement) an error such as may occur when two or more character traits are being rated, if an observer tends to give similar ratings to traits which do not necessarily go together; for example, an observer may think that a person who is industrious is also efficient, or that a person who is prompt is also industrious; these things may be, but are not necessarily, true.

error, maximum: the numerical value that no error involved in precise measurement can exceed, being equal to one-half the unit of measurement; for example, 0.005 is the maximum error in the measurement 3.72 in. *Syn.* **absolute error; apparent error; greatest possible error; tolerance.**

error, mean: *syn.* **deviation, average.**

error, mean absolute: *syn.* **deviation, average.**

error, mean square: *syn.* **variance.**

error, median: *syn.* **deviation, median.**

error, nonconstant: *syn.* **error, variable.**

error, normal curve of: *see* **curve, normal probability.**

error of a factor loading, standard: *see* **standard error of a factor loading.**

error of central tendency: the inclination of many observers charged with rating a group or individual on a particular quality to group their ratings close to the center of the scale.

error of estimate: (1) the amount by which the actual value of an observation differs from an estimated or computed value, or the deviation of a dependent variable from the regression line; *syn.* **error in estimation; error of prediction;** (2) in estimating an observed score, the error made in predicting the score on one form from the other form by using the least squares regression equation; in estimating a true score, the error made in attempting to predict the true score from the observed score.

error of estimate, standard: *see* **standard error of estimate.**

error of grouping: *syn.* **error, grouping.**

error of measurement: the difference between the actual measurement and that recorded by virtue of the unit being used (not because a mistake has been made); thus the error of measurement is related to the precision of measurement.

error of measurement, standard: *see* **standard error of measurement.**

error of observation: *syn.* **error of measurement.**

error of prediction: *syn.* **error of estimate.**

error of refraction: *syn.* **error, refractive.**

error of sampling: the chance deviation of a statistic from the true value of the parameter it is designed to estimate; the variation in a statistic due to the fact that the given observations are not perfectly representative but only a sample of a population. *Syn.* **sampling error.**

error of standards: the tendency of some observers to overrate or underrate because of differences in their standards.

error of substitution: the error arising from the difference between two observed scores on parallel tests; in substituting a score on one test for a score on a parallel form of the test, the error is given by the formula $S_d = S_1 \sqrt{2(1 - r_{12})}$ where S_d is the standard error of substitution, S_1 is the observed variance of the test, and r_{12} is the test reliability or correlation of the two parallel forms.

error of the first kind: *syn.* **error, alpha.**

error of the second kind: *syn.* **error, beta.**

error, oral-usage: a mistake made in speaking, for example, a mispronunciation.

error, percent of: the relative error expressed as a percent. *See* **error, relative.**

error, persistent: *syn.* **error, constant.**

error, probable (PE): (1) a statistic of limited utility which is of such size that 50 percent of the cases in a normal distribution are included between points 1 PE below the mean and 1 PE above the mean; (2) (of a frequency distribution) 0.6745 of the standard deviation of the distribution; in a normal distribution, equal to the quartile deviation; (3) (of a statistic) 0.6745 of the standard error of the statistic. *Syn.* **probable deviation; probable discrepancy;** *dist. f.* **deviation, quartile.**

error, random: (1) an error ascribable to chance, without bias or system, such that the sum of a large number of such errors approaches zero; one of a type that in the long run does not materially alter the accuracy of a large number of observations; *syn.* **chance error; compensating error; fortuitous error; unbiased error; variable error;** *dist. f.* **mistake;** *contr. w.* **error, constant;** (2) (read.) one of the errors in oral reading which have no pattern, which are due to guessing; *contr. w.* **error, systematic** (2).

error, range of: the span of values between the maximum and minimum admissible values for a specified measurement or observation; for example, if a measurement is given as 2.6 in., the range of error would be 2.55 to 2.65 in.

error rate: in programmed instruction generally, the percentage of incorrect responses on an item, a set of items, or a whole program; a relatively low error rate—though programmers do not agree on the range that is low—is a necessary but by no means sufficient condition for a program to be considered acceptable, since spuriously low error rates are too easily attained by adding irrelevant easy items, testing with a pretrained population, removing *terminal items,* etc.

error, refractive: a defect of the refractive mediums of the eye resulting in failure of the light rays to be brought to a single focus exactly on the retina; includes *myopia, hyperopia, presbyopia,* and *astigmatism. Dist. f.* **eye defect; visual defect.**

error, relative: (1) the difference between an observed (or obtained) value of a quantity and the theoretically true value, divided by the theoretically true value; *contr. w.* **error, absolute; error, apparent;** (2) the ratio of the absolute error to the accepted value of the measurement.

error, residual: the actual or observed value of a single measurement minus a computed value regarded as the most probable; the most probable value is often the arithmetic mean of a number of similar measurements or a value obtained from a regression equation, the residual then being a deviation from the mean or from the regression line or plane. *Syn.* **error of estimate; residual;** *dist. f.* **error, true.**

error, reversal: *syn.* **reversal.**

error, root-mean-square: *syn.* **deviation, root-mean-square.**

error, rounding: the error resulting from dropping certain less significant digits in a numeral and applying some adjustment to the more significant digits retained; sometimes called *round-off error.*

error, sampling: *syn.* **error of sampling.**

error, speech: *see* **speech error.**

error, standard: the estimated *standard deviation* of the values of a score or statistical measure that would be obtained if the measurement were repeated over and over again.

error, subjective: an error due to the conscious or unconscious bias of a person making observations or working with data.

error, systematic: (1) (math.) *syn.* **error, constant;** (2) (read.) one of the mistakes that consistently conform to a pattern or principle, such as errors in sounding vowel sounds; (3) (meas.) an amount of invalid variance due to individual differences in test-wiseness or to cheating, which affects test validity or a response set.

error, true: the difference between the observed value of an item and its true value; not obtainable practically, since true value is a theoretical concept. *Dist. f.* **error, residual.**

error, unbiased: *syn.* **error, random** (1).

error, variable: the deviation of obtained scores or measures from their respective true values, as a result of the operation of random factors that affect in varying degree and direction individual scores or measures; a concept which cannot be computed for any single value, but which (by definition) equals zero when the number of values is infinitely large. *See* **error, compensating.**

error variance: *see* **variance, error.**

errorless learning: *see* **learning, errorless.**

errors, nonessential: (fact. anal.) errors arising from (*a*) the guessing of communalities, (*b*) the use of correlations that have some members missing, (*c*) the incompleteness of factor extraction, and/or (*d*) the presence of computational mistakes.

errors, rater: errors arising from (*a*) central tendency, that is, tendency of a rater to avoid using the extreme positions on a rating scale, (*b*) generosity or leniency, the practice of rating everyone average or above on a rating scale, (*c*) logical fallacy, the tendency for raters to rate a person similarly on characteristics which the rater feels should go together, (*d*) proximity, the tendency of raters to describe behaviors which appear close together on the printed sheet more nearly alike than they do behaviors which are physically separated by some distance, and (*e*) stereotyping, rating a person according to one's preconceived notions or biases about the certain group to which the ratee belongs.

eructatio nervosa (e·ruk·tā'shi·ō nĕr·vō'sa): (Lat., lit., "nervous belching") belching as sometimes used by children to annoy parents or as an attention-getting mechanism.

eructation: belching.

eschatology (es·ka·tol'ə·jē): the portion of theological dogmatism dealing with finality, such as death and the end of time.

esophoria (es'ō·fō'ri·ə): (1) a type of *heterophoria* characterized by a tendency of the eyes to turn inward when the extrinsic muscles are relaxed; (2) a postural position of the eyes inward when fusion is broken. *Contr. w.* exophoria; hyperphoria.

esoteric services: *see* services, esoteric.

esotropia: a manifest turning inward of the eye; also called *convergent* (or *internal*) *strabismus, convergent squint, cross-eye. Contr. w.* exotropia; hypertropia.

esprit de corps (es·prē' də kōr'): (Fr., lit., "spirit of the body") the enthusiasm, loyalty, and oneness of a group.

essay: a short, nonfictional literary production on any subject; in the writing done in schools, may be synonymous with article, theme, or composition.

essay examination: *see* examination, essay.

essay test: *see* test, essay.

essence: that which makes a thing what it is; distinct from any accidental characteristics that it may possess; the basic character or structure of an entity independent of its physical existence.

essential: (1) loosely, whatever is regarded as principal or most important; (2) strictly, in many philosophies and especially in that of Aristotle, whatever pertains to the essence of something; *see* essence.

essential unity: *see* unity.

essentialism: the doctrine that there is an indispensable common core of culture (certain knowledges, skills, attitudes, ideals, etc.) that can be identified and should be taught systematically to all, with rigorous standards of achievement, it being regarded as a definite adult responsibility to guide education in this direction; presupposes not that individual pupil freedom is to be dismissed but rather that such freedom is to be made an aim or achievement instead of a means of education. *Syn.* philosophy of constant fundamentals.

essentially military college: *see* college, essentially military.

essentially military school: a residential school the primary purpose of which is educational but which is organized on a military basis and in which the student is at all times subject to a prescribed military discipline and uniform is the required dress; the term derives from the type of organization rather than from the basic purpose.

establishment in agriculture: a status of relative stability in an agricultural occupation (production or nonfarm agriculture), whether as owner, employee, or manager; the goal of vocational education in agriculture in the high school.

establishment, service: *see* service establishment.

establishment, the: a term used to designate the *status quo* or the traditional structure of an institution.

establishment trainer: *see* training sponsor, distributive education.

estate tax: *see* tax, estate.

estimate: *n.* the value arrived at by rough calculation or assumed to be approximately correct on the basis of one or more known and related values.

estimate: *v.* (1) (math.) to arrive at a value either by inspection without calculating the result or by a rough calculation; (2) (stat.) to use any statistic derived from a sample to infer the value of a parameter in the universe from which the sample was taken or the value of a statistic derived (or to be derived) from another sample.

estimate of error: *see* error, estimate of.

estimate, probability: the likelihood that a given event will or will not occur.

estimate, regression: *see* regression estimate.

estimate, standard error of: *see* standard error of estimate.

estimate, unbiased: an estimate of a population parameter such that its mean value over infinite samples equals the parameter; thus, the standard deviation is a biased estimate of the corresponding parameter since it is a consistent underestimate of that value.

estimates, matched regression: *see* matched regression estimates.

estimation: (1) *syn.* estimate *n.*; (2) the act or process of making an estimate.

estimation, interval: *see* interval estimation.

estoppel: a bar raised by the law which prevents a person from allowing or denying a certain fact because of his previous statements or conduct.

eta (ē'ta; ā'ta): (1) the lowercase Greek letter η which is used as the symbol for the correlation ratio; (2) sometimes used as synonymous with the term correlation ratio. *See* correlation ratio.

etching: one of the intaglio printing methods of the graphic arts from grooves scratched with a pointed instrument through an acid-resistant ground covering a plate; grooves thus exposed are incised by acid when the plate is immersed in an acid bath, the depth of each groove being regulated by the length of time the plate remains in the bath.

eternal-truths argument: *see* argument, eternal-truths.

ethical character: *see* character, ethical.

ethical education: *see* moral education.

ethical freedom: *see* freedom, ethical.

ethical guidance: *syn.* guidance, moral.

ethical instruction: *see* instruction, ethical.

ethical judgment: *see* judgment, ethical.

ethical nihilism: *see* nihilism, ethical.

ethical sense: (1) the capacity to judge the moral quality of acts; *syn.* moral sense; (2) as developed by English and Scottish philosophers of the seventeenth and eighteenth centuries, a theory of moral judgments opposed to rationalism and holding that such judgments are formed by direct intuition rather than by appraisal of the component values.

ethical standards: *see* standards, ethical.

ethics: (1) the moral obligations and responsibilities which are accepted by a particular society or group in a society; (2) the study of human behavior not only to find the truth of things as they are but also to inquire into the worth or goodness of human actions; the science of human conduct; concerned with judgments of obligation (rightness and wrongness, "oughtness") and with judgments of value (goodness and badness). *See* moral.

ethics, algedonic: *syn.* ethics, pleasure-pain.

ethics, business: the branch of ethics that deals with business relationships; seldom taught as a separate subject in secondary school or college, but often stressed in the teaching of business subjects, especially salesmanship, retailing, advertising, business law, and business finance. *See* ethics.

ethics, code of: *see* code of ethics.

ethics, counseling: standards providing for resolution of conflicts between a counselor's responsibility to his client and his responsibility to society.

ethics, dualistic: two different and sometimes even conflicting sets of standards for determining conduct.

ethics, educational: the principles and standards of desirable conduct expected of members of the teaching profession toward others in all situations affecting education.

ethics, hedonistic: a system of ethics that defines the good in terms of pleasure alone.

ethics, humanistic: the theory that the true norms and proper goals of conduct are to be found in the physiological, psychological, and social well-being of the individuals who compose a society.

ethics, idealistic: the theory that the true norms and proper goals of conduct are found in human perfection, both personal and social, with special emphasis on the superorganic, rational, and spiritual elements involved. *Contr. w.* ethics, materialistic.

ethics, materialistic: the theory that the true norms and proper goals of conduct are physiological well-being, material comfort, and sensuous pleasure. *Dist. f.* Epicureanism; *contr. w.* ethics, idealistic.

ethics, pleasure-pain: a system of ethics that defines the good in terms of pain and pleasure considered as contrasting qualities of experience; to be contrasted with hedonistic ethics, which defines the good in terms of pleasure alone. *Syn.* ethics, algedonic; *see* hedonism.

ethics, professional: the general principles of right and wrong conduct as applied to the special problems of a profession; this is in distinction to, but not separate from, the general problems of personal and social ethics.

ethics, relativistic: the theory that we cannot justifiably assume universally valid moral principles; that an ethical code is a human contrivance subject to time, place, person, and circumstance; and that history shows it always to have been so regardless of various and sundry claims to the contrary.

ethics, selling: a branch of business ethics dealing with the relationship of salespeople to their customers, to their competitors, to their employers, and to one another; seldom taught as a separate subject in secondary school or college, but given increased stress in such courses as salesmanship, advertising, and retailing. *See* **ethics.**

ethics, situational: a contemporary system of ethics which has obtained considerable popularity in liberal theological circles and which stresses the demands of the situation rather than the force of absolute principle in the determination of right conduct, the principle of love being always normative; this school of thought is sometimes called "the new morality."

ethics, teachers': *see* **ethics, professional.**

ethnic dance: *see* **dance, ethnic.**

ethnic group: *see* **group, ethnic.**

ethnocentrism: the centering upon race as a chief interest or end; regarding one's own race or ethnic group as the center of culture; opposed, with respect to focus of interest and predominant attention, to viewpoints termed theocentric, humanistic, naturalistic, idealistic, etc.

ethnogeography: the study of the distribution of races geographically and their relation to environmental factors.

ethnography: a branch of anthropology dealing with the origins and developments of the various human races.

ethnology: that branch of anthropology which divides and classifies human beings into distinctive groups and analyzes their cultures; the study of ethnic groups and their differences.

ethnomusicology: study of the tribal, folk, and art music of societies outside Western civilization, that is, non-Western music described in terms of Western concepts of musical coherence. *Syn.* **comparative musicology.**

ethnopsychology: study of the psychological behavior of persons living in different cultures.

ethnosociology: use of ethnographic methods in the study of comparative cultures; the study of the evolution of cultures as pursued by ethnographers.

ethography: descriptive study of moral attitudes, manners, and customs of mankind.

ethology: the study of customs, mores, and manners, especially a consideration of the ways in which they are formed, grow, and decay, and an analysis of their effectiveness.

etiological: pertaining to investigation of the cause of some state, for example, of a disability.

etiology (ē·ti·ol′ə·jē): a part of medical, behavioral, and other sciences dealing with the causes of symptoms.

etiquette: conventional rules of behavior or conduct acceptable in a given society.

ETV: *see* **television, educational.**

etymology: the study of the origin, derivation, and history of words.

etymology, folk: the process by which an unfamiliar or foreign word becomes transformed so that it appears to be related to a familiar word.

Euclidean geometry: *see* **geometry, Euclidean.**

Euclidean space: *see* **space, Euclidean.**

eudaemonism (ū·dē′mən·iz′m): the ethical theory derived from Aristotle that happiness, well-being, and self-realization constitute the highest good; pleasure is thus excluded directly but may be a by-product of the real good. *Contr. w.* **hedonism.**

eugenic: tending to improve the inherited qualities of future generations. *Ant.* **dysgenic.**

eugenics: that branch of science which aims to improve the human race through controlled heredity.

Euler circles technique: (math.) circles or any simple closed curves used to illustrate sentences having the form "All *A* is *B*," "No *A* is *B*," "Some *A* is *B*," or "Some *A* is not *B*," in order to test the validity of inferences drawn from such sentences; the technique is credited to Leonhard Euler.

euphoria (ū·fō′ri·ə): (1) a feeling of well-being; (2) an exaggerated sense of health and physical ability. *Ant.* **dysphoria.**

eurythmics: a system of combined muscular and musical instruction developed by Émile Jaques-Dalcroze; unites education in musical theory with bodily movements and is intended to make feeling for rhythm a physical experience; teaches the interpretation through bodily movements of musical compositions, especially those employing complex rhythms.

euthenics (ū·then′iks): the science or art of improving the environment or living conditions; the providing of plenty and well-being to improve the social group or race.

evaluation: (1) the process of ascertaining or judging the value or amount of something by use of a standard of appraisal; includes judgments in terms of internal evidence and external criteria; (2) (psych.) the process of determining the relative significance of phenomena of the same sort in terms of some standard; (3) the consideration of evidence in the light of value standards and in terms of the particular situation and the goals which the group or individual is striving to attain; (4) a judgment of merit, sometimes based solely on measurements, such as those provided by test scores, but more frequently involving the synthesis of various measurements, critical incidents, subjective impressions, and other kinds of evidence weighed in the process of carefully appraising the effects of an educational experience.

evaluation, billet: the determination of the level of difficulty and responsibility of a military billet. *See* **analysis, billet; billet.**

evaluation board, flying: (mil. ed.) a board of investigating officers that examines and evaluates the professional qualifications and proficiency of rated flying personnel and makes recommendations regarding the future utilization of persons who appear before the board.

evaluation, building: *see* **building evaluation.**

evaluation, context: a method of evaluation by describing individually and in relevant perspectives the major subsystems of the context by comparing actual and intended inputs and outputs of the subsystems and by analyzing possible causes of discrepancies between actualities and intentions, the objective being to define the operational context, to identify and assess needs in the context, and to identify and delineate problems underlying the needs; employed in relation to the decision-making process for deciding upon the setting to be served, the goals associated with meeting needs, and the objectives associated with solving problems, that is, for planning needed changes.

evaluation, cooperative: *syn.* **grading, cooperative.**

evaluation, counselor: the process of judging measurable progress toward stated counselor aims and objectives by established criteria.

evaluation criteria: (1) the standards against which a person, a group, a procedure, or an instrument may be checked; (2) the factors considered by an accrediting agency in analyzing the status of an educational institution to determine whether it shall be accredited; *see* **accreditation; criterion.**

evaluation, curriculum: the assessment of learning activities within a specific instructional area for the purpose of determining the validity of objectives, relevancy and sequence of content, and achievement of specified goals; leads to decisions associated with planning, programming, implementing, and recycling program activities.

evaluation cycle: (mil. ed.) the cycle which begins with the initial determination of educational objectives for a particular course and ends with a final evaluation of its effectiveness.

evaluation, faculty: the process of ascertaining or judging the value, through appraisal, of the persons responsible for administration and instruction in a school, college, or university. *See* **evaluation** (3).

evaluation, field: (mil. ed.) evaluation of the effectiveness of course materials prepared by the United States Air Force or other educational agency through visits to installations using the materials or through questionnaires answered by students, instructors, or administrative personnel.

evaluation, group: (couns.) a method of changing an individual's behavior from less desirable to more desirable; group forces that cause the individual to resist change in the first place; that is, the group pressures that encourage him to adhere to a given group norm are used to move the individual to this new level of behavior.

evaluation, guidance program: determination of the worth and outcomes of guidance efforts through the application of sound research procedures in securing the data.

evaluation, health: *see* **appraisal, health.**

evaluation, informal: appraisal of an individual's status or growth by means other than standardized instruments.

evaluation, input: a method of evaluation which consists in describing and analyzing available human and material resources, solution strategies, and procedural designs for relevance, feasibility, and economy in the course of action to be taken, in order to identify and assess system capabilities, available input strategies, and designs for implementing the strategies; in relation to the decision-making process, a method for selecting sources of support, solution strategies, and procedural designs, that is, for programming change activities.

evaluation, institutional: the process of studying and analyzing the strengths and weaknesses of an educational institution, often for the purpose of determining whether it shall be accredited.

evaluation instrument: any of the means by which one obtains information on the progress of the learner and the effectiveness of instruction; quantitative and qualitative data, objective measures, subjective impressions, tests, observations, anecdotal records, case studies, and sociometric methods may all serve as instruments for deciding whether instructional objectives have been attained.

evaluation, job: any objective technique for determining the relative functional worth of a job in a classification or hierarchy of jobs and its corresponding monetary worth; a research technique rather than a bargaining technique; the results of job evaluation may be used in collective bargaining.

evaluation, medical: (spec. ed.) determination of the nature and extent of the disability of the handicapped child (one step in determining eligibility), appraisal of the general health status of the individual in order to determine his capacities and limitations and to ascertain if physical restoration services might remove, correct, or minimize the disability condition, and contribution of a sound medical basis for selection of a rehabilitation objective.

evaluation of guidance: *see* **evaluation, guidance program.**

evaluation of supervision: *see* **supervision, evaluation of.**

evaluation period: *see* **period, evaluation.**

evaluation, postbroadcast: the act or process of judging the merits of a radio or television program after it has been presented to a pupil-teacher audience as an aid to instruction; intended, theoretically, to be used for the improvement of future broadcast lessons.

evaluation, prebroadcast: the process of judging the merits of a projected radio or television program prior to its formal presentation over the air, as at a rehearsal, with a view to improving it; sometimes resorted to in the case of educational broadcasts.

evaluation, prevocational: assessment of an individual prior to his beginning a job or reaching the age at which employment is possible.

evaluation, process: a method of evaluation by monitoring an activity's potential procedural barriers and remaining alert to unanticipated ones; its objective is to identify or predict defects in the procedural design or its implementation and to maintain a record of procedural events and activities; in relation to the decision-making process, employed for implementing and refining the program design and procedure, that is, for effecting process control.

evaluation, product: a method of evaluation by defining operationally and measuring criteria associated with the objectives, by comparing these measurements with predetermined standards or comparative bases, and by interpreting the outcome in terms of recorded input and process information; its objective is to relate outcome information to objectives and to context, input, and process information; in relation to the decision-making process, employed as a means for deciding whether to continue, terminate, modify, or refocus a change activity and for linking the activity to other major phases of the change process, that is, for evolving change activities.

evaluation, program: *see* **evaluation, radio.**

evaluation program: *see* **program, evaluation.**

evaluation, psychological: (1) the use of tests and other observational techniques to assess and rate the ability, achievement, interest, or personality of an individual; (2) results from a synthesis of psychometric data and information obtained during interviewing, counseling, and other aspects of the rehabilitation process; not an isolated service but closely related to counseling and all other rehabilitation services.

evaluation, pupil: a process in which a teacher commonly uses information derived from many sources to arrive at a value judgment; may or may not be based on measurement data; includes not only identifying the degree to which a student possesses a trait or to which his behavior has been modified but also evaluating the desirability and adequacy of these findings.

evaluation, radio: the act of judging the merits and faults of a radio program.

evaluation scale: *see* **scale, evaluation.**

evaluation, self-: *see* **self-evaluation.**

evaluation, subjective: an evaluative score of a student's answers to essay test questions or to his performance in other situations, the score assigned being determined by the personal opinion and judgment of the scorer.

evaluation, teacher: an estimate or measure of the quality of a person's teaching based on one or more criteria such as pupil achievement, pupil adjustment, pupil behavior, and the judgment of school officials, parents, pupils, or the teacher himself.

evaluation, test: the process of determining the merit of a test on the basis of such characteristics as validity, reliability, ease of administration and scoring, adequacy of norms, availability of equivalent or duplicate forms, and ease of interpretation. *See* **analysis, item.**

evaluative checklist: *syn.* **checklist, teacher-evaluation.**

evaluative labeling: naming that implies a favorable or unfavorable judgment of that which is named; diagnostic terms, for example, tend to be negatively evaluative in that they imply abnormality. (Names of speech disorders may be regarded as negatively evaluative labels and consequently as conducive to varying degrees of maladjustment on the part of the person whose speech is so labeled.)

evaluative method: (res.) the procedures in a study that has evaluation as its chief purpose and that in most cases includes some definite fact finding, through observation, and that involves the careful description of aspects to be evaluated, a statement of purpose, frame of reference, and criteria for the evaluation, and the degrees or terms that are to be employed in recording judgments. (Checklists, score cards, questionnaires, and rating scales are devices often employed in the evaluation of ability, aptitude, personality, etc., and sometimes for evaluating, indirectly, the institutions or practices that contributed to the observed results. The routine use of such instruments does not in itself, however, constitute research.)

evaluative therapy: *syn.* **therapy, general semantic.**

evening class: *see* **class, evening.**

evening class, agricultural: *see* **class, adult agricultural.**

evening college: *see* **college, evening.**

evening counseling program: *see* **program, evening counseling.**

evening course: *see* **course, evening.**

evening distributive education class, adult: *see* **class, adult evening distributive education.**

evening industrial class: *see* **class, evening industrial.**

evening industrial school: *see* **class, evening industrial.**

evening school: (1) in general, an institution, public or private, that offers an organized program of courses, at hours other than those commonly used for elementary and secondary school classes, for persons not engaged in full-time schooling; (2) more specifically, an adjunct of the public elementary and secondary school, offering continuation classes, vocational training, and avocational and recreational activities to adults; sometimes known as *community school, opportunity school, adult center, people's college, people's university, leisure hour school,* etc. (In some states attendance at such schools is accepted as meeting the part-time or continuation-school requirements on the part of employed youth.)

evening school, agricultural: *see* **class, adult agricultural.**

event: (math.) in the study of probability, some set of outcomes of an experiment; for example, in throwing a single die, throwing a "five" would be an event.

event-sampling: (couns.) collection of a series of anecdotes concerning a counselee, written at definite selected intervals during the day or week to accumulate data concerning contacts, behavior, and interest; based on observation, the recorded events should represent typical behavior and should be interpreted or evaluated as such. *See* **anecdotal method.**

events, antecedent: *see* **antecedent events.**

events, equiprobable: *see* **equiprobable events.**

evidence: (philos.) that which is submitted to one's judgment as the grounds or warrant for an asserted belief or idea.

evidence, admissible: (law) evidence presented or introduced in a legal proceeding; acceptable evidence used in adjudication.

evocative use of language: *see* **language, evocative use of.**

evolution: (1) (math.) the process of extracting roots; *contr. w.* **involution;** (2) (philos.) the theory that the universe is the result of a process of natural development; various species are viewed as the result of growth, change, modification, and adaptation rather than as a result of specific acts of deliberate creation.

evolution, cultural: a gradual change, over a relatively long period of time, of some or all of the features which make up *culture. Contr. w.* **revolution, cultural.**

evolution, determinate: variation of an organism *from generation to generation along a particular line, producing new types irrespective of the effect of natural selection or other external factors.

evolution, emergent: in conformity with a principle, the consistent progression of universal phenomena, but with the qualification that each new stage could not have been predicted from the laws of the preceding stages; the term, while used mainly in reference to biological change, can also be applied to cultural change; in the former the change is by mutation and in the latter the modification is based on the combination of cultural traits which provides a brand-new definition of the situation.

evolution, functional: the differentiation and outward growth of a staff function from the chain of command to which it is attached and the development of staff components. *See* **functions, staff.**

evolution, mental: the progressive increase and refinement of mental function seen in the evolutionary animal scale. *See* **mental;** *dist. f.* **development, mental.**

evolutionary instrumentalism: *see* **instrumentalism, evolutionary.**

evolutionary naturalism: *syn.* **humanism, scientific.**

evolutionism: (1) the theory that the universe is and has been the result of continuing evolutionary processes; no explanation of it is necessary outside these processes; *see* **creationism;** (2) in social and educational theory particu-

larly, the view that change is development, whether conceived as linear, circular, or spiral, which takes place gradually and not by leaps and bounds.

Ex libris: *see* **bookplate.**

ex officio (eks o·fish'i·ō): (Lat., lit., "by reason of the office") used of an officer whose position by statute automatically makes him holder of another office or member of a board with all rights and responsibilities of other members unless otherwise specified; for example, in some states the governor or the state superintendent of public instruction is ex officio a member of the state board of education.

ex officio member: usually, a person who is a member of a board of education or similar body by virtue of holding an elective or appointive office, sometimes by virtue of former membership in the board or group.

ex parte (eks pär'tə): (Lat., lit., "of the one part") applied to actions taken by or with the knowledge of only one party, with respect to matters involving two or more adversary parties; emanating from or relating to one side only, implying bias, for example, ex parte testimony.

ex post facto law: *see* **law, ex post facto.**

exact number: *see* **number, exact.**

exaggerations: (art ed.) in a child's drawing, special emphasis on parts that are important to him through his autoplastic experiences, his value judgments with regard to certain parts, or through their emotional significance to him; proportions of value.

examen pro facultate docendi (eks·ä'men prō fak'əl·tä'tə dō·sen'dī): (Lat., lit., "examination before the teaching staff ") the examination required of the Prussian teachers of the *Gymnasium* beginning in 1810, administered at the Universities of Berlin, Breslau, and Königsberg.

examination: (ed.) any process for testing the ability or achievement of students in any area; in ordinary speech, the terms *examination* and *test* are frequently used as synonyms; if a distinction is to be made, an examination should be regarded as more comprehensive and complex than a test. *See* **test.**

examination, admission: a test used as a whole or partial basis for admission to a school, to a division of a school, to a profession, or to any selected group; occasionally used by American colleges before permission to matriculate is granted.

examination, civil service: an examination for any government service except the military, naval, legislative, or judicial; widely used by the Federal government in selecting and promoting its employees; used less widely as the examination given by local boards of education to applicants for teaching and other positions.

examination, college board: *see* **college boards.**

examination, college entrance: *see* **examinations, entrance.**

examination, comprehensive: *syn.* **test, comprehensive achievement.**

examination, contemporary affairs: a test or other measuring instrument devised to determine a person's knowledge and awareness of present-day events or conditions and of their implications for education.

examination, content: a test designed to measure achievement or proficiency in a particular body of subject matter, for example, American history. *Syn.* **subject examination.**

examination, credit by: *see* **credit by examination.**

examination, dental: an examination of the teeth by a dentist or an oral hygienist.

examination, discussion: *syn.* **examination, essay.**

examination, ear: a complete examination of the appearance and function of the ear, including audiometric tests to determine the presence or absence of pathological conditions and hearing impairment.

examination, entrance: a verbal, written, or performance test which precedes the acceptance of an applicant into a specific job, field, or institution of learning.

examination, essay: a term frequently applied to written examinations of the discussion type, in which pupils are asked to discuss, summarize, outline, criticize, compare, reorganize, evaluate, state, show, analyze, etc.; usually implies that the scoring is done subjectively.

examination, external: a test or series of tests administered to students of an educational institution independently of the school and its staff and also scored independently, so that the competence of the students is not certified either by the particular school attended or by the completion of a certain number of years of attendance but rather by an independent judging agency.

examination, eye: a complete examination of the appearance and functioning of the eye, usually with dilation, including inspection of the interior of the eye, to determine the presence or absence of pathological conditions and refractive error. *Dist. f.* **assessment, eyesight.**

examination, final: a test given at the conclusion of a course or at the end of a period of instruction such as a year, a semester, or a quarter.

examination for certification: *see* **certification, examination for.**

examination, formal: strictly, any examination conducted formally, with strict regulations relating to such matters as time limits, seating arrangements, prevention of cheating, etc.; sometimes loosely used to designate the traditional or *essay* type of examination.

examination, graduate record: an examination, set by an outside agency, widely used by higher education institutions to determine, in part, the qualification of candidates for admission to graduate study.

examination, health: a physical examination given by a doctor of medicine to discover the health status of a person; usually recorded along with a health history and an account of tests and immunizations.

examination, leaving: an examination administered to pupils at the leaving of a particular level of education. (In most European countries it is given at the end of both the elementary and the secondary levels.)

examination, medical: an examination by a physician to determine the health status of a person.

examination, mental: determination of the relative strength of intellectual ability in terms of a standard.

examination, old-type: a somewhat vague term used to designate the essay examination when compared with the objective test or so-called new-type examination.

examination, physical: an examination for the purpose of determining the individual's general health condition and of discovering defects or disturbing conditions of any kind.

examination, psychological: *see* **evaluation, psychological** (1).

examination, qualifying: (1) a battery of achievement and aptitude examinations given to determine the adequacy of a student for continued work in a professional preparation program; may be given at specified stages, as when the student is applying for admission to the institution, is beginning work in the laboratory school, or is applying for a teaching certificate; (2) a battery of oral or written examinations that must be passed for admission to candidacy for a graduate degree.

examination report: *see* **report, examination.**

examination schedule: a timetable indicating day, time of day, and place for the administration of examinations.

examination, short-answer: *syn.* **test, objective.**

examination, state board of: *see* **board of examination, state.**

examination, subject: *syn.* **examination, content.**

examination, teacher: (1) a battery of educational tests, either written or oral, given under the auspices of the state or of some subdivision of the state, to ascertain the breadth and depth of a teacher's preparation, qualifications, and training to teach in certain fields; (2) any test or battery of tests designed to measure the preparation or qualifications of a teacher or prospective teacher for teaching in general or in a restricted area.

examination, traditional: *syn.* **examination, essay.**

examinations, board: a term used freely in schools and departments of music in institutions of higher learning to refer to short recital performances by student musicians before a board of examiners; the board of examiners will usually include the student's teacher and selected members of the music faculty; the board's evaluation partly determines the student's earned grade in applied music. *Syn.* **jury examinations.**

examinations, college entrance: (1) *syn.* **examinations, prematriculation;** (2) examinations used to determine whether college students transferring from one institution to another have gained the minimum mastery of subject matter required for admission. *See* **admission requirements.**

examinations, jury: *syn.* **examinations, board.**

examinations, prematriculation: aptitude or achievement tests administered by an educational institution to candidates before they have been officially admitted and registered for the purpose of determining whether they meet admission requirements and, in some cases, to classify and place them in required subject-matter classes.

examinee: a person examined or questioned by means of a test, interview, or questionnaire.

examiner: one who administers examinations or tests.

examiner, psychoeducational: one who appraises the mental endowment and the educational attainments of children, particularly for the purpose of diagnosing learning difficulties and outlining remedial treatment.

examiners, state board of: *see* **board of examiners, state.**

examiners, state board of educational: *see* **board of examination, state.**

example: (1) a number situation for which the arithmetical operation to be performed is indicated by signs or some form of directions; (2) a problem solved for illustrative purposes.

exceptional: descriptive of a pupil who displays a deviation from the normal by a considerable amount in respect to any one of a number of traits. *See* **atypical.**

exceptional child: *see* **child, exceptional.**

exceptional-child psychology: *see* **psychology of exceptional children.**

exceptional children in special classes or schools, percentage of: *see* **percentage of exceptional children in special classes or schools.**

exceptional children, industrial arts for: *see* **industrial arts for exceptional children.**

exceptional children, school for: *see* **special school.**

exceptional children, teacher of: any of a variety of teachers assigned to the instruction of children having exceptional needs due to deviations in physical, mental, or emotional status; special qualifications for such assignment are implied but not universally insured.

exceptionality, area of: that area in which a pupil's characteristics, skills, behavior pattern, and/or performance deviate significantly from the mean of the normal sample or population; such areas constitute the scope of the field dealing with children who require special education services.

exceptionality, multiple: deviation above or below the so-called normal in more than one area.

exceptionality, physical: an outward feature of an individual which deviates from the so-called average.

excess cost: *see* **cost, excess.**

exchange classes: *see* **classes, exchange.**

exchange concerts: *see* **concerts, exchange.**

exchange, cultural: reciprocal visits by people, singly or in groups, trading of exhibits, and performances of artists from two or more countries for the purpose of enhancing appreciation of the cultures involved.

exchange, farm youth: *see* **International Farm Youth Exchange.**

exchange grants, educational: the general program of the Federal government under which the State Department administers the reception and placement of foreign students, teachers, professors, and specialists in this country and the sending of similar American personnel to foreign countries under the terms of the Fulbright Act, the Smith-Mundt Act, and other laws.

exchange, international educational: any systematic interchange of pupils, teachers, administrative personnel, equipment, or ideas pertaining to education between countries. *See* **exchange, cultural; exchange of students, international; exchange of teachers, international; exchange program, Fulbright.**

Exchange, International Farm Youth: *see* **International Farm Youth Exchange.**

exchange of students: a process whereby two students or two classes from different schools exchange their respective school schedules for a limited period of time; in individual cases, the time period is usually a school year; for entire classes, the exchange period is a week or month; for example, a sociology class from a large city and one from a central rural school exchange home and school schedules for 1 week.

exchange of students, international: (1) arrangements made between schools, colleges, or universities in different countries to exchange a number of students for a limited time, with full academic credit to be given by the home institution; (2) a government-sponsored acceptance of foreign students by colleges and universities in various countries, usually limited to 1 year, under the terms of such legislation as the Fulbright Act, the Smith-Mundt Act, or the Finnish Debt Law. *Syn.* **student exchange.**

exchange of teachers, international: a program of interchange of teachers between countries under the sponsorship of both governmental and private agencies. (The United States Information and Educational Exchange Act yearly arranges for the exchange of teachers between the United States and Great Britain and several other countries. The U. S. Office of Education and the Department of State also arrange for the exchange of a considerable number of teachers. Private agencies sponsoring such interchange programs include the National Education Association, 4-H Clubs, National Grange, Kiwanis, Rotary, YWCA, and the AFL-CIO.)

exchange professor: *see* **professor, exchange.**

exchange program, Fulbright: a program initiated by an act of the 79th Congress; provides for the exchange of students, teachers, lecturers, research scholars, and specialists between the United States and designated countries; financial implementation of the act is effected by the use of funds derived from the sale of surplus properties left in designated countries at the close of World War II; the purpose of the act is to further international good will and understanding; all forms of study and research are included; supervised by a Board of Foreign Scholarship composed of 10 prominent American educators and educational administrators, which is responsible to the Department of State; the cooperating agency, known as the Conference Board of Associated Research Councils, supervises exchange projects on the university-lecture and postdoctoral research level.

exchange program, service academy: *see* **program, service academy exchange.**

exchange, student: *syn.* **exchange of students, international.**

exchange teacher: a teacher brought into a school system from another system for a limited period of time (usually 1 year), to replace a teacher who likewise has temporarily left his regular position to teach in another school system.

exchanges: copies of student publications from other schools and colleges received by the staff of a student publication in exchange for copies of its own.

excise tax: *see* **tax, excise.**

exclusion: the act of refusing to permit a youth to enroll or of forcing him to withdraw after having been enrolled in an educational institution.

exclusion, school: *see* **exclusion.**

exclusion, temporary: (1) an order refusing a pupil the right to participate in the work of the school for a limited period of time; (2) an order granting a pupil permission to remain out of school for a limited period.

exclusivism: a designation applied to any philosophy of education which fails to comprehend life as a whole and which presents a partial or exclusive pattern of education in which some aspects of life and nature are selected for undue emphasis while others are excluded; the Roman

Catholic philosophers desire Catholic Universalism in education and consider education without religion to be exclusivism.

excursion, school: *syn.* **field trip.**

excuse slip: (1) an administrative form used to explain a pupil's absence from his regular school assignment; (2) a statement written by the pupil or by his parents explaining the pupil's absence or tardiness.

excused absence: *see* **absence, excused.**

executed contract: *see* **contract, executed.**

execution: (1) the process for putting into effect the decree of a court; (2) the enforcement of such a decree by arrest of the person or seizure of the property of a debtor; (3) a judicial writ by which an officer is empowered to put a judgment into effect.

executive delegation: *see* **delegation, executive.**

executive development program: *see* **program, executive development.**

executive function: *see* **function, executive.**

executive officer: an educational administrator concerned with putting into effect a program, policy, or regulation, with power to give orders and directions to others; for example, the superintendent of schools is an executive officer, though much of his work may be advisory and may be thought of as staff rather than line service.

executive routine: *see* **routine, executive.**

executory contract: *see* **contract, executory.**

exemplar: one who serves as a model (a good example) of the behavior or attitudes valued by a social group.

exempted village district: *see* **district, exempted village.**

exemption: (1) freedom from any charge, duty, burden, or liability; (2) the varying degree of immunity of schools and colleges to taxation; (3) those conditions under which youths are freed from the requirements of the state's compulsory school-attendance laws (equivalent schooling, physical inability, mental inability, lawful employment, etc., are examples of the more common exemptions; poverty and distance from school used to be generally accepted exemptions, but they are being rapidly dropped from the statutes).

exemption census file: *see* **census file, exemption.**

exemption from school: *see* **exemption** (3).

exemption, homestead: (1) special privileges or exemptions (often from taxation) granted to owners of residences or homesteads; (2) a law exempting a homestead from attachment or sale under execution for general debts.

exemption, tax: a freedom from taxation enjoyed by the Federal government, the states, and religious, educational, and charitable corporations under certain conditions based on fundamental law or statutes.

exercise: (1) *syn.* **exercise, test;** (2) (math. and mus.) that which provides opportunity for practice in the application of principles and the building of skills; (3) (mil. ed.) a naval maneuver, drill, or operation for training purposes.

exercise, action: a reading exercise requiring some type of overt response, such as demonstration, construction, or drawing, that can be checked objectively.

exercise, classification: a task given to an examinee to assign each item or specimen given to the appropriate category or class or to decide whether a particular item does or does not belong in a particular class; for example, a vocabulary exercise in which the pupil is required to arrange words according to similarities and differences in form or meaning.

exercise, command and staff: (mil. ed.) an exercise conducted entirely on a discussion basis, without deployment of actual forces.

exercise, command post: (mil. ed.) an exercise involving the commander, his staff, and communications within and between headquarters.

exercise, conditioning: (phys. ed.) an exercise used for attaining a single objective, such as building cardiovascular endurance, increasing specific strengths or flexibilities, etc.

exercise, developmental: a problem, example, theorem, or assignment, or a set of these, used for the purpose of aiding the pupil to arrive at desired conclusions or to attain desired proficiencies.

exercise, dictation: words, phrases, sentences, or paragraphs read to and written by the pupil for the purpose of providing practice or testing on spelling or on certain aspects of language, such as capitalization and punctuation.

exercise, experimental: a problem, example, theorem, or assignment used to furnish a basis for discovering, through individual effort, relationships or principles that might provide a better understanding of material currently being studied or to be presented subsequently; also used to refer to a set of such problems, examples, etc.

exercise, field: (mil. ed.) an exercise conducted in the field under simulated war conditions, in which troops and armament of one side are actually present while those of the other side may be imaginary or in outline. *See* **exercise, command and staff; exercise, command post; maneuver, field.**

exercise, formal: an exercise or activity that is part of a highly organized performance and is carried on with the idea that improvement in this activity will improve the total performance.

exercise, interpretation: (lang.) (1) an exercise in expression; (2) practice material involving communication of ideas rather than translation.

exercise, law of: *syn.* **law of disuse.**

exercise, learning: a task assigned to a class or individual as a means of promoting learning, for example, a lesson to be studied, an essay to be composed, or a map to be drawn.

exercise, map: an exercise in which a series of military situations is stated and solved on a map.

exercise, matching: (1) (testing) an exercise based upon two lists of statements, terms, or symbols; the examinee's task is to match an item in one list with the one most closely associated with it in the other; (2) (read.) a reading exercise in which the reader is required to match words, words and pictures, or words and definitions as a means of indicating his grasp of meaning.

exercise, passive: exercise of part of a patient's body accomplished by the therapist or by use of some apparatus with no active contraction of the involved part by the patient.

exercise, phonics: instructional materials which are based on the phonetic principle that all written language symbols may be transformed into human speech sounds.

exercise, physiology of: *see* **physiology of exercise.**

exercise, practice: (1) the trials necessary for learning or competence; (2) (testing) a sample item or items at the beginning of a test designed to familiarize the examinee with the type of task presented and the mode of response expected throughout the tests.

exercise, pronunciation: (1) material used to provide practice in the pronunciation of words; (2) an important activity used in connection with the teaching of a spelling lesson or a speech lesson in which the words are correctly pronounced by teacher and pupils.

exercise, resistive: active exercise accomplished by the patient with application of additional resistance, whether manual or mechanical.

exercise, skimming: (read.) training in scanning or partial reading, for the purpose of getting the gist of the meaning, selecting some special item, or as a device for increasing the rate of reading.

exercise, terrain: (mil. ed.) an exercise in which a stated military situation is solved on the ground, the troops being imaginary and the solution usually being in writing.

exercise, test: a structural unit of a test for which a single set of directions is provided; unlike a test *item*, ordinarily requires more than one response.

exercise, vocabulary: (1) a teaching or learning experience that concentrates on word recognition and word mean-

ing; (2) a device such as the matching, completion, or multiple-choice test, which measures power in word discrimination.

exercises, chapel: *see* **chapel exercises.**

exercises, context: phrases, sentences, or paragraphs containing the words of a spelling lesson, to be used as a test or as practice material.

exercises, graduation: special ceremony at an educational institution marking the completion of a course of study for certain students, at which certificates and/or degrees are offered. *See* **graduation.**

exercises, joint: (mil. ed.) exercises in which two or more of the armed services take part. *See* **operation, combined.**

exercises, spiritual: (1) ascetic practice of meditation designed to bring individuals closer to God, used regularly or on special occasions such as *retreats;* (2) the specific rules and meditations developed by St. Ignatius Loyola for the purposes of spiritual growth.

exhaust ventilation: *see* **ventilation, exhaust.**

exhaustion, heat: *see* **heat exhaustion.**

exhibit: a collection of objects and materials arranged in a setting in order to convey a unified idea; often displayed for educational purposes.

exhibit, art: *syn.* **exhibition, art.**

exhibit, mathematics: *see* **mathematics exhibit.**

exhibitionism: (1) exaggerated effort to attract attention; (2) an immodest exposure of the body or parts of the body.

exhortation: a special plea or urging, used often by spokesmen for the church as a technique for developing character among believers.

existence, generic traits of: a term used to indicate several pairs of diametrically opposed attributes of ultimate reality, either pole of which pairs may be postulated as universal or permanent.

existential psychology: *see* **psychology, existential.**

existential quantifier: *see* **quantifier.**

existentialism: the theory in modern philosophy that man has no fixed nature and that he shapes his being by the choices he makes as he lives; both Protestants and Catholics as well as secularists have participated in its development, for example, Tillich, Marcel, Sartre; technically, the philosophical theory that existence precedes essence (Heidegger). *See* **essence.**

existentialism in counseling: a counseling theory which emphasizes that a person's identity, or awareness of himself, is a basic antecedent of his behavior and that man must be understood as being and becoming.

exit: (1) a door or other means of egress from a building, room, or enclosed area; (2) in programmed instruction, a means of stopping iterative action, as through the use of a test in a repeated loop of operations in a program; the place in the routine which serves as the stopping point.

exit interview: *see* **interview, exit.**

exogenous: due to causes external to the developing organism itself; when applied to mental retardation, due to an injury to or an infection of the brain.

exogenous feeblemindedness: *see* **feeblemindedness, exogenous.**

exogenous mental retardation: *see* **mental retardation, exogenous.**

exophoria: (1) a type of *heterophoria* characterized by a tendency of the eyes to turn outward when the extrinsic muscles are relaxed; (2) the postural position of the eyes outward when fusion is broken. *Contr. w.* **esophoria; hyperphoria.**

exotropia: abnormal turning outward from the nose of one or both eyes; also called *divergent squint, divergent* (or *external*) *strabismus,* or *walleye. Contr. w.* **esotropia; hypertropia.**

expanded notation: *see* **notation, expanded.**

expanding family: *see* **family, expanding.**

expansibility: (1) the characteristic of a school building which makes possible or convenient the construction of building additions in such manner that they may become an integral part of the building, for example, a blank wall and absence of windows on one end, or location of stairs elsewhere at the end on which an addition may be desired; possible need for an addition is recognized at the time the building is constructed; (2) the characteristic of a school site dependent upon the availability of additional land for development of school grounds.

expansion, curriculum: *see* **curriculum expansion.**

expectancy: a term descriptive of a predicted level of success, such as an expectancy level of performance in arithmetic as predicted from a pupil's mental age, or an expectancy quality or level of performance as a teacher as predicted from known qualifications of a candidate.

expectancy, ability: *see* **ability expectancy.**

expectancy, mental: (testing) the ability of a listener to anticipate the words, phrases, and thoughts of the speaker, thus giving an inflated intelligibility score.

expectancy norms: *see* **norms, expectancy.**

expectancy table: *see* **table, expectancy.**

expectation discrepancy: (spec. ed.) the difference between the expectations concerning the behavior and adjustment of a person with a disability and the apparent behavior and adjustment, that is, what is observed in the subject.

expectation, mathematical: *syn.* **value, expected.**

expectations, emerging: (admin.) tentative predictions of the events which will occur in education.

expectations of supervision: *see* **supervision, expectations of.**

expected value: *see* **value, expected.**

expediency, philosophy of: an implicit or explicit tendency to believe that whatever course of action solves a problem for the moment is to be preferred to other considerations.

expendable funds: *see* **funds, expendable.**

expenditure, capital: expenditure for other than operating or expense accounts. *See* **capital investment; capital outlay.**

expenditure, current: any outlay or liability that is payable immediately or in the near future out of current resources, as distinguished from a long-term liability to be met out of future resources.

expenditure, funded: an actuarially sound plan for the disbursement of funds, such as certain retirement programs. *See* **retirement program, actuarially sound.**

expenditures: if the accounts are kept on the accrual basis, a designation for total charges incurred, whether paid or unpaid, including expenses, provision for retirement of debt not reported as a liability of the fund from which retired, and capital outlays; if the accounts are kept on the cash basis, the term covers only actual disbursements for these purposes.

expenditures per pupil in ADA, annual current: (pupil accounting) the annual current expenditures (including expenditures for administration, instruction, attendance and health services, pupil transportation services, operation of plant, maintenance of plant, and fixed charges) divided by the average daily attendance for the year. *See* **attendance, average daily.**

expenditures per pupil in ADM, annual current: the annual current expenditures (including expenditures for administration, instruction, attendance and health services, pupil transportation services, operation of plant, maintenance of plant, and fixed charges) divided by the average daily membership for the year. *See* **membership, average daily.**

expense: the cost of goods delivered or services rendered for the operation of an institution, whether actually paid or unpaid.

expense, current: charges incurred, whether paid or unpaid, for operation, maintenance, interest, and other charges that are presumed to benefit the current fiscal period.

expense, nonoperating: expense incurred in relation to operation of properties or exercise of functions not used in the supplying of service.

expense, operating: expense incident to the maintenance of an enterprise, the rendering of service, and the collection of revenue.

expense order: *see* **order, expense.**

experience: (1) the acquisition of knowledge, attitudes, or skills through one's own perception and participation, or knowledge, attitudes, or skills so acquired; (2) (philos.) the context of the life process as distinct from the order of things in themselves or the realm of essences or reality; the process of interaction between a human being and his physical and cultural environment; in nonempirical or rationalistic philosophies, experience, as opposed to true knowledge, involves sense perception, habit, impulse, and emotion—hence, although it may tell us something about our practical affairs, it is not a reliable source of knowledge of universal principles or essences; in empirical philosophies, the inclusive matrix of human action and thought; experience, as the basis or context of all knowledge, involves the process of seeing relationships between what one does or plans to do and the consequence of doing it so that these connections may be used in guiding subsequent experiences.

experience-activity method: a method of teaching beginning reading that utilizes as reading material children's experiences formulated in their own language.

experience, aesthetic: that phase of experience dealing essentially with the perception, interpretation, and enjoyment of beauty; differentiated from nonaesthetic experience by its emphasis on intrinsic values. *See* **appreciation, aesthetic.**

experience, appreciational: (art ed.) the phase of the art experience characterized by interpretation, appraisal, contemplation, and enjoyment of objects of art or of art expression. *See* **appreciation, art; experience, art.**

experience approach: *see* **approach, experience.**

experience, art: participation of the pupil in creative and appreciational art activities. *See* **activity, art; art education; curriculum, art.**

experience balance, Rorschach: *see* **balance, Rorschach experience.**

experience-centered teaching: *see* **teaching, experience-centered.**

experience chart: *see* **chart, experience.**

experience, cognitive: reflective thinking or inquiry that is based on primary experience, locates within it that which is doubtful or problematic, and by selective use of verifiable hypotheses leads to the realignment of activity toward chosen ends. *See* **experience, primary.**

experience, compensatory language: *see* **language experience, compensatory.**

experience, constructive: in art education, participation of the pupil in various hand and machine crafts.

experience, consummatory: (1) that phase of experience in which things are had and enjoyed as intrinsically worthwhile, as distinct from the preparatory, instrumental, or mediate aspects of experience; (2) in John Dewey, the aesthetic component of primary experience in which each step forward fulfills what went before and foreshadows throughout a sense of fulfillment; *see* **experience, primary.**

experience, continuity of: *see* **continuity of experience.**

experience, creative: (1) art experience characterized by actual application of techniques and the making of original products, rather than by examining, studying, and appreciating works of art; (2) experience characterized by the production of original rather than copied or imitated forms.

experience curriculum: *see* **curriculum, experience.**

experience, design: (art ed.) (1) planning structural forms, for example, the relationships of line and mass in painting or architecture; (2) creating unified expression in any medium of art; (3) creating surface decoration; (4) the second stage in the development of a unit of teaching in art, the preceding stage being *orientation. See* **design; experience, art.**

experience, direct: in a learning process, actual practice with real things in a true-to-life situation; for example, one may learn to sell by working in a store. *Contr. w.* **experience, vicarious.**

experience, distributive education supervised occupational: on-the-job experience of a worker in a specific distributive occupation, in which he learns the skills and knowledges required by that occupation, under the supervision of an employer, a training sponsor, and/or the teacher-coordinator.

experience, education as the continuous reconstruction of: *see* education as the continuous reconstruction of experience.

experience, educative: (1) any interaction of the individual with his environment, resulting in modification of the individual's attitudes, knowledge, or values; commonly implies desirable changes according to the values of the group; *see* continuity of experience; interaction of experience; (2) (couns.) the total school experience from which the student derives and alters some basic attitudes, abilities, and behavior.

experience, enrichment of: *see* enrichment of experience.

experience, extension of: the development of meanings previously more or less strange to the learner (one of the values claimed for the reading and study of literature).

experience, field: *see* experience, field laboratory.

experience, field laboratory: actual practice away from the college campus, within schools or their environment, in dealing with educational problems; part of the program offered by a teacher education institution, usually conducted in schools that are not formally under the direct control of or affiliated with, the teacher education institution; usually more limited, incidental, and less formal and concentrated than the extended internship; sometimes refers to practice in supervision, administration, or guidance. *Comp. w.* field work.

experience, functional: (art ed.) the application of art concepts and fundamental understandings to the solution of problems—specifically, those involving aesthetic or artistic judgment—encountered either in the classroom or in life. *See* activity, art; art concept.

experience, glyphic: *see* art, glyphic.

experience, graphic: *see* art, graphic.

experience impact: the total effect of sensory impressions, level of interaction, and focus of interest associated with a given instructional activity.

experience in distribution, business: on-the-job experience in a distributive occupation as a wage earner.

experience, interaction of: *see* interaction of experience.

experience, learning: a puposeful activity that has meaning to students at their developmental level, carried through to completion and evaluated.

experience, mathematical: contact with ideas, situations, or problems which are mathematical in nature.

experience method: *syn.* experience-activity method.

experience, motor-constructive: experience characteristic of art, crafts, and industrial arts; activities requiring muscular-mental coordination and involving the planning and building of objects through the use of materials and tools, as distinguished from such activities as drawing and painting, for example, the designing and building of a coffee table.*See* curriculum, art; experience, art; handcraft; industrial arts.

experience, number: experience through activities which promote the concept of number; most frequently refers to the concept of *cardinal number.*

experience of form, autoplastic: graphic representation of intense bodily feelings, sensations, and experiences, such as muscular and kinesthetic sensations, tensions, pressure, pain, temperature, deformity, acts of stretching, screaming, chewing, etc., especially discernible in the art activity of *haptic* individuals. *See* haptic type.

experience, patterns of: *see* patterns of experience.

experience, prereading: planned experiences that prepare a child for systematic reading instruction; may include activities designed to develop auditory and visual discrimination, verbal facility, interpreting pictures, and a keen interest in reading.

experience, primary: in the philosophy of John Dewey and in experimentalism generally, the basic quality of life in its raw concreteness, a process of "beings and havings," "doing and undergoing," "suffering and enjoying"; to be distinguished from cognitive experience and reflection. *See* experience, cognitive.

experience, reading: (1) experience gained through the act of reading as contrasted with that gained through listening, observing, or other physical participation; (2) a unique experience peculiar to reading that can be gained in no other way.

experience, reconstruction of : *see* reconstruction of experience.

experience records: *see* records, experience.

experience, religious: *see* religious experience.

experience schedule: *see* schedule, experience.

experience, secondary: *syn.* experience, cognitive.

experience, success: attainment of a desired end through the direct observation of or participation in an activity; in the case of the educable mentally retarded child, involves a day-to-day program which presents him with short-range as well as long-range tasks in which he succeeds.

experience, tectonic (tek·ton'ik): that part of the art experience characterized by work in building or construction. *See* arts, industrial; experience, motor-constructive.

experience unit: *see* unit, experience.

experience-unit program: *see* program, experience-unit.

experience, vicarious: experience acquired not by direct, concrete, personal, or firsthand means but indirectly through the report of another person or group; the experience of one person or group as represented by symbols, usually words, and hence available to another.

experience with limits: *see* limits, experience with.

experience, work: (bus. ed.) a school-sponsored learning experience in an occupational area for persons preparing for full-time employment, conducted in connection with a course of study, where the student spends a part of his time on an actual job in a regular business or industry.

experiences, contrived: learning experiences designed to simulate real-life situations, often using real things or effective substitutions for real things for verisimilitude.

experiences, distributive education participating: learning experiences which focus on activities of distributive occupations and decision-making situations in distribution.

experiences, guided laboratory: (teacher ed.) professional laboratory experiences in which preservice or in-service teachers or interns have available the guidance of a more mature professional worker to help them in their selection of activities and interpretation of experiences.

experiences, home (and community): *see* home (and community) experiences.

experiences, integrated: learning experiences which are so related that they tend to unify knowledge.

experiences, professional laboratory: (teacher ed.) those contacts with children, youth, and adults which are provided through observation, participation, and teaching, and which make a direct contribution to the understanding of learners and their guidance in individual and group teaching-learning processes.

experiential background: the sum total of empirically obtained knowledge in the life of an individual.

experiential continuum: a term used to describe a series of ongoing experiences characterized by the following conditions: (*a*) the present experience gains meaning from and enhances the meaning of previous experiences; (*b*) the present experience is a potential for a more enriching future experience; (*c*) thinking occurs within and following the experience which reconstructs the individual's values and alters the direction of future experiences. *See* continuity of experience.

experiment: (1) the trial of a planned procedure accompanied by control of conditions and/or controlled variation of conditions together with observation of results for the purpose of discovering relationships and evaluating the reasonableness of a given hypothesis; (2) an integral part of any learning process, usually with less conscious attention to the elements listed under (1) and containing more of the trial-and-error element; (3) the administration, under controlled conditions, of treatments to a group or groups that have been specifically constituted for the purpose, and the analysis of the effects produced or induced in the subjects or units as a result.

experiment, classroom: (1) an experiment confined within the limits of a classroom or classrooms; (2) an experiment in which a classroom is employed as the basic sampling unit. *Contr. w.* **experiment, laboratory.**

experiment, controlled: an experiment in which factors other than the experimental factor are controlled or held constant for all experimental groups.

experiment, group: (1) an experiment involving the use of a relatively large number of persons as the treatment group; (2) an experiment involving the use of two or more treatment groups.

experiment, laboratory: (1) an experiment under the more strictly controlled conditions of the educational or psychological laboratory or clinic, as contrasted with an experiment under the practical limiting conditions existing in regularly established classrooms; frequently performed on one person or on a very small number of persons; *contr. w.* **experiment, classroom;** (2) (sci. ed.) an experiment performed with apparatus and materials manipulated by an individual student or a small group to find either a qualitative or a quantitative answer to a problem through procedures deliberately designed to produce the interaction of some agency under our control with the system or object we are studying.

experiment, methods: (1) strictly, an experiment in which the variable being studied is the teaching procedure, while an effort is made to hold constant the content presented for learning; (2) broadly, any experiment testing the effect on educational outcomes of any factor related to or incorporated into the instructional program.

experiment, multiple-variable: an experiment in which the effects of two or more factors are studied simultaneously, as in factorial design. *See* **design, factorial.**

experiment, one-group: an experiment in which a single group is subjected to a given set of conditions for a given time period and a description obtained of the final status of the group; or the same group may be subjected successively to two or more different treatments and the effects or relative effects observed.

experiment, open-ended: experimentation in which the student reports in his own manner, draws his own conclusions, makes his own predictions, etc.

experiment, partner: an experimental technique characterized by the observation and analysis of the behavior exhibited by persons as they work in pairs in some activity.

experiment station: a farm or plot of ground properly equipped for carrying out experiments in agriculture, engineering, mining, or other kinds of applied research. *See* **experimental farm; experiment station, agricultural.**

experiment station, agricultural: an organization, usually a department of a land-grant college, established to conduct research in agriculture, home economics, and related areas, and to disseminate the information for public consumption.

experiment, verification: a laboratory exercise, as used in science teaching, which is a repetition of an experiment already performed by scientists with, of course, the expectation of similar results; illustrates the thesis in science that any experimental evidence must meet the test of replication in other laboratories, with the experimenters using the same or similar equipment or techniques.

experimental behavior disorder: *syn.* **neurosis, experimental.**

experimental cabinet: a room or chamber designed to exclude or to control external stimuli in investigations of the behavior of human subjects and animals.

experimental coefficient: *see* **coefficient, experimental.**

experimental control: *see* **control, experimental.**

experimental data: *see* **data, experimental.**

experimental deafness: *see* **deafness, experimental.**

experimental design: *see* **design, experimental.**

experimental education: (1) the type of education offered by experimental schools, characterized by practices different from those of the typical public or private school, perhaps based on an essentially different philosophy of education; the program may be so arranged as to fit into

the pattern of a number of formal experiments, though usually the appraisal of the undertaking is informal and may be unprovided for; the experimental character may consist largely in frequent change in the program of work as the need for modifications is sensed by the schoolworkers through direct contact and group discussion; (2) courses of instruction offered in the professional education of teachers, administrators, or research workers, covering experimental methods of educational research.

experimental error: *see* **error, experimental.**

experimental exercise: *see* **exercise, experimental.**

experimental extinction: *see* **extinction, experimental.**

experimental factor: *see* **factor, experimental.**

experimental farm: a farm of an agricultural college devoted to experiments in agriculture. *See* **experiment station; experiment station, agricultural.**

experimental geometry: *see* **geometry, informal.**

experimental group: *see* **group, experimental.**

experimental inquiry, methods of: *see* **methods of experimental inquiry.**

experimental introspection: *see* **introspection, experimental.**

experimental method: (1) a method or procedure involving the control or manipulation of conditions for the purpose of studying the relative effects of various treatments applied to members of a sample, or of the same treatment applied to members of different samples; (2) the method or procedure by which the effect of a single designated factor is studied by applying it to one individual or group and not to another, or by varying the factor under controlled conditions.

experimental method, controlled: *see* **experimental method.**

experimental method, uncontrolled: a research method in which no deliberate effort is made to control extraneous variables, but in which an attempt is made to determine cause(s) for phenomena from data obtained in more or less natural settings; for example, *all* pupils may be given a school attitude inventory, and an attempt then made to determine behavioral correlates; a preliminary research method, rather than a definitive one.

experimental neurosis: *see* **neurosis, experimental.**

experimental phonetics: *see* **phonetics, experimental.**

experimental psychology: *see* **psychology, experimental.**

experimental research: *see* **research, experimental.**

experimental research report: *see* **report, experimental research.**

experimental school: an elementary or secondary school, frequently connected directly or indirectly with a teacher education institution or a large city school system, in which new teaching methods, new organizations of subject matter, psychological hypotheses, personnel practices, and advanced theories based on the findings of psychologists, educational philosophers, and a growing number of educational scientists are tested; may also be used as a model, practice, or demonstration school.

experimental science: *see* **science, experimental.**

experimental study: *see* **study, experimental.**

experimental test: *see* **test, experimental.**

experimental treatment: a deliberate variation or series of variations in any factor of which the influence on some measurable trait or performance is to be evaluated by means of an experiment.

experimentalism: an empirical philosophical position which holds that experience is the sufficient source of ideals, values, and methods of knowing, that reality is this world of man's experience, that knowledge is hypothetical, that the verifiable procedures of scientific inquiry are our greatest resource for controlling experience, that values and morality are empirical and social rather than absolute and inscrutable. *See* **humanism, scientific; instrumentalism; pragmatism.**

experimentation, animal: controlled laboratory studies in which animals are used to demonstrate a theory, principle, or mode of behavior; carried on primarily in conjunction with classes in agriculture, biology, nutrition, and psychology; chickens, white rats and mice, hamsters, and guinea pigs are most frequently used.

expert, reading: *see* **reading expert.**

expiation: (psych.) action performed to lessen sense of guilt.

explanation: (1) in science, the act or process of making phenomena intelligible with reference to their setting in a larger body of systematic and coherent relations; whereas description is usually the mere delineation of observed instances, qualities, or properties, together with their definition and classification, explanation places the individual facts in a deductive system in terms of which they assume meaning; (2) in metaphysics, teleological interpretation with reference to final causes and ultimate purposes on the part of nature itself; whereas scientific explanation attempts to discover causes of events, metaphysical explanation seeks to discover reasons for events.

explanatory hypothesis: *see* **hypothesis, explanatory.**

exploration: (ind. arts) the seeking of insight and knowledge having industrial significance through a wide range of laboratory experiences, contact with a wide range of materials, and the study of various industrial occupations.

exploration, career: *see* **career exploration.**

exploratory course: *see* **course, exploratory.**

exploratory language: *syn.* **language study, exploratory.**

exploratory language study: *see* **language study, exploratory.**

exploratory method: a method of organizing the program of studies that provides children with the opportunity for free experimentation.

exploratory movement: any movement of reaching or manual or oral manipulation that serves to acquaint the young infant with the characteristics of objects.

exposition: (lang. arts) *see* **writing, expository.**

expository writing: *see* **writing, expository.**

expressed class limit: *syn.* **class limit, apparent.**

expressed interest: *see* **interest, expressed.**

expression: (1) the act of reading or speaking in such a manner as to place proper emphasis on related words and word groups and thus reveal meaning; (2) the art of effective speech; (3) (mus.) that part of music which is not expressed by musical symbols but which includes all the nuances of dynamics, tempi, accent, touch, etc., which the artist performer combines to create living music.

expression, aesthetic: expression that is intended to please and gratify rather than serve a useful purpose; expression that produces beauty in words; expression in taste or in various art forms.

expression, art: (1) the release of feelings through art; (2) the result of one's thoughts made manifest in a work of art.

expression, extrapunitive: *see* **extrapunitive expression.**

expression, intrapunitive: *see* **intrapunitive expression.**

expression, manual: that phase of the child's motor activity in which use is made of the hands in creative and imitative work through such mediums as paints, clay, blocks, and sand, as a means of expressing ideas, feelings, and impressions; serves both as a stimulus for thinking and as a way of expressing and clarifying thought. *See* **expression, motor.**

expression, motor: a generic term designating all bodily means by which children express ideas and feelings, for example, *dancing, dramatic* or *imitative play,* and various forms of manual play expression such as drawing, modeling, and block construction. *See* **expression, manual.**

expression, nonvisual: *see* **haptic type.**

expression, oral: the special techniques or characteristics of communication by word of mouth.

expression subject: *see* **subject, expression.**

expression unit: *see* **unit, expression.**

expression, visual: *see* **visual type.**

expressionaire: a form of questionnaire designed to elicit a fairly free expression of opinions, attitudes, and/or other personal reactions on indicated topics; much the same as an opinionaire. *See* **opinionaire.**

expressional fluency: *see* **fluency, expressional.**

expressional skill: *see* **skill, expressional.**

expressionism: an early twentieth century style characterized by emotional extremes achieved through distortion, twisted space, intensity of color, and bold linear movements which artists used as a means of projecting tragic themes and often critical comments upon some aspect of reality; Max Beckmann, Georges Rouault, and Oskar Kokoschka were representative of this style.

expressionism, abstract: *see* **action painting.**

expressions, emotionally loaded: statements containing words that express, and tend to produce in others, convictions and their consequent forms of action, sometimes obscuring the effort to achieve reliable knowledge or rational belief.

expressive activity: *see* **activity, expressive.**

expressive aphasia: *syn.* **aphasia, motor-expressive.**

expressive movements: *see* **movements, expressive.**

expressive oligophasia: *see* **oligophasia, expressive.**

expressive symbol: *see* **symbol, expressive.**

expressive therapy: *see* **therapy, expressive.**

expulsion: the act of forcing a pupil to withdraw from school; applies particularly to cases of extreme misbehavior or incorrigibility where the youth is ejected under pressure of school authority.

expulsion, teacher: the dismissal by proper legal authority of the teacher before the expiration of his contract.

extended-day sessions: *syn.* **sessions, staggered.**

extended employment: a period usually of 2 weeks to 3 months beyond the regular school term (provided by some schools having home economics departments); during this time the teacher supervises home experiences of the students, makes visits to homes in the community, works with adults or out-of-school youth, or carries on other activities which may improve the program of education for home living; the teacher involved with job-training programs holds meetings with the advisory committee, makes contacts with cooperating employers, and confers with parents to gain their approval and cooperation.

extended family: *see* **family, extended.**

extended school day: *see* **school day, extended.**

extended school program: *see* **program, extended school.**

extended school services: *see* **program, public service; service, public.**

extended service: (bus. ed.) a period, usually four weeks or more beyond the regular school term, during which the teacher-coordinator engages in coordination activities relative to the administration and promotion of his program.

extended use of bus: *syn.* **vehicle, nonroutine use of.**

extension: the motion of straightening a part of the body that is in *flexion.*

extension agency, state library: an organization created or authorized by a state to promote library service in the state by the establishment, organization, and supervision of public and, sometimes, school libraries and by the lending of books and other material to libraries and to communities without libraries, for example, library commissions and state libraries.

extension agent: an official representative of the state land-grant institution and the U.S. Department of Agriculture who assists the people in carrying on educational programs normally to improve rural life, but increasingly in urban interest as well. *Syn.* **county agent;** *see* **extension worker, county.**

extension agent, agricultural: *see* **extension worker, county.**

extension, agricultural: the diffusion of agricultural and related knowledge concerning rural life through demonstrations, extension meetings, directed group study and discussion, bulletins, reading courses, and sometimes agricultural institutes and short courses.

extension bureau, university: an administrative unit in a university extension division, usually designed to promote one type of educational interest such as parent-teacher relations, adult education, audiovisual aids to secondary schools, and library extension.

extension center: *see* **center, extension.**

extension center, university: *syn.* **center, extension.**

extension class: *see* **class, extension.**

extension class, trade: *see* **part-time trade extension class.**

extension clinic: *see* **clinic, mobile.**

extension, cooperative: out-of-school education cooperatively provided by governmental units and land-grant institutions for the purpose of offering through demonstrations, publications, and other means useful and practical information on agriculture, home economics, and related subjects but increasingly on broader educational subjects which may or may not be agriculturally related.

extension course: *see* **course, extension.**

extension course program, Army: *see* **program, Army extension course.**

extension course, United States Air Force: *see* **course, United States Air Force extension.**

extension credit: *see* **credit, extension.**

extension department: *see* **department, extension.**

extension, director of: *see* **director of extension.**

extension, director of agricultural: *see* **director of agricultural extension.**

extension division: one of the administrative units of a university, ranking roughly with such other units as a resident school or college, which utilizes the staff and faculties of the other units as well as its own for the administration of university extension services.

extension division, agricultural: a division of a college teaching agriculture that offers extramural teaching by members of the college staff and shares in administering county programs of agricultural extension conducted through county agricultural agents (agricultural extension agents or agricultural extension advisers).

extension education: a service by which the resources of an educational institution are extended beyond its confines to serve a widely diversified clientele within the state or region regarded as the constituent area of the institution; may include a wide range of activities such as evening classes, short courses, exhibits, TV courses, correspondence course conferences, seminars, and institutes.

extension education, Jewish: usually applied to various forms of informal and off-campus educational programs.

extension, educational: organized programs of education offered to students and other citizens away from the campus; includes formal classes in various communities at night or on Saturdays, radio and television programs, lectures, demonstrations, and other forms of instruction.

extension, general: extension services of universities, colleges, and schools directed to both rural and urban populations but in subject matter and type other than agricultural. *See* **extension, university.**

extension high school: *see* **high school, extension.**

extension, home economics: formal and informal programs of information, demonstration, and instruction projected into rural and urban communities by the land-grant colleges and universities and other agencies concerned with problems of production, consumption, and family life.

extension homemaker club: *see* **club, extension homemaker.**

extension in agriculture, cooperative: *see* **extension service in agriculture and home economics, cooperative.**

extension, international home economics: the staff or unit within the *Federal Extension Service* which deals with international extension programs in home economics. *See* **Agricultural Development Service, International.**

extension, kindergarten: (1) the adaptation and use of kindergarten principles and procedures in nursery and primary schools that tend to articulate child education as a process of continuous growth, not merely by instruction but more particularly by purposeful and varied activities in an educational environment appropriate to age-level interests and needs of young children; *syn.* **junior first grade; preprimary class;** (2) progress in the establishment of kindergartens marked by three periods of growth: (*a*) a period of establishment of kindergartens by pioneer advocates (1855-1880); (*b*) a period of establishment of

kindergartens as a means of improving social conditions for underprivileged children by philanthropic groups, churches, and associations (1880-1890); (*c*) a period of incorporation of kindergartens in public school systems beginning about 1890.

extension, library: the promotion of libraries and wider library service by state, local, or regional agencies.

extension library service: *see* **library service, extension.**

extension of experience: *see* **experience, extension of.**

extension, overseas: (1) college or university programs abroad set up during wartime by the Department of Defense with the cooperation of American universities and local agencies and military installations; (2) similar programs abroad have been administered by the universities of California, Maryland, and Louisiana, and by American International College.

extension program, distributive education adult: *see* **program, distributive education adult extension.**

extension program, home economics: *see* **program, home economics extension.**

extension reeducation: *see* **reeducation, extension.**

extension service: *see* **extension, cooperative; extension, university; extension service, cooperative.**

extension service, cooperative: a governmental agency cooperatively financed by the Federal, state, and local governments and cooperatively administered by the U.S. Department of Agriculture, the state land-grant institutions, and county governing bodies for the purpose of diffusing among the people useful and practical information in agriculture, home economics, and related subjects through demonstrations, publications, and other means. *See* **extension, cooperative.**

Extension Service, Federal: a branch of the U.S. Department of Agriculture which serves as an administrative, supervisory, and educational unit to aid the state and international extension services; interprets area, national, and international situations and helps in organizing programs and producing educational materials to aid in the implementation of projects.

extension service in agriculture and home economics, cooperative: instruction and educational demonstrations in agriculture, home economics, and related areas; staff are a part of the designated land-grant college of the state with the responsibility of disseminating educational information to the public, while the U.S. Department of Agriculture, the state legislature, and county and city governments allocate the resources for educational work; sometimes referred to as *cooperative extension work* or *cooperative extension in agriculture.*

extension service, state: (1) a system of statewide contacts and activities maintained by educational and governmental institutions and agencies to further participation in adult and extension education; (2) the designation of the agricultural and general extension systems.

extension specialist: a subject-matter specialist who assists extension agents in improving the teaching of adults and who serves as a bridge between his university academic departments and field extension workers.

extension, trade: instruction designed to supplement or extend the trade knowledge or skill, or both, of employed workers in industry.

extension, university: (1) in general, a historical development and contemporary process by which institutions of higher learning develop, in widening geographical areas, educational services for groups, individuals, associations, and institutions; (2) specifically, the program of formal academic instruction, credit and noncredit, offered by the faculty of a college or university, on or off the campus, in classes and by correspondence, to persons unable to carry the usual program of full-time resident students; includes also a varied program of informal services through such procedures as lectures, library loans, audiovisual aids, school contests, conferences, institutes, demonstrations, short courses, forums, advisory services, publications, and radio and television broadcasts. *See* **extension division; service, public** (2).

extension work: instructional activities of a college or university other than those connected with the instruction of students on the campus; involves correspondence study, classes given for part-time students off the campus or at unusual hours on the campus, and similar instructional arrangements. *See* **extension service in agriculture and home economics, cooperative.**

extension work, cooperative: *see* **extension service in agriculture and home economics, cooperative.**

extension worker, county: an employee in a county who carries on cooperative extension work in agriculture and related subjects in accordance with the Smith-Lever Act (1914) and supplementary legislation; there are three types of county extension workers: (1) the *agricultural agent*, who devotes his efforts principally to agricultural matters and to working with agricultural workers and youth and is usually in charge of the cooperative extension program in agriculture in the county; (2) the *home demonstration agent*, who devotes her efforts to problems of home economics, rural family living, and community life; and (3) the *Four-H Club agent*, who devotes his efforts to the development of 4-H clubs. (These agents represent the land-grant college of the state and the U.S. Department of Agriculture, and practically all full-time extension agents hold appointments with the U.S. Department of Agriculture as well as with the land-grant college of the state.) *See* **extension agent.**

extensionalization: (1) the relating of verbal statements or other symbols to facts or reality; (2) defining terms nonverbally by "acting out," exhibiting, or pointing to what they represent; (3) the general process of abstracting by going from nonverbal experience or observation to descriptions and generalizations, and then rechecking the generalizations against further experience or observations, revising generalizations accordingly, etc. *See* **abstraction, levels of; therapy, general semantic.**

extensive enrichment: *see* **enrichment, extensive.**

extensive method: a teaching method in which reference is made by the teacher to a number of illustrations or applications in order to convince students of the importance of a generalization, as well as to explain its meaning.

extensive reading: *see* **reading, extensive.**

extensive sampling: *see* **sampling, extensive.**

extensive study: *see* **study, extensive.**

exteriorization: the process by which an image or impression that is in the percipient's mind becomes a phantasm outside his body. *Syn.* **externalization.**

external audit: *see* **audit, external.**

external controls: *see* **controls, external.**

external criticism: *see* **criticism, external.**

external environment: *see* **environment, external.**

external examination: *see* **examination, external.**

external frame of reference: *see* **frame of reference, external.**

external memory: *see* **memory, external.**

external storage: *see* **storage, external.**

external strabismus: *syn.* **exotropia.**

external student: *see* **student, external.**

external testing program: *see* **program, testing.**

external validation: *see* **validation, external.**

externality of relations: the doctrine that asserts the possibility of terms being related without having their characteristics altered by this relation; for example, according to realism, being known does not affect the nature of the object known; opposed to *internality of relations.*

externalization: *syn.* **exteriorization.**

externi (eks·těr'nī): (Lat., lit., "outsiders") a name applied to boys who entered a monastic school of the Middle Ages but who did not expect to enter the monastic order and therefore were considered outsiders.

exteroceptor: a sensory nerve terminal that is stimulated by the immediate external environment, such as those in the skin and mucous membranes.

extinction: the process by which the repeated response to a conditioning stimulus reduces the response to a minimum.

extinction, experimental: disappearance of a response after prolonged application or repetition of the eliciting stimulus; usually applied to the disappearance of a conditioned response when the unreinforced conditioned stimulus is successively presented.

extinctive inhibition: *see* **inhibition, extinctive.**

extraclass activities: *see* **activities, extraclass.**

extract: *v.* in automatic data processing, to obtain parts of a word or field as specified by a control (filter) word or field; to unpack.

extracurricular activities: *syn.* **activities, extraclass.**

extracurricular art: *see* **art, extracurricular.**

extracurricular program: *see* **program, extracurricular.**

extraempirical: pertaining to a realm that lies beyond the limits of ascertained facts, such as future existence, purely personal religion, etc. *See* **faith.**

extrainstructional load: total load incident to all activities other than that directly related to teaching classes; includes sponsoring and coaching clubs, teams, and other organizations, supervising study halls, committee work, etc. *Syn.* **extrateaching duties.**

extramural athletics: *see* **athletics, extramural.**

extramural class: *see* **class, extramural.**

extraneous movement: in reading, a movement of the eye, head, lips, or any muscles of the body in a manner not essential or helpful to the reading process as such.

extrapolation: in general, any process of estimating values of a function beyond the range of available data; as applied to test norms, the process of extending a norm line beyond the limits of actually obtained data in order to permit interpretation of extreme scores; this extension may be done mathematically by fitting a curve to the obtained data or, as is more common, by less rigorous methods, usually graphic. *Comp. w.* **interpolation.**

extrapunitive expression: reaction to frustration in which others are blamed for the difficulty, as contrasted with *intrapunitive* (self-blaming) *expression.*

extrapunitiveness: direction of aggression toward the environment.

extrateaching duties: professional responsibilities and duties which fall upon a teacher but are neither directly connected with nor in preparation for the teaching act.

extremely gifted: *see* **gifted, extremely.**

extremes: (1) the outside limits of a statistical series; the highest and lowest magnitudes of a statistical series; (2) (math.) the first and last terms of an expression in the general form $a:b::c:d$, or $a/b = c/d$.

extrinsic ability: *see* **ability, extrinsic.**

extrinsic-dualistic organization of supervision: *see* **supervision, extrinsic-dualistic organization of.**

extrinsic method: an instructional method (often involving drill) that directs the pupil's interest toward extraneous goals rather than toward the intrinsic worth of the material being studied.

extrinsic motivation: *see* **motivation, extrinsic.**

extrinsic programming: *syn.* **programming, linear.**

extrinsic value: *see* **value, extrinsic.**

extroversion: a general attitude or group of traits characterized by a predominant interest in the external world and social life and a correspondingly diminished concern for fantasies, reflections, and introspections. *Contr. w.* **introversion.**

extrovert: a person characterized by *extroversion.*

eye contact: looking at the person or persons whom you are teaching or with whom you are talking.

eye coordination: (1) the functioning of the two eyes in attaining a single image in reading or other visual activities; (2) the cooperation of the two eyes in seeing; (3) the positioning of the two eyes in an orbit to maintain macular fusion. *See* **eye-muscle coordination.**

eye defect: any nonpathological structural defect of the eye, including refractive errors. *Syn.* **ocular defect;** *see* **vision, defective.**

eye dominance: *syn.* **eye preference.**

eye, dominant: the eye that leads in reading and seeing; the fixing eye. *Syn.* **leading eye; master eye.**

eye enucleation: surgical removal of the eyeball.

eye examination: *see* **examination, eye.**

eye fixation: a stop of the eye in reading which allows it to react to the printed stimuli; fixations account for 92 to 94 percent of reading time. *See* **fixation, binocular; fixation pause.**

eye-hand coordination: ability to use the eyes and hands together in such acts as fixating, grasping, and manipulating objects.

eye-hand dominance: *see* **dominance, eye-hand.**

eye-hand span: (typewriting) the distance, as measured in number of words, between the word that a typist is reading and what is being typewritten; usually varies from 1 to 1½ words.

eye movement: (1) changes in the position of the eyeball brought about by the activity of the external eye muscles; described as fixation, convergence, divergence, elevation, depression, pursuit, nystagmus, etc.; (2) the left-to-right progression of the eyes along a line of print (including fixations and the movement between fixations) and the return sweep to the beginning of the next line.

eye-movement camera: *syn.* **oculophotometer.**

eye-movement photography: *see* **photography, eye-movement.**

eye-movement record: *see* **record, eye-movement.**

eye movements, coordinated: associated movements where both eyes move simultaneously.

eye-muscle balance: the normal condition of the eyes in which the large, or extrinsic, muscles that control the movement of the eyeball in the socket direct the eyes in the correct visual angle.

eye-muscle coordination: (1) the normal condition of the normally functioning eye, in which the muscles that control vision work in balance; (2) ability to make the eyes work together in harmony without any deviation of either eye from the normal visual angle.

eye physician: *syn.* **ophthalmologist.**

eye preference: a tendency toward use (typically unconscious) of a "preferred" eye when sighting objects, looking through small apertures, winking, etc. *Syn.* **eyedness; eye dominance;** *see* **laterality.**

eye record: *see* **record, eye.**

eye regression: *see* **regression, eye.**

eye-rest period: *see* **period, eye-rest.**

eye span: the amount of material grasped during one fixation pause of the eyes, measured in terms of either letters or letter spaces.

eye-voice span: (oral read.) the distance, usually measured in number of letters, between the word being spoken and the word on which the eyes are focused. (The voice lags behind the eyes.)

eyedness: *see* **eye, dominant; eye preference.**

eyedness, left-: the tendency for the left eye to assume the major function of seeing, being assisted by the right eye; usually associated with left-handedness.

eyedness, right-: the tendency for the right eye to assume the major function of seeing, being assisted by the left eye; the most common type of *eyedness*, usually associated with right-handedness.

eyesight assessment: *see* **assessment, eyesight.**

eyesight conservation: *syn.* **sight conservation.**

eyesight test: *syn.* **test, vision.**

eyestrain: a condition of the eye caused by overuse, uncorrected refractive error, or external conditions such as glare.

eyewink reflex: *syn.* **reflex, corneal.**

F: *see* **ratio, F; variance, analysis of.**

F distribution: *see* **distribution, F.**

f. number: (photog.) the numerical expression of the "speed" of a lens, representing the ratio between the diameter of the aperture and the focal length of the lens; thus the speed of a lens having a maximum aperture 1 inch in diameter and a focal length of 4 inches would be expressed as f. 4; likewise, the speed of the lens at smaller apertures would be indicated similarly, a ½-inch-diameter aperture, in this case, being expressed as f. 8. *See* **f. system; lens speed; t-stop.**

F ratio: *see* **ratio, F.**

f. system: (photog.) the most commonly used method of designating, not only the maximum "speed" of a lens, but also the speed of the various apertures to which the lens diaphragm may be set; based upon f. numbers, the succession of f. numbers frequently being chosen so that each aperture marked admits approximately twice as much light as the next smaller aperture, for example, f. 4, 5.6, 8, 11, 16, 22, 32, etc. *See* **f. number.**

F test: *syn.* **variance, analysis of.**

fables test: *see* **test, fables.**

fabrication: *syn.* **confabulation.**

facade: (couns.) a term used to indicate a superficial problem presented by a counselee, that is, a problem which he can discuss more freely in place of a problem which is more revealing of his true feeling about himself and others.

face sheet: a form, usually constituting the first page, used in a case study and on which essential details for identification of the case are placed. *See* **case study.**

face-to-face group: *see* **group, face-to-face.**

face validity: *see* **validity, face.**

face value: (1) *syn.* **midpoint;** (2) apparent value or worth.

facet: (1) a side of an area, such as a facet of a gem; (2) in language, one aspect of the complex, such as reading, writing, speaking, or listening.

facial reaction: *see* **reaction, facial.**

facial vision: *syn.* **perception, object.**

facilitation: the reinforcement of one stimulus-response mechanism by another, such that a response of heightened intensity is made to the first, though the second is not active; for example, a dog that has shown no interest in eating his dinner may begin to eat greedily when another dog approaches.

facilitation, social: (1) such augmentation of the efficiency of a performance as may result from having it take place in a social setting, that is, in the presence of other people; (2) the effect of contributory social stimuli on the response to a stimulus or situation, whether through increasing the readiness to respond or through augmenting the intensity of the response; for example, a shy child responds eagerly to an invitation to play ball because other children are already playing the game. *Contr. w.* **inhibition, social.**

facility, guidance: one of the physical objects used by the counselor in the guidance program, such as a room or office with functional equipment, games, etc.

facility, instructional: *see* **equipment, instructional.**

facility, residential school: *see* **school facility, residential.**

facility, residential treatment: a residential institution in which the major focus is on treatment (medical, psychological) as distinguished from instruction.

facility, school: *see* **school facility.**

facility, special: general designation for any one of a variety of agencies providing specialized aid in areas such as education, adjustment, speech, and occupational training through evaluation, training, and followup support.

facsimile: (1) in communications, an electronic system for transmitting pictures and graphic materials over very high frequency air waves; (2) in general, a precise, usually photographic, reproduction of an original document.

facsimile transmission: a method of transmitting graphic data (printed matter, drawings, photographs) by means of radio or telegraph.

fact: that which is analyzed out of the flux of experience and is recognized as the coercive aspect of the situation; an event or relationship indicated as the ground upon which a meaningful statement is judged to be true; examples are (*a*) a discriminated item in sense experience, as "The pointer on this dial coincides with this point on the scale"; (*b*) an interpreted item in sense experience, as "That sound is the fire alarm"; (*c*) a statement of invariable relationship, as "All gold is malleable"; (*d*) those things in time and space, with their relationships, in virtue of which a proposition is true, as "These findings indicate that the consolidation of these school districts is economically desirable."

fact density: relative number of facts per unit of presentation time; usually applied to motion pictures, television programs, and other presentations of fixed duration.

fact-finding study: *see* **study, fact-finding.**

fact, scientific: a statement of existence or of performance that is identifiable in experience; fact is in contrast with fancy.

factor: (1) (stat.) a cause or determiner, which may be unique to one variable or common to several variables, that may be used to account for the correlations among a set of variables; *see* **factor analysis;** (2) in mental measurement, a hypothetical trait, ability, or component of ability, that underlies and influences performance on two or more tests and hence causes scores on the test to be correlated; refers, strictly, to a theoretical variable, derived by a process of factor analysis, from a table of intercorrelations among tests, but is also commonly used to denote the psychological interpretation given to the variable, that is, the mental trait assumed to be represented by the variable, such as verbal ability, numerical ability, etc.; (3) (math.) a divisor; the natural number *m* is a devisor of the natural number *n* if there is exactly one natural number *c* such that $n = mc$; the definition can be appropriately altered for integers and polynomials.

factor analysis: (1) in general, any of several methods for analyzing the relationships among a set of values within a matrix; (2) as most commonly used, any of several methods for analyzing tests or the correlations of tests for one of two purposes: (*a*) to describe the test correlations with the smallest possible number of factors or (*b*) to discover the nature of the underlying processes that determine the test performances; these two purposes frequently lead to different factorial methods and different factorial results; (3) also used as a method for analyzing the criterion to determine what types of tests should be stressed in order to improve prediction; (4) any of several methods for analyzing the correlations of (*a*) individuals on tests, (*b*) tests on individuals, (*c*) individuals on different administrations, (*d*) different administrations on individuals, (*e*) tests on different administrations, or (*f*) different administrations on tests; generally used in studies of the composition of individual personality.

factor analysis, Hotelling-Kelly method of: a method closely related to Thurstone's centroid solution; the factors, geometrically, are as the axes of ellipsoids of uniform density which pass through the centers of gravity of both the test and residual configurations. *See* **centroid method.**

factor analysis, inverse: *syn.* **factor analysis, transposed.**

factor analysis, inverted: *syn.* **factor analysis, transposed.**

factor analysis, obverse: *syn.* **factor analysis, transposed.**

factor analysis, reading: the use of the factor-analysis technique to verify factors believed to be elements in the complex we call reading; used by Davis and Langsam.

factor analysis, substrata-: *see* **analysis, substrata-factor.**

factor analysis, transposed: analysis of a correlation matrix whose entries are obtained by correlating people or occasions instead of tests. *Syn.* **inverse factor analysis; inverted factor analysis; obverse factor analysis;** *see* **P-technique; Q-technique.**

factor, bipolar: a factor having both positive and negative loadings of appreciable magnitude.

factor, common: (1) a factor which at least partially accounts for the variance of two or more variables in a set under consideration and thus accounts for part of the correlation among such a set; may be a general or a group factor; *contr. w.* **factor, specific;** (2) in transfer of training, a term given to each of a group of mental processes of the same general type; emphasizes the view that transfer is broad and dependent upon relationships among the kinds of subject matter evoking the similar mental processes. *See* **transfer of training.**

factor-covariance matrix: *see* **matrix, factor-covariance.**

factor, experimental: any factor or condition that is deliberately varied or deliberately held constant in an experiment in order that its effect may be studied or ruled out of consideration.

factor fixation: the act or process of defining rotated factors by direction cosines in relation to a reference system; rotation involves both "finding" and "fixing."

factor, general: a factor that is present in the variances of all the tests in a battery; the first factor extracted from a set of positively correlated tests by (*a*) any of the centroid methods of factoring; (*b*) by the bifactor method; (*c*) by Hotelling's iterative process; or (*d*) by Spearman's tetrad methods. (The general factors determined by these methods from any particular correlation matrix are not the same factor.) *See* **g-factor.**

factor, group: a factor that is present in the variances of more than one test in a battery but not in all.

factor invariance: *see* **invariance, factor.**

factor loading: (1) entries in a factor matrix; (2) the saturation of a test or measure with a factor; (3) for orthogonal factors, the correlation of any particular test with the factor being extracted; in this case, the factor loading may also be interpreted as the square root of the variance of test *j* attributable to that factor.

factor loading, standard error of a: *see* **standard error of a factor loading.**

factor matrix: *syn.* **factorial matrix.**

factor, nonexperimental: any factor not deliberately introduced or varied in an experiment but that may be present.

factor of intelligence: *see* **intelligence, factor of.**

factor, overlapping specific: *syn.* **factor, group.**

factor pattern: (1) a factor matrix in which are recorded the existence and sign of each significant loading only; (2) for a single variable, its profile of factor loadings.

factor, primary: a trait corresponding to the primary vector. *See* **vector, primary.**

factor, randomized: any factor or condition assigned by chance methods to groups or individuals in an experiment.

factor, religious: a variable of influence relating to religious commitment or belief.

factor, repeatable: an experimental factor or variable all levels of which may be administered to the same subject with meaningful results.

factor resolution: the particular factors adopted for a given test configuration when the axes are rotated to some specific position.

factor, selective: the component of a total situation that is the primary factor on which selection depends.

factor, specific: a factor that is present in only one test of a battery; the square of the specific-factor loading of a test is equal to the difference between the reliability of the test and its communality.

factor, substrata: (read.) a somewhat fixed and organized body of knowledge thought to be a part of a working set of systems which are aspects of neurological structure; these can be assembled and ordered in a patterned fashion to support an intellectual task, such as reading. *See* **reading, dynamic substrata-factor theory of.**

factor, trend: an experimental factor for which the criterion means vary according to some pattern (for example, linear, parabolic) from level to level of this factor.

factor, unipolar: a factor having only positive or only negative loadings.

factor, unique: a factor that is involved in the variance of only one test in a battery; a combination of the specific and error factors of a test.

factored test: *see* **test, factored.**

factorial design: *see* **design, factorial.**

factorial design, complete: *see* **design, complete factorial.**

factorial design, incomplete: *see* **design, incomplete factorial.**

factorial matrix: a table in which are given the factor loadings of each factor. *Syn.* **factor matrix.**

factorial structure: the combination of the test vectors and the reference vectors for a test battery.

factorial validity: *see* **validity, factorial.**

factorization, diagonal method of: a simple method of extracting factors from a correlation matrix of any size; the first axis is placed so that it is collinear with the first test vector, the second axis is placed orthogonal to the first, and so on; limited in value since it requires very accurate estimates of the communalities.

factorization, group method of: a variant of the centroid method in which the successive axes are passed through the centroid of a subgroup of tests, selected for high intercorrelations, taken from a total correlation matrix. *See* **centroid method.**

factors, cooperative: two or more factors that load similarly and substantially the same group of items, but in different proportions.

factors, first-order: factors obtained directly from the intercorrelation of tests or variables. *See* **factors, second-order.**

factors, mental: (1) a concept relating to mental organization which has largely replaced the concept of *mental faculties* in contemporary psychology; the concept is more in accord with present knowledge and more amenable to scientific study; (2) any or all of the factors emerging from a *factor analysis.*

factors, nonchance: variables that are joined together in a causal relationship.

factors, second-order: factors among factors, that is, factors obtained from the correlations of oblique first-order factors. *See* **factors, first-order.**

factory method: (ind. arts) the organization and administration of school experience according to trade and industrial mass production. *Syn.* **production method.**

factory training: *syn.* **training, plant.**

factual book: *see* **book, factual.**

faculties, mental: a concept used to describe mental functioning; various lists of faculties have been drawn up, but each has emphasized the idea of unitariness of the various faculties; this concept led eventually to the view of *formal discipline* in education. *See* **discipline, mental.**

faculty: (1) the body of persons responsible for instruction and administration in a school, college, or university; (2) the teachers of an educational institution; (3) a branch of learning or instruction in a university, as the faculty of arts and sciences or the faculty of law; (4) (psych.) *see* **faculties, mental.**

faculty adviser: *see* **adviser, faculty.**

faculty athletic committee: *see* **athletic committee, faculty.**

faculty council: an organization of representatives of the faculty of a higher education institution which meets at prescribed times and under prescribed rules to consider and act on matters relating to policy making, administration, and operation of the institution, typically primarily academic (educational, instructional) but frequently also of a wider nature depending on the rules of the council or practices of the institution. *Syn.* **faculty senate.**

faculty counselor: *see* **adviser, faculty.**

faculty director: one responsible for supervision and professional leadership of the staff of an educational institution. *See* **faculty.**

faculty evaluation: *see* **evaluation, faculty.**

faculty, graduate: teachers at a college or university whose main duties involve the teaching of students who possess the bachelor's or first professional degree.

faculty load: *see* **load, faculty.**

faculty meeting: a gathering of some or all of the educational staff members of a school for the purpose of discussing professional problems, hearing announcements, receiving instructions, planning studies or committee activities, planning the school's program, determining or recommending policies, or listening to reports or addresses.

faculty member: a staff member of an educational institution who is engaged in instructional, research, or related educational activities.

faculty promotion: *see* **promotion, faculty.**

faculty psychology: *see* **psychology, faculty.**

faculty rank: *see* **rank, faculty.**

faculty recruitment: *see* **recruitment, faculty.**

faculty remuneration: *see* **remuneration, faculty.**

faculty senate: *syn.* **faculty council.**

faculty solution: *see* **solution, faculty.**

faculty sponsor: a teacher who is responsible for the leadership or supervision of a specified activity (usually extraclass) included in the educational program.

faculty-student ratio: (1) the ratio of the number of teachers and administrators of a school to the number of students enrolled in the school; (2) the quotient resulting from the division of the number of students by the number of instructors and administrators; thus, if a faculty numbers 100 and the students 2,000, the ratio is 1:20.

faculty theory: the theory that mind is composed of certain distinct faculties, or abilities, that are capable of being trained through specific exercises; the basis of *faculty psychology,* now largely discredited.

faculty turnover: *see* **turnover, teacher.**

fade-in: (1) a motion-picture technique used to minimize the abruptness with which a picture appears on the screen, the scene appearing dimly at first and then increasing to normal brightness; (2) the technique by which the volume of sound is gradually increased from zero to normal intensity; used in starting programs and as a transitional device in conjunction with *fade-outs* for dramatic effect.

fade-out: (1) a motion-picture technique used to minimize the abruptness with which a scene ends, the scene becoming increasingly dim until it disappears; (2) the technique by which the volume of sound is gradually reduced from normal to zero amplitude and/or intensity; used in terminating programs and as a transitional device in conjunction with *fade-ins* for dramatic effect.

fader: an electronic control that progressively decreases the intensity of an image picked up by a TV camera; this procedure can be continued until the image on the screen disappears entirely or the process can be reversed to fade in another image.

fading: in programmed instruction, the gradual removal of the prompts in a sequence of items teaching a particular topic; sequences typically begin with highly prompted items and end with unprompted terminal items; sometimes used as a synonym of *vanishing. See* **prompt.**

faience (fā·äns′): an earthenware ceramic decorated with opaque colored glazes.

failure, pupil: lack of success on the part of a pupil in the accomplishment of a school task, whether a small unit, such as an individual project, or a large unit, such as the work of a school subject or grade; often implies nonpromotion of the pupil.

failure, reading: inadequate and/or insufficient growth in the cognitive and affective areas related to reading.

failure, scholastic: (higher ed.) (1) marks in a subject or in a number of subjects below the level required by faculty regulation for continued residence or for graduation; (2) achievement at a level below the student's potentialities.

failure, school: *syn.* **failure, pupil.**

failure, subject: deficiency or nonattainment on the part of a pupil in a given subject, usually resulting in nonpromotion.

failure, teacher: lack of success on the part of an instructor in performing his assigned duties.

fair operative production standard: *see* **production standard, fair operative.**

fair, science: *see* **science fair.**

fair trade law: *see* **law, fair trade.**

faith: belief or trust in persons, doctrines, moral principles, spiritual realities, ideals, etc., whether proved or not, often incapable of proof, as a basis for action; usually nonrational and emotional, a priori; the will to believe (James); sometimes identified with an entire religious position, such as "the Methodist faith," or "the Catholic faith."

faith, good: *see* **good faith.**

fake: (journ.) a piece of journalistic writing that lacks factual foundation or perverts the facts it presents (colloquial).

faked stuttering: *see* **stuttering, pseudo.**

faking: *see* **stuttering, pseudo.**

faking use key: a means for arriving at a score indicating the extent to which a person has responded as do malingerers, that is, has faked on the explicit instructions from the experimenter.

faking, use of: (testing) (1) the tendency to select responses to a test which will place one in an unfavorable light; may range from simulation of mental deficiency or emotional disturbance to ineptitude on certain tests in classification batteries; (2) the tendency to select, either consciously or unconsciously, the responses on a self-report inventory which the subject feels will make him appear in a more favorable light.

fallacy: (1) an error in reasoning due to failure to conform to the principles of valid inference; (2) an untrue statement arrived at through an error in reasoning.

fallacy, genetic: the error that can be made in judging or explaining anything, especially a human being or a human institution, solely or almost solely in terms of its origin or of its early genesis.

fallacy, mathematical: a false conclusion derived from spurious calculations, illogical deductions, or pseudohypotheses.

fallacy of ambiguity: lack of clarity as to the meaning of a proposition due to vagueness of stipulation, slurring over distinctions, or other confusion in language; common fallacies of ambiguity include *accent; amphiboly; composition; division; equivocation.*

fallacy of begging the question: arguing toward a conclusion which is unwarrantedly assumed in the premise, as "Liberty is to be prized because liberty means freedom and freedom ought to be cherished." *See* **reasoning, circular.**

fallacy, particularistic: a form of illogical reasoning that is favorable to a specific cause or interest.

fallacy, reductive: the unwarranted simplification of causal explanations resulting from ignoring the interaction of interdependent variables and stressing one variable as the causal principle, as when individual behavior and social processes are presumably explained without reference to the interactions between them.

fallibism: in modern American philosophy, the theory that human knowledge is never absolute but is characterized by uncertainty and indeterminacy; developed systematically by Charles Sanders Pierce. ("There are three things to which we can never hope to attain by reasoning, namely, absolute certainty, absolute exactitude, absolute universality.")

false accuracy: *see* **accuracy, false.**

false guidance: *see* **guidance, pseudo.**

false positives: (testing) persons who would not have been accepted on the basis of their test performance but who would have succeeded had they been selected.

false principles: *see* **principles, false.**

false vocal cords: *see* **vocal cords, false.**

falsetto: a method of singing adopted by male singers permitting them to extend their range above the upper limits of their normal voice; these notes are generally inclined to be weak, lacking in dramatic expressiveness, and often nasal in character.

familial: pertaining to, of, or characteristic of a family; descriptive of that which occurs in members of the same family (may be environmental as well as hereditary).

familial mental deficiency: *see* **deficiency, familial mental.**

familial mental retardation: *see* **mental retardation, familial.**

familiarization training: *see* **training, familiarization.**

family: (1) (sociol.) a basic, primary social group, composed of a man (or a group of men) and a woman (or a group of women), their progeny, and possibly other members of the household; the structure varies from monogamy to various types of polygamy; the functional organization varies from patriarchy, through equalitarianism, to matriarchy; personnel inclusion varies from immediate biological relatives to the clan (Roman gens); (2) (biol.) a group of related biological beings classified above a genus and below an order; (3) (census) a group of two or more persons related by blood, marriage, or adoption and residing together; *dist. f.* **household;** (4) (read.) a combination of consonants and vowels which represents the sound of the human voice in speaking a word; in phonics, such families as "at," "and," "end," and the like are taught as aids to the recognition of words and are called "end phonograms"; all words formed on the phonogram "at" belong to the "at family"; *see* **phonics; phonogram.**

family allowance: (1) that money or means of subsistence, above salary, granted to an employee for maintenance of dependents; (2) (social work) amount granted from public or private funds for maintenance of a family in need of outside aid.

family approach: *see* **program, family-centered; teaching, family-centered.**

family autobiography: *see* **autobiography, family.**

family biography: *see* **autobiography, family.**

family budget: *see* **budget, household.**

family census: *see* **census, family.**

family census file: *see* **census file, family.**

family census record: *see* **census record, family.**

family-centered program: *see* **program, family-centered.**

family-centered teaching: *see* **teaching, family-centered.**

family, conjugal: a form of family organization in which the typical household consists only of parents and their dependent children. *Syn.* **nuclear family;** *contr. w.* **family, extended.**

family, consanguine: *see* **family, extended.**

family constellation: *see* **constellation, family.**

family, contracting: the stage in the family cycle when family size decreases because the children are leaving home.

family counseling: *see* **counseling, family.**

family cycle: sociological concept of the stages through which the typical family passes; engagement, husband and wife only, young children, adolescent children, launching of children, and old age.

family developmental theory: concept of the family as a group of interacting personalities with changing needs and desires that must be satisfied within the resources of the family group.

family education: (1) formal preparation included in the curriculum of schools, religious organizations, or other welfare associations for the purpose of effecting better parent-child, child-child, and parent-parent relationships; (2) informally acquired learnings, within the home, of pertinent data and techniques of family living.

family, elementary: a group of persons composed of husband and wife and their children.

family, expanding: the stage in the family cycle when children are being born or adopted.

family, extended: a form of family organization consisting of blood relatives and their several *nuclear family* units. *Syn.* **consanguine family;** *contr. w.* **family, conjugal.**

family health: an area of study in home economics emphasizing nutrition, emotional health, prevention of illness, safety in the home, and the care of the sick and the convalescent in the home.

family history: (1) record of pertinent data regarding the relatives and home associations of the student; (2) that part of a case study of a family, as used by researchers, social workers, or other professionally interested investigators, which includes pertinent data relative to the development of the family unit in question and which is necessary for a study of the total situation of the individual members of a family.

family, indigent: *see* **indigent family.**

family information: objective, statistical data regarding the number in a family, their ages, occupations, national origin, color, place of birth, and other such pertinent data.

family, job: *see* **job family.**

family-life education: (1) in the broad sense, education that is designed to promote satisfying and successful family living, offered at any level from preschool to adult, in separated courses or integrated; (2) in a restricted sense, a special program or course of instruction, usually at secondary, college, or adult level, to prepare youth or adults for successful marriage and parenthood; focused upon (*a*) the understanding of human personality and behavior as related to the development of emotional maturity and satisfying family relationships as well as physical well-being, and (*b*) the development of skills essential to effective family participation.

family, matriarchal: a family pattern in which the mother or grandmother is the dominant figure who provides a behavior model, values, and attitudes to the young of both sexes.

family, nuclear: *syn.* **family, conjugal;** *contr. w.* **family, extended.**

family, occupational: *see* **job family.**

family of orientation: a household in which the individual has the role of offspring and sibling as opposed to the roles of spouse and parent.

family of procreation: a household or family in which the individual has the roles of spouse and parent.

family, patriarchal: a family pattern in which the father or other male figure is the dominant person in decision making and leadership.

family planning: the regulating of birth by married persons so that responsible parenthood may be exercised in terms of personal resources, social conditions, and the demands of the situation; such practices are approved by most churches today, although the Roman Catholic church sets down stringent conditions as to licit means and conditions. *See* **birth control.**

family relations: processes whereby members of a family unit teach or learn human biological and social relationships within the family.

family relations, psychology of: that psychological investigation and body of information which concerns itself with the peculiar psychical processes and responses present in the intimate, primary relationships that exist within the membership of a household.

family relationships: (1) those problems of association and interaction present within the membership of a household unit and between these individuals and relatives

with whom they have social contacts; (2) the phase of home economics concerned with the solution of problems arising between members of the family group.

family romance: (psychoan.) the Oedipus situation through which it is alleged all persons pass. *See* **complex, Oedipus.**

fan-shaped distribution: *see* **distribution, fan-shaped.**

fanaticism: unreasonable zeal or bigotry; excessive enthusiasm for a cause or interest.

fantasy: a realm not completely distinct from reality in the young child's experience; his *play* may be viewed partly as a product of his imagination; his growing insistence on realism in his play indicates his gradual awareness of a difference between reality and fantasy which is more than playacting or making believe, since the young child is living the roles he assumes.

fantasy, punishment: a fantasy of an unpleasant consequence of wish-fulfillment; the subjective motive for inhibition or repression of a wish.

fantasy, stories of: stories in which the impossible occurs, but often within the boundaries of everyday realities.

fantasy, thematic: the orderly procession of ideas clustered about a central theme in a daydream.

far space: *see* **space, far.**

far vision: *syn.* **vision, distance.**

Farband Shule (fär′bänt shōo′lə): *n. fem.; pl.* . . . **Shulen;** (Yiddish, lit., "Alliance school") a school maintained by the Jewish fraternal order called "The Labor Zionist Alliance"; a supplementary school in which both Yiddish and Hebrew are taught and the orientation is Zionist. *See* **Yiddish school.**

farm and home planning: *see* **planning, farm and home.**

farm bureau: a county organization of farmers maintained to improve their economic status and social welfare.

farm, experimental: *see* **experimental farm.**

farm, laboratory: *see* **laboratory, land.**

farm laboratory: *syn.* **shop, agricultural.**

farm mechanics education: *see* **agricultural mechanics education.**

farm practice, supervised: *see* **program, supervised agricultural experience; program, supervised farming.**

farm practice, supplementary: a phase of supervised practice in vocational agriculture concerned principally with the introduction of new farming practices and the acquisition of new farming skills, providing experience on the home farm in addition to that afforded by agricultural production and improvement projects. *See* **program, supervised farming.**

farm project: *see* **project, farm.**

farm residents, rural: *see* **population, rural farm.**

farm, school: *see* **laboratory, land.**

farm school: (1) a school for farmers or prospective farmers; (2) *syn.* **parental school.**

farm shop: *syn.* **shop, agricultural.**

Farm Youth Exchange: *see* **International Farm Youth Exchange.**

farming, establishment in: *see* **establishment in farming.**

farming program, supervised: *see* **program, supervised farming.**

farsightedness: *syn.* **hyperopia.**

fartlek training: *see* **training, fartlek.**

fast forward: on a recorder, tape movement control which permits fast winding of the tape to facilitate location of a specific portion that has not yet been played; the speed of this movement varies considerably in different kinds of recorders.

fast motion: a technique used in motion pictures to cause movement on the screen to appear faster than normal; accomplished either by slowing down the camera in taking the scene or by speeding up the projector in showing the scene.

fatalism: (philos.) (1) the belief that all events are predetermined and inevitable, the result of fate; (2) the acceptance of and submission to all occurrences and events as being predetermined and inevitable and not subject to human will or efforts to modify.

father complex: *see* **complex, father.**

father figure: a person or divinity who for an individual actually or imaginatively plays a needed authoritarian role in providing security and sanctions for conduct.

father fixation: *see* **fixation, father.**

father, foster: *see* **foster father.**

Fathers of the Church: a popular title applied to those early church (before the sixth century) ecclesiastics who are especially revered for the orthodoxy of their doctrine, the holiness of their lives, and the wide acceptance of their teachings.

fatigue: a decrease in function or efficiency as a result of activity.

fatigue, auditory: the effect by which one sound makes a second one less audible by preceding it in time. *Syn.* **acoustic trauma; after-effect masking; residual masking; temporary hearing loss.**

fatigue, operational: combat fatigue; breakdown after months or years in military service, characterized by restlessness, insomnia, nightmares, irritability, stomach disorders, startle reactions, and "nervousness."

faulty emphasis: (1) speech characterized by a pattern of pitch and intensity variation, or accent, such as to produce relative distortion of meaning; (2) distribution of the relative stress on sounds and words to produce a pattern not characteristic of the speech being used, as in foreign accent or dialect, although the meaning may or may not be distorted.

fauvism (fō'vi•zəm): an early twentieth century style in painting which attempted to increase the emotional power of subject matter by high intensity nonrealistic color, bold outlines, and strongly patterned shapes; the term originated from the French "les fauves" (lā'fōv'), meaning "wild beasts," which was applied to the painters because of their distortions of natural appearances; among these painters were Henri Matisse, Maurice Vlaminck, and Alfred Derain.

favorable seat: a seat located in the front center of a classroom and recommended for seating a pupil with impaired hearing. *Syn.* **advantageous seat.**

fear: an acute affective upset characterized by an impulse to flee or escape from the inducing situation; to be distinguished from *anxiety*, which is involuntary.

feasance: in law, the performance of an act or duty. *Contr. w.* **malfeasance; misfeasance; nonfeasance.**

feasibility study: *see* **study, feasibility.**

feature profile test: *see* **test, feature profile.**

Fechner's law: *see* **law, Fechner's.**

Federal aid to education: *syn.* **aid for education, national.**

Federal and state school food service: *see* **school food service, Federal and state.**

Federal control: any control exercised by the Federal government over expenditure of funds, school operation, or instruction in local school districts; ordinarily restricted to the supervision of programs financed wholly or in part by the Federal government.

Federal degree-granting institution: *see* **institution, Federal degree-granting.**

Federal Extension Service: *see* **Extension Service, Federal.**

Federal grant: *see* **grant, Federal.**

Federal junior college: *see* **junior college, Federal.**

Federal rehabilitation agency: one of the "helping service" agencies of the U.S. government, presently combined under social and rehabilitation services; includes vocational rehabilitation and services for the aging.

Federal reservation: public lands held by the Federal government for a particular purpose and not intended to be disposed of.

Federal scholarship program: *see* **scholarship program, Federal.**

Federal school: a school operated by the Federal government, such as the United States Military Academy,

Haskell Institute (for Indians), and schools for the natives of Alaska.

Federal school lunch program: *see* **program, Federal school lunch.**

Federal support: *see* **support, Federal.**

federation, student: a state or national organization of students in colleges and universities specifically intended to further the interests of students, usually in one or more specialized problem areas; not prevalent in the United States.

fee: (1) an amount of money payable for professional services or for the enjoyment of some privilege for a designated period of time; ordinarily used in education to designate a general or specific charge to the student in an educational institution or a charge for admission to various scholastic or recreational activities, for example, tuition fee, locker fee, laboratory fee; (2) an estate of inheritance in land, at common law.

fee, activity: *syn.* **tax, blanket.**

fee, conditional: a fee restricted to some particular heirs and excluding all others. *See* **fee** (2).

fee, determinable: *syn.* **fee, qualified.**

fee, incidental: (1) a blanket payment or charge, arbitrarily fixed by a governing body to cover contingencies not immediately foreseen; (2) the designation of a fee to be paid by students in certain institutions that legally or for some other reason are prevented from charging "tuition" fees.

fee, qualified: a fee that has some qualification annexed to it and that terminates whenever the qualification terminates; a school district that holds title to property only so long as it is used for school purposes is said to have a qualified fee. *See* **fee** (2).

fee, remitted: (1) a fee that is returned or restored in consideration of some attainment or service; (2) a form of grant-in-aid to a student that permits him to enjoy institutional privileges without the payment of all the fees usually required. *See* **fee** (1).

fee simple: an absolute inheritance, clear of any condition, limitation, or restriction to particular heirs; the highest estate known to the law and necessarily implies absolute dominion over the land. *See* **fee** (2).

fee, student: a fixed charge paid by students for enjoyment of stated privileges, such as attendance at athletic and other events.

feeblemindedness: (1) a generic term, primarily legal in nature, formerly used to describe all levels of mental retardation; *comp. w.* **oligophrenia;** (2) a term formerly used technically in England as a synonym of mental retardation when present to a mild degree. *See* **retardation, mental.**

feeblemindedness, endogenous: (1) mental deficiency (accompanied by social inadequacy) due to germinal, or intrinsic, causes, that is, inherited deficiency; (2) also used by some to designate the "garden variety" of mental deficiency due to inheritance or to inferior environmental conditions, excluding only the cases arising from brain injury.

feeblemindedness, exogenous: (1) mental deficiency (accompanied by social inadequacy) due to brain injury or infection of the brain before, during, or after birth; (2) all instances of mental deficiency not included in the endogenous category; *see* **feeblemindedness, endogenous** (2).

feeblemindedness, progressive: *see* **mental retardation, progressive.**

feeblemindedness, pseudo: *see* **mental retardation, pseudo.**

feeblemindedness, subcultural: *syn.* **mental retardation, subcultural.**

feed reel: *see* **reel, supply.**

feedback: (1) error-correcting information returned to the control center of a servomechanism (or to the nervous system and brain of a living organism) enabling it to offset deviations in its course toward a particular goal; (2) in programmed instruction, information received by the student immediately after each of his responses to the programmed material; *see* **confirmation** (4); (3) knowledge obtained from tryout of programmed materials that may be used by the programmer in making subsequent revisions; (4) the interchange of information on the part of human beings in a communication or problem-solving situation; (5) (audiovis. instr.) the pickup of sound, produced by an audio-system speaker, by a microphone attached to that speaker and the recycling through the same speaker of the sound, which thus grows ever louder.

feedback, acoustic: leakage of sound from the receiver to the microphone.

feedback, auditory: a person's ability to hear his own vocalizations and speech; an essential part of linguistic development.

feedback, kinesthetic: stimulation of proprioceptors by each voluntary response of an organism and by some involuntary ones; induces the capacity to feel the movements of parts of the body through the functioning of the nerve endings situated in them; used, for example, by the deaf as a means of controlling the organs of articulation. *See* kinesthetic method (2).

feedback loops of concern: linguistic statements and expressive gestures—anything, indeed, that indicates to the communicator how the communicatee responds to his message, and anything that indicates to the interpreter the intent of the communicator in producing the message.

feedback, negative: reciprocal interaction of parts of a dynamic system such that increasing output of part of the system so affects input as in turn to decrease output of another part.

feedback, positive: reciprocal interaction of parts of a dynamic system such that increasing output of part of the system so affects input as in turn to increase output of another part.

feedback, psychological: the process whereby the individual gains information concerning the correctness of his previous responses in order that he can adjust his behavior to compensate for errors; involves a complex interaction between motives, goals, and information regarding progress toward these goals; a more inclusive expression than *knowledge of results,* which it is tending to replace.

feedback schedule: *see* reinforcement schedule.

feedback, sensory: an internal awareness resulting from the reception of self-activated sensory impulses.

feeder route: the designation of a short side route covered by a small bus or automobile for the purpose of bringing pupils from a side road to the main bus line.

feeding, cafeteria: an experiment in which young infants or other animals are given free access to a variety of foods rather than a fixed balanced diet; self-selection indicates that organismic hungers lead, over a period of time, to a balanced diet.

feeding, chain: a time-saving process of feeding envelopes into the typewriter in a continuous line, either by (*a*) back-feeding, whereby the first envelope is fed into the typewriter until about one-half inch of the bottom of the envelope shows behind the platen and then the top of the second envelope is placed between the platen and the bottom of the first so that as the first envelope is removed the third is fed into the typewriter, and so on, or (*b*) front-feeding, whereby the envelope just addressed is rolled back until about one inch of the top edge is free; the next envelope is then inserted face up between the platen and the top edge of the addressed envelope and rolled back into typing position, and so on.

feeding, self-demand: *see* schedule, self-demand.

feeling of helplessness: *see* helplessness, feeling of.

feeling of inadequacy: *syn.* inferiority feeling.

feeling tone: *syn.* affective tone.

feelings, bodily: *see* experience of form, autoplastic.

fellow: (1) the holder of a fellowship; (2) a member of a learned literary or scientific society; (3) in some universities, a member or trustee of the corporation.

fellowship: in education, a grant of money and/or professional position awarded on the basis of good scholarship, character, leadership, professional promise, and sometimes financial need, as an aid to an individual toward further educational endeavors. *See* scholarship (3).

fellowship, youth: *see* youth fellowship.

felt need: something regarded as either desirable or necessary by the individual concerned, as distinct from something which, whether desirable or not, is not recognized as such by the individual in question; for example, "He needs a bath" expresses a need felt by the speaker but not necessarily by the person spoken of.

felt needs: *see* needs, felt.

felt-tipped lettering pen: *see* lettering pen, felt-tipped.

feltboard: a display board made of cardboard or thin wood and covered with felt or similar cloth; pictured symbols to be displayed on it are backed with similar materials or with sandpaper and adhere to it; when flannel is used, the display board is called *flannelboard* or *flannelgraph.*

female seminary: *see* seminary, female.

fencing: an individual sport, a form of dueling, in which two opponents use foils, epees, or sabres; contestants wear masks, jackets, and gloves; a fencing bout takes place between two persons on a paved or turf strip or on a mat; may be included in class work, intramurals, and recreation programs serving all age levels and both sexes. *Syn.* foiling.

fenestration: (1) the plan for natural lighting or the adequacy and condition of windows in a school building; their size, arrangement, types, quality of glass, number, etc.; (2) an operation for the treatment of otosclerosis by which a new oval window is made in place of the one which has sealed.

feral child: *see* child, feral.

Fernald-Keller approach: *see* approach, Fernald-Keller.

fertility, differential: difference in changes in the birth rate between many population elements of the nation, states, regions, types of community, socioeconomic statuses.

fertility ratio: *see* ratio, fertility.

festination: (spec. ed.) an inability to control the timing of acquired automatisms, such as walking or talking; the act begins slowly, apparently with a delay of volition, then becomes faster and faster until the very speed renders coordination impossible, and the process stops.

fetish: an object presumed to possess magical power and supposed to protect its owner from injury or death; reliance upon such charms has its origin in the untutored imagination of primitive man, but it survives in modern civilized society.

fetishism: (1) belief in and use of objects, usually inanimate, thought to be the habitat of spirits and to have magic power; (2) the use of objects thought likely to appease the ire of a god or spirit; (3) (psychol.) a compulsive employment of inanimate objects such as clothing or a lock of hair for the attainment of sexual satisfaction; (4) (vernacular) blind devotion to an idea or reverence for an object with sentimental value.

feudal training: *see* training, feudal.

fibroplasia, retrolental: an eye defect frequent in babies born two or more months prematurely, characterized by growth of opaque fibrous tissue behind the crystalline lenses of the eyes; the largest single cause of blindness in children during the period 1945-1955.

fiction, career: *see* career fiction.

fiction, historical: (lang. arts) fiction for children and young people which, at its best, reflects an accurate picture of the people, the setting, and the character of the time about which it is written.

fiction, occupational: *see* career fiction.

fiction, regional: (lang. arts) fiction written for children and young people which realistically and sympathetically depicts life in various sections of the country.

fictionalized biography: *see* biography, fictionalized.

fidelity: (audiovis. ed.) the degree of exactness or faithfulness with which any sound is duplicated or reproduced.

fidelity bond: *see* bond, fidelity.

fiducial level: *syn.* confidence level.

fiducial limits: *syn.* confidence limits.

fiducial probability: *see* probability, fiducial.

fiduciary: (legal) holding, held, or founded, in trust; of the nature of a trust.

field: (1) (ed.) a broad area of knowledge within which an accredited degree is awarded; (2) the situation, context, or effective environment in which a particular object or event occurs and in interaction with which it is perceived, described, and made meaningful; (3) (stat.) one or more columns on a punch card, representing a single variable; (4) for computers, a set of one or more characters treated as a whole; (5) (math.) a unit of information; (5) (math.) in algebra, a particular kind of mathematical system; *see* **field properties; group** (4); **mathematical system.**

field agent: an individual representing a school for the purpose of securing enrollments.

field ball: a game, devised by L. R. Burnett, played between teams of 11 players, resembling basketball played on a soccer field with a soccer ball; points are scored by throwing the ball through the goal, kicking the ball at any time being forbidden.

field captain: (phys. ed.) the player who acts as captain of a team on the field during play.

field, card: in data processing, a set of card columns, either fixed as to number and position or, if variable, then identifiable by position relative to other fields.

field, data: *see* **data field.**

field day: a day on which the pupils of one or more schools engage in organized outdoor sport and play activities, especially track and field events, usually on a competitive basis.

field, depth of: *see* **depth of field.**

field distribution: *see* **distribution, field.**

field evaluation: *see* **evaluation, field.**

field events: events in a track meet including, usually, the running high jump, running broad jump, discus throw, shot-put, pole vault, and javelin throw.

field exercise: *see* **exercise, field.**

field experience: *see* **experience, field laboratory.**

field forces: in Lewin's theory, the strength of drive (as distinguished from need) in the psychological environment of the individual or group.

field hockey: *see* **hockey, field.**

field house: a large building with a high vaulted roof and, usually, a dirt floor; used for athletic activities in inclement weather.

field instruction: *see* **instruction, field.**

field laboratory experience: *see* **experience, field laboratory.**

field lesson: *see* **lesson, field.**

field maneuver: *see* **maneuver, field.**

field manual: *see* **manual, field.**

field, number: *see* **number field.**

field observation: *see* **observation, field.**

field, occupational: a broad area of occupations that require, for their successful pursuit, similar abilities, aptitudes, and vocational-interest patterns.

field of concentration: (teacher ed.) the particular area of work selected by a student for primary specialization in his professional and academic (subject-matter) preparation for the teaching profession. *See* **major, broad-fields; major, departmental.**

field of concentration, major: a single broad field of subject matter in which the senior college or graduate school student specializes, with emphasis on depth of penetration of the subjects involved.

field of interest: (1) the particular subject or group of related subjects in the curriculum that a teacher likes and is best prepared to teach; (2) the subject or group of related subjects that a pupil or student chooses of his own accord.

field of special preparation: *see* **field of concentration; major, broad-fields; major, departmental.**

field of study, major: a principal subject of study in one department or field of learning, in which a student is required or elects to take a specified number of courses and credit hours as a part of the requirement for obtaining a diploma or degree.

field of study, minor: a subject of study in one department or broad field of learning in which the student is required

or elects to take a specified number of courses or hours, fewer than required for a major field; implies less intensive concentration than in the major field.

field of vision: the entire area that can be seen without shifting the gaze. *Syn.* **visual field.**

field of vision, binocular: the combined fields of the two eyes, which overlap centrally and extend 160 to 180 degrees horizontally. *See* **field of vision.**

field of vision, peripheral: that outermost area of the retina in which there are rods but no cones; while differences of brilliancy are perceptible, colors are indistinguishable in this area.

field, phenomenological: everything, including itself, experienced by an organism at any moment; emphasis is upon the external world as experienced by the reacting organism, not as it is in the abstractions of physical science; objects physically present but not perceived are not part of the phenomenological field, and objects not physically present but thought about are. *Syn.* **phenomenal field.**

field practice: *syn.* **field work** (3).

field properties: characteristics of the mathematical system called a field, such as, (a) at least two elements in the set, (b) two binary operations defined on the set, (c) the set closed under both operations, (d) both operations commutative, (e) both operations associative, (f) one operation, called multiplication, distributing over the other, called addition, (g) identity elements for both operations in the set, (h) an additive inverse for each element in the set, and (i) a multiplicative inverse for each element except the additive identity in the set.

field properties, law of: *see* **law of field properties.**

field selection: *see* **selection, field.**

field study: *see* **study, field.**

field theory: a general term used to classify those psychological systems in which behavior is considered the result of various forces generated within a specific situation; to be contrasted with atomistic theories in which conduct is traced to a single isolated cause. *See* **atomism, psychological.**

field theory of learning: *see* **learning, field theory of.**

field theory, topological: a theory developed by Kurt Lewin, a psychologist involved in research with children, in which he refers to intelligence not as a property of the nervous system but of the way the world appears to people—its qualities, flavors, meanings, and possibilities for action; if the theory should be adopted, the goal of education would become that of making people more intelligent by teaching them what the environment consists of and how it operates, and how they can interact with it.

field training: *see* **training, field.**

field trip: a trip arranged by the school and undertaken for educational purposes, in which students go to places where the materials of instruction may be observed and studied directly in their functional settings; for example, a trip to a factory, a city waterworks, a library, a museum, etc. *Syn.* **instructional trip; school excursion; school journey;** *see* **plant tour.**

field trip, aerial: the utilization of aircraft for the purpose of conducting an educational field study.

field trip, industrial: *see* **industrial field trip.**

field unit analysis: *see* **analysis, field unit.**

field, utilization: *see* **utilization field.**

field work: (1) work, commonly of a practical nature, carried on outside an office, institution, or center of administration; (2) administrative or consultative services given by representatives of an organization to individuals, groups, or organizations in geographical locations away from the main office of the serving organization; (3) educational experience, sometimes fully paid, acquired by college students in a practical service situation; the terms *field laboratory experience* and *student teaching* are most commonly used for preservice levels, whereas *internship plan* and field work are more commonly used at graduate student levels.

field work educational method: *syn.* **instruction, field.**

field work, mathematics: *see* **mathematics field work.**

fieldworker: (1) one engaged in field work; *see* **field work;** (2) an educational officer or teacher employed by a governmental or private agency or by a school or college to organize and conduct such activities as advisory work, consultations, surveys, investigations, research, classes, and training courses in places outside the institution or center of administration; (3) a special agent or teacher employed in college or university extension outside the institution or center of administration.

FIFO: an accounting term used in connection with a value control of inventories; an acronym for "first in, first out," that is, the first item stored is the first item issued. *See* **LIFO.**

fifth year: a fifth year of collegiate study beyond high school required in preparation for teaching, supervising, or administering in specific fields; may lead to the master's degree or, sometimes, bachelor of education.

figurative art: *see* **art, figurative.**

figure-background disturbance: *see* **disturbance, figure-background.**

figure-copying test: *see* **test, figure-copying.**

figure drawing: *see* **drawing, figure.**

figure, father: *see* **father figure.**

figure-ground: pertaining to a phenomenon evidenced in the tendency of highly shaped configurations to stand out as figures and the rest of the perceptual image to fall into the background; figure-ground phenomena are related to the focus and periphery of awareness and are of particular interest to gestalt psychologists. (That which is figure may under certain circumstances become ground.)

figure-ground discrimination: *see* **discrimination, figure-ground.**

figures, ambiguous: (1) drawings which contain figures that are susceptible of being perceived in more than one way; (2) (gestalt) a field capable of momentary reorganization so that when one figure holds the focus of attention all else falls into ground and, upon a shift in perceptual attention, ground becomes figure and figure ground.

figures, rectilinear: figures consisting of or bounded by straight lines, such as triangles, squares, parallelograms, etc.

file: a set of records on a common subject and usually organized or ordered on the basis of some combination of items of data uniformly found in all the records of the file, such as a date.

file, disk: a secondary storage device employed in computer operation; consists of one or more plates attached to a rotating spindle which permits reading and writing heads to pick up or record information on thin magnetic film on the plate surfaces; access time is relatively slow but transfer rates high once the information has been reached. *See* **page.**

file, enlisted personnel schools: a computerized Bureau of Naval Personnel data bank of enlisted members in formal courses at all levels; linked in the Manpower and Personnel Management Information System with computerized control of Navy Enlisted Classification assignments; provides timely training data for planners and programmed rating managers and replaces various manual reports.

file, item: a filing system to enable the teacher to arrange test items for easy reference and to allow quicker, more efficient test construction; each item is typed on an *item card.*

file, line: a file for computerized data consisting of lines of from 1 to 255 characters, or *bytes;* the lines are identified by line numbers.

file, memory: *see* **memory file.**

file, sequential: in automatic data processing, a set of records, each of which may be from 1 to 32,767 characters, or *bytes,* in length; the set may be read only in sequence, not being randomly accessible by record number.

filing: a system used to arrange and store materials such as papers, booklets, records, film, or other data according to the designation by which it will be sought; the material may be sorted and filed in alphabetic, numeric, geographic, or subject sequence in order to present ready and easy access to the information.

filing, alphabetic: *see* **filing plan.**

filing, classified: *see* **filing plan.**

filing, coded: *see* **filing plan.**

filing, office machines, and general office clerical occupations training: *see* **training, filing, office machines, and general office clerical occupations.**

filing plan: (couns.) a plan or system of filing occupational information; several methods are presently being used, including, among others, the alphabetical plan, which is the simplest until it outgrows itself (approximately 100 folders), the classified plan, which uses 75 to 600 major headings under each of which may be filed information on many related occupations, and the coded plan, which utilizes code numbers from the *Dictionary of Occupational Titles and Codes,* Part II, from which teachers may create their own files.

filing plan, Bennett: in occupational guidance, a variation of the alphabetic filing plan; subject headings are adapted from the *Dictionary of Occupational Titles* but not code numbers; materials are filed under 270 subject headings with 501 labels for cross reference; headings are in red and blue capital letters, respectively, filed in single alphabetical list, and numbered consecutively, with 58 headings for supplement.

filing plan, chronicle: a system used for filing unbound occupational information, using code numbers and occupational titles which are similar to, but not always identical with, those in the *Dictionary of Occupational Titles;* 10 major occupational groups, from "professional" to "unskilled" are divided into 106 occupational divisions, within which folders are provided for 215 occupational titles, selected on the basis of the availability of unbound career literature. *See* **filing plan, Missouri.**

filing plan, Missouri: a method of filing unbound occupational information; 325 subject headings are used, grouped under eleven school subjects—agriculture, art and drawing, commercial, home economics, industrial arts, language arts, mathematics, music, physical education, science, and social science. *See* **filing plan, chronicle.**

filing plan, New York State: a method, based on the *Dictionary of Occupational Titles,* of filing unbound occupational information used in occupational guidance; code numbers and occupational titles are similar to, but not identical with, those in the *D.O.T.;* 12 major occupational groups from professional to semiskilled occupations are divided into 111 occupational divisions, within which are 200 occupational titles; the 12 groups and the 111 divisions use the 3-digit code of the *D.O.T.,* the 200 occupational titles use the 5-digit and 6-digit codes.

filing plan, S.I.C.M.: a method of filing based on the *standard industrial classification manual* but with its own code numbers; occupational information is filed as it describes an industry rather than an occupation.

filing plan, S.R.A.: a method of filing occupational information already prepared by Science Research Associates in a career information kit which is available as a collection of 700 publications on occupations filed in 194 coded and labeled folders in a portable file.

film: (photog.) (1) a thin, flexible, transparent strip made of nitrocellulose or cellulose acetate and coated with a light-sensitive emulsion, whether developed and printed or not; (2) a motion picture or filmstrip.

film, acetate-base: a type of photographic film the base of which consists of cellulose *acetate;* used for practically all 8- and 16-mm films as well as for the 35-mm film used in 2-by-2-inch slides and filmstrips.

film, career: *see* **film, occupational.**

film cement: a solution of cellulose acetate dissolved in acetone, used to cement two pieces of film together in making a splice.

film chain: the part of a television system which includes the slide and motion-picture projectors connected optically to a television camera.

film, classroom: a motion picture employed as an instructional device or material. *Syn.* **film, educational.**

film clip: a brief, filmed sequence used generally on television without having titles or special effects.

film, color: photographic film designed to yield either a positive image in a close approximation of the colors of the original subjects or a negative image in colors complementary to those of the original subject, from which a positive print can be made.

film depository: any agency engaging in the distribution of motion pictures.

film, diapositive: *syn.* **film, positive** (2).

film, documentary: *see* **documentary.**

film, educational: *syn.* **film, classroom.**

film, eight-millimeter: a motion-picture film 8-mm (approximately $\frac{3}{10}$ inch) wide, perforated along one edge only; perforations are the same size as in 16-mm film, with twice the number of perforations per foot.

film footage: in the United States and some other countries, length of motion-picture film, expressed in the English system with the foot as the basic unit; width, or gauge, of film, however, is universally expressed in the metric system.

film gate: *see* **gate, film.**

film humidification: *see* **humidification, film.**

film index: *syn.* **film speed** (1).

film, industrial: a type of sponsored film produced by or for an industrial or commercial agency for advertising or public relations purposes. *See* **film, sponsored.**

film, instructional: any film planned and produced for use as an aid to or a means of teaching.

film library: *see* **library, film.**

film loop: *see* **loop, continuous.**

film, magnetic: a sprocketed synchronous acetate-base film with a magnetic coating, available from stock in 35-, 17½-, 16-, and 8-mm sizes, which resembles the commonly known ¼-inch tape varieties, but through the use of sprockets can be synchronized with a silent film during the editing process.

film, magnetic-striped: 8-mm, 16-mm, 35-mm, 65-mm, or other motion-picture film to which a strip of magnetizable material is added which will accept sound impulses in the form of magnetic variations.

film manual: a sheet or booklet containing printed suggestions for the use of an educational film, usually consisting of description of the film content, suggested techniques of use, objectives to be attained, etc. *Syn.* **film study guide.**

film, negative: a film that after being exposed in a camera, is developed so that the photographically recorded image appears reversed as to light and shade, that is, light or white sections of the photographed scene appear dark or black in the negative, and vice versa.

film, nitrate-base: a type of photographic film the base of which consists of nitrocellulose. *Dist. f.* **film, acetate-base; film, safety.**

film, occupational: a film, motion-picture or filmstrip, which presents information about the duties of various occupations, including training requirements of apprentices.

film, positive: (1) photographic film, generally of the process type, used for preparing positive transparencies (diapositives) from negatives; (2) black-and-white or color film that, after being exposed in the camera, is developed directly into a positive (usually by means of a chemical reversal) without the intermediate step of making a master negative; often called *reversal film, reversible film,* or *diapositive film.*

film, public relations: (1) a film produced in or by a school for the purpose of interpreting all or part of the school program to the public; (2) a film produced by or for an industrial, commercial, or service agency for the purpose of interpreting the aims and methods of its program to the public.

film, reading: a motion-picture film to be used to increase the speed of reading; the reading material is exposed from left to right in a line of print in such a manner as to guide the eye in reading and to hasten the process of recogni-

tion; believed by some to increase the width of the span of recognition; developed at Harvard University and at the State University of Iowa.

film, reversal: *see* **reversal film.**

film, reversible: *syn.* **reversal film.**

film, safety: *syn.* **film, acetate-base.**

film sensitivity: *syn.* **film speed** (1).

film, shading: textures and patterns printed on acetate sheets having adhesive backing for adhering to cardboard, paper, acetate, or film.

film, silent: a motion-picture film on which no sound track has been recorded; generally, it is 16-mm and has sprocket holes on both edges; silent speed for projection of 16-mm film is 16 frames per second.

film, single concept: usually an 8-mm film in cartridge form which ranges from three to six minutes in length; as used in home economics instruction, each such film stresses one technique for which portrayal of motion is essential, for example, applying a zipper in clothing, bathing the baby, or making the bed.

film, sixteen-millimeter: motion-picture film 16 mm (approximately $\frac{3}{5}$ inch) wide; used widely for educational purposes and for amateur motion-picture making.

film, slide: *see* **slide film.**

film slide: *see* **slide, film.**

film, sound: a motion-picture film with self-contained sound track (optical or magnetic); a 16-mm sound film has sprocket holes on one edge only; it projects properly at 24 frames per second.

film speed: (1) the degree to which a film is sensitive to the action of light, which determines the length of exposure required at a given aperture; measured by the amount of light necessary to produce a negative of a given density under standardized conditions of development; variously expressed in degrees Scheiner, Weston, H. and H., DIN., etc.; *syn.* **film index; film sensitivity;** (2) the speed, as measured in frames per second, with which a motion-picture film moves past the aperture of a motion-picture camera or projector, commonly 16 frames per second for silent pictures, 24 for sound pictures, and 30 for sound pictures projected on television.

film splicer: *syn.* **splicer.**

film, sponsored: a film produced by or for any agency for the principal purpose of advocating a point of view or course of action, usually distributed free or for a small service charge. *Dist. f.* **film, industrial.**

film, stereoscopic: film exposed in matching pairs of frames of which one frame represents the right-eye view of the scene, the other the left-eye view; a slight but definite difference in angle of view, or parallax, between right- and left-eye versions of the scene provides a realistic depth perception cue when, simultaneously viewed, the right-eye positive picture is presented exclusively to the viewer's right eye and the left-eye positive is presented exclusively to his left.

film study guide: *syn.* **film manual.**

film, test: a standardized motion picture especially designed for testing the video and audio performance of projection and/or recording equipment; usually contains such things as test patterns, sustained tones, music, and dialogue.

film test: *see* **test, film.**

film, thirty-five-millimeter: photographic film having a width between sprocket holes of 35 mm (approximately 1⅖ inches); used for professional, theatrical motion pictures, as well as for miniature still cameras of the Leica type and for certain identification cameras, for filmstrips and for 2-by-2-inch slides. *See* **filmstrip, double-frame; filmstrip, single-frame.**

film, training: (1) a film produced with an instructional objective; may be synonymous with *educational* or *instructional film,* but sometimes is solely for instruction in skills; (2) a military term for instructional films.

filming, multicamera: recordings of the same action with two or more cameras operated at the same time and located at different positions in relation to the subject.

filmograph: a motion picture consisting of a sequential arrangement of individual still pictures, that is, a film without photography of live action.

films for deaf, captioned: motion picture films for the deaf provided through the efforts of the United States Office of Education to expand educational provisions in all groups of exceptional children; films have superimposed explanatory notes as is done with films having dialogue in a foreign language.

filmstrip: a length of 35-mm or 16-mm film containing a succession of still pictures intended for projection one at a time in the same way as slides are shown; some filmstrips are equipped with a tape or a recording that contains not only the narration but also a subsonic signal that activates a solenoid to advance the filmstrip to the next picture on cue; also called *strip film* or *slide film*.

filmstrip, double-frame: a series of pictures aligned lengthwise along 35-mm film, each one being equal in size to a 2-by-2-inch slide; the film is inserted in the projector horizontally.

filmstrip projector: *see* **projector, filmstrip.**

filmstrip, single-frame: a series of pictures oriented horizontally across the width of 35-mm film and of such a size that two adjacent pictures (or frames) equal the area of one 2-by-2-inch slide.

filmstrip, sound: *see* **filmstrip.**

final ability: *see* **final status.**

final art product: *see* **art product, final.**

final blend: *see* **blend, final.**

final-blend theory: a theory holding that the most effective approach to independent word recognition is to blend the end consonant or consonants with the preceding vowel, for example, the blending of *atch* in the word *catch. See* **initial-blend theory.**

final cause: *see* **cause, final.**

final draft: *see* **draft, final.**

final examination: *see* **examination, final.**

final position: the location of a sound occurring at the end of a word. *Dist. f.* **initial position; medial position.**

final report: *see* **report, final.**

final status: the condition or relative position of an individual or group with respect to a certain characteristic or ability at the conclusion of an experiment.

finance, educational: the science and practice of raising and expending revenue for education; the management of monetary affairs for schools.

finance, mathematics of: *see* **mathematics of finance.**

finance officer: a vice presidential level officer in a higher education institution whose responsibility is that of raising or supervising the raising of funds for the support of the institution. *See* **development** (4).

finance, public: the financial operations of both central and local government.

financial ability: *see* **ability, financial.**

financial ability, measure of: any calculable measure of the financial resources of a fund-raising school agency used for the purpose of comparing the capability of such agency to support an educational program with other similar agencies; for example, income per inhabitant, income per child, value of taxable property per child, etc.

financial accounting: *see* **accounting, financial.**

financial administration: *see* **administration, financial.**

financial aid: *see* **aid, financial.**

financial analysis: *see* **analysis, financial.**

financial campaign: a connected series of operations involving publicity and intensive canvass to bring about some desired financial result, such as increasing endowments or raising current or building funds.

financial effort: *see* **effort, financial.**

financial foundations: (1) those services and commodities available potentially for the operation of financial machinery, municipal enterprises, or other agencies; (2) agencies to which sums of money have been committed

by philanthropists and which are responsible for the disbursement of resources from the fund for the objects for which it was created.

financial management: *see* **management, financial.**

financial office employee: *see* **employee, financial office.**

financial report: a statement or series of statements concerning the financial operations of an activity, agency, or concern for a given period and its financial position at the close of that period. (Many different kinds of financial reports are prepared in local school systems. Most common are the *balance sheet*, which lists assets in the debit column, and equities, or liabilities and surplus, in the credit column; the statement of receipts and disbursements, or income and expenditures; the statement of bonded indebtedness, or bonds outstanding; the statement of sinking fund assets; the statement of school-plant assets, that is, land, buildings, and equipment, usually listed at acquisition value; the comparative statement of operations; the budget; the monthly recapitulation of unexpended budget balances. Financial reports are usually presented in the form of tables, which may be supplemented by explanations, interpretations, and graphs.)

financial report, state public schools: (1) a fiscal accounting made by the officials charged with general supervision of the schools of a state; (2) a formal and official written statement of the receipts and expenditures for the operation and maintenance of schools, demanded of local officials in city, county, and district schools according to state law.

financial support: *see* **support, financial.**

findings: (res.) the results of data gathering and analysis, usually involving a certain amount of interpretation.

fine and industrial art: *see* **art, fine and industrial.**

fine art: *see* **art, fine.**

fine-art music: *see* **music, fine-art.**

fine arts: *see* **arts, fine.**

fine motor activity: *see* **activity, fine motor.**

finger alphabet: *see* **alphabet, finger.**

finger gymnastics: physical exercises for the fingers, performed in a typewriting class and intended to make the fingers stronger or more supple.

finger movement: the use of the fingers or fingers and thumb in forming the letters in writing. (All writing may be done with the exclusive movement of the fingers, or such movement may be restricted largely to the formation of the smaller strokes or part strokes.)

finger painting: painting executed by applying a specially prepared, somewhat thick water paint to the painting surface and making designs with the fingers and hands; frequently rhythmic and abstract in nature; especially suitable as an aesthetic experience for young children.

finger play: a dramatization of a verse or poem with appropriate finger movements, used as an attention-getting device with young children.

finger pointing: keeping track of words in reading by placing the finger under each word as it is read (often a symptom of reading difficulty).

finger reaches: (typewriting) direction or path of movement made by fingers above or below the home keys of the typewriter.

finger reading: *see* **reading, finger.**

finger reading, electronic: *see* **reading, electronic finger.**

finger spelling: *see* **spelling, finger.**

finger stroking: (typewriting) *see* **stroking.**

finger-thumb opposition: the use of the thumb in opposition to the fingers in handling an object; first observable in infants about the fourth month, with proficiency by the seventh month; indicative of the degree of motor development.

fingering: a patterned selection and use of fingers in the playing of an instrument, for example, third space C sharp is fingered valves 1 and 2 on the cornet; the C major scale on the piano is fingered 1 2 3 1 2 3 4 5.

fingering chart: *see* **chart, fingering.**

finite: in general, subject to the restrictions of space, time, and circumstance; in physics, having bounds or limits; in mathematics, capable of being completely counted. *Contr. w.* **infinite.**

finite mathematical system: *see* **mathematical system, finite.**

finite population: *see* **population, finite.**

finite set: *see* **set, finite.**

finite universe: *syn.* **population, finite.**

fire alarm: *see* **alarm system.**

fire door: a metal door used to separate a fire-well from the interior of the building, or a room or section of the building from other parts of the building; often fitted with a wire glass section as a protection against breakage of the glass from heat.

fire drill: training in or rehearsing the procedures to be used in the event of a fire, such as practice in the systematic, safe evacuation of the children and teachers from a school building upon the sounding of the fire alarm; legally required as a means of preventing panic, injury, and loss of life in the event of fire.

fire escape: a provision made for rapid evacuation of the upper stories of a building when egress may be shut off by fire and smoke through the lower stories and the stairways; the most common form is a flight of steel steps leading from the doors or windows of upper stories to the ground; other means are steel ladders and chutes leading from the upper stories to the ground.

fire extinguisher: a portable apparatus for extinguishing fires; generally based on the action of various chemical compounds and/or gases. *See* **fire extinguisher, chemical.**

fire extinguisher, chemical: an apparatus designed to extinguish fires by chemical action; there are four commonly used types: (*a*) a portable tank with containers for soda and acid; when the tank is inverted, the chemicals unite, generate pressure, and shoot out in a stream through a hose; (*b*) a tank with a built-in pump, containing carbon tetrachloride, to be squirted into a fire; (*c*) a small glass globe containing carbon tetrachloride, to be thrown into a fire; and (*d*) a tank (to be suspended at points of fire hazard) containing carbon tetrachloride or carbon dioxide gas under pressure and having nozzles sealed with an alloy such as Wood's alloy, which melts at about 150°F from the heat of the fire, permitting the chemicals to spray out and smother the fire.

fire fighter: (voc. ed.) a worker who controls and extinguishes fires, protects lives and property, and maintains equipment as a volunteer or employee of city, township, or industrial plant.

fire hazard: any condition that is a potential cause of fire, such as defective electric wiring, electric flatirons or hot plates in use, heating pipes or smoke flues near joists, inadequate provision for the removal of ashes from the furnace and furnace room, the storage of wastepaper or oily rags, coal in a bin during the summer, and scores of other similar conditions.

fire-prevention education: a course of instruction at any age or grade level designed to provide education for the prevention of fires.

fire protection: (1) measures taken to protect a building from fire by eliminating fire hazards or by provisions for extinguishing fires; (2) provisions for warning and for the saving of lives in case of fire, such as fire gongs, fire escapes, or exits; (3) insurance against financial loss through loss of or damage to a building or equipment as a result of fire.

fire resistant: the quality of any substance (or type of construction) that can be ignited only with great difficulty and that is consumed slowly when ignited.

fire-resistive building: *see* **building, fire-resistive.**

fire-resistive construction: *see* **construction, fire-resistive.**

fire stairs: stairs leading from upper stories of a building to the lowest story, made of incombustible materials, such as concrete and iron, completely enclosed, and set off from the corridors of the building by steel doors fitted with wire glass.

fire stop: any space in a building (for example, between floors and walls) filled with noncombustible material, to prevent the spread of fire.

fireproof construction: *see* **construction, fireproof.**

fireproof-structure building: *see* **building, fireproof-structure.**

firewell: an inside fire escape made of metal, concrete, or other fireproof material, located at the end of a section of a school building, set off from the interior of the building by tight fire doors at each floor to prevent the entrance of smoke and flames; used instead of an outside fire escape. *See* **fire escape.**

first-aid certificate: *see* **certificate, first-aid.**

first-aid kit: a container used for carrying sterile medical supplies and essential equipment for rendering emergency treatment.

first cause: *see* **cause, first.**

first-cause argument: *see* **argument, first-cause.**

first classman: a cadet who is in his fourth year at a service academy; a senior.

first draft: *see* **draft, first.**

first grade, junior: *syn.* **extension, kindergarten** (1).

first-level schooling: *see* **schooling, first-level.**

first moment: (1) (of a frequency distribution) the sum of the products of each separate frequency and its deviation from the point used as the origin, divided by the number of observations or cases (the first moment of any frequency distribution about its mean is zero); (2) (of a frequency distribution) the sum of the products of each separate frequency and its deviation from the point used as the origin; (3) (of a frequency) the product of the frequency and its deviation from the point selected as the origin.

first-order correlation coefficient: *see* **coefficient, first-order correlation.**

first-order factors: *see* **factors, first-order.**

first-order gifted: *see* **gifted, first-order.**

first-order interaction: *see* **interaction, first-order.**

first principles: *see* **principles, first.**

first-time student: *see* **student, first-time.**

fiscal: of or pertaining to finances and financial matters in general and particularly to the period for which the financial program is set up.

fiscal adequacy: (1) financial productivity; (2) that property of a system of taxation through which the public authorities are provided immediately and ultimately with a supply of revenue sufficient to enable the state to discharge the functions for which the government has assumed responsibility; (3) the characteristic of a system of taxation that reflects the ability of the system to raise sufficient revenues for the needs of the government.

fiscal control: the power or authority to regulate financial matters.

fiscal machinery: (1) the means, appliances, and arrangements specifically designed for matters entailing the conduct of money; (2) the procedures followed in the operation of financial administration.

fiscal monopoly: *see* **monopoly, fiscal.**

fiscal period: any period at the end of which a governmental unit or private corporation determines its financial condition and the results of its operations and closes its books. (The period is usually a year, though not necessarily a calendar year.)

fiscal year: a period of 1 year (not necessarily corresponding with the calendar year), at the end of which financial accounts are reckoned, balanced, and settled and reports are made; usually ends on June 30 or Dec. 31 unless otherwise stipulated. *See* **school year.**

fiscally dependent system: a school system in which the board of education cannot make estimates and decisions on financial matters without the approval of and control by municipal authorities.

fiscally independent system: a school system in which the state has delegated to the board of education complete authority in all matters pertaining to the financial management of public schools, the board having the power to determine the amount of the budget and to levy or cause to be levied taxes to raise the required funds.

Fisher's t: *syn.* **test, t.**

Fisher's z: the inverse tangent transformation of the product-moment correlation, having a normal sampling distribution and a standard error determined entirely by the number of paired observations involved; must be used when r is to be used in further mathematical computations; mathematically equal to $\frac{1}{2} [\log_e (1 + r) - \log_e (1 - r)]$. *Syn.* **z transformation;** *dist. f.* **z score** (completely unrelated except for the similar symbol).

fit: *n.* (stat.) conformity to some standard, for example, the conformity of an observed distribution to a theoretical distribution.

fit: *v.* (stat.) to construct or select a curve or function to represent a set of empirical observations and to adjust the curve or function to the observations by some definite method.

fit, best: (1) the fit of a straight line or curve to a set of observations in such a manner as to conform to some criterion of goodness of fit; (2) the fit of a line (straight or curved) to a set of observations in such a manner that the sum of the squares of the deviations of the original observations from the line is a minimum. *Syn.* **closest fit.**

fit, closest: *syn.* **fit, best.**

fitness, muscular: optimum amount of muscular strength needed to meet individual requirements of daily activity, emergency physical activity, and occasional prolonged periods when adequate nutrition and hours of rest are reduced.

fitness, organic: effect of cultivation of physical, mental, emotional, social, and spiritual qualities that best serve the potentialities of the individual, both as a person and as a citizen. *See* **fitness, physical.**

fitness, physical: a condition of bodily health, resistance to disease, muscular strength, endurance, and skill that permits sustained, strenuous, and efficient muscular activity.

fitness, recreational: an individual condition that allows for sufficient skill in a variety of activities that are enjoyable to the participant.

Fitzgerald key: a device used for teaching language to the deaf, introduced by Edith Fitzgerald in 1926 and designed to aid in the systematic presentation of language to deaf children.

five-channel punched tape: *see* **tape, five-channel punched.**

five formal steps: *see* **Herbartian method.**

five W's: a term used to designate the typical content of the lead of a news article—the answers to the reader's expected questions, who, what, when, where, and why.

five-year high school: *see* **high school, five-year.**

fixation: (1) (psych.) the mechanism by which the first form of response to be reinforced persists, owing to its initial advantage; (2) a condition of arrested development at a particular growth stage; it may show itself as an actual halt in the development process or as an inclination to regress to a particular point as a defense against anxiety; (3) *syn.* **fixation pause;** (4) the postural position of the eyes that maintains the visual axes on the object of regard; (5) (photog.) the process by which the visible image formed in development is rendered relatively permanent by chemical means, through the process of dissolving silver salts present in the emulsion that have not been affected by light during exposure.

fixation, binocular: (1) the act of focusing both eyes on the same point in space; (2) the normal pause of both eyes, as in reading, for the purpose of perception.

fixation, child-parent: an excessive attachment of a child to a parent or an exaggerated emotional child-parent relationship, either of love or hate, which generally results in partial or total failure of the child to become a biosocially mature individual according to cultural prescriptions which determine, on an age-sex basis, what is and what is not acceptable behavior.

fixation drill: *see* **drill, fixation.**

fixation, factor: *see* **factor fixation.**

fixation, father: (1) *syn.* **complex, Electra;** (2) an exaggerated emotional attachment to the father, either of love or of hate; the fixation itself is an arrestment of emotional development on an infantile level.

fixation frequency: *see* **frequency, fixation.**

fixation, law of: the principle that if learning is carried far enough beyond the threshold it will become permanent.

fixation, libidinal: (psychoan.) arrest in psychosexual development, usually because of faulty guidance or some psychological shock blighting personal relationships.

fixation, mother: (1) *syn.* **complex, Oedipus;** (2) overattachment to the mother; (3) retention for an abnormally protracted period of relationship of attachment to and dependence on the mother, which in its pattern and degree is characteristic normally of younger persons; (4) exaggerated emotional relationship to the mother, whether of love or of hate.

fixation, parent-child: (1) excessive attachment of parent to child or of child to parent; (2) a form of aberrancy of affection displayed by the parent for the child at a time when such behavior is considered both inappropriate and detrimental to the child.

fixation pause: a cessation of movement of the eyes, as in reading, for the purpose of perception. *Syn.* **fixation.**

fixation point: any point in space upon which one or both eyes are sharply focused when the eyes are motionless; the point of regard.

fixation process: (1) (vision) those muscular movements, especially of convergence and accommodation, as a result of which rays of light are so directed on the retina as to secure clearest vision; (2) (psych.) the process by which an act or function reaches its static or final form.

fixation time: (1) the time consumed in reading by pausing to fix the eye upon the unit of recognition, commonly a word part, a word, or a word group; (2) the duration of the fixation in reading measured in seconds or fractions of seconds.

fixation to schema: *see* **schema, inflexible.**

fixed assets: *see* **assets, fixed.**

fixed-association test: *syn.* **test, controlled-association.**

fixed charges: a financial accounting classification which includes expenditures that are more or less regular and continuous and under which are found expenditures for such items as rents, insurance, and taxes.

fixed collection: a collection of books sent from a central agency, such as a library commission or a central school-system reservoir, that remains as a unit wherever it is sent. (If sent to a school, it may also be known as a *fixed unit* or fixed classroom collection.)

fixed do (dō): a system of sight singing in which C is uniformly called do, D is re (rā), etc., the various scales being sung in terms of these established names; the system is aimed at developing a sense of absolute pitch and is most popular in France and Italy. *See* **pitch, absolute; solfeggio;** *contr. w.* **movable do.**

fixed idea: a persistent idea that tends to recur and dominate the consciousness. *See* **obsession.**

fixed increment drill: *see* **drill, fixed increment.**

fixed point arithmetic: *see* **arithmetic, fixed point.**

fixed point of referral: an arrangement for the performance of central clearinghouse functions; an organized procedure related to processing information regarding characteristics and needs of patients or clients; may involve a central *referral clinic. See* **clearinghouse, information.**

fixed program computer: *see* **computer, fixed program.**

fixed salary schedule: *see* **salary schedule, fixed.**

fixed service, instructional television: *see* **television fixed service, instructional.**

fixed-solution problem: *see* **problem, fixed-solution.**

fixed unit: *syn.* **fixed collection.**

fixed value: *see* **value, fixed.**

fixed word length: *see* **word length, fixed.**

fixedness, functional: (Duncker) in problem solving, the perception of an object such as a pair of pliers only in this sense and not, for example, as a paperweight or as a weight to make a pendulum.

fixtures: articles permanently attached to various parts of buildings, such as electric lighting devices, lavatories, drinking fountains, shelves, and counters.

flaccid paralysis: *see* **paralysis, flaccid.**

flannel chart: *see* **feltboard.**

flannelboard: *see* **feltboard.**

flannelgraph: *see* **feltboard.**

flarimeter: a device for measuring ability to hold the breath against a known resistance, with the glottis open throughout the blow.

flash card: a small card of heavy cardboard having on it written or printed letters, words, phrases, numerals, or combinations of numerals for computation; used as an aid to learning, the teacher holding each card up for the class to see for a brief interval.

flash-card drill: *see* **drill, flash-card.**

flash device: any instrument or machine that exposes printed matter to a reader or readers under time control.

flash meter: *see* **tachistoscope.**

flash synchronizer: *syn.* **synchronizer.**

flashback: motion-picture and television technique of recreating an event independent from normal time sequence; for example, a flashback to the protagonist's seventeenth birthday party, etc.

flashing stop lights: signal lights operating intermittently to warn motorists that a school bus is going to stop, or has stopped, to load or discharge pupils.

flashing turn signals: *see* **turn signals.**

flat: (1) that musical sign (♭) which indicates that the pitch of a note is to be lowered by a semitone; (2) a term descriptive of faulty intonation, that is, playing or singing slightly below the correct pitch; (3) (school finance) a term meaning "without accrued interest added"; for example, bonds in default may be sold flat.

flat distribution: *see* **distribution, flat.**

flat grant fund: a financial grant made to schools on the basis of student enrollment, attendance, or membership, without consideration of the size or financial conditions of the community.

flat-pattern design: *see* **design, flat-pattern.**

flat picture: a print, sketch, photograph, map, chart, etc., that is intended to be viewed directly or projected in an opaque projector.

flat response: *see* **response, flat.**

fleet school ashore: training activities assigned to the command of fleet commanders-in-chief to provide refresher and team training to fleet personnel, officers and enlisted, who normally are members of ship's company; may include class A, B, and C courses in some cases. *See* **Navy enlisted school.**

FLES: an acronym formed from "foreign languages in the elementary school"; includes the teaching of any foreign language within or in conjunction with the curriculum of the elementary school.

Flesch readability formula: *see* **readability formula, Flesch.**

Flesch reading ease formula: *see* **formula, Flesch reading ease.**

flexibility: (1) ease of movement in joints of the body allowing a good range of movement of the body parts; (2) ability to change behavior in accord with changed needs and situations; (3) a creativity factor wherein the subject's ability to detect hidden figures is measured; a good performance on such measures requires freedom from persistence of approaches, permitting a restructuring of the given stimuli; (4) the characteristic of school design which facilitates making changes in the use to which the plant is put.

flexibility of buildings: the adaptability of buildings to various uses as needs change, for example, the possibility of turning laboratories into shops, shops into classrooms, or a gymnasium into an auditorium, enlarging or dividing rooms by relocating partitions, etc.

flexibility of taxation: the extent to which a tax system can be changed or modified to meet changed conditions, especially expanding or contracting public income; the opposite of rigidity in taxation.

flexible classification: *see* **classification, flexible.**

flexible daily program: *see* **program, flexible daily.**

flexible grading: *see* **grading, flexible.**

flexible-modular scheduling: *syn.* **scheduling, modular.**

flexible promotion: *see* **promotion, flexible.**

flexible scheduling: *syn.* **scheduling, modular.**

flexible time schedule: *see* **time schedule, flexible.**

flexion: the motion of a part of the body in folding back upon itself, for example, the bending of the arm at the elbow or the bending forward of the spine.

flight, check: in Air Force usage, (1) a flight on which a pilot or another aircrew member or members are checked for proficiency in the performance of their duties; also called *check ride* or *check-out-flight; syn.* **proficiency flight;** (2) a flight made in an aircraft to determine whether the coverage of a given radar installation has altered.

flight instruction: *see* **instruction, flight.**

flight laboratory: *see* **laboratory, flight.**

flight, proficiency: (1) a flight made by a pilot or another aircrew member or members to improve proficiency; (2) *syn.* **flight, check.**

flight school: a school which provides instruction to potential pilots in flying aircraft.

flight, simulated: (1) the flight of a spacecraft or other vehicle as shown by projected artwork depicting environment, movement, controls, etc.; (2) the experience of enduring the conditions of a real flight by means of a *simulator* or *ground trainer.*

flight surgeon: *see* **surgeon, flight.**

flight test: *see* **test, flight.**

flight trainer: *see* **trainer, flight.**

flight training program: *see* **program, flight training.**

flip chart: *see* **chart, flip.**

float: (school admin.) the amount of inventory of a material part or product that is in stores and/or in production between two points in its processing.

float time: *syn.* **time, lead.**

floating debt: *see* **debt, floating.**

floating point arithmetic: *see* **arithmetic, floating point.**

flocking: used with *feltboard*, a backing for cutouts; usually a mass of synthetic flakes or fibers sprayed from a can or gun, which stick to paper and will adhere to felt.

floor: (1) the bottom part of a room or corridor on which one walks or stands; made of various materials, such as wood, linoleum, cork, rubber tile, mastic, asphalt tile, etc.; (2) a base, as from which computations are made.

floor area, classroom: the size of floor in a classroom or in all classrooms of a building or a number of buildings; expressed as the number of square feet of floor surface. *See* **classroom size.**

floor layer: (voc. ed.) a worker who applies blocks, strips, or sheets of shock-absorbing, sound-deadening, or decorative coverings on ground surfaces, walls, and cabinets.

floor machine: an article of equipment operated by an electric motor and having a round block to which various attachments may be fastened for rotary motion in scrubbing, sanding, waxing, or polishing floors.

floors, preservation of: *see* **preservation of floors.**

floriculture education: (1) a program of instruction and on-job experiences offered as a part of vocational education in agriculture at the high school and postsecondary school levels and designed to prepare and upgrade students for employment at the nonprofessional level in floriculture jobs involving the handling, care, arranging, and marketing of floral plants and flowers; (2) a program of instruction offered in colleges and universities to prepare professional workers in floriculture.

flow chart: *see* **chart, flow.**

flow diagram: *see* **diagram, flow.**

fluctuation of attention: variation in perception or concentration in carrying on a uniform task, as indicated by variation in performance.

fluctuation of sampling: variation in a statistical constant when its value is determined from successive samples of the same size chosen by the same method from the same group; irregular variation causing statistical results based on a sample to differ from those based on other samples and those applicable to the universe.

fluency: smoothness and rapidity in reading, uninterrupted by failures in recognition or other faults.

fluency, associational: (1) (psych.) the speed and to some extent the quality of association of ideas, facts, and concepts; (2) (testing) ability to name synonyms for a given word or to generate adjectives to complete a simile.

fluency, expressional: (testing) an ability measured by a test of four-word combinations in which the subject writes four connected words, the first letters of which are given.

fluency, ideational: (testing) ability to name things which belong in a certain class, such as things which will burn, or to list different uses for a common object.

fluency, word: (testing) ability to generate a number of words beginning with the same letter or prefix or rhyming in a certain way.

fluid ability: *see* ability, fluid.

fluid duplicator: *syn.* duplicator, direct-process.

fluid power: (ind. arts) the study of hydraulics and pneumatics, including power conversion, transmission, and utilization in both stationary and mobile installations.

fluorescent chalk: *see* chalk, fluorescent.

fluteolet: *see* recorder (2).

flutter: undesirable movement in the recording of a picture or sound which lessens the fidelity of the record. (In the case of pictures, flutter can occur during exposure of the film in the camera, during the printing process as the image is transferred from one piece of film to another, or in the projector while a print is shown on the screen. Flutter in sound may vary in volume or it may be aperiodic, depending on its origin, which is usually the erratic or aperiodic motion of some mechanical component involved in recording or reproducing the sound.) *See* wow.

flutterboard: a plank used as a support for the body in practicing a swimming kick.

flying classroom: *see* classroom, flying.

flying evaluation board: *see* evaluation board, flying.

flying rings: a piece of gymnastic apparatus consisting of a pair of rings suspended shoulder distance apart.

flying training: *see* training, flying.

flying training, advanced: *see* training, advanced flying.

flying training, basic: *see* training, basic flying.

flying training, graduate: *see* training, advanced flying.

flying training, undergraduate: *see* training, basic flying.

FM radio: *see* modulation, frequency.

focal distance: *syn.* focal length.

focal epilepsy: *see* epilepsy, Jacksonian.

focal length: the distance from the optical center of the lens to the plane in which infinitely distant objects are brought into sharpest focus; more specifically, the distance from the optical center of a lens to the point at which parallel rays passing through the lens will converge at a point. *Syn.* focal distance.

focus: *n.* the point at which converging light intersects after refraction. *See* focal length.

focus: *v.* to adjust a lens so as to achieve a sharp image at the focal plane.

focus, depth of: *syn.* depth of field.

focus of infection: any tissue or organ in the body in which infection is present and serving as a potential source for the spreading of the infection to other parts of the body.

focused interview: *see* interview, focused.

focusing: (couns.) the act or process of establishing a satisfactory psychological relationship between an individual and his environment.

focusing, binocular: *syn.* accommodation, binocular.

fog count: *see* count, fog.

foil: *syn.* distractor.

foiling: *see* fencing.

folding over: (art ed.) in children's drawings, a space concept in which objects are drawn perpendicularly to the base line, even when objects appear to the observer to be drawn upside down; a space concept which places the self at the center of things.

folk dance: *see* dance, folk.

folk education: (1) education relating to the arts and culture of the folk, that is, the masses of the people; (2) vocational and cultural education for young people and adults, directed toward appreciation of commercial and national enterprises.

folk etymology: *see* etymology, folk.

folk high school: *see* high school, folk.

folk music: *see* music, folk.

folk school: (1) the elementary public school in German-speaking countries, the "Volksschule," founded in the sixteenth century to provide a curriculum including both practical studies and Protestant religious instruction taught in vernacular German instead of Latin; now administered by either municipalities or states, the folk school is coeducational, begins with age 6, and offers instruction for 8 or 9 years according to state; at age 10, if the child passes satisfactorily a set examination, he may transfer to the *Gymnasium* or other secondary school; religion is still included in the curriculum, taught as a special subject according to the child's religious preference; (2) a term applied also in Scandinavian countries to the primary school, not to be confused with the folk high school of Denmark and other Scandinavian countries, which is of secondary-collegiate rank; *see* high school, folk.

folk song: *see* song, folk.

folk tale: *see* tale, folk.

folklore: (1) the surviving beliefs, customs, myths, and traditions passed on and perpetuated by a people; (2) a branch of either comparative sociology or cultural anthropology that studies the lives and customs of peoples as revealed in their surviving beliefs, customs, myths, and traditions.

folkways: standardized patterns of behavior common to the members of a society and having some degree of traditional sanction for their continued usage.

follow-through on observation: *see* observation, follow-through on.

Follow Through program: *see* program, Follow Through.

Follow Through Project: *see* Project Head Start.

follow-up: (1) the process by which information as to the present status in an area of concern to the guidance or personnel services of an educational institution is obtained from a student or former student; (2) (bus. ed.) an organized plan for ascertaining the employment and educational status of graduates from vocational programs in order to establish the relationship between employment and the vocational training received.

follow-up activities: *see* activities, follow-up.

follow-up, purchase: *see* purchase follow-up.

follow-up, questionnaire: *see* questionnaire follow-up.

follow-up record, guidance: *see* record, guidance follow-up.

follow-up study: *see* study, follow-up.

followership: the role of an individual as a follower in a group.

food habit: *see* habit, food.

food management, production, and services program: *see* program, food management, production, and services.

food service: an institutional program providing for the control and supervision of food planning and preparation; typically this program is noncommercial and provides for frequent health inspections and the employment of trained dietitians. *See* program, Federal school lunch.

food service, Federal and state school: *see* school food service, Federal and state.

food service management: *see* management, food service.

foods instruction: *see* instruction, foods.

foods laboratory: *see* laboratory, foods.

foot mechanics: (1) the posture or alignment of the bones of the foot; (2) the functioning of the feet in locomotion.

foot-rule correlation: *syn.* **Spearman's foot-rule method of gains.**

foot-rule formula: *see* **Spearman's foot-rule method of gains.**

foot-rule method: *syn.* **Spearman's foot-rule method of gains.**

foot travel: a term sometimes applied to orientation and mobility of the blind, aided by the use of the long cane or touch technique and/or by dog guides.

foot writing: *see* **writing, foot.**

footage, film: *see* **film footage.**

football: a competitive contact team sport in which 6, 8, or 11 persons play on a field 360-by-160-feet or smaller, depending on the number of players on a team; various types of this sport are soccer, rugby, tackle football, and touch football.

footcandle: the illumination falling on a spherical surface one foot distant from a point light source of one standard candle intensity; also expressed as the illumination on a surface one foot square when the uniformly distributed luminous flux has a value of one lumen.

footcandle meter: an instrument that measures light in terms of footcandle power, used frequently in measuring the illumination of schoolrooms.

footedness: preference for either the right or the left foot in tasks performed with one foot, such as kicking a ball or operating a treadle, or in the more difficult or skilled parts of tasks requiring the use of both feet. *See* **laterality.**

forbidden code: *see* **code, forbidden.**

forced-choice item: *see* **item, forced-choice.**

forced-choice rating: *see* **rating, forced-choice.**

forced-choice rating scale: *see* **rating scale, forced-choice.**

forced-choice technique: *see* **item, forced-choice.**

forced-choice test: *see* **test, forced-choice.**

forced competition: *see* **competition, forced.**

forced frame: *see* **frame, forced.**

forces, aggressor: *see* **aggressor forces.**

forces, field: *see* **field forces.**

forcing: the use by stutterers of excessive muscular tension in speaking; the attempt literally to force a word out by muscular exertion.

forcing method: (read.) a method of teaching reading in which all children are forced to learn to read regardless of their readiness to learn (Anderson and Dearborn).

fore-exercise: a preliminary or trial exercise intended to acquaint the testee with the correct procedure to be followed in the actual test. *Syn.* **pretest** (1); **test, practice** (1); **test, preliminary** (1).

fore-question: a question introduced before an illustration, example, or unit of work to guide attention in reading, observation, or study.

forearm movement: a writing movement made by the forearm with the elbow joint as the pivot.

forecast: an estimate of a future trend, event, or magnitude, on the basis of previous experience. *Syn.* **prediction.**

forecast, population: a method of forecasting school enrollment by means of a forecast of total population; useful as a test of the reasonableness of other projections.

forecasting efficiency: *see* **index of forecasting efficiency.**

foreign acquisition program, Library of Congress: *see* **program, Library of Congress foreign acquisition.**

foreign broadcast: *see* **broadcast, foreign.**

foreign dialect: *see* **dialect, foreign.**

foreign language arts: *see* **language arts, foreign.**

foreign language house: at some colleges and universities, a house or other quarters maintained by a foreign language department where students of the language may meet regularly to converse in the language during meals and free time with their instructors and other native speakers of the language; the interior decor usually conveys the atmosphere of the country or countries where the language is spoken; various programs offer opportunities for the students to experience the culture of the country.

foreign language test, graduate school: *see* **test, graduate school foreign language.**

foreign-language workshop: *see* **workshop, foreign-language.**

foreign news: (journ.) a study, generally at college level, consisting of an analysis of the methods of gathering the news of other countries for the American press and transmitting it in spite of governmental and technical problems of communication.

foreign service school: a school for the training of consular and other foreign service employees.

foreign student: *see* **student, foreign.**

foreign-student adviser: *see* **adviser, foreign-student.**

foreman: a man who supervises work and workers on the job.

foreman, instructor: *see* **instructor foreman.**

foreman training: *syn.* **training, foremanship.**

foremanship training: *see* **training, foremanship.**

forensic club: *see* **club, forensic.**

forest, school: a wooded area available to the school for the laboratory study of the natural life it maintains or is capable of maintaining. *See* **nature trail.**

forestry education: (1) a program of instruction and on-job experiences offered as a part of vocational education in agriculture at the high school and postsecondary school levels and designed to prepare and upgrade students for employment at the nonprofessional level in forestry production and in wood products and wood utilization businesses; (2) a program of instruction offered in colleges and universities to prepare professional foresters.

forewoman: a woman who supervises work and workers on the job.

forfeiture of salary: the withholding or denial, for established violation of contract, of a portion of contractual payment that was to have been made for services rendered.

forgetting, curve of: *see* **curve of forgetting.**

form: (1) the shape, contour, or configuration of an object, whether two- or three-dimensional, by which it can be recognized or distinguished, exclusive of consideration of its color or substance; in two dimensions, includes surfaces, areas, shapes, silhouettes, and planes; in three dimensions includes volume, mass, and shape; (2) (math.) a polynomial function of two or more variables in which all terms are of the same degree; (3) (math.) a symbolic expression that typifies the representation of a mathematical entity or structure; (4) a relatively invariable, set pattern for the execution of a work of art, such as the sonnet form, the rondo, the triolet, the sonata, and the round; *see* **art form;** (5) the study of plan or design in musical compositions; often linked with analysis as a subject of instruction; *see* **analysis** (9); (6) such aspects of language study as the spacing and placing of the parts of a letter, report, or composition on paper and the accepted procedure in making introductions; (7) (lang.) such aspects of composition as balance, contrast, symmetry, and the relation of the parts to the whole; (8) (philos.) that characteristic of a thing identical with its essence, which distinguishes it from the substance that constitutes it; that which gives shape and appearance; (Plato) a transcendent, eternal idea (disputed by some scholars); (9) (of a test) an edition or version; usually one of several alternate forms designated by letter, date, or numerals and/or a word signifying its level (for example, Adult Form B); form designations may be used to indicate whether scored by hand or machine.

form adaptation: *see* **adaptation, form.**

form, art: *see* **art form.**

form, autoplastic experience of: *see* **experience of form, autoplastic.**

form board: the general term for a number of devices used in administering standardized performance tests, for example, a board with holes arranged in a geometrical pattern, into which the testee is required to fit pegs.

form-board test: *see* **test, form-board.**

form, brief: *see* **brief form.**

form class word: *see* **word, form class.**

form, clearance: *syn.* **release form.**

form concept: *see* schema.

form, derivative: *see* derivative form.

form discrimination: *see* discrimination, form.

form distribution chart: *see* chart, form distribution.

form-experimental stage: (art ed.) the second stage in the young child's creative development, following the manipulative stage and preceding the early expressive stage; naming of what is painted does not yet occur, but purpose seems discernible as far as organizing forms is concerned, so that normally there is ability to balance and unify masses of color. *See* early expressive stage; manipulative stage (2).

form flow diagram: *see* diagram, form flow.

form, individual record: *see* record form, individual.

form, inflected: *see* inflected form.

form letter: *see* letter, form.

form, parent-consent: *see* parent-consent form.

form procedure chart: *see* chart, form procedure.

form, release: *see* release form.

formal approach: (lang.) a procedure in teaching language usage that relies primarily on rules, technical terminology, mechanized drill, and deductive methods.

formal arithmetic: *see* arithmetic, formal.

formal cause: *see* cause, formal.

formal course: *see* course, formal.

formal discipline: *syn.* discipline, mental.

formal dramatics: *see* dramatics, formal.

formal drill: *see* drill, formal.

formal education: (1) any training or education that is conventional, given in an orderly, logical, planned, and systematic manner; thus, formal education is said to end with school attendance; (2) in a derogatory sense, any educational program that is confined to the experiences of the students within the classroom itself, failing to make use of the student's incidental and varied experiences outside the classroom.

formal examination: *see* examination, formal.

formal exercise: *see* exercise, formal.

formal geometry: *see* geometry, formal.

formal grammar: *see* grammar, formal.

formal gymnastics: *see* gymnastics, formal.

formal handwriting drill: *see* drill, formal handwriting.

formal implication: *see* implication.

formal intelligibility: *syn.* intelligibility, structural.

formal logic: *see* logic, formal.

formal mathematics: *see* mathematics, formal.

formal operations stage of development: *see* stage of development, formal operations.

formal organization: *see* organization, formal.

formal plan of instruction: in general, any method of teaching done in accordance with prescribed rules, especially those relating to the manner in which learning material is organized and presented; often used to signify a method of instruction utilizing the *five formal steps* of Herbart.

formal prompt: *see* prompt, formal.

formal proof: *see* proof, formal.

formal reading inventory: *see* inventory, formal reading.

formal recitation: *syn.* recitation, formalized.

formal steps: *see* Herbartian method.

formal study: *see* study, formal.

formal subject: *see* subject, formal.

formal system: (math.) *syn.* deductive system.

formal training: *see* training, formal.

formal viewpoint: (art ed.) that viewpoint in which content is not given importance and in which nonaesthetic qualities are excluded; also, art values are thought of here as removed from the values of common living and as beyond the grasp of ordinary man. *Contr. w.* genetic viewpoint (3).

formalism: educational practice determined more by evident factors, such as institutions, class timetables, distinct subject-matter areas, rigid discipline, and emphasis on grades or marks, than by less tangible factors, such as objectives, motivation, sensitivity to the learner, and relation to the social process; a tradition that occasioned the rise of *progressive education* as a revolt.

formalized recitation: *see* recitation, formalized.

formation, concept: *see* concept formation.

formative period: a period (sometimes hypothetical) in early growth during which the course of development or behavior is most susceptible to modification through environmental influences and the main lines or limits of subsequent growth, development, or learning are determined.

forming products: the third stage in the development of a unit of teaching in art, the preceding stages being *orientation* and *design*.

forms, alternate: *syn.* equivalent forms.

forms, comparable: *syn.* equivalent forms.

forms, duplicate: *syn.* equivalent forms.

forms, equivalent: *see* equivalent forms.

forms, parallel: *syn.* equivalent forms.

forms, similar: *syn.* equivalent forms.

formula: a general answer, rule, or principle usually written in symbols, as, for example, the formula for computing the area of a circle, $A = \pi R^2$.

formula, algebraic: an equation which identifies the interrelationship of two or more variables and which can be written using only the notation of elementary algebra, as, for example, $d = rt$.

formula, assign-study-recite: *see* assign-study-recite formula.

formula, Brown-Spearman: *syn.* Spearman-Brown prophecy formula.

formula, Brown's: *syn.* Spearman-Brown prophecy formula.

formula, correction-for-chance: *see* correction-for-chance formula.

formula, Dale-Chall readability: *see* readability formula, Dale-Chall.

formula, derivation of *a*: *see* derivation of *a* formula.

formula, Devereaux readability: *see* readability formula, Devereaux.

formula, difference: (1) any formula for computing the Pearson product-moment correlation by the use of differences rather than products of the paired observations; (2) any formula that is a function of the differences between corresponding scores in two variables; (3) any formula based on finite differences.

formula, Douglass: *see* Douglass formula for teaching load.

formula, empirical: a formula which expresses the observed results of experimentation.

formula, Flesch readability: *see* readability formula, Flesch.

formula, Flesch reading ease: a style of newspaper or periodical writing, popularized during the 1940s in books by Rudolph Flesch and imitators, to make reading easier for the less educated; usually involved short words, short sentences, and personal, pictorial, or emotional appeals.

formula, fundamental: (1) a formula pertinent to the foundation of the science in question; (2) a formula that serves as the basis of a system.

formula, Gompertz: a formula used in the measurement of growth or in the study of growth data ($Y = Ki^{rt}$, where Y = ordinate, K = maximum growth, i = initial growth, r = rate of growth, and t = time).

formula, grading: (read.) *syn.* formula, readability.

formula, Gray-Leary readability: *see* readability formula, Gray-Leary.

formula, Lewerenz readability: *see* readability formula, Lewerenz.

formula, Lorge readability: *see* readability formula, Lorge.

formula, open-end: *see* open-end formula.

formula, product: any method of calculating the Pearson product-moment correlation which makes use of product moments. *Contr. w.* formula, difference; formula, sum.

formula, prophecy: *syn.* **Spearman-Brown prophecy formula.**

formula, readability: *see* **readability formula.**

formula, Richards's: *see* **Richards's formula.**

formula, rule-of-five: a method of estimating the grade level at which a pupil has the intellectual capacity to function by subtracting 5 from the mental age of the pupil ($GC = MA - 5$). *See* **age, mental.**

formula, S-O-R: an expansion of the simpler S-R formula, meaning "stimulus-organism-response," the three elements of any act of animal or human behavior, which recognizes that the nature of the *organism*, especially its past experiences, attitudes, etc., act to modify or mediate the perception of the stimulus and the precise nature of the response, either of which may be covert or overt; in contrast to the S-R formula, the S-O-R formula recognizes the existence of individual differences, for whatever reason they may exist. *See* **formula, S-R.**

formula, S-R: the basic formula (stimulus-response) used to represent the two major elements in any simple or complex act of animal or human behavior, the "S" designating the stimulus, or cause of action, and the "R" designating the response, either of which may be covert or overt. *See* **formula, S-O-R.**

formula, scoring: *see* **scoring formula.**

formula, Spearman-Brown prophecy: *see* **Spearman-Brown prophecy formula.**

formula, sum: any method of computing the Pearson product-moment correlation from the sums, rather than the products, of the paired observations. *Contr. w.* **formula, difference; formula, product.**

formula translation: *see* **FORTRAN.**

formula, Washburne-Vogel readability: *see* **readability formula, Washburne-Vogel.**

formula, Yoakam readability: *see* **readability formula, Yoakam.**

formulas, Kuder-Richardson: *see* **Kuder-Richardson formulas.**

formulation: the organization of all the pertinent components of any particular project into a clear and concise pattern.

FORTRAN: an automatic symbolic coding language used in programming computational applications; an acronym formed from FORmula TRANslator. *See* **COBOL.**

fortuitous error: *syn.* **error, random.**

forum: a form of adult education utilizing a lecture or lectures and providing an opportunity for audience participation and discussion. *See* **panel** (1).

forum, neighborhood: a discussion group usually confined to a relatively local clientele.

forum, open: an organized meeting for the purpose of platform presentation of controversial issues, followed by informal debate and discussion in which all may participate.

forum, radio-television: a broadcast adapted to the discussion of current problems, in which speakers present their viewpoints and members of the studio audience then participate by asking questions, raising objections, etc.

forum, supervisory: an assembly of members of an educational organization where interaction may take place among them for the purpose of maintaining, enhancing, or changing the goals of the organization.

forum, symposium: a symposium, followed by audience participation in free discussion, presided over by a chairman.

forward branching: *see* **branching, forward.**

forward slant: writing that has a slope of more than 90 degrees with the preceding line of writing, with the up and down strokes extending to the right of the vertical above the line and to the left of the vertical below the line.

FOSDIC: an acronym formed from Film Optical Sensing Device for Input to Computers; an input method of photoelectrically reading microfilms of special documents to produce a magnetic tape; documents are business forms on which information has been coded as dark marks in certain positions; the method was developed by the United States Census Bureau to bypass the manual preparation both of punched cards and of magnetic tape.

foster child: *see* **child, foster.**

foster father: a man carrying out the paternal role with respect to a child who is not his own offspring.

foster home: a specially selected home, other than his own, in which a child may be placed for rearing, with or without adoption.

foster-home placement: the assignment of children to private homes not those of their natural parents.

foster mother: a woman carrying out the maternal role with respect to a child that is not her own offspring.

foster parent: a person who legally and officially assumes the responsibility of rearing a child and who takes the place of the child's natural parents.

foundation: the base structure upon which the superstructure of a building is erected.

foundation adviser: *see* **adviser, foundation.**

foundation, ecclesiastical: any of a number of incorporated charitable funds of an established church.

foundation, educational: a philanthropic foundation devoted to an educational purpose. *See* **foundation, philanthropic.**

foundation grant: *see* **grant, foundation.**

foundation, philanthropic: a legally chartered, eleemosynary fund, administered by a separate and independent board of control and of which the income or principal (or both) is dedicated to promoting the well-being of mankind; includes *educational foundations.*

foundation program: *see* **program, foundation.**

foundation school, Jewish: a Jewish day school starting with nursery education and continuing through the second or third grade of the elementary school. *See* **bet ha-yeled.**

foundation, semidetached: a foundation which is an integral part of some institution such as a college or hospital but of which the trustees, while connected with and subordinate to the parent institution, exercise some measure of autonomy in administering the foundation; the income and/or principal of the foundation is used by or through the institution with which it is affiliated; adopted as a legal device by many universities for pooling the income from the research activities of professors for use in further research.

foundations, financial: *see* **financial foundations.**

foundations of education: that part of the teacher-education curriculum which deals deliberately with a study of the social forces, institutions, and human relations which undergird formal education; writings in such disciplines as history, economics, sociology, psychology, political science, anthropology, geography, and philosophy serve as the basis for study and discussion. (Implicit in the focus on social, historical, philosophical, and psychological foundations of education is the assumption that the intellectual disciplines do not become meaningfully related to general education unless and until deliberate attention and scholarship are directed to the problem.) *See* **social foundations of education.**

foundations of education, social: *see* **social foundations of education.**

foundling: an infant found after its unknown parents have abandoned it.

four causes: *see* **causes, four.**

Four Freedoms: freedom of expression, freedom of religion, freedom from want, and freedom from fear; the realization of these freedoms everywhere was declared an objective of United States foreign policy by President Franklin D. Roosevelt in his message to Congress in 1941.

Four-H Club: the name, coined from the words "head," "heart," "hand," and "health," for the groups of rural boys and girls organized under the cooperative extension service in agriculture and home economics for improvement in farm and home practices and development of leadership.

Four-H Club agent: *see* **extension worker, county.**

Four-H Club project: *see* **project, Four-H Club.**

four-phase drill: *see* **drill, four-phase.**

four-quarter plan: *see* **quarter system.**

four-year college: *see* **college, four-year.**

four-year high school: *see* **high school, four-year.**

four-year junior college: *see* **junior college, four-year.**

four-year reorganized high school: *see* **reorganized high school, four-year.**

four-year teachers college: *see* **teachers college, four-year.**

fourfold table: *see* **table, fourfold.**

fourth classman: a cadet who is in his first year at a service academy; a freshman.

Fowler phenomenon: *syn.* **recruitment factor.**

foyer: a waiting place, usually at the entrance or side of an auditorium; a lobby. *See* **lobby.**

fractional anticipatory goal response: *see* **response, fractional anticipatory goal.**

fractional special class: *see* **class, fractional special.**

fracture: the breaking of a bone.

frame: *n.* (1) in programmed learning, each separate presentation of a small basic unit of material; *see* **item;** (2) in machine teaching terminology, each complete stimulus-response sequence of a pattern drill; (3) one picture in a series comprising a motion picture or filmstrip; *see* **filmstrip, double-frame; filmstrip, single-frame;** (4) a device used in teaching the structure of language to show membership of a word in a grammatical class; takes the form of a blank to be filled in; for example, a noun would be any word or group of words able to fit in the frame "The (—) is/are very large."

frame: *v.* to adjust the relative position of the aperture and the film in a motion-picture projector or camera or a filmstrip projector so that the top and bottom edges of each frame will coincide with the top and bottom edges of the aperture.

frame building: *see* **building, frame.**

frame, criterion: *see* **frame, terminal.**

frame, forced: in programmed instruction, a stimulus frame presented to the student forcing him to respond correctly because of the obvious nature of the answer.

frame of reference: (math.) (1) a figure consisting of a line or lines used as axes and a point or points of reference; (2) (philos.) a system of basic principles, concepts, and values, carefully organized and critically examined, in accordance with which an individual or group formulates hypotheses and collects and interprets data, plans, and acts; *see* **Weltanschauung.**

frame of reference, external: emphasis on objective reality in attempting to understand another individual by viewing him without empathy, as an object. *Comp. w.* **frame of reference, internal.**

frame of reference, internal: all the realm of experience available to the awareness of the individual at a given moment; includes the full range of sensations, perceptions, meanings, and memories available to consciousness. *Comp. w.* **frame of reference, external.**

frame sentence: *see* **sentence, frame.**

frame, terminal: in programmed materials, a frame at the end of a sequence of teaching frames which requires the student to perform free of any prompts, thus providing practice of what has been learned and simultaneously testing the effectiveness of the sequence. *Syn.* **criterion frame; criterion step.**

framer: a button, lever, or knob that controls the centering of the frame of film in the aperture of a motion-picture or filmstrip projector.

frames per second: the number of frames of motion-picture film that passes the film aperture per second in a motion-picture camera or projector, according to the speed at which the camera or projector is set to run.

framework, conceptual: *see* **conceptual framework.**

frameworks of society: a term used as a synonym for *social institutions.*

framing words: (read.) identifying a group of words by placing one hand or finger at each end of the group.

franchise tax: *see* **tax, franchise.**

Franciscan education: a type of teaching provided by the Franciscan Order, founded by St. Francis about 1212; the teaching was similar to that of the Dominican Order except that it was directed more to preaching, missions, and public service and was more democratic.

fraternal twins: *syn.* **twins, dizygotic.**

fraternity: a group of male students associated through common interests, either social or professional; may or may not include common living quarters; designated usually by means of Greek initial letters and with secret ritual; usually affiliated with other chapters on a national basis. *See* **sorority.**

fraternity, college: an essentially exclusive, self-perpetuating group, established in colleges and universities, that selects its members from an undergraduate school or department and that organizes the group life of its members as a factor contributing to their educational program, with especial emphasis on personal development and social competency. *Syn.* **social fraternity;** *see* **fraternity.**

fraternity, educational: (1) the members of the teaching profession, considered collectively; (2) a fraternity primarily interested in advancing the cause of education.

fraternity, honor: *syn.* **honor society.**

fraternity, honorary: a fraternity for which students qualify by meeting certain scholastic, and sometimes social, standards; usually restricted to students (men or women or both) in the professional school of a university.

fraternity house: a building containing sleeping and living rooms, devoted to use as living quarters for men students belonging to a particular social fraternity.

fraternity, professional: a self-perpetuating, specialized fraternity that limits its student membership to a specific field of professional education, maintains essentially exclusive membership in that field, and organizes its group life specifically to promote professional competency and achievement within its field; established in colleges and universities offering courses leading to recognized degrees in the given field, such as dentistry, education, or law.

fraternity, recognition: *syn.* **recognition society.**

fraternity, social: *syn.* **fraternity, college.**

traudulent school: a nonaccredited school making unsupported and exaggerated claims as to its educational program and offering certificates and degrees to individuals without requiring class work or the usual accomplishments to which the certificate or degree is presumed to certify.

free academy: *see* **academy, free.**

free association: *see* **association, free.**

free-association test: *see* **test, free-association.**

free composition: *see* **composition, free.**

free conference: *see* **conference, free.**

free-creative activity: *see* **activity, free-creative.**

free education: education provided at public expense, without-charges for tuition to the recipient or his parents.

free elective: *see* **elective, free.**

free-expression method: (art ed.) that practice in which choice of subject, materials, and ways of using materials is entirely in the hands of the child and the emphasis shifts from product to process. *Contr. w.* **directing method; eclectic method.**

free-field audiometry: *see* **audiometry, free-field.**

free-field hearing testing: *see* **testing, free-field hearing.**

free-floating anxiety: *see* **anxiety, free-floating.**

free imagery: *see* **imagery, free.**

free period: *see* **period, free.**

free play: *see* **play, free.**

free reading: *see* **reading, free.**

free-reading period: *see* **period, free-reading.**

free-response drill: *syn.* **drill, rejoinder.**

free-response test: *see* **test, free-response.**

free retirement system: *see* **retirement system, free.**

free school: (1) as commonly used, any school that does not require the individual to pay tuition, for example, any school supported by public taxation; (2) in colonial America, a philanthropically supported school that was neither a pauper school nor a tuition-supported school; (3) in the early national period, a school provided by philanthropic individuals organized as a free school society. (The *Free School Society* of New York City, organized in 1805 by DeWitt Clinton, is a notable example.)

Free School Society: a society incorporated in the state of New York in 1805 at the request of private persons to provide education for poor children not provided for by any religious society. (The society opened its first school in 1806 and was granted aid by both state and city.)

free textbook: *see* **textbook, free.**

free university: *see* **university, free.**

free will, doctrine of: (1) the theory that human action and volition are not compelled by an external agency or completely determined by habit or past conditioning; (2) the theory that denies universal immanent causation; (3) the theory which holds that man is free to choose to act in accordance with one among several alternatives open to him, in modern terms more likely called *freedom of choice* or *moral freedom.*

freedmen education: the opportunities for education offered to freed black persons before, during, and immediately after the Civil War; at first offered solely by benevolent freedmen aid societies, then from 1865 to 1872 with Federal government aid, and after 1872 again by benevolent societies.

freedom: (1) *syn.* **liberty;** (2) independence; self-sufficiency; (3) (philos.) the autonomy or self-determination of rational beings, meaning the ability of man to think, will, and act at least partially in terms of reasonable ideals and not to be completely forced to each thought or action by biological mechanisms and environmental stimuli.

freedom, academic: the opportunity for the teacher to teach, and for the teacher and the student to study, without coercion, censorship, or other forms of restrictive interference. *See* **freedom, intellectual.**

freedom, degree of: *see* **degree of freedom.**

freedom, ethical: freedom of the individual to make choices between alternative values and principles of right and wrong.

freedom, intellectual: the absence of restraint or of arbitrary limitations on the exercise of the intellectual capacities; the exercise of unfettered and unrestricted thought.

freedom, moral: *see* **free will, doctrine of.**

freedom of choice: *see* **free will, doctrine of.**

freedom of contract: the right of a worker to work under whatever conditions and for whatever wages he wishes to accept.

freedom of inquiry: exemption from interference by authorities or other power in the search for and the sharing of knowledge in any field.

freedom of the press: (1) the right of the press to publish whatever its editors consider proper, without official restraint prior to publication; (2) the right of the press to publish whatever its editors consider proper without fear of reprisals from advertisers, pressure groups, or officials.

freedom school: a school or class outside the regular school system in which black or other minority-group children are taught about their cultural heritage; organized by minority groups in the inner city on occasions when strikes or other problems prevent their children from attending the public school.

freehand drawing: *see* **drawing, freehand.**

frenum (frē′nəm): (properly, *frenum linguae*) a convective fold of mucous membrane that ties the front part of the tongue to the floor of the mouth, limiting tongue movements. (Extreme limitation in movement results in tongue-tie.) *See* **tongue-tie.**

frequency: (1) the number of occurrences in a unit of time; (2) the number of occurrences of any given value or set of values; a test score of 78 is said to have a frequency of 6 when that score is earned by 6 of the students in the group tested; (3) pitch of a sound (or an electronic signal) measured in cycles per second.

frequency, cell: the number of observations or measures in one of the cells of a double-entry table.

frequency chart: *syn.* **graph, frequency.**

frequency, class: *syn.* **class size** (2).

frequency coefficient: *syn.* **frequency, relative.**

frequency count: (lang.) a tabulation of the relative frequency or use of individual vocables or idioms with a view to presenting and teaching the most widely used words or expressions in a foreign language.

frequency, cumulative: an entry in a column or row consisting of the frequencies for all scores or class intervals up to and including the one corresponding to the entry; when the addition of frequencies starts at the upper end (rather than the lower end, as is more common) of the frequency distribution, the cumulative frequency is the total number of frequencies down to and including the frequency for the corresponding entry; useful in the computation of percentile ranks.

frequency curve: *see* **curve, frequency.**

frequency, diagonal row: the sum of frequencies of all cells in a designated diagonal row of a two-way table; used, rarely, in the computation of a correlation coefficient from a scatter diagram.

frequency diagram: *syn.* **graph, frequency.**

frequency discrimination: *see* **discrimination, frequency.**

frequency distribution: *see* **distribution, frequency.**

frequency distribution, grouped: a frequency distribution in which different successive scores are grouped into classes.

frequency, fixation: the number of times the eye fixes on a line of writing or print in reading; usually three to five fixations per line in the case of good adult readers.

frequency function: *see* **function, frequency.**

frequency graph: *see* **graph, frequency.**

frequency histogram: *syn.* **histogram.**

frequency, law of: *syn.* **law of disuse.**

frequency list: an arrangement of words or expressions showing the number of times they occur in a given number of running words and often the number of different types of representative subject matter in which they are used; the arrangement may be alphabetical or in ascending or descending order of frequency of occurrence.

frequency, marginal: the sum of the frequencies in one of the columns or in one of the rows of a double-entry table; marginal frequencies are customarily at the foot of the respective columns and at the right of the respective rows.

frequency modulation: *see* **modulation, frequency.**

frequency, percentage: the frequency of a class in a frequency distribution, expressed as a percentage of the total frequency; 100 times the relative frequency; sometimes called *percentage weight.*

frequency polygon: *see* **polygon, frequency.**

frequency, radio: part of the electromagnetic spectrum where bands of frequencies, or channels, are allocated for radio and television use.

frequency range: *see* **range, frequency.**

frequency rating: (lang.) a statistical expression, usually in the form of a ratio, that indicates the proportionate number of times a given factor occurs in a representative sample of running words.

frequency ratio: (lang.) a statistical expression showing the proportionate frequency of a given term in specified material as compared with the frequency shown in some standard tabulation.

frequency-recency theory of fixation: *see* **law of disuse; law of recency.**

frequency rectangle: a rectangle used to represent the frequencies of a given class of data, having a base proportional to the width of the class interval and an area proportional to the frequency; the graph formed by placing all the frequency rectangles in order is a *histogram*.

frequency, regression: the number of times the eye regresses in a line of printed matter or in a unit of a certain size. *See* **regression** (3) and (4); *contr. w.* **frequency, fixation.**

frequency, relative: the frequency of a given score or class interval in a frequency distribution expressed as a proportion of the total frequency. *Syn.* **frequency coefficient.**

frequency response: *see* **response, frequency.**

frequency-response range: *see* **range, frequency-response.**

frequency study: *see* **study, frequency.**

frequency surface: (1) the surface formed if the frequencies of the pairs of values in a scatter diagram are plotted in the third dimension and then connected; *syn.* **correlation surface;** (2) the area under any given probability curve, usually the normal probability curve.

frequency table: *see* **table, frequency.**

frequency, threshold: *see* **threshold frequency.**

frequency total: the number of observations or measures in the sample; the sum of all the individual frequencies; represented by N or *number*.

frequency, ultrahigh (UHF): wavelengths reserved for commercial and educational television which lie in the wave bands of 300 to 3,000 megacycles; UHF includes channels 14 to 83, and is less powerful than very high frequency.

frequency, variate: *syn.* **class size** (2).

frequency, very high (VHF): wavelengths reserved for commercial and educational television which lie in the wave bands of 30 to 300 megacycles; VHF includes channels 2 to 13 and is more powerful than ultrahigh frequency.

frequency, video: the range obtained from scanning by a TV camera tube, with the highest value restricted to 4 megacycles; does not include provision for sound or audio components.

frequency word list: *see* **word list, frequency.**

fresco: painting on freshly applied moist lime plaster with pigments suspended in a water vehicle; a medium especially prominent during the Middle Ages and the Renaissance.

fresh-air room: a classroom in which the windows are kept open in all but the most inclement weather and in which instruction is provided for tuberculous, anemic, frail, undernourished, or other groups of physically handicapped children; this type of health therapy is no longer commonly used, being replaced by classes for crippled children only.

freshman: a student in the first year of work of a bachelor's degree program normally requiring 4 years for completion.

freshman, college: a student regularly enrolled in the first year of a university or college.

freshman orientation: *see* **freshman week.**

freshman week: a week, usually the one preceding the date for regular registration, which is set aside for the introduction and orientation of freshman students to the college environment; activities include convocations, testing, physical examination, registration, and social events.

Freudianism: Freud's theory of psychoanalysis, based upon a biologic, genetic approach to personality and characterized by a division of mental life into classificatory *id, ego,* and *superego* functions.

friar: in the Roman Catholic Church, a member of the mendicant orders; one whose ministerial tasks, such as preaching in foreign missions, require him to spend time away from the undisturbed seclusion of the religious house.

friar orders: Roman Catholic mendicant orders founded during the thirteenth century whose aims were to save souls, strengthen the Church, and control education; chief among them are the Franciscans and Dominicans. *See* **order, religious.**

friend: (1) a person for whom one has affectionate feelings and from whom one receives appreciation and interested support; (2) an intimate who seeks one's welfare; (3) one who, motivated through personal appreciation of another, attempts to further and protect the latter's welfare.

friendly suit: *see* **suit, friendly.**

friendship: a relation of reciprocal attachment and mutually protecting interest between two or more persons.

frieze: a decorated horizontal band in architecture which may be carved or painted or both.

frigidity: decrease or absence of sexual desire; sexual indifference.

fringe benefit: *see* **benefit, fringe.**

fringer (frin′jər): a person who is neither genuinely accepted nor clearly rejected in a social group.

Froebelian (frö·bel′i·ən) **gifts:** play materials for a kindergarten, formerly considered essential, recommended by Friedrich Froebel (1782–1852), and consisting of six sets arranged in ascending order of complexity, beginning with colored worsted balls and progressing through such objects as cubes, squares, and blocks; intended to furnish a series of exercises in forms of utility, artistic forms, geometric forms, and lessons in number for the first period of infant school life.

Froebelian (frö·bel′i·ən) **occupations:** organized series of handwork activities for applying the principle suggested by Froebel's gifts, and composed of various manipulative activities, such as perforating, sewing, drawing, intertwining, weaving, folding, cutting, and clay modeling.

Froebelian kindergarten: *see* **kindergarten, Froebelian.**

Froebel's (frö′bəls) **games:** games originated by Froebel, for developing the limbs and senses of the child and for guiding and stimulating his awakening mind.

front view, mixture of profile and: *see* **profile and front view, mixture of.**

frontality: in sculpture, the characteristic of facing directly forward; a principle found in Egyptian, archaic Greek, and other early stages of culture.

frottage (fro·täzh′): a technique of achieving an image or textural surface by rubbing with a crayon, pencil, or other drawing tool on paper placed over various textured surfaces; a technique employed especially by the surrealist Max Ernst in an attempt to evolve subconscious imagery.

frustration: emotional tension resulting from the blocking of a desire or need or attempted mode of reaction.

frustration-aggression hypothesis, Yale: the view that an interruption of a series of acts leading toward a satisfying goal may result in the arousal of aggressive behavior.

frustration reading level: *see* **reading level, frustration.**

frustration threshold: the point at which an individual feels or shows frustration over an inability to achieve an objective.

frustration tolerance: the nature, degree, and duration of stress that an individual can tolerate without undergoing serious personality decompensation.

frustration, tolerance for: the ability to withstand egothreatening aspects generated when the individual is prevented from reaching a goal.

fugue (fūg): (1) (psych.) a state in which the subject forgets his identity and flees from an environment to which he cannot adjust, orientation usually being regained after varying periods of time; (2) (mus.) a composition of contrapuntal nature, based on a short theme which is restated, "imitated," by other voices in close succession, and repeated throughout the piece; *see* **counterpoint.**

fuguing tunes: vigorous, spirited early American hymns having a contrapuntal imitative section somewhat suggestive of a fugal exposition; originally spelled "fuging" tunes. *See* **counterpoint.**

Fulbright Exchange Program: *see* **Exchange Program, Fulbright.**

Fulbright scholar: *see* **Exchange Program, Fulbright.**

full arm movement: a type of movement used in handwriting in which the whole arm moves as a lever, the shoulder joint being used as a pivot.

full day of attendance: *see* **attendance, full day of.**

full professor: *see* **professor.**

full-time equivalency: the amount of time spent or required in a less than full-time activity divided by the amount of time normally spent or required in a corresponding full-time activity during the regular school term; usually expressed as a decimal fraction to the nearest tenth.

full-time equivalency of assignment: *see* **assignment, full-time equivalency of.**

full-time National Guard training: *see* **training, full-time National Guard.**

full-time pupil: *see* **pupil, full-time.**

full-time student equivalent: (1) one student carrying a full, normal academic load; (2) the amount of service rendered by an institution expressed in terms of the number of students carrying a full, normal academic load, plus the appropriate fraction for each student carrying less than a full load.

full-time student teaching: *see* **student teaching, all-day.**

full-time substitute teacher: *see* **substitute teacher, full-time.**

full-time teacher: a teacher who devotes the entire school day to teaching or supervision, or both.

full-track head: *see* **head, full-track.**

full-track tape: *see* **tape, full-track.**

full-tuition pupil: *see* **pupil, full-tuition.**

function: *n.* (1) a part of a process, action, or operation that belongs to or is charged to a particular thing, person, or group of persons in order that the overall process, action, or operation may be accomplished as planned; (2) the appropriate or assigned duties, responsibilities, missions, or tasks of an individual, office, or organization; (3) (math.) given two sets *A* and *B*, a function from *A* to *B* is a correspondence that assigns to each member of set *A* exactly one member of *B*; set *A* is called the *domain* of the function and set *B* is called the *range*; a function is in one variable, two variables, etc., according to whether the members of the domain are single objects, ordered pairs, ordered triples, etc.

function, communal: equivalent to popularizing function, but emphasizing especially service to the community. *See* **function, popularizing.**

function concept: (1) the notion of interdependent relationship; (2) (math.) the set of understandings associated with the term function. At one time the term referred to recognition of the way or ways in which two related quantities change; for example, as the size of an angle increases from 0 to 90°, its sine increases but its cosine decreases; *see* **function (3).**

function, counselor: one of the activities performed by a counselor in the enactment of his role as consultant, referral agent, counselor, and coordinator of resources.

function, discriminant: an equation that indicates how to combine a set of variables to give a total score or scores that will show the maximum difference or discriminative power between two or more groups.

function, executive: (admin.) supervisory activities concerned with the allocation of tasks to the various offices within a system.

function, frequency: a mathematical function used to describe or represent a frequency distribution.

function, guidance: the function of taking a scientific interest in the traits, abilities, and personal welfare of the student, of helping him to organize his studies and his personal life effectively, of making his school and life experience profitable to him to an optimum degree, of assisting him to fit into his place after leaving the school or college, whether in a higher educational institution, in a life occupation, or in a way of life.

function, judicial: (admin.) the act or process of making a judgment; in the process of supervision, a supervisor's making a judgment about the quality of the teacher with emphasis on the personality of the individual and not on the teaching act as such; also includes inspection of the instructional program designed to ensure that specific requirements are met.

function, locomotor: *see* **locomotor function.**

function of board, proprietary: *see* **board, proprietary function of.**

function of education, telic: *see* **telic function of education.**

function, office: *see* **office function.**

function, popularizing: (jun. coll.) the function of extending education of a general nature to secondary school graduates who for geographical or economic reasons could not otherwise obtain it and of giving similar benefits to mature residents of the community.

function, preparatory: (jun. coll.) the function of giving 2 years of college work, equivalent to that offered in the freshman and sophomore years of standard universities, that will adequately prepare students for upper division specialization in the university. *See* **function, transfer; function, university parallel.**

function, salvage: (school admin.) the work of collecting, reclaiming, reworking, and disposing of scrap and waste materials; includes also a staff responsibility for the reduction of the amount of such materials that are produced; a staff function of *supply. See* **staff functions.**

function, stores: (school admin.) the function of supply responsible for the custody and safekeeping of all inventories of materials or supplies not charged directly to some department or order.

function, supply: (school admin.) the work of providing the requisite materials in the proper quantities at the proper time and place and at the lowest cost consistent with the specified quality; includes the functions of procurement, maintenance, and disbursement of inventories.

function, supportive: (admin.) the performance of all tasks in a manner and to a purpose that will uphold and strengthen other personnel in achieving the results properly expected of each as incumbent of a post in the organization.

function, t: *syn.* **distribution t;** *see* **ratio, t; redundancy.**

function, terminal: (jun. coll.) the function of giving specific preparation along vocational lines for occupations at the semiprofessional and other levels that will qualify students for immediate places in specific life occupations and of giving general education for citizenship and for life to other students who cannot continue their formal education beyond the junior college.

function, transfer: (jun. coll.) equivalent to *preparatory function,* but preferred by some, especially in the Eastern states, because of the confusion of the term *preparatory* with the preparatory schools primarily engaged in preparing students for entrance as freshmen to 4-year colleges and universities.

function, university parallel: (jun. coll.) equivalent to *preparatory function,* but preferred by many junior and community colleges because of the confusion in usage of the term *preparatory.* (Practically all public junior colleges in California use the term university parallel to indicate curricula paralleling those of the first two years of the university.)

function word: *see* **word, function.**

functional: pertaining to operation or action but not to structure or substance.

functional activities: *see* **activities, functional.**

functional amnesia: *see* **amnesia, functional.**

functional analysis: *see* **analysis, functional.**

functional approach: (1) a method of introducing new subject matter by evaluating its usefulness and teaching its use to the learners; (2) a particular technique of individual counseling wherein the practical value of advice is stressed.

functional approach to trigonometry: *see* **trigonometry, functional approach to.**

functional arithmetic: *see* **arithmetic, functional.**

functional art: *see* **art, functional.**

functional autonomy of motives, hypothesis of: the hypothesis (advanced by G. W. Allport) that, while the origins of the motives of adults may be traced to childhood experiences or later experiences, these motives become more or less independent of their origins and are able to initiate behavior in their own right.

functional blindness: *syn.* **blindness, psychic.**

functional centers: the major language activities in which people engage, such as conversation, letter writing, or storytelling.

functional centralization: *see* **centralization, functional.**

functional classification: *see* **classification, functional.**

functional competence: *see* **competence, functional.**

functional curriculum: *see* **curriculum, functional.**

functional deafness: *syn.* **deafness, psychic** (1).

functional defect: any disability ascribable not to organic defects but to lack of skill or to psychological causes.

functional dependence: *see* **dependence, functional.**

functional design: *see* **design, functional.**

functional differentiation: *see* **differentiation, functional.**

functional disorder: (1) a disorder resulting from a psychological cause without any known or discernible alteration of physical structure, for example, hysterical blindness; (2) a disorder in the function of an organ or part brought about by another function, for example, heart palpitation brought on by indigestion.

functional education: education for which there is an anticipated application, which thus assumes that the learner has immediate meaning, translatable into action, for his learning activities.

functional equipotentiality: *see* **equipotentiality, functional.**

functional evolution: *see* **evolution, functional.**

functional experience: *see* **experience, functional.**

functional fixedness: *see* **fixedness, functional.**

functional grammar: *see* **grammar, functional.**

functional grammar method: a method of learning correct usage in language by observation of forms, constructions, and idioms in their natural setting in connected text, with appropriate exercises in imitation, completion, transposition, etc., only as the need arises in the daily work of the student or group.

functional graph: *syn.* **graph, mathematical.**

functional information: a type of knowledge or understanding that functions—that is, acts effciently—in meeting specific classroom or life needs. *See* **experience, functional.**

functional integration: *see* **integration, functional.**

functional intelligibility: *see* **intelligibility, functional.**

functional knowledge: *see* **knowledge, functional.**

functional literacy: *see* **literacy, functional.**

functional mathematics: *see* **mathematics, functional.**

functional method: (bus. ed.) a method of teaching shorthand devised by Louis A. Leslie in 1934 and based upon the concept that shorthand is a language art; stresses the reading-writing approach to shorthand in context rather than isolated rules and word lists.

functional organization: *see* **organization, functional.**

functional problem unit: *syn.* **unit, experience** (1).

functional psychology: *see* **psychology, functional.**

functional reading: *see* **reading, functional.**

functional reading chart: *see* **reading chart, functional.**

functional relation: (1) a term emphasizing that some relation also happens to be a function; (2) a term meaning that two or more natural phenomena are so regularly related that this relationship may be expressed as a function. *See* **function.**

functional relationship: *syn.* **functional relation.**

functional school: (mil. ed.) in the Navy and Marines, organized activities that provide training for personnel, often in a team situation, in the performance of specialized tasks or functions that are not normal to rating training of enlisted personnel; also, professional training of officers providing instruction on weapons of new or advanced design that have not yet reached universal fleet usage.

functional speech disorder: *see* **speech disorder, functional.**

functional swimming: *see* **swimming, functional.**

functional theory: (mus. ed.) a theory designed to fulfill the individual specific functional needs of the various types of musicians, whether they are performers, composers, musicologists, or teachers.

functional theory of mind: *see* **mind, functional theory of.**

functional thinking: *see* **thinking, functional.**

functional training: *see* **training, functional.**

functional unit: *syn.* **unit, activity; unit, experience** (2).

functional vision: *see* **vision, functional.**

functional weight: *syn.* **weight, effective.**

functional writing: *see* **writing, functional.**

functionalism: (1) the doctrine, distinctly biological in approach, that the mental processes should be regarded as functions, or operations, of the organism in its adaptation to and modification of its environment; the psychological basis of *pragmatism* and *instrumentalism* in philosophy; a protest against *structuralism*, for which the problem of psychology is the analysis and description of the states of consciousness; (2) (art ed.) a theory that architecture and objects of useful purpose should be designed in close coordination with their use and with the materials from which they are made; according to this precept, form is subordinate to function.

functioning content: the portion of the material presented in a course that can be applied by the learner.

functions, discretionary board: *see* **board functions, discretionary.**

functions, junior college: the distinctive aims or purposes of junior colleges. *See* **function, guidance; function, popularizing; function, preparatory; function, terminal; function, university parallel.**

functions, mandatory board: *see* **board functions, mandatory.**

functions, ministerial board: *see* **board functions, ministerial.**

functions of secondary education: ways in which the secondary school operates to contribute to the achievement of the objectives of secondary education.

functions, staff: *see* **staff functions.**

fund: a sum of money or other resources (gross or net) set aside for the purpose of carrying on specific activities or attaining certain objectives in accordance with special regulations, restrictions, or limitations and constituting an independent fiscal and accounting entity.

fund, alumni: money raised by collection of funds, usually annual, from almuni of a higher education institution for the general support of the institution or for specified activities.

fund, capital: (1) the available pecuniary resources of a person or corporation; especially, those assets of which the principal or interest (or both) is earmarked for specified purposes; (2) in corporate philanthropy, often used as roughly synonymous with *fund.* (The capital fund includes endowment, if any, plus other expendable assets.)

fund, college loan: *see* **loan fund, college.**

fund, community: (1) money raised by public contributions in an organized fund drive to finance local service institutions on basis of need; (2) a general plan for collection and disbursement of funds to participating agencies, also called *community chest.*

fund, contingent: that item designated in a budget for the purpose of meeting unforeseen needs.

fund, endowment: a fund the principle of which must be maintained inviolate but the income of which may be expended subject to such restrictions as may have been specified in the creation of the fund.

fund, equalization: a fund levied by a state to make more equitable the financial burden of school costs for the various administrative units and to make available, in each administrative unit, a mandated, acceptable minimum program of education on the basis of a uniform local tax effort.

fund, general: the fund that is available for any legally authorized purpose.

fund, imprest: a sum of money to be used for minor disbursements, the amount of the fund being fixed. (The fund is reimbursed by other funds of the enterprise for payments made from it, the vouchers then being surrendered.)

fund, loan: a fund the principal of which is loaned to qualified beneficiaries and when repaid is available for loan to others.

fund, permanent: (1) an amount of money of which the principal is stable but the interest is made available, for example, a permanent school fund; (2) a sum of money or securities permanently set aside as an investment, the principal of which is inviolate, but the interest may be expended, for example, a trust fund.

fund, replacement: (pup. trans.) money set aside for the specific purpose of purchasing new school buses as old ones are discarded.

fund, reserve: an amount set aside to provide for anticipated future expenditures or losses. *See* **reserve, insurance; reserve, interim.**

fund, retirement: the money set aside by professional organizations, insurance companies, or civil authorities for the purpose of providing retirement allowances for participants.

fund, revolving: a working fund of fixed sums provided to enable a cycle of operations to be carried out. *See* **fund, working capital.**

fund, sinking: a fund established by periodic contributions and earnings on these to provide for the retirement of the principal of term bonds and other bonds specified to be retired from such funds.

fund, state distributive common school: a fund, held by the state for annual distribution to the local school administrative units within the state, that has been received as the income derived from investments of a permanent fund or has been set aside for such distribution out of current taxes. *See* **fund; fund, permanent** (1).

fund, state general: usually one of the established funds in the state treasurer's accounts in which a number of expense items are included and to which all moneys returned to the state and not otherwise earmarked are credited.

fund, state school: a fund held by a state government to be used for the support of schools or a particular class or type of school.

fund, working capital: a fund established to finance activities, usually of a manufacturing or service nature, such as shops and garages, asphalt plants, and central purchases and stores departments; sometimes called *revolving fund.*

fundamental assumption: *see* **assumption, fundamental.**

fundamental education: (1) that course of study or set of experiences that is considered to be a basic minimum for adequate performance in some defined area, such as citizenship or scholarship; (2) (adult ed.) *see* **adult basic education.**

fundamental formula: *see* **formula, fundamental.**

fundamental laws of algebra: *see* **algebra, fundamental laws of.**

fundamental motive: *see* **motive, fundamental.**

fundamental movement: *see* **movement, fundamental.**

fundamental operation: traditionally, one of the operations of addition, subtraction, multiplication, and division; today addition and multiplication are frequently taken as fundamental with subtraction and division derived as inverse operations.

fundamental process: *syn.* **fundamental operation.**

fundamental processes: the basic skills or abilities in reading, arithmetic, language, or writing.

fundamental research: *syn.* **research, basic.**

fundamental rhythm: rhythmic expression through familiar everyday movements common to children, each type of movement following a set basic pattern, for example, skip, run, walk, march, etc. (The accompanying instrument sometimes follows the child's natural rhythm; at times the child adjusts his motion to fit the steady rhythm of the accompanying instrument.)

fundamental skill: *see* **skill, fundamental.**

fundamental subject: *see* **subject, fundamental.**

fundamental theology: *see* **apologetics.**

fundamental theorem of arithmetic: *see* **arithmetic, fundamental theorem of.**

fundamental tone: *see* **tone, fundamental.**

fundamentalism: the theory that knowledge, value, and reality are reducible to certain fundamental laws or principles; in religion, the rigid, dogmatic, literal interpretation of the biblical scriptures.

fundamentals: (1) (curric.) the basic essentials of a curriculum; also, the major permeating concepts and structure of a subject-matter field or area of living; (2) (phys. ed.) the basic motor skills in activities or sports.

fundamentals of arithmetic: *see* **mathematics, fundamentals of.**

fundamentals of mathematics: *see* **mathematics, fundamentals of.**

fundamentals, philosophy of constant: *syn.* **essentialism.**

funded expenditure: *see* **expenditure, funded.**

funding bond: *see* **bond, funding.**

funding debt: *see* **debt, funding.**

funds, agency: (1) funds consisting of resources received and held by the municipality as an agent for certain individuals or governmental units, for example, taxes collected and held by the municipality for a school district; (2) funds received and held by institutions as custodians, such as funds of student organizations and funds deposited with institutions by students and faculty members.

funds, allocation of book: *see* **book funds, allocation of.**

funds, annuity: funds acquired by an institution subject to annuity agreements or through bequests providing for annuity payments. *See* **annuity agreement.**

funds, apportionment of school: *see* **apportionment of school funds.**

funds, current: money and other resources expendable for operating purposes, either restricted or unrestricted.

funds, expendable: funds the principal of which may be expended.

funds in trust: funds held and administered at the direction of the donor by a trustee for the benefit of an institution.

funds, matching of: *see* **matching of funds.**

funds, restricted: funds that are restricted by outside agencies or persons as to use as contrasted with funds over which the institution has complete control.

funds, scholarship: usually, endowment funds, the investment earnings from which are awarded to students who achieve the specified required minimum record and who possess other specified characteristics, sometimes including financial need.

funds, trust: generally, funds to which title is held by one party, the trustee, for the benefit of another, the beneficiary. (Endowment funds of educational institutions are sometimes called trust funds, although the institution is often both trustee and beneficiary of endowment funds.)

furnace room: *syn.* **boiler room.**

furniture: articles such as desks and chairs. *See* **equipment;** *dist. f.* **fixtures.**

furniture, classroom: the articles in a classroom, such as desks, chairs, tables, and cases.

furor: extreme and violent outbreaks of anger without adequate cause, sometimes seen in epileptics.

Fürstenschulen (fyr'stən·shōō'lən): (Ger., lit., "princes' schools") boarding schools for princes founded in Germany during the sixteenth century; they were under special princely government and patronage and their aim was to train directly for leadership in state and church.

fused course of study: *syn.* **course of study, integrated.**

fused curriculum: *see* **curriculum, fused.**

fused program: (art) *syn.* **program, integrated** (2) and (3).

fusion: (1) the combining of units of subject matter from different fields to bring into relief their interrelationships; (2) the method of selecting or organizing subject matter into broad fields.

fusion, auditory: the act or process of blending separate sounds into words.

fusion, binaural (bin·ô'rəl): the mental process of combining the sounds heard by both ears into a single, blended impression.

fusion, binocular: *syn.* **fusion, visual.**

fusion course: *see* **course, fusion.**

fusion of partial impressions: in creative activity, arriving at an experience of the whole by blending into a single image a series of numerous partial impressions; refers especially to the fusing of partial tactile impressions of the blind.

fusion plan: (1) (curric.) *syn.* **curriculum, fused;** (2) (spec. ed.) a plan whereby children enrolled in special classes due to exceptional educational needs are integrated on a part-time basis into regular classes for the purpose of social interaction and reduction of stigmatizing effects of the special class.

fusion, visual: the combining of the images from the two eyes into a single impression.

future book: (journ.) a chronological list of coming events that may suggest assignments for articles in a student publication.

Future Business Leaders of America: an organization, national in scope, of students of business education in high schools and colleges; aims at the furtherance of better leadership opportunities for young people employed in the field of business.

Future Farmers of America (FFA): an organization sponsored by vocational agriculture teachers and designed to stimulate interest in rural life, to develop concern for the basic problems of farmers, and to study the personal satisfactions and social significance of farming as a career.

Future Homemaker's degree: *see* **degree, Future Homemaker's.**

Future Homemakers of America (FHA): a national organization of junior and senior high school students who are or have been members of homemaking classes; composed of local chapters that are affiliated with the state and national organizations; designed to stimulate interest in homemaking as a career and to provide opportunities to gain skills, insights, and competencies in solving problems of home and family life.

future need: (lang.) an item that the pupil will need in the future, such as a word the pupil will need to know how to spell as shown by an analysis of adult writing.

Future Teachers of America: an organization sponsored by the National Education Association and state educational organizations to encourage secondary school youth to study education, to participate in some teacher activities, and to consider teaching as a professional career; at the local school level, meetings and organization are similar to those of other clubs in the extraclass activities of the school.

futurism: (1) (mus.) a movement launched in 1912 by Francesco Pratella (1880-1955) to catch the spirit of the machine, factories, railways, battleships, etc.; the movement was later realized by Luigi Russolo (1885-1947) with the aid of especially constructed noise-producing instruments; (2) (art) an early twentieth century style in painting and sculpture in which artists attempted to capture the effect of objects in movement by showing successive instants in the motion of such forms as people walking, locomotives and automobiles moving, animals running, etc.; Umberto Boccioni, Marcel Duchamp, Balla, and Severini were among the originators of the style.

g-factor: the general factor in Spearman's two-factor theory of intelligence, regarded as being a psychoneural element or determiner fundamental and common to all the correlated abilities of a given person, as distinguished from the s-, or specific, factors, which were said to vary in the same person for special and unrelated abilities. *See* **factor, general; s-factors; two-factor theory.**

gain: (1) an increase in amount, magnitude, or degree of a given ability, trait, or characteristic; (2) in an experiment, the measured increment for an individual or a group in some factor as the result of a certain treatment; (3) sometimes used to designate any change, whether an increment or a decrement, the direction of the change being specifically indicated, as positive gain, negative gain, or zero gain; (4) the ratio between the input and output levels of sound equipment; gain is increased by means of an amplifier.

gain, auditory: *see* **auditory gain.**

gain score: *syn.* **score, change.**

gait, ataxic: the characteristic walk of a patient afflicted with ataxia; the foot is raised very suddenly, often abnormally high, and then jerked forward and brought to the ground again with a stamp and often heel first; by adoption of a broad base, effort is made to counteract the unsteadying effects of this style of progression. *See* **ataxia.**

gait, dromedary: in walking, a twisting movement of the extremities, lordosis, and spine twisting; clownish contortions resembling a camel's walk.

gait, high steppage: a gait characteristic of some handicapped, in which, since the patient wishes to avoid tripping from his toes catching the ground, the foot is raised high, then thrown forward, striking the ground forcibly as if the patient were continuously stepping over obstacles in his path.

gait, proper normal: procedure in walking whereby the person bears the weight momentarily on the heel and then upon the outer border of foot; the heel is next raised and the weight put on the toes, and finally the body is lifted over the tips of the toes.

gait, reeling: walking on a broad base; best described as a drunken gait.

gait, scissors: a gait disturbance caused by the fact that spasticity of the muscles holds the thighs in adduction, causing the legs to draw together.

gait, spastic: a gait in which the patient has difficulty in bending his knees and drags his feet along as if they were glued to the floor, the toes scraping the ground at each step; the foot is raised from the ground by tilting the pelvis and the leg is then swung forward so that the foot describes an arc, crossing the other foot in a "scissors" manner.

gait, waddling: a gait like that of a duck; the body is usually tilted backwards, there being a degree of lordosis present, the feet are planted rather widely apart, and the body sways more or less from side to side as each step is taken; the heels and the toes tend to be brought down simultaneously; the chief peculiarities of this gait are due to a difficulty in maintaining the center of gravity of the body because of weakness of the muscles of the back; it is met in pseudohypertrophic muscular dystrophy and congenital dislocation of the hip.

galvanic skin response: *see* **psychogalvanic skin response.**

game: (phys. ed.) a crystallized form of play patterns.

game, academic: *syn.* **game, simulation.**

game contract: *see* **contract, game.**

game, dynamic air war: *see* **war game, dynamic air.**

game, group: a crystallized form of play patterns in which more than two individuals are involved.

game, lead up: a physical activity which requires the use of facilities and physical skill found in an organized sports game; specifically related to the fundamental technique and skills of a game of higher organization, complex rules, and use of strategy in competition.

game of low organization: (1) a simple game, such as tag, having only a few easy rules; (2) a game requiring a minimum of skill and motor coordination, such as London Bridge.

game, reading: *see* **reading game.**

game, rhythmic: *see* **rhythmic game.**

game, simulation: specially designed activities providing opportunities to practice certain components of life itself by providing a set of players, a set of allowable actions, a segment of time, and a framework within which the action takes place; this leads students to active assimilation of information in order to carry out action toward relevant goals. *Syn.* **academic game.**

game, singing: *see* **singing game.**

game, spelling: *see* **spelling game.**

game theory: a branch of mathematics dating from 1928 in which general winning strategies for games played by two or more people, such as matching pennies, card drawing, etc., are studied as mathematical models for the competitive aspects of economics and warfare.

game, tone: *see* **tone game.**

game, war: *see* **war game.**

gaming: an educational technique in which the student is presented with a situation involving choice and in which there are differential risks; customarily, the choices are made in a simulated real-life situation and the situation changes dynamically as influenced by the choices, which then produce some type of payoff, such as a reward or deprivation, dictated either by chance or by the choice of strategies made by the student. *See* **simulation.**

gamma hypothesis: *see* **hypothesis, gamma.**

gang: a group of persons tied together by common goals or common feelings of inadequacy, having self-imposed discipline and usually a leader.

gang-age developmental stage: *see* **developmental stage, dawning-realism.**

gang punch: *see* **punch, gang.**

gang shower: a type of gymnasium shower bath in which the temperature of the water in all showers is controlled from a central mixing valve.

Ganser's syndrome (sin'drōm; sin'drə·mē): a syndrome of senseless speech and behavior, seen in hysteria and prison psychosis, and characterized by foolish acts and senseless answers to questions; for example, the patient may hold a spoon by the bowl, a picture upside down, etc. *See* **syndrome.**

gap: minute distance between the poles of a recording head; the shorter the gap, the higher the *frequency range* of the recorder at a given tape speed.

gap, achievement: *see* **achievement gap.**

gap, cultural: *see* **cultural gap.**

garage, bus: (1) a building used for the housing of buses; (2) a building used for inspecting, servicing, and repairing buses.

garage, maintenance: a school-bus garage used for the work of inspecting, servicing, and repairing buses as well as for the general upkeep of the appearance of the vehicles.

garage, repair: *syn.* **garage, maintenance.**

garage, storage: a building used for housing school buses when they are not in use.

garbage: in computer terminology, unwanted and meaningless information in the computer memory.

garden maze: a performance test for 4- to 5-year-old children of which the problem is to reach the center of the garden by paths arranged in the form of a maze; resembles the Porteus maze.

garden, school: *see* **school garden.**

garnishee: *see* **garnishment.**

garnishment: legal obligation placed upon money owed to a person by a third party (the *garnishee*) by, for example, an employer on money from the paycheck of his employee.

Gary plan: the first permanent plan of platoon school organization, initiated in 1908 in Gary, Indiana, by Superintendent William Wirt, on the basis of his earlier experiments in Bluffton, Indiana; based on the following scheme of organization: the school was divided into two platoons, each platoon containing half the classes of each grade; continuous utilization of all school facilities was secured by having one platoon do classroom work while the other engaged in activities involving the use of the auditorium, shops, gymnasiums, and playfields, the two platoons alternating throughout the day; all teaching was departmentalized by subject field.

gate: a computer circuit with several inputs and one output which operates so that a specified condition exists on the output line if and only if some specified combination of conditions is met on the input lines; a logic element. *See* **operation, logic.**

gate, aperture: the part of a motion-picture projector consisting of the aperture plate, which determines the exact framing of the image on the screen, and the aperture shoe, a pressure shoe that holds the film snugly against the aperture plate during projection; not to be confused with *camera gate*. the motion-picture framing device.

gate building: a test of behavior in which the subject is asked to build with blocks a gate similar to a model constructed by the experimenter.

gate, camera: a device in a motion-picture camera which frames the pictures. *Contr. w.* **gate, aperture.**

gate, film: a mechanism covering the film channel of a motion-picture (or filmstrip) projector; may be opened to insert or remove the film from the projector or to clean the film channel, guides, pressure plate, and aperture.

Gauss' curve (gous): *syn.* **curve, normal probability.**

Gauss-Laplace curve (gous la·plas'): *syn.* **curve, normal probability.**

Gaussian curve (gous'i·ən): *syn.* **curve, normal probability.**

gavotte: (mus.) a relatively short dance form in four-four meter, often with an upbeat of two quarter notes, and often with phrases which begin and end in the middle of the musical measures.

Gebrauchsmusik (gə·brouKHs' mōō·sēk'): (Ger., lit., "utility music," "workaday music") music for amateurs as opposed to music for art's sake. (A twentieth-century revival of interest in music of this type by serious composers is generally credited to Hindemith.)

G.E.D. test: *see* **test, general educational development.**

Gemara (gə·mä'rä): (Aramaic, lit., "study") that part of the Talmud which consists of analysis of the Mishnah, the discussions and deductions made in the Babylonian and Palestinian academies during the third to the fifth centuries A.D.; serves as the core of the course of study in Yeshivot and other Orthodox religious schools. *See* **Mishnah; Talmud; Yeshivah.**

gene: the ultimate physical unit of heredity, thought to be carried in the chromosome and transmitted in the germ cell from parent to offspring. *Syn.* **factor** (1); *see* **allelomorph; character; chromosome.**

general ability: *see* **ability, general.**

general achievement test: *see* **battery, achievement; measurement, multiple.**

general achiever, high: *see* **achiever, high general.**

general administration: *syn.* **administration, educational** (1).

general aid: *see* **aid, categorical.**

general area shop: *see* **laboratory, comprehensive general industrial arts.**

general attitude: *see* attitude, general.

general business: *syn.* training, junior business.

general business education: *syn.* business education, basic.

general clerical test: *see* test, general clerical.

general clerk: *see* clerk, general.

general college: *see* college, general.

general control: (1) an item, listed in a school budget under the general heading of expenditures, that includes outlays for the administrative direction of the school system; (2) services, functions, and expenditures related to salaries and other expenses of the school board, the superintendent, the secretary, school election, attendance and school census, and similar services; (3) one of the component functions that must be carried on in maintaining an educational program, for example, instruction, plant operation, etc.

general course: *see* course, general.

general education: (1) those phases of learning which should be the common experience of all men and women; (2) education gained through dealing with the personal and social problems with which all are confronted; purposes and programs of general education may be described with reference to three different and in some respects opposing philosophical foundations: (*a*) rationalism, (*b*) neohumanism, and (*c*) naturalism or instrumentalism.

general education mathematics: *see* mathematics, general education.

general educational development test: *see* test, general educational development.

general extension: *see* extension, general.

general factor: *see* factor, general.

general fund: *see* fund, general.

general fund, state: *see* fund, state general.

general home economics: *see* home economics, general.

general homemaking: *see* homemaking, general.

general hygiene: *see* hygiene, general.

general industrial arts: *see* industrial arts, general.

general industrial arts, comprehensive: *see* industrial arts, comprehensive general.

general industrial arts laboratory: *syn.* laboratory, composite industrial arts; laboratory, comprehensive general industrial arts.

general industrial arts laboratory, comprehensive: *see* laboratory, comprehensive general industrial arts.

general industrial arts, limited: *see* industrial arts, limited general.

general intelligence: *see* intelligence, general.

general intelligence test: *see* test, general intelligence.

general laboratory training: *see* training, general laboratory.

general language: *see* language, general.

general library: *see* library, general.

general mathematics: *see* mathematics, general.

general metals: *see* technology, metal.

general methods course: *see* course, methods.

general military science curriculum: *see* curriculum, general military science.

general military training: *see* training, general military.

general music: *see* music, general.

general objective: *see* objective, general.

general obligation bond: *see* bond, general obligation.

general occupational competencies: *see* competencies, general occupational.

general principles, transfer of: *see* transfer of general principles.

general psychology: *see* psychology, general.

general quarters drill: *see* drill, general quarters.

general related learnings: *syn.* competencies, general occupational.

general science: *see* science, general.

general science education: education in science directed at all citizens assuming that all will need scientific knowledge to function well in our culture and make adequate decisions in the process of everyday living regardless of what area of life is entered professionally; based on predication of the impermanence of facts and the open-endedness of data, concepts, and generalizations.

general semantic therapy: *see* therapy, general semantic.

general service school: a school operated by the Army for training commissioned officers in the technique and tactics of associated arms, the conduct of field operations of divisions, corps, armies, and higher echelons, strategy, tactics, and logistics of large operations, joint operations of the Army and Navy, industrial mobilization, and wartime procurement of military supplies. *Syn.* staff school; *dist. f.* special service school.

general shop: *see* industrial arts, general; laboratory, comprehensive general industrial arts.

general superiority: *see* superiority, general.

general supervisor: *see* supervisor, general.

general survey test: *see* test, general survey.

general welfare: *see* welfare, general.

generalist: (1) in the supervision of instruction, a supervisor who has the technical ability to coordinate the various elements or diversities of a broad program of studies and has developed or is conversant with several different skills, fields, and aptitudes necessary to the improvement of instruction; (2) in guidance, one who counsels with the greater number of students, though not with all of them, or who may offer guidance applicable to all individuals.

generalization: (1) the process of forming a general conclusion applicable to a class of data or a total situation on the basis of a number of specific instances, or the statement of a general conclusion so formed; *syn.* induction; (2) (psych.) the state of widespread involvement of an organism in response to stimuli; applies to lack of specificity of sensory-motor mechanisms, whether incident to maturational or to learning sequences; *see* generalized-to-specific; (3) (math.) a statement which is true in more than one situation; for example, the Pythagorean theorem, a generalization for all right triangles, or the statement "2 + 3 = 5," a generalization of many physical situations.

generalization, associative: *syn.* generalization, stimulus.

generalization, deliberate: a term referring to the view that little or no transfer of training takes place except when conscious effort is made by student and/or teacher to effect the transfer.

generalization, descriptive: a statement specifying the traits characteristic of a species or class of phenomena; a proposition involved in judgments of fact or theory as opposed to normative generalizations involved in judgments of practice.

generalization, law of: the principle that as a factor, element, or quality is identified or discovered in a variety of situations it tends to be identified less and less with specific or particular situations; thus the spread of training is the result of the power of generalization.

generalization, normative: a way of doing things, one which has been found to be dependable for directing conduct toward desired outcomes; its function is to tie practical situations together in general classes or types; a rule or principle of human conduct, a moral principle, a generalization about the way things should be done.

generalization, response: the phenomenon resulting when a given stimulating condition, connected with a particular response, will elicit other responses that are related or functionally equivalent to the original response.

generalization, stimulus: a term used to describe the fact that a response which has been conditioned to or somehow associated with a given stimulus may be elicited by other similar stimuli, the magnitude and frequency of such generalized responses depending upon the similarity between the originally conditioned stimulus and the stimulus to which the response is generalized.

generalization, theoretical: a statement defining the characteristic features of a given class, relations among classes, or between two or more variables.

generalization, transfer through: *see* **transfer through generalization.**

generalization, validity: *see* **validity generalization.**

generalized growth curve: *see* **curve, generalized growth.**

generalized item: *see* **item, generalized.**

generalized other: the social group as it becomes organized in the experience of the individual subject; developed by George H. Mead, an important theoretical tool in social psychology and social philosophy for the analysis of personality and mind in their social context.

generalized response: *see* **response, generalized.**

generalized-to-specific: a principle of development according to which an organism at first manifests extensive responses to stimuli, the responses showing progressive restriction or localization as development and refinement proceed.

generating routine: *see* **routine, generating.**

generic: (1) pertaining to a group of closely related species having in common characteristics differing greatly from those of other species; (2) having a general application.

generic traits of existence: *see* **existence, generic traits of.**

generosity: liberality in sharing one's possessions, ideas, interests, sympathies, etc.

genes, complementary: genes that produce a similar character when inherited separately but that, when inherited together, produce a distinct and different character.

genesis: (1) the beginning, or the process of coming into being; (2) (relig.) the biblical theory or story of creation.

genetic: (1) of or pertaining to the origins (particularly ontogenetic) of a phenomenon, state, or condition; (2) pertaining to the developmental precursors of a given phenomenon, state, or condition; *see* **genetic viewpoint; psychology, genetic;** (3) pertaining to heredity, particularly to the genes constituting the elementary "carriers" or "determiners" of heredity.

genetic-developing method: a theory of method evolved by Froebel and elaborated by Susan Blow that analyzes the procedure in learning as follows: (*a*) the act; (*b*) observation of the act; (*c*) analysis of the nature of the act from the point of view of significance, consequences, implications, and relations; not generally followed today.

genetic fallacy: *see* **fallacy, genetic.**

genetic method: (1) the method of study or investigation that aims to throw light on a given state or condition (especially a psychological state) by tracing the developmental precursors; (2) any method helping to identify or discover the role of heredity, and particularly of genes or specific hereditary determiners, in the causation of a given state or condition; sometimes restricted to the method of experimental breeding, as distinguished from cytological or evolutionary investigation.

genetic method, cross-sectional: a technique for studying simultaneously different groups of subjects at different ages of development with a view to ascertaining what is typical behavior at various stages of development. *See* **genetic method; genetic method, longitudinal.**

genetic method, longitudinal: a technique for studying a single individual or a group of individuals which is based on regular, relatively frequent, and repeated measurements, conducted over a time period for the purpose of studying trends of development. *See* **genetic method; genetic method, cross-sectional.**

genetic psychology: *see* **psychology, genetic.**

genetic sequence: *syn.* **developmental sequence** (2).

genetic society: *see* **society, genetic.**

genetic surgery: selective breeding of humans to control heredity.

genetic theory: (1) any theory relating to the developmental course of a phenomenon, state, or condition; *see* **genetic method; psychology, genetic;** (2) any theory relating to the role of heredity, and particularly to the role or action of genes; (3) broadly, any theory of origins (used in

this sense, the term seems too inclusive and vague to be of real service in the scientific vocabulary).

genetic theory of language: a theory suggesting that human language originated as spontaneous articulation rather than as conscious imitation.

genetic viewpoint: (1) the developmental viewpoint, which stresses the developmental precursors of a given state or condition, viewing these precursors as probable important contributory causes; *see* **development; psychology, genetic;** (2) the viewpoint concerned with the role of heredity, and particularly of genes or specific hereditary determiners, in the causation of a given state or condition; (3) (art ed.) that viewpoint which emphasizes the relatedness of art and life and its accessibility to all men, and which considers matter, form, and content as inseparable and interdependent; *contr. w.* **formal viewpoint.**

genetics: the systematic study of the laws governing biological inheritance.

genital character: *see* **character, genital.**

genital eroticism: *see* **eroticism, genital.**

genital erotism: *syn.* **eroticism, genital.**

genital growth: *see* **growth, genital.**

genital level: (psychoan.) a stage in psychosexual development in which the erotic drive is alleged to stem primarily from the genitals and to be directed to another person, instead of to one's own body or ego.

genius: (1) a person of exceptionally high mental ability, frequently evidenced by superior powers of invention or origination or by exceptional performance in some special skill, such as music, art, or mechanics; (2) exceptional ability, as defined above. (No specific level of ability has been universally accepted as indicative of genius, although an IQ of 140 or more has sometimes been used as an arbitrary standard.)

genotype (jen'ō·tip): the inherited or genetic constitution of an organism, including all hereditary characteristics and traits, whether latent or manifest, but excluding all attributes resulting from environmental influences. *See* **constitution** (2), (3), and (4); *contr. w.* **phenotype.**

genre (zhä'nrə): art which is concerned with scenes of everyday life, usually interpreted in a somewhat realistic manner.

genteel tradition: *see* **tradition, genteel.**

gentlemanly education: a type of education growing out of the Renaissance; mainly for the wealthy and upper classes, it was supposed to inculcate good manners and behavior appropriate to a gentleman; later characteristic of British public (that is, private) schools.

geo-board: a device consisting of a wooden board with regular rows and columns of protruding nails; by putting rubber bands over the nails geometric shapes such as triangles, trapezoids, etc., can be shown.

geocentric philosophy: *see* **philosophy, geocentric.**

geographical center: (stat.) the mean of a specified area (such as a nation, state, county, city, or school district) so defined that any plane having the shape of the area would balance at this point; mathematically similar to the *mean center of population*, except that units of area are employed instead of units of population (that is, the geographical center is not weighted by population). *Syn.* **mean center of area.**

geography: the science of the earth, including a study of land, water, air, the distribution of plant and animal life, man and his industries, and the interrelations of these factors.

geography, business: *syn.* **geography, commercial.**

geography, commercial: the phase of the science of geography that treats of the distribution of industry, the commerce of different localities with one another, and the various agencies and routes for carrying on trade. *Syn.* **business geography; industrial geography.**

geography, cultural: *see* **anthropogeography.**

geography, economic: an area of study dealing with the geographical factors influencing the economic development of a region, state, nation, etc., and including consideration of such factors as geographical position, climate, accessibility, natural resources, physiography, population, and presence or absence of competition with other areas.

geography, human: the study of the distribution of man and human societies in relation to the total conditions of the physical environment.

geography, industrial: *syn.* **geography, commercial.**

geography, linguistic: the study and recording of the dialects of native speakers in different regions.

geography, locational: a concept of geography that stresses the location of the natural and man-made physical features of the earth.

geography, military: the specialized field of geography dealing with natural and man-made physical features that may affect the planning and conduct of military operations.

geography, physical: the science or study of the features, changes, and interactions of earth in regard to land, water, and air; commonly divided into *geomorphology, oceanography,* and *climatology.*

geography, place: a concept of geography that stresses the description of landscape and the memorizing of many geographic facts, such as the names of capes, mountains, rivers, and capitals.

geography, political: (1) the branch of geography that deals with the relationship between the political activities of man and his physical environment; (2) a study that attempts to show the part that natural environment is playing in the development of nations.

geography, regional: (1) an areal and interareal study concerned with the relationships between specific peoples and the regions which they inhabit; (2) the study of geographical relations between regions or areas displaying similar characteristics.

geography, social: the study of the distribution of human groups on the earth in relation to the geographical environment (particularly climate, soil, topography, and natural resources).

geography, type: a concept of geography which stresses the study of similar communities and similar regions throughout the world.

geological science: *see* **science, geological.**

geology. *see* **science, geological.**

geometric addend code: *syn.* **code, geometric.**

geometric average: *syn.* **mean, geometric.**

geometric code: *see* **code, geometric.**

geometric illusion: a geometric configuration that makes certain relationships in the picture appear distorted or that seems to contradict established theorems or accepted hypotheses.

geometric mean: *see* **mean, geometric.**

geometric progression: *see* **progression, geometric.**

geometrical code: *syn.* **code, geometric.**

geometry: the study of the properties, relations, and measurement of spatial configurations.

geometry, affine (af·fin'): a kind of transformation geometry in which parallelism and linearity but not necessarily distance and angle measure are the invariants; *Euclidean geometry* is a special case of affine geometry.

geometry, analytic: geometry studied algebraically by identifying points with pairs of real numbers (plane analytic geometry) or with triples of real numbers (solid analytic geometry), using coordinate axes; it is then possible to represent lines, planes, circles, etc., with equations and prove theorems by algebraic computation; the method was developed by Descartes.

geometry, articulation of plane and solid: the fusion of the subject matter of the geometry of three dimensions with that of the plane to form a unified treatment.

geometry, Cartesian: *see* **geometry, analytic.**

geometry, coordinate: *syn.* **geometry, analytic.**

geometry, demonstrative: *syn.* **geometry, formal.**

geometry, descriptive: the grammar of graphic language; the three-dimensional geometry forming the background

for the practical applications of the language and the means through which many of its problems can be solved graphically.

geometry, Euclidean: (1) classical plane geometry, deriving from Euclid's elements, which has as one postulate, "Given a line *l* and a point *P* not on line *l*, there is exactly one line through *P* parallel to *l*" (or some logically equivalent version); (2) a subgeometry of *affine geometry* in which perpendicularity is an invariant. *See* **geometry, non-Euclidean.**

geometry, experimental: *syn.* **geometry, informal.**

geometry, formal: geometry studied as a deductive system, that is, by specifying axioms, establishing careful definitions, and then proving theorems. *Syn.* **demonstrative geometry.**

geometry, humanized: a treatment of the subject matter of geometry in which an effort is made to relate the instructional material more closely to the life of the pupil.

geometry, incidence: those topics in geometry which relate to intersections and to subset relations, as, for example, consideration of the number of points which two lines may have in common or the number of lines which two points may have in common.

geometry, informal: geometry as taught or learned through exploration and experimentation in such activities as folding paper, drawing diagrams, constructing with ruler and compass, etc. *Syn.* **experimental geometry; intuitive geometry;** *contr. w.* **geometry, formal.**

geometry, intuitive: *syn.* **geometry, informal.**

geometry, inventional: *syn.* **geometry, experimental.**

geometry, Lobachevskian: *see* **postulate, parallel.**

geometry, metric: (1) formal geometry in which congruence is defined in terms of measure; for example, two line segments are congruent if they have the same length; *contr. w.* **geometry, synthetic;** (2) geometry in which measurement aspects are emphasized through derivation and computation with formulas, etc.

geometry, non-Euclidean: geometry based on an axiom about parallel lines which is different from Euclid's, one consequence of this difference being that in non-Euclidean geometry the sum of the measures of the angles of a triangle is not 180°. *See* **postulate, parallel.**

geometry, nonmetric: geometry in which topics not involving measure are studied, as, for example, ideas of inside and outside, separation, and betweenness; usually studied informally at the elementary school level.

geometry, observational: geometry that is studied by means of observations, measurements, and experiments.

geometry, plane: a geometry of two-dimensional space; concerned primarily with the logical proof of propositions dealing with the relationships between points and lines in a space of two dimensions.

geometry, practical: (obs.) topics in geometry which would be useful in shop, a trade, etc. *See* **mathematics, trade.**

geometry, projective: a kind of *transformation geometry* in which lines and intersections are invariants but distance, parallelism, and perpendicularity are not; since distance and angle measure are not preserved, the subject is free of number and for this reason has been called *pure geometry;* an example of a projective transformation obtains by considering possible shadows of a circle projected onto a piece of cardboard.

geometry, pure: *syn.* **geometry, projective.**

geometry, Riemannian: *see* **postulate, parallel.**

geometry, solid: a geometry of three-dimensional space; concerned primarily with the logical proof of propositions dealing with relationships between points, lines, and surfaces in a space of three dimensions.

geometry, synthetic: (1) formal geometry in which congruence and betweenness are taken as undefined terms, as in Euclid; *contr. w.* **geometry, metric;** (2) formal geometry in which algebraic methods are not used; *contr. w.* **geometry, analytic;** (3) a synonym for formal geometry of any kind. *See* **geometry, formal.**

geometry, transformation: the study of geometric properties, such as angle measure, parallelism, etc., which remain invariant under different kinds of transformations (rotation, projections, etc.) and of the theorems provable under the ensuing restrictions; for example, theorems about congruent triangles cannot be proved if distance is not invariant.

geometry, vector: Euclidean geometry studied by considering points as vectors and using the algebra of vectors in the proofs of theorems. *See* **vector.**

geomorphology (jē'ō·môr·fol'ə·ji): (1) the phase of physical geography that deals with the form of the earth, the general configuration of its surface, the distribution of land and water, and the changes that take place in the evolution of land forms; (2) the investigation of the history of geologic changes through the interpretation of topographic forms.

Geophysical Year research program, International: *see* **International Geophysical Year research program.**

geophysics: the physics of the earth and its environment, that is, earth, air, and, by extension, space.

geopolitics: a study of the relation of the politics, foreign and domestic, of a people to its physical environment.

George-Barden Act: a Federal law enacted in 1946 that provides for "the further development and promotion of vocational education in the several states and territories" in vocational programs which meet certain minimum standards in agriculture, home economics, distributive education, trade and industrial education, and vocational guidance.

George-Deen Act: Federal legislation passed in 1936 supplementing and expanding the activities of public vocational education in the states and territories as set up under the Smith-Hughes Act of 1917; superseded by the George-Barden Act.

geriatrics (jer·i·at'riks): the study of the clinical problems of elderly people.

German gymnastics: *see* **gymnastics, German.**

German reform method: *syn.* **phonetic method** (2).

germinal factor: any one of the structures in a reproductive cell that govern the inheritance of characters. *See* **chromosome; gene.**

germinal period: that portion of prenatal existence beginning with fertilization of the ovum by the spermatozoon and ending upon implantation of the fertilized ovum in the uterus (1 to 2 weeks in man).

gerontology (jer·on·tol'ə·ji): the scientific study of the phenomena of old age.

Gerstmann's syndrome: *see* **syndrome, Gerstmann's.**

gestalt (gə·shtält'): *Pl.* **gestalten;** (Ger., lit., "configuration," "total structure," "form," or "shape") a term designating an undivided articulate whole that cannot be made up by the mere addition of independent elements, the nature of each element depending on its relationship to the whole; as a theory of perception which places stress upon structural unity, the wholeness by which consciousness gives order to experience; gestalt, in art, implies the structural wholeness of a work of art as well as the unity of the experience of it.

gestalt psychology: *see* **psychology, gestalt.**

gestalt theory of learning: *see* **learning, gestalt theory of.**

gestaltism: *see* **configuration; gestalt.**

gestation: (1) the process of embryonic development; (2) the time elapsing between fertilization and birth; the period of pregnancy.

gesture language: *see* **language, gesture.**

ghetto: (It.) (1) historically, the section of a city to which Jewish people were restricted for residence; (2) the section of a city in which members of a racial minority group are segregated; in America the term is used loosely to designate any sizeable area in any city which is characterized by a high degree of poverty and a high percentage of Negro or Puerto Rican population.

ghetto school: a public school which is attended wholly or almost exclusively by minority group children located in the inner city.

G.I. Bill of Rights: one of several acts of the U.S. Congress during World War II and thereafter to provide Federal government aid and other benefits to veterans of the military services, including vocational and other educational courses at approved educational or training institutions.

gift: (1) a voluntary and absolute conveyance of a thing of value without consideration of money or blood; usually, a face-to-face transfer that does not involve the formal legal action customary in endowments and other forms of trust funds; (2) any ability possessed by a person to a high degree, frequently manifested by achievement without apparent effort.

gift tax: *see* **tax, gift.**

gifted child: *see* **child, gifted.**

gifted, extremely: a small fraction of the gifted group who have an exceedingly high level of ability and whose potential powers should enable them to make original and significant contributions to the welfare of their own and succeeding generations.

gifted, first-order: the highest 1 percent of the intellectually gifted.

gifted, mentally: (1) (as applied to a child or youth) possessing high intellectual ability, with mental age well in advance of the norm, and consequently a high IQ; (2) (as applied to an adult) possessing intellectual ability well above the average.

gifted, second-order: the upper 10 percent of the intellectually gifted excluding the highest 1 percent who are designated *first-order gifted.*

gifted underachiever: a child with high intellectual ability who does not achieve on a level commensurate with his ability.

giftedness: a trait in an individual whose performance in a potentially valuable line of human activity is normally consistently remarkable.

gifts for buildings: donations of money, securities, or property for sale, given to an educational institution for the purpose of financing the construction of buildings.

gill: a measure of the arithmetic speed of an automatic computer, defined as the time required for a computer to do $A + B = C$, store C, $C + D + E = F$, store F, $G \times H = K$, store K, when all access is to the fastest internal storage used in the computer in question and full words of data are used; for a one-address computer with only one constant access storage device (such as magnetic cores), a gill is equal to 10 times the average operation time.

Gillingham method: a synthetic method of word identification prescribed for use in remedial reading instruction; uses the auditory, visual, and kinesthetic sense avenues and involves eight teaching processes or linkages; also called Gillingham-Stillman method.

gingerbread: fancy trimmings and other useless parts of buildings, indicating excessive expenditures for parts that are designed solely or mainly for show.

Gini's mean difference (jē'nēz): *syn.* **mean difference.**

girls' counselor: *see* **dean of girls.**

Girls' State: a program of education in state government for girls sponsored by the American Legion Auxiliary; under this plan, girls are sent to the state capital for approximately 1 week, during which time they are organized into political parties, hold elections, make appointments, and conduct affairs of state relative to pertinent problems actually confronting the state.

gland type: a type of habitus, temperament, diathesis, etc., supposedly caused by the overactivity or underactivity of one of the endocrine glands. (NOTE: This is a loose term, since the endocrine glands are not independent of one another and a given gland may secrete a variety of hormones that differ in their effects. In general, too, a variety of factors other than glandular are likely to be at least partly responsible for the so-called "gland type.") *See* **endocrine gland; habitus.**

glare recovery: the adjustment of the eye to see objects or details under low illumination after it has been subjected to a relatively very bright light.

glare resistance: the ability to see objects or details in low illumination when there is a relatively very bright spot (usually a light source) near by in the field of vision.

glarometer (glär·om′ə·tər): an instrument for measuring (*a*) glare resistance and/or glare recovery, and (*b*) the degree of contrast between the brightnesses of objects or areas near each other in the field of vision. *See* **glare recovery; glare resistance.**

glass area: the total area of the windowpanes of a given room, with allowance for the impeded or nonuseful area of glass; a measurement used particularly in relation to floor area.

glass-beaded screen: *syn.* **screen, beaded.**

glass-block lighting: thick nontransparent glass blocks, above window areas, that admit light without glare.

glass-block walls: sides or partial sides of buildings made of nontransparent glass blocks instead of brick, wood, or other building materials.

glass harmonica: *see* **harmonica, glass.**

glass slide: *see* **slide, lantern.**

glaze: (1) finely ground particles of clay applied to ceramic forms for the purpose of decoration and protection of the object; when fired this glaze becomes vitrified, smooth, and permanently fused with the clay; (2) in painting, glaze is a transparent or translucent color applied to modify the effects of the painted surface.

glazier: a person whose work is concerned with preparing and setting glass in structures, using bolts, screws, grinding and buffing wheels, glass-cutting tools, and other materials and devices.

glee club: a vocal group, specializing in part singing, with the primary purpose of enjoyment and entertainment; may be limited to either sex, or many comprise mixed voices.

gliding motion: a handwriting movement characterized by a smooth sideward movement to the right or left along a horizontal or near-horizontal line.

global IQ: a single score which represents the overall intellectual ability of the individual. *Comp. w.* **score, global.**

global score: *see* **score, global.**

global scoring system: *see* **scoring system, global.**

glockenspiel (glok′ən·spēl′): a musical instrument, composed of a series of flat metal bars tuned to the chromatic scale, and played with one or two hammers. *See* **melody bells.**

glossary: a listing and definition of terms in a special subject field.

glossolalia (glos′ə·lā′li·ə): a condition characterized by senseless repetition of words or phrases having no relation or only slight relation to a given situation.

glossophobia (glos′ə·fō′bi·ə): *syn.* **laliophobia.**

glottal fry: a tickerlike continuous clicking sound produced by the vocal cords.

glottal stop: a sound produced in speaking some languages by closing the vocal cords at the beginning of a syllable and suddenly releasing the air with an explosive effect, thus preventing elision or slurring of the syllable with the preceding one; also called glottal catch, glottal click, and glottal plosive.

glyphic art: *see* **art, glyphic.**

glyphic experience: *see* **art, glyphic.**

Gnosticism: a type of syncretistic religious thought originating in pre-Christian times and prominent in the early Christian era, its chief doctrine being that salvation was not attained through faith but by esoteric knowledge of higher religious and philosophical truths; broadly it was an attempt to harmonize Greek mythology with New Testament teachings; many different forms developed, both pagan and Christian, each distinguished by the element predominant in its particular synthesis; considered a heresy by the orthodox.

goal: a substance, object, or situation capable of satisfying a need and toward which motivated behavior is directed; achievement of the goal (sometimes called a reward or incentive) completes the motivated act.

goal, academic: the aspiration of a student in terms of academic achievements, that is, level of grade achievement, scholarship, honorary awards, or degrees.

goal card, Bronxville: an instrument for reporting pupil progress, consisting of a card on which is given an objective statement of fundamental skills acquired by the child or a statement of the child's progress toward acquisition of such skills; freely supplemented by objective tests and interviews with parents.

goal determination: as used in guidance, choice of a response which depends upon the extent to which the results will measure up to the person's expectation; a person sees in each situation possible sources of satisfaction and ways of making progress toward desired goals and is aware of the many outcomes that can be attained, some tangible, some social, some connected with maintaining and enhancing self-respect. *See* **aspiration level.**

goal-directed activity: *see* **activity, goal-directed.**

goal, directional-process: an object toward which an organism strives with conscious or unconscious purpose that guides activities toward a specified end.

goal gradient: *see* **gradient, goal.**

goal-gradient hypothesis: *see* **hypothesis, goal-gradient.**

goal model: *see* **model, goal.**

goal, occupational: *see* **occupational objective.**

goal-seeking method: a procedure in which teacher and students work together to determine desired goals, to plan how to attain them, and to evaluate progress toward them.

goal, vocational: the occupation for which the pupil or student is seeking to qualify by means of training.

goals of counseling: *see* **counseling, goals of.**

Goldammer's Manual: an English translation of Froebel's "Mutter-Spiel und Koselieder" made by the Misses Lord and published during the decade 1870–1880. *See* **mother play.**

golden mean, Aristotle's: the claim that any virtue falls midway between the vices of excess and deficiency, as, for example, that courage falls midway between cowardice and foolhardiness.

golf: a game played usually over an 18-hole course in which a small hard ball is propelled by one of a choice of clubs into the holes; strokes are scored for each hole; the winner is declared by the least number of strokes over the entire distance of the course.

Gompertz formula: *see* **formula, Gompertz.**

goniometer: (phys. ed.) an instrument used to measure the range of motion of a joint.

good citizenship: cooperation in the activities of the group to which one belongs, and the fulfilling of obligations to that group.

good faith: attitude the law attempts to set in employer-employee discussions; indicates the presence of common goals and objective discussion.

good-faith check: *see* **check, good-faith.**

good life: a delineation of the pattern of values which as realized renders a life admirable according to some criterion of value. *See* **value.**

good-work report: *see* **report, good-work.**

Goodenough scale: *see* **scale, Goodenough.**

goodness: (1) (ontological) a quality of being toward which a thing tends for the completion of its own being; a being is good insofar as it fulfills its definition and possesses all the qualities proper to it; (2) (moral) a quality that places a being or an act in conformity with moral law.

goodness, doctrine of native: *see* **native goodness, doctrine of.**

goodness of fit: the extent to which a particular function coincides with a series of observations; the extent to which a series of obtained measures agrees with a series of theoretical measures. *See* **chi-square test of goodness of fit.**

goods, capital: those economic goods or forms of wealth used in the production of *consumer goods.*

goods, consumer: economic goods or wealth produced for direct consumption, not for the production of other goods. *Comp. w.* **goods, capital.**

goods, durable consumer: consumer goods that are used for a long period of time, such as a refrigerator.

goods, nondurable consumer: consumer goods that are used in a relatively short period of time, such as food.

Gothic art: *see* **art, Gothic**.

Gouin Series: *see* **action series**.

governing board: an officially constituted group of persons charged with the overall responsibility for the control and management of the affairs of one or more educational institutions; usually delegates executive functions to appointed administrators and deals primarily with matters of policy. *See* **board of control; board of trustees; regent; school board**.

government: (1) an organized mechanism through which a state or a people formulates and executes its will; (2) a mode or form of governing, such as totalitarian, communistic, or democratic government; (3) a field of social study dealing with the structure and administration of any community organized for political purposes.

government, constitutional: a type of government in which the principles determining its specific character and the extent and mode of exercise of its powers are definitely prescribed, reduced to a precise written statement, and embodied in an instrument or instruments that are not subject to abrogation or amendment except according to certain specified formalities.

government library: *see* **library, government**.

government, republican form of: government by representatives chosen by the voters of a state.

government, student: *see* **student government**.

governmental immunity: *see* **immunity, governmental**.

gown: (1) the faculty and administrators, collectively, of a college or university; (2) the robe of the academic costume; *see* **academic costume**.

grace: according to Christian teaching, a supernatural gift of God's beneficence gratuitously bestowed upon man for the purpose of fitting him to live the Christian life here and now and ultimately for life eternal with God.

gradation: (1) the process of assigning data to the levels or categories to which they belong; (2) the process of assigning a pupil to a particular school grade; *syn.* **classification** (2); (3) the arrangement and presentation of material according to its difficulty, its logical relation with other material, and its place in a planned program.

grade: (1) a major division of the instructional program of an elementary school or secondary school, representing the work of one school year; (2) a group or unit of pupils working at the same year level of the curriculum; (3) a rating or evaluation of a pupil's achievement (and, sometimes, of his character traits or behavior), often expressed on a letter scale, as A, B, C, D, F, or in percentages; *syn.* **mark** (the latter is preferred as less ambiguous).

grade-a-year integration: *see* **integration, grade-a-year**.

grade, advanced: any grade of the elementary school above the intermediate level.

grade average: *see* **average, grade**.

grade card: *syn.* **report card**.

grade, centesimal: a test score in terms of percentage correct (or percentage wrong). *Contr. w.* **rank, percentile**.

grade combination: (1) the act or process of creating a unit of the school system (such as a junior high school) by the uniting of pupils from two or more grades under a separate administrative organization, which frequently also involves the use of a separate building; (2) the act or process of uniting two or more grades for purposes of joint instruction.

grade-distribution chart: *see* **chart, grade-distribution**.

grade, elementary: a division of elementary school work that normally requires 1 year to complete.

grade equivalent: (1) a converted score expressed in terms of a scale in which the grade is a unit of measurement and indicating the grade level of the group for which the score is typical or average; for example, a grade equivalent of 6.4 is interpreted as the fourth month of the sixth grade; *dist. f.* **age equivalent**; (2) any symbol used in place of a

numerical score or mark; thus A may replace or stand for the mark 90.

grade group: *see* **group, grade**.

grade, health: a medical rating of the health condition of a person at a given time.

grade, intermediate: *syn.* **elementary grade, intermediate**.

grade, intermediate elementary: *see* **elementary grade, intermediate**.

grade, junior first: *syn.* **extension, kindergarten** (1).

grade label: *see* **label, grade**.

grade level: a measure of educational maturity stated in terms of the school grade attained by an individual pupil or a group of pupils at a given time.

grade-level supervision: *see* **supervision, grade-level**.

grade library: *syn.* **library, classroom** (1).

grade norm: *see* **norm, grade**.

grade of certificate: *see* **certificate, grade of**.

grade organization: *see* **organization, grade**.

grade placement: (1) the allocation of pupils to a specified grade, year, or level of schoolwork; (2) the assignment of certain learning experiences, books, or subjects to a particular, appropriate school grade.

grade placement score: *syn.* **score, grade**.

grade point: numerical evaluation of scholastic achievement based upon a formula of equivalents that grants credit varying with the grade attained, as, for example, 6 points for A, 5 for B, etc., with zero or negative points for failure.

grade point average: *see* **average, grade point**.

grade point ratio: *syn.* **average, grade point**.

grade point system: *syn.* **point system** (2).

grade, prefirst: *syn.* **extension, kindergarten** (1).

grade, primary: any one of the first three grades of an elementary school.

grade progress: *see* **progress, grade**.

grade-progress survey: *see* **survey, grade-progress**.

grade-progress table: *see* **table, grade-progress**.

grade record: *see* **record, grade**.

grade record, permanent: *see* **record, permanent grade**.

grade-retention-rate method: a method of forecasting school enrollment which depends upon the relationship of grade-to-grade enrollment throughout the system as indicated by grade statistics for a number of years. *See* **enrollment, projected school**.

grade school: *syn.* **elementary school**.

grade score: *see* **score, grade**.

grade skipping: *see* **skipping** (1).

grade standards: *syn.* **promotion standards**.

grade, subject: *syn.* **score, grade**.

grade teacher: (1) one who instructs the pupils of one or more grades in a graded school, whether in academic or in special subjects; (2) an older designation for any elementary school teacher.

grade, upper elementary: *see* **elementary grade, upper**.

grade variate correlation: *see* **correlation, grade variate**.

graded approach: a method of teaching by which new subject matter is introduced by successively more difficult steps, usually beginning with steps that are easy for the learner.

graded book list: *syn.* **book list** (3).

graded map: *syn.* **cartogram**.

graded reader: *see* **reader, graded**.

graded school: (1) (originally and historically) a school in which each class or progress group had a teacher and classroom of its own; (2) (since the adoption of the grading system even in one-room schools) a school in which the materials of instruction are organized according to grade or year level of difficulty and interest and in which the pupils are organized into grades or year groups according to their progress in schoolwork.

graded student teaching: *see* **student teaching, graded**.

graded textbook: *see* **textbook, graded.**

graded vocabulary: *see* **vocabulary, graded.**

grades, telescoping: *see* **telescoping grades.**

grades, the: an older term designating the elementary school.

gradient: (physiol.) a gradation of responsiveness in a given direction in an organism, owing to the fact that certain tissues or portions of an organism are more responsive to stimulation than others because of graded rates of development or metabolism.

gradient, goal: (1) a term applied to the phenomenon of increasing readiness to learn and ease of learning as the learner perceives progress toward his goal; (2) (psych.) the increased excitatory level that appears as an organism approaches his goal in space and time, shown by a greater speed of locomotion, a stronger pull against a spring, or in any other way.

gradient, growth: the structuralization of transitional conditions between two states of organismic development.

gradient-shifts, maturational: a concept used to describe the hypothesized shifts that take place in most children from a preferred dominant but not exclusive use of the tactile-kinesthetic and motor modes of learning to the auditory and then to the visual mode as they mature from infancy through childhood into adolescence and adulthood; individual differences in rate and degree of the shifts are then postulated as one of the causes of individual failures in learning when teaching activities are restricted to a single mode of presentation. *See* **equipotentiality, functional.**

grading: (1) the process of placing a child in a school grade in which he is able to cope successfully with the scholastic tasks that have been prescribed for that grade; (2) *see* **marking system.**

grading, cooperative: the joint appraisal of the status or progress of an individual or group by the teacher and a member of the class or other group or joint appraisal by more than one teacher. *Syn.* **cooperative evaluation.**

grading, flexible: the process of fitting the work of the school to the child's abilities and needs with little or no regard to the grade in which a given subject is learned.

grading formula: (read.) *syn.* **formula, readability.**

gradualism: (1) the doctrine that development tends to proceed basically through fine, slight, or insensible gradations, rather than by sudden and extensive shifts or spurts; *contr. w.* **saltation;** (2) the doctrine that progress is better achieved by slow, tentative, regular, minute changes than by sudden, radical, and sweeping changes.

graduate: *n.* an individual who has satisfactorily completed all requirements of an educational program and has been awarded a diploma or certificate attesting to this.

graduate assistant: *syn.* **assistant.**

graduate curriculum: *see* **curriculum, graduate.**

graduate degree: *see* **degree, graduate.**

graduate, distinguished: a distinguished Air Force cadet who graduates and is commissioned in the Air Force. *See* **cadet, distinguished Air Force.**

graduate, distinguished military: an individual so designated by the professor of military science, who (*a*) has been designated a distinguished military student and has maintained the required academic standards, (*b*) has completed the advance course, senior division, Reserve Officers' Training Corps, including training at a Reserve Officers' Training Corps camp, and (*c*) has graduated with a baccalaureate degree or has a statement from the head of the institution that all requirements for a baccalaureate degree have been completed and that the degree will be conferred at the next regular commencement.

graduate education: *syn.* **study, graduate.**

graduate faculty: *see* **faculty, graduate.**

graduate flying training: *see* **training, advanced flying.**

graduate, high school: a person who has completed a course of study at a secondary school and has received a diploma attesting to this fact.

graduate library school: *see* **library school, graduate.**

graduate pilot training: *see* **training, advanced pilot.**

graduate reading room: *see* **reading room, graduate.**

Graduate Record Examination: *see* **Examination, Graduate Record.**

graduate school: an organization, usually a major division of a university, that administers programs for degrees beyond the bachelor's or the first professional degree and that may also have responsibility for administering research programs carried on by faculty members.

graduate school foreign language test: *see* **test, graduate school foreign language.**

graduate student: *see* **student, graduate.**

graduate study: *see* **study, graduate.**

graduated: (stat.) *syn.* **continuous.**

graduated curve: *syn.* **curve, smoothed.**

graduated data: *syn.* **data, continuous.**

graduation: (1) the process of receiving formal recognition from the school or college authorities, as by the granting of a diploma or degree, for completing a major unit of the educational system, such as the high school course or the 4-year college course; (2) the ceremony at which diplomas or degrees are conferred upon pupils or students who have completed a major unit of the educational system; *syn.* **commencement;** (3) (stat.) *syn.* **smoothing.**

graduation exercises: *see* **exercises, graduation.**

graduation program: *see* **program, graduation.**

graduation requirements: specifications of minimum educational achievement and other qualifications necessary for the granting of a specified degree by an institution's governing board; stated generally in terms of semester or quarter hours, sometimes in terms of units or credits in certain subject-matter fields, semesters or quarters of residence, or minimum grade, work, or mastery or, in some colleges, in terms of comprehensive examinations covering major areas of study.

Graeco-Latin square: *see* **square, Graeco-Latin.**

grainy: (photog.) the quality of a negative or positive in which the image is made up of relatively distinct dots, caused by excessive clumping of the silver granules in the emulsion.

gramian matrix: *see* **matrix, gramian.**

grammar: (1) strictly, the study of the phonology, inflections, and syntax of a language; (2) as commonly used, the part of language study that pertains to the different classes of words, their relations to one another, and their functions in sentences.

grammar, descriptive: the newer types of grammar which describe the way languages work rather than state rules for their use.

grammar, formal: logically organized principles and rules relating to the subject of English grammar.

grammar, functional: (1) those aspects of grammar which are actually helpful to the pupil in improving his speech and writing; (2) the designation of a method of learning correct usage in language through activity rather than through reference to rules.

grammar method: a method of teaching foreign languages in which much reliance is placed on the study of the formal grammatical relationships within the language, frequently involving the memorizing of logically organized blocks of subject matter such as declensions and conjugations, the study of rules of grammar and syntax, and drill, frequently written, on the material studied; ordinarily also involves the use of translation from the vernacular into the foreign language, and vice versa, both orally and in writing.

grammar, prescriptive: grammar which gives rules for correctness in writing and speaking.

grammar school: (1) historically, a shortened popular designation of the English grammar school of colonial times; (2) popularly and loosely, a term used to designate an elementary school.

grammar, traditional: the formal grammar usually taught as a combination of definitions, classification of sentence elements, and adherence to grammatical rules as applied to usage.

grammar, transformational: study of language which identifies the structural relationships of sentences.

grammar-translation method: a method of language teaching stressing the structure of the foreign language and translation from the foreign language into the vernacular and vice versa.

grammatical clue: *see* **clue, grammatical.**

grammatical error: *see* **error, grammatical.**

grammaticus (grə·mat′i·kəs): the master of an ancient Greek "higher elementary" school who instructed boys up to 16 in grammar, reading, and literature, introducing the students to the cycle of studies embraced in the trivium and quadrivium. *See* **quadrivium; trivium.**

grammatist: a teacher in an elementary school of ancient Athens in which young Greek boys learned to read, write, and count. (By the close of the fifth century B.C. it was usual for the grammatist to give more advanced instruction in addition to the original offerings.)

grand mal (gräN′ mal′): (Fr., lit., "great sickness") an epileptic seizure in which there is loss of consciousness and generalized tonic-clonic convulsions; the most severe type of epilepsy in which there is a sudden loss of consciousness with falling, which sometimes causes physical injuries; immediately following this phase, the muscles of the body stiffen out but usually for less than 1 minute, followed by spasms or violent jerking of muscles, excess salivation, and changes of color and breathing rate; ensuing coma or deep sleep may last from a fraction of an hour to several hours. *See* **epilepsy; petit mal.**

grandfather clause: a provision of law exempting certain parties from increased standards of a new law; often used in statutes governing certification, contract, and retirement requirements.

grant: (1) strictly and originally, a gift of real property from the sovereign power to a natural or legal person for use in purposes likely to benefit the general public; (2) a contribution by a governmental unit to another unit, often by a larger unit to a subordinate one, ordinarily to aid in the support of a specified function (for example, education) but sometimes also for general purposes; (3) an appropriation of funds made by a foundation to a recipient; the amount and purpose of the funds and the period of time during which they are expendable are usually specified.

grant, conditional: an allocation of money for specific purposes by a higher unit of government to a smaller unit; use of the grant is subjected to supervision.

grant, Federal: any donation or gift of property or money made by the Federal government.

grant, flat: a grant distributed to all recipients on an invariable basis. *See* **distribution, flat.**

grant, foundation: (1) financial support given, usually by the state government, for the whole or partial payment of costs involved in maintaining a prescribed uniform basic school program in a local school administrative unit; (2) a gift of money made by a philanthropic foundation or agency, as by the Carnegie Foundation for the Advancement of Teaching.

grant, general: a grant authorized (*a*) to one or more recipients for a continuing purpose and/or (*b*) to a number of recipients for a purpose common to all.

grant-in-aid: (1) a financial grant, frequently in the form of periodic payments, made by a government or agency to another government or agency or to an individual, by way of assistance for a general or special purpose; for example, a grant by the Federal government to the states for the promotion of vocational education; usually requires a preliminary or matching contribution and the meeting of certain stipulations by the receiver of the grant; *syn.* **subsidy; subvention;** (2) in student personnel work, a sum of money given to a student by an educational institution for conducting a specific project or for an immediate financial emergency; sometimes given outright; *see* **grant-in-aid, athletic.**

grant-in-aid, athletic: *syn.* **scholarship, athletic.**

grant, monetary: a gift of money for a particular purpose.

grant, per capita (Federal): financial assistance provided by a Federal agency to a state or local agency on the basis of the number of people residing in the state or locality.

grant, scholarship: *syn.* **scholarship** (3).

grant, special: a grant authorized for the accomplishment of a particular work or project, usually to be completed within a specified time.

grant, state: a sum of money or other property (such as land) given by the state government to some institution or agency.

grants, educational exchange: *see* **exchange grants, educational.**

graph: *n.* (1) a series of lines or areas and/or pictorial representation depicting numerical data for making comparisons and showing relationships; (2) (math.) a drawing which shows the relationship between two sets of numbers; *see* **graph, line; graph, relative bar;** (3) (math.) a means of representing some quantity by a geometric object such as representing a complex number by a point in the plane.

graph: *v.* to represent by a graph. *See* **graph** *n.*

graph, area: a graph in which quantities are expressed in variations of a real size or proportions of the area of a single plane figure.

graph, arithmetic: *syn.* **chart, arithmetic.**

graph, bar: (1) a pictorial representation of the proportionate relationship of two or more items; the method used is to draw rectangles of equal width whose lengths are related in the same way as the items represented by each rectangle or bar; the bars may be horizontal or vertical, but each bar is distinct, that is, does not have a common side with other bars, though all have their base on a common line; *syn.* **relative bar graph;** (2) a means of representing a whole (usually expressed as 100 percent) by a single bar subdivided into parts to show the proportional composition of the whole; (3) any representation or comparison of statistical data by means of a series of bars or rectangles.

graph, belt: *syn.* **chart, band.**

graph, broken-line: *syn.* **graph, line.**

graph, cartoon: *syn.* **graph, pictorial.**

graph, circle: a circle used to display the distribution of a total into its subparts; the circle, representing 100 percent, is divided into regions by drawing lines from the center to the circumference, thus creating a picture of a pie cut into slices; each region bears the same relationships to the whole circle as the item represented does to its total; generally used for visual display of such items as budgets, but always restricted to proportions of the total; often referred to as a *pie graph.*

graph, column: *syn.* **diagram, column.**

graph, correlation: *syn.* **diagram, scatter.**

graph, cumulative frequency: *syn.* **ogive.**

graph, double logarithmic: a graph drawn in the plane using perpendicular axes, each of which is marked with a logarithmic scale. *Syn.* **double logarithmic chart;** *see* **graph, logarithmic;** *dist. f.* **graph, semilogarithmic.**

graph, frequency: any graph showing the frequency of occurrence of observations in the various class intervals; may be either a *histogram* or a *frequency polygon. Syn.* **frequency chart; frequency diagram; simple frequency graph.**

graph, functional: *syn.* **graph, mathematical.**

graph, historical: *syn.* **historigram.**

graph, hundred percent bar: a method for geometrically comparing parts of a whole to the whole; the whole is represented by the length of a rectangle, the *bar,* while the parts are represented by the lengths of sections of the rectangle.

graph, line: a graph made up of a line or series of lines to show fluctuation in data; magnitudes or frequencies are represented by the distance of points on the line or lines above the base; various types of lines, as dotted, broken, colored, etc., are used to indicate classes or quantities being represented; useful in picturing change and predicting possible trends. *Syn.* **broken-line graph.**

graph, logarithmic: (1) a graph in which the quantities are expressed as logarithms of numbers; (2) a rectangular coordinate graph having the abscissa and/or the ordinate constructed on a logarithmic scale such that the distance between any two marks on the scale is proportional to the difference between the logarithms of the numbers which the lines represent. *Syn.* **logarithmic chart;** *see* **graph, double-logarithmic; graph, semilogarithmic.**

graph, map: a graph in the form of a map, dealing with geographical or other data, that uses various symbols or devices such as colors, shading, or crosshatching to show differences of phenomena, for example, a map showing the successive western frontiers of the United States from 1800 to 1900, or one showing the distribution of production of corn, wheat, and sugar beets.

graph, mathematical: a diagram designed to show the functional relationships between two or more variables. *Syn.* **functional graph;** *dist. f.* **graph, statistical.**

graph, multiple picture: a graphic representation in which numerical values are represented by pictures.

graph paper: *syn.* **cross-section paper.**

graph, percentile: *syn.* **curve, percentile.**

graph, pictorial: a graph in which quantity is indicated by a number of equal-sized pictorial symbols known as pictograms or pictographs. *See* **pictograph.**

graph, pictorial bar: a pictorial graph in which the pictures appear either in horizontal or in vertical bar formation.

graph, picture: *syn.* **graph, pictorial.**

graph, pie: *syn.* **graph, circle.**

graph, profile: *syn.* **chart, profile;** *see* **profile; psychograph.**

graph, relative bar: *syn.* **graph, bar.**

graph, semilogarithmic: a graph drawn in the plane using perpendicular axes, only one of which is marked with a logarithmic scale. *Syn.* **semilogarithmic chart;** *see* **graph, logarithmic;** *dist. f.* **graph, double logarithmic.**

graph, simple frequency: *syn.* **graph, frequency.**

graph, statistical: a graph that gives a diagrammatic representation of a set of statistics.

grapheme: a letter symbol which stands for a speech sound.

graphic art: *see* **art, graphic.**

graphic arts: *see* **art, graphic.**

graphic experience: *see* **art, graphic.**

graphic item counter: *see* **counter, graphic item.**

graphic materials: instructional materials conveying meaning largely through line representations or symbols that are nearer to reality than verbal symbols, such as maps, charts, diagrams, posters, cartoons, and graphs.

graphic method: any method of problem solving which uses graphs; for example, simultaneous equations in mathematics are often solved by graphic methods.

graphic rating scale: *see* **rating scale, graphic.**

graphic scale: *see* **scale, graphic.**

graphic score: *see* **score, graphic.**

graphic training aids: *see* **training aids, graphic.**

graphic vocabulary: *see* **vocabulary, graphic.**

graphical analysis: *see* **analysis, graphical.**

graphical comparison: use of the various graphical representations such as *circle graph, line graph, relative bar graph,* to show relationships between two or more items; most commonly encountered is the construction of two line graphs using the same base lines (or axes); certain inferences may be more obvious from this procedure than they would be from examination of the numerical data.

graphical representation: *see* **graphic method.**

graphics: (1) pictorial arts involving such reproductive methods as engraving, etching, lithography, photography, serigraphy, and woodcuts; (2) printmaking methods.

graphics, computer: *see* **computer graphics.**

graphological structure: *see* **structure, graphological.**

graphomania (grafʹō·māʹni·ə): an obsessive impulse to write. *Dist. f.* **graphorrhea.**

graphorrhea (grafʹō·rēʹə): the writing of disconnected words or phrases, often long lists of isolated words, that convey no meaning; occasionally seen in catatonia. *Dist. f.* **graphomania.**

graphovocal method: a remedial reading procedure in which a child is taught to write and pronounce words as a method of developing ability to recognize them as symbols for sounds.

grasping reflex: *see* **reflex, grasping.**

grass drills: physical conditioning exercises such as rolling and crawling done on the ground.

gratuitous instruction: *see* **instruction, gratuitous.**

gravity ventilation: *see* **ventilation, gravity.**

Gray-Leary readability formula: *see* **readability formula, Gray-Leary.**

gray scale: *see* **scale, gray.**

Great Books: any of several lists of books in the fields of theology, philosophy, science, history, biography, and creative literature considered by their compilers to be the best works in these fields; the general underlying philosophy of those using them in education has been that, since the Great Books deal with the fundamentals and experiences of mankind, the study of them provides the liberal education necessary for all those who pursue higher education; espoused in America by Robert Hutchins, Mortimer Adler, Mark Van Doren, and others.

Great Books program: *see* **program, Great Books.**

Great Decisions program: *see* **program, Great Decisions.**

"great issues" course: *see* **course, "great issues."**

great-man theory: the theory which assumes that all events of social and historical significance are brought about largely through the influence of notable persons and can best be studied through acquiring a knowledge of such leaders and their lives.

greatest possible error: *syn.* **error, maximum.**

Greco-Latin square: *see* **square, Graeco-Latin.**

Greek art: *see* **art, Greek.**

green room: (mus.) a room, which may or may not be decorated with green as its predominant motive, to which a performer or group of performers retire after a concert or recital to receive congratulations on the success of the event. *Syn.* **reception room.**

gregariousness: (1) the tendency habitually to live or move in groups rather than alone; (2) fondness for the company of one's kind; sociability, sometimes carried to extremes. *See* **herd instinct.**

grid: a lattice with only a finite number of lines or points. *See* **lattice** (1) and (2).

grid, answer: *see* **answer grid.**

grid, Wetzel: *see* **Wetzel grid.**

grief: a persistent affective state arising from loss of a valued object; regarded either as a nonadjustment within the person or as an outer manifestation of such nonadjustment.

grievance: in the field of collective negotiations between teachers and administration, a charge that the collective agreement is being violated or misinterpreted.

grievance procedure: (school admin.) a formal procedure for handling employee dissatisfaction resulting from some conflict of interests, either personal or organizational; the objective in setting up such a procedure is greater assurance that such conflicts will be resolved amicably, justly, and quickly.

grip age: *see* **age, grip.**

gross correlation: *syn.* **correlation, total.**

gross correlation coefficient: *syn.* **coefficient, total correlation.**

gross motor activity: *see* **activity, gross motor.**

gross receipts: total, or aggregate, receipts, without any deduction.

gross receipts tax: *see* **tax, gross receipts.**

gross score: *see* **score, gross.**

gross teacher turnover: *see* **turnover, gross teacher.**

gross words: according to the international typewriting contest rules, the total number of standard words typed by a person in a given length of time. *See* **net words; standard word** (2).

ground rules: *see* **rules, ground.**

ground school: for students in flight training, a program of classroom instruction in the theoretical aspects of flying and in related subjects, given either prior to or concurrently with their actual flight experiences; in the military services, a school providing such training for a candidate for an aeronautical rating.

ground trainer: *see* **trainer, ground.**

groundkeeper: *see* **grounds keeper.**

groundmen: workmen employed to care for grounds or campus, to tend the trees, shrubs, grass, and other vegetation, and to keep the land free from trash.

grounds: (1) the land belonging to a university, college, or school that surrounds the buildings of the institution; *see* **campus;** (2) (philos.) premises, the basic beliefs, assumptions, or evidences on which an argument or belief rests.

grounds keeper: (voc. ed.) a person who maintains landscapes and property, public or private, through the performance of a variety of tasks; also called *groundkeeper*, especially with reference to a sports field.

group: *n.* (1) a number of individuals, items, or observations for experimentation or analysis; (2) the total number of observed values of a quantitative variable, or the total number of categories of a qualitative variable; *syn.* **statistical group;** *dist. f.* **class** (7); (3) two or more persons in social interaction; *see* **group, social;** (4) a particular kind of *mathematical system;* the requirements are (*a*) one well-defined binary operation under which the set is closed, (*b*) associativity of the operation in the set, (*c*) an identity element in the set for the operation, and (*d*) an inverse in the set for each member of the set; if the operation is also *commutative,* the group is called a *commutative* or *Abelian* group; *see* **law, commutative;** *comp. w.* **field** (5); **field properties.**

group: *v.* (1) to classify or gather individual measures into classes or groups; (2) to classify pupils (or other individuals) into more or less homogeneous groups for purposes of instruction, testing, or experimentation; *see* **grouping** (2).

group, Abelian: (math.) a type of mathematical system named for Niels Abel (died 1829), a Norwegian mathematician. *See* **group** *n.* (4); **group, commutative.**

group action: *see* **action, group.**

group activity: *syn.* **action, group.**

group atmosphere: *see* **atmosphere, group.**

group atmosphere, autocratic: *see* **atmosphere, autocratic group.**

group atmosphere, democratic: *see* **atmosphere, democratic group.**

group audiometer: *syn.* **audiometer, phono.**

group auditory training equipment: *see* **auditory training equipment, group.**

group, average-ability: those pupils falling within an arbitrarily or functionally determined range on each side of a mean or median measure of ability. (The intelligence quotient range of approximately 90 to 110 includes the average mental ability group.)

group behavior: *see* **behavior, group.**

group, business and office occupational: students who have a goal of being employable in a specific business and office occupation after graduation from high school.

group, buzz: (1) one of several small groups within a larger class or group which assembles usually after a general session for the purpose of discussing a presentation, analyzing a problem, or preparing questions for the larger group; (2) a technique used by discussion leaders and adult educators to involve all members of a meeting in intimate participation in the procedures and discussion pursued, the members being divided into small discussion groups often with a leader or recorder who writes down suggestions to be presented later to the entire membership of the meeting.

group-centered instruction: *see* **teaching, nondirective.**

group, child study: a group of adults interested in the guidance of children, who gather regularly for systematic study of the many factors that influence the growth and development of children, for example, principles of child development, parental attitudes and practices, etc.

group, class: a group of pupils forming one section within a given grade.

group climate: *syn.* **atmosphere, group.**

group, coacting: *syn.* **group, secondary.**

group cohesion: *see* **cohesion, group.**

group, commutative: *see* **group** *n.* (4).

group composition: *see* **composition, group.**

group conference: *see* **conference, group.**

group, congeniality: a group which is formed and persists simply because friendships arise out of repeated associations and shared interests or experiences. *See* **club.**

group consciousness: an awareness on the part of members of a group of common characteristics, interests, and standards of behavior.

group, control: (1) the one of two or more groups that is not subjected to the experimental factor or condition introduced into the treatment of the experimental group; (2) the group with which the experimental group or groups are compared.

group counseling: *syn.* **counseling, multiple.**

group, criterion: (1) a group whose response is taken as a basis of reference for interpreting the response of another (usually smaller) group or of an individual; for example, a group whose scores on a test are used as norms; *syn.* **norm group;** (2) a standard population.

group, culture: (1) any large or small aggregation of persons, whether organized or not, of which the members have some common interests or characteristics that bring them into physical or intellectual contact and communication; (2) a group with a common set of concepts, usages, and techniques for satisfying basic needs, that is, with a common social heritage of major proportions.

group, derivative: *syn.* **group, secondary.**

group development: (1) the actual developmental stages in the growth of the group over a period of time from an undifferentiating body to one with increasing ability to discriminate and select and to utilize its resources fully in implementation of its goals; (2) the application of research in *group dynamics* to facilitate growth and development of the group.

group development therapy: *see* **therapy, group development.**

group difference: *see* **difference, group.**

group-directed-work supervisor: *see* **supervisor, group-directed-work.**

group disapproval: (1) the censure of the actions, attitudes, or manners of one or more members of a group by the other members of the group; (2) disapproval expressed as group consensus.

group, discussion: a relatively small number of persons who meet to study and discuss portions of subject matter of mutual interest, usually under the guidance of a leader.

group discussion: *see* **discussion, group.**

group discussion, leaderless: *see* **discussion, leaderless group.**

group dynamics: *see* **dynamics, group.**

group elective: *see* **elective, group.**

group, encounter: a relatively small group characterized by intimate, direct, and often intense social interaction.

group, ethnic: a fairly distinct cultural group, whether racial, national, or tribal.

group evaluation: *see* **evaluation, group.**

group experiment: *see* **experiment, group.**

group, experimental: (1) the one of two or more groups that is subjected to the experimental factor or condition, the effect of which it is the purpose of the experiment to discover; *contr. w.* **group, control;** (2) loosely, any of the groups in an experiment.

group, face-to-face: a primary group, having social control over individuals through direct influence and interaction. *See* **group, primary.**

group factor: *see* **factor, group.**

group game: *see* **game, group.**

group, grade: the pupils enrolled in or belonging to one of the grades in an elementary school.

group guidance: *see* **guidance, group.**

group-guidance course: *see* **course, group-guidance.**

group guidance, organization for: *see* **organization for group guidance.**

group hearing aid: *see* **hearing aid, group.**

group, home-room: the class group while under the supervision of a single teacher responsible for all or the majority of the activities participated in by the class.

group, homogeneous: (1) a group having a much higher degree of similarity among its members in respect to a given trait or complex of traits than is found in a random sampling; (2) a group having relatively little variation.

group, in: (1) a group in which one has a feeling of belonging; (2) a group in which one belongs and whose customs and habits are shared and which is characterized by "we" as opposed to "they." *Syn.* **we group;** *contr. w.* **group, out.**

group instruction: *see* **instruction, group.**

group, instructional: a group of pupils chosen in such a manner that instruction can be carried on expeditiously.

group intelligence quotient: *see* **quotient, group intelligence.**

group intelligence scale: *see* **scale, group intelligence.**

group interval: *syn.* **interval, class.**

group interview: *see* **interview, group.**

group leader: a director and teacher of all involved with the group and its problems in common; generally accountable for performance of the group.

group living: in home economics education, a number of persons living together and sharing the responsibilities for the household operation and for social activities; example is the home management house (or apartment) for home economics students. *See* **home management house.**

group, low-income: the currently used term acceptable to that group in our society which has previously been referred to as *culturally deprived group, disadvantaged group,* etc.

group, marginal: (1) group that lives "on the fringe" of the culture pattern of an area because its cultural heritage is rooted in a different social background; (2) group that is no longer physically a part of its "culture of origin" and for which accommodation to the dominant culture in its place of residence is not yet accomplished.

group, membership: (1) a group that is distinguished by its common alliance in any organization with respect to a particular social project; (2) a list of the members of any lodge, association, club, or formalized movement.

group method of class scheduling: *see* **scheduling, group method of class.**

group method of factorization: *see* **factorization, group method of.**

group method, remedial: a method of assisting pupils weak in a particular subject by organizing them into special groups for remedial instruction.

group, minority: one of the groups classified according to race, religion, or nationality whose membership is less than 50 percent of a given population.

group, modal age: *syn.* **group, modal age-grade.**

group, modal age-grade: the group of pupils included in the age range of 12 months within each grade which shows the greatest concentration of cases. *Syn.* **modal age group.**

group motivation: *see* **motivation, group.**

group, norm: *syn.* **group, criterion.**

group, normalization: the group (believed to be representative of the population) that is used in determining the

norms for the test; not the group used in trying out procedures for practicality, though that is necessary for standardizing; the norms can be determined only after the procedures have been stabilized.

group orientation: *see* **orientation, group.**

group, out: (1) that group of persons toward whom we feel a sense of fear, dislike, and avoidance, and toward whom we have no sense of loyalty or cooperation; (2) any group that happens to be apart from or opposed to the particular in group in question; *see* **group, in.**

group pacing: *see* **pacing, group.**

group, parallel: (1) one of two or more groups equivalent in certain characteristics; (2) one of two or more groups all of which are subjected to the same experimental procedures.

group, parent study: a group of parents of school-age children formed to study, with professional assistance, the special problems that arise for them, their children, or the school in providing the best educational opportunities for their children both in the formal school institution and in the out-of-school experiences in the community.

group, peer: usually interpreted as people who are similar in developmental level; occasionally refers to persons similar in respect to other qualifications, such as status or education.

group pickup: *see* **pickup, group.**

group, pilot: *syn.* **group, practice.**

group plan, cooperative: *see* **cooperative group plan.**

group planning: *see* **planning, group.**

group, play: (1) a group organized by the children themselves spontaneously or by teachers for various play activities; (2) a group of preschool-age children who meet for half-day sessions under the supervision of one or more parents.

group, postprimary: *syn.* **elementary grade, intermediate.**

group, practice: a preliminary group on which an experimental procedure or setup is tested; a trial or tryout group. *Syn.* **pilot group.**

group, preprimary: *syn.* **extension, kindergarten** (1).

group, preprimer: *syn.* **extension, kindergarten** (1).

group, pressure: a group of persons bound by common interests that attempts, by use of a variety of coercive measures, to influence others to adopt its programs or purposes.

group, primary: (1) the family; (2) a small, intimate face-to-face grouping having a feeling of oneness and mutual understanding; *see* **group, face-to-face.**

group process: (1) the method whereby a cohesive group forms; (2) the interaction occurring at a given moment within a group; (3) the pattern of interaction within a group; its way of functioning.

group processes: a series of actions in which attention is focused upon relationships among members of a group as they strive to achieve a common goal or to solve a common problem.

group productivity: the degree to which a group does what it hoped to do or what someone else hoped it would do; may be measured internally or externally.

group psychotherapy: *see* **therapy, group.**

group, racial: (1) a group of persons bound together by consciousness of membership in the same race; (2) less strictly, an aggregate of people belonging to a given race.

group, radical: a group that has an antagonistic attitude toward the prevailing order and is favorable to drastic changes therein.

group reading inventory: *see* **inventory, group reading.**

group recorder: *see* **recorder, group.**

group, reference: (1) the group to which a person aspires and with which he identifies himself but to which he does not actually belong; he thinks and acts in terms of the standards, attitudes, values, and status aspirations of the groups with which he identifies himself; (2) a defined collection of individuals whose test scores are used in establishing test norms.

group role: in the social structure or framework within which an individual may find a place as a member of a group, one of a series of behaviors or functions that occur within the group situation; may be specified by certain rank position or may arise internally from the personality of the group member and the group task.

group, rural youth: *see* **rural youth group.**

group scale: *see* **scale, group.**

group, secondary: the larger, more formal, more contractual, and as a rule less influential group.

group, social: two or more persons in a state of contact and interaction in which each person stimulates the response of the other.

group, statistical: *syn.* **group** *n.* (2).

group, steering: *syn.* **committee, steering.**

group structure: the way in which the relational patterns among members of a group are manifested in terms of friendship, interaction, morale, leadership, and other role behaviors of group members.

group, study: a group of students, ordinarily small in number, organized for independent study.

group, T-: *see* **T-group.**

group-task roles: behavior expected by society of a given group, especially the family.

group test: *see* **test, group.**

group therapy: *see* **therapy, group.**

group therapy, nondirective: *see* **therapy, nondirective group.**

group, transition: *see* **transition group.**

group tryout: *see* **tryout, group.**

group, we: *syn.* **group, in.**

group work: an educational process in which the members of a group, working cooperatively rather than individually under the guidance of a leader, formulate and work toward common objectives.

group work agency: *see* **agency, group work.**

group work, social: group approaches used as constructive forces for the improvement of pupils' social relations. *See* **group role.**

group, zero: the untreated group used in the zero-group technique. *See* **zero-group technique.**

grouped frequency distribution: *see* **frequency distribution, grouped.**

grouping: (1) (stat.) the act or process of combining all the observations that fall within a given range, bounded by the class limits, into a single group, which is then usually treated either as if all the observations in the group had the same value or as if the observations were distributed evenly over the interval; (2) the process of classifying pupils for instructional purposes; applied to class groups or intraclass groups; (3) formerly used synonymously with *grading;* (4) (sp.) the act of placing together related words for purposes of presentation to pupils according to some standard such as common difficulty, meaning, or word building.

grouping, ability: grouping of pupils within classes or schools on the basis of some measured mental ability.

grouping, balanced: formation of instructional groups in which the top or bottom sections are balanced out to ensure that sufficient bright or slow-learning pupils will be assigned to the teacher to form teachable subgroupings within the class.

grouping, class: the act or procedure of dividing the pupils of a class into two or more groups on the basis of interest or ability, for the purpose of adapting instruction.

grouping error: *see* **error, grouping.**

grouping, heterogeneous: the classification of pupils for the purpose of forming certain groups having a high degree of dissimilarity.

grouping, homogeneous: (1) the classification of pupils for the purpose of forming instructional groups having a relatively high degree of similarity in regard to certain factors that affect learning; (2) the procedure of organizing data in subject-matter fields or areas of experience into groups or divisions, the parts of which are relatively

alike in respect to one or more characteristics, such as degree of difficulty, usefulness, or appeal to pupils.

grouping, interclass: a plan for instruction in reading in which elementary children in the same school who are reading at the same level go to a specific room to work with the same teacher who teaches all of them at the appropriate level; called the Joplin plan because of its use in the Joplin, Missouri, schools.

grouping, intraclass: the process of dividing pupils into instructional groups within a given class or section.

grouping, sociometric: division of members of a group into subgroups on the basis of a *sociogram.*

grouping symbol: (math.) a pair of parentheses, brackets, braces, etc.

grouping, team: *see* **learning, team.**

grouping, tripartite: the process of dividing pupils into three graded sections according to ability (fast, average, and slow or X, Y, and Z groups). *Syn.* **XYZ grouping.**

grouping, XYZ: *syn.* **grouping, tripartite.**

groups, comparable: (1) two or more samples (usually of the same size), each similarly chosen from the same total population and hence supposed to be essentially similar; (2) two or more samples selected in such a manner as to ensure comparability on some basis, for example, two stratified samples.

groups, equivalent: groups having the same distribution on one or more variables; usually, groups so selected that corresponding measures of central tendency, variability, and form of distribution differ by amounts smaller than might reasonably be accounted for by random sampling fluctuations. (Groups are equivalent not in general but only in regard to specific variables.)

growth: the gradual or not so gradual increase in size of an organism or its parts or an analogous progressive increase in ability to perform. *See* **learning; maturation.**

growth, accretionary: growth characterized exclusively by increment of existing substance, structure, or function; purely quantitative growth; growth marked by absence of qualitative changes, changes in quantitative relations among elements, or changes in organization (integration). *Contr. w.* **growth, developmental.**

growth, aesthetic: (art ed.) in children's drawings, sensitivity to the integration of all experiences concerning thinking, feeling, and perceiving; manifested by increased concern of the child for organization in thoughts or feelings or in the expression of them by spaces, lines, textures, and colors.

growth, anatomical: changes with age in size, shape, number, complexity, etc., of bodily structures.

growth, atypical: growth differing from that considered normal for or characteristic of a particular organ or organism.

growth, cognitive: growth in the child's thought process which hinges particularly on self-regulation by the child and occurs when he perceives a mismatch between beliefs which relate to the same concept and strives to reconcile them as a means of regaining equilibrium.

growth components, integration of: *see* **integration of growth components.**

growth, creative: (art ed.) in children's drawings, the child's power to use freely the components of aesthetic, social, perceptual, physical, emotional, and intellectual growth and to apply them for an integrated effort; creative growth is shown by the independent and original approach evidenced in the child's work.

growth curve: *see* **curve, growth.**

growth curve, generalized: *see* **curve, generalized growth.**

growth, developmental: growth characterized by such features as differentiation or emergence of new characters, changes in quantitative relations among elements, or changes in organization (integration), with or without accretion or simple quantitative augmentation. *See* **development; growth;** *contr. w.* **growth, accretionary.**

growth, differential: (1) development marked by differences in rate or nature of growth among constituent elements of some complex structure, function, or capacity; (2) development in which associated organs, functions, habit systems, attitudes, etc., begin to develop at somewhat different times or continue development at different rates, proceed possibly in different directions, etc.; not synonymous with *dysplasia,* which denotes an unusual, anomalous, or abnormal degree of differential development and refers to the finished product rather than to the process of growth. Not inherently opposed to *integration of development.*

growth, education as: *see* **education as growth.**

growth, educational: changes in the number of skills or in amount of knowledge or information as a result of educational procedures, either self-directed or administered by others.

growth, emotional: (art ed.) an increasing power and freedom of the child in his drawings to identify himself with his work, evidence being found in the drawings in the inclusion of experiences of the self and in the absence of purely objective reports and stereotyped repetitions.

growth, genital: changes with age in size, shape, position, etc., of the organs of sex.

growth gradient: *see* **gradient, growth.**

growth, harmonious: normal growth of all parts in relation to one another, without anomalies or abnormalities.

growth, horizontal: (1) changes with age in breadth of shoulders, hips, etc., contrasted with increase in length measurement (the term is currently used mainly in factor analysis studies); *contr. w.* **growth, lineal;** (2) increase in the number of acts of the same difficulty at the command of the individual; *contr. w.* **growth, vertical.**

growth, inner: a nonscientific term referring either to inferred changes in mental or "moral" organization not manifested in overt behavior or to the unknown neural changes that presumably constitute the physiological basis for some observed behavior change. (Because of its loose meaning and the impossibility of objective verification, the use of this term in scientific discussion is to be deprecated.)

growth, intellectual: (art ed.) in a child's drawings, the child's increasing awareness of himself and his environment, seen in one form in the details of which he can think.

growth, lineal: changes with age in length measurements as contrasted with increase in breadth of shoulders, hips, etc. (The term is currently used mainly in factor analysis studies.)

growth, linguistic: the development in a person of increased power in the use of language.

growth, lymphoid: changes with age in the size of the lymphatic glands, spleen, tonsils, etc.

growth, mental: change in mental abilities, activities, attitudes, etc., characteristic of advance in age.

growth, neural: changes with age in the number of nerve cells or the length or the complexity of nerve fibers.

growth, occupational: growth of pupils in maturity of vocational understanding and in development of attitudes in harmony with every changing demand of our modern social and economic life.

growth pattern: *see* **pattern, growth.**

growth, patterning of: *see* **patterning of growth.**

growth, patterns of: *see* **patterns of growth.**

growth, perceptual: (art ed.) refers broadly to the cultivation and growth of the child's senses; children making intensive use of perceptual experiences include in their drawings kinesthetic sensations, tactile and visual experiences, and also a sensitive awareness of shapes, their colors, and the environment that surrounds them.

growth, physical: changes with age in both lineal and horizontal growth accompanied by the development of muscles, fatty tissues, and organs of the body. *See* **growth, horizontal** (1); **growth, lineal.**

growth, physiological: changes with age in the functioning of body structures.

growth potential: an attribute or quality in a person that indicates he will improve himself in knowledge, judgment, or skill in such a way as to become a more effective and valued member of his organization.

growth, professional: (ed.) increase in subject-matter knowledge, teaching skill and efficiency, and insight into educational problems, with a concomitant increase in success as a teacher.

growth, psychological: (guidance) change or gain in learned patterns of personal-social adjustment.

growth, saltatory: rapid growth; growth characterized by sudden spurts as contrasted with smooth and steady maturation.

growth, skeletal: changes with age in size, number, texture, etc., of the bony structures of the body.

growth, social: (art ed.) in a child's drawings, concerns the child's ability to identify himself with the needs of others, often manifested by his close feeling of self-identification with his own experiences and also with those of others and by spatial correlations in his drawings.

growth, spiritual: progress in the education of the soul, that is, the development of the inner life through ascetic discipline.

growth, trunk: changes with age in the size, shape, texture, and complexity of the body tissues comprising the thorax and abdomen.

growth unit: *see* **unit, growth.**

growth, vertical: increase in the ability to perform acts more difficult than those previously performed. *Contr. w.* **growth, horizontal** (2).

growth, vocational: *see* **growth, occupational.**

growth, zero population: *see* **zero population growth.**

Grube method (grōō′bə): a method of teaching arithmetic developed in Germany by Grube in 1842 and first introduced into the United States by Louis Soldan of St. Louis in 1870; based on intensive drill in each number combination taken separately and on the study of number "families," for example, all those combinations which make 6, such as 2×3, $4 + 2$, $10 - 4$, $36 \div 6$.

guaranteed loan program: *see* **program, guaranteed loan.**

guaranteed wage plan: (school admin.) any of a number of plans for stabilizing employee purchasing power by assuring some continuation of wage payments during unemployment over some period of time; may be accomplished by regularizing employment, regularizing employee earnings, providing reserves for the payment of supplementary unemployment compensation, or by some combination of methods. *See* **salary.**

guardian: an adult legally responsible for the care and management, both as to person and property, of a minor or of a person who for whatever reasons (such as age, feeble-mindedness, or insanity) has been legally judged unable to manage his own affairs.

"guess who" technique: the presentation of descriptive sketches, photographs, or voice recordings to a group of subjects for purposes of individual or group identification.

guessed average: *see* **average, guessed.**

guessed mean: *syn.* **average, guessed.**

guessing, correction for: *see* **scoring formula.**

guidance: (1) the process of assisting an individual to understand himself and the world about him and to gain a knowledge of the implications of this understanding for educational progress, career development, and personality fulfillment; (2) a form of systematic assistance (aside from regular instruction) to pupils, students, or others to help them to assess their abilities and liabilities and to use that information effectively in daily living; *see* **student-personnel work;** (3) the act or technique of directing the child toward a purposive goal by arranging an environment that will cause him to feel basic needs, to recognize these needs, and to take purposeful steps toward satisfying them; (4) a method by which the teacher leads the child to discover and make a desired response of his own will. *See* **counseling.**

guidance, abortive: guidance that fails to fulfill desired specific functions or asserted objectives; sometimes inaccurately referred to as *pseudo guidance, false guidance,* or *quack guidance.*

guidance, adjustive phase of: the phase of guidance that aims to help the individual to make the optimal adjustment to educational and vocational situations.

guidance, adult: systematic assistance given to mature persons in the analysis of experience and personal problems with a view to developing self-direction and aiding the individual to make adjustments.

guidance, agricultural: that phase of guidance, both group and individual, which provides information about and experiences in agricultural occupations, both nonfarm and farm, job selection, placement, and follow-up.

guidance and special services, director of: *see* **director of guidance and special services.**

guidance and testing, coordinator of: *syn.* **director of guidance.**

guidance and testing, supervisor of: *syn.* **director of guidance.**

guidance, art: (1) provisions for educational and vocational experience through observation of and participation in various phases of art; (2) direction of student interest into art or into active participation in art activities.

guidance, career: (1) career planning based on a student's values, needs, interests, and abilities and involving various informational resources; (2) (mil. ed.) the evaluation of the qualifications of Air Force military persons by interviewing, counseling, testing, or other valid techniques in order to recommend assignment to a career field.

guidance center: *see* **center, guidance.**

guidance center, community: a cooperative venture among various community agencies such as chamber of commerce, merchants, business associations, and manufacturers, established for the purpose of identifying and organizing information about the needs of youth and of the community; desired outcomes of this program are to make better use of the individual in the community and to help the student utilize community resources.

guidance, centralized: an organizational approach to guidance services utilizing professionally prepared counselors, test administrators, social workers, and other highly qualified personnel in specific, defined, coordinated positions to help solve pupil problems. *See* **guidance, decentralized.**

guidance, child: (1) the process of helping children to meet and master developmental tasks; (2) clinical assistance to maladjusted children.

guidance, classroom: the directing of the pupil in class on the basis of knowledge gained from the pupil's cumulative record and classroom performance for the purpose of fitting him for efficient citizenship.

guidance clinic: *see* **clinic, guidance.**

guidance clinic, child: *see* **clinic, child guidance.**

guidance clinic, educational: *see* **clinic, educational guidance.**

guidance committee: *see* **committee, guidance.**

guidance consultant: *see* **consultant, guidance.**

guidance, continuing: guidance that extends over a period of years (from 3 to 6 years).

guidance, continuous: the concept that organized guidance services are an essential and integral part of the total educational program and a continuing process for all boys and girls extending from kindergarten through the twelfth grade to college.

guidance, coordinator of: *see* **coordinator of guidance.**

guidance council: a system-wide representative staff group whose responsibility is to provide leadership for guidance and other pupil personnel services of the school system; its functions are (*a*) to provide leadership for the planning and conduct of investigative studies and to make recommendations to the director of pupil personnel, (*b*) to advise how the results of a study may be used to improve the school program, (*c*) to serve as a channel for staff proposals or complaints, (*d*) to consider the school system's plans for the evaluation of its pupil personnel services, (*e*) to receive and study the proposals of the pupil personnel staff as to their various functions and duties, (*f*) to be involved in the planning of the school

system's program of public relations, (*g*) to assist in developing and applying plans for the identification, recruitment, and placement of new pupil personnel staff members, and (*h*) to advise the director of pupil personnel and his staff as he makes recommendations regarding budget, facilities, and other resources. *Syn.* **pupil-personnel council;** *see* **committee, guidance.**

guidance council, student: a group of students, working with a faculty guidance committee, who contribute ideas for the improvement of the student activity program, suggestions regarding orientation of new students, and ways of publicizing and evaluating the existing guidance program and services.

guidance counseling: *syn.* **counseling.**

guidance counselor: *syn.* **counselor.**

guidance course: *see* **course, guidance.**

guidance, cultural: the process of learning the folkways and other accepted modes of behavior of a given culture from elders and others involved in the culture.

guidance, curriculum: assistance given the pupil in finding the most satisfactory offerings or groups of subjects to fit his proposed course of study and special needs.

guidance, decentralized: an organizational approach to guidance services in which all personnel, both teachers and administrators, perform the guidance function within the roles historically assigned to them; specialists are used only in a supporting role. *See* **guidance, centralized.**

guidance, developmental: (1) a concept of guidance as a continuing process which stresses help to all students in all areas of their vocational, educational, and personal-social experiences at all stages of their lives; (2) a program and process aimed at facilitating human development and changing human behavior, based on the assumption that clients are capable of choosing the desired directions of their own development.

guidance, diagnostic technique in: *see* **diagnostic technique in guidance.**

guidance director: *syn.* **director of guidance.**

guidance, director of: *see* **director of guidance.**

guidance dismissal blank: a form given to the pupil immediately prior to his leaving school, intended as a means of clearing him with his homeroom and subject teachers; blanks provide for the signature of each teacher, for comments concerning the pupil's interests and special abilities, and for statements of recognition of the pupil's release from the school and from each department of the school. *Syn.* **check-out card; school-leaving card.**

guidance, distributive phase of: *see* **distributive phase of guidance.**

guidance, educational: guidance which aids the pupil and his parents in relating his interests, aptitudes, and abilities to current educational and vocational opportunities and requirements. *See* **counseling, educational.**

guidance, elementary school: guidance which seeks to improve the adjustment of children in the elementary school to their immediate environment, with special reference to their emotional and social relationships, to the end that they may be free to develop to the limit of their individual capacities for well-balanced maturity.

guidance, ethical: *syn.* **guidance, moral.**

guidance, evaluation of: *see* **evaluation, guidance program.**

guidance facility: *see* **facility, guidance.**

guidance, false: *see* **guidance, pseudo.**

guidance follow-up record: *see* **record, guidance follow-up.**

guidance function: *see* **function, guidance.**

guidance, group: (1) those activities of a guidance nature which are carried on in groups to assist members to have those experiences desirable or even necessary for making intelligent vocational and social decisions; *see* **conference, guided;** (2) arriving at individual or group decisions by conferring with a group that has a common core of problems or characteristics.

guidance, health: those functions which will help an individual to take developmental, preventive, remedial, or corrective measures resulting in the fullest use of his health potential.

guidance, home: guidance given the pupil by his parents, other members of the family, or, in the case of home-bound children, by a *homebound teacher.*

guidance, homeroom: the provision of guidance-related activities, usually by a classroom teacher, for a designated group of students who meet regularly and consider various problems which may be personal, social, or vocational in nature; techniques such as checklists, discussions, sociodrama, and role-playing are used. *See* **advisership, homeroom.**

guidance information: *see* **information, guidance.**

guidance, information-centered: a type of counseling based on data regarding the individual, including his family, health, achievements, aptitudes, interests, occupational and educational goals, and work experiences, gathered by means of testing, autobiography, anecdotal records, and rating scales.

guidance instruction, humanized: a guidance program that seeks thorough understanding of the difficulties of the individual student and, by a sympathetic attention to his problems, is able to bring about adjustments when ordinary procedures would not suffice.

guidance, interpretative: assistance which results when one trained person, who personally knows the student, individually coordinates all the known information about the child and then communicates it to interested authorized persons.

guidance inventory: *see* **inventory, guidance.**

guidance level: the basis on which adjustment is made, such as the social, civic, economic, vocational, ethical, or physical basis, or chronological age.

guidance, moral: guidance that assists the individual to establish priorities in the face of demands from personal needs, social customs, and basic principles of conduct which may be required either by conscience or by external authority.

guidance, negative: guidance that consists of advising the student about vocations he should not choose or things he should not do as contrasted with suggesting vocations that he should choose, etc. *Contr. w.* **guidance, positive.**

guidance, nursery: the act or process of directing the behavior of very young children into socially acceptable channels by means of nursery supervision.

guidance, occupational: a function of a vocational guidance program which supplies individuals with an inventory of their abilities, aptitudes, and interests as they relate to occupations of interest to them; presents facts about jobs and occupational fields, requirements of various occupations, and employment possibilities; may include arranged experiences in order to help students select a vocation more intelligently. *Comp. w.* **guidance, vocational.**

guidance, organized: a planned program for carrying out guidance activities in a more extended way than through incidental interviews and general classroom guidance.

guidance, orientation: a function of student personnel work dealing specifically with guidance of the student during the period of transition from secondary school to college and during the early adjustment to college.

guidance outcomes: *see* **outcomes, guidance.**

guidance, personal: the phase of guidance that aims to assist an individual with respect to personal habits, attitudes, and intimate personal problems. *See* **guidance, social-personal.**

guidance personnel: *see* **personnel, guidance.**

guidance, placement: guidance with reference to seeking or accepting a position.

guidance placement: *see* **placement, guidance.**

guidance, positive: guidance characterized by constructive suggestions for achieving success. *Contr. w.* **guidance, negative.**

guidance, post-high school: sources of advice after high school graduation.

guidance, pre-high school: those phases of a guidance program which are concerned with the orientation and counseling of young persons, generally graduates of the

eighth grade and junior high school, prior to their entrance into general and special high schools; may include talks given before groups of pupils, trips to the general and special high schools, and individual meetings.

guidance, precollege: *see* **counseling, precollege.**

guidance, preventive: a guidance program emphasizing the use of tools and techniques which will discover in advance and treat the areas in which a particular student might have difficulty.

guidance, problem-centered: a program of services specifically designed to improve the adjustment of individual pupils by giving primary attention to "crisis situations" and to the discovery of minor obstacles to be overcome as a preventive measure against the creation of major problems.

guidance program: *see* **program, guidance.**

guidance program evaluation: *see* **evaluation, guidance program.**

guidance project: *see* **project, guidance.**

guidance project, demonstration: *see* **project, demonstration guidance.**

guidance, pseudo: incomplete, incorrect, or false suggestions or advice in which the scientific approach or procedures recognized as sound are not used; sometimes called *quack guidance.*

guidance, pupil: counseling and otherwise guiding persons enrolled in schools.

guidance, quack: (1) *syn.* **guidance, pseudo;** (2) inaccurate *syn.* **guidance, abortive.**

guidance questionnaire: *see* **questionnaire, guidance.**

guidance readiness: *see* **readiness, guidance.**

guidance, reading: directing the choice of books by readers in accordance with their interests and abilities through personal advice or printed lists.

guidance records: *see* **records, guidance.**

guidance research: *see* **research, guidance.**

guidance room: a room equipped for and devoted to the guidance or counseling of pupils.

guidance, school: assistance given schoolchildren and youth in developing to their maximum potential commensurate with their individual needs, interests, and abilities.

guidance seminar: *see* **seminar, guidance.**

guidance service: the guidance facilities of the school system made available to the community.

guidance services: *see* **services, guidance.**

guidance services, director of: *see* **director of guidance.**

guidance, social: the phase of guidance that attempts to assist persons or groups in their adjustments to the mores and practices of society and to help them develop satisfactory relationships with their fellows.

guidance, social-civic-moral: (1) direction of the individual to help him adjust to group mores; (2) assistance given to individuals to further their adjustment to group values.

guidance, social-personal: the use of available resources to meet the emotional, intellectual, and social weaknesses of the individual.

guidance specialist: a staff member who is properly prepared through a counselor education program and certificated for some phase of guidance work.

guidance, state supervisor of: *see* **supervisor of guidance, state.**

guidance, teacher: (1) a program organized to advise and assist teachers in their duties; may include suggestions on how to deal with individual students or with whole classes and may provide information on job opportunities, community resources, and student test scores; (2) activities of a guidance nature provided by a classroom teacher, especially in connection with a homeroom guidance program; *see* **guidance, homeroom.**

guidance teacher: *see* **counselor, teacher.**

guidance technique, diagnostic: *see* **diagnostic guidance technique.**

guidance techniques: those methods which are used in assisting a person to plan his life and solve his problems, such as interviews, case studies, case histories, testing of abilities, testing of achievements, analyzing data, and using the social service facilities of the community.

guidance, vocational: the process by which persons are assisted in a selection of occupations and of adequate vocational training or retraining for them which is realistic in the light of actual or anticipated opportunities for gainful employment and suited in each case to the counselee's interests, needs, and ability to benefit from such training. *See* **counseling, vocational.**

guidance, vocational curriculum: guidance through the systematic arrangement of courses and learning experiences which are designed to help students as they make choices of occupations, work activities, and training that are suitable to their abilities, interests, and needs.

guidance worker: one who has been assigned the responsibility in a school system for the carrying out of all or a part of the guidance services.

guide: a device used in primary reading to help the child "keep his place" and to make the return sweep from one line to the next; also called *line marker;* usually made out of a strip of cardboard.

guide, broadcast-lesson: *see* **broadcast-lesson guide.**

guide, correspondence study: *see* **correspondence study guide.**

guide, curriculum: *see* **curriculum guide.**

guide dog: one of the dogs trained as mobility aids for blind persons and either purchased by the individual or supplied by a special philanthropical organization for this service to the blind.

guide, library: *see* **library guide.**

guide, literature: *see* **literature guide.**

guide, observation: *see* **observation guide.**

guide, occupational: a resource for occupational information published in a two-section pamphlet form for an individual occupation; contains job description and a summary of labor market information.

guide, study: *see* **study guide.**

guide word: *see* **word, entry.**

guided conference: *see* **conference, guided.**

guided discovery: *see* **teaching, discovery.**

guided discussion: *see* **discussion, guided.**

guided independent study: *see* **instruction, individualized.**

guided laboratory experiences: *see* **experiences, guided laboratory.**

guided reading: *see* **reading, guided.**

guided study: *syn.* **study, directed; study, supervised.**

guided teaching: *syn.* **teaching, directed.**

guiding question: *see* **question, guiding.**

guild: (1) originally, a medieval association of a semireligious nature from which developed later a number of types of *guilds,* both religious and secular; among the latter were the trade and merchant guilds, the main object of which was the maintenance of certain rights and privileges of their members; (2) an organization formed by employers, masters, and apprentices in a particular trade for their mutual protection and welfare.

guild school: a type of school organized and supported by merchant and craft guilds during the later Middle Ages with the revival of business and industry in the cities of Europe; priests often were employed to offer elementary and sometimes secondary instruction.

guilt: unpleasant feeling of sinfulness arising from behavior or desires contrary to one's ethical principles; involves both self-devaluation and apprehension growing out of fears of punishment.

guilt complex: *see* **complex, guilt.**

gustation: the sense of taste, localized in receptors for sweet, sour, salt, and bitter, which are found in the membranous covering of the tongue and soft palate.

gymnasial training: *see* **training, gymnasial.**

gymnasium: (1) a large room devoted to physical education activities, including systematic physical exercise and the playing of indoor games; (2) a building devoted to physical education or indoor games; usually contains a playing floor, dressing rooms, shower room, staff offices, examining rooms, etc.

Gymnasium (gim·nä′zē·ŏŏm): *n. neut.; pl.* **Gymnasien** (gim·nä′zē·ən); (1) type of secondary school in Germany and some other countries in which German, Latin, Greek, and mathematics are stressed; (2) general name for all secondary schools that prepare for the university in German-speaking countries.

gymnasium-auditorium: a dual-purpose room designed for use as both auditorium and gymnasium; some equipment remains stationary and other equipment requires removal from the room as the use is changed.

gymnasium, double: a gymnasium that can be divided by folding doors to make two gymnasiums, frequently one for boys and the other for girls; can also be used as a single gymnasium for exhibition basketball games and the like.

gymnasium frame: a series of pieces of playground apparatus built of joined iron piping, including, for example, swings, horizontal bars, and ladders.

gymnasium, intramural: a gymnasium used for physical games or sports among students of a university or college and not for varsity sports, that is, games or sports with students of other institutions.

gymnasium, outdoor: a section of a playground equipped with gymnastic apparatus and covered for protection from the weather.

gymnast: (1) in ancient Greece, one who trained professional athletes; (2) one who teaches or is expert in gymnastic exercises.

gymnastic apparatus: *see* **apparatus, gymnastic.**

gymnastic game: any one of a number of simple team games especially suitable for use in a gymnasium.

gymnastics: exercises such as calisthenics and apparatus activities as distinguished from dancing, games, and athletics.

gymnastics class, individual: *syn.* **class, remedial** (2).

gymnastics, corrective: a program of exercises and activities designed to correct poor body mechanics. *See* **gymnastics, individual; gymnastics, remedial; physical education, corrective.**

gymnastics, formal: calisthenic exercises done in response to commands and apparatus exercises in which a set artificial form is prescribed. *Contr. w.* **gymnastics, natural.**

gymnastics, German: exercises such as calisthenics and apparatus activities adapted from those of Germany and introduced into the United States in the latter part of the nineteenth century. *See* **gymnastics.**

gymnastics, individual: special exercises, with or without apparatus, to be performed by an individual either to correct some physical deformity or to improve or develop physical condition, for example, foot exercises to remedy fallen arches or calisthenics to build up musculature.

gymnastics, natural: body movements characteristic of untutored spontaneous responses to life situations.

gymnastics, remedial: a remedial class program which is intended to minimize the handicapping consequences of orthopedic disability in children.

gymnatorium: a combination *gymnasium* and *auditorium* used for physical education performance and school assemblies.

gyp school: a nonaccredited educational institution that cheats its students by charging excessive prices for a shoddy education. *Contr. w.* **accredited school.**

habilitation: (1) the act or process of training to do something for the first time without any previous point of reference; (2) in Germany the acquisition of the right to teach at any institution of university rank; restricted to those with the doctor's degree and including in addition a scientific paper, a trial lecture, and a colloquium with members of the department; a public lecture by the candidate is also part of the process.

habit: (1) an act, movement, or pattern of behavior that through practice has become easy and familiar, and is performed without conscious thought, hesitancy, or concentration; (2) (gestalt) a form or pattern of action that through individuation and constancy of conditions has become dominant and stereotyped; (3) an acquired predisposition to ways or modes of response, not to particular acts except as, under special conditions, these latter express a way of behaving; (4) as a goal of foreign-language instruction, the facility to use a language actively at conversational speed without concentrating on the units of the language or its grammar but only on the message to be conveyed.

habit-family hierarchy: *see* **hierarchy, habit-family.**

habit, food: the accustomed eating of a particular kind of food or an acquired attitude toward or against some food.

habit, religious: the characteristic and distinctive dress or garb worn by a nun, monk, or brother.

habit spasm: a ticlike, recurrent, meaningless contraction of a muscle or group of muscles that is essentially a mannerism rather than a true tic.

habit, speech: *see* **speech habit.**

habit strength: a construct of Hull's learning theory which postulates that the strength of a given response is a product of previous reinforcements, the strength of the reinforcer, and temporal factors such as time between a response and reinforcement. *See* **reinforcement; reinforcer.**

habit, transfer of: *see* **transfer of habit.**

habits, reading: *see* **reading habits.**

habits, study: *see* **study habits.**

habitual disorder: *see* **disorder, classroom.**

habitual truant: *see* **truant, habitual.**

habitus (hab'i·təs): type of body build or external bodily conformation (such as pyknic, athletic, asthenic, linear, ectomorphic, or dysplastic). (Formerly, habitus usually implied a permanent, inherent type of bodily form, but the best current usage avoids commitment with regard to permanence or causal basis. Constitutional habitus is the same as habitus, except for a lingering connotation of inherited determination.)

Haftarah (häf·tä·räh'): *n. fem.; pl.* Haftarot (häf·tä·rōt'); (Heb.) (1) the portion of the Prophets read on the Sabbath and festivals, following the reading of the assigned portion of the Torah, chosen because it is linguistically or ideationally related to the portion read from the Torah; (2) the portion of the Prophets read by the boy on the Sabbath of his *bar mitzvah. See* **maftir.**

haiku (hī'koo): a form of Japanese poetry, borrowed by Western writers, in which a great deal of subtle meaning is expressed in three lines containing five, seven, and five syllables respectively; children in America and other lands have often been able to use the general form in original writing.

hair space: *see* **space, hair.**

half day of attendance: *see* **attendance, half day of.**

half-day session: *see* **session, half-day.**

half grade: a division of schoolwork that normally requires one-half year, or one semester, to complete.

half-time teacher: a teacher who devotes half the school day to the school activities assigned to him.

half-track head: *see* **head, half-track.**

half-track monaural tape: *see* **tape, dual-track monaural.**

half-track recorder: *syn.* **recorder, dual-track.**

half-track stereo tape: *see* **tape, two-track stereo.**

halftone subjects: printed illustrations consisting of uniformly spaced dots of varying size which blend together and convey shades of gray.

halfway house: a social agency, supported either charitably or from tax funds, for ex-drug addicts or alcoholics who have recently stopped using drugs or alcohol and who need constant supervision and group support so as not to start again.

hall: (1) any university or college building devoted to a special purpose; (2) a part of a name of a building of a university or college, as, for example, in Holmes Hall; (3) a passageway or corridor with doors opening into rooms.

hall patrol: a system of preserving order and quiet in hallways while pupils pass from one class to another or during lunch or recreation periods, etc.; sometimes organized for specific purposes such as the prevention of theft from lockers; duties may be assigned to teachers or pupil monitors.

hall, recitation: a room seating a large number of students that is devoted, usually, to class lectures. (The term is derived from the recitation method of class procedure, now obsolescent.)

hall, residence: *syn.* **dormitory.**

hallucination: a false sensory perception relating to any one of the special sense organs, for example, hearing, seeing, or feeling something that does not exist. *Dist. f.* **illusion.**

hallucination, induced: a hallucination brought on by means of suggestion, as in hypnosis.

hallucinosis, acute (ha·lū'si·nō'sis): a severe mental disorder in which imaginary voices are heard, often accusing or threatening in character; accompanied by acute anxiety but without clouding of consciousness.

halo effect: a bias in ratings arising from the tendency of a rater to be influenced in his rating of specific traits by his general impression of the person being rated.

ham: (slang) (1) an ineffective or amateur actor; (2) an amateur who operates radio sending and receiving apparatus as a hobby.

Hamiltonian philosophy of law: *see* **philosophy of law, Hamiltonian.**

hand-and-eye dominance: *see* **dominance, hand-and-eye.**

hand dynamometer: *see* **dynamometer, hand.**

handball: a game played by players batting a small rubber ball against the wall of a one- or four-wall court; object is to cause the ball to rebound in such a manner that the opponent cannot return it before the second bounce.

handbook: (1) a publication, usually prepared by the students, that presents in ready reference form important facts intended to help the student adjust himself more quickly to school or college life; (2) in guidance, refers to the *Occupational Outlook Handbook,* which attempts to give an overview of a job.

handbook, custodian's: *syn.* **handbook, janitor's.**

handbook, instructor: a book designed for use of an instructor which contains the material forms and other matter pertinent to a course of instruction.

handbook, janitor's: a manual of instructions for school-building janitors containing information pertaining to their work and instructions as to the manner in which their duties are to be performed; commonly published by state departments of education and by larger school districts. *Syn.* **custodian's handbook.**

handbook, pupil: *see* **pupil handbook.**

handbook, student: a special bulletin containing information about the college and designed to aid in orienting the new student; includes such topics as tuition and living costs, curricula available, personnel services provided, and the major student organizations and activities.

handbook, teacher's: a typed, mimeographed, or printed booklet for teachers containing general information concerning such matters of local school organization and administration as the marking system, attendance and tardiness, the school calendar, teachers' meetings, records and reports, course of study, textbooks, supplies, equipment, and miscellaneous school policies.

handcraft: productive creative work done by hand with the aid of simple tools and machines. (The term is now coming into general use by art educators and is regarded as an improvement over *handicraft*.) *Syn.* **craft.**

handedness: preference for either the right or the left hand in tasks demanding the use of one hand or in the more difficult or skilled parts of tasks demanding the use of both hands. *See* **laterality.**

handedness, left-: dominant or preferred use of the left hand in functions involving the use of a single hand. [Anomalies of reading and writing (mirror image writing, slanted writing, etc.) are frequently present.] *See* **handedness, right-; laterality.**

handedness, right-: dominant or preferred use of the right hand in functions involving the use of a single hand.

handedness test: *see* **test, handedness.**

handicap: (1) a defect in physique, intellect, or behavior; (2) any abnormality that renders achievement more difficult.

handicap, auditory: *see* **handicapped, hearing.**

handicap, language: (1) a defect in language that interferes with oral or written expression or reading; (2) sometimes synonymously used with reference to non-English-speaking handicaps.

handicap, mental: a condition involving subaverage general intellectual functioning.

handicap, multiple: two or more disabling conditions present in the same individual.

handicap, orthopedic: a crippling condition generally associated with diseases of bones, joints, tendons, and muscles; includes neurological conditions which tend to prevent movement.

handicap, personality: a marked defect in self-concept which tends to interfere with learning in school.

handicap, visual: an incapacity for specific visual tasks due to impairment of one or more of the visual organs; persons with a visual handicap may be described as either partially seeing or blind.

handicapped, academically: a term descriptive of students whose school achievement has failed to live up to their expectancy level to such a degree that physicians, psychologists, and/or educators feel that they would benefit from special considerations, special services, or a special curriculum in their daily school routine; also called *educationally retarded.*

handicapped, acoustically: *syn.* **handicapped, hearing.**

handicapped, auditorily: *syn.* **handicapped, hearing.**

handicapped child: *see* **child, handicapped.**

handicapped child, educationally: *see* **child, educationally handicapped.**

handicapped child, perceptually: *see* **child, perceptually handicapped.**

handicapped, creative activity of: *see* **therapy, creative.**

handicapped, educable mentally: *syn.* **mentally retarded, educable.**

handicapped, hearing: having defects of hearing which impede ability to respond to environmental sounds, speech, and pure tone; inclusive term covering both hard

of hearing and deaf. *Syn.* **acoustically handicapped; auditorily handicapped.**

handicapped, intellectually: those individuals who lack the ability to learn or achieve in school at the normal level. *See* **retardation, mental.**

handicapped, mentally: having a mind or mental powers that lack maturity or are deficient in such measure as to be a hindrance to achievement; a term employed by some educators to refer to the entire range of mentally subnormal children. *See* **retardation, mental.**

handicapped, multiple: descriptive of an individual who, by reason of two or more body dysfunctions or impairments, may often have to bear personal and social burdens that cannot be resolved. *Syn.* **multihandicapped.**

handicapped, neurologically: descriptive of children who are crippled by a condition of the central nervous system, such as epilepsy, cerebral palsy, postencephalitis, or postmeningitis. *Comp. w.* **handicapped, orthopedically.**

handicapped, orthopedically: descriptive of crippled children disabled by non-central-nervous-system conditions, such as poliomyelitis, tuberculosis of the spine, fractures, or burns. *Comp. w.* **handicapped, neurologically.**

handicapped, physically: as applied to a child, having a physical defect of such seriousness as to interfere with or render more difficult normal progress in the regular school program.

handicapped psychology: *syn.* **psychology, exceptional-child.**

handicapped, severely: descriptive of an individual who is disabled to such a degree that achievement is unusually difficult or impossible; the severely handicapped generally cannot be rehabilitated through the usual procedures and facilities established for general community use.

handicapped, socially: socially maladjusted; a term now increasingly applied to those with personality disturbances.

handicapped, trainable mentally: *syn.* **mentally retarded, trainable.**

handicapped, visually: a nonspecific term applying both to the blind and to the partially seeing.

handicraft: *see* **handcraft.**

handrail: a rail at the side or middle of stairs designed for grasping to prevent stumbling and falling in walking up or down stairs.

handwork: *see* **handcraft.**

handwriting: the act of placing or inscribing characters on a surface by hand with the aid of a marking instrument such as pen or pencil; differentiated from drawing, which deals with pictorial characters, from writing, which may include typewriting and penmanship, and from chirography and calligraphy, which emphasize artistic or skillful effects.

handwriting chart, self-corrective: *see* **chart, self-corrective handwriting.**

handwriting drill, formal: *see* **drill, formal handwriting.**

handwriting reversal: any type of handwriting product that evidences a tendency on the part of the writer to write backwards; may consist in writing the last letter of a word first, the next to the last letter second, etc., or may be the writing of individual letters or words from right to left instead of from left to right. *See* **mirror script.**

handwriting scale: *see* **scale, handwriting.**

handwriting system, Zaner-Bloser: a system created by C. P. Zaner providing for large writing in primary grades with a reduction in size of writing in grade 3 and above.

handwriting, vertical: handwriting characterized by downstrokes that are perpendicular to the line of writing.

hanger: (1) an enlarged coat hanger with suspended metal clips from which gymnasium uniforms are hung for storage; (2) a wire frame with a built-in receptacle at the bottom used for storing gymnasium uniforms.

Hanseatic centers: areas in the Hanseatic towns of northwestern Europe in which schools were established under municipal auspices; the schools were especially designed for the needs of the commercial classes.

happening: (art) usually applied to activities associated with art experiences in a situation created in time and space and in which those persons attending or viewing become participants in the created occurrence; a mid-twentieth-century movement variously labeled happenings, assemblages, and environments. *Syn.* **environmental art.**

haptic: pertaining to the sense of touch in its broadest sense.

haptic color: *see* **color, haptic.**

haptic image: the image produced through autoplastic sensations, such as body feelings and muscular sensations, and their emotional effects on the individual.

haptic perception: *see* **haptic type.**

haptic type: a reference to the individual who is mainly concerned with the body-self; primarily a subjective type, feeling the self as the true actor of the picture; concerned with muscular sensations, kinesthetic experiences, touch impressions, and all experiences placing the self in value relationship to the outside world. *Syn.* **nonvisual type.**

hard copy: (data processing) information recorded in a form which is easily readable, usually in numbers and letters, as opposed to such items as paper tape or cards, electronically prepared tape, or other materials requiring machine application.

hard of hearing: having defective hearing that is, however, functional for the ordinary purposes of life (sometimes with the use of a hearing aid). *See* **hearing loss, moderate.**

hard of hearing child: *see* **child, hard of hearing.**

hard palate: the hard portion of the roof of the mouth supported by the maxillary and palatine bones. *Dist. f.* **soft palate.**

hardware: (1) the mechanical, magnetic, electrical, and electronic devices from which computers or other instruments are constructed; (2) the technological equipment or machinery, such as television cameras and monitors, tape recorders, and computers, which serve as *media* for instructional purposes but which of themselves have no specific content; a given item of hardware is capable of carrying a variety of educational messages depending on the content (*software*) it is used to convey.

harmonic: a component of a complex tone whose frequency is an integral multiple of the fundamental frequency of the complex tone.

harmonic, aural: harmonic generated in the auditory mechanism.

harmonic average: *syn.* **mean, harmonic.**

harmonic dictation: *see* **dictation, harmonic.**

harmonic mean: *see* **mean, harmonic.**

harmonic progression: *see* **progression, harmonic.**

harmonic sensitivity: the ability to compare and judge musical chords, especially with reference to their progressions; measured in various music tests. *See* **consonance, sense of.**

harmonic sequence: *syn.* **progression, harmonic (2).**

harmonic series: sum of the terms of a harmonic sequence.

harmonica, glass: a musical instrument, invented by Benjamin Franklin in 1763, in which a series of glass disks are affixed to a horizontal rod which is turned by a foot treadle; the lower edges of the disks are partly submerged in water, and the sound is produced by a delicate friction of the fingers.

harmonics: (1) the partials of the fundamental waveform which give musical instruments their distinguishing tone quality; (2) technical procedures, and the notation thereof, for playing these partials on a musical instrument. *Syn.* **partials.**

harmonious development: *see* **development, harmonious.**

harmonious growth: *see* **growth, harmonious.**

harmony: the science and art of the combination of tones sounded simultaneously, dealing with the construction, interrelation, and sequence of chords; a major subject of study in musical theory.

harmony, keyboard: *see* **keyboard harmony.**

harp, aeolian: a long, narrow box with six or more strings stretched lengthwise over two different bridges; the strings differ in thickness and tension and are activated by the free flow of an air current, from an open window, for example; from the Greek Aeolos, god of the winds.

hash: in automatic data processing, unwanted data or data left in a storage device from other applications or other runs; also known as garbage.

hash total: in automatic data processing, a check total computed by adding together all digits or all numbers comprised in a group of words or fields; the digits or numbers are added without respect to their identification, meaning, or significance.

Haskalah (häs′kä·lä′): *n. fem.* (Heb., lit., "enlightenment") a nineteenth-century movement among East European Jews, known as Maschilim, which attempted to break up the isolation of Jewish life and to impart Western culture to the masses in respect to language, dress, and taste; has had a profound influence on the philosophy of Jewish education and on the curriculum of the Jewish school.

Hatch Act: an act of Congress approved Mar. 2, 1887, for establishing agricultural experiment stations in connection with land-grant institutions and providing support for them.

Hawthorne effect: increase in motivation deriving apparently from an increase in a group's morale because the group perceives itself as receiving special treatment or consideration; first observed by Roethlisberger and his associates at the Hawthorne plant of the Western Electric Company, where various incentives were used to attempt to increase production; the effect in educational experimentation is a difficult one to control and it is likely that many studies of new teaching methods gain much or some of their presumed superiority not from the method itself but from this effect. *See* **Pygmalion effect.**

Hayes Binet scale: *see* **scale, Hayes Binet.**

hazardous occupation: *see* **occupation, hazardous.**

hazards, transportation: *see* **transportation hazards.**

hazing: harassment by abusive or ridiculous treatment, usually inflicted by students upon new students or new members in a specific group of students.

head: (tape recorder) small ring-shaped electromagnet across which the tape moves to provide the energy which magnetizes the iron oxide coating on the tape into special patterns.

head alignment: *see* **alignment, head.**

head counselor: *syn.* **director of guidance.**

head demagnetizer: hand-held electromagnet used to neutralize the unwanted residual magnetism built up and retained in recording heads.

head, dual-track: head having two separate pole pieces, each covering about half the width of the tape so that recording or playback of one or both channels (separately or concurrently) is accomplished with the tape moving in a single direction; can be used for single-channel, dual-channel, or stereophonic recording; also called two-track, twin-track, or double-track.

head, erase: electromagnet which erases or rearranges any magnetic pattern on the tape before a new recording is made.

head-feet representation: *see* **representation, head-feet.**

head, full-track: head with a gap covering almost the entire width of the tape; used for a single-channel recorder.

head, half-track: head which records and plays back about one-half of the width of the tape; can be reversed to obtain use of the second half; used for single-channel recorders.

head-mouth orientation: *see* **orientation, head-mouth.**

head movement: the movement of the head instead of the eyes in reading, a sign of ineffective eye-movement habits.

head noises: *see* **tinnitus.**

head of college residence: *see* **director of dormitory.**

head, playback: electromagnet which converts the signal on the recorded tape into electrical impulses which are then amplified and reproduced as sound by a loudspeaker or headphones.

head pulleys: a device for exercising the muscles of the neck consisting of a head harness attached to a cord running over pulleys and fixed to adjustable weights.

head, quarter-track: head having two pole pieces which cover the first and third quarters of the tape; the second and fourth quarters are recorded by turning the tape over; many stereophonic recorders now use this type.

head, recording: electromagnet which converts the amplified audio information from the microphone into a succession of magnetic fields that rearrange the magnetic patterns of the iron oxide particles on the tape as it passes the gap; the same head is often used for playback.

Head Start Project: *see* **Project, Head Start.**

head tax: *syn.* **tax, capitation.**

head teacher: (1) usually, the teacher responsible for the instructional activities and minor administrative procedures in a given department or subject; *syn.* **teacher in charge;** (2) in early childhood education, the teacher responsible for planning and carrying through the major portion of the program developing strong home-school relations; suggested training includes a B.S. degree in *early childhood education* or equivalent. *See* **aide; assistant, nursery school; associate; director, nursery school; teacher-intern.**

head tone: *see* **tone, head.**

head voice: *see* **voice, head.**

heading, box: *see* **box heading.**

heading, brace: *see* **brace heading.**

heading, column: *see* **column heading.**

heading, stub: *syn.* **stub (1).**

heading, subject: *see* **subject heading.**

headmaster: (1) the principal of a private or public secondary school; (2) historically, the administrative head of an academy (a private or quasi-public secondary school); (3) sometimes used to designate the principal of a public elementary school.

headphone: a device consisting of one or two telephone receivers connected to a headband for individual listening to audio sources such as intercommunication circuits; some headphones are equipped with a small microphone to permit two-way communication; also called *headset.*

headset: *see* **headphone.**

health: (1) the condition of a human organism which measures the degree to which its aggregate powers are able to function so as to bring physical, social, and emotional well-being; (2) as applied to a teacher, a level of physical fitness sufficient to ensure efficient performance of his teaching duties without obvious danger to his own physical well-being or to that of his pupils.

health appraisal: *see* **appraisal, health.**

health center: *syn.* **clinic, health.**

health certificate, compulsory: a statement by a physician setting forth facts concerning the physical condition of a pupil; generally required if the pupil is to be exempt from attendance at school because of poor health; required in most states if a pupil is to be certificated for work.

health certificate, teacher's: a statement required from a legally licensed physician indicating the teacher's physical condition, to be issued only after a thorough physical examination.

health, civic: a healthy condition or situation in community civic affairs growing out of efficient administration and community effort and interest.

health clinic: *see* **clinic, health.**

health, community: (1) the status of health of the people of the community as measured by selective mortality and morbidity data and other indices; (2) measures designed for the protection of the health of the people of the community.

health coordinator: *see* **coordinator, health.**

health council: a committee composed of school personnel, pupils, parents, community physicians, dentists, representatives of local health agencies, and public health personnel with the purpose of developing community understanding and cooperation in support of a school health program.

health counselor: *see* **counselor, health.**

health director's annual report: *see* **report, health director's annual.**

health education: the phase of education in which factual, authentic material pertaining to health and health practices and attitudes is presented.

health education, public: *see* **public health education.**

health evaluation: *see* **appraisal, health.**

health examination: *see* **examination, health.**

health, family: *see* **family health.**

health grade: *see* **grade, health.**

health guidance: *see* **guidance, health.**

health history: the part of the health record of a person that has to do with discovering and recording past illnesses and any other factors affecting his growth and development during infancy and childhood.

health-improvement class: *see* **class, health-improvement.**

health inspection: (elem. ed.) a routine health check on children in the classroom for the purpose of screening out those children who reveal symptoms of communicable diseases or other illness; an early part of the daily program in all elementary classrooms, preferably taking place as the children enter the room.

health instruction: *see* **instruction, health.**

health, mental: wholesomeness of mind, analogous to the wholesomeness of body implicit in physical health; extended in modern usage to include all aspects of the adequacy of personality integration. *See* **hygiene, mental.**

health museum: *see* **museum, health.**

health physics: *see* **physics, health.**

health problem, chronic: a disorder in health which persists over a long period.

health program: a planned organization of the resources of the school, usually involving also those of the home and community, in order to promote desirable knowledge, habits, and attitudes about health for the purpose of improving the health conditions of the pupils and of their environment; usually implemented by such means as periodic physical examinations, classes in health and hygiene, nutrition programs, and the regulation of health conditions within the school as well as by attempts to enlist the cooperation of the home and of community agencies.

health program, student: a school or college program for the protection and improvement of the health of students.

health record: *see* **record, health.**

health report: *see* **report, health.**

health report, monthly: *see* **report, monthly health.**

health screening: *see* **screening, health.**

health service, director of: *see* **director of health service.**

health service, student: a medical clinic established by the college for the diagnosis and treatment of physical and mental disorders; financed by a special fee paid by all students and entitling them to specified services.

health services, school: basic medical services provided in educational settings by certified medical personnel, such as a nurse and consulting physician; usually included are examination, screening, and referral functions. *See* **fixed point of referral.**

health, social: *syn.* **social harmony.**

health specialist: a trained worker whose services relate to some aspect of health education or health preservation.

health staff: *see* **staff, health.**

health status: the health condition of an individual as related to physical difficulties, emotional disturbances, evidence of immunizations, and number and kinds of accidents and illnesses.

health suite: a set of rooms equipped and used for the purpose of the physical examination and first aid or medical treatment of children; may contain such units as waiting room, examining room, dental room, infirmary, or some combination of these and other rooms.

health supervision: *see* **supervision, health.**

health survey: *see* **survey, health.**

healthful school living: a general designation of all aspects of school environment influencing the health of teachers and pupils.

hearing acuity: *syn.* **acuity, auditory.**

hearing aid: any device which amplifies or focuses sound waves in the listener's ear; usually refers to the various types of wearable amplifiers which operate with miniature loudspeakers in the ear or oscillators on the head.

hearing aid, group: (spec. ed.) equipment by means of which sounds are amplified so that a group can hear the natural voice or sounds.

hearing aid, monaural: a hearing aid which has only one transmitting channel.

hearing, binaural: hearing with two ears; made possible by the independent functioning of each ear and the existence of separate, though interconnected, pathways from each ear to the brain; the phenomenon most characteristic of binaural hearing is ability to localize the direction from which a sound comes. *See* **localization, auditory.**

hearing clinic: *see* **clinic, hearing.**

hearing comprehension level: *see* **comprehension level, hearing.**

hearing, conservation of: *see* **conservation of hearing.**

hearing, cross: hearing which occurs when sound is applied to one ear, by either an air-conduction or a bone-conduction transducer, and excitation of the other ear is produced by conduction across the bony structure of the skull.

hearing, defective: *see* **hearing loss.**

hearing defects: *see* **hearing loss.**

hearing discrimination: the understanding or perceiving of what is heard.

hearing handicapped: *see* **handicapped, hearing.**

hearing impairment: the most general term for malfunction of the auditory mechanism; does not distinguish either the anatomical area primarily involved or the functional nature of the impairment.

hearing impairment, acquired: hearing loss resulting from damage to hearing that was formerly normal. *Syn.* **adventitious hearing impairment.**

hearing impairment, central: an impairment in hearing of which the cause is located somewhere in the central nervous system.

hearing impairment, conductive: *see* **deafness, conduction.**

hearing impairment, congenital: hearing loss present at the time of birth; may be either hereditary or acquired.

hearing impairment, hereditary: hearing loss resulting from a defect in the genes at the time of conception.

hearing, informal: a hearing held without formality or ceremony, usually in school, for the purpose of settling routine attendance, discipline, or educational problems.

hearing level: for speech, the difference in decibels between the speech level at which the average normal ear and a particular ear reach the same intelligibility, often arbitrarily set at 50 percent. *See* **hearing loss** (2).

hearing loss: (1) the symptom or condition of impaired hearing, particularly impairment of the sensitivity of hearing as tested by either pure tones or speech; (2) the ratio, expressed in decibels, of the threshold of hearing of an ear at a specified frequency to a standard audiometric threshold; *hearing threshold level* or *hearing level* should always be used instead of hearing loss when a numerical value in decibels is given; (3) a change for the worse in an individual's threshold of hearing. *See* **percent loss of hearing.**

hearing loss, conductive: the type of hearing loss caused by a plugging of the external ear canal, restriction of the free movement of the eardrum, or restriction of the movement of the bones in the middle ear. *Comp. w.* **hearing loss, perceptive; perceptive impairment.**

hearing loss, marked: average loss of 55 or 60 to 65 or 75 decibels; people with such a hearing loss are borderline between hard of hearing and deaf.

hearing loss, mixed: a combination of conductive with sensory-neural hearing loss.

hearing loss, moderate: a loss of 25 to 50 or 55 decibels in the speech range in the better ear; a person with such a loss is classified *hard of hearing.*

hearing loss, nerve-type: *see* **hearing loss, perceptive.**

hearing loss, noise induced: loss of hearing acuity caused by frequent exposure to high-intensity sounds, which damages portions of the inner ear.

hearing loss, perceptive: the type of hearing loss resulting from pathology in the inner ear and in the cranial nerve and its primary auditory nuclei; also called *nerve-type hearing loss.* *See* **hearing loss, conductive.**

hearing loss, profound: a loss of from 70 or 75 decibels (in the speech range) up to the inability to distinguish more than one or two frequencies at the highest measurable intensity in the better ear.

hearing loss, slight: average losses of 20 decibels or less in the speech range in the better ear; people with such a hearing loss are borderline between those with normal hearing and those with significantly defective hearing.

hearing loss, temporary: *syn.* **fatigue, auditory.**

hearing, monaural: the process, function, ability, or power of perceiving sound through only one auditory mechanism, or car.

hearing, normal: the hearing of a group of individuals of both sexes whose ears on otological inspection show no indications of present or past otological disease or anatomical deviation that might interfere with acoustic transmission, who have no history of past otological disease or abnormality, who are between the ages of adolescence and old age (approximately 15 to 65 years), who have no hearing complaints, and who understand and cooperate in the test of hearing that may be applied.

hearing, normal threshold of: in testing hearing acuity, the minimum intensity of the tone which elicits responses on 50 percent of the trials; the manner of listening (open acoustic field or under an earphone) and the place and method of measuring the sound pressure level must be defined; there are thus many different values for the normal threshold of hearing.

hearing, official: a hearing before the juvenile court of which a formal record is made and kept. *Contr. w.* **hearing, informal.**

hearing on charges: a hearing at which an accused teacher or other school employee has an opportunity to answer charges that have been preferred against him; includes the introduction of evidence, the argument, and the decree; used particularly in tenure disputes; corresponds to a trial in cases of law.

hearing, percent loss of: *see* **percent loss of hearing.**

hearing, primitive level: the awareness on the unconscious level of the environment of sounds surrounding us.

hearing recruitment: a sudden sensation of loudness, at levels 15 or 20 decibels above his threshold, experienced by a patient who may barely hear a sound at full or normal loudness; the effect upon him is a sudden, perhaps severe, increase in sound pressure.

hearing, residual: the measurable or usable hearing remaining in the acoustically handicapped.

hearing, symbolic level of: the process of oral communication as a function of the hearing mechanism.

hearing test: *see* **test, hearing.**

hearing testing, free-field: *see* **testing, free-field hearing.**

hearing threshold level: *see* **hearing loss** (2).

hearing threshold, pure-tone: that intensity of pure tones at a given frequency which can just barely be heard; in hearing measurement terms this is at a 50 percent criterion level.

heartometer: an apparatus designed to record on a paper disk measurements of heart action said to indicate its functional efficiency.

heat exhaustion: a condition of the body in which excessive temperature cannot be dissipated by the human organism, with resulting loss of energy and weakness.

heating, direct: a system of heating in which heat rays or hot air come from a source within the room or a heating plant located elsewhere.

heating, indirect: a system of heating in which air is first heated from coils through which steam or hot water flows and then passes by gravity or is forced by fan through a room or building.

heating plant: the furnaces, boilers, vacuum pumps, condensing pipes, transmission lines, radiators, valves, fans, motors, etc., used for the heating of buildings.

heating plant, central: a heating plant that furnishes hot water or steam to all or a large number of the buildings of a university, college, or school.

heating plant, separate: a heating plant used to heat a single building; separate from the central heating plant and often located at some distance from the university or college campus.

heating, radiant: heating by means of rays proceeding from a central source within the room, such as a steam or hot water radiator or a stove.

heating, radiant panel: (1) heating by means of hot water circulated through pipes embedded in concrete slabs in floors, ceilings, or walls; (2) heating by means of electric wires so embedded.

Herbartian steps: *see* **Herbartian method.**

hebephrenia (hē′bə·frē′ni·ə): a type of schizophrenia characterized by silliness, diminished emotional reactions, and the tendency to withdraw from reality.

hebetude (heb′ə·tūd): mental dullness, drowsiness, or lethargy.

Hebrew high school: *see* **high school, Hebrew.**

Hebrew school: a Jewish religious school in which Jewish values are taught from original sources in the Hebrew language; called Hebrew school because of the stress placed on the study of the Hebrew language and literature.

Hebrew school, afternoon: *see* **Hebrew school.**

Hebrew teacher's certificate: *see* **certificate, Hebrew teacher's.**

hectograph: a device for making copies of writings, drawings, etc., in which the original is transferred to a gelatinous surface; reproductions are made from this.

heder (Khe′der): *n. masc.; pl.* **hadarim** (Khä·dä·rim′); (Heb., lit., "room") an elementary school supported by the tuition fees paid by parents, with a program of instruction confined to Jewish religious subjects such as the Prayer Book, Bible, Talmud, Shulhan Arukh, etc.; at one time the dominant type of Jewish school in eastern Europe; transplanted to the United States by immigrants from eastern Europe and gradually transformed into a weekday supplementary school.

heder metukan (Khe′der mə·tōōk·kän′): *n. masc.; pl.* **hadarim metukanim** (Khä·dä·rim′ mə·tōōk·kä·nim′): (Heb., lit., "a modernized school") a type of school, with emphasis on the study of Hebrew as a living language, which came into existence in eastern Europe toward the end of the nineteenth century as a result of the impact of modernism and Zionism; it exerted considerable influence on the development of the heder and subsequently on American Jewish education.

hedge school: a term that originated in Ireland during the eighteenth century and denoted one of the proscribed gatherings of Roman Catholic children and their teachers during the repression of the Roman Catholic schools under the penal laws; the classes were held in open fields, generally near a hedge for shelter, hence the name; later the name was often applied to any poor school taught in an irregular manner or place. *Syn.* **adventure school.**

hedonia (he·dō′ni·ə): a condition characterized by abnormal animation and cheerfulness.

hedonic tone: the feeling tone of experience; the pleasurable or unpleasurable complement of experience.

hedonics (he·don′iks): a branch of psychology dealing with the nature, origin, effects, and relationship of pain and pleasure.

hedonism: in general, the theory that pleasure is the highest good; psychological hedonism is the theory that all human behavior is guided by the desire to avoid pain and achieve pleasure; ethical hedonism is the theory that pleasure is the only intrinsic good for man; one of the best known exponents in the modern historical era was Jeremy Bentham. *See* **Epicureanism.**

Hegelian dialectic: *see* **dialectic, Hegelian.**

Hegelianism (hə·gā′li·ən·iz′m; hə·jē′-): the philosophy of Hegel (1770–1831), an attempt to combine in one closely reasoned system the modern insistence on subjectivism, freedom, nature, and the temporal with the classical and medieval emphasis on objectivity, universality, purposiveness, and the eternal; regards spiritual activity as an absolute that is the ultimate basis of all being and meaning, the reality of which is an eternal enriching of its own self-knowledge, this enrichment taking place only as the absolute externalizes itself in nature and finite minds and thus makes possible its infinite and eternal process of enriched return to itself; regards existence as change, change as evolution, evolution as history, history as thinking, and thinking as eternal Being (Existence); regards all logic and all changes as dialectical in nature. *See* **dialectic.**

height age: *see* **age, height.**

height-weight index: *see* **index, height-weight.**

height-weight ratio: the ratio of the standing height of an individual to his weight.

Hellenism: (1) the type of culture, represented by the ideals of the classical Greeks, as in their regard for athletic vigor and grace, their cultivation of the arts and sciences, their devotion to civic-social organization, and their social and ethical attitudes; (2) adoption of the Greek language and thought, and conformity to Greek ideals.

Hellenistic art: *see* **art, Hellenistic.**

Hellin's law: *see* **law, Hellin's.**

helots: serfs of ancient Sparta attached to the landed estates of the Spartans, to whom they rendered a fixed portion of the produce of the land they worked.

helper: a person who assists a skilled worker in a particular trade at a wage usually higher than that of an apprentice, and who thus is afforded an opportunity to "pick up" the trade.

helping teacher: a term often applied earlier in this century to supervisory teachers and still applied in some rural areas to a teacher or supervisor whose task is to assist classroom teachers, especially new and inexperienced ones, to improve their teaching techniques; duties may also include rendering aid in planning work, in developing the course of study, and in promoting community relationships.

helplessness, feeling of: a personality trait, often an unconscious insecurity, related to personality structures (Rorschach).

hematophobia (hē′mə·tō·fō′bi·ə; hem′a-): morbid fear of blood.

hemianopsia (hem′i·ə·nop′si·ə): blindness in one-half the field of vision of one or both eyes.

hemicrania (hem′i·krā′ni·ə): (1) a neurotic condition characterized by severe recurrent headache affecting one side of the head; (2) a form of migraine.

hemiplegia: a neurological disorder characterized by paralysis of one side of the body.

hemophilia (hē′mə·fil′i·ə; hem′a-): a condition characterized by failure of the blood to clot and manifested by profuse and uncontrollable bleeding even from the slightest wounds; inherited by males through the mother as a sex-linked character. (Most hemophiliac children require a home teacher.)

henotheism: belief in a god but not necessarily to the exclusion of belief in the existence of other gods.

Heraclitean (her'ə·klī·tē'ən; -klī'tē-): (1) strictly, pertaining to the philosophy of Heraclitus of Ephesus (about 500 B.C.), according to which everything was thought to change continuously according to an unchanging law of purposeless circularity, the motive force being the tension of opposites; (2) in common usage, pertaining to the idea that things are in flux, that all is relative. *Syn.* **Heraclitic.**

Heraclitic: *syn.* **Heraclitean.**

Herbartian method: the five teaching steps advocated by Johann Friedrich Herbart (1776–1841), dogmatized by his followers, and widely accepted in teacher education in the nineteenth and early twentieth centuries; the five steps are: (*a*) preparation, (*b*) presentation, (*c*) comparison and abstraction (association), (*d*) generalization, and (*e*) application. *Syn.* **five formal steps;** *dist. f.* **Morrison plan.**

Herbartian movement: the development and extension of Herbart's psychology and methodology. (Representatives of Herbartianism in Germany during the last quarter of the nineteenth century were Stoy, Dörpfeld, Ziller, and Rein. In the United States, under the leadership of De Garmo, the McMurrys, and others, Herbartianism exerted an influence on educational theory and practice second only to that of Pestalozzianism, reaching its climax in the closing decade of the last century.)

herd instinct: (1) the reputed tendency of animals and human beings to group or "herd" together; (2) the tendency of the individual to acquire the culture ways of his group.

hereditarian: a person who places emphasis on the role of heredity in human development; sometimes implies an unfair depreciation or denial of historical, cultural, geographic, climatic, or other factors.

hereditary: pertaining to that which is inherited. (Usually refers to biological inheritance.) *See* **heredity; inheritance.**

hereditary hearing impairment: *see* **hearing impairment, hereditary.**

heredity: a general term denoting the orderly biological process by which an organism produces other organisms of comparable structure; includes the idea of factors that bring about resemblance between offspring and ancestors as well as considering the mechanical details of the transmission of characters through factors in the germ plasm. *See* **constitution** (2), (3), and (4); **environment; gene; inheritance** (2).

heredity, social: the transmission of cultural traits from the social forms, such as groups and institutions, to the young.

heredoconstitutional (her'ə·dō-): referring to the *genotype*, or those elements in the individual's constitution which have been derived from inherited factors. *See* **constitution** (2), (3), and (4).

heritage: the hereditary endowment; the totality of characters and traits that have been received through the process of hereditary transmission. *See* **heredity; heritage, social; inherit.**

heritage, social: the aggregate or complex of customs, ideas, ways of life, usages, organizations, institutions, and instruments that serves as the base for the culture of a group and is passed on and perpetuated, with some modification, from generation to generation.

heteroclisy: (of a double-entry table) the property of being composed of arrays that are not all *equally asymmetric,* or the property of being composed of arrays that are not all *symmetric. Contr. w.* **homoclisy.**

heteroclitic: (in a double-entry table) composed of arrays that are not *equally asymmetric,* or composed of arrays that are not *symmetric;* arrays may be nomic or anomic, depending upon the system or regularity of change in symmetry. *Contr. w.* **homoclitic.**

heterogeneity: when applied to the individuals in a group or the items in a test, refers to the degree to which they are different or unlike. *Ant.* **homogeneity.**

heterogeneous grouping: *see* **grouping, heterogeneous.**

heterogeneous test: *see* **test, heterogeneous.**

heterograde: (said of statistical data) varying in magnitude, grade, or intensity. *Contr. w.* **homograde.**

heterograde statistics: *see* **statistics, heterograde.**

heterokurtic: (said of a double-entry table) composed of arrays that do not all have the same degree of kurtosis. *Contr. w.* **homokurtic.**

heteronomy: state of being subject to the law of another; not self-governing or self-determining. *Contr. w.* **autonomy.**

heteronym: a word with the same spelling as another but having a different pronunciation and meaning, such as *lead,* the name of the metal, and *lead,* the verb "to conduct." *Dist. f.* **homograph.**

heterophoria (het'ər·ō·fō'ri·ə): a latent imbalance of the external muscles of the eyes, as opposed to *heterotropia,* which is a manifest imbalance.

heteroscedastic (het'ər·ō·skə·das'tik): (said of a double-entry table) composed of arrays having unequal variability and hence different standard deviations or, more generally, of arrays having different frequency distributions. *See* **scedasticity;** *ant.* **homoscedastic.**

heteroscedasticity (het'ər·ō·skə·das'tis'i·ti): unequal variability or, more generally, dissimilarity of frequency distributions of the arrays of a double-entry table. *See* **scedasticity;** *ant.* **homoscedasticity.**

heterosexuality: (1) ability to love one of the opposite sex; (2) a condition characterized by sexual interest in a member or members of the opposite sex.

heterotropia (het'ə·rō·trō'pi·ə): a manifest deviation of the axis of the eyes, making single binocular vision impossible; fixation is maintained with either eye but not simultaneously with both. *Syn.* **squint; strabismus.**

heterozygous (het'ər·ō·zī'gəs): containing both the dominant and the recessive genes for any given character or two different genes of a related series. *See* **allelomorph; dominant;** *contr. w.* **homozygous.**

heuristic (hū·ris'tik): having to do with the art of discovery; in learning and problem solving, pertaining to those methods by which one finds and applies strategies that may transfer across tasks; in computerized data processing, pertaining to a processing procedure which may not always yield the desired output. *See* **algorithm** (2).

heuristic argument: *see* **argument, heuristic.**

heuristic learning: *see* **learning, heuristic.**

heuristic method: *syn.* **problem method** (1).

heuristic program: *see* **program, heuristic.**

heuristic set: *see* **set, heuristic.**

hi-fi: *see* **high-fidelity.**

Hi-Y club: an organization for high school boys sponsored jointly by the school and the YMCA, housed usually in the school building, and having as goals the development of character and good citizenship.

hidden tax: *see* **tax, hidden.**

hierarchical order: (fact. anal.) the order characteristic of a correlation matrix when the rows of the matrix are proportional; in such a case the columns are also proportional, and the correlations can then be accounted for by a single general factor. (This property of certain correlation matrices was first noted by Spearman in 1904 and was the starting point for the development of factor analysis, first in terms of a single general factor and later in terms of any number of factors.) *See* **tetrad difference; two-factor theory.**

hierarchical theory: a theory of which the component laws are presented as deductions from a small set of basic principles.

hierarchy: any graded organization, whether mental, physical, or social, in which each rank (except the highest) is subordinate to the ranks above. *See* **hierarchical order.**

hierarchy, educational: the chain-of-command, line-of-authority channels of communication in the school system.

hierarchy, habit-family: arrangement in order of likelihood of occurrence of the responses which have become habitual reactions to a given stimulus situation or goal.

hierarchy, occupational: a ranking of the various occupational groups in terms of some characteristic (for example, average intelligence, income, social esteem). *See* **occupational level.**

hierarchy of control: as used in supervision of instruction, vertical levels of control in an organization with each level determining the degree of autonomy allowed the role incumbent.

hierarchy of development: the ranked or ordered stages of a developmental sequence considered as a whole.

hierarchy of values: *see* **values, hierarchy of.**

hieratic writing: *see* **writing, hieratic.**

hieroglyph: one of the characters used in *hieroglyphics;* in general, any pictorial symbol or pictorial mark used to represent spoken language.

hieroglyphics (hī'ər·ə·glif'iks): the picture writing of the ancient Egyptians in which two types of characters were used: (*a*) *ideographic* characters representing objects or symbolic ideas associated with objects; (*b*) *phonetic* characters representing the sound of single letters or of syllables.

Hieronymians (hī'ər·ə·nim'i·ənz): *syn.* **Brothers of the Common Life.**

high-fidelity (hi-fi): *adj.* descriptive of a recording or reproduction of the full audio range of a signal with a minimum of distortion.

high general achiever: *see* **achiever, high general.**

high-grade mentally defective child: *see* **mentally defective child, high-grade.**

high school: the school division following the elementary school, comprising most often grades 9 to 12 or grades 7 to 12 and sometimes including grades 13 and 14. *Syn.* **secondary school.**

high school, academic: a secondary school that emphasizes nonvocational subjects, particularly those thought to constitute preparation for schools and colleges of arts and sciences.

high school, accredited: a secondary school that has been designated by an accrediting agency as meeting accepted standards or criteria of quality. (The agencies that accredit high schools are the regional accrediting associations, the state departments of education, and certain of the state universities. In practice, an accredited high school in many states indicates a secondary school whose graduates are accepted for admission to the state university.)

high school, agricultural: (1) a school of secondary grade established and maintained by a county, district, or state, or by a combination of these, to provide theoretical and practical training in agriculture, generally employing a large corps of instructors who specialize in various branches of agriculture and having extensive equipment such as buildings, lands, animals, and machinery; (2) a rural secondary school in which agriculture is one of the major courses of instruction.

high school, business: a public high school that emphasizes business or commercial curricula, in contrast to high schools that offer academic as well as commercial curricula. *Syn.* **commercial high school; high school of business.**

high school, central: *syn.* **high school, union.**

high school, commercial: *syn.* **high school, business.**

high school, community: (1) a secondary school with a curriculum designed to meet the specific needs of the community which it serves as determined by a study of the community by professional and lay members of the community; (2) sometimes used as a rather ambiguous synonym for union high school; this use is rare. *See* **high school, union.**

high school, comprehensive: a secondary school that includes both general education courses and specialized fields of study in its program and thus offers academic, commercial, trade, and technical subjects. *Contr. w.* **high school, specialized.**

high school, county: a school of secondary level established and maintained by a county, open to pupils from the county at large except from districts maintaining their own high schools.

high school, diocesan: a secondary school operated by the Roman Catholic Church under the jurisdiction of the diocese authority and open to the children of one or several parishes.

high-school diploma, differentiated: *see* **diploma, differentiated high-school.**

high-school diploma, uniform: *see* **diploma, uniform high-school.**

high school district: a district organized and administered to provide education on the secondary level only. (The boundaries of a single elementary or common school district may be coterminous with those of a high school district, but more often two or more elementary or common school districts are in whole or in part included within the territory covered by a high school district.)

high school district, superimposed: a high school district organized for the purpose of supporting and administering a union high school. *See* **high school, union** (1).

high school district, union: in some states legally termed a partially consolidated district or a district consolidated for high school purposes only.

high school equivalency certificate: *see* **certificate, high school equivalency.**

high school, extension: a secondary school operated at times other than those during which the high schools are regularly operated, for example, an evening high school, a summer high school, etc.

high school, five-year: a school composed of five grades, usually grades 8 to 12 or, in 11-year systems, grades 7 to 11; applied rarely to a school of grades 10 to 14.

high school, folk: (1) a type of postprimary "people's college" started in Denmark (1851) by N. F. S. Grundvig for youth, especially of the rural and working classes, not selected for academic secondary schooling; later spread to other Scandinavian countries and still very common although declining in influence; (2) a school for adults patterned after the Scandinavian programs of study for townspeople and rural groups, aimed at improving the economic and cultural conditions of these people, with programs of study closely related to their needs through a cultural curriculum rather than one narrowly practical and vocational. *Comp. w.* **folk school** (2).

high school, four-year: a high school of four grades, usually grades 9 to 12 or, in 11-year systems, grades 8 to 11.

high school, four-year reorganized: *see* **reorganized high school, four-year.**

high school graduate: *see* **graduate, high school.**

high school, Hebrew: a continuation school for graduates of the weekday elementary Hebrew schools, offering a course of intensive Hebrew studies including Biblical, rabbinical, medieval, and modern literature, religious doctrine and ritual, Jewish history, and problems of Jewish life.

high school, incomplete regular: a secondary school which offers less than 4 full years of work beyond grade 8 in a school system that is organized in such a manner that nursery, kindergarten, or grade 1 through grade 8 constitute the elementary grades; sometimes called *truncated high school.*

high school, junior: *see* **junior high school.**

high school, junior-senior: a reorganized secondary school, usually comprising grades 7 to 12, and separated into an upper (or senior) and a lower (or junior) division, which frequently are housed in different wings or parts of the building and administered somewhat separately. (The junior division frequently has an assistant principal and teachers assigned primarily to its pupils.) *Dist. f.* **high school, six-year** (1).

high school, manual-training: an obsolete type of secondary school or program, found in the latter part of the nineteenth century, offering courses in shopwork and mechanical drawing in addition to many regular high school subjects and usually omitting the classics. (The first such school was sponsored by a group of businessmen in St. Louis in 1880.)

high school, multiple-purpose: *syn.* **high school, comprehensive.**

high school, occupational: *see* **high school, vocational.**

high school of business: *syn.* **high school, business.**

high school postgraduate: *see* **postgraduate, high school.**

high school principal: *see* **principal, high school.**

high school, public: a high school supported and controlled by the people, nonsectarian, open to all, and making no tuition charge.

high school, reorganized: *see* **reorganized high school.**

high school, rural: a school of secondary level established in the open country or in a small town or village; may or may not be jointly administered with a contributory elementary school or schools; often designated a rural high school by state law and made eligible for special state aid.

high school, senior: *see* **senior high school.**

high school, six-year: (1) a secondary school (not divided administratively on a junior and senior basis) that incorporates six grades, usually grades 7 to 12, administered under one principal and having a faculty organized to serve all six grades; *syn.* **undivided high school;** (2) a junior-senior high school in which grades 7 to 9 form a junior unit and grades 10 to 12 form a senior unit, both units being housed, usually, in the same building, often with separate principals (frequently teachers employed for one unit are not expected to teach in the other division); (3) a junior-senior high school in which grades 7 and 8 form the junior unit and grades 9 to 12 form the senior unit.

high school, specialized: a secondary school of which the educational program is designed especially for pupils training for specific vocations or fields of specialized interest, for example, an *agricultural high school, commercial high school,* or *trade high school. Contr. w.* **high school, comprehensive.**

high school standards, state: criteria used in judging the quality of a high school or of its program of studies for the purpose of determining approval.

high school student: *see* **student, high school.**

high school, summer: a secondary school operating during the summer vacation period only.

high school, technical: a name sometimes given to a vocational high school, although the word *technical* is in many parts of the country now restricted to use at the post-high school level. *See* **high school, vocational.**

high school, three-three junior-senior: *syn.* **high school, junior-senior.**

high school, township: a high school that serves and is supported by the citizens of a township, the term *township* being used to designate a governmental subdivision of the county. (The board that governs the township high school is often independent of the board that governs the elementary school or schools of the area.)

high school, trade: a high school of which the primary function is the teaching of skilled or semiskilled trades with only such nontrade subjects as bear on the understanding and mastery of the trade itself; frequently limited to the teaching of one trade or a group of closely allied trades. *Dist. f.* **high school, vocational.**

high school, traditional: (1) a high school composed of grades 9 to 12 (or 8 to 11); (2) a high school that is characterized by a philosophy, programs, and practices of long standing and in which there is little tendency toward innovation or experimentation.

high school, truncated: *see* **high school, incomplete regular.**

high school, two-year reorganized: *see* **reorganized high school, two-year.**

high school, undivided: *syn.* **high school, six-year** (1).

high school, undivided five-year: *syn.* **high school, five-year.**

high school, union: (1) a high school with an attendance area comprising two or more elementary school districts; financed and administered separately from the elementary districts and governed by a governing board which may be entirely different from any of the elementary boards, may be composed of the combined elementary boards, or may be composed of representatives from each of the elementary boards in the union high school district; (2) a high school jointly supported and administered by two or more school districts, which, however, maintain separate elementary schools; *syn.* **central high school; high school, community** (2).

high school, university: a secondary school, usually on a university campus, used for experimental, participation,

demonstration, or practice-teaching purposes in the preparation of secondary school teachers, supervisors, and principals. *See* **laboratory school.**

high school, vocational: a high school offering training in one or more skilled or semiskilled trades or occupations, along with certain related subjects, as well as a wide variety of elective nonrelated subjects having general rather than purely vocational value; the name is in general use throughout the United States, although in some sections the vocational high school is called *occupational high school,* in some others *technical high school. See* **vocational school, area;** *dist. f.* **high school, trade.**

high-speed printer: *see* **printer, high-speed.**

high-speed reader: *see* **reader, high-speed.**

high steppage gait: *see* **gait, high steppage.**

higher-decade addition: *see* **addition, higher-decade.**

higher education: instruction offered to persons of considerable intellectual maturity, usually requiring previous preparation through the secondary school; in terms of the institution common to the United States, higher education includes all education above the level of the secondary school given in colleges, universities, graduate schools, professional schools, technical institutes, teachers colleges, and normal schools. (The junior college is considered an institution of higher education by some authorities, and by others it is considered a part of secondary education.)

higher-level work skill: *see* **skill, higher-level work.**

higher mental process: *see* **mental process, higher.**

higher-order interaction: *see* **interaction, higher-order.**

hiking: taking organized long walks especially for pleasure and/or exercise.

Hillel Foundation: a foundation established by the Jewish fraternal order B'nai B'rith for the purpose of providing social, fraternal, religious, and educational opportunities of a formal and informal character to Jewish students in American colleges and universities.

Hindu-Arabic numerals: *see* **numerals, Hindu-Arabic.**

hirsutism: hairiness.

histogram: a graphic representation of the frequency distribution of a continuous variable consisting of a series of rectangles of widths proportional to the widths of the class intervals and of areas proportional to the frequencies represented; thus, when the class intervals are equal, the heights of the different rectangles are also proportional to the frequencies represented. *Syn.* **block diagram** (2); **frequency histogram;** *dist. f.* **graph, relative bar; historigram;** *contr. w.* **polygon, frequency.**

histogram, frequency: *syn.* **histogram.**

histogram, percentage: a histogram in which the frequencies represented are expressed as percentages.

histogram, solid: a three-dimensional figure showing the frequency distribution of a double-entry table, each cell frequency being represented by a solid rectangular column proportional in volume (and also in height if the class intervals are equal) to the frequency represented.

histology: a branch of anatomy that deals with the minute structure of animal and plant tissues as discernible with the microscope.

historical approach: (1) a method of teaching in which new subject matter or ideas are introduced through discussion or exposition of their historical origin; (2) a technique of individual counseling in which a person's problems are traced through their origin and development in his behavior.

historical chart: *syn.* **historigram.**

historical criticism: *see* **criticism, historical.**

historical data: *see* **data, historical.**

historical distribution: *see* **distribution, historical.**

historical fiction: *see* **fiction, historical.**

historical graph: *syn.* **historigram.**

historical method: (1) the process of discovering, recording, and interpreting facts having historical significance, involving collection, arrangement, criticism, and synthesis of the data into an acceptable whole and subsequent interpretation of the data; (2) the investigation of biological evolution by comparison of the temporal succession of life forms.

historical musicology: *see* **musicology, historical.**

historical realism: *See* **realism, historical.**

historical research: *see* **research, historical.**

historical school of economics: *see* **economics, historical school of.**

historical series: *syn.* **series, time.**

historical study: *see* **study, historical.**

historical variable: *see* **variable, historical.**

historical variation: *see* **variation, historical.**

historigram (his·tŏr′i·gram): a graph depicting the changes of a variable over a period of time; the ordinates are proportional to the values of the variable, and the time intervals are plotted as abscissas. *Syn.* **historical chart; historical graph;** *dist. f.* **histogram;** *contr. w.* **polygon, frequency.**

historiography (his·tō′ri·og′rə·fi): the study, criticism, and evaluation of historical writing in terms of accepted canons of historical writing and research; usually includes a study of the background and training of the historian.

historiography, naturalistic school of: a school of thought that bases its interpretation of events on the concept of a chain of causes and effects; also known as *humanistic, secular,* and *scientific.*

history: (1) a systematically arranged, written account of events affecting a nation, social group, institution, science, or art, usually including an attempted explanation of the relationships of the events and their significance; (2) the science or field of study concerned with the recording and critical interpretation of past events; generally divided into ancient history, medieval history, and modern history, with many subdivisions, such as United States history. *See* **history as actuality; history as knowledge; history as record; history as thought.**

history, ancient: a systematic account of events generally considered as covering the period from the time of the first written records down to the dissolution of the Roman Empire; often includes some study of preliterary history. *See* **history, medieval; history, modern.**

history as actuality: a term used to designate the concept that history consists of actual, existing facts and conditions, past and present, whether recorded or not.

history as knowledge: a term used by some authors to designate the concept that history is a collection of proved and generally accepted facts.

history as record: a term used by some writers to designate the concept that history consists of records of the past, such as signs, symbols, monuments, documents, and state papers, that convey information about the past.

history as thought: a term used by some authors to designate the concept that history consists of the selection, arrangement, and interpretation of facts taken from records of past events.

history, case: *see* **case history.**

history, church: a record of the events in the life of the Christian community and of the reciprocal influence of church and society from the inception of the church to the present time.

history, commercial: a branch of history, frequently offered in college and occasionally offered in secondary school, that deals with the history of business, commerce, transportation, and communication.

history, constitutional: the study of the legal aspects of government, including its origin, development, and present status.

history, contemporary: (1) the record of the events, facts, developments, trends, and leading personalities of the present; (2) the events, facts, developments, and trends themselves.

history cycle: a period of time during which a motif evolves in human activity, reaches its culmination, and terminates—a concept entertained by many but one that is far from universally accepted among scholars.

history, economic: (1) a record of the means by which men have made their living; (2) a branch of general institutional history concerned with the economic aspects of the social institutions of the past.

history, family: *see* **family history.**

history, medieval: that part of general history lying between ancient and modern history; convenient limits are the dissolution of the Roman Empire and the fifteenth century.

history, modern: the history of recent centuries; usually thought of as beginning with the Renaissance and extending to the present.

history, music: the study of music in Western civilization, generally, from the Greeks to the present; a required year's course in all programs of study in nearly all schools and departments of music in institutions of higher learning.

history of art: as a school subject, the study of an organized body of materials dealing with art expression through the ages, with specific periods or schools of art in their relation to the general development of art, and with the lives and works of artists having historical significance, such a study being undertaken with a view to increasing and enriching the student's appreciation of art works, whether old or new, and to supplying him with a historical perspective by which to see and understand better the current tendencies in art.

history of education: a division of history concerned primarily with the history and development of educational theories and practices from the earliest period to the present.

history of journalism: a systematic journalistic course, usually advanced, in the history and development of the newspaper and other periodicals in the United States, Great Britain, and other countries, designed to give understanding of present journalistic problems and policies.

history, political: (1) a phase or division of general institutional history concerned with the activities of political parties, elections, party principles, and party control of government; (2) a record of the development of a political party or parties.

history, school: *see* **school history.**

history, social: (1) a record of the unique social experiences of a person and his adjustment to them; (2) the approach to history which lays particular stress upon the social life, social trends, and social institutions and social organizations of people.

history, social case: *see* **history, social** (1).

history, world: a running record of the development of civilizations from the earliest stages to the present.

hitchhiking: a mental process of developing new or additional ideas which are stimulated by or derived from a previous idea. *See* **brainstorming.**

hitching: a form of locomotion occurring when the child has attained a sitting posture; the direction of movement is backward.

hobby: *see* **avocation.**

hockey, field: a field-type game in which 11 players on each team use hockey sticks to propel a small white leather-covered ball; played in the United States primarily by girls and women at the high school and college levels; sometimes referred to as hurley, shinny, or bandy.

hockey, ice: a team sport played on an ice hockey rink by six players on ice skates; object of the game is to drive a rubber puck, using a wooden hockey stick, into the opponent's goal.

holder, copy: *see* **copy holder.**

holding power: the power of the school to hold pupils in school until graduation.

holding power, annual: in pupil accounting, the percent that the number of pupils in end-of-year membership represents of the number of pupils for whom the school is arithmetically accountable for the period from July 1 of one year to June 30 of the next.

holding power, cumulative: the percentage that the number of graduates forms of the total number of pupils for whom the class is arithmetically accountable on June 30 of the graduating year.

holiday, school: a day on which school is not conducted either because of legal provisions or because of designation by the board of education as a holiday; since such days are not considered as days in session, the pupils are considered as being neither present nor absent on school holidays. *See* **days in session.**

holism: (1) an approach to life science based on the belief that understanding of organisms depends greatly upon studying the whole organism and its properties as a whole as well as upon the more familiar analytical method; (2) that philosophy of higher education and student-personnel work which maintains that education is and must be concerned with the whole man, his mental, physical, emotional, and spiritual development. *See* **gestalt; psychology, gestalt.**

Hollerith card: a punch card suitable for actuating a Hollerith machine.

Hollerith machine: any one of a variety of electrically actuated sorting, tabulating, and other special statistical machines designed to work with punch cards; based on the original invention and patents of Prof. Herman Hollerith. *See* **tabulating machine;** *dist. f.* **Powers machine.**

Hollerith system: a method of encoding *alphanumeric* information onto cards.

hollow building blocks: *see* **blocks, hollow building.**

hollow-square arrangement: (home ec.) arrangement of equipment on four sides of a square space in an all-purpose homemaking room or foods laboratory; has been replaced for the most part by the unit kitchen arrangement. *See* **unit kitchen.**

holophrase (hol'ə·frāz): a single word used to express the more complex thought of a phrase.

home, adoption: *see* **adoption home.**

home agent: *see* **extension worker, county.**

home (and community) experiences: meaningful learning experiences related to school instruction which are planned, carried on outside the classroom, and evaluated under the guidance of teachers, parents, or other adults; they may merely provide more practice of certain skills than is feasible or seems justified in the classroom, or they may involve a group of related activities which require careful planning and apply principles and techniques already learned to solving problems of personal, family, or community life.

home-and-family-life education: *see* **family-life education.**

home-and-school visitor: a trained attendance worker employed by the attendance department of a school and serving to coordinate the work of the school with that of the home with a view to bringing about mutual understanding and cooperation in matters of school attendance. *See* **supervisor, attendance.**

home art: *see* **art, household; interior decoration.**

home, boarding: *see* **boarding home.**

home, broken: *see* **broken home.**

home call: a visit to the natural or legal residence of a child by a pupil-personnel worker, an attendance officer, or a teacher for counseling or home-school planning for services.

home-call report: *see* **report, home-call.**

home-condition report: *see* **report, home-condition.**

home contact: any means of connection or communication between school and home, such as a written report or visit by a teacher.

home demonstration agent: *see* **extension worker, county.**

home demonstration club: *see* **club, extension homemaker.**

home demonstration program: *see* **program, home economics extension.**

home, detention: *see* **detention home.**

home duties: (1) those lesson assignments which pupils must perform at home; *syn.* **homework;** (2) any task or responsibility imposed by parents on their children.

home economics: (1) college instruction offered at the undergraduate and graduate levels to prepare students for homemaking and for a variety of professional fields, such as teaching, dietetics, management, food service, certain business careers, home economics extension, and research; (2) a discipline that draws from the biological, physical, and social sciences and the humanities the content needed to help people solve problems of food, clothing, shelter, and relationships and that deals with the development of understandings, skills, and attitudes essential to the improvement of the ways of living of individuals, families, and community groups. *See* **family-life education; home economics education; homemaking education.**

home economics adult work: *see* **homemaking education, adult.**

home economics, boys': courses dealing with personal and home-living problems, planned to meet the needs of boys.

home economics, college of: *see* **college of home economics.**

home economics core: courses deemed necessary for all home economics majors irrespective of their professional goals.

home economics education: professional courses offered at the senior college and graduate levels for prospective teachers and teachers in service in the field of home economics.

home economics extension: *see* **extension, home economics.**

home economics extension, international: *see* **extension, international home economics.**

home economics extension program: *see* **program, home economics extension.**

home economics, general: a specific college program leading to a bachelor's degree but not involving preparation for professional work other than homemaking.

home economics instruction, comprehensive: *see* **instruction, comprehensive home economics.**

home economics, occupational programs in vocational: *see* **programs in vocational home economics, educational.**

home economics program, vocational: *see* **program, reimbursed consumer and homemaking education.**

home economics, state supervisor of: *see* **supervisor of home economics, state.**

home economist: one who holds a bachelor of science or bachelor of arts degree or an advanced degree with a major in one of the fields of home economics.

home education: education in the home, usually referring to preschool or early childhood education and occasionally to the education directed by the school for homebound pupils. *Dist. f.* **homemaking education; home practice; home study; homework.**

home, foster: *see* **foster home.**

home furnishings, equipment, and services program: *see* **program, home furnishings, equipment, and services.**

home guidance: *see* **guidance, home.**

home improvement project: *see* **project, home improvement.**

home instruction: *see* **instruction, home.**

home investigation: the act of gathering data concerning the home of a given child.

home, juvenile detention: *see* **detention home.**

home management: an area of study dealing with the problems involved in making the best use of the human and material resources of the home so as to ensure the optimum development of the family, both as a group and as individuals, in their relationships with one another and with society.

home-management house (or apartment): a special dwelling, with furnishings and arrangement approximating a modern home, where home economics students, under faculty direction, participate in group living for a period of time. *See* **group living.**

home management services program: *see* **program, home management services.**

home membership, worthy: competence in discharging the duties and responsibilities of a member of a home, involving relations with others, homemaking, consumer business activities, child training, etc.; one of the aims or objectives of education as stated by various authorities.

home, parental: *see* **parental home.**

home pickup: *see* **pickup, home.**

home practice: (home ec.) *see* **home (and community) experiences.**

home project: (home ec.) *see* **home (and community) experiences.**

home reading: *see* **reading, home.**

home reading course: *see* **course, home reading.**

home report: *syn.* **report to parents.**

home rule: local self-government; autonomy.

home rule, theory of: educationally, the theory that control by local, representative, nonpartisan boards of education ensures that the voice of the people will be directly reflected in the modeling of local educational policies; home rule is therefore in contrast to state or Federal control over local policy decisions.

home-school-community relations: mutually helpful relationships among home, school, and community in the interests of child welfare.

home-school contact: a general term used to designate many of the different ways a parent might have contact with the school, for example, parent-teacher conference or phone calls between the home and school.

home-school relations: relationships between the school and its staff members and the parents of the children in the school with particular regard to the ways in which the school staff and parents work together in helping pupils to derive maximum benefit from their educational experiences.

home-school telephone: *see* **telephone, home-school.**

home science: *see* **science, household.**

home shop: a space or room at home equipped for constructional, mechanical, and allied activities for the purpose of maintaining the home and its equipment or serving recreational and/or vocational interests.

home study: any study done at home outside school hours; includes work on school assignments, community projects, and strictly individual problems.

home study course: *see* **correspondence course.**

home study, supervised: home study directed or supervised by the teacher in such a way as to aid the student in getting successful results.

home teaching of the blind: assistance and instruction by a trained teacher in adjustment to the conditions imposed by blindness, rendered in the home to blind persons; usually includes instruction in braille, handcrafts, travels, and orientation.

home visit: a home call to assist the counselor to an improved understanding of the home environment, including parental attitudes toward their children and toward learning.

home visitation: *see* **visitation, home.**

home visiting: visits by teachers to the homes of pupils for the purpose of knowing them in their home environment and of strengthening the bond between home and school.

home-visitor counselor: *see* **counselor, home-visitor.**

home workshop: *see* **workshop, home.**

homebound child: *see* **pupil, homebound.**

homebound instruction: *syn.* **instruction, home;** *see* **homebound teacher; pupil, homebound.**

homebound program: *see* **program, homebound.**

homebound pupil: *see* **pupil, homebound.**

homebound teacher: a teacher who carries instruction to the child who is physically unable to attend school.

homemaker club, extension: *see* **club, extension homemaker.**

homemakers: married or single men or women who carry major responsibilities for the establishment and maintenance of a home.

homemaking: the courses or units of instruction in home economics emphasizing acquisition of knowledge and development of understanding, attitudes, and skills relevant to personal, home, and family life; this is one phase of the vocational home economics program. *See* **program, reimbursed consumer and homemaking education.**

homemaking center: *see* **center, homemaking.**

homemaking cottage: *see* **center, homemaking.**

homemaking education: a program of instruction and organized experiences offered at the high school level, designed to help students solve problems of personal and family life and to assume homemaking responsibilities. *See* **family-life education; home economics; home economics education; program, reimbursed consumer and homemaking education.**

homemaking education, adult: instruction offered to men and women who are concerned with problems of family life; may be offered to organized classes or to informal groups. *See* **adult education.**

homemaking, general: a term used to designate a high school program that is not organized to meet requirements set up by the state board for vocational education.

homemaking-problems clinic: *see* **clinic, homemaking-problems.**

homemaking skill: *see* **skill, homemaking.**

homemaking unit: a suite of rooms consisting of laboratories and a model house used for the teaching of homemaking subjects.

homemaking, vocational: a term applied to the homemaking phase of the vocational home economics program, some vocational home economics departments offering only the homemaking program while others include preparation for both homemaking and gainful employment. *See* **program, reimbursed consumer and homemaking education.**

homeroom: (1) in a semidepartmentalized school (usually an elementary school), a room presided over by a single teacher to which a class is assigned as a group, to which the class reports morning and afternoon for checking attendance and hearing announcements in which instruction is given having general educational value as distinguished from instruction in specific subjects, and to which the class "belongs"; (2) in a completely departmentalized school, a room presided over by a single teacher to which a class is assigned for purposes of checking attendance and similar administrative details and in which educative homeroom activities may or may not be carried on.

homeroom adviser: *syn.* **homeroom teacher.**

homeroom advisership: *see* **advisership, homeroom.**

homeroom group: *see* **group, homeroom.**

homeroom guidance: *see* **guidance, homeroom.**

homeroom program: *see* **program, homeroom.**

homeroom subject: *see* **subject, homeroom.**

homeroom teacher: a teacher who is assigned to a homeroom to which pupils report during the day for administrative purposes, who is responsible for some formal records relating to the pupils, and who often serves as the pupils' counselor, advising on such matters as schedule planning, course planning, extraclass activities, vocations, health, leisure-time activities, and social behavior. *Syn.* **homeroom adviser.**

homestead exemption: *see* **exemption, homestead.**

homestead tax: *see* **tax, homestead.**

homework: school assignments to be completed out of regular school hours at the residence of the pupil. *Dist. f.* **home duties** (2); **home study.**

homiletics: the art of writing and delivering sermons.

homoclisy: (of a double-entry table) the property of being composed of arrays that are all of *equal asymmetry;* or, the property of being composed of *symmetric* arrays. *Contr. w.* **heteroclisy.**

homoclitic: (in a double-entry table) composed of arrays that are *equally asymmetric,* or composed of *symmetric* arrays. *Contr. w.* **heteroclitic.**

homogeneity: as applied to the individuals in a group or the items in a test, refers to the degree to which they are similar or alike. *Ant.* **heterogeneity.**

homogeneity reliability: *see* **reliability, homogeneity.**

homogeneity test: *see* **test of homogeneity.**

homogeneous: the property of possessing homogeneity. *See* **homogeneity.**

homogeneous group: *see* **group, homogeneous.**

homogeneous grouping: *see* **grouping, homogeneous.**

homogeneous special class: *see* **class, homogeneous special.**

homogeneous test: *see* **test, homogeneous.**

homograde: (said of statistical data) expressed in only two categories; for example, presence or absence. *Contr. w.* **heterograde.**

homograph: a word that is the same in spelling as another word but differs in origin, in meaning, and sometimes in sound, for example, *tear* (differing in sound) and *bear* (the same in sound). *Dist. f.* **heteronym.**

homokurtic: (said of a double-entry table) composed of arrays that all have the same degree of kurtosis. *Contr. w.* **heterokurtic.**

homonym (hom′ə·nim; hō′mə-): a word having the same pronunciation as another but a different origin, meaning, and, often, spelling, for example, *there* and *their*, *ate* and *eight*, and *here* and *hear*.

homophony (hō·mof′ə·ni; hom′ə·fō′ni): music containing a melody with a chordal accompaniment. *Contr. w.* **polyphony.**

homoscedastic (hō′mō·skə·das′tik): (said of a double-entry table) composed of arrays all of which have equal variability and hence the same standard deviation or, more generally, which have the same frequency distribution except for their means. *Ant.* **heteroscedastic.**

homoscedasticity (hō′mō·skə·das′tis′i·ti): the property of a double-entry table composed of arrays all of which have equal variability and hence the same standard deviation or, more generally, which may be represented by the same frequency distribution except for means. *Ant.* **heteroscedasticity.**

homozygous (hō′mō·zī′gəs): having a pair of identical genes for any given character, arising from the union of two germ cells alike with respect to a given gene. (The *homozygous* organism therefore transmits an identical gene for the character in question to each and all of its germ cells.) *See* **dominant; gene; inbreed;** *dist. f.* **monozygous;** *contr. w.* **heterozygous.**

homunculus theory (hō·mung′kū·ləs): the ancient theory (now discarded) that the child is a miniature adult.

honesty: the quality of being fair, impartial, and unwilling to deceive or take advantage of others.

honesty, intellectual: that quality which induces a person to have full regard for the scholarly handling of ideas as is appropriate to a society committed to the process of free inquiry, to state fully his real views, to examine the full range of alternatives, to become aware of his own intellectual and cultural motivations, to question his own assumptions, and to change his most cherished opinions if more reasonable ones are discovered.

honor code: *see* **code, honor.**

honor fraternity: *syn.* **honor society** (1).

honor points: numerical values assigned to teachers' marks, for example, 3 honor points per credit of A, 2 per credit of B, 1 per credit of C, 0 per credit of D, and − 1 per credit of F; designed to quantify quality of achievement as opposed to amount of credit.

honor roll: a list published each school term or year by a school, college, or university showing the students who have achieved a set academic standard. *Syn.* **dean's list.**

honor society: (1) an association that receives into membership persons who have achieved high scholarship and who in addition fulfill the society's established requirements of distinction in some broad field of education and culture or in general scholarship; established only in 4-year degree-granting colleges or universities accredited by the Association of American Universities or by the appropriate regional accrediting agency; *see* **fraternity; honor society, leadership; honor society, scholarship; honor fraternity;** (2) in the secondary school, an organization of students selected primarily on the basis of schol-arship and also on the basis of leadership and citizenship; its functions are to stimulate scholarship, leadership, and citizenship and to act as an agency for assuming responsibility for some specific problems assigned to it by its sponsor, the faculty, or the administration of the school.

honor society, leadership: an association that bases eligibility and election to membership primarily on desirable and constructive all-round leadership in student affairs and superior scholarship. *See* **honor society.**

honor society, national: an organization established under the auspices of the National Association of Secondary School Principals and designed to honor outstanding scholastic achievement by senior high school students; members are elected from the junior and senior classes, usually by secret vote of the faculty; no more than 15 percent of a graduating class is eligible, and members must be chosen from the upper one-third of the class.

honor society, national junior: an organization similar to the national honor society but designed for ninth-grade students.

honor society, scholarship: an association that bases eligibility and election to membership primarily on the attainment of a high standard of scholarship and admits only persons who have achieved high scholarship. *See* **honor society.**

honor student: one whose academic achievement is at or above a level specified in faculty regulations, usually an average mark of B in all subjects.

honor system: as applied to the administration of tests, a system under which students are required to be individually responsible for their own honesty and avoidance of cheating.

honorary degree: *see* **degree, honorary.**

honorary fraternity: *see* **fraternity, honorary.**

honorary society: an organization that elects to membership students who have outstanding records of scholastic achievement, student activities, or both; frequently confined to students in a particular field of work.

honorary sorority: *see* **sorority, honorary.**

honors class: *see* **class, honors.**

honors course: *see* **course, honors.**

honors system: a system existing in a few colleges and occasionally in secondary schools which provides *honors courses* for honor students and establishes other latitudes in course registration, attendance, and individual study so as to permit unusually able students to learn faster and more intensively and extensively than in traditional courses. *See* **course, honors;** *dist. f.* **honor system.**

hood: a heavy cloth band, widening into a long hood hanging down the back, worn on the neck and shoulders of a college or university graduate, over the gown; lined with specific colors to indicate the institution granting the degree; its shape indicates the level of the degree, that is, bachelor, master, or doctor. *See* **academic costume.**

hook-and-loop board: *see* **board, hook-and-loop.**

hooky: a word used in the popular expression playing hooky for the act of playing truant.

Hoover technique: *see* **cane technique.**

hopper: in data processing, the input receptacle on the card feed of a machine.

horizontal advancement: *see* **advancement, horizontal.**

horizontal articulation: *see* **articulation, horizontal.**

horizontal bar: a steel or wood bar about 1¼ inch in diameter, fixed parallel to the floor and adjustable at distances above the floor; used for gymnastic exercises.

horizontal cooperation: *see* **cooperation, horizontal.**

horizontal enrichment: *see* **enrichment, horizontal.**

horizontal growth: *see* **growth, horizontal.**

horizontal inventory: *see* **inventory, horizontal.**

horizontal occupational mobility: *see* **occupational mobility, horizontal.**

horizontal organization: *see* **organization, horizontal.**

horizontal social mobility: *see* **social mobility, horizontal.**

horizontal treadmill: *see* **treadmill, horizontal.**

horme (hôr′mē): urge to action.

hormic energies: propelling forces behind goal-directed actions.

hormic psychology: *see* **psychology, hormic.**

hornbook: a device once used in colonial America and elsewhere for teaching the alphabet and primary reading and for religious instruction; consisted of two sheets of printed or written material glued to either side of the blade of a paddle-shaped piece of wood and protected by thin layers of transparent cow horn.

horology: the principles and art of constructing instruments for indicating time.

horse, long: *see* **horse, side.**

horse, side: a piece of heavy gymnastic apparatus having two pommels and designed for vaulting and arm-support exercises; without pommels the apparatus becomes a *long horse.*

horseshoe pitching: a game played by two or four players who pitch horseshoes (two each player) from one stake to another, 40 feet apart; points are scored according to the position of the shoe in relation to the stake.

hospital birth certificate: *see* **certificate, hospital birth.**

hospital class: *see* **class, hospital.**

hospital instruction: *see* **instruction, hospital.**

hospital library: *see* **library, medical.**

hospital pupil: *see* **pupil, hospital.**

hospital school: a hospital or guesthouse providing shelter, physical care, and instruction for children, the earliest known school of this type being found among the Eastern Christians in Pontus in the fourth century; later became common in Europe, particularly in England.

hospital teacher: a teacher who instructs hospitalized pupils.

hospital teaching program: *see* **program, hospital teaching.**

hosteling: educational or recreational travel under one's own power, usually by young hikers or cyclists, for the purpose of getting acquainted with a particular geographical area and its people. *See* **youth hostel** (2).

hostility: antagonism; animosity; an unfriendly attitude; if undue and almost automatic, may be indication of paranoid trend or imaginary persecution feeling; a personality trait typically recognized in socially maladjusted children.

Hotelling-Kelly method of factor analysis: *see* **factor analysis, Hotelling-Kelly method of.**

hours of work: (voc. ed.) the total amount of time worked, expressed in terms of hours per day or hours per week. *See* **working hours.**

house, foreign language: *see* **foreign language house.**

house, fraternity: *see* **fraternity house.**

house organ: a company news publication distributed among the employees of a firm to maintain their interest, loyalty, and cooperation.

house plan: the organization of a large college or university into smaller communities, each usually having its own residence hall, common dining room, library, and athletic program.

house-tree-person test: *see* **test, house-tree-person.**

household: as defined by the Bureau of the Census for the 1970 census includes all the persons who occupy a house, room, group of rooms, or apartment that constitutes a dwelling unit; a household may contain more than one family.

household art: *see* **art, household.**

household budget: *see* **budget, household.**

household equipment: the designation of a course in home economics dealing with the selection, use, and care of equipment used in the home.

household equipment instruction: *see* **instruction, household equipment.**

household equipment laboratory: *see* **laboratory, household equipment.**

household mechanics: unspecialized practical activities or construction and maintenance activities centering in the home; frequently included as an area of industrial arts programs.

household science: *see* **science, household.**

housekeeping corner: a space in the classroom where material and equipment are arranged to provide opportunity for dramatic play and the reliving of the home activities familiar to the child prior to school entrance.

housekeeping duties: responsibilities assumed by primary teachers for keeping their rooms clean, neat, and attractive; for example, keeping cupboards orderly, providing and arranging potted plants, etc.

housemother: (1) an adult woman who serves in the capacity of chaperon and adviser to a college club, fraternity, or sorority; (2) a matron in a boarding home or "cottage plan" type of institution.

housing: (1) provision of buildings for various uses at a university, college, or school; (2) provision of dormitories and of living quarters for staff members and students; (3) (ind. arts) a curriculum area designed to develop both a technical knowledge of the problems of planning, buying, constructing, and maintaining a unit dwelling and a social understanding of the universal problem of shelter.

housing and home furnishings program: *see* **program, housing and home furnishings.**

housing bureau: an office that arranges for living quarters for students and for faculty members and other employees.

housing, cooperative: (1) as related to education, a system of housing, usually under general college supervision, in which students are responsible for the financing and administration of living costs, each paying a proportionate share of expenses and sometimes sharing in the work; (2) a housing project owned and operated as a cooperative enterprise by the tenants.

housing loans, college: Federal loans, authorized by Title IV of the Housing Act of 1950, made to educational institutions for construction of housing for students and faculties.

housing projection: *see* **projection, housing.**

housing, teacher: (1) living accommodations for teachers provided by the agency supporting a school; *see* **teacherage;** (2) dwelling quarters for teachers.

how-to-study course: *see* **course, how-to-study.**

human behavior: *see* **behavior, human.**

human communication: *see* **communication, human.**

human dignity: the doctrine that the individual is not to be treated as a mere means to some end but is to be regarded as an end in himself; thus he is not a thing but rather a person with inalienable natural rights and privileges.

human ecology: *see* **ecology, human.**

human engineering: *see* **engineering, human.**

human geography: *see* **geography, human.**

human infant: *see* **infant.**

human nature: (1) the characteristics that we have learned from the group as a result of group socialization; (2) those qualities which mark us as human, apart from physical form.

human nature as depraved: *see* **depraved, human nature as.**

human nature as deprived: *see* **deprived, human nature as.**

human paleontology: *see* **paleontology, human.**

human relations: the social interaction which takes place between people and the influence which persons have on one another; also refers to the scientific study of this influence or interaction as it occurs.

human relations education: the teaching of skills in personal relationships, the understanding of drives and motivations, and the interdependence of all people in a democratic society. *See* **intercultural education; intergroup education;** *dist. f.* **group development.**

human relations laboratory training: *see* **training, human relations laboratory.**

human resource development program: *see* **program, human resource development.**

human resources: all the physical, intellectual, and spiritual energies, abilities, capacities, and ideals of an individual or a society.

human schema: *see* **schema, human.**

human society: *see* **society, human.**

humanism: (1) historically, the literary phase of the Western Renaissance that sought to recover the spirit and values of the ancient Greeks and Romans through a recovery of their literature; (2) natural humanism is the philosophical theory that emphasizes human values; it is generally antimetaphysical; (3) rational humanism is the philosophical theory that emphasizes the unique nature of man's rational faculties; it is generally sympathetic to metaphysics.

humanism, classical: the medieval movement away from authoritative *scholasticism* and toward revived independent study of literae humaniores, namely, the Greek and Latin classics. *See* **humanities** (3); **Renaissance.**

humanism, literary: a movement, led by Irving Babbitt, Paul Elmer More, and Norman Foerster, which affirms a classical type of liberal education, the constant exercise of the active will, the balanced cultivation of the faculties, and a final appeal to intuition in the search for truth.

humanism, new: any one of the contemporary neohumanistic theories that seek to recover the spirit and values of the ancient Greeks and Romans or to emphasize the human qualities of the individual over all aspects of social or group interaction.

humanism, rational: a position (exemplified by R. M. Hutchins) in which appeal is made to the nature of man as man, rather than as a member of a society, as the ultimate source of educational authority; the cultivation of latent rational faculties through an education ordered by first principles rather than by factors of time and place. *See* **Great Books.**

humanism, scientific: a movement of modern thought, also called *empirical* or *evolutionary naturalism* or *humanistic naturalism,* in which man is interpreted as a biosocial organism, capable, through the use of intelligence, of directing his institutions and creating a humane civilization; also emphasizes the universal applicability of the methods of experimental inquiry, and holds that truth, reality, etc., are human values to be judged by reference to consequences humanly experienced. *See* **pragmatism.**

humanistic naturalism: *syn.* **humanism, scientific.**

humanistic realism: *see* **realism, humanistic.**

humanistic school of historiography: *see* **historiography, naturalistic school of.**

humanistic sciences: *see* **sciences, humanistic.**

humanitarianism: (1) any view based principally on interest in human values; (2) benevolence; a regard for the welfare of human beings; (3) a religious cult substituting faith in man for faith in God; (4) a theological doctrine denying the divinity of Christ.

humanities: (1) a term used currently by many schools and colleges in the United States to designate comprehensive courses in literature, language, art, philosophy, religion, and history, thus distinguishing the humanities from social science and the natural sciences; (2) whatever concerns man as distinct from physical nature, especially as expressed most adequately in the great or classic achievements of humanity in literature and art; (3) as used in the Renaissance period, the term designated the "more human letters" of recently revived Greek and Latin writers in contrast to the theological letters of the medieval schoolmen; (4) frequently has been used to designate courses in, or the study of, classical languages (Latin and Greek) and classical literature and art; (5) today the term *humanities* includes also the masterpieces of modern literature, art, and science, as being equally "creations of the free spirit of man."

humanized geometry: *see* **geometry, humanized.**

humanized guidance instruction: *see* **guidance instruction, humanized.**

humash (khōōm·mäsh′): *n. masc.;* (Heb., lit., "a fifth") a designation for one or all of the five books of Moses; constitutes a basis subject of study in most schools offering an intensive program of Jewish education.

humidification, film: the process of controlling relative humidity for optimum safety in film storage.

humidity: loosely and commonly used as a synonym for relative humidity. *See* **humidity, relative.**

humidity, absolute: the actual amount of water vapor present in a given volume of air, the quantity of water being directly proportional to and dependent on the constancy of the air's temperature and of other factors, such as its movement.

humidity, relative: the ratio of the amount of water vapor present in a volume of air at a given temperature to the maximum amount of water vapor that could be contained in that volume of air at that temperature.

humidor: (photog.) a container for films, especially motion-picture films, that is equipped to maintain the humidity within proper limits for optimum film preservation.

hundred percent bar diagram: *see* **graph, hundred percent bar.**

huskiness: a voice quality rough in tone and generally characterized by relatively low pitch.

hybrid test: *see* **test, hybrid.**

hydrography: the science which deals with the measurements and description of the physical features of the oceans, seas, lakes, rivers, and their adjoining coastal areas, with particular reference to their use for navigational purposes. *Comp. w.* **hydrology.**

hydrology: the study of water, including its various forms and properties, its distribution in oceans, lakes, streams, underground formations and glaciers, and in the atmosphere, and of the hydrologic cycle. *Comp. w.* **hydrography.**

hygiene: (1) the study of physical health and of the factors affecting it, both favorable and adverse, as applied both to individuals and to groups such as the school, community, or nation; (2) a term used somewhat generally to designate the body of knowledge and principles relating to healthful conditions of learning and teaching, both in the physical and in the mental sense; (3) (kind.-prim. ed.) instruction in simple, functional matters relative to health, cleanliness, and wholesome living on a level suitable to young children, particular emphasis being placed on healthful eating, sleeping, and toilet habits, care of the teeth, eyes, nose, ears, nails, and hair, guidance in correct posture, safety precautions, play activities, and development of emotional stability in meeting difficulties.

hygiene, community: the science or procedure of maintaining health in a community.

hygiene, general: the study of health and prevention of disease, and the formation of proper health habits.

hygiene, mental: (1) a humanitarian movement started by C. W. Beers in 1909 for the purpose of improving the conditions in hospitals for the insane and subsequently concerned with all aspects of mental health; (2) the establishment of environmental conditions, emotional attitudes, and habits of thinking that will resist the onset of personality maladjustments; (3) the study of principles and practice in the promotion of mental health and the prevention of mental disorder; for educators, the role of teachers and schools in safeguarding and promoting good mental and emotional climate in the development of children.

hygiene of instruction: a term used formerly to denote the area of health education relating to the daily planned teaching program, the physical condition of classrooms, school organization, and administrative procedures as they affect the health of pupils. *See* **healthful school living.**

hygiene, personal: the study and application of preventive medicine and of physiology for the preservation of the health of the individual.

hygiene, sex: the study of the health of the organs of reproduction, of healthy sexual adjustment, and of venereal diseases and their prevention and cure.

hygiene, social: (1) sanitation and health measures affecting the group, whether community, city, state, nation, etc.; (2) often used as a synonym for *sex hygiene.*

hygienist, mental: a specialist with psychological training in the fields of learning, individual differences, measurement, and the helping process who understands identification (especially of exceptional children), remediation, and treatment of individuals. *See* **psychologist, school.**

hylomorphism: a theory advanced by Aristotle to resolve the form-and-matter dualism of Plato by viewing reality as consisting of a single cosmic order of increasing perfection from matter upward to form.

hypacusis (hip·ə·kū′sis): any threshold shift in hearing which is potentially correctable by either medical or prosthetic techniques to a practical hearing level.

hyperactive child: *see* **child, hyperactive.**

hyperactivity: (1) a characteristic of the constitutionally active child who often meets restrictions with antagonism and needs space and opportunity for muscular activity to prevent chronic hostility patterns; (2) chronic aggressive reaction pattern due to brain damage.

hyperdistractibility: a highly inadequate attention span resulting in inability to focus attention selectively on one major aspect of a situation, making it the foreground, instead of shuttling back and forth among inconsequential details; the two types are (*a*) *external*, inability of the child to learn the lesson being put on the blackboard because his attention is preempted by the movement of chalk, and (*b*) *internal*, exemplified by the child who repeatedly interrupts his seat work to ask irrelevant questions.

hyperesthesia (hī′pər·es·thē′zhi·ə; -zi·ə): a condition characterized by acute and excessive sensibility to stimulation.

hyperkinesis: excessive mobility or motor restlessness.

hyperkinetic child: *see* **child, hyperkinetic.**

hypermetropia (hī′pər·mə·trō′pi·ə): *syn.* **hyperopia.**

hypermnesia: a state in which recall and memory are heightened; may describe unusual mental ability within an individual either as a trait or as a transient condition brought about usually by strong emotion.

hyperopia: a refractive error in which, because the axis of the eyeball is too short or the refractive power of the lens weak, the point of focus for rays of light from distant objects is behind the retina. *Syn.* **farsightedness.**

hyperphoria (hī′pər·fō′ri·ə): *syn.* **squint, vertical.**

hyperplane, coordinate: (fact. anal.) the space of *r*-1 dimensions, orthogonal to a reference vector; an extension of the geometric concept of the plane defined by any two coordinate axes in three-dimensional space.

hyperpnea (hī·pərp·nē′ə): increased volume of breathing per minute. *Syn.* **hyperventilation.**

hyperprosexia: abnormal absorption of the attention by a single stimulating condition together with inability to ignore the stimulus.

hypersensitivity: a reaction to criticism due to a lack of self-assurance; may be an indication of personality problems.

hypertonicity: excessive muscular tension; characteristic particularly, but not exclusively, of the speech musculature in varying degrees in stuttering, spastic speech, and certain voice disorders.

hypertropia (hī′pər·trō′pi·ə): *syn.* **squint, vertical.**

hyperventilation: *see* **hyperpnea.**

hypnagogic (hip′nə·goj′ik): pertaining to the interval preceding sleep.

hypnoanalysis: a psychiatric method of treating a patient psychoanalytically by hypnosis, thus gaining more direct access to repressed materials and unconscious conflicts.

hypnopompic (hip′nə·pom′pik): pertaining to the state of awakening from sleep.

hypnosis: a state of increased suggestibility resembling normal sleep or stupor, induced by suggestion of the hypnotizer with the cooperation of the subject.

hypnotherapy: treatment of a patient with hypnosis either to obtain additional diagnostic information or to alter behavior through *abreaction* or posthypnotic suggestion or both.

hypo: a colorless, crystalline salt used as a fixing agent in photographic processing (sodium thiosulfate, $Na_2S_2O_3$); usually applied to the complete fixing solution.

hypochondria (hī′pō·kon′dri·ə; hip′ō-): a morbid concern about one's health; unfounded belief that one is suffering from a malady or that a body part or system is more impaired or diseased than is actually the case.

hypochondriasis (hī′pō·kon·dri′ə·sis; hip′ō-): a mental disorder characterized by *hypochondria.*

hypomania (hī′pō·mā′ni·ə; hip′ō-): a mild degree of excitement of the manic-depressive type.

hypophoria (hī′pō·fō′ri·ə; hip′ō-): a deviation of the visual axis of one eye downward when fusion is broken.

hypophrenia (hī′pō·frē′ni·ə; hip′ō-): feeblemindedness; *see* **retardation, mental.**

hypothecation of endowment: the practice of pledging principal in order to secure nearly equivalent sums for current expenses or capital outlay. (At the beginning of the twentieth century, a majority of American college endowment funds had been thus "borrowed" by their own trustees, but the practice of hypothecating endowment has since been so frowned upon that it is now the rule for endowments to be kept inviolate and productively invested.)

hypothesis: (1) an informed guess about the solution to a problem or about a general rule which describes the common elements characterizing a series of instances; *see* **assumption; postulate; premise; presupposition;** (2) (math.) the sentence *p* in a sentence of the form "If *p*, then *q*"; *contr. w.* **conclusion** (2).

hypothesis, alpha: Knight Dunlap's term for the principle that the occurrence of a response increases the likelihood that the response will occur again when there is the same stimulus.

hypothesis, beta: Knight Dunlap's term for the principle that the occurrence of a response has no effect on the probability that response will occur again when there is the same stimulus; sometimes confused with *gamma hypothesis.*

hypothesis, continuity: (1) the hypothesis that in discrimination learning each trial adds an additional bit of information; *see* **learning, discrimination;** (2) (spec. ed.) the supposition that emotional disturbance in a child is symptomatic of a continuing psychological process that may lead to adult mental illness.

hypothesis, descriptive: a statement that names, defines, or classifies something that is observed and seeks to relate the present object of concern to other things observed and described.

hypothesis, explanatory: a tentative, guiding idea that seeks to account for an event by exhibiting its relationships with wider principles or theoretical considerations in terms of which the observed event becomes comprehensively understood.

hypothesis, gamma: Knight Dunlap's term for the principle that the occurrence of a response lessens the likelihood that the response will occur again when there is the same or a very similar stimulus; this principle has been utilized practically in the elimination of errors in speech and typing; sometimes confused with *beta hypothesis.*

hypothesis, goal-gradient: a theory that as an organism approaches its goal in space and time there is an increased excitatory level revealed, for example, by a greater speed of locomotion. *See* **gradient, goal.**

hypothesis, null: (stat.) (1) the hypothesis that two or more treatments are equally effective; (2) the hypothesis that corresponding parameters of two or more populations are equal; (3) the hypothesis that a population parameter is of a specified exact value. *See* **analysis, sequential.**

hypothesis, Orton: *see* **Orton hypothesis.**

hypothesis, prerecognition: the theory that the stronger the hypothesis, the less the appropriate information necessary to confirm it.

hypothesis, statistical: a hypothesis that is precisely stated so as to be suitable for testing, for acceptance or rejection, on the basis of experimental findings; may or may not be a null hypothesis. *See* **hypothesis, null.**

hypothetical construct: *see* **construct, hypothetical.**

hypothetical proposition: *see* **proposition, hypothetical.**

hypothymia (hī′pō·thī′mi·ə): a condition characterized by reduced capacity for emotional response.

hypothyroidism mental retardation: *see* **mental retardation, hypothyroidism.**

hysteria: a functional nervous disorder of varying manifestations characterized by episodes of emotion, inappropriate reactions, and transient disorders of motor, sensory, or special sense nerves; variable mental symptoms may also appear.

hysteria, anxiety: a form of hysteria in which anxiety is a prominent symptom and physical symptoms are less evident. *Dist. f.* **neurosis, anxiety;** *contr. w.* **hysteria, conversion.**

hysteria, conversion: a psychoneurosis in which a painful emotional idea becomes converted, after repression, into a physical symptom such as paralysis or anesthesia.

hysterical amblyopia: *see* **amblyopia, hysterical.**

hysterical blindness: *syn.* **blindness, psychic.**

hysterical deafness: *syn.* **deafness, psychic** (1).

hysterical paralysis: *see* **paralysis, hysterical.**

IAL: *see* **language, international algebraic.**

ice hockey: *see* **hockey, ice.**

ice skating: *see* **skating, ice.**

iconoclasm: historically, the struggle against religious images; in general, the process of opposing or destroying cherished beliefs or of exposing them as illusions or shams.

iconography: collective term for images in art which carry specific symbolic meanings.

id: (psychoan.) an alleged area of the personality, unconscious, operating in accordance with the pleasure principle, and supposed to be the major source of the drive of the individual; instinctual forces in the human being demanding gratification of instinctual needs, etc. (Represented in the id are the biological determinants of behavior, the unconscious biological residue of previous experiences and repressed impulses. Impulses originating in the id may be tempered by the *ego* or *superego*.)

I.D. number: one of the identification numbers assigned users in a computing center; consists of a certain number of characters and may be used with a *password*.

ID ratio: *see* **ratio, ID.**

idea: (1) (epistemology) the immediate or only object of knowledge, or the instrument of knowledge; (2) (logic) an insight (generally vague) into the intelligizing principle or meaning structure of a system; a guide to inquiry, quasi-independent of the knower; (3) (metaphysics; idealism) underlying, ultimate forms of reality, such as "justice" or "beauty"; (4) (psych.) a thought or concept, or a complex of mental images.

idea, compulsive: an imperative idea that dominates consciousness against the will, often with a dynamic urge toward some undesirable act, such as suicide.

idea, innate: an idea which, according to Plato, is inborn; a theory repudiated by Locke. *See* **idea** (3).

idea, item: a statement identifying some knowledge, understanding, ability, or characteristic reaction of the examinee from which a test item can be formulated; the manner in which the basis for a test item is to be cast into an actual item.

ideaism: *see* **idealism, Platonic.**

ideal: a standard of perfection or excellence that serves as an aim for human attainment or realization, whether or not conceived as attainable.

ideal climate of classroom: *see* **climate of classroom, ideal.**

ideal, ego: *see* **ego ideal.**

idealism: broadly, any system of thought or practical view emphasizing mind or spiritual reality as a preeminent principle of explanation; "the conclusion that the universe is an expression of intelligence and will, that the enduring substance of the world is of the nature of mind, that the material is explained by the mental, in contrast with all those systems of thought that center in nature,

such as *naturalism,* or in man, such as *humanism"* (H.H. Horne); obtains more determinate meaning when qualified, for example, *Platonic idealism, objective idealism,* etc.

idealism, epistemological: the philosophical belief that all knowledge, or all knowledge of the external world, is ultimately limited to and dependent on what is perceived in consciousness; espoused by George Berkeley (1685-1753) and David Hume (1711-1776) among others; sometimes termed *psychological positivism.* See **idealism, subjective.**

idealism, monistic: a philosophical conception of the universe that regards mind as the ultimate reality and ideas that are objectively embodied in the universe as the ultimate objects of perception.

idealism, objective: a theory which holds that (*a*) external nature is real but to be identified with the thought or activity of the world mind, and (*b*) finite minds are parts (modes, moments, projections, appearances, members) of the world mind or absolute mind. *See* **Hegelianism.**

idealism, personal: a modern term applied to any theory of philosophy which holds that personality is the supreme value in life and is the key to all reality and value.

idealism, Platonic: the conception that "reality" consists of transcendent universals, forms, or ideals, which are the objects of true knowledge, while "appearance" consists of human sense impressions which are like shadows or imitations of ideas; involves the belief that there exists, ulterior to all finite existence, an order of form (ideas, patterns, deity, etc.) that is real, eternal, self-explanatory, self-moving, intelligible, and purposeful, on which all finite beings and activities, including human knowledge and morality, are dependent both for their existence and for their meaning; sometimes referred to as *ideaism.*

idealism, subjective: (1) (epistemological) the theory that the existence of an object is dependent upon its being known; *see* **idealism, epistemological;** (2) (cosmological) the theory that nature is merely the projection of the finite mind and has no external, real existence (*solipsism,* if limited to one single mind); (3) (ontological) the theory that reality consists entirely of subjects, that is, possessors of experience, whether God or men, and that selves are the primary factors in art, education, religion, science, logic. *Contr. w.* **independence, principle of.**

idealistic ethics: *see* **ethics, idealistic.**

idealistic metaphysics: *see* **metaphysics, idealistic.**

idealization, cultural: a trait, value, behavior pattern, or a way of life that is idealized or held in high esteem in a culture.

ideas, imperative: thoughts, usually absurd or unnecessary, that persist in consciousness against the will of the subject.

ideas of reference: the delusional belief that others are talking about one or making references to one in other ways.

ideation: the process of forming, entertaining, and relating ideas in the mind.

ideational culture: *see* **culture, sensate.**

ideational fluency: *see* **fluency, ideational.**

ideational learning: *see* **learning, ideational.**

identical elements: a term used to explain the view that transfer from one situation to another results because of identical or common factors (conditions, contents, etc.) which exist in the two situations, the amount of transfer varying according to the number of common factors involved; as originally formulated by Thorndike, such transfer involved identical neural pathways. *See* **neural path.**

identical-elements test: *see* **test, identical-elements.**

identical twins: *syn.* **twin, monozygotic.**

identification: (1) the appropriation into the self of the characteristics of an admired group or person; (2) the act or process of classifying the self with a group or person, usually those admired; (3) the act of gaining satisfaction through the achievements of the persons or groups with whom one has classified himself; (4) the process in the child's early development whereby he accepts wishes and demands of grownups he loves. (The formation of a wholesome set of ideals results from association and emotional identification; also, by identification with a parent's illness, psychosomatic illness in the child can be produced; loss of a parent may deprive the child of certain automatic identification, resulting in psychological harm.) *See* **introjection.**

identification test: *see* **test, identification.**

identity: (1) an equation which is true for all replacements of the variable or variables in the set under consideration, such as $a - (-b) = a + b$, an identity in the set of real numbers; (2) a mathematical closed sentence which expresses an equality which is true, such as $5 = 5$ or $\sqrt{12} = 2\sqrt{3}$.

identity, cognitive: *see* **law of identity.**

identity, law of: *see* **law of identity.**

identity matrix: *see* **matrix, identity.**

identity, partial: (transfer of training) a view that transfer occurs because of minute elements or characteristics of perception or adjustment that are identical with those previously encountered.

identity, personal: the unity of personality over a period of time.

ideogram: a simple line drawing representing an idea which the student must then put into words; a device used in foreign language instruction.

ideograph (ĭ′dē·ə·graf): a type of character, used in ancient Egyptian hieroglyphics and in Chinese writing, that represents the object it pictures or an idea associated with that object.

ideology (ī·di·ol′ə·jē): an ideal, belief, doctrine, or an aggregate of ideals, beliefs, or doctrines held by a person, group, or society.

ideoplastic art: *see* **art, ideoplastic.**

idiocy: among the mentally retarded population, includes persons who are incapable of ordinary reasoning or rational conduct; a condition showing mental age on the Binet scale not exceeding 2 years.

idioglossia: *syn.* **idiolalia.**

idiographic activity: *see* **activity, idiographic.**

idiographic data: *see* **data, idiographic.**

idiographic method: (ed. psych.) study of the laws and principles governing one individual, as contrasted with *nomothetic methods,* by which groups of people are studied.

idiographic representation: *see* **representation, idiographic.**

idiolalia: (1) unintelligible speech caused by sound substitutions, omissions, and transpositions; (2) a language invented by a child which is based on a formula and is rarely entirely original. *Syn.* **idioglossia.**

idiom: an expression of which the meaning does not appear directly from the ordinary signification of the words in the combination but is attached to them by conventional usage, so that the expression can seldom be literally translated into another language.

idiom count: a statistical study of the number of times certain expressions peculiar to a language occur in an indicated number of running words.

idiomatic style: a term descriptive of music conceived for, and thus only effective when rendered by, a specific instrument or group of instruments.

idiot: a person with the greatest degree of *mental retardation;* the term has been used to describe the intelligence level of persons obtaining IQ scores below 25 or 30.

idiot savant: a person who is idiotic in some respects but has some special faculty well developed, such as memory or aptitude for mathematics or music.

IDP: *see* **data processing, integrated.**

IGY: *see* **International Geophysical Year research program.**

illegal work: *see* **work, illegal.**

illegible writing: *see* **writing, illegible.**

illiteracy: (1) strictly, complete inability to read and write; (2) more broadly, inability to read and write sufficiently well to meet the needs of adult life; a relative term usually implying comparison of the individual's ability to read and write with the average ability found at his social or economic level; (3) failure to learn to read through lack of educational opportunity. *Ant.* **literacy.**

illiteracy, percentage of: as defined by the United States census, the number of persons unable to read or write in each 100 persons of the general population above 10 years of age.

illiterate: a person who is 10 years old or more and who can neither read nor write.

illness, mental: illness manifested by the emotional disturbances observed in the extremely disturbed child; may be recognized by symptoms of extraordinary aggression or withdrawal, the child requiring highly modified programs or institutional treatment before being able to function in the general framework of school classes.

illuminant-stable color-vision test: *see* **test, illuminant-stable color-vision.**

illumination: (read.) the amount of light that is reflected from the printed page. (It is believed that at least 10 to 12 footcandles of light are essential for comfortable reading.)

illumination, building: (1) the natural or artificial light of a building; (2) the measured candlepower of the light admitted through windows or produced by artificial means.

illumination, level of: the amount of light on a given surface, usually measured in footcandles.

illusion: the false interpretation of a real sensory impression, as a shrub mistaken for an animal. *Dist. f.* **hallucination.**

illusion, geometric: *see* **geometric illusion.**

illusionism: in art, the characteristic of appearing natural; found in some Roman mural painting, Dutch still life painting of the seventeenth century, etc. *See* **trompe l'oeil.**

illustrated lesson: *see* **lesson, illustrated.**

illustration, technical: the study of the techniques of presenting information graphically by various means to illustrate or clarify verbal or written description.

illustrative material: (1) any material or apparatus that is used by an instructor to clarify points in teaching; (2) concrete objects or materials used in teaching home economics to facilitate understanding and to aid in building standards and in developing judgment and appreciation, for example, articles of clothing, swatches, charts, pictures, posters, labels, animals, food, etc.

image: (1) (psychoan.) *syn.* **imago;** (2) (psych.) a form of centrally aroused experience, bearing a resemblance in structure to a perception.

image, activation of passive: bringing forth from the mind by stimulation those images or some of them which are known but not used, especially through individual experiences.

image, active: (art ed.) the image we can recall at will; in a child's drawings, only the active image is used, the image that he has at his disposal during the act of drawing.

image, auditory: the mental reconstruction of a hearing experience or the mental combining of separate hearing experiences.

image, body: a conceptual construct of one's own body as it relates to orientation, movement, and other types of behavior. *Syn.* **body schema.**

image congruency: in group dynamics, the achievement of agreement, first, of a person's image of himself with his ideal of himself and the superimposition of both of these images on the person he really is; and, second, agreement among the images others have of him, their ideal images, and his real self.

image, eidetic (ī·det'ik): a visual afterimage distinguishable by a greater vividness and prolongation than those of ordinary afterimages; common among children, but rare after the adolescent period.

image, haptic: *see* **haptic image.**

image, latent: the invisible scene on an exposed film before development by chemical processes.

image, passive: (art ed.) the image we have but cannot use because we cannot recall it; the child knows more than he draws; he recognizes fingers and even fingernails, but they may be only his passive image if he omits them in his drawings.

image, self-: *see* **self-image.**

image, visual: the mental reconstruction of a visual experience, or the result of mentally combining a number of visual experiences.

imagery, auditory: the interpretation, as a phase of a mental reaction, of words or other sounds heard.

imagery, free: in counseling, the results elicited from the client when the counselor asks him to relax as completely as possible and to report to the counselor the visual images that occur; the technique has the effect of reducing contact with reality, which diminishes the controlling functions of the ego and allows unconscious material to be expressed.

Imagery, kinesthetic: (1) imagery related to muscular sensation and the sensation involved in movement; (2) in reading, the imagery that results from tracing or writing a word symbol while sounding the word or saying its letters.

imagery, pitch: the ability to form mental images of various tonal effects from music notation without actually hearing the music; measured in certain music tests.

imagery, tonal: the ability to hear musical tones in imagination.

imaginary companion: an imagined person with whom one pretends to associate and whose character is sufficiently stable from day to day or moment to moment to be a recognizable entity; an experience especially common among children.

imaginary journey: a method of teaching and learning by which imaginary trips, excursions, etc., are taken; a device used especially in geography and sometimes in history and other social studies; may designate one of a variety of practices that range in quality and purpose from those approximating the preliminary reconnaissance survey, as used in geographical research, to pretended sightseeing trips.

imaginary number: *see* **number, imaginary.**

imaginary playmate: *see* **playmate, imaginary.**

imagination: (1) the ability or power to form a mental image or symbol, to engage in fantasy or creative play, or to express or characterize something that has been remembered or experienced; (2) the ability to confront and deal with a problem.

imagination, space: *see* **space imagination.**

imago (i·mā'gō): (psychoan.) an idealized memory of a beloved person, as of a father or mother, existing uncorrected since childhood.

imago, mother: (1) the idealized conception, originating largely in childhood, that the individual has of his mother; (2) the mother influence which the individual carries within him and of which he is usually in large measure unaware.

imbalance, lateral: (1) a condition of the eyes in which the muscles are not equally strong and hence tend to pull the eyes sidewise, either inward or outward, from the true line of vision; (2) a horizontal deviation of the visual axes from parallelism when fusion is broken.

imbalance, muscle: (1) the tendency of one set of opposing muscles to act more strongly than the other; (2) a lack of equilibrium in the external muscles of the eye, which may cause the eye to diverge outward, upward, inward, or in any direction in which one or more muscles may pull. *See* **heterophoria.**

imbalance, racial: *see* **racial imbalance.**

imbalance, vertical: (1) a condition of the eyes in which the muscles are not equally strong and hence tend to pull the eyes upward or downward out of the true line of vision; (2) a vertical deviation of the visual axes from parallelism when fusion is broken.

imbecile: an archaic term used to describe a mentally retarded person of trainable level with an IQ score of from 25 or 30 to 50.

imbecile, moral: an individual of extremely low grade intelligence who is incapable of making moral judgments. *See* **delinquent, defective.;** *dist. f.* **psychopath.**

imitation: (1) the conscious or unconscious patterning of such *gestalten* as acts, feeling, attitudes, achievements, and possessions after some model; it may be used (*a*) as a means to an end other than mere reproducing, as in learning to pronounce words by imitation for the sake of communication, and (*b*) as an end in itself, that is, parrotlike repetition; all repetitions that are performed by the child on a level foreign to his own thinking, perceiving, and feeling, such as repetition of patterns seen in coloring books and in many workbooks; *ant.* **self-expression;** (2) a method of teaching style and techniques in English composition by close adherence to the style and techniques of chosen literary models; (3) a method used by the foreign language student to develop speaking skills of near-native quality by using a native speaker as a model.

imitative composition: *see* **composition, imitative.**

immaturity: (1) a state of less than final or adult development of a cell, a particular structure, or the organism as a whole; (2) the state of growing and maturing at a slower rate and reaching pubescence later than normally expected; both mental and physical growth may be influenced in this way, sometimes causing undue anxiety for both child and parent.

immediacy: direct awareness, without intermediate symbolic or conceptual intervention; may pertain to *primary experience,* out of which concepts arise.

immediate: (1) (art) acting or being without the intervention of another object, cause, or agency; (2) in artistic or aesthetic experience, descriptive of the apprehension of the qualities of objects or phenomena for their intrinsic worth, without judging or considering them according to criteria or principles.

immediate access: *see* **access, immediate.**

immediate aim: *see* **aim, immediate.**

immediate memory: *see* **memory, immediate.**

immediate objective: *see* **objective, immediate.**

immediate playback: *see* **playback, immediate.**

immunity, board: *see* **board immunity.**

immunity, governmental: a common-law principle that it is not in the public interest for the government to be the defendant in a civil suit except where waived or permitted by law; also known as *sovereign immunity* and *tort immunity.* See **respondeat superior, doctrine of.**

immunity, sovereign: *see* **immunity, governmental.**

immunity, tort: *see* **immunity, governmental.**

immunization: the development of immunity or protection against a disease by inoculation, vaccination, or other means.

immunological panel: *see* **panel, immunological.**

impact, experience: *see* **experience impact.**

impact of tax: *see* **tax, impact of.**

impacted area: a geographical area designated for allocation of Federal funds for elementary and secondary education which contains a school district with a high percentage of children whose families live in Federal housing and do not pay property taxes to support the local school system.

impaired, mentally: *syn.* **handicapped, mentally.**

impaired, visually: *see* **handicapped, visually.**

impairment: (spec. ed.) anatomical and/or physiological abnormality or loss.

impairment, hearing: *see* **hearing impairment.**

impairment, perceptive: *see* **perceptive impairment.**

impairment, physical: a physical condition which may adversely affect a pupil's normal progress in the usual school program; examples are asthma, epilepsy, cerebral palsy, diabetes, an allergy, a heart condition, a crippling condition, a physical developmental problem, and an impairment of sight, hearing, or speech.

impairment, residual: the disability remaining after recovery from a disease or operation.

impartiality: an attitude of approach to a subject or problem which forbids predetermination of conclusions and requires the patient withholding of judgment until all relevant data have been considered; both a teaching and a learning attitude, it need not necessitate elimination of convictions or loyalties but does require frank acknowledgment of these and willingness to reexamine them.

impasse: in the course of collective negotiations between teachers and administration, a persistent disagreement that continues after normal negotiation procedures have been exhausted.

imperative: a state that arises in any situation at that point at which conditions are in such serious contradiction with the values held by individuals and/or groups that the discipline of practical judgment requires action if the individual or group is to maintain integrity; such action brings changes both in the situation and in the character of those acting. *See* **moods of judger.**

imperative, categorical: in the ethics of Immanuel Kant (1724-1804), the absolute or unconditioned moral law or principle which is inherently right apart from any particular circumstances or consequences; as expressed by Kant, "Act so that the maxim of thy will can always at the same time hold good as a principle of universal legislation."

imperative ideas: *see* **ideas, imperative.**

imperative, practical: one of the two fundamental moral principles of Kant in which man is enjoined to act as if all other men are worthy ends in themselves; literally, "So act to treat humanity, whether in thine own person or in that of any other, in every case as an end withal, never as means only." *Contr. w.* **imperative, categorical.**

implementation pattern: (admin.) the relationship between line and staff specialists integrated to fulfill an organizational goal.

implication: the relation involved in certain propositions so connected with other propositions that the latter necessarily follow from the former; thus, implication is involved if propositions are so related that one set cannot be true unless another is also true; this relationship is often called *formal* or *strict implication.* (In various works in mathematical logic, the phrase "formal implication" is given a highly technical meaning which it is impractical to detail here.)

implication, double: *see* **sentence, biconditional.**

implication, statement of: (math.) a compound sentence in which the logical connective is "If . . ., then . . ."; for example, "If x is an even number, then x^2 is an even number."

implicit behavior: *see* **behavior, implicit.**

implicit contrast item: *see* **item, implicit contrast.**

implicit response: *see* **response, implicit.**

implicit speech: *see* **speech, implicit.**

implied authority: *see* **authority, implied.**

implied contract: *see* **contract, implied.**

impossible question test: *see* **test, impossible question.**

impression: (philos.) *see* **atomism, logical.**

impressionism: (1) (art) a late-nineteenth-century style which reached its peak between 1870 and 1890 in France; artists working in this style sought to capture the momentary effects of nature by applying small dabs of varied, intense colors to the canvas; emphasis was placed upon sensuous qualities, fleeting impressions of light over forms, and the instantaneity of the appearances of objective reality; leaders of the style were Claude Monet, Camille Pissarro, Alfred Sisley, Edouard Manet, and Auguste Renoir; (2) (mus.) a style of musical composition of the late nineteenth and early twentieth centuries represented by Ravel and Debussy; stressed color effects, atmosphere, shifting and wispy tonality, and vagueness; examples are nocturnes, fêtes, images.

impressions, fusion of partial: *see* **fusion of partial impressions.**

imprest fund: *see* **fund, imprest.**

imprint: the name of the publisher of a book together with the place and date of publication, generally printed on the title page, occasionally elsewhere in the book. *Comp. w.* **colophon.**

improper conduct: *see* **conduct, improper.**

improper subset: *see* **subset.**

improvement, capital: improvements to existing fixed assets; loosely, the acquisition of additional fixed assets.

improvement of instructional program: *see* **instructional program, improvement of.**

improvement over chance: *see* **index of forecasting efficiency.**

improvement project: *see* **project, improvement.**

improvement, speech: *see* **speech improvement.**

improvement, supervisory: whatever can be done to promote the effectiveness of the supervisory program of an organization so as to increase its value in terms of influencing others to achieve the goals of the organization.

improvements: (1) (in relation to expenditures) all expenditures for additions to plant that increase its value; (2) (as an asset account) all plant assets other than equipment.

impulse: a sudden impelling force or mental feeling that urges onward to action.

impulse shopper: a consumer who buys irrationally without consideration for need or alternatives.

impulsion: a morbid impulse to perform certain unnecessary or disagreeable acts.

impulsive action: *see* **action, impulsive.**

impulsive buying: purchasing on the spur of the moment without regard to need or alternatives.

in absentia (in ab·sen'shi·ə): (Lat., lit., "in absence") not in residence; (1) descriptive of the practice of permitting special and extension students to complete some of the work for a diploma or degree away from the college or school seat; (2) descriptive of a degree awarded to a nonresident student. *See* **credit, residence; student, external.**

in-and-outer class: *see* **class, in-and-outer.**

in-classroom supervision: *see* **supervision, in-classroom.**

in group: *see* **group, in.**

in lieu tax: *see* **tax, in lieu.**

in-line data processing: *see* **data processing, in-line.**

in loco parentis (in lō'kō pə·ren'tis): a Latin phrase meaning "in place of the parent"; in contemporary educational parlance this refers to the school's position in determining the amount of supervision given a student away from home.

in re (in rē): (Lat., lit., "in the matter of ") a phrase used in court titles and designating a type of case.

in-school instruction: *see* **instruction, in-school.**

in-school radio listening: *see* **radio listening, in-school.**

in-service counselor training: *see* **training, in-service counselor.**

in-service education: efforts to promote by appropriate means the professional growth and development of workers while on the job; in supervision of teaching, one of the major tasks; includes planned and organized effort to improve the knowledge, skill, and attitudes of instructional staff members to make them more effective on the job; illustrative are activities such as role-playing, intervisitation, demonstrations, and laboratory sessions. *See* **program, staff development.**

in-service program: *see* **program, in-service.**

in-service supervision: *see* **supervision, in-service.**

in-service teacher education: *see* **in-service education.**

inaccessibility: a condition resembling apathy or stupor in which the subject's attention cannot be attracted nor can responses be obtained.

inactive census file: *see* **census file, inactive.**

inactive duty: duty credited to a member of the Air Force Reserve for taking short periods of training, as on weekends or nights, without going on active duty. *See* **training, inactive duty.**

inactive duty training: *see* **training, inactive duty.**

inadequacy, feeling of: *syn.* **inferiority feeling.**

inappropriate vocational choice: *see* **vocational choice, inappropriate.**

inarticulateness: (1) inability to express ideas, thoughts, etc., in spoken language; (2) a persistence into later childhood or adulthood of the speech and voice characteristics found normally in children up to 6 years of age. *See* **speech, infantile.**

inbreed: to mate closely related members of a species. *See* **homozygous.**

inbreeding: (higher ed.) employment of excessive proportions of a higher education institution's own graduates, especially doctoral graduates, as members of the faculty.

incentive rate of pay: *see* **pay, incentive rate of.**

incentives: the factors and forces that incite or motivate one to action.

incidence geometry: *see* **geometry, incidence.**

incidence of retardation: *see* **retardation, incidence of.**

incidence of tax: *see* **tax, incidence of.**

incident, critical: *see* **critical incident.**

incident light: *see* **light, incident.**

incidental approach: a method of teaching arithmetic which is based on the idea that children can learn arithmetic through informal contacts with numbers in the course of varied classroom activities, its chief value being in supplying a motive and thereby arousing an interest in learning.

incidental disorder: *see* **disorder, classroom.**

incidental fee: *see* **fee, incidental.**

incidental learning: *see* **learning, incidental.**

incidental sample: *see* **sample, incidental.**

incidental study: *see* **study, incidental.**

incidental teaching: *see* **teaching, incidental.**

incipient: relating to the first stages or the beginning of a process.

incipient disorder: *see* **disorder, classroom.**

inclusive range: *see* **range.**

incoherent speech: *see* **speech, incoherent.**

income, current: all receipts or accruals, if accounts are kept on the accrual basis, during the current fiscal period that are expendable for the general operations of an institution or for designated, specific activities. (Receipts for plant additions and receipts to be added to the principal of any funds are not included under this term.) *See* **accrual basis.**

income, disposable: the total amount of income received by the consumer after deductions for social security tax and income taxes.

income, endowment: the net earnings (usually calculated on an annual basis) of a permanent fund; the sum that may be devoted to the cause for which the endowment was established.

income, money: the money (in dollars) one receives. *See* **income, disposable; income, psychic; income, real.**

income, psychic: (consumer ed.) the satisfaction which the goods and services one purchases will yield.

income, real: the amount of goods and/or services that can be purchased with the money income. *Syn.* **effective purchasing power.**

income tax: *see* **tax, income.**

incommensurable: (math.) a term descriptive of two measurable quantities which are not integral multiples of the same unit of measure; for example, a distance of $\sqrt{2}$ is not commensurable with a distance of 3. *Contr. w.* **commensurable.**

incompatible offices: two offices that cannot lawfully be held concurrently by the same person, either because of constitutional or statutory prohibition or by virtue of a court decision to the effect that such a situation would be contrary to public policy.

incompetent: the legal designation of a person who is mentally abnormal and hence is unable to take the responsibility of executing valid legal instruments and of managing his property.

incomplete block design: *see* **design, incomplete block.**

incomplete factorial design: *see* **design, incomplete factorial.**

incomplete-man test: *see* **test, incomplete-man.**

incomplete regular high school: *see* **high school, incomplete regular.**

inconsistent statistic: *syn.* **statistic, inefficient.**

incoordination, binocular: imbalance in vision. *See* **imbalance, lateral; imbalance, muscular; imbalance, vertical.**

incoordination, motor: faulty use of the muscles, with the result that they hinder one another rather than work together effectively and smoothly. *Syn.* **muscular incoordination.**

incoordination, muscular: *syn.* **incoordination, motor.**

incorporated college: *see* **college, incorporated.**

incorporation: (1) (psych.) the process of responding to the assumed or inferred responses of another to a situation as if the responses were one's own; (2) the intimate mixing of particles of different bodies so as to constitute a practically homogeneous mass.

incorrigible: one who is incapable of being corrected or reformed in his present situation and under his present control.

incorrigible child: *see* **child, incorrigible.**

increase-by-one method: a method of finding the quotient figure in division in cases where a two-figure (or larger) divisor is used; for example, where a two-figure divisor ends in 1, 2, 3, 4, or 5, by using as a trial divisor the first figure of the divisor; where a two-figure divisor ends in 6, 7, 8, or 9, by using the first figure of the divisor increased by 1; sometimes referred to as the *two-rule method. Dist. f.* **apparent method.**

increment: (1) (math.) a change, either positive or negative, in the value of a variable; (2) increase, usually referring to salary schedule steps.

increment, automatic annual: annual salary increases based on seniority rather than measures of merit.

incremental validity: *see* **validity, incremental.**

incubation: in problem solving or creative thought, the period of quiescence during which no apparent attention is devoted to the problem but in which it is assumed important unconscious mental events are occurring.

inculcation: the act or process of impressing pinciples, etc., on the mind by persistent and insistent urging or teaching.

indebtedness, bonded: *syn.* **debt, bonded.**

indecision, vocational: the inability of a student to arrive at a choice of his vocation.

indefinite tenure: *see* **tenure, indefinite.**

indenture: a legal contract; especially, an apprenticeship agreement. (Historically, a contract written in duplicate to be cut apart or otherwise divided along an indented line.)

indentured servant: a person who came to one of the American colonies bound out to a master for a period of 4 to 7 years to pay for passage from England. (These servants included craftsmen, laborers, political offenders, criminals, abducted children, and so-called "schoolmasters.")

independence: (1) a character pattern involving the requirement that a person learn to express his own will and to act spontaneously upon impulse while retaining a balance of self-control and conventionality; its achievement, involved in the process of growing up, requires years of growing, experimenting, and guidance; (2) lack of a causal relation between or among phenomena. *Ant.* **dependence**.

independence, principle of: the doctrine of independent reals; the realist believes that things exist independent of knowledge or experience; knowing, an act of association and interpretation, does not change the thing known. *See* **idealism, subjective**.

independence test: *syn.* **test of independence**.

independent block: *see* **block, independent**.

independent board of education: *see* **board of education, independent**.

independent junior college: *see* **junior college, independent**.

independent observation: *see* **observation, independent**.

independent reading: *see* **reading, independent**.

independent reading level: *see* **reading level, independent**.

independent school district: *see* **district, independent school**.

independent study: *see* **study, independent**.

independent study center: *syn.* **center, study**.

independent study, guided: *see* **instruction, individualized**.

independent variable: *see* **variable, independent**.

independent work: (elem. ed.) activities that the child performs with a minimum of teacher supervision. *See* **period, independent work**.

independent work period: *see* **period, independent work**.

indeterminacy: in the philosophy of experimentalism, a crisis situation in which there is hazard with respect to events that may follow, yielding the impression that something is wrong and that something must be done to restore equilibrium.

indeterminate appropriation: *see* **appropriation, indeterminate**.

indeterminate assignment: *see* **assignment, indeterminate**.

indeterminate transfer: *see* **transfer, indeterminate**.

indeterminism: a particular position concerning cause-and-effect relationships according to which there is no fundamental necessity in the sequence of cause and effect; the position that novelty, freedom, and chance characterize the relation of events as well as, if not more than, cause and effect. *Ant.* **determinism**.

index: *n.* (1) an alphabetically arranged list of the items or subjects in a book or paper in which the location of each item is indicated by page or other serial device (for example, section numbers); (2) (couns.) a book or pamphlet which helps an individual find the necessary educational or occupational information in which he has an interest; (3) (stat.) a variable or composite of variables employed to represent in quantitative form the changes in a trait (from case to case or from one value to another value of some independent variable); used as practically synonymous with *variable*, but acknowledges an awareness of lack of complete or perfectly faithful measurement of the trait it represents; *see* **index number**.

index: *v.* (stat.) to represent changes in a trait through the use of an index; roughly to measure, appraise, or assess; ordinarily used for quantitative changes only.

index, ability: (1) an index number computed to show the relative ability of a given area to support education; (2) a numerical device used to show the relative ability of

states and school districts to support education, the number being computed on the basis of various weighted factors.

index, age-grade: an individual's actual test achievement expressed in terms of school grade levels of attainment characteristic of the average pupil in those grades.

index, anthropometric: a number expressing a significant measure or the relationship between measures of two or more body structures in man, for example, the ratio of the length of the skull to its breadth (*cephalic index*); used to evaluate the status of growth (*maturity*) of an individual, to classify man in terms of origin, race, etc.

index, aptitude: (1) an index of an individual's aptitude, especially in reference to aptitude clusters; *see* **score, stanine**; (2) an index derived from a cluster of nine aptitude tests administered to airmen in the Air Force to indicate general learning ability or likelihood of success in administrative, mechanical, or electronics career fields.

index, athletic: a numerical value or figure derived from a combination of measurements having prognostic value with respect to ability in competitive games and sports; used in the classification of boys and girls into groups for athletic competition.

index, athletic-strength: a numerical value derived from one or more tests of muscular strength and used as an indicator of athletic ability.

index, author: a card index in a library which arranges the titles of books and other printed matter according to the authors' names in alphabetical order. *See* **index, subject**.

index, cephalic: a formula expressing the ratio of one diameter to another in measurements of the head. *See* **index, anthropometric**.

index, citation: a directory of cited references in which each reference is accompanied by a list of source documents which cite it. *See* **citation** (3).

index, class: *syn.* **mark, class**.

index, classification: a number assigned to all pupils falling into a particular category, as determined by various criteria, and used to form relatively homogeneous groups for athletic or other activities, a different number being assigned to each category; generally used only when classification is based on tested factors.

index, consumer price: an index published by the Bureau of Labor Statistics showing fluctuations in the cost of living.

index, Cornell: a revision of a psychiatric screening questionnaire used in World War II, in which 101 questions were used to assess the presence or absence of abnormality.

index, correlation: *syn.* **index of correlation**.

index, cost-of-living: a composite number designed to indicate the general level of living costs at a given date; usually expressed as a percentage against a base of 100.

index counter: *see* **counter, index**.

index, deterioration: an index suggested by the observation that the amount of age decrement varied with the subtest; tests requiring utilization of past learning showed less decline than those involving speed, new learning, and the perception of new relations in verbal and spatial content.

index, differentiation: an indication of the degree to which individual test items discriminate among students in designated criterion groups; sometimes called *discrimination index* or *validity index*.

index, discrimination: *see* **index, differentiation**.

index, film: *syn.* **film speed** (1).

index, height-weight: a measure of physical development derived from the *height-weight ratio*.

index, key-word-in-context (KWIC index): a document index in alphabetic order by title key word; each document is entered once for each of its significant title words, the key words being aligned on a particular column so that their alphabetic sequence may be easily observed. *Syn.* **permutation index; permuted index; permuted-title index; rotational index; subject-in-context index**; *see* **index, key-word-out-of-context**.

index, key-word-out-of-context (KWOC index): a permuted index in which the key word is placed in a left-hand column, the whole title being printed out to the right, with or without full bibliographic reference. *See* index, key-word-in-context.

index, KWIC: *see* index, key-word-in-context.

index, KWOC: *see* index, key-word-out-of-context.

index, laterality: a measure of relative sidedness with especial reference to hand usage.

Index Librorum Prohibitorum (in'deks lĭ·brō'rəm prō·hib'i-·tō'rəm): (Lat., lit., "list of forbidden books") a list of books that the Roman Catholic Church condemns as being detrimental to faith or morals; frequently shortened to Index.

index, national pupil-teacher: (1) a formula expressing a ratio between pupils and teachers for use in administering or devising a state-aid system for schools; (2) the formula devised by the National Survey of School Finance (1932) for determining allotments of teachers or weighted pupil units to schools.

index number: (1) broadly, any composite used to represent change in a (complex) trait; as such, it is practically synonymous with *index*; (2) more narrowly, a number or a series of numbers used to indicate level of value in comparison with a given level taken as standard, for example, cost-of-food index; *see* base; (3) (math.) one of a set of numbers used to assign an order to the members of some other set; for example, if t_1, t_2, t_3,... represent the elements of some set, the numbers 1,2,3,... are index numbers; (4) (math.) an integer used with a radical sign to indicate what root is sought; for example, 3 is the index number in $^3\sqrt{8}$.

index of brightness (IB): a rarely used measure of mental ability suggested by Otis for use with his general intelligence scales; secured by calculating the difference between a subject's test score and the score that is normal for a person of his chronological age, this difference being then added algebraically to 100; strictly comparable to the IQ only when the IB equals 100.

index of consistency: *syn.* coefficient of reliability.

index of correlation: a measure of relationship between a dependent and an independent variable, based on the closeness with which the data can be represented by some curve; the square root of the ratio of the variance of points on the curve of regression of the dependent on the independent variable to the variance of the dependent variable; always exceeds the coefficient of correlation but cannot be greater than the correlation ratio. *Syn.* correlation index; *dist. f.* correlation coefficient; correlation ratio.

index of determination: the square of the index of correlation, giving the proportion of the variance of a dependent variable which is accounted for by its relationship to the independent variable. *See* index of correlation; *dist. f.* coefficient of determination.

index of difficulty: (1) a mathematical expression that indicates the relative difficulty of a book or a part of a book, based on some formula derived from statistical measurement; developed by a number of experimenters, among them Patty and Painter, Lewerenz, Washburne, Gray, and Yoakam; (2) (stat.) any numerical designation of the ease or difficulty of a test item; (3) (stat.) the percentage of examinees passing a given test item; (4) (stat.) the percentage of examinees failing a given test item.

index of discrimination: (1) a numerical designation of the extent to which a test item discriminates among subjects or examinees of varying ability; (2) any of the many indices which may be derived from item analysis.

index of dissimilarity: the expression by a formula of the extent of dissimilarity between the profiles of two individuals on a battery of subtests.

index of forecasting efficiency: an expression $(1 - \sqrt{1 - r^2})$ showing by what ratio the scores predicted by the regression equations are better than guessing each score at the mean; the proportion by which the standard error of estimate is reduced below the original standard deviation. (When applied, the numerical value obtained is often referred to as *improvement over chance*,

efficiency of prediction, or *forecasting efficiency*.) *Syn.* coefficient of correspondence; predictive index.

index of nondetermination: ($100k^2$); the percentage of the variance of one variable which is not accounted for by a second variable with which it is correlated to some degree; $100 \times k^2$, the coefficient of nondetermination where k is the coefficient of alienation, $1 - r^2$. *See* coefficient of alienation.

index of precision: h; a measure of the extent to which a given set of observations cluster about their mean; expressed as $1/(\sigma\sqrt{2})$, where σ = standard deviation.

index of relevance: an estimate of the extent of agreement between "true" test scores and "true" criterion scores consisting of the square root of the ratio of that part of the "true" criterion variance that is determined by the "true" test variance to the total "true" criterion variance.

index of reliability: (1) theoretically, the correlation between true and obtained scores on a test, or the probable correlation between one test and the average of an infinitely large number of parallel tests; (2) practically, the square root of the reliability coefficient; useful in test construction as a statement of highest coefficient of validity that can possibly be obtained for a test with a given reliability coefficient. *Dist. f.* coefficient of reliability.

index of variability: *syn.* deviation standard.

index, periodical: (1) an index, usually arranged by author and subject, to materials in a group of periodicals; most widely used in this country are *Readers Guide to Periodical Literature* (indexing largely general periodicals published in America), *Education Index* (indexing periodicals in the education field), and *International Index to Periodicals* (indexing largely scholarly and foreign periodicals); there are many specialized indexes to periodicals in particular areas and subject fields; (2) an index to a volume or series of volumes of a single periodical.

index, permutation: *syn.* index, key-word-in-context.

index, permuted: *syn.* index, key-word-in-context.

index, physical-fitness: a measure of physical fitness which indicates the immediate ability of the individual for physical activity; derived from comparing an achieved strength index (SI) with a norm based upon the individual's sex, weight, and age. (An index of 100 is considered average.)

index, ponderal: the ratio of height to weight.

index, predictive: *syn.* index of forecasting efficiency.

index, readability: a composite score designed to indicate the level of difficulty, usually measured in terms of school grades, of a piece of reading matter.

index, reading: a device for indicating whether a reader is reading up to capacity; invented by Marion Monroe.

index, recovery: (phys. ed.) a standard used to rate how effectively the individual returns to normal respiration and pulse rate after exercise.

index register: *see* B-register.

index, replacement: *syn.* reproduction rate, net.

index, rotational: *syn.* index, key-word-in-context.

index, social service: *see* social service index.

index, strength: a score obtained from combining several tests of muscular strength in accordance with a specific formula, which includes weight and height. *See* test, physical-capacity.

index, subject: (1) the library catalog of books which is arranged alphabetically by subjects rather than by authors; (2) (read.) an index of the subject matter to be found in school readers, developed by Eleanor Rue.

index, subject-in-context: *syn.* index, key-word-in-context.

index, transportation saturation: a figure that represents the extent of existing pupil-transportation services compared with complete transportation service; usually the ratio between the number of pupils actually transported and the number that would be transported as the result of an objectively defined basic program.

index, validity: *see* index, differentiation.

indexed address: *see* address, indexed.

Indian school: a school maintained by the Federal government for the education of Indians.

indicated operation: a mathematical process that is implied or suggested by signs or symbols.

indictment: (school law) a written accusation against one or more persons of a crime of a public nature, referred to and presented upon oath by a grand jury.

indifferents: a group of persons who show little interest and little response either in their acceptance or rejection of an idea or in their carrying out of a plan; persons who do otherwise acceptable work and yet do not contribute to the goals of the educational system.

indigenous sound: on a sound film, the sound that is an integral part of the scene being shown on the screen, as differentiated from that which is commentary or background music.

indigent child: *see* **child, indigent.**

indigent clothing record: *see* **record, indigent clothing.**

indigent family: a family that is destitute and lacks all means of living with any degree of comfort.

indigent supplies: all supplies provided for indigent families.

indirect address: *see* **address, indirect.**

indirect approach: *see* **approach, indirect.**

indirect control: *see* **control, indirect.**

indirect correlation: *syn.* **correlation, negative;** *see* **correlation (1).**

indirect curve: *syn.* **undercurve.**

indirect heating: *see* **heating, indirect.**

indirect lighting: *see* **lighting, indirect.**

indirect measurement: *see* **measurement, indirect.**

indirect method: (1) a method of teaching by which the ultimate objectives are reached by a somewhat oblique or roundabout course rather than by the most direct and obvious route; thus, mensuration might be taught indirectly through the calculations performed by a class in planning a school garden; (2) (math.) a method of reaching a desired conclusion through the process of investigation and elimination of all other mutually exclusive possibilities; (3) a method of character education by which attempts are made to teach ethical and moral principles and practices by guidance of young people's discussions and choices in real or lifelike situations.

indirect method of difference: *see* **method of agreement and difference.**

indirect movement: any handwriting movement involving the making of a curve in a counterclockwise direction; sometimes called a *reverse curve.*

indirect objective: *see* **objective, indirect.**

indirect operating cost: *see* **cost, indirect operating.**

indirect oval: handwriting drill that consists in constructing either retraced or running ovals by a counterclockwise movement. *Contr. w.* **direct oval.**

indirect preparation: *see* **Montessori method.**

indirect projection: *syn.* **projection, rear-screen.**

indirect proof: *see* **proof, indirect.**

indirect reasoning: *see* **indirect method (2).**

indirect teaching: *see* **teaching, indirect.**

individual: (1) (stat.) any object or person measured or enumerated; (2) a member of a group, as distinguished from the group.

individual adaptation: *see* **adaptation, individual.**

individual analysis: *see* **analysis, individual.**

individual assessment: *see* **assessment, individual.**

individual-centered supervision: *see* **supervision, individual-centered.**

individual centers: living areas or arrangements within a home economics department approximating physical home environment. *See* **unit arrangement.**

individual choice behavior: *see* **behavior, individual choice.**

individual class: *see* **class, individual.**

individual conference: *see* **conference, individual.**

individual counseling: *see* **counseling, individual.**

individual curriculum: *see* **curriculum, individual.**

individual decision: *see* **decision, individual.**

individual differences: *see* **differences, individual.**

individual differences, adaptation of schools to: *see* **adaptation of schools to individual differences.**

individual differences, adjustment to: *see* **adjustment to individual differences.**

individual gymnastic class: *syn.* **class, remedial.**

individual gymnastics: *see* **gymnastics, individual.**

individual instruction: *see* **instruction, individual.**

individual-instruction plan: *syn.* **Winnetka plan.**

individual interview: *see* **interview, individual.**

individual inventory: *see* **inventory, individual.**

individual mental test: *see* **test, individual mental.**

individual method: (mus. ed.) *syn.* **private method.**

individual occupational training: *see* **training, individual occupational.**

individual-progress plan: a plan that permits each pupil to progress at his own rate, promotion taking place at any time during the school year provided only that the work of, or equivalent to, the preceding grade has been completed.

individual promotion: *see* **promotion, individual.**

individual psychology: *see* **psychology, individual.**

individual reading: *see* **reading, individual.**

individual record form: *see* **record form, individual.**

individual spelling demon: *see* **spelling demon, individual.**

individual spelling list: *see* **spelling list, individual.**

individual sport: *see* **sport, individual.**

individual study plan: *see* **study plan, individual.**

individual technique: *see* **interview technique.**

individual test: *see* **test, individual.**

individual training: *see* **training, individual.**

individual training, advanced: *see* **training, advanced individual.**

individual transporation: *see* **transportation, individual.**

individual variability: *see* **variability, individual.**

individual word list: *see* **word list, individual.**

individual worth: *see* **worth, individual.**

individualism: (1) a tendency to follow the inclinations and interests of the self as well as to seek to be different from others; (2) the doctrine which holds that the chief end of society is the promotion of individual success and welfare; (3) the theory that the welfare of society is best served by permitting individuals or groups to give direction to their lives and activities with a minimum of social or governmental interference.

individualism, rugged: *see* **rugged individualism.**

individuality: that characteristic of a human being which is influenced by organic, mental, and emotional behavior and which varies quantitatively and qualitatively in different individuals.

individualization: the development of characteristics, through learning and maturation, which differentiate one individual from another.

individualization, creative-activity: *see* **instruction, individualized.**

individualization, diversified-activity: *see* **instruction, individualized.**

individualization of instruction: *see* **instruction, individualized.**

individualized dictation: *see* **dictation, individualized.**

individualized instruction: *see* **instruction, individualized.**

individualized reading: *see* **reading, individualized.**

individualized spelling: *see* **spelling, individualized.**

individualized study: *see* **study, individualized.**

individually paced instruction, computer-assisted: *see* **instruction, computer-assisted individually paced.**

individually prescribed instruction: *see* **instruction, individually prescribed.**

individuation: the maturation of local behavior patterns within and their emergence from the larger behavior patterns of an organism.

indoctrination: (1) in the broadest sense, the attempt to inculcate beliefs, a possible concomitant of any learning situation; in narrower terms, the attempt to fix in the learning mind any doctrine, social, political, economic, or religious, to the exclusion of all contrary doctrines, and in a manner preventing serious comparison and evaluation; (2) (mil. ed.) the act of imbuing or instructing a person with the doctrine considered relevant to the understanding of a concept or to the carrying out of an operation, as in an indoctrination center, course, lecture, training, etc.; *see* **doctrine.**

indoctrination change: *see* **change, indoctrination.**

indoctrination, civic: the act of instilling in learners or listeners a particular civic *ideology* or doctrine.

induced hallucination: *see* **hallucination, induced.**

induction: classically, a method of reasoning by going from the particular to the general, that is, by making generalizations of varying degrees of probability concerning all members of a class from observation of particular instances, usually carefully selected samples; *perfect induction* sums up but does not go beyond the facts observed on examination of all the entities of a collection. *See* **reasoning, inductive; induction, mathematical;** *contr. w.* **deduction; Baconian method.**

induction loop system: an amplification system by which signals transmitted from a group amplifier are received by hearing aids using the magnetic induction process.

induction, mathematical: a specific form of argument used when an assertion is to be proved true for all natural numbers or for a collection indexed by the natural numbers; the form of the argument is to show that the assertion is true for the first number or the first case and then that whenever it is true for some number or case, it must of necessity be true for the succeeding number or case.

induction, negative: (neurol.; behav. psych.) a term introduced by Hering and Sherrington and adopted by Pavlov to describe the effect of intensification of inhibition following a period of excitability.

induction of teachers: *see* **induction process.**

induction, positive: (neurol.; behav. psych.) a term introduced by Hering and Sherrington and adopted by Pavlov to describe the effect of increased excitability manifested by heightened response when a reaction takes place after a period of inhibition.

induction process: (admin.) the introduction of new staff members into the school system beginning with the announcement of a vacancy and continuing until the staff member is well oriented to his position.

induction, staff: *see* **staff induction.**

induction test: *see* **test, induction.**

inductive approach: *see* **inductive method.**

inductive attack: *see* **inductive method.**

inductive lesson: *see* **lesson, inductive.**

inductive method: (1) a method of study, research, or argument based on reasoning from particular cases to a general conclusion; (2) a method of teaching based on the presentation to the learner of a sufficient number of specific examples to enable him to arrive at a definite rule, principle, or fact; in programmed instruction this procedure of presenting first the examples and then the rule is called *EGRUL;* (3) a procedure, formerly used in teaching foreign languages (sometimes still used in teaching Latin), in which a prose passage was studied word by word without previous instruction in rules, conjugations, declensions, etc., each point of grammar being taken up as it was encountered in the passage read and rules formulated to cover the particular cases encountered, these rules being gradually expanded and rendered more general as the students progressed with their knowledge of the language.

inductive presentation: in language instruction, postponement of the presentation of formal grammar until the student has been exposed to a quantity of linguistic patterns from which he formulates the grammar rules.

inductive proof: *see* **induction, mathematical.**

inductive reasoning: *see* **reasoning, inductive.**

inductive study: *see* **study, inductive.**

inductive teaching: *see* **teaching, inductive.**

industrial art: *see* **art, industrial.**

industrial art school: a school that specializes in the training of students for employment as artists in the industries. (Such artists are often called stylists or industrial designers.)

industrial arts: (1) those occupations by which changes are made in the forms of materials to increase their value for human use; (2) an area of education dealing with socioeconomic problems and occupational opportunities, involving experience with a wide range of materials, tools, processes, products, and occupations typical of an industrial and technological society; (3) a phase of the educational program concerned with orienting individuals through study and experience to the technical-industrial side of society for the purpose of enabling them to deal more intelligently with consumer goods, to be more efficient producers, to use leisure time more effectively, and to act more intelligently in regard to matters of health and safety, especially as affected by industry; (4) the study of industrial technology, its origins, development, and advance, its technical, social, economic, occupational, cultural, and recreational nature and influences, through research, experiment, design, invention, construction, and operation with industrial materials, processes, products, and energies, for the purposes of acquainting the student with technological culture and aiding him in the discovery and development of his native potential therein; (5) organized study of the knowledge or practice within that subcategory of the economic institution of society known as industry; (6) a curriculum area in general education in which students may create, experiment, design, and plan while dealing with issues related to technology. *Dist. f.* **art, industrial.**

industrial arts, comprehensive general: a course that provides facilities for a combination of pupil experiences in a variety of industrial arts subject fields in a single course, including two or more activities in areas such as drafting, woodwork, metalwork, and electricity.

industrial arts consultant, elementary school: *see* **consultant, elementary school industrial arts.**

industrial arts education: (1) the preparation of teachers in the field of industrial arts; (2) education that takes place through industrial arts. *See* **industrial arts.**

industrial arts, elementary: that phase of the elementary school curriculum which provides the child with opportunities for exploration, manipulation, experimentation, and planning in the use of tools, materials, and techniques appropriate to converting materials to serve useful purposes; planned activities and experiences include (*a*) the construction of projects related to and reinforcing the elementary school subject matter and projects related to recreational and personal purposes, (*b*) a study of industry with emphasis on its organization, materials, processes, occupations, products, and problems, and their effect on man's past and present cultures, and (*c*) those classroom activities for the child directed toward understanding things technical, mechanical, and industrial.

industrial arts, elementary school: *see* **consultant, elementary school industrial arts; industrial arts, elementary.**

industrial arts for exceptional children: a program of instruction through industrial arts activities for elementary and/or secondary school pupils with exceptional needs, such as the physically handicapped, the mentally deficient, the emotionally maladjusted.

industrial arts, general: a unified industrial arts program involving the study of two or more separate and somewhat distinct aspects of industry and technology; learning experiences include activities such as experimenting, designing, constructing, evaluating, and using a variety of tools, materials, and processes; formerly called *general shop.*

industrial arts laboratory: *see* **laboratory, industrial arts.**

industrial arts laboratory, composite: *see* **laboratory, composite industrial arts.**

industrial arts laboratory, comprehensive general: *see* **laboratory, comprehensive general industrial arts.**

industrial arts laboratory, diversified-activity: *syn.* **laboratory, composite industrial arts.**

industrial arts laboratory, general: *syn.* **laboratory, composite industrial arts; laboratory, comprehensive industrial arts.**

industrial arts, limited general: a course that provides facilities for pupil experiences in a number of closely allied activities; for example, a graphic arts course may include hand composition, presswork, silk screen process work, linoleum block printing, simple photography, paper and ink making, etc.

industrial arts mathematics: *see* **mathematics, industrial arts.**

industrial arts shop: *see* **laboratory, industrial arts.**

industrial arts teacher education: *see* **teacher education, industrial arts.**

industrial classification manual, standard: *see* **manual, standard industrial classification.**

Industrial Classification, Standard: *see* **Standard Industrial Classification.**

industrial design: *see* **design, industrial.**

industrial education: a term used to designate various types of education concerned with modern industry, industrial arts, technical education and apprenticeship training, and vocational-industrial education in both public and private schools.

industrial field trip: a trip through an industrial plant, a business concern, or a construction project taken by a class for the purpose of observing mechanical operations, equipment, products, and working conditions.

industrial film: *see* **film, industrial.**

industrial geography: *syn.* **geography, commercial.**

industrial literature: *see* **literature, industrial.**

industrial praxiology: *see* **praxiology, industrial.**

industrial recreation: *see* **recreation, industrial.**

industrial school: a residential school, usually for one sex only, for the education and supervision of delinquents committed by a juvenile court, the school in most states having legal custody until the delinquent becomes of age; a euphemism for the older term *reform school.*

industrial technician: *see* **technician, industrial.**

industrial technology: *see* **technology, industrial.**

industrially disabled: *see* **disabled, industrially.**

industries, ceramic: those industries utilizing earthy, inorganic, nonmetallic materials that are usually subjected to a high temperature during manufacture or use, such as abrasives, Portland cement and concrete, cement-lime-gypsum, structural clay products, carbon and graphite, electronic and technical ceramics, glass, glazes, gypsum, porcelain enamels, processed minerals, whitewares, and stone.

industries, laboratory of: *see* **laboratory of industries.**

industry: (1) the combination of organizations and facilities that, through the effective coordination of capital, management, and labor, produces goods to meet the needs and desires of society; (2) a program of study in industrial arts dealing with the various phases of a given industry or group of industries as it affects man.

industry, aerospace: the industry primarily engaged in manufacture of aircraft, guided missiles, and spacecraft, that is, both air and space vehicles and, in addition, their related components and parts.

industry, American: the prime source of industrial arts subject matter; consists of those enterprises in the United States involved in the production of goods and/or the providing of personal or technical services; sizes range from the small job shop to the large corporation and methods vary from the use of custom techniques to mass production.

industry, cement: industry engaged in the manufacture of a powder made from alumina, silica, lime oxide, and magnesia burned together in a kiln and finely pulverized and used as an ingredient of mortar and concrete.

industry, construction: organizations concerned with carrying out various types of projects, such as bridges, via-ducts, piers, buildings, highways, streets, pipelines, railroads, river and harbor projects, sewers, tunnels, and waterways.

industry, electronics: (voc. ed.) industry concerned with design, development, and manufacture of components such as semiconductor devices, thermionic valves, cathode ray tubes, special components for computers and resistors and capacitors and the manufacture of these components into many types of equipment, for example, radio and television receivers, communication equipment, specialized control apparatus, and computers.

industry, machinery: the group of establishments engaged in manufacturing machinery and equipment other than electrical equipment and transportation equipment.

industry, manufacturing: a basic division of industry which is concerned with the transformation of organic and inorganic substances, according to an organized plan and with division of labor, into new products, which may be finished or semifinished.

industry, telephone communications: companies primarily engaged in furnishing telephone communication service by placing the parties in vocal conversation with each other.

ineducable and untrainable mentally retarded: *see* **mentally retarded, Grade IV.**

ineducable mentally retarded: *see* **mentally retarded, ineducable.**

inefficient statistic: *see* **statistic, inefficient.**

inequation: (math.) an *open sentence* involving an inequality, such as $x + 2 < -1$.

infancy, human: *see* **infant.**

infant: (1) a person from birth to about 6 years; (2) a person during the prenatal and suckling periods; (3) a person during the suckling period; *contr. w.* **fetus;** (4) (law) a minor.

infant behavior: *see* **behavior, infant.**

infant, premature: an infant born before term; viable prematures are those which have the possibility of living, and nonviable are those too immature to live.

infant school: a type of public primary school first introduced in the United States in Boston about 1816 and intended to give instruction in reading and writing to children 4 to 7 years of age in preparation for admission to the city's grammar schools. (Originated by Jean Frédéric Oberlin in 1769 at Walbach, France, and later adopted and further developed by Robert Owen in New Lanark, Scotland, whence it spread to the United States.) *Syn.* **primary school.**

infant school society: an organization (of a type first constituted in London in 1824) formed for the purpose of popularizing and establishing infant schools and training teachers for such schools. (The society founded in New York City in 1827 furnished the means of instructing poor children between 3 and 6 years of age and was the forerunner of the primary department of the public schools.)

infant test: *see* **test, infant.**

infantile amnesia: *see* **amnesia, infantile.**

infantile behavior: *see* **behavior, infantile.**

infantile complex: *see* **complex, infantile.**

infantile complexes: (psychon.) a broad term including both the Oedipus and the Electra complexes.

infantile paralysis: *syn.* **poliomyelitis.**

infantile sexuality: (1) (psychoan.) a condition in psychosexual development, obtaining normally in the first year or two of life, in which erotic satisfaction is derived from the stimulation of certain cutaneous zones such as the lips as well as from the genitals or from certain visceral processes such as elimination; (2) a condition defined in terms of the operation of the sexual instinct in early life and of the effects of its operation.

infantilism: the state in which an adult manifests physiological and psychological characteristics of an immature person.

inference: (1) commonly and loosely, the act of obtaining a judgment or logical conclusion from given data or premises; (2) more precisely, a psychological or temporal process by which the mind passes from a proposition accepted as true to another proposition believed to be so connected to the first as to make the latter true; *dist. f.* **implication.**

inference, rules of: a collection of statements giving conditions under which logically valid conclusions can be drawn; exact lists will vary, but common to all would be the *rule of detachment* (*modus ponens*), which states "*Q* is a valid conclusion from *P* and '*P* implies *Q*' ", and the *rule of contraposition* (*modus tollens*), which states "not-*P* is a valid conclusion from not-*Q* and '*P* implies *Q*'."

inference, statistical: (1) the conclusions drawn about a population or populations on the basis of findings from one or more samples; (2) the act or process of making decisions based on the results of an experiment.

inferential method of character measurement: *see* **measurement, inferential method of character.**

inferior: below the average; below par.

inferior normal: an individual who is normal in some respects but slightly inferior in others; often used to designate the lowest division of a group considered to be of "normal" intelligence.

inferiority complex: *see* **complex, inferiority.**

inferiority feeling: (1) a controlling emotional attitude due to actual or imagined inadequacy; (2) a feeling of helplessness incident to infancy and childhood and reinforced by physical limitations and by failure to gain control of environmental situations; popularly confused with *inferiority complex. Syn.* **feeling of inadequacy.**

inferred causal method: *see* **causal-comparative method.**

infinite: (1) not subject to the restrictions of space, time, and circumstances; without limits or bounds; inexhaustible; not capable of being counted; *contr. w.* **finite;** (2) (math.) descriptive of the measure of a set if the measure exceeds any prescribed number, no matter how large.

infinite population: *see* **population, infinite.**

infinite sequence: *see* **sequence, infinite.**

infinite set: *see* **set, infinite.**

infinitesimal: *n.* loosely, a quantity that is so small as to be negligible, that is, insignificant in size.

infinitesimal: *adj.* (math.) descriptive of that which has a measure whose absolute value is smaller than any prescribed positive (real) number. *Contr. w.* **finite** (2).

infinity: distance, space, time, or quantity without limits or bounds.

infirmary: a hospital or a place offering some hospital services, usually associated with a particular organization or institution such as a college.

inflected form: a form of a word made up of a root word plus an inflectional ending or suffix; for example, *cars* is an inflected form of *car.*

inflection: the pattern of rise and fall of pitch in continuous phonation; used to give shades of meaning to words and phrases.

inflexible schema: *see* **schema, inflexible.**

influencing: as an administrative function, the task, after setting up an operative staff, of superimposing on the staff a supervisory staff capable of influencing the operative group toward a pattern of coordinated and effective behavior.

influential, community: *see* **community influential.**

informal course: *see* **course, noncredit.**

informal dramatics: *see* **dramatics, informal.**

informal education, Jewish: a program of informal Jewish educational activities, social, cultural, and recreational, conducted by synagogues, community centers, and schools, the purpose of which is to enrich the education of pupils attending religious schools as well as to provide a minimum program of Jewish education for adolescents and young people not attending any Jewish religious school.

informal evaluation: *see* **evaluation, informal.**

informal geometry: *see* **geometry, informal.**

informal hearing: *see* **hearing, informal.**

informal notice: a nonconventional note or notice inviting one to an informal hearing or calling some event or matter to the attention of teachers or pupils.

informal organization: *see* **organization, informal.**

informal reading inventory: *see* **inventory, informal reading.**

informal reading test: *see* **test, informal reading.**

informal test: *see* **test, informal.**

informant: (1) in linguistic study or language teaching, a person who acts as an authentic source of information about a language or its culture; (2) a speaker who has native fluency in a language and is used as a *model* for imitation by students learning to speak the language although the class is conducted by another person who is a trained teacher.

information: (1) knowledge about anything expressed in a symbolic form; in strict usage, information differs from *data* in its news value; information is that part of data that is of most interest to the data user; in common usage, data and information are often interchangeable terms; (2) a purely quantitative property of an ensemble of items that enables categorization or classification of some or all of them; (3) (legal) an accusation; (4) in data processing, data to be used by a computer; (5) in information theory, the amount of uncertainty reduced by a unit in a message, usually expressed in *bits;* (6) in military and civilian intelligence, unevaluated material of every description from observations, reports, rumors, imagery, and other sources which, when processed , may produce intelligence; *see* **intelligence** (5).

information analysis center: a formally structured organizational unit specifically (but not necessarily exclusively) set up for the purpose of acquiring, selecting, storing, retrieving, evaluating, analyzing, and synthesizing data and/or information in a clearly defined specialized field so as to present pertinent material in an authoritative, timely, and useful form.

information and education program: *see* **program, information and education.**

information blank, pupil: *syn.* **data blank, pupil.**

information center, education: *see* **center, education information.**

information-centered guidance: *see* **guidance, information-centered.**

information clearinghouse: *see* **clearinghouse, information.**

information communication training: *see* **training, information communication.**

information, comparable: (couns.) items of information which can be compared and combined as recorded because they are based on the same definitions.

information, compression of: *see* **compression of information.**

information, confidential: (couns.) *see* **communication, confidential; communication, privileged.**

information, consumer: (1) information of importance to consumers, provided by governmental agencies, private agencies, and educational institutions; concerned with money, credit, insurance, buying procedures, specifications of products, and the working conditions under which goods are produced; (2) information printed on labels and tags concerning the product.

information dissemination: the distribution of documents or information to interested persons, usually specialists in particular subject fields.

information, educational: (couns.) valid and usable data about all types of present and probable future educational or training opportunities and requirements, including curricular and cocurricular offerings, requirements for entrance, and conditions and problems of student life.

information, family: *see* **family information.**

information, guidance: information useful to pupils disseminated through the guidance services of the school; consists primarily of information about occupations, training programs, and community agencies.

information, item of: *see* **item of information.**

information, merchandise: *see* **merchandise information.**

information, occupational: *see* **occupational information.**

information, official: (mil. ed.) information which is owned by, produced by, or subject to the control of the United States government.

information-processing theory: a theory according to which the human being, like the computer, is viewed as a communication channel with a capacity for storing information and a repertoire of strategies or response patterns which process stored and incoming information; incoming information is identified and decoded, then related to already available information and used as a basis for producing an appropriate output.

information, product: *see* **merchandise information.**

information, related: *see* **related information.**

information requirements: (data processing) the actual or anticipated questions which may be posed to an information system.

information retrieval: (1) the recovering of desired information from a collection of documents or other graphic records; (2) in automatic data processing, the process of storing large quantities of information and of selectively producing this information under computer control.

information retrieval system: a system for locating and selecting certain records relevant to a given information requirement from a file of such material.

information retrieval system, dial-access: a system involving two or more receivers (students) who are able to select and receive one of two or more stored programs (audio and/or visual) from a source which is at a location different from that of the receivers, the transmission from the source to the receiver being wholly or in part electronic; selection is made on a dial similar to a telephone dial.

information science: *see* **science, information.**

information, selective dissemination of: *see* **dissemination of information, selective.**

information service: (1) in general, any extension of means of distributing factual or propagandistic materials; (2) the efforts of newspapers, radio and television programs, foundations, schools, colleges, universities, and libraries to furnish condensed answers to questions or to meet individual requests for special information; *see* **library, package;** (3) (couns.) *see* **service, informational.**

information services: *see* **services, information.**

information sheet: (voc. ed.) a form of instruction sheet bearing a written explanation or description of terms, machines, materials, facts, processes, etc., that are important for the understanding of a job.

information, social: (couns.) valid and usable data about the opportunities and influences of the human and physical environment which bear on personal and interpersonal relations and which will help a student to understand himself better and to improve his relations with others; also called *personal-social information.*

information sources, occupational: *see* **sources, occupational information.**

information system: the network of all communication methods within an organization; a means of providing information for decision making, evaluation of results, and knowledge about an organization and its environment through the acquisition, transmission, processing, storage, manipulation, and conversion of data. *See* **science, information.**

information system management: *see* **management, information system.**

information test: *see* **test, information.**

information theory: (1) an interdisciplinary study (not a theory) dealing with the transmission of *messages* or *signals* or the communication of *information* and drawing upon *communications theory*, which includes much from physics and engineering, linguistics, psychology, and sociology; (2) the study of the communication process in all its aspects; a body of mathematical results concerning a quantity called *information*—a measure of the amount of knowledge contained in a proposition or a message; (3) in automatic data processing, the mathematical theory concerned with information rate, channels, channel width, noise, and other factors affecting information

transmission; (4) (couns.) a theory that the choice of strategy in certain counseling situations is implicitly capable of mathematical solution and that, since the problem is subject in principle to rational analysis, the choice is not to be based on doctrine, philosophical grounds, or temperamental preference; *syn.* **communication theory;** *see* **decision theory.**

information, trade: *syn.* **related information.**

information, vocational: facts and figures given to job candidates allowing them to decide if they are interested in specific fields of work, telling them how they can become trained in those particular areas, and indicating what the outlook is for future employment.

informational approach: a method of teaching that consists in supplying information for the purpose of building a background and facilitating instruction.

informational service: *see* **service, informational.**

infraction: (1) the act of breaking or violating laws, rules, regulations, customs, etc.; (2) substitution which is made in terms of behavior and goals that do not conform to custom.

infrahuman: a term referring to a live animal other than a man, used in life science experiments.

infrared: (1) that invisible part of the spectrum whose rays have wavelengths longer than those of the red part of the visible spectrum; (2) (photog.) a special type of film that is sensitive to the infrared rays.

infrastructure: the underlying foundation or basic framework of an organization or system.

infused virtues: *see* **virtues, infused.**

inherit: (1) (genet.) to receive, via the germ plasm, potential or actual characters which are present in a parent or were present in a more remote ancestor and which are available for transmission in the reproductive process; *see* **character** (4); (2) (sociol.) to acquire the traditions and customs of the group by the process of learning or imitation (social inheritance); *see* **cultural background.**

inheritance: (1) in general, anything received from an ancestor; (2) (genet.) traits or characteristics received by the offspring from its parents in the course of reproduction, in accordance with the laws of hereditary biologic transmission. *See* **inherit; Mendel's law.**

inheritance, blending: that type of inheritance in which the F_1 generation shows a character intermediate between the parental types in any given respect and in which definite segregation does not appear in the F_2 generation; may be shown to be due either to lack of dominance or to multiple factors independently inherited. See **character** (4).

inheritance, collateral: (genet.) the inheritance of a given characteristic or set of characteristics from a common ancestor by collaterally related members of the same family, as when two cousins inherit a characteristic from one of their common grandparents. (Ordinarily used in connection with recessive rather than dominant characteristics.)

inheritance, law of ancestral: the postulate, formulated by Francis Galton (1822-1911), that one quarter of any individual's characteristics are derived from each parent, one-sixteenth from each grandparent, etc.

inheritance, maternal: (genet.) that which is inherited from the mother and not affected by inheritance from the father. *Contr. w.* **inheritance, paternal.**

inheritance, paternal: (genet.) that which is inherited from the father and not affected by inheritance from the mother. *Contr. w.* **inheritance, maternal.**

inheritance tax: *see* **tax, inheritance.**

inheritance, two-factor: inheritance of characters that depend for their formation on the combined effect of genes situated at two loci. See **genes, complementary.**

inhibition: the blocking, restraint, or arrest of a function, especially a nerve or mental function.

inhibition, conditioned: *syn.* **inhibition, differential.**

inhibition, differential: (neurol.; behav. psych.) a term used by Pavlov to describe the effect, manifested under certain conditions, by which one of two stimuli inhibits a conditioned response to the other. [An organism may be taught to discriminate between two stimuli, such as tactile stimulation of the right foot (S_1); and of the left foot (S_2); a conditioned response R is set up to one of these stimuli and reinforced; no reinforcement is given when both stimuli are administered together; the conditioned response R will now be given to S_1 but not to S_1S_2 since S_2 appears to inhibit response to S_1] *Syn.* **conditioned inhibition.**

inhibition, extinctive: the concept devised by Pavlov to explain the extinction of conditioned reflexes, according to which inhibitory responses are assumed to be set up through independent neural paths, ultimately causing the original conditioned reflexes to disappear.

inhibition, Muller-Schumann paradigm of: *see* **associative inhibition, Muller-Schumann paradigm of.**

inhibition, proactive: (1) the interference with the learning or subsequent retention of a new task occasioned by the previous learning of another task; *syn.* **transfer, negative;** (2) Underwood and others restrict this term to the phenomenon of negative transfer occurring in the following research design:

I Rest		Learn A	Rest	Recall and Relearn A
II Learn B	Learn A	Rest	Recall and Relearn A

where I represents the Control group. II the experimental group.

inhibition, reciprocal: elimination or weakening of old responses by substitution of new ones; as employed in a therapeutic technique developed by Wolpe, a patient's anxiety is reduced through counterconditioning; the process involves the use of relaxation procedures and a list of cues that elicit anxiety in rank order of strength. *See* **therapy, aversion.**

inhibition, reproductive: the decrement in retention following the association of a common stimulus with two different responses in succession.

inhibition, retroactive: a decrement in the retention of an act attributable to the learning of a second act between the time of the original learning and its recall. *Syn.* **interference effect.**

inhibition, social: such deterioration or decrement in the efficiency of performance as may result from having it take place in a social setting, that is, in the presence of other people. *Contr. w.* **facilitation, social.**

inhibition, visual: (1) the inhibition resulting from the inability to use the eyes effectively for observation, found in the extreme in later blinded people who long to use their eyes but are unable to do so; (2) a term referring to a situation in which artists who would like to base their creation on visual observation are inhibited through adherence to a cultural pattern that emphasizes other means of expression.

inhibitory conditioning: *see* **conditioning, inhibitory.**

initial ability: *see* **initial status.**

initial blend: *see* **blend, initial.**

initial-blend theory: a theory which holds that natural phonic blending consists in combining the initial consonant or consonants with the following vowel to produce a fundamental sound, such as *ca* in *catch*. *See* **final-blend theory.**

initial certificate: *see* **certificate, initial.**

initial condition: *see* **condition, initial.**

initial contract: *see* **contract, initial.**

initial entry student: *see* **student, initial entry.**

initial interview: *see* **interview, initial.**

initial position: the location of a sound at the beginning of a word. *Dist. f.* **final position; medial position.**

initial status: the condition or position of an individual or group with respect to ability or certain characteristics immediately prior to the beginning of an experiment or a directed learning program.

initial teaching alphabet: *see* **alphabet, initial teaching.**

initial test: *see* **test, initial.**

initialism: the first letters of the words making up the title of an organization and not forming a single word, an acronym, but spoken separately as an abbreviated name

for the organization; for example, FDA, FCC, TWA. *Comp. w.* **acronym.**

initialization: in a computer program, setting variables and control indicators in a program to their starting values.

initiating structure: in setting up an administrative procedure, the arrangements resulting from the leader's behavior in delineating the relationship between himself and the members of the group and in endeavoring to establish well-defined patterns of organization, channels of communication, and ways of getting the job done.

initiating tasks: (admin.) identifying, announcing, and encouraging the performance of tasks.

initiation ceremonies: formal introduction by preliminary instruction or initial ceremony into some position, office, or society; among the primitives these were known as puberty rites. *See* **puberty rites.**

initiatory activities: *see* **activities, initiatory.**

injunction: a writ or process, granted by a court of equity, whereby a party is required to do or refrain from doing certain acts; fulfillment may be enforced by fine or imprisonment, and violation constitutes contempt of court.

injunction, temporary: an injunction granted at the beginning of a suit to restrain the defendant from doing some act, the right to which is in dispute; may be discharged or made permanent according to the result of the case after the rights of the parties are determined.

injury, birth: *see* **birth injury.**

injury, brain: *see* **brain injury.**

ink-blot test: *see* **test, ink-blot.**

innate: inherited. *Dist. f.* **connate.**

innate idea: *see* **idea, innate.**

innate intelligence: *see* **intelligence, innate.**

innate perversity: *see* **perversity, innate.**

innatism: the philosophical theory that knowledge is present in the mind at birth.

inner city school: technically, any school located in a long-established city as opposed to being in one of the newer surrounding suburban school systems; in practice the term is used only for those schools within the city located in predominantly low socioeconomic areas. *Syn.* **central city school.**

inner conflicts: *see* **conflicts, inner.**

inner-directed orientation: *see* **orientation, inner-directed.**

inner-directed supervisor: *see* **supervisor, inner-directed.**

inner growth: *see* **growth, inner.**

inner monastic school: *see* **monastic school, inner.**

inner pronunciation: *see* **pronunciation, inner.**

inner speech: *see* **speech, inner.**

innocent realism: *see* **realism, innocent.**

innovation: the introduction of a new idea, method, or device in curriculum, educational administration, etc.

inorganic chemistry: *see* **chemistry, inorganic.**

input: (1) in a computer, an electrical connecting device, such as a jack, which carries the incoming signal; also the incoming signal itself; (2) (communications theory) the energy entering a system from without; in a communications system, that which acts on a receiver; (3) (data processing) any data in any of several possible forms which are introduced into and acted upon by the calculator to produce a particular result; also, information transferred from auxiliary or external storage into the internal storage of a computer. *Comp. w.* **output.**

input data: *see* **data, input.**

input device: (data processing) any device for entering data and/or instructions into a computer.

input evaluation: *see* **evaluation, input.**

input output device, magnetic-tape: a device which can either record or read information on magnetic tape. *Syn.* **tape drive.**

input unit: the functional unit which takes into the automatic computer information from outside the computer.

inquiry approach: (1) in general, a mode of investigation which rests on conceptual innovation, proceeds through uncertainty and failure, and eventuates in knowledge which is contingent, dubitable, and hard to come by; (2) (sci. ed.) a particular technique or strategy for bringing about learning of some particular science content by encouraging a student to be inquisitive and curious and to ask questions and try to find answers for himself; (3) a problem-solving approach to a set of learning activities, in which each newly encountered phenomenon becomes a challenge for thinking; begins with a careful set of systematic observations, proceeds to design the measurements required, clearly distinguishes between what is observed and what is inferred, invents interpretations which are, under ideal circumstances, brilliant leaps but always testable, and draws reasonable conclusions.

inquiry, freedom of: *see* **freedom of inquiry.**

inquiry, logic of: *see* **logic of inquiry.**

inquiry, methods of experimental: *see* **methods of experimental inquiry.**

inquiry station: *see* **station, inquiry.**

inquiry training: *see* **training, inquiry.**

insanity: (1) (law) any condition of mental disorder or of serious mental deficiency that renders the individual incompetent to act in accordance with legal and conventional standards; (2) popularly, any serious mental disorder, though preferred usage would restrict the meaning to (1).

insanity, moral: a condition, associated with mental illness, which is described as an inability to conform to recognized legal or moral standards.

insertion: (1) the act of supplying letters, syllables, and words that are not in the text in oral reading; (2) a letter, syllable, or word added by the reader in oral reading.

inside millage: *see* **millage, inside.**

insight: (1) sometimes considered as sudden, unmistakable, and immediate apprehension of the real; in modern science, the spontaneous occurrence of a fertile idea, or a restructuring of the situation, following at least some, and usually considerable, analysis; (2) a term used primarily by gestalt psychologists to account for transfer that is due to an understanding of basic principles, modes of attack, or any other type of nonspecific transfer; *see* **transposition** (1); (3) (couns.) self-knowledge or understanding that aids in evaluation of one's own mental ability, physical reactions, and personal abilities.

insight, mathematical: that which occurs when all the various elements of a quantitative situation are grasped in their relation to each other and to the whole situation.

inspection, boiler: *see* **boiler inspection.**

inspection, building: (1) examination of buildings during construction to determine whether they are being built in accordance with plans and specifications; (2) examination of buildings to determine whether they meet existing standards of health, safety, and suitability for educational use; (3) examination of buildings and equipment when in use to determine whether proper care and attention are being given to maintenance and operation.

inspection district: *see* **district, inspection.**

inspection, health: *see* **health inspection.**

inspection, medical: a program of health examination of school children by physicians and assisting nurses and teachers.

inspection trip: a trip through an industrial plant, a business concern, or a construction project, taken by a class for the purpose of observing mechanical operations, equipment, products, and working conditions.

inspectional supervision: *see* **supervision, inspectional.**

inspector: (1) an official who examines critically one or more aspects of the school and its program, such as instructional activities, building, health, playground, or budget; *contr. w.* **supervisor;** (2) sometimes, an official from a state department or college accrediting board who visits schools for the purpose of rating them.

instability, emotional: (1) a condition characterized by unnatural fluctuations of mood, ranging from animation to sadness or despondency; (2) the condition (due to physical or mental factors) of being unable to achieve normal control of one's emotions; abnormal excitability.

installment buying: *see* **credit, installment.**

installment credit: *see* **credit, installment.**

instinct: the psychic representation of somatic processes; local sensations resulting from cellular activities, thence carried to the mind and producing psychological feeling; energy released by physiochemical processes of the body causing tension until gratified; these instinctual forces are called the *id.*

instinct, herd: *see* **herd instinct.**

instinct, life: in Freudian psychology, the portion of the *id* or *libido* directed toward constructive ends. *Syn.* **eros;** *contr. w.* **thanatos, the death or destructive instinct.**

instinct theory: generally considered as the theory that the organism by its original nature is equipped with mechanisms that regulate those complex forms of behavior characteristic of the species and which adapt it to its environment.

institute: (1) a separate institution or organization designed to establish a relatively limited area of research or education, as the Institute for Advanced Study or Massachusetts Institute of Technology; (2) an arrangement for lectures and discussion sessions on a limited subject or theme, usually more intensive than a *convention* or *conference.*

institute, adult: *syn.* **institute** (2).

institute, art: an organization for the preservation and display of works of art and for recreational and educational purposes, sometimes embracing art classes or an art school. *See* **academy of fine arts.**

institute, county: a teachers' conference or convention sponsored by an educational official of the county or state for the purpose of promoting the professional development of teachers in service. *See* **institute, teachers'.**

institute, district: (1) a teachers' conference or convention sponsored by a school district for the purpose of promoting the professional development of teachers in service; (2) an established organization or society for the promotion of some educational purpose or work, membership being drawn from within the territorial limits of the district.

institute, mechanics': an adult institute sparked by the founding of workers' institutes in England in 1823, by the Franklin Institute in Philadelphia in 1824, and by the Boston Mechanics' Institution in 1826, and designed to provide libraries, lecture series, scientific collections, and periodicals containing up-to-date information on subjects calculated to aid mechanics in their vocations; also called mechanics' society.

institute, normal: a 4- to 6-week professional training school with a fairly continuous staff and a program including a review of common branches and methods of teaching; common in many states in the mid-nineteenth century; now practically nonexistent. *Contr. w.* **institute, teachers'.**

institute of technology: an institution of higher education offering instruction in applied sciences and technology, especially in the various fields of engineering.

institute, teachers': (1) short-term professional training schools for employed teachers conducted prior to the Civil War on a voluntary basis, later with state recognition and support in most states; provided courses lasting 2 to 8 weeks, including teaching methods and common-school subjects; *see* **institute, normal;** *contr. w.* **normal school;** (2) a conference of teachers, usually in county or rural districts, lasting one day to several days, for the purpose of discussing educational problems and hearing inspirational lectures; attendance by teachers is usually required.

institute, technical: *see* **technical institute.**

institute, workers': a series of lectures, consultations, and discussions on economic industrial, and labor problems and relations; usually held at a college or university under the joint auspices of the institution and labor organizations.

institution: (1) an established complex or pattern of social or culture traits that has some degree of permanence even though the individuals within it may change; (2) an organization, such as a school, church, or hospital, designed to serve some social purpose or end.

institution, civic: *see* **institution, social.**

institution, community: *see* **community institution.**

institution, corrective: an institution to which children and/or youth are committed for the correction of inappropriate patterns of social behavior.

institution, endowed: a school or other institution (museum, church, research foundation) enjoying the benefits of income from capital assets.

institution, Federal degree granting: one of the Federal military educational institutions to which the U.S. Congress has granted the right to confer bachelor's and/or master's and doctor's degrees, including the U.S. Air Force Academy, the U.S. Naval Academy, the U.S. Naval Postgraduate School, the U.S. Coast Guard Academy, the U.S. Merchant Marine Academy, and the Resident College, U.S. Air Force Institute of Technology, Air University.

institution management: *see* **management, institution.**

institution of higher learning: a college, university, or similar institution offering academic instruction suitable for students who have completed secondary schooling or its equivalent; also called institution of higher education.

institution, public: an establishment or corporation owned by or operated for the benefit of the group as a whole, such as a foundation, charitable enterprise, school, or college.

institution, residential: a facility (public or private) operated for the purpose of serving health, education, or welfare needs of persons whose circumstances require that they reside on a full-time basis within that facility.

institution, social: (1) an identifiable pattern of group behavior, established or recognized by custom or choice and having a certain degree of permanence, for example, *government,* commerce, manufacturing, *education,* etc.; (2) the organization developed to carry on the institution, for example, Congress, the lumbering business, the *school system,* etc.

institution, state: any public institution supported and controlled by the state and serving an area of the state or the entire state, for example, *universities,* hospitals, *industrial schools, trade schools,* and *special schools* for the feebleminded, the insane, the blind, the deaf, the crippled, etc.

institution, state teacher education: a general term used to designate any institution supported by the state in which the training of elementary or secondary school teachers takes place.

institution, teacher education: any educational institution concerned with the conduct of activities regarded as significant in the professional education of teachers and whose program is given appropriate recognition by state agencies that certify teachers; institutions included are teachers colleges, normal schools, and universities and colleges that have teacher education programs.

institution, terminal: a school intended primarily for the education of those who will go no further in their institutional education.

institutional administration: *see* **administration, institutional.**

institutional approach: *see* **approach, institutional.**

institutional camp: *see* **camp, institutional.**

institutional care: *see* **care, institutional.**

institutional control: *see* **control, institutional.**

institutional decision: *see* **decision, institutional.**

institutional evaluation: *see* **evaluation, institutional.**

institutional population: *see* **population, institutional.**

institutional quality, criteria of: standards for judging the educational effectiveness of an institution, established in terms of goals to be achieved.

institutional research: *see* **research, institutional.**

institutional teacher placement bureau: *syn.* **placement bureau, teacher.**

institutionalism: (1) the upholding of the validity or sanctity of institutions; (2) a school of thought in economics principally concerned with the normative study of present economic institutions, without any attempt to evaluate them in terms of desirability; *see* **economics, historical school of.**

institutionalization: the firming up of a complex of behavioral or culture traits so that it has a tendency to persist or to become an institution; the organization of labor is a good example.

instruction: (1) loose *syn.* **teaching;** (2) in a precise sense, the kind of teaching that obligates the instructor to furnish the learner with some lasting direction and is accountable for pupil performances commensurate with precise statements of educational objectives; (3) (mil. ed.) a serially numbered directive issued by commanders ashore and afloat; may contain policies, procedures, orders, doctrine, and information of a continuing or permanent nature; *see* **notice;** (4) (data processing) a command or direction put into a computer that tells it what to do and what to work with; *see* **code, operation; command; memory.**

instruction, adaptation of: *see* **adaptation of instruction.**

instruction area: the part of the area of a building devoted to the actual instruction of students, as distinguished from the area devoted to auxiliary purposes. *Syn.* **instruction space.**

instruction, audiovisual: (1) that branch of pedagogy concerned with the production, selection, and utilization of materials of instruction that do not depend solely on the printed word; (2) instruction in which a great variety of illustrative materials such as visual slides, films, models, records, tape recordings, and specimens may be utilized as aids in pupil understanding or appreciation. *See* **audiovisual education.**

instruction, block of: *see* **block of instruction.**

instruction, business and office education preemployment: *see* **instruction, business and office education preparatory.**

instruction, business and office education preparatory: instruction which prepares students for entry and advancement in a business and office occupation or in an occupation requiring business and office-education competencies.

instruction, business and office education related: that instruction necessary for in-depth training of vocational business and office education students; includes content other than business subject areas and uses the block-of-time approach. *See* **block of time; business and office education, intensive; program.**

instruction by subjects: the practice of organizing the auxiliary information of a trade into courses of instruction and teaching it by subjects separate from the shop practice work.

instruction, catechumenal (kat'ə·kū'mən·əl): a type of rudimentary instruction given to the early Christian converts to train them in the essentials of a religious life and church customs and practice.

instruction, class: the act or process of teaching a class of pupils or students. *Contr. w.* **instruction, individual.**

instruction, classroom: (1) direction or teaching through the medium of the school, college, or university; (2) knowledge imparted in the classroom by way of lecture, recitation, or discovery through purposive activity.

instruction, closed loop: a teaching system in which feedback from the evaluation of student performance is used to improve the instructional methods and learning environment.

instruction, clothing: instruction given in home economics courses applying the principles of art and science to the area of clothing; relates to the selection, purchasing, and maintenance of clothing and fabrics as well as the techniques of clothing construction and alteration.

instruction, comprehensive home economics: instruction which derives content from a combination of various areas of home economics and emphasizes basic principles and interrelationships among these areas.

instruction, computer assisted: an automated instructional technique in which automatic data processing equipment is used (*a*) to control the presentation of stimuli to a student, (*b*) to accept and evaluate the student responses, and (*c*) based on that interaction, to present further stimuli calculated to shape the student responses in the desired manner; the student uses a terminal directed by computer that may be in the same room or some distance away; the terminal is generally equipped with information display and student response devices.

instruction, computer assisted individually paced: a development of computer-assisted instruction in which the equipment, methodology, and program of instruction are designed to permit accomplishment of education or training by an individual student at his own learning rate.

instruction, correspondence: (1) a system of teaching by mail and other media conducted by an educational, governmental, or business institution or agency; (2) the actual teaching done by the teacher, instructor, or professor who has charge of the work of the correspondence student, correcting his lesson reports and directing his further study.

instruction, differential: *see* **instruction, individualized.**

instruction, differentiated: teaching in accordance with the individual's level of achievement and needs at that level, utilizing class, small-group, and individual activities. *See* **curricula, differentiated.**

instruction, director of: *see* **director of instruction.**

instruction, distributive education correlated: the result of combining and correlating learning experiences acquired both in the distributive education classroom and at the training station in the community.

instruction, distributive education post-high school: *see* **distributive education, postsecondary.**

instruction, distributive education preemployment: *see* **instruction, distributive education preparatory.**

instruction, distributive education preparatory: whether under the project plan or as part of the cooperative plan, instruction which prepares youth or adults for entry into and advancement in a distributive occupation or an occupation requiring distributive competencies.

instruction, distributive education programmed: a self-instructional training method in which part of the training can be accomplished outside the formal classroom setting.

instruction, distributive education related: *see* **instruction, distributive education preparatory.**

instruction, dual: (mil. ed.) flight instruction given with the aid of dual flight controls.

instruction, elementary: (1) instruction given in the elementary school grades; (2) instruction in the first principles of any body of subject matter.

instruction, ethical: instruction having to do with morality and good conduct. *Syn.* **moral instruction.**

instruction, field: educational experiences provided in a situation where the student takes an active role in working in a particular area outside his school to further his understanding of that area. *Syn.* **fieldwork education method.**

instruction, flight: a program to teach the techniques of flying aircraft; much of the instruction takes place while the plane is actually in flight.

instruction, foods: instruction given in home economics courses relating food to health and nutrition; includes food needs, dietary patterns for individuals and families, food selection and purchasing, and meal planning and preparation.

instruction for homebound pupil: *see* **instruction, home.**

instruction, formal plan of: *see* **formal plan of instruction.**

instruction, gratuitous: charitable education, one form of which was developed by St. Jean Baptiste de la Salle and the Brothers of the Christian Schools for the education of the poor in elementary schools; beginning in France during the seventeenth century, the movement spread to different parts of Europe and later to America.

instruction, group: (1) the act of attempting to teach a number of persons the same thing at the same time; (2) the instruction of group members in their different but interdependent roles, as in the case of a football team.

instruction, group-centered: *see* **teaching, nondirective.**

instruction, health: presentation of authentic health information for the purpose of developing habits and attitudes that promote good health.

instruction, home: individual teaching in the child's home under the jurisdiction of an itinerant teacher; in special education for the handicapped, school-like instruction by a regularly certified teacher in the child's home during the period when he is judged unable to attend school; in some instances such instruction is augmented by telephone communication between the classroom and the pupil or by other means. *Syn.* **instruction, homebound;** *see* **pupil, homebound.**

instruction, homebound: *syn.* **instruction, home;** *see* **homebound teacher; pupil, homebound.**

instruction, hospital: the school-like instruction of a pupil or pupils offered in a hospital because of the physical inability of the pupil to attend school.

instruction, household equipment: instruction in home economics dealing with the selection, use, and care of equipment used in the home.

instruction, in-school: instruction received by a pupil within the school plant.

instruction, incidental: *syn.* **teaching, incidental.**

instruction, individual: (1) the organization of instructional materials in a manner that will permit each student to progress in accord with his own abilities and interests; (2) the provision of instructional guidance and assistance to individual pupils in accord with their needs.

instruction, individualization of: *see* **instruction, individualized.**

instruction, individualized: a type of teaching-learning in which the teacher gives consideration to the individual learner; examples are (*a*) *guided independent study,* which permits pupils at any grade level in any subject area to work on their own at their own pace under the guidance of a teacher; (*b*) *diversified-activity individualization,* which allows the pupil to repeat activities, using multiple materials or experiences until he demonstrates adequate mastery; (*c*) *creative-activity individualization,* which permits the pupil to engage in choice-making in studying problems and to plan his own activities, choose between various approaches, and correlate results from other curriculum areas.

instruction, individually prescribed (IPI): an instructional system based on the principles of programmed learning, in which each student directs his own program of study based on teacher-prepared (or teacher-pupil prepared) daily prescriptions of study materials and activities; progress is noted through observation and curricula-embedded tests (short tests to determine mastery of a specific objective within the learning continuum) and through diagnosis of the pupils' performance according to a behavioral map of areas of the elementary school curricula.

instruction, instrument: a program which teaches an airplane pilot to control an aircraft by reference to instrument indications.

instruction, job: instruction on the job given in order to enable the worker to do the assigned task.

instruction, learner-centered: *see* **instruction, programmed.**

instruction line: a continuous line drawn through a list of teaching units that indicates the order in which the units will be presented to the learner.

instruction, materializing: the act of producing instructional materials, educational toys, or responsive environments that incorporate specific instructional functions or learning tasks. *See* **teaching, mediated** (2).

instruction materials, programmed: instructional materials prepared specifically to employ programmed instructional techniques, such as text, tapes, films and film strips, slides, scripts for live presentations, etc. *See* **hardware; software.**

instruction, mechanistic: any teaching procedure in which the pupil is viewed as raw material awaiting manipulation by the teacher.

instruction, mediated: *see* **teaching, mediated.**

instruction, medium of: *see* **medium of instruction.**

instruction modification: the changing of one or more of the parts of any given instruction, by means of computer operations specified in other instructions, when they are executed by the computer; often called *address modification* because the operand addresses are the most commonly modified.

instruction, monitorial: *see* **Lancastrian system.**

instruction, moral: *syn.* **instruction, ethical.**

instruction, mutual: *see* **Lancastrian system.**

instruction, nondirective: *see* **teaching, nondirective.**

instruction, occupational: (spec. ed.) the teaching of specific vocational skills in a high school program for the mentally retarded.

instruction, oral: teaching done through the medium of speech.

instruction, organization for: *see* **organization for instruction.**

instruction package, programmed: all the components of a specific unit of programmed instruction, including the instructional materials, learning aids, instructor guide or manual, pre- and post-tests, validation data, description of intended student population, and learning objectives. *See* **hardware; software.**

instruction, preventive reading: reading instruction designed to prevent reading retardation or disability; prevention is an essential function of the basal reading program.

instruction, programmed: instruction utilizing a workbook, textbook, or mechanical and/or electronic device programmed to help pupils attain a specified level of performance by (*a*) providing instruction in small steps, (*b*) asking one or more questions about each step in the instruction and providing instant knowledge of whether each answer is right or wrong, and (*c*) enabling pupils to progress at their own pace, either individually through self-pacing or as a team through group pacing. *Syn.* **autoinstruction; automated teaching;** *see* **conditioning, operant; pacing; program.**

instruction, programmed reading: instruction in reading by means of materials that present exercises in very small steps along with correct answers, so that the pupil can proceed independently and at his own rate.

instruction, recordings: (audiovis. ed.) instruction provided primarily through the medium of tape recordings or other recording media.

instruction, regimented: teaching children of the same grade without making any attempt to meet individual differences; assumes that those children reaching a given grade have the same achievement level and needs.

instruction register: (data processing) the register that stores temporarily the instruction currently being executed by the automatic computer control unit.

instruction-related activities: *see* **activities, instruction-related.**

instruction, related technical: (voc. ed.) instruction that includes those facts or general principles that one must know in order to plan and do a job.

instruction-relatedness: (1) the degree to which activities of personnel in the school setting have a direct influence upon the accomplishment of the major instructional goals of the school; (2) one of the two dimensions defining the major functions of the school operation. *Comp. w.* **pupil-relatedness.**

instruction, religious: the teaching of the tenets of a given faith or the teaching of commonly accepted values based upon religious conviction.

instruction, remedial: specific instruction based on comprehensive diagnostic findings and intended to overcome any particular learning deficiency of a pupil. *See* **adult basic education; teaching, remedial.**

instruction, resident: instruction given in the buildings on the campus of an educational institution.

instruction room: *see* **classroom; classroom, regular.**

instruction, school-home telephone: a device that permits conversations between those in the classroom and the homebound pupil, usually considered an adjunct to home instruction.

instruction, sectarian: the teaching of the tenets or doctrines of a particular religious faith.

instruction sheet: any of a variety of single-purpose, single-sheet or multiple-page guide sheets designed to give the learner certain detailed information or instruction about a task to be performed or a learning activity to be undertaken, for example, information sheet, assignment sheet, drill sheet, self-test sheet, operation sheet, job sheet; usually teacher-made or locally produced; in industrial arts and science such sheets utilize to a high degree graphic illustration of the learning activities recommended. *Syn.* **instructional sheet** (2).

instruction, simulator: instruction given in a mock-up of air or space vehicles to simulate actual conditions that will be experienced by an astronaut or pilot; an example is the Command Module Simulator located at Cape Kennedy, Florida, for the purpose of training astronauts for flight to the moon.

instruction, small-group: organization of subgroups within a class for the conduct of teaching-learning according to (*a*) interest in particular problems or activities, (*b*) specific skills, (*c*) social needs, such as security, affection, or a sense of belonging, or (*d*) educational needs, based on a concept, content, or achievement.

instruction, socialized: teaching in which class members participate in lesson planning, discussion, and activity, in contrast to teaching in which the teacher is active and the class members are relatively passive.

instruction space: *syn.* **instruction area.**

instruction, specific related: (voc. ed.) those concepts, skills, and attitudes needed by the individual student-learner to handle the duties and responsibilities at his training station and to prepare for advancement toward his career objective.

instruction, standard practice: (school admin.) a written description of what is regarded, at the moment, as the best method of executing a kind or type of project; this method is also called *standard office practice, standard office procedure,* or *standard operating procedure.*

instruction, student-centered: a characteristic of *programmed instruction* which, for one example, strives to take into consideration all pertinent student personality factors, such as differences in aptitude, background knowledge, and motivation. *See* **instruction, programmed.**

instruction, supervised correspondence: *see* **correspondence study, supervised.**

instruction, supplementary: (bus. ed.) instruction in such fields as business and office education; distributive education for adults or out-of-school youth wishing to refresh, update, or upgrade competencies needed in their employment; usually provided on a part-time basis.

instruction, textiles: the teaching of science and art as related to textile fibers and the fabric made from them; includes dyeing processes, woven and applied design, and selection, use, and care of different fabrics.

instruction time: the time a teacher gives to pupils during class or directed study periods.

instruction, unit of: *see* **unit, teaching.**

instruction, vernacular: *see* **vernacular instruction.**

instruction, visual: instruction in which a great variety of illustrative materials such as visual slides, films, models, and specimens may be utilized as aids in pupil understanding or appreciation; not to be confused with sight saving. *See* **sight conservation.**

instruction, voice: lessons designed to train a vocalist in proper and effective methods of singing with maximum resonance, projection, clarity, beauty, and control.

instructional adjustment: *see* **adjustment, instructional.**

instructional aid: any of the devices which assist an instructor in the teaching-learning process by simply presenting supporting or supplementary material, usually intermittently; they are not self-supporting. *Comp. w.* **instructional media.**

instructional consultant: *see* **consultant, instructional.**

instructional control: (1) the supervisory direction, coordination, and articulation of the curriculum of the school and of the methods and materials used in teaching; (2) discipline resulting from the interest and active participation of the class in the material being studied, as contrasted with externally enforced discipline.

instructional costs: *see* **costs, instructional.**

instructional curricular event: *see* **curricular event, instructional.**

instructional equipment: *see* **equipment, instructional.**

instructional facility: *see* **equipment, instructional.**

instructional field, special: one of the separate fields into which instruction is divided, such as home economics, industrial arts, music, agriculture, art, business education, etc., as distinguished from the academic fields.

instructional film: *see* **film, instructional.**

instructional group: *see* **group, instructional.**

instructional level, postsecondary: an instructional program designed for students who have completed high school and graduation requirements; includes technical-vocational, junior college, and two-year university programs as well as regular college and university curricula.

instructional material: any device with instructional content or function that is used for teaching purposes, including books, textbooks, supplementary reading materials, audiovisual and other sensory materials, scripts for radio or television instruction, programs for computer-managed instruction, instruction sheets, and packaged sets of materials for construction or manipulation.

instructional material, nonproduction: (voc. ed.) all material, apparatus, and equipment used in connection with the teaching of a lesson off the job and not used for production purposes.

instructional materials center: *see* **center, instructional materials.**

instructional materials director: *syn.* **director, audiovisual.**

instructional materials, kit of: *see* **kit of instructional materials.**

instructional media: devices and other materials which present a complete body of information and are largely self-supporting rather than supplementary in the teaching-learning process. *See* **educational media;** *comp. w.* **instructional aid.**

instructional method: *syn.* **teaching method.**

instructional objective: *see* **objective, instructional.**

instructional order: the sequence in which a teacher presents lessons or jobs in order to ensure the most efficient results from the teaching process.

instructional outcomes: *see* **outcomes, instructional.**

instructional practices: *see* **teaching technique.**

instructional process: the methods of instruction used to bring about desired change or learning.

instructional product: *see* **product, instructional.**

instructional program: *see* **program instructional.**

instructional program, counseling: *see* **program, counseling instructional.**

instructional program, improvement of: the subjection of instructional procedures to change, facilitating movement toward better outcomes; also involves the selection and use of techniques that provide an evaluation of the results of the teaching-learning activities.

instructional program, purpose of: (admin.) standards by which educational change should be designed and the quality of the instructional program assessed.

instructional programmer: *see* **programmer, instructional.**

instructional reading level: *see* **reading level, instructional.**

instructional service: a general term inclusive of classroom teaching and the supervision and administration of instruction.

instructional sheet: (1) (home ec.) in clothing instruction, directions which are included in all commercial patterns to explain the order of cutting and construction of garments; (2) *syn.* **instruction sheet.**

instructional staff: *see* **staff, instructional.**

instructional supplies: *see* **supplies, instructional.**

instructional system: (1) a plan or structure containing a collection of interrelated components that are designed to achieve a specific set of instructional objectives; (2) (mil. ed.) the use of all possible elements that may function to promote learning, such as textbooks, chalkboards, still and motion pictures, radio, television, audio tapes, programmed instructions, teaching machines, models, displays, square or round classrooms, air conditioning, field trips, and museums; specially developed by the Air Force Academy in harmony with the concepts of weapon systems.

instructional system, programmed: *see* **programmed instructional system.**

instructional systems engineering: *see* **engineering, instructional systems.**

instructional technology: *see* **technology, instructional.**

instructional television: *see* **television, instructional.**

instructional television fixed service: *see* **television fixed service, instructional.**

instructional test: *see* **test, instructional.**

instructional trip: *syn.* **field trip.**

instructional unit: *see* **unit, instructional.**

instructions, course: *see* **course instructions.**

instructor: (1) a teacher with the responsibility for instructing students in their progress toward specific educational objectives; (2) (obs.) one who imparts knowledge; (3) in colleges and universities, a teacher holding a rank below that of an associate professor.

instructor, aerospace education: (mil. ed.) the senior retired Air Force commissioned officer employed by the secondary school to supervise the Air Force Junior Reserve Officer Training Corps program at the host school.

instructor, call: one of a number of selected workers of advanced skill in a department of an industrial concern who is available for instructing new workers and who may be called upon for the purpose when the occasion arises.

instructor, distributive education, adult: a competent teacher, such as a full-time teacher or a capable businessman, who is employed to instruct adults in occupational skills and knowledges necessary to perform efficiently in distributive education.

instructor foreman: a foreman who, in addition to his supervisory duties, instructs other workers in trade skills and knowledge.

instructor-foreman course: *see* **course, instructor-foreman.**

instructor handbook: *see* **handbook, instructor.**

instructor, hourly rate: an instructor who is paid at a specified rate for each instructional hour of teaching; usually a competent person in his field employed to teach a course.

instructor pilot: *see* **pilot, instructor.**

instructor, water safety: a classification of achievement in the teaching of aquatic activities.

instrument, data-gathering: *syn.* **schedule, data-gathering** (1).

instrument, evaluation: *see* **evaluation instrument.**

instrument instruction: *see* **instruction, instrument.**

instrument, preband: *syn.* **instrument, preorchestral.**

instrument, preorchestral: a simple musical instrument built on the same principles as an orchestral instrument but less complex, so that it can be played with much less instruction and digital dexterity; may be of the percussion, whistle, or keyboard type. *Syn* **preband instrument;** *see* **class, preinstrument; instruments, classroom; recorder** (2).

instrument storage room: a room connected with a music practice room, used for the storage of band or orchestra instruments.

instrumental class: *see* **class, instrumental.**

instrumental conditioning: *see* **conditioning, instrumental.**

instrumental drawing: *see* **drawing, instrumental.**

instrumental learning: *see* **learning, instrumental.**

instrumental value: *see* **value instrumental.**

instrumentalism: (philos.) according to John Dewey, the theory that mind and ideas are instruments in the service of the organism; in educational philosophy, the theory that subject matter is primarily extrinsic in value and is to be used to modify life rather than to be assimilated for its own sake. *See* **experimentalism; pragmatism.**

instrumentalism, evolutionary: a term suggested by Jerome Bruner as an evaluation criterion for educational progress in the ability of students to use the instruments, tools, and technologies of a developing society to expand their own mental powers.

instrumentation: (1) the distribution of instruments within an orchestra or band; (2) the study of the selection and use of musical instruments in composing music for an orchestra or band and in preparing music for performance by an instrumental group for which it was not originally designed; *syn.* **orchestration;** (3) (ind. arts) the study of devices necessary to observe and control both manufacturing processes and the performance of mechanical and electrical machinery, including the science of measurement as well as the conversion and recording of physical, chemical, and mechanical state and condition into sensible information; (4) in research, employment of physical means such as tools or devices that apply known physical principles to increase the experimenter's perception of natural or manipulated phenomena or to perform his experiments.

instruments, brass: those musical wind instruments having a cup mouthpiece and made of brass or other metal, such as a trombone, tuba, trumpet, French horn, bugle, etc.; often referred to simply as "brasses".

instruments, classroom: (mus. ed.) a collection of bells, drums, sticks, song flutes, and related melodic and harmonic instruments, which are manufactured specifically for the public classrooms of the nation.

instruments, drawing: *see* **drawing instruments.**

instruments, keyboard: a generic term used by musicians to cover all musical instruments, regardless of tone-generating principles, that are played from a keyboard; this term thus includes pianos, organs, harpsichords, clavichords, celestas, and the modern electronic instruments built with white and black keys in the traditional arrangement.

instruments of diagnosis: *see* **diagnosis, instruments of.**

instruments, percussion: those musical instruments that are struck or shaken to produce sound; there are two types (*a*) those producing definite pitches—timpani, glockenspiel, bells, xylophone, marimba, chimes, and (*b*) those of indefinite pitch—snare drum, bass drum, tambourine, castanets, etc.

instruments, pupil-centered: *see* **pupil-centered instruments.**

instruments, sociometric: *see* **sociometric instruments.**

instruments, stringed: musical instruments having stretched strings as sound-producing agents; although including piano, harp, and violin, the term generally refers to members of the violin or violin-type family, which often are referred to simply as "strings."

instruments, valve: all brass instruments (except the bugle and trombone) provided with valve mechanisms that make possible all the tones of the chromatic scale.

instruments, woodwind: musical instruments having as a sound generator either a reed, single or double, or a mouth hole which sets into vibration an enclosed column of air; examples are flute, clarinet, oboe, bassoon, etc.

insurable value: *see* **value, insurable.**

insurance: a contract, usually called a policy, whereby one party undertakes to indemnify another for a loss caused by the occurrence of a specified event or events, provided the insured pays a premium as stipulated in the policy.

insurance, accident: a contract whereby one party undertakes to indemnify or guarantee another against loss from an unplanned event resulting in death, injury to persons, or damage to property.

insurance, building: protection, upon payment of a premium, against financial loss from destruction or partial destruction of buildings by fire, tornado, or other means.

insurance, cooperative purchasing of: *see* **cooperative purchasing of insurance.**

insurance register: a book or card file in which is kept a systematic record of all essential details of all insurance policies carried.

insurance reserve: *see* **reserve, insurance.**

insurance, social: various measures used by government or voluntary organizations to provide for members of low-income groups in case of sickness, old age, unemployment, accident, and invalidism.

insurance, state: a form of mutual insurance of state property, organized in some states, by which a reserve fund is maintained under authority and control of the state and operated in much the same manner as a regular private company and in which public school districts are usually eligible to participate.

insurance, teacher: a plan of insurance designed especially to protect teachers from loss of earning power through illness or accident, as well as to guarantee the payment of a sum to a specified beneficiary in the event of death.

intaglio printing: *see* **printing, intaglio.**

intangible personal property: *see* **property, intangible personal.**

integer: one of the numbers belonging to the set $\{..., -3, -2, -1, 0, +1, +2, +3,...\}$.

integer, negative: an integer less than zero in value, for example, -1, -2, etc.

integer, positive: an integer greater than zero in value, for example, $+1$, $+2$, etc.

integral class boundary: *syn.* **class limit, apparent.**

integral class limit: *syn.* **class limit, apparent.**

integral domain: *see* **mathematical system** (1).

integral number: *syn.* **integer.**

integral unit: the designation of a school bus whose body and chassis were constructed by the same manufacturer and assembled and sold as a unit.

integrated course of study: *see* **course of study, integrated.**

integrated curriculum: *see* **curriculum, integrated.**

integrated data processing: *see* **data processing, integrated.**

integrated experience approach: an approach to instruction that involves the teacher in identifying as clearly as possible those responses, attitudes, concepts, ideas, and manipulative skills to be achieved by the student and then in designing a multifaceted, multisensory approach that will enable the student to direct his own activity to attain these objectives; the program of learning is organized in such a way that students can proceed at their own pace, filling in gaps in their background information while omitting the portions of the program which they have covered at some previous time.

integrated experiences: *see* **experiences, integrated.**

integrated mathematics: *syn.* **mathematics, integrated.**

integrated personality: *see* **personality, integrated.**

integrated plan: a plan for teaching office practice by which the group of pupils is organized as a business office with the various duties of the office being performed in rotation by the pupils; models of business papers are used and the work is carried on as it would be in an actual office.

integrated program: *see* **program, integrated.**

integrating course: *see* **program, common-learnings** (2).

integration: (1) the condition of an organism in which there is continuous interactive adjustment of the physiological (glandular and chemical), physical (neuromuscular), emotional, and mental processes (internally and externally) with the environment, resulting in a state free from conflict and strain; *see* **personality, integrated;** (2) the process or practice of combining different school subjects and presenting them as aspects of one unifying project or activity, for example, the teaching of geography, history, art, English, and arithmetic in a study of the Panama Canal.

integration course: *see* **course, integration.**

integration, functional: (school admin.) the reverse of the process of functional differentiation; tends to take place with a decline in the volume of a company's business. *Contr. w.* **differentiation, functional.**

integration, grade-a-year: a plan for gradually breaking racial isolation in schools which calls for integrating one grade per year; such plans usually call for beginning with the first grade and working to the twelfth, or beginning with the twelfth and working to the first.

integration method: *see* **integrative method.**

integration of behavior pattern: coordination or organization of behavioral elements, parts, or segments into a more or less unified response; the term is usually employed in connection with motor components but is sometimes extended to include the associated neurological, physiological, attitudinal, etc., aspects of a response. *See* **integration** (1); **integration of development;** *dist. f.* **integration, total; total pattern.**

integration of development: the process by which functions or stimuli of a lower, simpler order become organized and unified to form new units of a higher order.

integration of growth components: the fusion of the aesthetic, emotional, intellectual, perceptual, physical, and social growth components into a unity in which the single components lose their identity; this *integration* occurs in the individual.

integration of personality: the developmental process by which the individual's major drives and values are coordinated and made to reinforce each other.

integration plan: *see* **curriculum, integrated.**

integration, racial: participation of nonwhite and white students and staff in the same school activities; includes cocurricular and school-related activities. *See* **desegregation.**

integration, reflex: the organization of specific innate responses into coordinated patterns.

integration, social: (1) harmonious personal adjustment of the individual to the standards, demands, and responsibilities of the group of which he is a part; (2) the fusion or harmonious interrelation of the values and functions of two or more persons or groups to make them an identifiable entity.

integration, total: (neonate behav.) that organization of behavior in which all muscles that by virtue of maturation, are capable of responding participate in a response. *See* **total pattern.**

integrative action: (1) the coordinating of specific responses into unified patterns; (2) the systematic organization of units into a meaningful constellation.

integrative behavior: *see* **behavior, integrative.**

integrative classes: *see* **classes, integrative.**

integrative method: one of the philosophic approaches to generalized truth, representing synthesis, that is, the thoughtful interrelating of findings of many scientific studies in such a way as to examine the validity of their conclusions in the light of a larger pattern or theory, and at the same time to formulate and examine the tenability of a larger pattern of interpretation and make any necessary tentative or hypothetical modifications in it.

integrator: (data processing) a mechanism for continuously adding up a quantity being measured over a period of time.

integrity: the quality of consistent moral soundness. *See* **character.**

intellect: a term that implies the faculty point of view as a designation of the so-called power to integrate experience. *See* **faculties, mental; intelligence.**

intellectual ability: *see* **ability, intellectual.**

intellectual capacity: *see* **capacity, mental.**

intellectual freedom: *see* **freedom, intellectual.**

intellectual growth: *see* **growth, intellectual.**

intellectual honesty: *see* **honesty, intellectual.**

intellectual maturation: *see* **maturation, intellectual.**

intellectual maturity: *see* **maturity, intellectual.**

intellectual performance: *see* **performance, intellectual.**

intellectual powers: *see* **powers, intellectual.**

intellectual rigor: *see* **rigor, intellectual.**

intellectual virtues: *see* **virtues, intellectual.**

intellectualism: the cognitive activity of the mind at the abstract and the higher conceptual levels. *Ant.* **activism.**

intellectualization: the process of reasoning abstractly, as in forming concepts or judgments.

intellectually handicapped: *see* **handicapped, intellectually.**

intelligence: (1) the ability to learn and to criticize what is learned; (2) the ability to deal effectively with tasks involving abstractions; (3) the ability to learn from experience and to deal with new situations; (4) as commonly used in measurement and testing, a degree of ability represented by performance on a group of tests selected because they have proved their practical value in the prediction of success in academic work and in some vocations; (5) (mil. ed.) the product resulting from the collection, evaluation, analysis, integration, and interpretation of all information concerning one or more aspects of foreign countries or areas, which is immediately or potentially significant to the development and execution of plans, policies, and operations.

intelligence, abstract: the ability to make effective use of abstract concepts and symbols in thinking and in dealing with new situations; involves the ability to generalize and a high degree of skill in nonmechanical, verbal thinking; for example, the type of intelligence displayed by the philosopher or mathematician. *Contr. w.* **intelligence, concrete.**

intelligence, adult: the capacity to adjust to situations in a mature way.

intelligence, animal: (1) the adaptive mental capacities of infrahuman species; that quality of response which enables animals to adjust to new situations, attend to significant stimuli, find solutions to problems, profit from experience, etc; (2) the quality of mental processes which causes animal-like responses of human beings to stimuli, for example, simple, automatic, unplanned, or unimaginative adaptive reactions that seem to be intuitive rather than logical.

intelligence, artificial: (1) a feigned, assumed, or imitation capacity for knowledge and understanding; not a genuine ability to apprehend the interrelationships between facts presented and arrive at a desired result; *see* **idiot savant;** (2) computer and related techniques as used to supplement the intellectual capabilities of man.

intelligence, athletic: a term, not in common usage, to indicate a composite conception of traits and qualities necessary for the exercise of motor skills involved in sports; relates particularly to the ability to reach high performance levels.

intelligence, average: (1) the mean or median of the population in general on a measure of brightness or mental maturity (an IQ of 100 is generally accepted as representing average brightness; a mental age of 16 years has been accepted by some as representing average mental maturity for adults, although a mental age of 13 years 5 months, based on Army Alpha test results during World War I, is often used as an indication of average adult mental maturity); (2) the mean or median intelligence, in terms either of brightness or of mental maturity, of any group of persons. *See* **age, mental; intelligence; quotient, deviation intelligence.**

intelligence, basic: the native capacity for adaptive responses; that capacity for correct discrimination, attention, and adjustment to situations which is prerequisite to learning and general mental development.

intelligence, biological: (1) the capacity to react successfully to an immediate stimulus; (2) mental functioning (or the type of functioning measured by a given test) determined and limited by the native constitution of the individual.

intelligence, borderline: (1) a level of mental development found in a person who is not readily classified as either normal or feebleminded; ordinarily used to describe the intelligence of those higher-grade feebleminded who, under proper social conditions, could make adequate adjustments to many life situations and would not need to be institutionalized; (2) a degree of ability represented by an IQ between 70 and 80.

intelligence, coefficient of (CI): *syn.* **coefficient of brightness.**

intelligence, cognitive: that mental functioning involved in perceiving, knowing, and understanding; sometimes measured through the use of problems involving relationships; sometimes restricted to performance in perceptual tasks.

intelligence components: any of the parts into which intelligence in general may be analyzed, for example, power, range, and speed, or memory, imagination, attention, comprehension, and reasoning, or group, specific, and general factors.

intelligence, conative: that aspect of mental functioning associated with motivation, or volition, as contrasted with affection or cognition; one of the main areas of intelligence not governed mainly by reasoning and examination of relationships. *Contr. w.* **intelligence, cognitive.**

intelligence, concrete: the capacity to manipulate objects to meet novel situations effectively; the term (as used in education) indicates the capacity to do work involving principally manipulation of objects, such as shopwork, mechanics, or sewing. *Contr. w.* **intelligence, abstract.**

intelligence, constancy of: (1) continuation at the same or very nearly the same relative level of general ability throughout one's developmental period and into adulthood until the period of decline; (2) in terms of *intelligence quotient* (IQ), an expected probable variation of about five points from one's average performance.

intelligence distribution: *see* **distribution, intelligence.**

intelligence, effective: the mental processes that can be utilized in dealing with concepts and situations; intelligence that can be put to work in solving problems or in adjusting to the environment; may be limited by emotional or physiological conditions.

intelligence, factor of: a component part of intelligence in general, such as Spearman's *g-factor*, one of Thurstone's *primary mental abilities*, a group factor, the speed factor, etc.; any of several differentiable mental abilities.

intelligence, general: the general ability or capacity for adjustment possessed by the individual in contrast to his specific, special, or relatively independent abilities. (One of the most characteristic features of the concept is the theory that, regardless of its exact nature, general intelligence not only remains relatively constant but also appears as a common factor in instances of special abilities.) *See* **two-factor theory.**

intelligence, innate: a person's potentiality for developing a certain level of ability, so far as that level is determined or limited by genetic factors.

intelligence, job: practical knowledge and understanding pertaining to one's job.

intelligence, level of: area, position, rank, or degree of mental ability.

intelligence, measured: the intellectual level indicated by a test but not necessarily the optimal level that may be recorded on another occasion.

intelligence, mechanical: (1) general capacity for dealing with mechanisms, tools, and materials; (2) ability to solve problems involving the use or interaction of tools, materials, and mechanisms.

intelligence, nonintellective: successful response to a stimulus without mental or cognitive behavior; the type of thinking that produces habits, instincts, or reflex actions, the nonrational components or determiners of performance in tests of intelligence.

intelligence, optimum: (1) superior mentality; the fullest development of mental capacity; (2) that amount of intelligence most advantageous for effective functioning in a particular environment, situation, or occupation.

intelligence, practical: intelligence centering about judgments of practice; intelligence concerned with what to do in situations primarily involving choice and evaluation, with discrimination among values in a situation.

intelligence quotient: *see* **quotient, deviation intelligence; quotient, ratio intelligence.**

intelligence quotient, deviation: *see* **quotient, deviation intelligence.**

intelligence quotient, group: *see* **quotient, group intelligence.**

intelligence quotient, ratio: *see* **quotient, ratio intelligence.**

intelligence scale: *see* **scale, intelligence.**

intelligence, social: (1) the ability to adjust oneself to the social environment and to act for its improvement; (2) an individual's ability to deal effectively with social relationships and with novel social situations.

intelligence test: *see* **test, intelligence.**

intelligence test, general: *see* **test, general intelligence.**

intelligence test, nonverbal: *see* **test, nonverbal intelligence.**

intelligence test, verbal: *see* **test, verbal intelligence.**

intelligence testing, brain-wave: *see* **testing, brain-wave intelligence.**

intelligibility, conceptual: *syn.* **intelligibility, structural.**

intelligibility, formal: *syn.* **intelligibility, structural.**

intelligibility, functional: a term used in organic philosophy of education to indicate comprehensibility of a practical operation or knowledge of activities of doing, as distinct from *theoretical intelligibility* or knowledge of organized subject matters in themselves; the union of the two is requisite for *organic intelligibility. Syn.* **operational intelligibility;** *see* **intelligibility, organic.**

intelligibility, operational: *syn.* **intelligibility, functional.**

intelligibility, organic: a term used in organic philosophy of education to denote the total comprehensibility of any significant unit of reality for knowing or learning; theoretically, the summation of all the partial intelligibilities in terms of total comprehension.

intelligibility, structural: a term used in organic philosophy of education to indicate comprehensibility of form of an entity as distinct from its function; refers to the "knowability" of a thing in terms of its *being,* in terms of parts and their relationships to each other and to the whole. *Syn.* **conceptual intelligibility; formal intelligibility; theoretical intelligibility.**

intelligibility, theoretical: *syn.* **intelligibility, structural.**

intensity: (1) a measure of energy in sound, speech, music, etc.; *see* **decibel;** (2) (photog.) a chemical process to increase the image of a negative with below normal density.

intensity discrimination: *see* **discrimination, intensity.**

intensity, law of: *see* **law of intensity.**

intensity, sense of: *syn.* **discrimination, intensity.**

intensive business and office education: *see* **business and office education, intensive.**

intensive course: *see* **course, intensive.**

intensive curriculum: *see* **curriculum, intensive.**

intensive enrichment: *see* **enrichment, intensive.**

intensive language program: *see* **program, intensive language.**

intensive language training: *see* **training, intensive language.**

intensive part-time class: *see* **part-time class, intensive.**

intensive reading: *see* **reading, intensive.**

intensive sampling: *see* **sampling, intensive.**

intent, occupational: *see* **occupational objective.**

intentional learning: *see* **learning, intentional.**

inter-African studies: *see* **studies, inter-African.**

interaction: (1) (philos.) a relation between more or less independent entities in which reciprocal influences of one upon the other are possible; (2) in philosophy of education, the view that the growth of personality and character, that is, education, is a product of continuously related forces of nature and nurture; that deliberate education is the effort to stimulate and direct this process (Dewey); (3) in experimentation, the condition resulting when the effect of one factor or condition is dependent on the presence or absence of another factor or condition; for example, if the effect of the size of type on reading rate is dependent on style of type used, there is an interaction between size and style.

interaction analysis: *see* **analysis, interaction.**

interaction, circular: a social stimulus-response mechanism in which the acts of each participant become a part of the total stimulating situation so that each individual's response is not only elicited by the common stimulus but also determined in part by the responses of others in the group.

interaction, conversational: issuance of a series of commands by the user of a computer at a remote terminal, the successive commands often based on the computer's response to previous commands by the user. *Contr. w.* **job, batch.**

interaction, first-order: the interaction between two variables or two main effects. *Syn.* **simple interaction;** *see* **variance, interaction.**

interaction, higher-order: the interaction between three or more variables.

interaction of experience: a meaningful exchange between the purposes and capacities of an individual and a selected set of conditions in an environment (Dewey). (An experience, to be educative, must be more than mere activity or happenings. A boy, for example, does not learn from cutting himself with his jackknife unless he relates his purposes—a sharp blade, an object to be shaped, an unprotected finger.)

interaction, second-order: the interaction between three variables, that is, the tendency for the interaction between two variables to differ for various values of a third variable. *Syn.* **triple interaction;** *see* **variance, interaction.**

interaction, simple: *syn.* **interaction, first-order.**

interaction, social: the mutual stimulation of one person by another and the responses that result; the mutual modification of the behavior of individuals in social contact.

interaction, third-order: *see* **variance, interaction.**

interaction, triple: *syn.* **interaction, second-order.**

interaction variance: *see* **variance, interaction.**

interactional change: *see* **change, interactional.**

interactionism: the theory that the mind and body are two different aspects of reality which can and do interact with one another and which influence one another. *Comp. w.* **epiphenomenalism; parallelism.**

interactive score units: *see* **score units, interactive.**

interarea specializations: *see* **specializations, interarea.**

iterative loop: in computer operations, a repeated group of instructions in a routine.

intercalation: the interposition of words or sounds between syllables, words, or phrases.

interchange of teacher: the temporary reciprocal replacement of an instructor of one school system or building with an instructor from another school system or building.

interclass correlation: *see* **correlation, interclass.**

interclass grouping: *see* **grouping, interclass.**

interclass visitation: *syn.* **intervisitation.**

intercollegiate athletics: *see* **athletics, intercollegiate.**

intercollegiate competition: *see* **competition, intercollegiate.**

intercom: a two-way sound system for direct, live conversation, usually between teacher and student in the language laboratory.

intercommunication line: usually, the audio connection between the television director and the members of the crew; in some closed-circuit applications, talk-back audio lines installed to permit verbal interchange between students and teachers in remote classrooms and the TV teacher.

intercommunity: the quality of belonging or pertaining to two or more communities; shared participation; the sharing of something in common.

intercorrelation: any of the $n(n-1)/2$ different correlations that are possible among n variables; for example, among the variables, A, B, C, and D, the following intercorrelations can be obtained: r_{AB}, r_{AC}, r_{AD}, r_{BC}, r_{BD}, r_{CD}.

intercorrelation coefficient: *see* **coefficient, intercorrelation.**

intercorrelation, positive: *syn.* **positive correlation;** *see* **correlation (1).**

intercorrelation table: *see* **table, intercorrelation.**

intercultural education: education designed to reduce actual and possible intercultural tensions, bias, prejudice, and discrimination, and by constructive programs of appreciation for group differences to promote full and equal participation in the life of a community; in schools, emphasis is placed on direct experiences which give children the chance to live, work, and play together regardless of differences in religious, racial, and ethnic groups. *See* **human-relations education; intergroup education.**

intercultural studies: *see* **studies, intercultural.**

interculturation: the process of bringing differing cultures into contact with one another for purposes of mutual understanding, appreciation, and influence, with a view toward instilling and developing feelings that encourage more constructive relationships among the individuals who make up the various culture groups.

interdisciplinary: involving professional groups from various subject-matter fields.

interdisciplinary approach: a method of study by which experts, or the best research workers from many different fields of learning, are brought together in the examination of a particular problem that is relevant to all their approaches; for example, a child-development problem may be studied by a team composed of psychologist, doctor, social psychologist, educator, psychiatrist, and sociologist.

interdisciplinary course: *see* **course, interdisciplinary.**

interest: (1) a subjective-objective attitude, concern, or condition involving a percept or an idea in attention and a combination of intellectual and feeling consciousness; may be temporary or permanent; based on native curiosity, conditioned by experience; (2) the holding of an attitude or feeling that objects are of consequence or concern to oneself; any preference displayed when choices are available; (3) sums paid by the borrower to the lender for the use of money, expressed in terms of percent per unit of time.

interest, center of: *see* **center of interest.**

interest, community: *see* **community interest.**

interest, doctrine of: a doctrine based on ideas of Rousseau and Pestalozzi, formulated by Herbart, and espoused by DeGarmo and Dewey with some modifications; holds that the interests of the learner should be considered and utilized in determining both the content and the methods of instruction; in some usages, interest as a basis for learning is opposed to effort in that either subject matter is to be made interesting or an act of effort on the part of the learner is called for; in other usages, interest and effort are interrelated functions of purposive activity, both being involved in a persistent reach for an object of concern.

interest, expressed: verbal profession of interest in an object, activity, task, or occupation.

interest finder: a questionnaire designed to discover the preferred activities of adults or young people, the results being frequently used as a basis for planning educational programs for the respondents.

interest group: an organization of persons pursuing a common interest.

interest group, pupil: a number of students who have a common purpose.

interest, inventoried: (testing) a list of activities and occupations for which the subject indicates preferences; scored by a system of experimentally determined weights. *See* **interest, tested.**

interest inventory: *see* **inventory, interest.**

interest, manifest: interest displayed by participation in an activity or occupation.

interest, occupational: *see* **occupational interest.**

interest pattern: a characteristic group of likes and dislikes for persons in the same occupation or class, typically revealed by an interest test. *See* **test, interest.**

interest, public: when human acts have public consequences of sufficient magnitude to warrant some official control, then public interest emerges; opposed to private interest. (Distinctions between private schools and public schools, private roads and public highways, .private power and public power suggest the difficulty of defining the sensitive relationship between private and public interest and the official controls that are desirable.)

interest test: *see* **test, interest.**

interest, tested: interest as measured by objective tests as differentiated from inventories, which are based on subjective self-estimates. *See* **interest, inventoried.**

interest theory of value: *see* **value, interest theory of.**

interest, vested: an interest that has become a complete and consummated right because of its distinguished or ancient origin or because of the prestige of its advocates, for example, the interest of the church in education; often opposed, at least in part, to the *public interest.*

interests, avocational: those pursuits or hobbies which are distinct from the regular work or occupation of the individual and which are followed for recreational purposes.

interests, reading: the types of reading matter that attract and hold a reader.

interests, sex: (1) interest held by an individual or group in the sex organs and processes; (2) sometimes used loosely to designate the interest of members of one sex in the members of the other sex.

interests, vocational: *see* **vocational interests.**

interfaith relations: *see* **relations, interfaith.**

interfamily environmental differences: *see* **environmental differences, interfamily.**

interference: (sp.) the influence of previous learning that leads one to spell a word incorrectly; one of the common causes of error in spelling.

interference effect: *syn.* **inhibition, retroactive.**

interference, linguistic: previous knowledge of one's native language, which is thought to inhibit the learning of certain features of a *target language.*

interfixation movement: the movement made by the eyes between the fixation pauses in reading.

interfraternity council: a legislative and advisory body composed of representatives of college social fraternities and of the college administration; in some institutions there are two councils, one for social and one for professional fraternities.

intergenerational occupational mobility: *see* **occupational mobility, intergenerational.**

intergrade: a term used to describe those who fall in the graduated series between the strongly right-handed and the strongly left-handed; employed in the same sense with respect to eyedness.

intergrade interval: the difference in average test scores of pupils in successive school grades.

intergroup contest: *see* **contest, intergroup.**

intergroup education: a term broadly applied to educational activities in schools, churches, and adult programs organized to improve democratic human relations and intercultural understandings within a subcultural system, to promote full citizen rights for all minority groups, and to reduce interpersonal and group prejudice. *See* **human-relations education; intercultural education;** *dist. f.* **dynamics, group; group development.**

intergroup education in cooperating schools: a project sponsored by the American Council on Education (1945-1948) for developing materials, techniques, and institutional emphases in public schools for the improvement of human relations and for intercultural and intergroup understandings.

intergroup relations specialist, school: *see* **specialist, school intergroup relations.**

interim reserve: *see* **reserve, interim.**

interinstitutional cooperation: *see* **cooperation, interinstitutional.**

interior architecture: *syn.* **interior design.**

interior building decoration: *see* **decoration, interior building.**

interior decoration: nearly synonymous with *interior design* but a less respectable term, implying a superficial treat-

ment; often used by persons engaged in this profession who lack art training.

interior design: the planning, furnishing, and decorating of interiors or of a specific room or rooms of a house, church, theater, hotel, or other building; sometimes called *interior architecture. See* **art, household.**

interiorization of control: the transfer of the locus of control of a person's behavior from an external authority, such as a parent or teacher, to processes within the person. *See* **superego.**

interiorized stuttering: *see* **stuttering, interiorized.**

interjectional theory of speech: the theory that speech originated with the spontaneous utterance of exclamations.

interlace: (data processing) to assign addresses, codes, etc., in a nonsequential pattern selected usually to increase the speed of computer operation.

interlibrary center: *see* **center, interlibrary.**

interlibrary loan: *see* **loan, interlibrary.**

interlocking item: *see* **item, interlocking.**

interlocutory: incident to a suit still pending, descriptive of an order or decree, made during the progress of the case, which does not amount to a final decision.

intermediate administrative unit: *see* **administrative unit, intermediate.**

intermediate algebra: *see* **algebra, intermediate.**

intermediate class: *see* **class, intermediate.**

intermediate district: *see* **district, intermediate.**

intermediate elementary grade: *see* **elementary grade, intermediate.**

intermediate grade: *syn.* **elementary grade, intermediate.**

intermediate school: (1) a school that enrolls pupils in intermediate grades, usually comprising the fourth, fifth, and sixth years of schoolwork; (2) formerly used also as synonymous with *junior high school,* especially when the school included only grades 7 and 8. *Comp. w.* **middle school.**

intermediate service unit: *syn.* **center, educational service.**

intermediate unit: *see* **unit, intermediate.**

intermission activities: *see* **activities, intermission.**

intermittent reinforcement: *see* **reinforcement, intermittent.**

intermittent truancy: *see* **truancy, intermittent.**

intern: (1) one who, upon completion of the required course of study for a professional degree, serves in a hospital, clinic, or office in preparation for independent practice; (2) a professionally trained young librarian who is working in a library for a specified period in order to receive planned and supervised training that allows the application of theory to actual, varied practice.

intern supervisor: *see* **supervisor, intern.**

intern teacher: a teacher whose teaching assignment and in-service professional growth plan conform to an internship plan of a college or of the local school system or of both; such plans usually provide for a major portion of the day, usually for a full school year, with supervision by the college or university personnel as well as by local supervisors, and occasionally with additional provision for parallel course work and college credit; intern teachers are college graduates, usually paid by the school districts though on a lower basis than regular teachers. *See* **apprentice teacher.**

intern teaching: *see* **intern teacher.**

intern, urban teaching: a college senior or college graduate appointed to an urban school system and assigned to a selected classroom teacher or to a teaching team; works with individuals, groups, or the class as a whole and also performs clerical duties; he may or may not be paid for this but if he performs satisfactorily he will go on to a classroom of his own where he will then be a first-year teacher.

internal accounting: *see* **accounting, internal.**

internal audit: *see* **audit, internal.**

internal check: a system under which the accounting methods and details of an institution are so laid out that the accounts and procedures are not under the absolute control of a single person but the work of one employee is a check on that of another.

internal consistency: *see* **consistency, internal.**

internal consistency, coefficient of: *see* **coefficient of internal consistency.**

internal consistency reliability: *see* **consistency, internal.**

internal controls: *see* **controls, internal.**

internal criticism: *see* **criticism, internal.**

internal environment: *see* **environment, internal.**

internal frame of reference: *see* **frame of reference, internal.**

internal memory: *see* **memory, internal.**

internal migration: *see* **migration, internal.**

internal morality: *see* **morality, internal.**

internal motivation: *see* **motivation, internal.**

internal organization: *see* **organization, internal.**

internal strabismus: *syn.* **esotropia.**

internal testing program: *see* **program, testing.**

internal validation: *see* **validation, internal.**

internality of relations: *see* **externality of relations.**

internalization: acceptance by the individual of attitudes, principles, codes, or sanctions that become a part of himself in forming value judgments and in determining his conduct.

internalized action: *see* **action, internalized.**

International Agricultural Development Service: *see* **Agricultural Development Service, International.**

international agricultural education: *see* **agricultural education, international.**

international algebraic language: *see* **language, international algebraic.**

international broadcast: *see* **broadcast, international.**

international consultant: *see* **consultant, international.**

international education: (1) the study of educational, social, political, and economic forces in international relations, with special emphasis on the role and potentialities of educational forces; (2) international programs to further mutual understanding by means of exchange of instructional materials, techniques, students, teachers, and technicians; (3) *syn.* **comparative education.**

international educational exchange: *see* **exchange, international educational.**

international exchange of students: *see* **exchange of students, international.**

international exchange of teachers: *see* **exchange of teachers, international.**

International Farm Youth Exchange: a program sponsored by the *cooperative extension service in agriculture and home economics* and financed from private funds, in which young people with farm experience in the United States live with farm families in other countries and young people from other countries live in farm homes in the United States for a period of several months.

International Geophysical Year research program: a program in which the countries of the earth pool their research efforts to learn more about the earth and its environment; the IGY occurs during the period of maximum sunspot activity.

international home economics extension: *see* **extension, international home economics.**

international house: a dormitory maintained for the convenience of students from foreign lands, usually admitting a limited number of others desiring to achieve mastery of foreign languages and acquaintance with representatives of foreign cultures.

international performance scale, Leiter: *see* **scale, Leiter international performance.**

international phonetic alphabet: *see* **alphabet, international phonetic.**

international relations: (1) the sphere of political, economic, and social intercourse or connections among nations and sovereign states; (2) the body of practices, precepts, and customs controlling the conduct of intercourse among nations in time of peace and war.

international studies: *see* **studies, international.**

interni (in·tẽr′nī): a name applied to boys who entered the monastic schools of instruction of the Middle Ages in order to prepare to become monks. *Syn.* **oblati; scholastici;** *contr. w.* **externi.**

internship, administrative: service in preparation for a position as an educational administrator; usually under the supervision of a university and a practicing administrator in the field; consists of a wide variety of experiences in educational administration undertaken in one or more schools or school districts; the intern usually receives a stipend for his work.

internship, counseling: a phase of supervised practice during which laboratory skills, such as testing, interviewing, and recording, are developed.

internship plan: (1) the curricular provision for internship experience in a particular educational field; (2) (teacher ed.) a plan whereby a graduate of a 4-year teacher-training institution is employed by a school system at a small salary for a period of time during which he is given an opportunity to participate in many phases of the work of the school system; frequently his practical work in the school system is correlated with further work at, and/or guidance by, the teacher-training institution from which he graduated; sometimes this correlated activity is regarded as graduate work and receives credit toward an advanced degree; *syn.* **apprentice teaching;** *see* **apprentice teacher** (2).

internship program: *see* **program, internship.**

intercentile range: *see* **range, intercentile.**

interpersonal adjustment: *syn.* **adjustment, social.**

interpersonal relationship: *see* **relationship, interpersonal.**

interpersonal relationships: the reciprocal influences that individuals exert upon one another in primary social groups.

interpoint braille: *see* **braille, interpoint.**

interpolated learning: *see* **learning, interpolated.**

interpolated mode: *see* **mode, interpolated.**

interpolation: (meas.) in general, any process of estimating intermediate values between two known points; as applied to test norms, refers to the procedure used in assigning interpreted values, for example, grade or age equivalents, to scores between the successive average scores actually obtained in the standardization process. *Comp. w.* **extrapolation.**

interpolation methods: methods by which values of a variable may be determined when they lie between two successive entries in a table of numbers.

interpret: (data processing) a machine operation to convert the punched data in a card to one of two printed lines (or both) on the face of the card.

interpretation: (1) (philos.) an explanation or exposition of meaning from a given point of view or school of thought; the meaning given to something within the context of a theory or philosophy of education; (2) in public relations, exposition of the school program; description of the purposes, conditions, activities, and needs of the school; (3) (mus.) that element of a musical performance which is contributed by the personal and creative ideas and tastes of the performer.

interpretation, art: *see* **art interpretation.**

interpretation, educational: *syn.* **interpretation** (2).

interpretation exercise: *see* **exercise, interpretation.**

interpretation of education, social: *see* **social interpretation of education.**

interpretation, oral: in speech instruction, the use of audible symbols and visible bodily action to transmit to an audience the meaning intended by the author of a selection.

interpretation, reading: an aspect of understanding what is read in which the reader goes beyond directly stated facts therein to include reasoning, making comparisons, relating to personal experience, etc.

interpretation, social: *see* **social interpretation.**

interpretation, test: *see* **test interpretation.**

interpretative dance: a form of the dance in which the dancer's movements portray some conception of a theme, act, thought, or musical composition.

interpretative guidance: *see* **guidance, interpretative.**

interpretative mode: *see* **mode, interpretative.**

interpreter: (1) one who translates orally for a person speaking in a different language; (2) (data processing) a machine or other device that reads information which has been punched into cards and prints it in legible form, usually onto the card itself in specified rows and columns.

interpretive projective method: *see* **projective method, interpretive.**

interpretive reading: *see* **reading, interpretive.**

interpretive rhythms: *see* **rhythms, interpretive.**

interpretive routine: *see* **routine, interpretive.**

interpretive test: *see* **test, interpretive.**

interpupillary distance: the distance in millimeters from the center of the pupil of one eye to the center of the pupil of the other eye; regarded as a factor in reading maturation.

interquartile range: *see* **range, interquartile.**

interrater reliability: *syn.* **coefficient, objectivity.**

interrelated program: *see* **program, interrelated.**

interscholastic athletics: *see* **athletics, interscholastic.**

interscholastic competition: *see* **competition, interscholastic.**

interschool contest: *syn.* **competition, interschool.**

interschool visiting: *see* **visiting, interschool.**

intersection of sets: *see* **sets, intersection of.**

interservice course: *see* **interservice school.**

interservice education: military education which is provided by one service to members of another service. *See* **military education; training, military.**

interservice school: a school utilized by two or more services/agencies which is administered by a coordinating service/agency and which presents a curriculum developed in coordination with the participating services and approved by the coordinating service; an *interservice course* is similar in all respects.

interservice training: *see* **training, interservice.**

interval: *syn.* **interval, class.**

interval, centile: one of the 100 successive intervals in a frequency distribution, each containing 1 percent of the observations or cases; one of the 100 ranges of scores cut off by the 99 percentile points. *Syn.* **centile range; percentile interval; range, percentile.**

interval, class: any one of a number of ranges representing a subdivision of the quantitative scale on which data are distributed and which is sufficiently narrow so that the cases that fall within its limits may, for practical purposes, be regarded as having the same value, the midpoint of the class interval; the scale distance between the lower and upper real limits of a class; often called *step* or *step interval. See* **class** (7).

interval, confidence: *syn.* **region, acceptance.**

interval, decile: one of the 10 successive intervals in a frequency distribution containing exactly one-tenth of the observations or cases; one of the 10 ranges of scores cut off by the nine deciles. *Syn.* **decile range.**

interval estimation: the calculation of an interval on the scale of values of a statistic such that the probability of its containing the parameter is known. *See* **region, acceptance.**

interval, group: *syn.* **interval, class.**

interval, median: the class interval of a frequency distribution which contains the median.

interval, modal: (1) that class interval of a frequency distribution which contains the mode; (2) the class interval containing the greatest number of cases. *Syn.* **modal range.**

interval, percentile: *syn.* **interval, centile.**

interval, promotion: *see* **promotion interval.**

interval, quartile: one of the four successive intervals in a frequency distribution containing exactly one-fourth of the observations or cases; one of the four ranges of scores cut off by the three quartiles. *Syn.* **quartile range.**

interval, quintile: one of the five successive intervals in a frequency distribution containing exactly one-fifth of the observations or cases; one of the five ranges of scores cut off by the four quintiles. *Syn.* **quintile range.**

interval scale: *see* **scale, interval.**

interval, score: *syn.* **subinterval.**

interval, step: *syn.* **interval, class.**

interval, tertile: one of the three successive intervals in a frequency distribution, each containing exactly one-third of the observations or cases; one of the three ranges of scores cut off by the two tertiles.

interval training: *see* **training, interval.**

intervening variable: *see* **variable, intervening.**

intervention: any action on the part of an organism that serves to change the relative position of the objects or forces of the environment and of the organism itself, thus bringing new stimuli to bear upon the organism.

interventionist school: a point of view in economic thought that takes a position between the doctrines of the capitalist school and the socialist school, considering these as extremes and believing in the necessity of moderate regulation and restriction of the principal agencies of production and distribution of wealth.

interview: a face-to-face meeting of two or more persons for the purpose of eliciting through consultation certain types of information.

interview, analytic: a fact-finding or fact-reviewing conference between a person and a counselor or committee, for example, a committee conference with a candidate to advise him with reference to admission or promotion in a teacher education program.

interview, counseling: a counseling session that starts from the information elicited and proceeds with guidance, counseling, or psychological treatment.

interview, depth: an interview concerned with the structure of motivation or the dynamic structure of the individual, for example, in the form of anxieties, frustrations, fears, motives, values, sentiments, hopes, attitudes, and prejudices.

interview, employment: a face-to-face questioning procedure that seeks to obtain facts from an applicant that will assist in determining his qualifications for a particular job.

interview, exit: a one-to-one counselor-student interview concluding a student's in-school experience for the purpose of administrative clearance and a determination of the student's future plans.

interview, focused: an interview centered on the subjective experiences of persons exposed to a preanalyzed situation such as viewing a film or hearing a radio program.

interview, group: (couns.) a multiple-client interview that can provide the counselee with his best opportunity for obtaining a cross-sectional view. *Syn.* **assembly consultation.**

interview, individual: a conference between a counselor and one person.

interview, initial: the first regularly scheduled interview that takes place between a counselor and a student who has recently enrolled in the school.

interview, life-space: a way of handling life conflicts of the child therapeutically, in close proximity to the time and place where they occurred.

interview, personal: *syn.* **interview, individual.**

interview, progress: a regularly scheduled pupil-counselor interview held at some time other than that of entering or leaving school, used primarily to discuss and evaluate the past growth of the pupil and his present condition and to make plans for his immediate future.

interview, psychiatric: an interview by a psychiatrist usually complementing information from a battery of psychological tests, investigations into family life and family background, agency and school reports, etc.; the psychiatrist's diagnosis and interpretation of the child's behavior are often used as an aid for proper placement in special classes or in an institution or as an aid to disposition by court or agency.

interview, structured or unstructured: *see* **structured.**

interview, teaching: a method of instruction which uses interviewing techniques to draw upon the specialized knowledge, experiences, or opinion of an expert in order to satisfy planned student learning outcomes.

interview technique: (1) a method used in a conference between an interviewer and one person in which an attempt is made, by direct questioning, to draw information from the respondent; (2) a method used in a conference between a counselor and one or more persons in which an attempt is made, by indirect means, to lead the individuals to direct their thoughts to an awareness of personal problems and to possible solutions; *see* **counseling, individual; counseling treatment.**

intervisitation: the exchange of classroom visits by teachers within a given school or school system; a specific supervisory activity usually associated with in-service education programs; involves individual or small group arrangements for observing classroom instruction in order to identify practices for adoption; frequently includes a follow-up interview with the teacher being observed and a discussion among observing teachers directed by the supervisor in charge.

intonation: (1) the general rise and fall of pitch and loudness during a number of successive phonations; (2) tone patterns characteristic of a language; (3) the degree of accuracy with which a musical performer plays or sings in tune.

intraclass correlation: *see* **correlation, intraclass.**

intraclass grouping: *see* **grouping, intraclass.**

intracollege transfer: *see* **transfer, intracollege.**

intrafamily environmental differences: *see* **environmental differences, intrafamily.**

intragroup sampling differences: *syn.* **variance, within-group.**

intramural athletics: *see* **athletics, intramural.**

intramural board: an official supervisory body composed of members of, and dealing with matters concerning, a single college or university.

intramural council: the committee that sets policies and settles questions involved in the intramural athletic program of a school.

intramural gymnasium: *see* **gymnasium, intramural.**

intramural manager: a person, usually a student, who assists in managing intramural athletic contests. *Syn.* **student manager; undergraduate manager.**

intramural sports: *see* **sports, intramural.**

intraorganizational power: *see* **power, intraorganizational.**

intrapunitive expression: placing blame for frustration upon self. *Contr. w.* **extrapunitive expression.**

intrastaff relationships: (admin.) the relationships of the members of the line-and-staff organization to one another in performing their responsibilities for leadership.

intravariability: variability within an individual; usually based on standard scores made by the individual on each of several tests.

intrinsic ability: *see* **ability, intrinsic.**

intrinsic method: a procedure in teaching reading that secures practice in word recognition and other skills by having the pupil read connected material in its natural setting; sometimes involves directive exercises or tests on the material read.

intrinsic motivation: *see* **motivation, intrinsic.**

intrinsic phonics: *see* **phonics, intrinsic.**

intrinsic programming: *see* **programming, intrinsic.**

intrinsic validity: *see* **validity, intrinsic.**

intrinsic value: *see* **value, intrinsic.**

introduction: the beginning of a unit of work during which the teacher helps the pupils to formulate objectives, plan their attack, and get a mental set conducive to study.

introduction card: *see* **card, introduction.**

introduction to business: *syn.* **training, junior business.**

introductory course: *see* **course, introductory.**

introjection: (1) (psych.) identification with a person or object so that the person or object seems peculiarly a part of the self; *contr. w.* **projection** (3) and (4); (2) (philos.) a theory which assumes that perceptions are images of the objects perceived.

introspection: the act of studying one's own thoughts, motives, and feelings; self-analysis.

introspection, experimental: a mode of investigation by which subjects are exposed under controlled conditions to selected situations or stimuli, such as combinations of colors, musical cadences, scents, or words, and each observes and reports the mental states or reactions evoked in himself.

introspective psychology: *see* **psychology, introspective.**

introversion: a trait complex, probably of diverse genetic origin, characterized by a tendency to shrink from social contacts, by a preference for covert and symbolic as opposed to overt activities, by great personal sensitiveness, and by a proneness to autistic thought. *Contr. w.* **extroversion.**

introversion-extroversion test: *see* **test, introversion-extroversion.**

introvert: a person characterized by *introversion.*

intuition: (1) (Descartes) apprehension unmediated by complex inferential procedures; simple ideas, as in Locke, relatively simple relations (taller-than, between, to-the-right-of, etc.), as in James and Russell, are all apprehended intuitively; in education, step-by-step methods, where the pupil apprehends each step like a "simple idea," use cartesian intuition; (2) (Bergson) "instinctive sympathy," a nonconceptual, imaginative self-projection into the creative life of what one is studying, so as to experience its significance directly from the inside; foreign languages, poetry, painting, and music, when taught by the *direct method*, use bergsonian intuition; (3) (Dewey) a suggestion, a hint, which may through intellectual analysis become an idea; (4) sometimes used to refer to the immediate or primary aspects of experience as distinct from the reflective, derived, or analytic; *see* **experience, primary.**

intuitional method: a method or technique used in teaching mathematics and in problem solving, involving emphasis on spontaneous insight into numerical, geometrical, or factual relationships.

intuitive geometry: *see* **geometry, informal.**

intuitive teaching: *see* **teaching, intuitive.**

invalidism: the condition of being disabled to some degree by ill health.

invariance, factor: factor consistency in a population; thus, the factor content of a test should be invariant for a given population when analyzed in successive batteries having the same sets of factors.

invariant: (math.) a property or object which does not change under some transformation; for example, if the plane is rotated about some point P, the point P is an invariant point (remains fixed) and the property of distance is invariant (the distance between two points of the plane is not changed by the rotation). *Contr. w.* **variant.**

inventional geometry: *syn.* **geometry, experimental.**

inventoried interest: *see* **interest, inventoried.**

inventory: (1) in the field of evaluation, a test or checklist used to determine the subject's or examinee's ability, achievement, aptitude, interest, or likes, generally in a limited area; (2) a number of questions, tasks, or other stimuli designed more to provide a comprehensive description of some aspect of an individual's characteristics than to provide a quantitative measurement of one of those aspects.

inventory, academic: (sec. ed.) a summary of programs for the academically talented students within a given school; contains data on the extent to which more talented students take more challenging courses.

inventory, adjustment: usually a self-report instrument on which the subject checks or describes his personal and social problems; differs from a *personality questionnaire,* which is concerned with beliefs, attitudes, etc., whereas the adjustment inventory is concerned with problems; used in preference to the terms *mental health analysis, mental-hygiene inventory,* or *temperament test,* which are regarded unfavorably by clinicians as too emotionally loaded. *See* **inventory, personality; test, personality.**

inventory blank, pupil: *see* **data blank, pupil.**

inventory, classroom: a detailed enumeration of the equipment and supplies assigned to a classroom.

inventory control: *see* **control, inventory.**

inventory controlling accounts: *see* **accounts, inventory controlling.**

inventory, equipment: a list of stored items of equipment on hand, items being added to the list as articles are acquired and deducted as articles are used or otherwise disposed of; may be made at intervals, or may be a continuing inventory.

inventory, formal reading: an analysis of the reading status of a pupil based on observation of his performance in oral and silent reading.

inventory, group reading: the use of group tests to identify the reading achievements or interests of children; to be contrasted with individual reading inventories.

inventory, guidance: a summarized appraisal of the guidance program according to predetermined criteria.

inventory, horizontal: (1) an evaluation of an individual's characteristics or attainments at a given age; (the position of the child with respect to various norms may be indicated by means of a *profile* or *psychograph*); (2) a listing of an individual's traits as observed at a single level of development.

inventory, individual: information compiled in an effort to serve the educational needs of pupils and to aid in self-understanding for the pupil; a functional, accurate and up-to-date record easily accessible to those who are authorized to use it; vital, pertinent information about the student that will aid the school to meet the needs of each student in his educational program and will supply all staff as well as the student and his parents with any information that will promote better understanding of the student and his problems and aid them in working with the student.

inventory, informal reading: an analysis of a child's reading abilities or disabilities based on observation of his reading performance and without the aid of objective check lists or inventory blanks.

inventory, interest: (1) a series of questions concerning the objects or activities which the individual likes, prefers, or in which he has an interest; (2) a checklist used to determine the interests of children or adults; the results of such inventories are often employed by reading specialists to motivate retarded or reluctant readers; (3) in vocational guidance, an instrument on which the individual indicates his liking for or interest in various kinds of job activities.

inventory, materials and supplies: a detailed list showing quantities, descriptions, and values of goods held for use by the institution in central storerooms or in service departments or for sale in supply stores.

inventory, mental-hygiene: *see* **inventory, adjustment.**

inventory, perpetual: a record which shows constantly, as of current date, the descriptions, quantities, and values of items of property and in which entries are made of additions, withdrawals, and current holdings.

inventory, personality: (1) a measuring device for determining an individual's personal characteristics such as his emotional adjustment or tendencies toward introversion or extroversion; may be arranged for self-rating or for rating by other persons; (2) self-rating questionnaires that deal not only with overt behavior but also with the subject's feelings about himself, other persons, and his environment, resulting from introspection. *Syn.* **personality questionnaire;** *see* **inventory, adjustment.**

inventory, phonetic: (1) a list of the phonetic elements known or unknown to the reader; (2) a checklist used to determine the student's knowledge of phonetic elements; (3) a diagnostic device used in a reading class, laboratory, or clinic, to determine phonetic deficiency.

inventory, progress: (1) the result of making and interpreting a grade-progress table; (2) an appraisal involving such factors as age-grade and age-grade-progress relationships, nationality, health, promotions, and failures.

inventory, property: a detailed list showing descriptions, quantities, and values of property.

inventory, psychoneurotic: a personality questionnaire designed to reveal neurotic trends in the subject.

inventory report: *see* **report, inventory.**

inventory, speech: analysis or detailed description of a person's speech, in terms of its differentiating characteristics with regard to articulation, phonation, breathing, syntactical organization, vocabulary, rhythm, etc.

inventory, structured: a personal-report type of scale so designed that the pupil must respond to each item in one of the two or more prescribed ways; to be contrasted with *unstructured inventory* in which his responses are not so limited.

inventory, study-skills: an identification of study skills through observation or measurement for the purpose of finding the strengths and weaknesses of an individual or a group.

inventory test: *see* **test, inventory.**

inventory, textbook: a detailed record showing descriptions, quantities, value, and disposition of textbooks owned by a school.

inventory, unstructured: *see* **inventory, structured.**

inverse correlation: *syn.* **negative correlation;** *see* **correlation** (1).

inverse factor analysis: *syn.* **factor analysis, transposed.**

inverse matrix: *syn.* **matrix, inverse of a.**

inverse of a matrix: *see* **matrix, inverse of a.**

inverse operation: *see* **operation, inverse.**

inverse relation: *syn.* **negative correlation;** *see* **correlation** (1).

inverse relationship: *syn.* **negative correlation;** *see* **correlation** (1).

inverse sine transformation: *syn.* **transformation, angular.**

inverse statement: *see* **statement, inverse.**

inverted factor analysis: *syn.* **factor analysis, transposed.**

investigation: *see* **research, investigative.**

investigative research: *see* **research, investigative.**

investment ledger: an accounting record of invested funds.

invisible control: *see* **control, invisible.**

invisible disability: *see* **disability, invisible.**

invitational supervision: *see* **supervision, invitational.**

invitational supervisory visits: *see* **supervisory visits, invitational.**

involuntary client: *see* **client, involuntary.**

involution: the process of evaluating a number expressed as a positive integral power of another, for example, 2^{53}. *Contr. w.* **evolution.**

involvement, ego: *see* **ego involvement.**

involvement, supervisory: *see* **supervisory involvement.**

inward vocalization: *see* **vocalization, inward.**

I/O: abbreviation for input-output. *See* **input; output.**

ipsative measurement: *see* **measurement, ipsative.**

ipsative score: *see* **score, ipsative.**

ipsative score units: *see* **score units, ipsative.**

IQ: *see* **quotient, deviation intelligence; quotient, ratio intelligence.**

IQ, global: *see* **global IQ.**

iris: a colored circular membrane, suspended behind the cornea and immediately in front of the lens, which regulates the amount of light entering the eye.

iris diaphragm: *see* **diaphragm, iris.**

irradiation: (1) the spreading discharge, following stimulation, of neural impulses from few to many neurons, by means of which the stimulation of a receptor gives rise to widespread motor activity; (2) a term used by Pavlov to describe the diffusion of a nervous impulse upon reaching the cerebral cortex, the excitation spreading from its center, or point of origin, over the cortex, with diminishing intensity the farther it spreads. (Pavlov identified the converse situation as *concentration.*)

irrational number: *see* **number, irrational.**

irregular replies: replies to a questionnaire or a test item not anticipated or not provided for by the coding manual or scoring key.

Ishihari color plates (ish′i·hä′rē): a set of standardized color plates printed in an overall pattern of squares, dots, etc., of different sizes and colors, so arranged that figures or letters are formed in the pattern and will be visible to persons with normal vision, but not to those who are color-blind.

isochron: a unit of mental growth that is based on equal time units; equal to one-hundredth of the age range involved in growth of any special mental ability from zero ability to the physiological limit of performance. *See* **scale, isochron; score, isochron.**

isochron scale: *see* **scale, isochron.**

isochron score: *see* **score, isochron.**

isokurtic: (said of an array of a double-entry column) having no skewness. *Contr. w.* **allokurtic.**

isolate: an individual who is neither selected nor rejected by other participants in group activity; information of this nature is often elicited by means of appraisal techniques such as *sociometry;* the individual may be well adjusted or not, depending upon other variable factors.

isolate, social: a sociometric term denoting a person chosen by no other member of a social group on a particular criterion. *See* **sociometric technique.**

isolated pupils: *see* **pupils, isolated.**

isolation: a method of organizing curriculum materials into subjects that maintain individuality without making any attempt to integrate them with other subjects. *See* **subjects taught in isolation.**

isolation cabinet: a cabinet used in the study of the neonate to facilitate control of humidity, temperature, sight, sound, and other variables.

isolation rigidity: *see* **rigidity, isolation.**

isometric chart: *see* **chart, isometric.**

isometric contraction: *see* **contraction, isometric.**

isomorphic model, theoretical: *see* **model, theoretical isomorphic.**

isomorphism: (1) literally, the state of having the same form; the belief that the same laws which govern organization of forces in the external world also govern such organization within the nervous system and that hence there is an actual physical correspondence between the item perceived and the force-field in the brain as it is perceived; (2) (math.) a relation between two mathematical systems when the only difference between them is the manner in which the objects of the system and the operations are represented; for example, the addition equation $3 + 2 = 5$ could be represented in the rationals as $3/1 + 2/1 = 5/1$, a difference in representation only.

isopleth: a straight line that is used to connect corresponding values on the three (or more) scales of a nomograph; a straight line which, when passing through points on any two scales of a nomograph, will pass through the corresponding point on the third scale. *See* **nomograph.**

isotonic contraction: *syn.* **contraction, phasic** (1).

it: (phys. ed.) the chaser or the chased in games of simple organization.

ITA: *see* **alphabet, initial teaching.**

italic writing: *see* **writing, italic.**

item: (1) in programmed instruction, a segment of material which the student handles at one time; may vary in size from a single incomplete sentence, question, or instruction to perform some response up to a sizable paragraph; in almost all programming methods, it will require at least one response and will provide for knowledge of results before the student proceeds to the next item; (2) in test contruction, any single fact, part, or unit that is or can be isolated for examination or measurement.

item, alternate-response: an item to which the examinee is asked to respond by choosing one of two suggested answers, for example, a *true-false item. See* **test, alternate-response.**

item, analogy: multiple-choice and completion-item varieties in which the pupil is asked to complete analogies started in the item stems.

item analysis: *see* **analysis, item.**

item, augmenting: in programmed instruction, an item which supplies new information but does not require the student to make a relevant response.

item, best-answer: a variety of the multiple-choice form of test item consisting of a stem followed by two or more responses that are correct or appropriate in varying degrees, the examinee selecting the best response.

item card: *see* **card, item.**

item characteristic curve: *see* **curve, item characteristic.**

item classification: *see* **classification, item.**

item, completion: a type of test item to which the examinee responds by filling a blank or blanks with the words, numbers, or phrases that he believes will correctly complete the meaning.

item correlation: *see* **correlation, item.**

item count: *syn.* **response count.**

item count statistics: *see* **statistics, item count.**

item counter, graphic: *see* **counter, graphic item.**

item, culture-fair: (1) an item of an intelligence or achievement test which is not biased in favor of one or more of several socioeconomic groups; (2) an item of an intelligence or achievement test which is equally difficult and equally valid when used with different national groups or with persons from different levels of society.

item, delayed review: in programmed instruction, an item which allows for spread of practice time; differs from other items only in terms of time of presentation.

item, dovetailing: in programmed instruction, an item which requires the student to make separate responses to separate stimuli which otherwise may become confused.

item, enumeration: a completion item variety in which the pupil is asked to list or enumerate specified types of names, events, or other terms. *See* **item, completion.**

item, essay test: an item of either (*a*) the extended response type, an open-ended item intended to test students' ability to organize, to evaluate, to write clearly, and to be creative, or (*b*) the restricted response type, an essay item in which the perimeter of the pupil's response is well defined, a specific problem being presented.

item file: *see* **file, item.**

item, forced-choice: (1) technically (and more properly), a special type of item in which the alternatives (*a*) have equal preference or favorability value (that is, each alternative is considered equally favorable or has been selected equally often by a typical group), but (*b*) have different ability to discriminate among examinees on some test variable; this type of item is used increasingly often on attitude, interest, and personality tests because of the item's tendency to reduce an examinee's ability to fake desired results; (2) popularly (but improperly) any type of item in which the examinee is required to select one or more of the given alternatives, for example, *multiple-choice item.*

item, generalized: in programmed instruction, an item which summarizes the common characteristics of several specific items which have already been presented to the student.

item, implicit contrast: in foreign language instruction, oral material used for a type of phonetic discrimination test in which students are given items and asked whether the words they hear are identical or different.

item, interlocking: in programmed instruction, an item requiring the student to review the established skills while new information is being presented to him.

item, lead in: in programmed instruction, an item which does not require new information or rehearsal of the skill where a problem is restated. *Contr. w.* **item, interlocking.**

item, multiple-choice: a test form in which the item stem is followed by two or more responses and the examinee selects the correct or best response. *See* **test, multiple-choice.**

item, multiple-response: a variety of the multiple-choice form of test item in which more than one of the provided responses may be correct and the examinee is instructed to mark all correct responses. *See* **test, multiple-response.**

item, obvious: an item which gives the subject little difficulty in guessing the significance his response to it will have. *Contr. w.* **item, subtle.**

item of information: (guidance) a descriptive heading under which is recorded information about pupils.

item, recall: an item that requires the examinee to supply the correct answer from his own memory or recollection, as contrasted with a *recognition item* in which he need only identify the correct answer.

item, recognition: a type of test item, such as true-false, multiple-choice, or matching, to which the examinee responds by selecting the best or correct answer from among several given.

item, restated review: in programmed instruction, an item which requires a rehearsal of the skill when a problem is restated.

item, rote review: in programmed instruction, an item which presents a problem identical to one presented previously.

item sampling: *see* **sampling, item.**

item, specifying: in programmed instruction, an item exemplifying a general rule or principle.

item stem: *see* **stem** (3).

item, stub: *syn.* **stub** (1).

item, subject-matter: in programmed instruction, an item which is classified in accordance with its subject matter content.

item, substitution: in foreign language instruction, an item which is to replace another word or lexical unit in a given statement on a substitution test.

item, subtle: an item to which the subject, in responding, will have difficulty in guessing the significance of his response; scoring weights of such items have been empirically derived. *Contr. w.* **item, obvious.**

item, tab: in programmed instruction, an item which requires the student to pull a tab in order to indicate his response rather than to write out his answer or to select from a choice of responses in the frame.

item, terminal: in programmed instruction, a test item containing no prompts and placed far enough from the training sequences to measure more than immediate memory. *See* **behavior, terminal.**

item trace line: *see* **trace line, item.**

item, transformation: a test item used in foreign language teaching, which requires the student to perform a gram-

matical transformation according to instructions, such as negation of a statement, change in number, mood, voice, tense, etc.

item, true-false: a type of test item in which the examinee indicates whether a statement is true or false. *See* **test, true-false.**

item validity: *see* **validity, item.**

item weighting: *see* **weighting, item.**

iteration: (data processing) repetition of part of a program.

iterative: *adj.* (data processing) describing a procedure or process which repeatedly executes a series of operations until some condition is satisfied.

iterative method of factoring: a method of factoring a matrix, devised by Hotelling, by which the principal axes solution can be obtained directly from the matrix.

iterative procedure: (math.) repetition of a sequence of steps with one or more variables being assigned different values for each step; these values may be developed by the procedure itself; an example is Newton's method of successively approximating square root by division in which each step yields a new trial divisor for the next; on a computer the repetition may be stopped by the procedure itself or on the basis of previously programmed numerical checks of its progress.

ITFS: *see* **television fixed service, instructional.**

itinerant teacher: a teacher who travels to two or more schools or to homes and hospitals to teach certain pupils. *Syn.* **circuit teacher.**

itinerant teacher plan: *see* **plan, itinerant teacher.**

itinerant teacher trainer: (agric. ed.) a traveling employee of a teacher-training institution or state board for vocational education who provides individual and group instruction for employed vocational teachers either in the schools in which these teachers are employed or at nearby centers.

ITV: *see* **television, instructional.**

ivory tower: a figure of speech referring to the state of mind of an individual, usually a scholar, who supposedly is not aware of what is going on in the world outside his field of particular interest.

ivri (iv'rə): *adj.* (Heb., lit., "Hebrew") a Yiddish expression for the reading of prayers with or without comprehension.

ivrit bi-ivrit (iv'rit bə iv'rit): (Heb., lit., "Hebrew by means of Hebrew") teaching the Hebrew language by means of the natural or direct method without recourse to the vernacular as an aid.

Ivy League: an association of eastern colleges and universities organized for athletic contests, primarily football; composed of Brown, Columbia, Cornell, Dartmouth, Harvard, Princeton, University of Pennsylvania, and Yale.

J

J curve: *see* **curve, J.**

J-shaped curve: *see* **curve, J-shaped.**

jack: receptacle for a plug connector which leads to the input or output circuit of a tape recorder or other audio device; standard phone plugs and jacks are used in most language laboratory systems; special jack boxes afford several outlets so that several headphones may be plugged in together.

jack, microphone: receptacle for connecting a microphone into a sound system.

jack panel: *see* **plugboard.**

jack, speaker: receptacle for connecting a speaker to a sound system.

jacket, book: *see* **book jacket.**

Jacksonian epilepsy: *see* **epilepsy, Jacksonian.**

Jacksonianism: the social, political, economic, and educational traditions and practices growing out of the rise of the common man and the extension of democratic concepts symbolized by the election of Andrew Jackson to the presidency of the United States in 1828.

jactitation: morbid restlessness or tossing about.

Jaeger measure: *see* measure, Jaeger.

Jaeger test: *see* measure, Jaeger.

janitor: a man employed to care for or to assist in caring for a building, such care including numerous cleaning jobs within a building and often custodial and police duties in the protection of property.

janitor-engineer: (1) a man employed for cleaning, heating, ventilating, and performing custodial duties in a school building; *syn.* custodian; janitor; (2) a person who performs both janitorial and engineering functions. *See* staff, janitorial-engineering.

janitorial-engineering staff: *see* staff, janitorial-engineering.

janitorial service: services related to school-building operation such as cleaning, care of equipment, general care of the physical plant, and policing. *Syn.* custodial service.

janitorial supplies: *see* supplies, janitorial.

janitors' equipment: tools, apparatus, and machines used by janitors in their work of cleaning and caring for the heating, air conditioning, and lighting of school buildings, for example, floor and radiator brushes, chamois skins, pails, mops, vacuum cleaners, eraser cleaners, floor machines, coal trucks, and pipe wrenches.

janitor's handbook: *see* handbook, janitor's.

janitors' supplies: supplies used up by janitors in their work, such as soap powder, ammonia, varnish, disinfectant, deodorant, and floor dressing.

janitors' training course: *see* course, janitors' training.

janitress: a woman who performs cleaning duties in a school building; a charwoman, cleaning woman, or matron.

jaywalker: (colloquial) a pedestrian who disobeys traffic regulations or safety rules by walking out into vehicular traffic from between parked cars, by crossing the street midblock, by cutting diagonally across a street or intersection, or by disregarding warning signs, signal lights, or traffic policemen.

jealousy: (1) resentment and envy because of a loved one's actual or believed appreciation of or attention to another person; (2) suspicious watchfulness; distrust of others, coupled with envy.

Jeanes teacher: at one time a supervisor of Negro rural schools in selected counties of the Southern states jointly employed by the county superintendent of schools, the state Negro rural school supervisor, and the Southern Education Foundation.

jeeped receiver: *see* receiver, jeeped.

Jeffersonian philosophy of law: *see* philosophy of law, Hamiltonian.

Jena method (yā'nä): a method of teaching lipreading originated by Karl Brauckmann of Jena, Germany, based on the kinesthetic sense (that is, sensations of movement), on the theory that if a person without hearing makes the same speech movements as a speaker he will have the same speech sensations and will understand him.

jerkiness: (speech) (1) lack of rhythm in speaking; (2) spasmodic speech; (3) speech characterized by halting and forced interruptions in phrasing.

Jesuit college: *see* college, Jesuit.

Jesuit Society: officially, the Society of Jesus; a Roman Catholic religious society founded in 1534 by Ignatius Loyola and approved by Pope Paul III in 1540; members take vows of poverty, chastity, and obedience; in addition, they are bound to render entire submission to papal authority and are forbidden to fill any of the higher offices of the Church.

Jewish all-day school: *see* day school, Jewish.

Jewish center: a communal building where informal educational, cultural, and recreational activities are provided for Jewish children, youth, and adults; may function in connection with a synagogue or as an independent communal organization; supported partly through membership and participation fees and partly from central communal funds.

Jewish communal Sunday school: *see* Sunday school, Jewish communal.

Jewish communal weekday school: *see* weekday school, Jewish communal.

Jewish community center school: *see* community center school, Jewish.

Jewish congregational Sunday school: *see* Sunday school, Jewish congregational.

Jewish congregational weekday school: *see* weekday school, Jewish congregational.

Jewish conservative religious school: *see* religious school, Jewish conservative.

Jewish day school: *see* day school, Jewish.

Jewish education: instruction in the religion, history, language, literature, culture, and traditions of the Jewish people. (In America children of the Jewish faith usually receive their formal Jewish education in Sunday schools; in Hebrew schools, which conduct classes after regular public school hours; or in day schools.)

Jewish extension education: *see* extension education, Jewish.

Jewish foundation school: *see* foundation school, Jewish.

Jewish informal education: *see* informal education, Jewish.

Jewish junior congregation: *see* congregation, Jewish junior.

Jewish Orthodox religious school: *see* religious school, Jewish Orthodox.

Jewish Reform religious school: *see* religious school, Jewish Reform.

Jewish religious school: *see* religious school, Jewish.

Jewish Sabbath school: *see* Sabbath school, Jewish.

Jewish secular school: *see* secular school, Jewish.

Jewish Sunday school: *see* Sunday school, Jewish.

Jewish supplementary education: *see* supplementary education, Jewish.

Jewish weekday school: *see* weekday school, Jewish.

J.I.T.: *see* training, job-instruction.

job: (1) a task performed by a student in order to develop skill or to "try out" the application of a principle; (2) a unit of a trade or task done by a worker in return for pay; an employment classification; (3) a contract or unit of work in the Dalton plan to be completed in a given time; (4) (voc. ed.) a specific, assigned task which provides the media by which the student practices and develops skills for an occupation.

job analysis: *see* analysis, job.

job-analysis approach: *syn.* occupational approach.

job-analysis technique: an approach to curriculum building based on the analysis of the major and minor duties of a particular occupation and the knowledge, habits, and skills required for success in it, accompanied by the development of appropriate instructional units to train persons for the occupation in question.

job, batch: an entire task submitted for computer processing; submitted as decks of punched cards to be read into the computer in groups; also called batch-made job. *Contr. w.* interaction, conversational.

job breakdown: the complete analysis of the skill and knowledge components required in a specific job.

job classification: a classification of jobs into types and categories, with a statement of requirements for each of the jobs in terms of training, personal characteristics, and experience.

job competencies, specific: *see* competencies, specific job.

Job Corps center: *see* center, Job Corps.

Job Corps program: *see* program, Job Corps.

job cost sheet: a record for use in school-plant maintenance on which are entered data pertaining to each major repair job, such as dates, description of the job, its location, workmen, the cost and amounts of materials used, and the cost of labor.

job counseling: *see* counseling, job.

job, dance: a term used by professional musicians to refer to a contract, formal or informal, verbal or written, in which an agreement is made to provide music for dancing.

job description: (bus. ed.) a written statement of the various operations and duties, equipment, methods, working conditions, responsibilities, and other essential factors concerned in a job; also, a job summary, usually based on a job analysis of detailed working conditions, promotional status, worker requirements, etc.; includes a summary of the education, experience, and training the worker must possess in order to qualify for employment.

job development: (voc. ed.) provision of satisfactory work opportunities through opening jobs to more people by removal of artificial barriers to employment and by *job redesign* or job creation.

job evaluation: *see* **evaluation, job.**

job family: (couns.) a cluster of jobs that are similar in terms of activities or skills required; also called *occupational family.*

job instruction: *see* **instruction, job.**

job-instruction training: *see* **training, job-instruction.**

job intelligence: *see* **intelligence, job.**

job judgment: the ability, developed as a result of experience, to make correct decisions in matters relating to one's job.

job-knowledge test: *see* **test, job-knowledge.**

job layoff: (voc. ed.) cessation of employment of a worker, usually temporary, because of slack in production or other reasons; generally involves also cessation of pay to the worker.

job, manipulative: a unit of work including a series of operations necessary for its completion.

job-opportunity card: *see* **card, job-opportunity.**

job plan sheet: a procedure blank to be filled out by the student, listing in sequence the principal steps necessary to perform a job, as well as the necessary tools and materials, to guide the learner in doing the assigned task.

job rating: *see* **rating, job.**

job, real: an actual work job that is representative of or approximates a *type job* in its characteristics.

job redesign: (voc. ed.) revision of a specific duty, role, or function of a worker in relation to the type or content of the job.

job-relations training: *see* **training, job-relations.**

job rotation: (1) the procedure of moving qualified workers from job to job, as a means of broadening their experience, developing versatility and skills, and avoiding boredom; (2) the procedure in cooperative vocational programs of allowing students to work in several different jobs with a cooperating employer during the school year in order to give them a wide basis of experience and training in the field.

job satisfaction: (voc. ed.) the quality, state, or level of satisfaction which is a result of various interests and attitudes of a person toward his job.

job seeker: (voc. ed.) a person actively interested in finding employment; includes the unemployed and may also include a person already employed but who is searching for another or better job.

job series: in counseling, a printed source of information that offers broad coverage of an entire occupational area, giving brief accounts of all job opportunities in the field.

job sheet: a written instruction sheet usually presenting directions, references, and questions designed to assist the learner in mastering an assigned job.

job, specialized: a task that involves only a limited range of activities in which the worker receives specific training; may involve low or high skill.

job specification: a carefully prepared written description of all the important characteristics and requirements of a job and of the qualities and qualifications which a worker should possess in order to perform effectively a given job in a standard manner; the qualities and abilities are usually expressed in terms of minima.

job sponsor: *see* **training sponsor, distributive education; training sponsor, business and office education.**

job supervisor: *see* **training sponsor, distributive education; training sponsor, business and office education.**

job, technical: (1) a piece of work necessary for getting out a production job, for example, mathematical computa-

tions, measurements, reading blueprints, etc., in connection with a given piece of work; (2) a job involving an appreciable amount of technical or scientific knowledge, for example, that of laboratory assistant.

job training: *see* **training, job.**

job training standards: (mil. ed.) training guides in outline form which identify the elements of an Air Force specialty that the trainee must master; they also state the specific levels of achievement the trainee must attain in each element.

job, type: a real or imaginary job matching exactly the specifications for any degree of difficulty on a difficulty scale. *See* **job, real.**

Johnson-Neyman method: (stat.) a method for matching two samples in subgroups on some trait related to the independent variable of an experiment.

joined prefix: *see* **prefix, joined.**

joined suffix: *see* **suffix, joined.**

joint airborne training: *see* **training, joint airborne.**

joint apprenticeship council: *see* **apprenticeship council, joint.**

joint contract: *see* **contract, joint.**

joint-contributory retirement system: *see* **retirement system, joint-contributory.**

joint course: *see* **joint school.**

joint exercises: *see* **exercises, joint.**

joint fund: combined state and Federal, local and Federal, or local, state, and Federal moneys available for use in vocational education.

joint method: *syn.* **method of agreement and difference.**

joint method of agreement and difference: *see* **method of agreement and difference.**

joint operation: *see* **operation, joint.**

joint ownership: (pup. trans.) an arrangement by which the school-bus body is owned by the school district or some other municipal unit and the chassis by a private individual.

joint planning: planning that is done through the combined efforts of two or more agencies, used frequently when the planning is done cooperatively by an agency representing a state and by another representing the Federal government, as in the case of programs of vocational education.

joint scale: *see* **scale, joint.**

joint school: (mil. ed.) a school utilized by two or more services that has a joint faculty and a director (commandant) who rotates among the services and is responsible, under the direction of the Joint Chiefs of Staff, for the development and administration of the curriculum; a *joint course* is similar in all respects.

joint school district: *see* **district, joint school.**

joint training procedures: *see* **training procedures, joint.**

joint union junior college: *see* **junior college, joint union.**

joint vocational school: *see* **vocational school, area.**

joint vocational school district: *see* **vocational school, area.**

jointure: act of combining by contract two or more school districts on a temporary basis; has particular reference to Pennsylvania.

journal, anecdotal behavior: a chronological recording of significant behavior of a pupil observed from day to day by competent observers; often a part of the pupil's total cumulative record; sometimes called *behavior journal.*

journal approach: the method of teaching principles of bookkeeping and accounting by starting with a consideration of original entries for transactions and following through the various steps of the cycle in chronological order.

journal, behavior: *see* **journal, anecdotal behavior.**

journal, teacher's: a term used among early American schoolmen to describe what would correspond to the school *register* of today.

journalese: a colloquial term for faulty journalistic writing that is characterized by clichés, incorrect syntax and grammar, and uncouth expressions.

journalism: (1) a blanket term for all activities concerned with the production of newspapers, magazines, and other periodicals; (2) the designation of special, professionalized training in the kinds of writing, judgments, and procedures involved in the production of periodicals, radio and television news broadcasts, etc.; (3) the designation of a high school course—nontechnical and nonvocational—that helps students to use mediums of communication intelligently, to gather facts objectively and accurately, and to produce worthwhile student publications efficiently; often termed *journalistic writing* or *news writing.*

journalism, collegiate: a blanket term for all the journalistic and publication activities carried on by students at the university, college, or junior college level.

journalism, community: a collegiate analysis of the distinctive problems of smaller local newspapers, including 11,000 rural or suburban weeklies and 1,500 dailies of less than 25,000 circulation.

journalism, comparative: a systematized study of the newspaper press of various countries, involving the characteristic current aspects and historical background.

journalism, history of: *see* **history of journalism.**

journalism, nonprofessional: a program in journalism, usually at the secondary or collegiate level, that is cultural rather than vocational in aim; may refer to study of the newspaper as a propaganda device, the reading of newspapers, analysis of journalistic styles, etc.

journalism, scholastic: a blanket term for all the journalistic and publication activities carried on by students at the high school or junior high school level, including the preparation, publishing, and managing of newspapers, magazines, yearbooks, and handbooks.

journalism, technical: analysis of and practice in popular periodical writing on scientific, industrial, commercial, and other technical subjects.

journalistic writing: (1) a branch of study in English composition that utilizes the subject matter, form, and incentives of newspaper and other periodical writing; (2) a general term used by Hyde to designate school activities and courses concerned with the preparation and publication of student newspapers, yearbooks, etc., below the level of professional courses in journalism; *syn.* **news writing.**

journalize: (1) to record financial transactions or narrative transactions in the book of original entry; (2) to record debits and credits.

journey, school: *syn.* **field trip.**

journeyman: a worker who has satisfactorily completed his apprenticeship and is classified as a skilled worker in his trade. *See* **training, apprentice.**

journeyman teacher: an instructor with a minimum of 2 or 3 years of experience as a novice teacher who, although a regular appointee, still has a probationary status.

J.R.T.: *see* **training, job-relations.**

Judaism (jōō′də·iz′m): the sum total of Jewish beliefs, practices, and culture; there are four main religious varieties of Judaism—Orthodoxy, Conservatism, Reconstructionism, and Reform or Liberal Judaism.

judger, moods of: an expression borrowed from grammar and syntax and having much the same meaning in the analysis of practical judgment; the moods (indicative, optative, imperative, interrogative, and contemplative) refer to the varying transfers and attitudes operative in judgment.

judgment: (1) the decision or sentence of the law given by a court of justice or other competent tribunal as the result of proceedings instituted there for the redress of an injury; (2) a final decision entered in a book of judgments under the signature of the judge or, as in many jurisdictions, under the signature of the clerk; (3) the transformation of an antecedent, existentially indeterminate, or unsettled situation into a determinate one (Dewey); an act of assertion or denial.

judgment, aesthetic: *see* **aesthetic judgment.**

judgment by default: a judgment rendered by a court for the plaintiff when the defendant fails to put in an appearance in court in response to proper notice.

judgment, declaratory: a declaration of a court that concerns the rights of parties to a case or an opinion of a court which does not order the performance of any act.

judgment, ethical: a practical judgment respecting conduct, a judgment of what is better or worse, of ends, values, and future consequences in terms of norms and principles.

judgment, moral: *see* **moral judgment.**

judgment, practical: a judgment that involves the character of the judger, which (*a*) clarifies the meaning of a problematic situation, (*b*) proposes a course of action, (*c*) reconstructs the character of the judger in accordance with the requirements of the situation as judged; to be distinguished from theoretical judgment or judgments of fact that are neutral with respect to the character of the judger.

judgment scale of products: *syn.* **scale, product.**

judgment, value: *see* **value judgment.**

judgmental character: the expression of the habitual methods by means of which a judger deals with problematical situations—situations that are confused, indeterminate, unsettled.

judgmental research: *see* **research, judgmental.**

judicial citation: *see* **citation, judicial.**

judicial function: *see* **function, judicial.**

judicial law: *see* **law, judicial.**

judo: method of wrestling or fighting without weapons, of Chinese-Japanese origin, in which an opponent uses weight, strength, and body position to gain advantage; a highly specialized sport with a definite system of etiquette, forms, and throws. *See* **aikido; jujitsu; karate.**

jujitsu: a means of self-defense of Japanese origin in which the object is to injure the opponent. *See* **aikido; judo; karate.**

jump: (computer operation) *see* **command, transfer.**

jump and reach: an athletic event in which the performer jumps vertically and reaches up simultaneously; used as a test to measure the height of the vertical jump and as a fair measure of general motor ability. *Syn.* **Sargent jump.**

jumper cord: *see* **patch cord.**

jumping-off point (j.o.p.): the point of transition from the preparation step into the presentation step of the Allen four-step lesson.

juncture: (lang. arts) a combination of pause, change in pitch, and degree of stress which marks the end of phrases, clauses, or sentences.

June Week: the week prior to graduation at a service academy of a cadet class, honoring the graduates with parades, awards, and social events and climaxed by graduation ceremonies followed by the presentation of diplomas and commissions to the graduates.

jungle gym: mazelike apparatus of vertical and horizontal ladders used for climbing activities; steel construction commonly found outdoors in elementary schools; wooden construction formerly found indoors in kindergartens.

junior business training: *see* **training, junior business.**

junior civic organization: *see* **civic organization, junior.**

junior college: (1) generally, a 2-year institution of higher learning; a question has been raised about whether it should be classified as an extension of secondary education or as a part of higher education; sometimes regarded as a "feeder" for 4-year colleges or universities; grants an associate in arts degree in most cases; *see* **junior college, two-year;** (2) an educational institution requiring for admission as a regular student completion of the tenth grade of a standard high school or its equivalent; *see* **junior college, four-year;** (3) an educational institution offering 3 years of work; *see* **junior college, three-year.**

junior college, branch: a junior college operated as a branch of a college or university and located on a different campus from the parent institution.

junior college certificate: *see* **certificate, junior college.**

junior college, church-related: *syn.* **junior college, denominational.**

junior college, county: a publicly controlled junior college, maintained by a county. (In California it may serve the area of a county not already organized into a junior college district.)

junior college, denominational: a junior college under denominational control, influence, affiliation, or auspices. *Syn.* **church-related junior college.**

junior college, district: a publicly controlled junior college organized in a separate district. (Such a district may coincide with a city or high school district, may consist of two or more city or high school districts, as in California or Texas, or may consist of an entire county or two or more adjacent counties, as in Mississippi.)

junior college, Federal: a publicly controlled junior college conducted under the auspices of the Federal government, for example, the Canal Zone junior college conducted under the auspices of the Department of Defense.

junior college, four-year: a junior college that includes, in addition to the freshman and sophomore years, the last two high school or preparatory school years organized and operated as a single unit; in public school systems usually a part of a six-four-four system. *See* **six-four-four plan.**

junior college functions: *see* **functions, junior college.**

junior college, independent: (1) a junior college that is independent of any institution of higher learning; *contr. w.* **junior college, branch;** (2) a private junior college not related to any church or church group; *contr. w.* **junior college, denominational.**

junior college, joint union: a district junior college serving a district composed of two or more contiguous high school districts located in adjacent counties. (Provided for by state law in California.)

junior college, local: a public junior college controlled by a local board of education; not a state or separate district junior college.

junior college movement: a term embracing the growth, development, and status of the junior college in all its branches, especially during the twentieth century.

junior college, municipal: a junior college maintained by a municipality. (Synonymous with *local junior college;* the term *municipal* is commonly used in Texas and Oklahoma.)

junior college, private: a junior college whose control is vested in a board of control (commonly known as a *board of trustees*), a single person, or a number of persons not selected by public vote or appointed by public officials.

junior college, proprietary: a private junior college whose control is in the hands of a proprietor or proprietors on a commercial or profit-making basis, usually without an elected board of trustees.

junior college, public: a junior college whose control is vested in a board (variously known as a *board of trustees, board of education, school board,* etc.) elected by the voting public or appointed by the governor or other public official; usually includes the state type of junior college. *See* **junior college, state.**

junior college, state: a junior college controlled by a state appointed or elected board of control; usually established by special act of legislature; includes both branch and independent types. [Ordinarily, junior colleges are divided into the two coordinate types, public and private, but Koos regularly uses three coordinate types, state, public (district, municipal, local, but not state), and private.] *See* **junior college, public.**

junior college, three-year: a junior college that, in addition to the freshman and sophomore years, has added a third year, either the junior year of college or the senior year of high school.

junior college, two-year: a junior college consisting of the freshman and sophomore college years; the prevailing type, including more than 90 percent of the junior colleges of the United States.

junior college, union: a district junior college serving a district composed of two or more contiguous high school districts in the same county.

junior congregation, Jewish: *see* **congregation, Jewish junior.**

junior division: *see* **division** (2).

junior-executive training course: *see* **course, junior-executive training.**

junior first grade: *syn.* **extension, kindergarten** (1).

junior high school: usually, a school that enrolls pupils in grades 7, 8, and 9; less commonly, grades 7 and 8 or 8 and 9; may be a separate school or the lower part of a junior-senior high school; if separate, sometimes spoken of as a "segregated junior high school."

junior high school counselor: *see* **counselor, junior high school.**

junior high school, segregated: *see* **junior high school.**

junior high school student: *see* **student, junior high school.**

junior kindergarten: *see* **kindergarten, junior.**

junior national honor society: *see* **honor society, national junior.**

junior placement: *see* **placement, junior.**

junior placement service: *see* **placement service, junior.**

junior ROTC: *see* **ROTC, junior.**

junior safety council: *see* **safety council, junior.**

junior school: a term loosely used, sometimes referring to a school housing only grades 4, 5, and 6 and sometimes referring to a junior high school.

junior-senior high school: *see* **high school, junior-senior.**

junior-senior high school, three-three: *syn.* **high school, junior-senior.**

junior town meeting: an organization for the encouragement of the discussion of important current issues and problems by young people, especially school classes and other school groups.

junior undergraduate library school: *see* **library school, junior undergraduate.**

junior unit: *see* **unit, junior.**

junior varsity: *see* **varsity, junior.**

junior worker: *see* **worker, junior.**

junior year abroad: a year spent by American students in residence in a college or university abroad, with credit toward graduation from their own institutions.

juridical method: a system of studying political science which places heavy reliance on a legal approach that regards the state as an entity with a personality, a will, and rights and interests of its own.

jurisdiction: geographical or topical area over which a court has judicial authority. *See* **venue.**

jurisprudence: the science of law; a body of law.

jurisprudence, comparative: study of the principles of legal science by comparing them with the various systems of law.

jury examinations: *syn.* **examinations, board.**

just noticeable difference: *see* **difference, just noticeable.**

justification records: *see* **records, justification.**

justify: in computer operations, to line up with the left or right edge of something, as the significant contents of an accumulator with one end of the accumulator.

juvenile aid bureau: a separate division or bureau within the police department which handles all cases involving juveniles who come to the attention of the police.

juvenile book: *see* **book, juvenile.**

juvenile court: *see* **court, juvenile.**

juvenile delinquency: *see* **delinquency, juvenile.**

juvenile delinquent: *see* **delinquent, juvenile.**

juvenile detention home: *see* **detention home.**

juvenile diagnostic center: *see* **center, juvenile diagnostic.**

juvenile offender: *see* **offender, juvenile.**

juvenile police: *see* **police, juvenile.**

juvenile probation: *syn.* **probation** (3).

K-units scaling: *see* **scaling, K-units.**

kainophobia (kī'nō·fō'bi·ə): a morbid dread of new situations or new things.

Kalamazoo case: a Michigan legal case (Stuart v. School District No. 1 of the Village of Kalamazoo, 30 Mich. 69) in which, in answer to a citizen who sued to prevent the use of public funds for secondary education, the Michigan Supreme Court decided in 1874 that there was nothing in the constitution or in the laws of Michigan to indicate that the school districts were restricted in the branches of knowledge or the grade of instruction offered and supported by public funds; several other states had similar cases, all of which were victories for the middle level of society, who favored the establishment of the American public high school at the expense of the working classes and poor who were generally opposed.

kaleidoscope: an instrument containing glass or mirror reflecting surfaces which produce a variegated changing pattern when viewed against light or focused on outside objects.

karate (kə·rä'tē): (Japanese, lit., "empty hand") the art of defending oneself in struggle to the point of maiming or killing by the use of head, body block, feet, and sharp cutting hand movements, with accuracy, precise timing, and good body movements for quick action and muscle control; used in self-defense to gain maximum results with minimum effort. *See* **aikido; judo; jujitsu.**

Kelly-Salisbury method: (stat.) an iterative method of obtaining regression weights.

Kelvin scale: *see* **scale, Kelvin.**

Keren Ami (kär'ən ä'mē): *n. fem.* (Heb., lit., "fund of my people") a children's ongoing fund-raising activity in Jewish religious schools, camps, and community centers in which the children participating are usually organized into a quasi-junior community, a Keren Ami Council, that decides democratically how the funds which have been collected should be distributed; aims to educate Jewish children to accept responsibility for Jewish community needs (physical and spiritual) and to participate intelligently in Jewish group life.

kernel sentence: *see* **sentence, kernel.**

kernicterus mental retardation: *see* **mental retardation, kernicterus.**

kerygma (ke'rYg·mä): (Gr., lit., "announcement") a proclamation or public announcement, which, in Christianity, refers specifically to the "Good News" or Gospel; preaching as contrasted with teaching. *See* **didache.**

key: (1) *syn.* **key, answer;** (2) the legend indicating the significance of various symbols, crosshatchings, kinds of lines, etc., in a given map, diagram, etc.; (3) a lever on a musical instrument which causes a specific tone to be produced; (4) (mus.) the basic pitch around which all musical resources will gravitate; a musical composition is often said to be in the key of C, or the key of F major, or the key of G minor, thus setting up a host of interrelated melodic and harmonic considerations; (5) a computer word or field which determines the position of a record in a sorted sequence; (6) a lever on a manually operated machine, such as a typewriter.

key, answer: (1) a device on which are recorded the right (or wrong) responses for a given test or by which the test may be otherwise scored; commonly furnished with objective tests to facilitate objective scoring; *syn.* **scoring key;** (2) a manual in which are recorded right answers to questions in an accompanying textbook.

key card: a master punch card, such as an IBM card, that contains (in coded form) the identifications of several variables, and possibly also their categories, especially if the latter are irregular; used with accounting machines for guiding subsequent punching, sorting, and tabulating operations.

key, coding: a list of the categories of expected data (such as the various possible answers to a question), together with the appropriate code numbers or symbols allotted each; employed as an aid in coding data for efficient subsequent filing or tabulation.

key, decoding: *syn.* **code, decoding.**

key, empirical: a device on which are recorded the right answers of a test based not on the judgments of the test constructor but on the differences between the answers actually given by individuals belonging to different criterion groups, such as good or poor students, friendly or hostile students, etc.; the responses are often weighted so as to maximize the difference between the chosen criterion groups.

key, faking use: *see* **faking use key.**

key, Fitzgerald: *see* **Fitzgerald key.**

key, pronunciation: the aid to pronunciation of words found in a dictionary in which the sounds of vowels and consonants are indicated by means of diacritical marks.

key punch: a machine for punching data into punch cards for use on an accounting machine; usually designed to record numerical data, but may be designed for alphabetical data as well. *See* **tabulating machine.**

key punch, printing: a card-punching machine used in data processing that prints every letter or number on the card as it is being punched.

key, scoring: *see* **key, answer.**

key, stencil: a scoring key which, when positioned over an examinee's responses, either in a test booklet, or more commonly, on an answer sheet, permits rapid identification and counting of all right (or wrong) answers; sometimes shortened to *stencil.*

key, strip: a scoring key arranged so that the answers for items on any page or in any column of the test appear in a strip or column that may be placed alongside the examinee's responses for easy scoring.

key-verify: (data processing) to use the punch-card machine known as a *verifier,* which has a keyboard, to make sure that the information supposed to be punched in a punch card has actually been properly punched; the machine signals when the punched hole and the depressed key disagree.

key word: *see* **word, key.**

key-word-in-context index: *see* **index, key-word-in-context.**

key-word-out-of-context index: *see* **index, key-word-out-of-context.**

keyboard harmony: the study, at the piano or some other keyboard instrument, of the structure, relation, and progression of chords.

keyboard instruments: *see* **instruments, keyboard.**

keyboard, simplified: (typewriting) rearrangement of characters of the typewriter, devised by Dvorak and Dealey in 1932, to provide better balance of stroking loads between the two hands; based upon the relative strength of various fingers and the relative frequency of use of the various keys.

keystone effect: an out-of-square image on a projection screen, resulting when the plane of the screen and the plane of the projected material are not parallel to each other.

kickout: in automatic data processing, a rejection, under the control of the program, of erroneous or invalid input data.

Kiddie Klimb: the trade name for climbing apparatus composed of one slanted, one horizontal, and two vertical ladders; commonly found in kindergartens.

kindergarten: an educational setup or section of a school system, devoted to the education of small children, usually from 4 to 6 years of age; characterized by organized play activities having educational, socializing values, by opportunities for self-expression and training in how to work and live together harmoniously, and by an environment, materials, curriculum, and program carefully selected to provide for child growth and development.

kindergarten curriculum: see **curriculum, kindergarten.**

kindergarten extension: see **extension, kindergarten.**

kindergarten extension certificate: see **certificate, kindergarten extension.**

kindergarten extension class: see **class, kindergarten extension.**

kindergarten, Froebelian (frø·bel'i·ən): a kindergarten for the training of young children between 3 and 7 years of age, in which Froebel's gifts, games, and occupations are employed and in which teaching methods are based on Froebel's principles and theories of education popular in the later nineteenth century.

kindergarten, junior: a kindergarten that enrolls the younger kindergarten pupils; if a school provides kindergarten experience for children 4 and 5 years of age, those 4 years old might be placed in the junior kindergarten.

kindergarten-primary department: see **department, kindergarten-primary.**

kindergarten-primary unit: see **unit, kindergarten-primary.**

kindergarten, senior: the second semester or second year of kindergarten experience immediately preceding entrance into first grade.

kindergarten, traditional: originally, the form of kindergarten procedure based on the theories and practices of Froebel; in more recent years the term connotes such formal, organized procedures as morning circle, highly organized singing games, use of patterns for handwork, and formal dramatization of stories. (Such procedures are in contrast to those of the modern kindergarten, which are based on research findings of studies in child growth and development.)

kindergarten-training school: (1) an institution specializing in the preparation of teachers for the kindergarten; (2) a laboratory school or affiliated school in a teacher-preparing program responsible for the instruction of children in the kindergarten; used for student teaching purposes.

kindergarten-visiting program: see **program, kindergarten-visiting.**

kinds of transfer: see **transfer, kinds of.**

kinematics: the geometry of motion that includes displacement, velocity, and acceleration without regard for the forces acting on a body.

kinescept: a sensory form of movement created by kinesthetic perception of a *kinestruct.*

kinescope: syn. **recording, kinescope.**

kinescope recorder: see **recorder, kinescope.**

kinescope recording: see **recording, kinescope.**

kinesia: see **kinetosis.**

kinesiologic analysis: see **analysis, kinesiologic.**

kinesiology: the scientific study of leverage and muscular action in movements of the body.

kinesthesia (kin'əs·thē'zhi·ə; -zi·ə; kī'nəs-): *alt. sp.* **kinesthesis** (-thē'sis); the sense by which weight, motion, and position of the body in space are recognized, through the stimulation of special sense receptors located in the muscle tissues, tendons, and joints, the stimuli being the movements of the muscles and parts; syn. **muscle sense;** (2) the capacity of the organism to maintain an awareness of position in space and to recall patterns of movement from previous experience for use in resolving continuing demands; see **awareness, kinesthetic.**

kinesthesis: syn. **kinesthesia.**

kinesthetic-auditory associations: see **associations, kinesthetic-auditory.**

kinesthetic awareness: see **awareness, kinesthetic.**

kinesthetic feedback: see **feedback, kinesthetic.**

kinesthetic imagery: see **imagery, kinesthetic.**

kinesthetic memory: impulses stored in the cortex which allow the performer mentally to perform the act; depending upon the degree to which execution parallels memory, success may be judged before the end result is visualized.

kinesthetic method: (1) a method of teaching the child to read number concepts and to spell by tracing with his finger the written forms of words or by writing and at the same time sounding the words written; syn. **tracing method;** (2) a technique for the treatment of faulty speech by attempting to make the speech-defective person conscious of the movements and positions of the speech organs necessary for correct speech production, by means of auditory, visual, and kinesthetic impressions.

kinesthetic perception: see **perception, kinesthetic.**

kinesthetic sense: syn. **muscle sense.**

kinesthetic-tactual method: a method of teaching the deaf that combines a kinesthetic technique similar to that of the *Jena method* with stimulation and training of the sense of touch.

kinesthetics: in foreign language instruction, the use and study of body movements and gestures in conjunction with speech.

kinestruct: *n.* (phys. ed.) the dynamic, somatic form created by the structural masses of the body in motion; the visually perceivable form of the movement experience.

kinestructure: the act of creating a kinestruct. See **kinestruct.**

kinetic art: see **art, kinetic.**

kinetic reversal: see **reversal, kinetic.**

kinetics: the study of motion which incorporates the concepts of mass, force, and energy as they affect motion.

kinetosis: any disorder caused by unaccustomed motion; sometimes called *kinesia.*

Kinzie method: a method of teaching lipreading, introduced by Cora Kinzie and Rose Kinzie, combining certain principles of the *Müller-Walle (Bruhn)* and *Nitchie* methods.

kippah (kip'pä): *n. fem.; pl.* **kippot** (kip'pōt); (Heb., lit., "skull cap") a skull cap worn by boys and men of Orthodox and Conservative persuasions during sessions at the religious school, synagogue services, and the reading of sacred texts; it is sometimes called by the Yiddish name *yarmelke.*

kit: a collection of pertinent materials gathered and integrated into an instructional unit; for example, a textbook, filmstrips, and a tape recording integrated into one basic unit; more recent and complex applications of this concept are to be found in *systems approach* and in *systems design.*

kit of instructional materials: (1) a packaged set of materials including such items as a teacher's guide, master copies for duplicating such as instruction sheets, films for projection, recordings, samples or models, etc., for the teacher's use in planning and teaching a unit; (2) a packaged assembly of learning materials, probably one set for each pupil, to provide practice in manipulation or other tasks under teacher direction; (3) a set of self-teaching materials. See **kit of learning materials.**

kit of learning materials: (1) a packaged set of materials to be used by an individual pupil for mastering tasks after they have been demonstrated and explained by the teacher; (2) a set of self-teaching materials that invite manipulation and exploration and have been organized to be meaningful and evaluative for the individual learner without need for teacher explanation, supervision, or appraisal.

kit, science: see **science kit.**

kitchen, unit: see **unit kitchen.**

Klang association (kläng): (Ger., lit., "sound" or "tone") association of words by reason of superficial tonal resemblances; common to manic excitement and catatonia.

kleptomania (klep'tō·mā'ni·ə): the impulse, often habitual and irresistible, to steal petty or useless articles that are not disposed of for profit; implies mental disorder.

kleptomaniac: a person afflicted with *kleptomania*.

knee-jerk reflex: *syn.* **reflex, patellar.**

knothole league baseball: *see* **baseball, little league.**

knowledge: (1) the accumulated facts, truths, principles, and information to which the human mind has access; (2) the outcome of specified, rigorous inquiry which originated within the framework of human experience and functions in human experience; (3) the product of the operation of man's intellect, either within or apart from human experience; (4) the recall of specifics and universals, or the recall of a pattern, structure, or setting; for measurement purposes, the recall situation involves mostly bringing to mind the appropriate material, with major emphasis on the psychological processes of remembering, the problem in a knowledge test situation being that of finding in the problem or task the appropriate signals, cues, and clues which will most effectively bring out whatever relevant knowledge is filed or stored.

knowledge, coherence theory of: the theory that knowledge is derived from the process of reasoning from a unified and rational universe.

knowledge, contextual theory of: the theory that man cannot apprehend absolute truth; therefore truth or knowledge is always relative to the quality of his experience.

knowledge, copy theory of: a phrase indicating that the mind's way of getting to know is that, via the sensations, it gets a reflection or copy of the outside world as this world is and that the outside world is not changed by the process of securing this reflection; a term used by some to designate the theory of knowledge that the realists and idealists do or must espouse.

knowledge, functional: a term sometimes used to distinguish knowledge which has immediate rather than delayed usefulness or assured rather than doubtful usefulness.

knowledge, object of: *see* **object of knowledge.**

knowledge of progress: in learning, knowledge afforded the learner, by any means, of the progress and improvement he is making as he practices a new skill or acquires new knowledge.

knowledge of results: in learning, information as to whether or not a response is correct and whether progress or improvement is being made; as applied in programmed instruction, immediate confirmation for the student of each of his responses; if his response is correct, he proceeds with the program; if incorrect, he is informed at once. *See* **confirmation** (4); **feedback** (2); **feedback, psychological.**

knowledge, presentative theory of: the theory that knowledge is gained through direct sense perception of an object. *Contr. w.* **knowledge, representative theory of.**

knowledge, recall: knowledge that can be defined in terms of itself and voluntarily remembered and used whenever the need arises. *Dist. f.* **knowledge, recognition.**

knowledge, recognition: knowledge that functions in perceptual responses and in comprehension but that cannot be voluntarily recalled and actively used whenever the occasion arises, for example, the child's knowledge of words as judged by his comprehension of the words used by other people. *Dist. f.* **knowledge, recall.**

knowledge, representative theory of: the theory that sense perception is only a representation of reality and that therefore knowledge is based on that which transcends sense perception. *Contr. w.* **knowledge, presentative theory of.**

knowledge, revelation theory of: the theory that man's knowledge comes through revelation from some divine source.

knowledge, scientific: *see* **scientific.**

knowledge, spectator theory of: the doctrine that the true and valid object of knowledge is that which has being prior to and independent of the operations of knowing, the act of knowing being the mirroring or beholding of reality without anything being done to modify its antecedent state.

knowledge test: *see* **test, knowledge.**

Knowledge, Tree of: a picture of a tree showing the main root as representing mathematics and the other roots and branches representing the basic and applied sciences, thus suggesting the basic importance of mathematics in its relation to other fields of study.

Kolmogorov-Smirnov method: (stat.) a nonparametric test of the differences between distributions based on a comparison of cumulative frequencies.

kolytic (kō·lit′ik): pertaining to checks or hindrances to reaction to a stimulus.

Koran (ko·rän′; kō′ran; kō′rən): the sacred book of the Mohammedans.

Kuder-Richardson formulas: formulas for estimating the reliability of a test from information about the individual items in the test, or from the mean score, standard deviation, and number of items in the test; permit estimation of reliability from a single administration of a test without the labor involved in dividing the test into halves, so that their use has become common in test development; not appropriate for estimating the reliability of speed tests.

kurtosis (kěr·tō′sis): as compared with that of the normal frequency curve, the relative degree of flatness or peakness of the part of a frequency curve that lies near the mode. *See* **leptokurtic; mesokurtic; platykurtic.**

KWIC index: *see* **index, KWIC.**

KWOC index: *see* **index, KWOC.**

kymograph, phonetic (kī′mə·graf): an apparatus consisting of a revolving drum covered with smoked paper, on which various vibrations and movements occurring in speech may be recorded for analysis and measurement.

L-method: a shortcut method for selecting a small number of variables from a larger number such that the criterion correlation for the selected variables combined at gross-score weights approximates the multiple correlation of all the variables with the criterion.

La Porte basket system: *see* **basket system, La Porte.**

label: in data processing by computer, an identifier; in either human or machine language, for example, a magnetic tape label identifying the tape or an address identifying a storage location.

label, grade: (consumer ed.) a letter, number, word, or phrase that gives an over-all rating to a commodity.

labial: *n.* a consonant articulated mainly by the lips, for example, the consonants *m, p,* and *b.*

labialism: substitution of labials for other consonants.

lability: apathy, flatness of effect, irritation, frequent emotional upsets, catastrophic reactions, brief depression, crying, etc.

labor college: *see* **college, labor.**

labor economics: *see* **economics, labor.**

labor education: instructional programs for union members, offered by colleges, universities, and unions, which emphasize topics and subjects relevant to union membership but which may also involve exposure to such areas as the liberal arts, parliamentary procedure, and public speaking.

labor force nonparticipants: (voc. ed.) persons who are not in the labor force, that is, who are neither working nor looking for work; includes primarily those who keep house, are still in school, or are unable to work because of long-term physical or mental illness, and also retired persons and certain others.

labor requisition: *see* **requisition, labor.**

labor school: a school maintained for laborers; usually a night school, maintained by labor unions or organizations.

labor supply: a summation of available labor in a given field or in all fields; consists not only of the size of the labor force and its age distribution, but also of its skills, geographic location, number of hours members work in a year, the intensity of effort they are willing to put forth, the training and experience they bring to their jobs, and their potential for employment under specified conditions.

labor turnover ratio: *see* **turnover ratio, labor.**

labor union: *see* **union, labor.**

laboratory: (1) a room or rooms appropriately equipped and used for scientific experimentation and research by a research staff of a university; (2) a room or rooms appropriately equipped and used by students for the study of some branch of science or the application of scientific principles; (3) (ind. arts) an activity area; preferred to the term "shop"; for example, industrial arts laboratory, laboratory of arts and industry, industries laboratory; (4) (teacher ed.) any teaching-learning situation where prospective or in-service teachers may conduct scientific observation of student learning and teaching or conduct action research into teaching practice.

laboratory, agriculture: *syn.* **laboratory, land.**

laboratory approach: in supervision of instruction, a way of working with teachers for in-service education purposes to develop new insights or skills; involves reaction to a simulated problem, recording of reactions, analysis and feedback, and follow-up discussion leading to the drawing of generalizations.

laboratory, audioactive: a type of language laboratory adapted for repetition exercise, in which the student may listen, speak, and hear his own voice amplified through a headset. *Contr. w.* **laboratory, audiopassive.**

laboratory, audiopassive: the simplest type of language laboratory or exercise in which the student listens and responds aloud without the use of a microphone or headset. *Contr. w.* **laboratory, audioactive.**

laboratory block: an allotted period of the school year, normally 6 weeks, which provides a pattern for laboratory investigation of a specific science subject by the student.

laboratory, carpentry: a laboratory equipped and used for instruction in carpentry.

laboratory, child development: the nursery school, kindergarten, and infant laboratory frequently serve as the laboratory for child development classes; day-care centers, play schools, and home experience may be supplementary, or they may serve when the former are not available. *See* **development, child.**

laboratory, child study: a place for studying the child under controlled conditions and for putting into practice experimental programs involving the child's behavior and learning. *Syn.* **child study clinic.**

laboratory, classroom-: *see* **classroom-laboratory.**

laboratory, clothing: (home ec.) a room provided for the study of clothing, containing sewing equipment and illustrative and reference materials.

laboratory collection: *see* **collection, laboratory.**

laboratory, combination: a broadcast language laboratory with a small number of fully equipped library-type booths.

laboratory, composite industrial arts: a laboratory providing the activities, tools, materials, experiences, and con-

sumers' goods necessary for a broad program of industrial arts. *Syn.* **laboratory, diversified-activity.**

laboratory, comprehensive general industrial arts: a space specifically designed and equipped for several types of instructional activities in two or more subject areas of industrial arts, and usually taught by one teacher; typically, may provide instructional experiences in drawing, metals, woods, and electricity/electronics, or in manufacturing, construction, graphics, power, and electricity/electronics; to be distinguished from special forms of unit laboratories such as general woods laboratory, general metals laboratory, etc. *Syn.* **laboratory, general industrial arts;** *see* **laboratory, composite industrial arts.**

laboratory, conventional: the common form of language laboratory containing program sources and control panels at a teacher console and student booths with headphone-microphone combinations and tape recorders.

laboratory course: *see* **course, laboratory.**

laboratory, crafts: a laboratory equipped and used for the teaching of skilled hand occupations or arts.

laboratory, curriculum: a facility where special assistance is provided to members of instructional staffs in planning and preparing for instruction; among materials usually available for reference and use are representative textbooks, curriculum guides, sample teaching units, tests, and selected audiovisual equipment and supplies.

laboratory, curriculum materials: a department within a library, or a separate unit within a school or college, organized to provide teaching aids for students such as elementary and/or secondary school textbooks, courses of study, tests, sample units, pamphlet materials, a picture file, film strips, slides, and other materials which may be helpful to the teacher in the preparation of a unit of work. *Syn.* **curriculum library; curriculum materials center; instructional materials center; textbook library.**

laboratory demonstration: *see* **demonstration, laboratory.**

laboratory, dial access: a type of language laboratory that utilizes telephone dials and switches to connect a program source to any given student booth; also referred to as dial laboratory.

laboratory, distributive education: a classroom equipped with store fittings such as wall display units, three-way mirror, showcase, wrapping counter, cash register, display window, and other typical store materiel. *Syn.* **merchandising laboratory; model store; retailing laboratory; retail selling laboratory.**

laboratory, diversified-activity industrial arts: *syn.* **laboratory, composite industrial arts.**

laboratory, electronic learning: basically, a series of tape recorders, earphones, and microphones, connected by wire to a console where switches permit the instructor to communicate with all students simultaneously, with groups of selected students, and with one student, individually; in some laboratories, each student may have his own individual master tape to which he listens, orally responds, and sometimes (according to instructions) records his oral responses; the student's desk is isolated by sound dampened panels, a microphone, and earphones; recently, instead of isolation panels, remotely controlled recorders have been installed for improved instruction; visual materials, also, may be presented either to the entire group or to each student individually; utilized for the teaching of foreign languages, reading, spelling, grammar and punctuation, music appreciation and criticism, English literature, social studies, stenography, and speech.

laboratory, English: in composition instruction, an arrangement whereby pupils may practice writing, reading, or speaking with opportunities to give and receive in-class help on an individual or small-group basis.

laboratory experiences, guided: *see* **experiences, guided laboratory.**

laboratory experiences, professional: *see* **experiences, professional laboratory.**

laboratory experiment: *see* **experiment, laboratory.**

laboratory, farm: *syn.* **shop, agricultural.**

laboratory farm: *see* **laboratory, land.**

laboratory, flight: a familiarization program of laboratory instruction dealing with the various aspects of flying and air travel; takes place mainly during flight in an airplane; often offered as part of an aerospace education workshop.

laboratory, foods: (home ec.) a room provided and equipped for the study of foods and nutrition, containing food preparation and serving equipment and illustrative and reference materials.

laboratory, general industrial arts: *syn.* **laboratory, comprehensive general industrial arts;** *see* **laboratory, composite industrial arts.**

laboratory, household equipment: space provided and equipped with laundry appliances and other small household appliances to be used for teaching and demonstration; may be annexed to or a part of the clothing and foods laboratories.

laboratory, industrial arts: a space designed and equipped specifically as an activity area with emphasis on the experimental research and development types of instructional activities such as creating, designing, synthesizing, and applying theories, principles, and concepts dealing with the development of insights and understanding of technology; preferred to the term *shop* in, for example, general drafting laboratory, general metals laboratory, power technology laboratory, automotives or transportation laboratory, wood technology laboratory, etc.

laboratory, land: a plot of land or a farm controlled by the school which is used to demonstrate and practice activities relating to the production and handling of plants and animals and their products; often used in the instructional program in vocational education in agriculture. *See* **demonstration plot, agricultural.**

laboratory, language: a special facility used particularly in the aural-oral method of language teaching; often each learner has a separate booth connected with a central station which can receive his speech, record it for him to play back, and also provide him other "listening" models of the language. *See* **laboratory, electronic learning.**

laboratory, mathematics: an area specially equipped for the teaching of mathematics; equipment sometimes found there includes calculating devices, models, surveying equipment, specially marked chalk boards, desks and tables, etc.

laboratory, mechanics: a general term applying to laboratories designed, equipped, and used for instruction in any trade or mechanic art.

laboratory, merchandising: *syn.* **laboratory, distributive education.**

laboratory, metal: a laboratory equipped with tools and apparatus for instruction in metalwork.

laboratory method: the instructional procedure by which the cause, effect, nature, or property of any phenomenon, whether social, psychological, or physical, is determined by actual experience or experiment under controlled conditions.

laboratory, mobile: (1) a type of language laboratory in which all necessary functioning parts may be carried or rolled from room to room and set up quickly; (2) a portable industrial arts equipment unit, carried on a truck or trailer, providing facilities for industrial arts experiences for pupils in schools having limited laboratory facilities.

laboratory nursery school: *see* **nursery school, laboratory.**

laboratory of industries: (ind. arts) a space or room, or a number of rooms, adequately equipped with tools, materials, visual aids, and machines characteristic of several phases or forms of industry.

laboratory, outdoor science: *syn.* **center, nature.**

laboratory, piano class: a room in which from 6 to 24 electric or electronic pianos are arranged in clusters of 4 to 6 pianos each, with a master control panel containing a piano, a series of separate channels, and related gear; the master teacher guides the piano students' skill practice in all manner of innovative teaching techniques, including prepared tapes, recorded examples, etc.; the piano class laboratory is employed widely for training musicians to a functional piano facility; soloists are universally trained in the traditional one-to-one method of the private lesson. *See* **electropiano system.**

laboratory plan: a form of school organization in which pupils of grade 4 and above study each subject in a separate designated classroom, called a *laboratory*, under a teacher specialist, each pupil usually progressing at his own rate, as, for example, in the Dalton laboratory plan.

laboratory, print: a laboratory appropriately equipped for printing or for instruction in printing.

laboratory, reading: (1) a special classroom or library which contains materials of particular usefulness in teaching reading, especially to pupils who need remedial help; *see* **center, reading;** (2) a commercially prepared collection of graded selections designed for individual reading practice in development of reading skills.

laboratory, regional educational: an educational laboratory, one of the geographical educational centers for converting basic research into classroom practice after screening and pilot studies; originally funded by the Federal government Title IV, Elementary and Secondary Education Act for promoting educational change, especially for disadvantaged pupils.

laboratory, remote: a language laboratory controlled and programmed from a location some distance away.

laboratory, retail selling: *syn.* **laboratory, distributive education.**

laboratory, retailing: *syn.* **laboratory, distributive education.**

laboratory, safety: (safety ed.) a workroom devoted to the study of safety problems.

laboratory, school: a room or other portion of a school building in which teachers and pupils may carry on experiments; commonly, a special room in the school containing special apparatus and equipment for use in performing experiments or exercises and working out problems.

laboratory school: an elementary or secondary school in which part or all of the teaching staff consists of cadet or student teachers and the control and operation of the school rests with an institution that prepares teachers. *Syn.* **model school** (2); **practice school** (2); *see* **demonstration school; elementary school, university; experimental school; high school, university; training school.**

laboratory school, university: *see* **university school.**

laboratory, space: (1) a space vehicle carrying sensing and measuring instruments, recording equipment, radio-transmitting equipment, and other related instruments, used as a means of obtaining scientific data on conditions in the upper regions of the earth's atmosphere or in space; may be manned or unmanned; (2) a vehicle that simulates the conditions of a space vehicle.

laboratory space: the area of a building or a college plant devoted to laboratories.

laboratory, statistical: a workroom in which statistical operations are performed; often contains electric and/or electronic calculators, scoring machines, and/or machines for sorting and tabulating data.

laboratory teacher: (teacher ed.) a teacher in a *laboratory school.*

laboratory, teaching materials: a place in the school where teaching aids and materials can be produced, used, or borrowed.

laboratory technique: (sci. ed.) a learning situation in which students work individually or in small groups, using a variety of equipment and materials, for the essential purpose of understanding principles, gaining experimental evidence, solving problems, and acquiring manipulative skills.

laboratory training, general: *see* **training, general laboratory.**

laboratory training, human relations: *see* **training, human relations laboratory.**

laboratory, typographical: a journalistic laboratory provided with printing equipment used to train journalism students in the problems of typography, rather than to produce finished printing.

laboratory unit: (ind. arts) a space designed and equipped to provide study and experience in a single industrial activity and/or material, for example, plastics laboratory, woodworking laboratory, electronics laboratory, automotives laboratory, etc.

laboratory, vocational: a laboratory designed, equipped, and used for instruction in some vocation.

laboratory, wireless language: a type of language laboratory employing radio broadcast instead of wired connections from the program source to student headphones.

laboratory, woodworking: a laboratory equipped and used for the teaching of woodworking.

laboratory work: learning activities carried out by pupils or students in a laboratory devoted to the study of a particular subject (such as physics, botany, zoology, or chemistry) and involving the practical application of theory through observation, experimentation, and research.

laches (lach'ez; lach'iz): (Old Fr. *laschesse*, lit., "negligence") delay; tardiness in asserting a right or privilege, especially in instituting a court action, as in the case of a teacher on permanent tenure who is unlawfully dismissed and is entitled to reinstatement but who fails to institute appropriate action until after an extended period of time has elapsed and whose right may be held to have been extinguished by his own laches.

lack of affect: *see* affect, lack of.

lack of stamina: a condition, usually curable in children, characterized by impaired vitality or endurance, making it difficult for the individual to carry consistently and continuously a full schedule of work.

lacrosse: a Canadian Indian game played on any large field by two teams of ten players each; the game is played by passing a white rubber ball back and forth among the players by means of a crosse, a light wood stick with a meshed net, triangular in shape at one end, until a goal is scored by throwing the ball into the goal with the crosse.

ladder system: a system of education in which the various levels of the school system are open to virtually all the graduates of the next lower school; this is a characteristic of the American public school system. *See* educational ladder.

lag, culture: *see* culture lag.

laggard: (1) a pupil who is not mentally defective but who is overage and lags behind the rest of his chronological age group; (2) sometimes but less frequently, synonymous with *mental defective*.

lagging community: *see* community, lagging.

laissez faire (le'sā' fār'): (Fr., lit., "leave alone," "allow to do") (1) a term that came into use in the eighteenth century as a slogan by those who urged that governments should make little attempt to direct the opinions and actions of their citizens; (2) the idea or theory that personal and group welfare are best achieved by the competitive pursuit of enlightened self-interest; especially applied to economic behavior.

laissez-faire system: any regime in which the policy of noninterference prevails.

laity: (1) all the people of the Christian churches who are not ordained ministers and, by implication, lack the expert knowledge of the clergy; (2) in the Roman Catholic Church, members of the church who do not possess authority; Catholic Church membership is composed of *clergy* and laity; (3) by extension, those persons unqualified to speak or to judge in all the various specialized fields of knowledge.

laliophobia (lā·li·ə·fō'bi·ə): a morbid aversion to or fear of speaking.

lallation (la·lā'shən): (1) faulty articulation of *l* and *r* sounds, particularly the type of distortion due to sluggish or inadequate tongue movement; (2) broadly, any defective articulation of certain sounds in the production of which the tongue plays a major part, including, in addition to *l* and *r*, the following: *n, t, d, k, g;* (3) repetition of a sound or syllable in an essentially meaningless manner (rare). *Syn.* lalling.

lalling: *syn.* lallation.

lalopathy: any speech disorder. *Syn.* logopathy.

lalorrhea (lal'ə·rē'ə): a disorder of speech marked by a continuous flow of words, often without meaning.

lambda coefficient: *see* coefficient, lambda.

lambda matrix: *see* matrix, lambda.

Lancasterian: a spelling variant of *Lancastrian.*

Lancastrian model school: a type of school established in the United States during the early part of the nineteenth century to demonstrate the Lancastrian method of monitorial instruction; frequently used as institutions for training teachers for Lancastrian schools.

Lancastrian system: a method of organizing for mass instruction; originated by Joseph Lancaster (1778-1838), an English Quaker schoolmaster; based on the use of abler pupils as *monitors* who, after learning the lesson from the master, taught small groups of fellow students; introduced into the United States in 1806 in New York City and adopted widely; finally abandoned in 1853. *Syn.* monitorial system.

land economics: *see* economics, land.

land grant: a gift or endowment in the form of land made by a government to aid a particular service or activity, often in support of public education.

land-grant college: *see* college, land-grant.

land-grant university: *see* university, land-grant.

land laboratory: *see* laboratory, land.

landmark: (spec. ed.) for the visually handicapped, any familiar object, sound, odor, temperature, or tactile clue that is easily recognized and has a known location in the environment. *See* reference point.

lands, state school: *see* state school lands.

landscaping: (1) the process of planning and planting trees, shrubs, and grass on the grounds or campus; (2) those parts of the grounds or campus of a school or college which have been tastefully planted to trees, shrubs, and grass.

language: (1) a code for conveying the thoughts and feelings of one individual to another which has been accepted and is mutually understood by both; may be (*a*) oral, through the articulation of vocal sounds into words and then the grouping of words into statements, (*b*) written, through an arrangement of symbols roughly approximating the sounds that one makes in speaking, or (*c*) gestural, through body movements; (2) (data processing) any system of characters used to represent instructions and/or data so that the instructions and data are understandable to both computer and operator.

language ability, receptive: *see* decoding, visual.

language activities: *see* activities, language.

language, American English: spoken and written English as it has developed in America; differs at times from British English in meanings of certain words and phrases, in pronunciation, and in grammatical construction.

language analysis: *see* analysis, language.

language and area center: *see* center, language and area.

language aptitude: *see* aptitude, language.

language, artificial: a language constructed with the express purpose of affording a universal means of communication for speakers of different languages; for ease in learning, the structure and pronunciation are made as simple as possible and the vocabulary is spelled phonetically and based on words with roots common to many languages; an example is Esperanto.

language arts: (1) the verbal skills used in communicating and expressing ideas; (2) a group of school subjects, the chief purpose of which is to teach control and proficiency in the use of the English language; commonly includes reading, language (oral and written), speech, spelling, and handwriting; includes the fields of radio, television, and motion pictures.

language arts education: an area of study dealing with problems of method and curriculum in English and foreign languages.

language arts, foreign: an area of study concerned with the social and cultural applications of the ability to read, write, or speak foreign languages.

language, basic: that language which is sufficient merely to communicate fundamental ideas.

language, common business oriented (COBOL): a specific language by which business data processing procedures may be precisely described in a standard form; intended not only as a means for directly presenting any business program to any suitable computer, for which a compiler exists, but also as a means of communicating such procedures among individuals. *See* **common-language media.**

language, common machine: machine-sensible information representation which is common to a related group of data processing machines; distinguishing characteristic is that, generally, one line of coding specifies one instruction to the computer; examples are the codes for data recording on paper tape, punched cards, and magnetic tape.

language, compiler: for an electronic computer a well-defined language closely related to the language in which a problem is originally stated, such as English or mathematics; used to write programs for the computer which are then automatically translated by a *compiler* into a machine language program.

language, computer: *syn.* **language, machine.**

language, decision: in automatic data processing, a programming language using decision tables. *See* **table, decision.**

language development: *see* **development, language.**

language, evocative use of: a nonreferential use of language; language use which calls up feelings and emotions; use of language which calls attention to the wholeness of experience.

language experience approach: an integrated language arts program which builds upon the interrelationship between and among reading and the related language arts of writing, speaking, and listening; use is made of individual and group compositions as reading materials in the language experience approach to the teaching of reading.

language experience, compensatory: a planned program to increase the extent and precision of vocabulary of children with a limited linguistic background.

language, exploratory: *syn.* **language study, exploratory.**

language, general: the study of the origin and development of human language, modes of expression, and characteristics of various groups of languages, with a more detailed study of typical languages.

language, genetic theory of: *see* **genetic theory of language.**

language, gesture: a method of communication by means of symbolic movements or positions of the hands, limbs, or body.

language handicap: *see* **handicap, language.**

language, international algebraic (IAL): the forerunner of *ALGOL.*

language laboratory: *see* **laboratory, language.**

language laboratory operation, library system: operation of a language laboratory on an individual study basis with students using separate tape programs as they would books.

language laboratory, wireless: *see* **laboratory, wireless language.**

language learning level: *see* **level, language learning.**

language, machine: a language for writing instructions in a form to be executed directly by the computer. *See* **language, compiler;** *contr. w.* **coding, symbolic.**

language, machine oriented: (1) a language designed for interpretation and use by a machine without translation; (2) a system for expressing information which is intelligible to a specific machine, such as a computer or class of computers; such a language may include *instructions* that define and direct machine operations, and *information* to be recorded by or acted upon by these machine operations; (3) the set of instructions expressed in the number system basic to a computer, together with symbolic operation codes with absolute addresses, relative addresses, or symbolic addresses, that is, labels indicating various information storage arrangements.

language of art: a metaphorical phrase indicating the expressive quality of art and implying that the elements of art, such as line, color, and texture, arranged according to aesthetic principles, produce a composition that may be interpreted or "read."

language pattern: *see* **pattern, language.**

language, philosophy of: a philosophical investigation taking its departure from the phenomenon called language, which is taken to mean any use of signs and symbols constituting *communication.*

language, procedure oriented: a machine independent language which describes how the process of solving the problem is to be carried out.

language proficiency test: *see* **test, language proficiency.**

language, program: *syn.* **language, programming** (2).

language program: *see* **program, language.**

language program, intensive: *see* **program, intensive language.**

language, programming: (1) the original form in which a program is prepared prior to processing by the computer; (2) a language used by programmers to write computer routines; also called *program language.*

language, psychology of: *see* **psycholinguistics.**

language-rhythm clue: *see* **clue, language-rhythm.**

language, Romance: any of the languages that have evolved from Latin—Italian, French, Spanish, Portuguese, Swiss Romansch, Romanian.

language, second: that language of a bilingual person which is not the so-called mother tongue in which he has from childhood usually expressed his thoughts and feelings.

language, secret: the preadolescent modifications of the language forms of the culture to render them unrecognizable except to the initiate; for example, Pig Latin, Tut-A-Hash, Opish, etc.

language, sign: (1) a means of communication by the use of gesture; (2) more specifically, a highly developed system of conventionalized gestures used in communication with the deaf or among the deaf themselves as a substitute for speech; *contr. w.* **finger spelling.**

language skill: *see* **skill, language.**

language, source: the original form in which a program is prepared prior to processing by the machine.

language study, exploratory: preliminary study of one or more foreign languages, with a view to discovering the student's language interests and abilities. *Syn.* **exploratory language.**

language symbol: *see* **symbol, language.**

language, symbolic: a language which is a translation to be fed into a computer of the language in which the user has written his source program.

language, target: a foreign language that is being learned or taught.

language test, graduate school foreign: *see* **test, graduate school foreign language.**

language training, intensive: *see* **training, intensive language.**

language usage: *see* **usage, language.**

languages, classical: traditionally, ancient Latin and Greek.

Lanham Act: a Federal emergency act passed in 1941 providing appropriations for public works including the construction, maintenance, and operation of child-care centers, schools, and recreation centers, especially in Federal housing projects; has been superseded by other legislation.

lantern: *syn.* **projector, lantern-slide.**

lantern slide: *see* **slide, lantern.**

lantern-slide projector: *see* **projector, lantern-slide.**

Laplace-Gaussian curve (la·plas' gous'i·ən): *syn.* **curve, normal probability.**

Laplacian curve (la·plas'i·ən): *syn.* **curve, normal probability.**

large-block-of-time organization: *syn.* **schedule, large-block-of-time.**

large-block-of-time schedule: *see* **schedule, large-block-of-time.**

large-fund plan: (1) a plan for distributing state aid to school districts by granting money in large or relatively large amounts, with no differentiation made in terms of the difference in taxpaying ability of the districts receiving the money; (2) a plan that does not attempt directly to equalize ability to support schools through recognition of variation in the taxpaying ability of local school districts but rather achieves its results by providing a relatively large amount of money to all districts, usually on a uniform basis of aid or as a flat grant; (3) a plan that provides for complete state support of the state minimum program of education.

large muscle equipment: *see* **equipment, large muscle.**

large sample theory: the group of related concepts which describe or refer to the properties of all those sampling distributions which are large enough to possess approximately the characteristics of a distribution with known mathematical properties; usually the normal probability distribution, but occasionally some other.

large-type book: *see* **book, large-type.**

large-type print: *see* **reading materials, large-type.**

large-type reading materials: *see* **reading materials, large-type.**

larynx: the organ of voice; the structure located at the upper end of the trachea, containing the vocal cords and composed of cartilages, muscles, and membranes.

latchkey child: *see* **child, latchkey.**

late bloomer: *see* **child, morning-glory.**

latency of response: *see* **response, latency of.**

latency period: (psychoan.) a period in psychosexual development, normally from about 5 or 6 years to puberty, in which infantile sexual aims or urges are sublimated and seem relatively dormant.

latent: (1) not presently manifest, but potentially able to develop; (2) (genet.) referring to traits or characters not visible in the individual, but for which genes exist in the germ plasm.

latent achiever: *see* **achiever, latent.**

latent class: *see* **class, latent.**

latent continuum: *see* **continuum, latent.**

latent image: *see* **image, latent.**

latent learning: *see* **learning, latent.**

latent structure: *see* **structure, latent.**

lateral: pertaining to one side.

lateral dominance: *see* **dominance, lateral.**

lateral enrichment: *syn.* **enrichment, horizontal.**

lateral imbalance: *see* **imbalance, lateral.**

lateral lisp: *see* **lisp, lateral.**

lateral space: the distance between the points of the small u; used as a norm in handwriting.

lateral swing: a handwriting movement characterized by a sweeping curve, either convex or concave, to the right and left; used as a drill in securing relaxation and motor control.

laterality: (1) sidedness; preferential use of one hand rather than the other (particularly in tasks demanding the use of one hand only), one eye rather than the other (as for initial sighting), one foot rather than the other (as in kicking a ball); a combination of the three factors, eyedness, handedness, and footedness; (2) assumed dominance of the left over the right cerebral hemisphere, or vice versa, with respect to motor functions of the individual.

laterality index: *see* **index, laterality.**

Latin grammar school: a secondary school, emphasizing Latin and usually Greek, the purpose of which was to prepare youths for the universities; first formed by the Romans in imitation of certain Athenian schools, nearly extinct during the Middle Ages, and strongly revived during the Renaissance, spreading to most European countries and to colonial America. (Usually known by different titles in different countries, such as *court school* in Italy, *college* in France, *Gymnasium* in Germany, and *public school* in England.)

Latin square: *see* **square, Latin.**

Latin squares, orthogonal: *see* **squares, orthogonal Latin.**

lattice: (1) a network of equally spaced horizontal and vertical lines in the plane or in space; (2) the points of intersection only of such a network of lines; sometimes

known as *lattice points;* (3) in algebra, a particular kind of mathematical system.

lattice, dynamic: a representation in graphic form of the relationships among various goal-seeking behaviors.

Laubach reading method: *see* **reading method, Laubach.**

launching stage: the period in the family cycle when the children leave home.

lavaliere (lä·va·li'ɔr): (audiovis. ed.) the pendant microphone which may be hung around the neck of a speaker appearing on radio or television.

lavatory: (1) a fixture consisting of a bowl on a pedestal or attached to the wall, for washing the face and hands; (2) the room in which such fixtures stand.

law: the basic concept under which any organization operates to produce a harmony in activity.

law, all-or-none: the principle of nerve or muscle cell action which states that the magnitude of the neural impulse and the extent of the muscle twitch are independent of the magnitude of the stimulus, which is triggerlike in its action; subliminal stimuli, repeated, may summate until an impulse is initiated or a contraction ensues.

law, associative: (math.) the pattern illustrated by $a * (b * c) = (a * b) * c$, where a, b, and c, represent members of a set and $*$ a particular operation defined on that set; if the pattern fits for every three members of a set, the operation is said to be associative in that set; for example, addition in the set of integers is associative since $a + (b + c) = (a + b) + c$ for any three integers chosen as a, b, and c.

law, Bernoulli's: *syn.* **Bernoulli's theorem.**

law, business: (1) the branch of law that regulates business transactions; (2) a subject taught in secondary school and college, dealing with the laws governing business and emphasizing contracts and their special applications, as in the sale of goods, bailments, insurance, leasing and sale of real estate, partnerships, and corporations. *Syn.* **commercial law.**

law, cancellation: for real numbers, one of two laws, the additive cancellation law, which states that if $a + b = a + c$, then $b = c$, and the multiplicative cancellation law, which states that if $a \times b = a \times c$ and $a \neq 0$, then $b = c$ (a, b, and c, being real numbers).

law, canon: *see* **canon law.**

law, commercial: (obsoles.) *syn.* **law, business.**

law, common: legal principles derived from Anglo-Saxon custom; the "unwritten" law.

law, commutative: (math.) the pattern illustrated by $a * b = b * a$, where a and b represent members of a set and $*$ a particular operation defined on that set; if the pattern fits for every pair of members of a set, the operation is said to be commutative in that set; for example, addition in the set of integers is commutative, since $a + b = b + a$ for every pair of integers chosen as a and b.

law, directory: a statute or part of a statute interpreted as imposing a duty upon an officer or board, but in a somewhat less imperious sense than does a *mandatory* statute; thus, the obligation may be absolute unless circumstances make it apparently unwise or untimely; or subsidiary details prescribed as to the manner of execution of a mandatory duty may be adjudged to be of such small consequence as to be nonessential and construed to be directory only and not mandatory. (Violation of a directory statute does not usually render a transaction null and void, as does violation of a mandatory statute.)

law, distributive: the pattern illustrated by $a * (b \cdot c) = (a * b) \cdot (a * c)$ and $(b \cdot c) *_a = (b * a) \cdot (c * a)$, where $*$ b, and c, represent members of some set and $*$ and $\cdot$ two particular operations; if the first pattern fits for every three members of a set, the operation $*$ is said to be left-distributive over 0 in that set; if the second pattern fits, the operation $*$ is said to be right-distributive over 0 in the set; multiplication in the integers is both left- and right-distributive over addition, because $a(b + c) = (ab) + (ac)$ for every three integers chosen as a, b, and c; however, in the set of positive rational numbers, division is right-distributive but not left-distributive, since $(6 + 8) \div 2 = (6 \div 2) + (8 \div 2)$ but $2 \div (6 + 8) \neq (2 \div 6) + (2 \div 8)$.

law, Emmert's: a law which states that the projection distance and the original stimulus distance determine and are directly proportional to the size of the afterimage.

law, ex post facto: (Lat., lit., "after the fact") generally, a law which makes an act illegal prior to the adoption of the law.

law, fair trade: a Federal, state, or local law which establishes a minimum price for a specific product or service.

law, Fechner's: a restatement of Weber's law, more elegant but less usable; it now reads, "The sensation is proportional to the logarithm of the stimulus"; where C is the constant, the equation takes the form: sensation equals log stimulus.

law, frontier of: a current social issue for which differing decisions-in-law may be found; for example, civil rights cases.

law, Hamiltonian philosophy of: *see* **philosophy of law, Hamiltonian.**

law, Hellin's: a law according to which the frequency of triplets, quadruplets, quintuplets, etc., in a large population, may be predicted quite accurately if the frequency of twins and the total number of births in this population for the same period are known; the number of births B is divided by the number of twins T to give P; then B/P^2 = number of triplets, B/P^3 = number of quadruplets, B/P^4 = number of quintuplets; predictions according to this principle have proved remarkably accurate.

law, judicial: that body of knowledge which has accumulated through decisions of the courts.

law library: *see* **library, law.**

law, mandatory: a statute imposing a duty upon an officer or board in such manner that the obligation is absolute and unequivocal, as distinguished from a permissive or directory law, either of which leaves something to the discretion of the officer or board. (Use of the words *shall* or *must* in the statute normally indicates that it is mandatory, but this is not an infallible test. Violation of a mandatory statute renders a transaction null and void.)

law, moral: *See* **moral law.**

law, natural: *see* **natural law.**

Law of 1647: *see* **Deluder Act.**

law of ancestral inheritance: *see* **inheritance, law of ancestral.**

law of assimilation: *syn.* **generalization, stimulus.**

law of averages: the statistical law that the stability of a statistic tends to increase as the number of observations on which it is based is increased.

law of belonging: a term proposed by Thorndike (1931) to describe the relationships between the elements of a sentence; things that belong together are more easily remembered than things that do not; separate elements take on or have belongingness to the degree that their temporal or spatial occurrence presents to the learner an integrated whole, that is, the perceived meaning (set, attitude, and the relative shifts of such) as well as the strength of long-standing associations is involved.

law of context: the principle that words, phrases, or statements take on meaning in relation to the situation in which they are found.

law of contiguity: a principle of learning which states that if a stimulus and a response occur closely together, in time they become maximally associated.

law of contradiction: one of the so-called laws of thought. *See* **contradiction, principle of.**

law of convention: a regulation imposed upon men and society that is man-made.

law of developmental direction: *see* **developmental direction, law of.**

law of disuse: a law of learning which states that the less frequently a connection between a situation and a response is exercised, the more difficult it will be to recall the connection, other things being equal. *Syn.* **law of exercise; law of frequency; law of repetition.**

law of economy: *syn.* **law of parsimony.**

law of effect: the principle that associations between a stimulus and a response are strengthened when the response is successful or rewarding, but not weakened when the response leads to unpleasant consequences.

law of error: *see* **error, law of.**

law of exercise: *syn.* **law of disuse.**

law of field properties: a system of concepts and explanations referring to general and specific characteristics of psychosocial fields or environments of individuals or groups.

law of fixation: *see* **fixation, law of.**

law of frequency: *syn.* **law of disuse.**

law of generalization: *see* **generalization, law of.**

law of identity: the first of the three laws of reason, formulated propositionally (logically) as "A is A," and metaphysically as "Whatever is, is"; to be distinguished from the principle of *cognitive identity* which refers to the sameness between concepts and things.

law of intensity: a law of learning which holds that a vivid, dramatic, or exciting learning experience teaches more than a routine or boring experience; for example, a student can gain more from seeing the play "Macbeth" performed than from just a reading of it.

law of least action: the principle that an action or a response, to occur at all, follows that path or course resulting in the least expenditure of energy per unit of time, under the existing conditions; based (a) on the well-known fact that otherwise the path or course would be indeterminate and unpredictable and (b) on empirical evidence.

law of mass action: (Lashley) a law which states that the efficiency of performance of any complex activity is reduced in proportion to the amount of brain injury, or mass of cortex destroyed, and is not dependent upon the integrity of any particular region.

law of parsimony: the position of William of Ockham (flourished about 1300 A.D.) that understanding becomes clearer as a variety of effects can be explained with very few principles and, conversely, understanding of phenomena is least complete when a different principle is required to explain every observation. *Syn.* **law of economy; Occam's razor.**

law of primacy: a law of learning which states that anything learned first often creates such a strong impression as to be almost unshakable; for the teacher, this means that what he teaches must be right the first time, and for the student, what he learns first must be right; thus if a piano pupil learns incorrect finger positions, his teacher will have a difficult task unteaching the bad habits and reteaching good ones.

law of readiness: a principle advanced by Thorndike, which may be stated briefly as follows: When an individual is ready to act in a particular way, it is satisfying to do so, and annoying not do to so; conversely, when an individual is not ready to act in a particular way, to do so is annoying.

law of recency: a law of learning which states that, other factors being equal, things most recently learned will be most effectively recalled.

law of repetition: *syn.* **law of disuse.**

law of similarity: *syn.* **generalization, stimulus.**

law of single variable: *see* **single variable, law of.**

law of statistical regularity for large numbers: *see* **statistical regularity for large numbers, law of.**

law of the press: laws and court decisions involving publications, concerning libel, contempt of court, right of privacy, constitutional guarantees, freedom of the press, copyright, etc.

law, positive: *see* **moral law.**

law, school: that branch of law which relates to schools and school districts.

law school: a school or college, formerly frequently independent but now almost universally a part of a university, which prepares students who have completed baccalaureate programs to be attorneys; formerly the typical degree granted was *bachelor of laws* (LL.B.) but current trend is to award *doctor of jurisprudence* (J.D.).

law, scientific: a statement of relations accepted as invariable within the range of usual observations; the term is not entirely acceptable in science, for it carries the anthropomorphic connotation of compulsory behavior. *See* principle, scientific.

law, statutory: that body of knowledge arising from the passing of bills by the legislative branch of government.

law, substantive: law, the purpose of which is the setting of duties and rights.

law, sumptuary: any law, the purpose of which is restraint of luxury and excessive expenditure.

law, Weber's: in comparing magnitudes we perceive the ratio of the magnitudes of the stimuli rather than the arithmetical difference; the general equation is: $\Delta s/s$ equals W, where delta is the increment of the stimulus, and W is the so-called Weber fraction.

lawful employment: *see* legal work.

laws, consumer: laws passed to protect the consumer, such as pure food and drug laws, meat inspection laws, and truth in lending and truth in packaging laws.

laws of the Twelve Tables: a set of Roman laws, adopted in 451 and 449 B.C., and subsequently used in Roman schools as textual content in teaching reading and writing.

lay: *syn.* secular.

lay advisory committee: *syn.* advisory committee.

lay leader: *see* leader, lay.

lay reader: *see* reader, lay.

lay teacher: a teacher in a religious school who is not a member of a sisterhood or brotherhood or of the clergy.

layout: (1) a comprehensive provision and arrangement of facilities; (2) (gymnastics) a position of the body in which the body is fully extended; (3) (audiovis. ed.) a visualized plan for a display, poster, bulletin board, publication, or chalkboard presentation; usually done to scale and with sufficient detail to indicate how the final product will appear.

layout, plant: (school admin.) the function of determining the physical relationships between the operations that must be performed on parts and assemblies and such physical performance factors as plant equipment, storage areas, materials handling equipment, and other facilities; a function of process planning.

layout sheet, operation: *see* operation layout sheet.

lead: (typography) a thin strip of metal used in printing to separate lines of type; when the word lead is used alone, it usually means a two-point lead.

lead in item: *see* item, lead in.

lead time: *see* time, lead.

lead up game: *see* game, lead up.

leaded: pertaining to printed matter having leads between the lines; the number of leads determines the space between the lines.

leader: (photog.) blank film or tape attached to the beginning or end of a reel of film or tape; used in threading the projector, camera, or recorder.

leader, Academy: the leader specified by the Academy of Motion Picture Arts and Sciences as standard for motion-picture prints for distribution in theaters and television stations, and commonly placed on 35- and 16-mm film by request; use of this leader permits smooth, unnoticeable changeovers from one reel to another during the running of the film. *See* leader.

leader, adult: a person whose primary responsibility is to help the members of a group work together effectively for the achievement of group goals. *See* leader, lay.

leader, community: *see* community leader.

leader, group: *see* group leader.

leader, lay: a participant in a group or organization who is appointed or otherwise selected to assume the primary responsibility of helping other participants to work together effectively in achieving group or organizational goals. *See* leader, adult.

leader, recognized: (group development) a person who is perceived by an individual or the group as being able to help provide the means they desire to use to identify or attain their goal. *Dist. f.* leader, status.

leader, status: a person who by reason of appointment, election, or title is identified as a leader within the structuring of a group or a public; to be contrasted with natural leader. *Dist. f.* leader, recognized.

leader status: *see* status, leader.

leader tape: *see* tape, leader.

leaderless group discussion: *see* discussion, leaderless group.

leaderless psychodrama: *see* role-playing, leaderless.

leaderless role-playing: *see* role-playing, leaderless.

leadership: (1) the ability and readiness to inspire, guide, direct, or manage others; (2) the role of interpreter of the interests and objectives of a group, the group recognizing and accepting the interpreter as spokesman.

leadership camp: *see* camp, leadership.

leadership honor society: *see* honor society, leadership.

leadership, permissive: (admin.) leadership by a person based on both power and ability to lead but with emphasis on the power of position which is implied but not directly used.

leadership, persuasive: (admin.) leadership by a person based on ability, understanding, and sensitivity rather than on power of position to accomplish the desired ends.

leadership style: mode of performance of an educational official; often used in reference to a school principal, whose performance may be judged according to various models, such as (*a*) the charismatic leader, who is interested in keeping attention focused primarily on himself, (*b*) the authoritarian leader, who claims his power not through personal endowments but through his office, and (*c*) the therapeutic leader, who frequently finds it difficult to make decisions for fear of hurting someone's feelings.

leadership, supervisory: *see* supervisory leadership.

leadership training: *see* training, leadership.

leading eye: *syn.* eye, dominant.

leap meter: a device that records the height of a vertical jump.

learned behavior: *see* behavior, learned.

learned response: *syn.* response, acquired.

learner, alien: *see* student, foreign.

learner-centered instruction: *see* instruction, programmed.

learner, slow: (1) a child who exhibits slight intellectual retardation, requires adaptations of instruction, and is slightly below average in learning ability; usually remains in regular class; (2) in terms of intelligence quotient (IQ), a pupil who falls within the range from 75 to 89. *See* mental retardation, degree of; retardation, mental.

learner, student: *syn.* trainee, student.

learning: change in response or behavior (such as innovation, elimination, or modification of responses, involving some degree of permanence), caused partly or wholly by experience, such "experience" being in the main conscious, but sometimes including significant unconscious components, as is common in *motor learning* or in reaction to unrecognized or subliminal stimuli; includes behavior changes in the emotional sphere, but more commonly refers to the acquisition of symbolic knowledge or motor skills; does not include physiological changes, such as fatigue, or temporary sensory resistance or nonfunctioning after continued stimulation. *Contr. w.* maturation.

learning ability: *see* ability, learning.

learning, abstract: learning not associated with any particular object or any concrete experience, involving adequate responses in situations concerned with concepts and symbols.

learning, acquiescent: that kind of learning which is passive in nature, the senses and the mind being passive functions that receive or absorb the stimulation of the objective world; learning concerned with conserving the past rather than active participation in reconstructing experiences.

learning, all-or-none: learning considered as taking place in a single trial.

learning aptitude: *see* **aptitude, learning.**

learning, associate: that which is learned incidentally or by implication or connection.

learning, association theory of: *see* **psychology, association.**

learning, associational: the acquiring of response patterns through their perceptual or meaningful connection with other facts and situations. *See* **connectionism; psychology, association.**

learning, book: the form of experience that is obtained vicariously through reading.

learning capacity: *see* **capacity, learning.**

learning center: *see* **center, learning.**

learning, collateral: *syn.* **learning, concomitant.**

learning, concomitant: learning in a casual manner, without the intent to learn. *Syn.* **collateral learning.**

learning, cooperative: changes in behavior resulting wholly or in part from shared experiences of two or more persons.

learning curve: *see* **curve, learning.**

learning-curve score: *see* **score, learning-curve.**

learning, cyclical motor: changes in ability to control muscles of the body characterized by spurts toward more mature behavior with temporary regression.

learning, developmental factors in: the acquisition of new skills, concepts, etc., in view of development which may be considered as a continual, orderly sequence of conditions that creates actions, new motives for actions, and eventual patterns of behavior.

learning difficulty: (sp.) the degree to which a given word is hard to learn to spell; determined by the amount of time or effort required for learning the word or by the percentage of pupils who learn the word under normal conditions.

learning, directed: learning guided and aided by the teacher, generally by means of suggestions, outlines, or problems.

learning disability: *see* **disability, learning.**

learning, discovery: (1) an instructional procedure which involves (*a*) some teaching act, formal or informal, in which learning takes place, (*b*) confrontation of learners with problem situations that create bafflement and start the process of inquiry, (*c*) possibly, withholding certain kinds of information and certain kinds of generalizations to challenge search behavior and to preserve the opportunity for autonomous exploration and experimentation, (*d*) the act of discovery or the moment of insight when the learner grasps the organizing principle so that he sees the relationships among the facts before him, understands the cause of the phenomenon, and relates what he sees to his prior knowledge, and (*e*) verbalization of a generalization based on principles, rules, ideas, and underlying generalizations; (2) broadly, the learning of principles or concepts which occurs as a generalization of experiences by the individual learner in the absence of direct telling by someone else; may be one of the consequences of so-called inductive or Socratic teaching; some believe it to be of greater transfer value and retained better than passive or reception learning.

learning, discrimination: a form of perceptual learning in which the individual can differentiate between different stimuli that in more difficult cases are quite similar; for example, a child must learn to discriminate between the sounds *pin, pen,* and *pan,* all of which to the untrained ear may be very similar. *See* **hypothesis, continuity.**

learning disorder: *see* **disorder, learning.**

learning, distributed: (1) the technique or method of learning by practicing or studying at definite and stated intervals in contrast to spending the same amount of time on the material all at one time; introduction of rest periods into the practice required for learning; (2) a principle of learning according to which there is evidence that on some types of material fewer repetitions are required when practice is distributed over a longer period of time.

learning environment: *see* **environment, learning.**

learning, errorless: the aim in some forms of programmed learning whereby the attempt is made to present material

in small steps with a high degree of redundancy so that learning is virtually errorless.

learning exercise: *see* **exercise, learning.**

learning experience: *see* **experience, learning.**

learning, field theory of: a theory of learning that emphasizes response to wholes or the effect of the whole upon the response to a part. *See* **learning, gestalt theory of.**

learning, gestalt theory of: a theory of learning that originated in Germany in the early twentieth century; introduced into the United States in the 1920s, it defines learning as the reorganization of the learner's perceptual or psychological world—his *field. See* **gestalt.**

learning, heuristic: a method of learning in which the student has the basic responsibility for solving problems that confront him; the term is rarely used in the United States. *See* **development method; discovery learning; problem method.**

learning, ideational: learning concerned with ideas, concepts, and mental associations, as distinguished from motor learning.

learning, incidental: learning that occurs in addition to what is specifically motivated or directed by means of explicit instructions to learn.

learning, instrumental: connotes learning at a time when it is functional and the learner recognizes a need for it.

learning, intentional: purposive learning according to a predetermined pattern. *Contr. w.* **learning, incidental.**

learning, interpolated: (1) learning that is inferred as having occurred between two states of observed development; (2) the process of acquiring additional knowledge and skills between two observed stages of learning.

learning kit: *see* **kit of learning materials.**

learning laboratory, electronic: *see* **laboratory, electronic learning.**

learning, latent: learning without apparent motivation or reinforcement, where a relatively long period of time elapses between the stimulus and the response or before the awareness of learning as evidenced by performance.

learning, mass: a situation in which the learning process involves a large number of people at the same time, as, for example, a television audience.

learning materials, kit of: *see* **kit of learning materials.**

learning, motor: learning in which the learner achieves new facility in the performance of bodily movements as a result of specific practice; may be known to be accompanied or preceded by ideas, or may be apparently independent of ideas; to be distinguished from improvement of function resulting from maturation. *Contr. w.* **learning, ideational.**

learning, operational: a change in performance resulting from practice or experience.

learning opportunities: the means available in the school curriculum through which the students learn; examples are experiences such as individualized instruction, small-group instruction, team teaching, interaction processes between teacher and learner, and background referents which include knowledge, society, and the learner himself.

learning outcome, desired: *see* **outcome, desired learning.**

learning, paired-associate: learning in which elements (words, designs, things, etc.) when learned in pairs become associated so that when one is presented as a stimulus, the other is recalled.

learning, part: the act or process of acquiring mastery of a whole unit by dividing it into parts and learning each separately. *Contr. w.* **learning, whole.**

learning, perceptual: learning that takes place largely or entirely through the senses.

learning plateau: a period during which there is no evidence of progress in learning. *See* **curve, learning.**

learning, process: behavior change concerned mainly with the acquisition of new strategies and methods.

learning, programmed: *see* **instruction, programmed.**

learning, pursuit rotor: learning in the measurement of which the individual is asked to trace with a stylus a relatively fast-moving target; learning is measured by the total time spent in contact with the target during successive practice periods. *See* **pursuitmeter.**

learning, rational: the acquiring of skills and information that fit into or agree with larger, universally or generally accepted experience patterns, with the emphasis on the discovery of new relations.

learning readiness: *see* **readiness, learning.**

learning resources center: *see* **center, learning resources.**

learning, rote: (1) acquiring the ability to reproduce meaningless materials such as digits or nonsense syllables; (2) learning by memorizing, with little attention to meaning.

learning, serial-anticipation: the most frequent method of presentation of verbal materials wherein the individual is presented with a series of items, one at a time, and is asked to associate each item with that following so that he can anticipate each succeeding item.

learning, serial verbal: the technique of presenting verbal materials as a series of items to be learned.

learning set: *see* **set, learning.**

learning, social: knowledge or skills that are acquired by the individual in the process of adjusting to a social environment.

learning station: *see* **station, learning.**

learning strategies: rules, principles, and procedures acquired in learning, often discovered by the learner himself and applicable in other learnings. *See* **learning to learn.**

learning, team: (1) a learning procedure consisting of two or three pupils working together without the teacher; (2) use of a tutorial group with one pupil acting as teacher for several others. *Syn.* **team grouping.**

learning to learn: an effect noted when the learning of successive tasks of the same type is accompanied by an increase in the speed of learning; a phenomenon usually mediated through some improvement in methods of work. *Syn.* **deuterolearning.**

learning, trial-and-error: a mode of learning in which the learner tries various responses in a somewhat random fashion until one response or combination of responses happens to succeed or bring satisfaction; this response or combination of responses is more frequently repeated with increasing sureness in subsequent trials, while the unnecessary or failing responses are gradually lessened in their frequency of occurrence.

learning unit: *syn.* **unit** (1) and (2).

learning, verbal: the process of acquiring the language skills necessary to respond adequately in a situation requiring the communication of thought.

learning, visual: any learning that takes place through sense impressions gathered through the eyes.

learning, whole: the act or process of acquiring mastery of a whole unit by going over all the material from beginning to end repeatedly until it is learned. *Contr. w.* **learning, part.**

learnings, common: *see* **common learnings.**

learnings, consumer: economic knowledge, attitudes, understandings, and skills acquired and developed by the consumer for use in his daily life.

learnings, general related: *syn.* **competencies, general occupational.**

learnings, occupational relations: *syn.* **competencies, general occupational.**

leased bus: *see* **bus, leased.**

least action, law of: *see* **law of least action.**

least noticeable difference: the least difference in the strength of a stimulus or of a response that an observer or tester is capable of detecting.

least squares, method of: a method of fitting a curve to a series of quantitative data so that the sum of squares of deviations from the curve is a minimum.

leather: (ind. arts) the study of leather and related materials including the tools and processes used to produce leather products; learning experiences generally include experimenting with, designing, constructing, and evaluating products.

leave of absence: an authorized extended absence of a teacher from a school system that does not affect tenure or contract. *See* **sabbatical teaching year.**

leave, sabbatical: *see* **sabbatical teaching year.**

leaver, school: *syn.* **dropout; early school leaver.**

leaving examination: *see* **examination, leaving.**

lectern: a reading desk in a church used especially for reading lessons from the Bible during the course of a worship service. *See* **pulpit.**

lection: *see* **lesson** (4).

lecture: a method of teaching by which the instructor gives an oral presentation of facts or principles, the class usually being responsible for taking notes; usually implies little or no class participation, such as questioning or discussion during the class period.

lecture bureau: an organization, usually proprietary, that provides the services of lecturers, musicians, and entertainers for forums, clubs, and institutes.

lecture course: *see* **course, lecture.**

lecture-demonstration method: an instructional procedure in which the verbal message is accompanied by the use of apparatus to illustrate principles, determine or verify facts, clarify difficult parts, or test for comprehension of the material under discussion.

lecture method: an instructional procedure by which the lecturer seeks to create interest, to influence, stimulate, or mold opinion, to promote activity, to impart information, or to develop critical thinking, largely by the use of the verbal message, with a minimum of class participation; illustrations, maps, charts, or other visual aids may be employed to supplement the oral technique.

lecture room: a room for class lectures, equipped with tablet armchairs or other types of seats. (Science lecture rooms are often provided with seats in tiers, rising toward the rear of the room, to give a better view of processes and results in lecture demonstrations.)

lecture series: (1) a series of public addresses or classroom presentations by a speaker or group of speakers, dealing with a number of related or associated topics; (2) a technical term used in the university extension field to designate a regular succession of meetings for enrolled groups among whom some may be given academic credit upon examination.

lecturer: a member of a faculty, usually without professorial status, employed for a limited time to offer instruction or to lecture to a class or group of students but not to carry out all the functions of a regularly employed member of the faculty. *Contr. w.* **lecturer** (Education in England and Wales).

ledger: a book in which are entered, individually or in summary, all transactions recorded in the journals, under appropriate accounts.

ledger approach: *syn.* **account approach.**

ledger, stores: *syn.* **record, balance-of-stores.**

left-eyedness: *see* **eyedness, left-.**

left-handedness: *see* **handedness, left-.**

left-to-right progression: *see* **progression, left-to-right.**

leg length: the total height minus the sitting height, one of the especially significant anthropometric measures.

legal absence: *see* **absence, legal.**

legal blindness: *see* **blindness, legal.**

legal disability: lack of legal capacity to perform an act.

legal education, continuing: *see* **continuing professional education.**

legal liability: *see* **liability, legal.**

legal manual: *see* **manual, legal.**

legal notice: an official statement sent by the school authorities to the parents or guardian in cases of a child's (or children's) inexcusable absence from school, in which a warning is given as to final consequences of failure to attend school.

legal person: the natural persons who make up a corporation, regarded collectively. *See* **corporate body.**

legal remedy: a remedy at law, as distinguished from a remedy in equity; a suit or proceeding in a court of justice; the means or method by which one may recover his rights or redress his wrongs; for example, the ordinary legal remedy for breach of a private contract is a judgment for damages, while the equitable remedy, if available, is a decree of specific performance.

legal residence: the officially recognized place of abode or address of a person, whether the person is actually and currently living there or not. (In the case of a child, the home of his parents or guardian.)

legal work: those activities in which youths of given ages may engage for pay according to current legislation, state or Federal. (In occupations governed by interstate commerce, these activities are fairly well defined; in other occupations, the activities are as varied as are the requirements of the child-labor laws of the 50 states.)

legasthenia (leg′əs·thē′ni·ə): a condition chracterized by inability to associate meanings with or to derive meanings from printed or written symbols; generally due to a lack of training rather than to a physical or mental defect.

legibility: the quality of handwriting that makes it easily readable, due to uniformity in slope, spacing, alignment, and distinct letter form.

legislation, permissive: *see* **permissive legislation.**

legislation, recreation: the legal authority for the operation of public recreation programs granted to local communities by Federal or state governments.

legislation, social: *see* **social legislation.**

legislative control of curriculum: the power of the state legislature to prescribe the nature of school studies permitted or made obligatory in the schools of the state.

legislative power, delegation of: *see* **delegation of legislative power.**

legislative reference library: *see* **library, legislative reference.**

Lehr- und Lernfreiheit (lär ōōnt lärn′frī′hĭt): (Ger., lit., "teaching and learning freedom") a principle, first promulgated by Gundling at the University of Halle in 1711, that some claim, but others doubt, is the basis for what is now known as *academic freedom,* or the right to be free to discover and follow the truth wherever it may lead.

leisure: time beyond that required, organically, for existence and subsistence; time to choose—discretionary time, when the feeling of compulsion should be minimal.

leisure hour school: *syn.* **evening school** (2).

leisure reading: *see* **reading, leisure.**

Leiter international performance scale: *see* **scale, Leiter international performance.**

length cue clue: *see* **clue, length cue.**

length of route, one-way: (pup. trans.) the distance from the point where the first pupil boards the bus, by way of designated roads, to the point where the pupils are discharged, usually at a school.

lens, anamorphic: a lens designed to distort an image in a systematic way, usually by means of an element or elements having cylindrical rather than the usual spherical surfaces; the object usually is to obtain a wide-screen image by projecting such a picture through a correcting lens having the same characteristics as the lens used on the camera.

lens, camera: a special type of transparent substance, usually glass, ground so as to focus light rays onto a film.

lens, projection: a special type of transparent substance, usually glass, ground so as to focus light rays coming from a projector onto any desired surface.

lens speed: the ability of a lens to pass light; a fast lens would be rated f. 1.4; a much slower lens might be designated as f. 8; the larger the f number, the slower the lens. *See* **f. number.**

lens, telephoto: a camera lens which permits a closer view of a subject than would be obtained by a normal lens from the same position.

lens turret: a revolving lens mount for the rapid changing of lenses on a camera.

lens, zoom: a camera lens of variable magnification which permits a smooth change of subject coverage between distance and close-up without changing the camera position.

lenticular screen: *see* **screen, lenticular.**

leptokurtic (lep′tō·kēr′tik): a term describing a frequency curve that is more highly peaked than the normal probability curve. *See* **kurtosis.**

leptokurtosis (lep′tō·kēr·tō′sis): the quality of being leptokurtic. *See* **leptokurtic.**

lesion, brain: *see* **brain lesion.**

"less than" ogive: *see* **ogive, "less than."**

lesson: (1) a short period of instruction devoted to a specific limited topic, skill, or idea; (2) the materials to be studied before or during such a period; (3) what is learned during such a period of instruction; (4) (relig. ed.) a portion of the Bible read in the course of a church service for the edification of the congregation, often serving as the basis of subsequent explication in sermon or homily; *syn.* **lection.**

lesson assignment: *see* **assignment, lesson.**

lesson, broadcast: a radio or television program intended specifically as a medium of instruction for classroom use; logically involves preparation, listening, and follow-up procedures. *See* **broadcast, classroom; lesson, demonstration.**

lesson, broadcast demonstration: (1) a broadcast of actual classroom procedure, usually produced as a public relations program in order to keep parents informed about what happens in a school; (2) a carefully planned model lesson, broadcast as a means of motivating the use of better instructional procedures by teachers in service.

lesson, deductive: a type of lesson developed by the deductive method in which the class draws inferences from generalizations and then consults books to determine how closely the inferences approach the facts; used frequently in geography and history. *Contr. w.* **lesson, inductive.**

lesson, demonstration: the learning and instruction activities that are used in a demonstration class for observation by a group of prospective or experienced teachers. *See* **class, demonstration.**

lesson, derived: a lesson based on another lesson previously studied by or presented to the class.

lesson, developmental: a lesson based on either the inductive or the deductive method.

lesson, disciplinary: a type of lesson, advocated by early twentieth century writers on educational methods, to be given regularly at a definite period of the school day and designed to prevent or correct "wrong" attitudes and actions or to encourage or establish "right" behavior; based on developing approved attitudes or actions through (*a*) the exemplary conduct of the teacher; (*b*) selective control of the ideas with which the pupils come into contact; or (*c*) stimulation, suppression, or redirection of the pupils' action through rewards and punishments.

lesson, field: a lesson for student teachers or prospective or experienced teachers conducted through the use of the facilities of schools not under the direct control of the teacher-education institution. *See* **experience, field laboratory; observation, field.**

lesson guide, broadcast-: *see* **broadcast-lesson guide.**

lesson, illustrated: a teaching or learning unit in which comprehension is facilitated through the use of pictures, recordings, samples, or *realia.*

lesson, inductive: a type of lesson in which a number of particular cases are presented to the class, with a view to having the class develop a generalization or rule to cover all the particular cases; applicable to such studies as grammar, foreign languages, mathematics, and the sciences. *Contr. w.* **lesson, deductive.**

lesson, model: *syn.* **lesson, demonstration.**

lesson, music: an appointment between teacher and pupil during which the teacher listens to the music prepared by the pupil and guides and adjusts the pupil's interpretation, technical delivery, etc.

lesson objective: *see* objective, lesson.

lesson observation criteria: *see* criteria, lesson observation.

lesson period: *see* period, lesson.

lesson plan: a teaching outline of the important points of a lesson arranged in the order in which they are to be presented; may include objectives, points to be made, questions to ask, references to materials, assignments, etc.

lesson, practice: the class activities of one period of instruction conducted by a student teacher himself as part of the student-teaching program.

lesson, radio: a lesson, conducted in a classroom or assembly hall, in which the principal activity consists in listening to a radio program; traditionally involves three steps: (*a*) preparation, (*b*) listening, and (*c*) follow-up; may also include note taking by the pupils and activity on the part of the teacher, for example, pointing to places on maps, etc.

lesson, radio demonstration: *syn.* lesson, broadcast demonstration.

lesson, review: a lesson in which the class period is devoted to a reexamination of a large unit of work or body of material, generally before formulating final generalizations or as preparation for a test.

lesson, socialized: a lesson in which the teacher enables the students to discuss a problem informally among themselves or to dramatize it in the form in which it is found in life situations.

lesson, technical: a lesson on some phase of mathematics, science, drawing, etc., related to a given trade or occupation.

lesson, telecast: a televised broadcast lesson. *See* lesson, broadcast.

letter: an athletic award, the initial letter or letters of a school or college, to be worn on a sweater; denotes recognition of participation in an interscholastic or intercollegiate sport; sometimes also given as recognition of participation in debate or music or for success in scholarship in secondary schools.

letter, ascending: a letter that projects above the line in writing or printing, such as *l, h, k, b, d;* believed by some to be used by the reader in differentiating one word from another in visual analysis of word form.

letter, correctable: *see* correctable letter.

letter, descending: a letter that projects below the line in writing or printing, such as *y* or *g.*

letter, form: (bus. ed.) a letter prepared for use in situations that recur frequently; duplicated or printed in advance of intended use.

letter form: the way in which individual letters are written, usually in terms of comparison with an ideal or normal form.

letter, mailable: *see* mailable letter.

letter phonics: *see* phonics, letter.

letter phonogram: *see* phonogram, letter.

letter styles: (bus. ed.) distinct, recognized patterns or forms of business letters, such as idented, block, modified block, etc.

lettering pen, felt-tipped: a felt-tipped pen used for making charts, posters, labels, etc.

letters: a term sometimes used as part of the title of the liberal arts college of a university, such as college of arts and letters, or college of letters and science; in some universities refers to a special division, department, college, or school where the main concern is the advanced study of literature, *belles-lettres. See* college, liberal arts.

letters, dominant: letters in a word which theoretically give the major clues to its identity and recognition; consonants are said to be more dominant than vowels.

level: (1) (linguistics) the height to which the voice rises or falls in speaking; *see* pitch; stress; (2) (ed.) a stage of learning such as beginning, intermediate, or advanced.

level, application: *see* application level.

level, aspiration: *see* aspiration level.

level, basal reading: *see* reading level, basal.

level, capacity reading: *see* reading level, capacity.

level, checking: *see* checking level.

level, confidence: *see* confidence level.

level, fiducial: *syn.* confidence level.

level, grade: *see* grade level.

level, guidance: *see* guidance level.

level, hearing: *see* hearing level.

level, hearing comprehension: *see* comprehension level, hearing.

level, hearing threshold: *see* hearing loss (2).

level, independent reading: *see* reading level, independent.

level indicator: in an audio system, an electronic or electromechanical device for indicating signal intensity; most often a *VU meter,* a magic eye, or a neon bulb.

level, instructional reading: *see* reading level, instructional.

level, language learning: a stage in the study of a language; for example, children starting a language are said to be at the beginning level; the foreign language program in the elementary school may be considered the beginning or elementary level; the work of *FLES* "graduates" who continue a foreign language at the secondary school may then be termed the intermediate or secondary level.

level of address: *see* address, level of.

level of comprehension test: *see* test, level of comprehension.

level of confidence: *syn.* confidence level.

level of development: *see* development, level of.

level of difficulty: *see* difficulty, level of.

level of hearing, symbolic: *see* hearing, symbolic level of.

level of illumination: *see* illumination, level of.

level of intelligence: *see* intelligence, level of.

level of probability: *syn.* confidence level.

level-of-proficiency scaling: *see* scaling, level-of-proficiency.

level, postsecondary instructional: *see* instructional level, postsecondary.

level, probable capacity: *see* capacity level, probable.

level, reading: *see* reading level.

level, sensation: *see* sensation level.

level, significance: *see* significance level.

level, skill: *see* skill level.

leveling: (psych.) in perception or retention, reproduction of an object with greater symmetry or better form than it actually has. *See* sharpening.

levels of abstraction: *see* abstraction, levels of.

levels of attainment: *see* attainment, levels of.

levography: (as used by Strack) *syn.* mirror script.

Lewerenz readability formula: *see* readability formula, Lewerenz.

Lexian distribution: *syn.* distribution, Lexis.

Lexian ratio: *syn.* ratio, Lexis.

lexical listening: *see* listening, lexical.

lexical meaning: *see* meaning, lexical.

lexicography: the art of compiling dictionaries or the principles involved in this pursuit; includes listing of terms in a language and description of their meanings either in the same language or in translation into another language.

lexicology: that branch of learning dealing with the derivation, meaning, and use of words.

lexicon: a dictionary; used especially for a dictionary in which the terms listed are in Greek, Latin, or Hebrew.

Lexis distribution: *see* distribution, Lexis.

Lexis ratio: *see* ratio, Lexis.

liabilities: debts or other legal obligations arising out of transactions in the past that must be liquidated, renewed, or refunded at some future date. (NOTE: The term should be confined to items payable but not necessarily due; it does not include encumbrances.)

liability: actual or implied standard of conduct or responsibility under the law.

liability, board: a term used in reference to the fact that school boards, in their corporate capacity, are not liable in damages for injuries resulting from the torts of their officers, employees, or agents.

liability, contingent: an obligation which is not now fixed and absolute but which will become so in the case of some future and uncertain occurrence.

liability, legal: legal obligation usually stated in terms of money.

liability, personal: a term meaning, in general, that school board members are not personally liable for the torts of the district, or of the district's employees and agents; they have been held personally liable, however, when they acted in bad faith, with malice, from corrupt motives, with fraud, or when they exceeded their authority; courts have also held them liable where they failed or refused to perform ministerial or discretionary duties, and where they improperly performed ministerial duties that were imposed upon individual officers.

liability, school: the legal responsibility of the teacher, school board, or any of the officers or agents of a school in case of accidents occurring in the school, on the school property, or in activities under school supervision conducted away from school property.

liability, teacher: a term referring to the fact that teachers, like all other individuals, are liable in damages to pupils injured as a result of their tortious acts.

liability, tort: *see* **liability, board; liability, personal; liability, teacher; tort.**

libel: (law) any statement or representation, published without just cause or excuse, or by pictures, effigies, or other signs, tending to expose another to public hatred, contempt, or ridicule; also, the act, tort, or crime of publishing this. *Comp. w.* **slander.**

liberal adult education: *see* **adult education, liberal.**

liberal arts: (1) the branches of learning that constitute the curricula of college education as distinct from technical or professional education; *see* **letters;** (2) in earlier times, the branches of higher learning, so designated because among the Romans they were regarded as arts befitting freemen (artes liberales). *See* **liberal arts, seven.**

liberal arts college: *see* **college, liberal arts.**

liberal arts, seven: the standard medieval curriculum, divided into two parts: the *trivium,* or elementary group of three studies (grammar, rhetoric, and logic or dialectic), and the *quadrivium,* or higher group of four studies (arithmetic, geometry, astronomy, music).

liberal education: (1) in the philosophy of Aristotle, the education which one growing up to be a freeman needs in order to bring his manhood and freedom to perfection— education cultivating his soul's powers to perform "leisure" activities judged desirable for their own sake, like contemplation of scientific and philosophic truth, rather than activities of "occupation" or "recreation," judged desirable for the sake of something else to which they lead; (2) in the Middle Ages, the education then thought most effective for cultivating such powers—education in the *seven liberal arts;* (3) in the philosophy of John Dewey, liberating education—whatever education actually accomplishes, liberation for the students being educated, as judged by observable consequences in the quality of their future experience, rather than by any supposition that certain subjects of study always possess more power of liberation than others; (4) in contemporary nonphilosophic usage, any education accepted as relatively broad and general, rather than narrow and specialized, and as preparation for living rather than for earning a living, such as that offered by academic high schools or by liberal arts colleges.

liberalism: (1) an attitude favorable to moderate change and reform; (2) an attitude reflecting belief in individual liberty and substantial limitation of the powers of government; *contr. w.* **conservatism; radicalism;** (3) a social and political position that advocates intelligent governmental action for mental, physical, and social welfare, whether through limitations on government and industry, or through governmental support of welfare measures, or through government ownership of resources and means

of production (Liberal Party of New York); (4) the philosophy of education that advocates freedom of thought and speech and the development of the individual along the lines of his greatest interest and aptitude; (5) a movement in recent Protestantism emphasizing intellectual liberty and the ethical and spiritual content of Christianity; utilizes modern experimental methods in religious education (Soares, Bower, Elliot, Harkness); (6) the educational philosophy that the mind is liberated through disciplinary studies like those of the classical curriculum, especially logic, mathematics, formal languages, and metaphysics.

liberty: (1) freedom from all restraints that are not voluntarily assumed, but not to be construed as license to interfere with other people's liberty; (2) the right to move in space, to pursue self-chosen activities, and to express personal opinions.

liberty within limits: *see* **Montessori method.**

libidinal fixation: *see* **fixation, libidinal.**

libido (li•bī′dō, -bē′-): (1) lust or passion; (2) the sexual appetite; (3) (psychoan.) the energy derived from the life and death instincts; (4) (psychoan.) the energy released by operation of the sexual instinct.

libido, ego: *see* **ego libido.**

librarian assignment, school: *see* **assignment, school librarian.**

librarian certification: *see* **certification, librarian.**

librarian, class: *syn.* **librarian, classroom.**

librarian, classroom: a pupil or student appointed to keep in order the books on deposit in a classroom library and to issue them to readers or to serve as a representative of the classroom library in its relations with the school library. *Syn.* **class librarian.**

librarian, nonprofessional: a library staff member who has not successfully completed a prescribed course of study in an accredited library school. *See* **librarian, professional.**

librarian, professional: a term usually employed to distinguish a library staff member who has successfully completed a prescribed course of study in an accredited library school from those members of the library staff who have not had this formal training in the theory and practice of librarianship.

librarian, research: a member of a university library staff, holding one of the positions established experimentally by the Carnegie Corporation, who devotes his time to assisting faculty members in their research, the results of which are to be published.

librarian, school: a person, usually one trained in library science, who has charge of the school's library.

librarian, teacher: a person engaged part time in classroom teaching and part time as librarian, whose basic training and experience are in classroom teaching and who has also some training in library work.

librarian's certificate: *see* **certificate, librarian's.**

librarianship: a profession concerned with organizing collections of books and related materials in libraries and with placing these resources at the service of readers and other users.

library: (1) a building or room equipped for housing books and other materials of communication and for reading, listening, or viewing purposes; (2) an information center, audiovisual center, or instructional materials center the function of which is to collect and acquire information systematically and classify and store it, and, upon demand, retrieve it and assist in adapting it to the use to be made of the information; (3) a collection of books of various kinds; (4) a collection of films, recordings, etc.

library acquisition: *see* **acquisition, library.**

library adult education: *see* **adult education, library.**

library, adult education by public: *see* **adult education by public library.**

library agency, state: *see* **library commission.**

library association: *see* **association, library.**

library, audiovisual: a repository for equipment and materials that deal principally with learning by seeing and/or hearing such as pictures, films, records, etc.

library, authority: (mil. ed.) a library that maintains a collection of laws, regulations, orders, letters, etc., of a military service.

library automation: *see* **automation, library.**

library binding: *see* **binding, library.**

library, branch: (1) a building in which books are housed separately from the main library; (2) a collection of books housed at a place other than the main, or central, library.

library building: *see* **building, library.**

library card: *see* **card, library.**

library, Carnegie: any of the public library buildings donated by Andrew Carnegie to communities throughout the United States, Canada, and the British Isles. (Because of uniformity of architecture, this type of building is frequently referred to as a Carnegie library.)

library catalog: *see* **catalog, library.**

library, central: (1) a main library, as contrasted with a branch library; (2) a relatively large collection of books housed in one room of a school for the use of the whole school, as contrasted with the smaller collections housed in individual classrooms.

library, centralized: a collection in one building or room of all the books and other communicative materials of an educational institution.

library, children's: a library particularly for children, with books suited to younger readers.

library, circulating: one of the small groups of books and other materials owned by a county school district and sent in rotation to various schools of the district.

library circulation: *see* **circulation, library.**

library, classroom: (1) a semipermanent or a temporary collection of books deposited in a schoolroom by a public or a school library; *syn.* **classroom collection; classroom deposit; grade library; school deposit; schoolroom library;** (2) a group of books from a college library sent to a classroom for use by instructors and students.

library club: *see* **club, library.**

library collection: a collection of books on a particular subject.

library, college: (1) a library forming an integral part of a college, organized and administered to meet the needs of its students and faculty; (2) in a university library system, a library with a collection of books related to the work of a particular college and administered separately by the college or as a part of the university library.

library commission: (1) an organization created by a state to promote library service within the state by the establishment, organization, and supervision of public and, sometimes, school libraries and by the lending of books and other material to libraries and to communities without libraries (the term *state library agency* is replacing this term); (2) occasionally, a local library board.

library committee: (1) an unofficial group formed to create, support, or expand a library, or used for advisory purposes; (2) in a college or university library, a faculty committee to advise the librarian on matters of policy and board procedure.

library consultant: *see* **consultant, library.**

library cooperation: *see* **cooperation, library.**

library, county: a centrally administered library within a county, having such branches and depositories, library truck service, or other supplementary services as will best enable it to reach all the people within the county; commonly supported in whole or in part by county tax levy or from general funds.

library, curriculum: *syn.* **laboratory, curriculum materials.**

library, decentralized: a number of separate collections (called libraries) of the books belonging to an educational institution, grouped according to subject matter and housed separately in the various faculties, departments, or rooms of the institution. (Thus, in a university, there may be a law library, a medical library, etc.; in an elementary school, there may be a first-grade library, a fifth-grade library, etc.)

library, departmental: the library of a department or school of a university or college, such as a law library, an education library, or an engineering library; may be part of either a centralized or a decentralized library system.

library, depository: a library that receives a complete file of the documents of a particular governmental unit (national, state, etc.).

library, district: *syn.* **library, regional** (1).

library, divisional: (1) one of several libraries organized on broad subject lines within the total college or university library system; common subject divisions are the humanities, the social sciences, and science and technology, in each of which departmental lines are minimized in the interest of broader subject interests; (2) in some colleges or universities, used to describe libraries of departments, schools, or colleges.

library, dormitory: a library in a residence hall of a college or university that provides students with recreational reading and, sometimes, reference books and books for required reading.

library education: education or training of library personnel, including professional and nonprofessional personnel and technical aides.

library equipment: *see* **equipment, library.**

library extension: *see* **extension, library.**

library extension agency, state: *see* **extension agency, state library.**

library, film: an organized collection of motion pictures and other films, photographs, slides, and other photographic items for public or private use.

library for the blind: a distributing agency that lends embossed books and talking books to blind persons within a given area under a free mailing permit.

library, general: (1) a library not limited to a particular field or special subject; (2) the main library of a university library system.

library, government: a library in a government department or office, related to the needs of the government agency in the composition of its collections and in its service functions.

library, grade: *syn.* **library, classroom** (1).

library guide: a handbook designed to acquaint users with the functions and facilities of the library, containing such information as rules and regulations, location of rooms, library hours, services and resources of the library, and suggestions concerning the nature and use of the card catalog, indexes, and reference works.

library, hospital: *see* **library, medical.**

library hour: *see* **period, library.**

library, law: a library concerned specifically with providing information and service to users interested in legal materials and practice.

library, legislative reference: a library providing assistance in problems of government and legislation, especially in connection with proposed or pending legislation, sometimes including the drafting of bills.

library logistics: *see* **logistics, library.**

library, medical: a library devoted to information and related services in the science and practice of medicine.

library, occupational information: a file and catalog of occupational materials of a varied character, such as pamphlets, college and university catalogs, mimeographed documents, magazine articles, and unbound materials in heavy manila folders.

Library of Congress classification: *see* **classification, Library of Congress.**

Library of Congress foreign acquisition program: *see* **program, Library of Congress foreign acquisition.**

library, package: a compact collection of magazine clippings, pamphlets, bulletins, reports, and occasionally books, sent by mail or otherwise distributed for loan by libraries, library commissions, university extension divisions, and Federal government agencies. *See* **information service.**

library period: *see* **period, library.**

library program: *see* **program, library.**

library, public: a library that serves all residents of a community, district, or region and receives all or part of its financial support from public funds.

library reading room: *see* **reading room, library.**

library, reference: (1) a library with either a general collection or a collection limited to a special field, organized for consultation and research, and generally noncirculating; (2) a library whose books may not be taken from the library.

library reference service: *see* **reference service, library.**

library, regional: (1) a public library serving a group of communities, or several counties, and supported in whole or in part by public funds from the governmental units served and/or from the state or province; sometimes known as *district library;* (2) 28 distributing libraries for the Library of Congress in lending Braille, Moon-type, or talking-book records to the blind; *see* **library for the blind.**

library report: *see* **report, library.**

library, research: a library provided with specialized material, where exhaustive investigation can be carried on, in a particular field, as in a technological library, or in several fields, as in a university library.

library routine: *see* **routine, library.**

library, rural school traveling: a collection of books, art, phonograph records, and similar learning aids (usually purchased and sent out by the state, county, or district or by the extension departments of state universities or other agencies) that may be subscribed for by the individual schools in the area served. (A school, as a rule, receives several such collections during the year, keeping each for a limited period of time.)

library, school: (1) an instructional space designed or adapted as a place for study and reading and for the custody, circulation, and administration of a collection of books, manuscripts, and periodicals kept for the use of the student body but not for sale; study carrels and audiovisual, storage, and other service areas opening into and serving as adjuncts to a particular library are considered parts of the library area; (2) in a university, a collection of books and other materials related to the work of a particular school or college, administered separately by the school or college or as part of the university library.

library school: a professional school, department, or division organized and maintained by an institution of higher education for the purpose of preparing students for entrance into the library profession.

library, school branch: a library agency in a school building, administered by a public library and/or a board of education for the use of students and teachers and, frequently, for adults of the neighborhood.

library, school district: (1) formerly, a tax-supported library established in a school district for the use of schools and free to all residents of the district; *syn.* **district library;** (2) a public library established and financially supported by action of a school district for the use of all residents of a district and supervised by a local board of education or by a separate library board under the board of education.

library school, graduate: (1) a school for education in librarianship that has met minimum standards of the Board of Education for Librarianship of the American Library Association by being connected with a graduate degree-conferring institution and meeting requirements with respect to faculty, curriculum, and other factors; offers at least a basic professional program for librarianship covering a minimum of five academic years of study beyond the secondary school; *see* **library school, type I; library school, type II;** (2) less exactly, a school for education in librarianship requiring a college degree for entrance; (3) the library school of the University of Chicago, which requires for admission an approved bachelor's degree or its equivalent, 1 year of training in a library school, and other requisites and offers advanced work leading to the degrees of master of arts and doctor of philosophy.

library school, junior undergraduate: a school for education in librarianship that met minimum standards of the Board of Education for Librarianship of the American Library Association from 1925 to 1933 by being connected or affiliated with an approved library, college, or university, requiring for entrance 1 year of college work, and meeting other requirements with respect to faculty, curriculum, and other factors. *See* **library school, type III.**

library school, senior undergraduate: a school for education in librarianship that met minimum standards of the Board of Education for Librarianship of the American Library Association from 1925 to 1933 by being connected with a degree-conferring institution, requiring for entrance 3 years of college work, and meeting requirements with respect to faculty, curriculum, and other factors.

library school, type I: a school for education in librarianship, accredited by the Board of Education for Librarianship of the American Library Association, that is part of a degree-conferring institution, requires at least a bachelor's degree for admission to the first full academic year of library science, and/or gives advanced professional training beyond the first year.

library school, type II: a school for education in librarianship, accredited by the Board of Education for Librarianship of the American Library Association, that is part of a degree-conferring institution, requires for admission 4 years of appropriate college work, and gives only the first full academic year of library science.

library school, type III: a school for education in librarianship, accredited by the Board of Education for Librarianship of the American Library Association, that is part of a degree-conferring institution or of a library or other institution approved by the board for giving professional instruction, does not require 4 years of college work for admission, and gives only the first full academic year of library science.

library, schoolroom: *syn.* **library, classroom** (1).

library science: *see* **science, library.**

library service, adult: special arrangements through which reading materials and advisory services are provided for mature persons by schools and universities through extension of library privileges to individuals and selected groups.

library service, extension: in a university or college, the supplying of books and reference aid to organizations and individuals outside the campus by the general library or a library connected with an extension department.

library services: *see* **services, library.**

library services, school: *see* **services, school library.**

library, special: a service organized to make appropriate information available to a particular organization or limited group; its chief functions are: (*a*) to survey and evaluate current publications, research in progress, and the activities of individual authorities; (*b*) to organize pertinent written and unwritten information; and (*c*) to assemble from within and without the library both publications and data and to disseminate this information, often in abstract or memorandum form appropriate for individual use; types of special libraries having various policies, methods, and collections, are: (*a*) the special-organization library, serving a corporation, a nonprofit organization, governmental body, etc., and maintained by the organization; (*b*) the special branch of a public library, serving certain occupational groups; (*c*) the special-subject library, serving students, professional groups, members, or the general public, on a given subject.

library stacks: *see* **stacks, library.**

library standards: *see* **standards, library.**

library, state: a library maintained by state funds for the use of state officials and citizens of the state; it provides service to public libraries, elementary and secondary schools, colleges and universities, and state institutions of various types.

library study hall: *see* **study hall, library.**

library survey: *see* **survey, library.**

library system language laboratory operation: *see* **language laboratory operation, library system.**

library table: *syn.* **reading table.**

library, tape: a collection of recordings of radio or other programs on magnetic tape; usually available for rerecording or reproduction.

library technical services: *see* **services, library technical.**

library technician: *see* **technician, library.**

library, textbook: (1) a library or library collection made up of samples of a great variety of textbooks, current and/or historical; (2) *syn.* **laboratory, curriculum materials.**

library, theological: an organized collection of books and other educational materials relating specifically to theology or to religion generally, normally housed at a theological college or seminary.

library training class: *see* **class, library training.**

library, transcription: a collection of recordings of music, historic occasions, speeches of famous personages, educational materials, etc., considered worthy of being preserved for the future.

library, traveling: a small collection of selected books sent by a central library agency for the use of a branch, group, or community during a limited period.

library unit: (1) a group of books sent to a classroom from a central school reservoir collection; (2) that component of a teaching machine used to store the program; *see* **selector unit** (2).

library, university: (1) a library or a system of libraries established and maintained by a university to meet the needs of its students and faculty; (2) the central library of such a system.

library workroom: a room used for the repair and rebinding of books.

libretto: the text (the book) of an opera, oratorio, etc.

license fee: a charge fixed by law for the use of a privilege or for the securing of a license under the control of the government.

license, permanent: *syn.* **certificate, permanent.**

license, projectionist's: legal permit usually issued by the state government giving qualified persons the right to operate motion-picture projectors.

license, provisional: *syn.* **certificate, provisional.**

license, teacher's: *syn.* **certificate, teacher's.**

license, teaching: *syn.* **certificate, teacher's.**

licensing: recognition by a state that an individual has met minimum requirements, as set by the state, for a position such as elementary teacher, secondary principal, or counselor, and permission granted by the state to the individual to practice the profession for which he has met the minimum requirements.

licentia docendi (li·sen'shi·ə dō·sen'dī): (Lat., lit., "license for teaching") in medieval universities the license that was bestowed upon teachers by the church.

lid reflex: *syn.* **reflex, corneal.**

lied (lēt): *pl.* **lieder** (lē'dər); (Ger., lit., "song") in German Romantic music, from about 1825 to 1900, an art song. *See* **song, art** (2).

lien: an enforceable claim of high rank against the property of a debtor; may come into existence either by virtue of common law or by statute and either by operation of law or by agreement of the parties; in school law, most frequently occurs under state statutes providing for mechanics' and materialmen's liens, by which claimants who have furnished labor or materials for a school-building contractor who has failed to pay them may perfect a prior claim to sums due the defaulting contractor.

life-adjustment education: educational opportunities designed to equip all American youth to live democratically with satisfaction to themselves and profit to society as home members, workers, and citizens; this program, while concerned with all youth, has a special importance for those whose objectives are less well served by our schools than objectives of preparation for either a skilled occupation or higher education; commonly employed in reference to the movement growing out of the Prosser resolution at the American Vocational Association in 1946 and as sponsored by the U.S. Office of Education.

life age: *syn.* **age, chronological.**

life curriculum: *see* **curriculum, life.**

life expectancy: the expectation of life at birth, based on computations of the average length of the total life-span.

life, good: *see* **good life.**

life-history report: *see* **report, life-history.**

life instinct: *see* **instinct, life.**

life of buildings: the length of time buildings can be used with safety and with satisfactory results for educational purposes, sometimes estimated at 75 years, though there are wide variations; depends on the quality of construction and the rapidity of change in the type of work undertaken in the building. [Many college buildings are being so well constructed (University of Chicago survey) that they are likely to be obsolete long before they have deteriorated.]

life science: *see* **science, life.**

life-situations approach: an approach to curriculum building founded on basic learning experiences that recur throughout life.

life situations, persisting: a concept referring to the situations that recur in the life of the individual in many different ways as he grows from infancy to maturity, such as getting along with others, managing money, meeting health needs, etc.; thus curriculum builders who organize instruction around persisting life situations argue that these situations not only have present meaning but also will take on new meanings as the individual matures.

life, social: *see* **social life.**

life space: the total environment in a person's life, including any persons who influence him or whom he influences.

life-space interview: *see* **interview, life-space.**

life space, psychological: the totality of facts that determine the behavior of the individual at a given moment; total psychological environment.

life-space survey: *see* **survey, life-space.**

life state certificate: *see* **certificate, life state.**

life-style: a term used by Adler to describe the manner in which an individual strives for security and adaptation to the environment.

life teaching certificate: *see* **certificate, life state.**

LIFO: an accounting term that is used in connection with a value control of inventories; an acronym for "last in, first out," that is, the last item stored is the first item issued. *See* **FIFO.**

lifting machine: a colloquial synonym for *dynamometer, back-and-leg.*

light adaptation: *see* **adaptation, light.**

light control: (1) methods architects prescribe to regulate light from sources outside a room; (2) (audiovis. ed.) devices by which rooms are darkened for projection of images on a screen.

light control, automatic: control of illumination by a photoelectric cell that switches artificial lights on or off in order to maintain any desired level of lighting. *Syn.* **photoelectric light control.**

light control, photoelectric: *syn.* **light control, automatic.**

light, incident: (photog.) light falling upon a subject, as distinguished from reflected light or light cast back from a subject.

light-line system: a shorthand system that does not use thickening or shading of the lines, for example, Gregg shorthand.

light meter: a device incorporating a photocell connected to a calibrated meter to read directly in *footcandles;* used to check light levels in a scene or set to be televised or photographed.

light perception: *see* **perception, light.**

lighting, artificial: (1) the illumination of a room or building by electricity or other means than natural daylight; (2) (photog.) illumination for photographic purposes by means of photoflash, photoflood, or other types of artificial lighting.

lighting, bilateral: the admission of light from two sides of a room.

lighting, direct: illumination in which the major portion of the light falls directly on the surface to be illuminated; usually applied only to artificial illumination.

lighting, glass-block: *see* **glass-block lighting.**

lighting, indirect: a type of illumination in which 90 percent or more of the light is directed toward the ceiling for diffused reflection over the room area.

lighting, natural: lighting by daylight, as opposed to artificial lighting.

lighting standards: *see* **standards, lighting.**

lighting, unilateral: illumination from one direction only, as from windows on one side of a room.

likelihood ratio test: *see* **test, likelihood ratio.**

limen (lī'mən): (Lat., lit., "threshold") *syn.* **threshold.**

limit, integral: *syn.* **class limit, apparent.**

limit, score: *syn.* **class limit, apparent.**

limitation, mental: *see* **mental limitation.**

limited age-and-schooling certificate: *see* **age-and-schooling certificate, limited.**

limited certificate: *syn.* **certificate, provisional.**

limited general industrial arts: *see* **industrial arts, limited general.**

limited tax bond: *see* **bond, limited tax.**

limited vision: *see* **partially seeing.**

limits, experience with: (math.) activities, problems, etc., selected to develop the students' concept of limit in the mathematical sense, as limit of a sequence, limit of a function, etc., for example, by presenting situations in which there is an intuitive idea of "getting closer and closer to."

limits, fiducial: *syn.* **confidence limits.**

limits, probability: *syn.* **confidence limits.**

limits, tolerance: *syn.* **confidence limits.**

line: (stat.) *syn.* **row.**

line administration: *see* **administration, line.**

line-and-staff administration: *see* **organization, line-and-staff.**

line-and-staff organization: *see* **organization, line-and-staff.**

line, base: *see* **base line.**

line file: *see* **file, line.**

line graph: *see* **graph, line.**

line-item appropriation: *see* **appropriation, line-item.**

line, item trace: *see* **trace line, item.**

line length: the length of a line of printed or written material, as measured in inches, millimeters, or letter spaces; regarded as a significant factor in ease and speed of reading. (Ninety millimeters is thought to be the maximum line length for effective reading of printed material.)

line marker: *syn.* **guide.**

line, norm: *see* **norm line.**

line, number: *see* **number line.**

line of means: a line joining the actual means of the several successive columns or of the several successive rows of a double-entry table. *Syn.* **empirical regression line.**

line of regression: *syn.* **regression line.**

line of relation: (1) *syn.* **regression line;** (2) *syn.* **curve, correlation.**

line-of-sight: a term popularly employed to describe transmission characteristics of UHF television channels and other high-frequency bands; such frequencies are usually limited in transmission range by straight-line distances between the radiating antenna and the receiving antenna; natural or man-made obstructions existing between the sending and receiving positions further limit coverage.

line of vision: a line extended from the eye of the writer to the horizontal writing surface, which should be parallel to or should coincide with the angle of slant of the writing.

line of writing: the base horizontal line upon which all small letters rest and above and below which all up-and-down strokes extend.

line officer: *see* **administration, line.**

line organization: *syn.* **administration, line.**

line polygon: *syn.* **polygon, frequency.**

line printer: *see* **printer, line.**

line production method: (ind. arts) the organization and administration of school experience according to mass production methods. *See* **mass production method.**

line title: *see* **title, line.**

line, trace: *syn.* **trace line, item.**

lineal growth: *see* **growth, lineal.**

linear: (1) (stat. or math.) capable of being satisfactorily represented in graphical form by a straight line; having changes in one variable proportional to those in the other variable; *syn.* **rectilinear;** *contr. w.* **curvilinear;** (2) *see* **programming, linear.**

linear algebra: *see* **algebra, linear.**

linear correlation: *syn.* **correlation, rectilinear.**

linear correlation ratio: *see* **correlation ratio, linear.**

linear feet of seating space: *see* **seating space, linear feet of.**

linear motion: *see* **movement, rectilinear.**

linear programming: *see* **programming, linear.**

linear regression: *see* **regression, linear.**

linear regression equation: *see* **regression equation, linear.**

linear relation: *syn.* **correlation, rectilinear.**

linear relationship: *syn.* **correlation, rectilinear.**

linear representation: *see* **representation, linear.**

linear transformation: *see* **transformation, linear.**

linearity: the characteristic of being linear; the state or condition of being capable of representation by a straight line. *Syn.* **rectilinearity;** *contr. w.* **curvilinearity.**

linearity, test for: *see* **test for linearity.**

lines of progression: planned avenues of promotion in industry, both within departments and among departments.

lingual: *n.* one of the sounds formed with the aid of the tongue.

lingual: *adj.* pertaining to or formed by the tongue.

linguistic analysis: *see* **analysis, linguistic.**

linguistic analysis, comparative: *see* **analysis, comparative linguistic.**

linguistic approach: an approach to beginning reading instruction distinguished by the systematic control of the introduction of sound and letter relationships; use of a sight vocabulary and picture clues to meaning as in traditional basal reader approaches are not aspects of most linguistically based programs for beginning reading.

linguistic geography: *see* **geography, linguistic.**

linguistic growth: *see* **growth, linguistic.**

linguistic interference: *see* **interference, linguistic.**

linguistic psychology: *see* **psycholinguistics.**

linguistic test: *see* **test, linguistic.**

linguistics: the study of the nature and use of language.

linguistics, descriptive: the description of the regular patterns of a language system.

linguistics, diachronic: historical study of a language, especially through description of its sounds in successive periods of its development. *Contr. w.* **linguistics, synchronous** (2).

linguistics, mathematical: the study of language through the application of mathematical principles.

linguistics, structural: the study of the complex patterns of sounds, inflections, and word arrangements of language.

linguistics, synchronous: (1) the teaching of different linguistic elements at the same time and in relation to each other; (2) description of a language, especially its sounds as they occur in any one historical period; *contr. w.* **linguistics, diachronic.**

Link trainer: *see* **trainer, Link.**

linkage: the association of two or more characters in inheritance that sometimes results from the location in the same chromosome of the several determining genes. *See* **chromosome; gene.**

linkage group: a set of two or more characters in inheritance resulting from the location in the same chromosome of the several determining genes.

linkage, optimal: in communication theory, the best connections between the elements in the communicative act.

linoleum cut: (art) a method of printing in which the drawing or pattern to be produced is incised or cut away from a flat linoleum block; the remaining raised surface is inked and produces the image when pressed on paper or other absorbent material.

lip movement: *see* **movement, lip.**

lip sync: *see* **lip synchronization.**

lip synchronization: (lip sync) the production of a film or kinescope with recorded sound track that is synchronized with the spoken words of the person or persons involved in the film; films that do not incorporate lip sync might have a narrator's voice recorded on the film.

lipreading: *see* **reading, lip-.**

lipreading, context method of: a method of teaching lipreading in which the overall content of speech, rather than isolated words or sentences, is stressed. *See* **Nitchie method.**

lipreading methods: *see* **audiovisual-kinesthetic method; Bruhn (Müller-Walle) method; Jena method; Kinzie method; Nitchie method; visual-hearing method.**

lisp, lateral: (1) defective production of the *s* sound, characterized by an emission of air through either side or both sides of the mouth, as in the substitution of *sh* for *s;* (2) a severe form of nervous lisping accompanied by facial contortions. *See* **lisping.**

lisp, nasal: a strong fricative sound produced by forcing air through the nasal passages when a voiceless *m* or *n* is substituted for *s;* usually occurs when *s* precedes *m* or *n,* as in *small* or *snare.*

lisp, occluded: substitution of *t* for *s,* as in *tay* for *say;* referred to as occluded because the airstream is more nearly shut off than in the substitution of *th* for *s.* *See* **lisping.**

lisping: defective articulation of *s, z,* and *zh,* with substitution of *th* as in *thing* and *th* as in *there,* for example, *thun* for *sun, thebra* for *zebra, chairth* for *chairs. Syn.* **paralalia.**

lisping, neurotic: (1) any articulatory defect caused by or closely related to a personality maladjustment; (2) faulty production of the fricatives, particularly the *s* sound, as in *thaw* for *saw,* due to the retention of generally infantile social reaction tendencies.

list, dean's: *syn.* **honor roll.**

listeners' group: an organized group that meets to hear radio or television broadcasts and discuss the subjects presented.

listening: in guidance, the art of paying close attention to the conversation of another person or persons in order to obtain selectively verbal and nonverbal clues to behavior patterns, explicit or implicit.

listening, assigned: listening, outside of school hours, to broadcasts and/or recordings considered to be of sufficient educational value to be a worthwhile complement to the instructional process.

listening comprehension: *see* **comprehension, listening.**

listening comprehension test: *see* **test, listening comprehension.**

listening, critical: listening to analyze but not mentally argue with a teacher or lecturer during his presentation.

listening, lexical: a multisensory approach to auditory training made up of four main highly complex factors—language, hearing, reading, and speech.

listening, visual: the process used by the hearing-impaired individual of viewing the speaker's lip movements with the intent to understand his thoughts; attention is directed toward comprehension rather than mere recognition.

listening vocabulary: *see* **vocabulary, listening.**

literacy: (1) strictly, the bare ability to read and write; (2) more broadly, ability to read and write at the level of the average fourth-grade pupil. (The term is relative and usually implies the comparison of the individual's ability to read and write with the average ability found at his social or economic level.) *Ant.* **illiteracy.**

literacy, economic: *syn.* **competency, economic.**

literacy, functional: demonstrated ability to read and write.

literacy, mathematical: *see* **mathematical literacy.**

literacy test: *see* **test, literacy.**

literacy, visual: intelligent, critical response to visual stimuli, such as television programs, motion pictures, paintings, etc.

literal address: *see* **address, literal.**

literal comprehension: *see* **comprehension, literal.**

literal number: *see* **number, literal.**

literary analysis: *see* **analysis, literary.**

literary censorship: *see* **censorship, literary.**

literary humanism: *see* **humanism, literary.**

literary material: (1) reading matter of distinct literary merit; (2) poetry and prose of the essay or story type, as contrasted with factual or informational prose.

literary reader: *see* **reader, literary.**

literature: the written or printed productions of a country or a period, but more especially that written or printed matter which has high quality and style; sometimes used to designate any body of printed or written matter whether of quality or not, such as the *literature of education.*

literature appreciation: *see* **appreciation, literature.**

literature, children's: (1) published reading material of a superior quality written for children by expert writers; (2) published reading materials of a superior and lasting quality accepted by children and read by them with pleasure; (3) all printed material available for the use of children.

literature, classical: literature that has stood the test of time and is regarded as of the highest excellence; sometimes used to designate the literature of the ancient world, Greek, Roman, and Oriental.

literature, comparative: the study of diverse literatures and their interrelations leading to an understanding of literature as a totality in spite of the natural language differences.

literature guide: a reference work designed to be used as a key to the literature and bibliographic tools of a specific discipline.

literature, industrial: (couns.) a body of writing published about careers in industry; can be general or specific as well as persuasive or strictly informative; the specific, strictly informative type is usually preferred in guidance.

literature, music: the various forms of musical composition (sonata, symphony, oratorio, etc.) in the music of Western civilization; subject of a required year's course in nearly all programs of study in the schools or departments of music in institutions of higher learning.

literature, occupational: (couns.) pamphlets, brochures, leaflets, and books containing adequate, well-written, valid, and reliable information concerning various jobs in order to assist people in choosing desirable occupations and to ensure the future for the professional, occupational, or industrial groups.

literature, official training: *see* **training literature, official.**

literature program: *see* **program, literature.**

literature, recruitment: as used in guidance, literature designed to recruit youth into a particular occupational field.

literature search: *see* **search, literature.**

lithography: in graphic arts, a method of printing from greased lines on a stone or metal plate, based on the fact that grease and water do not ordinarily mix.

litigation: a contest in court; a suit of law.

litterator (lit'ər·ā'tŏr): one who taught boys between the ages of 7 and 12 in the lower or strictly elementary Roman school.

litteratus (lit′ər·ā′təs): a teacher in a Roman school in which all the liberal arts were taught.

little league baseball: *see* **baseball, little league.**

little red schoolhouse: a symbol for the predominantly rural, subject-centered, but intimate schooling typical of the elementary education of earlier times in the United States; generally identified with nostalgic feelings, homely virtues, the three R's, and limited education.

Little Schools of the Port-royalists: schools of the type first founded at the convent of Port Royal, near Paris, France, in 1643 by the followers of Cornelis Jansen; operating on the principle of strict supervision, each school took only 20 to 25 pupils and provided a master to take charge of each group of 5 or 6 boys; children entered at the age of 9 or 10 and usually remained through the period of adolescence.

little theater: (1) a community dramatic organization of amateurs that produces plays; may occasionally employ professional directors and actors; (2) a program in dramatics sponsored by an adult education agency; may include aid to community groups in play production.

live census file: *see* **census file, live.**

"live" program: *see* **program, "live."**

livesaver: (phys. ed.) in a swimming program, a person prepared and certified in lifesaving and thus capable of making a water rescue.

living, area of: *see* **area of living.**

living, associational: (1) the application or use of response patterns through their insightful or meaningful connection with other facts and situations; (2) a procedure in which members of a social unit live and learn together, as in a camp.

living center: *see* **center, living.**

living room dialogues: *see* **dialogues, living room.**

load, aggregate: the total of all school duties assigned to a given teacher.

load card: *see* **card, load.**

load, case: *see* **case load.**

load, class: the total of a teacher's responsibility for classroom instruction; total number of classes or pupils taught by a teacher.

load, daily: the total load of the teacher during a typical school day.

load, extrainstructional: *see* **extrainstructional load.**

load factor: any factor that is considered in determining a teacher load; for example, time required per week, diversity of subjects, size of classes, type of subject, extraclass duties, etc.

load, faculty: the total amount of time spent by faculty members of a school or school system in fulfilling the services specified in the contract.

load, measurable: the part of the required work of a teacher that can be measured by means of a suitable formula, such as the *Douglass formula.*

load, passenger: the maximum number of pupils riding on the school bus on a given bus route.

load pressure: the difficulties encountered in performing the assigned or voluntary duties of a teacher in connection with his schoolwork; measured in terms of distribution of classes, the amount and time of fieldwork, the amount of laboratory work, the nature of subjects taught, and the need for special preparation. (Some of the load may not lend itself readily to measurement.)

load, pupil: the median number of pupils met by a teacher for instructional purposes.

load routine: *see* **routine, load.**

load, service: the teaching load plus all extraclass, community, and administrative activities in which a teacher participates.

load, student: the number of courses, credits, or hours for which the student is registered; sometimes includes, also, extraclass activity and approximation of time required for study. *See* **program, student.**

load, study: the number of hours of study required per unit of time, such as a day or week.

load, supervisory: the total number of activities or units of time for which a supervisor is expected to provide his service.

load, teacher: the total of the teaching load plus the load incident to all the other duties of the teacher in the school. *See* **load, teaching.**

load, teacher-hour: the number of hours (60 minutes each) of actual instruction done by a teacher per unit of time, as per day or per week, multiplied by the number of pupils taught.

load, teaching: load of a teacher or teachers incident to teaching; in terms of the *Douglass formula* for measuring the teaching load, a unit of teaching load is the load imposed by the teaching of a class of 25 students for a period of 50 minutes, requiring in addition to class time 34 minutes for preparation, the marking of papers, and other duties directly related to the teaching of the class.

load, total time: the total amount of time in terms of hours or minutes per week given to all work done in connection with the teacher's curricular and extraclass activity.

load, work: *see* **work load.**

loaded miles: *see* **miles, loaded.**

loading: the act of taking pupils onto the school bus.

loading area: a portion of property designated for use of pupils getting on or off school buses.

loading, educational: a characteristic of tests according to which they can be arranged along a spectrum from measurement of educational achievement (maximal educational loading) to independence of specific instruction (minimal educational loading); tests with maximal educational loading can be used to predict future school achievement while those with minimal educational loading can be used to assess potentialities or compare individuals with diverse educational and cultural backgrounds.

loading, factor: *see* **factor loading.**

loading station: *syn.* **school-bus stop.**

loading, zero: a factor loading so small that it is regarded as a chance deviation from 0.0.

loan, classroom: a small collection of books, usually material on a current school project, sent to a classroom for a limited period by a public or a school library.

loan fund: *see* **fund, loan.**

loan fund, college: the money set aside for lending to students who meet various requirements for such financial aid; generally, this is a temporary aid and carries stipulations for later refund; loan fund origin may be individual, local, state, or Federal.

loan, interlibrary: loans of library materials to other libraries.

loan, National Defense student: a loan available to high school graduates accepted for enrollment by colleges and universities or to college students already enrolled in full-time or at least half-time courses who need financial help for educational expenses; often called *NDEA loan. See* **National Defense Education Act.** (More recently the National Direct Student Loan.)

loan, NDEA: *see* **loan, National Defense student.**

loan program, guaranteed: *see* **program, guaranteed loan.**

loan, short-term: *see* **short-term loan.**

loan, student: financial assistance, from government or university funds, enabling students to enter college and pursue their courses to a successful conclusion; may be based on tuition charged and fees collected by an institution and must be paid back by the student. *See* **loan fund, college;** *contr. w.* **scholarship** (3).

loans, college housing: *see* **housing loans, college.**

Lobachevskian geometry: *see* **geometry, Lobachevskian.**

lobby: an open space within a building, often furnished with seats, used for waiting or relaxing. *See* **foyer.**

local autonomy: (ed.) the power the state grants to local school districts to make many of their own decisions, administer their own schools, etc. *See* **autonomy of school district.**

local control: (1) *syn.* **autonomy** (3); (2) *syn.* **autonomy of school district.**

local director of vocational education: *see* **director of vocational education, local.**

local initiative: (1) the freedom and willingness of a local community to move beyond the established minimum educational level set by the state government; (2) local independence to decide and act, especially in matters of school support.

local junior college: *see* **junior college, local.**

local norm: *see* **norm, local.**

local production center: *see* **center, local production.**

local relief: money or other assistance granted by a state government for use by a local government in order to reduce the burden of local taxes.

local school administration: *see* **administration, local school.**

local school administrative unit: *see* **administrative unit, local school.**

local school district: *see* **district, local school.**

local school unit: *see* **unit, local school.**

local support: *see* **support, local.**

local tax: *see* **tax, local.**

local tax leeway: *see* **tax leeway, local.**

local teacher: a faculty member who was educated in the school or school system in which he is teaching or who was a resident of the community in which he is teaching when employment was accepted.

local teachers' association: *see* **teachers' association.**

local-unit ventilation: *syn.* **ventilation, unit-system.**

localism: a word, phrase, or pronunciation peculiar to a given locality; usually not accepted as good English.

localization, auditory: the process of identifying the direction from which a sound comes; an association accomplished by the cephalic reflex, which consists of turning the glance toward the presumed source of sound until the characteristics of the sound are equal for the two ears.

localization, sound: *syn.* **localization, auditory.**

localization, spatial: the location by the observer of objects in space resulting from the integration of a series of visual impressions.

localized pattern: those responses which are restricted to specific segments of an organism, as opposed to the total pattern involving the whole organism.

localizing response: *see* **response, localizing.**

location: (1) (read.) the finding of reading material by the use of either the book index or the library index or by skimming within the book itself; a skill often demanded in the study type of reading but equally important in finding material for pleasure reading; (2) in automatic data processing, any physical place in a storage device which is used for storing a word or field and which usually has an address.

location, storage: *see* **storage location.**

locational geography: *see* **geography, locational.**

lock step in education: a term used to describe the rigid system of controlling the progress of a pupil through school grade by grade, regardless of his ability to make more rapid progress.

lock-step study pace: the uniform pace imposed on foreign-language students by a prerecorded tape program which does not allow for individual differences in optimal learning rates between students.

locker: a compartment for holding clothing that may be locked by the user; placed in locker rooms or in corridors of a building. (Each compartment having a door is considered one locker.)

locker, basket-type: one of a number of small open-top boxes, about 9 inches wide, 12 inches long, and 8 inches high, made of heavy wire mesh and used for storing individual gymnasium costumes. *Dist. f.* **locker, box.**

locker, box: one of a series of small metal cabinets used for the storage of gymnasium costumes and for the safekeeping of street clothing during exercise periods.

locker room: a room fitted with compartments for holding clothing; may be connected with a gymnasium room or provided for the use of students attending classes. *See* **dressing room.**

lockout: (data processing) the time interval in the cycle of an input or output device during which the rest of the automatic computer is prevented from having access to the contents of part or all of storage.

loco parentis: *see* **in loco parentis.**

locomotor activity: *see* **activity, locomotor.**

locomotor control: *see* **control, locomotor.**

locomotor coordination: *see* **coordination, locomotor.**

locomotor function: the operation of any organic mechanism which enables an organism to travel from place to place.

log, daily: a precise record kept by a student of all his activities during a day including the time at which an activity occurred and the amount of time spent on the activity; in some cases includes the student's response or reaction to a given activity. *See* **schedule, daily.**

logarithm: the logarithm of a number N to a base b is the exponent of the power to which it is necessary to raise b to give N; for example, since $10^2 = 100$, the logarithm of 100 (to the base 10) is 2.

logarithmic average: *syn.* **mean, geometric.**

logarithmic chart: *syn.* **graph, logarithmic.**

logarithmic graph: *see* **graph, logarithmic.**

logarithmic mean: *syn.* **mean, geometric.**

logarithmic scale: *see* **scale, logarithmic.**

logarithmic transformation: *see* **transformation, logarithmic.**

logger: an instrument used in research that automatically records events and physical processes, usually in a chronological manner.

logic: (1) in general, scientific (or systematic) study of the general principles on which validity in thinking depends; deals with propositions and their inferential interrelations; (2) the science of inference and proof; (3) the science of implication; (4) in computer operation, the process of determining by deductive reasoning the means for obtaining a desired result from a given set of conditions.

logic blocks: *see* **blocks, attribute.**

logic, formal: a systematized method of reasoning based on a kind of deductive argument, the *syllogism*, consisting of two related premises and a conclusion, as, "All mammals breathe by lungs. The whale is a mammal. Therefore, the whale breathes by lungs"; defined by Aristotle as "discourse in which certain things being posited, something else than what is posited necessarily follows merely from them." *See* **logic, symbolic.**

logic, mathematical: *syn.* **logic, symbolic.**

logic of analogy: a form of logic based on the inference from known resemblances to other resemblances not directly known.

logic of inquiry: (1) in Dewey, the theory that logical forms accrue to subject matter when the latter is subjected to controlled inquiry, such logical forms being operational in nature; conceives logic as a process of inquiry or investigation wherein acquiring is always secondary and instrumental to the act of inquiring; (2) a process of investigation that will be successful enough both to gather material in a rational way and to allow for complete coverage of the subject in order to reach valid conclusions.

logic operation: *see* **operation, logic.**

logic, sophistic: a logically arranged but fallacious argument which may be based on a false premise, ignore essential known facts, or draw a conclusion either not based on the facts or not based on all the facts concerned.

logic, symbolic: the study of the logic of statements (conditions for truth and falsity, equivalence, etc.) according to their form and not their content, the statements being represented by symbols such as p, q, etc., and the logical connectives *and, or, if . . . then, if and only if,* and *not* also represented by symbols, the general results then derived being applicable to all statements having certain forms; sometimes called *formal logic.*

logical approach to a subject: organization of an area of knowledge according to a structure inherent in the subject; for example, the division of chemistry into organic and inorganic; antithetical to a psychological approach which organizes a subject to match the understanding of the learner, postponing logical organization to a more advanced stage of comprehension.

logical atomism: *see* **atomism, logical.**

logical diagram: *syn.* **chart, flow.**

logical empiricism: *see* **empiricism, logical.**

logical error: *see* **error, logical.**

logical mathematics: *see* **mathematics, logical.**

logical method: (1) in general, the procedure of making generalizations from observed data (induction) or of drawing conclusions about particular instances from accepted premises (deduction); (2) (ed.) the process (as applied to instruction, selection and arrangement of materials, etc.) by which, from the point of view of a specialist in the subject matter, the simplest elements of the subject of study are introduced first, additional elements being systematically added to build up a complex whole; does not, usually, make allowance for individual differences among learners.

logical operation: *see* **operation, logic.**

logical organization: an arrangement (as of materials for study, courses of a curriculum, or topics of an outline) that exhibits the part-whole relation of a logical system in which parts and whole imply one another; usually starts with the logically simplest parts, that is, the elementary concepts, and proceeds gradually to the more complex.

logical positivism: *see* **positivism, logical.**

logical thinking: *see* **thinking, logical.**

logical validity: *see* **validity, logical.**

logistics, library: the procuring, cataloging, housing, and distribution of books and other library materials.

logology: a term used by Stumpf to designate the science of the relationships among ideas.

logomania (log'ō·mā'ni·ə): *syn.* **logorrhea.**

logopedics: the science of speech defects and their treatment.

logorrhea (log'ə·rē'ə): excessive and continuous speech; may be incoherent. *Syn.* **logomania.**

logos (lŏ'gos): (Gr., lit., "word," "speech," "reason") (1) (philos.) the principle of rational order conceived as part of nature; (2) (theol.) the second person of the Trinity, the Son as divine reason.

logospasm: spasmodic utterance of words.

Lollards: (1) certain heretics in the Netherlands in the fourteenth century; (2) the adherents or followers of the doctrines and practices of John Wycliffe in England and Scotland in the fourteenth and fifteenth centuries; they opposed episcopal licensing of teachers and founded schools run by unlicensed teachers, one of several acts and beliefs which the Crown and Papacy objected to and punished.

long division: *see* **division, long.**

long horse: *see* **horse, side.**

long-play record: *syn.* **record, microgroove.**

long-term borrowing: the process of obtaining money by loan for a long period of time. (In school finance, the issuance of school bonds for a period of 25 years would be long-term borrowing.)

longitudinal genetic method: *see* **genetic method, longitudinal.**

longitudinal representation of growth: the continuous record of growth for one individual, as contrasted with cross-sectional views of growth.

longitudinal scribbling: *see* **scribbling, longitudinal.**

longitudinal seating: *see* **seating, longitudinal.**

longitudinal study: *see* **study, longitudinal.**

look-and-guess method: *syn.* **sight method.**

look-and-say method: *syn.* **sight method.**

loop: (1) the slack film left above and below the gate of a motion-picture projector or camera to permit the film in the gate to move intermittently while the rest of the film moves at a constant speed; (2) for computers, a coding technique whereby a group of instructions is repeated with progressive modification of some of the instructions within the group and/or with modification of the data being operated upon until an exit condition is reached; *see* **iterative loop;** (3) in algebra, a particular kind of *mathematical system.*

loop, continuous: film or tape recording spliced for continuous playing without rethreading.

loop, iterative: *see* **iterative loop.**

loop letters: those handwritten letter forms which involve the use of a complete doubling or fold, as in *b, e, f, g, h, j, k, l,* etc.

looping, bypass: *see* **bypass looping.**

loops of concern, feedback: *see* **feedback loops of concern.**

Lorge readability formula: *see* **readability formula, Lorge.**

loss, hearing: *see* **hearing loss.**

loss of hearing, percent: *see* **percent loss of hearing.**

loss, onset of: a rather general reference to the period of time when first a physical or mental deviation from the norm took place.

loss, sensory-neural: a hearing impairment due to abnormality of the sense organ, the auditory nerve, or both.

losses: the designation in child accounting of cases of transfer to other institutions and permanent withdrawals from the school district, including all pupils discharged (*a*) to other institutions, (*b*) to other school corporations, (*c*) to other school districts, (*d*) for employment, (*e*) because of marriage, (*f*) because of death, (*g*) because of being over or under the compulsory school age, (*h*) because of graduation from high school, and (*i*) by process of law for reasons of misbehavior, physical deficiency, or mental incompetence.

lost-time accident: *see* **accident, lost-time.**

loudness discrimination: *see* **discrimination, intensity.**

loudness, recruitment of: *syn.* **recruitment, auditory.**

loudspeaker: device for converting electrical currents into sound waves.

low-grade mentally retarded: *see* **mentally retarded, Group IV.**

low-income group: *see* **group, low-income.**

low-power telecasting: *see* **telecasting, low-power.**

low-speed record: *syn.* **record, microgroove.**

low vision: *see* **vision, low.**

low-vision aid: *see* **aid, low-vision.**

low-vision child: *see* **child, low-vision.**

lower division: the name used in some universities for the freshman and sophomore years organized as a distinct unit for all freshmen and sophomores.

lower mental process: *see* **mental process, lower.**

lower school: a school whose curricular offering is preparatory to or below that of another school; for example, the elementary school is a lower school to the high school.

lowered vitality case: a person with a severe cardiac condition who has no visible signs of physical handicap but who is sometimes transported to an orthopedic school and, by stretching a point, can be brought under a subclass of orthopedically handicapped since heart muscles are affected.

lowest common denominator: *see* **denominator, lowest common.**

loyalty: a value concept which implies that allegiance to an idea, individual, or group has priority over all other values.

loyalty, consumer: the tendency of consumers to be loyal to a particular place of business; the degree of store loyalty is related to geographic area and to economic, educational, and occupational factors.

loyalty oath: an oath required by some state legislatures and boards of education as a prerequisite to employment; often made a part of a teacher's contract; various criteria of loyalty are established, usually including the teaching of love and respect for the country and its flag, upholding the Constitution of the United States, and not teaching any social, political, or economic theories opposed to the government of the United States; often including criteria for determination of disloyalty and consequent termination of employment, such as membership in organizations or other groups considered subversive. (As of October 1970 the Civil Service Commission has ruled loyalty oaths unconstitutional and deleted them from Federal employment application forms.) *Syn.* **teachers' oath;** *see* **affirmation; oath of allegiance.**

luah (lōō'äkh): *n. masc.; pl.* **luot** (lōō·khōt'); (Heb., lit., "calendar") a Jewish calendar indicating in some cases corresponding dates of the Jewish lunar and the civil solar calendar.

Lubavitcher school: a type of day school (organized by the late Rabbi Schneur Zalmen Miladi, known as the Lubavitcher rabbi) which offers a program of Jewish instruction that stresses piety, the study of Talmud, and a certain type of ethical literature. *See* **day school, Jewish.**

ludi magister (lū'dī ma·jis'tər): *syn.* **litterator.**

ludus (lū'dəs): an elementary "play" or "exercise" school, dating from the first century of the Roman republic, supplementing the more informal training of the home and offering instruction in reading, writing, and rudimentary calculation.

lumen: a unit for the measurement of light, being the light emitted in a unit solid angle by a uniform point source of one international candle.

lump-sum appropriation: *see* **appropriation, lump-sum.**

lunacy: a broad term implying mental unsoundness; now little employed except in legal documents. *See* **insanity; psychosis.**

lunar age: *see* **age, lunar.**

lunch, midmorning: part of the daily nursery school and kindergarten program which gives a light food menu to the children; important for values of nourishment and socialization.

lunch per day, average number of pupils served: *see* **average number of pupils served lunch per day.**

lunch program, Federal school: *see* **program, Federal school lunch.**

lunch program, state school: *see* **state school lunch program.**

lunch, school: noon meal brought from home in a lunchbox or sack and eaten in a space provided by the school; may be supplemented with food and/or beverages purchased in the *school cafeteria* or *school lunchroom.*

lunchroom: a room in a school building in which pupils eat lunches carried from home, in part carried and in part purchased, or entirely purchased, and which may either be self-service or provide dining-room service. (Federal funds are often furnished to help support a lunch program.) *See* **cafeteria, school.**

lunger: a leather belt to each side of which rope handles are attached by swivel couplings; worn by tumblers in learning acrobatic exercises.

lycée (lē·sā'): a secondary school in French-speaking countries, state owned and managed and financially self-supporting, in contrast to the collège (kō·lāzh'), which is set up and operated by the city but with personnel appointed and paid by the state. *See* **college** (3).

lyceum (lī·sē'əm): (1) the gymnasium on the east side of Athens where Aristotle taught; sometimes used as a synonym for his school of thought; closed at the same time and for the same reason as the Academy; *see* **academy** (1) and (2); a type of general adult education developed especially in the United States for instruction through lectures and entertainments; usually given in series, sometimes employing chautauqua and forum methods; *see* **chautauqua; forum.**

Lyceum Movement: (1) an organization founded by Josiah Holbrook at Millbury, Massachusetts, in 1826 for the purpose of improving town and village schools according to a uniform plan; in 1831 a similar movement was begun on a national scale for the improvement of the common schools and the general diffusion of knowledge and though it waned after 1839, many state organizations continued to function; (2) in later years, a movement similar to the *chautauqua.*

lymphoid growth: *see* **growth, lymphoid.**

Machiavellian (mak'i·a·vel'i·an): descriptive of any theory derived from the views of Niccolò di Bernardo Machiavelli (1469-1527), especially the political principle according to which every act of the state (or statesman) is permissible, particularly in foreign relations, if it is advantageous for one's own country.

machine address: *see* **address, machine.**

machine age: (1) a period characterized by extensive and increasing use of power-driven machinery in economic production; (2) the century or more following the Industrial Revolution.

machine, calculating: a machine for performing arithmetic computation; more frequently used for small desk models which add, subtract, multiply, and divide. *See* **computer, digital.**

machine, computer-based teaching: a machine capable of presenting information to learners and providing responses to questions on the information for the learners, including a system of reacting to the learners' responses with some form of immediate *feedback.*

machine, electronic: a machine, such as a computer, which uses the flow of electrons for its operation rather than using mechanical or electric mechanisms.

machine language: *see* **language, machine.**

machine language, common: *see* **language, common machine.**

machine, magnetic-ink character-recognition (MICR): (data processing) a machine for reading characters, usually numbers, which have been printed in magnetized ink, for example, the account number printed along the bottom of most bank checks. *Syn.* **magnetic-ink scanner.**

machine method: *syn.* **punch-card method.**

machine oriented language: *see* **language, machine oriented.**

machine, pacing: a mechanical device using shutters, films, or short-exposure contrivances which regulate the speed or "pace" of reading by exposing or covering a portion of the print at a predetermined speed.

machine pacing: *see* **pacing** (2).

machine process chart: *see* **chart, machine process.**

machine program: *see* **program, machine.**

machine, punch-card: *syn.* **tabulating machine** (2).

machine-readable cataloging: *see* **cataloging, machine-readable.**

machine-scorable test: *see* **test, machine-scorable.**

machine scoring: *see* **scoring, machine.**

machine shop: *see* **shop, machine.**

machine shorthand: *see* **shorthand, machine.**

machine, talking-book: *see* **talking-book machine.**

machine, teaching: *see* **teaching machine.**

machine, test-scoring: *see* **test-scoring machine.**

machine tool: type of apparatus, usually power-driven, designed for shaping solid work by tooling, either by removing material, as in a lathe or milling machine, or by subjecting it to deformation, as in a punch press.

machine tool operator: (voc. ed.) a person who tends any variety of mechanized equipment, such as lathes, drill presses, milling machines, grinders, or special machinery; prepares machines for the purpose of machining metal workpieces to specifications on production basis.

machine translation: *see* **translation, machine.**

machine word: *see* **word, machine.**

machinery industry: *see* **industry, machinery.**

machinery maintenance worker: (voc. ed.) a person who repairs and maintains, according to blueprints and other specifications, production machinery and equipment such as lathes, drill presses, and broaching, milling, and screw machines; uses hand tools, power tools, and precision-measuring instruments.

machinist: (voc. ed.) a person who sets up and operates machine tools and fits and assembles parts to make or repair metal parts, mechanisms, tools, or machines, applying knowledge of mechanics, shop mathematics, metal properties, and layout machining procedures.

macrocephaly (mak′rō·sef′ə·li): excessive enlargement or growth of the head; usually accompanied by feeblemindedness or idiocy. *Contr. w.* **microcephaly.**

macrocommand: in computer programs, a symbolic command or instruction that is translated into two or more machine language instructions (often an entire subroutine) by the translator program; also called *macroinstruction.*

macrocosm: the larger of two entities or parts of which the smaller is in some or all respects analogous to the larger, for example, our solar system as the macrocosm and the atom as the smaller entity, the *microcosm.*

macroeconomic theory: *see* **microeconomic approach.**

macroinstruction: *see* **macrocommand.**

macron: a short horizontal mark placed over a vowel to indicate the long sound.

macrophotography: the science or technique by which small subjects (such as insects) are photographed with a greater degree of enlargement than is possible by ordinary photographic methods; usually refers to still photography. *Syn.* **tabletop photography;** *comp. w.* **microphotography.**

macrosplanchnic: describing or designating a body build in which the volume of the trunk has developed in excess of the limbs so as to give a high morphological index. *Syn.* **pyknic;** *see* **body builds, classification of;** *contr. w.* **microsplanchnic.**

macrostatistics: statistics based on many observations; statistical methods appropriate to use when the number of observations is very large (say, in excess of 100).

Madisonian philosophy of law: *see* **philosophy of law, Hamiltonian.**

maftir (mäf′tir): *n. masc.* (Heb.) the concluding portion in the reading from the *Torah* at the Sabbath and festival services in the synagogue.

magazine: (1) a student periodical in booklet form, usually more literary in tone and more attractively printed and appearing less frequently than the student newspaper; an early form of student publication in many schools and colleges; (2) (photog.) a metal compartment for housing film, in either a motion-picture projector, a motion-picture camera of the magazine type, a 35mm still camera of the Leica type, or a cut-film camera of the reflex or press type; (3) (audiovisual) a container for film, slides, or filmstrips, usually embodying a transport mechanism designed for controlled exposure; most magazines are built to integrate with specific equipment, with drive mechanisms mechanically coupled.

magic square: *see* **square, magic.**

magister scholarum (mə·jis′tər skə·lä′rəm): (1) (Lat., lit., "master of schools") classically applied on the continent of Europe, particularly in Germany, to an administrative official who served as superintendent of schools in a specified geopolitical area; in contemporary Germany the function is served by a *Schulrat* whose duties are similar but whose geographical area of jurisdiction has been foreshortened; (2) (Lat., lit., "master of pupils") a teacher in a cathedral school who ranked next to the bishop and dean.

magnetic board: *see* **board, magnetic.**

magnetic chalkboard: *see* **chalkboard, magnetic.**

magnetic core: powdered magnetic oxide pressed into the shape of a doughnut and capable of being magnetized in either of the two circumferential directions; those used in computer storage units are about the diameter of a pencil lead.

magnetic core storage: *see* **storage, magnetic core.**

magnetic disk: *see* **disk, magnetic.**

magnetic disk storage: *see* **storage, magnetic disk.**

magnetic drum: *see* **drum, magnetic.**

magnetic drum storage: *see* **storage, magnetic drum.**

magnetic film: *see* **film, magnetic.**

magnetic-ink character-recognition machine: *see* **machine, magnetic-ink character-recognition.**

magnetic-ink scanner: *see* **machine, magnetic-ink character-recognition.**

magnetic sound projector: *see* **projector, magnetic sound.**

magnetic sound recording: *see* **sound recording, magnetic.**

magnetic-striped film: *see* **film, magnetic-striped.**

magnetic tape: *see* **tape, magnetic.**

magnetic tape input output device: *see* **input output device, magnetic tape.**

magnetic tape storage: *see* **storage, magnetic tape.**

magnetic tape strip storage: *see* **storage, magnetic tape strip.**

magnetic thin-film storage: *see* **storage, magnetic thin-film.**

magnitude: size or the property of having size, such as area, volume, or length; for example, the magnitude of a vector is its length.

mailable letter: a typewritten letter that is suitable to send out, depending on the standards of the sender; in general, a letter that would be satisfactory to the average businessman when judged for accuracy of transcription and neatness and accuracy of typing. *Dist. f.* **correctable letter.**

mailable transcript: *see* **transcript, mailable.**

main effect: *see* **effect, main.**

main title: *see* **title, main.**

mainstream: (spec. ed.) that part of the total public school program not concerned with special education services for exceptional children.

maintaining stimulus: *see* **stimulus, maintaining.**

maintenance: the repair and upkeep of tools, equipment, and property.

maintenance, bus: *see* **bus maintenance.**

maintenance, cost of: *see* **cost of maintenance.**

maintenance department: *see* **department, maintenance.**

maintenance garage: *see* **garage, maintenance.**

maintenance of buildings: the repair and replacement of worn-out parts of the plant.

maintenance of the school plant: the continuous processes of restoration of any piece of property, whether grounds, buildings, or equipment, as nearly as possible to the original condition of completeness or efficiency, either through repairs or by replacement with property of equal value and efficiency.

maintenance, preventive: (1) the maintenance of a computer system which attempts to keep equipment in top operating condition and to preclude failures during production runs; (2) (pup. trans.) regular servicing and inspection of school buses according to a predetermined mileage plan in order to discover mechanical difficulties.

maintenance shop: *see* **shop, maintenance.**

maintenance staff: *see* **staff, maintenance.**

major adviser: *see* **adviser, major.**

major, broad-fields: a field of major concentration that includes courses from related subjects or departments. (Science, social studies, and language arts are broad-fields majors, whereas history, physics, and literature are *departmental,* or *subject, majors.*)

major, departmental: in teacher education, the group of courses selected from a department's offering, and sometimes from related departments, as a requirement for specialization in preparation for teaching in that area or as professional preparation for graduation or certification. *Syn.* **subject major.**

major determinant: *see* **determinant, major.**

major diagonal: *see* **diagonal, major.**

major field of concentration: *see* **field of concentration, major.**

major field of study: *see* **field of study, major.**

major-minor system: the practice of establishing definite requirements for degrees or graduation in terms of academic major and minor fields at the secondary or college level, a definite number of courses, credits, or hours being required for the different major or minor fields of study in respective academic areas.

major professor: *syn.* **adviser, major.**

major seminary: *see* **seminary, major.**

major sort: *see* **sort, major.**

major, subject: *syn.* **major, departmental.**

major work class: *see* **class, major work.**

make-a-picture-story test: *see* **test, MAPS.**

make-believe: (journ.) the designation of class exercises involving the writing of news articles about imaginary events; used in journalistic writing classes.

make-up class: *see* **class, make-up.**

maladaptive behavior: *see* **behavior, maladaptive.**

maladjusted: descriptive of an individual characterized by inability to adapt his behavior to the conditions of his environment.

maladjusted child: *see* **child, maladjusted.**

maladjusted child, socially: *see* **child, socially maladjusted.**

maladjustment: any mild disturbance of the personality in which there is difficulty in securing a satisfactory adjustment to the environment, particularly to other persons.

maladjustment, educational: (student-personnel work) (1) any discrepancy between the vocational needs of the individual and his training program; (2) scholastic achievement below the minimum established through faculty regulations for continued residence and graduation; (3) achievement below that expected in view of a student's aptitude.

maladjustment, emotional: a condition in which the person's emotional state does not permit satisfactory reaction to existing environmental factors or interpersonal relationships.

maladjustment, personality: failure of an individual, through inherent weakness or faulty development, to adapt his behavior to the demands of the environment.

maladjustment, social: (1) inability, varying in degree, to accept and behave in accordance with the forms and values of the society in which one lives; (2) inability of a social system to function efficiently because of lack of integration of the parts; (3) inability to satisfy a desire for the enjoyment of social experiences or to associate satisfactorily with groups engaging in social and recreational activities. *Contr. w.* **adjustment, social.**

maladjustment, teacher: a lack of proper adaptation of an instructor to his status of employment, environment, or living conditions.

maladjustment, vocational and educational: (student-personnel work) a state of dissatisfaction caused by discrepancies between the student's interests, personality, and abilities and those required by the vocation he has chosen or by the subjects he is studying.

malbehavior: action that interferes with harmonious interpersonal relations or action that is not appropriate to the situation.

malfeasance: the commission of an illegal act. *Comp. w.* **misfeasance; nonfeasance.**

malformation: any type of abnormal growth or development in any part of the body.

malice: (legal) the state of mind manifested by a deliberate intent to commit an unlawful act; used especially in the expression "malice aforethought."

malicious mischief: the willful and unlawful injury to or destruction of the property of another with the malicious intent to injure the owner.

malingering: feigning illness or disability.

malnourished child: *see* **child, malnourished.**

malnutrite (mal'nū·trīt): any individual suffering from malnutrition. (The term has not been widely accepted.)

malnutrition: poor nutrition resulting from an imbalance between the body's supply and demand for nutrients; may result from undereating, overeating, poor assimilation of food, or a diet poor in quality; differs from *undernourishment* in that malnutrition may contribute to overweight or obesity with concomitant health or nutritional disorders.

malocclusion: faulty occlusion of the teeth resulting in an abnormal bite, caused by missing teeth, crowded teeth, widely spaced teeth, and so on.

malum in se (mā'ləm in sē): *pl.* **mala in se;** (Lat., lit., "bad in itself") a term used in reference to a contract that, although not prohibited in law, is for some reason invalid.

malum prohibitum (mā'ləm prō·hi'bi·təm): *pl.* **mala prohibito;** (Lat., lit., "bad because prohibited") a term used in reference to a contract that is invalid because it is prohibited by positive law.

man, animalistic nature of: *see* **nature of man, animalistic.**

man process chart: *see* **chart, man process.**

man-to-man rating scale: *see* **rating scale, man-to-man.**

management: a distinct process consisting of planning, organizing, actuating, and controlling the work of others, performed to determine and accomplish objectives.

management aide: (voc. ed.) a person who assists residents of public and private housing projects and apartments in relocation, provides information concerning regulations, facilities, and services, and maintains records for the owner and management.

management, behavior: *see* **behavior modification.**

management, financial: (school adm.) the work of planning, organizing, and controlling the provision and use of the company's capital within the limits of delegated responsibility and authority.

management, food service: the designation of a college course of study in home economics dealing with the problems relating to the planning, purchasing, preparing, serving, and selling of foods in quantities greater than those needed by a family. *See* **management, institution.**

management, information system: a communications process in which data are recorded and processed for operational purposes.

management, institution: a broad field of study which includes not only food service management but also personnel management and financial and legal management for the operation of restaurants, hotels, motels, and other large institutions. *See* **management, food service.**

management, money: *see* **money management.**

management of change: *see* **change, management of.**

management of information system: programming of the computer so that it will manage the student's learning, then test, and on this basis make decisions on its own as to what the student should do next; the computer thus may plan a complete learning sequence to obtain an objective and select the instructional tasks to this end.

management, records: (school admin.) the practice of preventing unnecessary forms and reports from being established, destroying papers that are no longer necessary, and streamlining present records.

management, school: the administration and direction of the school, with special emphasis on such matters as discipline, availability of supplies, care of building and grounds, and physical comfort.

management, scientific: (school admin.) application of scientific approach and systematic problem-solving techniques to management problems.

management, shop: *see* **shop management.**

management training: *see* **training, management.**

management training course: *see* **course, management training.**

manager, organization: (phys. ed.) a person, such as a student, appointed to manage a team representing some organization or group in intramural athletics.

managerial approach: a broad term including such specific means of presentation in the teaching of bookkeeping as the *balance sheet* and *equation approaches.*

managerial authority: *see* **authority, managerial.**

mandamus (man·dā′məs): a command issued by a superior court and directed to an inferior tribunal, corporation, or public officer to enforce the performance of some public duty.

mandated minimum program level: *see* **program level, mandated minimum.**

mandatory admission: *see* **admission, mandatory.**

mandatory board functions: *see* **board functions, mandatory.**

mandatory law: *see* **law, mandatory.**

manerkon: (1) a three-dimensional model of a frequency surface; (2) a general formula that gives the probability distribution of the dependent variable as predicted by a number of independent variables.

maneuver: (mil. ed.) a tactical exercise carried out at sea, in the air, on the ground, or on a map in imitation of war.

maneuver, air: (1) maneuver conducted by an air force to evaluate and test its equipment, doctrine, tactics, techniques, and state of readiness; (2) maneuver of an aircraft in flight, especially to avoid enemy gunfire or an enemy attack or to gain a tactical advantage in air-to-air combat.

maneuver, field: a maneuver in the field in which two opposing forces conduct operations under simulated combat conditions in order to test and evaluate combat or operational readiness. *See* **exercise, field.**

mania: a mental disorder characterized by excitement, irritability, talkativeness, and overactivity.

manic-depressive psychosis: *see* **psychosis, manic-depressive.**

manifest interest: *see* **interest, manifest.**

manila tagboard: large stiff sheets of pulpboard, usually made of oak content, used for construction and chart activities in primary grades; also known as *oak tag. See* **bristol board.**

manipulation: the act of handling objects in a constructive, exploratory, or exploitative way; in a restricted sense, this implies changing the form or the position of the object or material by the use of the hands; in a more general application, it refers to the action of any part of the body upon objects, such as oral manipulation, manipulation by feet, toes, etc.

manipulative approach: (1) an approach to human behavior appearing to be characterized by attempts to influence or control it; (2) a teaching method which utilizes the activity of *manipulative participation* in order to facilitate behavioral modifications in the learner; used generally with very young children, but also frequently useful with emotionally disturbed older learners.

manipulative equipment: *see* **equipment, manipulative.**

manipulative job: *see* **job, manipulative.**

manipulative participation: (kind.-prim. ed.) a learning activity by which pupils take part in the study of how common objects are made by handling certain raw materials (such as clay and wood), experimenting with them, learning their characteristics, and constructing simple objects from them.

manipulative play: the initial, most immature stage of the child's play activity with materials, in which the child merely moves, lifts, places, fingers, or handles materials without purposing to construct.

manipulative skill: *see* **skill, manipulative.**

manipulative stage: (1) a short period in babyhood during which the infant begins to reach, grasp, hold, and exploit objects and during which his interest in this type of activity is high; usually ends about the time the baby begins to creep; (2) (art ed.) the first stage in the young child's creative development, preceding the form-experimental and early expressive stages; during this stage the child may seem to be making meaningless daubs, but steady improvement and control occur as his familiarity with materials and tools increases; *see* **early expressive stage; form-experimental stage.**

manipulatory control: *see* **control, manipulatory.**

mannerism: (art) a characteristic of the High Renaissance, baroque, and rococo periods in which figures are elongated or affected in pose, gesture, and action.

mannerism, blind: *see* **blindism.**

manual: (1) a booklet or leaflet describing a test, a book, or a series of tests or books, indicating the use of the materials described and, in the case of tests, sometimes suggesting remedial procedures to be followed; (2) a term frequently used as part of the title of early American school textbooks, for example, Jesse Hopkins' "The Patriot's Manual," published in 1828, a textbook in civil government.

manual activity: *see* **activity, manual.**

manual alphabet: *syn.* **alphabet, finger.**

manual arts: *see* **arts, manual.**

manual arts shop: obs.; *see* **laboratory, industrial arts.**

manual, coding: (1) a manual of instruction to coders, usually with examples; (2) a collection of the coding keys used in an investigation.

manual dexterities: *see* **dexterities, manual.**

manual expression: *see* **expression, manual.**

manual, field: (mil. ed.) a manual containing instructional, informational, and reference material relative to military training and operations.

manual-labor movement: a movement to establish schools combining manual labor with schooling; based on a Pestalozzian principle, developed by Fellenberg beginning in 1806 at Hofwyl, Switzerland; widely adopted in the United States in several types of schools, such as polytechnic institutes and industrial schools for Negroes; a notable derivative was the Tuskeegee Institute of Alabama.

manual, legal: a manual concerning school law that should be available to all teachers; a guide to help them in legal matters within the school district.

manual, merchandise: a booklet based upon a study of some product or products sold by a distributive organization and constructed by distributive education students under the supervision of the teacher or coordinator.

manual method: (1) a formal, logical method of teaching shorthand, based on study of the shorthand alphabet and the rules governing the formation and use of shorthand characters, followed by application of the rules in writing from dictation and reading; (2) *syn.* **manualism.**

manual operation: a method of advancing film through some motion-picture cameras and projectors by means of a hand knob.

manual skill: *see* **skill, manual.**

manual, standard industrial classification: a Federal government publication which lists industrial occupational information based on the Standard Industrial Classification system.

manual, stenographers' reference: a reference book designed to improve the efficiency of office workers who need a quick, concise answer to problems involving grammar, letter styling, capitalization, writing numbers, or some office procedure or practice; also called reference manual, stenographic manual, etc.

manual, store: a student-constructed booklet based upon the student's job and his employing firm.

manual, teachers': a guide containing teachers' aids, references, and related topics of interest in a given subject-matter field, prepared to aid instructors in that field; usually arranged for use with a specific text.

manual, technical: (mil. ed.) a manual providing detailed treatment of specific subjects considered necessary for the full accomplishment of required training.

manual training: *see* **training, manual.**

manual-training high school: *see* **high school, manual-training.**

manualism: a method of instruction for the deaf in which the chief element is communication by means of *finger spelling* and *sign language;* also utilizes writing. *Syn.* **manual method;** *contr. w.* **reading, lip; speech education.**

manufacturing: (ind. arts) the study of the technology and the socioeconomic contributions of industries concerned with the creation of durable consumer products; learning experiences are developed around functions or concepts of industry and include research and experimentation, product design and development, fabrication (custom and mass), packaging, and distribution.

manufacturing industry: *see* **industry, manufacturing.**

manuometer: an instrument used to record strength of grip.

manuometer push and pull apparatus: an instrument attached to a manuometer to record arm and shoulder strength.

manuscript form: standards for the placing and spacing of written material on paper.

manuscript writing: *see* **writing, manuscript.**

map, chromosome: (biol.) a chart or diagram illustrating the linkage groups of the genes and their relative positions on the chromosome. *See* **chromosome; gene; linkage.**

map, circle: *syn.* **map, single-dot.**

map, cognitive: a construct in Tolman's learning theory; the structure of the individual's pattern of expectations about cause-and-effect relationships; used especially in handling the phenomena dealing with latent learning, vicarious trial and error, searching for the stimulus, hypotheses, and spatial orientation.

map, contour: a three-dimensional representation of a typographic map in which varying points of elevation are represented by heights corresponding but not necessarily proportional on the three-dimensional map.

map, crosshatch: a statistical map in which varying quantities are shown by different types of crosshatching and/or shading.

map, curriculum: (1) a chart or flow diagram that traces the developmental sequence from entering behaviors to terminal behaviors in a training program or shows the chain of interdependent learning tasks that the students will need to master; (2) a visual representation of the sequenced activities and student performances as structured into a curriculum design.

map diagram: *syn.* **graph, map.**

map, dissected relief: a map with raised features and removable political subdivisions for educational use with the blind or the partially seeing.

map, dot: a map on which dots placed at a given location represent the magnitude or frequency of the variable represented; may be a single-dot map or a multiple-dot map. *Syn.* **dot chart; dot diagram;** *see* **map, multiple-dot; map, single-dot.**

map exercise: *see* **exercise, map.**

map, graded: *syn.* **cartogram.**

map graph: *see* **graph, map.**

map, multiple-dot: a dot map in which the number of dots placed at a given location represents the magnitude or frequency of the variable represented. *See* **map, dot;** *Contr. w.* **map, single-dot.**

map, pin: a map on which various quantities or magnitudes, distributed geographically, are represented by movable pins inserted in appropriate material. *See* **map, dot.**

map, rate: a map indicating rate of change or growth.

map reading: *see* **reading, map.**

map, single-dot: a dot map in which the size of the dot placed at a given location represents the magnitude or

frequency of the variable represented. *See* **map, dot;** *contr. w.* **map, multiple-dot.**

map, social-base: (1) a map indicating by means of shading and code community socioeconomic and general cultural structure, such as type of buildings and homes, location of schools, churches, recreational facilities, civic centers, population density, etc.; (2) a map of the dominant demographic and social characteristics of a particular group, institution, or population.

map, statistical: *syn.* **cartogram.**

map, transportation: *see* **transportation map.**

map, window: a translucency placed upon a window to be illuminated by the daylight.

mapping: a correspondence established between the members of one set and the members of another, usually synonymous with *function* and *transformation;* for some writers, the term mapping carries a geometric connotation, in contrast to any algebraic description which might be given for the correspondence. *See* **function; transformation.**

MAPS test: *see* **test, MAPS.**

marble board test: *see* **test, marble board.**

MARC: *see* **cataloging, machine-readable.**

marching (stride or rhythmic): (phys. ed.) translatory movement using a regular measured step.

marginal activity: *see* **activity, marginal.**

marginal disease: *see* **disease, marginal.**

marginal frequency: *see* **frequency, marginal.**

marginal group: *see* **group, marginal.**

marginal training: *see* **training, marginal.**

marginal vocabulary: *syn.* **vocabulary, potential.**

marine school: *syn.* **nautical school.**

marionette: a puppet moved by string, by wire, or occasionally by a rod; manipulated from above, as distinguished from puppets, which are moved from below. *See* **puppet.**

mark: (1) a value or rating which indicates how a performance is to be valued; especially, a rating of schoolwork given by the teacher; (2) a rating of achievement assigned on the basis of some scale, such as a percentage scale, A, B, C, D, F scale, etc.; *syn.* **grade** (3).

mark, achievement: a measure intended to show the degree of attainment or proficiency resulting from instruction in a given school subject or area of study.

mark, admissible: *see* **admissible mark.**

mark, average: the mean or median of the distribution of marks actually assigned to a group of pupils.

mark, class: the midpoint of a class interval; the value halfway between the upper and the lower class limits. (In a double-entry table, the class mark of an array is called its type.) *Syn.* **class index.**

mark, relative: (1) an achievement mark that represents the amount achieved by one pupil as compared with that achieved by other pupils in the same class, grade, or school group; (2) an achievement mark expressed in relation to any standard, such as a percentage, a percentile, or a grade based on some predetermined scale, such as the familiar A, B, C, D, F system of marking.

mark-sensing: (1) in testing, a machine-scoring system which uses an electrical contact of the marks made by the student to sense these responses for scoring purposes; (2) in data processing, the sensing of discretely placed graphite marks on a card to cause the punching of data by the machine.

mark-sensing equipment: *see* **equipment, mark-sensing.**

mark, term: a mark or rating assigned to a pupil at the end of a school term as a measure of his accomplishment during the period in question; usually a composite measure consisting of an average of test marks and of teachers' estimates of all verbal or written work by the pupil.

mark, word: *see* **word mark.**

marked hearing loss: *see* **hearing loss, marked.**

marker: *syn.* **guide.**

markers: manipulative materials that can be used to objectify numbers; for example, pieces of cardboard or small wooden sticks may be used to demonstrate the meaning of counting.

markers, method of coincidental: *see* **coincidental markers, method of.**

marketing: an area of study, taught in secondary schools and colleges, dealing with the flow of goods and services from the producer to the consumer; the broadest of the distributive subjects, embracing salesmanship, advertising, and retailing.

marketing research: *see* **research, marketing.**

marking, dual: grading by giving two marks for each subject, one for achievement and the other for effort, improvement, or growth in terms of potential.

marking, selective: a procedure in marking compositions in which the teacher concentrates on a few weaknesses rather than commenting on a large number of errors.

marking system: the method used for recording and reporting the achievement of pupils in school studies.

marks, distribution of: *see* **distribution of marks.**

marriage counseling: *see* **counseling, marriage.**

marriage, preparation for: instruction and/or counseling offered at the senior high school or college level or to adult groups, focused upon relationships and responsibilities associated with married life; also, instruction provided by the clergy or other authorized teachers to individuals preparing for holy matrimony, that is, marriage witnessed by the church.

married-woman teacher: any married but not widowed or divorced woman employed as a teacher, generally with the exception of married women entirely dependent on their own financial resources.

Marxian psychology: *see* **psychology, Marxian.**

masculine protest: (1) (psychoan.) the wish of a female to be a male, or the wish on the part of a male to escape any suggestion of femininity, believed by psychoanalysts to be a universal experience; (2) (individual psych.) the desire for masculinity because femininity is interpreted by the individual as inferior or because of social institutions favoring masculinity.

masculinity: male characteristics such as aggressiveness, which are generally regarded as opposed to feminine passivity; social responses indicative of the male; sometimes used with the connotation that masculine feelings are superior and feminine feelings inferior.

mask: *n.* in photography, a frame of cardboard or other substance used to confine the picture area of slides or transparencies and to give support to the projection material in the slide.

mask card: a punch card employed in conjunction with any individual original punch card to prevent a portion of the latter from reproducing when it is being automatically duplicated.

masking: (1) the act of isolating an area of a picture by placing a border around it; (2) (photog.) the act of deliberately or accidentally allowing objects near or attached to the camera (such as a sunshade) to obscure part of the field of view of the camera.

masking, after-effect: *syn.* **fatigue, auditory.**

masking, auditory: a partial or complete obscuring of a tone based on the principle that a sound ceases to be audible in an ear if that ear is stimulated at the same time by another sound that has louder components within the same or a somewhat lower band of frequencies than itself. *See* **noise, white.**

masking, residual: *syn.* **fatigue, auditory.**

mass action, law of: *see* **law of mass action.**

mass-action theory: a theory holding that behavior is developed as the result of specific patterns of response emerging by individualization from the primitive, undifferentiated actions of the organism.

mass activity: *see* **activity, mass.**

mass athletics: *see* **athletics, mass.**

mass education: (1) universal schooling of all children, under public support; (2) the process of educating children or adults in large groups; once applied to the Lancastrian system of regimenting hundreds of pupils in classes; (3) a loose term applied to various large-scale activities (such as those of the press, motion pictures, radio, television, libraries, and museums) aimed at disseminating information to or influencing the opinion of the general public; education presented in a popular way to large unorganized groups.

Mass Education Movement: a movement originally developed by James Yen, a Yale graduate, attempting to make all China literate, partly through utilizing the specially prepared "Thousand Character Readers," which contain the basic 1,300 characters essential to ability to read vernacular Chinese.

mass learning: *see* **learning, mass.**

mass media: the instruments of communication that reach large numbers of people at once with a common message, for example, books, magazines, television, radio, motion pictures, etc., in contrast to the means employed for limited communication, as with a specific student or group of students.

mass production method: the manufacture of articles or products in large quantities; usually involves the principle of interchangeable parts.

mass psychology: *see* **psychology, mass.**

massed practice: *see* **practice, massed.**

master: an original recording or the machine on which this recording is played in order to produce copies on a *slave unit.*

master antenna system: an arrangement designed to eliminate need for individual antennas for each television receiver; antennas are arranged to pick up television signals in a given service area and are connected to an amplification and distribution network to provide optimum signals to multiple locations within one or more buildings.

master card: *see* **card, master.**

master class: *see* **class, master.**

master clock: a clock usually located in or near the principal's office which governs the ringing of bells to announce the beginning and close of class periods; also called *program clock. See* **clock-and-bell system.**

master conference group: *see* **conference group, master.**

master degree in cursu: *see* **degree in cursu, master.**

master device: in technology, a device which has control over several others or which produces the original taped material; for example, master tape, program, console, switch, duplicator, etc.; *slave* sometimes designates another device controlled by a master device.

master eye: *syn.* **eye, dominant.**

master list: (1) a comprehensive compilation of materials such as test items and vocabulary lists from which may be drawn such samples as are desired; (2) a form of matching test consisting, not of parallel columns but of one set of items preceding another with which they are to be matched.

master mechanic: a worker who has sufficient skill and experience in a trade to do all the jobs involved in the trade and who is considered to be an authority on problems that might arise in the trade.

master of arts (M.A.): (1) the degree now usually given in the United States to university students who have completed certain requirements embracing at least 1 year's work above the baccalaureate degree; (2) historically, a degree granted to advanced students in the medieval universities in Europe who majored in the faculty of arts rather than in the higher faculties of theology, law, and medicine.

master of arts degree in education (M.A.): a degree representing an advanced stage of professional educational preparation, approximately equivalent to the *master of education degree,* commonly granted upon completion of a year of graduate study beyond the baccalaureate degree in a teacher-education institution, with major specialization in courses in education or in teaching fields and frequently requiring the writing of a thesis or essay: semester hour requirements vary somewhat depending on the institution granting the degree. *See* degree, master of education; master of science degree in education.

master of education degree: *see* degree, master of education.

master of music degree: *see* degree, master of music.

master of novices: (R.C. ed.) the religious to whom is committed the training of the novices and the government of the novitiate of a religious order or congregation.

master of science degree in education (M.S.): approximately equivalent to the *master of arts degree in education. See* degree, master of education; master of arts degree in education.

master plan of work: *see* operation layout sheet.

master scale, attitude: *see* scale, attitude master.

master tape: *see* tape, master.

master teacher: (1) a teacher in the elementary or secondary schools who, because of advanced professional preparation, appropriate teaching experience, and superior professional skill, is qualified to assist in the education of student teachers and interns for the educational profession; *dist. f.* critic teacher; (2) a teacher recognized as possessing exceptional ability in the art of teaching.

master's degree: *see* degree, master's.

master's thesis: *see* thesis, master's.

mastery formula: a term used by Morrison to designate an instructional procedure recommended for securing mastery of subject matter and defined as "pre-test, teach, test the result, adapt procedure, teach and test again to the point of actual learning."

mastery test: *see* test, mastery.

mastery unit: *see* unit, mastery.

masturbation: manipulation of the genitals to the point of orgasm; may also be psychic, namely, through the thinking of lascivious thoughts to the point of orgasm.

mat hooks: iron arms fastened to a wall from which gymnasium mats are hung.

matched-dependent behavior: *see* behavior, matched-dependent.

matched groups: two or more groups of individuals that are alike as groups with respect to one or more designated characteristics.

matched groups, method of: any method of equating groups for some trait or combination of traits, usually on the basis of nearly equal means and standard deviations.

matched regression estimates: a method used in the analysis of covariance when the categorical trait is dichotomous.

matched sample: *see* sample, matched.

matching: in some teaching machines, a procedure whereby the student, after writing his response, moves a lever which exposes the correct answer with which the student then compares his own response.

matching, basis of: the characteristic or instrument used to match or equate groups in group experimentation.

matching exercise: *see* exercise, matching.

matching of funds: provision of money in accordance with the Federal requirement that, for each dollar of Federal money expended, the state or community or both must provide similar though not in all cases equivalent funds for the same purpose for expenditure under public control.

matching test: *see* test, matching.

matching, variable: that type of matching of local expenditures with state or national funds in which the percentage of local expenditure matched varies according to certain criteria established by the matching agency.

material, art: *see* art material.

material, audiovisual: *syn.* aid, audiovisual.

material, case: *see* case material.

material cause: *see* cause, material.

material, contrived: *see* contrived material.

material, instructional: *see* instructional material.

material science: *see* science, material.

material, source: *syn.* source, primary.

material, support: *see* support material.

materialism: (1) historically, the view that only matter is real and that in the last analysis all reality (including mind, idea, and purpose) is reducible to matter in motion; (2) modern materialism (Sellars, McGill, Farber) asserts an emergent and behavioral theory of mind, a conception of matter as developed by modern science, an optimism regarding scientific method and its control of nature, and a synoptic view of man and the universe, implicit in contemporary science; it rejects vitalism, general teleology, dualism, reductionism, terminal skepticism, supernaturalism, and contemporary fainthearted naturalism; (3) *syn.* materialism, dialectical.

materialism, dialectical: a philosophical school founded by Marx and Engels; its *ontology* contains two principles: *materialism*, the theory that the observable world, material nature, exists in its own right and that science has proved mind to be purely a function of matter, and dialectic, the theory that all things are dynamically interconnected, change is universal, and everything real has within itself opposing factors (thesis, antithesis) whose movement necessarily changes it to something else (synthesis), which in turn becomes the thesis of a new movement; epistemologically, the philosophy holds that *knowledge* must necessarily be the product of investigation of the histories of things, and of the factors, internal and external, involved in the changes taking place. *See* dialectic; Hegelianism.

materialistic epistemology: *see* epistemology, materialistic.

materialistic ethics: *see* ethics, materialistic.

materialistic metaphysics: *see* metaphysics, materialistic.

materialistic monism: *see* monism, materialistic.

materializing instruction: *see* instruction, materializing.

materials, algebra experience: *see* algebra experience materials.

materials and supplies inventory: *see* inventory, materials and supplies.

materials, basal-reader: *see* basal-reader materials.

materials bureau: a center established within a school system where curricula materials, visual aids, and other concrete materials and teaching aids are on file and accessible for use by teachers, supervisors, and administrators; may provide facilities and staff for experimentation and evaluation of media programs, conduct workshops in use of new technological teaching aids, etc.; may be divided into a library for books and printed materials and a media center. *Syn.* materials center.

materials center: *syn.* materials bureau.

materials center, instructional: *see* center, instructional materials.

materials, concrete: (arith.) actual objects that are used with pupils in activities and which provide opportunity for the development of number concepts; for example, two halves of an apple might be used to illustrate the concept that two halves are equal to one whole.

materials, didactic: *see* Montessori method.

materials, graphic: *see* graphic materials.

materials, nongraded: (spec. ed.) curriculum materials which are specially devised to meet the unique needs of pupils with various special learning problems.

materials orientation: *see* orientation, materials.

materials preparation center: *see* center, local production.

materials, programmed instruction: *see* instruction materials, programmed.

materials, representative: *syn.* materials, semiconcrete.

materials, self-managed: a term used with reference to instructional materials or learning kits which are designed so that students can be instructed and can learn without teacher intervention or with a minimum of teacher guidance.

materials, self-teaching: instructional materials designed to induce learner curiosity or behavior and to give the learner cues as to the success of his trials; for example, sets for assembly by children which are self-correcting in revealing misfits, programmed materials which give confirmation, and self-tests which provide scoring keys. *See* instructional materials, programmed; workbook, programmed.

materials, semiconcrete: (arith.) symbols and small objects, uninteresting in themselves, used to represent in a simple form the basic ideas of a number situation; for example, dots, circles, sticks, etc. used to clarify addition and subtraction. *Syn.* representative materials.

materials, source: publications and audiovisual supplies and equipment used to extend and enrich the educational experiences of the learners. *See* materials center.

materials, structural: *see* arithmetic, structural.

materials, supervision: in supervision of instruction, those items prepared or acquired to facilitate the supervisory task.

materials, supplementary reading: *see* reading, supplementary.

materials support occupations training: *see* training, materials support occupations.

materials, visual: those instructional materials which communicate primarily through sight; written and printed materials, projected pictures, charts, maps, objects, specimens, and the like.

maternal behavior: *see* behavior, maternal.

maternal deprivation: *see* deprivation, maternal.

maternal impressions, doctrine of: the doctrine, now regarded as unfounded and untenable, according to which the specific psychological experiences of the expectant mother produce physical modifications or determine aptitudes or disabilities in the developing fetus.

maternal inheritance: *see* inheritance, maternal.

mathematical analysis: *see* analysis, mathematical.

mathematical appreciation: *see* appreciation, mathematical.

mathematical concept: *see* concept, mathematical.

mathematical crutches: a term used for any mnemonic aids in arithmetic.

mathematical education: *see* mathematics education.

mathematical enrichment: *see* enrichment, mathematical.

mathematical equipment: *see* equipment, mathematical.

mathematical expectation: *syn.* value, expected.

mathematical experience: *see* experience, mathematical.

mathematical fallacy: *see* fallacy, mathematical.

mathematical graph: *see* graph, mathematical.

mathematical induction: *see* induction, mathematical.

mathematical insight: *see* insight, mathematical.

mathematical linguistics: *see* linguistics, mathematical.

mathematical literacy: state of being informed in those basic principles and techniques which constitute functional competence in mathematics.

mathematical logic: *syn.* logic, symbolic.

mathematical meanings: *see* meanings, mathematical.

mathematical model: (1) a mathematical system whose essential features characterize one or more physical situations; a simple example is the natural number system in which the equation $3 + 2 = 5$ characterizes physical situations in which a set of two objects is joined to a set of three objects, the sets having no elements in common; (2) a diagram or object made of wood, plastic, etc., which represents a mathematical object, as, for example, a model of a cube.

mathematical needs: the mathematical computational skills, knowledge, understanding, and attitudes required to achieve a given set of objectives of an individual or of a particular population.

mathematical operation: *see* operation, mathematical.

mathematical phase: *see* phase, mathematical.

mathematical proof: *see* proof, mathematical.

mathematical readiness: *see* readiness, mathematical.

mathematical reasoning: *see* reasoning, mathematical.

mathematical recreation: *see* recreation, mathematical.

mathematical relation: *see* relation, mathematical.

mathematical sentence: *see* sentence, mathematical.

mathematical skill: *see* skill, mathematical.

mathematical system: (1) a set of elements together with an equivalence relation, one or more binary operations, and the properties of these operations; mathematical systems are classified according to the number of operations and the properties of the operations; some common systems are groups, rings, integral domains, fields, and vector spaces; (2) *syn.* deductive system.

mathematical system, finite: a mathematical system which has only a finite number of elements, such as *modular arithmetic.*

mathematical table: *see* table, mathematical.

mathematical understanding: *see* meanings, mathematical.

mathematics, agricultural: mathematics that relates to problems in agricultural activities, both nonfarm and farm.

mathematics, applied: (1) school mathematics in which the topics are selected for and the teaching aimed at some particular use of mathematics, as, for example, *consumer mathematics, business arithmetic,* and *trade mathematics;* (2) topics in mathematics which are relevant to the theory of other disciplines and which are studied for this reason.

mathematics aptitude test: *see* test, aptitude.

mathematics, basic: *syn.* mathematics, general.

mathematics, business: *see* mathematics, applied.

mathematics club: *see* club, mathematics.

mathematics, computational: that phase of mathematics which emphasizes the operational skills only.

mathematics, computer: (1) mathematics relevant to the operation of electronic computers; (2) a course in which such mathematics is studied.

mathematics, concrete: mathematics dealing with the problems and concepts that arise within the experience of the individual.

mathematics, consumer: those branches and skills of mathematics useful to the individual in his affairs as a consumer in situations such as installment buying, paying taxes, etc. *See* mathematics, applied.

mathematics, cultural: mathematics that stresses the heritage which the subject contributes to the development of civilization.

mathematics education: a new discipline or specialization which has emerged from mathematics and education; interest of educators in this field is typically focused on research, theory, and development of mathematics teacher-training programs, mathematics curricula, and mathematics instruction; sometimes referred to as *mathematical education.*

mathematics exhibit: a display of mathematical books, tools, devices, or models for the purpose of stimulating interest in mathematics.

mathematics fieldwork: experiences based on generalizations in geometry, adapted from surveying techniques, and primarily concerned with both direct and indirect measurement problems of terrain; often designed to demonstrate the application of geometry theorems or to develop the theorems as intuitive generalizations; instruments typically used are plane table, alidade, sextant, transit, hypsometer, angle mirror, tape measure, and ranging poles.

mathematics, formal: (1) with reference to pedagogy, mathematics presented in a sequence chosen for its logical consistency and completeness, the method of presentation often expository and the content largely restricted to one particular branch of mathematics; (2) *syn.* deductive system; mathematical system (2).

mathematics, functional: (1) mathematics of which the content is useful to an individual or group of individuals; (2) mathematics which an individual understands well enough so that he can apply it to other situations as needed.

mathematics, fundamentals of: (1) in some contexts, the concepts, ideas, etc., necessary for a full understanding of some branch of mathematics; (2) the basic skills of some branch of mathematics, possession of which may or may not be accompanied by understanding; (3) concepts or skills which must be acquired first in the study of some branch of mathematics, for example, learning to·count as fundamental to learning the addition facts.

mathematics, general: a term usually referring to a course which is remedial in nature and emphasizes computational facility; such a course may or may not include applications. *Syn.* **basic mathematics; integrated mathematics.**

mathematics, general education: a program in mathematics that is designed to contribute to the development of those abilities, understandings, attitudes, and behavior patterns which should be the common experience of all educated men and women; not to be confused with *general mathematics.*

mathematics, industrial arts: mathematics used in mechanical or industrial activities or in training for such activities.

mathematics, integrated: (1) topics in mathematics united into one common discipline; (2) topics in mathematics articulated with topics in some other discipline, as, for example, mathematics integrated with science; (3) *syn.* **mathematics, general.**

mathematics laboratory: *see* **laboratory, mathematics.**

mathematics, logical: mathematics developed through sound reasoning or in accordance with the inferences reasonably to be drawn from previously established mathematical facts or principles.

mathematics, modern: (1) a term used to describe recent curricular innovations in precollege mathematics; (2) mathematics developed since the late nineteenth century; (3) college courses such as *abstract algebra* and *topology;* (4) from the point of view of the history of mathematics, mathematics which has been axiomatized and/or has a convenient notation.

mathematics, nontraditional: those high school courses in mathematics, such as *general mathematics, integrated mathematics,* etc., which are not restricted to a given branch of mathematics as are algebra, plane geometry, trigonometry, etc.

mathematics of finance: the study of the theory of such problems as depreciation, investment, insurance, capitalized costs, etc.

mathematics of investment: the study of the theory of interest, annuities, and other forms of investments.

mathematics, preparatory: mathematics that is necessary to prepare for a specific educational goal or purpose.

mathematics, prerequisite: that mathematical knowledge and understanding necessary for entrance into a specific program in mathematics or another area of activity.

mathematics, pure: mathematics which is studied as a *deductive system* and without regard for immediate applications to the physical world.

mathematics, recreational: *see* **recreation, mathematical.**

mathematics, refresher: a course in mathematics in which the primary objective is the systematic review of mathematical concepts and/or skills supposedly acquired previously.

mathematics, secondary: the mathematics curriculum of grades 7 to 14.

mathematics, sequential: an organization of mathematics curriculum in which each topic is a prerequisite for the content of some succeeding topic or topics.

mathematics, socialized: mathematical subject matter treated in such a way that it is closely related to experiences of people.

mathematics, socioeconomic: *syn.* **mathematics, socialized.**

mathematics, structure in: the patterns to be found in all of mathematics; may be simple—as, for example, the pattern characterizing partitive division problems—or so-phisticated, such as the concept of algebraic structure.

mathematics, survey: a brief course in mathematics designed to give the student a general idea of various fields of mathematics such as trigonometry, calculus, and algebra.

mathematics, terminal: any mathematics course intended as the last formal contact with the subject for some group of students.

mathematics, theoretical: a term sometimes used as a synonym for *pure mathematics* and sometimes to indicate a dimension of abstractness for either pure or *applied mathematics;* in the latter meaning the emphasis is on generality, that is, obtaining results which could be extended to diverse classes of problems.

mathematics, trade: mathematics related to a particular trade, for example, sheet-metal mathematics. *See* **mathematics, applied.**

mathematics, traditional: mathematics as taught at the precollege level prior to the late 1940s.

mathematics, vocational: *see* **mathematics, trade.**

mathematics workshop: *syn.* **laboratory, mathematics.**

matriarchal family: *see* **family, matriarchal.**

matrices, progressive: *see* **test, progressive matrices.**

matriculation: the formal process, completed by registration, of being admitted as a student to the rights and privileges of membership in a college or university. (In some institutions, *admission* implies only that certain courses may be pursued; *candidacy,* that certain or all requirements preliminary to approval for pursuit of a degree have been met; matriculation, usually, that all such requirements have been met.)

matrix: *pl.* **matrices;** a rectangular array of numbers, prices, measures, etc., usually enclosed in either parentheses or square brackets; in practical problems, a convenient method of recording information, with suitable coding of the rows and columns; in mathematics, with certain restrictions placed on the kind of number allowed in the matrix, matrices are studied as elements in a *mathematical system;* while a fundamental relationship exists among the symbols used, a matrix has no quantitative value as does a determinant. *See* **determinant.**

matrix algebra: *see* **algebra, matrix.**

matrix, correlation: a table of intercorrelations of n tests; a correlation matrix is square with n rows and n columns and is symmetric about the principal diagonal, since $r_{jk} = r_{kj}$.

matrix, covariance: a matrix whose elements are the covariances of the variables represented by its rows and columns.

matrix, diagonal: a square matrix having zeros in all positions except those on the principal diagonal.

matrix, element of a: a single entry in a matrix.

matrix, factor-covariance: a matrix each element of which is the product of the factor loadings of the item in whose row and column it appears.

matrix, gramian: a matrix, such as a correlation matrix, in which the entry a_{ij} in the ith row, jth column, is the same as that in the jth row, ith column (a_{ji}), and in which all principal minors have a value greater than or equal to zero.

matrix, identity: a matrix in which the elements of the principal diagonal are equal to 1.0 and all other elements are 0.0.

matrix, inverse: *syn.* **matrix, inverse of a.**

matrix, inverse of a: a square matrix, denoted M^{-1}, related to a given matrix M in such a way that the products $(M^{-1})(M)$ and $(M)(M^{-1})$ are both equal to the identity matrix. *Syn.* **inverse matrix.**

matrix, lambda: (λ) the matrix of cosines that is used in rotating a factor matrix to a new position in the search for simple structure. *See* **matrix, transformation** (2).

matrix, multitrait-multimethod: (testing) systematic experimental design for an approach to validation that requires the assessment of two or more traits by two or more methods.

matrix, product: a matrix showing the result of multiplying factor loadings of variables.

matrix, rank of: the numbers of rows (or columns) of the largest square matrix within the given matrix whose determinant does not equal zero; in factor analysis, the rank of the correlation matrix is theoretically equal to the number of common factors among the tests.

matrix, reduced correlation: the matrix of intercorrelations with the diagonal entries depressed from unity to the communalities.

matrix, residual: (fact. anal.) a new matrix obtained by abstracting variance due to one or more factors from a given matrix.

matrix, square: any rectangular array of numbers in which there are the same number of rows and columns, regardless of what the numbers may mean.

matrix, transformation: (1) a matrix of relations by which a set of points (x) may be changed into a new set of points (y); (2) (fact. anal.) a matrix of cosines between reference vectors and factor axes, used in making a rotation; *see* **matrix, lambda.**

matrix, triangular: a matrix containing all zeroes in the portion above and to the right or below and to the left of the principal diagonal.

matrix, unrotated: the matrix of factor loadings directly obtained by one of the factorization methods.

matrix, V: a factor matrix of structure values obtained in rotation to simple structure; may be used with a subscript (as V_3 matrix) showing the number of rotations already performed; for example, V_0 is the unrotated matrix.

matron: (1) a woman who has charge of a dormitory, especially of the working force in a dormitory; (2) a woman who has charge of rest rooms in a high school; (3) a janitress or cleaning woman; (4) a noncertificated person employed as an attendant to assist with the self-care of crippled or severely retarded children in special classes. *See* **teacher aide.**

matron, parental-home: the woman in charge of a parental home who functions as the mother for the youths housed there. *See* **parental home.**

matte screen: *see* **screen, matte.**

matter: (1) that which occupies space and constitutes the substance of the physical universe, in distinction from idea or spirit; *see* **materialism;** (2) in the philosophy of Aristotle, the material cause, the physical or nonphysical substratum which is something potentially, in distinction from and always relative to form which must combine appropriately with matter to constitute anything actually; *see* **cause, material; form** (8).

matter and motion: in classical (Newtonian) physics, the conception that reality, that is, *nature,* is "essentially a realm of masses, moving according to mathematical laws in space and time, under the influence of definite and dependable forces." *See* **mechanism.**

maturation: (1) changes in the characteristics of an organism resulting from intrinsic (anatomic, physiological, and neurological) development, with or without the aid of autogenous development; to be distinguished from changes due to special experience or learning; (2) the process of cellular, organic, and functional development of an organism.

maturation division: the variety of cell division in which only one member of each chromosome pair in the parent cell is given to each one of the daughter cells, thus producing cells with only half the number of chromosomes common to the species; a necessary step in the formation of gametes, or mature fertilizable germ cells. *See* **chromosome; mitosis.**

maturation, intellectual: the process of developing to higher degrees the rational, conceptual, and logical powers. *See* **growth, mental; intellectualization.**

maturation, reading: (1) full growth in reading; the stage at which the reader achieves complete adaptation in reading; (2) a state of readiness for reading as a result of physical, mental, and emotional development.

maturational gradient-shifts: *see* **gradient-shifts, maturational.**

maturity: the stage at which development has reached its maximum and growth has ceased; applied to cells, organs, functions—both physical and mental—and entire organisms.

maturity, consumer: the difference in group attitudes toward shopping, dependent upon age, income, social class, education, intelligence, shopping experience, and occupation.

maturity, emotional: the emotional pattern of an adult who has progressed through the inferior emotional stages characteristic of infancy, childhood, and adolescence and is now fitted to deal successfully with reality and to participate in adult love relationships without undue emotional strain.

maturity, intellectual: the state of having attained full development of one's mental capacity.

maturity, mental: (1) the stage of mental growth attained at a given age; (2) the stage of complete mental growth, beyond which no further growth takes place. *See* **growth, mental.**

maturity, moral: that stage of development when an individual or a group is able, through reasoned judgment of what is right and proper, to implement principles of ethical conduct in accordance with individual or group potentialities, and in line with cultural expectations; an end product of the sum total of numerous processes of acculturation.

maturity, physiological: the condition of final or highest development of an organ or function.

maturity, professional: (1) of an individual, a state or condition in his development which is perceived by members of his society to be of value to himself and of service to others; (2) of a group, an advanced state of an occupational group of people who (a) render an important social service, (b) control and discipline their own ranks, (c) possess unique expertise in knowledge, behavior, or both, and (d) consider their contribution to society as being vital to its survival.

maturity, psychological: *syn.* **maturity, social.**

maturity, sexual: the stage of life at which the reproductive organs function normally.

maturity, social: the degree to which an individual has acquired the social and socialized behaviors that are usual and expected for his age or for his age and status; or the social behavior characteristics of the supposedly typical adult member of a society. *See* **intelligence, social.**

maturity status: the degree to which cellular, organic, and functional development has been completed.

maturity, vocational: the level of development of the individual, either physical or emotional or both, that will equip him for the work, occupation, or profession to which he feels he is called and for which he considers himself fitted.

maxim, pragmatic: *see* **pragmatic maxim.**

maximum capacity of laboratory: *see* **capacity of laboratory, maximum.**

maximum compulsory school age: *see* **compulsory school age, maximum.**

maximum error: *see* **error, maximum.**

maximum likelihood method: a procedure for factor analysis which provides the best fitting factor matrix for a given number of factors; the goodness of fit to the correlation matrix can then be tested rigorously by chi square.

maximum likelihood statistics: *see* **statistics, maximum likelihood.**

maximum performance test: *see* **test, maximum performance.**

maze: a series of pathways, some of which lead to blind alleys while others lead to a goal; a device frequently used to test human or animal ability to learn from experience.

maze running: (phys. ed.) running in single file in circles and other patterns.

maze test: *see* **test, maze.**

McCollum case: a case originating in Champaign, Illinois, in which the United States Supreme Court ruled that the practice of excusing children from their classes so that they might attend classes of their choice in religious instruction was illegal when such classes were held in public school buildings.

McDade plan: a plan similar to the Winnetka plan but utilizing shorter units of individualized instructional material so organized that they may be adapted to the program of any pupil.

meal basis: method of teaching foods and nutrition by emphasizing the planning, preparing, and serving of meals rather than the preparation of isolated food products.

mean: a measure of central tendency; (1) strictly, any one of several calculated averages, including the arithmetic mean, the geometric mean, and the harmonic mean; (2) as commonly used, a synonym for arithmetic mean; *see* **mean, arithmetic.**

mean absolute error: *syn.* **deviation, average.**

mean, arithmetic (M or X): a measure of central tendency which is obtained from the sum of the measures, observations, magnitudes, items, or scores in a statistical series, divided by their number, or frequency; often shortened to *mean. Syn.* **arithmetic average; average; mean (2).**

mean, assumed: *syn.* **average, guessed.**

mean center of area: *see* **geographical center.**

mean center of population: a point representing a mean derived from cases (commodities, etc.) distributed geographically, so taken that the aggregate of distances from any straight line through the point to all the cases will algebraically total zero; the point at which a plane with the population distributed over it would balance when each case has equal weight. (This is the center usually calculated by the U.S. Census Bureau and referred to by the Bureau as the *center of population.*) *See* **geographical center;** *dist. f.* **mean center of area; median center of population.**

mean, contraharmonic: a measure of central tendency, seldom used, obtained by dividing the sum of the squares of the observations by the sum of the observations; expressed by the formula $\Sigma X^2 / \Sigma X$.

mean deviation: *syn.* **deviation, average.**

mean difference: the mean of the absolute values of all the $N(N-1)/2$ differences that can be found among N quantities; a measure of dispersion approximately equal to $\sigma\sqrt{2}$ in a normal distribution. *Syn.* **Gini's mean difference.**

mean discrepancy: *syn.* **deviation, standard.**

mean, doctrine of the: (Aristotelian ethics) the "golden mean" is the "middle" between excess and defect relative to that rational moderation of the passions which is most conducive to happiness; opposed to the notion that happiness lies either in total repression of the passions or in their unregulated expression; hence the mean is proportional, not arithmetical.

mean error: (1) strictly, an average deviation taken about the mean; (2) *syn.* **deviation, average;** (3) sometimes incorrectly used as a synonym for standard deviation; *see* **deviation, standard.**

mean, geometric (GM): a measure of central tendency which is equal to the Nth root of the product of N values, or the antilogarithm of the arithmetic mean of the logarithms of the observations; for example, the geometric mean of the series 5, 10, 15, would be $3\sqrt{5 \times 10 \times 15}$; used in averaging rates of change, ratios, etc. *Syn.* **geometric average; logarithmic average; logarithmic mean.**

mean, guessed (GM): *syn.* **average, guessed.**

mean, harmonic: (M_H) a measure of central tendency especially adapted to averaging such data as time rates and consisting of the reciprocal of the arithmetic mean of the reciprocals of the individual measures; thus, the harmonic mean of the series 2, 5, 10, 20 would be found as follows:

$$M_H = 1 \div \frac{\frac{1}{2} + \frac{1}{5} + \frac{1}{10} + \frac{1}{20}}{4} = 1 \div \frac{17}{20 \times 4}$$
$$= \frac{80}{17} = 4.7, \text{ approximately.}$$

Syn. **harmonic average.**

mean, logarithmic: *syn.* **mean, geometric.**

mean of extremes: *syn.* **value, midrange.**

mean, quadratic: *syn.* **root mean square.**

mean, simple arithmetic: *syn.* **mean, arithmetic.**

mean square contingency coefficient: *syn.* **coefficient of contingency.**

mean square deviation: *see* **variance.**

mean square error: *syn.* **variance.**

mean, true: a theoretical value consisting of the arithmetic mean of the measures which might be obtained if a whole universe were being observed on some variable.

mean, unweighted arithmetic: the arithmetic mean of a series of observations each of which is given the same weight as any other. *Syn.* **arithmetic mean; mean with equal weights; simple arithmetic mean; unweighted arithmetic average;** *contr. w.* **mean, weighted arithmetic (1).**

mean variability: *syn.* **deviation, average.**

mean variation: *syn.* **deviation, average.**

mean, weighted arithmetic: (1) an arithmetic mean in which the various items are assigned varying weights or importances; *syn.* **weighted arithmetic average; weighted mean;** *contr. w.* **mean, unweighted arithmetic;** (2) loosely used to designate an arithmetic mean in which the various magnitudes are weighted in proportion to their frequency of occurrence.

mean with equal weights: *syn.* **mean, unweighted arithmetic.**

mean, working: *syn.* **average, guessed.**

meaning: an ambiguous term commonly used in four main senses: (1) intention or purpose; (2) designation or reference; (3) definition or translation; (4) causal antecedents. (These senses are themselves not unambiguous.)

meaning associations: *see* **associations, meaning.**

meaning attack: (read.) an attack on meaning rather than on the form of words; use of the context in identifying the meaning of words.

meaning background: the experience, either direct or vicarious, which a reader or listener draws upon in attaching meanings to the words he reads or hears.

meaning clue: *see* **clue, meaning.**

meaning, contextual theory of: the theory that meaning is formal; that is, a symbol gets its meaning from precisely the context in which it occurs, no specific context being specifiable beforehand.

meaning, lexical: the meaning in a language that is expressed by words rather than by means of structure, function words, or intonation.

meaning of meaning: a theory or theories derived from systematic inquiry into situations where meaning is supposed or claimed to reside; results from an attempt to "dissect and ventilate" meaning.

meaning, operational: that meaning of a symbol which is wholly constituted by the actions called out in behalf of the symbol; thus, in scientific research, the meaning of a hypothesis is determined by the experimental procedures employed in the development and testing of the hypothesis.

meaning, stipulation of: the task of a speaker or writer to use words so that he specifies what he is talking about and so that his usage conforms as closely as possible to the customary.

meaning theory of perception: the implication that perception is the first step in differentiating a factor from the undifferentiated sensory mass in which it is found or in identifying a common factor in a series of different sensory experiences, differentiation leading to identification, classification, and generalization, hence meaning.

meaning unit: *see* **unit, meaning.**

meaning vocabulary: *see* **vocabulary, meaning.**

meaningful approach: a method of teaching arithmetic which provides pupils with a series of experiences in which they are certain to have numerous contacts with uses of arithmetic in daily life and to have the opportunity to develop an understanding of the mathematical basis of the uses of numbers; a planned, systematic, and sequential program that emphasizes both the mathematical and the social phases of arithmetic.

meaningful code: *see* **code, meaningful.**

meaningful code number: *see* **code number, meaningful.**

meanings, mathematical: the basic structure that gives significance to all computational skills, informational concepts, and logical abstractions which constitute the subject matter of mathematics as an essential field of knowledge.

meanings, plural: (Dolch) a number of meanings for words having one spelling.

meanings, variant: semantic variations in the meanings of words; multiple meanings of a single word.

means-ends relationship: in the philosophy of experimentalism, outcomes or purposes (as ends in view) are meaningful when related to the means for their achievement, and the method used for the attainment of an end defines the meaning and worth of the end; means and ends are thus integrally interrelated but not identical. *See* consequences.

measurable load: *see* load, measurable.

measure: *n.* (1) any standard or unit, whether commonly accepted or arbitrarily established, with reference to which something may be evaluated or an estimate made of its value; (2) *syn.* observation (3); (3) *syn.* statistic (1); (4) a number assigned to an entity to quantify intuitive ideas of "more than" and "less than" when that entity is compared with others of the same type, as, for example, assigning "4 hours" as a measure of time to compare it with other periods of time.

measure: *v.* (1) to determine the quantity, quality, or value of anything, whether exactly or approximately, with reference to some standard; (2) to determine how many times a unit quantity is contained in another quantity.

measure, approximate: the result of the determination within a certain degree of accuracy of the ratio of one quantity to another of the same kind.

measure, continuous: (1) one of a number of items or observations that differ by infinitely small increments, for example, an observation of the weight of an animal; (2) any measure of a continuous variable. *See* variable, continuous; *ant.* measure, discrete.

measure, criterion: (1) a measure listing specific behaviors implied at each level of proficiency, identified and used to describe the specific tasks a student must be capable of performing before he achieves one of these knowledge levels; it is in this sense that measures of proficiency can be criterion-referenced; (2) a measure which provides information as to the degree of competence attained by a particular student which is independent of reference to the performance of others; (3) a score in the criterion or dependent variable; a score, measure, or observation on the variable that is to be predicted by means of a regression equation; *syn.* score, criterion.

measure, derived: any measure computed from a given set of data. *Syn.* transmuted measure; rough *syn.* derived score.

measure, discrete: one of a number of items or observations that differ by clearly defined steps without intermediate values, for example, the number of children in a classroom; any measure of a discrete variable. *Syn.* point measure; *see* variable, discrete; *contr. w.* measure, continuous.

measure in normal units: *syn.* score, standard.

measure in standard units: *syn.* score, standard.

measure, Jaeger (yā′gər): a test for near vision composed of lines of reading matter printed in a series of various sizes of type. *See* assessment, eyesight.

measure, norm-referenced: a measure which indicates a student's relative standing along the continuum of attainment; provides little or no information about the degree of proficiency exhibited by the tested behavior in terms of what the individual can do; tells that one student is more or less proficient than another but does not tell how proficient either of them is with respect to the subject-matter tasks involved.

measure, obtained: any measure that has been derived from operations performed on raw data.

measure of central tendency: a statistic calculated from a set of observations or scores and designed to typify or represent that series; an average, for example, the *mean, median, geometric mean, mode,* etc.

measure of covariation: *syn.* measure of relationship.

measure of dispersion: a statistic calculated from a set of observations or scores and designed to show the extent to which the individual observations or scores are concentrated about or scattered from the mean or some other measure of central tendency, for example, the *standard deviation, average deviation, quartile deviation, variance,* etc. *Syn.* measure of precision; measure of variability; measure of variation; *dist. f.* coefficient of dispersion.

measure of precision: *syn.* measure of dispersion.

measure of relationship: a general term, sometimes used as a synonym for coefficient of correlation. *See* coefficient, correlation.

measure of skewness: *syn.* coefficient of skewness.

measure of variability: *syn.* measure of dispersion.

measure of variation: *syn.* measure of dispersion.

measure, point: *syn.* measure, discrete.

measure, predictive: (1) a score or measure that can be used in the prediction of another score or measure (for example, a particular score on a mechanical-aptitude test used as a basis for predicting success in an automotive trades course); (2) a correlational relationship between two series of scores or measures that makes possible the prediction of a value on one scale from a known value on the other scale. *See* regression equation, linear.

measure, qualitative: the degree of presence or absence of a trait or characteristic without reference to the amount.

measure, radian: a measure for angles; one radian is the measure of an angle with its vertex at the center of a circle and intercepting an arc whose length equals the radius of the circle.

measure, reduced: *syn.* score, reduced (1).

measure, sigma: *see* score, standard.

measure, standard: *see* score, standard.

measure, transmuted: *syn.* measure, derived.

measure, true: *syn.* score, true.

measure, unit of: *see* unit of measure.

measured intelligence: *see* intelligence, measured.

measurement: (1) the comparison of a quantity (exhibited by a particular case) with an appropriate scale for the purpose of determining (within the limits of accuracy imposed by the nature of the scale) the numerical value on the scale that corresponds to the quantity to be measured; *see* scale; *dist. f.* enumeration; (2) the term commonly applied to examining persons by giving some form of test; *dist. f.* evaluation; (3) process of obtaining a numerical description of the extent to which a person (or thing) possesses some characteristic.

measurement, accuracy in: a term used to describe the size of the *relative error;* the smaller the relative error, the more accurate the measurement. *See* error, relative; *contr. w.* measurement, precision in.

measurement, anthropometric: a measure of the dimensions, proportions, or other characteristics of a structure of the human body or of the body as a whole, for example, height, weight, the length of the nose, etc.

measurement, criterion: measurement of a psychological trait in a real-life situation such as a classroom; used to establish the validity of instruments.

measurement, criterion-referenced: measurement, against a standard of achievement, of how well a student can perform; represents an absolute grading system; that is, "yes, he can"; "no, he can't"; whether the instructional objectives require the standard to be related to the group or to success on the job, the test should allow for prediction; the instructor may require all students to get certain questions correct, an absolute standard; from this criterion he can accurately predict future success on the job. *Ant.* measurement, norm-referenced.

measurement, direct: measurement made by direct comparison of the object to be measured with a unit (or a collection of units assembled), such as measuring length with a ruler or yardstick or the capacity of a container by counting the number of cups of water required to fill it. *Contr. w.* measurement, indirect.

measurement, educational: (1) a broad term for the general study and practice of testing, scaling, and appraisal of aspects of the educational process for which measures are available and of the individuals undergoing the educational process; includes the theory of test and scale construction, validation and standardization, interpretation of test results, objective and subjective evaluations, and the application of statistical techniques to the interpretation of obtained measures; (2) the end product obtained through applying a measure to any aspect of the educational process or the individuals undergoing it; thus, a particular test result, an appraisal of the adequacy of a school building, or the determined weight of a pupil would be an educational measurement.

measurement, error of: *see* **error of measurement.**

measurement, indirect: (1) (math.) measurement of quantities such as time, temperature, and velocity which are determined by actually measuring some other quantity and then converting; for example, a thermometer is scaled so that the height of the column of mercury is converted to degrees of temperature; mathematical computations using formulas are also considered to be forms of indirect measurement, as in computing the height of a flagpole from the length of its shadow; (2) in intelligence testing, the estimation of intelligence by measuring its manifestations, such as ability to learn. *Contr. w.* **measurement, direct.**

measurement, inferential method of character: evaluation of specific traits of character in accordance with performance on a test or group of tests designed to reveal the extent of presence of each trait.

measurement, ipsative: measurement of the variation of an individual about his own mean, reflecting relative strengths and weaknesses for that individual alone; differences in scores cannot be interpreted normatively since each score may be related to a different mean.

measurement, mental: (1) the recording of performances in numerical terms by means of a mental test regarded as a scale; (2) the quantitative determination or estimation of any psychological function, trait, or disposition; the determination of the response strength of a habit, of the strength of a person's attitude, etc.

measurement, methods-time (MTM): analysis of procedure or operation into basic motions and assignment of a predetermined standard to each motion. *See* **study, motion; study, time.**

measurement, multiple: the securing of more than one measure of an individual or group of individuals through the use of more than one test; the separate tests employed are usually called a *battery* and are designed to accomplish a single measurement objective or a closely related set of measurement objectives.

measurement, norm-referenced: measurement in which test items are modified and changed to ensure that a normal distribution occurs. *See* **distribution, normal;** *ant.* **measurement, criterion-referenced.**

measurement of attention: *see* **attention, measurement of.**

measurement, personality: a general area of testing, investigation, and study concerned with the qualitative and quantitative measurement of various aspects of the personality, such as attitudes, character traits, interests, emotional stability, or neurotic tendencies.

measurement, precision in: a term used to indicate the size of the unit of measurement; the smaller the unit of measurement, the more precise the measurement. *Contr. w.* **measurement, accuracy in.**

measurement, social: the application of tests, scales, statistical analysis, and other measuring techniques and instruments to group phenomena such as association in groups, attitudes of persons toward values, social status, social adjustment, etc. *See* **sociometry.**

measurement, standard: measurement under standardized conditions, that is, with standardization of such factors as directions to the examinees, time allotment, method of scoring, interpretation of scores, etc.

measurement, standard error of: *see* **standard error of measurement.**

measures, comparable: two or more measures expressed in terms of the same unit and with reference to the same zero point, or origin, for example, two or more measures expressed in inches, in mental ages, or in z scores.

measures of utilization: *see* **utilization, measures of.**

mechanic, all-round: a trained individual possessing the skills and knowledges necessary to do practically all the jobs within a specified trade or occupation.

mechanic arts: *see* **arts, mechanic.**

mechanic, refrigeration: (voc. ed.) a worker who is one of the trained personnel who install and repair refrigerating and cooling systems.

mechanical ability: *see* **ability, mechanical.**

mechanical ability test: *see* **test, mechanical aptitude.**

mechanical aptitude: *see* **aptitude, mechanical.**

mechanical aptitude test: *see* **test, mechanical aptitude.**

mechanical arithmetic: *see* **arithmetic, mechanical.**

mechanical calculation: *see* **computation, mechanical.**

mechanical comprehension: *see* **comprehension, mechanical.**

mechanical computation: *see* **computation, mechanical.**

mechanical design technician: *see* **technician, mechanical design.**

mechanical drawing: *see* **drawing, mechanical.**

mechanical intelligence: *see* **intelligence, mechanical.**

mechanical pitcher: *see* **pitcher, mechanical.**

mechanical reading: *see* **reading, mechanical.**

mechanical scoring: *syn.* **scoring, machine.**

mechanical tabulation: *see* **tabulation, mechanical.**

mechanical ventilation: *see* **ventilation, mechanical.**

mechanics: (lang.) such aspects of language study as correct, conventional usage of words, capitalization, certain items of punctuation, and letter forms.

mechanics, agricultural: *see* **agricultural mechanics education.**

mechanics, body: *see* **body mechanics.**

mechanics' institute: *see* **institute, mechanics'.**

mechanics laboratory: *see* **laboratory, mechanics.**

mechanics, quantum: the science which includes the study of behavior of electrons and nucleons, the duality of energy and matter (wave and particle models), relativity, statistical and wave mechanics, and all aspects of quantum theory. (Electromagnetic radiation consists of small packets called quanta, according to the theory which hence is called the quantum theory.)

mechanics shop: *see* **shop, mechanics.**

mechanism: (philos.) a position according to which reality is similar to a machine, physical in substance and deterministic in character, operating with strict efficiency within a framework of relations, such as cause and effect, and not dependent upon spirit.

mechanism, adjustment: *see* **adjustment mechanism.**

mechanism, pollyanna: *see* **pollyanna mechanism.**

mechanism, sweet lemon: *see* **sweet lemon mechanism.**

mechanistic approach: (social studies) the viewpoint according to which nature as a whole and the processes of life are thought to be machinelike and mechanically necessitated and capable of explanation by the laws of physics and chemistry and which, in its intention to find immediate and efficient rather than final origins, processes, and goals for human life, is allied to *materialism.*

mechanistic instruction: *see* **instruction, mechanistic.**

mechanization of administration: the exercise of direction, management, and control as if done by a machine, automatically or through habit, without special thought for each separate problem.

media: *see* **medium.**

media, common-language: *see* **common-language media.**

media, educational: *see* **educational media.**

media, instructional: *see* **instructional media.**

media, mass: *see* **mass media.**

media, new educational: *see* **educational media, new.**

medial position: the location of a sound occurring in an intermediary position in a word. *Dist. f.* **final position; initial position.**

medials: body types with about equal components of endomorphy, mesomorphy, and ectomorphy. *See* **ectomorph; endomorph; mesomorph.**

median (Md; Mdn): the point on the scale of a frequency distribution at which or below which (also, at which or above which) 50 percent of the observations occur; used as a measure of central tendency; synonymous with 50th percentile, 2d quartile, and 5th decile.

median age: *see* **age, median.**

median center of population: a point representing a median derived from cases (for example, persons, commodities, etc.) distributed geographically, so taken that the aggregate of the distances from the point to all the cases will be a minimum, that is, less than a similar (or corresponding) aggregate for any other point that might be taken. (It is not given by the intersection of two perpendicular median lines.)

median, crude: *syn.* **median, rough.**

median deviation: *see* **deviation, median.**

median error: *syn.* **deviation, median.**

median interval: *see* **interval, median.**

median, modified: the arithmetic mean of the middle three, four, or more cases of a frequency distribution.

median, rough: the midpoint of the interval in which the median occurs. *Syn.* **crude median.**

mediate value: *see* **value, instrumental.**

mediated instruction: *see* **teaching, mediated.**

mediated teacher: a teacher whose instructional efforts are presented to students through media, outside the classroom as well as within the classroom situation. *Dist. f.* **classroom teacher.**

mediated teaching: *see* **teaching, mediated.**

mediation: (1) (admin.) in the course of collective negotiations between teachers and administration, a process by which a third party attempts to assist the negotiators to reach an agreement; *see* **arbitration;** (2) (psych.) a process whereby certain variables intervene between the stimulus and the response; various theories of learning and behavior postulate different intervening variables, called *mediators,* such as subvocal verbal symbols and fractional or covert responses.

mediational response: *see* **response, mediational.**

mediator: in communication theory, the system that intervenes between the receiver and the transmitter; combines the functions of destination and source. *See* **mediation** (2).

medical college: *see* **college, medical.**

medical education, continuing: *see* **continuing professional education.**

medical evaluation: *see* **evaluation, medical.**

medical examination: *see* **examination, medical.**

medical examination, state: examination of school enrollees or employees under authorization or compulsion of the state by a recognized practitioner in the medical profession.

medical examination, teacher's: an investigation of the health and physical condition of a teacher or prospective teacher, made by an examiner usually approved by the medical profession, to determine whether health standards for employment are met.

medical inspection: *see* **inspection, medical.**

medical library: *see* **library, medical.**

medical professional training: *see* **training, medical professional.**

medical record technician: *see* **technician, medical record.**

medical report: *see* **report, medical.**

medical school, proprietary: a medical school owned by one or more proprietors and usually operated as a profit-making business; no such schools are now in existence.

medical service: a program providing services of physicians, nurses, and sometimes other health workers to care for the health of students or some other group of persons.

medical training, aerospace: *see* **training, aerospace medical.**

medicine, space: a branch of aerospace medicine concerned specifically with the health of persons who make or expect to make flights into space beyond the sensible atmosphere; frequently used as a unit of instruction in an aerospace education program.

medicine, sports: a branch of science which appropriates from many other scientific areas those aspects which relate directly to biomedical facts, consequences, and problems pertinent to man's engagement in sports, games, recreation, and rehabilitation.

medieval culture: *see* **culture, medieval.**

medieval history: *see* **history, medieval.**

meditation: (relig. ed.) (1) the practice of mental prayer whereby the individual contemplates the divine with a view to progress in his devotion to God; (2) a devotional talk (often given in connection with a retreat or a quiet day) designed to deepen the spiritual life; *see* **retreat.**

medium: *pl.* **media;** in certain uses, **mediums;** anything intervening, such as a carrier or transmitter in, for example, communications, or the means by which a process is rendered. *See* **medium of instruction.**

medium, art: *see* **art medium.**

medium of instruction: the principal mode by which the plan of instruction is mediated to the learner, including face-to-face instruction by a live teacher (in school or out of school) or mediated teaching via prerecorded tapes or records, books, instruction sheets, correspondence or computer-assisted instruction, television, or some other audiovisual means or combination of means. *Dist. f.* **instructional media.**

meet: an athletic contest comprising a series of separate events and lasting 1 day or more.

meeting, adjourned: *see* **adjourned meeting.**

meeting, board: *see* **board meeting.**

meeting, school-board: *syn.* **board meeting.**

meeting, special: (school admin.) a board of education meeting in which only the items mentioned in the notice of the meeting can be acted upon. *See* **board meeting.**

meeting, training: *see* **training meeting.**

megalomania: a condition characterized by overestimation of self with delusions such as those of grandeur, wealth, position, and importance.

megaphonia: undue loudness of voice.

megrim: *syn.* **migraine.**

meiosis (mī·ō′sis): *alt. sp.* **miosis;** (1) the division of the germ cells, preceding the formation of gametes, in which the number of chromosomes is reduced to half the somatic number; (2) a decrease in the intensity of existing symptoms.

melamed (mə·läm′ed): *n. masc.; pl.* **melamdim** (mə·läm′-dim); (Heb., lit., "teacher") a teacher in a *heder,* the old traditional Jewish school.

melancholia (mel′ən·kō′li·ə): mental derangement or psychosis characterized by excessive gloom and depression.

melioration: the process of bettering economic or other conditions without the expectation of more than moderate results.

meliorism: the view that the world can be made better through our efforts; belief in progress; the view that man, by taking thought and by bringing intelligence to his problems, can improve his lot and that of his community.

melleiren (mel·i′rēn): a term used to refer to the Spartan youth at 18, when he began his training for warfare. *See* **eiren.**

melodic dictation: *see* **dictation, melodic.**

melody bells: a diminutive glockenspiel used in primary music classes for matching tones and recognizing and reproducing melodies; may be constructed by pupils; sometimes used in a rhythm band. *See* **glockenspiel; rhythm band.**

melting-pot theory: the theory that people of various nationalities and races will, when living in close association, modify their cultural identities and become assimilated into one group.

member, board: *syn.* **school-board member.**

member, ex officio: *see* **ex officio member.**

member, school-board: *see* **school-board member.**

membership: the number of pupils enrolled in a school or class at any time; computed by taking the number of pupils who enrolled on the opening day of school, deducting those who later dropped out, and adding those who enrolled after the first day. (It is no longer regarded as good practice to drop students temporarily from the roll for absence due to sickness or other causes, since to do so results in an artificially high attendance rate.)

membership, aggregate days: the sum of the days present and absent of all pupils when school is in session during a given reporting period; only days on which the pupils are under the guidance and direction of teachers should be considered as *days in session.*

membership, average: *see* **membership, average daily.**

membership, average daily (ADM): the aggregate of the daily membership for the school year divided by the actual number of days school was in session; a measure of the average resident pupil load in terms of actual in-school attendance; will always be less than enrollment, owing to absences. *Syn.* **average daily enrollment; average membership; average number belonging.**

membership being provided appropriate special education, percentage of total: *see* **percentage of total membership being provided appropriate special education.**

membership, day of: for a given pupil, any day that school is in session from the date the pupil presents himself at school and is placed on the current roll until he withdraws from membership in the class or school.

membership group: *see* **group, membership.**

membership in special classes and/or special schools: the number of pupils on the current roll of special classes and/or special schools as of a given date.

membership, percentage in: *see* **percentage of age group in all schools; percentage of age group in public schools.**

membership, percentage of change in: *see* **percentage of change in membership from previous year.**

membership, percentage of total excess public school: *see* **percentage of total excess public school membership.**

membership, professional education staff per 1,000 pupils in average daily: *see* **professional education staff per 1,000 pupils in average daily membership.**

memorandum, training: *syn.* **contract, cooperative student.**

memoriter method (mə·mor′i·tər): any method of teaching in which pupils or students are expected to commit to memory the subject matter taught or which places undue emphasis upon rote learning.

memorization: commitment to memory; a mental process involving recall.

memory: (1) knowledge or awareness of something previously known or experienced accompanied by consciousness that one has had the previous knowledge or experience; (2) (data processing) a device consisting of electronic, electrostatic, electrical, hardware, or other elements into which data may be entered and stored and from which data may be obtained as desired; (3) the erasable storage in any given computer.

memory, auditory: power of (*a*) recognition, (*b*) voluntary recall, and (*c*) (at maximum efficiency) reproduction in speech or by other means of sound quality, intensity, pitch, and rhythm. *See* **memory, tonal.**

memory capacity: in computer operations, the amount of information which a memory device can store.

memory drawing: *see* **drawing, memory.**

memory dump: *see* **storage dump.**

memory, external: storage of data on a device which is not an integral part of a computer.

memory file: in computer operations, a large bank of memory cores where information is stored.

memory-for-design test: *see* **test, memory-for-design.**

memory, immediate: the recall of learned materials with the minimum lapse of time after learning.

memory, impersonal: conceptions arising from the "collective unconscious" (Jung); connections between the individual psyche and any particular racial or ancestral heritage; the function of recalling the archetypes of the race; unconscious retention in the memory of content of racial origin.

memory, internal: storage devices, usually high-speed, that are an integral physical part of the automatic computer.

memory, kinesthetic: *see* **kinesthetic memory.**

memory location: a position within a computer's storage device. *See* **storage device;** *comp. w.* **storage location.**

memory method: a method of teaching children to read by having them memorize stories, sentences, or word groups without paying special attention to recognizing the individual words.

memory, musical: *syn.* **memory, tonal.**

memory, personal: judgments concerning one's own past experience.

memory span: the compass of the memory; the number of items that can be reproduced correctly after a single presentation; commonly measured in tests of intelligence by repetition of digits, words, or sentences.

memory span, auditory: the number of related or unrelated items that can be recalled immediately after one hearing.

memory, tonal: the ability to recall patterns of tones; measured in various music tests, generally by requiring a comparison of two series of tones. *Syn.* **musical memory.**

memory unit: storage unit of the computer where information can be introduced and later extracted.

memory, visual: memory of things seen. *Contr. w.* **memory, auditory.**

menarche (mə·när′ki): the first appearance of menstruation.

menarchial age: *see* **age, menarchial.**

Mendel's law: the basic principles of inheritance enunciated by Gregor Johann Mendel (1822–1884), Austrian botanist, which are as follows: (*a*) that characters exhibit alternative inheritance; that is, the factors that govern the production of a given character (for example, color) exist in dominant and recessive forms, and the recessive form appears only when its factor is not paired with and overcome by the corresponding dominant factor; (*b*) that each reproductive cell receives only one member of each pair of genes (determinant factors) present in the other cells of the organism and therefore contains but half of the species number of genes (or chromosomes); (*c*) that the reproductive cells combine at random to produce new individuals. (These principles explain the observation that in the progeny of hybrid matings characters tend to appear in certain predictable ratios, such as 3:1, 1:2:1, 1:1, provided that the progeny are sufficiently numerous.) *See* **chromosome; dominant; gene; maturation division.**

men's counselor: *syn.* **dean of men.**

mensuration: (1) the study or process of measurement; (2) a branch of geometry dealing with the determination of length, area, angle, and volume relationships.

mental: pertaining to the mind and its functions; variously interpreted as (*a*) conscious; (*b*) a generic term embracing conscious and unconscious; (*c*) roughly synonymous with responsive; and (*d*) synonymous with psychic.

mental abilities, primary: *see* **abilities, primary mental.**

mental ability: *see* **ability, mental.**

mental ability, superior: *see* **intelligence.**

mental activity: *see* **activity, mental.**

mental age: *see* **age, mental.**

mental alienation: a generic term for unsoundness of mind.

mental apparatus: (psychoan.) the hypothetical arrangement of the psyche for purposes of description and interpretation; assumed to consist of the *id,* the *ego,* and the *superego.*

mental blocking: *see* **blocking, mental.**

mental capacity: *see* **capacity, mental.**

mental competition: *see* **competition, mental.**

mental deafness: *syn.* **deafness, cortical.**

mental decay: the progressive loss of mental function, as in senescence or dementia. *See* **mental;** *contr. w.* **development, mental.**

mental defect: *see* **defect, mental.**

mental defective: *see* **defective, mental.**

mental defective, certifiable: a medicolegal term referring to a person who meets legal criteria with reference to being mentally retarded to a given degree. *See* **retardation, mental.**

mental defective, certified: *syn.* **mental defective, certifiable.**

mental deficiency: *see* **retardation, mental.**

mental deficiency, borderline: *see* **defective, borderline.**

mental deficiency, familial: *see* **deficiency, familial mental.**

mental degeneration: *syn.* **mental decay.**

mental deterioration: *syn.* **dementia.**

mental development: *see* **development, mental.**

mental deviate: (1) a person who differs to a considerable degree from the average in any psychological characteristic or trait; (2) a person who is distinctly above or below average in intelligence. *See* **atypical.**

mental differences: *see* **differences, mental.**

mental discipline: *see* **discipline, mental.**

mental disease: *syn.* **psychosis.**

mental dullness: *see* **mentally retarded.**

mental evolution: *see* **evolution, mental.**

mental examination: *see* **examination, mental.**

mental expectancy: *see* **expectancy, mental.**

mental factors: *see* **factors, mental.**

mental faculties: *see* **faculties, mental.**

mental growth: *see* **growth, mental.**

mental growth, dimensions of: *see* **dimensions of mental growth.**

mental growth unit: *see* **unit, mental growth.**

mental handicap: *see* **handicap, mental.**

mental health: *see* **health, mental.**

mental health analysis: *see* **inventory, adjustment.**

mental hygiene: *see* **hygiene, mental.**

mental-hygiene inventory: *see* **inventory, adjustment.**

mental hygienist: *see* **hygienist, mental.**

mental illness: *see* **illness, mental.**

mental limitation: a limitation of intelligence due to a lack of normal mental development rather than to a mental disease or a deterioration.

mental maturity: *see* **maturity, mental.**

mental-maturity age: *syn.* **age, mental.**

mental measurement: *see* **measurement, mental.**

mental mechanism: a mental reaction that functions in maintaining internal composure and normal behavior. (The mental mechanisms are innumerable, including repression, compensation, defense reactions, etc.)

mental overageness: the state of being older mentally than is normal for a given grade; for example, if mental ages of 6 and 6½ years are normal for entering grade 1B, a child with a mental age of 7 on entering this grade would be a half-year overage mentally.

mental philosophy: *see* **philosophy, mental.**

mental process: (1) any activity modified, directed, controlled, or conditioned by experience; (2) the subjective accompaniment, or "field property," of certain processes of the neuromuscular system.

mental process, abnormal: any mental process that diverges markedly from those commonly met within the species, for example hallucinations, delusions, delirium, etc.

mental process, higher: one of the more complex forms of mental activity involving highly organized processes, usually with an element of conscious control, as in reasoning, memory, imagination, aspiration, or voluntary attention. *Contr. w.* **mental process, lower.**

mental process, lower: one of the more elementary forms of mental response following more or less directly upon stimulation with a minimum of conscious control, as in sensation and simple feelings of pleasantness or unpleasantness. *Contr. w.* **mental process, higher.**

mental ratio: *syn.* **quotient, intelligence.**

mental retardation: *see* **retardation, mental.**

mental retardation, apparent: *see* **mental retardation, psychogenic.**

mental retardation, cerebral trauma: an etiological classification including those cases occurring during the birth process in which the mental retardation is primarily the result of cerebral injury.

mental retardation, congenital cerebral maldevelopment: an etiological classification of mental retardation including all conditions, acting at any time during prenatal life, which have interfered with the normal development of the central nervous system and which thus are directly responsible for the mental retardation; includes Mongolism, cranial anomalies, phenylketonuria, congenital ectodermoses, cerebral palsy, skeletal defects, prenatal infections, and other forms.

mental retardation, degree of: quantification of grades of retardation, from slight to great, based on psychological evaluation, including tests, observations, histories, and related findings concerning maturation, learning capacity, and social adjustment; degree of retardation is relative to cultural norms, demands, or stresses and hence modifiable. *See* **mentally retarded, Group I; mentally retarded, Group II; mentally retarded, Group III; mentally retarded, Group IV.**

mental retardation due to convulsive disorders: an etiological classification where the causative factor or factors originate in the epileptic state itself and lead to mental retardation.

mental retardation, endogenous: mental deficiency in those cases where biological factors have resulted in an impairment of the central nervous system; a genetic retardation.

mental retardation, exogenous: mental retardation occurring after birth.

mental retardation, familial: mental retardation dependent upon multiple causative factors of which the most distinctive is an inherited subaverage intellectual status or inadequacy; the term used to describe the largest segment of the retarded population who exhibit a fairly uncomplicated picture of borderline to mild mental subnormality; differs from other hereditary conditions associated with mental retardation in that the latter represent as a rule clearly abnormal or pathological genetic factors, arising originally through mutations and not present in the normal population, genetically speaking.

mental retardation, hypothyroidism: an etiological classification including cases of congenital cretinism and of myxedema causatively related to the mental retardation.

mental retardation, kernicterus: an etiological classification descriptive of the cerebral abnormalities resulting from isoimmunization due largely to the Rh or other blood factors.

mental retardation, mild: degree of mental retardation of individuals with IQ ranging from 55 to 69. *See* **mentally retarded, educable.**

mental retardation, postnatal cerebral infection: an etiological classification referring to mental retardation resulting from cerebral abnormalities following infectious processes directly involving the brain and occurring at any time after birth.

mental retardation, profound: a term indicating mental retardation where there is minus 5.00 standard deviation with IQ below 25. *See* **mentally retarded, custodial; mentally retarded, dependent.**

mental retardation, progressive: mental deficiency from arrested mental development that is continuing and increasing in severity. *Syn.* **progressive feeblemindedness.**

mental retardation, progressive neuronal degeneration: an etiological classification of mental retardation including a number of specific conditions having in common the presence of a degenerative process involving any part of the central nervous system.

mental retardation, pseudo: assumed appearance of mental deficiency which seems, falsely, to be caused by arrested mental development.

mental retardation, psychogenic: mental retardation in which causative agents are primarily environmental factors which may be psychological, sociological, or even physical, as in the case of the hard of hearing or the blind; a condition in which the individual is mentally retarded, has adequate genetic endowment as regards intelligence with no evidence of prenatal or postnatal cerebral injury or maldevelopment and with normal cerebral dynamics physiologically. *Syn.* **apparent mental retardation.**

mental retardation, severe: retardation of the totally dependent child who is unable to be trained in total self-care, socialization, or economic usefulness and who needs continuing help in taking care of his personal needs.

mental retardation, subcultural: mental deficiency where the causative factors are in the social, economic, cultural, and psychological realms; a type of exogenous or environmental retardation. *Syn.* **subcultural feeblemindedness.**

mental states, doctrine of: *see* **mind, mental states doctrine of.**

mental test: *see* **test, mental.**

mental test, individual: *see* **test, individual mental.**

mentalism: (1) (philos.) the doctrine that mind is a fundamental reality; (2) an area or school of psychology concerned with the introspective examination of conscious states.

mentally advanced: above the average group in intelligence. *Contr. w.* **mentally retarded.**

mentally defective child, high-grade: a child who is mentally retarded to a moderate degree. *See* **mental retardation, degree of; retardation, mental.**

mentally deficient: a generic term frequently used to describe persons at all levels of mental retardation.

mentally deficient, education of: *syn.* **mentally retarded, education and training of.**

mentally deficient, school for the: *syn.* **school for the mentally retarded.**

mentally gifted: *see* **gifted, mentally.**

mentally gifted child: *see* **child, gifted.**

mentally handicapped: *see* **handicapped, mentally.**

mentally handicapped, educable: *syn.* **mentally retarded, educable.**

mentally handicapped, trainable: *syn.* **mentally retarded, trainable.**

mentally impaired: *syn.* **handicapped, mentally.**

mentally retarded: subject to mental retardation. *See* **retardation, mental.**

mentally retarded, biologically: persons whose retarded functioning may originate either from biological factors which influence the biochemistry and structural organization of the organic neural matrix or from experiential factors which influence the organization of function within the nervous system during postnatal maturation in infancy and childhood.

mentally retarded, borderline: a person who is operating intellectually at the adaptive level of impairment I, with an IQ range of 70 to 84.

mentally retarded child: *see* **child, mentally retarded.**

mentally retarded child, educable: *see* **child, educable mentally retarded.**

mentally retarded child, trainable: *see* **child, trainable mentally retarded.**

mentally retarded, cultural familial: persons with a condition of mental retardation caused by a complex interaction of environmental and hereditary factors; usually in the *educable mentally retarded* range, exhibiting no cerebral pathologic condition but having at least one parent or sibling in whom there is evidence of retarded intellectual functioning.

mentally retarded, custodial: persons with the grossest form of mental retardation, usually requiring 24-hour-a-day care, with IQ below 30.

mentally retarded, dependent: *see* **mentally retarded, custodial.**

mentally retarded, educable: mentally retarded individuals with an IQ within the 50–75 range; imagination is lacking and ideation marked by rigidity; such persons do not exhibit any unusal or erratic behavior, are not necessarily marked by any special physical stigmata, and are almost indistinguishable from the normal population; literacy is up to fourth- or fifth-grade levels; if appropriate educational techniques are employed, they can be made reasonably socially adequate, so that a diagnosis of mental retardation would be inappropriate if made in adult life.

mentally retarded, education and training of: the application of specialized teaching techniques and method to content and materials suitable to the realization for mentally retarded pupils of the generally accepted aims and objectives of education and training; may be carried on in special classes of an ordinary school, in a special school within a larger system, or in a special institution, and may be differentiated for different degrees of retardation. *See* **school for the mentally retarded.**

mentally retarded, Group I: those mentally retarded persons who are just below the average range; this group has been called *borderline, slow-learning,* or *educable mentally retarded;* requires special education and training.

mentally retarded, Group II: those mentally retarded persons who can acquire minimum functional literacy; this group has often been termed *moron, high-grade,* or *educable.*

mentally retarded, Group III: persons who are mentally retarded to such a degree that although they may be trained to perform some personally and socially useful functions they cannot acquire functional literacy; this group has been called *imbecile, middle-grade, trainable, etc.*

mentally retarded, Group IV: mentally retarded persons of such a degree of retardation as to be unable to profit from education or training; this group has been variously termed *idiot, low-grade,* and *ineducable and untrainable.*

mentally retarded, ineducable: persons at an intellectual and social maturity level below the educable range of functioning.

mentally retarded, ineducable and untrainable: *see* **mentally retarded, Group IV.**

mentally retarded, low-grade: *see* **mentally retarded, Group IV.**

mentally retarded, middle-grade: *see* **mentally retarded, Group III.**

mentally retarded, mildly: individuals whose IQs range from 60 to 80 approximately and who are capable of becoming literate and of sustaining themselves with only minimal assistance.

mentally retarded, moderately: individuals whose IQs range from 40 to 60 approximately; many are capable of achieving partial self-support in a sheltered workshop situation and a few in cooperative employment.

mentally retarded, school for the: *see* **school for the mentally retarded.**

mentally retarded, trainable: mentally retarded individuals who may be trained to perform some personally and socially useful operations, but who cannot acquire functional literacy. *See* **mental retardation, degree of; retardation, mental;** *contr. w.* **mentally retarded, educable.**

mentally subnormal: *see* **subnormal, mentally.**

mentally superior: *see* **superior, mentally.**

mentally superior, education of the: the provision of materials and methods of instruction suitable for pupils of high or superior intelligence, by means of such techniques as (a) enrichment of course of study; (b) acceleration, that is, rapid promotion; (c) adaptation of subject matter through individual instruction; (d) homogeneous grouping; and (e) special classes for superior pupils.

mentally superior, school for the: *see* **school for the mentally superior.**

merchandise information: an area of study in the distributive education curriculum concerned with textiles and nontextiles.

merchandise manual: *see* **manual, merchandise.**

merchandise sales manual: *see* **manual, merchandise.**

merchandising: (1) strictly, the act or process of deciding on the kind, quality, quantity, and price of goods to be offered for sale so as to meet consumer demands; (2) the designation of a course offered in secondary schools and colleges, often loosely applied to a course in salesmanship.

merchandising laboratory: *syn.* **laboratory, distributive education.**

merchandising, visual: *see* **display.**

merchant, cooperating: an employer of students enrolled in the cooperative part-time training program in distributive education.

merchants' advisory committee: *syn.* **committee, distributive education advisory.**

merge: in automatic data processing, to file together two decks of cards in the same sequence order in a *collator.*

merge sort: *see* **sort, merge.**

merit rating: *see* **rating, merit.**

merit scale: *syn.* **scale, quality.**

Merit Scholar: *see* **Scholar, Merit.**

merit system, teacher: a plan by which promotion, increase in pay, and general advancement within a school system are determined by the degree of efficiency with which the teachers perform their duties; may be combined with other plans, such as experience or training evaluation, in arriving at salary increases or promotion. *See* **efficiency bar** (Education in England and Wales).

merit-type salary schedule: *see* **salary schedule, merit-type.**

mesokurtic (mes′ō·kẽr′tik; mē′sō-): a term which describes a frequency curve that has the same degree of peakedness as does the normal probability curve. *See* **kurtosis.**

mesokurtosis (mes′ō·kẽr·tō′sis; mē′sō-): the quality of being mesokurtic. *See* **mesokurtic.**

mesomorph: an individual characterized by solid musculature, good-sized bones, and strong and athletic build.

message: any thought or idea expressed briefly in a plain or secret language, prepared in a form suitable for transmission by any means of communication; in communication theory, an ordered selection from an agreed set of signs intended to communicate information.

metabolic rate, basal (BMR): *see* **metabolism, basal.**

metabolism (me·tab′ə·liz′m): the total of all physical and chemical processes required by the living organism for its maintenance; a balance or equilibrium between *anabolism* (the processes of assimilation and regeneration) and *catabolism* (the processes of excretion and degeneration) acting on the cells of the body, a favorable balance being necessary for the maintenance of life.

metabolism, basal: the minimum of the energy expended by an individual in maintaining the vital and vegetative functions of the body; determined by measuring the amount of heat produced by the body after a fast of 14 to 18 hours and a period of complete rest—but not sleep—of at least ½ hour; expressed in calories per hour per square meter of body surface. *Dist. f.* **metabolism.**

metal laboratory: *see* **laboratory, metal.**

metal shop: *see* **shop, metal.**

metal technology: *see* **technology, metal.**

metalcraft: the art or skill of working with metal, especially those activities in which metal is used in an artistic manner; may include jewelry making, enameling, metalfoil work, ornamental ironwork, metal smithing, and metal spinning. *Syn.* **art metalwork;** *see* **art metals.**

metallurgical technician: *see* **technician, metallurgical.**

metallurgy: that aspect of metal technology primarily concerned with the chemical and physical properties of metal.

metals, general: *see* **technology, metal.**

metalwork, art: *syn.* **metalcraft.**

metalworker: (voc. ed.) a person employed in the field of casting, cutting, forming, shaping, and treating metal.

metalworking: (1) producing objects out of metal or that aspect of metal technology focused on the praxiology in the metals field; (2) a study of the processes of reduction and refinement of metallic ores and the characteristics and uses of metals, with development of skill and facility in casting, cutting, forming, shaping, fabricating, and treating metal.

metamathematics: a formalized theory of proof devised by David Hilbert and his followers; the purpose was to investigate the consistency of the logical structure of ordinary mathematics; describes and investigates formal mathematical systems as systems of symbols independent of the interpretation of the symbols.

metaphysics: (1) the science of being as being; the science of first principles and the causes of things; the science that knows to what end each thing must be done (Aristotle); *see* **cosmology; ontology;** (2) inquiry into the "generic traits manifested by all existence of all kinds without differentiation into physical and mental" (Dewey).

metaphysics, dualistic: a position that reduces all reality to two independent, irreducible, and mutually exclusive substances or categories such as mind and matter, possibility and actuality, the real and the ideal, etc.

metaphysics, idealistic: the theory which holds that the nature of reality is of the nature of mind (ultimate reality being accorded only to ideas, concepts, and like "universals") and which accepts the teleological theory that the order of reality is due to purpose; postulates the existence of finite minds and an Infinite Mind, the Infinite Mind being regarded as the ultimate explanation of all things.

metaphysics, materialistic: in general, that view about the nature of ultimate reality (ontology) which affirms that matter alone is real as opposed to the view that *mind* is the ultimate category. *See* **materialism; mechanism.**

metapsychology (met′ə·sī·kol′ə·ji): speculative psychology; philosophical speculation concerning the mind, its origin, function, structure, etc., and similar matters that cannot be proved by experience.

meteorology: the science of the atmosphere, including all the aspects of matter-energy exchange; involves the study of the weather and climate, including humidity, temperature, atmosphere pressure, air masses and motion, clouds, precipitation, and interrelationships on both local and global scales; usually taught as a program on the university level.

meter, footcandle: *see* **footcandle meter.**

meter, light: *see* **light meter.**

method: (1) an established or systematic order for performing any act or conducting any operation; (2) the relationship established by an educational institution with a group of participants for the purpose of systematically diffusing knowledge among them.

method, ABC: *see* **ABC method.**

method, academic: *see* **academic method.**

method, acoustic: *see* **acoustic method.**

method, activity: *see* **activity method.**

method, alphabet: *syn.* **ABC method.**

method, analytic: *see* **analytic method.**

method, anecdotal: *see* **anecdotal method.**

method, apparent quotient: *see* **apparent quotient method.**

method, apprentice: *see* **apprentice method.**

method, audio-active-compare: *see* **audio-active-compare method.**

method, audiolingual: *see* **audiolingual method.**

method, audiotutorial: *see* **audiotutorial method.**

method, audiovisual-kinesthetic: *see* **audiovisual kinesthetic method.**

method, aural-oral: *see* **oral-aural.**

method, Baconian: *see* **Baconian method.**

method, Beacon reading: *see* **reading method, Beacon.**

method, biographical: *see* **biographical method.**

method, Bruhn: *see* **Bruhn method.**

method, Calvert: *see* **Calvert method.**

method, case: *see* **case method.**

method, case-history: *syn.* case method.

method, case-study: *syn.* case method.

method, casework: *see* casework method.

method, cathartic projective: *see* projective method, cathartic.

method, causal-comparative: *see* causal-comparative method.

method, class-descriptive: *see* class-descriptive method.

method, clinical: *see* clinical method.

method, coach and pupil: *see* coach and pupil method.

method, combined: *see* combined method.

method, conference: *see* conference method.

method, constitutive projective: *see* projective method, constitutive.

method, constructive projective: *see* projective method, constructive.

method, contrasting pairs: *see* contrasting pairs method.

method, controlled experimental: *syn.* experimental method.

method, Craig: *see* Craig method.

method, critical-incidents: *see* critical-incidents method.

method, decomposition: *see* subtraction, methods of.

method, deductive: *see* deductive method.

method, demonstration: *see* demonstration method.

method, demonstration-lecture: *see* demonstration-lecture method.

method, demonstration-performance: *see* demonstration-performance method.

method, descriptive: *see* descriptive method.

method, didactic: *see* didactic method.

method, directing: *see* directing method.

method, directive: *see* directive method.

method, discovery: *see* discovery method.

method, distributive education cooperative: *see* cooperative method, distributive education.

method, distributive education project: *see* project method, distributive education.

method, doing: *see* doing method.

method, eclectic: *see* eclectic method.

method, ensemble; *see* ensemble method.

method, evaluative: *see* evaluative method.

method, experience: *syn.* experience-activity method.

method, experience-activity: *see* experience-activity method.

method, experimental: *see* experimental method.

method, forcing: *see* forcing method.

method, free-expression: *see* free-expression method.

method, functional: *see* functional method.

method, Gillingham: *see* Gillingham method.

method, goal-seeking: *see* goal-seeking method.

method, grade-retention-rate: *see* grade-retention-rate method.

method, Grube: *see* Grube method.

method, Herbartian: *see* Herbartian method.

method, heuristic: *syn.* problem method (1).

method, idiographic: *see* idiographic method.

method, increase-by-one: *see* increase-by-one method.

method, indirect: *see* indirect method.

method, inductive: *see* inductive method.

method, inferred causal: *see* causal-comparative method.

method, integration: *see* integrative method.

method, interpretive projective: *see* projective method, interpretive.

method, Jena: *see* Jena method.

method, Johnson-Neyman: *see* Johnson-Neyman method.

method, Kelly-Salisbury: *see* Kelly-Salisbury method.

method, kinesthetic: *see* kinesthetic method.

method, Kinzie: *see* Kinzie method.

method, Kolmogrov-Smirnov: *see* Kolmogrov-Smirnov method.

method, Laubach reading: *see* reading method, Laubach.

method, line production: *see* line production method.

method, logical: *see* logical method.

method, look-and-guess: *syn.* sight method.

method, look-and-say: *syn.* sight method.

method, manual: *see* manual method.

method, mass production: *see* mass production method.

method, maximum likelihood: *see* maximum likelihood method.

method, Montessori: *see* Montessori method.

method, Müller-Walle: *see* Müller-Walle method.

method, multiple-appraoch: *see* multiple-approach method.

method, multiple-group: *see* multiple-group method.

method, multiple-ratio: *see* multiple-ratio method.

method, natural: *see* natural method.

method, Nitchie: *see* Nitchie method.

method, nomothetic: *see* nomothetic method.

method, nonoral: *see* nonoral method.

method, noun-unit: *see* noun-unit method.

method, object-descriptive: *see* object-descriptive method.

method, objective: *see* objective method.

method, observational: *see* observational method.

method of agreement: a method for discovering causal relations, formulated by John Stuart Mill as follows: "If two or more instances of the phenomenon under investigation have only one circumstance in common, the circumstance in which alone all the instances agree is the cause (or effect) of the given phenomenon." *See* methods of experimental inquiry.

method of agreement and difference: a method for discovering causal relations, formulated by John Stuart Mill as follows: "If two or more instances in which the phenomenon occurs have only one circumstance in common, while two or more instances in which it does not occur have nothing in common save the absence of that circumstance, the circumstance in which alone the two sets of instances differ is the effect, or the cause, or an indispensable part of the cause, of the phenomenon"; also called *indirect method of difference* and *joint method of agreement and difference. See* methods of experimental inquiry.

method of board selection, ward: *see* board selection, ward method of.

method of character measurement, inferential: *see* measurement, inferential method of character.

method of clothing construction, Bishop: *see* clothing construction, Bishop method of.

method of coincidental markers: *see* coincidental markers, method of.

method of concomitant variations: a method for discovering causal relations, formulated by John Stuart Mill as follows: "Whatever phenomenon varies in any manner whenever another phenomenon varies in some particular manner is either a cause or an effect of that phenomenon, or is connected with it through some fact of causation." *See* methods of experimental inquiry.

method of difference: a method for discovering causal relations, formulated by John Stuart Mill as follows: "If an instance in which the phenomenon under investigation occurs, and an instance in which it does not occur, have every circumstance in common save one, that one occurring only in the former, the circumstance in which alone the two instances differ is the effect, or the cause, or an indispensable part of the cause of the phenomenon." *See* methods of experimental inquiry.

method of discriminant function: *see* discriminant function, method of.

method of factorization, diagonal: *see* factorization, diagonal method of.

method of factorization, group: *see* factorization, group method of.

method of gains: *syn.* Spearman's foot-rule method of gains.

method of least squares: the method of finding the value of a statistic or the equation of a line or curve such that the sum of the squares of the deviations of the observations about the point or line is a minimum. (Such statistics as the arithmetic mean, partial regression coefficients, and regression lines are obtained by the method of least squares.)

method of lipreading, context: *see* **lipreading, context method of.**

method of matched groups: *see* **matched groups, method of.**

method of reliability, odd-even: *see* **reliability, split-halves.**

method of residues: a method for discovering causal relations, formulated by John Stuart Mill as follows: "Subduct from any phenomenon such part as is known by previous inductions to be the effect of certain antecedents, and the residue of the phenomenon is the effect of the remaining antecedents." *See* **methods of experimental inquiry.**

method of successive residuals: *see* **successive residuals, method of.**

method, office: *see* **office method.**

method, oral: *see* **oral method.**

method, Orff: *see* **Orff method.**

method, overlearning: *see* **overlearning method.**

method, parallel forms: *see* **parallel forms method.**

method, pedagogical: *see* **teaching technique.**

method, philosophical: *see* **philosophical method.**

method, pickup: *see* **pickup method.**

method, postulation: *see* **thinking, postulational.**

method, problem: *see* **problem method.**

method, problem-solving: *see* **problem-solving method.**

method, progressive choice: *see* **progressive choice method.**

method, project: *see* **project method.**

method, projective: *see* **projective method.**

method, pure-part: *see* **pure-part method.**

method, quartimax: *see* **quartimax method.**

method, question-and-answer: *see* **question-and-answer method.**

method, ramifying linkage: *see* **ramifying linkage method.**

method, refractive projective: *see* **projective method, refractive.**

method, remedial group: *see* **group method, remedial.**

method, résumé: *see* **résumé method.**

method, Rochester: *syn.* **combined method** (1); **simultaneous method.**

method, scientific: *see* **scientific method.**

method, sectional-view rotation: *see* **rotation method, sectional-view.**

method, showing: *see* **telling method.**

method, sight-word reading: *see* **reading method, sight-word.**

method, simultaneous: *see* **simultaneous method.**

method, single-plane rotation: *see* **rotation method, single-plane.**

method, sociological: *see* **sociological method.**

method, Socratic: *see* **Socratic method.**

method, song: *see* **song method.**

method, split-halves: *see* **reliability, split-halves.**

method, split-test: *see* **reliability, split-halves.**

method, study-test: *see* **study-test method.**

method, submatrix: *see* **submatrix method.**

method, survey: *see* **survey method.**

method, syllabic: *see* **syllabic method.**

method, synthetic: *see* **synthetic method.**

method, tachistoscopic: *see* **tachistoscopic method.**

method, tactile-kinesthetic: *see* **kinesthetic method.**

method, task: *see* **task method.**

method, telling: *see* **telling method.**

method, test-study: *see* **test-study method.**

method, test-study-test: *see* **test-study-test method.**

method, tracing: *syn.* **kinesthetic method** (1).

method, uncontrolled experimental: *see* **experimental method, uncontrolled.**

method, vibration: *see* **vibration method.**

method, visual-hearing: *see* **visual-hearing method.**

method, Wherry-Doolittle: *see* **Wherry-Doolittle method.**

method, Wherry-Doolittle multiple correlation test selection: *see* **test selection method, Wherry-Doolittle multiple correlation.**

method, whole-word: *syn.* **whole method; word method;** *see* **whole-part-whole-method.**

method, word-and-sentence: *see* **word-and-sentence method.**

methodology: (1) the science of methods or principles of procedure; (2) the theory of the nature, place, and kinds of method used in teaching; (3) attention to method; procedure according to method.

methodology, democratic: procedures (educational, political, social) that provide for the participation of all relevant individuals, on the basis of respect for individuality and for individual ideas, in problems of common concern; procedures that honor difference among individuals, institutions, and ideas, and have faith in compromise as a means of securing unity.

methodology of change: *see* **change, methodology of.**

methods, algebraic: *see* **algebraic methods.**

methods, autoinstructional: *see* **autoinstructional methods.**

methods course: *see* **course, methods.**

methods, dramatic: methods of teaching that are based upon the assumption that pupils learn best by doing; examples are acting out plays, acting a story or part of a story, demonstrating a process or procedure.

methods experiment: *see* **experiment, methods.**

methods in transfer, equivalent: *see* **equivalent methods in transfer.**

methods, interpolation: *see* **interpolation methods.**

methods, lipreading: *see* **audiovisual-kinesthetic method; Bruhn (Müller-Walle) method; Jena method; Kinzie method; Nitchie method; visual-hearing method.**

methods, Monte Carlo: mathematical methods making use of the theory of probability and random numbers.

methods of experimental inquiry: four inductive methods for discovering causal relations among phenomena, plus a fifth combining two of the others, formulated by John Stuart Mill in his "System of Logic." *See* **method of agreement; method of agreement and difference; method of concomitant variations; method of difference; method of residues.**

methods of subtraction: *see* **subtraction, methods of.**

methods of teaching art: *see* **art, methods of teaching.**

methods of transfer: *see* **transfer, methods of.**

methods, pupil-centric: methods of teaching that focus attention upon the interests and needs of pupils, such as laboratory and project methods.

methods study: *see* **study, methods.**

methods, teacher-centric: methods of teaching that stress the activities of teachers in directing learning, such as the lecture method and the recitation.

methods-time measurement: *see* **measurement, methods-time.**

meticulosity: a condition marked by extreme orderliness; abnormal need for spatial regularity.

metric geometry: *see* **geometry, metric.**

metric system: a system of weights and measures based on units of 10, designed by the French Academy of Science and adopted by the Constituent Assembly of France near the beginning of the French Revolution; the basic unit is the meter (approximately 39.37 inches), and other units such as the gram and the liter are defined in terms of that.

metro district: *see* **district, metro.**

metronome: a mechanical or electrical device used to indicate tempi, that is, pulsations, beats per minute, which are indicated in music by symbols such as MM ♩ = 120, meaning 120 pulses (quarter notes) per minute; by turning the selector knob of the metronome to 120, the exact tempo can be established.

metronoscope: a mechanical flash device that exposes successive phrases and lines of print at varying speeds.

metropolitan population: see **population, metropolitan.**

metropolitan statistical area, standard (SMSA): a type of area defined by the Bureau of the Census for the 1970 census report; consists of a county or group of counties containing at least one city of 50,000 population plus any adjacent counties which are metropolitan in character and economically and socially integrated with the central county or counties; in New England, towns and cities rather than counties are the units used in defining SMSAs. See **central city.**

metropolitan type vehicle: see **vehicle, metropolitan type.**

mezzo-soprano: a female voice intermediate between soprano and contralto, with a range from about A below middle C to A two octaves higher.

microcard: a card on which a large volume of printed materials has been condensed to extremely small size by photographic processes; microcard material is read with the aid of a microcard reader, which magnifies the minute printing.

microcephaly: a genetically caused abnormality consisting in having an abnormally small head; usually applied only when smallness is so grave as to be associated with marked mental deficiency or, in an adult, when the cranium of less than 1,350 cubic centimeters capacity. *Contr. w.* **macrocephaly.**

microchronometer: an instrument used with motion studies of an operation to indicate time intervals.

microcinematography: *syn.* **cinemicrophotography.**

microcopy: reading material, such as books, newspapers, or documents, photographed and reproduced in positive on strips of film 16 mm or 35 mm wide; intended for projection in a *microprojector.*

microcosm: the smaller entity or model of the macrocosm-microcosm relationship. See **macrocosm.**

microeconomic approach: (school finance) a study of economics in terms of individual areas of activity; the opposite of the *macroeconomic theory,* which approaches the system as a whole.

microfiche: a 4 × 6 inch sheet of transparent film on which are pages of information optically reduced at a ratio of 24 to 1, so that the sheet can contain 70 to 90 pages, arranged in a grid pattern by rows; a special machine, called a reader, is needed to blow up the miniaturized pages so that they may be read. *Comp. w.* **ultramicrofiche.**

microfilm: film upon which, by photographic processes, printed and other materials are reproduced as minute images on the film and may be observed through a special magnifying viewer or by projection. See **microfilm reader.**

microfilm reader: apparatus with a built-in screen or viewing glass arranged to magnify microfilm so that it can be read comfortably at eye distances and without the use of hand magnifying glasses.

microform: a generic term describing any miniaturized form containing microimages, such as a microcard, microfilm, microfiche, etc.

microgroove record: see **record, microgroove.**

microimage: a microproduction of an object such as printed matter, a document, an engineering drawing, or other publication or graphic matter.

micromotion study: see **study, micromotion.**

microopaque: an opaque microform, such as a microcard, microprint, or microtape.

microphone: device for converting the kinetic energy of sound waves into variations of electrical current; available in various designs and pickup or directional patterns, with accessories of stands, clips, etc., for support and manipulation.

microphone jack: see **jack, microphone.**

microphonia: undue softness of voice; "thin tone."

microphotography: still or motion-picture photography of minute objects through the lens system of a microscope. *Syn.* **photomicrography;** *comp. w.* **macrophotography.**

microprint: a reproduction of printed or other graphic matter in reduced size, to be read by a magnifying instrument.

microprogram: a special command repertoire for an automatic computer that consists only of basic elemental operations which the programmer can combine into commands to suit his own convenience and in terms of which he would then program.

microprogramming: see **programming, micro.**

microprojector: a special projector designed to enlarge and project microscopic transparencies such as microscope slides or sections of microfilm for viewing by whole classes or even by large audiences. See **projector, microslide.**

microreader: a device for enlarging and displaying a microimage.

microscope projector: *syn.* **projector, microslide.**

microsecond: one millionth of a second; a term used for timing operations in computerized data processing; written μs. See **millisecond; nanosecond.**

microslide projector: see **projector, microslide.**

microsplanchnic: describing or designating a body build in which the individual has a small trunk with long limbs so as to give a low morphological index. See **body builds, classification of;** *contr. w.* **macrosplanchnic.**

microteaching: a scaled-down teaching encounter that has been developed at Stanford University to serve (*a*) as a preliminary experience and practice in teaching, (*b*) as a research vehicle to explore training effects under controlled conditions, and (*c*) as an in-service training instrument for experienced teachers; usually 5 minutes in length, involving no more than eight students; often recorded on videotape for analysis.

microwave relay: a series of high-frequency directional transmitters and receivers strategically spaced to permit the successive reception and retransmission of radio and television signals through space between widely separated points.

middle-class bias in teaching: see **bias in teaching, middle-class.**

middle-grade mentally retarded: see **mentally retarded, Group III.**

middle grades: a term commonly applied to grades 4, 5, and 6, or to any two of these grades, in an elementary school.

middle-level occupation: *syn.* **semiprofession.**

middle school: a school administrative unit typically between the primary elementary unit and the last or secondary unit in the school system; in one form of organization includes in one school children of approximate ages 10 to14 from the conventional grades 5 to 8, making possible a primary school for kindergarten through grade 4 and a 4-year high school for grades 9 through 12; viewed as serving a transitional function from childhood to adolescence; seeks to overcome the rigidity of departmentalization, the pressures of intraschool competition, and the tensions of older adolescent functions commonly found in the conventional *junior high school.*

midmanagement: a group of junior administrators through which the coordination responsibilities are executed; also, the stratum of *management* immediately below top management.

midmeasure: *syn.* **midscore.**

midmorning lunch: see **lunch, midmorning.**

midparent: (biol. and psych.) the mean or average of the weighted values of any given character found in both parents.

midpoint: the value of a variable midway between the real upper and the real lower limits of a class interval. *Syn.* face value; midvalue.

midrange value: see **value, midrange.**

midscore: (1) the middle score when an odd number of scores are arranged in ascending or descending order; (2) the arithmetic mean of the two middle scores when an even number of scores are arranged in ascending or descending order. *Syn.* **midmeasure;** *dist. f.* **median.**

midshipman: a student naval officer enrolled at the United States Naval Academy or in the Navy ROTC. *See* **cadet; candidate, officer; trainee, officer.**

midspace: *see* **space, mid.**

midvalue: *syn.* **midpoint.**

migraine: a periodic headache usually unilateral and characterized by gastric, vasomotor, and visual disturbances.

migrant child: *see* **child, migrant.**

migrant child center: *see* **center, migrant child.**

migrant student: *syn.* **student, transfer** (1).

migration, internal: migration within the country from state to state, county to county, rural area to urban area, etc.

migration, net: the difference between the number of people who move into an area and the number who move out during a specified period of time.

migration, pupil: the movement of pupils from schools to other schools located in different administrative areas or units. *Dist. f.* **transfer** (3).

migration, teacher: the moving of teachers from one independent school, school system, or state to another. *See* **turnover, teacher.**

mike boom: a means of suspending a microphone over a scene in television or motion-picture production.

mil: one-thousandth of an inch; tape thickness is usually measured in mils.

mild deficiency: *see* **deficiency, mild.**

mild mental retardation: *see* **mental retardation, mild.**

mildly mentally retarded: *see* **mentally retarded, mildly.**

mile, bus: the travel of 1 mile by a school bus.

mile, pupil: a unit of school transportation service, consisting of the movement of one child a distance of 1 mile.

mile, seat: a unit of pupil-transportation service consisting of the movement of a seating space for one pupil a distance of 1 mile. (Thus, if a school bus having 30 seats travels 1 mile, the amount of service is 30 seat miles.)

mileage allowance: the amount of money allowed attendance workers or other field officers for each mile traveled in making their daily calls and visits.

mileage, daily: the total number of miles a given school bus is driven in a given day.

mileage, deadhead: the distance a school bus travels without passengers. *Syn.* **empty mileage.**

mileage, empty: *syn.* **mileage, deadhead.**

miles, aggregate pupil: the sum of the distances traveled by individual pupils in a school bus.

miles, loaded: the distance in miles a school bus travels along its route while one or more pupils are riding.

miles, one-way: *syn.* **length of route, one-way.**

miles, one-way loaded: the distance in miles a school bus travels one way on either a circuit route or a straight-line route while transporting pupils to or from school.

milieu, social (mē·l'yø′): the aggregate of all the external social conditions and influences that affect the life, development, and behavior of individuals, groups, nations, and cultures; as such it differs from the *environment* which is a broader term and actually includes the social milieu.

milieu space: *see* **space, milieu.**

militancy, teacher: the term applied to the movement of teachers, from the 1960s on, to organize more effectively, have a greater voice in making educational policy, and take collective action to achieve their ends.

military: (1) of or pertaining to soldiers, arms, war; according to the methods of war or armies, as in *military training* and *military discipline;* (2) of or pertaining to activities of the United States Armed Forces in the broad sense or to the United States Army in the restricted sense; (3) occasionally used to describe a machinelike school organization or a severe, rigid, and authoritative type of school discipline.

military academy: *see* **academy, military.**

Military Assistance Grant Aid training: *see* **training, Military Assistance Grant Aid.**

Military Assistance Program Grant Aid trainee: *see* **trainee, Military Assistance Program Grant Aid.**

Military Assistance Program Supported Third Country training: *see* **training, Military Assistance Program Supported Third Country.**

Military Assistance Sales trainee: *see* **trainee, Military Assistance Sales.**

military climatology: *see* **climatology, military.**

military course, advanced: the second half of the course of study designed for students of senior ROTC units, generally taken in the junior and senior years of college, and for which enrollment is limited, selection being made from applicants who have completed the basic course; students who satisfactorily complete the advanced course are eligible for a commission as second lieutenant in the Reserve Officers' Corps, Armed Forces of the United States.

military course, basic: the first half of the course of study designed for students of senior ROTC units, or the entire course for junior ROTC units; in the senior units it is generally taken in the freshman and sophomore college years and is intended to be preparatory to the advanced course; for many students, it is a terminal course, inasmuch as it is the only course required in schools having compulsory military training. (Registration in or completion of the basic course does not affect the students' civilian status.)

military courtesy: the system of the conventions of military life, especially as they pertain to the conduct and relationships between and among persons having military status; the basic feature of military courtesy is the showing of proper respect, for example, to one's superior officers or to the flag.

military discipline: *see* **discipline, military.**

military drill: *see* **drill, military.**

military education: the systematic instruction of individuals in subjects which will enhance their knowledge of the science and art of war.

military education, professional: the systematic acquisition of theoretical and applied knowledge of particular significance to the profession of arms; involves the acquisition of knowledge, skills, and attitudes which are requisite to military professionalism and which form the core of understanding which must be common to all officers, regardless of military service or of the specialized activities in which they are engaged; includes knowledge of military arts and sciences and the development of Command and Staff expertise in both peace and war; directed toward a thorough understanding of national goals and objectives and the ways and means of using military force to achieve them.

military geography: *see* **geography, military.**

military graduate, distinguished: *see* **graduate, distinguished military.**

military occupational specialty code: *see* **code, military occupational specialty.**

military occupational specialty evaluation test: *see* **test, military occupational specialty evaluation.**

military school: an establishment whose primary purpose is the education and training of cadets or of officers, noncommissioned officers, and men of the armed services, such as post schools, garrison schools, and service schools.

military science: (1) a generic term designating general and technical courses offered by the military department of a college or university to ROTC students; the designation of the department offering such courses; *syn.* **military science and tactics;** (2) the academic subdivision in a college or university which includes all ROTC activities at the institution; (3) the science of war as applied to the art of war, embracing tactics and strategy, including naval and air force operations.

military science and tactics: *syn.* **military science.**

military science curriculum, general: *see* **curriculum, general military science.**

military student, distinguished: *see* **student, distinguished military.**

military track: running, jumping, and throwing exercises, resembling track and field athletics, suitable for use with large numbers of individuals for purposes of developing physical fitness.

military training: *see* **training, military.**

military training, basic: *see* **training, basic military.**

military training, compulsory: at one time required enrollment of all freshman and sophomore men, unless specially excused, in the *basic military courses* in colleges and universities having ROTC units. (Almost all land-grant institutions and many other schools having ROTC units have had this requirement.)

military training, general: *see* **training, general military.**

military training, universal: *see* **training, universal military.**

mill: (voc. ed.) an equipped building or group of buildings in which raw material is worked or processed, by workmen using simple operations, into a form ready for the manufacturer, for example, a steel or flour mill.

millage, inside: under provisions of the constitution of the State of Ohio, any amount inside the maximum which a taxing district may levy without the vote of the people; such millage is divided among different political divisions, including the school district, for operation of those divisions; for example, with a 10-mill inside levy, the county may receive 2 mills, the township 2 mills, the school district 4 mills. *Contr. w.* **millage, outside.**

millage, outside: in taxing for school purposes, any millage that the school district needs in excess of the inside millage; must be voted on by the people. *See* **millage, inside.**

millisecond: one thousandth of a second; a term used in timing operations in computerized data processing; written *ms. See* **microsecond; nanosecond.**

mimeographed newspaper: *syn.* **newspaper, duplicated.**

mimetic: descriptive of those infantile responses which are said to be expressive of affective states; for example, the wry face evoked by quinine stimulation in the mouth being mimetic of unpleasantness. *See* **movements, expressive.**

mimetic activities: *see* **activities, mimetic.**

mimetics (mi·met′iks; mī·met′-): the acting out of a particular skill or action without equipment.

mimicry-memorization (mim-mem): a primary feature of the teaching sequence followed in the behavioral-structuralist approach to language teaching; continued imitation of spoken utterances required of the student to the point of total and instant recall.

mind: (1) a collective term for all forms of consciousness or intelligence; sometimes contrasted with *soul;* (2) a human being thought of as an intellectual force; (3) the total of an individual's mental faculties; (4) reflective behavior; (5) a characteristic mode of thought, as "the Greek mind"; (6) the spirit or intelligence that pervades the universe as opposed to matter.

mind, absolute: in Hegelian philosophy, the view that the universe, including man and all his works, is mind; each thing on earth is a concretion of the absolute mind, and history is the absolute mind expressing itself in time; absolute mind, in this view, is *all.*

mind, absorbent: *see* **Montessori method.**

mind-body problem: the problem stated as, "How, when mind is looked upon as a substance or a series of mental states, does mind influence and direct body? Since mind and body are utterly different, whence man's apparent individual unity?" [The history of philosophy since Descartes (*see* **Cartesianism**) reveals many different doctrines fashioned to resolve the mind-body problem. British empiricism and Kantian philosophies deal with it. In large part, the literature of what philosophers call *epistemology* is concerned with this problem.]

mind, collective: (1) consensus; (2) the sum of those similar mental processes among the members of a group that result in concerted action; (3) an alleged mind that inheres in each group and is different from the minds of the individuals composing the group or from their mind aggregate. *Dist. f.* **group consciousness.**

mind, crowd: *see* **crowd mind.**

mind, emergent theory of: the view that reflective behavior has evolved within the natural, physical-biological-psychological order of things, as opposed to supernaturalism; that the mental is continuous with, yet genuinely different from, the nonmental, as opposed to *dualism;* and that language and culture are key processes in the explanation of the rise of mental behavior in social interaction. *See* **mind, functional theory of.**

mind, functional theory of: the view that "mind" is a way of behaving in which an inhibited or obstructed act is analyzed and reconstructed through the use of significant symbols and behavior is reconstructed toward chosen ends. *See* **symbol; thinking, reflective.**

mind, mental states doctrine of: the view that mind is neither a substance nor a function but a series of ideal or "ideaing" experiences; these do not necessarily involve action or behavior, but they may be acted upon; the mental states have integrity and consistency within and among themselves; they may or may not refer to an independent "outside" world. *Contr. w.* **mind, functional theory of; mind, substantive theory of.**

mind, substantive theory of: the view that "mind" is an entity, a nonspatial, nonmaterial substance, as distinct from a name referring to a way of behaving; this spiritual substance operates according to its own distinctive laws just as material substance operates according to the laws of mechanics; learning is a process of developing that which is already there implicit within the mental substance.

miniature camera: a camera using narrow film of 35 mm width or less.

miniature painting: (1) a painting in an illuminated book or manuscript, usually produced in very small scale and minute detail; a technique commonly used in the medieval and Gothic periods; (2) a portrait painted in very small scale, often on ivory or metal; flourished especially in England in the eighteenth century.

minimal addend code: *see* **code, minimal addend.**

minimal art: *see* **art, minimal.**

minimal pairs: two words which are phonetically identical except for one sound feature; the difference in these sound features is the difference in phonemes. *See* **contrasting pairs method; phonemic contrast.**

minimum access programming: *see* **programming, minimum latency.**

minimum administrative unit: *see* **administrative unit, minimum.**

minimum compulsory school age: *see* **compulsory school age, minimum.**

minimum elementary school attendance unit: *see* **attendance unit, minimum elementary school.**

minimum essentials: rough *syn.* **fundamentals of arithmetic.**

minimum individual training: *see* **training, combat readiness.**

minimum latency programming: *see* **programming, minimum latency.**

minimum production: *see* **production, minimum.**

minimum program: *see* **program, minimum.**

minimum program level, mandated: *see* **program level, mandated minimum.**

minimum program, state: *see* **program, minimum.**

minimum salary schedule, state: *see* **salary schedule, state minimum.**

minimum salary, state: *see* **salary, state minimum.**

minimum school tax: *see* **tax, minimum school.**

minimum school term: *see* **school term, minimum.**

minimum school year: *syn.* **school term, minimum.**

minimum standards: *see* **standards, minimum.**

minimum term of school: *syn.* **school term, minimum.**

minimum transportation: *see* **transportation, minimum.**

minimum transportation program: *see* **program, minimum transportation.**

minimum wage, teachers': (1) the lowest salary that may be paid to a teacher under an established salary schedule; (2) the lowest salary that should be paid to a teacher in order to maintain a defined standard of living.

minister: (relig. ed.) any person authorized to carry out any of the various functions of the church; commonly used with specific reference to the ordained clergy.

ministerial board functions: *see* **board functions, ministerial.**

ministerial duty: *see* **duty, ministerial.**

ministry: (relig. ed.) (1) collectively, the clergy; (2) the general service function of the church as well as the specific offices and functions of those authorized to serve the church, for example, a teaching or healing ministry.

ministry, teaching: one of the several functions or special offices of the church described in the Bible and perpetuated down through the ages into modern times.

minor: (1) formerly any person who had not attained the age of 21, at which time full civil rights were granted; (Federal law and some states have lowered the legal age for voting); (2) *syn.* **field of study, minor.**

minor adviser: *see* **adviser, minor.**

minor field of study: *see* **field of study, minor.**

minor seminary: *see* **seminary, minor.**

minor sort: *see* **sort, minor.**

minority group: *see* **group, minority.**

minority group child: *see* **child, minority group.**

minority representation: (1) the right that is allowed to minority groups by some societies to participate in the society's councils; (2) the right by which minority parties are allowed a number of seats in a representative body.

minus time: *see* **time, minus.**

minutes: the record of the proceedings of a meeting of a board, committee, or conference, usually prepared by a secretary or clerk and formally approved at the succeeding meeting of the same body; may vary from a complete stenographic transcription of every word uttered at the meeting to a bare series of notations of the motions made and the disposition thereof and of resolutions adopted.

miosis: *see* **meiosis.**

mirror drawing: *see* **drawing, mirror.**

mirror image: the image of an object or symbol seen reversed, as though in a mirror; believed by some to be caused by interference between the hemispheres of the brain.

mirror-image television: *see* **television, mirror-image.**

mirror reading: *see* **reading, mirror.**

mirror script: handwriting produced by writing from right to left, so that what is written becomes legible when read from the reflection in a mirror; may be a sign of abnormality, or may occur as a result of forcing a left-handed person to use the right hand. *Syn.* **levography.**

mirror writing: *syn.* **mirror script.**

misappropriation: use for a wrong purpose, usually of money.

misarticulation of program: a failure of two educational programs or two or more aspects of a program to be adequately consistent, interlocked, or supportive. *Ant.* **articulation, program** (1).

misbehavior: (1) behavior that does not contribute to the goals of the group; (2) nonconformity to rules and standards, such as antagonism, nonparticipation, or overt rebellion.

miscellaneous office occupations training: *see* **training, miscellaneous office occupations.**

misconduct: any behavior on the part of a pupil, a teacher, or other individual in more or less variance from an approved or expected pattern; may be only thoughtless or indiscreet action, or a flaunting of rule or tradition, or a malicious or pernicious or aggressive challenging of authority.

misconduct of pupil: violation of implied or established rules governing pupil behavior in school.

misconduct of teacher: (1) actions unbecoming a teacher or tending to degrade the teaching profession; (2) actions of a teacher, either in school or in public, not in conformity with codes of professional ethics; (3) actions of a teacher that violate the mores of the community in which the teacher works. (Sometimes used in a legal sense as a reason for dismissal.)

misdemeanor: (law) any crime or indictable offense of lower consequence than a felony; usually separated by a dollar value of statutory description.

misfeasance: improper performance of a normally legal act. *Comp. w.* **malfeasance; nonfeasance.**

misfit in society: *see* **neurotic character.**

Mishnah (mish'nə): *n. fem.; pl.* **Mishnayot** (mish·nä·yōt'); (Heb., lit., "study") a collection of Jewish laws, compiled, edited, and codified in Palestine by Rabbi Judah the Prince about the year 200, governing the religious, legal, economic, and social life of the Jew; served for centuries as a basis for subsequent talmudic discussions and analyses; a basic subject in schools offering an intensive program of Jewish education.

missal Latin: (R.C. ed.) the designation of a type of elementary instruction in Latin based on the study of the vocabulary and forms encountered in the missal.

missing-parts test: *see* **test, missing-parts.**

mission, Air Force Junior ROTC: *see* **Air Force Junior ROTC mission.**

mission, Air Force Reserve Officers' Training Corps: *see* **Air Force Reserve Officers' Training Corps mission.**

mission school: a school operated by a religious body as a part of its missionary effort.

Missouri filing plan: *see* **filing plan, Missouri.**

mistake: (stat.) an error in calculation or interpretation of data not ascribable to chance but the result of carelessness, forgetfulness, etc. *Dist. f.* **error, constant; error, random** (1).

mister: the form of address in the Air Force Officer Training School, the Naval Officer Candidate School, and the United States Naval Academy, used in addressing naval officers up to the rank of Commander; also, students in the United States Military Academy and the United States Air Force Academy are addressed orally as *mister* or *cadet* interchangeably, *mister* being the commoner or preferred address.

mistress of novices: *see* **master of novices.**

mitosis (mi·tō'sis): the act of cell division, by which any living cell gives rise to two cells resembling itself; to be distinguished from *maturation division*, a special type of mitosis.

mix: in audio reproduction, to combine sound from two or more sources into a single recording (or output), usually with adjustment of tonal quality and/or relative volume level.

mixed cerebral dominance: *see* **cerebral dominance, mixed.**

mixed deafness: *see* **deafness, mixed.**

mixed dextral: a person who is right-handed and left-eyed.

mixed hearing loss: *see* **hearing loss, mixed.**

mixed-relations test: obsolescent *syn.* **test, analogies.**

mixed sinistral: a person who is left-handed and right-eyed.

mixed slant: the characteristic of handwriting in which the upstrokes and downstrokes show no uniformity of slant and no regular order of change of slant.

mixer: a device which permits the combining of two or more input signals at the same time into a recorder or audio system at the level desired.

mixer, audio-video: *see* **audio-video mixer.**

mixer, electronic: a control mechanism through which a number of sound-producing units can be fed in order to combine voice, music, or sound effects at desired recording levels onto a single tape or film sound track.

mixture of plan and elevation: *see* **plan and elevation, mixture of.**

mixture of profile and front view: *see* **profile and front view, mixture of.**

Mizrachi school (miz·rä·khe'): (Heb., lit., "pertaining to the East or the Orient") a day school under the sponsorship of the National Council for Torah Education of Mizrachi, an orthodox Zionist group; Mizrachi schools stress both traditional Judaism and the importance of modern Israel in the spiritual life of the Jew.

M.L.A. qualifications: see **qualifications, M.L.A.**

mnemonic device (nə•mon′ik): any artificial device, such as a familiar or striking formation of words, an acronym, a jingle, etc., to aid the learner in retaining memorized information.

mnemonic notation: see **notation, mnemonic.**

mnemonic symbol: see **symbol, mnemonic.**

mob: an assembly of people acting in a violent and disorderly manner intent on breaking the law and causing injury and/or destruction of property. *Comp. w.* **crowd.**

mob psychology: see **psychology, mob.**

mobile: a construction or sculpture, frequently of wire and sheet metal shapes, with parts that can be set in motion by air currents; innovated about 1930 by artist Alexander Calder; a form of *kinetic art. See* **stabile.**

mobile classroom: see **classroom, mobile.**

mobile clinic: see **clinic, mobile.**

mobile counseling center: see **counseling center, mobile.**

mobile laboratory: see **laboratory, mobile.**

mobile school: a school equipped to be transported to the pupil.

mobile testing unit: see **testing unit, mobile.**

mobile training assistance: see **training assistance, mobile.**

mobile training detachment: see **training detachment, mobile.**

mobile training team: see **training team, mobile.**

mobile training unit: see **training unit, mobile.**

mobile unit: a piece of equipment capable of being moved from place to place, usually on wheels and often self-powered; in broadcasting, transportable equipment in truck or trailer for radio or television broadcasting from the scene of an event, which is to be distinguished from remote-control broadcast by wire or satellite.

mobility: (1) the capacity for being moved with relative ease; for the human being, this implies an interaction with his surroundings, influencing as well as being influenced by his environment; (2) (spec. ed.) the ability to move oneself from one's present position to one's desired position in another part of the environment.

mobility, horizontal occupational: see **occupational mobility, horizontal.**

mobility, horizontal social: see **social mobility, horizontal.**

mobility, intergenerational occupational: see **occupational mobility, intergenerational.**

mobility, occupational: see **occupational mobility.**

mobility of the blind: see **mobility.**

mobility, promotional occupational: see **occupational mobility, promotional.**

mobility ratio: the ratio of the number of newly employed teachers to the total number of teachers.

mobility, vertical social: see **social mobility, vertical.**

mobilization course: see **course, mobilization.**

Möbius band: see **Moebius strip.**

mock broadcast: a learning activity considered especially effective in motivating better work in English, in which pupils prepare a script, rehearse, and act out a program as though it were to be broadcast; sometimes involves the use of an actual microphone connected with a public address system.

mock firing: a complete dry run of the operations connected with the firing and launch of a missile except that the engines are not actually fired, the object being to train personnel, develop procedures, and check out equipment.

mock-up: an edited version of working parts or systems of an object, so constructed as to emphasize a particular part or function of the real thing, for example, a transparent model of an engine and a replica of a spacecraft made of wood with or without functioning engines, etc.

modal: (stat.) pertaining to the mode.

modal age: see **age, modal.**

modal age-grade group: see **group, modal age-grade.**

modal age-grade norm: syn. **norm, age-at-grade** (1).

modal age group: syn. **group, modal age-grade.**

modal age norm: syn. **norm, age-at-grade** (1).

modal-age norms: see **norms, modal-age.**

modal average: syn. **mode** (4).

modal divergence: the difference between the mean and the mode.

modal interval: see **interval, modal.**

modal range: syn. **interval, modal.**

modality, sense: see **sense modality.**

modality, sensory: (read.) the avenue of perception used—visual, auditory, or kinesthetic—in achieving language skills.

mode: (1) the form or manner, as in "mode of communication" or "teaching mode"; (2) a popular fashion or practice; (3) (philos.) the actual determination of a thing (substance), which thing is in its nature indifferent to this or that determination; for example, when a coin's position on a table is changed, each position gives a different mode to the coin, yet the coin is indifferent in its nature to various positions; (4) (*Mo*) the most frequently occurring value in a frequency distribution; the highest point on a distribution curve; syn. **modal average.**

mode, apparent: syn. **mode, crude.**

mode, associative: one of the modes of knowing, involving the acquiring of response patterns through the association of one fact, element, or situation with another.

mode, computed: syn. **mode, refined.**

mode, crude: the midpoint of the class interval containing the greatest number of observations in a distribution. *Syn.* **apparent mode;** *contr. w.* **mode, refined.**

mode, interpolated: the mode often used in badly skewed distributions where the midpoint of the interval with the greatest frequency is not a good estimate; usually computed from the formula $Mo = l + \left(\dfrac{fa}{fa+fb}\right)i$, where l is the exact lower limit of the modal class interval, fa the frequency in the interval immediately above, fb the frequency in the interval immediately below, and i the size of the class interval.

mode, interpretative: one of the modes of knowing involving elaboration and explanation, usually within some frame of reference, leading to insights, conclusions, generalizations, etc. *See* **mode** (3).

mode, refined: an estimate of the value of the mode in the universe from which a given sample is drawn, usually made by the use of the theoretical mode, but may be made by other methods. *Syn.* **computed mode;** *contr. w.* **mode, crude.**

mode, relative: (1) the value of the observation, measure, or score that occurs more frequently than any of the other values near it; (2) the abscissa corresponding to any ordinate of a fitted frequency curve that is higher than the ordinates adjacent to it.

mode, replicative: one of the widely used modes of knowing involving repetition, reproduction, or subdivision. *See* **mode** (3).

model: (1) a pattern of something to be made or reproduced; (2) an example for imitation, such as a standard of performance; for example, in foreign-language instruction, the speech of a native speaker presented in the classroom for imitation during practice by the language students; (3) a graphic or three-dimensional scale representation of an object, principle, or idea; (4) (guidance) a set of interrelated factors or variables which together comprise elements which are symbolic of a social system; may be either verbal or mathematical.

model, analog: a model system or representation by which the operation of a physical system may be studied; *analogs* are commonly electrical networks which may be adjusted so that current measurements may be used to indicate the performance of mechanical systems, hydraulic systems, or larger electrical networks; *analog computers* differ essentially from *digital computers* because analogs are built or connected to operate like the system being studied, while digital computers operate only on numbers, and the problem to be solved must be presented in numerical form. *See* **computer, electronic digital.**

model, behavior: (couns.) any model image or role which may be promoted by counselors for emulation by counselees in order to help them develop strong ego identities and learn how to make purposive decisions.

model, communication: *see* **communication model.**

model, conceptual: a likeness that aids one in understanding a structure or a process; used by scientists when the phenomena studied would otherwise be indescribable or incomprehensible.

model, cultural: *see* **cultural model.**

model, developmental: in guidance, a framework for studying expected behaviors at various stages as an individual moves from childhood to maturity. *See* **task, developmental.**

model, disclosure: *syn.* **model, analog.**

model, goal: as used in guidance, a model for achieving mature behavior which may be socially oriented or individually oriented.

model lesson: *syn.* **lesson, demonstration.**

model, mathematical: *see* **mathematical model.**

model, role: *syn.* **role** (2).

model, scale: a likeness of the material object, system, or process which it represents and which preserves the same relative proportions of its parts. *See* **model, analog.**

model, scaled: a three-dimensional replica of an article or object made according to regularly graded proportions, for example, an architectural model of a structure made to the scale of 1 inch = 1 foot.

model school: (1) originally, an elementary school connected with an early American normal school or supported by a local public school district, in which normal school students observed and practiced teaching methods; *see* **Lancastrian model school;** (2) *syn.* **laboratory school;** (3) narrowly, a school maintained by a teacher education institution or a public school system in which approved methods of instruction or management may be observed by students and visiting educators but in which there is no provision for practice teaching.

model, search: a stage in problem solving involving the analysis of what is given and what is required.

model set: a set of bookkeeping records showing transactions recorded in the journal, the ledger, and the financial statements to illustrate the complete bookkeeping cycle and used as a guide for bookkeeping students.

model, statistical: a standard against which relative data may be compared, for example, the normal probability curve.

model store: *syn.* **laboratory, distributive education.**

model, theoretical: a model which has only the properties assigned to it by the model maker and which need have no close concrete counterpart; although it bears no close resemblance to familiar things, it must describe a phenomenon so that it becomes comprehensible.

model, theoretical isomorphic: a theoretical model which maintains the existence of a one-to-one correspondence between the concepts and assumptions of the theoretical model and the observed world; the relationships in each also take the same form.

modeling: (1) demonstrating or acting according to model performance or procedure; (2) a method of instruction that motivates learning and gives it direction by using respected persons to model desired behavior; (3) the act of forming a three-dimensional figure in a plastic, malleable material such as clay or wax, the resulting figure being either retained as the end product or used as a model or form for the making of a reproduction in plaster, terra cotta, bronze, marble, stone, or wood; (4) that quality of a painting, drawing, photograph, or other two-dimensional representation in which an effect or illusion of the third dimension is achieved through the use of such

means as lighting, contrast, color, perspective, and control of dark-light values.

moderate hearing loss: *see* **hearing loss, moderate.**

moderate realism: *see* **realism** (1).

moderately mentally retarded: *see* **mentally retarded, moderately.**

moderator variable: *see* **variable, moderator.**

modern dance: *see* **dance, modern.**

modern history: *see* **history, modern.**

modern language aptitude test: *see* **test, modern language aptitude.**

modern languages: a term collectively applied to the study of pronunciation, grammar, composition, and reading of foreign languages in contemporary use, as contrasted with that of the ancient languages commonly called the *classical languages.*

modern mathematics: *see* **mathematics, modern.**

modern school: a school in which up-to-date educational procedures are applied.

modernism: a designation of any one of the theories or beliefs of a modern era as opposed to a differing interpretation in a previous era.

modification, address: *see* **instruction modification.**

modification, behavior: *see* **behavior modification.**

modification, instruction: *see* **instruction modification.**

modified median: *see* **median, modified.**

modified platoon plan: *see* **alternate school.**

modified raw score: *see* **score, modified raw.**

modular arithmetic: *see* **arithmetic, modular.**

modular scheduling: *see* **scheduling, modular.**

modulation: (mus.) the process of changing from one key to another.

modulation, amplitude (AM): the system of radio transmission based on varying the amplitude of the power output while the frequency remains constant. *Contr. w.* **modulation, frequency.**

modulation, frequency (FM): a system of staticless radio transmission based on a reversal of the usual system (*amplitude modulation*) in that the power output remains constant while fluctuations created at the microphone vary the frequency of the waves. *Contr. w.* **modulation, amplitude.**

module: (1) a unit of time in the school day; varies in length from 15 to 30 minutes usually; classes may meet for one or several modules in a flexible scheduling system of organization; (2) a group of students who follow the same course of instruction in a flexible scheduling system of organization; (3) (school admin.) a standard or unit of measurement employed in presenting a plan or design, usually on a small scale.

module, proficiency: a term for the hundreds of study guides being developed in a program, Federally funded, to modernize the training of elementary education teachers; by using the module suited to him, each student will advance at his own best rate through bypassing unnecessary instruction and satisfying his particular needs, and he will thus in individual cases be able to earn his degree in a considerably shorter time.

module, schedule: one of the periods of teaching activity scheduled in units of time such as 15, 20, 30, or 45 minutes; subjects taught are scheduled in multiples of the shortest unit, with some requiring more modules than others.

module, source: *see* **program, source.**

modulus: (1) a measure of dispersion, expressed as $\sigma\sqrt{2}$, where σ = standard deviation; the index of precision is the reciprocal of the modulus; (2) the distance on the nomographic scale corresponding to a unit difference in logarithms; the distance on a nomographic scale from the point representing one number to the point representing a number ten times as great; (3) *see* **arithmetic, modular.**

Moebius strip: *alt. sp.* **Möbius** (mœ′bi·əs); a strip of paper given half a twist and then, with the ends fastened together, fashioned into a surface having one continuous side; named after the mathematician August Möbius who discovered it; also called *Moebius* (or *Möbius*) *band.*

molar behavior: *see* **behavior, molar.**

molar behaviorism: *see* **behaviorism, molar.**

molecular behavior: *see* **behavior, molecular.**

molecular behaviorism: *see* **behaviorism, molecular.**

molecular biology: *see* **biology, molecular.**

moment: the arithmetic mean of some power of deviations of the measures in a frequency distribution, the deviations having been measured from zero, from the mean, or from some other origin.

moment, teachable: *see* **teachable moment.**

momism: a term applied to attitudes of young people, particularly boys, who are overly dependent upon and dominated by their mothers.

monad: a self-enclosed unit of reality comparable to an atom except that atoms are physical; a concept used by Leibnitz in a theory embracing different levels of monads, ranging from the lowest, in which there is only subconscious perception, to the soul and the mind, which possess memory, discrimination, self-consciousness, and the power of logical reasoning.

monastic school, inner: a medieval school operated within the confines of a monastery for the general education and religious training of youths who intended to enter the monastic or clerical life.

monastic school, outer: a medieval school operated in conjunction with a monastery for the general education and religious training of youths who did not intend to enter monastic life.

monasticism: a movement that aims at higher Christian perfection through self-denial and asceticism of its members, who live in seclusion according to rule under religious vows.

monaural: *adj.* pertaining to any recording or audio presentation, with one or more microphones, which is recorded or broadcast on only one track.

monaural hearing: *see* **hearing, monaural.**

monaural hearing aid: *see* **hearing aid, monaural.**

monaural recording: *see* **recording, monaural.**

monetary grant: *see* **grant, monetary.**

money income: *see* **income, money.**

money management: determination of how to use one's money, based on predetermined values and priorities.

mongolism: a type of moderate mental retardation, identified by Langdon Down, which is characterized by physical stigmata resulting in appearance somewhat resembling the mongolian; a congenital condition of cerebral maldevelopment in connection with which errors in chromosome structures have been identified; also called *Down's syndrome.*

mongoloid: a person characterized by congenital idiocy with marked liveliness and imitativeness, a flattened skull, oblique eyeslit, mobile hips, and shortness of thumbs and of the little fingers, the special characters of *cretinism* being absent.

monism: the metaphysical theory that all reality is reducible to a single substance.

monism, materialistic: (1) the theory that mind is merely a more complex form or manifestation of matter and should not be regarded as essentially different from matter; (2) the metaphysics that admits but one form of ultimate reality and regards this as being some form of matter.

monistic idealism: *see* **idealism, monistic.**

monitor: *n.* (1) a person—generally a pupil-assistant—to whom is assigned the responsibility of performing or overseeing the performance of some routine task, such as directing traffic on the stairs of the school building, erasing the blackboard, collecting papers, or distributing books; *see* **monitor system;** (2) a more mature or a more capable pupil who assists a teacher in class instruction and room management; characteristic of the monitorial system developed by Bell and Lancaster during the late eighteenth and early nineteenth centuries. *See* **Lancastrian system.**

monitor: *v.* (1) to check recorded or transmitted signals in the process of broadcasting, recording, etc.; (2) in electronic learning laboratories, to listen to the sound signal as it is being recorded or played back; also, to listen to students through the intercom during listen-speak practice or during recording and playback of student practice responses; (3) in computer operation, to execute a program under the control of an executive routine capable of controlling the execution of a number of different programs one immediately after the other, including the cleanup and restart between each program, thus relieving the operating personnel of some control functions and reducing computer idle time.

monitor system: a plan by which a staff of pupils in school and classroom is selected to perform special duties assigned to it. *See* **monitor.**

monitor, viewing: a high-definition TV viewer connected directly to the camera output; does not incorporate channel selector components or audio components; in some closed-circuit applications, used where high definition in the reproduced image is necessary. *See* **camera chain.**

monitorial school: *see* **Lancastrian system.**

monitorial system: *syn.* **Lancastrian system.**

monitoring: in the language laboratory, listening in to the student's oral responses to taped exercises without his knowledge.

monitoring audiometry: *see* **audiometry, monitoring.**

monk: a person who withdraws from society and earthly activity and joins a community so that he may devote his time to prayer, contemplation, and manual labor; he normally spends all his time within the walls of the monastery.

monochorionic twins (mon′ō·kō·ri·on′ik): *syn.* **twins, monozygotic.**

monochrome: a picture, drawing, painting, etc., in shades of a single color.

monocountry studies: *see* **studies, mononational.**

monocular regression: *see* **regression, monocular.**

monocular vision: *see* **vision, monocular.**

monograph: a systematic and complete treatise on a particular subject, usually detailed in treatment but not extensive in scope; need not be bibliographically independent.

monograph, occupational: *see* **occupational monograph.**

monograph, research: a published paper, usually in the form of an enlarged bulletin or small book, reporting a study of some particular subject; a research report dealing with a single problem.

monoideism (mon′ō·ri·dē′iz′m): (1) the theory, advanced by René Descartes (1596-1650), that an idea unrelated to other ideas exercises an unusually powerful force in the mind; (2) an unreasonable harping on a fixed idea.

monolingual: able to speak and understand only one language, the mother tongue. *Contr. w.* **bilingual; multilingual.**

monologue, collective: a stage of speech development in which the child talks mainly to himself; used by Piaget to describe one of the stages in child thinking where there is no real interchange of ideas.

monomania (mon′ō·mā′ni·ə): domination by a fixed idea or obsession in a person who shows no other mental disorder.

mononational studies: *see* **studies, mononational.**

monophobia: morbid fear of being alone.

monophony: music consisting of single-line melodies only. *Contr. w.* **homophony; polyphony.**

monoplegia: paralysis which afflicts one limb. *See* **hemiplegia; paraplegia; quadriplegia; triplegia.**

monopoly, fiscal: a form of government industry deliberately planned to secure revenue from the monopoly of the sale of certain articles or services, for example, the postal service, lotteries, and tobacco and salt monopolies in European and Asiatic countries.

monoptometer (mon'op•tom'ə•tər): an optical device, developed by F. H. Lund and used for determining eye dominance.

monosignificant symbol: *see* **symbol, monosignificant.**

monosyllabic word: *see* **word, monosyllabic.**

monotheism: the doctrine or belief that there is but one God.

monotone: an individual who appears unable to sing a succession of tones of varying pitch and who, when he attempts to sing, sings tones all of one pitch. (The condition was formerly but is no longer regarded as incurable.)

monotonic: a sequence of numbers is said to be monotonic if the numbers are arranged so that each is larger (or smaller) than the one preceding it in the sequence.

monotonous phonation: *see* **phonation, monotonous.**

monozygotic (mon'ō•zī•got'ik): *var.* **monozygous.**

monozygotic twins: *see* **twins, monozygotic.**

monozygous (mon'ō•zī'gəs): (genet.) arising from one and the same ovum by division after fertilization; individuals resulting from such a division (twins, triplets, etc.) being genetically identical, that is, carrying identical gene structures. *Syn.* **monozygotic;** *see* **twins.**

montage: (1) in motion picture editing, the technique of cutting together a number of scenes that are either joined by straight cuts, dissolves, or other effects to give an overall impression; also, the printing of several scenes together in the same composition by the use of traveling mattes and an optical printer; (2) *syn.* **photomontage.**

Monte Carlo methods: *see* **methods, Monte Carlo.**

Montessori method: the method developed by Dr. Maria Montessori, an Italian psychiatrist and educator, for the education of children from birth to maturity, with special emphasis on the years of early childhood and featuring special techniques and materials to develop the child's senses and intellect along with a new philosophical viewpoint regarding the nature of children; includes emphasis on (*a*) the ability of the child's *absorbent mind* to absorb his culture and to select pertinent parts, unconsciously before age three, consciously thereafter, (*b*) *intrinsic motivation* through use of the child's innate curiosity and delight in discovery, (*c*) teaching through *daily living activities* concerned with care of self and environment, (*d*) *indirect preparation,* that is, activities that prepare the sensorimotor pathways for the future, for example scrubbing as preparation for writing, (*e*) *didactic materials* in graded series, and (*f*) *liberty within limits,* that is; freedom to choose between things which are in themselves good.

monthly health report: *see* **report, monthly health.**

monthly percent of attendance: *see* **attendance, monthly percent of.**

monthly report: *see* **report, monthly.**

moods of judger: *see* **judger, moods of.**

Moon type: a system of printing for the blind, devised by William Moon (1818–1894) and consisting of raised lines in the form of angles and curves, the outline of some letters resembling that of roman capitals; largely superseded by braille, but proves useful for older persons unable to learn braille.

moonlight school: classes held in the evenings for adults, often in public school buildings, in isolated regions such as the Kentucky mountains; usually designed to promote literacy and community welfare.

moot: (legal) academic or hypothetical, rather than pertaining to actual litigants.

moral: (1) a term used to delimit those characters, traits, intentions, judgments, or acts which can appropriately be designated as right, wrong, good, bad; in this meaning, moral is opposed to amoral; (2) a term also used to designate the right or good over against the wrong or bad, in relation to some criterion of obligation; in this meaning, moral is an antonym of immoral. (Since moral in sense 1 includes both moral in sense 2 and its opposite, the term is slippery and its educational usage is dogged with ambiguity.)

moral adjustment: *see* **adjustment, moral.**

moral age: *see* **age, moral.**

moral and spiritual values: *see* **values, moral and spiritual.**

moral authority: *see* **authority, moral.**

moral basis of public education: the system of morality which public education is designed fundamentally to propagate, sometimes identified in America as *democratic morality;* most vigorously urged by those who see the basic aims of the school in character development over against intellectual development and who are at the same time concerned to assert the moral foundations of a secular school. *See* **character education; morality; morality, civic.**

moral behavior: *see* **behavior, moral.**

moral character: *see* **character, moral.**

moral code: *see* **code, moral.**

moral concept: an idea or mental pattern that may be used as a criterion for discriminating between right and wrong.

moral defective: a person who, because of abnormal physical or mental conditions, is not accountable in matters of morality.

moral development: *see* **development, moral.**

moral deviate: a person who differs from the norm in respect to morality, whether toward "better" or toward "worse."

moral education: either formal or incidental instruction in morals or rules of conduct. (In countries with a recognized state religion and in parochial schools, this may be included in *religious instruction;* in countries where there is no state religion, such instruction may be part of *character education* or *citizenship education.*) *See* **training, moral.**

moral freedom: *see* **free will, doctrine of.**

moral guidance: *see* **guidance, moral.**

moral imbecile: *see* **imbecile, moral.**

moral insanity: *see* **insanity, moral.**

moral instruction: *syn.* **instruction, ethical.**

moral judgment: a judgment involving choice among principles, policies, or courses of action and involving also some criterion of right conduct; the judgment may involve primarily the selection and application of the right principle, or it may involve choice among or resolution of conflicting principles of morality. *See* **judgment; judgment, ethical; morality.**

moral law: any rule of right or wrong conduct or principle of obligation; may be regarded as derived from divine revelation, human intuition, the application of human intelligence, or human custom; to be distinguished from *positive law* or law enacted into statute by government.

moral maturity: *see* **maturity, moral.**

moral philosophy: *see* **philosophy, moral.**

moral sanction: *see* **sanction, moral.**

moral sense: *syn.* **ethical sense** (1).

moral strength: the capacity to seek and to live by standards of good conduct.

moral theology: *see* **theology, moral.**

moral training: *see* **training, moral.**

moral values: *see* **values, moral and spiritual.**

moral virtues: *see* **virtues, moral.**

morale: (1) a courage, faith, and personal integration maintained in the face of adversity; (2) group solidarity maintained in the face of threatening forces; (3) general level or tone of the attitudes of personnel of an institution; *see* **esprit de corps.**

morale, school: (1) the spirit of confidence characterizing the students of a school; (2) the fusing of wishes and attitudes into dominant group attitudes, making it possible for the school population to act with unity in certain areas.

morale survey: *see* **survey, attitude.**

morale, teacher: (1) the collective feelings and attitudes of a teacher group as related to their duties, responsibilities, goals, supervisors, and fellow workers; (2) state of mind of a teacher with respect to his work; may be influenced by such factors as salary adequacy, tenure conditions, sick leave and pension benefits, degree of participation in policy making and administration, opportunities for advancement, and the intelligence and constructiveness of supervision.

moralism: (1) a maxim or saying embodying a moral truth; (2) moral teaching or counsel; inculcation of morality; moralizing; (3) practice of morality as distinct from religion; the leading of a moral life as distinguished from a religious life.

moralistic attitude: (1) the tendency to identify morality with the process of controlling the behavior of others by coercive treatment, shaming the offender for his misconduct and blaming him for his evil intentions; (2) the tendency to mouth platitudes and to fail to see through a haze of abstract principles (whether utilitarian, religious, rationalistic, or other such principles) to the actual, concrete human situation.

morality: (1) a system of principles (or a code) of right and wrong conduct, actual or idealized, as in *democratic morality, Christian morality*, etc.; (2) conformity in behavior to some principle or code of right or good conduct, as in expressions like "training for morality." *See* **code, moral; moral; morals.**

morality, civic: a system of duties or responsibilities governing the members of a state, or of civil society otherwise named, as distinct from the duties and responsibilities of members of religious communities or of other communities to which the rules of civil society are thought not to apply. *See* **morality.**

morality, conventional: at the level of individual conduct, a morality that conforms to the customary codes of conduct of some group; at the level of self conscious philosophizing, a morality that finds in the mores of some social group the ultimate touchstone of rightness in any formulated code or maxim of conduct. *See* **code, moral; morality; morality, reflective; mores.**

morality, critical: *see* **morality, reflective.**

morality, democratic: *see* **moral basis of public education.**

morality, dynamic: adherence to the ethical belief that moral standards are not fixed and unchanging but relative and contingent, constantly varying according to culture, place, and time.

morality, internal: conformity to standards of conduct as a result of pressures arising from within the self; an existential conviction as to the values of that to which one conforms.

morality, reflective: at the level of individual conduct, a morality which finds in some criticized and reformulated version of customary morality the guide to right choice and conduct; at the level of self-conscious philosophizing, a morality that finds in the processes and products of intellectual criticism the touchstone not only of right choice or conduct but of the rightness or wrongness of the mores as well; sometimes referred to as *critical morality. See* **morality; morality, conventional.**

morals: (1) in a society, the basic values used in choosing among alternative life values; (2) actual customs more or less fully evaluated and rationalized according to some principle of right and wrong; in the middle classes of American society, especially sexual and property customs; (3) in the individual, the virtues or other elements that make up *morality.*

morals, Christian: those qualities which place human acts in conformity with the Judaeo-Christian tradition, namely, the Ten Commandments and the Two Commandments of the New Law: "Love God" and "Love your neighbor as yourself."

morals, natural: those qualities which place an act in conformity with natural law, that is, law arising from reason alone, not revelation.

"more than" ogive: *see* **ogive, "more than."**

mores (mō'rēz): the fundamental and relatively inflexible folkways or moral customs of a people, generally accepted as traditional and necessary to the well-being of the group.

Morgan's canon: *see* **law of parsimony.**

morning exercises: activities such as singing or saluting the flag conducted during the first few minutes of the school day. *Syn.* **opening exercises.**

morning-glory child: *see* **child, morning-glory.**

Moro reflex: *see* **reflex, Moro.**

moron: a mentally defective person, usually having a mental age of 8 years or upward or, if a child, an IQ of 50 or more; as a rule, the upper limit should be an IQ of 69, but this limit should not be adhered to in cases where medical, social, and other factors clearly indicate that the patient is mentally defective; designates any mental defective above the grade of *imbecile. See* **imbecile; mentally retarded, Group II.**

morpheme: a basic, indivisible language unit which carries meaning in a language.

morphogenesis: development of form in structure in the whole course of development during an individual's life history or in regeneration of an organism.

morphological analysis: *see* **analysis, morphological.**

morphology: (1) the study of form or shape without reference to composition or substance or to function; (2) (lang.) a branch of study dealing with language form and structure, including the origin and function of inflectional forms.

Morrill Acts: the first Morrill Act, passed by Congress in 1862, granted public lands for the establishment of colleges; new states as well as old states were eligible to participate; without excluding the sciences and the arts, it specified instruction in agriculture, mechanic arts, and military science; the second Morrill Act, passed in 1890, provided for an annual appropriation of money to each such land-grant college; later amendments increased the original amounts.

Morrison plan: a five-step instructional plan advocated by H. C. Morrison consisting of (*a*) exploration, in which are determined the pupil's apperceptive background and mastery of the unit of work; (*b*) presentation, in which the teacher gives a general overview of the whole unit of work; (*c*) assimilation, in which pupils actively investigate and study the unit and pass a mastery test; (*d*) organization, in which the class gathers together the argument of the unit into a logical, coherent outline; and (*e*) recitation, in which pupils who have mastered the unit give a series of talks, the teacher and class acting as audience. *Comp. w.* **Herbartian method.**

Mort plan: a state aid plan designed by Paul Mort under which a state would pay, as state aid, the difference between the need of a district (as expressed in terms of the cost of the minimum program, in unit costs, usually "classroom units") and the ability of a district (as expressed in terms of the actual or hypothetical yield of a uniform local tax at some fixed rate).

mortality, educational: the extent to which students fail to complete the school program, dropping out before graduation. *See* **dropout.**

mortality rate, age-specific: the number of deaths during the year per thousand persons in specific age groups.

mortality, student: the rate or amount of withdrawal of students from a college; includes those dropped for reasons of scholarship or discipline and voluntary withdrawals due to financial or other causes.

mortality, teacher: (1) the loss of teaching personnel from all causes during a given period; *see* **turnover, teacher;** (2) the death rate of those engaged in teaching.

mortarboard: common name for the academic cap with the stiff square top.

mortmain control (môrt'mān): (Fr. *mort,* "dead," + *main,* "hand"; lit., "dead-hand control") the control by the stipulations of the founders of an endowment or other wealth funded in perpetuity, especially when such control severely or unduly limits the trustees in their efforts to administer the endowment according to the spirit rather than the letter of the bequest. *Syn.* **dead-hand control;** *see* **cy pres, doctrine of.**

mosaic method of class scheduling: *see* **scheduling, mosaic method of class.**

mosaic plan: the most commonly used procedure for the construction of the general daily school schedule; employs each class section as a unit to be fitted into a schedule.

mosaic test: *see* **test, mosaic.**

Mosely commission of inquiry: *see* **commission of inquiry, Mosely.**

mother book: the English version of the title of a work by Pestalozzi intended to teach mothers how to observe and teach their children; devoted largely to a description of Pestalozzi's method of *object teaching.*

mother complex: *see* **complex, mother.**

mother fixation: *see* **fixation, mother.**

mother, foster: *see* **foster mother.**

Mother Goose: the designation or title of a number of collections of old English rhymes, first compiled and published in London about 1760 by John Newbery, formerly used extensively as nursery and kindergarten rhymes and primary reading material. (The rhymes are of obscure origin and meaning, but it is believed that some were originally intended as stories for young children, while others embodied moral precepts or political satires written and circulated long before their compilation by Newbery. Newbery apparently took his title from that of a collection of fairy stories that enjoyed enormous popularity, anonymously written by the French writer Charles Perrault and published in 1697 under the title *Contes de ma Mère l'Oye*, literally, *Stories of My Mother Goose.*)

mother imago: *see* **imago, mother.**

mother play: the English version of a term introduced by Froebel to designate little rhymes, games, and songs of his composition intended to be used by the mother to occupy and entertain her child while she was engaged in other activities; first published in 1843 in a collection entitled *Mutter-Spiel und Kose-Lieder (Mother Play and Child Songs);* translated into English under the title *Goldammer's Manual. See* **Goldammer's Manual.**

mothers, room: *see* **room mothers.**

mother's school: (1) as proposed by Comenius (1592–1670), the teaching to be given by the mother in the home before the children entered the vernacular school at 6 years; (2) a school established in 1911 by Mary L. Read to provide theoretical instruction and practical experience for young women in the care and training of babies and small children under home conditions.

motility: general movement or activity of a living form, such as the locomotor activity of spermatozoa or of the fetus after quickening, or the movements of the young postnatal infant which occur without apparent external stimulation.

motion and time study: *see* **study, motion and time.**

motion, linear: *see* **movement, rectilinear.**

motion picture: a series of still pictures taken in sequence which, when projected intermittently upon a screen, give the illusion of continuous action.

motion-picture director: *see* **director, motion-picture.**

motion picture, educational: *syn.* **film, classroom.**

motion-picture methods: *see* **audiovisual-kinesthetic method; visual-hearing method.**

motion picture, occupational: a motion picture designed primarily to present job characteristics, indicate specific tasks within a given industry, and denote possibilities of future employment based on demands of the given industry in relation to school achievement and individual aptitudes.

motion-picture projector, synchronized: *see* **projector, synchronized motion-picture.**

motion picture, theatrical: any motion picture designed primarily for use in commercial motion-picture theaters or on entertainment broadcasts.

motion study: *see* **study, motion.**

motion unit: a single, continuous movement of some working element of the human body that has definite starting and stopping points.

motivated schoolwork: *see* **schoolwork, motivated.**

motivating device: any technique or situation used in teaching for the primary purpose of stimulating interest and augmenting effort on the part of the pupils. *See* **motivation; motivation, extrinsic; motivation, intrinsic; motive.**

motivation: (1) (psych.) broadly considered, the process of arousing, sustaining, and regulating activity, a concept limited to some aspect such as the energetics of behavior or purposive regulation; (2) the practical art of applying incentives and arousing interest for the purpose of causing a pupil to perform in a desired way; usually designates the act of choosing study materials of such a sort and presenting them in such a way that they appeal to the pupil's interests and cause him to attack the work at hand willingly and to complete it with sustained enthusiasm; also designates the use of various devices such as the offering of rewards or an appeal to the desire to excel. *See* **motivating device; motivation, extrinsic; motivation, intrinsic; motive.**

motivation, achievement: (1) a combination of psychological forces which initiate, direct, and sustain behavior toward successful attainment of some goal which provides a sense of significance; no single measurable factor seems to account for it; measurement is in terms of construct validation of interrelated scholastic, societal, and individual factors; *syn.* **achievement need;** (2) an incentive variable used in research to indicate the relationship between individual reaction to *discovery learning* and other learning theories or techniques.

motivation, external: environmental determinants of behavior, including a perceived goal-object (such as food when hungry) and social incentives (such as a word of praise). *Contr. w.* **motivation, internal.**

motivation, extrinsic: the use of rewards or punishments external to intrinsic interests in the material itself in the attempt to control behavior. *See* **motivating device; motivation; motive;** *contr. w.* **motivation, intrinsic.**

motivation, group: aims or purposes that are held in common by the members of a group.

motivation, internal: physiological drives and purposes that are located within the organism. *Contr. w.* **motivation, external.**

motivation, intrinsic: (1) determination of behavior that is resident within an activity and that sustains it as with autonomous acts and interests; *contr. w.* **motivation, extrinsic;** (2) *see* **Montessori method.**

motivation, personal: one of the physical, intellectual, or psychological needs of an individual which cause him to act in a certain way.

motivation, radio: any instructional plan that definitely utilizes radio for the creation of interest in the process of learning.

motivation research: *see* **research, motivation.**

motivation, scholastic: the intensity of a student's efforts and desires to achieve a certain level of marks and a general educational objective.

motivation techniques: any methods designed to facilitate work and learning, for example, the use of a reading-progress chart in the classroom.

motivation, unconscious: any mental process the existence of which we are obliged to assume (because, for instance, we infer it in some way from its effects) but of which we are not directly aware; the process whereby we are motivated without actually being aware of the stimuli.

motive: (1) broadly considered, any impulse, drive, attitude, whether conscious or not, that arouses, sustains, or regulates behavior; (2) an acquired disposition that is goal-directed as distinct from an unlearned physiological drive; (3) an internal motivation, such as an intention to act or a physiological drive, as distinguished from an incentive, which is external. *See* **drive; incentives.**

motive, basic: an impulse, driving force, tendency, or motor attitude which is an inherent part of a person.

motive, economic: *see* **economic motive.**

motive, fundamental: an impulse, driving force, tendency, or motor attitude essential in producing behavior or attitudes.

motive question: *see* **question, motive.**

motor: *adj.* pertaining to a muscle, nerve, or center that effects or produces movement.

motor ability: *see* **ability, motor.**

motor-ability age: *see* **age, motor-ability.**

motor ability, test of: *see* **test of motor ability.**

motor achievement test: *see* **test, motor achievement.**

motor activity: *see* **activity, motor.**

motor activity, fine: *see* **activity, fine motor.**

motor activity, gross: *see* **activity, gross motor.**

motor-activity principle: a basic principle of the Froebelian kindergarten, based on the theory that children learn and acquire information, understanding, and skills through motor activities in which they are naturally interested, such as building, constructing, modeling, painting, running, and singing.

motor adaptability: the facility with which an individual can successfully accomplish various operations involving strength, muscular coordination, or speed of reaction.

motor apraxia: *see* **apraxia.**

motor capacity: *see* **capacity, motor.**

motor condensation: (behav. psych.) the telescoping or simplification of a compound movement by the elimination of unnecessary components.

motor-constructive experience: *see* **experience, motor-constructive.**

motor control: the ability to control and direct the voluntary muscles of the body.

motor control, general: ability to coordinate and direct the muscles of the body.

motor coordination: *see* **coordination, motor.**

motor development: *see* **development, motor.**

motor diffusion: widespread rather than localized muscular activity of the organism. *See* **activity, mass; generalization (2); irradiation.**

motor educability: *see* **educability, motor.**

motor encoding test: *see* **test, motor encoding.**

motor expression: *see* **expression, motor.**

motor-expressive aphasia: *see* **aphasia, motor-expressive.**

motor fitness: the condition of muscular strength, endurance, and skill that makes an individual ready for performance of bodily activities. *See* **physical fitness.**

motor incoordination: *see* **incoordination, motor.**

motor learning: *see* **learning, motor.**

motor pattern: a movement or a series of movements for a purpose; provides the basis for meaningful orientation and the foundation for more complex learnings.

motor performance: a relatively short-term aspect of movement behavior marked by movement oriented toward the execution of an identifiable task.

motor planning: *see* **planning, motor.**

motor process: a generic term embracing efferent neural processes and the effector activities excited thereby.

motor proficiency: effective chain of motor response, increased proficiency in motor change brought out by practice refinement of motor ability to perform a skill. *See* **ability, motor.**

motor quotient: *see* **quotient, motor.**

motor response: *see* **response, motor.**

motor rhythm: the ability to perform body movements in time to a designated rhythm.

motor sequence: successive stages in the infant's development of motor control that normally follow a regular order.

motor set: readiness to react, with attention or observation focused on the movement to be made rather than on the sensory source of the signal stimulus.

motor skill: *see* **skill, motor.**

motor skills, basic: *syn.* **movement, fundamental.**

motor, synchronous: an electric motor running at a speed proportional to the frequency of the operating current.

mount: (1) the material to which photographs, graphic materials, models, etc., may be attached for purposes of handling and preservation; (2) *see* **mounting.**

mount, dry: a picture mounted by use of a thermal-seal process.

mount, wet: a flat picture or other illustration mounted on a heavy cardboard backing with an adhesive such as rubber cement.

mounting: (1) the process of affixing models and specimens to a base for purposes of display; (2) the process of affixing pictures on a backing material for purposes of handling, preservation, or display; (3) the process of affixing transparencies in an aperturelike frame for purposes of projection and/or preservation.

mounting, permanent: the application of rubber cement to the back of a flat material to be mounted and also to the cardboard backing, then permitting the two surfaces to dry before joining them together; or the use of dry-mount tissue placed between the material and the cardboard, with heat and pressure being applied to seal the layers together.

mounting, temporary: application of rubber cement to the back of an illustration or lettering and immediate placement on a cardboard backing while the cement is still wet.

mouth-orientation response: *see* **response, mouth-orientation.**

movable do (dō): a system for teaching tonal relationships in singing in which a single set of Italian syllables indicates the tones of the scale for all keys, the syllables being shifted in position on the staff as the key is changed; the key signature determines the position of do, and accordingly of all the syllables, since their internal relationships remain constant regardless of key. (The system is aimed at developing a feeling for tonality or relative pitch and is most popular in England and the United States.) *See* **sol-fa; sol-fa syllables; solmization;** *contr. w.* **fixed do.**

movable school: a school, frequently located in a sparsely settled, open-range country, housed in a building small enough to be moved to a new location from time to time.

movable seating equipment: *see* **seating equipment, movable.**

movement, aesthetics of: *see* **eurythmics.**

movement, ballistic: movement that is initiated by a muscular contraction, followed by muscular relaxation, thus permitting movement to continue by the momentum started; a rapid movement of limbs started by the driving muscles (prime movers) but completed by their own momentum.

movement, basic: *syn.* **movement, fundamental.**

movement, consumer: the drive to develop effective, responsible consumers through consumer information and education, and through consumer organizations and Federal, state, and local legislation.

movement, cooperative: *see* **cooperative movement.**

movement, curvilinear: all translatory, nonrectilinear movement; moving an object in a curved but not necessarily circular pathway.

movement, ecumenical: *see* **ecumenism.**

movement education: (phys. ed.) the study of human motion involved in positive experiences concerned with body mechanics and basic movement pattern with the application of these in fundamental motor activity.

movement, fundamental: (phys. ed.) basic skill patterns which are common to all movement activities. *Syn.* **basic motor skills; basic movement.**

movement, lip: the use of the lips in silent reading; an immature habit which should disappear as the reader grows in reading skill but often characterizing the reading of those who read poorly.

movement, Perry: *see* **Perry movement.**

movement, reciprocating: repetitive movement as illustrated by a bouncing ball.

movement, rectilinear: (phys. ed.) the linear progression of an object as a whole, with all its parts moving the same distance in the same direction at a uniform rate of speed.

movement, scientific: *see* **scientific movement.**

movement, supervised-study: *see* **supervised-study movement.**

movement, survey: *see* **survey movement.**

movement, translatory: the movement involved in transferring an object as a whole from one location to another.

movement, youth: *see* **youth movement.**

movements, expressive: response patterns, usually of the facial musculature, which are interpreted as evidence of emotional experience.

movie sound audio channel: *see* **audio channel, movie sound.**

movigenics: the study of the origin and development of patterns of movement in man and the relationship of these movements to learning efficiency; movigenic theory rests on 10 postulates dealing with man as a moving being within a spatial world and forms the basis for a curriculum designed to achieve movement efficiency. *See* **awareness, body; balance, dynamic; bilaterality; planning, motor.**

moving school: a type of school, common in New England in the eighteenth century, held for a few months at a time in different parts of a township in order to secure equality of convenience for pupils.

ms: *see* **millisecond.**

μs: *see* **microsecond.**

MSA: *see* **analysis, multiple scalogram.**

MTM: *see* **measurement, methods-time.**

Muller-Schumann paradigm of associative inhibition: *see* **associative inhibition, Muller-Schumann paradigm of.**

Müller-Walle method (mYl'ər vä'lə): a method of teaching lipreading, originated by Julius Müller of Germany and introduced into the United States by Martha E. Bruhn, that, with some modifications, is often called the *Bruhn method* on this continent.

multiaddress computer: *see* **computer, multiaddress.**

multibase arithmetic blocks: *see* **blocks, multibase arithmetic.**

multiblock trade: *see* **trade, multiblock.**

multicamera filming: *see* **filming, multicamera.**

multichannel recording: *see* **recording, multichannel.**

multidimensional attitude: *syn.* **attitude, complex.**

multidimensional development: *see* **development, multidimensional.**

multidisciplinary team: representation on a group of two or more professional disciplines for purposes of achieving coordinated, complementary support functions.

multiethnic reader: *see* **reader, multiethnic.**

multigraph: machine for printing letters, etc., which has type similar to that of a typewriter.

multihandicapped: *syn.* **handicapped, multi.**

multilingual: having equal facility in the use of several languages. *See* **bilingual; trilingual;** *contr. w.* **monolingual.**

multimedia approach: use of a variety of selected and appropriate audiovisual materials to provide interrelated learning opportunities; also, use of more than one medium for instruction on a given subject or in a given time period. *See* **cross-media approach.**

multimedia center: *syn.* **center, instructional materials.**

multimodal: having more than one mode; sometimes indicates that the observations are not drawn from a homogeneous population or that more than one class of data has been included. *Dist. f.* **bimodal;** *contr. w.* **unimodal.**

multiphasic personality test: *see* **test, multiphasic personality.**

multiple-answer test: *syn.* **test, multiple-response.**

multiple-approach method: an approach to the teaching of foreign languages postulating the need for using many different methods and types of work.

multiple bar chart: *see* **chart, multiple bar.**

multiple birth: the birth of more than one offspring from a single pregnancy; appears, in the case of human beings, to be characteristic of some families, though not proved to be of hereditary origin. (The products of a multiple birth—twins, triplets, quadruplets, etc.—may be any combination of identical or fraternal multiples.) *See* **twins.**

multiple-car driving range: *see* **driving range, multiple-car.**

multiple-categoried data: *see* **data, multiple-categoried.**

multiple-causation concept: *see* **concept, multiple-causation.**

multiple-choice item: *see* **item, multiple-choice.**

multiple-choice item analysis: *see* **analysis, multiple-choice item.**

multiple-choice test: *see* **test, multiple-choice.**

multiple coefficient: *syn.* **coefficient of multiple correlation.**

multiple correlation: *see* **correlation, multiple.**

multiple correlation coefficient: *syn.* **coefficient of multiple correlation.**

multiple correlation, coefficient of: *see* **coefficient of multiple correlation.**

multiple correlation ratio: *see* **ratio, multiple correlation.**

multiple correlation test selection method, Wherry-Doolittle: *see* **test selection method, Wherry-Doolittle multiple correlation.**

multiple counseling: *see* **counseling, multiple.**

multiple-course plan: an enrichment plan of promotion in which the rate of progress for all pupils in a grade is kept fairly constant but in which the courses are different, with minimum, average, and maximum amounts of work.

multiple curriculum organization: *see* **curriculum organization, multiple.**

multiple disability: *see* **disability, multiple.**

multiple-dot map: *see* **map, multiple-dot.**

multiple exceptionality: *see* **exceptionality, multiple.**

multiple-factor analysis: any method of factor analysis that assumes the possibility of more than one common factor in the relations of a battery of tests; a generalization of the original two-factor theory in which it was assumed that the battery had only one common factor plus specific factors, one for each test. *See* **bifactor method; centroid method; principal component; two-factor theory.**

multiple-factor method: a method of predicting population that assumes that a prediction based on a large number of economic and social factors closely associated with growth of population is more reliable than a prediction based on a single index and that factors having positive correlation with increase of population in the past will continue to be closely related to growth of population in the future. (Only factors whose average increment of increase falls within one standard deviation of the mean of the mean increments of all the factors employed are used.) *Syn.* **economic-factor method.**

multiple factors: pairs of genes (factors) that produce similar or supplementary effects; used in a broad sense to indicate any or all factors combining to produce a single result.

multiple frequency table: *see* **table, multiple frequency.**

multiple-group method: (fact. anal.) a variation of the centroid method, distinguished from it mainly in that several factors (rather than only one) may be extracted simultaneously. *See* **centroid method.**

multiple handicap: *see* **handicap, multiple.**

multiple-headed school system: *see* **administrative organization, multiple type of.**

multiple line of approach: *syn.* **multiple-approach method.**

multiple linear regression equation: *syn.* **regression equation (1).**

multiple measurement: *see* **measurement, multiple.**

multiple picture graph: *see* **graph, multiple picture.**

multiple prediction: *see* **prediction, multiple.**

multiple-purpose high school: *see* **high school, multiple-purpose.**

multiple-question sociogram: *see* **sociogram, multiple-question.**

multiple-ratio method: a short-cut method for selecting a small number of tests from a larger number so as to give a criterion correlation only slightly lower than the multiple correlation of all the tests with the criterion; usually, the approximation is only slightly lower than the multiple correlation for the selected variables.

multiple regression equation: *syn.* regression equation, partial.

multiple-response item: *see* item, multiple-response.

multiple-response test: *see* test, multiple-response.

multiple-room department: *see* department, multiple-room.

multiple route: *see* route, multiple.

multiple scalogram analysis: *see* analysis, multiple scalogram.

multiple scoring: *see* scoring, multiple.

multiple supervision: *see* supervision, multiple.

multiple therapy: *see* therapy, multiple.

multiple track: *see* track, multiple.

multiple-track curriculum: *see* curriculum, multiple-track.

multiple type of administrative organization: *see* administrative organization, multiple type of.

multiple use: use of a particular part of a school plant for more than one purpose, for example, use of a room for teaching both physical and biological sciences or both mathematics and science.

multiple-variable experiment: *see* experiment, multiple-variable.

multiplexer: in computer operation, a buffer capable of coordinating, within limits, several inputs or outputs or data movements.

multiplexing: simultaneous transmission of two or more messages on a single channel; also, division of a transmission facility into two or more channels.

multiplexing, signal: a method for the mixing of several signals for transmission over a single system; *microwave relays* are often multiplexed to carry video and audio signals simultaneously; the device is called the *signal multiplexer.*

multiplication facts: the list of statements which give the products of all pairs of numbers chosen from the set {0,1,2,3,4,5,6,7,8,9}; earlier literature lists 100 such facts; contemporary programs stress the commutativity of the operation, the role of 1 as the identity element, and the special products with 0 in order to reduce the number of facts to be learned to 36.

multiplication facts, primary: *syn.* multiplication facts.

multiplicative cancellation: *see* law, cancellation.

multiply handicapped: *see* handicapped, multiply.

multiplying constant: *see* constant, multiplying.

multiplying punch: *see* punch, multiplying.

multipurpose room: a room in a school building designed for multiple utilization, such as a *lunchroom-gymnasium* or a *cafetorium. Syn.* combination room.

multisensory phonics: *see* phonics, multisensory.

multistage sampling: *see* sampling, multistage.

multitape recording: *see* recording, multitape.

multitrack programming: *see* programming, multitrack.

multitrait-multimethod matrix: *see* matrix, multitrait-multimethod.

multivariate analysis: *see* analysis, multivariate.

multivariate selection: *see* selection, multivariate.

municipal bond: *see* bond, municipal.

municipal camp: *see* camp, municipal.

municipal college: *see* college, municipal.

municipal control: control (of varying degrees) exercised over the schools by the municipal authority, existing when the board of education is appointed in whole or in part by municipal authority, when school buildings are directly maintained by the municipal authority, but more particularly when school revenues are determined or approved by the municipal authority.

municipal corporation: *see* corporation, municipal.

municipal corporation, quasi: *see* corporation, quasi.

municipal junior college: *see* junior college, municipal.

municipal lodge: a recreation unit owned by a municipality, usually located outside the city limits and used as a center for recreation activities.

municipal park: a recreation center operated by a municipality; implies landscaped areas with little provision for specific recreational activities.

municipal recreation: *see* recreation, municipal.

municipal recreation center: *see* recreation center, municipal.

municipal teachers' college: *see* teachers' college, municipal.

municipal university: *see* university, municipal.

mural: a painting on a wall surface applied either directly or on material attached to the wall, such as canvas, paper, wood, etc.; murals traditionally illustrate a story or historical event but have frequently been nonrepresentational in contemporary usage.

murder board: (mil. ed.) a naval term referring to an informal group before whom a speech or presentation is rehearsed.

muscle-bound: pertaining to a condition in which the overdevelopment and decreased elasticity of the muscles limit joint flexibility; sometimes a misnomer used to describe excessive strength accompanied by massive amounts of muscular tissue.

muscle imbalance: *see* imbalance, muscle.

muscle sense: the sense by which one is aware of the movement, position, or posture of muscles and bodily members (without the use of other senses, such as sight), through stimulation, possibly mechanical, of sense organs in the muscles, joints, and tendons. *Syn.* kinesthetic sense; proprioceptive sense.

muscle tonus: *see* tonus, muscle.

muscle training: *see* training, muscle.

muscular balance: the condition in which one eye continues to fixate when fusion of the images is made impossible; for example, when one eye is covered.

muscular coordination: *see* coordination, muscular.

muscular dystrophy: *see* dystrophy, muscular.

muscular endurance: *see* endurance, muscular.

muscular fitness: *see* fitness, muscular.

muscular incoordination: *syn.* incoordination, motor.

muscular movement: (1) a handwriting movement involving muscles of the whole arm, the large cushion, or muscle pad, and of the front forearm acting as the fulcrum, and in which finger movements are very slight; (2) a handwriting movement involving the free coordinated action of the gross muscles of the arm as distinguished from finger movements and wrist movements.

muscular strength: (1) the force that a voluntary muscle or group of muscles can exert against a resistance in one maximum effort; measured in units of pounds; (2) (spec. ed.) a movigenic term which indicates the capacity of the organism to maintain an adequate state of *muscle tonus,* power, and stamina to meet the daily demands appropriate to body size and chronological age.

museum: (1) a building or room used to preserve and exhibit collections of objects of interest in such fields as science, literature, and art; (2) the collection exhibited in such a room or building.

museum, commercial: (1) a collection of objects of permanent interest to teachers and students of business; may include specimens of raw materials, parts of manufactured products, and finished goods arranged systematically, as well as appliances used in business offices and stores and specimens of business forms, business letters, and advertisements; (2) a room or building in which such a collection is kept.

museum education: (1) those changes brought about in the individual through ideas suggested or communicated by museum materials and their arrangement; (2) the formal or informal educational program carried on by museums.

museum, health: a museum devoted to the display of pictures, charts, models, instruments, and other items relating to health.

music: traditionally, music has been (*a*) the organization of tones expressive of, and stimulating to, human feelings, (*b*) the art and science of creating and delivering these tones, and (*c*) the written or printed form of these tones; however, the music of modern composers, such as Cage and Stockhausen, is often deliberately not organized, not expressive of human feelings, and occasionally, not written in any form recognizable to even the most advanced professional musicians.

music, absolute: music conceived solely in terms of tonal material and formal organization, having no intentional descriptive or extramusical meaning. *Contr. w.* **music, program.**

music, adolescent: the music practiced and cherished by the adolescent subculture in Western society; folk music, jazz, rock 'n' roll, and their derivatives, which have grown into an enormous commercial enterprise in contemporary society.

music, aesthetics of: *see* **aesthetics of music.**

music agnosia, auditory: *see* **agnosia, auditory music.**

music, aleatory: music composed so as to permit the performer to rearrange at will certain elements of the musical materials; from *aleai* (Gr., lit., "dice"). *Syn.* **chance music.**

music, applied: (1) musical performance; (2) vocal and instrumental music considered as subjects of instruction. *Contr. w.* **theory** (2).

music appreciation: *see* **appreciation, music.**

music aptitude: *see* **aptitude, music.**

music aptitude test: *see* **test, music aptitude.**

music, art: music conceived purely in terms of its intrinsic aesthetic value, as opposed to popular and commercial music conceived for financial returns or for social utility; often referred to as "classical" or "serious" music. *See* **music, fine-art;** *contr. w.* **music, commercial; music, folk.**

music, background: music incidental to a drama, film, broadcast, reading, television show, etc., which serves to create and sustain a mood suitable to the action or text; the music plays a subordinate role.

music camp: *see* **camp, music.**

music, chamber: instrumental music performed in a small room or hall (chamber) and requiring but one player per part, for example, a string quartet or a woodwind quintet.

music, chance: *syn.* **music, aleatory.**

music, choral: music intended for group singing in concert style.

music, classical: (1) art music (fine-art music) as distinguished from folk music, jazz, popular music, etc.; (2) a musical style, as contrasted with romantic music; (3) music of the period 1750-1820, the period of Mozart, Haydn, Beethoven et al.

music clinic: *see* **clinic, music.**

music club: *see* **club, music.**

music, commercial: music conceived for monetary returns. *Contr. w.* **art music.**

music, community: musical activities designed to secure the interest and participation of large groups of people of varied ages in a given locality.

music, computer: (1) music composed with decisions as to the "proper" collection of musical components being made by an automatic high-speed digital computer which is instructed to select and reject the musical components on the basis of the mathematical probabilities of the components' appearance and arrangement in a given style period; (2) music composed with the use of a computer to try out various new possibilities for combining sounds which are not otherwise readily conceptualized in a composer's mind.

music, concrete: music in which natural sounds and noises—the wind, a motor accelerating, a door slamming, etc.,—are recorded on tape and then treated in various ways (the tape is played slower, or faster, or backwards, or certain frequencies are removed, or certain frequencies are amplified); a composition is then created from this palette of raw sound materials.

music conductor: *see* **conductor, music.**

music consultant: *see* **consultant, music.**

music, contest: *see* **music contest.**

music contest: a musical performance in which participants, either individuals or groups, are compared as to merit, and in which recognition in the form of awards is given to those judged best; may be local, regional, national, or international in coverage; frequently requires the performance of specified musical works, or works selected from a prepared list (called, thus, the *contest music*) and usually employs judges of acknowledged professional distinction. *See* **competition festival.**

music, creative: (mus. ed.) music instruction emphasizing originality and initiative, as in composing music and text and developing rhythmic activities.

music director: *see* **director, music.**

music, dodecaphonic: music composed in the 12-tone technique developed by Arnold Schoenberg (1874-1951) in which each of the 12 separate tones in the vocabulary of Western music is considered to be free and nonfunctionally related to its 11 neighboring tones. *Syn.* **serial music; twelve-tone music.**

music drama: *see* **drama, music.**

music editing: *see* **editing, music.**

music education: the science and art of the teaching of music.

music, elective: music courses in which enrollment is optional.

music, electronic: musical composition in which the sounds are generated electronically or in which natural sounds are recorded and then modified electronically.

music festival: a series of musical programs presented in close succession and regarded as a unit; often confined to music of a single type, as choral or band, or music by a single composer. *See* **competition festival.**

music, fine-art: a term coming into the literature to denote that music of Western culture hitherto called *art music*, or *classical music;* useful because it permits a distinction between that music (Beethoven, Brahms et al.) and new forms of art music (Dave Brubeck, Duke Ellington et al.).

music, folk: (1) music attributed to the people of a certain race, nationality, or location, the actual composer being unknown; may be a product of collective or cooperative composition; seldom recorded by its originators, and usually found in more than one version; (2) musical compositions expressive of popular feeling, yet having a known composer, for example, the songs of Stephen Foster. *See* **song, folk.**

music, general: that part of the program of musical instruction intended for all members of the student body of a school, usually embracing a variety of musical experiences.

music history: *see* **history, music.**

music lesson: *see* **lesson, music.**

music literature: *see* **literature, music.**

music methods class: *see* **class, music methods.**

music, philosophy of: *see* **musicology, historical; philosophy, applied.**

music practice room: (1) a room devoted to the purpose of practice or rehearsal by band, orchestra, or other group of music students; (2) a small room, often made soundproof, devoted to practice by individual pupils on the piano, violin, or other musical instrument.

music, program: music linked by title or explanatory notes to events, scenes, or moods. *Contr. w.* **music, absolute.**

music, public school: the entire curriculum and program for teaching music in public schools.

music reading: *see* **reading, music.**

music school: (1) (mus. hist.) a type of school common in the city-states of Greece, which the boy attended first to recite poetry and, after his thirteenth year, for a special music course on either the seven-stringed lyre or the flute; (2) a school that specializes in teaching music.

music, serial: *syn.* **music, dodecaphonic; music, twelve-tone.**

music, sociology of: *see* **sociology of music.**

music test: *see* **test, music.**

music theory: *see* **theory** (2).

music therapy: *see* **therapy, music.**

music, twelve-tone: *syn.* **music, dodecaphonic; music, serial.**

musical ability: *see* **ability, musical.**

musical ability test: *see* **test, music aptitude.**

musical analysis: *see* **analysis, musical.**

musical comedy: a term used by historians of American music to refer to works of George M. Cohan, George Gershwin, Rodgers and Hart et al., as distinctly American; to be contrasted with *operetta,* also called *comic opera,* a distinctly European import.

musical composition: *see* **composition, musical.**

musical memory: *syn.* **memory, tonal.**

musical therapy: *syn.* **therapy, music.**

musicality: developed proficiency in music; sometimes used synonymously with *musical ability. Syn.* **musicianship;** *see* **aptitude, music.**

musician, amateur: a person who performs (or, rarely, composes) music for social and recreational reasons rather than for reasons of a professional career and its attendant financial and psychological returns; properly used, the term amateur does not refer to inferior levels of proficiency.

musicianship: *syn.* **musicality.**

musicology: the study of music by the methods of history, science, and philosophy; makes use of findings and procedures from all scholarly and scientific fields of research. *See* **ethnomusicology; musicology, historical.**

musicology, comparative: *see* **ethnomusicology.**

musicology, historical: by far the most common and widely practiced branch of musicology; indeed, the term *musicology,* by itself, is frequently used in reference to what is more accurately and properly termed historical musicology; the many other areas of musicological study are generally entitled quite specifically *aesthetics of music,* or *acoustics, philosophy of music,* etc. *See* **ethnomusicology; musicology.**

mutation: a sudden variation in species character that is inheritable because of a change in the determining gene structure; may be the result of a change in a single gene or of chromosome rearrangement, etc. *See* **sport.**

mutation, somatic: a nonheritable mutation occurring in a somatic (bodily, nongerminal) cell. (In order to be observed or detected, the mutation must have occurred sufficiently early in development to permit manifold multiplication of the mutated cell.) *See* **mutation.**

mutism: a symptom arising from disorders of either attention or association or of volition, or of reactions (as a form of negativism), or having a hysterical or delusional basis; manifested by not speaking when reasonably expected to speak.

mutual-benefit retirement system: *syn.* **retirement system, contributory.**

mutual choices: *see* **choices, mutual.**

mutual instruction: *see* **Lancastrian system.**

mutual reinforcement: a term used in the "organic philosophy of education" which indicates the reciprocal relationships of various educational processes; examples of such relations are conceptual and perceptual, systematic instruction and functional experience, and academic and life activities.

mutuality: the feeling of belonging to a group and working cooperatively in a relationship of shared experiences; also applied to relationship between spouses.

muzak: a commercial industry which sells background music to hospitals, hotels, public buildings, etc.; a central station produces all the music for a given geographic area, and this music is transmitted over normal electric wires.

myatonia: deficiency or absence of muscular tone.

myogenic: of muscle or originating in muscle rather than in neural tissue; refers to movements of muscles without intervention of neural innervation.

myogram: a graphic record of muscle contractions. *See* **electromyogram.**

myograph: an instrument for recording muscle contractions: also called *electromyograph.*

myope (mī′ōp): one who is myopic, or nearsighted.

myope class: *see* **class, myope.**

myope school: a type of school organized in England in 1908 for the education of children suffering from severe or progressive myopia.

myopia (mī·ō′pi·ə): a defect of refraction in which the axis of the eyeball is too long or the refractive power of the lens too strong, with the result that the focal image is formed in front of the retina. *Syn.* **nearsightedness.**

myotonia: increased muscular irritability and contractility with decreased power of relaxation; tonic spasm of muscle.

mysophobia (mis·ə·fō′bi·ə): morbid fear of dirt or dread of being contaminated.

mysticism: a doctrine which asserts that, inasmuch as reality is an absolute, ineffable unity which cannot be apprehended by discursive reasoning or described by language, apprehension of the real can be achieved only through a suprarational union, more or less complete, of the knower and the known.

myth: a story, common to primitive peoples, often quite complex in plot and symbolism, which is intended to explain many of the basic problems and customs of human existence as well as the incidence of natural phenomena; cherished and elaborated in literature by later generations and even analogously created in advanced civilizations. *See* **tale, folk.**

myth, cultural: (1) a myth that interprets or reveals a particular culture or civilization; (2) the belief that one culture is superior to others by reason of divine gift, biological factors, or historical claims; (3) a story dealing with some animal, man, or god who is a hero because he has imparted the arts of life to man; origin of the myth is unknown; myth is perpetuated in a group from one generation to another.

mythology: the branch of human knowledge dealing with the stories a people tell about their origin and their prehistoric development.

mythomania (mith′ō·mā′ni·ə): an abnormal tendency to exaggerate and to report imaginary events. *Syn.* **pathological lying.**

N: symbol for number; usually, the total number of observations, scores, or cases involved in a study; sometimes, the number of observations, scores, or cases in any single sample or group; used in contradistinction to *n. See* **n.**

n: symbol for number; (1) the number of observations, scores, or cases in a subgroup or subsample; (2) the number of degrees of freedom involved in a statistic.

naevoid amentia: *see* **amentia, nevoid.**

naïve realism: *see* **realism, naïve.**

naming of scribbling: *see* **scribbling, naming of.**

nanosecond: one billionth of a second; written *ns;* a term used for timing operations in computerized data processing. *See* **microsecond; millisecond.**

narcism: *var.* **narcissism.**

narcissism (när·sis′iz′m): (1) an abnormal tendency to derive sexual gratification from admiration of one's own body; (2) love of the ego; considered by psychoanalysts as the normal manifestations of libidinal wishes which do not require giving pleasure to another for full gratification.

narcissistic object choice: the choice of a love object largely on the basis of characteristics similar to those with which the self is or was identified.

narcoanalysis: probing or exploring unconscious mental processes while the patient is under the influence of a narcotic. *See* **narcosynthesis.**

narcolepsy: a condition in which the subject is constantly falling asleep; sleep attacks may come at any time of the day under any circumstances.

narcosis: a condition in which automatic activities and normal responsiveness to stimuli are greatly reduced as a result of narcotic drugs.

narcosynthesis: treatment for various psychoneurotic states; a form of psychotherapy; a barbiturate drug, sodium pentothal or sodium amytal, is given intravenously until a semi-narcosed state is induced, during which patients are able to relive traumatic experiences with release of powerful and intense emotions.

narcotics education: the study of the nature and effects of narcotics upon the human body and upon society; usually sponsored, supervised, and directed by an agency centered in the state department of education.

narration: *syn.* **commentary.**

narration drill: *see* **drill, narration.**

narrative of transactions: a statement or explanation of transactions to be recorded by a student of bookkeeping or accounting; used as a substitute for original business papers or vouchers. *Syn.* **bookkeeping narrative.**

narrator: *syn.* **commentator.**

NASA Spacemobile program: *see* **program, NASA Spacemobile.**

nasal: *n.* one of the sounds formed by using the tongue and palate to direct the sound into the nose, such as *m*, *n*, and *ng.*

nasal lisp: *see* **lisp, nasal.**

nasality: a characteristic of speech in which vowel sounds are produced with an excessive amount of nasal resonance.

natatorium (nā′tə·tō′rē·əm): an indoor swimming pool.

National Achievement Scholarship Program: *see* **Program, National Achievement Scholarship.**

National Defense Education Act (NDEA): an act of the U.S. Congress, passed in the postsputnik era (1958), authorizing Federal funds for educational purposes in the form of loans and grants; provided funds for strengthening specific educational offerings in science, mathematics, and foreign languages in both public and private schools on the basis of national interest.

National Defense student loan: *see* **loan, National Defense student.**

National Forest Reserve Fund: a fund established by Federal law in 1908 that is made up of 25 percent of the money received from forest reserves during any fiscal year, the money being distributed to the states in which the reserves are located and the states then distributing the money to the counties in which the reserves are located for the support of roads and schools.

National Guard, Active: those units and members of the Army and Air National Guard of the several states, the Commonwealth of Puerto Rico, and the District of Columbia which are Federally recognized in accordance with law and which are authorized to have equipment and to engage in regularly scheduled training activities other than Federal service.

national honor society: *see* **honor society, national.**

National Merit Scholarship Program: *see* **Program, National Merit Scholarship.**

national norm: *see* **norm, national.**

national norms: *see* **norms, national.**

national philosophy: *see* **philosophy, national.**

national pupil-teacher index: *see* **index, national pupil-teacher.**

national school-bus chrome: *syn.* **school-bus chrome.**

national school volunteer program: *see* **program, national school volunteer.**

national teachers' association: *see* **teachers' association, national.**

National Youth Administration (NYA): a Federal emergency agency operating from 1935 to 1943 for young men and women in two areas of assistance: (*a*) persons from 18 to 25 years of age not attending school were given vocational and educational guidance and part-time jobs; (*b*) persons from 16 to 25 years of age attending school were given part-time jobs related to their school work in the nature of working scholarships.

nationalism: devotion to, advocacy of, or emphasis upon the values, interests, unity, or independence of a nation, often in distinction from emphasis upon sectional, international, or other values.

native character: *syn.* **trait, native.**

native endowment: *see* **endowment, native.**

native goodness, doctrine of: the position that man by nature is good and society alone makes him bad; affirms the spontaneous development of native organs and faculties; suggests a laissez-faire education in which the innate goodness will emerge. *Contr. w.* **depraved, human nature as.**

native student: *see* **student, native.**

native trait: *see* **trait, native.**

nativistic: referring generally to views which hold that ideational and perceptual elements are innate in their origin. *Contr. w.* **empirical.**

natural aristocracy: *see* **aristocracy, natural.**

natural change: *see* **change, natural.**

natural competition: *see* **competition, natural.**

natural gymnastics: *see* **gymnastics, natural.**

natural increase, rate of: the difference between the birth rate and the death rate for a given year; this provides a rough measure of the rate of natural increase or decrease in the population.

natural law: in general, refers to a law that is binding prior to and apart from any civil enactment or social convention; more specifically, and varying significantly in meaning according to the philosophical system from which it is taken, it may refer to (1) the order of the universe, sometimes conceived as a revelation of God's reason or will (stoicism); (2) the law binding men in a "state of nature" prior to the formation of society (Hobbes, Locke); (3) the immutable and universal dictates of reason known through an abstract consideration of man's nature or essence (rationalism); (4) those relatively few universal moral judgments which express the exigencies of man's nature as discovered in an analysis of his basic drives and inclinations, especially his inclination to be reasonable in his conduct (Scholasticism).

natural lighting: *see* **lighting, natural.**

natural method: (1) any method of teaching theoretically based on child nature or on the laws of learning; (2) a method of foreign-language teaching based on the theory that one should learn a new language as a child learns the mother tongue; instruction is by means of conversation in the foreign language, the study of grammar being introduced very late in the course, if at all; (3) a method of teaching language to deaf children which is based upon the premise that, for language to be meaningful, it must be directly related to ideas and concepts derived from children's interests and experiences.

natural morals: *see* **morals, natural.**

natural number: *see* **number, natural.**

natural philosophy: *see* **philosophy, natural.**

natural punishment: *see* **punishment, natural.**

natural realism: *syn.* **realism, common-sense.**

natural resources: those aspects or elements of man's environment such as climate, mineral deposits, and water power that render possible or facilitate the satisfaction of human wants and the attainment of social objectives.

natural rights: inalienable rights of man as man, that is, as an individual human being, asserted as both fact of nature and as absolute value, so that men could not give them up or governments infringe them; codified in the English Bill of Rights, in the French Declaration of the Rights of Man and the Citizen, in the first ten amendments to the Constitution of the United States, also called the Bill of Rights.

natural science: *see* **science, natural.**

natural selection: *see* **selection, natural.**

natural sign: *see* **sign, natural.**

natural weight: *see* **weight, natural.**

naturalism: (1) the philosophic point of view that considers mental phenomena, and particularly moral values, as natural phenomena, to be interpreted in the same way as the phenomena of natural science; (2) the educational point of view that stresses, as the goal of education, the development and expansion of what is natural in man, as opposed to discipline and the cultivation of an imposed set of standards and values; (3) (art) a style in which some aspect of reality is projected with very little interpretation, intensification, or modification on the part of the artist; in the mid-nineteenth century, a style which attempted to report reality as it appeared, without idealization, and which deliberately sought the commonplace for subject matter; Gustave Courbet was representative of this style.

naturalism, empirical: *see* **experimentalism; humanism, scientific; instrumentalism; pragmatism.**

naturalism, evolutionary: *syn.* **humanism, scientific.**

naturalism, humanistic: *see* **humanism, scientific.**

naturalistic school of historiography: *see* **historiography, naturalistic school of.**

naturally weighted: (stat.) of or pertaining to any datum or series of data having natural weight. *See* **weight, natural.**

nature: (1) the sum total of the phenomena of the physical world; (2) (biol.) the innate character of an organism; the inherent factors producing human character.

nature center: *see* **center, nature.**

nature conservation center: *syn.* **center, nature.**

nature, human: *see* **human nature.**

nature-nurture: a term most commonly used in reference to the problem of whether differences in the development of an organism are more directly traceable to inherent constitution or to environmental factors.

nature of man, animalistic: the concept that man shares with animals his activations of behaviors that serve homeostatic ends, such as his satisfaction of the need for nutritional restoration, elimination, etc., and the need to reproduce the species and propagate his kind.

nature of proof: *see* **proof, nature of.**

nature, original: the inborn or hereditary characteristics of a person or other organism; contrasted with acquired traits as developed by environment; basis of much controversy as to modifiability; all education depends upon potential modifiability.

nature study: (1) an objective study of objects or phenomena of nature, usually with particular reference to living things; (2) a school program for the study of nature in elementary schools supported in part by Froebel's theories of moral training and influenced by the romanticism of American literary men of the nineteenth century; the aim was to instill aesthetic and emotional values, especially a "love of nature"; taught in an effort to make life on the farm more attractive; psychological support was derived in part from teleological interpretation of nature and from theories of mental training; the methods of nature study were challenged on the basis of theory and the term has gradually been replaced by science, specified for the elementary school.

nature trail: (sci. ed.) a marked trail through a natural area with identifications and descriptions of objects of interest and concern. *See* **forest, school.**

naturism (nā'tūr·iz'm): the worship of nature, of the powers of nature, or of spiritual beings thought to direct the permanent or periodically recurring phenomena of nature.

nautical arts: *see* **arts, nautical.**

nautical school: a school to prepare young men for a seafaring career in a licensed capacity.

naval aviation officer candidate: *see* **candidate, naval aviation officer.**

naval aviation school: one of a group of schools conducted by the Naval Aviation Schools Command for officer candidates in subjects such as flight preparation, survival training, instructor training, officer indoctrination, and midshipman indoctrination.

naval science and tactics: the Navy counterpart of the Army's *military science and tactics. See* **military science.**

naval training school: a school operated by the Navy for training officers and/or enlisted personnel; in the case of officers, for qualification in a special line of endeavor; in the case of enlisted personnel, for qualification to a rating or for advancement to a higher rating.

navigation: science of determining the position of a ship.

navigation, aerospace: a course taught in aerospace programs dealing with the art or practice of directing the movement of an aerospace vehicle from one point to another; usually implies the presence of a human being acting as navigator, aboard the craft.

navigation, air: the art, science, or action of plotting and directing from within an aircraft its movement through the air from one place to another.

navigation, celestial: *see* **astronavigation.**

Navy enlisted classification code: *see* **code, Navy enlisted classification.**

Navy enlisted school: one of various categories of schools and courses designed and maintained to assist the forces afloat by giving instruction and training to enlisted personnel which, because of the time allowed and facilities available, can be given more advantageously ashore; they are divided into the following classes: *Class A—* designed to provide the basic technical knowledges and skills in a specific rating; *Class B—*designed to provide the advanced technical knowledges and skills in a specific rating; *Class C—*designed to train personnel in a particular skill or technique which in general is peculiar to any one rating or to train enlisted personnel in a particular skill or technique not peculiar to any one rating, for example, *instructors school;* such schools at a naval establishment are Class C-1 schools; those at a civilian manufacturing plant are Class C-2 schools; *Class P—* designed to conduct training at a preparatory level for a group of ratings, such as the Class P Electricity and Electronics School; curricula of Class A,B,C, and P schools are normally under the direct control of the Chief of Naval Personnel or the comparable command for aviation or medical training, but there are some A,B, or C schools or courses in *fleet schools* and *functional schools. See* **Navy officer school.**

Navy enlisted scientific education program: *see* **program, Navy enlisted scientific education.**

Navy officer school: Navy schools established for officer candidate training, special courses of instruction, postgraduate training, instruction for higher command, and officer special qualifications training. *See* **Navy enlisted school.**

NDEA: *see* **National Defense Education Act.**

NDEA loan: *see* **loan, National Defense student.**

near point of accommodation: the nearest point at which the eye can perceive an object distinctly; varies according to the power of accommodation of the individual eye.

near point of convergence: the nearest single point at which the two eyes can direct their visual lines, normally about 3 inches from the eyes on the midline between them.

near space: *see* **space, near.**

near vision: *see* **vision, near.**

nearsightedness: *syn.* **myopia.**

necessitarianism: a term used by Huxley and others in place of the term *determinism.*

necessity: an unbreakable connection between events, causes and effects, acts, truths, laws, etc.; a relentless sequence that is certain and determined, not to be set aside; there are different kinds of necessity, such as physical, logical, and moral.

necrophobia: morbid fear of death.

need: (psych.) a requirement of the organism for survival, growth, reproduction, health, social acceptance, etc. *Dist. f.* **drive.**

need, achievement: *see* **motivation, achievement.**

need dispositions: individual tendencies to orient and act with respect to objects in certain manners and to expect certain consequences from these actions.

need, educational: specific knowledge, skill, or attitude which is lacking but which may be obtained and satisfied through learning experiences.

need, felt: *see* **felt need.**

need, status: *see* **status need.**

needs, basic: those needs which everyone has regardless of age, sex, or station in life, such as sense of personal worth, status, recognition, love, a sense of belonging, and attainment of some measure of success in one's efforts, as well as physical requirements; as defined by authors—psychological social scientists or educators—these needs often serve as a basis for determining logically the kind of general education program necessary to satisfy them.

needs, consumer: goods and services that consumers individually or collectively must have to maintain a reasonable standard of living.

needs, ego: the need for a sense of security and the need for recognition as a person of worth or importance.

needs, felt: the doctrine that feeding schedules, items of nutrition, and curricular content should be determined by self-selection, according to the desires of the child; one of the principal tenets of progressive education. *See* **felt need.**

needs, mathematical: *see* **mathematical needs.**

needs of child: those experiences and attentions which satisfy the physical, biological, intellectual, personal, and social requirements of a child.

needs, pupil: the requirements for optimal development of the pupil—intellectual, physical, moral, emotional, and social—both in relation to his present interests, abilities, and level of achievement and in relation to the probable future demands of the individual and of society.

needs, social: dynamic entities motivating and directing individuals in a goal object.

needs theory: the belief that unmet emotional needs tend to produce such reactions as aggression, submission, withdrawal, or psychosomatic symptoms of illness.

needs, viscerogenic: needs which spring from the body's tissues and organ deficits, such as hunger.

negation: given a statement *p*, the negation of *p* (symbolized by "-*p*") is a statement which is true when *p* is false and false when *p* is true; for example, the negation of "All cats are black" is "Some cats are not black."

negation drill: *see* **drill, negation.**

negative: (1) (_) (stat.) a value less than zero, however small; any value to the left of or below an assumed origin; *contr. w.* **positive** (3); (2) *see* **film, negative.**

negative acceleration: *see* **acceleration, negative.**

negative adaptation: *see* **adaptation, negative.**

negative afterimage: *see* **afterimage, negative.**

negative association: *see* **association, negative.**

negative attack: a conference device in which the leader seems to favor the "wrong" side in order to stimulate thinking.

negative character trait: *see* **character trait, negative.**

negative conditioning: *syn.* **conditioning, inhibitory.**

negative correlation: *syn.* **indirect correlation; inverse correlation;** *see* **correlation** (1).

negative criticism: *see* **criticism.**

negative discrimination: *see* **discrimination, negative.**

negative feedback: *see* **feedback, negative.**

negative film: *see* **film, negative.**

negative gain: *see* **gain** (3).

negative guidance: *see* **guidance, negative.**

negative induction: *see* **induction, negative.**

negative integer: *see* **integer, negative.**

negative number: *see* **number, negative.**

negative practice: a treatment of undesirable behavior by voluntary repetition of the behavior that is to be eliminated, largely for purposes of bringing the undesirable behavior to the level of consciousness.

negative reinforcement: *see* **reinforcement, negative.**

negative relation: *see* **correlation** (1).

negative relationship: *see* **correlation** (1).

negative skewness: *see* **skewness, negative.**

negative suggestibility: *syn.* **contrasuggestibility.**

negative suggestion: a suggestion that tends to inhibit an act, process, or response.

negative transfer: *see* **transfer, negative.**

negative transference: *see* **transference, negative.**

negativism: (1) a mode of behavior frequently found in young children (sometimes in adults) and characterized by marked resistance to suggestion or by behavior that is the opposite of that suggested; may be present generally or only with respect to certain types of behavior; may also be present only with respect to certain individuals, as in the case of a normally tractable child who refuses to obey a particular person; sometimes called *active negativism; syn.* **contrariety** (1); **contrasuggestibility;** (2) the inhibition of or resistance to normal human activities such as eating, dressing, listening, looking; sometimes called *passive negativism;* (3) a condition, symptomatic of catatonia, in which speech and behavior are the opposite or reverse of what is normally done or called for in a given situation.

neglect case: (obs.) a vulgarism for a case involving a neglected child. *See* **child, neglected.**

neglected child: *see* **child, neglected.**

negligence: failure to act as a reasonably prudent person would act under the particular circumstances.

negligence, actionable: the nonperformance of a legal duty by the failure to act as a prudent person or the failure to exercise an ordinary amount of care, thus resulting in a damage to another. *See* **negligence.**

negligence, comparative: that doctrine in the law which compares the degree of negligence of the parties involved.

negligence, contributory: failure by an injured person to use ordinary care, which is a concurrent cause with the negligence of the injurer in producing the injury.

negligence, simple: negligence which is neither gross nor wanton but merely a failure to exercise ordinary care.

negotiate: to transact business; to bargain or trade; to conduct communications or conferences.

negotiations, collective: (school admin.) a process whereby the teaching staff as a group and their employers make offers and counteroffers in good faith on the conditions of their employment relationship for the purpose of reaching a mutually acceptable agreement.

negotiations, professional: *see* **collective bargaining.**

neighborhood: (1) a local area characterized by a high degree of intimacy among its inhabitants; (2) a local urban area in which the inhabitants have general community interests without necessarily knowing one another personally; *see* **community** (2).

neighborhood concert: *see* **concert, neighborhood.**

neighborhood forum: *see* **forum, neighborhood.**

neighborhood playground: *see* **playground, neighborhood.**

neighborhood school: a school all or most of whose pupils come from the immediate geographic area in which the school is located; the concept of neighborhood schools has a long history in the United States, but it is opposed by some people because it has been used to bolster de facto segregation in many cities. *Contr. w.* **community school; educational park.**

Neighborhood Youth Corps: a year-round work-training program for disadvantaged young people from low-income families; provides useful hometown work experience in public, private, and commercial settings, also counseling, remedial education, and health services as necessary; a program of the Office of Economic Opportunity, delegated to the U.S. Department of Labor for administration.

Neo-Realism: a philosophical revolt of the early twentieth century against absolute idealism, and distinguished by assertions that (*a*) objects can exist independently of a knowing consciousness; (*b*) the object to be known is given directly to consciousness (epistemological *monism*); (*c*) sensations are neither physical nor mental but are neutral entities becoming one or the other in certain contexts; represented in England by G. E. Moore, Bertrand Russell, and others, in the United States by R. B. Perry, E. B. Holt, W. T. Marvin, W. P. Montague, W. B. Pitkin, E. G. Spaulding, and others.

Neo-Scholasticism: *see* **Scholasticism.**

Neo-Thomism: a modern philosophical movement in the Roman Catholic Church, characterized by a return to the philosophical principles of St. Thomas Aquinas (1225–1274) in the light of modern scientific discoveries and modern culture; received its inspiration from an encyclical letter (*Aeterni Patris*) of Pope Leo XIII in 1879; some modern Thomists are Maritain, Gilson, Yves Simon, and Garrigou-Lagrange.

neobehaviorism: emphasis upon the observable response as in older *behaviorism* but with less antipathy toward words such as *mind, conscience,* etc.

neoclassicism: an art style occurring at the end of the eighteenth century and the beginning of the nineteenth which reasserted the principles of restraint, clarity, and economy of means such as characterized the best of ancient Greek and Roman art; in this recurrence of classicism, subject matter was often based upon ancient Greek and Roman myth, legend, and history; Jacques-Louis David was representative of this style.

neoimpressionism: an artistic movement of the late nineteenth century based largely on the work and theories of the French painter Georges Seurat; Seurat sought to consolidate the spontaneous effects of color and light with a new sense of space and a more structural rhythmic design; it was one phase of the general reaction against the impersonal objectivity of the impressionism of Pissarro, Sisley, and Renoir in the 1870s; the movement was closely associated with the theory of pointillism. *See* **impressionism; pointillism.**

neologism: (1) a word or expression not generally accepted due to its recent coinage; (2) coining of new words or the use of an old word with a new meaning; (3) (psych.) any newly coined term, often meaningless to the hearer, formed by condensation or displacement of letters or syllables; characteristic of the speech of young children and psychotics and sometimes of the speech in dreams.

neonatal (nē′ō·nā′təl): pertaining to the child during the first month after birth.

neonate (nē′ō·nāt): the child from birth to 1 month of age.

neoplasticism: the severely nonobjective style of the early twentieth century, which placed emphasis upon the purely formal aspects of the visual arts, line, shape, color, and space, with no object meaning implied or symbolized; the work of Piet Mondrian is representative of this style.

Neoplatonism: a transcendental religious phase of Hellenic philosophy whose chief representative was Plotinus (A.D. 205–270); Neoplatonist teachers encourage pupils to withdraw from interactivity with sense-perceivable "things" to rational contemplation of their laws or ideal forms and eventually toward mystical, suprarational union with the ultimate source of value and existence, called by Neoplatonists "The One."

nepotism (nep′ə·tiz′m): favoritism shown to relatives; bestowal of patronage by reason of relationship rather than of merit. (Many states have statutes forbidding nepotism in the employment of teachers. The provisions of these statutes vary greatly, and in general their enforcement is thought to be lax, though the courts construe them strictly when cases are brought before them.)

nerve deafness: *see* **deafness, nerve.**

nerve-type hearing loss: *see* **hearing loss, perceptive.**

nervous child: *see* **child, nervous.**

nervous system, autonomic: the nonmyelinated peripheral part of the nervous system of mammals that regulates the involuntary responses concerned with the nutritive, vascular, and reproductive activities.

nervous system, central: the brain and the spinal cord.

nervous system, cerebrospinal: the nerve system consisting of the brain, spinal cord, incoming nerves from the sense organs, and the nerves that go out to the striped muscles.

nervous system, sympathetic: the part of the autonomic nervous system lying in the middle of the body; the thoracicolumbar system.

net bonded debt: *see* **debt, net bonded.**

net, communication: *see* **communication net.**

net correlation: *syn.* **correlation, partial.**

net correlation coefficient: *syn.* **coefficient of partial correlation.**

net effect: (experimentation) the result that remains of a given treatment after due allowance has been made for the initial ability and/or the influence of extraneous factors and errors.

net enrollment: *see* **enrollment, net.**

net enrollment, city: *see* **enrollment, city net.**

net enrollment, state: *see* **enrollment, state net.**

net income allocation: the apportionment or distribution of the net income among the states entitled to levy a tax on it or with respect to it, by means of statutory formula, administrative determination, or separate accounting.

net migration: *see* **migration, net.**

net reproduction rate: *see* **reproduction rate, net.**

net table: *syn.* **abac.**

net teacher turnover: *see* **turnover, net teacher.**

net words: according to the international typewriting contest rules, the total number of *standard words* typed by a person in a given length of time minus deductions for errors in spelling and other mistakes. *See* **gross words; standard word** (2).

network, nomological: *see* **nomological network.**

neural growth: *see* **growth, neural.**

neural path: (psych.) a term originally used by Thorndike to designate individual or particular nerve fibers presumably involved in the completion of a given stimulus-response bond and hence fundamental to the concept of identical elements in transfer; a view not prevalent in contemporary psychology.

neurasthenia (nū′rəs·thē′ni·ə): nervous exhaustion; a psychoneurosis in which weakness and fatigue are prominent symptoms.

neurogram (nū′rō·gram): *syn.* **engram.**

neurological disability: *see* **disability, neurological.**

neurological organization: the theory that an individual's development of mobility, vision, audition, and language parallels and is functionally related to his anatomical progress.

neurologically handicapped: *see* **handicapped, neurologically.**

neurologist: a physician who devotes the greater part of his time to the study and treatment of diseases of the nervous system.

neuromuscular activity: *see* **activity, neuromuscular.**

neuromuscular coordination: *see* **coordination, neuromuscular.**

neuromuscular disability: *see* **disability, neuromuscular.**

neuromuscular organism: the complex structure of the nerves and muscles and the interdependent and subordinate elements of nerves and muscles whose relations and properties are largely determined by their function.

neuromuscular physiology: *see* **neurophysiology.**

neuropath (nū′rō·path): one who suffers from a functional nervous disorder.

neurophrenia: a disturbance of the central nervous system, to be differentiated from *exogenous mental retardation,* in which the intellectual impairment is primary and the social and other accompaniments are secondary, and from *cerebral palsy*, in which the motor impairments are primary and the other involvements are secondary, by a brain injury resulting in minimal physical involvement with a syndrome of behavior disturbances and in distorted intellectual functioning which is defective rather than deficient; prognosis is usually favorable. (The term has not been widely accepted.)

neurophrenic child: *syn.* child, brain-injured.

neurophysiology: the science dealing with functions of the nerves of living organisms; also called *neuromuscular physiology.*

neuropsychiatry (nū′rō·sī·kī′ə·tri; -psī·kī′-): the assumed division of medical science that includes neurology and psychiatry; not a scientific term, though in common use.

neurosis: mental disorder of varying degrees of severity, often characterized by tics, mannerisms, obsessions, phobias, anxiety, hysterical behavior, or neurasthenic exhaustion, and for which, usually, no organic basis can be found; less severe than a psychosis, and usually not of sufficient seriousness to warrant treatment of the individual in an institution for the mentally deranged. *Contr. w.* **psychosis.**

neurosis, anxiety: (1) a functional disorder of the nervous system characterized by objectively unfounded dread, fear, or feeling of insecurity; (2) a strong emotional attitude in which unfounded fear or dread predominates. *Dist. f.* **hysteria, anxiety.**

neurosis, compensation: *syn.* neurosis, traumatic.

neurosis, compulsion: a neurosis whose most conspicuous symptoms are compulsions which seriously impair the fulfillment of mature objectives; closely related to obsessional neurosis. *See* **neurosis, obsessional.**

neurosis, experimental: an experimentally induced emotional state characterized by chaotic behavior, loss of control, inhibition, and other manifestations roughly analogous to those found in clinical conditions; used as a means of studying the factors responsible for natural neuroses and the techniques applicable to their alleviation or cure. *Syn.* **experimental behavior disorder.**

neurosis, obsessional: a neurosis characterized by the presence of obsessional ideas.

neurosis, traumatic: a condition following injury or fright, as in accidents or war, which presents physical signs that are motivated emotionally; characterized especially by inhibition of function and a marked tendency to repeat consciously the emotions of the trauma, often reproducing portions of it in hallucinations or catastrophic dreams accompanied by intense anxiety; an example is shell-shock. *Syn.* **compensation neurosis.**

neurotic: *n.* (1) a person afflicted with *neurosis;* (2) a person of unbalanced judgment; one whose actions are prompted by the passions or emotions rather than by the dictates of calm reasoning; (3) a drug or other substance affecting the nervous system.

neurotic: *adj.* (1) of or pertaining to a *neurosis;* (2) relating or referable to a nerve or the nervous system; (3) having a morbid or mentally unhealthy tendency; (4) having an effect upon the nervous system (for example, a drug).

neurotic anxiety: *see* anxiety, neurotic.

neurotic character: the character of a person who is prone to act out his impulses without regard to rules and regulations laid down by society; unlike the *psychotic,* his behavior is never quite bizarre enough nor the disorganization in thinking and behavior serious enough to warrant commitment to a mental hospital; sometimes called *neurotic personality* or *misfit in society. Comp. w.* **personality, psychopathic.**

neurotic child: *see* child, neurotic.

neurotic lisping: *see* lisping, neurotic.

neurotic personality: *syn.* neurotic character.

neutral syllable: a single syllable to which all the tones of a song or vocal exercise are sung, for example, *oh, ah, la. See* vocalization.

neutrality: the state of not taking sides on debatable issues; often incorrectly identified with *objectivity,* which calls for the pursuit of evidence to its logical conclusions while guarding against subjective bias; hence it is logically possible to take a stand on an issue while defending the *objectivity* of that position, whereas by definition neutrality rules out the taking of a stand.

nevoid amentia: *see* amentia, nevoid.

new educational media: *see* educational media, new.

New England primer: *see* primer, New England.

new humanism: *see* humanism, new.

New Jersey plan: a program of education of visually handicapped children in that state under the direction of a commission for the blind rather than a residential school and public school integration, public school classes, or out-of-state residential school provisions have been made on a case-analysis basis. *See* **Oregon plan.**

new-type test: an obsolescent synonym for objective test. *See* test, objective.

new word: *see* word, new.

New York Point: obsolete form of writing for the blind.

New York State filing plan: *see* filing plan, New York State.

Newbery medal awards: *see* awards, Newbery medal.

news release: a statement or other information released or given out to newspapers, radio, or television for distribution to the public, often for public relations purposes.

news writing: *syn.* journalistic writing (2).

newspaper: a periodical printed in the format of a few large folded sheets, devoted primarily to news and other material of general interest, numbered serially, and published at stated intervals, usually daily or weekly in the commercial field but perhaps fortnightly or monthly in the scholastic field.

newspaper, children's: (1) a school paper written by children and ordinarily mimeographed or hectographed; (2) a weekly paper of current events designed and printed for children.

newspaper, duplicated: an inexpensive form of student newspaper consisting of a number of sheets duplicated— as by mimeographing—from typewritten pages; sometimes called *mimeographed newspaper.*

newspaper, mimeographed: *syn.* newspaper, duplicated.

newspaper, school: a newspaper produced by the school, often as an opportunity for the stimulation and publication of students' writing and as a means of communication with the community.

newsprint: blank paper of the sort on which newspapers are usually printed but used in the schools for writing or as easel paper for painting or drawing.

night blindness: *see* blindness, night.

night school: *see* evening school.

nihilism, ethical (nī′ə·liz′m; nī′hi-): a doctrine that denies the validity of all distinctions of moral value.

Nine Classics: the Five Classics and Four Books of the ancient Chinese, consisting chiefly of the teachings of Confucius and his followers, records of historical events, and collections of ancient documents and Chinese ballads.

nine-year school: a school for children of elementary and junior high school age, which normally requires 9 years to complete the work provided.

nirvana principle (nir·vä′nə): the thesis that it is universal for living forms to desire the cessation of the adjusting, tension, and striving by which life is maintained and to reduce ultimately to the more stable inorganic states.

nisus (nī′səs): (1) in its more common context in biology, the tendency of an organism to strive against obstacles; (2) in evolutionary theory, the potentiality toward emergence into new forms; (3) sometimes used in philosophy to denote the implicit urge of the self outward beyond itself toward self-realization.

Nitchie method: a method of teaching lipreading originated by Edward B. Nitchie and stressing practice in grasping the thought of whole sentences.

nitrate-base film: *see* film, nitrate-base.

no data (ND): a phrase used to indicate that no answer or no answer that can be standardized has been received to a questionnaire or test item; such responses must be tabulated in order to account for the entire number of cases in the distribution.

no-failure program: *see* **program, no-failure.**

nocturnal enuresis: *see* **enuresis.**

noetic: cognitive; conceived by reason alone rather than by empirical processes.

noise: (communication theory) (1) disturbances which do not represent any part of the messages from a specified source; (2) anything that introduces extraneous variability into a communication process or that raises the entropy or reduces the information, that is, the difference between input and output generated by random error in the communication system itself.

noise induced hearing loss: *see* **hearing loss, noise induced.**

noise, white: multifrequency sound; often used for auditory masking. *See* **masking, auditory.**

nomic: (1) a heteroclitic system of arrays (differing in skewness) in which the skewness of the arrays changes systematically with the position of the array; *contr. w.* **anomic** (1); (2) a heteroscedastic system of arrays (differing in variability) in which the standard deviation of the arrays changes systematically with the position of the array; *contr. w.* **anomic** (2).

nominal scale: *see* **scale, nominal.**

nominal weight: *see* **weight, nominal.**

nominalism: (1) the metaphysical doctrine that universals such as dog, redness, etc., are conventional names of classes of objects and have no real existence in themselves or in the objects which they characterize; (2) the epistemological doctrine that we can perceive only particular images and that a universal is, therefore, an abstraction from a set of such images. *Contr. w.* **realism** (1).

nominating technique: (meas.) a rating technique in which the rater selects or names the person in a small population who seems best to conform to a certain criterion, for example, the most popular in the group; the combination of many such ratings is used to characterize both the group structure and the personality of the individuals.

nomogram: *syn.* **nomograph.**

nomograph: a chart consisting of three lines or possibly curves (usually parallel) graduated for different variables in such a way that a straightedge cutting the three lines gives the associated values of three variables; for example, a nomograph can be so made that when a straightedge joins numbers on two lines, the third line will give the sum of those numbers. *See* **isopleth.**

nomographic: pertaining to the graphic methods used to represent the relations between several variables upon a plane surface.

nomography: a development of graphic methods which permits the representation of the relations between several (usually three) variables upon a plane surface; the act or process of graphic computation.

nomological network: in construct validity, the interlocking system of laws which constitute a theory; such laws may relate (*a*) observable properties or quantities to each other, (*b*) theoretical constructs to observables, or (*c*) different theoretical constructs to one another.

nomothetic: pertaining to the normative dimension of activity in a social system; comprises three major elements: institution, role, and expectation.

nomothetic method: (ed. psych.) study of the laws and principles governing groups of persons, as contrasted with the *idiographic method* by which individuals are studied singly.

non compos mentis (non kom'pəs men'tis): (Lat., lit., "not sound as to mind") a legal term signifying *demented.*

non-English transition group: *see* **transition group, non-English.**

non-Euclidean geometry: *see* **geometry, non-Euclidean.**

non sequitur (non se'kwi·tər): (Lat., lit., "it does not follow") the fallacy of drawing a conclusion that does not logically follow from the premises, even though the premises themselves may be true, for example, "The

student studied diligently. Therefore, he should not receive a failing grade."

nonacademic: (1) (sec. ed.) pertaining to fields other than English, foreign languages, history, economics, mathematics, and science; (2) (higher ed.) pertaining to noninstructional activities; (3) pertaining to capacities and interests in subjects involving primarily, but not exclusively, the managing of people or things; (4) (spec. ed.) pertaining to a child who is not able to participate in a regular academic program, usually because of limited mental ability. *See* **academic.**

nonalternate cooperative plan: *see* **cooperative plan, nonalternate.**

nonattendance: the failure to attend school on the part of any child whether enrolled in school or not.

nonattendance permit: (1) an authorization by the school authorities for a youth to cease attending school; (2) an administrative form used in granting a pupil the right to be absent (*a*) for a given day or period or (*b*) from a given class or classes for a given day or period.

noncallable bond: *see* **bond, noncallable.**

noncentral t distribution: *see* **distribution, noncentral t.**

noncertified: a descriptive term usually referring to one who does not need a state-approved certificate or license as a prerequisite to holding a job.

nonchance factors: *see* **factors, nonchance.**

noncollege-bound student: *syn.* **student, noncollege-preparatory.**

noncollege-preparatory student: *see* **student, noncollege-preparatory.**

nonconformist: (1) one who refrains from following or refuses to follow a pattern of behavior which is generally accepted, advocated, or used by his associates; (2) one who shows extreme individuality; (3) one who is unbound by convention and tradition or who defies authority; (4) one who challenges accepted beliefs or principles. (The term may be employed in either a complimentary or a derogatory sense, hinging on the way it is used and the point of view of the one who uses it.)

nonconstant error: *syn.* **error, variable.**

noncontinuous series: *syn.* **series, discrete.**

noncontributory retirement system: *see* **retirement system, noncontributory.**

noncourse activities: *see* **activities, noncourse.**

noncredit: without credit; pertains to certain types of instruction, such as correspondence and short courses that are not specifically acceptable for credit toward an academic degree or diploma.

noncredit class: *see* **class, noncredit.**

noncredit course: *see* **course, noncredit.**

nondenominational college: *see* **college, nondenominational.**

nondenominational university: *see* **university, nondenominational.**

nondetermination, coefficient of: *see* **coefficient of nondetermination.**

nondetermination, index of: *see* **index of nondetermination.**

nondirective counseling: *syn.* **counseling, client-centered.**

nondirective group therapy: *see* **therapy, nondirective group.**

nondirective teaching: *see* **teaching, nondirective.**

nondirective therapy: *see* **therapy, nondirective.**

nondurable consumer goods: *see* **goods, nondurable consumer.**

noneducational organization: *see* **organization, noneducational.**

nonessential errors: *see* **errors, nonessential.**

nonexperimental factor: *see* **factor, nonexperimental.**

nonfarm agricultural occupation: *see* **agricultural occupation, nonfarm.**

nonfarm population, rural: *see* **population, rural nonfarm.**

nonfarm residents, rural: *see* **population, rural nonfarm.**

nonfeasance: omission to perform a required duty. *Comp. w.* **malfeasance; misfeasance.**

nonfluency: relative lack of smoothness or regularity in the flow of speech. (Normal nonfluency is to be distinguished from *stuttering.*)

nonfood assistance program: *see* **program, nonfood assistance.**

nongraded class: *see* **class, ungraded.**

nongraded materials: *see* **materials, nongraded.**

nongraded school: (1) a school which groups its students according to academic ability, disciplinary problems, and mental and physical capabilities rather than strictly by grade and age, each student progressing at his or her own rate; (2) a school in which grade labels are not applied to the students and in which instruction is given on an individual basis; (3) a novel form of school which dispenses with all criteria except achievement scores for assignment of pupils to groups, called *phases;* the plan is to permit learners to work at their own rates within their own levels of competency and to allow them to go through high school, obtaining education of a quality best fitted to their individual needs; (4) a school that has gone far beyond eliminating annual promotions, grouping students subject by subject on the basis of achievement, or making local curriculum revisions as a contribution to the nongraded approach; uses *team teaching,* flexible scheduling, technical devices, and teaching-learning methods that deal with independent study, large-group instruction, and small-group instruction. *Syn.* **ungraded school;** *see* **center, study.**

nonintellective intelligence: *see* **intelligence, nonintellective.**

nonlaboratory course: *see* **course, nonlaboratory.**

nonlanguage test: *syn.* **test, nonverbal** (2).

nonlinear: *syn.* **curvilinear.**

nonlinear correlation: *syn.* **correlation, curvilinear.**

nonlinear regression: *see* **regression, nonlinear.**

nonlinear relation: *syn.* **correlation, curvilinear.**

nonlinear relationship: *syn.* **correlation, curvilinear.**

nonlinearity: *syn.* **curvilinearity.**

nonliterate: *syn.* **primitive man.**

nonmajor: a person enrolled for course work in a given field but not following the prescribed curriculum leading to a degree or certificate in that field.

nonmembership: (1) the status of one who has never been enrolled in a given school or school system; (2) the status of one who has been dropped permanently from membership in a given school or school system; (3) (obs.) the status of one who has been dropped temporarily from membership in a given school or school system.

nonmetric geometry: *see* **geometry, nonmetric.**

nonmetropolitan population: *see* **population, nonmetropolitan.**

nonobjective method: a procedure in research depending primarily on logical speculation in making evaluations or drawing conclusions.

nonobjectivism: in the visual arts, the absence of any reference to objects beyond the formal elements of line, shape, color, texture, and space.

nonoperating expense: *see* **expense, nonoperating.**

nonoral method: a method of teaching reading developed by McDade in Chicago; emphasizes the suppression of inner speech in silent reading by avoiding all oral reading in the early stage of teaching children to read.

nonparametric methods: *syn.* **statistics, nonparametric.**

nonparametric statistics: *see* **statistics, nonparametric.**

nonparametric test: *see* **test, nonparametric.**

nonparticipant observation: *see* **observation, nonparticipant.**

nonpartisan board election: *see* **election, nonpartisan board.**

nonproduction instructional material: *see* **instructional material, nonproduction.**

nonprofessional journalism: *see* **journalism, nonprofessional.**

nonprofessional librarian: *see* **librarian, nonprofessional.**

nonprofessional personnel: *see* **paraprofessional.**

nonpromotion: failure of a pupil to be promoted to the next higher grade at a regular promotion period.

nonpublic school: any private, parochial, or other school that is not public in nature and is not supported by public funds.

nonpublic schools, percentage of pupils in: *see* **percentage of pupils in nonpublic schools.**

nonrandom sample: a sample that is selected on some basis other than chance alone.

nonreader: one who is unable to read even after more or less extended instruction.

nonrecognition: (read.) failure to identify word symbols with their pronunciation and meaning.

nonreservation boarding school: *see* **boarding school, nonreservation.**

nonresident: (1) a pupil not living with his father, mother, or guardian and who, therefore, is not living at his legal residence; (2) a pupil residing outside a given school district; (3) a pupil living in a school district and receiving benefit of school privileges for whom legal residence has not been established.

nonresident pupil: *see* **nonresident.**

nonresident student: *see* **student, nonresident.**

nonresident tuition: *see* **tuition, nonresident.**

nonreturns: (1) youths of census age who have disappeared and for whom no data can be secured; (2) pupils of the previous semester who have not enrolled during the current semester.

nonrevenue: not from tax sources.

nonrevenue receipts: *see* **receipts, nonrevenue.**

nonroutine use of vehicle: *see* **vehicle, nonroutine use of.**

nonschool activities: *see* **activities, nonschool.**

nonsectarian college: *see* **college, nonsectarian.**

nonsectarian school: a school open to general admission irrespective of adherence to any sect or religious beliefs.

nonsense rhyme: a verse or jingle without meaning whose appeal to children is in the sound and rhythm of the words.

nonsense syllable: a combination of letters that can be sounded but carries no meaning.

nonsense word: *see* **word, nonsense.**

nonsigner clause: a provision of the fair trade laws whereby the moment one seller signs a contract agreeing to sell only at the stipulated price, all other sellers, whether partners to the contract or not, are bound.

nonspecific transfer: *see* **transfer, nonspecific.**

nonstandard age-and-schooling certificate: *see* **age-and-schooling certificate, nonstandard.**

nonstandard dialect: *see* **dialect, nonstandard.**

nonsynchronous projector: *see* **projector, synchronized motion-picture.**

nontax revenue: *see* **revenue, nontax.**

nonteaching personnel: *see* **personnel, nonteaching.**

nontechnical: a term frequently applied to practical arts education in which stress is laid on development of manipulative skill, with minor emphasis on the scientific principles involved.

nontest techniques: (couns.) means of observing and appraising a child's progress with the assistance of anecdotal records, rating scales, cumulative records, pupil data questionnaires, autobiographies, sociometric techniques, and case studies.

nontraditional mathematics: *see* **mathematics, nontraditional.**

nontransportation zone: any area in which resident pupils are not entitled to transportation.

nontuition pupil: *see* **pupil, nontuition.**

nonuniform scale: *see* **scale, nonuniform.**

nonvanishing determinant: *see* **determinant, nonvanishing.**

nonvariable attribute: *syn.* **category.**

nonverbal awareness: *see* **awareness, nonverbal.**

nonverbal communication: *see* **communication, nonverbal.**

nonverbal intelligence test: *see* **test, nonverbal intelligence.**

nonverbal thinking: *see* **thinking, nonverbal.**

nonvisual expression: *see* **haptic type.**

nonvisual type: *syn.* **haptic type.**

nonvocational: a term used to describe practical arts activities valued for their contribution to general education rather than designed to train persons for wage-earning occupations.

nonvocational agriculture: *see* **agriculture, nonvocational.**

nonwestern studies: *see* **studies, nonwestern.**

norm: (1) the standard or criterion for judgment; (2) in axiology, a standard for judging value; (3) in logic, a rule of valid inference; (4) in psychology, a single value or range of values constituting the usual performance of a given group; any measure of central tendency or a range of values on each side of that measure; the range to be included in the norm is arbitrary but is usually no greater than twice the standard deviation; (5) in philosophy, an ideal of excellence.

norm, adaptive-behavior: a standard of behavior, representing average performance at a given age level, by means of which the degree of adjustment of the individual may be determined.

norm, age: (1) a statement of the mean or median achievement, intelligence, or other characteristic of a group of pupils of a designated chronological age; (2) the chronological age corresponding to a particular score on a standardized test and representing the typical life age of individuals achieving that score.

norm, age-at-grade: (1) a norm based on a population of pupils who are at grade for their age, that is, the sample has been selected by omitting pupils who are above or below the normal age for their grade; *syn.* **modal age-grade norm; modal age norm;** (2) average test scores for pupils in different age groups within the same grade.

norm, age-behavior: typical behavior at a specific age level.

norm, behavior: (1) the typical level of behavior, quantitative or qualitative, found for and expected of individuals who are members of a specified sex, age group, or cultural group; the term may be applied to the typical behavior of any specified group; (2) a culturally prescribed course of action that is to be followed in a given situation.

norm, composite: a statement representing typical performance, usually in terms of the mean or median for a specified group of pupils, or a total score obtained by optimum or arbitrary weighting of two or more component scores. *See* **norm.**

norm, development: the level of structural growth or performance that the average or typical child attains at a given chronological age.

norm, grade: (1) the mean or median achievement of pupils in a given school grade on a given standardized test; (2) the average status of pupils in a given grade in regard to a single factor, such as weight or height.

norm group: *syn.* **group, criterion.**

norm line: a smooth curve drawn through the mean or median scores of successive age or grade groups or through percentile points for a single group.

norm, local: a locally established numerical basis for interpreting the test scores attained by pupils in a particular institution, curriculum, or locality.

norm, modal age: *syn.* **norm, age-at-grade** (1).

norm, modal age-grade: *syn.* **norm, age-at-grade** (1).

norm, national: a basis for interpreting test scores based on the scores attained by pupils taken as a representative nationwide sample.

norm, percentile: (1) a point on a scale of measurement defined by the percentage of cases in a large representative sample or population obtaining a score equal to or less than the value at that point; (2) *pl.* a set of values, usually in tabular form, indicating for each integral score on a test the percentage of cases in a given group who fall at or below that point. *See* **norms.**

norm, probability of success: a norm that indicates, for a group of persons who obtained a specified score, the likelihood of achieving a defined degree of success in a designated activity; such norms are determined by following up groups of persons achieving the specified score under similar conditions of testing.

norm, rate: an expression of the median or typical performance of a group of pupils in reading, handwriting, etc., in terms of amount accomplished in a specified time.

norm, reading: the average reading score achieved by children of a certain age or grade level.

norm-referenced measure: *see* **measure, norm-referenced.**

norm-referenced measurement: *see* **measurement, norm-referenced.**

norm, ridge-route: (1) the level of accomplishment of a normative sample of pupils all of whom are within a 12-month range of the chronological age showing the greatest concentration of pupils in each grade; (2) a norm representing the mean or other average performance of modal age-grade groups; *see* **group, modal age-grade.**

norm, stanine: *see* **score, stanine.**

normal: (1) typical; conforming to a norm, type, or standard; (2) distributed in the shape of the normal probability curve $y = \dfrac{N}{\sigma\sqrt{2\pi}}\, e - \dfrac{x^2}{2\sigma^2}$.

normal age: *see* **age, normal.**

normal behavior: *see* **behavior, normal.**

normal, borderline: descriptive of the intelligence of children who obtain IQ scores of from 70 to 80 or from 75 or 80 to 90.

normal capacity of school plant: *see* **capacity of school plant, pupil.**

normal child: *see* **child, normal.**

normal college: (obs.) *see* **normal school.**

normal college, state: (obs.) *syn.* **teachers college, state.**

normal course: *see* **course, normal.**

normal curve: *syn.* **curve, normal probability.**

normal curve of error: *syn.* **curve, normal probability.**

normal department: *see* **department, normal.**

normal distribution: *see* **distribution, normal.**

normal, dull: *see* **dull normal.**

normal frequency curve: *syn.* **curve, normal probability.**

normal frequency distribution: *syn.* **distribution, normal.**

normal gait, proper: *see* **gait, proper normal.**

normal hearing: *see* **hearing, normal.**

normal institute: *see* **institute, normal.**

normal probability curve: *see* **curve, normal probability.**

normal progress: *see* **progress, normal.**

normal sampling distribution: *syn.* **distribution, normal.**

normal school: (in the United States) formerly the name of an institution for the education of teachers; prior to 1900 usually a secondary school, training common school teachers, with a program including a review of common school subjects, some high school subjects, and the theory, practice, and observation of teaching; after 1900 normal schools gradually became higher institutions but usually did not grant degrees; the name originated in France, was popularized in New England by educational reformers around 1835, and was formally adopted as the designation of Massachusetts teacher-training institutions in 1838; gradually spread to other parts of the United States. *See* **university, normal.**

normal school, state: historically, an institution maintained by the state which usually offered a 1- to 2-year course of training in the science and art of teaching and sometimes operated a high school department for the secondary education of its pupils. *See* **normal school; teachers college, state.**

normal threshold of hearing: *see* **hearing, normal threshold of.**

normal training class: *see* **class, normal training.**

normal university: *see* **university, normal.**

normal university, state: *see* **university, normal.**

normal vision: *see* **vision, normal.**

normality: (1) distribution in conformity with the normal probability curve; (2) the quality of conformance to or lack of significant departure from the norm; *see* **norms;** (3) ability to adjust oneself adequately, physically, mentally, morally, socially, and economically, to situations in one's environment, exhibiting appropriate response to varying situations.

normalization: the procedure involved in establishing norms for standardized tests. *See* **group, normalization; norm; test, standardized.**

normalization group: *see* **group, normalization.**

normalize: (1) to modify values, as test scores, so that the distribution of values more closely approximates a normal probability distribution; (2) (fact. anal.) to divide each of a set of numbers by the square root of the sum of the squares of all the numbers in the set, so that the sum of squares of the new set is 1.00; (3) (computer operation) to adjust to standard, as the value of the exponent and the shift position of the mantissa in floating-point operations; also, to suppress leading zeros in the printout of words.

normalized child: *see* **child, normalized.**

normalized standard score: *see* **score, normalized standard.**

normate: (1) to supply for a raw score its approximate equivalent from a norm table; for example, to supply the corresponding mental age for each possible raw score; (2) to supply a numerical score for a qualitative or coded score in order to secure some end other than mere coding; for example, to maximize a validity coefficient or to rectify a curvilinear regression line; (3) to supply for qualitative answer categories numerical scores in proportion to some significant quantitative index applying in common to all categories; for example, to supply quantitative scores for the reported occupations of persons in proportion to the extent to which the several occupations respectively send their children to college.

normative: (1) in accordance with the normal; (2) at the norm for a given age, grade, sex, region, etc.; (3) (philos.) concerning a judgment of value. *Comp. w.* **descriptive.**

normative crib: *syn.* **clinical crib.**

normative data: *see* **data, idiographic.**

normative generalization: *see* **generalization, normative.**

normative philosophy: *see* **philosophy, normative.**

normative score: *see* **score, normative.**

normative study: *see* **study, normative.**

normative survey: *syn.* **study, fact-finding.**

norms: standards or criteria; for example, test norms give information about the performance of a particular group on a particular test and thereby provide a set of criteria against which can be compared the performance of any individual taking that particular test.

norms, difference: bases for comparisons of pupil achievement founded on the difference between observed and predicted accomplishments on a test.

norms, expectancy: any of various methods for adjusting achievement test norms with respect to mental ability and chronological and/or other characteristics of the person or persons to whom the tests are given. *See* **score, anticipated-achievement grade-placement.**

norms, modal-age: norms based on the performance of pupils of modal age for their respective grades, which are thus free of the distorting influence of underage or overage pupils.

norms, national: units used as national reference groups to assess comparatively other groups or individuals. *See* **norm, national.**

norms, percentile-age: tables based on the performance of a defined age group by means of which test scores can be converted into percentile ranks; used in determining relative placement of pupils in appropriate age groups. *See* **norm; norm, age; norm, percentile.**

norms, percentile-grade: tables based on the performance of a defined grade group by means of which test scores can be converted into percentile ranks; used in determining relative placement of pupils in appropriate grade groups. *See* **norm; norm, grade; norm, percentile.**

norms, standard-score: tables by which standard scores can be converted to percentile ranks, age or grade equivalents, or some other type of derived score having the desired meaning. *See* **norm, age; norm, grade; norm, percentile.**

norms, suitability of: the appropriateness of a norming group for a test for the particular group to be tested.

North Denver plan: an instructional plan inaugurated in North Denver, Colorado, by J. H. Van Sickle in 1898, by which a minimum study requirement was made for all pupils, but more capable pupils were permitted to move more rapidly and were given increased assignments.

Northampton chart: *see* **chart, Northampton.**

Northwest Ordinance of 1787: *see* **Ordinance of 1787.**

nosomania (nos'ō·mā'ni·ə): (1) a morbid dread of disease; (2) an obsession in which a person suffers from an imaginary disease.

nosophobia (nos'ō·fō'bi·ə): a morbid dread of becoming ill, usually of being afflicted with a particular disease.

nostalgia: a state of mind characterized by a desire to return to one's home, to one's native land, or to the conditions obtaining earlier in one's life.

not-being: (philos.) *see* **becoming; being.**

notation: (1) (mus.) the representation of musical sounds by written or printed characters designed to indicate both pitch and duration; (2) (math.) the symbols agreed upon to represent objects and operations in any branch of mathematics; (3) (libr. sci.) an arbitrary set of symbols which represent the classes of books, manuscripts, etc., and subdivisions of classes, providing a convenient means of reference to the arrangement of the library classification.

notation, author: *see* **book number.**

notation, dance: use of symbol or word to describe a dance movement.

notation, expanded: in a system of numeration which has the properties of additivity and place value, the representation of a number as a sum involving powers of the base; for example, 342 in expanded notation would be $3 \cdot 10^2 + 4 \cdot 10^1 + 2 \cdot 10^0$.

notation, mnemonic: (libr. sci.) a notation in which the same elements always indicate the same meaning wherever they appear in a classification scheme.

notation, scientific: a method of writing real numbers in an abbreviated form by expressing a number as the product of a number between 1 and 10 and a power of 10; for example, 25,000,000 becomes 2.5×10^7, 314 becomes 3.14×10^2, 2.1 becomes 2.1×10^0, and 0.21 becomes 2.1×10^{-1}. *Syn.* **standard notation.**

notation, Snellen: *see* **Snellen notation.**

notation, standard: *syn.* **notation, scientific.**

note, bond anticipation: (school admin.) a short-term note sold in anticipation of a bond issue by which these notes are to be repaid.

notebook, career: *see* **career notebook.**

notice: (mil. ed.) in the Navy, a specially numbered announcement or one-time directive, issued by a commander ashore or afloat, using the same numbering system as an instruction but not having its legal force. *See* **instruction** (3).

notice, board meeting: a public announcement giving the time and place of a school board meeting and often listing topics to be discussed at the meeting; state laws often require notice for special meetings such as budget hearings and stipulate the time of giving notice and the contents of the announcement.

notice, election: a public announcement listing such information as the date, time, and place of an election and a description of the issues involved in the election; such notice is usually prescribed by state law which often stipulates the time of giving notice and details concerning the contents of the announcement.

notice to parents: an administrative form used to notify parents of the absence of a pupil from school.

noumenon (nōō'mə·non): (new Lat., from Gr. *nooumenon*, lit., "thing perceived") the inner essence of anything, or of reality; the thing-in-itself; that which is the source of our sensory impressions of an object and of which our sensations are only evidences or representations. *Ant.* **phenomenon.**

noun-unit method: a teaching technique used in the early stages of foreign language instruction, wherein single visual objects are used in sentences to enable the student to grasp the pronunciation and fundamental linguistic features of the language at the outset of instruction.

nous (noōs): (Gr., lit., "mind") generally, reason; specifically, that faculty of mind capable of apprehending first principles, forms, and eternals; in this latter sense it partakes of the divine.

novelty seeking: tendency for organisms to prefer that which is new and unique when given a choice of objects to perceive or explore.

novice: one who has been accepted by a religious community and is serving a probationary period of not less than 1 year to determine his or her personal fitness for the religious life.

novice teacher: an instructor who has had no previous experience in classroom instruction and whose appointment is on a probationary basis.

novitiate: (1) a period of probation before admission to a religious community; (2) a part of a convent or monastery set aside for the exclusive use of the novices.

NROTC (Naval Reserve Officer Training Corps): *see* **program, Naval Reserve Officer Training Corps.**

ns: *see* **nanosecond.**

nuclear family: *syn.* **family, conjugal;** *contr. w.* **family, extended.**

nuclear science: *see* **science, nuclear.**

nucleonics: the science and technology of nuclear energy and its applications.

nuisance: in law, an act that unlawfully results in harm, inconvenience, or damage.

nuisance, abatable: (school law) that which annoys or disturbs another and under law may be enjoined.

nuisance, attractive: a legal term to designate a hazard or danger having the power or quality of appealing to, drawing, or interesting persons so that they may encounter the danger involved.

null hypothesis: *see* **hypothesis, null.**

null set: *see* **set.**

number: a symbol, or concept, used to express a measure of size or quantity.

number, abstract: a term, now infrequently used, meaning number as contrasted with number of units; thus 3 is considered to be an abstract number whereas 3 inches is not. *Contr. w.* **number, concrete.**

number, approximate: (1) a number that records the result of a measurement or a series of measurements, arrived at as the result of a finite number of steps in a process that may demand a greater number of steps, or a number that results from applying the fundamental operations of arithmetic to any such numbers; (2) *syn.* **round number;** (3) any number resulting from measurement rather than counting.

number, author: *see* **book number.**

number belonging: (1) *syn.* **enrollment** (2); (2) the number of children in a given school area, based on state census.

number belonging at date: *syn.* **enrollment** (3).

number belonging, average: *syn.* **membership, average daily.**

number, binary: *see* **number system, binary.**

number, book: *see* **book number.**

number, call: *see* **call number.**

number, cardinal: a number which denotes the numerousness of the membership of some set; such a number may be finite or infinite.

number, class: *see* **class number.**

number combination: (1) in a context such as "combinations of 10," one of the addition facts in which a given number (10 in this case) is the sum; (2) *syn.* **number fact.**

number, complex: a number of the form $a + bi$ where a and b are real numbers and $i = \sqrt{-1}$ such that $i^2 = -1$.

number, composite: an integral number that has integral factors other than itself and unity, for example, $6 = 3 \times 2$. *Contr. w.* **number, prime.**

number, compound: a number composed of more than one unit, for example, 3 feet 2 inches.

number concept: *see* **concept, number.**

number, concrete: a term, now infrequently used, meaning a number in conjunction with some unit, for example, 3 dogs. *Contr. w.* **number, abstract.**

number corner: center of interest in an elementary school classroom for discovering number values and working with study-type aids and games.

number, counting: one of the numbers 1,2,3,4, . . .; zero may or may not be included, according to the taste of the writer. *See* **number, natural.**

number, denominate: a number used in conjunction with some unit of measure, such as 6 hours or 4 feet.

number, directed: a term used to denote a real number (frequently an integer), especially with reference to a number line, when direction from the origin is emphasized.

number, exact: a number that represents the true value of some quantity; usually the result of accurate counting; it may also result from computation with such numbers.

number experience: *see* **experience, number.**

number, f.: *see* **f. number.**

number fact: any one of the addition, subtraction, multiplication, or division facts. *See* **number combination.**

number fact, denominate: any fact involving the relations between measures, for example, 2 pints = 1 quart.

number field: any set of numbers such that the sum, difference, product, or quotient (except by 0) is a number of the set.

number game: a game for the purpose of increasing skill in number fundamentals, most of the activity involved working directly toward that end.

number, I.D.: *see* **I.D. number.**

number, imaginary: (1) a complex number which has the form $(0,b)$ or $0 + bi$; in this meaning, frequently called *pure imaginary;* (2) any complex number in which $b \neq 0$ in either the form (a,b) or the form $a + bi;$ (3) any *complex number* (not good usage).

number, index: *see* **index number.**

number, integral: *syn.* **integer.**

number, irrational: (1) a real number which cannot be represented by a pair of integers in the form a/b ($b \neq 0$); for example, π and $\sqrt{2}$; (2) equivalently, a number represented by a nonrepeating infinite decimal. *Contr. w.* **number, rational.**

number line: a line, frequently a ray, on which points are associated with numbers in a way which is consistent with the natural ordering of those numbers.

number, literal: a letter used to represent a number; in practice, the term frequently means parameter, the domain being a set of numbers. *See* **parameter.**

number, natural: one of the numbers 1,2,3, . . . or 0,1,2,3, . . .; some writers use the term as synonymous with *counting number* and some choose one term for the set with zero and the other term for the set without zero.

number, negative: a number less than zero; for example, -12 degrees means 12 degrees below zero.

number, ordinal: a number that indicates the relative position of a particular object in some ordered arrangement, as, for example, first, second, third. *Contr. w.* **number, cardinal.**

number, positive: a number greater than zero; for example, $+12$ degrees means 12 degrees above zero.

number, prime: a natural number greater than 1 which has exactly two factors, as, for example, 5, whose only factors are 5 and 1; the number 1 is neither prime nor composite. *Contr. w.* **number, composite.**

number, pupil: *see* **pupil number.**

number, pure imaginary: *see* **number, imaginary.**

number, rational: a nonnegative number consisting of an infinite class of fractions obtained by putting with the fraction p/q all fractions m/n for which $p \times n = q \times m$, for example, $\{2/3, 4/6, 6/9, \ldots\}$; (2) a real number whose infinite decimal expansion either terminates or repeats.

number, real: (1) the union of the set of rational numbers and the set of irrational numbers; (2) those numbers named by infinite decimals.

number, round: *see* round number.

number, rounded: *syn.* round number.

number sentence: *see* sentence, number.

number, signed: a directed number for which the point of reference is zero. *See* number, negative; number, positive.

number singing: *see* singing, number.

number system: a set of numbers together with one or more binary operations defined on the set and the properties of these operations (commutativity, associativity, etc.), such as the system of integers.

number system, binary: a number system, used in many electronic computers and in information theory, which, unlike the usual *decimal system,* with its nine digits and a zero, has only one digit, 1, and a zero; thus, the first ten whole numbers of the binary number system (with their everyday equivalents in parentheses) are: 0 (0), 1 (1), 10 (2), 11 (3), 100 (4), 101 (5), 110 (6), 111 (7), 1000 (8), 1001 (9), 1010 (10). *Comp. w.* **decimal system; duodecimal system.**

number system, octal: a number system based on a radix of 8.

number theory: the branch of mathematics in which are studied properties of the integers such as factorization, divisibility, and the indentification of primes.

number, triangular: a natural number is so called if the objects in a set of that size can be arranged in a triangular array with one object in the first row, two in the second, three in the third, etc.; thus, 1,3,6,10, etc., are triangular numbers.

numeral: a term for *number,* although more commonly used to designate a *symbol* for a number, as XVI or 237.

numeral, binary: *see* number system, binary.

numerals, Arabic: *see* numerals, Hindu-Arabic.

numerals, Hindu-Arabic: the symbols 1,2,3,4,5,6,7,8,9, and 0, originated by the Hindus and introduced into the Western world by the Arabs.

numerals, Roman: the symbols I, V, X, L, C, D, and M, and combinations of these symbols, used by the Romans in writing numbers.

numeration base: *see* base, numeration.

numeration system: a systematic scheme for assigning individual names to the counting numbers such as the Roman numerals, the Egyptian hieroglyphic system, or the Hindu-Arabic system; in an *additive numeration system* the values assigned to the different numerals are to be added, as in the Egyptian and Hindu-Arabic systems, while in a *place value numeration system* the value assigned to a symbol is determined by its position in the numeral.

numeration system, octal: an additive place value system of numeration which has 8 as its base; uses only the digits 0,1,2,3,4,5,6, and 7.

numeric: consisting only of symbols representing numbers.

numerical adequacy: *see* adequacy, numerical.

numerical analysis: *see* analysis, numerical.

numerical control: *see* control, numerical.

numerical control system: (voc. ed.) a system which encompasses the conjunction of a machine and a read-in mechanism, input circuits, data storage, interpolation mechanism, position or command read-out mechanisms, control units, prime movers, closed loop servosystems, and appropriate feedback devices; not all of these components need be present.

numerical count: a rhythmic count used in handwriting and handwriting drills consisting of the counting of strokes or stroke combinations, accent or emphasis being placed where needed and changes in rhythm being clearly indicated.

numerical deviation: *syn.* **deviation, absolute.**

numerical rating scale: *see* rating scale, numerical.

numerical test: *see* test, numerical.

numerical trigonometry: *see* trigonometry, numerical.

numerical unity: *see* unity.

numerical value: *see* value, numerical.

numerology: the assignment of mystical significance to numbers and number relations.

numismatics: the systematic study of collections of paper money, coins, and medals or other tokens and the history of coinage.

nun: a member of a religious order for women who has taken vows for life; in common speech, nuns are also often called Sisters; nuns are found in large numbers in the Roman Catholic Church, in smaller numbers among Anglicans, Orthodox, and European (Continental) Protestants.

nunnery school: a girls' school conducted in the Middle Ages by nuns; a girls' academy or seminary.

nurse, public health: a nurse who, in addition to basic professional training, is taught to use concepts of human growth, development, and behavior in order to recognize developmental health needs; learns how to use existing community health services, and for school nursing learns the nature of the educational setting and how to select and use processes appropriate to the roles assumed by the school nurse.

nurse, public school: a nurse employed by the board of education of a public school system who gives part or full time to health work in the school system.

nurse, school: a medically certificated professional nurse providing basic medical services to schoolchildren, usually under direction of a consulting physician.

nurse, visiting: (1) a nurse who spends only a part of her time in a given school; (2) a nurse who travels about from one home or school to another in the course of her work.

nursery: (1) in age classification of children, the age group before kindergarten; (2) the room used for children in this age group.

nursery, day: *see* day nursery.

nursery education: provision for the physical, motor, health, nutritional, intellectual, aesthetic, emotional, and social development of the preschool child.

nursery guidance: *see* guidance, nursery.

nursery, parent-cooperative: *see* nursery school, cooperative.

nursery school: a school which offers a valuable supervised educational experience for 3- and 4-year-old children; gives the child the opportunity to learn to use his body, to express himself, to cope with his own feelings and emotions, to develop relationships within his peer group, and to satisfy his curiosity; each nursery school program is adapted to the child.

nursery school, church sponsored: a nursery school for which a church provides financial or other support for a half-day or all day care; may be parochial.

nursery school, community: a school for children 2 to 5 years of age; organized, sponsored, and often operated under community auspices; may function as a play school with little emphasis on the total developmental processes of the child, or as a nursery school, focusing on the intellectual, social, emotional, and physical development of the child. *See* **nursery school; play school.**

nursery school, cooperative: the term *cooperative* implies that each parent contributes services and/or time to the nursery school program, thereby providing the opportunity for many children to participate in an educational program within the financial possibility of the family's income; often it serves a twofold purpose, providing an intensive program of parent education as well as worthwhile educational experiences for the children; some cooperatives are operated by parents under church sponsorship, others are neighborhood or community ventures sponsored by parents only; most provide for a director qualified in early childhood education who is assisted by the parents (who, in turn, receive guidance and supervision from the director); sometimes called *parent-cooperative nursery.*

nursery school, day: a nursery school the aim of which is to provide an environment in which a child may develop during the hours his parents, for some reason, are unable to care for him; usually supported by the community chest, endowments, and donations; fees are based on size of the family, their income, and their ability to pay.

nursery school director: *see* **director, nursery school.**

nursery school, laboratory: a nursery school which is designed for participation of teachers-in-training and for observation of child behavior.

nursery school, private: a nursery school or day care center sponsored by a private group or individual and not dependent on community moneys for operation.

nursery word: a sound or combination of sounds uttered by a baby as an expression of a need or an emotion.

nurse's annual report: *see* **report, nurse s annual.**

nurse's monthly report: *see* **report, nurse's monthly.**

nurses, registration of: the licensing of nurses according to the laws of a state; recognition of professional competence by a licensing statutory agency.

nursing school: a school or college, formerly typically associated with a hospital but now increasingly a division of a university, which prepares students to be nurses; programs come in a number of different forms, including 2-year programs in junior colleges, 3-year registered nurse (R.N.) programs in some hospitals associated with medical schools, and 4-year programs typically culminating in the degree of *bachelor of science in nursing* or

bachelor of nursing (B.S.N. or B.N.); schools of nursing of large universities also typically offer graduate study leading toward the master's degree; few doctoral programs in schools of nursing are in existence.

nutrition: (1) the science of nourishing the living organism, that is, of providing adequate food for its growth, maintenance, and repair; (2) a physical state depending, among other things, on an adequate diet, assimilation of foods eaten, and desirable food habits.

nutrition class: *see* **class, nutrition.**

nutrition education: a program of instruction in schools or through health and welfare organizations to improve the nutritional status of the individual and the family; may be formal instruction in the classroom or community adult programs; television and/or radio programs are also used.

nutrition program: *see* **program, nutrition.**

nutritional deficiency: *see* **undernourishment.**

nutritional status: the health condition of an individual in relation to his nutrition, determination of which involves a study of the individual's clinical history, hereditary background, and peculiarities of structure and function.

NWPM: (net words per minute) the typewriting rate per minute when there is a 10-word penalty for each error. *Dist. f.* **CWPM.**

NYA: *see* **National Youth Administration.**

nyctophobia (nik′tō·fō′bi·ə): morbid fear of darkness or night.

nystagmus: involuntary movement of the eye which may be lateral, vertical, rotary, or mixed.

Ø: in handwritten work, the letter O, distinguished from the number 0 by drawing a vertical slant through the letter.

O-technique: (fact. anal.) the transpose of *P-technique;* involves the correlations of occasions for a series of tests for one individual, indicating the extent to which two or more occasions covary over a series of tests for one person.

oak tag: *syn.* **manila tagboard.**

Oakland plan: an enrichment plan that originated in Oakland, California, providing homogeneous grouping of pupils for slow, average, and rapid progress, special opportunity and atypical classes, and an enriched program for the more capable pupils.

oath, ephebic: *see* **ephebic oath.**

oath, loyalty: *see* **loyalty oath.**

oath of allegiance: an oath to bear true allegiance to a particular government or sovereign; an oath or affirmation of loyalty, usually to a government. *See* **loyalty oath.**

oath, teachers': *see* **loyalty oath.**

obedience: compliance in action with the dictates or desires of an authority, such as that of a parent or teacher.

obesity: an excessive accumulation of fat in the body, usually caused by overeating but sometimes the result of a glandular or metabolic disturbance.

object: (vis. ed.) anything removed from its natural setting and brought in its entirety into the schoolroom for study. *Dist. f.* **model.**

object-descriptive method: in programmed instruction, presentation to the learner of material in frames displaying a single, complete object the characteristics of which are to be studied in detail, for example, display of front, back, sides, top, and bottom of a painted Greek vase. *Contr. w.* **class-descriptive method.**

object of knowledge: broadly speaking, anything toward which the consciousness is directed, either cognitively or conatively; more specifically, that which receives cognizance by the mind of the subject or knower; usually the antithesis of *subject* in philosophical contexts; an *object* can be sensible or nonsensible, that is, perceptual, conceptual, or symbolic.

object perception: *see* **perception, object.**

object program: *see* **program, object.**

object teaching: *see* **teaching, object.**

objectification of character: the process in which one's character becomes for him an object for analysis, judgment, or reconstruction.

objectify: to make a phenomenon apparent to the senses so that different competent observers would agree on its character and status.

objective: *n.* aim, end in view, or purpose of a course of action or a belief; that which is anticipated as desirable in the early phases of an activity and serves to select, regulate, and direct later aspects of the act so that the total process is designed and integrated.

objective: *adj.* (1) impersonal, impartial, free of bias or idiosyncrasy; (2) pertaining to the object itself as it exists independent of the knowing mind; (3) relating to that which is reliably known through public demonstration or verification.

objective achievement: *see* **achievement, objective.**

objective approach: an introduction to the study of a topic or a subject through the study of facts not influenced by the judgment or personal bias of the individual.

objective camera angle: *see* **camera angle, objective.**

objective, career: *see* **occupational objective.**

objective criteria: *see* **criteria, objective.**

objective, educational: *see* **objective** *n.*

objective, general: a goal or aim stated for education in general, for a school division, or for a subject in general. *Dist. f.* **objective, specific.**

objective idealism: *see* **idealism, objective.**

objective, immediate: purposes to be realized directly through teaching processes. *Contr. w.* **objective, ultimate.**

objective, indirect: (voc. ed.) a secondary objective, sometimes as important as the main objective.

objective instruction: *syn.* **teaching, objective.**

objective, instructional: (mil. ed.) a definitive learning specification in behavioral terms; it states exactly what the student should be able to do after having received the instruction.

objective, lesson: the focal point for everything in a properly planned lesson; the purpose and goal of the lesson and therefore the prime criterion for the lesson's content, methods, approach, and activities; it is indicative of the behavior changes desired in the learner.

objective method: procedure in investigation, study, teaching, or application based on the use of accurately ascertained data, from the determination and interpretation of which any purely personal opinion or preconceived idea is excluded.

objective, occupational: *see* **occupational objective.**

objective score: *see* **score, objective.**

objective, specific: a goal or aim serving as a guide for a teaching unit, directed toward the eventual achievement of a general objective, and stating, preferably in exact terms, the results that may be expected from that particular unit of instruction; thus, ability to conjugate certain verbs in certain tenses might be the specific objective of a particular teaching unit in Spanish, contributing to the attainment of the *general objective* of ability to read, write, speak, and understand Spanish. *Dist. f.* **outcome.**

objective stage of color: *see* **color, objective stage of.**

objective teaching: *see* **teaching, objective.**

objective, tentative career: a student's tentative plan of the sequence of jobs, positions, and occupations through which he intends to progress through his working life.

objective test: *see* **test, objective.**

objective, ultimate: the final valued results that one seeks to achieve by means of a purposive educative process. *Contr. w.* **objective, immediate.**

objectives approach: a method of attack on the problem of curriculum revision in which, by considered judgment, a list of objectives is compiled, stating in as exact terms as possible the skills, abilities, knowledges, characteristics, and attitudes that the schools should develop in their graduates to equip them for a wholesome and productive life; materials for study in the schools are then selected on the basis of their probable contribution to the attainment of these objectives.

objectives, behavioral: the aims or objectives of education stated as actual performance criteria or as observable descriptions of measurable behavior.

objectives, civic: goals set for attainment in respect to civic affairs; often used to designate the aims of education for effective citizenship.

objectives, collateral: (school admin.) those values that the organization is expected or required to inculcate in individuals or groups other than customers or the organization itself; these fall broadly into two categories: personal and social.

objectives in education, specific: (transfer of training) a concept based primarily upon the view that the mind is made up of myriad stimulus-response bonds; thus, transfer is seen as depending upon specific identities rather than on any type of generalization or even on general principles.

objectives, primary service: (school admin.) those values whose creation and distribution constitute the primary mission of the particular organization; for example, the primary objectives of the business organization are those economic values with which it serves its customers—salable values for the most part.

objectives, reading: *syn.* **aims, reading.**

objectives, secondary: (school admin.) values that the organization or its components need to enable personnel to accomplish the mission of the group; the immediate objectives of staff departments.

objectives, seven cardinal: *see* **seven cardinal objectives or principles.**

objectives, social: the aims of a group; the values defined by a group as worthy aspirations for its members.

objectivism: the theory that exact or relatively exact standards can be found by which educational facts and processes may be weighed, tested, or otherwise impersonally established and determined.

objectivity: (1) a criterion for reliable knowledge calling for the exhibition of evidence so that the knowledge claim can be verified by other competent inquirers; this criterion involves (*a*) in the "precision sciences" the rigorous exclusion of the desires, hopes, and fears of men in the interest of knowing the nature of events as such without reference to their meaning for or bearing on other human purposes, and (*b*) in the social sciences, or in inquiry where ends and purposes are themselves at stake, the clear and precise statement of the values, choices, or purposes preferred together with the grounds for the preference and a regard for the full range of alternatives and related considerations; (2) (testing) the extent to which the instrument is free from personal error (personal bias), that is, subjectivity on the part of the scorer.

objectivity coefficient: *see* **coefficient, objectivity.**

oblati: *syn.* **interni.**

oblique: (1) descriptive geometrically of two vectors separated by an angle other than a right angle; (2) descriptive of two sets of data which are correlated. *Contr. w.* **orthogonal.**

obliterative subsumption: *see* **subsumption, obliterative.**

observation: (1) (res.) the act or process of observing (usually complex) conditions or activities as a means of gathering descriptive or quantitative data; (2) (res.) a verbal, numerical, or coded datum recorded as representing a condition or aspect of behavior; especially, a value expressed in relation to a scale, such as a measurement or test value; (3) (stat.) the value derived for a given time, place, object, or event through calculation of a statistical index or index number; *syn.* **measure;** (4) (art. ed.) the ability to see analytically, in detail; directed perception, which is almost entirely an acquired skill; its use arises from the individual's desire to record his sense impressions, to clarify his conceptual knowledge, and to build up his memory.

observation, approaches to: (couns.) various techniques which one may use when observing students, such as diary description, specimen description, time sampling, trait rating, and field unit analysis.

observation class: *see* **class, observation.**

observation course: *see* **class, observation.**

observation, dimensions of: (couns.) characteristics of the observational method which include exhaustiveness, inference, discreteness, size of unit, and applicability; if one dimension is used each time an observation takes place, there will be less chance for generalization.

observation, directed: observation guided by a specialist or an experienced teacher for the purpose of improving understanding; study and evaluation of that which is observed.

observation dome, Gesell: domelike chamber for observation and motion-picture photography of the responses of infants to test situations; the dome is composed of a one-way screen with provision for simultaneous cinematic records taken from different angles.

observation, error of: *see* **error of measurement.**

observation, field: a method of study and learning whereby the participants visit the area or activity under consideration.

observation, follow-through on: (couns.) evaluation of the observation process whereby one is able to see if the behavior or situation has real meaning, whether it is consistent, and whether the student needs further help from someone on a counseling basis.

observation guide: in supervision of instruction, an instrument designed to guide the observer as he studies instructional activities in the classroom, providing for systematic recording of observed evidence in some structured format. *Syn.* **observation schedule;** *see* **schedule, data-gathering.**

observation, independent: an observation or measurement that is not influenced in any way by any other observation or measurement. *Syn.* **observation, random.**

observation, nonparticipant: a setting in which the investigator does not share in the life and activities of the group under study but observes and records conditions or behavior, as in a classroom, a school administrator's office, a police station, or a court.

observation of instruction: (1) the act of examining classroom teaching by visitation, a supervisory procedure used to obtain information, to evaluate the work of teachers and pupils, to analyze classroom activities, and to diagnose teacher and pupil difficulties; (2) (teacher ed.) the act of seeing or studying the activities of teaching and learning in an actual school situation in order to secure a more realistic or meaningful conception of educational problems, appraise the work of teachers in action, or provide for feedback to be used in the development of an improvement program; also, the process of analyzing the playback of film or video tape recordings of one's own teaching to study one's teaching style and interaction with pupils; *dist. f.* **supervision.**

observation, one-way vision: a technique of observation by which the observer can watch the subject without the latter knowing that he is being watched; especially useful in studies of infant and child behavior; depends on the use of various devices, such as *one-way vision screen* and the *one-way vision mirror.*

observation, paired: the difference between two paired observations taken as values of the variable to be considered.

observation, participant: a setting in which the investigator commonly lives with or shares in the life and activity of the group under study, as in observing the life and behavior of hoboes or musicians; the investigator may have disguised himself in such a manner as to be accepted as a member of the group, although his role playing may not require him to carry out exactly the same activities as the other members of the group in order to be accepted as a participant observer.

observation, pre-student-teaching: an orientation program of observation in public or private schools designed for prospective student teachers; usually includes observing classwork, interviewing pupils, and participating in discussions with teachers.

observation, random: *syn.* **observation, independent;** *see* **independence.**

observation schedule: *syn.* **observation guide.**

observation school: *syn.* **demonstration school.**

observation song: *see* **song, observation.**

observation, supervisory: observation by a member of the supervisory staff involving systematic viewing and recording of events for purposes of either appraising the work of the teacher or providing feedback to assist him in his improvement.

observation, task: observation of a particular task by an educational systems designer to secure data to guide construction of applicable portions of a curriculum.

observational data: *see* **data, observational.**

observational geometry: *see* **geometry, observational.**

observational method: (meas.) any one of a number of techniques and procedures for assisting the observer to make more complete and accurate observations, such as aiding the study of individual personality characteristics by directing attention to the behavior of the individual in a given setting or environment, to teacher-pupil interactions, etc.; devices employed include specially prepared charts or checklists for the recording of behavior, the clinical crib, the *one-way vision screen,* concealed automatic motion-picture cameras, and sound recording apparatus. *See* **analysis, interaction; sampling, short-time; study, observational; study, time sampling.**

observational reading: *see* **reading, observational.**

observational schedule, classroom: *see* **schedule, classroom observational.**

observational study: *see* **study, observational.**

observatory: a building equipped with a telescope and other instruments for observation of natural phenomena, as in astronomy or meteorology.

observed score: *syn.* **score, raw.**

observer, process: the group member whose role is (*a*) to observe, generally or specifically, the way in which the group functions, its patterns of interrelationship, and the direction of group movement and (*b*) to present to the group when requested his observations and analysis of its process; also referred to as observer.

observer training: *see* **training, observer.**

obsession: an uncontrollable impulse to dwell on a particular train of thought or to perform some useless action.

obsessional behavior: *see* **behavior, obsessional.**

obsessional neurosis: *see* **neurosis, obsessional.**

obsolescence: the condition of being inadequate according to present standards; may be the condition of a building, an accounting system, a method of teaching, etc.

obsolescence, planned: the manufacture of products in such a way as to serve the consumer no more than 5 years, requiring replacement at that time by newer and presumably better models.

obsolescence, skill: *see* **skill obsolescence.**

obstacle course: an arrangement of walls, fences, ladders, ditches, and other obstacles used in conditioning troops and for developing speed and agility.

obstacle perception: *syn.* **perception, object.**

obstacle sense: *syn.* **perception, object.**

obstruction deafness: *syn.* **deafness, conduction.**

obtained measure: *see* **measure, obtained.**

obtained score: *syn.* **score, raw.**

obverse factor analysis: *syn.* **factor analysis, transposed.**

obvious item: *see* **item, obvious.**

ocarina: one of a family of small, egg-shaped terra-cotta musical instruments in character somewhat resembling the tonette. *See* **tonette.**

Occam's razor: *alt. sp.* **Ockham's razor;** *syn.* **law of parsimony.**

occluded lisp: *see* **lisp, occluded.**

occlusion: (1) shutting in or out by closing a passage, as the occlusion of the breath stream in the process of speaking; (2) the manner in which the teeth fit together when the jaws are closed.

occupation: the series of duties and responsibilities undertaken and related activities performed by an individual to accomplish a goal and/or for financial reward.

occupation, distributive education entry: the type of position which may require no previous work experience in that particular occupation and is related to the student's tentative career objective in distribution and marketing.

occupation, hazardous: a category of jobs that demand a higher degree of muscular coordination, stability, maturity of judgment, or resourcefulness in meeting emergencies than is usually found in the young worker; examples are mining, construction, and agriculture.

occupation, middle-level: *syn.* **semiprofession.**

occupation, nonfarm agricultural: *see* **agricultural occupation, nonfarm.**

occupation, off-farm agricultural: *syn.* **agricultural occupation, nonfarm.**

occupational adjustment: *see* **adjustment, occupational.**

occupational analysis: *syn.* **analysis, job.**

occupational approach: a method of attack on the problem of selecting materials for curriculum revision (especially those relating to the occupational or vocational training of pupils) in which analysis is made of the abilities, skills, and knowledge actually used by adults engaged in the particular occupations or vocations for training in which the curriculum is designed. *Syn.* **job-analysis approach.**

occupational aspiration: (voc. ed.) a goal-directed attitude which involves conception of the self in relation to a particular level of the occupational prestige hierarchy.

occupational biography: *see* **biography, occupational.**

occupational brief: (couns.) a relatively brief statement (3,000 to 5,000 words) about an occupation describing its history, the work performed, hours, requirements, wages, working conditions, and methods of entry, and usually supplying other reference sources; also called occupational file. *Comp. w.* **occupational monograph.**

occupational choice: *see* **choice, occupational.**

occupational competencies, general: *see* **competencies, general occupational.**

occupational competencies, specific: *see* **competencies, specific occupational.**

occupational counseling: *syn.* **counseling, vocational.**

occupational curriculum: *syn.* **curriculum, vocational.**

occupational dangers: specific chances for injury or disease that are inherent in a particular occupation; to be distinguished from general occupational hazards resulting from carelessness or indifference as to the safety of workers.

occupational description: printed material which describes the principal employment opportunities of an occupation in one or several industries; may include a brief account of the industry or industries.

occupational education: curriculum emphasis, used with mentally retarded groups, which is built around the achievement of social and vocational competence.

occupational experience, distributive education supervised: *see* **experience, distributive education supervised occupational.**

occupational experience education: *see* **work experience education.**

occupational family: *see* **job family.**

occupational fiction: *see* **career fiction.**

occupational field: *see* **field, occupational.**

occupational film: *see* **film, occupational.**

occupational goal: *see* **occupational objective.**

occupational group, business and office: *see* **group, business and office occupational.**

occupational growth: *see* **growth, occupational.**

occupational guidance: *see* **guidance, occupational.**

occupational guide: *see* **guide, occupational.**

occupational hierarchy: *see* **hierarchy, occupational.**

occupational high school: *see* **high school, vocational.**

occupational information: (1) (couns.) valid and usable data about positions, jobs, and occupations, including duties, requirements for entrance, conditions of work, rewards offered, advancement pattern, existing and predicted supply of and demand for workers, and sources for further information; *see* **sources, occupational information;** (2) (spec. ed.) that part of a work-study curriculum which stresses specific information and knowledge about occupations suitable for the mentally retarded.

occupational information library: *see* **library, occupational information.**

occupational information sources: *see* **sources, occupational information.**

occupational instruction: *see* **instruction, occupational.**

occupational intent: *see* **occupational objective.**

occupational interest: special curiosity, attention, or concern with regard to general types of positions or jobs.

occupational level: the position of an individual's occupation in a scale of occupations graded on an economic, social, or intelligence basis. *See* **hierarchy, occupational.**

occupational literature: *see* **literature, occupational.**

occupational mobility: (voc. ed.) the pattern of changes in occupation taking place in a society; changes between the occupation of father and son, movement in and out of an occupational position, changes from one job to another within a community, from one job to another between communities, and from one type of job to another within or between communities.

occupational mobility, horizontal: a pattern of movement from occupation to occupation at the same level of income, prestige, or responsibility.

occupational mobility, intergenerational: changes in occupational levels from grandparents to parents and to their children.

occupational mobility, promotional: the series of job changes a worker goes through during a working career.

occupational monograph: (couns.) a long, detailed statement (6,000 to 10,000 words) about an occupation, describing its history, the work performed, hours, requirements, wages, working conditions, and methods of entry, and usually supplying other reference sources. *Comp. w.* **occupational brief.**

occupational motion picture: *see* **motion picture, occupational.**

occupational objective: in business and office education and in distributive education, a current career goal selected by the student, the preparation for which is the purpose of his vocational instruction in one of these fields.

occupational orientation: *see* **orientation, occupational.**

occupational placement: *see* **placement service.**

occupational preparation: *see* **preparation, occupational.**

occupational program: *see* **program, occupational.**

occupational programs in vocational home economics: *see* **programs in vocational home economics, occupational.**

occupational psychology: *see* **psychology, occupational.**

occupational rating scale: *see* **rating scale, occupational.**

occupational relations learnings: *syn.* **competencies, general occupational.**

occupational research: *see* **research, occupational.**

occupational specialty code, military: *see* **code, military occupational specialty.**

occupational specialty evaluation test, military: *see* **test, military occupational specialty evaluation.**

occupational standard: *see* **standard, occupational.**

occupational study: *see* **study, occupational.**

occupational survey: *see* **survey, occupational.**

occupational survey, community: *see* **survey, community occupational.**

occupational test: *see* **test, occupational.**

occupational therapist: *see* **therapist, occupational.**

occupational therapy: *see* **therapy, occupational.**

occupational training: *see* **training, occupational.**

occupational training, cooperative: *see* **training, cooperative occupational.**

occupational training, individual: *see* **training, individual occupational.**

occupational workshop: *see* **workshop, occupational.**

occupations: a course of study involving a comprehensive survey of occupations designed to give the student vocational information, to assist him in selecting and preparing for a vocation, and to give him an opportunity to study problems that confront workers.

occupations class: *see* **class, occupations.**

occupations, construction: vocational activities dealing with the erection of buildings and other structures on a site, such as the occupations of carpenter, mason, structural steel worker, electrician, plumber, excavator, and environment control occupations.

occupations, data processing: vocational activities concerned with electronic and electromechanical machines that record, store, process, and transcribe data from punchcards, paper tape, magnetic tape, or other sources.

occupations, distributive: *see* **distributive occupations.**

occupations, electrical: vocational activities relating to the electric power generation, transmission, and distribution in industrial, commercial, and domestic applications and the installation and maintenance of electrical and communications systems and of other electrical equipment and components.

occupations, Froebelian: *see* **Froebelian occupations.**

occupations, paramedical: those jobs concerned with or supplementing the work of medical personnel, having a secondary relation to medicine.

occupations, related: those occupations defined in the *Dictionary of Occupational Titles* that are directly related to the major fields of business and office occupations under the 14.000 series listed therein. *See* **business and office education, intensive; code DOT; office education, cooperative; training, occupational.**

occupations, service: those occupations which have as their primary purpose the rendering of personal service to the customer or maintenance of existing equipment.

occupations training, accounting and computing: *see* **training, accounting and computing occupations.**

occupations training, business data processing systems: *see* **training, business data processing systems occupations.**

occupations training, materials support: *see* **training, materials support occupations.**

occupations training, miscellaneous office: *see* **training, miscellaneous office occupations.**

oceanography: the study of the sea, embracing and integrating all knowledge pertaining to the sea's physical boundaries, the chemistry and physics of sea water, and marine biology.

octal number system: *see* **number system, octal.**

octal numeration system: *see* **numeration system, octal.**

octile: (rare) one of the seven points measured along the scale of a plotted variable which divide the frequency distribution into eight intervals, each containing exactly one-eighth of the observations or cases.

ocular: pertaining to the eye. *Syn.* **ophthalmic;** *dist. f.* **optic.**

ocular defect: *syn.* **eye defect.**

ocular dominance: *syn.* **eye preference.**

ocular-neck reflex: *see* **reflex, ocular-neck.**

ocular pursuit: the following of a moving object by means of successive fixations of the eyes.

oculist: *syn.* **ophthalmologist.**

oculo-cephalo-gyric response: *see* **response, oculo-cephalo-gyric.**

oculomotor: (lit., "eye-moving") pertaining to eye-movement behavior.

oculomotor process: any of the motor processes involved in eye movement and in the focusing and adjusting of the eyes in the act of seeing.

oculophotometer: a portable instrument for photographing the movements of both eyes during reading; more recently known as the *ophthalmograph.*

oculus dexter (ok′ū·ləs dek′stər): (O.D.) (Lat.) right eye.

oculus sinister (ok′ū·ləs sin′is·tər): (O.S.) (Lat.) left eye.

oculus uterque (ok′ū·ləs ū·têr′kwə): (O.U.) (Lat., "each eye") both eyes.

O.D.: *see* **oculus dexter.**

odd-even method of reliability: *see* **reliability, split-halves.**

odd-even scores: *see* **scores, odd-even.**

Oedipus complex: *see* **complex, Oedipus.**

off-campus school: *syn.* **affiliated school.**

off-campus student teaching: *see* **student teaching, off-campus.**

off-farm agricultural occupation: *syn.* **agricultural occupation, nonfarm.**

off-line: detached from and operating independently of the automatic computer; sometimes incorrectly used to mean delayed time. *See* **data processing, delayed-time;** *contr. w.* **on-line.**

off-line data processing: *see* **data processing, off-line.**

off-line equipment: *see* **equipment, off-line.**

offender, juvenile: a juvenile who exhibits misconduct but who has not been legally classified as a delinquent.

office administration: *see* **administration, office.**

office bulletin: *see* **bulletin, office.**

office education, cooperative: terminal program designed for above-average business students whereby they attend school a half day and work in a cooperating local business firm a half day with pay; emphasizes the individual skills, knowledges, and attitudes in the office occupations area; object is to graduate an office worker already adjusted to the business world.

office employee, educational: *see* **employee, educational office.**

office employee, financial: *see* **employee, financial office.**

office function: (bus. ed.) the ability of an office normally to provide proper and adequate information to the right person, on time, and in proper form.

office-machines course: *see* **course, office-machines.**

office method: the sequence and manner of work performance used by an individual office worker to make each element of the office task as efficient as possible.

office occupations: occupations associated with the management and operation of offices, especially those involving skills such as typewriting, stenography, and accounting.

office occupations training, miscellaneous: *see* **training, miscellaneous office occupations.**

Office of Economic Opportunity program: *see* **program, Office of Economic Opportunity.**

office organization: the arrangement, space allocation, and working plans for the conduct of work in the office of a school principal or administrative head of a school system.

office practice: a course in the field of business education taught in secondary school or in college and intended to perfect business students in the methods and practices of business offices; may include practice in preparing office forms and in operating office machines.

office practice room: a room fitted with machines and equipment for use by office practice classes.

office practice, standard: *see* **instruction, standard practice.**

office practice typewriting: *see* **typewriting, office practice.**

office procedure: a series of related clerical steps, usually performed by more than one person, which constitute an established and accepted manner of performing a major phase of office activity.

office procedure, standard: *see* **instruction, standard practice.**

office reports: a general term for reports issued from the office of the administrative head of a school or school system.

office routine: a preplanned method of doing certain clerical work in the office which implements office operation and production; geared to reduce waste of time and extra effort for both the secretary and the executive.

office, school: *see* **school office.**

office-style dictation: *see* **dictation, office-style.**

office system: a network of procedures which are integrated and designed to carry out a major activity; the composite of many different information activities contributing to the end result, including personnel, forms, records, machines, and equipment.

office work: *syn.* **clerical work** (1).

officer, administrative: *see* **administrative officer.**

officer, admissions: *see* **admissions officer.**

officer advanced training: *see* **training, officer advanced.**

officer, attendance: *see* **attendance officer.**

officer basic technical training: *see* **training, officer basic technical.**

officer, cadet: *see* **cadet officer.**

officer candidate: *see* **candidate, officer.**

officer candidate, naval aviation: *see* **candidate, naval aviation officer.**

officer, court: *see* **court officer.**

officer, de facto: one who is in actual possession of an office without lawful title. *Comp. w.* **de jure officer.**

officer, de jure: one who has just claim and rightful title to an office, although not necessarily in actual possession thereof. *Comp. w.* **de facto officer.**

officer, finance: *see* **finance officer.**

officer lateral training: *see* training, officer lateral.

officer, line: *see* administration, line.

officer, placement: *see* placement officer.

officer, probation: *see* probation officer.

officer, public information: *syn.* director, public relations.

officer, school: *see* school officer.

officer, staff: *see* staff officer.

officer, student: *see* student officer.

officer supplemental training: *see* training, officer supplemental.

officer, tactical: *see* tactical officer.

officer trainee: *see* trainee, officer.

officer training school: (1) an Air Force school for giving basic military training leading to a commission; (2) loosely, an officer candidate school. *See* candidate, officer; trainee, officer; *contr. w.* academy, service.

officer, truant: *see* truant officer.

officer's data card: *see* card, officer's data.

officers qualification code number: *see* code number, officers qualification.

officers training school program: *see* program, officers training school.

offices, incompatible: *see* incompatible offices.

official, athletic: *see* athletic official.

official hearing: *see* hearing, official.

official information: *see* information, official.

official training literature: *see* training literature, official.

offset: *syn.* photolithography.

offset annual: *see* annual, offset.

offset yearbook: *syn.* annual, offset.

ogive (ō′jĭv; ō·jĭv′): an S-shaped curve that is a graphic representation of a cumulative frequency distribution, the frequencies being expressed in terms of either the percentages or the actual numbers of observations; may be plotted so that each ordinate expresses either the percentage or number of observations below or the percentage or number of observations above the corresponding value on the abscissa. *Syn.* cumulative frequency curve; cumulative frequency graph; cumulative percentage curve; *contr. w.* graph, frequency.

ogive, "less than": a cumulative frequency curve so drawn that any ordinate shows the number or percentage of the observations with variate values that are less than the corresponding value of the abscissa. *Contr. w.* ogive, "more than."

ogive, "more than": a cumulative frequency curve so drawn that any ordinate shows the number or percentage of the observations with variate values that are more than the corresponding value of the abscissa. *Contr. w.* ogive, "less than."

old-field school: a type of rural elementary school common in the South before 1850, deriving its name from the fact that often the schoolhouse was built on a worn-out field. *See* charity education (2).

old-type examination: *see* examination, old-type.

olfactory ability: *see* ability, olfactory.

olfactory awareness: *see* awareness, olfactory.

olfactory discrimination: *see* discrimination, olfactory.

olfactory sense: the sense of smell.

oligophasia, central: a disorder of symbolization caused by imperfection of auditory-perceptual or other perceptual and sensory-motor schemata, so that a symbolic schema of language cannot be clearly evolved.

oligophasia, expressive: a disturbance in the process of recognizing and forming phonemic patterns and in transferring them to the executive organs of speech.

oligophasia, receptive: a disturbance in auditory perception so that foreground and background relations cannot be clearly recognized.

oligophrenia: mental retardation of various levels; a term used especially in French and German research on this subject. *See* retardation, mental; *comp. w.* feeblemindedness.

oligophrenia, phenylpyruvic: *syn.* phenylketonuria.

ombudsman: (Swedish, lit., "representative") an official who represents the rights and interests of citizens who find themselves victims of bureaucratic complexity, mismanagement, ineptitude, or lack of responsiveness; though the office of ombudsman was first established in Scandinavia, many industrialized countries including the United States have begun instituting such offices; they are also found in some higher education institutions.

omission: (1) leaving out one or more sounds or letters in pronouncing or writing a word, as *histry* for *history* or *to* for *too;* (2) any sound, letter, or group of letters omitted; (3) (art ed.) in children's drawings, the neglect or omission of parts that are either suppressed or unimportant.

omnibus test: *see* test, omnibus.

omnipotence stage of development: *see* stage of development, omnipotence.

on-call supervision: *syn.* supervision, invitational.

on-campus student teaching: *see* student teaching, on-campus.

on-job training, agricultural: *see* training, agricultural on-job.

on-line: directly connected to and operating under the control of the automatic computer, in contrast to independent operation; sometimes incorrectly used to mean real time. *See* data processing, real-time; *contr. w.* off-line.

on-line data processing: *see* data processing, on-line.

on-line equipment: *see* equipment, on-line.

on-the-job sponsor: *see* training sponsor, business and office education; training sponsor, distributive education.

on-the-job trainer: *see* training sponsor, business and office education; training sponsor, distributive education.

on-the-job training: *see* training, on-the-job.

on-the-job training, dual channel concept of: *see* training, dual channel concept of on-the-job.

on-the-job training, veterans': *see* veterans' on-the-job training.

on-the-spot broadcast: *see* broadcast, on-the-spot.

one-address computer: *see* computer, one-address.

one-egg twins: *syn.* twins, monozygotic.

one-group experiment: *see* experiment, one-group.

one-hand alphabet: *see* alphabet, finger.

one-room school: a school, usually rural, in which the pupils in a number of grades or groups are housed in a single room.

one-tailed test: *see* test, one-tailed.

one-teacher school: an individual school for which one teacher is employed; may encompass the elementary grades or at one time the complete 12 grades.

one-to-one correspondence: *see* correspondence, one-to-one.

one-way length of route: *see* length of route, one-way.

one-way loaded miles: *see* miles, one-way loaded.

one-way vision booth: a booth from which the observer can see and hear the subject without being seen, the observer being concealed behind a one-way vision screen.

one-way vision mirror: a partly silvered mirror that can be seen through from the back; used in the *photographic dome* and the *one-way vision booth.*

one-way vision observation: *see* observation, one-way vision.

one-way vision screen: a screen of wire mesh or lightweight cloth brightly lighted on the subject's side but dark on the observer's side; used in the *one-way vision booth* and the *photographic dome.*

onomatopoeic theory (on′ə·mat′ə·pē′ik): the theory that language had its origin in the imitation or reproduction of natural sounds, as illustrated by such words as *buzz* and *hum.*

onomatopoeic word: *see* word, onomatopoeic.

onomatoschematic theory: the theory suggested by Holmes (1953) that words bearing some configurational resemblance to their meaning, for example, *zigzag, bed, look,* etc., are easier to read than are other words that do not bear such resemblance.

onset of loss: *see* **loss, onset of.**

ontogenesis (on'tō·jen'ə·sis): *syn.* **ontogeny.**

ontogenetic: of or pertaining to development during the life history of the individual.

ontogenetic activities: *see* **activities, ontogenetic.**

ontogenetic zero: the point of genesis of the individual; the moment a particular ovum is fertilized by a given spermatozoon.

ontogeny (on·toj'ə·ni): development of the individual of a species from conception onward. *Syn.* **ontogenesis;** *dist. f.* **phylogeny.**

ontological analysis: *see* **analysis, ontological.**

ontological argument: *see* **argument, ontological.**

ontology: (1) the theory of being or ultimate reality; (2) the science of existence in general.

op art: *see* **art, op.**

opaque effect: any technique used in motion-picture production to begin, end, or join scenes with the aim of producing an impression of emphasis.

opaque projector: *see* **projector, opaque.**

open-account credit: *see* **credit, open-account.**

open admission: *see* **admission, open.**

open-air class: *see* **class, open-air.**

open-air school: *see* **class, open-air.**

open book test: *see* **test, open-book.**

open-circuit: descriptive of broadcast situations where programs are radiated for reception by any listener or viewer within range of the station; applies to commercial and educational television and radio stations.

open classroom: *see* **classroom, open.**

open-end drama: *see* **drama, open-end.**

open-end formula: (school finance) a formula which pays out a total of state aid to meet the formula requirements, whatever that amount may be; appropriations are made in terms of "so much as is necessary to meet the requirements" rather than in terms of specific dollar amounts that may not be exceeded.

open-end question: *see* **question, open-end.**

open-end table: *see* **table, open-end.**

open-ended experiment: *see* **experiment, open-ended.**

open-ended problem: *see* **problem, open-ended.**

open-ended program: *see* **program, open-ended.**

open enrollment: *see* **enrollment, open.**

open forum: *see* **forum, open.**

open meeting: an educational meeting open to the general public, in contrast with one limited to a certain group such as the leader-training meetings sponsored by the cooperative extension service.

open-mindedness: a characteristic willingness to think through a situation without prejudice.

open sentence: *see* **sentence, open.**

open set: *see* **set, closed** (2).

open shop: *see* **shop, open.**

open society: a type of society that deliberately seeks its own improvement through the free use of knowledge and invention; has own distinctive group of procedures and relevant morality; sees free inquiry and criticism as indispensable and specifically legalizes them; sees itself as necessarily pluralistic, with minorities having an indispensable and creative role; sees change as natural and as opportunity for growth and progress; sees democracy as dependent upon such open inquiry, pluralism, etc., and education as a major instrument. *Contr. w.* **totalitarianism.**

open stacks: *see* **stacks, library.**

open syllable: *see* **syllable, open.**

open tournament: a tournament in a particular sport in which the entries are not limited by certain eligibility rules.

open university: *see* **university, open.**

open-window ventilation: *syn.* **ventilation, window.**

opening exercises: *syn.* **morning exercises.**

opera: a musical drama in which the characters act their parts and sing their lines to the accompaniment of an orchestra; in grand opera, generally, every word is sung; light or comic operas usually have spoken dialogue; the operas of Richard Wagner are grand opera of the highest intensity. *See* **drama, music.**

opera, chamber: an opera of very modest dimensions, requiring but few participants as soloists, chorus, or orchestra and needing no elaborate staging; an intimate music drama in contrast to the colossal productions of the nineteenth century.

opera, comic: *syn.* **operetta;** *contr. w.* **musical comedy.**

opera, rock: a term used, somewhat pretentiously, to refer to a musico-dramatic production of some length which has all the characteristics of a Broadway musical with rock 'n' roll as the musical substance throughout.

operand: (1) (math) a number on which mathematical operations are performed; (2) in data processing, one of the numbers a computer is to select to operate on; located in the storage unit; *see* **address.**

operant behavior: *see* **behavior, operant.**

operant behavior theory of reading: *see* **reading, operant behavior theory of.**

operant conditioning: *see* **conditioning, operant.**

operating cost: *see* **cost, operating.**

operating cost, direct: *see* **cost, direct operating.**

operating cost, indirect: *see* **cost, indirect operating.**

operating expense: *see* **expense, operating.**

operating ratio: in automatic data processing, the ratio obtained by dividing (*a*) the total number of hours of correct computer operation, including time when the program is incorrect through human mistakes and including time the computer is idle during scheduled work hours and capable of correct operation, by (*b*) the total number of hours in (*a*) plus the hours of all maintenance work, scheduled and unscheduled, and plus the hours of all *down time,* excluding maintenance time.

operation: (1) (voc. ed.) a definite set of machine-tool or hand-tool steps forming a convenient "work unit"; generally considered the smallest practical unit for trade or job-analysis work; *see* **unit operation;** (2) (data processing) any action or process, such as recording, sorting, calculating, storing, retrieving from storage, etc.

operation and maintenance score card: *see* **score card, operation and maintenance.**

operation bootstrap: *see* **bootstrap, operation.**

operation, calculating: a term including the arithmetic operations of addition, subtraction, multiplication, and division.

operation chart: *see* **chart, operation.**

operation code: *see* **code, operation.**

operation, combined: (1) an operation conducted by forces of two or more allied nations acting together for the accomplishment of a single mission; (2) an operation or exercise carried out by different units of a mixed force, as in Army combined training; *see* **training, combined.**

operation, cost of: *see* **cost of operation.**

operation, dual system of: the practice of using a school bus or fleet of buses to serve two or more schools which operate on different time schedules, or to transport elementary and secondary school pupils to the same or different schools on different time schedules. *See* **route, multiple.**

operation flow chart: *see* **chart, operation flow.**

operation, fundamental: *see* **fundamental operation.**

operation, inverse: (math.) an operation sometimes explained at the elementary level as an "undoing" or "doing the opposite" of some other operation; for example, separating (subtraction) is the opposite of joining (addition); more formally, an operation which can be defined in terms of that operation and its inverse elements; thus, for integers, subtraction is defined as adding the inverse, for example, $a - b = a + (-b)$.

operation, joint: an operation or exercise carried out by two or more military services of the United States, such as a joint air campaign of Army, Navy, and Air Force units; sometimes loosely used in the sense of combined operation. *See* **operation, combined.**

operation layout sheet: a form for collecting and recording the basic information concerning product and process that is necessary for manufacturing purposes; should be in a form that will facilitate its use by the production control department and the production line organization; known as a *master plan of work, routing sheet,* etc.

operation, logic: (data processing) any noncomputational operation of a computer, such as comparing, selecting, extracting, etc.; also called *logical operation.*

operation, logical: *see* **operation, logic.**

operation, manual: *see* **manual operation.**

operation, mathematical: a function which assigns an appropriate element (number, set, etc.) to each member of some other set (call it S); if S consists of single elements, the operation is unary; if the elements of S are ordered pairs, the operation is binary, etc.

operation of buildings: the work connected with the heating, ventilating, lighting, cleaning, policing, and general care of buildings; janitorial, engineering, and custodial work connected with the use of buildings.

operation of school plant: (finance) an accounting classification that includes all payments involved in keeping the physical plant open and ready for use, such as those for heating, lighting, and cleaning.

operation process chart: *see* **chart, operation process.**

operation, real-time: the use of the computer as an element of a processing system in which the times of occurrence of data transmission are controlled by other portions of the system or by physical events outside the system and cannot be modified for convenience in computer programming.

operation, school-plant: the keeping of the physical plant of a school in condition for use, involving work such as cleaning, heating, ventilating, and lighting. *See* **cost of operation.**

operation sheet: (voc. ed.) (1) written instructions arranged in a logical and sequential order, usually for the accomplishment of some unit part of a job requiring manipulative skills; (2) a factory production method sheet on which materials and steps of an assigned task are listed.

operation, staff: (school admin.) advisory and facilitating activities to make the work of others more effective.

operation staff: *see* **staff, operation.**

operation time, average: in automatic data processing, the mean time of nine additions and one multiplication; the concept in this form properly applies only to one-address computers. *See* **gill.**

operation, well-defined: a binary operation in which each pair of elements is associated with a unique third element; some writers also require closure; for example, addition in the integers is well defined since $3 + 4$ names one and only one integer; analogous definitions can be made for well-defined unary, tertiary, etc., operations. *See* **closure.**

operational balance: *see* **balance, operational.**

operational definition: *see* **definition, operational.**

operational fatigue: *see* **fatigue, operational.**

operational intelligibility: *syn.* **intelligibility, functional.**

operational learning: *see* **learning, operational.**

operational meaning: *see* **meaning, operational.**

operational order: *see* **order, operational.**

operational pattern of supervision: *see* **supervision, operational pattern of.**

operational readiness test: *see* **test, operational readiness.**

operational readiness training: *see* **training, operational readiness.**

operational test and evaluation: *see* **test and evaluation, operational.**

operational testing: *see* **testing, operational.**

operational training: *see* **training, operational.**

operational validity: *see* **validity, operational.**

operationalism: a philosophical point of view in which meaning is determined by the operations carried out in behalf of a word; thus, "simultaneous" means precisely the operations carried out in establishing events as simultaneous occurrences; operationalism has it that meaning of ideas is determined not by what we say or think about them but by what we do about them; ideas acquire meaning by virtue of the operations performed in their name, and their meaning is restricted to these operations.

operationism: (1) the interpretation of human behavior by its effects on the environment; (2) an analysis of the individual in action with special emphasis on the results or function of his acts.

operations analysis: *see* **analysis, operations.**

operations research: *see* **research, operations.**

operative authority: *see* **authority, operative.**

operative control: *see* **control, operative.**

operetta: a theatrical production of the comic-opera type, light and sentimental in nature and written in a popular vein; contains spoken dialogue interspersed with songs, dances, and scenes; typified by the works of Gilbert and Sullivan and Victor Herbert. *Syn.* **comic opera;** *contr. w.* **musical comedy; opera.**

ophidiophobia: extreme fear of snakes.

ophthalmia (of·thal'mi·ə): any inflammation of the eye, particularly one involving the conjunctiva.

ophthalmic (of·thal'mik): *syn.* **ocular.**

ophthalmic telebinocular: *see* **telebinocular.**

ophthalmograph camera: *syn.* **oculophotometer.**

ophthalmologist (of'thal·mol'ə·jist): a physician who specializes in the diagnosis and treatment of diseases and refractive errors of the eye. *Syn.* **eye physician; oculist.**

ophthalmology (of'thal·mol'ə·ji): the branch of medical science that deals with the anatomy, physiology, and pathology of the eye.

ophthalmoscope (of·thal'mə·skōp): an instrument with a perforated mirror, used in examining the interior of the eye.

opinion: (1) in popular usage, a belief, judgment, idea, impression, sentiment, or notion that has not been conclusively proved and lacks the weight of carefully reasoned judgment or certainty of conviction; taken broadly, it represents probability rather than knowledge; (2) the official view of an attorney general or other administrative official; rationale for a judge's decision; (3) *see* **opinion, public** (1).

opinion poll: *see* **poll, opinion.**

opinion, public: (1) the average judgment or consensus of the individuals of a society regarding certain social problems or objects; (2) the designation of a systematic journalistic course involving the review and correlation of background courses in the social studies to show the influence of the press in the formation and guidance of public opinion.

opinion scale: *syn.* **scale, attitude.**

opinionaire: a type of questionnaire designed to elicit opinions or attitudes, in contrast to objective facts; much the same as an *expressionaire.*

opportunism: acting in a given circumstance without reference to principles, standards, values, ideals, ultimate consequences, or any other external measure of significance beyond the gaining of some immediate end.

opportunistic supervision: *see* **supervision, opportunistic.**

opportunities, equal: *see* **equal opportunities.**

opportunities, learning: *see* **learning opportunities.**

opportunity class: *see* **class, opportunity.**

opportunity room: a room in which special instruction is provided for pupils who are handicapped or retarded mentally, physically, or educationally.

opportunity school: (1) an evening school aimed at providing educational opportunities needed or desired by the adult population of a community, such as formal college work, secondary education, literacy instruction, job training, etc.; (2) (spec. ed.) a segregated school for exceptional children.

opposites test: *see* test, opposites.

optic: pertaining to vision or to the science of optics. *Dist. f.* ocular; ophthalmic.

optic angle: *see* visual angle.

optical axis: the central line of vision; a straight line passing through the center of curvature of the lens and cornea.

optical character reader: *see* reader, optical.

optical defect: any malfunction or malformation of the organs of sight that interferes with or prevents normal vision.

optical reader: *see* reader, optical.

optical scanner: in data processing, the electronic process of reading or recognizing written symbols by reflecting light from the written page through an optical system to a light-sensitive device that converts the reflected energy into electrical impulses which may be transmitted as a digital representation of the information on the written page.

optical sound recording: *see* sound recording, optical.

optical sound track: sound which has been recorded and/or printed on photographic film by exposing and processing the light-sensitive sound track area. *See* variable area track; variable density track.

optician: one who makes or deals in eyeglasses and/or other optical instruments and who fills prescriptions for glasses. *Dist. f.* oculist; ophthalmologist; optometrist.

optifying: the act of translating sensory impressions, other than visual ones, into visual imagery, for example, translating impressions tactually perceived in darkness into visual images.

optimal linkage: *see* linkage, optimal.

optimal weight: *see* weight, optimal.

optimum age: *see* age, optimum.

optimum intelligence: *see* intelligence, optimum.

optimum step size: *see* step size, optimum.

option: (1) (testing) a set of alternative answers to a multiple-choice test item; (2) (curric.) *syn.* elective; (3) an agreement permitting one to buy or sell the thing named within the time and on the terms stipulated.

option, pass-fail: *see* pass-fail option.

options, transfer: *see* transfer points.

optometrist: one skilled in the measurement of the refraction of the eye for the prescription of eyeglasses. *Dist. f.* oculist; ophthalmologist; optician.

optometry: (1) the measurement of defects in the eye due to errors of refraction which may be corrected by glasses and without the use of drugs; (2) the art and science of visual care; especially the art and science of visual training for the development of visual skills and visual achievement.

opus: *pl.* **opera;** (Lat., lit., "work") (mus.) this term, when coupled with a number, indicates the chronological position of a particular piece within the total output of a composer; for example, "Opus 1" indicates the first composition, though these numbers are not always reliable, since they often apply to the date of publication rather than the date of composition; the term is abbreviated "op."; the plural is not to be confused with the singular opera, a music drama. *See* opera.

oracy: a word coined in 1965 to indicate the skills of speaking and listening, analogous to the term *literacy*, referring to reading and writing.

oral: in the teaching of the deaf, using the spoken word and understanding the spoken word by speech reading, without the aid of artificial appliances.

oral assignment: *see* assignment, oral.

oral-aural: pertaining to speaking and hearing, as applied to language teaching. *Syn.* audiolingual.

oral character: *see* character, oral.

oral composition: *see* composition, oral.

oral English: *see* English, oral.

oral erotic: (psychoan.) (1) characterized by the stimulation of erotic feeling or urges through oral mechanisms, especially the oral food-imbibing processes; (2) pertaining to the earliest stage of libidinal development in which it is alleged that satisfaction is derived chiefly through the processes of sucking and oral stimulation.

oral eroticism: *see* eroticism, oral.

oral expression: *see* expression, oral.

oral inaccuracy: a speech defect characterized by careless, slovenly articulation and occasional haphazard omission of consonants, particularly final consonants. *See* articulatory defect.

oral inactivity: lack of adequate movement of lips, tongue, and jaw in the process of speaking; may result in defective articulation, defective voice quality, or both.

oral instruction: *see* instruction, oral.

oral interpretation: *see* interpretation, oral.

oral-language activity: *see* activity, oral-language.

oral method: (1) a method of teaching reading based on oral response to the printed symbol as the chief means of checking the reader's ability to recognize and pronounce words; (2) a method used in the development of oral reading ability; (3) a method of teaching the deaf by means of the spoken word, without using sign language or finger spelling. *See* reading, lip.

oral reading: *see* reading, oral.

oral-reading scale: *see* scale, oral-reading.

oral-reading test: *see* test, oral-reading.

oral recall: *see* recall, oral.

oral stage of development: *see* stage of development, oral.

oral teaching: *see* teaching, oral.

oral test: *see* test, oral.

oral-usage error: *see* error, oral-usage.

oral vocabulary: *see* vocabulary, oral.

oralism: a method of instruction for the deaf in which the chief means of communication is lipreading and talking.

Oratorian: a member of a Roman Catholic order called the *Oratory*, first founded in Italy in the sixteenth century, and established as a teaching order in France in 1611. (The principal work of the order was the education of candidates for the priesthood. It also offered education of a general type in colleges which it established throughout France.)

oratorio: a long choral composition with instrumental accompaniment and with a text presenting a story or central theme, usually Biblical; performed in concert style without stage setting, costumes, or dramatization. *See* cantata.

orchestra: an instrumental ensemble, typically comprising the four sections of string, woodwind, brass, and percussion instruments and led by a conductor.

orchestra, chamber: an orchestra of small proportions, possibly 25 to 30 players, as contrasted with a full symphony orchestra of about 100 players.

orchestra, civic: an ensemble of strings, winds, and percussion drawn from the amateur musicians in a given area; the avowed purpose is social and recreational as well as musical.

orchestra, toy: *syn.* rhythm band.

orchestration: *syn.* instrumentation (2).

order: (1) (in reference to correlation coefficients, regression coefficients, etc.) strictly, the number of variables held constant in any partial correlation coefficient or partial regression coefficient; as commonly used, the number of variables minus two involved in any correlation coefficient or correlation-related statistic; for example, r_{xy} is a *zero-order* correlation coefficient, $b_{xy \cdot z}$ is a *first-*

order regression coefficient, etc.; (2) (of a matrix) a description of the size of the matrix; thus, a matrix of *m* rows and *n* columns is said to be of *order m* by *n*.

order effect: *see* **effect, order.**

order, expense: (school admin.) an order issued for work in connection with the repair and maintenance of plant and equipment or for other work whose cost cannot be charged directly to a production order.

order, hierarchical: *see* **hierarchical order.**

order of merit: any rank or set of ranks based on a good-bad continuum. *See* **rank order.**

order-of-merit value: *see* **value, order-of-merit.**

order, operational: (school admin.) an order that authorizes action.

order, rank: *see* **rank order.**

order, religious: (R.C. ed.) a body of men or of women who take vows of poverty, chastity, and obedience and who choose to live a community life of worship and service; members are involved in all levels of education as well as other areas of social service. *See* **community** (3).

order, technical: (school admin.) an order that authorizes the use of specified methods and standards for a designated purpose under specified conditions; does not authorize action. *See* **order, operational.**

ordered pair: (math.) a pair of elements symbolized by (*a,b*), (*x,y*), etc., to which order is assigned, that is, *a* and *x* are the first members, *b* and *y* the second; thus (2,4) is not the same as (4,2) since the order is reversed.

ordered series: *see* **series, ordered.**

ordinal number: *see* **number, ordinal.**

ordinal scale: *see* **scale, ordinal.**

ordinance: (1) a local law or regulation enacted by a municipal government or board of aldermen for the government of the municipality; (2) any rule or regulation adopted by a local board of education for the government of a school district.

Ordinance of 1785: an act, known as the *Survey Ordinance,* adopted by the Congress of the Confederation providing for the disposal of public lands in the Western Territory and reserving one section (640 acres) of every township for the endowment of schools within that township.

Ordinance of 1787: an act, known as the *Northwest Ordinance,* adopted by the Federal government providing for the governing of the Northwest Territory, declaring "Religion, morality, and knowledge being necessary for good government and the happiness of mankind, schools and the means of education shall forever be encouraged," and setting aside the sixteenth section of land in every township in the territory for the support of schools.

ordinate: the second of the pair of numbers assigned a point in the plane when *Cartesian coordinates* are used. *See* **coordinate; coordinate system.**

Oregon plan: a program of education of visually handicapped children utilizing the residential school for the elementary grades or until the pupil can be integrated in public school classes. *See* **New Jersey plan.**

Orff method: (mus. ed.) a group of principles deriving from the teaching techniques of the German composer-teacher Carl Orff; improvisation early in the exposure, extensive use of pentatonic scales, and much work with percussion instruments characterize the system.

organ of Corti: the sense organ of hearing.

organic chemistry: *see* **chemistry, organic.**

organic-efficiency test: *see* **test, organic-efficiency.**

organic fitness: *see* **fitness, organic.**

organic intelligibility: *see* **intelligibility, organic.**

organic paralysis: *see* **paralysis, organic.**

organic philosophy of education: a philosophy of education, systematically formulated, which endeavors to reconcile and harmonize the valid conceptions and principles of conflicting philosophies and theories around an organic core.

organic psychosis: *see* **psychosis, organic.**

organic reading disability: *see* **reading disability, organic.**

organic set: a preparation of the organism to respond in a specific manner, for example, a determination to take a trip one week hence; more broadly, any disposition, expectancy, or readiness to respond to a situation. (Distinctions have been drawn among goal set, situation set, task set as determined by instruction, and problem set.)

organic sign: *see* **sign, organic.**

organic speech disorder: *see* **speech disorder, organic.**

organic systems: (sci. ed.) the study of systems essential to life processes, such as the circulatory, respiratory, digestive, excretory, nervous, skeletal, and reproductive systems.

organic unity: *see* **unity, organic.**

organism: any living individual capable of maintaining existence as a unitary system, whether plant or animal; may be unicellular, as in the case of the amoeba and paramecium, or multicellular, as in the case of fish, insects, and mammals.

organism, neuromuscular: *see* **neuromuscular organism.**

organismic age: *see* **age, organismic.**

organismic concept of development: (1) a view emphasizing the essential unity or inseparable wholeness of development; (2) (psych.) the concept that local patterns of behavior, such as reflexes, emerge through maturation as recognizable entities from the total organismic pattern; *see* **gestalt.**

organismic psychology: *see* **psychology, organismic.**

organismic sociology: *see* **sociology, organismic.**

organismic supervision: *see* **supervision, organismic.**

organization: (1) the process (or result) of arranging interdependent elements into a functional or logical whole; (2) (read.) the process of selection, evaluation, and arrangement of ideas encountered in material read; (3) the step in the *Morrison plan* when teacher and pupils arrange assimilated materials so as to solve the problems set for study.

organization by cycles: a plan of subject-grade placement and of curriculum organization by which the pupils repeat the study of a subject or topic at two or three different grade levels, each time at a higher level of difficulty. *Syn.* **concentric-circles plan; spiral method;** *see* **curriculum, spiral.**

organization chart: *see* **chart, organization.**

organization, community: *see* **community organization.**

organization, curriculum: *syn.* **curriculum design.**

organization, departmental: the organization of subjects for instruction and the assignment of teachers on the basis of broad areas of knowledge, for example, English, social studies, art, music, physical education, and business subjects.

organization, divided: *syn.* **administration, dual type of.**

organization, divisional: a plan of organization involving the separation of the administrative unit into divisions for the purpose of planning and carrying on the activity of the unit. *See* **division** (1) and (4).

organization, double-headed: *syn.* **administration, dual type of.**

organization, double-headed plan of administrative: *syn.* **administration, dual type of.**

organization, dual: *syn.* **administration, dual type of.**

organization for group guidance: the organization or plan within a school for the formation of instructional groups.

organization for instruction: the framework within which teachers are free to work with children; consists of all the elements which when pieced together form this organizational framework.

organization, formal: (school admin.) a system of rules and positions arranged in a hierarchical order and officially established for the performance of one or more tasks.

organization, functional: a plan of school management based primarily on a clear formulation of the aims and purposes of the school and the operations required to meet these aims and purposes; the plan is implemented by staff members chosen for their ability to perform the operations that contribute toward the realization of the purposes.

organization, grade: (1) the organization of the school curriculum into year-long groups of subject offerings, each year's work comprising a grade; (2) the manner in which a school system organizes its attendance units, such as 8–4, 6-4-4, etc.; (3) a type of school organization in which for the purpose of facilitating instruction children are classified as to grade level or year level on the basis of certain criteria (chronological age, mental age, organismic age).

organization, horizontal: any plan by which provision is made in the secondary school program for offering subjects and training to meet the specialized needs and interests of pupils; may be based on the planned sequences of studies in various specialized fields within the curriculum of a comprehensive high school or on the organization of specialized high schools, such as agricultural, commercial, trade, and academic high schools.

organization, informal: (school admin.) a system of interpersonal relations which forms to affect decisions made in a *formal organization* setting.

organization, internal: the organization within a single school as opposed to organization involving several schools or a system.

organization, large-block-of-time: *syn.* **schedule, large-block-of-time.**

organization, line: *syn.* **administration, line.**

organization, line-and-staff: a system of educational administration that fixes a definite line of authority and responsibility from the superintendent through subordinates to all school employees and presumably also provides for specialized planning or supervisory officers who constitute the administrative staff.

organization manager: *see* **manager, organization.**

organization, neurological: *see* **neurological organization.**

organization, noneducational: any group of persons united for some purpose other than the discussion of policies, practices, and methods related to teaching, the course of study and/or training, or the implementation of the same.

organization, personnel: *see* **personnel organization.**

organization, radial: (1) a plan of organization in which cooperating schools are located some distance from and surrounding a central administrative unit which provides certain services for the cooperating schools; (2) a plan of organization in which a central administrative unit administers a number of outlying schools.

organization, school: the structure, framework, or arrangement within which teachers, pupils, supervisors, and others operate to carry on the activities of the school.

organization, secondary school: (1) any plan followed in assigning school grades to the secondary school administrative unit, such as the 8–4 plan or the 6–3–3 plan; (2) the arrangement of the offerings of the school into subject-matter departments or specialized fields of work to facilitate planning and administering both the program of studies and the work of pupil guidance; (3) the division of the program of secondary education among the various comprehensive and specialized high schools of a school system; (4) the method followed by a state in determining the local authority for the establishment and support of secondary schools.

organization, staff: *see* **staff organization.**

organization structure: a framework of relationships among similar functions, physical factors, and personnel that is set up to facilitate the accomplishment of some mission by promoting cooperation and facilitating an effective exercise of executive leadership.

organization, student: an officially recognized student group designed to conduct a program or manage an enterprise appealing to students; programs may be social, recreational, intellectual, fraternal, or political in content and emphasis.

organization, supervisory: (1) a group of persons united for the purpose of improving supervision; (2) the structure to provide supervision for a school or school system.

organization, teachers': *see* **teachers' association.**

organization, unit: (1) in school administration, the type of organization where one individual administers the whole organization, as contrasted with *multiple-type administrative organization* where two or more executives are coordinate administrators; (2) in curriculum, the organization of the instructional program into units of work such as subject-matter units, center-of-interest units, experience units, process units, and other unit types.

Organization, United Nations Educational, Scientific, and Cultural: *see* **UNESCO.**

organization, vertical: a plan of organization involving units made up of parts of several successive grades, as opposed to horizontal organization involving all of a small number of grades; usually applied to supervision in a subject field throughout several or all grades in the system.

organization, youth: an organization of young persons to promote some youth movement.

organizational classification: *see* **classification, organizational.**

organizational climate: *see* **climate, organizational.**

organizational pattern of supervision: *see* **supervision, organizational pattern of.**

organizational training: *see* **training, organizational.**

organized classwork: *see* **classwork, organized.**

organized-facts policy: the policy of publishing all the facts of a given situation, organized for ready understanding and suitable emphasis.

organized guidance: *see* **guidance, organized.**

organized play: *see* **play, organized.**

organizer, advance: *see* **advance organizer.**

organogenesis: pertaining to the origin and development process of any part of an organism performing some definite function.

organogeny: *see* **organogenesis.**

organs, speech: *see* **speech organs.**

orientation: (1) the act of determining one's course or position, whether literally, as in finding the direction of the compass in which to go, or figuratively, as in adjusting to a confusing situation or coming to an understanding of a problem; (2) determination of the relations of objects or data to one another; (3) capacity to estimate oneself correctly in the environment with reference to location, persons who should be recognized, and approximate time; (4) the process of making a person aware of such factors in his school environment as rules, traditions, and educational offerings for the purpose of facilitating effective adaptation; (5) a preliminary program of instruction to prepare cooperative part-time students in vocational education for entry into the world of work; (6) (couns.) a program to help pupils prepare for and adjust to new situations as they progress through school, as from home to kindergarten, to elementary school, to junior high school, to senior high school, and on to college or employment; (7) (art ed.) *see* **forming products;** (8) with the handicapped, the process of utilizing the remaining senses in establishing one's position and relationship to all other significant objects in one's environment; *syn.* **spatial orientation.**

orientation and mobility specialist: *see* **specialist, orientation and mobility.**

orientation, attitudinal: the realization of the attitudinal variance of client, community, and counselor; an adjustment of counselor, client, or guidance program to attitudes displayed in a specific situation.

orientation, building: (spec. ed.) the process by which a visually impaired person learns the physical layout of a systematically assembled structure for the purpose of functional mobility.

orientation course: *see* **course, orientation.**

orientation course, educational: *see* **course, educational orientation.**

orientation day: a day on which students visit their new schools, students leaving old schools are visited by counselors and teachers, conferences are held with parents and students, and students receive printed material in order to provide an introduction to a new situation.

orientation, directional: (read.) the understanding that in reading English and other modern European languages the eye must move from left to right rather than, as in Hebrew, from right to left; the adjustment of the reader to this left-to-right direction in reading, as contrasted with *directional confusion,* the lack of such adjustment.

orientation, efficiency: in supervision of instruction, an attitude resulting in a period of pressurized influence on teaching procedures by experts who were efficiency oriented. (Supervision during the period of 1876 to 1936 was generally an inspectorial function, and administration was concerned primarily with business management.)

orientation, family of: *see* **family of orientation.**

orientation, freshman: *see* **freshman week.**

orientation, group: a method by which students having a common problem may work together in charting a course for meeting the problem; the initial step in *group guidance* (a continuous process).

orientation guidance: *see* **guidance, orientation.**

orientation, head-mouth: the movement of the head of the young infant toward the site of contact stimulation of facial areas and the opening of the mouth to grasp the stimulating object.

orientation, inner-directed: a set toward a certain stimulus, or a predisposition toward certain behavior patterns determined by an early-instilled value system.

orientation, materials: (audiovis. instr.) a program through which teachers and other patrons are informed about the types of materials, equipment, other facilities, and services available to them; may consist of formal demonstrations, conferences, or workshops, or of informal activities such as personal contacts or the writing of memoranda.

orientation, occupational: (spec. ed.) a specific phase of a work-study program that emphasizes the subjective aspects of work in preparation for actual on-the-job experience.

orientation of buildings: *see* **orientation, school** (1).

orientation program: *see* **freshman week; orientation** (4) and (5).

orientation, room: the process of familiarizing a blind person with the layout of the room so that he will be able to find his way about the room unassisted. *See* **orientation** (8).

orientation, school: (1) the placement of buildings in correct relationships to other buildings on the school site or campus with reference to points of the compass, or the direction in which school buildings or classrooms face; (2) programs to acquaint new students and faculty with the facilities of their school.

orientation, social: adjustment to one's position in relation to society, environment, and associates.

orientation, spatial: the ability to orient oneself in space.

orientation, teacher: a school program, preceding the opening of classes, in which new teachers and the more experienced staff personnel meet and discuss new and old aspects of school life; new teachers are made aware of the facilities of the school, its rules and regulations, and the need for discipline and proper personal appearance; senior teachers are encouraged to search for improvements in their approach to the students by employing new and effective methods of teaching, where possible; also referred to as staff orientation and faculty orientation.

orientation week: *syn.* **freshman week.**

origin: (1) in data processing by computer, the absolute address used as a reference point for relative addresses; (2) (math.) on a number line the point selected to represent zero; when graphing in the plane or in three space, the common point of intersection of the axes.

origin, arbitrary: (1) (M') any point that is used as a zero point and from which all values on the scale are measured as deviations; thus, in calculating such measures as the arithmetic mean and the standard deviation, the midpoint of a class interval, either near the center or toward the lower end of the frequency distribution, is often taken as an arbitrary origin; *syn.* **working origin;** *see* **average, guessed;** (2) (math.) a synonym of *origin,* merely underscoring the fact that the origin is always chosen arbitrarily.

origin, working: *syn.* **origin, arbitrary.**

original enrollment: *see* **enrollment, original.**

original entry: *see* **entry, original.**

original nature: *see* **nature, original.**

original registration: *syn.* **enrollment, original.**

original score: *syn.* **score, raw.**

original sin: (1) the first sin committed by Adam; (2) the sin of Adam as transmitted, by natural generation, to all his descendants. (The effects of original sin are variously understood in the different Christian theologies. Roman Catholicism sees its effects mainly as the deprivation of gifts such as sanctifying grace, original justice, given to Adam, while human nature itself remains intact. Traditional Protestantism held that by it human nature was totally depraved. Liberal Protestantism tends to eliminate the doctrine entirely.)

original source: *syn.* **source, primary.**

ornamental horticulture education: a program of instruction and on-job experiences offered as a part of vocational education in agriculture at the high school and postsecondary levels and designed to prepare and upgrade students for employment in ornamental horticulture jobs in floriculture, turf management, grounds care, greenhouse work, nursery work, landscaping, and arboriculture; (2) a program of instruction offered by colleges and universities to prepare professional workers in ornamental horticulture.

orphism: an early twentieth century style in painting which placed primary emphasis upon color, attempting to achieve dynamism through color tensions; Robert Delaunay and Stanton MacDonald-Wright were among the innovators of the style. *Syn.* **synchromism.**

Ortho-Rater: a visual screening device for use with children and adults; screens for visual acuity, binocular coordination, and depth perception.

orthodontia (ŏr'thō·don'shi·ə; -ti·ə): (1) the practice of straightening the teeth and jaws and correcting faulty alignment, malocclusion, etc., by surgical or mechanical means; (2) the study of structural dental relationships and their development.

Orthodox religious school, Jewish: *see* **religious school, Jewish Orthodox.**

orthogenesis, theory of (ŏr'thō·jen'ə·sis): a theory of biological evolution which holds that variation in successive generations of an organism follows some predetermined line or order of nature, in accordance with the developmental potentialities of the organism, and irrespective of natural selection, specific environmental influences, etc.

orthogenic: pertaining to the amelioration of mental handicaps through educational, medical, and surgical treatment, the stimulation of mental growth, and the development of desirable traits of personality. *Contr. w.* **orthopedic.**

orthogenic class: *see* **class, orthogenic.**

orthogonal: (1) for lines and planes, perpendicular; curves are called orthogonal if their tangents at a point of intersection are perpendicular; (2) descriptive of two tests or sets of data when they are uncorrelated.

orthogonal axes: *see* **axes, orthogonal.**

orthogonal Latin squares: *see* **squares, orthogonal Latin.**

orthogonal planes: *see* **planes, orthogonal.**

orthographic chart: *see* **chart, orthographic.**

orthography: spelling according to standard usage; the study of spelling.

orthography, traditional: (t.o./TO) the usual 26-letter alphabet as distinguished from modified alphabets. *See* **alphabet, initial teaching.**

orthopedic: pertaining to the prevention and correction of deformity, especially in children. *Contr. w.* **orthogenic.** (NOTE: Derived from the Greek *orthos,* "correct," "straight," *pais, paidos,* "child." Not to be confused with words compounded with the Latin root *ped-* from *pes, pedis,* "foot.")

orthopedic class: *see* **class, orthopedic.**

orthopedic deformation: *see* **deformation, orthopedic.**

orthopedic handicap: *see* **handicap, orthopedic.**

orthopedic school: a school for crippled children providing transportation, specialized equipment, special education, medical direction, and physical, occupational, and/or speech therapy as needs indicate; vocational guidance and training are added at the secondary level.

orthopedically handicapped: *see* **handicapped, orthopedically.**

orthopedics: the branch of medicine concerned with the bones, joints, and muscles, and with correcting deformities in them.

orthophoria (ŏr′thŏ·fō′ri·ə): (1) the normal condition of the eyes in which the eye muscles are in correct balance; (2) the parallel postural position of the visual axes when fusion is broken.

orthopsychiatry (ŏr′thŏ·sī·kī′ə·tri; -psī·kī′-): guidance or clinical practices based on the combined findings of psychiatry, pediatrics, psychology, and social work.

orthoptic training: *see* **training, orthoptic.**

orthoptics: the science concerned with rendering visual reactions and responses correct and efficient, usually by some form of exercise or training. *See* **training, orthoptic.**

orthoscopic representation: *see* **representation, orthoscopic.**

Orton hypothesis: *strephosymbolia* (twisted symbols) resulting from a comparable intermixture of control in the two hemispheres of the brain in those areas which subserve the visual or reading part of the language function and are normally active only in the dominant hemisphere. *See* **cerebral-dominance theory.**

O.S.: *see* **oculus sinister.**

oscilloscope: a test instrument, similar in some respects to a TV receiver, that shows visual patterns of voltage and current characteristics.

ossicle: a small bone; any one of the chain of three bones in the middle ear.

Oswego Movement: the introduction into and development throughout the United States of formalized methods of Pestalozzian object teaching during the three decades after 1860; received its name from Oswego, New York, where this system of teaching first attracted national attention and where the first normal school for training teachers in the system was established. *See* **teaching, object.**

Oswego plan: *syn.* **teaching, object.**

other, generalized: *see* **generalized other.**

otherworldly: descriptive term applied by empirical philosophies to knowledge of that which transcends experience, which knowledge they claim is so removed from the conditions of reliable human knowing that its pursuit is fruitless as a source of guidance for human affairs.

otologist (ō·tol′ə·jist): a physician who specializes in diseases of the ear; preferred to the term *aurist.*

otosclerosis: a disease which results in a pathological growth of bone tissue around the footplate of the stapes in the oval window; a common etiology of *conductive deafness.*

O.U.: *see* **oculus uterque.**

out group: *see* **group, out.**

out-of-class activity: *see* **activity, out-of-class.**

out-of-classroom supervision: *see* **supervision, out-of-classroom.**

out-of-school activities: *syn.* **activities, nonschool.**

out-of-school activity: *see* **activity, out-of-school.**

out-of-school radio listening: *see* **radio listening, out-of-school.**

out-of-school youth: persons under 21 years of age, excluding children below school age, who (*a*) are not elementary or secondary pupils and (*b*) are not taking courses for college credit toward degrees or equivalent certificates; a pupil is not considered to be an out-of-school youth when he is not attending school during a vacation period.

outbuildings: buildings located on the school grounds for the purpose of providing facilities not available in the regular school buildings, such as fuel houses, "teacherages," garages, stables, outdoor toilets, and separate gymnasiums.

outcome: change in behavior resulting from learning; not to be confused with *objective,* which is a desired result.

outcome, desired learning: a necessary and specific component part of a lesson objective; sometimes referred to as *subobjective* or *subgoal;* a statement of one of the desired changes in student behavior for a given lesson; a criterion for planning, conducting, and evaluating a lesson.

outcomes, guidance: changes achieved in the behavior of individuals and of groups through application of guidance principles and services.

outcomes, instructional: outcomes that result from the instructional program, planned in terms of pupil growth in all areas.

outdoor education: an approach to teaching and a process through which learning experiences in all areas of the educational curriculum are provided and in which natural, community, and human resources beyond the traditional classroom are utilized as a motivation for learning and a means of broad curriculum enrichment and vitalization; direct firsthand learning opportunities involve the teacher and student in ecological explorations of the environment to develop and/or improve the knowledge, understanding, attitude, behavior, appreciations, values, skills, and stewardship responsibility of the learner; education in, for, and about the physical and biotic environment is emphasized in order to achieve a wide variety of educational goals.

outdoor gymnasium: *see* **gymnasium, outdoor.**

outdoor learning center: *syn.* **center, nature.**

outdoor play area: (phys. ed.) an open-air facility, either marked or unmarked, that is used for physical activities.

outdoor science laboratory: *syn.* **center, nature.**

outer monastic school: *see* **monastic school, outer.**

outlet, tension: *see* **tension outlet.**

outline: a sequential enumeration in condensed form of the main ideas and supporting details of material read or of material to be used in writing or speaking.

outline, correspondence: *see* **syllabus, correspondence.**

output: (1) (communications theory) the signal emitted by a source; in the case of an animal, overt behavior which acts as a signal for another animal or which acts upon a nonliving communications system; (2) (electronic) signal delivered from any audio device; also a jack or connector that feeds the signal to another piece of equipment; (3) (data processing) any media which contain the finished product (or partially finished product) of a calculating machine process. *Comp. w.* **input.**

output data: *see* **data, output.**

output equipment: *see* **equipment, output.**

output unit: a computer unit that delivers information from within the computer to the outside.

outside millage: *see* **millage, outside.**

outward vocalization: *see* **vocalization, outward.**

oval drills: *syn.* **ovals.**

ovals: a type of handwriting drill in which the learner makes designs shaped like the letter O, usually retracing the pathway a number of times; designed to give the writer training in motor control and coordination in rounding curves. *Syn.* **oval drills.**

overachievement: a level of accomplishment which extends above and beyond the level of expectation as indicated by a comprehensive assessment of an individual's potentiality. *Contr. w.* **underachievement.**

overage: older chronologically than is normal for entering a given grade.

overage certificate: *see* **certificate, overage.**

overage class: *see* **class, overage.**

overage in grade: an administrative term used to describe a pupil who is significantly older chronologically than is normal for pupils in his same grade.

overageness: the state of being *overage.*

overcompensation: the exaggeration of a trait in order to overcome a real or imagined inferiority.

overcrowding: (pup. trans.) the practice of transporting in a school bus more pupils than the bus is designed to carry.

overcurve: any curve in handwriting made in a clockwise direction, that is, a convex arc made by moving upward toward the right and then downward. *Syn.* **direct curve.**

overexpectation: the setting of goals that are far beyond the potential of the handicapped.

overexposure: exposure of film more than is necessary to yield a negative of normal contrast, shadow detail, and density. (Indicated in the case of a negative by a general density and exceptionally heavy deposits of silver in the highlights and in the case of a positive print from reversal film by paleness and lack of detail in the highlights.)

overflow: in computer operation, in a counter or register, the production of a word or field which has more admissible marks than the capacity of the counter or register; for example, in adding two numbers, each 10 characters long and hence within the capacity of a 10-character register, the result may be a sum 11 characters long, which is beyond the capacity of the register; the character lost may be either the most or least significant of the number.

overgrown child: *see* **child, overgrown.**

overhead projector: *see* **projector, overhead.**

overhead transparency projector: *see* **projector, overhead.**

overlapping: (1) the extent to which scores or observations in two distributions fall within the same range; sometimes measured by the percentage of one set of scores that exceeds the mean or median of the other set; (2) (art ed.) the visual impression of a foreground object partly covering one behind it.

overlapping debt: *see* **debt, overlapping.**

overlapping specific factor: *syn.* **factor, group.**

overlay: (1) in computer operation, a segment of a program read into storage on top of (and hence obliterating) other parts of the same program; use of overlays is a technique for conserving on the use of storage and usually is limited to rarely used parts of a program; (2) one or more additional transparent sheets with lettering or other matter that may be placed over a base transparency or an opaque background for use in a projector or over a map or chart to show details either not appearing or requiring special emphasis on the original.

overlearning: learning as a result of more or longer practice than would be needed for immediate recall or for immediate performance at a given level of skill; regarded as necessary to ensure delayed recall following disuse; for example, in foreign language study, the process of learning a word, phrase, or utterance to the point of automatic and total recall through frequent repetition.

overlearning method: a teaching method which utilizes the psychological principle of *overlearning* in order to achieve some specific educational objective, such as to overcome an emotional or psycholinguistic disorder.

overload: more volume than can be handled adequately without distortion in audio equipment.

overload principle: a principle applied to improve strength, muscular endurance, or circulorespiratory function by subjecting the individual to a workload greater than that to which he is accustomed. *Syn.* **overloading;** *see* **exercise, conditioning; physiology of exercise.**

overloading: (1) (pupil trans.) the practice of placing a greater weight of body and passengers on the chassis of the school bus than the gross vehicle weight for which the chassis was designed; *see* **capacity, weight;** (2) (phys. ed.) *see* **overload principle.**

overprompting: in programmed instruction, inclusion in a text of frames of an excessive number of *prompts,* so that the student is likely to become overly dependent on program-supplied responses, making *weaning* more difficult.

overprotection: the sheltering of one individual by another to such a degree that opportunity to experience the hazards and discomforts considered necessary for normal development is denied.

overpunch: a punched hole in a card that distinguishes alphabetic and special character symbols from numeric symbols; also known as a *zone punch. See* **punch, X.**

overseas extension: *see* **extension, overseas.**

overseer: a device used for purposes of diagnosis and supervisory guidance in handwriting; consists of a model or copy printed or written on a transparent sheet, such as a sheet of celluloid, in order that the model may be superimposed on the written form for examination and comparison.

overstudy: the expending of too much time and effort in study, generally implying that the learner has become inefficient.

oversupply, teacher: the situation resulting when the number of legally qualified and certified teachers available for appointment exceeds the number of positions that are available.

overt behavior: *see* **behavior, overt.**

overt response: *see* **response, overt.**

overture: (1) an instrumental work serving as an introduction to a larger composition such as an opera; (2) a concert instrumental piece patterned after an opera overture but complete within itself and not serving as an introductory piece to a more extended composition.

overview: a clear layout of the organizational pattern to be followed during a presentation, given as a part of the introduction to a speech or teaching exercise; briefly describes the content and procedures to be followed for the remainder of the speech or lesson; can include the desired learning outcomes to be developed during the lesson.

own story: (couns.) the statement of a youth whose problem is being studied; should relate to the problem and be of use in the solution of the problem.

ownership, joint: *see* **joint ownership.**

oxygen debt: (phys. ed.) the amount of oxygen required in the postexercise recovery period to reverse the anaerobic reactions of the exercise period; quantitatively, the difference between the oxygen requirement of a task and the oxygen intake during performance of the task. *See* **physiology of exercise; reaction, anaerobic.**

p

P-technique: (fact. anal.) correlating a group of tests over a series of occasions for one person; indicates covariation of traits in time. *See* **factor analysis, transposed.**

P.A. system: *see* **public-address system.**

pace setters: (1) time schedules, devices such as reading pacers or model school demonstrations, or human models that provide an advanced standard for gauging performance and rate of achievement; (2) (bus. ed.) certain typists who are somewhat more skillful than other nearby students and therefore are used to set the pace or speed goal of the timed writings.

paced-practice mode: a mode of operation of a teaching machine in which a timer limits the time for presentation of the program items or the time for response to them.

pacer, reading: *see* **machine, pacing.**

pacing: (1) the act of directing the performance of an individual or class by indicating the speed to be achieved, in order to increase or decrease the rate of accomplishment; (2) in programmed instruction, the rate at which the student proceeds through a given number of items; the usual procedure is *self-pacing* in which the student reads and responds at his own rate; if materials are presented to a group, the time allowed for input and for response must be standardized through *group pacing;* a few devices such as reading accelerators control the individual student's pace by *machine pacing,* moving on to the next item irrespective of the student's behavior; (3) in individualized reading, development of reading skills and interests at the child's own rate rather than at a rate predetermined for any individual or for an entire group.

pacing, automatic test: use of an automatic multiple-choice synchronized testing machine, such as Edex, which registers results of questions of a graphic nature on student digital counters.

pacing, group: a procedure in programmed instruction in which students progress in lockstep (together) toward the same objectives; frequently helps where intragroup discussions can contribute to the learning process and is sometimes desirable for administrative reasons in place of self-pacing. *See* **pacing, planned; self-pacing.**

pacing, machine: *see* **pacing** (2).

pacing machine: *see* **machine, pacing.**

pacing, planned: a technique of programmed instruction which calls for (*a*) *self-pacing* in the accomplishment of instructional units, where practicable, so as to allow for individual differences; (*b*) *group pacing,* where there should be an exchange of ideas, discussions, debate, or cooperative endeavor; and (*c*) responding within specific time limits if the learning situation demands speed as a requirement, such as typing, field-stripping a rifle, or answering questions in a foreign language.

pacing, self: *see* **self-pacing.**

pack: in automatic data processing, to combine two or more words or fields into one; for example, (District) 782 and (Territory) 671 into 782671.

package library: *see* **library, package.**

package, programmed instruction: *see* **instruction package, programmed.**

packet record: *see* **packet record system.**

packet record system: a collection of cards, usually fitted into a small folder, used for keeping the school's cumulative record of the most essential information pertaining to each pupil; generally employed from the first to the twelfth grade, although at times containing preschool and postschool information; contents include family information, health information, intelligence status, school history (both academic and extracurricular), and vocational goals and interests.

paddle tennis: *see* **tennis, paddle.**

paedogogus (pē′dǝ·gog′ǝs): (Lat., lit., "boy leader") the slave, unfitted by age or physical disability for other duties, who accompanied the young Athenian boy to school, carrying his lyre, cloak, etc.; this functionary had complete charge of the boy's morals and behavior and could enforce his discipline by whipping.

paedotribe (pē′dǝ·trīb): one who gave regular physical training or supervision in gymnastics to older boys in ancient Athens.

pagan school: a Roman secular school of the sixth century that taught the literature and knowledge of the earlier Greeks and Romans, in contrast to the Christian schools, which taught chiefly religion.

page: in computerized data processing, a unit in core, drum, or disk data storage devices; consists of 4,096 bytes of computerized information; number of pages in each memory unit varies; in some disk packs, for example, the capacity is over 7,000 pages.

paidology (pā·dol′ǝ·ji; pī·dol′): *alt.* **pedology.**

pain, threshold of: *see* **threshold of pain.**

painting: (1) the art of graphic expression in which objects seen or imagined are represented and in which ideas and feelings are given form by laying pigments on a surface with a brush or other implement; (2) any work of art so produced. (Pigments commonly used include water color, oil, tempera, enamel, acrylics, or other media in which a vegetable or mineral color base is impregnated with a vehicle such as water, oil, acrylic acid, or varnish.)

painting, action: *see* **action painting.**

painting, finger: *see* **finger painting.**

painting, miniature: *see* **miniature painting.**

pair: *v.* to match or equate two individuals (usually, several sets of two individuals) in terms of some appropriate factor or combination of variable factors employed in an experiment. *See* **group, parallel.**

paired-associate learning: *see* **learning, paired-associate.**

paired associates: (1) in correlation, pairs of individual cases from the two variables under consideration; (2) pairs of stimuli between which a subject must form correct associative connections in order to make correct responses.

paired comparison: (1) a method of indicating preferences in which an individual compares each member of a series in turn with each other member with respect to a given quality, indicating his preference in each pair, until the members are arranged in a graded series; (2) a method of measuring an individual's ability to discriminate between (or his preference for one of) two samples of work with respect to a given quality, as in art judgment tests.

paired-comparison rating: *see* **rating, paired-comparison.**

paired-comparisons scale: *see* **scale, paired-comparisons.**

paired observation: *see* **observation, paired.**

paired sample: *see* **sample, paired.**

paired sentence drill: *see* **drill, paired sentence.**

palace school: a school in the palace of a ruler for princes, princesses, and others connected with the court. (The most famous was Charlemagne's school taught by Alcuin, in which the ruler and the queen as well as others were taught.)

palatal: *n.* one of the sounds formed between the tongue and the palate, such as *k, g, y,* and *x.*

palate: the roof of the mouth, consisting of the forward hard part, or hard palate, and the back soft part, which is the *velum,* or soft palate.

palatogram (pal'ə·tə·gram'; pə·la'-): a recording of the contact made by the tongue on the roof of the mouth in the production of a sound, usually accomplished by placing a thin plate covered with chalk against the roof of the mouth and observing the places where the chalk is removed when the sound is spoken.

paleography: the systematic study of the remains of ancient writing on various types of material—papyrus, vellum, metals, pottery, stone, etc.; aims include decipherment of content, dating, and determination of source. *See* epigraphy.

paleontology, human: a science, based on fossil remains, which is concerned with investigating the development of the human being through past geological periods. *See* anthropology (1).

palestra (pə·les'trə): an Athenian elementary school where boys were given physical training.

palindrome (pal'in·drōm): a word that is meaningful whether read from right to left or from left to right, for example, *was* and *no.*

paliphrasia (pal'i·frā'zhi·ə): a condition characterized by frequent repetition of words or phrases in otherwise coherent speech.

palmar: pertaining to the palm of the hand.

palmar reflex: *see* reflex, palmar.

Palmer method: a method of handwriting, first presented in 1888, that stresses a script style, model letter forms, and a free-flowing muscular forearm movement.

palsy, birth: *see* birth palsy.

palsy, cerebral: *see* cerebral palsy.

pan: the motion-picture production technique of swinging the camera vertically and/or horizontally from a pivot point.

Pan-African studies: *see* studies, Pan-African.

Pan-Hellenic Council: a title given to a legislative and advisory body composed of representatives of college social sororities and of the college administration.

pancommunistic studies: *see* studies, pancommunistic.

panel: (1) a group of three to six persons having a purposeful conversation on an assigned topic with or without active participation by the audience; the panel is usually seated at a table in full view of the audience; *dist. f.* **symposium;** (2) in programmed instruction, a section of material available to the student while he is working through more than one item; the section may include texts, diagrams, maps, globes, and laboratory equipment; in a programmed textbook a panel is a single level in the horizontal format; thus, such a text may have three panels on a page—levels A, B, and C.

panel, consumer-acceptance: a group of lay persons who are asked to rate a given product in terms of their degree of liking for it.

panel, control: *see* control panel.

panel, display: *syn.* console.

panel, distribution: in a language laboratory, the control panel where all circuits terminate and from which signals are distributed to selected receivers in the booths assigned to students.

panel, immunological: a phrase, introduced by George Draper, designating as complete as possible a compilation of the disease susceptibilities and disease resistances of an individual.

panel, psychological: *see* psychological panel.

panel, reactor: a second panel group that supplements the first panel by making additional contributions to the subject under discussion and directing questions to members of the first panel before audience participation.

panel, sounding: *syn.* panel, reactor.

panic door: a type of door, used in schools and other public buildings, designed to unlock and open outward when a release bar across the door is pushed.

panic lock: a fire-exit bolt or latch on a door that releases the door and permits it to open outward when pressure is applied to the releasing device.

panning: *see* pan.

panorama: an extended picture or construction showing a continuous scene; for example, a sweeping view such as would result from *panning* in motion-picture production.

Pan's pipes: a simple wind instrument made of several hollow reeds of varying length fastened side by side and played by blowing across their open ends; can be prepared and played by young children.

pansophism (pan'sə·fiz'm): (1) the doctrine that all knowledge contains a unifying principle of wisdom; (2) the idea of Comenius (1592–1670) that there is a universal method of teaching or learning, and identified by him with the order of nature.

pantheism: the doctrine or teaching that everything in the universe partakes of the essential nature of God and has no existence apart from him; the essential immanence of God in the created universe.

pantograph: a lever-type device for enlarging or reducing diagrams to any predetermined scale by tracing the original under one point and duplicating it at the other point in suitable proportion.

pantomime test: *see* test, pantomime.

pantomimic speech: *see* speech, pantomimic.

pantophobia (pan'tə·fō'bi·ə): morbid anxiety and apprehension concerning what may happen.

papal encyclical: *see* encyclical, papal.

paper-and-crayon behavior: *see* behavior, paper-and-crayon.

paper-and-pencil test: *see* test, paper-and-pencil.

paper, construction: *see* construction paper.

paper-folding behavior: *see* behavior, paper-folding.

paper-form board: a test device composed of simple figures. *See* test, form-board; test, paper-form board.

paper-form board test: *see* test, paper-form board.

paper position: the angle at which the paper on which handwriting is being done is placed before the writer.

paper, reference: *see* reference paper.

paper tape: *see* tape, punched paper.

paperback: a type of book published in soft covers, recently widely available for elementary, junior, and senior high school students as well as for university students.

papier-mâché (pā'pər ma·shā'; pa·pyä' ma·shā'): (Fr., lit., "chewed paper") (art) (1) a light modeling material composed of shreds of wastepaper or newspaper and paste; (2) a process of making forms by building up layers over a structural framework, often used in art activities to make masks, figures, animal forms, etc.

parabolic classroom: *see* classroom, parabolic.

paracusia (par'ə·kū'si·ə): *alt. sp.* paracusis; any disorder of the sense of hearing.

paradigm (pa'rə·dīm): (1) a representation, a model of a theory, an idea, or a principle; (2) a pattern of procedure; (3) in foreign language instruction, an illustration of all the inflectional changes a word may undergo; to be used as a model for all similarly inflected words.

paradox: a statement that seems to be either self-contradictory or absurd but which in fact expresses a profound truth.

paragraph comprehension: *see* comprehension, paragraph.

paragraph meaning: the central idea of the paragraph as distinguished from the details of which the paragraph is composed.

paragraph-meaning test: *see* test, paragraph-meaning.

paragraph reading: *see* reading, paragraph.

paragraphia (par'ə·graf'i·ə): a disorder characterized by writing wrong words or letters; due to a limited lesion of the visual work center.

paralalia (par'ə·lā'li·ə): *syn.* lisping.

paralexia (par'ə·lek'si·ə): disturbance or impairment of the ability to comprehend printed or written words and sentences.

parallax: the apparent displacement of an object in relation to its background due to observation of the object from more than one point in space, such as the discrepancy between the fields defined by the viewfinder and the lens of a camera.

parallel access: *see* **access, parallel.**

parallel bars: a gymnastic apparatus having two bars or poles parallel to each other and about shoulder distance apart, adjustable as to height and distance apart.

parallel-course plan: *syn.* **parallel-curriculum plan.**

parallel-curriculum plan: an administrative plan by which the pupils of an elementary school are divided into a fast group and a slow group, the former covering the elementary school curriculum in 6 years, the latter in 8 years. *Syn.* **parallel-course plan**; *see* **Cambridge plan; Portland plan.**

parallel-form reliability: *syn.* **reliability, alternate-form.**

parallel forms: *syn.* **equivalent forms.**

parallel forms method: a method used for determining the reliability of a test by correlating the scores made on two approximately equivalent forms of the test. *See* **reliability.**

parallel group: *see* **group, parallel.**

parallel play: *see* **play, parallel.**

parallel postulate: *see* **postulate, parallel.**

parallel proportional profile: *see* **profile, parallel proportional.**

parallel track: *see* **track, parallel.**

parallel training: *see* **training, parallel.**

parallelism: the theory that bodily and mental changes are concomitant, every change in the body being accompanied by a corresponding change in mind but neither change being the cause of the other.

parallelism, psychological: *syn.* **dualism, psychophysical.**

parallelism, social and educational: harmony of the content of the educational program and current social ideals.

paralysis: partial or complete loss of ability to move voluntarily a part or member of the body normally under voluntary control.

paralysis, cerebral spastic: *see* **cerebral spastic paralysis.**

paralysis, flaccid: a disturbance of muscle function in which joint motion in the direction of contraction does not exist, the muscle is lifeless and flabby, and all attempts at direct stimulation fail.

paralysis, hysterical: apparent loss of the power to move a part of the body with no apparent defect in the motor nerve system. *See* **pseudoparalysis.**

paralysis, infantile: *syn.* **poliomyelitis.**

paralysis, organic: paralysis due to a defect either in the paralyzed organ or in the nerve supplying it.

paralysis, progressive: increasing loss of ability to move voluntarily a part or member of the body.

paralysis, spastic: one of the major diagnostic classifications of *cerebral palsy* caused by damage in the prerolandic area of the cerebral motor cortex and distinguished by the stretch reflex and by hyperirritability of the muscle(s) to normal stimuli.

paralyzed, educationally: *see* **educationally paralyzed.**

paramedical occupations: *see* **occupations, paramedical.**

parameter (pə·ram'ə·tər): (1) in general, any measure of function of a hypothetical and, perhaps, infinite population, for example, the true mean, true variance; (2) any measure of function of a real, finite population, for example, the mean test score of all 10-year-old pupils in a given school district etc.; *ant.* **statistic;** (3) (math.) in an expression, a variable to which a value is assigned which does not change while other variables in the expression take on values selected according to some particular sequence; for example, in the general form for the equation of a line, $y = mx + b$, m and b are parameters.

parameter difference: *see* **difference, parameter.**

paramnesia: distortion of memory or false recognition.

paranoia (par'ə·noi'ə): a mental disorder characterized by systematized delusions of grandeur or of persecution and in which hatred is present; one of several forms of paranoid *dementia* or *schizophrenia.*

paranoiac (par'ə·noi'ak): one who suffers from paranoia. (In the milder forms, the paranoiac may appear to be a "crank"—an erratic person or one with an impractical mission to fulfill.)

paranoid personality: *see* **personality, paranoid.**

paranoid psychosis: *see* **psychosis, paranoid.**

paraphasia (par'ə·fā'zhi·ə; -fā'zhə): a speech disorder caused by a brain lesion, characterized by mispronunciations, misuse of words, and errors of grammar and syntax.

paraphemia (par'ə·fē'mi·ə): a condition characterized by distorted speech, lisping, or other disorders of enunciation.

paraphonia (par'ə·fō'ni·ə): a condition allied to but less pronounced than *aphonia* and characterized by weakness of voice.

paraphrenia (par'ə·frē'ni·ə): (1) a mental disorder related to paranoid *dementia praecox* but with mild manifestations; (2) as used by Freud, synonymous with *dementia praecox.*

paraplegia (par'ə·plē'ji·ə): paralysis of the legs and lower part of the body. *See* **hemiplegia; monoplegia; quadriplegia; triplegia.**

parapraxis (par'ə·prak'sis): erroneous mental and emotional functioning resulting in minor errors, slips of the tongue and pen, forgetting to carry out intentions, etc.

paraprofessional: in conjunction with the instructional staff of an educational institution, an assistant from a group of technicians selected to do such parts of the teacher's work as reading and evaluating some student themes in English, science, social studies, etc., criticizing and evaluating some student work in the creative and practical arts, conferring with students on their work and reporting back to teachers on its quality, and serving as laboratory, library, and materials center assistants and supervisors; often part-time workers, men and women occupied outside the institution in other vocations as well as housewives. *Syn.* **nonprofessional, subprofessional;** *see* **aide, teacher.**

parasitology: the science dealing with animals that live on or in another larger animal, called the host, with benefit to one or both organisms involved.

parathymia (par'ə·thī'mi·ə): a somewhat loose general term designating any psychosis in which uncontrolled or poorly controlled emotions are the dominant feature.

parent: (1) an organism that has produced issue or descendants; (2) an adult legally responsible for a minor; implies blood relationship as well as legal relationship; *comp. w.* **guardian.**

parent-child fixation: *see* **fixation, parent-child.**

parent-child relations: the relationships, mutually or individually experienced, such as those of ascendance, submission, fear, hate, dependence, loyalty, ambivalence, distrust, and faith, that may exist between parent and child.

parent-child relationship: the relatively stable set of feelings which parent and child have established toward each other; the behavior of the child to the parent and the parent to the child as this behavior is modified through interaction.

parent-consent form: a form that is signed by parents giving permission to have their child enrolled in the distributive education program or in some other program.

parent-cooperative nursery: *see* **nursery school, cooperative.**

parent counseling: *see* **counseling, parent.**

parent education: a phase of adult education dealing with child care and the improvement of family living.

parent-figure: a person who represents a parent to an individual even though he may in no way have taken over that role.

parent, foster: *see* **foster parent.**

parent population: *see* **population, parent.**

parent-student-counselor conference: *see* **conference, parent-student-counselor.**

parent study group: *see* **group, parent study.**

parent study program: *see* **program, parent study.**

parent-substitute: an adult who takes on the role of a parent.

parent-surrogate: an adult who is designated to take on the role of a parent.

parent-teacher association: an organization, composed of teachers and parents of children of a school or community, the purpose of which is to improve the effectiveness of the school as a social and educational agency; may or may not be affiliated with the national and state councils of the Parent-Teacher Association (PTA) which has definite bylaws and objectives followed by all local units. *See* **home and school association** (Ed. in Canada); **parent-teacher association** (Ed. in England and Wales).

parent-teacher conference: *syn.* **conference, teacher-parent.**

parent-teacher-student conference: *see* **conference, parent-teacher-student.**

parent-volunteer: a parent who volunteers time or services in or for the school.

parent-volunteer coordinator: *see* **coordinator, parent-volunteer.**

parental authority: *see* **authority, parental.**

parental behavior: *see* **behavior, parental.**

parental consent: *see* **consent, parental.**

parental consent form, cooperative office education: *see* **consent form, cooperative office education parental.**

parental consent form, distributive education: *see* **consent form, distributive education parental.**

parental home: a unit of a school system to which minor children (usually boys) are committed by a juvenile court and where they are kept in residence and supervised for correction of delinquent tendencies. (The children may be sent to a nearby public school, or instruction may be given within the confines of the parental home.)

parental-home matron: *see* **matron, parental-home.**

parental letter: a letter written to inform the parent of the school progress of a pupil; sometimes used as a substitute for or as a supplement to the *report card.*

parental school: an institution, usually located on a farm, where socially handicapped youths are retained on a 24-hour basis and where an attempt is made to reproduce home conditions and an extensive educational program is provided, very similar in objectives to that of a *parental home.* Syn. **farm school; twenty-four-hour school.**

parental transportation: *see* **transportation, parental.**

parenthood, planned: broadly, the practice of any measures aimed at birth control, but especially within the family structure; the term is used as the abbreviated title of two organizations working in this field: the London-based International Planned Parenthood Federation, founded in 1952, and the United States-based Planned Parenthood-World Population, founded in 1921.

parents as resources: (couns.) parents serving as supportive, consultative, referral, and service agents in the guidance program; consultation, referral, and direct service by parents become especially necessary as the school counselor recognizes that changes in environmental emphasis in the home are necessary if the youngster is to effect an adequate adjustment to his self-development and self-planning.

Parents' Confidential Statement: a detailed questionnaire completed by the parents of a scholarship applicant which covers the financial condition of the family; used by the College Scholarship Service and participating schools to analyze the family's financial condition and to determine an estimate of the amount the parents could be expected to contribute toward college expenses.

parents, report to: *see* **report to parents.**

paresis (pə·rē′sis; par′ə-): a partial motor paralysis.

parish: (1) an administrative unit of a diocese under the spiritual care of a priest (who is responsible in turn to the ordinary, that is, the diocesan bishop); (2) in the state of Louisiana, a political subdivision corresponding to a county in other sections of the country or to a town in New England states.

parish school: (1) a school conducted by a local priest in a parish church during the Middle Ages in Europe, in which choirboys were taught singing and the pronunciation and sometimes the reading of Latin; the forerunner of the *parochial school;* syn. **song school;** (2) syn. **parochial school.**

parish superintendency: *see* **superintendency, parish.**

parish superintendent: *see* **superintendent, county.**

parishad: an institution of higher learning attended by the Brahmans in ancient India.

park, educational: *see* **educational park.**

parking area: a section of school or college grounds set aside for the parking of automobiles by visitors, staff, or students.

parochial school: (1) strictly, a school supported by a *parish* and serving the children of the parishioners; (2) loosely, a school conducted by some church or religious group, usually without tax support; (3) (R.C. ed.) an educational institution under the auspices of the Roman Catholic Church; may be at any level from kindergarten through secondary; usually characterized by open-admissions policy, that is, attendance open to all regardless of race, creed, or nationality; a superintendent of education, appointed by the bishop of the diocese, is chief school official of all schools in the diocese, with local pastor/-board of education responsible for educational program, staff, etc., of each school; faculty includes men and women of religious orders, lay members of the Roman Catholic Church, and also non-Catholic personnel; curriculum parallels that of the public schools where demanded by state agencies, its content and methods being local or diocesan decisions. *See* **parish school.**

parochialism: the practice of viewing issues from a narrow and provincial perspective.

parsimony, law of: *see* **law of parsimony.**

part correlation: *see* **correlation, part.**

part correlation coefficient: *syn.* **coefficient of part correlation.**

part learning: *see* **learning, part.**

part method: any teaching procedure in which activities are analyzed into parts that are practiced until skill has been acquired in the parts, these skills being finally combined into a complete activity.

part singing: *see* **singing, part.**

part song: *see* **song, part.**

part-time age-and-schooling certificate: *see* **age-and-schooling certificate, part-time.**

part-time class: (1) a type of class provided in vocational education programs permitting students to divide their time between formal education and working experience in business or industry; (2) a short-unit course, under the supervision of the local board of education and the district coordinator, given to employed workers who may leave their daily employment for brief periods of instruction during their working hours; (3) preemployment training given to persons selected for work in distributive occupations; (4) a class for distributive personnel which is taught during the normal working day on an in-store basis for one organization or in a central location for personnel of several organizations.

part-time class, agricultural: *syn.* **class, young-farmer** (1).

part-time class, cooperative: a class, organized in accordance with the provisions of the Smith-Hughes, George-Deen, or George-Barden Acts, which provides each pupil with an opportunity to work on a regular schedule of hours in a business, professional, or industrial establishment in addition to the hours he spends in school.

part-time class, discontinuous: a day or evening class organized to be operated during an entire school year and offering instruction relating to some trade or occupation to young workers who are employed in juvenile occupations and who wish to enter occupations having greater opportunities for advancement.

part-time class, intensive: a day or evening class organized to give instruction over a period of 2 to 5 months, following which students are placed at work in the trades or industries with advanced standing, frequently with a higher rate of pay than would be the case without such training.

part-time employment: *see* employment, part-time.

part-time general continuation class: *see* continuation class, part-time general.

part-time pupil: *see* pupil, part-time.

part-time school: (1) a school where pupils attend half time and are employed half time; pupils usually work in pairs and alternate in attending school and being employed; *syn.* **cooperative school;** (2) a school whose pupils are employed full time and attend school at night or at other hours of unemployment; (3) a school where pupils attend 4 to 8 hours weekly on the employer's time; *syn.* **continuation school.**

part-time school record: *see* record, part-time school.

part-time student: one not carrying a full-time load in terms of study and courses; applied to extension students, special students, and other unclassified persons who follow school or college courses by mail, in evening classes, in general or university colleges, or occasionally in a portion of the required certificate- or degree-carrying curricula.

part-time student teaching: *see* student teaching, block plan of.

part-time teacher: a teacher who devotes less than full time to instruction and to the work incidental to teaching.

part-time trade extension class: a class conducted by a public school offering part-time instruction relating to a particular trade. (To meet state and Federal standards, the students must be employed in the trade to which the instruction is related, and classes eligible for reimbursement from certain Federal vocational funds must meet for a minimum of 144 clock-hours per year.)

part-time trade-preparatory school or class: a school or class of less than college grade established on a part-time basis by a public school to give instruction to persons of 14 to 18 years of age who wish to enter a trade. (To meet state and Federal standards, classes must meet for a minimum of 144 clock-hours per year.)

part-whole correlation: *see* correlation, part-whole.

partial correlation: *see* correlation, partial.

partial correlation coefficient: *syn.* **coefficient of partial correlation.**

partial correlation ratio: *see* ratio, partial correlation.

partial-fact policy: the policy of selecting the facts to be presented to the public according to the effect desired.

partial identity: *see* identity, partial.

partial impressions, fusion of: *see* fusion of partial impressions.

partial investigation sampling: *see* sampling, partial investigation.

partial probability: *see* probability, partial.

partial regression: *see* coefficient of partial regression.

partial regression coefficient: *syn.* **coefficient of partial regression.**

partial regression equation: *see* regression equation, partial.

partial σ: *syn.* **standard error of estimate.**

partial segregation: *see* segregation, partial.

partial-sightedness: *see* partially seeing.

partial-tuition pupil: *see* pupil, partial-tuition.

partially blind: *see* partially seeing.

partially seeing: descriptive of those whose visual limitation interferes with their learning efficiency to such an extent that they require special teaching services and aids if they are to attain performance standards appropriate for normally sighted students of comparable ability but who rely on vision as a chief channel of learning and use of print as the primary mode of reading.

partially seeing class: *see* class, partially seeing.

partially sighted: *syn.* **partially seeing.**

partially sighted equipment: *see* equipment, sight-saving.

partials: *syn.* **harmonics.**

participant: (adult ed.) any person who takes part in an adult educational program designed to improve his knowledge, skills, or attitudes.

participant observation: *see* observation, participant.

participating experiences, distributive education: *see* experiences, distributive education participating.

participation: the act, on the part of a student of education, of assuming various responsibilities in the classroom as an introduction or prerequisite to actual teaching, as, for example, the collection of reference materials, the supervision of seatwork, and the correction of test papers.

participation chart: *see* chart, participation.

participation, pupil: activity on the part of the pupil that is under the guidance of the teacher and is directed toward the achievement of some skill.

participation schedule: *see* schedule, participation.

participation training: *see* training, participation.

participative administrator: *see* administrator, participative.

particular: relating to an individual entity; pertaining to the quality of individualeness, making generalizations inapplicable to solitary units of any kind, as contrasted with the common characteristics of the members of a classification because of which generalizations can be made and the units can be grouped within one class. *Ant.* **universal.**

particularistic fallacy: *see* fallacy, particularistic.

partner experiment: *see* experiment, partner.

parts of speech: in the study of traditional grammar, a classification of the words of a language in terms of function and use; for example, English is classified into eight parts of speech: noun, pronoun, verb, adverb, preposition, adjective, conjunction, and interjection; modern grammar classifies the parts of speech according to distribution.

parturition: the act of giving birth to young.

pass: *n.* one reading of input data by a computer, usually as part of a run.

pass-fail option: (1) a choice of course mark or grade open to students of some higher education institutions in certain restricted circumstances in place of more common grades of A,B,C,D, or F; (2) an option to receive a mark of pass or fail in a class typically established in response to protests against the limitations and misuse of more common marking systems.

passage, directed: in foreign-language teaching, an oral or written narrative, dialogue, or anecdote presented to the student who must then alter and restate each statement by some preassigned criterion. *See* answer, directed.

passenger load: *see* load, passenger.

passing score: *syn.* **score, cutting.**

passive exercise: *see* exercise, passive.

passive image: *see* image, passive.

passive image, activation of: *see* image, activation of passive.

passive negativism: *see* negativism (2).

passive recreation: *see* recreation, passive.

passive technique: a method used in the counseling interview, according to which the counselor listens and, if he speaks, only repeats or emphasizes what the counselee has said, thus allowing the counselee to be the active agent and to work out his own solution.

passive vocabulary: *see* vocabulary, passive.

passivity: instinctual needs requiring the reduction of initiative in the behavior of the object.

password: any combination of one to six characters used together with an *I.D. number* and often changed in order to prevent an unauthorized user of the I.D. number from gaining access to a computer.

paste-up: the combination of illustrations and lettering, each unit of which is rubber-cemented in position on paper or cardboard by a temporary method.

pastoral counseling: *see* counseling, pastoral.

pastoral psychology: *see* **psychology, pastoral.**

patch: in computer operation, a correction made to a program and usually inserted into the control sequence by unconditional transfers of control.

patch cord: connecting cable with a plug on each end for convenience in connecting two pieces of audio equipment such as a tape recorder and a record player, which are thus connected for transference of electrical impulses in order to make a recording; also, one of the wires used on *plugboards*, as on punched card machines. *Syn.* **jumper cord.**

patch test: *see* **test, patch.**

patellar reflex: *see* **reflex, patellar.**

paternal inheritance: *see* **inheritance, paternal.**

path, neural: *see* **neural path.**

pathogenic (path'ō·jen'ik): productive of or causing marked symptoms of disease.

pathography (path·og'rə·fi): an account or description of a disease.

pathological lying: *syn.* **mythomania.**

pathological type: a term used by E. O. Lewis and others as a synonym for clinical type. *See* **clinical type.**

pathology: the branch of medicine concerned with structural and functional changes caused by disease.

pathology, speech: *see* **speech pathology.**

patriarchal family: *see* **family, patriarchal.**

patrimony: (1) strictly, an estate inherited from one's father or other ancestor; (2) anything derived from one's father, ancestors, etc., for example, a craft handed down from father to son.

patrol, pupil: an organization of pupils who assist other pupils in complying with safety regulations on school buses for transported pupils, at crosswalks and intersections for those who walk, and on school grounds for all pupils.

patrology (pa·trol'ə·ji): an area of Roman Catholic religious education concerned with the study of the writings of the Fathers of the Christian church.

patron: (1) a parent or guardian of a child in a private (independent) school; (2) often used to refer to any citizen residing in a local school district, as a local school patron.

pattern, action: *see* **action pattern.**

pattern, behavior: *see* **behavior pattern.**

pattern block play: *see* **play, pattern block.**

pattern, career: *see* **career pattern.**

pattern, culture: *see* **culture pattern.**

pattern, developmental: a genetic sequence of morphological or behavioral change, for example, the *cephalocaudal* sequence, the development of *prehension*, etc. *See* **developmental sequence; genetic sequence.**

pattern discrimination: *see* **discrimination, pattern.**

pattern drill: *see* **drill, pattern.**

pattern, factor: *see* **factor pattern.**

pattern, growth: a method of presentation, usually by means of graphs or other data, of variations in growth curves for different types and groups of children.

pattern, implementation: *see* **implementation pattern.**

pattern, interest: *see* **interest pattern.**

pattern, language: a recurring arrangement of sounds, forms, words, utterances, or sentences in a language; other sounds, words, or forms that fit into the slots of a known pattern permit speakers to create infinite numbers of additional utterances. *See* **slot.**

pattern, motor: *see* **motor pattern.**

pattern of behavior: *syn.* **behavior pattern.**

pattern of supervision: *see* **supervision, pattern of.**

pattern of supervision, organizational: *see* **supervision, organizational pattern of.**

pattern, perceptual: *see* **perceptual pattern.**

pattern practice: a drill or exercise designed to give learners intensive repetition of a language item; the practice may consist of repetition of a model, or it may involve substitutions, additions, deletions, or combinations of words in the model or pattern being learned. *See* **pattern, language.**

pattern, response: *see* **response pattern.**

pattern, S-R linkage: *see* **S-R linkage pattern.**

pattern, sentence: *see* **sentence pattern.**

pattern similarity, coefficient of: *see* **coefficient of pattern similarity.**

pattern song: *syn.* **song, observation.**

pattern, sound: a combination of different sounds as they occur in words, such as similar beginnings, similar endings, rhymes, etc.

pattern, speech: *see* **speech pattern.**

pattern stage in block building: the stage of block-play development in which the child repeats a design, for example, repeating scallops or piling the same kinds of blocks together, or makes a balanced symmetrical arrangement of several blocks.

pattern, startle: *see* **startle pattern.**

pattern, stuttering: *see* **stuttering pattern.**

pattern, total: *see* **total pattern.**

patterned-string test: *see* **test, patterned-string.**

patterning of behavior: *see* **behavior, patterning of.**

patterning of growth: the tendency for growth to occur in distinctive or individual modes or patterns.

patterns of experience: constituents of experience having effects on one another.

patterns of growth: (read.) the characteristics of the growth curves of different children in graphs developed from scores made on analytical tests.

Patty Hill blocks: *see* **blocks, Patty Hill.**

pauper education: education given in lieu of public instruction to the children of the poor by the state or by charitable institutions. (The practice was largely discontinued as public schools arose.)

pauper school: *syn.* **charity school.**

pause: (read.) (1) the typical halting of the eye at a line of reading matter to bring a portion of the line into fixation for reading; (2) a stop in oral reading either for the purpose of indicating a division of thought or owing to some lack of recognition or interruption of thought.

pay-as-you-go plan: a method of financing school building programs providing either that a single tax large enough to pay for the required property shall be levied and collected during the same year in which the buildings are built and equipped or that a certain portion of the school taxes shall be put aside each year to form a building fund sufficient to pay for new sites and buildings as needed.

pay, base rate of: a rate which tends to approximate the going rate of pay in the community or the industry for people who are basically qualified for the particular class of work; frequently the starting rate of a new employee.

pay, incentive rate of: (school admin.) the percentage rate above base pay that should be earned by the average employee, who has been properly selected and trained for his work, when he meets a fair standard of performance.

pay load: pupils transported by the school bus.

pay, premium: *see* **premium pay.**

paying apprentice: *see* **apprentice, paying.**

Payne Fund Studies: a series of 12 studies of the influence of motion pictures upon children and youth made by the Committee on Educational Research of the Payne Fund; the studies were designed to secure authoritative and impersonal data that would make possible a more complete evaluation of motion pictures and their social potentialities.

payroll: a record showing payments due individual persons for personal services rendered. (While there is a wide variety of forms for such records, the following items are usually included: name of each person, classification of service, salary or wage scale, actual time and data of service, place of service, absences, deductions in pay for absence or pensions, and signature of approving officer.)

Peace Corps: an agency of the United States, established March 1, 1961, by President John F. Kennedy; now a permanent agency under the Department of State, its purpose is to enable experienced Americans to share their knowledge in education, agriculture, health, trade, technology, and community development with nations trying to build their own pools of trained manpower.

Pearson coefficient of relative variation: *see* **coefficient of relative variation, Pearson.**

Pearson product moment coefficient of correlation: *see* **coefficient of correlation, Pearson product moment.**

Pearsonian measure of asymmetry: a coefficient of skewness equal to the arithmetic mean minus the mode, divided by the standard deviation; expressed by the formula $(M - Mo)/\sigma$.

peccatophobia (pek′ə·tō·fō′bi·ə): a condition characterized by morbid anxiety about committing trifling sins or social errors.

pedagogical method: *see* **teaching technique.**

Pedagogium: a class established at Halle in Germany by August Hermann Franke (1663–1727) to prepare teachers for his and other schools; this pedagogical class was composed of the most gifted and pious of his theological students.

pedagogy: (1) the art, practice, or profession of teaching; (2) the systematized learning or instruction concerning principles and methods of teaching and of student control and guidance; largely replaced by the term *education.*

pedagogy of action: the science or procedure of teaching through purposeful activities, analyzable into the following steps, each of which involves initiation, evaluation, and choice by the child: (*a*) purposing—setting up of goals; (*b*) planning—preparing means necessary to realize the goals; (*c*) execution—performing the means; (*d*) judging—evaluating the extent of realization of the goals and the process. *See* **activism.**

pedagogy, therapeutic: correction of disabilites, particularly in the academic area, through specialized educational techniques.

pedantry: bookishness or ostentatiousness with respect to learning. (Applied to scholarship, it denotes preoccupation with minute matters of no practical significance. In the teacher, it denotes rigid insistence on formalism in instructional procedures often to the detriment of the pupil's genuine development as a person.)

pedestrian signal: a device other than a sign, using a light that flashes or otherwise changes or having moving parts, by which foot traffic is warned or is directed to take some specific action.

pediatric speech clinic: *see* **clinic, pediatric speech.**

pediatrician (pē′di·ə·trish′ən): a physician who is a child specialist.

pedology (pe·dol′ə·ji): the study of the complete child, his life, growth, ideas, and very being; places emphasis on the learner and his capacities and needs.

pedophilia (ped·ō·fil′i·ə): the desire on the part of adults for sexual relations with children.

peephole method: a procedure devised by Miles for directly observing eye movements in reading by looking through a peephole in a card while the subject reads material written or printed on the opposite side of the card.

peer acceptance: *see* **acceptance, peer.**

peer group: *see* **group, peer.**

peer relationships: *see* **relationships, peer.**

peer teaching: *see* **teaching, peer.**

pegboard: *see* **board, peg.**

pegboard test: *see* **test, pegboard.**

pellet: a small round object used in tests of development in infants and in animal experimentation. *See* **behavior, pellet-and-bottle; reinforcement, contingencies of.**

pellet-and-bottle behavior: *see* **behavior, pellet-and-bottle.**

pellet prehension: *see* **prehension, pellet.**

pen, felt-tipped lettering: *see* **lettering pen, felt-tipped.**

pencil-writing frame: a board having horizontal ridges, channels, wires, or strings to guide the pencil writing of persons unable to see. *Syn.* **pencil-writing grille.**

pencil-writing grille: *syn.* **pencil-writing frame.**

pendency: state of being undetermined or not yet decided, as, for example, the pendency of a suit at law.

penmanship: (1) the art of handwriting or of practicing writing with a pen or other instrument; (2) the style of writing used, emphasis being placed on the beauty of the product.

penmanship, shorthand: the individual's own style or manner of writing shorthand. (Ideally, the student should write compact, legible notes with minimum motion and maximum fluency.)

pension: a retirement program financed by the employer or by both employee and employer. *See* **annuity.**

pension system: *syn.* **retirement system, free.**

pension, teacher's: financial provision, whether a lump sum or a life annuity, based on the salary level and number of years of service, paid to a teacher upon retirement from the profession or from a given school system.

pension-type retirement system: *syn.* **retirement system, free.**

Pentateuch (pen′tə·tūk): the first five books of the Old Testament, namely, Genesis, Exodus, Leviticus, Numbers, and Deuteronomy, considered collectively.

pentathlon (pen·tath′lon): five athletic exercises, the basis of both the Spartan and the Athenian physical curriculum; included running, leaping, throwing the discus, casting the javelin, and wrestling.

people's college: *syn.* **evening school** (2).

people's university: *syn.* **evening school** (2).

pep rally: a student gathering, usually under the direction of cheerleaders, for the purpose of developing school spirit and encouraging teams prior to an athletic event.

per capita grant (Federal): *see* **grant, per capita (Federal).**

per capita tax: *syn.* **tax, capitation.**

per capita unit: *see* **unit, per capita.**

per pupil cost: *see* **cost, per pupil.**

per pupil cost of a building: *see* **cost of a building, per pupil.**

perceived self: *see* **self, perceived.**

percent loss of hearing: an estimate of the amount of hearing loss in a given case, obtained by averaging the loss at different frequencies.

percent of average development: *see* **development, percent of average.**

percent of error: *see* **error, percent of.**

percent of utilization: *see* **utilization, percent of.**

percentage: (1) that portion of the subject matter of arithmetic which is concerned with the development and use of the concept of *percent;* (2) that part of a number found by taking a certain rate percent of the number; for example, 15 percent of 60 is 9; the rate percent is 15, the percentage is 9.

percentage correct score: *see* **score, percentage correct.**

percentage, cumulative: the percentage of observations falling at or below any given point in a frequency distribution. *Syn.* **centile; percentile;** *contr. w.* **frequency, cumulative.**

percentage error: *see* **error, percentage.**

percentage frequency: *see* **frequency, percentage.**

percentage histogram: *see* **histogram, percentage.**

percentage in membership: *see* **percentage of age group in all schools; percentage of age group in public schools.**

percentage misfit: a rough method of measuring goodness of fit, obtained by summing the differences, irrespective of sign, between the frequencies expected and the observed frequencies and expressing this sum as a percentage of the total frequency.

percentage of absence: (pupil accounting) the average daily absence during a given reporting period divided by the average daily membership for the period, expressed as a percentage; the aggregate days absence divided by the aggregate days membership, expressed as a percentage.

percentage of age group in all schools: (pupil accounting) the number of resident pupils of a given age group, for example, 14 to 18 years of age, entered in all public and nonpublic schools divided by the total number of residents within the age group and expressed as a percentage.

percentage of age group in public schools: the number of resident pupils of a given age group, for example, 14 to 18 years of age, entered in public schools divided by the total number of residents within the age group and expressed as a percentage.

percentage of attendance: the average daily attendance during the given reporting period divided by the average daily membership for the period and expressed as a percentage; the aggregate days attendance divided by the aggregate days membership expressed as a percentage.

percentage of change in membership from previous year: (1) (for a given date) the change of membership from a given date in one year to a corresponding date the following year divided by the membership as of the first date and expressed as a percentage; (2) (for a period of time) the change of average daily membership from a given period of time in one year to a corresponding period of time the following year divided by the average daily membership during the first period of time and expressed as a percentage.

percentage of exceptional children in special classes or schools: the number of resident exceptional children entered in special classes or schools divided by the total number of resident children identified as exceptional and expressed as a percentage.

percentage of high school graduates who completed courses in various subject areas: the number of pupils in a given high school graduation group who completed courses in each of the number of specific subject areas divided by the total number of pupils in the group and expressed as a percentage.

percentage of pupils currently members of classes in various subject areas: the number of pupils in a given school group who are members of classes in each of the number of specific subject areas divided by the total number of pupils in the group and expressed as a percentage.

percentage of pupils in nonpublic schools: the number of pupils of a given age group or type of instructional organization entered in nonpublic schools divided by the total number of pupils in this age group or type of instructional organization entered in all schools and expressed as a percentage.

percentage of pupils making normal progress: the number of pupils making normal progress during a given reporting period divided by the membership at the close of the period and expressed as a percentage.

percentage of pupils not promoted: the number of pupils who, at the close of a given reporting period (usually a regular school term), are reassigned to the same grade divided by the membership at the close of the period and expressed as a percentage; pupils in ungraded classes are not considered not promoted unless (and until) they are asked to spend more than the usual amount of time in such classes; pupils not promoted are sometimes called pupils retained.

percentage of pupils participating in various activities: the number of pupils who, during a given reporting period, for example, a given regular school term, take part in each of a number of specific activities divided by the average daily membership of pupils in the group and expressed as a percentage.

percentage of pupils promoted: the number of pupils promoted during or at the close of a given reporting period (usually a regular school term) divided by the membership at the close of the period and expressed as a percentage; for reporting purposes, pupils in ungraded classes who have made satisfactory progress may be considered separately, or they may be considered promoted.

percentage of pupils transported at public expense: the average daily membership of pupils transported at public expense divided by the average daily membership of the reporting unit and expressed as a percentage.

percentage of pupils withdrawing: (by type of withdrawal) the number of pupils withdrawing from school during a given regular school term in each of the four principal categories of withdrawal (for example, transfer, completion of schoolwork, dropout, and death) divided by the total number of pupils withdrawing and expressed as a percentage.

percentage of school-age population in public (or nonpublic) elementary and secondary schools: number of resident pupils of compulsory school-attendance age entered in public (or nonpublic) elementary and secondary schools divided by the total number of residents of compulsory school-attendance age and expressed as a percentage.

percentage of total excess public school membership: total excess membership in public schools divided by the normal pupil capacity of accessible publicly owned school plants in use and expressed as a percentage.

percentage of total membership being provided appropriate special education: the number of pupils who have been identified as exceptional by professionally qualified personnel, and who are being provided appropriate special education, divided by the total membership and expressed as a percentage; these pupils may be considered also in small groups according to type of exceptionality, blind, deaf, mentally retarded, etc.

percentage of transported pupils riding a given distance: the average daily membership of pupils who ride a given distance (for example, 5, 10, 15, and 20 miles) divided by the average daily membership of pupils transported and expressed as a percentage; may be determined as of a given date or on the basis of averages for a given reporting period.

percentage of transported pupils riding a given time: the average daily membership of pupils who ride a given time (for example, 30 minutes, 1, 1½, or 2 hours) divided by the average daily membership of pupils transported and expressed as a percentage; may be determined as of a given date or on the basis of averages for a given reporting period.

percentage pie diagram: *syn.* **graph, circle.**

percentage, standard error of: *see* **standard error of percentage.**

percentage weight: *syn.* **frequency, percentage.**

percentile: (1) one of the 99 point scores that divide a ranked distribution into groups or parts, each of which contains 1/100 of the scores or persons; the points are located to coincide with the obtained score below which in each division 1/100 of the cases fall; (2) (for example, P_1, P_{10}, P_{37}, P_{90}) a point on a scale of test scores or other measures below which a given percentage of the measures fall and above which the complementary proportion of measures fall; designated by the percentages of cases lying below it; thus, 37 percent of the measures fall below P_{37} (the thirty-seventh percentile) and 63 percent above it. *Syn.* **centile;** *dist. f.* **grade, centesimal; interval, centile; rank, centile.**

percentile-age norms: *see* **norms, percentile-age.**

percentile band: (meas.) the range of score values within which the theoretical true value of an actual score is likely to fall; usually defined by plus and minus one standard error of measurement on both sides of the obtained score.

percentile curve: *see* **curve, percentile.**

percentile-grade norms: *see* **norms, percentile-grade.**

percentile graph: *syn.* **curve, percentile.**

percentile interval: *syn.* **interval, centile.**

percentile norm: *see* **norm, percentile.**

percentile range: *see* **range, percentile.**

percentile rank: *see* **rank, percentile.**

percentile score: *see* **score, percentile.**

percentile, standard error of: *see* **standard error of percentile.**

perception: (1) in its most limited sense, awareness of external objects, conditions, relationships, etc., as a result of sensory stimulation; (2) a continuous process of integration of present and past sensory impressions; (3) more broadly, awareness of whatever sort, however brought about.

perception, auditory: the ability to hear sounds; in reading, the ability to hear the vowels and consonants in words that differentiate one word from another.

perception deafness: *see* **deafness, perception.**

perception, depth: the ability to perceive the solidity of objects and their relative position in space. *See* **vision, stereoscopic.**

perception, development of: the establishing, through maturation and learning, of a knowledge of objects and of spatial, temporal, and social relations.

perception, haptic: *see* **haptic type.**

perception, kinesthetic: (read.) identification and recognition of a word through tracing or writing, involving the sense of touch and the motor accompaniments of writing. *See* **kinesthesia.**

perception, light: visual awareness of light.

perception, object: the ability to perceive obstacles without the use of sight and to judge accurately their distance; also called *facial vision, obstacle perception,* or *obstacle sense.* (It was found that audition is the necessary and sufficient condition for object perception, that pitch is the auditory dimension involved in the perception, and finally that high audible frequencies of approximately 10,000 H2 and above are necessary stimulus conditions.)

perception, obstacle: *syn.* **perception, object.**

perception, selective: a mode of response in which the observer's set or purpose and background of experience become the major determiners of the stimuli to which he responds. *See* **apperception; attention.**

perception, space: the apprehension of objects as they actually exist or as they appear in the perspective of the printed page.

perception span: *syn.* **perceptual span.**

perception, tactile: the capacity of the organism to gain information from cutaneous contact through active or passive touching; also called *tactile awareness.*

perception time, total: the total time used in fixation of the eyes in reading as computed from an ophthalmograph record; the total duration of the fixations of the eyes in reading a unit of reading matter.

perception, types of aesthetic: *see* **aesthetic perception, types of.**

perception, visual: recognition through visual clues of the orientation of figures in space, for example, the distinction between right- and left-sided right-angle triangles, between a foreground figure and a confusing background, etc.

perception, visual-auditory: (read.) the perception of a word through the use of both visual and auditory clues occurring simultaneously.

perception, word: (1) the act of seeing or perceiving words, as contrasted with perception of other objects in nature; (2) the seeing and identifying of words as wholes, as contrasted with letter perception or the perception of parts of words or small word groups.

perceptive hearing loss: *see* **hearing loss, perceptive.**

perceptive impairment: degeneration of the sensory structure located in the inner ear.

perceptual cue: *see* **cue, perceptual.**

perceptual development: *see* **development, perceptual.**

perceptual discrimination: *see* **discrimination, perceptual.**

perceptual disturbance: *see* **disturbance, perceptual.**

perceptual equipment: *see* **equipment, perceptual.**

perceptual growth: *see* **growth, perceptual.**

perceptual learning: *see* **learning, perceptual.**

perceptual-motor behavior: *see* **behavior, perceptual-motor.**

perceptual-motor coordination: *see* **coordination, perceptual-motor.**

perceptual pattern: a concept emphasizing the effect on sensory perception that one aspect of externality has on another.

perceptual span: (1) the horizontal extent of interpretation with the eye (monocular) or eyes (binocular) fixed on one point; (2) the number of words, figures, or other items that can be interpreted in a single fixation. *Syn.* **perception span; span of recognition; visual span.**

perceptual span, absolute: the maximum number of words (or letters) that the individual can perceive during a very short exposure of the tachistoscope or fall chronometer; exceeds the actual span used in reading.

perceptual span, relative: the number of words or letters that are seen during each pause or fixation as one reads, which constitutes the span actually used in ordinary reading; sometimes less than half the *absolute perceptual span.*

perceptual speed: *see* **speed, perceptual.**

perceptually disabled child: *see* **child, perceptually disabled.**

perceptually handicapped child: *syn.* **child, brain-injured.**

perceptually impaired child: *syn.* **child, brain-injured.**

percussion: *see* **instruments, percussion.**

percussion band: *syn.* **rhythm band.**

percussion instruments: *see* **instruments, percussion.**

percussion orchestra: *syn.* **rhythm band.**

perennialism: in twentieth-century educational philosophy, the theory that the structure of the universe implies a body of truth and knowledge that is not subject to the erosion of cultural evolution; truth and knowledge so conceived are permanent and universal and therefore should constitute the essence of education; vocational and professional studies in this view are necessarily predicated upon a prior mastery of the permanent, liberal studies; Robert Maynard Hutchins is the most eminent exponent of this position; although not identical with Roman Catholic educational philosophy, there is a large area of overlap.

Peretz Shule (per'ets shoo'lə): *n. fem; pl. . . .* **Shulen;** the name given to the *Arbeiter Ring Shulen* in 1951 in honor of the hundredth anniversary of the birth of the Yiddish and Hebrew writer Isaac Leib Peretz. *See* **Arbeiter Ring Shule.**

perfect correlation: *see* **correlation, perfect.**

perfect pitch: *syn.* **pitch, absolute.**

perfectionism: a psychological defense mechanism by means of which the individual hopes to escape blame or criticism through doing every thing "perfectly."

performance: actual accomplishment as distinguished from potential ability.

performance audit: *see* **audit, performance.**

performance budget: *see* **budget, performance.**

performance contracting: *see* **contracting, performance.**

performance, counselor: *see* **counselor performance.**

performance criteria: *see* **contracting, performance.**

performance, intellectual: (1) an action in which excellence or superiority depends primarily on abstract mental ability; (2) any action requiring the manipulation of abstract concepts or mental manipulation of any sort; (3) the display of intellect or the use of the higher thought processes such as memory, perception of meanings, or reasoning; (4) a response in which truth or the right answer is arrived at through covert behavior.

performance levels: the stages of performance that the average or typical child attains at successive age levels.

performance, motor: *see* **motor performance.**

performance rating: *see* **rating, performance.**

performance scale: *see* **test, performance.**

performance scale, Leiter international: *see* **scale, Leiter international performance.**

performance test: *see* **test, performance.**

performer's certificate: *see* **certificate, performer's.**

perimacular vision: *syn.* **vision, peripheral (2).**

perimeter wiring: a broadcast antenna installed around the walls of a classroom which is used as a limited-range broadcast laboratory.

period, accounting: *see* **accounting period.**

period, activity: a unit of time in the daily schedule, occurring on one or more days of the week, in which no classes are scheduled, the time being devoted to various nonclass activities, sometimes including home-room meetings and assemblies.

period, browsing: *see* **period, free-reading.**

period, budget: *see* **budget period.**

period, circumpuberal: the period near or about the time when the reproductive organs mature sufficiently to become capable of procreation.

period, class: (1) a portion of a school day set aside for a designated teaching activity; (2) the time assigned to a class for a particular division of work, whether recitation or preparation.

period, conference: (1) a class period devoted to discussion of study problems on the part of the teacher and pupils as a means of bringing about better personal and educational understanding; (2) a period during which students, as individuals or groups, may have the undivided attention of the teacher for discussion of pertinent problems.

period, conversation: a period giving children an opportunity for free exchange of ideas and for extending and refining their language habits; characterized by freedom and spontaneity in speaking, genuine motives for speaking, and provision for audience situations.

period, detention: (1) the time during which a child has been retained in a detention home prior to a court hearing; (2) the school period during which pupils attend detention hall or detention room for disciplinary purposes or remedial assistance or to make up work lost by absence.

period, developmental: an age characterized by distinctive structural or functional emergents, such as prenatal period, period of the neonate, period of adolescence, etc.

period, developmental reading: a period of reading instruction in which direct attention is given to teaching or developing some ability or skill in order to increase achievement in reading; a basal reading instruction period.

period, directed-study: a period of the day set aside for study under the direction of the teacher or with the use of study guides.

period, discussion: (1) a period following individualized study in which the problems or topic studied are discussed; (2) (kind.-prim. ed.) a short session before, during, or after an activity to provide an opportunity for pupils to tell what they have been doing in block play, construction, or other activities, to seek suggestions from the group for improvement, and at the same time to explain their plans for carrying out "next steps."

period, double: a period of twice the standard length for the school, for example, 90, 100, or 110 minutes, employed principally for laboratory or shop instruction.

period, evaluation: a short session, either during the progress or after the completion of an activity, that provides an opportunity for the individual pupil or the group to appraise the adequacy of accomplishment in terms of the outcomes desired.

period, eye-rest: a school session or interval in class routine devoted to activities other than those requiring close eye use.

period, fiscal: *see* **fiscal period.**

period, free: an obsolescent term designating the time in a regular school day during which a teacher or a pupil has no definitely assigned duties.

period, free-reading: a class period when voluntary reading is allowed in a classroom or in a school library; sometimes called *browsing period.*

period, independent work: a period planned for primary children while the teacher is busy helping another part of the class; provides opportunity for the child to become dependable, to develop desirable social habits in a natural social situation, to exercise self-control, to develop initiative and creative ability, to follow his interests and creative abilities, to broaden his interests, and to practice skills.

period, lesson: (1) a definite portion of time in the day given to the instruction or study of a particular subject or to the practice of a specific skill that is to be mastered; (2)

a period for group instruction as a scheduled part of a school program; in this sense, synonymous with *class period.*

period, library: a time set aside in the daily or weekly program in which pupils have the opportunity to engage in free reading in a library, to browse among the books and periodicals, and to be taught the techniques of using a library; also called *library hour.*

period of decision: *see* **developmental stage, period-of-decision.**

period of reasoning: *see* **developmental stage, pseudorealistic.**

period, planning: a part of the school day used by teacher and pupils in planning future work or new undertakings.

period, practice: the time spent in familiarizing a subject or subjects with an experimental procedure, the results of which do not form a part of the data to be interpreted.

period, preparation and conference: a period in the school day that the teacher can spend away from children in preparing, planning, gathering instructional supplies, and conferences with colleagues and parents.

period, promotion: *see* **promotion period.**

period, recitation: (1) in general, a period of time scheduled for a class meeting; (2) in conventional schools, a period characterized by a formal procedure of the question-answer type during which information learned from reading is recalled.

period, release: that part of the school day during which public school children are permitted to attend religious instruction classes conducted under the auspices of their particular denomination.

period, reporting: the period of time for which a report is prepared as, for example, the school year, regular school term, semester, or marking period.

period, rest: a time during the school day set aside or given to a teacher or pupil for rest or relaxation.

period, "show and tell": *syn.* **sharing time.**

period, study: an interval of time on the regular daily program set aside for study.

period, teaching: *syn.* **period, class.**

period, training: days or weeks devoted to instruction and preparation of players expecting to enter athletic contests.

period, unassigned: a part of the school day not devoted to a given subject during which the student may pursue work of his own choosing.

period utilization: *see* **utilization, period.**

period, work: a period in which children, through their own planning, executing, and judging, seek to satisfy needs by engaging in some form of activity—construction, painting, modeling, creative verbalization or writing, problem solving, special training, etc.—the object being to accomplish work planned by themselves under teacher guidance.

periodic rating: *see* **rating, periodic.**

periodic report: *see* **report, periodic.**

periodic review: *see* **review, periodic.**

periodical: a publication issued at regular or irregular intervals, each issue normally being numbered consecutively; distinguished from other serials in that the process of publication is continuous with no predetermined termination. *See* **serial.**

periodical index: *see* **index, periodical.**

Peripatetic School (per'i•pə•tet'ik): (from the Greek *peripatein*, "to walk about") a name given to the school conducted by Aristotle because he paced back and forth, followed by his auditors, in the walks of the Lyceum.

peripatologist: *syn.* **specialist, orientation and mobility.**

peripatology: the art and science of aiding a blind or severely visually impaired individual to make full use of his remaining senses and to use those aids, methods, services, and skills which enable him to move about with confidence, safety, and purpose.

peripheral deafness: *see* **deafness, peripheral.**

peripheral field of vision: *see* field of vision, peripheral.

peripheral nerves: a general term for both the sensory and the motor nerves, which, respectively, connect the receptor organs (eyes, ears, etc.) and the effector organs (hands, limbs, etc.) with the spinal cord or brain.

peripheral speech mechanism: all structures involved in the production of speech except the brain and the spinal cord; principal divisions are the breathing mechanism (lungs, trachea, respiratory muscles), the mechanism of phonation (the larynx with its accessory muscles), the articulatory mechanism (jaw, tongue, lips, hard and soft palate), and the resonators (pharynx, oral and nasal cavities).

peripheral vision: *see* vision, peripheral.

Perkins Act: *see* Vocational Education Act of 1963.

permanent age record: *see* record, permanent age.

permanent census file: *syn.* census file, dead.

permanent certificate: *see* certificate, permanent.

permanent cumulative record: *syn.* cumulative record.

permanent disability: *see* disability, permanent.

permanent fund: *see* fund, permanent.

permanent grade record: *see* record, permanent grade.

permanent license: *syn.* certificate, permanent.

permanent mounting: *see* mounting, permanent.

permanent professor: *see* professor, permanent.

permanent record card: *see* record card, permanent.

permanent record system: *see* record system, permanent.

permanent salary schedule: *see* salary schedule, permanent.

permanent school census card: *see* census card, permanent school.

permanent school census record: *see* census record, permanent school.

permanent substitute: *see* substitute, permanent.

permanent teacher: a teacher who, by virtue of certification and tenure, is entitled to continue in his position until retirement or removal from his position for due cause.

permanent tenure: *syn.* tenure, indefinite.

permanent withdrawal notice: (1) an administrative form used by a school or school system to notify those concerned that a pupil has been legally withdrawn from a particular school (the withdrawal is permanent in that the present intent is that he will not return to this school); (2) an administrative form used to signify that a pupil is not only withdrawing permanently from a particular school but that he is withdrawing permanently from school.

permissive: giving freedom to act without interference or censure.

permissive atmosphere: *see* atmosphere, permissive.

permissive counseling: *see* counseling, permissive.

permissive discussion: *see* discussion, permissive.

permissive leadership: *see* leadership, permissive.

permissive legislation: (1) historically, the legal permission for a particular district or municipality to do certain things not generally granted to all districts of a state (in the field of education this legislation usually granted the right to certain cities, often as a result of petitions, to establish public schools and to tax the public for their maintenance); (2) a grant of power to enable but not to compel any school district to do certain things. *See* permissive powers of school board.

permissive powers of school board: those responsibilities or powers that the school board is authorized by constitutional, statutory, or state administrative provision to exercise or engage in if it judges it desirable to do so, for example, the power of the school board in some states to establish kindergartens or junior colleges. *Dist. f.* board functions, mandatory.

permissiveness: the condition of interpersonal relationships within situational limits that permits freedom of expression to another person because of respect for his uniqueness and personal needs.

permit, employment: *see* employment permit.

permutation: any one of the possible arrangements of a given number of objects taking a stated number of the objects at a time; for example, there are six permutations of the items *a*, *b*, and *c* taken three at a time: *abc, acb, bac, bca, cab,* and *cba. Dist. f.* combination.

permutation index: *syn.* index, key-word-in-context.

permuted index: *syn.* index, key-word-in-context.

pernicious disorder: *see* disorder, classroom.

perpetual debt: *see* debt, perpetual.

perpetual inventory: *see* inventory, perpetual.

perpetual tournament ladder: *syn.* challenge tournament.

Perry movement: the name given to a philosophy of the teaching of mathematics, fostered by John Perry of England and E. H. Moore in America, which was concerned with a departure from the sequential pattern of courses and a correlation of mathematical subject matter in which attention to the experimental and intuitional aspects was emphasized as well as the applications of mathematics; a forerunner of the *general mathematics* curriculum.

perseity (pər·sē'i·ti): (from the Latin *per se*, lit., "through itself") the conception of self-included existence; intrinsically in, by, or of itself; according to C. S. Peirce, in one sense *per se* refers to the essence of anything, as "John is per se John"; in another sense, it refers to whatever is involved in the definition of anything, as "John is per se an animal," that is, that he is an animal is implied in the word *John*.

perseveration: (1) the phenomenon of persistence of sensation, as in the case of color sensation after the withdrawal of the color stimulus; (2) the tendency of an idea, sensation, feeling, emotion, or pattern of behavior to recur or to continue, once begun, and run a temporal course; (3) the abnormal tendency of the individual to continue an activity after the removal of the stimulus or after it is appropriate to go on to a new task.

persistence, academic: a measure, usually in school years, of the extent to which students continue their residence in college; usually employed in conjunction with measures of general scholastic aptitude.

persistence in school: the continuance on the roll of pupils who have once been enrolled. (A measure of persistence is the ratio between all those who enroll in grade 1 for a given year and those of this group who are retained in successive years thereafter.)

persistence of vision: a time-lag effect between visual stimulation of the eye and cessation of response to that stimulation; with the average screen illumination used in motion pictures, the critical frequency above which the average eye can detect no sensation of flicker is approximately 16 intermissions of illumination per second, and rates above this frequency appear to be continuous.

persistence test: *see* test, persistence.

persistent error: *syn.* error, constant.

persisting life situations: *see* life situations, persisting.

person, resource: *see* resource person.

personal-adjustment counselor: *syn.* counselor, personal.

personal adviser: *syn.* counselor, personal.

personal appraisal: *see* appraisal, personal.

personal audit: *see* audit, personal.

personal counselor: *see* counselor, personal.

personal culture: *see* culture, personal.

personal data sheet: *see* data sheet, personal.

personal economics: *syn.* economics, consumer.

personal guidance: *see* guidance, personal.

personal-history blank: a record form on which can be maintained a cumulative record of individual history—background, growth, behavior, etc.—over a period of some years, most frequently the elementary school and secondary school years.

personal history questionnaire: *see* questionnaire, personal history.

personal hygiene: *see* hygiene, personal.

personal idealism: *see* **idealism, personal.**

personal identity: *see* **identity, personal.**

personal interview: *syn.* **interview, individual.**

personal liability: *see* **liability, personal.**

personal memory: *see* **memory, personal.**

personal motivation: *see* **motivation, personal.**

personal-problems-of-living curriculum: *see* **curriculum, personal-problems-of-living.**

personal profile: *see* **profile, personal.**

personal property: *see* **property, personal.**

personal property, intangible: *see* **property, intangible personal.**

personal property, tangible: *see* **property, tangible personal.**

personal regimen: a phase of home economics in which pupils study and put into practice procedures pertaining to personal development, especially in its relation to home living and other social contacts.

personal service record: *see* **record, personal service.**

personal-social information: *see* **information, social.**

personal theme: *see* **theme, personal.**

personal-use bookkeeping: *see* **bookkeeping, personal-use.**

personal-use typewriting: *see* **typewriting, personal-use.**

personalism: *syn.* **idealism, personal.**

personality: the total psychological and social reactions of an individual; the synthesis of his subjective, emotional, and mental life, his behavior, and his reactions to the environment; the unique or individual traits of a person are connoted to a lesser degree by *personality* than by the term *character.*

personality adjustment: *see* **adjustment, personality.**

personality age: *see* **age, personality.**

personality, anal: *syn.* **character, anal.**

personality, authoritarian: a personality type postulated by psychologists to describe the individual who is rigid, antidemocratic in his verbal attitudes, and primitive and rejecting in his reaction to reference groups unlike his own.

personality, autistic (â·tis'tik): a type of personality characterized by social withdrawal and by the tendency to live in a thought world whose form is largely a function of the individual's desires rather than of any realistic appreciation of the conditions actually obtaining in the world.

personality, compulsive: a personality type characterized by strong urges to do, say, or think in rigidly prescribed ways, without a feeling of personal freedom of choice.

personality counseling: *see* **counseling, personality.**

personality defect: a deficiency in the individual's capacity to conform to an expected level or pattern of total behavior.

personality development: *see* **development, personality.**

personality, dimension of: *see* **dimension of personality.**

personality disturbance: any disorder in the organization of traits, needs, or habits making for maladjustment.

personality, dual: a mental disorder characterized by disturbed consciousness in which the individual leads two lives alternately, each phase being consecutive but neither personality being fully aware of the experiences of the other.

personality handicap: *see* **handicap, personality.**

personality, integrated: an active, adapting personality, characterized by unity of action, in which the responses of the various parts have meaning only in terms of their relation to the functioning of the whole; that is, a personality in which all the tensions and forces that play a part in human life work together in harmony with the purposes, desires, and needs of the individual concerned.

personality, integration of: *see* **integration of personality.**

personality inventory: *see* **inventory, personality.**

personality maladjustment: *see* **maladjustment, personality.**

personality measurement: *see* **measurement, personality.**

personality, neurotic: *syn.* **neurotic character.**

personality, paranoid (par'ə·noid): an abnormal psychic condition in which two or more relatively distinct sets of experiences, such as emotions, ideas, and habits, reveal themselves in the same individual, especially when under hypnotic influence or other abnormal conditions.

personality, psychopathic: a diagnostic term used variously by different psychiatrists; designates special types of abnormal personality, with or without definite psychosis, characterized predominantly by a profound disregard of social institutions and/or morals and a marked incapacity to restrain antisocial impulses, though intellectually there is normal awareness of the laws and mores and of the consequences of their violation.

personality questionnaire: *syn.* **inventory, personality.**

personality rating scale: *see* **rating scale, personality.**

personality, schizoid: the kind of personality ascribed to individuals whose attitudes and behavior are characterized by introversion and seclusiveness.

personality structure: the relatively permanent organization of behavioral traits which serve as the basis for regularities in behavior in a given individual.

personality structure, basic: according to Kardiner's theory, basic attitudes and values which are fundamentally the same in personality types produced by various cultures.

personality study: *see* **study, personality.**

personality test: *see* **test, personality.**

personality test, multiphasic: *see* **test, multiphasic personality.**

personality type: a construct according to which individuals with a certain outstanding trait or cluster of traits are considered as belonging together for descriptive purposes, for example, *introvert, extrovert.*

personalized reading: *see* **reading, personalized.**

personalizing of the curriculum: *see* **curriculum, personalizing of the.**

personification of color: *see* **color, personification of.**

personnel: individuals connected with a particular institution considered collectively, whether employees or students.

personnel administration: *see* **administration, personnel.**

personnel and placement bureau, director of: *syn.* **director of guidance.**

personnel, auxiliary: assistants to members of the school staff, including such persons as *teacher aides* and *paraprofessionals;* may perform a variety of helpful services to assist the professional teacher with clerical duties, such as preparing report cards, mimeographing, processing library books, etc., with housekeeping, such as cleanup after art classes and preparation of displays, with supervision of halls, lunchroom, and playground, with audiovisual equipment, and with community relations.

personnel, certificated: all school personnel, instructional or noninstructional, whose employment requires certification or licensing by the appropriate (usually state) governing agency. *See* **certificate, administrative; certificate, teacher's.**

personnel classification: *see* **classification, personnel.**

personnel classification and selection: *see* **classification and selection, personnel.**

personnel department: *see* **department, personnel.**

personnel, director of: *see* **director of personnel.**

personnel, education: the administrative and supervisory officials and teachers employed in a school system in order to carry on the educational program.

personnel, employee: persons who assist in the operation of an institution, for example—in the case of an educational institution—administrators, teachers, clerks, custodians, janitors, maintenance men, elevator operators, matrons, and any others who may be employed in or by the institution.

personnel, guidance: the body of persons, taken collectively, which has as its primary function the provision of guidance services.

personnel, instructional: all the teachers of a school, school system, college, or other educational institution. *See* **faculty.**

personnel management: *syn.* **administration, personnel.**

personnel, nonprofessional: *see* **paraprofessional.**

personnel, nonteaching: employees of a school system who have no duties pertaining to instruction.

personnel organization: (1) in industry, the organization of all workers for most effective production; (2) as applied to industrial arts education, the organization of pupils within the shop or laboratory in such a manner as to ensure maximum educational returns, often with a student superintendent (or equivalent), assistant superintendent, foreman, and student workers.

personnel, paraprofessional: *see* **paraprofessional.**

personnel, public health: individuals who provide health services to the public.

personnel, pupil: all children who are enrolled in or who are members of a school.

personnel record: (1) the record of a student or pupil systematically kept by the guidance officer; *see* **case record; cumulative record;** (2) a set of records containing data relative to all the employees of a school system or educational institution and including such items as background, experience, and progress of each person, position held, remuneration, and occupational success.

personnel record, cumulative: a continuous record, kept up to date, of the student's scholastic progress, personal characteristics and experiences, family background, aptitudes, and interests.

personnel, school: *syn.* **personnel, education.**

personnel selection: *see* **selection, personnel.**

personnel service: (1) organized programs of assistance, advice, or the provision of certain materials to personnel employed by a school system; (2) organized programs of assistance to students in the solution of personal problems; includes counseling, testing, health programs, etc.

personnel study: *see* **study, personnel.**

personnel, subprofessional: *see* **paraprofessional.**

personnel, supervisory: all school personnel officially assigned to assume responsibilities for any of the tasks of supervision; such personnel often include principals, supervisors, department chairmen, consultants, directors, and other persons with various supervisory titles.

personnel, training, and related occupations training: *see* **training, personnel, training, and related occupations.**

personnel work, student-: *see* **student-personnel work.**

personnel worker: (couns.) *see* **pupil-personnel worker.**

perspective: (1) the apparent relation between objects, as to position and distance, as seen from any given viewpoint; (2) the art or science of depicting this relation on a flat surface; (3) the capacity to view things in their spatial and distal relations.

perspective, aerial: the art or science concerned with the expression of distance in two-dimensional pictures by means of gradations of light, color, distinctness, etc.

perspective drawing: *see* **drawing, perspective.**

perspective of value: *see* **space, haptic.**

persuasion, community of: an uncoerced holding of belief, feeling, purpose, and direction in common; a communion of means and ends; democratic cooperation; consensus; opposed to physical compulsion, compromise, exploitation, and excommunication. *See* **consensus.**

persuasive leadership: *see* **leadership, persuasive.**

persuasive value: *see* **value, persuasive.**

PERT: an acronym signifying Program, Evaluation, and Review Technique; a set of principles, methods, and techniques for planning programs in relation to objectives, interrelating and controlling variables of time and resources, scheduling events and activities, and replanning research or developmental programs; a PERT diagram is used to show in network form the sequences and interrelationships of the events and activities from the beginning of a project to the end.

perversion: (1) a turning about or reversal of an impulse or function; (2) (psychiatry) usually, sexual practices that tend to deviate from the usual or normal.

perversity, innate: a turning from the truth or right, a tendency that has existed in one from birth, the idea being accepted that we are born with this fault.

Pestalozzian method: *see* **Pestalozzianism.**

Pestalozzianism (pes'tə·lot'si·ən·iz'm): a system of educational doctrines and practices developed by the Swiss educator Johann Heinrich Pestalozzi (1746-1827) and his followers, conceiving of education as continuous development of the mind through exercises graded from sense impressions gained from object lessons to the apprehension and application of abstract ideas, this development being attended by a progressive, harmonious functioning of the mind in all its capacities of action or expression. (For purposes of instruction, study material in any particular field was analyzed into its simplest elements, mastery of which was to be accompanied by synthesis. Discipline was characterized by sympathy and kindness.)

petit mal (pe'ti mal): (Fr., lit., "small sickness") a transient clouding of consciousness in epilepsy, lasting 5 to 30 seconds, with or without minor movements of head, eyes, and extremities and loss of muscular control. *See* **epilepsy; grand mal.**

Petites Ecoles (pə·tēt'zä·kal'): (Fr., lit., "little schools") *see* **Little Schools of the Port-royalists.**

petition: (legal) written application or prayer to the court for the redress of a wrong or the grant of a privilege or license.

Petty school: a type of school, named for its advocate, the Englishman Sir William Petty (1623-1687), that admitted all children, the poor gratuitously; pupils were taught how to earn something toward their living as well as to read and write. (In America the *dame school* was sometimes called a Petty school.)

phallic phase: that stage of sexual development in which the penis or clitoris is the zone of maximal sensory pleasure but in which tender objects—love and the pleasure of another—are not essential for maximal gratification.

phallic primary: (psychoan.) preoccupation with the penis in the period of transition from infantile sexuality, that is, preoccupation with the erotic stimulations deriving from the penis as well as with the questions of the causes concerning its absence (in females) and the possibility of its loss.

phantasy: *see* **fantasy.**

pharynx (far'ingks): the passage between the larynx and the oral and nasal cavities; at the upper end it is continuous with the oral and nasal cavities and at the lower end with the larynx and esophagus.

phase: (1) a stage of growth; (2) a subdivision of an area of subject matter, such as physical care of children; (3) *see* **nongraded school.**

phase, mathematical: (arith.) experiences in arithmetic provided for the purpose of helping the pupil understand the internal structure of arithmetic and develop the ability to perform various number operations skillfully and with understanding; considered to be one of the aspects that is included in the *meaningful approach* to the teaching of arithmetic.

phase sequence: *see* **sequence, phase.**

phase, social: (arith.) those experiences in arithmetic provided for the purpose of helping the pupil develop the ability to apply quantitative procedures effectively in social situations in life outside the school; considered to be one of the aspects that is included in the *meaningful approach* to the teaching of arithmetic.

phasic contraction: *see* **contraction, phasic.**

phenomena, qualitative: (art) the characteristics of objects in the natural environment or life situations in which one perceives or apprehends them as they are presented; the subtleties of colors, sounds, shapes, or movement, etc., as they provide aesthetic pleasure without being identified by concepts of artistic value or judgment.

phenomenal field: *see* **field, phenomenological.**

phenomenal self: *see* **self, phenomenal.**

phenomenalism: the doctrine that phenomena are the only sources of knowledge, the only realities. *See* **positivism.**

phenomenological: pertaining to a point of view in studying the learning process which seeks to identify the ways in which pupils themselves perceive the teaching-learning situation.

phenomenological field: *see* **field, phenomenological.**

phenomenology: a theoretical point of view that advocates the study of phenomena or direct experience taken naïvely or at face value; the view that behavior is determined by the phenomena of experience rather than by external, objective, physically described reality.

phenomenon: (1) a fact, occurrence, or circumstance that is open to observation; (2) (philos.) an immediate object of awareness in experience; Kant distinguishes between phenomena, things as we see them, and noumena, things as we apprehend them by pure reason, as they really are. (Comte founded positivism on the acceptance of phenomena, positive facts, and the rejection of speculation about their causes and origins.) *Ant.* **noumenon.**

phenotype (fē′nō·tīp): the appearance or total manifest attributes of an individual as produced and modified by the environment or external life situation. *See* **constitution;** *contr. w.* **genotype.**

phenylketonuria (PKU): a congenital faulty metabolism of phenylalanine because of which phenylpyruvic acid appears in the urine; ascertainable in the newborn; often associated with mental defects; also called *phenylpyruvic amentia* or *phenylpyruvic oligophrenia.*

phi coefficient: *see* **coefficient, phi.**

phi coefficient, standard error of: *see* **standard error of phi coefficient.**

philanthropic board: (1) strictly, the group of trustees of a philanthropic corporation; (2) a colloquial synonym for *philanthropic foundation;* (probably derived from the titles of two early and widely known philanthropic foundations, the Southern Education Board and the General Education Board); *see* **foundation, philanthropic.**

philanthropic charter: *see* **charter, philanthropic.**

philanthropic education: a term used to designate the various charitable efforts in England during the eighteenth and early nineteenth centuries to provide the rudiments of education for the children of the poor through charity schools, Sunday schools, schools of industry, etc.

philanthropic foundation: *see* **foundation, philanthropic.**

philanthropic founder: the individual or group donating the property or securities that implement the legal incorporation called a *philanthropic foundation.*

philanthropists (fil′ən·throp′i·nists): a group who patterned their educational doctrines after those of the Philanthropinum founded by the German, Johann Bernhard Basedow (1723-1790); their doctrine emphasized the study of gardening, agriculture, animal culture, geography, nature study, and gymnastics.

Philanthropinum (fi·lan′thrə·pi′nəm): one of the schools of the philanthropists (the first of which was established by Basedow in 1774 at Dessau, Germany), which attempted to apply the educational theories of Rousseau to school practice. *See* **philanthropists.**

philanthropy: (1) love of mankind; (2) the act of making a donation for a humanitarian cause by either gift or bequest.

philanthropy, college: a gift or endowment made to a college, frequently for some specified purpose.

philanthropy, educational: an expression of the altruistic spirit by giving wealth or services for the support or benefit of education.

philanthropy, student: an obsolescent term designating the philanthropic provision for loan funds, scholarships, fellowships, and other means of offering financial assistance to students.

philately (fi·la′tə·lē): the collecting and study of postage stamps and stationery marked with postal cancellations.

philistinism: a derogatory term used to designate an attitude of unenlightenment, opposition to progress or progressive ideas.

philology: the study of language, its history, origin, laws, development, and relationships; the scientific study of language.

philosophical analysis: *see* **analysis, philosophical.**

philosophical method: an approach to truth or value that rests principally on deliberative or rational processes, utilizing the results of observational research in so far as possible, and concerned with such purposes as (*a*) testing the consistency of findings; (*b*) integrating sets of findings into larger patterns of thought, possibly thus arriving at new truths or producing new theories to be checked; *see* **integrative method;** (*c*) determining values or goals, such as the essential criteria of a "good life"; (*d*) examining and formulating the basic postulates of research and science; and (*e*) establishing the characteristics of acceptable logic.

philosophical school: (1) one of the groups following the different philosophies in ancient Athens; among them were the Platonists, Peripatetics, Epicureans, Stoics, Skeptics, and Gnostics; (2) loosely, any system or "type" of philosophy, such as *naturalism, idealism, realism.*

philosophy: (1) (common sense) an integrated personal view that serves to guide the individual's conduct and thinking; (2) the science that seeks to organize and systematize all fields of knowledge as a means of understanding and interpreting the totality of reality; usually regarded as comprising logic, ethics, aesthetics, metaphysics, and epistemology; (3) a habit of mind in the exercise of which one tends not to take the conventional and customary for granted but always to see possible alternatives (Dewey); (4) in military usage, a body of beliefs or principles that give to the person who entertains them a certain bias for doing certain things and not doing others, or for doing something in a particular way.

philosophy, analytical: a nonmetaphysically oriented branch of philosophy that seeks to expose ambiguities and illogical uses of educational terms that lead to conceptual confusion in both theory and practice.

philosophy, anthropocentric: the philosophy that assumes man to be the central fact of the universe, to which all other facts have reference.

philosophy, applied: a term covering such fields as the philosophy of history, the philosophy of religion, and the philosophy of education, in which philosophy is "applied" to the subject matter of other disciplines. *Contr. w.* **philosophy, pure.**

philosophy, armchair: a term of disparagement signifying any purely theoretical philosophy not based on experience, reality, investigation, or experiment.

philosophy, educational: *see* **philosophy of education.**

philosophy, geocentric: a system of thought based on the concept of the earth as the center or central concern in the universe.

philosophy, mental: the philosophy of mind, or the theory concerning the reality of the ego and its place in the system of phenomena; closely allied to *psychology.*

philosophy, moral: an older term for ethics or theory of values; also, a broad term covering the philosophy from which the social sciences were to develop, that is, politics, economics, and sociology.

philosophy, national: a philosophy that is essentially based on a national cultural group and is primarily intended to support the aspirations of that group; may place emphasis on the importance of the nation at the expense of other values.

philosophy, natural: an analogous term to *moral philosophy;* it covered broadly the philosophy from which the natural sciences, particularly physics and chemistry, were to develop; it dealt primarily with the natural phenomena of the objective world, seeking general principles under which all facts could be explained.

philosophy, normative: a philosophy that lays down principles regulative of men's thoughts, feelings, and actions; philosophy in so far as it sets up norms or standards of human living.

philosophy of Catholic education: the philosophical position at the basis of the Roman Catholic educational system which holds that the educative process is properly directed to the maturation of the human person, based on a positive acceptance of the dignity of man, his free acceptance of social responsibilities and moral values, and his knowledge of and adherence to the Christian message as exemplified in the teachings in the gospels of Jesus Christ; this philosophy further holds that such unique objectives are best achieved in an atmosphere which specifically prepares the learner to accept these beliefs concerning the nature of man and which provides for practice and growth in self-directedness, based on knowledge of the proximate and ultimate goals of man and of the relationships between his goals and those of the community of mankind. *See* **Catholic education.**

philosophy of constant fundamentals: *syn.* **essentialism.**

philosophy of education: a careful, critical, and systematic intellectual endeavor to see education as a whole and as an integral part of man's culture, the more precise meaning of the term varying with the systematic point of view of the stipulator; any philosophy dealing with or applied to the process of public or private education and used as a basis for the general determination, interpretation, and evaluation of educational problems having to do with objectives, practices, outcomes, child and social needs, materials of study, and all other aspects of the field.

philosophy of education, organic: *see* **organic philosophy of education.**

philosophy of expediency: *see* **expediency, philosophy of.**

philosophy of John Dewey: a pragmatic philosophy of education, formerly known as instrumentalism but now generally called experimentalism, that avoids the metaphysical and holds that both knowledge and value are instrumentally determined; broadly naturalistic, humanistic, and biologically derived; strongly oriented toward democracy; educational ideas follow those of Rousseau, Pestalozzi, Froebel, and others; profoundly influenced the progressive education movement in the United States. *See* **experimentalism; instrumentalism; pragmatism.**

philosophy of language: *see* **language, philosophy of.**

philosophy of law, Hamiltonian: advocacy of a liberal interpretation of law according to which, for example, a subordinate level of a hierarchy may do anything that is reasonable and not prohibited by a superior level, such as Congressional power under the Constitution or local school board authority under state law; the Jeffersonian-Madisonian philosophy opposes this, calling for strict construction of Constitution and statutes, according to which a branch or level of government may do that for which it finds specific authorization or clear inference or implication, its discretionary powers being limited.

philosophy of music: *see* **musicology, historical; philosophy, applied.**

philosophy of science: *see* **science, philosophy of.**

philosophy, practical: those philosophical disciplines, such as ethics and aesthetics, which study the attainment of some good through doing or making. *Contr. w.* **philosophy, speculative.**

philosophy, pure: a term, derived from the division of the sciences of Christian Wolff (1679–1754), used to designate both speculative and practical philosophy as opposed to applied philosophy. *See* **philosophy, applied; philosophy, practical; philosophy, speculative.**

philosophy, social: (1) a branch of philosophy dealing with the study of social institutions, customs, and other phenomena of societal life and with their ethical implications; the philosophical aspect of sociology; (2) a systematized and more or less integrated viewpoint or body of doctrines concerning societal life, the state, the citizen, and related problems, for example, democracy, socialism, communism, fascism, etc.

philosophy, speculative: those philosophical disciplines, such as metaphysics, philosophy of nature, theory of knowledge, whose immediate and intrinsic goal is simply to know and understand reality. *Contr. w.* **philosophy, practical.**

phlegmatic: pertaining to a temperament characterized by indifference, passivity, and apathy.

phobia: psychoneurotic anxiety, experienced when some special object or situation, such as a certain street or the darkness, is encountered.

phobia, school: a generalized irrational anxiety expressed in deterioration of self-control when in school or when forced to attend school.

phobophobia (fō′bō·fō′bi·ə): a psychoneurotic condition marked by the fear of experiencing fear or anxiety.

phonation: (1) the production of vocal sound; (2) the functioning of the larynx in the production of the voice.

phonation, defective: *see* **disorder, voice.**

phonation, monotonous: a manner of speaking in which the usual rise and fall of pitch and intensity are relatively lacking.

phonation, prolonged: (1) an abnormally long duration of vocal tones, characteristic of conditions caused by certain lesions in the central nervous system; (2) any long-extended voiced sound.

phonation, staccato: (1) a vocal tone of abnormally short duration, characteristic of the speech of certain persons with lesions of the central nervous system or with personality disorders; (2) any vocal tone of short duration.

phone: a speech sound as a physical occurrence without reference to its fitting into the structure of a language. *See* **distribution, phonetic.**

phoneme (fō′nēm): (1) a single speech sound; (2) a group of slightly varying forms of what is generally considered to be one speech sound but that vary according to stress, rate of articulation, adjacent sounds, etc.; for example, the r sounds in *rat, dry, very,* and *borrow* though somewhat different in manner of production and in sound, all belong to the r phoneme; (3) in linguistic analysis, a family of sounds in a given language which are related in character and are used in such a way that no one member of the family ever occurs in the same phonetic context as another member.

phoneme-grapheme relationship: the relationship of consonant or vowel sounds to the written symbol. *See* **grapheme; phoneme.**

phonemic alphabet: *see* **alphabet, phonemic.**

phonemic contrast: a sound contrast that changes meaning in spoken language. *Contr. w.* **phonetic contrast.**

phonemic discrimination drill: *see* **drill, phonemic discrimination.**

phonemic spelling: *see* **spelling, phonemic.**

phonetic alphabet: *see* **alphabet, phonetic.**

phonetic alphabet, international: *see* **alphabet, international phonetic.**

phonetic analysis: *see* **analysis, phonetic.**

phonetic aptitude: *see* **aptitude, phonetic.**

phonetic contrast: sound contrast that may or may not change meaning in spoken language. *Contr. w.* **phonemic contrast.**

phonetic distribution: *see* **distribution, phonetic.**

phonetic elements: the parts of words (single letters, letter combinations, or syllables) standing for sounds that, blended together, result in pronunciation of the words.

phonetic inventory: *see* **inventory, phonetic.**

phonetic kymograph: *see* **kymograph, phonetic.**

phonetic method: (1) a technique of correcting articulatory defects that involves the teaching of appropriate positions of tongue, lips, jaw, and soft palate; *syn.* **phonetic placement method; placement method;** (2) a method of teaching foreign languages in which much reliance is placed on the study of phonetics to facilitate the accurate rendition of foreign sounds; usually involves instruction in the scientific principles of the production of sounds (position of lips, tongue, and teeth, breath control, etc.) and practice in transcribing foreign sounds in phonetic symbols such as those of the international phonetic alphabet; may be combined with any other method for teaching foreign language, such as the *inductive method, translation method, grammar method,* or *direct method.*

phonetic placement method: *syn.* **phonetic method** (1).

phonetic script: a system of spelling (sometimes with additional symbols such as those in the alphabet of the International Phonetic Association) in which each letter always represents the same special sound.

phonetic sight word: *see* **word, phonetic sight.**

phonetic spelling: *see* **spelling, phonetic.**

phonetic transcription: the precise recording of speech by means of a system of written characters, each character representing a single speech sound.

phonetic word: *see* **word, phonetic.**

phonetically balanced word list: *see* **word list, phonetically balanced.**

phonetics: (1) the science of speech sounds; (2) the analysis of words into their constituent sound elements. *See* **phonics.**

phonetics, experimental: the study of the acoustical properties of speech sounds and the physiological mechanisms by which they are produced.

phonic method: a method of teaching reading based on the analysis of words into their basic speech sounds.

phonic strip: a list of phonograms arranged vertically on a card or paper and used for drill in phonic recognition.

phonics: (1) phonetics as applied to the teaching of reading; (2) the use of speech sounds, and letters that represent speech sounds, in the teaching of reading as a means of helping the pupil achieve independence in the recognition of words.

phonics, analytic approach to: an approach to teaching phonics through the analysis of words for the purpose of developing phonic generalizations.

phonics exercise: *see* **exercise, phonics.**

phonics, intrinsic: phonics based on the phonetic elements met in words that are used in context, as contrasted with phonics based on isolated lists of words that are unrelated to any present context.

phonics, letter: that kind of phonics which emphasizes the sound of letters rather than the sound of groups of letters or phonic *families.*

phonics, multisensory: an approach to teaching phonics by establishing associations between sound and letter symbols through the use of the senses.

phonics, synthetic approach to: an approach to phonics instruction in which the sound of letters and groups of letters is taught prior to the actual reading of whole words and sentences; an early use of this approach was made in the Pollard reading method (about 1889). *See* **reading method, Beacon.**

phono audiometer: *see* **audiometer, phono.**

phonogram: (1) a letter or group of letters used to represent a speech sound; (2) phonetic symbol; (3) a diagram indicating the position of the tongue, lips, jaw, or soft palate (or any combination of these) for the production of a speech sound.

phonogram, compound: a phonic element made up of more than one letter which does not make a word in itself, such as *sl, str, ing, ight, ay,* or *ou.*

phonogram, letter: a phonic element of a word consisting of a single consonant.

phonogram, word: a small word that serves as an element in a larger word, such as *at* and *an.*

phonograph: a machine for reproducing sounds from records. *See* **playback equipment.**

phonograph audiometer: *syn.* **audiometer, phono.**

phonography: (1) the writing of sounds by phonetic symbols, as by the use of the international phonetic alphabet; (2) *syn.* **shorthand.**

phonology: the study of the history and theory of speech sounds and sound changes.

phonovisual chart: *see* **chart, phonovisual.**

phoria: *syn.* **heterophoria.**

photism (fō′tiz′m): a sensation of color visually perceived when another special sense organ is stimulated, as that of hearing, taste, or smell. (A familiar example is "seeing stars" upon receiving a blow on the head.)

photo-offset-lithography: *syn.* **photolithography.**

photocopy: *v.* to produce by a photographic process with reproduction machines copies of hand-drawn or printed materials, including pictures; such copies are termed photocopies.

photoelectric cell: (1) a light-sensitive unit that, when used in a motion-picture projector, receives light directed through the sound track from the exciter lamp and translates it into electrical impulses that, after amplification, produce sound in the loudspeaker; *syn.* **phototube;** (2) the activating mechanism found in many exposure meters by means of which light striking the cell is translated into electric current, which activates a movable pointer, from which the correct exposure and aperture combination may be determined.

photoelectric light control: *syn.* **light control, automatic.**

photoengraving: engraving by the aid of photography.

photoflash: a bulb emitting an intense light in a very short interval of time; used for photographic purposes.

photoflood: a bulb emitting a sustained intense light; used for photographic purposes.

photogenic: *adj.* descriptive of a subject that photographs very well.

photogram: (1) a pictorial photograph; (2) a survey picture or map derived from aerial photography; (3) a silhouette effected by exposing photograph paper or film to light while opaque articles are shielding selected parts.

photogrammetry: the art or science of aerial cartography.

photographic dome: the arched dome of a room equipped with a one-way vision screen and concealed cameras, used for observing and photographing infant behavior.

photographic duplication: *see* **duplication, photographic.**

photography: (ind. arts) the study of the tools, materials, and processes used in photography with emphasis on industrial uses; learning activities include experiences using cameras, developing negatives, and making contact prints, enlargements, and mountings.

photography club: *see* **club, photography.**

photography, eye-movement: a technique employed in the study of eye movements in reading. (While the subject reads, light is reflected from the cornea of each eye and registered by means of an optical apparatus upon light-sensitive material; the basic principle of the *ophthalmograph.)*

photography, slow-motion: a technique employed in motion-picture photography to reproduce on the screen motion that is slower than the original; to accomplish this, the film is exposed at a rate faster than normal and is projected at a normal rate.

photography, tabletop: *syn.* **macrophotography.**

photography, time-lapse: (1) a motion-picture technique used for visualizing normally invisible slow processes; in the original photography a greater than normal time interval elapses between exposures of successive frames; projection at normal projection speed results in an apparent speed-up of the action; the degree of the speed-up effect achieved depends on the time interval between successive exposures when the original is made; (2) in still photography, the technique of taking a number of separate still pictures of a process, each exposure being separated from the preceding one by a uniform lapse of time, which may vary from seconds to hours; makes possible the presentation of a slow process in a series of pictures of selected stages in which change can be clearly seen.

photolithography: (1) (art) the process of printing on a photographically prepared surface on which the image to be printed is ink-receptive and blank areas are ink-repellent; (2) (ind. arts) the study of the technology of graphic reproduction from a flat surface or plate prepared photomechanically; learning experiences include design, hot and/or cold composition, paste-up, camera and darkroom techniques, platemaking, and offset press-work; also called *photo-offset-lithography* or *offset.*

photometer (fō·tom′ə·tər): *syn.* **light meter.**

photomicrography: *syn.* **microphotography.**

photomontage: a composite photograph made by cutting out parts of several pictures and pasting them together to form a single composition or by printing different parts of several negatives on a single sheet of photographic paper to form a single composition. (In the case of photomontages made by cutting and pasting, the composite photograph resulting may be retouched and rephotographed to make the final print.) *See* **montage.**

photomural: a large-scale photograph mounted directly on a wall.

photophobia (fō′tō·fō′bi·ə): a condition characterized by extreme sensitivity and consequent aversion to light.

photostat: (1) type of camera for making copies of any flat printed surface directly on specially prepared paper; (2) the finished print from a photostat machine.

phototube: *syn.* **photoelectric cell** (1).

phrase: (mus.) a term denoting a division or section of a melodic line which compares with a sentence in speech; not used with exactness or uniformity.

phrase comprehension: *see* **comprehension, phrase.**

phrase meaning: the idea for which a phrase stands as a whole, as distinguished from the ideas suggested by the separate words that compose it.

phrase method: a method of teaching children to read by the study of phrases or word groups.

phrase reading: *see* **reading, phrase.**

phrasing: (shorthand) the writing together of the outlines for two or more words.

phrenology: the theory, fairly widely accepted in the mid-nineteenth century, that the human mind is composed of sections or faculties that are correlated with specific sections of the brain and that the shape of the skull is of significance in the study of the brain.

phylogenesis (fī′lō·jen′ə·sis): *syn.* **phylogeny.**

phylogenetic: of or pertaining to development through the different phyla or within the life history of the race.

phylogenetic activities: *see* **activities, phylogenetic.**

phylogeny (fī·loj′ə·ni): evolutionary or racial development of a related group of organisms or of some structure or function of the group. *Syn.* **phylogenesis;** *dist. f.* **ontogeny.**

physical-ability test: *see* **test, physical-ability.**

physical activity: *see* **activity, physical.**

physical and health education: coordinated school programs of physical education and health education, with an implied exception of health service. *See* **health education; physical education.**

physical anthropology: *see* **anthropology, physical.**

physical capacity: *see* **capacity, physical.**

physical-capacity test: *see* **test, physical-capacity.**

physical chemistry: *see* **chemistry, physical.**

physical culture: a term once used to indicate a program of activities for bodily development. *See* **physical education; training, physical.**

physical defect: a maldevelopment or markedly subnormal development of some part of the body.

physical development: *see* **development, physical.**

physical education: the program of instruction and participation in big-muscle activities designed to promote desirable physical development, motor skills, attitudes, and habits of conduct. *Dist. f.* **training, physical.**

physical education, adapted: a program of individually prescribed exercises or activities designed for those who need special programs. *See* **physical education, corrective.**

physical education, corrective: a program of special exercises and activities designed to remedy postural defects and other conditions calling for careful development of special muscle groups. *See* **gymnastics, individual; gymnastics, remedial.**

physical education, developmental: the practice of physical education designed to increase muscular strength, flexibility, coordination, and cardiorespiratory and muscular endurance of handicapped children.

physical education director: *see* **director of physical education.**

physical educator: a professional worker in physical education, particularly one who has received some professional recognition.

physical-efficiency test: *see* **test, physical-efficiency.**

physical examination: *see* **examination, physical.**

physical exceptionality: *see* **exceptionality, physical.**

physical fitness: *see* **fitness, physical.**

physical-fitness index: *see* **index, physical-fitness.**

physical geography: *see* **geography, physical.**

physical growth: *see* **growth, physical.**

physical impairment: *see* **impairment, physical.**

physical panel: a phrase, introduced by George Draper, designating a complete assembly or compilation of the physical or external-anatomical characteristics of an individual.

physical plant: the land, buildings, and improvements of campuses, farms, athletic fields, and other plots used for the activities of a university, college, or school; includes buildings for instruction and administration, libraries, gymnasiums, dormitories, power plants, and other buildings and the equipment and furniture of such buildings.

physical-plant additions: expenditures for the acquisition of land, buildings, improvements other than buildings, and equipment acquired for the permanent possession of an educational institution. (Real property that represents the investment of endowment or other funds is not included under this term.)

physical plant administration: *see* **administration, physical plant.**

physical plant, value of: *see* **value of physical plant.**

physical-record system: a plan for keeping an account of physical data about pupils; includes the physical record plus routines necessary to make this record and keep it up to date.

physical recreation program: *see* **program, physical recreation.**

physical science: *see* **science, physical.**

physical-skill test: *see* **test, physical-skill.**

physical space: *see* **space, physical.**

physical therapist: *see* **therapist, physical.**

physical therapy: *syn.* **physiotherapy.**

physical time: *see* **time, physical.**

physical training: *see* **training, physical.**

physical working capacity: *see* **capacity, physical working.**

physically below-par child: *see* **child, physically below-par.**

physically defective: *see* **defective, physically.**

physically handicapped: *see* **handicapped, physically.**

physician, eye: *syn.* **ophthalmologist.**

physician, school: a medically certified general practitioner or pediatrician working in an educational setting on a full- or part-time basis; may have involvement in direct student service and general health education.

physician's certificate: *see* **certificate, physician's.**

physicotheological argument: *see* **argument, physicotheological.**

physics: the branch of *physical science* that is concerned with matter and energy, including the study of phenomena associated with mechanics, heat, wave motion, sound, electricity, magnetism, light, and atomic and nuclear structure.

physics, health: the science concerned with recognition, evaluation, and control of health hazards from ionizing radiation.

physics, solid state: the study of the structure and the properties of solids such as crystals, alloys, superconductors, semiconductors, and plastics; includes theoretical aspects of transistors, lasers, and ceramic devices.

physics, space: a study of mechanics, heat, light, and their relations and reactions under space flight conditions.

physiography: (1) a study dealing primarily with the nature of the surface of the land and with the relation of air and water to it; (2) sometimes regarded as *physical geography* or *geomorphology.*

physiologic time: *see* **time, physiologic.**

physiological age: *see* **age, physiological.**

physiological drive: *syn.* **drive** (1).

physiological growth: *see* **growth, physiological.**

physiological maturity: *see* **maturity, physiological.**

physiological panel: a phrase, introduced by George Draper, designating a complete assembly or compilation of the characteristics of an individual with respect to physiological functioning (such as digestive efficiency, sensory acuity, and exercise tolerance).

physiological psychology: *see* **psychology, physiological.**

physiological reaction: *see* **reaction, physiological.**

physiological test: *see* **test, physiological.**

physiological training: *see* **training, physiological.**

physiology: the science dealing with the study of the functions of tissues and organs.

physiology, neuromuscular: *see* **neurophysiology.**

physiology of exercise: the study of human functions under the stress of muscular activity.

physioplastic art: *see* **art, physioplastic.**

physiotherapy (fiz'i·ō·ther'ə·pi): the treatment of disability, injury, and disease by nonmedical means, involving the use of massage, exercise, heat, light, water, and electricity (except Roentgen rays, radium, and electrosurgery). *Syn.* **physical therapy.**

physique: the body's structure and the appearance it displays in performance; also called build or constitution.

Piagetian concept: *see* **concept, Piagetian.**

piano class laboratory: *see* **laboratory, piano class.**

pica (pī'ka): (1) a size of type equal to 12-point square; pica type is 12-point type; 6 picas approximate 1 inch; 1 pica equals 6 point measures or $\frac{1}{6}$ inch; (2) a term used for large typewriter type in which there are 10 spaces to a horizontal inch; (3) a form of perverted appetite characterized by the ingestion of dirt, soot, plaster, hair, paint, and similar inedible items; in children it usually develops in the second or third year of life.

pickup: a cartridge containing the stylus (needle) and sensitive component for creating electric current; a term sometimes applied loosely to the tone arm and cartridge of a phonograph.

pickup arm: the part of a disk record player which supports the push-up head; usually counterweighted to produce correct stylus pressure.

pickup, group: a system of transportation in which children walk to and from loading stations located at suitable intervals along the route.

pickup head: that portion of a sound reproducing system (such as a disk or tape record player) which converts the recorded sound into variations in electrical current.

pickup, home: a system of transportation in which each child is carried to and from that point in the public highway directly in front of his home.

pickup method: unorganized learning by trial and error on the job, the learner "picking up" his knowledge and skill chiefly by watching others.

pickup service: a service, provided by the attendance department, that consists in calling at schools at regularly stated hours for the purpose of collecting investigation reports, which are then conveyed to the attendance center for distribution to the attendance officers.

pictogram: *syn.* **pictograph;** *see* **graph, pictorial.**

pictograph: (1) a picture reduced to its essentials in order to create a symbol that graphically defines an object or idea in the simplest possible way; used in posters and *pictorial graphs;* (2) *syn.* **graph, pictorial.**

pictorial bar graph: *see* **graph, pictorial bar.**

pictorial drawing: *see* **drawing, pictorial.**

pictorial graph: *see* **graph, pictorial.**

pictorial test: *see* **test, pictorial.**

picture book: *see* **book, picture.**

picture clue: *see* **clue, picture.**

picture-completion test: *see* **test, picture-completion.**

picture dictionary: *see* **dictionary, picture.**

picture, flat: *see* **flat picture.**

picture graph: *syn.* **graph, pictorial.**

picture-meaning test: *see* **test, picture-meaning.**

picture, still: *see* **still picture.**

picture story book: *see* **book, picture story.**

picture study: *see* **study, picture.**

picture transfer: *see* **transfer, picture.**

picture tube: that part of the television receiver from which the video signal is viewed. *See* **kinescope recording.**

picture vocabulary test: *see* **test, picture vocabulary.**

pie graph: *syn.* **graph, circle.**

Pietism (pī'ə·tiz'm): the attitude of a Protestant element in Germany in the seventeenth century, which emphasized conversion, personal religious experience, and humanitarian reforms rather than theological reasoning. (The effects of this attitude on education, in spite of fanatical opposition to worldliness, generally were favorable to intelligent comprehension, practical studies, popular schools, and attention to individuality.)

pigments, polymer: *see* **acrylics.**

pilot group: *syn.* **group, practice.**

pilot instructor: a pilot appointed as an instructor in a particular type of aircraft in which he is qualified to check out other pilots.

pilot light: a small electric light attached to a motion-picture or other type of projector and illuminating its controls for the convenience of the operator.

pilot program, distributive education: *see* **program, distributive education pilot.**

pilot school: a school designed to pioneer on a small scale in the development or testing of an idea or educational program in order to see if it is workable and warrants wider adoption.

pilot, student: (1) in the Army when used individually denotes a commissioned officer, a warrant officer, or a warrant officer candidate who is undergoing initial entry training in one of the aviator training programs conducted by the Army Aviation School; a student pilot is not a rated aviator; (2) used collectively to denote all initial entry students undergoing training in the Army Aviation School; (3) in the Air Force an officer, usually a second lieutenant, undergoing pilot training; *syn.* **pilot trainee; undergraduate pilot;** (4) *see* **candidate, naval aviation officer.**

pilot study: *see* **study, pilot.**

pilot trainee: *syn.* **pilot, student** (3).

pilot training: *see* **training, pilot.**

pilot training, advanced: *see* **training, advanced pilot.**

pilot training, basic: *see* **training, basic pilot.**

pilot training, graduate: *see* **training, advanced pilot.**

pilot training, primary: *see* **training, primary pilot.**

pilot training, undergraduate: *see* **training, basic pilot.**

pilot transition training: *see* **training, pilot transition.**

pilot, undergraduate: in the Air Force an officer, usually a second lieutenant, undergoing pilot training. *See* **candidate, naval aviation officer; pilot, student; trainee, pilot.**

pilpul (pil'pool): *n. masc.* (Aramaic, lit., "disputation") a method of critical analysis for the purpose of interpreting the Talmudic text and deriving deductions from all its implications; used in a derogatory sense to describe hairsplitting casuistry.

pin map: *see* **map, pin.**

pincer prehension: *see* **prehension, pincer.**

pipe trenches: tubes or tunnels usually constructed of concrete, connecting buildings with a separate heating plant, containing heating pipes and sometimes water pipes; the tubes or tunnels are usually large enough to permit a man to walk upright through them.

pitch: (1) a qualitative dimension of hearing related to the highness or lowness of tones and correlated with the frequency of vibration of the sound waves making up the stimulus, higher frequencies yielding higher pitches; frequency is measured in cycles per second and pitch in mels or intervals of the musical scale; (2) (for. lang.) a tonal aspect of speech which may distinguish meaning in certain languages; (3) in general, a quality of a speaker's voice.

pitch, absolute: a highly developed sense of tonal memory, which is evidenced by a person's ability to name the pitch of any tone or combination of tones without previously hearing any tone or tones that might be used for reference; ability to sing any designated pitch. *Syn.* **perfect pitch;** *see* **pitch, relative.**

pitch discrimination: *see* **discrimination, pitch.**

pitch imagery: *see* **imagery, pitch.**

pitch pipe: a small pipe of wood or metal used to determine pitch; may be restricted to a single tone, or may produce all tones of a chromatic scale. *Comp. w.* **tuning fork.**

pitch pipe, chromatic: a pitch pipe that produces all the tones of a chromatic scale. *See* **pitch pipe.**

pitch-range audiometer: *syn.* **audiometer, pure-tone.**

pitch, relative: ability to judge or recall musical intervals, that is, the differences in pitch between successive tones. *See* **pitch, absolute.**

pitch-tone audiometer: *syn.* **audiometer, pure-tone.**

pitcher, mechanical: a machine that uses the strength of a spring or the compression of an explosion of air to hurl a ball at a desired speed in a decided direction; may replace a human pitcher in training players of baseball.

place geography: *see* **geography, place.**

place-study habit: the habit of studying in a certain place, as in a room equipped with conveniences for study.

place value: *see* **value, place.**

place value chart: *see* **chart, place value.**

place value numeration system: *see* **numeration system.**

placeholder: a symbol which holds the place for a numeral, as in "□ + 4 = 13"; the term parallels the number-numeral distinction; in this context placeholder is associated with *numeral, variable* with number. *Contr. w.* **variable.**

placement: (couns.) the assignment of a person to a suitable class, course, job training institution, or educational institution in accordance with his aims, capabilities, readiness, educational background, and aspirations.

placement, advanced: the status accorded a student who is admitted to an institution of higher education with educational attainment credited to him beyond the minimum required for admission; usually shortens the time necessary to complete diploma or degree requirements. *Syn.* **advanced standing.**

placement bureau: a college or university agency primarily concerned with assisting recent graduates to obtain full-time employment; sometimes also concerned with assisting students in college to find part-time work and with helping alumni to transfer to new positions. *Syn.* **appointments bureau.**

placement bureau, alumni: a college or university agency organized to assist alumni to obtain full-time employment and to transfer to new professional positions.

placement bureau, teacher: (1) a department of a teacher-education institution that aids the graduates of the institution in obtaining teaching positions and endeavors to help the employers make appropriate personnel selections; not to be confused with a teacher placement agency operated as a private business; (2) a division of a state department or a teachers' association or agency that helps teachers obtain positions. *Syn.* **bureau of teacher recommendations; institutional teacher placement bureau.**

placement card: a card bearing information relating to the employment of a person, such as amount of general education, vocational training, test data showing abilities, position held, and reasons for leaving.

placement, child: (1) the finding of employment for a child of employable age; (2) the act of placing a child in the school grade or special class that seems best adapted to his needs; (3) the act of placing a child in a home for adoption.

placement, college: a service to the college student which assists him in planning his next step whether it be in employment or future educational pursuits. *See* **placement bureau.**

placement, coordinator of: *see* **coordinator of placement.**

placement counselor: *see* **counselor, placement.**

placement credentials: *syn.* **record, placement.**

placement decision: *see* **decision, placement.**

placement, director of: *syn.* **coordinator of placement.**

placement, educational: assistance afforded the student with the aims both of promoting maximum scholarship and of providing help in projecting his plans toward future training for vocation and life; includes aid in course planning.

placement for experience, agricultural: *see* **training, agricultural on-job.**

placement, guidance: assistance given the counselee in orientation and adjustment as he moves from one school stage to the next, as from junior to senior high school or from high school to college or job.

placement guidance: *see* **guidance, placement.**

placement, junior: securing part-time, full-time temporary, or permanent jobs for young persons usually up to 19 years of age; performed either by the schools or by a public employment agency, an attempt being made to help individuals make adjustments and work out their vocational plans.

placement method: *syn.* **phonetic method** (1).

placement, occupational: *see* **placement service.**

placement of building: (1) the situation of a building on the site or campus; (2) determination of the location or orientation of a building.

placement officer: one who provides a job placement service for students and graduates; counsels students regarding job opportunities, vocational choice, and desirable qualifications; develops job openings through employer contacts.

placement officer, student-employment: *syn.* **placement officer.**

placement record: *see* **record, placement.**

placement, residential school: legal action of placing an individual in a protected environment; may be long-term or short-term. *See* **state school.**

placement secretary: *syn.* **placement officer.**

placement service: an essential element of the guidance program concerned with assisting students to progress in employment or further education; *occupational placement* involves both part-time placement for those still in school and full-time placement for those who leave school; *educational placement* has to do with specialized and technical training opportunities as well as with academic institutions; the service is offered both in secondary schools and in institutions of higher education.

placement, student: (1) student-personnel service which is responsible for part-time or full-time employment of students and, sometimes, alumni of that particular institution; (2) the function of selecting students and arranging for their employment in suitable positions in the business and office occupations, the distributive occupations, or other areas of cooperative vocational education; (3) (couns.) the act of placing a person where he should be in accordance with his capabilities, aims, readiness, educational background, and aspirations.

placement, teacher: the process by which teachers obtain teaching positions.

placement test: *see* **test, placement.**

plaintiff: one who commences a suit or action in law.

plan: (art ed.) the top view of an object.

plan, academical: *see* **academical plan.**

plan and elevation, mixture of: (art ed.) the representation of both top and side views in children's drawings; created by the feeling of equal ties to both. *See* **representation, space-time.**

plan, battery: *see* **battery plan.**

plan book: a book of forms designed for the recording of systematic statements of teaching activities scheduled for a designated period of time, such as the day, the week, or the month.

plan, business and office education training: *see* **training plan, business and office education.**

plan, contract: *see* **contract plan.**

plan, cooperative group: *see* **cooperative group plan.**

plan, cooperative training: *syn.* **contract, cooperative student.**

plan, correlation: *see* **course of study, correlated.**

plan, distributive education cooperative: *see* **cooperative plan, distributive education.**

plan, distributive education project: *see* **project plan, distributive education.**

plan, filing: *see* **filing plan.**

plan, four-quarter: *see* **quarter system.**

plan, fusion: *see* **fusion plan.**

plan, guaranteed wage: *see* **guaranteed wage plan.**

plan, individual study: *see* **study plan, individual.**

plan, internship: *see* **internship plan.**

plan, itinerant teacher: a plan in which a teacher not regularly assigned to a school or class gives special help, at regular intervals, to children in various schools or classes, for example, to the blind child enrolled in a regular class in his home school. *See* **circuit teacher** (2).

plan, New Jersey: *see* **New Jersey plan.**

plan of alternation: *syn.* **alternation of grades.**

plan-of-search test: *see* **test, ball-and-field.**

plan of teaching, pyramid: *see* **teaching, pyramid plan of.**

plan of work: (Cooperative Extension Service) annual statement of specific activities and educational programs proposed by state or county personnel which is required by Federal legislation.

plan, Oregon: *see* **Oregon plan.**

plan, preceptorial: *see* **preceptorial plan.**

plan, remedial-teacher: *see* **remedial-teacher plan.**

plan, rotation: *see* **rotation plan.**

plan, St. John's: *see* **St. John's plan.**

plan, state: *see* **state plan.**

plan, study-work: *see* **study-work plan.**

plan, three-two: *see* **three-two plan.**

plan, training: *syn.* **contract, cooperative student.**

plan, unit progress: *see* **unit progress plan.**

plan, voucher: *see* **voucher plan.**

plane: (art) (1) the surface, usually with no elevations or depressions, on which a drawing, painting, or watercolor is produced; (2) the illusion created within a space on which points of distance are shown as in visual perspective; the overlapping of shapes, colors, or lines to produce an illusion of depth within an essentially flat composition.

plane geometry: *see* **geometry, plane.**

plane trigonometry: *see* **trigonometry, plane.**

planes, orthogonal: two or more planes passing through the same point and so related that each plane is perpendicular to all the remaining planes.

planetology: the study and interpretation of surface markings of planets and satellites; usually taught as a part of a course on space biology at the university level. *See* **biology, space.**

planned change: *see* **change, planned.**

planned curriculum, pupil-teacher: *see* **curriculum, pupil-teacher planned.**

planned economy: *see* **economy, planned.**

planned obsolescence: *see* **obsolescence, planned.**

planned pacing: *see* **pacing, planned.**

planned parenthood: *see* **parenthood, planned.**

planning, career: *see* **career planning.**

planning center: *see* **center, planning.**

planning, cooperative: process by which a group works together to determine goals, selects experiences that may help it reach the goals, and decides how to appraise its progress toward them.

planning, family: *see* **family planning.**

planning, farm and home: assistance offered by the Cooperative Extension Service to farm families in utilizing their total resources to study their own situations, set goals for improvements, and plan how to increase family satisfactions and personal development as well as improve farming practices.

planning, group: the process by which a group determines together its plan of activities, leadership roles, and member responsibilities; in classroom instruction, group planning might involve (*a*) the teacher making all the decisions and assigning the responsibilities to the group of pupils, (*b*) the group making all the decisions without teacher help, or (*c*) the teacher working with the group to help them reach decisions. *See* **planning, cooperative; planning, teacher-pupil.**

planning, motor: the capacity of the organism to plan a movement pattern prior to execution in order to meet the demands of the task.

planning of buildings: (1) the laying out of a scheme or order of building; (2) the determination of what shall be included in the blueprints and specifications for buildings. *See* **building specifications; program, building.**

planning period: *see* **period, planning.**

planning, program: *see* **program planning.**

planning-program-budgeting analysis: *see* **analysis, planning-program-budgeting.**

planning service, educational and occupational: a guidance service in which the pupil and his parents are aided in relating his interests, aptitudes, and abilities to current and future educational and occupational opportunities and requirements by a guidance worker who provides a carefully planned sequence of assistance including interviews, group discussions, special programs, etc.; this service also helps the pupil learn how to apply for admission to higher educational institutions and how to plan the financing of his further education; constitutes far more than a means of providing the student with pertinent educational and occupational literature in that it also involves working with him to plan a program for advanced educational or career entry which will further his self-actualization.

planning sheet: a prepared form to aid pupils in learning how to organize their work effectively.

planning, teacher-pupil: the instructional planning, evaluating, and replanning in which the teacher ideally encourages pupil participation commensurate with the learner's maturity, understanding, and sense of responsibility, and with its instructional value for him; full cooperative planning is the ideal. *See* **planning, cooperative; planning, group; teaching, pupil-centric.**

planning, teacher-pupil-parent: group effort by teachers, pupils, and parents to identify problems and needs and to plan appropriate learning experiences.

plant: (1) a term designating the physical property of an institution or industrial organization—land, buildings, improvements other than buildings, and equipment—used for institutional or industrial purposes; (2) a specific part of a general plant, or a separate enterprise, devoted to the production of some form of service, such as a power plant, gas plant, or heating plant.

plant addition: a building added to the physical plant or a new section attached to a building.

plant-construction progress report: *see* **report, plant-construction progress.**

plant consultant, school: *see* **consultant, school plant.**

plant costs: *see* **costs, plant.**

plant employees' contract: *see* **contract, plant employees'.**

plant endowment: *see* **endowment, plant.**

plant facilities: the devices or features of a physical plant that make for more efficient or more economical care or use, such as central vacuum-cleaning systems, furnace stokers, a hot-water system leading to all buildings, or electrical service.

plant layout: *see* **layout, plant.**

plant, school: *see* **school plant.**

plant tour: (couns.) a planned and guided trip to the physical plant of some organization in order to obtain occupational, educational, or social information. *See* **field trip; plant.**

plant training: *see* **training, plant.**

plant valuation: *see* **valuation, plant.**

plant, value of physical: *see* **value of physical plant.**

plantar reflex: *see* **reflex, plantar.**

plastic: capable of being molded or otherwise deformed.

plastic art: *see* **art, plastic.**

plasticity: the absence of rigid or complete predetermination of development; susceptibility to change or redirection by internal or external environmental factors. *See* **plasticity of development.**

plasticity of development: the susceptibility to change of developmental processes or growth trends, in response to changes in external or internal environment.

plastics technology: *see* **technology, plastics.**

plateau: a real or apparent temporary halt or leveling off in the measured progress of a particular aspect of learning or growth.

platen: a flat plate designed to press something or to be pressed against, such as the flat surface or platform in the opaque projector on which materials to be projected are placed or the roll against which the paper in a typewriter is held in position to receive typing.

Platonic idealism: *see* **idealism, Platonic.**

Platonic realism: *see* **realism** (1).

Platonism: the idealist attitude that sees through facts to their underlying "idea"; in education, the Platonist sees in each pupil his immanent "idea" ("ideal pattern"); the teacher stimulates the pupil to awaken to his potentialities and to direct his life accordingly, realizing "the best that is in him."

platoon plan, modified: *see* **alternate school.**

platoon school: the general designation of any school in which the platoon plan of organization is used, that is, a school in which two roughly equivalent groups of pupils, called platoons, alternate in studying the tool subjects in home rooms and in engaging in activities in special rooms and on the playgrounds. *See* **Gary plan.**

platykurtic (plat'i·kĕr'tik): a term describing a frequency curve that is flatter (that is, less peaked) than is the normal probability curve. *See* **kurtosis.**

platykurtosis (plat'i·kĕr·tō'sis): the quality of being platykurtic. *See* **platykurtic.**

plausible alternative: *syn.* **distractor.**

plausible wrong answer: *syn.* **distractor.**

play: any pleasurable activity carried on for its own sake, without reference to ulterior purpose or future satisfactions.

play accessories, block: *see* **block play accessories.**

play area, outdoor: *see* **outdoor play area.**

play, associative: (1) play involving cooperation and competition; (2) play related to other aspects of society in addition to the recreational.

play, block: (1) (city block) play in an area, usually square in shape, marked off by streets on all sides; (2) (child play) use of pieces of wood or plastic, sometimes cube-shaped and numbered or lettered, to pile up or build things without need of fastenings; (3) (sports) a procedure of hindrance or interference to halt or impede the progress of a player or ball.

play, children's: (1) freedom of action among children, for pleasure and amusement; (2) directed or undirected activity of children having to do with the development of conduct; (3) an exhibition by or for children of some action or story on the stage.

play diagnosis: *see* **diagnosis, play.**

play, directed: the activities of children during play movements when regulated by supervisors.

play, dramatic: an activity carried on by a child or group of children consisting in the reliving or dramatization in an appropriate setting of a direct or vicarious experience, through personal identification with the character or characters involved; for example, a group of children may enact an adult life activity such as conducting a store or a historical incident such as the surrender of Lee to Grant.

play, free: the spontaneous and independent play that grows out of the child's natural urge to be active; teacher guidance gives direction and form to the play through the selection and arrangement of materials and equipment.

play group: *see* **group, play.**

play lot: a small recreation ground, usually a quarter to a half block in size, intended for use by small children.

play method: a teaching method in physical education in which instruction is given in the form of games, relays, or contests.

play, organized: (1) any play activity planned in advance, controlled by rules, as in a game, and supervised to ensure the participation of all players; (2) group play conducted in accordance with recognized rules, such as baseball.

play, parallel: an intermediate stage between purely solitary play and cooperative play, in which a child plays near another child, both using the same materials in approximately the same way but with no active cooperation and no attempt to achieve a common goal.

play, pattern block: the stage of block-play development in which the child purposefully or accidentally places the blocks in a definite pattern or series of pattern forms.

play school: (1) a neighborhood or community program usually sponsored by a civic club, an organized group of parents, a church, or as part of a program of recreation; emphasis is on group play, which is not usually interpreted as being a part of the continuous educational plan for young children; (2) an organized experience, usually lasting for a short time, to provide opportunities for high school and college students to observe and work with a small group of young children in a supervised situation.

play street: a roadway physically blocked and marked as closed to through traffic, used by children for playing purposes.

play, supervised: play activities under the direction and oversight of a supervisor to secure full and fair participation of all players.

play, systematized: a basic principle of the Froebelian kindergarten, based on the theory that participation by the kindergarten child in traditional or conventional systematized games brings him enjoyment and results in knowledge, skill, and moral development.

play technique: a psychotherapeutic method for special use with children; by allowing freedom of the child's play activity within a defined setting, the therapist is able to clarify and analyze emotional problems. *See* **role playing.**

play therapy: *see* **therapy, play.**

play, water: in early childhood education, any creative activity in which water is used as the principal medium.

playback: reproduction of the sound previously recorded.

playback equipment: an electromechanical device for the reproduction of sound from electrical transcriptions, phonograph records, etc.; for school use, usually portable so that it may be moved from room to room, and for broadcasting stations, generally stationary.

playback head: *see* **head, playback.**

playback, immediate: a new development in recorders for language learning that consists of playing back each segment (variable lengths) of program stimulus and student response immediately after the student response without rewinding the tape or reversing its direction.

playback, tape: *see* **tape playback.**

playday: a day given over to play contests or athletic sports, each participating team being composed of players from different schools; for either sex or for both sexes, and intended to prevent intense rivalry between schools.

playfield: a suitable area used for physical education activities such as games and sports. *Syn.* **athletic field.**

playground: outside areas set aside and equipped for recreational activities; usually a part of the grounds; sometimes on the building roof.

playground activity: *see* **activity, playground.**

playground apparatus: such equipment as swings, climbing poles, teeterboards, bars, and giant strides on which children play.

playground commission: a committee or board of citizens organized to promote and control public recreation in a city.

playground director: *see* **director, playground.**

playground, district: a recreation ground of such size as to accommodate athletic fields for youth and adults and so serve a relatively large area in a community.

playground, neighborhood: a playground designed to serve a limited area in a city and used mainly by young children.

playground sunshade: *see* **sunshade, playground.**

playground supervision: *see* **supervision, playground.**

playground supervisor: *see* **supervisor, playground.**

playmate, imaginary: in the child's imagination, an identity or domain, human, animal, or inanimate, occurring especially at ages 4 to 5; sometimes born of a special need in a child's life for a friend, a scapegoat, an extra conscience, a model, or a haven.

playroom: a room or small gymnasium in a school used for physical education classes or for free play.

playwriting, creative: (1) playwriting done in creative writing classes; (2) the composing of plays by children, sometimes not written down but "made up" in the course of dramatic action.

plea in abatement: an answer by a defendant to a plaintiff's allegations which is not directed to the merits of the case and, if successful, defeats the action in question but does not prevent the plaintiff from bringing another action for the same cause.

pleasantness: (1) an affective experience associated with acceptance; (2) an attitude of accepting the stimulus object. *Contr. w.* **unpleasantness.**

pleasure-pain ethics: *see* **ethics, pleasure-pain.**

pleasure principle: an instinct theory, the principle that pleasure results from reduction of instinctual tension, that all psychological processes are determined by the desire for maximal pleasure and minimal pain, and that immediate gratification regardless of future consequences is normally characteristic of the instincts when not controlled by an organized and mature ego.

plebeian: of or pertaining to the Roman plebs or commons; hence of or pertaining to the common people.

pledge of employer: (1) an administrative form used by school authorities that must be signed by an employer before a youth can be granted a work permit by which the employer promises to hire the youth for specified work and to return the age-and-schooling certificate at the end of the youth's employment; (2) the promise made by the employer in signing the above-defined pledge.

pledge of employment: *syn.* **pledge of employer.**

pledging: the process of admitting a student as a neophyte in a fraternity or sorority; a declaration of intention on the part of the student to join and of the fraternity or sorority to accept.

plenary: absolute, full, final, complete.

plenum ventilation: *see* **ventilation, plenum.**

plosive consonants: consonant sounds that are made by stopping the air exhaled with the lips or tongue and releasing it abruptly, as in *p, k, b, t, d, g.*

plot: *n.* a scatter diagram, contingency table, or chart on which certain data have been indicated by tally marks, dots, or other symbols.

plot: *v.* (1) to locate and mark, as in filling in a contingency table, one tally or dot representing each observation; (2) to locate a point or set of points in space by using a coordinate system; to each point is assigned a set of numbers called *coordinates;* for example, a given longitude and latitude locate a particular point on the earth; *see* **coordinate system.**

plot, polar coordinate: any point that has been located with reference to an origin and reference vector.

plugboard: a wired panel, often removable, which is sometimes used to regulate and edit the handling of information done by a machine. *Syn.* **control board; jack panel; terminal board.**

plural meanings: *see* **meanings, plural.**

pluralism: a position stressing multiplicity as contrasted with unity and duality; for example, reality is many, not just one or two; metaphysical pluralism is the antithesis of *monism,* quantitatively and qualitatively, in its conception of reality; social pluralism emphasizes the multiplicity and variety of groups constituting society.

pluralism, cultural: (1) the social philosophy which emphasizes that the culture of countries such as Canada and the United States is the product of the cultures of the varied immigrant groups which people them; (2) the social philosophy which urges that immigrant groups retain their cultural heritage (in consonance with the limitations or features of the new environment) and thus contribute to the richness and variety of the country to which they have come; (3) the peaceful coexistence of subgroups having different *culture patterns* within one social-economic-political group.

pluralism of groups: divergence of groups and of group interests, ideas, standards, and codes, such as the frequent divergence between codes of business and political practice and the codes of civics generally adopted in the schools.

pluralsignificant symbol: *see* **symbol, pluralsignificant.**

Pocket-Tutor: a self-scoring device which allows students to take tests and, while doing so, to keep at a question until they get the right answer.

point: a unit equal to $1/72$ inch, used in measuring the size of type; thus, 18-point type has capital letters $1/4$ inch high and small letters in proportion.

point biserial correlation: *see* **correlation, point biserial.**

Point Four Program: *see* **Program, Point Four.**

point, grade: *see* **grade point.**

point measure: *syn.* **measure, discrete.**

point, reference: *see* **reference point.**

point, sample: *see* **sample point.**

point, scale: *see* **scale point.**

point scale: *see* **scale, point.**

point score: *syn.* **score, raw.**

point, significance: *see* **significance point.**

point system: (1) a manner of scoring a test so that credit for performance on items is given in terms of points or units of a score rather than in terms of age or other derived scores; (2) a manner of grading in which grade points or quality points are assigned to each grade; *syn.* **grade point system;** (3) a plan of awarding points to individual students for participation in extraclass activities; employed for the purposes of (*a*) restricting and distributing participation, and (*b*) assigning credit for participation.

point, zero: *see* **zero point.**

pointillism: (art) (1) the practice or technique of applying dots of color to a surface so that from a distance they blend together; (2) a scientific study of color mixtures which grew out of the impressionist movement, an approach practiced predominantly by French artists Georges Seurat and Paul Signac.

points, configuration of: *see* **configuration of points.**

points, lattice: *see* **lattice** (2).

Poisson distribution: *syn.* **distribution, Poisson sampling.**

Poisson sampling distribution: *see* **distribution, Poisson sampling.**

polar coordinate plot: *see* **plot, polar coordinate.**

polar forces: opposed yet related social forces that undergo constant change and modification, for example, authority and freedom, liberty and discipline, individual rights and social obligations, etc.

polarity: (biol.) a characteristic common to all higher organisms in which the head end of the body tends to show a higher rate of metabolism than the other parts; expressed in the *law of cephalocaudal development* and in the *law of developmental direction.* (This tendency continues in the more complicated integrations taking place in the head-end ganglions along with the specialized sensory end organs located close to them; the most highly developed regions of this kind result in the human brain with the higher associations located in the frontal regions, resulting in the relationships often spoken of as higher, as opposed to lower, centers.)

polarization: division of group members into opposing poles on a particular issue.

polarized projection: *see* **slide, still-motion.**

police education: a form of education that prepares a person for entrance into police work or gives added instruction to employed law-enforcement officers for purposes of promotion.

police, juvenile: policemen who work specifically with juveniles; usually plainclothes officers who are specifically trained for work with children.

police power: (1) the inherent power of a government to maintain the general security and safeguard the public morals, health, safety, and convenience, even at the expense of infringing the private right of the citizen to conduct himself and use his property in such manner as he may see fit; (2) the residuum of unallocated powers reserved to the states by the Tenth Amendment of the Federal Constitution; one of these is the governmental authority to conduct a system of public education.

policy: a judgment, derived from some system of values and some assessment of situational factors, operating as a general plan for guiding decisions regarding the means of attaining desired objectives.

policy, ad hoc: *see* **ad hoc.**

policy, administrative: *see* **administrative policy.**

policy board: *syn.* **board of control.**

policy, educational: *see* **educational policy.**

policy formulation: a function of policy making which has to do with the selection and statement of the principles and rules of action that are to govern a particular type of activity.

policy making: (1) the act of establishing principles to serve as guides for action; (2) a function of an individual or body of individuals legally endowed with the authority or to whom has been delegated the responsibility to establish policies.

policy, promotion: *see* **promotion policy.**

policy, social: *see* **social policy.**

poliomyelitis: a virus disease which is contagious and, in the paralytic form, produces acute inflammation or destruction of the gray matter of the spinal cord, resulting in paralysis of one or more parts of the body; colloquially called polio. *Syn.* **infantile paralysis.**

poliomyelitis, bulbar: acute anterior poliomyelitis, an infectious disease of viral origin; in this form there are weaknesses and malfunction of the muscles supplied by the lower cranial nerves and most commonly impairment of facial movements, phonation, and swallowing.

political activity: (1) any action having to do with matters pertaining to government; (2) behavior calculated to advance the interests of a political party, cause, or candidate.

political economy: *see* **economy, political.**

political education: (1) education designed to develop understanding of governmental problems and ability to participate in political life; conducted by means of informal discussion, lectures, reading materials, and political activity; (2) education involving indoctrination by the state.

political geography: *see* **geography, political.**

political history: *see* **history, political.**

political party: an organization concerned exclusively with advocating and supporting some program of action in governmental affairs.

political science: *see* **science, political.**

politics: (1) the science dealing with the organization, regulation, and administration of a political state; (2) partisan political activity.

poll, opinion: a survey of public opinion based on a sampling, subject to statistical treatment.

poll tax: *see* **tax, poll.**

pollyanna mechanism: the attempt to believe that "all is well" despite one's actual dissatisfaction. *See* **sweet lemon mechanism.**

polychoric correlation: *see* **correlation, polychoric.**

polycultural studies: *see* **studies, polycultural.**

polyglot dictionary: *see* **dictionary, polyglot.**

polygon, frequency: a graphic representation of a frequency distribution, constructed by plotting each frequency as an ordinate above the midpoint of its class interval and then connecting these plotted points by straight lines; by custom, points showing a frequency of zero are plotted for one additional class interval at each extreme, thereby permitting the polygon to be formed by starting at the base line and returning to the base line. *Syn.* **line polygon;** *see* **table, frequency;** *contr. w.* **histogram; historigram.**

polygon, line: *syn.* **polygon, frequency.**

polylogia (pol'i·lō'ji·ə): excessive speech; loquacity.

polymer pigments: *see* **acrylics.**

polynomial curve: *see* **curve, polynomial.**

polyphony (pō·lif'ə·ni; pol'ə·fō'ni): music resulting from the simultaneous combination of several melodic lines. *Contr. w.* **homophony; monophony.**

polysyllabic word: *see* **word, polysyllabic.**

polytechnic school: a school offering instruction in a number of applied sciences and practical arts.

polytheism: the doctrine of or belief in a plurality of gods. *See* **monotheism.**

ponderal index: *see* **index, ponderal.**

pontifical university: *see* **university, pontifical.**

pony: *see* **crib.**

pool deck: the walk or runway surrounding a swimming pool.

pool hook: a long pole with a large metal hook on one end, used to rescue swimmers from a pool in case of emergency. *Syn.* **rescuing pole.**

pooled rating: *see* **rating, pooled.**

poop sheet: in the Air Force, a slang term for a bulletin, memorandum, or the like containing information or instructions.

poor laws: various laws enacted both in England and in America, before the establishment of free education, to provide for the education of the children of the poor.

poor-work report: *see* **report, poor-work.**

pop art: *see* **art, pop.**

popular control: *see* **control, popular.**

popular election: *see* **election, popular.**

popularity: a state of being liked by the members of a group.

popularizing function: *see* **function, popularizing.**

population: (1) the total group which is of interest or concern; as commonly used in testing, the totality about which statistical inferences are to be made and from which a sample is taken; (2) (stat.) *syn.* **universe.**

population, adult: population over 14 years of age (United States census usage).

population, finite: a universe consisting of a finite and often a known or specified number of possible individuals; for example, the number of male collies registered with the AKC is a finite population when the universe to be sampled is defined as "male collies registered with the AKC," but only a sample (biased) of populations defined as "all male collies," "all collies registered with the AKC," or "all dogs in the United States." *Syn.* **finite universe.**

population forecast: *see* **forecast, population.**

population growth, zero: *see* **zero population growth.**

population, infinite: a population in which the number of possible measurements or observations is unlimited (either actually or theoretically.) *See* **population.**

population, institutional: the number of persons confined in institutions, as reported by the U.S. Census Bureau.

population, mean center of: *see* **mean center of population.**

population, median center of: *see* **median center of population.**

population, metropolitan: as defined for the U.S. Census of 1970, that part of the total population residing in *standard metropolitan statistical areas.*

population, nonmetropolitan: as defined for the United States Census of 1970, that part of the total population residing outside *standard metropolitan statistical areas.*

population, parent: any population from which samples may be drawn, not necessarily a population that has a normal distribution. *See* **population.**

population prediction: *see* **prediction, population.**

population projection, single-year-of-age: *see* **projection, single-year-of-age population.**

population, pupil: the number of pupils enrolled in schools in a given area (school system, state, nation).

population, rural farm: as defined for the U.S. Census of 1970, all persons not part of the urban population and residing on farms of 10 or more acres from which sales of farm products amounted to $50 or more the previous year or residing on farms of less than 10 acres from which such sales amounted to $250 or more; those who rent a house on a farm but who do not use any of the land for farming are excluded from rural farm population.

population, rural nonfarm: as defined for the U.S. Census of 1970, all persons residing in rural territory but not on a farm worked as an economic enterprise. *Comp. w.* **population, rural farm.**

population, school: the total number of different pupils enrolled in a school during a given term.

population, standardization: *see* **standardization population.**

population trend projection: *see* **projection, population trend.**

population, urban: as defined for the United States Census of 1970, all persons residing in areas determined to be *urbanized areas* or *urban places* outside urbanized areas; formerly called *urban residents.*

Populist: originally, an adherent of the People's Party, which was prominent in the United States about 1892; by derivation, an advocate of the extensive invasion of the field of private enterprise by government.

porcelain: (art) a fine ceramic ware that is hard, translucent, white, sonorous, and nonporous and usually consists essentially of kaolin, quartz, and feldspar.

portable building: *see* **building, portable.**

Portland plan: a parallel-course plan according to which bright pupils may complete the work of the elementary school curriculum in a minimum of 6 years while slower pupils are permitted to take 8 years to cover the same work, transfer from one course to the other being made possible at 1- and ½-year intervals.

posit: to set forth as a fact or principle; to affirm; to postulate; to assume as real or conceded.

position, administrative: *see* **administrative position.**

position analysis: *see* **analysis, job.**

position-automatic salary schedule: *see* **salary schedule, position-automatic.**

position average: *see* **average, position.**

position, Category I: (mil. ed.) a position which is required by law or army policy to be filled by individuals who possess graduate training in a relevant field of study; such positions may be supervisory or nonsupervisory.

position, Category II: (mil. ed.) a position in which the major, or most significant, duties cannot be performed except by individuals who possess qualifications that can normally be acquired only by completion of graduate training in a relevant field of study.

position, Category III: (mil. ed.) a position which must be filled by individuals who are required to exert direct technical supervision, of second line or higher level, over military and/or civilian personnel who are required to possess graduate training.

position, Category IV: (mil. ed.) a position which should be filled by individuals who possess sufficient knowledge of a specific field of study to permit effective staff planning, coordination, and command advisory service.

position, Category V: (mil. ed.) a position in which graduate level training is desirable in order to permit effective planning and coordination and to afford prestige in dealing with other military services, governmental agencies, educational institutions, private concerns, and representatives of foreign governments.

position in sibship: the ordinal position of a child among the children in a family.

position-merit salary schedule: *see* **salary schedule, position-merit.**

position salary schedule: *see* **salary schedule, position.**

position, student: *see* **student station.**

position, supervisory: *see* **supervisory position.**

position-type salary schedule: *syn.* **salary schedule, position.**

position, typing: *see* **typing position.**

position writing: in shorthand, the indication of vowels and occasionally of consonants by the relation of a character or outline to the line ruled on the paper.

positive: (1) a print or transparency that reproduces with relative accuracy the tones of the original subject with reference to light and dark; (2) a color print or transparency that reproduces with relative accuracy the color relationships of the original subject; (3) (stat.) a value greater than zero (or some other origin however small); *contr. w.* **negative** (1).

positive acceleration: *see* **acceleration, positive.**

positive adaptation: *see* **adaptation, positive.**

positive afterimage: *see* **afterimage, positive.**

positive association: *see* **association, positive.**

positive behavior: *see* **behavior, positive.**

positive character trait: *see* **character trait, positive.**

positive correlation: *see* **correlation** (1).

positive criticism: *see* **criticism.**

positive discrimination: *syn.* **discrimination** (2).

positive feedback: *see* **feedback, positive.**

positive film: *see* **film, positive.**

positive gain: *see* **gain** (3).

positive guidance: *see* **guidance, positive.**

positive induction: *see* **induction, positive.**

positive integer: *see* **integer, positive.**

positive intercorrelation: *syn.* **positive correlation;** *see* **correlation** (1).

positive law: *see* **moral law.**

positive number: *see* **number, positive.**

positive regard, unconditional: *see* **regard, unconditional positive.**

positive reinforcement: *see* **reinforcement, positive.**

positive relationship: *syn.* **correlation, positive;** *see* **correlation** (1).

positive response: *see* **response, positive.**

positive skewness: *see* **skewness, positive.**

positive teaching: *see* **teaching, positive.**

positive transfer: *see* **transfer, positive.**

positive transference: *see* **transference, positive.**

positively accelerated curve: *see* **curve, positively accelerated.**

positivism: (1) historically, a philosophical trend, based on the thought of Auguste Comte (1798–1857) that sought a unified view of phenomena, both physical and human, through the application of the scientific method; his theory of three historic stages in philosophy includes first, the theological, depending on supernatural and divine beings for explanation of phenomena; second, the metaphysical, depending on rational entities as explanatory principles; third, the positive, in which facts and their relations are understood in their empirical certainty; (2) the view that knowledge is limited to observable facts and their interrelations and that metaphysics and a disciplined method for dealing with values is impossible; (3) a method of dealing with a problem, whereby one acts in the manner in which a typical contemporary scientist deals with his problems of research (Richard von Mises).

positivism, logical: a philosophical movement that holds scientific method to be the basis of knowledge and emphasizes the analysis of language as a method of unifying and clarifying science; also known as *logical empiricism,* and is part of the broader movement known as *scientific empiricism.*

positivism, psychological: *see* **idealism, epistemological.**

post-high school guidance: *see* **guidance, post-high school.**

post-high school instruction, distributive education: *see* **distributive education, postsecondary.**

postbroadcast evaluation: *see* **evaluation, postbroadcast.**

postdoctoral education: study beyond the doctorate, for the further training of scientists or scholars and the advancement of research.

postentry education: education an employee receives outside working hours, aimed at his advancement or preparation for a new position.

poster: a placard, usually pictorial or decorative, utilizing an emotional appeal to convey a message aimed at reinforcing an attitude or urging a course of action.

postfix: *syn.* **suffix.**

postgraduate education: formal education for *graduate students;* usually identified with higher education beyond the baccalaureate degree, but also applicable in some secondary schools where students holding the high school diploma may enroll for additional secondary school courses past requirements for graduation. *See* study, graduate; *dist. f.* postdoctoral education.

postgraduate, high school: a pupil who, after graduating from high school upon completing grade 12, enters a secondary school for additional schoolwork.

postgraduate study: *see* **study, postgraduate.**

Postimpressionism: a style following the Impressionist movement of the late nineteenth century and continuing into the early twentieth century; extended the break from traditional and neoclassic trends toward greater freedom in presentational techniques and emotional interpretation; artists of this period included Paul Cézanne, Edgar Degas, Vincent Van Gogh, Paul Gauguin, and others.

postlingual deafness: *see* **deafness, postlingual.**

postmortem routine: *see* **routine, postmortem.**

postnatal: subsequent to birth. *Contr. w.* **prenatal.**

postponement: any activity used by stutterers for the purpose of concealing or minimizing their difficulties and that serves to delay the attempt to say a feared word. (Fear of stuttering may be so great that the stutterer is unwilling at the moment to attempt the word, or he may feel that after a slight delay he can say the word without difficulty.)

postponement of admission: practice of delaying enrollment of children beyond the general permissive or compulsory school age; an administrative practice usually dependent upon the recommendation of a school psychologist.

postprimary group: *syn.* **elementary grade, intermediate.**

postpubescent: of or pertaining to the early adolescent period immediately following puberty.

postremity theory: the theory that the last thing an organism does in a given situation will be done (most probably) when the situation occurs again.

postschool census file: *see* **census file, postschool.**

postschool record: *see* **record, postschool.**

postsecondary distributive education: *see* **distributive education, postsecondary.**

postsecondary education, agricultural: programs of instruction and on-job experiences at the thirteenth and fourteenth grade levels provided by vocational education in agriculture departments in area vocational schools, junior colleges, and community colleges.

postsecondary instructional level: *see* **instructional level, postsecondary.**

postsputnik era: the period of time following the 1957 launching by the Soviet Union of Sputnik, the first artificial earth satellite, extending through the subsequent United States and Soviet launchings into space, and culminating in the recent (1969–1972) lunar landings by the United States astronauts, first men on the moon.

postulant: one who has expressed the desire to join a religious order; a candidate for admission to community life, who serves a period of probation rarely exceeding 6 months, living as a guest at the convent or monastery.

postulate: *n.* (1) (math.) a mathematical statement which in a deductive system is assumed without proof; gives a property which objects in the system have without defining those objects; for example, "A line is a set of points" gives a property of lines but does not define them; *syn.* **axiom;** (2) (logic) a term borrowed from geometry and referring to that which is self-evident, possible, and necessary to the proof of a proposition; it is not contradicted by any principle of fact; it is slightly broader than *premise,* including constructions as well as theoretical propositions; *see* **assumption; premise; presupposition.**

postulate: *v.* to state as an accepted principle an assertion to be used as a basis for drawing inferences.

postulate, parallel: an assumption made by Euclid about parallel lines; a common version (not Euclid's) is "Given a line and a point not on the line, there is exactly one line containing the given point and parallel to the given line"; the non-Euclidean geometries substitute another postulate for this; for *Riemannian geometry* this postulate asserts that there is no line through the point parallel to the given line, while for *Lobachevskian geometry* the postulate asserts that there are at least two.

postulation method: *see* **thinking, postulational.**

postulational thinking: *see* **reasoning, axiomatic.**

posture: certain orientation of the body in space, or parts of the body in relation to other parts, which opposes gravity and involves mechanisms for maintaining or restoring balance.

posture, arm-hand: *see* **arm-hand posture.**

posture education: the process of learning the best adaptation of the bearing or position of the body as a whole within the limits of one's natural skeletal frame.

posture scale: *see* **scale, posture.**

posture score: *see* **score, posture.**

postvisitation conference: *see* **conference, postvisitation.**

potential deafness: *see* **deafness, potential.**

potential dropout: *see* **dropout, potential.**

potential, growth: *see* **growth potential.**

potential vocabulary: *see* **vocabulary, potential.**

potentiality: in the philosophy of Aristotle, (1) the mode of being of whatever could be, but in fact is not, actualized; (2) a capacity to act as originative source of change in another thing, or to be acted upon and change, belonging to a species by virtue of the kind of matter it is made of (for example, the capacity of man to become educated), or to an individual by virtue of the kind of development his powers have had (for example, the teaching skill of Socrates).

pottery: (1) ceramic wares made of clay that have been dried and hardened by firing; usually they have a vitreous glaze applied to the surface; (2) the activity of making such objects, frequently included in school art courses; (3) a place where earthen pots are made. *See* **ceramics.**

poverty area: as defined for the United States Census of 1970, those *census tracts* and minor civil divisions (townships, municipalities, towns, election districts, boroughs, etc.) or census county divisions where there is an incidence of poverty at least $1\frac{1}{4}$ times the national average.

poverty clause: an exception in compulsory school attendance laws that provides for those children whose services are needed to support the family.

poverty program: *see* **program, poverty.**

powdered tempera: *see* **equipment, early childhood education.**

power: (math.) the number of times a quantity is to be multiplied by itself; for example, X^2 is the second power of X and is equal to X times X; X^4, the fourth power, equals X times X times X times X.

power amplifier: *see* **amplifier, power.**

power curve: a graphic curve that shows the probability of rejecting a null hypothesis when it is really true.

power, discretionary: the power to act, not arbitrarily but with considered judgment regarding possible options.

power, effective purchasing: *syn.* **income, real.**

power function: *see* **power curve.**

power, intraorganizational: (school admin.) the activity of those who are moving other men to act in relation to themselves or in relation to organic or inorganic objects; the force underlying ordered interactions among members of an organized group.

power plant: (1) a building or buildings containing the heating equipment of a school or other institution; (2) the power and heating equipment itself; (3) equipment for the production of electricity; (4) all mechanical apparatus required to provide light, heat, and power.

power, police: *see* **police power.**

power, public: *see* **public power.**

power, purchasing: *see* **purchasing power.**

power reading: *see* **reading, power.**

power scale: *see* **scale, power.**

power score: *see* **score, power.**

power, student: student participation, authority, control, and influence on college campuses; a rallying cry of student activists. *See* **activism** (5); **activist, student.**

power technology: *see* **technology, power.**

power test: *see* **test, power.**

power, typing: *see* **typing power.**

powers, appetitive: *see* **appetitive powers.**

Powers card: a data card of the punch-card type suitable for actuating a Powers (mechanical) statistical or accounting machine.

powers, delegated: powers based on the authority of a person who is delegated or commissioned to act in the stead of another.

powers intellectual: the various capabilities or diverse functions that comprise the overall operation of intelligence; the intellect in its various manifestations and operations, including abstraction and generalization, reasoning and inference, intuition, memory, and imagination. *See* **factor analysis.**

Powers machine: any one of a number of sorting, tabulating, and other special statistical machines designed to be activated by punch cards; originally manufactured and leased by the Powers Tabulating Machine Co. and later by Remington Rand, Inc. *See* **tabulating machine;** *dist f.* **Hollerith machine; International Business Machines.**

powers of school board, permissive: *see* **permissive powers of school board.**

powers, reserved: powers not delegated by the states to the Federal government.

practical arts: *see* **arts, practical.**

practical arts education: a type of functional education predominantly manipulative in nature which provides learning experiences in leisure-time interests, consumer knowledge, creative expression, family living, manual skills, technological development, and similar areas of value to all.

practical geometry: *see* **geometry, practical.**

practical imperative: *see* **imperative, practical.**

practical intelligence: *see* **intelligence, practical.**

practical judgment: *see* **judgment, practical.**

practical nurse education: a program offering training in approved schools which leads to licensure as practical or vocational nurse.

practical philosophy: *see* **philosophy, practical.**

practical problem: *syn.* **problem, real.**

practical validity: *see* **validity, practical.**

practice class: *see* **class, practice.**

practice cottage: a dwelling, housing a home economics department, in which homemaking is taught.

practice, directed: a specific supervisory activity usually associated with in-service education programs; involves individualized or small-group supervision in which a supervisory person guides and assists a staff member who is undertaking to employ new skills.

practice, distributed: that schedule of practice in which separate trials are followed by rest periods or periods of other kinds of activities. *Syn.* **spaced practice;** *contr. w.* **practice, massed.**

practice effect: *see* **effect, practice.**

practice exercise: *see* **exercise, practice.**

practice group: *see* **group, practice.**

practice, home: (home ec.) *see* **home (and community) experiences.**

practice house: *syn.* **home-management house.**

practice lesson: *see* **lesson, practice.**

practice, massed: arrangement of learning material either in its presentation or during study so that there are few or no intervals of rest or spaces between successive periods of practice. *Contr. w.* **practice, distributed.**

practice material: (1) an exercise, based on the use of a skill or technique, given to pupils or students to enable them to master the skill or technique involved; (2) an item or exercise (to which the correct answer is usually self-evident) provided in an objective test as an illustration of how to proceed in answering the exercise that follows.

practice mode: a mode of operation of a teaching machine in which the student continues to make responses to a frame until he makes the correct response; after each response he is told whether it is correct or not. *Syn.* **correction procedure.**

practice, pattern: *see* **pattern practice.**

practice period: *see* **period, practice.**

practice sales talk: a teaching procedure in which one student acts as a salesperson while another student or the teacher takes the part of a prospective customer, the student thus securing practice in demonstrating articles, in meeting objections, in using correct English, and in applying the principles of courtesy and tact; used by teachers of salesmanship in secondary schools and colleges to develop in students the personal qualifications and skills needed by salespeople.

practice school: (1) generally, an elementary or secondary school used by a teacher education institution for giving students an opportunity to practice and observe teaching methods under the supervision of trained teachers; *see* **model school** (1) and (2); (2) narrowly, a school in which students of a teacher education institution practice teaching methods (usually the practice of methods and procedures advocated by the institution is implied); *see* **laboratory school; model school.**

practice school, rural: (1) a school located in a rural community or on the campus of a teacher-education institution and organized like a rural school to provide opportunity for practice teaching as a part of the preparation of rural school teachers; (2) a one- or two-teacher school, consolidated school, or village school not maintained by a teacher education institution but used by such an institution for practice teaching.

practice, service: *see* service practice.

practice, spaced: *see* practice, distributed.

practice supervision: *see* supervision, practice.

practice teacher: *see* teaching, practice.

practice teaching: *see* teaching, practice.

practice test: *see* test, practice.

practice work: (1) *syn.* fieldwork (3); (2) (voc. ed.) operations or elements of jobs (usually performed on scrap material) to supplement experience or production jobs in developing manipulative skills.

practices, adoption of: *see* adoption of practices.

practices, instructional: *see* teaching technique.

practicum (prak'ti·kəm): (1) a course of instruction aimed at closely relating the study of theory and practical experience, both usually being carried on simultaneously; (2) an academic exercise consisting of study and practical work; (3) supervised experience in counseling through such procedures as role-playing, recorded interviews, abstraction, analysis, and supervisory evaluation with interviewing techniques.

practicum, counseling: *see* counseling practicum.

pragmatic maxim: the maxim, first formulated by C. S. Peirce, that "in order to ascertain the meaning of an intellectual conception one should consider what practical consequences might conceivably result from necessity from the truth of that conception; and the sum of these consequences will constitute the entire meaning of the conception."

pragmatics: a branch of the study of signs, dealing with their uses and effects. *Comp. w.* semantics; syntactics.

pragmatism: (1) the philosophical position, founded in the United States by Charles S. Peirce and continued by John Dewey, and given a different, more psychological interpretation by William James, which holds that the meaning of an idea consists in the conduct it designates, that all thought distinctions consist in possible differences in practice, that thinking is a functional process for guiding action, and that truth is a social value which ideas earn as they are verified by competent inquirers in the open forum of thought and discussion; (2) sometimes loosely and erroneously thought to be the doctrine that a narrowly practical interest or view should predominate, that ends are denied or reduced to the status of means, that an idea which works or is personally satisfying is therefore true.

pragmatism, social: the belief that a value has its meaning in terms of its effect on such aspects of group life as interaction, culture, and the satisfaction of the needs of the group members.

Prägnanz (präg·nänts'): (1) the most characteristic shape or form an object can take (Wertheimer); (2) the tendency of memory traces of perceptual figures to change in the direction of a "better" gestalt, which results in a reduction of stress (Kohler, Kofka).

praxiology: (1) the organized, disciplined study of the principles of the practices of man which ultimately affect individual and social human behavior; (2) a distinct, developing body of knowledge which is being tested in practice and codified; (3) a proposed science of conduct and its disorders. *See* arts, industrial; praxiology, industrial.

praxiology, industrial: that subcategory of praxiological knowledge which is derived from the study of industrial management and production practices.

prayer: (1) (relig.) the effort of the individual to enter in communion with God through adoration, thanksgiving, confession, and supplication; this "lifting up the mind to God" may be with or without words, public or private, corporate or individual; (2) (legal) the part of a complaint that asks for relief.

prayer decisions: court decisions relating to prayer and Bible-reading ceremonies in public schools in the United States of America; for example, *Engel v. Vitale,* 370 U.S. 421 (1962) and *School District, Abington Township v. Schempp; Murray v. Curlett,* 374 U.S. 203 (1963); the former ruled against the State Board of Regents's recommended prayer for public school classrooms in New York, the latter declared unconstitutional a state law

requiring the reading of at least ten verses from the Holy Bible in public school classrooms in Pennsylvania; in actual practice, the reading of the scriptures was often followed by the recitation of the Lord's Prayer.

pre-high school guidance: *see* guidance, pre-high school.

pre-student-teaching observation: *see* observation, pre-student-teaching.

preadolescence: that period of life comprising the years just prior to pubescence or the very early stages of pubescence.

preamplifier: in an audio system, an amplifier designed to increase the strength of weak signals to a suitable level for further amplification by a power amplifier while preserving the quality and integrity of the original signal.

preaudit: an audit performed on the items of a budget to determine if contemplated expenditures are duly authorized or legal.

preband instrument: *syn.* instrument, preorchestral.

prebroadcast evaluation: *see* evaluation, prebroadcast.

precane technique: any of the techniques used by blind individuals to afford maximum protection, efficiency, and safety when moving about without the use of a mobility aid such as the long cane.

precept: a commandment, directive, order, or mandate; not to be confused with *concept.*

preceptor: (1) a member of the faculty, of any rank, at Princeton University, who directs the study of one or more small groups in a course, usually holding a weekly conference with each group; (2) a practicing physician who accepts an undergraduate medical student as an assistant and gives him personal training in the practice of medicine.

preceptorial plan: a plan of instruction at Princeton University under which small groups of students were assigned to faculty members to hold conferences with the groups to direct their reading and study.

précis (prā·sē'; prā'sē; pres'ē): a summary or digest (not, however, in outline form) of the most important parts of a work, such as a book or article, utilizing wherever possible the style and choice of words of the original.

precision: (1) (math. meas.) the degree of refinement with which a measurement is made; the smaller the unit of measure, the greater the precision (3.25 inches, correct to the nearest hundredth of an inch, is more *precise* than $3\frac{1}{4}$ inches, correct to the nearest fourth of an inch); (2) the exactness of a statement; (3) (exper.) the degree to which observed differences in criterion measures are due only to the variations in conditions deliberately introduced or prearranged by the investigator; (4) an estimate of the confidence that may be placed in an obtained statistic or of the divergence of the sample from the corresponding parameter; *see* coefficient, confidence; error, standard.

precision in measurement: *see* measurement, precision in.

precision, index of: *see* index of precision.

precocious child: *see* child, precocious.

precocity: mental or physical growth greatly in advance of that characteristic of a given age.

precoded answer categories: alternative answers to an item of a questionnaire, rating scale, or test that are labeled (precoded) with code numbers or addends; for example (code numbers precede the voting boxes), What is your sex? Check (√) one.

1] ☐ Male
2] ☐ Female

precoding: the act or process of assigning code symbols, usually numbers, to various categorized responses that a person may make in completing a questionnaire, rating scale, or test. *See* precoded answer categories.

precollege counseling: *see* counseling, precollege.

precollege guidance: *see* counseling, precollege.

precurrent response: *see* response, precurrent.

predelinquent: (1) one who is inclined to fail in duty or to offend by neglect or violation of duty or law; (2) one who sympathizes with delinquents or who boasts or threatens that he will perform delinquent acts; (3) one who shows tendencies toward antisocial behavior, owing to inherent characteristics or environmental conditions or to a combination of both.

predestination: the doctrine that every event in the life of man, including his final or eternal destiny, is predetermined by a higher order or being.

predicament, egocentric: *see* **egocentric predicament.**

predicate: *n.* (1) in formal logic, a sentence containing zero or more variables; (2) in mathematics, thought of as representing an *open sentence;* thus the logic of predicates translates to the logic of open sentences; *see* **sentence, open.**

prediction: *syn.* **forecast.**

prediction, actuarial: *syn.* **prediction, statistical.**

prediction, clinical: prediction of academic achievement, based upon case data and subjective judgments formed from an interview as well as upon the statistical significance of objective test data accumulated concerning the individual.

prediction, comparative: prediction of the absolute level of performance in each of several tasks.

prediction, differential: prediction of differences in achievement levels attained in pairs of school subjects or fields of endeavor, as contrasted with general prediction of success in a single activity or in several activities combined.

prediction, educational: a probability statement of the degree of scholastic success likely to be achieved by a student, judgment being based on the case-study method, with particular emphasis on the results of scholastic aptitude test scores.

prediction, efficiency of: *see* **index of forecasting efficiency.**

prediction, error of: *syn.* **error of estimate.**

prediction, multiple: prediction of the value of a criterion variable on the basis of known values on two or more measures (predictor variables). *See* **variable, predictor.**

prediction, population: the forecast of the number of persons expected to inhabit a given region (city, county, etc.) during one or more years in the future.

prediction, statistical: determination of the most probable level of success in a given task, based upon values of one or more independent variables, usually tests of previous success in similar tasks; for example, prediction of a student's academic achievement by means of mathematical equations utilizing the results of aptitude tests and/or marks in subjects previously studied. *Syn.* **actuarial prediction.**

predictive efficiency: a measure of the proportion of correct predictions a test makes possible. *See* **index of forecasting efficiency.**

predictive index: *syn.* **index of forecasting efficiency.**

predictive measure: *see* **measure, predictive.**

predictive validity: *see* **validity, predictive.**

predictive value: loose *syn.* **validity** (2).

predictor variable: *see* **variable, predictor.**

predisposition: the inherited capacity of an individual to develop a certain trait or attribute. (The capacity is transmissible genetically, but the attribute or trait does not necessarily appear unless the proper constitutional and environmental factors coexist.)

preeducation curriculum: *see* **curriculum, preeducation.**

preeducation sequence: *syn.* **curriculum, preeducation.**

preemployment counseling: *see* **counseling, preemployment.**

preemployment instruction, business and office education: *see* **instruction, business and office education preparatory.**

preemployment instruction, distributive education: *see* **instruction, distributive education preparatory.**

preemployment training: *see* **training, preemployment.**

preemployment training, distributive education: *see* **instruction, distributive education preparatory.**

preentry education: all the education and training a person has had prior to employment.

prefect of studies: a minor official in a Roman Catholic school who has charge of curricular assignments or other delegated authority.

preference: favorable evaluation of some object, course of action, method, end, or such, as compared to other possibilities that are rejected; a selection that may be intellectual or emotional in origin, that is always volitional at least in the act of choosing, and that concerns any of the value realms such as aesthetics or morals.

preferential voting: a system of voting in which the voters indicate their preference among candidates for an office so that, if no candidate receives a majority of first choices, the one receiving the greatest number of first and second choices together is nominated or elected.

prefirst class: *see* **class, kindergarten extension.**

prefirst grade: *syn.* **extension, kindergarten** (1).

prefix: a letter, syllable, or word which has a sense of its own and is placed at the beginning of a word or word *root* and fused with it, thereby changing the word's meaning, for example, *n* in *none, per* in *perform, out* in *outrage. See* **suffix.**

prefix, disjoined: (shorthand) the beginning of a word, consisting of one or more letters or syllables, which is not joined to the main part of the word because it has its own symbol.

prefix, inseparable: a prefix which does not exist as a separate word; for example, *se* in *a secluded grove.*

prefix, joined: (shorthand) one or more letters united with the beginning of a word, which in shorthand are joined to the main part of the word, for example, *after. dis. per, pur,* or *pro.*

prefix, separable: a prefix that can also exist free; for example, "the oncoming summer," "summer is coming on."

preflight aeronautics: *see* **aeronautics, preflight.**

preflight school: (mil. ed.) a school at which preflight training is carried out. *See* **aeronautics, preflight.**

preflight training: *see* **training, preflight.**

preformation: the doctrine that the various organs and parts of an organism exist in rudimentary form in the germ cell and that development is merely the subsequent unfolding of what was already present in miniature.

preformistic: referring to those views which hold that the patterning of physical traits and motor functions is determined by the germ plasm.

pregenital: (psychoan.) prior to the age of puberty; applied to the stage of sexuality in children prior to the centering of erotic interest in the genitals.

pregenital character: *see* **character, pregenital.**

pregenital sexuality: *see* **sexuality, pregenital.**

prehensile: adapted or fit for grasping objects.

prehension: (1) the act of seizing, grasping, or picking up an object; (2) (T. Brameld) unity, organic wholeness, of natural events; a unified type of awareness preceding and succeeding *apprehension. See* **apprehension** (1).

prehension, pellet: the act of grasping and picking up a small pill from a flat surface; used as a measure of motor coordination in infants.

prehension, pincer: the use of the thumb and first finger in opposed position for grasping or picking up an object; usually develops in infants between 7 and 12 months.

prehensory behavior: *see* **behavior, prehensory.**

prehistoric art: *see* **art, prehistoric.**

preinduction training: *see* **training, preinduction.**

preinstrument class: *see* **class, preinstrument.**

prejudice: an uncritical opinion or attitude held without regard for, or in spite of, evidence, grounds, or considered judgment.

prejudice, race: *see* **race prejudice.**

prekindergarten: planned education for preschool children, especially ages 3 and 4. *See* **early childhood education; preschool education.**

preliminary budget: *see* **budget, preliminary.**

preliminary control: *see* **control, preliminary.**

preliminary report: *see* **report, preliminary.**

preliminary test: *see* **test, preliminary.**

prelingual deafness: *see* **deafness, prelingual.**

prematriculation examinations: *see* **examinations, prematriculation.**

premature infant: *see* **infant, premature.**

prematurity, traumatic: birth before the normal time brought on by wound or injury.

premise: one of the two propositions called major and minor premises from which a third called the *conclusion* is derived or inferred; these three propositions form the *syllogism* which is the center of all formal logic. *See* **assumption; postulate; presupposition.**

premium pay: (voc. ed.) a sum in addition to regular compensation which is paid because of unusual circumstances such as overtime, or Sunday and holiday work, because the work is of a particularly hazardous or unpleasant nature, because the employee receiving the bonus possesses unusual ability or skill, or because the employee has produced above a specified minimum level of productivity.

prenatal: prior to birth. *Contr. w. postnatal.*

prenatal behavior: *see* **behavior, prenatal.**

prenatal clinic: *see* **clinic, prenatal.**

prenatal influence: any factor operating to modify or alter development during the period of intrauterine existence. *See* **maternal impressions, doctrine of.**

preoperational period: (Piaget) the stage in a child's mental development, in middle childhood, in which he is able to use symbols and to foresee consequences but cannot readily handle abstractions.

preorchestral instrument: *see* **instrument, preorchestral.**

preparation: (1) a step in Herbart's *five formal steps* in which the instructor motivates the subject or unit by appropriate historical or other data calculated to arouse interest in the unit; (2) a step in a directed-study plan in which the teacher attempts to set the stage or arouse an interest in something that is to be studied (often known as the building of background).

preparation and conference period: *see* **period, preparation and conference.**

preparation-automatic salary schedule: *see* **salary schedule, preparation-automatic.**

preparation, class: (1) the planning and work by a teacher prior to and for teaching one or more sections of a class; (2) study by students in preparation for a class meeting.

preparation for marriage: *see* **marriage, preparation for.**

preparation, indirect: *see* **Montessori method.**

preparation-merit salary schedule: *see* **salary schedule, preparation-merit.**

preparation, occupational: (home ec.) the courses or units in vocational home economics or technical schools emphasizing acquisition of knowledge and development of understanding, attitudes, and skills in the field of home economics necessary for gainful employment; learning activities and experiences are oriented toward the development of competencies essential for entry into a chosen occupation or for acquiring new or additional competencies for upgrading occupational proficiency.

preparation, professional: the total formal preparation for teaching that a person has completed in a teacher education institution; more usually it is understood to include, in addition, the aggregate of his experience in positions involving educational activities.

preparation, special-field: a teacher's preparation in one of the *special instructional fields,* as distinguished from his preparation in an academic field.

preparation, subject-matter: the preparation that a teacher has had in college or university in the academic areas, such as English, biology, history, and mathematics, in which he plans to teach.

preparatory classes: *see* **instruction, distributive education preparatory.**

preparatory function: *see* **function, preparatory.**

preparatory instruction, business and office education: *see* **instruction, business and office education preparatory.**

preparatory instruction, distributive education: *see* **instruction, distributive education preparatory.**

preparatory mathematics: *see* **mathematics, preparatory.**

preparatory motion: the handwriting motion that precedes the actual contact of the pen with the paper.

preparatory program, agricultural: *see* **program, agricultural preparatory.**

preparatory school: a school the purpose of which is the preparation of students for entrance to another educational institution; usually refers, in the United States, to a private secondary school preparing students for college.

preparatory school, private: a nonpublic school at the secondary level, usually one specializing in preparation for college.

prepared environment: *see* **environment, prepared.**

preparental education: training in such subjects as child psychology, nutrition, and health given to prospective parents with a view to increasing their efficiency as parents.

preprimary class: *syn.* **extension, kindergarten** (1).

preprimary education: an early childhood education program emphasizing the training, education, and total development of the child. *See* **kindergarten; nursery school.**

preprimary group: *syn.* **extension, kindergarten** (1).

preprimer: a beginner's reading book, consisting of single-line sentences and limited to a very small vocabulary.

preprimer class: *syn.* **extension, kindergarten** (1).

preprimer group: *syn.* **extension, kindergarten** (1).

preprimer type: large type commonly used in preprimers, generally 18 point or 24 point.

preprint: a document which is distributed in advance of its presentation or publication. *Comp. w.* **reprint.**

preprofessional training: *see* **training, preprofessional.**

prepuberal dip (prē·pū′bər·əl): deceleration in growth just prior to the adolescent spurt, one of the significant indications of pubescence.

prepubescent: of or pertaining to the period of late childhood just preceding puberty.

prereading class: *see* **class, prereading.**

prereading experience: *see* **experience, prereading.**

prereading program: *see* **program, prereading.**

prerecognition hypothesis: *see* **hypothesis, prerecognition.**

prerecorded tape: *see* **tape, prerecorded.**

preregistration: advance registration for participation in a particular program, workshop, or course, completed on payment of fees either immediately or during a final registration period just prior to the start of the activity.

prerepresentative drawing: *see* **drawing, prerepresentative.**

prerequisite: (1) a course that must be satisfactorily completed before enrollment will be permitted in an advanced or succeeding course; (2) any requirement that must be satisfied as a preliminary to a course or to any end or event (thus, swimming requirements may be a prerequisite to a course in lifesaving, or a speech course may be prerequisite to participation in school radio programs).

prerequisite mathematics: *see* **mathematics, prerequisite.**

prerequisites, college: the educational background and personal qualities of a prospective student which are required by a college for admission to a specific program or class, for example, the 16 *Carnegie units.*

presbycusia: *see* **presbycusis.**

presbycusis (prez′bi·kū′sis): the gradually increasing loss of hearing acuity associated with advancing age.

presbyopia (prez′bi·ō′pi·ə): (lit., "old sight") a restriction of accommodation due to inelasticity of the lens of the eye, developing with advancing age; distant objects can be seen clearly, but no distinct picture of nearby objects can be obtained.

preschematic developmental stage: *see* **developmental stage, preschematic.**

preschool census file: *see* **census file, preschool.**

preschool child: *see* **child, preschool.**

preschool class: *see* **class, preschool.**

preschool clinic: *see* **clinic, preschool.**

preschool curriculum: *see* **curriculum, preschool.**

preschool education: the method and theory of guiding young children in a group, generally referring to education demonstrated in *nursery schools;* emphasis is placed on developing capacities of the individual and on helping him to meet his problems.

preschool period: a term that refers usually to that period in the child's life when he is between 2 and 5 years of age.

preschool teacher: a person trained in child development or early childhood education who is involved in a program for preschool children in nursery school, kindergarten, or a day care center; may be assisted by nonprofessional workers.

preschool training for the deaf: *see* **training for the deaf, preschool.**

preschool vocabulary: *see* **vocabulary, preschool.**

preschooler: a child below kindergarten age.

prescription: (teacher ed.) faculty determination of the specific subjects and sequences of curricula that a student is to follow in preparing to become a teacher. (Prescription is opposed to election, which allows a student to choose from specific courses and to determine the sequence in which he will take the courses.)

prescription, curriculum: *see* **curriculum prescription.**

prescriptive grammar: *see* **grammar, prescriptive.**

prescriptive teaching: *see* **teaching, prescriptive.**

presecondary schooling: *syn.* **elementary education.**

preselection: (mil. ed.) the process of testing and observing individuals for those qualities desired in astronauts prior to their selection for training.

presentation: (1) a step in the Morrison plan of directing learning or study, involving the motivation of the study of a subject by a clear definition of the unit and by presenting a setting for the unit to arouse interest in the subject; (2) one of Herbart's *five formal steps.*

presentative theory of knowledge: *see* **knowledge, presentative theory of.**

presenting complaint: *see* **complaint, presenting.**

preservation of floors: the treatment of wood floors, or floors of other material, with some material that will prevent excessive wear from shoes and abrasives; floor preservatives may be various kinds of wax or oil and wax combined.

preservice education: the academic and professional work in high school, normal school, college, teachers college, or university that a person has done before employment as a teacher.

preservice preparation: *syn.* **preservice education.**

preservice selection: *see* **selection, preservice.**

preservice supervision: *see* **supervision, preservice.**

presession conference: *see* **conference, presession.**

president: the principal administrative officer of an institution of higher education.

President's Commission on Higher Education (1947): a committee of educators and civic leaders organized by presidential order to examine the functions of higher education and the means by which they can best be performed; report titled *Higher Education in American Democracy,* 1947.

press: the publications of a country taken collectively; often refers specifically to newspapers.

press club: *see* **club, press.**

press conference: *see* **conference, press.**

press, law of the: *see* **law of the press.**

press, university: a publishing establishment connected with a university and especially concerned with the publishing of scholarly works.

Pressey device: a multiple-choice device dating from the 1920s which presented questions either on a rotating drum or on separate sheets; the student selected an alternative and pressed a corresponding key; the machine was coded so that if the student's response was correct, the device advanced to the next question; if the response was incorrect, an error was tallied, and the device remained set for the question until the correct response was given; the device provided a raw score and an items analysis or error count.

pressure area: the phase of the professional work of a teacher that presents the greatest amount of difficulty or that makes heavy demands on his time and energy.

pressure, boiler: *see* **boiler pressure.**

pressure cooker approach: in early childhood education, an approach produced by Carl Bereiter together with philosopher Siegfried Englemann for teaching language and arithmetic skills to culturally disadvantaged 4- and 5-year olds; by employing a drill method the researchers aim at enabling disadvantaged children to start first grade on an equal footing with more privileged children. *See* **Project Head Start.**

pressure group: *see* **group, pressure.**

pressure pattern: the manner in which the different factors of the teacher load vary in weight in the case of an individual teacher or group of teachers.

prestige: special distinction in a social group, usually attributable to family connections, accomplishments, or the possession of goods valued highly by the group.

presupposition: a somewhat broader term than *premise;* that which is assumed or supposed as antecedent to the desired result of a course of reasoning; it is thus logically and causally necessary, although it may be merely a conjecture or presumption. *See* **assumption; postulate; premise.**

preteaching conference: *see* **conference, preteaching.**

pretest: (1) *syn.* **fore-exercise;** (2) a test given in order to determine the status of the testee or group in regard to some skill, aptitude, or achievement, as a basis for judging the effectiveness of subsequent treatment; (3) a tryout of some measuring instrument or piece of equipment in advance of its regular use.

pretraining selection: *see* **selection, pretraining.**

pretranscription training: *see* **training, pretranscription.**

prevention, dropout: *see* **dropout prevention.**

preventive discipline: *see* **discipline, preventive.**

preventive guidance: *see* **guidance, preventive.**

preventive maintenance: *see* **maintenance, preventive.**

preventive reading instruction: *see* **instruction, preventive reading.**

preventive teaching: *see* **teaching, preventive.**

preview: a preliminary showing of a motion picture or filmstrip, usually for the purpose of criticism, appraisal, and preparation for use.

prevocational activities: *see* **activities, prevocational.**

prevocational agriculture: *see* **agriculture, prevocational.**

prevocational course: *see* **course, prevocational.**

prevocational education: (1) an educational program, usually in the junior high school, providing general industrial arts and other experiences for exploratory and guidance purposes rather than preparation for a specific occupation; intended to lay a foundation for future vocational choice with understanding; (2) the first phase of a high school work-study program which offers students the opportunity to evaluate their abilities as workers and to become familiar with job requirements.

prevocational evaluation: *see* **evaluation, prevocational.**

price index, consumer: *see* **index, consumer price.**

priest: (1) a minister of sacred worship, found in almost all the great religions, and usually a person directly involved with the offering of sacrifices; (2) any member of the Christian church who, by virtue of this membership, shares in the priesthood of Christ, commonly called "the priesthood of all believers"; (3) the clergy in those churches stressing Catholic continuity through Apostolic succession; such priests are ordained especially to preside at the celebration of the Eucharist, to preach and to teach, and to administer the other sacraments including that of Penance (forgiveness of sins). *See* **minister; rabbi.**

prima facie (pri′mǝ fā′shi·ē): (Lat., lit., "at first appearance") (1) said of evidence that is subject to the possibility of being modified or completely overthrown after more thorough examination has been made and additional evidence, less obvious but perhaps more weighty, has been adduced; (2) said of the minimum evidence that will uphold a verdict as a matter of law.

primacy, law of: *see* **law of primacy.**

primal horde: the hypothetical organization of the human family before primitive clans developed.

primary ability: *see* **ability, primary.**

primary Air Force specialty code: *see* **code, primary Air Force specialty.**

primary amentia: *see* **amentia, primary.**

primary arithmetic: *see* **arithmetic, primary.**

primary class, ungraded: *see* **class, ungraded primary.**

primary correlation: *see* **correlation, primary.**

primary drive: *see* **drive, primary.**

primary education: that division of the elementary school including grades 1 to 3; devoted primarily to instruction in fundamental skills and the development of social attitudes necessary for democratic living.

primary emotion: *see* **emotion, primary.**

primary experience: *see* **experience, primary.**

primary factor: *see* **factor, primary.**

primary facts: the simplest arithmetic number combinations in addition, subtraction, multiplication, and division, such as the 100 facts in addition secured by pairing for purposes of addition the digits 0, 1, 2, . . . , 9, in every possible way.

primary flying training: *see* **training, primary flying.**

primary grade: *see* **grade, primary.**

primary group: *see* **group, primary.**

primary mental abilities: *see* **abilities, primary mental.**

primary multiplication facts: *syn.* **multiplication facts.**

primary pilot training: *see* **training, primary pilot.**

primary qualities: the properties, attributes, or characteristics of a body, such as figure, size, and position, which are necessary and sufficient to define the body, as distinct from *secondary qualities* such as color or taste, which do not necessarily identify and differentiate the body. (John Locke made the now classic argument that the primary qualities inhere in the object, while the *secondary qualities* are modes of perception induced in the observer by the object.)

primary reading retardation: *see* **reading retardation, primary.**

primary room: a room in which children of the primary grades are taught.

primary school: (1) a school that enrolls pupils in the first two, three, or four grades or years of school; may include preprimer groups; (2) a school of a type that sprang up about 1800, enrolling 30 to 40 pupils between the ages of 4 and 7 or 8; publicly supported and administered by a primary school committee.

primary service objectives: *see* **objectives, primary service.**

primary source: *see* **source, primary.**

primary substance: *see* **substance (2).**

primary subtraction facts: *see* **subtraction facts.**

primary training: *see* **training, primary.**

primary unit: *see* **unit, primary.**

primary vector: *see* **vector, primary.**

prime number: *see* **number, prime.**

prime-number code: *see* **code, prime-number.**

primer: (1) the first book after the *preprimer* in a basic reading series; (2) a simple, easy reading book intended for children in the early first grade.

primer, Columbian: a small (84-page) modernized and secularized imitation of the New England primer with each letter of the alphabet illustrated; printed in 1802.

primer, New England: a famous primer, composed of religious subject matter, published in Boston about 1690 and used extensively as the first book for teaching children to read in colonial America.

primer type: large type, usually 18 point, used in primers.

primitive art: *see* **art, primitive.**

primitive education: the system of learning, both formal and informal, in which primitive man acquires the skills and knowledge pertinent to the society in which he lives; primitive education tends to be more informal in character than education in the civilized societies but operates as a very effective instrument in the transmission of the social heritage.

primitive level hearing: *see* **hearing, primitive level.**

primitive man: man at the early stages of his cultural development and previous to the time when he could write records of his own experiences or progress. *See* **nonliterate.**

primitivism: the theory and tendency to believe that the simple, uncomplicated past contained the good; usually accompanied by the desire to return to it; evidenced today in the inability of many people to accept the complexities and realities of twentieth-century life; its political and religious expressions (frequently synonymous) tend to be hysterical and hence irrational.

prince school: one of the several types of schools that arose during the Renaissance, also known as a *Fürstenschule;* these schools were modeled on the court schools of Italy and were intended to educate leaders in church and state. *See* **Fürstenschulen.**

principal: the administrative head and professional leader of a school division or unit, such as a high school, junior high school, or elementary school; a highly specialized, full-time administrative officer in large public school systems, but usually carrying a teaching load in small ones; in public education, usually subordinate to a superintendent of schools. *See* **headmaster;** *contr. w.* **principal, supervising.**

principal, assistant: an officer who is designated as an assistant to the principal of a school and whose specific powers and duties vary according to the local situation.

principal axes: (fact. anal.) a set of orthogonal axes in which one axis (the major principal axis) is so located that the sum of the squares of the factor loadings is a maximum and some other axis (the mean principal axis) is so located that the sum of the squares of the factor loadings is a minimum. (The major principal axis defines that factor which accounts for the maximum possible part of the variance of the test battery, the first two principal axes account for the maximum possible part of the variance that can be described by two factors, etc.)

principal axes solution: (fact. anal.) that factor resolution of a matrix in which each successive reference axis is located so as to maximize the sum of squares of factor loadings or test projections.

principal, building: the person designated as the administrative officer in charge of a particular school building.

principal component: (fact. anal.) (1) a factor loading determined by one of the principal axes; (2) the factors determined by the principal axes.

principal diagonal: *see* **diagonal, principal.**

principal, district: an administrative or supervisory officer who is responsible in specified matters for the conduct of all the schools or the schools of a certain type within a geographical division of the township, county, city, or other such unit. *Syn.* **district superintendent.**

principal, elementary school: an administrative and supervisory officer responsible for an elementary school; usually limited to a single school or attendance area; may or may not engage in teaching.

principal, high school: an administrative and supervisory officer in charge of a high school, giving to administrative duties full time in large public schools and usually carrying a teaching load in small ones.

principal sequence: the subject field in which the student concentrates or specializes. *Syn.* **major, departmental;** *see* **field of concentration.**

principal, special school: the administrative head of a school for handicapped children or other school organized for any special purpose.

principal, supervising: (1) in some states, the executive head of all but the largest school systems; *syn.* **superintendent of schools;** (2) a school principal who has 75 percent or more of his time free from classroom teaching duties; (3) a person who takes charge of the more important details of administration and supervision of a group of city schools, usually assisted by a vice-principal in each school. *Contr. w.* **principal.**

principal, supervisory role of: that aspect of the principal's behavior pattern directed toward providing leadership to teachers and other educational workers in the improvement of instruction.

principal-teacher organization: (1) an organization of which a principal and the instructors in his school compose a unit; (2) an organization of which principals and instructors of more than one school compose the unit.

principal, teaching: a school principal who has less than 75 percent of his time free from classroom teaching duties.

principal's annual report to superintendent: *see* **report to superintendent, principal's annual.**

principal's monthly report to superintendent: *see* **report to superintendent, principal's monthly.**

principal's office record: *see* **record, principal's office.**

principal's office record card: *see* **record card, principal's office.**

principle: (1) originally, a temporal or normative priority (from the Latin *principium,* lit., "beginning"); hence, the first proposition of an argument, upon which other propositions depend for their validity; now used to signify a generalized statement through which otherwise unrelated data are systematized and interpreted; (2) a statement of policy by which individual decisions and cases are judged in a consistent and critical manner.

principle, conservation: *see* **conservation principle.**

principle of bipolarity: *see* **bipolarity, principle of.**

principle of contradiction: *see* **contradiction, principle of.**

principle of contrariety: *see* **contrariety, principle of.**

principle of economy: *syn.* **law of parsimony.**

principle of independence: *see* **independence, principle of.**

principle of least squares: the principle that the most probable value to be obtained from a series of observations or measurements is that value about which the sum of squares of the deviations is a minimum. *See* **method of least squares.**

principle of pupil activity: *see* **pupil activity, principle of.**

principle, overload: *see* **overload principle.**

principle, teaching: a concept or generalization that serves as a guide to teachers in directing learners toward the attainment of educational goals and objectives.

principles, art: *see* **design principles.**

principles, cardinal: *see* **seven cardinal objectives or principles.**

principles, complementary: *see* **complementary principles.**

principles, design: *see* **design principles.**

principles, false: general judgments from which further judgments are derived or which govern human action but which do not conform to the nature of reality.

principles, first: (Scholasticism) (1) in knowledge, general judgments from which new knowledge is derived through reasoning or new experience; first principles are not themselves derived from previous general judgments; each demonstrative science has its own first principles; however, human knowledge considered absolutely has, as its first principle, knowledge gained in immediate experience; (2) in being, the ultimate cause, God, from which all things draw their existence.

principles, scientific: a group of generalizations based on observations, all consistent within the limits of observational error, that scientists often accept as equivalent to facts. *See* **fact.**

principles, seven cardinal: *see* **seven cardinal objectives or principles.**

principles, ultimate: (1) in knowledge, the same as *first principles;* (2) in being, any source of being or action which, from a given standpoint, is primary; thus God, from the standpoint of Scholasticism, is the ultimate principle of all reality.

print: (1) a positive reproduction of a motion or still picture on an opaque or transparent photographic material; *ant.* **negative;** (2) a shortened form for *blueprint* or *black line print.*

print, answer: the first combined picture and sound print of a finished film in release form; it is usually studied carefully to determine whether further changes are required prior to release printing.

print, black line: *see* **print.**

print, composite: a positive motion picture print containing both the picture and the sound.

print laboratory: *see* **laboratory, print.**

print, large-type: *see* **reading materials, large-type.**

print, release: a composite print of a motion picture or filmstrip, including both picture and sound (unless it is a silent film), available for exhibition on standard projection equipment.

print through: in tape recording, transfer of the magnetic field from layer to layer of tape on the reel during storage, resulting in echo sounds on portions of the tape.

print, work: *see* **workprint.**

printer, high-speed: a printer which operates at a speed more compatible with the speed of computation and data processing so that it may operate on line; at the present time a printer operating at a speed of 250 lines per minute, with 100 characters per line, is considered high-speed.

printer, line: (data processing) a printer mechanism that prints complete multicharacter lines of printing, one after the other.

printing calculator: *see* **calculator, printing.**

printing, intaglio (in·tal'yō): printing done from a plate in which the image is incised into the surface of the printing plate; the engraving or incised figure is in stone or other hard material and the impression from the incised surface yields the image.

printing key punch: *see* **key punch, printing.**

printing, silk screen: a process for producing original color prints by pressing pigments through a silk screen (a finely woven material stretched over a wooden frame similar to a picture frame) which has a stencil or block-out solution applied; a graphic technique by which many impressions can be made. *Syn.* **serigraphy.**

printout: human language output produced by a computer, usually by means of a printer.

printscript: a style of handwriting that consists in the use of modified forms of the printed letter, simplified and without ornamentation, the letters in a word not being connected by strokes.

prison education: a program of activities designed to rehabilitate adult prisoners so that they will return to society with a more wholesome attitude toward living, with a desire to conduct themselves as good citizens, and with the skill and knowledge that will enable them to maintain themselves economically.

prison school: a systematic set of educational activities conducted in a prison for its inmates. (Most state and Federal penitentiaries and reformatories operate such schools.)

privacy, audio: *see* **audio privacy.**

private business school: *syn.* **college, business.**

private camp: *see* **camp, private.**

private college: *see* **college, private.**

private denominational education: *see* **church school.**

private education: (1) education other than that provided by an agency of government, at all levels from nursery school through university (the auspices are various, as proprietary, church, trade union, charitable); (2) more narrowly, education provided in private secondary schools, when not otherwise specified; (3) instruction provided in the home by tutors and governesses.

private junior college: *see* **junior college, private.**

private method: (mus. ed.) procedures designed for use in teaching one person at a time, in individual music lessons. *Syn.* **individual method;** *see* **class method; ensemble method; lesson, music.**

private nursery school: *see* **nursery school, private.**

private ownership: a plan under which a school bus is owned and operated by an individual or corporation rather than by the public school district.

private preparatory school: *see* **preparatory school, private.**

private residential school: *see* **residential school, private.**

private school: a school that does not have public support and that is not under public control.

private school, Roman Catholic: *see* **parochial school.**

private school teacher: an instructor in a school organized and administered under a private charter rather than under public school laws.

private seminary: *see* **seminary, private.**

private teachers college: *see* **teachers college, private.**

private university: *see* **university, private.**

private vocational school: *see* **vocational school, private.**

privately controlled college: *see* **college, private.**

privately controlled university: *see* **university, private.**

privately owned bus: *see* **bus, privately owned.**

privatism: a term used by Riesman to describe a form of behavior in which a person, feeling impotent in the face of the many demands and expectations he does not understand, develops those aspects of his life he does understand and over which he exercises a measure of control.

privilege tax: *see* **tax, privilege.**

privileged communication: *see* **communication, privileged.**

pro-rata tuition: *see* **tuition, pro-rata.**

proactive inhibition: *see* **inhibition, proactive.**

probabilism: the theory that absolute knowledge is impossible and that the probabilities of science are our best guides to life.

probability: (1) a branch of mathematics which deals with the chance of the occurrence of some event or sequence of events; (2) a mathematical statement of the chance of an event happening; for example, in the toss of a fair coin the probability of heads occurring on a single toss is 0.5.

probability, a posteriori: probability derived from experience; the limiting value of the ratio of the actual number of occurrences of a given event to the number of possible occurrences of that event (the total number of observations) when the latter number becomes very large. *Syn.* **chance; empirical probability; probability;** *contr. w.* **probability, a priori.**

probability, a priori: the probability of the occurrence of a given event, deduced by reasoning or from a mathematical model rather than from experience. *See* **ratio, probability;** *contr. w.* **probability, a posteriori.**

probability, a priori existence: the relative frequency with which any one of the possible causes of an event occurs before the observed event happens.

probability, compound: the probability associated with a combination of two or more events; for example, if two fair coins are tossed, the probability of getting either two tails or one head and one tail is compound.

probability curve: *see* **curve, probability.**

probability distribution: *see* **distribution, probability.**

probability estimate: *see* **estimate, probability.**

probability, fiducial: a statement of probability based on the fiducial (or confidence) limits of an experiment. *See* **confidence level; confidence limits.**

probability function: any mathematical function used to represent a distribution of probabilities; frequently used to refer to the normal probability curve.

probability integral: the integral of a probability function between any two limits; usually refers to the area under a probability curve between any two given abscissa values.

probability, level of: *syn.* **confidence level.**

probability limits: *syn.* **confidence limits.**

probability of compound events: *syn.* **probability, compound.**

probability of success norm: *see* **norm, probability of success.**

probability, partial: the probability that, in a series of mutually exclusive events, a given event will happen and all others will fail to happen.

probability ratio: *see* **ratio, probability.**

probability sample: *syn.* **sample, stratified.**

probability, simple: the ratio of the number of times a particular event can occur to the number of times that all events of the class can occur. *Contr. w.* **probability, compound.**

probability, total: the sum of the probabilities associated with each possible outcome of an idealized experiment; by convention this sum is 1.

probability value: *see* **value, probability.**

probable capacity level: *see* **capacity level, probable.**

probable deviation: *syn.* **error, probable.**

probable discrepancy: *syn.* **error, probable.**

probable error: *see* **error, probable.**

probation: (1) the act of giving a pupil a chance to "prove" himself, as by permitting him to enter a higher grade or to advance in a school subject under supervision or on the understanding that he must fulfill certain stipulated conditions as to achievement and behavior; (2) the act of suspending disciplinary action, such as expulsion, pending good behavior on the part of the pupil; (3) (juvenile court) the act of suspending sentence against a delinquent and placing him on parole, that is, "on his word," on the understanding that he is to report regularly to the court or to a representative of the court, such as a probation officer, no further legal action being taken so long as the youth's behavior is satisfactory.

probation, academic: *syn.* **probation, scholastic** (2).

probation card: a daily written statement testifying to the attendance and good behavior of a pupil on probation, obtained from the school and submitted at regular intervals by the pupil to the attendance officer who is in charge of the pupil's case; usually resorted to only when the pupil is quite unreliable.

probation, juvenile: *syn.* **probation** (3).

probation officer: a state or local official who is responsible for the supervision of persons on probation and to whom the latter must report at regular intervals.

probation, pupil: *see* **probation** (1) and (2).

probation pupil: (1) a pupil placed on probationary promotion; (2) a pupil enrolled in school but under the supervisory control of a probation officer from the courts.

probation report, pupil: (1) a statement relating to a pupil on probation, prepared for the information of the parent, the principal, the court, or any other person or agency concerned; (2) a statistical summary of data concerning all pupil probationers.

probation, scholastic: (1) *syn.* **probation** (1); (2) a trial period, usually one quarter or semester, in which the student must improve his academic achievement to avoid being dropped from college.

probation student: *syn.* **student, conditioned.**

probation, teacher: a trial period, usually of 3 to 5 years' duration, during which a teacher may give practical proof and actual demonstration of his efficiency before being tendered a permanent contract.

probationary promotion: *see* **promotion, probationary.**

probationary teacher: an instructor employed for a trial period (commonly 3 to 5 years) to prove his ability before appointment to a permanent position.

problem: (1) any significant, perplexing, and challenging situation, real or artificial, the solution of which requires reflective thinking; (2) a perplexing situation after it has been translated into a question or a series of questions that help to determine the direction of subsequent inquiry (Dewey); (3) (math.) a question whose answer requires reasoning from given elements to unknowns according to some set of definitions, axioms, and rules.

problem, abstract: a problem dealing with content that is or seems to be in no way related to the life experience of the individual encountering the problem.

problem, adjustment: *see* **adjustment problem.**

problem analysis: *see* **analysis, problem.**

problem, behavior: (1) loosely, any youth who has caused trouble; (2) any child whose behavior is abnormal, regardless of whether he is unruly or unusually quiet and sensitive; (3) any situation that so effects a child that his behavior becomes abnormal; (4) any problem presented by the abnormal behavior of a child.

problem behavior: *see* **behavior, problem.**

problem, case: the particular problem of an individual for which a *case study* is to be made and a solution sought.

problem-centered curriculum: *see* **curriculum, problem-centered.**

problem-centered guidance: *see* **guidance, problem-centered.**

problem child: *see* **child, problem.**

problem, community-centered: (couns.) a behavior problem which has its cause and contributing conditions centered in the pupil's community life; examples of these are population trends, racial integration, urban and suburban and rural movements, crime, and delinquency.

problem, concrete: a problem arising from some physical or practical situation.

problem, conditions of a: *see* **conditions of a problem.**

problem, detour: one of the problem situations devised by gestalt psychologists to reveal the presence or absence of insight in the organism; the goal is seen and known to the subject but the direct course to the goal is barred by an obstacle; the organism is said to have insight into the problem if it detours the obstacle without benefit of training or specific learning.

problem, double-alternation: a problem situation that may be solved only by responding twice in one way and then twice in another way; for example, the *RRLL* response required in the temporal alley maze.

problem, dropout: *see* **dropout problem.**

problem, fixed-solution: any problem for which there is one right answer and generally one standard procedure for arriving at this answer. *Contr. w.* **problem, open-ended.**

problem method: (1) a method of instruction by which learning is stimulated by the creation of challenging situations that demand solution; *syn.* **heuristic method;** (2) a specific procedure by which a major problem is solved through the combined solutions of a number of smaller related problems.

problem, mind-body: *see* **mind-body problem.**

problem, open-ended: a problem for which there are many answers. *Contr. w.* **problem, fixed-solution.**

problem, practical: *syn.* **problem, real.**

problem, race: *see* **race problem.**

problem, real: a problem arising from an actual situation or practical experience of the person encountering the problem. *Syn.* **practical problem.**

problem scale: *see* **scale, problem.**

problem situation: a situation calling for an adjustment in which the nature or form of the adjustment is not obvious; a question for which the answer must be sought by reflective thinking and possibly by securing additional information or experience.

problem, social: *see* **social problem.**

problem solving: a process employed by all people at all levels of maturity of discovering or educing new relationships among things observed or sensed; the process includes conscious or subconscious assumption, or *hypothesis,* of a possible relationship within a simple or complex system of thought and understanding, and means to test through experience the acceptability of the assumption; the process is equivalent to *research* when

there is refinement of the system and of process in stating and investigating the hypothesis; the solution of a problem by an individual implies discovery of a relationship that is accepted as adequate by the individual; the further testing of a solution is through search for agreement with further experience and with the discoveries of other investigators. *See* **problem.**

problem-solving ability: *see* **ability, problem-solving.**

problem-solving behavior: *see* **behavior, problem-solving.**

problem solving, cooperative: efforts to find a solution of a common problem by pooling the ideas of two or more persons or groups.

problem-solving debate: *see* **debate, problem-solving.**

problem-solving method: a manner of dealing with that which is problematic; a method involving clear definition of the problem confronted, formation of a hypothetical solution (hunch or suggestion), deliberate test of a hypothesis until evidence warrants its acceptance. *See* **scientific method.**

problem, two-step: a verbal problem in arithmetic which is solved with two operations; for example, finding the total cost of three items at 15 cents and two items at 20 cents, each requiring both addition and multiplication.

problem unit: *see* **unit, problem.**

problem unit, functional: *syn.* **unit, experience** (1).

problem, verbal: *syn.* **problem, written.**

problem, word: *syn.* **problem, written.**

problem, written: a problem so stated in words (rather than in symbols) that the operations necessary for solving the problem must be determined.

problem, youth: the set of difficulties growing out of inadequacies of adjustment on the part of the young people of a society or arising because of the failure of the society to provide adequate facilities for education, recreation, etc.

problematic situation: a situation characterized by a question mark, one that is "snarled up"; a situation in which what is already known is insufficient to permit an adequate response; a situation that prior habit cannot command, which demands a directing hypothesis before search for resolving experience or knowledge can be initiated (Dewey).

problems, consumer: the problems encountered in managing and using personal income; the problems of the individual involving money, credit, buying, investing, etc.; the problems of consumers as groups, including distribution of national income and consumer legislation and its enforcement.

procedural flow chart: *see* **chart, procedural flow.**

procedure: (data processing) a written (and often flow-charted or process-charted) description of a system.

procedure, accounting: *see* **accounting.**

procedure, accrediting: *see* **accrediting procedure.**

procedure, cloze: *see* **cloze procedure.**

procedure, conference: *see* **conference procedure.**

procedure, grievance: *see* **grievance procedure.**

procedure, office: *see* **office procedure.**

procedure-oriented language: *see* **language, procedure-oriented.**

procedure, residual: *see* **residual procedure.**

procedure, search: *see* **search procedure.**

procedures, joint training: *see* **training procedures, joint.**

process, algebraic: *see* **algebraic methods.**

process approach: an approach to science instruction in which children learn generalizable process skills that are behaviorally specific but which carry the promise of broad transferability across many subject matters; it adopts the idea that novel thought can be encouraged in relation to each of the processes of science, such as observation, inference, communication, measurement, etc.

process, building-up: *see* **synthetic method** (5).

process chart: *see* **chart, process.**

process chart, man: *see* chart, man process.

process, choice-making: *see* choice-making process.

process, climate setting: *see* climate setting process.

process, cognitive: the method or procedure of knowing or of attaining knowledge.

process, cultural: *see* cultural process.

process, dialectical: *see* dialectical process.

process, diffusion: *see* adoption of practices.

process evaluation: *see* evaluation, process.

process, group: *see* group process.

process, induction: *see* induction process.

process, instructional: *see* instructional process.

process learning: *see* learning, process.

process observer: *see* observer, process.

process of supervision: *see* supervision, process of.

process, reading: *see* reading process.

process, social: *see* social process.

process unit: *see* unit, process.

process, value-evaluating: *see* value-evaluating process.

process, working: *see* working process.

processes, fundamental: *see* fundamental processes.

processes, group: *see* group processes.

processing, automated data: *see* data processing, automated.

processing, data: *see* data processing.

processing, electronic data: *see* data processing system, electronic.

processing unit, central: *see* unit, central processing.

procreation, family of: *see* family of procreation.

proctor: one who assists in the administration of examinations and in the supervision of the examinees.

procurement: (school admin.) the work of securing the materials and supplies for production and the conduct of the business of an organization; may be accomplished by manufacture or by purchase; a function of supply. *See* function, supply.

prodigy: a person excessively advanced beyond the norm; usually applied to cases of exceptionally high intelligence or extreme talent of a particular sort, as in music or art.

producer services: *see* services, producer.

product, art: *see* art product.

product deviation: *see* deviation, product.

product evaluation: *see* evaluation, product.

product, final art: *see* art product, final.

product formula: *see* formula, product.

product information: *see* merchandise information.

product, instructional: in supervision of instruction, the desired change of learning resulting from instruction.

product matrix: *see* matrix, product.

product moment: the product of paired observations when each observation is measured from zero or some other origin. *See* moment.

product moment coefficient of correlation: *syn.* coefficient of correlation, Pearson product moment.

product research: *see* research, product.

product scale: *syn.* scale, quality.

production committee: *see* committee, production.

production director: (1) a broadcast-station staff member having the responsibility of preparing and putting programs on the air; (2) a member of the staff of an educational institution responsible for the general direction of educational broadcasts, often in close connection with the staff of a local station.

production method: *syn.* factory method.

production method, line: *see* line production method.

production method, mass: *see* mass production method.

production, minimum: technique of producing motion pictures with a limited quantity of relatively low-cost equipment and with limited use of professional production personnel.

production project: *see* project, production.

production standard: (bus. ed.) the number of acceptable work units to be completed within a given time under specific conditions; sometimes used in the business office to evaluate the production of certain office workers, usually those performing routine tasks.

production standard, fair operative: (school admin.) a standard rate of performance for an operation or larger undertaking that can be met continuously, over an extended period of time, without detriment to the health or well-being of the employee.

production technician: *see* technician, production.

production unit: (bus. ed.) a block of work involving integrated skills which is to be completed under conditions approximating those found in the business office; the quality of the work performed and the time required to complete the unit are taken into account in the teacher's evaluation of the completed unit.

productive-enterprise project: *syn.* project, production.

productivity: (school admin.) relation between input of some economic or other resource and the output of a product.

productivity, group: *see* group productivity.

profession: an occupation usually involving relatively long and specialized preparation on the level of higher education and governed by its own code of ethics.

professional: *n.* one who has acquired a learned skill and conforms to ethical standards of the profession in which he practices the skill.

professional areas: a breakdown of duties within a vocation.

professional attitude: *see* attitude, professional.

professional cabinet: (elem. ed.) an advisory group, consisting of teachers representing the various grade levels and other school employees, chosen by the principal to confer with him concerning the more important questions of school policy.

professional certificate: *see* certificate, professional.

professional code of ethics: *see* code of ethics, professional.

professional course: *see* course, professional.

professional curriculum: *see* curriculum, professional.

professional days: days taken off by teachers and other professionals for meetings similar to those held by labor unions; may be used as a special strike strategy, that is, as a substitute for an illegal formal strike.

professional education: *see* course, professional; curriculum, professional; preparation, professional; teacher education.

professional education, continuing: *see* continuing professional education.

professional education courses: courses that deal with the study of the history, philosophy, psychology, content, methods, etc., of education.

professional education staff per 1,000 pupils in average daily membership: the number representing the total full-time equivalency of professional education assignments in a school system during a given period of time multiplied by 1,000 and divided by the average daily membership of pupils during this period. *See* assignment, professional educational.

professional educational assignment: *see* assignment, professional educational.

professional ethics: *see* ethics, professional.

professional fraternity: *see* fraternity, professional.

professional growth: *see* growth, professional.

professional information: information about a profession, such as the history, personnel, institutions, publications, research, trends, organization, and legal aspects of the profession.

professional laboratory experiences: *see* experiences, professional laboratory.

professional librarian: *see* librarian, professional.

professional maturity: *see* maturity, professional.

professional military education: *see* military education, professional.

professional negotiations: *see* **collective bargaining.**

professional preparation: *see* **preparation, professional.**

professional reading: *see* **reading, professional.**

professional sanctions: *see* **sanctions, professional.**

professional school: (higher ed.) a higher education institution preparing students directly for the practice of a profession; traditional professional schools are those of law, medicine, and theology (or divinity) which, together with dentistry, prepare students who have completed baccalaureate programs; others include agriculture, business, education, engineering, home economics, library science, nursing, and social service, all of which typically offer undergraduate professional study as well as, in many cases, graduate study.

professional sorority: *see* **fraternity, professional.**

professional specialization: *see* **specialization, professional.**

professional status, teacher's: (1) the degree to which a teacher has attained the specialized competence, attitudes, and recognition that characterize the professions in general; (2) the extent of professional preparation, experience, and success in teaching; (3) the rank or recognition a teacher has achieved in the profession; (4) the status of the teacher among the members of other professions.

professional subject: *see* **subject, professional.**

professional supervision: *see* **supervision, professional.**

professional test: *see* **test, professional.**

professional training: *see* **training, professional.**

professionalization of subject matter: (teacher ed.) the presentation of academic materials or subject-matter content in such a way as to indicate how the material and the methods of instruction related to it can be adapted for use in classroom teaching.

professionalization of teaching: the concern with the vocation of teaching so that it may increasingly become and be known as a profession rather than a craft; this involves, among other things, distinctive expertness and high competence resulting from theoretical study and knowledge as well as practical mastery of pedagogical techniques.

professor: a teacher of the highest academic rank in an institution of higher education. [Within the staff different grades are usually recognized, as *full professor* (designated as *professor*), *associate professor*, and *assistant professor*, in descending order.] *See* **rank, faculty.**

professor, adjunct: a professor appointed for a specific purpose, restricted by length of appointment, type of duties, etc.; frequently on a part-time basis.

professor, assistant: *see* **professor.**

professor, associate: *see* **professor.**

professor, clinical: a faculty member of a teacher education institution who assumes responsibility for the clinical practice of student teachers or interns in particular subject fields of the secondary or elementary school; usually a specialist in a subject field and/or at a certain level of school instruction; frequently teaches methods courses as well.

professor, distinguished: (1) a rank granted by some higher education institutions for service and performance clearly exceeding that of the customary full professorship; (2) a generic term to denote special recognition for outstanding professors, frequently taking in addition the name of the philanthropist who donates the funds for the professorship or the name of someone the philanthropist wishes honored; sometimes called *research professor* or *university professor.*

professor, exchange: a professor who has temporarily exchanged his position with a professor in the same field in another institution. (In international arrangements, exchange assignments are not necessarily on a reciprocal basis.)

professor, full: *see* **professor.**

professor, major: *syn.* **adviser, major.**

professor of aerospace studies: the senior Air Force commissioned officer assigned to command a detachment or a subdetachment of the AFROTC and given the academic rank of professor by the host institution; formerly *professor of air science.*

professor of education: a professor whose major assignment is in teaching courses in education, such as methods of teaching and history of education.

professor of military science: (1) senior officer detailed by the Department of the Army for duty with a civilian educational institution for the purpose of supervising instruction in authorized military subjects; (2) senior military instructor provided by the educational institution and approved for the purpose of supervising instruction in authorized military subjects, by the Department of the Army for duty with the civilian educational institution sponsoring National Defense Cadet Corps units.

professor of naval science: the senior naval commissioned officer assigned to command a naval ROTC unit and given the academic rank of professor by the host institution.

professor, permanent: (mil. ed.) a professor having tenure authorized by Title 10, United States Code, appointed by the President by and with the advice and consent of the Senate; usually serves as head of an academic department in a service academy; military experience, effectiveness, research experience, and publications are the factors which will be evaluated for each nominee.

professor, refugee: a professor from a foreign country, now teaching in an American college or university, who left his native land because of political pressures from Nazi, Fascist, Communist, or similar dictatorial powers.

professor, research: *see* **professor, distinguished.**

professor, tenure associate: a faculty member in a service academy, other than a permanent professor, on an extended tour of duty; up to 10 percent of total faculty strength, exclusive of permanent professors assigned, may be offered tenure to meet the need for an expanded faculty with no diminution of the desired proportion of earned doctorates; in general, must have completed 10 years of service, possess a doctorate, and have taught at least 4 years, 2 at the academy.

professor, university: *see* **professor, distinguished.**

professor, visiting: (1) an exceptionally well-qualified college or university faculty member who holds or is qualified to hold the rank of professor but who for some reason, typically age, is not given regular faculty status and rank, including tenure, when he is first appointed; requires annual reappointment; (2) sometimes designates, as the title implies, someone from outside the institution who is a visiting or temporary professor for a year or two.

proficiency: (1) the degree of ability already acquired; (2) ability of acceptable degree, generally of a high degree, for a kind of task or for a vocation; (3) skill in a comprehensive sense, including not only motor or manual activities but also activities such as competence in language, bookkeeping, economics, mathematics, etc.

proficiency flight: *see* **flight, proficiency.**

proficiency module: *see* **module, proficiency.**

proficiency, motor: *see* **motor proficiency.**

proficiency, social: *see* **intelligence, social.**

proficiency test: *see* **test, proficiency.**

proficiency test, language: *see* **test, language proficiency.**

proficiency training: *see* **training, proficiency.**

profile: any graphic technique, usually a line diagram, that indicates the relative position of one person or a group on each of several tests or other measures or that reveals the measured characteristics of an inanimate object of scientific scrutiny, for example, the profile of a test item; three major characteristics of profiles are (*a*) level of performance as shown by the average height of the graph, (*b*) variability, or the extent of intraindividual differences between tests, and (*c*) shape, the difference between profiles after level and variability have been accounted for. *Syn.* **profile graph;** *see* **chart, profile.**

profile analysis: *see* **analysis, profile.**

profile and front view, mixture of: (art ed.) the tendency in children's drawings to represent both side and front view simultaneously in one symbol. *See* **representation, space-time.**

profile chart: *see* **chart, profile.**

profile, diagnostic: a graphic representation showing the characteristics of the subject in a test situation.

profile, education: a graphic representation of those abilities, achievements, and personality characteristics derived from the records of students of known achievement in a particular subject, course of study, or college.

profile graph: *syn.* **chart, profile;** *see* **profile; psychograph.**

profile number: (1) a code number employed to identify a profile distinctively as to general shape or type; (2) the sum of the addends appropriate to the several geometrically recorded statuses, on different tests or variables, of an examinee who has been representatively measured.

profile, parallel proportional: a proposed criterion for determining the rotated positions of factors, in which the rotation should be done so as to get maximum agreement among all studies being conducted. *Syn.* **simultaneous simple structure.**

profile, personal: a graphic portrayal of the strengths and weaknesses of one individual's personality traits as ascertained by a certain set of procedures.

profile, psychic: *see* **chart, profile; psychograph.**

profile, reading: a graph showing a reader's scores on an analytical reading test, indicating both strengths and weaknesses.

profile test: *see* **test, profile.**

profile, training: *see* **training profile.**

profile, vocational-ability: a graphic representation of abilities, achievements, and personality characteristics of youth in school and of adults in comparison with known degrees of success in a particular job or vocation.

profound hearing loss: *see* **hearing loss, profound.**

profound mental retardation: *see* **mental retardation, profound.**

progeny: offspring; issue; descendants.

prognosis: (1) (stat.) the act or process of predicting the value of a dependent variable by means of known values of one or more independent variables; (2) prediction of the duration, course, and outcome of a certain process or activity, especially of a disease but also of an individual's academic career or, in counseling, of the adjustment problems of a particular student.

prognosis, clinical: *see* **prediction, clinical.**

prognosis, differential: *syn.* **prediction, differential.**

prognosis, educational: prediction of an individual's probable upper level of general or specific learning and his probable quality of achievement; usually based upon objective tests of ability and of learning, as in arithmetic, reading, etc.

prognosis of success: *see* **prediction, clinical.**

prognosis, vocational: an estimate of the future vocational success of an individual or group of individuals based on past performances or scores on suitable predictive measures.

prognostic test: *see* **test, prognostic.**

program: *n.* (1) a plan of procedure; (2) (voc. ed.) all the courses in one field of study, such as business education or industrial trades, organized to fulfill the same general objectives and conducted along similar lines; (3) a set of in-sequence, coded instructions for a digital computer, sometimes known as a routine or a subroutine; (4) in programmed instruction, a sequence of carefully constructed items leading the student to mastery of a subject with minimal error; empirical evidence of the effectiveness of each teaching sequence is obtainable from the performance records of students; *see* **programming, intrinsic; programming, linear;** (5) (adult ed.) a series of learning experiences designed to achieve within a specified period of time certain specific instructional objectives for an adult or group of adults.

program: *v.* to plan the procedures for solving a problem; may involve the analysis of the problem, preparation of a flow diagram, preparing details, testing, developing subroutines, and, in addition, allocation of storage locations, specification of input and output formats, and the incorporation of a computer run into a complete data processing system.

program, A-S-T: *see* **assign-study-recite formula.**

program, accelerated: (1) the more rapid advancement of superior children through the school grades by means of extra promotions; *contr. w.* **program, enrichment;** (2) courses in colleges and universities leading to bachelor's and professional degrees in less than normal time; used in order to meet the shortage of trained manpower during the emergency of World War II and to meet the needs of superior students.

program, action-pattern: a supervisory program carried on in accordance with a standard model or design for supervision in a school system. *See* **supervision, pattern of.**

program, activity: *syn.* **curriculum, activity.**

program, ad lib: a broadcast program produced without script, in which the participants say what they please within previously prescribed limitations as to good taste, subject to be discussed, etc.

program, adult development: any program of activities designed for the education and/or recreation of the adult members of a given population.

program, adult reading: an instructional program intended for the improvement of the reading skills of adults; included are programs for illiterate adults, speed reading courses, general developmental courses, and remedial instruction.

program, advanced placement: a program, adopted in 1956, under which high school students can gain college credit for special courses; a national committee provides course descriptions and consultative service to participating high schools and grades the special examinations required by colleges for placement and credit. *See* **advanced standing.**

program, advisory: a plan for providing adequate counseling service for pupils or students by various advisers within a specified educational unit.

program, aerospace studies: (1) a series of studies concerned with aerospace science, aerospace power, aviation and space operations, and their implications; (2) a departmental name assigned to the Air Force ROTC program on a college campus; almost all academic courses in Air Force ROTC are listed in college catalogs as aerospace studies courses under the Department of Aerospace Studies.

program, Agency for International Development (AID): one of the programs of an agency of the Federal government established in 1961 to provide technical assistance to other countries in the fields of education, health, housing, and agriculture, whereby training may be in the country involved or in the United States or a combination of the two; may be operated through the Department of Agriculture or the Department of Health, Education, and Welfare; however, the resources and services from other Federal agencies and private enterprise are utilized as far as possible.

program, agricultural occupation experience: *see* **program, supervised agricultural experience.**

program, agricultural preparatory: a program of instruction and on-job experiences offered in vocational education in agriculture at the high school and postsecondary school levels to prepare students for employment in any occupation requiring knowledge and skill in agricultural subjects.

program, agricultural school laboratory experience: an experience program to simulate on-job training; used in vocational education in agriculture to supplement experiences received by students in supervised on-job employment. *See* **program, supervised agricultural experience.**

program, agricultural supervised occupational experience: *see* **program, supervised agricultural experience.**

program, agricultural supplemental: a program of instruction offered in vocational education in agriculture at the high school and postsecondary school levels to upgrade workers employed in occupations requiring knowledge and skill in agricultural subjects. *See* **agricultural education** (1).

program, Air Force Junior Reserve Officer Training Corps: a 3-year program offered with the approval of the U.S. Air Force to acquaint high school students with the aerospace age, to develop informed citizens, strengthen character, promote an understanding of the role of the citizen soldier in a democratic society, and motivate students for careers in the U.S. Air Force.

program, Air Force Reserve Officer Training Corps: an educational program on collegiate campuses sponsored by the Air Force ROTC to provide instruction, motivation, and experience to young men in their progressive development as career officers for the U.S. Air Force.

program, airman career: a program in the U.S. Air Force which continually evaluates job performance and provides additional study and training to overcome any deficiency and to ensure progress in appropriate military skills through training in special upgrade courses; ensures full utilization of personnel through training and assignment in the career fields in which they have the greatest interest and aptitude insofar as compatible with air manpower requirements. (Note: the term *airman* is not used to designate an officer.)

program, airman education and commissioning: an Air Force program whereby airmen with a minimum of 30 semester or 45 quarter hours of transferable college credit may complete the work toward a degree so as to qualify for entry into the officer training school.

program, Armed Forces education: the designation for those programs conducted by the U.S. Armed Forces which tend to be more complex than *training programs* and with learning outcomes more general in nature, a smaller number of participants, and no extensive facilities beyond classrooms and laboratories. *Dist. f.* **program, Armed Forces training.**

program, Armed Forces training: the designation for those programs conducted by the U.S. Armed Forces which develop specific skills, are job-oriented, and usually deal with large numbers of personnel and expensive equipment and facilities. *Dist. f.* **program, Armed Forces education.**

program, Army extension course: a program which provides a method for personnel of all components of the Army to further their military education by using correspondence study methods.

program, Army Junior Reserve Officer Training Corps: a training program offered in some high schools wherein students learn drill, weaponry, and tactics and are motivated for officer training in the Army.

program, Army Reserve Officer Training Corps: a program offered in some colleges and universities which leads to an Army commission; cadets are taught drill, tactics, missilery, and logistics.

Program, Army Specialized Training: *see* **Army Specialized Training Program.**

program, Army training: minimum essential training for units and individuals of the active Army and Reserve components as outlined in a Department of the Army publication; prescribes subjects, hours to be devoted to each subject, and applicable supporting Army Subject Schedules; lists essential study references and training aids for subjects not covered by Army Subject Schedules.

program articulation: *see* **articulation, program.**

program, assembly: a program produced usually by the student body for its membership, often thought of as a supplementary group-learning experience.

program, athletic: (1) a plan for supporting and conducting the athletics of a school; (2) a scheduled athletic exhibition.

program, audience-participation: a broadcast in which members of the audience may participate, for example, a *radio forum.*

program, balanced: (1) an art-education program in which balance is attained among such characteristic experiences as creative, appreciational, and functional or, in a unit of instruction, between general and technical infor-

mation and directed and creative activity; (2) (home ec.) a program of study in which the various aspects of homemaking are given consideration in proportion to their importance to society and to the needs of the group participating in the work.

program, balanced reading: a reading program in which basal reading, recreatory reading, curricular or study reading, and corrective reading instruction are stressed, each according to its importance, and no aspect of the program is overemphasized to the neglect of any other.

program, basal reading: a sequential, systematic program using a series of basic reading texts and related materials.

program, basic: *see* **basic program.**

program, bootstrap commissioning: a commissioning program established by the U.S. Air Force in 1968 for career airmen having three or more years of college credits; selected applicants up to the age of 34 may apply for temporary duty up to 1 year to complete their degree requirements and assignments to officer training school upon graduation; selected airmen who already have a degree are assigned directly to officer training school. *See* **bootstrap, operation.**

program, bracero (brə·se′rō): (Span., lit., "laborer") any of the social and educational programs, usually Federally funded and mostly located in Texas, New Mexico, Arizona, and California, for itinerant unskilled laborers of Mexican descent; the workers are known as *braceros.*

program, branching: *see* **branching.**

program, breakfast: a Federal school food service program through which breakfasts are made available free or at reduced cost to children in schools located in economically depressed areas or to those who must travel long distances to school; Federal cash reimbursement is provided. *See* **school food service, Federal and state.**

program, building: a complete plan that is being followed or is to be followed in the construction of buildings, providing for both present and future development and expansion.

program card: a form for an individual student on which are entered the subjects for which he is enrolled and the time and place of meeting of the sections to which he has been assigned.

program, Civil Air Patrol Cadet: a program of study at the high school level stressing the various areas of aerospace education, military leadership, moral development, and physical fitness with special reference to the problems and challenges of aviation and space; sponsored by the Civil Air Patrol, an auxiliary of the U.S. Air Force.

program, civilian institutions: a program administered by the Air Force Institute of Technology of Air University, whereby certain selected officers of the Air Force are assigned a duty station at an academic university or industrial plant where they receive professional education or on-the-job training.

program, classroom: a schedule showing the major activities to be carried on in the classroom and the hour and day on which each is to be undertaken; may cover the period of a day, week, month, semester, or school year; generally limited, however, to a relatively short period.

program clock: *see* **master clock.**

program, college work-study: a combination of employment and scholastic activities at the higher level of education; usually supervised by the educational institution. *See* **program, work-study; Upward Bound.**

program, common-learnings: (1) a program based upon the unspecialized knowledge, skills, and understandings that are required in common by all citizens to enable them to live together effectively, regardless of origins, goals, and individual differences; (2) a "core" or "unified-studies" program that correlates and fuses general education as presented in the school curriculum, especially at secondary school level; other terms include *basic socialization courses, basic education, stem courses, integrating courses;* (3) a program at the secondary school level using a large block of time during which youth study their personal-social-community problems so as to meet their common needs for present and future citizenship.

program, community: classes and less formal educational activities in which many agencies, including the school, cooperate to improve home and community life.

Program, Community Action (CAP): a community-based and -operated program dealing with the critical needs of the poor within the community or area, thus enabling individuals of all ages to obtain the knowledge, skills, motivations, and opportunities needed for them to become fully self-sufficient; planned, coordinated, evaluated, and administered by a group of elected or duly appointed citizens, representing a specific area or a state, with the power to enter into contracts with public or private nonprofit agencies and organizations to assist in the development of programs for the poor in urban and rural areas.

program, control tower operator training: an educational and training program approved and supervised by the Federal Aviation Administration at certain specified Federally approved airports for the purpose of training persons to become airport control tower operators; includes studies and experience in the use of civil air regulations and radar; successful completion of the program leads to an airport control tower operator's certificate.

program, cooperative: an organizational pattern of instruction which involves regularly scheduled part-time employment and which gives students an opportunity to apply classroom learnings in practice; enables them thus to develop occupational competencies through training on jobs related to their occupational interests. *See* **cooperative plan, distributive education.**

program, cooperative work experience: *syn.* **cooperative education.**

program, core: (1) the part of the whole educational program that presents those areas in which learning is essential for balanced living on the part of the majority of individuals; (2) in the junior high school and in some senior high schools, a portion of the curriculum organized into units which, centered about the needs, interests, and problems of youth, are considered so valuable that all should pursue them whether they are organized on the subject basis, correlated, or fused; units may be presented by one, two, or even three teachers working closely together in planning; usually the class period is longer than the normal 45 to 60 minutes, and in the majority of cases social studies are the heart of the units.

program, corrective: a plan for providing corrective gymnastics.

program, counseling: the phase of the school program that provides opportunity for individual students to receive counsel or advice in making a choice or arriving at a decision in educational, vocational, or social matters.

program, counseling instructional: a special educational program designed to incorporate opportunities for peer interaction with guided learning.

program, curricular reading: a planned procedure for teaching children to read the materials of the content subjects in the curricular fields.

program, curriculum: *see* **curriculum program.**

program, daily: (1) a chart or general plan of action by which the different activities of the curriculum involving pupils, teachers, and other school personnel are accorded a sequence and location; (2) a daily chart or plan for the activities of a classroom or teacher.

program, day care: includes such facilities as family daytime homes and group programs in day care or child development centers, nursery schools, day nurseries, and kindergartens; planned for hours before and after school and weekdays when school is not in session; provides educational experiences and guidance, health, and social services as needed by the child and his family; aims to safeguard the children, help parents maintain the values of family life, and prevent family breakdown.

program, day school: (spec. ed.) a program of studies taught during the day in a school where the pupils are not boarded. *See* **day school, special.**

program, defensible minimum: (1) the unit cost of a program of public education that people living in districts of average wealth have found themselves willing and able to support; usually figured by states and in terms of cost per pupil or classroom unit; (2) a unit-cost figure accepted as a reasonable expenditure for public education in a given community, state, or country.

program development: *see* **program planning.**

program, disadvantaged youth (DAVY): (bus. and office ed.) a clerical services program providing training in the skills of general business and office education for culturally, socially, and economically disadvantaged youth, with emphasis on remedial education.

program, distributive education adult extension: an organized program of distributive education offered to adults engaged in or preparing for distributive occupations away from a campus.

program, distributive education pilot: an experimental program concerned with processes and instructional materials to meet changing needs of students, teachers, and/or employers.

program, distributive occupations: commonly called *cooperative training,* this type of program covers work experience and training in trade and industrial occupations, in distributive occupations, and in office occupations; usually open to juniors and seniors for a 1- or 2-year period, the program is supervised by a *coordinator* who selects the students, places them on the job, provides classroom instruction related to the job experiences, and works closely with the employer to ensure that adequate training is provided; intent of the program is to fit the student for a job in the occupational field which he has elected.

program, diversified: a program adapted to meet the differing instructional needs of individuals.

program, diversified occupations: a high school course in which students are given supervised work experience, in any one of a variety of occupations, combined with related classroom instruction.

program, dropout: activities which are designed to reduce the rate of dropout and to encourage the return of those who have left an educational institution before graduation.

program, education: (mil. ed.) a program which tends to be more complex than a training program and of which the learning outcomes are more general in nature; also usually smaller in size and does not require extensive facilities beyond classrooms and laboratories. *Contr. w.* **program, training.**

program, education services: a program conducted at most Air Force installations under which airmen may take a very large variety of courses, on-base, off-base, or by correspondence, such as training leading to completion of work toward a high school education.

program, educational: *syn.* **program, school** (1).

program, educational development: a program at some universities which provides academic, personal, and financial counseling plus student and professional tutors and special services to handicapped students—such as members of minority groups, those with financial problems, and the physically handicapped—who must be already accepted for admission.

program, elective: (1) that part of a student's total schedule of courses where he elects to enroll in courses of his own choosing, as contrasted with that part of his total schedule filled by required courses; (2) those courses offered by a school in which enrollment is by student choice rather than by requirement.

program, enriched: a project which lends itself well to group activities in which gifted children can match wits and share ideas with other able learners; also permits individual specialization based on specific talent and interest.

program, enrichment: (1) extension of the curriculum to provide additional educational opportunities for gifted and bright children; *see* **enrichment, curriculum** (2); (2) compensatory education as part of the school program, consisting of field trips and after-school and Saturday programs; (3) (mil. ed.) a program in the Air Force Academy or a professional military school designed to encourage a student by giving him the opportunity to take elective courses beyond the prescribed curriculum and to concentrate in a major area of his interest.

program enrichment: *see* **enrichment, program.**

program, evaluation: the testing, measuring, and appraisal of the growth, adjustment, and achievement of the learner by means of tests and many nontest instruments and techniques.

program evaluation: *see* **evaluation, radio.**

program evaluation and review technique: *see* **PERT.**

program, evening counseling: a program of counseling services often provided for out-of-school youth and adults who are considering or already participating in an adult education program during the evening hours.

program, executive development: (school admin.) a program for the self-development of promising candidates for general executive responsibilities.

program, experience-unit: a program in reading described by Bond in which the material read is assembled around a unit of experience and from many sources, rather than from a single basal reader.

program, extended school: a program which provides special offerings for deprived children, outside regular school hours and commonly with special Federal or state support; includes such areas as supplementary and remedial instruction, pupil and family counseling, and health and welfare services directed toward overcoming learning handicaps.

program, extracurricular: (1) a program of out-of-class pursuits, usually supervised or financed by the school, in which pupils enjoy some degree of freedom in selection, planning, and control (for example, athletics, dramatics, orchestra, school publications, student government, civic-social-moral clubs, etc.); (2) a program of school activities not falling within the scope of the curriculum, when *curriculum* is interpreted as "the body of courses offered in an educational institution" (note that, although extracurricular program generally denotes out-of-class school activities, those who use *curriculum* to designate the entire offering of the school include extracurricular activities in the regular curriculum and emphasize that such activities should grow out of and thus enrich the class activities). *See* **activities, extraclass.**

program, family-centered: a program that focuses attention upon the problems and welfare of the individual in relation to the entire family in all stages of development and recognizes the varied goals and patterns of family life.

program, Federal scholarship: *see* **scholarship program, Federal.**

program, Federal school lunch: a program set up by the Federal government to provide aid in giving pupils an adequate lunch while at school; consists of a well-balanced, nutritionally adequate, low-cost meal providing at least one-third of the child's daily nutritional requirements; can be a hot or cold meal served on a plate or tray or in a box or bag; cash reimbursement and commodities donated by the U.S. Department of Agriculture are made available. *See* **school food service, Federal and state.**

program, flexible daily: a tentative time schedule of the activities for a school day, subject at any time to change, in order that more or less time may be devoted to any one activity as circumstances may dictate or that activities not originally planned may be incorporated into the day's work.

program, flight training: a training program approved and supervised by the Federal Aviation Administration for the purpose of training airplane pilots and enabling them to qualify for various airplane pilot's licenses, including the civilian private pilot's license and the commercial pilot's license; such programs are conducted at a Federally approved airport and frequently in connection with a university program of aviation or aeronautics.

program, Follow Through: a program focused primarily upon children in kindergarten or elementary school who were previously enrolled in *Project Headstart* or similar programs; included are comprehensive services in education, health, nutrition, and social development as well as parent participation activities; funded by the Office of Economic Opportunity through the Secretary of Health, Education and Welfare.

program, food management, production, and services: a two-year post-high school terminal program in home economics which prepares students for employment in commercial food services or other agencies; includes supervisory positions or serving as assistants in nursing homes, school lunch programs, hospitals, child care centers, or homes for the elderly.

program, foundation: (1) a term used by authorities in school finance to describe the minimum program of education that should be accepted as a basis for equalization in a state-aid or Federal-aid program; (2) the basic educational program that should be guaranteed under the state or Federal program of school support; (3) a given expenditure in dollars per weighted student or classroom unit per year accepted as a minimum in a state-aid or Federal-aid program; (4) the program of activities sponsored by an educational foundation, as, for example, the Rockefeller Foundation.

program, fused: (art ed.) *syn.* **program, integrated** (2) and (3).

program, graduation: (1) the program of events at the commencement exercises of a school; (2) a program of various events of the senior class toward the end of their last year in school, including commencement exercises, senior program, senior picnic, baccalaureate sermon, etc.

program, Great Books: (1) a program of study, as at St. John's College, Annapolis, organized around the systematic reading and group discussion of a selected list of classics, or "great books"; (2) a national movement in adult education to encourage the creation of a large number of small, intimate adult discussion groups to discuss the "great books" and possible modern applications.

program, Great Decisions: an annual educational program sponsored by the Foreign Policy Association and designed to encourage citizens in their own communities to review the key foreign policy decisions facing the nation and people.

program, guaranteed loan: a program carried out by means of legislation in a number of states which has made it possible for banks to offer low interest rates for college loans.

program, guidance: the part of the pupil personnel services program which is concerned with increased student understanding of himself and his relationship to the world around him.

program, health: *see* **health program.**

program, heuristic: a routine by which the computer attacks a problem by a trial-and-error approach, frequently involving the act of learning.

program, home demonstration: *see* **program, home economics extension.**

program, home economics extension: programs of home economics and other fields related to family and community life, organized under the Cooperative Extension Service; formerly called *home demonstration program*. *See* **extension, home economics; extension service in agriculture and home economics, cooperative; extension worker, county.**

program, home furnishings, equipment, and services: a vocational or technical program in home economics which prepares for gainful employment in areas related to home furnishings and equipment, including demonstration of equipment, custom making of accessories for the home, or assisting interior decorators or designers.

program, home management services: a course of study in home economics in high school and technical institutes which prepares for gainful employment as aides or assistants in homemaking services or for institutional housekeeping in hotels, motels, and public housing.

program, homebound: a program designed to provide continuing educational experiences for children who cannot attend school.

program, homeroom: (couns.) a type of group counseling in which the homeroom teacher often assumes the role of counselor during that period of the day designated as homeroom.

program, hospital teaching: a program designed to provide for the continuation of a sequential school experience during the time a child is in the hospital.

program, housing and home furnishings: an area of study in home economics related to the home and its furnishings; housing, with its various ramifications, is considered, as well as interior decoration and the selection of furniture and furnishings, to meet the needs of the family.

program, human resource development: a program whereby the concerted efforts of individuals, groups, agencies, and organizations are utilized to improve the social, economic, and educational levels in rural or urban areas in a community, county, state, or wider area; may be developed by a county extension service.

program, in-service: a school or community teacher-training plan that may include such activities as seminars, workshops, bulletins, television, or films for individuals who are already teaching; the program is designed to increase their competency or to bring them abreast of new developments.

program, information and education: (mil. ed.) a service at certain military installations that assists officers and airmen to increase their knowledge and education in academic, vocational, and general knowledge studies; also, to promote good morale, disseminates information about the nation, current affairs, and the mission of the Armed Forces.

program, instructional: (1) an outline of the contemplated procedures, courses, and subjects offered by a school over a given period of time (a semester or year); (2) a statement or description of the proposed instructional activity over a given period of time, especially the daily arrangement of teacher-pupil activities; (3) that which is being taught or has been taught by the school or teacher in question, and the manner of instruction.

program, integrated: (1) a plan of instruction in which the traditional boundaries between subject fields are largely ignored and which is based on the development of study units and broad learning experiences in which cogent material from a number of fields is brought to bear on the main problem of each study unit or learning experience; (2) a school art program in which art functions as an integral part of the total curriculum, thus contributing its share to the integration of pupil personality; (3) an art program in which several areas of the fine arts are fused together or integrated for purposes of study; for example, music, literature, painting, sculpture, and architecture may be studied together—without regard for subject-matter boundaries—basic principles, forms, or type of expression common to all being stressed; *syn.* **fused program;** *see* **integration.**

program, intensive language: a program for the study of a foreign language to which the student devotes many hours a day so that he may, through constant, concentrated attention, acquire speaking, reading, and writing fluency within a limited period of time; an example is the program set up by the United States military to prepare selected men for posts in foreign countries where they must use the local language. *See* **Army Specialized Training Program; training, intensive language.**

program, International Geophysical Year research: *see* **International Geophysical Year research program.**

program, internship: a program in which, during the first 2 or 3 years of a teacher's career, he is considered an intern (in the same sense as a medical intern), practicing his profession under the close supervision of a critic teacher and a supervising teacher from his college or university and attending seminars in the area of diagnostic and remedial techniques in his teaching field; when the program is completed he has earned his master's degree and then takes a state examination, administered by the profession, for a state license to practice as a teacher. *See* **apprentice teacher; teacher education, in-service; training, in-service.**

program, interrelated: (adult distributive ed.) a program in which courses for the five groups (*a*) nonvocational on the secondary level, (*b*) cooperative part-time on the level of grades 12 to 14, (*c*) salespersons, (*d*) junior executives, buyers, and department heads, and (*e*) owners, managers, and executives are treated as a whole so that the trainee gets a complete view of his entire field.

program, Job Corps: a national training program made possible by the Economic Opportunity Act of 1964; provides basic education, job-skill training, and work experience to disadvantaged young men and women aged 16 to 22 who are out of school; women members of the Job Corps receive training in home and family life also; all participants are assigned to one of three types of training centers. *See* **Center, Job Corps.**

program, kindergarten-visiting: a plan or arrangement by which children who are to enroll in a kindergarten during the following year are permitted to visit the kindergarten on certain days for purposes of orientation.

program, language: in the field of language arts, a school program intended to promote understanding of the structure and meaning of language as well as its effective use.

program language: *see* **language, programming** (2).

program level, mandated minimum: the amount which shall be spent by a local school district for every pupil in average daily membership.

program, library: a term used in computerized data processing for those items in a software collection of standard and proved routines and subroutines by which problems may be solved on a given computer.

program, Library of Congress foreign acquisition: a program in effect since 1958 under which the Library of Congress has been authorized by an act of the Eighty-third Congress in 1954 to carry on programs abroad for the acquisition of publications; countries included are the United Arab Republic, Indonesia, India, Pakistan, Israel, Poland, Burma, Yugoslavia, and Ceylon.

program, literature: planned procedures in providing learning experiences in literature for pupils at a given level.

program, "live": a broadcast transmitted while it is being produced as contrasted with one consisting of previously prepared recordings. *Contr. w.* **program, transcribed.**

program, machine: a sequence of step-by-step operations which is to be performed by the computer in order to solve a problem.

program making: (1) the act or procedure of arranging school activities into a workable schedule; (2) the act or procedure of constructing a daily or weekly schedule of classes in various studies and activities.

program, minimum: (1) a level of education, usually expressed in terms of a unit cost, below which a local school district cannot or should not go in the maintenance of schools; (2) an expenditure level for schools adjudged to be the lower limit in terms of adequate educational returns.

program, minimum transportation: transportation service that the school district is required to provide, as established by statute or practice.

program, misarticulation of: *see* **misarticulation of program.**

program music: *see* **music, program.**

program, NASA Spacemobile: a traveling lecture-demonstration program used mainly in schools, colleges, and universities to inform students, teachers, and segments of the general public about the major accomplishments and future objectives of the National Aeronautics and Space Administration; utilizes launch vehicle and spacecraft models, visual aids, and special electronic devices and is conducted by a science educator specially trained by the National Aeronautics and Space Administration.

Program, National Achievement Scholarship: annual competition for outstanding Negro students offering more than two hundred 4-year college scholarships with stipends related to need; administered by National Merit Scholarship Corporation. *See* **Scholar, Merit.**

Program, National Merit Scholarship: the program of Science Research Associates Inc., an organization that provides a battery of tests optimally suited to selecting a small percentage of college scholarship recipients from among high school students who have some hopes of obtaining a scholarship; a test battery, administered to second-semester juniors and first-semester seniors in March by the individual school, gives seven scores, including English usage, mathematics usage, social studies reading, natural sciences reading, word usage, a selection score, and composite (average).

program, national school volunteer: an advisory service established by the Public Education Association of New York City, Inc., with funding from the Ford Foundation, to help school systems and community groups either to organize school volunteer programs or to expand and strengthen existing programs.

program, Naval Junior Reserve Officer Training Corps: a training program offered in some high schools wherein students learn the basics of ship handling and naval weaponry. *See* **ROTC, junior.**

program, Naval Reserve Officer Training Corps: a program offered at many colleges and universities which leads to a Navy or Marine Corps commission; midshipmen learn navigation, aerodynamics, missilery, and other disciplines related to a naval career. *See* **ROTC, senior.**

program, Navy enlisted scientific education (NESEP): a program conducted in certain colleges and universities for selected Navy enlisted personnel leading to appointment to a commission.

program, no-failure: an educational program designed to eliminate pupil failure through the use of such procedures as adjustment of courses of study to individual needs, pupil grouping, teacher marks indicating stage of progress, pupil guidance, orientation classes, and prognostic and diagnostic testing.

program, nonfood assistance: a Federal school food service program designed to assist schools located in economically hard-pressed areas to purchase food service equipment to facilitate providing food for schoolchildren; Federal funds are provided on a matching basis. *See* **school food service, Federal and state.**

program, nutrition: (1) a program sponsored and conducted by a school for the purpose of raising the nutritional level among pupils; usually involves weighing and measuring pupils, determining their food habits, discovering cases of malnutrition, and providing extra nourishment—often in the form of midmorning lunch—for those pupils found to be malnourished; in larger schools, especially secondary schools, may also involve the operation of a school cafeteria; (2) a phase of the Head Start program which involves not only the children but also the parents; *see* **Project Head Start.**

program, object: for computers, a program produced by some translation process, as by the use of a compiler routine, from a *source program;* an object program need not be in a machine language but often is.

program, occupational: (1) in general, an educational program which provides the student with facts, concepts, principles, and skills which can be utilized in a specific type of work or vocation; also assists a student with limited educational ability to find employment at the unskilled level; job placement combined with school work and helping the student become a productive citizen are the objectives of the program; (2) a postsecondary instructional program, extending not more than 3 years beyond secondary school, which is designed to prepare the student for immediate employment in an occupation or cluster of occupations; not designed as the first 2 or 3 years of liberal arts education or of preprofessional training, though the credits earned are creditable toward an associate degree; in certain higher education institutions where the credits earned are acceptable, in whole or in part, toward a bachelor's degree, the program may be classified as an *open-ended program;* where there are not normally creditable to the bachelor's degree, the occupational program may be classified as a *terminal program.*

program of activity: the chronological arrangement of anticipated or planned teacher and pupil participation in any specific unit of schooltime.

program of studies: (1) a number of courses properly organized into learning units for the purpose of attaining specified educational objectives; may include out-of-school activities sponsored by the school; (2) a descriptive listing of courses being offered; sometimes used as a synonym for school program. *See* **program, school.**

program, Office of Economic Opportunity: one of the Federal programs, educational as well as noneducational, of an office established to augment the fight against poverty in the United States. *See* **Project Head Start; program, Job Corps; program, college work study; program, Follow Through; program, work experience and training; Vista.**

program, officers training school: (mil. ed.) a precommission program of the Air Force to which selected college graduates are assigned based on their academic specialties and Air Force needs; graduates of the program are appointed second lieutenants.

program, open-ended: a program of instruction, at the postsecondary instructional level, of an occupational or other terminal nature, designed, often in cooperation with one or more 4-year colleges or universities, so that credits earned may be applicable, at least in part, toward a bachelor's degree.

program, orientation: *see* **freshman week; orientation** (4) and (5).

program, parent study: that aspect of a special education program for the mentally retarded which involves the education and counseling of parents in respect to the problems of their retarded children.

program, physical recreation: an arranged or organized activity which is active or physical in nature and develops one's muscles, stimulates the circulatory system, aids the digestive system, and helps to improve the nervous system; voluntarily engaged in during leisure and primarily motivated by the satisfaction or pleasure derived from it.

program planning: a process by which the nature and sequence of future educational programs are determined. *Syn.* **program development.**

program, Point Four: a Federal program of giving educational and technical assistance to foreign countries in need of and asking for such aid; the name is derived from one of the points in the foreign policy program outlined by President Truman in his 1948 inaugural address; since 1964 this program has been the responsibility of the Federal Agency for International Development (AID). *See* **program, Agency for International Development.**

program, poverty: a somewhat vague designation for any of the several Federally sponsored activities, initiated in the 1960s, which were designed to reduce the amount and level of poverty in the United States; these programs have been housed in several Federal agencies, most of them, however, in the Office of Economic Opportunity of the Department of Health, Education, and Welfare.

program, prereading: an organized program of activities designed to prepare a child for learning to read.

program, psychoeducational: a system of investigation of the psychological problems involved in education together with the practical application of psychological principles to education.

program, public service: any one of various types of extension activities of schools, libraries, colleges, and universities directed to persons other than the immediate students and patrons by such means as radio and television, lectures, courses, information services, book loans, conferences, leadership training, community affairs, publications, etc.; a phase of university extension. *See* **extension, university.**

program, pupil: an administrative form, used in the principal's office, on which is indicated the pupil's hourly schedule for a given term or semester.

program, pupil-personnel: any authorized program administered by or under the supervision of a professional staff member connected with the pupil personnel services.

program, reading: a planned instructional program in reading, as contrasted with incidental teaching of reading or with unskilled and unplanned reading instruction.

program, reimbursed: a program in such fields as business and office education, distributive education, and home-making that meets the requirements of a particular state for reimbursement from Federal and/or state funds.

program, reimbursed consumer and homemaking education: a home economics program that meets the requirements of a particular state as indicated in an approved state plan for reimbursement from Federal vocational funds; two types of programs are included, namely, preparation for meeting consumer problems and for homemaking and preparation for gainful employment in areas utilizing the specialized knowledge and skills of home economics. *See* **consumer and homemaking education; homemaking.**

program, remedial reading: an organized instructional program based on comprehensive diagnosis and designed to correct or eliminate factors contributing to inadequate or faulty reading development and to increase efficiency and accuracy in reading.

program, Reserve Officer Training Corps: *see* **program, Air Force Reserve Officer Training Corps; program, Army Reserve Officer Training Corps; program, Naval Reserve Officer Training Corps.**

program, retraining: a program of courses that provides instruction serving to prepare persons for entrance into a new occupation or to instruct workers in new, different skills demanded by technological changes in their trades.

program, school: (1) the entire offering of the school, including the out-of-class activities, and the arrangement or sequence of subjects and activities; *syn.* **educational program;** (2) *syn.* **program of studies.**

program, school milk: a program through which extra milk is provided at a reduced charge to supplement the diets of many school children; Federal cash reimbursement is available. *See* **school food service, Federal and state.**

program, school recreation: a program, sponsored by an educational institution, teaching the arts of leisure and providing recreation opportunities within the framework of the school program.

program, school safety: instruction and services provided in a school to prevent accidents.

program, school volunteer: a structured activity to bring into the schools during the school day men and women of all ages and backgrounds who, after orientation and training, agree to serve on a regular schedule a minimum of a half day per week under the direction and supervision of a member of the professional staff; the school volunteer may relieve the teacher of noninstructional chores, work with an individual child or a small group, or enrich the curriculum beyond what the schools are able to provide. *See* **paraprofessional.**

program, science: all science within a curriculum that is related by previous planning to the teaching of science.

program, selective training and retention: in the Navy, a program for the selective training and retention of quali-fied, career-motivated, first-cruise personnel through various reenlistment incentives.

program selector switch: *see* **switch, program selector.**

program, sequential reading: a reading program designed for an extended period of time or for several grade levels which provides for presentation of reading instruction on an ordered continuum.

program, service academy exchange: annual program en-abling students at the four national service academies to visit other academies to compare their training and curricula.

program, social-action: a plan for reducing a social prob-lem through the influencing of public opinion and/or legislation.

program, social-recreation: a program of leisure-time ac-tivities, such as party games and social dancing, partici-pated in by both boys and girls.

program, source: in computerized data processing, a user program before it is translated; also called *source deck* or *source module.*

program source: *see* **source, program.**

program, special-education: (1) a program pertaining to the organization and administration of services for handi-capped children; (2) the instructional offerings in schools or classes for handicapped children.

program, special-events: a broadcast of some event that is either important or unusual and is therefore considered worthy of being presented to the public.

program, sponsored: a broadcast paid for or sponsored by any institution for the purpose of advertising a product or service.

program, staff development: all efforts of school officials to recruit, select, orient, assign, train, or reassign staff members so as to provide the best possible staff for the operation of the schools; generally used to include both staffing and in-service education.

program, state-financed: *see* **state-financed program.**

program, state minimum: *see* **program, minimum.**

program, state school lunch: *see* **state school lunch program.**

program, stored: in computer operation, a set of directions representing a program read into storage from input and expressed in the same type of symbols as used to express the operand data.

program structure: (school finance) strictly output-ori-ented classifications of government expenditures, instead of traditional classifications by function or agency; pro-gram structure lists and interrelates all programs de-signed to achieve a broad common objective. *See* **analysis, planning-program-budgeting.**

program, student: a student's daily sequence of class attendance in different school studies, extraclass activi-ties, and any other definitely scheduled work assign-ments; usually pictured as a weekly unit in chart form.

program, student health: *see* **health program, student.**

program, study: (1) a definite organized plan allotting a certain time for study in and/or out of school; (2) a plan of study set up by a person who must prepare himself as either a student or a teacher for mastery of a field.

program, study-reading: *syn.* **program, curricular reading.**

program, supervised agricultural experience: experience under school direction and related to classroom instruc-tion; comprises on-the-job employment in agricultural firms, production projects, improvement projects, the introduction and use of approved practices, and the acquisition of agricultural skills; provided in nonfarm agricultural firms or on farms. *See* **project, agricultural.**

program, supervised farming: a combination of integrated farm-practice activities carried on by a student in voca-tional education in agriculture who is preparing to farm; often not a part of the program of students in vocational education in agriculture, especially at the eleventh to fourteenth grade levels, who are preparing for nonfarm agricultural occupation. *See* **program, supervised agricul-tural experience.**

program, supervisory: (1) a system of planned activities directed toward maintaining or changing the school operation in such ways as to influence directly the attainment of the instructional goals of the schools; (2) a system of planned activities directed toward improving the instructional program by curriculum revision, in-service education, and program evaluation.

program, sustaining: a program not paid for by a sponsor, but put on the air as a service by the broadcasting station, such as early morning instructional broadcasts on televi-sion.

program, symbolic: a program written for the computer in a symbolic language such as *FORTRAN.*

program, terminal: (1) a unified series of courses that is intended to be complete in itself; (2) at the high school level, a curriculum provided for those who may not continue their formal education beyond the high school; (3) at the postsecondary instructional level, a program of instruction that is completed in less than 4 years and is designed to provide general education or occupational training for individuals who are not planning to enter a bachelor's degree program; credits earned in such a program normally are creditable toward an *associate degree.*

program, testing: a broad term to designate any organized plan for systematically carrying out evaluative procedures in a school or school system or among different school systems; involves the selection, administering, scoring, and interpretation of tests (usually objective tests) and generally implies that a relatively large number of pupils or students are being tested; in an *external testing program,* usually statewide or nationwide, tests are chosen and prepared by someone other than the classroom teacher for administration to students; an *internal testing program* consists of tests prepared by the classroom teacher.

program, total-life-span: (spec. ed.) a program based on the concept of providing a continuum of medical, psychological, and educational services for the mentally retarded from birth through adulthood.

program, trade preparatory: education to prepare for entrance into useful employment in an industrial occupation and provide an opportunity to continue a general education. See **part-time trade preparatory school or class.**

program, training: (1) an educational program for which the instruction aims at student competency and mastery of clearly specified skills and tasks and is expected to maintain at least minimum levels of proficiency for each trainee; see **training;** (2) (voc. ed.) a detailed set of directions covering the procedures for organizing and conducting an industrial course of training; includes statements covering location of classes, selection and number of trainees, description and length of courses, instructor selection, physical facilities and supplies, and supervisory duties; the responsibility of coordination between industry and school is also clearly defined; (3) (mil. ed.) a program which develops specific skills and is job-oriented; it is likely to deal with large numbers of personnel and expensive equipment and facilities; *contr. w.* **program, education.**

program, transcribed: a radio broadcast produced by playing electrical transcriptions previously made. *Contr. w.* **program, "live."**

program, transfer: a program of instruction, at the postsecondary instructional level, yielding credits which are normally acceptable by 4-year colleges and universities at full (or virtually full) value toward a bachelor's degree.

program, uniform: a term designating the organized scheme of activities constituting the *core curriculum* of the Froebelian kindergarten.

program, U.S. Military Academy preparatory training: preparatory training at the U.S. Military Academy Preparatory School for officers, warrant officers, and enlisted men on active duty who hold letters of appointment issued by the Department of the Army for possible admission to the U.S. Military Academy.

program, utility: a standard routine used to assist in the operation of the computer.

program utilization: *see* **utilization, radio.**

program, vocational consumer and homemaking: *see* **program, reimbursed consumer and homemaking education.**

program, vocational home economics: *see* **program, reimbursed consumer and homemaking education.**

program, weekly: (1) a time schedule made up by a teacher, showing the time to be devoted to each of the several activities, areas of study, etc., in which the class is to engage during the period of a week; (2) a time schedule of all the activities of a school, both those included in the curriculum and those which may be considered as extraclass, covering a period of 1 week.

program, wilderness survival: a program carried on in a forested, mountainous, uninhabited area to train groups of youths in active self-reliance; at the end of the program each youth demonstrates his ability to maintain himself for a certain period alone in the wilderness; has been used as a remedial program in Canada for young drug addicts.

program, work-experience: (spec. ed.) a specific phase of the high school *work-study program* for the retarded which provides opportunities for on-the-job training and evaluation.

program, work experience and training: a program funded by the Department of Health, Education, and Welfare

under delegation of authority to the Office of Economic Opportunity for the purpose of increasing the employability of unemployed, needy persons; offers adult basic education equivalent to high school education, vocational training, and on-the-job experiences; a wide variety of training programs are provided, especially in the health occupations and the service trades such as food handling and building maintenance.

program, work-study: (1) a plan—primarily funded by the Federal government under terms of the Economic Opportunity Act of 1964, extended by the Higher Education Act of 1965, and administered by individual higher education institutions—for providing part-time work either at the institution or in community agencies for full-time students who qualify on the basis of low economic status; (2) in the high school, educational experience in which the student spends a certain number of hours a day in classes in the school, acquiring basic learnings, and a specified number of hours working for some company or tradesman, generally on a salary basis; the actual work experience is administered jointly by the school and the employer; *see* **cooperative education;** (3) a high school program for the educable mentally retarded that combines actual work experience with classroom instruction related to the world of work.

program, YMW: assistance offered by the cooperative extension service and certain other groups to young men and women from 18 to 30 years of age; formerly called the Rural Youth program; the present name is a shortened form of young men's and women's program.

programmed instruction: *see* **instruction, programmed.**

programmed instruction, distributive education: *see* **instruction, distributive education programmed.**

programmed instruction materials: *see* **instruction materials, programmed.**

programmed instruction package: *see* **instruction package, programmed.**

programmed instructional system: the product of an integrated relationship of all subdivisions of an instructional unit using the principles of programmed instruction, involving the materials, their presentation devices, student activity, and the live instructor, all aligned to establish proper functional continuity toward the successful achievement of previously defined instructional objectives.

programmed learning: *see* **instruction, programmed.**

programmed reading instruction: *see* **instruction, programmed reading.**

programmed school: *syn.* **alternate school.**

programmed text: *see* **text, programmed.**

programmed textbook: *see* **textbook, programmed.**

programmed workbook: *see* **workbook, programmed.**

programmer: (1) (programmed instruction) the person responsible for the design of items and sequences in a program; may be either a psychologist working with a subject-matter expert who delineates the content or a subject-matter specialist trained in programming techniques; (2) the individual who prepares instruction sequences and who develops the step-by-step operations which are to be performed by the computer in order to solve a problem; (3) (data processing) a person who creates, evaluates, and/or corrects programs used in electronic data processing. See **program; programming.**

programmer, instructional: a person who analyzes training objectives and then prepares instructional material utilizing the principles of programmed learning.

programming: (1) the building of material to be learned into logical, sequential steps or frames; (2) preparation of a computer to perform various operations upon data put into it, for example, laying out a *block diagram,* coding, testing the program for accuracy, etc.

programming, absolute: with computers, the use of a machine language, in contrast to a symbolic language.

programming, computer: (1) the setting up of a computer to solve a problem; the *programmer* begins by pressing a key that clears the machine of any stored information left over from previous problems, then presses a key indicating to the computer that he is about to enter data, thus priming the computer for action; then pressing a key (or keys) identifying a particular storage location, called an *address*, within the machine, he inserts his first data which, by pressing still another key, he causes to be shifted into the selected location; next he commands the machine to take the data from the location and to apply the result to an output register or storage location from which the value can be automatically typed out on the keyboard; (2) the breakdown of a problem of any complexity into a program which consists of a series of instructions usually expressed in a compiler code; *see* **compiler.**

programming, criterion: a method of programmed instruction which consists both of *content* to be learned and *instructions* to the student to do such things as examine a blueprint, see a motion picture, or read something in a book; when done, student returns to program, where he makes a response to the criterion frame or test; depending on analysis of test results, he is directed to new material or remedial material if needed, and so on.

programming, eclectic: programming not committed to a particular school of programming; the resulting programs may contain *ruleg* and *egrul* sequences, *multiple-choice* and *constructed-response* items, *branches* and *linear* sequences.

programming, extrinsic: *syn.* **programming, linear.**

programming, intrinsic: a programming technique characterized by relatively lengthy items, *multiple-choice* responses, and consistent use of *branching;* if, after reading the information section of each item, the student selects the correct response to the question based on the material, he is sent to an item presenting new information; if he selects an incorrect alternative, he is sent to an item which provides information as to why his choice was incorrect; to the extent that the programmer has correctly predicted the possible responses that the student population will make, the program taken by each student is under the control of his own responses, and will differ for students of differing abilities. *See* **book, scrambled;** *contr. w.* **programming, linear** (2).

programming language: *see* **language, programming.**

programming, linear: (1) a mathematical process for selecting the "best" course of action in problems of a particular type arising in industry which are characterized by having many variables (time, cost, number of machines which can be used, etc.), with maximal or minimal restrictions on the variables (machine A cannot be used more than 4 hours per day, etc.); (2) in programmed instruction, a technique whereby set sequences of items present information in small units and require a response from the student at each step; the steps are so designed that errors will be minimal for even the slower students in the target population; every student does each item in the program, his progress differing only in the rate at which he proceeds through the sequence; *constructed responses* are demanded of the student most of the time; *syn.* **programming, extrinsic;** *contr. w.* **branching; programming, intrinsic.**

programming, micro: the technique of using a certain special set of instructions for an automatic computer that consists only of basic elemental operations.

programming, minimum access: *see* **programming, minimum latency.**

programming, minimum latency: in computer programming, arranging instructions and other data in a cyclic storage device so that the average realized access time is close to the minimum access time; usually achieved by interlacing instructions and operand data, both separately and together.

programming, multitrack: a method of programmed instruction that employs more than one version or *track;* all tracks teach the same objectives, but presentation varies to accommodate students of different ability levels or degrees of prior knowledge or skill. *See* **track system.**

programming, symbolic: in computer programming, the use of arbitrary symbols (often mnemonic) to represent addresses and commands in order to facilitate programming work.

programs in vocational home economics, occupational: three types of programs in vocational home economics directed toward gainful occupations include: (1) the high school program; (2) the technical school post-high school program; and (3) the adult program for training or retraining individuals for wage earning. *See* **consumer and homemaking education; preparation, occupational.**

progress, academic: the progress made by a pupil in achievement in the school subjects as measured by various tests, teachers' marks, and teachers' judgment.

progress, accelerated: *syn.* **acceleration.**

progress, age-grade: (1) pupil progress measured in grades as compared with age; (2) advancement in school measured by the ratio of grade attained to grade expected at the child's age.

progress chart: *see* **chart, progress.**

progress, continuous: continual progression from one stage to the next in difficulty; applied to a reading program in which a number of stages of reading achievement are developed and through which the pupil must progress in a continuous fashion.

progress distribution chart: *see* **chart, progress distribution.**

progress, grade: the rate of a pupil's progress through the school grades, either rapid, normal, or slow. *See* **acceleration** (1); **progress, normal** (1); **progress, slow.**

progress interview: *see* **interview, progress.**

progress inventory: *see* **inventory, progress.**

progress, knowledge of: *see* **knowledge of progress.**

progress, normal: (1) the process of completing the school grades at a normal rate of one per year; (2) progress that keeps pace with growth toward mental maturity.

progress, rapid: *syn.* **acceleration** (1).

progress, rate of: (1) the rapidity with which a pupil completes the various grades, measured in terms of the amount of acceleration or retardation; (2) (of a school system) a measure based on the percent of acceleration, retardation, and normal progress among the pupils enrolled in the school system.

progress record, pupil: *see* **record, pupil progress.**

progress report: *see* **report, progress.**

progress report, school: *see* **report, school progress.**

progress, school: *see* **progress, rate of.**

progress sheet: (mil. ed.) a training aid that records progress made in certain requirements by a group of men.

progress, slow: the process of completing the school grades at a rate of less than one per year.

progress, social: *see* **social progress.**

progress survey: *syn.* **inventory, progress.**

progress, theory of: during the Enlightenment in Europe the belief that natural law makes progress inevitable, that knowledge is power, that man can remake his world; dominant in early history of the United States (Thomas Jefferson, public education movement). *See* **meliorism.**

progression, arithmetic: a sequence in which the difference between each term and its predecessor is a constant; for example, 2, 7, 12, 17, ...

progression factor table: *see* **table, progression factor.**

progression factors: causes of difficulty involved in the progress of learners that must be recognized in organizing a sequential course of training.

progression, geometric: a sequence in which the ratio of each term to its predecessor is a constant; for example, 2, 4, 8, 16, ...

progression, harmonic: (1) a sequence in which the terms are reciprocals of the terms of an *arithmetic progression;* for example, 10, 5, $3\frac{1}{3}$, $2\frac{1}{2}$, 2, . . . , since the reciprocals $\frac{1}{10}$, $\frac{2}{10}$, $\frac{3}{10}$, $\frac{4}{10}$, $\frac{5}{10}$, . . . form an arithmetic progression; (2) (mus.) a series of shifts in the vertical harmony of a musical composition; for example, moving from the chords C to F, to G, and back to C; *syn.* **harmonic sequence.**

progression, left-to-right: movement of the eyes from left to right in reading the printed or written line. *See* **orientation, directional.**

progression of training: see **training, progression of.**

progressive: *n.* one who advocates change in the direction of improvement rather than adherence to tradition merely for the sake of tradition.

progressive choice method: a procedure for teaching beginning reading which is based upon the learning of selected individual letters followed by reading of words formed from these letters previously learned; the "choices" of words to be recognized are thus limited at first and later enlarged as more words and letters are learned.

progressive choice reading materials: see **progressive choice method.**

progressive deafness: see **deafness, progressive.**

progressive digiting: *syn.* **digiting.**

progressive education: the designation of an educational movement that protested against formalism; arising in Europe and America during the last two decades of the nineteenth century, its extent was marked in 1919 by the formation of the Progressive Education Association; associated with the philosophy of John Dewey, it emphasizes commitment to the democratic idea, the importance of creative and purposeful activity, the real life needs of students, and closer relations between school and community.

progressive feeblemindedness: see **mental retardation, progressive.**

progressive matrices test: see **test, progressive matrices.**

progressive mental retardation: see **mental retardation, progressive.**

progressive neuronal degeneration mental retardation: see **mental retardation, progressive neuronal degeneration.**

progressive paralysis: see **paralysis, progressive.**

progressive school: a type of transitional school that departs from the traditional procedures by varying degrees, usually organized on an activity-subject-matter basis.

progressive slant: a type of slant in handwriting in which there is a regular change throughout a line of writing, for example, from an almost vertical slant to an extreme forward slant.

progressive tax: see **tax, progressive.**

progressivism: in twentieth-century educational philosophy the theory that education is an instrument in the service of man, that academic values are primarily extrinsic and therefore functional, that content and subject matter should be modified as man's knowledge of himself and his world changes, and that all expressions of absolutistic thinking are impediments to progress; postulated upon a biological, naturalistic theory of man, upon a dynamic rather than a static theory of the universe, and upon modern psychology—particularly upon the dynamic and functionalistic schools of thought; sometimes erroneously equated with the theory of *laissez faire;* John Dewey is the most eminent exponent of this position.

project: a significant, practical unit of activity having educational value and aimed at one or more definite goals of understanding; involves investigation and solution of problems and, frequently, the use and manipulation of physical materials; planned and carried to completion by the pupils and teacher in a natural, "real-life" manner.

project agreement: a contract between the U.S. Department of Agriculture and a land-grant college which covers objectives, procedures, and plans for carrying out educational activities in a given subject-matter area when both Federal and state funds are used.

project, agricultural: a production agriculture activity or a work experience in a nonfarm agricultural occupation conducted primarily for educational purposes and under school supervision, through one or more complete natural cycles or for a relatively long period, by a person enrolled in a class in agriculture. See **supervised agricultural experience; project, improvement; project, production; program.**

project, appreciation: an experience in which the purpose is mainly aesthetic in that children enjoy and appreciate rather than construct, produce, create, or engage in problem solving.

project-centered teaching: see **teaching, project-centered.**

Project, Citizenship Education: see **Citizenship Education Project.**

project, class: an instructional project carried out by an entire class under school supervision and usually on school property.

project, cooperative: (home ec.) (1) a project in home economics planned and carried out at home by two or more members of a family under the guidance of one or more teachers; (2) a project relating to home economics and planned and carried out at school by individuals from two or more groups under the guidance of one or more teachers.

project curriculum: *syn.* **curriculum, classroom activities.**

project, demonstration guidance: a study which seeks to discover what the school could do to work to better advantage with certain groups; for example, a demonstration guidance project carried on in New York at the junior high school level attempted to find out how guidance could better serve the urban disadvantaged pupil.

project, distributive education: a combination of organized learning activities related to an individual's distributive occupational interests; the length of time to complete the project depends upon the nature of the project and the ability of the individual learner.

project, farm: a business venture for profit involving a series of farm jobs following a production cycle in a farm enterprise, or an undertaking involving a series of farm jobs designed to improve the real estate value of the farm or the efficiency of the farm business as a whole, carried on as a fundamental part of the student's supervised farming program in vocational agriculture, under the supervision of the teacher of vocational agriculture.

Project Follow Through: see **Project Head Start.**

project, Four-H Club: work experience related to the farm or to home and family living carried on by an individual member of a Four-H Club, a group of members, or such a club working collectively. See **Four-H Club.**

project, guidance: an extended plan for developing a certain phase of a guidance program, such as making a follow-up survey of the previous year's graduates.

Project Head Start: a Federal preschool child development program of the Office of Economic Opportunity which provides a comprehensive program of education, medical care, social services, and nutritional help for preschool children from disadvantaged backgrounds; programs are organized and administered by local communities, which must provide the facilities for a child development center; has been continued into elementary school by a similar program called *Project Follow-Through.* See **center, child development; child, preschool; pressure cooker approach.**

project, home: (home ec.) see **home (and community) experiences.**

project, home improvement: any community development and home economics extension project related to the improvement and management of the home, especially in poverty areas and in developing nations; includes the improvement both of sanitary conditions and practices affecting the family's health, and of housing and home facilities through the use of local inexpensive materials.

project, improvement: a project conducted by a student in vocational agriculture, not primarily for the purpose of an immediate or direct financial return but to improve the agricultural business, either nonfarm or farm. *Contr. w.* **project, agricultural.**

project method: a method of teaching in which students individually or in groups accept an assignment to gather and integrate data relative to some problem and are then free to fulfill the requirements independently of the teacher, who furnishes help only when necessary. *Syn.* **self-directed study;** see **activity method; study, independent.**

project method, distributive education: a means by which classroom instruction is correlated with a series of group and/or individually designed learning activities and projects related to a student's occupational interest.

project plan, distributive education: an organizational pattern of instruction which involves a series of selected learning activities or projects related to the fields of marketing, merchandising, and management and specifically related to a student's occupational interest.

project, production: a possible type of activity in a supervised agricultural experience program. *See* **agricultural production education; program, supervised agricultural experience.**

project, productive-enterprise: *syn.* **project, production.**

project, school-store: an actual store set up within the school for the dual purpose of selling merchandise in demand by the students and providing retail training for classes in salesmanship and merchandising.

project sheet: a form of instruction sheet containing complete directions, with references, for the use of learners in carrying out an assigned project.

project, study: a unit of study involving the solving of a problem in its natural setting, usually including the planning, collection, and organization of both oral and written data, sometimes resulting in a definite overt piece of work such as a paper or physical product. *See* **contract** (2).

project talent: a comprehensive and detailed study of students being conducted by the University of Pittsburgh and American Institutes for Research for the purpose of accumulating data concerning abilities in the light of personal and social needs and in terms of the social context in which the students live and learn; in the spring of 1960, a 2-day battery of tests and questionnaires was administered to about 440,000 students in grades 9 through 12 in 1,353 public, private, and parochial schools in various parts of the United States; a series of follow-up studies has been planned for 1, 5, 10, and 20 years after each of the classes in the sample graduates from high school.

project, talented youth: a project organized to assemble existing research results in this field, to assist school systems in conducting their own research for finding and developing talented children, and to study the nature of talent itself.

project training: *see* **training, project.**

projected school enrollment: *see* **enrollment, projected school.**

projection: (1) (vis. ed.) the process of causing to be reflected from a screen an image of a film, plate, or opaque object; (2) (photog.) the process of throwing the image of a negative on a sensitized printing surface, as in enlarging or reducing; (3) (psych.) the mechanism by which the ego relieves itself of blame by placing the burden of responsibility or blame on another person or object; (4) (psych.) the act of locating the source of a stimulus in space or within the observer's body (for example, hunger in the stomach, sound as a point in space, etc.); (5) (map making) representation of the terrestrial or celestial sphere on a plane surface; (6) (math.) a projective transformation; *see* **geometry, projective;** (7) (math.) a vector whose initial and terminal points are respectively the projections of the initial and terminal points of a given vector.

projection areas of the brain: *see* **brain, projection areas of.**

projection, census class: one of the four commonest methods used to project future enrollments and determine the space needs of school buildings. *See* **enrollment, projected school.**

projection, continuous: *see* **reel, continuous projection.**

projection, employment: *see* **employment projection.**

projection, housing: a method of forecasting school enrollment involving contingency estimates of residential development, redevelopment, etc. *See* **enrollment, projected school.**

projection, indirect: *syn.* **projection, rear-screen.**

projection lens: *see* **lens, projection.**

projection of test vector: *see* **test vector, projection of.**

projection, polarized: *see* **slide, still-motion.**

projection, population trend: a total population forecast on some basis of past population trends; from this total population forecast for the community is derived an enrollment estimate by means of a ratio based on past experience, such as the average ratio or trend in the ratio of school enrollment for 10 years back. *See* **enrollment, projected school.**

projection, rear: a method of projecting images onto the back of a translucent screen, used for background in television and motion-picture production as well as in display projection.

projection, rear-screen: for this procedure, the projector, located behind a translucent screen, is placed in front of the viewers; it may be housed in a self-contained unit or in a projection room; because a mirror system adapted to the projector bends the beam and reverses the image from left to right, the procedure is also called *indirect projection.*

projection receiver: *see* **receiver, projection.**

projection reel, continuous: *see* **reel, continuous projection.**

projection, retention ratio: a method of estimating future enrollments which relies on a dependable record of resident births and the enrollment history of the district schools and which has been found to reflect community characteristics with considerable accuracy; it consists of two determinations: first, a way is found to estimate the future enrollments of a convenient primary grade (for example, grade 2) and, second, this grade enrollment is projected to successive years by a series of grade-survival or retention ratios established from experience. *See* **enrollment, projected school.**

projection, single-year-of-age population: the population at some future date classified by each year of age, that is, under 1 year, 1 year, 2 years, 3 years, etc.

projectionist club: *see* **club, projectionist.**

projectionist's license: *see* **license, projectionist's.**

projective geometry: *see* **geometry, projective.**

projective method: a method of obtaining information which avoids as much as possible any structuring of the situation, so that the response made by the subject will be close to his real feelings and will not reflect the biases or prejudices implicit in the structuring itself of the directive items; the externalizing of images and ideas through the use of such devices as the Rorschach test, the thematic apperception test, etc. *See* **test, Rorschach; test, thematic apperception.**

projective method, cathartic: a method of inferring personality traits from the subject's affective reactions to situations; for example, he comments on stories, expresses feelings while modeling clay, etc.

projective method, constitutive: a method of inferring personality aspects from the way the subject imposes structure on relatively less structured material; for example, the subject models clay, draws a person, copies designs, attributes organization to blots on the Rorschach test.

projective method, constructive: a method of inferring personality aspects from the subject's organization of materials into larger patterns; for example, the subject completes sentences, arranges forms into mosaics, plays roles, etc.

projective method, interpretive: a method of inferring personality aspects from the subject's ascription of meanings to relatively clearly structured situations; for example, the subject tells stories about pictures in the thematic apperception test.

projective method, refractive: a method of inferring personality aspects from samples of the subject's conventional modes of communication, such as handwriting or speech.

projective technique: (1) *syn.* **projective method;** (2) a technique in testing a subject by giving the testee material with which to work creatively; for example, the tester presents an ambiguous stimulus and asks the subject what he sees in it or what he thinks will happen next; these interpretations are regarded as projections of the subject's unconscious wishes, attitudes, and conceptions of the world.

projective test: *see* **test, projective.**

projector: a device that projects images of motion-picture film, plates, opaque objects, or slides on a reflecting surface or screen so as to produce an enlarged image for group use.

projector, carbon arc: a projector that is illuminated by an electric spark between two rods of carbon; also, a projector with a hot, bright light.

projector, filmstrip: projection instrument designed to accept 35-mm filmstrips vertically or horizontally; often equipped with an adapter to accept slides; models are available with manual advance and/or remote control. *See* **filmstrip, double-frame; filmstrip, single-frame.**

projector, lantern-slide: a projection instrument designed to accept standard $3\frac{1}{4} \times 4$ inch lantern slides and occasionally $2\frac{1}{4} \times 2\frac{1}{4}$ inch slides with the provision of a special adapter; this projector, still popular, was the forerunner of the *slide projector* and the *filmstrip projector*.

projector, magnetic sound: a motion-picture projector capable of showing motion-picture film which has either an optical or a magnetic sound track.

projector, microscope: *syn.* **projector, microslide.**

projector, microslide: a device combining a microscope with a projector by means of which the enlarged images of microscopic objects or organisms may be projected upon a screen. *Syn.* **microscope projector.**

projector, nonsynchronous: *see* **projector, synchronized motion-picture.**

projector, opaque: a device arranged to project images picked up by reflecting light from the surface of opaque graphics, such as pictures, drawings, and printed and typed material; it is not necessary to employ slides or other transparencies with this unit; as part of a multiplexer arrangement, the *Telop* feeds projected images to the TV camera.

projector, overhead: machine for projecting the highly illuminated image of transparent material by use of lenses and special mirrors; differs from regular straight-line projectors inasmuch as light is reflected from a lower mirror up through the transparency on a flat platform to a tilted upper mirror and then to the screen; placed in front of the audience, it may be used in a semidarkened or completely lighted room.

projector, overhead transparency: *see* **projector, overhead.**

projector, silent: a device for projecting silent motion pictures. (Sound motion pictures usually cannot be projected on silent projectors without severe damage to the film.)

projector, slide: a device for showing images of positive or negative transparencies on a screen; consists, in its simplest form, of a lamp in a housing, a condensing lens to direct the light from the lamp through the positive, and a lens to focus the image of the positive on a screen.

projector, sound: a device for projecting the pictures and reproducing the sound of a sound motion picture. (Silent pictures may also be projected on a sound projector, but sound pictures may not be projected on most silent projectors without ruining the films.)

projector, stop-motion: a projector designed with speed controls and a stop-start mechanism so that images can be projected at variable speeds or held immobile.

projector, synchronized motion-picture: a motion-picture projector that is specially equipped with a speed and shutter mechanism compatible with the television frame and scanning system; use of *nonsynchronous projectors* ordinarily results in interference patterns on the reproduced images.

prolongation: (1) that form of stuttering in which the sound being spoken is abnormally prolonged, generally with noticeable muscular strain; (2) a voluntary prolonging of a sound, without strain, sometimes employed in the treatment of stuttering, on the assumption that the stutterer's emotionality, anxiety, and straining reactions are thus reduced. *See* **stuttering; stuttering, pseudo.**

prolonged phonation: *see* **phonation, prolonged.**

promoted, percentage of pupils: *see* **percentage of pupils promoted.**

promoting teacher: a teacher who, at regular periods for promotion, advances her pupils to the next higher grade or year of work.

promotion: (1) the act of shifting a pupil's placement from a lower to a higher grade; (2) advancement in position or salary of school personnel; *see* **promotion, faculty.**

promotion, academic: (1) in a broad sense, the process by which a student is passed on to the next school grade or academic level; (2) in a narrow sense, promotion based upon academic achievement, as contrasted with *automatic promotion* or school advancement on the basis of age, social group, or factors other than scholarship.

promotion, accelerated: promotion of a pupil at a faster rate than usual; if a pupil receives an accelerated promotion, he thereby condenses or omits time customarily spent in a given grade or course.

promotion, annual: advancement of a pupil at yearly intervals from a lower to a higher grade.

promotion, automatic: *syn.* **promotion, continuous.**

promotion, conditional: *syn.* **promotion, probationary.**

promotion, continuous: a theory or practice of school promotion according to which all pupils are advanced on the basis of chronological age. *Syn.* **automatic promotion;** *dist. f.* **promotion, continuous progress.**

promotion, continuous progress: a theory or practice of providing an ungraded curriculum and interage groupings within which individual promotions in schools are based on a whole matrix of factors such as physical, emotional, and social factors as well as on intellectual, chronological, and achievement changes. *Dist. f.* **promotion, continuous.**

promotion, double: a promotion of two grades at one time.

promotion, enrichment plan of: *see* **differentiated-course plan; multiple-course plan.**

promotion, faculty: an advance in salary, rank, position, or responsibility of a member of the instructional, supervisory, or administrative staff of an educational institution or school system.

promotion, flexible: a plan for the advancement of a pupil from one grade to a higher one when he is ready and able to advance, as opposed to a regular promotion interval.

promotion, individual: promotion from one class or grade to another for an individual child at a time other than a usual promotion period.

promotion interval: the time that elapses between promotion periods.

promotion period: the time of year at which the change in pupils' grade placement is usually made.

promotion policy: the plan followed by a school for the promotion and placement of children.

promotion, probationary: an arrangement by which a pupil is promoted to the next higher grade on a trial basis in order that his progress and adjustment may be observed; if these are satisfactory, the pupil is retained in the higher grade.

promotion, quarterly: the plan of advancement or promotion on a quarterly basis.

promotion, rapid: *see* **promotion, double.**

promotion, selective: *see* **selective retention.**

promotion, semester: *syn.* **promotion, semiannual.**

promotion, semiannual: the practice of promotion of pupils at each half-year or semester interval.

promotion, special: (1) a promotion, whether in a grade or school subject, made at any time other than a usual promotion period; (2) *syn.* **promotion, probationary.**

promotion standards: minimum standards set up by the school for pupils to achieve in order to be promoted. *Syn.* **grade standards.**

promotion, subject: a system of promotion by subject, as opposed to promotion by grade, the pupil being allowed to advance only in those subjects in which he does satisfactory work and being obliged to repeat those subjects in which he fails.

promotion survey: *see* **survey, promotion.**

promotion, teacher: (1) an advance in salary, rank, or responsibility of a member of the instructional staff of an educational institution or school system; (2) selection of classroom teachers for a demonstration school or college position or for an administrative post.

promotion, trial: *syn.* **promotion, probationary.**

promotional occupational mobility: *see* **occupational mobility, promotional.**

prompt: *n.* a stimulus added to the terminal stimulus to make the correct response more likely while the student is learning; may be pictorial or verbal and may vary in strength, that is, in the probability with which it will evoke the correct response from a given population; used synonymously with *cue* and is generally synonymous with the nontechnical term *hint;* a distinction between *prompt* and *cue* is made by some writers; prompt describes the functions of a model of the response which the student copies, while a cue is a hint of a weaker sort, not a stimulus to be imitated; in programmed materials, the portion of a teaching frame which helps the student to respond appropriately, such as multiple-choice items instead of blanks to fill in.

prompt: *v.* to whisper to the language learner a word, expression, or utterance that appears to be causing him difficulty; prompting should be done quickly and unobtrusively in order to retain the brisk or smooth pace of a drill.

prompt, emphasis: in programmed instruction, one of the cues or stimuli employed to ensure that a response will be correct; usually a word or phrase underlined or written in capital letters.

prompt, formal: in programmed instruction, a prompt which provides knowledge about the form of the expected response, such as number of letters or sound pattern prompted by a rhyme.

prompt, sequence: in programmed instruction, the presentation of items in a certain series, then the request for one or more that have been removed from the sequence.

prompt, thematic: in programmed instruction, a hint with meaningful associations with the expected response, such as "man's best friend" to elicit the response "dog" or "the Louvre" for "Paris."

prompting: in programmed learning, the use of *cues,* various forms of redundancy, or other means of providing the learner with directional aid in his study.

prompting, response: a laboratory technique in which a student is given a stimulus (a word or picture), is told the correct response (prompted), and repeats the response after the prompter. *See* **prompt.**

pronated: (1) pertaining to feet the soles of which are rotated outward so that the individual stands or walks on the inner borders; (2) pertaining to the hand when it has been rotated so that the palm is facing downward.

pronation: (handwriting) the turning of the hand toward the position in which the palm is down.

prone: lying face downward.

prone behavior: *see* **behavior, prone.**

pronumeral: (math.) a placeholder; a term introduced by the University of Illinois Committee on School Mathematics to emphasize the similarity of the role of a symbol x in a mathematical sentence such as $x = 7$ to that of a pronoun in an English sentence such as "He is president of the class." *See* **placeholder.**

pronunciation: the manner of uttering words, with reference to the pattern of accent, choice of phonemes, vowel quality, and syllable length employed; to be distinguished from *articulation,* which refers to production of individual sounds.

pronunciation, colloquial: familiar and conversational pronunciation of educated persons when speaking in everyday situations.

pronunciation, correct: the pronunciation commonly used by educated speakers of a given region.

pronunciation exercise: *see* **exercise, pronunciation.**

pronunciation, inner: subvocal speech carried on during silent reading.

pronunciation key: *see* **key, pronunciation.**

pronunciation unit: *see* **unit, pronunciation.**

proof: in logic, a connected piece of reasoning by which a proposition is said to be "proved" when shown to follow upon other propositions already accepted as true, especially if these are shown to be the direct, positive, and sufficient evidences of the given proposition's truth, and no alternative interpretation of the evidence is apparent.

proof, analytic: (1) a proof which relies almost exclusively on algebraic manipulation, such as proofs of theorems in analytic geometry; (2) a proof making use of the limiting processes of the calculus. *See* **analysis** (1), (2), (3), and (4); **analysis, mathematical.**

proof, constructive: a proof in which some object (line, number, etc.) is shown to exist by demonstrating a process for finding it; for example, proving that every angle has a bisector by describing how to select a ray with the necessary properties.

proof, deductive: (1) a proof in which the argument proceeds according to the rules of inference of logic; *syn.* **direct proof;** (2) sometimes, *syn.* **proof, formal.**

proof, direct: *see* **proof, deductive** (1).

proof, formal: (1) a mathematical proof within a deductive system which proceeds according to some acceptable pattern such as mathematical induction, deductive proof, etc.; (2) sometimes used to mean a written proof in a particular form (reason for every statement, use of connecting words, etc.).

proof, indirect: (1) (logic) a method of argumentation that proceeds to the establishment of a particular proposition through the refutation of all other mutually exclusive possibilities. *See* **indirect method;** *contr. w.* **proof, direct;** (2) (math.) a proof which shows that if a theorem is not true, that is, if its negation is true, there is an inconsistency in the axiom system by virtue of a contradiction with either a previous theorem or an axiom; (3) sometimes used to mean a proof of the contrapositive of a theorem.

proof, inductive: *see* **induction, mathematical.**

proof, mathematical: an argument employing valid reasoning which shows some general mathematical assertion to be a necessary consequence of accepted premises which may be formalized as axioms, theorems, etc., or, especially at more elementary levels, specified as rules, laws, etc.

proof, nature of: the characteristics of argumentation used in deriving desired conclusions from accepted hypotheses.

proof of age: *see* **age, proof of.**

proof, synthetic: a proof which does not rely on algebraic methods. *See* **synthetic method;** *contr. w.* **proof, analytic.**

proofreading: *see* **reading, proof.**

propaedeutic (prō′pə·dū′tik): a preliminary study that serves as an introduction to some higher branch of learning.

propaganda: (1) an attempt to influence the actions, thoughts, and emotions of people or to secure acceptance of a belief, attitude, doctrine, or principle; (2) a doctrine spread by concerted effort; (3) secret or clandestine spreading of doctrines, ideas, information, or gossip with a view to assisting, impeding, or injuring the interests of a person, institution, or cause.

propaganda analysis: *see* **analysis, propaganda.**

propensity: (1) an inborn tendency; a natural proclivity; (2) condition of being favorably disposed.

proper subset: *see* **subset.**

property, abandonment of: *see* **abandonment of property.**

property accounting: *see* **accounting, property.**

property classification: the act or process of developing categories for the grouping of property, in order that the taxes may be differentiated in each category.

property, intangible personal: noncorporeal property rights which are evidenced by claims, stocks, bonds, mortgages, notes, contracts, etc.

property inventory: *see* **inventory, property.**

property, personal: tangible forms of wealth possessed by a person but not permanently affixed to land or buildings.

property, real: immovable property consisting of land, buildings, and permanent fixtures.

property register: (1) an official record book listing the taxable property within a governmental unit; (2) an official record of property owned by a governmental unit.

property, school: *see* **physical plant; school plant.**

property, symmetric: *see* **symmetric property.**

property, tangible personal: movable wealth, such as household furniture, farm machinery, automobiles, farm animals, jewelry, etc.

property tax: *see* **tax, property.**

property, transitive: *see* **transitive property.**

prophecy formula: *syn.* **Spearman-Brown prophecy formula.**

prophylaxis: (1) (theory of discipline) that kind of discipline which emphasizes the preventive element rather than the punitive element of treatment; the person administering the discipline is more concerned with prevention of wrongdoing than he is with punishment for wrongdoing; (2) (read.) the prevention of retardation or disability in reading.

proponent: (mil. ed.) a school which has been assigned responsibility for developing and reviewing instructional material which is primary to its area of academic interest but which is also presented at one or more other schools.

proportion: (math.) a sentence which asserts the equality of two ratios, as $\frac{1}{5} = \frac{2}{10}$.

proportional sample: *see* **sample, representative** (1).

proportional selection: *see* **selection, proportional.**

proportional taxation: *see* **taxation, proportional.**

proportioned selection: *syn.* **selection, proportional.**

proportions of value: (art ed.) a term referring to sizes that are determined by the artist's or child's subjective relationship to his environment and not directly by visual experiences; omissions of unimportant and exaggerations of important parts that arise from such value judgments.

proposal, curriculum: *see* **curriculum proposal.**

proposition: (1) (math.) in classical Euclidean geometry, a statement to be proved; classified as either a *theorem* or a *problem* (that is, a construction); (2) (logic) a mental entity composed of concepts in relation such that it is true or false, potentially or actually; an instrument of knowing, usually distinguished both from judgment as the mental act of assertion or denial and from the material signs, oral or written, in terms of which it is expressed.

proposition, categorical: the simplest form of assertion or denial, consisting of a subject term, about which something is asserted, and a predicate term, which asserts something about the subject, connected by a copula, represented by some form of the verb "to be," as "A dog is an animal."

proposition, disjunctive: a proposition taking the form of "not both . . . and . . ." in which it is stated that all the possibilities it lists (its disjuncts) may be false, but that all cannot be true because at least one must be false; for example, "A school cannot both be child-centered and place exclusive emphasis upon subject matter."

proposition, hypothetical: a conditional or implicative proposition taking the form of "If . . . then . . ." wherein the "if" introduces a hypothesis or condition, called the antecedent, and the "then" introduces the conclusion, called the consequent.

propositions, contradictory: specifically, two sentences one of which is the negation of the other; generalizing, a set of sentences such that all cannot be simultaneously true and all cannot be simultaneously false. *See* **negation.**

propositions, contrary: *see* **propositions, contradictory.**

propositus (prō·pŏz′ĭ·tŭs). (biol.) the individual whose ancestors or progeny (or both) are being traced.

proprietary accounts: those accounts necessary to reflect the assets and liabilities and displaying the results of operations in terms of revenue, expenditure, surplus, or deficit.

proprietary function of board: *see* **board, proprietary function of.**

proprietary junior college: *see* **junior college, proprietary.**

proprietary medical school: *see* **medical school, proprietary.**

proprietary school: a private school conducted for profit and serving the educational needs of business and industry, professional training, and many areas of a social and cultural nature.

proprioceptive sense: *syn.* **muscle sense.**

proprioceptor: a sensory receptor which receives and transmits impulses from the muscles, tendons, and joints.

proscenium: that part in a theater which includes a portion of the stage between the curtain and drop scene and the orchestra, sometimes also including the curtain and its arch.

proselyting: (athletics) the practice of inducing boys to attend a school for the purpose of playing on its athletic teams.

prospectus: a booklet containing descriptive material designed to enlist interest in an institution by setting forth salient facts. *See* **catalog.**

prosthesis: an appliance used to compensate for the absence of a natural body appendage, such as a false finger, hand, arm and hand, foot, foot and leg, or other compensating appliance.

prosthetic appliance: *see* **prosthesis.**

protagonist: central character in a dramatic production with whom the audience identifies itself.

protection, consumer: provision for the welfare of the consumer by supplying him with reliable information regarding the purchase of goods and services. *See* **information, consumer.**

protective reflex: *syn.* **reflex, defense.**

protective tenure: *syn.* **tenure, indefinite.**

Protestantism: (1) a religious reform movement beginning early in the sixteenth century, constituting a revolt against many of the practices and beliefs of the medieval Western Church and ending in a separation from that Church; this movement, commonly called the *Reformation,* led to a variety of church groups differing from one another on many points but holding to certain basic principles—for example, supremacy of the Bible, justification by faith alone, and universal priesthood of all believers—and united in opposition to the medieval Church and until quite recent times to the post-Tridentine Roman Catholic heir to that Church; advocated instruction in reading for everyone and made use of vernacular versions of the Bible and church services; (2) loosely used, especially in the United States and other English-speaking countries, a term descriptive of any branch of Christianity not in communion with the Pope, the supreme head of the Roman Catholic Church.

protocol: (sci. ed.) a "first draft" of an experience later to become formalized knowledge; facts function as protocols against which scientific theories and all other kinds of conjectures are ultimately tested.

protocols for counseling: *see* **counseling, protocols for.**

Protometer: an instrument developed by Ellis Freeman and designed for rapid and comprehensive testing of vision; gives data on monocular acuity, binocular acuity, and muscle balance for both distance and near vision.

protopathic sensibility: *see* **sensibility, protopathic.**

protoplasm: the complex chemical compound that is the basis of all living matter and is capable of the typically "vital" functions of metabolism, growth, and reproduction. (While the chemical elements entering into its composition are known, its structure is so complex that at present little is known about it.)

provisional certificate: *see* **certificate, provisional.**

provisional license: *syn.* **certificate, provisional.**

provisional try: *see* **try, provisional.**

provost: (1) originally, a chief academic or educational administrator in a higher education institution; (2) recently used, but rarely, to denote the chief administrator on an individual campus of a multicampus institution; *see* **chancellor;** (3) recently and more commonly, a high administrative officer in some American universities, above the rank of *dean* of a particular college unit, in charge of educational activities under the *president.*

proxemics: a field of study concerned with the amount of space people need around them for humane living, the so-called "space bubble," which may vary greatly from culture to culture or even from location to location within a culture.

proximate aim: *see* **aim, proximate.**

proximate cause: *see* **cause, proximate.**

proximodistal development, law of (prok'si•mō•dist'əl): the tendency for anatomical and early motor development to proceed from proximal to distal regions, or from the main axis of the body to more remote segments or members. *See* **proximodistal direction;** *dist. f.* **cephalocaudal development, law of.**

proximodistal direction: from the midline of the body outward toward the extremities of the fingers and toes.

proxy: authority to act for another, as in voting; a person thus authorized to act for another.

prudence: a virtue of the reasoning power, usually acquired through much experience, which enables one to judge correctly his moral obligations in a given situation, after giving careful consideration to all the contingent circumstances and possible effects of his actions; sometimes, practical sagacity.

pseudo feeblemindedness: *see* **mental retardation, pseudo.**

pseudo guidance: *see* **guidance, pseudo.**

pseudo mental retardation: *see* **mental retardation, pseudo.**

pseudo replication: (1) the division into subsets of the data collected from a single experiment so that each subset may be viewed as the result of a repetition of the basic experiment; (2) any of the subsets of data thus organized.

pseudo retardation: *see* **mental retardation, pseudo.**

pseudo stuttering: *see* **stuttering, pseudo.**

pseudocode: a series of commands or instructions, used by programmers in writing a program, which have the form of regular commands or instructions but the function of defining operands, specifying origins, or otherwise directing the translation process; a human or machine translation or interpretation is required before a program incorporating pseudocodes can be used by an automatic computer. *Comp. w.* **macrocommand.**

pseudogifted child: *see* **child, pseudogifted.**

pseudoinstruction: *see* **pseudocode.**

pseudoparalysis (sū'dō•pə•ral'ə•sis): false paralysis; apparent loss of muscular power without true paralysis, marked by defective coordination of movements or by the repression of movement.

pseudorealistic developmental stage: *see* **developmental stage, pseudorealistic.**

pseudorealistic representation: *see* **developmental stage, pseudorealistic.**

P.S.G.R.: psychogalvanic skin response. *Syn.* **response, galvanic skin.**

psychasthenia (sī'kas•thē'ni•ə; psī'kas-; sī'kas•thə•nī'ə): a complex condition, described by Janet, that is marked by morbid anxiety, fixed ideas, phobias, doubts, and feelings of unreality.

psychiatric clinic: *see* **clinic, psychiatric.**

psychiatric interview: *see* **interview, psychiatric.**

psychiatric social worker: *see* **social worker, psychiatric.**

psychiatrist (sī•kī'ə•trist; psī•kī'-; sī'ki•at'rist): a physician whose specialty is the diagnosis and treatment of mental disorders.

psychiatrist, school: a physician qualified to diagnose and treat mental illnesses to whom students who remain resistant to counselor aid should be referred; provides intensive, individual psychiatric studies of such children; the resulting information is used to aid understanding by teachers, administrators, pupil-personnel workers, and parents.

psychiatry: that department of medicine which studies and treats mental disease and mental aspects of organic disease as well as problems of personal adjustment.

psychic blindness: *see* **blindness, psychic.**

psychic deafness: *see* **deafness, psychic.**

psychic determinism: *see* **determinism, psychic.**

psychic income: *see* **income, psychic.**

psychic profile: *see* **chart, profile; psychograph.**

psychical deafness: *syn.* **deafness, psychic.**

psycho-asthenics (sī'kō•as•then'iks; psī'kō-): the body of knowledge pertaining to mental deficiency and the feebleminded.

psychoacoustics: the experimental study of sound sensations and their relation to sound stimuli.

psychoanalysis: a technical method devised by Sigmund Freud for investigating the deeper regions of the mind by the study of normal and abnormal reactions and unconscious mental processes.

psychoanalytic theory in counseling: a counseling approach which stresses that one's personality is a system composed of id, ego, and superego and a result of genetic relationship between ego functions in later life and those of infancy and childhood.

psychobiology: an approach to human behavior in which the individual is studied in relation both to his past experiences and to the environment in which he is called upon to adjust.

psychodrama: (couns.) a diagnostic and therapeutic device whereby two or more persons are assigned roles to play in a situation which, as described to them, frequently involves frustration or conflict; each actor attempts to assume the role so completely that he will have the feeling of experiencing and reacting to a situation as he would in real life; spontaneous action and expression by participants should bring release from the effects of conflict and frustration.

psychodrama, leaderless: *see* **role-playing, leaderless.**

psychodynamics: mental processes viewed as a system of motivational forces leading to action, change, and development.

psychoeducational: pertaining to the psychological aspects of the learning process in general or of progress and adjustment in school or course.

psychoeducational clinic: *see* **clinic, psychoeducational.**

psychoeducational examiner: *see* **examiner, psychoeducational.**

psychoeducational program: *see* **program, psychoeducational.**

psychogalvanic: pertaining to a phenomenon, discovered independently by Fere (1888) and Tarchanoff (1890), characterized by the fact that an emotional change is accompanied by an alteration in the electrical potential between points on the skin. *See* **response, galvanic skin.**

psychogalvanic reflex: *syn.* **psychogalvanic skin response.**

psychogalvanic skin response (P.S.G.R.): (1) decreased electrical resistance of the skin, due to physiological activities under the control of the autonomic nervous system, following sensory or ideational excitation; (2) increase in the electromotive force of the skin under conditions similar to (1); (3) a procedure for hearing testing which consists in conditioning a child to respond to sound as he normally does to an electric shock, thus providing a means of measuring his involuntary responses to sound.

psychogalvanic skin response audiometry: *see* **audiometry, psychogalvanic skin response.**

psychogalvanometer: a device for detecting or measuring the *psychogalvanic skin response.*

psychogenesis (sī'kō•jen'ə•sis; psī'kō-): (1) the study of the beginning and development of mental functions; (2) a somewhat inexact term, depending in part on inference, designating the experiential factor in behavior; as ordinarily used, refers to behavior of which the particular pattern has been determined wholly or in part by individual experience that has given rise to "sets," attitudes, prejudices, conditioned reactions, habits, and similar "learned" behavior tendencies.

psychogenic: (1) caused by psychological factors; of psychological origin; (2) pertaining to the evolution of the mind.

psychogenic deafness: *see* **deafness, psychic.**

psychogenic mental retardation: *see* **mental retardation, psychogenic.**

psychograph: a printed graph or profile upon which are plotted in diagrammatic form the psychological traits of an individual. *Comp. w.* **profile.**

psycholinguistics: the discipline concerned with the study of the relations between communications or messages and the cognitive or emotional states of the persons who communicate; specifically, the study of language as related to the general or individual characteristics of the users of language, with emphasis upon underlying causes of language behavior and its effects on other activities of the person, thus having implications for other fields of psychology; an interdisciplinary field. *Syn.* **linguistic psychology; psychology of language.**

psycholinguistics, developmental: that area of *psycholinguistics* which deals with investigation of the acquisition and growth of power in language on the part of the native speaker.

psychological approach: (1) a method of teaching in which new subject matter and ideas are presented in a manner appropriate to the way in which the pupil learns and through situations that are meaningful to him; (2) a technique of individual counseling that takes account of the way in which the counselee learns and identifies problems and presents advice through situations that are meaningful to him. *See* **child-experience approach; functional approach;** *contr. w.* **logical method.**

psychological atmosphere: *see* **atmosphere, psychological.**

psychological atomism: *see* **atomism, psychological.**

psychological block: *see* **block, psychological.**

psychological climate: *syn.* **atmosphere, psychological.**

psychological clinic: *see* **clinic, psychological.**

psychological control: *see* **control, psychological.**

psychological counselor: *syn.* **counselor, personal.**

psychological determinism: *see* **determinism, psychological.**

psychological diagnosis: *see* **diagnosis, psychological.**

psychological disengagement: *see* **disengagement, psychological.**

psychological evaluation: *see* **evaluation, psychological.**

psychological examination: *see* **evaluation, psychological (1).**

psychological feedback: *see* **feedback, psychological.**

psychological growth: *see* **growth, psychological.**

psychological life space: *see* **life space, psychological.**

psychological maturity: *syn.* **maturity, social.**

psychological method: a direct method of foreign-language teaching in which series of sentences on everyday life are presented orally, with the object of enabling the pupil or student to associate each new word with a mental picture or to grasp the logical relation of ideas.

psychological panel: a phrase, introduced by George Draper, designating as complete as possible a compilation of the psychological characteristics of an individual (such as intelligence, sensory acuity, emotional stability, interests, etc.).

psychological positivism: *see* **idealism, epistemological.**

psychological reeducation: *see* **reeducation, psychological.**

psychological service: in guidance, those services involving the intensive, individual psychological study of children. *See* **psychologist, school.**

psychological services: *see* **services, psychological.**

psychological test: *see* **test, psychological.**

psychologist: (1) one trained in psychology who is able to conduct research in this field or to apply the science in professional practice; (2) (couns.) *syn.* **counselor, personal.**

psychologist, clinical: a specialist with a Ph.D. in clinical psychology who concerns himself with persons suffering from emotional disorders.

psychologist, consulting: (1) a psychologist who acts as an expert adviser to his clients in matters pertaining to psychological problems; usually, a specialist in a particular area, such as clinical, industrial, business, advertising, or educational psychology, his competence depending on sufficient knowledge of the special area so that he can exercise guidance in the solution of the psychological problems involved; (2) a diplomate of the American Board of Examiners in professional psychology.

psychologist, counseling: a professional psychologist who specializes in counseling; his training equips him to deal with personal problems not classified as mental illness,

though they may be sequels or corollaries of mental or physical illness, for example, the academic, social, or vocational problems of students. *See* **psychology, counseling.**

psychologist, school: a school staff member with specialized training in psychological procedures and techniques (preferably holding at least an M.A. degree in psychology) who provides intensive, individual psychological studies of pupils; the resulting information and understandings are used in consultation and follow-up services with children, parents, teachers, and other professional workers in the school and in the community. *See* **hygienist, mental.**

psychologist, visiting: a psychologist who devotes time to the treatment of schoolchildren either under contract with a local school system or after referral of children to him by school authorities.

psychology: the study of adjustments of organisms, especially the human organism, to changing environment.

psychology, abnormal: the branch of psychology that treats of abnormal behavior, abnormal mental processes, and abnormal reactions to situations, involving conflict between the intellect and the emotions. *See* **abnormal.**

psychology, Adlerian: theory of personality and system of treatment developed by Alfred Adler, contemporary and at one time a coworker of Sigmund Freud; essential elements of his theory are a life-style developed by each individual as he strives to find a place of significance for himself in a world that often gives him feelings of inferiority and inadequacy.

psychology, adolescent: the study of the behavior of human beings during the period of adolescence, dealing with such topics as adolescent interests, physical and mental growth, ideals and morals, causes of unintelligent and delinquent behavior, adjusting the school and the home to the adolescent, and organizing a community for adolescent welfare.

psychology, analytic: (1) the systematic study of human behavior by selecting the major factors, arranging them in order, then separating them into their parts and considering their relations to each other and to the field of psychology as a whole; (2) in a special sense, the psychological system of Carl Jung, which emphasizes the urges toward growth, action, food, comfort, and reproduction in human life.

psychology, association: a view that mental states become integrated as a result of being contiguous in either time or space. *Syn.* **associationism;** *see* **learning, associational.**

psychology, child: the portion of the field of psychology that investigates the behavior and development of the individual prior to the age of maturity and applies those facts and principles necessary to the understanding of the child.

psychology, clinical: a form of applied psychology that aims to define the behavior capacities and personality characteristics of an individual through methods of measurement, analysis, and observation and on the basis of these findings makes recommendation for management of the individual or carries on educational, counseling, and psychotherapeutic procedures.

psychology, comparative: the study of the behavior and development of organisms other than man; originally embraced also the study of development in children whose behavior was compared with that of adults, but this usage is not now widespread.

psychology, counseling: the application of the methods of general psychology to the study of individuals; overlaps extensively the field of *clinical psychology;* traditionally more concerned with vocational and educational psychological counseling than with therapeutic counseling; recently, the distinction has become less apparent; however, *counseling psychologists* are more often employed in schools, industries, and various community activities, while *clinical psychologists* are professionally engaged in clinics and hospitals.

psychology, crowd: (1) that branch of social psychology or sociology which treats of the behavior and reactions of crowds; (2) the psychology of individuals acting in "crowd" situations.

psychology, depth: (Freudian psych.) a system of psychology that seeks to explain human emotional reactions through the study of underlying unconscious mechanisms.

psychology, developmental: the branch of psychology concerned with the course or progressive stages of behavior, considered phylogenetically and ontogenetically, and including both the phases of growth and of decline; broader in meaning than *genetic psychology*, though the terms are frequently used interchangeably.

psychology, dialectical: *syn.* **psychology, Marxian.**

psychology, differential: that branch of psychology dealing with differences or variations in traits among different individuals or groups or with differences within the same individual and studying these differences with respect to the effects of various factors, including sex, age, socioeconomic status, racial origins, heredity, environmental factors, and motivating factors. See **psychology, individual.**

psychology, dynamic: a form of psychology concerned largely with human motivation and explanatory principles derived in good part from psychoanalysis, such as unconscious motivation, repression, compensatory adjustment, etc. See **psychodynamics.**

psychology, educational: (1) the investigation of the psychological problems involved in education, together with the practical application of psychological principles to education; (2) a study of the nature of learning.

psychology, ego: a branch of psychoanalysis originating from a greater emphasis on ego defenses and resistances in the analysis of neurosis and in the process of psychoanalysis.

psychology, exceptional-child: *see* **psychology of exceptional children.**

psychology, existential: analysis of human behavior in terms of what is actual or objective as opposed to what is possible or ideal.

psychology, experimental: study through laboratory techniques of those phases of human behavior that can be so investigated.

psychology, faculty: a term that derives from an attempt by Wolff (1912) to analyze conscious experiences in terms of a mind (soul) endowed with certain faculties or "potencies of action"; Wolff sought to establish a relationship between the location in the soul of a faculty and its ability to re-present specific elements of the universe.

psychology, functional: the science of human behavior concerned with the conditions, utility, consequences, applications, and values of acts in adjustments to environment.

psychology, general: the study of all phases of human behavior from all points of view; presents elementary, essential, and universal principles, rather than intensive studies of particular periods or particular applications or the development of principles from a particular point of view.

psychology, genetic: a branch of psychology concerned with the origins and course of behavior of organisms in their development toward maturity; frequently restricted to the study of human childhood and adolescence, though theoretically inclusive also of infrahuman species; sometimes used synonymously with *developmental psychology*, of which it is a part. See **genetic method.**

psychology, gestalt (gə•shtält′): (Ger., lit., "form," "structure") a system of psychology which holds that experiences should be studied not in segregated parts but as units, and which maintains that the organism always reacts as a whole, regardless of specific stimuli.

psychology, handicapped: *syn.* **psychology, exceptional-child.**

psychology, hormic: the psychology of William McDougall, which emphasizes the purposive, or goal-seeking, phases of behavior.

psychology, individual: (1) the branch of psychology that deals with differences among individuals; (2) the name given by Alfred Adler to his variation of psychoanalytic theory, which emphasizes individual differences in ways of striving toward recognition and improved status. See **psychology, differential;** *contr. w.* **psychology, general.**

psychology, introspective: (1) a system of psychology based on trained self-observation as advocated by E. B. Titchener; (2) *syn.* **psychology, existential.**

psychology, linguistic: *see* **psycholinguistics.**

psychology, Marxian: a dialectical, materialistic interpretation of behavior that features economic factors as the primary determinants of human nature.

psychology, mass: (1) the study of human behavior as it is modified through the influence of group contacts or associations; (2) in a more limited sense, the modifications of conduct in large group contacts as in mob action, crowd hysteria, etc., including such modifications occurring as the result of propaganda.

psychology, mob: a special type of behavior and mental activity as exhibited by groups of persons under the influence of strong emotional excitement, usually characterized by lack of deliberation and sense of responsibility; more extreme than *crowd psychology.*

psychology, occupational: study of the mental states and processes of a person dealing with a job or of the mental requirements for a specific occupation.

psychology of development: the study of development as related to psychological factors.

psychology of exceptional children: the application of psychology to the study of the nature and needs of physically, mentally, and socially exceptional children.

psychology of family relations: *see* **family relations, psychology of.**

psychology of language: *see* **psycholinguistics.**

psychology of religion: *see* **psychology, religious.**

psychology, organismic: the interpretation of behavior in terms of the structure and function of the organism as a whole; emphasizes the role of the anatomical and physiological backgrounds in the interpretation of conduct and assumes that the directive forces for all reactions follow generalized laws of energy systems and that the organism and its environment constitute an integrated system.

psychology, pastoral: a field of study devoted to the training of pastors to help people help themselves through the process of gaining understanding of their inner conflicts.

psychology, physiological: the study of the functions of the parts and organs of an organism as they affect its integrating of experience.

psychology, purposive: any system of psychology that emphasizes purposiveness or goal orientation. See **psychology, hormic.**

psychology, religious: the study of the religious motivations and behaviors of individuals made from the standpoint of the science of psychology. *Syn.* **psychology of religion.**

psychology, social: (1) the study of the behavior of groups; (2) the study of the influence of the group on the development of personality; (3) the study of social interaction. See **sociology.**

psychology, structural: *syn.* **psychology, existential.**

psychology, topological: psychological research that utilizes mathematical topology, or the science of nonmetric space.

psychomathematics: the psychology of mathematics learning.

psychometric sign: *see* **sign, psychometric.**

psychometrics: (1) the branch of knowledge that is concerned with the development and application of mathematical and statistical methods for the measurement of psychological traits and analysis of psychological data; encompasses such areas of study as test theory, psychological scaling theory, and latent trait analysis; (2) psychological testing; measurement by means of psychological tests; (3) measurement in psychology. *Syn.* **psychometry.**

psychometrist: one who administers, scores, and interprets psychological tests.

psychometrist, school: a school staff member with special training in psychological testing procedures and techniques who is responsible for testing in connection with case studies of individual pupils.

psychometry: *syn.* **psychometrics.**

psychomotor: *adj.* pertaining to muscular action which follows directly from a mental process; important in vocabulary proficiency, the performing arts, and sports.

psychomotor epilepsy: *see* **epilepsy, psychomotor.**

psychomotor skill: *see* **skill, psychomotor.**

psychomotor test: *see* **test, psychomotor.**

psychoneurosis: *syn.* **neurosis.**

psychoneurotic child: *see* **child, psychoneurotic.**

psychoneurotic inventory: *see* **inventory, psychoneurotic.**

psychonomics: the science concerned with the psychological laws relating the mind to the environment, both internal and external; now used in such a general way that it is almost equivalent to *experimental psychology.*

psychopath: a person having a pathological instability of character but with no other apparent disorder and, frequently, with unimpaired intellectual functions.

psychopathic personality: *see* **personality, psychopathic.**

psychopathology: the study of abnormalities of mind and personality.

psychopathy (sī·kop′ə·thi; psī·kop′-): (1) mental disorder; any distortion of mental processes resulting from the unsatisfactory resolution of conflicts within the self; (2) (obs.) the science or system of treating disease by means of mental influence.

psychophysical: of or pertaining to the functional quantitative relation between stimuli and the ensuing discriminatory motor responses.

psychophysical dualism: *see* **dualism, psychophysical.**

psychophysical parallelism: *syn.* **dualism, psychophysical.**

psychophysical test: *see* **test, psychophysical.**

psychosemantics (sī′kō·sə·man′tiks; psī′kō-): an approach to language study that stresses not a formal attack but rather insights into the past and present ways of thinking and giving meaning in a language.

psychosexual immaturity: the persistence in adult life of the sexual attitudes, emotions, and behavior of childhood and adolescence.

psychosexuality: the psychological or emotional aspects of sexuality.

psychosis: a major or generalized mental disorder characterized by persistent and extensive ignoring of reality and one's surroundings, usually accompanied by seriously disordered behavior; may be organic or psychogenic in origin; usually of sufficient seriousness to warrant treatment of the individual in an institution for the mentally deranged. *Contr. w.* **neurosis.**

psychosis, affective: a mental disorder characterized by disturbance mainly in the emotional sphere, for example, *manic-depressive psychosis.*

psychosis, epochal: any one of a number of psychoses occurring typically at the principal epochs of life, for example, at puberty or at the menopause.

psychosis, manic-depressive: a type of mental disorder in which periods of activity alternate with periods of depression and retardation.

psychosis, organic: any psychosis resulting from a pathological disorder of the central nervous system, for example, delirium tremens. *See* **psychosis, toxic.**

psychosis, paranoid: a psychosis whose most conspicuous feature is the presence of delusions that certain people are plotting, persecuting, or disloyal.

psychosis, senile: mental disorder attributable to the onset of old age.

psychosis, toxic: any organic psychosis resulting from poisoning by toxic agents. *See* **psychosis, organic.**

psychosocial adjustment: *see* **adjustment, psychosocial.**

psychosomatic (sī·kō·sō·mat′ik): pertaining to the relationship of bodily symptoms that arise on the basis of psychological factors.

psychosomatic-experience blank: inventory of items referring to physical complaints and other reactions attributable to personal adjustment difficulties.

psychosurgery: brain surgery performed in the treatment of mental and emotional disorders.

psychotherapeutics (sī′kō·ther′ə·pū′tiks; psī′kō-): the treatment of mental disorders through mental influences; includes suggestion, psychoanalysis, and mental training.

psychotherapy: those processes directed by a professional individual skilled in psychological techniques toward improvement of a client who needs help to remedy a defined pathological condition.

psychotherapy, client-centered: *see* **counseling, client-centered.**

psychotherapy, group: *see* **therapy, group.**

psychotic: caused or affected by a psychosis. *See* **psychosis.**

psychovisual efficiency: sight utilization as affected by such factors as motivation, reaction to environment, and attitude.

puberty: the period of life or stage of development at which the reproductive organs mature and become capable of functioning and the secondary sex characteristics develop; the physiological stage marking the beginning of adolescence.

puberty praecox (prē′koks): the abnormally early development of sex organs and functions.

puberty rites: short courses in tribal lore given by elders or medicine men of certain primitive peoples to test obedience and self-control in the adolescent boys of the clan; they include instruction concerning spirits, totem animals, religious ceremonies, clansmen's obligations, and fasting; the candidates are usually mutilated or marked in some way. *See* **initiation ceremonies.**

pubescent spurt: increase in rate of growth in an individual who is just reaching or who has just reached the period at which the generative organs become capable of exercising the function of reproduction.

public-address system: a device for conveying sounds by wire over relatively short distances and amplifying them to more than their original volume; consists of a microphone for picking up the sound, an electrical amplifying unit using vacuum tubes, and one or more loudspeakers; may be centralized, as in the case of a public-address system installed in a school with a microphone in the principal's or superintendent's office and speakers in the classrooms, or portable, for use in auditoriums, on athletic fields, etc.; often includes an electric phonograph by which records and transcriptions may be played over the system; commonly shortened to *P.A.* or *P.A. system.*

public affairs education: (adult ed.) those educational programs designed to develop understanding and knowledge of public issues and problems facing the country and its citizens domestically and internationally in political, economic, and social areas.

public bond: *see* **bond, public.**

public borrowing: money secured for public use by means of a governmental bond issue or other debt-incurring method.

public corporation: *see* **corporation, public.**

public credit: *see* **credit, public.**

public education: usually, the educational programs sponsored by the state, by counties, by school districts, etc., for the pupils in the elementary and secondary schools; may include adult or vocational education. (Sometimes used in contrast with private and parochial education and sometimes to differentiate elementary and secondary education from higher education.)

public education, moral basis of: *see* **moral basis of public education.**

public finance: *see* **finance, public.**

public health education: organized activities carrying on a process of changing or maintaining personal and community health goals and directed toward promoting, maintaining, and improving the health and well-being of the population at a given time and place.

public health nurse: *see* **nurse, public health.**

public health personnel: *see* **personnel, public health.**

public health services: *see* **services, public health.**

public high school: *see* **high school, public.**

public information officer: *syn.* **director, public relations.**

public institution: *see* **institution, public.**

public interest: *see* **interest, public.**

public junior college: *see* **junior college, public.**

public libraries, state and local: *see* **library, public.**

public library: *see* **library, public.**

public library, adult education by: *see* **adult education by public library.**

public opinion: *see* **opinion, public.**

public ownership: (pup. trans.) a plan under which a school bus is owned and operated by a board of education, a municipality, a state, etc.

public power: (1) the inherent power of a government to maintain the general security and safeguard the public morals, health, safety, and convenience, even at the expense of infringing upon the private rights of individuals; an exception to the right of the citizen to conduct himself and use his property in such manner as he may see fit; (2) the residuum of unallocated powers reserved to the states by the Tenth Amendment of the Federal Constitution; one of these powers is the governmental authority to conduct a system of public education.

public recreation: *see* **recreation, public.**

public relations: the formal activity of improving the relations of a school or college with its special public or with the general public. See **public school relations.**

public relations broadcasting: *see* **broadcasting, public relations.**

public relations director: *see* **director, public relations.**

public relations film: *see* **film, public relations.**

public school: (1) a school, usually of elementary or secondary grade, organized under a school district of a state, supported by tax revenues, administered by public officials, and open to all; (2) in England, one of approximately 200 prestigious private schools whose headmasters belong to the Headmasters' Conference.

public school adult education: *see* **adult education, public school.**

public school doctor: *see* **doctor, public school.**

public school, endowed: a public school receiving a considerable portion of its operating budget from invested funds that must be held in perpetuity. See **endowment.**

public school music: *see* **music, public school.**

public school nurse: *see* **nurse, public school.**

public school relations: (1) an activity concerned with giving information to the public about the school or creating goodwill for the school; (2) a condition of mutual understanding that subsists between school and community. (Public school relations and publicity are often used synonymously. Publicity, however, refers more particularly to informational output, while public school relations includes the bringing of institutional policies into harmony with public opinion.)

public school relations agency: any instrumentality or medium used for disseminating information about the school, such as the press, the radio, television, or school demonstrations.

public school relations agent: a person connected with or recognized by a school or school system who engages in the dissemination of school news or, more generally, in the creation of goodwill.

public school teacher: any properly qualified person employed as an instructor in a public school system.

public service: *see* **service, public.**

public service occupations, training for: *see* **training for public service occupations.**

public service program: *see* **program, public service.**

public service vehicle: *see* **vehicle, public service.**

public support: *see* **support, public.**

public support and control: (voc. ed.) a rule for reimbursement from Smith-Hughes and George-Barden funds that all vocational education programs must be administered through public agencies.

public teachers college: *see* **teachers college, public.**

public vocational school: *see* **vocational school, public.**

Public Works Administration: an agency of the Federal government during the depression years of the 1930s, the function of which was to encourage public works, such as the construction of school buildings, with a combination of Federal and local or state financial assistance; the agency enforced certain controls over the projects it aided, such as specification of the kind and quality of materials used, standards of workmanship required, and the method of employment of labor.

publication adviser: *syn.* **adviser of publications.**

publication, school: (1) any printed or mimeographed yearbook, or annual, handbook, magazine, or newspaper that is edited and managed by a group of pupils or students under the auspices of a school or college; (2) any publication of a school.

publication sponsor: *syn.* **adviser of publications.**

publication, student: *syn.* **publication, school** (1).

publication supervisor: *syn.* **adviser of publications.**

publicity: (1) activities and materials designed to bring public notice and attention to an institution; (2) releases to periodicals concerning the activities of an institution or of its members.

publicity campaign: a concerted effort, of limited duration, to gain public support; in relation to the school, usually conducted to secure additional revenue or continuance of the present amount of revenue.

publicity device: a means of diffusing information.

publicity, educational: the diffusion of information concerning the educational program through various media of communication.

publicly owned bus: *see* **bus, publicly owned.**

Pueblo plan (pweb'lō): a grouping plan according to which pupils are organized into relatively small, homogeneous ability groups which are permitted to work and progress at their optimum rate; individual work with a minimum of teacher assistance is stressed. See **individual-progress plan.**

pugging: a process of mixing, stirring, and refining wet clay for use in ceramics and pottery making.

pulpit: a stand, often elevated, for the preaching of sermons usually delivered by the clergy in church buildings during services of worship. See **lectern.**

pulse-ratio test: *see* **test, pulse-ratio.**

punch card: *see* **card, punch.**

punch-card equipment: mechanical or electronic equipment that uses cards in which holes have been punched in predetermined positions to write data in codified form.

punch-card machine: *syn.* **tabulating machine** (2).

punch-card machine, alphabetic: any punch-card machine that, in addition to handling numbers, will also handle letters of the alphabet. *Syn.* **alphameric punch-card machine.**

punch-card machine, alphameric: *syn.* **punch-card machine, alphabetic.**

punch-card method: a method of recording and tabulating data in which the data are coded, the code numbers punched in cards, and the cards run through any one or a combination of several machines that sort, count, multiply, tabulate, etc. *Syn.* **machine method.**

punch-card unit: *syn.* **record, unit** (2).

punch, gang: *v.* to punch identical or constant information into all of a group of punch cards.

punch, multipying: a machine that automatically multiplies two or more factors previously punched into a punch card and automatically punches the resulting product into the card, or which cumulates products from a number of cards and punches their sum into another card or prints their sum on a paper form.

punch, reproducing: a machine that, among other operations, automatically duplicates a punch card from another employed as a pattern.

punch, summary: a machine that automatically punches a punch card for all members (or a predeterminable specified portion) of a series of summaries as they automatically accumulate in a tabulating machine.

punch tape: *see* **tape, punch.**

punch, X: on some punched cards, a hole in the row above the zero row; loosely, an *overpunch.*

punch, Y: on some punched cards, a hole in the row nearest the top of the card; also known as a 12 punch.

punch, zone: *syn.* **overpunch.**

punchboard: *see* **autotutor.**

punched paper tape: *see* **tape, punched paper.**

punched tape, five-channel: *see* **tape, five-channel punched.**

punching machine: a machine for punching holes into punch cards. *See* **punch card.**

punishment: unpleasant experience consequent on a certain course of behavior and mediated by an external agent or by the self acting as agent in the hope of providing retribution or of discouraging the repetition of the behavior. *Contr. w.* **reward.**

punishment, corporal: disciplinary action involving the infliction of physical pain upon one person by another, although physical contact is not necessary. *See* **hazing.**

punishment, natural: the theory or practice of controlling pupils through reliance or emphasis on the direct consequences of specific acts, in contrast to use of intentionally imposed penalties or rewards. (Injury resulting from carelessness and ostracism for violation of group standards are examples of natural punishment.)

punishment phantasy: *see* **fantasy, punishment.**

punitive discipline: *see* **discipline, punitive.**

pupil: (1) one who attends a kindergarten or a school of elementary level; (2) one who attends a school of secondary level (in this sense, *pupil* often is replaced by *student*); (3) a person (child or adult) studying under the relatively close supervision and tutelage of a teacher.

pupil accountability: *see* **accountability, pupil.**

pupil accounting: *see* **accounting, pupil.**

pupil achievement: *see* **achievement, pupil.**

pupil activity: *see* **activity, pupil.**

pupil activity, principle of: the principle that children learn most readily and retain longest those things which they learn by themselves of their own accord through manipulation, experimentation, and active participation, as contrasted with vicarious or externally motivated learning; does not preclude guidance by the teacher, but does preclude teacher domination.

pupil adjustment: *see* **adjustment, pupil.**

pupil-adjustment service: an area of pupil-personnel services designed to improve the pupil-school relationship; includes services of psychologists, psychiatrists, physicians, dentists, visiting teachers, and special teachers.

pupil age: *see* **age, chronological.**

pupil, atypical: a pupil revealing one or more physical, mental, or behavioral characteristics which are markedly different from those of the mean of his chronological age group.

pupil, backward: a child who fails to make progress in accordance with the desired and accepted school schedule; usually 1 to 3 years retarded in grade placement; also used, particularly in English writings on mental retardation, to designate the slow learner.

pupil, boarding: a tuition pupil who resides in a *boarding home* during the school week and in his own home on weekends; for example, a deaf child who resides beyond ordinary commuting distance from the special classes for the deaf in which he is enrolled.

pupil capacity of school plant: *see* **capacity of school plant, pupil.**

pupil-centered instruments: the more formal of the guidance tools, such as standardized tests, autobiographies, sociometric devices, and interviews, which cannot function without the pupil's participation; however, although he knows he is participating, the pupil may have no knowledge of why the instrument is being employed and he has no direct part to play in the functioning of statistical techniques.

pupil-centric methods: *see* **methods, pupil-centric.**

pupil-centric teaching: *see* **teaching, pupil-centric.**

pupil classification: *see* **classification, pupil.**

pupil classification, vertical: *see* **classification, vertical pupil.**

pupil-clock-hour: one hour spent in class or laboratory by one pupil; a unit of measurement formerly widely used in measuring and determining the teaching load of a given teacher or department; also sometimes employed as a unit in measuring costs of instruction. (A class of 25 pupils meeting five 45-minute periods a week would involve a load of $25 \times 5 \times \frac{3}{4} = 375 \div 4 = 93\frac{3}{4}$ pupil-clock-hours.)

pupil cost: *see* **cost, pupil.**

pupil council: a representative group of pupils to which is delegated the responsibility for managing certain specified school activities; a student legislative body.

pupil, culturally disadvantaged: the pupil, one or more years behind his age group in school, who is characterized by an inadequate self-image, frequent tardiness, absenteeism or truancy, inability to communicate adequately for school routine, retardation in reading, poor performance on tests, and hostility to authority.

pupil cumulative record card: *see* **record card, cumulative.**

pupil data blank: *see* **data blank, pupil.**

pupil density: (pupil accounting) *see* **pupils per square mile.**

pupil driver: *see* **driver, pupil.**

pupil, elementary: *see* **pupil, elementary school.**

pupil, elementary school: a child enrolled in a course of study normally encompassed by grades 1 through 6.

pupil evaluation: *see* **evaluation, pupil.**

pupil, full-time: a pupil who is carrying a full course load as determined by the state or the local school system.

pupil, full-tuition: a public-school pupil, usually a nonresident of the school district, for whom the maximum allowable tuition is paid; may also be applied to private school pupils.

pupil guidance: *see* **guidance, pupil.**

pupil handbook: a publication giving the new pupil information about school activities, traditions, students' clubs, and school policy as well as other data concerning the institution he is attending.

pupil helper: *syn.* **monitor.**

pupil, homebound: a pupil who is not able to attend regular school classes because of some handicap or illness and is confined to his home.

pupil, hospital: a pupil who is confined to a hospital and must receive instruction from a hospital teacher.

pupil information blank: *syn.* **data blank, pupil.**

pupil interest group: *see* **interest group, pupil.**

pupil inventory blank: *see* **data blank, pupil.**

pupil load: *see* **load, pupil.**

pupil management: the act or process of controlling pupils and maintaining discipline among them while in school.

pupil migration: *see* **migration, pupil.**

pupil mile: *see* **mile, pupil.**

pupil mobility: the degree to which pupil migration takes place; the rate or amount of pupil migration.

pupil movement: the passage of children, singly and in groups, from place to place on school property.

pupil needs: *see* **needs, pupil.**

pupil, nonresident: *see* **nonresident.**

pupil, nontuition: a pupil, usually a resident of the school district, for whom no tuition is paid.

pupil number: a number assigned to a pupil by the school system for identification and record-keeping purposes.

pupil, part-time: a pupil who is carrying less than a full course load as determined by the state or the local school system.

pupil, partial-tuition: a pupil for whom tuition which is less than the maximum or full amount is paid.

pupil participation: *see* **participation, pupil.**

pupil patrol: *see* **patrol, pupil.**

pupil personnel: *see* **personnel, pupil.**

pupil-personnel council: *syn.* **guidance council.**

pupil personnel, director of: *see* **director of pupil personnel.**

pupil-personnel program: *see* **program, pupil-personnel.**

pupil-personnel record: *syn.* **record, pupil.**

pupil-personnel service: *syn.* **guidance.**

pupil-personnel services: *see* **services, pupil-personnel.**

pupil-personnel services, director of: *see* **director of pupil-personnel services.**

pupil-personnel work: *syn.* **guidance.**

pupil-personnel worker: one who serves as a guidance counselor, school psychologist, visiting teacher, or school social worker.

pupil population: *see* **population, pupil.**

pupil portraits: a series of short characterizations of real or hypothetical pupils; used frequently in classroom reputation tests, which require that the pupils in a class shall specify which, if any, of their classmates each portrait characterizes.

pupil-principal ratio: *see* **ratio, pupil-principal.**

pupil, probation: *see* **probation pupil.**

pupil probation: *see* **probation** (1) and (2).

pupil probation report: *see* **probation report, pupil.**

pupil-professional educational staff ratio: *see* **ratio, pupil-professional educational staff.**

pupil progress: *see* **progress, rate of.**

pupil progress record: *see* **record, pupil progress.**

pupil-rating scale: *see* **scale, pupil-rating.**

pupil record: *see* **record, pupil.**

pupil record form: *syn.* **record form, individual.**

pupil-relatedness: the degree to which activities of personnel in the school setting have a direct influence upon the pupils; one of the two dimensions defining the major functions of the school operation. *Comp. w.* **instruction-relatedness.**

pupil, resident: a pupil residing within the local school administrative unit.

pupil, retarded: a pupil who exhibits some degree of mental retardation and lack in adaptive behavior. *See* **retardation, mental.**

pupil-school librarian ratio: *see* **ratio, pupil-school librarian.**

pupil self-activity: *syn.* **activity, pupil.**

pupil self-government: *see* **student government.**

pupil, slow: a pupil who is incapable of keeping up in a regular class; frequently 1 to 2 years retarded in academic grade placement.

pupil station: *see* **station, pupil.**

pupil-station utilization: *see* **utilization, pupil-station.**

pupil-teacher index, national: *see* **index, national pupil-teacher.**

pupil-teacher planned curriculum: *see* **curriculum, pupil-teacher planned.**

pupil-teacher ratio: *see* **ratio, student-teacher.**

pupil-total-staff ratio: *see* **ratio, pupil-total-staff.**

pupil, transfer: a pupil who severs his connections with a class, grade, or school in order to transfer to another class, grade, or school; includes pupils who transfer or are promoted from an elementary school to a secondary school or from a junior high school to a senior high school.

pupil transfer: *see* **transfer, pupil.**

pupil transportation: *see* **transportation, pupil.**

pupil transportation service: *see* **service, pupil transportation.**

pupil transportation, state aid for: *see* **aid for pupil transportation, state.**

pupil, transported: as used in pupil accounting, a pupil who is transported to and from school at public expense.

pupil, tuition: an administrative term to describe a pupil attending an educational program of the public school system for which a tuition charge is made, either due to the nonresident status of the pupil or to the special nature

of the administrative unit providing the program, such as a board of cooperative educational services. *See* **tuition, nonresident.**

pupil turnover: *see* **turnover, pupil.**

pupil, unclassified elementary: in pupil accounting, an elementary school pupil who is not classified according to grade.

pupil, unclassified secondary: a secondary school pupil who is not classified according to grade.

pupil unit: *see* **unit, pupil.**

pupil, unrelated: *see* **student, foreign.**

pupillary reflex: *see* **reflex, pupillary.**

pupils, isolated: those children who live in remote or inaccessible places.

pupils per acre: the average daily membership of a school divided by the total number of developed and undeveloped acres in the school site.

pupils per square mile: the total number of resident pupils who live in a given attendance area or administrative unit divided by the number of square miles in the attendance area or administrative unit; also referred to as *pupil density.*

pupils withdrawing, percentage of: *see* **percentage of pupils withdrawing.**

pupils' workshop: *see* **workshop, pupils'.**

puppet: a small-scale figure of a human or other animal form, often constructed with jointed limbs, of materials such as papier-mâché, wood, and cloth; manipulated directly by hand or sometimes with a rod or stick from below; used in art education for children's dramatic play and expression. *See* **marionette.**

purchase contract: *see* **contract, purchase.**

purchase follow-up: the function of assuring the delivery of a shipment of purchased materials at the time and place specified.

purchase of care: (spec. ed.) a system of service availability based on a single agency having funds and authority to purchase services from any source considered best able to provide that service component.

purchase order: a document that authorizes the delivery of specified merchandise or the rendering of certain services and the making of a charge for them.

purchasing: (school admin.) the function of securing from vendors, or other outside sources, the proper quantities of whatever materials and supplies are wanted by the organization; these items are purchased with due regard for requirements as to the time, place, and rate of delivery, the specified quality, and the lowest price that is consistent with the preceding requirements or others that may be set up. *See* **receiving.**

purchasing agent: a designated person who has the authority to order the purchase of supplies and equipment for an institution or school system.

purchasing, centralized: the system of making all purchases through a central office or department, common to many of the larger school districts in which a purchasing department buys all supplies and materials for all divisions of the school system.

purchasing committee: an organized group of persons in whom is vested the authority for making or authorizing purchases.

purchasing department: *see* **department, purchasing.**

purchasing power: the amount of goods and/or services that can be obtained by a consumer with his disposable income.

purchasing power, effective: *syn.* **income, real.**

Purdue pegboard test: *see* **test, Purdue pegboard.**

pure ego: *see* **ego, pure.**

pure geometry: *syn.* **geometry, projective.**

pure imaginary number: *see* **number, imaginary.**

pure line: a strain of individuals of which all members carry essentially the same gene structure (that is, are homozygous), so that each generation tends to resemble closely the preceding one. *See* **homozygous.**

pure mathematics: *see* **mathematics, pure.**

pure-part method: a method of sequencing programmed instruction in which each part is first learned separately to a criterion of mastery; subsequently, all the parts are repeated until the whole has been brought to the criterion already achieved by each separate part.

pure philosophy: *see* **philosophy, pure.**

pure research: *syn.* **research, basic.**

pure science: *ant.* **science, applied.**

pure-tone audiometer: *see* **audiometer, pure-tone.**

pure-tone hearing threshold: *see* **hearing threshold, pure-tone.**

purism: a twentieth-century theory and practice in art that reduces natural appearances to geometric simplicity or essential qualities of form, color, and composition. *See* **neoplasticism.**

puritanism: (1) serious love of virtue and purity; self-mastery in thought, speech, and acts, and in avoidance of all idleness; the position which holds that strong character and wise behavior come from strict adherence to established rules; that wisdom directs the disciplining of desire by hard work and exercise rather than by reflection; "if any will not work, neither let him eat"; that every man has a calling, has God's work to do; (2) (cap) the beliefs and practices of a group of English Protestants who, during the Reformation, opposed tradition and formal usage and advocated simpler forms of faith and worship than those prevailing in the English church of the time; emphasis was placed on such virtues as self-reliance, thrift, industry, and initiative, but the movement eventually was characterized by unnatural self-denial and oversevere discipline.

purity, test: *see* **test purity.**

Purkinje phenomenon (poor'kin·ye): the phenomenon of more rapid loss of brightness by long wavelength colors than shorter wavelength colors under decreased illumination; for example, in bright light, red appears brighter than blue, while, in dim light, blue appears brighter than red.

purpose: *n.* (1) an objective or end in view which is projected throughout the aspects of an activity and serves to motivate and direct it by providing a criterion as to the selection, interpretation, and evaluation of what is relevant; (2) (school finance) designation of type of improvement to be financed by bond issue.

purpose: *v.* to act knowing what one is about, to plan consciously, to choose knowingly goals that satisfy one's needs and interests, and to devise means to achieve the ends in view.

purpose of instructional program: *see* **instructional program, purpose of.**

purposeful activity: *see* **activity, purposeful.**

purposive action: action motivated by and directed toward a desired end or goal.

purposive activity: *syn.* **activity, purposeful.**

purposive psychology: *see* **psychology, purposive.**

purposive sample: *see* **sample, purposive.**

pursuit rotor learning: *see* **learning, pursuit rotor.**

pursuitmeter: an apparatus designed to measure progress in learning to maintain contact with a point on a bar that travels in one plane but in an irregular path and at varying speeds determined by the machine but unknown to the subject.

push-and-pull apparatus, manuometer: *see* **manuometer push-and-pull apparatus.**

push-and-pull drill: a type of handwriting exercise in which the learner retraces up- and downstrokes of a specified length, with the purpose of gaining motor control and precision in alignment and slant.

push-up: *syn.* **dip.**

puzzle-block test: *see* **test, puzzle-block.**

pycnoepilepsy: *syn.* **pyknolepsy.**

Pygmalion effect: the hypothesis that teacher expectancy (a form of experimenter bias) affects pupil performance. *See* **Hawthorne effect.**

pyknic: *syn.* **macrosplanchnic.**

pyknic type: *see* **body builds, classification of.**

pyknolepsy: a condition characterized by frequent attacks of an epileptic nature but of slight severity and of very short duration; during the seizure the child stops whatever he is doing and makes a few aimless and unrelated movements before proceeding as if nothing had happened; the child does not fall or injure himself and there may be a large number of such attacks (50 or more) during a single day. *Syn.* **pycnoepilepsy.**

pyramid building: (phys. ed.) the forming by a group of students of a pyramidlike human structure with one person at the top and all other participants gradually tapering to the sides.

pyramid plan of teaching: *see* **teaching, pyramid plan of.**

pyramid story: a scholastic designation for the typical outline of a newspaper article in which the most interesting parts are crowded toward the beginning.

pyromania (pī'rō·mā'ni·ə): a morbid impulse to start fires and to destroy buildings or property by fire.

pyrophobia (pī'rō·fō'bi·ə): a morbid fear of or anxiety about fire.

Q-sort: a personality inventory in which the subject (or someone making judgments about him) sorts a considerable number of statements into categories that represent the degrees to which the statements apply to him; each statement thus gets a score indicating relative strength within the individual of the quality or trait it represents.

Q-technique: (1) (in correlation) a process in which the scores on many tests for pairs of people are correlated; inverse correlation or obverse correlation, the transpose of *R-technique;* correlation of a pair of people over a number of tests; (2) a method of factorial analysis in which Q-technique correlations are used; (3) *syn.* **Q-sort.** *See* **factor analysis, transposed.**

quack guidance: *syn.* (1) **guidance, pseudo;** (2) **guidance, abortive.**

quadrangle: an open court, in the form of a rectangle, with university, college, or school buildings on all sides.

quadrant: any one of the four parts of a plane formed by the intersection of two mutually perpendicular lines or axes.

quadrant seating plan: *see* **seating plan, quadrant.**

quadratic mean: *syn.* **root mean square.**

quadriplegia: paralysis of the four extremities. *See* **hemiplegia; monoplegia; paraplegia; triplegia.**

quadriserial r: *see* **r, quadriserial.**

quadrivium (kwod·riv'i·əm): (Lat., lit., "four ways," "four roads") the designation of the four higher studies or disciplines of the medieval curriculum, namely, arithmetic, geometry, astronomy, and music. *See* **liberal arts, seven;** *dist. f.* **trivium.**

quadrupedal locomotion: locomotion involving the use of all four limbs.

quadruplets: four offspring born at the same birth. *See* **multiple birth.**

qualification card, soldier's: *see* **card, soldier's qualification.**

qualification code number, officers: *see* **code number, officers qualification.**

qualification standard: (mil. ed.) a description of the knowledge, abilities, and skills required to predict potential for successful performance of the duties of a class of positions as well as a means for determining that applicants possess this potential.

qualification, teacher: the education, experience, and physical, social, and mental characteristics of an instructor that determine his fitness for an educational position.

qualifications, M.L.A.: standards of preparation for modern foreign language teachers prepared by the steering committee of the Foreign Language Program of the Modern Language Association of America; teachers are rated as superior, good, or minimal in the skills of aural understanding, speaking, reading, writing, and language analysis.

qualified fee: *see* **fee, qualified.**

qualifying examination: *see* **examination, qualifying.**

qualitative: distinguished by differences in attributes rather than by numerical differences; differing in kind rather than in amount. *Contr. w.* **quantitative.**

qualitative change: a change in the nature or function of a structure or of the organism as a whole.

qualitative environment: *see* **environment, qualitative.**

qualitative measure: *see* **measure, qualitative.**

qualitative phenomena: *see* **phenomena, qualitative.**

qualitative series: *see* **series, qualitative.**

qualities, primary: *see* **primary qualities.**

qualities, secondary: *see* **secondary qualities.**

quality control: *see* **control, quality.**

quality decision: the judicial function in supervision in appraising the choices made by others in the administrative hierarchy.

quality discrimination: *see* **discrimination, quality.**

quality point average: *syn.* **average, grade point.**

quality scale: *see* **scale, quality.**

quality series: *syn.* **rating scale, descriptive.**

quantification: the act or process of assigning, either arbitrarily or rationally, numerical values to observations that are commonly qualitative. *See* **code** *v.*

quantifier: (math.) one of the two phrases used to distinguish conditional and identical *open sentences;* the existential quantifier (symbol ∃) asserts "there is" or "there exists," as, for example, "There is a number x such that $x = 2$"; the universal quantifier (symbol ∨) asserts "for every . . ." or "for all . . .," as in the expression "For every $x, x + 2x = 3x.$"

quantitative: concerned with measurement.

quantitative change: a change in the size of a structure or in the number of structures.

quantitative method: a method of research based on the collection and statistical analysis of numerical data. *Syn.* **statistical method.**

quantitative research: *see* **research quantitative.**

quantitative scale: *syn.* **rating scale, numerical.**

quantitative series: *see* **series, quantitative.**

quantity: that which may be measured or counted or which may be subjected to the fundamental laws of numerical computation.

quantity distribution: *see* **distribution, quantity.**

quantum mechanics: *see* **mechanics, quantum.**

quantum meruit (kwon'tǝm mer'ū·it; mer'ŏŏ-): (Lat., lit., "as much as he deserved") the principle of fair and equitable recompense for services rendered; applied legally when a person employs another to do work for him without any stipulation as to compensation, in which case the law presumes a promise from the employer to the workman that he will pay for his services as much as he may deserve or merit; also applied when a party has received and been enriched by goods for which he is not legally bound to pay the agreed price.

quantum valebant (kwon'tǝm va·lē'bant): (Lat., lit., "as much as they were worth") a term used in legal pleadings, founded on an implied promise on the part of the defendant to pay the plaintiff as much as the goods were reasonably worth.

quarantine: the isolation of any person suffering or convalescing from acute contagious disease.

quarter credit hour: *see* **credit hour, quarter.**

quarter hour: (higher ed.) 1 hour a week of lecture or class instruction for one quarter, or its credit equivalent of laboratory, fieldwork, or other type of instruction.

quarter system: a method of dividing the school year into four terms usually with 11 weeks per term of instruction, including final examination; in higher education, three quarters constitute the work of the academic year; the summer quarter is sometimes subdivided into terms of shorter length. *Comp. w.* **semester; trimester.**

quarter-track head: *see* **head, quarter-track.**

quarterly promotion: *see* **promotion, quarterly.**

quartile: one of the three points, measured along the scale of a plotted variable, that divides the distribution into four parts, each including 25 percent of the frequency; thus, the first quartile (Q_1) is the 25th percentile, the second quartile (Q_2) is the median, and the third quartile (Q_3) is the 75th percentile. *Dist. f.* **interval, quartile.**

quartile deviation: *see* **deviation, quartile.**

quartile deviation, standard error of: *see* **standard error of quartile deviation.**

quartile interval: *see* **interval, quartile.**

quartile measure of dispersion: *syn.* **deviation, quartile.**

quartile range: *syn.* **interval, quartile.**

quartile, standard error of: *see* **standard error of quartile.**

quartimax method: (fact. anal.) an analytical solution for orthogonal simple structure programmed for electronic computers by Wrigley.

quasi contract: *see* **contract, quasi.**

quasi corporation: *see* **corporation, quasi.**

quasi municipal corporation: *see* **corporation, quasi.**

quaternion: (1) a set of four persons, things, or parts; (2) a term used in reference to a mathematical system created by W. R. Hamilton which satisfies all axioms for a field except the *commutative law* of multiplication.

Queen of the Sciences: an identifying phrase, attributed to the mathematician Gauss (1777–1855), frequently used in reference to mathematics.

question-and-answer method: a method both of instruction and of oral testing based on the use of questions to be answered by the pupils.

question, guiding: a question used by the teacher to guide the pupil in reading through a sentence or longer unit; used especially in beginning reading to focus the child's attention on the meaning.

question list: *syn.* **questionnaire.**

question, motive: a question that is designed to arouse a motive for reading a passage or larger unit.

question, open-end: a semistructured technique for probing associations connected with a specific area; a sentence-completion test used in a clinical setting; after a suggestive start the subject is expected to finish the sentence; for example, "Because success . . ." or "A thing to ponder is . . ."

question, tag: a secondary cue question commonly used in *analogy drills* to elicit a given response.

question, thought: (1) any question for which an adequate answer ordinarily requires deliberation; (2) a question not ordinarily answerable in terms of everyday verbal habits; (3) a question not concerned primarily with skills or with knowledge of ordinary facts.

questionnaire: a list of planned written questions related to a particular topic, with space provided for indicating the response to each question, intended for submission to a number of persons for reply; commonly used in normative-survey studies and in the measurement of attitudes and opinions.

questionnaire, attitude: a series of questions focused on one or more specified attitude objects and designed to obtain a measure of the attitude or attitudes in question.

questionnaire, depth-essay: a technique for probing the motivational elements that underlie preferences, attitudes, decisions, or behavior; an open-end question or statement that the subject expands into a written essay, usually of specified length. *See* **question, open-end.**

questionnaire follow-up: a survey or study of individuals after they leave the guidance services; may include interviews, opinions, questionnaires, or checklists; one of the services undertaken in order both to find further opportunities for serving the student and to determine the reach, influence, and value of the school program as a means toward the improvement of the school.

questionnaire, guidance: a series of written questions to be answered in writing by present or former students, requesting information significant in the guidance of individuals or in formulating a program of guidance.

questionnaire, personal history: (couns.) a questionnaire which provides information about a child's home life and family background, his special abilities, health, hobbies, and interests, and the way in which he spends time outside class. *See* **theme, personal.**

questionnaire, personality: *syn.* **inventory, personality.**

questions, study: *see* **study questions.**

queuing theory: in automatic data processing, a form of probability theory useful in studying delays or lineups at servicing points.

quickening procedure: in programmed instruction, giving the student knowledge of the results of his response while he is still in the process of making it; for example, telling him while he is still in the process of writing a response word that it is incorrect.

quiet day: *syn.* **retreat.**

Quincy plan: an early plan of school reorganization based on the example of German pedagogy and carried out in the last two decades of the nineteenth century in the elementary schools of Quincy, Massachusetts, at the suggestion of Charles Francis Adams and through the efforts of Superintendent Francis W. Parker (1837–1902); marked by informal teaching, flexible daily programs, and the fusion of such subject-matter fields as reading, writing, grammar, spelling, history, and geography into the areas of reading and writing; a precursor of modern progressive education.

quintile: one of the four points, measured along the scale of the plotted variable, that divides the distribution into five parts or intervals, each including 20 percent of the frequency; thus, the first quintile is the 20th percentile, the second quintile is the 40th percentile, etc. *Dist. f.* **interval, quintile.**

quintile interval: *see* **interval, quintile.**

quintile range: *syn.* **interval, quintile.**

quintiserial r: a statistic to estimate the linear correlation of a continuously measured variable with a variable that is expressed in five classes.

quintuplets: five offspring born at the same birth. *See* **multiple birth.**

quirk: an odd or eccentric mental reaction; a deviation from the usual or normal attitude.

quiz: a popular term used to designate a test, especially a relatively short test, given periodically to measure achievement on material recently taught or on any small, newly completed unit of work.

quo warranto (kwō wă·ran′tō): (Lat., lit., "by what warrant") a form of action at law based on a writ inquiring into the right of a public officer to hold his office, the right of a board to continue the exercise of its powers, or the right of a corporation to continue to enjoy the privileges of its charter. (As a result of a successful action in quo warranto, a court may order an officer or board ousted or the charter of a corporation forfeited.)

quorum: the number of persons belonging to a legislative assembly, a corporation, society, or other body whose presence is required for the transaction of business.

quota: (1) a predetermined enrollment figure for a given course, curriculum, or institution beyond which candidates for admission will not be accepted (used in connection with *selective admission*); (2) a specific limitation on the number of persons admitted for preparation or permitted to graduate as teachers, used as a basis for regulating the supply of teachers.

quota-control sampling: *see* **sample, stratified.**

quota sample: *syn.* **sample, stratified.**

quotient: (meas.) an indication in a single numerical index of the relative position of a pupil on two related age scales; usually obtained by dividing one such age by another.

quotient, accomplishment (AQ): *syn.* **quotient, achievement.**

quotient, achievement: an index of achievement calculated by dividing a student's achievement age by his mental age; hence essentially a ratio of scores on two kinds of tests, achievement and aptitude; presumably shows how the student's actual achievement compares with his potential achievement. *Syn.* **accomplishment quotient; attainment quotient; educational ratio;** *dist. f.* **quotient, educational.**

quotient, arithmetic: *see* **quotient, subject.**

quotient, athletic: a number obtained by dividing an achieved score in athletic events by a score representing a measure of general athletic ability.

quotient, attainment (AQ): rare *syn.* **quotient, achievement.**

quotient, developmental (DQ): the ratio between a pupil's developmental age and the developmental age typical for a pupil of his chronological age.

quotient, deviation intelligence (DIQ): a measure of intelligence based on the extent to which an individual's score deviates from a score that is normal for the individual's age; it is a standard score, not a quotient, with an arbitrarily assumed mean, usually 100, and a standard deviation, usually 15 or 16, for all age levels. (Though a misnomer, the term *quotient* is still used here because of the common usage of the abbreviation *IQ*.) *See* **quotient, ratio intelligence.**

quotient, educational (EQ): the quotient obtained by dividing educational age by chronological age and multiplying by 100; shows a pupil's achievement as compared with the average achievement of pupils of his own age. *Dist. f.* **ratio, educational.**

quotient, group intelligence: (1) an intelligence quotient obtained from a group intelligence test rather than from an individual intelligence test; (2) an aggregate intelligence quotient for a group obtained by dividing the sum of the mental ages by the sum of the chronological ages.

quotient, intelligence (IQ): *see* **quotient, deviation intelligence; quotient, ratio intelligence.**

quotient, motor: a measure of relative level of motor achievement obtained by dividing a measure of motor achievement by a comparable measure of ability to achieve.

quotient, ratio intelligence (IQ): a measure for expressing level of mental development in relation to chronological age; obtained by dividing the mental age (as measured by a general intelligence test) by the chronological age and multiplying by 100; the chronological age is often fixed at a certain maximum, most commonly 16 years, when growth of intelligence due to maturation has been assumed to cease, so that a testee whose actual age was greater than this would still be assigned an age of 16 years; maximum chronological age for different tests varies from about 14 to 18 years; formerly a commonly used scale, now largely replaced by a standard score scale, the deviation intelligence quotient. *See* **quotient, deviation intelligence.**

quotient, reading: a quotient made by dividing the reading age by the mental age; an index of the reader's capacity to read.

quotient score: *see* **score, quotient.**

quotient, social (SQ): the ratio between a pupil's social age, as obtained from such an instrument as the Vineland Social Maturity Scale, and his chronological age.

r: symbol for Pearson product moment coefficient of correlation. *See* **coefficient, correlation.**

R: symbol for the multiple coefficient of correlation, usually with subscripts showing the variables involved, for example, $R_{1.23}$. *See* **coefficient of multiple correlation.**

r, quadriserial: a statistic used to estimate the linear correlation of a continuously measured variable with a variable that is expressed in four classes. *Comp.* **quintiserial r.**

R-score: (rare) a transformed standard score with a mean of 50 and a standard deviation of 20.

R-technique: (fact. anal.) the correlation of a series of tests or items administered to a sample of persons on a single occasion; indicates the extent to which the tests covary over a series of persons under one condition. *See* **factor analysis, transposed; Q-technique.**

rabbi (rab′ī; rab′i): (Heb., "teacher") a title designating an ordained religious spiritual leader and teacher of a Jewish congregation; originally used as a title describing those well-versed in Jewish learning, authorized to teach Torah and to adjudicate on the basis of Jewish law.

rabbinical school: *see* **synagogue school.**

race: a large division of the human family possessing a common ancestry and more or less common distinguishing physical traits.

race differences: *see* **differences, race.**

race prejudice: (1) a biased, unfavorable attitude toward a race; (2) a biased attitude toward a race, whether favorable or unfavorable.

race problem: the difficulties of social and other adjustments growing out of the presence of two or more races in the same community.

race suicide: the falling off in the birth rate resulting from the refusal to propagate and assume the responsibilities of parenthood.

rachitis: *syn.* **rickets.**

racial balance: a term, the precise meaning of which varies according to individuals and groups employing it, but usually implying one of the following: (*a*) racial composition of a subgroup directly proportional to the racial composition of the whole society; (*b*) any racial composition which approximates the condition described in (*a*) above; (*c*) a racial composition of 50 percent black and 50 percent white; (*d*) any significant trend away from total or nearly total racial segregation. *Contr. w.* **racial imbalance.**

racial-difference hypothesis: (1) the hypothesis that certain races are innately superior or inferior in physique, intellectual capacity, traits of personality and character, and special aptitudes; (2) the theory that differences in racial physical traits are associated with differences in psychological traits. [Neither (1) nor (2) has been shown to have scientific validity.]

racial discrimination: *see* **discrimination, racial.**

racial doctrine: *see* **racism.**

racial group: *see* **group, racial.**

racial imbalance: a condition existing in a social institution, such as a church or school, when the social composition is significantly different from the proportions to be expected from those of the social order of which the institutions are a part. *Contr. w.* **racial balance.**

racial integration: *see* **integration, racial.**

racial toleration: *ant.* **race prejudice** (1).

racism: the assumption of inherited superiority and purity of certain races; often such assumptions are made the basis of discriminatory practices. *See* **discrimination** (3); **discrimination, racial.**

radar astronomy: *see* **astronomy, radar.**

radial organization: *see* **organization, radial.**

radian measure: *see* **measure, radian.**

radiant heating: *see* **heating, radiant.**

radiant panel heating: *see* **heating, radiant panel.**

radiation chemistry: *see* **chemistry, radiation.**

radical: (math.) the indicated root of a number, such as $\sqrt{3}$, $\sqrt[3]{x^2}$, etc.

radical empiricism: *see* **empiricism, radical.**

radical group: *see* **group, radical.**

radicalism: an attitude antagonistic to the prevailing order and commitment and favorable to drastic change. *Contr. w.* **conservatism; liberalism.**

radio, AM: *see* **modulation, amplitude.**

radio and television education: the utilization of broadcasting in the area of education, both public and private; includes the broadcasting of programs by educators or for educational purposes, the production and utilization of programs within classrooms, public relations broadcasting by educators or in behalf of educational interests, and commercial programs with educational motives that may be assigned to pupils for out-of-school listening and observing.

radio-appreciation course: *see* **course, radio-appreciation.**

radio class: *see* **class, radio.**

radio demonstration lesson: *see* **lesson, broadcast demonstration.**

radio educator: *see* **educator, radio.**

radio evaluation: *see* **evaluation, radio.**

radio extension course: *see* **course, radio extension.**

radio, FM: *see* **modulation, frequency.**

radio forum: a radio program adapted to the discussion of current problems in which speakers present prepared papers, after which members of the studio audience participate by asking questions, raising objections, etc.

radio frequency: *see* **frequency, radio.**

radio lesson: *see* **lesson, radio.**

radio lesson guide: material prepared in advance of a radio lesson for the purpose of aiding preparation, listening, and follow-up of the broadcast; frequently includes a bibliography, questions, and comments.

radio listening, in-school: the classroom or auditorium activity of listening to broadcasts specially prepared for school use or considered sufficiently important to warrant taking time that otherwise would be devoted to more traditional instructional activities.

radio listening, out-of-school: the activity of listening to radio programs at home, whether as a school assignment or merely by the choice of the pupil; sometimes assigned as homework.

radio motivation: *see* **motivation, radio.**

radio news writing: the preparation of news for radio broadcast.

radio-phonograph combination: a device consisting of a radio and phonograph having a common audio amplifier and loudspeaker.

radio-production class: *see* **class, radio-production.**

radio program, educational: *see* **broadcast, educational.**

radio round table: a broadcast in which three or more participants discuss informally, presumably without script, the topic selected for discussion.

radio script: (1) strictly, the written material prepared in advance and read aloud by participants in radio broadcasts; (2) a simulation of a professional radio script prepared for use in a mock broadcast; *see* **mock broadcast.**

radio station, educational: a transmitter operated by an educational institution or group for the purpose of broadcasting to the public or to certain segments of the public; a station that has as its sole purpose educational broadcasting.

radio teacher: a broadcaster of radio lessons; one who is specially trained to include within a relatively brief period on the air the essentials of subject matter in an instructional period.

radio-television forum: *see* **forum, radio-television.**

radio unit: *see* **unit, radio.**

radio utilization: *see* **utilization, radio.**

radio work sheet: mimeographed or printed information, including instructions, suggested exercises, and/or questions to be answered, prepared in advance of a radio broadcast intended specifically for classroom listening.

radio workshop: *see* **workshop, radio.**

radioactive tracer: a radioactive isotope which, when injected into a chemically similar substance or artificially attached to a biological or physical system, can be traced by radiation detection devices.

radiochemistry: the study of radioactive substances and phenomena, including all applications of radioactive isotopes to chemistry; may be used synonymously with *radiation chemistry;* a more general field is nuclear chemistry. *See* **science, nuclear.**

radioecology: the body of knowledge concerning the effects of radiation on species of plants and animals in natural communities and the formal study of this field.

radiographer: (voc. ed.) a term used in industry for a technician who controls radiography equipment to take x-ray photographs (radiographs) of metal castings, weldments, metal samples, pipes, machinery, and structural members to detect flaws, cracks, porosity, and presence of foreign objects.

radiography: the technique of making photoshadowgraphs of objects which are transparent to alpha rays and x-rays but opaque to visible light.

radiology: the science which deals with the use of all forms of ionizing radiation in the diagnosis and treatment of disease. *See* **radioactive tracer.**

radix: (1) the quantity of characters for use in each of the digital positions of a numbering system; for example, the decimal system with the numerals 0 through 9 has a radix of 10, the binary system with only the characters 0 and 1 has a radix of 2, the octal system with characters 0 through 7 has a radix of 8, etc.; (2) the base of a system of logarithms.

raffia work: a creative handcraft that involves the making of mats, baskets, purses, hats, slippers, etc., using raffia alone or in combination with reed or string.

ragged school: a school "for poor and neglected children," based on the Pestalozzian principle that society must be regenerated through education, the first school of the type having been founded by Pestalozzi at Neuhof, Switzerland, in 1774 and the first one in the United States by Edward A. Sheldon in Oswego, New York, in 1848; a forerunner of the present free, public, elementary school.

raised line drawing: *see* **drawing, raised line.**

rally, pep: *see* **pep rally.**

ramifying linkage method: a method used in group, grouping, or multiple-group methods of factoring, of obtaining clusters from a matrix of correlations.

ramp: a sloping trafficway connecting separate levels.

random: chance; without bias.

random access: *see* **access, random.**

random access storage: *see* **storage, random access.**

random activity: *see* **activity, random.**

random articulation: *see* **articulation, random.**

random error: *see* **error, random.**

random mailing list: a list of names selected at random from a longer list and employed for the purpose of sampling, as in questionnaires.

random movement: *see* **activity, random.**

random numbers: digits so arranged that any number has an equal chance of being chosen; in practice, usually read in any predetermined order from a table of random numbers.

random numbers, table of: a table containing numbers that have been drawn or selected in a strictly chance fashion; useful in research studies that involve randomization.

random observation: *syn.* **observation, independent;** *see* **independence.**

random replication design: *see* **design, random replication.**

random sample: *see* **sample, random.**

random selection: *see* **selection, random.**

randomization: the act or process of distributing a certain variable in relation to certain categories in a purely chance fashion; may involve use of a table of random numbers.

randomize: to distribute a certain factor in relation to certain categories in a purely chance fashion.

randomized block design: *see* **design, randomized block.**

randomized design, simple: *see* **design, randomized simple.**

randomized factor: *see* **factor, randomized.**

randomized groups design: *see* **design, randomized groups.**

range: (1) a measure of dispersion that is equal to either (*a*) the difference between the largest and smallest observed values of a variable or, preferably, (*b*) the difference between the largest and smallest observed values plus one; this latter measure is often referred to as the *inclusive range;* (2) (math.) *see* **function; relation** (4); (3) occasionally, *syn.* **domain** (2).

range, audibility: *syn.* **range, audio-frequency.**

range, audible frequency: the sounds lying between and including those of highest and lowest frequency that the average human ear can hear; measured in cycles per second. (Sounds from 20 to 20,000 cycles are usually audible to the normal human ear.)

range, audio-frequency: *syn.* **range, audible frequency.**

range, average: the deviations on both sides of the mean which, by common agreement, are near enough to the mean to be best represented by its characteristics; widely applied in such expressions as "children in the average range of intelligence."

range, centile: *syn.* **interval, centile.**

range, class: *syn.* **class limits.**

range, decile: *syn.* **interval, decile.**

range, dynamic: the range between the softest and loudest sounds a tape recorder can reproduce without significant distortion, measured in decibels and expressed as a ratio. *Comp. w.* **range, frequency.**

range, effective: a crude measure of dispersion that is equal to the range of a series of observations after scattered items (as test scores) widely removed from the others have been eliminated.

range, frequency: range between the highest and lowest pitched sounds a recorder or sound system can reproduce at a usable output, or volume level. *Comp. w.* **range, dynamic; response, frequency.**

range, frequency-response: the sounds lying between and including the highest and lowest frequencies that a sound recording and/or reproducing system or component can record or reproduce.

range, inclusive: *see* **range.**

range, interpercentile: the range of scores between two percentile points that are equidistant from the 50th percentile, for example, the range of scores between the 91st and the 9th percentiles.

range, interquartile: a measure of dispersion equal to the difference between the first and third quartiles; the distance from the 25th to the 75th percentile. *Dist. f.* **deviation, quartile; range, semi-interquartile.**

range, modal: *syn.* **interval, modal.**

range of error: *see* **error, range of.**

range, percentile: (1) the difference between any two specified percentiles; (2) *syn.* **interval, centile.**

range, quartile: *syn.* **interval, quartile.**

range, quintile: *syn.* **interval, quintile.**

range, reading: (1) the extent of a person's reading experiences; (2) the range of scores in a reading test; *see* **range.**

range scale: *see* **scale, range.**

range, semi-interquartile: *syn.* **deviation, quartile.**

range, speech: *syn.* **speech area.**

range, visual: *see* **visual range.**

range, vocal: *see* **vocal range.**

ranger exercises: physical conditioning exercises resembling movements executed by infantry in ground maneuvers, such as zigzag running and falling to the ground on command.

rank: (1) (stat.) the position of an observation, score, or individual in relation to the others in the group according to some character such as magnitude, quality, or importance; usually indicated by a number; thus, the highest item may be given a rank of 1, the second a rank of 2, etc.; (2) (math.) a term describing a property of determinants or matrices; it is the highest order of the nonvanishing minors in the determinant or matrix.

rank, average: the rank of the observation that is at the middle of the group when the observations are arranged in order of magnitude.

rank, centile: *syn.* **rank, percentile.**

rank, composite: a single indication of position obtained by combining the separate simple or weighted ranks already secured for several traits.

rank correlation: *see* **correlation, rank.**

rank correlation coefficient: *see* **coefficient, rank correlation.**

rank, decile: the relative position or magnitude of an observation in a distribution, expressed in terms of the ordinal number corresponding to the decile interval in which the observation is found. *See* **interval, decile.**

rank difference: the difference between the ranks of an individual in two variables; the rank of one individual on a variable minus the rank of another individual on the same variable.

rank difference correlation coefficient: *see* **coefficient, rank difference correlation.**

rank difference correlation coefficient, standard error of: *see* **standard error of rank difference correlation coefficient.**

rank, faculty: the status of a faculty member in a college or university in relation to other staff members of the same educational institution as, for example, *professor, assistant professor,* and *instructor.*

rank of matrix: *see* **matrix, rank of.**

rank order: (1) the distribution of a series of observations that have been arranged according to their relative magnitudes or positions, that is, from highest to lowest or from lowest to highest; (2) the relative magnitude or position of any single observation in a series.

rank-order rating: *see* **rating, rank-order.**

rank, percentile: (1) a derived score stated in terms of the percentage of examinees in a specified group who fall below a given score point; (2) the relative position of a case in a distribution, expressed in terms of the ordinal number corresponding to the centile interval in which the case is placed; *syn.* **centile rank;** *see* **percentile;** *dist. f.* **range, percentile.**

rank-product method of correlation: a method of correlation somewhat similar to Spearman's rank difference correlation, but depending upon the product of the ranks. *Contr. w.* **coefficient, rank difference correlation.**

rank sum method of correlation: a method of correlation somewhat similar to Spearman's rank difference method, but depending on the sums of the ranks. *Contr. w.* **coefficient, rank difference correlation.**

ranking: the act or method of relative marking according to which all variate values are arranged in rank order. *See* **rank.**

ranks, analysis of variance by: a method used for making an analysis of variance by placing the observations in rank order; has the advantage of not depending on the assumptions of homogeneity of variance or of normality of variance, but the disadvantage of being a less efficient test than analysis of variance based on the magnitudes of the observations when the above assumptions can be met.

rapid progress: *syn.* **acceleration** (1).

rapid promotion: *see* **promotion, double.**

rapport (ra·pōrt'; Fr., ra·pŏr'): interpersonal relationship of mutual confidence and trust, such as is to be achieved and maintained in the counseling interview.

rapport, emotional: (1) the reactions of an individual when he responds appropriately to emotional situations; (2) response with emotional interest to appropriate environmental situations.

Rashi (rä'shē): (1) an abbreviation for the name of a famous scholar of the eleventh century, Rabbi Shlomo Itzchaki (Solomon, son of Isaac), the author of the most widely used set of commentaries on the Bible and the Talmud; (2) the commentaries on the Bible and the Talmud prepared by Rashi; (3) a subject included in the curriculum of Jewish schools which stress the study of the Bible and the Talmud.

rate: (mil. ed.) identifies personnel occupationally by pay grade; within a *rating,* a rate reflects levels of aptitude, training experience, knowledge, skills, and responsibilities; for example, "boatswain's mate" is a rating, whereas "boatswain's mate third class" is a rate within a rating.

rate, basal metabolic: *see* **metabolism, basal.**

rate, base: *see* **base rate.**

rate bill: an assessment on parents for partial school support, the amount being in proportion to the number of their children attending school. (Rate bills supplied school revenue in some of the older states before school taxes came into common use.)

rate, birth: *see* **birth rate.**

rate, completion: *see* **completion rate.**

rate, dropout: *see* **dropout rate.**

rate, error: *see* **error rate.**

rate map: *see* **map, rate.**

rate norm: *see* **norm, rate.**

rate of development: *see* **development, rate of.**

rate of natural increase: *see* **natural increase, rate of.**

rate of pay, base: *see* **pay, base rate of.**

rate of pay, incentive: *see* **pay, incentive rate of.**

rate of progress: *see* **progress, rate of.**

rate of response: *see* **response, rate of.**

rate pair: a pair of natural numbers used to represent a rate or comparison situation; for example, the pair 1/5 represents the rate on a scale drawing where 1 inch represents 5 feet.

rate score: *see* **score, rate.**

rate test: *syn.* **test, speed.**

rater errors: *see* **errors, rater.**

ratification, doctrine of: a legal principle that a school district may ratify a contract that is for some reason invalid, provided that it could legally have made the contract in the first instance.

rating: (1) an estimate, made according to some systematized procedure, of the degree to which an individual person or thing possesses any given characteristic; may be expressed qualitatively or quantitatively; (2) (mil. ed.) an enlisted career field in the Navy and Marine Corps which requires related aptitudes, knowledge, training, and skills; a petty officer always serves in a rating while a nonpetty officer who has had special training or experience or has demonstrated qualifications for a petty officer grade may be designated striker for a particular rating and thus be assigned duties in that occupational career field; *see* **striker.**

rating, advancement in: (mil. ed.) promotion of an enlisted man.

rating, aeronautical: one of several ratings conferred by competent authority upon a member of the Air Force who has completed the requisite training and has obtained the requisite competence in a given aspect of flying, such as bombardment, navigation, radio, radar, gunnery, and engineering.

rating, behavior: the assignment of a rank, score, or mark to the response of an individual in an experimental or observational situation.

rating chart: *syn.* **rating scale.**

rating device: an instrument used to evaluate or score subjectively a person's character, personality, special ability, or other quality in terms of a list of specific traits that compose or characterize the quality.

rating, efficiency: *syn.* **rating, merit.**

rating, forced-choice: a method of rating in which the rater is forced to choose between descriptive phrases that appear of equal value for selection by the rater but that are different in validity or discrimination value for a criterion.

rating, job: a rating, usually in terms of level of skill involved or quality of performance required, assigned to a particular job; usually the outgrowth of a *job analysis.* *See* **job classification.**

rating, merit: an evaluation of the effectiveness of teaching, supervision, or administration, based on a definite scale or collection of items accepted as legitimate measures for such purposes.

rating of sociability: *see* **sociability, rating of.**

rating of teaching, composite: the combined evaluation of instruction based on the results of observations and ratings made by different persons as, for example, the combined ratings of the principal, supervisor, and superintendent.

rating, paired-comparison: a method of rating in which each individual, object, or attribute is judged in turn as better or worse than every other one in the group; these judgments are then manipulated so that each object of comparison is assigned a scale value. *See* **paired comparison.**

rating, performance: (1) that process during which a time-study analyst compares the performance or effective effort of the operator under observation with the observer's own concept of proper performance in relation to a bench mark, that is, some reference point; *see* **study, motion and time;** (2) a performance number which represents the degree of effectiveness of the performance.

rating, periodic: (1) an analysis of the qualifications of employed workers made at intervals to gather reliable information for promotion purposes; (2) an analysis of the departments of a company or industry made at intervals to ascertain its current output status as compared with past records.

rating, pooled: a composite rating of a stimulus or characteristic that has been ranked or otherwise rated by a number of judges; may represent either weighted or unweighted averaging of ranks by such means as Thurstone's law of comparative judgment.

rating, rank-order: a method of rating in which objects, persons, or attributes are placed in serial order in accordance with the rater's judgment of the degree to which a stated or defined quality is present.

rating scale: a device used in evaluating products, or attitudes, or other characteristics of persons rated. (The usual form is an evaluation chart carrying suggestive points for checking.)

rating scale, art: (1) a scoring device for measuring achievement in the visual arts, generally in the fields of design and representation; usually consists of a graded set of standardized design specimens or drawings ranging in score points from 0 to 100; (2) a validated score sheet for rating achievement in art discrimination or appreciation. *See* **test, art-appreciation.**

rating scale, cumulated points: a unique scoring device in that the score for an object or individual is the sum or average of a number of points, weighted or unweighted; resembles psychological tests except that the points are derived from human judgments.

rating scale, descriptive: a device for making and recording subjective estimates as to the degree to which a thing (a

school building, for example) or an individual possesses each of a number of specific traits, the judgment for each trait being recorded by checking one of several descriptive statements, such as "(*a*) Very lazy," "(*b*) Somewhat lazy," "(*c*) Of average drive," "(*d*) More industrious than most people," "(*e*) Exceedingly industrious." *See* **rating scale, graphic.**

rating scale, forced-choice: a device in which the rater is asked not whether the ratee has a certain trait or to what degree, but whether he has more of one trait than another of a pair, one of which is valid for predicting some total quality and the other not, both appearing about equally favorable or unfavorable.

rating scale, graphic: a device intended to facilitate the making and recording of subjective estimates as to the degree to which a thing (a school building, for example) or an individual possesses each of a number of specific traits, the judgment for each trait being recorded by making a mark at an appropriate position on a line of which the two extremes represent the lowest and highest degrees of the trait, such as "Extremely dishonest" and "Scrupulously honest." *See* **rating scale, descriptive.**

rating scale, man-to-man: a rating device by which a person is rated by comparison with other persons known to the rater. (The mechanism for the rating may be one of ranking the persons on the trait or traits in question, or assigning numbers of points to each, or locating the persons in terms of described amounts of each trait.)

rating scale, numerical: a device for making and recording a subjective judgment as to the position of an individual or item in relation to a prearranged scale of values; typically consists of a list of traits or characteristics for each of which a numerical value or weight is assigned, representing the maximum degree of the trait or characteristic; the rater is instructed to assign for each trait or characteristic a number from 0 up to and including the maximum value given, representing the degree to which the individual or item is judged to possess the trait in question.

rating scale, occupational: (1) a scale by which a person is rated in terms of his probable success or interest in various occupations; (2) a scale by which the component factors in an occupation are rated and classified.

rating scale, personality: a device used in evaluating individual personality traits and characteristics.

rating scale, standard: any of those scales which provide for the rater several standard specimens, usually objects of the same kind as those to be rated and with preestablished scale values; previously calibrated on a common scale of excellence by some scaling method such as equal-appearing intervals or paired comparison. *See* **scale, equal-intervals; scale, paired comparisons.**

rating scale, teacher: a device for comparing the apparent performance of one teacher with that of other teachers or with some accepted standards.

rating sheet: *syn.* **rating scale.**

rating, somatotype: a series of three numbers indicating the amount of endomorphy, mesomorphy, and ectomorphy in an individual's type of body build.

rating, stanine: *see* **score, stanine; stanine.**

rating, teacher: the systematic evaluation of the work of an instructor in relation to such factors as achievement, personality, and participation in extraclass activities and community affairs.

rating, trait: a recording of the existence of a personal characteristic rather than its process during observation of various dimensions of behavior. *See* **observation, approaches to.**

ratio: (1) the indicated quotient of two numbers or quantities; (2) an ordered set of two or more numbers which represent the relative sizes of certain numbers or quantities, as 1/60, used to represent the relative sizes of 1 inch and 5 feet, or 3:4:5, to represent the relative sizes of the three sides of a particular right triangle.

ratio, accomplishment (AR): rare *syn.* **quotient, achievement.**

ratio, achievement (AR): *syn.* **quotient, achievement.**

ratio, association-sensory: A/S ratio; ratio between the amount of brain tissue that is associative in nature and the amount of sensory tissue.

ratio, attainment (AR): rare *syn.* **quotient, achievement.**

ratio, brightness: *see* **brightness ratio.**

ratio chart: *see* **chart, ratio.**

ratio, correlation: *see* **correlation ratio.**

ratio, counselor-pupil: *see* **counselor-pupil ratio.**

ratio, critical (CR): the difference between two comparable statistics divided by the standard error of that difference; mathematically equal to *t*, but providing a less rigorous test of significance than does *t*. *Syn.* **significance ratio;** *see* **standard difference; statistically significant differences; test, t.**

ratio delay study: *see* **study, ratio delay.**

ratio, educational (ER): *syn.* **quotient, achievement.**

ratio, F: the ratio of the larger to the smaller of two independent estimates of variance; the distribution of this ratio is known under the assumption that both estimates of variance arise from the same normally distributed population. *See* **variance, analysis of.**

ratio, faculty-student: *see* **faculty-student ratio.**

ratio, fertility: the ratio of children to women, for example, the number of children under 10 years of age for each 100 women between the ages of 20 and 45 years. *See* **birth rate, crude.**

ratio, grade-point: *syn.* **average, grade point.**

ratio, ID: in supervision of instruction, a ratio computed for characterizing teacher behavior based on the observed indirect/direct teacher behaviors when accepting students' ideas; encouraging and questioning are characterized as indirect while lecturing, criticizing, etc. are characterized as direct behavior.

ratio intelligence quotient (IQ): *see* **quotient, ratio intelligence.**

ratio, labor turnover: *see* **turnover ratio, labor.**

ratio, Lexian: *syn.* **ratio, Lexis.**

ratio, Lexis: the ratio σ/σ_B where σ = standard deviation of the series of obtained frequencies, and σ_B = theoretical standard deviation, $\sqrt{Npq}$; a criterion for determining whether an observed distribution is a Bernoulli distribution, a Poisson distribution, or a Lexis distribution; when equal to 1.00, distribution has normal dispersion. *Syn.* **Lexian ratio.**

ratio, mental: *syn.* **quotient, intelligence.**

ratio, multiple correlation: a measure of the nonlinear relationship between a dependent variable and a number of independent variables; the ratio of the standard deviation of the weighted means of the values of the dependent variable to the original standard deviation of the dependent variable, where there is a cell for every possible combination of scores on the independent variables and where each mean is weighted according to the number of observations on which it is based; always equals or exceeds the multiple correlation coefficient. *Dist. f.* **multiple-ratio method.**

ratio of correlation: *syn.* **correlation ratio.**

ratio of scholarship: the quotient of commensurate measures of the scholastic ability or achievement of two persons.

ratio, operating: *see* **operating ratio.**

ratio, partial correlation: a measure of the correlation of one variable with a second, the influence of others being removed, when the interrelationships of the variables are nonlinear; a measure similar to the partial correlation coefficient but based on correlation ratios instead of correlation coefficients.

ratio, probability: a fraction, the numerator of which is equal to the number of ways of obtaining the desired outcome and the denominator of which is equal to the number of total possible outcomes when all outcomes are equally likely and mutually exclusive; for example, ½ is the probability ratio of an unbiased coin falling heads.

ratio, pupil-classroom teacher: (1) the number of pupils in membership, as of a given date, divided by the number representing the total full-time equivalency of classroom

teaching assignments serving these pupils on the same date; (2) the average daily membership of pupils for a given period of time divided by the number representing the total full-time equivalency of classroom teaching assignments serving these pupils during the same period.

ratio, pupil-counselor: (1) the number of pupils in membership, as of a given date, divided by the number representing the total full-time equivalency of counseling assignments serving these pupils on the same date; (2) the average daily membership of pupils, for a given period of time, divided by the number representing the total full-time equivalency of counseling assignments serving these pupils during the same period.

ratio, pupil-principal: (1) the number of pupils in membership in the elementary and secondary schools of a school system, as of a given date, divided by the number representing the total full-time equivalency of school direction and management assignments serving these pupils on the same date; (2) the average daily membership of pupils in the elementary and secondary schools of a school system, for a given period of time, divided by the number representing the total full-time equivalency of school direction and management assignments serving these pupils during the same period.

ratio, pupil-professional educational staff: (1) the number of pupils in membership in a school system, as of a given date, divided by the number representing the total full-time equivalency of all professional educational assignments in the school system on the same date; (2) the average daily membership of pupils, for a given period of time, divided by the number representing the total full-time equivalency of all professional educational assignments in the school system during the same period.

ratio, pupil-school librarian: (1) the number of pupils in membership in a school system, as of a given date, divided by the number representing the total full-time equivalency of school librarian assignments serving these pupils in school libraries on the same date; (2) the average daily membership of pupils, for a given period of time, divided by the number representing the total full-time equivalency of school librarian assignments serving these pupils in school libraries during the same period.

ratio, pupil-teacher: *see* **ratio, student-teacher.**

ratio, pupil-total staff: (1) the number of pupils in membership in a school system, as of a given date, divided by the number representing the total full-time equivalency of all staff assignments in the school system on the same date; (2) the average daily membership of pupils in a school system, for a given period of time, divided by the number representing the total full-time equivalency of all staff assignments in the school system during the same period.

ratio scale: *see* **scale, ratio.**

ratio score: *see* **score, ratio.**

ratio, selection: the proportion of those who are accepted to all individuals examined in a given situation; other factors remaining the same, the practical validity of a test or test battery is increased by lowering the ratio.

ratio, significance: (1) *syn.* **ratio, critical;** (2) *syn.* **t ratio.**

ratio, standard: *syn.* **difference, standard.**

ratio, student-teacher: an index of the number of pupils per teacher in a school or a school system; the ratio used to evaluate the teaching load of a school or a school system; however, it does not accurately indicate the number of pupils that the average teacher has in a classroom.

Ratio Studiorum (rā'shi·ō stū·di·ō'rəm): (Lat., lit., "method of studies"); Part Four of the constitution of the *Society of Jesus,* consisting of detailed directions to Jesuit teachers and school officials on the organization and administration of schools and on classroom practices and methods; this work by Saint Ignatius Loyola, first published in 1586, was revised in 1599 and remained relatively unaltered as the basis of Jesuit education until the early part of the twentieth century.

ratio, subject (SR): a rarely used index of achievement in a given school subject; secured by dividing a pupil's subject age by his mental age and multiplying by 100. *See* **quotient, achievement.**

ratio, success: percentage of those selected for a program who successfully complete the program, course, etc.

ratio, t: the ratio of the difference between two statistics to the standard error of the difference; mathematically equal to the *critical ratio*, but providing a more critical test of significance. *Syn.* **significance ratio; t;** *see* **distribution, t; test, t.**

ratio, type-token: (read.) the relation between the number of different words and the number of running words, computed by dividing the number of running words into the number of different words.

ratiocination: formal reasoning; reasoning that is deliberately controlled by the rules of logic.

rational: (1) reasonable in thought and speech; (2) logical, in a formal sense; (3) pertaining to beliefs that in content are in accordance with, although not necessarily the product of, reason.

rational being, character of man as: (1) a composite substance which, in addition to being material, has reason, that is, a synthesis of will and intellect; the latter two terms refer to "faculties" in a dynamic sense, not as in *faculty psychology;* (2) in some forms of naturalism, human nature interpreted as that component of nature which has become reflective and self-conscious through the processes of significant communication and cultural interaction.

rational counting: *see* **counting, rational.**

rational humanism: *see* **humanism, rational.**

rational learning: *see* **learning, rational.**

rational number: *see* **number, rational.**

rational spelling: *see* **spelling, rational.**

rationale: a synoptic exposition or the gist of principles, procedures, or axioms underlying or constituting the foundation of human enterprise, especially of scientific work or experimentation.

rationalism: (1) the philosophical doctrine that reason can be a source of knowledge and that truth can best be established by a process of deduction from a priori principles independent of experience (in this sense the term is opposed to *sensationalism* and *empiricism*); (2) in theology, the attitude holding that religious belief must stand the test of human reason and be in harmony with it (in this sense, it is opposed to *mysticism* as well as to *dogmatism* and *revelation*, although it should be noted that medieval scholasticism held that the content of revealed faith is reasonable).

rationalization: a plausible explanation given to himself or to others by a person to account for his own beliefs or behavior, though these may be based on motives not apparent to the rationalizer.

raw data: *see* **data, raw.**

raw score: *see* **score, raw.**

raw score, corrected: *see* **score, corrected raw.**

raw score, modified: *see* **score, modified raw.**

reach, grasp, and release: normal control of voluntary muscles to reach for, take, hold more than momentarily, and then let go of an object.

reaction: response to a stimulus; any mental and emotional state brought about by a situation.

reaction, acquired: *syn.* **response, acquired.**

reaction, alarm: *syn.* **reaction, emergency.**

reaction, anaerobic: (phys. ed.) change occurring in the absence of oxygen.

reaction, approach: a positive or adient response through which an organism approaches the goal object. *See* **adient;** *contr. w.* **reaction, avoidance.**

reaction, avoidance: (1) a negative or abient response through which an organism escapes contact with a threatening object; (2) specifically, in stuttering, a refusal to attempt a feared word, whether by substituting another word, remaining silent, or other means, in an apparent attempt to avoid expected stuttering. *Contr. w.* **reaction, approach.**

reaction, balancing: the automatic postural response that maintains any natural position of the body.

reaction, catastrophic: abnormal emotional response completely out of proportion to the stimulus or situation precipitating the outburst.

reaction, circular: a series of two or more responses that are reciprocally instigated and maintained.

reaction, conditioned emotional: an emotional response resulting from conditioning; for example, an adult may fear the dark as a result of having been frightened in the dark during childhood; a person may take a seemingly undue amount of pleasure from hearing a particular tune, as a result of having first heard the tune during a moment of particular happiness or satisfaction.

reaction, defense: *syn.* **defense mechanism.**

reaction, delayed: any response that occurs only after an appreciable interval of time from the moment of its initiation by a stimulus.

reaction, differential: *syn.* **response, differential.**

reaction, differentiated mimetic: one of the various responses of the infant that are said to be indicative of the presence of and to vary with the different mental states.

reaction distance: the distance traveled by a neural impulse during the time between a sensory stimulus and the response to it.

reaction, emergency: the response of the sympathetic nervous system, the adrenal glands, and other structures to a threatening situation, mobilizing energies of the body for vigorous and prolonged struggle such as that demanded in a crisis. *Syn.* **alarm reaction.**

reaction, facial: a change in pattern of tonus or posture of the muscles of the face resulting in a change of expression; illustrated by the facial models of Pierdit, Feleky, and others.

reaction formation: the formation of attributes that control repressed impulses in order to prevent their recognition by the ego. (This is accomplished by developing desirable traits to conceal undesirable ones, for example, by replacing sadistic traits with pity.)

reaction, physiological: the change in an organ of the body or in the body as a whole as a result of stimulation.

reaction time: the time elapsing between a sensory stimulus and the response to it; may be used to characterize the response as elicited automatic behavior.

reactionary: *n.* one who "reacts" against the failures and tragedies of our age by favoring the beliefs about reality, knowledge, and value that he finds fundamental to an earlier age.

reactive depression: *see* **depression, reactive.**

reactor panel: *see* **panel, reactor.**

read in: in computer operation, to place words or fields in storage at specified addresses. *See* **read out** v. (1).

read-out: *n.* in programmed instruction, the operation of sensing and/or perceiving what is displayed; an activity of an individual or of a group; with the group, it can be simultaneous or distributed in time, all together or scattered in smaller groups in many locations; task involvement during read-out is another consideration, that is, the act of responding to a *display* by identifying information content and interpreting its significance. *See* **display** v.

read out: v. (1) in computer operation, to copy words or fields from specified addresses in storage into an external storage device, or to output words by copying them from specified addresses in storage; *see* **data, output; read in;** (2) (programmed instruction) *see* **read-out** n.

readability: the quality of a piece of reading matter that makes it interesting and understandable to those for whom it is written, at whatever level of educational experience.

readability formula: (1) a technique for determining the difficulty of reading materials, generally taking into account vocabulary and sentence length, though additional aspects are included in different formulas; (2) a style of writing, popularized by Rudolph Flesch and imitators, formerly employed to provide easier reading especially for the less educated; *see* **formula, Flesch reading ease.**

readability formula, Dale-Chall: a formula devised by Edgar Dale and Jeanne Chall which measures readability in terms of number of easy words and number of simple sentences in a given unit of reading material.

readability formula, Devereaux: a formula intended to measure readability of written material in terms of word difficulty (the average number of letters, numerals, punctuation marks, etc.) and sentence length.

readability formula, Flesch: a formula devised by Rudolph Flesch which measures readability in terms of several factors in a regression equation, including an interest factor.

readability formula, Gray-Leary: a formula for measuring the readability of reading matter involving the use of several factors in a regression equation; used only for measuring the difficulty of adult reading matter.

readability formula, Lewerenz: a formula devised by A. S. Lewerenz involving the use of factors in a regression equation.

readability formula, Lorge: a formula developed by Irving Lorge involving the factors in a regression equation, including a measure of vocabulary difficulty and sentence length.

readability formula, Washburne-Vogel: one of the first readability formulas; developed by Carleton Washburne and Mabel Vogel and involving the use of several factors in a regression equation.

readability formula, Yoakam: a formula devised by G. A. Yoakam for measuring the readability of reading material; based upon the weight of the vocabulary in a given unit of running words as determined by the serial numbers of words in Thorndike's *Teacher's Wordbook of 20,000 Words.*

readability index: *see* index, readability.

readability score: *syn.* index, readability.

readability test: *see* test, readability.

reader: a device used to enlarge a microcard, microfilm, or microprint to readable size.

reader, basal: a textbook, usually part of a graded series, used for instruction in reading. *Syn.* basic reader.

reader, basic: *syn.* reader, basal.

reader, beginning: a pupil who is in the preprimer stage of reading development or at the reading-readiness stage.

reader, character: (data processing) a machine that can automatically read data typed or printed on documents and convert it into *machine language.*

reader, context: (1) a reader who depends on the context, or setting, of words as a means of recognizing their form, rather than on visual or phonetic analysis; (2) a rapid reader, somewhat careless of details, who concentrates on meaning rather than on form.

reader, controlled: a filmstrip projector with special films, presenting connected reading material with a device for covering and then exposing words from left to right.

reader, graded: a textbook designed for instruction in reading at a particular level.

reader, high-speed: (data processing) a reading device capable of being connected to a computer so as to operate on-line without seriously holding up the computer; examples are a card reader reading more than 250 cards per minute or a device which reads punched paper tape at a rate greater than 50 characters per second. *See* data processing, on-line.

reader, lay: a helper, not a teacher, but competent in English, who assists the English teacher in reading and evaluating pupils' compositions.

reader, literary: a book of reading selections chosen for their excellence of expression and general interest.

reader materials, basal-: *see* basal-reader materials.

reader, microcard: *see* microcard.

reader, microfilm: *see* microfilm reader.

reader, multiethnic: a basal reader which presents in pictures and in text members of the various races of mankind.

reader, optical: a test-scoring machine which senses by a photoelectric process the responses marked by the examinee on a special answer sheet; the machine then prints the score on each answer sheet and/or punches the score on an IBM card.

reader, optical character: *see* reader, optical.

reader, reluctant: a child who is a capable learner and reader but who is not inclined to read.

reader, retarded: a child who is reading below his capacity to read; however, a child who is not reading up to grade level is not necessarily *retarded.*

reader service: the use of a sighted person to read to a handicapped person.

reader, study: a reading book constructed for the purpose of developing basic reading abilities and having content representative of subjects the pupils are studying in school.

reader, supplementary: a reading book used to supplement basic instruction and give additional reading experience and practice.

reader, work-type: a school reader made up of factual material designed to teach children work-type, that is, study reading.

reader's adviser: *see* adviser, reader's.

readiness: willingness, desire, and ability to engage in a given activity, depending on the learner's level of maturity, previous experience, and mental and emotional set.

readiness, auditory: sufficient maturity in auditory discrimination for an individual to understand the meaning of words.

readiness, client: (couns.) a state or condition of the client that makes it possible for him to engage profitably in the counseling process.

readiness curriculum: *see* curriculum, readiness.

readiness, dictionary: an understanding of the concepts and skills necessary for functional and efficient use of the dictionary.

readiness, guidance: a state of receptivity to counsel or adjustment on the part of a pupil or student.

readiness, law of: *see* law of readiness.

readiness, learning: the level of development at which an individual has the capacity to undertake the learning of a specified subject of study; usually the age at which the average group of individuals has the specified capacity (such as *reading readiness*).

readiness, mathematical: readiness to learn a mathematical topic a student has reached when he has acquired the background of knowledge and skill on which development of the topic is based; frequently includes the factors of maturation and motivation.

readiness, reading: attainment of the levels of interest, experience, maturity, and skills which enable the learner to engage successfully in a given reading task; often used to indicate the preparedness of a child for beginning formal reading instruction.

readiness test: *see* test, readiness.

readiness, writing: the condition of physical and mental maturity and of personal interest that indicates that an individual is prepared to profit from handwriting instruction.

reading ability: *see* ability, reading.

reading accelerator: one of the various pacing devices designed to provide reading rate training for competent readers.

reading achievement: *see* achievement, reading.

reading, adult: (1) difficult reading material or material that, by reason of its content, is not suitable for children; (2) mature reading procedures.

reading age: *see* age, reading.

reading aims: *see* aims, reading.

reading analysis: *see* analysis, reading.

reading, applied: the utilization of attained reading skills in reading situations other than those contrived specifically for reading skill development.

reading approach: (shorthand) a method of teaching that begins with a period of reading shorthand outlines without attempting to write them, in order to familiarize the student with the correct forms; characteristic of the *functional method* and of some forms of the *direct method* of teaching shorthand.

reading aptitude: *see* **aptitude, reading.**

reading-aptitude test: *syn.* **test, reading-capacity.**

reading, assimilative: a type of reading in which the reader concentrates on grasping the literal meaning without evaluation of or reflection on the significance of the ideas.

reading, associational: reading involving higher mental processes and bringing past experience to bear on the vicarious experience provided by reading.

reading, audience: oral reading in which the pupil reads to a group who acts as an audience.

reading, basal: reading aimed at the systematic development of reading ability by means of a series of books or other materials especially suitable for each successive stage of reading development. *See* **reader, basal;** *comp. w.* **reading, basic.**

reading, basic: reading related to any of a number of reading skills essential to continuous growth and development in general reading achievement; includes any reading methods and materials to develop basic reading skills; a more generic term than basal reading. *See* **reading, basal.**

reading, beginning: reading at the early first-grade level; the reading activities that occur first in teaching children to read.

reading behavior: *see* **behavior, reading.**

reading, Bible: (1) historically, the reading aloud of selected portions of the Bible at a stated time during the school day; carried on at present in some private schools and, until the middle of the twentieth century, in a considerable number of public schools also; (2) (relig. ed.) *see* **reading, Scripture.**

reading bulletin board: *syn.* **reading chart, functional.**

reading capacity: *see* **capacity, reading.**

reading-capacity test: *see* **test, reading-capacity.**

reading center: *see* **center, reading.**

reading certificate: *see* **certificate, reading.**

reading chart: a large sheet of paper or cardboard on which is printed simple reading material in large letters; intended to be hung on a wall and used for initial instruction in reading.

reading chart, functional: (prim. ed.) a wall chart or posted notice containing short, simple, and meaningful sentences giving facts having significance and utility to the pupils, for example, assignments of various pupils to various duties, information or news about school events and happenings, etc.

reading, choral: *see* **choral speaking.**

reading circle: a group of persons organized for the purpose of reading and discussing books. *Syn.* **reading club.**

reading circle, teachers': a type of organization, usually affiliated with state teachers' associations, which prepared systematic courses of study covering professional and academic subjects to guide reading of employed teachers; diplomas and certificates awarded at the end of the courses, usually on the basis of state examinations, were recognized by the departments of education in some states in renewing and granting teaching licenses; had period of greatest importance between 1890 and 1920.

reading clinic: *syn.* **center, reading.**

reading club: *see* **club, reading.**

reading, collateral: (1) reading material related to the main topic or theme being studied, as distinguished from the textual or basic material of the assignment; (2) reading relating to a subject that supports and enriches or broadens the experience of the reader. (Sometimes used as a synonym for *supplementary reading.*)

reading-comprehension test: *see* **test, reading-comprehension.**

reading, concert: oral reading by the teacher and child together with the purpose of calling the attention of the child to his reading errors.

reading, concerted: *see* **choral speaking.**

reading consultant: *see* **consultant, reading.**

reading, content: reading of books that contain needed information, such as textbooks or reference books on geography, history, or science; to be contrasted with the reading of books for recreation or fun only.

reading, controlled: reading done at a controlled rate through the use of such devices as a *tachistoscope*, reading film, or other pacing device.

reading coordinator: *see* **coordinator, reading.**

reading, corrective: class instruction in reading planned for pupils with specific reading difficulties and carried on by the classroom teacher in the regular classroom situation. *See* **reading, remedial.**

reading counselor: *see* **counselor, reading.**

reading course: *see* **course, reading.**

reading, creative: the type of reading in which the reader is able to create new meanings out of his imagination from the words he reads; in a sense all reading is creative.

reading, critical: reading in which the reader evaluates content in terms of its authenticity, beauty, usefulness, or some other criterion.

reading, cultural: reading carried on for improvement of the reading tastes and interests of the reader and for the purpose of acquiring general knowledge.

reading, curricular: reading that is done in connection with curricular study.

reading, developmental: reading instruction aimed at the orderly, sequential development of reading skills as they are related to the needs of the learner.

reading, devotional: books and other meditative reading materials used to enrich one's spiritual life by providing a deeper understanding of the divine.

reading diagnosis: *see* **diagnosis, reading.**

reading difficulty: (1) a specific lack of skill that prevents the pupil from reading effectively; (2) the degree of difficulty with which a selection or book is read by a given pupil or group; determined by consideration of various factors such as the vocabulary, sentence structure, figurative language, sentence length, etc., of the material in relation to the age and intelligence of the proposed reader or readers.

reading disability: lack of ability to read due to some physical, mental, or other cause, ranging from partial to complete inability to read; a handicap in reading.

reading disability, developmental: reading disability of individuals who exhibit no gross clinical findings related to psychological, physiological, and/or neurological disorders but who do have a basic defect in their manifest ability to integrate concepts with symbols.

reading disability, organic: reading difficulty of children who have abnormality in one or more areas subject to the classical neurological examination of cranial nerves, muscle tone and synergy, and deep and superficial reflexes.

reading disability, specific: failure to learn to read with normal proficiency despite conventional instruction, a culturally adequate home, proper motivation, intact senses, normal intelligence, and freedom from possible neurological defect.

reading distance: the distance from the eyes to the point at which the eyes converge in reading; commonly found to be between 14 and 16 inches among adults and 10 and 13 inches among children.

reading, dynamic substrata-factor theory of: (Holmes, 1948, 1953) a theory proposing that reading is a dynamic and complex act compounding and recompounding for each new and/or different reading task an appropriate integration of a multiplicity of related and underlying subabilities; some key concepts postulated are an integrating principle, a functional equipotentiality, cognitive working systems of subabilities, predominant use of preferred modes (tactile-kinesthetic, motor, auditory, and visual) of functioning in different learning situations, maturational gradient-shifts, and the constant interaction of the whole and its parts. *See* **factor, substrata.**

reading, early: reading skills developed before a child enters school and receives systematic and formal teaching.

reading ease formula, Flesch: *see* **formula, Flesch reading ease.**

reading, electronic finger: finger reading by the blind through translation of written or printed material by an electronic scanning device into impulses conveyed in a tactile form corresponding to the shape of the letters of the ordinary alphabet.

reading experience: *see* **experience, reading.**

reading expert: a person well versed in all aspects of reading instruction; a research expert in reading who is regarded as an authority on the psychology and pedagogy of reading.

reading, extensive: (1) wide reading, covering much material; (2) rapid reading for main thought rather than for detail or mechanics of expression. *Contr. w.* **reading, intensive.**

reading factor analysis: *see* **factor analysis, reading.**

reading failure: *see* **failure, reading.**

reading film: *see* **film, reading.**

reading, finger: methods of touch reading used by the blind.

reading, free: reading done at the child's own option and during time that is not allotted to other schoolwork.

reading, functional: purposive reading activities evolving from daily classroom activities; for example, reading in a science book to check an observation, reading in a health book to learn how to care for a pet, reading notices on the bulletin board, etc.

reading game: an exercise in reading that is appealing to the play interests of the child; for example, Wordo, alphabet wheels, Reado, etc.

reading guidance: *see* **guidance, reading.**

reading, guided: reading supervised and aided by the teacher.

reading habit: an acquired predisposition to engage in the act of reading, select for reading a particular type of material, and perform the reading act in a specific or idiosyncratic way.

reading habits: patterns of reading behavior which have become habitual and are performed without hesitation.

reading, home: reading done out of school for pleasure, appreciation, or information.

reading improvement: horizontal and/or vertical growth in the cognitive and affective areas related to reading.

reading, independent: reading which a pupil is able to do without assistance from a teacher.

reading index: *see* **index, reading.**

reading, individual: reading done by a pupil as an individual reader rather than as a member of a reading group.

reading, individualized: reading taught through providing a number of books from which the child selects those he wants to read and is able to read, proceeding at his own pace; diagnosis of needs and needed instruction are given during an individual conference. *Contr. w.* **reading, individual.**

reading information: (1) facts concerning how to read that enable the individual to carry on the act of reading more effectively; (2) facts concerning books and other reading materials that enable the individual to locate reading materials.

reading instruction, preventive: *see* **instruction, preventive reading.**

reading instruction, programmed: *see* **instruction, programmed reading.**

reading, intensive: (1) reading confined to a limited amount of material; (2) careful reading with attention to details of grammar, meaning, mechanics of expression, etc. *Contr. w.* **reading, extensive.**

reading interests: *see* **interests, reading.**

reading interpretation: *see* **interpretation, reading.**

reading, interpretive: reading which requires additional skills beyond literal comprehension, for example, understanding of the implied and symbolic meanings contained in writing and the ability to draw inferences, predict outcomes, and relate to personal experience. *See* **reading, creative; reading, critical.**

reading inventory, formal: *see* **inventory, formal reading.**

reading inventory, group: *see* **inventory, group reading.**

reading inventory, informal: *see* **inventory, informal reading.**

reading knowledge: the level of efficiency in reading a foreign language required for advanced courses or degrees, normally acquired in about three college semesters, and usually tested by an examination in the translation of excerpts from books or articles in the student's general or specific field.

reading laboratory: *see* **laboratory, reading.**

reading ladder: an arrangement of books for reading instruction by theme and level of difficulty.

reading, leisure: reading that is done for relaxation or amusement or is guided by interests other than those relating to educational or vocational obligations. *Syn.* **recreational reading.**

reading level: the level of achievement reached by a reader, generally defined in terms of grade or stage of growth, for example, the reading-readiness level, the first-grade level, etc.

reading level, basal: the level at which a pupil can read basal reading material; generally designated by grades such as fifth-grade level.

reading level, capacity: the level at which a reader exercises all the reading ability for which he has capacity.

reading level, frustration: generally described as the level of difficulty in reading at which a pupil experiences numerous errors in pronunciation, shows tension, and has a low level of comprehension of what he has read.

reading level, independent: a term used by Betts to describe a level at which a reader can read without aid from a teacher or other adult in word recognition and in the identification of meaning.

reading level, instructional: the level of difficulty sometimes described as one at which a pupil reads orally with few errors, without tension, and with approximately 75 percent comprehension; at this level instruction, rather than independent reading, is indicated.

reading, lip: (usually written as "lipreading") the process of understanding what is said by another person by observing visual cues such as movements of facial muscles, particularly the lips; an art frequently acquired by the deaf and the hard of hearing. *Syn.* **speech reading;** *see* **lipreading methods;** *contr. w.* **manualism.**

reading list: a selected, often annotated, list of books or of books and articles suggested for reading and study. *Syn.* **reference list; reference reading list.**

reading, map: the interpretation of maps, as in geography.

reading materials, large-type: books, newspapers, etc., printed in 18 or larger point type of clear, simple design; produced especially for partially seeing pupils.

reading materials, progressive choice: *see* **progressive choice method.**

reading maturation: *see* **maturation, reading.**

reading, mechanical: (Heb. ed.) (1) phonetic reading of a Hebrew text (usually the prayer book) without concern for meaning; (2) the study of the Hebrew characters and vowel points.

reading method: a method of language teaching in which oral work, grammar, and composition are regarded merely as aids to reading for comprehension at sight.

reading method, autoinstructional: teaching procedures in which the reading activities are presented to the student by a machine.

reading method, Beacon: a procedure in teaching reading based on a synthetic approach to phonics; the learner begins with letter sounds, then blends these sounds into larger word parts and entire words. *See* **phonics, synthetic approach to.**

reading method, Laubach: a method for teaching reading originally developed for use with illiterate Filipinos; literacy materials developed on the Laubach principle are characterized by the use of key words and word configuration to represent the various sounds of a language; the system has been identified with the expression "Each one teach one."

reading method, sight-word: teaching beginning reading by having the pupil learn a number of words "at sight" before doing any kind of word analysis.

reading, mirror: reading from right to left.

reading, music: the act of rendering by voice or instrument the musical sounds called for in printed notation.

reading norm: *see* **norm, reading.**

reading objectives: *syn.* **aims, reading.**

reading, observational: light, fluent reading such as is used in reading a story or the newspaper. *Contr. w.* **reading, work-type.**

reading, operant behavior theory of: the view that reading involves bringing the linguistic behavioral unit under the control of textual stimuli; the ability to read is a tendency to behave in certain ways under suitable circumstances involving a verbal, nonauditory stimulus.

reading, oral: the act of reading aloud.

reading pace: the rate or speed of reading.

reading pacer: *see* **machine, pacing.**

reading, paragraph: reading in which emphasis is placed upon paragraph meaning as contrasted with word or sentence meaning; the reading of paragraphs as measured by such tests as those of Gates.

reading period, developmental: *see* **period, developmental reading.**

reading, personalized: an approach to reading instruction in which the child reads material of his own choice; the teacher gives individual and group instruction in needed skills.

reading, phrase: reading that consists in recognizing and pronouncing word groups rather than complete sentences; a type of drill exercise.

reading, power: achievement in speed of comprehension beyond what is normally expected for a student at his given age and grade level.

reading process: the act of reading, involving primarily the recognition of printed symbols and the meaningful reaction of the reader to these symbols; such reaction may include the reader's interpretation, appraisal, and attitudinal responses as determined by his purposes and needs.

reading, professional: (ed.) reading relating to education in general or to one's field of specialization and that, directly or indirectly, increases one's skill, knowledge, and efficiency as an educator.

reading profile: *see* **profile, reading.**

reading program: *see* **program, reading.**

reading program, adult: *see* **program, adult reading.**

reading program, balanced: *see* **program, balanced reading.**

reading program, basal: *see* **program, basal reading.**

reading program, curricular: *see* **program, curricular reading.**

reading program, remedial: *see* **program, remedial reading.**

reading program, sequential: *see* **program, sequential reading.**

reading, proof: reading the printer's copy, or proof, of a manuscript to make sure that the printed copy follows the written copy exactly; involves the use of proof marks to indicate needed corrections; usually written "proofreading."

reading quotient: *see* **quotient, reading.**

reading range: *see* **range, reading.**

reading rate: speed of reading; usually measured in terms of the number of words or letters recognized and comprehended per minute or per second.

reading readiness: *see* **readiness, reading.**

reading-readiness activities: *see* **activities, reading-readiness.**

reading-readiness test: *see* **test, reading-readiness.**

reading record: *see* **record, reading.**

reading, recreational: *syn.* **reading, leisure.**

reading, recreatory (rek′rē·ə·tō·ri): reading for sheer enjoyment.

reading, reference: that type of reading activity in which the materials read are chosen from a bibliography or reference list, as contrasted with the reading of a textbook as the chief source of ideas.

reading, reflective: (1) thoughtful reading in which the reader seeks to grasp not only the literal meaning but also the ideas suggested by the writer's words; (2) reading undertaken for the purpose of solving a problem or difficulty.

reading, remedial: in reading instruction, activities planned for individuals or groups of pupils in order to provide for both the diagnosis of reading difficulties and their correction; usually carried on in a special remedial class. *See* **Gillingham method.**

reading, required: reading prescribed by the teacher or course of study.

reading research: *see* **research, reading.**

reading retardation, cholinesterase theory of: the theory proposed by Donald E. P. Smith that the chemicals, cholinesterase (ChE) and acetylcholene (ACh), control the transmission of nerve impulses from neuron to neuron.

reading retardation, primary: condition of children whose reading skills are significantly below age and grade norms. *See* **reading disability.**

reading retention: *see* **retention, reading.**

reading, rhythm: (1) reading that is timed by a metronome or by a device like the metronoscope; (2) performance of rhythm patterns that are presented either monotonically or melodically, by clapping, tapping, voice, or instrument.

reading room, graduate: a reading room in a university library for the use of advanced students, with a collection of special value for research.

reading room, library: a room in or supervised by a library, in which library users read or study.

reading scale: *see* **scale, reading.**

reading school: a type of school above the primary grades, ordered established in Boston in 1789 to offer elementary subjects including spelling, reading, English grammar, and composition to pupils of 7 to 14 years of age; also sometimes loosely applied to any colonial school in which the letters or reading were taught, such as the *dame school.*

reading, Scripture: (1) (Heb. ed.) a periodic public reading from the Pentateuch and selected chapters of the Prophets; conducted as a part of the Jewish religious service on the Sabbath and on certain holidays; forms a basis for individual or group study and review at home and in the Jewish school for both children and adults; (2) a practice, common to most Christian groups, of reading portions of the Bible, either publicly or privately, for the edification and education of those assembled; *comp. w.* **Bible reading.**

reading, sentence: (1) reading that is confined to sentences, as in the preprimer and early primer; a normal stage in learning to read; (2) reading that, in expression and comprehension, proceeds sentence by sentence, without consideration of the larger units, especially the paragraph.

reading sequence: a series of related sentences that, linked together, express a central idea.

reading series, basal: a set of books issued by a publisher as texts for systematic instruction in reading; usually includes a reading-readiness book, a preprimer, a primer, and the first to sixth readers. (More recently, basal readers have been developed for junior and senior high school classes.)

reading, sight: (1) the act of recognizing and pronouncing words and sentences in meaningful contexts without previous preparation; (2) performance of music from its notation without previous preparation through practice or repeated hearings.

reading, silent: reading done without audible vocalization.

reading, single: the act of reading a selection in a straight-forward fashion without rereading and regressing.

reading skill: *see* **skill, reading.**

reading skill, specialized: *see* **skill, specialized reading.**

reading span: the number of words in a line of reading material perceived in a single fixation.

reading, speech: *syn.* **reading, lip.**

reading stage: a period of development in reading generally less than a grade in length, for example, the pre-primer stage, primer stage, and first-reader stage.

reading, study: *syn.* **reading, work-type.**

reading, study-type: *syn.* **reading, work-type.**

reading, subvocal: *syn.* **speech, inner.**

reading, supplementary: reading material (books, maga-zines, or fugitive materials), aside from basal texts, used for the purpose of enriching the materials of instruction or for furnishing additional practice in reading; generally easier to read than textbook materials.

reading survey: *see* **survey, reading.**

reading table: a table on which books suitable for free or independent reading are kept. (In primary classrooms, easy picture books, preprimers, and simple primer mate-rials are generally kept on the reading table.) *Syn.* **library table.**

reading test, analytical: *see* **test, analytical reading.**

reading test, binocular: *see* **test, binocular reading.**

reading test, diagnostic: *see* **test, diagnostic reading.**

reading test, informal: *see* **test, informal reading.**

reading, therapeutic: the perusing of materials chosen to help in uncovering conflicts and giving interpretations and guidance. *See* **bibliotherapy.**

reading therapy: *see* **therapy, reading.**

reading time, total: the amount of time taken to pause or fix the eye in reading plus the time taken in movements and return sweeps.

reading unit: *see* **unit, reading.**

reading vocabulary: *see* **vocabulary, reading.**

reading, voluntary: (1) reading done at one's own volition; (2) *syn.* **reading, free.**

reading, word-by-word: an ineffective type of oral reading characterized by pauses between words.

reading, word-form: identifying words by shape or con-figuration rather than by analysis and synthesis; used more by adult readers, according to Anderson and Dear-born.

reading, work-type: purposeful reading directed toward the mastery of ideas or the solving of problems.

readmission: the act of re-enrolling a pupil after he has been dropped from the school roll.

real class boundary: *syn.* **class limit, real.**

real class limit: *see* **class limit, real.**

real income: *see* **income, real.**

real job: *see* **job, real.**

real-life situation: any situation commonly met by pupils in and outside school and used in planning the school program.

real number: *see* **number, real.**

real problem: *see* **problem, real.**

real property: *see* **property, real.**

real-time data processing: *see* **data processing, real-time.**

real-time operation: *see* **operation, real-time.**

real weight: *syn.* **weight, effective.**

realia (rē·ā′li·ə): tangible objects and/or specimens such as cocoa beans, ore samples, etc.

realism: (1) (ancient and medieval philos.) the theory that universals have being independent of, antecedent to, and more real than the specific individual instances in which they are manifested; in this form the theory is known as *Platonic realism;* when the theory holds that universals, though not independent of individual things, nevertheless constitute part of their real structure, it is called *moderate*

or *Aristotelian realism; contr. w.* **nominalism;** (2) (modern philos.) the doctrine that the object of knowledge is distinct from the process of knowing, exists indepen-dently of it, and that its nature and properties are not constituted or affected by its being known; *see* **Neo-Realism; realism, classical; realism, critical;** *contr. w.* **ideal-ism;** (3) the educational movement away from the ex-treme verbalism prevalent in the schools after the Ren-aissance; demanded that education concern itself with realities and not merely with words; (4) a philosophy holding that the aim of education is the acquisition of verified knowledge of the environment and adjustment to the environment; recognizes the value of content as well as of the activities involved in learning, and takes into account the external determinants of human behavior; advocates freedom of the individual limited by consider-ation of the rights and welfare of others.

realism, Aristotelian: *see* **realism** (1).

realism, classical: modern versions of the Platonic and Aristotelian doctrines which assert (*a*) that the cosmos consists of real, substantial entities existing in themselves and ordered to one another by real, extramental relations; (*b*) that these entities can be known, at least in part, as they really are; (*c*) that there are intelligible structures of human nature and human groups which when grasped can provide valid principles for the guidance of individ-ual and social action.

realism, common-sense: a doctrine associated with Thomas Reid (1710–1796) and the Scottish school, which held that mind and matter were real substances, both distinct from the "ideas" that suggested them; epistemo-logically the doctrine is dualistic with an *idea* being referred to an external object in the act of knowing, although primary qualities are supposed to be presented directly to the mind.

realism, critical: a philosophical doctrine advanced in America about 1920 by George Santayana, A. K. Rogers, A. O. Lovejoy, R. W. Sellars, J. B. Pratt, Durant Drake, and others, which emphasized the representational char-acter of sense perception; it held that although physical objects exist independently of the mind, they are known through sense data, or *sensa,* which are numerically distinct from both object and the mind. *Contr. w.* **Neo-Realism.**

realism, historical: in contrast to modern realism, the theory that ideas or universals are as real as or more real than particulars. *See* **nominalism.**

realism, humanistic: an educational movement that arose in the sixteenth and seventeenth centuries as a protest against the extreme verbalism of *classical humanism;* resembled humanism in that it upheld the study of ancient languages and culture, but would have this study pursued for information on life and nature, the realities, rather than for form and literary style; sometimes referred to as *verbal realism.* [Erasmus (1466–1536) and John Milton (1608–1674) are representative humanistic real-ists.]

realism in art: fidelity in art and literature to nature or to real life and to accurate representation without idealiza-tion, distortion, or imaginative exaggeration.

realism, innocent: (1) the notion that whatever is directly presented to the subject in perception carries no sign which guarantees that the perception of it will be true, that is, it is innocent of its truth or falsity state as cognition; (2) used as equivalent to the position of *naïve realism* (Samuel Alexander); *see* **realism, naïve.**

realism, moderate: *see* **realism** (1).

realism, naïve: the precritical or preanalytical belief that objects exist in the manner disclosed to us by sense perception, especially that primary, secondary, and terti-ary qualities are where they are perceived to be, namely, in the object. *See* **realism, innocent** (2).

realism, natural: *syn.* **realism, common-sense.**

realism, Platonic: *syn.* **realism** (1).

realism, scientific: (1) the belief that natural science pro-gressively discloses the true nature of an independent physical world; (2) the doctrine that scientific knowledge provides a stable content for the curriculum as well as a model for pupils' thinking.

realism, sense: the doctrine that an objective world with sense qualities exists independent of cognition and that sensory experience yields direct and verifiable knowledge; applied to education by way of emphasis on sense training, the study of the physical environment, and the use of concrete objects as illustrative materials in teaching.

realism, social: (1) a somewhat aristocratic educational movement of the sixteenth and seventeenth centuries which held that education should equip the student for a happy and successful life as a man of the world; stressed modern languages, travel, and a study of contemporary institutions, and regarded the classical languages and culture as more or less trivial [Montaigne (1533-1592) was its outstanding representative]; (2) belief that persons and groups constitute values real and independent in themselves.

realism, verbal: *see* realism, humanistic.

realistic choice: *see* choice, realistic.

realistic color: *see* color, realistic.

realistic representation: *see* realism in art.

realistic story: a simple narrative in which the child's immediate experiences are reflected and in which the characters solve their difficulties and secure their pleasures without the aid of magic or the supernatural.

reality: a metaphysical or ontological concept of being, and hence dependent for its meaning on the metaphysical or ontological position held; the physical as opposed to consciousness; actuality; that which has actual existence and is not imaginary, fictitious, or an appearance merely. (As actually used, the word frequently constitutes a problem for semanticists.)

reality simulation: *see* simulation, reality.

reality testing: *see* testing, reality.

reality, ultimate: a hypothetical entity or entities that underlie or are a phase of the phenomena of experience and of which the latter are but the superficial manifestations; variously conceived and described depending upon the school of philosophy represented; the most common entities are the natural order, the supernatural order, the thing in itself, the world of ideas and ideals, sense experience and thought, matter, spirit, matter and spirit, and a space-time integration or combination which is not itself space-time.

rear projection: *see* projection, rear.

rear-projection screen: *see* screen, rear-projection.

rear-screen projection: *see* projection, rear-screen.

rearrangement test: *see* test, rearrangement.

reason: a term used for a function of knowing, a faculty of knowledge, or an object of comprehension: (1) as a function of knowing, reason may refer to a process of drawing inferences by combining concepts or propositions to reach truth discursively; or of intuiting truths immediately and nondiscursively; or of judging well in discriminating good from evil, truth from falsity, beauty from ugliness; or of grasping natural knowledge (as distinguished from revealed knowledge grasped by faith); or of discovering within itself, by reflection, innate ideas whose meaning, and first principles, whose truth, can be established apart from experience; or of comprehending directly the reality underlying appearances or the absolute underlying accidents; or, in a problematic situation, of solving the problems and thereby resolving the situation; or reason may refer to the whole constellation of higher mental processes; (2) as a faculty of knowledge, reason may refer to a special faculty with power to perform one of the foregoing functions, or to a general faculty with power to perform several of them, or to all the higher mental capacities; (3) as an object of comprehension, reason may refer to the principles of orderliness which make things understandable, to the ratio or relationship constituting a mathematical progression; or to the theoretical explanation that enlightens men's minds by leading them to understand something (in contrast to its efficient cause or a logical demonstration concerning it); or to the legitimate motive, or justification, for doing something; or to the intelligence or order pervading minds collectively, nature, or the universe, and thereby

fitting whatever it pervades to be comprehended by functions or faculties of men's reason.

reasonable doubt: *see* doubt, reasonable.

reasonable result: (math.) a value within the realm of common sense or practical possibility.

reasoning: the development of the meaning content of ideas through operating with symbols constituting propositions so that the propositions stand in serial order constituting argument or discourse.

reasoning, abstract: the act or process of arriving at conclusions through the use of symbols or generalizations rather than concrete data.

reasoning, accuracy in: *see* accuracy in reasoning.

reasoning, analogous: reasoning based on the assumption that if two situations are alike in certain respects, they are alike in other respects also; for example, if B has property P and A is like B in some ways, then A also has property P. *See* analogy.

reasoning, analytical: *see* analysis, mathematical.

reasoning, arithmetic: (1) mathematical reasoning applied to topics in arithmetic; (2) sometimes used to mean the ability to solve by reasoning a verbal problem in arithmetic.

reasoning, axiomatic: deductive reasoning within the framework of an axiom system, that is, using a fixed set of premises and no others when the premises have been chosen to characterize some physical or mathematical situation. *Syn.* postulational thinking; *see* deductive method.

reasoning, circular: arguing in a circle by assuming a premise that can be proved only by the conclusion, as "Conscience is a proper guide for conduct and we know this is true because our conscience tells us so." *See* fallacy of begging the question.

reasoning, deductive: reasoning based on the rules of inference of logic, for example, knowing that given A one always has B, and not having B, thus concluding that it cannot be the case that one has A. *See* deduction; deductive method.

reasoning, direct: *see* direct method (3).

reasoning, discursive: thinking that is characterized by or resultant from the examination of particulars or the consideration or analysis of that which is involved.

reasoning, eclectic: reasoning by selecting elements from two or more divergent systems, doctrines, or theories.

reasoning, indirect: *see* indirect method (2).

reasoning, inductive: (1) (logic) reasoning that proceeds from known data to a generalization, such as a theory or hypothesis that will explain the evidence at hand; (2) (math.) reasoning based on the assumption that if something is observed or known to happen in some finite number of cases, then it will always happen; for example, observing that $3 \times 4 = 4 \times 3, 6 \times 7 = 7 \times 6$, etc., leads to the generalization that multiplication for the counting numbers is always *commutative. See* induction.

reasoning, mathematical: reasoning which is either completely deductive or uses *inductive* or *analogous reasoning* to form hypotheses which are then subjected to deductive reasoning for confirmation or rejection. *See* deduction.

reasoning, period of: *see* developmental stage, pseudorealistic.

reasoning, scientific: (1) the act or mental process of inferring relationships among facts or phenomena, of weighing and evaluating evidence, and of coming to a conclusion; (2) the process of eliciting from hypotheses certain implications that are susceptible of confrontation with such factual situations as pointer readings, scales, etc.; (3) an examination of factual information and the relationship of fact as a basis for this or that practical action; (4) *syn.* reasoning, inductive.

reasoning, syllogistic: (1) literally, reasoning carried on by means of syllogisms; (2) usually used more loosely (since very little actual reasoning is carried on in strictly syllogistic form) to refer to reasoning carried on by any deductive process or by rhetorical devices that could readily be transformed into syllogisms if certain premises that "seem to go without saying" were made explicit. *See* syllogism.

reasoning, synthetic: *see* **synthetic method.**

reasoning test: *see* **test, reasoning.**

recall: (1) the procedure by which the qualified electors of a given district may remove from office those officials who have been elected by the electors of the same district; in education most often used in the case of elected school board members; (2) the reproduction of former knowledge or experience that may not be identified or recognized as something previously known or experienced.

recall, delayed: the recall of learned material after a lapse of time.

recall item: *see* **item, recall.**

recall knowledge: *see* **knowledge, recall.**

recall, oral: an exercise in which the pupil is required to read a selection one or more times and then recount in his own words all that he can recall of the material read.

recall test: *see* **test, recall.**

recall, written: an exercise in which the pupil is required to read a selection one or more times and then write out all that he can recall of the material read.

recapitulation: (biol.) the condensed process of repeating the history of the race during the life history of the individual.

recapitulation theory: the theory that "ontogeny repeats phylogeny," or that the development of the individual is characterized by a sequence of structures or behavior observable in the phylogenetic development of the species; usually restricted mainly to the period of embryological development or early childhood; sometimes extended to include *cultural recapitulation theory* or *culture-epochs theory.*

receipt by transfer: *see* **received by transfer.**

receipts: cash received; to be distinguished from income in that the latter may include items that have accrued but have not been received.

receipts, nonrevenue: receipts that involve an obligation that must be met at some future date and that may or may not result in a decrease in the amount and value of school property, for example, receipts from loans, sale of bonds, insurance adjustments, sale of property, etc.

receipts, revenue: cash receipts that do not result in increasing school indebtedness or in decreasing school assets, for example, receipts from taxes and state appropriations.

receipts, revolving fund: *syn.* **advancements.**

received by transfer: a phrase designating a pupil who has come to a school or school system by transfer from another school or school system within the same state. *Syn.* **transfer in.**

receiver: (communications theory) that which transforms a signal into a message.

receiver, direct-view: a television receiver typical of most home-type receivers where the image to be viewed is formed directly on the inside surface of the kinescope or picture tube.

receiver, jeeped: (audiovis. ed.) a regular television receiver that has been modified to permit it to be used as a monitor for direct-video purposes in a closed-circuit system; accomplished through bypassing most of the circuit elements and feeding the picture signals directly into the video amplifier; when this is done it is necessary to provide a separate audio source; some receivers on the market can be used conventionally or jeeped according to need.

receiver, projection: a television set with a small but high-intensity picture tube which operates through an optical system to project images which are viewed on a screen; some recent developments employ different approaches to achieve this effect.

receiving: (school admin.) the function of properly inducting into the plant all materials received from vendors or other outside sources; includes the work of handling, recording, reporting, and moving incoming materials; a phase of the supply function. See **purchasing.**

receiving teacher: the designation of any teacher to whom a new pupil or class is being assigned or to whom a new pupil or class has been assigned for the first time.

recency, law of: *see* **law of recency.**

reception room: (1) room connected with the administrative office of a school, in which persons wishing to see the principal or other school official may wait to be received; (2) *syn.* **green room.**

receptive aphasia: *syn.* **aphasia, sensory-receptive.**

receptive language ability: *see* **decoding, visual.**

receptive oligophasia: *see* **oligophasia, receptive.**

recess, school: a period of rest from regular schoolwork during which children may engage in recreational activities largely of a physical sort.

recess supervision: *see* **supervision, recess.**

recidivism (rə·sid'ə·viz'm): a return to criminal acts or behavior after attempts at cure or reformation.

recidivist: one who continually returns to criminal acts or behavior despite efforts at reformation; specifically, in the United States, one who has served or is serving a second term in prison.

recipient: (res.) one who receives a questionnaire to be filled in. *Contr. w.* **respondent.**

recipient responsibility: *see* **responsibility, recipient.**

reciprocal inhibition: *see* **inhibition, reciprocal.**

reciprocal interweaving, principle of: the developmental sequence through which opposing muscle systems are organized into progressively more complex coordinations; it involves the reciprocal innervation of antagonistic muscle groups and the integration of muscle systems on both sides of the organism.

reciprocal training: *see* **training, reciprocal.**

reciprocal transformation: *see* **transformation, reciprocal.**

reciprocating movement: *see* **movement, reciprocating.**

reciprocity in teacher certification: recognition by certifying authorities of a certificate or license issued by some other certifying authority.

recital: *see* **concert.**

recital, chamber: *see* **concert.**

recitation. (1) traditionally, a learning exercise and teaching procedure in which students repeat orally or explain material learned by individual study or previously presented by the teacher and reply to questions asked by the teacher or instructor; (2) in the modern school, those parts of the instructional unit devoted to evaluation, checking, reporting, summarizing, or free expression.

recitation, choral: repetition of any language material by the entire class or by a group speaking together; where feasible, choral recitation should always precede individual recitation. *Syn.* **concert recitation.**

recitation, concert: *syn.* **recitation, choral.**

recitation, formalized: recitation organized and carried out more or less rigidly according to set forms of rules (often authoritatively prescribed).

recitation hall: *see* **hall, recitation.**

recitation method: a plan of teaching that stresses the oral repetition or explanation by pupils of lessons learned by individual study; may also include much oral review of previously learned material and answering questions asked by the teacher; does not necessarily imply verbalism or rote learning.

recitation period: *see* **period, recitation.**

recitation room: obsolescent *syn.* **classroom.**

recitation, socialized: learning through participation of pupils in group activities, with such objectives as stimulating interest and reflective thinking, learning how to attack problems, supplementing knowledge with facts necessary for understanding, learning techniques of critical evaluation, developing ability in creative expression, developing wholesome social attitudes, and training in cooperative effort and in techniques of organizing and expressing ideas and of group thinking.

recitation teacher: *syn.* **classroom teacher.**

recitation, textbook: an oral class exercise in which the main effort is centered in checking pupils on the mastery of textbook material.

recognition: the process of perceiving words in reading and associating meaning with word symbols. *Syn.* **word recognition.**

recognition day: a day at the end of the school year when promotions are made, with exercises giving appropriate recognition to the pupils' accomplishments.

recognition fraternity: *syn.* **recognition society.**

recognition item: *see* **item, recognition.**

recognition knowledge: *see* **knowledge, recognition.**

recognition society: an association that receives into membership persons of achievement in a given course, department, or special field of study or interest such as accountancy, architecture, biology, electrical engineering, history, language, mathematics, or speech and who are definitely above average in general scholarship and actively interested in a specific field; established only in 4-year degree-granting colleges and universities; differs from the *honor society* in that its field is specialized and its standards of eligibility and election to membership may be more flexible. *Syn.* **recognition fraternity;** *see* **fraternity.**

recognition span: (read.) (1) the amount of material recognized at each fixation pause; (2) the number of words and letters with which the reader can associate meaning during one fixation of the eyes.

recognition test: *see* **test, recognition.**

recognition vocabulary: *see* **vocabulary, recognition.**

recognition, word: *syn.* **recognition.**

recognized leader: *see* **leader, recognized.**

recommended cost: *see* **cost, recommended.**

reconditioning: the process of reestablishing a conditioned reflex or response that has ceased to operate, whether by reason of its having been experimentally extinguished or negatively adapted or owing to disuse; sometimes used to signify the process of reestablishing an original, unlearned reflex or response, but in this case the term unconditioning is to be preferred as less ambiguous. *See* **unconditioning.**

reconditioning training, advanced: *see* **training, advanced reconditioning.**

reconstruction of belief: reorganization of one's system or set of opinions and judgments, involving a change of the intensity of conviction and/or of the relationship of beliefs with respect to any aspect of existence.

reconstruction of experience: the use of critical or reflective thinking to examine and evaluate present and past experiences so that one may exercise the freedom of intelligence in planning, choosing, and directing more meaningful future experiences.

reconstruction of experience, education as the continuous: *see* **education as the continuous reconstruction of experience.**

reconstruction, social: *see* **social reconstruction.**

reconstructionism: *syn.* **social reconstruction.**

record: a group of words or fields on a related subject, for example, the memorandum of an employee's employment history.

record, absence: systematically kept data showing the frequency, the date, the cause, and the disposition of cases of absence; usually kept on cards 4 by 6 inches, one for each child who has been absent, the cards being retained by the assistant principal or other official responsible for improving attendance at the school.

record, academic: the official marks assigned to a student in the subjects in which he has been registered, including a record of any action taken by the faculty in the case of students with marks of failure in these subjects; sometimes includes a record of official disciplinary action for scholastic or other reasons.

record, activity: a permanent record of a student's extraclass activities, used in conjunction with the cumulative or permanent record. *See* **activities, extraclass.**

record, anecdotal: a series of notes containing exactly what a child said or did in concrete situations; as observations are accumulated, a variety and continuity of information yielding a picture of the child's behavior patterns, development in various directions, interests, attitudes, strengths, and problems can be seen. *Syn.* **descriptive record.**

record, attendance: collected data relative to the attendance of each pupil, showing daily absence and tardiness; in elementary schools, generally kept in the teacher's register and, in secondary schools, in the teacher's classbook or (more frequently) in registers or on individual cards in the principal's office.

record, balance-of-stores: a perpetual inventory record; may also be called *stores ledger, stock record,* etc. *See* **inventory, perpetual.**

record, baptismal: recorded data concerning the baptism of a child; usually includes a statement of the date of birth. *See* **certificate, baptismal.**

record, behavior: (couns.) a complete observational description of the counselee in the classroom, on the playground, in the cafeteria, and in similar unstructured situations; also called *behavior-description record.*

record, behavior-description: *see* **record, behavior.**

record, birth: *syn.* **record, permanent age.**

record book, teacher's class: a book in which the teacher records the entry, withdrawal, absence, tardiness, and school marks of each pupil.

record card, attendance: the form on which is entered the attendance record of the pupil.

record card, cumulative: *see* **cumulative record card.**

record card, permanent: a printed form used to record the most essential information about each pupil, generally employed from the first to the twelfth grade, although at times containing preschool and postschool information; includes permanently valuable information pertaining to family, health, intelligence status, vocational plans, personal development, academic transcript, extraclass activities, etc.

record card, principal's office: a card on which the principal keeps the record of a pupil. *See* **record, principal's office.**

record, case: all the pertinent facts about an individual in collected and recorded form.

record, cumulative: *see* **cumulative record.**

record, daily: data that the teacher is required to record daily in the class register; usually includes daily information about attendance, absence, and tardiness; may include daily achievement, health data, standard test results, and other desired information.

record, descriptive: *syn.* **record, anecdotal.**

record, diary: *syn.* **record, anecdotal.**

record, dictation: a phonograph record used as a teaching aid to build speed in shorthand and for practice and makeup work of students; recordings on belts, wire, or tapes may also be used for shorthand dictation.

record, discipline: a systematic collection of data concerning the date, nature, and cause of all instances of misbehavior on the part of a pupil and the action taken in each case; kept in the office of the school official responsible for the maintenance of discipline within the school.

record, dismissal: (1) a written account of the major facts surrounding dismissal of a school employee; in the case of a permanent teacher, ordinarily includes the charges and a record of the hearing and of the action taken; (2) a formal accounting, filed in the accounting office, of all individuals discharged from a school system or institution.

record, eye: a printed form used for noting the results of eye examinations or eyesight tests and giving recommendations for medical treatment.

record, eye-movement: (1) a photographic record of eye movement produced by the ophthalmograph or other photographic apparatus; (2) a statistical record of a reader's eye movements made by means of observation with a mirror or by the Miles peephole method.

record folder, cumulative: *see* **cumulative record folder.**

record form, cumulative: *see* **cumulative record form.**

record form, individual: a record form used for pertinent information, such as test performance, about a single pupil in contrast to the *school register,* or *class book,* which is a record form used for a group of pupils. *Syn.* **pupil record form.**

record form, pupil: *syn.* **record form, individual.**

record, grade: a record, compiled and kept by an instructor, of the marks and other measures of achievement that he assigns to the pupils or students whom he teaches; may be in loose-leaf or grade-book form; may cover a semester or an entire school year; used at all levels of education.

record, guidance follow-up: (1) a form letter or blank sent out periodically to a former pupil or student who is now engaged in an occupation, for the purpose of discovering his progress or difficulties; (2) the record derived from information given on such a blank.

record, health: a record which provides specific information about one's height, weight, vision, hearing, teeth, physical disabilities, vaccinations, disease, treatments, and referrals by the school doctor or nurse and also lists other health information about students.

record, high-speed: a cylinder or disk on which sound has been recorded at the speed of 78 revolutions per minute and which may be played back at the same speed on a suitable machine. *Contr. w.* **record, microgroove.**

record, indigent clothing: data concerning the receipt of clothing by pupils unable to buy it for themselves; includes name of pupil, date of receiving, amount of clothing received, reason for providing it, and other pertinent facts.

record keeping: (1) the act or procedure of recording financial transactions, as distinguished from interpreting them; (2) a beginning course in the more elementary, routine phases of bookkeeping, sometimes offered for students who lack the qualifications for success as bookkeepers or accountants.

record-keeping approach: a broad term including such specific methods of presentation in teaching bookkeeping as the *journal* and *account approaches.*

record, long-play: *see* **record, microgroove.**

record, low-speed: *syn.* **record, microgroove.**

record, microgroove: a phonograph disk, commonly called *long-play,* the grooves of which have been cut to utilize a .001-inch-diameter stylus in playback.

record of withdrawals: recorded data showing the date and cause in each case of the withdrawal of a pupil from school.

record, packet: *see* **packet record system.**

record, part-time school: data concerning pupils in part-time schools; in general, similar to the school record used in regular, or full-time, schools.

record, permanent age: systematically compiled data relating to date and authority for the date of birth of the pupil, occasionally kept on cards, one for each pupil. (Sometimes referred to as a *birth record,* it is quite generally a part of such records as the pupil's cumulative record, the principal's office record, and the census record.)

record, permanent cumulative: *syn.* **cumulative record.**

record, permanent grade: (1) a systematic collection of data on the school marks of each pupil, covering a period of years and frequently kept in the principal's office; (2) a systematic collection of data on the school marks for an entire class group; kept permanently in some schools; (3) a systematic collection of data concerning a grade group for a given year; may contain school marks, a record of activities, and other information concerning such a group of pupils.

record, personal service: (school admin.) a history of an employee's service with an organization that is sufficient to supply a basis for executive decisions concerning problems affecting the employee personally; may be part of a personnel record.

record, personnel: *see* **personnel record.**

record, placement: a formal set of papers including records of experience and training, recommendations, and vital statistics pertaining to the professional qualifications of a candidate for employment; usually assembled by a placement or employment office and used by employing officers for evaluation and selection of personnel; constitutes a permanent professional file for registrant in some cases; also called *placement credentials. See* **placement service.**

record, postschool: (1) data assembled about a youth after he has left school; (2) the form, card, folder, or booklet that contains data concerning the afterschool career of a youth; frequently of use in vocational guidance and job placement.

record, principal's office: the record of a pupil that is kept by the principal of a school as a permanent part of the school's property and that never leaves the school. (If during his school life a pupil enrolls in a dozen schools, there will be a dozen principal's office records for that pupil, on cards, sheets, or folders or in individual books.)

record, pupil: any systematic collection of data regarding a pupil; may deal with his physical, mental, social, or moral attitudes, abilities, or capacities and with his environment, whether home, out-of-home, or school; may be used by teachers, principals, superintendents, attendance workers, visiting teachers, health officers, etc.

record, pupil-personnel: *syn.* **record, pupil.**

record, pupil progress: systematically organized information and data indicating the attainments of a pupil in a particular subject or in all his educational work.

record, reading: (1) a written list of the books that have been read by a pupil; (2) the past performance of a pupil in reading as indicated by a series of marks in reading.

record, safety: (1) a mark of achievement as a result of the safe transportation of pupils, that is, without accidents or injury; (2) an official written account for each driver or for a transportation system as a whole, including accidents, injuries, or other matters pertaining to the safe transportation of pupils.

record, school: a systematic collection of data relative to schools, usually preserved for a considerable period of time; generally made and retained by the office using it.

record, score: a record of the score of athletic contests.

record, service: an enlisted man's document recording his conduct, performance of duties, results of tests, etc.

record sheet: (testing) a separate sheet for recording the frequencies of correct responses or the examinees' scores on a test.

record, stock: *syn.* **record, balance-of-stores.**

record system, attendance: a plan for keeping an account of the attendance of pupils; includes the record of attendance, as well as those routines necessary to make this record and to keep it up to date.

record system, permanent: a plan for keeping indefinitely an account of many kinds of data about pupils; includes the record forms plus all devices that a school system may use as means of reporting data so that they can be made a part of the permanent record.

record, tardiness: recorded data showing the frequency, the date, the cause, and the disposition of cases of tardiness. *See* **record, absence.**

record, time-sample: a series of reports or anecdotes, written at definite times, which are used for gathering data to study behavior. *See* **sampling, short-time; study, time sampling.**

record, transfer: (1) a record of the change of pupils from one "teacher grade" to another; (2) a record of the change of pupils from one school to another within the system; (3) a record of the change of pupils from one school system to another.

record, truancy: recorded data concerning the time, cause, and disposition of cases of truancy.

record, unit: (1) a physically separate record that is similar in form and content to other records with which it is grouped, for example, a summary of a particular employee's earnings to date; (2) a record in such form as a Hollerith card, a line of printing, or a length of magnetic tape called a block; *see* **block** (3); **card, punch.**

recorded book: *see* **book, recorded.**

recorder: (1) any device for recording audio signals on disk, magnetic tape, or photographic film; (2) a whistle-type flute that is end-blown and has a soft, slightly reedy tone; though an instrument of the Middle Ages, currently very popular as a simple instrument for amateurs and as a preband instrument; *syn.* **blockflöte;** *see* **instrument,**

preorchestral; (3) a person who notes down what happens in a conference or other group meeting to afford a basis for later discussion or action; *see* **recorder, group.**

recorder, cassette: an audio recording and playback device distinguished by its small size, portability, relatively low price, and simplicity of operation, utilizing magnetic tape in a sealed plastic *cassette* as the recording medium.

recorder, disk: a device that reproduces sound on disks surfaced with acetate or another plastic substance, in which grooves may be cut containing the physical representation of vibrations created by sound; a stylus vibrates to cut the signal and the groove.

recorder, dual-track: a tape recorder utilizing a recording head that covers half the tape width, thus making it possible to record one track on one direction of the tape and a second track on the other direction after the reels have been turned over. *Syn.* **half-track recorder.**

recorder, group: the member of a discussion group assigned the task of maintaining a continuous record of the content of the discussion, including topics, differences, agreements, points of confusion, etc., and who is responsible for reporting this information as needed to facilitate the group's progress toward its goals.

recorder, half-track: *syn.* **recorder, dual-track.**

recorder, kinescope: a device with which a film recording is made of a television program; the film camera records the images directly from the face of a TV tube.

recorder, tape: a machine, sometimes called a recorder-reproducer, which can record sound impressions magnetically on a long strand of metallic-coated plastic tape and then play them back; contains recording and playback amplifiers and heads; the heads may be full-, half-, dual-, or quarter-track. *See* **recorder, cassette.**

recorder, video tape: a device to record both the audio and video signals of a television production on a special magnetic tape which can be played back to reproduce the entire program.

recorder, wire: a machine for recording magnetically sound impressions on a long strand of fine wire; the recorded material may then be played back for listening.

recording: a cylinder, disk, tape, or wire on which sound has been recorded with relative permanency, so that the sound may be recreated by playing the recording on a suitable machine.

recording, binaural: a recording made simultaneously on two tracks of a tape with two separate microphones and electronic circuits; a stereo recording. *Comp. w.* **recording, monaural.**

recording, disk: the ordinary phonograph record, a flat disk varying from 6 to 17 inches in diameter and played at varying revolutions per minute.

recording, dual tape: usually a stereophonic (dual-track) recording system adapted so that two separate channels—program signal and student signal in an electronic learning laboratory—are recorded simultaneously or sequentially on two separate tracks of the same tape; special switches and circuitry allow the student channel to be rerecorded without erasing the program channel.

recording head: *see* **head, recording.**

recording, kinescope: a film recording of a television program; sometimes called a *telefilm.*

recording, magnetic sound: *see* **sound recording, magnetic.**

recording, monaural: a recording made on a single track as opposed to one made on two or more tracks simultaneously using two separate microphones.

recording, multichannel: a tape recording on which several signals are recorded and retrievable, in turn or simultaneously.

recording, multitape: (1) simultaneous transmission over a conduit, called a channel, of recorded messages from several program sources to selected student positions in the language or other learning laboratory network; (2) that property of a multitrack recorder permitting several different signals or channels to be recorded or played back simultaneously but separately.

recording, optical sound: *see* **sound recording, optical.**

recording, stereo: *see* **recording, binaural.**

recording, stereophonic: a sound recording made with two (or more) separate microphones attached to independent electronic circuits and reproduced correspondingly through separate amplifier circuits to give the illusion of three-dimensional sound.

recording studio: an acoustically insulated room in which taped programs are prepared using an open microphone.

recording system, uniform: a system of records adapted for use by all the school districts of the country or of a state, or of any relatively large administrative unit.

recording, tape: a recording of sounds in the form of magnetic patterns on iron-oxide-coated plastic or paper-based tape.

recording, television: a television program photographed on film either for a permanent record or for presentation at a later time; called a *kinescope recording* if recorded directly from the picture tube.

recording, thermoplastic: a process which combines the processing speed and versatility of magnetic recording and the storage capacity of photography; it can concentrate 100 times as much information in a given space as can magnetic recording, records almost instantaneously, and will produce pictures in color or black and white, but it does not require chemical processing and can be erased and reused as desired; presently under experimental development by General Electric.

recording, video tape (VTR): (1) recording and reproducing television picture tube signals on standard—but highest quality—magnetic tape such as Instrumentation tape; it is extremely difficult to design a tape recorder capable of handling wide-frequency range up to 4 million cycles per second; usually several magnetic tracks are recorded side by side on a ½-inch tape at a considerably higher speed than used in home recording, each track recording a certain range of frequencies; improved quality and lower operating cost are expected to enable it to replace movie film for television use; (2) the material recorded on such tape, to be reproduced in audiovisual form on a television receiver.

recording, wire: a recording of sounds in the form of magnetic patterns on steel wire.

recordings instruction: *see* **instruction, recordings.**

records, child-accounting: records maintained by the school as a part of its child-accounting activities, particularly those dealing with attendance, census, and enrollment.

records, confidential: (couns.) information gathered and maintained by and for qualified staff members whose consultation will benefit the client; all such data are guarded against exposure to other than qualified personnel.

records, efficiency: (voc. ed.) data collected to discover the best procedure for improving any piece of work.

records, experience: charts or other hand-printed or written materials which constitute written records of excursions, observations, and other experiences of a group of children.

records, guidance: a part of the total school records system from kindergarten through the twelfth grade; kept basically to give an account of activities performed and to form a basis for assisting pupils in the process of development; utilized by counselors to improve self-understanding on the part of the pupils, to interpret pupil characteristics to parents, to motivate learning and adjustment, and to further the adaptation of the curriculum to individual and group needs.

records, justification: collected information that may be used to justify such steps as the expenditure of funds, the continuance or the closing of a class, or the ordering of equipment.

records management: *see* **management, records.**

records, transportation: *see* **transportation records.**

recovery, glare: *see* **glare recovery.**

recovery index: *see* **index, recovery.**

recovery time: (phys. ed.) a phase of muscular contraction in which the muscle fibers return to a resting state.

recreation: a worthwhile, socially accepted leisure experience that provides immediate and inherent satisfaction to the individual who voluntarily participates in the activity.

recreation, campus: planning of recreation experiences, to be carried on under auspices of the educational institution, that will enable students to learn a variety of skills in activities that reflect valuable contemporary recreation interests.

recreation center, municipal: a building and grounds serving as a community center devoted to various forms of public recreation under trained leadership and operated as a unit in a city public recreation program.

recreation, co-ed: the participation of both sexes in an activity voluntarily engaged in during leisure and primarily motivated by the satisfaction or pleasure derived therefrom.

recreation, commercialized: a provision for public recreation made by private enterprise; the primary concern is the profit of the enterprise.

recreation commission: a committee or group given authority as a policy-forming and controlling body for the guidance of public recreation in a specific community or district.

recreation, community: play activities, including enjoyment and appreciation of the arts, sciences, crafts, etc., sponsored or engaged in by a community acting collectively.

recreation council: *syn.* **recreation commission.**

recreation department: *see* **department, recreation.**

recreation, industrial: organized leisure-time activity programs for employees of industrial firms.

recreation leader: one who directs play activities. *See* **director, playground.**

recreation legislation: *see* **legislation, recreation.**

recreation, mathematical· puzzles, games, tricks, etc., based on certain mathematical concepts, principles, or techniques.

recreation, municipal: an organized program of public recreation maintained as a function of a municipal government.

recreation park: a beautiful area used as a city park and recreation grounds. *See* **municipal park.**

recreation, passive: leisure-time activities not involving stimulating physical exercise.

recreation program, physical: *see* **program, physical recreation.**

recreation program, school: *see* **program, school recreation.**

recreation, public: leisure-time activities organized for the benefit of the public.

recreation service: the provision of finances, facilities, and staff for conducting a program of public recreation.

recreation worker: a trained leader of recreation activities.

recreational activity: *see* **activity, recreational.**

recreational approach: (read.) presentation of a literary selection to a class by treating the selection as something to be read and enjoyed rather than as something to be studied.

recreational facility: an area or a building, pool, or other permanent construction used for recreation purposes.

recreational fitness: *see* **fitness, recreational.**

recreational mathematics: *see* **recreation, mathematical.**

recreational reading: *syn.* **reading, leisure.**

recreational sports: *see* **sports, recreational.**

recreational therapy: *see* **therapy, recreational.**

recreatory reading: *see* **reading, recreatory.**

recruit: (mil. ed.) a newly enlisted man, one who is still in a training activity.

recruit training: *see* **training, recruit.**

recruiting: (1) (student-personnel work) procedures involving the search for college graduates who qualify for employment in an industrial or business organization; (2) (higher ed.) a program of personal solicitation and

enrollment of new students in a college; (3) efforts of a private educational institution to secure enrollments by means of a field agent; *see* **field agent;** (4) securing players for school or college athletic teams by offering inducements.

recruitment: the sudden building up of the sensation of loudness, once the threshold of hearing has been crossed.

recruitment, auditory: a phenomenon observed in ears with hearing loss caused by damage to the inner ear, in which intense sounds are heard with normal or near-normal loudness despite a loss of acuity to fainter sounds. *Syn.* **recruitment of loudness.**

recruitment factor: the contribution made by *recruitment of loudness* to the overall sensitivity of a hard-of-hearing ear. *See* **recruitment, auditory.**

recruitment, faculty: the process by which qualified persons are informed of positions available on the teaching staff of an educational institution and their potential interest is assessed; in order to accomplish these ends, there must be (*a*) lines of communication by which an opening may come to be known to qualified personnel and (*b*) a means of contact through which the interest of qualified personnel may come to be known to the school.

recruitment, hearing: *see* **hearing recruitment.**

recruitment literature: *see* **literature, recruitment.**

recruitment of loudness: *syn.* **recruitment, auditory.**

recruitment, student: in business and distributive education, techniques employed to interest students in programs in these fields.

recruitment, teacher: the process of attracting and persuading capable persons to prepare for and to enter the teaching profession; usually associated with such appeals to high school graduates and college students.

rectangular coordinate paper: *see* **coordinate paper.**

rectangular distribution: *see* **distribution, rectangular.**

rectilinear: (1) capable of being represented graphically by a straight line; (2) presumed to be straight, in the absence of good evidence to the contrary; (3) data lying on a line without detectable curvature; (4) data, the regression line which is straight within an acceptable degree of probability. (The less precise term *linear* is commonly used as a synonym.)

rectilinear correlation: *see* **correlation, rectilinear.**

rectilinear movement: *see* **movement, rectilinear.**

rectilinear regression: *syn.* **regression, linear.**

rectilinear relation: *syn.* **correlation, rectilinear.**

rectilinear relationship: *syn.* **correlation, rectilinear.**

rectilinearity: *syn.* **linearity.**

rector: (1) a priest in the churches of the Anglican communion who has charge of a parish; (2) a priest in the Roman Catholic church who has charge of a congregation, religious house, or seminary; (3) in many European countries, the head of a school, college, or university.

recycling: in programmed instruction, a machine function which returns the student to a previous part of the program.

red tape: computer operations which do not directly contribute to useful data handling, such as extracting of fields, verifying the identification of the input, etc.; in general, the setup (including initialization) and cleanup operations in a program.

redevelopment, urban: *see* **urban renewal.**

redintegration: the act or process of recalling an entire experience through revival by association of ideas relating to an element or portion of that experience. *Comp. w.* **reintegration.**

reduced correlation matrix: *see* **matrix, reduced correlation.**

reduced measure: *syn.* **score, reduced** (1).

reduced score: *see* **score, reduced.**

reductio ad absurdum (re·duk'shi·ō ad ab·sër'dəm): (Lat., lit., "reduction to the absurd") proving a proposition by showing contradiction between its negation and other propositions previously proved or taken for granted, or proving the negation of a proposition by showing contradiction between the proposition and other propositions previously proved or granted.

reduction, cue: *see* **cue reduction.**

reduction, data: *see* **data reduction.**

reductive fallacy: *see* **fallacy, reductive.**

redundancy: (information theory) (1) (of a source) broadly, a property given to a source through an excess of rules (syntax) making it increasingly likely that mistakes in reception will be avoided; (2) that property of a message which reduces the error of prediction for a given event to less than chance through presentation of information about what will come next; also called *t function;* (3) more broadly in current usage, any properties of a message with built-in repetition.

redundant check: *see* **check, redundant.**

reeducation: (1) learning again material that has been forgotten; (2) establishing a new relationship because of some physical, mental, or emotional handicap.

reeducation, auditory: retraining in the interpretation of speech sounds, especially as given to persons with partial deafness, whose residual hearing has become less serviceable through disuse or failure to listen.

reeducation, extension: organized instruction designed for postgraduate professional groups, such as short courses for doctors, bankers, social workers, dentists, or alumni groups. *See* **college, alumni.**

reeducation, psychological: a process involving interaction between a psychologist and client through which undesirable patterns of behavior are replaced by desirable ones.

reel: (1) a circular spool intended to hold a length of magnetic tape or motion-picture film; (2) a unit of measurement of the length of motion-picture films, as follows: (*a*) in the 35-mm size, 1,000 feet of film, running for approximately 11 minutes with sound or 15 minutes without; (*b*) in the 16-mm size, 400 feet of film, running for approximately 11 minutes with sound or 15 minutes without; (*c*) in the 8-mm size, 200 feet of film, running for approximately 8 minutes (silent only).

reel, continuous projection: a device for repetitive showing, without interruption for rethreading, of a loop of film.

reel, supply: a spool which supplies film or tape as it is being recorded or played back; also called *feed reel.*

reel, take-up: a spool which receives film or tape as it is being recorded or played back. *See* **reel, supply; take-up.**

reeling gait: *see* **gait, reeling.**

refectory: a school dining room.

referee: *see* **athletic official.**

reference book: *see* **book, reference.**

reference department: *see* **department, reference.**

reference group: *see* **group, reference.**

reference, ideas of: *see* **ideas of reference.**

reference library: *see* **library, reference.**

reference library, legislative: *see* **library, legislative reference.**

reference list: *syn.* **reading list.**

reference manual, stenographer's: *see* **manual, stenographer's reference.**

reference paper: (composition) a written paper for which the organization of information is required; more formal term is research paper.

reference point: (spec. ed.) a familiar object, sound, odor, temperature, or tactual clue the exact location of which in the environment is known but is more difficult to recognize or perceive than a landmark; used in relation to orientation and mobility for visually limited individuals.

reference reading: *see* **reading, reference.**

reference reading list: *syn.* **reading list.**

reference service, library: the phase of library activity concerned with direct, personal aid to persons in search of information, and various library activities aimed at making information available to library users.

reference system: (math.) lines, or points and lines, used to locate any point or line in a plane or in space.

reference, teacher: (1) a testimonial concerning the professional qualifications of a teacher; (2) a person who is in a position to furnish a statement regarding the professional qualifications of a teacher.

reference vector: *see* **vector, reference.**

reference work: (1) the phase of library work that is directly concerned with assistance to readers in securing information and in using the resources of the library in study and research; (2) the work of a reference department.

referent: that which a sign refers to, stands for, or denotes; used especially of a physical or imagined thing, event, quality, etc.

referential analysis: *see* **analysis, referential.**

referral: (couns.) the act of transferring an individual to another person or agency for specialized assistance not available from the original source.

referral clinic: *see* **clinic; fixed point of referral.**

referral, fixed point of: *see* **fixed point of referral.**

referral form from school to attendance bureau: the standard form by means of which cases for investigation are referred by the schools to the attendance department and which has space for recording the cause of absence, the person or persons interviewed, the pupil's name, birth date, and address, the parents' names, the pupil's complete attendance record to date of issuance, and other relevant information.

referral resources: *see* **resources, referral.**

referral services: *syn.* **counseling, auxiliary services.**

refined death rate: *syn.* **death rate, corrected.**

refined mode: *see* **mode, refined.**

refixation: a fixation of the eye which occurs in reading after the reader has regressed and then returned to the place from which he moved backward.

reflect: (fact. anal.) to reverse the direction of measurement of a test or factor by interchanging positive and negative ends of a variable or factor and to make the corresponding changes in the signs of the correlations and factor loadings.

reflection coefficient: *see* **coefficient, reflection.**

reflective action: *see* **action, reflective.**

reflective morality: *see* **morality, reflective.**

reflective reading: *see* **reading, reflective.**

reflective study: *see* **study, reflective.**

reflective thinking: *see* **thinking, reflective.**

reflex: any constant response that is inherited or present at birth and that follows stimulation of a sensory area connected to the responding mechanism by means of a direct neural pathway; sometimes, but less accurately, considered to be any mechanically determined response. *Syn.* **reflex response.**

reflex, acquired: *syn.* **reflex, conditioned.**

reflex, association: a term used by Bekhterev as a synonym for conditioned reflex. *See* **reflex, conditioned.**

reflex, Babinski: (1) in strict usage, the extension of the big toe upon stimulation of the sole of the foot; (2) loosely, the extension and "fanning" of all the toes. (The reflex is said to be physiological in young infants and pathological in adults.) *Syn.* **Babinski sign.**

reflex, bladder: the involuntary emptying of the bladder. (With suitable training the child by the age of 2 years develops control in the sense of adequate temporal anticipation of the event and ability to control the reflex voluntarily.) *Syn.* **urinary reflex; vesical reflex.**

reflex, chain: a series of integrated reflexes that occur successively following elicitation of the first of the series.

reflex, clasping: *syn.* **reflex, Moro.**

reflex, cochlear-palpebral: closure or tightening of the eyelids in response to sudden or intense auditory stimuli.

reflex, compensatory: an automatic righting movement following any movement that has thrown the body or a part of it out of equilibrium.

reflex, compound: any reflex that may be analyzed into physiological components, all of which may be conditioned or inhibited simultaneously and none of which may be conditioned or inhibited without a secondary influencing of the other components.

reflex, conditioned: a reflex elicited by a stimulus that originally was incapable of causing this reaction but that has been substituted for the originally adequate stimulus by a process of association; thus, a given stimulus S_1 produces a reflex R; another stimulus S_2 will not produce R; by presenting S_1 and S_2 simultaneously, S_2 can be made eventually to call forth R. (The original experiments on conditioned reflex were performed on dogs by a Russian physician, Pavlov, about the beginning of the twentieth century.) *Contr. w.* **reflex, unconditioned.**

reflex, conjunctival: *syn.* **reflex, corneal.**

reflex, corneal: the wink normally caused by touching the eyeball. *Syn.* **conjunctival reflex; lid reflex.**

reflex, Darwinian: a grasping response of the newborn infant; evoked by suspending the child with palms in contact with a bar or rod.

reflex, defense: a protective movement brought about by a stimulus, for example, blinking, the withdrawal of the part of the body affected, or the pushing away of the stimulating object; does not include learned defensive behavior. *Syn.* **protective reflex;** *dist. f.* **defense mechanism.**

reflex, delayed: a reflex that follows the presentation of a stimulus only after a period of time has elapsed, rather than taking place immediately.

reflex, eyewink: *syn.* **reflex, corneal.**

reflex, grasping: (1) involuntary flexing of fingers of the human infant in response to stimulation of the palm of the hand during the first 6 months; contact or pressure stimulation produces closure of the fingers upon the palm; *see* **reflex, palmar;** (2) pull upon the palm or fingers evokes a tendon reflex; *see* **reflex, Darwinian.**

reflex integration: *see* **integration, reflex.**

reflex, knee-jerk: *syn.* **reflex, patellar.**

reflex, lid: *syn.* **reflex, corneal.**

reflex, Moro: the arms and legs of the young infant are drawn up in a pattern described as the clasping or embrace reflex; aroused by various stimuli but described by Moro as occurring when the supporting surface is jarred. *See* **response, startle.**

reflex, ocular-neck: the bending of the neck backward when an infant's eyes are stimulated by a flash of light.

reflex, palmar: an involuntary flexing of the fingers of the infant in response to stimulation of the palm of the hand; sometimes applied to the grasping response of the infant; observed by Hooker in the fetus as early as $11\frac{1}{2}$ weeks.

reflex, patellar: contraction of the quadriceps femoris muscle upon striking the patellar tendon after flexing the knee at a right angle and relaxing the leg. *Syn.* **knee-jerk reflex.**

reflex, plantar: one of a variety of responses evoked when the sole of the foot is stimulated. *See* **reflex, Babinski.**

reflex, protective: *syn.* **reflex, defense.**

reflex, psychogalvanic: *syn.* **psychogalvanic skin response.**

reflex, pupillary: reflex constriction or dilation of the pupil of the eye normally consequent to sudden change of illumination intensity; produced by action of the circular and radial muscle fibers of the iris.

reflex response: *syn.* **reflex.**

reflex, search: *syn.* **response, mouth-orientation.**

reflex, static: a postural response of the body as a whole, oriented in reference to gravity or other forces.

reflex, tactuopalpebral: closure of the eyelids upon contact stimulation of the eyelids or adjacent areas.

reflex, trace conditioned: *see* **conditioned reflex, trace.**

reflex, Umklammerung (ōōm·kläm′ər·ōōng): *syn.* **response, startle.**

reflex, unconditioned: an innate, natural, and unlearned response to a given type of stimulus, for example, the eyewink reflex as called forth by a touch on the cornea or eyelash. *Contr. w.* **reflex, conditioned.**

reflex, urinary: *syn.* **reflex, bladder.**

reflex, vesical: *syn.* **reflex, bladder.**

reflex, visuopalpebral: closure of the eyelids upon stimulation of the eye by a flash of light.

reflexes, concatenated: *see* **reflex, chain.**

reflexive thinking: *see* **thinking, reflexive.**

reflexogenous zone: an area of the body surface in which all points are essentially equivalent for the arousal of a given reflex. *Syn.* **stimulogenous zone.**

reflexology: a study of behavior based on neural foundations; a dominant note in Russian psychology represented by Pavlov and Bekhterev.

Reform religious school, Jewish: *see* **religious school, Jewish Reform.**

reform school: a correctional penal institution (frequently state operated), in which an effort is made to educate, rehabilitate, and correct the maladjustments of youths, usually delinquents, with whom the ordinary public schools have been unable to deal successfully. *Syn.* **reformatory;** *comp. w.* **Borstal institution** (Education in England and Wales).

reformatory: *syn.* **reform school.**

reformatory education: a type of character education provided for delinquents, with a view to character reformation and preparation for earning a living by legitimate means.

refraction: (1) the bending of light rays as they pass obliquely from one medium to another of different density; (2) the bending of the light rays that enter the eyeball so that they converge upon the retina; (3) the power of the spectacle lens (as stated in terms of spheres, cylinders, and prisms) needed to correct errors of refraction in the eye; (4) a term used to describe that part of an eye examination made to determine the power of the artificial lens (glasses) required to neutralize the so-called "error of refraction."

refraction, error of: *syn.* **error, refractive.**

refractive error: *see* **error, refractive.**

refractive projective method: *see* **projective method, refractive.**

refresher course: *see* **course, refresher.**

refresher mathematics: *see* **mathematics, refresher.**

refresher training: *see* **training, refresher.**

refresher training, reserve: *see* **training, reserve refresher.**

refrigeration mechanic: *see* **mechanic, refrigeration.**

refugee child: *see* **child, refugee.**

refugee professor: *see* **professor, refugee.**

refunding: the act of replacing an existing loan or fund by a new loan or fund.

refunding bond: *see* **bond, refunding.**

refunds: obligations to pay back money resulting from payments erroneously made to the school, including overpayments of tuition, fees, tax money, etc.

regard, unconditional positive: a therapist's or counselor's attitude that expresses a warm caring for one's client and involves acceptance of the client's expression of painful, fearful, and/or abnormal feelings as well as of his expression of positive, mature, confident, and social feelings; additionally, it involves an acceptance of and a caring for the client as a separate person, with permission for him to have his own feelings and experiences and to find his own meanings in them. *See* **acceptance; counseling, client-centered; therapy, client-centered.**

regenerate: (data processing) to read information out of a storage unit and then, after amplification, to read it back into the same storage location.

regeneration, social: *see* **social regeneration.**

regent: ordinarily, a member of the controlling board of a state institution or of a state educational system vested with the corporate powers assigned by constitution or legislature to this board.

regimented instruction: *see* **instruction, regimented.**

region, acceptance: the range of values within which an unknown parameter is most likely to be located; therefore, in a statistical study, values that fall within this range call for the acceptance (rather than the rejection) of a null hypothesis; set off from the rejection region or critical region by the confidence limits, which values are fixed by the confidence level. *Syn.* **confidence band; confidence belt; confidence interval;** *see* **confidence level; confidence limits;** *ant.* **region, rejection.**

region, critical: *syn.* **region, rejection.**

region of rejection: *syn.* **region, rejection.**

region of significance: *syn.* **significance region.**

region, rejection: the region in the sampling distribution of a statistical test (for example, t, F, x^2) which is beyond the arbitrarily chosen confidence limits, thereby justifying the rejection of a null hypothesis; thus, the area beyond any selected confidence level. *Syn.* **critical region;** *see* **confidence level;** *ant.* **region, acceptance.**

region, significance: *see* **significance region.**

regional accrediting association: *see* **accrediting association, regional.**

regional agent: a Federal employee engaged in supervisory and inspectional activities and assigned to a region or group of states, active especially in vocational education and in vocational rehabilitation of the physically disabled.

regional association of colleges and secondary schools: an organization made up of representatives of both secondary schools and higher institutions from a group of states, for the consideration of common problems, usually maintaining an accrediting procedure applicable both to secondary schools and to institutions of the collegiate type, such as the North Central Association of Colleges and Secondary Schools.

regional conference: *see* **conference, regional.**

regional dialect: *see* **dialect, regional.**

regional education conference: *see* **conference, regional education.**

regional educational laboratory: *see* **laboratory, regional educational.**

regional fiction: *see* **fiction, regional.**

regional geography: *see* **geography, regional.**

regional library: *see* **library, regional.**

regional school: a school established to serve a region of wider geographical area than the usual civil or educational unit; usually offers specialized educational services that cannot be provided economically in small schools in each of which only a few pupils would need the specialized training.

regionalism: (social studies) the study of the social-economic-political-geographical-historical aspects of different sections of the United States or of any country or of the world.

register: *n.* (1) *syn.* **attendance register;** (2) the various ranges of the human voice, such as head voice, chest voice, etc., determined by quality of sound and the method of its production; (3) in automatic data processing, the hardware for storing a *word* temporarily, usually in the arithmetic and logic unit and not in the storage unit.

register: *v.* (pupil accounting) to enroll officially in a school program.

register, attendance: *see* **attendance register.**

register, average daily: in some states, the average number of pupils on record each day as enrolled in a school. *See* **attendance register.**

register, base: *see* **B-register.**

register, control: *see* **instruction register.**

register, index: *see* **B-register.**

register, instruction: *see* **instruction register.**

register, teachers': (1) a record kept of the name, age, sex, race, and address of each teacher employed by the employing unit and of the class, grade, and basis of the certificate held; (2) occasional *syn.* **record book, teacher's class.**

register, teacher's daily: *syn.* **record book, teacher's class.**

registered bond: *see* **bond, registered.**

registered warrant: *see* **warrant, registered.**

registrar: an official, usually at the college or university level, who is responsible for maintaining records on students.

registration: *syn.* **enrollment.**

registration, continuous: a system by which each pupil is permanently on the school register, instead of being registered anew each year. (Under a system of continuous registration a child who registers in the first grade in September, 1971, would be on the school register automatically at the beginning of school in September, 1972, unless for some legal reason he had withdrawn from school. If, therefore, he is not at school at the opening session in 1972, he is regarded as enrolled but absent. In order to make such registration effective, a continuous school census becomes a necessity.)

registration form: a form for an individual student on which are to be entered the subjects for which the student registers for the coming or current semester, usually providing a place for the signed approval of student, parent, and counselor.

registration, original: *syn.* **enrollment, original.**

registration, teacher: the enrollment of a person as a teacher, as one possessing a teacher's certificate, or as an applicant for a position.

registration, total: the sum of all original registrations for all schools of the area for which total registration is desired, each pupil being counted only once.

registry for the blind, central: a written record of all of the legally blind persons who are known to reside within a state.

regnancy: (psych.) the smallest unit of experience that can be classified as a *gestalt.*

regression: (1) (stat.) the tendency for observations that show a high deviation from the mean and a low degree of variability among themselves in regard to one trait to display wider variability and markedly less deviation (on the average) from the mean in a second trait; (2) the psychological mechanism of retreat from difficulties of the adult world of reality to an imaginary world patterned on an earlier, more comfortable mode of life, as in childhood; normally seen in adults as play and make-believe; (3) (read.) a movement of the eyes backward from right to left along the line of type being read; *dist. f.* **return sweep;** (4) an error in silent or oral reading in which the reader retraces or goes back over what he has been reading; *dist. f.* **return sweep;** (5) (meas.) the tendency for predicted scores to lie closer to the mean that do the scores used to predict them when the two are correlated and expressed on the same standard score scale.

regression, binocular: *syn.* **regression** (3) and (4).

regression coefficient: *syn.* **coefficient of regression.**

regression, coefficient of: *see* **coefficient of regression.**

regression curve: *syn.* **curve, correlation.**

regression, curvilinear: *syn.* **regression, nonlinear.**

regression effect: the tendency for predicted scores to fall toward the mean so that it is never possible to predict scores as high or low as will actually be attained; the result is to present a distribution of predicted scores which is more constricted in dispersion than is true of actually obtained scores; the lower the value of r_{xy}, the narrower will be the distribution of predicted scores compared with actual scores.

regression equation: (1) an equation for predicting the most probable value of one variable, Y, from the known value of another variable, X, or for computing the amount of change in Y for a unit change in X (this is called the regression equation of Y on X, whereas, if the independence-dependence relationship is reversed, the regression equation is that of X on Y); expressed, in the case of linear regression, by the formulas

$$\overline{X} = r_{xy}\frac{\sigma_x}{\sigma_y}(Y - M_y) + Mx$$

$$\overline{Y} = r_{xy}\frac{\sigma_y}{\sigma_x}(X - M_x) + My$$

where r_{xy} equals the coefficient of correlation, σ_x and σ_y

are the standard deviations, and M_x and M_y are the means of the two distributions; *syn.* **multiple linear regression equation;** (2) *syn.* **regression equation, partial.**

regression equation, linear: a formula based on the means and standard deviations of the distributions of two related variables and on the rectilinear correlation coefficient between the two variables that is used in estimating the most probable value on one variable from a known value on the other variable. *See* **regression equation** (1).

regression equation, multiple linear: *syn.* **regression equation** (1).

regression equation, partial: a linear equation for predicting a criterion or dependent variable from two or more independent variables, the coefficients of the independent variables being so chosen as to make the sum of the squares of the differences between the actual and the predicted values of the dependent variable a minimum; an equation expressing the relation between a dependent variable and a number of independent variables. *Syn.* **multiple regression equation; regression equation** (2).

regression estimate: the prediction of unknown values of one variable from known values of another variable or other variables.

regression estimates, matched: *see* **matched regression estimates.**

regression, eye: a return of the eye to a previously fixated syllable, word, or phrase for a repeat fixation. *See* **eye fixation.**

regression frequency: *see* **frequency, regression.**

regression line: the line that describes the relationship between two variables; the locus of the regression equation; the line that is the best fit to the means of the columns (or rows) of a double-entry table. *Syn.* **correlation line; line of regression; line of relation.**

regression line, empirical: *syn.* **line of means.**

regression, linear: the kind of relationship that exists when, for both variables, the locus of the average of one variable corresponding to successive values of the other variable is a straight line. *Syn.* **rectilinear regression;** *contr. w.* **regression, nonlinear.**

regression, monocular: a backward movement of one eye from right to left along the same line of print.

regression, multiple: a statistical method that uses the values of two or more variables to predict the values of another variable. *See* **coefficient of multiple correlation.**

regression, nonlinear: regression in which some curve other than a straight line describes the relationship between two variables. *Syn.* **curvilinear regression; skew regression;** *contr. w.* **regression, linear.**

regression, partial: *see* **coefficient of partial regression.**

regression, rectilinear: *syn.* **regression, linear.**

regression, skew: *syn.* **regression, nonlinear.**

regression weight: *syn.* **coefficient of regression** (1).

regressive movement: *syn.* **regression** (3) and (4).

regressive tax: *see* **tax, regressive.**

regrouping: for the decimal system of numeration, expressing one 10 as ten 1s, one 100 as ten 10s, etc., or vice versa; the term is now used to replace the words *borrowing* and *carrying* in subtraction, for example, as being more descriptive of the processes involved. *See* **decomposition method; equal additions method.**

regular class: *see* **class, regular.**

regular classroom: *see* **classroom, regular.**

regular or nonemergency certificate: *syn.* **certificate, standard.**

regular teacher: a teacher devoting full time to instruction, not serving a probationary or practice-teaching period; one officially recognized as a full-time staff member.

regulation, state: one of a body of rules existing to govern the operation of schools, usually having the force of law, but distinguished from law or statute in being enacted by a state board of education rather than by a legislative body. *See* **administrative code.**

regulations, transportation: *see* **transportation regulations.**

regulatory tax: *see* **tax, regulatory.**

regurgitation: the bringing up of ingested food materials by reverse peristalsis; common in young infants and utilized by adult members of some species of birds to feed their young.

rehabilitation: (1) the act or process of putting into good repair or of restoring to a previous good state; for example, the act of repairing or improving a school plant; (2) the act or process of restoring a person to economic self-sufficiency through education or retraining, often of a vocational nature, or of assisting a person, by whatever means, to make a fresh start after previous failure and to succeed in his new life pattern; (3) restoration to a satisfactory physical, mental, vocational, or social status after injury or illness, including mental illness; the status need not be the same as that preceding the injury or illness.

rehabilitation agency, Federal: *see* **Federal rehabilitation agency.**

rehabilitation, aural: *see* **reeducation, auditory.**

rehabilitation center: *see* **center, rehabilitation.**

rehabilitation, civilian: practical and effective retraining for physically disabled persons for the purpose of returning them to self-sustaining employment. (May include surgical and therapeutic treatment and other medical care, as well as retraining and measures aimed at occupational adjustment.)

rehabilitation counseling: *see* **counseling, rehabilitation.**

rehabilitation counselor: *see* **counselor, rehabilitation.**

rehabilitation, dropout: programs designed to assist individuals who have left educational institutions prior to graduation; these efforts may be directed toward reentry into an educational institution and/or toward suitable employment.

rehabilitation training center: *see* **training center, rehabilitation.**

rehabilitation, vocational: the continuous and coordinated process which strives toward the adaptation and readaptation of disabled persons to suitable employment and which involves early and effective treatment through provision of such medical, psychological, social, educational, vocational, and placement services as may be necessary to individual circumstances to restore or preserve the ability of disabled persons to engage in such employment.

reimbursable class: *see* **class, reimbursable.**

reimbursed consumer and homemaking education program: *see* **program, reimbursed consumer and homemaking education.**

reimbursed course: *see* **course, reimbursed.**

reimbursed program: *see* **program, reimbursed.**

reimbursement: funds made available to educational units (local or state) from larger educational units (state or Federal) to pay in part the costs, already incurred, of vocational or other special educational programs; usually, as in the case of services for exceptional children, the amount is based on excess cost differentials in accordance with appropriate statutes and regulations.

reinforced edition: *syn.* **edition, school.**

reinforcement: (1) strengthening of a conditioned response by reintroducing the original unconditioned stimulus; (2) increase in response strength when that response leads to the reduction of a drive; derived from Thorndike's law of effect; *see* **habit strength; law of effect;** (3) in the foreign language laboratory, reexposure to the desired linguistic utterance to allow the student to compare his response with the correct response and thus to strengthen the likelihood that he will master the correct response.

reinforcement, autogenous (â·toj′ə·nəs): the strengthening of an imperfectly established behavior pattern or stabilization of a recently established one by untutored, "natural" trials or exercise, that is, trials or exercise stimulated by normal physiological and environmental factors. *See* **development, autogenous.**

reinforcement, contingencies of: conditions under which reinforcement will be given; for example, a reinforcer such as a food pellet will be achieved only when the animal used in some experiment presses a lever three times; pressing the lever is the contingency.

reinforcement, continuous: *see* **reinforcement.**

reinforcement, decremental: presentation of reinforcers at a decreasing rate and/or quantity.

reinforcement, direct: *see* **conditioning, operant.**

reinforcement, emotional: (1) the effect of the immediate emotional state of the organism on the response of the organism to a stimulus or situation in increasing the energy of the response; thus, a man who is already angry may respond violently to a given situation, whereas he would respond mildly to the same situation were he in a calm frame of mind; (2) the effect of an already established emotional set regarding a given type of stimulus in increasing the energy of the response to a stimulus of that type; thus, the dog lover, who has a positive emotional set toward dogs, may show a strong approach response upon seeing a dog.

reinforcement, intermittent: a schedule of reinforcement in which groups of nonreinforced trials are interspaced within some regular pattern of reinforcement.

reinforcement, mutual: *see* **mutual reinforcement.**

reinforcement, negative: increase in response strength (usually some kind of avoidance response) occurring when the organism's response leads to decrease of an aversive external stimulus. *See* **reinforcement** (2).

reinforcement, positive: increase in response strength brought about by the kinds of reinforcers that satisfy drives.

reinforcement schedule: the rate and temporal pattern used in giving reinforcers to an organism, such as fixed ratio, variable ratios, etc.

reinforcement, secondary: *see* **reinforcer, conditioned.**

reinforcement theory in counseling: *see* **counseling, reinforcement theory in.**

reinforcement, verbal: words in any form (spoken, heard, seen, written, or thought) which reward a response or strengthen the connection between stimuli and responses.

reinforcer: in *operant conditioning*, the actual stimulus that strengthens a response; may be tangible (candy) or intangible or social (praise).

reinforcer, conditioned: a reinforcer in the form of a secondary type of stimulus such as money, poker chips, bonds, etc., which come to have the properties of an original reinforcer such as food. *Syn.* **secondary reinforcement.**

reinstatement: (1) the act of readmitting a pupil to a class after he has dropped it or been suspended from it; (2) the act of readmitting a pupil to school after he has been suspended for a limited period while still being retained on the roll.

reinstatement, teacher: the restoration to position of a teacher who has been suspended or discharged.

reintegration: the act of restoring one to unity with self or environment after disorientation. *Comp. w.* **redintegration.**

reject: an individual who is disliked by others, as indicated by sociometric techniques.

rejected student: *see* **student, rejected.**

rejection: (1) hostility; (2) a state of desiring to be freed from or to have no identification with; for example, a parent's rejection of a child.

rejection of true hypothesis: *syn.* **error, alpha.**

rejection region: *see* **region, rejection.**

rejection, region of: *syn.* **region, rejection.**

rejoinder: (1) a reply to a question, statement, or action; (2) (for. lang. instr.) may be another question, statement, or an utterance of any kind. *See* **drill, rejoinder.**

rejoinder drill: *see* **drill, rejoinder.**

relata (re•lā′tə): elements as distinguished from the bonds that relate them. *See* **relation.**

related art: *syn.* **art, applied.**

related blocks: (ind. ed.) two or more blocks of a trade having certain common factors of knowledge and skill.

related career areas: *see* **career areas, related.**

related information: (ind. ed.) trade knowledge necessary for a thorough understanding of the equipment, tools, materials, processes, and skills of a given trade. *Syn.* **trade information.**

related instruction, business and office education: *see* **instruction, business and office education related.**

related instruction, distributive education: *see* **instruction, distributive education preparatory.**

related instruction, specific: *see* **instruction, specific related.**

related learnings, general: *syn.* **competencies, general occupational.**

related occupations: *see* **occupations, related.**

related quantities: (1) quantities that have like properties or characteristics; (2) quantities that change together.

related subject: *see* **subject, related.**

related technical instruction: *see* **instruction, related technical.**

relation: (1) any bond or connection that renders one entity in any way relevant to another; (2) (logic) a property of propositions that permits the inference of the truth or falsity of one of them from the truth or falsity of the other or others; (3) one of the categories listed by Aristotle; (4) (math.) any *subject* of a set of ordered pairs; may be chosen arbitrarily or according to some meaningful description such as "the first member of the pair divides the second," or "the first member is parallel to the second;" if the set from which a relation is chosen is denoted by "$A \times B$," the set A is called the *domain* of the relation, the set B the *range.*

relation, functional: *see* **functional relation.**

relation, mathematical: a relation expressing symbolically the correspondence between two or more sets of data or configurational patterns.

relation, self-other: *see* **self-other relation.**

relational thinking: *see* **thinking, relational.**

relations, business-labor: that field of personnel management which deals with the relations between the personal interests of employees, the service objectives of the business organization, and the personal interests of the owners of the business.

relations, externality of: *see* **externality of relations.**

relations, family: *see* **family, relations.**

relations, home-school: *see* **home-school relations.**

relations, human: *see* **human relations.**

relations, interfaith: contacts, both formal and informal, between various groups (religious communities) to promote the common good or to develop mutual understanding.

relations, internality of: *see* **externality of relations.**

relations, international: *see* **international relations.**

relations, student teacher: the associations the student teacher has in a clinical assignment with pupils, parents, colleagues, community representatives, etc. and, more importantly, the close ties between the student teacher and the supervising teacher and the college supervisor.

relations, test of: *see* **test of relations.**

relations, university: activities of a higher education institution connected with disseminating news and information and conducting public relations. *See* **director, public relations.**

relationship: an association or connection in some known and definite manner, thereby providing a basis for transfer of training. *See* **generalization, response; generalization, stimulus; insight.**

relationship, authoritative: *see* **authoritative relationship.**

relationship, cause-effect: *see* **cause-effect relationship.**

relationship, client-counselor: *see* **counseling relationship.**

relationship, counseling: *see* **counseling relationship.**

relationship, functional: *syn.* **functional relation.**

relationship, interpersonal: the intercommunication between the minds of two or more persons; may be mutually facilitating or mutually frustrating.

relationship, means-ends: *see* **means-ends relationship.**

relationship, parent-child: *see* **parent-child relationship.**

relationship, phoneme-grapheme: *see* **phoneme-grapheme relationship.**

relationship, situation-response: (1) the balance between the stimulus pattern that affects an individual at a given moment and during the receptive period and his reaction to the stimulus; (2) the relationship between two or more persons in the same general social setting.

relationship, somatopsychological: the effect on the psychological situation of a person of certain variations in physique that influence the effectiveness of his body as a tool for actions or serve as a stimulus to himself or others.

relationship, spatial: *see* **correlation, spatial.**

relationship, student-college: interaction between student and faculty member or between student and administration; may be harmonious or conflicting.

relationship, subject-object: *see* **subject-object relationship.**

relationship, superordinate: the relationship between one person in a school system and another in a lower position, such as that of the principal to the teacher.

relationship, supervisory-teacher: *see* **supervisory-teacher relationship.**

relationship, therapeutic: a counseling atmosphere created by a therapist that will produce desired results; some therapists advocate a relationship that permits the client much freedom, with the therapist intervening as little as possible; others stress greater activity and interventions on the part of the therapist.

relationship therapy: *see* **therapy, relationship.**

relationships, color and object: *see* **color, objective stage of.**

relationships, family: *see* **family relationships.**

relationships, interpersonal: *see* **interpersonal relationships.**

relationships, intrastaff: *see* **intrastaff relationships.**

relationships, means-ends: *see* **means-ends relationships.**

relationships, peer: relationships with individuals of one's own group; commonly used to indicate especially relationships with a child's or youth's own age group.

relative accuracy: *see* **error, relative.**

relative address: *see* **address, relative.**

relative bar chart: *syn.* **graph, bar.**

relative bar graph. *syn.* **graph, bar.**

relative dispersion: *syn.* **variability, relative.**

relative error: *see* **error, relative.**

relative frequency: *see* **frequency, relative.**

relative humidity: *see* **humidity, relative.**

relative mark: *see* **mark, relative.**

relative mode: *see* **mode, relative.**

relative perceptual span: *see* **perceptual span, relative.**

relative pitch: *see* **pitch, relative.**

relative variability: *see* **variability, relative.**

relative variation, Pearson coefficient of: *see* **coefficient of relative variation, Pearson.**

relativism: a theory taking its cue from the assumption that truth is a property of an interpretation which an observer makes of an object or an event, that truth is relative to or dependent upon observer, observed, and conditions of the observation; a *field* theory. *Contr. w.* **absolutism.**

relativistic ethics: *see* **ethics, relativistic.**

relativistic thinking: *see* **thinking, relativistic.**

relativity, theory of: (philos.) the doctrine that the actual nature and meaning of any thing or situation are relative to its connection with other things or situations and that its nature and meaning may be discovered only by consideration of its position and relations within the system of which it is a part.

relator: a private person upon whose behalf a public officer, such as an attorney general, files information in the case of an action in *quo warranto.*

relaxation therapy: *see* **therapy, relaxation.**

relay: (phys. ed.) organized game or competitive activity between groups that requires the participants of each "side" to perform the same action in turn.

relay, microwave: *see* **microwave relay.**

relearning: learning again what had once been learned and is now forgotten or partly forgotten.

release form: the form used to obtain written permission for use either of pictures taken of persons or of their copyrighted materials. *Syn.* **clearance form.**

release from school: the administrative form used to certify that a child may legally withdraw from school; completed by an authorized school official, usually by the ranking head of the attendance department, under authority delegated to him by the superintendent of schools.

release period: *see* **period, release.**

release print: *see* **print, release.**

release therapy: *see* **therapy, release.**

released time: time granted by public schools to their pupils for the express purpose of attending religious classes conducted under the auspices of their respective denominations or faiths.

relevance: (1) pertinence to a situation, relation, issue, or concern which for any reason is in the focus of attention; significantly related to the problem at hand, or to the problems with which people are struggling in a given period; some different kinds of relevance are logical, moral, cultural, religious; (2) (testing) an estimate that reflects the closeness of agreement between what the test measures—other than chance—and the function it is designed to measure; differs from validity in that validity includes reliability.

relevance, ego: *see* **ego relevance.**

relevance, index of: *see* **index of relevance.**

reliability: (1) worthiness of dependence or trust; (2) (meas.) the accuracy with which a measuring device measures something; the degree to which a test or other instrument of evaluation measures consistently whatever it does in fact measure; *see* **coefficient of equivalence; coefficient of internal consistency; coefficient of reliability; coefficient of stability;** *dist. f.* **validity.**

reliability, alternate-form: the closeness of correspondence, or correlation, between results on alternate (that is, equivalent or parallel) forms of a test; thus, a measure of the extent to which the two forms are consistent or reliable in measuring whatever they do measure, assuming that the examinees themselves do not change in the abilities measured between the two testings. *Syn.* **parallel-form reliability;** *see* **coefficient of reliability; equivalent forms; error, standard; reliability.**

reliability coefficient: *syn.* **coefficient of reliability.**

reliability, coefficient of: *see* **coefficient of reliability.**

reliability, content: (meas.) the consistency with which a test measures whatever it measures; may be estimated by a reliability coefficient based on (*a*) split halves, (*b*) alternate forms, or (*c*) internal consistency.

reliability, homogeneity: agreement on the same occasion and with the same people (commonly, of single items) in the same test; agreement among parts of a test (or battery) designed to measure some one thing.

reliability, index of: *see* **index of reliability.**

reliability, inter-rater: *syn.* **coefficient, objectivity.**

reliability, internal consistency: *see* **consistency, internal.**

reliability, odd-even method of: *see* **reliability, split-halves.**

reliability, parallel-form: *syn.* **reliability, alternate-form.**

reliability, retest: a method of estimating the reliability of a test by correlating the scores made by the same individuals on two administrations of the test.

reliability, Rulon formula for: a formula for estimating the reliability of a test, used especially with IBM test-scoring equipment.

reliability, sample: *syn.* **reliability (2).**

reliability sample: *see* **sample, reliability.**

reliability, scorer: evidence that the same test responses will be similarly scored by different scorers or by the same scorer at different times.

reliability, split-halves: reliability of a test or other variable measured by splitting it into comparable halves (usually the odd-numbered items and the even-numbered items), correlating the scores of the two halves, and applying the Spearman-Brown prophecy formula to estimate the correlation between the entire test (or other variable) and a comparable alternative form; properly applied only when the respective means and variances are equal and when the test is a power test rather than a speed test; *odd-even method of reliability*, *split-halves method*, and *split-test method* are also terms used to indicate reliability arrived at through this method.

reliability, stability: reliability of a test as determined by the method of correlating the scores made by the same individuals on two administrations of the test.

reliable: in testing, having a satisfactory degree of consistency from sample to sample or from trial to trial. *See* **reliability;** *dist. f.* **valid.**

reliable sample: *see* **sample, reliable.**

relief bus: *see* **bus, relief.**

relief map, dissected: *see* **map, dissected relief.**

relief teacher: *syn.* **substitute teacher.**

religion: (1) an inclusive system of beliefs and practices which involves men in association with one another and/or with the transcendent or holy, ordinarily manifested in organized social groups exhibiting common creedal formularies, cultic worship, and codes of conduct; (2) the study of man's encounter with that which is viewed as divine or as ultimate reality.

religion, comparative: the systematic study of the creedal formulations, cultic practices, and codes of conduct of the various religions of the world.

religion, psychology of: *see* **psychology, religious.**

religious art: *see* **art, religious.**

religious brotherhood: *see* **brotherhood, religious.**

religious community: *see* **community** (3).

religious conflict: sharp disagreement or open clash between churches or individuals, often arising from differences in teachings or practices.

religious counseling: *syn.* **counseling, pastoral.**

religious counselor: *see* **counselor, religious.**

religious discrimination: *see* **discrimination, religious.**

religious education: education directed specifically to the inculcation of religious and moral values and ordinarily sponsored by a church or other religious agency.

religious education, adult: *see* **adult education, religious.**

religious education director: *see* **director, religious education.**

religious experience: the encounter between the individual and a transcendent power (or believed-in "holy other"), realized through private prayer, sacramental worship, or other spiritual encounters.

religious factor: *see* **factor, religious.**

religious habit: *see* **habit, religious.**

religious instruction: *see* **instruction, religious.**

religious order: *see* **order, religious.**

religious psychology: *see* **psychology, religious.**

religious school, Jewish: a religious school affiliated with a congregation; the major congregational movements in American Jewish life are Conservatism, Orthodoxy, Reform, and Reconstructionism.

religious school, Jewish Conservative: a religious school affiliated with the Conservative wing in Judaism; this wing stresses "continuity in change," that is, it allows for continuing changes in the patterns and forms of Jewish ritual and observance (provided that the new forms are recognizable outgrowths of the old) and, at the same time, tries to preserve the persistent traditions and historic continuity of Judaism.

religious school, Jewish Orthodox: a religious school affiliated with the Orthodox wing in Judaism which stresses the traditional interpretation of Judaism and of the Jewish ritual observances as prescribed by the *Shulhan Arukh*, the traditional code of Jewish law.

religious school, Jewish Reconstructionist: a religious school affiliated with the Reconstructionist wing in Judaism which stresses in the curriculum the totality of the Jewish experience, religion not being taught as a separate subject but as that complex of concepts and values which pervades the entire Jewish civilization—language, land, history, traditions, laws, etc.; follows a naturalistic interpretation of the Bible and of the role of the Jewish people in history, with an evolutionary interpretation of Jewish practices and emphasis upon the need to adjust to changing conditions; stresses both the Land of Israel as potential spiritual center of world Jewry and the spiritual possibilities of the Diaspora, with special concern for the structure of the Jewish community as the framework within which the Jew finds spiritual fulfillment.

religious school, Jewish Reform: a religious school affiliated with the Reform wing in Judaism which recognizes the nonbinding character of traditional Jewish ritual and ceremonial practice and stresses the right of each generation to interpret Judaism in its own way and to revise the patterns and forms of Jewish observance and ritual as considered necessary in the light of new conditions.

religious society for education: a philanthropic society organized under church auspices primarily to offer some type of education; for example, the Society for Promotion of Christian Knowledge formed in England in 1699.

religious superior: the head or governor of a religious house, who has authority over others by virtue of rank and whose term of office is usually limited to a period of years prescribed by the rules of the order to which he belongs.

religious training: *see* **training, religious.**

religious vocation: *see* **vocation, religious.**

reluctant reader: *see* **reader, reluctant.**

remedial adviser: *syn.* **counselor, personal.**

remedial arithmetic: *see* **arithmetic, remedial.**

remedial class: *see* **class, remedial.**

remedial counselor: *syn.* **counselor, personal.**

remedial education: *see* **adult basic education; teaching, remedial.**

remedial game: a reading exercise that appeals to the child as fun and that is used for corrective purposes.

remedial group method: *see* **group method, remedial.**

remedial gymnastics: *see* **gymnastics, remedial.**

remedial instruction: *see* **instruction, remedial.**

remedial-period plan: a plan that consists in assigning certain periods to each teacher to be spent in remedial work with a group of pupils needing such assistance.

remedial practice: *syn.* **drill, corrective.**

remedial reading: *see* **reading, remedial.**

remedial reading class: *see* **class, remedial reading.**

remedial reading program: *see* **program, remedial reading.**

remedial reading vocabulary: *see* **vocabulary, remedial reading.**

remedial speech: *see* **speech, remedial.**

remedial teacher: a teacher who has the special responsibility of doing all the remedial teaching in a school; usually distinguished from a special classroom teacher in that instruction is carried on with individuals or small groups for short-term intervals, focusing on learning problems believed to be reversible and short-term in nature.

remedial-teacher plan: a plan of remedial instruction that assigns to a single teacher the responsibility for carrying on remedial work either in a school or in a certain division of a school.

remedial teaching: *see* **teaching, remedial.**

remedial vision training: *syn.* **training, orthoptic.**

remediation: corrective teaching. *See* **teaching, remedial.**

rememoration: the relearning of material previously committed to memory.

reminiscence: (1) return of memories from past experience; (2) in learning, an increase in measured recall after a short period without practice.

remission: the abatement for a short period of the symptoms of disease; in cases of mental derangement, a lucid interval.

remitted fee: *see* **fee, remitted.**

remodeling of buildings: the alteration or making over of buildings for the purpose of better adaptation of assigned floor area to instructional purposes.

remote batch mode computing: *see* **computing, remote batch mode.**

remote broadcast: *syn.* **broadcast, on-the-spot.**

remote broadcasting: *see* **broadcast, on-the-spot.**

remote center for student teaching: an affiliated school a considerable distance from a teacher education institution, where student teaching is done, usually during a period of continuous absence from the training institution.

remote control: any mechanical or electrical installation which makes possible the control, operation, and adjustment of such devices as projectors, cameras, tape recorders, electronic learning laboratories, and audio and video systems from adjacent or remote areas by means of special switches and electrical relays.

remote-control broadcast: *see* **broadcast, remote-control.**

remote-control broadcasting: *see* **broadcasting, remote-control.**

remote laboratory: *see* **laboratory, remote.**

remote space: *see* **space, remote.**

remoting, data: *see* **data remoting.**

remuneration, faculty: the compensation paid to teachers for services rendered while employed in a school, school system, or institution of higher education.

Renaissance: a movement or period of vigorous artistic and intellectual activity; the transitional movement in Europe between medieval and modern times, beginning in the fourteenth century in Italy and lasting into the seventeenth century; marked by a humanistic revival of classical influence expressed in a flowering of the arts and literature and by the beginnings of modern science.

renewal, urban: *see* **urban renewal.**

renewals: expenditures necessary because of depreciation and wear to restore buildings and make improvements on equipment without increasing their value. (Any amount by which their value is increased over the original by such renewals should be treated as physical plant additions.)

rental book: *see* **book, rental.**

renunciation: in psychoanalytic theory, refusal of the *ego* to seek the satisfactions demanded by the *id.*

reopener: a provision calling for reopening a current contract at a specified time for negotiations on stated subjects, such as salary increases, pensions, health and welfare benefits, etc.

reorganization, school: (1) a change in the internal organization of a school, as from the eight-four to the six-three-three plan; (2) a change in the geographic area included in an attendance area or administrative unit; *see* **annexation; consolidation** (2).

reorganization, school district: *see* **school district reorganization.**

reorganization, secondary school: (1) the departure from the traditional eight-four, seven-four, or seven-five plan of school organization, involving the shortening of the period of elementary education and the recognition of an upper and lower division of the period of secondary education; involves the adoption of the six-three-three, six-six, six-four-two, six-four-four, or some similar plan; (2) with respect to curriculum, adjustment of secondary education to the maturational level of the pupils, usually by beginning secondary education at an earlier grade than that provided for in the traditional eight-four, seven-four, or seven-five plan, and involving also changes in matters of objectives, adjustment of the curriculum to individual differences, and the closer articulation of secondary education both with elementary and with higher education.

reorganized elementary school: *see* **elementary school, reorganized.**

reorganized high school: *see* **reorganization, secondary school.**

reorganized high school, four-year: a high school of four grades, not grades 9 to 12 or 8 to 11 in an 11-year school system, but some such combination as 7 to 10 or 8 to 11 in a 12-year school system.

reorganized high school, two-year: a 2-year secondary school that has developed out of the change from an eight-four or seven-four plan of organization, usually made up of grades 8 to 9, though the term may well be applied to a school of grades 9 to 10 or grades 11 to 12. (Perhaps incorrectly, the term is frequently applied to a school made up of grades 7 to 8 or 6 to 7 and possessing many of the characteristics of a junior high school.)

reorganized school: a somewhat ambiguous synonym for consolidated school. *See* **consolidated school.**

reorganized school, six-year: a secondary school including six grades, usually grades 7 to 12.

reorganized secondary school: *syn.* **reorganized high school;** *see* **reorganization, secondary school.**

repair garage: *syn.* **garage, maintenance.**

repair inspector's report: *see* **report, repair inspector's.**

repairs: (1) the restoration to a serviceable or operating condition of buildings, mechanical equipment, furniture, books, etc., that have been damaged or worn by use; (2) expense necessary because of damage to and ordinary wear and tear of buildings, improvements other than buildings, and equipment to restore them to a condition suitable for use or occupancy. *Syn.* **maintenance.**

repeatable factor: *see* **factor, repeatable.**

repeater: a pupil who has repeated or is currently repeating the work of a grade or part of a subject at some designated level of difficulty.

repeater screen: *see* **screen, repeater.**

repetition for self-assurance: (art ed.) the type of repetition that is the result of a natural desire to feel mastery and control; such repetition occurs especially in children's drawings during the schematic developmental stage; this is not rigid repetition but shows changes whenever a special experience incites them. *See* **developmental stage, schematic; schema** (2).

repetition, law of: *syn.* **law of disuse.**

repetition, stereotyped: *see* **repetition for self-assurance.**

repetition stuttering pattern: *see* **stuttering pattern, repetition.**

repetitious speech: *syn.* **cataphasia.**

replacement drill: *see* **drill, replacement.**

replacement fund: *see* **fund, replacement.**

replacement index: *syn.* **reproduction rate, net** (2).

replacement training center: *see* **training center, replacement.**

replacement training unit: *see* **training unit, replacement.**

replacement value: *see* **value, replacement.**

replacements: expenditures as a result of which plant assets are replaced by assets of the same kind or performing the same function and having the same value. (If the asset acquired has a greater value, the difference in cost should be treated as a *capital outlay.*)

replicate: to repeat or reproduce; in research to perform the identical operations on a number of different groups, as, for example, when the research design is such that only a small number of cases or observations can be included in a single replication, but when larger numbers of cases or observations will permit more precise statistical tests of significance.

replication: (1) the act or process of subdividing a major experiment into a number of parts, each of which is carried out under essentially similar conditions, but with the different parts so arranged in space or time as to reduce errors due to extraneous factors; (2) one of the subdivisions of a major experiment as in 1 above; (3) a copy or duplicate; in research, any one of several identical studies made in order to increase the number of cases or observations to the point where statistical testing is feasible; *see* **replicate.**

replicative mode: *see* **mode, replicative.**

report: an oral or written account usually of an official character, such as the return of a committee or officer to a superior or an account rendered to a board, a committee, or the public. (Unlike a *record*, a report is not a primary, but a derived, statement.)

report, accident: (1) an administrative form on which school accidents are reported to the central office; (2) a written account by a teacher or other employee to a principal, a principal to his superior, or a superintendent to a board of education giving details concerning an accident occurring in school or on the way to or from school.

report, age-grade: a statistical summary of pupils showing the numbers in each grade or half grade that corresponds to their age and the numbers retarded or accelerated chronologically.

report, age-grade-progress: a statistical summary of pupils showing for each grade the number of pupils of different ages and the number of pupils who have spent different numbers of terms in school.

report, annual: a report issued according to tradition and legal stipulation by the responsible school officer at the end of the fiscal year or school year, for purposes of record and interpretation of the schools to the public; may contain data or progress accounts on finance, matériel, personnel, and instruction, according to legal requirements and local policy; serves as a means of reporting stewardship, for a recapitulation of the fiscal condition of the school system, and for relating the more important educational problems to their financial aspects.

report, annual tabulation: an annual statistical summary of a number of reports handled by an attendance department; includes totals by grades, causes of absence, number of times each case was reported, etc.

report, annual transportation: a summary report prepared by an official in charge of transportation; may include such data as number of pupils transported, routes taken, traffic conditions, discipline of pupils, number of buses in service, condition of buses, days of service, number of schools to which transportation was provided, bus insurance, and other matters pertaining to the transportation of pupils; may be supplemented by explanations, interpretations, graphs, and suggestions for the improvement of service.

report, attendance: (1) a public, written statement made by the proper school officials concerning the presence, absence, and tardiness of pupils during a given period of time; (2) a written report made by a teacher to the principal or other designated officer concerning the presence, absence, and tardiness of pupils in that teacher's classes during a given period of time.

report, board committee: a report prepared by a subcommittee of a board of education for the board as a whole.

report, book: (1) a report usually employed in extensive reading to summarize the results of such reading; (2) *syn.* **review, book.**

report, business: an executive report dealing with business activities relating to finance, school plant, or supply services.

report, cafeteria: a report by the manager of the cafeteria stating existing conditions as to finances, service, food, equipment, and needs.

report card: formal, written notification to parents and/or guardians reporting achievement or progress of a student in various aspects of the school program; may include such items as subject-matter achievement, pupil's attitudes, effort, and attendance. *Syn.* **grade card.**

report, case: an individual report presenting information about a developing young person who has been observed over a period of time, including any available data on school achievement, results of tests administered, and similar pertinent items of information; should not be confused with *case history* or *case study.*

report, class: a report, complete up to the date of issuance, containing information concerning the progress of a class taught by a particular teacher.

report, clinical: a description of the performance of an individual on tests and in other situations when behaviors are observed and specific traits can be inferred so that the whole individual may be better understood.

report, comprehensive student: (couns.) a method of summarizing data about an individual by giving a cumulative picture of the total personality in full-length study of the individual that shows his development and the interrelations of the factors governing his current status. *See* **case history; case study.**

report, consolidated: a summary of the data and statistics of several individual reports on the same general subject.

report, corporal-punishment: an administrative form on which information relative to corporal punishments is sent to the central office.

report, custodian's: an account prepared by the custodian relating to the maintenance of the school plant, including information on work done and general existing conditions and recommendations for repairs, improvements, and equipment.

report, dental: a report made by the school dentist in which he states the number of patients treated in a given period, nature of the work done (including actual dental work, demonstrations to pupils, etc.), anticipated needs for the coming period, requests for material and supplies, and suggestions for the improvement of service.

report, descriptive: a report that recounts, characterizes, or classifies material; an enumeration of the essential qualities of a subject.

report, dismissal: *syn.* **record, dismissal** (1).

report, driver's daily: a written statement prepared daily by a school bus driver giving statistical information, time schedule, pupils transported, condition of bus and roads, etc.

report, examination: a report of ratings attained by students in an examination.

report, experimental research: a recapitulation of controlled research, giving purpose, defining terms, outlining the study, noting results, and carrying a bibliography.

report, final: a report made at the termination of a project, program, term, semester, or school year.

report, financial: *see* **financial report.**

report, good-work: an intraschool form used by a teacher for reporting satisfactory scholarship or school progress.

report, health: (1) a statement relative to the physical condition of a pupil, based on a report from a physician, sent to parents, teachers, or school officials; (2) a statistical or descriptive statement issued by the school health department showing in general the health conditions in the schools; data may cover personnel, plant, or both.

report, health director's annual: a comprehensive yearly report of the health status of pupils and employed personnel and of the conditions of school buildings conducive or detrimental to good health; usually includes recommendations for improvement.

report, home-call: (1) a printed administrative form used by the attendance division in making its summary report on home calls; (2) a verbal or written statement of findings, activities, and recommendations in connection with a visit to a pupil's home by an authorized person.

report, home-condition: an administrative form used by the attendance division in describing the social and economic status of a pupil's home.

report, inventory: a report giving details as to amount, kind, and condition of supplies, textbooks, and equipment on hand.

report, library: (1) any report of the activities, procedures, or statistics of a library; may deal with a wide variety of topics, such as acquisition and circulation of books and other materials, analysis of book stock, complete or partial inventories, costs, methods, personnel, and services; (2) a report assigned as part of class work in a school or college, requiring extensive use of library facilities and materials.

report, life-history: an account of the development of an individual or of the use of some object, such as a building or an item of equipment.

report, medical: a report by a medical officer giving the health status of pupils and other personnel and stating number and types of examinations, plant inspections, and visits; may include recommendations for improvement.

report, monthly: a monthly summary of activities by a pupil, teacher, principal, or other worker or group of workers responsible for carrying out a program in a school or school system.

report, monthly health: a report prepared by a health official to define the health status of pupils and teachers and the sanitary conditions of a school; includes recommendations for improvement of conditions.

report, nurse's annual: a report prepared by a school nurse at the end of the fiscal or school year; includes data on the general health of pupils, examinations, special cases, assistance to school physicians, home visits, and other information within the purview of the department.

report, nurse's monthly: a monthly summary of all matters within the jurisdiction of the school nurse; includes information pertaining to examinations, assistance given the school physician, home visits, special cases, and group instruction.

report of visits, supervisor's annual: a yearly recapitulation of the supervisor's visits to schools, teachers visited, recommendations made to teachers, suggestions and recommendations to the superintendent, special programs, educational progress, and matters pertaining to special departments.

report of visits, supervisor's monthly: a written account giving such information as the number of schools visited during a month by the supervisor, the groups and teachers observed, recommendations to teachers for improvements, recommendations to the superintendent about the work of teachers, and other information relating to the special field of work.

report, periodic: a report issued regularly for a stated period, such as a day, week, month, or year.

report, plant-construction progress: a report showing the stage of completion of a construction job, usually including the percentage of completion under each class of work, weather conditions, and number and classification of workers, correlated with the contractual completion dates; photographs taken at various stages of progress are often included.

report, poor-work: an intraschool form used by a teacher for reporting unsatisfactory scholarship or school progress.

report, preliminary: a preparatory or introductory report, frequently tentative in nature.

report, progress: a report submitted prior to the completion of a task or program for the purpose of defining the stage to which it has advanced. *See* **report, plant-construction progress; report, school progress.**

report, pupil probation: *see* **probation report, pupil.**

report, repair inspector's: a report to the superintendent of buildings making specific recommendations for repairs or for the approval or rejection of repairs made.

report, scholarship: a report summarizing the scholarship record of an individual or group.

report, school: (1) a form or blank for recording data concerning a group of pupils, for transmission from one school official to another; usually intended for temporary use, but occasionally filed and retained for a number of years; (2) a report about a pupil, sent by the school to the parents; *see* **report to parents.**

report, school progress: a report that summarizes the rate of advancement of pupils from grade to grade, usually by means of an account of the numbers making normal progress, accelerated progress, and retarded progress.

report, semester: a report issued at the end of each semester.

report, sick: notification of the illness of a pupil sent by the teacher to the principal, medical officer, school nurse, or board of health.

report, Spahr: a study of technical institutes made under the auspices of the Society for the Promotion of Engineering Education (now the American Society for Engineering Education) in 1931.

report, special: a report issued on demand or as the occasion warrants.

report, state: *see* **state report.**

report, state school: (1) in general, a school report, whether compiled by local school districts for the state office, by state departments of education for the Federal office, or by state departments of education for the use of the local school districts within the state; (2) more specifically, a report prepared by the chief state school officer. [Most important is the biennial report, submitted, usually, in the form of a communication to the governor of the state; commonly includes (*a*) a list of state educational officials; (*b*) a report of progress made by the schools of the state; (*c*) recommendations for executive and legislative action; (*d*) reports of administrative subdivisions of the state department of education; (*e*) a report dealing with institutions of higher education; and (*f*) a statistical section, including a classified summary of the receipts and disbursements of school districts, the value of school property, apportionment of state and Federal funds, and numerical data concerning pupils and teachers.]

report, statistical: a report devoted largely to the statistical presentation of facts.

report, student: (1) any report originating with a student; (2) a report dealing with students.

report, superintendent's: an executive report prepared by the superintendent of schools for the board of education or, in some states, for the state school authority.

report, survey: a report that summarizes the findings and recommendations of a school survey.

report, tardiness: (1) a report submitted to a principal by a teacher, consisting of a summary of cases of tardiness in his classes over a specified period; (2) a report made by a principal in summarizing the tardiness statistics in his school for a term or a year.

report, teacher: (1) any report prepared by a teacher, usually for the principal or superintendent; (2) a report concerning a teacher or teachers.

report, teacher-observation: a written or oral account of a teacher's work by a principal, supervisor, or other visitor, giving information as to teaching techniques, classroom management, and similar problems; suggestions for improvement or commendation for work well done may be included.

report, teacher's daily absence and tardiness: a report of the number of pupils absent and tardy at a given session or period, usually rendered at the beginning of each daily session or period.

report, technical: a report giving details and results of a specific investigation of a scientific or technical problem.

report, theoretical research: a report not concerned with materials, apparatus, or method, but one that states the purpose of an investigation, defines the terms employed, shows reason for undertaking the study, reviews previous investigations, and indicates the limits set by the investigator.

report to attendance officer, employer's: (1) a report by an employer giving such information about student employees as type and amount of work done, regularity of attendance, industry, punctuality, and attitude; (2) legal acknowledgment of employment or discharge of an employee who is a minor.

report to bureau, attendance officer's: an account of the activities of the attendance officer submitted to the attendance bureau, giving such data as number of cases investigated and reasons for absences; submitted daily or at other stated intervals.

report to parents: a statement to parents concerning the progress made by their children in school, whether by use of school marks or by teacher-parent conferences.

report to principal, attendance officer's: a written account submitted to the principal, giving the reasons for absences of pupils; information about such matters as disposition of each case may be included.

report to superintendent, principal's annual: a written report prepared by a principal at the end of the academic year; may include data as to educational progress, anticipated needs for the coming year, pupil enrollment, transfers, general health conditions, health of pupils and other personnel, and other matters pertaining to the interests of the school.

report to superintendent, principal's monthly: an account rendered each month by a principal to a superintendent, covering school enrollment, health of pupils and personnel, general health conditions prevailing in the school, repairs, supplies, educational progress, and proposals for future programs.

report, transfer: notification of the transfer of a pupil from one school or class to another, usually transmitted directly but sometimes sent through the office of attendance or that of the superintendent of schools.

report, transportation: a report prepared at periodic intervals by the driver of a school bus or other agent for the principal or superintendent, giving number of pupils transported, routes taken, traffic conditions, discipline of pupils, number of buses in service, condition of buses, number of days of service, and other pertinent information.

report, truancy: a report of the cases of unauthorized or illegal absence from school; may be (a) a report of individual truancy by a teacher to the principal, (b) the principal's report to the attendance officer, or (c) a summary report of the attendance officer to the chief attendance officer or to the superintendent.

report, wage-and-hour: a form used to record the wages earned and the total hours worked by cooperative part-time students in business and office education, distributive education, or other areas of vocational education.

reporting course: see course, reporting.

reporting period: see period, reporting.

reporting practice: the procedure by which a school reports pupil achievement to parents.

reporting system: (1) the method adopted by a school system for reporting pupil progress to parents; (2) a plan adopted by a school, a district, or a state for collecting and compiling statistical data from its various administrative units. (Though each of the 50 states has a different reporting system, efforts have been made, with considerable success, to harmonize these systems with respect to definition of terms and classification of items, in order to improve the trustworthiness of statistical comparisons between states and to give greater accuracy to summaries derived from the state reports, such as the Biennial Survey of Education, compiled by the U.S. Office of Education.)

reporting, test: see test reporting.

reporting unit: see unit, reporting.

reports, office: see office reports.

repoussé work (rə·pŌŌ·sā′): metal, formed, shaped, or ornamented with patterns in relief, made by hammering or pressing on the reverse side.

representation: any reproduction such as a drawing, painting, photograph, or model intended to resemble, to represent, or to be a likeness of an object, person, scene, etc.; drawing, modeling, or construction in which a likeness of something is made, either in two or in three dimensions.

representation, dramatic: a learning experience that involves planning, action, and evaluation by the group.

representation election: see election, representation.

representation, graphical: see graphic method.

representation, head-feet: (art ed.) a child's first symbol of a man in which he draws a circular shape or scribble for the head and longitudinal lines for the legs; such a representation shows his way of satisfying his desire for establishing a relationship between his drawing and a man.

representation, idiographic: (art ed.) representation according to knowledge rather than visual reference.

representation, linear: (for. lang.) lines drawn to reflect the intonation pattern of a given utterance.

representation, minority: see minority representation.

representation, orthoscopic: (art ed.) the drawing of the preferred view or of that view most indicative of the object.

representation, pseudorealistic: see developmental stage, pseudorealistic.

representation, realistic: see realism in art.

representation, space-time: (art ed.) the tendency in children's drawings to represent several time phases in one space, such as different actions, different time sequences, plane and elevation, side view and front view, or inside and outside.

representation, x-ray: (art ed.) the type of representation in which the child depicts the inside and outside of objects simultaneously, usually because the inside and outside were both important in the experience underlying the representation.

representational stages in child art: syn. art, developmental stages in child.

representative data: see data, representative.

representative drawing: see representation.

representative materials: syn. materials, semiconcrete.

representative sample: see sample, representative.

representative stage: that period in the development of the child's ability to draw when he attempts to draw objects as he sees them; usually occurs after the fifth or sixth year.

representative supervision: see supervision, representative.

representative symbol: syn. symbol (5).

representative theory of knowledge: see knowledge, representative theory of.

representativeness: (1) as applied to a test, the degree to which it samples every aspect of the field or outcome to be tested; (2) as applied to sampling, the degree to which the sample possesses essentially the same characteristics as the total population or universe from which it is taken.

repression: according to psychoanalytic theory, the unconscious mechanism of rejection by the ego of perceptions and ideas having painful and disagreeable content.

reprint: a book, document, or article from a larger publication reprinted for distribution subsequent to its original publication.

reproducer, card: see card reproducer.

reproducibility: the property of a test whereby it is possible to predict the subject's response to any item if his total score is known; perfect reproducibility is as rare as perfect correlation and depends on it. See coefficient of reproducibility.

reproducing punch: see punch, reproducing.

reproduction rate, net: (1) another measure, in addition to the rate of natural increase, of the extent to which a given population is growing; it represents the number of daughters that would be born to 1,000 newly born girls if the birth and death rates of a given year were assumed to continue through their child-bearing period; (2) the ratio which the fertility ratio of a given population must bear to the mortality rate so as to produce an exactly stable population; syn. replacement index.

reproductive inhibition: see inhibition, reproductive.

republican form of government: see government, republican form of.

reputation: the estimation of a person's character on the part of those with whom he comes in contact.

reputation test: see test, reputation.

required course: syn. constant n. (4).

required reading: see reading, required.

required subject: syn. constant n. (4).

requisition: a demand or request for specified articles or services, usually from one department to the purchasing officer or to another department.

requisition, labor: (school admin.) an authorization and request for the employment section of the personnel department to procure certain personnel for the current needs of a department or other organizational component.

requisition order: a list of equipment and supplies requested by a teacher or school official for use in a classroom or school building.

requisition order, classroom: an official itemized list of instructional supplies desired by a teacher and submitted to one in line of authority for consideration and approval.

requisition, stores: (school admin.) a clerical instrument that conveys written authority for the withdrawal of materials or supplies from an organization's stores.

rerouting: the act of changing the regular operating circuit of a school bus.

resatellization: in personality theory, the idea that after the child has broken away from satellizing with his parents, he resatellizes, that is, identifies, with his age mates. *See* **desatellization; satellization.**

rescission: the termination of a contract, usually because of fraud.

rescuing pole: *syn.* **pool hook.**

research: (philos.) careful, critical, disciplined inquiry, varying in technique and method according to the nature and conditions of the problem identified, directed toward the clarification or resolution (or both) of a problem. (Philosophical dimensions or aspects of research have to do with locating hidden assumptions, presuppositions, and value judgments implicit in the treatments of problems, with criteria of evaluation and of admissible evidence, with selection of methods appropriate to various investigations, and with the basis for selection and interpretation of data, etc.) *See* **problem.**

research, action: a firing-line or on-the-job type of problem solving or research used by teachers, supervisors, and administrators to improve the quality of their decisions and actions; it seeks more dependable and appropriate means of promoting and evaluating pupil growth in line with specific and general objectives and attempts to improve educational practices without reference to whether findings would be applicable beyond the group studied.

research, analytical: research that has for its purpose the discovery of the composition and structure of a given case, object, or variable. (Practically all research is analytical to a large extent; a number of types of research may be regarded as highly analytical, especially case study.)

research and development: includes basic and applied research and their utilization; in industry and in the professions, basic and applied research and development are closely interrelated.

research and experimentation: (ind. arts) an individual-centered method of teaching industrial arts with the scientific method of problem solving being the principal element and student curiosity the key motivating stimulus.

research, applied: research derived from fundamental or basic research and directed toward demonstrating that the findings from fundamental research may be applied in new and presumably useful processes.

research, basic: research directed toward correlating sense experience with a total structure of thought and understanding in such a way that the resulting coordination is complete and convincing; description of natural phenomena. *Syn.* **fundamental research; pure research.**

research, biblical: the scholarly study of the forms, origins, texts, etc., of the books of the Bible, using critical methods of investigation similar to those employed in the fields of history and literature.

research bureau: *syn.* **bureau of research.**

research, consumer: research conducted by governmental agencies, producers, private research agencies, or individuals to determine (*a*) the needs and desires of consumers, (*b*) the proper specifications of products for specific purposes, and (*c*) the relative efficiency of specific products to satisfy consumers' wants, with reference also to their relative cost.

research, curriculum: a process of systematic investigation and evaluation in the selection and placement of school material, activity, and experience.

research, deliberative: investigation that involves examination and evaluation of findings (often diverse and conflicting) of a number of studies or of various points of view concerning values or interpretations; the procedure involves discussion or active interchange of opinion, with a presumed progressive clarification of issues and values,

with the purpose of arriving at tenable conclusions. *See* **research, synthetic.**

research, director of: *see* **director of research.**

research, educational: study and investigation in the field of education or bearing upon educational problems. *See* **bureau of research; research.**

research, endowment of: *see* **endowment of research.**

research, experimental: research study in which experimentation is the principal method involved.

research, fundamental: *syn.* **research, basic.**

research, guidance: the systematic attempt to solve problems pertaining to guidance through the use of recognized research procedures.

research, historical: the type of research that has as its chief purpose the ascertaining of facts that fit into a significant time sequence and the relationships among these facts; usually concerned in a broad way with some delimited subject, delineating each aspect of the subject as it throws light on other aspects or on the general story; normally concerned with causes, but these may have to be imputed. (The term implies that a story will be reconstructed from observations that were not made especially for the purpose of the study; sources must be discovered and evaluated as to authenticity and accuracy.)

research, institutional: research conducted on a campus and designed to improve understanding of the institution and its operation. *See* **bureau of research.**

research, investigative: research that has for its purpose the discovery of conditions or causes of conditions that exist or have recently existed at a particular time and place; a loose term, implying concern with phenomena of local or temporary character, in contrast to *experimental research* designed to discover universal or permanent generalizations.

research, judgmental: research that devolves upon judgment. *See* **research, deliberative; research, synthetic.**

research librarian: *see* **librarian, research.**

research library: *see* **library, research.**

research, marketing: the application of scientific principles to observational, experimental, historical, and survey methods in a careful search for more accurate knowledge of consumer and market behavior so that more effective marketing and distribution may be developed.

research method: an instructional procedure the desired outcomes of which are achieved by setting up situations in such a form that the student gathers and organizes information, draws his own conclusions on the basis of data, and compares his results with those obtained by other investigators.

research monograph: *see* **monograph, research.**

research, motivation: a technique whereby a search is made for consumers' hidden hopes and aspirations and deeply imbedded anxieties and fears which advertisers can use; employed by nearly every major industry which engages psychologists to pierce consumers' minds and recommend advertising themes.

research, occupational: in guidance, the systematic collection of facts about employment and employment opportunities for the purpose of presenting an accurate picture of the availability, requirements, location, outlook, and remuneration to those seeking jobs.

research, operations: (1) a scientific method of providing executives with a quantitative basis for decisions regarding the operations under their control; (2) (mil. ed.) the analytical study of military problems, undertaken to provide responsible commanders and staff agencies with a scientific basis for decision on action to improve military operations; also known as operational research and operations analysis; (3) in computerized data processing, the use of analytic methods adapted from mathematics for solving operational problems.

research problem: a question accepted and stated for the purpose of guiding research directed toward its solution; must be delimited with respect to time, space, institutions, etc.

research, product: (curric.) research in the field of curriculum aimed at the systematic improvement of school programs and materials that are reproducible.

research professor: *see* **professor, distinguished.**

research program, International Geophysical Year: *see* **International Geophysical Year research program.**

research, pure: *syn.* **research, basic.**

research, quantitative: research involving determination (as precise as practicable) of number and amount, as opposed to unsupported assumptions concerning quantity.

research, reading: investigations into the psychology and pedagogy of reading.

research, scientific: a searching for new relations within a total structure of thought and understanding (for example, a theory of learning) and for a correlation of discoveries in a way that is in agreement with the total of observed properties or behaviors; an assumed relation stated as hypothesis gives specificity and direction to the search. *See* **research, applied; research, basic.**

research, service: investigations, generally of the survey or experimental types, conducted by teachers, supervisors, or a designated group to improve school practices and procedures.

research, small-group: empirical and experimental work by sociologists and other social scientists on interpersonal statics, structure, interaction, and change within and among small groups; a field of research that overlaps practical educational enterprises such as group dynamics, leadership training, and community services.

research, synthetic: research of the deliberative type that has for its purpose the synthesis of findings originating in a number of different studies and perhaps emanating from diverse schools of thought; involves comparison, evaluation, and interpretation, usually with respect to a larger frame of reference that will permit reconciliation of conflicts or inconsistencies and impart new meaning to the whole. *Contr. w.* **research, analytical.**

resentment: an emotional reaction characterized by animosity or indignation aroused by an act or attitude on the part of another that concerns the individual.

reservation boarding school: *see* **boarding school, reservation.**

reserve: an amount set aside out of surplus to cover such items as outstanding orders, working capital, depreciation, renewals and replacements of plant, and other contingencies.

reserve, depreciation: a fund set aside to replace assets that are reducing in value owing to obsolescence and wear and tear through use; usually a percentage fixed in advance. *See* **reserve.**

reserve duty training: *see* **training, reserve duty.**

reserve fund: *see* **fund, reserve.**

reserve, insurance: (1) funds set aside to cover losses that may occur by fire or other hazard, used in some larger cities in lieu of regular insurance polices; (2) an amount set aside out of surplus, estimated as the sum necessary at any given time to meet all claims that might be made against insurance policies currently in force.

reserve, interim: a reserve fund to meet expenditures during a period prior to the receipt of revenues. (School taxes are frequently paid at a certain time, whereas expenditures are more or less regular; it is frequently necessary, therefore, to provide funds during the interim before the next tax collection date.)

Reserve Officers' Training Corps (ROTC): an organization provided for under the National Defense Acts of 1916 and 1920 with amendments and more recently by the Reserve Officers' Training Corps Vitalization Act of 1964; composed of students taking military training in civilian educational institutions in which ROTC units have been established; training qualifies selected students on graduation for appointment as officers in the various branches of the United States military forces. (Strictly speaking, ROTC applies to Army-controlled units, AF-ROTC to Air-Force-controlled units, and NROTC to Navy-controlled units, but except where the distinction is important ROTC includes all three units.)

reserve refresher training: *see* **training, reserve refresher.**

reserved powers: *see* **powers, reserved.**

residence: (1) personal presence in a fixed and permanent abode; (2) the abode where one actually lives.

residence assistant: *see* **assistant, residence.**

residence center: *see* **center, residence.**

residence counselor: *see* **counselor, residence.**

residence credit: *see* **credit, residence.**

residence, director of: *syn.* **director of dormitory.**

residence hall: *syn.* **dormitory.**

residence, head of college: *see* **director of dormitory.**

residence house: a building devoted to use as living quarters for students and containing sleeping rooms, library, clubrooms, and sometimes a dining room. *See* **dormitory; fraternity house; hall, residence; sorority house.**

residence requirements: the minimum period during which one must be in attendance at a college or university in order to receive a degree from it.

residence, rural-urban: (pupil accounting) a category used for pupils who have two permanent residences, one in an unincorporated area and one in a population center of 50,000 or more.

resident: a person who resides in a place. (A child is considered a resident of a school district "if he has gone there in good faith for the purpose of acquiring a home and not for the purpose of taking advantage of school privileges.")

resident child: *see* **child, resident.**

resident children per square mile: in pupil accounting, the total number of resident children, by age, who live in a given attendance area or administrative unit, divided by the number of square miles in the attendance area or administrative unit.

resident college: *see* **college, resident.**

resident instruction: *see* **instruction, resident.**

resident pupil: *see* **pupil, resident.**

resident student: *see* **student, resident.**

resident teacher: *syn.* **supervising teacher.**

residential adult center: *see* **center, residential.**

residential adult school: *see* **center, residential.**

residential center: *see* **center, residential.**

residential college: *syn.* **college, resident.**

residential conference: *see* **conference, residential.**

residential institution: *see* **institution, residential.**

residential school: a boarding school generally thought of as offering services to blind or other atypical children of school age, having a curriculum similar to that of the public elementary and high schools but employing special teaching methods and equipment.

residential school facility: *see* **school facility, residential.**

residential school for the blind: a boarding school for blind and in some cases also for partially seeing children of school age, having a curriculum similar to that of the public elementary and high schools but employing special teaching methods and equipment.

residential school for the deaf: a self-contained educational program which provides a complete educational and boarding school program for the hearing handicapped.

residential school placement: *see* **placement, residential school.**

residential school, private: a boarding school for deaf, blind, or otherwise handicapped children, operated on a private or nonpublicly supported basis.

residential treatment facility: *see* **facility, residential treatment.**

residents, rural farm: *see* **population, rural farm.**

residents, rural nonfarm: *see* **population, rural nonfarm.**

residents, urban: *see* **population, urban.**

residual: *syn.* **error, residual.**

residual error: *see* **error, residual.**

residual hearing: *see* **hearing, residual.**

residual impairment: *see* **impairment, residual.**

residual masking: *syn.* **fatigue, auditory.**

residual matrix: *see* **matrix, residual.**

residual procedure: a method of estimating migration for intercensal periods for small geographic areas, that is, by subtracting from the net population change between two census dates an estimate of the excess of births over deaths during the period.

residual variance: *see* **variance, residual.**

residual vision: *see* **vision, residual.**

residues, method of: *see* **method of residues.**

resignation: (1) the act of resigning, or giving up, as a claim, possession, office, or the like; (2) the attitude of being resigned or submissive to a situation that the individual does not resent or attempt to change.

resignation, teacher's: the premature termination by a teacher of a teaching contract, either according to law or with the consent of the employing authority.

resistance: (1) in general, the tendency to respond in an opposite direction from that of an applied force; may be physical or mental; *contr. w.* **conductivity;** (2) according to psychoanalytic theory, an unconscious force within the mind that accomplishes repression and also prevents repressed ideas from becoming conscious; commonly manifested in the forgetting of dreams.

resistance, glare: *see* **glare resistance.**

resistant behavior: *see* **behavior, resistant.**

resistive exercise: *see* **exercise, resistive.**

resolution: ability of a TV system to distinguish and reproduce fine detail in the subject picked up by the camera.

resolution, bond: *see* **bond resolution.**

resolution, factor: *see* **factor resolution.**

resonance: (1) (speech) the amplification of a tone or of any component of a complex tone as a result of the vibration of air within a cavity such as the mouth or nose; loosely, a rich, vibrant quality of voice; (2) in a general educational sense, the total response process of an open-minded and sympathetic teacher to pupils.

resonance tone: *see* **tone, resonance.**

resonator: (in speech) any of the throat, mouth, or nasal cavities that may act to amplify any of the components of vocal sounds.

resource center, learning: *see* **center, learning resource.**

resource development program, human: *see* **program, human resource development.**

resource person: (1) (in teaching) any individual identified as a potential resource to a classroom group by reason of that person's special knowledge or experience, as, for example, a fire chief for a first-grade class or a local politician for a course in government; (2) a person who has had special training and/or significant experience in the subject under consideration by a group and who serves the group by furnishing authoritative information when called upon to do so; *dist. f.* **leader, recognized; recorder** (3); (3) a consultant, representing a highly specialized field, who is called in by a curriculum workshop to help integrate his specialty with the solution of the curriculum problem at hand.

resource room: (spec. ed.) an organizational plan in which children are registered with regular teachers who assume the major responsibility for their education; the resource room and resource room teacher are utilized as the need arises.

resource room teacher: a teacher who provides an instructional program for individuals or small groups of exceptional children (primarily partially sighted but also auditorily impaired and other handicapped individuals) who attend a resource room on a part-time basis.

resource teacher: (1) a teacher specializing in one subject field (such as music, science, or physical education) who teaches on an itinerant basis, usually in elementary grades, to supplement instructional offerings of the regular classroom teachers in self-contained classroom situations; (2) a supervisor who works primarily with inexperienced teachers to assist them in developing teaching plans, materials, and procedures, often using demonstrations and directed practice sessions; sometimes assigned to a single elementary building rather than serving on a central staff; sometimes a part-time teacher and part-time supervisor.

resource unit: (1) a comprehensive collection of suggested learning and teaching activities, procedures, materials, and references organized around a unifying topic or learner problem, designed to be helpful to teachers in developing their own teaching units appropriate to their respective classes; includes more than any one teacher could implement; typical content: desired outcomes, typical learner experiences, suggestions for starting, developing, and concluding the unit, evaluation, and reference lists for pupils and teachers; *dist. f.* **unit, teaching;** (2) a collection of suggestions for materials, activities, experiences, sources of aids, etc., with emphasis on the learner, and possibly designed for the learner's use or for use in guiding the study of a group of learners in their problem solving; in this sense resource unit and *teaching unit* may be identical; (3) (sci. ed.) the accumulation in one place (notebook, filing-cabinet drawer, shelf) of all the resources that could be used for teacher and student experiences in connection with one of the major units into which a course or area has been organized.

resource-use education: a reality-centered concept of education which assumes that the learning process is given vitality by the utilization of community resources in the educational program; any community institution, individual, organization, landmark, or material object can be considered a resource if it has use in enhancing the social understanding of the pupil; schools engaging in resource-use learning tend to survey, appraise, and catalog the resources in the community, which are then used when appropriate for the established educational purposes.

resources, community: (couns.) those agencies and forces which affect children directly or indirectly and which an effective school program can tap for cooperative assistance although they are generally outside the control of school boards or school administrators. *See* **resources, referral.**

resources, parents as: *see* **parents as resources.**

resources, referral: (couns.) individuals, clinics, and community agencies to which students might be sent for specialized service.

respiration: (phys. ed.) a body process that provides oxygen for metabolism of the body cells and eliminates the carbon dioxide resulting from oxidation.

respiration, artificial: maintenance of respiratory movements by artificial means.

respiratory type: a type of habitus characterized by a long chest, a strongly developed nose, a voluminous cavity in the upper jaw, and large accessory cavities in the skull, the whole supposedly reflecting adequacy of respiratory functions. *See* **habitus.**

respondeat superior, doctrine of (rə·spon'de·at sū·pē'ri·or): (Lat., lit., "let the superior answer") a legal doctrine to the effect that the master is liable in damages for the torts, negligence, and frauds of his servant when they are committed in the course of his employment; this doctrine, however, does not apply to the state and such of its agencies as school districts.

respondent: (1) any recipient of a questionnaire who actually replies to the questionnaire; (2) (legal) the one making an answer in a court action.

respondent behavior: *see* **behavior, respondent.**

respondent conditioning: *see* **conditioning, classical.**

responding, controlled: a characteristic of programmed instruction that requires continuous or frequent responses from each student.

response: (1) any implicit or overt change in an effector organ (a muscle or a gland) consequent to stimulation; (2) a subject's answer to a test item or question.

response, acquired: any response that has been learned by an organism, as contrasted with one that has been inherited. *Syn.* **learned response;** *see* **character, acquired; hierarchy, habit-family;** *contr. w.* **reflex.**

response, adequate: any response to any signal the consummation of which is biologically and/or psychologically favorable to the organism and which results in a significant change or even ablation of the instigating stimulus. (Such response may establish a new or restore an old state of equilibrium. The act conforms to the prodrome, or set, that precedes instigation. It need not be useful, beneficial, or protective in a biosocial sense.)

response, aesthetic: an emotional reaction in the presence of beauty, generally considered to be a favorable one.

response, affective: an emotional response to music or any other sensory experience.

response, amplitude of: the strength of a response; for example, in Pavlovian conditioning the number of drops of saliva would be a measure of the amplitude of the conditioned response.

response, antedating: a response that has occurred ahead of the time when it occurs in a particular sequence of acts. *Syn.* **anticipatory response.**

response, anticipated: (mil. ed.) (1) an expected answer to a lead-off or follow-up question asked by the leader of a guided discussion; (2) a term that the instructor includes in a list of possible responses to his lead-off and follow-up questions in the belief that it should be discussed by the students if they are to develop an understanding of the subject of the guided discussion.

response, anticipatory: *syn.* **response, antedating.**

response, arousal: the response of a sleeping or relaxed person to the stimulus of suddenly being awakened or forced to act upon some emergency, especially as this response is measured in psychological or physical tests given to astronauts.

response bias: the effects of measurement artifacts on the average responses of a group of people; one example is the effect of guessing on the values of items when subjects are required to attempt all items.

response, conditioned: a response to a conditioned stimulus.

response, constructed: in programmed instruction, a student's effort to complete a sentence, solve a problem, or answer a question; a model of the response may be provided for the student to copy, but as long as he writes, says, or thinks it rather than selects it from a set of alternatives, the response is constructed. *Comp. w.* **response, multiple-choice.**

response, consummatory: the final response of an organism to a situation by means of which the maintaining stimuli are removed, by altering either the external situation or the internal state of the organism; for example, the consummatory response of copulation reduces the appetitive tension of the organism and brings about a cessation of mating behavior.

response count: an indication of the frequency with which one or more of the answer options for an objective test item were chosen by examinees in a particular group. *Syn.* **item count;** *see* **analysis, item.**

response, covert: an act or behavior that cannot be directly observed but is inferred from subsequent behavior or from subjective reports, as, for example, covert trial and error in which the person thinks of various possibilities to solve a problem without actually performing the acts; sometimes a fractional portion of such covert behaviors may be observed, as when a person moves his lips or changes his posture, or when a lower mammal adopts a postural set; this latter phenomenon has been called *vicarious trial and error* (VTE) by Tolman.

response device: an object used in instruction, such as a typewriter, which provides for practice but not for controlled input of information; stimulus may be provided by the teacher. *Comp. w.* **stimulus device; stimulus-response device.**

response, differential: a response that is particularized, being made to a particular stimulus but not to a different stimulus or to a slightly different stimulus of the same general type. (For example, an animal may first be trained to respond in a certain way to the sound of a whistle and later, by a further process of conditioning, to

respond only to a certain tone of the whistle, with increasingly finer differentiation in tone until a limit is reached.)

response differential: a learned discrimination whereby the organism makes a response to only one stimulus where before he had made the response to one or more similar stimuli.

response, diffused: a response that spreads to or involves most of the motor segments of an organism, for example, the responses of the vegetative, or autonomic, nervous system of the body. *See* **activity, mass.**

response, directed: *syn.* **answer, directed.**

response, egocentric: a response with a distinct reference to the subject's self, as found, for example, in the word-association test.

response, electrodermal (E.D.R.): *syn.* **response, galvanic skin;** *see* **psychogalvanic skin response.**

response, flat: ability of an audio system to reproduce all tones (low and high) in their proper proportion; a sound system might be specified as having an essentially flat response, plus or minus two decibels, from 75 to 9,000 cycles per second.

response, fractional anticipatory goal: a reaction in the conditioning chain that occurs earlier as time progresses; the organism seems to ready itself posturally and to makes responses that are a fractional part of the later total response.

response, frequency: the output level of a recorder or sound system within a narrow range of volume levels over a specific range of frequencies, which is usually charted in the form of a curve; more specific than *frequency range* and includes the plus or minus decibel rating, which shows the flatness.

response, galvanic skin: *see* **psychogalvanic skin response.**

response generalization: *see* **generalization, response.**

response, generalized: (1) a response involving the whole organism rather than a single part; (2) a response other than that originally called forth by a stimulus and consisting of a number of separate responses occurring more or less simultaneously or in concatenation.

response, implicit: (behav. psych.) a response so limited in scope or magnitude that it can be detected by an observer only with the aid of precision instruments.

response, latency of: measure of the delay between a stimulus and the occurrence of a response; a broader term than *reaction time*, which is usually restricted to automatic elicited behavior.

response, learned: *syn.* **response, acquired.**

response, localizing: movements that orient the organism with reference to the stimulus site; for example, eye and head movements to a moving light or object or to a source of auditory stimuli, or movements of hands or feet toward an area of contact stimulation of the body.

response, mediational: an instance of active decision-making and higher mental activity, believed by some behavior theorists to be important determinants of much human behavior, which frequently involves language behavior although the language may not be spoken or overt; for example, labeling two situations, such as crossing the street and playing with a ferocious dog, both as "dangerous," which increases the probability of a like response in these dissimilar situations; or identifying two similar appearing men with the differing labels "father" and "uncle," which increases the probability of a dissimilar response.

response, motor: the physical capacity of an individual to react to a stimulus.

response, mouth-orientation: the turning of the head and opening of the mouth on the part of young infants in response to stimulation of face or lip areas. *Syn.* **search reflex.**

response, oculo-cephalo-gyric: the eye and head turning movements of an organism to a moving light within the visual field; one of the postural components of primary attention. *See* **response, localizing.**

response, overt: (behav. psych.) an act or movement of an organism that may be noted by an observer using only his unaided sense organs.

response pattern: (1) (scoring) a set of specified responses to a group of items which has significance over and above that provided by a weighted sum of scores for the group of items; (2) the simultaneous or successive shortening or extension of muscle groups that provides a qualitatively and quantitatively distinct form of act or movement; the pattern may comprise both overt and implicit components.

response, positive: (1) a response to a written question that seems to indicate that the subject has read and reacted to it (as contrasted with leaving the answer space blank, which carries no clue as to whether the question was not read or was read but not answered); (2) *see* **adient.**

response potential: an inference that within the habit system of an organism there exists the capacity for various behaviors that may not be evident except when the proper stimulus situation occurs.

response, precurrent: any one of a number of responses of an organism preceding and leading up to the final, or consummatory, response; for example, the hungry animal sniffs the odor of food, salivates, runs toward the food, licks his lips, etc., prior to the consummatory response of eating.

response prompting: *see* **prompting, response.**

response, psychogalvanic: *see* **psychogalvanic skin response.**

response, rate of: measures of frequency of some bit of behavior; such measures may be used in operant conditioning to determine the effectiveness of a *reinforcer. See* **conditioning, operant.**

response, reflex: *syn.* **reflex.**

response, serial: a complex response consisting of several components—compatible acts or movements—performed in series. (In the case of a serial response constituting a skilled action, there is a certain telescoping, or overlapping, of the component actions, so that one action is anticipated or begun before the preceding one is completed, thus resulting in a reduction of the time required for the serial response.)

response set: certain test-taking attitudes which might obscure or distort the traits that the test was designed to measure; for example, social desirability, evasiveness, tendency to answer "yes" or "true" regardless of item content, or tendency to utilize extreme response categories.

response, startle: a response pattern involving much of the musculature of the body, released by stimuli such as sudden dropping, jarring, or loud sounds; the constellation of reflexes that follow the startle pattern; identified with fear and with the *Moro reflex* by some, while others differentiate it from the latter. *Syn.* **Umklammerung reflex;** *see* **startle pattern.**

response style: a reliable source of variance in individual differences which is an artifactual product of measurement methods and is at least partially independent of the trait which the measurement methods are intended to measure.

response, sucking: movements of the lips and tongue that enable the young of mammals to grasp the nipples and to create the negative pressure that draws milk from the mammary glands of the mother.

response, swimming: (1) the locomotor responses that enable the child to move forward when placed in water; (2) the term sometimes applied to the movements of trunk, arms, and legs of the child while progressing in a prone position; (3) a term used to describe various patterns of aquatic locomotion in other organisms, as, for example, the primitive locomotor response of the salamander, described by Coghill as basic to later terrestrial responses.

response system: generally, the aggregate of neural, muscular, and glandular structures that serve as the mechanism of behavior; specifically, the complex of organic circuits active in any movement. (Lack of fixity and interchangeability are highly characteristic; for example,

in the failure of the extrinsic muscles to move the eyes, the muscles of the neck become oculomotor substitutes.)

response system, sensory: a set of parts that begins with the ability to see, hear, feel, taste, and smell and results in an answer by word or act.

response system, student: *see* **student response system.**

response, trial: a random effort the results of which are not known at the time the effort is made.

response, unconditioned: behavior that already exists at the beginning of a period of learning or conditioning. *See* **reflex, unconditioned.**

responsibilities, supervisory: *see* **supervisory responsibilities.**

responsibility: the obligation that an individual assumes when he accepts a general work assignment or job, to perform properly the functions and duties that have been assigned to him, to the best of his ability, in accordance with the directions of the executive to whom he is accountable; the right that corresponds to this obligation is *authority.*

responsibility, recipient: in supervision of instruction, the duty of those who are supervised to understand the roles and relationships in the supervisor-teacher interaction and to report conscientiously successes and failures in teaching practice.

responsibility, self-: *see* **self-responsibility.**

responsibility, social: *see* **social responsibility.**

responsibility, ultimate unit of: the obligation of an operative employee for the proper performance of the work assignments that constitute his job.

responsive environment: *see* **environment, responsive.**

ressentiment: a term introduced by Friedrich Nietzsche which approximates the meaning of the English term "resentment" but differs from it by being less conscious, specifically focused, psychological, and more social; defined by Friedenberg and others who use the term as a kind of free-floating ill temper.

rest period: *see* **period, rest.**

rest room: a room devoted to rest or recreation, provided for the use of students or teachers; usually furnished with lounges, easy chairs, and a table or tables.

restart: in automatic data processing, to go back to a specific planned point in a routine for the purpose of rerunning the portion in which the error occurred.

restated review item: *see* **item, restated review.**

restoration class: *syn.* **class, adjustment.**

restricted elective: *see* **elective, restricted.**

restricted funds: *see* **funds, restricted.**

restricted universe: *see* **universe, restricted.**

result, approximate: *see* **approximate result.**

result demonstration: *see* **demonstration, result.**

resultant variable: *syn.* **variable, dependent.**

results, knowledge of: *see* **knowledge of results.**

results, test: *see* **test results.**

résumé (rā′zū·mā′): a synopsis of the events or ideas, or both, of a literary work.

résumé method: a technique for developing reading comprehension of a foreign language, requiring the student to write short résumés of assigned reading selections according to a definite plan for the general idea and reading for details.

retail selling: (1) the selling of merchandise in small quantities to the ultimate consumer; (2) a subject taught both in secondary school and in college that deals with the principles of salesmanship applied to the work of salespeople in retail stores.

retail selling laboratory: *syn.* **laboratory, distributive education.**

retail selling unit: *syn.* **store unit, distributive education.**

retail training: *see* **training, retail.**

retailing: *syn.* **retail selling.**

retailing laboratory: *syn.* **laboratory, distributive education.**

retardate: an all-inclusive term indicating an individual with an intellectual function level from the educable mentally retarded to the dependent mentally retarded.

retardation, academic: *syn.* **progress, slow.**

retardation, apparent mental: *see* **mental retardation, psychogenic.**

retardation, cholinesterase theory of reading: *see* **reading retardation, cholinesterase theory of.**

retardation, degree of mental: *see* **mental retardation, degree of.**

retardation, educational: failure to develop as rapidly or as far as the average in scholastic ability.

retardation, endogenous mental: *see* **mental retardation, endogenous.**

retardation, exogenous mental: *see* **mental retardation, exogenous.**

retardation, familial mental: *see* **mental retardation, familial.**

retardation, incidence of: the proportion of nonpromotions which occurs in a school grade.

retardation, mental: a term referring to that group of conditions characterized by (*a*) slow rate of maturation, (*b*) reduced learning capacity, and (*c*) inadequate social adjustment, present singly or in combination, and associated with intellectual functioning which is below the average range, usually present from birth or early age; incorporates all that has been meant in the past by such terms expressing degrees of mental retardation as mentally deficient, borderline, feebleminded, high-grade, middle-grade, and low-grade, slow learner, mentally defective, moron, imbecile, and idiot. *See* **mental retardation, degree of.**

retardation, mild mental: *see* **mental retardation, mild.**

retardation, primary reading: *see* **reading retardation, primary.**

retardation, profound mental: *see* **mental retardation, profound.**

retardation, progressive mental: *see* **mental retardation, progressive.**

retardation, pseudo: *see* **mental retardation, pseudo.**

retardation, psychogenic mental: *see* **mental retardation, psychogenic.**

retardation, severe mental: *see* **mental retardation, severe.**

retardation, social: failure to attain as satisfactory social relationships as would be normally expected at a given age or under given circumstances.

retardation, subcultural mental: *see* **mental retardation, subcultural.**

retarded, biologically mentally: *see* **mentally retarded, biologically.**

retarded, borderline mentally: *see* **mentally retarded, borderline.**

retarded child: *see* **child, retarded.**

retarded child, educable mentally: *see* **child, educable mentally retarded.**

retarded, cultural-familial mentally: *see* **mentally retarded, cultural-familial.**

retarded, custodial mentally: *see* **mentally retarded, custodial.**

retarded, dependent mentally: *see* **mentally retarded, custodial.**

retarded, educable mentally: *see* **mentally retarded, educable.**

retarded, educationally: *see* **handicapped, academically.**

retarded, ineducable and untrainable mentally: *see* **mentally retarded, Group IV.**

retarded, ineducable mentally: *see* **mentally retarded, ineducable.**

retarded, low-grade mentally: *see* **mentally retarded, Group IV.**

retarded, mentally: *see* **mentally retarded.**

retarded, middle-grade mentally: *see* **mentally retarded, Group III.**

retarded, mildly mentally: *see* **mentally retarded, mildly.**

retarded, moderately mentally: *see* **mentally retarded, moderately.**

retarded pupil: *see* **pupil, retarded.**

retarded reader: *see* **reader, retarded.**

retarded, trainable mentally: *see* **mentally retarded, trainable.**

retention: (psych.) the result of an excitation, experience, or response, occurring as a persisting aftereffect, that may serve as the basis for future modification of response or experience; regarded as one of the necessary factors in the determination of habit formation and memory.

retention curve: *see* **curve, retention.**

retention ratio projection: *see* **projection, retention ratio.**

retention, reading: the ability to retain both words and their meanings; one of the major factors in reading.

retention, selective: (1) the practice on the part of teacher-training institutions of retaining only the most promising candidates for the teaching profession and of dropping those of less promise from the curriculum or institution; a phase of preservice selection; (2) the continuing assessment of school counselors-to-be, the purpose being the derivation of possible future activities to be included in their guidance preparation programs.

retention, teacher: (1) continued employment of an instructor from one school year or other contractual period to the next; (2) the extent to which employment of a given group of teachers is continued; *see* **turnover, teacher.**

retest: (1) a second or later examination in which the procedures are comparable with those used in an earlier examination; (2) a later examination using an alternative or equivalent form of the test employed earlier; (3) a reexamination using exactly the same procedures, test forms, or standardized instruments employed in a preceding examination.

retest reliability: *see* **reliability, retest.**

reticular formation: small clumps of cell bodies embedded in fibers of the brain near the thalamic area; the function of the reticular formation seems to be involved in the maintenance of an optimal level of *arousal.*

retired teacher: a teacher who has left the educational field permanently after having taught a specified number of years or upon having reached a certain age.

retirement allowance: money paid to teachers, supervisors, and administrative officers who have been removed, usually because of age, from active service.

retirement base: the part of earned income upon which the retirement allowance is computed.

retirement board, teacher: a committee that assumes the responsibilities for effectively carrying out the laws or regulations governing teacher retirement funds.

retirement, compulsory: the automatic removal from active service of all persons in a given classification at a specific chronological age.

retirement fund: *see* **fund, retirement.**

retirement program, actuarially sound: a retirement program or investment program in which the eventual payments are covered by the current and/or predicted income; such plans are funded; that is, the money is available to pay the obligations when they come due rather than being provided by following a bookkeeping procedure through which the money is appropriated regularly to pay such obligations.

retirement, state plan for teacher: *see* **retirement system, statewide.**

retirement system: a plan by which persons, either because of disability or age or having rendered a specified number of years of service as required by law, are obliged or permitted to leave their positions of employment, usually with a guarantee of an income for the duration of life. *See* **retirement system, contributory; retirement system, free; retirement system, joint-contributory; retirement system, noncontributory; retirement system, pension-type; retirement system, statewide.**

retirement system, contributory: a system by which teachers contribute a certain percentage of their earnings during their years of service and, upon retiring from teaching, receive an annual income as long as they live in proportion to the amount paid into the fund and the number of years spent in service; frequently shortened to contributory system or contributory plan. *Syn.* **mutual-benefit retirement system;** *dist. f.* **retirement system, joint-contributory.**

retirement system, free: a system by which retired teachers are paid a small pension from funds supplied entirely by the state or by the employing authority; frequently shortened to free system or free plan. *Syn.* **pension system; pension-type retirement system.**

retirement system, joint-contributory: a system by which teachers, upon retiring from service, are paid an annual income until death out of funds accumulated partly through regular contributions of teachers while in service and partly from public moneys; frequently shortened to joint-contributory plan or joint-contributory system. *Dist. f.* **retirement system, contributory; retirement system, mutual-benefit.**

retirement system, mutual-benefit: *syn.* **retirement system, contributory.**

retirement system, noncontributory: a plan for fully providing retirement funds from sources other than contributions from the teachers, supervisors, or administrative officers of a school system.

retirement system, pension-type: *syn.* **retirement system, free.**

retirement system, statewide: a retirement plan, typically established by state statute, that enables all teachers in public schools of the state to participate in a plan for providing retirement allowance for those released from active service because of age.

retirement, teacher: the permanent withdrawal of a teacher from active participation in educational activities by reason of age or of length of service.

retraction: the act of retracting or drawing back, as a retraction of the muscles after amputation.

retrad: in or toward the rear.

retraining program: *see* **program, retraining.**

retreat: (relig. ed.) a period of time, usually several days, spent in silence (although this practice is often relaxed), in which the individual seeks to deepen his spiritual life through meditation, prayer, etc.; most often under the direction of a retreat conductor. *Syn.* **quiet day; day of recollection.**

retrieval: (data processing) the act or process of searching in a computer's storage unit to locate the required data, select them, and remove them from storage.

retrieval, information: *see* **information retrieval.**

retrieve: for communication, to carry out the operations preparatory for display of a stored message; these operations include initiation of the retrieval process and transportation of the message from the point of storage to the point of display.

retroactive amnesia: *syn.* **amnesia, retrograde.**

retroactive inhibition: *see* **inhibition, retroactive.**

retrodeviation: any backward displacement; a retroflexion or retroversion.

retrograde amnesia: *see* **amnesia, retrograde.**

retrogression: *syn.* **regression** (2).

return sweep: the movement of the eyes from the end of one line of print or writing to the beginning of the next line.

returnee, dropout: *see* **dropout returnee.**

revelation: (1) the communication by God of truths (especially about God Himself and man's destiny) to man; (2) the body of truths thus communicated; revelation may be natural, that is, through the created world, or supernatural, that is, by a special intervention of God, as in prophecy, inspiration of scriptures, or special internal inspiration.

revelation theory of knowledge: *see* **knowledge, revelation theory of.**

revenue: additions to cash or other current assets that are expendable and do not increase any liability or reserve.

revenue bond: *see* **bond, revenue.**

revenue, nontax: the income of a government derived from public utilities, municipal enterprises, customs duties, or other nontax sources.

revenue receipts: *see* **receipts, revenue.**

reverence: profound respect or admiration.

reversal: the tendency to read from right to left, causing the reader to reverse the order of letters, to confuse one letter with another, or to mix the order of letters in words, which results in mistaking one word for another. *See* **reversal, kinetic; reversal, static; strephosymbolia.**

reversal error: *syn.* **reversal.**

reversal film: a film upon which the negative image has been reversed, or changed to a positive image; usually motion-picture film.

reversal, handwriting: *see* **handwriting reversal.**

reversal, kinetic (ki‧net'ik): (1) a confusion of directional sequence in the reading of a word, for example, reading "felt" as "left" or the reverse; (2) the mental confusion of a word with another word made up of the same letters in a different order.

reversal, static: the confusion of letters of similar or identical form normally distinguished by their spatial orientation, for example, confusion of the letters *n, u, p, q, b*. and *d*.

reversal tendency: a tendency of immature children to reverse or confuse letters and word forms.

reversible film: *syn.* **reversal film.**

reversion: the reappearance of a character present in an ancestor but not present in the generation just preceding. *Dist. f.* **atavism.**

review: (1) reexamination of material previously presented or studied; (2) (journ.) a critical report of a current book, play, musical event, or motion picture.

review, aperiodic: in programmed instruction, spacing of review materials at irregular intervals in the program. *See* **seeding** (1).

review, book: an oral or written evaluation of a book, usually dealing with its style, content, and literary or informational value.

review item, restated: *see* **item, restated review.**

review lesson: *see* **lesson, review.**

review of literature: (1) a survey of the printed material dealing with or bearing on a given subject or problem; (2) a summary embodying the findings of such a search. *Comp. w.* **study, summary.**

review, periodic: in programmed instruction, spacing of review materials at regular intervals in the program. *See* **seeding** (1).

review, rote: in programmed instruction, repetition, usually out of sequence, of a frame presented earlier in the program; useful mainly where sheer memorization of verbal material is desired.

revision, curriculum: *see* **curriculum building.**

revocation, certificate: *see* **certificate revocation.**

revolution, cultural: rapid change of some or all of the features which make up *culture. Contr. w.* **evolution, cultural.**

revolving fund: *see* **fund, revolving.**

revolving-fund receipts: *syn.* **advancements.**

revolving staff: *see* **staff, revolving.**

reward: pleasant, satisfying experience consequent upon a certain course of behavior and mediated by an external agent or by the self, acting as agent, in the hope of encouraging the repetition of the behavior. *Contr. w.* **punishment.**

reward for effort: a term designating the principle that the state or other central educational authority should render financial assistance to subordinate units in proportion to the amount of educational effort expended by them as a means of encouraging local school systems and educational institutions to exceed the minimum legal requirements.

rewind: *n.* a device (sometimes incorporated into a projector or recorder, sometimes separate) used for winding film or tape from one reel to another, thus returning material to the supply reel.

rewind: *v.* to return recording tape or projection film from take-up reel to supply reel after playback or projection.

rheostat: a variable-resistance device used to change the amount of current that flows through any electrical instrument and that is used, on some motion-picture projectors, to control the speed with which the film passes through the projector.

rhetor (rē'tŏr): in ancient Greece and later in the Roman Empire, a teacher who conducted a school for those who aspired to public office. *See* **rhetorical school.**

rhetoric: the art of effective speech or writing.

rhetorical school: a type of school, originating in ancient Athens and later prevalent in the Roman Empire, that was intended primarily to train young men in rhetoric and oratory with a view to preparing them for careers in public life.

rhetorician: a professor or teacher of the art of rhetoric (especially in ancient Greece and Rome).

rheumatic fever: a chronic infection of the connective tissues of the body, affecting the joints, heart, and blood vessels; the specific cause of this disease is unknown, but in most cases it follows a streptococcus infection.

rho (rō): a letter of the Greek alphabet (P, ρ); the lower-case letter ρ is frequently used as a designation for a rank difference correlation coefficient, and is occasionally used to represent the product-moment correlation when it is regarded as a parameter. *See* **coefficient, rank difference correlation.**

rho coefficient: *syn.* **coefficient, rank difference correlation** (1).

rhythm: (1) the capacity of the organism to synchronize patterns of movements according to situational demands, thus achieving harmony, grace, and optimum use of movement; (2) (mus.) the organization of successive sounds in terms of their time relations and accents.

rhythm band: a group of young children performing with primitive toy instruments, usually of the percussion class, ordinarily with a piano part or phonographic recording supplying the essential musical structure. (The instruments used, such as drums, cymbals, triangles, sand blocks, sticks, bells, and jingle sticks, are frequently of the children's own construction.) *Syn.* **percussion band; percussion orchestra; rhythm orchestra; toy band; toy orchestra.**

rhythm, biologic: *see* **biologic rhythm.**

rhythm clue: *see* **clue, rhythm.**

rhythm, defect of: *see* **defect of rhythm.**

rhythm discrimination: *see* **discrimination, rhythm.**

rhythm, fundamental: *see* **fundamental rhythm.**

rhythm orchestra: *syn.* **rhythm band.**

rhythm reading: *see* **reading, rhythm.**

rhythm, speech: *see* **speech rhythm.**

rhythmic action: a sustained action pattern within which a regular beat or cadence can be defined. *Contr. w.* **arrhythmia; dysrhythmia.**

rhythmic dictation: *see* **dictation, rhythmic.**

rhythmic drill: *see* **drill, rhythmic.**

rhythmic game: the child's reproduction through bodily movements of different rhythms and tempi suggested by music.

rhythmical drill: *see* **drill, rhythmical.**

rhythmical movement: (1) any handwriting movement made in tempo with a set rhythm, as in the successive strokes; (2) a characteristic of handwriting in which there may be no evidence of a definite time rhythm but in which there is evidence of the adjustment of the rate of movement of the writing instrument to the curvature of the arc of the curve being constructed.

rhythmics: movements and dance activities done to music or rhythmical sounds; a term used especially in reference to such activities for young children.

rhythms: *see* **rhythmics.**

rhythms, interpretative: rhythmic movements in which children express in their own way whatever the music, song, or activity suggests to them.

Richards's formula: a method, devised by C. R. Richards, of analyzing the factors contributing to the efficiency of a worker, according to which the efficiency of the worker varies as the sum of his manipulative skill, technical knowledge, job intelligence, job judgment, and shop morale.

rickets: a disease of infancy and childhood resulting from a deficiency in the diet or a failure to assimilate either vitamin D or minerals (calcium or phosphorus) essential to the hardening of growing bones, which therefore bend under the stress of muscular action or weight bearing. *Syn.* **rachitis.**

ridge-route norm: *see* **norm, ridge-route.**

riding time: the amount of time a pupil spends riding a bus to or from school, that is, the minutes from the time when he boards the bus until he is discharged.

Riemannian geometry: *see* **geometry, Riemannian.**

right-eyedness: *see* **eyedness, right-.**

right-handedness: *see* **handedness, right-.**

right of attendance: (1) the legal right to attend school; (2) lawful permission to attend school.

right, vested: a right that has, legally, so completely and definitely accrued and has so long been considered as belonging to one that it cannot be impaired.

right-wrong test: *see* **test, alternate-response; test, true-false; test, yes-no.**

rights-minus-wrongs formula: a formula used in computing the score on multiple-choice or true-false tests in an attempt to compensate for guessing on the part of the examinee; may be expressed as follows:

$$\text{score} = R - \frac{W}{N-1},$$ where R = number of right answers, W = number of wrong answers, and N = number of alternatives in an item. *See* **correction-for-chance formula.**

rights, natural: *see* **natural rights.**

rigid constitution: *see* **constitution, rigid.**

rigidity: (1) stiffness; immobility; tonic contraction of muscles; (2) (psych.) lack of ability to shift attention; *see* **meticulosity; perseveration;** (3) a diagnostic classification of cerebral palsy.

rigidity, isolation: adjustive mechanism in which the individual pauses from further perception or movement.

rigor: (math.) the quality of an argument that stresses completeness, exactness, and preciseness.

rigor, intellectual: strict intellectual exactitude or discipline; to be able to engage in rigorous intellectual discipline is to control one's thinking without leniency or exception, to follow the discipline of an accepted theory of logic with the utmost consistency.

rings: (phys. ed.) gymnastic apparatus upon which stunts are performed. *See* **apparatus, gymnastic.**

risers and treads: the parts of stairs; the risers are the vertical parts, the treads are the horizontal parts or steps of the stairs.

risk, alpha: probability of rejecting a hypothesis that is really true.

risk, beta: probability of accepting a hypothesis that is really false.

rivalry: conscious competition between individuals of about equal ability. *See* **competition.**

rivalry, sibling: competition without direct conflict between brothers and/or sisters for specific objects or distinctions considered desirable by the individuals concerned.

road emergency: *see* **emergency, road.**

road test: *see* **test, road.**

Rochester method: *syn.* **combined method** (1); **simultaneous method.**

rock opera: *see* **opera, rock.**

rocking board: an apparatus similar to a seesaw; a board seating two children, resting on two wide curved rockers; usually found in nursery school or kindergarten.

rococo art: *see* **art, rococo.**

Rogerian: a term used to designate the principles and work of Carl Rogers, usually as it pertains to *client-centered therapy.*

role: (1) the characteristic behavior shown by an individual within a given group; (2) the behavioral patterns of functions expected of or carried out by an individual in a given societal context.

role, group: *see* **group role.**

role model: *syn.* **role** (2).

role-playing: (1) the assuming, either overtly or in imagination, of the part or function of another or others; originally used by G. H. Mead as a tool in the philosophical analysis of personality and society, the concept of role-playing now has important theoretical and practical applications in psychotherapy, group dynamics, and education; *see* **character-impersonation sale;** (2) (couns.) a method for developing insights into human relationships by acting out certain behavior in situations that are similar to real life; (3) an instructional technique involving a spontaneous portrayal (acting out) of a situation, condition, or circumstance by selected members of a learning group.

role-playing, leaderless: (1) a projective technique wherein the subject is asked to dramatize meaningful situations which are relatively unstructured and in which the leader is passively observant; also called *leaderless psychodrama;* (2) role-playing carried out without the fusing influence of a leader; usually a nonproductive situation lacking in group growth through interaction.

role, senior teacher: *see* **senior teacher role.**

role shift: a counseling technique that involves persuading the client to try out a new pattern of behavior so that some information about it can be gained.

role, supportive: the provision through various means of either material or moral support to those primarily responsible for the achievement of the purpose in question.

role theory: a theory assuming the prediction of an individual's behavior in a specific social system.

roles, group-task: *see* **group-task roles.**

roll: the list of pupils who are officially registered as belonging to a given class or school.

roll, honor: *see* **honor roll.**

roll, school: a list of the names of the pupils who are entered or enrolled in a school.

roller skating: *see* **skating, roller.**

rolling motion: a handwriting movement of a circular or wavelike character produced by rolling the arm on the muscle pad of the forearm.

Roman alphabet, augmented: *see* **alphabet, initial teaching (ITA).**

Roman art: *see* **art, Roman.**

Roman numerals: *see* **numerals, Roman.**

romance, family: *see* **family romance.**

Romance language: *see* **language, Romance.**

Romanesque art: *see* **art, Romanesque.**

romanticism: (1) a term for a movement in the arts which represents a return to nature, an exaltation of the senses and the emotions over the intellect, a revolt against *realism;* (2) often used in education to refer to a school of philosophy which, to the user of the term, appears to ignore the realities of life and of educational problems; (3) the view that the spontaneous occurrences of the natural man are good and morally superior to the products of human association, as in Rousseau, Wordsworth, and some modern interpretations of child development; (4) (art) an attitude in art which gives emphasis to emotion, individualism, and heroism; typified by extremes of light and dark, spiral and circular movements, dramatic gesture, merging forms, and highly emotional, often tragic,

themes; Eugene Delacroix and Theodore Gericault were the predominant romanticist painters of the first half of the nineteenth century.

roofer: (voc. ed.) a worker who covers roofs with roofing materials other than sheet metal, such as composition shingles or sheets, wood shingles, or asphalt and gravel, to make them waterproof.

room, accessory: *see* **accessory room.**

room, audiovisual: *see* **audiovisual room.**

room, browsing: *see* **browsing room.**

room, combination: *syn.* **multipurpose room.**

room, community: *see* **community room.**

room, conference: *see* **conference room.**

room, control: *see* **control room.**

room, emergency: *see* **emergency room.**

room, fresh-air: *see* **fresh-air room.**

room, green: *see* **green room.**

room, guidance: *see* **guidance room.**

room, instruction: *see* **classroom; classroom, regular.**

room, instrument storage: *see* **instrument storage room.**

room, library reading: *see* **reading room, library.**

room mothers: interested mothers who serve as coordinators between PTA and the classroom teacher; they encourage parent participation in PTA and in room functions such as excursions, parties, and Open House.

room, multipurpose: *see* **multipurpose room.**

room, music practice: *see* **music practice room.**

room, office practice: *see* **office practice room.**

room, opportunity: *see* **opportunity room.**

room orientation: *see* **orientation, room.**

room, reception: *see* **reception room.**

room, resource: *see* **resource room.**

room schedule: *see* **schedule, room.**

room, science: *see* **science room.**

room, shower: *see* **shower room.**

room, sight-saving: *see* **sight-saving room.**

room, special: *see* **special room.**

room, special-instruction: *see* **special-instruction room.**

room, typewriting: *see* **typewriting room.**

room, ungraded: *see* **class, ungraded.**

rooming-in: (1) practice of allowing the mother to care for the newborn infant in her hospital room following delivery, as contrasted with nursery isolation of the baby; (2) practice of allowing a family member to stay in the hospital to help care for young children who are under medical care or following surgery, as a means of reducing shock of hospitalization.

root: that element of a word which remains after all prefixes, suffixes, or inflectional endings have been removed; an irreducible base from which words relating to the same idea are derived.

root mean square: the square root of the arithmetic mean of the squares of the observations, items, or scores; may be expressed by the formula $\sqrt{\Sigma X^2/N}$. *Syn.* **quadratic mean.**

root-mean-square deviation: *see* **deviation, root-mean-square.**

root-mean-square deviation about the median: *see* **deviation about the median, root-mean-square.**

root-mean-square error: *syn.* **deviation, root-mean-square.**

ropes: (phys. ed.) gymnastic apparatus attached to a high support and made of strands of natural or artificial fibers twisted or braided together. *See* **apparatus, gymnastic.**

Rorschach experience balance: *see* **balance, Rorschach experience.**

Rorschach test: *see* **test, Rorschach.**

roseola: (1) a rose-colored rash or eruption; (2) *see* **rubella.**

rotary gang: an industrial learner group that remains constantly of the same size, though composed of persons in various stages of learning, new members being inducted to replace those whose training is completed.

rotation: (1) the act of turning about an axis passing through the center of a body, as rotation of the eye, rotation of the arm; (2) (fact. anal.) the process of moving factor axes and their hyperplanes around the origin in order to allow points to fall in these hyperplanes, thereby obtaining the most useful set of loadings for interpretation.

rotation, job: *see* **job rotation.**

rotation method: a procedure, commonly used in laboratories, by which the students work individually but on different problems, rotating the problems until each student has completed all of them. (In this way, more work can be done with limited apparatus.)

rotation method, sectional-view: (fact. anal.) any rotation method in which graphing of two-dimensional cross sections of the factor space is used to help in finding the best locations for hyperplanes for each factor.

rotation method, single-plane: (fact. anal.) a method of rotation in which each hyperplane and its reference vector are fixed independently of the other reference axes.

rotation plan: (bus. ed.) a system for moving students from one station to another in *secretarial-practice* and *office-machines courses.*

rotation technique: *syn.* **design, counterbalanced.**

rotational index: *syn.* **index, key-word-in-context.**

ROTC: *see* **Reserve Officers' Training Corps.**

ROTC advanced training: *see* **training, ROTC advanced.**

ROTC cadet: *see* **cadet, ROTC.**

ROTC, junior: under the authority of Public Law 88-647, as amended, those units of the Army, Navy, Marine Corps, and Air Force Reserve Officers' Training Corps established at public and private secondary educational institutions offering as part of their curriculum a course of military instruction for a minimum of 3 years as prescribed by the secretary of the military department concerned.

ROTC, senior: under the authority of Public Law 88-647, as amended, those units of the Army, Navy, and Air Force Reserve Officers' Training Corps organized in colleges and universities offering, as part of their curriculum, a 2-year or 4-year course of military instruction, or both, which the secretary of the military department concerned prescribes. (NOTE: the Marine Corps has no senior ROTC units.) *See* **training, ROTC advanced.**

rote counting: *see* **counting, rote.**

rote learning: *see* **learning, rote.**

rote review: *see* **review, rote.**

rote review item: *see* **item, rote review.**

rote song: *see* **song, rote.**

rough check: *see* **check, rough.**

rough median: *see* **median, rough.**

round: in archery, a prescribed number of arrows shot in succession at prescribed distances.

round number: (1) an approximation obtained by rounding off a given number; *see* **rounding off;** (2) an estimated number, approximately correct for a specified number of significant figures.

round-off error: *syn.* **error, rounding.**

round robin: a form of tournament in which each contestant or team plays every other contestant or team entered.

round table: a discussion in a group small enough for all to participate and in which all present are on a basis of equality; a member of the group is given the responsibility of raising the opening question, keeping the discussion to the point, and summarizing from time to time the progress of the group in thinking through the question.

rounded number: *syn.* **round number.**

rounding: (1) (math.) the process of dropping one or more digits to the right of a specified digit in a number, the digit to the extreme right of those which are retained being adjusted in accordance with specified rules; for example, rounding both 825 and 815 to 820 by employing the rule that if a 5 is dropped, the last nonzero digit retained should be even; if it is odd, it is to be increased by 1; (2)

in speech instruction, the act of placing the lips in a circular or round position in order to pronounce a certain sound.

rounding error: *see* **error, rounding.**

rounding off: the process of expressing a number to a desired lesser degree of precision or to a specified smaller number of significant figures; accordingly, a number may be rounded off to the nearest hundredth, nearest tenth, nearest integer, etc.

roundup: an organized plan for promoting health examinations of children about to enter the public schools for the first time.

route, circuit: a school-bus route that begins and ends near the school.

route description: a written record of the route and trip of each school bus, usually identifying the roads traveled, turns, stops, and scheduled time of departure and arrival at the beginning and end of the route and at the pupil stations.

route, multiple: a school-bus itinerary in which a number of children are transported to school, the bus completely unloaded, and a different group of pupils subsequently transported. (For example, a bus may first bring to school those children living to the east of the school, then bring in those living to the west; or, in the case of joint ownership of one bus by two schools, the bus may first bring the children to school *A,* then perform the corresponding service for school *B.*) *Syn.* **dual routing.**

route, shoestring: *syn.* **route, straight-line.**

route, single: the travel of a school bus in which the entire morning service consists of one trip. *See* **bus trip.**

route, straight-line: a school-bus route in which the bus proceeds toward the school from a point some distance away from the school. *Syn.* **shoestring route;** *contr. w.* **route, circuit.**

routine: as used in data processing by automatic computer, a program or a part of a program, consisting of two or more instructions that are functionally related, arranged as a set in proper sequence to direct the computer to perform a desired operation or sequence of operations.

routine activities: *see* **activities, routine.**

routine chart: *syn.* **chart, procedural flow.**

routine, compiling: a routine by means of which a computer can translate a source program into an object program by assembling and copying from other programs stored in a library of routines; also called compiler routine. *See* **program, object; program, source.**

routine, diagnostic: a routine designed to locate either a malfunction in the computer or a mistake in coding.

routine, executive: a routine designed to control the execution of other routines in data processing by automatic computer.

routine, generating: in data processing, a form of *compiling routine,* capable of handling less fully defined situations of more limited scope, as, for example, sorting situations.

routine, interpretive: an *executive routine* which, during the course of data-handling operations, translates a stored macrocoded program into a machine code and at once performs the indicated operations by means of subroutines.

routine, library: in automatic data processing, any of a collection of standard and fully debugged programs, routines, and subroutines by means of which many types of problems and parts of problems can be processed or handled.

routine, load: a routine which causes a computer to read a program into storage, sometimes punched into a load card.

routine, office: *see* **office routine.**

routine, post-mortem: a routine that produces a record of machine conditions and contents when the control sequence of some other routine is broken.

routine, trace: in data processing by automatic computer, a routine which follows the control sequence instruction by instruction, usually producing a print-out reporting the consequences of each instruction.

routine, utility: in automatic data processing, a routine to perform functions auxiliary to the running of other programs; examples are *storage dump* routines and *bootstrap* routines.

routing: (school admin.) that phase of process planning which determines where the operations on a part or assembly shall be performed.

routing of buses: the determination of routes to be followed by buses in providing transportation for pupils; usually involves determining places of residence of pupils to be transported, the possible routes a bus may take, and the capacity of the buses necessary to transport the pupils on each route, and the assignment of buses and drivers.

routing sheet: *syn.* **operation layout sheet.**

row: (stat.) any line of cells (or the entries therein) from left to right in a scatter diagram or table. *Syn.* **line;** *see* **diagram, scatter.**

row switching: *see* **switching, row.**

rubella: German measles; also called epidemic roseola.

rugged individualism: belief in the merits of relying on one's own individual resources as opposed to the reliance on the resources of the group; Herbert Hoover and Ayn Rand are representative exponents of this belief.

rule, administrative: *see* **administrative rule.**

rule of contraposition: *see* **inference, rules of.**

rule of detachment: *see* **inference, rules of.**

rule of ejusdem generis: *see* **ejusdem generis, rule of.**

rule-of-five formula: *see* **formula, rule-of-five.**

rule of life: a fixed way of directing one's personal religious life, including the practice of such ascetical exercises as Bible reading, self-examination, meditation, confession, alms giving, and similar forms of spiritual discipline.

RULEG: in programmed instruction, a systematic technique for construction of programmed sequences according to which all verbal subject matter is classified into (*a*) RUs, a class including definitions, formulas, laws, etc., and (*b*) EGs, a class including descriptions of physical events, theorems, statements of relationships between specific objects, etc.; the latter provide examples (EGs) of the former class; programmers are to introduce new information according to the formula "RU, EG, incomplete EG," the student's response being the completion of the incomplete example; for instance, the student could be given a spelling rule and a correctly spelled example of it and be required to spell a second such word. *See* **deductive method;** *contr. w.* **EGRUL.**

RULEG procedure: in programmed learning, the procedure whereby the learning sequence provides first a rule and then an example of that rule.

rules, ground: in Montessori terminology, rules limiting human group and individual behavior stated in such a way that a child can understand them and check for himself whether he is obeying them.

rules of Benedict: the constitution established by St. Benedict in 529 to govern the lives and activities of the monks under his direction. (Rules affecting education required each monk to devote about 7 hours each day to labor and about 2 hours to reading.)

rules of inference: *see* **inference, rules of.**

Rulon formula for reliability: *see* **reliability, Rulon formula for.**

run: (data processing) (1) the performance of one program on a computer, thus the performance of one routine, or several routines linked so that they form an automatic operating unit, during which manual manipulations by the computer operator are zero or at least minimal; (2) the time necessary for the computer to execute the program.

run: *v.* to operate an automatic computer.

run-on sentence: *see* **sentence, run-on.**

run-together sentence: *syn.* **sentence, run-on.**

runaway: a child who leaves school and home without the knowledge of teachers or parents.

runaway file: a record, so organized as to facilitate regular checking, kept for children of compulsory school age reportedly away from their designated home and school without the approval of parent or guardian.

running oval: a formal handwriting-drill exercise consisting in making successive connected ovals, of either the direct or the indirect type.

running space: (handwriting) spaces between letters in words, and spaces between words.

running words: the total number of words in a passage, made up of the different words plus their repetitions; a number used as a base for relative error, that is, errors per hundred words, or for measures of reliability, such as prepositions per hundred words, etc.

running writing: *syn.* **writing, cursive.**

rural adult education: *see* **adult education, rural.**

rural child: *see* **child, rural.**

rural community: the people in a local area who live on dispersed farmsteads or in a hamlet or village of less than 2,500 population that forms the center of their common interests. *See* **community** (2).

rural dropout: *see* **dropout, rural.**

rural education: (1) those phases of education which deal with the peculiar conditions, opportunities, and problems of people living on dispersed farmsteads or in hamlets or villages of less than 2,500 population; (2) the act or art of developing and cultivating through education the various physical, intellectual, aesthetic, and moral faculties and the economic and social welfare of persons living in rural communities; (3) the totality of information and qualities acquired through instruction and training that further the physical, mental, moral, and social development of persons living in rural communities; (4) an organized body of knowledge and theory dealing with the principles and practices of learning and teaching in rural communities.

rural farm population: *see* **population, rural farm.**

rural farm residents: *see* **population, rural farm.**

rural high school: *see* **high school, rural.**

rural nonfarm population: *see* **population, rural nonfarm.**

rural nonfarm residents: *see* **population, rural nonfarm.**

rural practice school: *see* **practice school, rural.**

rural school: (1) a school that may include the elementary grades or the high school grades, or both, under the administrative supervision of county, district, or other superintendent of schools, and that is located in the open country or in a village or town of fewer than 2,500 population; (2) a one- or two-teacher elementary school located in the open country; *see* **district school** (2).

rural school district: *see* **district, rural school.**

rural school plant: *see* **school plant, rural.**

rural school superintendent: *see* **superintendent, rural school.**

rural school supervision: *see* **supervision, rural school.**

rural school system: *see* **school system, rural.**

rural school teacher: (1) a person who instructs in a school located in the open country or in a village or town of fewer than 2,500 population; (2) a person who instructs in a one- or two-teacher school located in the open country.

rural school traveling library: *see* **traveling library, rural school.**

rural sociology: *see* **sociology, rural.**

rural-urban residence: *see* **residence, rural-urban.**

rural youth: *see* **youth, rural.**

rural youth group: an organization of rural young people, usually 16 to 24 years of age, conducted for educational, social, and recreational purposes.

rushing: (colloquial) the competition of fraternities and sororities for new members. (At most colleges there is a scheduled rushing period during which the competing organizations are open to inspection by prospective initiates.)

s-factors: the *specific factors* in Spearman's two-factor theory of intelligence, regarded as being psychoneural elements or determiners of special, specific abilities (such as deductive thinking or high jumping) and alleged to vary in the same individual according to the special abilities in question; distinguished from the g-, or general, factor, which is regarded as being fundamental and common to all abilities in the same individual. *See* **g-factor; two-factor theory.**

S-O-R formula: *see* **formula, S-O-R.**

S-R formula: *see* **formula, S-R.**

S-R linkage pattern: a programmed learning task designed to develop in one or more of four ways—one-to-one, one-to-many, many-to-one, or many-to-many linkages between stimuli and responses; for example, teaching that 2 + 6 = 8 and 3 + 5 = 8 illustrates a many-to-one S-R linkage pattern, where the same response is made to two different stimuli; teaching symptom-cause relationships in medical diagnosis is an example of the many-to-many S-R linkage. *See* **formula, S-R.**

Sabbath school, Jewish: a religious school which meets only once a week on the Jewish Sabbath for the purpose of providing a program of religious instruction for Jewish children.

sabbatical leave: *see* **sabbatical teaching year.**

sabbatical teaching year: a plan for providing teachers with an opportunity for self-improvement through a leave of absence with full or partial compensation following a designated number of consecutive years of service (originally, after 6 years).

saccadic (sə·kad′ik): discontinuous; jerky.

saccadic movement: the rapid movement of the eyes in changing from one fixation point to another.

Sacramento plan: a modified platoon plan of school organization instituted in the Sacramento, California, schools by Superintendent Charles C. Hughes.

safety committee: any kind of group dealing primarily with any aspect of safety.

safety council: an organized group working to reduce the number and seriousness of accidents in a community by means of a program of education, engineering, and enforcement of safety rules.

safety council, junior: a self-governing organization of school pupils the purpose of which is to promote safety among pupils, especially while under school jurisdiction.

safety education: (1) education for effective living in relation to the physical and health hazards of modern society; current school programs deal with safety as related to the following areas: home, school, traffic (including school transportation), fire, industry, rural, civil defense, and recreation; (2) (ind. arts) instruction in the safe use of tools and machinery and in preventive maintenance, inspection, and safe operation of automobiles, small engines, outboard motors, etc.

safety education, driver: *see* **driver safety education.**

safety engineering: the art and science by means of which trained specialists attempt to remove the physical causes of accidents through scientific study, systematic control, and special construction.

safety film: *syn.* **film, acetate-base.**

safety laboratory: *see* **laboratory, safety.**

safety patrol: a group of pupils who assist in instructing and directing pupils in safe conduct in assembly, shop, gymnasium, corridor, playground, fire drill, school-bus, or outdoor traffic situations.

safety program, school: *see* **program, school safety.**

safety record: *see* **record, safety.**

safety school: an educational institution which teaches the causes and prevention of accidents.

safety, school-bus: the procedure and practices for the prevention of bus accidents.

safety training, bicycle: *see* **training, bicycle safety.**

safety zone: a designated area in which children are given some protection from physical harm, particularly from traffic hazards.

salable skills: *see* **skills, salable.**

salary: (school admin.) the total amount regularly paid or stipulated to be paid to an individual, before deductions, for personal services rendered while on the payroll of the school district; payments for sabbatical leave are also considered as salary.

salary differential: *see* **differential, salary.**

salary, forfeiture of: *see* **forfeiture of salary.**

salary increment: an increase in salary awarded as one of a series of additions to the salary levels of the schedule.

salary-ratio formula: a salary formula that utilizes the years of training, degrees held, and a limited number of years of teaching experience in determining salaries to be paid to the members of a regular teaching staff or to school administrators, or both.

salary schedule: a planned scheme for determining the amount of salary to be paid to a particular employee or class of employees, or a written presentation of such a scheme.

salary schedule, fixed: an established plan for paying salaries to teachers, supervisors, and administrative officers according to a definite scale of increases depending on length of service and/or professional preparation.

salary schedule, merit-type: a plan of paying salaries to teachers, supervisors, and admininstrators involving increases in salary on the basis of proficiency rather than length of service.

salary schedule, permanent: a fixed salary scale usually based on the amount of training and the number of years of teaching experience.

salary schedule, position: a plan adopted by a board of education for the adjustment of salaries of employees according to the position held, for example, elementary school teacher, secondary school teacher, principal, supervisor, etc.

salary schedule, position-automatic: a salary schedule for school employees in which the compensation varies with the type of school in which the person works, salary increments being otherwise uniform and automatic.

salary schedule, position-merit: a salary schedule for school employees in which the compensation varies with the type of position or school in which the person works and in which increments are determined on the basis of merit.

salary schedule, position-type: *syn.* **salary schedule, position.**

salary schedule, preparation-automatic: a salary schedule for teachers in which the compensation varies with the amount of preparation required, salary increments being otherwise automatic.

salary schedule, preparation-merit: a salary schedule for teachers in which the compensation varies with the amount of preparation required and in which increments are determined on the basis of estimated merit as a teacher.

salary schedule, single: a plan by which the same salary is paid to all teachers in a school system who have the same amount of professional experience and preparation and who are given comparable teaching responsibilities.

salary schedule, state minimum: a legally established schedule that provides gradations in salary according to length of service and years of teaching, below which no district may contract to pay salaries to teachers.

salary, state minimum: a legally established minimum specified salary that must be offered teachers in all school districts.

salary, supermaximum: a salary beyond the regular maximum salary of the schedule, granted for superior teaching service or for the assumption of additional responsibilities.

sale, character-impersonation: *see* character-impersonation sale.

sales tax: *see* tax, sales.

salesmanship: (1) the art of persuading others to purchase goods or services; (2) a subject, taught both in secondary school and in college, that deals with the principles used in successful salesmanship. (NOTE: The modern course in salesmanship emphasizes ethics and service to customers and discourages high-pressure selling.) *Dist. f.* **merchandising.**

salient variable similarity: *see* similarity, salient variable.

sally port: a long, open porch or passageway, extending along the side or end of a building or connecting buildings.

saltation: (1) the act of leaping, especially as in *chorea*, or the dancing that sometimes accompanies it; (2) development marked by sudden and extensive shifts or spurts, especially when such shifts or spurts are caused by sudden transformations in the chain of causal factors rather than by gradual "closure," or completion, of underlying mechanisms essential to the particular development; *contr. w.* **gradualism.**

saltatory growth: *see* growth, saltatory.

salvage function: *see* function, salvage.

same-group procedure: a one-group research method by which the same persons are made to serve both as the experimental and as the control group, by comparing progress for a given period of time when an experimental variable is present with progress over an equivalent period of time when the experimental variable is absent.

same-or-opposites test: *see* test, same-or-opposites.

sample: *n.* a finite number of observations, individuals, or units selected from those which comprise a particular universe for the express purpose of making an inference about the universe; often assumed to be representative of the total group, or universe, of which it is a part; a general term referring to a group selected by any means to represent a population, for example, *random sample, cluster sample, stratified sample,* etc.

sample: *v.* to select a set of cases or observations on some predetermined basis from a larger, perhaps infinite, number of possible observations or cases that are similar in some respect. *See* sample *n.*

sample, accidental: *syn.* sample, incidental.

sample, adequate: a sample large enough to ensure the accuracy required for some designated purpose; one composed of sufficient cases to bring the sampling error within a specified magnitude. (NOTE: Adequacy of size does not ensure representativeness or freedom from bias.)

sample, biased: a sample that is not representative of the universe from which it is drawn; a sample affected by a constant error of whatever sort.

sample, cluster: any one of a number of relatively small groups of individuals or geographical clusters of individuals into which the population is divided; the clusters may be selected randomly or selected carefully to be representative collectively of the population, this latter procedure being used by some market research agencies because of the economy of obtaining several interviews from adjacent homes within each of the various clusters.

sample, correlated: *see* sample, matched; sample, paired.

sample, incidental: a group used as a sample solely because it is readily available. *Syn.* accidental sample.

sample, matched: (1) as commonly used, a sample drawn by selecting cases each having (within limits) the same

variate values in the control variables as do corresponding cases in another sample; (2) a sample so selected as to match another sample in mean and variance on some characteristic pertinent to a study.

sample, paired: a sample drawn by selecting for every individual of a certain kind in an experimental group a similar one in the control group, with pairing done on the basis of some trait or traits known to correlate with the criterion variable, thereby controlling one or more extraneous factors. *See* sample, matched.

sample point: *see* sample space.

sample, probability: *syn.* sample, stratified.

sample, proportional: *syn.* sample, representative (2).

sample, purposive: a sample arbitrarily selected because it is known to be representative of the total population; frequently used in prediction of election results following an intensive study of opinions of voters in a representative or "key" ward, precinct, county, etc.

sample, quota: *syn.* sample, stratified.

sample, random: a sample selected in such a way as to guarantee equal probability of selection to all possible samples of this size that could be formed from the members of the universe involved; if the universe is large, a sample selected in such a way as to guarantee to each member an equal probability of selection. *Syn.* **simple random sample.**

sample, reliability: the sample or group of subjects on which the reliability of a test is determined; used to estimate the appropriateness of a test for a particular group to be tested.

sample reliability: *syn.* reliability (2).

sample, reliable: any sample so selected and of such size that it and other samples of the same size, similarly selected, have essentially the same characteristics.

sample, representative: (1) a sample possessing the same characteristics as the population with reference to some variable other than, but thought to be related to, the one under investigation; (2) sometimes used to refer to a stratified sample in which the subsample numbers are proportional to the size of the strata; *syn.* **proportional sample.**

sample, simple random: *syn.* sample, random.

sample space: a model of an idealized experiment in which each possible outcome of the experiment is represented by a unique point called a *sample point;* one of the primitive (undefined) notions in probability theory. *See* value, probability.

sample, standardization: a term used to refer to that part of the reference population which is selected for use in norming a test.

sample, statistical: *syn.* sample.

sample, stratified: a sample obtained by dividing the entire population into categories or strata according to some factor or factors and sampling proportionately and independently from each category, sampling within a category usually being done randomly. *Syn.* **probability sample; quota sample.**

sampling: the act or process of selecting a limited number of observations, individuals, or cases to represent a particular universe. *See* universe.

sampling, acceptance: selection of individual items (usually, manufactured products) to be tested for the purpose of deciding whether to accept or reject all the items in the finite population from which the sample was taken; used frequently in industry.

sampling, area: selection of individual subjects on the basis of place of residence or employment; used frequently in market research.

sampling, cumulative: *see* analysis, sequential.

sampling differences, within-group: *syn.* variance, within-group.

sampling distribution: *see* distribution, sampling.

sampling error: *syn.* error of sampling.

sampling, extensive: in achievement testing, the covering of a variety of topics and subtopics, the topics not necessarily being covered in great detail.

sampling, fluctuation of: *see* **fluctuation of sampling.**

sampling, intensive: in achievement testing, the practice of covering a topic or topics in great detail. *Contr. w.* **sampling, extensive.**

sampling, item: a procedure for estimating test-norm distributions by administering a different sample of items from the test to each of a set of examinee samples as opposed to administering the entire test to each of a sample of examinees.

sampling, multistage: sampling carried out in successive stages; for example, selecting several clusters randomly from each of a number of stratified clusters.

sampling, partial investigation: a series of observations or measurements drawn from the upper or lower part of a distribution derived from part of a universe.

sampling, quota-control: *see* **sample, stratified.**

sampling, sequential: *see* **analysis, sequential.**

sampling, short-time: method developed by Olson to improve observation of behavior of children, especially of social behavior; trained observers record all acts of children under observation during fixed periods of time. *Syn.* **sampling, time;** *see* **record, time-sample;** *contr. w.* **anecdotal method.**

sampling, time: *see* **record, time-sample; sampling, short-time; study, time sampling.**

sampling unit: one of the units formed by the subdivision of the material to be sampled, the basis of an actual sampling procedure.

sanatorium class: *see* **class, sanatorium.**

sanction: (1) a principle of morality that urges or makes binding an action, duty, or judgment because of consequences; (2) an influence which, when internalized, helps the individual determine moral choices.

sanction, moral: that which urges or makes binding a moral action or judgment upon one as a duty; that which brings it about that, in contrast to doing one's duty for duty's sake, one is made to do good through the action of consequences, which, according to Bentham, may be physical, political, popular, or religious, and which produces either pain or pleasure.

sanction, teaching: *see* **teaching sanction.**

sanctions, professional: a technique developed by the National Education Association as an alternative to strikes; may include any one or combination of the following: public declaration of unsatisfactory working conditions; recommendation that members of the profession refuse to accept employment in the area; censure, suspension, or expulsion of members who accept jobs in the area; campaign to mobilize public opinion and political action to bring about change.

sand craft: modeling and working sand as a play activity.

sand play: a technique that provides an opportunity for observing the behavior of the child in a controlled situation and according to which the child is supplied with sand, stones, and water and permitted to do as he wishes.

sand table: (1) a table with raised edges or a portable tray device with raised edges containing sand used to set up model villages and displays, demonstrate map concepts, etc.; (2) (mil. ed.) a scale model of an amphibious assault landing beach used for training purposes.

sanitarian: a public health worker, not an engineer, whose duties involve inspecting sanitary facilities and giving related public health instruction.

sanitary facilities: (1) the equipment and building parts for keeping a building clean or the facilities for personal cleanliness, such as vacuum cleaners, floor machines, sinks, lavatories, cleaning tools, and mirrors; (2) interior or exterior provision of toilets.

sanitation, building: (1) the condition of a building or buildings with respect to cleanliness; (2) the cleaning of buildings, or provisions for keeping them in a clean condition.

Santa Barbara plan: an enrichment plan originating in Santa Barbara, California, according to which the pupils of each grade were homogeneously grouped into three sections and the work adjusted in amount and difficulty to the abilities of each group; class promotions were made three times a year, while individual promotions could be made at any time.

Sargent jump: *syn.* **jump and reach.**

satellite college: *see* **college, satellite.**

satellite communication: *see* **communication, satellite.**

satellization: in Ausubel's personality theory, the stage in ego development in which a child identifies with his parents or, later, a peer group in order to gain greater security, approval, and satisfaction of needs.

satiation: (psych.) complete gratification of a drive such as hunger.

saturated test: *see* **test, saturated.**

saturation: (stat.) the degree to which a trait includes or subsumes another; hence, the extent to which variation in one trait represents (and is accounted for by) variation in another.

satyriasis (sat·ə·rī′ə·sis): an exaggerated degree of sexual desire in the male.

save harmless: law or guarantee giving respondeat superior protection to public employees when accused of civil negligence. *See* **respondeat superior, doctrine of.**

savings bank, school: an agency organized and administered by school officials for the receipt of small savings from pupils for deposit in a bank; intended to promote habits of thrift in children.

saxette: a simple wind instrument, used in preinstrument classes.

scale: (1) a system of marks in a predetermined order and at a known interval; most commonly employed as graphs, rulers, etc., as an aid in measurement and comparison of various quantities; (2) a series of numbers, such as norms, percentile scores, grade equivalents, or age equivalents, the values of which take significance from their derivation; (3) a test having items arranged in order of difficulty, a *scaled test;* (4) a series of graded specimens (such as samples of handwriting, woodworking, or composition) arranged in order of merit and/or level of difficulty, usually having derived (somewhat arbitrary) numerical values, and used for comparison with similar products as a means of grading student achievement; (5) a series of discriminating statements or questions intended to reveal certain attitudes or personality characteristics of the respondent, for example, a personality scale; the individual items of such a scale may, in scoring, be assigned various weights according to the particular purpose for which the scale is being scored; *see* **rating scale, personality.**

scale, achievement: *syn.* **test, achievement.**

scale, age: a test in which the items are arranged in groups on the basis of the earliest age at which a group of typical, normal pupils can answer those items correctly.

scale analysis: *syn.* **analysis, scalogram.**

scale, analytical: *syn.* **test, diagnostic.**

scale, arithmetic: any scale in which equal numerical intervals are represented by equal linear intervals; a scale of which the successive points of division are equidistant. *Contr. w.* **scale, logarithmic; scale, nonuniform.**

scale, art rating: *see* **rating scale, art.**

scale, attitude: an attitude-measuring instrument the units of which have been experimentally determined and equated; designed to obtain a quantitative evaluation of an attitude; to be distinguished from *attitude questionnaire,* in which there is no such rational equality of units.

scale, attitude master: a type of attitude scale devised to measure attitude toward any one of a large number in a class of attitudes, such as any racial or national group, any social institution, any proposed social action.

scale, Binet-Simon: (1) a famous early intelligence test constructed by Binet and Simon, arranged in the form of an age scale; (2) any of the revisions of the early Binet-Simon scale, or any test constructed according to the same principles and procedures.

scale, building: an instrument for assigning a quantitative value to a school building to indicate the degree to which it meets certain educational and structural criteria; may consist of a list of suitable criteria with specific details, each section or subdivision of the scale having a stated maximum value, which is an arbitrary or empirically determined number, and the total or maximum usually being a convenient number like 1,000; the person using the scale indicates for each item the degree to which a part or aspect of the building is judged to satisfy the criterion. *See* score card, building.

scale, C: *see* C scale.

scale caption: one of the items or subdivisions of a rating scale. *See* rating scale.

scale, composition: a series of sample compositions arranged in order at measured intervals according to excellence and used as a device for judging the quality of compositions, especially in surveys and other large-scale pieces of research.

scale, continuous: (1) a rating scale along which only selected points are given, but in which a continuum is assumed so that judges may indicate their ratings at any point; (2) a scale representing a continuous variable.

scale, cumulative: a scale in which the items can be arranged in an order so that a testee who responds positively to any particular item also responds positively to all items of lower rank order; designed to ensure that test items be approximately along a single dimension, that is, test the same thing.

scale, developmental: (1) a test, check list, or inventory for use in measuring or estimating the stage of development of individuals, often with special reference to physiological aspects of development; (2) a carefully prepared arrangement of items in a sequence for quantifying, placing, and improving the interpretation of observational or other data insofar as they pertain to a certain aspect of development.

scale, diagnostic: (1) a diagnostic test; a test that is arranged with items in order of increasing difficulty, and one that yields several different scores considered to be useful in diagnosing level of proficiency in one or more types of tasks; (2) a scale that measures one or more abilities and provides one or more scores, while indicating types of errors made, with indications of source of error and procedures for use in remedial instruction.

scale, difficulty: (1) a test designed to determine the maximum level of performance of which an individual is capable; consists of items arranged in ascending order of difficulty, the increment from item to item being, preferably, approximately constant; (2) a series of tasks arranged in order of difficulty (or a series of tasks the difficulty of each being known) from which a selection may be made to prepare a test; (3) (voc. ed.) a list of the jobs in a block, arranged in order from the easiest to the most difficult; *see* block.

scale, discrete: (1) a scale representing a discrete variable; (2) a rating scale on which are given only selected points or intervals, one of which must be selected by the judges, no intermediate selection being allowed.

scale, drawing: a uniformly marked or graduated wood or plastic measuring rule used in architectural or mechanical drawing to draw objects to scale; also used in measuring objects and scaled drawings; some scales in common use are architect's, engineer's, mechanical draftman's, and decimal scales.

scale, emotional-maturity: a standardized instrument for measuring a person's level of emotional maturity by comparing his score on the scale with norms based on samplings of children of various ages and of adults. *See* inventory, personality.

scale, equal-intervals: (1) a set of items selected, usually from a larger, previously scaled set, so that the scale intervals between items are equal; (2) a scale constructed by having judges sort attitude statements toward an object on a favorable-unfavorable continuum so that the intervals between sets of statements seem equal to the judge.

scale, evaluation: an instrument of appraisal in which the person or thing being appraised for a given trait or traits is rated on a prepared scale, or continuum, such as the increasing amount in a characteristic or trait, covering the range through which the trait might be found or appraised.

scale, Goodenough: a scale used in measuring intelligence; the subject is asked to draw a man, and the product is evaluated on the basis of developmental data. *See* test, draw-a-man.

scale, graphic: a rating scale on which each trait is represented by a line, the various degrees of the trait being indicated by descriptions, explanations, or illustrations at different points on the line; the extent to which the individual possesses the trait is noted by a mark at the appropriate place on the line.

scale, gray: (1) variations in value from white, through shades of gray, to black on a television screen; the gradations approximate the tonal values of the original image picked up by the TV camera; some systems are capable of producing a relatively high number of gradations whereas others may be rather limited; (2) a strip of paper or film which has a graduated series of tones from white to black.

scale, group: a questionnaire type of test (like the personality inventory) that can be administered to a group of testees; it is not a *scale* in the sense of a *rating scale,* nor does it deal necessarily with the measurement of a group but rather with a number of individuals simultaneously.

scale, handwriting: a schema, usually in the form of a chart, containing samples of handwriting arranged in order from poor to good quality, each having an assigned value as determined by the qualified judgments of experts or by objective measurement; usually accompanied by norms of quality and rate of writing.

scale, Hayes Binet: a collection of Binet tests used to assess blind children.

scale, intelligence: an instrument used to provide a measure of intelligence, constructed in accordance with the scale principle, often having exercises of increasing difficulty corresponding to levels of mental ability; loosely used as a synonym for *intelligence test.*

scale, interval: a scale in which the assignment of values to the scaled items implies the existence of a constant unit of measurement; the zero point, however, is arbitrarily determined.

scale, isochron: a scale, used in the measurement of mental ability, that is based on isochron, or equal-time, units ranging from 0 to 100. *See* isochron; score, isochron.

scale, joint: a scale in which both the positions of items to which persons are responding and the positions of the persons themselves are considered.

scale, Kelvin: a scale developed by Lord Kelvin (1824–1907) for measuring the color temperature of light.

scale, Leiter international performance: a nonverbal mental age scale consisting of 68 items, constructed with the assumption that ability to deal with new situations is a good criterion of intelligence; the scale, constructed by Leiter, is intended for the age range from 2 to 18 years.

scale, logarithmic: an assignment of numbers to points of a line so that distances on the line correspond to the logarithms of the numbers rather than to absolute value; for example, on a uniform scale the distance from 2 to 3 would be the same as the distance from 3 to 4; on a logarithmic scale the distance from 2 to 3 is greater than the distance from 3 to 4.

scale, merit: *syn.* scale, quality.

scale model: *see* model, scale.

scale, nominal: a scale in which the measurement consists only of classifying the items into two or more categories; no determination of their magnitudes is involved.

scale, nonuniform: a scale having unequal units, so constructed that the successive possible values are not equidistant; a scale in which first differences are not constant, for example, a *logarithmic scale. Contr. w.* scale, arithmetic.

scale, opinion: *syn.* scale, attitude.

scale, oral-reading: a type of reading test consisting of selections of increasing difficulty to be read aloud, used to determine the upper limits of a person's oral-reading power.

scale, ordinal: a scale in which the scaled items are assigned values that permit placing them only in relative rank order, with no implication as to the distances between positions.

scale, paired-comparisons: a scale constructed by presenting all possible pairs of a set of statements to subjects and having them judge the relative degree of favorability of each statement; in this way all the statements can be arranged along a continuum from unfavorable to favorable.

scale, performance: *syn.* **test, performance.**

scale, personality rating: *see* **rating scale, personality.**

scale, point: a measuring device so arranged that the score is indicated in terms of points or units of the scale rather than in terms of age or other derived scores; most commonly used to designate certain intelligence scales.

scale point: one of a number of points dividing the continuum thus marked off for rating or ranking purposes. *See* **scale, continuous.**

scale, posture: a graded series of silhouettes of standing posture used as a basis for rating the posture of individuals.

scale, power: an ability test, administered without a time limit (or with a very generous time limit), in which the items are arranged in order of increasing difficulty. *See* **test, power.**

scale, problem: the name for an early type of achievement test in arithmetic problem solving in which each problem had a determined difficulty value. *See* **test, scaled.**

scale, product: *syn.* **scale, quality.**

scale, pupil-rating: a personal-report type of instrument on which the teacher periodically or on request records judgments about the pupil.

scale, quality: (1) a series of typical specimens of such things as handwriting, composition, or drawings of a particular subject, arranged in an order of merit, usually with a numerical value assigned to each; used as a standard of comparison for rating the quality of work of other examinees; *syn.* **product scale;** (2) a scale in which the successive steps or units are qualities rather than quantities.

scale, quantitative: *syn.* **rating scale, numerical.**

scale, range: a test covering a wide variety of different subjects, intended to measure the breadth of a person's ability, skill, and knowledge.

scale, rating: *see* **rating scale.**

scale, ratio: a scale having equal units throughout the range of the scale and for which zero represents complete absence of the property being measured.

scale, reading: a type of reading test consisting of materials arranged in ascending order of difficulty, as contrasted with one that is of the same difficulty throughout.

scale, self-rating: a rating scale by means of which a person rates himself on the traits included in the scale; may deal with character ratings, teaching ability, etc.

scale, Snellen: a series of scientific measurements to which a Snellen test chart is drawn, according to which the height of each letter subtends a visual angle of 5 minutes at the distance at which the normal eye should distinguish the letter and the width of the component limbs of the letter subtends a visual angle of 1 minute, which is the minimum visual angle for the normal eye; the scale is used as a screening device in determining visual acuity relative to a distance of 20 feet. *See* **chart, Snellen; notation, Snellen.**

scale, social-competency: a scale designed to measure an individual's ability to maintain satisfactory relationships with others.

scale, social-development: a scale of age norms established for the appearance of social traits in children.

scale, social-distance: a scale originated by E. S. Bogardus for measuring the degree to which representatives of different ethnic groups are accepted by other individuals and groups; the degree of acceptance is judged in terms of the distance one would want to keep between himself (as a representative of one group) and a representative of

another group; for example, on the scale one may indicate the "closeness" or "farness" of a representative of an ethnic group by indicating how far socially one would accept him; at one extreme, exclude him from the country, or at the other extreme, go so far as to admit him to kinship by marriage.

scale, social maturity: a scale employed as a test purporting to quantify social maturity, usually based on age increments; scores may be expressed in age norms, quotients, or point scales.

scale, source: a series of items of graded difficulty from which tests can be constructed, for example, a *spelling scale.*

scale, spelling: a list of words arranged in order according to spelling difficulty; used as a source of words for making spelling tests.

scale step: one of a number of equal intervals on the continuum marked off by scale points for rating or ranking purposes. *See* **scale, continuous.**

scale, summated ratings: a scale so constructed that subjects state their degree of agreement with a statement in one of five categories from "strongly disagree" to "strongly agree"; these categories of responses are weighted in such a way that the "strongly agree" response will have the most weight.

scale, T: *syn.* **score, T.**

scale, unidimensional: a scale on which a person with a more favorable attitude score than another person must also be just as favorable as or more favorable than the other person in his response to every statement in the set of items.

scale, uniform: *syn.* **scale, arithmetic.**

scale value: the value assigned to a particular response in a test, examination, questionnaire, etc.

scale, vocabulary: a list of words that a subject is asked to define, usually arranged in order of increasing difficulty.

scale, Wechsler: a series of about 10 point scales used for measuring intelligence; the *Wechsler scale* for use with children from 4 through 7 years of age is called WPPSI, that for persons 5 through 15 is called WISC, and that for persons 16 years of age and older is called WAIS; derived from the *Wechsler-Bellevue scale.*

scale, Wechsler-Bellevue: a scale, with verbal and nonverbal components, constructed to reveal the pattern of an individual's mental functioning; purports to assess the strengths and weaknesses and general level of development of adults and adolescents.

scaled drawing: *see* **drawing, scaled.**

scaled model: *see* **model, scaled.**

scaled scores: *see* **scores, scaled.**

scaled test: *see* **test, scaled.**

scaling: the procedure or process of determining numerical values to be assigned to statements, test items, compositions, handwriting specimens, etc., or to the number of such statements, test items, etc., that are correct or that follow a given rule of classification. (The resulting values are called *scale values.*)

scaling, K-units: a method of establishing units of measurement in academic traits over a range of many grades, where the trait under consideration is assumed to be distributed as a Pearson type III curve in each grade.

scaling, level-of-proficiency: a procedure for defining a score scale in terms of the level of difficulty of test material at which an examinee can attain a given proportion of correct responses.

scaling, successive-intervals: a method of scaling in which judges sort attitude statements on a favorable-unfavorable interval continuum and from which the scale values are defined as the medians or means of the cumulative proportion distributions as projected on the psychological continuum.

scalogram: a graphical representation of the presence or absence of a response in each of an ordered set of response categories by each of an ordered set of persons, designed to aid in determining whether a characteristic scale pattern emerges.

scalogram analysis: *see* **analysis, scalogram.**

scalogram analysis, multiple: *see* **analysis, multiple scalogram.**

scalogram board: a board with movable rows and columns devised by L. Guttman to test unidimensionality of attitude. *See* **Cornell technique.**

scan: (data processing) to examine every reference or entry in a file as a part of a retrieval scheme.

scanner: in computer operation, an instrument which automatically interrogates the state of various conditions and initiates action in accordance with the information obtained.

scanner, magnetic-ink: *syn.* **machine, magnetic-ink character-recognition.**

scanner, optical: *see* **optical scanner.**

scanning: (1) in reading, the rapid perusal of written material, sometimes used as a strategy for making later reading of the material more efficient; (2) in perception, the searching of a perceptual field in order to pick out salient elements in it.

scanning speech: *see* **speech, scanning.**

scapegoat: a person or group that becomes the object of displaced aggression and frustration.

scatter: *syn.* **dispersion.**

scatter analysis: *see* **analysis, scatter.**

scattergram: *syn.* **diagram, scatter.**

scatterplot: *syn.* **diagram, scatter.**

scatterpoint: *syn.* **diagram, scatter.**

scattter diagram: *see* **diagram, scatter.**

scedasticity (skə·das'tis'i·ti): a term referring to the variability or similarity of the distributions within each of the arrays of a double-entry table. *See* **heteroscedasticity; homoscedasticity.**

scene: the basic element that makes up the visuals of an audiovisual material; each separate picture or amount of motion-picture footage exposed when the release button is pushed and then released. *See* **shot.**

schedule: (1) an arrangement for recording various types of data for particular study or investigation; (2) a written plan indicating the time for carrying out each step of an operation.

schedule, building work: a plan for the care and/or operation of school buildings, arranged by time of day or week and by time required to complete each separate job.

schedule, class: *syn.* **schedule, room.**

schedule, classroom: *see* **schedule, room.**

schedule, classroom observational: a schedule planned to collect the needed data for a classroom observational study; three observers record behaviors on three different sections of the schedule, the procedure being as follows: (*a*) a team of observers visit a classroom together, each recording on a different section; (*b*) one observer visits the classroom alone, recording on a different section; (*c*) one observer visits a classroom and tallies on each section in turn for a brief period; the recorded observations must show which of certain incidents specified beforehand have occurred during each period of observation and how often.

schedule, daily: a detailed timetable for opening and closing each class section during the day, usually also indicating the teacher assigned, the section, and the room in which it will meet.

schedule, data-gathering: (1) a form or outline used as a guide in gathering data; for example, (*a*) a printed form such as a checklist or rating scale on which the research worker may record his observations; (*b*) a blank, such as a questionnaire, rating scale, etc., used by the research worker to record information, opinions, or ratings from others; (*c*) a memorized outline or procedure used to guide interrogation in personal interviews; (*d*) (sometimes) a test; *syn.* **data-gathering instrument;** (2) a timetable including deadlines for completion of the several stages of an investigation.

schedule, debt-maturity: *see* **debt-maturity schedule.**

schedule, examination: *see* **examination schedule.**

schedule, experience: a part of the training plan in the cooperative part-time distributive education program which describes and lists, in schedule form, the jobs a student worker will perform during his employment in a retail, wholesale, or service establishment.

schedule, feedback: *see* **reinforcement schedule.**

schedule, large-block-of-time: a term applied to a type of school organization in which one teacher is responsible for the learning activities of a group of students for 2 or more hours during each day, as contrasted with a teacher-per-period schedule; such block scheduling is common in elementary schools and in core curriculum patterns in secondary schools; enables teachers to know students better, facilitates guidance, provides the longer periods of time considered necessary for problem-centered and unified subjects teaching. *Syn.* **large-block-of-time organization.**

schedule module: *see* **module, schedule.**

schedule, observation: *syn.* **observation guide.**

schedule of activities: the plan, program, or time sequence according to which activities of any sort take place.

schedule of work processes: the list of job skills and procedures to be performed by the student worker as he learns the occupation in a cooperative work-experience program.

schedule, participation: (sec. ed.) an instrument for diagnosing the student's activity participation by compiling the extent of participation, range of leadership, range of activities, and the relationship of the activities in terms of social prestige. *Comp. w.* **chart, participation.**

schedule, reinforcement: *see* **reinforcement schedule.**

schedule, room: a plan for the use, by various classes, of rooms of a university, college, or school for the different periods of each day and for the several days of the week; usually produced in tabular form.

schedule, salary: *see* **salary schedule.**

schedule, self-demand: pediatric practice of feeding or nursing an infant according to interpretations of the child's crying rather than according to a predetermined time- or clock-hour schedule.

schedule, state minimum salary: *see* **salary schedule, state minimum.**

schedule, study: (1) a definite listing of the time and place to study; (2) a program indicating the subject to be studied at a given time or place.

schedule, time: *see* **time schedule.**

scheduled supervisory visits: *see* **supervisory visits, scheduled.**

scheduling: (school admin.) that function of control which determines when or at what rate the principal phases of the plan must be completed to meet the final time objectives of the project or program; supplies the timing that is necessary for an effective coordination of action.

scheduling, all-school: scheduling that is necessary because all the pupils are involved, such as all-school lunch schedules, and that supersedes the daily programs of classroom teachers.

scheduling, block method of class: *syn.* **scheduling, group method of class.**

scheduling by computer: (admin.) the use of a computer to assign students and teachers into rooms, classes, and proper periods in the school schedule.

scheduling, flexible: *see* **scheduling, modular.**

scheduling, flexible-modular: *see* **scheduling, modular.**

scheduling, group method of class: the method of scheduling classes by blocks of students who stay together through two or more different class periods in different subjects as an identifiable group; more common in lower secondary grades where few if any elective subjects are offered or made available to the majority of students. *Syn.* **block method of class scheduling.**

scheduling, modular: an arrangement of periods scheduled in *modules* of time, as 15, 20, 30, 40 + minutes, where the basic module is 15 minutes; those subjects that require a great deal of time, such as science or math, are scheduled in multiple modules and those that require less, such as art, are scheduled for fewer modules, thus allowing for various time allotments for various subjects; also called *flexible scheduling, flexible-modular scheduling*. See **module, schedule.**

scheduling, mosaic method of class: a method of class scheduling that contrasts with the regularly recurring pattern of the *block method* and is most frequently used where many single sections of courses must be included as electives for many students; such staggered subject schedules when seen on the schedule board resemble a mosaic.

schema (skē'mə): (1) a drawing, sketch, or diagram, preliminary to more detailed representation; *see* **drawing, prerepresentative; drawing, schematic;** (2) the concept in children's drawings which through repetition gains general validity.

schema, body: *syn.* **image, body.**

schema, color: (art ed.) individualized color relationships as seen in children's drawings based upon fundamental first experiences which through repetition obtain general validity; for example, the sky is blue, the trees are green, regardless of differences seen in nature; deviations are based upon significant emotional experiences with color. *See* **developmental stage, schematic.**

schema, deviation from: (art ed.) in children's art, the tendency, particularly during the schematic stage (7 to 9 years), to manifest a particular experience by changing the schematic representation; three principal forms deviation takes are (*a*) exaggeration of important parts, (*b*) neglect or omission of unimportant or suppressed parts, and (*c*) change of symbols of emotionally significant parts.

schema, human: (art ed.) the concept of a "man" or a "woman" which incorporates all the child's active knowledge about man and which through repetition becomes the general concept of man for a particular child; *schemas* are highly individualized; the term has special significance for the period from 7 to 9 years of age.

schema, inflexible: (art ed.) the same schema meaninglessly repeated; indicates inability to use the schema flexibly.

schema, spatial: the representation of space or spatial relationship which through repetition obtains general validity; the *base line* is the most common spatial schema of children between 7 and 9 years.

schemata: Piaget's term for the sensory-motor coordinations present within the child at birth.

schematic developmental stage: *see* **developmental stage, schematic.**

schematic drawing: *see* **drawing, schematic.**

schematograph (skē·mat'ə·graf): a device used in recording posture by tracing the outline of a person in reduced form.

scheme, classification: *see* **classification scheme.**

schizoid (skiz'oid): pertaining to or resembling schizophrenia, for example, a schizoid personality. *Syn.* **schizophrenic.**

schizoid personality: *see* **personality, schizoid.**

schizophrenia (skiz'ə·frē'ni·ə): a term used to designate the early stages of dementia praecox or a mental disorder displaying some of the symptoms of dementia praecox; sometimes loosely used as a synonym for *dementia praecox.*

schizophrenic (skiz·ə'fren'ik): *syn.* **schizoid.**

schizotonia (skiz'ə·tō'ni·ə): division of the influx of tone to the muscles, so that, for instance, the flexor groups of the arm become hypertonic, while in the leg the extensors become hypertonic.

schola cantorum: *see* **singing school** (1).

scholar: (1) a student or pupil; (2) a student who holds an academic scholarship; (3) one who, by long-continued systematic study, especially in a university, has gained competent mastery of one or more of the highly organized academic studies; more narrowly, one who has acquired detailed knowledge, skill in investigation, and powers of critical analysis in a special field; (4) a literate person; specifically, one who can read and write.

scholar, Fulbright: *see* **Exchange Program, Fulbright.**

Scholar, Merit: a second-semester junior or first-semester senior in high school who has taken the National Merit Scholarship Qualifying Test and has satisfied the requirements; school records, biographical forms, and confidential financial information forms are submitted to the National Merit Scholarship Corporation and college scholarships are then awarded.

scholarship: (1) the quality of achievement of a student in one or more of his studies; (2) comprehensive mastery of an area of knowledge including understanding; (3) a stipend and/or special recognition given to a student for certain types of proficiency, such as academic or athletic, or as encouragement toward high achievement; *syn.* **scholarship grant;** *see* **fellowship.**

scholarship ability: *see* **ability, scholarship.**

scholarship aid: *see* **scholarship** (2).

scholarship, athletic: a financial grant for further education for those proficient in some sport; usually covers entire costs unless the athlete stops participating in the sport; also called *athletic grant-in-aid.*

scholarship committee: (1) a group of members of the instructional and administrative staffs whose duty is to review the scholastic records and sometimes the financial need of students to whom honors, prizes, and money may be awarded; (2) a committee of the faculty assigned responsibility for reviewing standards of scholastic requirements and students' records with a view to maintaining desirable standards.

scholarship funds: *see* **funds, scholarship.**

scholarship grant: *syn.* **scholarship** (3).

scholarship honor society: *see* **honor society, scholarship.**

scholarship program, Federal: a proposed program of Federal scholarships and fellowships.

Scholarship Program, National Achievement: *see* **Program, National Achievement Scholarship.**

Scholarship Program, National Merit: *see* **Program, National Merit Scholarship.**

scholarship, ratio of: *see* **ratio of scholarship.**

scholarship report: *see* **report, scholarship.**

scholarship service, college: a service of the College Entrance Examination Board in Princeton, New Jersey, which provides a financial aid manual that serves as a guide to colleges awarding scholarships, although colleges are in no way compelled to follow the judgment of the staff providing this service; the manual suggests that a family with an income of x dollars and y responsibilities should be able to contribute z dollars annually to a child's education; the staff of the Scholarship Service works out the formula for the individual family and each recommendation so made is derived from a multiplicity of facts and figures.

scholastic: *n.* (1) (usually cap.) an exponent of *Scholasticism*, the chief Christian philosophy of the Middle Ages, or any philosopher or theologian of the Middle Ages; *syn.* **Schoolman;** (2) (R.C. ed.) originally the headmaster of a cathedral school; later, a title given to headmasters generally; (3) (R.C. ed.) in the Society of Jesus, a student who has completed 2 years as a novice and has taken the simple perpetual vows, following which he teaches or studies philosophy and theology; in other religious orders, a student for the priesthood.

scholastic: *adj.* used in denoting relationship to school, for example, scholastic average, scholastic achievement.

scholastic-aptitude test: *see* **test, scholastic-aptitude.**

scholastic defective: *see* **defective, scholastic.**

scholastic discipline: *see* **discipline, scholastic.**

scholastic failure: *see* **failure, scholastic.**

scholastic journalism: *see* **journalism, scholastic.**

scholastic motivation: *see* **motivation, scholastic.**

scholastic probation: *see* **probation, scholastic.**

scholastic test: *see* **test, scholastic.**

scholasticate: a home of higher studies for Jesuit scholastics. *See* **scholastic** *n.* (3).

scholastici: *syn.* **interni.**

Scholasticism: the theory dominant during the medieval period which sought to subordinate philosophy and science to theology and which relied heavily upon deductive logic; St. Thomas Aquinas and Duns Scotus were perhaps its most eminent exponents; it is vigorously reasserting itself as *Neo-Scholasticism.*

scholasticus (skō·las′ti·kəs): *syn.* **scholastic** *n.*

school: (1) an organized group of pupils pursuing defined studies at defined levels and receiving instruction from one or more teachers, frequently with the addition of other employees and officers, such as a principal, various supervisors of instruction, and a staff of maintenance workers; usually housed in a single building or group of buildings; (2) a division of the school organization under the direction of a principal or head teacher (to be distinguished from the school building, which may house more than one school); (3) a major subdivision of a university, offering a curriculum to which admission can be had usually only after some study in a college of arts and sciences and which leads to a technical, professional, or graduate degree; (4) occasionally used to designate a group of subjects organized to a definite end, as a school of civil engineering in a college of engineering; (5) a common body of beliefs and assumptions held by authoritative scholars in philosophy, theology, science, economics, etc., for example, the Marxist school, the Freudian school.

school accident: *see* **accident, school.**

school, accredited: *see* **accredited school.**

school, accredited elementary: *see* **elementary school, accredited.**

school adjustment: *see* **adjustment, school.**

school administration: *see* **administration, educational (1).**

school administration, state: *see* **administration, state school.**

school admission age: *see* **age, school admission.**

school, adult: *see* **adult school.**

school-affiliated club: *see* **club, school-affiliated.**

school, afternoon Hebrew: *see* **Hebrew school.**

school age: *see* **age, school.**

school age, compulsory: *see* **age limit, compulsory-attendance.**

school-age population, percentage of: *see* **percentage of school-age population in public (or nonpublic) elementary and secondary schools.**

school, agricultural: *see* **agricultural school.**

school, agricultural evening: *see* **class, adult agricultural.**

school aid: *see* **aid, school.**

school, all-year: *see* **all-year school.**

school, alternate: *see* **alternate school.**

school, Amish: *see* **Amish school.**

school architect: *see* **architect, school.**

school, area vocational: *see* **vocational school, area.**

school, Army: *see* **Army school.**

school, art: *see* **art school.**

school ashore, fleet: *see* **fleet school ashore.**

school attendance, age of compulsory: *see* **age of compulsory school attendance.**

school attendance area: *see* **attendance unit (2).**

school attendance, compulsory: *see* **attendance, compulsory school.**

school attorney: *syn.* **attorney, board.**

school band: *see* **band, school.**

school, basic training: *see* **basic training school.**

school, Binet: *see* **Binet school.**

school board: the school district agency created by the state, but generally popularly elected, on which the statutes of the state or commonwealth place the responsibility for conducting the local public education systems; individual members have no authority unless it is delegated to them, power being vested in the board only when it acts as a body; control is exercised through vote by which administrative officers are selected and discharged and rules, regulations, and policies are established; the board usually has power to levy local taxes for education either after the approval of other governmental agencies or independently. *See* **board of control; board of education; board of trustees; governing board; school committee.**

school board, district: *see* **district school.**

school-board meeting: *syn.* **board meeting.**

school-board member: a citizen elected or appointed in a manner prescribed by law to serve for a limited number of years on the policy-making board of the school district. (Legally, a school-board member has power to act only as a member of the board when it is in session. Specific duties may be assigned a member by vote of the board.)

school, boarding: *see* **boarding school.**

school boundary: *syn.* **boundary line.**

school boycott: a form of protest in which parents withhold their children from school or in which the students of a school refuse to attend the school.

school, branch: *see* **branch school.**

school branch library: *see* **library, school branch.**

school broadcast: *see* **broadcast, school.**

school building authority: *see* **authority, school building.**

school building service facilities: *see* **building service facilities, school.**

school-building standard: *see* **standard, school-building.**

school building, useful life of: *see* **building, useful life of school.**

school bus: *see* **bus, school.**

school-bus accident: *see* **accident, school-bus.**

school-bus accident, associated-type: *see* **accident, school-bus, associated-type.**

school-bus chrome: a light orange color defined by the National Bureau of Standards and adopted by most states as the required color for official vehicles that transport school children; often called *national school-bus chrome.*

school-bus patrol: *see* **patrol, pupil.**

school-bus safety: *see* **safety, school-bus.**

school-bus stop: a designated place along a route where one or more pupils get on or off the school bus.

school, business: *syn.* **college, business.**

school cafeteria: *see* **cafeteria, school.**

school calendar: a calendar of a school year, showing all school functions and teaching days, holidays, etc.

school camp: *see* **camp, school.**

school cannery: a building owned or leased by a school with equipment for preserving and processing foods; used primarily for instruction in canning and processing of foods but sometimes available for community use.

school, catechumenal: *see* **catechumenal school.**

school, cathedral: *see* **cathedral school.**

school census: *see* **census, school.**

school census age: *see* **age, school census.**

school census, continuous: *see* **census, continuous school.**

school center: the location of one or more schools, whether elementary or secondary, or both.

school, central city: *syn.* **inner city school.**

school, centralized: *syn.* **consolidated school.**

school, chantry: *see* **chantry school.**

school, charity: *see* **charity school.**

school child: *see* **child, school.**

school, child-centered: *see* **child-centered school.**

school, church: *see* **church school.**

school, civilian contract: *see* **civilian contract school.**

school clerk: *see* **clerk, school.**

school code: *see* **code** *n.* **(2).**

school code, state: *see* **code** *n.* **(2).**

school, combined: *see* **combined school.**

school committee: (1) the local board or committee on which the statutes of the state or commonwealth place the responsibility for conducting the local public education system; may be appointed or elected and may be responsible in varying degrees to the local government authorities; a term employed largely in some of the New England states, in others a similar board being generally known as the *school board* or *board of education*; *see* **town system**; (2) historically, the committee of the local town or city council to which matters pertaining to education were referred.

school, community: *see* **community school.**

school, community nursery: *see* **nursery school, community.**

school, community-unit: *see* **community-unit school.**

school, consolidated: *see* **consolidated school.**

school, continuation: *see* **part-time school** (2).

school control: the exercise of directive or restraining influence over a school or over the pupils of a school.

school, cooperative: *see* **part-time school** (1).

school cooperative: *see* **cooperative, school.**

school, cooperative nursery: *see* **nursery school, cooperative.**

school cooperative service organization: *syn.* **center, science teaching.**

school, correspondence: *see* **correspondence school.**

school counselor: *see* **counselor, school.**

school counselor certification: *see* **certification, school counselor.**

school credits: *see* **credits, school.**

school, day: *see* **day school.**

school day: the portion of the calendar day during which school is in session; typically contains 5½ hours of instruction time, beginning at 9 A.M. or earlier and closing at 4 P.M. (frequently earlier), with 1½ hours or less of intermissions.

school day, extended: a school day with separate times for different groups of pupils to start and end their daily sessions in the same school plant; for example, high school juniors and seniors begin their session at 7:30 A.M. and the freshmen and sophomores begin their session at 8:30 A.M.—the session for juniors and seniors ending 1 hour prior to the time the session ends for the freshmen and sophomores. *Comp. w.* **sessions, staggered.**

school, day nursery: *see* **nursery school, day.**

school decentralization: *see* **control, community.**

school, defense: *see* **defense school.**

school delinquent: *see* **truant.**

school, demonstration: *see* **demonstration school.**

school, denominational: *see* **church school.**

school department: *syn.* **department, school-libraries.**

school, departmental: *see* **departmental school.**

school, dependents': *see* **dependents' school.**

school deposit: *syn.* **library, classroom** (1).

school-development council: *see* **council, school-development.**

school, diocesan: *see* **diocesan school.**

school direction and management assignment: *see* **assignment, school direction and management.**

school, dissenter: *see* **dissenter school.**

school district: *see* **district, school.**

school district, consolidated: *see* **district, consolidated school.**

school district, cooperating: *see* **district, cooperating school.**

school district, independent: *see* **district, independent school.**

school district, joint: *see* **district, joint school.**

school district library: *see* **library, school district.**

school district, local: *see* **district, local school.**

school district reorganization: the act of legally changing the designation of a school district; changing the geographical area of a school district or incorporating a part or all of a school district with an adjoining district.

school districts, joint vocational: *see* **vocational school, area.**

school, divided: *see* **divided school.**

school, divinity: *syn.* **theological school.**

school dollar: a device used to indicate the percentage distribution of school funds among the several services and agencies of the school or school system; based on the concept that if one dollar constituted the total cost of maintaining a school, the dollar could be divided in such a way as to indicate the proportional part that each particular service or agency within the school would cost. (For example, if teachers' salaries constitute 75 per cent of the total cost of operating a school, one might refer to the fact that 75 cents of the school dollar goes for teachers' salaries.)

school, duplicate: *syn.* **alternate school.**

school duplicate collection: a collection of books for boys and girls of elementary and junior high school age, duplicating books in a children's department of a public library and used by the library to supply books for schoolroom use.

school, elementary: *see* **elementary school.**

school engineer: *see* **engineer, school.**

school enrollment, projected: *see* **enrollment, projected school.**

school enrollment status: *see* **enrollment status.**

school entrance age: *syn.* **age, school admission.**

school enumeration: *see* **census, school.**

school, evening: *see* **evening school.**

school exclusion: *see* **exclusion.**

school excursion: *syn.* **field trip.**

school, exemption from: *see* **exemption** (3).

school, experimental: *see* **experimental school.**

school facility: a building or site belonging to or used by a school or school system for school purposes.

school facility, residential: a building or site belonging to or used by an educational institution in which pupils are boarded and lodged as well as taught.

school, farm: *see* **farm school.**

school farm: *see* **laboratory, land.**

school, flight: *see* **flight school.**

school, folk: *see* **folk school.**

school food service, Federal and state: a food service program for schools administered by the United States Department of Agriculture at the Federal level and by the Department of Education in each state; four types of programs available are the school lunch program, the milk program, the breakfast program, and the nonfood assistance program. *See* **program, breakfast; program, Federal school lunch; program, nonfood assistance; program, school milk.**

school for crippled children: a special school administered for crippled children only, the term "crippled" being interpreted to include cardiac children.

school for exceptional children: *see* **special school.**

school for the blind, residential: *see* **residential school for the blind.**

school for the deaf, residential: *see* **residential school for the deaf.**

school for the mentally deficient: *see* **school for the mentally retarded.**

school for the mentally retarded: a school devoted entirely to the education and training of the mentally retarded, utilizing and emphasizing special techniques, methods, and materials applicable to such pupils; such schools may be located within a larger system or operated as public or private boarding schools with the 24-hour day supervised. (Use of the term "school for exceptional children" in this instance is an unwarranted restriction of the term *exceptional*.)

school for the mentally superior: a type of school devoted entirely to the education of pupils of high intelligence, presumably permitting more complete and effective organization of methods and materials for this purpose than is provided in an ordinary school.

school, foreign service: *see* **foreign service school.**

school forest: *see* **forest, school.**

school, fraudulent: *see* **fraudulent school.**

school, freedom: *see* freedom school.

school, functional: *see* functional school.

school funds, apportionment of: *see* apportionment of school funds.

school garden: a plot of ground devoted to the growing of vegetables or flowers and managed by the children of the school under the direction and guidance of the teacher or school supervisor; emphasis is on the science involved in the growing of plants, in soil preparation and maintenance, and in the control of pests.

school, ghetto: *see* ghetto school.

school, grade: *syn.* elementary school.

school, ground: *see* ground school.

school guidance: *see* guidance, school.

school, gyp: *see* gyp school.

school health service: *see* health service, school.

school health services: *see* health services, school.

school, Hebrew: *see* Hebrew school.

school, high: *see* high school.

school history: record of past achievements and previous experiences in school.

school-history blank: a form used to tell the story of a pupil's progress during the years he spends in school; may be one of two types: (*a*) a form kept by the pupil in which he assumes the responsibility for recording from time to time significant items of school progress, personal-social development, attitudes, interests, aptitudes, etc.; (*b*) a form maintained by the school as a record of the pupil's continuing development to be used, first, as a sound basis for guidance and, second, as a record to send to an employer, to another school, or to some other agency, to serve as a guide in the understanding, treatment, and placement of the pupil.

school holiday: *see* holiday, school.

school-home instruction: *see* instruction, school-home telephone.

school, hospital: *see* hospital school.

school housekeeping: activities connected with keeping the school building and premises clean, neat, attractive, and comfortable.

school, incomplete regular high: *see* high school, incomplete regular.

school, inner city: *see* inner city school.

school intergroup relations specialist: *see* specialist, school intergroup relations.

school, intermediate: *see* intermediate school.

school, interservice: *see* interservice school.

school, Jewish all-day: *see* day school, Jewish.

school, Jewish communal Sunday: *see* Sunday school, Jewish communal.

school, Jewish communal weekday: *see* weekday school, Jewish communal.

school, Jewish community center: *see* community center school, Jewish.

school, Jewish congregational Sunday: *see* Sunday school, Jewish congregational.

school, Jewish congregational weekday: *see* weekday school, Jewish congregational.

school, Jewish Conservative religious: *see* religious school, Jewish Conservative.

school, Jewish day: *see* day school, Jewish.

school, Jewish foundation: *see* foundation school, Jewish.

school, Jewish Orthodox religious: *see* religious school, Jewish Orthodox.

school, Jewish Reform religious: *see* religious school, Jewish Reform.

school, Jewish religious: *see* religious school, Jewish.

school, Jewish Sabbath: *see* Sabbath school, Jewish.

school, Jewish secular: *see* secular school, Jewish.

school, Jewish weekday: *see* weekday school, Jewish.

school, joint: *see* joint school.

school, joint vocational: *see* vocational school, area.

school journey: *syn.* field trip.

school, labor: *see* labor school.

school, laboratory: *see* laboratory school.

school laboratory experience program, agricultural: *see* program, agricultural school laboratory experience.

school lands, state: *see* state school lands.

school, law: *see* law school.

school law: *see* law, school.

school leaver: *syn.* dropout.

school-leaving age: *see* age, school-leaving.

school-leaving card: *syn.* guidance dismissal blank.

school librarian: *see* librarian, school.

school librarian assignment: *see* assignment, school librarian.

school libraries department: *see* department, school libraries.

school, library: *see* library school.

school library: *see* library, school.

school library services: *see* services, school library.

school library supervisor: *see* supervisor, school library.

school-life activities: *see* activities, school-life.

school, lower: *see* lower school.

school, Lubavitcher: *see* Lubavitcher school.

school lunch: *see* lunch, school.

school lunch program, Federal: *see* program, Federal school lunch.

school lunch program, state: *see* state school lunch program.

school management: *see* management, school.

school, middle: *see* middle school.

school milk program: *see* program, school milk.

school, Mizrachi: *see* Mizrachi school.

school, mobile: *see* mobile school.

school, model: *see* model school.

school, monitorial: *see* Lancastrian system.

school month: usually construed to be 20 school days, or 4 weeks of 5 days each.

school morale: *see* morale, school.

school, mother's: *see* mother's school.

school, music: *see* music school.

school, naval aviation: *see* naval aviation school.

school, naval training: *see* naval training school.

school, Navy enlisted: *see* Navy enlisted school.

school, Navy officer: *see* Navy officer school.

school, neighborhood: *see* neighborhood school.

school newspaper: *see* newspaper, school.

school, night: *see* evening school.

school, nongraded: *see* nongraded school.

school, nunnery: *see* nunnery school.

school nurse: *see* nurse, school.

school, nursery: *see* nursery school.

school, nursing: *see* nursing school.

school of business: *see* business, college of.

school of early childhood: a generic term embracing the educational provisions made for children of 2 to 8 years of age, depending on local school-entrance requirements; includes the nursery, kindergarten, and primary school, and is characterized by socialized learning through meaningful, interesting, and vital experiences.

school of education: *see* institution, teacher education.

school of engineering: *see* college of engineering.

school of law: *see* law school.

school of nursing: *see* nursing school.

school of social service: *see* social service, school of.

school of the air: (1) the name given to a number of organized series of radio and/or TV programs intended to supplement classroom instruction; frequently sponsored and controlled by institutions of higher education and public school systems, both state and city; (2) an adult education or public relations project utilizing radio and/or TV broadcasting as the means of reaching the intended audience and sponsored by an educational institution.

school of three R's: a type of school that developed in the United States during the colonial period, teaching "reading, 'riting, and 'rithmetic" and later forming the basis for the elementary school.

school office: the general office of the school; a center providing services to the on-going program of the school.

school officer: (1) sometimes used to refer to a member of the administrative personnel of a school system; (2) may refer to any of those designated by statute as the officers of the board of education.

school, officer training: *see* **officer training school.**

school, old-field: *see* **old-field school.**

school, one-teacher: *see* **one-teacher school.**

school, open-air: *see* **class, 'open-air.**

school, opportunity: *see* **opportunity school.**

School Ordinance of Joshua Ben Gamala (gä·mä′lä): the earliest known provision for compulsory education, an ordinance issued in Palestine during the first century, making it obligatory for boys to enter school at the age of 6 or 7 years and for teachers of young children to be appointed in each district and each town.

school organization: *see* **organization, school.**

school orientation: *see* **orientation, school.**

school, orthopedic: *see* **orthopedic school.**

school, parental: *see* **parental school.**

school, parish: *see* **parish school.**

school, parochial: *see* **parochial school.**

school, part-time: *see* **part-time school.**

school, pauper: *see* **charity school.**

school personnel: *syn.* **personnel, education.**

school, philosophical: *see* **philosophical school.**

school phobia: *see* **phobia, school.**

school physician: *see* **physician, school.**

school, pilot: *see* **pilot school.**

school placement service: *see* **placement service.**

school plant: (1) the physical property belonging to a school; consists of grounds, buildings, and equipment; (2) the physical property belonging to a school district. *See* **physical plant.**

school plant consultant: *see* **consultant, school plant.**

school plant, pupil capacity of: *see* **capacity of school plant, pupil.**

school plant, rural: the rural school building and the furniture, equipment, outbuildings, and grounds of the school.

school, play: *see* **play school.**

school population: *see* **population, school.**

school, practice: *see* **practice school.**

school, preflight: *see* **preflight school.**

school, private: *see* **private school.**

school, private residential: *see* **residential school, private.**

school, private vocational: *see* **vocational school, private.**

school, professional: *see* **professional school.**

school program: *see* **program, school.**

school program, extended: *see* **program, extended school.**

school progress report: *see* **report, school progress.**

school property: *see* **physical plant; school plant.**

school, proprietary: *see* **proprietary school.**

school psychiatrist: *see* **psychiatrist, school.**

school psychologist: *see* **psychologist, school.**

school psychometrist: *see* **psychometrist, school.**

school, public: *see* **public school.**

school, public vocational: *see* **vocational school, public.**

school publication: *see* **publication, school.**

school publicity: *see* **publicity.**

school record: *see* **record, school.**

school recreation program: *see* **program, school recreation.**

school, reform: *see* **reform school.**

school register: *see* **register** (1) and (2).

school reorganization: *see* **reorganization, school.**

school report: *see* **report, school.**

school republic: a term sometimes used to designate the student self-government of a school; used by W. L. Gill in 1896 to characterize such an organization in a New York City school.

school, residential: *see* **residential school.**

school, residential adult: *see* **center, residential.**

school roll: *see* **roll, school.**

school, rural: *see* **rural school.**

school, safety: *see* **safety school.**

school safety program: *see* **program, school safety.**

school secretary: *see* **secretary, school.**

school, secular: *see* **secular school.**

school, segregated special: *see* **special school, segregated.**

school senate: (elem. ed.) a pupil government body, composed of the presidents of the various pupil organizations of the school, such as the home-room civic clubs and the school councils, and intended to coordinate the various pupil activities and to promote a democratic pupil participation in the development and enforcement of school policy.

school, service: *see* **service school.**

school services: the functions served by the school, for example, educational, guidance, extraclass, and community service functions.

school services, extended: *see* **program, public service; service, public.**

school session: *see* **session, school.**

school, Sholom Aleichem: *see* **Sholom Aleichem school.**

school shop: *see* **shop, school.**

school, singing: *see* **singing school.**

school social service: *see* **social service, school.**

school social services: the services which the school extends to its pupils in an attempt to make them more receptive to learning; direct aid to pupils in the form of food, clothing, medical care, dental services, and other services ministering to their physical needs.

school social worker: *syn.* **visiting teacher.**

school society: *see* **society, school.**

school, society-centered: *see* **society-centered school.**

school, sociological: *see* **sociological school.**

school solution: *syn.* **solution, faculty.**

school, song: *syn.* **parish school** (1).

school, special: *see* **special school.**

school, special day: *see* **day school, special.**

school, specialist: *see* **specialist school.**

school staff: *see* **staff, school.**

school, standard: *see* **standard school.**

school standards: *see* **standards, school.**

school, state: *see* **state school.**

school-store project: *see* **project, school-store.**

school, storefront: *see* **storefront school.**

school-study council: *syn.* **council, school-development** (1).

school-subject unit cost: *see* **unit cost, school-subject.**

school, suburban: *see* **suburban school.**

school, summer: *see* **summer school.**

school support: *see* **support, school.**

school survey: *see* **survey, school.**

school system: all the schools operated by a given board of education or central administrative authority.

school system, city: the organization of all schools within a city school district, controlled and administered by the district.

school system, county: a local educational unit, coterminous with the governmental unit known as the county and having a board of education and a chief executive officer administering the schools for the county as a whole. *See* **county unit.**

school system, multiple-headed: *see* **administrative organization, multiple type of.**

school system, rural: a term loosely used to embrace all the schools, elementary and secondary, of a county, township, or other type of local district serving principally the children living in rural communities.

school system, state: the aggregate of educational institutions organized under the constitution and laws of the state, administered under the general supervision of the state department of education, deriving their financial support, at least in part, from the state, and usually referred to as *public schools,* to distinguish them from private institutions of learning; usually includes kindergartens, elementary schools, high schools, junior colleges, teacher-education schools, a state university, and an agricultural and mechanical arts college; tax-supported and free to the public below the junior college level.

school system, unit-headed: *see* **administrative organization, unit type of.**

school tax: *see* **tax, school.**

school term: a major subdivision of the school year, often concluded by examination periods and, perhaps, by promotion. (Commonly, there are two school terms per *school year.*)

school term, minimum: the shortest period each year during which the public schools of a state or other administrative unit may remain in session under the provisions of the law. (The actual school term may not be less than the minimum school term, but may exceed it.) *Syn.* **minimum school year; minimum term of school.**

school term, summer: the school term taking place in the summer during the period between the end of one regular school term and the beginning of the next regular school term.

school, theological: *see* **theological school.**

school, township: *see* **township school.**

school township: (1) a political township organized as a local unit of school administration; (2) a geographical area under the jurisdiction of the township board of education; sometimes irregular in boundary and size, but generally a rectangle 36 square miles in area.

school, trade: *see* **trade school.**

school, traditional: *see* **traditional school.**

school, training: *see* **training school.**

school, traveling: *see* **mobile school.**

school, truncated high: *see* **high school, incomplete regular.**

school trustee: *see* **trustee, school.**

school trustee, district: *see* **district school.**

school, twelve-month: *syn.* **all-year school.**

school, twenty-four-hour: *see* **twenty-four-hour school.**

school, ungraded: *see* **nongraded school.**

school, ungraded primary: *see* **ungraded primary school.**

school union: a joining of two or more local school units (district, township, or town, for example) for some educational purpose such as maintenance of an enlarged attendance unit, supervisory unit, or administrative unit or for the provision of special services.

school, university: *see* **university school.**

school, university laboratory: *see* **university school.**

school, university training: *see* **university school.**

school, vacation: *syn.* **summer school.**

school, vacation Bible: *see* **vacation church school.**

school, vacation church: *see* **vacation church school.**

school, vocational: *see* **vocational school.**

school volunteer program: *see* **program, school volunteer.**

school volunteer program, national: *see* **program, national school volunteer.**

school week: typically, a period of 5 days, namely, Monday through Friday, during which school is in session.

school, welfare: *see* **welfare school.**

school, work-study-play: *syn.* **platoon school.**

school year: (1) that period of time during which the school offers daily instruction, broken only by short intermission periods; varies according to location and legal stipulation, 32 to 40 weeks being approximately the range of the typical school year; (2) the 12-month period of time denoting the beginning and ending dates of the year used for school accounting purposes, usually from July 1 to the following June 30.

school year, compulsory: the length of time or the period in the regular school year during which youths of the district are required to attend school.

school year, minimum: *syn.* **school term, minimum.**

school, Yiddish: *see* **Yiddish school.**

schoolboy patrol: a group of boys who assist those responsible for the safety of children on the way to and from school and, frequently, within the school grounds.

schoolhouse: a school building used for general educational purposes.

schoolhousing: the building provisions made by a school system for the education of children.

schooling: individual training or education received at an educational institution, military or civilian.

schooling, first-level: a term used by some specialists in comparative education to indicate the stage of schooling referred to in America as *elementary school* because the terms *primary school, elementary school,* and *secondary school* do not universally mean the same things. *See* **schooling, second-level; schooling, tertiary.**

schooling, second-level: a term used by some comparative educators to indicate the stage of education following *first-level schooling,* usually beginning at about ages 11 to 13, and preceding *tertiary schooling* or higher education; roughly synonymous with the term *secondary education* as used in the United States. *See* **schooling, first-level; schooling, tertiary.**

schooling, tertiary: (1) a term used by some comparative educators to designate higher education and related postsecondary schooling; (2) third-level schooling. *See* **schooling, first-level; schooling, second-level.**

Schoolman: *syn.* **scholastic** *n.* (1).

schoolmaster: (obsoles.) (1) a man who presides over, directs, disciplines, and teaches a school; (2) one of the masters or preceptors of a school; (3) a private tutor.

schoolroom library: *syn.* **library, classroom** (1).

schools file, enlisted personnel: *see* **file, enlisted personnel schools.**

schools, standardization of: *see* **standardization of schools.**

schoolwork, motivated: a phrase employed to designate intrinsically motivated school activity; schoolwork designed to coincide with the pupil's motives and interests, so that it appeals to the pupil, seems desirable in itself, and is undertaken and completed willingly, without external coercion. *See* **motivation.**

schulflöte: a simple wind instrument, similar in type and purpose to the *blockflöte. See* **recorder** (2).

Schulrat (shōōl'rät): *see* **magister scholarum.**

science: (1) activity carried on as an effort to make the diversity of our sense experiences correspond to a logically uniform system of thought; in this activity, experiences are correlated with a previously constructed theoretic structure of thought and understanding in an effort to make the resulting coordination in agreement with all observed properties or behavior; (2) in the personal experiences of an individual, science is an activity by means of which the person seeks to relate his current sense experiences to his total structure of understanding in a manner that is in agreement with all his pertinent observations of properties and behaviors; such activity is believed to be inherent in the behavior of individuals at all levels of maturity; the individual gains, through practice, in his ability to correlate his current experience with his previously conceived structure of understanding however naïve or sophisticated that structure may be; (3)

organized knowledge gained through science as activity, frequently used with a qualifying adjective to indicate a special branch of study, for example, *biological science, physical science,* or *social science.*

science, aerospace: a subject or curricular program dealing with the various scientific aspects of aviation and space exploration and travel.

science, applied: (1) utilized or practiced knowledge of facts, laws, and/or proximate causes, gained and verified by exact observation and logical thinking; also, the application of universal knowledge; (2) any branch of science employed for a particular purpose, pursued for some end outside its own domain, whether in a distinctly utilitarian way or as an aid to some other branch, as *applied mathematics* or *applied biological science; contr. w.* **pure science;** (3) sometimes, science concerned with concrete problems of data rather than with fundamental principles, as distinguished from abstract or theoretical science.

science, applied biological: (1) organized knowledge at an application level about living things; includes botany, zoology, and related sciences; description of living things in terms of origins (evolution), structure (morphology), function or operation (physiology), interrelations with environmental components (ecology), and areas of specialization derived from these; (2) (agric. ed.) a program of instruction and on-job experiences for students preparing for employment in jobs involving work with living plants and animals and their products; often included in curricula in vocational education in agriculture.

science, basic: general facts and principles that are fundamental to the study of specialized fields of science.

science, behavioral: any science devoted to the study of human and lower animal behavior as it occurs in their respective environments; included are *psychology, sociology,* and *cultural anthropology.*

science, biological: organized knowledge about living things; includes botany, zoology, and related sciences; description of living things in terms of origins (evolution), structure (morphology), function or operation (physiology), interrelations with environmental components (ecology), and areas of specialization derived from these.

science building: *see* **building, science.**

science, consumer: those phases of science needed by or useful to the consumer, including the operation and repair of simple household equipment, care and preservation of food and clothing in the home, identification of materials through simple tests, effects of soaps, detergents, bleaches, and softeners used in laundry processes, and sewage disposal and purification of water supply.

science corner: a center of interest in the elementary school classroom for observing nature and experimenting in science.

science, domestic: *see* **science, household.**

science, earth: a science derived mainly from geology and meteorology.

science, earth and space: (sci. ed.) facts, concepts, and principles of geology, astronomy, meteorology, oceanography, and space exploration all of which are interrelated in the study of the natural environment of both earth and space.

science, economic: the accumulated, systematized body of knowledge relating to man's production and utilization of natural resources and other goods and services; earlier restricted to "goods" having exchange value.

science education: (1) education in natural science; education by means of which a person gains in ability to relate his experience with natural events or things in such a manner as to make up, what is for him, a comprehensive and logically uniform system of thought or theoretic structure; (2) an area of professional education including facilities, curriculum, and teacher education as these relate to education in science. *See* **scientific method.**

science, elementary: (1) a selection of scientific facts and principles presented in such a way as to be understood and appreciated by persons with meager experience in science; (2) science taught in the elementary school.

science, experimental: scientific facts and principles developed through the collection and interpretation of data from observation and experiment, in contrast with scientific concepts developed by purely theoretical or philosophical means.

science fair: (1) (sci. ed.) a collection of student exhibits, each of which is designed to show a biological, chemical, physical, or technical principle, a laboratory method, or some procedure for industrial development; (2) an orderly collection for public display of anything that can be fitted into the broad concept of any branch of any pure or applied science.

science, general: (1) facilities and plans for teaching science in grade 9 or in grades 7, 8, and 9; (2) subject matter selected, and organized for use in instruction, from the several areas of special science, by the criterion of immediate usefulness in personal and social relations of day to day; (3) the extension of elementary school science into the grades of the secondary school; *see* **science in the elementary school;** (4) an extension into upper grades of high school, frequently called advanced general science or advanced science; (5) may be used to describe a major in college.

science, geological: the organized body of knowledge or field of study dealing with the history of the earth, with those forces or agencies acting on the earth (such as volcanic action and erosion), with certain types of rocks and minerals, and particularly with the evidences of such history as are revealed in rock formations and earth strata.

science, household: (1) a phase of home economics relating chiefly to the selection and preparation of food; *obsoles. syn.* **science, domestic;** (2) a course in science the content of which is selected on the basis of its potential values for the planning and maintaining of a home; *syn.* **home science.**

science in general education: (1) a term distinct from *general science* in that it implies that science is an integral part of a total plan of general education; *see* **general education;** (2) science in its significant applications in personal and social problems with which all people in a democratic society are confronted; *see* **science.**

science in the elementary school: (1) facilities and plans for teaching science from kindergarten through the first six or eight grades; (2) the learning gained by children (*a*) through activities in which they correlate ideas from sense experience to make up a more comprehensive pattern of thinking and (*b*) through use of this pattern in making decisions; the accumulated learnings include background of generalizations, principles, and facts related to their own pertinent experiences; (3) *syn.* **science, elementary** (2).

science, information: the systematic investigation of the properties and behavior of information and the forces governing its flow, including study of its generation and methods of information storage, retrieval, and use; may utilize computer technology in the support of management systems and their organizational structure. *See* **information system.**

science laboratory, outdoor: *syn.* **center, nature.**

science, library: the knowledge and skill by which printed or written records are recognized, collected, organized, and utilized.

science, life: sometimes used synonymously with *biological science,* at other times to distinguish between the systematic study of plants and animals and the study that includes the above plus *psychology.*

science, material: study of the properties of matter from an atomistic point of view; the materials include metals, ceramics, and synthetic plastics.

science, military: *see* **military science.**

science, natural: organized opinion and understanding that have been gained through sense experience about events or things; it includes both biological and physical science and stands in contrast to social science and political science.

science, nuclear: the study of areas such as the structure of the nucleus, radioactivity, energy-mass equivalence, radiation detection and measurement, and energy effects produced when nuclear particles are disturbed by external forces.

science of education: a systematized body of knowledge dealing with the quantitative and objective aspects of the learning process; employs instruments of precision in submitting hypotheses of education to the test of experience, frequently in the form of experimentation.

science, philosophy of: a study of the method common to all the sciences, of the fundamental concepts resulting from the use of this method, of the generic traits of existence implied by these concepts, and of the basis for a unity of science.

science, physical: (1) organized knowledge about physical composition and structure of phenomena; includes chemistry, physics, astronomy, geology, meteorology, and areas of specialization derived from these; (2) process of relating quantitative and qualitative descriptions of physical phenomena related to time, space, mass, or derived concepts in a manner that is in agreement with all observed properties of these phenomena.

science, political: (1) a field of social studies having for its purpose the ascertaining of political facts and arranging them in systematic order as determined by the logical and causal relations that exist among them; concerned with political authority in all its forms, and dealing with them historically, descriptively, comparatively, and theoretically; (2) a division of social study concerned with government, its origin, development, geographical units, forms, sources of authority, powers, purposes, function, and operations.

science program: *see* **program, science.**

science, pure: *ant.* **science, applied.**

science room: a room equipped with science apparatus and devoted to instruction or research in one or more science subjects.

science service center: *syn.* **center, science teaching.**

science, social: (1) the branch of knowledge that deals with human society or its characteristic elements, as family, state, or race, and with the relations and institutions involved in man's existence and well-being as a member of an organized community; (2) one of a group of sciences dealing with special phases of human society, such as economics, sociology, and politics; (3) a term sometimes applied to the scholarly materials concerned with the detailed, systematic, and logical study of human beings and their interrelations. *Dist. f.* **social studies.**

science, space: a special discipline concerned with the techniques and methods of obtaining knowledge on space and on the particles, bodies, structures, and photons that move in space, as well as with the classification of knowledge obtained; a science derived mainly from astronomy.

science survey course: *see* **course, science survey.**

science teaching: providing situations favorable to learning science; the term is applicable to three different types of situation and correspondingly different types of learning outcomes: (a) formal or mental discipline; (b) preparation for college; (c) helping others to correlate sense experiences of immediate personal and social interest, to make up a more comprehensive pattern of thinking, and to use this pattern in making what is for them pertinent decisions.

science teaching center: *see* **center, science teaching.**

science, trade: science related to a particular trade, for example, automotive science.

science, unified: (sci. ed.) a structured, broad area sequential program in science where interpretive generalizations essential to the basic understanding of all science form the organizing core of study and where content is drawn in as needed regardless of subject matter boundaries.

sciences, humanistic: physical and social sciences in which the teaching of systematic science is humanized by attention to its historical growth and regional applications.

scientific: relating to methods in discovery and organization of knowledge gained through experience; pertaining to empirical knowledge as contrasted with rational knowledge. *See* **science.**

scientific attitude: *see* **attitude, scientific.**

scientific empiricism: *syn.* **empiricism, logical.**

scientific fact: *see* **fact, scientific.**

scientific humanism: *see* **humanism, scientific.**

scientific keyboard: an arrangement of the keys of a typewriter that takes into account letter frequencies, word patterns, and the stroking abilities of the various fingers.

scientific knowledge: *see* **scientific.**

scientific law: *see* **law, scientific.**

scientific management: *see* **management, scientific.**

scientific method: (1) a method of correlating sense experience and already accepted or established thought; *see* **problem solving;** (2) in special areas of research, it includes the use of instruments applicable in a particular area for controlled observations and experimentation, the use of techniques, particularly mathematical, to give precise description of things observed, and the description of possible or probable relations as a means to further discovery; (3) in relatively unspecialized activity, it refers (a) to methods used in relating sense experience to the system or pattern of thought held by an individual and (b) to the use of objective, and in some measure, quantitative criteria for estimating the validity of the accepted relation, such as criterion of prediction; *see* **science education;** (4) procedures or operations used to acquire and systematize knowledge concerning things and phenomena experienced in observation and experiment, or to test hypotheses (propositions) or assertions about the empirical world.

scientific movement: (1) an educational movement begun in the United States by J. M. Rice about 1900; his studies directed national attention to the feasibility of objective and exact measurement and statistical study in education; it was an attempt to apply scientific methods to the problems of education, such as testing, curriculum development, methods, etc.; (2) the advancement of trends in thinking favorable to pragmatism and empiricism as contrasted with scholasticism and rationalism; *see* **science.**

scientific notation: *see* **notation, scientific.**

scientific principles: *see* **principles, scientific.**

scientific realism: *see* **realism, scientific.**

scientific reasoning: *see* **reasoning, scientific.**

scientific research: *see* **research, scientific.**

scientific school of historiography: *see* **historiography, naturalistic school of.**

scientific society: an organization or group formed primarily to further scientific discovery and the popularization of science. (The American Philosophical Society, founded by Benjamin Franklin in 1779, became the parent of numerous other scientific societies, including the American Association for the Advancement of Science, formed in 1848).

scientific supervision: *see* **supervision, scientific.**

scientific test: *see* **test, scientific.**

scientific thinking: *see* **thinking, scientific.**

scientism: (1) an overemphasis on and extreme faith in the method of science, as distinct from a recognition of metaphysics or of theology as the keystone of all knowledge; the hopeful notion that we can learn from science the goals of human life and of organized society; (2) a devotion to the methods, mental attitudes, and doctrines that are appropriate to science, usually culminating in some type of naturalistic speculation.

scissors gait: *see* **gait, scissors.**

Scopes vs. State: a Tennessee case in which it was held that a state law prohibiting the teaching of evolution was constitutional. (This case became well known largely because of the attorneys pitted against each other—William Jennings Bryan and Clarence Darrow.)

scorability: a criterion used in judging tests; refers to the degree of objectivity possible, directions provided, time involved, and simplicity of procedure.

score: *n.* (1) the numerical evaluation of the performance of an individual on a test; (2) unless otherwise specified, used synonymously with *raw score.*

score: *v.* to obtain or assign a numerical value.

score, accuracy: the number or proportion of items in a test that are correctly answered by the person tested.

score, achievement: the score made by a pupil on a subject-matter test or scale.

score, affective: the score on a test or scale designed to measure emotional characteristics, indicating the extent to which the testee is emotionally disturbed by certain words or experiences.

score, age: the score of a pupil in terms of the chronological age level for which his performance is typical; usually pertains to a score on a mental test or achievement test. *See* **norm, age.**

score, age-at-grade: the score of an individual in terms of age-at-grade norms. *See* **norm, age-at-grade.**

score, anticipated-achievement grade-placement: a concept used by the California Test Bureau to indicate the average grade-placement score made on an achievement test by pupils having a specified mental age and grade placement.

score, Army standard: a standard score with a mean set at 100 and a standard deviation of 20; raw scores on Army personnel measuring instruments are usually converted to Army standard scores which state the individual score in relation to the scores of the standard reference population. *See* **score, standard.**

score, ascendance: the rating obtained on an ascendance-submission scale such as that developed by Jock and others at Iowa.

score, attitude: a quantitative score on an attitude scale; also, with less logical basis, often used to designate quantification on attitude questionnaires.

score, average: (1) the sum of the scores in a distribution divided by the number of scores, that is, the arithmetic mean of the scores in a distribution; (2) the median, mode, geometric mean, or any other measure of central tendency of a group of scores.

score, building: the value (usually numerical) assigned to a building after it has been rated by means of a building score card.

score, C: *see* **C score.**

score card: a standardized rating scale printed in a compact form and used in special areas, as in evaluating school buildings or textbooks; usually provides for numerical scoring. *See* **score card, building.**

score card, building: a device for rating or measuring the adequacy, desirability, etc., of a building; based on an analytic division of a building into its main features, with provisions for assigning a score to each division and arriving at a composite or total score.

score card, operation and maintenance: a score card designed to measure the approach to assumed perfection of the various elements of operation and maintenance of the physical plant of an educational institution; based on judgment guided by standards; for example, the Engelhardt-Reeves-West score card of the North Central Association.

score, change: measured amount of change in an individual on some trait or variable due to treatment or instruction. *Syn.* **difference score; gain score.**

score, cluster: a standard score for an individual on a particular cluster of tests, obtained by weighting each test in the cluster so as to maximize the correlation of the weighted sum of scores with the cluster components.

score, composite: (1) a summation of weighted scores or observations secured from two or more tests of the same or similar functions for a given individual; (2) the central tendency of scores obtained from different tests; (3) any combination of scores obtained from different tests.

score, comprehension: an index (usually numerical) of the degree to which a pupil or student manifests understand-ing of material read or heard, as indicated by his test performance. *See* **test, comprehension.**

score, content standard test: a number that indicates the percent of a systematic sample from a defined domain of tasks which an individual has performed successfully; the part of the test score that is not related to the scores of other examinees and which indicates, not how many of his peers a student can excel, but what he can do to surpass them.

score, correct-principle: a type of score used in certain mathematics tests, consisting in the number of times that the correct mathematical principles have been used in solving the problems presented in the tests, without consideration of the correctness of the answers given.

score, corrected raw: a raw test score based on some formula other than number of items right or number of items wrong.

score, criterion: *syn.* **measure, criterion** (3).

score, critical: *syn.* **score, cutting.**

score, crude: (1) *syn.* **score, raw;** (2) occasionally used to designate a score based on a relatively inexact measuring instrument or a score that represents a rough approximation of the true score.

score, cutting: a score that divides those individuals earning scores above and below it into two groups with reference to some purpose or criterion. *Syn.* **critical score;** *rough syn.* **passing score.**

score, derived: (1) the score resulting when a raw score is converted to some system of comparable measures, preferably a system having a standard reference point and equal units, such as a *T score* or a *z score;* permits the comparison of derived scores from one test with derived scores from other tests; (2) any score that has been converted from one unit into its equivalent in terms of another unit, such as a raw score converted into percentages or into letter marks.

score, deviate: *syn.* **deviate** (2).

score, deviation: an individual test score expressed in terms of units determined by the spread or scatter of a group of such test scores.

score, difference: *syn.* **score, change.**

score, difficulty: a statement of the highest level of difficulty on a given variable at which the testee has performed with a certain specified degree of accuracy.

score, discrepancy: (1) any score stated in terms of deviation from some reference point, usually the mean; (2) *syn.* **error, residual.**

score, gain: *syn.* **score, change.**

score, global: a single score, based on heterogeneous test materials, that is judged to provide a meaningful over-all measure of a specified characteristic.

score, grade: a derived score that expresses the ability or achievement of a pupil in terms of the grade level for which his performance is typical; thus, a grade score of 6.2 indicates that the pupil is achieving at a level equal to that of the typical sixth-grade pupil in the second month of the school year. *Syn.* **grade-placement score.**

score, grade-placement: *syn.* **score, grade.**

score, graphic: a score represented by a line, bar, or diagrammatic figure on a chart or diagram of scores.

score, gross: a score expressed in terms of the original units of measurement; thus, all raw scores and certain derived scores, such as ages, are gross scores. *Contr. w* **score, derived; score, standard; score, transmuted.**

score interval: *syn.* **subinterval.**

score, ipsative: a value showing an individual's standing on a test in relation to his own standing on other tests; such scores vary around the individual's own mean and are in a form readily adaptable to Q-technique correlations. *See* **Q-technique.**

score, isochron: a score representing any special mental ability of an individual at a given time on an isochron scale; isochron scores of 0 and 100 represent, respectively, no ability and ability at the physiological limit of performance, while an isochron score of 50 is midway between these two extremes. *See* **isochron; scale, isochron.**

score, learning-curve: a score that indicates directly the proportion of complete mastery attained in terms of the typical time required to reach a specified level as compared with the typical time required to reach complete mastery.

score limit: *syn.* **class limit, apparent.**

score, modified raw: a raw test score based on some formula other than number of items right or number of items wrong.

score, normalized standard: a score, like other *standard scores*, having a predetermined mean and standard deviation; derived in a way that makes the distribution of standard scores approximately normal, regardless of the shape of the distribution of raw scores on which it was based.

score, normative: any score expressing an individual's standing in relation to a tested (or *normative*) group; familiar examples are standard scores, IQs, percentile ranks, etc. *Rough syn.* **score, derived**, *contr. w.* **score, ipsative.**

score, objective: a mark or rating given for performance on an objective measuring instrument or on a part thereof. *See* **test, objective.**

score, observed: *syn.* **score, raw.**

score, obtained: *syn.* **score, raw.**

score, original: *syn.* **score, raw.**

score, passing: *syn.* **score, cutting.**

score, percentage-correct: a derived score (type 1 A) which expresses the examinee's performance as a percentage of the maximum possible score; frequently overlooked is the fact that such scores are more a function of item difficulty than a true measure of an examinee's absolute performance.

score, percentile: a percentile corresponding to a given raw score in a frequency distribution; a given score expressed as a percentile rank. *See* **rank, percentile.**

score, point: *syn.* **score, raw.**

score, posture: an evaluation of body carriage expressed in terms of a numerical score or letter grade.

score, power: a test score indicating the level of difficulty of the most difficult item, or more often, the number of items in a scaled test that a pupil answers correctly. *See* **test, power.**

score, quotient: a score that expresses a person's performance in comparison with his supposed ability to perform as indicated by his chronological or mental age.

score, rate: an expression of an individual's speed of performance, usually stated in terms of the number of items or units of work done in a given time; less frequently stated in terms of the amount of time required to complete a given amount of work. *Syn.* **speed score.**

score, ratio: a score similar to a quotient score; usually, a score derived by dividing an achievement score expressed in terms of age by mental age and multiplying by 100. *See* **score, quotient.**

score, raw: a score obtained on a test as determined by the performance itself, to which no correction or modification of any kind has been applied other than the possible addition or subtraction of a constant score. *Syn.* **crude score** (1); **obtained score; original score;** *see* **score, corrected raw; score, gross.**

score, readability: *syn.* **index, readability.**

score reading: the visual and mental interpretation of the score of a musical composition, carried on either while listening to its performance or in order to hear the composition in imagination; a subject of instruction in some institutions for music education.

score record: *see* **record, score.**

score, reduced: (1) a score from which a constant, such as the mean, has been subtracted; *syn.* **reduced measure;** (2) sometimes an observation expressed in terms of measures of central tendency and variability of a defined population or sample, for example, a *standard score, T score,* or *sigma score.*

score, sensed-difference: a score on a scale where differences in test scores of individuals are proportional to the

differences between the same individuals in the characteristic measured, as sensed by competent judges.

score, sigma: *see* **score, standard.**

score, speed: *syn.* **score, rate.**

score, standard: a derived score on a test or other measuring device expressed in terms of the mean and standard deviation of the distribution of scores made on this test; this may be (*a*) a score in which the deviation from the mean is expressed as a multiple of the standard deviation, and the direction of the deviation by a positive or negative sign; known also as *z score, sigma score, standard measure* or *sigma measure;* mean and range sometimes taken as 5 and as 0 to 10, respectively, in order to eliminate negative signs; (*b*) a score that indicates the position of a given raw score in the group by fixing the mean of the distribution at 50 and expressing deviations from the mean in units of one-tenth the standard deviation (T score); or (*c*) a score derived by multiplying the standard score as defined in *a* by any constant and algebraically adding it to any other constant. *See* **deviation, standard; score, T; sigma; z score.**

score, stanine: a normalized score on a nine-point one-digit scale in which the successive score values represent intervals of one-half of a standard deviation with the middle interval set at 5, and in which the proportion of examinees at each score is the proportion of the normal curve area corresponding to the interval; a type of derived score, used originally in testing in the U.S. Air Force; score 1 represented the lowest 4 percent, score 2 the next 7 percent, score 3 the next 12 percent, scores 5, 6, 7, 8, and 9 represented the next 17, 20, 12, 7, and 4 percents, respectively. *See* **stanine.**

score, T: (1) a standard score with a mean of 50 and a standard deviation of 10 which is a linear transformation of the raw score; may be found by the formula

$$T = 10 \frac{X - M}{\sigma} + 50,$$ where X = raw score, M = mean,

and σ = standard deviation; (2) a normalized standard score with a mean of 50 and a standard deviation of 10; distribution is normalized by assigning values based on percentile equivalents of normal-curve z-score values. *Syn.* **T scale.**

score, test: a measure of the performance of an individual or group on a particular examination; usually expressed numerically in terms of the number of correct responses made, or transmuted into the units of an appropriate scale.

score, transmuted: a score expressed in terms of a scale different from the one on which it was obtained, for example, a *z score* derived from a *raw score,* a score obtained by finding the reciprocal of the raw score, etc. *Contr. w.* **score, gross; score, raw.**

score, true: (1) the value of an observation entirely free from error; (2) the mean of an infinite number of observations of a quantity. *Syn.* **true measure.**

score, ungrouped: (1) any score of a variable in which the class interval is equal to the smallest unit in which the data are customarily expressed; (2) a score on a variable in which the class interval is the same as the unit in terms of which the data have been obtained.

score units, interactive: psychological or sociological scores that are not relative to any other organism's scores but are expressed directly in physical units describing the extent of interaction with the environment; this includes all raw scores.

score units, ipsative: units expressed as standard scores based on a distribution of test scores made by one individual rather than on a distribution of scores on a single variable made by many different people; thus, all persons have the same mean and standard deviation for their scores.

score, z: *see* **z score.**

scorer reliability: *see* **reliability, scorer.**

scores, comparable: scores stated in terms of the same unit and based on the same reference point; hence subject to interpretation by the use of the same method.

scores, conversion of: *see* **conversion of scores.**

scores, distribution of: *see* **distribution of scores.**

scores, equated: derived scores that are comparable from test to test.

scores, odd-even: scores that result from scoring separately the even-numbered items and the odd-numbered items of a test, usually as a first step in computing test reliability by the split-halves method.

scores, scaled: (1) derived scores expressed, not in terms of age, grade, or percentile rank, but in terms of units of standard deviation of the scores for the original group (members of this group having been selected with a view to forming an average group); (2) any of several systems of scores (usually similar to standard scores) used in (a) articulating different forms, editions, and/or levels of a test or (b) developmental research.

scores, undistributed: (1) scores that do not discriminate between different degrees of ability; for example, perfect and zero scores on a test are undistributed scores because they do not differentiate among the varying abilities of those who obtained them; (2) scores that have not been arranged in order of magnitude or in a frequency table.

scoring: the act or process of evaluating responses to test situations or evaluating characteristics of whoever or whatever is being rated.

scoring, differential: the technique of scoring the same test or questionnaire in two or more different ways in order to obtain two or more scores that have different meanings; commonly used with interest inventories.

scoring formula: (1) any formula by which a test (usually, but not always, an objective test) is scored; (2) most frequently used is $X = R$ or $X = W$, where X = raw score, R = number of items right, and W = number of items wrong; (3) may involve a so-called *correction for guessing* which makes an allowance for differences in number of items not answered. *See* **correction-for-chance formula.**

scoring key: *see* **key, answer.**

scoring, machine: the scoring of tests by means of electrical, optical, and other devices that eliminate or minimize the handwork usually involved in marking, counting, and assembling credits. *Syn.* **mechanical scoring.**

scoring, mechanical: *syn.* **scoring, machine.**

scoring, multiple: a system of scoring in which different scoring keys are provided for the same items, each key being calibrated for measuring a different trait or capacity; for example, the scoring used in the Bernreuter personality inventory and Strong's vocational interest blank for men.

scoring system, global: evaluation of the total oral response given by a student of a foreign language rather than one or two aspects of his verbal performance in the target language.

scoring table: *see* **table, scoring.**

scoring, weighted: the assignment to each answer choice to a test item of a number of scoring points, called a *weight,* proportional to its value in assessing or predicting the criterion.

scotomization: mental blindness to one's faults or errors; the disposition to deny or to deprecate whatever tends to belittle the self.

scotophobia (skot′ə·fō′bi·ə; skŏ′tə-): morbid dread of darkness or night.

scouting: (1) the activities of the Boy Scouts and Girl Scouts; (2) making reconnaisance trips for the purpose of finding desired persons or information or materials; (3) the act of securing information about an opponent prior to an athletic contest.

Scouts, Boy: an organization for boys founded in England in 1908 to promote good citizenship through a program of activities that has now become very extensive; the movement spread to America and to other countries of the world.

Scouts, Girl: an organization for girls having its beginnings in Savannah, Georgia, in 1912, and having headquarters in New York City since 1916; similar in purpose to the *Boy Scouts.*

scrambled book: *see* **book, scrambled.**

scrambled text: *see* **book, scrambled.**

screen: the prepared surface on which images are projected, whether for motion-picture or slide projection; may be portable and designed to be rolled up on a spring roller or may be permanently fastened to a wall or frame.

screen, aluminum: a projection screen having the reflecting surface coated with aluminum paint.

screen, beaded: a projection screen whose surface consists of innumerable, minute glass beads; at a limited angle it gives a high quality reflection. *Syn.* **glass-beaded screen.**

screen, daylight: a projection screen so constructed that clear images from a projector are visible in an undarkened room; *beaded and lenticular screens* are often placed in this category.

screen, glass-beaded: *syn.* **screen, beaded.**

screen, lenticular: a silver projection screen with tiny corrugations on its surface to increase the brilliance of the image.

screen, matte: a projection screen with a flat, even surface and a dull finish that provides an even brilliance at all viewing angles; most effective in well-darkened viewing areas.

screen out: to separate, by a process of testing, those members of a group who may have a particular defect or deficiency (for example, a hearing loss, a deviation from 20/20 vision, or low academic aptitude), or those in whom the presence of tubercle bacilli is discovered from those who do not have that same defect or deficiency. *See* **screening; test, screen.**

screen, rear-projection: a translucent projection screen, used by placing the projector behind the screen and projecting the pictures through it.

screen, repeater: (audiovis. ed.) basically, one of a series of monitors which are connected in multiples to reproduce the images picked up by the television cameras; can be made by modifying regular television receivers.

screen test: *see* **test, screen.**

screen, translucent: *syn.* **screen, rear-projection.**

screen, white: a projection screen with the reflection surface having a flat white finish.

screening: (1) the act or process of administering a *screen test* and applying its results; *see* **screen out; test, screen;** (2) (spec. ed.) the process of selecting certain pupils who appear to be disturbed and significantly deviant; not intended to take the place of diagnosis or classification; leads the teacher to refer to competent specialists those children who could benefit most from diagnosis.

screening audiometry: *see* **audiometry, screening.**

screening, health: the cursory examination of physical, mental, social, and emotional aspects of an individual, designed to reveal deviations from the normal but not diagnostic in intent or result.

screening test: *syn.* **test, screen.**

scribble drawing: *see* **scribbling, circular; scribbling, longitudinal; scribbling, naming of; scribbling, uncontrolled.**

scribbling, circular: (art ed.) usually at the age of 2½ to 3½ after the child has assured himself through longitudinal scribbling, his urge for variation leads him to employ the whole arm in a more complex circular motion, which is called circular scribbling.

scribbling developmental stage: *see* **developmental stage, scribbling.**

scribbling, longitudinal: (art ed.) usually at the age of 2 years the child indicates through repeated longitudinal motions his ability for motor coordination; these motions are called longitudinal scribbling.

scribbling, naming of: (art ed.) the stage wherein a child identifies his scribbled lines with various objects, actions, or experiences gives rise to naming of scribbling; it is indicative of the change from kinesthetic to imaginative thinking.

scribbling stage: *see* **developmental stage, scribbling.**

scribbling, uncontrolled: (art ed.) the type of lines resulting from uncontrolled motions, usually the first stage of scribbling of the child from 2 to 3 years, indicating mere enjoyment of motor activity.

scribe: in ancient Egypt and Babylonia and among the Hebrews, a person of professional or semiprofessional status who performed clerical work, taught, or expounded the law. (Among the ancient Hebrews the scribe was also an authority in religious matters.)

script: a set of written specifications for the production of a motion picture, television program, or another type of presentation; includes narration and presentation layout. *See* **storyboard.**

scriptorium (skrip·tō′ri·əm): a writing room in a monastery of the early Middle Ages, devoted to the copying of manuscripts by the monks or nuns.

Scripture reading: *see* **reading, Scripture.**

scriptures: (1) the sacred writings of any people, such as the Persian scriptures; (2) (usually cap.) the sacred writings of Christendom, the Bible; (3) a quotation, passage, or text from the Bible; (4) figuratively, something regarded as a sacred record.

scuba diving: *see* **diving, scuba.**

sculpture: (1) the art of expressing ideas and representing forms in three dimensions rather than in a single plane, through the use of hard materials or of plastic materials rendered hard, such as stone, metal, wood, clay, wax, and cement, or of soft materials such as wire, paper, styrofoam, etc., and of such processes as cutting, carving, chiseling, modeling, casting, and assemblage or construction; (2) an object so produced.

scum gutter: a drainage gutter at the level of the surface of the water in a swimming pool.

SD: *see* **deviation, standard.**

sea daddy: an informal term used by Navy personnel to designate an older man who takes a recruit or young officer in hand and teaches him his trade or profession.

search, binary: *see* **binary search.**

search, literature: (libr. sci.) a systematic, exhaustive search for material related to a specific problem or subject.

search model: *see* **model, search.**

search procedure: in seeking material through information retrieval systems, the operation to determine whether certain information is in storage, the manner in which it is organized, and where it is located; as information is stored in a wider diversity of forms, the problem of search becomes increasingly complex; also needed in the search procedure is the inclusion of such considerations as the character of the audience for whom the message is designed and the task it proposes to do.

search reflex: *syn.* **response, mouth-orientation.**

seasonal sequence: adaptation of instruction in vocational agriculture to current conditions and activities on the farms of the community.

seasonal unemployment: *see* **unemployment, seasonal.**

seat mile: *see* **mile, seat.**

seating capacity: the number of students that can be seated in a classroom, auditorium, or other room of a building or in an entire building; sometimes computed as the number of seats actually installed in the unit under consideration, and sometimes by dividing the total amount of floor area by the number of square feet allowed for each seat.

seating chart, classroom: a sheet of paper, chart, or diagram on which is shown the location of the seat of each pupil in the room, with space for writing in the name of each pupil.

seating equipment, movable: seats and desks so designed that they may be moved from place to place at will, as opposed to the older type of seating equipment that is fastened permanently to the floor.

seating equipment, stationary: classroom furniture, such as seats and desks, that is fastened to the floor and cannot be moved about at will, as opposed to the more modern, movable equipment.

seating, longitudinal: an arrangement of bench-like seats running lengthwise in the school bus, usually located at side walls and center.

seating plan, diagonal: a method of placing the seats and desks in a classroom suggested by H. E. Bennett, the seats being arranged in rows diagonally across the room so that light from the windows comes over each pupil's left shoulder.

seating plan, quadrant: a way of arranging the seats and desks in a classroom proposed by H. E. Bennett, according to which the desks are placed in four concentric arcs and part of a fifth, the teacher's desk being at the right front corner of the room as the center of each arc and there being an aisle and cross passages 18 inches wide.

seating space: the area provided for seating each passenger of a school bus; usually 13 inches wide by 14 inches deep.

seating space, linear feet of: in a school bus, the number of feet in the lengthwise measurement along the forward edge of the seat cushion.

seatwork: any work or activity that the child may carry on at his desk or table without supervision.

second classman: a cadet who is in his third year at a service academy; a junior.

second language: *see* **language, second.**

second-level schooling: *see* **schooling, second-level.**

second moment: (1) (of a frequency distribution) the sum of the products of the separate frequencies by the squares of their deviations from the point used as origin, divided by the number of observations or cases (the second moment of a frequency distribution about its mean is its variance, whose square root is the standard deviation); (2) (of a frequency distribution) the sum of the products of the separate frequencies and the squares of their separate deviations from the point used as the origin; (3) (of a frequency) the product of that frequency and the square of its deviation from the point selected as the origin.

second-order drive: *see* **drive, second-order.**

second-order factors: *see* **factors, second-order.**

second-order gifted: *see* **gifted, second-order.**

second-order interaction: *see* **interaction, second-order.**

second wind: (phys. ed.) a physiological phenomenon, typified by the feeling of relief upon making the necessary metabolic adjustments to a heavy endurance load.

secondary agricultural education: *see* **agricultural education, secondary.**

secondary amentia: *see* **amentia, secondary.**

secondary clue: *see* **clue, secondary.**

secondary correlation: *see* **correlation, secondary.**

secondary drive: *see* **drive, secondary.**

secondary education: a period of education planned especially for young people of ages approximately 12 to 17, in which the emphasis tends to shift from mastery of basic tools of learning, expression, and understanding to the use and extension of the tools in exploring areas of thought and living, and in exploring and acquiring information, concepts, intellectual skills, attitudes, social, physical, and intellectual ideals, and habits, understandings, and appreciations; often differentiated in varying degrees according to the needs and interests of the pupils; may be either terminal or preparatory.

secondary experience: *syn.* **experience, cognitive.**

secondary group: *see* **group, secondary.**

secondary mathematics: *see* **mathematics, secondary.**

secondary objectives: *see* **objectives, secondary.**

secondary pupil, unclassified: *see* **pupil, unclassified secondary.**

secondary qualities: the sense qualities (color, taste, sound) that John Locke and others held to belong to the object only when we perceive it, whereas primary qualities (extension, motion) are real in that they belong to the thing even when we do not perceive it. *See* **primary qualities.**

secondary reinforcement: *see* **reinforcer, conditioned.**

secondary school: *syn.* **high school.**

secondary school counselor: *see* **counselor, secondary school.**

secondary school organization: *see* **organization, secondary school.**

secondary school reorganization: *see* **reorganization, secondary school.**

secondary school, reorganized: *syn.* **reorganized high school.**

secondary school student: *see* **student, secondary school.**

secondary sex character: *see* **character, secondary sex.**

secondary shop: *see* **shop, secondary.**

secondary source: *see* **source, secondary.**

secret language: *see* **language, secret.**

secretarial accounting: *see* **accounting, secretarial.**

secretarial-practice course: *see* **course, secretarial-practice.**

secretarial training: *see* **training, secretarial.**

secretary of board of education: the person charged by law with the keeping of the official minutes or record of the transactions of the board and with other duties prescribed by law; in some states he must be a member of the board; in others the superintendent or other nonmember is designated or may act as secretary; sometimes called clerk. *See* **clerk, school.**

secretary, placement: *syn.* **placement officer.**

secretary, school: an educational office employee responsible for the management of a school or school system office; usually assigned directly to one or more administrative officers; duties include secretarial work as well as office management and often the conducting of certain activities of the school such as the collection of various funds.

secretary to the principal: an educational office employee with responsibilities for managing the office of a school principal; duties often include maintaining certain school records, conducting certain financial business, and directing all other secretarial work in the school.

secretary to the superintendent: an educational office employee with responsibilities for managing the office of a superintendent of schools; duties often include direct responsibility for maintaining school board records.

sectarian college: *see* **college, sectarian.**

sectarian instruction: *see* **instruction, sectarian.**

section: a distinct part of a school grade or class group.

section, duplicate: one of two or more classes in a given subject offered in the same semester and following the same course of study.

sectional teachers' meeting: *see* **teachers' meeting, sectional.**

sectional-view rotation method: *see* **rotation method, sectional-view.**

sectioning, class: dividing a single class in a given grade or subject into two or more sections based on the pupils' ability to learn, in order to permit differentiation of instruction; a method employed where homogeneous grouping into separate classes is not possible; also employed by those who are opposed to homogeneous grouping and believe each class should represent a "cross section" of abilities, with instructional adaptations made within each class.

secular: (1) used in the church for priests, not members of monastic orders nor bound by their rules; also called *lay;* (2) more commonly, nonreligious; not sacred; opposed to *supernatural;* without religious ties or observances; may be applied to schools, curriculum, and way of life (for example, nationalism, society, science, industrialism, political and economic aspects of life, etc.); a secular viewpoint forces lessening of men's loyalties to the church. (A person may support secular public schools, however, who otherwise accepts the religious point of view.)

secular school: a school which has no ties with churches or other religious groups and which does not support any particular religious philosophy.

secular school, Jewish: a type of school that developed in eastern Europe and in America during the second decade of the present century; it offers a program of Jewish studies which emphasizes the study of the Hebrew or Yiddish language and literature and reduces to a minimum the teaching of religious rituals and practices. *See* **Sholom Aleichem school; Yiddish school.**

secular school of historiography: *see* **historiography, naturalistic school of.**

secularism: (1) an all-inclusive, nonreligious view of life; finds security in obedience to natural law; holds that man directs his own destiny; does not recognize such conceptions as sin, regeneration, grace, etc.; (2) historically, the separation of education and other cultural aspects of society from church influence, beginning largely with the Renaissance. *See* **humanism, scientific.**

secularization: the removal of religious control from schools or of religious materials from the curriculum.

secured credit: *see* **credit, secured.**

security: (1) the feeling of personal worth, self-assurance, confidence, and acceptance by the group, developed in the child through giving him ample recognition, by paying attention to his needs, and by enabling him to become aware of his own abilities; (2) (in testing) the act or process of taking all steps necessary to keep a test or set of tests from becoming available to individuals who may later take the test or tests, and of not permitting any form of cheating before, during, or after the taking of the tests.

security, social: *see* **social security.**

seder (sā'dēr): (Heb., lit., "order," "arrangement") the traditional ritual ceremony performed on the first two evenings of Passover, commemorating the exodus of the Jews from Egypt.

seeding: (1) in programmed instruction, the insertion of review materials at intervals in a program; these reviews may be either regularly spaced (periodic) or irregularly spaced (aperiodic); (2) (phys. ed.) the plan or procedure of placing the better players in a tournament in such an order that they will not meet until the final round of competition.

seeing, constructive: seeing that is constructed out of successive partial impressions, usually found in partially blind persons.

Seeing Eye: a philanthropic organization (founded 1929) which trains dog guides as mobility aids for blind persons.

seeing, partially: *see* **partially seeing.**

segment: in computer operation, a portion of a program, often used as an *overlay,* consisting of one or more complete routines.

segmental activity: *see* **activity, segmental.**

segregated junior high school: *see* **junior high school.**

segregated special school: *see* **special school, segregated.**

segregation: (1) (genet.) the process by which differing characters present in the grandparents (P^1 generation) reappear in the grandchildren (F^2 generation) after having been submerged in the parents (F^1 generation); (2) the separation from an otherwise mixed group of individuals having a given characteristic; hence, the assignment of Negro and white pupils and/or school officials to separate schools or classes, etc.

segregation, de facto: racial separation not directly guaranteed by laws, but which exists in fact and which is maintained by housing patterns, gerrymandered school district lines, and social class barriers; before the 1970s characteristic of the school systems of most American cities. *Contr. w.* **segregation, de jure.**

segregation, de jure: racial separation directly guaranteed by laws as in South Africa today or in America from the late 19th century (Plessy *v.* Ferguson, 1896) until after the mid-twentieth century (Brown *v.* Board of Education, Topeka, 1954). *Contr. w.* **segregation, de facto.**

segregation of ability: the classing or grouping of individuals according to their power to perform specific acts, and the provision of differentiated instruction fitted to the aptitudes and capacities of each group and of each member of the group.

segregation, partial: the regular scheduling of children from different grades together for part of the school day to meet special educational needs; used frequently in special educational provisions for hearing handicapped, speech handicapped, visually handicapped, and gifted children.

seizure, Jacksonian: *see* **epilepsy, Jacksonian.**

selection: (1) (genet.) a natural or artificial process tending to prevent some individuals or groups from surviving and propagating, at the same time allowing others to do so; (2) (read.) choice of a unit of reading material pertinent to the problem at hand; (3) (voc. ed.) the assignment of students by a teacher-coordinator or a vocational instructor for a vocational program based on their occupational intent, vocational interests, skills, attitudes, and abilities to succeed in the particular program; *see* **teacher-coordinator.**

selection, artificial: the process by which desirable traits are consciously chosen by man for perpetuation, as in livestock and plant breeding. *See* **selection; selection, natural.**

selection by design: *syn.* **selection, proportional.**

selection, field: (data processing) the channeling of differing data locations into one field for printing, punching, or accumulation.

selection, multivariate: selection of a group of subjects on the basis of their homogeneity on more than one test. *See* **selection, univariate.**

selection, natural: the evolutionary theory that viability of various traits and structures comes about by the utility of those traits in the struggle for survival.

selection, personnel: (elem. and sec. ed.) the process of assessing candidates for teaching positions and nonprofessional employment; handled either by the central administration or by selection committees, of which the school principal is often a member, frequently with staff participation in evaluation of professional candidates.

selection, preservice: any process by which certain persons are prevented from entering the teaching profession while certain others are encouraged to enter it; includes selective admission to teacher-education curricula or institutions, selective retention or promotion in these curricula or institutions, certification requirements, and recruitment of promising candidates for the profession.

selection, pretraining: any phase of preservice selection operating prior to the candidate's period of professional specialization. *See* **selection, preservice.**

selection, proportional: a method of selecting a sample by taking the same proportion of each of a number of categories into which the total or universe may be divided, the resulting sample being called a *stratified sample* or *probability sample.* *Syn.* **proportioned selection; selection by design.**

selection, proportioned: *syn.* **selection, proportional.**

selection, random: the process of obtaining a random sample. *See* **sample, random.**

selection ratio: *see* **ratio, selection.**

selection, social: the process by which participation in social interaction results in the selection of persons, customs, and institutions possessing certain kinds of aptitudes for survival and use.

selection, teacher: *see* **selection, personnel.**

selection test: *see* **test, selection.**

selection, univariate: the selection of a group of subjects on the basis of their homogeneity in a single test; Godfrey Thomson has investigated how such selection would modify the results of a factorial analysis of a test battery.

selective admission: *see* **admission, selective.**

selective dissemination of information: *see* **dissemination of information, selective.**

selective factor: *see* **factor, selective.**

selective listening: listening either in school or at home to particular radio programs recommended by school authorities as having educational value.

selective marking: *see* **marking, selective.**

selective perception: *see* **perception, selective.**

selective promotion: *see* **selective retention.**

selective retention: *see* **retention, selective.**

Selective Service test: *see* **test, Selective Service.**

selective system: (sec. ed.) the organization of the European secondary school which selects children between the ages of ten and twelve for study in a fixed curriculum; similar to the arrangement of the New England Latin schools. *See* **academy** (1).

selective thinking: *see* **thinking, selective.**

selective training and retention program: *see* **program, selective training and retention.**

selectivity: the practice of using the best evidence available and of exercising discriminating judgments in making choices.

selector unit: (1) that component of a teaching machine which compares the pupil's response with the correct response; *see* **comparator;** (2) the component of a teaching machine that picks items to be presented from the *library unit.*

self-acceptance: (1) seeing oneself as one really is; accepting and understanding one's interests, needs, and abilities; (2) seeing oneself as being accepted by others; being one of and conforming to the group.

self-activity: the type of activity that has its origin, direction, and determination within the conscious subject or agent who acts; it is contrasted both with natural activity below the conscious level and with activity resulting from external force or pressure; learning is, at least in part, a form of self-activity.

self-actualization: A. Maslow's term to describe the process of becoming integrated to the point of developing capacities and of accepting one's motives and goals in life.

self-adjustment: (1) full understanding in relating feelings toward self as well as toward others; (2) a continuous process of maintaining harmony among the attributes of the individual and the environmental conditions that surround him.

self-administering test: *see* **test, self-administering.**

self-analysis: an attempt to understand one's own behavior, one's abilities and disabilities, and one's motivations.

self-appraisal: (1) a student's evaluation and understanding of his interests, aptitudes, abilities, personal adjustment, and personal character; (2) knowing oneself, one's capabilities and limitations; for example, knowing what one can offer a prospective employer.

self-assurance: *syn.* **self-confidence.**

self-awareness: an aim in *sensitivity training* whereby the individual has the opportunity to see himself as he is seen by others, to examine his motivations, to compare his perceptions with those of others, to control his feelings under group pressure, and to study the kinds of roles he tends to take in a group.

self-check: in computer operation, a redundant symbolization; for example, a number incorporating a check digit.

self-concept: the individual's perception of himself as a person, which includes his abilities, appearance, performance in his job, and other phases of daily living.

self-confidence: faith in one's own ability.

self-confrontation technique: presentation, via video tape recording, of a student's performance in a role-playing situation.

self-confrontation television: *see* **television, mirror-image.**

self-congruence: the state in which self-experiences are accurately symbolized in the self-concept in such a way that one is freely, deeply, and acceptably oneself, with one's actual experience of his feelings and reactions matched by an accurate awareness of these feelings and reactions as they occur.

self-conscious: (1) having a tendency to be aware of the self when reacting or performing, especially in the presence of others; (2) having a tendency to pay attention to or be preoccupied with the reactions of others to oneself, particularly when these reactions are thought to be evaluative.

self-consciousness: (1) (philos.) awareness of one's self as an object of knowledge; being able to see one's self "from the outside"; an ability to know that distinctive organization of roles and statuses which is called personality by taking the role of other individuals and of groups of others toward one's self; awareness of self as a distinct and continuing center of purposeful activity, or as a spiritual reality; (Hegel) the participation of the selfhood of the human individual in the "absolute self"; (2) a state in which one is overly aware of self and unduly sensitive to the reactions of others.

self-contained classroom: *see* **classroom, self-contained.**

self-control: (1) the application by an individual of his own values, ideals, or judgment to his behavior; (2) the willingness and ability to curb or restrain or guide one's present impulses by giving consideration to future consequences; (3) the tendency and ability to hold to a deliberately chosen course of action or to refrain from diversionary or unacceptable courses of action by choice rather than from compulsion or fear. *See* **discipline** (2).

self-correction: (for. lang. instr.) a fundamental aspect of the learning process with *pattern drills* in which the student notices discrepancies between his own response and the correct response and presumably is able to correct his response in a subsequent frame.

self-corrective handwriting chart: *see* **chart, self-corrective handwriting.**

self-critique: critique by a student of his own performance, especially when recorded on video tape, thus allowing immediate playback and critique under supervision of instructor. *See* **self-confrontation technique.**

self-defense activities: *see* **activities, self-defense.**

self-demand feeding: *see* **schedule, self-demand.**

self-demand schedule: *see* **schedule, self-demand.**

self-determinism: the theory that man's actions are determined by his own nature, character, or volition rather than by external determinants. *See* **determinism; free will.**

self-directed study: *syn.* **project method.**

self-discipline: control of conduct exercised not by an external authority but by the learner who accepts a task as his own, including whatever effort is involved, and controls his activities accordingly. *See* **discipline.**

self-education: the act of inciting and effecting growth and development of oneself through one's own motivation. (A person chooses himself the stimuli to which he will attend; he determines within himself the kind and intensity of the remolding of himself that goes on.)

self, emerging: an evolutionary concept which holds that the individual is continuously rebuilding the self through interaction with the surrounding culture and that nothing is predetermined at birth or at any subsequent period; what the individual accepts out of each experience is built into the self and, in turn, affects the emerging culture.

self-esteem: the judgment and attitude an individual holds toward himself.

self-evaluation: making a judgment about oneself or about some characteristic of oneself.

self-evident: pertaining to that which needs no verification or proof because a clear and attentive mind perceives it so distinctly that it cannot be doubted; known intuitively; descriptive of the universal a priori principles from which other truths can be deduced—upon which all knowledge is based.

self-examination: (relig. ed.) a spiritual inventory made periodically by an individual, consisting of a careful scrutiny of past thoughts and acts as a prelude to a change in behavior; a necessary step in character formation and in spiritual growth.

self-expression: expression of thoughts, feelings, or percepts of an individual according to his own level of development.

self-government, pupil: *see* **student government.**

self-guidance: the endeavor of the individual to direct himself, using his own knowledge, experiences, and self-judgment as a basis.

self-help: the act of carrying out a task without outside assistance.

self-ideal: a person's view of what he aspires to be or believes he ought to be. *See* **ego ideal.**

self-identification: (art ed.) (1) the ability to put oneself into the place of the subject matter and the medium of one's own creation, that is, to feel like being a part of the representation and also to feel like the medium, such as wood, which "likes to show its grain and has a special ability" to bend, etc., or like water color, which "loves to merge" with other colors on the basis of its fluidity; (2) the ability to understand and feel the creative needs of children during the different stages of development; (3) the ability to appreciate a work of art on the basis of identification with both the individual needs of the appreciator and the intentions of the artist.

self-image: the perceptual component of self; the image one has of the appearance of his body; the picture one has of the impressions he makes on others.

self-instructional center: *see* **center, self-instructional.**

self-insurance: the setting aside of a reserve fund to cover the eventuality of loss sustained by fire or other hazard instead of the more common practice of purchasing a policy from an established insurance company.

self-judgment: approbation or disapprobation of an individual by himself.

self-liquidating bond: *see* **bond, self-liquidating.**

self-managed materials: *see* **materials, self-managed.**

self-marking test: *see* **test, self-marking.**

self-monitoring: the act of listening to one's recorded or simultaneous live responses to linguistic drills. *Comp. w.* **monitoring.**

self-monitoring system: equipment in an electronic learning laboratory which permits the student to hear his own voice performance whether simultaneously through activated headphones or delayed through playback of his recording.

self-motivation: determination of behavior in which the welfare of one's self is an important factor and in which there is ego involvement.

self-other relation: a relation producing *self-consciousness* which is developed in social situations that require the individual to become aware of self through identifying himself with the full range of consequences which follow as he puts his choices into action, a continuing relation that results in a potentially expanding self.

self-pacing: an arrangement, particularly in programmed instruction, whereby provision is made for the individual student to set his own schedule for learning or rate of achievement and to monitor his own progress. *See* **pacing, group; pacing, planned.**

self, perceived: the view a person has of himself.

self-perception: *see* **self-analysis; self-awareness; self-concept.**

self, phenomenal: all those aspects of the phenomenal field which the individual experiences as part of himself.

self-possession: (1) the ability to marshal one's resources, mental, emotional, and physical, for effective use in any emergency; (2) composure; (3) a feeling of assurance that one can remain in command of himself and not be driven by external forces.

self-psychology: the view that psychology must be defined by reference to the self or person and that mental activity or behavior can only be understood in terms of the varying attitudes or changes in the self.

self-rating scale: *see* **scale, self-rating.**

self-rating, teacher: the introspective comparison by a teacher of himself with other teachers or with a known standard.

self-realization: the development of one's immanent potentialities of character and intelligence by identifying oneself imaginatively with the spirit of the best that has been said, thought, and done, and acting accordingly; some authorities understand these potentialities in an abstractly ideal sense which transcends verifiability in everyday biological experience. *Comp. w.* **social-self-realization.**

self-responsibility: the trait that grows with the opportunities to share in a democracy mutual tasks for the orderliness and welfare of the group as well as for personal independence.

self-study: a process, terminating in a written report and usually fulfilling stated guidelines, which a higher education institution carries out, frequently to fulfill requirements of a regional accrediting association.

self-sufficient: (1) able to take care of one's own needs without the support of others; (2) not dependent on the companionship and services of others.

self-teaching: learning carried on by the learner without the intervention of a live teacher.

self-teaching materials: *see* **materials, self-teaching.**

self-test: a test that can be self-administered and also scored by the pupil; often included with *self-teaching materials.*

self-testing activities: *see* **activities, self-testing.**

self theory in counseling: a counseling approach that stresses the counselee's ability to determine the issues discussed and to solve his own problems and establishes a warm, permissive, and accepting climate which permits the counselee to explore his self-structure in relation to his unique experience and thus enables him to face his unacceptable characteristics without feeling threatened and anxious, so that he moves toward acceptance of himself and his values and is able to modify or change those aspects of himself which he thinks need modification.

self-understanding: the student's adequate and realistic self-concept based upon a knowledge of as many facts and factors as he can obtain about himself. *See* **self-perception.**

selling ethics: *see* **ethics.**

selling, retail: *see* **retail selling.**

semanteme: an image or idea word; the element of a word that indicates its general meaning; an element of a word that provides basic images and ideas.

semantic analysis: *see* **analysis, semantic.**

semantic approach: a method of teaching correct usage in language utilizing the psychology of meaning rather than formal grammar.

semantic conditioning: *see* **conditioning, semantic.**

semantic counseling: *see* **counseling, semantic.**

semantic differential: C. Osgood's technique for measuring the connotative meaning of words by using a scale of bipolar adjectives to rate a given term such as mother, school teacher, communism, etc.

semantic therapy, general: *see* **therapy, general semantic.**

semantics: (1) a general theory of signs and their referents; signs that constitute language are the central concern of some semanticists while others have interested themselves in the semantics of the symbols of art, ritual, etc.; (2) the logical analysis of language.

semantogenic (sə·man'tō·jen'ik): originating in semantic reaction; resulting from evaluations made of experiences. (Semantogenic disorders are inadequate or maladjustive reaction tendencies determined by the ways in which events or experiences are interpreted, evaluated, judged, etc.)

semasiology (sə·mā'si·ol'ə·ji): a study of the development and changes in the meanings of words; practically synonymous with *semantics.*

semeiotics: *see* **semiotics.**

semester: half of an academic year, usually 16 to 18 weeks.

semester credit hour: *see* **credit hour, semester.**

semester hour: 1 hour a week of lecture or class instruction for one semester or its credit equivalent of laboratory field work, or other types of instruction.

semester promotion: *syn.* **promotion, semiannual.**

semester report: *see* **report, semester.**

semi-interquartile range: *syn.* **deviation, quartile.**

semiannual promotion: *see* **promotion, semiannual.**

semiconcrete materials: *see* **materials, semiconcrete.**

semicontrolled composition: *see* **composition, semicontrolled.**

semideaf: an obsolete term, formerly used by educators of the deaf to designate pupils with partial hearing.

semidepartmentalization: a plan of school organization in which the work is partly departmentalized, as in platoon schools, each teacher instructing pupils in more than one subject but not in all subjects.

semidetached foundation: *see* **foundation, semidetached.**

semilogarithmic chart: *syn.* **graph, semilogarithmic.**

semilogarithmic graph: *see* **graph, semilogarithmic.**

semimute: an obsolete term, formerly used to designate persons with partly intelligible speech acquired before the loss of hearing.

seminar: an instructional technique common in but not limited to higher education in which a group of students engaged in research or advanced study meets under the general direction of one or more leaders for a discussion of problems of mutual interest. *See* **colloquium.**

seminar, guidance: a class in counseling philosophies, techniques, and procedures for advanced students of counseling psychology.

seminar room: (1) a small room in a college or university library in which selected material on a given subject is placed temporarily for the use of a group engaged in special study or research; (2) a room in a college or university library in which a large part of its collection in a particular field is placed for the convenience of advanced students and faculty; (3) a room designated primarily for use by seminar groups.

seminar, teachers': *see* **seminar.**

seminary: a school of secondary or higher grade usually designed to serve a particular rather than a general purpose; for example, *female seminaries* during the first half of the nineteenth century in the United States served only girls, *teachers' seminaries,* particularly in Prussia near the middle of the nineteenth century, trained only teachers, and *theological seminaries* even now train only students for the ministry.

seminary, female: a secondary school for girls in the United States during the nineteenth century.

seminary, major: (R.C. ed.) a church-operated college devoted to training for the priesthood and usually offering a course extending over 6 years, during which philosophy and theology are studied.

seminary, minor: (R.C. ed.) a church-operated preparatory school where young men planning to enter the priesthood follow a course of secondary education.

seminary, preparatory: (R.C. ed.) a secondary school where students may test their vocation for priesthood.

seminary, private: a seminary operated under ecclesiastical authority but not controlled by a diocese.

seminary, teachers': a term used to designate an early type of teacher-training institution. (One of the first teacher-training schools, established in Reims, France, in 1685, was known as a *seminary,* as were many such schools subsequently established in Germany.)

seminary, theological: *syn.* **theological school.**

semiotics (sē·mi·ot'iks): *alt. sp.* **semeiotics;** the systematic study or philosophy of signs and symbols as they function in languages both natural and artificial; includes *semantics, syntactics,* and *pragmatics.*

semiprofession: an occupation ordinarily requiring as preparation a course of training approximately 2 years in length, with a high school education or its equivalent as a prerequisite; a *middle-level occupation* intermediate between a trade and a profession.

semirural school: a rarely used, somewhat loose term designating a school in which a considerable percentage of the students are from a rural community.

semiskilled: (mil. ed.) qualified to assist a skilled specialist, but not so skilled as to work without supervision.

semiskilled trade: *see* **trade, semiskilled.**

semistate certification system: *see* **certification system, semi-state.**

semivowel: a speech sound that has the nature of a vowel but, like a consonant, does not form a separate syllable, for example, English *y* in *young* and *w* in *twin.*

senate, faculty: *syn.* **faculty council.**

senescence: (1) most generally, the period of decline for a given function, skill, structure, etc.; more commonly, the age period (in human beings, usually considered to be from about 60 years onward) when physical and mental capacities have, on the average, already definitely declined from maximum level and are continuing their involutionary course; (2) the process of normal decline for a given function, skill, structure, etc., associated with or due to advancing age.

senile psychosis: *see* **psychosis, senile.**

senior college: *see* **college, senior.**

senior high school: the upper part of a divided reorganized secondary school, comprising usually grades 10 to 12 or 9 to 12.

senior high school counselor: *see* **counselor, senior high school.**

senior high school, three-year: a secondary school composed of the three upper high school grades, usually grades 10 to 12.

senior kindergarten: *see* **kindergarten, senior.**

senior ROTC: *see* **ROTC, senior.**

senior teacher role: in team teaching, the part played by an experienced, mature master teacher who coordinates and leads a team in his area of specialization.

senior undergraduate library school: *see* **library school, senior undergraduate.**

senior unit: *see* **unit, senior.**

sensa: *n. pl.* qualities by which we describe what we perceive, for example, redness, loudness, hardness, fragrance; in various theories they are held to be mental, physical, neither, or both.

sensate culture: *see* **culture, sensate.**

sensation: a stimulus conveyed to the brain by a sensory nerve.

sensation area, auditory: *see* **auditory sensation area.**

sensation level: the sound-pressure level required to make any frequency barely audible to the average normal ear.

sensation unit: *see* **decibel.**

sensationalism: (philos.) that theory of knowledge which holds that the mind is natively empty, a *tabula rasa,* upon which impressions are left by the processes of sense perception, following which complex ideas may be developed by the mind (*concepts* follow *percepts*); refutes the doctrine of innate ideas and rationalism as a theory of knowledge; a kind of extreme empiricism, developed from Locke's *Essay* by Condillac.

sense experience: the direct experiences or results of the stimulation of the special sensory endings, such as warmth, bitter taste, or blackness.

sense, kinesthetic: *syn.* **muscle sense.**

sense modality: a specific sensory entity such as vision, hearing, etc.

sense, muscle: *see* **muscle sense.**

sense, obstacle: *syn.* **perception, object.**

sense of consonance: *see* **consonance, sense of.**

sense of intensity: *syn.* **discrimination, intensity.**

sense of pitch: *syn.* **discrimination, pitch.**

sense of rhythm: *syn.* **discrimination, rhythm.**

sense of time: *syn.* **discrimination, time.**

sense, olfactory: *see* **olfactory sense.**

sense, proprioceptive: *syn.* **muscle sense.**

sense realism: *see* **realism, sense.**

sense, visceral: *see* **visceral sense.**

sense, visual: *see* **visual sense.**

sensed-difference score: *see* **score, sensed-difference.**

sensibility: responsiveness to external stimuli; capacity to experience sensations or emotion.

sensibility, epicritic: the neural capacity to distinguish among slight variations of pressure, temperature, and other sensory modalities. *Dist. f.* **sensibility, protopathic.**

sensibility, protopathic: the neural function of responding only to painfully intense, undifferentiated, or crude sensory stimulation. *Dist. f.* **sensibility, epicritic.**

sensitive zone: an area of the body surface that is markedly sensitive to tactile stimulation. *See* **erogenous zone.**

sensitivity: (stat.) the power of an experiment to sense or detect a difference between the true value of a parameter and the value hypothesized for it when such a difference exists.

sensitivity, diagnostic: in sensitivity training, a term used by guidance specialists to refer to the process of coming to see more clearly what happens in a small group and how "what happens" can be influenced.

sensitivity, film: *see* **film speed** (1).

sensitivity, harmonic: *see* **harmonic sensitivity.**

sensitivity, social: perceptual skill that makes one aware of another's feelings even though the cues to such feelings are weak or disguised.

sensitivity training: *see* **training, sensitivity.**

sensory acuity: *see* **acuity, sensory.**

sensory aid: *see* **aid, sensory.**

sensory aphasia: *syn.* **aphasia, sensory-receptive.**

sensory capacity: *see* **capacity, sensory.**

sensory compensation: *see* **compensation, sensory.**

sensory contacts: those experiences by which children become acquainted with objects or ideas through the use of their senses, for example, the baby's experience in feeling, tasting, smelling, and seeing its hand.

sensory deprivation: *see* **deprivation, sensory.**

sensory-discrimination test: *see* **test, sensory-discrimination.**

sensory education: in Montessori usage, educational activities to refine the senses (auditory, visual, gustatory, olfactory, tactile) to higher sensitivity and to develop the capacity to appreciate fine differences in stimuli.

sensory feedback: *see* **feedback, sensory.**

sensory modality: *see* **modality, sensory.**

sensory-motor process: matching sensory data to motor data.

sensory-neural deafness: *see* **deafness, sensory-neural.**

sensory-neural loss: *see* **loss, sensory-neural.**

sensory-receptive aphasia: *see* **aphasia, sensory-receptive.**

sensory response system: *see* **response system, sensory.**

sensory threshold: a range on a continuum of qualitatively or quantitatively equal steps of discrimination produced by relatively proportional increments of stimulus intensity. [The lower limit of the threshold range (RL_l) is the point of first appearance of the specified quality as the stimulus intensity is increased above some subliminal value by equal increments. At such intensity the qualitative discrimination can be made half the time. The upper limit (RL_u) is the point of maximal intensity change which yet fails to increase the frequency of positive judgments of the quality.]

sensory training: *see* **training, sensory.**

sensuous: (art) (1) a term descriptive of impressions or imagery addressing the senses; (2) relating to or providing pleasure or delight in qualities of color, sound, texture, or artistic form, including bodily ease or movement; (3) pertaining to pleasure of the senses for its own sake.

sentence: (1) a word or number of words arranged grammatically and syntactically to form a full unit of expression of thought or feeling; (2) *see* **sentence, mathematical.**

sentence, biconditional: (math.) a compound sentence where the two parts are joined by the logical connective "if and only if". *Syn.* **double implication.**

sentence building: an area of language study dealing with (*a*) the combining of words to form sentences; (*b*) the formation of compound tenses, phrases, and clauses; (*c*) the nature and use of concord, or agreement; (*d*) the relationship of sentence components; (*e*) differences between regular and irregular sentences.

sentence, closed: a mathematical sentence whose empirical truth or falsity can be determined under the conventional meanings attached to the symbols; examples are $2 < 7$, 2 is a prime number, and $\pi < 3.15$.

sentence completion: a projective technique in which the subject is instructed to finish incomplete sentences or stories.

sentence, compound: (math.) two mathematical sentences joined by one of the logical connectives; these are "and", "or", "if . . . then", "if and only if", "not".

sentence comprehension: *see* **comprehension, sentence.**

sentence, dehydrated: sequences of words which, when organized by the student into proper agreement and word order, will form a complete sentence.

sentence, directed: an oral or written exercise in which the language student performs a grammatical transformation according to directions. *See* **transformation, chain.**

sentence, frame: (math.) an open sentence in which a square, triangle, or circle is used as placeholder, for example, $\Box + 3 = 7$.

sentence, kernel: (lang. arts) a basic pattern sentence from which other sentence forms may be developed through transformational procedures such as changes in word order, tense, or expansion.

sentence, mathematical: any expression of a mathematical relation such as set membership, equality, congruence, order, and the like; not necessarily a sentence in the formal grammatical sense.

sentence meaning: the idea for which the entire sentence stands; to be distinguished from the ideas suggested by the parts separately.

sentence method: (1) a method of teaching reading in which the whole sentence, instead of a word, phrase, or letter, is presented as a unit; (2) a method of teaching shorthand in which new words are first presented in sentences rather than as isolated words.

sentence, number: (math.) a sentence that makes an assertion about order or equality for numbers, for example, $-3 - 2$ or $x + 2 = 1$.

sentence, open: (math.) a mathematical sentence whose empirical truth or falsity cannot be determined; examples are "$x + 3 = 7$", "ABC is a triangle", and "p is an open sentence." *Contr. w.* **sentence, closed.**

sentence pattern: one of the recurring patterns of words in the order familiar in English sentences, for example, noun-verb, noun-verb-object, or noun-verb-adverb.

sentence reading: *see* **reading, sentence.**

sentence, run-on: two or more sentences lacking appropriate relationship and incorrectly given in the form of one sentence.

sentence, run-together: *syn.* **sentence, run-on.**

sentence sense: the ability to recognize a group of words that forms a sentence, as distinguished from a group of words that does not form a sentence or a group of words that forms more than one sentence.

sentence, single-word: a form of expression characteristic of early speech development in which a single word is used to express a complete thought, for example, "Go" meaning "I want to go outside." *Syn.* **word sentence.**

sentence, topic: a sentence in a paragraph that shows what the paragraph is about.

sentiment: an affective and therefore noncognitive response, more permanent but weaker than emotion, usually associated with a rationally known motive or value, for example, the sentiment of patriotism is associated with duty to one's country; a sentiment differs from an emotion only in degree and involves a predisposition to a given emotional response.

sentinel: (automatic data processing) a symbol identifying or indicating the beginning or end of a word, field, record, block, or file.

separate: *n.* a *reprint* or special copy of an article, chapter, or other part of a larger publication; distinguished from a pamphlet in having been issued originally in a larger publication.

separate heating plant: *see* **heating plant, separate.**

separate school: (1) a school set apart from the regular school system or the main educational group by a unique course of study, separate administration, etc.; (2) a racially segregated school.

separation of church and state: the traditional American principle that society's institution of government should not be used as an instrument for furthering the ends of any sect of institutionalized religion and, conversely, that no sect of institutionalized religion should be used for furthering the ends of government; this principle, embodied in the First Amendment to the Constitution of the United States and in other governmental documents, prohibits the establishment of a state church and ensures to the individual the right to the free exercise of his religion.

Sephardit (sə·fär′dit): (from Heb., Sepharad, "Spain"; lit., "Spanish pronunciation") a way of pronouncing Hebrew characteristic of the Jews of Spain, Portugal, Italy, Turkey, Holland, and wherever Jews from these countries have settled; the form of pronunciation adopted in modern Israel and gaining increased acceptance in other countries where Jews live. *See* **Ashkenazit.**

sequence: (1) a division of a motion picture made up of one or more scenes comprising a major thought unit within the whole motion picture; somewhat analogous to a paragraph of a written composition; (2) (math.) a set of elements, numbers, or terms that are ordered in a consistent manner, such as in increasing magnitude.

sequence, behavior: term applied by Margaret Mead to the successive responses of children in a given social situation such as weaning, reactions to sibling, etc.

sequence, control: *see* **control sequence.**

sequence, developmental: *see* **developmental sequence.**

sequence effect: *see* **effect, sequence.**

sequence, genetic: *syn.* **developmental sequence** (2).

sequence, infinite: (math.) a set of symbols arranged in an ordered one-to-one correspondence with the positive integers; frequently symbolized by $a_1, a_2, a_3, \ldots$; in practice these symbols usually represent elements chosen from some particular set.

sequence, phase: (D. O. Hebb) the neural correlate of a concept or group of concepts; each simple perception becomes a *cell assembly;* these assemblies are linked together in phase sequences.

sequence, preeducation: *syn.* **curriculum, preeducation.**

sequence prompt: *see* **prompt, sequence.**

sequence, stable: a serial-learning task in which the order of stimuli and responses remains fixed and predictable; for example, learning the letters of the alphabet.

sequence, subject: *see* **subject sequence.**

sequence, systematic: *see* **systematic sequence.**

sequence, unstable: arbitrary and unpredictable order between items in a paired-associates learning task such as learning a French-English vocabulary. *Comp. w.* **sequence, stable.**

sequencing: in programmed learning, the attempt to arrange materials in the proper order for optimum efficiency in learning.

sequencing ability: *see* **ability, sequencing.**

sequential analysis: *see* **analysis, sequential.**

sequential approach: in composition, instruction in planning writing activities so as to provide pupils with a helpful basis of skills needed for new tasks.

sequential file: *see* **file, sequential.**

sequential mathematics: *see* **mathematics, sequential.**

sequential pattern: a plan of organization and order of presentation of curriculum materials as between school grades (grade placement) or within a grade, a subject, or a series of these; determined by a wide variety of theories, such as those concerning the abilities, interests, experiences, and needs of pupils, etc.

sequential reading program: *see* **program, sequential reading.**

sequential sampling: *see* **analysis, sequential.**

serial: *n.* a publication issued in several parts, usually at regular intervals, and as a rule intended to be continued indefinitely, for example, periodicals, annuals, proceedings, and transactions.

serial access: *see* **access, serial.**

serial-anticipation learning: *see* **learning, serial-anticipation.**

serial bond: *see* **bond, serial.**

serial music: *syn.* **music, dodecaphonic; music, twelve-tone.**

serial number: a natural number; one of the numbers of our number system assigned seriatim, or in turn, to a particular object, quality, or class, usually for purposes of identification; in such use it is a *code;* if the cases have previously been arranged in order according to some specified characteristic, the serial number becomes a rank (provided the numbers began with 1).

serial response: *see* **response, serial.**

serial verbal learning: *see* **learning, serial verbal.**

series: the indicated sum of a sequence of numbers, for example, $1 + 3 + 5 + 7 + \ldots$.

series, broken: *syn.* **series, discrete.**

series, categorical: a series in which the divisions refer to qualitative differences in things, for example, typewriters of different makes.

series, continuous: a series of observations in which the various possible values of the variable may differ by infinitesimal amounts; a series in which it is possible for frequencies to occur at any intermediate value within the range of the series. *Contr. w.* **series, discrete.**

series, discrete: a series in which frequencies can occur only at certain variate and not at intermediate values. *Syn.* **broken series; noncontinuous series;** *contr. w.* **series, continuous.**

series, historical: *syn.* **series, time.**

series, noncontinuous: *syn.* **series, discrete.**

series, ordered: a series in which the values of a variable are arranged according to magnitude or to some ordered principle such as merit, value, etc.

series progression: (voc. ed.) an order of job instruction secured by teaching all the jobs in one block before proceeding to the next block.

series, qualitative: a series in which the basis of classification is a set of attributes rather than a numerical series, for example, *very blond, medium blond, brown, dark brown, black. Contr. w.* **series, quantitative.**

series, quality: *syn.* **rating scale, descriptive.**

series, quantitative: a statistical series in which classification is numerical rather than on the basis of attributes. *Contr. w.* **series, qualitative.**

series, temporal: *syn.* **series, time.**

series, time: a sequence of values corresponding to successive points or periods of time; the numerical record of the values of a variable at a number of successive points or intervals of time; for example, the population of the United States given at 10-year intervals from 1850 to 1950. *Syn.* **historical series; temporal series.**

serigraphy: *syn.* **printing, silk screen.**

sermon: an address or homily normally given by a clergyman during a service of worship to instruct in religion or morals.

service: the performance of a task for the benefit of others whether voluntarily, by request, or to fulfill a social need.

service academy: *see* **academy, service.**

service academy exchange program: *see* **program, service academy exchange.**

service, call-in: *see* **call-in service.**

service center, educational: *see* **center, educational service.**

service club: *see* **club, service.**

service, college scholarship: *see* **scholarship service, college.**

service, community: *see* **community service.**

service, counseling: *see* **counseling service.**

service course: *see* **course, service.**

service, day care: *see* **day care service.**

service department: *see* **department, service.**

service door: *see* **door, service.**

service, educational and occupational planning: *see* **planning service, educational and occupational.**

service equipment: *see* **equipment, service.**

service establishment: (distrib. ed.) a business firm classified as a distributive business which offers services rather than products to the customer.

service, extended: *see* **extended service.**

service, extension: *see* **extension, cooperative; extension service, cooperative; extension, university.**

service facilities: the service fixtures and equipment of a building, such as the water system, electric lighting equipment, vacuum cleaners, and scrubbing machines.

service facilities, school building: *see* **building service facilities, school.**

service, food: *see* **food service.**

service, information: *see* **information service.**

service, informational: in guidance, providing valid information about the educational, occupational, and social aspects of the present and probable future environment of students; also called *information service. Comp. w.* **services, information.**

service, library reference: *see* **reference service, library.**

service load: *see* **load, service.**

service occupations: *see* **occupations, service.**

service, personnel: *see* **personnel service.**

service, placement: *see* **placement service.**

service practice: (mil. ed.) part of the training program for artillery units consisting primarily of practical problems in the preparation, execution, and conduct of fire with service or target practice ammunition.

service, psychological: *see* **psychological service.**

service, public: (1) activities designed to reach the general population in the public interest; (2) activities of educational institutions not classified as formal teaching and training. *See* **program, public service.**

service, pupil-personnel: *syn.* **guidance** (2).

service, pupil transportation: *see* **transportation service, pupil.**

service, reader: *see* **reader service.**

service record: *see* **record, service.**

service record, personal: *see* **record, personal service.**

service research: *see* **research, service.**

service room: a room in a school building used to render some form of service, for example, a storeroom, a lunchroom, a health clinic.

service school: (mil. ed.) a school which presents a curriculum developed and approved by a service to meet a military education and training requirement of that service.

service shopping: a method of checking the efficiency of salespeople by which the store itself or some outside agency hires people to act as customers in the store and to observe and report on the efficiency, honesty, and service of the persons who waited on them.

service, student health: *see* **health service, student.**

service test: *see* **test, service.**

service, testing and measurement: *see* **testing and measurement service.**

service trade: *see* **trade, service.**

service unit, intermediate: *syn.* **center, educational service.**

service, visual education: *see* **visual education service.**

service, vocational: *see* **vocational service.**

service, welfare: *see* **welfare service.**

services, ancillary: *see* **ancillary services.**

services and activities, distributive education ancillary: services and activities which are provided to assist in the development, improvement, support, and upgrading of the developmental and operating phases of the distributive education program; examples are vocational guidance, vocational teacher education, research, experimental programs, administration, supervision, and evaluation.

services, attendance: *see* **attendance services.**

services, audiovisual: services for instructional staff members and for pupils such as preparing, caring for, and making available to members of the instructional staff the equipment, films, transparencies, tapes, scripts, and other similar materials, whether maintained separately or as a part of an instructional materials center; included are facilities for the audiovisual center and related work-study areas, related equipment and supplies, and services provided by audiovisual personnel.

services, clinical: *see* **clinical services.**

services, consultative: guidance services provided through the assistance of specialists equipped to act as consultants in particular fields, for example, psychologists, psychiatrists, physicians, nurses, social workers, and individuals with special knowledge of vocations and placement. *See* **resources, community; resources, referral.**

services, contracted: those services rendered to a school system through contract or other agreement with a firm, company, individual, or other educational agency or institution; such services being performed by a person or persons not on the school staff.

services, crippled child: agencies' offerings of grant-in-aid programs providing medical and related services to crippled children; administered by the state health department in most states.

services, director of guidance: *see* **director of guidance.**

services, distributive education consultancy: services rendered by a person or persons specifically qualified in specialized areas of marketing and distribution and designed to assist administrators and teachers in preparing instructional programs and materials.

services, employment: public or private services for job finding and placement; if a general agency function, usually does not include training and follow-up; if a Federal-state program (administered by state employment service agencies), serves employers and unemployed individuals and includes guidance and placement of handicapped persons.

services, esoteric: areas of education in which specialists offer expertise gained by highly technical training.

services, extended school: *see* **program, public service; service, public.**

services, guidance: a system of services designed to assist the individual in developing an understanding of himself and his environment and in realizing more satisfactorily his potentialities; these functions are understood to include generally an individual inventory, educational, occupational, and social information, counseling, placement, and follow-up.

services, information: (couns.) those services which are responsible for selecting, collecting, organizing, and disseminating information to the student and his parents; generally handle materials that promote understanding of the educational program, of various educational and vocational opportunities for students, and of the requirements related to school and career choices; social-personal information is also included; information services also assist pupils in making appropriate choices, decisions, and adjustments. *Comp. w.* **service, informational.**

services, library: activities inherent in obtaining, organizing, preparing, and servicing library materials for use.

services, library technical: services involving the operations and techniques for acquiring, recording, and preserving materials; also called *library technical activities, library technical operations, and library technical processes.*

services, producer: (voc. ed.) those services that business firms, nonprofit institutions, and government provide and usually sell to the producer rather than to the consumer.

services, psychological: those professional services relating to the appraisal and interpretation of the intellectual, emotional, and social characteristics of children. *See* **services, pupil-personnel.**

services, public health: health-related services of training or direct treatment available through Federal, state, county, or city medical and other health programs, for example, public health nursing programs and crippled children's division activities.

services, pupil-personnel: those aids to pupil and teacher that give added help to the pupil in his learning experiences; carried on by the school counselor, school nurse, school psychologist, school social worker, and other psychological and health service personnel.

services, referral: *syn.* **counseling, auxiliary services.**

services, school: *see* **school services.**

services, school health: *see* **health services, school.**

services, school library: selection, acquisition, preparation, catologing, and circulation of books and other printed materials to pupils and staff; planning the use of the library by pupils, and instructing pupils in their use of library books and materials, whether maintained separately or as a part of an instructional materials center; included are facilities for the library materials center and its related work-study areas, related equipment and supplies, and services provided by school library personnel.

services, social: those services providing support in psychosocial areas, frequently as a component of pupil-personnel service structure.

services, state employment: publicly supported programs for job finding and personnel placement; usually do not provide training or follow-up. (In 1954, the need for special attention to the placement of the severely handicapped, including those with emotional disabilities, was recognized in the establishing of special placement officers in the employment service who give their entire time to the placement of the severely disabled, making contact with employers in the field and giving personal assistance to the disabled applicant.)

services, structured community: *see* **community services, structured.**

services, student-personnel: the specific services exclusive of classroom teaching provided for college and university students.

services, tutorial: private instruction by a teacher or student to an individual or small group of students.

servomechanism: a control device or system whose operation depends upon the difference between its own output and the desired output which is then indicated by a signal; to be distinguished from simpler regulators and timing devices that operate on fixed cycles without error-sensing feedback from the output.

session, all-day: a school program designed for the entire school day, usually extending from 9 A.M. to 12 NOON and from 1 to 3:30 P.M.

session, buzz: *see* **buzz session.**

session, curtailed: a school session with less than the number of hours of instruction recommended by the state education agency.

session, days in: days on which the pupils of a school are under the guidance and direction of teachers.

session, half-day: a school program designed for one-half of a full-time school day, usually resulting in a telescoped offering adjusted to a half-day schedule.

session, school: the period of time during the school day when a given group of pupils is under the guidance and direction of teachers.

sessions, double: a school day with separate sessions for two groups of pupils in the same instructional space, for example, one room used by one fourth-grade class in the morning and by another fourth-grade class in the afternoon or one school building used by high school juniors and seniors during a morning session and by freshmen and sophomores during an afternoon session.

sessions, extended-day: *syn.* **sessions, staggered.**

sessions, staggered: units of instructional time scheduled to begin at various periods of the day or on alternate days to allow for more effective use of school personnel and facilities. *Syn.* **sessions, extended-day.**

set: *n.* (1) a condition of readiness for some specific act or form of behavior that facilitates the activity; (2) a predisposition toward specific kinds of behavior or goals or both; often used as a synonym for *attitude; see* **organic set;** (3) (math.) an undefined term used to mean any collection of objects which need have no common property other than that of belonging to the set; a set is well-defined if it is possible to tell for a given object whether or not it belongs to the set; for example, the set "all positive even numbers" is well-defined, the set "all voters" is not; a set with no members is called the *empty set* or the *null set;* (4) (programmed instruction) a series of frames in the program dealing with one information unit.

set, Cartesian: a set whose members are ordered pairs obtained from two other sets in the following way: to form the Cartesian set from sets A and B (denoted by the symbol $A \times B$), each member of set A is paired in turn with each member of set $B;$ the Cartesian set $B \times A$ would be formed by pairing each member of set B in turn with each member of A.

set, closed: (1) in algebra, a set which has the closure property under a given operation; (2) in topology, a set that contains all its limit points; for example, a circle is a closed set whereas the interior of a circle is not.

set, countable: a set which is either finite or which can be placed in one-to-one correspondence with the set of positive integers; the set of letters in the English alphabet, the set of all integers, and the set of even integers are examples. *Syn.* **denumerable set.**

set, denumerable: *syn.* **set, countable.**

set, empty: *see* **set.**

set, equivalence class: a set all of whose members are related by some equivalence relation, such as a set of natural numbers (1, 4, 7, 10, 13, . . .) having the same remainder on division by 3.

set, finite: (1) a set in which there is some counting number or zero that is its cardinal number or, equivalently, which cannot be placed in one-to-one correspondence with any proper subset of itself; (2) a set that has some real number that can be assigned as its measure.

set, heuristic: the attitude of willingness on the part of a counselee to accept the major share of the responsibility for the progress of a counseling relationship.

set, infinite: a set which can be placed in one-to-one correspondence with a proper subset of itself, as, for example, the counting numbers which can be placed in a one-to-one correspondence with the even counting numbers.

set, learning: the acquisition of an approach to learning or problem solving that increases efficiency across various tasks. *See* **learning to learn.**

set, null: *see* **set.**

set, open: *see* **set, closed** (2).

set, response: *see* **response set.**

set, solution: the set of all those members of the universal set that make an open sentence true; sometimes called the *truth set* for the sentence.

set theory: the study of sets within the framework of a deductive system; for example, in a theory of sets the existence of an empty set would be logically deduced from axioms, that is, proved as a theorem rather than being accepted as the name for a certain kind of set. *See* **set.**

set, transfer of: *see* **transfer of set.**

set, truth: *see* **set, solution.**

set, universal: (math.) the set from which subsets are to be selected for a particular problem; for example, in probability a *sample space* is the universal set for the selection of events and in algebra the integers might be chosen as the universal set for selection of solution sets of open sentences. *See* **domain** (2); **sentence, open.**

set, well-defined: *see* **set.**

sets, complementary: two subsets having no members in common but whose union is the universal set.

sets, disjoint: sets that have no elements in common; for example, the set of positive integers and the set of negative integers.

sets, equipollent: *syn.* **sets, equivalent.**

sets, equivalent: two sets that have the same number of members; more precisely, two sets whose members can be placed in one-to-one correspondence; equal sets are always equivalent but equivalent sets need not be equal.

sets, intersection of: the intersection of two sets A and B is a set whose members are those elements that belong to both A and $B;$ if A and B have no elements in common, their intersection is called the *null set.*

settlement: (1) a group of social workers, instructors, physicians, etc., in an underprivileged neighborhood in residence together or closely associated and conducting classes, clinics, and other activities for community welfare; (2) an agreement to which two parties in a dispute come, as in teacher negotiations or a court case.

seven cardinal objectives or principles: commonly used inaccurately to refer to the seven objectives set forth in a bulletin, *The Cardinal Principles of Secondary Education,* formulated by a committee of the National Education Association and published in 1918 by the U.S. Bureau of Education; the seven objectives: command of the fundamental processes, worthy home membership, vocational efficiency, citizenship, worthy use of leisure, ethical character, and health.

Seven Cardinal Virtues: *see* **virtues, cardinal.**

Seven Deadly Sins: according to the medieval Church, pride, envy, avarice, anger, lust, gluttony, sloth. *See* **virtues, cardinal;** *contr. w.* the **Seven Cardinal Virtues.**

seven-four plan: the administrative organization of the educational program of a school system into an elementary school of 7 years (grades 1 to 7), exclusive of kindergarten, and a secondary school of 4 years (grades 8 to 11).

seven liberal arts: *see* **liberal arts, seven.**

severance tax: *see* **tax, severance.**

severe mental retardation: *see* **mental retardation, severe.**

severely handicapped: *see* **handicapped, severely.**

sewing: (home ec.) work done on cloth or other fabrics with a needle and thread by hand (hand sewing) or by machine (machine sewing); used in the construction of clothing or the making of furnishings for the home.

sewing machine operator: (voc. ed.) a worker who operates single- or multiple-needle sewing machines in the manufacture of clothing, tents, awnings, tarpaulins, leather goods, etc.

sex behavior: *see* **behavior, sex.**

sex difference: *see* **difference, sex.**

sex education: (1) education dealing with the processes and problems of reproduction; (2) education designed to provide the individual with understanding and control of his sex impulses and behavior; (3) education dealing with the principles of both individual and group problems stemming from the biological fact that there are two basic types of human being, male and female.

sex hygiene: *see* **hygiene, sex.**

sex interests: *see* **interests, sex.**

sex linkage: the phenomenon of the association of a hereditary character with sex, such that the character will appear in only one sex but will be recessive in and transmitted by the other, as in the case of hemophilia and color blindness.

sex-linked character: *see* **character, sex-linked.**

sextile: (rare) any of the five points measured along the scale of the plotted variable which divide the frequency distribution into six parts, each containing exactly one-sixth of the observations or cases.

sexual maturity: *see* **maturity, sexual.**

sexuality, pregenital: those aspects of infantile sexuality which antedate object love and whose maximal gratification is ante-erotic gratification and its conscious derivative.

sfumato (sfoo·mä'tō): (It., lit., "misty") a term used particularly during the high Renaissance to describe paintings and drawings that are soft and atmospheric in execution; works of Leonardo da Vinci have been so described.

sgraffito (z'gräf·fē'tō): an art technique; the application of ink, then crayon, and finally the scratching off of crayon with a short pointed instrument to create design.

shading: the thickening of a shorthand character representing a surd to make it represent the corresponding sonant; for example, in Pitman shorthand the character for *t* is shaded to represent the sound of *d.*

shading film: *see* **film, shading.**

shadow area: a geographical area where a community does not receive satisfactory signals from television stations on certain channels because of natural barriers, such as mountains and terrain variations.

shadowing: *see* echo speech technique.

shape: (meas.) the residual information in the score set after equating profiles for both elevation and scatter.

shape discrimination: *see* discrimination, shape.

shaped note: (obs.) a musical note the shape of which indicates its pitch; used in some early American singing schools.

shaping behavior: *see* behavior, shaping.

shared tax: *see* tax, shared.

shared time: *see* enrollment, dual.

sharing time: time when children discuss experiences and/or objects brought to the classroom; valuable in the primary school for language growth, socialization, discovery of children's interests, and growth in general information.

sharp: (1) a musical symbol indicating the raising of a note by one half step, that is, by a semitone; (2) a term descriptive of faulty intonation, caused by playing or singing slightly above the correct pitch. *Contr. w.* flat.

sharpening: in perception and the retention of perceived figures (or abstractions in the case of conceptualization) sharpening has occurred when on successive reproductions of the original material there is a tendency to overemphasize and make clearer and more prominent various details of the original, as contrasted with leveling; the concepts "leveling" and "sharpening" are important explanatory ideas for qualitative changes in memory. *See* leveling.

sheet, assignment: *see* assignment sheet.

sheet, data: *see* data sheet.

sheet, face: *see* face sheet.

sheet, information: *see* information sheet.

sheet, instruction: *see* instruction sheet.

sheet, instructional: *see* instructional sheet.

sheet, job: *see* job sheet.

sheet metal: (ind. arts) the study of the operation, problems, and related information concerned with forming and fabricating sheet metal products.

sheet, operation layout: *see* operation layout sheet.

sheet, personal data: *see* personal data sheet.

sheet, planning: *see* planning sheet.

sheet, poop: *see* poop sheet.

sheet, progress: *see* progress sheet.

sheet, project: *see* project sheet.

sheet, rating: *syn.* rating scale.

sheet, routing: *syn.* operation layout sheet.

sheet, tabulation: *see* tabulation sheet.

sheet, tally: *syn.* tabulation sheet.

sheet, tear: *see* tear sheet.

sheet, work: *see* worksheet.

shelf list: a record of the books and other materials in a library arranged in the order in which they stand on the shelf, that is, in the order of their class and book numbers.

shelter: (pup. trans.) a building where pupils may gather while waiting for a school bus.

sheltered workshop: *see* workshop, sheltered.

shelters, air-raid: areas of the school building designated by Civilian Defense as the safest place in the event of bombing.

Sheppard's correction: *see* correction, Sheppard's.

Shield's method: (R.C. ed.) fundamentally, a method of teaching religion that correlates other branches of learning with religious instruction.

shift: in automatic data processing, to move the admissible marks in a word or field one or more places to the left or right; in the case of a number, this is equivalent to multiplying or dividing by a power of the radix.

shift, sound: *see* sound shift.

shifting, associative: *see* associative shifting.

shifting of tax: *see* tax, shifting of.

shifts, maturational gradient-: *see* gradient-shifts, maturational.

shock therapy, electroconvulsive: *see* therapy, electroconvulsive shock.

shoestring route: *syn.* route, straight-line.

Sholom Aleichem school (shō'lom ä·lā'khem): a secular Jewish school named after a Yiddish writer and humorist which emphasizes the study of the Yiddish language and literature. *See* Arbeiter Ring Shule; Farband Shule; secular school, Jewish; Yiddish school.

shop: a term used, rather commonly and somewhat loosely, to refer to study or instruction in wood- or metalwork or other industrial laboratory skills and procedures; used also to refer to the laboratory and equipment used. *See* laboratory, industrial arts.

shop, agricultural: a shop equipped with appropriate apparatus and tools for performing miscellaneous adjustment, maintenance, and repair work of a mechanical nature involved in agricultural occupations; used for instruction in certain courses in agriculture. *Syn.* agricultural mechanics shop; farm laboratory; farm shop; *contr. w.* agriculture laboratory; laboratory farm; laboratory, land.

shop, closed: the operation of a computer facility where programming service to the user is the responsibility of a group of specialists.

shop, composite: *see* laboratory, composite industrial arts.

shop, comprehensive: *see* laboratory, comprehensive general industrial arts.

shop, diversified-activity: *see* laboratory, composite industrial arts.

shop, farm: *syn.* shop, agricultural.

shop, general: *see* industrial arts, general; laboratory, comprehensive general industrial arts.

shop, general area: *see* laboratory, comprehensive general industrial arts.

shop, industrial arts: *see* laboratory, industrial arts.

shop, machine: a school laboratory equipped with assorted machinery generally representative of the machine metals trade; a *laboratory unit* in machine metals.

shop, maintenance: a shop, equipped with machines or tools, devoted to the repair of furniture and fixtures and to the preparation of materials for the repair of buildings.

shop management: (voc. ed.) principles and practices of efficient direction of people, activities, and use of facilities in the operation of a *school shop.*

shop, manual arts: (obs.) *see* laboratory, industrial arts.

shop, mechanics: a shop used for the repair or construction of building parts or equipment.

shop, metal: a shop equipped with tools and apparatus for metalwork; used by maintenance workmen.

shop, open: the operation of a computer facility where computer programming, coding, and operating can be performed by any qualified employee of the organization.

shop, school: (voc. ed.) a special classroom designed, or provided with special built-in equipment, for vocational or trade learning activities in such fields as mechanics, machine tools, sheet metal work, woodworking, electrical trades, radio, plumbing, masonry, aviation, printing, refrigeration, air conditioning, baking and other commercial food preparation, cosmetology, and agriculture.

shop, secondary: in connection with the maintenance of school buses, a subshop equipped for regular servicing and minor repairs of vehicles as opposed to the central shop or maintenance garage where major repair work can be done.

shop, unit: *see* laboratory unit.

shopper, impulse: *see* impulse shopper.

shore line: (spec. ed.) the border or edge of a sidewalk; a term used in teaching the blind to walk alone.

short-answer test: rough *syn.* test, objective.

short course: *see* course, short.

short cuts in mathematics: simplified and contracted methods of performing mathematical operations; for example, to multiply by 25, first multiply by 100, and then divide by 4.

short division: *see* **division, short.**

short-essay test: *see* **test, short-essay.**

short exposure: the designation of a technique for increasing speed of recognition in reading, in which flash cards are presented briefly or words (or characters) are flashed on a screen for brief intervals by means of a projector having a lens fitted with a mechanical shutter of the type used on hand cameras.

short-exposure apparatus: a device for controlling the exposure of letters, syllables, words, or phrases for different intervals of time for reading purposes, for example, the *tachistoscope*, the *metronoscope*, or the *flash meter*.

short-period note: (1) a written promise to pay at the end of a short period of time; (2) a written agreement acknowledging a debt that falls due in a short time, for example, in 60 days.

short-term bond: *see* **bond, short-term.**

short-term loan: (1) a loan made for a short period of time and usually evidenced by a note or warrant payable; may be unsecured or secured by specific revenues to be collected; usually repayable during the fiscal year in which it is made; (2) (student aid) a money loan to the student by the college and payable before the end of the school year, before graduation, or at a specified time following graduation and at a specified rate of interest.

short-time sampling: *see* **sampling, short-time.**

short-unit course: *see* **course, short-unit.**

short-wave broadcasting: *see* **broadcasting, short-wave.**

shortage of teachers: a situation in which the available supply of trained and legally licensed teachers is less than the number of vacancies.

shorthand: a method of writing rapidly by substituting symbols for longhand letters, syllables, or words. *Syn.* **phonography.**

shorthand, machine: a rapid method of writing by substituting symbols and letter combinations for letters and words, in which a machine is used for recording the message instead of a pen or pencil.

shorthand penmanship: *see* **penmanship, shorthand.**

shorthand, simplified: 1949 revision of the 1929 Gregg system of shorthand, devised by Leslie and Zoubek; alphabet remains the same but many of the special outlines, seldom-used shortcuts, and exceptional rules have been eliminated; many more words now written in their full phonetic form.

shot: (1) a single run of the camera; (2) the piece of film resulting from such a run; systematically joined together in the process of editing, shots are synthesized first into *scenes*; the scenes are joined to form *sequences*, and the *sequences* in turn are joined to form the entire film; in the technique of photography, there are various types of shots, such as close-up, long shot, running shot, etc.

"show and tell" period: *syn.* **sharing time.**

shower room: a room with shower equipment (individual or gang) for the use of students; usually located in a gymnasium or field house.

showing method: *see* **telling method.**

shrinkage: (in a multiple correlation coefficient) (1) an estimate of the amount by which a multiple correlation coefficient should be reduced to offset the effect of chance factors in the particular sample on which it is based; (2) the amount by which a multiple correlation, obtained on one sample, is reduced when computed on another sample.

Shulhan Arukh (shōōl·khän′ ä·rōōkh′): *n. masc.* (Heb., lit., "a set table") designates the code of laws and regulations governing the traditional Jewish way of life, compiled and edited by Joseph Caro during the sixteenth century; the official code of Orthodox Jewry.

shutter: (1) the device on a camera that may be made to open for a predetermined length of time to permit light to pass through the lens and strike the film, thus exposing the film; (2) the mechanism in a motion-picture projector that passes in front of the film during the instant that one frame is moving out of the gate and the next film is moving into the gate.

shyness: reticence in social situations, exemplified by the withdrawn child who is reluctant to answer questions or take part in classroom activities. *Dist. f.* **bashfulness; timidity.**

sib: *syn.* **sibling.**

sibilant: a consonant characterized by a hissing sound. (The English sibilants are *s, z, sh,* and *zh.*)

sibling: one of two or more children who is biologically defined as brother or sister, either full or half.

sibship: the relationship existing among two or more children of the same parents, though not necessarily of the same birth or sex.

S.I.C.: *see* **Standard Industrial Classification.**

sick leave: a grant of legitimate absence from regular duties because of illness.

sick leave, state-wide provisions for: provisions by state law, now common in many states, for granting legitimate absence from regular duties for personal or family illness, with or without pay.

sick report: *see* **report, sick.**

S.I.C.M. filing plan: *see* **filing plan, S.I.C.M.**

siddur (sid′ōōr): *n. masc.* (Heb., lit., "order," "arrangement") the prayerbook used as a standard textbook for teaching pupils to read and become familiar with the daily, Sabbath, and festival prayers.

side horse: *see* **horse, side.**

sidedness: *syn.* **laterality** (1).

sieve of Eratosthenes: a procedure for generating prime numbers in order or for testing a number to see if it is prime; the process begins by listing the natural numbers from 2 to any desired number, crossing out every second number after 2, every third number after 3, every fifth number after 5, etc.; the numbers not crossed out are not divisible by any number (except 1) smaller than themselves.

sight: the sense by means of which the position, color, and shape of objects are perceived through the medium of light waves reflected from the objects to the eye. *Syn.* **vision.**

sight check: *see* **check, sight.**

sight conservation: a general term for those activities involved in the deliberate effort to conserve and/or improve the eyesight and eye health of individuals or groups; a term used by the medical profession in the prevention of blindness; formerly used to refer to the education of the partially seeing. *Syn.* **conservation of vision; sight saving.**

sight-conservation class: *see* **class, sight-conservation.**

sight method: a method of teaching reading based on recognition and pronunciation of whole words without any attempt to teach word analysis and synthesis.

sight reading: *see* **reading, sight.**

sight-saver type: *see* **book, large-type.**

sight saving: *syn.* **sight conservation.**

sight-saving class: *see* **class, partially seeing.**

sight-saving equipment: *see* **equipment, sight-saving.**

sight-saving room: a room especially constructed to admit much natural light and with especially strong artificial lighting and equipped with desks and instruction equipment, including books, especially designed for children having very poor sight. *See* **class, sight-saving.**

sight singing: performing vocal music from notation without previously hearing the tones played or sung.

sight-singing class: *see* **class, sight-singing.**

sight utilization: (spec. ed.) in the education of the partially seeing, the act of using residual vision to the greatest degree possible.

sight vocabulary: *see* **vocabulary, sight.**

sight vocabulary, basic: *see* **vocabulary, basic sight.**

sight word: *see* **word, sight.**

sight word, phonetic: *see* **word, phonetic sight.**

sight-word reading method: *see* **reading method, sight-word.**

sighted guide technique: use by a blind person of a sighted guide whose elbow he grasps lightly for the purpose of interpreting the environment.

sighted, partially: *syn.* **partially seeing.**

sigma (sig'mə): a Greek letter, used in the lower case (σ) as the symbol for *standard deviation;* used in the upper case (Σ) as the symbol for *summation.*

sigma measure: *see* **score, standard.**

sigma score: *see* **score, standard.**

sigma value: *see* **score, standard.**

sigmatism (sig'mə·tiz'm): defective rendering of the sounds *s* and *z.*

sign: (1) in general, an indicator; (2) any object or event—especially an action, or the direct result of an action—perceived as having a significance beyond itself; for example, the blush of embarrassment, the slouched posture of fatigue or boredom; (3) a stimulus that substitutes for another in evoking a response, such as a conventional gesture standing for a word or words or for an idea, as nodding for "yes" and the sign language of the deaf. *Comp. w.* **signal; symbol.**

sign, artificial: that which is representative by virtue of agreement in use; for example, a flag may be a sign for approaching storm.

sign language: *see* **language, sign.**

sign, natural: that which is representative of a thing by virtue of a connection between them; for example, smoke is a natural sign of fire.

sign, organic: the symbol for a response on the Rorschach test which refers to the symptoms of organic pathology.

sign, psychometric: (meas.) a characteristic of an item, empirically derived, which distinguishes between two or more groups; thus, the surface content of an item is irrelevant to what one wishes to measure since the main interest in the item is whether it distinguishes between the empirically defined groups.

sign test: *see* **test, sign.**

signal: (1) a sign communicated by one person to another in order to indicate that the time and place for a certain action are at hand; (2) (radio and TV broadcasting) the waves, impulses, sounds, pictures, etc., transmitted or received; the wave that modulates the carrier wave.

signal multiplexer: *see* **multiplexing, signal.**

signal multiplexing: *see* **multiplexing, signal.**

signal system, warning: *see* **warning signal system.**

signed number: *see* **number, signed.**

significance: (philos.) loosely, the meaning or import of a statement; more precisely, that which is indicated by or is to be inferred from a *sign,* thus, the significance of smoke (as a thing) is "fire—over there"; to be distinguished from *meaning,* which is mediated by symbols rather than signs and which involves implication rather than inference, thus, the *meaning* of smoke (as a word) may be "prosperity," "health hazard," etc.

significance level: a probability value determining the region of rejection of a hypothesis or the number of rejections of a true hypothesis out of 100 cases. *See* **confidence level.**

significance limits: *syn.* **confidence limits.**

significance point: a point on the scale of values of a test statistic such that the probability of the statistic exceeding this value is some arbitrarily preestablished amount.

significance ratio: *syn.* **ratio, critical.**

significance region: the region of rejection of a hypothesis which may be located in either or both tails of the sampling distribution. *Syn.* **critical region; region, rejection; region of significance.**

significance, social: *see* **social significance.**

significance standards: the probabilities commonly associated with confidence limits or significance points; usually 0.01 or 0.05.

significance, statistical: the property of having low probability of occurrence on the basis of chance alone, thereby likely occasioned by factors other than chance; not necessarily synonymous with practical significance.

significance, test of: *see* **test of significance.**

significant difference: *see* **difference, significant.**

significant difference, statistically: *see* **difference, statistically significant.**

significant digit: *syn.* **significant figure.**

significant figures: digits that affect the accuracy of measurement. *See* **rounding off.**

significant, statistically: *see* **statistically significant.**

significant symbol: *see* **symbol, significant.**

silent film: *see* **film, silent.**

silent projector: *see* **projector, silent.**

silent reading: *see* **reading, silent.**

silent-reading ability: *see* **ability, silent-reading.**

silent-reading test: *see* **test, silent-reading.**

silent speed: the normal speed at which a motion-picture camera or projector is operated in making or showing silent films, approximately 16 to 18 frames per second. *See* **sound speed.**

silhouettograph: a cameralike device that takes a picture of anterior-posterior posture on ruled sensitized paper.

silk-screen printing: *see* **printing, silk-screen.**

similar forms: *syn.* **equivalent forms.**

similarities test: *see* **test, similarities.**

similarity: (1) (math.) the property in two figures of having the same shape but not necessarily the same size; thus congruence is a particular case of similarity; (2) (meas.) a quality measurable only with respect to specified dimensions or complex characteristics; between persons or profiles cannot be validly reduced to a single index since it loses much of the information in the score set; a high index of correlation between two persons might indicate they are unusually alike or might indicate that they possess in common only the characteristics most humans have.

similarity, law of: *syn.* **generalization, stimulus.**

similarity, salient variable: (*S*) a measure of the likelihood of obtaining by chance a given degree of similarity in factor patterns from two different researches.

simple arithmetic mean: *syn.* **mean, unweighted arithmetic.**

simple code: *see* **code, simple.**

simple correlation: *see* **correlation, simple.**

simple effect: *see* **effect, simple.**

simple frequency graph: *syn.* **graph, frequency.**

simple frequency table: *syn.* **table, frequency.**

simple interaction: *syn.* **interaction, first-order.**

simple negligence: *see* **negligence, simple.**

simple probability: *see* **probability, simple.**

simple random sample: *syn.* **sample, random.**

simple randomized design: *see* **design, simple randomized.**

simple-recall test: *see* **test, simple-recall.**

simple sample: *syn.* **sample, random.**

simple structure: (fact. anal.) the position of factor axes and their hyperplanes for which the maximum number of points possible has been rotated into each hyperplane.

simplification: (1) the act or process of rendering anything less complex, or the result of such a process; (2) the act or process of simplifying a mathematical expression or operation, as in simplifying the fraction $\frac{8}{64}$ to $\frac{1}{8}$.

simplified keyboard: *see* **keyboard, simplified.**

simplified run test: *see* **test, simplified run.**

simplified shorthand: *see* **shorthand, simplified.**

simplified spelling: *see* **spelling, simplified.**

simulaid: (safety ed.) a first-aid model and teaching device used to give students firsthand life-like learning experiences.

simulated environment: *see* **environment, simulated.**

simulated flight: see **flight, simulated.**

simulation: (1) in learning and training, making the practice and materials as near as possible to the situation in which the learning will be applied; for example, *microteaching* wherein student teachers actually teach a small group in a laboratory setting; (2) an initiative type of data processing in which an automatic computer is used to implement an information model of some entity such as a chemical process; information enters the computer to represent the factors entering or affecting the real process and the computer then produces information that represents the results of the process, with the processing done by the computer representative of the process itself; (3) the use of role-playing by the actors during the operation of a comparatively complex symbolic model of an actual or hypothetical social process; usually includes gaming and may be all-man, man-computer, or all-computer operations; see **gaming.**

simulation, driving: see **driving simulation.**

simulation game: see **game, simulation.**

simulation, reality: any contrived experience planned so as to give the illusion of real experience; illustrative are training materials and devices used in driver training, laboratory sessions, demonstrations, and sociodrama.

simulator: in aerospace research, a machine or apparatus that creates a set of conditions considered to be the same as those existing in an environment into which a person, animal, or thing is expected to go, as a *simulator* for training an astronaut for a space environment.

simulator, aircraft: an Air Force synthetic trainer that very closely simulates the real thing; the instructor observes pilot or crew trainees perform various procedures which, if erroneous, can be corrected immediately by "freezing" the simulator; after correction, simulator is "unfrozen" and trainee resumes pursuit of desired lesson objectives, thus achieving near error-free behavior.

simulator instruction: see **instruction, simulator.**

simulator, space: in aerospace research, any apparatus or laboratory that simulates the conditions of space.

simulcast: the simultaneous transmission of the same program over a pair of AM and FM stations or over both a radio station broadcasting the audio portion and a television station sending out the complete program.

simultaneous method: (1) a system of teaching, first introduced by Comenius in the seventeenth century, by which a group of pupils could be taught at the same time; was developed further a half century later by the Brothers of the Christian Schools, and finally popularized and made a permanent school practice by Pestalozzi; (2) syn. **combined method** (1).

simultaneous simple structure: syn. **profile, parallel proportional.**

simultaneous translation: see **translation, simultaneous.**

sine correction (sī'nə): (*S̄* or *S.C.*) without correction; said of vision without glasses. *Contr. w.* **cum correction.**

singer's node: syn. **singer's nodule.**

singer's nodule: a swelling or growth on the vocal cords caused by strain or overuse of the voice. *Syn.* **singer's node;** see **chorditis nodosa.**

singing, community: informal singing after a banquet, during a camp meeting, on a bus trip, and the like.

singing game: a rhythmic game, usually accompanied by singing, that has a set pattern to be learned, for example, "Did You Ever See a Lassie?" "The Farmer in the Dell," etc.

singing, number: the singing of the tones of the scale in terms of number designations; intended to develop a feeling for relative pitch. (The numerals most commonly used correspond to the sol-fa syllables, 1 being used for do, 2 for re, etc.). *See* **sol-fa; sol-fa syllables.**

singing, part: the singing of a *part song,* that is, the simultaneous performance of the various parts of voice lines of a composition written for two or more separate voices, for example, soprano and contralto.

singing school: (1) a European school, under religious auspices, and flourishing from about the fifth to the

sixteenth centuries; the most famous examples are the *scholae cantorum* of Rome, in which Gregorian plain song was developed; (2) (United States, nineteenth century) a group of adults organized to receive instruction in singing and to sing for pleasure, usually meeting in a district or village schoolhouse.

singing, unison: the rendition of a song by a group of singers, all of whom sing the same melody, or voice line. *Comp. w.* **singing, part.**

singing voice: the range, quality, and other characteristics of the voice a person uses in singing.

single-answer test: see **test, single-answer.**

single-block trade: see **trade, single-block.**

single-concept film: see **film, single-concept.**

single-course plan: a plan for pupil promotion in which course requirements are kept fairly constant but the rate of progress is varied to permit the most capable pupils to complete the work of the elementary school in the shortest time.

single-dot map: see **map, single-dot.**

single-frame filmstrip: see **filmstrip, single-frame.**

single-framing: exposing one frame at a time on motion-picture film, as opposed to continuous exposure (8 frames per second or faster).

single-period plan: a plan for supervised or directed study in which all recitation and study activities are carried on in the same period.

single-plane rotation method: see **rotation method, single-plane.**

single reading: see **reading, single.**

single route: see **route, single.**

single salary schedule: see **salary schedule, single.**

single-session day: a school day uninterrupted by a lunch period, usually from 8:30 A.M. to 1 P.M.; rarely found today.

single tax: see **tax, single.**

single-teacher-per-class plan: syn. **single-teacher-per-grade plan.**

single-teacher-per-grade plan: a school organization plan in which only one teacher is assigned to each grade or group and each pupil has therefore only one teacher.

single track: see **track, single.**

single-track tape: see **tape, full-track.**

single variable, law of: the rule of experimentation that, if the treatments applied to equivalent groups or individuals differ in only one respect, any resulting differences in effects may be ascribed to the single respect in which the treatments differ; or the corollary that, if identical treatments are applied to groups that differ in only one respect, differences in effects may be ascribed to the one respect in which the groups differ.

single-word sentence: see **sentence, single-word.**

single-year-of-age-grade specific enrollment rate: see **enrollment rate, single-year-of-age-grade specific.**

single-year-of-age-population projection: see **projection, single-year-of-age-population.**

singleton: a singly born individual as contrasted with one of a set of twins, triplets, etc.

sinistral: *n.* one who uses the left eye as the leading eye in reading.

sinistral: *adj.* (1) left; pertaining to the left side of the body; (2) referring to a movement or tendency toward the left, for example, a backward slant in handwriting, or reverse writing.

sinking fund: see **fund, sinking.**

sinking fund bond: see **bond, sinking fund.**

Sins, Seven Deadly: see **Seven Deadly Sins.**

sister: a woman who has consecrated her life to God and who has taken on herself a permanent commitment to serve the needs of individuals or society; sisters live a community life centered around liturgical worship, teach in parochial schools and other educational institutions (public and private), and also serve in other areas where dedicated, professional women are found.

site: (1) the location of buildings, as of a university, college, or school; (2) the local position of a single building on the grounds or campus.

site, building: the grounds on which buildings are situated; includes grounds belonging to the institution in the same plot, but not occupied by buildings. (For university and college buildings, the site is the campus or the position of a single building on the campus.)

sitting height: the stature of the body measured from the plane surface on which the subject is sitting erect to the top of the head.

situation: a stimulus in its total setting; frequently used as equivalent to environment; transactionally, as used by Arthur F. Bentley and John Dewey, the "more general, and less clearly specified range of the named phase of fact."

situation, problematic: *see* **problematic situation.**

situation, real-life: *see* **real-life situation.**

situation-response relationship: *see* **relationship, situation-response.**

situation, social: *see* **social situation.**

situational analysis: *see* **analysis, situational.**

situational ethics: *see* **ethics, situational.**

situational test: *see* **test, situational.**

situations, persisting life: *see* **life situations, persisting.**

six-four-four plan: the administrative organization of the educational program of a school system into an elementary school of 6 years, exclusive of kindergarten (grades 1 to 6), a middle school of 4 years on the secondary level (grades 7 to 10), and an upper secondary school of 4 years (grades 11 to 14), which represents an extension of the traditional upper two high school years to include the junior college years (grades 13 and 14) as an integral part of the school.

six-four-two plan: the administrative organization of the educational program of a school system into an elementary school of 6 years, exclusive of kindergarten (grades 1 to 6), a junior high school of 4 years (grades 7 to 10), and a senior high school of 2 years (grades 11 and 12).

six-grade elementary school: *syn.* **elementary school, six-year.**

six-six plan: the administrative organization of the educational program of a school system into an elementary school of 6 years, exclusive of kindergarten (grades 1 to 6), and a secondary school of 6 years (grades 7 to 12), the secondary unit being organized either as a *junior-senior high school* or as a *six-year high school.* See **high school, junior-senior; high school, six-year.**

six-three plan: a plan of school organization that includes 6 years of work at the elementary level and 3 years of work at the junior high school level.

six-three-three plan: the administrative organization of the educational program of a school system into an elementary school of 6 years, exclusive of kindergarten (grades 1 to 6), a junior high school of 3 years (grades 7 to 9), and a senior high school of 3 years (grades 10 to 12).

six-year elementary school: *see* **elementary school, six-year.**

six-year high school: *see* **high school, six-year.**

six-year reorganized school: *see* **reorganized school, six-year.**

sixteen-millimeter film: *see* **film, sixteen-millimeter.**

sixteenth section: the square mile in a township set aside as a source of funds for educational purposes, as provided for in the Survey Ordinance of 1785 for the Northwest Territory. (Beginning with the admission of Ohio as a state in the Union, Congress granted the sixteenth section of every township of this territory to be used for education.)

sixth sense, blind: *see* **blind sixth sense.**

siyum ha-sefer (sē·ūm′ hä·sä′fer): *n. masc.* (Heb., lit., "completion of the book") a traditional celebration customarily arranged by students, both young and old, upon completing their study of a book of the Bible or a tractate of the *Talmud.*

size discrimination: *see* **discrimination, size.**

skating, ice: an activity in which individuals propel themselves on skates with blades over frozen surfaces.

skating, roller: an activity in which individuals propel themselves on skates with wheels over hard surfaces.

skeletal age: *see* **age, skeletal.**

skeletal growth: *see* **growth, skeletal.**

skepticism: (1) an attitude promoting a proneness to question the truth or validity of the accepted beliefs of one's culture especially when these beliefs are founded in supernaturalism; (2) in more philosophical circles, the term is often used as a synonym of *agnosticism*, indicating man's inability to know ultimate reality or to know anything completely; (3) a term often used to indicate man's tendency or obligation to test all propositions and hypotheses either by further rationalism or by further experimentation.

sketching: making a rough drawing, a *sketch*, representing the chief features of an object or subject, often intended as a preliminary study or quick, spontaneous composition.

skew: asymmetry of a frequency distribution or frequency curve, as manifested by a greater range of values in the cases lying on one side of the mode than in those lying on the other. *Syn.* **asymmetry** (2); *see* **skewness, negative; skewness, positive;** *contr. w.* **symmetry.**

skew correlation: *syn.* **correlation, curvilinear.**

skew regression: *syn.* **regression, nonlinear.**

skewed distribution: *see* **distribution, skewed.**

skewness, coefficient of: *see* **coefficient of skewness.**

skewness, negative: strictly, the characteristic of a frequency distribution or frequency curve in which the sum of the cubes of the deviations of the observations from the mean is negative, that is, in which there is a greater range of values below the measure of central tendency than above it; apparent upon visual inspection of a frequency curve if the curve is unsymmetrical and has a long tail extending to the small, or negative, values without a corresponding tail extending to the large, or positive, values; in negative skewness, the mode and median are greater than the mean. *Contr. w.* **skewness, positive.**

skewness, positive: strictly, the characteristic of a frequency distribution or frequency curve in which the sum of the cubes of the deviations of the observations from the mean is positive, that is, in which there is a greater range of values above the measure of central tendency than below it; apparent upon visual inspection of a frequency curve if the curve is unsymmetrical and has a long tail extending to the large, or positive, values without a corresponding tail extending to the small, or negative, values; in positive skewness, the mode and median are less than the mean. *Contr. w.* **skewness, negative.**

skewness (Sk): the extent to which a frequency distribution or curve departs from a symmetrical shape; the state or quality of a frequency distribution or frequency curve in which the sum of the cubes of the deviations of the observations from the mean differs from zero. *Syn.* **asymmetry;** *contr. w.* **symmetry.**

skiing: (1) (snow) propelling oneself smoothly over snow on a pair of wooden or fiber glass skis that are approximately three inches wide and from six to seven feet long; (2) (water) planing over water on a pair of skis selected in relation to the weight of the performer; the skier is towed by a boat.

skill: (1) anything that the individual has learned to do with ease and precision; may be either a physical or a mental performance; (2) (orthopedic) manipulative proficiency in hand, finger, foot, and eye coordination.

skill, art: dexterity in performance with an art medium or mediums. See **art medium; art technique.**

skill, basic: *syn.* **skill, fundamental.**

skill, communicative: one of the four skills in communication: they are listening, speaking, reading, and writing.

skill, expressive: competency in expressing concepts and feelings with force, vividness, clearness, or other desirable qualities.

skill, fundamental: a skill that is basic to the mastery of a school subject, such as addition or subtraction in arithmetic.

skill, higher level work: a skill such as learning to learn, profiting from warm-ups, using *brainstorming* or *heuristic* procedures to solve problems, in short, any skill with high transfer value to a variety of special skills.

skill, homemaking: the ability to deal with all needs of the family; includes home management, care of the children, feeding and clothing the family, and the establishment of attitudes and practices conducive to the development of good family relationships.

skill-improvement practice: *syn.* **drill, corrective.**

skill, language: demonstrated competency in the use of language.

skill level: level of proficiency required for performance of a specific military job and at which an individual qualifies in that occupational specialty.

skill, manipulative: (ind. arts) proficiency in handling or operating tools or machines, in planning or investigating processes, or in designing, shaping, forming, or fabricating various objects.

skill, manual: proficiency with respect to muscular coordination of the hands and fingers.

skill, mathematical: ability to use the operational techniques of mathematics; for example, computation, induction, deduction, and abstraction.

skill, motor: reasonably complex movement behavior.

skill obsolescence: lack of or deficiency in currently required knowledge or skill.

skill, psychomotor: a muscular proficiency or dexterity believed to ensue from conscious mental activity. *See* **psychomotor.**

skill, reading: an ability that is essential to successful performance in reading, such as word recognition, comprehension, organization, or remembrance.

skill, specialized reading: a specific skill needed in reading in the content fields, such as map reading, reading of graphs, recognition of technical vocabulary, etc.

skill, speech: skill in the use of oral language or of language generally.

skill, study: any special ability used in study, such as reading, outlining, summarizing, or locating material.

skill subject: *see* **subject, skill.**

skill, teaching: the ability to promote learning, developed through appropriate preparation and experience and facilitated by natural aptitude. *See* **teacher; teaching.**

skill test: *see* **test, skill.**

skill, trade: (1) the ability to perform the manipulative operations connected with a given trade; (2) the ability to perform a certain manipulative operation connected with a given trade.

skill training: *see* **training, skill.**

skill, unit: a simple, elemental, unrelated reaction or activity.

skill, visual: an element of visual achievement; a basic skill of the seeing mechanism such as visual acuity, stereopsis, or skillful eye movements.

skilled trade: *see* **trade, skilled.**

skills, basal study: *see* **study skills, basal.**

skills, basic motor: *syn.* **movement, fundamental.**

skills, comprehension: (read.) those abilities involved in understanding the printed page, such as ability to find the main point and supporting details, to follow a sequence, to anticipate events, to follow directions, and to draw an inference.

skills, dictionary: the abilities to find and use word meanings appropriate for interpreting the language structure.

skills, salable: skills and knowledges acquired by a student that meet acceptable standards for employment in a particular field.

skills, social: skills taught by peer groups that are necessary for social acceptance; what these skills are depends upon the cultural context of the particular group and upon its age level.

skimming: (1) a method of reading according to which the reader looks for certain items but does not read the complete text; (2) a method of reading according to which the reader attempts to get the general meaning without attention to details.

skimming exercise: *see* **exercise, skimming.**

skin diving: *see* **diving, skin.**

skin response, psychogalvanic: *see* **psychogalvanic skin response.**

skipping: (1) the omission of a grade or grades in the orderly progress upward through the grades of the school; thus, a pupil promoted from grade 3 to grade 5 is said to have skipped one grade; (2) the act of being absent from a given class without permission although in attendance at school for the day; (3) in programmed instruction, termination of a program prior to the final item of a subset and continuation by the student on the next set; skipping may be indicated when he has responded correctly on a key frame of the program.

slack-season course: *see* **course, slack-season.**

slander: (legal) the speaking of base and defamatory words which tend to the prejudice of the reputation, office, trade, business, or livelihood of another. *Comp. w.* **libel.**

slant: inclination of downward strokes from the vertical line of writing.

slate, braille: *see* **braille slate.**

slate, cubarithme: *see* **cubarithme slate.**

slate, school: a tablet of smooth slate enclosed in a wooden frame, used as a writing surface; used in American schools until the beginning of the twentieth century.

slate, Taylor: *see* **Taylor slate.**

slave: *see* **master device.**

slave unit: the recorder which is used to make a copy of a *master tape. See* **master device.**

slide: any positive transparency mounted individually for use in a projector or for viewing by transmitted light; includes positive films mounted between glass as well as those employing emulsion on glass.

slide carrier: the device on a slide projector that receives the slides and holds them between the light source and the projection lens so that the image may be thrown on the screen.

slide, film: a positive picture, in black and white or color, printed as a positive on film and either bound between two pieces of thin glass or mounted in a cardboard frame; frequently made from double-frame 35-mm film mounted between glass plates measuring 2 by 2 inches; intended for projection or viewing by transmitted light. *See* **filmstrip.**

slide film: *syn.* **filmstrip.**

slide, glass: *see* **slide, lantern.**

slide, lantern: a mounted plate, occasionally $2\frac{1}{4}$ by $2\frac{1}{4}$ inches but usually $3\frac{1}{4}$ by 4 inches, often glass enclosed, which may be handmade with pencil, crayon, or ink, or typed on special materials, or photographically processed; their larger transparent surfaces made lantern slides the most popular teacher-student produced projection medium until the advent of the overhead transparency. *Syn.* **glass slide.**

slide mask: an opaque mask, generally having a rectangular opening, that is permanently inserted in a slide binding to frame the picture on the screen.

slide projector: *see* **projector, slide.**

slide rule: an instrument consisting of a ruler and a medial slide (both usually, but not necessarily, graduated on a logarithmic scale), used for approximate computation.

slide, still-motion: a stationary slide or transparency with polarized overlay, used with a revolving disk at the overhead projection lens to simulate various forms of movement including linear motion, turbulence, radiation, blinking, and rotary motion; this technique also lends itself to display box animations and to *flow charts* of process.

slide, two by two: usually a positive picture, in black and white or color, printed as a positive on film and either bound between two pieces of thin glass or mounted in a cardboard frame; frequently made from double frame 35-mm film mounted between glass plates measuring 2 by 2 inches; intended for projection or viewing by transmitted light.

slight hearing loss: *see* **hearing loss, slight.**

slighting: careless omission or indistinct articulation of a speech sound, particularly a final consonant or a component of a blend of two or more consonants; for example, *singin'* for *singing.*

slot: in *pattern drills* used in foreign language instruction, the position of a word or phrase in an utterance that could be occupied by other words or phrases of the same class; for example, in "I'm going to the library," the slot "to the library" can be replaced by "to the store," "to the park," or "to the hospital."

slow learner: *see* **learner, slow.**

slow-learning child: *see* **child, slow-learning.**

slow-motion photography: *see* **photography, slow-motion.**

slow progress: *see* **progress, slow.**

slow pupil: *see* **pupil, slow.**

slow reading class: *see* **class, slow reading.**

sloyd: a system of manual training first introduced in 1858 as a part of elementary instruction in Finland, involving bench and metal work, wood carving, and basket weaving; it spread rapidly to Sweden and other countries, including the United States.

sluggish articulation: *see* **articulation, sluggish.**

slum: the district of a city characterized by poverty, squalor, high population density, and marginal living conditions.

small consistent differences: *see* **differences, small consistent.**

small-fund plan: a plan for state equalization of educational opportunities that requires a minimum amount of state money for its operation and provides that when a school district levies a specified local tax, the state will supplement its receipts by an amount sufficient to ensure the support of a minimum program.

small-group instruction: *see* **instruction, small-group.**

small-group research: *see* **research, small-group.**

small sample theory: the development of distributions of statistics (mean, standard deviation, etc.) which contain few (say, less than 25 or 30) cases. *Contr. w.* **large sample theory.**

smell box: a box containing a variety of materials with strong residual odors; used in early childhood education (1) as a medium for exploratory sensory experiences and (2) as a technique in the fostering of sex identification through association of masculinity or femininity with articles such as perfume or a cigar.

Smith-Hughes Act: the basic Federal vocational-education act, passed in 1917 and establishing the principles of Federal financial aid and cooperation with the states in promoting public vocational education of less than college level in agriculture, trades and industries, and home economics for persons 14 years of age or over. *See* **state board for vocational education.**

Smith-Lever Act: the agricultural extension act, approved by the U.S. Congress in 1914, which provided aid for "the diffusion among the people of practical information on subjects relating to agriculture and home economics and to encourage the application of the same."

Smith-Mundt Act: a Federal law authorizing the government to pay expenses of foreign students and leaders to study and to observe conditions in the United States and similarly to send American students and leaders abroad. *See* **exchange grants, educational; exchange of students, international; exchange of teachers, international; exchange program, Fulbright.**

smooth: (stat.) (1) free from irregularities of data; (2) (said of a curve) without sudden or erratic changes in slope.

smooth curve: *see* **curve, smooth.**

smoothed curve: *see* **curve, smoothed.**

smoothing: the application of any method or process (such as the use of moving averages, of a graduation formula, or of the freehand or other method of curve

fitting) intended to remove the irregularities arising from fluctuations of sampling, presumably without disturbing the characteristics that may be peculiar to the data investigated. *Syn.* **adjustment; graduation.**

Snellen chart: *see* **chart, Snellen.**

Snellen notation: a system of recording visual acuity based on the Snellen test chart; specifically, a symbol written like a fraction, in which the numerator equals the distance from the chart and the denominator the smallest line read correctly. (For example, $20/50$ indicates ability to read the 50-foot line of the Snellen test chart at a distance of 20 feet; $10/200$ indicates the ability to read the 200-foot line at a distance of 10 feet; $20/20$ is considered to represent normal visual acuity.)

Snellen scale: *see* **scale, Snellen.**

Snellen test: *see* **test, Snellen.**

snorkling: *see* **diving, skin.**

so-fa (sō'fä'): *var.* **sol-fa.**

soccer: a type of football game played with a round ball between two teams of 11 men on a large field, in which only the goal keeper can touch the ball with the hands or arms while in play; essentially a kicking game.

soccer water polo: a game played between two teams in the water with a tightly inflated ball, in which the object is to throw the ball into a net goal.

sociability: the ability of a person to communicate with others, especially in the nonvocational aspects of life.

sociability, rating of: (1) competent evaluation of a person's ability to attain an acceptable social status and the degree of his adaptation to or social adjustment in a group; (2) a rating of the degree to which a person seeks group contacts.

social: in its broader sense, pertaining to the interaction of organisms in groups; in its narrower sense, descriptive of the development of an individual's ability to get along with others.

social ability: *see* **ability, social.**

social acceptability: *see* **acceptability, social.**

social act, creative: behavior occurring in a group, characterized by originality in furthering the social purposes of the group.

social-action program: *see* **program, social-action.**

social activity: *see* **activity, social.**

social adaptation: *see* **adaptation, social.**

social adjustment: *see* **adjustment, social.**

social adviser: *syn.* **counselor.**

social age: *see* **age, social.**

social agency: *see* **agency, social.**

social altitude: position on the scale of social class.

social altruism: *see* **altruism, social.**

social and educational parallelism: *see* **parallelism, social and educational.**

social anthropology: *see* **anthropology, social.**

social anxiety: (1) Locke's notion that once the mind learns to relish social approval and has developed an apprehension of shame and disgrace, these become the most powerful incentives of life; (2) a feeling of apprehension common to large groups of people, caused by tension and lack of security.

social approach: a method of teaching arithmetic based on the idea that pupils should have a series of carefully planned experiences which are certain to provide numerous uses of arithmetic in daily life; there may be little if any provision for the development of understanding of the number system or the basic mathematical concepts.

social approval: *see* **approval, social.**

social aptitude: *see* **aptitude, social.**

social arithmetic: *see* **arithmetic, social.**

social aspects of education: (1) all phases of the educational enterprise in which group life and adjustment of the individual to it are concerned; (2) theoretical emphases on the culture as a source of or context for ideals, knowledge, and values in curriculum construction; (3)

aspects pertaining to group phenomena in the conduct of a school, for example, types of class organization, social climate, interpersonal relations. *See* **dynamics, group; sociodrama; sociometry.**

social attitude: *see* **attitude, social.**

social-base map: *see* **map, social-base.**

social behavior: *see* **behavior, social.**

social biology: *see* **biology, social.**

social business education: *syn.* **business education, basic.**

social capacity: *see* **capacity, social.**

social case history: *see* **history, social** (1).

social case work: *syn.* **case work** (2).

social caseworker: *see* **caseworker, social.**

social center: a place where people may come together for instruction, recreation, or other community activities; usually comprehensive in program and less formal than such institutions as churches or schools. *See* **social settlement.**

social change: evolution of society either toward or away from an improved state, the progression being cyclical (Sorokin) or passing through stages from birth to decay (Spengler); the ideal is that of gradually providing a better life for its members as against an unchanging embodiment of universals; theories of social change have varied from conservation and reaction, stressing stability and the preservation of values, through liberalism, which stresses evolution, directed or laissez-faire, and the emergence of new values, to radicalism, stressing rapid change even to the point of revolution. *See* **social reconstruction.**

social-civic-moral guidance: *see* **guidance, social-civic-moral.**

social class: a group of individuals in a society who accept each other as equals, the concept of equality being mediated by or hinging upon similarities in such respects as mode of living, behavior form, material possessions, status of ancestors, type of occupation, and amount and kind of education, as well as other prestige-yielding qualities; mobility into and out of a social class is possible; to be contrasted with caste, which is a stratum in a hierarchy of social esteem into which the individual is born and beyond which he usually may not seek a mate or have intimate social intercourse. *See* **caste system.**

social climate: that complex of tangible and intangible conditions which gives a group or situation its distinguishing atmosphere or stimulus value; the term is used with special reference to interpersonal relationships, attitudes, rules, and regulations which affect especially the tendency of the situation to be friendly and congenial or the opposite; those mores or interpersonal relationships which distinguish one group from another.

social cohesion: *see* **cohesion, group.**

social competence: the ability to maintain satisfactory relationships with others.

social-competency scale: *see* **scale, social-competency.**

social conditions: the economic, political, geographical, and other conditions or circumstances determining the quality and quantity of interaction of groups and cultural development.

social confusion: (1) unpredictable group interaction due to disorganized group culture; (2) the conflict in mores representing the transitional stage when a new social factor has not been integrated into life in a functional sense or when a traditional factor has been removed, breaking up the functional unity of the situation.

social conscience: *see* **conscience, social.**

social consciousness: (1) awareness of having responsibilities to and for the social group; (2) awareness of the self as a social being; (3) awareness of others and their interests as distinct from the self and its interests; (4) awareness of the ordered pattern of social institutions.

social consensus: (1) decisions that result from the conscious or rational deliberations of all members of a given social group; (2) an awareness of a commonness of sentiments, traditions, ideals, opinions, values, and definitions of situations.

social continuity: *see* **continuity, social.**

social contract: (1) in modern philosophy, a theory purporting to explain the origin of authority in society, that is, how men who are by nature free, equal, and independent came to accept the political power of other men (Hobbes, Locke, Rousseau); (2) in general, voluntary agreement of individuals to inhibit some of their individual desires in order to cooperate with others for the common good.

social control: *see* **control, social.**

social convention: a custom or way of acting, established through usage or general agreement, that is not of vital importance. *Contr. w.* **social institution.**

social counseling: *see* **counseling, social.**

social curriculum: *see* **curriculum, social.**

social dance: *see* **dance, social.**

social Darwinism: the adaptation of Darwin's theories of biological evolution to the social relationships of man; formulated by Herbert Spencer and espoused in the United States by William Graham Sumner.

social degeneracy: *see* **degeneracy, social.**

social desirability: (meas.) a dimension for describing the attribute of a personality statement or personality inventory item which indicates the desirability of endorsing the statement or item as true or not true of the subject; scale values of items in this dimension indicate the proportion of individuals who will say, in self-description, that the statement does describe them; items in a forced-choice inventory can be matched on their social desirability to control for this source of variation in test response; they can also be used as a measure of tendency to "fake good."

social development: *see* **development, social.**

social-development scale: *see* **scale, social-development.**

social disorganization: (1) a process of accelerated and abnormal breaking down or collapse of social institutions to such an extent that the former close correlation of personality and culture is destroyed, and a certain chaos or disorder arises in which old ways of doing have been lost and adequate new ways not yet developed; this process is indicated by increased rates of divorce and suicide, by political upheavals and revolutions, and by the failure or closing of schools, business enterprises, churches, etc.; usually occurs in times of rapid cultural change or as the result of wars, pestilence, or other natural or societal catastrophe; (2) the partial or complete failure of the members of a group or society to respond to common values that were formerly shared.

social distance: the degree of failure to accept an individual or group on terms of social intimacy.

social-distance scale: *see* **scale, social-distance.**

social dominance: *see* **dominance, social.**

social drama: *see* **sociodrama.**

social dynamics: *see* **dynamics, social.**

social education: (1) experiences, usually controlled, that improve the individual's ability to participate in group life; (2) education in school that aims to develop persons able to participate effectively in society.

social efficiency: (1) a type of social action which exhibits effective internal dynamics; (2) the effectiveness in a society in which the internal dynamics are such as to produce intended results.

social engineering: *see* **engineering, social.**

social facilitation: *see* **facilitation, social.**

social force: (1) the influence on the individual of stimuli of a social nature originating in or generated by other persons of the group; the stimuli themselves; (2) the influence on the individual or on society in general of the customs, traditions, ideas, taboos, etc., accepted by or common to the group, as distinguished from the nonsocial aspects of the environment; (3) the influence on the individual of the physical presence or memory of another person or persons; (4) any influence, stimulus, or power peculiar to the group rather than the individual. *See* **facilitation, social.**

social foundations: the group bases of an activity or institution.

social foundations of education: an approach to the study of education in which an analysis of the social forces, policies, and issues of a culture, with some attention to their historical roots, is used as a basis for considering the proper functions of the school; the consideration of educational programs and policies in the light of an interdisciplinary endeavor involving philosophical, psychological, sociological, historical, and anthropological understandings.

social fraternity: *syn.* **fraternity, college.**

social function: any natural or artificial process that produces social effects; in curriculum planning, the term is used to designate an area of activity common to group life in all cultures, for example, production, transportation, etc.

social-functions core curriculum: *see* **curriculum, social-functions core.**

social-functions procedure: a method of curriculum organization in which social functions (such as consumption or transportation, about which the activities of individuals and the plans and problems of the group tend to cluster) are used rather than subjects or other bases in defining areas of the curriculum. (First developed on a wide scale in the Virginia Course of Study, 1931–1934.)

social geography: *see* **geography, social.**

social group: *see* **group, social.**

social-group approach: a basis for or method of organizing the content of the social studies, based on the study and consideration of the social group. *See* **group, social;** *contr. w.* **biographical method** (2).

social group work: *see* **group work, social.**

social growth: *see* **growth, social.**

social guidance: *see* **guidance, social.**

social harmony: (1) a high degree of acceptance of identical values by the members of a group; (2) an adjustment in which the process of interaction is accommodation rather than conflict. *Syn.* **social health.**

social health: *syn.* **social harmony** (2).

social heredity: *see* **heredity, social.**

social heritage: *see* **heritage, social.**

social history: *see* **history, social.**

social hygiene: *see* **hygiene, social.**

social ideal: an aim or goal accepted by a group as worthy of exerting effort to attain.

social information: *see* **information, social.**

social inhibition: *see* **inhibition, social.**

social institution: *see* **institution, social.**

social insurance: *see* **insurance, social.**

social integration: *see* **integration, social.**

social intelligence: *see* **intelligence, social.**

social intelligence, curriculum for: *see* **curriculum for social intelligence.**

social interaction: *see* **interaction, social.**

social interpretation: an activity of the school, based on investigation and publicity, by which the home, school, and community each is kept aware of the needs, conditions, purposes, and values of the others; implies a state of interdependence among the three in which each contributes continuously to the social adjustment and reinforcement of the other two.

social interpretation of education: the view that, since education always serves to continue some way of life, its function is rooted in the particular cultural conditions of a time and a place rather than in an unchanging and absolute order which may be known apart from a social context.

social invention: the act of discovering or the discovery of any new social concept, instrument, or organization, as contrasted with the more common tendency of society to follow a traditional course.

social isolate: *see* **isolate, social.**

social learning: *see* **learning, social.**

social legislation: a term coined by William I of Germany in 1881 in an address before the Reichstag urging the enactment of a system of accident and health insurance; now refers to laws designed to ameliorate social ills and thus protect and improve the social position of those groups in society which, because of age, sex, race, national origin, or economic status, are not in a position to achieve healthful and decent living standards for themselves.

social life: a general term designating group life and institutional procedures.

social maladjustment: *see* **maladjustment, social.**

social maturity: *see* **maturity, social.**

social maturity scale: *see* **scale, social maturity.**

social measurement: *see* **measurement, social.**

social milieu: *see* **milieu, social.**

social mobility, horizontal: the possibility for people to move about within the same social-status level.

social mobility, vertical: the possibility for people to move up and down the social-status scale; a high degree of vertical social mobility is said to exist in a society or community in which it is relatively easy for people to move from one social status to another; a low degree, when the social-status scale tends to be rigid and people cannot move from one status to another.

social needs: *see* **needs, social.**

social objectives: *see* **objectives, social.**

social order, telic (tel'ik): any society deliberately established on the basis of and operating in accordance with a consciously conceived plan or theory, as opposed to a society that has developed somewhat haphazardly and that lacks a conscious, guiding principle. *Contr. w.* **society, genetic.**

social organization: (1) the definite system of relationships among the components of a group that makes it an identifiable entity; (2) an established group of persons; (3) the process of consolidating small groups having common interests into larger, purposive groups, for example, the organization of the 13 American colonies into the United States, or the organization of a number of different but related groups of wage workers into a trade union.

social orientation: *see* **orientation, social.**

social-personal guidance: *see* **guidance, social-personal.**

social phase: *see* **phase, social.**

social philosophy: *see* **philosophy, social.**

social policy: a long-range plan for social affairs in terms of which individual cases and particular events are judged; a statement of principle about common purposes or public events which influence the lives of all the people; an appeal to others for loyalty and support, claiming that selected interests or values should prevail over others; a point of view expressly urged by or implicitly involved in the statements or activities of groups or individuals.

social pragmatism: *see* **pragmatism, social.**

social pressure: (1) influence exerted by members of a society that tends to shape the convictions and valuations of other members of the group; (2) influence purposively exerted by certain members of a society to affect the decisions of others.

social problem: a question that arises from a social situation resulting from recurring and widely prevalent maladjustments and that thrusts itself upon the attention of the community, evokes agitation, calls for reform, and usually leads to attempts at societal solution. (Recognition of a problem by many usually involves conflict with groups that do not recognize the problem or do not wish change.)

social-problems core curriculum: *see* **curriculum, social-problems core.**

social process: (1) a dynamic, continuous, step-by-step transition of social phenomena from one condition to another, relatively automatically and spontaneously carried on as a result of the interaction and interrelation of social groups; *see* **social processes approach;** (2) the process by which beliefs and values which are merely individual become social.

social processes approach: one approach to curriculum development in which the scope of the curriculum is defined through analysis of the series of activities constituting group action.

social proficiency: *see* **intelligence, social.**

social progress: (1) social change or changes which enable human beings to lead the kind of life which promotes human excellence; (2) the change or changes in institutional relationships which free individuals and social groups from arbitrary restrictions in the free exchange and use of ideas, technological improvements, etc.

social psychology: *see* **psychology, social.**

social quotient: *see* **quotient, social.**

social realism: *see* **realism, social.**

social reconstruction: the belief that man can to a significant degree plan and control his society, that in a democratic society this should be done in the public interest, and that the schools have a significant part to play in the process; various emphases and varying degrees of radicalism have been stated (George S. Counts, William H. Kilpatrick, Theodore Brameld). *Syn.* **reconstructionism.**

social-recreation program: *see* **program, social-recreation.**

social regeneration: the mental or moral rehabilitation of persons to enable them to reenter normal social life.

social responsibility: (1) the duty of each person to try to understand what the common good is and to act in accordance with it; (2) the duty of a group to share in community undertakings in relation to the welfare of individuals.

social retardation: *see* **retardation, social.**

social room: a room devoted to social or community activities, such as conversation, singing, and dancing.

social science: *see* **science, social.**

social security: a policy or type of insurance intended to protect the individual and his home against misfortunes, whether of an economic or of a personal nature, often including some scheme of unemployment compensation, sickness and life insurance, maternity insurance, and a pension plan; may be supported by Federal, state, or private agencies, in cooperation with the individual.

Social Security Acts: a series of acts, the first of which was enacted by Congress in 1935, providing for a system of retirement and health benefits for many workers (and spouses) after they reach the age of 62 or 65 years.

social selection: *see* **selection, social.**

social-self-realization: harmony between individual needs, desires, and drives and social needs, desires, and drives. *Comp. w.* **self-realization.**

social sensitivity: *see* **sensitivity, social.**

social service activities: *see* **activities, social service.**

social service committee: a committee of school officials and interested civic leaders appointed by the superintendent of schools; functions as the executive and policy-setting body for the administration of a school social-service program to provide means for meeting the needs of indigent school children.

social service index: a file listing the cases with which a social agency is occupied or with which it has dealt, or a similar file in a social service exchange dealing with all the cases handled by the cooperating agencies.

social service, school: a service to supplement the work of the teacher; makes her work more effective both through helping her to better understand the children with whom she works and through offering direct help to children and their parents with problems which may interfere with successful school achievement.

social service, school of: a professional school of a university the main purpose of which is to prepare at the graduate level (typically for the master's degree) social workers who will administer and carry on the work of a social agency such as a department of social welfare, family service agency, etc.

social services: *see* **services, social.**

social services, school: *see* **school social services.**

social settlement: a service institution, generally located in an underprivileged neighborhood, established and maintained by more prosperous members of the community, frequently in connection with a church or similar organization, and intended to ensure educational, recreational, medical, and other assistance for the less prosperous inhabitants of the city. *See* **settlement.**

social significance: importance in terms of effect upon group life.

social situation: the totality of group influences, culture, interaction, status, and role impinging upon the individual and contributing to his definition of the situation and his corresponding behavior.

social skills: *see* **skills, social.**

social sorority: *see* **fraternity, college; sorority.**

social stability: the condition of steadiness or firmness of the social group because of commonly understood and accepted ideals, standards, and aspirations.

social statics: *see* **statics, social.**

social status: (1) social class; (2) position of an individual on a scale of social prestige; (3) (law) the legal rights, obligations, and privileges of an individual that result from family connections and relationships, age, sex, achievements, occupation, and prosperity.

social strategy: that plan of action which has as its objective the solution of social problems such as those arising from depressions, prejudices, wars, the relation of the individual to the group, etc.

social structure: *see* **structure, social.**

social studies: those portions of the subject matter of the *social sciences,* particularly history, economics, political science, sociology, and geography, which are regarded as suitable for study in elementary and secondary schools and are developed into courses of study, whether integrated or not, and of which both the subject matter and the aims are predominantly social; not to be confused with the social sciences or with subjects having a social aim but not social content (as in the case of courses in English, art appreciation, and personal health), nor to be confined to too narrow or rigid a combination of studies.

social telesis: a telic society in action, actually or ideally. *See* **social order, telic.**

social test: *see* **test, social.**

social transmission: the act or process of passing on the learning, culture, habits, traditions, arts, etc. commonly accepted or used by the group to the next and so to succeeding generations. *Dist. f.* **inheritance** (2).

social trend: a predominant tendency persisting over a relatively long time span and affecting the character of prevailing institutions or of a given period; some spirit of the times sufficiently a habit of action as well as of thought so that it is expressed in social events, for example, urbanization, decentralization, laissez-faire, or planning.

social understanding: the knowledge that one has of the forces in social groups that are molding public opinion; knowledge about society that the individual needs in order to live and work effectively in it; an understanding of the community pattern, its background, and its problems.

social utility: usefulness in fulfilling needs or desires of members of a society.

social values: *see* **values, social.**

social-values approach: a method of attack on the problem of curriculum revision in which the principal criterion for the selection of materials is whether the study of certain materials or subjects will result in outcomes held worthwhile by society.

social work: (1) programs and procedures for improvement of societal conditions affecting individuals or the family unit; includes both case work and group process; *see* **case work; case work, social; group process;** (2) in school guidance programs, special services provided for pupils who need assistance which cannot be given by teachers and counselors.

social worker, psychiatric: an individual specially trained in analysis and interpretation of social conditions in the home, school, and neighborhood.

social worker, school: *syn.* **visiting teacher.**

sociality: the disposition or tendency to associate with or identify oneself with others. (One of the tasks of educational theory is to explore the relations of sociality and *individuality,* including the problem of the degree to which and the senses in which they are (*a*) mutually exclusive, and (*b*) mutually complementary.)

socialization: (1) the process by which individuals and groups living in geographical proximity establish a relatively stable social order involving a common culture and a feeling of group unity; (2) the process of bringing the individual, particularly the child, to understand and accept the customs, standards, traditions, and culture of the group of which he is a member and to cooperate actively with that group; (3) the process of placing emphasis on the social aspects of any institution or activity, as contrasted with its individual aspects; an example is the socialization of instruction in physical education, by which emphasis is placed on pleasurable group contacts and social activity rather than on individual excellence of performance; (4) the process of changing an institution or activity with a view to making it applicable or beneficial to society as a whole rather than to individuals or small groups; an example is the socialization of the school, intended to make the school serve the educational needs of all the students, from all classes of society, rather than those of a small, elite group; (5) the process of educating boys and girls to the social side of modern living, for example, to recognized patterns of group behavior in dating a member of the opposite sex in connection with entertainment, dinner, a car ride, or dancing.

socialization change: *see* **change, socialization.**

socialization, child: *see* **child socialization.**

socialization course, basic: *see* **program, common-learnings (2).**

socialization of drives: *see* **drives, socialization of.**

socialization of education: (1) the introduction of discussion, student government, and other democratic procedures into the program of the schools; (2) the adaptation of the curriculum and the administration of the educational program to the effective meeting of social needs.

socialized bookkeeping: *see* **bookkeeping, socialized.**

socialized instruction: *see* **instruction, socialized.**

socialized lesson: *see* **lesson, socialized.**

socialized mathematics: *see* **mathematics, socialized.**

socialized procedure: *see* **socialization of education.**

socialized recitation: *see* **recitation, socialized.**

socialized school: (1) a school in which each person has a share in determining policies and administrative activities; (2) a school in which the curriculum and other phases of the program are highly adapted to meeting the educational needs of society.

socialized vocalization: *see* **vocalization, socialized.**

socially disadvantaged child: *see* **child, socially disadvantaged.**

socially handicapped: *see* **handicapped, socially.**

socially maladjusted child: *see* **child, socially maladjusted.**

societal: *syn.* **social.**

societal tension: a state of disequilibrium in a group or among groups.

society: (1) an enduring, cooperating social group (generally of human beings) so functioning as to maintain and perpetuate itself; (2) any group, but especially a nation, consisting of human beings who may be similar or different in race and culture, who have more or less clearly recognized common interests, and who cooperate in the pursuit of those interests.

society-centered curriculum: *see* **curriculum, society-centered.**

society-centered school: a school in which the philosophy, curriculum, and methods are focused more on the conditions, trends, and needs of society than on subjects or children.

society, child: *see* **child society.**

society, city school: *see* **city school society.**

society, classless: (1) an organized social group devoid of status, prestige, or power differentiations; (2) an unstratified society; (3) a concept of social organization, emphasized in the theories of Karl Marx, but now widely believed to be very rare if not absent among human societies.

society, comparative-education: *see* **comparative-education society.**

society, contemporary: a society existing during the same period of time as another society, event, etc.; especially, society functioning at the present time.

society editor: (school journ.) a member of a student publication staff who is responsible for personal items and for accounts of the social activities of students and faculty members.

society, educational: *see* **educational society.**

Society for the Propagation of the Gospel in Foreign Parts (SPG): a missionary body founded in England in 1701 by the Anglican Church; it was especially active in America in the Middle and Southern colonies, where SPG missionaries maintained schools for the primary purpose of teaching religion.

society, frameworks of: *see* **frameworks of society.**

society, genetic: a social order that has grown without conscious, purposeful planning. *Contr. w.* **social order, telic.** (No social order can be considered wholly genetic or telic.)

society, honor: *see* **honor society.**

society, honorary: *see* **honorary society.**

society, human: a relatively large *aggregate* having a common culture—habits, attitudes, values, and feelings of unity.

society, leadership honor: *see* **honor society, leadership.**

society, national honor: *see* **honor society, national.**

society, open: *see* **open society.**

society, scholarship honor: *see* **honor society, scholarship.**

society, school: interacting groups that make up the school population (pupils, teachers, administrators, classes, grades, sections, faculty, teams, clubs, committees, etc.) and that carry on the functions for which the school is organized.

society, telic: *syn.* **social order, telic.**

sociodrama: an experimental educational method utilizing role-playing or dramatic techniques in a contrived situation in which the individual participates not as himself but in the role of someone else, for the purpose of learning more about, and understanding better, various skills and attitudes in human relations. *See* **role-playing; psychodrama.**

socioeconomic approach: a method of attack on the problem of curriculum revision in which stress is placed on the study of existing social and economic problems, conditions, and trends as a means of deciding on the suitability of materials for instruction.

socioeconomic background: the background or environment indicative of both the social and economic status of an individual or group.

socioeconomic education: *syn.* **business education, basic.**

socioeconomic influences: the social and economic forces bearing upon an individual, group, institution, law, policy, etc.

socioeconomic mathematics: *syn.* **mathematics, socialized.**

socioeconomic status: *see* **status, socioeconomic.**

socioempathy: the process that causes a child to think, feel, and behave as though the characteristics of another person or group of people belonged to him. *See* **identification.**

sociogenesis: the science dealing with the origin and evolution of societies or of a particular community, society, or social unit.

sociogram: a graphic representation of the sociometric structure of a group; the structure of choice patterns is usually presented in the form of a diagram, with circles or triangles representing the group members; the choices are represented by lines drawn between the circles or triangles; the diagram thus shows the interactions preferred among individual members of the group.

sociogram, class: a chart or diagram showing the social relationships among members of a particular school class in terms of responses to specific stimulus questions.

sociogram, multiple-question: a chart or graph showing the social relationships among members of a group in terms of responses to two or more stimulus questions.

sociograph: a *matrix* presentation of data gathered by a *sociometric test;* this information may also be presented by use of a *sociogram. See* **sociometry.**

sociohistorical approach: a method of attack on the problem of curriculum revision in which the principal criterion for the selection of materials for study is the extent to which such topics or subjects have contributed to human progress in the past and their probable future importance.

socioindustrial competence: the ability to earn a living and to participate satisfactorily in family and civic life.

sociological age: *syn.* **age, social.**

sociological approach: the group viewpoint, or the consideration of the collective aspects of human behavior in undertaking a study or an activity.

sociological determination of curriculum: *see* **curriculum, sociological determination of.**

sociological method: an approach to the study of political science that recognizes that government and society are closely interrelated and therefore makes maximal use of findings in the field of social psychology in order to gain a better understanding of government, the degree to which it can function, and the extent of its influence.

sociological school: a mode of thinking and of interpreting social phenomena characteristic of the sociologist. *See* **sociology.**

sociology: (1) the science or study of human social grouping and behavior, regarded generally and collectively, and dealing particularly with the origins, development, purposes, functions, problems, adjustments, and peculiarities of human society; (2) the study of human beings living together in groups.

sociology, educational: a subarea of sociology which applies sociological knowledge and techniques to educational problems in the field of human relations; this area concerns itself with (a) community and school relations; (b) the role of the teacher in the community and school; (c) the role of the school in society; (d) social factors affecting the schools; (e) consequences for personality of modern educational practices; (f) modifications in curricular content in response to social pressure; (g) the understanding of our culture and its social trends in relation to both formal and informal educative agencies; (h) group process approach to education; (i) the utilization of research and critical thinking to define educational goals.

sociology of music: a relatively new field of inquiry into the sociological aspects of the music profession—rewards, relevance to the needs of society, perpetuation of the myth of the musician as an egocentric artist, and related concerns.

sociology, organismic: a view held by Comte and Spencer, among others, and now largely abandoned, that the group is like a biological organism and is subject to similar laws of development.

sociology, rural: a study of rural social life and organization, including (a) comparisons with city life and (b) the interrelations between rural and urban conditions.

sociology, urban: a study of urban social life and organization, including comparisons with rural and village life.

sociomatrix: a table in which sociometric choices and rejections are recorded; has vertical and horizontal columns which show the reaction of each person in the group to every other person.

sociometric grouping: *see* **grouping, sociometric.**

sociometric instruments: checklists, scales, and tests used to study the psychological reactions of human beings in relation to others.

sociometric technique: a device used for revealing the preferences, likes, dislikes, etc., of the members of a group; characterized by the procedure of obtaining from each member a statement as to which group members (usually two or three) he would prefer as cooperating participants in various activities or relationships, for example, as housemates, workmates, seatmates, or teammates; also used for revealing group structures and subdividing the group into various types of members, for example, leaders, isolates, rival factions, etc.; may employ a *sociogram* as illustration.

sociometric test: *see* **test, sociometric.**

sociometry: measurement of the interpersonal relationships prevailing among the members of a group; by means of sociometric devices, such as the *sociogram,* an attempt is made to discover the patterns of choice and rejection among the individuals making up the group—which ones are chosen most often as friends or leaders (*stars*), which are rejected by others (*isolates*), how the group subdivides into clusters or cliques, etc.; includes also methods and principles followed in making groups more effective in pursuing their goals and more personally satisfying to their members; may also include the evolution and organization of groups and the position of individuals within them.

socius (sō′shi·əs): the individual regarded as a basic social unit, having characteristics in common with other members of his group.

Socratic method: a process of discussion led by the teacher to induce the learner to question the validity of his reasoning or to reach a sound conclusion; the name derives from the strategy ascribed to Socrates (in Plato's *Dialogues*) in his role as intellectual midwife.

soft palate: a structure of membranes and muscles forming the back part of the roof of the mouth and attached to the bony hard palate, and capable of movement so as to shut off the nasal cavity from the mouth and throat cavities; to be distinguished from the *uvula,* which is attached to the posterior end of the soft palate. *Syn.* **velum.**

softball: an adapted baseball game; played with a smaller bat and a larger ball and in a smaller area than *baseball.*

software: (1) all nonhardware elements of a computer-based system, including written computer programs, flow charts, subroutines, and other items related to information systems; also, the package of programming support or utility routines which is provided (or available with) a given computer, generally including an *assembler,* a *compiler,* an operating system (or monitor), debugging aids, and a library of subroutines; (2) the educational stimuli or messages, such as a televised lecture, a teacher-prepared audio tape, or a programmed textbook, which provide the content of instruction to the student. *See* **hardware.**

sol-fa (sōl′fä′; sol′fä′): n. a system designating various tones, degrees of the scale, by syllable names rather than by letters or numbers; the syllables exemplify the position and function of the notes of the musical scale and thus aid in sight singing. *See* **fixed do; movable do; singing, number; solfeggio; solmization.**

sol-fa: v. to sing a musical passage, using *sol-fa* syllables.

sol-fa syllables: Italian terms designating (a) the tones of the chromatic scale or (b) the tones corresponding to the lines and spaces of the staff, and employed in teaching tonal relationships in singing. *See* **fixed do; movable do; sol-fa.**

sol-fa, tonic: an English system of teaching sight singing, employing a complicated notation based on the movable-do principle. *See* **movable do; sol-fa.**

soldier's qualification card: *see* **card, soldier's qualification.**

solenoid: an electromagnet which forces a piston to move by magnetic action when a current is introduced in order to activate a mechanical operation in a piece of electronic equipment.

solfège (sol·fäzh′): the French spelling of *solfeggio.*

solfeggio (sol·fej′ō): *pl.* **solfeggi** (sol·fej′ē); a vocal exercise intended to be sung to the *sol-fa syllables* or to a single syllable; may follow the *movable-do* or the *fixed-do* system.

solid geometry: *see* **geometry, solid.**

solid histogram: *see* **histogram, solid.**

solid state physics: *see* **physics, solid state.**

solipsism: (1) epistemologically, a theory that all knowledge begins with the self and all knowledges are but constructs of the self; (2) metaphysically, a theory that the whole of reality is comprehended within the mental activity of the individual.

solitary-play stage: an early stage in social development in which a child is absorbed in his own play interests and is apparently unaware of the activities of other children playing near him, to the point where he makes no overtures toward them.

solmization: the designation of the steps of a musical scale by syllables. *See* **sol-fa.**

solution: (1) the answer or result that satisfies the conditions of a given problem; (2) the process of finding the answer to a given problem.

solution, faculty: (mil. ed.) a fixed or official solution to a given problem adopted in military schools or staffs for the purpose of standardizing instruction and grading, or planning. *Syn.* **school solution.**

solution, principal axes: *see* **principal axes solution.**

solution, school: *syn.* **solution, faculty.**

solution set: *see* **set, solution.**

somatic: (1) of or pertaining to the body cells as distinguished from the germ cells; (2) pertaining to the framework of the body as distinguished from the internal organs.

somatic development: *see* **development, somatic.**

somatic mutation: *see* **mutation, somatic.**

somatopsychological relationship: *see* **relationship, somatopsychological.**

somatopsychology: the study of body forms (physique) and their correlation with personality traits.

somatopsychosis (sō′mə·tō·si·kō′sis; -psi·kō′-): (1) a term used by Southard to designate a type of mental disorder accompanying and showing symptoms of an organic disease; (2) any psychosis characterized by the delusion that one is afflicted with a physical disorder.

somatotomy (sō·mə·to′to·mē): (1) the science of the structure of the human body; (2) dissection.

somatotype: a classification of an individual according to body structure; thought by some to be indicative of personality characteristics.

somatotype rating: *see* **rating, somatotype.**

sonant: any speech sound in the normal production of which the voice plays a part, such as the sounds *b, v, w,* and *d. Contr. w.* **surd.**

sonata: a musical composition of three or four parts or movements for solo instrument, the form of which is the basis of the concerto, compositions for small instrumental ensembles, and the symphony.

song, action: a song used in the elementary schools for rhythmic muscular response or dramatization.

song, art: (1) a song in which the music is the artistic expression of individuals who are trained in music; (2) a composition for solo voice, with accompaniment, which derives from an extramusical source (a poem, a view, etc.) and which succeeds because of the special interdependence of the voice and the accompaniment. *See* **lied;** *contr. w.* **song, folk.**

song cycle: a collection of songs of related thought and character designed to form a musical whole.

song, folk: (1) a song originating with the common people that has been passed on from generation to generation until the identity of its composer or composers is lost; attuned to the characteristics and life of its race or nationality; essentially rhythmic and melodic, and extremely simple in its structural form; (2) a song as defined above, with a known composer. *See* **music, folk.**

song method: a procedure for teaching music notation through the analysis of songs that have been learned by rote. *See* **song, rote.**

song, observation: a short simple song taught to children by rote as a basis for instruction in reading music; usually restricted to the tones of the diatonic scale. *Syn.* **pattern song.**

song, part: a song intended to be sung in harmony by voices of different types, such as soprano, contralto, tenor, and bass.

song, pattern: *syn.* **song, observation.**

song, rote: a song taught by ear, that is, by having the learner imitate the teacher with no reference to textbook; most commonly employed in kindergarten and primary grades. *See* **song, observation.**

song school: *syn.* **parish school** (1).

song, study: a song designed to afford drill on tonal problems previously learned.

song, unison: a song appropriate for or used in unison singing. *See* **singing, unison.**

sonic spectacles: eyeglass frames for the blind equipped with three transducers across the bridge, each the size of a one-cent piece, the center one emitting a high-frequency sonic pulse which strikes objects in the wearer's path and gives off a sonic echo received by the other two transducers; the resulting vibration is transformed by a control pack on the wearer's belt into sound signals which are fed through tubes on the earpieces of the glasses to a tiny speaker over the wearer's ear; the signals vary according to the texture of the object and its location in relation to the wearer, its range being about 20 feet; though the blind still need a seeing-eye dog or a long cane, the spectacles afford them much greater mobility through recognition of the objects in their immediate environment; they "see" with their ears, for example, a bus stop sign, a brick building, a glass door, a lamppost, or hedges; developed by Leslie Kaye of Canterbury University in Christchurch, N.Z.

sophism (sof′iz′m): an argument embodying a subtle fallacy, intentionally used to deceive or resulting in unintentional deception.

sophist: originally (cap.), one of a group of Greek teachers of geometry, rhetoric, literary interpretation, and conduct who flourished during the fifth century B.C., some of whom became famous for their skill in disputation and for their ability to argue cleverly but fallaciously; they contributed much, however, to the development of higher education, their work resulting in the foundation of schools of rhetoric in Athens, which exercised a great influence on Greek and Roman literature; included among their number is Protagoras, who first systematized grammar; now usually applied in a derogatory sense to one who argues cleverly and convincingly but fallaciously.

sophistic logic: *see* **logic, sophistic.**

sophisticated system: (mil. ed.) a space or other system which is complex and intricate, makes use of advanced techniques, and requires special skills to operate.

sophronistes (sof′rə·nis′tēz): the title of the state official supervisor, or censor of morals, of adolescent youth in ancient Athens.

soprano: the musical term for the highest female voice; applied also to certain wind instruments, such as the *recorder,* to distinguish those which have a high or treble range.

SOPS: an acronym for *standard operating procedures. See* **instruction, standard practice.**

soroban: a Japanese *abacus;* the device uses sliding beads on vertical rods; above the horizontal bar there is one bead on each rod and below there are either four or five. *See* **abacus; suan pan.**

sorority: a group of women students associated through common interests, either social or professional; may or may not include common living quarters; designated usually by means of Greek initial letters and with secret ritual; usually affiliated with other chapters on a national basis. *See* **fraternity; fraternity, college.**

sorority, honorary: a sorority for which students qualify by meeting certain scholastic, and sometimes social, standards; usually restricted to students in the professional school of a university.

sorority house: a building used as living quarters by women belonging to a specific sorority. *See* **fraternity house; residence house.**

sorority, professional: *see* **fraternity, professional.**

sorority, social: *see* **fraternity, college.**

sort: (data processing) to arrange items of information according to rules dependent upon a key or field contained in the items or records; for example, to perform the operation called *digital sort* is to sort out first the keys on the least significant digit and then to resort on each higher order digit until the items are sorted on the most significant digit.

sort, block: (automatic data processing) to break a deck of data cards into decades by the highest order code digit so that smaller groups can be handled and the work expedited by more quickly feeding sequenced data to a succeeding procedure step.

sort, digital: *see* **sort.**

sort, major: the controlling or general order of items in a sequence; for example, a month's invoices could be sorted by customer and, within each customer group, by date; the sort by customer is the major sort, the sort by date the *minor sort.*

sort, merge: (data processing) to produce a single sequence of items, ordered according to some rule, from two or more previously unordered sequences without changing the items in size, structure, or total number, although more than one pass may be required for a complete sort; items are selected during each pass on the basis of the entire key.

sort, minor: the order of items within the homogeneous groups formed by a major sort. *See* **sort, major.**

sort, Q-: *see* **Q-sort.**

sorter: a machine designed to arrange punch cards in order or in classes according to the information that has been punched into them.

sorter-collator: (data processing) a special machine built to handle specific jobs of sorting and collating as determined by a code.

sorting machine: *syn.* **sorter.**

sorting test: *see* **test, sorting.**

soul: (1) (dualism) an animating principle or substance thought to be totally independent of the body; believed to be the source of all conscious operation and, usually, to be immortal; this immortality may be conceived of as a state of continued personal existence or as the absorption of the soul into God or a Universal Soul; (2) (Scholasticism) the ultimate source of all vital activity, especially of intellectual processes, which gives existence to the body and thus forms one substantial unity with the body; in this doctrine the human soul is considered as immortal, but always remains distinct from God and from other souls; (3) sometimes used to refer to any ultimate principle of activity in living beings.

sound, dental: *see* **dental sound.**

sound discrimination: *see* **discrimination, sound.**

sound-discrimination test: *see* **test, sound-discrimination.**

sound distortion: faulty production of a speech sound in which the sound is partly recognizable, although altered from its normal or usual form. *Dist. f.* **sound substitution.**

sound drum: that portion of the mechanism of a sound motion picture projector around which the film passes at the point where the sound is picked up; usually attached to a flywheel to stabilize the movement of the film through the projector at this point.

sound effect: a sound from any source other than the dialogue, narration, or music in an audio presentation which enhances the illusion of reality.

sound film: *see* **film, sound.**

sound filmstrip: *see* **filmstrip.**

sound gate: a part of the sound head of a sound projector that holds the film in proper position so that the sound track will pass over the sound aperture correctly.

sound leader: a piece of film attached to the beginning of a sound film, used for threading the projector so that when the actual sound film reaches the gate, it will be in frame and the projector will be running evenly at sound speed.

sound localization: *syn.* **localization, auditory.**

sound omission: complete failure to articulate a given speech sound in pronouncing a word, as in *pay* for *play.*

sound pattern: *see* **pattern, sound.**

sound projector: *see* **projector, sound.**

sound recorder: *see* **recorder** (1).

sound recording, magnetic: the process or product of recording sound in the form of magnetic patterns; usually in iron oxide. *See* **recording, tape.**

sound recording, optical: the process of recording sound in patterns of variable area or density on film by means of a galvanometer or light valve.

sound shadow: the false graphic representation of the hearing level of an ear caused by the crossover of amplified sound entering the other sound.

sound shift: a change in consonants that can be traced and observed in the historical development of a language.

sound spectrogram: a visible record, produced by the *sound spectrograph*, in which sound frequency is shown on the vertical axis, time on the horizontal axis, and intensity by variations in darkness of the pattern.

sound spectrograph: a machine which provides visible records of the frequency, intensity, and time of samples of speech.

sound speed: the normal speed at which a motion-picture camera or projector is operated in making or showing sound films, namely, 24 frames per second. *See* **silent speed.**

sound, stereophonic: sound produced from a number of separate speakers to create the effect of multidirectional sound.

sound-striping: *see* **film, magnetic-striped.**

sound substitution: an articulatory speech error consisting in replacing one speech sound with another, as in *wun* for *run.*

sound system, central: *see* **central sound system.**

sound tracing: a technique for teaching word recognition that consists in having the pupil trace the letters of a word while pronouncing it slowly and distinctly.

sound track: that portion of the motion-picture film on which the sound is recorded, normally one band in 16 mm along the edge opposite the sprocket holes; may be optical or magnetic, or both, and with stereo sound may have two or more tracks. *See* **variable area track; variable density track.**

sound track channel, movie: the thin strip along one side of a movie film where the sound accompanying the sequence is recorded by means of exposure to a lamp of fluctuating intensity; the sound-sending mechanism of the movie projector converts these fluctuations into electronic impulses.

sound track, optical: *see* **optical sound track.**

sound trap, acoustical: a system of baffles which captures and absorbs sounds with a minimum of reflection.

sound, voiced: *syn.* **sonant.**

sound, voiceless: *syn.* **surd.**

Soundex filing system: the trade name of a system of filing records and correspondence according to a simplified phonetic rendering of the names of persons, in which most of the vowels are omitted and like-sounding consonants are combined.

sounding panel: *syn.* **panel, reactor.**

soundproofing: the treatment of a room or other part of a building with sound-absorbing material so as to prevent (*a*) the reverberation of noises originating within the room, such as a library, or (*b*) the escape of noises from a room, such as a music practice room.

sour grapes: a mechanism for compensating by disparaging the goal that one is unable to attain; a type of rationalization in which envy or jealousy predominates.

source: in communications theory, that part of a communication channel where messages are assumed to originate, that is, where selective action is exerted upon an ensemble of *signs.*

source deck: *see* **program, source.**

source, documentary: *see* **document** (3).

source language: *see* **language, source.**

source material: *syn.* **source, primary.**

source materials: *see* **materials, source.**

source module: *see* **program, source.**

source, original: *syn.* **source, primary.**

source, primary: (hist. res.) a document, a relic, or oral testimony presenting firsthand evidence of a fact or event, for example, a legal document, a school building or school furnishings, or an account of an event by an eyewitness. *Syn.* **original source.**

source, program: in a language laboratory, any electronic device which produces a program of practice material for broadcast to student positions.

source program: *see* **program, source.**

source scale: *see* **scale, source.**

source, secondary: (hist. res.) a written or oral report or other source more than one step removed from the original fact or event, for example, a newspaper editorial by a special writer who has obtained his information from the eyewitness account of a newspaper reporter. *Contr. w.* **source, primary.**

sources, occupational information: printed materials and/-or audiovisual aids employed to give knowledge concerning vocational opportunities; job descriptions, occupational monographs, textbooks, abstracts, and briefs are types of printed matter; films, charts, records, tapes, and posters are among audiovisual aids used. *See* **occupational information.**

sources of legitimate authority: *see* **authority, sources of legitimate.**

sovereign immunity: *see* **immunity, governmental.**

space: (1) formerly conceived of as a property of the physical world independent of other properties and of an observer; in modern science, seen as part of the space-time relation; (2) (typography) blank type used to separate words.

space, affective: (art ed.) that space in a creative work which is feeling-toned, that is, of particular emotional significance.

space ambiguity: *see* **ambiguity, space.**

space biology: *see* **biology, space.**

space, common-factor: geometrical space of r dimensions, where r is the number of common factors which will account for the variance in a matrix of intercorrelations (within experimental error).

space education: (1) an educational program, subject, or curriculum encompassing a study of the various aspects of space science, exploration, and travel, and their significance in present-day life; (2) that branch of general education concerned with communicating knowledge, skills, and attitudes about space science and activities and their total impact on society today.

space, euclidean: (1) the familiar one- and two-dimensional space of ordinary experience; (2) more generally and with equality defined as identity, the set of all ordered n-tuples of real numbers for $n = 1, 2, 3, \ldots$; according to the value of n, there is euclidean 1-space, 2-space, etc.

space, far: the third zone of space, measured as a distance of from 17 to 30 feet; at a physical level of measurement this range was derived from the natural line of vision extending from the gravitational line to a point in space some 20 feet more or less distant from the erect individual. *See* **space, mid; space, near; space, remote.**

space, hair: a very thin space in printing that is usually one-half point thick.

space imagination: the ability to visualize correctly geometric figures and relations; often used to denote the ability to visualize correctly three-dimensional figures.

space laboratory: *see* **laboratory, space.**

space, life: *see* **life space.**

space medicine: *see* **medicine, space.**

space, mid: a distance extending from 2 to 16 feet from a person in all directions, approximating a general boundary within the spatial surround that can easily be managed by a few steps in any direction.

space, milieu: space of social identification; each milieu defines a pattern of spatial living, a code of behavior, and an achievement expectancy.

space, near: the distance of most school tasks; can be diagrammed with a boundary extending two feet away from the corporate midline in all directions, the distance of reach, grasp, and release and the performance area for manipulation.

space perception: *see* **perception, space.**

space, physical: the world of objects and events which appear in the energy surround in a never-ending stream of bombardment on the individual.

space physics: *see* **physics, space.**

space, remote: the fourth zone of space, which includes any distance beyond 30 feet extending into infinity; the space of landscape, farmland, sky, horizon, etc., where the absence of detail forces reliance upon generalities rather than specifics.

space, sample: *see* **sample space.**

space science: *see* **science, space.**

space simulator: *see* **simulator, space.**

space system: in aerospace activities, a total complex consisting of a space vehicle, the industrial base required to produce it, the operational facilities for its operation and maintenance, the command communications system for its operational control, the supply and transportation system for its support, the training facilities and instructors, and the people organized and trained to operate and maintain the vehicle.

space, test: geometric space of $(n + r)$ dimensions, where r is the number of common factors and n is the number of unique factors of all the tests of the battery.

space-time: formerly conceived as properties of the physical world independent of each other and of an observer; in modern science, measures of space and time are seen as relative to an observer and the coordinates he is using to take his measurements.

space-time representation: *see* **representation, space-time.**

space utilization: *see* **utilization, space.**

space, visual: (art ed.) the space of the objective environment that is influenced by conditions such as degree of light, clarity, and distance as perceived through the eyes.

spaced practice: *see* **practice, distributed.**

spaceflight: the flight of a man-operated or man-controlled vehicle or other device into or through space.

spacemobile program: *see* **program, NASA Spacemobile.**

spacing, variable: (typewriting) vertical spacing done by use of either the variable line spacer or ratchet release for typing on lines or intervals of spacing narrower or wider than the regular typewriter spacing.

Spahr report: *see* **report, Spahr.**

span, attention: *see* **attention span.**

span, auditory: *see* **auditory span.**

span, auditory memory: *see* **memory span, auditory.**

span, eye-hand: *see* **eye-hand span.**

span, eye-voice: *see* **eye-voice span.**

span, memory: *see* **memory span.**

span of control: *see* **control, span of.**

span of interest: the length of time during which a child's attention can be given to one activity without artificial stimulation.

span of recognition: *syn.* **perceptual span.**

span of supervision: *see* **control, span of.**

span, perception: *syn.* **perceptual span.**

spare bus: *syn.* **bus, relief.**

sparsity correction: *see* **correction, sparsity.**

spasm: a sudden, violent, involuntary, rigid contraction due to muscular action; when persistent, called tonic spasm; when characterized by alternate contraction and relaxation, called clonic spasm; attended by pain and interference with function, producing involuntary movement and distortion; the term is also used for a sudden but transitory constriction of a passage, canal, or orifice.

spasm pattern: *syn.* **stuttering pattern.**

spasmophemia: a disorder of speech caused by the lack of control of the muscles of the lips and/or jaws. *See* **dysphemia.**

spastic: one afflicted with *spasticity.*

spastic gait: *see* **gait, spastic.**

spastic paralysis: *see* **paralysis, spastic.**

spastic paralysis, cerebral: *see* **cerebral spastic paralysis.**

spastic speech: *see* **speech, spastic.**

spasticity: (1) a central nervous disorder characterized by muscular incoordination often manifested by a dragging gait with the toes turned inward, awkward use of the hands and arms, and facial distortion, especially of the mouth; may be accompanied by severe speech disorder owing to incoordination of the speech mechanism; (2) the condition of being subject to spasms, that is, sharp muscular contractions, such as facial tics, whether as the result of a nervous disorder or of habit.

spatial: relating to or involving space.

spatial arts: *see* **arts, spatial.**

spatial awareness: *see* **awareness, spatial.**

spatial correlation: *see* **correlation, spatial.**

spatial localization: *see* **localization, spatial.**

spatial orientation: *see* **orientation, spatial.**

spatial relationship: *see* **correlation, spatial.**

spatial schema: *see* **schema, spatial.**

spatial visualization: *see* **visualization, spatial.**

spatiography: a branch of learning descriptively treating the spatial environment.

S.P.C.K.: the Society for Promotion of Christian Knowledge, founded in 1699, chiefly for the purpose of teaching the catechism or elementary subjects relating to the principles of the Church of England to the children of the poor.

speaker: a device that converts electrical impulses into sound, reproducing speech, music, etc. *Syn.* **loudspeaker.**

speaker jack: *see* **jack, speaker.**

speakers bureau: a group formed in order to provide members, generally students, with opportunities to speak in public.

speaking, choral: *see* **choral speaking.**

speaking test, directed: *see* **test, directed speaking.**

speaking vocabulary: *syn.* **vocabulary, speech or oral.**

Spearman-Brown prophecy formula: a formula expressing the theoretical relationship between the length of a test and its reliability coefficient; used for estimating the reliability of a test when lengthened by the addition of items of the same type, level of difficulty, validity, etc.; may be written as follows: $r_n = \dfrac{nr_{12}}{1+(n-1)r_{12}}$, where r_{12} is the reliability coefficient of the original test (that is, the coefficient of correlation between equivalent forms 1 and 2 of the test) and r_n represents the reliability coefficient of a test n times as long but otherwise equivalent to it. *Syn.* **Brown's formula; Brown-Spearman formula; Brown-Spearman prophecy formula; prophecy formula; Spearman's prophecy formula.**

Spearman's foot-rule method: *syn.* **Spearman's foot-rule method of gains.**

Spearman's foot-rule method of gains: *(R)* a rough method of obtaining an estimate of the relationship existing between the rank orders of the observations of two variables, as, for example, the rank order of the pupils of a class in each of two examinations; consists in the application of the formula $R-1 = \dfrac{6\Sigma G}{N^2-1}$, in which ΣG equals the sum of the positive difference in rank (known as *gains*) for each pair of scores and N equals the number of pairs. *Syn.* **foot-rule correlation; foot-rule formula; foot-rule method; method of gains; Spearman's foot-rule method;** *dist. f.* **coefficient, rank difference correlation.**

Spearman's prophecy formula: *syn.* **Spearman-Brown prophecy formula.**

special ability: *see* **ability, special.**

special-ability test: *see* **test, special-ability.**

special aptitude: *see* **aptitude, special.**

special assessment: *see* **assessment, special.**

special assessment bond: *see* **bond, special assessment.**

special branch library: *see* **library, special.**

special center for the deaf: *see* **deaf, special center for the.**

special certificate: *see* **certificate, special.**

special class: *see* **class, special.**

special class, fractional: *see* **class, fractional special.**

special class, homogeneous: *see* **class, homogeneous special.**

special class, ungraded: *see* **class, ungraded special.**

special class unit: *see* **unit, special class.**

special classes, supervisor of: *see* **supervisor of special classes.**

special classroom: *see* **classroom, special.**

special day school: *see* **day school, special.**

special device: in naval training, a term covering synthetic training aids, teaching aids, research in human engineering, tactical evaluation, and training methods.

special education: the education of pupils (for example, the deaf, the blind and partially seeing, the mentally subnormal, the gifted) who deviate so far physically, mentally, emotionally, or socially from the relatively homogeneous groups of so-called normal pupils that the standard curriculum is not suitable for their educational needs and their variation presents unusual management problems to the school through its interference with the learning of others; carried on in special classes, through special curricula, and/or in special schools.

special-education aid: *see* **aid, special-education.**

special-education aide: *see* **teacher aide.**

special-education class: *see* **class, special-education.**

special-education classroom: *see* **classroom, special-education.**

special education, director of: *see* **director of special education.**

special education, percentage of total membership being provided appropriate: *see* **percentage of total membership being provided appropriate special education.**

special-education program: *see* **program, special-education.**

special-education teacher: a teacher of atypical children who has ability and preparation for the work (teacher of the blind, etc.). *Syn.* **special teacher** (3).

special-events program: *see* **program, special-events.**

special facility: *see* **facility, special.**

special-field preparation: *see* **preparation, special-field.**

special-fund doctrine: the principle or idea that a fund derived from a special tax on the local school unit for the support of schools is the best source of support for public education.

special help class: *see* **class, special help.**

special instruction room: (1) a room specially designed and equipped for the instruction of so-called special classes, usually consisting of ungraded children having very low or relatively low IQs; *see* **class, special** (1); (2) a room in a school building equipped to provide pupil experiences in areas of special interest or in areas that cannot be cared for properly in the regular classroom, for example, music room or art room.

special instructional field: *see* **instructional field, special.**

special-interest club: *see* club, special-interest.

special-interest course: *see* course, special-interest.

special library: *see* library, special.

special meeting: *see* meeting, special.

special methods course: *see* course, special methods.

special-organization library: *see* library, special.

special promotion: *see* promotion, special.

special report: *see* report, special.

special room: (1) any room in a school designated for a purpose other than as a classroom, such as a cot room for children's use in resting; (2) *see* classroom, special.

special school: (1) a school established for the purpose of caring for the educational needs of atypical children; offers special education to exceptional children of a single classification (blind for example or mentally retarded children) or to children with many different types of exceptionality; *see* special education; (2) a school that departs in character from the conventional graded school and high school, for example, a trade school or a school of fine arts.

special school district: *see* district, special school.

special school principal: *see* principal, special school.

special school, segregated: a school established for the purpose of providing for children with special instructional needs and organized in such a way as to emphasize segregation from regular schools and pupils in order to make better provision for those needs.

special service school: a school operated by the Army for training its personnel in the detailed techniques and tactics of all units of a particular arm or service, and the general techniques and tactics of associated arms. *Dist. f.* general service school; staff school.

special services, director of: *see* director of special services.

special services, director of guidance and: *see* director of guidance and special services.

special student: *see* student, special.

special subject: *see* subject, special.

special-subject library: *see* library, special.

special-subject supervision: *see* supervision, special-subject.

special supervisor: *see* supervisor, special.

special tax bond: *see* bond, special tax.

special teacher: (1) one who teaches or directs instruction in subjects for which regular teachers are not specially trained, for example, art, music, and physical education; *see* resource teacher (1); (2) in agricultural education, more commonly a teacher employed because the regular teachers lack time to teach classes in certain subjects in which they are, however, prepared; (3) in special education, one who teaches particular types of children or uses certain types of methods in which regular teachers are not specially trained.

special training: *see* training, special.

special transfer: *see* transfer, special.

specialist: a person who has studied and worked intensively in one field of knowledge and supposedly has thus attained a high degree of understanding and proficiency; in teacher education, there are specialists in subject matter as well as in fields related to the science and practice of education such as educational philosophy, educational psychology, methods of teaching, curriculum, and administration; in public school systems, there are often specialists in art, music, and physical education. *See* generalist.

specialist, child development: a person whose professional training has prepared him to understand and work with the changes that take place in a child as he passes from birth toward maturity; generally assumed to mean a specialist in the period from the end of infancy to the beginning of adolescence.

specialist, communications: *see* communications specialist.

specialist course: *see* course, specialist.

specialist, curriculum: *see* curriculum specialist.

specialist, extension: *see* extension specialist.

specialist, guidance: *see* guidance specialist.

specialist in education degree: *see* degree, specialist in education.

specialist, orientation and mobility: one who teaches handicapped persons the utilization of the remaining senses for optimum spatial orientation; for example, instructs blind and partially sighted persons in the use of the long cane utilizing the *touch technique* to afford safe, effective, and efficient independent movement. *Syn.* peripatologist.

specialist school: an Army school which does not conduct any officer career course; the Medical Service Veterinary School is an exception by reason of its close identification with a branch; such schools are the Aviation School, Civil Affairs School, Missile and Munitions School, Helicopter School, etc; joint and defense schools operated by the Army are specialist schools. *See* branch school; defense school; joint school.

specialist, school intergroup relations: an educator trained in the social sciences and in the philosophy of pragmatism as applied to community problems, whose primary task is to help improve the relations among groups within a school system.

specialist, subject-matter: (mil. ed.) a person who is considered proficient in a particular subject matter or skill area and who collaborates with writers of instructional materials to ensure accuracy and completeness of such materials.

specialist, teacher: a teacher whose major function is to provide consultative assistance to other teachers. *See* consultant, instructional.

specialist training, common: *see* training, common specialist.

specialization, broad-field: *see* field of concentration, major.

specialization of counselors: *see* counselors, specialization of.

specialization, professional: the part of formal teacher education that deals specifically with the history, personnel, institutions, publications, research, trends, organization (administrative, supervisory, and instructional), legal aspects, instructional and evaluative techniques, purposes, and practices of formal education.

specialization, subject: (teacher ed.) intensive study and work done by an individual in a specific subject in preparation for teaching that subject. (Such preparation is distinguished from the general education of teachers, which stresses orientation in many areas of human experience as a general background for teaching and as a broad base for specialization.)

specializations, interarea: specializations and related subspecializations common to two or more general areas of study and/or major academic fields; for example, biochemistry includes studies in the biological sciences and the physical sciences, which are considered to be two separate general areas of study.

specialized education: (1) education of the type that takes account of the individual differences of learners; (2) education that seeks to prepare individuals for specific types of occupation; *contr. w.* general education.

specialized high school: *see* high school, specialized.

specialized job: *see* job, specialized.

specialized reading skill: *see* skill, specialized reading.

specialized vocabulary: *see* vocabulary, specialized.

specialty, Air Force: *see* Air Force specialty.

specialty code, Air Force: *see* code, Air Force specialty.

specialty knowledge test: *see* test, specialty knowledge.

specialty-oriented student: *see* student, specialty-oriented.

specialty training standard: *see* training standard, specialty.

specific activity: *ant.* activity, mass (1).

specific aim: *see* aim, specific.

specific attitude: *see* attitude, specific.

specific determiner: *see* clue, specific determiner.

specific determiner clue: *see* clue, specific determiner.

specific elements in transfer: *syn.* identical elements; *dist. f.* transfer, nonspecific.

specific enrollment rate, single-year-of-age-grade: *see* enrollment rate, single-year-of-age-grade specific.

specific factor: *see* factor, specific.

specific intelligence test: *syn.* **test, aptitude.**

specific job competencies: *see* **competencies, specific job.**

specific objective: *see* **objective, specific.**

specific objectives in education: *see* **objectives in education, specific.**

specific occupational competencies: *see* **competencies, specific occupational.**

specific reading disability: *see* **reading disability, specific.**

specific related instruction: *see* **instruction, specific related.**

specific transfer: *see* **transfer, specific.**

specific variance: *see* **variance, specific.**

specification: (pup. trans.) a statement setting forth all details of construction of school buses including size, materials, shape, dimensions, quality, color, etc.

specification equation: *see* **equation, specification.**

specification, job: *see* **job specification.**

specifications, educational: detailed, precise, and expert presentation of what is needed in educational facilities, including equipment, classrooms, laboratories, curriculum, etc.

specifications, table of: *see* **table of specifications.**

specificity of development: independence or partial independence in the development of different structures or functions with respect to rate of growth, degree of development, period of initiation or termination of development, etc. *See* **dysplasia; growth, differential** (2); *contr. w.* **integration of development; organismic concept of development.**

specificity of traits, doctrine of: the teaching that human behavior consists of specific acts controlled by specific habits, as contrasted with the doctrine that behavior can be described in terms of general traits, such as honesty or carelessness.

specifying item: *see* **item, specifying.**

specimen: (1) a portion of a thing or a representative of a class of thing removed from its natural setting for analysis and study; (2) a standard of comparison used in a quality scale, such as one of a series of examples of handwriting arranged in order of merit; (3) the item to be judged by comparison with a quality scale.

specimen description: (guidance) a recording of particular behavior observed at a selected time and place; the nature of the behavior, however, is not observed in a selected way. *See* **observation, approaches to.**

spectacles, sonic: *see* **sonic spectacles.**

spectator, creator as: *see* **visual type.**

spectator theory of knowledge: *see* **knowledge, spectator theory of.**

spectrogram, sound: *see* **sound spectrogram.**

spectrograph, sound: *see* **sound spectrograph.**

speculative philosophy: *see* **philosophy, speculative.**

speech: a system of communication by means of symbolic vocal sounds.

speech area: the range of frequencies most important for the understanding of speech, roughly from 400 to 3,000 cycles per second. *Syn.* **speech range.**

speech audiometer: *see* **audiometer, speech.**

speech audiometry: *see* **audiometry, speech.**

speech block: a momentary failure to proceed with the act of speaking, characteristically accompanied by anxiety and tension; a symptom or type of stuttering. *See* **stuttering.**

speech center: the portion of the cerebral cortex believed to control the function of speech; specifically, the inferior portion of the third frontal convolution (Broca's area), usually in the left cerebral hemisphere, which is assumed to control the movements of the speech mechanism. *See* **Broca's area.**

speech clinic: *see* **clinic, speech.**

speech clinic, pediatric: *see* **clinic, speech, pediatric speech.**

speech, compressed: recorded speech which is processed to increase its speed without distortion of pitch; in some cases, words or parts of words are also omitted from compressed speech recordings; an educational timesaver allowing individuals to become exposed to pertinent points from a wide variety of recorded materials via dial-access information retrieval systems or in listening laboratories; also called *time-compressed speech.*

speech contest: speech performance in which speakers, either as individuals or as groups, are compared as to excellence and some recognition is given to those judged to be best.

speech correction: administration of special instruction designed to alleviate or eliminate speech disorders; in public schools and colleges, involves individualized instruction and work with small groups of pupils who have similar speech problems.

speech-correction class: *see* **class, speech-correction.**

speech defect: any imperfection in the sounding of words, phrases, and parts of words, including extreme difficulties such as stammering and minor difficulties such as mispronunciation and nasal voice.

speech, defective: speech that is inadequate to the point of rendering communication difficult or impossible.

speech, delayed: retarded speech development, usually the result of emotional blocking, understimulation, hearing deficiency, or mental deficiency. (Sometimes the term is used to designate only that speech retardation not demonstrably due to organic causes.)

speech disorder: *syn.* **speech defect.**

speech disorder, functional: faulty speech for which there is no apparent physical or physiological cause.

speech disorder, organic: faulty speech that has an observable physical cause, such as cleft palate or absence of frontal teeth.

speech education: the teaching of oral speech to the deaf with the purpose of developing intelligible or understandable speech and a pleasing voice suitable to the age and sex of the person.

speech, egocentric: a type of speech characterized by being self-centered.

speech error: any deviation from accepted normal speech production; may be classified as to the chief process involved, as breathing, articulation, phonation, or symbolization errors; mispronunciation is a speech error to be distinguished from articulatory errors, such as sound omissions, sound substitutions, or general articulatory inaccuracy.

speech habit: a customary practice in oral language, especially with respect to voice quality, enunciation, pronunciation, and articulation.

speech-hearing consultant: *see* **consultant, speech-hearing.**

speech, implicit: changes in the muscle action potential (MAP) of the speech musculature which accompany silent reading; MAP is premised on the principle that each muscle has a certain electrical potential and that this potential increases as the muscle contracts.

speech improvement: (1) administration of instruction designed to facilitate the development of increasingly adequate speech, the instruction not being limited to pupils with definite speech disorders; sometimes incorporated in reading or English classes, with additional special individual and group work for pupils having definite speech disorders; *dist. f.* **speech correction;** (2) the process of motivating and teaching the proper production of speech sounds and other proper speech behavior to a kindergarten or primary grade class as a whole; differentiated from more intensive corrective procedures with individuals or small groups apart from the regular class activities.

speech-improvement class: *see* **class, speech-improvement.**

speech, incoherent: speech in which the consecutive ideas expressed bear little or no relation to each other; a symptom of extreme emotion or of mental disorder.

speech, inner: a mental awareness of the implicit movements of the speech musculature; a pseudohearing of the sounds associated with the graphic symbols called words. *Comp. w.* **subvocalization.**

speech inventory: *see* **inventory, speech.**

speech or oral vocabulary: *see* **vocabulary, speech or oral.**

speech organs: consist of the lips, teeth, gums, hard palate, soft palate, tongue, and vocal cords.

speech, pantomimic: (1) nonverbal communication by means of gestures, facial expression, and movements; (2) the execution of the articulatory movements involved in speaking without vocalizing or whispering the sounds and words; used by some speech correctionists in the treatment of certain types of speech disorders.

speech, parts of: *see* **parts of speech.**

speech pathology: the study of the causes, symptoms, classification, and treatment of speech disorders.

speech pattern: (1) the ordered relations among the elements involved in a person's speech, as represented in the spatial or temporal order of their occurrence; (2) the more prominent characteristics of a person's speech, for example, jerkiness, monotony, etc.

speech range: *syn.* **speech area.**

speech reading: *syn.* **reading, lip.**

speech-reception threshold level: *see* **threshold level, speech reception.**

speech, remedial: instruction designed to alleviate or eliminate speech disorders. *See* **speech correction;** *dist. f.* **speech improvement** (1).

speech, repetitious: *syn.* **cataphasia.**

speech report: a type of newspaper account that reproduces in brief form parts of a public address; an exercise used in journalism classes.

speech rhythm: the pattern of recurrence of stressed syllables, pauses, long and short syllables, and inflections characteristic of spoken language.

speech, scanning: slow, deliberate speech in which each syllable is accented.

speech situation: (1) any instance of human social behavior involving spoken language; often used particularly to indicate public-speaking performances; (2) in remedial speech work, an assignment used chiefly in the treatment of stuttering, requiring that the student should engage in conversation or other socialized speech activity as opposed to drill or practice, on the assumption that by a series of these assignments the stutterer's objectivity, confidence, and skill in controlling his speech will be improved.

speech skill: *see* **skill, speech.**

speech, spastic: the manner of speech characteristic of persons afflicted with bilateral paralysis, or Little's disease; the voice is weak and strained, articulation is defective, sometimes to the point of being completely unintelligible, and the act of speaking is often extremely difficult and labored.

speech technique, echo: *see* **echo speech technique.**

speech test: *see* **test, speech.**

speech therapist: *see* **therapist, speech.**

speech therapy: *see* **class, speech therapy.**

speech therapy class: *see* **class, speech therapy.**

speech tic: an involuntary and localized spasmodic muscular twitching, usually of the facial muscles, accompanying the act of speaking.

speech, time-compressed: *see* **speech, compressed.**

speech tones: the tones most useful for speech, namely, those between 256 and 4,096 double vibrations per second.

speech training aid: any of the technical devices used to assist speech training, particularly with deaf or hearing-impaired individuals; the usual effect of such devices is to amplify or modify sounds presented to the trainee or to represent sounds visually. *Syn.* **voice training aid.**

speech tune: the combination of pitch, stress, and rhythm that distinguishes (*a*) the spoken language of one person from that of another and (*b*) one language from another.

speed drill: *see* **drill, speed.**

speed, film: *see* **film speed.**

speed, lens: *see* **lens speed.**

speed, perceptual: rapidity of verbal and/or oral response to space relations; generally associated with clerical activities.

speed score: *syn.* **score, rate.**

speed, silent: *see* **silent speed.**

speed, sound: *see* **sound speed.**

speed, tape: *see* **tape speed.**

speed test: *see* **test, speed.**

speedball: a game played by two teams on a field or grassy area in which two sides try to drive a ball through opposite goals by kicking or throwing; a combination of *soccer* (a type of *football*) and *basketball.*

speedwriting: (bus. ed.) a simplified system of writing using the longhand alphabet, usually in abbreviated form.

spelling algorithm: a set of rules for a phoneme that indicates which spelling of that phoneme should be used under various conditions of position, stress, and adjacent letters; usually applied to computer use. *See* **algorithm; phoneme.**

spelling, alphabet: spelling using the names of the letters rather than the sounds of the letters.

spelling, alphabetic: a method of word recognition that consists in naming or pronouncing the individual letters and fusing them into the whole word sound.

spelling bee: a game to encourage the correct spelling of words, involving a contest in which students (often arranged in teams) seek to spell correctly and with reasonable speed words named by the master of ceremonies, with elimination of individuals as the penalty for a misspelling, until only one person is left standing.

spelling conscience: sensitivity to correctness in spelling and pride in ability to spell correctly.

spelling consciousness: awareness of spelling errors.

spelling contest: *syn.* **spelling match.**

spelling demon: any word that is commonly and persistently misspelled by a large percentage of persons.

spelling demon, individual: a word frequently misspelled by a particular person.

spelling difficulty: the degree to which a word is hard to spell correctly; often determined by comparing a record of misspellings at various grade levels with frequency of use at these levels.

spelling, finger: the use of the manual alphabet to spell out words for the deaf. *See* **alphabet, finger.**

spelling game: a game activity designed to help children increase spelling skills, for example, the spelling bee, in which each child attempts to outspell the others in the group.

spelling, individualized: a method of teaching spelling in which the pupil studies only those words which he misspelled on a pretest. *See* **test-study method.**

spelling list, adult: a list of words that adults need to be able to spell.

spelling list, basic: (1) a list of the words that are thought to be most important for the pupil to learn to spell; (2) a list of the words to be taught in spelling in a given school; (3) a list of the words to be taught during definite spelling periods in the daily program; contrasted with words to be taught outside the spelling period when the need for them arises; (4) a list of words that a pupil must spell correctly in order to be judged proficient in spelling; for example, some secondary schools have a basic spelling list that a student must spell correctly in order to graduate.

spelling list, individual: a list made by each pupil of the words that are persistently difficult for him to spell or that he has misspelled.

spelling match: a contest to determine which of a number of contestants is the best oral speller; used to motivate the study of spelling. *Syn.* **spelling contest.**

spelling method: (1) a method of teaching word recognition by having the child first spell and then pronounce each word; (2) a technique used by the child in working out the pronunciation of a new word.

spelling need, adult: a word that adults need to be able to spell as shown by analyses of their writing.

spelling need, children's: a word that children need to be able to spell as shown by analyses of their writing. *Syn.* **children's present spelling need.**

spelling, phonemic: system of spelling words according to their sounds, using a phonemic alphabet. *See* **alphabet, initial teaching; Unifon.**

spelling, phonetic: the spelling of a word as it sounds, whether done inadvertently by analogy with other words, as writing *capten* for *captain*, or deliberately, by means of a system of sounds and symbols used to show pronunciation, as *hweil*, which is the word *whale* written in the international phonetic alphabet.

spelling, rational: (1) spelling a word correctly by using what one has learned about the spelling of other similar words; (2) spelling that is logical in the sense that it is phonetic.

spelling reform: any plan for presenting the spelling of English sounds consistently, generally by adding new symbols to represent specific sounds and/or omitting phonetically superfluous letters.

spelling scale: *see* **scale, spelling.**

spelling, simplified: an attempt to make English orthography more nearly phonetic and to make spelling a reliable clue to pronunciation, and vice versa; especially, spelling that discards silent letters.

spelling, structured approach to: a procedure for helping pupils to greater achievement in spelling by teaching them to know sounds of letter patterns and letter combinations through hearing the sound before studying a written form.

spelling, thematic approach to: the choice of words for spelling study from a reading selection which the pupil has previously read and discussed; the expectation is that meanings will thus be clarified and the use of the words will become clear to the pupil.

spelling vocabulary: *see* **vocabulary, spelling.**

spending, deficit: *see* **deficit spending.**

SPG: *see* **Society for the Propagation of the Gospel in Foreign Parts.**

spherical trigonometry: *see* **trigonometry, spherical.**

sphygmomanometer: (phys. ed.) an instrument for measuring arterial blood pressure in man.

spillover benefit: *see* **benefit, spillover.**

spiral approach: an approach to teaching mathematics in which topics are constantly reintroduced, each time with more sophistication and more emphasis on their interrelatedness with other topics in mathematics. *See* **organization by cycles.**

spiral curriculum: *see* **curriculum, spiral.**

spiral method: *syn.* **organization by cycles.**

spiral progression: (voc. ed.) an order of job instruction according to which all the jobs having the lowest level of difficulty in two or more blocks are taught, then all those jobs having the next higher level of difficulty, etc., until all the jobs in all the blocks have been taught.

spiral test: *see* **test, spiral.**

spirit duplicator: *syn.* **duplicator, direct-process.**

spiritual: (1) in soul-substance theories of mind-body relationship, the body is recognized as being composed of matter and the mind is, by contrast, of the spirit; the mind, being spiritual, has a higher origin and destiny than the body, which is material; the mind, a spiritual entity, or a soul-substance without material form, is designed to control and outlive the body; (2) in more naturalistic theories, pertaining to an ideal of development to be attained through the quality of personal-social experience; (3) pertaining to the ideas, beliefs, and faiths of religious and sectarian groups with respect to the Deity, the supernatural, life after death, etc.

spiritual director: *see* **director, spiritual.**

spiritual exercises: *see* **exercises, spiritual.**

spiritual growth: *see* **growth, spiritual.**

spiritual values: *see* **values, moral and spiritual.**

spirometer (spī·rom'ə·tər): a device for measuring the amount of air that can be expelled forcibly from the lungs following a complete inhalation.

splice: a lap joint made in motion-picture film by means of film cement; a butt joint made in magnetic tape, usually held together by pressured sensitive adhesive.

splicer: a device for aligning motion-picture film or magnetic tape during the process of splicing.

splint, dynamic: a support for a body part designed to encourage therapeutic exercise and functional use.

split catalog: *syn.* **catalog, divided.**

split growth: the tendency for the several growth processes to follow different curves.

split-half method: *syn.* **split-halves method.**

split-halves method: *see* **reliability, split-halves.**

split-halves reliability: *see* **reliability, split-halves.**

split-plot design: *see* **design, split-plot.**

split-rate bid: *see* **bid, split-rate.**

split-system ventilation: *see* **ventilation, split-system.**

split-test method: *see* **reliability, split-halves.**

spluttering: *syn.* **cluttering.**

spoken vocabulary: *syn.* **vocabulary, speaking.**

sponsor, on-the-job: *see* **training sponsor, business and office education; training sponsor, distributive education.**

sponsor, publication: *syn.* **adviser of publications.**

sponsor, student: *syn.* **Big Brother (2); Big Sister.**

sponsored film: *see* **film, sponsored.**

sponsored program: *see* **program, sponsored.**

spontaneous activity: *see* **activity, spontaneous.**

spontaneous behavior: *see* **behavior, spontaneous.**

spontaneous strategy: *see* **strategy, spontaneous.**

sport: (genet.) (obsolescent) an individual displaying a variation in species character. *See* **mutation.**

sport clinic: *see* **clinic, sport.**

sport, competitive: an athletic contest or game commonly played between teams each representing some organization, such as a school or college.

sport, dual: a recreational athletic activity that may be adapted for play by sides of one or two players.

sport, individual: a recreational game, activity, or athletic event designed for play by one person or by sides of one player each.

sports, carry-over: sports that can be participated in after school or college life is over.

sports, intramural: athletic activities participated in by teams organized within a school.

sports medicine: *see* **medicine, sports.**

sports, recreational: athletic activities of a type that may be participated in by adults either individually or in pairs, for example, golf, swimming, tennis, and badminton.

spot check: *see* **check, spot.**

Sprachgefühl (shprä KH'gə·fYl'): (Ger., lit., "feeling for language") the feeling, native or later acquired, for the properties and niceties of idiomatic usage.

spread: *syn.* **dispersion.**

spread, associative: *syn.* **generalization, stimulus.**

spread of effect: Thorndike's observation that the strengthening effect of a satisfying state of affairs following a response would spread to other contiguous stimulus-response pairs. *Comp. w.* **transfer of training.**

sprinkler system: a system for fire protection consisting of pipes with outlets just below the ceiling, extending at regular intervals (such as 8 feet) to all parts of a building or section of a building; the sprinkler system is attached to a water system so that water in the sprinkler system's pipes will be under continuous pressure; the outlets are sealed with material having a low melting point so that a fire, near its start, will cause sufficient heat (such as 160 degrees) to bring about the release of water which will sprinkle the interior beneath the outlet.

sprocket holes: rectangular holes in film; intended to engage the teeth of various sprockets and the claws of the intermittent mechanism, in order that the film may be transported through the camera and projector.

spurious correlation: *see* **correlation, spurious.**

SQ: *see* **quotient, social.**

SQ3R technique: a reading-study technique developed by F. P. Robinson in which the first step is to *s*urvey the material; the second is to establish a clear purpose for reading through raising *q*uestions to be answered, followed by *r*eading for research, *r*ecitation or *r*eport, and *r*eview.

squad: (phys. ed.) (1) all players practicing to become members of a team; (2) a unit of class organization.

square contingency: *syn.* **chi square.**

square, diagonal: a Latin square in which only a single symbol appears along any given negatively or positively sloping diagonal (but not along both).

square, Graeco-Latin: *alt. sp.* **Greco-;** (1) a square consisting of two superimposed Latin squares, one formed with Latin and the other with Greek letters in such a way that the same Latin letter is never paired more than once with the same Greek letter; used in a four-factor experimental design; (2) an experimental design in which each subject is exposed successively to the several experimental conditions in different sequence and also to the several treatments in a still different sequence; thus, each subject has a different order of both condition and treatment, and each condition-treatment combination appears only once; (3) an experimental design in which each subject is exposed to a different condition-treatment combination.

square, Latin: (1) a square configuration formed from one of *k* different symbols (usually Latin letters) arranged in *k* rows and *k* columns in such a way that the same symbol appears only once in each row or column; used in a three-factor experimental design as a scheme for organizing treatment groups to provide counterbalancing of main effects, but leads to a confounding of interaction effects with each other and may lead to a confounding of certain interaction effects with certain main effects; (2) a research design in which each experimental subject is exposed to each of the experimental conditions in a different order in an effort to counterbalance any differential effect in any of the possible orders of occurrence. *See* **square, Graeco-Latin.**

square, magic: a set of numbers arranged by rows and columns in a square, and so selected that the sums of the numbers in each row, column, and diagonal are equal.

square matrix: *see* **matrix, square.**

square root transformation: *see* **transformation, square root.**

squared paper: a special type of cross-section paper that is marked off in squares. *See* **coordinate paper.**

squares, orthogonal Latin: Latin squares which may be superimposed to form a *Graeco-Latin square.*

squaring off: (spec. ed.) the act of aligning and positioning one's body in relation to an object for the purpose of getting a line of direction and establishing a definite position in the environment.

squash racquets: a racquet game played in a four-walled court which is entirely enclosed; points are scored when the opponent fails to return a ball which has been legally played within the designated areas of the court.

squat-jump: an exercise used as a test of physical condition, involving starting in a walk-stand position, squatting on the heel of the back foot, jumping into the air, reversing position of feet, squatting again, and repeating as many times as possible.

squat-thrust: an exercise used as a test of agility, consisting in starting from a standing position, squatting with hands on the floor and thrusting both feet back to a support position on feet and hands with arms and trunk fully extended, returning to a squat and then to a stand, repeated as rapidly as possible in a given number of seconds. *Syn.* **Burpee.**

squint: *syn.* **heterotropia.**

squint, alternating: the alternating deviation of the visual axes from the object of regard. (Often both eyes have normal acuity, but fixation of the eyes alternates.)

squint, convergent: a defect of the eyes due to weakness in the external muscles and characterized by an inward turning of the eyes. *Syn.* **cross-eye; internal strabismus.**

squint, divergent: a defect of the eyes due to a weakness in the internal muscles and characterized by an outward turning of the eyes. *Syn.* **external strabismus; walleye.**

squint, vertical: (1) a condition characterized by an upward deviation of the visual axis on one eye; (2) a constant deviation of one visual axis upward, making fusion impossible. *Syn.* **hyperphoria; hypertropia.**

S.R.A. filing plan: *see* **filing plan, S.R.A.**

St. John's plan: a plan of curriculum and instruction at St. John's College, Annapolis, Maryland, based primarily on some 100 of the greatest books of Western thought, with considerable emphasis on the seminar method of instruction.

stabile: a small mobile mounted on a base; commonly constructed and displayed by primary children on their individual desks or tables in connection with units of work; the base, rather than the size, differentiates it from a mobile. *See* **mobile.**

stabilimeter: a platform so mounted that movement of any part in any direction may be recorded on a moving tape or other recording device; used in studying differential behavior in the newborn.

stability, coefficient of: *see* **coefficient of stability.**

stability, emotional: (1) the ability to control the emotions; (2) the lack of excess emotionality or of extreme or unusual variation in normal emotional characteristics and patterns of response; involves a satisfactory personal and social adjustment.

stability of function: (1) relative uniformity in speed, strength, skill, performance, etc., of a function in day-to-day or hour-to-hour observation or measurement; (2) maintenance of a reasonably uniform relative level of development (such as a percentile rank) in individuals upon reobservation or remeasurement after intervals of considerable length, such as several weeks, months, or years; (3) the limitation of the change of function to a gradual, systematic shift, as opposed to frequent or erratic deviations.

stability reliability: *see* **reliability, stability.**

stability, social: *see* **social stability.**

stability test: *see* **test, stability.**

stable sequence: *see* **sequence, stable.**

staccato phonation: *see* **phonation, staccato.**

stacker: in computer operation, the output receptacle for cards on a card feed.

stacks, library: (1) the shelves on which books are stored in a library; (2) the area in a library used for storing books. (Library stacks are either open, that is, arranged so that the user can go directly to the shelves to locate material he wishes to examine, or closed, that is, arranged so that the user of books must present a request for a particular book at the desk and have a library assistant procure the book for him.)

stadiometer (stā'di·om'ə·tər): a device for measuring standing or sitting height, consisting of a platform or box with a graduated upright and a sliding arm.

stadium: an oval-shaped structure with tiers of seats for spectators of outdoor athletic contests, such as *football, baseball,* or track events which are carried on in the enclosed area.

staff: (journ.) the group of students who (usually guided by a sponsor) perform the editorial and business tasks involved in producing a student newspaper, magazine, handbook, or yearbook.

staff authority: *see* **authority, staff.**

staff development program: *see* **program, staff development.**

staff functions: (1) (admin.) work that at some level has been differentiated from a line hierarchy of functions to render some service to the line organization or to some other staff group; the principal staff functions are investigation, analysis, interpretation, recommendation (including formulation of plans), coordination (including assistance in control), and facilitation; *see* **evolution; functional; organization; line-and-staff;** (2) in guidance, duties properly assigned so as to ensure that each staff member understands his role in the program; important for effective staff relationships and cooperation.

staff, health: the corps of workers engaged in carrying on a program for health promotion or health protection in a school, college, factory, or other organization.

staff induction: (admin.) the steps involved in securing, introducing, and confirming a new staff member in a position.

staff, instructional: all the members of a school staff who are occupied directly with teaching or with the supervision of instruction in the school.

staff, janitorial-engineering: the total number of janitors and engineers or janitor-engineers and janitresses or matrons employed to care for a school building.

staff liner: a device holding five pieces of chalk in such positions that the five-line musical staff can be drawn on the blackboard in one movement; usually constructed of wood and wire; sometimes called *board liner.*

staff, maintenance: the employees who keep buildings and equipment in repair, including various tradesmen, such as carpenters, painters, masons, tinsmiths, electricians, and plumbers.

staff meeting: (1) a meeting of the principal, teachers, and other schoolworkers for the consideration of professional problems; (2) a meeting of the workers of any division of school service to consider professional problems of their area.

staff officer: an educational administrator, frequently a specialist in his field, who serves as an adviser and produces needed information as a basis for judgment or action but is not responsible for making decisions effective; for example, the director of research in a city school system whose job may be the collection of information and solution of problems, or a supervisor whose job may be advising teachers and helping them to solve their problems.

staff, operation: employees whose duty it is to care for buildings and to keep them in a condition of cleanliness, comfort, and safety.

staff operation: *see* **operation, staff.**

staff organization: the plan according to which duties and responsibilities are assigned and executed by members of the school personnel and by groups of staff members organized for cooperative effort.

staff per 1,000 pupils in average daily membership, professional education: *see* **professional education staff per 1,000 pupils in average daily membership.**

staff, revolving: a type of student-publication staff in which duties are rotated so that each student in the group may hold several or all positions in turn for a limited period.

staff, school: all the personnel hired by a school to carry out the work of the school.

staff school: a general service school designed to train staff officers of the Armed Forces. *Syn.* **general service school;** *see* **service school.**

staff study: *see* **study, staff.**

staff supervision: *see* **supervision, staff.**

stage: a platform or dais in the front part of an auditorium from which dramatic plays are presented or from which public addresses are made.

stage design: *see* **design, stage.**

stage of development, anal: (psychoan.) the period in an infant's growth during which toilet training assumes importance in the development of personality.

stage of development, concrete operations: according to Piaget, the period in the child's mental development from preschool through upper elementary grades (about junior high school) in which analysis of situations and events is based largely upon present perceivable elements.

stage of development, desatellization: *see* **desatellization.**

stage of development, formal operations: according to Piaget, the final stage in mental development of the child in which he is able to use symbols and deal with abstractions.

stage of development, omnipotence: used to describe a period in the infant's personality development when he perceives himself as the center of the universe, with power over his parents who "bend" to his every wish.

stage of development, oral: the earliest stage of libidinal development in which it is alleged that satisfaction is derived chiefly through the processes of sucking and oral stimulation.

stage of development, preoperational: *see* **preoperational period.**

stage of development, resatellization: *see* **resatellization.**

stage of development, satellization: *see* **satellization.**

stages in child art, developmental: *see* **art, developmental stages in child.**

staggered sessions: *see* **sessions, staggered.**

stairwell: a fireproof stairway, usually equipped with doors opening at each floor, the doors being fitted with wire glass to prevent breakage if exposed to heat.

staleness: (phys. ed.) a decline in performance and some change in personality and behavior which an individual may feel after training intensely and incessantly.

stammering: *see* **stuttering.**

stamper: (colloquial) a person affected with locomotor ataxia; so called because of the peculiar stamping gait of those with that disease.

stance: the position of the feet and body in an athletic activity.

stand, demonstration: a metal or frame stand accommodating a typewriter for demonstrating various typewriting reaches and techniques.

standard: (1) a goal, objective, or criterion of education expressed either numerically as a statistical average or philosophically as an ideal of excellence; (2) any criterion by which things are judged. *Dist. f.* **norm.**

standard, academic: (1) officially accepted level of attainment of scholarly excellence; (2) officially accepted components of the curriculum that are maintained by all schools, such as mathematics, science, and the official language of the country.

standard certificate: *see* **certificate, standard.**

standard code: *see* **code, standard.**

standard conditions: *see* **conditions, standard.**

standard, course training: *see* **training standard, course.**

standard credit cost: *see* **cost, standard credit.**

standard cubic feet per student: the desirable number of cubic feet that should be allowed per student in a classroom, laboratory, or other room. (The standard cubic feet per student was formerly used in determining student capacity but has now generally been abandoned in favor of the square feet per student standard and the *student station* standard.)

standard deviation: *see* **deviation, standard.**

standard deviation about the median: a loose term for the root-mean-square deviation about the median. See **deviation about the median, root-mean-square.**

standard-deviation machine: a machine for computing the moments necessary to a solution of the standard deviation.

standard difference: *see* **difference, standard.**

standard, employability: *see* **employability standard.**

standard English: *see* **English, standard.**

standard English braille grade two: *see* **braille grade two, standard English.**

standard error: *see* **error, standard.**

standard error of a factor loading: a statistic that indicates the amount of sampling error in a factor loading.

standard error of a score: *syn.* **standard error of measurement.**

standard error of estimate: an expression of the reliability of the estimated values of a second variable that have been obtained from values of a known related variable through the application of a regression equation; may be estimated from the formula $\sigma_{xy} = \sigma_x \sqrt{1 - r^2{}_{xy}}$ in which σ_{xy} is the standard error of estimating x from y, while σ_x is the standard deviation of the variable x, and $r^2{}_{xy}$ is the square of the coefficient of correlation between x and y.

standard error of grouping: a measure of the amount of error introduced into statistical constants by grouping the data into class intervals. *Dist. f.* **standard error of sampling.**

standard error of measurement: (1) (σ_m) an estimate of the dispersion of a group of obtained scores from the corresponding true scores; may be estimated from the formula $\sigma_m = \sigma\sqrt{1 - r_{12}}$, in which σ represents the standard deviation of the distribution of obtained scores and r_{12} is the coefficient of reliability of the test from which the distribution of scores was obtained; *syn.* **standard error of a score;** *dist. f.* **standard error of estimate;** (2) an estimate of the standard deviation that would be found in the distribution of scores for a specified person if he were to be tested repeatedly on the same or a similar test (assuming no learning).

standard error of percentage: a statistic that estimates the divergence of a percentage of a sample from its parametric value, given by the formula $\sigma = 100 \sqrt{pq/n}$, where p is the proportion of some characteristic in a given class, q is equal to $1.00 - p$, and n is the number of cases in the sample. *See* **error, standard.**

standard error of percentile: a statistic that estimates the divergence of a percentile of a large sample from its parametric value, given by the formula $\sigma_p = \dfrac{1}{y} \sqrt{\dfrac{pg}{N}}$, where σ_p is the standard error of the percentile, y is the height of the ordinate at that centile point in a normal distribution, p is the proportion of frequencies above or below the centile point, q is equal to $1.00 - p$, and N is the number of cases in the sample. *See* **error, standard.**

standard error of phi coefficient: used as an estimate of whether an obtained phi correlation is significantly greater than zero. *See* **error, standard.**

standard error of quartile: a statistic that estimates the divergence of a quartile of a sample from its parametric value, given by the formulas σQ_1 or $\sigma Q_3 = 1.362\sigma/\sqrt{n}$, and σQ_2 or $\sigma mdn = 1.253\sigma/\sqrt{n}$, where σ = standard deviation of the distribution and n = number of cases in the sample. *See* **error, standard.**

standard error of quartile deviation: a statistic that estimates the divergence of the quartile deviation of a sample from its parametric value.

standard error of rank difference correlation coefficient: a statistic used to determine whether a *rank difference correlation* coefficient found is significantly greater than zero; usually found by treating the coefficient as an estimate of a product moment coefficient *(r).*

standard error of sampling: a measure of the discrepancies of the observed frequencies of a distribution from the frequencies of a theoretical curve or of a curve fitted to the observed frequency distribution. *Dist. f.* **standard error of grouping.**

standard error of the mean: the estimated standard deviation of the distribution of means of an infinite number of samples of N observations each, drawn independently at random from the same universe; thus, an estimate of the reliability of a mean based on the number of values and the standard deviation of the values; may be stated as $\sigma/\sqrt{N - 1}$, where σ = standard deviation and N = number of values in the distribution.

standard industrial classification manual: *see* **manual, standard industrial classification.**

Standard Industrial Classification (S.I.C.): a numerical system set up by the Federal government to classify different segments of industry according to products.

standard keyboard: the arrangement of the keys found at present on most typewriters, that is, an arrangement without regard to the stroking ability of various fingers and to balanced hand stroking of many common words.

standard measure: *see* **score, standard.**

standard measurement: *see* **measurement, standard.**

standard metropolitan statistical area: *see* **metropolitan statistical area, standard.**

standard normal curve: *syn.* **curve, unit normal.**

standard notation: *syn.* **notation, scientific.**

standard, occupational: an established measure for judging the quality of work performed in a trade or occupation.

standard office practice: *see* **instruction, standard practice.**

standard office procedure: *see* **instruction, standard practice.**

standard operating procedure: *see* **instruction, standard practice.**

standard practice instruction: *see* **instruction, standard practice.**

standard practice procedure: (school admin.) method of performing a basic administrative technique in order to facilitate control and coordination.

standard, production: *see* **production standard.**

standard, qualification: *see* **qualification standard.**

standard rating scale: *see* **rating scale, standard.**

standard ratio: *syn.* **difference, standard.**

standard regression coefficient: *syn.* **coefficient, beta regression.**

standard school: a school that has attained a certain predetermined level of accomplishment in such matters as curricular offering, preparation of teachers, and school buildings.

standard, school building: an established rule, model, or measure as applied to some specified detail in the construction and erection of a school building.

standard score: *see* **score, standard. .**

standard score, Army: *see* **score, Army standard.**

standard score, normalized: *see* **score, normalized standard.**

standard-score norms: *see* **norms, standard-score.**

standard, specialty training: *see* **training standard, specialty.**

standard supply list: a list of the supply items regularly furnished by the school; usually includes the name of the article, its code number, quantities, and cost.

standard task: *see* **task, standard.**

standard terminology: *see* **terminology, standard.**

standard test: rare *syn.* **test, standardized.**

standard, training: *see* **training standard.**

standard unit: *see* **unit, standard.**

standard unit of measure: *see* **unit of measure, standard.**

standard word: (1) a unit of 1.4 syllables devised in 1931 by Louis A. Leslie, and frequently used as the basis for measuring shorthand speed; (2) a unit of five strokes on the typewriter (whether on letter keys or on the space bar) used according to the international typewriting contest rules; thus *to a* is considered as one standard word, while *millionth* is considered as two standard words. *See* **gross words; net words.**

standardization of rural schools: the establishment of a definite level of school attainment through the adoption of certain minimum requirements authorized either by law or by the chief school administrative officer of the state, relating either to the physical plant, or to the management of the school, or to both. (Schools that meet the requirement are usually rewarded in one or more of the following ways: by receiving honorary mention in reports issued by the state department of education or by receiving tablets, certificates, or money appropriations from the state.)

standardization of schools: the act or process of requiring that all schools of a similar type shall meet a certain predetermined level or pattern of accomplishment in such matters as curricular offerings, preparation of teachers, and school buildings.

standardization of supplies: the process of selecting school supplies according to definite specifications; for example, a school may select two or three kinds of writing paper that it will purchase and use regularly in the future.

standardization of test battery: the assignment of a system of derived scores of the tests to facilitate interpretation of the tests in terms of reference populations.

standardization population: the total population from a sample selected to establish norms for a test.

standardization sample: *see* **sample, standardization.**

standardization, test: (1) the establishment of fixed procedures for administering and scoring a test; (2) the establishment of norms for a test. *See* **norm; normalization; test, standardized.**

standardize: (1) to transform a set of scores to a given mean and standard deviation; (2) to determine (presumably on the basis of empirical investigation) the exact procedures to be used in testing, the permitted variations in environmental conditions, and the method of scoring.

standardized death rate: *syn.* **death rate, corrected.**

standardized test: *see* **test, standardized.**

standardizing association: an organization that maintains an accrediting system. (The term is now generally considered outmoded, and the term *accrediting association* has replaced it.)

standards, achievement: specific levels of attainment or goals to be mastered in educational programs.

standards, building: accepted statements indicating what is desirable or ideal in a building serving a particular purpose; formulated to apply to various features of buildings, and intended to guide judgments in using a building score card. *See* **score card, building.**

standards, EIA: a set of criteria and standards worked out by research institutions to arrive at a working basis for commercial broadcast television equipment, both transmission and reception; equipment not meeting EIA standards cannot be used for conventional telecasting purposes. [The Electronics Industry Association (EIA), formerly known as RETMA, was responsible for activating this important work.]

standards, error of: *see* **error of standards.**

standards, ethical: standards concerning morals or the principles of morality; standards pertaining to right and wrong in the conduct of a particular profession.

standards for school buses: standards governing size, quality of construction, equipment and markings, and performance of buses.

standards, grade: *syn.* **promotion standards.**

standards, job training: *see* **job training standards.**

standards, library: performance standards which have been developed for library service, personnel, operations, equipment, and supplies.

standards, lighting: criteria for judging the adequacy and suitability of lighting arrangements, based on the amount, quality, and distribution of light that should be provided for rooms of various kinds; quantitative standards are usually stated in terms of footcandles at working surface levels; standards of quality and distribution are stated in terms of placement and arrangement of light sources, contrast brightness, and glare; standards of natural lighting are frequently expressed in terms of the ratio of window area to floor area, as 1:4 or 1:5, and also in terms of the ratio of height of top of window sash to width of room, as 1:2.

standards, minimum: formal statements of the lowest acceptable quality for various phases of the educational program, for example, the minimum standards that a local school unit must meet in relation to buildings, equipment, personnel, library facilities, curriculum, school hygiene, activities, etc., in order to qualify for state financial aid.

standards, promotion: *see* **promotion standards.**

standards, school: (1) criteria used in judging the quality of a school or of its program of studies, representing the judgment of the person or group making the appraisal and, frequently, the findings of objective tests and ratings; (2) requirements for credit in courses taken or for graduation from school; (3) goals or ideals of achievement accepted as worthy of attainment.

standards, significance: *see* **significance standards.**

standards, state: the level of quality on announced criteria or other qualifications that must be maintained by an institution in order to (a) be accredited by a state

accrediting agency or (b) receive, in some instances, financial aid from the state.

standards, state high school: *see* **high school standards, state.**

standing, advanced: *syn.* **placement, advanced.**

standing committee: a regularly constituted committee of a board of education (or a similar board) such as a committee on finance or buildings; usually appointed for a definite period of time.

Stanford-Binet test: *see* **test, Stanford-Binet.**

stanine: a term formed by the contraction of "standard nine"; any of the steps in a 9-point scale of normalized standard scores having a mean of 5 and a standard deviation of 2 with integral values ranging from 1 to 9; the stanine's chief advantages are (a) rough classification and (b) the occupying of only a single column when punched into a punch card. *See* **score, standard; score, stanine; sten.**

stanine norm: *see* **score, stanine.**

stanine rating: *see* **score, stanine; stanine.**

stanine score: *see* **score, stanine.**

star: in sociometry, a term used to designate a person who receives more than the average number of choices on the same criterion, such as working together, playing together, etc.

stare decisis (sta're də·sī'sis): (Lat., lit., "to stand by decided matters") a legal principle to the effect that a court's decision on a legal matter is the law until it has been changed by some competent authority.

start time: in automatic data processing, the time interval required to commence some physical motion, as the movement of magnetic tape past the read-write head.

starter: a sound, word, phrase, or gesture used by a stutterer in an apparent attempt to initiate speech, as in "I see the uh-boy." *See* **postponement.**

startle pattern: a quick response of the trunk, arms, and legs to sudden or intense stimuli (typically auditory); the movements of the arms and legs are predominantly flexor. *See* **response, startle;** *contr. w.* **reflex, Moro.**

startle response: *see* **response, startle.**

state: (1) the concept of a politically organized entity for the promotion of common ends and the satisfaction of common needs, having the characteristic of permanency regardless of internal changes of governmental forms; (2) a political body organized under one government, particularly one that is sovereign.

state adoption of textbooks: a practice in some states by which specific textbooks are either recommended or required by the state department of education for use in the public schools of the state. (In some instances, lists of books are approved, from which local authorities may make selections for local use.)

state agency: an office, branch, or department of state charged with performance of a specific function.

state aid: *see* **aid, state.**

state aid for pupil transportation: *see* **aid for pupil transportation, state.**

state and local public libraries: *see* **library, public.**

state athletic association: *see* **athletic association, state.**

state board for vocational education: a board created by a state legislature to cooperate with Federal authorities in administering the provisions of the *Smith-Hughes Act* and supplementary laws.

state board of control: *see* **board of control, state.**

state board of education: *see* **board of education, state.**

state board of educational examiners: *see* **board of examination, state.**

state board of examination: *see* **board of examination, state.**

state board of examiners: *see* **board of examiners, state.**

state certification: *see* **certification, state.**

state college: *see* **college, state.**

state compulsory attendance laws: *see* **compulsory education.**

state control: the authority vested in the state under the Tenth Amendment to the Federal Constitution to administer, supervise, and direct the schools of the state.

state-county certification system: *see* certification system, state-county.

state courses of study: *see* courses of study, state.

state curriculum: *see* curriculum, state.

state curriculum program: *see* curriculum program, state.

state department of education: *see* department of education, state.

state department supervision: *see* supervision, state department.

state director of vocational education: *see* director of vocational education, state.

state distributive common school fund: *see* fund, state distributive common school.

state economic area: *see* economic area, state.

state education association: an association of teachers and educational administrators of a state that has as its primary objectives the improvement of schools through instruction and organization and through keeping the public informed on educational problems, policies, and progress.

state employment services: *see* services, state employment.

state equalization program: *see* equalization program, state.

state equalized valuation: *see* valuation, state equalized.

state extension service: *see* extension service, state.

state-financed program: an educational program financed wholly or in part by state funds, such as, in some states, schools for the deaf and blind or other programs for exceptional children.

state general fund: *see* fund, state general.

state graded school: a graded school, located in a district that does not maintain a high school, with certain standards authorized by law and by regulations of the state superintendent of schools.

state grant: *see* grant, state.

state high school standards: *see* high school standards, state.

state institution: *see* institution, state.

state insurance: *see* insurance, state.

state junior college: *see* junior college, state.

state library: *see* library, state.

state library agency: *see* library commission.

state library extension agency: *see* extension agency, state library.

state medical examination: *see* medical examination, state.

state minimum program: *see* program, minimum.

state minimum salary: *see* salary, state minimum.

state minimum salary schedule: *see* salary schedule, state minimum.

state net enrollment: *see* enrollment, state net.

state normal college: obs. *syn.* teachers college, state.

state normal school: *see* normal school, state.

state normal university: *see* university, normal.

state plan: an agreement between a state board for vocational education and the U.S. Office of Education describing (*a*) the vocational education program developed by the state to meet its own purposes and conditions and (*b*) the conditions under which the state will use Federal vocational education funds. (Such conditions must conform to the Federal acts and the official policies of the U.S. Office of Education before programs may be reimbursed from Federal funds.)

state plan for teacher retirement: *see* retirement system, statewide.

state planning board: a committee of persons, usually officially appointed experts, to whom is assigned the function of formulating programs for future political, industrial, or other social action for the government or people of a state.

state public school supervisor: *see* supervisor, state public school.

state public schools financial report: *see* financial report, state public schools.

state regulation: *see* regulation, state.

state report: an annual statement by a state board of vocational education to the U.S. Office of Education concerning the work done and the receipts and expenditures of money, showing that Federal funds have been expended in accordance with the Federal acts and the official policies of the U.S. Office of Education, and that Federal funds have been matched by total state and local funds; includes a descriptive account of the progress of vocational education within the state.

state school: (1) an institution supported and controlled by the state and performing an educational function within the state, especially one serving peculiar functions not duplicated locally, as a teachers college, special school, etc.; usually distinguishes between institutions receiving total or major financial support from the state and those supported wholly or largely from local sources; (2) a public-supported specialized facility providing services, usually on residential, school-age basis, for a particular handicapping condition, for example, blindness, deafness; (3) a public-supported facility maintained for custodial care of residents on a long-term basis; (4) as used in comparative education studies, a secular school that receives the bulk of its financial support from the public treasury and is usually subject to some form of government inspection.

state school administration: *see* administration, state school.

state school code: *see* code (2).

state school fund: *see* fund, state school.

state school lands: lands held by the state, the proceeds from which are used for education.

state school lunch program: a lunch program financed partially by state and/or Federal governments.

state school report: *see* report, state school.

state school survey: *see* survey, school.

state school system: *see* school system, state.

state standards: *see* standards, state.

state superintendent: *see* superintendent of public instruction.

state supervision of schools: *see* supervision of schools, state.

state supervision of teaching: *see* supervision of teaching, state.

state supervisor, distributive education assistant: *see* supervisor, distributive education assistant state.

state supervisor of business and office education: *see* supervisor of business and office education, state.

state supervisor of distributive education: *see* supervisor of distributive education, state.

state supervisor of guidance: *see* supervisor of guidance, state.

state supervisor of home economics: *see* supervisor of home economics, state.

state supervisor of physical education: *see* supervisor of physical education, state.

state support: *see* support, state.

state syllabus in teacher education: a publication containing the essential regulations governing teacher preparation and certification in the particular state concerned.

state teacher certification: *see* teacher certification, state.

state teacher education institution: *see* institution, state teacher education.

state teachers' association: *see* teachers' association, state.

state teachers college: *see* teachers college, state.

state transfer system: a plan developed in some states to standardize and expedite the transfer of a pupil from one school to another or from one school district to another.

state unit: *see* unit, state.

state university: *see* university, state.

statement: (math.) *syn.* sentence, closed.

statement, inverse: (math.) given a statement of implication, "If *p*, then *q*," the inverse of that statement is "If not *p*, then not *q*"; for example, the inverse of the statement "If he is smart, he will pass" is "If he is not smart, he will not pass."

statement of implication: *see* **implication, statement of.**

statewide provisions for sick leave: *see* **sick leave, statewide provisions for.**

statewide retirement system: *see* **retirement system, statewide.**

static balance: *see* **balance, static.**

static contraction: *syn.* **contraction, isometric.**

static reflex: *see* **reflex, static.**

static reversal: *see* **reversal, static.**

statics, social: the search for a "permanent" social order adjusted to nature's "laws."

station, agricultural experiment: *see* **experiment station, agricultural.**

station, college-operated: a radio and/or television transmitter and studio operated by an institution of higher education; originally, and usually, a nonprofit station. *Dist. f.* **station, educationally operated.**

station, educational: an AM, FM, or TV nonprofit station broadcasting in the interest of cultural development; accepts no advertising.

station, educationally operated: a radio and/or television transmitter and studio operated by an educational group such as a university, college, high school, junior high school, elementary school, business college, trade school, or church or other religious group. *Dist. f.* **station, college-operated.**

station, experiment: *see* **experiment station.**

station, inquiry: the remote terminal device from which an inquiry into computing or data processing equipment is made.

station, learning: a physical location, such as a position on the control panel of a simulator or an assignment to a study carrel in the school library, where individual learning occurs, usually in connection with laboratory instruction that requires special materials, equipment, or individualized instruction.

station, loading: *syn.* **school-bus stop.**

station, pupil: a seat, chair, or location within a classroom, gymnasium, laboratory, etc., that can be used by a pupil engaged in an instructional activity.

station, student: *see* **student station.**

station, training: a specific area within a local business firm where the student in such areas as business and office education and distributive education receives on-the-job training that is coordinated with his training plan. *See* **cooperative education; job rotation; placement, student (2).**

station, university-operated: *see* **station, college-operated.**

station, waiting: a sheltered place along a bus route where pupils may wait for the school bus.

station, work: (1) an area equipped to provide working space and facilities for one student at any one time while he is engaged in an educational activity; *see* **station, pupil;** (2) (bus. ed.) *see* **station, training.**

stationary seating equipment: *see* **seating equipment, stationary.**

statistic: (1) a value or measure that describes or characterizes a particular series of quantitative observations, or that characterizes the universe from which the observations were drawn, or is designed to estimate the corresponding value in that universe; *syn.* **characteristic; statistical constant;** *ant.* **parameter;** (2) a summary value based on a sample; (3) a term sometimes used to designate any statistical item, observation, score, measure, or similar datum (a usage that results in ambiguity).

statistic, ancillary: a statistic that gives no information about the parameter being estimated, but that does help to determine (and possibly improve) its accuracy, for example, N, the number of cases or observations.

statistic, consistent: *syn.* **statistic, efficient;** *ant.* **statistic, inefficient.**

statistic, efficient: a statistic that, as the size of the sample is increased, approaches the true population value as a limit and has a normal distribution of error and a smaller standard error than any other measure that could be used

to estimate the true value of a particular statistical constant. *Syn.* **consistent statistic;** *contr. w.* **statistic, inefficient.**

statistic, inconsistent: *syn.* **statistic, inefficient;** *ant.* **statistic, efficient.**

statistic, inefficient: (1) a statistic that, as the size of the sample is increased, does *not* have a smaller standard error than that of any other measure that could be used to estimate the true value of the parameter of which it is an estimate; (2) a statistic that does *not* approach more nearly a correct or true value as the size of the sample is increased. *Syn.* **inconsistent statistic;** *ant.* **consistent statistic; statistic, efficient.**

statistical analysis: *see* **analysis, statistical.**

statistical class: *syn.* **class (7).**

statistical coefficient: *syn.* **coefficient.**

statistical constant: *syn.* **statistic (1).**

statistical control: *see* **control, statistical.**

statistical decision: *see* **decision, statistical.**

statistical graph: *see* **graph, statistical.**

statistical group: *syn.* **group** *n.* **(2).**

statistical hypothesis: *see* **hypothesis, statistical.**

statistical inference: *see* **inference, statistical.**

statistical laboratory: *see* **laboratory, statistical.**

statistical map: *syn.* **cartogram.**

statistical method: *syn.* **quantitative method.**

statistical model: *see* **model, statistical.**

statistical prediction: *see* **prediction, statistical.**

statistical regularity for large numbers, law of: the view that a moderately large number of items chosen at random from a very large group are almost certain, on the average, to have the characteristics of the larger group.

statistical report: *see* **report, statistical.**

statistical sample: *syn.* **sample.**

statistical significance: *see* **significance, statistical.**

statistical study: *see* **study, statistical.**

statistical test: *syn.* **test of significance.**

statistical universe: *syn.* **universe.**

statistical validity: *see* **validity, statistical.**

statistically significant: having a satisfactorily low probability, as shown by statistical procedures, of being due to chance factors; does not necessarily imply practical importance. *See* **significance level.**

statistically significant difference: *see* **difference, statistically significant.**

statistics: (1) the branch of science dealing with the classification and frequency of occurrence of different kinds of things or of different attributes of things, as a basis for induction and inference; (2) quantitative data affected to a marked extent by a multiplicity of causes; (3) a set of tools for summarizing and describing a set or sets of data and for the testing of hypotheses.

statistics, descriptive: statistics used only for the purpose of describing the sample from which they are derived and not for describing a parent population or universe. *Syn.* **summary statistics.**

statistics, distribution-free: *syn.* **statistics, nonparametric.**

statistics, enumeration: statistics based on the number of cases or items within successive class intervals or categories without regard to the values of the items therein; computation, therefore, is limited largely to counting or enumerating; common examples include the median, percentiles, chi square, binomial distribution, etc.

statistics, heterograde: observations of a given variable which show variations in magnitude or intensity. *Contr. w.* **statistics, homograde.**

statistics, homograde: observations of a variable that are expressed in only two categories. *Contr. w.* **statistics, heterograde.**

statistics, item count: test statistics which may be computed or estimated from counting plus simple arithmetic, for example, test mean, item difficulty index, item discrimination index, etc.

statistics, maximum likelihood: those statistics which provide the most efficient estimate of the corresponding parameters.

statistics, nonparametric: any of several statistics, either descriptive or sampling, which may be applied to a set of data without any assumption as to the shape of the distribution or distributions involved; generally used only when assumptions for more efficient statistics cannot be made, for example, *chi square, median, rank difference correlation coefficient, sign test. Syn.* **distribution-free statistics.**

statistics, summary: *syn.* **statistics, descriptive.**

status: (1) position within the social structure; (2) degree of acceptance or honor accorded an individual.

status, age-grade: the age (mental or chronological) of a child as compared with the normal age range established for the school grade in which he is enrolled.

status, developmental: the developmental attainment or level of the child; the prognostic significance of this depends upon how it compares with the norm for children of like chronological age.

status, health: *see* **health status.**

status, initial: *see* **initial status.**

status, leader: the position of the leader in a group as measured by the attitudes of his associates toward him.

status leader: *see* **leader, status.**

status need: the need of any individual for an acceptable position as indicated by the attitude of his associates toward him.

status, nutritional: *see* **nutritional status.**

status quo: the existing state of affairs, that is, the present condition of the economic structure, power structure, moral code, religious influences, etc.; usually associated with conservative and/or reactionary social theories.

status quo ante bellum: (Lat., lit., "the status in which before the war. . .") the status of affairs before the war.

status, social: *see* **social status.**

status, socioeconomic: the level indicative of both the social and the economic position of an individual or group.

statute: an act passed by a state legislature or by Congress.

statutory citation: *see* **citation, statutory.**

statutory law: *see* **law, statutory.**

steering committee: *see* **committee, steering.**

steering group: *syn.* **committee, steering.**

stem: (1) the root of a word, plus one or more derivational suffixes but no inflectional suffixes; *see* **root;** (2) the vertical stroke of a type face; (3) the part of a multiple-choice test item that sets the task, ordinarily an introductory question or incomplete statement; sometimes referred to as *premise;* (4) in connection with curriculum organization, used ordinarily to designate the required part of the curriculum, in, for example, the stem-elective type of curriculum organization; *see* **elective.**

stem course: *see* **program, common-learnings** (2).

stem-elective curriculum organization: *see* **stem** (4).

stem, item: *see* **stem** (3).

sten: any of the steps in a 10-point scale of normalized standard scores, so arranged that the mean forms the point of separation between scores of 5 and 6; otherwise identical with *stanine* with essentially the same advantages and limitations. *See* **score, standard; stanine.**

stencil: *see* **key, stencil.**

stencil duplicator: *see* **duplicator, stencil.**

stencil key: *see* **key, stencil.**

stenographers' reference manual: *see* **manual, stenographers' reference.**

stenographic, secretarial, and related occupations training: *see* **training, stenographic, secretarial, and related occupations.**

stenography: (1) as commonly used, the process of writing in shorthand and transcribing on the typewriter or in longhand; (2) etymologically, any system of brief, rapid writing; *syn.* **shorthand.**

Stenotype: (bus. ed.) trademark for a keyboard machine used to write phonetic shorthand by typing the symbols in single strokes.

step: (1) in programmed instruction, an indefinite, intuitive, but basic concept; a subject to be programmed is broken down into items; it is assumed that students cannot take later steps in a given sequence before taking the early steps and that each item represents progress in the student's mastery and an objective measure of the student's ability to respond correctly to the item; the size of the step is not necessarily related to the size of response or to the amount of material contained in an item; a programmer generally increases the number of items to reduce the size of the steps; *see* **programming, linear;** (2) *see* **interval, class.**

step, criterion: *syn.* **frame, terminal.**

step deviation: *see* **deviation, step.**

step interval: *syn.* **interval, class.**

step, scale: *see* **scale step.**

step size, optimum: in programmed instruction or in the systems approach applied to educational psychology, the biggest step a student can take toward achieving a particular learning objective; such a step is neither so small as to insult his intelligence nor so large as to cause frustration.

step well: a depressed box or well, inside the bus body, which constitutes a step when the service door is open.

step well guard panel: a vertical sheet of metal on the passenger side of the entrance to a bus and in front of the passengers in the first seat.

steps, Herbartian: *see* **Herbartian method.**

steps, teaching: *see* **teaching steps.**

stereo camera: *see* **camera, stereo.**

stereo recording: *see* **recording, binaural.**

stereo tape, (four-track): *see* **tape, stereo (four-track).**

stereognosis: perception of objects or forms by touch.

stereograph: a pair of photographs or transparencies for producing the illusion of three dimensionality when viewed by means of a stereoscope.

stereophonic sound: *see* **sound, stereophonic.**

stereopsis (ster′i•op′sis; stēr′i-): stereoscopic vision. *See* **vision, stereoscopic.**

stereopticon (ster′i•op′ti•kən; stēr′i-): obs. *syn.* **projector, lantern-slide.**

stereoscope: a device having two lenses through which the observer looks and a rack to hold a pair of specially prepared photographs of the same scene or object taken from points of view a little way apart (usually 2 to 3 inches) and mounted side by side; the combined image seen by the two eyes gives the effect of solidity and depth, as in normal binocular vision. *See* **camera, stereo;** *comp. w.* **telebinocular.**

stereoscopic film: *see* **film, stereoscopic.**

stereoscopic vision: *see* **vision, stereoscopic.**

stereotype (ster′i•ə•tīp′; stēr′i-): a fixed standardized conception of the attributes of a class of persons or social values that is not readily modified by evidence of its falsity; (2) a standardized pattern of response to specific objects and situations.

stereotype, emotional: response to different emotional stimuli with similar reactions that follow a rigid pattern, such as the euphoria of a manic patient in response to varying stimuli. *Syn.* **emotional stereotypy;** *see* **euphoria.**

stereotyped repetition: *see* **repetition for self-assurance.**

stereotypic behavior: *see* **blindism.**

stereotypy: (spec. ed.) frequent and mechanical recurrence without variation of movements of the body, speech forms, or postural mannerisms. *See* **blindism.**

stereotypy, emotional (ster′i•ə•tīp′i; stēr′i-; -i•ot′i•pi): *syn.* **stereotype, emotional.**

Stern blocks: *see* **arithmetic, structural.**

stigma: *pl.* **stigmata;** (spec. ed.) any mental or physical mark or peculiarity which aids in identification or in the diagnosis of a condition.

stigmata of degeneration (stig'mə·tə): a number of physical abnormalities frequently associated with a congenital lack of intellectual potentialities; sometimes considered indicative of defective or degenerate intelligence.

still: *syn.* **still picture.**

still-motion slide: *see* **slide, still-motion.**

still picture: a visual static representation of persons, objects, or views; to be distinguished from the motion picture in that no effort is made to portray ongoing motion, although the feeling of dynamic action may be suggested; to be distinguished from graphic representations in that the aim is to present objective reality rather than symbolisms or interpretations.

stimulability test: *see* **test, stimulability.**

stimulation: the process by means of which a receptor, or sense organ, is excited to its characteristic activity, which occasions neural impulses in its sensory nerve.

stimulation method: *syn.* **stimulus method.**

stimulation, supervisory: *see* **supervisory stimulation.**

stimulogenous zone: *syn.* **reflexogenous zone.**

stimulus: anything to which a sense organ is sensitive and which is capable of causing excitation of the sense organ; may be external to the organism, as in the case of light rays impinging upon the eye, or internal, as in the case of pressure of urine in the bladder.

stimulus, adequate: any stimulus that normally serves to excite a specific type of receptor. (To be "adequate" a stimulus must be of supraliminal intensity, must excite the receptor for a duration greater than a certain minimum, and must change from low to high intensity at a rate peculiar to each modality. The receptor must be in the excitatory phase at the moment of energy impact.)

stimulus, aversive: painful or unpleasant stimulus such as electric shock.

stimulus, compound: any stimulus comprising more than one component and involving several different senses or more than one phase of the same sense, for example, the stimulus to the taste buds of French dressing, involving both saline and sour taste components, or the highly compound stimulus presented to a person attending a symphony concert, involving auditory, visual, kinesthetic, and many other components.

stimulus, conditioned: a stimulus that is originally insufficient cause for a given response but that, through association (conditioning) with an unconditioned or sufficient stimulus, elicits a response that is appropriate to the unconditioned stimulus.

stimulus conditioning: *syn.* **generalization, stimulus.**

stimulus deprivation: *see* **deprivation, stimulus.**

stimulus device: an object used in instruction, such as a film, phonograph, etc., which presents information but makes no provision for responses from the student. *Comp. w.* **response device; stimulus-response device.**

stimulus, discriminative: a stimulus that through association controls the operant response. *See* **conditioning, operant.**

stimulus-field transfer: *see* **transfer, stimulus-field.**

stimulus generalization: *see* **generalization, stimulus.**

stimulus, maintaining: a stimulus that continues to activate the organism to respond as long as the response tendency persists and that is removed by the final act of consummation; for example, a wasp may make numerous and persistent responses to fill a hole in its nest, the hole serving as a maintaining stimulus.

stimulus material: words or nonsense syllables, usually in lists, or sentences used in remedial speech instruction by the stimulus method. *See* **stimulus method.**

stimulus method: a technique for the correction of articulatory defects that depends on the student's auditory perception of the correct manner of articulating the sound in which he is defective; involves training in sound discrimination and intensive repetition by the instructor of the sound to be corrected, followed by the student's attempt to produce the sound correctly. *Syn.* **stimulation method;** *dist. f.* **phonetic method** (1).

stimulus object: any object that may emit, reflect, or transmit the energy of excitation to a receptor. *See* **stimulus.**

stimulus-response device: in programmed instruction, an object, such as a *teaching machine,* which provides immediate reinforcement of the response to each stimulus. *See* **teaching machine;** *dist. f.* **response device; stimulus device.**

stimulus, subliminal: (1) a stimulus that cannot be discriminated under the conditions of the experiment; (2) a stimulus below the threshold of awareness, that is, one too weak to be specifically apprehended and reported but not too weak to be influential on conscious processes or behavior; the effects of such stimuli are also termed subliminal.

stimulus, supraordinate: a stimulus which gives the organism information about the relevant properties of a group of stimuli, for example, the color red, which signals danger in a number of stimulus situations.

stimulus, unconditioned: a stimulus that, independent of any training or conditioning, releases some specific response; for example, a touch on the cornea or eyelashes is the unconditioned stimulus for winking.

stimulus words: lists of words containing a given speech sound, used by the speech correctionist in remedial speech instruction by the stimulus method. *See* **stimulus method.**

stipulation of meaning: *see* **meaning, stipulation of.**

stitchery: a creative handcraft in which stitches of all kinds are applied to form a design; the stitches are varied in numerous ways to achieve certain effects, such as line, texture, color, or shape. *See* **handcraft.**

stock record: *syn.* **record, balance-of-stores.**

stockroom: a storeroom for educational or janitorial supplies that are frequently checked out for use. *See* **storeroom.**

stoicism: (1) a school of philosophy founded in Athens about 308 B.C., based on the teachings of Zeno; advocated the development of freedom from desire and external wants and indifference to pleasure and pain; (2) the attitude or outlook that places high value on man's inner or mental independence from all externals and on indifference to pleasure and pain.

stoneware: (art) an opaque pottery that is high-fired, well vitrified, and nonporous, that may be glazed, unglazed, or salt-glazed, and that is commonly made from a single clay; color and texture frequently resemble stone but may vary through all earth colors.

stop: the relationship between the focal length of a lens and the effective diameter of its aperture. *See* **f. number; t-stop.**

stop-go: a pattern of stuttering characterized by sudden discontinuance of the tenseness involved in trying to say a word, followed by the attempt to complete the word while relaxed; sometimes recommended in treating stuttering, on the grounds that it helps to avoid certain noticeable symptoms of stuttering.

stop lights, flashing: *see* **flashing stop lights.**

stop-motion projector: *see* **projector, stop-motion.**

stop time: in automatic data processing, the time interval required to bring to a halt some physical motion, as the movement of magnetic tape past the read-write head. *Syn.* **deceleration time.**

storage: (1) in information retrieval, the interval between the creation of the message as a unit, or as organized data or information, and its presentation to the senses of the individual; in direct speech or a live demonstration, the delay is zero; however, both events can be stored for delayed *readout* by appropriate methods; the information loss characteristic of the storage system and the space occupied by the stored information are significant factors; (2) in data processing, a method to keep data for future reference; in computer processing of symbols representing information, permanent storage on tapes, intermediate storage on drums, and rapid access storage on magnetic cores.

storage, auxiliary: a storage device in addition to the main storage of a computer, for example, magnetic tape, disk, or magnetic drum; usually holds much larger amounts of information than the main storage, and the information held is less rapidly accessible.

storage, buffer: use of equipment, in which information is assembled and stored temporarily, to link an input-output device to another input-output device or to the computer itself.

storage device: (data processing) any mechanism in which data and/or instructions may be stored.

storage device, computer: *see* **computer storage device.**

storage, disk: *see* **storage, magnetic disk.**

storage dump: a readout or printout of the contents of a storage device; usually only the contents of internal storage are dumped, and usually the readout is onto magnetic tape or punched cards, and the printout onto paper via a line printer or typewriter. *Syn.* **core dump; drum drump; memory dump.**

storage, external: storage devices physically separate from but connected to the automatic computer and holding information available to the automatic computer.

storage garage: *see* **garage, storage.**

storage location: (data processing) that part of a computer's storage unit which can be identified by an *address.* *Comp. w.* **memory location.**

storage, magnetic core: a storage device in which binary data are represented by the direction of magnetization in each unit of an array of magnetic material, usually in the shape of toroidal rings, but also in other forms such as wraps on bobbins.

storage, magnetic disk: a storage device or system consisting of magnetically coated disks, on the rotating surface of which information is recorded for storage in the form of magnetic spots arranged in a manner to represent binary data; these data are arranged in circular tracks around the disks, which are mounted on a vertical shaft, and are accessible to reading and writing heads on an arm which can be moved mechanically to the desired disk and then to the desired track on that disk; data from a given track are used or written sequentially as the disk rotates. *See* **binary system.**

storage, magnetic drum: (data processing) a computer storage device which stores data in the form of magnetic spots on the magnetically coated surfaces of a rotating cylindrical drum.

storage, magnetic tape: a storage device in which data are stored in the form of magnetic spots on metal or coated plastic tape; binary data are stored as small magnetized spots arranged in column form across the width of the tape; a read-write head is usually associated with each row of magnetized spots so that one column can be read or written at a time as the tape traverses the head.

storage, magnetic tape strip: a computer storage device in which data are recorded as magnetic spots on plastic or metallic tape.

storage, magnetic thin-film: a computer storage device in which data are stored on a very thin layer of magnetic material.

storage, random access: a storage technique in which the time required to obtain information is independent of the location of the information most recently obtained; access is usually relatively random; thus, magnetic drums are relatively nonrandom access when compared with magnetic cores for main storage but are relatively random access when compared with magnetic tapes for file storage.

storage room, instrument: *see* **instrument storage room.**

store manual: *see* **manual, store.**

store, model: *see* **laboratory, distributive education.**

store unit, distributive education: a classroom unit usually composed of four or more wall cases, a wrapping counter, a showcase, a display window, and a cash register; used for demonstration sales, practice in display, and various retail selling activities.

stored program: *see* **program, stored.**

storefront school: classes held in an available store fronting on the street, usually in the inner city.

storeroom: a room used for storing new or used equipment or supplies until they are needed for use or until they are to be otherwise disposed of. *See* **stockroom.**

stores department: a department set up for the purpose of maintaining central stocks of goods for issuance to the various departments of an institution; sometimes termed *storeroom.*

stores function: *see* **function, stores.**

stores ledger: *syn.* **record, balance-of-stores.**

stores requisition: *see* **requisition, stores.**

stories of fantasy: *see* **fantasy, stories of.**

story hour: (library ed.) a regularly scheduled program of story telling, the primary purpose of which is to interpret literature to children and to inspire them to read for themselves; carefully selected folk tales form the basis for many story-hour programs.

story-memory method: a combination method of teaching reading in which a story is told, memorized, and then read; used only in the beginning stages of teaching reading. *See* **memory method; story method.**

story method: (1) a procedure in teaching reading in which the story to be read is first narrated by the teacher; *see* **memory method; story-memory method;** (2) the presentation of factual material in story form.

storyboard: a series of sketches or pictures which visualize each topic or sequence in an audiovisual material to be produced; generally prepared after the *treatment* and before the *script.*

strabismus (strə·biz′məs): *syn.* **heterotropia.**

strabismus, convergent: *syn.* **esophoria.**

strabismus, divergent: *syn.* **exophoria.**

strabismus, external: *syn.* **exotropia.**

strabismus, internal: *syn.* **esotropia.**

straddle run: (phys. ed.) running with the feet wide apart.

straight bid: *see* **bid, straight.**

straight bond: *see* **bond, straight.**

straight-line relation: *syn.* **correlation, rectilinear.**

straight-line relationship· *syn.* **correlation, rectilinear.**

straight-line route: *see* **route, straight-line.**

stranger: (sociol.) (1) one who has come into face-to-face contact with the group for the first time; (2) one who is socially isolated from the group even though he is in regular contact with the people who make it up.

strategy: (mil. ed.) the art and science of developing and using political, economic, psychological, and military forces as necessary during peace and war, to afford the maximum support to policies, in order to increase the probabilities and favorable consequences of victory and to lessen the chances of defeat; includes military strategy and national strategy.

strategy, accommodation: *see* **accommodation strategy.**

strategy, divergent: a type or mode of artistic thinking that an artist or student employs in drawing, painting, or graphic processes, according to which the artist commences to work with single elements or precise detail but as he proceeds, the artwork undergoes unexpected changes as the artist alters his viewpoint, shifts his focus, adds detail, simplifies, and so on.

strategy, social: *see* **social strategy.**

strategy, spontaneous: (art) a type or mode of artistic thinking which an artist or student employs in drawing, painting, or graphic processes; the artist makes an organic statement suggestive of a whole picture devoid of detail; as he proceeds he continues to work on the whole problem as he feels it and to solve it through procedural experimentation.

stratification: (sociol.) (1) the separation of a community into a hierarchy of social classes, based on birth, wealth, or other factors; (2) the process of stratifying, or putting into class levels.

stratified sample: *see* **sample, stratified.**

Strauss syndrome: *see* **syndrome, Strauss.**

streaming: the practice in various countries of placing pupils in different groups, tracks, or streams according to aptitude and/or achievement; known in the United States as *homogeneous grouping. See* **grouping, ability; streaming** (Education in England and Wales).

streaming, autokinetic: *syn.* **autokinetic effect.**

street trade: *see* **trade, street.**

strength, ego: *see* **ego strength.**

strength, habit: *see* **habit strength.**

strength index: *see* **index, strength.**

strength, muscular: *see* **muscular strength.**

strength test: *see* **test, strength.**

strephosymbolia: reversal of words, phrases, or other symbols in reading. *See* **reversal.**

stress: (lang. arts) greater emphasis on some syllables or words over others; produced by pronouncing at greater length, with more energy, or at a higher pitch. *Contr. w.* **level** (1).

strict implication: *see* **implication.**

strike for: a Navy expression meaning to learn the trade of; for example, a man may strike for yeoman.

strike, teacher: a temporary cessation of work by teachers in order to express a grievance or enforce a demand.

striker: (mil. ed.) a member of the Navy enlisted personnel in the general apprenticeships at E-2 and E-3 levels who has received training at naval schools or aboard ship or has demonstrated significant qualifications in the duties of a particular rating and who is authorized to be specifically designated for advancement to that rating by the rating symbol; for example, BMSN, a designated *striker* in the boatswain's mate rating.

stringed instruments: *see* **instruments, stringed.**

strip film: *syn.* **filmstrip.**

strip key: *see* **key, strip.**

stroboscope: (1) a series of dots or parallel lines which appear to stand still when a turntable is rotating at the corresponding speed; (2) (mus.) an instrument that translates audible tones into visual terms, measuring the pitch level of a given tone through the position of a line of light on a scale marked to indicate frequency of vibrations; *syn.* **tonoscope.**

stroke volume: (phys. ed.) (1) an increase in blood circulation which increases the rate of transportation of oxygen, carbon dioxide, and the metabolites formed during muscular contraction; (2) the amount of blood leaving a ventricle at each beat of the heart.

stroking: finger movement on the keys of the typewriter; correct stroking technique includes attention to the quality, "feel," and speed of the stroking movements.

stroking, finger: (typewriting) *see* **stroking.**

structural analysis: *see* **analysis, structural.**

structural arithmetic: *see* **arithmetic, structural.**

structural intelligibility: *see* **intelligibility, structural.**

structural linguistics: *see* **linguistics, structural.**

structural psychology: *syn.* **psychology, existential.**

structuralism: the point of view, held by Wundt and Titchener, that experiences or mental states are made up of sensations, images or ideas, and feelings, as well as analysis of these elements, their attributes, and their ways of combining.

structure: (1) the framework of expectancies and limits in a situation; (2) (curric.) the organization of the cognitive composition of the respective subject-matter fields or school disciplines; *see* **cognitive structure.**

structure, age: *see* **age structure.**

structure, algebraic: *see* **algebraic structure.**

structure, art: *see* **art structure.**

structure, basic personality: *see* **personality structure, basic.**

structure, behavioral processes of: (couns.) the single segments of an individual that together constitute his total personality.

structure, cognitive: *see* **cognitive structure.**

structure, factorial: *see* **factorial structure.**

structure, graphological: written or printed word patterns.

structure, group: *see* **group structure.**

structure in mathematics: *see* **mathematics, structure in.**

structure, initiating: *see* **initiating structure.**

structure, latent: a system of parameters describing a set of observed responses to a group of items by a number of persons in terms of the coefficients of trace lines and the proportion of the group in each latent class. *See* **class, latent; trace line, item.**

structure, organization: *see* **organization structure.**

structure, personality: *see* **personality structure.**

structure, program: *see* **program structure.**

structure, simple: *see* **simple structure.**

structure, simultaneous simple: *syn.* **profile, parallel proportional.**

structure, social: the framework of customs, laws, beliefs, and institutions in which a society exists.

structured: a term applied to tests, inventories, interviews, and similar devices or situations, indicating that they are set up or handled so that the variety of responses which the subject can make is limited.

structured approach to spelling: *see* **spelling, structured approach to.**

structured community services: *see* **community services, structured.**

structured or unstructured technique: *see* **structured.**

structured test: *see* **test, structured.**

struggle, class: *see* **class struggle.**

stub: (1) the title of a row in a table; placed at the left of the corresponding row; *syn.* **stub heading; stub item;** *contr. w.* **caption;** (2) the vertical column at the left of a table, containing the titles of all the rows in a table; *contr. w.* **caption.**

stub heading: *syn.* **stub** (1).

stub item: *syn.* **stub** (1).

student: (1) one who attends an educational institution of secondary or higher level; (2) a person engaged in serious study, especially one doing independent study. *See* **pupil.**

student, able: a student of high learning ability, which is defined by some in its cognitive aspects, such as the ability to do abstract thinking, by others as an adaptive process of an individual to his total environment; also called gifted, or superior, student.

student accounting: *see* **accounting, student.**

student activism: *see* **activism, student.**

student activist: *see* **activist, student.**

student activities: *see* **activities, extraclass.**

student-activity adviser: *see* **adviser, student-activity.**

student, advanced: (1) a student who has been promoted to the next class or course in the sequence of classes or courses, without a unit of value or a certificate being awarded; (2) a student who has been placed in a more advanced section of the same activity or in a similar activity requiring a greater degree of ability for successful participation.

student adviser: *see* **adviser, student.**

student affairs, director of: (1) *syn.* **director of pupil personnel services;** (2) *syn.* **director of student personnel.**

student aid: *see* **aid, student.**

student assistant: (1) a student who assists in the performance of duties discharged by one or more of the nonstudent employees of the school; (2) a student employed part time usually in the library or laboratories of a university, college, or school to perform nontechnical or nonprofessional duties under the supervision of the professional staff; sometimes works voluntarily, but is usually paid on an hourly basis.

student award: *see* **award, student.**

student, beneficiary: one receiving financial aid disbursed through an institution, as through a scholarship or bursary.

student body: all persons enrolled for study at an educational institution, considered collectively.

student body activities: *see* **activities, student body.**

student-centered instruction: *see* **instruction, student-centered.**

student-centered teaching: *see* **teaching, nondirective.**

student-clock-hour cost: *see* **cost, student-clock-hour.**

student, college: an individual admitted to and enrolled as a student in any capacity in an institution of higher education.

student, college-bound: a high school student who has plans to attend college after graduating from a secondary school.

student-college relationship: *see* **relationship, student-college.**

student, commuting: a student who does not live on or near his college or university campus and who travels to and from day classes. *Syn.* **day student** (2).

student, conditioned: a student who, because of either deficient entrance credits or deficient performance, must make up work in a particular subject or raise his general scholastic average. *Syn.* **probation student.**

student, cooperative: (1) a student who attends a vocational school or class on a part-time basis and spends an approximately equal amount of time working in an industry or business pursuing his career goal; usually receives school credit and pay for his work; (2) a student who helps to defray part or all of the cost of a college education by working part time or during vacations in some occupation related to his major areas of study; in some cases the student may be employed by the institution that he is attending, either in some branch, department, or office or in an industry operated by or affiliated with the institution.

student cost: *see* **cost, student.**

student council: an agency of student government consisting of one or more faculty members and of student members elected on some sort of representative basis; its functions vary considerably from school to school but most typically are concerned with aspects of the extraclass program and with phases of school conduct and discipline; its decisions are generally subject to the authority of the faculty or of the principal; used in elementary, secondary, and higher schools.

student counseling bureau director: *see* **director, student counseling bureau.**

student counselor: *see* **counselor, student.**

student court: (1) an agency of pupil self-government; (2) a phase of pupil participation in school government in which selected pupils sit as a court of justice, hearing evidence and proposing penalties for pupil violations of the school's regulations; (3) an organization to handle minor disciplinary cases used sometimes as a teaching device, as in civics classes, or as an administrative means of delegating responsibility to students.

student-credit-hour: credit for one student under instruction for a period for which 1 hour of credit is granted.

student-credit-hour cost: *see* **cost, student-credit-hour.**

student, day: (1) a person who attends a regular day session in contrast to a person attending continuation school, evening school, or residential school; (2) *syn.* **student, commuting.**

student discipline: *see* **discipline, student.**

student, distinguished military: a military student, enrolled in the advanced course, Reserve Officers' Training Corps, at a college or university, who because of his high scholastic standing and leadership is recognized as outstanding by both the professor of military science and school officials.

student driver: *see* **driver, student.**

student-employment placement officer: *syn.* **placement officer.**

student exchange: *syn.* **exchange of students, international.**

student, external: a student who studies a curriculum and who may obtain a degree after comprehensive examinations without being in residence in the institution. (This practice is not common among institutions in the United States but is found in some institutions abroad.) *See* **in absentia.**

student federation: *see* **federation, student.**

student fee: *see* **fee, student.**

student, first-time: a student who, in a given semester, entered a college or university for the first time.

student, foreign: a student from a particular culture studying in and about another culture; also referred to as *alien learner,* or *unrelated pupil.*

student government: the control of extraclass activities, the maintenance of order, and the regulation of matters of conduct in school by elected representatives chosen from the student body by the students themselves, when this authority has been delegated to them by the school administration. *Syn.* **student self-government;** *see* **student council.**

student, graduate: a holder of the bachelor's or first professional degree who is enrolled in a college or university for additional courses within the field in which the degree was taken.

student guidance council: *see* **guidance council, student.**

student handbook: *see* **handbook, student.**

student health program: *see* **health program, student.**

student health service: *see* **health service, student.**

student, high school: a student enrolled in a course of study at a school offering courses in those grades above the junior high school level through grade 12; where there is no junior high school, a student enrolled in any of the grades 9 through 12.

student, honor: *see* **honor student.**

student-hour unit cost: *see* **unit cost, student-hour.**

student, initial entry: (mil. ed.) a commissioned officer, warrant officer, or warrant officer candidate who is undergoing training at the U.S. Army Aviation School that will lead to qualification as an Army aviator; can be refined further to initial entry fixed-wing student, or initial entry rotary-wing student, to denote the category of aircraft in which the individual will be qualified upon completion of his training.

student, junior high school: a student who attends a separately organized and administered secondary school intermediate between the elementary and senior high schools. *See* **junior high school.**

student learner: *syn.* **trainee, student.**

student load: *see* **load, student.**

student loan: *see* **loan, student.**

student loan, National Defense: *see* **loan, National Defense student.**

student manager: *syn.* **intramural manager.**

student, migrant: *syn.* **student, transfer.**

student mortality: *see* **mortality, student.**

student, native: a junior or senior student in a university who has spent his freshman and sophomore years in that same university; a term used for purposes of comparison in studies of the success of former junior college students (*transfer students*) enrolled in the upper divisions of universities.

student, noncollege-preparatory: a student who does not plan to attend college after high school graduation and who is enrolled in a program of studies oriented to post high school employment; also referred to as *noncollege-bound student.*

student, nonresident: (1) a student enrolled at a college or university for off-campus research, so that class attendance is not required; (2) a student enrolled at a state university or college or at a community college, who is not a bona fide resident of the state or area of the state served by that institution and who is usually required to pay an additional fee.

student officer: in the Air Force, a commissioned officer on duty as a student.

student organization: *see* **organization, student.**

student, part-time: *see* **part-time student.**

student-personnel coordinator: *see* **coordinator, student-personnel.**

student personnel, director of: *see* **director of student personnel.**

student-personnel point of view: a philosophy which stresses the total development of the student as a person rather than his intellectual development alone.

student-personnel services: *see* **services, student-personnel.**

student-personnel services director: *syn.* **director of pupil personnel services.**

student-personnel work: individual and group service in higher education primarily of a consultative nature; concerned with the total welfare of the student, such as educational and vocational counseling, student employment and housing services, student organization advisement and coordination. *See* **guidance** (2).

student philanthropy: *see* **philanthropy, student.**

student pilot: *see* **pilot, student.**

student placement: *see* **placement, student.**

student position: *see* **student station.**

student power: *see* **power, student.**

student, probation: *syn.* **student, conditioned.**

student program: *see* **program, student.**

student publication: *syn.* **publication, school** (1).

student recruitment: *see* **recruitment, student.**

student, rejected: a student toward whom hostility is directed, especially by the *peer group.*

student report: *see* **report, student.**

student report, comprehensive: *see* **report, comprehensive student.**

student, resident: (1) a full-time student at a college or university; (2) a student living in facilities provided by the institution or in off-campus facilities nearby; *ant.* **commuter;** (3) an in-state student at a state-supported institution or, in a municipal institution, a student whose legal residence is within boundaries set by the institution.

student resource center: *syn.* **center, study.**

student response system: a system allowing students to indicate answers to the instructor's questions in a classroom or learning laboratory or while using educational television; may provide instantaneous feedback to classroom or television instructor as well as a permanent record of responses.

student, secondary school: a student who attends a school comprising any span of grades beginning with the next grade following the elementary school and ending with or below grade 12, including the junior high school and other types of high school.

student self-government: *syn.* **student government.**

student, special: as commonly used, a college student who is not a candidate for a degree because he has not met specified requirements for admission to or continuance in the institution or because he does not wish to be a candidate for a degree. (NOTE: A distinction may be made between a special student in respect to whose entrance requirements there are certain irregularities and who accordingly may not proceed to a degree and an *unclassified student* whose status with respect to entrance requirements is satisfactory but who does not wish to proceed to a degree.)

student, specialty-oriented: (couns.) the student who is seeking noncollege educational training beyond high school, such as technical or vocational training.

student sponsor: *syn.* **Big Brother** (2); **Big Sister.**

student station: (1) in general, a place at which a student may be located, as a classroom seat, a laboratory seat, bench, or table, or a lecture-room chair; (2) in programmed instruction, a desk, table, or booth with equipment that enables the student to receive a program and to react to it; *syn.* **student position.**

student-station utilization: *see* **utilization, student-station.**

student teacher: a person enrolled in a school of education who has been assigned to assist a regular teacher in a real school situation.

student-teacher ratio: *see* **ratio, student-teacher.**

student-teacher relations: *see* **relations, student-teacher.**

student teaching: observation, participation, and actual teaching done by a student preparing for teaching under the direction of a supervising teacher or general supervisor; part of the preservice program offered by a teacher education institution. (Other terms sometimes used synonymously are practice teaching, directed teaching, and *supervised student teaching.*) *See* **teaching, directed; teaching, practice;** *dist. f.* **apprentice teaching; internship plan.**

student teaching, all-day: a student-teaching assignment in which the student teacher is assigned to a campus or off-campus school for the entire school day, usually daily and for a stipulated period of weeks; such assignment includes cocurricular activities and extraclass teacher duties in the school, with major reduction or cessation of all college classes and activities during the period of all-day student teaching; also called *full-time student teaching* in contradistinction to *part-time student teaching. Dist. f.* **student teaching, block plan of.**

student teaching, block plan of: a student-teaching schedule in which the student teacher is assigned for two or more periods daily to student teaching for a given number of weeks or semesters, in addition to a professional course or courses at the college; also called *part-time student teaching. Dist. f.* **student teaching, all-day.**

student-teaching center: *see* **center, student-teaching.**

student teaching, director of: *see* **director of student teaching.**

student-teaching facilities: the plant, equipment, instructional materials, and personnel available for the conduct of student-teaching activities in institutions that prepare teachers.

student teaching, full-time: *see* **student teaching, all-day.**

student teaching, graded: teaching activities that are systematically varied and increased in difficulty for the gradual induction of the student teacher into teaching; a common general pattern or sequence includes observation and participation prior to actual practice teaching.

student teaching, off-campus: student-teaching activities carried on in affiliated or cooperating schools that are not on the campus of an institution engaged in preparing teachers.

student teaching, on-campus: student teaching that is done in a campus laboratory school or in any other school staffed or administered by the college or university. *Contr. w.* **student teaching, off-campus.**

student teaching, part-time: *see* **student teaching, block plan of.**

student teaching, supervised: *see* **student teaching.**

student traffic: the movement of students about buildings and through corridors in passing from class to class.

student trainee: *see* **trainee, student.**

student, transfer: (1) a student who has withdrawn from one college and applies for admission to another; sometimes applied to students moving from one college to another within a university; *syn.* **migrant student;** (2) a junior college student who transfers to a 4-year college or university during or at the completion of his junior college course; the term is used in studies of the success of transfer students as opposed to native students; *see* **student, native;** (3) *see* **pupil, transfer.**

student, unclassified: a student whose status with respect to entrance requirements is acceptable but who, for whatever reason, is not pursuing a course leading to a degree. *Dist. f.* **student, special.**

student union: (higher ed.) an organization of students (often provided with a special building) concerned with student recreational, social, and governmental activities; supported by a fee levied on all students, and governed by a board composed, usually, of elected students and appointed faculty members. (This governing board organizes and provides special recreational programs supplemental to those sponsored by other student organizations.) *See* **building, student-union.**

student-union building: *see* **building, student-union.**

student, veteran: a term referring to a student attending any school under the terms of the GI Bill of Rights. *See* **GI Bill of Rights; veterans' education.**

student withdrawal: *see* **withdrawal.**

student worker: *syn.* **trainee, student.**

student's card: (1) in a public library, a borrower's card for the use of students, granting special privileges; (2) in some public libraries, a borrower's card issued for a limited period to out-of-town students attending school or college in the town.

students, exchange of: *see* **exchange of students.**

students, international exchange of: *see* **exchange of students, international.**

student's t: *syn.* **test, t.**

studies, area: *see* **area studies.**

studies, inter-African: investigations involving comparison and contrast between two African countries.

studies, intercultural: investigations involving two cultures, either within a single country or in different countries. *See* **educational studies, cross-cultural.**

studies, international: investigations and publications treating topics which cut across national boundaries. *See* **educational studies, cross-national.**

studies, mononational: investigations and publications which deal exclusively with issues and topics from a single country. *Syn.* **monocountry studies;** *see* **educational studies, cross-national.**

studies, non-Western: a not very precise term embracing any discipline concerned with the geographical area of the world outside Europe and North America; includes even such areas as Latin America, obviously partly Western, and frequently Russia, while excluding those areas where the traditional core of Western culture in Europe has dominated a society, such as Canada, the United States, and Australia.

studies, Pan-African: investigations dealing with all or most African countries or with issues and topics common to most African countries as opposed to those dealing with only one or a few countries. *Contr. w.* **studies, inter-African.**

studies, pancommunistic: investigations dealing with topics which cut across all or most of the communist bloc countries.

studies, polycultural: investigations involving several cultures, either within a country or in different countries. *See* **educational studies, cross-cultural.**

studies, program of: *see* **program of studies.**

studies, social: *see* **social studies.**

studio: (1) the workroom of an artist; (2) a classroom in which art work is carried on.

studio broadcast: *see* **broadcast, studio.**

studium generale (stū'di·əm gen'ər·ā'lē): (Lat.) usually, an unorganized group of teachers and scholars that assembled for study in the medieval universities of Italy, France, Germany, and England; also used to designate a school or place where students from all parts of the civilized world were received.

study: (1) application of the mind to a problem or subject; (2) a branch of learning; (3) an investigation of a particular subject, or the published findings of such an investigation.

study aid: *see* **aid, study.**

study, analytical: (1) purposeful mental activity involving breaking down a problem into its elements or logical parts; (2) selective thinking carried on in the solution of a problem; (3) an investigation or the published findings of an investigation, based on the reduction of a problem to its elements or logical parts and the examination of these elements in detail.

study area: *see* **area, study.**

study, biogenetic: genetic research with emphasis on biological factors, such as inheritance and maturation; in its general sense, research concerned with the development of organisms.

study, biographical: a historical study concerned with a person's deeds, behavior, successes, problems, etc., during his entire life or some selected portion of it.

study carrel: *see* **carrel.**

study, case: *see* **case study.**

study center: *see* **center, study.**

study, child: *see* **child study.**

study club: *see* **club, study.**

study coach: *see* **coach, study.**

study, community: an analysis of the work, amusements, reading, beliefs, and customs, or phases of these, of a whole community in an effort to understand community life and problems.

study, comparative: a term used loosely to indicate any study in which two or more cases or groups of cases are compared. (Experiments are comparative studies; but practically all research involves comparison, between contemporary groups, or with earlier groups, or with established norms or expectations.)

study, conducted: a rarely used, somewhat ambiguous synonym for supervised study. *See* **study, supervised.**

study, correlation: a study involving correlation, or one in which the correlation between two or more variables is prominent.

study, correspondence: *see* **correspondence study.**

study, cost-quality: a study of the operation of a school district wherein both the cost and the quality of the educational program are measured; theoretically provides a control for the study of comparative efficiency of school districts.

study, cross-section: (1) a status study concerned with conditions at a given point in time; (2) a study making one set of measurements of different children from each age level; the averages for the variables for each group are calculated and plotted to depict the general growth patterns of each variable over all the age levels; usually describes fewer factors than a longitudinal study, but includes more subjects. *Contr. w.* **study, longitudinal.**

study day: a day set aside for study activities to be carried on during the day as contrasted with night study.

study, deductive: study of the type in which the learner draws inferences or arrives at conclusions solely on the basis of previously accepted principles.

study, detached: a method of study which results in the individual's failing to see relationships among ideas, within a subject, and from one subject to another.

study, diagnostic: analytical study of a pupil's or group's activities in some field with the purpose of identifying strengths and weaknesses.

study, directed: any study procedure in which the pupil's learning efforts are guided toward the desired objectives rather than being left to chance; may involve teacher supervision and assistance or the use of specially prepared study materials, such as workbooks; may also include provisions for evaluation by the pupil of the work accomplished and means of measuring progress at regular intervals. *Syn.* **guided study.**

study, documentary frequency: an analysis of a specified body of published material (such as periodicals or textbooks) for the purpose of noting the frequency of occurrence of certain characteristics, such as topics treated, vocabulary characteristics, illustrations, and exercises.

Study, Eight Year: *see* **Eight Year Study.**

study, environment: *see* **environment study.**

study, experimental: a study in which the data are obtained solely or principally from experiment.

study, extensive: (1) the study involving the assimilation of a variety of materials, as contrasted with the intensive study of a limited amount of material such as is contained in a textbook; (2) wide or extended study over a considerable area.

study, fact-finding: an investigation designed and conducted to ascertain the facts concerning or the present status of an institution, situation, etc. *Syn.* **normative survey.**

study, feasibility: a study or survey to determine the practicability of instituting a program, course, or other proposed activity.

study, field: a study for which data are gathered from a source broader than a single classroom or, usually, than one school; may extend over an entire nation; used often in contradistinction to laboratory study, meaning that data are obtained from sources other than a laboratory.

study, follow-up: (1) (couns.) a study made in order to achieve one or more of the following purposes: (*a*) to determine the effectiveness of the guidance process, (*b*) to obtain a realistic picture of what lies ahead for present students, (*c*) to help former students reappraise their educational and vocational plans, (*d*) to appraise the school's program, (*e*) to obtain ideas for improving the program, and (*f*) to obtain information that the school requires to adapt its adult education program to meet more efficiently the needs of its former students and the community; (2) (mil. ed.) evaluation of progress of persons in jobs or training to which they have been assigned, on the basis of certain measuring instruments and procedures.

study, formal: (1) systematic study carried on under the direction of a teacher; (2) study directed by study exercises, books, or other aids to study, as contrasted with incidental or undirected study.

study, frequency: a study designed primarily to ascertain the number of occurrences of various specified objects or characteristics, within certain defined limits or conditions set for the study. (The term suggests that measurement is not a necessary or at least prominent part of the study and that the phenomena studied can be identified and classified largely without measuring.)

study, graduate: formal study pursued after receiving the bachelor's or first professional degree, usually for the purpose of obtaining a higher degree. *Dist. f.* **study, postgraduate.**

study group: *see* **group, study.**

study group, parent: *see* **group, parent study.**

study guide: a printed, written, or duplicated set of directions or questions for the use of pupils or students in independent study.

study guide, correspondence: *see* **correspondence study guide.**

study guide, film: *syn.* **film manual.**

study, guided: *syn.* **study, directed; study, supervised.**

study, guided independent: *see* **instruction, individualized.**

study habit: (1) the tendency of a pupil or student to study when the opportunity is given; (2) the pupil's or student's way of studying, whether systematic or unsystematic, efficient or inefficient, etc.

study habits: the basic features involved in the application of the mind to a problem or subject; the characteristic pattern which an individual follows in learning about things and people.

study hall: a room under the direction of one or more teachers where pupils are sent to study.

study hall, departmental: a special room in a departmentalized school to which pupils are assigned for study under the direction of a member of the department concerned.

study hall, library: a room used for the combined purposes of study and the storage and reading of books and other materials.

study-hall teacher: a teacher who, in addition to instructional responsibilities, has charge during one or more periods per day of a room used by students primarily for study and the preparation of assignments. (In a few cases full time is spent in supervising the study hall.)

study, historical: a study of events or conditions that fit significantly into a temporal sequence.

study, home: *see* **home study.**

study, incidental: (1) study not previously planned or systematically directed but carried on during some purposeful activity and owing to some stimulus arising from that activity; (2) study definitely planned but incidental to the accomplishment of some purpose.

study, independent: educational activity carried on by an individual seeking self-improvement, usually but not always self-initiated.

study, individualized: study activities that are differentiated to meet the needs of the student instead of being the same for all those in a study group.

study, inductive: study of the type in which the learner begins with specific data or hypotheses and through reasoning arrives at generalizations.

study load: *see* **load, study.**

study, longitudinal: a study that follows a case or group of cases over a period of time; includes genetic study, follow-up studies, growth studies, and experimental growth studies; its purpose may be to gather normative data on growth, to plot trends (as of attitudes), or to observe the effects of special factors (as in an experiment). *Contr. w.* **study, cross-section.**

study, methods: (school admin.) analysis of motions, materials, procedure, tools, and equipment used or to be used to perform a task in order to develop a way to perform the task more effectively.

study, micromotion: a technique that employs motion-picture photography, making it possible consequently to observe, record, and analyze the unit motions that are used in performing a piece of work together with the conditions immediately surrounding this work.

study, motion: a technique for the investigation, analysis, and study of the movements made by an operative in doing a piece of work. *See* **measurement, methods-time; microchronometer; study, micromotion.**

study, motion and time: a technique for investigating and analyzing the requirements for an effective, economical performance of a step or operation in an operative procedure.

study, nature: *see* **nature study.**

study, normative: a study of the cross-section or survey type designed to ascertain status, often especially the status of values or expectations, or norms (averages) of performance on tests, for the establishment of criteria.

study, observational: a study in which direct observation (usually of a complex situation such as of children in a group) is dominant or prominent in the gathering of data; may be longitudinal, in that it involves successive observations over a period of time, but is more generally normative.

study, occupational: (1) a collection of data concerning a specific occupation, gathered and analyzed according to accepted methods of research, for the purpose of supplying adequate and accurate information concerning the need for and supply of workers and the requirements of the job in terms of skills, knowledge, and personal characteristics; (2) a term also applied to study by students of an occupation or occupations in connection with a program of vocational guidance or in a regular class. *See* **survey, occupational.**

study outline: a skeleton arrangement of problems, topics, questions, or other data to be used by the pupil or student in the study of a subject, lesson, or unit of work.

study period: *see* **period, study.**

study, personality: the study of the components of personality and of its causal factors.

study, personnel: an intensive analysis of any or all phases of the characteristics or activities of the students or students and employees of an educational institution.

study, picture: (read.) utilizing pictures in any text as a means of (*a*) self-help in recognition of words and (*b*) aid to visualizing concepts presented in the text.

study, pilot: a preliminary study, generally conducted with a small group (or small groups), used in advance of a major or formal research project in order to try out techniques, procedures, methods, and/or instruments. *Syn.* **group, practice.**

study plan, individual: a plan to be incorporated in the master schedule of a high school, under which students engage in study activities as individuals or in groups of two or three, with teachers serving as consultants in conferences with the students when needed to clarify goals, content, and personal problems; students are provided with study areas, including some individual study booths, where they may read, listen to records and tapes, think, examine and analyze evidence, etc., thus taking progressively more responsibility for self-direction.

study, postgraduate: formal study carried on after having received the bachelor's or first professional degree; sometimes employed as a synonym for *graduate study,* but more correctly used to designate such study when carried on in short courses of a few days' or weeks' duration, rather than study of longer duration undertaken for the purpose of obtaining a higher degree. *See* **study, graduate.**

study program: *see* **program, study.**

study program, parent: *see* **program, parent study.**

study project: *see* **project, study.**

study questions: a series of problematic statements, directions, or thought-provoking questions given to the pupil or student to stimulate mastery of reading material.

study, ratio delay: (school admin.) a statistical technique for determining the frequency of each kind of delay for a class of work or machine; based on the statistical theory of *sampling.*

study reader: *see* **reader, study.**

study reading: *syn.* **reading, work-type.**

study reading program: *syn.* **program, curricular reading.**

study, reflective: the progressive mental reorganization of the experience secured by reading or direct experience, a process that constitutes true study as distinguished from rote memorizing and mechanical performance of routine tasks.

study schedule: *see* **schedule, study.**

study, self-directed: *syn.* **project method.**

study skill: *see* **skill, study.**

study skills, basal: the study skills that are common to all study situations as distinguished from specialized study skills peculiar to one type or area of study.

study-skills inventory: *see* **inventory, study-skills.**

study-skills test: *see* **test, study-skills.**

study song: *see* **song, study.**

study, staff: (mil. ed.) an analytical study prepared for a commander which normally includes five parts: the subject, the statement of the problem, the assumptions (sometimes augmented by a statement of criteria used), the discussion (sometimes with conclusions), and the action recommended; a similar study prepared for practice.

study, statistical: (1) a study involving statistical techniques; loosely, a quantitative study; (2) in a special sense, a study designed to evaluate or improve statistical techniques.

study, summary: a study designed to locate and summarize the treatises that have previously been prepared on a certain subject or problem; presumably involves some synthesis and interpretation and is therefore broader and more productive than the simple *review of literature.*

study, supervised: a procedure in which the teacher is available to answer questions and offer suggestions, as contrasted with the practice of requiring independent study by students without aid from the teacher. *Syn.* **guided study.**

study, supervised correspondence: *see* **correspondence study, supervised.**

study technique: a definite procedure used in study to accomplish a specific purpose, such as outlining, summarizing, or taking notes.

study, terrain: (mil. ed.) an analysis and interpretation of natural and man-made features of an area, their effects on military operations, and the effect of weather and climate on these features.

study-test method: a teaching procedure in which the assigned material is first studied in detail, after which a test is administered to determine the degree of mastery achieved; for example, spelling study in which words to be learned are studied by all pupils before a test is given. *Contr. w.* **test-study method.**

study, time: *see* **time study.**

study, time-motion: the systematic investigation of the motions and the time required to perform a specific operation; intent of the study is to increase efficiency of that operation.

study, time sampling: a method of observational study in which the reliability of an observation is obtained by observing the subject under controlled conditions on several occasions for short intervals of time.

study trip: *syn.* **field trip.**

study, type: a method of teaching involving a survey of typical examples of major units of content, as when students study typical models and apply the knowledge thus gained in comparisons and contrasts with other units; two stages of a type study are (*a*) concrete presentation and (*b*) comparison.

study-type reading: *syn.* **reading, work-type.**

study unit: *see* **unit, study.**

study, use: (libr. sci.) a study of the use by clientele, staff, or others of libraries, information sources, tools, and techniques.

study, word-frequency: an examination of a text or texts to determine the occurrence and the frequency of occurrence of the words employed, as a means of determining words to be taught.

study-work plan: an arrangement whereby students may combine work experience with their formal program of education. *See* **program, cooperative; program, work-study.**

stuttering: speech characterized by anxious expectation of difficulty in emitting sounds or words, by reactions of unusual strain or tension, and by one or more of the following: repetition or prolongation of speech elements (sounds, syllables, words, or phrases), interjection of superflous speech elements, silent intervals; sometimes used incorrectly to indicate the free, easy repetitions more or less characteristic of the speech of young children. (Stuttering is used synonymously with stammering, except by some writers who designate speech repetitions as stuttering and speech blocks or stoppages as stammering.)

stuttering, clonic (klon'ik): stuttering characterized mainly by the repetition of sounds or syllables, as in g-g-g-go or for-for-forward.

stuttering, interiorized: a form of stuttering behavior in which no visible contortions or audible abnormalities are shown but in which a hidden struggle, usually in the larynx or breathing musculature, is present; characterized by clever disguise reactions.

stuttering pattern: (1) the sequence of or ordered relations among the activities involved in a particular occurrence of stuttering; (2) any manner of stuttering prescribed for speech-correction purposes in order to eliminate certain stuttering symptoms by means of substitute reactions and to objectify the stutterer's attitude toward his speech difficulty.

stuttering pattern, repetition: (1) that form of stuttering in which sounds, syllables, or words are repeated, usually with more than usual muscular tension; (2) a type of stuttering, as defined above, sometimes employed voluntarily, without excess tension, in the treatment of stuttering, on the assumption that the emotionality and anxiety and straining reactions of the stutterer are thus reduced.

stuttering, pseudo: obsolete term for simulated or voluntary stuttering, performed deliberately or wilfully; sometimes employed in the treatment of stuttering on the assumption that it will increase the stutterer's understanding of his difficulty and the objectivity of his attitude toward it; may constitute malingering. (Sometimes referred to as *faking, faked stuttering,* or *cold stuttering.*) *Syn.* **voluntary stuttering.**

stuttering, voluntary: obsolete *syn.* **stuttering, pseudo.**

style, idiomatic: *see* **idiomatic style.**

style, leadership: *see* **leadership style.**

style, life-: see **life-style.**

style, response: *see* **response style.**

style sheet: a compact set of rules concerning capitalization, punctuation, abbreviations, figures, and similar usages, adopted to provide uniformity in a particular publication. *See* **style sheet, all-school.**

style sheet, all-school: a *style sheet* used as a guide in all publication activities and in English composition classes in a particular school. *See* **style sheet.**

style, teaching: *see* **teaching style.**

styles, letter: *see* **letter styles.**

styles of art: *see* **art, styles of.**

stylistics: the appreciation and study of the characteristics of artistic writing.

stylus: (1) a needle used in disk recording or playback; in the case of microgroove recording, standardized at a width of 0.001 inch diameter; on records making 78 revolutions a minute, standardized at 0.003 inch diameter; (2) in ancient times, an implement for writing on waxed tablets, with a sharp pointed end for writing and a blunt end for erasing.

stylus, braille: *see* **braille stylus.**

stylus maze: a complicated or confusing groove pattern cut into a wooden or composition base through which a subject attempts to trace his way with a pointed pencil-like object, without looking at the pattern.

suan pan: a Chinese abacus; the device uses sliding beads on vertical rods; above the horizontal bar there are two beads on each rod and below the bar there are five. *See* **abacus; soroban.**

sub specie aeternitatis (sub spē′shi·ē ē·tĕr·ni·tā′tis): (Lat., lit., "under the aspect of eternity") (1) from the viewpoint of that which is eternal in any body, namely, its essence, as opposed to the other aspect that any body has, that which is changing, temporal, transient (Spinoza); (2) in general, from a standpoint beyond time (when trying to understand anything in time from such a point of view).

subaverage: of a lower level or quality than some norm.

subbasement: stories of a building below the basement.

subcultural feeblemindedness: *syn.* **mental retardation, subcultural.**

subcultural mental retardation: *see* **mental retardation, subcultural.**

subcultural type: (1) a term used by E. O. Lewis and others to distinguish that major group of feebleminded persons whose physical appearance in no way differentiates them from normal persons; similar to endogenous or familial mental deficient; *contr. w.* **clinical type;** (2) those retarded individuals who do not and cannot share common cultural experiences.

subculture: a custom or customs characteristic of a subgroup, a part of a larger group or society whose members share a common culture.

subemployment: (voc. ed.) a summary measure of the total problem of unemployment and low earnings, designed to represent its compounded impact on the same disadvantaged groups and its effects in preventing several million workers and their families from sharing in the nation's economic prosperity; can be expressed in absolute numbers or as a rate.

subfreshman course: *see* **course, subfreshman.**

subgoal: *see* **outcome, desired learning.**

subgroup: a small instructional group within the classroom group.

subinterval: the range of values assumed to be included by a single score or observation in one class interval of a frequency distribution, when the observations are assumed to be distributed equally throughout the class interval; the distance from one item to the next within a class interval, assuming that the frequency in the class interval is evenly distributed throughout the class interval; for example, if there are 18 frequencies in a given class interval of width 5, the subinterval is five-eighteenths. *Syn.* **score interval;** *dist. f.* **interval, class.**

subject: (1) a division or field of organized knowledge, such as English or mathematics; (2) a selection from an organized body of knowledge for a course or teaching unit, such as the English novel or elementary algebra; (3) (philos.) *see* **object of knowledge;** (4) an individual who is being tested or subjected to experiment.

subject age: *see* **age, subject.**

subject articulation: *see* **articulation, subject.**

subject, basic: (1) a subject or one of several subjects considered absolutely essential in a given field as background preparation for further study in that field or as a necessary tool in learning other related subjects; (2) sometimes used to indicate one of those subjects which are essential to the *common learnings* that form the base upon which is built the good citizen in a democratic society; (3) one of the subjects which form the core of the social processes, such as family living, governing, appreciating, consuming, and communicating; to be distinguished from *common learnings,* or *core subjects,* in that a basic subject may or may not be required of every student. *Contr. w.* **subject, special.**

subject catalog: *see* **catalog, subject.**

subject catalog, classified: *syn.* **catalog, classified.**

subject coefficient: *see* **coefficient, subject.**

subject combination: the combining of certain subjects to facilitate integration of material across narrow subject lines (language-spelling-reading).

subject, common school: usually, a subject taught in a district or public elementary school, such as reading, writing, spelling, arithmetic, civics, history, or geography.

subject, content: a school subject in which the acquisition of information or knowledge is the chief aim, for example, history, geography, science, and civics. *Contr. w.* **subject, skill.**

subject, continuous-tone: *see* **continuous-tone subject.**

subject contrast: *see* **contrast, subject.**

subject, core: (1) a central subject (such as reading) that, because of its fundamental or key position, is adapted to the task of unification of the school program at a particular educational level; (2) a school subject that is considered so essential that every student is required to have instruction in it; (3) one of the required courses or subjects in a school program, about which are grouped the special subjects and electives.

subject course: *see* **course, subject.**

subject curriculum: *see* **curriculum, subject.**

subject difficulty: (1) the degree of effort involved in teaching or learning a particular subject, as expressed by the subject coefficient; (2) the degree to which a subject is difficult to master, as indicated by the percentage of failure or the marks obtained by pupils.

subject, disciplinary: *syn.* **course, disciplinary.**

subject, drill: during the early years of education in the United States, a subject of study usually considered basic and therefore often taught through "drill," that is, repetitive practice for automatic speed and accuracy; reading, writing, arithmetic, spelling, and grammar were viewed as drill subjects.

subject enrichment: *see* **enrichment, subject.**

subject examination: *syn.* **examination, content.**

subject, expression: a school subject or activity which is neither of the drill nor of the content type but the nature of which involves more creative expression, for example, music, drawing, play, gardening, and manual and domestic arts.

subject failure: *see* **failure, subject.**

subject field: (1) a body of knowledge organized under traditional school headings (such as English, arithmetic, history); (2) a body of knowledge broader than a *subject* such as third-grade spelling, eighth-grade arithmetic, or English history but less comprehensive than a *broad subject field* (such as social science, language arts, natural sciences).

subject, formal: a school subject (for example, penmanship, spelling, arithmetic, formal grammar) in which forms, traditional practices, or conventional facts are emphasized more than natural facts (as in science). *See* **subject, content.**

subject, fundamental: (1) a term formerly designating a school subject that gave a command over the written or printed expression of knowledge (for example, reading, writing, spelling, English composition, arithmetic, and grammar); (2) more recently, the term designates a subject that provides the student with the opportunity to acquire knowledges, skills, or appreciations essential for a successful life.

subject grade: *syn.* **score, grade.**

subject heading: a word or group of words expressing a subject under which all material dealing with the same theme is filed in a catalog, an index, or a bibliography.

subject, home-room: one of the subjects that pupils study under a home-room teacher in the home room of an elementary school organized for semidepartmentalized work.

subject-in-context index: *syn.* **index, key-word-in-context.**

subject index: *see* **index, subject.**

subject, logical approach to a: *see* **logical approach to a subject.**

subject major: *syn.* **major, departmental.**

subject matter: (1) the facts, information, knowledge, or content to be acquired by the learner in any course of study, that is, its basic substance, as distinguished from the methods, disciplines, and activities that give form to a course; the content of education as contrasted with the science or art of educating; (2) (art ed.) in creative activity, not such concrete matter as houses, trees, etc., but rather the individual's expression of his changing relationship to man and environment.

subject-matter approach: an approach to curriculum building which begins with the demands of logically organized bodies of subject matter, or with a set of preconceived ideas regarding facts, ideas, and principles to be learned, rather than with the needs of the learner and/or of the society.

subject matter, core: (1) the subject matter of all required courses and other nonelective constants that form the fundamental part of the curriculum; (2) the fundamental knowledge or learning material basic to any subject of study, as the concept of numbers and number relations in arithmetic; (3) sometimes, the subject matter involved in the core curriculum.

subject-matter department: *syn.* **department, academic.**

subject-matter item: *see* **item, subject-matter.**

subject-matter plan of organization: organization of course content on the basis of logical arrangement of subject matter, as contrasted with psychological arrangement or presentation.

subject-matter preparation: *see* **preparation, subject-matter.**

subject matter, professionalization of: *see* **professionalization of subject matter.**

subject-matter specialist: *see* **specialist, subject-matter.**

subject-matter test: *syn.* **test, achievement.**

subject-matter unit: *see* **unit, subject-matter.**

subject-object relationship: in the act of knowing, the kind of connection or relationship or togetherness that obtains between the knower and the known; this relationship could involve a process in which the nature of both the known and the object is being changed in the process, or it could involve a process that leaves both the subject and the object unchanged, depending upon one's epistemological presuppositions.

subject, professional: (1) any organized body of class or course work offered by a teacher education institution, the content of which deals primarily with educational problems; usually refers to courses in education; (2) an organized body of knowledge dealing with the principles and practice of a profession. *See* **course, professional.**

subject promotion: *see* **promotion, subject.**

subject ratio: *see* **ratio, subject.**

subject, related: (1) a classroom subject intended not to teach specific vocational skills but to increase the student's vocational knowledge, understanding, and ability in the field of distribution, for example, laws affecting stores, consumer economics, consumer demand, business English, etc.; (2) a subject that contains the associated trade information, trade mathematics, trade drawing, trade science, etc., necessary to intelligent performance in a given trade.

subject, required: *syn.* **constant** *n.* (4).

subject sequence: the arrangement of subject matter or courses in a definite order, as determined by either logical or psychological considerations.

subject, skill: (1) (bus. ed.) a subject integrating developed techniques, skill, and accuracy and calling for motor activity and clear thinking combined, such as typewriting or shorthand; (2) more generally, a school subject in which the acquisition of special skills is the chief aim, such as reading, penmanship, and arithmetic. *Contr. w.* **subject, content.**

subject, special: (1) a term formerly used in secondary education to designate subjects such as art, home economics, industrial arts, or music; (2) a subject introduced to meet the needs and interests of a particular group, such as the gifted, the retarded, or the handicapped.

subject specialization: *see* **specialization, subject.**

subject supervisor: *see* **supervisor, subject.**

subject, technical business: *see* **business subject, technical.**

subject, tool: a subject the study of which is necessary in order to study other subjects successfully; usually, a subject that involves the ability to use language and number.

subject, vocational: any school subject designed to develop specific skills, knowledges, and information that enable the learner to prepare for or to be more efficient in his chosen trade or occupation.

subject weight: *see* **weight, subject.**

subjective: (1) conditioned by the individual's temperament, biases, prejudices, and partialities; (2) not verifiable by other competent investigators since not susceptible to observational report, physical measurement, or other form of public record; (3) pertaining to the ego or to consciousness as the subject of experience, conditioned but not produced by external stimuli.

subjective camera angle: *see* **camera angle, subjective.**

subjective criteria: *see* **criteria, subjective.**

subjective data: *see* **data, subjective.**

subjective error: *see* **error, subjective.**

subjective evaluation: *see* **evaluation, subjective.**

subjective idealism: *see* **idealism, subjective.**

subjective method: method in which the use of data is supplemented, extended, or directed by the personal judgment, preference, belief, or hypothetical reasoning of the user.

subjective stage of color: *see* **color, subjective stage of.**

subjective test: *see* **test, subjective.**

subjectivism: (1) in theories about knowledge, the view that all one can ever know surely is limited to one's personal and private states of awareness and such realities as may be inferred from them; *see* **egocentric predicament; solipsism;** (2) any theory emphasizing the subjective elements of experience instead of its objective elements; (3) the ethical doctrine that defines good in terms of the attainment of states of feeling, usually pleasure or happiness; (4) preoccupation with mental and emotional states and with thought, as contrasted with preoccupation with objective, physical matters.

subjectivity: (1) the quality of dependence on judgment, personal opinion, or bias, rather than on impersonal, factual evidence; (2) the religious or philosophical doctrine that truth should be sought and tested by inner consciousness, conviction, or intuition of each individual, instead of by some objective criterion, such as history, logic, or tradition; (3) (meas.) an attribute of a test so constructed that different scores might be assigned by different but equally competent scorers and in the scoring of which the personal opinion, judgment, bias, etc., of the scorer would affect the score assigned; (4) a tendency to become centered in one's own feelings and thoughts, to see things exclusively from one's own viewpoint.

subjects, clerical: a general term for those areas of business education which prepare students to do clerical work in offices; included are typewriting, bookkeeping, statistics, accounting, business arithmetic, business English, filing, spelling, penmanship, and sometimes shorthand. *Contr. w.* **business subjects, social.**

subjects, distributive: those subjects designed to develop vocational skills in, impart vocational knowledge to, and provide proper ideals in those students preparing for or already engaged in distributive occupations, for example, salesmenship, retailing, advertising, marketing, sales-letter writing, sales management, and retail-store management.

subjects, halftone: *see* **halftone subjects.**

subjects taught in isolation: the usual school subjects, each taught by itself in a daily period specifically set aside for that purpose; the daily schedule consists of enough separate periods so that each subject may receive appropriate attention; the work in each subject proceeds in accordance with the logical and psychological arrangement of the content within that one subject and without consideration for what is taught the same children in other subjects.

sublimation: the act of directing an impulse from its primitive aim or goal into a channel having objectives of higher social value.

subliminal stimulus: *see* **stimulus, subliminal.**

submarginal district: *see* **district, submarginal.**

submaster tape: *see* **tape, submaster.**

submatrix method: any method of factor extraction (for example, the *multiple-group method*) which rearranges the order of the variables in the correlation matrix in order to bring clusters into district areas of the matrix and which then computes separately for those submatrices.

submissiveness: a trait characterized by a tendency to yield to and accept the leadership of others; compliance; meekness; obedience. *Contr. w.* **aggressiveness; ascendance.**

subnormal: (1) below the norm; *dist. f.* **abnormal;** (2) often used in referring to the group of persons who are subnormal in intelligence.

subnormal child: *see* **child, subnormal.**

subnormal, educationally: (British) *syn.* **mentally retarded, educable;** *see* **subnormal, mentally.**

subnormal, mentally: a generic British term indicating all levels of mental retardation. *See* **feeblemindedness; retardation, mental;** *comp. w.* **subnormal, educationally.**

subobjective: *see* **outcome, desired learning.**

subordinate relationship: the relationship between one person in a school system and another in a higher position, such as that of the teacher to the principal.

subordinate teacher: *syn.* **assistant teacher.**

subprofessional personnel: *see* **paraprofessional.**

subrogation: the substitution of one person for another with respect to the rights of the latter, as, for example, where a surety has paid the debts of another he may be entitled to subrogation to all the securities of the creditor.

subroutine: (data processing) a portion of a *routine* that instructs a computer to carry out some well-defined logical or mathematical operation; often written in relative or symbolic coding even if the routine is not; may be arranged so that the control transferred to it reverts, at the conclusion of the subroutine, to the master routine, which may make multiple use of the subroutine in order to avoid repetition of the same sequence of instructions; a subroutine may be a master routine with regard to a subsequent subroutine. *See* **compiler.**

subsample: a sample drawn from some subdivision of a population, for example, that part of a sample drawn from any one of the 4 years of high school when the groups representing all 4 years make up, collectively, the whole sample; part of a sample.

subscript: (math.) a symbol written to the right or left of and below some other symbol to give information relative to the context about order, position in an array, etc.; for example, in the symbol a_4, the subscript 4 might indicate that a_4 was the fourth term in some sequence; double subscripts are used to represent elements in a matrix, the first number denoting the row number and the second the column number; a_{24}, for example, is the element in the second row and fourth column. *See* **matrix.**

subscription television: *see* **television, subscription.**

subset: a set X is a subset of set A if all members of X are members of A; if there is some member of A which is not in X, then X is a *proper subset* of A; if there is no member of A which is not in X, then X is an *improper subset* of A.

subsidiary account: *see* **account, subsidiary.**

subsidization of athletes: compensating athletes for participating in athletic contests.

subsidy: *syn.* **grant-in-aid.**

subsistence: (1) that state of being attributed to concepts, numbers, and principles; (2) a state of being that is independent of specific spatial and temporal dimensions, as opposed to the sort of existence enjoyed by concrete physical objects; (3) the state of being sometimes ascribed to the neutral entities of the Neo-Realists and to the essences of Santayana.

subspecialization: (mil. ed.) a group of courses or academic or on-the-job professional experiences, associated with a given specialization; in most cases, the subspecialization will be neither identified nor reported but will be used to identify the types of courses or experiences that may be considered under, or which constitute, a specialization; exceptions are cases of graduate study in a definite type of research (such as aerodynamic loads or ballistics) or where current professional competence is established through either formal study or on-the-job experience to such an extent that the subspecialization can be readily identified.

substance: (1) that which exists in itself and not in something formally distinct from itself as a property or accident; for Descartes and Spinoza *in se* "in itself" became *a se* "by itself"; (2) that which is always a subject and never a predicate, that is, a *primary substance;* (3) the meaning or content of written or spoken language, as distinguished from its form of expression.

substandard certificate: *see* **certificate, substandard.**

substantive law: *see* **law, substantive.**

substantive theory of mind: *see* **mind, substantive theory of.**

substitute adjustment: *see* **adjustment, substitute.**

substitute behavior: *see* **behavior, substitute.**

substitute driver: *syn.* **driver, alternate.**

substitute, permanent: a teacher who is on a school's permanent list of substitute teachers.

substitute teacher: (1) one who occupies temporarily the position of an absent teacher, whether employed for a few days only or for an extended period of time; (2) a distinguishing term often associated with large school systems having local teacher-license examination and appointment listing, where *regular teachers* meet all license requirements and have year-long appointments as contrasted with substitute teachers who may be granted temporary exemption from full requirements and receive irregular employment varying from long-term assignments to day-to-day assignment to different schools; under this system a teacher from the substitute list who is assigned for a semester or a year to one school is called a *full-time substitute teacher. Dist. f.* **regular teacher.**

substitute teacher, full-time: (1) a teacher hired full time with no particular subject or grade assigned to him, but required to fill temporary vacancies caused by illness, etc., and when no such vacancies exist to help in some school department or school office; (2) *see* **substitute teacher** (2).

substitution: (1) an error in oral reading that consists of saying a word not actually in the context, for example, "can't" for "cat"; (2) the use of one sound or letter in the place of another in pronouncing or spelling a word, for example, saying "kin" for "can" or writing "tought" for "taught"; (3) (psych.) the act of replacing one thing by another, as developing success in athletics when distinction in scholarship is not attainable, the purpose being to avoid a sense of inferiority.

substitution, consonant: (read.) substituting one consonant for another at the beginning of a word that is already familiar in order to make a different word that is similar in form and sound except for the initial consonant; a technique taught to beginners to develop independence in word recognition.

substitution, error of: *see* error of substitution.

substitution item: *see* item, substitution.

substitution test: *see* test, substitution.

substitutional average: *syn.* average, abstract.

substrata-factor analysis: *see* analysis, substrata-factor.

substrata-factor theory of reading, dynamic: *see* reading, dynamic substrata-factor theory of.

subsumption, obliterative: the theory that new concepts when learned are often qualitatively changed by present cognitive structure, that all concepts must be fitted into category systems, and that when these systems are unstable and unclear the new concepts will also be unclear and undifferentiated. *See* inhibition, proactive.

subsumption system: D. Ausubel's phrase to describe any of the categories one uses to build a cognitive structure that will accommodate new concepts. *See* subsumption, obliterative.

subsystem: a component of a larger information system, often comprising two or more applications; that is, systems of problems to which a computer is applied, which may be either of the computational type wherein arithmetic computations predominate or of the data-processing type wherein data-handling operations predominate.

subtest: a part of a test, composed of similar items having a distinct purpose, for which a separate score may be provided.

subtitle: a word, phrase, or sentence that appears under or over a visual to explain, emphasize, or clarify a point.

subtle item: *see* item, subtle.

subtraction, comparative: (1) subtraction performed to compare two numbers; (2) a term used in classifying verbal problems in which the computation is subtraction; in contrast to "take-away" situations, comparative subtraction problems require an answer to a question of the type "How much larger (smaller) . . . ?", the idea being that one person's age, height, etc., cannot be removed, strictly speaking, from its relation to another's.

subtraction facts: the set of statements about differences which derive from the addition facts, as, for example, $17 - 9 = 8$ and $11 - 6 = 5$; the number of facts to be learned depends upon the way in which the addition facts are handled; earlier literature refers to a list of 100 (from $0 - 0 = 0$ to $18 - 9 = 9$). *See* addition facts.

subtraction, methods of: computational methods for subtraction, classified according to (*a*) the interpretation of the subtraction process as either *take-away subtraction* or as *additive subtraction*; for example, in the problem $12 - 8$ one may ask "12 minus (take-away) 8 is what?" or "8 plus (added to) what is 12?"; and (*b*) whether, in either of these two processes, the symbols are rewritten by *decomposition* or by *equal addition*; for example, $42 - 18 = N$ may be rewritten as (decomposed into) $(30 + 12) - 18 = N$, or, by equal addition of the number 10 to both minuend and subtrahend, as $(40 + 12) - (18 + 10) = N$. *See* complementary method, regrouping.

subtrainable: below trainable functioning level.

subtrait: a specific trait constituting a component of a broader or more significant trait; thus, the trait of respect for public property may be considered a subtrait of the broader characteristic of good citizenship.

suburban school: a school located in the population centers, usually incorporated townships, surrounding a city. *See* inner city school.

subvention: (1) *syn.* grant-in-aid; subsidy; (2) especially a governmental grant for literary, artistic, or scientific purposes, or other educational ends.

subvocal reading: *syn.* speech, inner.

subvocalization: observable movements of the speech musculature in which the intensity of the sounds uttered is below the threshold of normal hearing. *Comp. w.* speech, inner.

success experience: *see* experience, success.

success ratio: *see* ratio, success.

success, school: (1) the degree or measure of pupil achievement at school; (2) the amount and character of satisfactory accomplishment by a school as a whole.

successive-hurdles method: a method of selecting a group of persons for employment by requiring all subjects to take an initial examination, those who pass being then required to take a second examination, and so on successively, until only a predetermined number or percentage of the original applicants remain.

successive-intervals scaling: *see* scaling, successive-intervals.

successive residuals, method of: a shortcut method for selecting a small number of variables from a larger number so as to give a criterion correlation for the selected variables combined at gross-score weights that is only slightly lower than the multiple correlation of all the variables with the criterion; can be applied to either item or test selection.

sucking response: *see* response, sucking.

suffix: an affix, which when added to the end of a word or word root modifies its meaning, for example, -ment in "easement" and "condiment."

suffix, disjoined: in shorthand, a word ending that is not joined to the main part of the word, usually represented by an abbreviated shorthand symbol.

suffix, joined: one or more letters united with the end of a word which in shorthand are joined to the main part of the word.

suggestibility: (couns.) the tendency of individuals (especially children) to be swayed by the suggestions of those surrounding them; susceptibility to a group leader or other person.

suggestibility, negative: *syn.* contrasuggestibility.

suggestive question: a question that is so worded as to include the principal ideas of the problem and to lead the student to the correct solution through his own reasoning.

suicide, race: *see* race suicide.

suit, class: *see* bill, class.

suit, friendly: a lawsuit agreed to by two parties to obtain the opinion of the court in a doubtful question.

suitability of norms: *see* norms, suitability of.

suite, health: *see* health suite.

Sulpician method (sul·pish'ən): (R.C. ed.) a method of teaching religion developed by the priests of St. Sulpice in Paris, in which the teaching of the catechism text involves reading of the Holy Scriptures, recitation of prayers, singing of hymns, and listening to moral exhortations.

sum formula: *see* formula, sum.

summarizing: oral or written condensing of material read; generally recognized as a *study skill*.

summary: (1) an oral, written, or mental condensation, as of material read; (2) (legal) as adjective, immediate, provisional; without normal judicial protections.

summary punch: *see* punch, summary.

summary statistics: *syn.* statistics, descriptive.

summary study: *see* study, summary.

summated ratings scale: *see* scale, summated ratings.

summation: (Σ) addition; the formation of an aggregate or total; customarily indicated by the symbol Σ immediately preceding the symbol of the series to be summed; limits are sometimes indicated by placing the lower limit under

the Σ and the upper limit over the Σ; thus $< \sum\limits_{1}^{N} x^2$

indicates the summation of x^2 over the cases 1 to N; for example, ΣX means the sum of the X series, and ΣY^2

means the sum of the squared magnitudes of the Y series; also used in such forms as

$$\sum_{i=1}^{n} a_i x_i = a_1 x_1 + a_2 x_2 + a_3 x_3 + \cdots + a_n x_n,$$

$$\sum_{i=1}^{n} a_i x^i = a_1 x + a_2 x^2 + a_3 x^3 + \cdots + a_n x^n.$$

summer camp: *see* **camp, summer.**

summer church camp: *see* **camp, summer church.**

summer elementary school: *see* **elementary school, summer.**

summer high school: *see* **high school, summer.**

summer makeup class: *see* **class, summer makeup.**

summer reading club: *syn.* **club, reading** (2).

summer roundup: a plan or procedure for finding and bringing together groups of children during the summer; generally refers to the practice of bringing together preschool children for health examinations prior to their entering school.

summer school: a school conducted during the summer months while the regular school is not in session. *Syn.* **vacation school.**

summer school of the air: a series of radio programs broadcast during vacation period, as a means of maintaining the interest of children in school subjects, and to serve as a worthwhile summer activity; has been tested briefly in certain cities.

summer school term: *see* **school term, summer.**

summer session: *syn.* **summer school.**

summer term: *see* **school term, summer.**

summum bonum (sum'məm bō'nəm): (Lat., lit., "the highest good") the ultimate goal; justice, truth, wisdom, beauty, charity, and virtue are indicative of the many values that have competed for supremacy over all others as the summum bonum, the chief end and aim of existence.

sumptuary law: *see* **law, sumptuary.**

sumptuary tax: *see* **tax, sumptuary.**

Sunday church school: *see* **church school, Sunday.**

Sunday school: *syn.* **church school, Sunday.**

Sunday school, Jewish: a school held once a week on Sunday to provide religious instruction for Jewish children; sometimes loosely called a *Sabbath school.* (The term Jewish Sunday school was first applied to a school of this sort organized in Philadelphia by Rebecca Gratz in 1838.)

Sunday school, Jewish communal: a Jewish religious school conducted on Sunday morning by a central community agency, or by a membership association organized for the purpose of providing Jewish education, or by a national or local organization which, as one of its purposes, provides for religious education needs of the Jewishly unschooled.

Sunday school, Jewish congregational: a Jewish religious school conducted on Sunday morning under the auspices of a congregation.

Sunday-school movement: a movement to provide the elements of both secular and religious instruction on Sunday, mainly for the children of the poor. (The first Sunday school was established by Robert Raikes in Gloucester, England, in 1780, and the institution spread rapidly in England and later in the United States.)

Sunday-school society: an organization the purpose of which was to foster the opening and maintenance of Sunday schools and to prepare and publish appropriate teaching aids and materials for them. (The first society was formed in England in 1785, and similar societies were subsequently organized in the United States.)

sunshade, playground: a light structure consisting of a roof on standards, without walls, furnished with benches, to provide shade for pupils who become unduly hot while at play; commonly provided in certain hot climates of the United States.

superego: (psychoan.) that component of mental life, as distinguished from *id* and *ego*, which represents the internalization of parental or other external authority demands to control instinctual (id) impulses; analogous to the lay term *conscience.*

superimposed high school district: *see* **high school district, superimposed.**

superinstitutional control: *see* **control, superinstitutional.**

superintendency, parish: the county superintendency in Louisiana, where the governmental subdivision referred to in other states as a county is designated as a parish.

superintendent: (1) (school admin.) primarily a coordinating officer who marshals many functions and specialists toward the accomplishment of the system's goals; a generalist in all aspects of school operations, a specialist only in the skill of coordinating; may be called school coordinating officer; (2) (mil. ed.) the principal administrative officer of a service academy.

superintendent, assistant: a member of the administrative staff of a school system who assists and is responsible to the superintendent for the management of certain phases of the administration.

superintendent, associate: a school administrator whose duties and responsibility are shared with one or more officials; usually second to the superintendent in authority.

superintendent, building: (1) an executive officer supervising the operation and maintenance of buildings and the care of grounds of a university, college, school, or school system; (2) a person employed by the architect or contractor to supervise the construction of a new school building.

superintendent, county: a person appointed or elected for a term generally of 2 to 5 years to perform various duties and functions relating to the supervision and management of all public schools in the county or only part of the schools of the county; functions vary from state to state, ranging from those required as chief executive of the county board of education to statistical and clerical duties required as representative of the state department; has been called *county commissioner* in Michigan, *parish superintendent* in Louisiana, and *division superintendent* in Virginia.

superintendent, deputy: a school official subordinate to the superintendent (usually next in authority) and authorized to exercise the powers and carry the responsibilities of the superintendent in the latter's absence.

superintendent, district: *syn.* **principal, district.**

superintendent, division: *see* **superintendent, county.**

superintendent of buildings: *see* **superintendent, building.**

superintendent of buildings, grounds, and equipment: one whose duty it is to administer and supervise the work connected with the operation and maintenance of the physical plant of universities, colleges, or schools.

superintendent of education: one of several terms employed to designate the chief state school officer; used only in certain states and territories; a different term may be used for the same officer in another state.

superintendent of free schools: formerly the designation of the chief state school officer and executive head of the central educational authority of the state of West Virginia.

superintendent of public instruction: one of several terms employed to designate the chief state school officer; used in only certain states and territories; a different term may be used for the same officer in another state. *See* **commissioner of education; director of education.**

superintendent of schools: (1) the chief executive and advisory officer charged with the direction of schools in a local school administrative unit, as in a district, city, town, or township or in a county or state; *see* **superintendent of schools, city; superintendent of schools, county; superintendent of schools, state;** (2) the designation of the chief state school official and executive head of the central educational authority of several states and similar districts.

superintendent of schools, city: (1) the chief advisory and executive officer of a city school system, usually elected by the local board of education and responsible to it, with few of his powers defined by state statute; (2) the advisory and executive officer responsible for the more directly instructional and supervisory aspects of schools in cities that have a dual or multiple type of administrative organization.

superintendent of schools, diocesan: (R.C. ed.) the educational official appointed by the bishop of a diocese and charged with the direction of the schools within the diocese.

superintendent, parish: *see* **superintendent, county.**

superintendent, rural school: a person appointed by a board of education to administer a single rural school or group of rural schools.

superintendent, state: *see* **superintendent of public instruction.**

superintendent, supervisory role of: that aspect of the superintendent's behavior pattern directed toward providing leadership to teachers and other educational workers in the improvement of instruction.

superintendent's report: *see* **report, superintendent's.**

superior child: *see* **child, superior.**

superior mental ability: *see* **intelligence.**

superior, mentally: measuring 130 IQ or more on the Stanford-Binet test and showing advanced achievement.

superior public use: the principle on which is based the decision about whose claim is most important in eminent domain proceedings involving two governmental agencies. *See* **eminent domain.**

superiority, general: a factor in one of the theories of giftedness, namely, that the gifted person is an all-round superior person.

supermaximum salary: *see* **salary, supermaximum.**

supernatural: pertaining to that which is above or beyond nature or which transcends the natural; divine.

supernaturalism: a doctrine which holds that there is something in the world above the order of nature; the precise meaning depends upon the concept of *nature;* in Roman Catholic usage, *supernatural* refers to the action and effects of God beyond, relatively or absolutely, the power or due of creatures (thus, sanctifying grace, miracles, etc.); in the usage of materialists and naturalists, it refers to anything immaterial or beyond the methods of science (for example, the soul).

supernormal: considerably above the norm in physical or mental development, or both. *Dist. f.* **abnormal.**

superordinate relationship: *see* **relationship, superordinate.**

superstition: (1) fear of superhuman power; (2) irrational attitude of mind toward the unknown; (3) acceptance of beliefs or practices groundless in themselves and inconsistent with the degree of enlightenment reached by the community to which one belongs.

supervised agricultural activities: *see* **program, supervised agricultural experience.**

supervised agricultural experience program: *see* **program, supervised agricultural experience.**

supervised club activity: *see* **activity, supervised club.**

supervised correspondence instruction: *see* **correspondence study, supervised.**

supervised correspondence study: *see* **correspondence study, supervised.**

supervised farm practice: *see* **program, supervised agricultural experience; program, supervised farming.**

supervised farming program: *see* **program, supervised farming.**

supervised home study: *see* **home study, supervised.**

supervised occupational experience, distributive education: *see* **experience, distributive education supervised occupational.**

supervised occupational experience program, agricultural: *see* **program, supervised agricultural experience.**

supervised play: *see* **play, supervised.**

supervised student teaching: *see* **student teaching.**

supervised study: *see* **study, supervised.**

supervised-study movement: an agitation for supervised study which started in America in the first quarter of the twentieth century and continued during the 1920s and 1930s; later it received less emphasis.

supervised teaching: *see* **teaching, supervised.**

supervising architect: *see* **architect, supervising.**

supervising principal: *see* **principal, supervising.**

supervising teacher: an experienced teacher employed in the local school system to work with high school students and to supervise college students during their student-teaching experience. *Syn.* **cooperating teacher; resident teacher.**

supervision: (school admin.) that function of control which evaluates current action while in progress and assures that execution is taking place in accordance with plans and instructions; the only function of control that can lead directly to corrective action while execution is taking place.

supervision, allocation of: delegation of supervisory talent, authority, and responsibility for carrying out tasks in a manner which will be consistent with the best interests of the organization.

supervision as teaching: a supervisory theory derived from a concept of supervision as the teaching of teachers about teaching; in this concept procedural elements are similar to those which guide teachers in their work with students.

supervision, attendance: the process of promoting and enforcing satisfactory attendance. *See* **attendance enforcement.**

supervision, authority-centered: supervision perceived by the supervisor as based on authority, absolute principle, and line organization as a means of carrying out the instructional policy of the school system.

supervision, autocratic: dictatorial direction of the instructional activities of teachers.

supervision, cabinet plan of: a type of supervisory organization in which the principal confers with a cabinet composed of school officials who in addition to having certain administrative duties (such as acting as dean of girls or as director of extraclass activities) are also department heads responsible for the direction of instruction in their respective departments.

supervision, concepts of: ideas involved in the development of a consistent and comprehensive program which seeks to influence other persons in the achievement of appropriate selected instructional expectations of educational service.

supervision, contributory function of: *alt. sp.* **contributary;** performance of tasks under independent or prescribed controls that constitute assistance toward achievement of results appropriate to the purpose ascribed to the organization and assigned to specific line positions.

supervision, cooperative: a plan for improvement of instruction according to which teachers and supervisors are regarded as coworkers, the teachers participating in analyzing and determining such aspects of instruction as objectives, materials, and methods.

supervision, coordinate organization of: a plan according to which the principal authority for supervision and administration resides in the superintendent and his assistants, but a number of additional groups (such as the principals, subject-matter supervisors, and directors of supervisory agencies) are regarded as parallel and coordinate to one another, the functions, duties, and areas of responsibility of each being unequivocally defined; coordination of these several groups is effected by the efforts of the superintendent and his assistants, on the basis of democratic cooperation and frequent consultation among all groups.

supervision, core: supervision of instruction in a core-curriculum program. *See* **curriculum, core.**

supervision council: *see* **council, supervision.**

supervision, creative: a constructive plan or program for the improvement of instruction through the cooperative efforts of teachers and supervisors, in which initiative, imagination, originality, and experimentation are encouraged.

supervision, curriculum: processes used to evaluate the body of courses as well as planned school activities that are offered by an educational institution.

supervision, democratic: *syn.* **supervision, cooperative.**

supervision, departmental: a plan for the delegation of responsibility to each department head for the improvement of instruction within the departments, the principal coordinating the work of the several department heads.

supervision, dynamic: an orientation to the various tasks of supervision designed to change supervisory programs; emphasis is placed on discontinuity, disruption of existing practices, and the substitution of different practices. *Comp. w.* **supervision, tractive.**

supervision, evaluation of: appraisal of the processes and functions of supervision.

supervision, expectations of: anticipation of the outcomes of directive, inspectional, and evaluative processes of supervising.

supervision, extrinsic-dualistic organization of: a plan of supervision according to which overlapping authority is delegated by the superintendent to two groups consisting of the assistant superintendents, principals, and department heads, on the one hand, and the special supervisors or other directors of supervisory agencies on the other hand, both groups having supervisory and administrative authority. *See* **supervision, coordinate organization of; supervision, line-and-staff organization of.**

supervision, grade-level: a type of supervisory organization in which each supervisor is assigned to assist the teachers of a particular grade or restricted number of grades. *Dist. f.* **supervision, vertical.**

supervision, health: school procedures for observing pupil health conditions and for protecting the health of individual pupils.

supervision, in-classroom: visitation by the supervisor in the teacher's classroom while instructional activities are in process; a method for carrying out supervisory objectives, which is one of several means available for cooperative planning between supervisor and teacher. *Contr. w.* **supervision, out-of-classroom.**

supervision, in-service: learning how to supervise and how to be supervised while concurrently performing other duties within the school organization.

supervision, individual-centered: supervision based on the realization that individuals should carry out their own self-defined tasks with as little direct assistance as possible, thereby allowing for individual freedom, responsibility, and variety in reaching solutions to educational problems.

supervision, inspectional: a plan based on a narrow concept of supervision, usually limited to the rating of teachers and teaching on the basis of classroom visitation.

supervision, invitational: assistance in the improvement of instruction rendered to teachers on their own initiative or request. *Syn.* **on-call supervision.**

supervision, line-and-staff organization of: a plan of supervision providing for two groups of supervisory officers: (*a*) the line officers, such as the superintendent, principals, and department heads, to whom the teachers are directly responsible; (*b*) the staff officers, including special supervisors and directors of other services such as research and guidance, who have no direct authority over teachers but who provide assistance of an advisory nature, acting as consultants to the line officers. *See* **supervision, coordinate organization of; supervision, extrinsic-dualistic organization of.**

supervision materials: *see* **materials, supervision.**

supervision, multiple: simultaneous supervision by an instructor of the activities of more than one group of students; facilitated by the use of glazed partitions.

supervision of schools, state: the overseeing of schools within the state by persons vested with authority by the state; may involve qualification and certification of teachers, maintenance of adequate opportunities for all pupils, judicial powers, and various other responsibilities relating to a state program of education.

supervision of teaching, state: the act or process of overseeing the qualification and certification of teachers and of teaching methods within the schools of the state, carried on by persons acting under authority of the state.

supervision, on-call: *syn.* **supervision, invitational.**

supervision, operational pattern of: design achieved through the directed balancing of a number of processes of supervision; observed through varying degrees of supervisory behavior characteristics as the processes and components thereof are carried on. *See* **balance, operational.**

supervision, opportunistic: a type of supervision that takes advantage of circumstances, with little or no regard for basic principles or ultimate consequences; for example, congratulating a teacher on her work but providing no assistance in helping solve teacher problems.

supervision, organismic: supervisory activity carried on through an interrelated group of functions analogous to those of the human body.

supervision, organizational pattern of: the arrangement of tasks that permits supervision to be carried out.

supervision, out-of-classroom: observation which is indirect, that is, outside the classroom situation, and which provides information on the basis of which the supervisory purposes may be achieved or assessed. *Contr. w.* **supervision, in-classroom.**

supervision, pattern of: the dynamic structure of a supervisory organization, which results from the interaction of incumbents within their particular position and their assigned tasks as well as from the reciprocal relationship between them and individuals occupying adjacent roles; also called action pattern. *See* **program, action-pattern.**

supervision, playground: the act or procedure of overseeing and directing activities of pupils on the playground.

supervision, practice: course- or classwork in a teacher-preparing institution that requires students to assume some or all of the actual duties or responsibilities of a supervisor, presumably under the direction of a specialist in the field.

supervision, preservice: supervisory activities in which organization members become involved prior to fulfilling requirements for new roles.

supervision, process of: administrative behavior chosen by persons involved in supervisory responsibilities as they attempt to influence other persons and situations in achievement of major tasks; components of this behavior are directing and controlling, stimulating and initiating, analyzing and appraising, and designing and implementing.

supervision, products of: those outcomes of the educational process which are the direct result of supervisory efforts.

supervision, professional: supervisory activities of persons who have had specialized preparation in the field; based upon maturity and ethics as determined by the particular profession.

supervision, recess: the act or procedure of overseeing and directing activities of pupils when excused from regular schoolwork during the recess period.

supervision, representative: a plan for the delegation of some of the responsibility for improvement of instruction to teachers from various areas of the school curriculum; the principal usually coordinates the work of these individuals.

supervision, rural school: those professional activities concerned directly with the improvement of the instructional service in rural schools; may be performed by the principal, superintendent, or county superintendent or by a person specifically designated for that purpose.

supervision, scientific: improvement of instruction through the application of the scientific method; characterized by testing programs, collection of data from many sources, statistical analyses, and the substitution of factual evidence for subjective judgment.

supervision, span of: *see* **control, span of.**

supervision, special-subject: supervision of instruction within a specified field, such as art, music, physical education, or special education.

supervision, staff: provision of assistance of an advisory and consultative nature to line officers, such as superintendents, principals, and departmental heads, to whom the teachers are directly responsible.

supervision, state department: the act or function of directing, overseeing, overviewing, or consulting with local school boards, administration, teachers, or community members on general or specific educational topics, subject areas, or interest areas by members of the state educational agency.

supervision, supportive function of: the performance of all supervisory tasks in a manner and to a purpose that will uphold and strengthen other personnel in achieving results properly expected of each as incumbent of an organizational position; includes policy determinations and implementations dealing with the improvement of the instructional program and requires reciprocal support from recipients of supervision.

supervision, tasks of: an array of major goals or undertakings toward which the supervision program is directed; illustrative are developing curriculum, organizing for instruction, staffing for instruction, providing instructional materials, providing in-service education, and evaluating educational programs.

supervision, teacher: all efforts of designated school officials directed toward providing leadership to teachers in the improvement of instruction; involves the stimulation of professional growth and development of teachers, the selection and revision of educational objectives, materials of instruction, and methods of teaching, and the evaluation of instruction.

supervision, tractive: an orientation to the various tasks of supervision that stresses maintenance as distinguished from change in instructional practices; characterized by emphasis upon coordination, articulation, enforcement, and resistance. *Comp. w.* **supervision, dynamic.**

supervision, units of: *see* **control, span of.**

supervision, vertical: a type of supervisory organization in which subject supervisors assist teachers of all grades in the improvement of instruction. *Dist f.* **supervision, grade-level.**

supervision via radio: supervision of instruction carried on directly, through messages from state, county, or city school officials broadcast by radio to teachers and other schoolworkers, or indirectly, by the example of well-planned and expertly executed radio lessons.

supervisor: the professional person responsible for the promotion, development, maintenance, and improvement of instruction in a given field. *See* **consultant** (2); **coordinator** (5) and (6).

supervisor, activities: a teacher who directs and manages a nonclass activity of a school, such as the pep club, the school annual, etc.

supervisor, adult distributive education: a person employed by a local board of education or a tax-supported institution of higher learning for the purpose of organizing, promoting, and supervising training courses designed for instructing workers on a part-time or continuing basis.

supervisor, art: *syn.* **director, art.**

supervisor, attendance: (1) an attendance officer of a school system who is responsible for coordinating the work of a subgroup of attendance officers; (2) *syn.* **attendance officer.**

supervisor, business and office education area: *see* **supervisor, business and office education assistant state.**

supervisor, business and office education assistant state: a staff member of the state department of education whose duties include general supervision of business and office education in all state-supported schools.

supervisor, census: (1) a member of a school system's administrative staff who is responsible for the maintenance of the school census; (2) in a large city, the staff member responsible for the maintenance of the school census in one of the city's census districts.

supervisor, college: (teacher ed.) a staff member of the college or university who regularly visits or observes student teachers; supervisors are sometimes identified as *special supervisors* when they supervise in a special field or in certain subjects or grade levels, and as *general supervisors* when they supervise student teachers regardless of specialties; the college supervisor usually has additional responsibility for on-campus seminar or college courses. *Dist. f.* **critic teacher; supervising teacher.**

supervisor, community: (R.C. ed.) a person appointed by a religious order or community to exercise general supervision over instruction in the schools conducted by its members. *See* **community** (3); **order, religious.**

supervisor, curriculum: *syn.* **curriculum specialist.**

supervisor, departmental: the supervisor who is responsible for the instructional activities of a specific department; may be the head or chairman of the department in a single school, but in large school systems he frequently works in several schools.

supervisor, diocesan: (R.C. ed.) a person appointed by the diocesan superintendent of schools or by any other authority to exercise a supervisory function in the parish schools of the diocese, regardless of the particular religious order in charge of the schools. *Dist. f.* **supervisor, community.**

supervisor, distributive education area: *see* **supervisor, distributive education assistant state.**

supervisor, distributive education assistant state: a staff member of the state department of education whose duties include general supervision of distributive education in all state-supported schools.

supervisor, district: a supervisor who is responsible for the instructional activities of a given school district.

supervisor, elementary school: a person who devotes full time or more than half time to the supervision of instruction in one or more elementary schools.

supervisor, general: the supervisory officer who is responsible for all the instructional activities of a school system; often an assistant superintendent, director, or principal. (Usually a principal is general supervisor only in a school system having one or two school buildings.)

supervisor, group-directed-work: a person who subscribes to the idea that the most effective method for improving educational practice is through groups working together in identifying and solving problems.

supervisor, inner-directed: a supervisor who is able to perceive the immediate solution to educational problems by relying on his own wise judgment rather than on formal decision making at the organizational level.

supervisor, intern: a person who functions as an apprentice with a qualified supervisor in order to learn or master the elements and the functions of supervision.

supervisor, job: *see* **training sponsor, business and office education; training sponsor, distributive education.**

supervisor of audiovisual instruction: *syn.* **director, audiovisual.**

supervisor of business and office education, state: a member of a state department of education whose duties include general supervision of business and office education in all state-supported schools.

supervisor of distributive education, state: a member of the state department of education whose duties include general supervision of distributive education in all state-supported schools.

supervisor of guidance and testing: *syn.* **director of guidance.**

supervisor of guidance, state: an official of the state department of education who (*a*) visits and evaluates local school guidance programs; (*b*) enforces minimum certification requirements; (*c*) provides consultative services to local schools, including assistance in initiating, expanding, and evaluating local programs, helping schools establish in-service education programs in guidance and counseling, preparing and distributing pertinent literature to the schools, and assisting in the organization of local professional groups; (*d*) conducts research; and (*e*) performs miscellaneous related services, such as providing speakers and consultants to nonprofessional groups.

supervisor of home economics, state: a member of the state department of education whose responsibilities include the supervision of programs in home economics for homemaking and for gainful employment in state-supported junior and senior high schools as well as post high school technical programs and adult programs in home economics.

supervisor of nurses: an administrative official who directs activities of nursing personnel.

supervisor of physical education, state: a member of the state department of education whose duties include general supervision of health and physical education in all state-supported schools.

supervisor of practice teaching: *see* director of student teaching.

supervisor of publications: *syn.* adviser of publications.

supervisor of special classes: any school officer charged with the responsibility for the supervision and improvement of instruction and instructional materials within classes organized to serve exceptional children, such as the mentally retarded, physically handicapped, etc.

supervisor of student teaching: *see* director of student teaching.

supervisor, playground: (1) the administrative head of a playground system; (2) a person who supervises a particular activity, such as athletics, throughout a playground system. *Dist. f.* director, playground.

supervisor, publication: *syn.* adviser of publications.

supervisor, school library: a member of the staff of a library or of a local or state board of education who inspects school libraries and advises and directs the school librarians.

supervisor, special: any school officer charged with responsibility for the supervision and improvement of instruction and instructional materials within a specified field, such as music, art, physical education, or special education.

supervisor, state public school: a state-appointed or state-elected official, usually an assistant to the chief state school officer, charged with the improvement of instruction through school visitation.

supervisor, subject: one who supervises instruction in only one subject or in a few related subjects.

supervisor, training: *see* training sponsor, business and office education; training sponsor, distributive education.

supervisor's annual report of visits: *see* report of visits, supervisor's annual.

supervisor's monthly report of visits: *see* report of visits, supervisor's monthly.

supervisor's role: (1) those elements that constitute the talents and the professional repertoire of the supervisor; (2) those elements assigned to the supervisor as perceived by staff, others, or self.

supervisory and administrative management occupations training: *see* training, supervisory and administrative management occupations.

supervisory area: the particular subjects or activities within a school system in which a supervisor has responsibility for the improvement of teaching.

supervisory behavior: activities chosen by supervisors or the persons involved in supervisory responsibilities who set out to influence other persons and situations with respect to the task of directing the education of youth.

supervisory bulletin: a communication issued to teachers regarding such items as instructional procedures, materials, schedules, bibliographies, results of research, reports of committees, news items, and announcements.

supervisory capacity: the extent of the contributions that supervision can make toward the achievement of results appropriate to the purposes of an organization.

supervisory certificate: *see* certificate, supervisory.

supervisory climate: conditions prevalent that could possibly affect the processes involved in influencing others to strive to reach the goals set by an organization.

supervisory conference: *see* conference, supervisory.

supervisory effects: the results brought about by the efforts of those who try to influence others in the achievement of the goals set by an organization.

supervisory forum: *see* forum, supervisory.

supervisory improvement: *see* improvement, supervisory.

supervisory involvement: the inclusion of supervision within the complexities of the administrative structure under conditions which would require that a supervisor be a part of certain aspects of administration at all times.

supervisory leadership: showing an ability to lead and develop a program of meaningful supervision.

supervisory load: *see* load, supervisory.

supervisory observation: *see* observation, supervisory.

supervisory organization: *see* organization, supervisory.

supervisory personnel: *see* personnel, supervisory.

supervisory position: (1) a post that a supervisor holds in an organization, usually indicating an area of responsibility; (2) a way of thinking or a set of opinions about supervision.

supervisory program: *see* program, supervisory.

supervisory responsibilities: those areas or items in the educational program for which a supervisor is responsible and in which he is expected to account for his activities in an organized way; may include responsibilities assumed through appropriate delegation of authority.

supervisory role of principal: *see* principal, supervisory role of.

supervisory role of superintendent: *see* superintendent, supervisory role of.

supervisory role of teacher: *see* teacher, supervisory role of.

supervisory stimulation: the act or process of exciting to activity or growth or to greater activity or growth through the efforts of a supervisory officer in a professional capacity.

supervisory talent, allocation of: placement by chief administrators of supervisors in positions where their specialized service can be most appropriately used; also, the assumption by individual supervisors of the amount and kind of activity which they can reasonably manage and execute.

supervisory-teacher relationship: a state of affairs existing between persons having the professional responsibility of providing leadership for improvement of instruction on the one hand and the teacher on the other.

supervisory visits: attendance by a supervisory officer in a professional capacity at class sessions, individual conferences, or teachers' meetings or on inspectorial visits to school grounds, buildings, or activities; an outmoded term employed more often when supervision was regarded simply as a process of inspection and rating. *See* supervision; program, supervisory.

supervisory visits, invitational: attendance, upon request, by a supervisory officer in a professional capacity at class sessions or teachers' meetings or on inspectorial vists to school grounds, buildings, or activities.

supervisory visits, scheduled: attendance by a supervisory officer in a professional capacity at class sessions or teachers' meetings or on inspectorial visits to school grounds, buildings, or activities, according to a prearranged plan.

supinate: to turn the arm or hand so that the palm faces the front; also, to rotate the leg outward.

supine: lying on the back.

supine behavior: *see* behavior, supine.

supplementary education center: *see* center, supplementary education.

supplementary education, Jewish: Jewish education given after public school hours (Monday through Thursday) and on Sunday mornings, or on Sunday mornings only; the pupils attending such schools receive their general education in the public school.

supplementary farm practice: *see* farm practice, supplementary.

supplementary instruction: *see* **instruction, supplementary.**

supplementary reader: *see* **reader, supplementary.**

supplementary reading: *see* **reading, supplementary.**

supplementary reading materials: *see* **reading, supplementary.**

supplementary resource center: *syn.* **center, instructional materials.**

supplementary text: any textbook used in addition to the basic text for a course or subject.

supplies, art: materials employed in the visual and spatial arts that go into the product itself and are used in the process of creating the product, for example, pastels, paper, canvas, clay, paints, etc. *See* **art material; art medium.**

supplies, educational: articles or materials consumed in the course of use, such as ink, pencils, electric-light bulbs, and coal, as distinguished from relatively permanent articles of equipment that render service during a period of years, such as desks, carpets, window shades, and furnaces.

supplies, instructional: school supplies that are a direct aid to learning, such as paper, pencils, paste, scissors, and workbooks. *See* **supplies, educational.**

supplies, janitorial: articles and materials used by school custodians in cleaning, heating, and making replacements of parts of buildings and equipment. *See* **janitors' supplies.**

supplies, janitors': *see* **janitors' supplies.**

supply: (consumer ed.) the quantity of any goods that producers are willing to offer at various prices. *See* **demand.**

supply and demand, teacher: the ratio between the number of available teachers and the number of vacancies.

supply function: *see* **function, supply.**

supply, labor: *see* **labor supply.**

supply management: the practice of or organization for administering the requisitioning, procuring, and distributing of supplies for instructional and janitorial services.

supply reel: *see* **reel, supply.**

support agency, training: *see* **training support agency.**

support, Federal: financial support by the Federal government of educational programs and institutions; by some authorities the term is restricted to programs and institutions that are distinctly Federal in character and are Federally operated; quite commonly the term is loosely used as synonymous with *Federal aid.*

support, financial: money or money's worth provided for the operation, maintenance, and development of a school or other activity.

support, local: the financial provision for a school system supplied by a local administrative unit such as a school district.

support lying: (phys. ed.) a position used in floor or apparatus work in which the body is extended, partly lying, but with most of the weight supported by the arms.

support material: (mil. ed.) (1) verbal or visual connections between experiences and ideas being taught, including examples, comparisons, statistics, testimony, and definitions; (2) explanatory information which is used to clarify, prove, illustrate, or emphasize a point which a communicator wishes to make.

support, public: moral and/or financial support supplied by the public or its funds.

support, school: moral and/or financial support supplied for the operation and maintenance of schools by the public and its funds.

support stand: (phys. ed.) a position used in apparatus work in which the individual stands with most of the weight resting on the feet, but with shoulders above the apparatus and part of the weight supported on the hands.

support, state: (1) payment by the state government of a portion of the burden of cost of a governmental function, the balance being provided by local government; (2) assumption by the state government of a part of the cost of education.

supportive function: *see* **function, supportive.**

supportive function of supervision: *see* **supervision, supportive function of.**

supportive role: *see* **role, supportive.**

supportive therapy: *see* **therapy, supportive.**

supportive treatment: specialized treatment provisions applied as part of a general support program for persons with a major handicap or specifically to a secondary handicapping condition affecting learning, adjustment, or behavior.

suppression: periods of nonseeing in the structurally normal visual mechanism that result from an act of inhibition, a concession of the central nervous system to protect basic visual function; usually considered to be voluntary. *Syn.* **suspenopsia.**

suppression, alternating: alternate periods of nonseeing in the structurally normal visual mechanism, the signaling from one retina being inhibited or blocked while the signaling from the other retina reaches the level of interpretation. (The signaling from the two retinas is inhibited or blocked alternately.)

suppression, emotional: the voluntary restraint of the emotions or of overt emotional display under ordinary conditions of emotional stimulation.

suppressor test: *see* **test, suppressor.**

suppressor variable: *see* **variable, suppressor.**

supraordinate stimulus: *see* **stimulus, supraordinate.**

surd: a sound made by the obstruction of the breath in the mouth without the vibration of the vocal cords; for example, the sounds *k, p, t, wh. Syn.* **voiceless sound;** *contr. w.* **sonant.**

surety: one who has become legally liable for the debt or default of another; one bound with and for another who is primarily liable and who is called the principal obligor. (School fiscal officers are generally required to provide sureties for the faithful performance of their duties.)

surety bond: *see* **bond, surety.**

surface therapy: *syn.* **therapy, supportive.**

surgeon, flight: a physician specially trained in aviation medical practice whose primary duty is the medical examination and medical care of aircrew.

surgical technician: *see* **technician, surgical.**

surplus: the excess of the assets of a fund over its liabilities and liability reserves; or, if the fund has also other resources and obligations, the excess of resources over obligations. (The term should not be used without a properly descriptive adjective unless its meaning is apparent from the context; in institutional accounting, surplus is used to designate the excess of general current funds assets over liabilities of such funds.)

surplus property distribution: the act of allocating government surplus property among school districts.

surplus revenue deposit: the designation of a virtual gift to the various states of a monetary surplus accumulated by the U.S. Treasury Department, which was withdrawn from the United States Bank at the order of President Andrew Jackson and deposited in state banks in 1837, much of this money having been used thereafter for permanent school funds.

surrealism: an early twentieth century movement in art and literature in which artists attempted to express subconscious imagery through the use of fantastic or incongruous or unnatural juxtapositions and combinations of forms; Max Ernst, Salvador Dali, Giorgio de Chirico, and Marc Chagall, among others, are identified with this movement.

surrogate: a representation of a person which conceals from conscious recognition the identity of that person; for example, in a dream, a king may represent the dreamer's father.

survey: an investigation of a field to discover current practices, trends, and/or norms; may or may not include recommendations based on the data gathered. *See* **survey, school.**

survey, age-grade: the act of making and interpreting an age-grade table or of determining the number of pupils for each age in each grade.

survey, age-grade-progress: the act of making and interpreting both an age-grade table and a grade-progress table.

survey, attitude: any fact-finding, fact-collecting, and analytical technique that obtains and evaluates information concerning the attitudes of individuals and groups; the intent is to determine the level of morale within the organization to which they belong. Also called *morale survey.*

survey, behavior: a study that attempts to record the behavior of infants; it may be cross-sectional or longitudinal and employ ratings, systematic observations, measurements, and experiments; for example, Gesell's surveys leading to normative schedules of child behavior.

survey, building: a study of the physical plant of a school, college, or university, with respect to (*a*) effectiveness of operation and maintenance of the present plant, (*b*) utilization of existing buildings, (*c*) need for remodeling, improvement, and additions, and (*d*) estimated cost of improvements or additions and method of financing.

survey, community: (1) a fact-finding study of social conditions and resources, uses of community agencies, institutional practices, etc., as they exist at a given time in a given community; (2) (agric. ed.) systematic collection of data regarding farming conditions and practices and farm people in the school-patronage area, used to diagnose community needs, to provide teaching materials, and to evaluate progress in agricultural education.

survey, community educational: in its strictest sense, a study made to gather information for use by counselors, teachers, other adults, and students about training facilities in a particular geographical area; data about the various schools should include such basic items as identifying information (name of school, address, telephone number), curriculum, entrance requirements, fees, and scholarships available.

survey, community occupational: (couns.) a survey in the local community of the workers as well as their jobs, including investigation of the occupational distribution of the community's population, collection of specific information about particular occupations, and a check for local occupational trends which may be developing.

survey course: *see* **course, survey.**

survey course, science: *see* **course, science survey.**

survey, educational: *see* **survey, community educational.**

survey, employment: an investigation of the personnel requirements of local business and industrial establishments, often made by public schools or government agencies in connection with the organization of vocational classes.

survey, grade-progress: the act of making and interpreting a grade-progress table.

survey, health: an investigation of the health conditions prevailing among the persons enrolled in an educational institution or school system; is usually conducted at the beginning of each semester, and involves physical examinations by medical examiners and the recording of data concerning the health of each pupil or student.

survey, library: a scientifically conducted study of a library or group of libraries for the purpose of identifying areas of inadequacy and providing recommendations for improving library services.

survey, life-space: a basic concept of Kurt Lewin incorporating a study of the totality of coexisting facts that influence the behavior of an individual at a particular time; includes study of the structure and state of the person (P) and of the psychological environment (E).

survey mathematics: *see* **mathematics, survey.**

survey method: a research method that aims at ascertaining prevailing conditions; data are gathered through questionnaires, score cards, interviews, checklists, etc.; used for revealing status and central tendencies, making comparisons, making predictions, etc.

survey, morale: *see* **survey, attitude.**

survey movement: a movement in curriculum revision, beginning about 1910 and reaching its peak in the 1920s, for determining curriculum objectives through analytic surveys of human activities; initiated broad-scale curriculum studies to decide through surveys which materials should go into the curriculum; early in the movement, emphasized listings of specific objectives for generalized areas of human experience, but later stressed increased differentiation between objectives of individual development and those of general life activities; leaders associated with the movement include Bobbitt, Charters, Harap, Uhl, among others.

survey, normative: *syn.* **study, fact-finding.**

survey, occupational: (1) an investigation and evaluation to gather pertinent information about industries or occupations in an area, to determine the need for training, etc., for the purpose of improving or developing a vocational program; (2) (couns.) a study of occupational opportunities and employment trends, local or national, made by counselors or by student members of an occupations class. *See* **study, occupational.**

Survey Ordinance: *see* **Ordinance of 1785.**

survey, progress: *syn.* **inventory, progress.**

survey, promotion: an investigation of practices relative to promotion, including not only a grade-progress survey but also a study of factors used in determining promotion, causes of nonpromotion, plans for increasing promotions, etc.

survey, public opinion: a study of public sentiment carried out over a given area, usually with respect to a current question or problem of importance.

survey, reading: an investigation in which the reading abilities and habits of a school or class are studied through tests, inventories, observation, and the examination of records; an investigation of the reading abilities and habits of adults.

survey report: *see* **report, survey.**

survey, school: a study or evaluation of a school, a school system, or any part thereof; may be fact-finding, or may indicate the strong and weak features as judged by definite criteria; commonly concluded with suggestions for needed changes and/or recommendations for more desirable practices.

survey test: *see* **test, survey.**

survey, transportation: a complete study of pupil-transportation conditions and requirements.

survey unit: *see* **unit, survey.**

survey, vocational: *syn.* **survey, occupational.**

survey, vocational education: a study to obtain necessary information as a basis for the proper development of programs of vocational education. *See* **survey, occupational.**

suspenopsia: *syn.* **suppression.**

suspension: (1) the temporary, forced withdrawal of a pupil from school, resorted to by school officials for various disciplinary and other reasons; (2) temporary repeal of a law, practice, or privilege such as employment.

suspension, teacher: temporary severance of a teacher from his position by the employing authority; used occasionally as a disciplinary measure and also as an expedient while charges are being prepared against the teacher.

sustaining program: *see* **program, sustaining.**

swampland grant: the designation of a gift of swamplands, made by the Federal government to various states between 1849 and 1860 and used by many states to provide revenues for school purposes.

Swedish system: a system of exercises or of massage, modeled after Swedish procedures. (A term no longer widely used.)

sweep-check test: *see* **test, sweep-check.**

sweet lemon mechanism: an adjustive device or defense mechanism by which a person makes the unpleasant more acceptable through a form of rationalization—one in which he says, for example, "I know I failed but it's all for the best, as I'll make more money as a plumber than I will as a teacher." *See* **pollyanna mechanism.**

swimming, functional: swimming and other aquatic activities in which the objective is to acquire ability to handle oneself in any emergency in water. (Has special reference to swimming for military personnel.)

swimming pool: an indoor or outdoor basin or hollow space, walled with material such as tile, fire brick, or cement, which holds water for use in swimming.

swimming response: *see* **response, swimming.**

swimming, synchronized: rhythmic swimming movements performed in a definite pattern synchronized with a prescribed accompaniment. *Syn.* **water ballet.**

swinging voice test: *see* **test, swinging voice.**

switch: (data processing) (1) a physical device having two or more positions sensible by the computer; (2) an instruction in a program which is modified by the program to cause the computer to take alternative courses of action; usually an unconditional transfer or a NO OPERATION, the alternative condition (symbol value) of which is usually determined by one or more prior conditional transfers; for example, as a result of a conditional transfer, the computer might change at a later point in the control sequence a NO OPERATION to an UNCONDITIONAL TRANSFER, thus changing the course of subsequent processing.

switch, all-call: a switch on the control panel of a language laboratory which allows the teacher to speak to the entire group at one time.

switch, program selector: a switch at a student position in a language laboratory with which he selects the program he wishes to receive.

switcher, camera: a set of push buttons mounted on a box or panel that allows selection of the TV image from any of several cameras; the image can then be fed into a closed-circuit distribution system or to a broadcast transmitter.

switching, row: an arrangement on a distribution panel whereby a single switch programs an entire row of booths in a language laboratory.

syllabarium: *alt. sp.* **syllabary.**

syllabary: (1) in certain languages, a phonological way of writing syllables of words that notes the consonant articulations and indicates the vowels when necessary by a system of dots or other marks; (2) a table of syllables.

syllabic method: a method of teaching reading based on the study of the syllable as a word element.

syllabication: *syn.* **syllabification.**

syllabification: the act of dividing words into groups of letters constituting elements known as *syllables. Syn.* **syllabication.**

syllabize: (mus.) to substitute the syllable names for the letter names of tones. *See* **solmization.**

syllable: one or more speech sounds which represent a complete articulation or complex of articulation and form either a whole word or a unit of a word.

syllable, closed: a syllable ending in a consonant.

syllable, open: a syllable ending with a vowel, such as "so."

syllable-span test: *see* **test, syllable-span.**

syllabus: a condensed outline or statement of the main points of a course of study or of books or other documents.

syllabus, correspondence: *see* **correspondence study guide.**

syllogism (sil'ə·jiz'm): a formalized scheme of deductive reasoning, or of exhibiting deductive reasoning so clearly that its validity can easily be checked, consisting of two premises and a conclusion that must necessarily be true if both premises are true and having either the form "All *P*'s are *Q*'s; *x* is a *P*; therefore *x* is a *Q*"—as, for example, "All animals are mortal. All men are animals. Therefore, all men are mortal—or the form "All *P*'s are *Q*'s; all *Q*'s are *R*'s; hence all *P*'s are *R*'s," such as "All governors are men. All men are fallible. Therefore, all governors are fallible."

syllogism, deductive: *syn.* **syllogism.**

syllogistic reasoning: *see* **reasoning, syllogistic.**

symbol: (1) something that stands for an idea not intrinsically suggested by its form or character; thus, a word is a symbol that represents a sound combination to which we have attached meaning but has no meaning in and of itself; (2) (math.) a character, mark, or abbreviation representing an expression, quantity, idea, concept, or mathematical operation; (3) a character that represents a basic sound, as in phonetics; (4) a word that stands for an idea not literally represented by the word, such as "lily" for purity; (5) (art ed.) a sign representing an associative relationship with reality, such as a representation of reality in children's drawings exhibited in the use of lines, colors, and shapes having individual significance and referring to individual projections of creative and mental states; (6) (communications theory) a sign, producible by the person using it with the intent to modify the behavior of other persons in a specific direction; to be effective the sign must have the same meaning for the user as for the interpreter; *see* **sign** (3).

symbol, change of: (art ed.) in children's drawing, a term referring to the change of size and shape of emotionally significant parts of the symbol, such as exaggerated symbols for hands, which express reaching for something.

symbol-digit test: *see* **test, symbol-digit.**

symbol-E chart: *syn.* **chart, E.**

symbol-elaboration test: *see* **test, symbol-elaboration.**

symbol, expressive: (art ed.) that which not only suggests something else by reason of relationship, association, or convention, such as a cross for Christianity, but also has individual and emotional quality, such as a special symbol for crying eyes.

symbol, grouping: *see* **grouping symbol.**

symbol, language: a spoken sound or a written mark, such as a word, phrase, or sentence, that stands for a meaning intended by a speaker or writer.

symbol, mnemonic: a symbol chosen for the aid it affords to the human memory.

symbol, monosignificant: that symbol which points unambiguously to a simple referent or class of referents; for example, the symbols of science are regarded as monosignificant symbols.

symbol, pluralsignificant: that symbol the referent of which is deliberately vague or ambiguous; for example, the symbols of poetry are regarded as pluralsignificant symbols.

symbol, representative: (art ed.) *syn.* **symbol** (5).

symbol, significant: a symbol that calls out the same response in both self and others; a symbol which has a certain community of meaning; to be distinguished from a symbol to which a response, but not a self-conscious response, is possible.

symbolic coding: *see* **coding, symbolic.**

symbolic confusion: *see* **confusion, symbolic.**

symbolic development: *see* **development, symbolic.**

symbolic language: *see* **language, symbolic.**

symbolic level of hearing: *see* **hearing, symbolic level of.**

symbolic logic: *see* **logic, symbolic.**

symbolic program: *see* **program, symbolic.**

symbolic programming: *see* **programming, symbolic.**

symbolic thinking: *see* **thinking, symbolic.**

symbolism: (1) in general, the process, whether consciously or unconsciously carried out, of assigning broad meanings to specific things or ideas, so that the part comes to represent the whole; (2) (psychoan.) the result of unconscious thinking or of repressing an idea, desire, or the memory of an experience, so that an acceptable substitute is found and adopted to which is transferred and attached the original feeling, emotion, or concept, although one may not necessarily be aware of the transfer or of the real meaning of the substitute (according to Freudian psychology, many dreams have symbolic significance; thus, in Freudian theory, a child who hates his father may dream of killing a wolf, the wolf being, in this case, a symbol for the father); (3) a literary device consisting of veiled allusion, parallelism of thought, mixed metaphor, etc., with a view to suggesting more than is stated directly and of producing parallel meanings, the one written and explicit but of secondary importance, the other not stated but suggested, and of primary importance; (4) the use of conventional or traditional signs; the systematic employment of symbols.

symbolophobia (sim′bə•lō•fō′bi•ə): a morbid fear that one's speech or gestures may convey some symbolic meaning.

symbols of operation: abbreviations, marks, or characters that represent mathematical processes to be performed.

symmetric property: (math.) a property of a relation in a set if, whenever a is related to b, then b is also related to a; for example, for numbers the relations "is equal to" and "is not equal to" both have the symmetric property whereas the relation "is less than" does not.

symmetrical variable: *see* **variable, symmetrical.**

symmetry: (1) (math.) a property of some geometric figures; a figure is symmetric with respect to a point P if for every point A of the figure there is a point B of the figure such that P is the midpoint of the segment joining A and B; for example, a square is symmetric with respect to either diagonal, a circle with respect to any diameter; (2) of a frequency distribution, the state or quality of having equal frequencies at points equally distant above and below the mode; *contr. w.* **skew; skewness.**

sympathetic nervous system: *see* **nervous system, sympathetic.**

sympathism: a mechanism by means of which the individual unconsciously avoids a problem or obstacle by obtaining sympathy from others.

sympathy: (1) an emotion composed both of concern for others who are in difficulty or who are suffering and of some degree of feeling similar in kind to that of the sufferers under observation; *contr. w.* **empathy;** (2) concern for the sufferings of either the self or others; (3) a relationship among things so that what affects one affects the others; (4) a disposition to agree.

symphony: a musical composition in a series of related movements in the form of a sonata, for performance by an orchestra.

symposium: an instructional technique in which two to five persons qualified to speak with authority on different phases of the same topic or on closely related topics present a series of related speeches. *Dist. f.* **panel.**

symposium forum: *see* **forum, symposium.**

synagogue school: originally, the reading and study of the Torah in the synagogue under the direction of teachers who, about the time of Christ, became known as *rabbis.* (After the fall of Jerusalem, these schools commonly became known as *rabbinical schools.*)

synchromism: *syn.* **orphism.**

synchronization, lip: *see* **lip synchronization.**

synchronize: (1) in sound-picture production and projection, to make the required adjustments so that the sound and the corresponding action occur simultaneously; *see* **lip synchronization;** (2) to adjust a synchronizer (or the camera shutter with which a synchronizer is to be used), so that flash bulbs may be fired while the shutter is wide open during an instantaneous exposure; *see* **synchronizer.**

synchronized motion-picture projector: *see* **projector, synchronized motion-picture.**

synchronized swimming: *see* **swimming, synchronized.**

synchronizer: (1) an electrical or mechanical device intended to be attached to a camera shutter, by means of which it is possible simultaneously to make an instantaneous exposure and fire one or more flash bulbs; *syn.* **flash synchronizer;** (2) (data processing) an instrument which, when transmitting information from one device to another, compensates for a difference in rate of flow or time of occurrence of events.

synchronizer, flash: *syn.* **synchronizer.**

synchronous linguistics: *see* **linguistics, synchronous.**

synchronous motor: *see* **motor, synchronous.**

synchronous variation: *see* **variation, synchronous.**

synchrony: in programmed instruction, a method of presentation of items, in which both stimuli and responses change from item to item in the series or in which neither the stimulus nor the response changes from item to item (as in repetition). *Comp. w.* **asynchrony.**

syncopation: generally speaking, any deviation from the normal pulse of meter, accent, and rhythm; the misplacement of the strong and weak beats of an established rhythmic pattern.

syncope (sing′kə•pē): (1) a brief period of unconsciousness; a fainting; (2) the omission of one or more sounds from the middle of a word.

syncretic thought: *see* **thought, syncretic.**

syndrome (sin′drōm; sin′drə•mē): (1) a complex of symptoms that is typical of a given physical or psychological condition but lacks characteristic pathology; (2) a number of characteristic symptoms occurring together which help to explain one's behavior.

syndrome, chronic brain: *see* **brain syndrome, chronic.**

syndrome, Down's: *see* **mongolism.**

syndrome, Gerstmann's: a complex disorder of cerebral functions accompanying a lesion, classically giving rise to right-left disorientation, finger agnosia, dysgraphia, and dyscalculia.

syndrome, Strauss: a pattern of symptoms exhibited by certain children with learning disabilities, most of whom are mentally retarded although they can represent the full range of intelligence; includes primarily hyperactivity, uninhibited actions, perseveration, and perceptual disorders; though both behavioral and biological criteria identify this syndrome, it is not necessary to assume an etiology of neurological impairment.

synergetic: working together; said of muscles that cooperate in performing an action.

synergy: (1) cooperative interaction of various elements of a system; implies that the gains of coordinated efforts are greater than the sum of independent efforts; (2) in guidance, the total energy manifested by a group; the energy developed by the individuals working together.

synesthesia: linkage of two perceptual modalities, as, for example, provocation of the subjective auditory image of a fog horn or other deep tone by the color blue.

synonym: a word that has the same or nearly the same meaning as another word in the same language.

synoptic: affording an overall view; pertaining to a synopsis; descriptive of a statement of agreement on a broad basis, perhaps among views which in minor ways are divergent.

synoptic thinking: *see* **thinking, synoptic.**

syntactics: one division of the study of signs, dealing with the way in which signs of various classes are combined to form compound signs; it abstracts from the signification of the signs it studies and from their uses and effects. *Dist. f.* **pragmatics; semantics.**

syntality: (1) the total inferred attributes and behavioral characteristics of a group, corresponding to personality in an individual; the element within the group that develops out of the combined efforts of the leader and the group members in developing problem-solving skills and applying them to the solution of problems; (2) (school admin.) the abstract entity defined by measures of the accomplishment of the organization (or group) as an organization.

syntax: the area of grammatical study dealing with sentence structure and word relations as established by usage.

syntax count: a statistical study of the number of times different grammatical factors affecting structure and word order in language occur in a representative number of running words.

synthesis: (1) a putting together, after comparison and evaluation, of several sets of findings or points of view to evolve a general point of view embracing what appear to be the sound elements of the several sets; (2) (math.) a method of logical thought or mathematical procedure in which a structure of proof is built up from initial assumptions, the movement of thought being from the known to the unknown and from the simple to the complex; (3) (read.) putting together word parts in sounding a word; (4) (couns.) the process through which data collected about a counselee and his problem are organized to reveal assets and liabilities.

synthesis of partial impressions: *syn.* fusion of partial impressions.

synthesizing ability: *see* ability, synthesizing.

synthetic approach to phonics: *see* phonics, synthetic approach to.

synthetic geometry: *see* geometry, synthetic.

synthetic method: (1) a procedure in which principles, laws, or generalizations are developed as a result of the accumulation, classification, examination, verification, and evaluation of information, facts, results of experimentation, and observation of specific cases or instances; (2) a method of proof that consists in drawing a series of necessary conclusions until the desired conclusion is reached; (3) a method of proof that is entirely independent of algebraic or analytic techniques; (4) a method of teaching reading based on the mastery of progressively larger and more complex units, beginning with the letters of the alphabet, followed by the syllables, then with monosyllabic words through polysyllabic words, to phrases and whole sentences; (5) (art ed.) a creative approach consisting of adding parts or details together to make a whole; for example, a person modeling in clay may add the single parts, arms, head, legs, feet, etc., to the body instead of pulling them out from the original lump of clay; *ant.* analytic method (2).

synthetic proof: *see* proof, synthetic.

synthetic reasoning: *see* synthetic method.

synthetic research: *see* research, synthetic.

synthetic thinking: *see* thinking, synthetic.

synthetic validity: *see* validity, synthetic.

system: (1) in general, the structure of organization of an orderly whole, clearly showing the interrelationships of the parts to each other and to the whole itself; (2) in systems analysis, a combination of machine service, material service, and labor service to accomplish information handling operations, as, for example, the method of processing orders for merchandise; (3) hardware, such as an automatic computer system, or some item of software, as a compiling system; (4) in reference to a social organization of mankind, a portion of a total society, analogous to a system of the human body such as the circulatory system,

system, binary: *see* number system, binary.

system, binary number: *see* number system, binary.

system, blind-writing: *see* blind-writing system.

system, Borstal: *see* Borstal institution.

system, case: *see* case system.

system, caste: *see* caste system.

system, central nervous: *see* nervous system, central.

system, central sound: *see* central sound system.

system, channel: *see* channel system.

system, coordinate: *see* coordinate system.

system, counseling: *see* counseling system.

system, data-handling: *see* data-handling system.

system, decimal: *see* decimal system.

system, deductive: *see* deductive system.

system, dial-a-tape: *see* dial-a-tape system.

system, dial-access information retrieval: *see* information retrieval system, dial-access.

system, dual-track: *see* curriculum, multiple-track.

system, duodecimal: *see* duodecimal system.

system, electric: *see* electric system.

system, electronic data processing: *see* data processing, electronic.

system, grade point: *syn.* point system (2).

system, Hollerith: *see* Hollerith system.

system, honor: *see* honor system.

system, honors: *see* honors system.

system, induction loop: *see* induction loop system.

system, information: *see* information system.

system, information retrieval: *see* information retrieval system.

system, instructional: *see* instructional system.

system, ladder: *see* ladder system.

system, marking: *see* marking system.

system, master antenna: *see* master antenna system.

system, mathematical: *see* mathematical system.

system, metric: *see* metric system.

system, number: *see* number system.

system, numeration: *see* numeration system.

system, office: *see* office system.

system, point: *see* point system.

system, programmed instructional: *see* programmed instructional system.

system, quarter: *see* quarter system.

system, reference: *see* reference system.

system, response: *see* response system.

system, selective: *see* selective system.

system, self-monitoring: *see* self-monitoring system.

system, sensory response: *see* response system, sensory.

system, sophisticated: *see* sophisticated system.

system, sprinkler: *see* sprinkler system.

system, student response: *see* student response system.

system, subsumption: *see* subsumption system.

system, time-sharing: *see* time-sharing system.

system, track: *see* track system.

system, training records and information management: *see* training records and information management system.

system, value: *see* value system.

system, warning signal: *see* warning signal system.

systematic designs: *see* designs, systematic.

systematic error: *see* error, systematic.

systematic sequence: a set of items to be learned that are arranged in the order of their probable importance or in their logical or psychological order.

systematized play: *see* play, systematized.

systems analysis: *see* analysis, systems.

systems analysis, educational: the process of identifying goals, considering all facts and resources in alternative approaches, and giving serious thought to the relation between input and output.

systems and procedures analysis: *see* analysis, systems and procedures.

systems approach: an integrated, programmed complex of instructional media, machinery, and personnel whose components are structured as a single unit with a schedule of time and sequential phasing; purpose is to ensure that the components of the organic whole will be available with the proper characteristics at the proper time to contribute to the total system, and in so doing to fulfill the goals which have been established.

systems chart: *syn.* chart, procedural flow.

systems design: (ed.) a conceptual framework for planning, with orderly consideration of functions and resources, including personnel and technical facilities such as television, the kinds and amount of resources needed, and a phased and ordered sequence of events leading to the accomplishment of specified and operationally defined achievements; should provide a way of checking on the relation of performances of all components to factors of economy and should reveal any inadequacies of the several components, including the faults of timing and consequently of the entire system. *See* kit.

systems designer: one who is skilled in applying the concepts of programmed instruction and related techniques, especially in an *instructional system.*

systems engineer: one who studies problems in industry, science, business, and government, and then organizes electronic data processing techniques and machine systems to solve them; works at the source and with management in the organization concerned.

systems engineering: *see* engineering, systems.

systems, organic: *see* organic systems.

t: *syn.* **ratio, t.**

T account: a teaching device in business education used for sorting and classifying journal entries in bookkeeping and for analyzing financial forms in which the debits and credits are not readily apparent to the student; consists of two lines in the form of a T, the debit items being placed to the left of the vertical line, and the credit items to the right.

t distribution; *see* **distribution, t.**

t distribution, noncentral: *see* **distribution, noncentral t.**

t, Fisher's: *syn.* **test, t.**

T formation: a style of offensive play in football in which the quarterback lines up directly behind the center and the three backs somewhat on a line behind the quarterback.

t function: *syn.* **distribution, t;** *see* **ratio, t; redundancy.**

T-group: a term which originated through the activities of the National Training Laboratory, Bethel, Maine; refers to a group which has as its objective the mobilization of group forces to support the growth of members as unique individuals simultaneously with their growth as collaborators; influences among peers are paramount in this learning process; the T-group differs from the therapy group in that it tends to utilize data about present behavior and its consequences rather than delve into genetic causes, to deal with conscious and preconscious behavior rather than with unconscious motivation, and makes the assumption that persons participating are well rather than ill. *See* **dynamics, group; training, sensitivity.**

t ratio: *see* **ratio, t.**

T scale: *syn.* **score, T.**

T score: *see* **score, T.**

t-stop: a system of calibration to rate the speed of lenses which is based on actual light transmission and is beginning to be recognized as more realistic than the older f/stop system. *See* **f. number.**

t, student's: *syn.* **test, t.**

t test: *see* **test, t.**

tab item: *see* **item, tab.**

table: a collection of data in a form suitable for ready reference. *See* **tabulation.**

table, age-grade: a series of age distributions arranged in parallel columns, showing the number of pupils of various ages in each grade of the school or school system, a separate age distribution being included for each grade.

table, classification: a table used in tabulating observations, made by identifying the rows by the tens' digits and the columns by the units' digits; thus, a tally mark in row 3 and column 7 would denote an observation whose value is 37. *Syn.* **classifier.**

table, coding: a table that gives code symbols (usually numbers) that correspond to data in another form; used as an aid in converting data into code or, sometimes, for decoding.

table, contingency: a two-way frequency table showing the frequencies of occurrence of the classes indicated by the rows and the columns of the cells; the variables are usually both qualitative, but both may be quantitative, or one qualitative and the other quantitative. *Syn.* **cross-classification table.**

table, correlation: *syn.* **diagram, scatter.**

table, cross-classification: *syn.* **table, contingency.**

table, cumulative frequency: a table that shows the cumulative frequency for each class interval. *See* **frequency, cumulative.**

table, decision: in automatic data processing, an array that lists combinations of conditions and consequences.

table, displacement: a table presenting, often in the form of percentages, the degree to which the correlation between two variables indicates the two variables to be unrelated; such a table might show, for example, the chances in 100 that an individual's score on the second variable will be, relative to his score on the first variable, in the same tenth or will be displaced by one-, two-, three-, etc., tenths.

table, double-entry: any table in which the entries are identified by the values or headings of both the rows and the columns. *Syn.* **double-frequency table; double-rating table; table of double entry; two-way table.**

table, double-frequency: *syn.* **table, double-entry.**

table, double-rating: *syn.* **table, double-entry.**

table, expectancy: (1) a table which expresses the relation between two or more variables by stating the probability that individuals who belong to each of a set of subgroups defined on the basis of one or more variables will belong to each of a set of subgroups defined on the basis of another variable; *see* **table, displacement;** (2) a series of predictive levels of success in tabulated form, such as an expectancy level of performance in arithmetic as predicted from a pupil's mental age or an expectancy quality or level of performance of a teacher as predicted from known qualifications of a candidate.

table, fourfold: a table showing the frequency of occurrence of each of the four possible classes formed by two variables when each variable is divided into two classes.

table, frequency: a table showing the various classes of scores or observations or other data together with their frequencies, frequencies usually being shown by numbers. *See* **simple frequency table; variate frequency table;** *contr. w.* **table, cumulative frequency.**

table, grade-progress: a two-way table showing the relationship between the length of time pupils have been in school and their grade placement. *See* **table, age-grade.**

table, intercorrelation: a table showing all the $n(n-1)/2$ coefficients of correlation existing among a group of n variables. *Syn.* **matrix, correlation; table of intercorrelations.**

table, mathematical: information summarized in tabular form either for a particular problem or, more frequently, for general reference, such as a table of square roots or a table of logarithms.

table, multiple frequency: a table showing three or more variables, such as a tabulation of unemployed by age, sex, country of birth, and occupation.

table of double entry: *syn.* **table, double-entry.**

table of intercorrelations: *syn.* **table, intercorrelation.**

table of specifications: (testing) a table which includes a test outline specifying what proportion of the items shall deal with each content area and with each type of ability; may also include other specifications, such as the number of items in the test, the time to be allowed for its administration, and descriptions of kinds of items that will or will not be included in the test.

table of units: a device, first used by Pestalozzi in the teaching of arithmetic, consisting of boards divided into squares upon which were placed dots or lines concretely representing each unit up to 100; by means of this table of units the pupil obtained a clear idea of the meaning of the digits and the process of addition.

table, open-end: a frequency table in which one or both of the extreme classes are indefinite in extent, as "above 60" or "below 10."

table, progression factor: an orderly arrangement of the *progression factors* involved in a course of training.

table, scoring: any table used in converting scores into scale scores.

table, simple frequency: *syn.* **table, frequency.**

table, transformation: a table giving the values of the original scores and the corresponding transmuted scores. *Syn.* **transmutation table.**

table, transmutation: *syn.* **table, transformation.**

table, truth: in logic, a table set up to determine or exhibit those conditions which make a compound sentence true and those conditions which make it false. *See* **sentence, compound.**

table, two-way: *syn.* **table, double-entry.**

table, variate frequency: *syn.* **table, frequency.**

tabletop photography: *syn.* **macrophotography.**

taboo: a rigid traditional restraint, growing out of religion or custom, imposed by a society against a particular behavior believed to be wrong, improper, or dangerous.

tabula rasa (ta'bə•lə rā'sə): (Lat., lit., "a smoothed tablet") a theory developed by John Locke (1632-1704) that the mind is at birth a blank tablet and that the facts of sense experience (sense empiricism) are the means by which knowledge is attained. *See* **empiricism; knowledge, copy theory of; sensationalism.**

tabulate: to arrange and group data in order according to some prearranged system.

tabulating machine: (1) strictly, a machine activated by punch cards and designed to add the values that have been punched into the cards; usually also designed to list items and totals and to yield various cumulations and moments of series in printed form; may also, if it is of the alphabetical type, print verbal material that has been punched into the cards; *syn.* **tabulator;** (2) loosely, any one of several machines of the IBM or Remington Rand type, such as punches, sorters, or tabulators, used to facilitate the statistical treatment of data; *syn.* **punch-card machine.**

tabulation: (1) the act or process of grouping and classifying observations according to some prearranged system; (2) data grouped and classified in the form of a table.

tabulation, mechanical: automatic tabulation by a punch-card machine or other mechanical device.

tabulation report, annual: *see* **report, annual tabulation.**

tabulation sheet: a sheet for arranging and/or grouping data in order. *Syn.* **tally sheet.**

tabulation, test: a table of the scores made by a group of individuals, each score being represented in the table by a mark or tally.

tabulation tree: a method for tabulating with a single tally mark a compound pattern of responses to several items in a test or questionnaire; for example, the two classes male and female subdivide into white, Negro, and others, while each of the six classes (sex and color) subdivide into single and married; thus one tally mark in the appropriate box will indicate, for example, a married white male.

tabulator: *syn.* **tabulating machine** (1).

tachistoscope: attachment for or variation of the slide projector consisting of a diaphragm-type shutter for controlling illumination and duration of projected images of figures, words, silhouettes, etc.; used in the investigation and improvement of reading, spelling, and visual perception in general; also called *flash meter. See* **flash device.**

tachistoscopic method: a method of presentation of learning materials whereby an image is flashed on an overhead screen for 1/25th of a second and the student marks in workbook a symbol corresponding to the image flashed.

tachistoscopic technique: the presentation of words, phrases, sentences, numbers, or other graphic symbols by a tachistoscope, an optical instrument which flashes visual stimuli on a screen at controlled rates and areas of exposure.

tachylogia (tak'i•lō'ji•ə): *syn.* **tachyphemia.**

tachyphemia (tak'i•fē'mi•ə): a psychoneurotic speech disorder characterized by excessively and unnaturally rapid speech; a form of *dysphemia. Syn.* **tachylogia; tachyphrasia.**

tachyphrasia (tak'i•frā'zhi•ə; -zi•ə): *syn.* **tachyphemia.**

tackboard: (1) *syn.* **bulletin board;** (2) the narrow stripping of cork or composition materials usually located atop the classroom chalkboards or blackboards to provide a special surface for tacking display materials, or any similar stripping located elsewhere for tacking surfaces.

tactical officer: in a military training school or service academy, an officer in charge of those activities of the cadets or students that pertain to drill formations, instruction in the manual of arms, and other like military training exercises; popularly called "tac officer."

tactical training: *see* **training, tactical.**

tactile: *syn.* **haptic.**

tactile agnosia: *syn.* **astereognosis.**

tactile awareness: *see* **perception, tactile.**

tactile-kinesthetic method: *see* **kinesthetic method.**

tactile perception: *see* **perception, tactile.**

tactual: *syn.* **haptic.**

tactuality: a system for gaining information from the cutaneous surfaces of the body by means of active or passive contact; these surfaces receive various energy forms and channel the data to higher control centers for information processing.

tactuopalpebral reflex: *see* **reflex, tactuopalpebral.**

tag question: *see* **question, tag.**

tail: the part of the area of a frequency curve lying above or below any given value of the variable shown on the abscissa; as generally used, includes the area at one or both extremes and equals less than half the total area under the curve. *Contr. w.* **body.**

tailoring: (home ec.) a type of garment construction, typical for coats and suits, which requires the application of shaping principles not usually employed in the construction of dresses; such principles involve techniques of (*a*) strengthening certain edges, (*b*) stiffening certain portions, and (*c*) handling work so that the garment is molded or shaped as it is being constructed.

take: *n.* (shorthand) a dictation over a certain period of time at a stipulated speed.

take-away-carry method: *see* **subtraction, methods of.**

take-away method: *see* **subtraction, methods of.**

take-up: a mechanism which winds the tape or motion-picture film on the *take-up reel* after it has passed through the recorder or projector.

take-up reel: *see* **reel, take-up.**

tale, folk: a narrative which has been preserved through oral tradition, and which reflects the skill and artistry of an unknown representative (or representatives) of the common people of a region or a country. *See* **myth; tale, tall.**

tale, talking beast: a story, often a folk tale, in which animals speak and act as humans.

tale, tall: a folk tale expressing humor and exaggeration, generally having a strong "superhero" as a central figure who represents some area of American life and work, for example, Paul Bunyan, a lumberman, and Mike Fink, a keelboatman on the Mississippi. *See* **tale, folk.**

talent: capacity and ability in a special field, or natural aptitude capable of high functioning under training, as in visual art or music; does not necessarily imply a high degree of general intelligence.

talent agency: a promotion office for the distribution of publicity information and contract conditions for professional musicians, dancers, lecturers, and the like.

talent allocation: (admin.) the assignment of persons to the roles for which they have the best qualifications.

talent, project: *see* **project talent.**

talented child, academically: *see* **child, academically talented.**

talented youth project: *see* **project, talented youth.**

talk-back: use of an intercommunication system to provide voice contact between the television director and the crew or, in some closed-circuit applications, to permit students in remote classrooms to ask questions of the television instructor.

talk broadcast: *see* **broadcast, talk.**

talk, chalk: *see* **chalk talk.**

talking beast tale: *see* **tale, talking beast.**

talking book: *see* **book, talking.**

talking-book machine: a phonograph-record player specially designed to reproduce talking-book records and specially adapted for the use of the blind and other physically handicapped persons.

talking page: a trade name identifying an audiovisual device for individual learning that synchronizes a disk recording with the printed page and features easy random access to the sound by positioning an indicator to any place in the printed text.

talking typewriter: a computer-assisted machine which may be programmed to teach a variety of subjects, as well as reading and other language skills, through an electronic program presenting visual and vocal instruction while guiding the pupil's use of the typewriter keyboard; the pupil responds by depressing a typewriter key after computer-assisted questions are "spoken" by the machine; if he presses the wrong key, it locks and the computer tells him he is wrong.

tall tale: *see* **tale, tall.**

tally: *n.* a mark made in recording a count. *See* **tally** *v.*

tally: *v.* (1) to estimate; to count; (2) to make a tally, a score; (3) to make a mark connecting a group in counting, as a diagonal line through four vertical lines, made for each fifth count.

tally sheet: *syn.* **tabulation sheet.**

Talmud (tal′mŏŏd): *n. masc.* (Heb.) the body of Jewish civil and canonical law consisting of two parts: the *Mishnah*, the Jewish code of laws compiled by Rabbi Judah the Prince in Palestine about the year 220, and the *Gemara*, the analysis, discussions, and deductions of the Mishnah, made in the Babylonian and Palestinian academies during the third to the fifth centuries A.D.; serves as the core of the course of study in some Yeshivot and Orthodox day schools.

Talmud Torah (tal′mŏŏd tŏ′rä): *n. masc.; pl.* **Talmudei Torah** (tal·mŏŏ·dā′): (Heb., lit., "study of the Torah") a communal Hebrew school that provides a fairly intensive type of Jewish education after public school hours. *See* **weekday school, communal Jewish.**

Tanakh (tä·näkh′): (Heb.) an acronym for the three major divisions of the Hebrew Scriptures: Torah (Pentateuch), Neviim (the Prophets), and Ketuvim (the Writings); a major subject of study in the Jewish religious school.

tangible apparatus: devices, tools, or toys used in the education of the blind.

tangible personal property: *see* **property, tangible personal.**

tantra: one of the sacred writings of the worshippers in ancient India of Shakti, the female creative force personified.

tantrum: *see* **temper tantrum.**

tape breaking point: *see* **breaking point, tape.**

tape cartridge: a magazine or hard plastic case containing a reel or two of tape that is placed on a recorder without threading; reel-to-reel cartridges allow the tape movement to be controlled in either direction; endless-loop or continuous-loop cartridges can continue to play indefinitely but do not permit rewinding at will.

tape, change: in automatic data processing, a paper tape or magnetic tape carrying information that is to be used to update filed information (the filed information is often on a *master tape*).

tape deck: *syn.* **tape transport.**

tape drill: *see* **drill, tape.**

tape drive: *syn.* **tape transport.**

tape, dual-track monaural: tape which provides space for two full-length recordings, one on each half of the tape; the second track is played without rewinding by switching the position of the feed reel and the take-up reel and rethreading the machine; also called *half-track monaural tape* and *two-track monaural tape.*

tape, five-channel punched: (data processing) a serial or continuous form of record, punched in uniform communications code; five channels or positions are used in each column on the tape; frequently used as a master tape to enter nonvariable or repetitive information automatically in common machine language into data processing machines. *See* **tape, punch.**

tape, full-track: a monaural tape on which the recording covers the full width of the tape; also called *single-track tape.*

tape generation: one specified occasion in the numbered succession of times in which copies of a master tape are made from a previous copy.

tape, half-track monaural: *see* **tape, dual-track monaural.**

tape, half-track stereo: *see* **tape, two-track stereo.**

tape, leader: special nonmagnetic tape attached to ends of the tape that is used for recording, in order to identify and protect those ends.

tape library: *see* **library, tape.**

tape, magnetic: an acetate or plastic ribbon coated on one surface with tiny iron oxide particles; $1/4$-inch-width tape is ordinarily employed for magnetically recording audio for subsequent reproduction; special tapes of greater width are used for magnetic storage of data in computers; the most recent development is the 2-inch width used in videotape recording the entire television program, including the audio, video, and synchronizing and control signals.

tape, master: (1) in automatic data processing, a paper tape or magnetic tape carrying semipermanent information (such as a file of information); (2) the tape recording from which duplicates are made; frequently copied on metal disk records to insure the recorded material against loss by fire or by accidental exposure of the master tape to strong magnetic fields.

tape, paper: *see* **tape, punched paper.**

tape playback: a reproducer unit used only for playback of prerecorded tapes; it is not equipped to record.

tape, prerecorded: tape on which a program has already been recorded or duplicated for use.

tape, punch: a tape, usually paper, upon which data may be stored in the form of punched holes; hole locations are arranged in columns across the width of the tape; there are usually 5 to 8 positions (channels) per column with data represented by a binary coded decimal system; all holes in a column are sensed simultaneously in a manner similar to that for *punch cards.*

tape, punched paper: (data processing) a strip of paper on which data for subsequent processing are recorded by means of patterns of holes punched across the strip. *Syn.* **paper tape.**

tape recorder: *see* **recorder, tape.**

tape recorder, video: *see* **recorder, video tape.**

tape recording: *see* **recording, tape.**

tape recording, video: *see* **recording, video tape.**

tape, single-track: *see* **tape, full-track.**

tape speed: the movement of a tape past the recording head at a predetermined rate measured in inches per second (ips); the faster the speed, the better the audio quality or frequency response; standard speeds are $1\frac{7}{8}$ ips, $3\frac{3}{4}$ ips, $7\frac{1}{2}$ ips, 15 ips, and 30 ips; most standard recorders use $7\frac{1}{2}$ ips and $3\frac{3}{4}$ ips. (Note: Corresponding standard speeds in centimeters per second are 4.75, 9.5, 19, 38, and 76.)

tape, stereo (four-track): a single tape on which there are four separate tracks for recording; for stereo these tracks are recorded in pairs running in each of two directions, the first and third tracks being recorded in opposite directions; monaural four-track recordings are made one track at a time.

tape, sub-master: any copy of a *master* tape.

tape-to-card converter: *see* **converter, tape-to-card.**

tape transport: the mechanism which moves the tape past the heads of the recording apparatus; includes head assembly, motor, and controls for tape movement but does not normally refer to the electronic components which together with the transport mechanism constitute a tape recorder. *Syn.* **tape deck; tape drive;** *see* **input-output device, magnetic-tape; tape unit.**

tape, two-track monaural: *see* **tape, dual-track monaural.**

tape, two-track stereo: a recording tape with two separate parallel tracks both of which are recorded in the same direction; also called *half-track stereo tape.*

tape unit: a device consisting of a tape transport, controls, a set of reels, and length of tape which is capable of recording and reading information on and from the tape at the request of the computer under the influence of a program.

tape, video: a tape used to record picture and sound from television programs by a magnetic process; usually written *video tape.*

tapescript: the written text of that which is recorded on a tape for replay on a tape recorder.

tardiness: the act or state of being late; in school the term refers to a pupil's failure to be in a prescribed place, ready to begin work, at a prescribed time.

tardiness record: *see* **record, tardiness.**

tardiness report: *see* **report, tardiness.**

target culture: *see* **culture, target.**

target language: *see* **language, target.**

task analysis: *see* **analysis, task.**

task appraisal: (admin.) development and use of norms and tests which assess performance.

task, developmental: a task that arises at or about a certain time in the life of an individual; successful achievement leads to his happiness and success with later tasks, while failure leads to unhappiness in the individual, disapproval by his society, and difficulty with later tasks. *See* **task method.**

task method: a method of learning that involves use of a physical act called a *developmental task,* successful achievement of which leads to one's success with later tasks.

task observation: *see* **observation, task.**

task, standard: (for. lang.) questions and format of a test that are uniform for all taking the test.

task, visual: the work of the eyes in reading or in performing some other work requiring visual effort.

tasks checklist: *see* **checklist, tasks.**

tasks, initiating: *see* **initiating tasks.**

tasks of supervision: *see* **supervision, tasks of.**

taste, artistic: sensitivity to art form; taste implies power to discriminate among good, mediocre, and bad artifacts according to imposed standards and to make suitable choices according to a set of criteria; in art education the term is archaic. *See* **aesthetic judgment.**

taste discrimination: *see* **discrimination, taste.**

tau coefficient: *see* **coefficient, tau.**

tautology: in logical discourse, refers to a reiterated proposition equivalent in content to the original proposition; in some logical systems, taken to refer to propositions equivalent in logical force.

TAVOR aids: (for. lang. instr.) a commercial system of picture writing which when read tends to elicit specific linguistic responses.

tax: a compulsory charge levied by a governmental unit for the purpose of financing services performed for the common benefit. (Note: The term does not include specific charges made against particular persons or property for current or permanent benefits and privileges accruing only to those paying such charges, such as licenses, permits, and special assessments.)

tax anticipation: the practice of borrowing money for current expenditures in expectation of taxes to be collected.

tax anticipation notes: notes issued in anticipation of collection of taxes, usually retirable only from tax collections and, frequently, only from the proceeds of the tax levy whose collection they anticipate. *Syn.* **anticipation warrant.**

tax base: the value or unit to which the tax rate is applied to determine the tax due; in property tax, the base is the assessed valuation; in income tax, the base is net taxable income.

tax, blanket: (1) a uniform levy per month or year on the entire student body of a school or college to support one or more student publications and activities; (2) the share of a schoolwide fee assigned to publications or some other activity. *Syn.* **activity fee.**

tax capitalization: the act of determining the present worth of anticipated taxes on a property and adjusting the value of the property in accordance with such determination.

tax, capitation: any ungraduated tax levy on the individual, figured at so much per head or poll; the simplest form of personal taxation. *Syn.* **head tax; per capita tax; poll tax.**

tax commission: an official organization created for the purpose of administering the tax laws; sometimes given appellate jurisdiction.

tax, consumption: a tax on expenditures for consumer goods and services.

tax, corporation: any tax imposed on an industry organized as a corporation, such as a general property tax, a net profit tax, a gross earnings tax, or a franchise tax.

tax, corporation organization: a tax levied on a corporation for the privilege of incorporating; includes charter taxes, filing fees, capitalization taxes, initial fees, and franchise taxes.

tax, death: a form of levy, generally graduated as to rates, on property transferred at the death or in contemplation of the death of the owner.

tax, dedicated: *see* **tax, earmarked.**

tax delinquency: failure on the part of an individual, company, or corporation to pay taxes when due.

tax, direct: a tax that cannot be shifted from the original payer to the ultimate consumer of the good or service taxed.

tax, earmarked: a tax of which the revenues are designated for the financing of specific public services or projects.

tax, estate: a tax on the right to transmit property to heirs; the Federal death tax is an estate tax, assessed on the estate itself; the rate of tax depends on the size of the estate and not on the number or kinds of heirs. *Contr. w.* **tax, inheritance.**

tax, excise: a levy imposed on the sale of a particular commodity.

tax exemption: *see* **exemption, tax.**

tax, franchise: a levy imposed on the privilege to operate an enterprise or a public utility, granted by law to an individual or corporation.

tax, gift: a tax on the transfer of property by gift, under Federal law levied against the donor, under state laws against the donee; primarily a supplement to the *inheritance tax* to prevent easy evasion of death taxes.

tax, gross receipts: a tax based on total receipts from sales rather than on profits.

tax, head: *syn.* **tax, capitation.**

tax, hidden: an indirect tax which is incorporated in the price of the goods and services.

tax, homestead: a charge or pecuniary burden levied on the owners of residences used as homesteads.

tax, impact of: the immediate obligation of a tax or the immediate effect of the tax.

tax, incidence of: in general, the final resting place of a tax after all shifting of the burden has occurred.

tax, income: a tax imposed by the Federal government, most of the states, and some municipalities on the income of an individual, a firm, or a corporation; a *direct tax* levied on the *ability-to-pay tax theory.*

tax, inheritance: a tax collected from heirs on the right to receive an inheritance; the amount of the tax depends on the amount left by the deceased person to the heir and his family relation to the deceased.

tax, in lieu: (from the French *lieu*, meaning "place" or "stead") the designation of a tax theoretically regarded as a property tax but levied instead on some different base, such as gross earnings.

tax leeway, local: (1) freedom with respect to the limits of the local tax rate; (2) freedom in the establishment of tax rates or amount of taxes to be collected by the local government.

tax, local: a tax levied by a local administrative unit of government as distinguished from a state or Federal unit.

tax, minimum school: (1) the lowest legal tax that may be levied for schools; (2) the tax levied for the support of a *minimum school program.*

tax, per capita: *syn.* **tax, capitation.**

tax, poll: (1) *syn.* **tax, capitation;** (2) a tax levied at a flat rate per person; once required as a prerequisite to voting in some states.

tax, privilege: a government levy charged for a privilege granted by a state; a tax levied on a valid right to pursue an occupation, business, or profession; for example, a tax levied on the franchise of a railroad.

tax, progressive: (1) a tax levied at an increasing rate of taxation against income or property such that the rate increases as the tax base increases; (2) a tax whose effect is to take an increasingly larger percentage of income.

tax, property: a tax levied on real or personal property; usually based on a uniform and proportionate rate.

tax rate: the ratio of the tax to the tax base; the rate to be applied to the assessed value to determine the amount of tax.

tax rate, district: the amount of tax, expressed in terms of a ratio to assessed valuation, to be imposed on the taxable property in a district; usually expressed in mills per dollar, in cents per 100 dollars, or in dollars per 1,000 dollars of taxable property.

tax-rate structure: the method of application of the tax rate to the units of the tax base; may be proportional, graduated, progressive, degressive, regressive, apportioned, or percentaged.

tax reduction: the act or process of subtracting or abating an amount or item that is not subject to tax for some legal reason.

tax, regressive: (1) a tax against income or property where the rate of taxation diminishes with increases in the base; the rate of diminution may be constant, increasing, or decreasing; (2) a tax whose effect is to take a decreasing percentage of the income.

tax, regulatory: a tax used not only for purposes of public revenue but also to control by restriction economic development along any given line.

tax relief: the act of removing or transferring taxes in whole or in part from certain persons, classes of persons, properties, privileges, or governmental units to other persons, classes of persons, properties, privileges, or governmental units.

tax roll: the official list showing the amount of taxes levied against each taxpayer or property.

tax, sales: a tax levied upon a commodity at the time of sale; may be on specific commodities, such as liquor, gasoline, or tobacco, on all retail sales, or on all sales.

tax, school: a levy imposed for the support of schools.

tax, severance: a charge or levy imposed by a governmental unit, such as a state, for the removal by private enterprise of natural resources or raw materials from land or water under the jurisdiction of the unit.

tax, shared: a tax which one political unit (often a state) levies and collects and of which the proceeds are then shared in part with other political units (such as counties or cities) under a formula set by statute.

tax, shifting of: the process of passing the tax forward from one who pays the tax to a person such as the one who buys or uses the taxed article or service, for example, adding the gasoline tax to the price of the gasoline; a tax may also be shifted backward to the producer of the taxed commodity in the form of a lower revenue after taxes for the product or service purchased.

tax, single: a tax to be levied on a single object as the sole source of public revenue, especially by taking the entire economic rent of land. (The theory of a single tax on land was brought into prominence in the eighteenth century by the physiocrats and publicized in the late nineteenth century by Henry George.)

tax sources, earmarked: tax sources whose receipts are allocated by statute or otherwise for a particular use such as education.

tax, sumptuary: a tax designed to prevent the consumption of goods considered harmful to the health or welfare of society.

tax theory, ability-to-pay: the most common principle on which the tax burden is based; income, property, or consumption can be used as a basis for measuring the ability to pay, which, theoretically, is measured by sacrifice. *Comp. w.* **benefit theory of taxation.**

tax, use: a device to protect the sales tax from wholesale invasion; a state having a sales tax places a similar tax on the use of all articles on which no sales tax has been paid so that people are not encouraged to go out of the state to make tax-free purchases which they can then bring home.

tax, withholding: a method of collecting estimated income taxes as the income is earned rather than delaying payment until the end of the year; collected by deductions from payments due the taxpayer from employers.

taxation, benefit theory of: *see* **benefit theory of taxation.**

taxation, degressive: a tax structure according to which the size of the rate increases as the assessed amount decreases or diminishes as the assessed amount increases; taxation that discriminates either by degree or by value in favor of higher incomes against lower incomes.

taxation, diversity in: *see* **diversity in taxation.**

taxation, double: the act or process of levying taxes twice on the same taxable object or objects, whether by the same or by coordinate jurisdictions.

taxation, equity in: *see* **equity in taxation.**

taxation, flexibility of: *see* **flexibility of taxation.**

taxation, proportional: a system of imposing taxes in which the rate, expressed as a percentage, is uniform for each unit taxed.

taxes, commodity: taxes levied by both state and Federal governments on articles of trade or commerce, generally on some specific basis rather than on value; commodity taxes differ from a property tax only as to time of levy; the term includes customs, excise, and general sales taxes, for example, *liquor taxes* and *gasoline taxes.*

taxing limitations by state restrictions: restrictions placed upon the amount of taxes that may be levied by the local school districts; may be by state promulgation or more often by state legislation or state constitution; usually in terms of maximum millage that may be levied without popular approval although such restrictions may also be of an over-all nature including all taxes, both those levied with and those levied without popular approval.

taxonomy: a system of classification and the concepts underlying it.

taxonomy, business and office education: the department of knowledge that embodies the laws and principles of classification in the areas of business and office education with specific reference to the Dictionary of Occupational Titles. *See* **code, DOT.**

taxonomy, distributive education: the body of knowledge that encompasses the laws and principles of classification in the area of distribution and marketing.

taxonomy of counselor functions: the scientific classification of the duties and functions falling within the scope of the guidance counselor.

Taylor slate: a rigid frame, used in arithmetic by the blind, that has many rows of evenly spaced octagonal holes in which square types having a raised bar on one end and two points on the other are placed in different positions to represent the digits and zero; algebra type is also available. *Dist. f.* **cubarithme slate.**

teach-in: (higher ed.) a conference involving speeches and discussion, of one day or more in length, in which activists examine some controversial issue and attempt to arrive at conclusions concerning it. *See* **activist, student.**

teachable moment: that moment when the pupil recognizes a problem and conditions for learning are optimum.

teacher: (1) a person employed in an official capacity for the purpose of guiding and directing the learning experiences of pupils or students in an educational institution, whether public or private; (2) a person who because of rich or unusual experience or education or both in a given field is able to contribute to the growth and development of other persons who come in contact with him; (3) a person who has completed a professional curriculum in a teacher education institution and whose training has been officially recognized by the award of an appropriate teaching certificate; (4) a person who instructs others.

teacher absence: *see* absence, teacher.

teacher accountability: *see* accountability, educational.

teacher accounting: *see* accounting, teacher.

teacher, adjustment: *see* adjustment teacher.

teacher adviser: *see* adviser, teacher.

teacher, agricultural: *see* agricultural occupations teacher.

teacher, agricultural occupations: *see* agricultural occupations teacher.

teacher aide: *see* aide, teacher.

teacher, apprentice: *see* apprentice teacher.

teacher-aptitude test: *see* test, teacher-aptitude.

teacher, art: *see* teacher.

teacher, auxiliary: *see* teacher aide.

teacher, Bible: *see* Bible teacher.

teacher blue laws: *see* blue laws, teacher.

teacher, business: *see* business teacher.

teacher-centric methods: *see* methods, teacher-centric.

teacher-centric teaching: *see* teaching, teacher-centric.

teacher, certificated: *see* certificated teacher.

teacher certification: *see* certification, teacher.

teacher certification, state: the procedure by which the state department, or an agency thereof, authorizes the issuance of licenses or certificates that permit the individual holder to teach in the public schools of that state. *See* certification, state; certification, teacher.

teacher, circuit: *see* circuit teacher.

teacher classification: *see* classification, teacher.

teacher clerk: (1) a person with pedagogical training who is serving as a clerical worker in a school; (2) a clerical worker in the central office of a large school system who has charge of personnel records.

teacher, clinical: *see* clinical teacher.

teacher, cooperating: *syn.* supervising teacher.

teacher-coordinator: in fields such as business and office education and distributive education, a member of the school staff who teaches the related and technical subject matter involved in work experience programs and coordinates classroom instruction with on-the-job training; in cooperative office education he is responsible for administering the program and may or may not be responsible for the adult program in distributive education.

teacher, core: *see* core teacher.

teacher counselor: *see* counselor, teacher.

teacher, crisis: *see* crisis teacher.

teacher, critic: *see* critic teacher.

teacher education: (1) all the formal and informal activities and experiences that help to qualify a person to assume the responsibilities of a member of the educational profession or to discharge his responsibilities more effectively; (2) the program of activities and experiences developed by an institution responsible for the preparation and growth of persons preparing themselves for educational work or engaging in the work of the educational profession. *Syn.* teacher training.

teacher education curriculum: *see* curriculum, teacher education.

teacher education, director of: *see* director of teacher education.

teacher education, in-service: *see* in-service education.

teacher education, industrial arts: a college curriculum or program designed for the preparation of industrial arts teachers, leading to the bachelor's degree and involving both professional and technical course work.

teacher education institution: *see* institution, teacher education.

teacher education institution, state: *see* institution, state teacher education.

teacher educator: *see* educator, teacher.

teacher educator, business and office education: *see* educator, business and office education teacher.

teacher educator, distributive education: *see* educator, distributive education teacher.

teacher effectiveness: (1) the ability of a teacher to create a meeting and an interaction between the physical, intellectual, and psychological interests of the student and some given subject-matter content; the ability of the teacher to relate the learning activities to the developmental process of the learners and to their current and immediate interests and needs; (2) teacher behavior whether in a classroom or in relation to his or her faculty group; a basis for decisions as to award of tenure or continuing contract and for determination of worthiness for merit salary increases, though not as yet predictable or measurable by any definite criteria.

teacher efficiency: the degree of success of a teacher in performing instructional and other duties specified in his contract and demanded by the nature of his position.

teacher employment: *see* employment, teacher.

teacher evaluation: *see* evaluation, teacher.

teacher-evaluation checklist: *see* checklist, teacher-evaluation.

teacher examination: *see* examination, teacher.

teacher exchange: a placement bureau maintained by teachers' associations or by the various states or their educational institutions for the purpose of securing employment for the teachers who are registered with the exchange.

teacher federation: a group of affiliated local, state, or national teachers' associations, such as the Columbus (Ohio) Federation of Teachers, the Massachusetts Federation of Teachers, or the World Federation of Education Associations. (The American Federation of Teachers is affiliated with the American Federation of Labor and consists of state federations and local unions.)

teacher, full-time substitute: *see* substitute teacher, full-time.

teacher-grade: any aggregation of pupils reported on as a single group by the teacher; used as a unit in child accounting.

teacher, guidance: *see* counselor, teacher.

teacher guidance: *see* guidance, teacher.

teacher, half-time: *see* half-time teacher.

teacher, head: *see* head teacher.

teacher, helping: *see* helping teacher.

teacher, homebound: *see* homebound teacher.

teacher, homeroom: *see* homeroom teacher.

teacher, hospital: *see* hospital teacher.

teacher-hour load: *see* load, teacher-hour.

teacher housing: *see* housing, teacher.

teacher improvement: the professional betterment of teachers in service.

teacher in charge: *syn.* head teacher.

teacher in training: any individual who is enrolled and is participating in a program for the education of teachers or for the improvement of teaching skill, such a program being sponsored by a recognized teacher education institution.

teacher insurance: *see* insurance, teacher.

teacher, intern: *see* intern teacher.

teacher intern: a fifth-year teacher trainee involved in an off-campus in-service education experience.

teacher-intern: a staff member of a nursery school with duties very similar to those of an *associate* but with more involvement in diagnosis and planning; suggested training: B.A. or B.S. degree and enrollment in a college of teacher education or other institution which offers a program leading to certification. (In order to become certified by the American Montessori Society a teacher must first serve such an internship.) *See* **head teacher.**

teacher, itinerant: *see* **itinerant teacher.**

teacher, laboratory: *see* **laboratory teacher.**

teacher liability: *see* **liability, teacher.**

teacher librarian: *see* **librarian, teacher.**

teacher load: *see* **load, teacher.**

teacher-made test: *see* **test, teacher-made.**

teacher maladjustment: *see* **maladjustment, teacher.**

teacher, master: *see* **master teacher.**

teacher, mediated: *see* **mediated teacher.**

teacher migration: *see* **migration, teacher.**

teacher militancy: *see* **militancy, teacher.**

teacher morale: *see* **morale, teacher.**

teacher mortality: *see* **mortality, teacher.**

teacher-observation report: *see* **report, teacher-observation.**

teacher of exceptional children: *see* **exceptional children, teacher of.**

teacher orientation: *see* **orientation, teacher.**

teacher-parent conference: *see* **conference, teacher-parent.**

teacher placement: *see* **placement, teacher.**

teacher placement bureau: *see* **placement bureau, teacher.**

teacher, practice: *see* **teaching, practice.**

teacher preparation, in-service: *syn.* **teacher education, in-service.**

teacher, preschool: *see* **preschool teacher.**

teacher probation: *see* **probation, teacher.**

teacher promotion: *see* **promotion, teacher.**

teacher, public school: *see* **public school teacher.**

teacher-pupil conference: *see* **conference, teacher-pupil.**

teacher-pupil-parent planning: *see* **planning, teacher-pupil-parent.**

teacher-pupil planning: *see* **planning, teacher-pupil.**

teacher-pupil ratio: (1) the number of pupils in membership per classroom teacher; (2) the ratio of the number of teachers in a given school system to the number of pupils.

teacher qualification: *see* **qualification, teacher.**

teacher rating: *see* **rating, teacher.**

teacher rating scale: *see* **rating scale, teacher.**

teacher recruitment: *see* **recruitment, teacher.**

teacher registration: *see* **registration, teacher.**

teacher, regular: *see* **regular teacher.**

teacher, remedial: *see* **remedial teacher.**

teacher report: *see* **report, teacher.**

teacher requirements: *see* **qualification, teacher.**

teacher, resident: *syn.* **supervising teacher.**

teacher, resource: *see* **resource teacher.**

teacher, resource room: *see* **resource room teacher.**

teacher retention: *see* **retention, teacher.**

teacher retirement, state plan for: *see* **retirement system, statewide.**

teacher, rural school: *see* **rural school teacher.**

teacher selection: *see* **selection, personnel.**

teacher, special: *see* **special teacher.**

teacher specialist: *see* **specialist, teacher.**

teacher-sponsor: a teacher who advises and guides an activity group.

teacher status: the relative position of any instructor with respect to professional, legal, social, and other factors.

teacher strike: *see* **strike, teacher.**

teacher, student: *see* **student teacher.**

teacher, substitute: *see* **substitute teacher.**

teacher, supervising: *see* **supervising teacher.**

teacher supervision: *see* **supervision, teacher.**

teacher, supervisory role of: that aspect of the teacher's behavior directed toward assisting other teachers and educational workers in the improvement of instruction.

teacher supply: the number of teachers available for appointment who have valid, legal teaching certificates.

teacher technician: *see* **aide.**

teacher tenure: *see* **tenure, teacher.**

teacher, therapeutic: *see* **adjustment teacher.**

teacher trainer: *see* **educator, teacher.**

teacher training: *see* **teacher education.**

teacher-training course: *syn.* **course, professional.**

teacher training, director of: *syn.* **director of teacher education.**

teacher training, in-service: *syn.* **teacher education, in-service.**

teacher-training institution: *syn.* **institution, teacher education.**

teacher, traveling: *see* **traveling teacher.**

teacher turnover: *see* **turnover, teacher.**

teacher, visiting: *see* **visiting teacher.**

teacher work load: the responsibilities assigned to the teachers, including work involved in teaching classes, counseling, serving on committees, sponsoring clubs and other extraclass activities, etc. *See* **load, teacher; load, teaching.**

teacherage: a residence for a teacher or teachers located on or near the school grounds and owned or leased by the school district.

teachers' agency: a commercial employment agency that aids teachers in securing positions, the charge for such service being a certain percentage of the teacher's salary during the first year following placement.

teachers' association: a formalized group composed of teachers and other certificated personnel employed in a school district, state, or other area; may be established for various purposes, such as the advancement of teachers' welfare and the promotion of the cause of education; criteria for membership may be established consistent with the Civil Rights Act of 1964. *Syn.* **teachers' organization.**

teachers' association, local: a voluntary organization of teachers in a local district, county, or city; usually not affiliated with state or national education associations; primarily concerned with the improvement of the teachers' economic welfare, but also devoted to improving teaching efficiency, promoting educational reform, and conducting programs of social activities. (After 1870, many such associations were disbanded or reorganized, but since 1910 a large number have been established, especially in cities.

teachers' association, national: an organization of teachers that draws its membership from the nation as a whole.

teachers' association, state: an organization of teachers within a particular state that draws its membership from the state as a whole.

teachers' bonus: payment to teachers for summer-school attendance, travel, or outstanding achievement in addition to the contractual salary, or as an extra salary payment not provided for in the salary schedule or contract.

teacher's card: a special library borrower's card for teachers, giving certain extended privileges to meet their professional needs.

teacher's certificate: *see* **certificate, teacher's.**

teachers' club: *see* **club, teachers'.**

teachers college: (1) a degree-granting college specializing in the preparation of teachers and other education workers; (2) a college within a university that is responsible for the professional preparation of teachers. *See* **college of education;** *dist. f.* **normal school.**

teachers college, four-year: a teacher education institution supported by a state, county, or municipality or by private funds that offers 4-year curricula leading to standard bachelor's degrees.

teachers college, municipal: a teacher education institution supported by a municipality in connection with its public school system for the purpose of training teachers for its elementary and secondary schools; offers 4-year curricula leading to standard bachelor's degrees.

teachers college, private: a teachers college that receives its major financial support from other than state or local sources and that is not under the direct control of a state or local governmental agency.

teachers college, public: a teachers college supported by public funds. (May be a state teachers college, a municipal teachers college, or a college or school of education of a state university.)

teachers college, state: a teacher-preparing institution supported by the state to train elementary and secondary school teachers through 4-year curricula leading to standard bachelor's degrees or to professional degrees of baccalaureate ranking.

teacher's console: *see* **console, teacher's.**

teacher's contract: *see* **contract, teacher's.**

teacher's contract, abandonment of: *see* **abandonment of teacher's contract.**

teachers' convention: *see* **convention, teachers'.**

teachers' council: (1) a legislative or advisory body of teachers; (2) an organization composed of members elected by a given teaching staff for the purpose of participating in administration, promoting the welfare of teachers, and contributing to the advancement of education in general.

teacher's credential: *syn.* **certificate, teacher's.**

teachers' credit union: *see* **credit union, teachers'.**

teachers' curriculum: *syn.* **curriculum, professional.**

teacher's daily absence and tardiness report: *see* **report, teacher's daily absence and tardiness.**

teacher's daily register: *syn.* **record book, teacher's class.**

teacher's estimate: the judgment of a teacher concerning the achievement, ability, or capacity of a pupil.

teachers' ethics: *see* **ethics, professional.**

teachers' federation: a group of affiliated local, state, or national *teachers' associations.*

teacher's handbook: *see* **handbook, teacher's.**

teachers, induction of: *see* **induction process.**

teachers' institute: *see* **institute, teachers'.**

teacher's journal: *see* **journal, teacher's.**

teacher's license: *syn.* **certificate, teacher's.**

teachers' manual: *see* **manual, teachers'.**

teacher's medical examination: *see* **medical examination, teacher's.**

teachers' meeting: a gathering of instructors for a definite purpose; usually ordered and authorized by a superior authority. *See* **faculty meeting.**

teachers' meeting, sectional: (1) a meeting of teachers from within the boundaries of an area designated as a section for the purpose of improving instruction by professional contacts, discussions of mutual problems, and explanations of the work being done in various fields of instruction; (2) a meeting of a *teachers' association* held for the benefit of teachers in particular fields of instruction.

teachers' meeting via radio: a somewhat ambiguous term applied to the practice, adopted by some school systems and educational institutions, of having the superintendent or other official broadcast information or instructions to the entire teaching staff, as, for example, at the opening of each school term; principally a public relations technique.

teachers' oath: *see* **loyalty oath.**

teachers' organization: *see* **teachers' association.**

teachers other than classroom teachers per 1,000 pupils in average daily membership: the number representing the total full-time equivalency of teaching assignments minus the number representing the total full-time equivalency of classroom teaching assignments in a school system during a given period of time, multiplied by 1,000 and divided by the average daily membership of pupils during the period.

teachers per 1,000 pupils in average daily membership: the number representing the total full-time equivalency of teaching assignments in a school system during a given period of time, multiplied by 1,000 and divided by the average daily membership of pupils during this period.

teachers' reading circle: *see* **reading circle, teachers'.**

teachers' register: *see* **register, teachers'.**

teachers' seminar: *see* **seminar.**

teachers' seminary: *see* **seminary, teachers'.**

teachers' union: *see* **union, teachers'.**

teaching: (1) narrowly, the act of instructing in an educational institution; *syn.* **instruction** (1); (2) broadly, management by an administration of the teaching-learning situations, including (*a*) direct interaction between the teacher and the learner, (*b*) the preactive decision-making process of planning, designing, and preparing the materials for the teaching-learning conditions, and (*c*) postactive redirection (evaluation, redesign, and dissemination); (3) collectively, that which is taught, such as the teachings of a religious leader.

teaching aid: *see* **aid, teaching.**

teaching, all-day student: *see* **student teaching, all-day.**

teaching, apprentice: *syn.* **internship plan.**

teaching, Army method: *see* **Army Specialized Training Program.**

teaching assignment: *syn.* **assignment, teacher;** *dist. f.* **assignment, lesson.**

teaching assistant: (1) *syn.* **assistant teacher;** (2) (higher ed.) *see* **assistant.**

teaching, automated: *syn.* **instruction, programmed.**

teaching brother: (R.C. ed.) one who binds himself voluntarily by vows of poverty, chastity, and obedience and devotes his time to giving instruction in Roman Catholic schools or institutions of higher learning but who does not take holy orders.

teaching, cadet: *syn.* **internship plan.**

teaching certificate: *syn.* **certificate, teacher's.**

teaching, color: instruction in the field of color as an aspect of art expression, dealing with the creative and appreciative aspects of color; may include theory and practice through drawing, painting, and designing and the application of color to work in other fields; sometimes organized as a separate course of study, including such concepts as typical colors, color characteristics, color properties, color families, color harmony, and functional applications of color. *See* **color sensation; color theory; color wheel.**

teaching combination: the subjects or fields, such as English, chemistry, science, language, etc., in which a teacher is giving instruction simultaneously or in sequence during the school term.

teaching, concept: a method of teaching which emphasizes the usefulness of learning through the formation of consistent, generalized symbolic ideas; patterns of facts are stressed; as a response to the "knowledge explosion," aims at reducing the complexity of the environment, reducing the necessity of relearning at each encounter, and providing for direction, prediction, and planning; permits ordering of objects and events into classes and subclasses; may be conducted inductively, as by chemistry experiments, or deductively.

teaching, demonstration: teaching activities presented by skilled or experienced teachers for the purpose of illustrating educational materials, procedures, or techniques in connection with preservice or in-service education of teachers. *See* **class, demonstration.**

teaching device: a broadly inclusive term signifying any material or any means used by a teacher to promote, stimulate, or motivate learning, for example, textbooks, visual aids, models, projects, drills, reviews, outlines, discussions, etc.

teaching, diagnostic: the process of prescribing for pupils learning opportunities based on individually determined needs and objectives.

teaching, direct: an organization of instruction specifying definite items or skills to be taught at stated times and by systematic method. *Dist. f.* **teaching, incidental.**

teaching, directed: student teaching done under the guidance and supervision of a skilled or experienced teacher or supervisor. *Syn.* **guided teaching;** *see* **student teaching; teaching, practice.**

teaching, director of student: *see* **director of student teaching.**

teaching, discovery: any method of teaching purposefully organized to foster *discovery learning;* some writers distinguish between pure discovery and guided discovery, the distinction being in the amount of control exercised by the teacher over the direction taken by the student; in guided discovery the student is given less latitude in pursuing either false conjectures or directions irrelevant to the problem at hand.

teaching, effective: use of a plan for instruction or presentation which causes a desired change in the learners' behavior.

teaching, experience-centered: an effort to make learning more meaningful by correlating school, home, and community experiences.

teaching, family-centered: instruction that uses everyday problems and situations involving the entire cycle of family life and emphasizes the more intangible values as well as homemaking skills.

teaching fellow: the holder of a fellowship that requires some instructional activities.

teaching, graded student: *see* **student teaching, graded.**

teaching, guided: *syn.* **teaching, directed.**

teaching, incidental: the teaching of certain items or skills only as the need for them occurs in connection with other schoolwork or with the pupil's activities or interests. *Contr. w.* **teaching, direct.**

teaching, indirect: (1) any teacher activity that facilitates and contributes to learning but is not directly concerned with the teaching act; (2) the impact on or gains in learning of those who are not being taught directly but who identify with the students receiving direct instruction; a method of exploiting man's innate tendency to learn from modeling.

teaching, inductive: teaching in which generalizations are presented through a series of instances; students are encouraged to find and sometimes to state the "general idea" which applies to all of the cases.

teaching, intern: *syn.* **internship plan;** *see* **intern teacher.**

teaching interview: *see* **interview, teaching.**

teaching, intuitive: (kind.-prim. ed.) a method of teaching based on direct observation with accompanying discussion, followed by further discussion and reasoning about the ideas acquired by observation.

teaching license: *syn.* **certificate, teacher's.**

teaching load: *see* **load, teaching.**

teaching load, Douglass formula for: *see* **Douglass formula for teaching load.**

teaching load, equalization of: *see* **equalization of teaching load.**

teaching-load formula: any equation that attempts to measure the work of a teacher by giving consideration to factors believed to be involved in doing the work. *See* **Douglass formula for teaching load.**

teaching machine: a device that presents a program; the simplest form is a programmed text, the most sophisticated a computer; most machines control the material to which the student has access at any moment, preventing him from looking ahead or reviewing old items; many contain a response mechanism, that is, a tape on which the student writes, a keyboard, or selection buttons; some provision is made for knowledge of results, either by revealing the correct answer after the student responds or by advancing to the next item, thus signaling correct completion of the previous item; a few machines score responses and tabulate errors. *See* **stimulus-response device.**

teaching machine, adaptive: a teaching machine recently developed which will select the next step in a program on the basis of the student's response to the previous item. *See* **branching.**

teaching machine, computer-based: *see* **machine, computer-based teaching.**

teaching material: *syn.* **instructional material.**

teaching materials laboratory: *see* **laboratory, teaching materials.**

teaching, mediated: (1) in general, teaching that is conducted with communication media rather than the direct face-to-face interaction of the teacher with the student, for example, by print, film, recording, telephone, radio, television, or computer terminal; *syn.* **self-teaching;** *see* **materials, self-teaching;** (2) the process of designing the teaching-learning interactions and actually materializing the instructional decisions into any of the available modes of communication; this process takes place during the preactive phase of teaching, usually far in advance of the intended direct interaction of the learner with the mediated teaching.

teaching method: (1) a rational ordering and balancing, in the light of knowledge and purpose, of the several elements that enter into the educative process, the nature of the pupil, the materials of instruction, and the total learning situation; (2) a standard procedure in the presentation of instructional material and the content of activities, for example, the *Herbartian method,* the *Morrison plan,* etc. *Syn.* **instructional method.**

teaching, middle-class bias in: *see* **bias in teaching, middle-class.**

teaching ministry: *see* **ministry, teaching.**

teaching, nondirective: a technique whereby the instructor, as resource person, creates for the student an atmosphere of self-directed learning in order to encourage independent judgment, intellectual curiosity, strong motivation, and both subjective and objective evaluation; the target values therefore become self-understanding and growth in social, intellectual, and emotional patterns. *Contr. w.* **teaching, teacher-centric.**

teaching, object: a method of elementary school teaching derived from the work of Johann Heinrich Pestalozzi (1746-1827) in Europe and introduced into the United States in 1848 at the Westfield, Massachusetts, State Teachers College and in 1861 at Oswego, New York; based on the use and study of real objects, rather than textbooks, and characterized by oral instruction, careful planning of lessons, and the stimulation of student observation and inquiry; in practice, tended to become highly formalized and sterile. *See* **Oswego Movement.**

teaching, objective: (1) teaching in which the presentation and treatment of the subject are clearly defined and based as much as possible on factual material, with a minimum of subjective feelings and personal bias, and in which the evaluation of pupil achievement is made largely on a nonsubjective basis; (2) teaching based on concrete experiences and perceptions of sense or form rather than on abstractions and verbalization.

teaching, off-campus student: *see* **student teaching, off-campus.**

teaching, on-campus student: *see* **student teaching, on-campus.**

teaching, oral: a method of teaching an entire group of pupils by means of oral questioning and discussion as advocated by Pestalozzi, in contrast with an earlier method of individual recitation at the teacher's knee.

teaching order: a religious order whose members are primarily engaged in the work of conducting schools.

teaching, peer: working with others of similar developmental level to bring about change.

teaching period: *syn.* **period, class** (1).

teaching, positive: teaching a principle or other unit by means of an active attack rather than by a negative or passive approach.

teaching, practice: a term sometimes used to designate only those activities involved in actual teaching by a student teacher, as contrasted with student teaching, which may include observation and participation as well as *practice teaching*. See **participation; student teaching.**

teaching, prescriptive: (spec. ed.) a method of utilizing diagnostic information to modify educational programs for children with problems.

teaching, preventive: teaching intended to forestall or prevent the development of faulty habits or wrong learning.

teaching principal: *see* **principal, teaching.**

teaching principle: *see* **principle, teaching.**

teaching procedure: that which the teacher actually does, step by step, in any teaching-learning situation.

teaching, professionalization of: *see* **professionalization of teaching.**

teaching program, hospital: *see* **program, hospital teaching.**

teaching, project-centered: a method of presenting concepts of learning through practical experiences such as laboratory work.

teaching, pupil-centric: instructional methods or procedures developed with considerable regard for the interests, needs, meaningful problems, and learner participation of the learners involved as well as for the objectives of the school; logical organization of subject-matter and teacher-dominated activities are supplemented or replaced by psychologically appropriate, useful, and meaningful activities with respect to problems in which the learners are interested; examples are laboratory method, specialized discussion, pupil-teacher planning, cooperative procedures in learning. *Syn.* **group-centered instruction; nondirective instruction; student centered teaching;** *contr. w.* **teaching, teacher-centric.**

teaching, pyramid plan of: a teaching plan implemented by Pennsylvania State University; uses groups of 15 (6 freshmen, 6 sophomores, 2 juniors, and 1 senior who acts as group leader) in guided discussions; the group leader meets regularly with a faculty supervisor to define group objectives and issues to be considered and the techniques of small group leadership; promotes the systematic involvement of university students in teaching-learning functions with the goal of increasing motivation for academic development.

teaching, remedial: special instruction intended to overcome in part or in whole any particular deficiency of a pupil not due to inferior general ability, for example, remedial reading instruction for pupils with reading difficulties.

teaching sanction: (admin.) the authority under which teachers carry on the function of instruction.

teaching, science: *see* **science teaching.**

teaching sister: a nun who devotes her time to the instruction of the young in a convent school or parochial school. *See* **teaching brother.**

teaching skill: *see* **skill, teaching.**

teaching station: any one of a number of places or positions in a school or school system that require the services of a full-time teacher.

teaching steps: the sequence of activities prescribed for or planned by the teacher to arrive at instructional goals. *See* **Herbartian method; Morrison plan.**

teaching, student: *see* **student teaching.**

teaching, student centered: *see* **teaching, nondirective.**

teaching style: the characteristic manner in which a teacher conducts his interactions with his pupils.

teaching success: the extent of realization of instructional objectives as measured by the mental, physical, emotional, and social growth of the pupil. (Estimates of teaching success stem fundamentally from one's philosophy of education, out of which educational objectives are derived. Given a particular philosophy of education, the accuracy of such estimates depends on the measurability of achievement of the objectives and the quality of the measuring instruments.)

teaching, supervised: teaching that is directly observed by a supervisory teacher or administrative supervisor. *Syn.* **teaching, directed; teaching, guided.**

teaching, supervision as: *see* **supervision as teaching.**

teaching, teacher-centric: a method of teaching in which the teaching-learning situation is controlled primarily by the teacher, his ideas, his interests, and his plans.

teaching, team: (1) a type of instructional organization involving teaching personnel and the students assigned to them, in which two or more teachers are given joint responsibility for all or a significant part of the instruction of the same group of students; the team may include such assistants as auxiliary aides or student teachers; (2) a method whereby the teachers of adjoining rooms plan and work together so that pupils have a homeroom teacher and another teacher for other subjects.

teaching, team interim: teaching done by one who has completed the formal requirements for teaching and who is engaged in the first year of actual teaching as a member of a teaching team.

teaching technique: (1) a specific way of presenting instructional material or conducting instructional activities; (2) the teacher's manner and method of teaching.

teaching technology: all the artifacts and strategies used to aid in the teaching process, including media of instruction, learning laboratories, programmed learning, and teaching machines.

teaching, textbook: a method of teaching based mainly on the content and procedures of one or several textbooks.

teaching unit: *see* **unit, teaching.**

team game: any highly organized game or athletic sport played by teams of several players on a side, such as basketball, soccer, or hockey.

team grouping: *see* **learning, team.**

team interim teaching: *see* **teaching, team interim.**

team learning: *see* **learning, team.**

team, multidisciplinary: *see* **multidisciplinary team.**

team teaching: *see* **teaching, team.**

team training: *see* **training, team.**

tear sheet: a sheet or page torn from a publication, usually one containing an advertisement, and sent as proof of insertion to an advertiser; also supplied occasionally upon request in place of a *reprint*.

technical: pertaining to a mechanical or industrial art or applied science.

technical agriculture: *see* **agriculture, technical.**

technical analysis: *see* **analysis, technical.**

technical business subject: *see* **business subject, technical.**

technical consultant: *see* **consultant, technical.**

technical drawing: *see* **drawing, technical.**

technical education: (1) a type of education that emphasizes the learning of a technique or technical procedures and skills, and aims at preparing persons in the technical areas of distribution and marketing, in the more sophisticated areas of business and office education, etc.; originally did not lead to a degree or carry college credit but more commonly today involves transferable college credit and leads toward a 2-year associate degree; *see* **technical institute;** (2) those aspects of the program of *teacher education* which stress the use of special methods or techniques of teaching, such as the diagnosis of abilities and disabilities, remedial instruction, and test construction; *see* **course, professional.**

technical education, agricultural: an instructional program in agriculture and related disciplines designed to prepare technicians for nonfarm agricultural occupations and for production agriculture; a technician in agriculture is a semiprofessional, highly skilled worker located midway between the skilled person and the professional person in the developmental structure of jobs, in his work performance, and in his educational attainment; many technicians work in direct, supporting capacity with professional agriculturalists and agricultural scientists.

technical elite: *see* **elite, technical.**

technical high school: *see* **high school, technical.**

technical illustration: *see* **illustration, technical.**

technical information: (art. ed.) specific knowledge pertaining to the material, mechanical, and aesthetic aspects of art.

technical institute: an educational institution at the post-high school level which offers specialized education in one or more fields to prepare individuals for employment in positions which lie between those of the skilled worker or craftsman and the professional scientist or engineer; the programs may lead to the associate degree.

technical instruction, related: *see* **instruction, related technical.**

technical job: *see* **job, technical.**

technical journalism: *see* **journalism, technical.**

technical lesson: *see* **lesson, technical.**

technical manual: *see* **manual, technical.**

technical order: *see* **order, technical.**

technical professional education: *syn.* **technical education.**

technical report: *see* **report, technical.**

technical school: a school offering instruction in practical arts, usually below the level of higher education. *See* **high school, technical.**

technical services, library: *see* **services, library technical.**

technical training: *see* **training, technical.**

technician: (1) a person skilled or highly specialized in the method or practice of a particular trade, specialty, or the like, with special reference to mechanical details and the use of special techniques; one who has mastered the techniques of his art; (2) *see* **technical education, agricultural.**

technician, agricultural: *see* **technical education, agricultural.**

technician, electromechanical: a person who fabricates, tests, analyzes, and adjusts precision electromechanical instruments, such as temperature probes and aerodynamic probes, following blueprints and sketches, using hand tools, metalworking machines, and measuring and testing instruments.

technician, engineering: a graduate of a technical institute course of study qualified to carry out in a responsible manner either proved techniques which are common knowledge among those who are technically expert in a branch of engineering or those techniques which are specially prescribed by professional engineers; may also supervise work of others.

technician, industrial: a worker on a level between that of the skilled trade worker and the professional scientist or engineer.

technician, library: a member of the library and information personnel qualified to provide support to professional librarians and whose assignments may be more specialized than a clerical employee's or may involve more supervisory responsibilities.

technician, mechanical design: (voc. ed.) a subprofessional working in the technology concerned with the development, testing, evaluation, and design of machinery, equipment, instruments, and other mechanical devices prior to production and with the determination and design of the tooling required to manufacture a proposed product; may determine the suitability of design, materials, tooling, and fabrication methods and suggest modifications in design; may conduct performance and endurance tests of mechanically and electrically propelled devices, and determine weight and stress and strain of components.

technician, medical record: (voc. ed.) a worker who, under the supervision of the medical record librarian, a medical record committee, or a medical group supervisor, performs technical tasks associated with the maintenance and custody of medical records; certification depends upon graduation from an approved program, generally 9 months in length, and passing an accreditation examination.

technician, metallurgical: (voc. ed.) a worker who assists metal specialists by testing metals for strength and other characteristics, determining working characteristics, and designing and operating special laboratory equipment.

technician, production: (voc. ed.) a subprofessional working in the technology concerned with industrial engineering problems involving the efficient use of manpower, materials, and machines in mass production processes; may prepare layouts of machinery and equipment, plan the flow of work, investigate and analyze production costs, study different production methods, and develop recommendations pertaining to time allocations for production operations.

technician, surgical: (voc. ed.) an operating-room technician who performs a variety of tasks before and during the operation, for example, washing, shaving, and sterilizing operative area of the patient, cleaning the operating room, and assisting the surgeon with instruments and supplies.

technician, teacher: *see* **aide.**

technique: (1) a specific reproducible way of doing something, and therefore a predictably dependable process; (2) a process, manipulation, or procedure required in any art, study, activity, or production; (3) an instructional procedure designed to relate to the learner the material being presented in order to facilitate learning; (4) the ability of a human being to produce consistent results, for example, in music education, the ability to produce musical results with a given instrument such as the voice, the piano, or the violin, dependent on a variety of skills and their integration.

technique, action-potential: *see* **action-potential technique.**

technique, art: *see* **art technique.**

technique, cane: *see* **cane technique.**

technique, classroom: *see* **classroom technique.**

technique, cohort-survival: *see* **cohort-survival technique.**

technique, Cornell: *see* **Cornell technique.**

technique, critical-incidents: *see* **critical-incidents method.**

technique, delayed-response: *see* **delayed-response technique.**

technique, diagnostic guidance: *see* **diagnostic guidance technique.**

technique, double-testing testing: *see* **testing technique, double-testing.**

technique, echo speech: *see* **echo speech technique.**

technique, error-choice: *see* **error-choice technique.**

technique, Euler circles: *see* **Euler circles technique.**

technique, forced-choice: *syn.* **item, forced-choice.**

technique, "guess who": *see* **"guess who" technique.**

technique, Hoover: *see* **Hoover technique.**

technique, individual: *see* **interview technique.**

technique, interview: *see* **interview technique.**

technique, job-analysis: *see* **job-analysis technique.**

technique, laboratory: *see* **laboratory technique.**

technique, nominating: *see* **nominating technique.**

technique, O-: *see* **O-technique.**

technique, P-: *see* **P-technique.**

technique, play: *see* **play technique.**

technique, precane: *see* **precane technique.**

technique, program evaluation and review: *see* **PERT.**

technique, projective: *see* **projective technique.**

technique, Q-: *see* **Q-technique.**

technique, R-: *see* **R-technique.**

technique, Rogerian: *see* **counseling, nondirective.**

technique, rotation: *syn.* **design, counterbalanced.**

technique, self-confrontation: *see* **self-confrontation technique.**

technique, sighted guide: *see* **sighted guide technique.**

technique, sociometric: *see* **sociometric technique.**

technique, SQ3R: *see* **SQ3R technique.**

technique, structured or unstructured: *see* **structured.**

technique, tachistoscopic: *see* **tachistoscopic technique.**

technique, teaching: *see* **teaching technique.**

technique, touch: *see* **cane technique.**

technique, zero-group: *see* **zero-group technique.**

techniques, basal: *see* **basal techniques.**

techniques, conference: procedures used to stimulate discussion, in which the leader does not dominate the situation but encourages expression by each member of the group.

techniques, counseling: *see* **counseling techniques.**

techniques, guidance: *see* **guidance techniques.**

techniques, motivation: *see* **motivation techniques.**

techniques, nontest: *see* **nontest techniques.**

techniques of analysis: *see* **analysis, techniques of.**

techniques of diagnosis: *see* **diagnosis, techniques of.**

technocracy: (1) management of the whole of society by technical experts or in accordance with principles established by technicians; (2) a movement of the early 1930s which forecast economic doom unless certain economic institutions were abandoned and new principles of operation established, control to be in the hands of scientists and engineers.

technocratic change: *see* **change, technocratic.**

technological applications: (sci. ed.) the study of aspects of the earth and space sciences as oriented to the needs of individuals, industries, or government; includes applications in research, production, and human welfare.

technological education: that education which emphasizes the application of principles rather than their theoretical development.

technological unemployment: *see* **unemployment, technological.**

technology: (1) the systematic scientific study of technique; (2) the application of science to the solution of practical problems; (3) a systematic body of facts and principles comprehensively organized for a practical purpose; may include the principles of effective teaching; (4) the science or systematic knowledge of the industrial arts, especially as applied to manufacturing; (5) the material culture resulting from the combination of logic, mathematics, and science.

technology, drafting: *see* **drafting technology.**

technology, educational: (1) the application of scientific principles to the designing and implementing of instructional systems, with emphasis on the precise and measurable educational objectives, learner-centered rather than subject-centered orientation, strong reliance on educational theory to guide educational practice, validation of educational practices through empirical analysis, and the extensive use of audiovisual equipment in instruction; also used in a more limited sense to describe a reliance on equipment-oriented instructional techniques such as computer-assisted instruction, simulators, multimedia presentations, and media-based self-instruction; *see* **technology, instructional;** (2) a term applied to a 2-year post-high school terminal program which trains persons to assist teachers in kindergarten through grade 8.

technology, environmental: a 2-year post-high school terminal program emphasizing the knowledge and skills necessary for preparing the student to assist in occupations related to improving the community environment, for example, housing, sanitation, etc.

technology, industrial: that phase of technology employed to transform materials and energy. *See* **technology.**

technology, instructional: (1) the study of instruction and its techniques for the purpose of enhancing its systematic organization and dependability; (2) the comprehensive organization of principles, resources, personnel, and logistics that combine to produce gains in learning, there being several subordinate organizations such as behavior science technology, the technology of instructional materials and educational media, of behavior analysis and measurement, and of personnel management, including staff training and individualization of the curriculum. *See* **technique** (1).

technology, metal: the study of the production, processing, and transformation of metals into usable products with special emphasis on technical information; learning experiences generally include experimenting, designing, fabricating, forming, and evaluating metals and metal products; subject matter and learning activities are organized under this descriptive title and others such as general metals, metals, and metal machining (metals laboratory).

technology, plastics: (1) a category of information and skills concerned with the production, processing, and uses of plastics and related factors such as occupations, economics, and consumer information; subject matter and learning experiences are organized under various descriptive titles referring to plastics; (2) the study of the tools, materials, and processes used in several facets of the plastics industry; learning experiences include experimenting, designing, machining, fabricating, forming, and evaluating plastics and plastic products; (3) generic name for a technology employing a wide range of certain organic substances of high molecular weight, which at a suitable stage in manufacture can be molded, cast, or otherwise shaped, usually employing heat and pressure.

technology, power: the study of the source, generation, transmission, harnessing, controlling, and utilization of energy, usually with emphasis on internal combustion two-cycle and four-cycle engines, the automobile, and small engine industries; may also include the study of pneumatics, hydraulics, steam engines, reaction engines, steam, hydro, and gas turbines, and direct energy conversion; subject matter and learning experiences are organized under this descriptive title and others such as *automotive mechanics, power and automotive mechanics, power mechanics, power and transportation,* and *transportation.*

technology, teaching: *see* **teaching technology.**

technology, wood: the study of the wood manufacturing industries and the technology involved in the construction of buildings and the manufacture of articles made from wood and wood products; learning experiences usually include experimenting with, designing, and constructing wood products, evaluating woods and wood products, and using the tools, materials, and processes related to these industries; subject matter and learning experiences are organized under such titles as general wood laboratory, wood technology laboratory, and woodworking.

tectonic: pertaining to building or construction.

tectonic experience: *see* **experience, tectonic.**

Tele-class: a method of teaching homebound pupils as a group; the teacher uses an automatic dialer on his desk, and buttons on the telephone console enable him to talk to his whole class of homebound pupils or to each pupil privately; each pupil has his own telephone line at home, exclusively for the Tele-class, and may likewise be heard by the class or only by the teacher; he wears a light headset to keep his hands free for note taking, page turning, etc.

telebinocular (tel'ə·bin·ok'ū·lər; -bī·nok'ū-): an instrument resembling a stereoscope, mounted on a stand and used to test vision at ordinary reading distance to determine whether the reader has any difficulties of vision; also has remedial uses.

telecast lesson: *see* **lesson, telecast.**

telecasting: staging a program before the television cameras.

telecasting, low-power: operation, under amended rules of the Federal Communications Commission, of TV stations with as little as 100 watts of effective radiated power; prior to this ruling the minimum was 1,000 watts.

telecommunication: any transmission, emission, or reception of signs, signals, writing, images, and sounds of intelligence of any nature by wire, radio, video, or other electromagnetic systems.

telecourse: a full sequence of lessons offered over *closed-circuit* or broadcast television for credit or for auditing purposes; depending upon the individual institution sponsoring the activity, written requirements, reading assignments, and examinations are included.

telefilm: *see* **recording, kinescope.**

telelecture: an arrangement which brings a teacher or any lecturer to the classroom audience via regular telephone lines enabling the speaker to participate with several classes simultaneously at different locations; the installation may provide two-way communication between speaker and audience. See **blackboard by wire.**

telelesson: an Air Force term for a lesson specifically planned for presentation via television.

teleological argument: *see* **argument, teleological.**

teleology: (1) that character of causal action by which efficient (or mechanical) causes lead to a final end (cause); (2) in the philosophy of nature, teleology is the doctrine that there is some purpose, such as the will of God, directing the activity of all natural phenomena.

telephone communications industry: *see* **industry, telephone communications.**

telephone, home-school: two-way communication linking a homebound child with his regular classroom by telephone.

telephone instruction, school-home: *see* **instruction, school-home telephone.**

telephoto lens: *see* **lens, telephoto.**

telephotography: the technique in photography by which distant subjects are made to appear closer through the use of long-focus lenses.

teleprompter: a device originally designed to feed cues to television actors or teachers, now available also to speakers and lecturers; consists of a compact unit placed in front of the speaker which unrolls, at a speed controlled by the speaker or an assistant, words typed in letters eight times the size produced by a typewriter having pica type; using multiple units in synchronization, the speaker can apparently look directly at the audience as his own eyes travel back and forth from the teleprompters placed in front of and to the left and right of the lectern; recorders, projectors, and room lights can be turned off and on in synchronization with the speaker's delivery.

telescopic glasses: spectacles based on the principle of the telescope; occasionally prescribed for improving very poor vision that cannot be helped by ordinary glasses.

telescoping grades: a program for the gifted which enables a child to cover the same material as is offered in the regular curriculum but in a shorter period; an alternative to grade *skipping* which sometimes leaves a gap in a child's experience. See **skipping** (1).

telesis: *see* **social telesis.**

television: the transmission and reception by electromagnetic waves of moving visual images and of the sound produced by or accompanying them.

television class: *see* **class, television.**

television, closed-circuit (CCTV): a television system which limits distribution of an image to those receivers which are directly connected to the origination point by coaxial cable or microwave link.

television, educational (ETV): (1) noncommercial broadcasting (may not accept advertising) transmitting the broad range of educational, cultural, and entertainment programs and also programs designed for use by schools in connection with regular school courses; (2) any broadcast or *closed-circuit television* program related to some form of instruction or peripheral enlightenment.

television fixed service, instructional (ITFS): programming occupying the 2500 Megahertz band to provide educators with nonbroadcast, multiple-channel television service for transmission directly to schools.

television, instructional (ITV): lesson-planned programs, systematically developed and conducted largely in school systems or universities; may be offered on commercial television or ETV, UHF, ITFS, or standard microwave, open (broadcast) and/or closed-circuit television. See **television fixed service, instructional.**

television, mirror-image: the use of the video tape recorder to record and play back for self-critique. *Syn.* **self-confrontation television.**

television recording: *see* **recording, television.**

television, self-confrontation: *see* **television, mirror-image.**

television, subscription: a plan whereby a person selects and pays for the type of television program he desires; for example, a program may be delivered to the receiver in coded form and the subscriber is then charged for the decoding key required to unscramble the picture and sound.

telewriting: use of telephone lines for transmission of graphics to accompany audio information; provides visual displays of graphic material on a TV monitor or similar device in the classroom while simultaneously permitting two-way conversations between teachers and students at separate locations. See **telelecture.**

telic (tel'ik): tending toward an end or goal; purposive; sometimes used in connection with progress to mean purposed or planned progress, in contrast to progress that occurs by chance variation or survival.

telic function of education: a concept affirming the need for teachers and educators to play a directive role in shaping society on the basis of knowledge; held necessary since superstition, sentiment, and personal ambition have dominated our social goals; elaborated in detail and defended by Ross L. Finney.

telic social order: *see* **social order, telic.**

telic society: *syn.* **social order, telic.**

telling method: an educational procedure wherein the learners are given information orally in a classroom or lecturelike situation, with a minimum of learner participation except for listening; most frequently used with reference to elementary school instruction or in vocational education in place of the term *lecture method* and in contradistinction to the terms *showing method* and *doing method.*

Telop: *see* **projector, opaque.**

temper tantrum: a pronounced outburst of anger evoked when the young child is thwarted, particularly in social situations; sometimes related with other symptoms indicating a neuropathological condition.

tempera, powdered: *see* **equipment, early childhood education.**

temperament: the affective and emotional aspects of personality, with special reference to mood and degree of activity.

temperament test: *see* **inventory, adjustment.**

temperament trait: *see* **trait, temperament.**

temporal distribution: *syn.* **distribution, historical.**

temporal series: *syn.* **series, time.**

temporary certificate: *syn.* **certificate, emergency.**

temporary discharge: the temporary dropping of a pupil from the roll after a certain number of days of absence and pending his return to school; rapidly becoming obsolete. *Syn.* **temporary left;** *see* **dropping of pupils.**

temporary exclusion: *see* **exclusion, temporary.**

temporary hearing loss: *syn.* **fatigue, auditory.**

temporary injunction: *see* **injunction, temporary.**

temporary left: (obsolescent) *syn.* **temporary discharge.**

temporary mounting: *see* **mounting, temporary.**

temporary permit: a temporary authorization allowing a youth to work; usually given to permit the youth to work until the *age and schooling certificate* can be granted.

tenacity: a method of fixing belief by repeating constantly to oneself any answer one has chosen to a question, by dwelling on everything that may confirm one in this belief, and by rejecting anything that might shake its fixity, the basis of the rejection being emotional commitment to the belief.

tendency, actualizing: *see* **actualizing tendency.**

tendency, reversal: *see* **reversal tendency.**

tennis: a game played by two or four people with rackets and an elastic ball on a level court divided by a low net.

tennis, paddle: a game for two or four players using tennis balls or rubber balls and a solid paddle; the ball is struck back and forth over a net with a paddle into a specified court or area; the game is played like tennis.

tenor: the highest male voice (except that of a male soprano who uses a falsetto voice) with a range, usually of two octaves, from C below middle C to C above middle C.

tenotomy (te·not'ə·mi): the surgical cutting of a tendon for corrective purposes.

tensiometer, cable: a small apparatus designed to measure the pull on a wire cable; used in physical education in measurement of muscular strength.

tension: a state of biological and psychological readiness; preparedness to meet a real or imaginary situation with energy; manifested by increased muscular tone, heightened reflexes, and excitability of the cardiac and respiratory apparatus.

tension athetoid: *see* **athetoid, tension.**

tension control: (phys. ed.) regulation of the force which develops in a muscle when it is stimulated.

tension outlet: an opportunity for the child to release his feelings in a socially acceptable way.

tension, societal: *see* **societal tension.**

tentative career objective: *see* **objective, tentative career.**

tenure, academic: the means by which, or the conditions under which, college staff members hold their positions. *See* **tenure, indefinite; tenure, teacher.**

tenure associate professor: *see* **professor, tenure associate.**

tenure case: a dispute concerning the tenure rights of a school employee; may be heard by school authorities having judicial powers and either heard or reviewed by the courts.

tenure, indefinite: a system of school employment in which the teacher or other employee, having served a probationary period of a certain number of years, retains his position indefinitely and is protected in his position either by statute or by rule of the school board; dismissal of employees having such protection must follow certain specified procedures. *Syn.* **permanent tenure; protective tenure;** *see* **tenure, academic; tenure, teacher.**

tenure, permanent: *syn.* **tenure, indefinite.**

tenure, protective: *syn.* **tenure, indefinite.**

tenure, teacher: (1) the means by which a person holds a teaching position; *see* **contract, annual; tenure, indefinite;** (2) the length, usually expressed in years, of a teacher's service in a single position or school system; (3) the total time a teacher remains in the profession.

teratology: the branch of biology dealing with malformations and monstrosities in organisms.

term: (1) a period of time during which a school or other educational institution is open for instruction; may designate the *summer term*, or may be used as a synonym for *semester* or *school term;* (2) historically, any one of the two or three major periods during which school was in session, specifically referred to as the fall term, winter term, and spring term; *see* **school term; school year;** (3) (finance) a period of time; (4) (math.) in an equation, the entire quantity on either side of the equality sign; (5) (math.) of an expression, any quantity combined as a whole with other quantities by addition; for example, in $3x^2 + xy^2 - \dfrac{3x+1}{x-3} - 5$, the terms are $3x^2$, xy^2, and $\dfrac{3x+1}{x-3}$, and -5.

term bond: *see* **bond, term.**

term contract: *see* **contract, term.**

term mark: *see* **mark, term.**

term paper: an essay or written discussion of a subject in partial fulfillment of the requirements of a course.

term, school: *see* **school term.**

term, summer: *see* **school term, summer.**

term test: *see* **test, term.**

term, undefined: in a deductive system of mathematics, an object or idea for which no definition is given, as, for example, point or line in geometry; by placing no restrictions on such objects, the system has wider application since any object characterized by the axioms can then be assigned the names of the undefined terms.

terminal: (data processing) any type of hardware device permitting one- or two-way communication with a computer via communication lines.

terminal behavior: *see* **behavior, terminal.**

terminal board: *syn.* **plugboard.**

terminal cost: *see* **cost, terminal.**

terminal course: *see* **course, terminal.**

terminal education: a type and level of schooling beyond which pupils are not normally expected to take additional full-time schooling.

terminal frame: *see* **frame, terminal.**

terminal function: *see* **function, terminal.**

terminal institution: *see* **institution, terminal.**

terminal item: *see* **item, terminal.**

terminal mathematics: *see* **mathematics, terminal.**

terminal program: *see* **program, terminal.**

terminal session: a set of interactions with a computer, begun when a user has gained access from a remote terminal and ended when he signs off. *See* **interaction, conversational.**

terminal training: *see* **terminal education.**

terminology: the system of technical or special terms or expressions peculiar to a science, art, business, or special subject.

terminology, standard: (mil. ed.) words, terms, and phrases used in official directives; those in Naval Warfare Publications are considered the standard for all other naval and Marine Corps publications.

terrain exercise: *see* **exercise, terrain.**

terrain study: *see* **study, terrain.**

terrarium: (elem. ed.) a glass enclosure for growing plants; part of primary school science environment.

territorial board for vocational education: a board for vocational education acting for a territory instead of a state. *See* **state board of vocational education.**

tertiary schooling: *see* **schooling, tertiary.**

tertile: one of the two points measured along the scale of a plotted variable which divides the frequency distribution into three parts, each containing exactly one-third of the observations or cases.

tertile interval: *see* **interval, tertile.**

test: (1) a group of questions or tasks to which a student is to respond, the purpose being to produce a quantitative representation of the pupil trait that it is designed to measure; (2) a systematic procedure for comparing the behavior of two or more individuals; (3) (logic) any procedure or criterion used to determine the truth or falsity of a hypothesis.

test, ability: a nontechnical term usually applied to tests designed to measure intelligence or aptitude; ordinarily used with various modifying adjectives, for example, mechanical ability test or musical ability test.

test, abstract-reasoning: (1) a test of one of the abilities measured in the differential-aptitude test battery; a power test used for prediction of success in secondary schools; (2) any test of abstract-reasoning ability; any test designed to measure capacity for solving problems requiring facility in the use of abstract symbols.

test, absurdities: a test requiring the individual to detect an incongruity in a situation as described in word or picture.

test, academic-aptitude: a prognostic test designed to measure the fitness of the examinee to undertake and perform activities of an academic nature.

test, accomplishment: *syn.* **test, achievement.**

test, accuracy: a test in which time is not necessarily considered as a factor of performance, greatest emphasis being placed on the ratio of the number of exercises or items attempted to the number correctly completed.

test, achievement: a test designed to measure a person's knowledges, skills, understandings, etc., in a given field taught in school, for example, a mathematics test or an English test. (In practice, an achievement test may include measures of several types of subject matter and may yield separate scores for each subject; such a test is usually called an *achievement battery.*) *Syn.* **achievement scale; educational test.**

test age: *see* **age, test.**

test, alertness: a proposed but rarely used substitute for the term *intelligence test.*

test, alternate-response: a test made up of items which permit only two possible responses; the usual form is the familiar true-false test; similar alternate responses are right-wrong, correct-incorrect, yes-no, same-opposite. *See* **item, alternate response; test, recognition.**

test, analogies: a test designed to measure ability to perceive similarities and differences, or relationships, among figures and ideas; the subject is usually expected to supply the missing term or to select the proper response in such items as

         black : white = night : _____
         grass : green = coal : _____;

frequently used in general intelligence tests, less often in achievement tests.

test, analytical: (1) a test designed to serve as a basis for the analysis of skills or understandings underlying performance on the total test; usually providing, in addition to a total score, subscores that are less exhaustive measures of specific skills than a *diagnostic test* would yield; (2) an examination designed to reveal the factors involved in any mental ability.

test, analytical reading: a test used as an aid in revealing a person's specific abilities and difficulties in reading.

test, anchor: a test used in the development, for the several tests in a series, of a uniform system of interpreted scores, such that a given score on any one of the tests will always denote the same relative performance in a hypothetical population having a specified mean and standard deviation on an anchor test, the anchor test being a measure of mental ability or scholastic aptitude.

test and evaluation, operational: any program or project designed to obtain, verify, and provide data for conclusions about the suitability of operational systems, subsystems, equipment, concepts, tactics, techniques, and procedures.

test, antonym: a test requiring the giving of the opposites of a series of words or pictures.

test anxiety: fear of taking examinations; unpleasant emotional reaction elicited by anticipation of a testing situation; may have an effect on the test performance of the subject.

test, apprehension-span: a test designed to measure the amount of material (such as a series of numerals, letters, or words) that a person can grasp after seeing it once for a short time. *Syn.* **attention-span test.**

test, aptitude: a device used to assess a combination of native and acquired abilities which are considered indicative of future performance, for example, a *music-aptitude test* or a *mathematics aptitude test. Syn.* **capacity test; specific intelligence test;** *see* **test, prognostic; test, scholastic-aptitude;** *dist. f.* **test, general intelligence.**

test, Army Alpha: (1) a group intelligence test, largely verbal, designed for use in classifying draftees in the U.S. Army in World War I; (2) any of several revisions of the original Army Alpha test.

test, Army Beta: a group nonverbal intelligence test designed for use in classifying draftees in the U.S. Army in World War I; the test was designed for use with illiterate and non-English-speaking recruits and was considered as supplementary to the Army Alpha test.

test, Army training: as outlined in a Department of the Army publication, a test, under simulated combat conditions, of individuals and units up to and including battalions, battle groups, and air defense artillery brigades to ensure uniformity of training and to evaluate the ability of a unit to perform its assigned mission and the ability of the soldier to perform the minimum skills requisite to success in battle.

test, art-appreciation: a measuring device for the purpose of determining systematically and scientifically a person's ability to judge the significance and value of an art product. *See* **appreciation, art; rating scale, art.**

test, art-aptitude: a test designed to predict the extent to which a person may be expected to profit by special training in art.

test, articulation: an examination to determine the accuracy with which a person produces the various speech sounds singly or in connected speech; nonreaders' tests for young children and illiterates usually involve the naming of objects shown in a standard set of pictures; readers' tests usually involve the speaking of standard lists of words and the reading of prescribed phonetically edited sentences.

test, association: (1) in general, any test intended to measure the strength of different mental elements or determine the nature of the connections existing between them; (2) specifically, a test designed to measure the nature or speed of verbal responses made to verbal stimuli.

test, associative-learning: a test that measures the ability of the learner to associate meanings with words.

test, attention-span: *syn.* **test, apprehension-span.**

test, attitude: a test to measure the mental and emotional set or pattern of likes and dislikes held by an individual or group, often in relation to controversial issues, personal adjustments, etc.

test, audiometric: a test of auditory acuity performed by means of the *audiometer.*

test, auditory: any test designed to assess ability to hear, either generally or in such specific abilities as pitch and rhythm discrimination.

test, auditory decoding: a test designed to determine how well the child understands spoken language.

test, Aussage (ous'sä·gǝ): (Ger. lit., "testimony") the general designation of a type of test in which the testee is directed to observe a specified object or event for a given length of time and to report on his observation; scored in terms of accuracy and completeness of observation, honesty, memory, and verbal ability.

test, ball-and-chicken: delayed-response test of duration of retention of experience; first a rubber ball when squeezed causes a chicken to emerge; after a period of delay, a ball similar in appearance but without any chicken in it is presented to the child to determine from its behavior whether the child has any carry-over from the first ball; one of the Bühler-Hetzer tests.

test, ball-and-field: a test requiring the subject to trace the path he would follow to find a ball lost in a field; a type of *plan-of-search test,* used in measuring general intelligence.

test, Bartlett: a test of homogeneity of variance, that is, a test of the null hypothesis regarding the variances of k populations.

test, basic-skills: a standardized objective test designed to measure mastery of essential skills in basic school subjects, for example, the necessary skills in reading, language, arithmetic, work-study habits and techniques.

test battery, basic: *see* **battery, basic test.**

test, Behrens-Fisher: (stat.) a method for testing the significance of the difference between the means of two samples drawn from populations having unequal or unknown variances.

test, best-answer: a test composed of multiple-choice items so constructed that, while several of the suggested answers to each item may be partly correct, one suggested answer is definitely better than the others; used in testing in areas involving judgment, evaluating data, drawing inferences and conclusions, and exercising insight.

test, best-reason: a variety of the *best-answer* or *multiple-choice test,* so named because the responses to each item are phrased as reasons rather than as facts. *See* **test, multiple-choice.**

test, bifactor: an intelligence test from which two separate aspects of mental ability can be obtained. *See* **abilities, primary mental; battery, differential-aptitude.**

test, Binet: a series of items combined in an age scale for the measurement of intelligence, based on the test developed by Alfred Binet in 1905 in France. *See* **scale, Binet-Simon.**

test, Binet-Simon intelligence: *see* **test, Binet.**

test, binocular reading: a technique to test for the adequate operation of both eyes in reading.

test, Blakeman's: a statistical method of testing whether regression is linear, which amounts to determining whether there is a statistically significant difference between the square of the correlation ratio and the square of the coefficient of correlation, the regression being assumed to be nonlinear if the difference is statistically significant; expressed by the formula $N(\eta^2 - r^2) < 11.37$. *Syn.* **Blakeman's criterion.**

test blank: (1) a printed or mimeographed test or examination form on which the examinee is to place appropriate marks or record his responses or on which the examiner records the examinee's responses; (2) a blank for recording the responses of individuals who are examined according to a set routine.

test, block-design: a test of intelligence based on the assembling of painted cubes so as to form a pattern or design.

test, bone-conduction: a hearing test which makes it possible to compare the responses of the middle and inner ears; in this test, sound is transmitted through the temporal bone directly to the inner ear.

test, cancellation: a test intended to measure speed and accuracy in discriminating among forms, in which the subject usually is directed to cross out as quickly and accurately as possible certain specified letters, words, or forms scattered among others. *Syn.* **cross-out test.**

test, capacity: *syn.* **test, aptitude.**

test, card-sorting: a test requiring the subject to arrange a series of cards in piles or put them in boxes according to marks or signs such as numbers, letters, designs, or colors.

test, cardiovascular (kär'di·ō·vas'kū·lər): a type of measurement technique intended to supply information about the response of the heart to regulated amounts of exercise.

test, cause-and-effect: a test requiring the subject (*a*) to state a presumptive cause of a specified effect, or the reverse, or (*b*) when the test is in multiple-choice form, to choose the correct presumptive cause or effect.

test, CAVD: a group mental test of the power type, designed by E.L. Thorndike and intended to measure intellectual capacity through use of four types of subtests, namely, completion (C), arithmetic (A), vocabulary (V), directions (D).

test ceiling: (1) the upper limit of the quality of a characteristic that is being measured by a test; (2) the upper limit of ability that can be measured by a test; reached when individuals have abilities surpassing the highest performance level at which the test can make reliable discriminations. *See* **test floor.**

test, central-thought: a test that measures the ability to locate and understand the main idea in a paragraph or larger unit of thought.

test, cerebral dominance: *see* **test, Wada sodium amytal.**

test, change-sensitive: a test composed of items that measure change in a characteristic which is subject to alteration by educational practices; composed of items identified by test-retest procedures as sensitive to change in the desired direction; useful in measuring differential change in achievement, attitudes, and values.

test, channel-transportation: a test similar to a maze test, in which the subject must pursue a course along the proper channels to obtain a desired object.

test, character: any test designed to assess the ethical, volitional, or valuational aspects of personality, such as honesty, persistence, loyalty, and dominating values and ideals.

test, chi square: *see* **chi square.**

test, classification: (1) any test employed to group or classify pupils for purposes of instruction or to classify any examinees in regard to given abilities, aptitudes, or achievement; (2) an objective test of ability to discriminate and to perceive similarities, consisting of items such as the following:

> red, blue, hot, green, yellow
> 6, 2, 5, 4, 8
> run, play, happy, eat, swim;

the subject is instructed to select the term in each item that differs from the others or to select all the terms that are alike; somewhat similar to the *analogies test* in regard to the mental operations necessary for satisfactory performance.

test, classroom: a teacher-made or locally constructed test, either objective or of the essay type, for local classroom use. *See* **test, essay;** *contr. w.* **test, standardized.**

test, clerical: a test of capacity or ability to do such work as checking sums, filing, accounting, typewriting, and stenography.

test, clinical vision: *syn.* **test, vision.**

test, cloze: a test of reading made by replacing words in a regular sequence in a given passage with an underlined blank space in which the pupil writes the word he believes was deleted; the score is the number of words correctly supplied.

test, Cochran-Cox: a small sample approximate test of the significance of the difference between the means of two normally distributed populations that have different variances.

test, code: a test requiring the subject to write or translate a message in a given code, such as one based on parts of geometrical figures.

test, comparable: tests of different mental or physical characteristics that, like equivalent forms, yield scores in an indefinitely large sample of examinees at an appropriate age or grade level that have identical averages, distributions, and accuracy of measurement.

test, completion: a test requiring the subject to supply the missing part or parts in a series, whether numerical, verbal, pictorial, or graphic.

test, comprehension: (1) a test requiring the subject to interpret or pass judgment on a situation presented in language or pictures; frequently used as an exercise in mental tests; (2) a test designed to measure understanding of principles or relationships in a subject field; (3) in reading, a test to determine how much the subject understands of what he reads. *See* **score, comprehension.**

test, comprehensive achievement: (1) a test designed to measure proficiency in various areas of learning rather than in a single subject; (2) an inclusive, searching test in a given area or subject. *Comp. w.* **battery, achievement.**

test, controlled-association: a test requiring the subject to respond to a number of stimulus words by giving words having a specified relation to them; for example, a list of book titles might be given, the subject being instructed to supply the name of the author of each book. *Syn.* **fixed-association test;** *contr. w.* **test, free-association.**

test, cooperative: an inferential method of measuring the presence or extent of cooperativeness by comparing the extent of work performed for the group with that performed for the individual alone in a given period of time.

test, criterion: (1) the instrument used to measure the end result of a treatment or treatments being studied in an experiment; (2) an independent measure of an ability, quality, or trait that is used in judging the worth of a measuring instrument being evaluated; (3) in programmed instruction, a test of acquisition, if given immediately after a learning sequence, or of retention, if given considerably later; may involve only the material actually covered in the learning sequence or may involve extension, generalization, or application of the learned material, generally called *transfer; see* **behavior, terminal;** (4) (mil. ed.) a test of essential terminal behavior as called for by the statements of learning objectives; test items should measure the student's ability to behave in performance as he was taught during the course of instruction.

test, cross-out: *syn.* **test, cancellation.**

test, crucial: any test, such as an observation, criterion, or experiment, used to prove or disprove a given hypothesis.

test, culture-fair: a measurement device, such as an intelligence test, which has maximum freedom from verbal, conceptual, and emotional loadings as these differentiate among cultures. *Syn.* **culture-free test.**

test, culture-free: *see* **test, culture-fair.**

test, curriculum-embedded: a short test to determine mastery of a specific objective within the learning continuum; employed to monitor progress of pupils whose instruction is individually prescribed.

test, cycle: a test consisting of exercises or items differing in difficulty or perhaps in form or kind but so arranged that the variations occur in cycles; thus, if the numbers 1, 2, 3, and 4 represent the relative difficulty of the items (or four different kinds or forms of items), the test items might be arranged as follows: 1-3-2-4, 1-4-2-3, etc., or in any other regular order. *See* **test, spiral**.

test, deduction: a test requiring the subject to answer a question or find a relationship, depending on stated facts or conditions.

test, deterioration: a test employed to detect intellectual deterioration or impairment arising from a variety of possible causes.

test, dexterity: a test of the speed with which a person can perform such a routine motor task as fitting a certain number of pins into holes of appropriate size in a form board; used in the determination of aptitudes for certain trades. *See* **test, form-board**.

test, diagnostic: (1) an examination intended to measure achievement in a narrow subject field or in related subfields, particularly with a view to determining specific weaknesses of pupils as a basis for remedial measures; (2) an examination the results of which permit a broad, general diagnosis of pupil weaknesses and strengths; (3) (couns.) a standardized instrument for the identification of a specific characteristic or set of characteristics of the individual.

test, diagnostic reading: a test designed to reveal a person's specific abilities and difficulties in reading; used as a base for the diagnosis of the causal factors affecting his performance in reading. *Dist. f.* **test, analytical reading**.

test, differential-aptitude: a standardized objective test that measures separately several aspects of mental ability; each aspect, or aptitude, is scored separately and represented by a separate index of performance, on the theory that intelligence is not a unitary trait but rather is composed of various abilities. *See* **battery, differential aptitude**.

test, digit-span: a form of apprehension-span test involving ability to repeat series of numbers after auditory or visual presentation; the number of digits that the subject can remember and repeat is taken as his digit span.

test, digit-symbol: a timed test of performance thought to relate to mental functioning; an individual is required to match a given series of numbers with a given series of symbols, a particular number always being represented by a given symbol.

test, directed speaking: one of a variety of speaking tests in which a student orally alters an orally presented cue sentence according to directions given in advance.

test, directions: a test requiring the subject to perform a series of acts in a specified sequence, in response to instructions.

test, disarranged-sentence: (1) a test requiring the subject to arrange a jumbled group of words in order, to make a sentence; (2) a test requiring the subject to answer questions about or indicate the truth or falsity of a statement that must first be formed by rearranging a jumbled group of words.

test, distribution-free: *syn.* **test, nonparametric**.

test, dotting: a measure of speed and accuracy in which the subject is directed to make a series of dots with a pencil as rapidly as possible, the score on such a test being expressed usually in terms of the number of dots made in a given time and the accuracy with which they are placed.

test, double-tailed: *syn.* **test, two-tailed**.

test, draw-a-man: a drawing test used to assess psychomotor development and ability to observe details. *See* **behavior, draw-a-man**.

test, drivometer: a mechanical test devised to measure a person's reactions to traffic situations and his ability to manipulate the controls of a motor vehicle. *See* **drivometer**.

test economy: *see* **economy**.

test, educational: (1) *syn.* **test, achievement**; (2) any test used in connection with educational activity.

test efficiency: validity per minute of testing time.

test element: a general term for any of the items or tasks that constitute the content of a test.

test, empirical: a test constructed or selected for use largely on the basis of experience rather than on the basis of some well-defined theory.

test, employment: a test designed for the purpose of predicting a person's probable success in a given type of employment; frequently used to select the most promising of a number of applicants for employment.

test, end: a test given at the conclusion of a period of training or instruction.

test, equating: *syn.* **test, matching** (2).

test, essay: a type of examination in which the subject or examinee is asked to discuss, enumerate, compare, state, evaluate, analyze, summarize, or criticize; involves writing at specified length on a given topic involving the processes listed above.

test evaluation: *see* **evaluation, test**.

test exercise: *see* **exercise, test**.

test, experimental: activities, instituted by and performed under the guidance of a hypothesis, such that they will disclose the conditions, or complete and unify the order of facts, which will determine whether the hypothesis should be accepted or rejected.

test, eyesight: *see* **test, vision**.

test, F: *syn.* **variance, analysis of**.

test, fables: a test in which the subject is required to interpret fables read to him or by him; used as a part of the Stanford-Binet scale.

test, factored: a test battery for which several scores representing different factors of ability, established by factor analysis, are obtained.

test, feature profile: a test requiring the subject to put together blocks to represent the profile of a human face.

test, figure-copying: an evaluation designed to show visual perception by the way the subject can reproduce certain forms.

test, film: (1) an examination based on the content of a motion picture; (2) a film designed to present test items either in pictorial or in printed form.

test film: *see* **film, test**.

test, fixed-association: *syn.* **test, controlled-association**.

test, flight: a flight examination to evaluate the pilot's efficiency in flying the aircraft.

test floor: the level beneath which a test ceases to distinguish between actual differences in the variable being tested. *See* **test ceiling**.

test for attention: a term applied loosely to a number of tests assumed, without very clear evidence, to measure uniformity or "concentration" of attention; no longer commonly used.

test for linearity: a test to determine whether the line connecting the means of successive arrays is sufficiently straight to justify the use of a correlation coefficient rather than a correlation ratio. *Syn.* **test for rectilinearity**.

test for rectilinearity: *syn.* **test for linearity**.

test, forced-choice: a test in which a choice of two desirable answers is given for each item.

test, form-board: a test requiring the subject to make use of a form board, for example, to place blocks of various shapes in openings of corresponding shape or to arrange a group of blocks so as to fill an opening.

test, free-association: a psychological test in which a selected list of words is read or repeated to the subject, who is instructed to respond to each stimulus word instantly after hearing it by uttering the first word or phrase that comes to mind; scored in terms of speed of reaction and type of response; frequently used as a means of determining ideas associated with emotional disturbance, worries, hidden fears, etc. *Contr. w.* **test, controlled-association**.

test, free-response: a test in which each item appears as a direct question, a stimulus word or phrase, a specific direction, or an incomplete statement or question; the response must be supplied by the student rather than merely identified from a list of suggested answers supplied by the teacher; the response is usually short, preferably a single word or phrase.

test, general achievement: *see* **battery, achievement; measurement, multiple.**

test, general clerical: a combination of tests of intelligence, manual dexterity, mechanical aptitude, spatial visualization, and personality.

test, general educational development (G.E.D. test): a comprehensive test used primarily to appraise the educational development of adults who have not completed their formal high school education; through achievement of satisfactory scores adults may earn a high school equivalency certificate, qualify for admission to college or to more advanced educational or employment opportunities, or meet qualifications for admission to licensing examinations for certain occupations; tests are administered at official G.E.D. centers approved by state departments of education and also, to military personnel on active duty, through the U.S. Armed Forces Institute. *See* **certificate, high school equivalency.**

test, general intelligence: a nonspecific term designating a composite test made up of parts that have been found empirically to correlate well with some practical indirect measure of intellectual ability, such as success in school.

test, general survey: a test designed to measure knowledge, skills, or achievement in a relatively broad area, whether in a number of different subjects or in a number of different phases of a single subject; usually composed of a battery of subtests; often scored in terms of educational age or grade placement. (A composite score may be derived, or provision may be made, for showing subtest scores in the form of a profile.)

test, graduate school foreign language: a test designed to evaluate the foreign language reading proficiency of graduate-level degree candidates.

test, group: a test so constructed that it can be administered to a number of individuals at the same time. *Contr. w.* **test, individual.**

test, handedness: a test or battery of tests used to indicate right- or left-hand preference; usually indicated by performance in handwriting, tapping, throwing, gripping, sawing, etc.

test, hearing: any objective or subjective measure used to determine the acuity of hearing as a whole or for certain frequencies; for example, the *watch-tick test* and the *whisper test.*

test, heterogeneous: a test in which the different parts, whether through intent or accident, measure different traits; therefore, a test with low internal consistency.

test, homogeneous: (1) a test containing items that are similar in form and closely related in content; (2) a test measuring primarily a single ability or trait and, therefore, expected to be internally consistent; a test highly saturated with a single factor.

test, house-tree-person: a clinical projective test in which the individual is asked to make free-hand drawings of a house, a tree, and a person.

test, hybrid: a test of listening discrimination in writing, in which a student of a foreign language calls upon two or more skills at a time.

test, identical-elements: a test designed to simulate as nearly as possible elements of behavior that are practically identical with those found in the criterion behavior; for example, an identical-elements test of skill in shorthand might require the examinee to produce a typed business letter from shorthand notes made when a letter was dictated to him.

test, identification: a form of objective test in which things, ideas, concepts, locations, etc., are indicated by means of pictures or words and are to be named or otherwise identified by the person taking the test.

test, illuminant-stable color-vision: a type of color-vision test developed by Ellis Freeman, which, unlike previous color-vision tests, remains diagnostically stable despite variations in illumination.

test, impossible question: a test presenting 10 questions considered impossible to answer; during the test, notes are taken on each child's reaction to the frustrating situation to see whether different patterns of reaction can be detected.

test, incomplete-man: a test of intelligence in which the subject is shown an incomplete picture of a man and required to indicate what parts are missing; used at the 4- and 5-year levels of the Stanford revision of the Binet test.

test, individual: a test that can be administered to only one person at a time, usually because the subject's responses are oral or because the examiner must note down a rather careful description of them; especially common in testing oral-reading ability, speech, and general intelligence.

test, individual mental: one of the intelligence tests designed for use with one subject at a time.

test, induction: a test requiring the subject to make a generalized statement from facts presented verbally or concretely.

test, infant: any test of motor development and intelligence used with children up to the age of 3.

test, informal: the general designation of any test prepared by a classroom teacher for use in the local situation, as contrasted with a standardized test.

test, informal reading: a teacher-made test which may make use of recording the pupil's responses to passages in reading texts and/or maintaining checklists of reactions to various kinds of reading tasks.

test, information: a test designed to measure the subject's knowledge of facts; may cover various fields or a single restricted field.

test, initial: the first test in a series; frequently, a test given at the beginning of a period of instruction to determine the extent to which the subject of study has already been mastered.

test, ink-blot: a psychological test of which the principal materials consist of reproductions of ink blots on paper, usually black on a white background (but sometimes in colors), the subject being instructed to examine each figure and tell what it might be; commonly scored on the basis of type of response, for example, the *Rorschach test.*

test, instructional: a test designed principally as an aid in instruction or learning, rather than as a basis for evaluation; frequently designed to cover a unit or a limited portion of a course rather than the subject as a whole.

test, intelligence: an instrument used for measuring intellectual functioning, the ability to learn, or the ability to deal with new situations.

test, interest: a test or device used to measure a person's likes and dislikes; typically determines the extent to which a person's pattern of likes and dislikes corresponds to those of persons who are known to be interested in a given vocation, school subject, school curriculum, or other activity; usually lists numerous vocations, school subjects, activities, etc., the subject being instructed to indicate whether he likes, dislikes, or is indifferent to each one.

test interpretation: the process of communicating test results and relating the significance of test scores to clients, parents, teachers, employers, or other personnel.

test, interpretive: an achievement test in which there are several introductory selections of material in verbal, numerical, pictorial, or graphical form, each followed by a series of questions requiring various interpretations of the material presented.

test, introversion-extroversion: a test designed to measure the degree to which a person tends, in his attitudes and behavior, toward the reflective, self-centered type or toward the energetic, externally minded type.

test, inventory: a detailed coverage test designed to ascertain pupils' achievement levels or abilities in a given field; frequently used as a pretest to sample pupils' mastery of subject matter prior to a period of instruction.

test, Jaeger: *see* **measure, Jaeger.**

test, job-knowledge: (mil. ed.) a short multiple-choice test designed to measure knowledge acquired through actual experience or training in an Air Force specialty or related civilian occupation.

test, knowledge: any test designed to measure what an individual or group knows about a particular subject, as distinguished from an *aptitude test* or an *attitude test.*

test, language proficiency: an Air Force test designed to determine an individual's potential ability to understand, read, and write a particular foreign language.

test, level-of-comprehension: a test designed to measure the degree of difficulty of the most difficult reading material that a person is able to understand.

test, likelihood ratio: a criterion used in testing statistical hypotheses consisting of the ratio of the maximized likelihood for the sample over the possible values of the parameters specified by the hypothesis under test to the maximized likelihood for the sample over all possible values of the parameters.

test, linguistic: a test of comprehension and correct use of a language.

test, listening comprehension: any oral test designed to measure the extent and accuracy of a student's memory and correspondingly his total understanding of spoken utterances in a foreign language.

test, literacy: a test of ability to read and write.

test, machine-scorable: a test in which the examinee records his answers on separate answer sheets with a special electrographic pencil so that current flowing through the electrically conductive pencil marks enables the answers to be read on a suitably calibrated dial as a test score; by means of appropriate keys, the machine distinguishes between correct and incorrect answers and can combine them in groups to yield total or part scores, weighted scores, or corrected scores.

test, make-a-picture-story: *see* **test, MAPS.**

test, MAPS: (make-a-picture-story) a test wherein the individual is asked to create a story, using cardboard cutout figures as actors against a stage background.

test, marble board: a test designed to measure visual perception through motor performance; two identical cardboards are used, one by the examiner for constructing patterns of red and black marbles set in small holes, the other by the examinee, who is directed to make a pencil drawing of the pattern arranged on the examiner's board; used extensively in the study of the brain-damaged child.

test, mastery: a test designed to measure the knowledge and skills that every pupil of the class should have acquired; combines quality of a speed test in that item difficulty is uniformly low and of a power test in that it has liberal time limits.

test, matching: (1) a recognition form of objective test to which the pupil responds by attempting to match or pair the related items in two or more columns of related material; *see* **test, recognition;** (2) an examination that purports to measure variables considered important in influencing the results obtained from a study, the scores on this examination to be used by the investigator to divide the individuals into groups that will be relatively equal in regard to the variables measured; *syn.* **equating test.**

test, mathematics-aptitude: *see* **test, aptitude.**

test, maximum-performance: any test on which the examinee is directed, at least implicitly, to do the best job he can; for example, intelligence, aptitude, and achievement tests. *Contr. w.* **test, typical-performance.**

test, maze: a test requiring the subject to trace the most direct path to a specified goal through a figure that contains a number of blind alleys or false paths leading off from the true path.

test, mechanical-aptitude: a test of a person's potential ability to succeed in work or study involving the understanding and manipulation of machinery and mechanical devices.

test, memory-for-design: a type of subtest or item in which the individual is asked to reproduce from memory a design or figure seen briefly; this type of test has been much used in intelligence testing, for example, in the original Binet scale, in the Stanford-Binet, in the Wechsler test, and in the Cornell-Coxe performance-ability scale.

test, mental: a test used in mental evaluations. *See* **examination, mental.**

test, military occupational specialty evaluation: a test designed to evaluate individual knowledge and skills required in the performance of a military occupational specialty.

test, missing-parts: a test in which the subject is required to discover missing parts in a number of pictures of objects; used as an item in such intelligence tests as the Kuhlmann and revised Stanford-Binet.

test, mixed-relations: obsolescent *syn.* **test, analogies.**

test, modern language aptitude: a test designed to evaluate those areas of knowledge and ability essential for Air Force personnel to complete successfully formal courses in foreign languages.

test, mosaic: a type of projective test in which the individual is given a set of colored geometric shapes and is asked to make a pattern; it is intended to provide the examiner with insight into the quality of thought processes and with some information about personality dynamics.

test, motor achievement: those evaluative instruments which measure the capacity for accomplishment in a specific physical skill.

test, motor encoding: an obsolete title for a test which determines how well a child can express himself by gestures without vocal responses.

test, multiphasic personality: a test designed to measure various aspects of the personality.

test, multiple-answer: *syn.* **test, multiple-response.**

test, multiple-choice: a recognition type of test in which the subject is asked to choose for each item the one correct or best answer from several suggested answers. *See* **item, multiple-choice; test, recognition;** *dist. f.* **test, multiple-response.**

test, multiple-response: an objective test of the recognition type in which the subject is asked to select for each item two or more correct answers from a group of several suggested answers. *Syn.* **multiple-answer test;** *see* **item, multiple-response; test, recognition;** *dist. f.* **test, multiple-choice.**

test, music: a term used rather loosely to refer to measurement either of capacity for musical development (called, generally, a *music aptitude test*) or of achievement, knowledge, or proficiency (called, variously, an *audition,* a *board examination,* or, possibly, a *placement test*).

test, music aptitude: a test designed to predict the extent to which a person may be expected to profit by musical training; usually consists of measures of such basic functions as the ability to differentiate among tones, tempi, and rhythms and musical memory; sometimes loosely called *musical ability test.*

test, new-type: obsolescent *syn.* **test, objective.**

test, nonlanguage: *syn.* **test, nonverbal.**

test, nonparametric: any of several statistical tests that may be applied to a set of data without any assumption as to the shape of the distribution or distributions involved; generally used only when assumptions for more efficient statistical tests cannot be made, for example, *chi square.* *Syn.* **distribution-free test.**

test, nonverbal intelligence: a device used for measuring intelligence without the use of speech or language by examiner or subject; frequently tests requiring little speech or language are referred to as nonverbal; such tests indicate the ability to work efficiently to solve problems that do not involve verbal symbols.

test, numerical: (1) a test concerned primarily with abilities involved in the use of numbers; (2) a test of special ability in dealing with numbers and their interrelationships; (3) a subtest in a battery of intelligence tests, emphasizing thought in terms of numerical symbols, as contrasted with other subtests that involve primarily verbal concepts.

test, objective: a test so constructed that different scorers working independently will arrrive at the same or essentially the same score for a given performance; usually based on alternate-response, multiple-choice, matching, or completion-type questions; scored by means of a key of correct answers, any answer disagreeing with the key being regarded as wrong. *Syn.* **new-type test; short-answer test;** *see* **test, standardized.**

test, occupational: (1) a device for recording one's interests and comparing them with interests of those persons successfully engaging in a particular field of work; (2) a work sample used to judge future performance in a job.

test of association, corner: a nonparametric test of the existence of relations between two variables; involves counting the number of plots within certain prescribed locations of a scatter diagram.

test of balance: any test used to measure the factors involved in maintaining body equilibrium.

test of cooperativeness: *syn.* **test, cooperative.**

test of homogeneity: any test of the hypothesis that there is no real difference between the parameters corresponding to two or more statistics and that differences in the observed values of the statistics are ascribable to chance fluctuations in random sampling.

test of independence: any statistical test of the hypothesis that two or more variables are unrelated, for example, the *chi square test. See* **test of homogeneity.**

test of motor ability: a test including measurements of muscular movement, coordination, and/or ability. *See* **ability, motor.**

test of relations: statistical analysis to determine the relative significance of several variables.

test of sensory-motor coordination: any test used to measure bodily coordinations in motor skills requiring adjustments to moving objects.

test of significance: any statistical test (for example, t, x^2, or F) which may be applied to data to determine the likelihood of their having occurred as predicted by some hypothesis. *Syn.* **statistical test;** *see* **confidence level; hypothesis, null.**

test of timbre: *see* **discrimination, timbre.**

test of writing, dictation: a test of the pupils' ability to write when recording a passage spoken by the instructor, rather than when copying from printed or inscribed material.

test, omnibus: (1) a test containing items or exercises of various sorts, mixed together in regular or irregular order, instead of grouped in subtests each containing items or tasks of a single kind; thus, there may be an analogies exercise, a number-completion item, a vocabulary item, a general-information item, a second analogies exercise, etc.; (2) an achievement test covering several different fields of subject matter, such as English usage, spelling, arithmetic, and geography; not very commonly used in this sense.

test, one-sided: *syn.* **test, one-tailed.**

test, one-tail: *syn.* **test, one-tailed.**

test, one-tailed: a statistical test of significance involving only a single side (tail) of the sampling distribution; a test of a null hypothesis which precludes the possibility of a difference in one direction. *Syn.* **one-sided test; one-tail test; single-tailed test;** *dist. f.* **test, two-tailed.**

test, open book: a test during which the examinee may consult his textbook, reference books, or, sometimes, notes, the purpose being to emphasize command of knowledge as distinguished from recall of factual information.

test, operational readiness: (mil. ed.) a test and inspection to determine or prove the extent of the overall operational readiness of an organization. *See* **training, operational readiness.**

test, opposites: a test in which the subject is required to supply the antonyms, or opposites, of a given list of terms or to select them from a second list.

test, oral: a test in which both questions and answers are spoken rather than written.

test, oral-reading: a test that measures the ability of the reader to recognize and pronounce words in the natural context; may be a standardized test, or may consist of typical reading material at a specified level.

test, organic-efficiency: a test of functional efficiency of bodily organic systems, especially circulatory and respiratory; an older, nonscientific term applied to a test of the response of the heart to exercise. *See* **test, pulse-ratio.**

test pacing, automatic: *see* **pacing, automatic test.**

test, pantomime: a test conducted without the use of spoken or written language, directions being conveyed to the subject by means of gestures and illustrative language; used chiefly in measuring the abilities of persons who are unable to understand the language spoken by the examiner.

test, paper-and-pencil: (1) a test in which the subject indicates his responses by writing; (2) a conventional type of school examination not involving the use of mechanical and other apparatus but requiring pencils and paper; (3) a test requiring longhand writing, printing, or figuring, as contrasted with oral tests or performance tests.

test, paper-form-board: a test of mechanical ability and spatial relations requiring the subject to place back together disconnected parts of a figure or form printed on the test sheet.

test, paragraph-meaning: a test designed to measure ability to comprehend the central thought of a paragraph.

test, patch: a skin test for sensitivity of an individual to a test material; specifically, a test for detection of tuberculin sensitivity. (Gauze treated with tuberculin is brought into contact with an area of carefully cleansed skin and held in position by adhesive tape for 48 to 72 hours; the result is read as positive or negative depending on the degree of local reaction observed when the patch is removed.)

test, patterned-string: a test in which a desired object is fastened at the end of one of several strings that form crisscross patterns, the subject being able to gain the desired object only by selecting the string to which it is fastened; used with primates and young children.

test, pegboard: a time-limited test of finger dexterity, for use in vocational placement.

test, performance: (1) a test which attempts to measure intellectual ability by using a minimum of verbal directions and responses so as to avoid penalizing a subject with deficiencies in language ability resulting from hearing defects, foreign background, or other causes; (2) broadly, any test intended to measure actual accomplishment rather than potential ability or aptitude, regardless of how the subject is instructed to respond; (3) specifically, one half of a Wechsler test, which, when combined with the verbal scale score, yields a full scale score and IQ.

test, persistence: a test that measures the degree to which a subject will continue a given trend of behavior against opposing incentives or motives.

test, personality: a test designed to obtain and evaluate information about the trait patterns of individuals so that an assessment of an individual's character can be made.

test, physical-ability: a test designed to ascertain the fitness of the individual to participate successfully and safely in activities requiring physical exertion.

test, physical-capacity: a performance test designed to determine an individual's physical fitness and skill; usually based upon his performance in a number of subtests of strength, agility, and physical achievement for which standards have been established, results sometimes being expressed in terms of a strength index. *See* **index, strength.**

test, physical-efficiency: a test that shows the effective operation of bodily coordination, strength, and endurance as measured by a comparison of actual and possible results.

test, physical-skill: a test measuring ability in performance of some gross bodily motor activity such as throwing. *See* **test, achievement.**

test, physiological: any measure to determine the nature or degree of the functioning of a particular body structure, for example, an analysis of the blood or a test of basal metabolism.

test, pictorial: a test in which the use of pictures is emphasized as either a substitute for or a supplement to purely verbal devices. *Contr. w.* **test, performance; test, verbal.**

test, picture-completion: a test requiring the subject to supply the missing part of a picture by selecting and inserting a block on which the missing part appears or by sketching in the missing part.

test, picture-meaning: a test designed to show an individual's experiential background, his use of language, and his common understandings.

test, picture vocabulary: a set of pictures designed for estimating the size of one's vocabulary by requiring the testee to point to a picture that stands for a word pronounced by an examiner.

test, placement: (1) a test for the determination of ability or achievement in any given subject or skill; (2) in speech, a test consisting of oral reading and spontaneous speaking, designed to detect speech defects and by means of which speech defectives may be classified and so placed in appropriate groups for retraining; (3) (mus. ed.) a test of a musician's proficiency to determine his proper level of applied music study or a test of a vocalist's range and tone quality to determine his proper location in a choir; *see* **tryout.**

test, plan-of-search: *see* **test, ball-and-field.**

test, power: any test the content of which is arranged in order of increasing difficulty, intended to measure the level of maximum ability or achievement of the testee. Rough *syn.* **scaled test.**

test, practice: (1) *syn.* **fore-exercise**; (2) a test primarily intended to afford practice or drill in a given field rather than to measure knowledge or achievement; commonly used in arithmetic and, to some extent, in algebra, languages, and other subjects; sometimes used as a measure of aptitude for purposes of prognosis.

test, preliminary: (1) *syn.* **fore-exercise; practice test**; (2) a test given before the beginning of detailed study of material to be learned, used to discover the relative emphasis that should be given various aspects of the subject matter.

test, professional: an examination used for the purpose of estimating the quality of a teacher's professional preparation in subject matter or in content dealing specifically with education.

test, proficiency: a test which measures ability to perform some task that is significant in its own right, such as reading French, playing a piano; since one of the principal uses of such a test is to evaluate the performance of persons who have been given training in the task, these tests are often referred to as *achievement tests.*

test, profile: a test containing a series of subtests each of which is scored separately, so that the results can be exhibited graphically in such a way as to show an individual score on each.

test, prognostic: an instrument which seeks to test characteristics and interests to foretell areas best suited to future success.

test, progressive matrices: a nonverbal intelligence test of 60 graded designs (matrices) which the subject is asked to complete by selecting the correct one from a number of solutions offered; used in the attempt to measure Spearman's *g-factor*, a native, abstract ability.

test, projective: a global method of measurement of individual personality in which the presentation of a stimulus does not make manifest or only partially makes manifest the intent or nature of the response; the stimulus is usually unstructured and produces responses reflecting the person's own individuality; effective use requires much training.

test, psychological: (1) *syn.* **test, mental**; (2) rare *syn.* **test, attitude.**

test, psychomotor: in aviation medicine, any one of certain tests designed to measure an individual's psychological and motor reactions under normal and abnormal conditions.

test, psychophysical: (pup. trans.) a test of breadth of vision, judging distance, and reaction time given so that each driver may be aware of any personal limitations that might affect his ability to drive.

test, pulse-ratio: a test of the response of the heart to exercise, as measured in terms of pulse rate and expressed as a ratio between pulse rates before and after exercise, change of position, or other conditions.

test purity: the degree to which the test measures only one factor of mental ability.

test, puzzle-block: a test of ability to form the appropriate picture or object by combining blocks of various sizes and shapes in the proper manner; used in measuring mental ability and mechanical aptitude.

test, rate: *syn.* **test, speed.**

test, readability: any formula devised to estimate the difficulty or comprehensibility of any printed material; formulas generally utilize number of words per sentence, number of syllables per word, and number of words not on a general list and considered unfamiliar.

test, readiness: a test of ability to engage in a new type of specific learning; a specialized type of aptitude test most commonly devised for use in the primary grades. *See* **test, aptitude.**

test, reading-aptitude: *syn.* **test, reading-capacity.**

test, reading-capacity: a reading test that attempts to determine a child's capacity for reading; also called *reading-aptitude test.*

test, reading-comprehension: a test that measures the power to grasp meanings, as contrasted with a *rate test*, which measures speed of comprehension.

test, reading-readiness: (1) a test used to determine whether pupils have attained sufficient maturity to begin the study of reading (may include tests of vocabulary, visual and auditory discrimination, and motor coordination); (2) a test designed to determine whether pupils are ready for a given type of reading experience.

test, rearrangement: a form of objective test in which each item consists of several disarranged parts, which the subject is required to rearrange so as to form a correct and meaningful sequence.

test, reasoning: (1) a test of intelligence in which the subject is directed to draw inferences from statements; (2) a test of intelligence in which the subject is directed to select the most logical of a series of conclusions suggested to explain given data; (3) (arith.) a term frequently used to designate an old-type problem test in arithmetic.

test, recall: a test in which the subject is required to supply missing items of information, usually words, numbers, or phrases, to complete statements; strictly, a term which could be applied to the traditional essay-type examination; in common usage, however, restricted to the objective type of test. *See* **test, completion; test, simple-recall;** *contr. w.* **test, recognition.**

test, recognition: a test in which the subject is required to select the right answer to each question from among a number of answers given, of which one is correct. (Sometimes this procedure is reversed, the subject being instructed to select the incorrect answer or answers from among a number of responses.) *See* **test, alternate-response; test, matching; test, multiple-choice;** *contr. w.* **test, recall.**

test reporting: the feedback of test results to teachers and/or other professional persons or to students and their parents.

test, reputation: a test designed to determine the opinions of a group concerning certain persons, usually members of the group; members of a class may be asked, for example, to indicate which of their classmates they believe to be aptly characterized by any of a series of brief personality sketches.

test results: (1) the raw scores obtained from the administration of a test; (2) any meaningful statistical or verbal expressions of the raw scores of a test, whether arranged in a table of distribution for purposes of clarification or transmuted into derived scores utilizing some unit such as age, school grade, deviations from the mean, or percentile ranks.

test, right-wrong: *see* **test, alternate-response; test, true-false; test, yes-no.**

test, road: (1) a performance test to evaluate the skill of a driver; (2) a performance test to evaluate the performance of a vehicle under actual driving conditions.

test, Rorschach (rôr′shäkh): a test devised by the Swiss psychiatrist H. Rorschach (1884–1922), in which inferences concerning a personality are made on the basis of responses to a series of standardized, intrinsically meaningless ink blots, which the subject interprets according to what he "sees" in them; a variety of *ink-blot test. See* projective method.

test, same-or-opposites: a test in which the subject is instructed to indicate whether given pairs of words or other expressions are synonyms or antonyms, or in which by some similar procedure the subject is requested to recognize and indicate basic similarity or dissimilarity.

test, saturated: a test in which the items measure, to the highest degree possible, a particular test variable such as Spearman's g-factor, one of Thurstone's primary mental abilities, etc. *See* **abilities, primary mental; g-factor.**

test, scaled: a test in which the questions or items are arranged in ascending order of difficulty; usually so constructed that the increment is approximately constant from item to item. *See* **test, power.**

test, scholastic: a measuring instrument devised to determine student achievement in school subjects, generally in the academic subjects.

test, scholastic-aptitude: a test used to predict the facility with which the individual will progress in learning academic school subjects. *See* **test, aptitude; test, prognostic;** *dist. f.* **test, mental;** *contr. w.* **test, mechanical-aptitude.**

test, scientific: a test so constructed that it is adequate as an instrument for research, that is, one that is valid for the purpose for which it is to be used, yields objective data, is reliable, and can be administered, scored, and interpreted under standard conditions.

test score: *see* **score, test.**

test score, content standard: *see* **score, content standard test.**

test-scoring machine: any one of a number of different machines designed to score objective tests by mechanical, electrical, or optical means; usually necessitates the use of specially prepared answer sheets.

test, screen: a test designed to select from a group those individuals in a specified category, for example, a group intelligence test given to a group for the purpose of identifying those individuals having either subnormal or exceptionally high intelligence.

test, screening: *syn.* **test, screen.**

test, selection: any objective test in which the subject is instructed to choose and indicate one or more correct answers from among several answers suggested for each item.

test selection method, Wherry-Doolittle multiple correlation: a systematic way of calculating a multiple correlation coefficient by analytically selecting at once from many tests the best battery by adding them one at a time until a maximum R has been obtained.

test, Selective Service: a test formerly given to male college students under the auspices of the Selective Service System to determine whether the tested students should be inducted into the armed services immediately or after graduation; abandoned before 1970.

test, self-administering: any test whose written directions are so clear that the persons tested can proceed with a minimum of guidance, the test administrator having only to keep order and time the test.

test, self-marking: a test in which the first phase of scoring is done as the subject writes his responses; sometimes accomplished by means of a carbon sheet.

test, sensory-discrimination: a test requiring the subject to indicate the direction of a difference between two sensory stimuli (as two tones differing in pitch), for the purpose of determining how small a difference can be perceived.

test, service: a test designed to reveal the degree of cooperativeness, generosity, or altruism possessed by the subject, conducted usually by placing the subject in situations that provide opportunity to work for the welfare of others; the subject may also be placed in situations that offer occasion for contrasting his efficiency when working for a group and when working for his own interests.

test, short-answer: rough *syn.* **test, objective.**

test, short-essay: a series of questions to which the subject is asked to respond by writing a brief answer.

test, sign: a nonparametric test of the difference between paired observations; involves the number of paired observations in which the first member of the pair has a higher (or lower) value than the second member.

test, silent-reading: any test in which the subject makes no oral response but indicates his reactions to the test items by marking, checking, or writing.

test, similarities: (1) a test directing the subject to state the similarity between two or more named objects; (2) a test directing the subject to determine and indicate which of a number of words, signs, symbols, etc., are in the same category.

test, simple-recall: a memory type of objective test in which each item is to be answered by a single word recalled and written down or by a number obtained by computation. *See* **test, recall.**

test, simplified run: (phys. ed.) a test involving running a specified time and/or distance for measuring cardiorespiratory endurance.

test, single-answer: a type of objective test in which each item is to be answered by means of a single word, the correct word either to be recalled and written down or selected from among a list of suggested answers.

test, single-tailed: *syn.* **test, one-tailed.**

test, situational: controlled setups, where an individual is submitted to stimuli designed to elicit the kinds of behavior the tester wishes to observe, but in which the testee believes he is being tested for something else; the observer records the method of performance, the emotional content, and the amount achieved.

test, skill: (phys. ed.) an evaluative device used for measuring physical performance.

test, Snellen: a test, used to measure central vision, in which the subject stands a certain distance from a standard chart and reads the letters on the chart; based upon the fact that objects may be seen by the normal eye when they subtend an angle of 1 minute.

test, social: a measure of social aptitude.

test, sociometric: (1) a device on which members of a group record their preferences for associates in a specific activity; (2) a technique for revealing group structure and identifying subdivisions of the group and various types of group members, for example, leaders, isolates, rival factions, etc.

test, sorting: a performance test demanding discrimination of presented materials into categories; often used for normal subjects and also for individuals suspected of having brain damage; a test of "rigidity," brain damage, and an index of intelligence.

test, sound discrimination: a method of measuring ability to perceive differences between phonetic units or speech sounds; as usually administered, pairs of words or syllables are given and the subject is asked to determine whether the two members of a pair are alike or different.

test space: *see* **space, test.**

test, special-ability: a test designed to measure some special ability or restricted group of capacities.

test, specialty knowledge: a test designed to evaluate the knowledge required by Air Force specialties (jobs); scores are used with other pertinent information to assess the overall competence of airmen for award of an Air Force specialty.

test, specific intelligence: *syn.* **test, aptitude.**

test, speech: a test of ability to enunciate and pronounce correctly, used to determine speech defects or to measure progress in speech correction.

test, speed: a form of a test in which performance is measured by the number of tasks performed in a given time; it is assumed that the items are uniform in difficulty; primarily intended to yield a *rate score* that is not affected by other dimensions of pupil performance. *Syn.* **rate test.**

test, spiral: a type of cycle test, so arranged that there is an increase in difficulty in successive subtests or exercises. (Most spiral tests are not entirely regular or uniform in increase in difficulty.) *See* **test, cycle.**

test, stability: a simple and crude test of the adequacy of sampling, consisting in taking several approximately equal samples from the data and then deciding whether the statistics computed from these samples are reasonably similar, the size of the samples being increased, if necessary, until the successive samples are reasonably similar.

test standardization: *see* **standardization, test.**

test, standardized: a test for which content has been selected and checked empirically, for which norms have been established, for which uniform methods of administering and scoring have been developed, and which may be scored with a relatively high degree of objectivity.

test, Stanford-Binet: a revision of Binet's test by Lewis Terman and others at Stanford University; the most popular adaptation of the test in the United States.

test, statistical: *syn.* **test of significance.**

test, stimulability: a type of articulation test in which the individual is allowed to see and hear a sound as it is produced by the examiner before attempting to produce it himself. *See* **test, articulation.**

test, strength: a test designed to measure muscular strength; often designates a series of test items intended to measure general bodily strength rather than the strength of specific muscles.

test, structured: a test in which all subjects interpret the task in the same way. *See* **structured.**

test-study method: a teaching procedure in which a unit of study is preceded by a test on the material to be studied, as a means of determining the extent of pupil knowledge of the material and of avoiding the teaching of items with which pupils are already familiar. *See* **test, preliminary;** *contr. w.* **study-test method.**

test, study-skills: a test which measures selected study skills; more analytical than an ordinary *reading-comprehension test* and measuring somewhat different skills.

test-study-test method: (spelling) a procedure in spelling study in which words are dictated to pupils before the study of them; each pupil then studies the words missed in preparation for a final test.

test, subject-matter: *syn.* **test, achievement.**

test, subjective: a test, such as an essay test, that is scored on the basis of the scorer's personal judgment of the worth of each answer, rather than by reference to an objective scoring key; often used to designate the traditional type of examination. *See* **subjective;** *contr. w.* **test, objective.**

test, substitution: a test requiring the subject to substitute one set of symbols or characters for another according to a key.

test, suppressor: a test designed to have high correlation with a predictor test and low correlation with the criterion; such a test is used in a battery to improve prediction by suppressing some of the irrelevant variance of another test or tests. *See* **variable, suppressor.**

test, survey: a test that measures general achievement in a given subject or area, usually with the connotation that the test is intended to measure group status rather than to yield precise measures of individuals.

test, sweep-check: an audiometric method of screening out possible hearing-loss cases by testing for auditory response to different frequencies presented at a constant intensity level. *See* **audiometry, screening.**

test, swinging voice: a test in which speech is fed alternately to one ear and then to the other; the speech will be very intelligible if both ears are stimulated at about the same sensation level; if one ear is bad, however, the speech will lose much of its intelligibility.

test, syllable-span: a test in which groups of nonsense or other syllables are spoken by the examiner, the testee being required to repeat them immediately; the number of such syllables that the subject can remember and repeat is taken as his syllable span; used chiefly in individual intelligence tests. *Dist. f.* **test, digit-span.**

test, symbol-digit: a test in which the subject is asked to substitute an equivalent symbol (such as a letter or simple geometrical form) for each of a number of digits in accordance with a prearranged plan or key; thus the numbers 1 to 9 might be represented by the letters A to I, and the subject asked to replace the digits in a long series by their equivalent letters; a type of *substitution test* or *code test.*

test, symbol-elaboration: a projective-type test requiring the interpretation by the testee of symbols which are then to be combined by him into a fairly coherent whole.

test, t: a statistical test resulting in evidence for the acceptance or rejection of a null hypothesis; the ratio of a statistic to its standard error; t is mathematically equal to the critical ratio, but provides a more critical test than does the normal probability table. *Syn.* **Fisher's t; student's t;** *see* **distribution, t; ratio, t.**

test tabulation: *see* **tabulation, test.**

test, teacher-aptitude: a measuring instrument intended to determine a person's potential capacity for success in the teaching profession. *See* **aptitude.**

test, teacher-made: a test prepared by a teacher for her own classes. (While such a test lacks the advantages of standardization, it may better reflect the actual teaching purposes.)

test, temperament: *see* **inventory, adjustment.**

test, term: an examination, given at the close of a school term, that usually samples achievement in the entire term's work.

test, thematic apperception: one of the projective techniques characterized by obtaining from the person tested interpretations of a series of standardized pictures, these interpretations being then analyzed to reveal the projected values, motives, associative constellations, and complexes of the respondent.

test, threshold knowledge: a test which can assist an educational systems designer to identify those knowledges and skills which need not be taught, as in the programmed instructional framework; such tests are administered to only a sampling of prospective students to help discover what to put into a course of instruction.

test, timed: a test on which the subject may work only for a certain length of time, frequently having time limits for each part or section; usually scored on the basis of the amount of work, that is, the number of items, correctly completed during the allotted time. Rough *syn.* **rate test.**

test, trade: a test designed to measure ability in a given trade or vocation, usually based on performance in a sampling of actual processes or skills common to the trade or vocation in question.

test, triangle: a test devised by Gwyn requiring the subject to fit four triangular blocks into two openings, one a rectangle and the other a triangle.

test, true-false: a type of alternate-response test in which the subject indicates whether each of a number of statements is true or false. *See* **test, alternate-response.**

test, tuberculin: a diagnostic procedure, utilizing tuberculin, for the purpose of determining the presence or absence of tuberculosis infection. *See* **test, patch.**

test, tuning fork: in otology, the classic method of measuring, or more properly describing, hearing loss by noting the patient's responses to vibrating tuning forks; forks of various frequencies are selected for administering the standard test.

test, two-sided: *syn.* **test, two-tailed.**

test, two-tail: *syn.* **test, two-tailed.**

test, two-tailed: a statistical test of significance which includes both extremes (tails) of the sampling distribution; a test of a null hypothesis that two parameters are equal when the logical possibility exists for either parameter to be larger than the other. *Syn.* **double-tailed test; two-sided test; two-tail test;** *dist. f.* **test, one-tailed.**

test, typical-performance: any test designed to measure what an examinee is "really like" rather than any intellective or ability characteristic; includes tests of personality, attitude, interest, etc.; used in opposition to *maximum-performance test.*

test, uniform: *syn.* **test, speed.**

test, unit: an examination on a unit of work; used in many directed-study plans to test the pupils' assimilation and mastery of the unit experience.

test universality: consistency of a test across changes in culture.

test vector: *see* **vector, test.**

test vector, projection of: (fact. anal.) scalar product of a test vector with the unit vector along the axis upon which the test vector is projected (length of test vector $X \cos Y$, where Y is the angle between the test vector and the axis upon which it is being projected).

test, verbal: any test depending on written or spoken language, whether in administering or responding, or both.

test, verbal intelligence: a device used for measuring intelligence which requires speech and/or language ability by the person responding; such tests indicate the ability to work efficiently with verbal symbols.

test, verbal-reasoning: a type of subtest commonly used in group intelligence tests, employing verbal materials and designed to measure logical thought processes.

test, vision: an assessment or examination of one or more of the visual functions, such as central visual acuity, peripheral vision, or binocular vision.

test, visual: *see* **test, vision.**

test, visual-acuity: a test device designed to measure or examine visual acuity, for example the *Snellen test. See* **visual acuity.**

test, visual classification: (mil. ed.) intelligence test given at induction centers to men who do not speak English and to men who cannot read.

test, visual-haptic: a battery of seven tests which determines the degree to which a person has a preference for using his eyes or his body as the intermediary for his experiences; whether he has a preference for observation or for tactile and kinesthetic experiences. *See* **haptic type; visual type.**

test, vocabulary: (1) a word-recognition or word-pronunciation test; (2) a test in which the subject is given a graded series of words to define; frequently used as a measure of mental age.

test, vocational interest: a series of questions concerning the objects or activities for which an individual indicates preferences; high scores are indicative of behavior patterns which would enable the individual to succeed in an occupational field.

test, Wada sodium amytal: a method introduced by Wada in 1949 for determining cerebral dominance; a one-sided intracarotid injection of sodium amytal is carried in the carotid artery directly to the same side of the brain; if it is the side of the dominant hemisphere, there will rapidly be disturbance of speech and a feeling of depression; on the nondominant side, there will be euphoria instead of depression and no language disorder; in both instances, EEG and other neurological signs are unilateral. *See* **cerebral dominance.**

test, watch-tick: a quick method of testing hearing; a person with normal hearing can hear the tick of an Ingersoll watch 48 inches from his ear; also called watch test.

test, whisper: a method of screening for a hearing loss; the examiner whispers at a 20-foot distance from a pupil whose back is to the tester.

test, whole-meaning: a test that measures the power to grasp the central idea of a paragraph or larger unit of printed matter.

test, will-and-temperament: a test used to measure emotional reactions and traits such as speed of movement, flexibility, and speed of decision.

test-wiseness: a subject's capacity to utilize the characteristics and formats of the test and/or the test-taking situation to receive a high score; logically independent of the examinee's knowledge of the subject matter which the items are supposedly measuring; includes knowledge of strategies in using time, avoiding error, guessing, reasoning deductively, and using cues and specific determiners.

test, word-discrimination: a test designed to measure ability to differentiate words.

test, word-recognition: a test designed to measure the power of the reader to perceive and identify words with which he is familiar.

test, work-limit: a test providing sufficient time for all or nearly all the students to finish their work; sometimes scored on the basis of the time required by the examinee or examinees to complete all the tasks. *See* **test, power.**

test, work-sample: a performance test which provides a controlled tryout of the examinee's behavior under conditions as similar as possible to those he will encounter in a work situation.

test, yes-no: a type of alternate-response test in which the pupil gives affirmative or negative responses to questions or to statements. *See* **test, alternate-response.**

tested interest: *see* **interest, tested.**

testing: use of tests, usually some specific instrument or set of instruments to determine a certain quality or trait or a series of such qualities or traits.

testing, accountability: the attempt to monitor the academic results achieved by teachers in their instructional activities and the social and emotional impact of the school on the pupils through periodic sample testing by outside education experts or with specially constructed tests purchased from education industry firms. *See* **accountability, educational.**

testing and measurement service: the functions within the schools which are scheduled to assist pupils and/or staff to gain carefully designed samples of pupil behavior for pupil and staff benefit.

testing, brain-wave intelligence: testing, in the early 1970s on an experimental basis, which is based upon an assumed relationship between intelligence and the rate of speed with which brain waves respond to a flashing light flashed at random 100 times in 300 seconds; a computer records what happens after each flash and gives an accumulated report; the assumption is that the amount of electrical activity varies with the intelligence of the individual.

testing, cooperative: testing in which the construction, administration, and scoring (and the reporting on any one or more of these) are done on a cooperative basis.

testing, free-field hearing: a method of measuring auditory sensitivity by projecting either a live voice or a recorded voice or other sounds through a loudspeaker instead of through headphones worn by the person being tested; sound intensity is reduced to the threshold of perception and the actual intensity of the sound is measured after the subject has been removed from the field in order to eliminate the effect of absorption, reflection, and diffraction by the body.

testing, operational: a continuing process of evaluation which may be applied to either operational personnel or a situation to determine their validity or reliability.

testing program: *see* **program, testing.**

testing program, external: *see* **program, testing.**

testing program, internal: *see* **program, testing.**

testing, reality: the process of interpreting and verifying perceptual experience.

testing technique, double-testing: a situational test for determining cheating by administering equivalent forms of a test, one under supervised conditions and the other under unsupervised conditions.

testing unit, mobile: a sound-treated trailer which is used in some places for hearing-test administrations and which moves from community to community.

tests, articulated: a series of tests in which different levels of the test are used for different ages or grades and which have been constructed and standardized so that the same or comparable elements or objectives are measured in the overlapping ranges among the various levels of the test.

tests, employment: (mil. ed.) those tests needed by the commands to (*a*) obtain data that can be used to enhance the operational capability and utilization of existing forces and equipment, (*b*) develop the most effective tactics, techniques, and procedures for the use of existing forces and equipment, and (*c*) define or investigate operational problems associated with the use of existing forces and equipment.

tetherball: a game played with a ball attached by a rope (7 to 8 feet long) to a pole which is usually 10 feet high; players position themselves on opposite sides of the pole beyond a circle, 3 feet in radius from the pole as center; players hit the ball in an endeavor to wind it around the pole.

tetrachoric correlation: *see* **correlation, tetrachoric.**

tetrachoric correlation coefficient: *see* **coefficient, tetrachoric correlation.**

tetrad difference: an expression of the form $r_{ab}r_{cd} - r_{ac}r_{bd}$; in the correlation matrix, each of these is the determinant of a second-order minor that does not contain an element from the principal diagonal; when every tetrad of a set of correlations is equal to zero, hierarchical order is present and the correlations can be accounted for by a single common factor and a specific factor. *See* **hierarchical order; two-factor theory.**

tetraplegia (tet'rə‧plē'ji‧ə): paralysis of all four extremities; also called *quadriplegia.*

text: (1) *syn.* **textbook;** (2) main body of writing in a book, excluding introductory matter, supplementary matter, notes, etc.

text blindness: rare *syn.* **alexia.**

text, programmed: a book in which a program is printed in one of two typical formats: page-to-page or down-the-page; in the former, the student turns the page after each item, finding the answer and the next item on the following page; generally, items are arranged in levels; the student goes through the book doing all the items on one level, then repeats the process for each successive level; a down-the-page format requires the student to mask the answer column and in some cases everything but the item he is working on as he reads down the page; a programmed text almost always presents a *linear program.* *See* **instruction, programmed; book, scrambled.**

text, scrambled: *see* **book, scrambled.**

textbook: (1) any manual of instruction; (2) a book dealing with a definite subject of study, systematically arranged, intended for use at a specified level of instruction, and used as a principal source of study material for a given course.

textbook commission: a commission appointed, elected, or otherwise selected in a state, municipality, or school district with the legal responsibility for selecting textbooks for adoption in the schools of a given area. *See* **state adoption of textbooks.**

textbook-control commission: *syn.* **textbook commission.**

textbook, free: any textbook provided for pupil use without cost to the pupil.

textbook, graded: a textbook prepared especially for use in a specific grade.

textbook inventory: *see* **inventory, textbook.**

textbook library: *see* **library, textbook.**

textbook, programmed: a textbook or teaching machine laid out so that the student reads a frame and responds to questions on what hc has read, then turns the page and finds the correct answer; machine or book has been designed to solve the cheating problems in that pages cannot be turned out of sequence, making cheating as hard as learning; cost of machine is relatively low compared with a standard textbook.

textbook recitation: *see* **recitation, textbook.**

textbook, scrambled: *see* **book, scrambled.**

textbook teaching: *see* **teaching, textbook.**

textbooks, uniform: textbooks conforming to the same standard, usually one fixed for all the schools of a district or regional administrative division. (The standard may consist of a stipulation that particular books shall be used.)

textile school: a school organized for the purpose of preparing individuals for profitable employment and advancement in the clothing and allied trades.

textiles: (ind. arts) the study of the tools, materials, and processes used in the textile industry, including the source, preparation, and applications of fibers; learning experiences generally include experimenting, designing, weaving, and evaluating products made of a variety of fibers.

textiles and clothing: (home ec.) an area of study in which students learn to plan, select, buy, make, and care for clothing.

textiles instruction: *see* **instruction, textiles.**

thanatophobia (than'ə‧tō‧fō'bi‧ə): a morbid fear of death.

thanatos (thä'nə‧təs): (Gk., lit., "death") the death instinct, the destructive instinct in Freudian psychology contrasted with *eros,* the life instinct.

the establishment: *see* **establishment, the.**

theater art: *see* **art, theater.**

theatrical motion picture: *see* **motion picture, theatrical.**

theism: (1) a belief in the existence of a god or gods, especially of personal gods; (2) sometimes contrasted with deism. *See* **deism; henotheism; monotheism; pantheism.**

thematic apperception test: *see* **test, thematic apperception.**

thematic approach to spelling: *see* **spelling, thematic approach to.**

thematic fantasy: *see* **fantasy, thematic.**

thematic prompt: *see* **prompt, thematic.**

theme: (1) a generalization selected as the basis for an area of the curriculum or for a unit of study or activity; (2) (journ.) a unified scheme of content, tone, point of view, central idea, decorative or pictorial art, color, individuality, or originality, adopted to give coherence or continuity to a scholastic or collegiate yearbook; (3) an essay done as an educational exercise.

theme, personal: (couns.) an autobiography used as a guidance technique by classroom teachers for the purpose of writing themes in English classes and for providing personal information for use by the counselor. *See* **questionnaire, personal history.**

theme procedure: a method of curriculum development in which the curriculum is organized around certain of the more important generalizations employed by adults in interpreting contemporary life.

theme unit: *see* **unit, theme.**

theocracy: government either immediately under the direction of God or in the hands of his earthly representatives; a political theory holding that the ideal state is one in which a Supreme Being (God) rules the state through his earthly body (thc church).

theological education: precisely, the training of persons in studies associated with the doctrine of God, such as biblical and dogmatic studies, but frequently used to refer to the professional training of the clergy.

theological library: *see* **library, theological.**

theological school: a professional institution of higher learning, most often established for the training of the clergy and specializing in religious and moral fields of knowledge. *Syn.* **divinity school; theological seminary.**

theological seminary: *syn.* **theological school.**

theological virtues: *see* **virtues, theological.**

theology: systematically formulated beliefs or knowledge concerning God; the science of God.

theology, ascetic: the systematic study of the methods and rules of training the Christian in the knowledge and love of God, that is, progress in the spiritual life.

theology, fundamental: *see* apologetics.

theology, moral: the study of the growth of Christian character with special emphasis on the obtaining of personal holiness.

theomania: morbid concern about religious cults and emotionalized modes of worship.

theorem: (math.) in a deductive system, a sentence for which a proof is given; theorems usually give information applicable to a large number of instances as, for example, the Pythagorean theorem, which applies to any right triangle in the plane.

theorem, Bernoulli's: *see* Bernoulli's theorem.

theorem of arithmetic, fundamental: *see* arithmetic, fundamental theorem of.

theoretical: (1) pertaining to reflective thought that is detached from the pressure for immediate results in order to examine the relatedness of current practices and affirmed values; (2) pertaining to general concepts by which particular situations can be understood and adequately related; (3) impractical. (When theory and practice are viewed in opposition, theoretical considerations are tolerated but it is the practical man who gets things done.)

theoretical approach: speculative examination of issues; inquiry based on general principles or definitions, proceeding to interpretation in the light of these general ideas.

theoretical generalization: *see* generalization, theoretical.

theoretical intelligibility: *syn.* intelligibility, structural.

theoretical isomorphic model: *see* model, theoretical isomorphic.

theoretical mathematics: *see* mathematics, theoretical.

theoretical model: *see* model, theoretical.

theoretical research report: *see* report, theoretical research.

theoretical yield: (1) the amount of revenue that would be produced by a tax if all taxpayers were to pay their tax bills in full on the true value of all their taxable property; (2) the revenue of a tax at a constant rate on the full value of all taxable property.

theories, vocational: *see* vocational theories.

theory: (1) a set of assumptions or generalizations, supported by related philosophical assumptions and scientific principles and serving as a basis for projecting hypotheses which suggest a course of action; the hypotheses are then subjected to scientific investigation, the findings of which are evaluated in order to validate new scientific principles and philosophical assumptions; a symbolic construction; (2) (mus.) the study of the principles underlying musical structure, usually interpreted as including harmony, sightsinging, dictation, single and double counterpoint, canon, fugue, and form; orchestration may or may not be considered a theoretical study; *see* music, applied.

theory, ability-to-pay tax: *see* tax theory, ability-to-pay.

theory, administrative: *see* administrative theory.

theory, Americanization: *see* Americanization theory.

theory, atomistic: *see* atomistic theory.

theory, babble-luck: *see* babble-luck theory.

theory, behavior: *see* behavior theory.

theory, child benefit: *see* child benefit theory.

theory, communication: *see* information theory.

theory, communications: *see* communications theory.

theory, community: *see* community theory.

theory, concatenated: *see* concatenated theory.

theory, content: *see* content theory.

theory, counseling: *see* counseling theory.

theory course: *see* course, theory.

theory, cultural recapitulation: *see* cultural recapitulation theory.

theory, culture-epochs: *see* culture-epochs theory.

theory, decision: *see* decision theory.

theory, dissonance: *see* dissonance, cognitive.

theory, dominant-letter: *see* dominant-letter theory.

theory, double-aspect: *see* double-aspect theory.

theory, drive reduction: *see* drive reduction theory.

theory, family developmental: *see* family developmental theory.

theory, field: *see* field theory.

theory, functional: *see* functional theory.

theory, game: *see* game theory.

theory, great-man: *see* great-man theory.

theory, hierarchical: *see* hierarchical theory.

theory in counseling, behavioral: *see* behavioral theory in counseling.

theory in counseling, psychoanalytic: *see* psychoanalytic theory in counseling.

theory in counseling, reinforcement: *see* counseling, reinforcement theory in.

theory in counseling, self: *see* self theory in counseling.

theory, information: *see* information theory.

theory, information-processing: *see* information-processing theory.

theory, large sample: *see* large sample theory.

theory, macroeconomic: *see* microeconomic approach.

theory, mass-action: *see* mass-action theory.

theory, needs: *see* needs theory.

theory, number: *see* number theory.

theory of counseling, trait and factor: *see* counseling, trait and factor theory of.

theory of cultural change: *see* cultural change, theory of.

theory of elite: *see* elite, theory of.

theory of home rule: *see* home rule, theory of.

theory of identical elements: *see* identical elements.

theory of knowledge, coherence: *see* knowledge, coherence theory of.

theory of knowledge, contextual: *see* knowledge, contextual theory of.

theory of knowledge, copy: *see* knowledge, copy theory of.

theory of knowledge, presentative: *see* knowledge, presentative theory of.

theory of knowledge, representative: *see* knowledge, representative theory of.

theory of knowledge, revelation: *see* knowledge, revelation theory of.

theory of knowledge, spectator: *see* knowledge, spectator theory of.

theory of learning, association: *see* psychology, association.

theory of learning, field: *see* learning, field theory of.

theory of learning, gestalt: *see* learning, gestalt theory of.

theory of meaning, contextual: *see* meaning, contextual theory of.

theory of mind, emergent: *see* mind, emergent theory of.

theory of mind, functional: *see* mind, functional theory of.

theory of mind, substantive: *see* mind, substantive theory of.

theory of orthogenesis: *see* orthogenesis, theory of.

theory of progress: *see* progress, theory of.

theory of reading, dynamic substrata-factor: *see* reading, dynamic substrata-factor theory of.

theory of reading, operant behavior: *see* reading, operant behavior theory of.

theory of reading retardation, cholinesterase: *see* reading retardation, cholinesterase theory of.

theory of relativity: *see* relativity, theory of.

theory of sets: *see* set theory.

theory of taxation, benefit: *see* benefit theory of taxation.

theory of truth: *see* truth, coherence theory of.

theory of truth, correspondence: *see* truth, correspondence theory of.

theory of unity: Froebel's doctrine maintaining that the soul of man is a manifestation of nature and that the education of human beings requires the knowledge and appreciation of religion, nature, and language in their intimate, mutual interaction.

theory of value, interest: *see* **value, interest theory of.**

theory of values: *see* **ethics; philosophy, moral.**

theory, onomatoschematic: *see* **onomatoschematic theory.**

theory, postremity: *see* **postremity theory.**

theory, queuing: *see* **queuing theory.**

theory, recapitulation: *see* **recapitulation theory.**

theory, role: *see* **role theory.**

theory, small sample: *see* **small sample theory.**

theory, topological field: *see* **field theory, topological.**

theory, transformational: *see* **transformational theory.**

theory, true-score: *see* **true-score theory.**

theory, two-factor: *see* **two-factor theory.**

theory, value: *see* **value theory.**

theory, vestibule: *see* **vestibule theory.**

theory, yo-he-ho: *see* **yo-he-ho theory.**

theosophy: (1) any philosophy or religion that maintains the possibility of achieving a knowledge of God in mystical fashion through various practices; (2) the beliefs or doctrine of a particular sect, the Theosophical Society, derived largely from Buddhism and embracing many of its teachings.

therapeutic: healing; curing; correcting.

therapeutic counseling: *see* **counseling, therapeutic.**

therapeutic discipline: *see* **discipline, therapeutic.**

therapeutic pedagogy: *see* **pedagogy, therapeutic.**

therapeutic reading: *see* **reading, therapeutic.**

therapeutic relationship: *see* **relationship, therapeutic.**

therapeutic teacher: *see* **adjustment teacher.**

therapeutics: the body of knowledge pertaining to the treatment of disease, including the administration of medicines and the employment of physical or mental correctives.

therapist, occupational: professional personnel employed in hospital schools and/or classes and schools for crippled children; under medical direction emphasizes therapy to improve the use of the upper extremities.

therapist, physical: professional personnel employed in hospital schools and/or classes and schools for crippled children; under medical direction emphasizes therapy to improve the use of the lower extremities.

therapist, speech: a specialist who has the responsibility for diagnosing and carrying out corrective procedures for speech disorders.

therapy: (couns.) sociopsychological assistance or counseling which involves considerable involvement in personality restructuring and/or environmental change.

therapy, activity-group: a type of permissive play or club situation used to provide therapy for children of an age below middle adolescence who are experiencing behavioral and adjustment problems; usually not suitable for any adolescents with extreme problems of a neurotic or aggressive nature.

therapy, art: (1) (spec. ed.) the use of various art forms in the treatment of educationally handicapping disabilities; (2) (art. ed.) *see* **therapy, creative.**

therapy, attitude: that part of psychotherapy, or reeducation, that seeks to improve the general outlook on life.

therapy, aversion: a process of counterconditioning, using pain or other noxious stimulation, to treat nonadjustive, anxiety-reducing responses; in such counterconditioning the maladjustive responses, which previously served as anxiety reducers, now become the cues for anxiety increments.

therapy, behavior: a therapeutic treatment of a pupil using special methods, materials, or environmental manipulation intended to facilitate behavioral modifications in the pupil and thereby improve his learning potential.

therapy, client-centered: psychological counseling in which the therapist endeavors to keep the client expressing and exploring his attitudes as freely as possible; through this, the client becomes more understanding and accepting of himself and others. *Contr. w.* **therapy, directive.**

therapy, creative: the use of creative activity as a means of personality adjustment.

therapy, dance: the use of a form of rhythmic motor activity for improving a physical or emotional condition.

therapy, directive: the therapeutic approach in which the therapist takes an active role by aiding in the uncovering of conflicts and in giving interpretations and directive guidance. *Contr. w.* **therapy, client-centered.**

therapy, diversional: therapy consisting of suggestions or assistance given to the counselee for the beneficial use of activities with the aim of focusing the counselee's attention on specific activities so that he will be less preoccupied with problems.

therapy, educational: special educational practices conceived of as contributing to the treatment of some organic or functional disorder in the pupil; for example, remedial teaching of reading for the purpose, in part, of reducing reaction to frustration, or teaching of touch typing for the purpose, in part, of providing a compensatory skill for a visually handicapped pupil.

therapy, electroconvulsive shock: use of a high-frequency electric current applied to the head of a patient to produce convulsions and unconsciousness in the attempt to alter mood and emotional responses, particularly to improve the severely depressed person. *See* **electrotherapy.**

therapy, evaluative: *syn.* **therapy, general semantic.**

therapy, expressive: therapeutic method in which the patient is allowed free expression (through play, music, sociodrama, etc.), through which a resolution of conflicts is achieved to varying degrees; the therapist aids in creating a permissive atmosphere but plays a minimal part in the therapeutic process.

therapy, general semantic: a method of treatment based on the principles of general semantics as expounded by Alfred Korzybski; designed for the treatment of behavior disorders, language defects, speech difficulties, etc. *See* **abstraction, levels of; extensionalization.**

therapy, group: technique employed by qualified psychologists, psychiatrists, or psychoanalysts for assisting, chiefly through a process of group interaction and exploration in a permissive, cooperative atmosphere, relatively homogeneous groups of individuals into gaining insights and understandings of the probable causative background of the individual's present mental, emotional, and social conflicts; the goal sought is some degree of conflict resolution or better orientation for each member of the group. *Syn.* **group psychotherapy.**

therapy, group development: cooperative diagnosis, decisions, and actions toward group growth, resulting in the development of interrelationships in social experiences which may be therapeutic to individuals in the group.

therapy, multiple: a counseling technique which ordinarily employs two counselors with one client.

therapy, music: use of music in the treatment of persons suffering from physical, mental, or emotional disorders.

therapy, musical: *syn.* **therapy, music.**

therapy, nondirective: therapeutic approach that places primary responsibility for direction of therapy on the client (patient); utilizes the individual's drive toward adjustment and works toward freeing the individual for normal personality growth; emphasis on the individual rather than on the problem and on emotional rather than intellectual aspects of behavior.

therapy, nondirective group: therapy similar to *nondirective counseling* but focused more on basic personality restructuring in a group setting.

therapy, occupational: prescribed creative activity for patients physically or mentally handicapped, carried out under supervision for its effect in promoting recovery or rehabilitation following disease or injury.

therapy, physical: *syn.* **physiotherapy.**

therapy, play: the process of assisting a child through play to a better understanding, at his level of maturity, of his behavior or providing an outlet for maladjusted behavioral activities. *See* **therapy, recreational; therapy, release.**

therapy, reading: the use of reading as a means of relieving mental or emotional difficulties or disease.

therapy, recreational: a method of treatment based on the use of games, crafts, and other recreational activity; used in the treatment of mental, personality, and behavior disorders.

therapy, relationship: a method of treatment, developed in Philadelphia in the 1930s, in which the therapist represents variously to the client persons who have had a close relationship to the client, the solution of the client's emotional problems being facilitated thereby.

therapy, relaxation: a method of treatment that seeks to eliminate unnecessary muscular tensions and strains, using such techniques as light manipulation of the muscles, deep massage, alternate tensing and relaxing of muscles, concentration on peaceful thoughts and images, and listening to quiet music; used especially in cases of spastic paralysis, but also in cases of stuttering, voice defects, and personality maladjustment.

therapy, release: in guidance and counseling, a therapeutic treatment of mental or behavior problems in which the emphasis is on the encouragement of the client in the release of feeling and emotion, that is, in bringing into the open the thoughts, attitudes, feelings, and emotional impulses that are clustered around his problems and conflicts.

therapy, speech: *see* **class, speech therapy.**

therapy, supportive: therapeutic method emphasizing reinforcement of defenses and making them more effective; aids the repression rather than the "uncovering" of deep conflicts. *Syn.* **surface therapy.**

therapy, surface: *syn.* **therapy, supportive.**

theriomorphism (thĕr′i·ō·môr′fiz'm): the attribution to human beings of the characteristics of subhuman beings. *See* **anthropomorphism.**

thermoplastic recording: *see* **recording, thermoplastic.**

thesaurus: an alphabetical list of vocabulary terms authorized for use in an information retrieval system, each of which is accompanied, where relevant, by its related terms, references, and scope notes.

thesis: a systematic, written presentation of the results of study, investigation, or research; may be offered to satisfy in part the requirements for a degree. *See* **dissertation.**

thesis, doctoral: a thesis submitted in partial fulfillment of the requirements for a doctor's degree; the term thesis alone is more appropriately applied to the master's degree. *See* **dissertation.**

thesis, master's: a written report of some extensiveness submitted in partial fulfillment of the requirements for a master's degree.

thick voice: phonation characterized by a muffled, lifeless quality, and usually by pitch variation of less than average extent; usually accompanied by sluggish articulation.

thinking: (1) an unregulated flow of ideas or stream of images, impressions, recollections, and hopes sometimes indicated by the pleasantry "a penny for your thoughts"; *see* **thinking, autistic;** (2) an undisciplined guessing that treads lightly and superficially over grounds and evidence in an effort to reach a conclusion; (3) the contemplation of ideas, or meditation, without any endeavor to control nature or experience; (4) reflective, cognitive, or critical looking into something for the sake of establishing belief and controlling action; *see* **act of thought.**

thinking, abductive: the act of conceiving a hypothesis or developing a theory—often based on the use of data considered surprising.

thinking, analogical: thinking that proceeds on the assumption that if two or more things are similar in one or more respects they probably will agree in other respects; drawing conclusions about an unknown on the basis of its agreement with or resemblance to a known.

thinking, analytical: *see* **analysis, mathematical.**

thinking, autistic (â·tis'tik): (1) daydreaming or fantasy that serves to gratify wishes or desires not attained in the real world (poetry, wit, dreams, music may represent normal forms; pathological forms occur in schizophrenia and paranoid states); (2) a tendency to consider deep desires and wishes as being accomplished regardless of contradictions with reality.

thinking, axiomatic: *see* **reasoning, axiomatic.**

thinking chart: *see* **chart, thinking.**

thinking, conceptual: (1) the process of thinking in which abstract concepts are related without reference to concrete situations; (2) the manipulation of linguistic or mathematical symbols in terms of their inherent logical relations.

thinking, constructive: *syn.* **thinking, creative.**

thinking, convergent: a type of thinking appropriate for closed-solution-type (one-answer) problems whereby the individual attempts to operate according to prescribed and tested forms of analysis, method, and judgment. *Contr. w.* **thinking, divergent.**

thinking, creative: thinking that is inventive, that explores novel situations, that reaches new solutions to old problems, or that results in thoughts original with the thinker. *Syn.* **constructive thinking.**

thinking, critical: thinking that proceeds on the basis of careful evaluation of premises and evidence and comes to conclusions as objectively as possible through the consideration of all pertinent factors and the use of valid procedures from logic.

thinking, directed: thinking that is guided along particular lines with reference to some goal by the suggestions of another person.

thinking, divergent: mental activity directed to open-end kinds of problems for which there is no one correct answer; the more infrequent statistically a response is under these conditions, the more divergent is the thinking. *Contr. w.* **thinking, convergent.**

thinking, functional: the use of expressed or implied relationships in the process of drawing conclusions or making inferences.

thinking, logical: mental ability that allows one to proceed purposefully from the known to the unknown guided by objective rules and principles.

thinking, nonverbal: perception of a thought in consciousness before it is expressed verbally.

thinking, postulational: *see* **reasoning, axiomatic.**

thinking, reflective: active, persistent, and careful inquiry into any belief or knowledge claim in the light of the grounds and evidences that support it and the further considerations to which it leads (a pragmatic definition); the particular explanation of the nature of reflection or cognition varies with the philosophical assumptions of the person who uses the term: (*a*) in pragmatism, problem-solving, (*b*) in radical behaviorism, implicit movements of the throat and larynx; (*c*) in Thomism, abstracting and using essences to form ideas.

thinking, reflexive: mental activity in which the person introspects about his own thinking.

thinking, relational: (1) thinking in terms of relationships and interrelationships among things, beings, and ideas rather than thinking in terms of the nature or essence of things, beings, and ideas; (2) that process through which concentrated effort is made to isolate the essential characteristics of any property, technique, or concept and to detect any significant relationships that may exist among such fundamental characteristics so that generalizations may be made that will lead to significant abstractions; *see* **thinking, reflective.**

thinking, relativistic: thinking in terms of relationships and interrelationships with reference to conditions and situations, rather than thinking that regards relationships, ideas, and data as independent or absolute entities.

thinking, scientific: (1) thinking based upon ideas derived from sense experience; (2) a term that implies the correlation of single experiences with a logically uniform system of thought, or theoretic structure, in such a manner that the statement of relationship is complete and convincing; (3) thinking the purpose of which is to invent the intellectual tools and instruments for use in common-sense thinking.

thinking, selective: thinking that is delimited by the scope of the problem to be solved and in which elements germane to the problem are applied to its solution, while extraneous elements are discarded.

thinking, symbolic: thinking in terms of symbols and abstractions rather than in terms of concrete data, for example, the kind of thinking used in the solution of problems in algebra or geometry.

thinking, synoptic (si·nop'tik): thinking in terms of broad concepts; thinking that comprises, not only the whole and its parts, but also a wider set of facts pertinent to the whole.

thinking, synthetic: thinking that brings together from different sources data or ideas not previously related and combines or organizes them into logical unity.

thinking, visual: learning that can be acquired only visually rather than as a response to verbal instructions.

third classman: a cadet who is in his second year at a service academy; a sophomore.

third-order interaction: *syn.* **variance, interaction.**

third-world country: *see* **country, third-world.**

thirty-five-millimeter film: *see* **film, thirty-five-millimeter.**

"thirty-school" studies: a series of investigations, sponsored by the Progressive Education Association, of the effects of a variety of plans of curriculum experimentation on various aspects of pupil growth and on later achievement in college.

Thomism: a system of philosophy based on the teachings of St. Thomas Aquinas (1225-1274); its three fundamental principles are (1) being is transcendent; (2) God alone is pure Act; (3) absolute things are specified by themselves; relative things are specified by another.

thought, act of: *see* **act of thought.**

thought control: *see* **control, thought.**

thought question: *see* **question, thought.**

thought, syncretic (sin·kret'ik): thought characterized by inconsistency and by the reconciliation of incongruous ideas; common to the thinking of young children, owing to their limited experience and insufficiently logical organization of experiences.

thought unit: *see* **unit, thought.**

threading: the act of positioning film or magnetic tape in the appropriate mechanism so that it will be transported properly through the mechanism.

three-day drop: the act of dropping pupils from the roll after they have been absent for 3 days. (In certain school districts, the term means the dropping of pupils from the rolls for the entire period of absence after the first 3 days of absence.)

three-dimensional aid: *see* **aid, three-dimensional.**

three-dimensional diagram: *see* **diagram, three-dimensional.**

three R's: (1) formerly, reading, writing, and arithmetic; (2) now interpreted to include the areas of reading, phonics, arithmetic, language and grammar, penmanship, and spelling.

three-teacher school: a school for which three teachers are employed; may include either the elementary grades alone or both the elementary and some or all of the high school grades.

three-three junior-senior high school: *syn.* **high school, junior-senior.**

three-three plan: *see* **six-three-three-plan.**

three-track course of study: a course of study providing for instruction in a particular area on three distinct levels; affords greater individualization of instruction by offering modified curriculum content for the superior, average, and inferior pupils in each class group. *See* **two-track course of study.**

three-two plan: (engineering ed.) a coordinate arrangement between an engineering school and a college of liberal arts, under which a student attends the liberal arts college for 3 years and the engineering school for 2 years, which enables him to receive a bachelor's degree at the end of 4 years and a bachelor of science degree in engineering at the completion of the combined curriculum; similar arrangements have been applied to other professions but usually without formalized agreement.

three-year alternation plan: a plan by which three contiguous grades are combined into one group. *See* **alternation of grades.**

three-year junior college: *see* **junior college, three-year.**

three-year senior high school: *see* **senior high school, three-year.**

threshold: the level of stimulation necessary to produce a response, for example, the number of decibels needed before a person hears a sound or the number of lumens required before he sees something. *Syn.* **limen.**

threshold, audibility: the minimum effective sound pressure of a signal that is capable of evoking an auditory sensation in a specified fraction of the total trials in which the signal is presented; in classical psychophysical techniques, this criterion is usually set at one-half, or 50 percent, although most practical audiometric procedures set a criterion of 100 percent correct identification of the presence of the signal to establish threshold audibility. *See* **hearing threshold, pure-tone.**

threshold audiogram: *see* **audiogram, threshold.**

threshold, audiometric: *see* **audiometric threshold.**

threshold audiometry: *see* **audiometry, threshold.**

threshold, frequency: in measurement of hearing, the point at which the subject being tested consistently responds correctly to the sound stimulus at a specific frequency.

threshold, frustration: *see* **frustration threshold.**

threshold knowledge test: *see* **test, threshold knowledge.**

threshold level, hearing: *see* **hearing loss** (2).

threshold level, speech-reception: the hearing threshold for speech.

threshold of hearing, normal: *see* **hearing, normal threshold of.**

threshold of pain: in measurement of hearing, the point at which sounds are so powerful that they become painful to listen to; normally at an intensity of about 120 decibels.

threshold, pure-tone hearing: *see* **hearing threshold, pure-tone.**

threshold school: an industrial school organized exclusively for the preliminary training, or breaking in, of new employees other than apprentices. *Syn.* **vestibule school.**

thrift campaign: (1) a school-sponsored drive for the purpose of developing habits of thrift among the pupils in such matters as the use of money, time, and materials, the care of property, and the conservation of natural resources; (2) a special school-sponsored drive to collect old papers or other articles to sell so that money will be available to purchase something for the school.

thriftiness: economy and good management.

throatiness: a quality of voice characterized by a harsh or hoarse tone and, usually, low pitch; so called because the speaker seems to be talking "too far back in his throat" or to be "swallowing" his words.

throughput: in automatic computer operation, the highest quantity and quality of services for the greatest number of users, at reasonable cost.

throw: (photog.) the distance from the projector lens to the screen.

thumb apposition: the act of bringing the thumbs against the fingers in picking up or holding objects. (In the first few months of life infants use the five digits as a unit, but by the age of 5 or 6 months they separate the thumb from the other digits and use it counter to the fingers in picking up objects.)

thumb mark: an identification point drawn on, or a marking device pasted on, an upper corner (left or right) of a slide to insure consistent, proper insertion in the projector. *Syn.* **thumbspot.**

thumbspot: *syn.* **thumb mark.**

thumbsucking: (psychoan.) an autoerotic gratification that is an expression of infantile sexual cravings.

thwarting: a condition or circumstance in which attainment of a desired goal cannot be accomplished by means of the accustomed mechanisms of the individual.

tic: a twitching, especially of the facial muscles.

tic, speech: *see* **speech tic.**

ticket, activity: a ticket issued to or purchased by a high school or college student entitling the holder to certain privileges. *See* **book, activity.**

timbre (tim'bər; Fr., taʌ'br'): *syn.* **tone color.**

timbre discrimination: *see* **discrimination, timbre.**

time, acceleration: *see* **start time.**

time, access: *see* **access time.**

time allotment: the amount of time designated for a given activity.

time, available: *see* **up time.**

time, average operation: *see* **operation time, average.**

time block: *see* **block, time.**

time, blocked: *see* **blocked time.**

time budgeting: *see* **budgeting, time.**

time, cognitive: *see* **cognitive time.**

time-compressed speech: *see* **speech, compressed.**

time, cycle: *see* **cycle time.**

time data, engineered: standards or models set up for a job by a time-study engineer. *See* **time study.**

time, dead: that part of total *float* or *lead time* for a part of assembly which is not directly productive; includes the time during which work is moving between operations, waiting time at a machine for the next operation, and time used moving to and waiting for inspection, moving between departments, etc. *See* **time, lead.**

time, deceleration: *see* **stop time.**

time discrimination: *see* **discrimination, time.**

time, dismissed: *see* **dismissed time.**

time distribution: *syn.* **distribution, historical.**

time, down: *see* **down time.**

time, float: *syn.* **time, lead.**

time-lapse photography: *see* **photography, time-lapse.**

time, lead: the amount of time that is required between the initiation of an activity and its completion; a certain part, for example, may have a two-month lead time on the end of the assembly line. *Syn.* **float time;** *see* **time, dead.**

time, minus: the concept of regression, or negative time, involved in man's capability of returning to earlier stages of behavior under the duress of organic injury, illness, and extreme environmental stress.

time-motion study: *see* **study, time-motion.**

time, physical: time marked by the traditionally defined units, as clock time or calendar time.

time, physiologic: internal time, defined by the variegated rates occurring within the individual's corporal system.

time, released: *see* **released time.**

time, riding: *see* **riding time.**

time-sample record: *see* **record, time-sample.**

time sampling: *see* **record, time-sample; sampling, short-time; study, time sampling.**

time sampling study: *see* **study, time sampling.**

time schedule: (1) a written plan or statement, prepared in advance, showing the activities to take place during each portion of the school day, week, month, or year; (2) a plan of dividing the total time allotment for each school subject or activity into daily learning periods of suitable length; (3) a time arrangement for loading or unloading pupils at designated stops along the school bus route.

time schedule, flexible: a schedule that permits periods to be lengthened, shortened, combined, or shifted in time to meet the varying demands of activity.

time series: *see* **series, time.**

time, shared: *see* **enrollment, dual.**

time-shared computer: *see* **computer, time-shared.**

time, sharing: *see* **sharing time.**

time-sharing system: organization of the computer system's *software* so that several programs may be executed concurrently, though not simultaneously, instead of completing them one by one.

time, start: *see* **start time.**

time, stop: *see* **stop time.**

time study: analysis of a job to determine normal time required to complete it. *See* **study, motion.**

time-study habit: the habit of devoting oneself to study at certain regular periods that have been planned and set aside for that purpose. *See* **place-study habit.**

time, total perception: *see* **perception time, total.**

time, up: *see* **up time.**

time, word: *see* **word time.**

timed test: *see* **test, timed.**

timed writing: *see* **writing, timed.**

timidity: an attitude or mental set similar to bashfulness and shyness but somewhat more inclusive; manifested by avoiding reactions or fear in certain situations or as a general pattern of behavior, especially when the situation confronting the individual is new or strange. *Dist. f.* **bashfulness; shyness.**

title: *syn.* **caption.**

title, credit: *see* **credit title.**

title, end: the formal title which brings the audiovisual material to a conclusion.

title, line: the phrase or entry at the extreme left of any row in a table stating the nature or description of the other entries in the row.

title, main: the name of the production, shown at the start of an audiovisual material.

tobacco use education: the approach used to change smoking habits in adults and to prevent the use of tobacco among youth.

toe brace: an appliance for correction of flat foot and deformed toes.

toilet room: a room equipped with washbasins, mirrors, water closets, and, sometimes, urinals, for the use of students and teachers.

tokens: (Wendell Johnson) the running words in a unit of reading matter.

tol: a one-teacher school in India, dating from ancient times but still supported by the government; often surrounded by mud huts in which the students lived, tols became famous for their work in logic and law.

tolerance: (1) an attitude of forbearance, or willingness to consider without prejudice (but not necessarily to accept, reject, or approve) views, opinions, and situations with which one is not in full sympathy; also, an attitude of allowing the existence of such views, opinions, or situations; (2) (math.) *syn.* **error, maximum;** (3) (meas.) *see* **error, absolute.**

tolerance for ambiguity: *see* **ambiguity, tolerance for.**

tolerance for frustration: *see* **frustration, tolerance for.**

tolerance limits: *syn.* **confidence limits.**

tonal dictation: *see* **dictation, tonal.**

tonal gap: a range of pitches that a partly deaf individual does not hear, although he hears tones of higher or lower pitch. (The condition is presumably related to the functioning of the inner ear.) *Contr. w.* **tonal island.**

tonal imagery: *see* **imagery, tonal.**

tonal island: a range of pitches that a partly deaf individual can hear, although he is deaf to tones of higher or lower pitch. *Contr. w.* **tonal gap.**

tonal memory: *see* **memory, tonal.**

tonality: the feeling for key, that is, for the relationships of the various tones within a musical composition to the keynote, or tonic.

tone: (1) a sound or modification of a sound; any discrete vibration that can be perceived by the ear; (2) a sound of definite pitch; (3) the characteristic quality of the sounds produced by a given voice or musical instrument.

tone, chest: a vocal tone deriving a heavy quality from chest resonance. *See* **tone, head; voice, chest; voice, head.**

tone color: that difference between identical pitches sounded on unlike instruments, for example, on the flute and on the oboe; determined by the prominence of certain harmonics over the others; the clear flute quality, for example, results from the almost total absence of all harmonics except the first. *Syn.* **timbre**; *see* **discrimination, timbre.**

tone control: a device on a sound-reproducing or -amplifying instrument by which certain frequencies may be suppressed or increased in intensity, thus changing the character of the sound; for example, suppressing the higher frequencies will make the sound appear to have more bass, and vice versa; incorporated into most sound projectors, phonographs, radios, public-address systems, tape recorders, etc.

tone deafness: *see* **deafness, tone.**

tone discrimination: *see* **discrimination, tone.**

tone, fundamental: a vocal sound produced by an individual when the vocal cords are drawn almost together so that the air passing between them sets them in vibration and a sound results.

tone game: a play activity in which the child imitates or matches various musical tones without prescribed pitch or melodic restrictions, the purpose being to develop a tonal sense.

tone, head: (1) the type of tone obtained in that part of the vocal range (usually the middle and upper registers) suitable for head resonance; (2) any vocal production characterized by head resonance, for example, with the nasal cavities used as resonators. *See* **tone, chest; voice, chest; voice, head.**

tone limits, auditory: *see* **auditory tone limits.**

tone, muscle: *see* **tonus, muscle.**

tone, resonance: (1) a tone that is reinforced by sympathetic vibration of the air within the throat, mouth, or nose cavities; (2) loosely, a tone of rich, vibrant quality.

tonette: an inexpensive whistle-type instrument designed for beginning instrumental instruction; considered as a good preparatory instrument to the wood-winds because of certain similarities in fingering patterns. *See* **recorder** (2).

tongue depressor: a blade of metal or wood for holding the tongue down during examination of the throat or mouth; also used in certain types of corrective speech instruction as a means of indicating to the pupil the correct placement of the tongue for the production of particular sounds.

tongue-tie: a relatively rare condition in which the attachment between the tongue and the floor of the mouth is so short that it restricts and interferes with the movement of the tip of the tongue upward and thus interferes with the correct production of certain speech sounds.

tonic: pertaining to tone; producing normal tone or tension; characterized by continuous tension or contraction.

tonic sol-fa: *see* **sol-fa, tonic.**

tonic spasm: *see* **spasm.**

tonoscope: *syn.* **stroboscope.**

tonus, muscle: a slight, sustained contraction of a muscle which gives it a quality of firmness; serves the purpose of maintaining the body postures and of preventing the full weight of the body parts from falling on the ligaments; also called *muscle tone.*

tool subject: *see* **subject, tool.**

topic, art: *see* **unit, art.**

topic sentence: *see* **sentence, topic.**

topical unit: *syn.* **unit, theme.**

topics in creative expression: (art ed.) in creative activity, a term that relates to the changing needs of the child and not to subject matter and content specifically.

topics of information: (voc. ed.) items of basic information given to learners to broaden their understanding of a trade or occupation.

topological field theory: *see* **field theory, topological.**

topological psychology: *see* **psychology, topological.**

topology: a branch of mathematics which deals with those properties, primarily geometric, which remain unchanged when the figures are deformed in some pre-

scribed way; for example, a square and a circle are topologically alike, since either can be deformed into the other with an acceptable set of topological transformations.

Torah (tō'rä): (Heb., lit., "instruction") (1) in a limited sense, a designation for the Pentateuch; (2) in a somewhat broader sense, a concept encompassing all Biblical and Talmudic teaching; (3) in the widest sense, the entire body of Jewish knowledge and tradition, a way of life.

Torah Umesorah school (tō·räh' ōō·mə·sō·räh'): (Heb., lit., "Torah and Tradition") one of a network or chain of day schools that emphasizes orthodox teaching; they are conducted under the auspices of *Torah Umesorah,* an orthodox organization called *National Society of Hebrew Day Schools.*

torque weight training: *see* **training, torque weight.**

tort: (1) a private or civil wrong or injury, arising from some cause other than breach of contract; (2) the commission or omission of an act, by one without right, by which another receives some injury in person, property, or reputation; (3) any negligent or willful and wrongful act of school officers or employees by which pupils or other innocent persons are injured.

tort action: *see* **action, tort.**

tort feasor: wrongdoer under civil law.

tort immunity: *see* **immunity, governmental.**

tort liability: *see* **liability, board; liability, personal; liability, teacher; tort.**

tortious act: *see* **act, tortious.**

total blindness: *see* **blindness, total.**

total correlation: *see* **correlation, total.**

total correlation coefficient: *see* **coefficient, total correlation.**

total cost: *see* **cost, total.**

total enrollment: *see* **enrollment, total.**

total, frequency: *see* **frequency total.**

total integration: *see* **integration, total.**

total-life-span program: *see* **program, total-life-span.**

total pattern: (neonate behavior) the fundamental organization of neurally aroused responses in an organism, many specific responses individuating or emerging from this pattern.

total perception time: *see* **perception time, total.**

total probability: *see* **probability, total.**

total reading time: *see* **reading time, total.**

total registration: *see* **registration, total.**

total time load: *see* **load, total time.**

totalitarianism: (1) a theory of the state that calls for a highly centralized government controlled and operated by one party or group and controlling all important phases of individual and group life; (2) certain political practices designed to promote the "unity" of the state, such as means for controlling political organizations, expressions of opinion, and mass media of information and culture.

totem: any of a number of possible objects believed by primitive people to have a blood relationship with the tribe, the family, or some subgroup; can take the form of a plant although more generally symbolized by an animal.

totemism: a term that is applied to a wide variety of phenomena, ranging from the simple use of symbols, (such as college students speaking of themselves as "gophers"), to a group of practices emanating from the belief that some mystical relationship exists between a kinship group of humans and an animal, plant, or natural phenomenon such as the sun or wind.

touch football: a type of football that resembles American college football except that no tackling or blocking is allowed.

touch method: a method of teaching the blind that utilizes the sense of touch in the acquisition of knowledge, as in finger reading and the interpretation of embossed maps, educational models, and other materials.

touch technique: *see* **cane technique.**

touch typewriting: *see* **typewriting, touch.**

tour, plant: *see* **plant tour.**

tournament: a series of contests between players or teams following one of several patterns designed to produce a winner after giving each entry a somewhat equal opportunity.

tournament, elimination: a series of contests in which teams or players are bracketed in pairs and winners from each round of play are paired until a final match is played between the last two.

Tower Gym: a trade name for a square stationary tower with a platform on top, a rope ladder, and other climbing facilities; available in several sizes; nursery size commonly found both in nurseries and in kindergartens.

town council: the legislative body of a town.

town-gown: a term applied to a traditional, but usually fictitious or exaggerated, cleavage between the general inhabitants of a community (town) containing a college or university and the students, faculty, and administration of the educational institution (gown).

town meeting: (United States) a general assemblage of the people of a town; in New England and some of the Western states it constitutes the legislative body of the town; in other states it has smaller powers, sometimes only advisory.

town school committee: *see* **town system.**

town system: a type or form of school administration in which the school affairs of a New England town are managed by a central body elected by the people, generally known as the town school committee. (In many matters the power of the school committee is regulated by general state law.) *See* **school committee.**

town unit: *see* **unit, town.**

township high school: *see* **high school, township.**

township school: a school that serves and is supported by the citizens of a township, the term township being used to designate a governmental subdivision of the county

township school administration: *see* **administration, township school.**

township system: a type or form of school administration in which the township becomes the unit of administration; a single board of trustees or officers manages the school or schools of the township, subject in turn to the oversight of the county and state educational authorities. *See* **school township.**

township-unit consolidation: *see* **consolidation, township-unit.**

township-unit system: *see* **school township; township system.**

toxic deafness: *see* **deafness, toxic.**

toxic psychosis: *see* **psychosis, toxic.**

toxicophobia (tok'si·kō·fō'bi·ə): a morbid preoccupation with, and fear of, poison.

toy band: *syn.* **rhythm band.**

toy, educational: any play item which has value in developing physical or mental capacities and manipulative and motor skills, in addition to performing the usual function of pleasure or recreation.

toy instrument: a musical instrument suitable for use in a rhythm band. *See* **rhythm band.**

toy orchestra: *syn.* **rhythm band.**

trace conditioned reflex: *see* **conditioned reflex, trace.**

trace line: *syn.* **trace line, item.**

trace line, item: a graphical representation expressing the probability of a particular response to an item by a person in terms of the point at which he stands on a hypothetical continuum.

trace routine: *see* **routine, trace.**

tracer, radioactive: *see* **radioactive tracer.**

Trachtenberg method: a collection of rules for performing computation in arithmetic speedily and accurately, developed by Jakow Trachtenberg in the early 1940s; the rules are very specific, as, for example, the rule for multiplying by 11 and the rule for multiplying by 12, and all must be committed to memory.

tracing method: *syn.* **kinesthetic method** (1).

track: (1) a pattern of subject organization or of course sequences in a school; for example, at the beginning level in elementary school, there might be two tracks, one for very gifted children and the other for less able children; at the secondary level, there may be two or even three tracks, as, in foreign language instruction, in one track may be children who have studied the language, in a second those who show aptitude for it, and in a third those who have not made satisfactory progress in the elementary school and who need a special curriculum; *see* **track, parallel;** (2) in electronics, the path along a tape on which it is possible to record.

track and field: a sport in which the emphasis is placed upon those events that require sprinting, long distance running, relays, hurdles, high jumping, broad jumping, shot putting, discus throwing, and javelin throwing.

track athletics: *see* **athletics, track.**

track, multiple: in programmed instruction, a provision within the programmed material for allowing students to pursue alternative subdivisions of the program in accord with their successes or failures with earlier sections of the program sequence. *See* **branching;** *contr. w.* **track, single.**

track, optical sound: *see* **optical sound track.**

track, parallel: each of two or more sequential patterns in the curriculum, each directed usually toward a specific educational or occupational goal, which exists at a particular educational level.

track, single: in programmed instruction, a common set of programmed materials through which all students work. *See* **programming, linear;** *contr. w.* **track, multiple.**

track, sound: *see* **sound track.**

track system: (1) a term used in some high school curriculum programs to designate the various groupings; there are tracks for slow, average, and fast learners, thus meeting the individual needs of the pupils; (2) a plan to guide students, in accordance with both their abilities and their probable future destinations, into one of several series of high school courses; the various series include alternate courses in the same subject field, such as mathematics, or courses in different fields; the track for academically talented pupils, for example, includes no vocational courses and that for vocational pupils no foreign languages.

track, variable area: *see* **variable area track.**

track, variable density: *see* **variable density track.**

tractive supervision: *see* **supervision, tractive.**

trade: an occupation requiring specific manual or mechanical skills and training; a craft in which only skilled workers are employed.

trade analysis: *see* **analysis, trade.**

trade and industrial education: instruction which is planned to develop basic manipulative skills, safety judgment, technical knowledge, and related occupational information for the purpose of fitting persons for initial employment in industrial occupations and upgrading or retraining workers employed in industry.

trade and industrial education club: *see* **club, trade and industrial education.**

trade book: *see* **book, trade.**

trade book, children's: *see* **book, children's trade.**

trade classes, all-day: *see* **classes, all-day trade.**

trade course, unit: *see* **course, unit trade.**

trade drafting: *see* **drafting, trade.**

trade drawing: *syn.* **drafting, trade.**

trade education: *see* **trade and industrial education.**

trade extension: *see* **extension, trade.**

trade extension class: *see* **part-time trade extension class.**

trade high school: *see* **high school, trade.**

trade information: *syn.* **related information.**

trade mathematics: *see* **mathematics, trade.**

trade, multiblock: an occupation that can be divided into several blocks in order to effect a logical analysis. *Contr. w.* **trade, single-block.**

trade papers: (1) periodicals addressed to a specific industrial or commercial public; (2) the designation of a journalism course, generally at the college level, dealing with the writing and procedures involved in the publication of such periodicals.

trade-preparatory program: *see* program, trade-preparatory.

trade-preparatory training: *see* part-time trade-preparatory school or class.

trade school: a public or private vocational school that trains youth and adults in the skills, technical knowledge, related industrial information, and job judgment necessary for success in one or more skilled trades.

trade science: *see* science, trade.

trade, semiskilled: an industrial occupation requiring skill in a limited range of activities. *Contr. w.* **trade, skilled.**

trade, service: any occupation that has as its primary purpose the rendering of personal service to the customer or the maintenance of existing equipment.

trade, single-block: a trade in which all jobs can be included in one division, or block, for purposes of analysis. *Contr. w.* **trade, multiblock.**

trade skill: *see* skill, trade.

trade, skilled: an industrial occupation requiring a high degree of skill, usually in a wide range of related activities, and secured through a combination of job instruction, trade instruction, and work experience, such as apprenticeship or a cooperative industrial program. *Contr. w.* **trade, semiskilled.**

trade, street: one of the trades which are usually plied by children along city streets, for example, selling newspapers or shining shoes.

trade test: *see* test, trade.

trade training: *see* training, trade.

tradevman: in the Navy, a petty officer who operates and maintains training devices.

tradition: (1) a belief, practice, custom, etc., transmitted orally from generation to generation; (2) more generally, any belief, practice, custom, or convention that has its roots in the past.

tradition, genteel: the tradition in education that supports the Aristotelian theory of a classical education in the liberal arts as best suited for the gentleman; nineteenth-century British boys' schools were examples of this approach in the modern era.

traditional arithmetic: *see* arithmetic, traditional.

traditional curriculum: *see* curriculum, traditional.

traditional examination: *syn.* examination, essay.

traditional grammar: *see* grammar, traditional.

traditional high school: *see* high school, traditional.

traditional kindergarten: *see* kindergarten, traditional.

traditional mathematics: *see* mathematics, traditional.

traditional orthography: *see* orthography, traditional.

traditional school: a term presently used to refer to the typical American school of the late nineteenth and early twentieth centuries in which innovation and experimentation were minimal or to any school which is organized and operated in that style. *Contr. w.* **life-adjustment education.**

traditionally organized school: a school organized as part of the 8-4 plan and providing either 8 years of elementary work, 4 years of secondary work, or both.

traffic: (1) pedestrians, ridden or herded animals, and vehicles traveling on any highway; (2) persons moving along halls and stairways of a school building.

traffic pattern: established procedures for approaching, parking on, and leaving the school grounds, thereby making it unnecessary for the bus to be driven backward.

traffic safety training: *see* training, traffic safety.

traffic squad: *see* safety patrol.

trailing: use of the back of the fingers by the visually handicapped to follow lightly over a straight surface such as a wall, lockers, desks, or tables to determine one's place in space, to locate specific objectives, or to establish a parallel line of travel.

trainable mentally handicapped: *syn.* mentally retarded, trainable.

trainable mentally retarded: *see* mentally retarded, trainable.

trainable mentally retarded child: *see* child, trainable mentally retarded.

trainee: a person being trained; in a military sense, a person undergoing basic training or on-the-job training.

trainee, basic: an airman undergoing basic military training.

trainee, Military Assistance Program Grant Aid: a foreign national receiving training under the Grant Aid portion of Military Assistance Program training.

trainee, Military Assistance Sales: a foreign national receiving training conducted by the Department of Defense, on a reimbursable basis, at his country's request.

trainee, officer: the designation of a student in the Air Force Officer Training School. *See* cadet; candidate, officer.

trainee, pilot: *syn.* pilot, student (3).

trainee, student: a regularly enrolled secondary school student participating in a cooperative vocational program of training in an occupation of his choice with related classroom instruction. *Syn.* student learner; student worker.

trainer: (1) the person in charge of the program concerned with the care of minor athletic injuries and the physical condition of players on an athletic team; (2) (mil. ed.) a training device, such as an aircraft used in pilot training or a ground trainer; *see* trainer, ground; (3) (adult ed.) an instructional leader who plans and conducts a learning activity designed to help participants acquire information, skills, and attitudes in a particular content area; usually one conducting skill-training activities.

trainer, advanced: (mil. ed.) an airplane used for advanced flying training.

trainer, bench: (mil. ed.) a training device that can be or is set up on a bench for the trainee to examine and operate.

trainer, establishment: *see* training sponsor, distributive education.

trainer, flight: (mil. ed.) any training device that simulates certain conditions of actual flight, such as a *Link trainer.*

trainer, ground: (mil. ed.) any of several kinds of specially designed or modified apparatus or items of equipment in which a person on the ground may receive training in flying, gunnery, bombing, or other activities carried out in the air, under simulated conditions of flight.

trainer, Link: (mil. ed.) a ground trainer made by Link Aviation, Inc., as a trainer for pilots, especially for instrument flying.

trainer, on-the-job: *see* training sponsor, business and office education; training sponsor, distributive education.

trainer, teacher: *see* educator, teacher.

training: (1) the special kind of teaching and instruction in which the goals are clearly determined, are usually readily demonstrated, and call for a degree of mastery which requires student practice and teacher guidance and appraisal of the student's improved performance capabilities; (2) (mil. ed.) a process by which a crew or other group of persons gains unity by virtue of its members learning to do certain things together; (3) in a derogatory sense, a process of helping others to acquire skills or knowledge by rote, without reference to any greater framework of knowledge or comprehension.

training, academic: training done in a classroom or by supervised study, as distinguished from on-the-job training or operational training.

training, accident prevention: training to foster a safety-conscious attitude resulting in the habitual use of prophylactic measures to counteract the likelihood of a chance disaster.

training, accounting and computing operations: planned learning experiences, including courses and practical experiences concerned with systematizing information about transactions and activities into accounts and quantitative records and with paying and receiving money;

examples are training as bookkeepers, as cashiers, and as machine operators. *See* **taxonomy, business and office education.**

training, acoustic: *syn.* **training, auditory;** *see* **acoustic method.**

training, active duty for: full-time active duty for reserve personnel for training purposes in the military service of the United States, usually for a limited number of days or months; an example is the annual active duty for training, not to exceed 17 days, performed by many members of the Ready Reserve of the Reserve Components of the Armed Forces except the Army National Guard of the United States and the Air National Guard of the United States.

training, advanced flying: a late stage of flying training in any given specialty; sometimes referred to as *graduate flying training.*

training, advanced individual: (1) training given to enlisted personnel after completion of *basic training* in order to qualify them for the award of a military occupational specialty; (2) training conducted at training centers, Army service schools, and, when so directed, by United States Strategic Army Force units which qualifies an individual to perform in an entry or higher military occupational specialty.

training, advanced pilot: a late stage of pilot training, including training and instruction in flying a particular type of advanced aircraft and training designed to qualify pilots for performing duties as junior officers in Air Force units; sometimes referred to as *graduate pilot training.*

training, advanced reconditioning: refresher military training, common to all branches of the service, given to selected patients in certain hospitals and convalescent centers to prepare them to return directly to duty upon release from the hospital or center.

training, advanced unit: (1) applicatory training given during the final stages of unit training when small (company size) table of organization and equipment (TOE) units, organic to a parent TOE organization (battle group, battalion, etc.), are assembled and trained together to rehearse their role in the mission of the parent organization; (2) participation of separate companies and larger organizations in combined arms and service training.

training, aerospace: a process in which a person is trained in skills and responses considered necessary for an operator to carry out tasks and duties in developing or applying aerospace power.

training, aerospace medical: a very broad program conducted by the Aerospace Medical Division at Brooks Air Force Base, under the Air Training Command, emphasizing the biomedical problems connected with space travel; lectures in aerospace medicine form one aspect of the program, conducted as an interdisciplinary course, bringing together foremost authorities on topics of annual interest; papers are usually published in order to constitute an educational resource in libraries.

training agency: (mil. ed.) a command, bureau, or office exercising command of and providing support to some major increment of the Navy's total training effort.

training agreement: *syn.* **contract, cooperative student.**

training agreement, cooperative: *syn.* **contract, cooperative student.**

training, agricultural on-job: an integral part of a vocational education program in an agriculture; students are placed for supervised employment experiences in non-farm agricultural firms or in production agriculture.

training aid: (mil. ed.) any item which is developed and/or procured with the primary intent that it shall assist in training and the process of learning.

training aid equipment: equipment used to display training aids; includes items such as motion-picture projectors, overhead projectors, slide projectors, tape recorders/playback units, record players, opaque projectors, etc.

training aid, speech: *see* **speech training aid.**

training aid, voice: *see* **speech training aid.**

training aids, graphic: (mil. ed.) military instruction charts and posters, flat transparencies, and simple training devices produced through printing processes.

training and retention program, selective: *see* **program, selective training and retention.**

training, apprentice: an organized system for providing young people with the manipulative skills and technical or theoretical knowledge needed for competent performance in skilled occupations; involves a specified rotative series of experiences in such occupations and related studies at a vocational school.

training, area: (mil. ed.) instruction often given in conjunction with foreign language training to familiarize students with customs, courtesies, geography, history, and government of a nation or geographical area.

training, armory: training or duty other than full time performed at home station by units of the Army National Guard and the members thereof, in state status; for the purpose of benefits only, such duty is considered inactive duty training in Federal service.

training, Army school: training designed to produce a soldier with the maximum requisite technical knowledge and skills to perform as an effective member of a unit engaged in combat.

training, Army training center: training designed to produce a soldier who has the minimum requisite knowledge and skills to perform as a replacement in a unit engaged in combat.

training assistance, mobile: (mil. ed.) includes mobile training detachments, traveling teams, and contract technical services personnel used primarily for the training of foreign military personnel.

training, astronaut: training of personnel from various military services in spaceflight activities at such installations as NASA's Manned Spacecraft Center at Houston, Cape Kennedy, Vandenberg Air Force Base, California, and Brooks Air Force Base; involves such things as the physiology of closed environments, experience in the centrifuge, zero-G training, and all aspects of operating and flying in manned spacecraft. *See* **training, zero-G.**

training, athletic: a program of conditioning and care and prevention of athletic injuries.

training, auditory: training in the recognition and interpretation of common sounds in the environment, such as gross sound, musical sounds, and speech; may be an integral part of the reading-readiness program or of the remedial reading program; becomes an important aspect in the education of children with limited hearing, for whom auditory training is usually undertaken with amplified sound through the use of hearing aids. *See* **acoustic method.**

training, aural: *see* **training, auditory.**

training, auricular: *see* **training, auditory.**

training, aviation: (mil. ed.) *see* **air training command; naval aviation school.**

training base: (mil. ed.) those activities, facilities, equipment, and personnel which make up the Army training centers, Army schools and courses, and units specifically established or directed to conduct individual training on a recurring basis.

training, basic: (1) elementary training and instruction in the essential fundamentals of military service; (2) a short term for *basic flying training, basic military training,* or *basic pilot training.*

training, basic combat: training in basic military subjects and fundamentals of basic infantry combat given to newly inducted and enlisted Active Army and Reserve Components male personnel without prior military service.

training, basic flying: a stage of flying training in any given specialty between primary and advanced; sometimes referred to as *undergraduate flying training;* may be synonymous with *basic pilot training.*

training, basic military: military training given a person without previous or recent military training or experience.

training, basic pilot: a stage of pilot training between primary pilot training and advanced pilot training, comprising basic training and instruction in visual and instrument flying, together with academic and military instruction and training; sometimes referred to as *undergraduate pilot training* (UPT). *See* **pilot, undergraduate.**

training, bicycle safety: (phys. ed.) training in the knowledge and use of skills in manipulating a two-wheeled vehicle in such a manner as to avoid an accident or injury.

training bill: (mil. ed.) schedule and outline of training for a particular unit of men.

training, blind approach: (mil. ed.) in pilot training, training in making blind approaches to landing.

training boss: a worker assigned to train a group known in industry as a *training gang.*

training, business: *syn.* **training, junior business.**

training, business data processing systems occupations: planned learning experiences including courses and practical activities concerned with business data processing systems and operations, such as computer and console operations, programming, systems analysis, and other data processing systems occupations. *See* **taxonomy, business and office education.**

training, cadet: (nautical) training for a seafaring career in a licensed capacity, provided by the United States Maritime Corps or by a state maritime academy.

training center: (mil. ed.) a facility that instructs newly enlisted personnel in naval duties and customs.

training center, rehabilitation: an Army correctional facility used in periods of national emergency as a vehicle for rehabilitating and restoring prisoners to duty.

training center, replacement: (mil. ed.) a center for the training of replacements before they are permanently assigned.

training, certificate of approved: *see* **certificate of approved training.**

training, circuit: a conditioning, training, or teaching technique which utilizes a series of stations to develop motor patterns and skills and physical fitness.

training circular: (mil. ed.) a paper which promulgates training directives, policies, or information of an interim nature which require revision too frequently for inclusion in permanent training literature; also used to promulgate new training doctrine, tactics, or techniques, the immediate dissemination of which is essential.

training, citizenship: (1) generally, educational activity carried on in educational institutions designed to teach the information, attitudes, skills, etc., essential to good citizenship; (2) a program of education designed to prepare foreign-born adults for citizenship.

training, collateral: (mil. ed.) training in standard subjects, such as military, physical, security, weapons, and recognition training, given along with training in a career field.

training college: *syn.* **training school** (1).

training, combat readiness: (mil. ed.) the continuing flying training required of a rated person not on primary flying duty in order to maintain his flying proficiency; formerly called *minimum individual training.*

training, combative measures: (mil. ed.) training designed to assist an individual who is unarmed to protect himself in case of an attack by another individual armed with a pistol, knife, or club.

training, combined: (mil. ed.) training of any unit of the Army with the Army branch or branches with which it would normally cooperate, for example, combined training of artillery, engineers, infantry, armored units, and air units.

training command, air: *see* **air training command.**

training, common specialist: (mil. ed.) training in technical skills which are used in more than one military service.

training, continuation: (mil. ed.) (1) repeated collateral training; *see* **training, collateral;** (2) that military training which is received concurrently with basic technical or flying training courses conducted on Air Training Command bases; consists primarily of inspections, corrections, marching to and from classes, parades, reviews, ceremonies, and physical conditioning.

training, cooperative: *see* **cooperative plan, distributive education.**

training, cooperative occupational: a plan which correlates actual work experience in the community with classroom instruction under the supervision of a coordinator or teacher-coordinator who is occupationally qualified.

training coordinator: *see* **coordinator, training.**

training, corrective: *see* **gymnastics, corrective; gymnastics, remedial; physical education, corrective.**

training, counterinsurgency: (mil. ed.) instruction in the techniques of countering insurgent or guerrilla warfare, including an understanding of the causative factors.

training course, junior-executive: *see* **course, junior-executive training.**

training course, management: *see* **course, management training.**

training, crew: *see* **training, operational readiness.**

training, cross-: *see* **cross-training.**

training, cross-service: (mil. ed.) any education or training provided by the schools or other facilities of one service for students of other services.

training cycle, unit: (mil. ed.) the time provided in the unit training program from the start of basic individual training until the completion of the field exercise and maneuver phase in the case of units participating in maneuvers, or until the end of unit training for those units that do not participate in maneuvers. *See* **training, phases of; training, unit.**

training detachment, mobile: (mil. ed.) a mobile unit of a field training squadron or technical school controlled by Air Training Command; consists of a detachment commander and technically qualified instructors capable of providing on-site specialized technical training required to support a specific system located at the station of assignment.

training device: (mil. ed.) a device or item of equipment designed or modified for use by the trainee in training. *Dist. f.* **training aid.**

training, distributive education preemployment: *see* **instruction, distributive education preparatory.**

training, driver: *see* **driver, student.**

training, dual channel concept of on-the-job: (mil. ed.) a system of on-the-job training in which an airman takes a career development course to acquire the fundamental knowledges of his Air Force specialty, followed by (or simultaneously with) on-the-job training under the provisions of a job proficiency guide. *See* **course, career development.**

training, ear: (1) instruction designed to improve the individual's ability to distinguish one speech sound from another or correct some faulty production of any given sound; (2) training in discrimination between inflectional patterns, pitch levels, intensity levels, and other characteristics of speech; (3) process of teaching a child to use his hearing to the maximum extent throughout his education and in all the circumstances of his daily life; (4) (mus.) studies and exercises designed to train music students to recognize and describe the separate components of the music discipline—melodic intervals, harmonies, rhythmic patterns, etc.; no printed notation is provided, all work being done aurally; *see* **dictation** (2).

training, entrance: educational experiences provided for a new employee, designed to help him become adjusted to the particular organization, procedures, and personnel with which he is to work; may be casual or highly organized, and may range in length from a brief to an extended period of time. *Syn.* **vestibule training.**

training, ephebic (e·fē′bik): a 2-year period of cadet training, begun at the age of 18 years by the youth of ancient Athens and comprising the following stages: (*a*) 1 year in garrison at Athens; (*b*) transfer to a frontier fortress, after successfully passing a public examination in the use of arms; (*c*) granting of citizenship after a citizenship examination.

training equipment, group auditory: *see* **auditory training equipment, group.**

training, factory: *syn.* **training, plant.**

training, familiarization: (mil. ed.) individual training for personnel having a fundamental technical knowledge to acquaint them with a specific system; normal on-the-job training as known within the U.S. Air Force, without full qualification for the award of an *Air Force specialty code.*

training, fartlek: (Swedish, lit., "speed play") a method of training for the acquisition of an acceptable physical condition through a systematic program of running.

training, feudal: the training of youths of the nobility in Europe from the ninth to about the fourteenth century, with emphasis on developing the body and learning to fight, with little or no attention to academic accomplishments; in the course of training, the youth progressed through three stages, those of page, squire, and knight.

training, field: (mil. ed.) technical training conducted at the operational location on assigned aircraft, space and missile systems, and their associated direct support equipment, for maintenance and aircrew/operator personnel.

training, filing, office machines, and general office clerical occupations: planned learning experiences including courses and practical activities concerned with the recording and retrieval of data and also with classifying, sorting, and filing related records and other data; comprises training as duplicating machine operators, file clerks, general office clerks, and includes training for other filing, office machines, and general office clerical occupations. *See* **taxonomy, business and office education.**

training film: *see* **film, training.**

training, flying: (mil. ed.) training in the art or skill of manning or operating aircraft or aircraft equipment in any capacity; also includes certain courses which do not prepare personnel specifically for flying duties but rather for duties which involve flying skills or skills closely associated with flying; also called flight training.

training for citizenship: *see* **training, citizenship.**

training for public service occupations: education, usually of a preservice character, designed to provide firemen, policemen, tax assessors, welfare workers, or other publicly employed persons with broader or more highly specialized skills or knowledge relating to their duties.

training for the deaf, preschool: training in a school for 3- and 4-year old deaf children which places emphasis upon auditory training and language development.

training forces: a category of Army personnel consisting of (*a*) trainees, personnel assigned to training centers and other miscellaneous training activities for the purpose of receiving instruction, (*b*) students, personnel assigned to formal Army service schools and courses, schools of other services or allied armed forces, and joint colleges and projects, and personnel attending civilian institutions for the purpose of receiving instruction, excluding personnel on temporary duty, and (*c*) trainers, personnel who instruct or provide training advice to units or individuals or who provide essential administrative support in schools, training centers, military districts, and other miscellaneous training activities.

training, foremanship: training to prepare industrial workers as foremen or to improve foremen in industries. (The term is used especially with reference to a program of preparation maintained by subventions of the Federal government through the Smith-Hughes Act and subsequent legislation.)

training, formal: training authorized and approved by a competent authority and meeting certain fixed standards as to type of instruction, length of instruction periods, qualifications of instructor, etc.

training, full-time National Guard: full-time training duty performed by members of the Army National Guard in State status and under State control.

training, functional: (mil. ed.) training which prepares personnel as individuals or in groups to perform specialized duties.

training gang: a group to be trained or taught by an instructor, or *training boss.*

training, general laboratory: (mil. ed.) in Air Force usage, the exploration in depth of particular student interests related to important areas of learning in which maximum student participation in the group is encouraged.

training, general military: continuing training in subjects essential to a military career but separate and distinct from the primary duty of the individual or the primary mission of his unit; its purpose is to develop and enhance the individual's knowledge, skills, and understanding of why he fights, his basic aims, the nature, methods, and capability of the enemy, how to protect himself and his unit actively and passively, and how to care for his physical needs and maintain health and physical alertness.

training, graduate flying: *see* **training, advanced flying.**

training, graduate pilot: *see* **training, advanced pilot.**

training, gymnasial: physical and civic training given under the supervision of the state to youth between 16 and 18 years in ancient Athens, usually in gymnasiums just outside the city, and consisting in running, wrestling, boxing, riding horseback, chariot driving, singing, dancing, and instruction in civic matters.

training, human relations laboratory: the here-and-now experience in which each participant attempts to identify accurately how his behavior is perceived by others (and vice versa) through the process of verbal/nonverbal communications; as an atmosphere of trust develops, the individual's potential for growth in all his human relations is more fully achieved.

training, in-service: instruction provided employed persons on the job while they continue the normal performance of their occupational duties. *See* **in-service education.**

training, in-service counselor: a service by which counseling personnel may be provided with a planned program of continuous learning concurrent with their employment or by which students may prepare for counseling careers by supervised work experience.

training, inactive duty: training performed by Air Force Reservists while not on active duty for which point credit is authorized; includes unit training assemblies, training periods, instruction, preparation of instruction, appropriate duties, equivalent training, military flying duty, and completion of correspondence courses through the United States Air Force Extension Course Institute or other approved program. *See* **inactive duty.**

training, individual: (mil. ed.) training of an individual only, such as on-the-job training. *Dist. f.* **training, unit.**

training, individual occupational: training for a specific DOT title within an occupational cluster. *See* **code, DOT.**

training, information communication: learning experiences including courses and practical activities concerned with the distribution of information by mail, telephone, telegraph, and in person; for example, training as communication systems clerks and operators, correspondence clerks, mail and postal clerks, mail-preparing and mail-handling machine operators, and workers in other information communication occupations. *See* **taxonomy, business and office education.**

training, inquiry: method of teaching children how to seek information in order to solve problems or to explain a phenomenon that they do not understand.

training, intensive language: (mil. ed.) formal, full-time language instruction consisting of approximately 6 hours per day with a native-speaking instructor and 2 or more hours per day spent in outside study or language laboratory exercises.

training, interservice: military training which is provided by one service to members of another service. *See* **military education; training, military.**

training, interval: (phys. ed.) a system of conditioning in which repeated efforts of strenuous activity at a timed pace are alternated with measured recovery periods of low activity.

training, job: (1) vocational instruction for employed persons; (2) practical adult education for persons who desire immediate help in getting a job or improving their competence in an occupation.

training, job-instruction (J.I.T.): a training program organized under the Training-Within-Industry plan for the purpose of teaching the elements of individual instructional procedure to supervisors; used extensively in the adult distributive education program.

training, job-relations (J.R.T.): a training program organized under the Training-Within-Industry plan for the purpose of teaching the elements of good human relations to supervisors; used extensively in the adult distributive education program.

training, joint airborne: training operations or exercises involving airborne and appropriate troop carrier units; includes (a) air delivery of personnel and equipment, (b) assault operations by airborne troops and/or air transportable units, (c) loading exercises and local orientation flights of short duration, and (d) maneuvers/exercises as agreed upon by the services concerned and/or as authorized by the Joint Chiefs of Staff.

training, junior business: a beginning subject in the field of business, generally offered in the junior high school or in the first year of a 4-year high school; may be an exploratory subject intended to show whether students have the interests and abilities that would warrant their specializing in business work, or a foundation course in preparation for the later study of more advanced commercial subjects, especially bookkeeping; sometimes considered as a general information subject, which is required of all high school students, both commercial and noncommercial. *Syn.* **business training; elementary business; general business; introduction to business.**

training, leadership: instructional programs designed to assist adults to acquire the knowledge and abilities needed to inspire and guide others to participate in group activities such as community development; often organized by university extension and by voluntary associations.

training literature: (mil. ed.) that body of writings published for the primary purpose of informing all concerned as to doctrine, tactics, techniques, and procedures adopted for use in training individuals and units of the United States Army.

training literature, official: (mil. ed.) the media covered by this category are Army field manuals, training circulars, ROTC manuals and pamphlets, all published as Department of the Army documents.

training literature, unofficial: (mil. ed.) literature such as special texts published as service school documents to support resident or extension course instruction in a particular phase of a subject and training tests published by United States Continental Army Command.

training, management: instruction designed for managers at all levels in various forms of business and industrial organizations and normally offered by colleges, universities, and professional associations as well as by private firms.

training, manual: an earlier type of school laboratory activity usually restricted to fixed exercises in woodwork, metalwork, and mechanical drawing; strong emphasis was placed on tool exercises and manual skill; gave way first to *manual arts* and later to *industrial arts.*

training, marginal: training given in vocational education of less than college grade.

training, materials support occupations: planned learning experiences which include courses and practical activities concerned with (a) receiving, storing, issuing, shipping, requisitioning, and accounting for materials, (b) assigning locations and space to items, (c) physical handling of items, (d) preparing or committing stocks for shipment, (e) inventorying stock, (f) replenishing depleted items, and (g) filling orders. *See* **taxonomy, business and office education.**

training, medical professional: (mil. ed.) that training and education concerned with the health of individuals or the care and treatment of patients and which is presented by or under supervision or direction of physicians, dentists, veterinarians, nurses, Army Medical Specialists Corps officers and Medical Service Corps officers of the Allied Science field, optometrists, pharmacists, and sanitary engineers.

training meeting: a session at which local leaders or teachers are shown how to conduct demonstrations, discussions, or other educational activities with their local groups.

training memorandum: *syn.* **contract, cooperative student.**

training, military: (1) the instruction of personnel to enhance their capacity to perform specific military functions and tasks; (2) the exercise of one or more military units conducted to enhance their combat readiness. *See* **military education.**

training, Military Assistance Grant Aid: training provided under Military Assistance Program Grant Aid, conducted under the authority of the Foreign Assistance Act of 1961, as amended, for which the United States receives no reimbursement.

training, Military Assistance Program Supported Third Country: training provided not under United States supervision outside the continental United States in a country other than the country of program; may include United States assistance for costs of normal student travel and living allowance.

training, minimum individual: *see* **training, combat readiness.**

training, miscellaneous office occupations: planned learning experiences concerned with the facilitating functions such as training as collectors, hotel clerks, clerical technicians, credit clerks, and other occupations and areas of specialization related to office occupations not listed or classifiable in the other taxonomy categories. *See* **taxonomy, business and office education.**

training, moral: instruction and study that prepare the individual to choose between alternative values in accordance with those ethical standards which a society or one of its institutions, for example, the church, seeks to conserve or to promote.

training, muscle: carefully administered bodily exercise for the improvement of functional control.

training, observer: a planned program of training in a trade or occupation which is carried on by watching others.

training, occupational: (bus. and office ed.) training for a specific occupational area which has as its objective the eventual employment of a student in the area of his training, as opposed to general course approaches in business and office education. *See* **block of time; business and office education, intensive; instruction, business and office education related; office education, cooperative.**

training, officer advanced: formal training designed to facilitate the qualification of individuals in Air Force staff specialties; graduates are awarded the appropriate Air Force specialty code at the entry level.

training, officer basic technical: formal training leading to the award of a single operating or technical Air Force specialty code at entry level.

training, officer lateral: formal training leading to the award of an entry level Air Force specialty code by qualifying officers for lateral movement within a career field, or as an interim measure preceding a change in existing career structure, or to provide temporary personnel support of a lateral nature.

training, officer supplemental: formal training toward a portion of an Air Force specialty without change in Air Force specialty code.

training on location: (teacher ed.) a special form of in-service education provided for the teacher in the school in which he is employed.

training, on-the-job: supervision and other supplemental instruction furnished to a learner while he is employed as a beginner or trainee in the regular duties of a position or job.

training, operational: (mil. ed.) training, especially flying training, that prepares a person or group of persons for actual combat or other operations.

training, operational readiness: in Air Force training, that consolidated instructional period wherein personnel for operational units, already qualified in their respective specialties, are given integrated operational training by the designated command to perform the sequential duties and tasks prerequisite to efficient accomplishment of their assigned weapon system operational functions; also referred to as *crew training;* in the Army, the phase of training by units that have completed their formal training and are assigned responsibility for maintaining the highest state of combat proficiency in order to accomplish operational missions.

training, organizational: (mil. ed.) training in which an entire unit participates in order to improve team work. *See* **training, unit.**

training, orthoptic (ŏr·thop'tik): (1) exercise of the muscles of the eye for the development of eye coordination and correct vision; (2) the reeducation of the squinter to adequate binocular vision.

training, parallel: (mil. ed.) method of instruction in which an individual is given technical training, either basic or advanced, by another individual who is an expert.

training, participation: (adult ed.) an instructional program designed to help participants use the processes and procedures of group discussion and other educational procedures in order to learn effectively.

training period: *see* **period, training.**

training, personnel, training, and related occupations: planned learning experiences including courses and practical activities concerned with personnel administration of an organization and the facilitating functions of scheduling and conducting clerical work and management and operations of organizations; examples are training as educational and training assistants, interviewers, test technicians and personnel assistants, and training for other personnel training and related occupations. *See* **taxonomy, business and office education.**

training, phases of: (mil. ed.) the five formal phases of training covered by separate Army training programs: basic combat training, advanced individual training, basic unit training, advanced unit training, and field exercises and maneuvers training; a sixth phase, operational readiness training, is entered into as determined by major commanders.

training, physical: a program of exercises and other physical activities designed to improve physical development and condition and performance in motor skills. *Dist. f.* **physical education.**

training, physiological: (mil. ed.) training designed to acquaint flying personnel with the physiological problems of flight and to instruct them in methods of meeting and solving these problems.

training, pilot: the training and instruction given to certain student pilots, pilot trainees, or other persons in the art or skill of piloting heavier-than-air aircraft; usually divided into two or more stages. *See* **training, flying.**

training, pilot transition: in Air Force usage, the transition training given a pilot. *See* **training, transition.**

training plan: *syn.* **contract, cooperative student.**

training plan, business and office education: a description of training experiences and instruction the cooperative student has received or will receive from his job sponsor at the training station.

training plan, cooperative: *syn.* **contract, cooperative student.**

training, plant: any type of instruction given by the employer in his own industrial establishment during working hours.

training, preemployment: organized, brief, intensive instruction for entrance into employment in a specific job or retraining for workers leading to new duties or a new position.

training, preflight: the initial training given to an aviation cadet prior to flying training, to provide him with the fundamental training generally required for all Air Force officers.

training, preinduction: that training in the high school program which has made possible a more effective orientation of youth into the armed forces; in the social studies field this program usually has stressed such matters as a better understanding of America, faith in American ideals, civic responsibilities, opportunities in the military service for a career or for further education, the development of moral and spiritual values, and a greater degree of world geographic and political literacy.

training, preprofessional: a sequence of courses basic to specialized training for a profession.

training, pretranscription: special drill in the separate elements of shorthand, typewriting, and English that will later be needed to develop skill in transcription.

training, primary: (mil. ed.) in Air Force usage, short for *primary pilot training;* sometimes refers to *undergraduate flying training.*

training, primary flying: the initial stage of flying training in any given aircrew specialty; may be restricted to *primary pilot training;* also referred to as *undergraduate flying training.*

training, primary pilot: in the Air Force, the initial stage of pilot training, following preflight training and providing academic and military training and training in the fundamental principles of visual and instrument flying; sometimes referred to as *undergraduate pilot training* (UPT).

training procedures, joint: training procedures agreed to jointly by those service agencies charged with developing doctrine involving more than one service.

training, professional: (1) instruction and study that prepare one directly for the practice of a profession; (2) (mil. ed.) a formal resident course of general educational value which improves an officer's general qualifications and ability to perform commissioned duties but is not necessarily designed specifically to enable him to perform one or more of the tasks contained in an Air Force specialty description; includes courses conducted in military colleges and in the program of the Air Force Institute of Technology and in those colleges which advance the qualifications of officers whose specialties lie in the field of law, medicine, or theology.

training, proficiency: (mil. ed.) individual training, either formal or on-the-job, that enables an individual to maintain skill in an Air Force specialty.

training profile: a graphic description of training experiences and instruction the cooperative student has received or will receive from his job sponsor at the training station.

training program: *see* **program, training.**

training program, Armed Forces: *see* **program, Armed Forces training.**

training program, Army: *see* **program, Army training.**

training program, United States Military Academy preparatory: *see* **program, United States Military Academy preparatory training.**

training, progression of: the rotation of the student learner through the experiences outlined in the training agreement when established standards of skill and knowledge have been attained.

training, project: (voc. ed.) a participation experience which combines vocational instruction in the classroom with supervised and coordinated laboratory activities.

training, reciprocal: (mil. ed.) training provided by one foreign country to another with no Military Assistance Program funds involved; arranged by the countries concerned.

training records and information management system: (mil. ed.) in Naval usage, an automated data collection system for information on training of military and civilian personnel of the shore establishment.

training, recruit: (mil. ed.) training upon initial enlistment or induction which includes general indoctrination and prepares the recruit for early adjustment to military life by providing skill and knowledge in basic military subjects. *See* **training, basic.**

training, refresher: (mil. ed.) military training given a person after he has been inactive for a considerable period of time to freshen his skills and knowledge and bring him up to date in any given field.

training, religious: instruction in and study of the fundamentals of religious belief and practice in order to develop committed churchmanship among adherents of the faith.

training, remedial vision: *syn.* **training, orthoptic.**

training requirement: (mil. ed.) a requirement to train personnel in specified quantity to perform identified duties and thereafter to be available for assignment to the duties at a specified time.

training requirements, minimum essential: (mil. ed.) minimum levels of essential equipment required by a unit in conducting productive phased training.

training, reserve duty: (mil. ed.) any authorized training, instruction, or duty (other than active duty or active duty for training) performed with or without pay by members of the Reserve components.

training, reserve refresher: (mil. ed.) formal training for inactive-duty reservists to freshen and update their skills and knowledge in a given field associated with their Air Force specialty; students must possess the Air Force specialty code pertinent to the course or be in training towards that code; these courses are conducted by Air Training Command at the technical training centers.

training, retail: a term often used synonymously with *distributive education* but properly carrying the narrower interpretation of training for work in places of business where commodities are sold directly to the customer.

training, ROTC advanced: the training and instruction offered in the senior ROTC to students in the third and fourth years of a 4-year senior ROTC course of the Army, Navy, or Air Force, or the equivalent period of training in an approved 2-year senior ROTC course of the Army, Navy, or Air Force.

training school: (1) any institution of secondary or collegiate grade for the education of teachers (the term was frequently used in this sense during the nineteenth century; since mid-twentieth century it has become obsolete); (2) an elementary or secondary school, or both, connected with a teacher education institution and used to give student teachers opportunities for observation and practical experience in teaching classes under the supervision of a critic teacher; (3) sometimes used with a somewhat derogatory connotation to indicate a *model school* or *practice school* in which student teachers are taught to use fixed and formalized teaching methods; see **model school; practice school;** (4) a term formerly applied to rural high schools in the South; (5) sometimes used as a synonym for an institution or hospital for the mentally retarded; specifically, an institution emphasizing education and rehabilitation.

training school, basic: *see* **basic training school.**

training school, naval: *see* **naval training school.**

training school, university: *see* **university school.**

training, secretarial: instruction and practice in the duties performed by secretaries, given at the secondary or the college level.

training, sensitivity: a group technique the goal of which is to make people more sensitive to themselves and others and more aware of how they affect others and how others influence them. *See* **T-group.**

training, sensory: a series of planned experiences that offer abundant opportunity for use of the senses in the discrimination of sounds, colors, weights, forms, sizes, textures, tastes, odors, etc.

training, skill: vocational courses or portions of courses that have as their principal objective the development in the student of certain specific abilities that will have marketable value in business or industry.

training, special: (mil. ed.) formal training to qualify skilled level or supervisory/technician level personnel in maintaining and/or operating new or special equipment, such as a new and significantly different type of aircraft, or in new operational techniques and procedures.

training sponsor, business and office education: that person in a business establishment designated to be responsible for training and supervising the cooperative business and office education student on his job; works directly with the business and office education *teacher-coordinator.*

training sponsor, distributive education: the person in a distributive organization designated to be responsible for training and supervising the distributive education student on his job; works directly with the distributive education teacher-coordinator.

training standard: in Air Force usage, a standard of proficiency to be attained and maintained by members of a given unit, established to assure accomplishment of the mission.

training standard, course: (mil. ed.) an Air Training Command specialized publication which specifies the levels of performance and knowledge a student must possess upon graduation from a training course; lists the specific job elements and functional knowledges and specifies the level of proficiency required in each; the prime qualitative course control document.

training standard, specialty: (mil. ed.) a training control document used in the standardization and quality control of airman training; identifies general study references and contains a specification of subject knowledge levels, task knowledge levels, and task performance levels required for each skill level (3, 5, 7, 9) indicated by the corresponding Air Force specialty code. *See* **code, Air Force specialty.**

training station: *see* **station, training.**

training, stenographic, secretarial, and related occupations: planned learning activities which include courses and practical activities concerned with making, classifying, and filing records, including written communications, for example, training as an executive administrative secretary, a secretary-stenographer, and as a worker in other stenographic, secretarial, and related occupations. *See* **taxonomy, business and office education.**

training structure, Army: *see* **Army training structure.**

training supervisor: *see* **training sponsor, business and office education; training sponsor, distributive education.**

training, supervisory and administrative management occupations: learning activities and experiences such as (*a*) studying policies, organizational structures, and administrative practices, (*b*) reviewing periodic budgets submitted by operations personnel, (*c*) preparing reports summarizing findings and recommending changes in policy, organization, and administration to line management, (*d*) consolidating the budget estimates and preparing financial reports for consideration and action by upper echelons of management, and (*e*) supervising and coordinating activities, determining work procedures, and assigning duties. *See* **taxonomy, business and office education.**

training support agency: (mil. ed.) a command, bureau, or office responsible for supporting the training agencies by providing material and other forms of support within the cognizance of the command, bureau, or office involved.

training, tactical: training of troops in all phases of combat operations, including marches, security, offensive and defensive action, and withdrawals.

training, teacher: *syn.* **teacher education.**

training, team: (1) (Navy) training at sea or ashore in which an entire ship's company or a team, or a group that functions as a team, participates in order to improve its capability to perform its functions; examples are an antisubmarine warfare team or naval gunfire support team; (2) (Marine Corps) *syn.* **training, organizational.**

training team, mobile: a team consisting of one or more persons drawn from United States military service personnel resources and sent on temporary duty to a foreign nation to give instruction; the mission of the team is to provide a military service of the foreign nation with a self-training capability in a particular skill by training its instructor personnel.

training, technical: in the Air Force, technical, medical, and military training as distinguished from flying training.

training, terminal: *see* **terminal education.**

training test, Army: *see* **test, Army training.**

training, torque weight: improvement of the muscle's ability to move an anatomic lever or assist mechanical advantage in order to compensate for the diminishing force due to shortening of a muscle.

training, trade: (1) *syn.* **trade and industrial education;** (2) sometimes used to designate short trade education courses dealing with skills only.

training, trade-preparatory: *see* **part-time trade-preparatory school or class.**

training, traffic safety: training in the procedures and practices carried on in a community to prevent accidents in the street.

training, transition: (mil. ed.) individual training to qualify skilled personnel in the use of new or different types of equipment.

training, typing and related occupations: planned learning activities which include courses and practical experiences concerned with recording data, supervising and administering typing staffs and typing, and managing offices, for example, training as clerk typists, key punch and coding equipment operators, typists, and other typing and related occupations. *See* **taxonomy, business and office education.**

training, undergraduate flying: *see* **training, basic flying.**

training, undergraduate pilot: *see* **training, basic pilot.**

training, unit: (mil. ed.) phase of military training in which emphasis is placed upon training individuals to function as members of a team or unit; usually follows individual training (basic, technical, or specialist) and is generally conducted in the field under conditions which the unit would be likely to encounter in combat.

training unit, mobile: (mil. ed.) a set of system-oriented trainers, training aids, special tools, test equipment, and training accessories designed for portability and use in the field.

training unit, replacement: in the Air Force, a tactical unit responsible for training of replacement tactical aircrews.

training, United States military service funded foreign: training which is provided to foreign nationals in United States military service schools and installations under authority other than the Foreign Assistance Act of 1961.

training, universal military (UMT): a proposed program for the common defense and security of the United States that would provide for drafting into military service all men in the United States of a certain age, subject to certain physical and mental examinations, and for the training and service of such men for a period of time determined by law; in full, *universal military training and service.*

training, upgrade: (mil. ed.) the training of a person in a military career field leading to a higher grade.

training, vestibule: *syn.* **training, entrance.**

training, veterans' on-the-job: *see* **veterans' on-the-job training.**

training, visual: the teaching of visual skills to increase visual comfort and achievement. *Syn.* **visual reeducation.**

training, vocational: (1) *syn.* **vocational education;** (2) sometimes used to designate short vocational courses dealing with skills only; (3) on-the-job training and experiences which contribute to the student's preparation for occupational adjustment.

training, weight: systematic exercise with weights for the purpose of developing the body.

training within industry (T.W.I.): a program of instruction for persons in supervisory positions in business, industry, and the public service, designed to assist them in imparting information, giving instructions, handling personnel problems, and improving industrial processes.

training, zero-G: that phase of astronaut training concerned with activities to be performed in the weightless state characteristic of unpowered flight in orbit, in which the force of gravity is opposed or balanced by another and equal force, such as centrifugal force.

trait: (1) any attribute of an individual or thing; (2) a characteristic and relatively permanent mode of behavior, the outcome of hereditary and environmental factors; (3) (fact. anal.) a variable quality; an ability; (4) (stat.) a character or quality that is possessed by the different members of a group or class of objects or individuals; may vary in kind (as color may be divided into different colors and shades) or in degree or amount (as is the case with a quantitative trait such as height, weight, or intelligence); *comp. w.* **variable;** *dist. f.* **character trait;** (5) (genet.) *syn.* **character** (4).

trait and factor theory of counseling: *see* **counseling, trait and factor theory of.**

trait, autotelic: one of the traits central to the individual, such as his self concept, self-preservation tendency, etc.

trait, behavior: any action or behavior item that reveals some generalized pattern of perception and response with primary reference to the self; traits are always revealed by behavior, that is, by acts from which self-confidence or its lack can be inferred.

trait, character: *see* **character trait.**

trait cluster: the distinctive behavior pattern built up by the impact of experience on an individual's native endowments.

trait, cognitive: a well-defined reaction tendency observed in fields of behavior concerned with knowing and understanding, as contrasted with feeling or willing. *See* **affection** (1); **cognition** (1); **conation; trait.**

trait, common: a well-defined general reaction tendency, inferred from observed responses to many specific items within a class of stimuli.

trait, culture: relatively indivisible unit of a culture; examples are fire making with flints, an arrowhead, polygyny, etc.

trait, native: an inherited capacity or characteristic. *Syn.* **native character;** *contr. w.* **character, acquired.**

trait rating: *see* **rating, trait.**

trait, temperament: one of the characteristics of an individual's personality, concerned with emotional dispositions and reactions and contributing to the prevailing mood of a person.

trait transfer: *see* **transfer, trait.**

trait, unique: a variable that correlates zero (or nearly zero) with the other variables under consideration; a variable that is mathematically independent of the other variables being investigated; sometimes used as a synonym for *unique variable.*

traits of existence, generic: *see* **existence, generic traits of.**

trampoline: a piece of gymnastic apparatus consisting of a sheet of heavy canvas supported on all sides by many springs attached to a metal frame about 6 by 10 feet in size and about 4 feet above the floor; used for bouncing and tumbling exercises.

trance: a temporary mental state, resembling sleep, in which consciousness is partly or wholly lost.

transcend: (1) to surpass; to go beyond; to attain a higher quality; to achieve a better state of affairs; (2) to resolve a contradiction or ambiguity by going beyond it to a higher intellectual synthesis.

transcendent: (1) outside of, beyond, and above all possible human experience; unexperienceable; outside the realm of empirical knowledge; *dist. f.* **transcendental** (2); (2) as applied to ideal generalizations, pertaining to that which, according to some, transcends definite and particular operations yet may guide a people by being a symbol of hopes and aspirations, but which, according to others, is too vague or abstract to be given any immediate sensory content.

transcendental: (1) of or pertaining to *transcendentalism; see* **transcendentalism;** (2) in Kantian philosophy, pertaining to the a priori elements of experience such as space, time, and causality (what is beyond all experience is *transcendent;* what is a priori in all experience is transcendental); (3) applied as an adjective to "idealism," "realism," or other symbols, designating a point of view that seeks in general to restore moral and intellectual certitude from the relativism, radical empiricism, positivism, and nominalism regretfully found in pragmatism.

transcendentalism: (1) in general, the attempt to go beyond experience (or the belief in the possibility of doing so), to determine a priori the nature and the principles of human knowledge; (2) especially, the philosophy of Immanuel Kant (1724-1804) and his followers, which viewed a priori innate knowledge as the basis of sense experience and stated that that which can neither be experienced through the senses nor known through the understanding can nevertheless be thought or conceived; (3) the philosophy of Emerson and his followers, emphasizing the spiritual in both life and nature; (4) (theol.) the view that contrasts the absolute knowledge, power, and goodness of God with man's limited nature and holds that religious truth is grasped by intuition or mystical insight rather than by the ordinary processes of experience or reason.

transcribed program: *see* **program, transcribed.**

transcript: an official list of all courses taken by a student at a college or university, showing the final grade received for each course, with definitions of the various grades given at the institution; sometimes gives the names of the teachers; may also be issued by high schools.

transcript, acceptable: (bus. ed.) *syn.* **transcript, mailable.**

transcript, mailable: a term usually employed to identify a letter, transcribed from shorthand, which is acceptable by the dictator for his signature and mailing. (The ultimate aim of all transcription techniques is acceptability or mailability of transcript.) *Syn.* **acceptable transcript.**

transcription: (1) the act or process of reproducing in longhand or on the typewriter material taken from dictation in shorthand; the reproduction itself; (2) a phonograph recording originally designed for broadcast; as a convenience for radio-station scheduling, it provides approximately 15 minutes of time per side; the disk, approximately 16 inches in diameter, is played with a 3-mil stylus at a speed of 33 1/3 rpm; for school use, transcriptions are being replaced by long-playing records.

transcription library: *see* **library, transcription.**

transfer: (1) the act of a pupil in withdrawing from one grade, school, or system and enrolling in another grade, school, or system; (2) the work demanded of school officials in officially recognizing the withdrawal of a pupil from one school and his enrolling in another; (3) the movement of pupils from one school center to another within an administrative unit; (4) *syn.* **transfer of training;** *see* **behavior, terminal.**

transfer, associative: the tendency to transfer responses learned in one stimulus situation to other stimulus situations that are similar or associated.

transfer, bilateral: the effect of having previously learned a task with one body part (usually a hand or arm) on the learning of the same or a very similar task with the bilaterally opposite body part; for example, one who has already learned a given skill with the right hand should acquire the same skill with the left hand more readily than an individual without the previous learning.

transfer, block: in data processing by automatic computer, the movement of a group of words from one group of addresses to another group of addresses. *See* **address.**

transfer command: *see* **command, transfer.**

transfer, complex: transfer of training involving influence from more than a single source; except for some experiments or demonstrations, all transfer is probably complex.

transfer, conditional: an instruction which causes the automatic computer either to continue with the next instruction in the original sequence or to change control to some other stated instruction, depending upon the result of some logic operation.

transfer effect: the result of prior training on a new function (sensory or mental).

transfer, equivalent methods in: *see* **equivalent methods in transfer.**

transfer function: *see* **function, transfer.**

transfer in: *syn.* **received by transfer.**

transfer in language learning: (1) the application of techniques established in the mastery of one language to the study of a second language; (2) improvement observed in command and/or analysis of English as a result of training in a foreign language; (3) the influence of training in language on facility in another intellectual pursuit.

transfer, indeterminate: (1) *syn.* **transfer, zero;** (2) transfer existing in an amount too small to detect or determine; transfer that cannot be detected.

transfer, intracollege: the change made by a student from a sequence of courses that he has been following to another sequence within the same college.

transfer, kinds of: may refer either to statistical quantification of transfer or to different aspects of the stimulus-response bond involved in transfer; thus, transfer may be considered as (*a*) being positive, zero (or indeterminate), or negative, or (*b*) involving habits, modes of attack, stimulus or response generalization, etc.

transfer, methods of: a term referring to various explanations of how transfer is effected, for example, through identical elements, insight (involving functional equivalence), mechanical methods, etc.

transfer, negative: transfer of training in which the existence of one habit, skill, idea, or ideal retards or interferes with the acquisition, performance, or relearning of a similar characteristic. *Syn.* **proactive inhibition.**

transfer, nonspecific: the term describing the tendency for nonspecific factors (for example, principles or methods) acquired in one activity or situation to be elicited in a new (usually similar) activity or situation; transfer explainable in terms of method, system, principles, etc., rather than in terms of content.

transfer of abstract relationships: fundamentally, an idea that is associated with the process of *generalization* (either of stimulus or of response) and that emphasizes the possibility of transferring ideas and thoughts not immediately obvious to the senses.

transfer of credits: the act of reporting to a school the credits that a given pupil has earned in another school.

transfer of funds: the process by which money appropriated in the budget to one fund is transferred to another fund, such transfers being frequently necessary during the fiscal year but usually requiring formal approval of the school board.

transfer of general principles: (1) the tendency for the understanding of basic principles to influence the acquisition of new learnings; (2) the application to a new situation of the understanding of basic principles acquired in a previous situation.

transfer of habit: (1) the tendency for a practiced function to persist; perhaps related to functional autonomy; (2) the tendency for a practiced function to influence the formation and development of new functions; *syn.* **transfer of learning.**

transfer of learning: *syn.* **transfer of habit; transfer of training.**

transfer of modes of attack: the application of general methods of procedure to an activity or situation not encountered previously; an example of *nonspecific transfer.*

transfer of set: the tendency for *set* to facilitate or inhibit new learning.

transfer of students: *see* **pupil, transfer.**

transfer of training: the influence that the existence of an established habit, skill, idea, or ideal exerts on the acquisition, performance, or relearning of another similar characteristic; such influence may facilitate new learning (*positive transfer*), retard or inhibit new learning (*negative transfer*), or be of negligible effect on new learning (*zero* or *indeterminate transfer*).

transfer options: *see* **transfer points.**

transfer out: a pupil who has been enrolled in a given school center and who is being sent to another school center. (Such pupils are transfers out according to records of the sending school; they are *transfers in* according to records of the receiving school.

transfer phenomenon: *syn.* **transfer effect.**

transfer, picture: the transfer of printing ink from a magazine picture to a special acetate sheet after the two are sealed together with heat and pressure and then submerged in water to remove the paper.

transfer points: as used in comparative education studies, points in a school system at which pupils may change, without substantial loss of time and credits, from one course of study, stream, or type of school to another. *Syn.* **transfer option;** *see* **streaming.**

transfer, positive: transfer of training in which the existence of one habit, skill, idea, or ideal facilitates the acquisition, performance, or relearning of a similar characteristic.

transfer program: *see* **program, transfer.**

transfer, pupil: (1) change in a pupil's school enrollment or attendance from one school or administrative unit to another; (2) a pupil who has transferred his enrollment or membership from one school to another.

transfer pupil: *see* **pupil, transfer.**

transfer rate, annual: the total number of times pupils transfer within the school or school district during the regular school term divided by the total number of pupils who enter the school or school district during the term; when expressed as a percentage, the annual transfer rate indicates the proportion of pupil transfer within the school or school district in relation to the total number of pupils in the school or school district during the term.

transfer record: *see* **record, transfer.**

transfer report: *see* **report, transfer.**

transfer, special: (1) a pupil who is transferred to a school in a district other than the one in which he lives; (2) the act or process of making such a transfer.

transfer, specific: transfer of training in which the transfer is in terms of the subject matter or content rather than in terms of method, principles, etc.

transfer, specific elements in: *syn.* **identical elements;** *dist. f.* **transfer, nonspecific.**

transfer, stimulus-field: positive or negative transfer that is regarded as dependent upon recognized similarities in more or less complex patterns of experience (that is, perceptions or relations). *See* **generalization, stimulus; insight** (2); **transposition** (1).

transfer student: *see* **student, transfer.**

transfer system, state: *see* **state transfer system.**

transfer, teacher: the removal of a teacher from one position in a school system and his assignment to another position of the same or different rank within the same system.

transfer through generalization: a theory of transfer first proposed by Judd, whereby transfer occurs through generalizations or principles common to old and new tasks. *Syn.* **transfer of general principles;** *see* **transfer of abstract relationships.**

transfer, trait: a term used to emphasize transfer that involves the organization of cognitive and affective processes in regulating behavior.

transfer, unconditional: in computer operation, a command which causes the following instruction to be taken from an address other than the next one in the sequence.

transfer, unilateral: improvement in performance induced by practice of one part of the body on another part of the body on the same side, for example, effect on performance by the right foot through practice in the same or a similar task by the right hand.

transfer, zero: the situation in which the existence of one habit, skill, idea, or ideal has no observable influence upon the acquisition, performance, or relearning of a similar characteristic; although zero transfer can be observed practically, its existence cannot be demonstrated experimentally since it would involve proving a null hypothesis (an experimental impossibility).

transferability: agreement in score-meaning of the same test applied (on the same kind of occasion and under the same conditions) to different sets of people.

transference: (psychoanal.) the process whereby the analyst becomes the object of the patient's love or hate, through identification as a substitute for the original object; for example, the analyst is endowed with the qualities of the patient's father or mother; similarly, in guidance a relationship between the counselee and the counselor in which dissociated emotions that were formerly directed toward other situations, persons, or objects are activated and directed toward the counselor or therapist. *See* **countertransference.**

transference, mixed: a combination of positive and negative transference. *See* **transference, negative; transference, positive.**

transference, negative: a term used in psychoanalytic theory to refer to the transfer of aggression or hostility felt toward a person such as a parent or sibling, developed early in life, to another person encountered later in life; essential in psychotherapy, according to some views.

transference, positive: a term used in psychoanalytic theory to refer to the transfer of love for a person, developed early in life, to another person encountered later in life; essential in psychotherapy, according to some views.

transformation: (1) the act or process of changing a value from one unit of measurement to another, especially when done to modify the shape of a distribution of raw scores to make them more closely conform to some assumption involved in a statistical test of significance; usually performed to make the distribution of values approximate the normal probability distribution; (2) (math.) *syn.* **function** (3); **mapping.**

transformation, angular: a transformation into angles sometimes used with proportions; use is made of the formula $\phi = 2 \arcsin \sqrt{p}$. *Syn.* **arcsin transformation; inverse sine transformation;** *see* **transformation.**

transformation, arcsin: *syn.* **transformation, angular.**

transformation, chain: a type of drill employed in foreign language instruction in which each successive response is taken as a model for the following response; a fragment proposed by the master voice must be fitted into the last response in the correct place according to structure and meaning. *Comp. w.* **drill, transformation.**

transformation drill: *see* **drill, transformation.**

transformation geometry: *see* **geometry, transformation.**

transformation, inverse sine: *syn.* **transformation, angular.**

transformation item: *see* **item, transformation.**

transformation, linear: a transformation that can be accomplished through the use of a simple linear equation; for example $z = \dfrac{X - M}{\sigma}$, where $X =$ raw score, $M =$ mean, and $\sigma =$ standard deviation. *See* **transformation.**

transformation, logarithmic: a transformation of values into their respective logarithms. *See* **transformation.**

transformation matrix: *see* **matrix, transformation.**

transformation, reciprocal: a transformation of values into their respective reciprocals. *See* **transformation.**

transformation, square root: a transformation of values into their respective square roots; commonly used when observations are small integral values whose experimental errors have a Poisson distribution. *See* **transformation.**

transformation table: *see* **table, transformation.**

transformation, z: *syn.* **Fisher's z.**

transformational grammar: *see* **grammar, transformational.**

transformational theory: the theory that English grammar can be understood as a set of *kernel sentences* from which more complicated sentences may be built.

transformed correlation coefficient: *syn.* **Fisher's z.**

transiency of teachers: (1) the degree of permanency in specific positions for teachers as a group; (2) the permanence of tenure of educational personnel in a given position. (It is assumed that continued residence of a teacher in a community is necessary for effective adjustment, appreciation, and knowledge with respect to community conditions and needs.)

transient child: *see* **child, transient.**

transit-type vehicle: *see* **vehicle, transit-type.**

transition class: *see* **class, transition.**

transition group: (1) a group of children who have been in kindergarten for a year but are not yet ready for reading and who therefore are given enriching experiences for a period of time until they are ready to enter the first grade and undertake beginning reading; (2) a junior first-grade class for children who have outgrown the kindergarten activities but who apparently are not ready for regular first-grade work.

transition group, non-English: a postkindergarten class in which non-English-speaking children are stimulated through a variety of experiences and conversation relative to these experiences so that they may acquire an English vocabulary.

transition training: *see* **training, transition.**

transition zone: the interval between the point on the scale below which none pass a certain test item and the point on the scale above which all pass the item.

transitional: (1) pertaining to a state of transition, to passage from one place or state to another; (2) historically, in evolution, development, etc., pertaining to passage from one definable type, style, or stage to another; changing from an earlier to a later form.

transitional school: the designation of a school midway in philosophy and organization between the traditional and the extremely progessive, some elements of both being retained; usually has an activity and subject-matter program and an organization including both subject fields and units of work.

transitive property: (math.) a property which a relation may have, stated as follows: for members a, b, and c of the set on which the relation is defined, if a is related to b, and b is related to c, then a is related to c; for example, the relation "is less than" for numbers has the transitive property, since if $a < b$ and $b < c$, then $a < c$.

translation: the act of rendering into a given language material in another language, giving the closest possible idiomatic equivalents of the original words and phrases.

translation, algorithm: in automatic data processing, a specific, essentially computational, method for obtaining a translation from one language to another.

translation, machine: the use of computers to translate a text; the linguistic cues to the text are programmed so as to provide for the translating operation.

translation method: a method of teaching foreign languages in which the principal learning exercise consists in translating passages in the foreign language into the vernacular, and vice versa, both orally and in writing.

translation, simultaneous: an equivalent translation which seldom lags behind the utterances of the native speaker by more than a few seconds.

translator: (1) an electronic device capable of receiving a TV transmission from a VHF station and converting it for retransmission on a UHF channel; can also be used to pick up a program from a UHF channel and retransmit it on a different UHF channel; (2) a computer program, FORTRAN compiler, assembler, interpreter, etc., which accepts a *source program* as input and produces an equivalent *object program* as output; may announce errors in the source program, such as inconsistencies in the source deck, errors in format design, etc.; the translator makes it possible for the human nonspecialist to have much more direct access to the computer since the translator languages are far easier to work with than the binary codes required by the machine.

translatory movement: *see* **movement, translatory.**

translucent screen: *syn.* **screen, rear-projection.**

transmission: (communications theory) the processes by which a message passes from input to output; also, the average amount of information coming from the input which reaches the output.

transmission, cultural: *see* **cultural transmission.**

transmission, facsimile: *see* **facsimile transmission.**

transmission, social: *see* **social transmission.**

transmitter: (1) in broadcasting, a general term applying to the equipment necessary to radiate radio or television signals into space for reception at locations within the service area; (2) in communications theory, any means by which a message is encoded and started on its way through a channel.

transmutation equation: an equation stating the relationship between original scores and the transmuted scores.

transmutation of measures: the act or process of changing measures or scores from one basis to another, such as raw scores to ranks, standard scores, or percentile ranks.

transmutation table: *syn.* **table, transformation.**

transmute: to change any given variable from one basis to another, as from the original scores to ranks, standard scores, or percentile ranks.

transmuted measure: *syn.* **measure, derived.**

transmuted score: *see* **score, transmuted.**

transparency: transparent material designed for projection to facilitate enlargement of the image; originally associated with 2 × 2 inch and 3¼ × 4 inch slides, the term is now more popularly associated with 7 × 7 inch and 10 × 10 inch slides used with overhead projectors. *See* **overlay** (2); **projector, overhead.**

transparency projector, overhead: *see* **projector, overhead.**

transport, tape: *see* **tape transport.**

transportation: (ind. arts) an area of study dealing with the operating principles, design, construction, maintenance, and repair of transportation conveyances; generally includes automotives, aerospace and nautical conveyances, and related physical and chemical principles.

transportation area: *syn.* **transportation district.**

transportation contract: *see* **contract, transportation.**

transportation cost per pupil transported, average: the annual current expenditures for pupil transportation divided by the average daily membership of pupils transported.

transportation, director of: *see* **director of transportation.**

transportation district: an area from which pupils are brought to a school building.

transportation, eligible for: the designation applied to any child who may ride to school because of distance, traffic hazard, or physical disability.

transportation, emergency: pupil transportation provided under unusual circumstances at unscheduled periods.

transportation, individual: the provision of conveyance from home to school and return for children whose particular (usually handicapped) conditions demand personalized arrangements (usually by taxicab or other small vehicle).

transportation map: a large map of the area in which transportation is provided showing roads, location of pupils, bus routes, school buildings, and other information pertinent to the pupil transportation program.

transportation, minimum: transportation service that the school district is required to provide, as established by statute or practice; requirements are usually designated by an established distance from the school that pupils attend.

transportation, parental: pupil transportation supplied by the parent or guardian of the child.

transportation program, minimum: *see* **program, minimum transportation.**

transportation, pupil: the movement of school children from home to school and return by means of a conveyance of whatever sort, usually a bus, at public expense.

transportation records: records covering any or all phases of transportation, such as number of buses, cost of buses, costs of operation and repair of buses, pupils transported, route description, bus accidents and persons injured or killed, and other pertinent information.

transportation regulations: a set of rules or guides that determine (a) the manner in which school buses are to be operated, and (b) pupil responsibilities and conduct.

transportation report: *syn.* **report, annual transportation.**

transportation report, annual: *see* **report, annual transportation.**

transportation saturation index: *see* **index, transportation saturation.**

transportation service, pupil: those activities which have as their purpose the conveyance of pupils to and from school activities, either between home and school or on trips related to school activities.

transportation service vehicle: *see* **vehicle, transportation service.**

transportation, state aid for pupil: *see* **aid for pupil transportation, state.**

transportation survey: *see* **survey, transportation.**

transported at public expense, percentage of pupils: *see* **percentage of pupils transported at public expense.**

transported pupil: *see* **pupil, transported.**

transported pupils riding a given distance, percentage of: *see* **percentage of transported pupils riding a given distance.**

transported pupils riding a given time, percentage of: *see* **percentage of transported pupils riding a given time.**

transposed factor analysis: *see* **factor analysis, transposed.**

transposition: (1) a term used by gestalt psychologists to refer to the detection of repetition of common patterns of psychological events, as in the transposition of a melody; hence, one factor in *transfer of training;* (2) (math.) a term, not in correct usage, for a method of solving an algebraic equation by moving a term from one side of it to the other, accompanied by change in sign; (3) (math.) the interchange of two members of some arrangement; (4) (read.) the act of pronouncing a word out of its place in the context; a word pronounced by the reader out of its place in the context; exchanging the positions of two letters or sounds in a word, for example, *preform* for *perform.*

transvestitism (tranz·ves′ti·tiz′m): *syn.* **eonism.**

trauma (trâ′mə): (1) a wound or injury caused by violence such as striking, cutting, crushing, or other mechanical means; (2) a wound or injury to the body or mind.

trauma, acoustic: injury to the ear by a single brief exposure to sounds. *Comp. w.* **fatigue, auditory.**

trauma, birth: *see* **birth trauma.**

trauma, weaning: emotional disturbances resulting from the thwarting associated with being weaned.

traumatic constitution: a condition resulting from severe head injury, marked by instability of the emotions, change of character, and increased susceptibility to alcoholic poisoning.

traumatic dementia: *see* **dementia, traumatic.**

traumatic neurosis: *see* **neurosis, traumatic.**

traumatic prematurity: *see* **prematurity, traumatic.**

travel abroad, academic: travel outside one's home country by students or staff of schools or universities when undertaken primarily in pusuit of activities of an educational or research nature rather than a commercial or recreational nature.

travel, foot: *see* **foot travel.**

traveling clinic: *syn.* **clinic, mobile.**

traveling library: *see* **library, traveling.**

traveling library, rural school: *see* **library, rural school traveling.**

traveling rings: a series of five or six rings suitable for hanging onto and suspended about 6 feet apart in a row.

traveling school: *see* **mobile school.**

traveling teacher: (1) a person, usually a subject specialist, who has teaching assignments in more than one building; may be employed by one, two, or more school districts; (2) an itinerant instructor employed by a state department of education, health, or welfare to hold classes and demonstrations in local communities; (3) a staff or faculty member of a college or university who conducts credit or noncredit classes through extension services in local communities at varying distances from the seat of the institution.

treadmill, horizontal: an endless conveyor belt which is operated by an electric motor and provides sufficient space for walking or running; can be made to run at various speeds and inclinations; used for research in physical education.

treasurer: (school admin.) the principal line executive, usually, in the field of finance; he is immediately responsible for the provision, custody, and disbursement of funds on proper authority. *See* **administration, line; organization, line-and-staff.**

treatment: a brief written outline of a proposed cinematic or other rendition of a story. *See* **storyboard.**

treatment, counseling: *see* **counseling treatment.**

treatment facility, residential: *see* **facility, residential treatment.**

treatment, supportive: *see* **supportive treatment.**

Tree of Knowledge: *see* **Knowledge, Tree of.**

tremor: continuous, involuntary muscular trembling or spasm; may be limited to a small area of the body.

trend analysis: *see* **analysis, trend.**

trend chart: *see* **chart, trend.**

trend factor: *see* **factor, trend.**

trend, social: *see* **social trend.**

trespass: the unauthorized entry upon, taking of, or interfering with the property of another.

trial, abortive: a trial terminated without reaching a verdict.

trial-and-error learning: *see* **learning, trial-and-error.**

trial and error, vicarious: *see* **response, covert.**

trial promotion: *syn.* **promotion, probationary.**

trial response: *see* **response, trial.**

triangle: (sociometry) (1) a closed chain of interpersonal feelings among three persons; (2) a geometric figure in a *sociogram,* representing a male.

triangle test: *see* **test, triangle.**

triangular matrix: *see* **matrix, triangular.**

triangular number: *see* **number, triangular.**

tribunal: a court or quasi-judicial body; often implies more than one judge sitting on the bench.

trichopathophobia (trik′ō·path·ō·fō′bi·ə): anxiety about hair; especially a morbid concern about the presence or absence of hair on the face, chest, etc.

trichophobia (trik′ō·fō′bi·ə): morbid dread of touching fur or hair.

trichotomy (tri·kot′ə·mi): (1) a division of a distribution, variable, or other unit into three parts; (2) (math.) a property of the real numbers which states that for any two numbers *a* and *b,* exactly one of the following holds: $a = b$, $a < b$, or $a < b$.

tridimensional concept of educational administration: *see* **administration, tridimensional concept of educational.**

trigonometry: a branch of mathematics concerned with the study of the relations between the sides and angles of triangles, including the study of the trigonometric functions (sine, cosine, tangent) and their properties of periodicity, domain, range, related inverse functions, etc.

trigonometry, functional approach to: teaching the trigonometric functions as contrasted to teaching numerical trigonometry.

trigonometry, numerical: (1) those topics in trigonometry which are computational in nature, such as solving triangles; (2) derivation of the trigonometric functions from similar triangles.

trigonometry, plane: teaching the trigonometric functions (sine, cosine, tangent) relative to the plane.

trigonometry, spherical: the study of the trigonometric functions which derive from the geometry of the sphere; these are hyperbolic sine (sinh), hyperbolic cosine (cosh), and hyperbolic tangent (tanh).

trigraph, consonant: *see* **consonant trigraph.**

trilingual: having equal facility in the use of three languages. *See* **bilingual; multilingual;** *contr. w.* **monolingual.**

trimester: one of three equal portions of an academic calendar year; typically about 15 weeks in length; 3 trimesters correspond roughly to 4 quarters or to 2 semesters and a summer session of 8 to 12 weeks. *See* **academic year.**

trip, bus: *see* **bus trip.**

trip, double: the practice of assigning a bus to two separate routes. *Syn.* **route, multiple.**

trip, field: *see* **field trip.**

trip, industrial field: *see* **industrial field trip.**

trip, instructional: *syn.* **field trip.**

trip, study: *syn.* **field trip.**

tripartite grouping: *see* **grouping, tripartite.**

triphthong: a speech sound formed when sequences of three vowels are joined and function as a single syllable; for example, "ours" as pronounced by *r*-droppers, $a + oo + az$.

triple interaction: *syn.* **interaction, second-order.**

triplegia: paralysis of three extremities. *See* **hemiplegia; monoplegia; paraplegia; quadriplegia.**

triplets: three offspring born at the same birth. *See* **multiple birth.**

trivium (triv′ē·əm): (Lat., lit., "three ways," "three roads") the designation of the three basic studies or disciplines of the medieval curriculum, namely, grammar, rhetoric, and dialectic. *See* **liberal arts, seven;** *dist. f.* **quadrivium.**

trompe l'oeil (trōnp′loy′): (Fr., lit., "trick the eye") an extreme kind of naturalism in which the illusion of reality in the painting reaches a point of fooling the senses; found in some ancient Roman painting, some Dutch seventeenth-century still-life painting, early twentieth-century American lithographs, etc.

tropism: tendency to turn toward or away from a stimulus, for example, geotropism, the tendency of a plant to turn toward earth; negative heliotropism, the tendency of rats to turn away from light places.

trot: *see* **crib.**

trouble case: a problem involving nonattendance recorded by the attendance officer in case-history form and regarded as susceptible to satisfactory solution out of court. *Contr. w.* **court case.**

truancy: (1) deliberate absence from school on the part of the pupil without the knowledge and consent of the parent; (2) absence of a pupil from school for which no reasonable or acceptable excuse is given. (This latter concept broadens the definition considerably and makes it synonymous with *unexcused absence.*)

truancy, intermittent: the act of being truant at somewhat regular intervals.

truancy record: *see* **record, truancy.**

truancy report: *see* **report, truancy.**

truant: a youth who is absent from school without the knowledge and consent of his parents; legally defined, in some states, according to the frequency of occurrence of such absence; popularly, a youth who is absent from school without a valid excuse. *Syn.* **school delinquent.**

truant, committed: a truant sent by court action to a state industrial school or to a local parental or farm school.

truant, habitual: a child given to constant and continual absence from school without the knowledge or consent of his parents, the number of such truancies sometimes being specified as a means of determining legally when to consider a child a habitual truant, but with considerable variation from system to system. (Probably a habitual truant cannot be defined in terms of frequency of absence alone but must be considered psychologically and sociologically.)

truant officer: synonymous with *attendance officer* in some school systems. (In general, the term implies less training than is usually demanded of an attendance officer and has become obsolete.)

truck: *v.* to move a camera translationally in space as a shot proceeds, usually by means of a dolly or other vehicular camera support, in order to pace moving actors or objects while maintaining their image size. *See* **shot.**

true: (stat.) referring to a universe rather than to a sample; thus, true mean, true correlation, true difference, etc., are the values existing in the universe, as contrasted with corresponding values appearing in a sample.

true congenital deafness: *see* **deafness, true congenital.**

true correlation: *see* **correlation, true.**

true difference: *see* **difference, true.**

true error: *see* **error, true.**

true-false item: *see* **item, true-false.**

true-false test: *see* **test, true-false.**

true mean: *see* **mean, true.**

true measure: *syn.* **score, true.**

true regression curve: *see* **curve, true regression.**

true score: *see* **score, true.**

true-score theory: determination by complex statistics of what a person's *true score* would be if conditions were optimal and he performed at the maximum of his capabilities.

true valuation: *see* **valuation, true.**

true value: *see* **value, true.**

true variance: *see* **variance, true.**

truncated distribution: *see* **distribution, truncated.**

truncated high school: *see* **high school, incomplete regular.**

trunk growth: *see* **growth, trunk.**

trust: (1) an equitable right or interest in property distinct from the legal ownership thereof; (2) a property interest held by one person for the benefit of another. (School and college endowments are educational trusts held by their governing boards for the benefit of the public or some portion thereof properly designated as the clientele of the institution.)

trust, charitable: a trust dedicated to public eleemosynary purposes; usually free of the legal limitations imposed on private or commercial trusts, being granted longer life and exemption from taxation; is not usually, however, accorded all the immunities of a specifically chartered charitable corporation. *See* **charter, philanthropic; trust.**

trust, community: *see* **community trust.**

trust funds: *see* **funds, trust.**

trustee: (1) a person, whether real or juristic, to whom property is committed in trust; (2) one entrusted with the property of another. (The governing board of an educational institution or system, often called a *board of trustees,* constitutes in its collective entity a juristic person holding in trust the property and endowment funds of the institution.)

trustee, corporate: (1) a person who serves as a *trustee* of an incorporated commercial, philanthropic, or public trust; (2) a corporation that serves as a *trustee* for a person, an association, or another private corporation.

trustee, district school: *see* **district school.**

trustee, school: a person, selected under legal provision, usually chosen by popular election from the district at large for a term of 3 to 5 years to direct, with other members of a board of trustees, the program of education within the territorial limits of the school district.

truth: (1) the correspondence of a thought or judgment with reality, with an actual occurrence, or with natural processes; (2) the correspondence of a thought or idea with its own implications; (3) a state of coherence and correspondence of all the parts or subtruths of an idea, thought, or judgment, not only with themselves but also with the whole and with experience; (4) (pragmatism) that value which a proposition earns when it succeeds in inquiry, that is, when it becomes verified by the universal assent of competent inquirers.

truth, coherence theory of: the theory that a proposition is true if it has logical consistency with what is already known.

truth, correspondence theory of: the theory that a proposition is true if it conforms to the fact(s) that it asserts.

truth set: *see* **set, solution.**

truth table: *see* **table, truth.**

truthfulness: the quality of telling or reporting that which is accurate or correct.

try, provisional: in learning theory, the notion that in a problem situation an organism often tests out a response without a total commitment to the response until the consequences are observed.

tryout: (1) a trial contest to determine the physical fitness and ability of a student to participate in a certain event; (2) as used freely in schools of music, a test to determine a musician's proper assignment in a band, choir, or orchestra.

tryout course: *see* **course, tryout.**

tryout, group: tryout of programmed instructional materials on a group of students to determine how well they teach, what revisions are needed, and how best to use them in realistic training situations.

tube, cathode ray: (data processing) (1) an electronic vacuum tube containing a screen on which information may be stored by means of a multigrid modulated beam of electrons from the thermionic emitter; storage effected by means of charged or uncharged spots; (2) a storage tube; (3) an oscilloscope tube; (4) a picture tube.

tube, data-storage: *see* **data-storage tube.**

tuition: the amount of money charged by an educational institution for instruction, not including materials, books, or laboratory fees. *See* **tuition, nonresident.**

tuition academy: *see* **academy, tuition.**

tuition based on financial ability: a term often used to justify tuition fees lower than the regular rate but in keeping with the income of the payer. *See* **tuition, pro-rata.**

tuition fee: *see* **fee.**

tuition investigation: an investigation made under authority of the superintendent of schools of the residence status of any school child not living within the city or school district with either one or both parents. (Tuition investigations are required because of the ruling that only those children whose parents are residing within the school district are legally entitled to the privileges of the public schools in that district.)

tuition, nonresident: (1) a charge or fee paid for the privilege of school attendance in a district by residents outside the district; (2) in a state-supported institution of higher education, the fee charged students whose legal residence is not in that state.

tuition pay notice: a notice to the persons, other than parent or parents, with whom a child is living that tuition must be paid if the child is to be allowed to attend school in the district in which they live.

tuition payment plan, deferred: an arrangement whereby a matriculated college student whose tuition is beyond his or his family's means may contract to pay it in installments stretching through a term of his earning years after graduation, at a percentage based on the size of his income; a scheme under consideration by some private institutions of higher education as a check to the tendency of inflation to place a college education out of reach of worthy students for whom scholarships are inadequate or unavailable; there is a similar plan at public higher education institutions in California.

tuition, pro-rata (prō'rā'tə, -rä'tə): a fee for instruction determined by dividing the total operating expense of an institution by the number of students.

tuition pupil: *see* **pupil, tuition.**

tuition school: an independent or private school, attendance at which is in whole or in part conditioned on the payment of a fee.

tuition waived: a notice to a principal of a school that the payment of tuition has been waived by the superintendent of schools.

tumbling: gymnastic or acrobatic exercises principally involving throwing the body into the air; performed on the ground, usually with the protection of mats, by one or more performers.

tunes, fuguing: *see* **fuguing tunes.**

tuning fork: a two-pronged steel fork used to indicate absolute pitch; capable of producing nearly pure tones free of harmonics and having great permanence of pitch retention. *Comp. w.* **pitch pipe.**

tuning fork test: *see* **test, tuning fork.**

tunnel vision: *see* **vision, tunnel.**

turn signals: an electric warning signal system whereby the intermittent flashing of lights mounted on front and rear of a vehicle indicates to other drivers the intention to change course by turning to the right or left. *Syn.* **direction signals.**

turning point: the designation of the place at which a school bus regularly turns completely around and begins its trip back to the school.

turnover, faculty: *see* **turnover, teacher.**

turnover, gross teacher: the total turnover of a given teacher group during a stated period. *See* **turnover, teacher;** *contr. w.* **turnover, net teacher.**

turnover, net teacher: that part of the gross, or total, turnover represented by beginning teachers. *See* **turnover, teacher;** *contr. w.* **turnover, gross teacher.**

turnover, pupil: the proportion of pupils who leave a school during a term in relation to the total number of pupils in the school during a term.

turnover ratio, labor: a measure of the rate of separation of employees from an organization or some part of it.

turnover, teacher: the loss and subsequent replacement of teachers, usually expressed as the proportion of change in a specific teacher group during a stated time period, for example, 1 year. *See* **migration, teacher; turnover, gross teacher; turnover, net teacher.**

turntable: the rotating part of a phonograph upon which records are carried during play.

turnverein (tōōrn'fə·rīn): (Ger., lit., "gymnastic society") an association of gymnasts and athletes, particularly as sponsored by organizations whose members are of ethnic German origin; these clubs, brought to the United States by German immigrants and especially prominent toward the close of the nineteenth century, foster amateur gymnastics and athletics as well as concomitant social and educational activities.

tutor: (1) a member of the instructional staff who, through informal conferenees, instructs and examines students, sometimes while maintaining residence in a dormitory with the same students; (2) an undergraduate or graduate student selected and recommended by professors to assist students by means of private conferences.

tutorial: *n.* a process of instruction used in some colleges in which a *tutor* acts as general adviser to a small number of individuals and supervises the pursuit of knowledge in a specific subject area. *See* **class, tutorial; tutor** (1).

tutorial class: *see* **class, tutorial.**

tutorial plan: as developed at Harvard University, a plan for carrying out specific individual guidance through the assignment of students to individual instructors, whose responsibility it is to develop effective study habits in the student and relate his intellectual activities to his whole life; the plan involves weekly conferences, preparation for each conference usually consisting in the accomplishing of specific reading assignments and sometimes the writing of papers. (The tutorial plan of instruction has long been used in the colleges of Oxford and Cambridge Universities in England.)

tutorial-preceptorial plan: as developed at Colgate University, a plan of individual guidance involving the assignment of each incoming student to a general counselor (preceptor), who is concerned with the whole development of the student rather than instruction in any given subject; in the upper 3 years of enrollment, students are assigned to tutors whose responsibility it is to help students work out special problems of scholarship and research in certain designated areas.

tutorial services: *see* **services, tutorial.**

twelve-month school: *syn.* **all-year school.**

Twelve Tables, laws of the: *see* **laws of the Twelve Tables.**

twelve-tone music: *syn.* **music, dodecaphonic; music, serial.**

twenty-four-hour school: *syn.* **parental school.** (Found chiefly in the Far West.)

T.W.I.: *see* **training within industry.**

twins: a pair of offspring produced at a single birth in a species that usually brings forth only one offspring at a time; may be *monozygotic* or *dizygotic.*

twins, dizygotic (dī'zī·got'ik): twins resulting from the fertilization of two ova at the same time; may be dissimilar in sex and appearance. *Syn.* **fraternal twins; two-egg twins;** *contr. w.* **twins, monozygotic.**

twins, fraternal: *syn.* **twins, dizygotic.**

twins, identical: *syn.* **twins, monozygotic.**

twins, monochorionic (mon'ō·kō·ri·on'ik): *syn.* **twins, monozygotic.**

twins, monozygotic (mon'ō·zī·got'ik): twins resulting from the early complete division of a single fertilized ovum and who, accordingly, share the same heredity, are always of the same sex, and are in almost all instances closely alike in physical attributes. *Syn.* **identical twins; monochorionic twins; one-egg twins;** *contr. w.* **twins, dizygotic.**

twins, one-egg: *syn.* **twins, monozygotic.**

twins, two-egg: *syn.* **twins, dizygotic.**

two by two slide: *see* **slide, two by two.**

two-egg twins: *syn.* **twins, dizygotic.**

two-factor inheritance: *see* **inheritance, two-factor.**

two-factor theory: the theory that the correlations of a test battery can be described by a single factor common to all the tests and a factor specific to each test. *See* **tetrad difference.**

two-hand alphabet: *see* **alphabet, finger.**

two-room school: *see* **two-teacher school.**

two-sided test: *syn.* **test, two-tailed.**

two-step problem: *see* **problem, two-step.**

two-tailed test: *see* **test, two-tailed.**

two-teacher school: an individual school for which two teachers are employed; may include either the elementary grades alone or both the elementary and some or all of the high school grades; often used as a synonym for *two-room school.*

two-track course of study: a course of study designed to provide instruction in the same general area on two distinct levels, superior and average; affords greater individualization of instruction. *See* **three-track course of study.**

two-track monaural tape: *see* **tape, dual-track monaural.**

two-track stereo tape: *see* **tape, two-track stereo.**

two-way table: *syn.* **table, double-entry.**

two-year college: *see* **junior college, two-year.**

two-year junior college: *see* **junior college, two-year.**

two-year reorganized high school: *see* **reorganized high school, two-year.**

type: (1) (stat.) the class mark of an array in a double-entry table; *see* **mark, class;** (2) (biol.) a class of individuals or objects having in common certain distinguishing characteristics, by reference to which they may be classified; (3) (read.) one of the total of different words in a unit of reading matter.

type A construction: *see* **construction, type A.**

type B construction: *see* **construction, type B.**

type, body: the physique or build of a person when classified according to certain characteristics. *See* **body builds, classification of; somatotype.**

type C construction: *see* **construction, type C.**

type D construction: *see* **construction, type D.**

type E construction: *see* **construction, type E.**

type face: the surface of the type that actually comes in contact with the paper in printing.

type geography: *see* **geography, type.**

type, haptic: *see* **haptic type.**

type I library school: *see* **library school, type I.**

type II library school: *see* **library school, type II.**

type III library school: *see* **library school, type III.**

type job: *see* **job, type.**

type of certificate: *see* **certificate, type of.**

type size: size of the body rather than of the face of the type; the term point indicates size of the body, not of the face.

type study: *see* **study, type.**

type-token ratio: *see* **ratio, type-token.**

type, unstable: *see* **unstable type.**

type, visual: *see* **visual type.**

types of aesthetic perception: *see* **aesthetic perception, types of.**

types of children's drawing: *see* **drawing, types of children's.**

typescript: material written on the typewriter (a term coined by analogy with manuscript).

typewriter, automatic: a typewriter actuated from a master control unit which contains copy that is to be typed automatically in a large number of identically worded copies.

typewriter, braille: *see* **brailler.**

typewriting, office practice: a typewriting unit or course in which the major emphasis is placed on the development of typewriting skills and related knowledges required of office workers.

typewriting, personal-use: typewriting taught from the point of view of its usefulness to the average person, as in personal business and informal social correspondence and in writing school themes, without regard for its vocational applications; usually taught in high school and college as a comparatively short course of one or two semesters. *Contr. w.* **typewriting, vocational.**

typewriting room: an instruction room equipped with tables or desks on which are placed typewriters for use in practicing typewriting.

typewriting, touch: the method of typing in which all the fingers are used for striking the keys and the eyes are employed for reading copy only. *Contr. w.* **typewriting, visual.**

typewriting, visual: the method of typing in which the operator alternately watches the keys and the material being copied. *Contr. w.* **typewriting, touch.**

typewriting, vocational: typewriting taught with a view to its use for business or professional purposes, as in the occupation of stenographer or typist; includes intensive training in basic typing skills and instruction and practice in business and legal forms; usually taught in secondary schools as a relatively long course of two to four semesters and in colleges for two semesters. *Contr. w.* **typewriting, personal-use.**

typhlology: the science and art of work with the blind and the field of education which concerns itself with this science and art.

typical average: *see* **average, typical.**

typical child: *see* **child, typical.**

typical data: *syn.* **data, representative.**

typical-performance test: *see* **test, typical-performance.**

typing and related occupations training: *see* **training, typing and related occupations.**

typing, art: *see* **art typing.**

typing position: correct posture at the typewriter; recommended position specifications: about 6 to 8 inches of space between top of knee and frame of typewriter; front of body 8 to 10 inches from base of typewriter and slightly right of center of keyboard; fingers curved, wrists low; feet preferably on floor.

typing power: combination of high degree of typewriting speed and accuracy plus related understandings that makes for effective use of typewriting skill as demonstrated by master typists; involves the ability to type difficult material for long periods of time.

typographical laboratory: *see* **laboratory, typographical.**

typology (tī·pol′ə·ji): (1) the study of types of individuals and their systematic classification according to certain modes of behavior or physical characteristics or according to certain relationships between behavior and physical characteristics; (2) a multidimensional classification.

U-shaped curve: *see* **curve, U-shaped.**

U-shaped distribution: *see* **distribution, U-shaped.**

UHF: *see* **frequency, ultrahigh.**

ultimate: *n.* the extreme limit of actual or possible knowledge.

ultimate: *adj.* last; final; furthest removed; absolute.

ultimate aim: *see* **aim, ultimate.**

ultimate cause: *see* **cause, ultimate.**

ultimate class: *see* **class, ultimate.**

ultimate objective: *see* **objective, ultimate.**

ultimate principles: *see* **principles, ultimate.**

ultimate reality: *see* **reality, ultimate.**

ultimate unit of responsibility: *see* **responsibility, ultimate unit of.**

ultra vires (ul'trə vī'rēz): (Lat., lit., "outside the powers") applied to an action or decision of an officer, board, or corporation that is beyond the scope of authority belonging to such an officer or body. (Generally an ultra vires contract entered into by a board of education is not enforceable against the board, on the theory that those who deal with public bodies are bound to know the limits of their powers.)

ultrafiche: *see* **ultramicrofiche.**

ultrahigh frequency: *see* **frequency, ultrahigh.**

ultrahigh-frequency broadcasting: *see* **frequency, ultrahigh.**

ultramicrofiche (UMF): a 4- × 6-inch sheet of transparent film containing microdots, 3,200 to one transparency; when projected, each dot is a page or two of written material, so that one transparency holds the equivalent of five to seven volumes; also called *ultrafiche. Comp. w.* **microfiche; microfilm.**

UMF: *see* **ultramicrofiche.**

Umklammerung reflex (ōōm·kläm'ər·ōōng): *syn.* **response, startle.**

umpire: an official of a game charged with the responsibility of conducting the game in accordance with the rules.

UMT: *see* **military training, universal.**

unappropriated surplus: that part of surplus which has not been set aside for any specific purpose but remains available for any purpose to which surplus may be applied.

unary operation: *see* **operation, mathematical.**

unassigned period: *see* **period, unassigned.**

unauthorized contract: *see* **contract, unauthorized.**

unaware creation: *see* **creation, unaware.**

unbiased error: *syn.* **error, random (1).**

unbiased estimate: *see* **estimate, unbiased.**

unclassified: a term descriptive of governmental or civil service posts for which classification by competitive examination is not required; usually includes certificated, or licensed, professional employees for whom examinations are not needed and unskilled laborers for whom examinations would be impractical.

unclassified elementary pupil: *see* **pupil, unclassified elementary.**

unclassified secondary pupil: *see* **pupil, unclassified secondary.**

unclassified student: *see* **student, special.**

unconditional positive regard: *see* **regard, unconditional positive.**

unconditional transfer: *see* **transfer, unconditional.**

unconditioned reflex: *see* **reflex, unconditioned.**

unconditioned response: *see* **response, unconditioned.**

unconditioned stimulus: *see* **stimulus, unconditioned.**

unconditioning: the process of reestablishing an original, unlearned reflex or response and of eliminating a conditioned reflex or response (for example, if a child has been conditioned to fear the dark, unconditioning may be undertaken in order to extinguish the child's fear response and to restore his natural condition of being unafraid of the dark; accomplished by reinforcing the original, unlearned response, in this case, perhaps, by the association of pleasure and satisfaction with darkness, as by playing games in the dark); sometimes used to signify the reestablishment of a *conditioned* reflex, but in this sense the term reconditioning is to be preferred as less ambiguous. *See* **reconditioning.**

unconscious: (psychoan.) according to psychoanalytic theory, a hypothetical region of the mind where repressed concepts are lodged, supposedly not accessible to memory but susceptible of investigation by the technical procedure known as *psychoanalysis.*

unconscious motivation: *see* **motivation, unconscious.**

uncontrolled experimental method: *see* **experimental method, uncontrolled.**

uncontrolled scribbling: *see* **scribbling, uncontrolled.**

uncontrolled variable: *see* **variable, uncontrolled.**

uncorrelated: (1) not related; having a correlation coefficient of zero; unaffected by change in the size of another variable; *contr. w.* **correlated (1);** (2) not having a correlation coefficient computed; the degree of relationship, if any, not having been determined; *contr. w.* **correlated (2).**

undefined element: *see* **term, undefined.**

undefined term: *see* **term, undefined.**

underachievement: academic achievement at a level below the one expected on the basis of the student's performance on general aptitude tests and in the classroom. *See* **achiever, latent;** *contr. w.* **overachievement.**

underachiever: a person who falls below his capacity in school achievement.

underachiever, gifted: *see* **gifted underachiever.**

underage: younger chronologically than is normal for entering a given grade. *See* **age standard per grade.**

underclassman: a member of the freshman or sophomore class in an institution of college or high school level.

undercurve: any curve in handwriting made by a counterclockwise movement, that is, a concave arc made by moving downward toward the right and then upward. *Syn.* **indirect curve.**

underdeveloped countries: *see* **country, developing.**

underexposure: (photog.) exposure of light-sensitive film or paper for a length of time insufficient to yield a negative or print of normal contrast, shadow detail, and density. (Indicated in the case of a negative by a general appearance of "thinness," or paleness, and in the case of a positive print from reversal film by a general appearance of darkness.)

undergraduate: a student in an institution of higher education who has not yet taken the bachelor's, or first professional, degree in the field in which he is studying.

undergraduate flying training: *see* **training, basic flying.**

undergraduate library school, junior: *see* **library school, junior undergraduate.**

undergraduate manager: *syn.* **intramural manager.**

undergraduate pilot: *see* **pilot, undergraduate.**

undergraduate pilot training: *see* **training, basic pilot.**

undergraduate school: an instructional unit of a college or university offering a curriculum leading to the bachelor's degree, or the first professional degree.

undernourishment: a state of health due to improper food habits, inadequate diet, faulty assimilation, overactivity, or disease that frequently accompanies physical retardation; used loosely to denote a below-par physical condition; mistakenly used to designate the condition of a person of slight body build. *Syn.* **nutritional deficiency; undernutrition;** *comp. w.* **malnutrition.**

undernutrition: *syn.* **undernourishment.**

underprivileged: pertaining to one who is considered to have a lack of adequate material benefits.

underprivileged child: *see* **child, culturally deprived.**

understanding: the process of gaining or developing the meaning of various types of material or knowledge. *Comp. w.* **insight.**

understanding, mathematical: *see* **meanings, mathematical.**

understanding, social: *see* **social understanding.**

underweight: below the weight that is average for one's height, age, sex, and body build.

undeveloped countries: *see* **country, developing.**

undistributed scores: *see* **scores, undistributed.**

undivided five-year high school: *syn.* **high school, five-year.**

undivided high school: *syn.* **high school, six-year** (1).

uneducable and untrainable mentally retarded: *see* **mentally retarded, Group IV.**

unemployable teacher: a teacher disabled because of age, incompetence, or physical, mental, or social unsuitability for educational employment.

unemployment, cyclical: unemployment due to general inactivity of business during the depression phase of the business cycle.

unemployment, seasonal: displacement of workers caused by periods of business slackness (in some industries) due to seasonal factors such as weather conditions or social customs related to seasonal climatic changes.

unemployment, technological: (1) the temporary or permanent displacement of workers by the introduction of various technological improvements; (2) the number of job opportunities lost because of changing industrial techniques and other factors.

unencumbered balance: that portion of an appropriation or allotment not yet expended or encumbered.

UNESCO: the United Nations Educational, Scientific, and Cultural Organization, formed primarily to serve as a clearinghouse of information and ideas relating to education in the various member nations.

unexcused absence: *see* **absence, unexcused.**

unexpended balance: the portion of an appropriation or allotment that has not been expended.

ungraded class: *see* **class, ungraded.**

ungraded primary class: *see* **class, ungraded primary.**

ungraded primary school: a school having a flexible system of grouping in which children in the primary grades are grouped together regardless of age and in which extensive effort is made to adapt instruction to individual differences.

ungraded room: *see* **class, ungraded.**

ungraded school: *see* **nongraded school.**

ungraded special class: *see* **class, ungraded special.**

ungrouped: expressed in terms of the original units of a variable; not grouped into class intervals; having class intervals equal to the unit of measurement.

ungrouped randomized design: *see* **design, ungrouped randomized.**

ungrouped score: *see* **score, ungrouped.**

unidimensional attitude: *see* **attitude, unidimensional.**

unidimensional scale: *see* **scale, unidimensional.**

unified curriculum: *see* **curriculum, unified.**

unified district: *see* **district, unified.**

unified science: *see* **science, unified.**

unified-studies approach: a method of attack on the problem of curriculum reorganization in which an effort is made to achieve unification and integration of the educational program through breaking down the boundaries between related fields of study and effecting a fusion of such subject fields.

Unifon: a modified alphabet of 40 phonemes designed to simplify and reform spelling.

uniform accounting: *see* **accounting, uniform.**

uniform high school diploma: *see* **diploma, uniform high school.**

uniform-paper accounting: *see* **accounting, uniform-paper.**

uniform program: *see* **program, uniform.**

uniform recording system: *see* **recording system, uniform.**

uniform scale: *syn.* **scale, arithmetic.**

uniform school accounting system: *see* **accounting system, uniform school.**

uniform test: *syn.* **test, speed.**

uniform textbooks: *see* **textbooks, uniform.**

uniform vehicle code: *see* **vehicle code, uniform.**

uniformization: the transformation of scores or other values to ranks when the form of distribution of a variable is not known or is presumed not to be normal.

unilateral: of or pertaining to one side.

unilateral lighting: *see* **lighting, unilateral.**

unilateral transfer: *see* **transfer, unilateral.**

unimodal: (said of a frequency distribution or of a frequency curve) having only one mode; showing a tendency toward concentration at only one point or region; having only one peak. *Contr. w.* **bimodal; multimodal.**

union building: *see* **building, student-union.**

union catalog: *see* **catalog, union.**

union, credit: *see* **credit union.**

union high school: *see* **high school, union.**

union high school district: *see* **high school district, union.**

union junior college: *see* **junior college, union.**

union, labor: an organization of operative employees whose leaders are elected by and from their own number for the purpose of collective bargaining with employers and for other legitimate purposes the accomplishment of which will promote the interests of the employees.

union school district: *see* **district, union school.**

union, teachers': a local organization of teachers affiliated with organized labor, the purpose of which is the promotion of professional growth, economic welfare, security of tenure, and advancement of the general professional status of teachers.

union, teachers' credit: *see* **credit union, teachers'.**

unipolar factor: *see* **factor, unipolar.**

unique addend code: *see* **code, unique addend.**

unique code number: *see* **code number, unique.**

unique factor: *see* **factor, unique.**

unique trait: *see* **trait, unique.**

unique variable: *see* **variable, unique.**

uniqueness: that portion of the variance of a variable which is not accounted for by factors contained in any other variables in the set but which is associated with specific factors and error. *Ant.* **communality.**

unison singing: *see* **singing, unison.**

unison song: *see* **song, unison.**

unit: (1) a major subdivision of a course of study, a textbook, or a subject field, particularly a subdivision in the social studies, practical arts, or sciences; (2) an organization of various activities, experiences, and types of learning around a central problem, or purpose, developed cooperatively by a group of pupils under teacher leadership; involves planning, execution of plans, and evaluation of results; *see* **project;** (3) a basic measure used in calculating the amount of credit to be assigned to any particular course or the number of graduation credits earned by a pupil or student in completing a course; variously defined, as follows: (*a*) in secondary education, one unit equals approximately 120 hours of classroom or laboratory work in a given subject, which is the amount of time spent in a class that meets for one period daily during the entire school year; (*b*) in higher education, according to local usage, one unit may equal 1 hour of class or laboratory work per week during one term, semester, or school year; *syn.* **unit of credit; unit of work;** (4) (math.) (*a*) an identity element for multiplication and (*b*) in an integral domain, an element which divides the multiplicative identity.

unit, absorption: a unit of reading matter in basal reading in which there are no new and strange words and which the pupil can read with complete absorption in the meaning.

unit, activity: a large learning situation in which pupils are sufficiently interested to participate willingly and actively, usually in an informal group; intended to promote the social and educational development of the pupils and to motivate the incidental study of many different subjects necessary to the successful completion of the unit; for example, an activity unit on transportation in the third grade might be based on the activity of building models of trains, boats, wagons, etc., but arithmetic, measurement, vocabulary, history, and general science might be studied by the pupils in the course of the project. *Syn.* **broad unit; experience unit** (2).

unit, administrative: *see* **administrative unit.**

unit, appreciation: (arith.) a teaching or study unit on nondrill material intended to broaden the pupil's outlook, satisfy curiosity, give present enjoyment, and further the development of permanent interest in arithmetic.

unit, arithmetic: *see* **arithmetic unit.**

unit arrangement: (home ec.) an arrangement or plan by which laundry, sewing, or foods laboratory equipment is so placed that each grouping is a complete unit. (The equipment may or may not duplicate the home-kitchen type; but each unit is complete, and within it one or more students may carry out all the necessary activities.)

unit, art: an art experience or series of experiences having unity through being organized around some theme, activity, or concept.

unit assignment: *see* **assignment, unit.**

unit, attendance: *see* **attendance unit.**

unit blocks: *see* **blocks, unit.**

unit card: *see* **card, unit.**

unit, card punching: *see* **card punching unit.**

unit, card reading: *see* **card reading unit.**

unit, Carnegie: a standard of measurement for describing the secondary school subject-matter pattern that constitutes the entrance requirements of a college, defined originally by the Carnegie Foundation for the Advancement of Teaching; assuming 16 units of work in a 4-year secondary school pattern, the Carnegie unit represents a year's study in any subject (not less than 120 sixty-minute hours or their equivalent); thus secondary schools organized on any other than a 4-year basis can estimate their work in terms of the unit.

unit, central processing: the computer mechanism that can perform both calculations and such logical operations as comparing.

unit character: *see* **character, unit.**

unit, classroom: *see* **classroom unit.**

unit, competitive: an organization or group represented by a team in a program of competitive athletics.

unit construction: *see* **construction, unit.**

unit, control: *see* **control unit.**

unit-control system: (1) that system in which each state educational institution has its own board of education or board of regents; (2) the system by which vocational education is organized as a definite department of the regular school system and administered by the same personnel as the academic schools but is taught by a separate staff of qualified vocational teachers; the usual system in the United States; *contr. w.* **dual-control system.**

unit cost: a term used in cost accounting to denote the cost of producing a unit of product or rendering a unit of service.

unit cost of transportation: an average sum expended for a defined service, for example, *cost per bus per mile, cost per pupil per year,* etc.

unit cost, school-subject: the average amount of money per student that has been expended for one unit in a designated subject, for example, the cost of giving instruction for one school year to one student in English or the cost per clock-hour of instruction in geometry.

unit cost, student-hour: the average amount of money expended for some designated service per student per hour unit of credit earned; obtained by dividing the total expenditure by the total number of student credit hours.

unit covariance: *see* **covariance, unit.**

unit, display: *syn.* **console.**

unit, distributive education store: *see* **store unit, distributive education.**

unit, district: *syn.* **district, rural school.**

unit, experience: (1) (math.) a teaching or learning unit based on real-life situations familiar to the group and demanding applications of arithmetic; for example, a unit based on buying an automobile, or purchasing food for the family, in which judgment is a chief consideration; (2) *syn.* **unit, activity.**

unit, expression: any of a number of possible forms that attempts at expression may take; for example, sentence, paragraph, composition, essay, article, story, editorial, poem, novel, etc.

unit, functional: *syn.* **unit, activity; unit, experience** (2).

unit, functional problem: *syn.* **unit, experience** (1).

unit, generalization: *syn.* **unit, theme.**

unit, growth: a unit used for the measurement or description of maturation.

unit-headed school system: *see* **administrative organization, unit type of.**

unit heater and ventilator: *syn.* **ventilator, unit.**

unit, homemaking: *see* **homemaking unit.**

unit, input: *see* **input unit.**

unit, intermediate: (1) a division of the elementary school including grades 4, 5, and 6; (2) a building housing only the intermediate grades 4, 5, and 6.

unit, intermediate service: *syn.* **center, educational service.**

unit, junior: a unit division of a school or college including only the lower grade or grades enrolled in the school, for example, a unit made up of grades 7 to 9 in a 6-year secondary school or one made up of the lower 2 years of a college.

unit, kindergarten-primary: an organization, usually made up of the kindergarten and the first three grades, whose program is based on a unified course of study that articulates the school experiences of the kindergarten with those of the primary grades.

unit kitchen: (home ec.) space in an all-purpose homemaking room or a foods laboratory arranged and equipped as a family kitchen (except that the refrigerator and freezer serve several units) to facilitate teaching good work habits and management as well as food preparation. *See* **hollow-square arrangement.**

unit, laboratory: *see* **laboratory unit.**

unit, learning: *syn.* **unit** (1) and (2).

unit, library: *see* **library unit.**

unit, local school: a general term used to designate an attendance area, an administrative unit, or a fiscal unit for school purposes.

unit, mastery: a teaching unit so organized with subject matter and learning activities as to lead to the mastery of a definite major understanding. *Dist. f.* **mastery formula.**

unit, meaning: one of the parts of a word which gives a clue to its meaning, such as root, prefix, or suffix.

unit, memory: *see* **memory unit.**

unit, mental growth: a unit applied to the measurement of mental development in the attempt to substitute for mental age a measure that takes into account the fact that progressive reductions in amount of mental growth per year or other time unit occur as the individual develops from birth to maturity; used in computing percent of average development. *See* **age, mental; development, percent of average.**

unit, mobile: *see* **mobile unit.**

unit, mobile testing: *see* **testing unit, mobile.**

unit, motion: *see* **motion unit.**

unit normal curve: *see* **curve, unit normal.**

unit of competition: a division or basis from which to secure teams to compete in intramural athletics, such as a fraternity.

unit of cost: *see* **cost, unit of.**

unit of credit: *syn.* **unit** (3).

unit of instruction: *see* **unit, teaching.**

unit of measure: (1) a magnitude used as a unit, which is repeated or added to some point taken as the origin to form larger dimensions and subdivided (normally into equal parts) to form smaller dimensions; may be represented spatially on a scale of some measuring instrument (for example, a yardstick) or may be a statistically derived, perhaps normative, quantity (for example, a standard error unit or a standard score); in testing, the unit may vary in measured magnitude from time to time or from place to place on the same scale even though it is regarded as conceptually constant; *see* **scaling;** (2) by extension, a unit of enumeration or counting; for example, a test is generally scored by counting each correct item as one, the score so obtained being regarded as a *measure* of the examinee's standing on the characteristic (ability, aptitude, interest, etc.) measured by the test.

unit of measure, standard: (1) any officially designated and theoretically or actually uniform unit of measure; (2) the original, standard measure (where such exists) established and kept by the government, as the official yard, the official pound, etc., and used for checking the accuracy and uniformity of weights and measures in use; (3) *syn.* **score, standard.**

unit of need: (1) a standard of measurement in school administration representing a certain number of children in a school situation, as, for example, 35 children in average daily attendance; (2) a standard of measurement, sometimes expressed in dollars, of cost for educating some particular number of children.

unit of responsibility, ultimate: *see* **responsibility, ultimate unit of.**

unit of study: the unit of work that has been chosen for systematic directed study. *See* **unit.**

unit of work: *syn.* **unit** (3).

unit operation: a basic performance element of a job that occurs in the same form in many jobs; for example, straight turning, thread cutting, and taper turning are basic elements in many jobs of the machine trade.

unit organization: *see* **organization, unit.**

unit, output: *see* **output unit.**

unit, per capita: (1) a unit that represents one person; (2) a measure involving one individual, frequently used as a unit of cost.

unit, primary: (1) *syn.* **ungraded primary school,** (2) a building housing the primary grades.

unit, problem: a unit in which pupils study a particular problem which is either inherent in the subject matter as determined by adults or developed from the interests of the pupils.

unit, process: a unit of instruction based upon the processes of thinking, the patterns of thought involved in solving problems, in making judgments, in criticizing and evaluating propositions; examples are units of discovery, verification, decision making, criticism, etc. *Dist. f.* **unit, subject-matter.**

unit, production: *see* **production unit.**

unit progress plan: a type of organization in which curricular work is divided into large units of relatively long-term assignments as opposed to daily lessons; a plan intended to bring about greater individualization of instruction.

unit, pronunciation: the parts of a word which aid the reader to pronounce the word, generally the syllables in a multisyllabic word; these enable the reader to "sound out" the word.

unit, punch-card: *syn.* **record, unit** (2).

unit, pupil: a standard of measurement that represents the equivalent of one pupil constantly present in school. *See* **unit of need.**

unit, radio: an organization of extraclass radio activities within a school; includes directed and/or supervised listening, program evaluation, production, script writing, casting, direction, acting, and amateur technical experimentation and/or practice; sometimes functions as a club, the members exploring a variety of interests.

unit, reading: a number of selections on one topic which constitute a unified body of subject matter to be read.

unit record: *see* **record, unit.**

unit, reporting: in pupil accounting, the organizational unit submitting a report, namely, a state department of education, an intermediate administrative unit, a local basic administrative unit, or a school.

unit, resource: *see* **resource unit.**

unit, retail selling: *syn.* **store unit, distributive education.**

unit, sampling: *see* **sampling unit.**

unit, selector: *see* **selector unit.**

unit, senior: a unit division including only the upper grade or grades of the school, for example, a unit made up of the upper three grades of a 6-year high school or of the upper two grades of a 4-year college.

unit, sensation: *see* **decibel.**

unit shop: *see* **laboratory unit.**

unit skill: *see* **skill, unit.**

unit, slave: *see* **slave unit.**

unit, special class: a unit on which is based state support of local school district services for exceptional children, usually in terms of incidence of such children and a pupil-teacher ratio formula.

unit, standard: (1) a unit of measurement equal to the standard deviation (or a fraction of the standard deviation) and measured from the mean of the distribution, scores expressed in standard units being called *standard scores;* (2) a unit of measurement of definitely established magnitude such as a meter, gram, degree, or hour.

unit, state: a system in which educational functions are subject to one state authority.

unit, study: (1) the topic, subject, or unit of work that engages the student's effort and attention in study; (2) an integrated, comprehensive, and significant activity or experience in which the student is assimilating new knowledge or solving new problems; (3) an outline of a topic or of a division of a subject intended to guide the student in independent study.

unit, subject-matter: a selection of subject matter, materials, and educative experiences built around a central subject-matter area; to be studied by pupils for the purpose of achieving learning outcomes that can be derived from experiences with subject matter.

unit, survey: a unit, very broad in nature, that attempts to examine a whole area of human experience.

unit system: *syn.* **unit-control system.**

unit-system ventilation: *see* **ventilation, unit-system.**

unit, tape: *see* **tape unit.**

unit, teaching: (1) *see* **unit** (1) and (2); (2) the plan developed with respect to an individual classroom by an individual teacher to guide the instruction of a unit of work to be carried out by a particular class or group of learners; *dist. f.* **resource unit.**

unit test: *see* **test, unit.**

unit, theme: a unit of study based on a single central idea or topic.

unit, thought: a group of words that expresses a meaningful idea; commonly a phrase made up of two or more words that together carry a special meaning that they do not express singly.

unit, topical: *syn.* **unit, theme.**

unit, town: a school district, established and maintained as an attendance or administrative unit or both, that embraces the site on which a town is located and sometimes certain adjoining areas.

unit trade course: *see* **course, unit trade.**

unit trade school or class: a public school or class organized to fit persons for useful employment in a particular trade. (To meet Federal and state standards, the school or class must extend over a period of not less than 36 weeks per year, 30 hours per week, half the time to be allotted to productive work and the remaining time to be devoted to related general and social subjects. Learners must be 14 years of age or older.)

unit training: *see* **training, unit.**

unit training, advanced: *see* **training, advanced unit.**

unit training cycle: *see* **training cycle, unit.**

unit type of administrative organization: *see* **administrative organization, unit type of.**

unit ventilation system: *see* **ventilation, unit-system.**

unit ventilator: *see* **ventilator, unit.**

unit, vocational: a financial unit and program of study approved by the state department of education in accordance with the state's vocational plan. See **plan, state.**

unit, work: *see* **unit** (1) and (2).

unitarianism: a religious theory that emphasizes the unity of the Supreme Being (God), as contrasted with the trinitarian view of the deity as the Father, the Son, and the Holy Spirit.

unitary administrative system: *syn.* **administrative organization, unit type of.**

unitary weight: *see* **weight, unitary.**

United Nations Educational, Scientific, and Cultural Organization: *see* **UNESCO.**

United Service Organizations: *see* **USO.**

United States Air Force extension course: *see* **course, United States Air Force extension.**

United States Armed Forces Institute (USAFI): a correspondence and self-teaching organization established by the Department of Defense for servicemen on active duty anywhere in the world, covering elementary, secondary, and college subjects, including academic, technical, and vocational courses, with credits accepted by many schools and colleges toward graduation requirements; headquarters are in Madison, Wisconsin.

United States Commissioner of Education: the executive head of the U.S. Office of Education.

United States Continental Army Command: an arm of the U.S. Army which supervises Army branch and specialist schools. See **branch school; specialist school.**

United States Military Academy preparatory training program: *see* **program, United States Military Academy preparatory training.**

United States military service funded foreign training: *see* **training, United States military service funded foreign.**

United States Office of Education: a division of the Federal government, within the Department of Health, Education, and Welfare, established by Congress in 1867 for the purpose of advancing the cause of education throughout the nation; the Division of Vocational Education in the Office of Education is responsible for the administration of the vocational education acts, including the allocation of Federal funds to the states for vocational education.

uniterm: (libr. sci.) a single word used to describe the subject content of documents; usually coordinated with other terms used in information retrieval. See **descriptor; key word.**

units, interactive score: *see* **score units, interactive.**

units, ipsative score: *see* **score units, ipsative.**

units of supervision: *see* **control, span of.**

unity: (Thomism) that by which a thing exists undivided in itself and divided from others; this transcendental (existential) unity includes indivision and completeness, and is distinguished from *numerical unity*, which adds the

notion of extension or univocal order, and from *essential unity*, the self-consistency of any essence, which does not preclude existential multiplicity.

unity, organic: wholeness; the integration of all parts and elements into an inseparable oneness of interdependent parts, comparable to the way in which parts of a living organism are interdependent; in the arts, the structural unity which is comparable to the structural unity of a living thing.

univariate selection: *see* **selection, univariate.**

universal: *n.* (1) (philos.) a general term or characteristic of a thing such as "tableness" or triangularity as distinct from particulars such as "this table" or "the triangle which I just drew"; Platonic realists affirm the reality of universals; nominalists deny this and say universals are only names; *see* **nominalism;** (2) (sociol.) any of such ideas, habits, and conditioned emotional responses as are common to all sane, adult members of a particular culture.

universal decimal classification, (Brussels): *see* **classification, universal decimal (Brussels).**

universal education: any system of education that extends its opportunities to all youth regardless of race, color, creed, sex, or ability.

universal military service and training: *see* **training, universal military.**

universal military training: *see* **training, universal military.**

universal quantifier: *see* **quantifier.**

universal set: *see* **set, universal.**

universality, test: *see* **test universality.**

universe: (1) (stat.) the total or aggregate of all possible items of the class under consideration; the entire group of items or individuals or possible observations from which a sample is taken; may be finite or infinite; *syn.* **population; statistical universe;** (2) (math.) *syn.* **domain** (2); **set, universal.**

universe, finite: *syn.* **population, finite.**

universe, restricted: a universe which is limited to that part of the whole universe which logically would be expected to provide data congruent with the purpose of an investigator; for example, the restricted universe of male American athletes instead of the *whole universe* of the male population of the United States in a study of personality factors in male athletes. See **universe.**

universe, statistical: *syn.* **universe.**

universe, whole: *see* **universe.**

universitas magistrorum et scholarium (ū·ni·vēr′si·tas maj·is·trō′rəm et skō·lä′rē·ən): (Lat., lit., "a company of masters and scholars") a national group of students attending one of the larger medieval universities in Europe.

university: (1) an institution of higher education consisting of a liberal arts college, offering a program of graduate study, and having usually two or more professional schools or faculties and empowered to confer degrees in various fields of study (note that, in the United States, there is some confusion in the use of the terms university and college; some institutions of higher learning that are in reality colleges of liberal arts have been incorporated as *universities* and use the term in their names; some institutions incorporated as colleges are in reality universities containing graduate and professional schools in addition to colleges of arts and sciences); (2) an organization that includes the recognized secondary and higher educational institutions of a state and certain other institutions and agencies for education, for example, the University of the State of New York; (3) the institution of higher education that grew up in Europe in the late Middle Ages, from which all modern forms of higher education are descended; provided instruction in the seven liberal arts, medicine, law, and theology.

university branch: a unit of the university, located separately from the main physical plant but under the direction of the central university administration; a single university may have more than one branch; generally these do not encompass the university program as a whole but deal with a specific segment, such as the medical school, law school, 2-year college, etc.

university college: *see* **college, university.**

university community center: *see* **community center, university.**

university elementary school: *see* **elementary school, university.**

university, endowed: a university holding endowment funds or participating in income from funds held in trust for it.

university extension: *see* **extension, university.**

university extension bureau: *see* **extension bureau, university.**

university extension center: *syn.* **center, extension.**

university, free: instructional programs set up by dissident students and/or faculty members near some university centers as protests against alleged irrelevant educational programs in their respective institutions.

university high school: *see* **high school, university.**

university laboratory school: *see* **university school.**

university, land-grant: a university participating in the benefits of grants of land made in accordance with the first Morrill Act, approved July 2, 1862, and supplementary legislation; sometimes used to include all universities that have received grants of land from the Federal government.

university library: *see* **library, university.**

university mothers: a term applied to the universities of Bologna and Paris, which furnished the pattern for later medieval universities.

university, municipal: a university maintained by a municipality.

university, nondenominational: a university having no organic connection with a religious denomination or sect.

university, normal: (1) originally used as legal designation of the state teacher education institution established at Normal, Illinois, in 1857; (2) obs. *syn.* **teachers college;** (3) sometimes used in the latter part of the nineteenth century to indicate that the public or private teacher education institution so designated either was or was expected to become of collegiate rather than of secondary grade; *see* **normal school.**

university, open: the university or college viewed as an educational resource from which students of all ages may attain a degree by completing work at home, by correspondence, by TV, by attending classes, and then appearing for challenge examinations in areas of knowledge when they are ready; a type of university organization in the planning stage in the early 1970s for California state colleges.

university-operated station: *see* **station, college-operated.**

university, pontifical: a Roman Catholic institution of higher learning whose constitutions are formally approved by the Pope and whose specifically ecclesiastical faculties (namely, theology, canon law, and philosophy) are empowered to confer ecclesiastically recognized degrees, for example, the Catholic University of America.

university press: *see* **press, university.**

university, private: a university under control of a governing board independent of public governmental agencies except for charter and statutory limitations; more properly designated as a *privately controlled university.*

university professor: *see* **professor, distinguished.**

university relations: *see* **relations, university.**

university school: a school of elementary or secondary grade attached to a university for the purpose of providing facilities for the observation and demonstration of educational practices, for practice teaching by students preparing to teach, and for experimental work in education; sometimes called *university laboratory school* or *university training school. See* **elementary school, university; high school, university.**

university, state: a university controlled by a state; the term has been used within a state to designate the institution that centers its attention on undergraduate and graduate instruction in the liberal arts and in professional schools such as those of law, medicine, education, and commerce, which are based chiefly on the liberal arts program, in contrast to the land-grant college, which has emphasized agriculture, engineering, and professional curricula based chiefly on the sciences.

university, state normal: *see* **university, normal.**

university training school: *see* **university school.**

university, urban: a university located in and serving the needs of an urban community, but not necessarily a *municipal university.*

university week: a 1-week program of popular lectures, scientific demonstrations, health talks, concerts, plays, etc., produced under the auspices of a university as a part of its extension service. *See* **college, alumni.**

unlearned behavior: *see* **behavior, unlearned.**

unlearning: the learning of material or a skill that interferes with or is substituted for something that has already been learned.

unloading: (pup. trans.) the act of discharging pupils from a school bus.

unmoral: lacking any moral quality; not involving any moral distinctions; nonmoral; unable to distinguish right from wrong. *Syn.* **amoral;** *ant.* **moral.**

unofficial case: a case that has been brought before the attendance department or the juvenile court and that has been handled by an officer of the department or court but not in his official capacity as a representative of the department or court, no official record being kept of such a case.

unofficial hearing: the hearing of an unofficial case; used in disposing of minor offenses.

unorganized-facts policy: the policy of presenting all available data without organization or interpretation.

unpleasantness: (1) an affective experience associated with rejection; (2) an attitude of rejecting the stimulus object. *Contr. w.* **pleasantness.**

unrelated pupil: *see* **student, foreign.**

unreliability: (1) lack of consistency of observations of the same or similar events; inconsistency in the results of repeated applications of the same or comparable measuring devices to the same individuals; (2) divergence of a statistic from the corresponding true value; inconsistency of a given statistic from one sample to another. *Contr. w.* **reliability** (2).

unrotated matrix: *see* **matrix, unrotated.**

unrounding: in oral language practice, the act of changing a sound produced by rounding and protruding the lips to one that is produced without rounded or protruded lips.

unselected: (stat.) chosen at random; free from bias; not selected in such a manner as to tend to introduce constant errors.

unskilled occupation: work requiring little or no planned training.

unsociable: *syn.* **unsocial.**

unsocial: having a tendency to avoid interaction or participation with others. *Dist. f.* **antisocial; asocial.**

unstable child: *see* **child, unstable.**

unstable sequence: *see* **sequence, unstable.**

unstable type: the type of individual subject to emotional oscillations, easily elated or discouraged; a changeable, unsteady type.

unstructured: a term applied to tests, interviews, and similar devices, techniques, or situations which are used for measuring personality attributes, indicating that they are set up and handled so that the subject has almost unlimited freedom of choice in the responses he makes. *Ant.* **structured.**

unstructured inventory: *see* **inventory, structured.**

untrain: to develop skill in another direction or in another way.

unverbal awareness: *syn.* **awareness, nonverbal.**

unweighted: (stat.) (1) commonly applied (when equally weighted would be preferable) to any item having the same number of units allowed for its maximum (or mean) condition as any other item in the series; (2) commonly applied (when naturally weighted would be preferable) to a series of data to which no special coefficient greater than or less than unity has been attached. *See* **weight, equal; weight, natural.**

unweighted arithmetic average: *syn.* **mean, unweighted arithmetic.**

upgrade training: *see* **training, upgrade.**

upgrading: improvement on the job, in skills or knowledge or both, by means of systematic industrial arts courses or the study of related information.

upholstery: an industrial arts area, usually located in the general woods laboratory, concerned with the study of the style, design, tools, materials, and processes used in the construction and repair of upholstered furniture.

upkeep: (1) the keeping of buildings and equipment in good repair; (2) the condition of repair of buildings and equipment; (3) the cost of repair and/or maintenance.

upper elementary grade: *see* **elementary grade, upper.**

upper grades: the designation of grades 7 and 8 in the 8-year elementary school.

upperclassman: a member of the junior or senior class in an institution of college or high school level.

Upward Bound: a program designed to generate skills and motivation necessary for success in education beyond high school among young people from low-income backgrounds and to give them adequate secondary-school preparation; a cooperative program involving institutions of higher education and secondary schools; usually coordinated with activities of the Community Action Agencies and the Higher Education Act of 1965. *See* **program, college work-study; Program, Community Action.**

urban dropout: *see* **dropout, urban.**

urban places: as defined in the United States Census of 1970, all incorporated and unincorporated places of 2,500 population or more plus towns in New England, townships in New Jersey and Pennsylvania, and counties in other states which contain no incorporated municipalities and have a density of 1,500 or more persons per mile.

urban population: *see* **population, urban.**

urban redevelopment: *see* **urban renewal.**

urban renewal: the systematic rebuilding of decaying sections of population centers; the Federal, state, and municipal programs aimed at such rebuilding.

urban residents: *see* **population, urban.**

urban school: a school in a concentrated population area, as opposed to a rural or village school.

urban sociology: *see* **sociology, urban.**

urban teaching intern: *see* **intern, urban teaching.**

urban university: *see* **university, urban.**

urban youth: *see* **youth, urban.**

urbanized area: as defined for the United States Census of 1970, a city (or twin cities) of 50,000 or more population, that is, a *central city,* plus the urban fringe, the surrounding closely settled incorporated areas and unincorporated areas with a certain population density; contiguous urbanized areas with central cities in the same *standard metropolitan statistical area* are combined into one; established to distinguish the urban from the rural population in the vicinity of large cities and to exclude places which qualify as urban but are separated by rural areas from the urban fringe.

usable capacity: *see* **capacity, usable.**

USAFI: *see* **United States Armed Forces Institute.**

usage, language: common practices in the use of language especially ·as related to purposes to be served for the audience intended.

usage vocabulary: *see* **vocabulary, usage.**

use, multiple: *see* **multiple use.**

use of bus, extended: *syn.* **vehicle, nonroutine use of.**

use of language, evocative: *see* **language, evocative use of.**

use tax: *see* **tax, use.**

usher: the assistant to the master or head teacher in English and early American schools.

USO: United Service Organizations; a joint organization of character-building agencies and individual groups that established recreational centers during World War II in communities near Army and other service camps for the purpose of providing wholesome recreational and other facilities for service personnel on leave.

utilitarianism: (1) the doctrine that the criterion of right conduct is or should be grounded in the principle of utility, in that which will produce the greatest amount of pleasure or happiness; (2) the doctrine that regards adaptation to the goal of general happiness as the criterion of moral worth.

utility building: *see* **building, utility.**

utility program: *see* **program, utility.**

utility routine: *see* **routine, utility.**

utility, social: *see* **social utility.**

utilization during periods used: the ratio of the number of students occupying a given unit of the physical plant (such as a laboratory) when that unit is in use to the total number of student stations provided in that unit. (Thus, if 50 students occupy a laboratory having student stations for 100 students, the ratio would be 50:100, or 1:2, and the utilization 50 percent.)

utilization field: (mil. ed.) a grouping of Air Force officer specialties closely related on the basis of required skills and knowledge; a single specialty also may be a utilization field when it requires skills and knowledge of a highly specialized nature that are not directly related to those required by any other specialty. *See* **Air Force specialty.**

utilization, measures of: measures expressed in terms of the ratio (*a*) of the number of students using a room or a building to the number of student stations; (*b*) of the number of students using a room or building to the capacity as determined by dividing the number of square feet of floor area in the unit by the number of square feet considered necessary for each student. (Similar calculations for cubic feet are no longer used.) *See* **utilization, space; utilization of buildings; utilization of building space.**

utilization of building space: (1) the proportion of the area (termed space) in use for educational purposes as compared with the area of corridors, stairs, rotundas, etc., not considered as used; usually expressed as a percentage; (2) the proportion of time buildings are in use, or the ratio of actual room-hours of use to total possible room-hours of use. *See* **utilization, measures of; utilization, space; utilization of buildings.**

utilization of buildings: an expression in percent of the ratio of the number of students using all rooms of all buildings for all class periods of all days of a week to the total number of student stations in all rooms of all buildings for all class periods of all days of a week. (Other measures of utilization are capacity units expressed as square feet per student, such as 16 for classrooms and 25 for laboratories.) *See* **utilization, measures of; utilization, space; utilization, student-station; utilization of building space.**

utilization of classrooms: an expression in percent of the ratio of the number of students occupying classrooms of a building or buildings for all class periods of all days of a week to the total number of seats in classrooms (or capacity units expressed in terms of square feet or, formerly, of cubic feet in classrooms) for all class periods of all days of a week. *See* **capacity of classroom; utilization, percent of; utilization, student-station.**

utilization of dormitory: the ratio of the number of students housed in a dormitory to its student capacity, that is, to the number of students that the total number of rooms with beds are designed to accommodate.

utilization of library: a measure of the number of students using a library; may be expressed in terms of percentage of available seats occupied for all periods of all days of a week or in terms of the number of books and other materials used by students.

utilization, percent of: (1) an expression in percent of the ratio between the amount of time that a building or parts of a building are in use and the total time available for use; (2) an expression in percent of the ratio between the amount of time that student stations are in use and the total station-hours available for use.

utilization, period: the ratio of the number of instruction periods per week during which a room or all rooms of a building or school are used to the total number of instruction periods in the week; usually expressed in terms of percent of utilization.

utilization, program: *see* **utilization, radio and/or television.**

utilization, pupil-station: *see* **utilization, student-station.** (*Pupil* is substituted for *student* in speaking of the use of elementary school buildings.)

utilization, radio and/or television: (1) the act of using broadcasts as a part of the instructional program of a school; (2) the extent to which the radio and television are actually used in a school situation.

utilization, sight: *see* **sight utilization.**

utilization, space: the degree to which a room or building is used, or the actual amount of use compared with the total possible amount of use of such a unit.

utilization, student-station: the ratio of the number of student stations (seats and other places of work) used for all class periods to the total number provided for all class periods of all days of a week. *See* **utilization, measures of.**

utopia: (1) (cap.) a term coined by Sir Thomas More (1478-1535) as a play on words, having elements of the Greek "*eutopia*" (good place) and "*outopia*" (no place); used by More as the title of a book concerned with a mythical island kingdom where a perfect economic, social, and political system was enjoyed as a result of right education and wise government; (2) a generic term for ideal commonwealths or any situation where the conditions are ideal or perfect; frequently implies lack of practicality.

utterance: as used in language instruction, a group of speech sounds, no matter how small, which conveys meaning.

uvula (ū′vū·lə): the small fleshy mass hanging from the edge of the soft palate. *Dist. f.* **velum.**

V matrix: *see* **matrix, V.**

vacation Bible school: *syn.* **vacation church school.**

vacation church school: a school under church auspices, set up for a short period during the summer vacation, in which students pursue biblical and other religious subjects. *Syn.* **vacation Bible school.**

vacation school: *syn.* **summer school.**

vaccination affidavit: a statement certifying to the fact that a given youth has been vaccinated, giving the date and stating whether the vaccination was successful.

valence: (1) a term used by Lewin to signify the attracting (positive) or repelling (negative) value of an object or activity; (2) the relative combining or replacing capacity of an element or atom compared with that of an atom of hydrogen.

valid: measuring what it purports to measure; having a high correlation with a criterion. *Dist. f.* **reliable.**

valid excuse: a reason given for school absence that justifies that absence, such as personal illness, death in the immediate family, severe illness in the family, quarantine, necessary attendance in court, extreme poverty, observance of a religious holiday, or unusual weather conditions.

validation: the process of determining or of improving the degree of the validity of a measuring instrument.

validation, cross: *see* **cross validation.**

validation, discriminant: test validation requiring a low correlation between a test and other variables which logically have low relationship with the test; used, together with convergent validation, for testing the justification of novel trait measures, for validation of test interpretation, or for the establishment of construct validity, since tests can be invalidated by too high correlations with other tests from which they were intended to differ; demonstrates whether or not a test construct is completely or even largely redundant with other better established or more parsimonious constructs with which it should differ. *See* **validity, convergent.**

validation, empirical: *syn.* **validation, external.**

validation, external: determining the validity of a set of measures by comparing them with another set, the criterion, that has been independently obtained and is known (or believed) to approximate the true measure. *Syn.* **empirical validation.**

validation, internal: an attempt to determine or improve the validity of a test by studying the test items and the total makeup of the test.

validity: (1) the quality of being grounded on truth or fact; (2) in formal logic, the formal correctness of an inference which is drawn from a set of premises in a manner permitted by the laws of the logic, regardless of the truth or falsity of the premises; (3) in experimentalist logic, the strength and effectiveness of a proposition which, when used in a problematic situation, forwards inquiry by leading toward solution of the problems and a resolution of the entire situation; (4) (meas.) the extent to which a test or other measuring instrument fulfills the purpose for which it is used; usually investigated by an analysis of test content or by a study of relationships between test scores and criterion variables, independence of methods being a common denominator among the major types of validity excepting *content validity. Dist. f.* **reliability.**

validity coefficient: *syn.* **coefficient of validity.**

validity, coefficient of: *see* **coefficient of validity.**

validity, concurrent: (of a test) validity based upon correlation with a criterion variable that is measured at about the same time as the test is administered.

validity, construct: validity evaluated by investigating what qualities a test measures, that is, by determining the degree to which certain explanatory concepts or constructs account for performance on the test.

validity, content: validity demonstrated by showing how well the content of the test samples the class situations or subject matter about which conclusions are to be drawn; the test user wishes to determine how an individual performs at present in a universe of situations that the test situation is claimed to represent.

validity, convergent: (1) a type of test validity which requires a high correlation between a test and other variables which logically are related to the test; (2) confirmation by independent measurement procedures; *comp. w.* **reliability.**

validity, criterion-related: validity demonstrated by comparing the test scores with one or more external variables considered to provide a direct measure of the characteristic or behavior in question; may take the form of an expectancy table or, most commonly, a correlation relating the test score to a criterion measure; the test user wishes to forecast an individual's future standing or to estimate an individual's present standing on some variable of particular significance that is different from the test.

validity, curricular: evidence of test validity shown by agreement between test content and curricular content and test objectives and curricular objectives. *See* **validity, content.**

validity, differential: of a classification test, validity which depends on the difference between its correlation with each of the separate criteria to be predicted; in a two-criterion classification problem, for example, the ideal test would have a high correlation with one criterion and a zero correlation (or preferably a negative correlation) with the other criterion.

validity, empirical: (1) quality of a test of having definite and proved value for a given purpose; usually stated in terms of a correlation coefficient; *see* **validity** (4); (2) extent to which scores on a test agree with some outside criterion or some future measures of success.

validity evidence: information gathered to determine exactly what kind of inferences can be made from test scores.

validity extension: process by which test validity is checked against a new criterion as well as with a different population.

validity, face: a term which indicates a validity referring not to what a test actually measures but to what it appears, on the basis of a subjective evaluation, to measure; of all the concepts of validity, the least justifiable; valuable in the original writing of test items.

validity, factorial: the most sophisticated form of *content validity;* makes use of *factor analysis* to determine to what extent a given test measures certain content areas; factor analysis partitions the true score variance into subcomponents represented by a matrix of factor loadings which indicates the extent to which each factor is a subcomponent.

validity generalization: a process in which additional information is obtained by checking the effectiveness of the test on a differently defined population but using the same criterion as in the original study.

validity, incremental: (1) validity of a test stated in terms of some increment in productive efficiency over the information otherwise easily and cheaply available; *see* **base rate;** (2) the amount the test will add to or increase the validity of predictions made on the basis of data usually available.

validity index: *see* **index, differentiation.**

validity, intrinsic: (testing) a type of evidence of validity, based upon the fact that the items in a test are selected so as to simulate the criterion item that the test is used to predict.

validity, item: the discriminative value of an item; strictly, the correlation between an item and some criterion of performance. *See* **discrimination** (2).

validity, logical: an estimate of the *content validity* based on a comparison of the behavior demanded by the test with the behavior that, by a prior analysis, belongs to the variable to be measured.

validity, operational: the ability of a test or other measuring instrument to do some task, defined in terms of the operations that it actually performs; for example, a yardstick is operationally valid for linear measurement.

validity, practical: validity of a test as determined by its ability to predict within a certain sphere of behavior. *Syn.* **validity.**

validity, predictive: (of a test) validity based upon correlation with a criterion variable that is not available until some time after testing (as, for example, school grades).

validity, statistical: evidence of test validity expressed numerically, usually as a coefficient of correlation between scores on the test and another set of measures such as scores on another test, teachers' marks, or ratings by experts.

validity, synthetic: validity for which each predictor is validated, not against a composite criterion but against job elements identified through job analysis; the validity of any test for a given job is then computed synthetically from the weights of these elements in the job and in the test.

valuation: (1) the value or worth set upon an object; (2) the estimated worth of a property or other asset for a specific purpose, such as taxation.

valuation, assessed: *syn.* **value, assessment.**

valuation, building: estimation of the worth of a building or buildings in accordance with predetermined criteria, such as original cost, original cost less depreciation, or replacement value.

valuation, plant: (1) the value of a building (or group of buildings) as determined by its age and type, location, type of architecture, supplies, amount of time it is in use, equipment, and appurtenances thereto; implies educational adequacy or fitness for a given type of school; (2) *syn.* **value, assessment.**

valuation, state equalized: valuation of real property where state control is exercised to ensure that the rate of assessment is consistent throughout the state.

valuation, true: the price at which a given piece of property could be sold at the present time under actual sale conditions. (Not a precise term. In common usage it means real value as distinguished from a value shown by books or records.)

value: any characteristic deemed important because of psychological, social, moral, or aesthetic considerations; commonly used in the plural, as in counseling, to refer to built-in inner systems of beliefs from which one can gain security or support.

value, absolute: (math.) the distance of a number from the origin on a number line or, in the case of complex numbers, in the complex plane; thus the absolute value is never negative; it is zero for the number zero and positive for all nonzero numbers.

value, algebraic: a term usually employed in contexts in which it is important to know whether a number is positive or negative; in such contexts the term is used to distinguish a number from its absolute value. *See* **value, absolute.**

value, ambiguity: the various explicitly stated meanings of multisense concepts of worth or of vague value propositions.

value, approximate: a value that differs very little from the exact or accepted value.

value, arithmetic: *syn.* **value, absolute.**

value, assessment: the value placed on a building or other piece of real property for purposes of taxation.

value, assigned: a value given to or designated for a symbol or expression.

value, consummatory: value that serves to satisfy wants, needs, or demands, resulting in a feeling of satisfaction or fulfillment; value held not as a means but as an end, and hence distinguished from instrumental value. *See* **value, instrumental** (1).

value, cost: the value of a building or physical plant in terms of its original cost in dollars expended for its construction.

value, cultural: (1) value being a function of interest, the value of the arts is cultural if one's interest is primarily in refining his taste and developing his powers; if one's interest in carpentry, ceramics, etc., is technical, their value to him is, to that extent, technical-utilitarian; *see* **liberal education;** (2) a value as a norm or standard of desirability within a culture and interiorized within the individual through interaction with and critical study of his environment.

value-evaluating process: the method by which the individual determines the worthwhileness of his experiences in terms of his conceptual standards of behavior.

value, expected: (1) (of a statistic) the mean of the sampling distribution of a statistic; (2) (of a measure drawn at random from a universe) the mean value of the measures in the universe. *Syn.* **mathematical expectation.**

value, extrinsic: (1) a value considered as a means; (2) an entity's value as a means; (3) the value of an entity judged by the value of the consequences it produces.

value, face: (1) *syn.* **midpoint;** (2) the apparent value; value that is obvious.

value, fixed: a value that does not change during a particular discussion or operation. *Syn.* **constant.**

value, instrumental: (1) a value that has its ground in the consequences it produces; (2) (transfer of training) a method of work, mode of attack, etc., which, when possessed by an individual, can be used by that individual on numerous occasions and in varied situations, provided only that the individual can see its utility as applied to any given occasion or situation.

value, insurable: the present replacement value of property, minus noninsurable items and depreciation.

value, interest theory of: the theory of the nature of value contributed by Ralph Barton Perry asserting that any object whatsoever acquires value when any interest whatsoever is taken in it.

value, intrinsic: (1) a value considered as an end; (2) the value of an entity considered in itself; (3) a form of excellence judged worthy on its own account.

value judgment: (philos.) (1) a decision about the conditions and the results of experienced objects; (2) a decision concerning those factors which should regulate the formation of desires, affections, and enjoyments; usually distinguished from a judgment of fact or a judgment of practice. *See* **judgment, practical.**

value, mediate: *see* **value, instrumental.**

value, midrange: a crude measure of central tendency, obtained by taking the mean of the highest and lowest values of a series of observations. *Syn.* **mean of extremes.**

value-neutral: (fact or principle) *see* **descriptive.**

value, numerical: (1) a vague term usually with the meaning *absolute value;* (2) occasionally, a number associated with some quantity or object.

value of buildings per student: a measure, sometimes used for comparison among universities, colleges, or public school systems, obtained by dividing the total valuation of buildings by some measure of student population, such as total enrollment, number belonging as of a certain date, or average daily attendance. (Value of plant per student is a similar measure, but the dividend used is the value of the whole plant, including campus and equipment.)

value of equipment: the worth, in terms of money value, of articles or materials classified as equipment, variously figured as follows: (*a*) original cost, without increases for cost of repair and replacement but with deduction of losses; (*b*) original cost less depreciation of a determined percentage, such as 10 percent a year, plus cost of replacement; (*c*) appraisal, after inventory, of the worth of existing equipment.

value of physical plant: an amount representing the worth of buildings, equipment, and grounds determined by some measure of worth, such as original cost, original cost less depreciation, replacement cost, or assessed worth.

value, order-of-merit: the position of objects, persons, or attributes in a list arranged in serial order in accordance with the reader's judgment of the degree to which a defined quality is present; the value may be expressed in terms of rank, although Hull and others have proposed devices (assuming a normal distribution of stimuli rating) for translating the assigned ranks into scale values on the base line of the normal distribution area.

value, persuasive: (school admin.) influence of decisions of one jurisdiction in another jurisdiction.

value, place: the value associated with a digit by virtue of its position with respect to the units' place; for example, in the number 24.3, 2 denotes 20 units, 4 denotes 4 units, and 3 denotes 3/10 of a unit; or, in other words, 2 is in the tens' place, 4 is in the units' place, and 3 is in the tenths' place.

value, predictive: loose *syn.* **validity** (4).

value, probability: a number assigned to a sample point; for example, in a toss of a fair die the number assigned to the occurrence of throwing a five is 1/6.

value, proportions of: *see* **proportions of value.**

value, replacement: value expressed in terms of the amount of money required to reconstruct an identical building or buildings at a given time.

value, scale: *see* **scale value.**

value system: an inclusive set of deep-lying attitudes and beliefs that tend to direct the person's habitual responses in various situations.

value theory: (1) the theory of value, that is, *axiology;* (2) the doctrine that the realm of values has ontological or logical status superior to or prior to any other realm of philosophic investigation.

value, true: (stat.) (1) loosely, the correct value as contrasted with approximate value; (2) more strictly, the hypothetically exact value of a parameter of some universe.

values, art: *see* **art values.**

values, corresponding: values that are associated with each other through some indicated or expressed law of relationship.

values, culture: *see* **culture values.**

values, hierarchy of: a ranking of values or objectives in education according to some principle of order in which the objectives are so arranged that those below lead to and form a part of those above and all taken together present the aims of the philosophy of education under consideration.

values, moral: *see* **values, moral and spiritual.**

values, moral and spiritual: those principles and standards which, if accepted by the individual and applied in human behavior, exalt life and bring it into accord with approved levels of conduct; these principles, from the point of view of the naturalist, approach universality in their conception and acceptance by all mankind; to supernaturalists and idealists, they exist a priori to human experience.

values, social: aspects of human interactions that are regarded as being worthy, important, or significant for the proper functioning of group life; aspects that the members of society seek to conserve or promote.

values, spiritual: *see* **values, moral and spiritual.**

values, theory of: *see* **ethics; philosophy, moral.**

valve instruments: *see* **instruments, valve.**

vandalism: destruction of property through carelessness or displaced aggression.

vanishing: in programmed instruction, a term originally designating the removal of more and more of the components of a specific chain of responses; for example, a student might be asked in the first frame to fill in a few obvious letters in a poem, then more letters, then words, phrases, and whole lines; when all the components had been caused to vanish, the student would be reciting the whole poem; often synonymous with *fading,* although the process of withdrawing *prompts* is not strictly parallel to vanishing.

variability: (1) (biol. and psych.) the characteristic of being subject to change; the tendency or ability to change (in value, form, quality, etc.) with time or some other factor; (2) the spread or dispersion of scores, usually indicated by quartile deviations, standard deviations, range of 90 to 10 percentile scores, etc.; *see* **deviation.**

variability, absolute: (1) the extent of the deviations (expressed in terms of the original units of the distribution) of a series of observations or measurements from some measure of central tendency; (2) a measure of the scatter, or spread, of a series of test scores, defined either as a range between comparable points in the distribution or as a deviation from some measure of central tendency of the scores. *Contr. w.* **variability, relative.**

variability, coefficient of: *syn.* **coefficient of variation.**

variability, continuous: the characteristic of being subject to modification or change by increments that may be considered as subdivisible into an infinite number of parts, for example, change in size, volume, time, etc. *Contr. w.* **variability, discontinuous.**

variability, discontinuous: (1) the characteristic of being subject to modification or change by discrete amounts or indivisible units (for example, sex, marital status, number of children per family, etc.); *syn.* **discrete variability;** (2) (biol.) the characteristic of being subject to change by the production of discrete types with no intermediate forms. *Contr. w.* **variability, continuous.**

variability, discrete: *syn.* **variability, discontinuous** (1).

variability, index of: *syn.* **deviation, standard.**

variability, individual: variability that may be ascribed to any individual being measured rather than to the error of the measuring device.

variability, mean: *syn.* **deviation, average.**

variability, relative: (1) the variability of a series of observations relative to the magnitude of the observation; (2) a measure of dispersion expressed as a proportion (or percentage) of a measure of central tendency; *syn.* **relative dispersion.** *Contr. w.* **variability, absolute.**

variable: *adj.* exhibiting differences in magnitude; assuming a large number (often an infinite number) of values in different individual cases; occurring in various magnitudes in different cases. *Contr. w.* **constant** *adj.*

variable: *n.* (1) (stat.) any trait that changes from one case or condition to another; more strictly, the representation of the trait, usually in quantitative form, such as a measurement or an enumeration; (2) (math.) a symbol in a mathematical sentence which can be replaced by any member of some set called the *domain* of the variable; for example, the unknown in an algebra problem is represented by a variable, as is the symbol t in the function given by $f(t) = \sin t$; (3) in automatic data processing, a quantity which can assume any of the numbers of some set of numbers; (4) (curric.) *syn.* **elective.**

variable area track: any sound track recorded in the form of a modified photo-oscillographic trace more or less sharply divided longitudinally into two components, one essentially transparent. *See* **optical sound track.**

variable, causal: any variable that produces a change in another variable; an independent variable.

variable, complex: (1) (math.) a variable of the form $z = x + iy$ where $i = \sqrt{-1}$ and x and y take on real values; (2) (stat.) a concept or trait that is regarded as consisting of two or more simpler variables that are at least in part independent with respect to each other and that, to the extent that they can be identified and measured, can be used to represent it; for example, the trait represented by an index number, such as cost of living or retail prices, is a complex variable, measured or indexed through a weighted combination of constituent classes; common *syn.* **composite** (1).

variable, concomitant: any variable that varies concurrently with any other variable or composite, even though it is not necessarily causally related. *See* **correlation** (1).

variable, continuous: a variable capable, actually or theoretically, of assuming any value, as opposed to *discrete variable*, which may take only whole-number values; test scores are treated as being continuous, although they are less obvious examples than time, distance, weight, etc.

variable, controlled: a factor that is held constant (or as nearly constant as possible) or one for whose effect an allowance is made in statistical analysis, so that the effect of some other factor or factors may be isolated, measured, and evaluated. *Contr. w.* **variable, uncontrolled.**

variable, criterion: (1) the measured value of a factor that is under experimental investigation; (2) the dependent variable involved in a regression problem; *see* **variable, dependent.**

variable density: *see* **density, variable.**

variable density track: any sound track in which a recorded sound is represented as full-track-width density variations extending along the length of the track; in such a track the density range from a local maximal density to an adjacent minimal density is related to amplitude, while the spacing between adjacent local maximal (or minimal) densities is related to frequency. *See* **optical sound track.**

variable, dependent: (1) a variable whose magnitude depends on, or is a function of, the value of another variable (or other variables); a variable whose value is being estimated (for example, by regression techniques) from that of one or more independent variables to which it is related; when represented graphically, the y or vertical axis is conventionally used for the dependent variable; *syn.* **resultant variable;** *contr. w.* **variable, indepen-**

dent; (2) (math.) the variable which represents the quantity to be predicted in a particular problem from the formula used, all other variables being *independent*; sometimes used with reference to equations, sometimes with reference to functions.

variable, discontinuous: *syn.* **variable, discrete.**

variable, discrete: a variable in which the various possible magnitudes differ by clearly defined steps, often by unity, with no intermediate values being possible. *Syn.* **discontinuous variable;** *contr. w.* **variable, continuous.**

variable, distributive: a variable conceived as a continuum or series of classes along (or among) which cases are distributed; a quantitative or qualitative variable subdivided into various categories (classes) for the purpose of classifying observed data.

variable error: *see* **error, variable.**

variable, historical: a variable for which time is the basis of classification or the value of which changes with time.

variable, independent: (1) a variable to which values may be assigned at will; (2) the variable on which an estimation or prediction is based in a regression problem; (3) in the plural, often used to refer to variables that are uncorrelated; when represented graphically, the x or horizontal axis is conventionally used for the independent variable; (4) (math.) *see* **variable, dependent** (2).

variable, intervening: (1) a symbolic expression dealing with a set of experimental operations and serving as a methodological tool in the more advanced stages of theory construction; the simpler the symbolic shorthand, the more quantitative the expression, and the more specified the experimental operations, the greater the utility of the intervening variable; (2) (E/C, or Experimental/Control type) a symbolic expression more closely tied to a specified set of experimental operations than is a *hypothetical construct*, yet more flexible than the orthodox type of intervening variable; functions through the method of successive approximations as a means of clarifying semantic usage in the early stages of theory construction; *see* **construct, hypothetical;** (3) in guidance, a variable which has a functioning connection to a variable which has preceded or which follows.

variable matching: *see* **matching, variable.**

variable, moderator: a variable which correlates with the degree of predictability; any variable which has an effect upon the weighting of the original predictors of the criterion.

variable, predictive: the one of two related variables on which a known score is predictive of the position of the related score on the second variable; the independent variable in prediction. *See* **measure, predictive.**

variable, predictor: that observation or set of observations from which an estimate of the value of another variable can be made by the use of regression equations.

variable, resultant: *syn.* **variable, dependent.**

variable similarity, salient: *see* **similarity, salient variable.**

variable spacing: *see* **spacing, variable.**

variable, suppressor: a variable which, although not itself predictive of a criterion, can be used to increase the predictability of a second variable (usually through addition to or subtraction from that second variable).

variable, symmetrical: one of two or more variables that enter into a formula on the same basis; for example, in the formula for $r_{12\cdot3}$, variables x_1 and x_2 may be interchanged without affecting the result and hence are symmetrical variables.

variable, uncontrolled: any variable that may conceivably affect the results of an experiment but that is not taken into account in designing or in evaluating the results of an experiment. *Contr. w.* **variable, controlled.**

variable, unique: (1) a variable that enters into a formula on a different basis from the other variables; thus, in the formula for $r_{12\cdot3}$, x_1 and x_2 may be interchanged without affecting the value of the formula, but x_3 may not be interchanged with either x_1 or x_2 and hence x_3 is a unique variable; *contr. w.* **variable, symmetrical;** (2) sometimes used as a synonym for *unique trait.*

variable word length: *see* **word length, variable.**

variance (σ^2): a measure of variability equal to the square of the standard deviation; the second moment about the mean; the arithmetic mean of the squares of the deviations from the mean. *Syn.* **mean square error;** *see* **mean square deviation.**

variance, analysis of: an arithmetic procedure for treating the data for the criterion variable; it results in a partition of the total sum of squared deviations (of all observations) from the mean into sums of squares attributable to the various experimental effects, to the interaction among them, and to sampling error; thus it facilitates tests of the significance of these experimental and interaction effects. *See* **ratio, F.**

variance, between-group: in analysis of variance, the estimate of variance that is based on differences between (or among) the means of the several groups involved; commonly the numerator of the F ratio.

variance, common factor: *syn.* **communality.**

variance, error: (1) the variance of a sampling distribution; (2) in analysis of variance, the mean square that reflects only random effects and which is, therefore, used as the error term in tests of significance; *see* **variance, analysis of;** (3) in a set of test scores, the mean of the squared errors of measurement for each score in the set; the reliability of a set of test scores is sometimes defined as the proportion of the total score variance which is not error variance.

variance, interaction: (in analysis of variance) that part of the total variance which is attributable to the joint effect of two or more components or dimensions, rather than to any single component; for example, in a study involving several methods of study at each of several schools, the total variance may be divided into variances attributable to methods, schools, interaction (methods $\times$ schools), and within-class variances; first-order interaction involves interaction between two components, second-order interaction involves interaction among three components, etc. *Syn.* **interaction.**

variance, residual: a variance based solely on random or uncontrolled sources; a measure of the variance that remains after the elimination of difference attributable to experimental or controlled variables.

variance, specific: that portion of the reliable variance which does not correlate with any other variable, that is, which is attributable to abilities that are unique for the test in a given battery.

variance, true: individual differences in test scores that are attributable to true differences in characteristics under consideration.

variance, within-group: in analysis of variance, the estimate of variance that is based on variations within each of the several groups involved; almost invariably the denominator of the F ratio.

variant: a quantity that is not constant but is subject to change. *Contr. w.* **invariant.**

variant meanings: *see* **meanings, variant.**

variant, word: *see* **word variant.**

variate: (1) *syn.* **variable** *n.*; (2) the magnitude of a particular observation; a particular value of a variable; the value of a single observation or measurement of a variable; (3) an observation (or individual) that deviates from a norm.

variate frequency: *syn.* **class size (2).**

variate frequency table: *syn.* **table, frequency.**

variates, continuous: a set of observations in which the various possible values of the variable may differ by infinitesimal amounts.

variates, discrete: a set of observations in which the various possible values of the variable may differ by no less than a fixed amount, often unity.

variation: (1) (stat.) *syn.* **dispersion;** (2) (stat.) *syn.* **variability, absolute;** (3) (biol.) the appearance of significant differences between and among the members of the same species; *see* **mutation;** (4) (math.) a pattern of change in one or more quantities.

variation, average: *syn.* **deviation, average.**

variation, coefficient of: *see* **coefficient of variation.**

variation, combined: (math.) a pattern of change in one quantity resulting from the combined effect of changes in two or more other quantities.

variation, concomitant: *syn.* **correlation (1).**

variation, continuous: change from one value to another by infinitely small gradations. *Contr. w.* **variation, discrete.**

variation, discontinuous: *syn.* **variation, discrete.**

variation, discrete: change from one value to another by distinct increments or steps with no intermediate values. *Contr. w.* **variation, continuous.**

variation, historical: variation in magnitude or frequency with changes in time. *Contr. w.* **variation, synchronous.**

variation, mean: *syn.* **deviation, average.**

variation, synchronous: variation between or among items at the same moment; variation that is independent of time. *Contr. w.* **variation, historical.**

variations, method of concomitant: *see* **method of concomitant variations.**

varsity: an athletic team that represents a college or university in intercollegiate athletics; a first team.

varsity, junior: the first team among younger players, usually seventh to ninth graders in a high school or the freshmen in college, participating in an interschool or intercollege competitive sports program.

vector: (1) a line segment having both length and direction; useful in representing physical situations such as wind velocity; (2) an ordered pair, ordered triple, etc., of elements chosen from some field; useful in studying the general properties of vectors and vector spaces, that is, the algebra of vectors.

vector diagram: *see* **diagram, vector.**

vector geometry: *see* **geometry, vector.**

vector, primary: the line of intersections of all hyperplanes except that which is of immediate concern.

vector, projection of test: *see* **test vector, projection of.**

vector, reference: the normal to a hyperplane; hence, the normal to an $r - 1$ dimensional subspace in the common factor space. *Dist. f.* **vector, primary.**

vector, test: a vector used to represent a test or other variable, drawn from an origin to a point in r-dimensional space, the location of the point being determined by the loadings of the test on the common factors.

Veda (vā′də; vē′də): the name given by the Brahmans to the whole body of the most ancient sacred literature of the Hindus, the four holy books, Rig-Veda, Yajur-Veda, Sama-Veda, and Atharva-Veda, which are collections of hymns.

vegetarianism: the practice of living entirely on vegetables and fruits; a belief that killing animals is either undesirable or wrong is sometimes a corollary.

vegetative: referring to vital functions such as digestion, respiration, metabolism, etc.

vehicle, capacity of: *syn.* **capacity, bus; capacity, motor.**

vehicle code, uniform: the recommendations of the National Committee on Uniform Traffic Laws and Ordinances have served as guides to the states in the development and adoption of uniform practices in the operation of vehicles.

vehicle, metropolitan-type: a nonconventional type of bus with the motor under the driver, beside the driver, or toward the rear of the bus; distinguished by the location of the service door behind the front wheels of the vehicle. *Contr. w.* **bus, conventional-type;** *dist. f.* **vehicle, transit-type.**

vehicle, nonroutine use of: any use or trip made by a school bus for a purpose other than transporting pupils over a regularly scheduled route. *Syn.* **field trip;** *see* **instructional trip.**

vehicle of change: *see* **change, vehicle of.**

vehicle overcrowding: *syn.* **overcrowding.**

vehicle, public service: any vehicle that is used to serve or transport the general public, usually for a fare, for example, buses, trains, airplanes, etc.

vehicle, transit-type: a nonconventional type of bus having the motor under the driver, beside the driver, or toward the rear of the bus; distinguished by the location of the service door ahead of the front wheels of the vehicle. *Contr. w.* **bus, conventional-type;** *dist. f.* **vehicle, metropolitan-type.**

vehicle, transportation service: a service truck, gasoline truck, car, or other such vehicle not used for carrying pupils and used to service school buses along the route.

velum (vē'ləm): *syn.* **soft palate.**

venireman (və·nī'rə·mən): a person who has received a writ summoning him for jury duty.

Venn diagram: *see* **diagram, Venn.**

ventilation: the process of supplying and removing air by natural or mechanical means to and from any space; such air may or may not be conditioned.

ventilation, central fan: a system for circulating air through a building by means of a fan usually located in the basement.

ventilation, exhaust: a system of removing air from a room by means of a fan that draws the air out of the room, creating a slightly reduced pressure, which tends to be equalized by incoming air. *Contr. w.* **ventilation, plenum.**

ventilation, gravity: any system of ventilation that operates by displacement of warmer, lighter air by cooler, heavier air, as distinguished from ventilating systems that move air by mechanical means.

ventilation, local-unit: *syn.* **ventilation, unit-system.**

ventilation, mechanical: any system of ventilation that uses a fan either to force air into or to draw air out of a space.

ventilation, open-window: *syn.* **ventilation, window.**

ventilation, plenum: the forcing of air into a room or building so that the result is slightly denser air than the surrounding air of equal temperature; the air is forced by means of a fan either through ducts from a central compartment or by means of a unit ventilator located within each room.

ventilation, split-system: a heating system in which a plenum system is supplemented by direct radiation. *See* **ventilation, plenum.**

ventilation, unit-system: a system for circulating and heating air, in which separate ventilators are used for each room, each operated independently. *Syn.* **local-unit ventilation:** *see* **ventilator, unit.**

ventilation, window: ventilation through open windows, sometimes screened, sometimes equipped with deflecting boards, but with no fans or other mechanical aids.

ventilation, window-gravity: *see* **ventilation, gravity; ventilation, window.**

ventilator: (photog.) a device for air cooling the projection lamp and adjacent parts of a projector or enlarger.

ventilator, unit: equipment by means of which air is drawn into each room separately, passed over heating coils, and distributed through the room. *Syn.* **unit heater and ventilator.**

venue: geographic area, usually a county, of a court's *jurisdiction.*

verbal apraxia: *see* **apraxia, verbal.**

verbal attitude: *see* **attitude.**

verbal context clue: *syn.* **clue, context.**

verbal contract: *see* **contract, verbal.**

verbal intelligence test: *see* **test, verbal intelligence.**

verbal learning: *see* **learning, verbal.**

verbal problem: *see* **problem, written.**

verbal realism: *see* **realism, humanistic.**

verbal-reasoning test: *see* **test, verbal-reasoning.**

verbal reinforcement: *see* **reinforcement, verbal.**

verbal test: *see* **test, verbal.**

verbalism: (1) undue reliance upon words; the assumption that relationships suggested by facile habitual associations among words prevail in reality; (2) uncritical acceptance of definitions as if they were explanations; (3) wordy expression lacking meaning.

verbalization: the overt statement of thoughts in words.

verbigeration (vĕr·bij'ər·ā'shən): *syn.* **catalogia.**

verification: established truth; meaning or hypothesis as verified in consequence of a designed program of testing in which fact as come upon serves to check validity of hypothesis and fact is sought through the pursuit of implications of hypothesis. *See* **problem-solving method.**

verification experiment: *see* **experiment, verification.**

verification of address: (1) the designation of an administrative form used to verify the address of a pupil or family; (2) the act of gathering corroborating data relative to the pupil's address.

verification of birth date: (1) the designation of an administrative form used to verify the birth date of a pupil; (2) the act of gathering corroborating data relative to the pupil's date of birth, accomplished by interviewing a person qualified to furnish this information.

verification of case-history records: the act of gathering corroborating data relative to the facts contained in a case-history record; may involve a verification of birth date, employment, income, spelling of names, number in family, or any other pertinent matters.

verification of census information: the act of gathering corroborating data relative to the census data on a given family in order to determine which of two or more records that are in disagreement is correct. *Syn.* **callback.**

verification of return to school: (1) the designation of an administrative form used to verify the report that a pupil has returned to school; (2) a systematic checking by an attendance officer in the field and at a school to determine if children who have been absent from school have returned, through the issuance at regular intervals of a group of reports that require verification.

verifier: a device on which a record can be compared or tested for identity character-by-character with a retranscription or copy as it is being prepared. *See* **key-verify.**

verifying machine: a machine employed to locate the punching errors in individual punch cards, for example, an IBM *verifier.*

vernacular instruction: instruction in the native or common language rather than in a classical or learned language.

vernacular school: a school that developed during the latter part of the Middle Ages to teach the children of the common folk the language (vernacular) of the people rather than Latin.

verse choir: *see* **choir, verse.**

verse-speaking choir: *see* **choir, verse.**

vertical advancement: *see* **advancement, vertical.**

vertical articulation: *see* **articulation, vertical.**

vertical bar chart: *see* **chart, vertical bar.**

vertical cooperation: *see* **cooperation, vertical.**

vertical enrichment: *see* **enrichment, vertical.**

vertical growth: *see* **growth, vertical.**

vertical handwriting: *see* **handwriting, vertical.**

vertical imbalance: *see* **imbalance, vertical.**

vertical organization: *see* **organization, vertical.**

vertical pupil classification: *see* **classification, vertical pupil.**

vertical slant: the slant of writing in which the downstrokes are perpendicular to the line of writing.

vertical social mobility: *see* **social mobility, vertical.**

vertical squint: *see* **squint, vertical.**

vertical supervision: *see* **supervision, vertical.**

vertigo: a sensation of whirling or dizziness from over-stimulation of the semicircular canal receptor; often associated with disease of the ear and deafness.

very high frequency: *see* **frequency, very high.**

vested interest: *see* **interest, vested.**

vested right: *see* **right, vested.**

vestibule: a room or chamber between the outer door and the inside of a building.

vestibule class: *syn.* **extension, kindergarten (1).**

vestibule course: *see* **course, vestibule.**

vestibule school: *syn.* **threshold school.**

vestibule theory: a term applied critically to narrow viewpoints in program planning which regard one school as preparation for the next school level, as in the case of the high school viewed as a "passageway" to college, with all content decided in terms of preparation for college.

vestibule training: *syn.* **training, entrance.**

vestigial: pertaining to rudimentary structure or to a trace or relic; for example, the appendix is thought to be a vestigial organ.

veteran student: *see* **student, veteran.**

veterans' education: programs of education that are exactly the same as for the general public, except that the enrolled veterans of World War II, the Korean War, and later are given financial assistance by the Federal government in accordance with applicable laws.

veterans' on-the-job training: the plan by which a state department of education authorizes the establishment of certain kinds of educational programs to be carried on under proper supervision on the actual job to be studied, usually with some financial compensation and for the benefit of honorably discharged veterans of the armed services; ordinarily such educating agencies must be fully inspected and properly authorized, and are assisted financially according to a carefully adopted plan, under provisions of Public Laws 16 and 346, commonly known as the *GI Bill of Rights,* and subsequent provisions for Korean veterans and later service.

VHF: *see* **frequency, very high.**

viable: capable of living; usually applied to a normal newborn organism or to a fetus able to continue living outside the mother's body.

vibration method: a highly individualized method of teaching speech to the deaf, devised by Kate and Sophia Alcorn, which tries, mainly by means of the tactile sense, to present a pattern of speech which is natural and fluent.

vibrato (vĕ-brä'tō): a periodic pitch fluctuation in the production of a tone in singing or playing an instrument, often also present in speech under emotional stress; believed by some psychologists to be a factor in artistic musical performance.

vibrator, bone-conduction: *see* **bone-conduction vibrator.**

vicarious experience: *see* **experience, vicarious.**

vicarious trial and error: *see* **response, covert.**

vice-principal: an administrative officer who assists the principal by executing delegated responsibilities, such as supervisory or attendance functions. *Syn.* **assistant principal.**

video: the visual components of a television system.

video frequency: *see* **frequency, video.**

videotape: *see* **tape, video.**

videotape recorder: *see* **recorder, videotape.**

videotape recording: *see* **recording, videotape.**

viewer: a table-mounted or hand-held device used by one person or a group of persons to see a filmstrip, slides, overhead transparencies, or a motion picture; also useful in previewing or editing such visual material.

viewfinder: (1) (electronic) a small picture tube built into a television camera and connected to the pickup circuits, thus enabling the cameraman to see exactly what is being scanned by the camera; (2) (optical) a reflex optical arrangement that picks up the image from the lens of a television camera to provide the cameraman with an indication of the field of view of the camera.

viewfinder, camera: a camera component arranged to indicate the boundaries of the camera's field of view; an external viewfinder may be as simple as an open wire loop used with a properly spaced pupil for viewing, or it may be an elaborate optical device with provision for altering the boundaries of its field to correspond with the field of any of several camera lenses; external viewfinders, to be accurate, must be corrected for the parallax; this possible error in framing is obviated by that type of integral viewfinder which can be moved into position for viewing the field through the camera lens. *See* **parallax.**

viewing monitor: *see* **monitor, viewing.**

viewpoint, formal: *see* **formal viewpoint.**

viewpoint, genetic: *see* **genetic viewpoint.**

villein (vil'ən): a member of the lowest class of unfree persons during the prevalence of the feudal system, a feudal serf; not to be confused with villain, which, though an alternative spelling of the same word, is restricted to mean an ignoble or base-born person, a boor, peasant, or clown.

virtue: (1) in general, excellence of character or of habitual behavior; (2) in Thomism, a relatively permanent disposition of either the reasoning power or the will, usually acquired through repeated and conscious self-determination, by reason of which faculties are inclined to morally good objects and actions, as, for example, the will is inclined by the virtue of justice to respect for another's rights; (3) the quality through which one adheres to those social ideas and standards involving moral conduct.

virtues, acquired: those developed habits of character associated particularly with the cardinal virtues—justice, temperance, etc.—and which have as their object man's well-being in this life. *See* **virtues, cardinal;** *contr. w.* **virtues, infused.**

virtues, cardinal: a group of four virtues—courage, wisdom, temperance, and justice—as defined by the ancient Greeks; added to these by the medieval Church were the three—faith, hope, and charity—resulting in the term *Seven Cardinal Virtues.* *See* **Seven Deadly Sins; virtues, moral.**

virtues, infused: those elements of character which Christians believe to be direct gifts from God and without which the individual could not progress far toward union with God; the prime example would be the *theological virtues. Contr. w.* **virtues, acquired.**

virtues, intellectual: the intellectual habits that perfect man in knowledge; in theoretical knowledge, they are understanding, the knowledge of first principles, science, the knowledge of proximate causes, wisdom, the knowledge of first causes; in practical knowledge, they are art, right knowledge about things to be made, and prudence, right knowledge about things to be done.

virtues, moral: the habits that perfect man in goodness and hence lead to natural happiness; justice is concerned with rectifying the will; temperance and courage (fortitude) with the moderation of the appetites. (In the context of morality, "habit" is here to be conceived not merely physiologically but as a product of reason.) *See* **virtues, cardinal.**

Virtues, Seven Cardinal: *see* **virtues, cardinal.**

virtues, theological: the attributes of Christian character which are expressed through faith, hope, and love; these are made explicit in the epistles of St. Paul and are developed more fully in the *Summa* of St. Thomas Aquinas. *Comp. w.* **virtues, cardinal.**

virtuoso: a person with exceptional mastery as a performer and interpreter of music through a particular medium, as the voice, the piano, or the violin.

visceral sense: in aerospace usage, a sense related to the internal organs of the body that sets up emotional or instinctive responses as differentiated from rational responses.

viscerogenic needs: *see* **needs, viscerogenic.**

viscerotonic: producing normal tone or tension of the organs located in the four great body cavities.

visible control: *see* **control, visible.**

visible vocabulary: *see* **vocabulary, visible.**

vision: *syn.* **sight.**

vision, achromatic: *see* **blindness, color.**

vision, alternating: the act of seeing with one eye and then with the other rather than seeing with both together. *See* **squint, alternating; suppression, alternating.**

vision appraisal: the procedure of making a general examination and appraisal of an individual's vision through observation and the application of a battery of tests; frequently used as a screening technique by medical examiners in college health services; may include tests for central visual acuity, near vision, far vision, muscular balance, near point of convergence, visual field, and color vision as well as observations on personal and family history and on the manifest condition of the eyes.

vision, binocular: the use of the two eyes simultaneously to focus on the same object and to fuse the two images into a single image which gives a correct interpretation of its solidity and position in space. *See* **field of vision, binocular.**

vision, borderline: vision on the line of demarcation between the normal and the defective or between any two groupings; 20/200 vision in the better eye after maximal correction is generally regarded as borderline vision for acceptance in a class of partially seeing children or in a braille class.

vision, central: mental interpretation of light stimuli falling on the macula.

vision, color: (1) the visual perception of radiant energy of specified wavelengths; (2) the perception of differences in hue, brilliance (value), and saturation (chroma).

vision conservation: *see* **sight conservation.**

vision, defective: vision impaired so that it measures below normal, that is, below 20/20 on the Snellen scale; vision impaired in any of its functions, as manifested by imperfect depth perception, faulty muscular action, or poor peripheral vision. *See* **handicap, visual.**

vision, distance: ability to perceive objects at a distance (usually considered to be 20 feet or more) at which light rays entering the eye are approximately parallel. *Syn.* **far vision.**

vision, double: *syn.* **diplopia.**

vision, facial: *syn.* **perception, object.**

vision, far: *syn.* **vision, distance.**

vision, field of: *see* **field of vision.**

vision, functional: the manner in which an individual makes use of his sight in gaining information.

vision, limited: *see* **partially seeing.**

vision, low: visual acuity substantially below normal. *See* **vision, normal.**

vision, monocular: seeing with one eye only.

vision, near: perception of objects at normal reading distance, or about 14 inches from the eyes.

vision, normal: refractive condition of the eye such that when at rest, the image of distant objects is brought to a focus on the retina (Snellen 20/20). *See* **chart, Snellen.**

vision, perimacular (per′i·mak′ū·lər): *syn.* **vision, peripheral** (2).

vision, peripheral: (1) visual sensation resulting from images falling on the outer portions of the retina (when the eyes are directed straight ahead, peripheral vision is perception on the extreme edges of the visual field); (2) mental interpretation of light stimuli falling on the retina outside the 10 degrees surrounding the macula; *syn.* **perimacular vision.**

vision, peripheral field of: *see* **field of vision, peripheral.**

vision, persistence of: *see* **persistence of vision.**

vision, residual: the usable vision remaining in the visually handicapped.

vision, stereoscopic (ster′ē·ə·skop′ik; stēr′ē-): the perception of the third dimension, that is, depth, through binocular vision or by means of a stereoscope.

vision test: *see* **test, vision.**

vision test chart: *see* **chart, vision test.**

vision, tunnel: an eye defect in which the visual field is contracted to such an extent that only central visual acuity remains, thus giving the affected individual the impression of looking through a tunnel.

visitation, class: the practice of going to observe teachers at work teaching their classes; may be carried on by other teachers for purposes of improving their teaching techniques or by supervisors, principals, and superintendents as a supervisory practice.

visitation, home: (1) a visit to the home of a pupil by any member of the school staff with the purpose of improving home and school cooperation or of discussing a problem related to the school; (2) (bus. ed.) the practice of making visits to the homes of prospective student learners to orient the parents and students to the responsibilities involved in participation in the cooperative programs in such fields as business and office education and distributive education.

visitation, interclass: *syn.* **intervisitation.**

visiting: observation of the work of a teacher or supervisor; may or may not be announced, and may be made either on the invitation of teachers or on the initiative of supervisors.

visiting days: (1) days set aside for parents and others to visit the school, such as occur during Education Week or on school exhibit days; (2) days when teachers or pupils may go to see the work in other schools.

visiting, home: *see* **home visiting.**

visiting, interschool: a program set up in some schools whereby a teacher may visit for a day a class in another school for the purpose of observing teaching methods.

visiting nurse: *see* **nurse, visiting.**

visiting professor: *see* **professor, visiting.**

visiting psychologist: *see* **psychologist, visiting.**

visiting-student counselor: *syn.* **adviser, foreign-student.**

visiting teacher: a school staff member who works with individual children and their families when a child has difficulty, such as maladjustment, failure to learn, or nonattendance; this service supplements the contribution of the teacher and other school personnel and is carried out in cooperation with them; as a liaison service, it helps to integrate school and community services for the benefit of the child.

visitor, home-and-school: *see* **home-and-school visitor.**

VISTA: an acronym for Volunteers in Service to America; one of the antipoverty programs established by the Office of Economic Opportunity Act of 1964; sponsored by local agencies, public and private, state and local, for developing programs in rural areas, urban communities, on Indian reservations, among migrant workers, in Job Corps centers, and in other agencies or in institutions applying for the services of human talent to help overcome the handicaps of poverty; volunteers, who may be men or women over 18 years of age, including the elderly and retired, organize and help run remedial and adult education classes, health and sanitation programs, recreation activities, and other programs to meet the needs of the community or area.

visual acuity: clearness or keenness of vision, measured by the ability of the eye to resolve detail; quantitatively expressed in terms of *Snellen chart* and other measurements.

visual acuity test: *see* **test, visual acuity.**

visual afterimage: *see* **afterimage, visual.**

visual aid: *see* **aid, visual.**

visual analysis: *see* **analysis, visual.**

visual and motor coordination: *see* **coordination, visual and motor.**

visual and spatial arts: *see* **arts, visual and spatial.**

visual angle: (1) the angle included between the two lines drawn from the two extremities of an object to the optic center of the crystalline lens of the eye; (2) the angle which the optic axes of the eyes make with one another as they tend to meet at some distance before the eyes. *Syn.* **optic angle.**

visual apprehension: *see* **apprehension, visual.**

visual art: *see* **art, visual.**

visual-auditory association: (read.) the act or process of relating visual symbols to their corresponding sounds.

visual-auditory perception: *see* **perception, visual-auditory.**

visual axis: a straight line from the point on which the eye is focused, passing through the optical node, and ending at the point of sharpest vision on the retina; not necessarily the same as the *optical axis.*

visual classification test: *see* **test, visual classification.**

visual clue: *see* **clue, visual.**

visual color: *syn.* **color, realistic.**

visual comprehension: *see* **comprehension, visual.**

visual decoding: *see* **decoding, visual.**

visual defect: an imperfection of vision resulting from impairment of the eye, the optic nerve, and/or the visual area in the brain; may manifest itself as a reduction of central visual acuity, contraction of the visual field, muscular imbalance, color blindness, or ametropia.

visual difficulty: a problem in seeing that interferes with the normal use of the eyes, especially in reading or writing.

visual disability: a handicap in or incapacity for specific visual tasks due to impairment of one or more of the visual functions.

visual discrimination: *see* **discrimination, visual.**

visual drop-off: a change in appearance of a walking surface that is observable at night; a handicap in vision even for the normally sighted.

visual education: a broad term to describe all education based on the use of materials (other than books) that appeal directly to the sense of sight, such as charts, models, and still motion pictures.

visual education service: an organized plan, frequently operated by a school system, museum, library, college, or university, for providing and distributing visual aid materials and equipment for the use of schools and adult study centers; sometimes provides projectionists.

visual efficiency: (1) effectiveness of the individual's interpretation of light stimuli received through the eye; (2) the skill with which the seeing mechanism operates; (3) the capacity to perform specific visual tasks under varying environmental conditions.

visual expression: *see* **visual type.**

visual fatigue: (1) tiredness of the eyes from whatever cause, but especially from long application to close work, to strain induced by uncorrected visual defects, or to improper illumination; (2) any sensation of fatigue localized in or near the eyes, probably governed by the laws of referred pain. (There is ample evidence to indicate that whatever the mechanism of visual fatigue, it is located in the central nervous system, for the focusing and turning mechanisms of the eyes are relatively fatigueless.)

visual field: *syn.* **field of vision.**

visual fusion: *see* **fusion, visual.**

visual handicap: *see* **handicap, visual.**

visual-haptic test: *see* **test, visual-haptic.**

visual hearing: *syn.* **lipreading.**

visual hearing method: a method of teaching lipreading in which motion pictures serve as the basis of instruction. *See* **audiovisual-kinesthetic method.**

visual image: *see* **image, visual.**

visual impact: (mil. ed.) in Air Force usage, the quality of a visual stimulus which creates a strong, immediate, and lasting reaction on the part of the observer.

visual inhibition: *see* **inhibition, visual.**

visual instruction: *see* **instruction, visual.**

visual-kinesthetic associations: *see* **associations, visual-kinesthetic.**

visual learning: *see* **learning, visual.**

visual listening: *see* **listening, visual.**

visual literacy: *see* **literacy, visual.**

visual materials: *see* **materials, visual.**

visual memory: *see* **memory, visual.**

visual-memory span: (1) the extent of an individual's memory for visual symbols, such as letters, words, or other objects; (2) the number of items seen that can be recalled after a single presentation.

visual merchandising: *see* **display.**

visual-motor method: a method of teaching reading that emphasizes seeing or clearly visualizing a word, accompanied by the action of saying and writing it; used chiefly as a remedial procedure for pupils who have difficulty in word recognition.

visual perception: *see* **perception, visual.**

visual presentation: the introduction of an item or lesson to be studied by letting the pupil see it, for example, introducing the words of a spelling lesson by having the pupil look at them.

visual range: (mil. ed.) in aerospace studies, the distance at which the apparent contrast between a specified type of object and its background becomes equal to the threshold contrast of an observer.

visual reeducation: *syn.* **training, visual.**

visual sense: (mil. ed.) the sense of sight, subject to measurements for acuity, depth perception, color differentiation, etc.; important in the testing of astronauts before and after flights.

visual skill: *see* **skill, visual.**

visual space: *see* **space, visual.**

visual span: *syn.* **perceptual span.**

visual task: *see* **task, visual.**

visual test: *see* **test, vision.**

visual thinking: *see* **thinking, visual.**

visual training: *see* **training, visual.**

visual type: (art ed.) a term referring to the individual who is mainly concerned with his optical impressions, that is, with appearances, with differences of color, light and shade, with atmosphere, with perspective space; such a person looks at his work from outside and feels like a spectator.

visual typewriting: *see* **typewriting, visual.**

visualization: the act of forming and fixing a clear mental image of the form of an object.

visualization, spatial: visual relations of objects in space as they are visually manipulated.

visualization, word: ability of the student to see a written or printed word or phrase from his visual memory.

visually handicapped: *see* **handicapped, visually.**

visually impaired: *see* **handicapped, visually.**

visuopalpebral reflex: *see* **reflex, visuopalpebral.**

vital capacity: *see* **capacity, vital.**

vitalism (vī'təl·iz'm): the doctrine or theory that physical force and mechanical principles are inadequate to explain life processes, which are thought to be due to a living principle that transcends the physical and mechanical; advanced, among modern philosophers, by Bergson, who emphasized the *élan vital,* or "vital force."

vocabulary, active: the content and function words of a language which are learned so thoroughly that they become a part of the child's understanding, speaking, and later, reading and writing, vocabulary.

vocabulary, adult reading: the words commonly used only in adult reading material.

vocabulary, adult writing: (1) the words that adults use in writing; (2) the words that adults both understand and use in writing.

vocabulary, basic: the words and idioms considered essential for minimal use of a language.

vocabulary, basic-blend: a list of words that represent the basic phonetic blends commonly found in reading material.

vocabulary, basic reading: (1) the fundamental vocabulary essential to effective reading, common to all fields and subjects; (2) the vocabulary that is systematically taught in the basic reader, as contrasted with the vocabularies of supplementary readers and of the school subjects.

vocabulary, basic sight: the words taught so as to be instantly recognized as wholes in the early stages of learning to read and before the analysis of words is attempted.

vocabulary burden: (1) the general level of difficulty of the vocabulary in a particular piece of writing; (2) the number of unfamiliar words in relation to the total number of running words, especially in basic readers designed for the primary grades.

vocabulary, children's writing: (1) the words that children use in writing; (2) the words that children both understand and use in writing.

vocabulary, child's: the word stock of children at a given mental stage or grade level; hence, the vocabulary used in speaking to or writing for children.

vocabulary, comprehension: words having meaning when heard or seen even though not produced by the individual himself to communicate with others. (The child acquires understanding of many words before it can utter even one.) *See* **vocabulary, recognition.**

vocabulary, controlled: vocabulary selected and spaced in a basal reader or other textbook so as to control the number of new words to be learned by the child per unit of reading matter.

vocabulary density: a measure of the concentration of difficult words in a number of running words. (High vocabulary density is believed to be a cause of reading difficulty.)

vocabulary development: *see* **development, vocabulary.**

vocabulary diversity: a measure of the difference in the difficulty of words occurring in a piece of printed matter.

vocabulary entry: *syn.* **word, entry.**

vocabulary exercise: *see* **exercise, vocabulary.**

vocabulary, graded: a list of words that have been evaluated or measured and assigned to a certain grade or level of child development.

vocabulary, graphic: a term coined by Walter Sargent in 1916 to designate a method of teaching drawing by which a "vocabulary" of simple forms is acquired by pupils as a basis for graphic expression.

vocabulary, listening: the number of words an individual can understand when they are heard, as contrasted with *reading vocabulary,* the number of words that he can identify and understand by reading.

vocabulary, marginal: *syn.* **vocabulary, potential.**

vocabulary, meaning: (1) the words which one understands, the meaning of which one knows; (2) a list of the meanings represented by words in a given amount of material.

vocabulary, oral: the words a person employs in expressing himself orally.

vocabulary, passive: words that are rarely or never used in a person's speaking or writing but that he readily understands in reading and listening.

vocabulary, potential: words that the individual does not know but that he can interpret from their context or by reason of his background of knowledge. *Syn.* **marginal vocabulary.**

vocabulary, preschool: (1) the words used in speaking by children of the preschool age level; (2) a specific list of words known to be used and understood by preschool children.

vocabulary, reading: (1) the word forms that one recognizes when he sees them in print or writing; (2) the words that one understands when he sees them in print or writing; (3) a list of words that one needs to know in order to read.

vocabulary, recognition: those words which a person can recognize in context but that he may not be able to use in his own speech and writing.

vocabulary, remedial reading: a special list of words designed for use with children who have reading defects.

vocabulary scale: *see* **scale, vocabulary.**

vocabulary, sight: the words that the child immediately recognizes as he reads, without resort to word-analysis techniques.

vocabulary, speaking: *syn.* **vocabulary, speech or oral.**

vocabulary, specialized: the words in reading material which are important in particular fields of study as in science, mathematics, or the social studies.

vocabulary, speech or oral: words that a person uses actively in conversation. *Syn.* **vocabulary, speaking.**

vocabulary, spelling: (1) the words to be taught in spelling; (2) the words that one is able to spell correctly.

vocabulary, spoken: *syn.* **vocabulary, speech or oral.**

vocabulary test: *see* **test, vocabulary.**

vocabulary test, picture: *see* **test, picture vocabulary.**

vocabulary, usage: (1) vocabulary confined to words in general use; (2) a list including words and statements of their meaning in common usage.

vocabulary, visible: meanings of words interpaged with the text of foreign-language readers to obviate reference to a complete vocabulary.

vocabulary, writing: the words commonly used by a person writing; the commonest words used in writing are listed by Horn at 10,000, of which 4,000 are of greatest permanent value to children.

vocal bands: *syn.* **vocal cords.**

vocal compass: *syn.* **vocal range.**

vocal cords: the two muscular membranous bands in the voice box (larynx) that produce the fundamental voice sounds when they are placed in varying degrees of proximity and have air forced between them.

vocal cords, false: two folds located above and parallel to the vocal cords, probably playing no active role in normal production.

vocal range: the span between the lowest and highest tones that a given singer can perform. *Syn.* **vocal compass;** *see* **alto-tenor; baritone; bass; contralto; mezzo-soprano; soprano; tenor.**

vocalization: (1) the production of sounds by the vocal organs; the earliest vocalization is the birth cry, which is reflex in nature and devoid of symbolic or language function; (2) the exercise of the voice through singing vowel sounds; used for the improvement of vocal quality and skill, and also often practiced prior to public performance; (3) (linguistics) (*a*) transformation of a consonant to a vowel and (Hebrew and Arabic) (*b*) the indication of vowel sounds by vowel points called Masoretic points.

vocalization, inward: the act or process of "sounding" words mentally in silent reading.

vocalization, outward: the act or process of sounding words aloud in oral reading.

vocalization, socialized: a stage in the development of speech in the child, usually beginning about the fifth month, in which vocal sounds are used as a means of communication, though they are not yet formed into words.

vocation: a calling, as to a particular occupation, business, or profession.

vocation, blind-alley: any vocation that seems to contribute little of positive value to success in other vocations and that itself offers little or no possibility of advancement. (The term is a much-used misnomer, as many jobs with no apparent favorable outlet prove to be steppingstones to other seemingly unrelated jobs, tasks, or positions.)

vocation, religious: (R.C. ed.) commonly referred to as *vocation;* generally considered as a celibate life in a religious community dedicated to contemplative or apostolic pursuits.

vocational: pertaining to a vocation or occupation (for example, all gainful occupations and utilitarian labor, including homemaking).

vocational-ability profile: *see* **profile, vocational-ability.**

vocational adjustment: *see* **adjustment, vocational.**

vocational adjustment coordinator: *see* **coordinator, vocational adjustment.**

vocational adjustment counselor: *see* **counselor, vocational.**

vocational adviser: *see* **adviser, vocational.**

vocational agriculture: *see* **agriculture, vocational.**

vocational and educational maladjustment: *see* **maladjustment, vocational and educational.**

vocational and technical education: training intended to prepare the student to earn a living in an occupation in which success is dependent largely upon technical information and an understanding of the laws of science and technology as applied to modern design, production, distribution, and service.

vocational aptitude: *see* **aptitude, vocational.**

vocational arithmetic: *see* **arithmetic, vocational.**

vocational art: *see* **art, vocational.**

vocational blindness: *see* **blindness, vocational.**

vocational bookkeeping: *see* **bookkeeping, vocational.**

vocational choice: *see* **choice, vocational.**

vocational choice, inappropriate: (couns.) a choice of vocation not congruent with the student's interests or aptitudes or with known employment requirements and opportunities.

vocational civics: *see* **civics, vocational.**

vocational clinic: *see* **clinic, vocational.**

vocational consumer and homemaking program: *see* **program, reimbursed consumer and homemaking education.**

vocational coordinator: *see* **coordinator, vocational.**

vocational counseling: *see* **counseling, vocational.**

vocational counselor: *see* **counselor, vocational.**

vocational course: *see* **course, vocational.**

vocational curriculum: *see* **curriculum, vocational.**

vocational curriculum guidance: *see* **guidance, vocational curriculum.**

vocational development: *see* **development, vocational.**

vocational director: *see* **director, vocational.**

vocational education: a program of education below college grade organized to prepare the learner for entrance into a particular chosen vocation or to upgrade employed workers; includes such divisions as trade and industrial education, health education, agricultural education, business education, and home economics education; training or retraining (including field or laboratory work incidental thereto) is given in schools or classes under public supervision and control or under contract with a state board or local educational agency.

Vocational Education Act of 1963: (Perkins Act) Federal legislation designed to (*a*) extend present programs and develop new programs of vocational education, (*b*) encourage research and experimentation, and (*c*) provide work-study programs to enable youth to continue vocational education.

vocational education, adult: instruction on a part-time basis designed to develop skills, understandings, and attitudes, encompassing knowledge and information needed by adults or out-of-school youth over 16 years old to enter an occupation or make progress in employment on a useful and productive basis.

vocational education in agriculture: *see* **agriculture, vocational.**

vocational education, local director of: *see* **director of vocational education, local.**

vocational education, state board for: *see* **state board for vocational education.**

vocational education, state director of: *see* **director of vocational education, state.**

vocational education survey: *see* **survey, vocational education.**

vocational goal: *see* **goal, vocational.**

vocational growth: *see* **growth, occupational.**

vocational guidance: *see* **guidance, vocational.**

vocational guidance and placement, director of: *see* **director of vocational guidance and placement.**

vocational high school: *see* **high school, vocational.**

vocational home economics, occupational programs in: *see* **programs in vocational home economics, occupational.**

vocational home economics program: *see* **program, reimbursed consumer and homemaking education.**

vocational indecision: *see* **indecision, vocational.**

vocational-industrial club: *see* **club, trade and industrial education.**

vocational information: *see* **information, vocational.**

vocational-interest test: *see* **test, vocational-interest.**

vocational interests: (1) measured patterns of likes and dislikes that have been found experimentally to differentiate successful adults in one occupation from those in other occupations; (2) a feeling of liking associated with a reaction, either actual or imagined, to a specific area or field of an occupation.

vocational laboratory: *see* **laboratory, vocational.**

vocational maladjustment: *see* **maladjustment, vocational and educational.**

vocational mathematics: *see* **mathematics, shop; mathematics, trade.**

vocational maturity: *see* **maturity, vocational.**

vocational prognosis: *see* **prognosis, vocational.**

vocational rehabilitation: *see* **rehabilitation, vocational.**

vocational school: a school which is organized separately under a principal or director for the purpose of offering training in one or more skilled or semiskilled trades or occupations.

vocational school, area: a term currently coming into use for a vocational school at the secondary level which serves *joint vocational school districts,* set up so that each school district need not set up a vocational high school of its own; may be named in some places *joint vocational school. See* **high school, vocational.**

vocational school district, joint: *see* **vocational school, area.**

vocational school, joint: *see* **vocational school, area.**

vocational school, private: a school established and operated by an agency other than the state or its subdivisions and supported by other than public funds, which has as its purpose the preparation of students for entrance into or progress in trades or skilled occupations.

vocational school, public: a secondary school under public supervision and control and supported by public funds which provides instruction that will enable high school youth and adults to prepare for, enter, and make progress in a skilled trade or occupation of their choice.

vocational service: a counseling service in which the client is assisted in choosing a vocation and developing and carrying out a program to reach his vocational objective; or, if he has already made tentative vocational plans, he is assisted with the evaluation of these plans.

vocational subject: *see* **subject, vocational.**

vocational survey: *syn.* **survey, occupational.**

vocational theories: (couns.) theoretical models leading to statements of relationships believed to prevail and to underlie choice and progress in an occupation.

vocational trade and industrial education: the type of education that prepares persons for employment in a trade or industrial occupation or prepares employed persons in trade and industrial occupations for advancement through further training.

vocational training: *see* **training, vocational.**

vocational typewriting: *see* **typewriting, vocational.**

vocational unit: *see* **unit, vocational.**

vocationalism: a term used as an indictment of modern education, particularly the professional schools of the university, on the grounds that narrow vocational courses of study have diluted the pursuit of knowledge for its own sake and that triviality, isolation of content, and a narrowly practical interest have detracted from that study of general and fundamental principles which is the worthy object of university study (R. M. Hutchins).

voice, chest: that lower part of a vocalist's range which derives from chest resonance. *See* **tone, chest; tone, head; voice, head.**

voice, child: a voice with the light, flutelike quality characteristic of children up to the age of their voice change, usually at the age of 12 or thereafter.

voice class: *see* **class, voice.**

voice disorder: *see* **disorder, voice.**

voice, head: (1) that part of the vocal range suitable for producing a head tone; (2) a voice characterized by head resonance. *See* **tone, chest; tone, head; voice, chest.**

voice instruction: *see* **instruction, voice.**

voice placement: a devised imaginative concept of vocal production serving to divert the attention from certain physical areas where strain and tension, the main cause of faulty tone, exist; for example, by "placing the voice in the mask," that is, in the front of the mouth and nose, attention is diverted from the throat, making for a more relaxed condition in that area.

voice, singing: *see* **singing voice.**

voice training aid: *see* **speech training aid.**

voiced sound: *syn.* **sonant.**

voiceless sound: *syn.* **surd.**

voicing error: substitution of a voiced sound for its voiceless equivalent, or vice versa, as in *dok* for *dog, greaze* for *grease,* or *Chimmy* for *Jimmy.*

void: without legal right or benefit, as in the case of a void contract that is so defective that it cannot be remedied.

voidable: capable of being made void, as in the case of a contract that is not absolutely void but may be voided.

volition: any act of the will; an act of desire that involves tendency toward a known object; to be distinguished from an act of knowledge which, as such, does not involve tendency or an appetitive reaction; the act of the will is said to be free when it involves a choice of means to an end and where two or more efficacious means to the end are known. *See* **will.**

Volk Shule (folk shoo′lə): *n. fem.; pl.* **Volk Shulen;** (Yiddish, lit., "people's school") a type of daily afternoon Jewish school, of which Yiddish is the language of instruction and which is organized and maintained by the Jewish labor groups; has Zionist and socialist leanings; instruction is nonreligious but not antireligious in character.

Volksschule (folks′shoo·lə): *see* **folk school** (1).

volleyball: a game played by two teams of six or eight players on a side; each team occupies half the playing court which is divided by a net at midcourt; each team attempts to accumulate the greatest number of points by legally hitting the ball over the net so that the opponents will be unable to return it.

volume: an acoustic, rather than electrical, measurement which refers to the pressure of the sound waves in terms of dynes per square centimeter; the louder the sound, the greater the pressure; most technicians prefer to talk in terms of *decibels.*

volume control: a device on a sound-reproducing or - amplifying instrument for regulating the loudness of the sound.

volume indicator: *see* **level indicator.**

voluntarism: in metaphysics, the theory that emphasizes will or volition as distinct from reason or intellect in describing reality; Schopenhauer and William James are perhaps the most eminent exponents of this view.

voluntary reading: *see* **reading, voluntary.**

voluntary stuttering: *see* **stuttering, pseudo.**

volunteer: (spec. ed.) an individual contributing services without pay to a specialized program; usually an outsider or a member of the *paraprofessional personnel.*

volunteer program, national school: *see* **program, national school volunteer.**

volunteer program, school: *see* **program, school volunteer.**

Volunteers in Service to America: *see* **VISTA.**

voodoo: an African Negro religion, still practiced with some variation by Negroes in the Western Hemisphere, especially in Haiti and to some extent in the United States; based on serpent and phallus worship and involving sorcery with charms, amulets, secret nocturnal rites, etc.

voucher check: a check or written order for money, to which is attached a duplicate, or voucher, which may be used for filing purposes by the person receiving the check.

voucher, educational: *see* **voucher plan.**

voucher plan: a plan to distribute educational monies through issuance to parents directly of a *voucher* allocating public funds to pay the cost of their children's education in either a public or a private school of their choice; vouchers are regulated by a locally selected agency, which may be the current board of education augmented by members of alternative sources of education or may be a new board empowered to receive funds from the local school system and to disburse them to parents; the parents take the voucher to a school of their choice which then returns it to the agency which next sends the school a check equal to the value of the voucher. (The plan is intended to provide incentive to private as well as public schools to enroll some proportion of disadvantaged children; the Office of Economic Opportunity has sponsored an experimental application of the plan, restricted to the elementary school level, in one or two school systems, beginning in September of 1971.)

vow: (R.C. ed.) a free, deliberate promise made to God which is binding in conscience and must be fulfilled as promised; a simple vow is temporary in nature, and the release or dispensation by proper authorities is permitted; a solemn vow is the absolute and irrevocable surrender and acceptance of it by lawful authority.

vowel: a sound produced with a vibration of the vocal cords by the air passing relatively unobstructed through the oral part of the breath channel. *Contr. w.* **consonant.**

vowel digraph: *see* **digraph.**

vowel fracture: the diphthongization of a vowel due to the influence of neighboring sounds. *See* **diphthong.**

voyeurism (voi′ər·iz′m): sexual aberration in which sexual gratification is obtained by looking at sexual objects.

VTR: *see* **recording, videotape.**

VU meter: a volume unit meter, indicating by means of a moving needle the total voltage passing through an audio system, which is a relative indicator of volume level of the various sounds being recorded or played. *See* **level indicator.**

Vulgate: a Latin version of the Bible prepared in the fourth century by St. Jerome, so called from its common use in the Roman Catholic Church.

vulnerable child: *see* **child, vulnerable.**

Wada sodium amytal test: *see* **test, Wada sodium amytal.**

waddling gait: *see* **gait, waddling.**

wage-and-hour report: *see* **report, wage-and-hour.**

wage plan, guaranteed: *see* **guaranteed wage plan.**

WAIS: *see* **scale, Wechsler.**

waiting station: *see* **station, waiting.**

Walddorfschule (vält′dörf·shoo′lə): (Ger., lit., "woods-village school") a private secondary school patterned after the theories of Rudolf Steiner, founder and leader of the German anthroposophical movement; similar schools, called Waldorf schools, have been set up in the United States. *See* **anthroposophy.**

walking distance: *see* **distance, walking.**

wall card: a large card, used in teaching handwriting, that has letters in model form placed upon it, usually white on a black background, and is so located on the wall as to be visible from any part of the schoolroom.

wall weights: a piece of apparatus attached to a wall and equipped with ropes and handles designed to allow arm movements in lifting adjustable weights.

walleye: *syn.* **exotropia.**

walls, glass block: *see* **glass block walls.**

wanderlust: a powerful urge to wander, to travel from one place to another with no well-defined motive.

war game: (mil. ed.) a simulation, by whatever means, of a military operation involving two or more opposing forces, using rules, data, and procedures designed to depict an actual or assumed real-life situation.

war game, dynamic air: an air war game played on a machine having a number of electronic devices.

ward method of board selection: *see* **board selection, ward method of.**

wardrobe: a closet, compartment, or supplementary room attached to a classroom, used for the hanging or temporary storage of pupils' or teachers' outer garments.

warming up: that part of an increase in efficiency during the early part of a work period which is abolished by a moderate rest (say of 60 minutes); warming-up effects should show clearly in some individuals at or near the limit of practice and, in other persons, should compound with the effects of practice to make the rise in efficiency especially rapid in the first portion of a practice period; warming-up effects may transfer from one task to another.

warmth: (couns.) behavior exhibited by the counselor conveying cognitive understanding and feeling for the individual and his concerns.

warning flags and flares: devices used to inform approaching motorists that a vehicle has become inoperative in a location which presents a hazard to traffic and that special caution is needed.

warning signal system: (pup. trans.) a system of lights, bells, horns, buzzers, or other devices which indicates conditions representing a hazard to the pupils or to the vehicle.

warrant: (1) an order drawn by the legislative body or an officer of a governmental unit upon its treasurer directing the latter to pay a specified amount to the person named or to the bearer (it may be payable upon demand and then usually circulates in the same way as a bank check; or it may be payable only out of certain revenues when and if received and then does not circulate so freely); (2) an order for the treasurer to receive money; (3) a written document, generally issued by a court or other duly constituted authority, granting certain specific powers to the bearer, for example, a search warrant, a warrant of arrest, etc.

warrant officer candidate: *see* **candidate, warrant officer.**

warrant payable: (school finance) a warrant issued by the school board but not yet signed by the treasurer.

warrant, registered: a warrant that is registered by the paying officer for future payment on account of present lack of funds and that is to be paid in the order of its registration. (In some cases, such warrants are registered when issued; in others, when first presented to the paying officer by the holders.)

warranted assertibility: *see* **assertibility, warranted.**

washback: *see* **branching, backward.**

Washburne-Vogel readability formula: *see* **readability formula, Washburne-Vogel.**

Wassermann reaction (väs'ər·män): the accepted test applied to the blood or spinal fluid to determine the presence or absence of syphilis, the result being reported as plus or minus.

waste space: unfinished or unusable rooms, or space not serving either instructional or auxiliary purposes.

watch-tick test: *see* **test, watch-tick.**

watchmaker: (voc. ed.) a worker who repairs, cleans, and adjusts mechanisms of instruments such as watches, time clocks, and timing switches, using hand tools and measuring instruments. *See* **horology.**

water ballet: *see* **swimming, synchronized.**

water basketball: a game similar to basketball but played in the water.

water play: *see* **play, water.**

water polo: a game played with a partly inflated ball between teams, each of which endeavors to hit the opponents' goal with the ball.

water safety instructor: *see* **instructor, water safety.**

watered-down curriculum: *see* **curriculum, watered-down.**

waves, action-potential: neural impulses propagated along the neuronal axon as evidenced on electrical recording equipment, for example, contact electrodes, amplifier, and oscillograph.

waves, brain: (1) electrical changes in cortical potentials which have been shown to correlate with certain changes in or mental states of an individual; (2) *see* **electroencephalogram.**

wax tablet: a hollowed slab of wood filled with wax, used in ancient times in learning activities and in communication of ideas. *See* **stylus.**

we group: *syn.* **group, in.**

wealth: (1) anything that is economically useful, but particularly material objects or possessions; anything that has utility, that is, the ability to satisfy a human want; (2) the degree or extent to which a community, school district, person, etc., possesses things of value, power to purchase them, or control over them.

weaning: (1) the act of removing a child from the mother's breast or from the bottle through substitution of cup or glass for tendering him liquid nourishment; used metaphorically in a psychological sense to refer to the beginning of volitional independence; (2) in programmed instruction, training the pupil to make independent responses to stimuli which were previously accompanied by *prompts*; behavioral goal of the *fading* technique.

weaning trauma: *see* **trauma, weaning.**

Weber's law: *see* **law, Weber's.**

Wechsler-Bellevue scale: *see* **scale, Wechsler-Bellevue.**

Wechsler scale: *see* **scale, Wechsler.**

weed: *v.* (libr. sci.) to discard currently undesirable or unneeded materials from a library collection or file.

weekday church school: *see* **church school, weekday.**

weekday school, Jewish: a school providing religious instruction several days a week after public school hours, as distinguished from Sabbath or Sunday schools. *See* **weekday school, Jewish communal; weekday school, Jewish congregational.**

weekday school, Jewish communal: a Jewish religious school conducted after public school hours (Monday through Thursday), as well as Sunday morning, by a central community agency or by a membership association organized for the purpose of providing Jewish education; usually maintained in part by tuition fees and in part by community funds; frequently called Talmud Torah. *See* **Talmud Torah.**

weekday school, Jewish congregational: a Jewish religious school conducted after public school hours (2 to 5 days a week) under the auspices of a Conservative, Orthodox, or Reform congregation.

weekly program: *see* **program, weekly.**

weight: *n.* (1) the relative importance or relative value of an item entering into a computation; (2) the relative number of units allowed for different items, as for different sections of a test; (3) the coefficient applied to a score or other value entering into a total or average (in this sense usually called *nominal weight*); (4) the effect of an individual series in determining the position of a particular case in a composite of several series; (5) the extent to which a series contributes to the variability (usually the standard deviation or the variance) of a composite of several series. (Weight is always to be interpreted as relative to other weights; it has no absolute value.) *See* **unweighted; weight, arbitrary; weight, effective; weight, equal; weight, natural; weight, nominal.**

weight: *v.* (1) the act of determining the relative importance to be assigned to a given datum or result as compared with other data or results; (2) the act or process of assigning the weights thus obtained to the variables concerned.

weight age: *see* **age, weight.**

weight, apparent: the apparent importance of an element entering into the computation of any statistic. *Contr. w.* **real weight; weight, effective.**

weight, arbitrary: a nominal weight selected for some particular purpose, often when more correct weights cannot be ascertained, for example, weights assigned on the basis of individual judgment or equal weights imposed without consideration.

weight, beta: *syn.* **coefficient, beta regression.**

weight, beta regression: *syn.* **coefficient, beta regression.**

weight capacity: *see* **capacity, weight.**

weight, effective: (1) the actual weight of a series as measured by either (*a*) its (average) effect in determining the position of a particular case in a composite or (*b*) its contribution to the dispersion of the composite reflecting, in addition to nominal weight applied to equally dispersed series, the influence of correlation between the series; (2) the assigned weight of any individual item in a series, such as that of an item of an objective test or of a section of an essay test. *Syn.* **functional weight; real weight;** *see* **weight, nominal.**

weight, equal: (1) as applied to several items in a series or total, either the allowance of the same number of units for each item when the object or condition is at its maximum (or, possibly, at its norm) or the fact of equal variability of observed or derived scores for each item in the series or total; (2) as applied to several series, equal dispersion of all the series that are entered into a composite, a condition that may be brought about by applying the appropriate coefficients (such as the reciprocal of the standard deviation) to the various series of raw scores; series are ordinarily said to have equal weight when their variances are equal, even though their effective weights may vary, owing to the influence of correlation between the series. *See* **weight, effective.**

weight, functional: *syn.* **weight, effective.**

weight lifting: the lifting of weights in competition.

weight, natural: the relative weight that any series of raw data has, when it is entered into a composite, by virtue of the relation of its variance to the variances of the other series in the composite.

weight, nominal: (1) a coefficient applied to a datum or series of data in the raw form or to one of a number of equally weighted data or series in a composite; (2) the ratio of the variance of a series to the variance of other series in a composite.

weight, optimal: the weight of a variable combined with another variable (or variables) such that the weighted sum of the variables yields the maximum correlation with a criterion.

weight, percentage: *syn.* **frequency, percentage.**

weight, real: *syn.* **weight, effective.**

weight, regression: *syn.* **coefficient of regression** (1).

weight, subject: (1) one of the factors used in calculating teacher load, consisting of a measure of the amount of time needed by the teacher to prepare for a single period of instruction in a particular subject; expressed, in the case of the Douglass formula, as a number greater than, equal to, or less than 1.00, according to how the amount of time needed compares with that required to prepare for a section in mathematics, a foreign language, or the social studies; (2) a numerical value assigned to a school subject according to its difficulty or importance; used in determining how many periods a week shall be devoted to a given subject and what combination of subjects a pupil may study.

weight training: *see* **training, weight.**

weight, unitary: a nominal or natural weight of 1, indicating that a particular datum or series has a weight that is regarded as the unit weight, in terms of which other (smaller or larger) weights are expressed. *See* **weight, natural; weight, nominal.**

weighted: having been assigned numbers indicating the relative importance or value of each of the items entering into the computation of a composite or statistic. *Contr. w.* **unweighted.**

weighted arithmetic average: *syn.* **mean, weighted arithmetic** (1).

weighted arithmetic mean: *see* **mean, weighted arithmetic.**

weighted classroom unit: *see* **classroom unit, weighted.**

weighted credit: *see* **credit, weighted.**

weighted scoring: *see* **scoring, weighted.**

weighting, confidence: a special mode of responding to objective test items and of scoring these responses, the examinee being asked to indicate not only what he believes to be the correct answer to a question but also how certain he is of the correctness of his answer; intended to reduce the chance error component of a test score—especially in the test item most affected by guessing, the true-false item.

weighting, item: process of determining the proportion of the total score of a test that is to be gained by passing a particular item.

welding: (ind. arts) the study of the operations used in cutting and fabricating metal products by welding techniques.

welfare, child: *see* **child welfare.**

welfare class: *see* **class, welfare.**

welfare, consumer: the economic comfort and well-being of the consumer.

welfare, economic: *see* **economic welfare.**

welfare, general: a term providing one touchstone by which social and political arrangements are to be judged morally; related closely to the notion of the common good; in collectivist theories of politics, refers to that which qualitatively satisfies the general will somehow defined; in individualist theories of politics, often defined quantitatively as the greatest good of the greatest number of persons.

welfare school: a term used to designate schools conducted for children who are seriously maladjusted socially; the school, which has charge during the school day, may be maintained solely by the board of education or may be connected with a residential institution having charge during the full 24-hour day or with foster homes to which the juvenile court sends the children under its jurisdiction.

welfare service: (1) the organized group of activities developed by universities and colleges in the United States through their extension divisions in the interests of public welfare, such as the work of community surveys and organizations, municipal reference bureaus, and child-welfare promotion; (2) any organization, public or private, designed to improve health, morale, living conditions, etc., of certain groups in a community such as the poor.

welfare work: (1) organized charitable efforts on the part of the more prosperous element of a community to improve the living conditions, health, morale, etc., of the less fortunate members of the community, especially the poor; (2) in industry, any effort on the part of industrial corporations to assist their employees, as in improving their working conditions, home life, means of recreation, health, etc., such services not being demanded by law.

well-adjusted: tending to respond to one's environment in a way that is not harmful to oneself and to society and, in fact, is positively beneficial to oneself and to one's society.

well-baby clinic: *see* **clinic, well-baby.**

well-child clinic: *see* **clinic, well-child.**

well-defined operation: *see* **operation, well-defined.**

well-defined set: *see* **set.**

Weltanschauung (velt'än'shou·oong): (Ger., lit., "world view") a life conception or perspective.

West Point: the popular designation for the United States Military Academy, located at West Point, New York; hence, West Pointer, a graduate of, or cadet in, this academy.

Westfield plan: (teacher ed.) an arrangement first introduced in the State Teachers College at Westfield, Massachusetts, by means of which members of the senior class taking a professional course exchange places for a week with appropriate members of the previous year's graduating class who are employed in the area served.

wet carrel: *see* **carrel.**

wet mount: *see* **mount, wet.**

wetting the bed: *see* **enuresis.**

Wetzel grid: a chart devised by Wetzel which provides through successive measurements of height and weight an index of consistency of physical development.

WFF 'N PROOF: a series of games played with specially marked cubes to teach the principles of symbolic logic. *See* **logic, symbolic.**

Wherry-Doolittle method: a modified procedure for the solution of a multiple-regression problem; a method designed to meet the requirement of assembling a battery of tests to select personnel for some particular assignment.

Wherry-Doolittle multiple correlation test selection method: *see* **test selection method, Wherry-Doolittle multiple correlation.**

whipping post: a post, found both in and out of school, at which children were disciplined; more or less commonly used in early New England.

whisper, buccal: (spec. ed.) use in whispered speech of an accumulation of air in the mouth and pharynx instead of the normal use of the air expelled from the lung passages.

whisper test: *see* **test, whisper.**

white noise: *see* **noise, white.**

white screen: *see* **screen, white.**

whole child: *see* **child, whole.**

whole learning: *see* **learning, whole.**

whole meaning: (1) the general idea of an article, chapter, or large unit of reading matter; (2) the general significance of a large unit of thought as distinguished from the detailed items that support that thought. *Syn.* **central thought.**

whole-meaning test: *see* **test, whole-meaning.**

whole method: a method of teaching speech sounds by attempting to produce them correctly in words, as opposed to the *part method,* in which sounds are taught in isolation.

whole-part-whole method: a modern analytic-synthetic method of teaching children to read, beginning with whole words or sentences, followed by word analysis, and culminating in emphasis on reading by thought groups rather than word-by-word.

whole universe: *see* **universe.**

whole-word method: *syn.* **whole method; word method;** *see* **whole-part-whole method.**

wholesaling: (distrib. ed.) all activities in which goods are bought for business or institutional purposes as distinguished from personal or ultimate consumption.

wilderness survival program: *see* **program, wilderness survival.**

will: (1) a source of conscious tendency toward an object known as good and, sometimes, the power of the agent to direct himself toward a goal; (2) in faculty psychology, such as Scholasticism, the will is to be distinguished from the *intellect,* which is a faculty of knowing but, as such, does not initiate activity, and from the sense *appetites,* which are the sources of tendencies toward goods immediately perceived by the senses; the will is the source of tendency toward a good known intellectually, as, for example, one wills that justice prevail in his nation.

will-and-temperament test: *see* **test, will-and-temperament.**

will to refrain: the "constant exercise of the active will" that distinguishes man from beast and provides a check upon the impulses of sense, and even reason, and thus produces a spiritual self-discipline; radically opposed to utilitarianism, naturalism, and humanitarianism (Irving Babbitt). *See* **humanism, literary.**

window card: a piece of cardboard with a circular hole so placed as to show only a single letter at a time in one of the lines of the *Snellen chart.*

window deflector: *see* **deflector, window.**

window-gravity ventilation: *see* **ventilation, gravity; ventilation, window.**

window map: *see* **map, window.**

window ventilation: *see* **ventilation, window.**

Winnetka plan: a plan for individualizing instruction developed in 1919 by Carleton W. Washburne in the public elementary and junior high schools of Winnetka, Illinois; long in operation there, and widely copied; based on the following scheme: the curriculum is divided into two parts, namely, common essentials and social and creative activities; pupils work individually at their own rates on the first part, largely by means of workbooks, progressing only as rapidly as their abilities permit; in the social and creative activities, measurement of achievement is not attempted, and much group work is done.

wipe: a visual transition between film or television scenes by means of which the scene is caused not to fade out but to disappear progressively from a given point or line as if it were being wiped out as the next scene is wiped in.

wire recorder: *see* **recorder, wire.**

wire recording: *see* **recording, wire.**

wireless language laboratory: *see* **laboratory, wireless language.**

WISC: *see* **scale, Wechsler.**

withdrawal: (pupil accounting) (1) a pupil who has withdrawn from membership in a class, grade, or school by transferring, by completing schoolwork, by dropping out, or by dying; (2) leaving a class, grade, or school by transferring, by completing schoolwork, by dropping out, or by dying; the date of withdrawal from membership is the first day after the date of the last day of membership, if known; otherwise, the date of withdrawal is considered to be the date on which it becomes known officially that the pupil has left.

withdrawal rate, annual: (pupil accounting) the total number of times pupils withdraw from school during a given regular school term divided by the number of different pupils entering during the term, expressed as a percentage.

withdrawal, student: *see* **withdrawal.**

withdrawals, record of: *see* **record of withdrawals.**

withdrawing, percentage of pupils: *see* **percentage of pupils withdrawing.**

withdrawn behavior: *see* **behavior, withdrawn.**

withdrawn child: *see* **child, withdrawn.**

withholding tax: *see* **tax, withholding.**

within-group variance: *see* **variance, within-group.**

wolf-child: *see* **child, feral.**

women's counselor: *syn.* **dean of women.**

wood technology: *see* **technology, wood.**

woodcut: a graphic printing surface, a wooden block on which a drawing or pattern is cut; the raised surface is inked and its pattern transferred to paper or other material when pressure is applied.

woodwind instruments: *see* **instruments, woodwind.**

woodworking: (1) an activity including the designing, construction, finishing, and reclaiming of wood articles or structures; (2) an area of study relating to industries producing or using lumber.

woodworking laboratory: *see* **laboratory, woodworking.**

word: (1) the smallest unit of vocal expression which has meaning and communicates an idea when taken by itself; (2) in computerized data processing, (*a*) an ordered set of admissible marks of a definite length which has at least one meaning and which is stored, handled, and transferred within the computer as a unit and (*b*) an impulse that conveys a quantum of information; *see* **field** (4).

word, action: (1) a word that suggests physical action to the reader, such as *hop, skip, jump;* (2) a word that can be used as a flash-card word and responded to by action of the body rather than by speech.

word analysis: *see* **analysis, word.**

word-and-sentence method: a method of teaching reading in which whole words and sentences are memorized as a means of learning to read; Comenius (1592-1670) first suggested the word method, Farnham, in 1895, the sentence method.

word association: unreflective verbal responses to stimulus words. (Used in the controlled-association method of C. G. Jung, in which the subject responds to a list of words called out to him and the examiner studies the words found to be emotionally disturbing to the subject.)

word blindness: *syn.* **alexia.**

word building: a study of word formation and word families, and the construction of new words from familiar parts, as by adding prefixes or suffixes to familiar roots.

word-by-word reading: *see* **reading, word-by-word.**

word caller: (1) a reader who pronounces words individually, without intelligent grouping with regard to meaning; (2) a poor, inexpressive oral reader.

word comprehension: *see* **comprehension, word.**

word configuration: the general outline of a word or its peculiar features that distinguish it from other words.

word, content: a word that is used to describe a thing, an action, or a quality, such as *pencil, buy, yellow.* The vocabulary of a language is made up of thousands of content words. *See* **word, function.**

word count: a statistical study of the number of times different words occur in a representative number of running words.

word deafness: *see* **deafness, word.**

word discrimination: *see* **discrimination, word.**

word-discrimination test: *see* **test, word-discrimination.**

word element: (1) any part of a word that constitutes an irreducible minimum; a letter; (2) any part of a word that cannot be reduced for practical purposes, such as the suffix *ing;* (3) any part of a word, such as a phonogram or syllable, that aids the reader in understanding the pronunciation and meaning of the word.

word, entry: one of the words in a dictionary which are arranged in alphabetical order and printed in heavy type, marked for pronunciation, and defined; to be distinguished from *guide word,* which refers to one of those words which are at the top of each page to facilitate the search for entry words.

word family: (1) a group of words having a common root, such as *front, frontal, affront, confront, frontier;* (2) (phonics) a group of words having similar phonetic elements.

word, form class: (lang. arts) a word that fits interchangeably with others in a specific construction, such as "The boy runs," or "The boy eats"; the words runs and eats are the same form class.

word-form clue: *see* **clue, word-form.**

word-form reading: *see* **reading, word-form.**

word-frequency study: *see* **study, word-frequency.**

word, function: a word which does not describe a thing, quality, or action, but which is used only to convey grammatical relationships, such as prepositions (*of, into,* etc.) and auxiliary verbs (*will, may, can,* etc.). *See* **word, content.**

word game: an exercise in word recognition and meaning that is appealing to children as play, such as Wordo or the word wheel.

word, guide: *see* **word, entry.**

word, key: (1) a word which most accurately describes the significant meaning in a document (there may be more than a single key word); usually taken from the text or title to identify subject content; *see* **descriptor; uniterm;** (2) a marked word in the dictionary at the top or bottom of the page in a list which gives the key to interpretation of pronunciation symbols.

word knowledge: the number of words known for use in reading, writing, speaking, listening; levels of word knowledge include simple recognition, recall, extensiveness, and depth of memory. *See* **vocabulary, active; vocabulary, passive.**

word length: in computer operations, the number of admissible marks that constitute a field or word, often expressed in terms of the number of *bits* or decimal digits.

word length, fixed: in automatic data processing, a property of those machine words which always contain the same number of characters or digits.

word length, variable: in automatic data processing, a property of those machine words which may have a variable number of characters.

word list: a list of words which are essential for some teaching purpose such as developing pupils' ability to pronounce correctly, to read, and to spell.

word list, basic: (1) a list of words intended to express the concepts and needs of ordinary existence, for example, the list of 850 words known as *Basic English* compiled by C. K. Ogden; (2) a list of words in a certain area of knowledge or for a designated school grade, such as a vocabulary for a reading lesson or a list of the words to be taught in spelling.

word list, frequency: a list of words scientifically selected and arranged to indicate relative frequency of occurrence.

word list, individual: (spelling) a list of words, correctly spelled, which a pupil will use frequently.

word list, phonetically balanced: a list of monosyllabic English words containing the individual sounds of the language in the same proportions as in average connected speech and designed for use in speech audiometry.

word, machine: in automatic data processing, a unit of information consisting of a standard number of characters which a machine regularly handles in each transfer; has one addressable location.

word mark: in automatic data processing, an indicator to signal the beginning or end of a word. *See* **word** (2).

word meaning: the significance of a word, as distinguished from its form.

word method: (1) a method of teaching reading in which the words are first presented as wholes and later analyzed into parts, rather than presented as parts and then synthesized into wholes; (2) a method of teaching reading in which words are taught as wholes, as contrasted with the *alphabet method,* in which letters and syllables are taught first. *Contr. w.* **ABC method.**

word, monosyllabic: a word composed of a single syllable.

word, new: (read.) one of the words in a basal reading book which have not been met before by the child in reading; in the early grades, generally one to three words per page.

word, nonsense: a word made up of letters that can be sounded or pronounced but that carries no meaning.

word, onomatopoeic: a word that indicates its meaning by its sound, such as *buzz, patter,* and *hiss.*

word perception: *see* **perception, word.**

word, phonetic: a word that is pronounced wholly or in part according to phonetic principles.

word, phonetic sight: a phonetic word taught as a sight word, usually because there are few other words that contain the same phonetic element.

word phonogram: *see* **phonogram, word.**

word-picture approach: *see* **approach, word-picture.**

word-picture dictionary: a dictionary for beginning readers in which each word is accompanied by a picture that aids the child to determine the meaning of the word; usually made by the pupils themselves from words and pictures cut out from workbooks, magazines, etc.

word-picture game: (1) a reading game in which words are represented by pictures; (2) a game in which pictures are matched with words.

word, polysyllabic: a word composed of two or more syllables. *Contr. w.* **word, monosyllabic.**

word problem: *syn.* **problem, written.**

word recognition: *syn.* **recognition.**

word-recognition test: *see* **test, word-recognition.**

word salad: continuous speech, often carried on with great fluency, in which there is no sense or continuity of thought, although isolated parts may be intelligible; symptomatic of mental disorder. *See* **catalogia.**

word sentence: *syn.* **sentence, single-word.**

word, sight: a word memorized or recognized as a whole, rather than by its parts blended together to form the whole.

word sign: *syn.* **brief form.**

word, standard: *see* **standard word.**

word study: (1) analysis of the structure, meaning, and use of words; (2) an exercise in school in which words are subjected to analysis.

word time: in computer operation, the time required to move one word.

word variant: an inflectional form of a word which indicates change in meaning; a variant from the root form of a word.

word visualization: *see* **visualization, word.**

word wheel: a device for vocabulary or word-recognition drill, in which parts of words are so arranged on a wheel as to form entire words when the wheel is revolved.

words, correct: *see* **correct words.**

words, framing: *see* **framing words.**

words, gross: *see* **gross words.**

words in color: (read.) the use of a regular alphabet presenting in a separate color every consonant and vowel sound, irrespective of the letter or letter combinations representing the sound.

words, net: *see* **net words.**

work: (1) the product of a force and the distance through which the force is applied; for example, if a 1-pound weight is lifted a distance of 1 foot, the work performed is 1 foot-pound; (2) in human movement, energy expenditure from concentric or eccentric muscle contraction; (3) (voc. guid.) groups of tasks requiring performance for one's livelihood; (4) the necessary exertion of one's faculties to attain given goals.

work, case: *see* **casework.**

work center: (elem. ed.) an area in a classroom in which materials and equipment concerning a subject of study are assembled for the use of pupils.

work certificate: *syn.* **age-and-schooling certificate.**

work experience: *see* **experience, work.**

work experience, agricultural: *see* **training, agricultural on-job.**

work experience and training program: *see* **program, work experience and training.**

work experience education: employment undertaken as part of the requirements of a school course, designed to provide experiences in the chosen occupation which may or may not be supervised by a teacher, coordinator, or an employer. *Syn.* **occupational experience education;** *see* **cooperative education.**

work experience program: *see* **program, work experience.**

work experience program, cooperative: *syn.* **cooperative education.**

work, group: *see* **group work.**

work habit: procedure in learning activities that, through repeated use, has been established or has become semiautomatic or automatic.

work, illegal: in school law, those occupations in which youths are forbidden by state or Federal legislation to participate and which vary according to the age of the youth and according to the state in which he lives.

work, independent: *see* **independent work.**

work-limit test: *see* **test, work-limit.**

work load: (1) the intensity of work, usually expressed in terms of foot-pounds or kilogram-meters of work per minute; sometimes expressed in terms of the oxygen requirement per minute; (2) *syn.* **load, teaching.**

work load, teacher: *see* **load, teaching.**

work, office: *syn.* **clerical work.**

work period: *see* **period, work.**

work period, independent: *see* **period, independent work.**

work permit: a legal authorization permitting a child to work, and in this respect synonymous with *age-and-schooling certificate* but frequently less stringent.

work processes, schedule of: *see* **schedule of work processes.**

work, pupil-personnel: *syn.* **guidance.**

work record, distributive education: a form used to record dates of employment, hours worked, salary earned, and other data concerned with cooperative part-time students in distributive education.

work-sample test: *see* **test, work-sample.**

work skill, higher level: *see* **skill, higher level work.**

work, social: *see* **social work.**

work, social group: *see* **group work, social.**

work station: (1) *see* **station, work;** (2) (bus. ed.) *see* **station, training.**

work, student-personnel: *see* **student-personnel work.**

work-study-play school: *syn.* **platoon school;** *see* **Gary plan.**

work-study program: *see* **program, work-study.**

work-study program, college: *see* **program, college work-study.**

work-type reader: *see* **reader, work-type.**

work-type reading: *see* **reading, work-type.**

work unit: *see* **unit, learning.**

work, unit of: *syn.* **unit** (3).

work week: the total number of days or hours each week during which the teacher or other employee of the school system is at work.

work, welfare: *see* **welfare work.**

workbook: (1) a study or learning guide for pupils, often related to a particular textbook or to several textbooks; may contain exercises, problems, practice materials, directions for use, space for recording answers, and, frequently, means of evaluating the work done; (2) a supplementary or preparatory exercise or practice book in reading, used to give additional training not found in basic reading materials.

workbook, programmed: information in booklet form that has been prepared for students to do individual work in a subject; designed to reinforce previously taught information; the situation or problem is given, and after the student supplies an answer, he looks in the back of this booklet to check it; if he is correct, then and only then does he go to the next step; otherwise he goes back and tries working it again; the steps for presenting content and questions are in predetermined sequences.

worker, attendance: *see* **attendance worker.**

worker, curriculum: *syn.* **curriculum specialist.**

worker, distributive: a person employed in a distributive organization such as a retail, wholesale, or service establishment.

worker, entry: a person entering a particular occupation for the first time at a beginning level with minimum training, skills, and knowledge needed for average performance in a specific job-worker situation.

worker, guidance: *see* **guidance worker.**

worker, junior: a student employee under the distributive education cooperative part-time training program who is working in one of various retail, wholesale, or service establishments.

worker, personnel: *see* **pupil-personnel worker.**

worker, psychiatric social: *see* **social worker, psychiatric.**

worker, pupil-personnel: *see* **pupil-personnel worker.**

worker, school social: *syn.* **visiting teacher.**

worker, student: *syn.* **trainee, student.**

workers' education: instruction for mature workers developed especially in the United States and England by colleges, universities, and trade and industrial unions, chiefly for the benefit of union members; usually emphasizes labor economics and industrial relations. *See* **Workers' Educational Association** (Education in England and Wales); *comp. w.* **institute, workers'.**

workers' institute: *see* **institute, workers'.**

working capacity, physical: *see* **capacity, physical working.**

working capital: a reserve set aside, usually out of surplus, to finance such items as receivables and inventories.

working capital fund: *see* **fund, working capital.**

working hours: (voc. ed.) the specific hours during the day which are set for the worker while on the job. *See* **hours of work.**

working mean: *syn.* **average, guessed.**

working origin: *syn.* **origin, arbitrary.**

working process: (art ed.) the mental as well as physical activity in which the creator becomes involved when producing creatively. (In art education the process is of greater importance than the final product.)

working system, cognitive: *see* **cognitive working system.**

workmanship: technical skill applied to the execution of a piece of work.

workmen's compensation, teacher's: payments made to a teacher by his employer for an injury incurred, not necessarily arising out of the duties of the employment.

workprint: any picture or sound track print, usually a positive, intended for use in the editing process to establish through a series of trial cuttings the finished version of a film; the purpose is to preserve the original intact and undamaged until the cutting points have been established.

Works Progress Administration (WPA): a governmental work relief program established in 1935 for youth between the ages of 16 and 25 through which the Federal government cooperated with local communities in the construction of public buildings such as school plants.

worksheet: a form designed for the rapid and efficient recording of data, such as a form used for problem analysis.

workshop: an instructional method in which persons with common interests and problems meet with appropriate specialists to acquire necessary information and develop solutions through group study; usually residential and of several days' duration.

workshop, aerospace education: an aerospace educational program offered either for university credit or as a noncredit in-service course ranging in length of time from a few days to 5 or 6 weeks; usually a full-time program for teachers, it includes aerospace lectures and seminars with discussions of general aviation and space technology and their economic, political, and social effects; additional activities are science laboratories, flight laboratories, field trips to aerospace industries, airports, Air Force bases, and other aerospace installations; also includes professional activities in the development, coordination, and integration of aerospace insights and materials into the various areas of the school program.

workshop, art: a place for carrying on art activities, providing opportunity for students to explore the fields of the creative arts largely according to their major interests, without any set program.

workshop, career: (couns.) time set aside when students are provided with the opportunity to acquire practical information about jobs or training institutions directly from the persons in the community who know most about them; presents information on careers of interest and on local employment opportunities to the majority of the student body and provides an opportunity for students to meet and converse with the business and industrial leaders of the community who may be their future employers. *See* **career day.**

workshop, curative: a facility for the handicapped which is oriented specifically toward training and rehabilitation; generally provides both recreational and vocational services.

workshop, foreign language: a meeting of teachers of a foreign language, often in connection with a university summer session, where suggested solutions to problems in teaching the language are the subject of lectures, discussions, and demonstrations through the use of a model class of children; new techniques are demonstrated in concrete situations and opportunities are given to the workshop participants to put them into practice.

workshop, home: a space or room at home, equipped for constructional, mechanical, and allied activities, for the purpose of maintaining the home and its equipment or serving recreational and/or vocational interests.

workshop, mathematics: *syn.* **laboratory, mathematics.**

workshop, occupational: a specialized facility for occupational evaluation, training, counseling, and job placement; may provide internal term employment.

workshop, pupils': a place where pupils engage in activities specifically planned and organized by themselves under teacher guidance.

workshop, radio: a study group having as its purpose the application of theories to the actual production and utilization of broadcasts; may be connected with a college or university or with a public school system; sometimes regarded as a part of the curriculum, carrying academic credit, and sometimes as an extraclass activity.

workshop, sheltered: a nonprofit workshop conducted for the purpose of providing remunerative employment or rehabilitating activity for various physically, emotionally, and mentally handicapped workers suited for competitive employment; may provide for vocational evaluation and training.

world affairs education: curriculum and processes aimed at helping students develop the capacities to observe, analyze, evaluate, and participate in the global affairs of man and aiding them to view the world as a social system.

World Confederation of Organizations of the Teaching Profession (WCOTP): an international organization formed in 1952 by the merger of the World Organization of the Teaching Profession, International Federation of Teachers Associations, and the International Federation of Secondary Teachers; consists of a federation of 146 national organizations in 90 countries; aims to promote, through education, international understanding and goodwill, to improve teaching methods and professional training of teachers, to defend the rights of teachers, and to promote closer relationships between teachers in different countries.

world court: an international organization of judges and accompanying institutional forms for hearing cases presented from all over the world, primarily for the purpose of settling disputes between nations; reference is often made to the particular institution of this type that exists at The Hague, Netherlands, known as the Permanent Court of International Justice.

world history: *see* **history, world.**

world technique: a projective technique for differentiating retarded or neurotic from normal children, according to which the child is presented with 150 objects for constructing a town, village, farm, zoo, etc., and observations are made of his behavior.

worth, individual: (couns.) the concept that each person is of value.

worthy home membership: *see* **home membership, worthy.**

wow: a periodic disturbance in sound from a tape or record player; usually caused by regular variations in angular velocity of some mechanical component of the system. *See* **flutter.**

WPA: *see* **Works Progress Administration.**

WPM: (words per minute) in typewriting, speed of typewriting words per minute, each word averaging five strokes or spaces; in shorthand, speed of dictating or writing shorthand, each word having an average syllable intensity of 1.4.

WPPSI: *see* **scale, Wechsler.**

wrestling: an athletic contest between two individuals who start in an upright position and attempt to pin the shoulders of each other to the mat for one second.

wrist movement: a handwriting movement in which the emphasis is placed on the free movement of the hand, with the wrist joint as the pivot.

writ: a court order in written form.

write: in data processing, to store a number on the surface of a magnetic tape, a magnetic drum, or a cathode ray tube.

writing: the graphic representation of a language that follows some systematic order; pictures or graphic symbols are not considered a form of writing unless they form part of a system that can be grasped by any reader familiar with the system.

writing approach: a science-type learning of shorthand in which early writing is emphasized; an inductive-deductive writing approach through word lists, rules of joinings and abbreviating devices, and accuracy practices.

writing, ataxic (ə·tak′sik): the writing of one whose movements are characterized by spasmodic, irregular jerks and lack of motor coordination, owing to a pathological motor condition.

writing, automatic: (1) writing executed while the writer is in an unconscious state, as in a trance or under hypnosis; (2) writing executed skillfully, so that ideas may be recorded in an easy, fluent, and legible form without the attention being distracted by the writing process; acquired as a result of matured, habituated, muscular coordination; (3) (art) spontaneous and rapid drawing and painting by which the artist attempts to use chance effects for the discovery of new imagery; used principally by some of the early surrealists in a search for subconscious expression.

writing, backhand: writing that has a slope of less than 90 degrees with the preceding line of writing, with the up- and downstrokes extending to the left of the vertical above the line and to the right of the vertical below the line.

writing, blind: writing executed without the use of visual guides; usually refers to writing with the eyes closed or blindfolded (to relieve tension), though it may be used to designate the writing of those who lack vision.

writing, business: the style of writing commonly recommended and practiced for commercial purposes.

writing chart, creative: *see* **chart, creative writing.**

writing, coordinated: handwriting that shows smooth curves and transitions between arcs of curves, with no wavering of line or angularities, being indicative of a well-organized and -controlled interplay of the muscles of the arm, fingers, and wrist.

writing, creative: original prose or poetry composed by children and young people.

writing, cursive: writing that is characterized by running or flowing lines, with strokes joined within the word and angles rounded. *Syn.* **running writing;** *contr. w.* **printscript; writing, manuscript.**

writing, demotic: a simplified and cursive form of Egyptian hieroglyphic writing. *See* **hieroglyphics; writing, hieratic.**

writing devices, braille: equipment for the embossing of raised dots used in the braille system such as a slate and stylus or a *braillewriter.*

writing, dextral: writing done with the right hand.

writing, dictation test of: *see* **test of writing, dictation.**

writing, expository: writing which is designed to set forth or explain as distinguished from narrative writing or argumentation.

writing, foot: writing executed by the use of the feet, with the writing instrument held by the toes; sometimes performed as a trick of skill, but more frequently having practical values for those deprived of their arms.

writing, functional: a composition written to meet a specific purpose, such as a letter or a report; ordinarily used to indicate practical, factual prose.

writing, hieratic: an abridged and somewhat cursive form of Egyptian hieroglyphic writing which in later use was reserved for religious writings. *See* **hieroglyphics; writing, demotic.**

writing, illegible: handwriting that cannot be read or that can be read only with great difficulty owing to defects of form or construction.

writing, italic: a form of handwriting, a modification of an early style used in writing manuscripts; has received considerable attention in Great Britain.

writing, manuscript: handwriting that makes use of adaptations of the printed letter forms, as in printscript, but that permits of more ornamentation and free strokes than are used in the latter. *See* **printscript;** *contr. w.* **writing, cursive.**

writing, mirror: *syn.* **mirror script.**

writing posture: the position of the writer's body with regard to his seat, desk or table, and writing surface.

writing rate: the speed of handwriting, usually measured in terms of the number of letters written per minute.

writing, running: *syn.* **writing, cursive.**

writing school: a type of school, developed in America during the eighteenth century, in which writing and arithmetic were taught.

writing, timed: typewriting of straight copy or other material for a definite period of time to determine typewriting speed.

writing vocabulary: *see* **vocabulary, writing.**

written assignment: *see* **assignment, written.**

written problem: *see* **problem, written.**

written recall: *see* **recall, written.**

wrong answer, plausible: *syn.* **distractor.**

Wunderkind (vo͞on′də·kint): (Ger., lit., "wonderchild") *pl.* Wunderkinder (-kin′də); a child prodigy. *See* **prodigy.**

X-knee: knock-knee.

X punch: *see* **punch, X.**

x-ray representation: *see* **representation, x-ray.**

xenomania (zen′ō·mā′ni·ə): an unreasonable predilection for institutions, customs, and fashions that are foreign.

xenophobia (zen′ō·fō′bi·ə): an unreasonable fear of meeting strangers.

xerography: a dry copying process; a printing process that uses electrically charged particles to make a positive photographic contact print.

XYZ grouping: *syn.* **grouping, tripartite.**

Y punch: *see* punch, Y.

Y-Teens: an organization for high school girls sponsored jointly by the school and the YWCA; members are between the ages of 12 and 18 years; purpose is to promote understanding among girls of all races and religions; formerly called Girl Reserves.

Yale frustration-aggression hypothesis: *see* frustration-aggression hypothesis, Yale.

yardstick method: a procedure for constructing a high school schedule in which strips of cardboard of varying length or sticks (frequently yardsticks) are employed for the quick discovery of conflicts in student programs.

yarmelke (yär'mel·ke): *n. masc.; pl.* **yarmelkes** (yär'mel·kes); (Yiddish) *see* kippah.

yarn picture: a creative handcraft in which colored yarns are stitched to cloth to produce a picture or design. Needlepoint and crewel embroidery are techniques often used for this purpose.

Yates correction: *syn.* correction for continuity.

Yates correction for continuity: *see* correction for continuity.

year, academic: *see* academic year.

year, ecclesiastical: a period of time beginning with the fourth Sunday before Christmas; it is divided into seasons during which the Christian church commemorates the life and works of Christ.

year, fiscal: *see* fiscal year.

year, school: *see* school year.

yearbook: *syn.* annual.

yearbook, offset: *syn.* annual, offset.

yes-no test: *see* test, yes-no.

yeshivah (ye·shē'vä): *n. fem.; pl.* **yeshivot** (ye·shē'vōt); (Heb., lit., "session") (1) an institution for advanced study of talmudic and rabbinic law, with the authority to ordain qualified students for the rabbinate; (2) in the United States, this term also refers to an Orthodox Jewish elementary day school, known as *yeshivah ketana.*

Yiddish school: a Jewish school in which the language of instruction is Yiddish and which emphasizes primarily the study of the Yiddish language and literature. *See* **Arbeiter Ring Shule; Farband Shule; secular school, Jewish; Sholom Aleichem school.**

yield basis: *see* basis, yield.

yield, bond: *see* bond yield.

YMW program: *see* program, YMW.

yo-he-ho theory: the theory that language had its origins in the spontaneous vocalizations of primitive man while engaged in cooperative enterprises such as lifting or moving heavy objects.

Yoakam readability formula: *see* readability formula, Yoakam.

yoga: an ascetic practice, involving concentration and controlled physical posture, originating in Hinduism and diffusing to some Western circles, both secular and Christian; aims to provide complete control over mind and body.

young-farmer class: *see* class, young-farmer.

young-farmer group: a local organization of persons enrolled in part-time classes in vocational agriculture; devoted mainly to social and recreational activities.

young men's and women's program: *see* program, YMW.

youth: (1) a collective term for young people; (2) the period of life from puberty to maturity, usually from 12 or 13 to 21 years; may vary for each individual; (3) an individual of an age falling within this range.

Youth Corps, Neighborhood: *see* Neighborhood Youth Corps.

youth culture: *see* subculture.

youth, disadvantaged: *see* child, disadvantaged.

youth fellowship: a group of church-related young people who ordinarily meet together on a regular basis under church auspices for study, prayer, social service, and recreation.

youth group, rural: *see* rural youth group.

youth hostel: (1) a residence for students; (2) a type of low-cost lodging place for traveling young people, maintained by various organizations in America and in certain European countries; *see* hosteling.

youth movement: an activity or program of activities by or in behalf of the young people of a society.

youth organization: *see* organization, youth.

youth, out-of-school: *see* out-of-school youth.

youth problem: *see* problem, youth.

youth program, disadvantaged: *see* program, disadvantaged youth.

youth project, talented: *see* project, talented youth.

youth, rural: (pupil accounting) youth who reside in unincorporated areas.

youth, urban: (pupil accounting) youth who reside in population centers of 50,000 or more.

Z

Z: in handwritten work, the letter Z as distinguished from a number 2 by means of the short bar drawn across the letter.

z, Fisher's: *see* **Fisher's z.**

z score: a standard score in which the deviation of a raw score from the mean is expressed as a multiple of the standard deviation and the direction of its deviation by a positive or negative sign; may be expressed as, $z = \dfrac{X - M}{\sigma}$, where X = raw score, M = mean, and σ = standard deviation. *See* **score, standard.**

z transformation: *syn.* **Fisher's z.**

Zaner-Bloser handwriting system: *see* **handwriting system, Zaner-Bloser.**

Zeigarnik effect: *see* **effect, Zeigarnik.**

Zeitgeist (tsīt'gīst): (Ger., lit., "time spirit") (1) the spirit of the time; trend of taste and culture of a time; (2) (pol. philos., especially Hegelian) the consciousness that evolves out of the synthesis of communal and individual experience; the universal and moral order.

Zend-Avesta (zend'ə·ves'tə): a collection of all extant documents containing the sacred writings of the religion of Zoroaster, still the Bible and prayer book of the Parsis; it consists of the Yasna, the Vispered, the Vendidad, and the Khordah-Avesta.

zero correlation: *see* **correlation** (1).

zero discrimination: *see* **discrimination, zero.**

zero-G training: *see* **training, zero-G.**

zero gain: *see* **gain** (3).

zero group: *see* **group, zero.**

zero-group technique: a variation of the control-group technique in which usually three groups are used, namely, (*a*) the zero group, (*b*) the control group, and (*c*) the experimental group. [Following this technique, in an experiment to determine the relative merits of two methods of teaching, the zero group would be given a pretest and an end test but would receive no instruction; the control group would be given a pretest, instruction by one method, and an end test; the experimental group would be given a pretest, instruction by a second method, and an end test; the mean gain of the zero group (which may be interpreted as being due to maturation or practice effect or to factors other than those relating to specific instruction) would be taken as the zero point from which the effects of the treatments introduced in the control and experimental groups might be expressed in terms of percentage of gain or loss.]

zero loading: *see* **loading, zero.**

zero order: (referring to correlation coefficient, alienation coefficient, regression coefficient, etc.) having no secondary subscripts; based on two variables; for example, r_{12}, k_{25}, and b_{94} are all of zero order.

zero-order correlation: *syn.* **correlation, total.**

zero-order correlation coefficient: *syn.* **coefficient, total correlation.**

zero point: on a scale, the point separating positive scale values from negative scale values; may be arbitrary, that is, assigned according to convenience, or absolute, that is, having unique significance in reality.

zero population growth: a state of population stability in which the total number of deaths per unit of population equals the total number of births per unit of population.

zero transfer: *see* **transfer, zero.**

zoanthropy (zō·an'thrə·pi): a delusion that one has been changed into a beast or has been given the nature of a beast.

zone punch: *syn.* **overpunch.**

zone, transition: *see* **transition zone.**

zoning: a set of regulations governing land use of an incorporated or especially designated area.

zoom lens: *see* **lens, zoom.**

zoophobia (zō'ō·fō'bi·ə): an unreasonable fear of animals, usually harmless ones.

EDUCATION IN CANADA*

COORDINATOR: E. BROCK RIDEOUT, Ontario Institute for Studies in Education

A license: *see* **license, A.**

act: the designation of a piece of legislation passed by the Parliament of Canada or by a provincial legislature after it has received the assent of the Governor-General or the Lieutenant-Governor; examples are the Public Schools Act, the Cities Act. *See* **bill.**

administrator, business: *see* **business administrator.**

adviser, technical: (Que.) *see* **regional bureau.**

advisory board: (Man.) an advisory body required to consider and report on educational matters submitted to it by the minister of education and empowered to consider and report on other educational matters as it deems fit; known in Saskatchewan as the *educational council,* in Prince Edward Island as the *council of education,* and in Newfoundland as the *general advisory committee;* usually consists of both professional educators and laymen. *See* **advisory committee, general;** *dist. f.* **council of public instruction;** *comp. w.* **superior council of education.**

advisory committee, general: (Nfld.) a statutory advisory body required to consider, and make recommendations to the *Lieutenant-Governor in Council* concerning existing educational policy and the initiation of new policy; composed of the *Minister,* the *deputy minister,* the assistant deputy minister, the executive secretaries of the *denominational educational committees,* the heads of the various divisions of the *department of education,* and two members appointed by the Lieutenant-Governor in Council: one a representative of the Faculty of Education of the Memorial University of Newfoundland and the other of the Newfoundland Teachers' Association. *Comp. w.* **advisory board; superior council of education.**

aid to education, Federal: *see* **Federal aid to education.**

allowance, family: *see* **family allowance.**

allowance, youth: *see* **youth allowance.**

amalgamated school board: (1) (Nfld.) formerly a school board formed by the amalgamation of two or more denominational school boards in the same geographical area for the purpose of administering the schools of the amalgamating boards; usually united various Protestant denominations; now obsolete; *see* **district, integrated;** (2) (N.S.) a school board formed by the amalgamation of two or more existing school boards in the same geographical region and with a common area of interest; administers the schools of the amalgamating boards, the existing boards being eliminated; has jurisdiction over at least 10,000 pupils and operates or has access to a vocational school.

area superintendent, municipal: (Ont.) a supervisor of instruction employed by a *board of education* or *separate school board;* responsible to the board through the *director of education* or *superintendent of separate schools,* respectively. *Dist. f.* **area superintendent, provincial.**

area superintendent, provincial: (Ont.) formerly school inspector; now largely replaced by locally employed directors and superintendents; those remaining are usually attached to a regional office and are chiefly concerned with public school sections and separate school zones not included in a school division or county district combined separate school zone. *See* **inspector, school;** *dist. f.* **area superintendent, municipal.**

assistant superintendent of business affairs: *see* **business administrator** (1).

assistant superintendent of schools: (Que.) *syn.* **director of studies;** *see* **inspector, school.**

associate institution: *see* **private school.**

Atlantic Institute of Education: a proposed (1969) body corporate of the *Atlantic provinces* to promote cooperation among all institutions concerned with the education of teachers and to have authority to grant degrees, diplomas, and certificates in education; it is to be governed by the Academic Council of the Institute under the terms of the Atlantic Institute of Education Act; its creation is subject to acceptance by two or more of the Atlantic provinces.

Atlantic provinces: *see* **provinces, Atlantic.**

Atlantic Provinces Examining Board: a body composed of representatives of the universities and teachers' organizations of the four *Atlantic provinces* and of the *departments of education* of Nova Scotia and Prince Edward Island, which sets and marks high-school examinations; the examinations are at the *junior matriculation* and *senior matriculation* levels and are used by some private schools in New Brunswick as well as by the provincial school systems of Nova Scotia (senior matriculation level only) and Prince Edward Island (junior matriculation level only), in lieu of *departmental examinations. See* **provincial examinations.**

auxiliary class: (obs.), *see* **class, special** (1) (*see* main section of the Dictionary).

B. Ed. (bachelor of education): (1) (B.C., Alta., Sask., Que. Protestant) a first degree in education; *comp. w.* **B. Paed.** (2); (2) (Man., Ont., N.S., B.C. [1944–1956]) usually a second degree, indicating completion of a first bachelor's degree plus 1 or 2 years of teacher education; (3) (Nfld.) either (1) or (2).

B. Paed. (bachelor of pedagogy): (1) (Ont.) a graduate professional degree in education formerly granted by the Ontario College of Education after approximately 1 year of study to holders of a recognized bachelor's degree who have approved teacher-training and professional experience; (2) (Que.) an undergraduate degree granted by French-language universities to (*a*) a student who has successfully completed a 4-year program in academic and professional studies or (*b*) a student who has received a *diploma (brevet) class A* on completion of a 4-year program in a *normal school. Dist. f.* **B. Ped.**

B. Ped. (bachelor of pedagogy): (Man.) a degree granted to holders of a teaching certificate who have completed third-year university work (including the professional content required of a *B.Ed.);* when an approved first degree has been awarded, may be surrendered for a *B.Ed. See* **B.Ed.;** *dist. f.* **B. Paed.**

B. T. (bachelor of teaching): (1) (N.B.) a professional first degree granted to a teacher who completes a special 4-year university course (after *junior matriculation*); granted in three grades: elementary, industrial, and commercial; usually approximately 2 years' credit toward the 4-year course may be obtained by completion of a 2-year training program for industrial, commercial, or home economics teachers operated by the provincial *department of education;* (2) (Man.) a professional first degree in education granted to a person who completes a 3-year university course (after *senior matriculation*); designed especially for elementary-school teachers.

---

*Educational terms have not been included as entries in those cases where Canadian usage is the same as that defined in the main section of this dictionary.

bilingual school: a school in which French and English are in daily use for purposes of instruction.

bill: the term used, followed by a number, to refer to a proposed *act* of the Parliament of Canada or of a provincial legislature from the time it is introduced until it has received the assent of the Governor-General or the Lieutenant-Governor; for example, Bill 44, an act to amend the Secondary Schools and Boards of Education Act.

B.N.A. Act: The British North America Act, 1867, by which the Dominion of Canada came into being, and section 93 of which gives to the provinces exclusive power to make laws with respect to education; Canada's constitution.

board, advisory: *see* **advisory board.**

board, amalgamated school: *see* **amalgamated school board.**

board chairman: a school trustee (or commissioner in Quebec) who presides at meetings of the school board and has certain other duties as defined by statute. *See* **board of school commissioners; board of school trustees.**

board, divisional: *see* **divisional board.**

board of arbitration: (1) (Man.) a body appointed by the *Lieutenant-Governor in Council* to arbitrate disputes between teachers and trustees when, in the opinion of the minister, the dispute cannot be successfully settled by a *board of conciliation;* decision is binding on both parties; *comp. w.* **board of reference** (1); (2) (Sask.) a body appointed by the Minister to arbitrate disputes between teacher and trustee negotiation area salary committees; consists of a nominee of the school board area committee, a nominee of the teacher area committee, and a third person either nominated by the above-mentioned two nominees or by the minister, except that, if the committees agree to nominate jointly a single person, the minister appoints that person as the board.

board of conciliation: (Man.) a body appointed by the *Minister of Education* to settle disputes between teachers and the board of trustees of a *school district* or *school division. See* **board of arbitration** (1).

board of education: (1) (Ont.) a school board administering both public elementary and secondary education; *dist. f.* **public school board; separate school board;** (2) in other provinces, a term sometimes used unofficially as synonymous with *board of school trustees, public school board, school board,* etc., to signify the local education authority.

board of education, county: *see* **county board of education.**

board of education, district: *see* **district board of education.**

board of education, divisional: *see* **divisional board of education.**

board of reference: (1) (Alta., Ont., B.C., Nfld., Sask.) a statutory body to which are submitted disputes relating to the dismissal of a teacher by a board or the termination of a contract by a teacher; has power to direct the continuance or discontinuance of the contract; in Alberta, consists of three members appointed by the *Lieutenant-Governor in Council;* in Ontario, consists of a judge appointed by the *minister of education,* one appointee of the teacher, and one of the school board; in British Columbia, consists of a chairman nominated by the Chief Justice of the Province, one appointee nominated by the Provincial Teachers' Association, and one by the Provincial Trustees' Association; considers only appeals by teachers against dismissal, suspension, or transfer, referred to it by the *Council of Public Instruction* and recommends action to the latter; in Newfoundland, consists of a member of a school board, other than the employing board, appointed by the Minister, a member appointed by the Provincial Teachers' Association, and a chairman appointed by the other two members; in Saskatchewan, consists of a chairman nominated by the Attorney-General, a nominee of the teacher and a nominee of the board, all of whom are appointed by the *minister of education;* may make such order as in its opinion the circumstances warrant; *comp. w.* **board of arbitration** (1); (2) (Man.) a statutory body which deals with the transfer of land from one school district or school division to another.

board of school commissioners: (1) (Que.) generally the elected local education authority for the religious majority in the *school municipality; comp. w.* **board of school trustees;** (2) (N.S.) the name given to the local education authority of a city or town; usually composed of three appointees of the city or town council and two appointees of the *Lieutenant-Governor in Council.*

board of school trustees: (1) (Que.) the elected local education authority for the religious minority in the *school municipality; dist. f.* **board of school commissioners;** (2) in other provinces, roughly synonymous with the terms "school board" and "board of education." (The term "trustees" is used throughout all the provinces except Quebec to denote members of the local *school board.*)

board, public school: *see* **public school board.**

board, school: *see* **school board.**

board, separate school: *see* **separate school board.**

brevet: *see* **Class I diploma; Class II diploma; diploma Class A; diploma Class B.**

bureau régional: (Fr.) *see* **regional bureau.**

business administrator: (Ont.) (1) the officer of a school board directly responsible for its business affairs (plant, transportation of pupils, financial matters, etc.); sometimes called *superintendent* or *assistant superintendent of business affairs;* usually subordinate to, though sometimes coordinate with, the *director of education* or *superintendent of separate schools;* called *business manager* in Newfoundland, and *secretary-treasurer* in British Columbia; (2) an official of the department of education attached to a *regional office,* who represents the *department of education* in dealings with the boards of the region relating to school business matters (site and building approvals, *provincial grants,* attendance records, transportation contracts, etc.); usually called *regional business administrator.*

business manager: (Nfld.) *see* **business administrator** (1).

CAAT: *see* **college of applied arts and technology.**

canton: (Que.) *see* **township** (2).

Catholic committee (comité catholique): (Que.) a statutory body composed of five representatives each of the Catholic Church, teachers, and parents; makes regulations, with respect to the *Catholic system,* on all matters pertaining to religion and morals in connection with curricula, textbooks, teacher training and qualifications, diplomas, religious instruction, nomenclature of schools, etc.; its chairman (président) is ex officio a member of the *superior council of education. Comp. w.* **Protestant committee.**

Catholic system: informal term for that part of the system of public education in the province of Quebec that is under the direction of Catholics; consists of those *regional school boards, boards of school commissioners,* and *boards of school trustees,* and the schools they administer, that are under the direction of Catholics, together with the *Catholic committee* and those teacher-training institutions that prepare teachers for the Catholic schools. *See* **dissent; dissentient school; Protestant committee.**

CEGEP: (Que.) (Eng. sē'jep; Fr. sä·zhep′) universally used acronym for Collège d'Enseignement Général et Professionel (General and Vocational College); a two- or three-year postsecondary institution providing both preuniversity and vocational courses; normally follows the fifth year of secondary education (kind. + 6 elem. + 5 sec.); corresponds in some degree with the U.S. *junior college,* or *community college,* but is administered by a public corporation with finances derived from the provincial *department of education. Comp. w.* **college of applied arts and technology; public college; regional college.**

center: (Ont.) a geographical point used in determining the boundaries of a *separate school zone;* the most northern point of the *separate school site;* a board operating more than one school has a number of centers equal to the number of schools. *See* **zone, separate school.**

central Canada: *see* **provinces, central.**

central education authority: the policy-making authority in education at the provincial level; in most provinces the *Lieutenant-Governor in Council;* in British Columbia, the *council of public instruction.*

central provinces: *see* **provinces, central.**

certificate 1: (P.E.I.) a teaching certificate valid for grades 1 to 10; indicates completion of 2 years of teacher education beyond *junior matriculation;* made permanent after 2 years of successful teaching. *Comp. w.* **diploma Class B; elementary school teacher's certificate, standard 1; first class certificate; teaching license.**

certificate 2: (P.E.I.) *see* **standard certificate.**

certificate 3: (P.E.I.) a teaching certificate valid for grades 1 to 10; indicates completion of 4 years of education, including teacher education, beyond *junior matriculation;* made permanent after 2 years of successful teaching; corresponds to elementary-school teacher's certificate, standard 3, of Ontario.

certificate 4: (P.E.I.) *see* **certificate IV.**

certificate 5: (P.E.I.) *see* **certificate V.**

certificate 6: (P.E.I.) *see* **certificate VI.**

certificate A, standard: (Sask.) *see* **standard certificate A.**

certificate, Class I: (Que.) *syn.* **Class I diploma.**

certificate, Class II: (Que.) *syn.* **Class II diploma;** *see* **diploma (brevet), Class B.**

certificate, conditional: *see* **conditional certificate.**

certificate, first class: *see* **first class certificate.**

certificate, Grade I: (Nfld.) *see* **Grade I certificate.**

certificate, Grade II: *see* **Grade II certificate.**

certificate, Grade III: *see* **standard certificate A.**

certificate, Grade IV: (Nfld.) *see* **certificate IV.**

certificate, Grade V: (Nfld.) *see* **Grade V certificate.**

certificate, Grade VI: (Nfld.) *see* **certificate VI.**

certificate, Grade VII: (Nfld.) *see* **Grade VII certificate.**

certificate, high school assistant's: *see* **high school assistant's certificate.**

certificate, high school specialist's: *see* **high school specialist's certificate.**

certificate III: (N.B.) *see* **standard certificate A.**

certificate IV: (N.B.) a teaching certificate valid for all grades; indicates possession of an approved university degree; signifies completion of at least 4 years of education, including teacher education, beyond *junior matriculation;* called *certificate 4* in Prince Edward Island, and *Grade IV certificate* in Newfoundland; permanent when issued. *Comp. w.* **Class I diploma; diploma Class A; professional certificate.**

certificate, professional: *see* **professional certificate.**

certificate, provisional: *see* **provisional certificate.**

certificate, standard: *see* **standard certificate.**

certificate V: (N.B.) a teaching certificate valid for all grades; indicates completion of a minimum of 5 years of education beyond *junior matriculation;* signifies the possession of a postgraduate degree or equivalent; permanent when issued; called *certificate 5* in Prince Edward Island. *Comp. w.* **Grade V certificate; professional certificate.**

certificate VI: (N.B.) a teaching certificate valid for all grades; indicates completion of a master's degree by the holder of a *certificate V;* usually signifies at least 6 years of study beyond *junior matriculation;* permanent when issued; corresponds with *teaching certificate, Class VI,* of Nova Scotia, *certificate 6* of Prince Edward Island, and *Grade VI certificate* of Newfoundland.

certification committee, teachers': *see* **teachers' certification committee.**

chairman, board: *see* **board chairman.**

chancellor: the titular head of a university in some provinces; has chiefly ceremonial duties, the administration of the university being left to the president, the vice-chancellor, or, in French-speaking universities, the rector.

chief education officer: *see* **district superintendent** (2).

chief executive officer: (1) (Ont.) the chief education officer, through whom the other officials of a board report and who is responsible for executing the policies and programs of the board; the *director of education* in the case of a *board of education* and the *superintendent of separate schools* in the case of a *separate school board;* (2) (B.C.) used in the same sense as in Ontario but refers to a *district superintendent* of schools who has been designated as an executive officer by the *board of school trustees.*

chief inspector: (obs.), *syn.* **superintendent of schools, chief.**

chief superintendent of schools: *see* **superintendent of schools, chief.**

city school division: *see* **defined city.**

class, auxiliary: (obs.), *see* **class, special** (1) (*see* main section of the Dictionary).

Class I certificate: (Que.) *syn.* **Class I diploma.**

Class I diploma (brevet): (Que., Protestant system) a teaching certificate issued by the *department of education;* indicates that the holder has an approved first degree and 1 year of professional studies, or a *B.Ed.* degree; requires a minimum of 4 years of education beyond *junior matriculation;* valid for teaching in elementary and secondary grades; made permanent after 2 years of successful teaching. *Syn.* **Class I certificate;** *comp. w.* **certificate IV; diploma (brevet) Class A; professional certificate.**

Class II certificate: (Que.) *syn.* **Class II diploma;** *see* **diploma (brevet) Class B.**

Class II diploma: (Que.) *see* **diploma Class B.**

classical college (collège classique): (Que.) a private 8-year college to which students are usually admitted on completion of elementary school; through affiliation with a university, its graduates obtain bachelor's degrees in classical studies; supported in part by public funds.

collège classique: (Que.) *see* **classical college.**

Collège d'Enseignement Général et Professionel: *see* **CEGEP.**

college, district: *see* **regional college.**

college, general and vocational: (Que.) *see* **CEGEP.**

college of applied arts and technology (CAAT): (Ont.) one of a network of postsecondary institutions designed primarily to serve two classes of students: (*a*) graduates of high schools not wishing to attend university and (*b*) adults and out-of-school youth; under the administration of a board of governors but completely financed by the provinces; called *institute of technology* in some provinces. *Comp. w.* **CEGEP; public college; regional college.**

college, public: *see* **public college.**

college, regional: *see* **regional college.**

college, teachers': *see* **teachers' college.**

collegiate institute: a high school meeting certain minimum standards as to number and qualifications of teachers. (Although the term is still used, particularly in Ontario, it is of less significance than before 1920.)

combined separate school zone: *see* **zone, combined separate school.**

combined separate school zone, county: *see* **zone, county combined separate school.**

combined separate school zone, district: *see* **zone, district combined separate school.**

comité catholique: *see* **Catholic committee.**

commission scolaire régionale: *see* **school board, regional.**

committee, Catholic: *see* **Catholic committee.**

committee, denominational educational: *see* **denominational educational committee.**

committee, general advisory: *see* **advisory committee, general.**

committee, Protestant: *see* **Protestant committee.**

committee, teachers' certification: *see* **teachers' certification committee.**

composite school: a secondary school offering both the general, academic, or university entrance course and one or more commercial, technical, or other vocational courses; considered as 2 or more specialized schools under one administration. *See* **comprehensive school.**

comprehensive school: a secondary school offering individual programs of study with selections possible from general, academic, commercial, technical, and vocational options; staff and students are identified with school rather than with course; provides more flexibility in course structure than is customary in a *composite school. See* **polyvalent.**

conditional certificate: (Alta.) a teaching certificate valid for all grades in the province; indicates completion of 2 years of teacher education beyond *senior matriculation;* on completion of an additional year, becomes a *provisional certificate,* and on completion of the *bachelor of education* and 2 years of successful teaching, becomes a permanent *professional certificate. Comp. w.* **standard certificate A.**

conseil supérieur de l'éducation: *see* **superior council of education.**

consolidated school district: *see* **school district, consolidated.**

consultant, program: *see* **program consultant.**

coordinator, regional: *see* **regional bureau.**

council, county: *see* **county council.**

council, educational: (Sask.) *see* **advisory board.**

council, municipal: *see* **municipal council.**

council of education: (1) (Nfld.) a constituent part of the *department of education,* coordinate in responsibility with the *deputy minister of education;* composed of the minister, deputy minister, and the five denominational *superintendents of education;* the authority, subject to the minister, for all educational policy dealing with school boards, schools, and teachers under the Education Act; operates by unanimous consent, each superintendent thus having veto power; *dist. f.* **advisory board; council of public instruction;** *comp. w.* **superior council of education;** (2) (P.E.I.) *see* **advisory board.**

council of public instruction: (B.C.) the *central education authority* of the province, composed of the *minister of education* and the other members of the executive council (cabinet). *See* **Lieutenant-Governor in Council.**

county: (1) (Ont.) an intermediate unit of municipal government composed of the towns, villages, and townships, but not the cities and *separated towns,* located in one or more geographical counties; with the inclusion of cities and towns (except *defined cities*), constitutes the *school division* in that part of the province divided into counties; (2) (Que.) an intermediate unit of municipal government for the incorporated villages, parishes (paroisses), and townships (cantons), but not for the cities and towns, located in a geographical county; is also the basic unit of municipal government in those parts of the geographical county that are not incorporated as municipalities; (3) (Alta.) a basic unit of municipal and school government in some rural areas; *see* **county system of government;** (4) (N.S.) a political subdivision of the province, sometimes coterminous with the municipality.

county board of education: (Ont.) a school board having jurisdiction over all public elementary and secondary education in a *school division* composed of a county and all cities (except *defined cities*) and *separated towns* located within its boundaries; consists of from 14 to 20 members elected in such a way that both urban and rural areas are represented and both *public school electors* and *separate school supporters* have representation; members elected by separate school supporters do not vote on any matters exclusively affecting the public elementary schools. *Comp. w.* **district board of education.**

county combined separate school zone: *see* **zone, county combined separate school.**

county council: (1) (Ont., Que.) a governing body of a *county;* composed of designated members of the councils of the local municipalities composing the county; no longer has any significant powers or duties with respect to education; (2) (Alta.) the governing body of a *county* for all local purposes, including education; must appoint a school committee to administer the county schools; *see* **county school committee; county system of government.**

county school committee: (Alta.) a committee appointed by the county council (the local education authority) to administer the schools of the county; has all the powers of a local education authority except the power to borrow money, pass a bylaw, or do such things as are reserved to the council by a bylaw or by the *Lieutenant-Governor in Council.*

county system of government: (Alta.) a system of municipal government, patterned after the English system, in which the county council is responsible for all local

governmental functions, including education; the county council must appoint a municipal committee and a school committee to administer the municipal and school affairs of the county, respectively; fiscal control over both committees remains with the county council; the school committee may be augmented by the addition of representatives of independent districts which are then a part of the county for school purposes but not for municipal purposes; the county system of government may be adopted by a city or town, in which case the city or town is considered (for purposes of the County Act) as an *urban county. See* **county council; county school committee.**

crossing guard: a person stationed at major highway and street crossings to halt traffic so that children may cross; usually partially uniformed and carrying a whistle and "Stop" sign; usually employed by the police department on the request of the school board.

D. Paed. (doctor of pedagogy): the second, or higher, professional degree in education, formerly granted by the Ontario College of Education after approximately 1 year of study and the writing of a thesis to holders of the degree of *B. Paed.;* later replaced by the doctorate of education (Ed. D.), following completion of the *M.Ed.*

debentures, school: school bonds; issued in some provinces by the *municipal council,* in others by the local education authority; proceeds are applied to capital expenditure.

defined city: (Ont.) one of four large cities excluded by legislation from forming part of a county school division; constitutes a city school division. *See* **division, school.**

denominational educational committee: (Nfld.) one of several bodies outside of the department of education established by and representing a religious denomination or denominations; has the responsibility for making recommendations to the *Lieutenant-Governor in Council* concerning the establishment and alteration of school district boundaries, the selection and appointment of school board members, the development and administration of religious education, and the selection, training, and initial certification of teachers with respect to the schools of its particular denomination or group of denominations; required to employ an executive secretary who acts as the official channel between the committee and the minister and department and who is ex officio a member of the *general advisory committee* and of the *denominational policy commission;* the salaries of the executive secretaries, and other necessary expenses of the committees, are met in large part by provincial grants. *Comp. w.* **Catholic committee; Protestant committee.**

denominational policy commission: (Nfld.) an arm of the *department of education* composed of the *Minister* and *deputy minister of education* and the executive secretaries of the *denominational educational committees;* responsible for advising the *Lieutenant-Governor in Council* on all educational policy that affects any right or privilege of any religious denomination, particularly with respect to curriculum, textbooks, and teacher selection and training.

denominational school board: any school board operated by and for adherents of a particular religious denomination or group of religious denominations; thus any school board in Quebec or Newfoundland and any *separate school board* in Ontario, Alberta, or Saskatchewan.

department head: the chairman of a department in a *secondary school, junior high school,* or *senior public school.*

department of education: a department of the provincial civil service headed in all provinces by a *minister of education;* administers all publicly supported education; advises as to, and implements, the policy of the *central education authority.*

department of university affairs: (Ont.) a department of the provincial civil service headed by a *minister of university affairs;* administers government policies in regard to the expansion of and assistance to the universities of the province.

departmental examination: an examination set and marked by agents of the provincial *department of education;* in most provinces, used in the final year of high school; in some provinces, used in several high-school grades; now obsolete in Ontario. *See* **provincial examinations.**

deputy minister of education: a professional educator who, as the senior civil servant in the *department of education,* advises the minister on policy and administers the program drawn up by the legislature.

deputy minister of university affairs: (Ont.) the senior civil servant in the *department of university affairs;* advises the minister on policy and administers the policy of the minister.

diploma (brevet) Class A: (Que., Catholic system) a teaching certificate issued by the *department of education* indicating successful completion of at least 4 years of formal education beyond *junior matriculation;* by agreement between the department and French-language universities, results in the awarding of a *B. Paed.* degree if the education was obtained in a *normal school,* or may be granted to a *B. Paed.* graduate of a university; valid for teaching all grades of elementary and secondary school. *Comp. w.* **certificate IV; Class I diploma (brevet); professional certificate.**

diploma (brevet) Class B: (Que., Catholic system) a teaching certificate valid for grades 1 to 9; indicates completion of 2-years of teacher education beyond *junior matriculation;* called *Class II diploma (brevet)* in the Quebec Protestant system. *Comp. w.* **certificate 1; elementary school teacher's certificate, standard 1; first class certificate; teaching license.**

diploma, Class I: (Que.) *see* **Class I diploma.**

diploma, Class II: (Que.) *see* **Class I diploma; diploma Class B.**

diploma in education: (N.S.) teaching qualification obtained on completion of 3 years (junior diploma) or 4 years (senior diploma) of university study after *junior matriculation,* including a year of teacher education.

diploma, secondary school graduation: (Ont.) *see* **secondary school graduation diploma.**

diploma, specialist: (Que., Catholic system) *see* **specialist diploma.**

director-general of schools (directeur général des écoles): (Que.) the chief education officer of a *regional school board;* may have one or more *directors of studies* as his assistants. *Comp. w.* **director of education; district superintendent** (1); **divisional superintendent.**

director of education: (Ont.) the senior professional educator (chief education officer) and *chief executive officer* employed by the city, county, and district boards of education; appointment and dismissal are subject to the approval of the *minister of education;* has certain statutory powers and duties for which he is responsible to the minister as well as powers and duties delegated by his board.

director of education, regional: *see* **regional director of education.**

director of studies (directeur des études): (Que.) a professional educator employed by a *regional school board* or *board of school commissioners* to supervise the educational program of the board; used synonymously with *superintendent* or *assistant superintendent of schools. Comp. w.* **director of education; superintendent of public schools.**

director, regional: *see* **regional bureau.**

dissent: (Que.) procedure by which the Protestant or Catholic minority in a *school municipality* may establish a school or schools under its own board of trustees. *See* **board of school trustees** (1).

dissentient school (école dissidente): (Que.) a type of publicly supported school established by the religious minority, Protestant or Roman Catholic, in a *school municipality;* under the jurisdiction of an elected *board of school trustees. Comp. w.* **separate school;** *dist. f.* **parochial school.**

district board of education: (Ont.) a school board having jurisdiction over all public elementary and secondary education in a *school division* within a *territorial district,* established by *regulation* and composed of a number of cities, towns, villages, townships, and municipally unorganized territory; consists of from 5 to 20 members, depending upon population, elected in such a way that both urban and rural areas are represented and both *public school electors* and *separate school supporters* have representation; members elected by *separate sup-*

porters do not vote on any matters exclusively affecting the public elementary school. *Comp. w.* **county board of education.**

district college: *see* **regional college.**

district combined separate school zone: *see* **zone, district combined separate school.**

district, consolidated school: *see* **school district, consolidated.**

district, divisional: the term used in Alberta to specify one of the original school districts constituting a *school division* or *county;* its board has chiefly advisory powers except as to whether courses in French and/or religious instruction shall be given in the district school; where either of these courses is given, the district board has, in effect, power to appoint the teacher; such districts in Saskatchewan are simply referred to as "districts included in the unit"; may be a public school district or separate school district. *Dist. f.* **district, nondivisional;** *comp. w.* **school section** (2a).

district, educational: (Nfld.) *see* **educational district.**

district, inspectorial: *syn.* **inspectorate.**

district, integrated: (Nfld.) 1 of 20 units of school administration for children belonging to the Anglican Church of Canada, the United Church of Canada, and the Salvation Army religious denominations; administered by a school board appointed by the *Lieutenant-Governor in Council* on the recommendation of the *denominational educational committee* established by those denominations acting together. *See* **amalgamated school board** (1).

district, municipal: (Alta.) *see* **municipality, rural.**

district municipality: (B.C.) *see* **municipality, rural.**

district, nondivisional: in Alberta, a *school district* which has not been included in a *school division* or *county;* its board has the same status as the board of a *school division;* all cities and many towns are in this category, also most separate school districts, some *consolidated school districts* and a few isolated *rural school districts;* called "district not included in the unit" in Saskatchewan. *Dist. f.* **district, divisional.**

district, Pentecostal Assemblies of Newfoundland education: (Nfld.) *see* **Pentecostal Assemblies of Newfoundland educational district.**

district, Presbyterian educational: (Nfld.) *see* **Presbyterian educational district.**

district, Roman Catholic educational: (Nfld.) *see* **Roman Catholic educational district.**

district, rural: (Nfld.) *see* **municipality, rural.**

district, school: *see* **school district.**

district school: (N.S.) a public school in a *municipality* conducted for the education of pupils in two or more *school sections.*

district, Seventh Day Adventist educational: (Nfld.) *see* **Seventh Day Adventist educational district.**

district superintendent: (1) (B.C.) a provincially employed educator who administers the educational program of from 1 to 3 *school districts;* frequently also employed by the board of the district(s) as their *chief executive officer;* (2) (N.B.) the locally employed *chief education officer;* may be jointly employed by 2 or 3 boards; responsible to his board(s) for the operation of the public school education program and to the *regional superintendent of schools* for matters pertaining to *department of education* administration, control, and program; in New Brunswick the cost of education is entirely met from provincial resources; (3) (Nfld.) the locally employed chief education officer and usually chief executive officer of a school board.

district, territorial: 1 of 11 defined areas in Northern Ontario; for judicial purposes equivalent to a county but not constituting a municipality; may contain a number of cities, towns, villages, and organized townships, as well as unorganized townships and unsurveyed territory.

division, city school: *see* **defined city.**

division, multidistrict: (Man.) a *school division* having one board to administer all secondary education in the division but in which elementary education is administered by a number of elementary school boards; only 6 of the province's 47 school divisions were in this category on January 1, 1970.

division, school: (1) (N.S.) the territory under the jurisdiction of a school inspector; *see* **inspectorate;** (2) (Alta.) one of the large basic units of local school administration in those parts of the province not organized into counties or cities; contains from 50 to 100 *school districts;* (3) (Man.) the basic unit of administration for high-school purposes and usually for elementary school purposes; (4) (Ont.) the basic unit of local school administration for public elementary and secondary education in the *counties,* in the *defined cities,* and in designated areas in the *territorial districts; see* **county board of education.**

division, single-district: (Man.) a *school division* having but one school board to administer both elementary and secondary education; 41 of the province's 47 school divisions were in this category on January 1, 1970.

divisional board: the *school board* having jurisdiction over a *school division;* in Alberta, Ontario, and in *single-district divisions* in Manitoba, has responsibility for both elementary and secondary schools; in *multidistrict divisions* in Manitoba has responsibility for secondary education only. *See* **division, school.**

divisional board of education: (Ont.) a *county board of education,* a *district board of education,* or the *board of education* of a *defined city. See* **board of education; divisional board.**

divisional district: *see* **district, divisional.**

divisional superintendent: (Alta.) a provincially employed educator who administers the educational program of a *school division* and usually evaluates elementary and junior-high school programs in small *nondivisional districts* and in private schools surrounded by or near the division to which they are attached; called *unit superintendent* in Saskatchewan. *Dist. f.* **district superintendent** (2) and (3); *comp. w.* **district superintendent** (1).

Dominion Bureau of Statistics (DBS): a Federal agency administered under the Federal department of trade and commerce, the education division of which collects and disseminates statistical information respecting various aspects of education in Canada.

école de bonheur: *see* **family institutes.**

école dissidente: (Que.) *see* **dissentient school.**

école normale: *see* **normal school.**

Ed. D. (doctor of education): *see* **D. Paed.**

educable retarded pupil: an educable mentally retarded pupil. *See* **mentally retarded, educable** (*see* main section of the Dictionary).

education, Federal aid to: *see* **Federal aid to education.**

educational council: (Sask.) *see* **advisory board.**

educational district: (Nfld.) a district organization which reflects a system of denominational public schools; three of the educational districts are composed of the whole province, namely, those of the Presbyterians, of the Seventh Day Adventists, and of the Pentecostal Assemblies of Newfoundland; there are 15 Roman Catholic educational districts and some 20 integrated educational districts. *Syn.* **school district;** *see* **district, integrated.**

elementary school: (1) a school having a curriculum offering work in any combination of grades 1 to 8 or from preprimary grades to grade 8; (2) in some provinces, a school offering work only to grade 6; (3) (Que.) a *public school* offering work in any combination of grades from preprimary to grade 8 or a *separate school* offering work in any combination of grades from preprimary to grade 10.

elementary school teacher's certificate, standard 1: (Ont.) a certificate valid for the elementary (1 to 10) grades; indicates the completion of *senior matriculation* and 1 year in a teachers' college; completion of each 5 university subjects raises the standard 1 level so that standard 4 is reached when a bachelor's degree is obtained; made permanent after 2 years of successful teaching; analogous to certain certificates in other provinces. *See* **certificate 1; diploma class B; first class certificate; teaching license.**

elementary school teacher's certificate, standard 2: (Ont.) *see* **elementary school teacher's certificate, standard 1; standard certificate.**

elementary-school teacher's certificate, standard 3: (Ont.) *see* **certificate 3; elementary school teacher's certificate, standard 1.**

elementary-school teacher's certificate, standard 4: (Ont.) *see* **elementary school teacher's certificate, standard 1.**

examination board, high school: *see* **high school examination board.**

examination, departmental: *see* **departmental examination.**

examination, public: *see* **open house.**

examinations, provincial: *see* **provincial examinations.**

Examining Board, Atlantic Provinces: *see* **Atlantic Provinces Examining Board.**

executive officer, chief: *see* **chief executive officer.**

faculty of education: a university faculty concerned with the theory and practice of teaching and with the professional training of teachers and prospective teachers; may grant the degree of bachelor of education, bachelor of teaching, master of education, master of arts in education, and the doctorate in education, as well as various professional certificates.

family allowance: an allowance paid by the Federal government to mothers; amounts to $6 per month per child under 10 and $8 per month per child 10 to 15 years of age; discontinued if child ceases to attend school; nontaxable. *See* **youth allowance.**

family institutes (instituts familiaux): (Que.) private high schools for girls (grades 10 to 12) with a special emphasis on education for marriage and motherhood; established and operated by religious orders but assisted by grants from the province; popularly referred to as *schools of happiness* (écoles de bonheur).

Federal aid to education: support given by the Federal government to the provinces in the form of direct grants and tax abatements; the major item of Federal aid results from an agreement whereby the Federal government has undertaken to meet a minimum of 50 percent of the operating costs of public postsecondary educational institutions, including the *provincial universities,* through a combination of direct grants to the provinces and an abatement of 4 percentage points of the Federal provincial income tax and 1 percentage point of the Federal corporation income tax, which abatements are then levied by the provincial legislatures, collected (except in Quebec) by the Federal department of national revenue, and remitted to the provinces.

finance board, public school: *see* **public school finance board.**

financing, formula: *see* **formula financing.**

first class certificate: (Man.) a teaching certificate valid in the *elementary* and *junior-high school* grades; indicates completion of a minimum of *senior matriculation* and 1 year of teacher education; made permanent on completion of two approved courses, 2 years of teaching experience, and the recommendation of a *school inspector. Comp. w.* **certificate 1; diploma Class B; elementary school teacher's certificate, standard 1; teaching license.**

formula financing: a device for paying financial aid to universities by the use of a formula which weights students in different years and faculties in proportion to the ratios of the presumed unit costs of educating them.

general advisory committee: (Nfld.) *see* **advisory committee, general.**

general and vocational college: (Que.) *see* **CEGEP.**

Governor: (N.S.) *see* **Lieutenant-Governor.**

Governor-in-Council: (N.S.) *see* **Lieutenant-Governor in Council.**

grade: (1) strictly, a major division of the school, used for purposes of classification, instruction, and promotion, as in the United States; a year of the elementary school, junior high school, or high school; (2) an evaluation or rating, as on an examination.

Grade I certificate: (Nfld.) a teaching certificate valid for all grades; indicates completion of 1 year of approved teacher education beyond *junior matriculation.*

Grade II certificate: (Nfld.) a teaching certificate valid for all grades of the public school system; indicates completion of 2 years of approved teacher training following *junior matriculation;* permanent when issued. *Comp. w.* **teacher's license; teaching certificate, Class II.**

Grade III certificate: (Nfld.) *see* **standard certificate A.**

Grade IV certificate: (Nfld.) *see* **certificate IV.**

Grade V certificate: (Nfld.) a teaching certificate valid for all grades; indicates completion of a minimum of 5 years of education beyond *junior matriculation;* signifies an approved degree and 1 year of teacher education; called *teaching certificate, Class V* in Nova Scotia. *Comp. w.* **certificate V; Class I diploma; diploma Class A; professional certificate.**

Grade VI certificate: (Nfld.) *see* **certificate VI.**

Grade VII certificate: (Nfld.) a teaching certificate valid for all grades; indicates completion of at least 7 years of successful study beyond *junior matriculation,* possession of at least two university master's degrees, and the completion of at least 5 education courses. *Comp. w.* **teaching certificate, Class VII.**

graduation diploma, secondary school: (Ont.) *see* **secondary school graduation diploma.**

grants, legislative: *see* **school grants.**

grants, provincial: *see* **school grants.**

grants, school: *see* **school grants.**

headmaster: a term often used for the principal of a private secondary school.

health region: (Sask.) *see* **health unit.**

health unit: a term often used for the unit of administration for public health purposes when it is composed of several municipalities; in some provinces provides school health services; in British Columbia, its board includes members appointed by the school board or boards concerned; called *health region* in Saskatchewan.

high school assistant's certificate: (Ont.) professional qualification for teaching in high school granted to teachers who hold the bachelor's degree from an approved university and 1 year's training in an Ontario College of Education or its equivalent; first award is interim, and certificate is made permanent after 2 years' successful teaching experience; called *specialist diploma* in the Quebec Catholic system; to be distinguished from *professional certificate* as used in several provinces because the latter entitles the holder to teach in both elementary and high schools.

high school examination board: (Man.) a body composed of representatives of the *department of education,* the universities, and the teachers which superintends and controls examinations required for high-school graduation. *See* **departmental examination.**

high school inspector: an official of the Alberta department of education who supervises and evaluates, sometimes alone, and sometimes as a member of a team, the secondary schools of the province; called *high school superintendent* in Saskatchewan and *superintendent of high schools* in Prince Edward Island.

high school of commerce: a commercial high school operated by a *school board.*

high school, senior: *see* **senior high school.**

high school specialist's certificate: (Ont.) a certificate granted after 2 years of successful teaching experience to a teacher who has specialized in certain subject areas while taking a bachelor's degree at an approved university and a further year's training at an Ontario College of Education; qualifies holder for appointment as a department head in a secondary school. *Comp. w.* **high school assistant's certificate.**

high school superintendent: (Sask.) *see* **high school inspector.**

holiday, school: (1) a day during the school term on which school is not in session; (2) *pl.* **holidays;** refers to the longer periods of vacation between terms.

home and school association: the Canadian equivalent of the American *parent-teacher association;* in British Columbia and in the Quebec Catholic system, the latter term is used.

honor graduation diploma, secondary school: (Ont.) *see* **secondary school honor graduation diploma.**

inspector, high school: *see* **high school inspector.**

inspector of schools: *see* **inspector, school.**

inspector, school: (also called inspector of schools) (1) (Man., N.S.) an experienced educator employed by the provincial *department of education* originally to rate teachers, enforce school laws, and represent the *central education authority* in local school districts, but in recent years increasingly involved with supervision of instruction, in-service training of teachers, and liaison between the central and local authorities; called *district superintendent* in British Columbia, *divisional superintendent* in Alberta, *unit superintendent* in Saskatchewan, *regional superintendent* in New Brunswick and Newfoundland, *superintendent of schools* in Prince Edward Island, and *area superintendent* in Ontario; position has been abolished in Quebec; (2) (Ont.) an official of a large local school board, usually third or fourth in the administrative hierarchy of the board, whose duties are chiefly of an evaluative and supervisory nature related to the teaching-learning process; title being replaced by *area superintendent* in many instances.

inspectoral district: *syn.* **inspectorate.**

inspectorate: (obsoles.) (1) the schools under the jurisdiction of a *school inspector;* called a *school division* in Nova Scotia; *syn.* **inspectoral district; inspectorial district; superintendency;** (2) sometimes used to refer to the inspectors of a province collectively.

inspectorial district: *syn.* **inspectorate.**

institut familial: *see* **family institutes.**

institute, collegiate: *see* **collegiate institute.**

institute of technology: (N.S.) *see* **college of applied arts and technology.**

institution, associate: *see* **private school.**

integrated educational district: (Nfld.) *see* **district, integrated.**

intermediate school: *syn.* **senior public school.**

junior diploma: *see* **diploma in education.**

junior high school: a school forming a link between elementary and secondary education and usually consisting of grades 7 to 9; not common to all provinces. *See* **intermediate school; senior public school.**

junior matriculation: *see* **matriculation, junior.**

junior public school: (Ont.) an elementary school comprising kindergarten and grades 1 to 6 only; pupils proceed to a *senior public school* or *intermediate school.*

junior secondary school: (B.C.) *syn.* **junior high school.**

legislative grants: *see* **school grants.**

letter of authority: written order issued by the provincial *department of education* to persons with suitable academic and professional qualifications but who do not meet the requirements stated in provincial regulations for a teacher's certificate. *See* **letter of permission; letter of standing.**

letter of permission: written order issued by the provincial *department of education* permitting a board to employ as a teacher a person who has inadequate professional qualifications; valid only for 1 school year; sometimes called *teaching permit* or *permit.*

letter of standing: written order issued by a provincial *department of education* permitting the employment of a teacher certified in another province or country. *Comp. w.* **provisional certificate** (2).

license, A: (Nfld.) a teaching certificate valid for all grades; indicates completion of four-fifths of a year of approved teacher education beyond junior matriculation; permanent when issued. *See* **matriculation, junior.**

license, teacher's: *see* **teacher's license.**

license, teaching: *see* **teaching license.**

Lieutenant-Governor: the Sovereign's personal representative in a province; appointed by the *Governor-General in Council,* that is, by the Federal government; has no real power; called the *Governor* in Nova Scotia; to be distinguished from Lieutenant-Governor as used in the United States.

Lieutenant-Governor in Council: the executive arm of government of a province; the Lieutenant-Governor and the members of the executive council or cabinet; the Lieutenant-Governor himself has no voice in the decisions of the Lieutenant-Governor in Council; called *Governor-in-Council* in Nova Scotia. See **Lieutenant-Governor.**

M. Ed. (master of education): a professional degree indicating completion of teacher education, a university degree, successful teaching experience, and at least 1 year of postgraduate study, or equivalent summer-school study, in a *faculty of education.*

Maritime provinces: *see* **provinces, Maritime.**

matriculation, junior: informal term used particularly in interprovincial comparisons to signify successful completion of a high-school program leading either directly to a 4-year university arts and science degree program, or, on successful completion of a further year of high school (senior matriculation level), to a 3-year university arts and science degree program; indicates completion of the eleventh grade in Alberta, Saskatchewan, Manitoba, Quebec, Nova Scotia, and Newfoundland, and the twelfth grade in British Columbia, Ontario, New Brunswick, and Prince Edward Island. *Dist. f.* **matriculation, senior.**

matriculation, senior: informal term used particularly in interprovincial comparisons to signify successful completion of a high-school program which includes the first year of a 4-year university arts and science degree program; entitles the holder to enter the second year of such a program or the first year of a 3-year program; signifies completion of the twelfth grade in Alberta, Saskatchewan, Manitoba, Quebec, and Nova Scotia, and the thirteenth grade in Ontario and in a few school districts in British Columbia, Newfoundland, and New Brunswick; cannot be obtained in high school in Prince Edward Island. *Dist. f.* **matriculation, junior.**

metropolitan municipality: *see* **municipality, metropolitan.**

metropolitan school board: *see* **school board, metropolitan.**

metropolitan separate school board: *see* **school board, metropolitan separate.**

mill: one-tenth of a cent or one-thousandth of a dollar; unit of measurement used for calculating taxes on assessed property for educational and municipal services. *See* **mill rate, school.**

mill rate, school: the number of mills which the local government authority fixes annually as the rate of school taxation on each dollar of assessed value of real property.

minister of education: in all provinces, the political head of the public school system; an elected member of the legislature (called national assembly in Quebec) who has been raised to the executive arm of the provincial government, that is, to the cabinet, by the provincial premier or prime minister; functions as head of the *department of education;* in educational circles, usually referred to simply as "the Minister."

minister of education, deputy: *see* **deputy minister of education.**

minister of university affairs: (Ont.) an elected member of the legislature who has been raised to the executive arm of the provincial government, that is, to the cabinet, by the provincial prime minister; head of the *department of university affairs.*

minister of university affairs, deputy: *see* **deputy minister of university affairs.**

model school: (1) historically, a state professional school for the training of teachers for the third-class certificate; now obsolete; (2) a school under the direct control of a provincial department of education, usually at the elementary level, used as a laboratory school for purposes of demonstration or experimentation in methods of teaching; obsolescent, since this type of school has almost completely disappeared.

multidistrict division: *see* **division, multidistrict.**

municipal area superintendent: *see* **area superintendent, municipal.**

municipal council: the governing authority of a local *municipality;* in most provinces it is required to levy and collect school taxes; sometimes it has powers relating to

organization and alteration of units of local school administration, appointment of school trustees, issue of school debentures, location of school sites, and approval of the school budget.

municipal district: (Alta.) *see* **municipality, rural.**

municipal school board: the local education authority in a Nova Scotia *rural municipality;* composed of seven members, four appointed by the *municipal council* and three by the *Lieutenant-Governor in Council. Comp. w.* **county board of education; county school committee; divisional board.**

municipal school district: *see* **school district, municipal.**

municipality: (1) an area of which the governing body and/or the citizens have been incorporated by the provincial authorities; a city, town, borough, village, or *rural municipality;* (2) (N.S.) a *rural municipality.*

municipality, district: (B.C.) *see* **municipality, rural.**

municipality, metropolitan: (Ont., Man.) a new type of municipal unit, at present operating only in the Toronto and Winnipeg areas, which serves as a strong intermediate unit between the province and the local municipalities, in Toronto for both municipal and school purposes, but in Winnipeg for municipal purposes only. *See* **school board, metropolitan.**

municipality, regional: (Ont.) a new type of intermediate municipal corporation; composed of one or more *counties* together with the cities and *separated towns* which were located in the geographical county or counties; replaces the county as a municipal corporation and has broader powers with respect to the cities, towns, and boroughs composing it than did the *county. Comp. w.* **municipality, metropolitan.**

municipality, rural: (Sask., Man.) a municipality other than a city, town, borough, or village; called *district municipality* in British Columbia, *municipal district* or *county* in Alberta, *township* in Ontario, *parish* (paroisse), *township* (canton), or *municipality without designation* (sans designation) in Quebec, *municipality* in Nova Scotia, and *rural district* in Newfoundland; Prince Edward Island and New Brunswick do not have rural municipalities. *See* **municipality, urban.**

municipality, school: *see* **school municipality.**

municipality, urban: generally, an incorporated city, town, or village; in Ontario, includes a borough. *See* **municipality, rural.**

municipality without designation: (Que.) *see* **municipality, rural.**

nondivisional district: *see* **district, nondivisional.**

normal school (école normale): (Que.) a teacher-training institution offering 2 to 4 years of academic and professional education beyond grade 11 *(junior matriculation);* successful completion of 2 years entitles a student to the *diploma (brevet) Class B* or the *Class II diploma;* successful completion of the 4-year program leads to the *diploma (brevet) Class A* or *Class I diploma. See* **faculty of education; teachers' college.**

official trustee: a person appointed by the *central education authority* of some provinces to perform the functions of a local *school board* when a new school district has been erected until such time as a school board can be elected, or when an existing school board fails to act, is disqualified from holding office, or where it is impossible to get enough qualified persons to constitute a school board; becoming obsolescent with the growth of larger units of administration.

one session: in some provinces, a day on which a school operates only for the morning session, usually one hour longer than normal, and then allows the pupils to go home; usually resorted to when a bad rain or snow storm develops after the morning session begins; applies to all schools in a local school system; now obsolescent with the formation of large units of administration and regular school transportation systems.

Ontario Institute for Studies in Education (O.I.S.E.): an independent college affiliated with the University of Toronto which combines the functions of a university graduate school in education with those of a research and development institute; unique as a method of organization in higher education.

open house: the public display of the work of the school, often during Education Week; characterized by the visit of parents to the school either during the day or in the evening; called the *public examination* in New Brunswick.

order-in-council: an order having the full force of law issued by the *Lieutenant-Governor in Council* as a means of giving legal effect to a decision of the cabinet in areas not involving legislative action; in education, used chiefly to make appointments and pay out sums of money for extraordinary purposes.

parish (paroisse): (Que.) one of three types of rural municipality in that province; distinct from, though sometimes coterminous with, the ecclesiastical parish. *See* **municipality, rural.**

parochial school: a private school operated by a church or other religious group, usually Roman Catholic. *Dist. f.* **dissentient school; separate school.**

Pentecostal Assemblies of Newfoundland Educational District: (Nfld.) the unit of school administration for children of that religious denomination; coterminous with the provincial boundaries; administered by a school board appointed by the *Lieutenant-Governor in Council* on the recommendation of the *denominational educational committee* established by the denomination.

permit, teaching: *see* **letter of permission.**

polyvalent: (Que.) the French-language term for "comprehensive"; sometimes used in English-language translations of French-language documents, as in the expression "polyvalent school" where it is a synonym for *comprehensive school.*

prairie provinces: *see* **provinces, prairie.**

Presbyterian educational district: (Nfld.) the unit of school administration for children of that religious denomination; coterminous with the provincial boundaries; administered by a school board appointed by the *Lieutenant-Governor in Council* on the recommendation of the *denominational educational committee* established by the denomination or, in the absence of such committee, on the recommendation of the Minister. *See* **educational district.**

president: *see* **chancellor.**

président: *see* **Catholic committee.**

private school: a school not forming part of the publicly administered school system of a province; in some provinces, subject to registration and/or inspection by the *department of education;* in Alberta and Saskatchewan indirectly supported by public funds by the device of paying a small direct grant to parents sending a pupil to a private school; in Quebec many private schools have entered into agreements with *regional school boards* under which they achieve the status of an *associate institution* and are eligible for instruction fees payable by the regional board on behalf of pupils from the region who are pursuing work in the secondary grades (8 to 11) at the private school; such fees are in accordance with the agreement and are subject to approval by the *department of education.*

professional certificate: (western provinces) a teaching certificate issued by the provincial *departments of education* indicating that the holder has obtained at least the equivalent of a bachelor's degree at a university with professional teacher training either included or in addition; valid for teaching in all grades of the publicly supported system; permanent when issued in Saskatchewan but made permanent only after 2 years of successful teaching in the other three provinces.

program consultant: (Ont.) a member of the staff of a *regional office* with special capabilities in a program area (mathematics, science, English, classics, commercial subjects, etc.) who assists school boards and teachers in his subject specialty.

Protestant committee (comité protestante): (Que.) a statutory body composed of five representatives each of the Protestant denominations, teachers, and parents; makes regulations, with respect to the *Protestant system,* on all matters pertaining to religion and morals in connection with curricula, textbooks, teacher training and qualifications, diplomas, religious instruction, nomenclature of

schools, etc.; its chairman is ex officio a member of the *superior council of education. Comp. w.* **Catholic committee.**

Protestant separate school: *see* **separate school, Protestant.**

Protestant system: informal term for that part of the system of public education in the province of Quebec that is under the direction of Protestants; consists of those *regional school boards, boards of school commissioners,* and *boards of school trustees,* and the schools they administer that are under the direction of Protestants, together with the *Protestant committee* and those teacher-training institutions that prepare teachers for the Protestant schools. *See* **Catholic committee; dissent; dissentient school.**

province: 1 of the 10 political subdivisions of Canada; under the *B.N.A. Act,* has exclusive power to make laws respecting education; comparable to "state" in the United States.

provinces, Atlantic: the four most easterly provinces of Canada: New Brunswick (N.B.), Nova Scotia (N.S.), Prince Edward Island (P.E.I.), and Newfoundland and Labrador (Nfld.).

provinces, central: the provinces of Ontario (Ont.) and Quebec (Que.); sometimes referred to as *central Canada.*

provinces, Maritime: the provinces of New Brunswick (N.B.), Nova Scotia, (N.S.), and Prince Edward Island (P.E.I.); frequently referred to as *the Maritimes.*

provinces, prairie: the provinces of Alberta (Alta.), Saskatchewan (Sask.), and Manitoba (Man.).

provinces, western: the four most westerly provinces of Canada: British Columbia (B.C.), Alberta (Alta.), Saskatchewan (Sask.), and Manitoba (Man.); sometimes referred to as *western Canada.*

provincial area superintendent: *see* **area superintendent, provincial.**

provincial examinations: (N.S.) examinations set and marked by the *Atlantic Provinces Examining Board* at the Grade 12 *(senior matriculation)* level. (The Nova Scotia Grade 11 *departmental examination* was abolished, effective 1970.) *See* **Atlantic Provinces Examining Board; departmental examination.**

provincial grants: *see* **school grants.**

provincial university: a university either under the direct administrative and financial control of the provincial government or receiving the greater part of its funds from provincial sources; differs from a university which, though it receives a provincial grant, is independent of the state; the degree of provincial control varies with the province; most Canadian universities now fall under this heading, the chief exceptions being universities and colleges established and still administered by religious denominations. *See* **Federal aid to education.**

provisional certificate: (1) (Alta.) a certificate entitling a person to teach all grades in the province; indicates completion of 4 years of teacher education beyond *junior matriculation;* not permanent, but on completion of the bachelor of education becomes a *professional certificate; comp. w.* **certificate IV; diploma Class A; professional certificate;** (2) (Sask.) a certificate, valid for one year, issued to a person whose education has been completed wholly or in large part outside Canada, or to a person whose former certificate had previously been suspended or cancelled; may be exchanged for the appropriate regular certificate on the completion of 1 year of teaching satisfactory to the Minister and on the removal of any conditions attached to the provisional certificate; *comp. w.* **letter of standing.**

public college: (Alta.) a postsecondary institution financed by public funds, offering the first 2 years of a university general arts or science course as well as day and evening vocational courses. *Comp. w.* **CEGEP; college of applied arts and technology; regional college.**

public examination: *see* **open house.**

public school: (1) (B.C., Man., Que., N.B., N.S., P.E.I., Nfld.) any school supported by tax revenues and other public funds and open to all; (2) (Ont., Alta., Sask.) such a school attended only by children of parents who do not support a *separate school;* (3) (Ont.) an extralegal term sometimes used to denote an *elementary* as opposed to a *secondary school.*

public school board: (1) (Alta., Sask.) the elected *school board* having jurisdiction over a public school district; *see* **district, divisional; district, nondivisional;** (2) (Ont.) the elected school board having jurisdiction over a *school section;* now found only in those parts of northern Ontario not included in a *school division;* responsible only for elementary education. *Comp. w.* **board of education.**

public school elector: (Ont.) a person qualified to vote at school elections, not having signified that he is a *separate school supporter.*

public school finance board: (Man.) an agency of the provincial *department of education;* administers the provincial foundation program for elementary and secondary schools, paying to each *divisional board* the full amount of its calculated foundation program; receives 65 percent of its revenue from uniform *mill rates* of equalized assessment determined by it each year and paid to it by the municipalities of the province, which collect it, and the remaining 35 percent from the consolidated revenue of the province.

public school, junior: *see* **junior public school.**

public school section: (Ont.) *see* **school section** (1).

public school, senior: *see* **senior public school.**

pupil, educable retarded: *see* **educable retarded pupil.**

pupil, trainable retarded: *see* **trainable retarded pupil.**

recommendation: the system by which pupils are promoted from one grade to the next on the recommendation of the teacher, wholly on the basis of the year's work and without final written examinations; used in some provinces to include the various subjects of the school-leaving certificates of grades 11 and 12 (or grades 12 and 13 in the case of provinces having a 13-year system); pupils may be recommended for promotion in some subjects and not in others, depending on their year's work; if a student is not recommended in a particular subject, he may write a final examination in that subject and, if successful, still be promoted.

rector: *see* **chancellor.**

region, health: (Sask.) *see* **health unit.**

region, school: *see* **school region.**

région scolaire: *see* **school region.**

regional bureau (bureau régional): (Que.) one of the 9 decentralized organs of the provincial *department of education;* headed by a *coordinator* or *director* and composed of a number of *technical advisers,* specialists in school organization, curriculum, examinations, personnel management, financing, planning; responsible for the *regional school boards, boards of school commissioners,* and *boards of school trustees* within its administrative region. *Comp. w.* **regional office.**

regional business administrator: (Ont.) *see* **business administrator** (2); **regional office.**

regional college: (B.C.) a 2-year postsecondary institution offering both academic and technical programs and fulfilling transfer, terminal, and general education functions; administered by a board representing all the school districts in its region and financed by local taxation and government grants; called *district college* when operated by a single school board. *Comp. w.* **CEGEP; college of applied arts and technology; public college.**

regional coordinator: *see* **regional bureau.**

regional director: *see* **regional bureau.**

regional director of education: (Ont.) a professional educator in the employ of the department of education who, as head of a *regional office,* represents the department in working with school boards. *See* **regional office.**

regional municipality: *see* **municipality, regional.**

regional office: (Ont.) headquarters of 1 of the 10 educational regions into which the province has been divided for purposes of decentralizing the provincial *department of education;* is headed by a *regional director of education* with one or more assistants, together with a number of *provincial area superintendents* and *program consultants* and a *regional business administrator. Comp. w.* **regional bureau.**

regional school board: *see* **school board, regional.**

regional superintendent: (N.B., Nfld.) a provincially employed superintendent, the agent of the central authority in the field, whose duties relate primarily to upgrading education in the school districts of his superintendency in consultation with *district superintendents;* comparable to a *regional director of education* or a *regional coordinator* or *director* in other provinces. *See* **regional bureau.**

regulation: a rule or order, having the force of law, issued by a provincial cabinet minister; usually required to be approved by the *Lieutenant-Governor in Council;* must be within the power of the Minister to make as authorized by statute; usually must be registered and published in the official provincial gazette.

religious: (Fr. religieux, religieuse); *n.* informal designation for a teacher belonging to a religious teaching order; a teaching sister (religieuse) or brother (religieux), or a priest.

retarded pupil, educable: *see* **educable retarded pupil.**

retarded pupil, trainable: *see* **trainable retarded pupil.**

Roman Catholic educational district: (Nfld.) 1 of 15 units of school administration for Roman Catholics; administered by a school board appointed by the *Lieutenant-Governor in Council* on the recommendation of the *denominational educational committee* established by the Roman Catholic religious denomination. *See* **educational district.**

Roman Catholic separate school: *see* **separate school, Roman Catholic.**

rotary system: a system of operation of a school in which pupils are instructed by different teachers for different subjects, either by changing classrooms or by being visited by different teachers.

royal commission on education: a commission of inquiry into some or all aspects of education in a province; composed of one or more persons appointed by *order-in-council;* makes recommendations for action; all provinces have, from time to time, appointed royal commissions on education or on a specified aspect of education, such as the financing of education.

rural district: (Nfld.) *see* **municipality, rural.**

rural municipality: *see* **municipality, rural.**

rural school district: *see* **school district, rural.**

rural school section: *see* **school section, rural.**

school, bilingual: *see* **bilingual school.**

school board: unofficial designation for the body of persons charged with responsibility for the administration of education in a local unit of school administration. *See* **board of education; board of school commissioners; board of school trustees; divisional board; separate school board; school board, regional.**

school board, amalgamated: *see* **amalgamated school board.**

school board, denominational: *see* **denominational school board.**

school board, metropolitan: (Ont.) the *school board* having jurisdiction in the municipality of Metropolitan Toronto; an indirectly elected board having broad powers over both public elementary and secondary education in the City of Toronto and the five boroughs constituting the *metropolitan municipality;* approves the budgets of the six area boards and levies a uniform local *mill rate* on the equalized assessment of the metropolitan municipality to raise the local share of the combined budgets; receives the *school grants* payable on behalf of the area boards. *See* **school board, metropolitan separate.**

school board, metropolitan separate: (Ont.) the *separate school board* having jurisdiction over Roman Catholic separate elementary education in the municipality of Metropolitan Toronto. (There are no borough separate school boards.) *See* **school board, metropolitan.**

school board, municipal: *see* **municipal school board.**

school board, public: *see* **public school board.**

school board, regional: (1) (commission scolaire régionale) (Que.) the school board administering secondary education in one of the 64 *school regions* into which most of the province is divided; may by agreement perform some functions for the *school municipalities* within its boundaries; elected by and from a bureau of delegates composed of three commissioners or trustees from each *board of school commissioners* and *board of school trustees* having jurisdiction over elementary education in the region; 55 of the boards are Catholic and 9 Protestant; *see* **director-general of schools**; (2) (N.S.) the board that administers a regional school (usually a vocational high school) in a region consisting of a number of cities or towns and/or *municipalities.*

school board, separate: *see* **separate school board.**

school committee, county: *see* **county school committee.**

school, composite: *see* **composite school.**

school, comprehensive: *see* **comprehensive school.**

school, district: *see* **district school.**

school district: (1) (B.C., P.E.I., N.B.) the unit of administration for elementary and secondary education; varies in size from the rural district employing one teacher to a large district containing a city and surrounding rural territory; used in these provinces for all types of units of school administration; called *educational district* in Newfoundland; (2) (Alta., Sask.) the original unit of administration for elementary and secondary education; those that have become part of a *school division* or *county* in Alberta, or a *school unit* in Saskatchewan, are now residual districts with minimal functions; those that did not become part of the large units continue as basic units of administration; *see* **district, divisional; district, nondivisional;** (3) (Man.) the unit of administration for elementary education in a *multidistrict division;* (4) (Que.) one of the attendance areas into which a school municipality is divided. *See* **division, school; educational district; school municipality; school region; school unit; zone, separate school.**

school district, consolidated: a school district formed by the uniting of several rural school districts for the purpose of operating a single school; such districts represented the first attempts, in the first quarter of the twentieth century, to form large units of school administration; most such districts have now disappeared, having become part of the newer *school divisions, school regions, school units,* or other enlarged school districts; a few continue to exist independently in Alberta and Saskatchewan.

school district, municipal: (1) (Man.) a *school district* whose boundaries are coterminous with those of one municipality; (2) (B.C.) a *school district* containing one or more municipalities within its boundaries.

school district, rural: (1) a school district other than one composed of or containing a town, village, or city; (2) in British Columbia, a school district containing no territory organized under the Municipal Act. (Less than 1 percent of the area of the province is organized municipally but the whole province is divided into 84 school districts, 81 of which are rural and 3 unattached.) *See* **school district, municipal** (2).

school district, separate: (Alta., Sask.) a *school district* established by the religious minority (Catholic or Protestant) in a public school district; may join a *school division* or *county* (Alta.) or *school unit* (Sask.) or may elect to remain independent; most such districts, however, are in cities and large towns, which do not form part of the divisions, counties, or units. *See* **separate school;** *comp. w.* **zone, separate school.**

school division: *see* **division, school.**

school, elementary: *see* **elementary school.**

school grants: grants by the province to local or intermediate school administrative units for the support of the educational program; sometimes referred to as *legislative grants* or *provincial grants. Comp. w.* **aid, state** (*see* main section of the Dictionary).

school holiday: *see* **holiday, school.**

school inspector: *see* **inspector, school.**

school, intermediate: *syn.* **senior public school.**

school mill rate: *see* **mill rate, school.**

school municipality: (Que.) (1) the unit of administration for elementary school education in a *school region; comp. w.* **school district** (3); (2) the unit of administration for elementary and secondary school education in areas not included in a school region; *comp. w.* **division, single-district; school district** (1).

school of happiness (Fr. école de bonheur): (Que.) *see* **family institutes.**

school patrol: a group of responsible pupils selected to assist in seeing that other pupils exercise proper safety measures when using the streets on the way to and from school; frequently replaces the *crossing guard.*

school, private: *see* **private school.**

school, public: *see* **public school.**

school region (région scolaire): (Que.) the basic unit of administration for secondary education and, by agreement, for some aspects of elementary education. (The province is divided into 64 regions, 55 of which are under Catholic administration, the remainder under Protestant administration; excluded are the school commissions of greater Montreal and greater Quebec and some isolated Protestant school boards). *See* **school board, regional.**

school section: (1) (Ont.) formerly the basic unit of administration for public elementary education; now found only in those remote parts of northern Ontario not included in a *school division; see* **public school board;** (2) (N.S.) formerly, the basic unit of administration for elementary and secondary education; now of two types: (*a*) *rural school sections* and *village school sections,* which, although having their own boards for minor functions, are administered by the *municipal school board* in the rural municipality in which they are located, and (*b*) *urban school sections,* the basic units of administration in cities and towns; *comp. w.* **district, divisional.** *See* **school district; division, school; school region; school unit.**

school section, rural: (N.S.) a *school section* employing only one teacher.

school section, urban: *see* **school section** (2).

school section, village: (N.S.) a *school section* having more than one teacher, other than a section consisting of all or part of a city or town.

school, senior public: *see* **senior public school.**

school, senior secondary: (B.C.) *syn.* **senior high school.**

school, separate: *see* **separate school.**

school trustee: general term used to refer to a school board member; frequently shortened to *trustee. See* **board of school trustees.**

school unit: (1) a unit of local school administration; (2) (Sask.) official name of the large basic units of local school administration first established in 1946. *Comp. w.* **division, school** (2); **school region.**

secondary school graduation diploma: (Ont.) a certificate granted by the department of education on the recommendation of the principal of a secondary school, with the inspector's approval, to a candidate who has successfully followed a course of study throughout grades 11 and 12. *See* **matriculation, junior.**

secondary school honor graduation diploma: (Ont.) a certificate issued by the department of education to a student who successfully completes grade 13. *See* **matriculation, senior; secondary school graduation diploma.**

secondary school, junior: (B.C.) *syn.* **junior high school.**

secondary school, senior: (B.C.) *syn.* **senior high school.**

secretary-treasurer: *see* **business administrator** (1).

section, school: *see* **school section.**

senior diploma: *see* **diploma in education.**

senior high school: the designation of a school or subdivision of a school in which the upper high school grades are taught; occurs in school systems which have *junior high schools;* called *senior secondary school* in British Columbia.

senior matriculation: *see* **matriculation, senior.**

senior public school: (Ont.) an elementary school containing only grades 7 and 8; similar in purpose and method of operation to a *junior high school. Syn.* **intermediate school;** *comp. w.* **junior public school.**

senior secondary school: (B.C.) *syn.* **senior high school.**

separate school: a type of publicly supported school established and supported by the Roman Catholic or

Protestant minority in a *school district;* under the jurisdiction of an elected *separate school board;* found in Ontario, Alberta, and Saskatchewan. *See* **separate school, Protestant; separate school, Roman Catholic;** *dist. f.* **parochial school;** *comp. w.* **dissentient school.**

separate school board: (Ont., Alta., Sask.) an elected *school board* having jurisdiction over a *separate school district* or *separate school zone.*

separate school board, metropolitan: *see* **school board, metropolitan separate.**

separate school district: *see* **school district, separate.**

separate school, Protestant: a type of publicly supported school established and supported by the Protestant minority of ratepayers in a local school unit; gradually disappearing from the three provinces where it is found (Ontario, Alberta, Saskatchewan); can be established in Ontario only when the teacher in the public school is a Roman Catholic; in Alberta and Saskatchewan, found only in predominantly Roman Catholic *rural school districts.*

separate school ratepayer: (Sask.) *see* **separate school supporter.**

separate school, Roman Catholic: one of the schools operated by a Roman Catholic *separate school board;* established, supported, and attended by Roman Catholics; receives provincial aid under the same *regulation* as do public schools; in Alberta and Saskatchewan, provides the full range of elementary and secondary education; in Ontario, provides education from kindergarten to grade 10.

separate school site: (Ont.) (1) the parcel of land on part of which a separate school is located or has been located; (2) where a board does not operate a school, one parcel of land owned by the board; (3) where a board neither operates a school nor owns any property, any parcel of land approved by the *separate school supporters* for the purposes of determining the center of a zone. *See* **center.**

separate school supporter: (1) (Ont.) an elector who, or whose spouse, has elected to direct the school taxes in respect of the property he owns or rents to the support of a *separate school*—except in the case of the two *Protestant separate schools,* to a *Roman Catholic separate school; comp. w.* **public school elector;** (2) (Alta.) any Roman Catholic ratepayer in a *school district* in which the Roman Catholic minority has established a *Roman Catholic separate school district,* or any Protestant ratepayer in a *school district* in which the Protestant minority has established a *Protestant separate school district;* called *separate school ratepayer* in Saskatchewan.

separate school zone: *see* **zone, separate school.**

separated town: (Ont.) a town that is separated, for municipal purposes, from the county in which it is situated. *See* **county board of education.**

Seventh Day Adventist educational district: (Nfld.) the unit of school administration for children of that religious denomination; coterminous with the provincial boundaries; administered by a school board appointed by the *Lieutenant-Governor in Council* on the recommendation of the *denominational educational committee* established by the denomination, or, in the absence of such a committee, on the recommendation of the Minister. *See* **educational district.**

single-district division: *see* **division, single-district.**

specialist diploma: (Que., Catholic system) a teaching certificate valid for grades 7 to 12; indicates completion of a master's degree and 1 year of teacher education; permanent when issued.

standard certificate: (B.C.) a teaching certificate valid for the elementary grades; indicates completion of 3 years of teacher education and university education beyond Grade 12 (junior matriculation); equivalent to the *elementary school teacher's certificate, standard 2* of Ontario, the *provisional certificate* of Alberta, and *certificate 2* of Prince Edward Island.

standard certificate A: (Sask.) a teaching certificate valid for all grades; indicates completion of 2 years of teacher

education beyond *senior matriculation;* permanent when issued; equivalent to the *teaching certificate, Class III,* of Nova Scotia, the *Grade III certificate* of Newfoundland, *certificate III* of New Brunswick, and the *conditional certificate* of Alberta.

superannuation: retirement on pension.

superintendency: *syn.* **inspectorate.**

superintendent, district: *see* **district superintendent.**

superintendent, divisional: *see* **divisional superintendent.**

superintendent, high school: (Sask.) *see* **high school inspector.**

superintendent, municipal area: *see* **area superintendent, municipal.**

superintendent of business affairs: *see* **business administrator** (1).

superintendent of education: (B.C.) the executive officer, immediately below the *deputy minister of education,* responsible for the supervision and educational administration of the public school system. *Dist. f.* **superintendent of schools, chief.**

superintendent of high schools: (P.E.I.) *see* **high school inspector.**

superintendent of public schools: (Ont.) a professional educator who, under the *director of education,* is responsible for the academic administration and supervision of the elementary schools of a *board of education;* may have one or more *area superintendents* or *program consultants* under his direction.

superintendent of schools: (Que.) *syn.* **director of studies;** *see* **inspector, school.**

superintendent of schools, chief: generally the head of the inspectoral or supervisory staff of a *department of education;* has certain responsibilities as well for locally employed superintendents; so called only in Alberta, Saskatchewan, and New Brunswick; has other designations in other provinces.

superintendent of secondary schools: (Ont.) a professional educator who, under the *director of education,* is responsible for the academic administration and supervision of the secondary schools of a *board of education;* may have one or more *area superintendents* or *program consultants* under his direction.

superintendent of separate schools: (Ont.) a professional educator employed by a Roman Catholic *separate school board* of a large city or of a *county* or *district combined separate school zone* as its *chief executive officer;* may have one or more *area superintendents* or *inspectors* reporting to him. *See* **business administrator** (1).

superintendent, provincial area: *see* **area superintendent, provincial.**

superintendent, regional: *see* **regional superintendent.**

superintendent, unit: (Sask.) *see* **divisional superintendent.**

superior council of education (conseil supérieur de l'éducation): (Que.) an advisory body of 24 members established by statute to advise the minister of education on questions he submits or on other matters respecting education; must consist of at least 16 Catholics, 4 Protestants, and one person who is neither Catholic nor Protestant; meets monthly. *Comp. w.* **advisory board.**

teachers' certification committee: (Nfld.) a statutory body including the executive secretaries of the *denominational educational committees* with power, subject to the approval of the *Lieutenant-Governor in Council,* to make regulations dealing with academic and professional standards in the training and classification of teachers.

teachers' college: (Ont., N.S., N.B.) non-degree-granting institution at which elementary school teachers are trained, usually for a period of one year after *senior matriculation* or its equivalent. *See* **faculty of education; normal school.**

teacher's license: (N.B.) a teaching certificate valid for all grades of the public school system; indicates completion of a 2-year *teachers' college* program after *junior matriculation;* permanent when issued. *Comp. w.* **Grade II certificate; teaching certificate, Class II.**

teaching certificate, Class II: (N.S.) a certificate valid for all grades of the public school system; indicates 2 years of education beyond *junior matriculation*, one in completing *senior matriculation* at high school or university and one at *teachers' college* or in a *faculty of education;* made permanent after 2 years of successful teaching experience. *Comp. w.* **certificate 1; Grade II certificate; teacher's license.**

teaching certificate, Class III: (N.S.) *see* **standard certificate A.**

teaching certificate, Class IV: (N.S.) a teaching certificate valid for all grades; indicates completion of 3 years of university education and 1 year of teacher education beyond *junior matriculation;* usually signifies that the holder does not have an approved university degree. *Comp. w.* **certificate IV; provisional certificate** (1).

teaching certificate, Class V: (N.S.) *see* **Grade V certificate.**

teaching certificate, Class VI: (N.S.) *see* **Certificate VI.**

teaching certificate, Class VII: (N.S.) a certificate valid for all grades; indicates completion of 7 years of education beyond *junior matriculation;* usually signifies 1 year of additional study beyond the master's degree or 2 years of additional study beyond the bachelor's degree, together with 1 year of teacher education. *Comp. w.* **Grade VII certificate.**

teaching certificate, Class VIII: (N.S.) a certificate valid for all grades; indicates possession of a doctor's degree in a field of study related to elementary and secondary education in the province and 1 year of teacher education; signifies completion of at least 8 years of education beyond *junior matriculation.*

teaching license: (B.C.) a certificate issued after the completion of 2 years of teacher education beyond Grade 12 *(junior matriculation),* or 1 year beyond Grade 13 *(senior matriculation);* never made permanent; must be raised to a *standard certificate. Comp. w.* **certificate 1; diploma Class B; elementary school teacher's certificate, standard 1; first-class certificate.**

teaching permit: *see* **letter of permission.**

technical adviser: (Que.) *see* **regional bureau.**

technology, institute of: (N.S.) *see* **college of applied arts and technology.**

tender: an offer, usually written, to furnish materials or services for a specified sum of money. (School boards are generally required by law to secure competitive tenders before awarding building contracts or making major capital purchases.) *Syn.* **bid** (*see* main section of the Dictionary).

territorial district: *see* **district, territorial.**

the Maritimes: *see* **provinces, Maritime.**

timetable: (1) a schedule indicating the arrangements made for each class or student for every day in the school week; shows the subject to be taught in each period, the teacher responsible, and the classroom in which the lesson is given; (2) a similar schedule for each teacher. *See* **schedule, daily** (*see* main section of the Dictionary).

timetabling: the act of preparing a set of *timetables* for a school, particularly a junior high school, senior public school, or high school.

township: (1) (Ont.) the designation for a *rural municipality;* excludes incorporated towns and villages but may contain hamlets constituted as police villages for certain minor municipal functions; (2) (Que.) (canton) one of three types of *rural municipality,* found chiefly in the southeastern part of the province; (3) (Alta., Sask., Man.) a defined area of 36 square miles, 6 miles square.

trainable retarded pupil: a trainable mentally retarded pupil. *See* **mentally retarded, trainable** (*see* main section of the Dictionary).

trustee, official: *see* **official trustee.**

trustee, school: *see* **school trustee.**

unit, health: *see* **health unit.**

unit, school: *see* **school unit.**

unit superintendent: (Sask.) *see* **divisional superintendent.**

university affairs, department of: *see* **department of university affairs.**

university affairs, deputy minister of: *see* **deputy minister of university affairs.**

University Grants Commission: (Man.) a committee of senior education officials, established by *order-in-council;* allocates available funds to the three universities for both capital and current expenditures.

university, provincial: *see* **provincial university.**

Upper Canada: (1) historically, the present province of Ontario; (2) often used informally in the *Maritime provinces* to refer to the *central provinces.*

urban county: *see* **county system of government.**

urban municipality: *see* **municipality, urban.**

urban school section: *see* **school section** (2).

vice-chancellor: *see* **chancellor.**

village school section: *see* **school section, village.**

western Canada: *see* **provinces, western.**

western provinces: *see* **provinces, western.**

youth allowance: (1) a monthly payment of $10 made by the Federal government to mothers in all provinces and territories except Quebec on behalf of each child aged 16 or 17; requires proof that child is in full-time attendance at school; nontaxable; (2) (Que.) a similar payment made by the provincial government but, in effect, reimbursed by the Federal government through a tax-sharing arrangement. *See* **family allowance.**

zone, combined separate school: (Ont.) a large unit of administration for Roman Catholic *separate schools; see* **zone, county combined separate school; zone, district combined separate school.**

zone, county combined separate school: (Ont.) one of the two types of large units of administration for *Roman Catholic separate schools;* composed of all former *separate school zones,* or any such zones created in the future, whose *centers* lie within a county or designated group of counties; includes all zones which are cities or *separated towns* which are within but not part of the county or counties. *See* **county;** *comp. w.* **zone, district combined separate school.**

zone, district combined separate school: (Ont.) one of the two types of large units of administration for *Roman Catholic separate schools;* composed of all *separate school zones,* past, present, and future, whose *centers* lie within areas, designated by *regulation,* in the *territorial districts. Comp. w.* **zone, county combined separate school.**

zone, separate school: (Ont.) the unit of administration for *Roman Catholic separate schools;* in *urban municipalities* comprises the whole *municipality* and in rural areas those parcels of real property which lie within or partly within a 3-mile radius of a *center* or *centers. See* **center; separate school, Roman Catholic; zone, combined separate school; zone, county combined separate school; zone, district combined separate school.**

EDUCATION IN ENGLAND AND WALES

COORDINATOR: R. E. BELL, The Open University, Bletchley, Buckinghamshire

administration, divisional: *see* **scheme of divisional administration.**

administrative county: a division of England first established by the Local Government Act of 1888 when the whole of England and Wales was mapped into such counties; however, large towns (known as county boroughs) do not come under the jurisdiction of the administrative county in which they are situated; certain of the traditional counties are subdivided into administrative counties—Yorkshire, for example, into three, Sussex and Suffolk into two; the London area is organized on a quite . different basis. *See* **county borough; local education authority.**

adult education: those agencies and procedures intended to extend the period of education beyond the termination of formal training in school or university; includes the provision of any kind of general, cultural, or practical education that arises from the various interests and needs of adult life. *See* **further education; Workers' Educational Association.**

age, school-leaving: *see* **school-leaving age.**

agreed syllabus: a nondenominational program of religious instruction for schools, agreed on by the local education authority, church representatives, and teachers.

agricultural college: *see* **college, agricultural.**

aided school: a voluntary primary or secondary school maintained by the local education authority; under the Education Act of 1959, the managers or governors pay for repairs to the exterior of the building and for capital expenditure on alterations required by the authority, who do however pay all running costs; the managers have substantial rights over the appointment and dismissal of teachers and complete control of the school's religious policy. *Syn.* **grant-aided school;** *dist. f.* **assisted school.**

alderman: *see* **council member.**

all-age school: (1) a type of school providing special educational treatment for physically and mentally defective children who have attained the age of 5 years but have not attained the age of 17 years; (2) a type of school for children from 5 years to under 17 found particularly in rural areas that have not been reorganized in accordance with the Education Act, 1944.

all-through comprehensive education: *see* **comprehensive education, all-through.**

approved school: a school under the control of the Home Office, for persons under 16 years who may be sent there by a magistrate following their appearance in a juvenile court; such schools provide both therapy and a general education; under the Children and Young Persons Act of 1933 they replaced the *industrial school* for younger and the *reformatory school* for older delinquents. *Syn.* **Home Office school;** *see* **Borstal institution; detention center.**

art class: *see* **class, art.**

art school: a type of school officially classified as forming part of the system of "technical and further education" that offers full-time and part-time day and evening courses relating principally to the industrial and commercial branches of arts and crafts; may be a public institution under the supervision of the Department of Education and Science and the recipient of government grants or a privately operated institution that may or may not receive financial aid.

articles of government: rules that define the respective powers and functions of the local education authority, the governors, and the head teacher in the conduct of a secondary school. *See* **rules of management.**

assistant: a graduate appointed to secondary schools and universities through an arrangement between the British and continental governments in order to assist with conversation classes in modern languages; most assistants are French or German.

assisted school: a school assisted in part—though not fully maintained by—the local education authority. *Dist. f.* **aided school.**

attendance officer: an employee of the *local education authority,* responsible for the preparation of the school census and the investigation of absences.

bachelor of education degree: *see* **degree, bachelor of education.**

backward: a term often used to describe the slow learner, usually one whose intelligence quotient is between 70 and 84.

Barlow report: a report of the 1946 committee under Sir Alan Barlow on the future of scientific manpower.

Beloe report: report of a committee under Mr. R. Beloe set up in 1960 to investigate the examination system in secondary schools; this report led to the establishment of the *certificate of secondary education.*

bilateral school: a secondary school that offers a program related to any two of the three kinds of study—the academic, the technical, and the modern—in separate courses in the same school. *See* **multilateral school.**

binary system: the description used by the Department of Education and Science for the clear division of function and financing between the university sector on the one hand and, on the other, those areas of tertiary education directly controlled by the central and local government authorities. *See* **polytechnic; schooling, tertiary** (*see* main section of the Dictionary).

Board of Education: established in 1899 to replace the earlier Education Department and the Science and Art Department; chief functions were the distribution of governmental funds for education and the drafting of regulations under which such funds were distributed; was the national educational authority of England and Wales until replaced in 1944 by the *Ministry of Education* in which more comprehensive powers were vested. *See* **Committee on Education of the Privy Council; Department of Education and Science; Ministry of Education.**

board of governors: the governing body of a school with varied powers and make-up according to the nature and legal status of the school; for example, in the case of a secondary school, it is responsible for administering the *articles of government;* in the case of local education authority schools, the term *board of managers* is reserved for primary schools and the term *board of governors* for nonprimary establishments. *See* **articles of government.**

board of managers: *see* **board of governors.**

board, school: *see* **school board.**

board school: an obsolete term for an elementary school administered by a school board set up under the Education Act of 1870. *See* **school board;** *contr. w.* **boarding school.**

boarding school: a school in which pupils live and sleep.

Borstal institution: an institution, fully under central government control and run by the Home Office, offering a type of education aimed at developing intellectual interests and a sense of social responsibility and industry among delinquents over 16 years of age; sentence is for 2 years followed by a licensing period of a year during which the Borstal institution furnishes effective aftercare; name derived from village in Kent where first experiments were tried. *See* **approved school; detention center.**

Bryce Commission: a Royal Commission set up in 1894 to consider "the best methods of establishing a well-organized system of secondary education in England"; its report led to the establishment of the *Board of Education* and of *local education authorities. See* **Radcliffe-Maud Commission.**

bulge: any outstanding increase in the number of children of school age, particularly that occurring immediately after the 1939-45 war.

Burnham Committee: a permanent committee for adjusting primary and secondary teachers' salaries to the needs of the time.

bursar: (1) the administrative and financial officer of a large school or college; (2) the holder of one type of scholarship at a university.

Butler Act: the Education Act of 1944, whose major purpose was to provide secondary education for all with selection at "eleven plus" for allocation of children to *grammar, secondary modern,* or *technical* schools; responsible for the establishment of the secondary modern school which replaced the senior classes of the old elementary schools. *See* **Central Advisory Council; examination, eleven-plus.**

cadet corps: a military training organization attached to many (particularly public) secondary schools in which the teachers usually are given military rank; at one time, the term used was *officer training corps* but this term is now reserved for similar organizations in the universities.

captain: the chief pupil of a school or a house; sometimes elected but more often appointed by the school.

Central Advisory Council: an organization created by the Education Act of 1944 to supersede the Consultative Committee of the *Board of Education;* its function is to advise the Secretary of State for Education and Science, as it thinks fit, upon matters connected with educational theory and practice and to enquire into any questions referred to it by the Secretary; there is one council each for England and Wales consisting (in addition to the chairman) of 21 members and 18 members respectively; the members are of wide educational experience and represent varied interests; the chairman holds office for 3 years, ordinary members for 6, and one third retire every 2 years. *Dist. f.* **regional advisory council.**

central school: formerly a free selective school on the postprimary level offering a general curriculum with courses somewhat, but not strictly, vocational in nature; after the 1944 Act some central schools became technical schools, though others became new grammar schools. *See* **grammar school; technical school.**

certificate, higher school: a certificate formerly given to a person who passed the second or higher certificate examination taken by pupils remaining in a secondary school for 2 years of advanced work after passing the first or school certificate examination; has been replaced by the advanced level of pass of the general certificate of education. *See* **examination, general certificate of education.**

certificate, national: a certificate at two levels, ordinary and advanced, for proficiency in technical subjects; also called *national diploma.*

certificate of education, general: *see* **examination, general certificate of education.**

certificate of secondary education (C.S.E.): a certificate given to a person who has passed a less academic examination than that for the *general certificate of education* and designed after the *Beloe Report* of 1960 to provide a leaving examination for secondary modern and other less academically inclined pupils; unlike the general certificate of education examination which is organized by the universities, the C.S.E. examination is organized on a regional basis and teachers have a considerably greater say in the planning of the examination. *See* **examination, general certificate of education.**

certificate, professional nursery: an optional qualification for those having the care of preschool children.

certificate, school: a certificate awarded formerly to pupils in secondary schools who passed the first school certificate examination at about the age of 16; has been replaced by the general certificate of education. *See* **examination, general certificate of education.**

chancellor: the honorary rather than administrative head of a university. *See* **vice-chancellor.**

charity school: a type of school in England that provided education for the poor and became increasingly common during the eighteenth century; offered instruction in religion, reading, writing, and spelling, as well as some study of arithmetic as a practical course of training for domestic service; was usually supported by private contributions and controlled by some religious body.

chief education officer: an administrative head of the education committee of the *local education authority;* an experienced professional educator having functions and responsibilities analogous to those of a superintendent of schools in the United States. *See* **director of education.**

chief inspector: *see* **inspector, chief.**

chief inspector, senior: *see* **inspector, senior chief.**

chief medical officer: an officer responsible for the central supervision of the Schools Health Service (formerly the Medical Department of the Board of Education); as chief medical officer of the Ministry of Health, maintains a connection between the Ministry of Health and the Department of Education and Science. *See* **school clinic.**

child, defective: *see* **defective child.**

children's panels: new bodies of an advisory rather than a judicial nature which are to supplement though not replace juvenile courts under an Act of 1969; membership will not be confined to magistrates but will also include social workers and lay members with an interest in this field; certain cases which would previously have gone to the courts will now be dealt with by the panel instead.

city: in England this title does not necessarily indicate that a town is large; it is reserved for those towns which are (*a*) the seats of Anglican bishops whose seats were established before the nineteenth century or (*b*) towns of sufficient historical or economic importance to have had the title conferred on them by Royal Charter; thus it has no administrative significance since some cities are *county boroughs,* some are *municipal boroughs,* while some have no borough status at all.

City and Guilds Institute: an institute founded in 1879 by the Livery Companies of the City of London to encourage technical education and to award certificates for proficiency.

civic university: *see* **university, civic.**

Clarendon Commission: a Royal Commission of 1861 which reported on the future of the nine great public schools of England. *See* **public school.**

class, art: a class operated on a part-time or evening schedule, offering instruction in art.

class, nursery: a division of a primary school providing a program mainly for children between the ages of 3 and 5 years.

close exhibition: *see* **exhibition, close.**

close scholarship: *see* **scholarship, close.**

college: a term that for a long time retained the original meaning of its Latin origin *collegium,* an association, guild, or corporation established for any purpose and administered under common rules; from the Middle Ages on, the term gradually began to be applied more specifically to institutions for secondary or higher education, for example, Winchester College and Eton College at the secondary level and the colleges at Oxford and Cambridge at the higher level; does not have degree-conferring powers except in the case of St. David's College, Lampeter; the term is also used for certain professional bodies such as the Royal College of Surgeons which have surrendered much of their teaching function to the universities.

college, agricultural: an institution at the postsecondary level; financially aided by the Ministry of Agriculture and Fisheries; offers highly specialized courses in agricultural education to persons admitted from secondary schools, farm institutes, and other sources.

college, county: an institution proposed under the 1944 Act to be established by the local education authority in order to provide part-time education to persons above compulsory school age and under 18 years who are not in full-time attendance at an educational institution.

college, national: an institution established in the interest of the national economy to offer the highest levels of technical training to a limited number of persons from certain sections of industry.

college of education: a term now used in preference to *training college* or *teacher-training college* to describe a college outside a university where teachers are trained; most of its students follow a 3-year course of nongraduate training though specialist and general courses are also offered in some colleges to university graduates; in recent years some colleges have also taken over the responsibility for preparing students for the new Bachelor of Education degree, the foundation of which was recommended in the *Robbins report;* the degree, however, remains that of the local university rather than of the college, and the actual examinations are under the university's supervision. *Contr. w.* **institute of education.**

college of further education: a college established to meet local needs for further education; offers a program of full-time or part-time general or vocational education; includes the local *county college* in the same group of buildings; classified as central, branch, and local. *See* **evening institute.**

College of Preceptors: a nonresidential college in London founded in 1846 to improve the professional standards of teachers; has no official status but runs courses, certificate examinations, etc. for those wishing to improve their competence.

college, residential: an institution for adult education in rural areas to which students come for full-time study and which offers facilities for room and board, or means by which students may maintain themselves while in attendance; recognized by the Department of Education and Science and given financial and instructional assistance by the local education authorities; may be *county college, village college,* or *college of further education;* such colleges do not exist in large numbers.

college, Sixth Form: *see* **comprehensive education; comprehensive education using a Sixth Form college; Form.**

college, teacher-training: *see* **college of education.**

college, technical: an institution offering courses in the practical sciences and vocational subjects related to the industries of the area in which it is located; the college may embrace courses for students of secondary school age.

college, training: *see* **college of education.**

college, university: an institution that provides higher education but does not confer degrees; usually students in such institutions take the external examinations for degrees in the University of London but students at colleges in Wales take the examinations of the Federal University of Wales of which they are a part; many of the provincial universities began as university colleges and obtained charters as degree-granting universities later; the title "university college" also belongs to one constituent college at each of the Universities of Durham, Cambridge, London, and Oxford, but in these cases it in no way distinguishes it from the colleges of its universities and its functions are similar to theirs.

college, village: an institution established in a rural area as a community center for young people and adults; activities include a secondary school in addition to further education; such colleges are not commonly found except in Cambridgeshire where the system is highly developed.

Committee of Council: *see* **Committee on Education of the Privy Council.**

Committee on Education of the Privy Council: a committee organized in 1839 that consisted of four Ministers of the Crown, one of whom was the Lord President, who served as chairman, and a Permanent Secretary; dealt with matters concerning education in general and allocated governmental grants to elementary schools; was replaced in 1899 by the Board of Education; usually known as the *Committee of Council.*

common entrance examination: *see* **examination, common entrance.**

commoner: a member of an Oxford or Cambridge college who does not hold a college *scholarship* or *exhibition.*

comprehensive education: secondary education carried on in *comprehensive schools* and organized in systems varying from authority to authority.

comprehensive education, all-through: the comprehensive system in which a child remains in the same school from the age of 11 until he leaves.

comprehensive education, three-tier: the comprehensive system that involves the creation of a *middle school* for children aged 9-14 which acts as a transitional establishment covering part of the former primary and part of the former secondary course.

comprehensive education, two-tier: the comprehensive system in which the child transfers, or may transfer, to a different school at the age of 14. *See* **Leicestershire scheme.**

comprehensive education using a Sixth Form college: under such a scheme, either the academically distinguished or, in some places, all the remaining pupils age 16 transfer to a senior establishment run on more adult lines. *See* **Form; Form, Sixth.**

comprehensive school: a secondary school that combines every variety of academic, technical, and modern studies without arranging them in separate departments and for which there is no selection procedure on entry; ideally such a school would admit all the children of its age group from the surrounding area. *Contr. w.* **multilateral school.**

Consultative Committee: a group of advisers to the former Board of Education; first organized in 1900 under the Board of Education Act to represent the universities and other groups interested in education; duties were advisory and, when requested, investigatory; has been replaced by the *Central Advisory Council for Education.*

contributory service: teaching service on the basis of which the teacher contributes toward his pension and in terms of which the pension is assessed.

controlled school: a voluntary school entirely maintained by the *local education authority,* which controls the appointment of teachers and religious instruction from an agreed syllabus; certain rights are reserved to the managers or governors to preserve the original purpose for which the school was established. *See* **voluntary school.**

coopted members: those members of the education committee of the *local education authority* who have been invited to join the committee because of their personal qualities or expertise and not because they are members of the local education authority (that is, elected members of the County or County Borough Council) or because they have been officially nominated to represent some body such as a church or a teachers' organization. *See* **education committee; local education authority.**

corporation: a legal term used to denote a *municipal* or *county borough council.*

corporation school: *see* **council school.**

corps, cadet: *see* **cadet corps.**

council, county borough: *see* **county borough.**

Council for National Academic Awards: an autonomous body established by Royal Charter in 1964 with powers to award degrees, diplomas, certificates, and other academic awards to persons who have pursued courses approved by the council at establishments other than universities or who have carried out research under the auspices of such establishments.

council member: a member of any council, popularly elected for the general purposes of local administration; normally referred to as a "councillor;" includes all members of *county* and *county borough councils*, the senior members of which are given the title of "alderman."

council, municipal borough: *see* **municipal borough.**

council school: the term formerly applied to a public elementary school provided by the *local education authority;* replaced by the term *county school* or, in common parlance, by *corporation school* in county boroughs.

council secondary school: *see* **secondary school, council.**

county: *see* **administrative county.**

county borough: a large town which for purposes of local administration has been made completely independent of the *administrative county* in which it is situated; this independence does not prevent it from being also the site of the headquarters of an administrative county that has no control over it; county borough councils have all the powers of administrative counties and are their own *local education authority;* for example, in Carlisle are located the offices of two local education authorities, that of the county borough Carlisle itself and that of Cumberland Administrative County which has no say in the running of education in its own capital city. *See* **Radcliffe-Maud Commission;** *comp. w.* **county town; excepted district; municipal borough.**

county borough council: *see* **county borough.**

county college: *see* **college, county.**

county council: *see* **county borough; council member.**

county school: a primary or a secondary school other than a nursery or special school established and maintained by a *local education authority;* responsibility for the appointment of teachers rests with the local education authority and religious instruction is given according to an agreed syllabus; formerly called *council* or *provided school. Comp. w.* **controlled school; voluntary school.**

county town: a title conferred on the traditional capital of a county; may be a *municipal borough* or a *county borough.*

course, diploma: a course at a university or other institution of higher education which leads to the award of a diploma rather than a degree; formerly a diploma was usually awarded at the end of the year spent by graduates undergoing training in a university department of education, though the term "certificate" is now more often used, the term "diploma" being reserved for a more academic course on educational theory offered at some universities.

course, honors: an undergraduate course of a specialist kind involving study of a higher standard than that required in a constituent course of a general (or nonhonors) degree; most undergraduate courses at English universities are now of an honors type, and most students undertake the study of one subject only at this level. *See* **degree, honors.**

course, pass: (1) a university program of studies leading to the B.A. or B.Sc. pass degrees, nonspecialized and general in character, and approximately equivalent to the typical course for the A.B. or B.S. degrees in the United States; common also throughout the British Commonwealth of Nations and India; the adjective *pass* signifies that the student is obliged to obtain a certain minimum mark in each class (this minimum is somewhat lower than that required for the *honors course); see* **course, honors;** (2) a single class or subject of study constituting a part of the program of studies leading to a pass degree.

course, pilot: an experimental course tried out for observational purposes on a small sample group before being applied to a larger sample of the population.

course system, sandwich: a system whereby an apprentice spends his time partly in a job and partly in a university or other institution which offers training in the theory of the subject; normally the apprentice spends a period of weeks or months, full-time, in one sector and the other alternately.

crèche (kresh): a type of day nursery established to care for the preschool children of working mothers, usually upon the payment of a small fee; accepts children of 1 month to 3 years of age.

credit: a standard of successful performance on an examination in advance of the ordinary pass mark but ranking below a *distinction.*

Crowther report: a report of the *Central Advisory Council* in 1959, dealing with educational provision for young people between the ages of 15 and 18; recommended the raising of the age for compulsory education to 16.

day-release scheme: a scheme whereby young people are released by their employers during normal working hours and on a part-time basis for general education or vocational training related to their jobs.

dean: at Oxford and Cambridge, a college *fellow* who is responsible for the internal organization or discipline of the college; often a clergyman who is also responsible for the college chapel; in other English universities normally used for the head of a faculty.

defective child: a child suffering from any mental or physical disability.

degree, bachelor of education: a degree awarded on successful completion of a course for the training of teachers, with the work usually done in a college of education; it is of *general degree* level and the course usually lasts for four years.

degree, double honors: *see* **degree, joint honors.**

degree, general: a degree awarded on successful completion of a course, usually of three years, during which a number of subjects have been studied at a level lower than that demanded for the more specialized *honors degree.*

degree, honors: a degree awarded on the successful completion of an *honors course* which usually lasts for three years. *See* **tripos;** *comp. w.* **degree, general.**

degree, joint honors: a degree awarded on the successful completion of a course, usually of three years, in which two or occasionally three subjects have been studied at a level higher than that required for a *general degree* but covering less ground than that required for a single *honors degree. Syn.* **double honors degree.**

degree, Lambeth: a degree conferred by the Archbishop of Canterbury by virtue of the Papal rights which were deemed to have passed to him in the sixteenth century; candidates for the degree need not have attended any university courses.

demonstrator: a teacher or teacher's assistant, as in a medical or scientific school, whose duties consist in the demonstration of experiments, dissections, anatomical preparation, etc.

department, extramural: the department of a university that arranges lectures, concerts, etc., for general audiences outside the university; the country has been divided into regions for each of which a particular university has a special responsibility in this field of activity.

Department of Education and Science: the government body presided over by a Secretary of State which in April 1964 took over, among other responsibilities, those of the former *Ministry of Education;* responsible for schools in England and Wales and in addition for the University Grants Committee for the whole of Great Britain. *See* **Secretary of State for Education and Science.**

Department, Science and Art: a department of the central government established in 1853 for the encouragement of science; provided grants for schools and financial aid for special students in science; was replaced in 1899 by the then newly created *Board of Education.*

department, university training: *see* **institute of education.**

detention center: a center, set up by the Criminal Justice Act of 1948 and under the Home Office Prisons Department, offering a short course of intensive, military-style training, 8 to 12 weeks in duration, for young offenders aged 16 to 21 whose offenses or records are not considered serious enough for them to be sent to a *Borstal institution.*

diploma course: *see* **course, diploma.**

diploma, national: *syn.* **certificate, national.**

direct grant: *see* **grant, direct.**

direct-grant school: a school or institution that receives a grant direct from the Secretary of State for Education and Science to meet the cost of its educational services; used in particular for those independent secondary schools which receive the grant in exchange for an undertaking to accept a substantial number of pupils from the local education area in which it is situated, often at the expense of that authority who selects candidates on the basis of their secondary selection examination. *See* **Donnison Report.**

director of education: in certain local education authorities this term is used in place of *chief education officer.*

disabled person: a physically handicapped person who receives special educational training in preparation for employment.

distinction: *see* **credit.**

division, inspectional: *see* **inspectional division.**

divisional administration: *see* **scheme of divisional administration.**

divisional executive: an appointed body of persons aware of the needs of a community; exercises functions over one of the sections into which the area of a local education authority may be divided for efficient administration. *See* **education committee.**

divisional inspector: *see* **inspector, divisional.**

don: a teacher or tutor in a university; used particularly at Oxford and Cambridge.

Donnison Report: the report (1970) of a special committee appointed by the *Public Schools Commission* to deal with the future of the direct-grant schools and the independent day-schools and with their relationship to the rest of the educational system; recommended that the direct-grant system should be ended and that such schools should have the choice of either being completely maintained or being completely independent. *See* **direct-grant school; independent school.**

dormitory: in England, almost invariably a common bedroom rather than a building housing separate rooms.

double honors degree: *see* **degree, joint honors.**

dual system: arrangement whereby both the state and private or denominational voluntary bodies possess powers of control in the administration of education.

Duke of Edinburgh's Award: a scheme for recognizing proficiency in leisure time pursuits among young people leading to the award of bronze, silver, and gold medals for which definite standards are set by a body presided over by the Duke; established in 1954.

education, adult: *see* **adult education.**

education board, joint: *see* **joint education board.**

education committee: the board that represents a *local education authority,* responsible locally for the general administration of public education and for the exercise of the main powers of the local education authority with the exception of the right to raise rates and borrow money; consists of a committee of the local council—the chairman and the majority of the members being council members and the remainder being either representatives of the churches, teachers, and other interested parties or coopted members. *See* **coopted members; divisional executive.**

education, fundamental: *see* **fundamental education.**

education, further: *see* **further education.**

education, higher: *see* **higher education.**

education, infant: *see* **infant education.**

education, postprimary: *see* **postprimary education.**

education, primary: *see* **primary education.**

education, secondary: *see* **secondary education.**

educational settlement: a type of center for adult education through classes and discussion groups; recognized by the Department of Education and Science; aided through grants and teaching assistance by the local education authorities.

efficiency bar: restriction imposed at a point in the salary scale to be crossed for entry into higher salary grade only on proof of teacher's efficiency.

elementary school: prior to 1944, a free publicly operated school offering *primary* (to 11 years of age) and *postprimary* education (to the age of 14 years).

eleven-plus examination: *see* **examination, eleven-plus.**

endowed school: a school which benefits from endowments that have been bequeathed to it.

entrance examination, common: *see* **examination, common entrance.**

evening institute: a program of classes offered in the evening as part of a general program of adult education; founded on local initiative, the course of study being determined by local needs and interests. *See* **college of further education.**

evening school: a type of school conducted in the evening for the benefit of young people who have left day school and gone to work without completing their formal education; similar in scope and aims to the evening schools in the United States.

examination, common entrance: the examination taken, usually at the age of 13 and at a *preparatory school,* by candidates for places in *public schools.*

examination, eleven-plus: the examination, normally administered to pupils at the age of 10 or 11, whereby local authorities assigned them to either *grammar, secondary modern,* or *technical* schools; the form of the examination varied from area to area and some authorities took teachers' opinions into account in addition to the examination; however, under most authorities it took the form of a battery of objective tests in English, arithmetic (or mathematics), and verbal reasoning, prepared either by the National Foundation for Education Research or by Edinburgh University; the examination was largely swept away by the government's decision to change to a system of *comprehensive schools;* in certain localities it is still administered since local authorities have not as yet been compelled to abolish it; the Conservative Party has said that, if returned to power, they would revive it.

examination, first school certificate: *syn.* **examination, school certificate.**

examination, general certificate of education: in 1951 superseded the *school certificate* and *higher school certificate examinations;* candidates may take one or more subjects at ordinary, advanced, or higher levels; the examinations are organized not by Government but by the universities either individually or in groups, though an attempt is made to maintain nationally uniform standards. *See* **certificate of secondary education; examination, higher school certificate; examination, matriculation; examination, school certificate.**

examination, higher school certificate: before 1951, an examination given in the secondary school to pupils who had taken 2 years of advanced work in the Sixth Form and who held the first school certificate; it has been superseded by the advanced level of the general certificate of education examination. *See* **examination, general certificate of education.**

examination, intermediate: an examination given at provincial universities and the University of London at the end of the first year of a course of studies leading to a degree. (The possession of the advanced level of the general certificate of education is sometimes accepted as ground for exemption from the whole or part of this examination.)

examination, matriculation: an examination which must be passed before a candidate may matriculate at a University; most English students, however, are exempted from the examination on the basis of having passed the necessary parts of the *general certificate of education examination* and the matriculation examination has therefore been suspended in many universities.

examination, school certificate: prior to 1951, an examination given to pupils at the completion of their fifth year in a grammar school or their first or second year in a *public school,* that is, normally in their 16th or 17th year; served as a means of exemption from the matriculation examination for university entrance and, in many cases, as a school-leaving examination; it has been superseded, except for overseas candidates, by the ordinary level of the general certificate of education examination. *See* **examination, general certificate of education.**

examination, university entrance: *see* **examination, matriculation.**

excepted district: a large urban area which is not a *county borough* but which is given a certain degree of independence, under the county education authority, to run its own educational affairs; for certain purposes, however, it is still controlled by the county authorities and has not the complete independence of a county borough.

exhibition: a financial award made to a secondary or university student generally on the basis of competitive examinations.

exhibition, close: an award at a university or school which is not available to everyone but is restricted in some way, for example, to people born in a certain county, studying a certain field, etc.; normally slightly lower in status and monetary value than a close scholarship. *See* **scholarship, close;** *contr. w.* **exhibition, open.**

exhibition, open: an exhibition subject to no restriction of entry. *Contr. w.* **exhibition, close.**

extramural department: *see* **department, extramural.**

farm institute: an institution provided by the local education authority; offers full-time specialized technical training below that of the agricultural college to prospective farmers from about 18 years of age.

farmers' institute: *syn.* **farm institute.**

fellow: at Oxford and Cambridge, a senior member of a college who is usually a member of the college or university teaching staff or has an important part to play in the college community; elsewhere, the holder of a research appointment doing work at a very high level; also used to denote full or senior members of certain learned societies and colleges outside the universities.

finals: the examinations at the end of a university course.

first school certificate examination: *syn.* **examination, school certificate.**

Fisher Act: the Education Act of 1918 giving local authorities the power, which was largely ignored, to extend children's compulsory education beyond the age of 14.

Form: a unit of the secondary school system corresponding to a high school *grade* in the U.S.A. or Canada; Form I normally corresponds to ages 11 to 12, thus Form VI is composed of pupils 17 to 18 and over; except in a few schools, there is no Form VII, many pupils remaining in Form VI for the last two or three years of their school career; the ordinary level examination of the general certificate of education is usually taken in Forms IV or V and the advanced level after two years in Form VI. *See* **examination, general certificate of education.**

Form, Sixth: traditionally, the senior class of a secondary school in which pupils are normally pursuing courses of high academic content. *See* **Form.**

foundation governor: governor appointed in a voluntary secondary school by the founding body and not by the municipal authority; such governors form only a proportion of the governing body of a school. *Comp. w.* **foundation manager.**

foundation manager: manager appointed in a voluntary primary school by the founding body and not by the municipal authority; such managers form only a proportion of the body of management of a school. *See* **manager, voluntary school;** *comp. w.* **foundation governor.**

foundation school: a private school financed, in part at least, by endowments.

free place: obsolescent *syn.* **special place.**

free university: *see* **university, free.**

fundamental education: a type of mass education that aims to eliminate illiteracy and raise the standard of living in underdeveloped areas.

further education: a general term for the training offered in (*a*) *county colleges* (once these shall have been established) providing compulsory part-time education for young people under 18 years of age not in full-time attendance at a school or other educational institution and (*b*) a group of institutions and schools attended on a voluntary basis and operated under special regulations through the authority of a separate branch of the Department of Education and Science and the *local education authority;* intended to give training largely of a technical, vocational, and cultural type as a supplement to what is offered in primary and secondary schools; extends through a wide range of activities centering around preparation for work and learning for leisure. *See* **adult education.**

general certificate of education (G.C.E.): *see* **examination, general certificate of education.**

general degree: *see* **degree, general.**

general inspector: *see* **inspector, general.**

grammar school: the traditional form of secondary education for boys dating from medieval and Renaissance times with the study of Latin a basic component; in modern times, a school mainly academic in its orientation and preparation of its pupils for university, professional life, etc.; in this sense the term covers both day and boarding schools (independent as well as state-aided) offering such an education; however, in the twentieth century it has most often been used only of those schools in which boarders are in a minority and in which state-aided pupils play a significant part; for girls to attend grammar schools has been usual only during this century; entrance into such schools has depended on gaining high marks in the *eleven-plus examination* though the proportion of an age group entering grammar schools has varied from one local authority area to another; most of the state-aided grammar schools have now been incorporated into comprehensive schools. *See* **comprehensive school.**

grant-aided institution: an educational institution that receives direct grants from the Department of Education and Science and/or aid from a *local education authority* out of rate-fund moneys, that is, money raised by local rates.

grant-aided school: *syn.* **aided school.**

grant, direct: a grant of money paid by the Secretary of State for Education and Science directly to an institution for the purpose of educational services.

Greater London Council (G.L.C.): the governing body for the London area, including the former counties of London and Middlesex and parts of the surrounding counties; subdivided for certain purposes into a number of London Boroughs. *See* **local education authority.**

greats: *see* **literae humaniores; modern greats.**

Hadow report: a report issued in 1926 by the Consultative Committee of the Board of Education under the chairmanship of Sir Henry Hadow, entitled *The Education of the Adolescent.* [The Consultative Committee subsequently issued two other reports, *The Primary School* (1931) and *Infant and Nursery Schools* (1933); the three reports greatly influenced the subsequent reorganization of the traditional English elementary school, particularly at the postprimary level.]

hall of residence: a place of residence for students at universities other than Oxford, Cambridge, and Durham.

head teacher: a teacher in charge of a separate department of a public primary school or in charge of the whole school; often devotes some time to class instruction in addition to supervisory and administrative duties. *See* **headmaster.**

headmaster: strictly, the principal of a secondary school; also applied popularly to principals of elementary schools for whom the official designation in government regulations is *head teacher.*

Headmasters' Conference: a private organization which a limited number of headmasters are invited to join; membership normally implies that the headmaster's school is generally recognized to be a *public school* though membership is by no means restricted to boarding or even completely independent schools; criteria for selecting members include the size and quality of the *Sixth Form* and the number of ex-pupils at universities.

headmistress: a woman employed as the administrative head of a school.

high master: the title used instead of *headmaster* at St. Paul's School, London and at Manchester Grammar School.

high school: a type of grammar school, normally for girls, though the term is sometimes used for coeducational establishments. *See* **grammar school.**

higher education: prior to the Education Act 1944, a general term for the education provided in the secondary schools and universities; is still used to refer to postsecondary education of the university type.

higher school certificate: *see* **certificate, higher school.**

higher school certificate examination: *see* **examination, higher school certificate.**

His (Her) Majesty's Inspector: *see* **Inspector, His (Her) Majesty's.**

Home Office: a branch of the central government presided over by the Secretary of State (for the Home Department) and responsible, among other duties, for the control of various schools for delinquents. *See* **approved school.**

Home Office school: *syn.* **approved school.**

honors course: *see* **course, honors.**

honors degree: *see* **degree, honors.**

hospital special school: an institution established on hospital premises by the local education authority or a voluntary body to provide education for hospitalized children of school age.

housecraft: household science or home economics.

housemaster: a teacher in charge of a division of a school, called a "house," consisting of pupils of all ages; generally found in secondary schools and, occasionally, in primary schools. (Originated in boarding schools; applied to a teacher residing in a house or dormitory and responsible for the discipline, conduct, and advising of the boys living in the house or dormitory.)

independent school: a school that does not receive grants from the *local education authority* or direct aid from the Secretary of State for Education and Science yet provides a full-time program of education for five or more pupils of compulsory school age.

independent university: *syn.* **university, free.**

industrial school: formerly, a type of reform school for potential delinquents, either voluntarily maintained by a private association or publicly operated by a *local education authority,* aided by government grants and subject to governmental inspection; curriculum stressed practical trades and crafts; replaced by the *approved school.*

infant education: the type of education given in the *infant school;* aims at supplying what is essential for the child's healthy growth, physically, intellectually, spiritually, and morally, during the transitional stage from babyhood to childhood; curriculum consists of activity and experience rather than of knowledge to be acquired and facts to be stored and is intended to encourage the child to achieve control and orderly management of his energies, impulses, and emotions.

infant school: the lower division of the primary school; accepts pupils from 5 to 7 or 8 years; sometimes also provides for pupils under 5 years. *See* **junior school; primary school.**

Inner London Education Authority: *see* **local education authority.**

Inns of Court: collegiate institutions in London for the training of barristers.

inspection: the term used in England and Canada to designate the activities denoted in the United States by the term *supervision.*

inspection, subject: the intermittent observation and evaluation of formal instruction in a particular school subject. *See* **inspection.**

inspectional division: the area or district containing the schools under the jurisdiction of the inspector who carries out the duties pertaining to inspection.

inspector: an experienced educator employed either by the *local education authority* or by the Department of Education and Science to supervise and offer educational guidance in the schools under its jurisdiction. *See* **Inspector, His (Her) Majesty's.**

inspector, chief: one of the six supervisors appointed by order in council on the advice of the Secretary of State for Education and Science.

inspector, divisional: inspector in charge of one of the 10 inspectoral regions into which the country is divided; responsible for coordinating inspectoral duties in a division.

inspector, general: the one inspector responsible for the general inspection of a school from time to time.

Inspector, His (Her) Majesty's: an inspector appointed by the Secretary of State for Education and Science to conduct negotiations with the *local education authority* in accordance with the policy of the Department of Education and Science; gives educational advice in schools. *See* **inspector.**

inspector, senior chief: head of the entire unified inspectoral staff under whom are six chief inspectors and a number of divisional and staff inspectors.

Institute, City and Guilds: *see* **City and Guilds Institute.**

institute, evening: *see* **evening institute.**

institute, farm: *see* **farm institute.**

institute of education: a body, normally attached to a university, which supervises teacher training in the surrounding area; also provides specialist and other advanced courses on its own account for both students and serving teachers; not to be confused with the university's department of education the main task of which is the training of graduates for teaching; research is, however, carried on in both institutions. *Comp. w.* **college of education.**

instrument of government: a document that defines the terms under which the *board of governors* of a secondary school is formed.

instrument of management: a document that defines the terms under which the board of managers of a primary school is composed. *Comp. w.* **instrument of government; rules of management.**

intermediate examination: *see* **examination, intermediate.**

italic writing: *see* **writing, italic.**

joint education board: a board established as the *local education authority* of two or more municipal units permitted to unite to provide adequate educational facilities which, separately, they cannot afford.

Joint Four: a committee of the professional associations concerned with grammar school education: the Incorporated Association of Headmasters (I.A.H.M.), the Association of Headmistresses (A.H.M.), the Incorporated Association of Assistant Masters (A.M.A.) and the Association of Assistant Mistresses (A.A.M.). *See* **grammar school.**

joint honors degree: *see* **degree, joint honors.**

joint matriculation board: the school examination body of the Universities of Manchester, Leeds, Liverpool, Sheffield, and Birmingham.

junior school: the upper division of the primary school; accepts pupils from 8 to 11 years. *See* **infant school; primary school.**

junior technical school: a general term formerly applied to a number of schools that admitted pupils at the age of 13 years for a 3- or 4-year course and prepared them for a particular industry or group of related industries while continuing the pupils' general education; included junior commercial schools, junior art departments, nautical schools, and junior housewifery schools; by the Education Act 1944, became part of the secondary technical school system. *See* **secondary technical school.**

Lambeth degree: *see* **degree, Lambeth.**

L.E.A.: a commonly used abbreviation for *local education authority.*

leader, youth: *see* **youth service.**

lecturer: a teacher in higher education; in a university, most of the teachers have the rank of lecturer which comes below those of *professor* and *reader*, which are normally reserved for those who are either heads of departments or particularly distinguished in their field.

Leicestershire scheme: a two-tier system under which the child may decide at 14 either to transfer from the high school (which he has attended since 11) to an upper school where he would normally stay until the age of 18 to 19 or to remain in the high school which he would leave at the age of 15 to 16. *See* **comprehensive education, two-tier.**

literae humaniores (li'tə·rī hŏō·mä·nē·ō'räs): (Lat., lit., "more humane letters") the course for an *honors degree* in classics and philosophy at Oxford, commonly called "greats."

local education authority (L.E.A.): a county council or county borough council in its role as the body required to provide stipulated educational facilities in the area under its control; however, the *Greater London Council* is not the local educational authority; Central London (that is, those London Boroughs previously forming part of the old County of London) comes under a special authority, the *Inner London Education Authority*, while each of the boroughs not included in its area is its own local education authority.

manager, voluntary school: one of the board of managers of a *voluntary school;* this board consists of the foundation managers or trustees and representatives of the *local education authority* in the proportion of 4:2 except that this is reversed in the case of controlled voluntary schools. *See* **board of governors; controlled school; foundation manager.**

matriculate: (1) strictly and etymologically, to enter or enroll in an institution such as a school or university; (2) as commonly used, to fulfill the requirements for entrance into a university, especially by passing examinations.

matriculation board, joint: *see* **joint matriculation board.**

matriculation examination: *see* **examination, matriculation.**

middle school: *see* **comprehensive education, three-tier; comprehensive school.**

Minister of Education: formerly, the political head of the Ministry of Education; his duties have now been taken over by the *Secretary of State for Education and Science. See* **President of the Board of Education.**

Ministry of Agriculture and Fisheries: a department of the central government that, among its other duties, has general responsibility for the administration of agricultural education and maintains and gives financial assistance to special agricultural colleges for students beyond the usual school age.

Ministry of Education: formerly the government department responsible for overseeing the work of the *local education authorities* in England and Wales; established under the Education Act of 1944 to supersede the *Board of Education;* its duties are now undertaken by the *Department of Education and Science.*

minor authority: the authority for a noncounty borough or an urban district or rural parish controlling an area contained in the wider area of the administrative county.

modern greats: an honors examination at Oxford in philosophy, politics, and economics, commonly known as P.P.E. *See* **literae humaniores.**

modern school: *see* **secondary modern school.**

multilateral school: a secondary school that offers programs in the three kinds of studies—the academic, the technical, and the modern—in separate courses in the same school. *See* **bilateral school;** *dist. f.* **comprehensive school.**

municipal borough: a small town not large enough to be given the educational independence of a *county borough;* under the 1902 Act it was required to establish and maintain elementary schools in its area but this is now the responsibility of the *local education authority. Comp. w.* **county borough; excepted district; Part III authority.**

municipal borough council: *see* **municipal borough.**

national certificate: *see* **certificate, national.**

national college: *see* **college, national.**

national diploma: *syn.* **certificate, national.**

Newcastle Commission: a commission appointed in 1858 to investigate the state of elementary education; its findings led to the framing of the Education Act of 1870 and the system of free, compulsory schooling which developed in the years that followed.

Newsom Committee: a committee which reported in 1963 on the education of children of average and below average ability.

nonprovided school: formerly, a school which, though maintained by the *local education authority,* was not provided with its buildings by the authority. *See* **voluntary school.**

nursery certificate, professional: *see* **certificate, professional nursery.**

nursery class: *see* **class, nursery.**

nursery school: a school established by the local educational authority or voluntary bodies to provide daytime care for children of ages 2 to under 5 years whose working mothers desire the facilities; program emphasizes play, health care, and social development of pupils; eligible for maintenance or assistance grants.

nursery student: a probationary helper between the ages of 15 and 18 years in nursery institutions; supplements duties in nursery by further general and vocational education, thereby qualifying for a *professional nursery certificate.*

nursery training: a course given in a model nursery school in which the methods of dealing with very young children may be studied by prospective infant teachers.

officer training corps: *see* **cadet corps.**

open-air school: a type of special school developed for the education of physically debilitated children in order that they may continue their education while regaining their health and vitality; classes are held in the open air; children are well fed and warmly clad, and formal work is reduced and modified.

open exhibition: *see* **exhibition, open.**

open scholarship: *see* **scholarship, open.**

open university: *see* **university, open.**

outward bound school: a school normally providing short courses for a changing student population where, by emphasizing physically strenuous activities and ventures involving personal resources, the leaders hope to encourage self-confidence and a feeling for team work; these schools have been created largely by disciples of Kurt Hahn, the founder of Salem in Germany and Gordonstoun in Scotland, and are normally situated in wild, mountainous areas.

parent-teacher association: a voluntary, purely advisory body found in some—but by no means all—schools in England and Wales; has no statutory basis.

Parliamentary Secretary: a member of Parliament, appointed to serve the interests of the Department of Education and Science in the House of Commons, who frequently replies for the Secretary of State for Education and Science on points raised in debate; is *Undersecretary for Education,* but is not a professionally trained educator and does not return to a position in the Department of Education and Science when he ceases to be Parliamentary Secretary or a member of Parliament.

Part II authority: formerly the *local education authority* of a county or county borough; authorized, under Part II of the Education Act of 1902, to provide any type of education from nursery school up to and including adult education and to make grants to universities and other institutions of higher education; responsibilities were modified and the term no longer applied under the Education Act, 1944.

Part III authority: formerly the *local education authority* of an urban district or municipal borough, defined and authorized under Part III of the Education Act of 1902; was responsible for the administration and organization of nursery and elementary schools though permitted to cooperate with Part II authorities in the provision of postelementary education; was abolished under the Education Act, 1944.

pass course: *see* **course, pass.**

Permanent Secretary of the Department of Education and Science: the professional head of the Department of Education and Science permanently attached to the Department and under the Secretary of State for Education and Science; formulates and directs the policies of the Department subject to the sanction of the Secretary of State for Education and Science and exercises general supervisory and advisory functions in relation to the work of the Department.

pilot course: *see* **course, pilot.**

Plowden Committee: a committee appointed to investigate the future of primary education and reporting in 1966.

polytechnic: an establishment in which work of university standard is done, normally for the degrees of the *Council for National Academic Awards,* but which also carries on work of nonuniversity standard, is government financed, and is under (normally local) government control.

postprimary education: the education formerly offered in senior and central schools and in the postprimary departments of elementary schools for children over 11 years of age.

postprimary school: prior to 1944, a school for the postprimary education of children between the ages of 11 and 14 or, sometimes, 15 years; was a *central school,* or a *senior school,* or the postprimary department of an elementary school. *See* **secondary school.**

P.P.E.: *see* **modern greats.**

prefect: a senior pupil generally appointed to discharge certain duties with respect to student government of the school.

prep: (short for "preparation") a term used in grammar and public schools for work done at home or outside class.

preparatory school: a junior department of a public school or a separate institution, usually privately operated, having as its principal function the preparation of pupils for enrollment in an independent school at the secondary level; may be inspected by the Department of Education and Science and recognized as efficient, but does not receive grants; however, where suitable educational facilities do not otherwise exist, pupils may be assisted to attend by means of government grants. *See* **public school.**

President of the Board of Education: a former official designation of the political head of the central government organization for education; subsequently termed *Minister of Education,* a title which has now been replaced by *Secretary of State for Education and Science.*

primary education: in general, education up to about 11 years of age. *See* **primary school.**

primary school: any school for pupils of 5 to 11 years; divided into the *infant school* (5 to 7 years) and the *junior school* (8 to 11 years); may also include a *nursery class* for children of 3 to 5 years.

private school: a school, provided by a private individual or a group of private individuals, that receives no financial aid from either the local or the central education authority. (Such schools, if their proprietors or board of governors so desire, may be inspected by the local or central education authority.) *See* **independent school.**

professional nursery certificate: *see* **certificate, professional nursery.**

professor: *see* **lecturer; reader; regius professor.**

proprietary school: a privately owned school operated for private profit.

provided school: a primary school established and maintained by the local education authority; now called *county school.*

provincial university: *see* **university, civic.**

provost: (1) commonly, the head of an English college; (2) *see* **provost** (main section of Dictionary).

public school: a private boarding school, endowed and charging tuition fees, usually very exclusive, often of great antiquity, and traditionally academic in curriculum; noncoeducational; pupils usually admitted at about 13 years for a course on the secondary level in preparation for university matriculation. (NOTE: The designation *public* signifies, in this case, a privately operated school open to public patronage or with a wide public reputation.) *See* **Headmasters' Conference.**

Public Schools Commission: a Royal Commission reporting in 1969 on the ways in which the *public schools* and other independent boarding schools could be associated more closely with the general educational system. *See* **Donnison Report.**

qualified teacher: a teacher who, subject to certain provisions, has completed to the satisfaction of the Secretary of State for Education and Science an approved course of training for the teaching profession or who possesses such special qualifications as the Secretary of State for Education and Science may approve.

Radcliffe-Maud Commission: a Royal Commission reporting in 1969 on the boundaries and responsibilities of English local government outside London; proposed, among other things, the abolition of the existing distinction between *counties* and *county boroughs* and suggested a considerable redrawing of county boundaries.

reader: a university teacher of a rank immediately below that of *professor. See* **lecturer.**

reformatory school: formerly, a certified school for youthful offenders, where they were maintained, educated, and instructed in manual work; subject to ultimate control by the Home Office, publicly or privately operated; supported by parliamentary, council, and, in certain cases, borough council grants. *See* **approved school.**

regional academic board: an organization set up to deal with needs of advanced technology in a region and to coordinate programs of the local education authorities, the local universities, and industrial interests in meeting those needs.

regional advisory council: an organization established by the Secretary of State for Education and Science to deal generally with problems of *further education* in a region and to ensure and coordinate provision for local interests and needs. *Dist. f.* **regional academic board.**

regius professor: a university professor whose chair was founded by the Crown and who is appointed by the sovereign on the advice of the prime minister.

reserved place: a place, in excess of the free places, reserved in the upper section of a direct-grant secondary school for suitably qualified pupils; with the free places, should not exceed 50 percent of upper school admissions. *See* **free place; special place.**

reserved teacher: a teacher competent to give denominational religious instruction in *controlled* or *special agreement schools;* appointed by the *local education authority* after consultation with the managers or governors.

residential college: *see* **college, residential.**

revised code: a series of government instructions for the payment of money to schools which was issued in 1862 and was largely responsible for the notorious system of "payment by results", later abandoned.

Robbins Committee: a committee appointed to investigate the future of higher education, whose findings were published in 1963.

rules of management: rules made by a local education authority which define the respective powers and functions of the local education authority, the managers, and the head teacher in the conduct of a county or voluntary primary school. *Comp. w.* **instrument of management.**

sandwich course system: *see* **course system, sandwich.**

scheme of divisional administration: scheme for partitioning the area of an authority in divisions and appointing persons with special knowledge of the needs of the community for service on the *divisional executive* to which some functions of the local education authority are delegated; ensures that local circumstances are provided for.

scholarship, close: a scholarship at a university or school which is not available to everyone, for example, one restricted to people born in a certain county or, more often, to those who have attended a certain school. *See* **exhibition, close;** *contr. w.* **scholarship, open.**

scholarship, open: a scholarship subject to no restriction of entry. *See* **exhibition, open;** *contr. w.* **scholarship, close.**

school, aided: *see* **aided school.**

school, all-age: *see* **all-age school.**

school, approved: *see* **approved school.**

school, art: *see* **art school.**

school, assisted: *see* **assisted school.**

school attendance order: notification sent to parents by the *local education authority* requiring the child's enrollment and full-time attendance at school if the child is of compulsory school age.

school, bilateral: *see* **bilateral school.**

school, board: *see* **board school.**

school board: a local body which between 1870 and 1902 administered elementary education and was responsible for *board schools.*

school, boarding: *see* **boarding school.**

school, central: *see* **central school.**

school certificate: *see* **certificate, school.**

school certificate examination: *see* **examination, school certificate.**

school, charity: *see* **charity school.**

school clinic: a department of the school devoted to the medical inspection and treatment of school children; developed by the Board of Education (now Department of Education and Science) as part of the School Medical Service since 1907, and transferred to the Ministry of Health in 1919. *See* **chief medical officer.**

school, comprehensive: *see* **comprehensive school.**

school, controlled: *see* **controlled school.**

school, corporation: *see* **council school.**

school, council: *see* **council school.**

school, county: *see* **county school.**

school, direct-grant: *see* **direct-grant school.**

school, elementary: *see* **elementary school.**

school, endowed: *see* **endowed school.**

school, evening: *see* **evening school.**

school for defectives: a school for those who are markedly subnormal, especially with regard to mental and physical traits.

school, foundation: *see* **foundation school.**

school, grammar: *see* **grammar school.**

school, grant-aided: *syn.* **aided school.**

school, high: *see* **high school.**

school, hospital special: *see* **hospital special school.**

school, independent: *see* **independent school.**

school, industrial: *see* **industrial school.**

school, infant: *see* **infant school.**

school, junior: *see* **junior school.**

school, junior technical: *see* **junior technical school.**

school-leaving age: the age after which school attendance is no longer compulsory; all children have been required to attend school until the age of 15; it is planned to raise this to 16 in the academic year of 1972-3.

school meals services: the activities involved in giving meals or extra nourishment to school children; originally planned to provide free meals to undernourished children of the poor, now provided for a majority of children; administered by local education authorities under the Provision of Meals Act of 1906; attention is paid especially to the distribution of milk.

school, middle: *see* **comprehensive education, three-tier; comprehensive school.**

school, modern: *see* **secondary modern school.**

school, multilateral: *see* **multilateral school.**

school, nonprovided: *see* **nonprovided school.**

school, nursery: *see* **nursery school.**

school, open-air: *see* **open-air school.**

school, outward bound: *see* **outward bound school.**

school, postprimary: *see* **postprimary school.**

school, preparatory: *see* **preparatory school.**

school, primary: *see* **primary school.**

school, private: *see* **private school.**

school, proprietary: *see* **proprietary school.**

school, provided: *see* **provided school.**

school, public: *see* **public school.**

school, reformatory: *see* **reformatory school.**

school, secondary: *see* **secondary school.**

school, secondary modern: *see* **secondary modern school.**

school, secondary technical: *see* **secondary technical school.**

school, senior: *see* **senior school.**

school, special: *see* **special school.**

school, special agreement: *see* **special agreement school.**

school, technical: *see* **technical school.**

school, trade: *see* **trade school.**

school, vacation: *see* **vacation school.**

school, voluntary: *see* **voluntary school.**

Science and Art Department: *see* **Department, Science and Art.**

second master: the vice-principal of a *grammar* or *public school. See* **headmaster; high master.**

secondary education: full-time education suitable to the requirements of senior pupils whose ages range from 12 years to 19 years; under certain circumstances the beginning age may be about 10½ years; emphasis is on education suitable to the ability and aptitude of the pupil; consequently, secondary education embraces academic, modern, and technical education.

secondary modern school: a postprimary school that offers a general secondary education centering around the interests of the child; avoids the strict academic or technical bias.

secondary school: an institution established either by the county or by a voluntary body, offering a full-time program of education to pupils ranging from 11 to 18 years of age (more precisely 10½ to under 19); attendance has been compulsory up to 15, but by 1973 it is expected to be 16 years of age.

secondary school, council: a former type of school that offered a course parallel to that of the *grammar school* but had a practical or scientific bias.

secondary technical school: secondary school offering senior pupils a general secondary education linked with some branch of industry or commerce; formerly called *junior technical school.*

secretary for education: *syn.* **director of education;** *see* **chief education officer.**

Secretary of State for Education and Science: the political head of the *Department of Education and Science* who exercises the powers previously exercised by the *Minister of Education* but is also responsible for certain aspects of scientific, cultural, and university life that were never the responsibility of that minister; he is usually a member of the Cabinet. *See* **Parliamentary Secretary.**

secular instruction: education of a nonreligious nature.

senior chief inspector: *see* **inspector, senior chief.**

senior school: formerly a free nonselective school or a division of a school that offered postprimary education to pupils 11 to 14 or 15 years of age who were not proceeding to a secondary school; offered a program of general studies supplemented by courses of a vocational or technical bias.

set book: literary work prescribed for detailed study in a particular course.

setting: *see* **streaming.**

single school area: an area served only by a voluntary school, not by a county school or a controlled school. *See* **controlled school; county school; voluntary school.**

Sixth Form: *see* **Form, Sixth.**

Sixth Form college: *see* **comprehensive education using a Sixth Form college; comprehensive education; Form.**

special agreement school: a school that entered, under terms of the 1936 Act, into a special agreement with the *local education authority* whereby, in addition to the regular grants, the authority assumed a greater amount of the cost of extension and erection of new facilities for senior pupils; the 1944 Act permitted schools that failed to fulfill agreements made under the 1936 Act to do so.

special educational treatment: education given by special methods appropriate for the disability from which a pupil is suffering.

special place: the right awarded to a pupil, subsequent to the 1902 Act, to attend a *secondary* or *grammar school* with a total or partial exemption from fees; was awarded on the basis of competitive examination to those pupils judged to be most capable of profiting from the education offered; formerly called *free place. See* **reserved place.**

special school: a school established for the education of children who, by reason of some physical or mental defect, cannot be educated in an ordinary school.

special-subjects teacher: a teacher who, in addition to general professional training, has special qualifications to teach a subject not required of a teacher without such specific training, for example, a teacher of music.

speech day: the annual prize-giving ceremony at a *secondary school.*

Spens report: the report of a committee under Sir Will Spens (1938) whose findings greatly influenced the structure of secondary education in the Act of 1944.

streaming: the practice of segregating children into groups based on their general ability for instruction in all the school subjects, as opposed to the practice of *setting* whereby they are sorted into different groups for each subject in accordance with their ability in that subject alone.

subject inspection: *see* **inspection, subject.**

supplementary teacher: formerly a special grade of teacher in rural schools whose only qualification for employment was the approval of the *inspector.*

Taunton. Commission: a commission appointed in 1864 to investigate those areas of educational provision not covered by the *Newcastle* and *Clarendon Commissions;* in particular, it investigated secondary school provision and enabled suitable legislation to be framed which made it possible to reframe the regulations under which old established schools were operating often to the detriment of the education provided.

teacher, head: *see* **head teacher.**

teacher, qualified: *see* **qualified teacher.**

teacher, reserved: *see* **reserved teacher.**

teacher, special-subjects: *see* **special-subjects teacher.**

teacher, supplementary: *see* **supplementary teacher.**

teacher, temporary: *see* **temporary teacher.**

teacher-training college: *see* **college of education.**

teacher, uncertified: *see* **uncertified teacher.**

technical college: *see* **college, technical.**

technical school: a school on the secondary level offering a general secondary education supplemented by the study of the principles underlying various areas of work such as commerce, domestic science, engineering, and art. *See* **central school; secondary technical school.**

temporary teacher: a teacher, not fully qualified, employed by the Secretary of State for Education and Science on a temporary basis.

three-tier comprehensive education: *see* **comprehensive education, three-tier.**

trade school: a school for adolescents and adults, giving preparation for specific occupations requiring manual or mechanical skill, such as dressmaking, millinery, photography, or silversmithing; may or may not charge tuition fees.

training college: *see* **college of education.**

training department, university: *see* **institute of education.**

training, nursery: *see* **nursery training.**

treatment center: a medical clinic set up as a part of a school system by the local education authorities under the authority of the Minister of Health; provides for periodic medical inspection of both primary and secondary pupils and for the free treatment of physical disorders.

tripos: the name given to the honors degree examination at Cambridge.

tutorial instruction: a type of highly individualized instruction used in universities by which each student is assigned to a tutor (one of the teaching staff) with whom he consults at set intervals concerning studies that the student carries on independently. *Comp. w.* **class, tutorial** (*see* main section of Dictionary).

two-tier comprehensive education: *see* **comprehensive education, two-tier.**

UCCA: *see* **Universities Central Council on Admissions.**

uncertified teacher: a term formerly applied to a teacher who had graduated from high school, having passed the school certificate examination, but who held no certificate of professional training. *See* **temporary teacher.**

Undersecretary for Education: *see* **Parliamentary Secretary.**

Universities Central Council on Admissions: a body which, since 1962, has acted as a clearinghouse for applications for admission to university courses, candidates' applications being referred to the university of their second or third choice, etc., when a place is not available at the school of their first choice; usually known as *UCCA.*

university: an institution of higher education that has received a charter to grant degrees; may consist of a number of colleges, or may be a single institution.

university, civic: a university established through local liberality and civic-mindedness but not under civil or municipal control.

university college: *see* **college, university.**

university entrance examination: *see* **examination, matriculation.**

university, free: a proposed establishment being planned by academics, which would be free from all government subsidies and thus, they believe, free from government interference; also called *independent university.*

University Grants Committee: a committee consisting mainly of university representatives which is responsible for assessing the need and allocating the funds supplied by the central government for the general tasks and accommodation of the universities; acts as a buffer between university and government and thus prevents direct interference in university affairs.

university of the air: *see* **university, open.**

university, open: a university established by the government in 1968 in order to satisfy the need of those who desire a university education but are unable to regularly attend an institution; instruction is by means of radio and television, correspondence courses, and tutorial classes; an American credit system will operate and degree courses may thus be spread over a much longer period than is usual in English universities; sometimes (unofficially) referred to as the *university of the air. See* **tutorial instruction.**

university, provincial: *see* **university, civic.**

university training department: *see* **institute of education.**

vacation school: a type of school operated during the summer vacation; originally founded by social workers and philanthropic societies with the idea of counteracting the harmful effects of idleness and the influence of the city streets on children of school age.

vice-chancellor: the principal executive and academic head of a university responsible for the general administration of the university; an experienced educator selected at some universities for a period of 2 or 3 years or appointed at others on a permanent full-time basis. (The position of *chancellor* is somewhat of a sinecure, bestowed as an honor.)

village college: *see* **college, village.**

voluntary school: a school established and kept structurally in repair by a voluntary body, usually denominational, such as the Church of England. *See* **controlled school.**

voluntary school manager: *see* **manager, voluntary school.**

Workers' Educational Association: a voluntary organization, founded in 1903 by Albert Mansbridge, that cooperates with the universities in a program of adult education; provides a number of 1-year and terminal courses, and appoints full-time tutors in certain rural areas to organize adult educational projects.

writing, italic: a simplified form of handwriting, originated in Renaissance Italy and recently revived in English schools as a reaction against the copperplate style normally taught in schools.

Young Farmers' Club: a national organization of over 100 clubs, associated in a national federation, that is intended to stimulate an interest in agriculture and to supply pupils for the rural continuation courses in some areas.

youth leader: *see* **youth service.**

youth service: those organizations, whether run by a voluntary organization or the local authority, which cater to the moral, cultural, and recreational activities of young people outside the formal school structure; those holding posts of responsibility in it are known as *youth leaders.*